영어

2026학년도 대비
기출문제 해설집

문제편

2025학년도 27개 대학 43개 유형의 편입영어 기출문제 수록!

교육서비스 브랜드 대상

누적 32만부 돌파

2024 대한민국 브랜드 어워즈
대학편입교육 대상(한경비즈니스)
산출근거 후면표기

| 기출로 완성하는 합격 전략 김영편입 영어 기출문제 해설집 | 대학별 출제 문항 분류표 & 상위권 대학 심층 분석 수록 | 정확한 해설과 상세한 분석으로 문제 이해력 극대화 |

김앤북
KIM&BOOK

김영편입 컨텐츠평가연구소

김영편입 컨텐츠평가연구소는 편입 시험의 다양한 문제 유형과 난이도를 분석하여 수험생에게 올바른 학습 방향을 제시해 줄 목적으로 설립된 메가스터디의 부설 기관이다. 수십 년간 시행되어 온 대학별 편입 시험을 심층 분석하여 실전에 가까운 컨텐츠를 개발하고 있으며, 김영편입의 우수한 교수진과 축적된 컨텐츠를 기반으로 다양한 교재를 출판하고 있다.

주요 집필 교재

「김영편입 영어 시리즈」 이론서 / 기출 1, 2 단계 / 워크북 1, 2 단계
「김영편입 수학 시리즈」 이론서 / 워크북 / 공식집
「김영편입 연도별 기출문제 해설집 시리즈」 영어 / 수학 / 연고대
「MVP Starter」, 「MVP 시리즈 Vol. 1, 2」, 「해독제 Vol. 1, 2」 등

영어 기출문제 해설집
2026학년도 대비

초판1쇄 인쇄 2025년 6월 16일
초판1쇄 발행 2025년 6월 30일
편저 김영편입 컨텐츠평가연구소
기획총괄 최진호
개발/기획 이순옥, 신종규, 안진영, 김진희, 김형석
감수 류형동
디자인 김소진, 서제호, 서진희, 조아현
제작/영업 조재훈, 김승규, 정광표
마케팅 지다영

발행처 ㈜아이비김영
펴낸이 김석철
등록번호 제22-3190호
주소 (06729) 서울 서초구 강남대로 279, 백향빌딩 4, 5층
전화 (대표전화) 1661-7022
팩스 02)599-5611

ⓒ ㈜아이비김영
이 책은 저작권법에 따라 보호받는 저작물이므로 무단복제를 금지하며, 책 내용의 전부 또는 일부를 이용하려면 반드시 저작권자의 서면동의를 받아야 합니다.

ISBN 979-11-7349-059-0 13740
정가 49,000원

잘못된 책은 바꿔드립니다.

My rising curve with

김앤북
KIM & BOOK

합격

목표 달성
실전 감각 극대화
실전 적용
출제 패턴 파악
문제 풀이
탄탄한 기초
기초 학습
편입 도전

김앤북과 함께
나만의 합격 곡선을 그리다!

완벽한 기초, 전략적 학습, 확실한 실전
김앤북은 합격까지 책임집니다.

#편입 #자격증 #IT

www.kimnbook.co.kr

김앤북의 체계적인
합격 알고리즘

기초 학습 → 문제 풀이 → 실전 적용 → 합격

김영편입 영어

MVP Vocabulary 시리즈

MVP Vol.1   MVP Vol.1 워크북   MVP Vol.2   MVP Vol.2 워크북   MVP Starter

기초 이론 단계

문법 이론   구문독해

기초 실력 완성 단계

어휘 기출 1단계   문법 기출 1단계   독해 기출 1단계   논리 기출 1단계   문법 워크북 1단계   독해 워크북 1단계   논리 워크북 1단계

심화 학습 단계

어휘 기출 2단계   문법 기출 2단계   독해 기출 2단계   논리 기출 2단계   문법 워크북 2단계   독해 워크북 2단계   논리 워크북 2단계

교육서비스 브랜드
3년 연속 대상

2021 대한민국 우수브랜드 대상
2024, 2023, 2022 대한민국 브랜드 어워즈 대학편입교육 대상 (한경비즈니스)

실전 단계

연도별 기출문제 해설집 　　　　　　　　　TOP6 대학 기출문제 해설집

김영편입 수학

편입 수학 이론 & 문제 적용 단계　　　　　　　　　편입 수학 필수 공식 한 권 정리

미분법　　적분법　　선형대수　　다변수미적분　　공학수학　　　　　　공식집

편입 수학 핵심 유형 정리 & 실전 연습 단계　　　　　　　실전 단계

미분법 워크북　적분법 워크북　선형대수 워크북　다변수미적분 워크북　공학수학 워크북　　　연도별 기출문제 해설집

김앤북의 완벽한
단기 합격 로드맵

핵심이론 → 최신기출 → 실전적용 → 단기합격

자격증 수험서

| 전기기능사 필기 | 지게차운전기능사 필기 | 위험물산업기사 필기 | 산업안전기사 필기 | 전기기사 필기 필수기출 / 전기기사 실기 봉투모의고사 | 소방설비기사 필기 필수기출 시리즈 |

컴퓨터 IT 실용서

    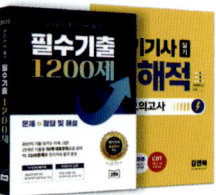 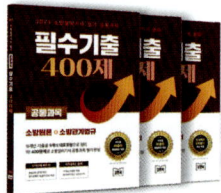

SQL | 코딩테스트 | 파이썬 | C언어 | 플러터 | 자바 | 코틀린 | 유니티

컴퓨터 IT 수험서

컴퓨터활용능력 1급실기 | 컴퓨터활용능력 2급실기 | 데이터분석준전문가 (ADsP) | GTQ 포토샵 | GTQi 일러스트 | 리눅스마스터 2급 | SQL 개발자 (SQLD)

영어

2026학년도 대비

기출문제 해설집

문제편

2025학년도 27개 대학 43개 유형의 편입영어 기출문제 수록!

PREFACE

김영편입 영어 2026학년도 대비 기출문제 해설집

기출로 완성하는 합격 전략

편입영어 시험은 대학에서의 학업 수행에 필요한 영어 능력을 평가하는 시험으로, 단순한 영어 실력뿐만 아니라 정해진 조건 안에서 주어진 문제를 빠르고 정확하게 해결하는 문제 해결 능력까지 함께 요구됩니다.

이러한 점에서 『김영편입 영어 2026학년도 대비 기출문제 해설집』은 가장 효과적인 실전 대비서입니다. 편입을 준비하는 수험생은 문제 유형과 난이도를 체계적으로 파악하고, 제한된 시간 안에 문제를 푸는 연습을 반복함으로써 실제 시험에 필요한 전략과 감각을 기를 수 있습니다.

『김영편입 영어 2026학년도 대비 기출문제 해설집』에는 총 27개 대학, 43개 유형의 최신 기출문제가 수록되어 있습니다. 각 문제마다 지문 해석뿐만 아니라 선택지 분석, 어휘 정리, 오답 해설까지 상세히 담아내어 수험생이 기출문제에 대한 실전 감각과 자신감을 함께 키울 수 있도록 구성했습니다.

또한, 영어 시험을 준비하는 자연계 수험생을 위해 인문계 문제 중 자연계에서 공통으로 출제되는 영어 문제에 대해서는 해당 문제 옆에 별도 표기를 하여 계열별 기출 문제를 쉽게 확인할 수 있도록 구성했습니다.

마지막으로 본 해설집의 집필에 도움을 주신 김영편입 구완석, 김응석, 배장현, 오수원, 윤상환 교수님께 감사의 마음을 전합니다.

김영편입 컨텐츠평가연구소

HOW TO STUDY

2025학년도 기출문제 분석

2025학년도 편입영어 시험은 문법의 비중이 줄고, 독해와 논리 영역이 강화되었으며, 어휘는 고난도로 출제되어 변별력을 높였다. 특히 독해는 전체 문항의 절반 이상을 차지하며, 내용일치, 글의 주제, 빈칸완성, 지시대상, 문맥상 부적절한 문장 또는 단어 고르기, 문장삽입, 단락배열 등 글의 전체적인 내용과 전개 흐름에 대한 이해를 묻는 문항이 주로 출제되었다. 전반적인 출제 유형과 평가 기조는 예년과 크게 다르지 않으며, 사고력을 기반으로 한 독해·논리 문항이 여전히 중심을 이루고 있다.

추천 학습법

1. 기출문제집에 수록된 모든 대학의 문제를 풀어보자!

기출문제는 대학별로 출제 유형과 난이도가 상이하므로, 초반에는 자신의 수준에 맞는 문제로 학습한 내용을 실제 문제에 적용해 보고, 점차 고난도 문제로 확장해 가는 단계별 학습이 효과적이다.

2. 실제 시험과 동일한 환경에서 풀어보자!

편입시험은 철저한 시간 관리가 중요하며, 배점이 높은 문항부터 푸는 전략이 유효하다. 실제 시험 환경에 익숙해지기 위해서는 기출문제를 활용한 반복 연습이 필수적이다.

3. 해설과 함께 철저히 복습하자!

정답을 맞혔다고 해서 반드시 이해하고 문제를 푼 것은 아니다. 우연히 맞힌 문항일수록 해설을 통해 출제 의도와 접근 방식, 선택지 간의 논리를 반드시 확인해야 한다. 특히 오답이나 확신 없이 고른 문항은 오답노트로 정리하며, 어휘·문법·논리·독해별 핵심 개념을 체계적으로 복습하는 것이 중요하다.

ZOOM IN 교재 활용법

문제편

HANKUK UNIVERSITY OF FOREIGN STUDIES

한국외국어대학교
- 2025학년도 T1-1 A형: 50문항 · 60분
- 자연계: 영어 25문항, 수학 20문항 · 90분
- 인문 · 자연계 공통 영어문제 별도* 표시

문항별 배점 01~13 1점 / 14~17 1.5점 / 18~30 2점 / 31~40 2.5점 / 41~50 3점

01~04 Choose the one that best completes the sentence.

01* Despite evidence to the contrary, he remained _____ in his beliefs.
① obdurate ② onerous
③ vestigial ④ tantamount

02* We wanted a buzzy atmosphere that represented that kind of vibrant, _____ nature.
① haughty ② rancid
③ myopic ④ clamorous

03* In an attempt to lure customers, companies go to great lengths to _____ their green policies.
① tout ② denude
③ censure ④ balk

04 The _____ hired by the television channels to give expert opinions professed themselves surprised by the election results.
① pundits ② lampoons
③ manifestos ④ amulets

• 제한 시간 및 문항 수, 문항별 배점 표기
실전과 같은 조건에서 문제를 풀 수 있도록, 문항 수와 제한 시간을 대학별로 표기했습니다.

문항 수: 50문항 | 제한시간: 60분

• 영역별 문항 수
목표 대학의 영역별 출제 비중을 확인하여 효율적으로 학습할 수 있습니다.

2025 한국외대 T1-1 A형 영역별 문항 수

구분	문법			어휘			논리완성	독해	생활영어	총 문항 수
	G/S, W/E	정비문	재진술	동의어	반의어	유추				
문항 수	4	2	2	9			4	29		50
백분율	8%	4%	4%	18%			8%	58%		100%

해설편

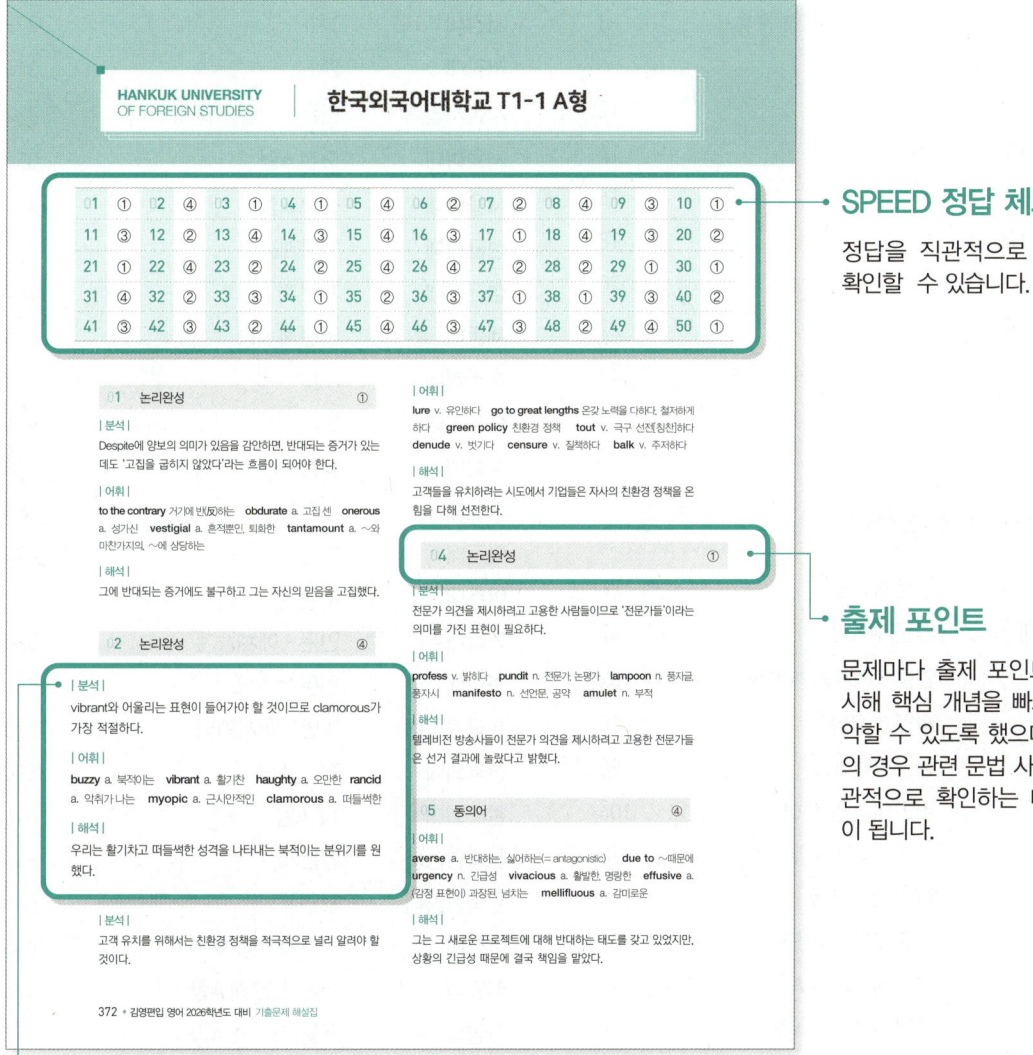

SPEED 정답 체크표
정답을 직관적으로 빠르게 확인할 수 있습니다.

출제 포인트
문제마다 출제 포인트를 표시해 핵심 개념을 빠르게 파악할 수 있도록 했으며, 문법의 경우 관련 문법 사항을 직관적으로 확인하는 데 도움이 됩니다.

정확한 해석과 상세한 분석
지문과 선택지 해석은 물론, 풀이 과정과 오답에 대한 설명까지 꼼꼼하게 담아 문제를 정확히 이해할 수 있도록 구성했습니다.

CONTENTS

문제편

2025학년도 기출문제 파트별 문항 분류표		8
상위권 대학 심층분석		
경희대학교		12
서강대학교		14
성균관대학교		16
중앙대학교		18
한국외국어대학교		20
한양대학교		22
2025학년도 대학별 문항 수 및 제한시간		24

2025학년도 기출문제

가천대	인문계 A형	26
가톨릭대	인문계 A형	42
건국대	인문·예체능계 B형	62
건국대	자연계 B형	80
경기대	일반편입 A형	90
경찰대	일반대학생 전형	104
경희대	인문·체육계열	128
경희대	한의학과 인문	146
고려대	세종 인문·자연계	154
광운대	인문계 1교시 A형	178
광운대	자연계 2교시 A형	194
단국대	인문계 오전	206
단국대	인문계 오후	222
덕성여대	1교시	238
덕성여대	2교시	252
명지대	인문계 오전	264
명지대	인문계 오후	282
서강대	1차	298
서강대	2차	314
서울시립대	인문·자연계열 II	332
서울여대	오전 A형	350
서울여대	정오 A형	364
성균관대	인문계 A형	378
성균관대	자연계 A형	402
세종대	인문계 A형	414
숙명여대	A형	432
숙명여대	B형	446
숭실대	인문계	460
숭실대	자연계	484
아주대	인문계	496
아주대	자연계	522
인하대	인문·예체능계	536
중앙대	인문계 A형	560
한국공학대	일반·학사편입	580
한국외대	T1-1 A형	596
한국외대	T2 A형	616
한국항공대	인문계	636
한국항공대	자연계	652
한성대	인문계 A형	664
한양대	서울 인문계 A형	684
한양대	서울 자연계 A형	702
홍익대	서울 인문계 A형	720
홍익대	서울 자연계 A형	736

해설편

2025학년도 기출문제

대학	구분	페이지
가천대	인문계 A형	6
가톨릭대	인문계 A형	17
건국대	인문·예체능계 B형	31
건국대	자연계 B형	43
경기대	일반편입 A형	49
경찰대	일반대학생 전형	58
경희대	인문·체육계열	75
경희대	한의학과 인문	86
고려대	세종 인문·자연계	91
광운대	인문계 1교시 A형	104
광운대	자연계 2교시 A형	117
단국대	인문계 오전	125
단국대	인문계 오후	134
덕성여대	1교시	144
덕성여대	2교시	152
명지대	인문계 오전	160
명지대	인문계 오후	171
서강대	1차	181
서강대	2차	191
서울시립대	인문·자연계열 II	201
서울여대	오전 A형	211
서울여대	정오 A형	221
성균관대	인문계 A형	231
성균관대	자연계 A형	246
세종대	인문계 A형	254
숙명여대	A형	266
숙명여대	B형	275
숭실대	인문계	284
숭실대	자연계	299
아주대	인문계	307
아주대	자연계	323
인하대	인문·예체능계	333
중앙대	인문계 A형	347
한국공학대	일반·학사편입	361
한국외대	T1-1 A형	372
한국외대	T2 A형	385
한국항공대	인문계	398
한국항공대	자연계	408
한성대	인문계 A형	416
한양대	서울 인문계 A형	428
한양대	서울 자연계 A형	440
홍익대	서울 인문계 A형	452
홍익대	서울 자연계 A형	462

ANALYSIS | 2025학년도 기출문제 파트별 문항 분류표

대학명		문법			어휘			논리완성	독해	생활영어	총 문항수
		G/S, W/E	정문/비문	재진술	동의어/숙어	반의어	유추			대화문	
가천대 [인문계 A형]	문항 수	3			8			11	18		40
	백분율	7.5			20			27.5	45		100
가톨릭대 [인문계 A형]	문항 수	5						15	20		40
	백분율	12.5						37.5	50		100
건국대 [인문·예체능계 B형]	문항 수	2			4			16	18		40
	백분율	5			10			40	45		100
건국대 [자연계 B형]	문항 수	2			5			3	10		20
	백분율	10			25			15	50		100
경기대 [일반편입 A형]	문항 수	10						20	10		40
	백분율	25						50	25		100
경찰대 [일반대학생 전형]	문항 수	4			5				30	1	40
	백분율	10			12.5				75	2.5	100
경희대 [인문·체육계열]	문항 수				8			5	27		40
	백분율				20			12.5	67.5		100
경희대 [한의학과(인문)]	문항 수				9			6	35		50
	백분율				18			12	70		100
고려대 [세종캠퍼스]	문항 수	8			5			7	20		40
	백분율	20			12.5			17.5	50		100
광운대 [1교시 A형]	문항 수		11					14	14	1	40
	백분율		27.5					35	35	2.5	100
광운대 [2교시 A형]	문항 수		7		2			10	10	1	30
	백분율		23.3		6.7			33.3	33.3	3.3	100
단국대 [인문계 오전]	문항 수	10			10				20		40
	백분율	25			25				50		100

대학명		문법			어휘			논리완성	독해	생활영어	총문항수
		G/S, W/E	정문/비문	재진술	동의어/숙어	반의어	유추			대화문	
단국대 [인문계 오후]	문항 수	10			10				20		40
	백분율	25			25				50		100
덕성여대 [1교시]	문항 수	6			4			6	17		33
	백분율	18			12			18	52		100
덕성여대 [2교시]	문항 수	5			6			5	17		33
	백분율	15			18			15	52		100
명지대 [인문계 오전]	문항 수	5			3			7	15		30
	백분율	16.7			10			23.3	50		100
명지대 [인문계 오후]	문항 수	5			3			7	15		30
	백분율	16.7			10			23.3	50		100
서강대 [1차]	문항 수	2						3	25		30
	백분율	7						10	83		100
서강대 [2차]	문항 수	3						2	25		30
	백분율	10						7	83		100
서울시립대 [인문·자연계]	문항 수	2			2	1		1	24		30
	백분율	7			7	3		3	80		100
서울여대 [오전 A형]	문항 수	10			5			12	13		40
	백분율	25			12.5			30	32.5		100
서울여대 [정오 A형]	문항 수	10			5			12	13		40
	백분율	25			12.5			30	32.5		100
성균관대 [인문계 A형]	문항 수	5			5			12	28		50
	백분율	10			10			24	56		100
성균관대 [자연계 A형]	문항 수	2			3			5	15		25
	백분율	8			12			20	60		100

ANALYSIS | 2025학년도 기출문제 파트별 문항 분류표

대학명		문법			어휘			논리완성	독해	생활영어	총 문항수
		G/S, W/E	정문/비문	재진술	동의어/숙어	반의어	유추			대화문	
세종대 [인문계 A형]	문항 수	30					5	10	15		60
	백분율	50					8.3	16.7	25		100
숙명여대 [A형]	문항 수				4			12	17		33
	백분율				12			36	52		100
숙명여대 [B형]	문항 수	4			3			9	17		33
	백분율	12			9			27	52		100
숭실대 [인문계]	문항 수	2			4			4	40		50
	백분율	4			8			8	80		100
숭실대 [자연계]	문항 수	2			4			4	15		25
	백분율	8			16			16	60		100
아주대 [인문계]	문항 수	4						10	36		50
	백분율	8						20	72		100
아주대 [자연계]	문항 수	4						3	18		25
	백분율	16						12	72		100
인하대 [인문·예체능계]	문항 수								40		40
	백분율								100		100
중앙대 [인문계 A형]	문항 수	3			7			14	14	2	40
	백분율	7.5			17.5			35	35	5	100
한국공학대 [일반·학사편입]	문항 수	8			5			12	15		40
	백분율	20			12.5			30	37.5		100
한국외대 [T1-1 A형]	문항 수	4	2	2	9			4	29		50
	백분율	8	4	4	18			8	58		100
한국외대 [T2 A형]	문항 수	4	2	2	9			4	29		50
	백분율	8	4	4	18			8	58		100

대학명		문법			어휘			논리 완성	독해	생활 영어	총 문항수
		G/S, W/E	정문 /비문	재진술	동의어 /숙어	반의어	유추			대화문	
한국항공대 [인문계]	문항 수	2			5			10	13		30
	백분율	6.7			16.7			33.3	43.3		100
한국항공대 [자연계]	문항 수	1			5			7	7		20
	백분율	5			25			35	35		100
한성대 [인문계 A형]	문항 수							10	35	5	50
	백분율							20	70	10	100
한양대 [서울 인문계 A형]	문항 수				6			13	16		35
	백분율				17			37	46		100
한양대 [서울 자연계 A형]	문항 수				6			10	19		35
	백분율				17			29	54		100
홍익대 [서울 인문계 A형]	문항 수	8			10			10	12		40
	백분율	20			25			25	30		100
홍익대 [서울 자연계 A형]	문항 수	6			9			4	6		25
	백분율	24			36			16	24		100

ANALYSIS | 상위권 대학 심층분석

경희대학교
- 인문·체육계열
- 40문항·90분

출제경향 및 난이도 분석

경희대 인문·체육계열 편입영어 시험은 객관식 5지 선다형 40문항·90분으로 진행 됐으며, 학부 과정에서 전공 서적을 영어로 이해할 수 능력을 측정하는 수준에서 문제가 출제됐다. 영역별 차등 배점이 적용됐으며, 특히 독해 영역의 배점과 문항 수의 비중이 높아, 제한시간 90분을 감안했을 때 독해 문제를 차분히 풀어 오답률을 낮추는 것이 관건이었다.

2023~2025학년도 경희대 영역별 문항 수 비교

구분	어휘	문법	논리완성	독해	합계
2023학년도	7	-	5	28	40
2024학년도	5	-	9	26	40
2025학년도	8	-	5	27	40

2025 경희대 영역별 분석

어휘

구분	2023	2024	2025
문항 수 (동의어)	7/40 (17.5%)	5/40 (12.5%)	8/40 (20%)

제시어와 의미가 가장 가까운 것을 고르는 동의어 유형 8문항이 출제됐다. 출제 어휘는 obviate(=eliminate), acquiesce(=assent), predilection(=partiality), brooding(=pensive), foreboding(=apprehension), impervious(=immune), dole out(=grant), inexhaustible(=indefatigable)이었다. 제시어와 보기가 모두 기출어휘에서 출제되어, 기출어휘를 충실히 공부한 수험생들은 대부분 정답을 고르는 데 어려움이 없었을 것이다. 다만, 5번의 경우 제시어 foreboding이 '나쁜 일이 일어날 것 같은 불길한 예감'을 의미해 '장래에 대한 우려'를 의미하는 apprehension을 정답으로 골라야 했지만, apprehension이 '이해', '체포'와 같은 다른 뜻으로도 쓰일 수 있어서, 정확한 의미를 알지 못할 경우 정답을 고르기 힘들었을 것이다.

논리완성

구분	2023	2024	2025
문항 수	5/40 (12.5%)	9/40 (22.5%)	5/40 (12.5%)

one-blank 유형 3문항, two-blank 유형 2문항이 출제됐다. one-blank 유형에서는 로맨스 장르가 감정을 불러일으킨다는 내용에서 conjure(상기시키다)를 고르

는 문제, 강의가 주제에서 이탈했다는 내용을 통해 digression(주제에서 벗어남)을 고르는 문제, 설치 과정이 복잡하고 여러 기관의 승인을 받아야 한다는 내용에서 cumbersome(번거로운)을 고르는 문제가 각각 출제되었으며, two-blank 유형에서는 미스터리를 풀려는 시도에서 theorize(이론화하다)를 고르고 성과 없이 끝나버렸다는 내용에서 perplexed(당황케 했다)를 고르는 문제, 객관적인 물증과 대조되는 주관적인 증거로서 confession(자백)을 고르고 자백에 대한 부연 설명으로 용의자의 admission(시인)을 고르는 문제가 각각 출제됐다. rather than(~하기 보다), hinge on(~에 달려 있다) 등의 제시어가 주어져 글의 전개 방향을 파악하는 데 중요한 단서로 활용되었다.

독해

구분	2023	2024	2025
지문 수	16	12	12
문항 수	28/40(70%)	26/40(65%)	27/40(67.5%)

독해는 총 27문항이 출제되어 전체 문항 수 대비 가장 높은 비중을 차지했다. 출제 유형으로는 빈칸완성, 글의 주제, 글의 제목, 내용일치, 내용추론, 문장삽입, 단락배열, 지시대상, 동의어 등 편입시험에서 자주 출제되는 유형이 골고루 포함되었는데, 특히 빈칸완성 문제가 압도적으로 많이 출제됐다. 지문의 내용을 살펴보면, 플라스틱 재활용의 현실적 어려움, 인류가 놓쳐왔던 열에너지, 인터넷 접속을 가능하게 하는 해저 케이블, 소비를 유도하는 계획된 노후화, 순수함을 상품화하는 디즈니, 프랑스 혁명의 배경, 유럽 경제와 이민자들의 관계, 선택을 유도하는 행동경제학, 지성인의 비판적 사고, AI 코딩 도우미가 바꿀 소프트웨어의 미래, 차이를 포용하는 현대 민주주의 등 다양하게 출제됐다. 「TIME」, 「The Economist」, 「Sapiens: A Brief History of Humankind」, 「Brave New World Revisited」, 「The Mouse that Roared: Disney and the End of Innocence」 등의 대중매체와 전문서적의 수준 높은 글에서 지문이 발췌됐다.

2026 경희대 대비 학습전략

경희대는 문항 수 대비 제한시간이 넉넉한 편이므로, 속도보다는 정확도에 중점을 두고 문제를 풀어 오답률을 줄이는 전략적 시간 안배가 필요하다. 어휘의 경우 기출어휘를 기본으로 하되, 다의어는 반드시 예문을 통한 문맥별 학습이 요구된다. 논리완성의 경우 평소에 연결사 전후로 글의 흐름이 어떻게 바뀌는지 파악하는 훈련을 해야 한다. 독해의 경우 시험에서 가장 높은 비중을 차지하므로, 유사 난도의 기출문제를 반복적으로 풀면서 문제풀이 스킬을 향상시켜야 한다.

ANALYSIS | 상위권 대학 심층분석

서강대학교

- 1차
- 30문항 · 60분

출제경향 및 난이도 분석

서강대학교는 '1차(일반편입(인문))'와 '2차(학사편입(인문), 일반[학사]편입(자연))'로 구분해 두 차례 편입영어 시험이 시행됐다. 지난해와 마찬가지로 30문항·60분으로 진행됐으며, 각 문제 당 난이도에 따라 차등배점을 부여했다. 서강대의 경우 매년 유형이 조금씩 바뀐다. 지난해와 마찬가지로 어휘는 출제되지 않았고, 문법과 논리완성의 비중이 감소했으며 독해의 비중이 증가했다.

2023~2025학년도 서강대 영역별 문항 수 비교

구분	어휘	문법	논리완성	독해	합계
2023학년도	2	6	4	18	30
2024학년도	-	4	6	20	30
2025학년도	-	2	3	25	30

2025 서강대 영역별 분석

문법

구분	2023	2024	2025
W/E	4	2	2
G/S	2	2	-
합계	6/30(20%)	4/30(13%)	2/30(7%)

밑줄 친 부분 중 어법상 옳지 않은 것을 고르는 Written Expression 유형 2문제가 출제됐다. 문법 문제의 비중이 4문제에서 2문제로 감소했고, 지난해에 새롭게 출제된 유형인 대화문에서 어법상 옳지 않은 것을 고르는 문제는 올해 출제되지 않았다. 출제된 문법사항으로는 동사를 수식하는 부사, 동명사를 수식하는 부사를 묻는 것으로 2문제 모두 형용사를 부사로 고치는 문제였다. 기본적인 문법 사항을 숙지하고 있고 문장구조를 파악할 수 있다면 정답을 고르는 데 어려움은 없었을 것이다.

논리완성

구분	2023	2024	2025
문항 수	4/30(13.3%)	6/30(20%)	3/30(10%)

단문의 어휘형 논리완성 3문제가 출제됐다. 논리완성 문제의 비중이 6문제에서 3문제로 감소했다. 'quick to believe'와 유사한 뜻인 'credulity(쉽게 믿음)'를 묻는 문제, 관용표현인 'beyond one's ken(지식의 범위 밖에 있는)'을 묻는 문제, 두 상반된 개

념이 함께 사용되어 모순을 이루는 것을 나타내는 'oxymoronic(모순(어법)의)'을 묻는 문제가 출제됐다. 빈칸을 전후로 빈칸을 추론할 수 있는 단서가 비교적 명확히 제시되었지만 난이도 높은 어휘들이 보기로 제시되어, 상당한 어휘실력이 요구됐다.

독해

구분	2023	2024	2025
지문 수	8	9	10
문항 수	18/30(60%)	20/30(67%)	25/30(83%)

문제의 난이도와 출제 유형은 지난해와 큰 차이가 없었지만, 독해 문제의 비중이 증가했다. 출제된 유형을 살펴보면 글의 요지, 글의 제목, 내용일치, 내용파악, 내용추론, 동의어, 지시대상, 저자의 어조, 빈칸완성, 문장배열 등 편입시험에 자주 출제되는 유형이 골고루 출제됐다. 특히 지문의 전체 내용을 파악해야 풀 수 있는 문제의 비중이 높았다. 지문의 내용을 살펴보면 그라이스(Grice)의 추론적 의사소통 모델, 플라톤(Plato)의 시 비평, 한강의 감각을 활용한 창작 과정에 대한 강연, 시어도어 루스벨트 섬(Theodore Roosevelt Island), 행복에 대한 대중의 관심 증가, 델포이 신탁(The Delphic Oracle)에 대한 현대의 지질학적 탐구, 18세기의 대중 콘서트, 문학 작품의 새로운 번역의 필요성, 핵실험 금지 조약이 환경 의식 형성에 미친 영향, 정신·육체 이원론이 인지 과학에 제기하는 도전 등이었다. 철학, 예술, 정치 등 학문적인 내용의 지문뿐만 아니라 최근 시사적인 내용의 지문이 다양하게 출제됐다.

2026 서강대 대비 학습전략

서강대의 최신 출제경향을 살펴보면 문법과 논리완성의 비중이 감소하고 독해의 비중이 증가하는 추세에 있다. 문법의 경우 문제의 길이가 긴 것이 특징이므로 문장 분석 능력이 요구된다. 논리완성의 경우 빈칸을 추론하기는 어렵지 않지만 보기의 어휘가 어렵게 출제되므로 중·상 수준의 기출어휘를 학습해야 한다. 독해의 경우 출제 비중과 배점이 높으므로 고득점을 얻기 위해서는 다양한 주제의 고급 독해지문을 학습하여 독해력 향상에 힘써야 한다. 또한 매년 문장배열 문제가 출제되고 있으므로 이 유형에 대한 연습을 해야 한다. 그리고 문제 유형이 자주 바뀌는 대학임을 감안할 때 올해 출제되지 않은 문제가 다시 출제될 수 있으므로 최소 3~5년의 서강대 기출문제를 풀고 출제된 모든 유형에 대한 대비가 필요하다.

ANALYSIS | 상위권 대학 심층분석

성균관대학교
- 인문계
- 50문항 · 90분

출제경향 및 난이도 분석

성균관대학교 편입영어 시험은 50문항·90분으로 진행됐다. 문제 유형과 난이도는 지난해와 비슷했으며, 각 문제는 난이도에 따라 차등 배점이 적용됐다. 논리완성의 경우 지난해에 비해 비중이 증가하고 주로 장문으로 출제되어 다소 어렵게 느껴졌을 것이다. 그리고 출제 비중이 가장 높고 문항 당 배점이 높은 독해 영역이 시험의 당락을 좌우했을 것으로 보인다.

2023~2025학년도 성균관대 영역별 문항 수 비교

구분	어휘	문법	논리완성	독해	합계
2023학년도	5	5	9	31	50
2024학년도	5	5	10	30	50
2025학년도	5	5	12	28	50

2025 성균관대 영역별 분석

어휘

구분	2023	2024	2025
문항 수 (동의어)	5/50(10%)	5/50(10%)	5/50(10%)

밑줄 친 어휘와 의미가 가장 가까운 것을 고르는 동의어 유형 5문제가 출제됐다. 출제된 어휘에는 precarious(=perilous), latch onto(=grasp), pay no heed to(=ignore), adjudicate(=determine), torturous(=agonizing)가 있었다. 제시어와 보기가 대부분 기출어휘로 출제되어 정답을 고르는 데 큰 어려움은 없었을 것으로 보인다. 그리고 지난해와 마찬가지로 숙어 및 관용어를 묻는 문제가 출제됐는데, 제시어의 의미를 알지 못해도 문맥을 통해 정답을 고를 수 있는 수준이었다.

문법

구분	2023	2024	2025
문항 수 (W/E)	5/50(10%)	5/50(10%)	5/50(10%)

밑줄 친 부분 중 어법상 옳지 않은 것을 고르는 Written Expression 유형 5문제가 출제됐다. 출제된 문법사항으로는 동격의 to부정사, 관사의 용법, 'neither A nor B'의 구문에서 동사의 수일치, 부정 부사구의 도치구문 등이 있었다. 문장의 구조가 복잡하지 않고 기본적인 문법사항을 묻는 문제가 주로 출제됐지만, to부정사와 관사 문제의 경우 세부적인 문법사항을 알고 있어야 정답을 고를 수 있는 까다로운 문제였다.

논리완성

구분	2023	2024	2025
문항 수	9/50(18%)	10/50(20%)	12/50(24%)

one-blank 유형으로 12문제가 출제됐다. 주로 한 단락 길이의 지문에서 빈칸에 적절한 것을 고르는 문제였는데, 문제를 풀 수 있는 결정적인 단서가 빈칸 앞뒤에 제시되어 문맥을 제대로 이해했다면 빈칸을 어렵지 않게 추론할 수 있었다. 예를 들면, 역접의 접속사 yet, still 등을 제시하여 반대되는 의미의 단어를 고르는 문제, 앞뒤 문맥을 파악하여 이를 설명하는 어구나 부연 설명하는 문장을 고르는 문제 등이 출제됐다.

독해

구분	2023	2024	2025
지문 수	17	16	14
문항 수	31/50(62%)	30/50(60%)	28/50(56%)

총 28문제가 출제되어 독해의 출제 비중이 가장 높았다. 출제된 유형을 살펴보면 글의 요지, 글의 제목, 내용일치, 내용파악, 부분이해, 빈칸완성, 지시대상, 문맥상 적절하지 않은 단어 고르기 등 편입시험에 자주 나오는 유형이 골고루 출제됐다. 지문의 내용을 살펴보면 국가수반 요리사의 외교적 역할, 넬슨 만델라의 아파르트헤이트 투쟁, 미국의 역사 교육과 시민 교육의 중요성, 인종차별 경험이 신체에 미치는 부정적인 영향, 기호와 소비의 상관관계, 질문 구성 방식이 부모에 대한 기억에 미치는 영향, 미국의 건국 원칙, AI에 대한 인식과 학습 능력의 영향, 공직 출마 연령 상한제, 루스벨트의 뉴딜 정책에 대한 반발, 예술과 인공지능의 창작 방식 차이, 포용적 정치 제도와 착취적 정치 제도, 방송 자막의 다양한 유형, 신경정신분석의 이론과 발전 등이었다. 학문적인 내용뿐만 아니라 최근 사회적으로 이슈가 되고 있는 내용 등이 다양하게 지문으로 활용됐는데, 특히 정치와 심리 관련 지문이 상당수 출제됐다.

2026 성균관대 대비 학습전략

성균관대는 유형의 변화가 크지 않으므로 기출문제를 통해 평가 요소를 확인하고 학습 목표를 설정하는 것이 중요하다. 어휘는 숙어 및 관용어 문제가 매년 꾸준히 출제되고 있으므로 이에 대한 대비가 필요하다. 문법은 기본적인 문법사항을 학습하고 문장의 구조를 파악하는 연습을 해야 한다. 논리완성은 한 단락 길이의 지문에서 문제가 출제되므로 앞뒤 문맥을 파악하여 빈칸을 추론할 수 있는 능력을 키우는 것이 중요하다. 독해는 학문적인 내용의 지문이 많이 출제되고 있으므로 다양한 분야의 지문을 통해 배경지식을 쌓아두는 것이 도움이 될 것이다.

ANALYSIS | 상위권 대학 심층분석

중앙대학교
- 인문계 A형
- 40문항 · 60분

출제경향 및 난이도 분석

중앙대학교 편입영어 시험은 40문항·60분으로 진행됐으며, 영역별로 차등 배점이 적용됐다. 지난해와 마찬가지로 관용어구를 알아야 풀 수 있는 생활영어 문제, No error 보기가 들어있는 문법 문제, 그리고 복잡한 구조와 긴 지문이 특징인 독해 문제가 출제됐다.

2023~2025학년도 중앙대 영역별 문항 수 비교

구분	어휘	문법	논리완성	독해	합계
2023학년도	9	3	14	14	40
2024학년도	9	3	14	14	40
2025학년도	9	3	14	14	40

2025 중앙대 영역별 분석

어휘&생활영어

구분	2023	2024	2025
동의어	7	7	7
생활영어	2	2	2
합계	9/40(22.5%)	9/40(22.5%)	9/40(22.5%)

동의어 문제에서는 waylay(=detain), diaphanous(=filmy), overweening(=presumptuous), wheedle(=inveigle), insouciant(=indifferent), spoliation(=pillaging)이 출제됐다. 대화의 흐름상 적절하지 않은 보기를 고르는 생활영어 문제에서는 관용어구의 이해도를 평가했는데, pave the way for something(~를 위한 길을 닦아 놓다), keep a high profile(주변의 이목을 끌다), too big for one's britches(자기 분수를 모르는), push the envelope(한계에 도전하다), put somebody on the spot(~를 곤혹스럽게 만들다) 등의 관용어구가 출제됐다.

문법

구분	2023	2024	2025
문항 수 (W/E)	3/40(7.5%)	3/40(7.5%)	3/40(7.5%)

문장의 밑줄 친 부분 중 문법적으로 적절하지 않은 보기를 고르는 Written Expression 유형이 3문항 출제됐다. 등위접속사에 의한 형용사의 병치, neither A nor B but C, 과거분사와 현재분사의 구분이 출제됐다.

논리완성

구분	2023	2024	2025
문항 수	14/40(35%)	14/40(35%)	14/40(35%)

한 문장으로 이루어진 짧은 문장에서 빈칸을 완성하는 어휘형 빈칸완성 8문항과 단락 길이의 문제에서 빈칸을 완성하는 논리형 빈칸완성 6문항이 출제됐다. 어휘형 빈칸완성 문제는 빈칸 전후로 단서가 비교적 명확하게 제시되어 빈칸에 들어갈 의미를 유추하는 데 큰 어려움이 없었지만, 보기에 제시된 고급어휘를 모르는 수험생들은 정답을 고르기 힘들었을 것이다. 논리형 빈칸완성 문제에서는 겉모습에만 치중하고 본질을 보지 못하는 사람들, 포착하기 어려운 노화과정, 초식성 곤충과 방어하는 식물의 전략, 비트코인과 전통 화폐의 차이점, 약물의 효과와 부작용 등 다양한 주제의 지문이 출제됐다.

독해

구분	2023	2024	2025
지문 수	9	8	8
문항 수	14/40(35%)	14/40(35%)	14/40(35%)

총 14문항이 출제됐다. 출제된 유형을 살펴보면 글의 제목, 글의 요지, 내용일치, 내용추론, 빈칸완성, 단락배열, 문맥상 적합하지 않은 문장 고르기 등 편입시험에 자주 출제되는 유형으로 구성되었다. 지문의 내용은 쇼팽이 상류 사회에 진출하는 과정, 문화적 차이가 논리적 추론에 미치는 영향, 세계관 전환과 지구과학의 발전, 철학자 칸트(Kant)가 남긴 유산, 영화편집이 만드는 시공간의 유연성, 사회인류학과 과학기술학의 가능성, 술의 흥망성쇠, 혈액은행 설립에 기여한 전쟁 등 다양한 주제를 다루었다.

2026 중앙대 대비 학습전략

동의어, 생활영어, 논리완성은 고급어휘와 관용어구 중심으로 출제되므로, 이에 철저히 대비해야 한다. 문법은 지엽적인 문법사항보다는 문장 구조를 정확히 분석할 수 있는지를 묻는 경향이 있으므로, 지문을 읽을 때 구조 파악 연습을 꾸준히 하고 모의고사를 통해 문제풀이 스킬을 쌓는 것이 중요하다. 독해는 긴 지문에 비해 문항 수가 적어 시간 관리가 어려울 수 있으므로, 서강대, 성균관대, 한양대 등 수준 높은 기출 지문으로 속독 훈련을 하는 것이 필요하다. 또한 배경지식은 문제 해결 시간을 단축하는 데 큰 도움이 되므로, 다양한 전문서적을 온·오프라인에서 꾸준히 접하는 습관을 들여야 한다.

ANALYSIS | 상위권 대학 심층분석

한국외국어대학교
- T1-1 A형
- 50문항 · 60분

출제경향 및 난이도 분석

한국외대 편입영어 시험은 50문항·60분으로 진행됐다. 문항별로 차등 배점이 적용됐으며, 독해 영역의 배점이 높았다. 전체 문항에서 독해가 차지하는 비중을 감안할 때, 짧은 시간 안에 독해 문제의 정확한 정답 도출이 요구되는 고난도 시험이었다.

2023~2025학년도 한국외대 영역별 문항 수 비교

구분	어휘	문법&재진술	논리완성	독해	합계
2023학년도	9	8	4	29	50
2024학년도	9	8	4	29	50
2025학년도	9	8	4	29	50

2025 한국외대 영역별 분석

어휘

구분	2023	2024	2025
동의어	5	5	5
문맥상 동의어	4	4	4
합계	9/50(18%)	9/50(18%)	9/50(18%)

동의어 문제로 averse(=antagonistic), insuperable(=impassable), diatribe(=denunciation), perspicuous(=lucid), conscientiously(=painstakingly)가 출제됐으며, 문맥상 동의어 문제로 leave(=entrust), quarter(=district), case(=lawsuit), due(=suitable)가 출제됐다.

문법&재진술

구분	2023	2024	2025
G/S	2	2	2
W/E	2	2	2
정비문	2	2	2
재진술	2	2	2
합계	8/50(16%)	8/50(16%)	8/50(16%)

문법에서는 세 가지 유형의 문제가 출제됐다. '문장 완성하기(빈칸에 알맞은 문법사

항을 보기에서 고르기)' 유형에서는 목적격 관계대명사의 생략, 'reprove A for B(A를 B의 이유로 꾸짖다)' 등을 물어보았고, '문장 내 오류 찾기(문장에서 문법적으로 적절하지 않은 보기를 고르기)' 유형에서는 주어와 동사의 수일치, 자동사로 오인하기 쉬운 타동사 등을 물어보았고, '비문 고르기(문법적으로 틀린 문장을 보기에서 고르기)' 유형에서는 'so much+비교급+a+명사(훨씬 더 ~한)', 부정의 부사어에 의한 도치 등을 물어보았다. 제시문의 의미를 파악한 뒤, 동일한 의미를 전달하는 문장을 고르는 재진술 문제는 총 2문항이 출제됐다.

논리완성

구분	2023	2024	2025
문항 수	4/50(8%)	4/50(8%)	4/50(8%)

단문의 어휘형 논리완성 4문항이 출제됐다. 문제의 내용을 살펴보면, 증거가 제시됐어도 수긍하지 않는 태도에서 obdurate(고집하는)를 고르는 문제, 북적이는 분위기에서 clamorous(떠들썩한)를 고르는 문제, 기업이 친환경 정책을 내세우는 상황에서 tout(선전하다)를 고르는 문제, 전문적인 의견을 제시한다는 내용에서 pundit(전문가)를 고르는 문제가 출제됐다.

독해

구분	2023	2024	2025
지문 수	12	12	12
문항 수	29/50(58%)	29/50(58%)	29/50(58%)

12지문에서 총 29문제가 출제됐다. 출제된 유형을 살펴보면, 글의 제목, 글의 주제, 내용일치, 내용추론, 빈칸완성, 부분이해, 글의 목적 등이 출제됐다. 출제된 지문의 내용을 살펴보면, 아침햇살로 여는 자연스러운 기상, 보행 친화적인 16세기 베네치아, 부모 세대와 달라진 자녀 세대의 수어, 2024년 옥스퍼드 올해의 단어로 선정된 Brain Rot, 유럽연합의 AI 법안 시행, 한강의 「채식주의자」 금서 지정을 둘러싼 논란 등이 출제됐다.

2026 한국외대 대비 학습전략

문맥상 동의어 문제의 경우, 다의어가 문장에서 어떻게 쓰이는지 영영 사전의 예문을 활용해 문장별로 달라지는 의미를 파악해야 한다. 재진술 문제의 경우, 관용어구나 난이도 있는 문법 구조가 자주 출제되므로, 어려운 표현들을 해석해 보는 습관을 들이는 것이 중요하다. 독해는 제한시간 대비 지문의 수가 많으므로, 시간을 정해놓고 지문을 속독하는 훈련을 해야 한다. 그리고 대중매체의 기사를 꾸준히 읽으면서 배경지식과 영어 표현력을 쌓는 것이 필요하다.

ANALYSIS | 상위권 대학 심층분석

한양대학교
- 서울 인문계 A형
- 35문항 · 60분

출제경향 및 난이도 분석

한양대 편입영어 시험은 35문항·60분으로 진행됐으며, 문항별 차등 배점이 적용됐다. 기본 배점은 문항 당 2점이지만, 논리와 독해 영역의 경우 배점이 3점과 4점인 문제가 다수 출제되었고, 두 영역이 전체 문항에서 대부분을 차지해, 지문을 정확히 읽고 정답을 도출하는 능력이 합격의 당락을 좌우했다.

2023~2025학년도 한양대 영역별 문항 수 비교

구분	어휘	문법	논리완성	독해	합계
2023학년도	6	1	16	17	40
2024학년도	8	-	7	20	35
2025학년도	6	-	13	16	35

2025 한양대 영역별 분석

어휘

구분	2023	2024	2025
문항 수(동의어)	6/40(15%)	8/35(23%)	6/35(17%)

밑줄 친 제시어와 의미가 가장 가까운 것을 고르는 동의어 유형 6문제가 출제됐다. 출제 어휘는 crucible(=trial), respite(=rest), protean(=mutable), cajole(=coax), forgo(=relinquish), beacon(=signal)이었다. 제시어와 보기가 모두 출제빈도가 높은 기출어휘로 구성되어, 기출어휘를 충실히 숙지한 수험생이라면 무난하게 정답을 고를 수 있는 수준이었다.

논리완성

구분	2023	2024	2025
문항 수	16/40(40%)	7/35(20%)	13/35(37%)

총 13문항이 출제됐다. 문제의 내용을 살펴보면, 지나치게 비위를 맞추려는 행동에서 obsequious(아첨하는)를 고르는 문제, 노골적인 차별 다음에 역접을 나타내는 but이 와서 insidious(은밀한)를 고르는 문제, 과학자의 이론이 무시 받았다는 내용에서 implausible(신빙성이 없는)을 고르는 문제, 세상으로부터 물러나 있다는 내용에서 seclusion(은둔)을 고르는 문제, 대중이 이해하기 어려운 수학모델을 사용했다는 내용에서 esoteric(난해한)을 고르고 역접을 나타내는 however가 와서 optimism(낙

관적인 태도)을 고르는 문제, 힘들이지 않고 매끄럽게 표현하는 발레의 이미지에서 어려운 상황을 능숙하게 처리하는 활동에도 '발레'라는 용어가 비유적으로 쓰일 수 있음을 고르는 문제, 문명의 지속적인 번영을 가능케 하는 적응력을 구체적으로 설명한 표현을 고르는 문제 등 다양한 문제가 출제됐다. 특히 빈칸에 적절한 보기로 긴 표현을 고르는 문제는 난이도에 비례해 높은 배점이 부여된 것이 특징이다.

독해

구분	2023	2024	2025
지문 수	13	16	13
문항 수	17/40(42.5%)	20/35(57%)	16/35(46%)

총 16문항이 출제됐다. 출제 유형으로는 글의 주제, 글의 요지, 글의 제목, 내용일치, 빈칸완성, 동의어, 글의 흐름상 적절하지 않은 단어 고르기 등 편입시험에서 자주 출제되는 유형이 골고루 포함되었는데, 특히 세부적인 내용파악보다는 전체적인 내용을 묻는 문제가 많이 출제됐다. 지문의 내용을 살펴보면 인간이 털을 잃은 이유, 멸종에 대한 윤리적 책임, 중앙은행과 복지국가와의 관계, 유토피아의 공간적 의미와 시간적 의미, 우주와 뗄 수 없는 인간의 운명, 네안데르탈인의 동굴벽화, 곤충의 영양분을 활용하는 식물의 전략, 2024년 문화 아이콘인 Brat의 상징적 의미, 수면 패턴의 발달과 변화, 미국 문화에서 숨어 있는 도시 혐오, 사회적 교정역할을 하는 웃음이론, 지루함이 주의력에 미치는 영향 등이 출제됐다. 「Stuff: Humanity's Epic Journey from Naked Ape to Nonstop Shopper」, 「Brilliant Green: The Surprising History and Science of Plant Intelligence」, 「The Science of Sleep: What It Is, How It Works, and Why It Matters」 등의 수준 높은 전문서적에서 지문이 발췌됐다.

2026 한양대 대비 학습전략

한양대 편입영어 시험은 지난해부터 문법 문제가 출제되지 않고, 동의어, 논리완성, 독해의 세 가지 유형으로 출제되고 있다. 특히 논리완성과 독해의 비중이 크므로, 한양대 과년도 기출문제를 비롯해 비슷한 난이도와 유형으로 구성된 성균관대 기출문제도 함께 풀어보는 것이 문제풀이 스킬을 향상시키는 데 도움이 될 것이다. 동의어 문제의 경우 기출어휘에서 크게 벗어나지 않는 범위에서 출제되므로, 기출어휘 중심으로 공부해야 하며, 논리완성과 독해의 경우 주로 학문적인 내용의 글에서 출제되는 것을 고려할 때 이런 전문분야의 문제를 풀기 위한 다양한 배경지식을 쌓아둘 필요가 있다.

2025학년도 대학별 문항 수 및 제한시간

대학명	계열	과목 및 문항수	제한시간
가천대	인문계	영어 40	60분
	자연계	수학 25	60분
가톨릭대	인문계	영어 40	90분
	자연계	영어 20, 수학 20	90분
건국대	인문·예체능계	영어 40	60분
	자연계	영어 20, 수학 20	60분
경기대	인문·예체능계	영어 40	60분
	자연계	영어 25, 수학 20	100분
경찰대	일반대학생 전형	영어 40	60분
경희대	인문체육계열	영어 40	90분
	한의학과 인문	영어 50	90분
	자연계	수학 30	90분
고려대[세종]	인문·자연계	영어 40	60분
광운대	인문계	영어 40	60분
	자연계	영어 30, 수학 25	100분
단국대	인문계	영어 40	60분
	체육교육/산업경영(야)	영어 30	60분
	자연계	수학 30	90분
덕성여대	인문·자연계	영어 33	50분
명지대	인문계	영어 30	60분
	자연계	영어 30, 수학 25	120분
서강대	인문계	영어 30	60분
	자연계	영어 30, 수학 20	120분
서울과학기술대학교	자연계	수학 20	100분
서울시립대	인문계	영어 30	60분
	자연계 I	수학 25	60분
	자연계 II	영어 30, 수학 25	120분
서울여대	인문·자연계	영어 40	70분
성균관대	인문계	영어 50	90분
	자연계	영어 25, 수학 20	90분
세종대	인문계	영어 60	100분
	자연계	수학 25	100분
숙명여대	인문계	영어 33	60분
	자연계	수학 20	60분
숭실대	인문계	영어 50	90분
	자연계	영어 25, 수학 25	90분
아주대	인문계	영어 50	90분
	자연계	영어 25, 수학 25	90분
인하대	인문계	영어 40	80분
	자연계	영어 20, 수학 30	120분
중앙대	인문계	영어 40	60분
	공학계열 (수학과 포함)	수학 30	60분
한국공학대	인문계	영어 40	60분
	자연계	수학 25	60분
한국외대	인문계	영어 50	60분
	자연계	영어 25, 수학 20	90분
한국항공대	인문계	영어 30	60분
	자연계	영어 20, 수학 20	90분
한성대	인문계	영어 50	90분
	자연계	영어 25, 수학 20	90분
한양대	인문계	영어 35	60분
	자연계	영어 35, 수학 25	130분
홍익대	인문계	영어 40	70분
	자연계	영어 25, 수학 15	70분

* 자연계 시험의 경우 대학별 학과에 따라 전형방법이 상이하오니 지원하는 대학의 모집요강을 반드시 참고하시기 바랍니다.

가천대학교

▶ 2025학년도 인문계 A형　▶ 문항 수: 40문항 | 제한시간: 60분

2025 가천대 인문계 A형 영역별 문항 수

구분	문법			어휘			논리완성	독해	생활영어	총 문항 수
	G/S, W/E	정비문	재진술	동의어	반의어	유추				
문항 수	3			8			11	18		40
백분율	7.5%			20%			27.5%	45%		100%

GACHON UNIVERSITY

가천대학교

2025학년도 인문계 A형: 40문항 · 60분

문항별 배점 01~08 1.2점 / 09~13 2.1점 / 14~21 2.4점 / 22~31 3.1점 / 32~40 3.3점

01~08 Choose the one that is closest in meaning to the underlined part.

01 Perhaps the Japanese commitment to collective values is an anachronism that does not fit with modern industrialism but brings economic success despite that collectivism. Collectivism seems to be inimical to the kind of <u>maverick</u> creativity exemplified in Benjamin Franklin and John D. Rockefeller.

① orthodox ② adulator
③ zealot ④ iconoclast

02 NFL football was unimaginably simpler back then. When Randy and I were twelve-year-old boys, we'd ride our bikes to the game and leave them outside the stadium, which of course wasn't the Superdome but the old, <u>rickety</u>, now demolished stadium, not far from our houses.

① decrepit ② rudimentary
③ exquisite ④ puerile

03 In the midst of blatant injustices inflicted upon the Negro, I have watched white churches stand on the sideline and merely mouth pious irrelevancies and <u>sanctimonious</u> trivialities.

① self-righteous ② ominous
③ self-contained ④ transient

04 ChatGPT returned a condensed and slightly reworded version of the paragraph. The <u>tweaked</u> version removed the French term *grande idée* and Americanized the British spelling of "marginalization," but otherwise wasn't obviously better.

① shortened
② censored
③ modified
④ transcribed

05 Bowen remembered the exhilaration whenever his submarine surfaced in open sea and he would emerge topside into the briny spray, <u>tethered</u> to the boat, taking in a view of nothing but water in every direction.

① anchored
② hanged
③ attached
④ immobilized

06 By shifting admissions criteria in this way, Conant hoped to realize Thomas Jefferson's dream of a natural aristocracy of talent, <u>culling</u> the smartest people from all ranks of society.

① winnowing
② defining
③ repudiating
④ rankling

07 Since 1947, the Japanese government has distributed a booklet to expectant mothers, encouraging them to record their journeys through pregnancy, delivery, and matrescence. Prepartum, women can <u>jot down</u> their diet and exercise regimes, and the details of their doctors' visits; after giving birth, they can note vaccination dates and developmental milestones.

① plan out
② lay out
③ copy down
④ write down

08 The diplomat used his negotiating skills to <u>finesse</u> credulous officials into releasing the backpackers who had crossed a borderline.

① mislead
② coerce
③ maneuver
④ cram

09~11 Choose the one that is grammatically INCORRECT.

09 What is a wedding for? This sounds like a question ① <u>in which</u> there ought to be an obvious answer, but when I posed it to a group of soon-to-be brides and ② <u>recently married</u> women with whom I met near the outset of my research for this book — the question came perhaps an hour, and a bottle of wine or two, ③ <u>into</u> a very lively conversation — the room fell momentarily silent, and then everyone broke into slightly ④ <u>embarrassed</u> laughter.

10 The trial that Cassy ① <u>is enrolled in</u>, which Barker co-leads, and another more-advanced trial run by BlueRock Therapeutics, a biotechnology firm based in Cambridge, Massachusetts, ② <u>gives</u> participants A9 progenitor cells derived from human ES cells. The BlueRock trial has reported preliminary results for its 12 participants. Two years in, the treatment ③ <u>has proved</u> safe and shown hints of efficacy in those ④ <u>receiving</u> the higher of two doses.

11 We didn't buy any Anne dolls, ① <u>nor</u> did we visit the Green Gables facsimile farmhouse, which — judging from online accounts of it — is as complete as Sherlock Holmes's digs on Baker Street, ② <u>contained</u> everything from the slate Anne broke over Gilbert Blythe's head to the brooch she was accused, wrongly, of losing. There's even a ③ <u>pretend</u> Matthew who gives you drives around the property, though he's not described as running to hide out in the barn at the approach of lady visitors, as the real Matthew ④ <u>would have done</u>.

12~14 Choose the most appropriate word or phrase for each blank.

12 It's said that nowhere in the United Kingdom _____ seventy miles from the sea, a fact I recall whenever I hear seagulls croaking overhead in North London's streets. Wherever you are on this island, you are near its margin, a coastline that is estimated to extend for about eleven thousand miles.

① you can never move evenly
② are you ever further than
③ you are never allowed to swim
④ are you ever invariably within

13 Microfiber synthetics have been taking the place of natural fibers in an ever-increasing number of clothes because they provide the same durability and deplete fewer natural resources. A shirt made of microfiber synthetics is, however, three times as expensive to produce as a natural-fiber shirt. It follows that the substitution of microfiber synthetic clothes for natural-fiber clothes is, at this time, not recommended from a financial standpoint. _____, the widespread substitution of microfiber synthetic clothes for natural-fiber clothes is currently economically unfeasible.

① In other words   ② In contrast
③ Fortunately   ④ Otherwise

14 When the question of tragedy in art is not at issue, we never hesitate to attribute to the person of high standing the very same mental processes as the lowly. And finally, if the exaltation of tragic action were truly a property of the high-bred character alone, it is inconceivable that the mass of mankind should cherish tragedy above all other forms, _____ be capable of understanding it.

① let alone   ② rather than
③ so as to   ④ more than

15~22 Choose the most appropriate word or phrase for each blank.

15 The Byzantine Empire preserved the last vestiges of the Roman Empire into the Middle Ages, although it developed a distinct culture of its own. As a successor of the Roman Empire, the Byzantines retained much of the legal and cultural scaffolding of Ancient Roman society, but some of these elements were subverted by facets of Greek culture, which became so pervasive that Greek ultimately replaced Latin as the officially endorsed language of the empire. This _____ of influences contributed to the uniqueness of the Byzantine Empire.

① innovation
② amalgamation
③ resuscitation
④ dispersion

16 The lizards snapped up insects that are so noxious that other potential predators avoid them. Among the lizards' prey were some beetles that they initially rejected because the insects were spraying their hot, irritant defense chemical at the time. Yet even these produced no apparent ill-effects, since the lizards, having eaten, proceeded on their way _____ enough.

① capriciously
② irksomely
③ nonchalantly
④ diffidently

17 The serious study of popular culture by intellectuals is regularly credited with having rendered obsolete a once-dominant view that popular culture is inherently inferior to high art. Yet this alteration of attitudes may be somewhat overstated. Although it is now academically respectable to analyze popular culture, the fact that many intellectuals feel compelled to rationalize their own penchant for action movies or mass-market fiction reveals, perhaps unwittingly, their continued _____ the old hierarchy of high and low culture.

① controversy over
② investment in
③ aversion to
④ misconception of

18 We can scorn the smug WASP blue bloods from Harvard and Yale — and certainly their era's retrograde views of race and gender — but their leadership helped produce the Progressive movement, the New Deal, victory in World War II, and NATO. After the meritocrats took over in the 1960s, we got _____ in Vietnam and Afghanistan, needless carnage in Iraq, the 2008 financial crisis, the toxic rise of social media, and our current age of political dysfunction.

① attainments
② quagmires
③ bayous
④ assemblages

19 A well-known quote from King Charles V of Spain suggests that some individuals have no difficulty keeping languages apart and even assign different functions to each. But most individuals do not have such control and are not so _____. Why one cannot keep languages apart and why the mixing and merging of various languages known and being learned occurs are issues at the heart of research on multilingualism.

① compartmentalized
② beguiled
③ imperceptible
④ disproportionate

20 Though many of her contemporaries found her odd, Kate Scott is now much admired for her _____ spirit, especially her willingness to reject prevailing feminine roles and to travel to foreign lands.

① forlorn
② desolate
③ modest
④ doughty

21 The Japanese author Marie Kondo famously instructed readers to pose the question, when deciding whether to hold on to an object, "Does this spark joy?" When she recommended that people dispose of books that did not spark joy, the _____ was so intense that Kondo was compelled to affirm publicly that she didn't hate books.

① backlash
② exoneration
③ acclaim
④ absolution

22

Beyond the wish to secure the right to live in the country I had long called home, there was another motivation behind my wish to become an American: the possibility that my family and I might, one day, leave. As a green card holder, I had only a(n) _____ right of residency in America. As a citizen, I would be able to leave the country and have the right to return at any time.

① inalienable
② provisional
③ equal
④ instantaneous

23~40 Read the following passages and answer the questions.

The director shoots Sue with slow panning close-ups over her scantily clad body. The camera is leery, obsessive, and hypersexual. It makes sense that Sue would be keen to flaunt her young and beautiful body. But it's less clear why the director is so intent on highlighting Sue's undeniable beauty in a film supposedly critiquing the film industry's obsession with it. The director Ⓐ_____ the history of exploitation of women's bodies rather than subverts it.

23 Which of the following is most appropriate for the blank Ⓐ?

① denies
② replicates
③ distorts
④ subdues

By one estimate, the average American spends a total of two and a half days every year looking for misplaced household items. More than a third of homeowners say their garage is Ⓐ too cluttered to use for parking. Eleven percent of us rent storage units. "There are now Ⓑ less storage facilities in the United States than Starbucks, McDonald's, Dunkin' Donuts, and Pizza Hut locations combined," Lane writes. This has all happened as the size of the typical American home increased: we somehow have Ⓒ more room and less space. One often quoted statistic is that the standard American household contains three hundred thousand items. It is hard to verify, but the fact that so many don't Ⓓ question it speaks volumes.

24 Which of the following underlined Ⓐ, Ⓑ, Ⓒ, and Ⓓ is NOT appropriately used?

① Ⓐ 　　　　　　　　② Ⓑ
③ Ⓒ 　　　　　　　　④ Ⓓ

The Bebop era, 1944-1955, represents for many the most significant period in jazz history. Some consider it the period when musicians began stressing artistic rather than commercial concerns, put innovation ahead of convention, and looked toward the future instead of paying homage to the past. Others view Bebop as jazz's ultimate dead end, the style that instituted solemnity and elitism within the jazz community, stripped jazz of its connection with dance, and made it impossible for anyone except dedicated collectors, academics, and other musicians to enjoy and appreciate the music. Each assessment contains enough grains of truth to merit closer, more extensive examination, and there have been many studies devoted to addressing and evaluating these contentions.

---

25 Which of the following is the most appropriate title of the passage?

① The stylistic change of Jazz
② The artistic significance of Bebop Jazz
③ The conflicting appraisal on Bebop Jazz
④ The contrary studies on Jazz

Once these disparate parts were held together by a common enemy, by the fault lines of world wars and the electrified fence of communism. With the end of the cold war, there was the creeping concern that without a focus for hatred and distrust, a sense of national identity would evaporate, that the left side of the hyphen — African-American, Irish-American — would Ⓐ_____ the right. And slow-growing domestic traumas like economic unrest and increasing crime seemed more likely to emphasize division than community. Today the citizens of the United States have come together once more because of the September 11 terror attacks. Terrorism has led to devastation — and Ⓑ_____.

26 Which of the following is most appropriate for the blanks Ⓐ and Ⓑ?

① underpin — stupor
② sublimate — angst
③ reinforce — accord
④ overwhelm — unity

Echinosorex gymnura, also known as the moonrat, is one of the many fascinating creatures that inhabit the jungles of Southeast Asia. A close relative of the hedgehog, the moonrat likewise belongs to the order *Insectivora* and the family *Erinaceidae*. However, the family then splits into the sub-family *Hylomyinae*, which contains three separate genera and eight distinct species. The appearance and habitat of the moonrat are actually far more similar to those of various members of the order *Rodentia*, though its eating habits are more in line with its fellow insectivores.

---

27 Which of the following best describes the author's tone?

① ambivalent   ② didactic
③ sullen   ④ incensed

Comfort was proclaimed as the privilege of royalty. Only the king might stretch his legs. We may feel sure, however, that he stretched them in a very majestic manner. At ordinary times the king was seated, it is true, but seated in a dignified and upright position; the appearance of majesty had to be kept up. The courtiers, meanwhile, kept up the appearances of Ⓐ_____, either standing, or else, if their rank was very high, sitting, even in the royal presence, on stools. What was true of the king's court was true of the nobleman's household; and the knight was to his dependants, the merchant was to his apprentices and servants, Ⓑ_____ the monarch was to his courtiers.

28 Which of the following is most appropriate for the blanks Ⓐ and Ⓑ?

① deference — what
② civility — so
③ piety — that
④ indignation — as

29~30

In Hollywood, the only roles offered to Jimmy O. Yang were goofy sidekicks and background parts, but even when he tried to make characters like Jian-Yang as rounded and complicated as possible, he felt he couldn't win. "I didn't understand the Ⓐ_____ Asian accents," he said. He gets why Asian Americans are sensitive to such portrayals, given Hollywood's long history of stereotyping, but some of the criticism, he said, felt "a little overblown and a little dumb." "There's a constant foreigner bit," he explained, referring to the industry's tendency to Ⓑ_____ Asian characters.

29 Which of the following is most appropriate for the blank Ⓐ?

① beef against
② soft spot for
③ propensity toward
④ break down of

30 Which of the following is most appropriate for the blank Ⓑ?

① aggrandize
② exoticize
③ idolize
④ pulverize

31~32

Throughout twentieth century, it was accepted as fact that cells in our brains, called neurons, do not regenerate. However, research by neurologist Gould's experiments on rats showed that even after suffering severe trauma, their brains were able to heal themselves by regenerating neurons. Gould's findings have Ⓐ_____ a flood of new research into applications that may take advantage of neurogenesis. One such study examines the role of reduced neurogenesis among individuals suffering from depression. It is speculated that neurogenesis may contribute to an explanation for the so-called "Prozac lag." As an antidepressant, the immediate boost of serotonin caused by Prozac should have had instantaneous mood elevating effects. However, patients suffering from depression only begin to experience mood elevation weeks after beginning treatment. The study speculates that during this period, the brain may be regenerating neurons.

31 Why did the author mention the "Prozac lag"?

① to raise a possible objection to a newly proposed theory
② to present a situation for which a new theory may serve an explanatory role
③ to suggest a counterexample that weakens a newly proposed theory
④ to provide evidence that a new theory may have unforeseen side effects

32 Which of the following is most appropriate for the blank Ⓐ?

① discharged
② exacerbated
③ deterred
④ incited

33~34

When I asked a few professors about A.I.-assisted writing, I was met with mixed feelings. One instructor told me that easy writing assignments, such as short response paragraphs that Ⓐ_____ students to complete their reading, are easily "GPT'd," and would likely need to be eliminated. But, for longer and more complex assignments, such as one's graduate-school paper on perspectivism, teachers seem to be discovering, to their relief, that "load sharing" with ChatGPT still requires students to think carefully and write clearly. It might make the process of completing an assignment feel less Ⓑ_____, but it's not a(n) Ⓒ_____ to receiving a higher grade.

33 Which of the following is most appropriate for the blank Ⓐ?

① forestall
② nudge
③ detract
④ bemuse

34 Which of the following is most appropriate for the blanks Ⓑ and Ⓒ?

① daunting — shortcut
② riveting — impasse
③ prohibiting — highway
④ gripping — bypass

35~36

In the late 1990s, a group of Italian researchers started a project to investigate longevity in Sardinia. The results were Ⓐ intriguing. Sardinia's centenarians were not evenly distributed across the island, the researchers found. Instead, there seemed to be a higher concentration in the province of Ogliastra, a central mountainous region. The province also boasted almost as many men who were older than 100 as women — a highly unusual finding, as women centenarians usually far outnumber men.

35 Which of the following is likely included as the researcher's initial expectation regarding centenarians in Sardinia?

① Centenarians would be evenly distributed throughout the island.
② Men would outnumber women among centenarians.
③ Centenarians would be primarily found in coastal regions.
④ The study would reveal significant disparities in lifespan across different regions of the island.

36 Which of the following is closest in meaning to the underlined Ⓐ?

① repulsive   ② unavoidable
③ interesting   ④ ungrounded

37~38

Art historians will often point to Courbet's *The Painter's Studio* as the vanguard of the modern art movement. The peculiar subtitle of Courbet's work, "Real allegory summing up a seven-year period of my life," confirms that Courbet was striving to do something strikingly original with his work. The argument has been made that the painting struck a blow for the independence of the artist, and that since Courbet's work, artists have felt freed from the societal demands placed upon their work. Paintings prior to Courbet's time were most often focused on depicting events from the Bible, history, or literature. With his singular painting, Courbet Ⓐ_____ the idea that an artist is capable of representing only that which he can experience through his senses of sight and touch.

37 Which of the following is most appropriate for the blank Ⓐ?

① promulgated　　② procrastinated
③ prostrated　　　④ procured

38 Which of the following can be inferred from the passage about Courbet?

① His painting inspired artists to focus on religious themes to discourage sacrilegious practices.
② His work diminished the importance of artistic technique.
③ His painting liberated artists from the constraints of traditional subject matter.
④ His work led to a decline in the appreciation of historical paintings.

39~40

Rachel Carson questioned human being/nature dualism. Whatever airs we might give ourselves, "we" were not distinct from "it": We were part of it, and could live only inside it. To think Ⓐ_____ was self-destructive:

The "control of nature" is a phrase conceived in arrogance, born of the Neanderthal age of biology and philosophy, when it was supposed that nature exists for the convenience of man. The concepts and practices of applied entomology date from that Stone Age of science. It is our alarming misfortune that so primitive a science has armed itself with the most modern and terrible weapons, and that in turning them against the insects it has also turned them against the earth.

One can criticize the metaphor — "Stone Age" people were much more in tune with the wholeness of the fabric of life than were the twentieth-century pundits Carson was up against — but the conclusion stands. If the only tool you have is a hammer, you see every problem as a nail. Carson was exploring other tools, and other ways of solving problems.

39 Which of the following is most appropriate for the blank Ⓐ?

① likewise
② discreetly
③ otherwise
④ independently

40 Which of the following CANNOT be inferred from the passage?

① Carson views the human attitude of dominance over nature as haughty and rooted in primitive thinking.
② Carson uses "Stone Age of science" metaphor to describe the unsophisticated mindset underlying the concepts of applied entomology.
③ "Stone Age of science" metaphor may be misleading as actual Stone Age people had likely more harmonious relationship with the nature than modern scientists Carson criticizes.
④ The author underscores Carson's reliance on a single perspective in human's relationship with the nature.

가톨릭대학교

▶ 2025학년도 인문계 A형 ▶ 문항 수: 40문항 | 제한시간: 90분

2025 가톨릭대 인문계 A형 영역별 문항 수

구분	문법			어휘			논리완성	독해	생활영어	총 문항 수
	G/S, W/E	정비문	재진술	동의어	반의어	유추				
문항 수	5						15	20		40
백분율	12.5%						37.5%	50%		100%

THE CATHOLIC UNIVERSITY OF KOREA

가톨릭대학교

- 2025학년도 인문계 A형: 40문항 · 90분
- 자연계: 영어 20문항, 수학 20문항 · 90분

인문 · 자연계 공통 영어문제 별도* 표시

01~05 빈칸에 들어갈 가장 적절한 표현을 고르시오.

01* Since most sociological research uses people as sources of information, sociologists need to be certain they are not invading their subjects' privacy; generally, they do so by assuring subjects of _____ and by guaranteeing the confidentiality of personal information.

① anonymity
② scrutiny
③ mobility
④ integrity

02 Extensive viewing of television violence may have a _____ effect on children. Children who watch violent TV programs many hours a week can be more aggressive and anxious.

① versatile
② mandatory
③ pernicious
④ benevolent

03 Genes and heritability play a part in why some people are at higher risk for an eating disorder, but these disorders can also _____ those with no family history of the condition.

① bolster
② exploit
③ afflict
④ remove

04. With billions of people online, ensuring that students use digital technology safely is _____, and while parental controls are a good start, students must learn to protect themselves.

① provocative
② dispensable
③ imperative
④ negligible

05. It turns out that the doctors often were not persuaded by the chatbot when it pointed out something that was at _____ with their diagnoses.

① stake
② fault
③ odds
④ a loss

06~10 빈칸에 들어갈 어법에 맞는 표현을 고르시오.

06. Modern rockets and space technology allowed scientists to send robot exploring machines to all the major planets in the solar system, _____ those previously distant and unknown worlds almost as familiar as the surface of the Moon.

① make
② made
③ makes
④ making

07. The coffee bushes grow for years without the need for farmers _____ the soil, and the surrounding vegetation offers valuable habitat to wildlife, especially birds.

① disturb
② disturbed
③ to disturb
④ disturbing

08 It was with the introduction of the foot-treadle machine in 1859 by the American inventor Isaac Singer _____ the sewing machine began to play a serious role both in the home and workplace.

① that
② what
③ who
④ whose

09* As cellulose is hard to digest, herbivores such as cattle and rabbits have relatively large, heavy digestive tracts _____ large amounts of plant material sit for long periods of time.

① which
② what
③ of which
④ in which

10* Over the past three years, the United States has enacted the Inflation Reduction Act, which _____ to pour hundreds of billions of dollars into low-carbon technologies like wind, solar and nuclear energy.

① expected
② has expected
③ expects
④ is expected

11~20 빈칸에 들어갈 가장 적절한 표현을 고르시오.

11 Rather than investing in expensive scientific equipment to predict earthquakes, perhaps scientists should spend more time watching their pets. Many researchers now believe that the behavior of certain animals might help them predict natural disasters. For instance, Chinese scientists in the 1970s thought that reports of farm animals running around in circles, and of dogs barking all night may indicate an impending natural disaster. They decided to evacuate the city of Haichin, which shortly afterwards was hit by a huge earthquake. Japanese scientists have also discovered that catfish become livelier several days before moderately strong earthquakes. Many scientists now accept that this cannot be _____. They believe the explanation may be linked to slight changes in the Earth's magnetic field.

① a pure coincidence
② an example of superpower
③ a natural disaster
④ detrimental to survival

12* Spacecraft missions throughout the solar system have resulted in a renaissance of interest and understanding about the formerly mysterious worlds (planets and moons) in this solar system. Celestial bodies once believed to have been life-bearing worlds have proven to be _____, while other worlds now hold out the promise of sustaining perhaps primitive forms of extraterrestrial life. Besides Mars, the leading candidate is the Jovian moon, Europa.

① disappointingly barren
② relatively fertile
③ surprisingly diverse
④ obviously static

13 The sciences were developing in most of Western Europe in the nineteenth century, particularly in England, France, and Germany. No one nation had a monopoly on the enthusiasm, conscientiousness, or optimism with which the tools of science were being applied to a variety of research problems. Yet, there was a significant difference between those nations. Science in France and England was limited to physics and chemistry, which could be approached quantitatively. Meanwhile, science in Germany included such areas as linguistics, history, archaeology, esthetics, logic, and even literary criticism. French and English scholars were _____ about applying science to the complex human mind. Not so the Germans, and they plunged ahead, unconstrained, using the tools of science to explore and measure all facets of mental life.

① skeptical
② unbiased
③ confident
④ enthusiastic

14* In Finland, saunas are located almost everywhere and play a role in the local social context. For example, they are often used as a gathering place for friends to discuss the local gossip and politics. The sauna _____. As an illustration, Finnish people may well have a beer as they cool off after a sauna and then call clients to finalize business deals. They may even discuss important issues that they have had difficulty resolving during the regular workday. There are saunas in other nations such as Sweden and Ireland. However, the distinction between the manifest or apparent functional roles and the latent, hidden, or symbolic roles of saunas in Finland is distinctive, if not unique, and beyond comparison.

① is frequently attached to homes
② is also used as a place to do business
③ turns into a holy place of equality
④ cherishes nature-focused values and customs

15 It's getting late in the evening, but you're feeling restless. You want to wind down after a long day by casually browsing your Instagram or Facebook feed when you're overcome by an all-too-familiar sensation. You see a friend has uploaded pictures of an elaborate dinner at a high-end restaurant. Another has recorded a beach sunset saturated with beautiful pastels. As you scroll through countless stories of your friends doing fun and impressive things, your restlessness grows. The emotions are hard to describe, but it feels like _____. It's an utterly empty feeling, and it's becoming increasingly common among social media users. This phenomenon is known as "the fear of missing out," or FoMO. With the social media's rise, the psychology of FoMO is gaining more attention in scholarly conversations because of its power to dominate the mental health of those who feel like they are on the outside looking in.

① a burst of excitement, joy, and contentment
② a weird mix of exclusion, self-loathing, and envy
③ a combination of fulfillment, relaxation, and satisfaction
④ a sense of indifference, self-respect, and independence

16 In the 21st century, most of the 17 countries in Latin America have celebrated their bicentennials. Compared with most of the developing world, Latin Americans have been independent for a long time. Yet _____. Among the countries in the region, some 250 constitutions have been written since independence and military coups have been alarmingly frequent. Since the 1980s, however, the trend has been toward democratically elected governments, the openings of markets, and broader popular participation in the political process. Where dictators once outnumbered elected leaders, by the 1990s each country in the region had a democratically elected president, except Cuba.

① political stability has not been a hallmark of the region
② a trend of left leaning politicians has been dominant
③ they have been frustrated by slow economic growth
④ there have been nagging disputes over international borders

17* Setsuko, a Japanese woman now living in the United States, had to spend several months in a hospital for a chronic illness. She became extremely depressed, to the point of feeling suicidal. Whenever the staff would ask her how she was feeling, Setsuko would answer that she was fine. The staff were unaware of her depression for weeks. It was not until she began to exhibit physical signs of depression that she was offered a psychiatric consultation. The problem was that Setsuko was culturally conditioned to be a good patient by not making a fuss or drawing attention to herself or embarrassing her family with complaints about being depressed, so she always reported that she was fine. The psychiatrist tried to explain to her that in this context a "good patient" was expected to discuss and report any and all problems or symptoms. Nevertheless, Setsuko still had to redefine her cultural role as a good patient in order to receive better health care. This case reminded us that both health care providers and patients _____.

① may operate out of an ethnocentric framework without realizing it
② should realize that treating patients is not always a matter of communication
③ must share a basic set of medical terms for effective communication
④ should be aware of restrictions in communicating health information to others

18* Pearl oysters filter water as they feed, with the result that the waters around a pearl farm are of exceptionally good quality. A single adult pearl oyster can filter up to 50 gallons of water per day and in doing so, remove a number of harmful pollutants from water including excess nitrogen. Excess nitrogen in sea water leads to the growth of algae, which lowers the oxygen levels in water, adversely affecting all marine life. Pearl oysters safely remove nitrogen from sea water during the filtration process and add it to their shell or tissues. This nitrogen helps oysters grow. Thus, pearl farms filter and purify sea water in their environment, which in turn leads to _____.

① an increase in algae blooms that help marine life
② reduced competition among marine species
③ making marine life healthier than before
④ decreased growth of pearl oysters due to nitrogen use

19. There are extreme difficulties in devising any objective criterion for distinguishing "original" thought from sufficiently sophisticated "parroting"; indeed, any evidence for original thought can be denied on the grounds that it ultimately was programmed into the computer. Alan Turing (1912-1954), an English mathematician, sidestepped the debate about exactly how to define thinking by means of a very practical, albeit subjective, test; if a computer acts, reacts, and interacts like a conscious being, then call it sentient. To avoid unfairly dismissing evidence of machine intelligence, Turing suggested the "imitation game," now known as the Turing test: A remote human interrogator, within a fixed time frame, must distinguish between a computer and a human subject based on their replies to various questions. The computer's performance in these tests reflects its "thinking" ability, determined by _____.

① how closely it resembles the parrot
② how objectively it describes the world
③ how effectively it mimics human emotions
④ how often it is mistaken for the human subject

20. Information has always played a central role in our economy — a simple fact that too often gets lost in all the hype about the information age. The total amount of information in existence hasn't expanded all that much in recent decades. What has changed is that the information _____. Many of the great technological advances of the twentieth century — telephones, radio, motion pictures, television, computers — have served to speed the flow and widen the availability of information. The arrival of the Internet is just the latest step — albeit a very big step — in a process that continues to unfold.

① has been mostly obtained on the Internet
② has become dramatically more accessible
③ can be recorded or stored in various forms
④ can be perilous to certain groups of people

21~30 다음 글을 읽고 물음에 답하시오.

> People who have never taken biology courses have been known to remark, "I don't want to lift weights, because if I build muscular tissue, I am afraid it will turn to fat when I stop lifting." Of course, muscular tissue is specialized for its contractile function, and does not "turn into" fat tissue, which is specialized for energy storage. As people age, skeletal muscles do atrophy or shrink over the years, while adipose tissue tends to grow. Some of these changes in body composition appear to be an inevitable part of the aging process. However, scientists believe much of the loss of muscular tissue can be prevented with enough exercise.

21 Which of the following is true?

① People ignorant of biology tend to think weight lifting doesn't help muscle building.
② The major function of muscular tissue is to preserve energy for our body.
③ It is not possible to stop the loss of muscular tissue by exercising enough.
④ The results of aging processes such as weakened skeletal muscles are unavoidable.

> In 1865 Gregor Mendel, an Austrian monk, wrote a paper that laid the foundation for modern genetics. Mendel was the first to demonstrate experimentally the manner in which specific traits are passed from one generation to the next and to use mathematics to analyze his data. He concluded that discrete, or distinct, hereditary units that passed from parent to offspring determined how traits were inherited. Mendel's findings were ahead of his time; their significance, and the hereditary elements he described, were not understood until the early 1900s, when the units became known as genes. In the monastery garden where he conducted his experiments, Mendel used the garden pea as his model organism. The plant is ideal genetic working material; it is easily raised and produces many progeny in a short time. It is also self-fertilizing, and its reproductive anatomy prevents accidental outside fertilization.

22* Which of the following is true about Mendel?

① While he presented what he had found in the mid 1800s, his theory was understood far later in the 20th century.
② At first he used the garden pea in his experiments, but later he used some other plants.
③ For him, the garden pea was ideal since it produced enough offspring, even though it was hard to breed.
④ The hereditary units he assumed are different from what the modern scientists call genes.

Everyone is overly busy during the holidays, and most of us want to spend our time shopping, decorating, or seeing friends and family, which leaves less time to cook healthy meals. Take defensive action several weeks ahead of time by cooking meals intended specifically for the freezer. You'll be thankful later when you can pop one of the meals into the microwave and turn your attention instead to writing out holiday cards with a personal message in each.

23* **What does this passage suggest?**

① To save our time during the holidays, it is a good idea to prepare microwavable meals.
② For your friends and family, holiday meals should be cooked in a more special way.
③ Give priority to preparing meals over shopping or seeing friends during the holidays.
④ Cooking healthy meals during the holidays usually requires a lot of time and energy.

In 1861, a fifty-one-year-old Frenchman named Leborgne was transferred to the clinical service of Paul Broca, a highly respected French physician. The long-suffering Leborgne had been hospitalized for at least two decades with a range of neurological ills, including epilepsy, loss of speech, and paralysis of his right side. Leborgne had been nicknamed Tan by the other patients because that was the only word he could say, and he repeated it over and over again. His ability to understand spoken language, however, was relatively unaffected. Leborgne had been a patient of Broca's for less than a week when he passed away. Examining Leborgne's brain afterward, Broca was at once struck by a rather large irregular lesion on the surface of the left frontal region. Located just behind the left temple, the portion of the brain is now commonly referred to as Broca's area. Today, neurologists classify a loss of language as an aphasia and the specific kind of language difficulty observed in Leborgne — a loss of fluent speech while retaining the ability to understand language — is known as Broca's aphasia.

24 **Which of the following is NOT true?**

① Leborgne suffered from neurological ills for at least 20 years.
② Leborgne's nickname reflects how limited his language ability was.
③ Leborgne was not able to understand language with loss of speech.
④ Broca's aphasia is a term that describes a specific kind of language difficulty.

A recent report from the McKinsey Health Institute found that one out of four employees worldwide experiences high rates of toxic behavior at work. While no work environment is perfect, a toxic workplace is defined as being disrespectful, discriminatory, distrustful and many times hostile. Ⓐ <u>Unfortunately, an unhealthy work culture negatively impacts employee productivity and well-being.</u> Ⓑ <u>What has changed since the pandemic is that employees are no longer willing to tolerate harmful work environments.</u> Ⓒ <u>In such a workplace, you might feel extreme tension, avoid speaking up for fear of retribution or even find yourself excluded from meetings for no reason.</u> Ⓓ <u>Even the U.S. surgeon general issued guidance stating that toxic work cultures are harmful to a worker's mental and physical health.</u> In fact, an MIT Sloan study revealed that a toxic workplace is the number one reason people are resigning. Workers don't just want a high salary, flexibility and work-life balance. They also want to feel psychologically safe at work.

25. Which order works best for the flow of the passage?

① Ⓐ-Ⓓ-Ⓑ-Ⓒ
② Ⓒ-Ⓐ-Ⓓ-Ⓑ
③ Ⓑ-Ⓓ-Ⓐ-Ⓒ
④ Ⓓ-Ⓐ-Ⓒ-Ⓑ

Penned by Aphra Behn, the first Englishwoman known to have earned a living through her writing, *Oroonoko; or, The Royal Slave* was published in 1688, at which time it was viewed as a progressive antislavery text. The novel follows an African prince as he is tricked into slavery by "civilized" English slave traders, and he ends up enslaved in a British colony in South America. There he's reunited with his love, whom he thought to have died at the hands of his former African king, and he is recognized by his enslaver to be of royalty and noble descent. However, acquiring his and his lover's freedom proves impossible after he is repeatedly told that the decision is not up to the enslaver but instead rests on the governor, who is back in England. The plot thus unravels in a tragic and grotesque resolution, leaving the reader questioning the morality as well as the rationality of the slave trade.

26. Which of the following doesn't seem to be included in Aphra Behn's novel?

① How Oroonoko became a slave and ended up in South America
② Where Oroonoko happened to meet his love again
③ How Oroonoko tried to regain his lover's freedom as well as his
④ Where Oroonoko met the governor and got set free

A seemingly innocuous plant, white snakeroot was responsible for the death of Abraham Lincoln's mother, Nancy Hanks. White snakeroot is a North American herb with flat-topped clusters of small white flowers and contains a toxic alcohol known as trematol. Unlike those who have died from directly ingesting deadly plants, poor Nancy Hanks was poisoned by simply drinking the milk of a cow that had grazed on the plant. Indeed, both the meat and milk from poisoned livestock can pass the toxin to human consumers. Symptoms of "milk poisoning" include loss of appetite, nausea, weakness, abdominal discomfort, reddened tongue, abnormal acidity of the blood, and death. Luckily farmers are now aware of this life-threatening hazard and make efforts to remove the plant from animal pastures.

27*. Which of the following is NOT true?

① The toxin in white snakeroot can transfer to humans through affected animal produce.
② Having "milk poisoning" can cause dizziness and imbalances in the body's chemistry.
③ Nancy Hanks consumed a small amount of concentrated trematol, which led to her demise.
④ Farmers are taking measures to protect livestock from white snakeroot exposure.

The term "vegetarian" didn't exist at the start of the Romantic era, but many literary figures of the time followed meatless diets. One of the characteristic ideas of the Romantic movement was a deep appreciation for the beauty of nature; for many Romantic intellectuals this was simply incompatible with eating meat. Mary Shelley, the author of *Frankenstein*, ate a meatless diet, and the book itself can be read as a kind of vegetarian manifesto. If you're familiar with the Frankenstein story from its film adaptations, you might recall that the monster is created using parts from human corpses. In the original, though, Shelley specifies that the monster's parts come not just from the dissecting room but from the slaughterhouse, a place she must have regarded with equal horror. Despite the terrifying circumstances of his creation, the monster lives harmoniously with nature, embracing vegetarianism like many Romantic intellectuals, saying, "I do not destroy the lamb and the kid to glut my appetite; acorns and berries afford me sufficient nourishment."

28 What can be inferred from the above passage?

① Shelley viewed meat consumption as a natural part of life that should be respected.
② The monster's harmony with nature is a direct critique of industrialization.
③ Shelley's description of monster creation highlights her disapproval of vivisection.
④ The monster's vegetarianism reflects Romantic ideals of harmony with nature.

The day following Thanksgiving — commonly referred to as Black Friday — has become one of the busiest shopping days of the year in the United States. National chain stores traditionally offer limited money-saving specials on a wide variety of goods in an effort to lure shoppers into stores. It is believed by many that the term Black Friday derives from the concept that businesses operate at a financial loss, or are "in the red," until the day after Thanksgiving, when massive sales finally allow them to turn a profit, or put them "in the black." However, this is untrue. A more accurate explanation of the term dates back to the early 1960s, when police officers in Philadelphia began using the phrase Black Friday to describe the chaos that resulted when large numbers of suburban tourists came into the city to begin their holiday shopping. The huge crowds created a headache for the police, who worked longer shifts than usual as they dealt with traffic jams, accidents, shoplifting, and other issues. Within a few years, the term Black Friday had taken root in Philadelphia. City merchants attempted to put a prettier face on the day by calling it "Big Friday."

29 Which of the following is NOT true about Black Friday?

① The negative image of Black Friday came from huge crowds and frenzied shopping.
② Black Friday originally referred to businesses' financial losses before the shopping rush.
③ The police coined the term Black Friday to describe the disorder caused by shoppers.
④ Merchants made some efforts to rebrand the day as Big Friday to improve its image.

When we think of the polar seas, we always envisage a very hostile environment mainly due to two factors: cold temperatures and rough weather with extreme storms. Because of these, we always think that life there must be very hard for the inhabitants. But how wrong we are! In this situation, we are taking the human viewpoint, and indeed, life for human populations in polar regions is very hard because we did not evolve there and are not adapted to the harsh environment. Life for the local inhabitants, however, is no harder than it is for a sturgeon fish to swim around in a coral reef. If we took that sturgeon fish and placed it in a polar sea, it would die in a short time from cold. But if we took a polar cod and placed it in water at a temperature of 8℃, it too would die, this time from heat shock. All animals, both warm-blooded and cold-blooded, have evolved to make the habitat their own.

30* What is the main point of the passage?

① The hostile environment for human populations in the polar areas might be improved in the near future.
② Contrary to our common belief, life for the sea animals in the polar areas is not really difficult.
③ The polar seas are extremely productive and support an immense array of life in high concentrations.
④ Physiologically, there is no big difference between warm-blooded and cold-blooded sea animals.

31~32 다음 글을 읽고 물음에 답하시오.

The scientific study of animal behavior is often called ethology, a term used first by a French zoologist in the 19th century. Ethology is derived from the Greek *ethos*, meaning "character." The word "ethics" is also derived from the same Greek word, which makes sense, because ethics is basically about how humans ought to behave. ⒶUnfortunately, the word "ethology" is also often confused with the word "ethnology" (the study of human peoples), with which it has nothing in common. ⒷFor whatever the reason, the word "ethology" is not used as much as it used to be, although there is still an active animal behavior journal bearing this name. ⒸInstead of "ethology," many authors now use the words "animal behavior" or "behavioral biology" when they refer to the scientific study of animal behavior. ⒹAnyhow, scientists (and amateurs) had studied animal behavior long before the word "ethology" was introduced. For instance, Aristotle had many interesting observations concerning animal behavior. The study of animal behavior was taken up more systematically, however, mainly by German and British zoologists around the turn of the nineteenth century.

31 Which of the following is true?

① We can replace ethnology with ethics in various contexts.
② The term ethology is no longer used to refer to animal behavior in today's academia.
③ Ethology and ethnology have much in common in their meanings.
④ Both ethology and ethics originated from the same Greek word.

32 Which is the best place for inserting the following sentence?

In fact, the very word processor with which we are writing this book keeps prompting us to replace "ethology" by "ethnology"!

① Ⓐ ② Ⓑ
③ Ⓒ ④ Ⓓ

33~34 다음 글을 읽고 물음에 답하시오.

> Ordinarily, artists do not work with ready-made parts, but with materials that have little or no shape of their own; the creative process consists of a long series of leaps of the artist's imagination and her attempts to give them form by shaping the material accordingly. The hand tries to carry out the commands of the imagination and hopefully puts down a brush stroke, but the result may not be quite what had been expected, partly because the image in the artist's mind is constantly shifting and changing, so the commands of the imagination cannot be precise. _____, the mental image begins to come into focus only as the artist 'draws the line somewhere.' That line then becomes part — the only fixed part — of the image. The rest of the image, as yet unborn, remains fluid. And each time the artist adds another line, a new leap of the imagination is needed to incorporate that line into her ever-growing mental image. If the line cannot be incorporated, she disregards it and puts down a new one.

33 Choose the best one for the blank.

① However
② In fact
③ As a result
④ For instance

34 What is the main point of the passage?

① The artist completes her image by a constant flow of impulses between her mind and the material.
② Artistic creation is an exact step-by-step description that rarely allows any leap of imagination.
③ Transfer and projection of an image from the artist's mind is both joyous and painful.
④ We must not confuse the making of an art work with manual skill or craftsmanship.

35~36 다음 글을 읽고 물음에 답하시오.

In the United States and abroad, wartime has long involved knitters. Especially before women were involved in combat, they were encouraged to support troops from home by knitting necessary items for soldiers such as socks and hats. Since knitting was a very common sight, nobody would think of knitting as a suspicious activity. However, knitting and espionage had a fascinating connection throughout history. During World War I, a Frenchwoman named Madam Levengle acted as a "yarn-equipped informant" helping the Allies. She would sit in front of her window and knit, watching the movements of German troops from her window. She would then tap her feet on the floor to send codes to her children, who pretended to do schoolwork as they recorded the information unnoticed by nearby German marshals. World War II also saw knitters playing secretive roles. One such knitter-spy was Phillyis Doyle, a secret agent for Britain. She parachuted into Normandy in 1944 and chatted with German soldiers, acting as a friendly helper. But then she knitted messages to the British, which they translated using Morse Code. Knitting coded messages is a form of steganography, which is a way to physically hide messages. A specific combination of knit and purl stitches could be translated into messages. While knitting coded messages was less common than using knitting to disguise suspicious activity, codes in knitting were still a threat. In fact, knitting's role in espionage was significant enough that the U.S. Office of Censorship banned mailing knitting patterns abroad during World War II, fearing they could hide military secrets.

35. What is the main purpose of the passage?
① To explain how soldiers used knitted items as a part of their wartime equipment
② To detail the lives of women involved in knitting projects during wartime
③ To describe how knitting became a banned activity due to lack of yarn during wartime
④ To explore how knitting was used as a disguise for espionage during wartime

36. Which of the following is NOT a way knitters supported war efforts?
① Creating essential items like socks and hats for soldiers
② Knitting coded message using specific stitches
③ Using knitting needles as concealed weapons
④ Monitoring and reporting enemy troop movements

[37~38] 다음 글을 읽고 물음에 답하시오.

The forerunners of the modern zoo, open to the public and grounded in science, took shape in the 19th century. Public zoos sprang up across Europe, many modeled on the London Zoo in Regent's Park. Ostensibly places for genteel amusement and edification, zoos expanded beyond big and fearsome animals to include reptile houses, aviaries and insectariums. Living collections were often presented in taxonomic order, with various species of the same family grouped together, for comparative study. The first zoos housed animals behind metal bars in spartan cages. But relatively early in their evolution, a German exotic animal importer named Carl Hagenbeck changed the way wild animals were exhibited. In his Animal Park, which opened in 1907 in Hamburg, he designed cages that didn't look like cages, using moats and artfully arranged rock walls to invisibly pen animals. By designing these enclosures so that many animals could be seen at once, without any bars or walls in the visitors' lines of sight, he created an immersive panorama, in which the fact of captivity was supplanted by the illusion of being in nature. Mr. Hagenbeck's model was widely influential. Increasingly, animals were presented with the distasteful fact of their imprisonment visually elided. Zoos shifted just slightly from overt demonstrations of mastery over beasts to a narrative of benevolent protection of individual animals. From there, it was an easy leap to protecting animal species. The "educational day out" model of zoos endured until the late 20th century, when zoos began actively rebranding themselves as serious contributors to conservation. Zoo animals, as this new narrative went, function as backup populations for wild animals under threat, as well as "ambassadors" for their species, teaching humans and motivating them to care about wildlife.

37 What is the best title for the passage?

① From Bars to Nature: The Evolution of Zoo Design
② Understanding the Role of Zoos in Science and Education
③ Wild Animals in Zoos: Ethics or Profits?
④ The Conservation Efforts of Zoos

38 Which of the following is true about the development of zoos over time?

① The earliest public zoos prioritized creating an illusion of freedom for the animals.
② Zoos originally focused on preserving endangered species and promoting conservation efforts.
③ A key innovation in zoo design involved replacing visible cages with hidden barriers like moats.
④ By the late 20th century, zoos abandoned their role as educational spaces for public engagement.

39~40 다음 글을 읽고 물음에 답하시오.

Ask a teenager about their day, and you'll likely hear a long list of classes, extracurriculars, and endless homework. This overloaded schedule often comes with visible anxiety: students pulling fire alarms during exams, breaking down in tears, or even fainting during tests. The relentless pressure to excel pushes many teens to sacrifice essentials like sleep, exercise, and downtime. It's no surprise, then, that over 25 percent of teens aged 13 to 18 develop diagnosable anxiety disorders, according to the National Institute of Mental Health. Even those without formal diagnoses often struggle to make it through the grueling school day. With mere minutes to shuffle between classes and little opportunity to recharge, our focus dwindles as the day drags on. Recess could be a powerful antidote to this unhealthy cycle. Research shows that physical activity boosts both physical and mental health, yet only 27 percent of high schoolers meet the recommended 60 minutes of daily exercise. If schools dedicated even a brief period to recess, students could relieve stress, sharpen their focus, and engage more fully in class. The benefits extend beyond physical movement; even those who opt not to run around would gain from a mental pause. Ⓐ <u>A short break to regroup could leave students feeling refreshed and ready to tackle academic challenges.</u> Ⓑ <u>In addition, mandatory free time could lead to increased trouble on campus if teens get bored and feel the need to "shake things up."</u> Ⓒ <u>Recess also fosters social and emotional connections that don't always happen in a formal classroom setting.</u> Ⓓ <u>It's a chance to blow off steam, recuperate from demanding classes, and bond with peers</u> — all of which are critical to mental well-being. Recess shouldn't be exclusive to younger kids; teens deserve the same opportunity to prioritize their mental health. After all, success in school isn't just about academics — it's also about fostering healthy, balanced lives.

39* Which of the following should be deleted for the flow of the passage?

① Ⓐ   ② Ⓑ
③ Ⓒ   ④ Ⓓ

40* What can be inferred about the author's perspective on the mental health of teens?

① Mental health issues among teens are overexaggerated.
② Schools should focus more on balancing mental health with academics.
③ Physical activity is a minor contributor to stress relief.
④ Students must learn to deal with and overcome academic pressure by themselves.

건국대학교

▶ 2025학년도 인문·예체능계 B형   ▶ 문항 수: 40문항 | 제한시간: 60분

2025 건국대 인문·예체능계 B형 영역별 문항 수

구분	문법			어휘			논리완성	독해	생활영어	총 문항 수
	G/S, W/E	정비문	재진술	동의어	반의어	유추				
문항 수	2			4			16	18		40
백분율	5%			10%			40%	45%		100%

KONKUK UNIVERSITY

건국대학교

2025학년도 인문·예체능계 B형: 40문항·60분

문항별 배점 01~20 2점 / 21~40 3점

01~04 밑줄 친 어휘와 의미가 가장 가까운 것을 고르시오.

01 Grassian does admit that Coupland is Canadian, but he insists that despite this geographical <u>aberration</u>, Coupland's writing appears almost indistinguishable from American fiction.

① expediency ② equilibrium ③ deviation
④ deterioration ⑤ hallucination

02 Slavery has been the norm in many societies throughout history, but in the modern world it has been <u>eradicated</u>, at least in its overt forms, in nearly every part of the world.

① manifested ② sophisticated ③ abolished
④ exemplified ⑤ revitalized

03 I can't quote the exact statistics for you <u>offhand</u>, but they're there for you to see in the report.

① interestingly ② immediately ③ insolently
④ invariably ⑤ inevitably

04 Small children can often feel supplanted in their parents' affections when a new brother or sister is born.

① stimulated ② repelled ③ replaced
④ supervised ⑤ supplied

05~18 빈칸에 들어갈 가장 적절한 단어를 고르시오.

05 To _____ is to be attracted by or to move in the direction of something or someone.

① garnish ② gulp ③ guide
④ generate ⑤ gravitate

06 To _____ is to be a perfect example of a quality or type of thing.

① exonerate ② exhibit ③ eject
④ epitomize ⑤ equalize

07 Albert Einstein stated that he would not have lent his _____ to the cause of the proponents of building the atomic bomb if he had known in advance that the Germans would not develop one.

① empathy ② fame ③ credibility
④ conscience ⑤ decree

08 Chemists _____ many organic compounds from petroleum, which is composed of the remains of microscopic marine organisms.

① construe ② synthesize ③ moderate
④ quantify ⑤ embody

09 The Hopi people of Arizona stress the institutions of family and religion. They emphasize a harmonious existence which makes the self-sacrificing individual the ideal. The Hopi individual is trained to feel his or her responsibility to and for the Peaceful People — the Hopi's own term for themselves. Fighting, bullying, and attempting to surpass others bring automatic _____ from the community.

① requisite ② rebuke ③ remission
④ reception ⑤ recount

10 Beliefs may agree with one another or they may clash. When beliefs clash, they induce an unpleasant state called cognitive _____, which the person tries to reduce.

① tranquility ② justification ③ distillation
④ suppression ⑤ dissonance

11 Anarchists believe that since people are autonomous agents, they should not allow themselves to be _____ by the restrictions of the state.

① emancipated ② constrained ③ deceived
④ circumvented ⑤ fascinated

12 The advent of three-dimensional printing has made once _____ fabrication of complicated plastic components possible for many individuals and companies.

① negligible ② ambiguous ③ lucid
④ illusive ⑤ implausible

13 There is a great sense of excitement in New York and it has a reputation for being 'the city that never sleeps'. The Big Apple', as it is sometimes called, feels alive, fast and at the centre of everything, with cars hooting, yellow taxis weaving through the traffic, brightly lit theatres, and restaurants busy late into the night. The city offers enormous _____. Some of the most expensive homes in the world are in New York City, but on the pavements outside are poor people without a home. It is possible to pay hundreds of dollars for a meal in a restaurant, or eat good, filling food for a couple of dollars from a street vendor.

① digression   ② contrasts   ③ harmony
④ opportunities   ⑤ enjoyment

14 At every step in our journey through life we encounter junctions with many different pathways leading into the distance. Each choice involves uncertainty about which path will get you to your destination. Trusting our intuition to make the choice often ends up with us making a suboptimal choice. Turning the uncertainty into _____ has proved a potent way of analyzing the paths and finding the shortcut to your destination. The mathematical theory of probability hasn't eliminated risk, but it allows us to manage that risk more effectively. The strategy is to analyze the possible scenarios that the future holds and then to see what proportion of them lead to success or failure.

① opportunities   ② practices   ③ purposes
④ numbers   ⑤ pictures

15 The mark of genius is the willingness to _____ not just the most likely solution. Reproductive thinking fosters rigidity. This is why we often fail when we're confronted with a new problem that appears on the surface to be similar to others we've solved, but is, in fact, significantly different. Interpreting a problem through your past experience will inevitably lead you astray. If you think the way you've always thought, you'll get what you've always gotten.

① explore all the alternatives
② value insignificant outcomes
③ respect others' exotic experiences
④ avoid misleading interpretations of others
⑤ stick to the most unique way of solving problems

16 All athletes can recall winning a big game or beating a tough opponent. Athletes also inevitably _____. Both successful and failing experiences offer feedback that can either help or hurt athletes' confidence. Optimistic and pessimistic athletes differ greatly in the kinds of feedback they more readily accept.

① envy other players' success
② experience setbacks and failures
③ accept all the results of the match
④ restrain negative attitudes to the opponents
⑤ try to show best plays in all of the matches

17 In the past there was little genetic pressure to stop people from becoming obese. Genetic mutations that drove people to consume fewer calories were much less likely to be passed on, because in an environment where food was scarcer and its hunting or gathering required considerable energy outlay, an individual with that mutation would probably die before they had a chance to reproduce. Mutations that in our environment of abundant food now drive us towards obesity, _____, were incorporated into the population. Things are of course very different now but the problem is that evolutionary timescales are long. It's only in the last century or so, approximately 0.00004 percent of mammalian evolutionary time, that we managed to tweak our environment to such a degree that we can pretty much eat whatever we want, whenever we want it.

① for example
② on the other hand
③ in sum
④ in other words
⑤ in consequence

18. In an experiment, subjects viewed a film of an automobile accident and then answered questions about events that did and did not occur in the film. For some questions, the English article *the* (the definite article) was used, as in "Did you see *the* broken headlight?" For other questions, the article *a* (the indefinite article) was used, resulting in questions like "Did you see *a* broken headlight?" Questions using *the* produced fewer "don't know" responses and more false recognition of events that had not occurred in the film than did questions using *a*. A similar result was observed when four-year-old children were interrogated about the contents of filmed commercials that had been presented a few moments earlier. "Did you see *the*....?" produced more false recognitions of objects that _____.

① they had often seen before
② matched their expectations
③ they did not like a lot
④ did not actually exist
⑤ they wanted to buy

[19~20] 밑줄 친 부분에 공통으로 들어갈 말로 가장 적절한 것을 고르시오.

19. Rigid school schedule and old-fashioned policies should not dictate the types of learning experiences students can and should have available to them today. Staying the course without adapting to bumps in the road will inherently result in failure. _____ avoids common pitfalls that disturb all types of change initiatives. Policies and normal procedures should act only to guide school function. They should not create a sterilized atmosphere where learning is anything but fun, relevant, or meaningful. It is more than OK to take a detour now and then to ensure that change is implemented strategically and with purpose. This will become a reality only if _____ is an embedded component of the school culture.

① rigidity ② reliability ③ normality
④ flexibility ⑤ sterility

20 The immune response is as self-sufficient as someone's heartbeat or breathing. Yet immunity as a built-in response has a gaping flaw in it. To find the flaw, pause and simply take a deep breath. Breathing is an automatic function, but you can step in and make it work willingly anytime you want. The same ability extends almost everywhere. You can _____ induce the stress response by going to a horror movie. You can alter your metabolism by exercising or changing your diet. The dividing line between what happens automatically and what happens _____ is not fixed. Choices matter, and thus the healing self comes into play. On its own the body knows how to survive; it's up to us to teach it how to thrive.

① reluctantly
② emphatically
③ forcibly
④ materially
⑤ voluntarily

21~22 밑줄 친 Ⓐ~Ⓔ 중 어법상 옳지 않은 것을 고르시오.

21 A tag question is appended to a declarative statement, as in "The light was green, wasn't it?" Typically, a tag serves as a request for confirmation of the Ⓐ <u>declarative</u>. In Brown's words, "The peculiar beauty of the English tag question is Ⓑ <u>that</u> it is semantically rather trifling, a request for confirmation, and it has such simple equivalents as *huh*? and *right*?" In fact, these simple tags are acquired very early by children, at about the time they use Ⓒ <u>two-word</u> utterances. Thus, while there are cases Ⓓ <u>which</u> tag questions do not solicit confirmation (e.g., Jackendoff's 1972 example: "Max certainly has finished eating dinner, hasn't he?," Ⓔ <u>said</u> with the falling intonation of a rhetorical question), for the most part they do ask for agreement.

① Ⓐ
② Ⓑ
③ Ⓒ
④ Ⓓ
⑤ Ⓔ

22 By the end of the century, the two fields of psychiatry and neurology had become Ⓐ <u>effectively</u> merged under the rubric of psychiatry. In both fields there Ⓑ <u>was</u> movement toward psychotherapy, a term coined by two Dutch psychiatrists in 1887. In moral therapy, stress was placed on Ⓒ <u>having</u> a therapeutic, one-to-one relationship between psychiatrist and patient in addition to the structured life of the asylum. Initially, neurologists thought Ⓓ <u>to cure</u> their patients by physical means, for example, by hosting excitable patients with cold water to soothe their supposedly overexcited nerves. However, neurologists began to recognize, with psychiatrists, that talking could help patients, Ⓔ <u>established</u> working relationships between doctor and patient.

① Ⓐ ② Ⓑ ③ Ⓒ
④ Ⓓ ⑤ Ⓔ

23~24 밑줄 친 Ⓐ~Ⓔ 중 문맥상 자연스럽지 않은 것을 고르시오.

23 Taking a long break in the middle of the day is not only healthier than the Ⓐ <u>conventional</u> lunch, it's apparently more Ⓑ <u>abnormal</u>. Sleep researchers have found that the Spanish biorhythm may be tuned more closely to our Ⓒ <u>biological</u> clocks. Studies suggest that humans are "biphastic" creatures, requiring days broken up by two periods of Ⓓ <u>sleep</u> instead of one "monophastic" shift. The drowsiness you feel after lunch comes not from the Ⓔ <u>food</u> but from the time of day.

① Ⓐ ② Ⓑ ③ Ⓒ
④ Ⓓ ⑤ Ⓔ

24 A key assumption in consumer societies has been the idea that "money Ⓐ <u>buys</u> happiness." Historically, there is a good reason for this assumption — until the last few generations, a majority of people have lived close to subsistence, so an Ⓑ <u>increase</u> in income brought genuine increases in material well-being (e.g., food, shelter, health care) and this has produced more happiness. However, in a number of developed nations, levels of material well-being have moved beyond subsistence to unprecedented Ⓒ <u>indigence</u>. Developed nations have had several generations of unparalleled material prosperity, and a clear understanding is emerging: More money does bring Ⓓ <u>more</u> happiness when we are living on a very low income. However, as a global average, when per capita income reaches the range of $13,000 per year, additional income adds relatively Ⓔ <u>little</u> to our happiness, while other factors such as personal freedom, meaningful work, and social tolerance add much more.

① Ⓐ ② Ⓑ ③ Ⓒ
④ Ⓓ ⑤ Ⓔ

25 다음 글의 제목으로 가장 적절한 것은?

One popular Victorian notion was that music gradually developed from adult speech through a separation of the prosodic elements from the syntactic. William Pole wrote in *The Philosophy of Music*: The earliest forms of music probably arose out of the natural inflections of the voice in speaking. It would be very easy to sustain the sound of the voice on one particular note, and to follow this by another sustained note at a higher or lower pitch. This, however rude, would constitute music. We may further easily conceive that several persons might be led to join in a rude chant of this kind. If one acted as leader, others, guided by the natural instinct of their ears, would imitate him, and thus we might get a combined unison song. Dr. Pole's original lectures, on which his book is based, were given in 1877, and bear the impress of their time, with frequent references to savages, barbarians, and the like. Although *The Philosophy of Music* is still useful, Pole shows little appreciation of the fact that music amongst pre-literate peoples might be as complex as our own.

① Philosophy Matters a Lot in Music
② How Music Evolves: A Possible Explanation
③ Imitation vs. Inflection: Two Elements of Music
④ W. Pole: A Revolutionary Figure in Music History
⑤ Why Appreciation of Music Influences Our Life

26 다음 글의 주제로 가장 적절한 것은?

If you look at the sky from a dark site, far from city lights, you can see the Milky Way arching over you, its diffuse stream of light interrupted by dark patches. These are interstellar clouds. The dust particles in them block starlight and make them opaque to visible light. Consequently, those of us who seek to observe star formation face a fundamental problem; stars cloak their own birth. The material that goes into creating a star is thick and dark; it needs to become dense enough to initiate nuclear fusion but has not done so yet. Astronomers can see how this process begins and how it ends, but what comes in the middle is inherently hard to observe, because much of the radiation comes out as far-infrared and submillimeter wavelengths where the astronomer's toolbox is relatively primitive compared with other parts of the spectrum.

① need to update the equipment to examine stars
② mysterious process of initiating nuclear fusion
③ difficulty in observing the formation of stars
④ limitations of astronomy in exploring the space
⑤ relationship between density and brightness of stars

27 다음 글의 요지로 가장 적절한 것은?

For teenagers and adults who want to learn new languages, baby studies may offer some useful tips. For one thing, researchers have found that it is far better for a language learner to talk with people who speak the language than to rely on educational CDs and DVDs with recorded conversations. When infants watched someone speaking a foreign language on TV, Patricia Kuhl, co-director of the University of Washington's Institute for Learning and Brain Sciences, found, they had a completely different experience than they did if they watched the same speaker in real life. With real speakers, the babies' brains lit up with electrical activity when they heard the sounds they had learned. "The babies were looking at the TV, and they seemed mesmerized," Kuhl says. Learning, however, did not happen. "There was nothing going on in their brains," she says. "Absolutely nothing."

① 어른들의 언어 습득과 아이들의 언어 습득은 전혀 다른 과정으로 볼 수 있다.
② 교육용 CD나 DVD를 활용한 언어 학습은 효율성이 매우 높은 학습 방법이다.
③ 어른들과의 상호작용을 통한 새로운 소리의 습득은 아이들 언어 습득의 출발점이다.
④ 아이들의 언어 습득은 녹음된 대화를 반복적으로 들을 때 가장 효과적으로 이루어진다.
⑤ 아이들이 언어를 습득하는 가장 좋은 방법은 실생활에서 사람들이 하는 말을 듣는 것이다.

28 글의 흐름상 다음 문장이 들어가기에 가장 적절한 곳은?

> This may be because additional food provides 'incorrect' cues to birds for timing of breeding.

In the UK, 40-50 percent of householders feed birds in their gardens, dishing out an estimated 50,000-60,000 tonnes of bird food each year. [A] Providing food in winter, when natural foods might be scarce, allows birds to survive food shortages, but it is not clear whether feeding year-round has a positive or negative effect on birds. [B] In the US, species that use bird feeders most frequently tend to be doing just as well as, or better than, species that use them more sporadically. [C] But some studies in the UK suggest that winter feeding can have a negative effect on following breeding performance, advancing laying date but decreasing clutch size and breeding success. [D] Feeders also change the evolution of birds, selecting for longer bills that are better at reaching the food inside, and changing migratory behaviour. [E]

① A   ② B   ③ C
④ D   ⑤ E

29 중세 융성기(High Middle Ages)의 유럽에 대한 다음 글의 내용과 일치하지 않는 것은?

In the early Middle Ages, Europe had a relatively small population. However, the population increased dramatically in the High Middle Ages, from 38 million to 74 million people. What caused this huge increase in population? It was mostly caused by the dramatic expansion in food production after 1000. The invasions of the early Middle Ages from outside had stopped and the peace and stability led to the increase of food-production. In addition, more land was cultivated as peasants of the eleventh and twelfth centuries cut down trees and drained swamps. By 1200, Europeans had more land for farming than they do today. Changes in technology also aided the development of farming. The High Middle Ages witnessed an explosion of labor-saving devices, which used the power of water and wind to do jobs once done by people or animals.

① 인구가 급속도로 증가하였다.
② 서기 1000년이 지나면서 식량 생산이 급증하였다.
③ 외세로부터의 침략이 멈추어 평화가 지속되었다.
④ 1200년 경의 경작지 면적은 현재의 절반 정도였다.
⑤ 수력과 풍력의 활용이 농업의 발달을 가져왔다.

30 밑줄 친 Ⓐ~Ⓔ 중 문맥상 자연스럽지 <u>않은</u> 것은?

The idea that enduring personality differences in temperament may have a significant influence on how people deal with short-term affective states has been around for a very long time. However, the Ⓐ <u>systematic</u> exploration of this relationship between state- and trait-aspects of affectivity and their links with social cognition has not been undertaken until quite recently. With the Ⓑ <u>accumulation</u> of experimental studies of affective influences on cognition, it became clear that many of these effects are highly dependent on personality and individual difference variables. For example, self-esteem and trait anxiety were found to have a Ⓒ <u>marked</u> influence on how people cognitively respond to short-term experiences of negative affectivity. Cheryl Rusting provides a comprehensive review and integration of the available evidence about the role of personality characteristics in Ⓓ <u>preventing</u> affective influences on cognition. According to the work reviewed by Rusting, some traits served to amplify affective reactions, whereas other traits tend to have exactly the opposite effect, attenuating and even Ⓔ <u>reversing</u> the cognitive consequences of affective states. Several recent experiments found that affect infusion into social cognition and behavior are significantly moderated by personality traits.

① Ⓐ ② Ⓑ ③ Ⓒ
④ Ⓓ ⑤ Ⓔ

31 밑줄 친 Ⓐ~Ⓔ 중 전체 흐름과 관계 없는 것은?

It's a sound you will probably never hear, a sickened tree sending out a distress signal. Researchers hypothesized that these sounds — vibrations produced by the surface of plants — were caused by a severe lack of moisture. Ⓐ They fastened electronic sensors to the bark of drought-stricken trees and clearly heard distress calls. Ⓑ According to one of the scientists, most parched trees transmit their plight in the 50- to 500-kilohertz range. (The unaided human ear can detect no more than 20 kilohertz.) Ⓒ Because some insects communicate at ultrasonic frequencies, they may pick up the trees' vibrations and attack the weakened trees. Ⓓ Researchers experimented on red oak, maple, white pine, aspen, and birch and found that all make slightly different sounds. Ⓔ With practice, scientists could identify the species of tree by its characteristic sound signature.

① Ⓐ ② Ⓑ ③ Ⓒ
④ Ⓓ ⑤ Ⓔ

32 다음 글의 내용과 일치하지 않는 것은?

Many species have languages; birds and baboons can warn others in their group of the approach of predators. But animal languages can share only the simplest of ideas, almost all of them linked to what is immediately present, a bit like mime. Several researchers have tried to teach chimps to talk, and chimps can, indeed, acquire and use vocabularies of one or two hundred words; they can even link pairs of words in new patterns. But their vocabularies are small and they don't use syntax or grammar, the rules that allow us to generate a huge variety of meanings from a small number of verbal tokens. Their linguistic ability seems never to exceed that of a two- or three-year-old human, and that is not enough to create today's world. Human language crossed a subtle linguistic threshold that allowed utterly new types of communication. Above all, human languages let us share information about abstract entities or about things or possibilities that are not immediately present and may not even exist outside of our imagination.

① 거의 모든 동물 언어는 지금 눈앞에 있는 것에 관한 것이다.
② 침팬지는 100개 혹은 200개의 어휘를 습득하여 사용할 수 있다.
③ 침팬지는 인간처럼 문법 규칙을 사용할 수 있다.
④ 침팬지의 언어 능력은 2세, 3세 인간의 언어 능력을 결코 능가하지 못하는 듯하다.
⑤ 인간의 언어는 추상적인 실체에 관한 정보를 공유하게 한다.

33~34 다음 글을 읽고 물음에 답하시오.

All design Ⓐ involves choice, and the choices often have to be made to satisfy competing constraints. Building a two-car attached garage beside a house Ⓑ that is only a single-car width from the property line presents a design problem with seemingly incompatible constraints. There are solutions but all involve compromise, which Ⓒ lead to a less than ideal solution. One would be to build the garage well behind the house, Ⓓ connected to it by a breezeway, but this would necessitate using considerable space in the backyard, where the driveway would have to be doubled in width, something that might be undesirable. Another solution would be to build a garage one car width wide but two car lengths deep. This two-car garage need not Ⓔ encroach upon the backyard at all, but it would necessitate moving one car whenever it blocked the exit of the other. The designer must always make choices within constraints, hard and soft.

33 윗글의 주제로 가장 적절한 것은?

① the necessity of compromise in design
② methods of separating competing constraints
③ the importance of using rich space in the backyard
④ efficient ways of building a two-car attached garage
⑤ the significance of adjusting incompatible constraints

34 밑줄 친 Ⓐ~Ⓔ 중 어법상 옳지 않은 것은?

① Ⓐ　　　② Ⓑ　　　③ Ⓒ
④ Ⓓ　　　⑤ Ⓔ

35~36 다음 글을 읽고 물음에 답하시오.

In the early 1800s, mathematician and physicist Joseph Fourier recognized that as the sun's energy or radiation passes through the atmosphere and strikes the Earth's surface, it heats up the planet. Without the atmosphere, though, the planet would regularly turn _____. Fourier was the first to recognize that the atmosphere insulates Earth from heat loss like a blanket. Then in 1859, scientist John Tyndall discovered something astonishing about one of the trace gases in our atmosphere — carbon dioxide. While the other major components of the atmosphere, nitrogen and oxygen, are essentially transparent to long-wave radiation, carbon dioxide is not. Carbon dioxide, along with water vapor, even in small quantities, absorbs long-wave energy, which is stored as heat. Several decades later, Swedish chemist Svante Arrhenius went further, suggesting that increased levels of carbon dioxide in the atmosphere could alter Earth's surface temperatures. Since that time, observations and experimental evidence have repeatedly confirmed these early discoveries.

35 빈칸에 들어갈 말로 가장 적절한 것은?
① frigid
② dry
③ active
④ oblique
⑤ extreme

36 윗글의 제목으로 가장 알맞은 것은?
① The History of Carbon Dioxide
② The Reason for Global Warming
③ The Role of Carbon Dioxide in the Atmosphere
④ The Relation of Carbon Dioxide to Long-wave Energy
⑤ Difference between Nitrogen or Oxygen and Carbon Dioxide

37~38 다음 글을 읽고 물음에 답하시오.

Risk plays an interesting role in terms of creative practice. Pushing the boundaries or breaking rules may Ⓐ <u>entail</u> risks. The results of this may be fruitful and Ⓑ <u>invigorating</u> but they may also be disastrous or wasteful. Flirting with risk means that the outcome is not guaranteed but also that aspirations go beyond the known and familiar, beyond the Ⓒ <u>extraordinary</u>. This pushing of boundaries takes place at many different levels from the production of single objects to a broader kind of experimentation with materials themselves, and it may therefore be identified as a mainstay of creativity at the everyday level. This kind of creative risk is illustrated by the comments made by a modern-day potter when confronted with a copy of the Skarpsalling vessel, usually considered the most beautiful and outstanding Neolithic vessel found in Denmark. In describing the vessel's Ⓓ <u>qualities</u> she said its shape was 'vibrating'. Asked to specify what she meant, she explained that the Neolithic potter had pushed the shape to its upmost, to just before it would Ⓔ <u>collapse</u>.

37 윗글의 주제로 가장 적절한 것은?

① impact of creativity in everyday life
② necessity of risk taking as creative practice
③ importance of breaking rules in modern pottery
④ use of creativity in the production of art works
⑤ danger of pushing boundaries beyond the known

38 밑줄 친 Ⓐ~Ⓔ 중 문맥상 자연스럽지 않은 것은?

① Ⓐ
② Ⓑ
③ Ⓒ
④ Ⓓ
⑤ Ⓔ

39-40 다음 글을 읽고 물음에 답하시오.

Visual attention works something like a spotlight, highlighting a part of a scene while leaving the rest obscured in darkness. Anxiety causes tunnel vision making it easier to focus on a threatening stimulus like a weapon. From an evolutionary perspective, this is _____. An ancient man spotting a lion in the distance while wandering on the savanna would want to keep the animal in keen focus and not be distracted by anything less dangerous. In the modern world, a modest dose of anxiety can help a student focus on preparing for an exam. A little anxiety can sometimes even help people solve problems — when analytic thought suffices. But if there is useful information outside of the spotlight of attention, then this narrowness comes at a cost. Focusing on a gun will lead you to the wrong conclusion if you can't broaden your attention enough to notice that it's a toy being carried by a child wearing a Halloween costume.

39 빈칸에 들어갈 말로 가장 적절한 것은?

① irreversible
② hilarious
③ logical
④ regressive
⑤ incredulous

40 윗글의 내용과 일치하지 않는 것은?

① 시각적 주의력은 보이는 것의 일부만 부각시킨다.
② 불안감으로 인해 위협적 자극에 쉽게 집중할 수 있다.
③ 현대사회에서 일정량의 불안은 문제해결에 도움이 될 수 있다.
④ 유용한 정보가 스포트라이트 밖에 있을 경우 시야를 확장할 수 있다.
⑤ 주의력이 충분히 확장되지 않으면 잘못된 결론에 이를 수 있다.

건국대학교

▶ 2025학년도 자연계 B형　▶ 문항 수: 영어 20문항, 수학 20문항　｜　제한시간: 60분

2025 건국대 자연계 B형 영역별 문항 수

구분	문법			어휘			논리완성	독해	생활영어	총 문항 수
	G/S, W/E	정비문	재진술	동의어	반의어	유추				
문항 수	2			5			3	10		20
백분율	10%			25%			15%	50%		100%

KONKUK UNIVERSITY

건국대학교

2025학년도 자연계 B형: 영어 20문항, 수학 20문항 · 60분

문항별 배점 01~20 2점

[01~05] 밑줄 친 어휘와 의미가 가장 가까운 것을 고르시오.

01 It is important to remember that authorities in the various fields of knowledge can be wrong; thus, their assertions should be examined <u>impartially</u> and not accepted uncritically.

① nervously ② miraculously ③ promptly
④ objectively ⑤ unanimously

02 Knowledge of the <u>nuances</u> of similar words allows a writer to choose the most appropriate word for each situation.

① details ② absurdities ③ conditions
④ contradictions ⑤ subtleties

03 In general, driving a motor vehicle in America is a widely <u>varied</u> skill. Every state has its own laws and guidelines on how to handle their cars.

① diverse ② respected ③ prevalent
④ prohibited ⑤ factual

04. A collection of signs that was nearly uniform was obtained from a new <u>delegation</u> of the Kaiowa, Comanche, Apache, and Wichita tribes.

① rebellion   ② reconciliation   ③ extinction
④ deputation   ⑤ prosperity

05. Wenders' belief that cinematography bears an <u>unimpeachable</u> witness to "things as they are" invokes a metaphysics of presence.

① irreproachable   ② inadvertent   ③ insincere
④ unpresumptuous   ⑤ unrepentant

[06~08] 빈칸에 들어갈 가장 적절한 단어를 고르시오.

06. A study of communities and brain size among living non-human primates reveals a strong _____ relationship between brain and social group size: the larger the brains, the bigger the social communities in which individuals live.

① problematic   ② negative   ③ physical
④ statistical   ⑤ biological

07. Hippocrates, the first physician, posited four body fluids ("humors") that when imbalanced produced various physical maladies. Hippocrates's theory, however, was more than just one that linked body fluids to diseases; it also included a role for emotion. The humoral imbalances thought to cause illness also, in his view, created characteristic and chronic emotional states — black bile led to sorrow, phlegm to sleepiness, blood to sanguine feelings, and yellow bile to anger — and thus Hippocrates linked affect and disease by virtue of their common antecedents. Hippocrates no doubt had the particulars wrong. Yet if we ignore the devil in the details and, instead, focus on the big picture, Hippocrates provides prescient guidance: He motivates to look for connections between _____.

*phlegm: 점액질, **bile: 담즙

① particular details and big picture
② emotion and humoral imbalance
③ diseases and personality type
④ blood type and personality
⑤ emotion and health

08 An ethical _____ sometimes faced by drug companies is whether they should sell drugs more cheaply in poor countries than in affluent countries, thus foregoing profits that would recompense them for the big cost of the research required to develop new drugs, or sell them at the market price and thus have sufficient funds to continue the development of new drugs.

① confinement   ② discrimination   ③ paradigm
④ dilemma   ⑤ pretext

(09~10) 밑줄 친 Ⓐ~Ⓔ 중 어법상 옳지 않은 것을 고르시오.

09 And here Ⓐ <u>lies</u> the rub for James. If emotions consist in our registration of the emotion-producing stimulus and in the bodily responses automatically Ⓑ <u>triggered</u> by the stimulus, then we may question if emotions actually cause behavior. If we feel Ⓒ <u>afraid</u> because we run away, then fear is not the cause of running away but a conscious state Ⓓ <u>what</u> comes along for the ride, as it were. The James-Lange theory of emotion seems Ⓔ <u>to be</u> quite consistent with the automation theory of the brain that James rejected.

① Ⓐ   ② Ⓑ   ③ Ⓒ
④ Ⓓ   ⑤ Ⓔ

10 One way Ⓐ <u>that</u> a writer can create engaging and entertaining articles Ⓑ <u>are</u> by learning to identify, write and place anecdotes. These tightly Ⓒ <u>written</u> mini-stories are delicious little bites that one editor describes Ⓓ <u>as</u> the "chocolate chips" of articles. They are as Ⓔ <u>much</u> at home in speeches, sermons, comedy monologues and books as they are in feature stories.

① Ⓐ   ② Ⓑ   ③ Ⓒ
④ Ⓓ   ⑤ Ⓔ

11 T. E. Lawrence에 대한 다음 글의 내용과 일치하지 않는 것은?

T. E. Lawrence (1888-1935) was an English soldier and writer. He began his career as an archaeologist, but in 1916 went to Saudi Arabia to plan and lead a successful military campaign against Turkish rule in the Middle East, as a result of which he became known as 'Lawrence of Arabia'. He described the campaign in his book *Seven Pillars of Wisdom* (1926). This brought him fame and a romantic reputation, but he disliked publicity and tried to escape it by twice changing his name. He died in a motorcycle accident in Dorset, England. The film *Laurence of Arabia* (1962) featured Peter O'Toole as Lawrence.

① 군인, 작가, 고고학자 등 여러 직업이 있었다.
② 터키가 중동 지역을 지배하는 것에 반대했다.
③ '아라비아의 로렌스'라는 별칭을 얻게 되었다.
④ 유명세를 싫어해서 두 차례 개명했다.
⑤ 1962년 오토바이 사고로 사망했다.

12 다음 글의 내용과 일치하지 않는 것은?

Our current medical world is based largely on averages. Not every drug, for example, works for every person, but if it works for even a moderate percentage of people, regulators often approve it. If you show up in a standard doctor's office with a condition that could be treated with the drug, generally there's a very simple way you find out if it works — by trying it. If you take the common blood thinner Warfarin and it helps, that proves it is right for your biology. If you are among the one in a hundred people from whom Warfarin causes internal bleeding and possibly death, you learn the opposite the hard way.

*Warfarin: 와파린(혈액 응고 저지제의 일종)

① 우리의 현재 의학계는 대부분 평균에 기초한다.
② 모든 약이 모든 사람에게 잘 맞는 것은 아니다.
③ 어떤 약이 대다수의 사람에게 효과가 있을 때 규제기관은 그 약을 승인한다.
④ 백 명 중 한 명은 와파린을 복용하고 죽을 수도 있다.
⑤ 어떤 질환이 어떤 약으로 치료될지를 알아내는 간단한 방법은 복용해보는 것이다.

13. 다음 글의 요지로 가장 적절한 것은?

Few accounts of early human evolution depict males being fathers or sons, and yet every single one of our male ancestors was both of those things. That's not to say that early human fathers put as much effort into hands-on child care as early human mothers did. But once the size of our ancestors' brains began to expand, it's likely that adult males began to live with mothers and children, and groups worked together to collect and prepare food. It seems to us that mothers would have needed help from adult males to get enough food for themselves and their larger-brained children. Chimp mothers are stretched to capacity finding enough food to keep their larger-brained babies alive. We reckon that australopithecine mothers could have managed if they had worked together and got help from their older children. But it's hard to see how mothers could find enough food to supply the calories needed to support the growth of even larger-brained youngsters while at the same time supporting their own larger brain. Males were the only possible source of the extra nourishment.

① 인류의 두뇌 크기의 발달은 충분한 영양분의 공급과 함께 이루어졌다.
② 초기 인류 사회에서 여성의 역할은 아이를 키우는 것에 한정됐다.
③ 초기 인류 사회에서 여성들은 협동 작업을 통해 아이들을 양육했다.
④ 인간의 초기 진화에서 남성은 추가적인 영양분 공급을 제공하는 역할을 했다.
⑤ 아이들의 두뇌 크기가 점점 커지면서 부모들은 점점 더 많은 식량을 찾아야 했다.

14 글의 흐름상 다음 문장이 들어가기에 가장 적절한 곳은?

A zebra is not very "typical" of all animals, especially if it has to serve as an example for insects, worms, and squid, as well as mammals.

Bacteria, like all other living organisms, live to multiply. ⒶThey will produce offspring as long as conditions allow, and they will adapt their lifestyle to the local conditions that apply, as long as this is within their capabilities. ⒷSome bacteria have a very limited repertoire of lifestyle possibilities, so that you always find them living in more or less the same conditions, whereas others are real universalists and can be detected in a variety of environments. ⒸIt would be silly to treat bacteria in general terms only, pretending they are all alike. ⒹLikewise, *E. coli*, which is probably the most generally known bacterial species, is not "typical" of all bacteria. ⒺWe can only pay respect to the true nature of bacteria if we recognize their diversity.

① Ⓐ ② Ⓑ ③ Ⓒ
④ Ⓓ ⑤ Ⓔ

15~16 다음 글을 읽고 물음에 답하시오.

In bipedal species, the big toe is no longer used for gripping, so it Ⓐ <u>aligns</u> more closely with the other toes, while the spine enters the skull from below, not from the back (get down on four legs and you'll understand why). Walking on two legs required rearrangements of the back, the hips, even the braincase. It also Ⓑ <u>favored</u> narrower hips, which made childbearing more difficult and dangerous and probably means that many hominins, like modern humans, gave birth to infants that were not yet Ⓒ <u>capable</u> of surviving on their own. That would have meant that their babies needed more parenting, which may have encouraged sociability and gotten hominin fathers more involved in child-rearing. There were many indirect effects of bipedalism, but we're not yet sure exactly why hominins became bipedal. Perhaps bipedalism Ⓓ <u>let</u> our ancestors walk or run farther in the grassy savanna lands that had spread around a cooling world in the past thirty million years. It also Ⓔ <u>restricted</u> human hands to specialize in manipulative tasks including, eventually, the making of tools.

*hominin: 호미닌(인간의 조상으로 분류되는 종족)

15 윗글의 내용과 일치하지 <u>않는</u> 것은?

① 두 발로 걷는 종에서 엄지발가락은 더 이상 움켜잡는 데 사용되지 않는다.
② 척추는 등쪽에서가 아니라 아래쪽에서부터 두개골로 들어간다.
③ 두 발로 걷는 것은 출산을 더 어렵고 위험하게 만들었다.
④ 호미닌 아버지들은 자녀 양육에 전혀 참여하지 않았을 수 있다.
⑤ 호미닌이 두 발로 보행하게 된 이유는 아직 확실하지 않다.

16 밑줄 친 Ⓐ~Ⓔ 중 문맥상 자연스럽지 <u>않은</u> 것은?

① Ⓐ ② Ⓑ ③ Ⓒ
④ Ⓓ ⑤ Ⓔ

17~18 다음 글을 읽고 물음에 답하시오.

The main meal of the day for most people is the evening meal, called *supper*, *tea*, or *dinner*. It is usually a cooked meal with meat or fish or a salad, followed by a sweet course. Some people have a *TV supper*, Ⓐ eaten on their knee while watching television. In Britain younger children may have tea when they get home from school. *Tea*, Ⓑ meaning a main meal for adults, is used especially in Scotland and Ireland; *supper* and *dinner* are more widely used in England and Wales. *Dinner* sounds more formal than *supper*, and guests generally receive invitations to 'dinner' rather than Ⓒ to 'supper'. In the US the evening meal is called *dinner*. It is usually eaten around 6 or 6:30 p.m. and often Ⓓ consist of dishes bought ready-prepared that need only to be heated. In many families, both in Britain and in the US, family members eat at different times and rarely sit down at the table together. Ⓔ Unless it is a special occasion, few people drink wine with dinner.

17 윗글의 내용과 일치하지 <u>않는</u> 것은?

① 'TV supper'란 TV를 보면서 먹는 저녁을 뜻한다.
② 웨일즈에서는 주로 저녁 식사를 'tea'라고 부른다.
③ 영국에서는 가족이 함께 식사하는 일이 흔치 않다.
④ 'supper'보다 'dinner'가 좀 더 격식있는 표현이다.
⑤ 미국의 저녁 식사는 이미 조리된 음식일 때가 많다.

18 밑줄 친 Ⓐ~Ⓔ 중 어법상 옳지 <u>않은</u> 것은?

① Ⓐ   ② Ⓑ   ③ Ⓒ
④ Ⓓ   ⑤ Ⓔ

19~20 다음 글을 읽고 물음에 답하시오.

> The trickster is a kind of hero, but Ⓐ he often does not seem very heroic. The trickster may have various names or various forms, but Ⓑ his predominant characteristic is guile in human relations. Typically, the trickster forges a contract with a dupe and then betrays Ⓒ him. He is a power broker who achieves his strength by violating the boundaries set by society. Or Ⓓ he tries to play a trick and is caught and disgraced. In this case, the trickster is also the dupe, and other characters in the story are seen as power brokers who punish Ⓔ him. Some stories represent a contest of two tricksters. Unlike European folktales, which usually have a happy ending, trickster stories typically end in disharmony. Many of the African-American folktales that did survive depict the adventures of a trickster whose behavior can be laughed at, yet learned from.
>
> *guile: 교활, **dupe: 얼간이

19 밑줄 친 Ⓐ~Ⓔ 중 가리키는 대상이 <u>다른</u> 하나는?

① Ⓐ ② Ⓑ ③ Ⓒ
④ Ⓓ ⑤ Ⓔ

20 윗글에 제시된 'trickster'에 대한 설명으로 올바른 것은?

① 그 어떤 영웅보다도 영웅적 면모가 두드러진다.
② 여러 이름만큼이나 다양한 성격적 특성이 있다.
③ 대체로 행복하게 끝나는 이야기의 주인공이 된다.
④ 때로 잔꾀를 부리다가 곤경에 처할 때도 있다.
⑤ 사회적 규범을 수호하여 권력을 얻게 된다.

경기대학교

● 2025학년도 일반편입 A형   ● 문항 수: 40문항 | 제한시간: 60분

2025 경기대 일반편입 A형 영역별 문항 수

구분	문법			어휘			논리완성	독해	생활영어	총 문항 수
	G/S, W/E	정비문	재진술	동의어	반의어	유추				
문항 수	10						20	10		40
백분율	25%						50%	25%		100%

KYONGGI UNIVERSITY

경기대학교

● 2025학년도 일반편입 A형: 40문항 · 60분

문항별 배점   01~10 2점 / 11~30 2.5점 / 31~40 3점

01~10 Choose the option that best completes each dialogue.

01 A: Why do I need to enter my phone number to sign up for this website?
B: It's just a way for them to _____ that you're a real person, not a bot.

① justify
② manifest
③ relate
④ verify

02 A: Who's going to be in charge of the new project?
B: The boss asked Tim to _____ responsibility for it.

① assume
② preserve
③ confront
④ challenge

03 A: How did you get that angry customer to calm down?
B: I managed to _____ her by giving her a discount.

① integrate
② attune
③ conform
④ placate

04 A: Did you know that job cuts were coming?
B: Not at all. I was completely _____ when I heard the news.

① flabbergasted
② whittled
③ admonished
④ consecrated

05 A: Why did the contract negotiations break down?
B: I blame the _____ of both parties. Neither would compromise.

① gallantry
② enthrallment
③ dormancy
④ intransigence

06 A: I'm stressed out about presenting in front of the class.
B: Just take a deep breath and remember to _____ your main points clearly.

① provoke
② encroach
③ articulate
④ delegate

07 A: Marie handles stressful situations really well.
B: I know. She always seems to _____ confidence.

① rescind
② exude
③ depose
④ dissipate

08 A: James Hardy has published so many novels in his short career.
B: I know. I can't believe how _____ he is.

① lenient
② irreverent
③ deferential
④ prolific

09 A: Would you like to become a manager someday?
B: Yeah. I'd really _____ the chance to lead my own team.

① abate
② anoint
③ relish
④ commend

10 A: The CEO saved the company from disaster.
B: Yes. She made some very _____ strategic decisions.

① vigilant
② shrewd
③ impudent
④ recalcitrant

11~20 Choose the option that best completes each sentence.

11 The dictator used national defense as a(n) _____ to justify a war of aggression that had actually been motivated by territorial ambitions.

① pretext
② imposition
③ epitome
④ venture

12 In an attempt to end the labor dispute, the government offered to make several _____.

① repercussions
② concessions
③ expeditions
④ premonitions

13 Bruce felt awful about spilling wine on Sara's new rug, though he had done so _____.

① inadvertently
② illustriously
③ inattentively
④ indiscreetly

14 To _____ a ComfyMan chair, pull the lever on the right side and lean back until the desired angle is reached.

① descend
② recline
③ reflect
④ curl

15 The company has a detailed _____ for handling customer complaints.

① transaction ② enterprise
③ procedure   ④ ratio

16 A skilled mediator can often _____ a tense situation before a full-on argument breaks out.

① defuse   ② exude
③ pamper   ④ obscure

17 The environmentalists were so _____ opposed to the construction of a hotel on the riverside that they staged sit-in protests at the building site.

① apathetically   ② blithely
③ presciently   ④ vehemently

18 Historical records suggest that much of the city burned to the ground in a massive _____ in the Middle Ages.

① secretion   ② emanation
③ conflagration ④ exoneration

19 Greater investment in social welfare programs is needed to _____ poverty in inner city neighborhoods.

① perturb   ② ameliorate
③ insinuate ④ ornament

20 Claims that the play *Pericles, Prince of Tyre* was written entirely by Shakespeare are _____, as evidence points clearly to there being another author.

① imperious
② clandestine
③ hypothetical
④ spurious

21~30 Choose the option that best completes each sentence.

21 The children _____ hardly believe their eyes when they saw the huge pile of gifts under the Christmas tree.

① should
② must
③ might
④ could

22 To reduce Cold War tensions, the US offered _____ in nuclear disarmament talks with the Soviet Union.

① engage
② engaged
③ engaging
④ to engage

23 The woman _____ as a waitress when she was discovered by a talent agent and offered a modeling job.

① was working
② had worked
③ has worked
④ has been working

24 A caricature is a type of depiction _____ the subject's physical features or other characteristics have been deliberately exaggerated.

① that
② which
③ in that
④ in which

25 In response to the economic crisis, lawmakers are considering _____ unprecedented stimulus measures.

① implemented ② to implement
③ having implemented ④ implementing

26 The monument was built _____ memory of the soldiers who had lost their lives during World War II.

① for ② in
③ from ④ about

27 After a song from his upcoming album was leaked online, the musician took steps to prevent _____ again.

① an incident from such happening
② such an incident from happening
③ an incident happening from such
④ happening from such an incident

28 _____ for his fine singing voice and strong stage presence, the actor excelled in the leading role throughout the musical's run.

① Selected ② Selecting
③ Having selected ④ To be selected

29 In response to the accident, the municipal government mandated that the company _____ employees with additional safety training.

① would provide   ② will provide
③ provided   ④ provide

30 The police chief pledged _____ to catch those responsible for the robbery.
① to do in his power was everything
② everything was in his power to do
③ to do everything in his power
④ everything to do in his power

31~40 Read the passage, question(s), and options. Then, based on the given information, choose the option that best answers each question.

> Abdominal bloating, heartburn, nausea, and gastrointestinal bleeding are signs that may all, individually or collectively, indicate the presence of a stomach ulcer. Ulcers often manifest early as bloating in the stomach area. Heartburn — a strong pain in the chest — is another possible ulcer symptom and should be checked by a doctor if it persists. Nausea and bleeding may also be indicative of an ulcer, particularly if the former is unexplained or the latter is accompanied by pain in the upper abdomen.

31 What is the main topic of the passage?
① Signs of ulcer treatment being effective
② Tests used to make accurate ulcer diagnoses
③ Indications of the possible presence of ulcers
④ Factors increasing the risk of developing ulcers

The medieval Faust legend — a story of a scholar who sells his soul to the devil in return for supernatural powers — has been recreated time and again. An example of this is the 1936 novel *Mephisto*, which is set in Nazi Germany. In this novel, the protagonist ingratiates himself with the Nazis to improve his social status. Another rendition is "The Devil and Daniel Webster," an American short story that was adapted into two films. In the best-known film adaptation of the story, a Depression-era farmer, out of fear of poverty, trades his soul for riches. Beyond these retellings, the Faust legend can be found in myriad cultural spaces, from opera and classical music to anime.

32 What is mainly being said about the medieval Faust legend?

① It has inspired numerous diverse adaptations.
② It resembles a large number of other legends.
③ Its source incorporated many cultural influences.
④ Its fame is based on the timeless nature of its story.

American artist Matthew Albanese is known for producing photographs of dramatic and oftentimes haunting landscapes. At first glance, these photographs appear to capture actual views of the natural world. However, upon closer inspection, these images take on an extraordinary, almost surreal quality. This effect is the result of Albanese's unique artistic process. Albanese starts by constructing miniature landscapes from random objects. Under carefully chosen lighting conditions, he then photographs these dioramas from creative angles, giving his small-scale models the appearance of reality. The real pleasure in his work comes when the curtain is pulled back, so to speak, and the viewer recognizes that the images represent stunning illusions.

33 What is mainly being stated about Albanese?

① His camera techniques reveal unusual aspects of nature.
② He simulates reality by using a unique artistic process.
③ His images are more realistic than actual photographs.
④ He makes common landscape views appear incredible.

All ants possess an acute sense of smell, enabling them to distinguish between numerous odors. Ants detect scents using their antennae, which are covered in a waxy coating composed of cuticular hydrocarbons (CHCs). These compounds serve primarily to stop the antennae from becoming dried out. Additionally, they help ants acquire important information from fellow colony members. When two ants touch antennae, each can smell the odor given off by the CHCs in the other's antennae. In some ant species, this odor is affected by environmental conditions. For example, an ant that spends time foraging in the sun will come to smell differently from one that remains in the nest. This information can help certain ant species coordinate their actions for the benefit of the colony.

34 According to the passage, what is the main function of CHCs?

① They keep ants' antennae from losing too much moisture.
② They enable ants to communicate about their activities.
③ They give each ant a unique individual odor.
④ They assist ants in recognizing others' roles in colonies.

35~36

During college, I was offered a part-time job at a plant nursery. Because the work seemed physically demanding, I wasn't looking forward to starting this job, but I accepted because the hourly pay rate was pretty good and because my dad said that the job would teach me responsibility. Although the first few days were tough, I quickly grew to enjoy taking care of the plants. Also, most of my coworkers were nice people, though I didn't exactly get along with all of them.

Eventually, I got really busy with school, and my grades started to fall, so I decided to quit my job to focus on my studies. However, I picked up some classes about plant science and later ended up switching my major. After I graduated, I got a full-time job back at the nursery, this time overseeing all aspects of the operations there. To my surprise, my part-time job had led me to a career!

35 Why did the writer stop working at the nursery?

① His pay was unsatisfactory.
② His coworkers were unfriendly.
③ He did not enjoy the nature of the work.
④ He was struggling to keep up with school work.

36 What can be inferred about the writer from the passage?

① His father got him the job at the plant nursery.
② He was pressured into working at the nursery.
③ His work at the nursery influenced his choice of major.
④ He regretted quitting his part-time job at the nursery.

37~38

In 18th-century Europe, the practice of reading in bed was frequently frowned upon. Newspapers even went so far as to portray it as a dangerous hobby, highlighting house fires that had been caused by people falling asleep in bed without extinguishing the candles that they had been using for reading. Although such incidents were exceedingly rare, reading in bed became synonymous with irresponsibility, danger, and moral failing.

Why was European society so troubled by reading in bed if it posed so little danger? Such reactions are common during periods of rapidly changing social norms. Before the 18th century, only those educated enough to read, wealthy enough to own books, and privileged enough to have personal space could consider reading a book in bed. As a result, reading was very much a communal activity for commoners, as was sleeping, since most families did not have the space to sleep separately. In the 18th century, this situation started to change. Standards of living improved, resulting in higher literacy rates, wider ownership of books, and greater space for sleeping alone — and reading in bed. As social norms were upended, many people naturally felt a sense of anxiety and reacted negatively.

37 What is the main topic of the passage?

① How the growth in popularity of reading in bed impacted society
② How people in the 18th century were dissuaded from reading in bed
③ Why many people used to have a negative perception of reading in bed
④ Why the most privileged people in society were opposed to reading in bed

38 Which of the following is NOT a change that occurred in the 18th century?

① Communal reading grew in popularity.
② Shared sleeping areas fell out of favor.
③ Literacy started to become more widespread.
④ Book ownership became increasingly common.

39~40

> Among the most controversial decisions made by US President Harry Truman was his decision to relieve General Douglas MacArthur of his command in 1951. The general had been in charge of US forces early on in the Korean War and had suffered setbacks at the hands of Chinese forces. While MacArthur wanted to strike Chinese forces directly, Truman was wary of a broader war and desired to bring peace to Korea through negotiations.
>
> American generals are expected to give presidents a frank assessment of military conditions and provide expert advice on military strategy. However, they are supposed to remain silent in public on overall military policy, as the president, in the role of commander-in-chief of the armed forces, is responsible for deciding on how to use the nation's armed forces. In defiance of this tradition, MacArthur openly advocated stronger US military action.
>
> The conflict between the two men came to a head in March of 1951, when MacArthur wrote a letter sharply critical of Truman to a Republican congressman. When this letter was read aloud in Congress, Truman felt that he had no choice but to act. Despite MacArthur's widespread popularity, Truman quickly conferred with other military leaders and replaced MacArthur with General Matthew Ridgway.

39 What issue initially caused the disagreement between Truman and MacArthur?

① Whether Truman should terminate diplomatic peace talks
② Whether MacArthur should publicly discuss military strategy
③ Whether the US should withdraw its armed forces in Korea
④ Whether the US should expand its military involvement in Asia

40 What can be inferred from the passage?

① Truman saw political risks in disciplining MacArthur.
② Most of Truman's generals opposed MacArthur's firing.
③ MacArthur fell out of public favor for attacking Truman.
④ Ridgway advocated expanding the war in Asia.

경찰대학

▶ 2025학년도 일반대학생 전형   ▶ 문항 수: 40문항 | 제한시간: 60분

2025 경찰대 일반대학생 전형 영역별 문항 수

구분	문법			어휘			논리완성	독해	생활영어	총 문항 수
	G/S, W/E	정비문	재진술	동의어	반의어	유추				
문항 수	4			5				30	1	40
백분율	10%			12.5%				75%	2.5	100%

KOREAN NATIONAL POLICE UNIVERSITY | 경찰대학

● 2025학년도 일반대학생 전형: 40문항 · 60분

[01~05] 밑줄 친 단어의 뜻과 가장 가까운 것을 고르시오.

01 A gunshot splashed the water high near the steamer, <u>ricocheted</u> towards the other flying ships to the north, and smashed a smack into matchwood.

① fizzled ② deflected ③ dripped
④ scorched ⑤ wobbled

02 It is hardly necessary to <u>enumerate</u> the authors to whom I am indebted.

① list ② ignore ③ abandon
④ confuse ⑤ disregard

03 Acquisition of a paradigm and of the more <u>esoteric</u> type of research it permits is a sign of maturity in the development of any given scientific field.

① obscure ② prevalent ③ permeable
④ translucent ⑤ outlandish

04 The girl was staring out through the open window with <u>dazed</u> horror in her eyes.

① clear ② stunned ③ vague
④ disinterested ⑤ indubitable

05 He became increasingly frustrated at not being able to express what he wanted to <u>convey</u> in letters that he wrote.

① relate ② imbibe ③ vouchsafe
④ dismiss ⑤ regurgitate

06 다음 대화의 빈칸에 들어갈 말로 가장 적절한 것은?

A: Did you see the email from the client about the project budget? They're asking for a detailed breakdown of every expense.

B: Yeah, I saw that. Honestly, I'm a bit skeptical. It feels like they're trying to find a reason to challenge our spending.

A: That thought crossed my mind, too. It's unusual for them to request such specific details all of a sudden.

B: When we respond, let's be careful. I don't want to come across as defensive, but we need to be clear that we've been managing the budget responsibly.

A: Agreed. We can start by laying out the numbers and then address any concerns they raise.

B: Thanks. We've stuck to the budget according to the agreement, so there shouldn't be any issues with how we've allocated the funds.

A: Exactly. But if they continue to push back, we might need to rethink some of our spending strategies.

B: I hope we can _____ without having to make any major adjustments. It's starting to feel like they're looking for ways to reduce costs wherever they can.

① hash things out
② throw in the towel
③ beat around the bush
④ burn the midnight oil
⑤ kick the can down the road

07 빈칸 Ⓐ, Ⓑ, Ⓒ에 들어갈 낱말로 가장 적절한 것은?

Some no doubt will argue that Roman art in any event scarcely merits serious consideration, and it is of course true that it was Ⓐ_____ indebted to the Greeks. Nevertheless, it did contribute original features of its own. Italian taste is secularly for the baroque; the Greek aim was rather to produce ideal types. The adjective "classical" Ⓑ_____ belongs only to Greek art. The practical nature of the Romans was reflected in their art. Instead of attempting to portray ideal beauty or abstract ideas, it tended to be realistic, representing various phases of everyday life. This led Roman artists to include subjects to which Greek artists were Ⓒ_____ indifferent, children for instance. It also explains why so much of Roman art is commemorative, and evolved forms, such as the continuous narrative picture, the better to describe outstanding exploits.

① strictly — ordinarily — heavily
② heavily — strictly — usually
③ usually — strictly — heavily
④ heavily — usually — strictly
⑤ usually — heavily — ordinarily

08 밑줄 친 부분 중 어법상 옳은 것을 고르시오.

Film and Politics in America developed from an interest both in the politics of the American film industry and in a generation of broadly social filmmakers ① <u>who</u> formative experiences were arguably those of the thirties, and who began working in Hollywood as directors in the forties. The object was to produce an empirically based book on the work of this group, ② <u>discussed</u> the films in broad historical context, and in particular with reference to the changing nature of the industrial and commercial process of filmmaking. What follows is a modest and by no means comprehensive attempt to discuss issues relating to the social and political content of American film — issues that ③ <u>have yet received</u> systematic study, at least for the period prior to the sixties. While there are clearly dangers ④ <u>in making</u> the individual filmmaker the focus, rather than the production system itself, and the broader codes and ideologies of film and their relationship to economic and political power, there are also some advantages of such an approach. The notion of a particular group provides a sample of films at the centre of the study that could then be examined in terms of ⑤ <u>that</u> Jim Cook and Alan Lovell see as the process in which this generation of artists 'negotiated' their relationships with the film industry.

09 밑줄 친 부분 중 어법상 옳은 것을 고르시오.

I accept the Nobel Prize for Peace at a moment when 22 million Negroes of the United States of America are engaged in a ① creatively battle to end the long night of racial injustice. I accept this award on behalf of a civil rights movement ② what is moving with determination and a majestic scorn for risk and danger to establish a reign of freedom and a rule of justice. I am mindful that only yesterday in Birmingham, Alabama, our children, crying out for brotherhood, ③ were answering with fire hoses, snarling dogs and even death. I am mindful that only yesterday in Philadelphia, Mississippi, young people seeking to secure the right to vote ④ were brutalized and murdered. And only yesterday more than 40 houses of worship in the State of Mississippi alone were bombed or burned because they offered a sanctuary to those who would not accept segregation. I am mindful that debilitating and grinding poverty ⑤ afflict my people and chains them to the lowest rung of the economic ladder.

10 밑줄 친 부분 중 어법상 옳지 않은 것을 고르시오.

Neurons are specialized for communication with each other. Unlike other cells in the body, nerve cells are ① excitable: They are powered by electrical impulses and communicate with other nerve cells through chemical signals. During the reception phase, neurons ② are taken in chemical signals from neighboring neurons. During integration, incoming signals are assessed. During transmission, neurons pass their own signals to yet other ③ receiving neurons. There are many types of neurons. *Sensory neurons* detect information from the physical world and pass that information along to the brain. To get a sense of how fast that process can work, think of the last time you touched something hot or accidentally ④ pricked yourself with a sharp object, such as a tack. Those signals triggered your body's nearly instantaneous response and sensory experience of the impact. The sensory nerves that provide information from the skin and muscles are called *somatosensory nerves*. *Motor neurons* direct muscles to contract or relax, thereby producing movement. *Interneurons* act as relay stations ⑤ facilitating communication between sensory and motor neurons.

11 밑줄 친 부분 중 어법상 옳지 않은 것을 고르시오.

What is Style? In reality the question is two-fold. One may have Style; and one may have a style. The former is general; the latter individual. The former can be taught and learned, for it is based on certain ① well-defined rules; the latter is personal — in other words, is not universally applicable. Not infrequently it is a particular application of those rules which gives the impress of originality. But correct taste must first be formed by the study of the noblest creations in the particular art that ② claims attention. In singing, as in the sister arts, the laws which govern Style must be apprehended and understood before Individuality can ③ be given full scope. Otherwise, ④ which to the executant would appear as original might, to correct taste and judgment, appear ridiculous and extravagant. A genius is sometimes eccentric, but eccentricity is not genius. Vocal students ⑤ should hear as many good singers as possible, but actually imitate none.

12~15 글의 흐름으로 보아 주어진 문장이 들어가기에 가장 적절한 곳을 고르시오.

12

Rather than tear down City Hall and replace it at an estimated cost of $500 million, officials are spending $153 million for a major rehabilitation of the eclectically styled 1928 landmark.

Like many structures in Los Angeles, the 30-story building millions know from the cop drama "Dragnet" has endured repeated hammering by earthquakes, particularly the January 17 Northridge event that measured 6.8 on the Richter scale. (①) A band of netting wrapped around L.A. City Hall prevents chunks of its fractured terra cotta exterior from falling to the street. (②) Inside the tower, stout steel rods stabilize the cracked walls of the evacuated 25th and 26th floors. (③) It will be the tallest office building ever to be retrofitted with earthquake-resistant features. (④) A major element of the project involves jacking up the steel-framed building's 430 vertical columns a few at a time, and inserting layered steel-and-rubber base isolators that will allow the entire structure to move laterally by as much as 18 inches. (⑤) A four-foot-wide underground moat around the building's perimeter will separate it from seismic motion in the surrounding earth.

13

Thus the tradition of English literature began, though the language of the church and of learning was still Latin.

A key cultural landmark in the Old English period had been the bringing of Christianity to the pagan Anglo-Saxons. (①) This was accomplished first by the mission of St. Augustine, who arrived in Kent from Rome with 40 monks in 597, and then by the efforts of Celtic missionaries originating in Ireland, who began their work in the north in the 620s. (②) By the end of the 7th century, all of England was effectively Christianized. (③) Nevertheless, echoes of the old pagan ways remained; the names of four weekdays, for instance, commemorate pagan gods — Tiw in Tuesday, Woden in Wednesday, Thor in Thursday, and Frig in Friday — and Easter is the name of an old pagan festival. (④) With Christianity came literacy, and Christian monks for the first time used the Latin alphabet to write down the English language in the early 7th century. (⑤) England in the later 7th and 8th centuries became renowned throughout Europe for its Christian scholarship.

14

This architectural treatment held its own through every change of taste until the second quarter of the present century.

In the middle ages, when warfare and brigandage shaped the conditions of life, and men camped in their castles much as they did in their tents, it was natural that decorations should be portable, and that the naked walls of the medieval chamber should be hung with arras, while a *ciel*, or ceiling, of cloth stretched across the open timbers of its roof. (①) When life became more secure, and when the Italian conquests of the Valois had acquainted men north of the Alps with the spirit of classic tradition, proportion and the relation of voids to masses gradually came to be regarded as the chief decorative values of the interior. (②) Portable hangings were in consequence replaced by architectural ornament: in other words, the architecture of the room became its decoration. (③) But since then various influences have combined to sever the natural connection between the outside of the modern house and its interior. (④) In the average house the architect's task seems virtually confined to the elevations and floor-plan.

(⑤) The designing of what are today regarded as insignificant details, such as mouldings, architraves, and cornices, has become a perfunctory work, hurried over and unregarded; and when this work is done, the upholsterer is called in to "decorate" and furnish the rooms.

15

Most people see the problem of love primarily as that of being loved, rather than that of loving, of one's capacity to love.

Is love an art? Then it requires knowledge and effort. Or is love a pleasant sensation, which to experience is a matter of chance, something one "falls into" if one is lucky? (①) Not that people think that love is not important. They are starved for it; they watch endless numbers of films about happy and unhappy love stories, they listen to hundreds of trashy songs about love — yet hardly anyone thinks that there is anything that needs to be learned about love. (②) This peculiar attitude is based on several premises which either singly or combined tend to uphold it. (③) Hence the problem to them is how to be loved, how to be lovable. (④) In pursuit of this aim they follow several paths. One, which is especially used by men, is to be successful, to be as powerful and rich as the social margin of one's position permits. (⑤) Another, used especially by women, is to make oneself attractive, by cultivating one's body, dress, etc.

16~19. 주어진 글 다음에 이어질 글의 순서로 가장 적절한 것을 고르시오.

16

On September 12, 1960, John F. Kennedy, the Democratic candidate for president, gave a speech in Houston, Texas, on the role of religion in politics. The "religious issue" had dogged his campaign.

A. "I believe in a president whose religious views are his own private affair," Kennedy stated. "Whatever issue may come before me as president — on birth control, divorce, censorship, gambling or any other subject — I will make my decision . . . in accordance with what my conscience tells me to be the national interest, and without regard to outside religious pressures or dictates."

B. Kennedy was a Catholic, and no Catholic had ever been elected president. Some voters harbored unspoken prejudice; others voiced the fear that Kennedy would be beholden to the Vatican in the conduct of his office or might impose Catholic doctrine on public policy.

C. Hoping to lay these fears to rest, Kennedy agreed to speak to a gathering of Protestant ministers about the role his religion would play in his presidency, should he be elected. His answer was simple: none. His religious faith was a private matter and would have no bearing on his public responsibilities.

① A — C — B
② B — A — C
③ B — C — A
④ C — A — B
⑤ C — B — A

17

Unlike most other terrestrial quadrupeds of America, so long as he could roam at will the buffalo had settled migratory habits.

A Thus it happened that nearly the whole of the great range south of the Saskatchewan was occupied by buffaloes even in winter. The movement north began with the return of mild weather in the early spring. Undoubtedly this northward migration was to escape the heat of their southern winter range rather than to find better pasture; for as a grazing country for cattle all the year round, Texas is hardly surpassed, except where it is overstocked.

B At the approach of winter the whole great system of herds which ranged from the Peace River to the Indian Territory moved south a few hundred miles, and wintered under more favorable circumstances than each band would have experienced at its farthest north.

C While the elk and black-tail deer change their altitude twice a year, in conformity with the approach and disappearance of winter, the buffalo makes a radical change of latitude. This was most noticeable in the great western pasture region, where the herds were most numerous and their movements most easily observed.

① A — C — B
② B — A — C
③ B — C — A
④ C — A — B
⑤ C — B — A

18

Sometimes the way to make progress on a topic is to turn your back on it for a few years. At least I hope so, because I have just returned to the frame problem after several years of concentrating on other topics.

A He insists that angels with all the time in the world to get things right would still be beset by the frame problem. I am not convinced; at least I don't see why this would be a *motivated* problem for such lucky beings — unless perhaps Satan offers them a prize for "describing the world in 25 words or less."

B It seems to me that I may have picked up a few odds and ends that shed light on the issues. Perhaps it is true, as Patrick Hayes has claimed, that the frame problem really has nothing directly to do with time pressure.

C I still see the frame problem as arising most naturally and inevitably as a problem of finding a *useful*, compact representation of the world — providing actual *anticipations in real time* for purposes of planning and control.

① A — C — B
② B — A — C
③ B — C — A
④ C — A — B
⑤ C — B — A

19

The allegations that the US government helped to cause 9/11 are reflected in conspiracy theories that one can easily find on Internet and social media. Large groups of concerned citizens — such as the "9/11-for-truth" movement — made documentaries, published books and articles, and organized rallies to convince the public that the US government is withholding the truth about these events.

A Other variants make allegations of a more active role for the US government and propose that public officials directly organized and carried out these attacks. These latter conspiracy theories often portray the 9/11 strikes as a "false-flag operation" — an attack that was designed to look as if it were carried out by other countries or organizations in order to justify far-reaching actions such as war.

B These false-flag 9/11 conspiracy theories are well known for claims such as that the airplanes were remote-controlled, that explosives caused the destruction of the Twin Towers, that the Pentagon was hit by a rocket instead of a passenger plane, and so on.

C Furthermore, there are many different variants of 9/11 conspiracy theories. The relatively "milder" variants propose that the US government is merely an accessary, and for instance assume that public officials knew that the terrorist strikes were coming yet deliberately failed to prevent them.

① A — C — B
② B — A — C
③ B — C — A
④ C — A — B
⑤ C — B — A

20~23 다음 글에서 전체 흐름과 관계 없는 문장을 고르시오.

20

It may seem that with scientific management there is not the same incentive for the workman to use his ingenuity in devising new and better methods of doing the work, as well as in improving his implements, that there is with the old type of management. It is true that with scientific management the workman is not allowed to use whatever implements and methods he sees fit in the daily practice of his work. ① Every encouragement, however, should be given him to suggest improvements, both in methods and in implements. ② And whenever a workman proposes an improvement, it should be the policy of the management to make a careful analysis of the new method, and if necessary conduct a series of experiments to determine accurately the relative merit of the new suggestion and of the old standard. ③ And whenever the new method is found to be markedly superior to the old, it should be adopted as the standard for the whole establishment. ④ Some workers prefer traditional methods due to the greater autonomy they experience compared to structured systems. ⑤ The workman should be given the full credit for the improvement, and should be paid a cash premium as a reward for his ingenuity. In this way the true initiative of the workmen is better attained under scientific management than under the old individual plan.

21
At the Smithsonian National Museum of African American History and Culture, curators engage with a public that brings varied relationships to the institution of American slavery. ① One challenge is to bring the scale of the institution, and its seeming distance in time, to life. ② Foregrounding the physicality of enslavement is a primary focus for exhibitions on the ground floor, where curators carefully arrange relics to demonstrate the constraints of enslavement on the individual man, woman, or child. ③ Tools used for physical confinement, instruments for punishment, and machines used to automate key features of preparing cash crops for markets are documented and exhibited alongside a carefully paced and curated narrative. ④ Slaveowners felt entitled to and often received compensation from local, colonial and state legislatures, especially in times of crisis — when enslaved women and men ran away, participated in rebellions or were executed for crimes. ⑤ The tools range from child-sized chattels to chains to a cotton gin. The narrative of African enslavement is delivered through citations from Thomas Jefferson's writing, alongside testimonials from individual slaves, who articulate their lived experience in regard to legislative decisions that render them property, rather than persons or citizens, in a newly born republic.

22
The rapid growth of industrialisation and urbanisation — the outward signs of modernity — encouraged the articulation of the nation as whole and unified in order that production and economic growth could develop around common goals, shared beliefs and a sense of cohesion. ① If in reality this never existed, there was a persistent emphasis upon the 'melting pot' as a way of bringing people together into the American nation. ② However, with the questioning of modernity and its values and the increasing rediscovery of ethnic, marginalised and minority histories in America, this semblance of unity has had to be revised. ③ Traditionally in America, male, white, heterosexual stories and versions of history have emerged as dominant ideological culture. ④ American identity is constructed through a wide range of competing forces or 'heterogeneous dialogues', as parts of 'the infinitely varied mutual contest of sameness and difference'. ⑤ The modern universalising tendencies that sought to identify national traits, beliefs and values and call them identity, can no longer be accorded under these conditions of 'reinterpretation, modification, transformation and challenge'. There is a tension between the conventional discourses of American identity and a series of counter-discourses that question and critique the neatness and stability of just such a view of identity.

23

It is said that Sisyphus, being near to death, rashly wanted to test his wife's love. ① He ordered her to cast his unburied body into the middle of the public square. ② Sisyphus woke up in the underworld; and there, annoyed by an obedience so contrary to human love, he obtained from Pluto permission to return to earth in order to chastise his wife. ③ But when he had seen again the face of this world, enjoyed water and sun, warm stones and the sea, he no longer wanted to go back to the infernal darkness. ④ It is during that return, that pause, that Sisyphus interests me. ⑤ Recalls, signs of anger, warnings were of no avail; many years more he lived facing the curve of the gulf, the sparkling sea, and the smiles of earth. A decree of the gods was necessary: Mercury came and seized the impudent man by the collar and, snatching him from his joys, led him forcibly back to the underworld, where his rock was ready for him.

24 다음 글의 제목으로 가장 적절한 것은?

T. H. Huxley and Matthew Arnold represent two sides of a neo-Kantian division of knowledge. On one side lies a concern for facts and on the other a concern with values. Interestingly, Arnold thought one of the main functions of literature was to enable people to accept the burden of the results of science. In the end, Huxley and Arnold agreed to differ and remained good friends. Looking back, however, we can see them as representatives of wider tendencies at work. Arnold was intent on securing a normative role for the humanities in the face of the relentless growth of science. Huxley was a champion of the emerging scientific meritocracy and the self-made entrepreneurs of industrial Britain. The group to which Huxley belonged, which included the physicist John Tyndall and the social philosopher Herbert Spencer, wanted to forge a new secular society based on the scientific understanding of nature. A culture based on science had to displace that based on religion, and to do so, religious claims had to be dismissed as false and the clerical and literary elite ousted from positions of influence. This was the manifesto announced by Tyndall in his famous "Belfast Address," given at the Meeting of the British Association for the Advancement of Science at Belfast in 1874. Tyndall's proposed solution was a demarcation: science to explain the natural world and the humanities to inform and nourish our moral life and to satisfy our spiritual yearnings.

① Cultural and Scientific Critics United by Faith
② Science Fiction: A Scientific Response to Religion
③ Science-Humanities Divide in 19th-Century Britain
④ Nature and Culture in 19th-Century British Thought
⑤ Tyndall's Belfast Address: Bridging Science and Religion

[25~29] 다음 글의 빈칸에 들어갈 말로 가장 적절한 것을 고르시오.

According to Heidegger, the whole of *Being and Time* is concerned with a single question — the question of the meaning of Being. But what does he mean by the term 'Being'? What, if anything, does it signify? It is no accident that Heidegger provides no clear and simple answer to this question — neither at the opening of his book nor at any later point within it; for, in his view, it will take at least the whole of his book to bring us to the point where we can even ask the question in a coherent and potentially fruitful way. Nevertheless, he also takes a certain, preliminary understanding of Being to _____; so it should be possible, even at this early stage, to indicate at least an initial orientation for our thinking.

25
① be absent in the way most of us behave
② lack completely in any meaningful manner
③ be irrelevant in pursuing his line of thinking
④ offer no clear answers to his ultimate questions
⑤ be implicit in everything human beings say and do

What is art really and why does it appear to be so tightly linked with what it means to be a human? We are the only mammal species that produces art, and while it is important to us, it is in no way necessary for our physical survival. Still, the examples are numerous on how humans have risked, even sacrificed, their lives for the right to express themselves artistically. Art comes in many forms, from literature with its prose and poetry to sculptures and paintings, movie making, the composition of music, but also bodily expressions such as dance. But what is it that we seem so eager to express through art? By studying the various artworks over the millennia, a few themes keep appearing, namely that of expressing the human condition and our sometimes anxious deliberations over life and death, including the existence of a soul and similar ethereal phenomena. These are typically depicted in a contemporary setting, sometimes through metaphors that in particular will resonate with its intended audience, which will come in variations, and the many manifests of art do take different shapes and forms over time, culture, and geography, and in the past at least, they also came with _____.

26 ① mandates of theatrical art compliance
② guidelines for cultural narrative expectations
③ standards of athletic performance evaluations
④ requirements of aesthetic minimum standards
⑤ conditions for environmental sustainability plans

The creed which accepts as the foundation of morals, Utility, or the Greatest Happiness Principle, holds that actions are right in proportion as they tend to promote happiness, wrong as they tend to produce the reverse of happiness. By happiness is intended pleasure, and the absence of pain; by unhappiness, pain, and the privation of pleasure. To give a clear view of the moral standard set up by the theory, much more requires to be said; in particular, what things it includes in the ideas of pain and pleasure; and to what extent this is left an open question. But these supplementary explanations do not affect the theory of life on which this theory of morality is grounded — namely, that pleasure, and freedom from pain, are the only things desirable as ends; and that all desirable things (which are as numerous in the utilitarian as in any other scheme) are desirable either for the pleasure inherent in themselves, or as means to _____.

27
① the promotion of pleasure and the prevention of pain
② the acquisition of wealth and the escape from poverty
③ the pursuit of knowledge and the avoidance of ignorance
④ the attainment of power and the liberation from oppression
⑤ the cultivation of virtues and the achievement of moral excellence

During the years of the July Monarchy (1830-48) and influenced by Louis-Philippe's more informal lifestyle and the devotion of the royal parents for their children, the ideal of family life had taken a strong hold on the public imagination and become the keystone of bourgeois society. The care and education of children and the development of the infant personality became a matter of great interest. This preoccupation with the family and the child's role in it continued in the Second Empire under Napoleon III (1852-70), who with his wife, the Empress Eugénie, cultivated an image of _____. The same phenomenon occurred in Britain, where prints of Queen Victoria and Pince Albert playing with their offspring adorned the walls of many homes. It is this period from 1850 onwards, a period noted for its economic prosperity, civic improvement, and bourgeois self-assurance, that can be regarded as the most fruitful in the development of children's literature in the nineteenth century. The novel of domestic realism, or the family novel, developed from the moral tale of the first half of the century and mirrored the development of the realist novel for adults.

28
① family intimacy
② a happy mother
③ a dominant family
④ a flourishing group
⑤ middle classes' desire

The Columbus myths enabled white Americans to find a beginning, to declare a courageous opening to their 'story'. It was part of the influential dream myth of origin so prevalent in America. F. Scott Fitzgerlad's *The Great Gatsby* is aware both of the power of American dreams and the problems of seeking them out in lived experience. The ideals of endless progress, self-creation, achievement and success — _____ incorporated in the spirit of Columbus — are played out in the figure of Jay Gatsby as seen through the eyes of Nick Carraway. The novel concerns itself with issues of identity and in particular with the temptation to believe in a 'dream' which is manifested in Gatsby's yearning for Daisy Buchanan, a woman he almost married in the past, who encompasses 'the endless desire to return to "lost origin", to go back to the beginning'.

29
① the frustrated plan
② the fulfilled scheme
③ the unattainable aim
④ the fruitless longing
⑤ the mythicised dream

30~32 Ⓐ, Ⓑ, Ⓒ의 각 네모 안에서 문맥에 맞는 낱말로 가장 적절한 것을 고르시오.

Before Lise Meitner and Otto Frisch discovered the process of fission in atomic nuclei in late 1938, most physicists believed that using nuclear physics for practical purposes like energy production and weapons was utterly impractical, and indeed some Ⓐ relished / abhored this lack of practical application of their work. But with the discovery of fission, all that changed. The nuclear physics community in the United Kingdom and the United States immediately began not only to speculate about but also directly to Ⓑ investigate / disregard whether fission opened the door to practical use, whether enough neutrons resulted from the fission of a uranium nucleus to support a chain reaction, and what sorts of materials could be used to increase the likelihood of a chain reaction. By December 1942, Italian physicist Enrico Fermi Ⓒ created / restrained the first self-sustained nuclear reaction in a laboratory at the University of Chicago.

30

	Ⓐ	Ⓑ	Ⓒ
①	relished	disregard	restrained
②	relished	investigate	created
③	abhored	disregard	restrained
④	relished	investigate	restrained
⑤	abhored	disregard	created

The aqueous rocks, sometimes called the sedimentary, or fossiliferous, cover a larger part of the earth's surface than any others. They consist chiefly of mechanical Ⓐ remnants / deposits (pebbles, sand, and mud), but are partly of chemical and some of them of organic origin, especially the limestones. These rocks are *stratified*, or divided into distinct layers, or strata. The term *stratum* means simply a bed, or any thing spread out or *strewed* over a given surface; and we infer that these strata have been generally spread out by the action of water, from what we daily see taking place near the mouths of rivers, or on the land during temporary Ⓑ inundations / precipitations. For, whenever a running stream charged with mud or sand, has its velocity checked, as when it enters a lake or sea, or overflows a plain, the sediment, previously held in Ⓒ dissolution / suspension by the motion of the water, sinks, by its own gravity to the bottom. In this manner layers of mud and sand are thrown down one upon another.

31

	Ⓐ	Ⓑ	Ⓒ
①	deposits	precipitations	suspension
②	remnants	precipitations	dissolution
③	deposits	inundations	dissolution
④	remnants	inundations	dissolution
⑤	deposits	inundations	suspension

There is no one best way to teach elementary Greek or to learn it. Any successful course will Ⓐ impinge / depend on a complex interaction among the classroom teacher, the textbook, and the students, with their varying learning-styles and differing degrees of dedication to a challenging project. *Introduction to Attic Greek* was inspired by Ⓑ frustration / satisfaction with a standard textbook and began several years ago as a typewritten manual prepared as part of an Undergraduate Instruction Improvement Project at the University of California, Berkeley. In my teaching I have worked with students of all levels and been keenly aware of the Ⓒ gaps / skills with which many students arrive at advanced undergraduate and graduate courses. In writing this book, it was my desire to provide to the mature college student a reliable and relatively complete presentation of ancient Attic Greek.

32

　　　Ⓐ　　　　Ⓑ　　　　Ⓒ
① impinge — satisfaction — gaps
② depend — frustration — gaps
③ impinge — satisfaction — skills
④ depend — satisfaction — skills
⑤ impinge — frustration — skills

33 다음 글의 주제로 가장 적절한 것은?

Having kept a sharp eye on philosophers, and having read between their lines long enough, I now say to myself that the greater part of conscious thinking must be counted among the instinctive functions, and it is so even in the case of philosophical thinking; one has here to learn anew, as one learned anew about heredity and "innateness." As little as the act of birth comes into consideration in the whole process and procedure of heredity, just as little is "being-conscious" OPPOSED to the instinctive in any decisive sense; the greater part of the conscious thinking of a philosopher is secretly influenced by his instincts, and forced into definite channels. And behind all logic and its seeming sovereignty of movement, there are valuations, or to speak more plainly, physiological demands, for the maintenance of a definite mode of life.

① the superiority of logical thinking
② the flaws of modern philosophical reasoning
③ the interplay of instinct and conscious thought
④ how philosophers use logic to override instinct
⑤ the role of education in enhancing philosophical logic

34 다음 글의 요지로 가장 적절한 것은?

Augustine writes that "to love is indeed nothing else than to crave something for its own sake," and further on he comments that "love is a kind of craving." Every craving is tied to a definite object, and it takes this object to spark the craving itself, thus providing an aim for it. Craving, or love, is a human being's possibility of gaining possession of the good that will make him happy, that is, of gaining possession of what is most his own. This love can turn into fear: "None will doubt that the only causes of fear are either loss of what we love and have gained, or failure to gain what we love and have hoped for." Craving, as the will to have and to hold, gives rise in the moment of possession to a fear of losing. As craving seeks some good, fear dreads some evil, and "he who fears something must necessarily shun it."

① Love is constantly bound by craving and fear.
② The trouble with human love is that it is beset by fear.
③ Love consists in having lost our good and in enduring the loss.
④ Love is not the lack of possessing but the safety of possession that is at stake.
⑤ The lasting enjoyment for its own sake cannot possibly be the proper object of desire.

35 다음 글의 내용과 일치하지 않는 것은?

Born into a wealthy Roman family, Marcus Terentius Varro led a long and adventurous life. After studying under the pre-eminent scholar Lucius Aelius Stilo, he travelled to Athens to study philosophy. Varro returned to fight on the losing side in one of the power struggles in which Caesar eventually triumphed. He was forgiven and rose to a position of prominence under Caesar's protection, then fell precipitously out of grace under Antony in 43 BCE. Varro escaped death, but suffered the destruction of his private library. He retired to spend the latter half of his life reading and writing, dying at age 89. Estimates vary, but on some accounts he produced 620 books — granted that most Roman books are the length of modern chapters. Varro wrote on virtually every topic: astronomy, geography, agriculture, mathematics, law, history, philosophy, and language. He also left behind poetry, speeches and letters.

① Varro studied philosophy in Athens.
② Varro fought on the losing side in a power struggle.
③ Varro was forgiven by Antony and rose to prominence.
④ Varro is thought to have produced over 600 books.
⑤ Varro wrote on astronomy, mathematics, and language, among other things.

36 다음 글의 내용과 일치하지 <u>않는</u> 것은?

Where a matter directly involves criminal issues, much of the practical investigation is carried out by the police on behalf of the criminal justice system, a system in which a coroner plays little part in most jurisdictions. In these circumstances, there is a practical basis for concluding that the pathologist in fact is carrying out a service for the police investigators. In reality, a criminal investigation involves many phases. Traditionally, the forensic pathologist was involved in that phase of an investigation that was centered on a death or injury, and in particular the examination of an injured or deceased person to ascertain the nature and cause of their injuries. In practice, however, forensic pathologists play a wider role in the criminal investigation. For example, they may become involved in the examination of scenes of death, or in the examination of suspects who may have inflicted injuries on the victim. They may evaluate medical records for medico-legal purposes, and examine the statements of other witnesses with regard to medical matters. In practice, therefore, forensic pathologists have a wider role than just dealing with suspicious deaths. The vast majority of autopsies conducted by forensic pathologists involve unconfirmed natural deaths which society requires to be scrutinized and confirmed. The investigation of non-suspicious natural deaths, fatal accidents, deaths from suicide and deaths from other forms of intentional and non-intentional injury forms the vast majority of their casework.

① The police carry out much of the investigation involving criminal issues.
② Forensic pathologists traditionally focused on the investigation of deaths or injuries.
③ Forensic pathologists are often involved in the examination of suspects and scenes of death.
④ The majority of autopsies performed by forensic pathologists involve unconfirmed natural deaths.
⑤ The investigation of suspicious deaths constitutes the vast majority of the casework handled by forensic pathologists.

[37~38] 다음 글을 읽고 물음에 답하시오.

　　Human society, then, unlike animal society is mainly a social heritage, created in and transmitted by communication. The continuity and life of a society depend upon its success in transmitting from one generation to the next its folkways, mores, technique, and ideals. From the standpoint of collective behavior these cultural traits may all be reduced to the one term "consensus." Society viewed abstractly is an organization of individuals; considered concretely it is a complex of organized habits, sentiments, and social attitudes — Ⓐ_____, consensus.

　　The terms society, community, and social group are now used by students with a certain difference of emphasis but with very little difference in meaning. Society is the more abstract and inclusive term, and society is made up of social groups, each possessing its own specific type of organization but having at the same time all the general characteristics of society in the abstract. Community is the term which is applied to societies and social groups where they are considered from the point of view of the geographical distribution of the individuals and institutions of which they are composed. It follows that every community is a society, but not every society is a community. An individual may belong to many social groups but he will not ordinarily belong to more than one community, except in so far as a smaller community of which he is a member is included in a larger of which he is also a member. Ⓑ_____, an individual is not, at least from a sociological point of view, a member of a community because he lives in it but rather because, and to the extent that, he participates in the common life of the community.

37 윗글의 제목으로 가장 적절한 것은?

① How Community Shapes the Individual
② The Social Inheritance of Human Society
③ Human and Animal Social Structures Compared
④ Understanding Society: From Tradition to Modernity
⑤ Communication and Culture in Animal and Human Societies

38 빈칸 Ⓐ, Ⓑ에 들어갈 말로 가장 적절한 것은?

　　　　Ⓐ　　　　Ⓑ
① in short — However
② that is — Namely
③ in short — Namely
④ that is — Otherwise
⑤ in addition — However

39~40 다음 글을 읽고 물음에 답하시오.

The exact phonological and grammatical reasons for the existence of gradation — a term characterizing the way in which the Indo-European vowels *e* and *o* once alternated with each other and with zero in different grammatical forms or word classes — are largely unknown. It is possible that the variation between *e* and *o* in the root is due to variation in the placement of the accent, while absence of stress correlates with the zero-grade. In the classical languages and in Germanic, gradation often signaled change from one word-class to another; it also regularly accompanied paradigmatic change. The major function of gradation within the Germanic languages was to mark person, number, and tense of a large class of verbs, traditionally referred to as *strong verbs*. Without familiarity with the phonetic changes from Indo-European to Present-Day English, through Germanic, Old, and Middle English, the original *e-*, *o-*, and zero-grades of the verbal allomorphs are not recognizable today; we have come to label these verbs "irregular."

Gradation in word derivation was also a common Germanic pattern which became less and less _____ in English, but not in the other Germanic languages. Still, there are some fossils of this pattern in Modern English, as in the verb-noun pairs: *do-deed*, *sing-song*, *break-breach*, and *bind-bond*. Historical phonetic processes have changed the initial vowel grades beyond recognition, though the semantic relationship between the members of these pairs is obvious to every speaker of English.

39 윗글의 빈칸에 들어갈 말로 가장 적절한 것은?
① scarce
② succinct
③ notorious
④ redundant
⑤ productive

40 윗글의 제목으로 가장 적절한 것은?
① Gradation in Germanic Languages
② Why We Should Use Strong Verbs
③ How Word Classes Are Determined
④ The Evolution of Classical Languages
⑤ Various Phonetic Changes in Old English

KYUNGHEE UNIVERSITY

경희대학교

▶ 2025학년도 인문·체육계열　▶ 문항 수: 40문항　｜　제한시간: 90분

2025 경희대 인문·체육계열 영역별 문항 수

구분	문법			어휘			논리완성	독해	생활영어	총 문항 수
	G/S, W/E	정비문	재진술	동의어	반의어	유추				
문항 수				8			5	27		40
백분율				20%			12.5%	67.5%		100%

KYUNG HEE UNIVERSITY

경희대학교

2025학년도 인문 · 체육계열: 40문항 · 90분

01~08 Choose the answer closest in meaning to the underlined word or phrase.

01 Thanks to the generous contribution made by the outgoing CEO, the need for year-end fundraising has been <u>obviated</u>. [1.7점]

① compromised ② eliminated ③ exasperated
④ supplanted ⑤ accelerated

02 Contrary to expectations that the upcoming year's budget would be rejected, the various political factions <u>acquiesced</u> and passed the budget in one vote. [1.7점]

① delineated ② prolonged ③ recuperated
④ assented ⑤ emerged

03 The author disclosed in an interview that she has a <u>predilection</u> for poetry even though her published works in recent years have leaned toward biographical fiction. [1.7점]

① aversion ② disdain ③ partiality
④ contempt ⑤ supposition

04 There have been hundreds of thousands of videos on TikTok about Jane Austen and her work — many of them about her brooding romantic hero, Mr. Darcy.

[1.7점]

① attractive   ② pensive   ③ untroubled
④ respectable   ⑤ buoyant

05 Airports are not scary. They are purposely bland, simple to navigate, reassuringly similar. What's scary is the uncertainty embedded in any journey, a vague foreboding that informed the theory of a flat earth, which merely assumed the horizon was exactly what it appears to be: a precipice.

[1.7점]

① apprehension   ② desiccation   ③ aspiration
④ devotion   ⑤ contradiction

06 Most of the water at the bottom of the North Pacific Ocean has not been exposed to sunlight in at least 800 years and some of it has been down there for two millennia. Accordingly, oceanographers have assumed the temperature of the bottom layer is stable, impervious to atmospheric warming.

[1.7점]

① sensitive   ② accessible   ③ susceptible
④ immune   ⑤ responsive

07 In Britain a surge in demand from foreign students has created a huge boom in postgraduate education. Universities there now dole out four postgraduate qualifications for every five undergraduate ones.

[1.7점]

① hoard   ② conceal   ③ withhold
④ relinquish ⑤ grant

08 Quincy Jones, one of the most important drivers of 20th century pop culture, died on Nov. 3 at 91. A music producer, composer, and executive, Jones served as the connective tissue between many eras and styles of music. With his golden ear, inexhaustible work ethic, and devotion to both music history and new technologies, he defined the center of American pop music for decades. [1.7점]

① indefatigable ② measurable ③ depletable
④ unifying ⑤ constrained

09~11 Choose the best answer for the blank.

09 Romance is, above all, an emotional composition. It's a magic trick that turns words on a page into pleasure chemicals in the brain. The tropes and traditions of the genre represent hundreds of years of practice not simply mimicking the sensation and aesthetics of longing and release but actually _____ them in the reader. For the spell to work, you need the readers' total trust. [1.7점]

① repelling ② smothering ③ conjuring
④ thwarting ⑤ obstructing

10 The students did not mind it when the professor wandered from the subject. His _____ were often more interesting and memorable than the topic of the day. [1.7점]

① incantations ② peripheries ③ digressions
④ altercations ⑤ modifications

11 A big increase in residential solar and energy storage would help local utilities better manage growing demand and spikes in use, but the process of getting new systems permitted remains _____. Most utilities don't incentivize it or make it easy to install new systems and the need to get approval from numerous entities, including power companies and local governments, doesn't help. [2점]

① hopeful ② exemplary ③ improvident
④ cumbersome ⑤ utilitarian

12~13 Choose the best answer for the blanks.

12 Who is Bitcoin's founder, Satoshi Nakamoto? The question has Ⓐ_____ and excited cryptocurrency fans ever since Bitcoin was created by someone with that username in 2009. Fans have endlessly Ⓑ_____, debated, and hunted for clues across the web while investigative journalists have tried to unwind the mystery with no success. The answer matters because Satoshi's ideas are imbued with near religious significance — and because whoever it is owns about $60 billion worth of Bitcoin, which would make them roughly the 25th richest person alive. [2점]

① muted — rescinded
② dismayed — confirmed
③ assured — diverted
④ confused — worshiped
⑤ perplexed — theorized

13 In some respects, Japan is a lenient place. It has a low crime rate and locks up far fewer citizens than other rich countries. Minor offenders who admit guilt and apologise are often freed with a stern warning. But when prosecutors decide to go after someone, they have extraordinary powers. Unlike in other rich countries, they rely heavily on Ⓐ_____, rather than physical evidence: nine out of ten cases in Japan still hinge on the suspect's Ⓑ_____ of guilt. [2점]

① confessions — admission
② witnesses — retaliation
③ investigation — rehabilitation
④ proof — denial
⑤ arrests — judgment

14~15 Read the passage and answer the questions.

> In 2020, to manage its own pollution problem, Fiji implemented a ban on single-use plastics. Water bottles were notably Ⓐ_____, mainly because access to clean drinking water is limited outside the main cities. But also because banning bottles would be impractical for a country that exports them. Under pressure for sustainability issues, Fiji Water, the island's largest exporter, has started a bottle-buyback program. However, only 23% of Fiji Water bottles are returned on Fiji. It's an Ⓑ_____ rate, but still better than the global plastic-recycling average. Fiji Water's voluntary program is a precursor to a countrywide bottle-deposit scheme under parliamentary review. Kinks are still being worked out. Five Fiji cents might be enough incentive for residents to return bottles if they live near collection centers, but probably not enough for Ⓒ_____ to bring their plastics to a centralized location.

14 Which of the following is most appropriate for the blanks Ⓐ and Ⓑ? [2점]

① recognized — admirable
② exempted — abysmal
③ excluded — artificial
④ included — acceptable
⑤ traded — exclusive

15 Which of the following is most appropriate for the blank Ⓒ_____? [3점]

① Fiji Water employees
② overseas importers
③ government officials
④ water bottle producers
⑤ remote island communities

16~17 Read the passage and answer the questions.

Throughout these long millennia, day in and day out, people stood face to face with the most important invention in the history of energy production — and failed to notice it. It stared them in the eye every time a housewife or servant put up a kettle to boil water for tea or put a pot full of potatoes on the stove. The minute the water boiled, the lid of the kettle or the pot jumped. Heat was being converted into movement. But jumping pot lids were an annoyance, especially if you forgot the pot on the stove and the water boiled over. Nobody saw their real potential.

A partial breakthrough in converting heat into movement followed the invention of gunpowder in ninth-century China. At first, the idea of using gunpowder to propel projectiles was so Ⓐ_____ that for centuries gunpowder was used primarily to produce fire bombs. But eventually — perhaps after some bomb expert ground gunpowder in a mortar only to have the pestle shoot out with force — guns made their appearance. About 600 years passed between the invention of gunpowder and the development of effective artillery.

16 Choose the best word for Ⓐ_____. [2점]

① spontaneous
② expedient
③ propitious
④ counterintuitive
⑤ incontrovertible

17 According to the passage, what did people fail to do for a long time? [3.3점]

① Record the history of energy
② Contain heat energy in cooking
③ Cultivate experts in fire bombs
④ Invent gunpowder for warfare
⑤ Convert one type of energy to another

18~19 Read the passage and answer the questions.

It was the opening days of 2022, in the aftermath of a huge volcanic eruption, when Tonga went dark. The underwater eruption severed internet connectivity, causing a communication blackout at just the moment that a crisis was unfolding.

When the undersea cable that provides the country's internet was restored weeks later, the scale of the disruption was clear. The lack of connectivity had hampered recovery efforts, while at the same time devastating businesses and local finances, many of which depend on remittances from abroad.

The disaster exposed the extreme vulnerabilities of the infrastructure that underpins the workings of the internet. "Contemporary life is really inseparable from an operational internet," says Nicole Starosielski, a professor at the University of California, Berkeley. In that way, it's very much like drinking water — a utility that underpins our very existence. Very few people understand what it takes for it to travel from Ⓐ_____. Modern consumers have come to imagine the internet as something unseen in the atmosphere — an invisible "cloud" just above our heads, raining data down upon us. "Because our devices aren't tethered to any cables, many of us believe the whole thing is wireless," says Starosielski, but the reality is far more extraordinary.

18 Which phrase best completes Ⓐ_____? [3점]

① takeoff to landing
② the epicenter to the eruption
③ crisis to recovery
④ a distant reservoir to our kitchen taps
⑤ invisible cloud to atmosphere

19 Which of the following is the main topic of the passage? [3.3점]

① Underwater volcanic eruptions
② Permanence of human existence
③ Hidden cables that power the internet
④ Threat to the source of drinking water
⑤ Consumer misuse of wireless devices

20~21 Read the passage and answer the questions.

A strategy used by manufacturers to deliberately design or produce products with a limited useful life is called planned Ⓐ_____. Examples include smartphones that are no longer supported with software updates after a few years, printers that use chips to limit the number of prints, and fashion trends that change rapidly, making previous styles seem outdated. Planned Ⓐ_____ is considered bad for several reasons: it leads to increased environmental waste as products are discarded more frequently; it forces consumers to spend money on new products more often; and it can contribute to Ⓑ_____, undermining efforts towards sustainability. Additionally, it can limit consumer choice by making it difficult or expensive to repair products, pushing consumers towards a cycle of constant consumption.

20 Which word best completes Ⓐ_____? [2점]

① efficacy
② obsolescence
③ publicity
④ summation
⑤ volatility

21 Which phrase is most appropriate for Ⓑ_____? [3점]

① frugal consumption practices
② comparative advantages
③ a culture of disposability
④ a desire for exclusivity
⑤ improved socioeconomic status

22~23 Read the passage and answer the questions.

The Walt Disney Company's attachment to the appeal of innocence provides a rationale for Disney to both reaffirm its commitment to children's pleasure and to Ⓐ_____ any critical assessments of the role Disney plays as a benevolent corporate power in sentimentalizing childhood innocence as it simultaneously Ⓑ_____ it. Stripped of the historical and social constructions that give it meaning, innocence in the Disney universe becomes an atemporal, ahistorical, apolitical, and atheoretical space where children share a common bond free of the problems and conflicts of adult society. Disney both markets this ideal and presents itself as a corporate parent who safeguards this protective space for children by magically supplying the fantasies that nourish it and keep it alive.

22 Choose the best answer for the blanks. [3점]

① sanction — customizes
② downplay — commodifies
③ embellish — dignifies
④ overstate — humanizes
⑤ accentuate — marketizes

23 What is NOT true according to the passage? [3.3점]

① The Walt Disney Company attaches itself to the appeal of innocence.
② Disney uses its corporate power to provide pleasure to children.
③ Disney's portrayal of innocence is rooted in historical and social contexts.
④ Childhood innocence serves as a crucial mechanism for Disney's commercialization.
⑤ Disney promotes an ideal protective space for children to play out their imaginative fantasies.

24~25 Read the passage and answer the questions.

The most immediate cause of the French Revolution, which began in the summer of 1789, was the government's financial crisis. ⒶBecause some of the wealthiest elements in the country were exempt from taxation, the state could not balance its budget. An important element in the French public debt was the expense incurred by helping the Americans in their revolt against England. ⒷFor years the enlightened advisers of the French king had endeavored to abolish the tax privileges of the clergy and the nobility, but these two orders had solidly resisted the efforts. ⒸThe king could proclaim the necessary laws, but the courts, completely controlled by the nobility, would never enforce them. ⒹThe result was an aristocratic revolt: the army officers and the king's officials in Paris and in the provinces refused to serve, and the whole state was brought to a halt. ⒺUnable to persevere in the attempt to reform, Louis XVI acceded to noble demand that, for the first time since 1614, a National Assembly be called to settle the nation's problems.

24 Choose the best place to insert the following sentence. [3점]

Finally, in 1788, the royal government simply abolished the old court system and created a new one.

① Ⓐ ② Ⓑ ③ Ⓒ
④ Ⓓ ⑤ Ⓔ

25 Choose what the underlined "the wealthiest elements" refers to in the passage above. [3점]

① the whole state
② the royal government
③ the National Assembly
④ the enlightened advisers
⑤ the clergy and the nobility

26~27 Read the passage and answer the questions.

As COVID-19 ravaged the world, a generation that had yet to experience a cataclysm of precisely this scale turned to art for insight into how we might survive it. Contemporary speculative fiction about lethal pathogens surged in popularity. Readers also turned to tales of pestilence past. But no dusty tome got a bigger boost than Giovanni Boccaccio's early-Renaissance classic *The Decameron*. Set amid the Black Death that decimated Europe in the mid-14th century, Boccaccio's masterpiece follows 10 young nobles fleeing an outbreak in Florence that would ultimately reduce the city's population by half. To pass the time in their rural idyll, they tell the stories that make up the bulk of the book — one apiece for 10 days, hence the title. The consensus interpretation of *The Decameron* is that it illustrates the power of storytelling to buoy us through history's horrors.

Kathleen Jordan, the creator of Netflix's *The Decameron*, came away from her pandemic-era reading of Boccaccio with a different understanding. What if, her black comedy proposes, the book's true timeless message is that whether they're Florentine aristocrats in 1348 or Manhattan financiers in 2020, the privileged will always blithely abandon their less fortunate neighbors when the plague comes to town? Jordan has stripped *The Decameron* of its stories, choosing instead to riff on the frame narrative. Somehow, her irreverence pays off. While successful on its own terms, the series also raises the question of which derivative works even deserve to be called adaptations.

26 Choose the best title for the passage. [3점]

① The Insensitivity of the Privileged
② The Rise and Fall of *The Decameron*
③ Human Endurance during Catastrophic Times
④ The Contemporary Revival of *The Decameron*
⑤ The Dangers of Adapting Classic Literature

27 Which of the following CANNOT be inferred from the passage? [3.3점]

① Giovanni Boccaccio wrote *The Decameron* during the Renaissance period.
② Boccaccio's *The Decameron* features Florentine aristocrats of the Black Death era.
③ Boccaccio's *The Decameron* gained renewed popularity during the COVID-19 pandemic.
④ Kathleen Jordan's version of *The Decameron* is a black comedy.
⑤ Kathleen Jordan's adaptation was faithful to Boccaccio's *The Decameron*.

28~29 Read the passage and answer the questions.

America was born a nation of immigrants. Modern Europe, much less so. Its history — at least over the past few hundred years — is one of countries built on comparatively Ⓐ_____ national cultures. The creation of the European Union has been a marvel of benevolent globalization in the sense that it brought together 28 of those nations into an economic and political alliance. While the European debt crisis has challenged the future of that union, it hasn't yet doomed it. Now, with the great migration, Europe faces a bigger crisis still — and it's one with profound implications for its culture and its economy.

The challenges of Germany's decision to take in hundreds of thousands of immigrants are enormous. But the benefits could be too. Economic growth is essentially productivity combined with workers — when numbers for both are rising steadily, countries prosper. Europe, which has been struggling to achieve even a percentage point of economic growth per year, is not doing well on either front. The continent has some of the lowest birthrates in the world. In Germany, the economic engine of Europe, the population is predicted to shrink from 81.3 million today to 70.8 million by 2060. If unchecked, that trend would Ⓑ_____ the country's welfare state and future economic growth. Other nations, like France and Spain, are in similar quandaries. Given that women in rich countries tend to have fewer children, the only way to achieve better demographics is immigration.

28 Which of the following best fits into Ⓐ and Ⓑ? [2점]

① homogeneous — devastate
② primitive — evaporate
③ bureaucratic — ameliorate
④ heterogeneous — postulate
⑤ revolutionary — cultivate

29 Which of the following is the most appropriate theme for the passage? [3.3점]

① Europe's low birthrates are disastrous.
② Migrants are detrimental to Germany's growth.
③ Migrants could be the key to a stronger economy for Europe.
④ The European debt crisis is destroying the European Union.
⑤ The European Union was created to achieve the goal of globalization.

30~32 Read the passage and answer the questions.

Behavioural economics is a well-established strand of research in which psychological insights are used to question human's ability to make "sound" decisions. Humans tend to make bad decisions, so the argument goes, because we do not like to exert ourselves, and we are thus inclined to choose the path of least resistance, often leading to less than Ⓐ_____ decision-making. This basic tendency is believed to manifest itself in decision moments to choose the easiest, or most popular option, and a tendency to rely on Ⓑ_____ impressions and emotions, rather than on Ⓒ_____ evaluations.

Behavioural economics was showcased once more in Richard Thaler and Cass Sunstein's 2008 book *Nudge: Improving Decisions about Health, Wealth, and Happiness*. What distinguished this book from earlier work in the field was that the authors went a step further, arguing that government can, and ought to take the lead in protecting citizens from their own pernicious Ⓓ_____. More specifically, Thaler and Sunstein argued for "soft paternalism," a new governance approach in which subtle changes in choice architecture are used to "nudge" citizens towards better choices, but without restricting choice.

30 Which order of words best fills the blanks Ⓐ_____ ~ Ⓒ_____? [3점]

① opportune — subjective — irrational
② ambiguous — objective — subjective
③ beneficial — immediate — optional
④ optimal — superficial — rational
⑤ capable — indifferent — succinct

31 Which word is most suitable for the blank Ⓓ_____? [2점]

① propensities   ② casualties   ③ injuries
④ obligations   ⑤ qualms

32 Which of the following can be inferred about the premise of behavioural economics? [3.3점]

① Decision-making is a basic human right.
② Behavioural economics is an emerging science.
③ Humans tend to choose the most challenging options.
④ Humans are prone to make erroneous decisions.
⑤ Governments need to take a forceful approach to influence sound decision-making.

33~35 Read the passage and answer the questions.

Unlike the masses, intellectuals have a taste for rationality and an interest in facts. Their critical habit of mind makes them resistant to the kind of propaganda that works so well on the majority. They regard over-simplification as the original sin of the mind and have no use for the slogans, the unqualified assertions, and sweeping generalizations which are the propagandist's stock in trade. Philosophy teaches us to feel uncertain about the things that seem to us self-evident. Propaganda, Ⓐ_____, teaches us to accept as self-evident matters about which it would be reasonable to suspend our judgment or to feel doubt. The aim of the demagogue is to create social coherence under his own leadership. The demagogic propagandist must therefore be consistently dogmatic. All his statements are made without qualification. There are no grays in his picture of the world; everything is either diabolically black or celestially white. In Hitler's words, the propagandist should adopt "a systematically one-sided attitude towards every problem that has to be dealt with." Ⓑ_____.

33 Which best fits in the blank Ⓐ_____? [2점]

① likewise
② nevertheless
③ surprisingly
④ as a consequence
⑤ on the other hand

34 Which sentence best fits in the blank Ⓑ_____? [3.3점]

① He must pay close attention to what opponents are saying.
② He must be careful to acknowledge human beings as individuals freely associating with other individuals.
③ He must consider alternative solutions to problems of the masses.
④ He must learn to fill in the gray areas to appeal to the masses by qualifying his statements.
⑤ He must never admit that he might be wrong or that people with a different point of view might be even partially right.

35 Which of these is NOT suggested in the passage? [3.3점]

① Intellectuals are not easily influenced by propaganda.
② Intellectuals follow the teachings of philosophy.
③ Philosophy teaches people to question the seemingly obvious.
④ Propagandists teach the masses to suspend judgment.
⑤ Propaganda relies on generalizations and absolute assertions.

36~37 Read the passage and answer the questions.

Just before Christmas in 2023, the small team at Cognition was struggling to set up a particularly complex data server for the San Francisco-based AI startup's fledgling coding assistant, Devin.

A As the AI sprung into action, it befuddled its creators. "It ran the most witchcraft, black-magic-looking commands," cofounder, Walden Yan, 21, recalls.

B They'd spent hours poring over installation documents and trying different commands but just couldn't get it to work. Tired and frustrated, they decided to see how Devin would handle it.

C Devin had deleted a faulty system file the team had overlooked, they realized. "That was the moment it really hit me how much software engineering is going to change," Yan says.

D For a time, it seemed Devin wouldn't do any better than they had. Then a server terminal light that had been red for hours turned green. The data server was up and running.

36 Put the sentences above into a logical order. [3.3점]

① A — C — D — B
② B — A — C — D
③ B — A — D — C
④ B — D — C — A
⑤ C — B — D — A

37 Which is true of 'Devin' according to the passage? [3점]

① It failed to start the data server.
② It took the grunt work out of coding.
③ It interfered with human coding processes.
④ It retained faulty system files in data servers.
⑤ It shifted the AI industry towards cost-cutting.

38~40 Read the passage and answer the questions.

Much of the contemporary literature on democracy and difference operates with notions of a more active and vigorous democracy that depends crucially on public debate. Rejecting both the false harmony that Ⓐ stamps out difference, and the equally false essentialism that defines people through some single, authentic identity, many theorists look to a democracy which _____ citizen participation, and requires us to engage and contest with one another. In a recent essay on feminism and democracy, Susan Mendus suggests that difference is the rationale for democracy and that "whereas traditional democratic theory tend to construe difference as an obstacle to the attainment of a truly democratic state, feminist theory should alert us to the possibility that difference is rather what necessitates the pursuit of democracy." In his work on multiculturalism, Charles Taylor also calls for a politics of democratic empowerment as the way of dealing with demand for equal recognition without thereby entrenching people in fragmented identities.

38 Choose the answer closest in meaning for Ⓐ**stamps out**. [2점]

① insinuates ② obliterates ③ embraces
④ exposes ⑤ inculcates

39 Choose the best word for the blank. [3점]

① maximizes ② precedes ③ impedes
④ deters ⑤ diminishes

40 What is true according to the passage above? [3.3점]

① Charles Taylor advocates for a politics of democratic empowerment that entrenches people in singular, fixed identities.
② Contemporary literature on democracy and difference supports a passive democracy that avoids public debate.
③ Embracing difference in democracy enhances participation and empowers diverse identities.
④ Democracy thrives by eliminating differences.
⑤ Asserting uniformity above difference is key to empowering diverse identities in democracy.

경희대학교

▶ 2025학년도 한의학과(인문) ▶ 문항 수: 50문항(인문·체육계열 중복 문제 제외 수록) | 제한시간: 90분

2025 경희대 한의학과(인문) 영역별 문항 수

구분	문법			어휘			논리완성	독해	생활영어	총 문항 수
	G/S, W/E	정비문	재진술	동의어	반의어	유추				
문항 수				9			6	35		50
백분율				18%			12%	70%		100%

KYUNG HEE UNIVERSITY

경희대학교

2025학년도 한의학과(인문): 50문항 · 90분

인문 · 체육계열 중복 문제 제외

07 Choose the answer closest in meaning to the underlined word or phrase.

07 Contemporary water treatment methods allow governments to treat water infested with potentially harmful bacteria and make it drinkable. While these methods make tap water entirely safe to drink, it is not practical to treat all of the world's surface water in this fashion. Thus, people who use untreated water for recreational purposes are at risk of <u>ingesting</u> harmful bacteria.   [1점]

① consuming
② maintaining
③ generating
④ producing
⑤ inspecting

11 Choose the best answer for the blank.

11 The liver is an internal human organ that is capable of natural regeneration of lost tissue. Even if the liver is impaired by excessive drinking or hepatitis, it can be easily restored after a short period of _____ or if the hepatitis is completely cured.   [1.3점]

① vitality
② mourning
③ continuity
④ abstinence
⑤ retention

16~17 Read the passage and answer the questions.

While previous generations may have seen dictionaries as Ⓐ_____ and defenders of "correct" language — that is no longer the case. Most major dictionaries are now focusing on describing the language people use while consciously leaving any possible stuffy scholarly objections at the door.

Back in 2007, the *Oxford English Dictionary* removed words describing nature such as acorn, dandelion, mistletoe, pasture, and willow from their junior edition aimed at school children. They replaced them with terms such as "blog," "broadband," "chatroom," "cut-and-paste," and "MP3 player," causing an uproar among parents. While some parents petitioned the dictionary to reinstate the outdoor words, other parents couldn't see a reason for the fuss. They argued that the less bulky the book was, Ⓑ_____ the kids would be to carry it around with them.

16 Which word is best for Ⓐ_____? [1.3점]

① opponents
② skeptics
③ custodians
④ forebears
⑤ philanthropists

17 Which phrase is best for Ⓑ_____? [2점]

① the less possibly
② the more likely
③ more or less
④ the least likely
⑤ less so

32~33 Read the passage and answer the questions.

> There are two basic concepts that you need to understand if you wish to be able to engineer biological systems: how information flows in biological systems and how this information flow is controlled. With an understanding of these concepts one can, in principle, apply engineering principles to the design and building of new biological systems: what we call synthetic biology.
>
> Biology is, of course, highly complex and there are important differences that distinguish it from other engineering disciplines. Firstly, biology is not programmed on a printed circuit board, so interactions cannot be programmed by their physical position; rather interactions are based on interactions between molecules that occur in the complex milieu of the cell. Secondly, biology is subject to natural selection, so that modifications which are <u>deleterious</u> to the cell will be selected against and competed out of the population. These evolutionary pressures are not applicable when building an aircraft, and so new definitions of robustness are relevant to biology. Other concepts such as complexity and emergent behavior may be familiar to engineers, but one must be aware of how they can arise in biology and what their effects may be.

32 Choose the answer that is closest in meaning to the underlined word, "deleterious." [2점]

① beneficial   ② deliberate   ③ damaging
④ flexible   ⑤ spontaneous

33 According to the passage, which is true about biology? [2.7점]

① It cannot be engineered into new systems.
② It is programmed on a printed circuit board.
③ It is contingent upon evolutionary pressures.
④ It is dissociated from complex and emergent behavior.
⑤ It is indistinguishable from other engineering disciplines.

42~44 Read the passage and answer the questions.

The Polynesian Islands are one of three major subregions that compose a large group of islands called Oceania in the central and southern Pacific Ocean. Unlike the dark-skinned people of short stature in the other subregions, the people of Polynesia are lighter-skinned and taller. [A] Although scientists today believe that Polynesia was colonized by cultures from South Asia, Europeans journeying through the Pacific in the late 1800s and early 1900s <u>articulated</u> a theory that the Egyptians had populated Polynesia. [B] They believed the Egyptians settled the islands because they were the only civilization existing at the time Oceania was believed to have been populated. [C] Researchers in the late 1970s pointed to the use of a layer of color applied to the eyes of some statues in Polynesia as evidence. [D] In addition, Polynesia's birdman ceremony has as its parallel the traditional ritual quest for the egg of Egypt's sun god, Ra. [E] However, vessel drift computer simulations based on ocean currents in the Pacific have proved that it was impossible for the Egyptians to have arrived at Polynesia even accidentally, and so Ⓐ_____.

42 Choose the most appropriate place to insert the following sentence. [3점]

Egyptians utilized the same technique in their sculptures to make them appear lifelike.

① [A] ② [B] ③ [C]
④ [D] ⑤ [E]

43 Choose the answer closest in meaning to the underlined word, "articulated." [2점]

① refuted ② reneged ③ proposed
④ distorted ⑤ misrepresented

44 Which is most suitable for Ⓐ_____? [2점]

① they couldn't have developed traditional rituals
② they couldn't have populated the islands
③ they could have been the first to discover the islands
④ they could have been colonized by regions of South Asia
⑤ they could have reached the European continent

45~47 Read the passage and answer the questions.

Just before Christmas in 2023, the small team at Cognition was struggling to set up a particularly complex data server for the San Francisco-based AI startup's fledgling coding assistant, Devin.

[A] As the AI sprung into action, it befuddled its creators. "It ran the most witchcraft, black-magic-looking commands," cofounder, Walden Yan, 21, recalls.

[B] They'd spent hours poring over installation documents and trying different commands but just couldn't get it to work. Tired and frustrated, they decided to see how Devin would handle it.

[C] Devin had deleted a faulty system file the team had overlooked, they realized. "That was the moment it really hit me how much software engineering is going to change," Yan says.

[D] For a time, it seemed Devin wouldn't do any better than they had. Then a server terminal light that had been red for hours turned green. The data server was up and running.

45 Put the sentences above into a logical order. [3점]

① [A] — [C] — [D] — [B]
② [B] — [A] — [C] — [D]
③ [B] — [A] — [D] — [C]
④ [B] — [D] — [C] — [A]
⑤ [C] — [B] — [D] — [A]

46 Choose the answer closest in meaning to the underlined word, "befuddled." [1.3점]

① exonerated   ② vindicated   ③ composed
④ undermined   ⑤ flustered

47 Which is true of 'Devin' according to the passage? [3점]

① It failed to start the data server.
② It took the grunt work out of coding.
③ It interfered with human coding processes.
④ It retained faulty system files in data servers.
⑤ It shifted the AI industry towards cost-cutting.

48~50 Read the passage and answer the questions.

Much of the contemporary literature on democracy and difference operates with notions of a more active and vigorous democracy that depends crucially on public debate. Rejecting both the false harmony that <u>stamps out</u> difference, and the equally false essentialism that defines people through some single, authentic identity, many theorists look to a democracy which Ⓐ_____ citizen participation, and requires us to engage and contest with one another. In a recent essay on feminism and democracy, Susan Mendus suggests that difference is the rationale for democracy and that "whereas traditional democratic theory tend to construe difference as an obstacle to the attainment of a truly democratic state, feminist theory should alert us to the possibility that difference is rather what Ⓑ_____ the pursuit of democracy." In his work on multiculturalism, Charles Taylor also calls for a politics of democratic empowerment as the way of dealing with demand for equal recognition without thereby entrenching people in fragmented identities.

48 Choose the answer closest in meaning for <u>stamps out</u>. [2점]

① insinuates   ② obliterates   ③ embraces
④ exposes   ⑤ inculcates

49 Which of the following best fits into Ⓐ and Ⓑ? [2.7점]

① maximizes — necessitates
② precedes — dissuades
③ impedes — bolsters
④ deters — entails
⑤ diminishes — dictates

50 What is true according to the passage above? [3점]

① Charles Taylor advocates for a politics of democratic empowerment that entrenches people in singular, fixed identities.
② Contemporary literature on democracy and difference supports a passive democracy that avoids public debate.
③ Embracing difference in democracy enhances participation and empowers diverse identities.
④ Democracy thrives by eliminating differences.
⑤ Asserting uniformity above difference is key to empowering diverse identities in democracy.

고려대학교

▶ 2025학년도 세종 인문·자연계   ▶ 문항 수: 40문항 | 제한시간: 60분

2025 고려대 세종캠퍼스 인문·자연계 영역별 문항 수

구분	문법			어휘			논리완성	독해	생활영어	총 문항 수
	G/S, W/E	정비문	재진술	동의어	반의어	유추				
문항 수	8			5			7	20		40
백분율	20%			12.5%			17.5%	50%		100%

KOREA UNIVERSITY

고려대학교

2025학년도 세종 인문 · 자연계: 40문항 · 60분

01~04 Choose the one that is grammatically incorrect. [각 1.5점]

01 Most people envy Mr. Buffett's success but tend ① <u>to overlook</u> his strong saving habits and simple life. He still lives in the house he bought in 1958. Only a couple of bedrooms and a racquet court ② <u>have added</u> over the years. ③ <u>Called</u> the "Oracle of Omaha," he strictly distinguishes speculators ④ <u>from</u> investors.

02 A fairy story, ① <u>as</u> distinct from a merry tale, or an animal story, is a serious tale with a human hero and a happy ending. The progression of ② <u>its</u> hero is the reverse of the tragic hero's: at the beginning he is ③ <u>either</u> socially obscure or despised as being stupid or untalented, lacking in the heroic virtues, but at the end, he has surprised everyone by demonstrating his heroism and ④ <u>win</u> fame, riches, and love.

03 Writing a story or a novel is one way of discovering sequence in experience.... Connections slowly emerge. Like distant landmarks you are approaching, cause and effect begin to align ① <u>themselves</u>, draw closer together. Experiences too indefinite of outline in themselves ② <u>to be</u> recognized for themselves connect and are identified as a larger shape. And suddenly a light is thrown back, ③ <u>as when</u> your train makes a curve, showing that there ④ <u>have been</u> a mountain of meaning rising behind you on the way you've come, and is rising there still, proven now through retrospect.

04

① <u>Rank</u> cities on the somewhat nebulous notion of "liveability" can bring out extreme reactions among our readers. Some question the relatively ② <u>lowly</u> position of vibrant metropolises like London or New York; others scoff at the sedate places that ③ <u>score</u> highly: cities like Copenhagen and Calgary appear in the top ten this year, as they have done for ④ <u>much</u> of the past two decades.

05~08 Choose the one that is grammatically correct for each blank. [각 1.5점]

05

_____ is that it does this without any nerves or muscles. This phenomenon has intrigued scientists for years as they try to determine how the animal is able to close its trap with such blinding dexterity.

① What most surprising is about is how the animal catches its prey
② How most surprising about is what the animal catches its prey
③ What is most surprising about how the animal catches its prey
④ How is most surprising is about what the animal catches its prey

06

If I happen to be entering a building behind some people who appear skittish, I may walk by, letting them clear the lobby before I return, _____ to be following them.

① so as not to seem
② not so as to seem
③ not so much as to seem
④ so much as not to seem

07

Perhaps all cultures in the world have had superstitions relating physical features of the body to personality traits. England is no exception, and had a large number of such beliefs in the past. People with red hair, for example, _____.

① had been believing to be naturally hot-tempered
② were believing to be naturally hot-tempered
③ had believed to be naturally hot-tempered
④ were believed to be naturally hot-tempered

08 The availability of technology has led some to argue that we are creating a generation of "worried well." Sometimes people use software that is not tested or scientific to research their symptoms. In people who are already anxious, this poor information can lead to worry. Generally, the more frightening an article is, _____.

① it is likely to get the more your attention
② the more of your attention it is likely to get
③ your attention it is more likely to get
④ it is likely to get your attention more

09~13 Choose the one that is closest in meaning to the underlined word. [각 1.5점]

09 Because framing has the power to subconsciously alter the way people think, many politicians use it to influence voters. Once frames have entered into the consciousness of a population, they cannot be changed right away. <u>Modifying</u> them takes a great deal of time and energy.

① Adjusting
② Consolidating
③ Generating
④ Dismantling

10 When a candidate tries to convey the impression that he is just like the great majority of people, many voters, unfortunately, are swayed by his folksy actions to the point of <u>disregarding</u> what is most important — the candidate's record.

① dominating
② commanding
③ neglecting
④ inspecting

11 The discovery of the Iceman in 1991 was an <u>unprecedented</u> event. A well-preserved body thousands of years old could provide a wealth of information never available before.

① impressive
② irresistible
③ unethical
④ unusual

12 A community that can meet many of its needs by using locally available natural, human, and financial resources will be less affected by the vicissitudes of the national and global economies.

① changes
② balances
③ deficits
④ variants

13 It's an approach that resonates equally with businessmen steeped in the win-win jargon of negotiations and politicians deep in the pragmatic you-scratch-my-back-I'll-scratch-yours conversations that make Washington run.

① romantic
② unreasonable
③ practical
④ insensible

14~20 Choose the most appropriate one for each blank.

14 The other day an acquaintance of mine, a gregarious and charming man, told me he had found himself unexpectedly alone in New York for an hour or two between appointments. He went to the Whitney and spent the "empty" time looking at things in solitary _____. For him it proved to be a shock as great as falling in love to discover that he could enjoy himself so much alone. [2점]

① grievance
② bliss
③ abstraction
④ introspection

15 Five score years ago, a great American, in whose shadow we stand, signed the Emancipation Proclamation. This _____ decree came as a great beacon light of hope to millions of Negro slaves who had been seared in the flames of withering injustice. It came as a joyous daybreak to end the long night of captivity. [2점]

① minor
② trivial
③ immaterial
④ momentous

16 Despite DNA fingerprinting's usefulness, significant issues _____ its success. Over the years, massive amounts of DNA evidence have been collected, but a lack of funding, qualified staff, and time has created huge backlogs of unprocessed information. DNA fingerprinting requires a high level of expertise and accuracy, and when testing is not properly carried out, violent offenders can go free to commit more crimes. The mishandling and possible contamination of evidence can still present major problems.

[2.5점]

① temper
② facilitate
③ legitimate
④ reinforce

17 Her early life showed clear signs of the formidable spirit and _____ within her. An energetic youngster, she learned to ski at the age of five, taking to the sport with unbridled enthusiasm and passion. Seven years later, she would be faced with the first of many obstacles in her life when she lost her leg to bone cancer. With _____ and fixed determination, she continued skiing and kept in shape by jogging with crutches. A year later, she won the downhill event in the world championships.

[3점]

① fragility — stubborn
② audacity — dependent
③ tenacity — resolute
④ flexibility — assertive

18 Some books are to be _____, others to be swallowed, and some few to be chewed and digested; that is, some books are to be read only in parts; others to be read, but not curiously; and some few to be read _____, and with diligence and attention.

[2.5점]

① tasted — wholly
② savored — rapidly
③ scanned — carefully
④ appreciated — precisely

19 Distrust of and distaste for "new fangled inventions" has a long history. English writers of the nineteenth century _____ the arrival of the railroad in their beloved lake country. Fifty years ago, H.L. Mencken recorded in characteristically _____ language his dislike for automobiles, photographs, and movies. [2.5점]

① praised — temperate
② acquiesced — bland
③ approved — sharp
④ denounced — pungent

20 The teacher needs to create clear boundaries for permissible behavior, while maintaining a relaxed, open environment for learning to take place. Teachers with easy-going personalities are often good at creating a positive learning environment, but if they are too _____, they can have major discipline problems. Teachers with strict personalities and teaching styles usually have better classroom discipline, but going too far with rules can have negative effects. When students make mistakes, overly-strict responses may create a _____ atmosphere which inhibits participation. [3점]

① restrictive — harsh
② lenient — tense
③ indolent — miserable
④ whimsical — stressful

21. Which of the following is the author's intention regarding the underlined part? [3점]

An offshoot of the environmental movement of the 1970s, ecotourism has come into its own over the past two decades. Thanks to an increasing awareness of environmental issues such as climate change, combined with a high demand among European and North American travelers for unspoiled locations, authentic cultural experiences, and recreational challenges, ecotourism is growing at a rate of 20 percent annually, making it the fastest-growing sector in the tourism industry. The International Ecotourism Society defines ecotourism as "responsible travel to natural areas that conserve the environment and the welfare of local people." The International Union for Conservation of Nature characterizes ecotourism as economically sustainable, ecologically sensitive, and culturally acceptable. Closely related is the concept of sustainable tourism identified in *Our Common Future*, a report to the 1987 World Commission on Environment and Development: <u>development that "meets the needs of the present without compromising the ability of future generations to meet their own needs."</u>

① to describe sustainable development as ecotourism's premise
② to suggest a potential disagreement between present and future generations
③ to illustrate ecotourism's attempt to promote tourism development
④ to blame present generations for not conserving nature for future generations

22 Which of the following is the main point of the Minnesota findings in the passage?

[3점]

> The genetic makeup of a child has a stronger influence on personality than child rearing, according to the first study to examine identical twins reared in different families. The findings shatter a widespread belief among experts and laypeople alike in the primacy of family influence and are sure to lead to fierce debate.
>
> The findings are the first major results to emerge from a long-term project at the University of Minnesota in which more than 350 pairs of twins went through six days of extensive testing that included analysis of blood, brain waves, intelligence, and allergies.
>
> For most of the traits measured, more than half the variation was found to be due to heredity, leaving less than half determined by the influence of parents, home environment and other experiences in life.
>
> The Minnesota findings stand in sharp contradiction to standard wisdom on nature vs. nurture in forming adult personality. Virtually all major theories since Freud have given far more importance to environment, or nurture, than to genes or nature.

① Research on genes brings about serious debates on the role of heredity.
② Education is more critical than heredity in forming children's personality.
③ An individual's personality and traits are more inherent than acquired.
④ The primacy of environment in shaping personality is appreciated again.

23
Which of the following is not a reason for piloting and the pilots' association being "things of the dead and pathetic past"? [3점]

> The pilots' association was the most compact monopoly in the world, perhaps, and seemed simply indestructible. And yet the days of its glory were numbered. First, the new railroad stretching up through Mississippi, Tennessee, and Kentucky, to Northern railway-centers, began to divert the passenger travel from the steamboats; next the war came and almost entirely annihilated the steamboating industry during several years, leaving most of the pilots idle and the cost of living advancing all the time; then the treasurer of the St. Louis association put his hand into the till and walked off with every dollar of the ample fund; and finally, with the railroads intruding everywhere, there was little for steamers to do, when the war was over, but carry freight; so straightway some genius from the Atlantic coast introduced the plan of towing a dozen steamer cargoes down to New Orleans at the tail of a vulgar little tugboat; and behold, in the twinkling of an eye, as it were, the association and the noble science of piloting were <u>things of the dead and pathetic past</u>!

① The pilots yearned for the revival of the steamboating industry.
② The railroad replaced the steamboats for passenger transport.
③ The steamboating business was almost destroyed by the war.
④ The steamers came to be used as cargo vessels after the war.

24
Which of the following cannot be inferred from the passage? [4점]

> Plutarch loved those who could use life for grand purposes and depart from it as grandly, but he would not pass over weaknesses and vices which marred the grandeur. His hero of heroes is Alexander the Great; he loves him above all other men, while his abomination of abominations is bad faith, dishonorable action. Nevertheless he tells with no attempt to extenuate how Alexander promised safe conduct to a brave Persian army if they surrendered, and then, "even as they were marching away he fell upon them and put them all to the sword," "a breach of his word," Plutarch says sadly, "which is a lasting blemish on his achievements." He adds piteously, "but the only one." He hated to tell that story.

① The author suggests that Plutarch could not overlook Alexander's faithlessness.
② The author considers that Plutarch was not fair in his writing about Alexander.
③ The author indicates that Plutarch was reluctantly speaking about Alexander's treatment of the Persians.
④ The author asserts that the Persians withdrew from the battlefield due to their trust of Alexander.

25 Which of the following is the most appropriate for the blank? [3점]

> Nevertheless, poetry and advertising have much in common. To begin with, they both make extensive use of rhyme and rhythm ("What's the word? Thunderbird!"). They both use words chosen for their affective and connotative values rather than for their denotative content ("Take a puff ... it's springtime! Gray rocks and the fresh green leaves of springtime reflected in a mountain pool.... Where else can you find air so refreshing? And where can you find a smoke as refreshing as Salem's?"). William Empson, the English critic, said in his *Seven Types of Ambiguity* that the best poems are ambiguous; they are richest when they have two or three or more levels of meaning at once. Advertising, too, _____, deliberately exploits ambiguities and plays on words: a vodka is advertised with the slogan "Leaves you breathless;" an automobile is described as "Hot, Handsome, a Honey to Handle."

① although surpassing poetry in the level of meaning
② although on an extremely grand level
③ although being confined to richness of imagery
④ although on a much more primitive level

26. Which of the following is the main goal of "a Learning Society"? [3점]

In a world of ever-accelerating competition and change in the conditions of the workplace, of ever-greater danger, and of ever-larger opportunities for those prepared to meet them, educational reform should focus on the goal of creating a Learning Society. At the heart of such a society is the commitment to a set of values and to a system of education that affords all members the opportunity to stretch their minds to full capacity, from early childhood through adulthood, learning more as the world itself changes. Such a society has, as a basic foundation, the idea that education is important not only because of what it contributes to one's career goals but also because of the value it adds to the general quality of one's life. Also at the heart of the Learning Society are educational opportunities extending far beyond the traditional institutions of learning, our schools and colleges. They extend into homes and workplaces; into libraries, art galleries, museums, and science centers; indeed, into every place where the individual can develop and mature in work and life. In our view, formal schooling in youth is the essential foundation for learning throughout one's life. But without life-long learning, one's skills will become rapidly dated.

① to make lifetime learning possible by extending educational opportunities
② to discover and develop one's ability while having a learning opportunity
③ to make traditional basic education available to everybody
④ to establish as many educational institutions as anybody can use

27. Which of the following is <u>not</u> mentioned about glacier retreat in the passage?

[4점]

> Global temperatures are rising as a result of carbon emissions that trap greenhouse gases in the atmosphere. And glaciers — large masses of ice at the Earth's poles and high up in the mountain ranges — are particularly affected by this global warming. The higher temperatures not only cause the glaciers to melt, they reduce the snowfall as well. Glaciers are formed when snow falls on existing snow, and the lower layer of snow is compressed, creating a large mass of ice. If some of the surface of the glacier melts during warmer weather, that's OK as long as more snow falls to replace what was lost. But continually warmer temperatures mean that more ice is melting and less snow is falling. As a result, the glacier cannot sustain its mass; in other words, it shrinks. We call this phenomenon "glacier retreat" because as its mass gets smaller, it seems to be retreating from the land it once covered.
>
> Why do retreating glaciers have scientists and environmentalists so concerned? First of all, most of the Earth's supply of fresh water is found in the form of glaciers. The normal melting of glaciers during seasons of warmer temperatures provides fresh water to people, animals, and plants. If the glaciers are not able to sustain their mass, there will be less fresh water available for people to drink and use for raising crops. This could spell disaster for human populations around the world.
>
> Furthermore, while the disappearance of glaciers would mean diminished fresh water supplies, the process of this disappearance is causing floods and rising ocean levels. Most glaciers are located at higher elevations because of the colder temperatures found there. So when the ice melts, gravity propels the water downward via rivers and streams. More melting means more water is entering the river system, which may be unable to bear the increased volume, resulting in flooding. Flooding, in turn, destroys property and crops and disrupts the equilibrium of ecosystems. Once the water reaches the sea, it raises the water level, threatening coastal settlements. In addition, seawater can get into the ground water supply, further diminishing fresh water supplies as the seawater contaminates the fresh water with salt.

① circumstances that cause it to happen
② its negative impact on global warming
③ its influence on global water supplies
④ the aftermath of its impact on the ocean

28 Which of the following is <u>not</u> a difference among the three primary headaches?

[3점]

> Currently, doctors classify headaches into two general types: primary and secondary. A primary headache is a condition suffered as only the headache itself. On the other hand, a secondary headache is one caused by another physiological condition, such as an infection or a tumor.
>
> For primary headaches, doctors have determined three possible causes. One kind of primary headache is caused by stress. Doctors usually call these tension headaches, and they are characteristically felt on both sides of the head as a dull, steady pain.
>
> Another kind of primary headache is the migraine headache. Exactly what causes these headaches is not well understood, but many experts believe it could be abnormal brain activity causing changes in the brain's chemistry and blood flow. For many people, migraines are triggered by certain stimuli, such as poor sleep or particular foods or smells. A sufferer usually feels intense pain on one side of the head and becomes sensitive to light and noise. If the migraine is severe, the sufferer may vomit repeatedly.
>
> The third kind of primary headache is known as the cluster headache. Cluster headaches typically occur around the same time each day for weeks or months at a time. The person suffering from this kind of headache usually feels pain on one side of her or his head, and the pain is centered around one of the eyes. Doctors do not know much at present about cluster headaches, but they seem to be more common among men and could be related to alcohol or other things that affect a person's blood flow.

① body parts where pain is felt
② regularity of the pain occurrence
③ irrelevance to another physiological condition
④ possible causes that trigger the pain

29. Which of the following is the main idea of the passage? [3점]

> Cultural clashes often result from misinterpreting contextual information. Different cultures place varying degrees of emphasis on certain contextual information gathered from the environment during communication.
>
> In this regard, there are generally two types of cultures: high-context cultures and low-context cultures. High-context cultures, like those in many East Asian and Middle Eastern countries, assign a lot of importance to the environment surrounding a message; consequently, the meaning of the message itself is often implicit. In order to understand what is being said, the speakers must first understand the situation and the participants' relationship to each other. These cultures place less value on the specific meaning of words and more on implied themes.
>
> In contrast, low-context cultures like Germany or America place more importance on the message itself, which is generally much more explicit. For low-context speakers, communication is more detailed and specific since external factors are not emphasized nearly as much. Every word is meaningful, and precision is often important.
>
> Contextual differences are often very apparent in the business world. For example, a business contract from Japan tends to be comparatively short while a contract from America is usually longer and much more detailed.

① There is a difference in the length of a business contract between countries depending on the importance of context.
② Understanding the situation and the participants' relationship is important during cross-cultural communication.
③ There is a difference in the degree of using contextual information during communication across cultures.
④ Differences in the importance of context cause misunderstandings in cross-cultural communication.

30 Which of the following is <u>not</u> a fact about medicinal leeches in the passage?

[4점]

> Leeches are a kind of worm from 1 millimeter to 5 centimeters long. They live all over the world. In general, leeches live in lakes and rivers. There are 650 kinds of leeches in the world. Only one kind is used in medicine. They are called medicinal leeches.
>
> Medicinal leeches live on the blood of other animals. They have suckers at both ends — one for feeding and one for holding on. Their saliva has three special chemicals that help them drink the blood. One is an anesthetic, which allows the leech to feed without hurting the animal. The second chemical makes the veins open wide, and the third makes the blood flow from the veins for a long time. A medicinal leech will drink 10 to 15 milliliters of blood at one time. This takes about 45 minutes. After the leech is full, it falls off. The bite will still bleed for another 24 hours because of the chemicals from the leech's saliva.
>
> Leeches have been used in medicine for over 3,000 years. Leeches were most popular in Europe in the early 1800s. At this time, people thought that too much blood in a person's body made the person sick. Doctors put three or four leeches on a patient's body. The leeches took out the extra blood. Leeches were used to cure many illnesses, from fevers to broken legs.
>
> Unfortunately, leeches often hurt more than they healed. For example, the Russian writer Nikolai Gogol was leeched because he had anemia, an illness caused by too *little* blood. He died a few days later. As we know today, blood is what helps the body heal, so removing blood from a sick person usually does not help. By the mid-1850s, people began to understand some of the problems with leeching, and it became unpopular.
>
> Today, doctors know more about leeches. They know when to use them and why. They understand that the chemicals in the leeches' saliva make leeches very useful in medicine. For this reason, the United States made it legal in 2004 to use leeches in reattachment surgeries.

① The parts that it has at both ends function differently while biting.
② Its saliva keeps an animal from feeling pain while feeding.
③ It was used to treat many illnesses in the past.
④ Treatment using it remains illegal in all countries.

31~32 Read the following passage and answer the questions. [각 3점]

Weather is what it's like outside from day to day. Is it sunny and hot? Is it rainy and cold? Is there a thunderstorm? Or is it just "normal?" Climate, on the other hand, is the pattern of weather for a region over a long period of time. For example, many deserts get rain every now and then, yet their "normal" pattern over a year's time is to be hot and dry.

Climate can be rated by different methods. Two of the most important are how much sun and rain a place gets and what kinds of plants grow there. Because of these, Earth has several different climate zones. A climate zone is a large area of land in which the weather follows the same pattern year after year. It can be based on different measurements. The best known climate zones are based on rainfall. Using the amount of rainfall a place can expect in different seasons, Earth has 8 climate zones.

The first zone is called the Equatorial Zone. It has rain in all seasons. This zone is named for the equator, the imaginary line that divides the world in half. The next is the Tropical Zone. There, it rains in summer but not in winter. Following this is a zone called Semiarid Tropical. That zone has only a little summer rain. The next two zones are similar — the Arid Zone is dry all year, while the Mediterranean Zone has winter rain, but a dry summer. Then comes the Temperate Zone. Like the Equatorial Zone, this zone gets rain in all seasons. Surprisingly, the Polar Zones, which lie at the northern and southern extremes of the planet, get hardly any rain or snow. They are just frozen all year.

Overall, climates vary from place to place because of five main factors — distance from the equator, height above sea level, surface features, distance from oceans and large lakes and the circulation of the atmosphere.

31 Which of the following is not a factor that determines climate zones?

① patterns of wind and air currents around a region
② universal features of weather recurring in different regions
③ measurement of rainfall or amount of sunlight in a region
④ locations and geographical features of regions on Earth

32 Which of the following is the zone that has the least amount of rainfall?

① the Temperate Zone
② the Mediterranean Zone
③ the Arid Zone
④ the Tropical Zone

33~34 Read the following passage and answer the questions. [각 3점]

As snow accumulates on a car windshield, it sticks to the cold surface of the window. When the driver turns the ignition and starts the car, the windshield begins to warm from the increased temperature in the car's interior. As the temperature rises, the snow on the windshield begins to thaw and slide off, sometimes in large chunks. Although the driver might not recognize it, an avalanche has just occurred on the windshield.

A windshield avalanche imitates what is known as a slab, or large scale, avalanche. However, it is not the deadly force of nature that occurs during an avalanche in a large area. A real avalanche is one of the most powerful natural events. Its formation depends upon three factors: snow, a sloped surface, and a trigger. A snowy slope with an angle between 30° and 45° is considered a potential avalanche site. The first day following a heavy, sudden snowfall over 12 inches is prime time for an avalanche to occur.

Several natural circumstances can cause an avalanche. An environment with forests is much safer than open terrain. The trees create a natural buffer to anchor snow and prevent it from causing an avalanche. Valleys or sloped areas are possible danger zones, as they can quickly accumulate large amounts of snow.

The condition of snow layers in a snowpack, or accumulation of snow, also influences the likelihood of an avalanche. In areas that are quite snowy, a snowpack consists of several layers of snow that have developed over time. The types of bonds throughout the snowpack's layers can determine whether an avalanche might occur. If the snow crystals do not create a strong bond, they create a weak layer in the snowpack. If the weak layer exists near the surface, it may cause a sluff, or small slide of dry, powdery snow. If the weakened layer is at the base of a snowpack, it can result in a deadly slab avalanche. _____.

33 Which of the following is not true in the passage?

① Slopes that are full of trees are less prone to avalanches.
② The occurrence of avalanches is subject to specific natural conditions.
③ Degrees of bonding in a snowpack's layers can influence the occurrence of avalanches.
④ The occurrence of avalanches can be ascribed to environmental crises.

34 Which of the following is the most appropriate for the blank in relation to "the snow on the windshield" in the passage?

① Avalanches are often initiated by specific natural factors under particular weather circumstances
② Snowpack stability depends on the influence of certain natural conditions, which can lead to avalanches
③ Dramatic changes in temperature also can cause melting in the snowpack, leading to weak bonds
④ The growing number of cars has precipitated global warming, which triggers avalanches

35~36 Read the following passage and answer the questions. [각 3점]

Rumor is the most primitive way of spreading stories — by passing them on from mouth to mouth. But civilized countries in normal times have better sources of news than rumor. They have radio, television, and newspapers. In times of stress and confusion, however, rumor emerges and becomes rife. At such times the different kinds of news are in competition: The press, television, and radio versus the grapevine.

Especially do rumors spread when war requires censorship on many important matters. The customary news sources no longer give out enough information. Since the people cannot learn through legitimate channels all that they are anxious to learn, they pick up "news" whenever they can and when this happens, rumor thrives.

Rumors are often repeated even by those who do not believe the tales. There is a fascination about them. The reason is that the cleverly designed rumor gives expression to something deep in the hearts of the victims — the fears, suspicions, forbidden hopes, or daydreams which they hesitate to voice directly. Pessimistic rumors about defeat and disasters show that the people who repeat them are worried and anxious. Optimistic rumors about record production or peace soon coming point to complacency or confidence — and often to overconfidence.

35 Which of the following is the topic of the passage?

① Fascination with rumors
② The nature of rumor
③ Breeding places of rumors
④ A case against rumor

36 Which of the following is not true in the passage?

① Rumors usually can be suppressed by censorship.
② People who repeat a rumor as truth want to do so in fear of the truth.
③ During wartime the regular sources of news present only limited information.
④ In times of stress, people frequently revert to primitive ways.

37~38 Read the following passage and answer the questions. [각 3점]

Likewise, in Washington, D.C., there is the Vietnam memorial. There are fifty thousand names listed — middle names, too — of American soldiers killed in Vietnam. Real human beings with names were killed and their breaths moved out of this world. There was the name of Donald Miller, my second-grade friend who drew tanks, soldiers, and ships in the margins of all his math papers. Seeing names makes us remember. A name is what we carry all our life, and we respond to its call in a classroom, to its pronunciation at a graduation, or to our name whispered in the night.

It is important to say the names of who we are, the names of the places we have lived, and to write the details of our lives. "I live on Coal Street in Albuquerque next to a garage and carried paper bags of groceries down Lead Avenue. One person had planted beets early that spring, and I watched their red/green leaves grow."

We have lived; our moments are important. This is what it is to be a writer: to be the carrier of details that make up history, to care about the orange booths in the coffee shop in Owatonna.

Recording the details of our lives is a stance against bombs with their mass ability to kill, against too much speed and efficiency. A writer must say yes to life, to all of life: the water glasses, the Kemp's half-and-half, the ketchup on the counter. It is not a writer's task to say, "It is dumb to live in a small town or to eat in a cafe when you can eat macrobiotic at home." Our task is to say a holy yes to the real things of our life as they exist — the real truth of who we are: several pounds overweight, the gray, cold street outside, the Christmas tinsel in the showcase, the Jewish writer in the orange booth across from her blond friend who has Black children. We must become writers who accept things as they are, come to love the details, and step forward with a yes on our lips so there can be no more noes in the world, noes that invalidate life and stop these details from continuing.

37 Which of the following is the title of the passage?

① The Significance of Name and Memory
② The Role of Writers
③ The Power of Details
④ The Importance of Observation

38 Which of the following is the main reason why the author believes it is important to capture details of daily life?

① Recording all the moments of life can be a way of enjoying life.
② Recording the details of life is necessary to be a writer.
③ Recording daily life can be a way of not denying life.
④ All the moments when we live now are very important.

39~40 Read the following passage and answer the questions. [각 3점]

Delivering medical supplies to hard-to-reach places has been an issue for years. Worldwide, more than two billion people lack access to essential life-saving supplies, such as blood and vaccines. In the African nation of Rwanda, for example, several remote health clinics do not have sufficient quantities of blood and other healthcare products. As a result, many people die of treatable illnesses.

A company called Zipline is trying to ① address this problem. It uses drones to transport medical supplies around Rwanda. In the past, it took hours for packages of medicines to reach some health clinics. However, a drone can now deliver medicine in 30 minutes. Thanks to this ② gradual healthcare service, fewer women suffer during childbirth and more children receive life-saving medicines.

Drones are also helping to protect vulnerable wildlife populations in parts of Africa and Asia. Every year, poachers kill thousands of elephants, rhinos, and other endangered animals. To stop them, the environmental organization World Wildlife Fund (WWF) is using drones. "Drones help us see things we can't," says Colby Loucks, who works for the WWF. For example, they can show where poachers are hiding and if they are carrying weapons. Drones are particularly helpful at night, when poachers tend to be most active. Fitted with infrared video cameras, drones can easily identify people and animals in the dark. These drones are not only helpful, they are ③ affordable. Drones with infrared cameras cost about $20,000 each — a fraction of the cost of other high-tech tools.

It is ④ ironic that a tool originally created for military use is increasingly being used to save lives instead of taking them. Drones have the potential to provide solutions that will benefit both humans and animals, says photographer and environmentalist Kike Calvo. "There's nothing that can replace a good scientist," he says. But with the help of drones, "researchers are empowered to carry out projects they've never imagined before."

39 Which of the following is <u>not</u> an advantage of using drones mentioned in the passage?

① delivering medical items fast to remote areas
② tracking enemies effectively during wartime
③ potential to be a powerful research tool
④ lower price than other high-tech tools

40 Which of the underlined words is <u>not</u> appropriate for the context?

① address   ② gradual

③ affordable   ④ ironic

광운대학교

▶ 2025학년도 인문계 1교시 A형 ▶ 문항 수: 40문항 | 제한시간: 60분

2025 광운대 인문계 1교시 A형 영역별 문항 수

구분	문법			어휘			논리완성	독해	생활영어	총 문항 수
	G/S, W/E	정비문	재진술	동의어	반의어	유추				
문항 수		11					14	14	1	40
백분율		27.5%					35%	35%	2.5%	100%

KWANGWOON UNIVERSITY

광운대학교

2025학년도 인문계 1교시 A형: 40문항 · 60분

01~02 빈칸에 들어가기에 가장 적절한 것은? [각 1.9점]

01 A: Let me have a cheeseburger, regular French fries and a large Coke, please.
B: Will that be all?
A: _____
B: Here or to go?
A: To go.

① That's it.
② Yes, I will.
③ I appreciate it.
④ You're welcome.
⑤ What do you mean?

02 The board of directors must _____ before making such a significant change to the company's strategic direction.

① promulgate   ② speculate   ③ advocate
④ validate   ⑤ deliberate

03~10 빈칸에 공통으로 들어가기에 가장 적절한 것은? [각 1.9점]

03 All payments are _____ upon satisfactory completion dates.
A British _____ was sent to assist the security forces.

① dependent   ② suitable   ③ concomitant
④ contingent   ⑤ congruent

04 The storm continued to _____ the coastal region for days.
    The past tragic events still _____ the old man's memories.

    ① haunt   ② persist   ③ conduct
    ④ occupy   ⑤ retract

05 There is a(n) _____ competition for places at the college.
    Tom is _____ as mustard on golf, but he's not a very good player.

    ① crucial   ② agile   ③ keen
    ④ solid   ⑤ hollow

06 He was sent to the _____ for armed robbery.
    It was the practice to _____ the sheep for clipping.

    ① jail   ② penitentiary   ③ lead
    ④ pen   ⑤ function

07 The scholar _____ dissected every nuance of the text.
    The detective _____ unraveled the complex web of deceptions.

    ① ostensibly   ② scrupulously   ③ perpetually
    ④ mischievously ⑤ anemically

08 He had a few medals and a _____ mouth.
    Steer clear of wearing white or _____ colors to avoid competing with the bride.

    ① foul   ② watery   ③ big
    ④ black   ⑤ loud

09 Many adolescents feel _____ to peer pressure.
The coastal regions are particularly _____ to the effects of climate change.

① congenial ② dissident ③ susceptible
④ adaptable ⑤ nonchalant

10 The artist's later works became increasingly _____ as he explored themes of mortality and existence.
The quantum mechanics equations remain _____ to most people without advanced mathematical training.

① dormant ② abstruse ③ moribund
④ ephemeral ⑤ amenable

11~14 어법상 가장 적절한 것은? [각 1.9점]

11 ① They accused him of being a traitor, which he was.
② This is not something what would disturb me anyway.
③ She's not the brilliant dancer who she used to be.
④ The book who you ordered last month has arrived.
⑤ The man, whom we hope will arrive soon, is trustworthy.

12 ① She has another's coat.
② Some of the rolls has been eaten.
③ All of boys want to become football players.
④ I'm having a drink. Would you like one too?
⑤ The cautious one can't be too careful, can the one?

13
① Strange that it turned out that way.
② Strangely, how she still likes him.
③ Longly his hair played in the breeze.
④ The man restrained the woman, aggressive.
⑤ She glanced with disgust at the cat, quiet.

14
① He is being tall.
② He was moving the town about.
③ He is being careful.
④ He walked the car past.
⑤ They took John to quickly.

15~21 어법상 적절하지 않은 것은? [각 2.3점]

15
① I had better go now.
② You had best forgot all about the whole thing.
③ I would sooner stay at home tonight.
④ He would rather not commit himself.
⑤ I'd rather you pulled an all-nighter for the exam.

16
① She found the most blackberries.
② He denied having taken the money.
③ This car isn't worth to be repaired.
④ It is suggested that he leave immediately.
⑤ She went so far as to claim she was innocent.

17 ① Down the hill rolled a ball.
② In the room slept Robin.
③ Around the fire danced the women.
④ Out of the barn ran a black horse.
⑤ In the garden Nik built a play house.

18 ① I'm flying to London first thing tomorrow morning.
② Bullets were hitting the street just feet away from us.
③ He waved his hand at me, obviously meaning me to leave.
④ I've only been to your old house once when you left it.
⑤ The stones came from a mill which formerly stood on this site.

19 ① Which country was she the president of?
② Of which country was he the president?
③ The president of which country was she?
④ What subjects are you interested in?
⑤ In what subjects are you interested?

20 ① We owe it to you that we got off so lightly.
② I take it you'll be accepting their offer.
③ This made me glad I'd stayed at home.
④ They regard it as a discourtesy that you didn't notify them earlier.
⑤ I find that he tried to retract his statement hardly surprising.

21
① I asked them if they'd like to stay to dinner.
② He wants to know if you'd mind moving your car.
③ It depends on if we have enough time left.
④ I don't know whether she'll accept the offer.
⑤ The question is whether guilt has been established beyond doubt.

22~24 빈칸에 들어가기에 가장 적절한 것은? [각 2.3점]

22 Modern urban planning increasingly emphasizes the importance of creating inclusive spaces that serve all members of society. The city's recently unveiled public transportation system represents a significant step forward in this direction. Designed to be _____ to individuals with various types of disabilities, the system incorporates features such as wheelchair-friendly ramps, tactile paving for the visually impaired, clear audio announcements in multiple languages, and easy-to-read digital displays, ensuring that public transport can be used comfortably by everyone.

① accessible   ② hostile   ③ detrimental
④ negligent   ⑤ averse

23 Suppose you are present in a packed arena watching your favorite team win a home game. As you roar along with your fellow fans, everyone's enthusiasm for the team spikes. At the same time, animosity for the opposing team and its fans intensifies. Your mood is elevated and your identity is _____. Cheering with fellow fans makes us feel good about ourselves.

① challenged   ② denied   ③ maintained
④ deteriorated   ⑤ affirmed

24 Even as China's diplomatic standing across much of the developed world declines, its economic centrality grows apace. Indeed, if they orient their collective agenda too narrowly around counterbalancing China's influence, they risk amplifying the differences between their approaches. There are at least some fronts, however, on which they will likely, and properly, pursue more widespread, sustained coordination in managing Beijing's _____, with global supply chains and technology standards being among the most significant.

① respect ② retreat ③ resistance
④ resurgence ⑤ restructuring

25~26 빈칸에 들어가기에 가장 적절한 것은? [각 2.9점]

25 Many organizations today are transitioning to cloud-based data storage solutions that offer enhanced security features and regular backups. These solutions provide various levels of protection for sensitive data. To ensure maximum data protection in their cloud environments, companies typically _____ encryption protocols, which serve as sophisticated security measures converting sensitive information into coded text that can only be decoded with specific authentication keys.

① evaluate the cost effectiveness of
② deploy these systems in parallel with
③ implement these features instead of
④ coordinate security assessments against
⑤ reduce their dependence based on

26 Fans are hung up on the possibility that the singers could be going with NewJeanz, the name under which the five members set up a new Instagram account and started uploading new content. Even The Boyz were getting ready to begin as The Boys just in case things went south. One Hundred Label filed for a trademark right on the name The Boys, when The Boyz members were still signed to IST Entertainment, but the patent hasn't been approved by the authority yet. NewJeans just started its legal dispute with ADOR, so using the name is _____ until the court delivers a decision.

① on cloud nine
② under the belt
③ out of the blue
④ up in the air
⑤ under influence

27 글의 내용과 가장 잘 부합하는 것은? [2.9점]

> The studio was filled with the rich odor of roses, and when the light summer wind stirred amid the trees of the garden, there came through the open door the heavy scent of the lilac, or the more delicate perfume of the pink-flowering thorn. From the corner of the divan of Persian saddle-bags on which he was lying, smoking, as was his custom, innumerable cigarettes, Lord Henry Wotton could just catch the gleam of the honey-sweet and honey-colored blossoms of a laburnum, whose tremulous branches seemed hardly able to bear the burden of a beauty so flamelike as theirs.

① Multiple flower fragrances fill the air.
② The scene is set in a winter afternoon.
③ The room has no connection to the garden.
④ Lord Henry Wotton is working in his garden.
⑤ Lord Henry Wotton is standing by the window.

28 밑줄 친 문장이 들어갈 가장 적절한 위치는? [2.9점]

> The shift to remote work has fundamentally changed how many companies operate. [A] Organizations have reported increased productivity and reduced overhead costs since implementing work-from-home policies. [B] Employees generally report higher job satisfaction and better work-life balance. [C] Many workers struggle with isolation and difficulty separating work from personal life. [D] Additionally, some managers find it challenging to maintain team cohesion and company culture in a virtual environment. [E]

This transition has not been without its complications.

① A ② B ③ C
④ D ⑤ E

29~30 글의 내용과 부합하지 않는 것은? [각 2.9점]

29

> Jane Austen's *Pride and Prejudice* opens in the rural village of Longbourn, where the Bennet family lives with their five unmarried daughters. Mrs. Bennet's greatest wish is to see all her daughters married, particularly as the modest family estate is to be inherited by a distant male cousin in the event of Mr. Bennet's death. When wealthy Mr. Bingley takes up residence in a nearby mansion, Mrs. Bennet is excited by the prospect of a possible marriage to one of her daughters. At a ball, Bingley takes an immediate liking to the eldest daughter, Jane. However, Bingley's friend, Mr. Darcy, initially snubs Elizabeth, the second eldest Bennet daughter, dismissing her as merely "tolerable." Elizabeth immediately develops a strong aversion to Darcy upon hearing this slight. Elizabeth's poor first impression of Darcy's pride is further reinforced by his subsequent behavior and his apparent role in separating Bingley from her beloved sister Jane.

① Mrs. Bennet's matrimonial concerns for her daughters are partly motivated by inheritance-related anxieties.
② Elizabeth's initial prejudice against Darcy stems both from his direct insult and his subsequent actions.
③ The social status of the Bennet family appears precarious due to the nature of their estate inheritance.
④ Mr. Bingley and Jane's potential relationship faces interference from Darcy's intervention.
⑤ The contrast between Bingley's and Darcy's first impressions of the Bennet sisters reflects their opposing personalities.

30

The Apollo 11 mission made history on July 20, 1969. After launching from Kennedy Space Center on July 16, the spacecraft entered lunar orbit three days later. While Michael Collins remained in the command module, Neil Armstrong and Buzz Aldrin descended to the moon's surface in the lunar module Eagle. Armstrong became the first human to step onto the moon, followed shortly after by Aldrin. The astronauts spent about two and a half hours exploring the lunar surface before returning to Earth, splashing down in the Pacific Ocean on July 24.

① The spacecraft entered lunar orbit three days after launch.
② All three astronauts landed on the moon's surface.
③ The spacecraft splashed down in the Pacific Ocean.
④ Armstrong was the first person to step onto the moon.
⑤ The lunar surface exploration lasted about two and a half hours.

31 글의 제목으로 가장 적절한 것은? [2.9점]

The discovery of the structure of DNA in 1953 by James Watson and Francis Crick marked a pivotal moment in scientific history, but one key contributor was initially overlooked. Rosalind Franklin's X-ray diffraction images of DNA provided crucial evidence for the molecule's helical structure, particularly her famous "Photo 51." However, Watson and Crick were shown this image without Franklin's knowledge or consent by her colleague Maurice Wilkins. When Watson and Crick published their groundbreaking paper in *Nature*, Franklin's contribution went unacknowledged. She died of ovarian cancer in 1958, possibly due to her extensive work with X-rays, and was thus ineligible for the Nobel Prize awarded to Watson, Crick, and Wilkins in 1962. Only in recent decades has Franklin's critical role been widely recognized.

① Watson and Crick's DNA Discovery
② The Structure of DNA Molecules
③ The Forgotten Hero of DNA Research
④ Nobel Prize Winners in Science
⑤ History of X-ray Crystallography

32~40 다음 글을 읽고 물음에 답하시오.

32~33

> Living in space poses unique challenges for astronauts' mental and physical well-being. The International Space Station (ISS) crew members must exercise for about two hours daily to prevent muscle atrophy and bone loss caused by microgravity. Besides physical health concerns, the isolation and confinement can _____ psychological stress. To address this, astronauts maintain regular video contact with their families and participate in various recreational activities. The crew also follows a strict daily schedule that includes scientific experiments, station maintenance, and designated rest periods. Despite these measures, extended stays in space can still affect sleep patterns and overall mental health, making careful monitoring essential.

32 빈칸에 들어가기에 가장 적절한 것은? [2.9점]

① take off
② cut down
③ give away
④ bring about
⑤ set aside

33 글의 내용과 부합하지 <u>않는</u> 것은? [3.1점]

① ISS crew members spend two hours exercising every day.
② The crew performs maintenance work on the space station.
③ The daily schedule includes time for conducting scientific research.
④ Astronauts can communicate with their families through video calls.
⑤ Extended space stays make a negligible impact on astronauts' sleep patterns.

34~35

In 1990, Patagonia made a donation to Planned Parenthood, angering Christian fundamentalists. The response was swift: calls for a boycott, threats of store pickets and a deluge of complaints to its call center that jammed its phone lines. The Ventura-based outdoor apparel retailer could have tried to placate the protesters. Instead, the company directed customer service representatives to respond: "Thank you so much for sharing your views. We want you to know that for every call like this we receive, we're donating an additional $5 to Planned Parenthood." Ⓐ"_____," recalled Vincent Stanley, Patagonia's director of philosophy. And the sales, as usual, kept chugging along. Politics has always been a minefield for businesses. But it used to be one they could avoid. Three decades ago, it was all but unheard of for a major consumer brand to stake out a position on a hot-button culture war issue. Today, they're increasingly finding such positions thrust on them by societal upheavals too big to simply ignore and activist customer bases demanding expressions of solidarity and meaningful action. The rise of Ⓑ"_____" has bred in younger consumers, particularly, an expectation that the companies seeking their dollars should share their values. Meanwhile, the hyper-partisan polarization of everything from sneakers to coffee means even "safe" causes can turn controversial in an instant, and silence is no refuge, with companies that avoid engaging on social issues apt to be tagged as complicit.

34 빈칸 Ⓐ에 들어가기에 가장 적절한 것은? [3.1점]

① The calls stopped pretty soon
② Calls of complaints increased rapidly
③ Societal pressure forces soared up
④ The sales department stop calling complaining customers
⑤ Silence on social issues risks complicity in a polarized world

35 빈칸 Ⓑ에 들어가기에 가장 적절한 것은? [3.1점]

① impatient customers
② political correctness
③ corrupted business
④ conscious capitalism
⑤ reckless complaints

36~37

Sustainable architecture has become increasingly important in modern urban development. It Ⓐ_____ environmentally responsible methods and materials throughout a building's lifecycle. These practices aim to reduce the environmental impact of buildings through better design, construction, operation, and maintenance. The benefits of sustainable architecture can be Ⓑ_____ various aspects of urban life. Energy-efficient buildings reduce power consumption and minimize waste. Green buildings often incorporate natural lighting and ventilation, which can improve occupants' health and well-being. Moreover, sustainable buildings frequently use renewable materials and are designed to minimize water usage. "The future of architecture lies in sustainability," says architect David Chen, who specializes in eco-friendly design. Many cities are now implementing regulations that require new buildings to meet specific environmental standards.

36 빈칸 Ⓐ와 Ⓑ에 들어가기에 가장 적절한 쌍은? [3.7점]

① works with — turned against
② comes from — divided into
③ gives up — looked into
④ moves toward — dealt with
⑤ relies on — observed in

37 글의 내용과 부합하지 않는 것은? [3.7점]

① Sustainable buildings are more expensive to construct than traditional buildings.
② Natural lighting and ventilation in green buildings can have positive health effects.
③ Energy efficiency is one of the key benefits of sustainable buildings.
④ Sustainable architecture considers environmental impact throughout the entire building lifecycle.
⑤ Cities are creating new regulations for environmental standards in buildings.

38-40

Here's an easy fix to polarization: Stop hating your political adversaries. But that's easier Ⓐ_____. Why do people despise those who are politically different from themselves? The answer lies with a widespread cognitive phenomenon called group polarization. When you talk only to those you agree with, or listen only to news that affirms your opinions, you become more radical in your beliefs. As people radicalize like this, they grow less able to comprehend opposing views, more likely to dismiss objections to their opinions and increasingly prone to regarding dissenters as incompetent and Ⓑ_____. Online environments function as immense polarization machines. They enable individuals to select their information sources and filter out challenging or unfamiliar messages. Many have suggested that people would become less polarized if they could only break out of their "echo chambers" and expose themselves to more diverse opinions. However, there's a crucial difference between prevention and cure. Diversifying your media diet could help to prevent group polarization, but it may not reverse the polarization once it has taken effect.

38 빈칸 Ⓐ에 들어가기에 가장 적절한 것은? [3.1점]
① felt than said
② said than done
③ tasted than said
④ seen than heard
⑤ done than mentioned

39 빈칸 Ⓑ에 들어가기에 가장 적절한 것은? [3.7점]
① immortal ② depraved ③ invincible
④ infuriated ⑤ deprived

40 글의 내용과 부합하지 않는 것은? [3.7점]
① Media diet is necessary to keep you from being polarized.
② Once polarization has occurred, it may be irreversible.
③ Online environments facilitate the proliferation of polarized discourse.
④ To avoid group polarization, consume a variety of news sources.
⑤ You should stay in echo chambers if you'd like to be less polarized.

KWANGWOON UNIVERSITY

광운대학교

▶ 2025학년도 자연계 2교시 A형   ▶ 문항 수: 영어 30문항, 수학 25문항 | 제한시간: 100분

2025 광운대 자연계 2교시 A형 영역별 문항 수

구분	문법			어휘			논리완성	독해	생활영어	총 문항 수
	G/S, W/E	정비문	재진술	동의어	반의어	유추				
문항 수		7		2			10	10	1	30
백분율		23.3%		6.7%			33.3%	33.3%	3.3%	100%

KWANGWOON UNIVERSITY

광운대학교

▶ 2025학년도 자연계 2교시 A형: 영어 30문항, 수학 25문항 · 100분

01~02 빈칸에 들어가기에 가장 적절한 것은? [각 2.8점]

01 A: How's your new business going?
B: To be honest, we're still _____.

① getting the boot
② crossing the line
③ learning the ropes
④ breaking bread
⑤ seeing through a ladder

02 I was trying to keep the party a secret, but Mel went and let the _____ out of the bag.

① dog
② cat
③ sheep
④ fish
⑤ monkey

03~08 빈칸에 공통으로 들어가기에 가장 적절한 것은? [각 2.8점]

03 Callie started feeding her _____ ideas, getting her to think there was something better out there for her.
He once again earned _____ applause from the audience.

① wild
② sound
③ mature
④ crazy
⑤ tamed

04 The pleasant aroma of fresh coffee _____ throughout the house.
Fear and panic _____ among the crowd when the fire alarm went off.

① moved ② fled ③ lingered
④ swept ⑤ transformed

05 Certain animals _____ to South America are endangered.
He grows a wide variety of both _____ and exotic plants.

① innovative ② inquisitive ③ ingenuous
④ indifferent ⑤ indigenous

06 The general's _____ enabled him to surprise the enemy.
The magician's trick turned out to be an elaborate _____.

① altercation ② tribulation ③ debacle
④ regression ⑤ artifice

07 The team has a plan to _____ a plane.
The _____ proclaimed that all states would have their own government.

① rent ② hire ③ charter
④ chapter ⑤ company

08 He was disappointed because the team _____ his brother.
The essay would be better if you _____ the first paragraph.

① left out ② tore down ③ stayed behind
④ dropped back ⑤ went against

09~10 밑줄 친 부분을 바꾸기에 가장 적절한 것은? [각 3.7점]

09 He seems to have some <u>inimical</u> feeling toward me.
① hospitable
② imitative
③ creative
④ hostile
⑤ amicable

10 The <u>upshot</u> of the matter was that they came to a compromise.
① total agreement
② final result
③ interim summary
④ brief wrap-up
⑤ unanimous decision

11~13 어법상 적절하지 <u>않은</u> 것은? [각 2.8점]

11 ① My brother is good at playing the piano.
② I have lived here since I was born.
③ His baggages have been lost at the airport.
④ Would you like some more coffee?
⑤ The girl wearing a red dress is my sister.

12 ① I have been to Paris three times.
② She hasn't finished her homework yet.
③ The movie was so interesting that I watched it twice.
④ Why did you go there by yourself?
⑤ He said that his business was as solid as rock.

13
① The book which I bought yesterday is interesting.
② Would you mind opening the window?
③ She speaks English as if she were a native speaker.
④ The book which cover is torn is mine.
⑤ The teacher made me study harder.

14~17 어법상 적절하지 않은 것은? [각 3.7점]

14
① It is high time we should go home.
② Only when he arrived did I leave the office.
③ Little did she know what would happen next.
④ Such was his anger that he couldn't speak.
⑤ Were I in your position, I would do the same.

15
① Can you give me a few nails? I need some.
② Do you have any knives? I need a sharp one.
③ I'd like some more colored paper, if you have any.
④ Shall I pass the butter? Or have you got one already?
⑤ I asked for a dozen tickets, but they couldn't spare many.

16
① Each of the students has finished the test.
② Whose book is laying on the table?
③ This is the man whom I met yesterday.
④ The teacher requested that we arrive early.
⑤ The city where I live is quite large.

17
① I used to know this area like the back of my hand.
② They stay away from high-fat food items like sweets.
③ Now that you have received this ad, you feel differently.
④ When you think about it, small talk is anything but small.
⑤ Had it not been for your help, I would fail.

18~20 빈칸에 들어가기에 가장 적절한 것은? [각 3.3점]

18 Almost everyone knows at least one language. Five-year-old children are nearly as proficient at speaking and understanding as their parents. Yet the ability to carry out the simplest conversation requires profound knowledge that most speakers are _____ of. This is true for speakers of all languages, from Albanian to Zulu. A speaker of English can produce a sentence having two relative clauses without knowing what a relative clause is.

① proud   ② full   ③ conscious
④ unaware   ⑤ skillful

19 The ancient Roman Forum has been meticulously preserved through the centuries, allowing modern visitors to experience its grandeur. Walking through the ruins today, with their towering columns and weathered stone pathways, visitors can witness the architectural elements that have inspired countless buildings worldwide. The detailed craftsmanship and monumental scale of these structures are _____ the immense power and sophistication of the Roman Empire at its height.

① indicative of   ② derivative of   ③ subordinate to
④ contingent on   ⑤ discrepant from

20 "Asian Americans are a deeply political group of folks in this country. We participated in the fight for civil rights in the 60s. Asian Americans were a part of what Cesar Chavez did. And this moment, as hard as it may seem, and as new as it may seem for some, is actually connected to a much _____. So, you know, we're doing this with history at our backs, and that's really exciting. I encourage folks to keep that in mind, especially when it gets hard."

① recent past
② habitual past
③ longer legacy
④ modern humanism
⑤ legendary profanity

21 글의 제목으로 가장 적절한 것은? [3.3점]

The number of stalking complaints filed with police more than quadrupled in one year. However, response measures for victims did not correspond with the sharp increase in cases. According to the report from the Police Science Institute (PSI), which analyzed the effectiveness of police response in protecting stalking victims under the current law, the enforcement of measures, such as separating perpetrators from victims, should be enhanced. The anti-stalking law delineates specific actions as stalking, encompassing activities such as approaching or following the victim, their partner or family; loitering near the victim's residence; and sending unsolicited objects, texts, words, pictures or videos through various communication channels.

① Declining Stalking Complaints
② Anti-stalking in Communication
③ PSI's Responsibility for Stalking
④ Stronger Measure against Stalking Necessary
⑤ Using New Media to Protect Stalking Victims

22 글의 내용과 가장 잘 부합하는 것은? [3.3점]

> The use of spices in medieval European cooking served multiple purposes beyond simply adding flavor. Wealthy hosts would serve heavily spiced dishes to demonstrate their prosperity, as spices were among the most expensive commodities of the time. Additionally, spices were believed to have medicinal properties according to the medical theories of the era. Medieval doctors prescribed specific spices to balance the body's "humors." Furthermore, in an age before refrigeration, strong spices could mask the taste of preserved meats that had begun to spoil, though historians now believe this was not their primary purpose.

① Spices were mainly used to preserve meat.
② Medieval doctors banned the use of spices in cooking.
③ Spices were considered luxury items in medieval Europe.
④ All spices were imported from neighboring countries.
⑤ Only rich people used spices in their daily lives.

23~25 글의 내용과 부합하지 않는 것은? [각 4.0점]

23

> An issue of central concern has been to determine which parts of the brain are responsible for human linguistic abilities. In the early nineteenth century, Franz Joseph Gall proposed the theory of localization, which is the idea that different human cognitive abilities and behaviors are localized in specific parts of the brain. For example, he proposed that language is located in the frontal lobes of the brain because as a young man he had noticed that the most articulate and intelligent of his fellow students had protruding eyes, which he believed reflected overdeveloped brain material. He also put forth a pseudoscientific theory called "organology" that later came to be known as phrenology, which is the practice of determining personality traits, intellectual capacities, and other matters by examining the "bumps" on the skull.

① Phrenology examines skull shapes.
② Gall was interested in localization of human bodies.
③ Protruding eyes were believed to reflect too big brain material.
④ Gall tried to develop a theory about personality and intelligence.
⑤ According to Gall, the frontal lobes of the brain are the locus of language.

24

One in six to seven Korean women in their 20s are underweight, and nearly half of women of underweight or normal weight in the same age group still try to lose even more weight. In contrast, the ratio of men in their 30s and 40s trying to lose weight has decreased despite the increasing prevalence of obesity. In addition, 15.1 percent of women aged between 19 and 29 were underweight in 2021 with a BMI (body mass index) less than 18.5. The ratio of underweight women of the same age stood at 14.8 percent between 2019 and 2021, up from the 12.4 percent tallied between 2016-2018. About 16.2 percent of these underweight women and 53.9 percent of women of normal weight attempted to lose weight.

① One in six to seven Koreans try to lose weight.
② The proportion of men in their 30s and 40s actively seeking weight loss has declined.
③ A significant proportion of women with normal weight still strives for weight reduction.
④ In 2021, 15.1 percent of women aged between 19 and 29 were with a BMI less than 18.5.
⑤ From 2016-2018 to 2019-2021, the proportion of underweight women increased by 2.4 percentage points.

25

Some 2,700 years ago in the ancient city of Samal, in what is now modern Turkey, an elderly servant of the king sits in a corner of his house and contemplates the nature of his soul. His name is Katumuwa. He stares at a basalt stele made for him, featuring his own graven portrait together with an inscription in ancient Aramaic. It instructs his family, when he dies, to celebrate "a feast at this chamber: a bull for Hadad Harpatalli and a ram for Nikarawas of the hunters and a ram for Shamash, and a ram for Hadad of the vineyards, and a ram for Kubaba, and a ram for my soul that is in this stele." Katumuwa believed that he had built a durable stone receptacle for his soul after death. This stele might be one of the earliest written records of dualism: the belief that our conscious mind is located in an immaterial soul or spirit, distinct from the matter of the body.

① Katumuwa was a man of the king of Samal about 2,700 years ago.
② The stele also instructs that a ram be given to Kubaba's soul.
③ This basalt stele could be the oldest written evidence of dualistic beliefs.
④ What Katumuwa was looking at was a basalt stele with his picture inscribed.
⑤ Dualism means that our consciousness is one thing but the matter of the body is another.

26~30 다음 글을 읽고 물음에 답하시오.

26~27

A search for the word *they* on Merriam-Webster's website turns up definitions for the personal pronoun, which saw a massive spike in lookups this year over last. Several months ago the dictionary added a definition for its 2019 Word of the Year that classified it as a functioning nonbinary pronoun. Merriam-Webster noted that the tiny, unassuming word had undergone a rather radical transformation in usage in recent years — and found itself at the heart of some wide-ranging cultural conversations in the process.

26 제목으로 가장 적절한 것은? [3.3점]

① Beyond *He* and *She*: The Story of *They*
② The Evolution of Personal Pronouns
③ The Impact of *She* on Language and Culture
④ A Reflection of Never Changing Gender Identities
⑤ The Rise of *They* as a Nonbinary Pronoun

27 밑줄 친 the tiny, unassuming word가 가리키는 것은? [4.3점]

① he
② she
③ they
④ person
⑤ people

28~30

Deep in the mountains of central Japan, there exists a centuries-old tradition of paper-making that continues to this day. The artisans who create washi, traditional Japanese paper, begin their work before dawn, when the mountain air is still crisp and clean. They harvest the inner bark of mulberry trees, carefully selecting only the strongest fibers. The process requires intense concentration and physical stamina. Each sheet is made by hand, with the artisan standing for hours in cold water, swaying back and forth as they mix the fibers with natural adhesives derived from local plants. Sometimes the weather is too warm, causing the fibers to decompose before they can be processed. Or the winter might be too harsh, freezing the water needed for production. Even when conditions are perfect, a moment's distraction can ruin an entire batch.

However, when everything aligns, the resulting paper possesses an almost magical quality — strong yet delicate, with a subtle sheen that seems to capture light itself. _____. Many practitioners speak of experiencing a deep sense of connection with their ancestors, who used the same techniques hundreds of years ago.

These artisans are more than just craftspeople; they are guardians of an endangered art form. Despite the availability of mass-produced paper, there remains a steady demand for high-quality washi among traditional artists, calligraphers, and collectors who appreciate its unique properties. Each sheet tells a story not just of the materials used to create it, but of the dedication and skill of the artisan who made it.

28. 글의 제목으로 가장 적절한 것은? [3.3점]

① Japan's Mountain Communities
② A Living Tradition of Craftsmanship
③ Modern Uses of Traditional Paper
④ The History of Japanese Paper
⑤ The Science of Paper-Making

29. 빈칸에 들어가기에 가장 적절한 것은? [4.3점]

① Each piece becomes a work of art in itself
② The market for traditional paper is shrinking
③ Most people in Japan are proud of their tradition
④ The process requires modern technology
⑤ The competition is becoming fierce

30 글의 내용과 부합하지 <u>않는</u> 것은? [3.3점]

① Traditional artists still value hand-made washi.
② The artisans stand in cold water while making paper.
③ The paper-making process starts early in the morning.
④ Weather conditions can affect the paper-making process.
⑤ The artisans use chemical adhesives to strengthen the paper.

단국대학교

▶ 2025학년도 인문계 오전 ▶ 문항 수: 40문항 | 제한시간: 60분

2025 단국대 인문계 오전 영역별 문항 수

구분	문법			어휘			논리완성	독해	생활영어	총 문항 수
	G/S, W/E	정비문	재진술	동의어	반의어	유추				
문항 수	10			10				20		40
백분율	25%			25%				50%		100%

DANKOOK UNIVERSITY

단국대학교

- 2025학년도 인문계 오전: 40문항 · 60분
- 체육교육 · 산업경영학(야): 영어 30문항 · 60분

공통 영어문제 별도* 표시

문항별 배점 01~30 2점 / 31~40 4점

01~10 밑줄 친 부분과 뜻이 가장 가까운 것을 고르시오.

01* Sit-down chain restaurants may be the <u>quintessential</u> American business, beginning with the expansion of Howard Johnson's after World War II as families got in the car and started to travel.

① representative ② abrupt
③ premeditated   ④ impetuous

02* In fact, the Nigerian government has campaigned for decades for the <u>restitution</u> of these culturally significant objects.

① repayment   ② recompense
③ restoration   ④ remuneration

03* The awards span various categories, including the Education Award for significant contributions to educational content and events and the Faculty Advisor Award for supporting and <u>fostering</u> student chapters.

① advising   ② leading
③ nurturing   ④ repressing

04. Even more <u>gruesome</u> are the methods used in the U.S. to kill millions of chickens and turkeys when bird flu is detected on a factory farm.

① ghastly
② efficacious
③ productive
④ frail

05. PFAS chemicals don't break down easily and have been linked to health issues, and <u>contamination</u> of soil and groundwater around the world.

① contemplation
② extent
③ pollution
④ suspension

06. His success is even more unusual because he is based in Africa, which lacks the East's and the West's well-resourced mechanisms for <u>promulgating</u> their creations.

① announcing
② expurgating
③ venerating
④ eradicating

07. A <u>perceptible</u> color difference is one that is so subtle that one has to look quite hard to see it.

① detectable
② practical
③ simple
④ intricate

08. The investigation also found that the board enjoyed a round of golf at a <u>prestigious</u> Beijing golf course, which has hosted several international golf tournaments.

① subsidiary
② national
③ presumptive
④ reputable

09 Greatness may evoke envy and <u>rancor</u> among those less great and misleadingly absolve others of their responsibilities.

① competition
② detestation
③ struggle
④ disunion

10* When we are in a state of painful loneliness, it is our bodies giving us information to find social support or do <u>reparative</u> work on our social ties.

① recuperative
② recumbent
③ reciprocal
④ recurrent

11~15 어법상 빈칸에 가장 적절한 것을 고르시오.

11* _____ her warmth and light firsthand, I know the energy she radiates in every room she enters.

① Having experienced
② Being experienced
③ To experience
④ Having been experienced

12* Since the operation two months ago, Samuel _____ to walk again. He can already take one or two steps unaided.

① has been learned
② has been learning
③ had been learning
④ had learned

13 Since _____ approach uses nor requires water as an application media for fluropolymer incorporation, then the environmental wastewater burden is eliminated.

① both
② either of
③ neither
④ none of

14* To understand how our social fabric has been transformed, think of marriage as an institution _____ upon by centripetal forces pulling inward and centrifugal forces pulling outward.

① acting
② acted
③ have been acting
④ have been acted

15 In the past few decades, the Palestinian vaccination effort was a success, in large part because of the ease _____ parents could take their children to hospitals for scheduled doses.

① with which
② whose
③ when
④ how

(16~20) 밑줄 친 부분 중 어법에 맞지 않은 것을 고르시오.

16* Not only ① did she have the internet on her side the second time around, ② in which helped more people ③ find the book, but ④ the world had also changed in other ways.

17* Protocols ① such as agar plate diffusion methods were ② less widely used as these qualitative protocols, while easy to conduct, yield data that are difficult ③ comparing and are ④ best designed for leaching technologies.

18* ① Instead of the quantitative liberalism of the 1930's, rightly ② dedicated to the struggle to ③ secure the economic basis of life, we need now a "qualitative liberalism" dedicated to ④ bettered the quality of people's lives and opportunities.

19 Power as a means of getting things ① done appeals to ② that which men share with brutes; to fear and to greed; power leads ③ those who wield it to desire it for its own sake, not ④ on the service it may render, and to seek its continuance in their own hands.

20 If you look at a map ① showing archaeological sites where ② remain and artifacts of human ancestors ③ have been found, you'll see sites linked to different species ④ clustering together in the same places.

21~22 다음 글을 읽고 물음에 답하시오.

Ice is frozen water. Glacial ice is quite different to more regular ice, including artificially made ice cubes. The compacted crystalline structure of glacial ice means that it absorbs every other colour (such as red and yellow light) in the spectrum apart from blue or turquoise. So the net effect is that it appears quite different to normal _____ ice, which reflects all visible light back without apparent preference. Blue light is the only form of light able to penetrate below its icy surface. What also makes glacial ice quite unlike ice cubes harvested from the freezer is that it will contain impurities such as rock, soil, plant and bacterial matter. It will be more than just simply frozen water.

But there is much more to it than that. Ice can take multiple crystalline forms, and it can resist the usual freezing point of 0°c (32°f) at lower pressures. It can carve and shape things like rock and soil, it can reflect back solar energy, it can float on water, and it plays a crucial role in the determining the Earth's energy balance. Ice never forgets its origins. It is a substance after all which is perfectly capable of turning back into water. If ice endures then it can shape-change. As a mover and shaker, it can excavate, spread and deposit. It can and does support life below and above its surface as fish, seals, polar bears, whales and smaller life such as algal meadows and microbes attest. Subglacial lakes buried under Antarctic glaciers and ice sheets are the latest extreme environment to attract scientific attention because of the possibility to investigate which microorganisms might endure.

21* Which is the most appropriate for the blank?

① translucent
② melting
③ sooted
④ angled

22* According to the passage, which is TRUE?

① Ice always remembers its origins.
② Ice cannot take diverse crystalline forms.
③ Ice cubes harvested from the freezer contain impurities.
④ Glacial ice is considered just simply frozen water.

23~24 다음 글을 읽고 물음에 답하시오.

A picture, so the saying goes, is worth a thousand words. But in a world in which millions of photographs are taken and uploaded every minute and we are exposed to a daily avalanche of pictures on our computer screens, what is the value of a single image? According to Martin Barnes, Senior Curator of photographs at the Victoria and Albert Museum in London, "Great photographs are like visual poetry. They neatly capture and express a situation or emotion that transcends the everyday." By capturing a single moment and holding it absolutely still, a photograph can convey a powerful idea in a universal language. But more than that, images can transport us to new places and help us see our lives from a different perspective. As National Geographic photographer Aaron Huey says, "Photography has the power to undo your assumptions about the world."

23 Which is NOT true about the photographs described by the author?

① We encounter a daily flood of images on our computer screens.
② Photographs can change our view of the world.
③ Photographs can offer a universal idea to the world.
④ Images can assist us to see our way of life from a different attitude.

24 Which is the closest meaning to the underlined part?

① accommodate   ② transform
③ fulfill   ④ realize

25~27 다음 글을 읽고 물음에 답하시오.

We constantly view the world around us through the lens of our thoughts. _____ seeing the world for what it is, we see things through our thoughts, memories, and emotions. This way of seeing things is a problem. We need to learn how to remove the lens we are looking through and see our thoughts rather than look at the world through our thoughts.

The first step in enjoying the present moment, whether we're gift-giving or having a cup of coffee, is to be fully connected to what we are doing and what is happening around us. Our attention is often focused on the past or the future. The past is full of regret; the future is usually linked to worry and concern. Connecting to the present means taking in our five-sense experiences with openness, curiosity, and willingness to experience whatever we experience.

When our mind is hooked to unhelpful thoughts, memories, emotions, and sensations, we need to learn how to let go of our struggle to control and avoid our discomfort. The moment we become reactive to uncomfortable memories, we make things worse, not better. Practice letting unwanted thoughts and emotions come and go without fighting against them. I like the metaphor of picturing thoughts and feelings as waves on a stormy sea. I can either fight waves on the surface or sink into the quietness of the water and notice them from a distance.

25 According to the passage, which is NOT true?

① The past and future are typically associated with positive feelings.
② Being connected to the present involves using all five senses actively.
③ Unwanted thoughts and emotions should be allowed to pass without resistance.
④ Our perception of the world is often filtered through our thoughts and emotions.

26 How does the author suggest we handle unhelpful thoughts and emotions?

① By intensifying our focus on them
② By revisiting painful memories frequently
③ By letting them come and go without resistance
④ By completely eliminating them from our minds

27 Which is the most appropriate for the blank?

① Because
② By
③ Despite
④ Rather than

28~30 다음 글을 읽고 물음에 답하시오.

What if there were a magic pill that could make you feel more in control of your life? In a sense, one already exists. Debbie Moskowitz, Ph.D., a psychology professor at McGill University in Montreal, recently discovered that upping the intake of tryptophan — the essential amino acid found in high-protein foods such as turkey and milk — may make people behave more <u>assertively</u>.

In her study, non-depressed people who took three grams of tryptophan for 12 days seemed more goal-oriented — making suggestions and placing demands on others — than did those who took a placebo. The subjects also acted less disagreeable and sarcastic. Moskowitz's findings lead her to believe that tryptophan works by maximizing the body's synthesis of serotonin, the neurotransmitter that acts as a natural antidepressant.

"Our bodies make enough serotonin so that most of the time we don't act submissive and quarrelsome," says Moskowitz. "But this study suggests that maximizing our serotonin with tryptophan will help us behave even more dominantly and less argumentatively, which can keep us feeling confident and help us accomplish our goals." Unfortunately, just upping your intake of high protein foods won't do the trick, because so many other amino acids in protein compete with tryptophan for transport to the brain. Instead, you need to take purified supplements that contain no other amino acids. But talk to your physician first, advises Moskowitz, because there have been contamination problems with tryptophan supplements in the past.

28. What is the main topic of the passage?

① The dangers of taking dietary supplements
② The effects of tryptophan on assertive behavior
③ The competitive absorption of amino acids in the brain
④ The relationship between diet and psychological well-being

29. Which is the closest meaning to the underlined part?

① sarcastically ② submissively
③ dominantly   ④ argumentatively

30. According to the passage, which is TRUE?

① Serotonin decreases when the intake of tryptophan increases.
② Most amino acids do not compete with tryptophan for brain transport.
③ Tryptophan supplementation was linked to more goal-oriented behavior in the study.
④ Eating high-protein foods is sufficient to increase tryptophan absorption in the brain.

[31~32] 다음 글을 읽고 물음에 답하시오.

> Society and the individual are inseparable; they are necessary and _____ to each other, not opposites. "No man is an island, entire of itself." in Donne's famous words. "Every man is a piece of the continent, a part of the main." That is an aspect of the truth. On the other hand, take the dictum of J. S. Mill, the classical individualist: "Men are not, when brought together, converted into another kind of substance." Of course not. But the fallacy is to suppose that they existed, or had any kind of substance, before being "brought together." As soon as we are born, the world gets to work on us and transforms us from merely biological into social units. Every human being at every stage of history or pre-history is born into a society and from his earliest years is moulded by that society. The language which he speaks is not an individual inheritance, but a social acquisition from the group in which he grows up. Both language and environment help to determine the character of his thought.

31 Which is the most appropriate for the blank?

① complementary   ② differentiated
③ satisfactory   ④ impartial

32 According to the passage, which is TRUE?

① Society and the individual usually exist like parallels which cannot be overlapped.
② If you don't see the social aspect of human beings, you are missing an important point of understanding them.
③ Men and language cannot be separated because they are helpful to each other.
④ Men are always transformed to a kind of social substance only when they have the will to do.

33~34 다음 글을 읽고 물음에 답하시오.

Identity will be the most valuable commodity for citizens in the future, and it will exist primarily online. Online experience will start with birth, or even earlier. Periods of people's lives will be frozen in time, and easily surfaced for all to see. Ⓐ_____, companies will have to create new tools for control of information, such as lists that would enable people to manage who sees their data. The communication technologies we use today are invasive by design, collecting our photos, comments and friends into giant databases that are searchable and, in the absence of outside regulation, fair game for employers, university admissions personnel and town gossips. We are what we tweet.

Ⓑ_____, all people would have the self-awareness to closely manage their online identities and the virtual lives they lead, monitoring and shaping them from an early age so as not to limit their opportunities in life. Of course, this is impossible. For children and adolescents, the incentives to share will always outweigh the vague, distant risks of self-exposure, even with salient examples of the consequences in public view. By the time a man is in his forties, he will have accumulated and stored a comprehensive online narrative, all facts and fictions, every misstep and every triumph, spanning every phase of his life. Even the rumors will live forever.

33 Which is the most appropriate for the blanks Ⓐ and Ⓑ?

① In response — Ideally
② However — In reality
③ In particular — However
④ On the contrary — Consequently

34 According to the passage, which is TRUE?

① It will be possible for online experience to start with birth in the future.
② The distant risks of self-exposure will outweigh the incentives to share for the youth.
③ Identity is not likely to exist primarily online for citizens in the future.
④ Our data are securely protected by the current communication technologies.

35~37 다음 글을 읽고 물음에 답하시오.

In 1810, a German physician named Samuel Hahnemann published an overview of his medical theories and research in a book titled *The Organon of the Healing Art*, which stated that consuming a substance that causes the symptoms of an illness could cure that illness. This was the birth of homeopathy.

A Ever since then, many people have tried this alternative treatment and found success with it. Often, homeopathic treatment is less expensive than conventional medicine is, since it is made from plants and other natural substances.

B Why shouldn't people be allowed to make their own health choices? They have this freedom in other aspects of their lives — for example, which school to send their children to — so why not in terms of their health care?

C Also, but perhaps less importantly, over 400 doctors in the United States regularly recommend homeopathic treatments. Since they are cheap and popular, I find it difficult to understand why Medicare and Medicaid do not fund them.

As for the critics who argue that homeopathy doesn't work, I could give hundreds of examples of patients who have been cured by my treatment. On top of that, there's plenty of research that shows the benefits it can bring.

Homeopathy _____ so long if it were complete nonsense. It has much more than just a placebo effect. Too much emphasis is sometimes put on providing "proof" of why something works. Belief is just as powerful.

35 According to the passage, which is NOT true?

① Conventional medical treatment costs more than homeopathic treatment.
② The treatment of a disease by taking substances causing symptoms of the disease is called homeopathy.
③ This alternative treatment has succeeded in treating many people.
④ Homeopathic treatment uses substances from plants and factitious resources.

36 Which is the most appropriate order for A, B, and C?

① B — A — C
② A — C — B
③ B — C — A
④ C — B — A

37. Which is the most appropriate for the blank?

① has survived
② should not have survived
③ might have survived
④ would not have survived

38~40 다음 글을 읽고 물음에 답하시오.

Stress has become so endemic that it is worn like a badge of courage. The business of stress reduction, from workshops to relaxation tapes to light and sound headsets, is booming. If ours is a culture without deep intimacy, then our relationship with stress is the exception.

The effects of stress are even more profound than imagined. It penetrates to the core of our being. Stress is not something that just grips us and, with time or effort, then lets go. It changes us in the process. It alters our bodies and brains.

We may respond to stress as we do an allergy. That is, we can become sensitized, or acutely sensitive, to stress. Once that happens, even the merest intimation of stress can trigger a cascade of chemical reactions in brain and body that assault us from within. Stress is the psychological equivalent of ragweed. Once the body becomes sensitized to pollen or ragweed, it takes only the slightest bloom in spring or fall to set off the biochemical alarm that results in runny noses, watery eyes, and the general misery of hay fever. But while only some of us are genetically programed to be plagued with hay fever, all of us have the capacity to become sensitized to stress.

38. What is the main idea of the passage?

① Stress is less harmful than previously believed.
② Only a few people are biochemically affected by stress.
③ Stress reduction methods are ineffective in the long run.
④ Stress is akin to a physical allergy in how our bodies respond to it.

39. Which is the closest meaning to the underlined part?
① ceases
② infiltrates
③ obstructs
④ precedes

40. According to the passage, which is TRUE?
① Stress only affects our physical state, not our mental state.
② Everyone is genetically programmed to suffer from hay fever.
③ Stress is easily overcome by most people without any long-term effects.
④ The body may become sensitized to stress, reacting strongly to even slight triggers.

단국대학교

▶ 2025학년도 인문계 오후　▶ 문항 수: 40문항 ｜ 제한시간: 60분

2025 단국대 인문계 오후 영역별 문항 수

구분	문법			어휘			논리완성	독해	생활영어	총 문항 수
	G/S, W/E	정비문	재진술	동의어	반의어	유추				
문항 수	10			10				20		40
백분율	25%			25%				50%		100%

DANKOOK UNIVERSITY

단국대학교

2025학년도 인문계 오후: 40문항 · 60분

문항별 배점 01~30 2점 / 31~40 4점

01~10 밑줄 친 부분과 뜻이 가장 가까운 것을 고르시오.

01 She won't initiate the mass <u>deportation</u> of undocumented immigrants, as Trump promises, or fire legions of civil servants and replace them with MAGA loyalists.

① invitation
② banishment
③ summon
④ deployment

02 If our doctors were <u>conspicuously</u> overworked according to our standards, it would be hard to get young people to choose that profession.

① randomly
② reciprocally
③ obviously
④ generously

03 Through nonviolent resistance the Negro will be able to rise to the noble height of opposing the unjust system while loving the <u>perpetrators</u> of the system.

① executors
② experts
③ governors
④ attorneys

04 First of all, the smaller population doesn't contain all the genetic material of the species as a whole. It's a <u>skewed</u> sample, so that soon the two populations are going to look recognizably different.

① clarified
② straightforward
③ fictitious
④ contorted

05 They have concentrated their criticism on the separation of powers which <u>hamstrings</u> the executive, blurs responsibility and accountability, and makes it impossible for the country to frame coherent policy.

① accommodates
② accelerates
③ provokes
④ cripples

06 The feedback relationship between the two sets of events is as <u>indubitable</u> as it was prolonged in time.

① disputable
② dubious
③ irrefutable
④ familiar

07 Thomas Alva Edison, the genius inventor, only attended school for three months before it was decided that he was too <u>fidgety</u> and distractable to fit in.

① avaricious
② impatient
③ keen
④ princely

08 I was underlined{exasperated} by the critics who assert that B.A. degree isn't worth a nickel in the pay envelope, and that a college education is no good.

① suffocated ② provoked
③ irritated ④ agitated

09 The underlined{downtrodden} population of one side resists the military occupation of the wealthier overload, but endures the bulk of the carnage.

① trampled ② dwindled
③ retained ④ bolstered

10 Last year, caregiver and domestic helper expenses increased by 50 percent and 37 percent, respectively, compared to 2016.

① approximately ② correspondingly
③ distinctively ④ quantitatively

11~15 어법상 빈칸에 가장 적절한 것을 고르시오.

11 The man wore a hat pulled down over his eyes and a large coat that _____ be covering something.

① seems to ② seemed to
③ will seem to ④ may seem to

12 Sensing and intuition refer to how people prefer to gather information about the world, _____ concrete information (sensing) or emotional feelings (intuition).

① in spite of
② as such
③ because of
④ whether through

13 Other less-than-orthodox treatments he recommends _____ activities that can help people feel in step with others, including dancing, drumming, and choir, as well as in step with themselves, such as yoga and breath work.

① include
② including
③ to include
④ includes

14 In a retail environment where consumers are faced with a dizzying array of products, this kind of service can combat what _____ as "the paralysis of choice."

① has referred to
② has been referred to
③ has been referring to
④ had referred to

15 The findings reveal that youngsters who spend 30 or more hours a week in group child care _____ academically than those cared for in other ways.

① score more higher
② score more highly
③ score higher
④ have scored high

16~20 밑줄 친 부분 중 어법에 맞지 않은 것을 고르시오.

16 ① People-pleasing usually stems from childhood ② as a result of some sort of trauma, often from ③ grown up with someone in your family who was particularly volatile, so you'd learn ④ to control people's reactions.

17 Most people have settled on describing them as tapestries or quilts, partly because ① those are the closest things the Western art traditions ② has to his giant, supple swaths, and partly because the amount of close-up handiwork ③ that goes into making them ④ is similar.

18 The book offered several helpful strategies ① to deal with procrastination, ② including breaking the task down into manageable chunks, starting small and ③ removed distractions such as ④ listening to music.

19 ① To force companies' hands, Forrest suggests that governments adopt legally binding carbon budgets, ② which would require all proposed projects ③ to be disclosed carbon intensities, and ④ be approved based on them.

20 Robbins cries one last time during our three hour conversation, ① as she speaks of a visitor center attendant in Iceland ② who recognized her voice ③ which she asked for directions to the bathroom, ④ burst into tears, and shared how her YouTube videos were a lifeline during a painful divorce.

(21~23) 다음 글을 읽고 물음에 답하시오.

It is a curious phenomenon of nature that only two species practice the art of war — men and ants, both of which, significantly, maintain complex social organizations. This does not mean that only men and ants engage in the murder of their own kind. Many animals of the same species kill each other, but only men and ants have practiced the science of organized destruction, employing their massed numbers in violent combat and relying on strategy and tactics to meet developing situations or to capitalize on the weaknesses in the strategy and tactics of the other side. The longest continuous war ever fought between men lasted thirty years. The longest ant war ever recorded lasted six-and-a-half weeks, or whatever the corresponding units would be in ant reckoning.

While all entomologists are agreed that war is instinctive with ants, it is encouraging to note that not all anthropologists and biologists are agreed that war is instinctive with men. Those who lean on experience, of course, find everything in man's history to indicate that war is locked up within his nature. But a broader and more generous, certainly more philosophical, view is held by those scientists who claim that the evidence of a war instinct in men is _____ and misleading, and that man does have within him the power of abolishing war. Julian Huxley, the English biologist, draws a sharp distinction between human nature and the expression of human nature. Thus war is not a reflection but the expression of man's nature. Moreover, the expression may change, as the factors which lead to war may change. "In man, as in ants, war in any serious sense is bound up with the existence of accumulations of property to fight about. As for human nature, it contains no specific war instinct, as does the nature of harvester ants. There is in man's makeup a general aggressive tendency, but this, like all other human urges, is not a specific and unvarying instinct; it can be molded into the most varied forms."

21 Which is the most appropriate for the blank?

① incomplete
② wholesome
③ reasonable
④ incorrupt

22 According to the passage, which is NOT true about Julian Huxley's argument?

① There are many elements for men which lead to war.
② There is no specific war instinct for men.
③ Men make war only for occupying the huge property of others.
④ Aggressive nature is one of all other human urges.

23 According to the passage, which is TRUE?

① The war instinct of men and ants cannot be discriminated.
② Men can have simultaneously both tendencies of war making and war abolishing.
③ Men's war instinct can have only a few forms of expression.
④ Social organizations are the only cause of war for men and ants.

24~25 다음 글을 읽고 물음에 답하시오.

> In addition to oxygen, the blood needs to carry a constant supply of glucose, or the muscles will run out of energy. This is especially true during exercise, when energy use is high. However, the body cannot store glucose or other sugars. Ⓐ_____, energy is stored as glycogen, a carbohydrate made up of many glucose molecules joined in long chains.
>
> The main store of glycogen in the body is the liver. When there is too much glucose in the blood (for instance, just after a meal), the liver takes up some glucose and turns it into glycogen. During exercise, when the glucose in the blood is quickly used up, the liver breaks down some of its glycogen to glucose and releases it into the blood.
>
> Muscles first use the glycogen stored in the liver during exercise. Then the body has to begin using its fat stores to supply the muscles. Ⓑ_____, the body cannot burn fats as quickly as sugars. Once the muscles start using fat, the athlete slows down.

24 Which is the most appropriate for the blanks Ⓐ and Ⓑ?

① Instead — However
② For example — Overall
③ Accordingly — Therefore
④ On the contrary — In addition

25 According to the passage, which is TRUE?

① The body can burn sugars faster than fats.
② Glucose or other sugars can be stored in the body.
③ The body first uses its fat stores to supply the muscles during exercise.
④ The blood takes up some glycogen and turns it into glucose.

26~27 다음 글을 읽고 물음에 답하시오.

Within the countries that provide free or public health care, there are many models. In some countries, consultations, treatment, and medicines are free to all citizens. This may be paid for directly by the government, perhaps funded by the country's valuable natural resources that the government owns. Other countries collect money from citizens through taxes based on their income. Workers pay according to how much they earn, and employers also make a contribution. Hospitals and other medical services are then provided and run by the government. There may also be some private medical services that people can choose to buy. The advantage of systems such as these is clear: free basic health care for all, <u>regardless of</u> income. However, it is a very expensive system and, as life expectancy and costs rise, many countries are facing either an unsustainable financial burden, or a drop in the quality of services and facilities provided.

26 Which is the topic of the passage?

① The functions of free or public health care
② Many models for free or public health care
③ Two effects of health care services
④ Advantages of public health care systems

27 Which is the closest meaning to the underlined part?

① in spite of
② in addition to
③ irrespective of
④ in relation to

28~30 다음 글을 읽고 물음에 답하시오.

Men who make money can't wait to marry. But well-to-do women are in no such hurry. Working women are 50 percent more likely to move in with their partner and 15 percent less likely to marry than women who lack a stable employment history. Men with money, however, are only 13 percent more likely to live with their partner before marriage, but 26 percent more likely to get hitched than men who earn an average salary.

Matin Clarkberg of Cornell University's Employment and Family Careers Institute examined data of people surveyed over a 14-year period — covering job history, income, and views on marriage. She notes that men feel ready to wed once they reach a high standard of living because they know they can fulfill the traditional role of breadwinner.

But financially secure women prefer _____, says Clarkberg, so they can focus on their careers without juggling domestic duties. "For women, marriage often entails hanging up the briefcase," she says. "Their housework goes up, and if there are children, the woman tends to become the primary caretaker." But, "cohabiting couples are usually more egalitarian." The live-in woman can devote herself to both the partner and the job.

28 What is the main topic of the passage?

① The career impacts of marriage on working women
② The influence of financial stability on the perspectives of marriage
③ The increasing tendency of men to live with their partners before marriage
④ The differences in household duties between cohabiting and married couples

29 What does Matin Clarkberg suggest about the traditional role of men in marriage?

① Men feel pressure to marry regardless of their financial situation.
② Men are ready to marry once they can fulfill the role of breadwinner.
③ Men are less interested in marriage when they have a high standard of living.
④ Men generally reject traditional roles in marriage.

30 Which is the most appropriate for the blank?

① cohabitation ② marriage
③ separation   ④ divorce

[31~33] 다음 글을 읽고 물음에 답하시오.

The concept of history as an escalator carrying man to perfection grew out of profound changes in the human situation and outlook beginning with the Renaissance. The first deep change was the rediscovery and development of science. Nature no longer seemed arbitrary or intractable. Governed by laws which could be discovered and then controlled, it was subject to mastery.

Once physical nature was seen to be lawful, it seemed natural to assume that human nature was too. As reason had disclosed the principles regulating the former, so would it (once it set itself to the job) lay bare the laws relating human life and how these too might be channeled toward man's well-being. The task might even prove not to be difficult. Voltaire wrote that, whereas it has taken centuries to learn a part of nature's laws, one day was sufficient for a wise man to learn the duties of man.

This extension of faith in reason's efficacy from physical to human nature marked the second attitudinal change in the modern world supporting the idea of progress. The Enlightenment's confidence in reason was astonishing and exhilarating. As Carl Becker has pointed out, the world on which the 18th century looked seemed almost new because so recently bathed with reason's light. It was a world in which everything seemed wonderfully clear and in focus, with details falling into place by the hour. The assurance with which the Encyclopedists ranged their guns of the intellect against the bastions of ignorance and superstition is almost breathtaking. Autonomous reason, backed by the universal assent of mankind, was to be the supreme authority. Mind was to be not just king; it was Messiah. Laggards might refuse to follow, but time would take care of them as it rolled inexorably on its upward way.

31 According to the passage, which is NOT true?

① The major transforming force of the Renaissance was science.
② The major transforming force of the modern world is reason.
③ Ignorance was a kind of enemy to the modern reason.
④ Superstition was regarded as one of wisdom in the modern world.

32 Which is the main idea of this passage?

① The significance of science and reason in the modern world
② The reason of the collapse of the modern world
③ Enlightenment and superstition
④ Mastering power of scientific technology

33 According to the passage, which is the logical ground of the underlined part of Voltaire's argument?

① A wise man is so clever to understand human beings.
② The similar law governs nature and human.
③ Human duties are so complicated to understand.
④ Human law is much more simple than nature's law.

34~35 다음 글을 읽고 물음에 답하시오.

In order to Ⓐ_____ the problems that drought can bring, there are several short- and long-term strategies that can be adopted. A range of policies designed to combat these problems exists at local, national, and international levels. As well as general issues related to this topic, there are specific recommendations that can be made in the case of Kenya, where drought has been a major problem in recent years.

Droughts frequently put millions of people at risk of food Ⓑ_____ in central Kenya. The area is so dry that it cannot support agricultural crops. There are few permanent rivers, and the seasonal waterways caused by flood waters in the rainy months disrupt transportation across the region. The people of this area mainly live off their cattle. Droughts can quickly kill off their animals, which eliminates their main source of income. Finally, because the area is so vast, infrastructure is under-developed, so access to the population is difficult.

34 According to the passage, which is NOT true?

① Several ways are being implemented to overcome the drought issues.
② Kenya is too dry for growing crops.
③ Kenya depends on livestock and agriculture for its livelihood.
④ Droughts can be the crucial reason causing the residents to lose their economic sources.

35 Which is the most appropriate for the blanks Ⓐ and Ⓑ?

① mitigate — insecurity
② define — uncertainty
③ diminish — abundance
④ expand — scarcity

36~37 다음 글을 읽고 물음에 답하시오.

The human child shows probably a greater variety of playful activities than any other young animal. He displays, for example, in addition to the fighting and hunting play which he shares with other animals, the activity of pulling things to pieces, which Groos calls *analytical play*.

He also shows *synthetic play* (with toy bricks or modelling clay) in which he builds up new things. These are clearly rehearsal of the adult behavior of curiosity and of construction respectively. Later, he may exercise himself in play which stimulates adult activities that are relatively distant from primitive forms of behavior, as for example, bartering, and even the carrying out of religious ceremonies.

Activities which fulfill Groos's definition of play do not, however, exhaust the list of rehearsal phenomena to be found in animal and human life. _____, for example, is an activity which is to some extent a rehearsal of the sexual act, and is indulged in for its own sake. It does not, however, belong to quite the same class as the fighting or hunting play of young animals, for it is an adult activity, leading up to and having an obvious function in the performance of the sexual act itself.

Other rehearsal phenomena discussed by Groos are the baby's exploratory movements of the hands, and his other activities which bring him new experimental sensations. We ought, probably, also to bring under the heading of rehearsal phenomena some of the infantile forms of emotional reaction which are regarded by the psychoanalysts as infantile elements from which the adult sex-instincts develop.

36 Which is the most appropriate for the blank?

① Courtship   ② Friendship
③ Membership   ④ Championship

37 According to the passage, which is TRUE?

① Play is the culture shared only by children.
② There are many kinds of play not having any rehearsal role.
③ Children's play can be a rehearsal developing into an adult's culture.
④ There is no connection between play and reality.

38~40 다음 글을 읽고 물음에 답하시오.

Virtual Reality (VR) and Augmented Reality (AR) are among the most recent developments in technologies of surveillance that date back to the video and photographic cameras, as well as audio-recording devices. Placing devices in our environment to watch and listen to us is nothing _____; what is novel is the intimate and pervasive relationship that these media technologies set up between users and their space around them. Earlier surveillance technologies were situated somewhere in the world and surveilled us from a vantage point, and even then, the sense that the space was watching us was uncanny enough. Countless spy and detective films feature planted recording devices. Directors of horror and suspense films treat the camera itself as a surveillance device to evoke a sense that the characters are under threat. But the film camera is necessarily only in one location at a time. AR and VR tracking and sensing technologies enlist the whole space to surveil us. They connect us to the space so that we become part of a unified system of mutual sensing and response.

When this works as intended, the space becomes responsive to our actions to achieve the task or create the experience intended. In a VR space, we look in one direction or another, and the system responds by drawing objects in the appropriate perspective. We reach out with our hand or a controller and can pick up virtual objects. In an AR space, the desired information appears in the right place at the right time. But we know that this interaction of tracking and sensing could be transmitted to a server on the internet and recorded. The space around us in that sense is not necessarily benign and cooperative; it may be appropriated to the interests of companies or governments. A rupture occurs when we feel that the space itself has become a surveillance device. Whether benign or threatening, the spaces of AR and VR awaken a sense of the uncanny. It may be a mild surprise at how responsive the space is or a stronger reaction to the threat that the space may pose.

38 Which is the topic of the passage?

① The doubtful aspect of VR and AR spaces as recent surveillance technologies
② The significance of VR and AR spaces as useful surveillance devices nowadays
③ How AR and VR tracking and sensing technologies connect us to the space
④ The way companies or governments use VR and AR technologies for their interest

39. According to the passage, which is NOT true?
① The space itself became a surveillance device due to earlier technologies.
② It is possible for the space to respond to our actions in the spaces of VR and AR.
③ Planted recording devices are featured in many spy and detective films.
④ Photographic cameras were also considered surveillance technologies.

40. Which is the most appropriate for the blank?
① new
② threatening
③ weird
④ expensive

덕성여자대학교

▶ 2025학년도 1교시 ▶ 문항 수: 33문항 | 제한시간: 50분

2025 덕성여대 1교시 영역별 문항 수

구분	문법			어휘			논리완성	독해	생활영어	총 문항 수
	G/S, W/E	정비문	재진술	동의어	반의어	유추				
문항 수	6			4			6	17		33
백분율	18%			12%			18%	52%		100%

DUKSUNG WOMEN'S UNIVERSITY

덕성여자대학교

2025학년도 1교시: 33문항 · 50분

01~02 Select the word that has the most similar meaning to the word in capital letters.

01 IMPROMPTU [2.8점]
① rehearsed
② spontaneous
③ rigid
④ scheduled

02 TENACIOUS [3점]
① impartial
② grudging
③ persistent
④ apathetic

03~04 Choose the answer that has the closest meaning to the underlined word.

03 She gave an <u>incredulous</u> look when she heard the unbelievable news. [3점]
① skeptical
② coerced
③ gullible
④ indifferent

04 In the gloomy poem, he <u>laments</u> the destruction of the countryside. [1.8점]
① celebrates
② mourns
③ ignores
④ wanders

05~10 Choose the best answer to complete each sentence.

05 The manager's decision was seen as _____, since it balanced the needs of the employees with the _____ of the company. [2점]

① swift — values
② inattentive — rules
③ thoughtful — priorities
④ arbitrary — goals

06 The artist's latest work is both _____ and _____, earning praise for its originality while sparking intense debates among critics. [2점]

① conventional — insipid
② derivative — foreseeable
③ obscure — irrelevant
④ provocative — innovative

07 Due to its immense historical value, the ancient artifact was carefully displayed in a climate-controlled glass case to ensure its _____ preservation for future generations. [2.8점]

① enduring
② careless
③ temporary
④ haphazard

08 The athlete's extraordinary skills were evident throughout the competition, but it was her _____ performance in the final event that earned her a standing ovation from the crowd. [2점]

① lackluster
② mediocre
③ flawless
④ chaotic

09 Despite the _____ conditions, the team managed to complete the project on time.

[2.2점]

① idyllic ② serene
③ irrelevant ④ trying

10 The lake was so _____ that you could see the fish swimming at the bottom.

[3.4점]

① radiant ② unanimous
③ limpid ④ exotic

11~13 Choose the best answer to make each sentence grammatically correct.

11 He traveled to _____ Paris last year and visited _____ Eiffel Tower.

[3.6점]

① - / the ② the / the
③ the / - ④ - / -

12 I wish I _____ more time to prepare for the test yesterday. [3.2점]

① have ② had
③ had had ④ will have

13 Neither of the options _____ acceptable to the committee. [3.2점]

① having been ② was
③ are ④ isn't

14~16 Identify the part where the English grammar is incorrect in the following paragraphs.

14 Maria enjoys painting in her free time because it <u>helps her to relax</u>. She often paints landscapes and sometimes portraits, but <u>she rarely shows</u> her works to anyone. Last week, she <u>decided to paint picture of</u> her neighborhood park, and she was <u>thrilled with the results</u>. [3.6점]

① helps her to relax
② she rarely shows
③ decided to paint picture of
④ thrilled with the results

15 The <u>complex nature</u> of quantum mechanics <u>requires scientists to approach</u> problems <u>with a high degree</u> of precision, making it one of the most challenging <u>field in physics</u>. [3점]

① complex nature
② requires scientists to approach
③ with a high degree
④ field in physics

16 After months of saving, <u>Daniel finally purchased his dream car</u>, a sleek red convertible. He couldn't wait to take it for a drive and show it off to his friends. On the first weekend, he invited his best friend, Liam, to join him for a road trip to the coast. <u>As they drove, Daniel noticed that the engine was making a strange sound</u>, but he decided to ignore it. However, <u>halfway through the trip, the car suddenly broke down, leaving them stranding</u> in the middle of nowhere. Daniel felt frustrated but grateful that <u>Liam stayed calm and called for assistance</u>. [3.4점]

① Daniel finally purchased his dream car
② As they drove, Daniel noticed that the engine was making a strange sound
③ halfway through the trip, the car suddenly broke down, leaving them stranding
④ Liam stayed calm and called for assistance

17~33 Read the following passages and answer the questions.

17~18

> Can the perception of a product be influenced by background music? In an attempt to address this inquiry, researchers conducted a study where participants were presented with slides featuring light blue or beige pens. Concurrently, pleasant or unpleasant music played while the participants viewed the pens. Later, when asked to select a pen as a gift, the majority chose the one they had observed while listening to the pleasant background music. Interestingly, many participants were not conscious of the impact of the music on their decision. A significant number stated that they were unaware of why they preferred one pen over the other pen.

17 What was the primary goal of the study mentioned in the passage? [3.2점]

① To determine the impact of music on memory
② To explore whether background music influences one's opinion of a product
③ To investigate why certain pen colors are more popular than others
④ To study the relationship between background music and one's favorite colors

18 Which of the following words best replaces "Concurrently" in the sentence? [2.8점]

① Simultaneously ② Formerly
③ Separately   ④ Subsequently

19~22

The term "cell" originates from the Latin "cellula," meaning a small room. An English polymath Robert Hooke coined the name since his observation of plant cells reminded him of monks' small rooms. Cells, the basic units of life, can be unicellular (e.g., bacteria) or multicellular (e.g., humans). Despite their diverse types, sizes, and functions, all cells share common features.

All cells have a protective cell membrane allowing the passage of microscopic molecules. With the exception of bacteria cells, all cells also have a nucleus which contains DNA and directs the cell's activities. Most cellular activities occur in the cytoplasm, a jelly-like material consisting of water and other substances.

Among the many kinds of cells, the two most familiar are animal and plant cells. Plant cells have a protective cellulose cell wall while animal cells do not. They also have chloroplasts for photosynthesis which converts sunlight into energy. Plant cells also contain large vacuoles which help maintain the shape of the cell.

Cells constantly reproduce and die, with about three billion human cells dying every minute. New cells emerge through division, starting with one cell duplicating its chromosomes. Cell growth and division occur between these stages. Powerful electron microscopes aid cell studies, magnifying cells over a million times. However, some cell parts remain invisible even with such technology, so video camera-enhanced images prove very useful for cytology development.

19 What process allows cells to constantly reproduce and replace dying cells? [3점]

① Photosynthesis
② Cellular respiration
③ Cell division
④ Nutrient processing

20 According to the passage, which of the following is true? [3.8점]

① All cells contain DNA.
② Powerful electron microscopes can view all cell parts.
③ The cytoplasm is a rigid structure.
④ The cell membrane regulates the passage of molecules.

21 What is the role of the nucleus in a cell? [3.4점]

① It stores energy for the cell.

② It directs cell activities.

③ It produces protein for the cell.

④ It magnifies cells over millions of times.

22 What is unique about plant cells compared to animal cells? [2.8점]

① Plant cells have a cellulose cell wall.

② Plant cells do not have a nucleus.

③ Plant cells lack cytoplasm.

④ Plant cells contain smaller vacuoles than animal cells.

23~25

We are not unlike a particular hardy crustacean. The lobster grows by developing and shedding a series of hard, protective shells. Each time it expands from within, the confining shell must be sloughed off. The lobster is left exposed and vulnerable until, in time, a new covering grows to replace the old. With each passage from one stage of human growth to the next, we, too, must shed a protective structure. We are left exposed and vulnerable — but also yeasty and embryonic again, capable of stretching in ways we hadn't known before. These sheddings may take several years or more. Coming out of each passage, though, we enter a longer and more stable period in which we can expect relative tranquility and a sense of equilibrium regained.

As we shall see, each person engages in the steps of development in his or her own characteristic step-style. Some people never complete the whole sequence. And none of us "solves" with one step — by jumping out of the parental home into a job or marriage, for example — the problems of separating from the caregivers of childhood. Nor do we "achieve" autonomy once and for all by converting our dreams into concrete goals, even when we attain those goals. The central issues or tasks of one period are never fully completed, tied up, and cast aside. But when they lose their primacy and the current life structure has served its purpose, we are ready to move on to the next period.

23. **According to the passage, which of the following is NOT true?** [3.8점]

   ① Humans gain complete autonomy by achieving their goals.
   ② Human growth can be described through an analogy.
   ③ Human sheddings may take numerous years.
   ④ Humans go through the developmental steps in their own ways.

24. **What happens to individuals during the transition from one stage of growth to the next?** [3.2점]

   ① They gain immediate stability and confidence.
   ② They feel insecure but are capable of growth.
   ③ They experience permanent equilibrium and tranquility.
   ④ They completely resolve all their past developmental issues.

25. **How does the passage describe the periods following a major developmental transition?** [3점]

   ① They are marked by ongoing instability and change.
   ② They produce a sense of equilibrium and calmness.
   ③ They require revisiting past issues to achieve closure.
   ④ They are characterized by rapid, successive transitions.

26~28

To say that Samuel Smith Old Brewery prides itself on tradition is to wildly understate the intensity of its chairman's longing for a different era. With over 200 pubs throughout the UK, his aim seems to be to build an entire world in which the past — or at least, his idealized picture of the past — is preserved just as it was. For decades, Smith has used his considerable personal means to pursue this vision. He seems to regard his properties as stage-sets, on which people — pubgoers, managers, local residents — must perform the roles he assigns to them, exactly as he directs. Where this is not possible, the premises' curtain instantly falls.

Inside the pubs, efforts to procure any snack, spirit or beer not made by Samuel Smith will prove futile. All beers on tap are brewed in Samuel Smith's Old Brewery, using water drawn from Yorkshire's magnesium limestone natural wells. Even the potatoes for the crisps in its pubs come from Yorkshire. The brewery keeps prices low. _____, In exchange for the savings, drinkers must submit to strict rules for how patrons should conduct themselves. The Samuel Smith website specifies that drinks should be enjoyed in a "responsible" manner. "Friendly pub conversation is encouraged" but swearing is forbidden. Televisions, laptops and mobile phones are banned. Customers who take out their phones for any reason other than to pay can expect a warning from the publican.

26 Which of the following best describes the chairman's approach to running the pubs? [3.2점]

① Encouraging innovation and creativity among pub managers
② Modernizing the pubs with the latest technology and other offerings
③ Allowing customers to make decisions about their behavior freely
④ Treating the pubs like historical landmarks where tradition must be preserved

27 Which word or phrase should fill the blank in the second paragraph? [3점]

① However
② Moreover
③ As a result
④ Likewise

28. What does "the premises' curtain instantly falls" most likely mean in the passage? [3.8점]

① The pub closes down if the chairman's rules cannot be followed.
② The chairman decides to renovate the premises for modern use.
③ The pub becomes a place for theatrical performances.
④ The pub stops serving Samuel Smith products temporarily.

29~31

Emma glanced out the window as the rain began to fall, drumming softly against the glass. She had planned to spend the day hiking in the nearby hills, where the autumn leaves were just starting to turn brilliant shades of red and gold. However, the dark clouds that had rolled in overnight had other plans. The forecast now warned of heavy rain and strong winds, and Emma reluctantly put her hiking boots back in the closet. Determined not to let the day go to waste, she lit a candle, brewed her favorite chamomile tea, and settled onto the couch with a thick, well-worn novel. The storm outside soon grew louder, with the wind howling and tree branches swaying in the gusts, but Emma felt cozy and safe in her little living room. She wrapped herself in a soft blanket and let herself be transported into the world of her book, a story she had loved since she was a child. Although she was disappointed to miss her hike, Emma couldn't help but feel grateful for the quiet, unexpected pause. The day might not have gone as planned, but it gave her the perfect excuse to slow down and enjoy the simple comfort of being indoors.

29. What does Emma's decision to stay indoors and enjoy her book reveal about her character? [3.4점]

① She does not enjoy outdoor activities.
② She is adaptable and makes the best of unexpected changes.
③ She enjoys reading above all other activities.
④ She is nostalgic and always dwells on the past.

30 What role does the storm play in the narrative? [3.6점]

① It creates a conflict that disrupts Emma's original plans and leaves her frustrated.
② It highlights Emma's tendency to avoid challenges and seek comfort.
③ It symbolizes the unpredictability of nature and Emma's fear of it.
④ It serves as a catalyst for Emma to appreciate the importance of relaxation.

31 Which of the following words best replaces "reluctantly" in the sentence? [3점]

① eagerly
② grudgingly
③ cautiously
④ indifferently

32~33

> Nowadays even your toaster can be programmed to work in response to a voice command, so it should be no surprise that cars have been assigned the task of driving for us. It seems futuristic, but it now seems certain that cars and trucks will become fully automated. Is this a good thing?
>
> Self-driving cars — also known as driverless or autonomous cars — can scan their immediate surroundings and navigate without any human intervention. The obvious benefit to this technology is convenience, but even if travel becomes faster and cheaper, a number of unresolved problems such as safety and liability make this innovation largely undesirable. There are no legal frameworks or government regulations for autonomous vehicles, and driverless cars open up a world of catastrophic possibilities for cybercriminals such as hackers or terrorists.
>
> There are clear advantages to automated features such as speed control or emergency braking, but those are fundamentally distinct from the technology of full automation. Driver-assisted technology is a beneficial goal for automotive engineers, but it's time to draw a line and insist that humans — not computers — should drive vehicles.

32 The author's main argument can best be summarized as _____ : [3점]

① Speed control and emergency braking demonstrate the need to switch to fully automated cars
② There are no laws that govern automated vehicles
③ The risks associated with self-driving cars far outweigh their benefits
④ Although convenient, self-driving cars would lead to an increase in terrorism

33 According to the reading, what's the difference between "automated features" and "full automation"? [3점]

① Automated features allow the driver to take a nap while in transit.
② Automated features offer assistance to a human driver, but full automation requires no driver.
③ Automated features are dangerous while full automation is relatively harmless.
④ Automated features rely less on human decisions than full automation.

DUKSUNG WOMEN'S UNIVERSITY

덕성여자대학교

▶ **2025학년도 2교시** ▶ **문항 수: 33문항** | **제한시간: 50분**

2025 덕성여대 2교시 영역별 문항 수

구분	문법			어휘			논리완성	독해	생활영어	총 문항 수
	G/S, W/E	정비문	재진술	동의어	반의어	유추				
문항 수	5			6			5	17		33
백분율	15%			18%			15%	52%		100%

DUKSUNG WOMEN'S UNIVERSITY

덕성여자대학교

2025학년도 2교시: 33문항 · 50분

01~03 Select the word that has the most similar meaning to the word in capital letters.

01 **VIVACIOUS** [3.2점]
① dull   ② solemn
③ lively   ④ colorful

02 **TRANSPARENT** [2.5점]
① reflective   ② opaque
③ difficult   ④ clear

03 **IMPARTIAL** [2.8점]
① obscure   ② fair
③ indifferent   ④ severe

04~08 Choose the best answer to complete each question.

04 She won the court case, but it was a _____ victory because she had to pay so much in legal fees. [4점]
① lyric   ② cynic
③ laconic   ④ pyrrhic

05 Many separated couples fight over _____ of their children. [3.5점]

① maternity   ② adoptability
③ custody   ④ lien

06 The scientist presented a(n) _____ explanation of the theory, making it easy for the audience to understand. [3.2점]

① cryptic   ② elusive
③ lucid   ④ contradictory

07 The engineer's design was _____, leaving no room for errors or oversights. [2.8점]

① meticulous   ② conspicuous
③ audacious   ④ awkward

08 Though the book was _____ with facts, its _____ style made it difficult for readers to stay engaged. [3.2점]

① sparse — simple
② filled — exciting
③ devoid — complex
④ packed — tedious

(09~11) Choose the answer that has the closest meaning to the underlined word.

09 The team worked tirelessly to <u>alleviate</u> the suffering caused by the natural disaster. [2.5점]

① worsen   ② relieve
③ prevent   ④ ignore

10 The general delivered an <u>impassioned</u> speech to rally his troops before the battle.
[2.8점]
① exceptional
② uninterested
③ emotional
④ indefinite

11 The child showed an <u>innate</u> talent for music, playing complex melodies at an early age.
[3.2점]
① acquired
② inherent
③ incidental
④ absolute

12~15 Choose the best answer to make each sentence grammatically correct.

12 _____ with a bill of $10,000, Ruth has taken an extra job.
[3점]
① Having faced
② Facing
③ Faced
④ Being facing

13 _____ of my twin sisters is willing to help our mother run the store.
[2.8점]
① Both
② Any
③ Neither
④ All

14 The factory _____ for several years when they began to refurbish it.
[3.5점]
① has deserted
② has been deserted
③ was being deserted
④ had been deserted

15 They arranged _____ to stay in London during the conference. [3.5점]

① Jim ② for Jim
③ Jim's ④ to Jim

16 Choose the answer that is NOT grammatically acceptable among the underlined.

16 ① <u>Much</u> too many students failed ② <u>the end-of-year</u> maths exam, ③ <u>which</u> was particularly ④ <u>challenging</u> this year due to the inclusion of advanced topics.

[2.5점]

17~33 Read the following passages and answer the questions.

> Shakespeare's plays have endured for centuries, captivating audiences with their timeless themes and complex characters. He wrote tragedies, comedies, and histories, each showcasing his mastery of language. Many scholars believe that his works also reflect the political and social concerns of his time. For instance, plays like *Macbeth* and *Hamlet* explore themes of power and corruption that resonate with the Elizabethan era.

17 Which of the following can be inferred from the passage? [2.5점]

① Shakespeare's works are influenced by the historical context of his time.
② Shakespeare wrote only tragedies and comedies.
③ Political themes are absent from Shakespeare's plays.
④ Audiences today fail to relate to Shakespeare's themes.

18~20

The development of electric vehicles (EVs) is a significant step toward reducing greenhouse gas emissions and combating climate change. EVs produce zero tailpipe emissions and are powered by electricity, which can be generated from renewable sources like solar and wind. As battery technology advances, EVs are becoming more affordable and capable of longer ranges, making them a viable alternative to traditional gasoline-powered cars.

However, challenges persist. The environmental impact of mining materials for batteries and the limited availability of charging infrastructure are major concerns. Policymakers and manufacturers must address these issues to ensure that the shift to electric vehicles is both sustainable and accessible.

18 According to the passage, one major advantage of electric vehicles is that they _____. [2.5점]

① produce zero tailpipe emissions
② eliminate the need for charging infrastructure
③ are entirely free of environmental impact
④ reduce the need for renewable energy sources

19 One challenge associated with electric vehicles is _____. [3점]

① the complete elimination of mining activities
② the limited availability of charging infrastructure
③ their inability to reduce greenhouse gas emissions
④ the lack of interest from policymakers

20 The tone of the passage can best be described as _____. [3.5점]

① celebratory   ② dismissive
③ foreboding   ④ cautious

21~23

Democracy requires critical thinking. Almost everyone agrees that the ability to read and write should be a fundamental human right, extended to everyone. We understand that a person who cannot read is in thrall to those who can. You cannot enter the developed world as a full human subject unless you can break and master the code of the word. Today, literacy doesn't stop with words and numbers. To enter social and political debates as a full participant, one must also break the thrall of the magic box and master its secrets. If we fail to adopt media literacy — a basic knowledge of how and why media images are chosen — as an essential goal of public cultural policy, we doom ourselves to be forever in the grip of the powerful interests who own and control the mass media.

The global proliferation of electronic mass media has excited deep feeling and passionate debate. Most alarming to observers around the world has been the Ⓐ_____ the mass media seems to breed in most people; it displaces and undermines social life, community activities, and other creative pursuits. We jokingly call it being couch potatoes.

As a society, we need to foster a more dynamic relationship between the citizenry and the media, one that does not stop when the program ends and the TV is turned off. For those who aspire to greater democracy in public life, our greatest challenge is transforming the media into a tool for democratic change.

21 Why is media literacy important according to the passage? [2.8점]

① It helps people become passionate and better writers.
② It allows people to critically evaluate media content.
③ It encourages people to watch more television.
④ It teaches the history of media development.

22 Which of the following best fills in the underlined blank Ⓐ? [3.5점]

① creativity   ② subjectivity
③ objectivity   ④ passivity

23 Which of the following is NOT true about media literacy according to the passage?
[3.2점]

① Media literacy is essential for participating in social and political debates.
② Media literacy helps people understand how and why media images are chosen.
③ Media literacy encourages people to become couch potatoes.
④ Media literacy is a goal of public cultural policy.

24~26

> Body Dysmorphic Disorder (BDD) is a mental health condition where an individual becomes excessively concerned with perceived flaws in their appearance, which may be minor or not observable to others. People with BDD often feel embarrassed, ashamed, and anxious about their appearance, leading them to avoid social situations. They may engage in repetitive behaviors such as mirror checking, excessive grooming, or seeking reassurance about their looks. These behaviors can consume significant time and cause distress, impacting daily functioning.
>
> The exact cause of BDD is unknown, but it is believed to result from a combination of genetic, environmental, and psychological factors. Bullying, teasing, or a history of mental health disorders in the family can contribute to the development of BDD. Symptoms typically begin in adolescence and can affect both men and women equally. Common areas of concern include the face, skin, hair, and body shape. Treatment for BDD often involves cognitive-behavioral therapy (CBT) and medication. CBT helps individuals challenge and change their distorted beliefs about their appearance, while medication can help manage symptoms of anxiety and depression associated with BDD. Early intervention is crucial for better outcomes, as untreated BDD can lead to severe emotional distress and even suicidal thoughts.

24 Which of the following is NOT mentioned as common behaviors exhibited by individuals with Body Dysmorphic Disorder (BDD)?
[2.5점]

① Excessive grooming and mirror checking
② Avoiding social situations
③ Seeking reassurance about their appearance
④ Bullying and teasing of the mentally disordered

25. Which of the following statements best describes the treatment approach for Body Dysmorphic Disorder (BDD)? [3점]

① CBT helps change distorted beliefs about appearance, while medication might manage anxiety and depression symptoms.
② Medication is the primary treatment, with CBT used only in severe cases requiring intensive treatment.
③ Treatment involves only medication, as CBT has not been proven effective for BDD.
④ Neither CBT nor medication is effective in treating BDD even in its early stages.

26. Which of the following best explains why early intervention is crucial for individuals with Body Dysmorphic Disorder (BDD)? [3점]

① Early intervention can prevent the development of other mental health disorders.
② Early intervention can reduce the risk of severe emotional distress and suicidal thoughts.
③ Early intervention ensures that individuals do not develop physical health problems.
④ Only early intervention can guarantee a complete cure for BDD.

27~29

As emerging algorithm-driven AI continues to spread, will people be better off than they are today? Some 979 technology pioneers, innovators, developers, business and policy leaders, researchers, and activists answered this question in a canvassing of experts conducted in the summer of 2020. The experts predicted networked artificial intelligence would amplify human effectiveness but also threaten human autonomy, agency, and capabilities. They spoke of the wide-ranging possibilities; that computers might match or even exceed human intelligence and capabilities on tasks such as complex decision-making, reasoning and learning, sophisticated analytics and pattern recognition, visual acuity, speech recognition, and language translation. They said "smart" systems in communities, in vehicles, in buildings and utilities, on farms and in business processes will save time, money, and lives and offer opportunities for individuals to enjoy a more customized future. Many focused their optimistic remarks on health care and the many possible applications of AI in diagnosing and treating patients or helping senior citizens live fuller and healthier lives. They were also enthusiastic about AI's role in contributing to broad public-health programs built around massive amounts of data that may be captured in the coming years about everything from personal genomes to nutrition. Additionally, a number of these experts predicted that AI would abet long-anticipated changes in formal and informal education systems. Yet, most experts, regardless of whether they are optimistic or not, expressed concerns about the long-term impact of these new tools on the essential elements of being human.

27 Which of the following is true about the future of AI, according to the text?

[3점]

① AI will only benefit a small group of people.
② AI might threaten human autonomy and agency.
③ AI will make everyone lose their jobs very soon.
④ AI might change the essential elements of human beings.

28 How do experts view the role of AI in healthcare and public health programs?

[2.5점]

① They believe AI will have no significant impact on healthcare.
② They think AI will only be useful in non-medical fields.
③ They all predict that AI will replace doctors entirely.
④ They are optimistic about AI's potential in healthcare.

29 Which of the following best describes the overall sentiment of the experts regarding the future of AI? [3.5점]

① complacent
② pessimistic
③ ambivalent
④ utopian

30~33

> Deforestation, the large-scale removal of trees, poses a significant threat to ecosystems, climate stability, and human health. Trees play a crucial role in absorbing carbon dioxide and other greenhouse gases, which helps mitigate the effects of climate change. Despite this, deforestation continues at an alarming rate, driven by activities such as agriculture, livestock grazing, mining, and logging. Since 1990, the world has lost over 420 million hectares of forest, with the most significant losses occurring in Africa and South America. This extensive deforestation contributes to global warming by releasing stored carbon dioxide back into the atmosphere, Ⓐ_____ the greenhouse effect.
>
> Moreover, deforestation disrupts the habitats of countless species, increasing the risk of zoonotic diseases as wildlife is forced into closer contact with human populations. This can lead to the emergence of new diseases that can spread to humans, posing serious public health risks. The loss of forests also affects local communities that rely on them for their livelihoods, including food, medicine, and shelter.
>
> Efforts to combat deforestation are underway, with initiatives such as rewilding and reforesting gaining traction. These efforts are essential for restoring biodiversity, stabilizing the climate, and achieving the climate goals set forth in the Paris Agreement. Rewilding involves allowing natural processes to restore degraded ecosystems, while reforesting focuses on planting trees to rebuild forests. Both approaches are critical for reversing the damage caused by deforestation and ensuring a sustainable future for the planet.

30 What are the main activities driving deforestation? [2.5점]

① Agriculture and livestock grazing
② Urban development and overtourism
③ Fishing and aquaculture
④ Industrial manufacturing and transportation

31 Which of the following best fills in the underlined blank Ⓐ? [4점]

① counterbalancing ② nullifying
③ exacerbating ④ undoing

32 According to the text, what are the potential public health risks associated with deforestation? [2.8점]

① Decreased availability of clean drinking water
② Increased levels of air pollution from industrial activities
③ Higher rates of skin cancer due to increased UV exposure
④ Increased risk of zoonotic diseases due to habitat destruction

33 What are the two main approaches mentioned to combat deforestation, and how do they differ? [3.2점]

① Urbanization and industrialization; urbanization focuses on building cities, while industrialization involves developing factories.
② Rewilding and reforesting; rewilding focuses on natural processes to restore ecosystems, while reforesting involves planting trees to rebuild forests.
③ Conservation and preservation; conservation focuses on sustainable use of resources, while preservation involves protecting areas from any human activity.
④ Recycling and reducing waste; recycling focuses on reusing materials, while reducing waste involves minimizing the production of waste.

MYONGJI UNIVERSITY

명지대학교

▶ 2025학년도 인문계 오전 ▶ 문항 수: 30문항 | 제한시간: 60분

2025 명지대 인문계 오전 영역별 문항 수

구분	문법			어휘			논리완성	독해	생활영어	총 문항 수
	G/S, W/E	정비문	재진술	동의어	반의어	유추				
문항 수	5			3			7	15		30
백분율	16.7%			10%			23.3%	50%		100%

MYONGJI UNIVERSITY

명지대학교

2025학년도 인문계 오전: 30문항 · 60분

문항별 배점 01~05 2점 / 06~15 3점 / 16~24 4점 / 25~26 5점 / 27~30 3.5점

01~03 Choose the one that has the closest meaning to the underlined word.

01 It is no secret that as muscles age, their cells lose the ability to <u>regenerate</u> and heal after injury.

① refresh
② redirect
③ recycle
④ recreate

02 The war-stricken country is in danger of becoming another failed state because civil society is <u>disintegrating</u> amid a proliferation of armed groups.

① struggling
② destroying
③ collapsing
④ neglecting

03 Under the selection pressure of cancer therapies, tumor cells undergo a <u>veritable</u> evolution to adapt to the changing conditions — and often escape the effects of therapy as a result.

① real
② swift
③ unbeatable
④ spontaneous

[04~05] Choose the one that best fills in the blank.

04 Unlike the most widely used reusable toothbrushes, a chewable toothbrush is _____. It is a miniature plastic molded toothbrush which can be placed inside the mouth and chewed like a chewing gum. While not commonly used, it is useful to travelers. It is spat out after use.

① generic
② disposable
③ common
④ prevalent

05 A significant change of World War II is that after the war many colonies were granted _____ and became independent nations.

① consent
② coalition
③ autonomy
④ acceptance

[06~10] Choose the part that is <u>not</u> grammatically acceptable.

06 In 1986, the Chernobyl nuclear disaster in Ukraine ① <u>dominated the world's</u> attention. As the magnitude of the catastrophe became apparent, ② <u>officials scrambled to</u> the critically essential task of containing the radiation. Lethal gamma rays from highly radioactive debris ③ <u>kept destroying</u> the robots deployed to clean up the mess. So thousands of heroic individuals became "Chernobyl liquidators," ④ <u>disposed of</u> the hazardous material in "shifts" of ninety seconds or less. People did what technology could not, at great personal risk.

07 The essence of humor is incongruity, ① <u>which is seen</u> at its crudest when someone slips on a banana-skin. Human beings are ② <u>meant to walk</u> upright; when they are suddenly thrown into a horizontal position, the instinct of a spectator is to laugh — unless the person has bothered to think how ③ <u>is it unpleasant</u> to fall, or ④ <u>how tedious and overworked</u> the banana-skin-type joke is.

08 There's plenty about the U.S.A. that will ① amaze and awe you. For instance, the current 50-star flag was designed ② as part of a high school project by 17-year-old Robert Heft. It was 1958, and there were only 48 states at the time, but Heft had a hunch Hawaii and Alaska would ③ soon be granted statehood. His teacher gave him a grade of B− but updated the grade to an A after Heft submitted his design to the White House, eventually leading to a call from President Eisenhower that it ④ had selected as the official U.S. flag.

09 The earliest substantial work in the field of artificial intelligence was done by ① the British logician and computer pioneer Alan Mathison Turing. In 1935 Turing described an abstract computing machine ② consisting a limitless memory and a scanner that moves back and forth through the memory, symbol by symbol, reading what it ③ finds and writing further symbols. The actions of the scanner are dictated by a program of instructions that ④ also is stored in the memory in the form of symbols.

10 It is impossible to begin this lecture ① without again expressing my deep appreciation to the Nobel Committee ② for bestowing me and the civil rights movement in the United States ③ such a great honor. Occasionally in life there are those moments of unutterable fulfillment which cannot be completely explained by those ④ symbols called words. Their meaning can only be articulated by the inaudible language of the heart. Such is the moment I am presently experiencing.

11~15 Choose the one that best fills in the blank.

11 No one can learn to write by reading any or even all of the how-to-do-it books available on the subject. Writing well enough to be readily understood is something anyone could do. The reason that not many do write well consistently is that most would-be writers are looking for the secret or the inspiration. About the first, they are misinformed; about the second, they are simply attempting to rationalize away laziness. There are no secrets. No one is inherently more talented than any other person to write in such a way as to be readily understood. Writing is like golfing or tennis or chess: you might have 'beginner's luck,' but consistently good performance requires study and practice. Writing well, like doing anything well, _____.

① requires effort
② requires aptitude
③ comes from inspiration
④ comes from extensive reading

12 Living creatures, which thrive all the most because of the slight changes in their environments, are likely to be destroyed if these changes come over them quickly on too large a scale. That is way some species of animals die out. The same thing applies to human creatures: _____.

① changes too abrupt and massive kill them
② slight changes can quickly accumulate over time
③ many homo species became extinct due to many slight changes
④ they will suffer extinction if slow yet constant global warming goes on

13 Washing your hands is a given if you want to avoid germs — but it's especially important after touching certain microbe magnets. Of course, it's impossible to keep your hands 100 percent germ-free at all times, but it's absolutely essential after touching certain things. For instance, these days you can use a debit or credit card for most purchases, but sometimes you just need to handle cash. When you do, be sure to wash your hands as soon as possible. Researchers tested $1 bills from a New York City bank and found hundreds of microorganisms, including bacteria, and DNA from pets and viruses. Similar research has shown some cash and coins even contain pathogens like E. coli and salmonella. Germs accumulate as the money is circulated. There is no way of knowing _____.

① which bank notes are most seriously germ-ridden
② which of the two — a bank note or a credit card — has more germs
③ how many germs are hiding in your wallet right now
④ how many years bank notes are circulated on average

14 If you desire to know or learn anything to your advantage, then take delight in being unknown and unrecognized. A true understanding and humble estimate of oneself is the highest and most valuable of all lessons. To take no account of oneself, but always to think well and highly of others is the highest wisdom. Should you see another person openly doing evil, do not on that account _____, for you cannot tell how long you will remain in a state of grace. We are all frail; consider no one frailer than yourself.

① follow what the person is doing
② stop learning from other people
③ regard yourself as liable to evil-doing
④ consider yourself better than the person

15 If we could only do as we pleased and get away with that without any censorious comments from our fellow creatures, there would be many more philandering husbands and wives than there are, many more girls wandering down the primrose path, many more neglected children and ill-kept houses. It is the knowledge that, if they give way to their natural impulses, they will be talked about, which gives many would-be sinners _____.

① the chance to think about gains and losses of being a good citizen
② the thought of consequences of the sins they have committed in secret
③ the fear that they would be hated if they do not hide the dirty secrets
④ the strength to resist the temptation to be as bad as they would like to be

16 Which of the following is <u>not</u> true of the passage?

> Have you noticed that 60 degrees doesn't feel the exact same in fall as it does in spring? The real-world number is officially known as the "feels-like temperature." The same temperature can feel completely different for a few reasons. First of all, higher humidity makes it feel warmer. Spring and summer are stickier. Extra moisture into the atmosphere raises the humidity and dew point. The dew point tells us how much moisture the air can hold before it feels muggy and when it's high, sweat doesn't evaporate as easily, making us feel warmer and more uncomfortable even at lower temperatures. In addition, the previous season matters. Your body gets acclimated to the season you just went through. If it's early fall and you're coming off hot summer temperatures, 60 degrees in the middle of the afternoon may be jarring enough to make you reach for a light jacket. On the other hand, spring's first 60s in the afternoon may make you so excited that you might celebrate by going outside without a jacket.

① Moisture in the air makes the feels-like temperature go up.
② Sweat evaporation becomes slower at a high dew point.
③ The dew point is invariable and unaffected by the season.
④ The feels-like temperatures are affected by our acclimated body.

17 Which of the following is the main topic of the passage?

> Humans, in their earliest years upon the earth, probably accepted everything about them without question. During cold and rainy times they felt uncomfortable — even miserable; during warm and sunny times they felt glad to be alive. But they never questioned why. When they became able to provide enough food, clothes and shelter for themselves and their family, however, there was some time left over to think. Slowly the words *why, what* and *how* came into their mind and into their speech. Why did the earth sometimes shake and tremble until trees fell and soil slid down the hillsides? Where did the sun and stars and planets come from? But there was no science to try to answer these questions. The laws of nature and the idea of cause and effect were unknown. There was no body of knowledge, no careful experiments and little careful observation. Everything that was puzzling, or could not be explained in another way, was said to be the work of some god or goddess.

① Humans' struggle to find food and reproduce
② Humans' cognitive development before scientific thinking
③ Natural disasters forcing humans to think scientifically
④ Scientific knowledge emancipating humans from superstition

18 Which of the following is the best title of the passage?

> When the first white people came to America, they found vast amounts of natural resources of tremendous value. Forests covered a large part of the nation; later gas, oil and minerals were found in unbelievable amounts. There was a great abundance of very fertile soil. Forests, prairies, streams and rivers abounded with wildlife. So vast were these resources that it seemed that they could never be used up. So, forests were destroyed to make way for farmland. Minerals and oil were used in great quantities to supply a young industrial nation. Mammals and birds were slaughtered for food and sport. Within a short time, the results were obvious. Floods caused millions of dollars' worth of damage yearly. The seemingly inexhaustible oil and minerals showed signs of depletion. Many of the rivers were made unfit for fish. Several species of birds disappeared, and some mammals seemed on the verge of going. In short, Americans soon came to realize that some sort of conservation program must be set up, if future as well as present Americans were to share in the resources that are the heritage of every American.

① Inexhaustibly Immense Natural Resources in America
② European Settlers in America and Unsurpassed Development
③ Consequences of Exploitation of American Natural Resources
④ Irreparable Damage on the Nature and Fall of American Civilization

19 Choose the sentence that does not belong to the passage.

There is an old saying that you are what you eat. A well-known psychiatrist recently said that people who are fighting depression should stop eating junk food. "Your gut health is critical to brain health," said the psychiatrist. "If you have, for example, an ultra-processed food diet, you have a dramatically increased risk of struggling with depression." ① The gut and brain constantly communicate through an intricate network of nerves and chemical signals. ② Human body, made up of diverse elements, the largest of which being water (about 42 liters), is a complex system composed of many different types of cells and organs. ③ For instance, the brain signals the gut to prepare for food digestion, while stress can trigger signals that cause gastrointestinal symptoms like nausea or diarrhea. ④ The gut microbiome — the collection of bacteria, viruses, and fungi in our digestive system — produces chemicals that can influence brain function and affect mood. Over 100 trillion microbes, primarily bacteria, make up the microbiome.

20 Which of the following best summarizes the main idea of the passage?

> Teaching was never a cakewalk — now add increased pressure from limited resources, low pay, heavy workloads, etc. It's no wonder teachers are burning out in record numbers. So how do you stay in a job that's so high-pressure while feeling underappreciated and overworked? You have to prioritize self-care. There are truly diverse ways teachers relax, recharge, restore, and come back to teach year after year. One teacher says, "I have a date night scheduled with my husband every Friday night. It gives me something to look forward to all week, and we have a rule that we don't talk about either of our jobs!" Another teacher says, "For me it's burlesque dancing. I take an adults-only dance class once a week and it is the highlight of my week. It's just so much fun and a great way to relax." Still another teacher says, "I go for a run. I come home feeling exhausted so you'd think running would be the last thing I'd want to do! I put my AirPods in and listen to podcasts and it's actually really energizing."

① Teachers have diverse ways to deal with work stress and replenish themselves.
② Teaching has become increasingly more complex and challenging recently.
③ Teachers feel that they are underappreciated, which undermines their morale.
④ Teachers need support and recognition so they can perform better at work.

21 Which of the following is the passage mainly about?

> I was diagnosed with panic disorder 20 years ago at age 19. I quickly learned that treating anxiety requires a maintenance plan — for life. My first panic attack came out of nowhere and left me breathless and scared in a bathroom stall — I felt helpless. I've learned to treat it like a sort of character trait — I'm free-spirited, funny, creative — and anxious. Because I have chronic anxiety and panic attacks, despite taking medication, I had to find a way to deal with anxiety to get my life back. I've found that dealing with my condition has made me a healthier person, and anxiety made me more creative. For instance, when my 12-year-old son was much younger, I would ease my anxiety by joining him to build with Legos, color, or sculpt with Play-Doh. Focusing on those tiny, bright bricks or shading in a cartoon character with a colored pencil distracted me and calmed me down. These days, I'm not ashamed to say I own adult coloring books and have sat at the kitchen counter during bouts of anxiety with my trusty colored pencils. I also write and paint with watercolors. "Engaging in a soothing activity like knitting or coloring is extremely helpful," says a mental health researcher. "The repetitive motions, exercised during an art project, engage parts of the cerebral cortex while relaxing the brain's fear center."

① I have become healthier through my efforts to change my personality traits.
② I could completely overcome my panic disorder with the help of coloring books.
③ Panic disorder can be effectively contained with the help of medication.
④ Engaging in repetitive, creative activities helps me deal with panic disorder.

22 Which of the following is the main message of the passage?

> For parents of estranged adults who are sad, or those pining away for the son or daughter who lays blame for everything that has ever gone wrong in their life, there comes a time when enough is enough. Routinely, I hear from mothers and fathers who for ten or twenty years have been neglected, blamed, ridiculed, ignored, or contacted only when the son or daughter needs money. Their self-esteem has taken a huge hit because of the estrangement from adult children. Many of the parents in these long-term estrangements cope well most of the time, but their emotions are triggered when a death or other life events cause contact and/or renew their pain. When that happens, they can go on for weeks feeling blue, reliving the early shock and bewilderment of estrangement, and even asking "Why?" all over again. You need to make a decision to change. Acknowledge all the hurt your son or daughter has caused, and decide not to allow it to shackle you anymore. Stop ruminating over the son you lost, questioning how he could do such a thing to his family, and feeling sad, and move forward.

① Estrangement by adult children is mostly caused by the parents' neglect.
② Pondering on causes of estrangement is the first step to a solution.
③ Determination for recovery is the best known solution for estrangement.
④ Shake off the guilt feelings for estranged adult children and move forward.

23 Choose the best order after the sentences in the box.

> It is a common saying that thought is free. A man can never be hindered from thinking whatever he chooses so long as he conceals what he thinks. The working of a person's mind is limited only by the bounds of the person's experience and the power of the person's imagination. But this natural liberty of private thinking is of little value.
>
> A Some have preferred, like Socrates, some would prefer today, to face death rather than conceal their thoughts. Thus, freedom of thought, in any valuable sense, includes freedom of speech.
>
> B It is unsatisfactory and even painful to the thinkers themselves, however, if they are not permitted to communicate their thoughts to others, and it is obviously of no value to their neighbors.
>
> C Moreover, it is extremely difficult to hide thoughts that have any power over the mind. If someone's thinking leads them to call in question ideas and customs which regulate the behavior of those about them, it is almost impossible for them, if they are convinced of the truth of their own reasoning, not to betray by silence, chance words, or general attitude that they are different from them and do not share their opinions.

① C — A — B
② C — B — A
③ B — C — A
④ B — A — C

24 Choose the best title for the passage.

> Even though milk has been found to be a lead food to cause inflammation, new research suggests dairy can, in fact, do the opposite. Specifically, a January 2023 study found that adding dairy to your cup of coffee may help reduce inflammation levels. Researchers looked at how polyphenols (antioxidants) would behave in the body when mixed with certain amino acids. The combination of coffee and milk fit the bill, with coffee having polyphenols and milk being a complete protein with all nine essential amino acids. The researchers realized that the polyphenols mixed with amino acids had a protective effect against inflammation found in immune cells. Inflammation occurs, in some cases, reacting to the effects of an unhealthy diet. Over time, inflammation can be detrimental, which is why eating a healthy diet full of anti-inflammatory foods is key for reducing the risk of chronic disease. Now it seems drinking coffee with milk can actually help.

① Milk Can Help Reduce Inflammation
② Coffee and Milk: A Perfect Combination
③ Coffee Fights Bacteria Causing Inflammation
④ Milk Causes Inflammation; Coffee Cures Inflammation

25 Which of the following is consistent with the passage?

> Counterfactual thinking is a concept in psychology that involves the human tendency to create possible alternatives to life events that have already occurred; something that is contrary to what actually happened. These thoughts consist of the "What if?" and the "If only..." that occur when thinking of how things could have turned out differently. A counterfactual thought occurs when a person modifies a factual prior event and then assesses the consequences of that change. For example, a person may reflect upon how a car accident could have turned out by imagining how some of the factors could have been different, for example, "If only I hadn't been speeding." These alternatives can be better or worse than the actual situation, and in turn give improved or more disastrous possible outcomes, "If I hadn't been wearing a seatbelt, I would have been killed". Counterfactual thoughts have been mostly shown to produce negative emotions; however, they may also produce functional or beneficial effects. There are two types of counterfactual thoughts: downward and upward. Downward counterfactuals are thoughts about how the situation could have been worse; and people tend to have a more positive view of the actual outcome. Upward counterfactuals are thoughts about how the situation could have been better. These kinds of thoughts tend to make people feel dissatisfied and unhappy; however, upward counterfactuals are the kind of thoughts that allow people to think about how they can do better in the future. These counterfactual thoughts, or thoughts of what could have happened, can affect people's emotions, such as causing them to experience regret, guilt, relief, or satisfaction.

① Counterfactual thinking normally leads to the feeling of relief.
② Counterfactual thinking can be helpful for future improvement.
③ Downward counterfactual thinking imagines a more desirable scenario.
④ Upward counterfactual thinking leads to regret or satisfaction.

26. Which of the following best summarizes the main idea of the passage?

The light and dark influences are related to the Earth's position and rotation. This has a more decisive factor on culture that many people overlook more than other geographical features. Cultures in Alaska, Scandinavia, and Northern Russia are significantly affected to extremes by the number of hours they have of light and dark in a day. They have both extremes. There are times when it is almost entirely dark or light depending on the time of the year. Many countries in polar regions have a culture that strongly depends on the season. They have to be resilient. For example, the Yakut people in Northern Russia have worked hard in the summer months to ensure everything goes according to plan with the harvests. They also have to ensure they are well equipped for brutal winters where it can be −40° Fahrenheit. Many people sometimes see people from these cultures as direct and occasionally harsh, as winter can be brutal and affect national stereotypes. On the other hand, one can look at cultures closer to the equator, where darkness and light do not vary as much. The amount of resting time and working time is the same year-round. The temperaments and traditions more or less remain constant throughout the rest of the year. One can see places such as Ecuador, Indonesia, and Uganda as examples. Punctuality is less key to these cultures. People in these regions are also perceived as more laid back than others who have fewer hours of daylight.

① Light and dark have significant influence on culture.
② The impact of temperatures on lifestyle has been underexplored.
③ People living in harsh environments tend to be highly cooperative.
④ Light and dark influences carry lesser importance than other geographical features.

27~28 Read the passage below and answer the questions that follow.

A white elephant is a possession that its owner cannot dispose of without extreme difficulty, and whose cost, particularly that of maintenance, is out of proportion to its usefulness. In modern usage, it is a metaphor used to describe an object, construction project, scheme, business venture, facility, etc. considered expensive but without equivalent utility or value relative to its capital (acquisition) and/or operational (maintenance) costs. The term derives from the sacred white elephants kept by Southeast Asian monarchs in Myanmar, Thailand, Laos and Cambodia. To possess a white elephant was regarded — and is still regarded in Thailand and Myanmar — as a sign that the monarch reigned with justice and power, and that the kingdom was blessed with peace and prosperity. Because these animals were considered sacred and laws protected them from labor, receiving a gift of a white elephant from a monarch was _____. It was a blessing because the animal was sacred and a sign of the monarch's favor, and a curse because the recipient now had an animal that was expensive to maintain, could not be given away, and could not be put to much practical use. In the West, the term "white elephant", relating to an expensive burden that fails to meet expectations, was first used in the 17th century. In modern usage, the term now often refers to an extremely expensive building project that fails to deliver on its function or becomes very costly to maintain. Examples include prestigious but uneconomic infrastructure projects such as airports, dams, bridges, shopping malls and football stadiums.

27 Which of the following best fits in the blank?

① simultaneously a blessing and a curse
② regarded as the gift of ultimate honor
③ the dream of anyone in the kingdom
④ considered a divine blessing for prosperity

28 Which of the following is <u>not</u> true of a 'white elephant', according to the passage?

① It carries generally a negative connotation in the West.
② Its meaning in English changed from positive to negative meanings.
③ Its original meaning originated from the conflicting cultural and practical values.
④ Its modern meaning emphasizes the inordinate cost as compared to its function.

29~30 Read the passage below and answer the questions that follow.

The practice of sexual cannibalism may sound like a horrific piece of fiction, but in fact this occurs in the behavioral repertoires of several animals. It refers to the eating of one's mate during courtship or copulation. Sexual cannibalism has been documented in several invertebrates, including arachnids, insects, and cephalopods. In some cases, it is rare within a species, whereas in others it is common.

[A] This is a question for evolutionary biologists who consider why a behavior occurs by examining how it benefits an individual's reproductive success. With respect to sexual cannibalism, the high cost to the individual male is obvious, but the evolutionary benefits to both him and his mate are not as clear.

[B] For females, consuming a male likely provides her with the benefits of added nutrition and energy that can be passed along to offspring. Studies have found that females who eat males go on to produce heavier egg cases with more numerous offspring.

[C] Generally, sexual cannibalism involves a female eating a male. The male's response in this interaction can vary dramatically between species. For example, the male redback spider sacrifices himself voluntarily. In contrast, the male giant Asian mantis does all it can to avoid being eaten; it leaps onto the female's back from a great distance and positions himself at an angle that makes an attack less likely. Why doesn't the redback spider do this?

Males that get eaten, in contrast, may benefit in several ways despite paying the ultimate price. Consider that some 80 percent of male redback spiders die without ever getting the chance to mate and produce offspring. Under such circumstances, a 65 percent chance of dying during mating may be worth the risk from an evolutionary fitness perspective.

29 Choose the best order after the passage in the box.

① [B] — [C] — [A] ② [B] — [A] — [C]
③ [C] — [A] — [B] ④ [C] — [B] — [A]

30 Which of the following is true according to the passage?

① Victims's behavior in sexual cannibalism widely varies by species.
② Sexual cannibalism is widely documented across species in animal kingdom.
③ Males and females in sexual cannibalism cooperate for best evolutionary benefits.
④ Evolutionary advantage of sexual cannibalism is clear for males and females.

명지대학교

▶ 2025학년도 인문계 오후　▶ 문항 수: 30문항 ｜ 제한시간: 60분

2025 명지대 인문계 오후 영역별 문항 수

구분	문법			어휘			논리완성	독해	생활영어	총 문항 수
	G/S, W/E	정비문	재진술	동의어	반의어	유추				
문항 수	5			3			7	15		30
백분율	16.7%			10%			23.3%	50%		100%

MYONGJI UNIVERSITY

명지대학교

2025학년도 인문계 오후: 30문항 · 60분

문항별 배점 01~05 2점 / 06~15 3점 / 16~24 4점 / 25~26 5점 / 27~30 3.5점

01~03 Choose the one that has the closest meaning to the underlined word.

01 The turbulent waters caused one of his oars to crack, which — without a motor or a sail — can be severely <u>detrimental</u> to his voyage.

① violent
② instrumental
③ exhausting
④ disadvantageous

02 The decision brings the military more in line with its veterans who have seen combat and found nothing <u>sublime</u> in war.

① glorious
② prosperous
③ conventional
④ humanitarian

03 Her writing style as a lower-court judge was explanatory, and with little rhetorical <u>embellishment</u>.

① illustration
② adornment
③ manipulation
④ complication

04~05 Choose the one that best fills in the blank.

04 The fighters for India's independence were being imprisoned by the British for acting under the inspirations of ideals to which, ironically, the British themselves officially _____ and which they took seriously for their own benefit, at home.

① assessed
② banned
③ subscribed
④ hypothesized

05 At the age of twelve years, the human body is at its most vigorous. It has yet to reach its full size and strength, and its owner his or her full intelligence; but at this age the likelihood of death is _____.

① plain
② least
③ predicted
④ undetermined

06~10 Choose the part that is not grammatically acceptable.

06 Every book has a skeleton ① hidden between its covers. Your job is to find it. A book comes to you with flesh on its bare bones and clothes over its flesh. It is all dressed up. I am not asking you to be impolite or cruel. You do not have ② to undress it or tear flesh off its limbs to get the firm structure that ③ underlie the soft. But you must read the book with X-ray eyes, for it is an essential part of your first apprehension of any book ④ to grasp its structure.

07 In his library at Monticello, Jefferson made hundreds of architectural drawings, ① all of which have been preserved. He must have had a great gift of concentration and a real love for his subject to be able to work in a room with such an outlook. And ② what energy he had for this precise and exquisite work was also devoted to riding over his estate, working in his garden, and ③ carry out correspondence with everyone from the Marquis de Lafayette to his youngest grandchild. "Something pursued with ardor" was Jefferson's prescription for life, and he got the last ounce of excitement and ④ interest out of everything that came to his notice.

08 According to the Anxiety and Depression Association of America, anxiety disorders are the most common mental illness in the United States, ① affecting 40 million adults in the United States, age 18 and older. What's more, women are twice as likely to be ② affected than men. Anxiety disorders develop from a complex set of risk factors, including genetics, brain chemistry, personality, and life events. "Anxiety can be a positive trait," says a health professional. "Someone who ③ worries about being on time or performing at a high level ④ often excels in various aspects of life, both professionally and personally."

09 Some people are ① proud of telling their own faults. They will tell that they are the silliest men in the world; that they ② cannot help speaking the truth, like children, in anybody's presence; that ③ they own it is a folly; that they have lost a lot of advantages by it; but that they cannot help it, even if you would give them a world of riches to prevent it; and that there is something in their nature ④ that hate insincerity and hypocrisy, etc.

10 The use of barter-like methods may ① date back to at least 100,000 years ago, though there is no evidence of a society or economy that relied primarily on barter. Instead, non-monetary societies ② operated largely along the principles of gift economy and debt. When barter did ③ in fact occur, it was usually between either complete strangers or potential enemies. Many cultures around the world developed the use of commodity money, i.e., the money whose value comes from ④ a commodity which it is made.

11~15 Choose the one that best fills in the blank.

11 Before the invention of the toothbrush, a variety of oral hygiene measures had been used and this has been verified by archaeological excavations. The _____ of the toothbrush is the chew stick. Chew sticks were twigs with frayed ends used to brush the teeth while the other end was used as a toothpick. The earliest chew sticks were discovered in Sumer in southern Mesopotamia in 3500 BC, in an Egyptian tomb dating from 3000 BC, and mentioned in Chinese records dating from 1600 BC.

① pinnacle
② predecessor
③ evidence
④ confirmation

12 The earliest surviving written literature is from ancient Mesopotamia. The *Epic of Gilgamesh* is often cited as the first great composition, although some shorter compositions have survived that are even earlier. Apart from its length, the *Epic of Gilgamesh* may be considered the earliest significant composition because of its _____. It is believed, for example, to have influenced other ancient literary works, including the *Iliad*, the *Odyssey*, Alexander romance literature, and the Hebrew *Bible*, all of which continue to have significant literary impact in their own right.

① enduring impact on literature through the ages
② beauty in literary style and complexity of plots
③ exquisite condition in which it was preserved
④ extraordinary length and meticulous attention to details

13 People who are habitually late should undertake at the earliest possible moment to mend their ways and make punctuality one of the main principles of their daily conduct. _____ as much a breach of etiquette as bad table manners or any other habit which is frowned on by the well-bred. Many young ladies consider it smart to keep their friends waiting. Such conduct is as inexcusable as it is rude. Whether you are to meet someone, appear at the family table, or keep a business appointment, remember that punctuality is decreed on all occasions.

① Tardiness is
② Formalities are
③ Conventions are
④ The code of conduct is

14 It was when I was at school, in the sixth, that I first realized the most important truth about myself, namely, that _____. The urge to go one better than the next person, which seems to dominate most people's lives in one way or another, is something I just didn't have built into me. As I think it over now, I can see just how much of a puzzle I was to my schoolmasters; in spite of the fact that I didn't cause much trouble and worked fairly steadily I was disliked by nearly all the teachers who had charge of me. I was incapable of absorbing the one lesson they were all put up there to teach — that life is competition.

① I'm a pacifist
② I'm a late-bloomer
③ I'm indomitable
④ I'm noncompetitive

15 Shun the gossip of people as much as possible, because discussion of worldly affairs, even though sincere, is a great distraction inasmuch as we are quickly ensnared and captivated by vanity. Many a time I wish that I had held my peace and had not associated with people. Why, indeed, do we converse and gossip among ourselves when we so seldom part without a troubled conscience? We do so because we seek comfort from one another's conversation and wish to ease the mind wearied by diverse thoughts. Hence, we talk and think quite fondly of things we like very much or of things we dislike intensely. But, sad to say, we often talk vainly and to no purpose. This external pleasure effectively bars our inward peace. Therefore, we must watch lest time pass idly. When the right and opportune moment comes for speaking, say something that will edify. For the benefit of your inward growth, _____.

① avoid idle talk with other people
② carefully choose a conversation partner
③ focus your thoughts on the topic
④ pursue your desires and aspirations

16 Which of the following is true of the passage?

> At a dinner in honor of Mark Twain, whose real name was Samuel Clemens, a member of the club which had invited him happened to resemble the guest of the evening. With the help of a 'make-up man', the resemblance was so increased that it was difficult to distinguish the original from his double. An innocent conspiracy was formed, and at the hour for sitting down at the table the double entered the dining room quickly and sat in the seat of honor, unsuspected by those at the table. A few minutes later, the true Mark Twain appeared. Everybody looked up in astonishment. Mark Twain himself was no less surprised, but he was equal to the occasion. "So, you're Mark Twain, are you?" he said. "Well, I'm glad to have caught you at last. Whenever I do anything good, you're sure to get the credit of it. Whenever I do anything bad, Samuel Clemens gets the blame. I was getting pretty tired of it, and I'm very glad to tell you so."

① Mark Twain was never surprised or embarrassed.
② Mark Twain handled a surprising situation very humorously.
③ Mark Twain's double was greatly disgraced by the occasion.
④ Mark Twain's host masterminded a malicious prank to hurt him.

17 Which of the following can be correctly inferred from the passage?

> Advances in medical science including antibiotics and vaccines as well as improved standards of living contributed to shifting the burden of illness from acute, infectious illnesses to chronic conditions. While advances in modern medicine have produced important treatments for chronic illnesses, most have resulted in 'halfway' technologies that extend life but do not cure the underlying disease. Examples include long-term renal dialysis for the treatment of kidney failure and, more recently, antiretroviral drugs that extend the lives of people with acquired immunodeficiency syndrome (AIDS). Chronic conditions are accompanied by a myriad of functional limitations and social support needs that fall outside the conventional definition of medical practice. Nurses, social workers, occupational therapists, physical therapists, and other nonphysician health professionals have demonstrated interest and expertise in helping the chronically ill and frail elderly manage the chronic conditions and medical treatments, thus creating new roles for themselves in the medical division of labor.

① Diverse non-medical occupations will replace physicians in the future.
② Cures for most formerly incurable diseases are to be found in the near future.
③ Underlying diseases will become increasingly serious through complications.
④ An increasing number of patients may live in chronic conditions in the future.

18 Which of the following is the main topic of the passage?

> People all over the world believe they've seen or heard a ghost, but there's no scientific evidence for spirits, hauntings or the paranormal. So, what's behind these "encounters"? Considering there's no scientific evidence that ghosts exist, why do some people think they've seen or heard them? A psychology professor recently wrote a book about the science of the paranormal and said ghost sightings are often "sincere misinterpretations of things that do have a natural explanation." "Just because you can't think of an explanation doesn't mean there isn't one," the professor told *Live Science*. He is a skeptic who explores non-paranormal explanations for ghostly encounters. These explanations include hallucinations, or perceptions of things that aren't there; false memories, or recollections of events that didn't happen; and pareidolia, or the tendency to see a face or something significant in an inanimate object or random pattern. The human brain is prone to missing things and misremembering events, and it can jump to conclusions when trying to understand an ambiguous experience. This is especially true when a person wants to believe they've seen a ghost or another legendary creature.

① The scientific explanation for 'ghost encounters'
② The clash between the scientific and the spiritual
③ The story of a psychologist who believe in ghosts
④ The science of the paranormal and memory failures

19 Choose the sentence that does not belong to the passage.

Imagine you have a train scheduled for 11 am, and you are stuck in traffic. You arrive at 11:30 and miss the train. You find out that the train left on time. Now, imagine your friend has another train scheduled at 11 am, and he is also stuck in traffic. He arrives at 11:30 and misses his train. He finds out that his train is 25 minutes late and departs at 11:25. Who will feel sadder? Research shows that 95% of people will answer that your friend will be more disappointed than you, because he just missed the train by 5 minutes. ① He will curse himself more than you do, and say: "What if I leave 5 minutes early? If I had reduced my shower time by 5 minutes, maybe I could have caught the train. If I had woken up earlier, I would be on my way now." ② Meanwhile, you will feel more at ease thinking about it, because there is no way to go back half an hour, and you will say to yourself, "Even if I had left 20 minutes earlier, I would still have missed the train." ③ You are very sad that you missed the train, and become even sadder because your friend also missed the train. ④ But the fact remains the same: You both were late and missed the train. But this shows that when we analyze something went wrong, we will create a scenario of "if only I...", depending on the opportunities we have. That's also the reason why a silver medalist will be sadder than a bronze medalist.

20 Which of the following is true of the passage?

The fight-or-flight also called 'hyperarousal' or the 'acute stress response' is a physiological reaction that occurs in response to a perceived harmful event, attack, or threat to survival. The theory states that animals react to threats with a general discharge of the sympathetic nervous system, preparing the animal for fighting or fleeing. This response is recognized as the first stage of the general adaptation syndrome that regulates stress responses among vertebrates. An evolutionary psychology explanation is that early animals had to react to threatening stimuli quickly and did not have time to psychologically and physically prepare themselves. The fight-or-flight response provided them with the mechanisms to rapidly respond to threats against survival.

① The fight-or-flight is partly physiological but largely psychological.
② The chances of survival with fight-or-flight are more or less the same.
③ Living organisms carefully evaluate options when confronted with a predator.
④ The fight-or-flight is a survival mechanism commonly found among vertebrates.

21 Which of the following is the passage mainly about?

Music is the arrangement of sound to create some combination of form, harmony, melody, rhythm, or otherwise expressive content. It is generally agreed to be a cultural universal that is present in all human societies. It is often characterized as a highly versatile medium for expressing human creativity. Diverse activities are involved in the creation of music, and are often divided into categories of composition, improvisation, and performance. Music may be performed using a wide variety of musical instruments, including the human voice. It can also be composed, sequenced, or otherwise produced to be indirectly played mechanically or electronically, such as via a music box, barrel organ, or digital audio workstation software on a computer. Music often plays a key role in social events and religious ceremony. The techniques of making music are often transmitted as part of a cultural tradition, and listening to music is a common means of entertainment.

① What are the characteristics of music?
② What are categories of musical activities?
③ What is the usefulness of music in society?
④ What is the relationship between music and culture?

22 Which of the following is the main topic of the passage?

Human evolution is the lengthy process of change by which people originated from apelike ancestors. Scientific evidence shows that the physical and behavioral traits shared by all people originated from apelike ancestors and evolved over a period of approximately six million years. One of the earliest defining human traits, bipedalism (the ability to walk on two legs) evolved over 4 million years ago. Other important human characteristics — such as a large and complex brain, the ability to make and use tools, and the capacity for language — developed more recently. Many advanced traits — including complex symbolic expression, art, and elaborate cultural diversity — emerged mainly during the past 100,000 years. Humans are primates. Physical and genetic similarities show that the modern human species, Homo sapiens, has a very close relationship to another group of primate species, the apes. Humans and the great apes of Africa — chimpanzees and gorillas — share a common ancestor that lived between 8 and 6 million years ago.

① Common ancestors of modern-day primates
② Emergence of bipedalism and language faculty
③ Humans' evolution from apelike ancestors
④ The place of origin of humans and their migration

23 Which of the following is not true of the passage?

> In the animal kingdom, speed can mean the difference between life and death. Predators use their speed to overtake and overpower their prey, while animals with few other defenses rely on speed to avoid becoming dinner. Here are some of the fastest animals in the world. Capable of going from 0 to 60 miles per hour in less than three seconds, the cheetah is considered the fastest land animal, though it is able to maintain such speeds only for short distances. Lions are also quite fast when hunting prey, with a top speed of about 50 miles per hour. However, the common prey of these African big cats can be pretty speedy as well. The springbok, for example, can reach 55 miles per hour when pursued, and the wildebeest has been clocked at 50 miles per hour. Whereas the cheetah is the fastest sprinter, the pronghorn is the fastest long-distance runner of the animal kingdom. It is capable of maintaining a speed of nearly 35 miles per hour over several miles and is even faster over shorter distances. During sprints to elude predators, pronghorns can hit top speeds of about 55 miles per hour thanks to special cushions on their hooves and the ability to take in large quantities of oxygen as they run.

① Springbok and pronghorn can outrun lions.
② Pronghorn is an easy prey for cheetah and lions.
③ Pronghorn is the fastest long-distance runner of land animals.
④ Cheetah is the fastest sprinter of all land animals.

24. Choose the best title for the passage.

You may have heard that some foods and drinks, such as grapefruit and alcohol, shouldn't be consumed with certain medications. But did you know that dairy products can also make some drugs less effective? This effect is particularly problematic for certain classes of antibiotics, which are drugs used to treat bacterial infections. Antibiotics taken by mouth, for example, need to be absorbed into the bloodstream to work effectively. But when taken with dairy products, such as milk, some antibiotics are not absorbed as they should be. For instance, one study found that the absorption of an antibiotic called demeclocycline into the bloodstream dropped by a staggering 83% when taken with milk, compared with water and a dairy-free meal. Another study showed that when another kind of antibiotics, ciprofloxacin, is taken with milk, levels of the drug in the bloodstream are about 30% to 36% lower than when it is taken with water.

① Do Not Take Antibiotics with Milk
② Do Not Orally Administer Antibiotics
③ No Grapefruit or Alcohol When Taking Antibiotics
④ Read Medicine Labels Before Taking the Medicine

25. Which of the following is not true of the passage?

One cannot doubt that the study of history makes people wiser. But it is indispensable to understand the limits of historical analogy. Most useful historical generalizations are statements about massive social and intellectual movements over a considerable period of time. They make large-scale, long-term prediction possible. But they do not justify small-scale, short-term prediction. It's because short-run prediction is the prediction of detail and there are simply too many variables to ensure exact forecasts of the immediate future. History, in short, can answer questions, after a fashion, at long range. Alas, policy makers are rarely interested in the long run and the questions they put to history are thus most often the question which history is least qualified to answer. Far from offering a short-cut to clear-sightedness, history teaches us that the future is full of surprises and outwits all our certitudes. If thirty years ago anyone had predicted that before the end of the decade of the forties Germany and Japan would be well on the way to becoming close friends and allies of Britain and the United States, the person would have been considered mad. If twenty years ago, as Russia and China were signing their thirty-year pact of amity and alliance, anyone had predicted that by the end of the fifties they would be at each other's throats, that person too would have been considered mad. The chastening fact is that many of the important events of our age were unforeseen: from the Nazi-Soviet pact and the Tito-Stalin quarrel of years ago to more recent events such as the anti-communist upsurge in Indonesia and the abrupt change in the relationship between the United States and Communist China.

① In general the study of history is beneficial.
② Short-term predictions from history cannot be accurate.
③ Predictions from history are useful only from a long-term perspective.
④ History tells us that nothing is predictable in life.

26. Which of the following best summarizes the main idea of the passage?

This new device can distinguish between different coffee blends or detect when food or drink may be on the verge of going bad. Have you ever wondered if that old carton of fruit juice in the back of your fridge is still safe to drink? A new "electronic tongue" could tell you. The system, powered by artificial intelligence (AI), can identify issues with food safety and freshness. It also offers a glimpse at how AI makes decisions, researchers reported in the journal *Nature*. To make the tongue, researchers used an ion-sensitive field-effect transistor — a device that detects chemical ions. The sensor collects information about the ions in a liquid and turns that information into an electrical signal that can be interpreted by a computer. "We're trying to make an artificial tongue, but the process of how we experience different foods involves more than just the tongue," said one of the authors. "We have the tongue itself, consisting of taste receptors that interact with food species and send their information to the gustatory cortex — a biological neural network." In the new system, the sensor acts as the tongue, while AI plays the role of the gustatory cortex, the brain region responsible for perceiving taste. The team linked the sensor to an artificial neural network, a machine learning program that mimics the way the human brain processes information, to process and interpret the data that the sensor collected. Initially, the researchers gave the neural network a handful of parameters to use when finding out how acidic a certain liquid was. Using those parameters, the neural network determined acidity with about 91% accuracy. When they let the neural network define its own parameters for the acidity analysis, its accuracy improved to more than 95%. They then tested the tongue on real-world beverages. The system could distinguish between similar soft drinks or coffee blends, assess whether milk has been watered down, and identify when fruit juice has gone bad. The device's decision is unreliable in some situations. "We figured out that we can live with imperfection," said one author. "And that's what nature is — it's full of imperfections, but it can still make robust decisions, just like our electronic tongue."

① An electronic tongue can make accurate decisions about food at all times.
② An electronic tongue works on exactly the same mechanisms as human tongues.
③ An AI-powered electronic tongue can detect taste differences and food conditions.
④ An AI-powered electronic tongue analyzes diverse nutrients in food for assessment.

27~28 Read the passage below and answer the questions that follow.

As a rule we greatly exaggerate children's interest in power struggle with us. We are so concerned about maintaining our power over them that we think they are equally concerned about taking Ⓐ it away from us. They are very much aware that they are powerless, and that we have great power over them. They don't like this, and in a vague way look forward to a time when Ⓑ it may not be true. But they are realistic enough to know that at the moment they are not going to be able to do much to change this. In any case, if they are to any degree healthy and happy, and have other things to do, they are busy living. They don't want to quarrel with us all the time. As long as we don't abuse our power intolerably, or weary the children with our constant struggles to assert Ⓒ it, most of them, most of the time, are willing, perhaps even too willing, to accept Ⓓ it. Most of the quarrels I've seen between adults and children are caused by the adults needlessly trying to prove to the children what they never suspected: that they are the boss.

27 Which one of the four occurrences of 'it' is different from others in what it refers to?

① Ⓐ
② Ⓑ
③ Ⓒ
④ Ⓓ

28 Which of the following is the main theme of the passage?

① Children know enough about what is wrong and what is right.
② Children are well aware that adults do not have authority over them.
③ Adults unnecessarily try to assert their power over children.
④ Adults are too realistic and children are too idealistic.

29~30 Read the passage below and answer the questions that follow.

> The Dunning-Kruger effect is a cognitive bias in which people with limited competence in a particular domain overestimate their abilities. It was first described by Justin Kruger and David Dunning in 1999. Some researchers also include the opposite effect for high performers: their tendency to underestimate their skills. In popular culture, the Dunning-Kruger effect is often misunderstood as a claim about general overconfidence of people with low intelligence instead of specific overconfidence of people unskilled at a particular task.
>
> [A] There is disagreement, however, about the causes of the Dunning-Kruger effect. Researchers are still exploring where the effect applies and how strong it is, as well as its practical consequences.
>
> [B] Other studies have been conducted across a wide range of tasks. They include skills from fields such as business, politics, medicine, driving, aviation, spatial memory, examinations in school, and literacy.
>
> [C] Numerous studies have been done. The Dunning-Kruger effect is usually measured by comparing self-assessment with objective performance. For example, participants may take a quiz and estimate their performance afterward, which is then compared to their actual results. The original study focused on logical reasoning, grammar, and social skills.
>
> For instance, inaccurate self-assessment could potentially lead people to making bad decisions, such as choosing a career for which they are unfit, or engaging in dangerous behavior. It may also inhibit people from addressing their shortcomings to improve themselves.

29 Choose the best order between the two passages in the box.

① [C] — [B] — [A]   ② [A] — [C] — [B]
③ [A] — [B] — [C]   ④ [C] — [A] — [B]

30 Which of the following is <u>not</u> true about the Dunning-Kruger effect, according to the passage?

① It is manifested with regard to diverse skills and capabilities.
② It is a form of bias occurring in evaluating other person's intelligence.
③ It is primarily about those with limited capabilities overestimating their skills.
④ Its force and the scope of its applicability have not yet been fully determined.

서강대학교

▶ 2025학년도 1차 ▶ 문항 수: 30문항 | 제한시간: 60분

2025 서강대 1차 영역별 문항 수

구분	문법			어휘			논리완성	독해	생활영어	총 문항 수
	G/S, W/E	정비문	재진술	동의어	반의어	유추				
문항 수	2						3	25		30
백분율	7%						10%	83%		100%

SOGANG UNIVERSITY

서강대학교

2025학년도 1차: 30문항 · 60분

01~03 Choose the answer that best completes the sentence.

01 Her _____ made her an easy target for scams, as she was quick to believe even the most outlandish of stories. [3점]

① frivolity
② solemnity
③ mendacity
④ credulity
⑤ humility

02 When the family doctor encountered symptoms he could not diagnose, he consulted a specialist, recognizing that the matter was beyond his _____. [3점]

① ken
② zone
③ mew
④ grip
⑤ span

03 Oratorio implies the sincere religious treatment of sacred subjects, such that non-sacred oratorio is generally qualified as secular oratorio: a piece of terminology that would, in some historical contexts, have been regarded as _____. [3점]

① plagiaristic
② oxymoronic
③ statutory
④ inopportune
⑤ syllogistic

04~05 Identify the grammatical error.

04 The rebel group that ① <u>toppled</u> former Syrian dictator Bashar al-Assad's regime now faces the challenge of ② <u>replacing</u> it. They've set up an interim government. Many people ③ <u>are waiting</u> to see what the rebel group will do ④ <u>different</u> than Assad. The challenge is to govern a ⑤ <u>devastated</u> country with many ethnic and religious groups.
[2점]

05 Civic engagement plays a vital role in shaping a strong and inclusive society. It is impossible for people to achieve dignity in the contemporary world ① <u>without active participating as citizens</u>. Voting, volunteering, and community organizing ② <u>are just a few ways</u> individuals can make a difference. By taking part in these activities, people ③ <u>not only improve their communities but also gain</u> a sense of purpose. Those who remain disengaged often miss out on opportunities to influence decisions ④ <u>that affect their lives</u>. Ultimately, a healthy democracy ⑤ <u>depends on</u> the involvement of its citizens.
[2점]

06 Reorder the following sentences to form a coherent passage. [4점]

> Ⓐ Relevance theory may be seen as an attempt to work out in detail one of Grice's central claims: that an essential feature of most human communication, both verbal and non-verbal, is the expression and recognition of intentions.
>
> Ⓑ According to the code model, a communicator encodes her intended message into a signal, which is decoded by the audience using an identical copy of the code.
>
> Ⓒ However, the linguistic meaning recovered by decoding is just one of the inputs to a non-demonstrative inference process which yields an interpretation of the speaker's meaning.
>
> Ⓓ In developing this claim. Grice laid the foundations for an alternative to the classical code model: an inferential model of communication.
>
> Ⓔ An utterance is, of course, a linguistically coded piece of evidence, so that verbal comprehension involves an element of decoding.

① Ⓑ-Ⓓ-Ⓐ-Ⓔ-Ⓒ
② Ⓐ-Ⓑ-Ⓓ-Ⓒ-Ⓔ
③ Ⓑ-Ⓐ-Ⓔ-Ⓓ-Ⓒ
④ Ⓐ-Ⓓ-Ⓑ-Ⓔ-Ⓒ
⑤ Ⓐ-Ⓒ-Ⓑ-Ⓓ-Ⓔ

07~08 Read the passage and answer the questions.

A monumental figure in the history of Western philosophy, Plato looms nearly as large in the history of European literary theory. Indeed, for many literary scholars he marks the beginning of the tradition of literary theory, although his choice of the dialogue format, in which historical personages convey particular arguments, suggests that the issue he raises had already been debated before he took them up — as do the extant fragments of the writings of the pre-Socratic philosophers. The several dozen dialogues attributed to Plato engage almost every issue that interests philosophers: the nature of being; the question of how we come to know things; the proper ordering of human society; and the nature of justice, truth, the good, beauty, and love. Although Plato did not set out to write systematic literary theory — unlike his student Aristotle, who produced a treatise on poetics — his consideration of philosophical issues in several of the dialogues leads him to reflect on poetry, and those reflections have often set the terms of literary debate in the West.

What binds together Plato's various discussions of poetry is a distrust of mimesis. According to Plato, all art — including poetry — is a mimesis of nature, a copy of objects in the physical world. But those objects in the material world, according to the idealist philosophy that Plato propounds, are themselves only mutable copies of timeless universals, called Forms or Ideas. Poetry is merely a copy of a copy, leading away from the truth rather than toward it. Philosophers and literary critics ever since, from Plotinus in the third century C.E. to Jacques Derrida in the late twentieth century, have wrestled with the terms of Plato's critique of poetry, revising it or attempting to point out inconsistences in his argument.

07 What is being said about Plato's use of the dialogue form? [4점]

① It shows a link between the pre-Socratics and 20th-century criticism.
② It was a landmark in the history of Western literary criticism.
③ It reveals that Plato was uninterested in the function of literature.
④ It makes the issues he addresses in them appear longstanding.
⑤ It was the motivation for Aristotle to write his treatise on poetics.

08. According to the passage, which statement is correct? [4점]

① Plato's role in European literary theory has been minor.
② Plato believed poetry lacks truth because it is a copy of a copy.
③ Plato first raised issues now perennial in Western philosophy.
④ Plato set out to write a systematic theory of literature.
⑤ Plato values mimesis over objects in the material world.

09~10 Read the passage and answer the questions.

Nobel laureate Han Kang spoke Saturday about how she employed all of her senses in the creation of some of her best known works. "When I write, I use my body," she said. "I use all the sensory details of seeing, of listening, of smelling, of tasting, of experiencing tenderness and warmth and cold and pain, of noticing my heart racing and my body needing food and water, of walking and running, of feeling the wind and rain and snow on my skin, of holding hands." In her lecture she expressed gratitude for those moments when she sensed that she was able to transmit those "vivid sensations" to her readers. "In these moments I experience ... the thread of language that connects us, how my questions are relating with readers through <u>that electric, living thing</u>," Han said as she finished her lecture. "I would like to express my deepest gratitude to all those who have connected with me through that thread, as well as to all those who may come to do so."

09. Which pairing is incorrect? [2점]

① of seeing — visual
② of listening — auditory
③ of smelling — olfactory
④ of tasting — gustatory
⑤ of feeling — kinetic

10 What is the author referring to in mentioning "that electric, living thing"? [2점]

① expressing gratitude
② noticing sensory details
③ vivid sensations
④ forming connections
⑤ the thread of language

11~13 Read the passage and answer the questions.

> Theodore Roosevelt Island, a living memorial to the 26th President of the United States, stands apart from the grand marble monuments of Washington DC's National Mall. Accessible only by footbridge from Virginia, this lesser-known retreat on the Potomac River offers serene woodsy trails leading to a statue of Roosevelt. Unlike the vast open spaces honoring presidents like Lincoln, Jefferson, and Washington, Roosevelt Island humbly celebrates nature and quietly commemorates Roosevelt's environmental legacy.
>
> Roosevelt, renowned for his conservation efforts and the Antiquities Act of 1906, expanded public lands and national forests, securing his place in environmental history. Yet, his legacy is intricate, entwined with imperialism and views on racial domination, reflecting broader American history and environmentalism's roots in Indigenous displacement and natural resource exploitation.
>
> Before its transformation into an urban wilderness honoring Roosevelt in 1940, the island had had a rich history — first, stewardship by the Nacotchtank tribe and then development by the Mason family who cultivated it into a prominent estate with the use of slave labor. This layered narrative of conservation, memorialization, and America's checkered past underscores the nuance of Theodore Roosevelt Island's monument to its complex namesake, inviting visitors to reflect on the interconnectedness of nature, history, and memory.

11 Which is correct according to the passage? [3점]

① Theodore Roosevelt Island was first located on the National Mall.
② The statue of Theodore Roosevelt is enmeshed in controversy.
③ Theodore Roosevelt is known for the 1906 Humanities Act.
④ The Masons superseded the Nacotchtank on Roosevelt Island.
⑤ Theodore Roosevelt's monument receives only few visitors.

12 What is implied about Theodore Roosevelt Island's design compared to other presidential monuments? [3점]

① It is grander than other memorials in Washington, DC.
② It emphasizes nature and environmentalism over politics.
③ It was designed primarily to be widely accessible.
④ It stresses military accomplishments over social issues.
⑤ It highlights the legacy of slavery in the United States.

13 In the context of the passage, which is the best synonym for "stewardship"? [3점]

① supervision　　② guidance　　③ cultivation
④ auspices　　　⑤ improvement

14~16 Read the passage and answer the questions.

What do I mean by "the happiness turn"? It is certainly the case that numerous books have been published on the science and economics of happiness, especially from 2005 onward. The popularity of therapeutic cultures and discourses of self-help have also meant a turn to happiness: many books and courses now exist that provide instructions on how to be happy, drawing on a variety of knowledges, including the field of positive psychology, as well as on readings of Eastern traditions, especially Buddhism. It is now common to refer to "the happiness industry": happiness is both produced and consumed through these books, accumulating value as a form of capital. Barbara Gunnell (2004) describes how "the search for happiness is certainly enriching a lot of people. The feel-good industry is flourishing. Sales of self-help books and CDs that promise a more fulfilling life have never been higher."

The media are saturated with images and stories of happiness. In the UK, many broadsheet newspapers have included "specials" on happiness and a BBC program, *The Happiness Formula*, was aired in 2006. This happiness turn can be described as international; you can visit the "happy planet index" on the World Wide Web and a number of global happiness surveys and reports that measure happiness within and between nation states have been published. These reports are often cited in the media when research findings do not correspond to social expectations, that is, when developing countries are shown to be happier than overdeveloped ones. Take the opening sentence of one article: "Would you believe it, Bangladesh is the happiest nation in the world! The United States, on the other hand, is a sad story: it ranks only 46th in the World Happiness Survey." Happiness and unhappiness become newsworthy when they challenge ideas about the social status of specific individuals, groups, and nations, often confirming status through the language of disbelief.

14 What is the passage mainly about? [3점]

① The UK's flourishing happiness industry
② The variety of knowledges in positive psychology
③ The media coverage of "the happiness turn"
④ Bangladesh as the happiest country in the world
⑤ Public interest in happiness being on the rise

15 Which best describes the author's overall tone in the text? [4점]

① critical and objective
② appreciative and supportive
③ condescending yet pleased
④ accusatory and indignant
⑤ pretentious yet sympathetic

16 According to the passage, which statement is incorrect? [4점]

① The rise of self-help discourses signals a shift toward prioritizing happiness.
② The happiness industry is currently making many people wealthy.
③ Global happiness surveys and reports are generally trustworthy.
④ Since "the happiness turn," happiness has become a quantifiable good.
⑤ Happiness is considered newsworthy when it contradicts social expectations.

17~19 Read the passage and answer the questions.

The Delphic Oracle was one of the most revered consultation sites of ancient Greece, renowned for its role in providing divine guidance. Located at Delphi, a sacred site dedicated to the god Apollo, the Oracle attracted people from all walks of life — kings, warriors, and common citizens — seeking answers to their most pressing questions. Central to this mystical tradition was the Pythia, the priestess of Apollo, who was believed to channel the god's voice while in a trance-like state. Her cryptic yet profound prophecies were seen as messages from the divine. Ancient writers such as Virgil and Plutarch spoke of the Oracle with reverence, portraying it as a direct link to the gods.

Modern science, however, offers a compelling explanation for the Oracle's seemingly supernatural abilities. Geologists have determined that Delphi is situated atop intersecting fault lines, areas prone to geological activity. These fault lines may have allowed gases, such as ethylene, to seep through the earth's surface. Ethylene is known to induce euphoria and altered states of consciousness, which could explain the Pythia's trance-like state during her prophetic rituals. This scientific perspective provides a rational basis for understanding how natural phenomena might have contributed to the Oracle's mystique.

The Delphic Oracle remains an enduring symbol of ancient spirituality, but its story also highlights the interplay between human beliefs and the natural world. By examining both historical accounts and modern geological insights, we gain a deeper appreciation for the ways in which mythology and science can intersect.

17 Which is the best title for the passage? [3점]

① The Pythia's Prophecies: A History of Ancient Greek Divination
② Ethylene and the Human Mind: A Study in Altered States
③ The Oracle's Whisper: Myth, Geology, and the Search for Truth
④ Exploring the Supernatural: Ancient Greek Beliefs and Practices
⑤ The Psychology of Prophecy: Understanding Ancient Beliefs

18 Based on the passage, which best describes the relationship between modern science and ancient belief in the Delphic Oracle? [4점]

① Modern science has debunked the ancient beliefs surrounding the Oracle.
② Modern science has provided a possible natural explanation for the Oracle.
③ Modern science has proved that the Oracle's prophecies were often accurate.
④ Modern science has dismissed the role of geology in the Oracle's previsioning.
⑤ Modern science has confirmed that the Pythia's trances were caused by ethylene.

19. Based on the passage, what can we infer about the ancient Greeks' understanding of the natural world and the divine? [4점]

① They believed that the natural world was totally separate from the divine.
② They understood the divine as intervening very directly in human affairs.
③ They were skeptical of supernatural claims and wanted rational explanations.
④ They felt that human sacrifice was the way to communicate with the gods.
⑤ They were aware of the geological factors involved in the Delphic Oracle.

20~21 Read the passage and answer the questions.

Ⓐ_____ One of the first rooms to be devoted to formal concerts was that opened in London by Thomas Hickford in 1711. From then on other custom-built concert halls and opera houses gradually started to appear all over Europe. German Ⓑ_____ of music built concert halls on a grand scale. At Schwetzingen, the Elector of Palatine built a new opera house capable of holding an audience of 5000, while Duke Karl Theodor of Württemberg bankrupted his entire principality to provide sensational opera productions at Mannheim. The Berlin Opera House was built by Frederick the Great of Prussia (1740-1786). A notable flautist and patron of music, Frederick was deeply immersed in French culture and maintained a French-speaking court. In London, purpose-built concert halls included Carlisle House, Soho Square (1764); the Pantheon, Oxford Street (1772); and the Hanover Square Rooms (1775). Throughout the 19th century the orchestras involved in London concerts contained so many of the same players that it would be difficult to describe each orchestra as different.

20. Choose the best sentence to complete Ⓐ. [3점]

① In the 17th century, concert halls were ubiquitous in Europe.
② Concert halls and opera houses in Europe have a century-long history.
③ Public concert halls were first founded by musicians in the eighteenth-century.
④ Public concerts as they are known today did not exist until the 18th century.
⑤ London was the center of music performances in the eighteenth-century.

21 Choose the best word for Ⓑ. [3점]

① composers　　② patrons　　③ princes
④ vanguards　　⑤ architects

22~24 Read the passage and answer the questions.

　The release of new translations of well-known literary works is more than just a matter of rewording old texts; it's an opportunity to reintroduce these works in ways that resonate with contemporary readers. Even the most iconic and frequently translated works can benefit from a fresh approach, as language, cultural context, and scholarly understanding continue to evolve. New translations of classic literary works are essential for _____.

　First, earlier translations are sometimes based on original editions that contain inaccuracies, which later research and textual scholarship have since corrected. As new discoveries about the source text emerge, these insights can lead to a more accurate and faithful representation of the original work. This ensures that the translation reflects the true intent of the author, rather than perpetuating lingering misconceptions or misinterpretations.

　Additionally, past translators were shaped by the cultural and social norms of their time, which could influence their interpretation of the text. Language that was once considered appropriate may now feel outdated, and expressions that were acceptable in one era may not resonate with modern sensibilities. Older translations might also have been altered to align with the values or expectations of their time, which can make them feel disconnected from the contemporary world.

　Furthermore, there is always room for improvement in translation. Even the best previous versions may not have fully captured the nuance of the work in its original language. A new translation allows for a fresh perspective, providing an opportunity to refine the text in ways that speak more directly to today's readers. By incorporating current translation techniques and cultural awareness, these versions can present a richer and more authentic experience.

　Ultimately, new translations breathe renewed life into familiar works, allowing them to be rediscovered and appreciated by modern readers. They offer updated perspectives and can highlight subtleties or meanings that were previously overlooked, ensuring that timeless works remain relevant and engaging for future generations.

22 Which best completes the missing thesis statement in paragraph one? [4점]
① clarifying intent, changing cultural context, and increasing appeal
② removing ambiguity, modernizing style, and making texts digestible
③ ensuring accuracy, maintaining relevance, and allowing richer nuance
④ reinterpreting themes, adjusting tone, and replacing expressions
⑤ preserving meaning, simplifying language, and updating references

23 According to the text, which might do harm to an author's "true intent"? [4점]
① inaccuracies from the source text
② poorly rendered new translations
③ social norms of the author's times
④ the sensibilities of modern readers
⑤ lack of appreciation and obscurity

24 In the context of the essay, which is the best synonym for "nuance"? [3점]
① subtlety   ② accuracy   ③ expediency
④ respectability   ⑤ equivalency

25~27 Read the passage and answer the questions.

The 1963 Nuclear Test Ban Treaty marked a pivotal moment not only in nuclear diplomacy but also in the growing global awareness of environmental consequences. By halting atmospheric nuclear testing, the treaty shed light on the far-reaching impacts of radioactive fallout and underscored the interconnectedness of human activity and the natural world. Signed by the three major nuclear powers of the time — the United States, the Soviet Union, and the United Kingdom — the treaty prohibited nuclear tests in the atmosphere, outer space, and underwater. However, underground testing was still permitted, reflecting the geopolitical realities of the Cold War and the continued desire for nuclear advancement.

The agreement emerged as a response to mounting public and scientific concerns over the widespread release of radioactive fallout, which had become a serious environmental pollutant during the surge of atmospheric nuclear testing in the 1950s and early 1960s. Fallout consisted of radioactive isotopes such as strontium-90 and cesium-137, which were carried by wind currents across vast distances, settling into soil, water, and vegetation. These isotopes posed severe risks to ecosystems and human health, infiltrating the food chain through contaminated crops, livestock, and water supplies. For instance, strontium-90, a particularly persistent isotope, was found to accumulate in bones and teeth, raising fears about long-term health consequences, including cancer and genetic mutations.

The scientific scrutiny surrounding radioactive fallout played a crucial role in elevating environmental consciousness. Research into the dispersion and effects of these radioactive particles revealed the delicate balance of ecosystems and the dangers posed by persistent pollutants. Scientists, environmentalists, and concerned citizens began to recognize the global nature of environmental threats and the need for international cooperation to address them.

Ultimately, the Nuclear Test Ban Treaty represented a turning point in the public's understanding of environmental stewardship. By directly addressing the environmental consequences of human activity, it laid the groundwork for future environmental movements. The treaty's success in limiting atmospheric pollution offered a powerful example of how scientific research, public awareness, and international collaboration could converge to mitigate a global crisis — an approach that would inspire later efforts to combat other environmental challenges, such as industrial pollution, deforestation, and climate change.

25 Which is the best title for the passage? [3점]

① Banning Atmospheric Tests: A Victory for Nuclear Disarmament
② Scientific Research and Public Concern: The Drive for a Nuclear Test Ban
③ The Legacy of the Nuclear Period: From Atomic Bombs to Environmentalism
④ From Fallout to Awareness: The Nuclear Test Ban Treaty's Environmental Legacy
⑤ The Dangers of Radioactive Fallout: Strontium-90 and its Impact on Human Longevity

26 Why was the 1963 Nuclear Test Ban Treaty considered a turning point? [4점]

① It represented a moment of international awareness of the impact of human activity on the environment.
② It brought to the fore the issue of nuclear disarmament and the need for international cooperation.
③ It gave rise to environmentalism as we know it today, most specifically in the climate change movement.
④ It was the first step toward preserving the integrity of space as a neutral international zone.
⑤ It launched effort to clean up the environment and eliminate the use of persistent pollutants.

27 What can be inferred from the passage? [4점]

① The nuclear test ban was the first major rift between science and environmentalism.
② The fallout from nuclear testing brought together environmentalism and science.
③ The power of vested interests over the autonomy of science is still an issue.
④ The nuclear test ban foreshadowed problems climate activists would face.
⑤ The issue of nuclear testing is likely to arise again as a major problem.

28~30 Read the passage and answer the questions.

The issue of mind-body dualism — the debate over how the "mind" interfaces with the physical brain — poses a fundamental challenge to modern cognitive science, which seeks to understand thought and mental organization as arising solely from physical phenomenon. From the musings of ancient philosophers like Plato to the pronouncements of modern thinkers such as René Descartes, the concept of mind-body dualism asserts that the "mind," being non-material and indivisible, cannot be fully explained by physical phenomena alone.

This philosophical position presents a significant obstacle to cognitive science's goal of explaining consciousness as the result of physical brain processes. If the mind operates on a plane separate from the physical, how can a science grounded in materialism reconcile the two? Philosopher David Chalmers further complicates this inquiry by distinguishing between the "easy" problems of cognitive functions — such as perception, memory, and decision-making — and the "hard" problem of consciousness. For example, Chalmers questions why subjective experience accompanies certain brain processes but not others, adding a layer of complexity to the debate.

Chalmers' analysis highlights a crucial issue: cognitive science can address the functional aspects of consciousness — how the brain processes information and enables behaviors — but it struggles to explain the experiential qualities of consciousness, the "what it's like" of being aware. This gap in understanding, often referred to as the "explanatory gap," remains a profound metaphysical quandary. Mind-body dualism, therefore, does not simply challenge the scope of cognitive science; by asserting the metaphysical uniqueness of the "mind," it _____.

28 Which is the best title for the passage? [4점]

① Cognitive Functions and Brain Processes: Understanding Perception, Memory, and Thought
② The Philosophy of Mind: Exploring Ancient and Modern Perspectives on Consciousness
③ The Hard Problem of Consciousness: Mind-Body Dualism's Challenge to Cognitive Science
④ Materialism and the Study of Mind: Physical Processes Can Account for Consciousness
⑤ The Science of Consciousness: Advances and Challenges in Today's Post-Cognitive Research

29 According to Chalmers, the greatest difficulty cognitive science faces is _____.
[4점]
① explaining how the brain processes information and enables behavior
② answering the challenges laid down by Plato and René Descartes
③ admitting that their inquiry falls outside the purview of science
④ convincing mind-body monists to reconsider their views
⑤ explaining the experiential aspect of consciousness

30 Choose the phrase that best completes the blank.
[4점]
① casts doubt on the work of Plato and Descartes
② calls into question its own relevance
③ opens a pathway for dialogue between the disciplines
④ solves the problem of the "explanatory gap"
⑤ strikes at the very foundation of the discipline

서강대학교

▶ 2025학년도 2차 ▶ 문항 수: 30문항 | 제한시간: 60분

2025 서강대 2차 영역별 문항 수

구분	문법			어휘			논리완성	독해	생활영어	총 문항 수
	G/S, W/E	정비문	재진술	동의어	반의어	유추				
문항 수	3						2	25		30
백분율	10%						7%	83%		100%

SOGANG UNIVERSITY

서강대학교

2025학년도 2차: 30문항 · 60분

01~02 Choose the answer that best completes the sentence.

01 The labor union says workers are walking off the job at some 300 out of over 10,000 stores across the U.S. as contract negotiations _____. [3점]

① dispel   ② falter   ③ bask
④ gall   ⑤ lull

02 The Duke fell in love with Elizabeth, but his early attempts to woo her were unsuccessful. Part of the problem was that he could not propose to a commoner, since, as the King's son, he could not place himself in a position in which he might be refused. For that reason, he sent a(n) _____ to her to ask on his behalf for her hand in marriage. [3점]

① interloper   ② peddler   ③ outrider
④ emissary   ⑤ despot

03~05 Identify the grammatical error.

03 GPT-3 was a watershed moment in AI due to ① its unprecedented size, featuring 175 billion parameters, which enabled ② it to execute a wide range of natural language tasks without extensive fine-tuning. This model was trained ③ using big data, allowing it to generate human-like text and ④ engage in conversation. It also had the ability ⑤ of performing few-shot learning, which demonstrated its usefulness in commercial AI applications such as chatbots and virtual assistants. [2점]

04 The airplane was ① scheduled to depart on time, but an unexpected issue caused a delay. Neither the pilots nor the mechanics ② was able to figure out what made the airplane display a warning message. Passengers waiting in the terminal ③ grew increasingly frustrated as the hours passed without updates. Finally, a senior engineer was ④ called in to assess the situation and discovered that a sensor had malfunctioned. After the repairs were completed, the airplane ⑤ was cleared for takeoff, and the passengers boarded with a mix of relief and lingering irritation.   [2점]

05 During World War One, artwork was employed by the US government for propaganda purposes, to encourage the American people ① to get behind the war effort. For example, impressionistic paintings by Childe Hassam, ② who featured city streets overflowing with American flags, were popularized to evoke patriotism in a nation teetering ③ on the edge of war. Later, to bolster a war-weary populace exhausted by combat, works by George Bellows depicting powerful scenes of the enemy's barbarity were ④ used to justify the sacrifices of war ⑤ as noble and necessary.   [4점]

06 Reorder the following sentences to form a coherent passage.   [4점]

> Ⓐ Likewise, ocean currents redistribute heat between land and water, but on a more regional scale.
> Ⓑ However, such variables alter, with changes attributable to the gradual shifting of tectonic plates.
> Ⓒ Over extended time spans, a number of nearly constant variables determine climate, including latitude, altitude, proportion of land to water, and proximity to oceans and mountains.
> Ⓓ Other climate determinants are more dynamic: the thermohaline circulation of the ocean, for example, leads to a 5°C (9°F) warming of the northern Atlantic Ocean compared to other ocean basins.
> Ⓔ Ultimately, the state of the climate is the result both of global long-term and regional dynamic factors.

① Ⓒ-Ⓐ-Ⓑ-Ⓓ-Ⓔ
② Ⓐ-Ⓑ-Ⓓ-Ⓒ-Ⓔ
③ Ⓒ-Ⓓ-Ⓐ-Ⓑ-Ⓔ
④ Ⓒ-Ⓑ-Ⓐ-Ⓓ-Ⓔ
⑤ Ⓒ-Ⓑ-Ⓓ-Ⓐ-Ⓔ

07~09 Read the passage and answer the questions.

Ancient Mesopotamian cultures, often overlooked in the broader narrative of medical history, demonstrated a surprisingly advanced understanding of psychological trauma, including symptoms that closely resemble modern post-traumatic stress disorder (PTSD). Recent research has uncovered evidence suggesting that Mesopotamians were aware of and addressed this condition long before the ancient Greeks, who are traditionally credited with the earliest descriptions of PTSD. This discovery challenges the conventional view of the Greeks as the pioneers in the field of mental health and highlights the complexity of early medical knowledge.

In Mesopotamia, trauma was viewed through a holistic lens, blending spiritual beliefs with treatments for both the mind and body. The Assyrians, one of the prominent civilizations of the region, documented symptoms in their medical texts that mirror those seen in PTSD today, such as recurring visions, nightmares, emotional distress, and agitation. These afflictions were often attributed to the restless spirits of slain enemies, a belief deeply rooted in the Mesopotamian understanding of the afterlife and spiritual forces.

To address these symptoms, Mesopotamian priests and healers employed a range of therapeutic practices. These included rituals and incantations aimed at appeasing the angry spirits, as well as medicinal remedies intended to calm the mind and restore balance to the body. The healing process was not limited to physical treatments; it also encompassed spiritual and emotional healing, underscoring the Mesopotamians' recognition of the interconnectedness of mind, body, and spirit.

While the methods used by the Mesopotamians are markedly different from modern approaches to mental healthcare, their efforts to alleviate trauma reflect an enduring human concern for the well-being of individuals affected by psychological distress. The ancient texts reveal a thoughtful and empathetic approach to healing, one that resonates with contemporary efforts to address mental health. These early contributions to the understanding and treatment of psychological trauma offer valuable insights into the history of mental healthcare, illustrating the long-standing human desire to understand and mitigate the impact of trauma on the mind.

07 Which is the best title for the passage? [3점]

① Ancient Mesopotamian Medicine: Treatments for Physical and Spiritual Ailments
② Spirits in Mesopotamia: Beliefs about the Afterlife and Their Influence
③ Before the Greeks: Mesopotamian Insights into PTSD-like Symptoms
④ Early Civilizations and Mental Health: A Comparative Study of Ancient Cultures
⑤ Mesopotamian Beliefs about the Mind and Body: A Holistic Approach

08 Based on the passage, it can be inferred that the Mesopotamian understanding of trauma differed from later, more traditionally recognized historical understandings (like the Greek perspective) primarily in its _____. [4점]

① emphasis on the interconnectedness of spiritual and physical health
② reliance on purely spiritual explanations for psychological distress
③ focus on the social and cultural context of traumatic experiences
④ development of complex diagnostic categories for forms of trauma
⑤ belief that trauma was temporary and treatable with simple remedies

09 What is meant by the phrase "the broader narrative of medical history" in paragraph one? [4점]

① the persistent belief that ancient medicine is inferior to modern medicine
② the stories and tales that give us insight into prehistoric medical techniques
③ the contradictions that riddle our understanding of ancient healthcare
④ the widely accepted body of facts that form the history of healthcare
⑤ the understanding that medical knowledge is being made into a story

10~12 Read the passage and answer the questions.

In the mid-nineteenth century, milk producers marketed their product to Americans by linking it to the idyllic purity of the countryside. The rural image of cows grazing on lush, green pastures and fresh milk flowing straight from the farm was carefully cultivated to appeal to urban consumers who associated the countryside with wholesomeness and health. However, the milk being sold at the time was often far from pure. Rapid urbanization and industrialization brought about a host of problems, including unsanitary milking practices, improper storage, spoilage, and widespread adulteration, such as watering down milk or adding substances like chalk to mask its poor quality.

Faced with growing public concerns over safety and quality, milk producers sought solutions in emerging scientific advancements. Scientists introduced methods such as pasteurization, which reduced bacteria and extended milk's shelf life, and improved techniques for storing and transporting milk under more sanitary conditions. These innovations not only made milk safer to drink but also allowed producers to rebrand their product. To distinguish it from unregulated competitors and justify a higher price, "improved" milk was "officially certified" as scientifically pure.

Over time, this shift had a significant impact on milk's image. While it had once been associated with the natural purity of the countryside, milk now became increasingly tied to the sterility and precision of the laboratory. The scientific processes that guaranteed milk's safety also reshaped its symbolism, turning it from a rustic staple into a product of modern industry and scientific progress.

10 Which is the best title for the passage? [3점]

① Milk's Rural Roots: A Look at 19th-Century Dairy Science
② Marketing Purity: How Science Transformed the Milk Industry
③ From Pasture to Product: The Journey of Milk to Consumers
④ The Power of Pasteurization: Ensuring Milk Safety and Longevity
⑤ Marketing the Modern Meal: How Advertising Shaped Food Choices

11 Which of the following is NOT a consequence of scientific methods being applied to milk? [3점]

① Milk was made safer to drink.
② Milk was able to be rebranded.
③ Milk was made more affordable.
④ Milk was associated with sterility.
⑤ Milk was linked with advancement.

12 What does the shift in milk's image from "natural purity" to "scientific progress" suggest? [3점]

① That milk was no longer associated with health.
② That scientific advancements made milk less nutritious.
③ That consumers preferred milk processed in labs.
④ That milk producers had improved traditional methods.
⑤ That pasteurization had no effect on food safety.

13~15 Read the passage and answer the questions.

In rural Texas in the years leading up to the Civil War, settlers faced harsh living conditions where survival was a daily struggle. Life expectancy was short, typically ranging between thirty-five and fifty years, due to a variety of factors. Contaminated water, infectious disease, and the constant dangers of childbirth or even simple injuries made life _____. With professional medical help scarce and often unreliable, families were forced to adopt a do-it-yourself approach to healthcare, relying on their own resourcefulness and what little knowledge they could cobble together.

Even when settlers sought professional help, the outcomes were often grim. Physicians, many of whom were minimally trained and sometimes battled personal demons like alcoholism, were ill-equipped to handle the realities of frontier medicine. Their medical arsenal was limited, ranging from rudimentary surgical knowledge to questionable treatments like "mercury purges." More often than not, these methods proved ineffective or, in some cases, harmful, leaving patients with little hope for recovery.

Compelled by necessity, settlers turned to home remedies and folk practices, though these too carried significant risks. Among the most unusual was the use of "mad stones" — peculiar objects believed to have curative powers, particularly for treating rabies and other similar ailments. Despite their popularity, these folk remedies often walked a fine line between traditional wisdom and dangerous quackery. They reflected the settlers' desperate search for health in a world where medical resources were scarce, and their hope for healing often led them down a path fraught with uncertainty.

13 Which is correct according to the passage? [4점]

① Life expectancy in post-Civil War Texas was from thirty-five to fifty years.
② Physicians in rural Texas were well trained but sometimes troubled.
③ Treatments such as mercury purges often left patients in perilous condition.
④ The use of "mad stones" sometimes caused patients to develop rabies.
⑤ Patients' best hope for healing from illness was usually to do nothing at all.

14 What does the use of "mad stones" suggest about settlers' approach to healthcare? [3점]

① They had easy access to reliable medical treatments.
② They were skeptical of traditional medicine.
③ They were desperate for effective health solutions.
④ They preferred to seek professional medical help.
⑤ They had advanced medical knowledge and practices.

15 Which word best fills the blank? [4점]

① contagious   ② uproarious   ③ pernicious
④ lugubrious   ⑤ precarious

16~18 Read the passage and answer the questions.

Urbanization has significantly influenced bird behavior, particularly altering birdsong as birds adapt to increasing noise levels. Over the past thirty years, researchers have documented changes in the songs of white-crowned sparrows in urban San Francisco. These changes reflect adaptations to persistent ambient noise from traffic, construction, and other human activities, highlighting broader implications for wildlife in human-altered landscapes.

In urban environments, birds that shift their vocalizations to higher frequencies can communicate more effectively amidst noise pollution, thereby improving their chances of survival and reproductive success. For white-crowned sparrows, the minimum frequency of their songs has risen over time, suggesting an evolutionary adjustment that allows their calls to stand out against the urban din. By contrast, in quieter rural areas, such adaptations are unnecessary, as evidenced by the stable song frequencies observed there. This phenomenon underscores the pressure for wildlife to adapt rapidly to human-driven environmental changes.

The study of the white-crowned sparrow exemplifies how even subtle shifts in human environments can profoundly influence animal behavior. This adaptation extends beyond individual survival; it also involves cultural transmission, as modified songs are passed down through generations, potentially giving rise to new dialects better suited to noisy urban life. The ongoing impact of urbanization on natural behaviors reveals the dynamic interplay between human activity and wildlife, emphasizing both the resilience of species and the challenges they face in an increasingly urbanized world.

16 Which is the best title for the passage? [4점]

① Singing in the City: How Urban Noise Affects Birdsong
② Bird Behavior: A Study of Adaptation and Survival in the City
③ The Effects of Pollution on Wildlife: The Impact of Human Activity on Nature
④ Evolutionary Adaptations in Birds: How Species Change Over Time
⑤ The White-crowned Sparrow: A Common Urban Species

17 According to the passage, what change has been observed in the songs of white-crowned sparrows in urban San Francisco? [4점]

① The complexity of their songs has decreased.
② The length of their songs has markedly shortened.
③ They have stopped using vocalizations altogether.
④ The minimum frequency of their songs has risen.
⑤ They have started mimicking traffic sounds.

18 Based on the information in the passage, it can be inferred that if urban noise levels were significantly reduced, the songs of white-crowned sparrows in San Francisco would likely _____. [4점]

① become much more complicated and various
② gradually shift back towards lower frequencies
③ become measurably higher in frequency over time
④ remain unchanged due to the nature of evolution
⑤ disappear entirely as they would serve no purpose

19~21 Read the passage and answer the questions.

Dirt is something in the wrong place at the wrong time. Dirt disgusts us because it appears where it shouldn't be — on the kitchen floor or under the bed. The very same objects (dust and grime) do not constitute dirt if they are in a different place. The meaning of dirt is dependent on its _____.

Mary Douglas, in her book *Purity and Danger*, examines the concept of dirt and pollution. She connects the dread of dirt to a fear of disorder. Removing dirt, on the other hand, is part of the establishment of an ordered environment. We make the environment conform to an idea, a sense of order. Dirt, she says, is "matter out of place," a definition that suggests simultaneously some form of order and a contravention of that order. Dirt, by its very definition, depends on the preexistence of a system, a mode of classification. Douglas makes this point well:

Shoes are not dirty in themselves, but it is dirty to place them on the dining table; food is not dirty in itself, but it is dirty to leave cooking utensils in the bedroom, or food bespattered on clothing; similarly, bathroom equipment in the drawing room; clothing lying on chairs; out-door things in-doors; upstairs things downstairs; underclothing appearing where over-clothing should be, and so on.

Dirt, then, is a mismatch of meanings — meanings that are erroneously positioned in relation to other things. Things that transgress become dirt — they are in the wrong place. Douglas's discussion of "matter out of place" provides a useful analytical tool for decoding the reactions to transgressions. Beliefs about dirt and pollution relate to power relations in society as they delineate, in an ideological fashion, what is out of place. Those who can define what is out of place are those with the most power in society.

19 What is the right word for the blank? [2점]

① location   ② territory   ③ landscape
④ status   ⑤ none of these

20 According to the passage, which statement is incorrect about dirt? [3점]

① Dirt reveals the underlying disorder in preexisting systems.
② Dirt is a substance that is in the wrong place.
③ Dirt disgusts us because it is connected to a fear of disorder.
④ Things that violate boundaries become dirt.
⑤ Ideas about dirt are closely tied to societal power dynamics.

21 Which statement is the author least likely to agree with? [3점]

① Gypsies are labeled deviant because their living spaces are identified as "disorderly."
② Graffiti is considered deviant because it is art placed where it should not be.
③ Place plays a significant role in the creation of norms of behavior.
④ The homeless are seen as abnormal because they lack conventional accommodations.
⑤ Hippies are disorderly and need help finding their place in society.

22~23 Read the passage and answer the questions.

I always think about climate justice as multitasking. We live in a time of multiple overlapping crises: we have a health emergency; we have a housing emergency; we have an inequality emergency; we have a racial injustice emergency; and we have a climate emergency, so we're not going to get anywhere if we try to address them one at a time. We need responses that are truly _____. So how about, as we decarbonize and create a less polluted world, we also build a much fairer society on multiple fronts?

Many environmentalists hear this and think: "Well, that sounds a lot harder than just implementing a carbon tax or switching to green energy." And the argument we make in the climate justice movement is that what we're trying to do is to build a power base that is invested in climate action. Because if you're only talking about carbon, then anybody who has a more immediate emergency — whether it's police violence, gender violence or housing precariousness — is going to think: "That's a rich person problem. I'm focused on the daily emergency of staying alive." But if you can connect the issues and show how climate action can create better jobs and redress gaping inequalities, and lower stress levels, then you start getting people's attention and you build a broader _____ that is invested in getting climate policies passed.

22 Choose the correct pair of words for the blanks in order. [3점]

① convivial — conclave
② intersectional — constituency
③ refractory — constitution
④ influential — convention
⑤ indispensable — confluence

23 Which is the best title for the passage? [4점]

① Combating Climate Change: Together with Social Justice
② Multiple Crises in Our Time: Climate Change Comes First
③ Achieving Climate Justice: It is More than Just a Carbon Tax
④ Emergencies in Our Time: More Pressing than Ever
⑤ Climate Policies: Sustainable Jobs, Sustainable Future

24~25 Read the passage and answer the questions.

Several years before the Holocaust, which eventually branded Western modernity as the distinctive bearer of collective trauma in the twentieth century, the most developed society outside the West had itself already engaged in systematic atrocities. In early December 1937, invading Japanese soldiers slaughtered as many as 300,000 Chinese residents of Nanking, China. Under orders from the highest levels of the imperial government, they turned out this massacre in six of the bloodiest weeks of modern history, without the technological aids later developed by the Nazis in their mass extermination of the Jews.

In contrast to the Nazi massacre, this Japanese atrocity was not hidden from the rest of the world. Indeed, it was carried out under the eyes of critical and highly articulate Western observers and reported upon massively by respected members of the world's press. Yet, in the sixty years that have elapsed since that time, the memorialization of the "Rape of Nanking" has never extended beyond the regional confines itself. The trauma contributed scarcely at all to the collective identity of the People's Republic of China, let alone to the self-conception of the postwar democratic government of Japan.

As the most recent narrator of the massacre puts it, "Even by the standards of history's most destructive war, the Rape of Nanking represents one of the worst instances of mass extermination." Yet, though it became "the forgotten Holocaust of World War II," and it remains an "obscure incident" today, the very existence of which is routinely and successfully denied by some of Japan's most powerful and esteemed public officials.

24 Which underlined word is incorrect?

① branded
② engaged
③ turned
④ elapsed
⑤ denied

25 What is the passage mainly about?

① the Rape of Nanking as an instance of genocide
② Japanese atrocities in Nanking during World War II
③ the forgotten cause of history's most destructive war
④ contrasting responses to World War II collective traumas
⑤ the banality of evil found both in Nazi and Japanese atrocities

26~27 Read the passage and answer the questions.

> Invertebrates are animals that do not have a backbone. Although many of them are small and therefore easily overlooked, they are immensely varied and wide-spread, accounting for about 97 percent of all known animal species. While vertebrates form a single phylum, invertebrates are an informal collection of more than 30, and the members of just one phylum — the arthropods — probably outnumber all other animals on earth. Invertebrates are found in every conceivable type of habitat, but they are most plentiful in the oceans, which is where animal life first arose. Invertebrates were the first animals to evolve, although exactly how this happened is not yet known. There is little doubt that their ancestors were single-celled, food-eating microorganisms, similar to extant protozoans, and many biologists think that at some point, groups of these began to form permanent symbiotic partnerships. When this occurred, animal life began.

26 Which statement is incorrect? [4점]

① The arthropods are possibly the most numerous creature on Earth.
② The number of invertebrates greatly exceeds that of vertebrates.
③ The progenitors of invertebrates were likely single-celled.
④ The invertebrates can be found all over the planet.
⑤ The protozoans were the first living creatures.

27 Which can be inferred from the passage? [3점]

① Vertebrates once greatly outnumbered invertebrates.
② Symbiosis among microorganisms produced invertebrates.
③ Invertebrates only survive in specialized habitats.
④ Many invertebrates are on the road to becoming extinct.
⑤ The vertebrates gave rise to the first invertebrates.

28~30 Read the passage and answer the questions.

> In the late 1960s, when computers were used almost exclusively in scientific or industrial applications, Honeywell offered an audacious new vision to the world. The Honeywell Kitchen Computer, priced at a staggering $10,600, was advertised as a "recipe selector" and held up as being every futuristic homemaker's dream.
>
> The reality, however, was less "space age" and more "marketing stunt." This computer was never meant for mass production, but rather to gauge consumer interest in something entirely new: home computing. Despite minimal sales and it being very impractical, the Kitchen Computer sparked something bigger.
>
> Tech visionaries like Gordon Bell saw it as a beacon, their imaginations ignited by the potential of computers in everyday life. They envisioned homes transformed by learning, organization, entertainment, and even automation. Though Honeywell's Kitchen Computer flopped commercially, it represented a crucial turning point.

28 Which is the best title for the passage? [3점]

① The Honeywell Kitchen Computer: A Marketing Stunt That Inspired a Revolution
② The Kitchen Computer: A Pioneer of Culinary Automation
③ A Technological Breakthrough: The Kitchen Computer's Impact on Food Preparation
④ The Kitchen Computer: A Potent Symbol of 1960s Optimism
⑤ Honeywell's Bold Gamble: Bringing Mainframe Power to the Home at a Fair Price

29 What can be inferred from the passage? [4점]

① The Kitchen Computer inspired Gordon Bell to invent the first true home computer.
② The Kitchen Computer "marketing stunt" severely damaged Honeywell's reputation.
③ Honeywell lost a lot of money manufacturing and promoting the Kitchen Computer.
④ Honeywell never expected that the "space aged" Kitchen Computer would sell well.
⑤ Gordon Bell believed that Honeywell compromised his vision of home computing.

30 From the direction of the last paragraph, what is likely to follow? [4점]

① An example of the Kitchen Computer sparking innovation
② A description of how Honeywell recovered its reputation
③ An argument in support of the importance of Gordon Bell
④ A comparison of the Kitchen Computers to similar devices
⑤ An opinion against "marketing stunts" and sales gimmicks.

# 서울시립대학교

▶ 2025학년도 인문·자연계열 Ⅱ   ▶ 문항 수: 30문항 | 제한시간: 60분

2025 서울시립대 인문·자연계열 Ⅱ 영역별 문항 수

구분	문법			어휘			논리완성	독해	생활영어	총 문항 수
	G/S, W/E	정비문	재진술	동의어	반의어	유추				
문항 수	2			2	1		1	24		30
백분율	7%			7%	3%		3%	80%		100%

서울시립대학교

2025학년도 인문·자연계열 II : 30문항 · 60분

01 밑줄 친 enigmatical와 의미가 가장 먼 것을 고르시오. [3점]

Artificial intelligence (AI) has evolved from simple rule-based systems to complex algorithms capable of learning and adapting. Early AI systems relied heavily on predefined rules and lacked the ability to handle enigmatical or unforeseen situations.

① unequivocal
② unstipulated
③ nebulous
④ intricate

02 밑줄 친 prescient와 의미가 가장 가까운 것을 고르시오. [3점]

Edison's genius lay in his ability to conceive of a fully developed marketplace, not simply a discrete device. He was able to envision how people would want to use what he made, and he engineered toward that insight. He wasn't always prescient (he originally believed the phonograph would be used mainly as a business machine for recording and replaying dictation), but he invariably gave great consideration to users' needs and preferences.

① precarious
② foregone
③ prerequisite
④ foresighted

03 밑줄 친 solace와 의미가 가장 가까운 것을 고르시오. [3점]

"Eat the Night" understands the lived-in comforts of a virtual space when compared to the horrors of the outside world. The film works best when it cogitates on this theme. For a younger generation becoming more isolated in a deteriorating environment with political unrest, it's not only understandable but necessary to seek <u>solace</u> mediated through the safety of a screen.

① condemnation ② consolation
③ allegation ④ application

04 다음 빈칸에 들어갈 단어로 가장 적절한 것을 고르시오. [3점]

"What is deviant behavior?" cannot be answered in a straightforward manner. Whether an act is labeled deviant or not depends on many factors, including location, audience, and the individual committing the act. Listening to music on the way to class is considered acceptable behavior. Listening to music during your lecture is considered rude. As norms vary across cultures and time, it makes sense that notions of deviance change also. In a time of war, acts usually considered morally _____, such as taking the life of another, may actually be rewarded. Whether an act is deviant or not depends on society's response to that act.

① unreliable ② reprehensible
③ susceptible ④ laudable

05 다음 글에서 문법적으로 가장 <u>어색한</u> 것을 고르시오. [3점]

Realism is a literary and artistic movement ① <u>that originated in the 19th century</u> and known for its objective depiction of ordinary life. It involves careful observation of detail and explores the complexities of human psychology. Rejecting romantic idealism, ② <u>realism aims to portray the world as it truly is</u>. It often talks about social concerns. ③ <u>It explores how industry and cities have impacted people and communities</u>. Overall, realism in literature is a literary movement ④ <u>that was emerged in the 19th century and aimed to capture life as it truly was</u>, depicting the ordinary, mundane, and often harsh aspects of human existence.

06
다음 글에서 문법적으로 어색한 것을 고르시오. [3점]

Apple is allowing anyone to access its Apple TV+ streaming service for free this weekend from January 3 to 5. The company made the announcement on Monday alongside a short video featuring its most popular TV shows, including "Severance," "Slow Horses," "Shrinking," and more. ① <u>It's worth noting</u> that this is the first time that Apple has offered something like this. The announcement comes a few days ② <u>after Apple TV+ began teasing</u> that it was planning to open up its content to non-subscribers. A weekend is enough time to binge-watch some of Apple's most popular shows, especially "Severance," which is returning ③ <u>for its highly anticipating second season on January 17</u>. ④ <u>Although Apple's tweet announcing the promotion says</u> Apple TV+ will be free to stream on January 4 and 5, Apple's official press release says it will be available free from January 3 to 5.

07~08
아래 지문을 읽고 문제에 답하시오.

An algorithm is a set of steps for solving a problem or accomplishing a task, used in both daily life and computer science. For example, making coffee or tying shoelaces involves following a Ⓐ <u>step-by-step</u> process, much like a computer executes algorithms. In computer science, algorithms are mathematical processes with a Ⓑ <u>finite</u> number of steps, essential for programs and applications like search engines, navigation systems, and music streaming. They instruct computers on what to do and how to do it, enabling tasks like Ⓒ <u>calculations</u>, data processing, and decision-making. Think of an algorithm as a recipe guiding a sequence of actions to achieve a specific goal. Like recipes that can vary but still produce chocolate chip cookies, different algorithms can solve the same problem using distinct approaches while delivering Ⓓ <u>inconsistent</u> results. Ⓔ_____.

07
Ⓐ~Ⓓ 중 가장 적절하지 <u>않은</u> 것을 고르시오. [3점]

① Ⓐ step-by-step ② Ⓑ finite
③ Ⓒ calculations ④ Ⓓ inconsistent

08 ⓔ에 들어갈 내용으로 가장 적절한 것을 고르시오. [3점]

① Algorithms can only be applied to theoretical problems, not practical applications
② The evolution of algorithms has made traditional programming methods obsolete
③ Versatile algorithms can result in constant outcomes, regardless of the problem or approach used
④ Developing algorithms requires an infinite number of steps to ensure functionality

(09~10) 아래 지문을 읽고 문제에 답하시오.

Stress has many wonderful attributes. It reminds us that we care; it connects us directly with the most challenging and important aspects of our lives. We aren't suggesting that Ⓐ_____, only that it can bring unexpected benefits, too, in the form of personal growth. Combining our years of experience conducting leadership seminars and teaching meditation and martial arts and exploring empirical research in the area of psychology, we have found that individuals who adopt a "stress-is-Ⓑ_____" mind-set in their lives show greater work performance and fewer negative health symptoms than those who adopt a "stress-is-Ⓒ_____" lens. Drawing on our work and research with executives, students, and professional athletes, we have devised a three-step approach to responding to pressure that we believe can help you harness the creative power of stress while minimizing its deleterious effects.

09 Ⓐ에 들어갈 가장 적절한 것을 고르시오. [3점]

① sustained stress does not take a toll
② moderate stress is better for personal growth
③ stress is not associated with performance
④ stress inspires highly-motivated individuals

10 Ⓑ와 Ⓒ에 들어갈 가장 적절한 것을 고르시오. [3점]

① debt — asset
② enhancing — debilitating
③ virtue — rectitude
④ malicious — beneficial

11~12 아래 지문을 읽고 문제에 답하시오.

Sinead Gleeson, an Irish writer, said "We have a tradition of bards and poets being taken seriously by the higher echelons of society. We're also a nation of storytellers. Even when we went through terrible times like the famine, poverty, and British colonization, people would do what was called 'ceilidh.' It's an Irish tradition of traveling to houses and telling stories. And much like once-colonized Korea, Ireland has undergone seismic sociocultural changes over the last 100 years — from its independence from the United Kingdom in 1921 to the sweeping forces of modernization and a gradual shift away from Catholic conservatism. These Ⓐ_____ have sparked a new wave of voices coming out of a place of silence."

This silencing was both linguistic and cultural. In the 19th century, the country's national primary education system banned the teaching and speaking of Irish in schools. The Catholic Church's predominant influence further enforced the social silence, especially among women, as infamously witnessed in the Magdalene Laundries, where thousands of unmarried mothers and other "fallen women" were incarcerated to work to wash away their sins. There's a lot of repressed trauma that modern contemporary Ireland is still very much working through, and some of them do that in their writing. Another Irish writer, Ronan Hession, observed that both Korea and Ireland appear similar in their histories, Ⓑ_____ beyond colonization and Ⓒ_____ intense modernization. In both Irish and Korean literature, you get this sense of what has been won and lost — people who have been left behind or marginalized, values that have changed, who is included in modernity and who is not.

11 Ⓐ에 들어갈 가장 적절한 것을 고르시오. [3점]

① democracies
② transformations
③ affiliations
④ relinquishments

12 Ⓑ와 Ⓒ에 들어갈 가장 적절한 것을 고르시오. [3점]

① moved — experienced
② having been moving — have experienced
③ have moved — are experiencing
④ having moved — experienced

13~14 아래 지문을 읽고 문제에 답하시오.

Match Group, the technology company with the world's largest portfolio of dating platforms, has announced it is increasing investment in artificial intelligence (AI) with new products coming in March 2025. An as yet unnamed AI assistant will perform core dating tasks such as selecting the photos that garner the most responses and recommend what prompts and information to put in a bio. It will also help users choose the perfect partner. The AI will conduct a spoken interview with the users to establish what they want to get out of their dating experience and suggest what messages to send to people they are matched with based on interests. The company has also said AI will provide "effective coaching for struggling users," which will include tips for people who are failing to meet matches about how to attract more attention to their profile.

13 밑줄 친 garner와 의미가 가장 가까운 것을 고르시오. [3점]

① sprinkle ② acquire
③ flutter   ④ garnish

14 윗글의 내용과 가장 거리가 먼 것을 고르시오. [3점]

① AI is expected to recognize users' preferences on dating.
② AI is expected to help users find a match on the platform.
③ AI is expected to generate photos for struggling users.
④ AI is expected to provide users with tips to allure others.

15~16 아래 지문을 읽고 문제에 답하시오.

Stanley Milgram's study, conducted in the early 1960s, is one of the most famous experiments in the field of social psychology. The experiment involved participants who were told they were part of a study on memory and learning. They were assigned the role of "teacher," while another individual, who was actually an actor (the "learner"), was strapped to a chair and told to memorize word pairs. The teacher's task was to administer increasingly severe electric shocks to the learner whenever they gave a wrong answer. The shocks ranged from 15 volts to 450 volts, with labels indicating dangerous levels of shock. The learner would intentionally give wrong answers, and as the shock intensity increased, the learner would scream in pain, eventually falling silent as the shocks became more intense. However, the learner was not actually receiving any shocks; the cries and silence were scripted to simulate the effects.

Milgram's central finding was that a surprising number of participants — over 60% — were willing to administer the maximum 450-volt shock, despite the apparent distress of the learner. Many participants showed signs of stress, such as sweating and nervous laughter, but they continued to obey the experimenter's instructions. Milgram's study revealed the extent to which ordinary individuals could deliver Ⓐ_____ actions when ordered by an authority figure, Ⓑ_____ the assumption that only inherently cruel people could engage in such behaviors.

15 윗글의 내용과 일치하는 것을 고르시오. [3점]

① People tend to obey an authority figure, even if their actions conflict with their personal conscience.
② Milgram's study faced significant ethical criticism, particularly regarding the psychological distress caused to participants.
③ If the shock intensity increases, the "learner" in the experiment increasingly gives wrong answers.
④ The "teacher" in the experiment was the actor fabricating the signs of stress to enhance the "learner" performance.

16 Ⓐ, Ⓑ에 들어갈 가장 적절한 것을 고르시오. [3점]

① moral — supporting
② detrimental — instigating
③ harmful — challenging
④ biased — insinuating

[17~18] 아래 지문을 읽고 문제에 답하시오.

The periodic table is, for many, the symbol of chemistry. It is a single image that contains all of the known elements in the universe combined into an easily readable table. There are many patterns present in the table as well. All of the elements seem to fit together and connect to form a readable table and, in turn, the image of chemistry. The idea of elements first came about in 300 B.C. The great Greek philosopher Aristotle conceived an idea that everything on earth was made up of these elements. In ancient times, elements like gold and silver were readily accessible, but the elements that Aristotle chose were earth, water, fire, and air.

In 1649, the idea of elements took a huge step when Hennig Brand was the first to discover a new element: phosphorous. Brand was an alchemist in search of the Philosopher's Stone, or an object that would turn any ordinary metal into gold. In his search, he tried everything, including distilling human urine. When that experiment was carried out, Brand found a glowing white rock. This was the new element he would call phosphorous. The alchemists and scientists of the enlightenment period added incredible amounts of knowledge to the ideas about elements. In 1869, there were already 63 elements that had been discovered. With each new element that was found, scientists began to realize that there were patterns developing and some started to put the elements into a table.

The modern periodic table differs in some ways from Mendeleev's original version. It contains more than 40 additional elements, and its rows are longer instead of being squeezed under one another in staggered columns. For example, Mendeleev's fourth and fifth rows are both contained in the fourth period of the modern table. This ends up placing gallium, not scandium underneath boron in the periodic table. This Ⓐ_____ is due to theory on the electronic structure of atoms, in particular ideas about orbitals and the relation of electronic configuration to the periodic table. The extremely important idea of vertical groups of related elements is still retained, as are Mendeleev's group numbers. The latter appears as roman numerals at the top of each column in the modern table.

17 Ⓐ에 들어갈 가장 적절한 것을 고르시오. [3점]

① rearrangement ② retention
③ impediment   ④ preservation

18 윗글을 읽고 유추할 수 있는 것을 고르시오. [4점]

① The periodic table has finalized all existing elements into a readable and systematic format.
② Mendeleev's original periodic table remains unchanged in the modern version.
③ Advances in electronic theory have influenced the modern structure of the periodic table.
④ Aristotle's four-element theory is directly reflected in the modern periodic table.

19~20 아래 지문을 읽고 문제에 답하시오.

> Climate change is a deeply controversial subject, despite decades of scientific research and a high degree of scientific consensus that supports its existence. One effect of climate change is more extreme weather. There are increasingly more record-breaking weather phenomena, from the number of Category 4 hurricanes to the amount of snowfall in a given winter. These extremes, while they make for dramatic television coverage, can cause immeasurable damage to crops, property, and even lives. So nearly 200 countries signed the Kyoto Protocol, a document intended to engage countries in voluntary actions to limit the activity that leads to climate change.
>
> There is, however, a lot of finger-pointing among countries, especially when the issue arises of who will be permitted to pollute. World systems analysis suggests that while, historically, core nations (like the United States and Western Europe) were the greatest source of greenhouse gases, they have now evolved into post-industrial societies. Industrialized semi-peripheral and peripheral nations are releasing increasing quantities of greenhouse gases, such as carbon dioxide. The core nations, now post-industrial and less dependent on greenhouse-gas-causing industries, wish to enact strict protocols regarding the causes of global warming, but the semi-peripheral and peripheral nations rightly point out that they only want the same economic chance to evolve their economies. Since they were Ⓐ_____ affected by the progress of core nations, if the core nations now insist on "green" policies, they should pay offsets or subsidies of some kind. There are no easy answers to this conflict. It may well not be "fair" that the core nations benefited from Ⓑ_____ during their industrial boom.

19 Ⓐ, Ⓑ에 들어갈 가장 적절한 것을 고르시오. [3점]

① unduly — ignorance
② improperly — controversies
③ moderately — knowledge
④ reasonably — enlightenment

20 윗글의 내용으로 유추할 수 있는 것을 고르시오. [4점]

① Semi-peripheral and peripheral nations argue that core nations are responsible for climate change.
② Semi-peripheral and peripheral nations question the science used as evidence for climate change.
③ Post-industrial economies increasingly rely on industries that produce greenhouse gases.
④ Green policies promote core nations' but not industrialized nations' economic development.

21~22 아래 지문을 읽고 문제에 답하시오.

Humans are tribal. We need to belong to groups. We crave bonds and attachments, which is why we love teams, fraternities, and family. Almost no one is a hermit. But the tribal instinct is not just an instinct to belong. Some groups are voluntary; some are not. But once people belong to a group, their identities can become oddly bound with it. They will seek to benefit their group mates even when they personally gain nothing. They will penalize outsiders, seemingly gratuitously. They will sacrifice for their groups.

Today, no group in America feels comfortably dominant. Every group feels attacked, pitted against other groups not just for jobs and spoils but for the right to define the nation's identity. In these conditions, democracy <u>devolves into</u> zero-sum group competition — pure political tribalism.

In our foreign policy, for at least half a century, we Americans have been spectacularly blind to the power of tribal politics. We tend to view the world in terms of territorial nation-states engaged in great ideological battles — Capitalism versus Communism, Democracy versus Authoritarianism, the 'Free World' versus the 'Axis of Evil.' Blinded by our own ideological prisms, we have repeatedly ignored more primal group identities. This blindness has been the Achilles' heel of U.S. foreign policy.

Domestically as well, elites in the United States have either not cared about or been remarkably oblivious to the group identities that matter most to large segments of ordinary Americans. The most important tribal identity missed by America's elites was the powerful antiestablishment identity forming within the working class that helped elect Donald Trump.

21 <u>devolves into</u>와 의미가 가장 가까운 것을 고르시오. [3점]

① descends into
② looks up to
③ evolves into
④ looks down on

22 윗글의 내용으로 유추할 수 없는 것을 고르시오. [4점]

① Tribal politics may have substantial influence in both domestic and international politics.
② American foreign policy has been dominated by tribal considerations.
③ Some tend to offend others for their primal group benefits.
④ Donald Trump won the presidential election in 2016 partly due to political tribalism.

[23~24] 아래 지문을 읽고 문제에 답하시오.

The common cold is caused by a variety of viruses, but rhinoviruses are the most common culprit. These viruses Ⓐ_____ the cells in your nose and throat and use them to produce more viruses. After a few days, your immune system notices and destroys it, but not before you infect, on average, one other person. After you fight off the infection, you are immune to that particular rhinovirus strain — an immunity that lasts for years.

If we are all put in quarantine, the cold viruses we carry would have no fresh hosts to run to. Could our immune systems then wipe out every copy of the virus? Before we answer that question, let's consider the practical consequences of this kind of quarantine. The world's total annual economic output is in the neighborhood of $80 trillion, which suggests that interrupting all economic activity for a few weeks would cost many trillions of dollars. The shock to the system from the worldwide "pause" could easily cause a global economic collapse.

A global quarantine brings us to another question: How far apart can we actually get from one another? The world is big, but there are a lot of people. If we divide up the world's land area evenly, there's enough room for each of us to have a little over 2 hectares each, with the nearest person 77 meters away. While 77 meters is probably enough separation to block the transmission of rhinoviruses, that separation would Ⓑ_____. Much of the world's land is not pleasant to stand around on for five weeks. A lot of us would be stuck standing in the Sahara Desert or central Antarctica.

A more practical — though not necessarily cheaper — solution would be to give everyone biohazard suits. Ⓒ_____. If rhinoviruses don't have enough humans to move between, they die out.

23 Ⓐ, Ⓑ에 들어갈 가장 적절한 표현을 고르시오. [4점]

① put out — result in danger
② cut off — go beyond the border
③ take over — come at a cost
④ get back at — lead to the answer

24 Ⓒ에 들어갈 내용을 순서대로 배열한 것을 고르시오. [4점]

Ⓐ Dr. Mackay, a virology expert, said that this idea is actually somewhat reasonable, from a purely biological point of view.
Ⓑ That way, we could walk around and interact, even allowing some normal economic activity to continue.
Ⓒ He said that rhinoviruses and other RNA respiratory viruses are completely eliminated from the body by the immune system; they do not linger after infection.
Ⓓ Furthermore, we don't seem to pass any rhinoviruses back and forth with animals, which means there are no other species that can serve as reservoirs of our colds.

① Ⓓ — Ⓑ — Ⓐ — Ⓒ
② Ⓑ — Ⓓ — Ⓒ — Ⓐ
③ Ⓐ — Ⓑ — Ⓓ — Ⓒ
④ Ⓑ — Ⓐ — Ⓒ — Ⓓ

25~26 아래 지문을 읽고 문제에 답하시오.

Democracy's global momentum peaked soon after the end of the Cold War. For the first time in history, systems in which people could choose and replace their leaders in free and fair elections became the Ⓐ_____ form of government. By 2006, about three-fifths of all countries met this standard.

[A] Protecting democracy against such forces will take strength, agility, and tenacity. The world's liberal democracies must enhance their external defenses and cooperate more closely to maintain an economic, military, and technological edge that denies antidemocratic adversaries the power to dominate global politics and undercut their rivals.

[B] Since then, democracy and freedom have been in steady retreat. The decline has been global. The changes have not always been disastrous, but they have been remarkably broad and persistent. The global outlook for democracy is clouded, if not downright disheartening. Political extremism, polarization, and distrust have been on the rise even in long-established liberal democracies.

[C] The challenges confronting democracy today are Ⓑ_____. Authoritarian regimes have gone on the offensive to discredit and destabilize free societies. That they do so out of fear and concern for their own legitimacy does not make their actions any less dangerous. Making matters worse, hostile autocracies are increasingly acting in concert in a malevolent axis that features China, Russia, and Iran at the center, joined by Cuba, North Korea, and others.

[D] At the same time, as underscored by the recent electoral gains of extremist populist forces on both the right and the left in France and Germany, democratic leaders cannot neglect their internal defenses. Emerging and mature democracies alike need strategies to counter the siren song of illiberal populism. Even a long-standing liberal democracy can turn toward autocracy if its government does not deliver effective policies to combat crime and terrorism, manage national borders, soothe societal divisions, and ensure broad access to economic opportunity and security.

25 Ⓐ와 Ⓑ에 들어갈 가장 적절한 것을 고르시오. [4점]

① predominant — formidable
② inherent — insignificant
③ premature — impressive
④ principal — inconsequential

26 A~D 문단의 순서 중 가장 적절한 것을 고르시오. [4점]

① A — B — D — C
② B — A — D — C
③ B — C — A — D
④ C — A — B — D

27~28 아래 지문을 읽고 문제에 답하시오.

NASA's Parker Solar Probe is a groundbreaking mission to dive into the sun's atmosphere, enduring extreme heat and radiation to give humanity its first-ever close-up Ⓐ_____ of a star's outer layers. Launched in 2018, the spacecraft is equipped with cutting-edge thermal engineering and instruments to study the sun's magnetic fields, plasma, energetic particles, and the solar wind.

The Parker Solar Probe's discoveries have already transformed our understanding of the sun and its influence on Earth. By answering long-standing questions — such as why the corona is hotter than the sun's surface and how solar wind accelerates — it provides critical data for predicting space weather. These insights protect satellites, power grids, and astronauts from solar radiation.

On December 24, 2024, Parker completed its closest-ever approach to the sun, passing just 3.8 million miles from its surface at a record-breaking speed of 430,000 miles per hour. The latest flyby marks the spacecraft's 23rd close flyby and brings it deeper into the corona than ever before. When data is returned, it will provide unprecedented details of the sun's behavior during its 11-year solar maximum. NASA confirmed the probe's health on December 27, 2024, when a beacon tone signaled its successful navigation through the sun's outer atmosphere.

It will continue its highly elliptical orbit, making two more close passes of the sun in March and June 2025. After completing its primary mission in June 2025, the probe will remain in orbit to conduct additional observations until its onboard fuel runs out. Without corrective thrusts, the solar wind will gradually push the spacecraft out of alignment with Earth, ending its ability to transmit data. When its mission concludes, nearly all of the probe will incinerate, leaving only its carbon heat shield to orbit the sun for potentially billions of years, until the very end of the solar system itself.

27 Ⓐ에 들어갈 가장 적절한 것을 고르시오. [3점]

① broadcasting
② sampling
③ networking
④ forecasting

28 윗글의 내용과 일치하는 것을 고르시오. [4점]

① The Parker Solar Probe is scheduled to return to Earth when it completes its task.
② The Parker Solar Probe will have made 23 close passes of the sun by June 2025.
③ The Parker Solar Probe will be mostly burnt up after finishing its duty.
④ The Parker Solar Probe has provided data covering the entire period of the solar maximum.

29~30 아래 지문을 읽고 문제에 답하시오.

Ⓐ Studies of genetic disorders also reveal that one cognitive domain can develop normally simultaneous with abnormal development in other domains. Children with Turner's syndrome (a chromosomal anomaly) reveal normal or advanced language simultaneous with serious nonlinguistic cognitive deficits. Similarly, the studies of the language development in children with Williams syndrome reveal a unique behavioral profile in which there appears to be a selective preservation of linguistic functions in the face of severe general cognitive deficits.

Ⓑ As children with Specific Language Impairment show, language may be impaired with general intelligence intact. But can language develop normally with general intelligence impaired? If such individuals can be found, it argues strongly for the view that language does not derive from some general cognitive ability. The question as to whether the language faculty from birth is domain specific — is in our genes — or whether it is derivative of more general intelligence is a controversial question receiving much attention and debate among linguists, psychologists, and neuropsychologists.

Ⓒ There are cases of children who had difficulties in acquiring language or are much slower than the average child. These children show no other cognitive deficits; they are not autistic or retarded and have no perceptual problems. They are said to be suffering from Specific Language Impairment.

⬜D The psychological literature documents numerous cases of intellectually handicapped individuals who, despite their disabilities in certain spheres, show remarkable talents in others. One has been reported about a severely retarded child, named Laura. She lacks almost all number concepts including basic principles, can draw only at a preschool level, and has an auditory memory span limited to three units. Yet, she produces syntactically complex sentences. She is one of many examples of children who display well-developed linguistic abilities and severe deficits in nonlinguistic cognitive development.

Thus, evidence from Specific Language Impairment and other genetic disorders, along with the asymmetry of abilities, supports the view of Ⓐ_____.

29 Ⓐ~Ⓓ 문단의 순서 중 가장 적절한 것을 고르시오. [4점]
① C — A — B — D
② B — C — A — D
③ A — D — C — B
④ C — B — D — A

30 Ⓐ에 들어갈 내용으로 가장 적절한 것을 고르시오. [4점]
① language ability as an independent brain module
② language as a reflection of general intelligence
③ language as a mixture of domain-specific and general cognitive abilities
④ language ability as a derivative result of universal cognitive perception

서울여자대학교

▶ 2025학년도 오전 A형 ▶ 문항 수: 40문항 | 제한시간: 70분

2025 서울여대 오전 A형 영역별 문항 수

구분	문법			어휘			논리완성	독해	생활영어	총 문항 수
	G/S, W/E	정비문	재진술	동의어	반의어	유추				
문항 수	10			5			12	13		40
백분율	25%			12.5%			30%	32.5%		100%

SEOUL WOMEN'S UNIVERSITY

서울여자대학교

2025학년도 오전 A형: 40문항 · 70분

문항별 배점 01~10 2점 / 11~30 2.5점 / 31~40 3점

[01~05] Choose the word that is closest in meaning to the underlined expression.

01 The Taiwanese director <u>reverently</u> follows the conventions of the genre that he says occupied a great deal of his movie-going life in '50s and '60s.

① derisively
② affectedly
③ deferentially
④ garrulously

02 A <u>doting</u> mother, Emma was far more likely to praise her son's crude attempts at art than to disparage them.

① docile
② obedient
③ tyrannic
④ affectionate

03 The medicine proved to be <u>potent</u>, alleviating the patient's pain.

① effective
② fragile
③ flawless
④ persistent

04 Most of our conversations were about <u>scarcity</u> and how things were tight.

① fright
② shortage
③ hardship
④ unrest

05 A district council leader has warned that proposals to <u>streamline</u> local government are a threat to democracy.

① relocate
② undercut
③ merge
④ rationalize

06~10 Choose the one that best completes the sentence.

06 The U.S. Securities and Exchange Commission advises investors to be _____ for possible signs of online investment fraud.

① vivacious
② alert
③ fervent
④ prolix

07 Please use a coaster under your glass in order to avoid _____ the wood furniture.

① marring
② aggrandizing
③ abating
④ miring

08 Machines are _____ more and more of the attributes we used to think of as uniquely human.

① taking on
② turning to
③ making up
④ running into

09 Universal Pictures announced this week that Christopher Nolan will be directing a cinematic _____ of "The Odyssey," an ancient poem believed to be written by Homer between 750 and 650 BCE.

① adjustment
② reparation
③ adaptation
④ commendation

10 By the summer of 2022, the majority of people had been fully vaccinated and accordingly all mandatory mask-wearing requirements _____ in most countries.

① lifted
② impaired
③ installed
④ decreed

11~15 Identify the one underlined word or phrase that should be corrected or rewritten.

11 The idea of human rights ① as fundamental rights ② is not without ③ their critics, even at this ④ otherwise receptive time.

12 It's one of ① the great injustices of this era ② that countries ③ contribute negligible amounts to global carbon emissions are now feeling ④ the most harrowing impacts of climate change.

13 The process ① which public or private lands ② are transformed ③ into park areas ④ is complex.

14 According to a new ① analysis from LinkedIn, which examined millions of jobs from January 2022 to July 2024, some of ② fast-growing jobs for 2025 ③ barely existed at ④ the turn of the century.

15 ① That we often derive sorrow from the sorrow of ② others, is a matter of fact ③ so obvious to require any ④ instances to prove it.

16~20 Choose the one that best completes the sentence.

16 Some people find the idea of seeking out emotional well-being _____.
① incredible appeal
② incredibly appeal
③ incredible appealing
④ incredibly appealing

17 The world is already facing _____ the Cornell agricultural economist Chris Barrett calls a "food polycrisis."
① with
② what
③ that
④ whether

18 _____ people see an advantage in moving to the city than they used to.
① Few
② A few
③ Fewer
④ A fewer

19 In 2016, she won the Man Booker International Prize for fiction for *The Vegetarian*, the first of her novels to be translated into English and _____ her major international breakthrough.
① consider
② considered
③ considering
④ was considered

20 New York City's _____ congestion pricing began on January 5, marking a new era for driving into Manhattan.
① long-awaiting
② awaiting-long
③ long-awaited
④ awaited-long

21~27 Choose the one that best completes the sentence.

21 Digital technology has eliminated the need for grand productions of old days in cinema. Crowds can be replicated, buildings reconstructed, and characters invented within the confines of the computer. Yet whether digital is aesthetically preferable to the old way is another matter entirely. *Gladiator* is a good instance that _____ as in *Ben Hur* (1959), and *Spartacus* (1960); its digital technique is remarkable but premature with its absence of dirt, natural movement, and human detail; its settings and supplements are too clean. Visually, the past never looked so perfect.

① digital productions cannot replace old ones
② digital technology can invoke new nostalgia
③ digital reproductions pay tribute to old epics
④ the past can be digitally replicated in aesthetically new ways

22 KEEP YOUR EDGE: Sologig.com reduces the pressure of marketing yourself and lets you focus on what you do best. Our job is to keep you in touch with your most important client and your next one as well. Being a Gold or Platinum Level member is the definitive way to stay ahead of your competition and promote your services to thousands of companies. Put simply, enhancing your Membership Level _____. A higher Membership Level ensures that your profile appears higher in an employer's search than those with lower service level memberships.

① improves your working competence to the utmost
② solidifies your relationship with other members
③ changes your view about job training methods
④ increases your visibility to potential customers

23 Man is a rational animal — so at least I have been told. Throughout a long life, I have looked diligently for evidence in favor of this statement, but so far I have not had the good fortune to come across it, though I have searched in many countries spread over three continents. On the contrary, I have seen the world _____.

① plunging continually further into madness
② left unassisted to face the mundane reality
③ stuck in the irresistible forces of reasoning
④ possessing strong desires and abilities to express rationality

24. Many animals and insects have an inborn ability to camouflage themselves in order to hide from prey or predators. Camouflage is a form of deception. It isn't in an animal's best interest to _____. The more it blends, the longer it lives.

① play dead
② live longer
③ draw attention to itself
④ avoid being noticed by others

25. For the majority of human history, most people didn't go to school. Formal education was a privilege for the Alexander the Greats of the world, who could hire Aristotles as private tutors. Starting in the mid-19th century, the United States began to establish truly _____. It was a social compact: the state provides public schools that are free and open to all. And children, for most of their childhood, are required to receive an education.

① universal and compulsory education
② privileged and accessible education
③ inclusive and vocational education
④ targeted and innovative education

26. The bacterium *Acinetobacter baumannii* is _____. The microorganism causes a range of infections, and its ability to survive drying up means it can persist for weeks on hospital air vents, computer keyboards and human skin. Its metabolic and genetic flexibility has allowed it to become resistant to the few antibiotics that can make it through its two protective cell membranes. Antibiotic-resistant microbes kill more than one million people each year. The global threat posed by *A. baumannii* has put the microbe high on the list of priority pathogens drawn up by the World Health Organization (WHO).

① a portrait of resilience
② a source of inspiration
③ a subject of controversy
④ a case of misunderstanding

27 The EU has fallen behind the US and Asia in recent decades in important digital technologies: semiconductor manufacturing has shifted to East Asia and Europe lacks any consumer-facing firms with the scale of America's digital monoliths. The EU sees this as a risk to Europe's autonomy, security and commitment to competitive markets. Its regulatory proposals and public investments are increasingly aimed at curbing the power of US tech giants while securing European leadership in emerging technologies. But China and the US also want sovereignty over how technology is regulated in their own jurisdictions and to control global technology standards. This poses threats to Europe's _____.

① engagement with global environmental issues
② prospects for regaining technological leadership
③ project to integrate all nations into a single market
④ endeavor to outsource semiconductor manufacturing

28~40 Read the following passages and answer the questions.

28~29

The word disability hints at something missing either fiscally, physically, mentally or legally. To be disabled evokes a marginalized place in society, culture, economics and politics. It is concentrated in some parts of the globe more than others, caused by armed conflict and violence, malnutrition, rising populations, child labour and poverty. Yet it is increasingly found to be everywhere as well, and disability affects us all, transcending class, nation and wealth. The notion of the TAB (Temporarily Able Bodied) recognizes that many people will at some point become disabled. Most impairments are acquired (97%) rather than congenital, and world estimates suggest a figure of around 500–650 million disabled people, or one in ten of the population. Currently, 150 million of these are children and it is estimated that 386 million of the world's working-age population are disabled. 88% live in the world's poorest countries and 90% of those in rural areas. People with impairments tend to be ignored, pitied, patronized, objectified and fetishized. And while impaired bodies and minds have always been part of everyday life, demeaning societal responses to impairment, which we can define as Ⓐ 'disablement' or 'disablism,' are historically and culturally relative.

28 Which of the following does the underlined Ⓐ refer to?

① Social discrimination of impairment
② Equal rights of people with impairment
③ Common features of disabled people
④ Cultural values of the TAB (Temporarily Able Bodied)

29 Which of the following is NOT discussed in the passage?

① The global nature of disability
② The impacts of disability upon economy
③ The social and economic context of disability
④ The size of the disabled population worldwide

[30~31]

Most persons are surprised, and many distressed, to learn that essentially the same objections commonly urged today against computers were urged by Plato in the *Phaedrus* and in the *Seventh Letter* against writing. Writing, Plato has Socrates say in the *Phaedrus*, is inhuman, pretending to establish outside the mind what in reality can be only in the mind. It is a thing, a manufactured product. The same of course is said of computers. Secondly, Plato's Socrates urges, writing destroys memory. Those who use writing will become forgetful, relying on an external resource for what they lack in internal resources. Writing weakens the mind. Today, parents and others fear that pocket calculators provide an external resource for what ought to be the internal resource of memorized multiplication tables. Calculators weaken the mind, relieve it of the work that keeps it strong. Thirdly, a written text is basically unresponsive. If you ask a person to explain his or her statement, you can get an explanation; if you ask a text, you get back nothing except the same, often stupid, words which called for your question in the first place. In the modern critique of the computer, the same objection is put, "Garbage in, garbage out." Fourthly, in keeping with the agonistic mentality of oral cultures, Plato's Socrates also holds it against writing that the written word cannot defend itself as the natural spoken word can: real speech and thought always exist essentially in a context of give-and-take between real persons. Writing is passive, out of it, in an unreal, unnatural world. So are computers.

30 What is the passage mainly about?

① A defense of writing

② A charge against writing

③ Differences between writing and computing

④ Comparisons between internal and external resources

31 According to the passage, which of the following is true?

① Socrates wrote the *Phaedrus*.

② Plato cherished external resources.

③ Unlike writing, computers are not passive.

④ Socrates favored spoken words.

32~34

In 2020 our school board announced it was eliminating the school's entrance exams and adopting new admissions requirements in an effort to increase the diversity of the student body. No one argued against such a noble goal but many of us had plenty to say about Ⓐ the method. It crushed the kids who had worked hard and sacrificed so much to gain entrance to the school based on merit. I was part of a group including parents, students and alumni that sued to reinstate merit-based admissions. The school board insists the new admissions requirements are based on merit. A federal judge ruled this year that the changes to the admissions requirements were "patently unconstitutional" and discriminatory to Asian American kids. We are confident we will prevail while the school board appeals the ruling.

Unfortunately, these misguided policies are spreading across the education landscape. In California, school districts are moving to decrease the number of D and F grades distributed and putting in place "equitable grading," like making a 50 (instead of a 0) the lowest grade a student can receive and allowing missed deadlines in new "reasonable late work policy" guidelines. School districts in other parts of the country are eliminating academically advanced programs and advanced placement classes. This race to the bottom doesn't help the young people it aims to uplift, including students with learning disabilities, people facing socioeconomic challenges and new English language learners.

32 What would be the best title of the passage?

① Success Stories in Education
② Equity Over Excellence in Education
③ Defending Merit in Education Policy
④ The Case for Diversity in Education

33 Which of the following is the author most likely to argue for?

① More generous grading
② A reasonable late work policy
③ Elimination of entrance exams
④ Academically advanced programs

34 Which of the following does the underlined ⓐ refer to?

① How to attract outstanding students
② How to improve the quality of education
③ How to enhance the diversity of the student population
④ How to assist students from disadvantaged backgrounds

35~36

In 1948 half a million workers were employed in mining coal; the great bulk of those jobs had disappeared by the early 21st century not because we stopped mining coal — the big decline in coal production, in favor first of natural gas and then of renewable energy, started only around 15 years ago — but because technologically advanced surface mining and mountaintop extraction made it possible to extract an increasing amount of coal with many fewer workers. It's true that the jobs that disappear in the face of technological progress have generally been replaced by other jobs. But that doesn't mean that the process has been painless. Individual workers may not find it easy to change jobs, especially if the new jobs are in different places. They may find their skills devalued; in some cases, as with coal, technological change can uproot communities and their way of life.

This kind of dislocation has been a feature of modern societies for at least two centuries. But Ⓐ <u>something new</u> may be happening now. In the past, the jobs replaced by technology tended to involve manual labor. Machines replaced muscles. On the one hand, industrial robots replaced routine assembly-line work. On the other hand, there has been ever-growing demand for knowledge workers, a term coined by Peter Drucker for people engaged in nonrepetitive problem-solving. Many people, myself included, have said that we're increasingly becoming a knowledge economy. But what if machines can take over a large chunk of what we have historically thought of as knowledge work?

35 What caused the large-scale disappearance of coal miners in the early 21st century?

① Exhaustion of coal reserves
② Decrease in miners' wages
③ A shift towards environment-friendly energy
④ Technological advancements in mining methods

36 Which of the following does the underlined Ⓐ refer to?

① The rise of a knowledge-based economy
② The arrival of an era of technology-driven knowledge work
③ The collaboration between human workers and industrial robots
④ The decrease of coal production in favor of clean energy resources

37~38

2024 was the hottest year on record, according to new data published by the Copernicus Climate Change Service. It was also the first year the planet surpassed the 1.5 degrees Celsius global warming target set forth in the Paris Climate Accord. But years from now, you're unlikely to remember 2024 as an especially hot year, because it will also be one of the coolest years of the rest of your life. As humanity keeps burning fossil fuels and heating up the Earth, your future self will look back on the present as a time of calmer weather, snowier winters, and milder temperatures. To children born today, the hotter, stormier climate conditions of the future will feel normal. This is due to a mind trick known as shifting baseline syndrome, which causes people to grow accustomed to whatever environmental conditions they're currently experiencing. The phenomenon can lead to a gradual erosion of society's environmental standards, whether those standards concern acceptable levels of air pollution or the number of fish in the sea. When it comes to climate change, shifting baseline syndrome may be causing society to normalize progressively hotter temperatures — and a host of other planetary impacts.

37 What is this passage mainly about?

① What has caused abnormal climate conditions so far
② What humans should do to cope with climate changes
③ How extreme the year 2024 was in terms of temperature
④ How people will feel about environmental crises in the future

38 According to the passage, shifting baseline syndrome may _____.

① affect children more easily than adults
② diminish people's willingness to combat climate change
③ enhance people's awareness of harsh environmental conditions
④ cause lawmakers to set stronger targets in conservation policies

39~40

Populist parties and political movements have risen or become stronger all over Europe in the aftermath of the European Union's financial crisis, the politics of austerity, and the increasing number of refugees and immigrants. This development has been similar in countries such as Greece and Spain where radical cuts to welfare transfers and services were implemented as a precondition for bailout loans but also in countries such as Finland, France, Germany, and the Netherlands that contributed to the bailout while struggling with the crisis themselves. Together, the downturn that was initiated by the crisis and its management created a reservoir of discontent, despair, and anger among many Europeans. These collective emotions have fueled protests against governments held responsible for unjustified and unpopular politics. The question is, why have these processes predominantly harbored support for the political right rather than the left that has traditionally benefited from wide-ranging social dissatisfaction?

39 What is this passage mainly about?

① The process and the result of bailout in Greece and Spain
② The failure of welfare systems in Central and Northern Europe
③ Different types of political populism in diverse European regions
④ The economic and psychological context for populist politics in Europe

40 According to the passage, which of the following is NOT true?

① Currently left-wing rather than right-wing populism prevails in Europe.
② The rise of populism in Europe is partly due to the EU's financial crisis.
③ In Greece and Spain welfare transfers and services were seriously reduced.
④ Traditionally it is the left that has thrived on people's social dissatisfaction.

서울여자대학교

▶ 2025학년도 정오 A형   ▶ 문항 수: 40문항 | 제한시간: 70분

2025 서울여대 정오 A형 영역별 문항 수

구분	문법			어휘			논리완성	독해	생활영어	총 문항 수
	G/S, W/E	정비문	재진술	동의어	반의어	유추				
문항 수	10			5			12	13		40
백분율	25%			12.5%			30%	32.5%		100%

SEOUL WOMEN'S UNIVERSITY

서울여자대학교
2025학년도 정오 A형: 40문항 · 70분

문항별 배점 01~10 2점 / 11~30 2.5점 / 31~40 3점

01~05 Choose the word that is closest in meaning to the underlined expression.

01 Evan and his people never learned why they shouldn't help each other although the devil in disguise tried to <u>infuse</u> the idea of competition into people.

① intrigue ② instill
③ inhibit ④ incur

02 Because of the <u>reticence</u> of the key witness, the case against the defendant collapsed.

① rebuke ② refutation
③ recession ④ reserve

03 They performed several experiments to <u>ascertain</u> whether the theory was valid.

① confirm ② inquire
③ applaud ④ foretell

04 Canada is preparing to retaliate with an <u>exhaustive</u> list of tariffs on American goods if Donald Trump follows through with his plans to add a steep 25% import tax on Canadian goods.

① definitive ② destructive
③ comprehensive ④ selective

05 The politician's <u>inflammatory</u> remarks caused a great deal of unrest among the public.

① soothing
② provocative
③ placid
④ arrogant

06~10 Choose the one that best completes the sentence.

06 A good performing actor must know how to _____ his dramatic role right at the moment, just like a jazz musician who plays to the moment at every concert.

① facilitate
② install
③ improvise
④ replicate

07 Without additional funding, it may not be _____ to build a new stadium for the Yankees on New York's West Side.

① feasible
② impassible
③ impetuous
④ dismal

08 Her presentation was so _____ that even the most complicated concepts were easy to understand.

① ambiguous
② convoluted
③ concise
④ rampant

09 Many rice growers use planes to _____ crop ripening by spraying hormones from the air.

① reap
② evict
③ hasten
④ confide

10 Different villages within a larger cultural unit are highly autonomous and there is no _____ structure of the whole.

① flimsy
② overarching
③ archaic
④ exquisite

11~15 Identify the one underlined word or phrase that should be corrected or rewritten.

11 Machines may not be alive, but the evolutionary pressures ① surrounding them are ② as intensely as ③ those in nature, and with ④ few of its constraints.

12 The age of A.I. ① forces us to more clearly distinguish the knowledge that is useful information ② with the humanistic knowledge ③ that leaves people wiser and ④ transformed.

13 ① What is happening ② in our schools ③ will shape what our future society ④ will look.

14 More than ① three-quarter of the population of Africa, which has already ② surpassed ③ one billion, cannot ④ afford a healthy diet.

15 Sudan's military and a powerful paramilitary have spent almost two years at war, ① with many ② tens of thousands civilians killed, and ③ close to twelve million people ④ displaced.

16~20 Choose the one that best completes the sentence.

16 The study cites affordable day-care facilities and stable economic growth _____ factors for raising the birth rate.

① of
② with
③ as
④ from

17 Why _____ hair looks shinier after a few weeks off shampoo?

① do some claim
② does some claim
③ do some claims
④ does some claims

18 The eating habits of tadpoles are _____ interest to many scientists.

① on
② in
③ of
④ as

19 November 1989 brought more shifts in the basic structure of the world system than _____ since the summer of 1945.

① were seen
② had seen
③ have been seen
④ had been seen

20 She began operating the site with a small team, _____ were, like her, militant anarchists.

① most members of it
② its most members
③ whose most of members
④ most of whose members

21~27 Choose the one that best completes the sentence.

21 It is now five years since Jacques Delors retired as the European Commission's president. The British tabloids no longer revile him; the battles with Margaret Thatcher have faded into EU folklore; and the all-night squabbles in Brussels are someone else's headache. So there is no obvious reason why a retired Frenchman of 75, though he looks a trim 60, should still command the attention of Europeans who count. And yet in the run-up to the EU summit that began in Nice on December 7th, he had ministers, civil servants and commissioners _____.

① trumpeting their victories
② supporting his presidency
③ straying from their offices
④ hanging on his every word

22 It is said that the lobster when washed ashore makes no effort to get back into the water, but waits for the sea to come to him. If it does well and good: if it does not, he simply dies. There are literally thousands of men who complain that no one helps them, and who frown upon the success of others as due wholly to good luck or the influence of friends. The time spent in lamenting their lot, _____, would yield splendid results and give them their proper place in the world.

① if wasted in dreaming
② if they blamed it on society
③ if applied to honest endeavor
④ if they were grateful to others

23 To an overwhelming degree, students today see college as job training, the avenue to a stable career. They are not wrong, given the 70 percent wage premium for 22- to 27-year-old workers with a bachelor's degree over those with only a high school diploma. This orientation, however, can close students off from learning things that _____.

① do not obviously help their job prospects
② are directly tied to their chosen career path
③ do not contribute to a well-rounded education
④ prepare them for the demands of the workforce

24 In the developed nations of the 21st century, convenience, more efficient and easier ways of doing personal tasks, has emerged as perhaps the most powerful force shaping our individual lives and our economies. This is particularly true in America, where, despite all the tributes to freedom and individuality, many believe that _____.

① convenience is in fact a supreme value
② the power of convenience is often overlooked
③ what seems convenient may actually be misleading
④ convenience can be compatible with freedom and individuality

25 People often blame the blue light from phones for difficulty in falling asleep, but experts say the issue is more complex. While blue light does affect our circadian rhythm, it's not just the color of the light, but also its brightness and exposure duration that matter. Stuart Peirson, a professor of circadian neuroscience, explains that both blue and red light can affect sleep by triggering receptors in our eyes. The problem _____.

① depends on whether the light is blue or red
② lies in the screen resolution and pixel density
③ is in part due to the type of content viewed on the screen
④ is how bright the light is or how long you are exposed to the light

26 About 40 pet dogs are taking part in a study to explore whether their brainwaves synchronize with those of their owners when the pair interact, a phenomenon previously seen when two humans engage with each other. The researchers behind the work say such synchronization would suggest person and pet are paying attention to the same things, and in certain circumstances interpreting moments in a similar way. In other words, owner and dog really are on the same wavelength. Dr. Valdas Noreika of the University of Cambridge said he got the idea for the study after working on similar experiments with mothers and their babies, where _____.

① such synchronization has also been seen
② human-dog synchronization has been affirmed
③ irregular synchronization patterns have been detected
④ facial rather than brainwave synchronization has been observed

27 Paris was the Hollywood of the nineteenth century, its novels were read and imitated everywhere — they even invented cinema there! No wonder they hate the other Hollywood, no one likes to give up symbolic hegemony; but no one keeps it by mere force of will either, and although France knows how to protect its own market (which was twice inundated by foreign films, in the 1920s and 1940s, and twice bounced back), there is no question of _____. Between 1986 and 1995, only four non-American films enjoyed a large international success: two British comedies, an Australian comedy, an American Italian melodrama. None of them was French. In fact, none was any different from the usual Hollywood fare.

① its developing diverse film genres
② its giving up its worldwide hegemony
③ its competing with Hollywood abroad
④ its maintaining a distinct cultural identity

28~40 Read the following passages and answer the questions.

28~29

This is to notify you of a change made by state law to your Medical Coverage. Beginning January 18, 2025, Blue Cross & Shield will no longer pay for day care services. These services are counseling services provided by Drug Treatment Centers. But if you are pregnant, this change does not apply to you during the time of your pregnancy or during the two months following the month in which your pregnancy ends. If you are under age 21, Blue Cross & Shield may continue as well to pay for these services until you reach age 21. If you are not pregnant (or recently pregnant) or under 21, you may call the Alcohol and Drug Program Administrator in your county to get information about getting other help to pay for these services, or to see if you can change to another drug treatment service which may be covered under Blue Cross & Shield. County Alcohol and Drug Program Administrators are listed in your telephone book white pages under County Government, Health Service.

Only the drug counseling services described above are being eliminated. All other services, including other Drug-related services, will continue as usual. If your provider denies or plans to discontinue your drug counseling services, but you think they should be provided because you are in one of the groups noted above, you may request a hearing by calling 1-800-923-3333.

28 Who is the notice trying to reach?

① Staff members in day care centers
② State lawmakers in the Health Committee
③ Counselors of County Government
④ Drug Treatment Center's counseling recipients

29 According to the passage, which of the following is NOT true?

① All of the drug counseling services are to be discontinued.
② The change does not apply to the minors who are pregnant.
③ The change does not concern females in the last period of pregnancy.
④ Blue Cross & Shield pays for the counseling services until minors get age 21.

[30~31]

What is certain is that baseball's antecedents go back to well before the *Mayflower*. Cricket, played since the sixteenth century in England and commonly in America until the nineteenth, appears to be the grandfather of all bat and ball games, but many others followed in both Britain and America over the next two centuries — *tipcat (or kitcat), bittle-battle, stick ball, one old cat, two old cat, three old cat,* and *base or base-ball*, among others. All involved the same principles of striking a ball with a stick or paddle and trying to traverse a defined path before being caught or thrown out by the fielding side. The first mention of baseball is found not in America but in Britain, in a children's book called *A Pretty Little Pocket Book, Intended for the Amusement of Little Master Tommy and Pretty Miss Polly*, published in London in 1744. But ball games by this time were already well rooted in America. The first mention of a bat in the context of American play is in 1734, and there are many references throughout eighteenth-century America to ball games and their implements. The Boston Massacre, for instance, was provoked in part by someone waving a tipcat bat in a threatening manner at the British troops, and soldiers at Valley Forge are known to have passed the time in 1778 by "playing at base."

30 What is the passage mainly about?

① The main rules of baseball
② An early history of baseball
③ Anecdotes concerning baseball
④ Baseball as a pastime in America

31 According to the passage, which of the following is true?

① It is not possible to trace a pristine form of baseball in the sixteenth century England.
② A baseball bat once triggered a political upheaval in London.
③ The first reference to baseball can be found in a children's book published in England.
④ Americans didn't have a fad for baseball in the eighteenth century.

32~33

For thousands of years, it was common in Western thought to imagine that there was an eternal war between reason and our emotions. In this way of thinking, reason is rational and sophisticated. Emotions are primitive, impulsive and likely to lead you astray. A wise person uses reason to override and control the primitive passions. A scientist, business executive or any good thinker should try to be objective and emotionally detached. Modern neuroscience has delivered a fatal blow to this way of thinking. If people thought before that passions were primitive and destructive, now we understand that they are often wise. Most of the time emotions guide reason and make us more rational. It's an exaggeration, but maybe a forgivable one, to say that Ⓐ this is a turnabout to rival the Copernican Revolution in astronomy. The problem is that our culture and our institutions haven't caught up with our knowledge. Today we still live in a society overly obsessed with raw brainpower. Our schools sort children according to their ability to do well on standardized tests, slighting Ⓑ the kind of wisdom held in the body that is just as important for navigating life. Our economic models are based on the idea that humans are rational creatures coolly calculating their self-interest.

32 Which of the following does the underlined Ⓐ refer to?

① That humans are rational
② That reason controls emotions
③ That emotions make us more rational
④ That reason and emotions cannot be divided

33 Which of the following is the underlined Ⓑ most likely to refer to?

① Passion
② Navigation
③ Self-interest
④ Raw brainpower

34~35

> In an A.I. world, college students should focus on developing skills that machines cannot replicate, making them more distinctly human. Classes that teach impersonal, linear, generalized thinking, which A.I. excels at, should be avoided. Instead, students should gravitate toward courses that foster distinctly human abilities. Children, according to Alison Gopnik, balance the obvious and the crazy when they create. They explore and innovate rather than simply imitating or absorbing data. Students should take classes, whether in coding or art, that nurture their imaginative abilities. A.I. excels at predictions, so students should develop contrarian, unconventional mentalities. They should learn about diverse worldviews from history, philosophy, and other cultures, which will be valuable in a world where conventional thinking is easily outpaced by A.I. Machines can analyze behavioral patterns, but they struggle with understanding individual experiences. Studying humanities, such as literature and history, allows students to better understand human perspectives, giving them a unique and valuable skill in an A.I.-driven world.

34 What would be the best title of the passage?

① What Humanities Can Teach A.I.
② How Humans Will Cooperate with A.I.
③ Why A.I. Will Not Replace Human Creativity
④ How Students Can Develop Human Skills in an A.I. World

35 Which of the following is the author NOT likely to recommend to college students?

① Exploration
② Pattern analysis
③ Literature and history
④ Unconventional worldviews

36~37

> Louisa Jaskulski died in her sleep in 2023 at 77, just a few days after having what seemed, at first, to be successful heart surgery. She was survived by four fan-tailed pigeons, three Amazon parrots, three lorikeets, a pair of finches, two desert tortoises, a bearded dragon, and a blue-tongued skink — all rescues. "For me, the connection to birds and reptiles goes way deep," she said in a 2020 interview. "When I look into the eyes of a parrot or finch or pigeon, or a lizard or snake or tortoise, I feel I am looking into the eyes of God." But when exotic pet owners die, where do their animals go? It's a common yet often excruciating challenge for those who keep exotic pets. Keeping the animals in the family is ideal, but there's no guarantee they'll want to take on the responsibility of being, essentially, an amateur zookeeper. Jaskulski left few concrete plans for who would inherit her animals — perhaps because she knew she could count on her animal rescue friends to sort it out. The hardest to place were the parrots and the tortoises, long-lived animals that can be demanding pets.

36 What is the passage mainly about?

① How to build a sympathetic relationship with animals
② How to become an ideal zookeeper raising exotic pets
③ How to save species in danger of extinction in your area
④ How to take care of the exotic animals that outlive their owners

37 According to the passage, which of the following is NOT true about Louisa Jaskulski?

① She underwent heart surgery a few days before dying.
② The birds and reptiles she had kept were all rescued animals.
③ She asked her animal rescue friends to keep her animals after her death.
④ She had a religious feeling when looking into the eyes of her exotic pets.

38~40

Coughing is an important reflex that protects the airway from dangers like noxious fumes, water, or bits of mis-swallowed food. The reflex is triggered by nerves that reach into the airway. These nerves are decorated with receptor proteins that react to everything from cold air to capsaicin, the chemical that makes peppers spicy. When an irritant triggers those receptors, nerves send signals up the vagus nerve to the brain that we experience as the urge to cough. From there, the brain sends commands back down to the airway to cough — or not. This detour to the brain is why there's a degree of conscious control in certain types of coughs. Scientists know about many different stimuli that can trigger a cough, but they still don't agree on the specific biological mechanisms that trigger coughing while we're sick, let alone in the weeks afterwards. While it may seem obvious coughing is meant to clear our throats of mucus, it's also possible that viruses trigger the reflex to help themselves spread. Many infections involve dry coughs that don't produce phlegm at all. And if we do ultimately cough to clear out our airway during an infection, that still wouldn't explain what exactly our nerves sense during an infection that triggers a cough.

38 What is this passage mainly about?

① The mechanism of coughing

② Stimuli that trigger coughing

③ Infections that involve coughing

④ Studies on the cure for coughing

39 According to the passage, scientists still don't agree on _____.

① which nerves are involved in coughing

② whether the brain has a role in coughing

③ what triggers coughing while we are sick

④ what function receptor proteins have in coughing

40 According to the passage, dry coughs during an infection suggest that _____.

① some chemicals in addition to the virus are triggering coughing
② coughing may be meant for something other than to clear out our airway
③ the viruses infecting our body and triggering coughing are not very powerful
④ the receptor proteins decorating the nerves around the airway do not work properly

성균관대학교

▶ 2025학년도 인문계 A형　▶ 문항 수: 50문항 ｜ 제한시간: 90분

2025 성균관대 인문계 A형 영역별 문항 수

구분	문법			어휘			논리완성	독해	생활영어	총 문항 수
	G/S, W/E	정비문	재진술	동의어	반의어	유추				
문항 수	5			5			12	28		50
백분율	10%			10%			24%	56%		100%

SUNGKYUNKWAN UNIVERSITY | 성균관대학교

2025학년도 인문계 A형: 50문항 · 90분

01~05 Choose one that is closest in meaning to the underlined expression.

01 The situation for U.S. equity markets is additionally <u>precarious</u> because those markets were closed on Thursday — the first full day of stock trading after Dubai's announcement — for American Thanksgiving. [1.9점]

① perilous
② guarded
③ definite
④ strong
⑤ moored

02 This diversification allows the newspaper to engage with readers in various ways, catering to different preferences and making it easier for audiences to <u>latch onto</u> its content. [1.9점]

① turn away
② release
③ despise
④ grasp
⑤ dishonor

03 During a dinner with my wife, my son and his wife and our two granddaughters at a beachside restaurant, I caught all of us looking at our phones as we waited for our food, <u>paying no heed to</u> the gorgeous scenery right in front of us. [1.9점]

① ignoring
② acknowledging
③ going over
④ dilating
⑤ outspreading

04 Some of the specifics still need to be worked out — how safe is "safe," how effective is "effective" — but those are the sorts of specifics that a prize committee can <u>adjudicate</u>. [1.9점]

① determine ② dissuade ③ dodge
④ repress ⑤ initiate

05 I think the world economy is recovering, although the process of recovery is a slow and <u>torturous</u> one. [1.9점]

① innocent ② agonizing ③ homogeneous
④ virtuous ⑤ delightful

06~10 Choose one that is either ungrammatical or unacceptable.

06 In Israel, the country's missile defense system, the Iron Dome, ① <u>autonomously</u> senses the threat of an ② <u>incoming</u> rocket and sends a warning to an operator, ③ <u>who</u> then ④ <u>gives</u> the command ⑤ <u>firing</u> a missile. [1.8점]

07 The ① <u>highly</u> competitive private clinics ② <u>would</u> generally offer ③ <u>whatever</u> therapies ④ <u>seemed</u> trendy — such as diet therapy ⑤ <u>in the</u> late nineteenth-century America. [1.8점]

08 He was travelling ① <u>on</u> the wrong visa, ② <u>despite</u> her ③ <u>having</u> obtained that visa for his previous trips to the United States to attend ④ <u>series of</u> similar ⑤ <u>events</u>. [1.8점]

09 ① Although neither Tanaka nor Ohasi ② assume a central role in the films ③ in which they appear, their presence onscreen is ④ nonetheless striking, especially ⑤ from our vantage point. [1.8점]

10 ① Not only ② does this not ③ involving any major repudiation of liberal thought, ④ but this kind of intervention ⑤ has a respectable pedigree in the thought of Adam Smith. [1.8점]

11~15 Choose one that is most appropriate for the blank.

11 The IUCN Red List now includes a handful of species that have been revived through conservation efforts, including the European white-tailed eagle and the Mekong catfish. Narrow corridors of protected habitat now connect nature preserves in South Africa, and similar corridors link up the coral reefs of the Bahamas, allowing species in the protected areas to move back and forth, exchange genes and sustain their _____. [2.0점]

① populations ② territories ③ originality
④ migration   ⑤ wilderness

12 The Armenians were active money brokers, borrowing cheaply in Macao and lending expensively in Canton; most Canton merchants were _____ on a large scale. Trade was fraught with risk but the Armenians showed that small itinerant traders could make a profit; they were determined and independent, and readily accepted by both Protestants and Catholics. [2.0점]

① self-sufficient ② prosperous ③ collateral-free
④ in debt   ⑤ in surplus

13 The chief task of casino design is to arrange the spatial relationships of surrounding areas, the shape and feel of the structural box that encloses the setting in such a way as to encourage machine gamblers' entry into _____ playing worlds. While players prefer gambling in bustling casinos, they want to be isolated in their own private, intimate world from the surrounding hubbub that attracted them in the first place. [2.0점]

① vibrant   ② noisy   ③ secluded
④ exposed   ⑤ communal

14 Officials and state media painted Western countries as hostile and subversive, and critics of the Kremlin were described as 'the enemy within' and collaborators with foreign powers. I began to spend much of my time reporting from courtrooms, charting Kremlin's increasing efforts to _____ all kinds of dissent. It was a dark period that opened with the shooting of one opposition politician, Boris Nemtsov, and covered the attempted assassination of another, Alexei Navalny, with a military-grade nerve agent. Navalny would die suddenly three years later, locked up in an Arctic prison camp for his politics. [2.0점]

① establish   ② stamp out   ③ build up
④ create   ⑤ praise

15 Much of the social and political theory in postwar America extended from the contributions of refugee scholars. In the ensuing years, the émigrés' theories of mass society became widely read and popularized as Americans sought to comprehend the dynamics of Cold War geopolitics abroad and dangerous mass tendencies hiding behind atomistic individualism at home. Thus, the mass emigration of European intellectuals in the 1930s and 1940s _____ in the postwar period. [2.0점]

① resulted in the distortion of American thought
② heightened the political tensions surrounding America
③ intensified Americans' sense of isolation amid the crowd
④ contributed to developing a new understanding of immigrants
⑤ had dramatic long-term effects on the shaping of American thought

16~19 Choose one that is most appropriate for the blank.

16 _____ can contribute to stories about the human condition under duress more fundamentally. Actors in fictions of an existential slant will struggle against injustice caused by bad people, a corrupt system, or a godless world. Few stories capture more brutally and forlornly the reality of political violence than Jean-Paul Sartre's "The Wall" set during the Spanish Civil War. A prisoner, Pablo Ibbieta, awaits execution and considers the value of life and whether it is worth betraying his principles to give the Fascists the information they want in exchange for his release. The exhausted Pablo does not relent until at the last minute he gives his captors false information about the location of a comrade they are hunting down, unaware that his friend has changed hiding places and has now been betrayed. Through its plot twist, a story about political violence acquires another dimension as a fable of existentialism and the human condition as a trap. [2.0점]

① Hate ② Contentment ③ Want
④ Courage ⑤ Dread

17 The Hollywood sign is perhaps the most conspicuous yet least-_____ landmark in the world. It is monitored 24 hours a day by motion sensors, high-definition cameras and the Los Angeles Police Department, which keeps watch from a TV tower on the hilltop. The public is only allowed to view the letters from nearby trails, though some people still try to scramble up the hill to reach them. [1.9점]

① liberal ② unobtrusive ③ subtle
④ accessible ⑤ conservative

18. This type of work is known as extreme event attribution. One common method compares two versions of the world. The first is the real world — where humans burning fossil fuels have caused global warming. The second is what the world would look like _____. Scientists estimate what that second, ideal world where humans dramatically diminish the use of fossil fuels would look like based on historical weather data and climate models. With some clever number-crunching, researchers can see how likely or severe a weather event is in each of those versions of the world. Hundreds of studies have probed the role of global warming in natural disasters. Many have found that climate change made extreme weather worse. [1.9점]

① in the near future
② in a brutal heat wave
③ without climate change
④ in any historical event
⑤ despite extreme weather events

19. The asteroid impact triggered rapid changes in the environment. This could have pushed some birds to evolve larger brains quickly. Parrots and members of the crow family have evolved some of the biggest brains of any bird. And larger brains relative to body size often suggest intelligence. The ancestors of parrots probably had large brains that helped them overcome challenges in their environment. After the asteroid impact, this would have allowed them to _____. Birds that learn how to open pinecones with their beaks, for instance, are more likely to survive than those that wait for a crop of berries that might never come. [1.9점]

① go way back in time
② repeat different sounds
③ conceal the target
④ learn from others how to sing or talk
⑤ outcompete other animals for resources

20~22 Choose one that is most appropriate for the blank.

20 So is the economy really doing well? Yes, by practically all measures. Inflation is down, unemployment is low, the dollar is strong and the stock market has soared. U.S. consumer sentiment recently ticked up again, suggesting Americans are feeling pretty good despite higher prices for everything from healthcare to Thanksgiving groceries. That positive consumer sentiment is especially justified when comparing the U.S. with other large, advanced economies. Europe is lagging, with Germany, its economic engine, flirting with a recession and struggling through a political crisis. The United Kingdom is facing a long-term decline, and Japan's aging population and low birth rates bode ill for its future. Even Canada, which usually does well when the U.S. does well, is feeling decidedly unwell these days, imperiling the regime of longtime Prime Minister Justin Trudeau. Still, as anyone familiar with investing has heard many times, past performance is _____. And, in fact, while the outlook for the U.S. economy is better than that of many other countries, it isn't exactly rosy.

[2.0점]

① remarkably resilient
② no indication of future results
③ showing first signs of stabilizing
④ accurately capturing what would happen in the future
⑤ affected chiefly by the stock market

21 Challengers are most successful and satisfied in companies that are hungry for change. Those could be firms in which strong traditions or a stretch of success has made people cautious or complacent. In such circumstances challengers have the most impact, and experience the fewest clashes with their executive teams. The most successful challengers are often protégés of CEOs who want "something different" and value professional expertise. It's worth noting that while many CEOs are uneasy being champions of this approach themselves, they do want it to be represented on their teams, so they hire challengers but don't give them enough support. That kind of ideological tokenism is a _____. And like custodians, challengers can fall out of favor when their work is no longer seen as constructively questioning the status quo but, rather, as a costly subversion.

[2.0점]

① recipe for failure
② learning by doing
③ holistic personal growth
④ property associated with the growth
⑤ desire to learn from the company's culture and habits

22 The USSR was an eager supplier of weapons and political support for many African nations fighting anti-colonialism wars in the 1960s and 1970s. Yet the Russian language didn't make a big foray into the African continent compared to French and English. When the anti-colonial struggles waned, local interest in the Russian language _____. "Moscow support ended at supplying weapons and training for anti-colonialism guerillas. Very few Africans, steeped in traditions of Arabic, English, and French colonialism, were eager to learn the Russian language," says political analyst Kimberly Mutandiro in South Africa. The fall of the Soviet Union, too, meant Moscow didn't have much money to spread its language projects across Africa — a vast continent of 52 countries — unlike in Central Europe and Eurasia, where Russian-language cultures were already rooted. [2.0점]

① practically ended
② started to flourish
③ solidified the diplomatic support
④ began to show sophisticated power
⑤ just started to grow

23~24 Choose the one that is inappropriate for the whole context.

23

The role of a head-of-state chef stands apart from virtually any other job in hospitality. Ⓐ Not least because there are real-world diplomatic implications. "The leader who arrives in your country and who wants to discover it, you can let them discover your culture through cuisines," says Laurent Billi, France's ambassador to Washington. He notes that a mistake during a bilateral meeting can quite literally cause a diplomatic incident while a positive experience can Ⓑ smooth over relations. Billi remembers having lunch with a particularly aggressive Asian foreign minister who insisted that western Europe was in decline and Asia was on the rise. By the second course and some French wine, the tone had Ⓒ a lingering effect. "Suddenly they were looking at France as a great power in terms of Ⓓ gastronomy. The mood and dynamic of the dinner changed after that moment," says Billi. Then there's the Ⓔ culinary diplomacy aspect: food gives world leaders and their staff a lasting impression of the country they're visiting, a responsibility that chefs from smaller countries in particular take to heart.

[2.1점]

① Ⓐ   ② Ⓑ   ③ Ⓒ
④ Ⓓ   ⑤ Ⓔ

24

Ⓐ Trace the life of Nelson Mandela in Cape Town during his drive to end apartheid, from recruiter for the armed Ⓑ resistance in the township of Nyanga to City Hall, where he addressed the public after his release from prison in 1990. Ⓒ Nowhere is Mandela's legacy felt more strongly than in a visit to Robben Island Museum, the onetime prison where he spent 18 of his 27 years of incarceration. With the floor for a bed and a bucket for a toilet, his small cell is a stark reminder of the Ⓓ nobility of apartheid and the triumph of the human spirit. Instead of breaking him, the experience transformed Mandela from revolutionary to Ⓔ revered statesperson.

[2.0점]

① Ⓐ ② Ⓑ ③ Ⓒ
④ Ⓓ ⑤ Ⓔ

25 The main point of the following passage would be _____. [2.1점]

One of the core purposes of education, both public and private, is to prepare students for civic life and to be effective citizens in our democracy. When students are unaware of our history and don't have a solid grasp of our fundamental political institutions, they're less prepared for civic life. There's broad consensus that American democracy is experiencing significant challenges, and it is hard to envision us overcoming those challenges unless citizens understand our political institutions and learn how to engage as participants in our civic life. It's also the case that the current moment is not the first time that American democracy has been threatened. An understanding of our nation's history cannot just equip students for civic life, but hopefully also give them a sense of optimism that we can rise to the challenge.

① Why do we need to study math and science?
② Should citizens really protect their freedoms in a democracy?
③ What is the potential problem associated with free election?
④ When did the U.S. teacher shortage start?
⑤ Why do U.S. history and civic education matter?

26. The underlined "this phenomenon" would mean that _____. [2.0점]

As scientific understanding in the fields of stress physiology and epigenetics grew over the next two decades, evidence for the weathering hypothesis began to mount. Researchers are increasingly discovering how the health effects of chronic exposure to discrimination within societies could help explain racial and ethnic disparities in health and disease outcomes that aren't accounted for by other factors. Living in a racist society can harm the health of all Black people, even those who don't directly experience racism, according to a public health researcher. "This is akin to other environmental risk factors for health, such as high levels of air pollution," Devakumar told the *Economist* in a 2020 interview. Early evidence for this phenomenon began to emerge in the 1990s.

① the exposure to economic disadvantage leads to favorable physical health outcomes
② the poverty has an influence on poor diet and poor nutrition
③ the stress of experiencing racism has a negative impact on the body
④ the high temperature ultimately contributes to racism
⑤ racism-related challenges do not influence our body and mind

27. The main point of the following passage would be _____. [2.0점]

The amount of popcorn you buy for a movie should probably depend on how much you enjoy popcorn, right? Maybe not. New research shows that people's consumption habits are surprisingly insensitive to their fondness for products. In fact, consumers themselves are bad at predicting how much their preferences will influence their consumption, assuming that if they like, say comedy specials, they'll watch more of them than they do of other offerings — for instance, sitcoms. In six studies researchers asked a total of 1,486 U.S. participants to rank their preferences for various items and estimate how much they'd consume of each in a given period. In one study they were asked how much they liked different flavors of jelly beans and how much of each they'd eat over the course of the experiment. Participants were then offered either their preferred jelly beans or another flavor, along with M&M's. At the end of the experiment, the differences in their consumption of preferred and nonpreferred items turned out to be negligible. And the result was the same in all the experiments, including a real-world study that found that people used the same amount of lip balm during a week whether they received a brand they liked or another one.

① The love for a certain product is not always a good thing.
② People overestimate how much their consumption is dependent on their preferences.
③ Shoppers should consider consumers' favorite products among other factors.
④ Consumers hated jelly beans because they were actually aware of the value.
⑤ Consumers tend to consider cheaper alternatives to their unfavorable products.

28~30 Read the following passage and answer the questions.

For many, deconstructing relationships and interactions with parents can be a mainstay of the therapeutic experience. Naturally, as part of this experience, therapists may ask questions about these important dynamics — normally in a neutral, Ⓐ_____ way, designed to ensure clients can make sense of things on their own terms. Therapists should beware, though: according to a new study from Lawrence Patihis and Mario E. Herrera, it isn't just negatively framed questions that can change how we feel about our relationships. Even positively framed questions could lead people to reappraise their relationship with their parents.

In their investigation, the team asked 301 US-based online participants to write a short passage, the topic of which changed depending on the condition they were in. For the first, they wrote about positive examples of their mother's warmth, competence, and love; in the second, examples of a lack of these qualities; in the third, negative examples of a teacher. Those in the fourth and final condition did not receive a writing prompt. All participants then completed measures on how they currently rated their mothers on traits like warmth and generosity, reported positive and negative memories of emotions towards their mother at different stages of childhood and in the present day, and rated their current mood. Analyses showed, perhaps unsurprisingly, that those who appraised their mother positively reported feeling significantly happier about their mother than those in the other conditions. Happiness was strongly associated with how positively participants saw their mother. This group also remembered feeling significantly happier towards their mothers during childhood. This suggests that reappraising one's parents can significantly impact your memories from childhood, Ⓑ_____ these effects were relatively short lived, lasting around four weeks.

We already know that memories are fallible, and that all sorts of factors can change the way we think or feel about something that's happened in the past. This study underlines that therapists should keep this in mind, and remain cautious of framing when discussing family relationships with clients. The team takes this one step further, and argues that clients should be informed at the outset of therapy about the potential for change in how they see their parents or others in their life.

28 The most appropriate words for the blanks Ⓐ and Ⓑ are _____. [2.0점]

① provocative — as a result
② non-leading — though
③ remarkable — in addition
④ emotional — moreover
⑤ impartial — consequently

29 According to the above passage, the author thinks that question framing can influence _____. [2.1점]

① the frequency of clinic visits
② different kinds of conditions
③ how people remember their parents during childhood
④ how people forget trivial things
⑤ rights and responsibilities of parents

30 Which is true of the above passage? [2.2점]

① Memories are inherently impeccable and intact.
② How participants appraised their mother affected their feelings about their mother.
③ The experiment only takes neutral examples of their mother's warmth into account.
④ Participants were always instructed to say something bad.
⑤ Participants were asked to anticipate their future mood in order to deconstruct relationships and interactions with parents.

31~32 Read the following passage and answer the questions.

Discussions about the fate of large empires are not new. They have been around as long as history books have been written. However, serious policy makers are now engaged in this type of active planning and strategizing within and outside the intelligence community. Around the world, America is seen as the global policeman. America did embrace this role, even though reluctantly, to the detriment of the nation's domestic agenda and often not without scorn from the rest of the world. Whereas the founders wanted no such dominion around the world, and instead believed in liberty, justice, and the pursuit of happiness for all, American policy makers today believe in some form of nation building, both through hard power and soft diplomacy, as part and parcel of their global purview.

In the coming decades, will America go into Islamic lands and try to wage war with those nations that harbor ill will against it and its allies? Although not a practical solution, this type of thinking is not uncommon among policy makers. They see no alternative to an all-out war with the Islamists or the extreme elements in Islamic societies. Can we achieve a middle ground, a compromise solution, and a breakthrough between the more moderate elements in Islam and American civilization? It will be a somber day when the American ideals of freedom, liberty, and equality are sacrificed at the altar of _____. America's founding principles would need a thorough going revision if America the majestic were to turn into a Roman fortress with security walls around its perimeter. America's ventures in Afghanistan are a perfect example of how attempts at nation building might over a longer duration drain the country of its precious resources in terms of human lives and capital as well as military reserves.

31 The most appropriate expression for the blank would be _____. [2.1점]

① the victory of Islamic societies
② nation building in foreign lands
③ a period of happiness and prosperity
④ the economic success of a country
⑤ the armed force from other parts of the world

32 According to the passage, which one is NOT relevant to others? [2.0점]

① nation building   ② justice   ③ liberty
④ equality   ⑤ the pursuit of happiness

33~35 Read the following passage and answer the questions.

People generally hold the view that mistakes help humans learn and grow, instead of interpreting errors as a sign of unchangeable defects. But they frequently think AI tools are rigid and not adept at adjusting and evolving — a belief that may stem from past experiences of machines as static devices that carry out limited functions.

Perceptions like that can diminish trust in the technology and create concerns about its efficacy in new scenarios. Studies have indicated, however, that consumer use of AI output rises when people are told that AI has the capacity for adaptive learning. Even nominal cues that imply learning potential, such as branding AI as Ⓐ "machine learning" instead of merely an "algorithm," have boosted engagement. Netflix frequently publicizes how its content recommendation algorithm continuously improves its selections as it collects more data on users' viewing habits. It reinforces that message by putting labels like "for you" on its recommendations and explaining that they were made "because you watched x," further reassuring users that the algorithm is considering their evolving preferences.

People who think that AI is inflexible may believe that it will treat every person identically, rigidly applying a Ⓑ one-size-fits-all approach. Indeed, the more distinctive consumers perceive themselves to be, the less likely they are to use AI. In one study, for instance, the more exceptional participants thought that their own ethical characteristics were, the more resistant they were to an AI system that assessed moral qualities. At the same time, there's a delicate balance between flexibility and predictability. Even though adoption often increases when companies highlight AI's ability to learn and evolve, if users feel that the outputs of the system are too unpredictable, the intervention could backfire. A more adaptable AI system is also riskier since it allows a greater spectrum of user interactions, some of which may not be captured in the data used to train the AI. When AI is more flexible, it increases the possibility that people will use it in inappropriate ways and that in those cases the algorithms might provide undesirable responses, creating new risks for users and companies alike.

33 The underlined Ⓐ "machine learning" may suggest that AI has a property of being _____.

[2.0점]

① too opaque
② counterproductive
③ emotionless
④ unaccommodating
⑤ flexible

34 The underlined Ⓑ"one-size-fits-all approach" suggests that people may think AI _____. [2.0점]

① ignores an individual's unique traits
② provides precise responses
③ shows a preference towards glaring consumers
④ is too expensive to purchase
⑤ has an ability to balance flexibility and predictability

35 According to the above passage, the author believes that _____. [2.2점]

① nominal cues in branding turn out to be insignificant
② moral qualities can never be assessed using AI systems
③ AI systems will not be able to handle any input
④ there is a trade-off between flexibility and predictability of AI systems
⑤ people experience difficulty in understanding the algorithm

36~37 Read the following passage and answer the questions.

Every democracy sets a minimum age for holding office. Some, such as France, are exceptionally liberal, allowing 18-year-olds to run for president, a position with near-monarchical powers. Others are more circumspect. Italy's president must be at least 50, even though the position is largely ceremonial. But no country sets an upper age limit for wielding power. Should they? Wisdom and experience count for a lot. But so do vitality, dynamism and fresh ideas. North Dakota is leading the charge: in June its voters approved a measure that sets a maximum age for representing the state in Congress. More widely, both Republicans and Democrats favour age limits for politicians and Supreme Court judges by overwhelming majorities, according to a survey by the Pew Research Centre. In Britain, the governing Labour Party has promised to impose a retirement age of 80 on members of the House of Lords, who are appointed for life.

It may sound reasonable for democracies to adopt age limits for those seeking elected office. But to do so would set a dangerous precedent. In a free society both the electorate, and the candidates they vote for, should be as broadly representative as possible on who can vote and whom they can vote for. The more governments impose limits on who can stand, the greater danger that such limits will be subject to political meddling. _____. The bar to imposing an age limit should thus be very high.

36
According to the above passage, imposing a maximum-age limit on elected politicians may _____. [2.1점]

① be an ideal solution for the country and politicians
② appear sensible, but may pose threats to democracy
③ indicate that politicians are public servants
④ influence the number of the relatively dangerous jobs
⑤ be the primary way to understand the symptom of deeper problems in the States

37
The most appropriate expression for the blank would be _____. [2.1점]

① Better just to let voters decide
② Age really matters in politics
③ Candidates are more intelligent than we think
④ There is a strong need to enshrine age limits into law
⑤ Supreme Court judges should be served until a designated age

38~40 Read the following passage and answer the questions.

> Despite garnering the support and appreciation of a majority of Americans, Roosevelt and his New Deal programs did inspire their fair share of outraged critics. The governor of Louisiana, Huey Long, made a national name for himself breaking his one-time support for Roosevelt and challenging his initiatives, which he saw as too subservient to the demands and desires of corporations and the wealthy. He offered instead his "Share Our Wealth" plan, which proposed to expropriate the wealth of the richest and redistribute it to the poor in the form of a $5,000 homestead and an annual income of $2,500. Roosevelt had an equally threatening enemy in the Michigan-based Catholic priest and radio personality Father Charles Coughlin, who ratcheted up the worry of his forty-five million largely white, working-class listeners into a full-scale panic with his anticommunist, anticapitalist, rabidly anti-Semitic diatribes, as he called for a "Christian front" to fight off these forces of evil. Because the hyperbole and hysteria of Long's and Coughlin's rhetoric exhibited more rancor and resentment than reasoned arguments, piecing together their logic is not easy. Nevertheless, they helped inspire sincere dread among their followers that the modern industrial state was horning in on their personal autonomy and _____ on precious liberties.

38 The most appropriate expression for the blank would be _____. [2.0점]

① elevating ② looking ③ focusing
④ trampling ⑤ smiling

39 According to the author, both Long's and Coughlin's criticism of Roosevelt was _____. [2.0점]

① persuasive ② self-effacing ③ judicious
④ constructive ⑤ unreasonable

40 According to the passage, which of the following is correct? [2.1점]

① Huey Long criticized Roosevelt throughout his career.
② Critics of Roosevelt helped uphold democracy.
③ Roosevelt and his New Deal programs garnered an overwhelmingly unfavorable reaction from the public.
④ Father Charles Coughlin revealed his antipathy to Jews.
⑤ The two critics' arguments were too logical to be criticized.

41~43 Read the following passage and answer the questions.

Art is notoriously hard to define, and so are the differences between good art and bad art. But let me offer a generalization: art is something that results from making a lot of choices. This might be easiest to explain if we use fiction writing as an example. When you are writing fiction, you are — consciously or unconsciously — making a choice about almost every word you type; to oversimplify, we can imagine that a ten-thousand-word short story requires something on the order of ten thousand choices. When you give a generative-A.I. program a prompt, you are making very few choices; if you supply a hundred-word prompt, you have made on the order of a hundred choices.

If an A.I. generates a ten-thousand-word story based on your prompt, it has to fill in for all of the choices that you are not making. There are various ways it can do this. One is to take an average of the choices that other writers have made, as represented by text found on the Internet; that average is equivalent to the least interesting choices possible, which is why A.I.-generated text is often really bland. Another is to instruct the program to engage in style mimicry, emulating the choices made by a specific writer, which produces a highly derivative story. In neither case is it creating interesting art.

I think the same underlying principle applies to visual art, although it's harder to quantify the choices that a painter might make. Real paintings bear the mark of an enormous number of decisions. By comparison, a person using a text-to-image program like DALL-E enters a prompt such as "A knight in a suit of armor fights a fire-breathing dragon," and lets the program do the rest. Most of the choices in the resulting image have to be borrowed from similar paintings found online; the image might be exquisitely rendered, but the person entering the prompt can't claim _____ for that.

41 The author believes that _____. [2.2점]

① A.I. can write fiction in a way similar to how humans do it
② A.I. can draw creative paintings on its own
③ A.I. generates both textual and visual content through statistical procedures
④ it is merely a human-oriented thought that A.I. cannot be a real writer or artist
⑤ human can collaborate with A.I. to create art by entering a well-crafted prompt

42 What does the underlined "highly derivative" mean? [2.1점]

① Every piece of art is, in essence, built upon previous works.
② What A.I. generates is nothing more than a mimicry of art.
③ The stories A.I. produces are identical to those written by human writers.
④ Although A.I. may not create interesting art, it does not mean it lacks originality.
⑤ The stories A.I writes result from a number of choices it makes.

43 Choose the most inappropriate word for the blank. [2.0점]

① originality   ② ownership   ③ civility
④ kudos   ⑤ credit

44~45 Read the following passage and answer the questions.

Political institutions determine who has power in society and to what ends that power can be used. If the distribution of power is narrow and unconstrained, then the political institutions are absolutist. In contrast, political institutions that distribute power broadly in society and subject it to constraints are pluralistic. Instead of being vested in a single individual or a narrow group, political power rests with a broad coalition or a plurality of groups. Max Weber provided the most famous and widely accepted definition of the state, identifying it with the "monopoly of legitimate violence" in society. Without such a monopoly and the degree of centralization that it entails, the state cannot play its role as enforcer of law and order, let alone provide public services and encourage and regulate economic activity. When the state fails to achieve almost any political centralization, society sooner or later descends into chaos. We will refer to political institutions that are sufficiently centralized and pluralistic as inclusive political institutions. When either of these conditions fails, we will refer to the institutions as extractive political institutions.

There is strong _____ between economic and political institutions. Extractive political institutions concentrate power in the hands of a narrow elite and place few constraints on the exercise of this power. Economic institutions are then often structured by this elite to extract resources from the rest of the society. Extractive economic institutions thus naturally accompany extractive political institutions. In fact, they must inherently depend on extractive political institutions for their survival. Inclusive political institutions, vesting power broadly, would tend to uproot economic institutions that expropriate the resources of the many, erect entry barriers, and suppress the functioning of markets so that only a few benefit.

44 What is most appropriate for the blank? [2.0점]

① discord ② synergy ③ similarity
④ antagonism ⑤ competition

45 According to the passage, which of the following is a characteristic of extractive political institutions? [2.1점]

① They are governed exclusively by a few elites.
② They strive to distribute resources to a broader population.
③ They are often accompanied by inclusive economic institutions.
④ They are pluralistic because power is distributed without constraints.
⑤ They eliminate entry barriers for newcomers in the market and society.

46~48 Read the following passage and answer the questions.

Most broadcast subtitles are prepared in advance, but there are also live subtitles (e.g. for news broadcasts or sports events) which are generally produced by respeaking: in a manner somewhat similar to simultaneous interpreting, a same-language subtitler listens to the audio stream and respeaks the words, for clarity and to remove background noise, into a high-quality audio system, and this 'clean' input is then processed by speech-to-text software, with real-time corrections keyboarded by the subtitler as necessary, for display on screen with just a slight delay to account for the production time.

There are significant differences between intralingual subtitles for accessibility purposes and interlingual subtitles done by organizations such as Netflix for people who are not hearing impaired but cannot understand the original language. Subtitling is always a matter of compromise between the conflicting requirements of Ⓐ_____ and Ⓑ_____ of information. When equality of access to information is the goal, the speech content of the broadcast will as far as possible be transcribed verbatim: any alterations would be confusing for lip-readers, and this kind of subtitle can also support viewers with reading difficulties, as well as language learners.

Accessibility subtitlers can use visual means to convey meta-information about the audio stream: for instance, changes of speaker may be indicated by different colored text, and other significant audio elements (sound effects) annotated in CAPITALS or [square brackets]. On the other hand, a hearing viewer using translated subtitles will typically not need colors or indication of background sounds, but will want a condensed version of the dialogue in their own language that they can read quickly and that distracts them as little as possible from following the video content.

46 The best title of the passage would be _____. [2.1점]

① The Secret of Interlingual Subtitle
② Differences Between Intralingual Subtitle and Interlingual Subtitle
③ Different Types of Subtitle
④ The Role of Subtitler
⑤ The Importance of Colored Text in Subtitle

47 The most appropriate words for the blanks Ⓐ and Ⓑ are _____. [2.1점]

① accessibility — variety
② readability — digression
③ quality — quantity
④ accuracy — necessity
⑤ completeness — concision

48 According to the passage, intralingual subtitles should be verbatim in order _____. [2.1점]

① to make equal access to information for all viewers
② to increase the quality of information
③ to better serve viewers who are not hearing impaired
④ to improve the ability of lip-readers
⑤ not to distract language learners' attention from the video content

49~50 Read the following passage and answer the questions.

Neuropsychoanalysis is a diverse, interdisciplinary field that comprises the efforts of researchers and clinicians within several branches of psychoanalysis, neuroscience and psychiatry to construct a shared space of inquiry in which to consider how empirical findings and neuroscientific theories can be enhanced by metapsychological knowledge derived from subjective, clinical observation and vice versa. It was named and constituted by a small group of researchers at whose heart lies the psychoanalyst and neuropsychologist Mark Solms.

The main neuropsychoanalytic claim is that consciousness must be understood as both affective and embodied and that the Freudian theory of the psychic apparatus, while falling short in bringing together mind, brain and body, nevertheless provides us with the foundations for such an understanding.

49 According to the passage, neuropsychoanalysis is NOT _____. [2.0점]

① a discipline that compromises the two different approaches
② a discipline with a balanced view of consciousness
③ a discipline partly built on Freud's theory
④ a discipline established solely by one prominent scholar
⑤ an interdisciplinary field

50 The underlined "vice versa" suggests that _____. [2.0점]

① psychoanalysis and psychiatry would benefit from the empirical knowledge provided by neuroscience
② neuroscience should not rely on subjective approaches to understanding the human mind
③ neuroscience and psychiatry are distinct disciplines
④ researchers and clinicians should cooperate with each other to better understand consciousness
⑤ clinical observation often provides a biased view of the human mind

성균관대학교

▶ 2025학년도 자연계 A형 ▶ 문항 수: 영어 25문항, 수학 20문항 | 제한시간: 90분

2025 성균관대 자연계 A형 영역별 문항 수

구분	문법			어휘			논리완성	독해	생활영어	총 문항 수
	G/S, W/E	정비문	재진술	동의어	반의어	유추				
문항 수	2			3			5	15		25
백분율	8%			12%			20%	60%		100%

SUNGKYUNKWAN UNIVERSITY | 성균관대학교

2025학년도 자연계 A형: 영어 25문항, 수학 20문항 · 90분

[01~02] Choose one that is either ungrammatical or unacceptable.

01 It refers to behavior that makes military life worse than it needs to be: petty ① harassment of the weak by the strong; open ② scrimmage for power and authority; sadism thinly ③ disguised as necessary discipline; a constant ④ paying off of old scores; and ⑤ insisted on the letter than the spirit of ordinances. [1.9점]

02 In a well-designed airport, travellers ① drifting toward their gate will always ② find the fast-food restaurants on their left and the gift shops on their right, because people will readily ③ cross a lane of pedestrian traffic to ④ satisfying their hunger but rarely to make an impulse ⑤ buy of a magazine. [2.1점]

[03~05] Choose one that is closest in meaning to the underlined expression.

03 Those who migrate out of poor countries today need to have the money to afford the cost of travel and have the grit required to overcome a system of immigration control typically loaded against them. [1.9점]

① property
② fortitude
③ connection
④ modesty
⑤ political influence

04 Ladies and gentlemen, the maiden voyage of our newest flagship deserves more pomp and circumstance than we can afford today. A <u>christening</u> of the ship will just have to be our reward for a safe return. [2.0점]

① farewell   ② arming   ③ sinking
④ launching   ⑤ cleaning

05 To maintain a professional relationship with my office colleagues, I like to keep them <u>at arm's length</u>. [2.1점]

① busy   ② distant   ③ friendly
④ supervised ⑤ curious

06~10 Choose one that is most appropriate for the blank.

06 Why study philosophy? Philosophy is to be studied, not for the sake of any definite answers to its questions, since no definite answers can, as a rule, be known to be true, but rather for the sake of the questions themselves; because these questions enlarge our conception of what is possible, enrich our intellectual imagination and _____ the dogmatic assurance which closes the mind against speculation.

[1.9점]

① enhance   ② expand   ③ appreciate
④ diminish   ⑤ elongate

07 If there is one thing that stands out about the human brain compared with those of other primates, it is its size. The human brain is up to three times larger in volume than the brains of chimpanzees and gorillas. Brain size is tightly correlated with body size in most animals. But humans _____. Our brains are much larger than expected given our body size. [1.9점]

① break the pattern
② are not primates
③ are above all creation
④ conform to the pattern
⑤ are much smarter than other animals

08 There were different types of colonization policies which created different sets of institutions. At one extreme, European powers set up extractive states, exemplified by the Belgian colonization of the Congo. These states did not introduce much protection for private property, nor did they provide checks and balances against government expropriation. In fact, the main purpose of the extractive state was to _____. [2.0점]

① favor the colony
② return natural resources to the colony
③ establish free, democratic states in Africa
④ promote economic growth of the colony
⑤ transfer the resources of the colony to the colonizer

09 If you ask a physicist how long it would take a marble to fall from the top of a ten-story building, he will likely answer the question by assuming that the marble falls in a vacuum. Of course, this assumption is false. In fact, the building is surrounded by air, which _____ the falling marble and slows it down. [2.1점]

① breaks
② vacuums
③ exerts friction on
④ increases velocity of
⑤ increases the choice of

10 Heavy drinking had become normalized during the pandemic. Excessive alcohol leads to arrhythmias, strokes and high blood pressure. It weakens the immune system and has been associated with an increased risk of certain cancers. But many of these effects take years to emerge. We know that alcohol use begins as a silent disease and only _____ years later in terms of chronic disease. [2.1점]

① rears its head
② chases its tail
③ becomes benign
④ buries its head in the sand
⑤ keeps its head under water

11~12 Read the following passage and answer the questions.

The economic analysis of immigration often comes down to a seductive _____. The world is full of poor people who want to earn more money; these poor people would obviously earn a lot more if they could find their way here, where things are clearly much better. Therefore, given half a chance, they will indeed leave wherever they are and come to our country, and this will drive down wages and make most of us already here worse off. What is remarkable about this argument is its faithfulness to the standard exposition of the law of supply and demand. People want more money and therefore will all go wherever wages are highest (supply goes up). As the demand curve for labor slopes down, the rise in the labor supply will lower wages for everyone. The migrants may benefit, but the native workers will suffer.

The logic is simple, seductive, and wrong. First, wage differences between countries actually have relatively little to do with whether or not people migrate. While there are obviously many people desperate to get out from wherever they are, the enduring puzzle is why so many others don't move when they can. Second, there is no credible evidence that even relatively large inflows of low-skilled migrants hurt the local population, including members of the local population most like the migrants in terms of skills. Indeed, migration seems to make most people, migrants and locals, better off. This has a lot to do with the peculiar nature of the labor market. Very little about it fits the standard story of supply and demand.

11 What is most appropriate for the blank? [1.9점]

① puzzle   ② service   ③ method
④ reasoning   ⑤ dilemma

12 According to the passage, the inflow of low-skilled migrants will _____.
[2.1점]

① hurt the local population
② only benefit the migrants
③ increase the wage difference between countries
④ benefit both migrants and the native workers
⑤ change the peculiar nature of the labor market

13~15 Read the following passage and answer the questions.

In the late 1990s, after nearly two decades of unprecedented growth in industrial manufacturing, China started to face a variety of pressing environmental challenges, including deteriorating surface water quality. To tackle China's severe water pollution problems, the central government installed several hundred state-controlled water quality monitoring stations along the major national river trunks.

The central government assigned abatement requirements to each province, and provincial governors were required to sign individual responsibility contracts with the central government, documenting their emission abatement plans and commitments in detail. Provincial governors further assigned strict abatement mandates to local government officials and used the water quality readings to help determine their promotion cases. Given such high-powered political incentives, large polluting industrial firms became the target of local government officials, because their emissions are the largest contributor to local water pollution. Many local governments, by threatening polluting firms with production suspension and temporary shutdown, coerced them to clean up their production processes and to _____. As a result, these regulated firms experienced a reduction in total factor productivity, which measures the amount of output obtained from a given set of inputs.

However, this political contract between central and local governments is undermined because of imperfect monitoring. Because rivers flow from higher to lower elevation, water quality monitoring stations can only detect emissions from upstream. Local government officials had strong incentives to regulate polluting firms in the immediate upstream of a monitoring station but little incentives to regulate polluting firms in the immediate downstream.

13 What is most appropriate for the blank? [1.9점]

① pollute the water
② increase their profit
③ increase pollution emission
④ avoid abatement requirements
⑤ invest in costly abatement equipment

14 According to the passage, which firm is most likely to experience the reduction in total factor productivity as a result of water regulation? [2.1점]

① all nonpolluting firms
② polluting firm in the immediate upstream of monitoring station
③ polluting firm in the immediate downstream of monitoring station
④ non-polluting firm in the immediate upstream of monitoring station
⑤ non-polluting firm in the immediate downstream of monitoring station

15 According to the passage, local government officials have political incentives to regulate polluting firms because _____. [2.0점]

① monitoring water quality is perfect
② rivers flow from higher to lower elevation
③ water quality readings determine their promotion cases
④ large firms' emissions do not contribute to local water pollution
⑤ local officials cannot regulate polluting firms in the downstream of a monitoring station

16~17 Read the following passage and answer the questions.

Higher productivity means more output from the same amount of input. Two main factors drive productivity growth: within-firm improvements and economy-wide allocative efficiency. Within-firm productivity gains are achieved through better technology, improved management practices, and innovative processes. Companies that adopt state-of-the-art technologies and attract top talent can significantly enhance their productivity. For example, a tech company that invests in cutting-edge research and development can create new products or improve existing ones, thereby expanding its market share and increasing its competitiveness.

_____ returns on investment in R&D are diminishing. For instance, in the semiconductor industry, more researchers are needed to double the density of chips. This trend also spans various sectors, including information and communications technology, where rapid gains have notably plateaued since the early 2000s. Therefore, it is imperative to look to other sources of enhanced productivity to sustain economic growth.

That brings us to the second major factor driving productivity growth, allocative efficiency. Economy-wide allocative efficiency is about how well an economy's resources are distributed across businesses for their most productive uses. Imagine an economy as a large farm. If the best land is used for growing the highest-value crops, the farm will be more productive overall. In the same way, if an economy's resources flow to the most innovative and efficient companies, those enterprises can grow and drive economic progress. This process ensures that the best businesses thrive, while less efficient ones exit the market.

16 What is most appropriate for the blank? [1.9점]

① Thus
② Fortunately
③ Sure enough
④ It is not true that
⑤ The problem is that

17 According to the passage, _____ is NOT a reason for the growth of productivity. [2.1점]

① innovation
② better technology
③ income equality
④ hiring talent workers
⑤ efficient allocation of resources

18~20 Read the following passage and answer the questions.

The incentives for CEOs (chief executive officers) and other leaders to stick around are material: assistants, chauffeurs, private jets and all. They are also psychological. People who reach the top of organizations do not often lack ego; the idea that someone else can do the job well may be hard to stomach. This is called "_____". The prospects of retirement can be particularly gruesome — this week, a farewell trip to Davos; next week, a strategic review of the spice rack.

If bosses are prone to misjudge when to quit, what can be done? Blunt instruments do exist, from mandatory retirement ages to explicit term limits. But strict rules have drawbacks, too. CEOs may be approaching their peak, not past it, at the time they are required to throw in the towel. Bosses approaching the end of their careers risk being seen as lame ducks. And the knowledge that the end is near can change a CEO's own behavior in potentially unhelpful ways. For instance, research suggests that firms run by bosses with short career horizons (i.e., less time to go until they retire) generate fewer big innovations. Another paper found that the likelihood a firm would be taken over jumped when a CEO was at retirement age. The bosses of target firms often lose their jobs; that is less of a concern when a career is winding down.

Rigid rules are not the best defense against people overstaying their welcome. Most important are institutional constraints on CEO power — most obviously, a board that has a mind of its own — and bosses with the self-awareness to recognize that everyone has a natural shelf life. One of the first questions to ask a would-be senior hire is how long they think they should last.

18 What is most appropriate for the blank?

① the law of extradition ② the aura of character ③ the law of ability
④ the law of reciprocity ⑤ the aura of indispensability

19 According to the passage, which one is NOT a disadvantage of using mandatory retirement ages for CEOs?

① CEOs may be constrained by the board of directors.
② CEOs may lose leadership power as they approach their retirement.
③ CEOs' performance may still be improving when they are forced to retire.
④ CEOs are less likely to make big innovations when they are about to retire.
⑤ CEOs with short career horizons may not aggressively defend against takeover.

20 According to the passage, _____ is a reason that CEOs misjudge when to retire.

[2.0점]

① strong ego
② takeover
③ innovations
④ explicit term limits
⑤ mandatory retirement ages

21~23 Read the following passage and answer the questions.

The periodic table lists 118 different chemical elements. And yet, for thousands of years, humans have really, really liked one of them in particular: gold. Gold has been used as money for millennia, and its price has been going through the roof. Why gold? Why not osmium, lithium, or ruthenium? We take the periodic table, and start eliminating anything that would not work as money. We first eliminate the elements that are gases. We also cross out the elements that are pretty _____: not all of them burst into flames (like Lithium), but sometimes they corrode and start to fall apart. In addition, we cross out the elements that are radioactive.

In this way, we are down from 118 elements to 30, and we have come up with a list of three key requirements: (1) Not a gas, (2) Does not corrode or burst into flames, and (3) Does not kill you. Now we add a new requirement: you want the thing you pick to be rare. This crosses off a lot of the boxes near the top of the table, because the elements clustered there tend to be more abundant. At the same time, you do not want to pick an element that is too rare. So osmium — which apparently comes to earth via meteorites — gets the axe. That leaves us with just five elements: rhodium, palladium, silver, platinum and gold. And all of them, as it happens, are considered precious metals. But even here we can cross things out. Silver has been widely used as money, of course. But it tarnishes. So it is not the best choice. Early civilizations could not have used rhodium or palladium, because they were not discovered until the early 1800s. That leaves platinum and gold, both of which can be found in rivers and streams. But if you were in the ancient world and wanted to make platinum coins, you would have needed some sort of magic furnace from the future. The melting point for platinum is over 3,000 degrees Fahrenheit. Gold happens to melt at a much lower temperature, which made it much easier for pre-industrial people to work with.

21 What is most appropriate for the blank? [2.1점]

① inactive ② reactive ③ expensive
④ cheap ⑤ nonresponsive

22 According to the passage, gold is a good choice for money because _____.
[2.0점]

① it is a gas
② it may corrode
③ it is radioactive
④ it does not tarnish like silver
⑤ it melts at a relatively higher temperature than platinum

23 According to the passage, osmium has NOT been used as money because _____.
[1.9점]

① it may vaporize
② it was discovered too late
③ it is too limited in supply
④ it may burst into flame
⑤ it may be dangerous to human health

24~25 Read the following passage and answer the questions.

In Africa, a generation of scientists is trying to break the stranglehold of the Anopheles mosquitoes that transmit the disease-causing parasite. Their weapon of choice is genomics. It is a challenge taken up by organizations like *Target Malaria*, a not-for-profit international research consortium. There, researchers' game plan is simple: reduce the population numbers of the mosquitoes, specifically those of three related species responsible for most malaria transmissions in Africa — Anopheles gambiae, Anopheles coluzzii and Anopheles arabiensis. To do so, they are looking to capitalize on a naturally occurring phenomenon, gene drive. Often described as "selfish genetic elements", taking the form of bits of DNA code, genes are driven when a gene that has a favorable effect becomes more prevalent in successive generations. Typically, with both humans and mosquitoes, offspring inherit two copies of any gene, one from each parent. As a result, there is a 50/50 chance of either of the two copies being passed on to later generations. Using gene drives, researchers are manipulating the bias that is introduced to that rate of inheritance so that a specific trait is nearly 100% guaranteed to be passed on.

Gene-drive malaria research takes on many forms. Two of the most popular are known as population replacement and population suppression. With population replacement, the aim is to modify the mosquitoes so that they are no longer _____ the malaria parasite. With population suppression, the goal is to reduce the mosquito population. The main strategy is to sterilize and reduce the number of female mosquitoes. The females transmit the malaria-causing parasite known as Plasmodium falciparum to humans, and the number of females determines the size of a mosquito population.

24 What is most appropriate for the blank? [1.9점]

① killed by ② reduced by ③ vectors of
④ enemies of ⑤ threats to

25 Which is true of the above passage? [2.1점]

① Only male mosquitoes transmit Plasmodium falciparum.
② There is only one way to perform gene-drive malaria research.
③ Genomics is ineffective in reducing the number of mosquitoes.
④ The aim of population suppression is to increase the mosquito population.
⑤ Reducing the number of female mosquitoes will reduce the mosquito population.

세종대학교

▶ 2025학년도 인문계 A형   ▶ 문항 수: 60문항 | 제한시간: 100분

2025 세종대 인문계 A형 영역별 문항 수

구분	문법			어휘			논리완성	독해	생활영어	총 문항 수
	G/S, W/E	정비문	재진술	동의어	반의어	유추				
문항 수	30					5	10	15		60
백분율	50%					8.3%	16.7%	25%		100%

SEJONG UNIVERSITY

세종대학교

▶ 2025학년도 인문계 A형: 60문항 · 100분

문항별 배점 01~10 2.8점, 오답 −0.7점 / 11~15 3.8점, 오답 −0.95점 / 16~30 3.2점, 오답 −0.8점
31~45 2.8점, 오답 −0.7점 / 46~60 4.2점, 오답 −1.05점

01~10 주어진 문장의 빈칸에 들어갈 가장 알맞은 단어를 고르시오.

01 Frightening and physically painful _____, such as those endured in rites of passage, will impact memory and belief.

① felicities
② stumps
③ ordeals
④ inversions

02 Will the border arrangements be eased, or will the borders lead to a real and tangible division by separating ethnic groups and _____ existing relations?

① hypnotizing
② severing
③ humidifying
④ swooning

03 Anyone who _____ the norm by refusing to follow traditional gender stereotypes is viewed askance and, in small and large ways, treated as an outcast.

① ingratiates
② romps
③ transgresses
④ lisps

04 Some researchers are exploring how the adolescent _____ for unrestrained risk-taking propels teens to experiment with drugs and alcohol.

① propensity
② rumination
③ proportion
④ rummage

05 His continuous and deliberate lies show a _____ disregard for the rule of law, as well as a contempt for the values of honesty and fairness.

① cellular
② sooty
③ brazen
④ monastic

06 Today, thankfully, women tennis players are not _____ by long, heavy skirts and high-necked blouses.

① encumbered
② foraged
③ fluttered
④ equivocated

07 There may be too much bad blood, too much suspicion and too much anger on both sides to turn the _____ around.

① anatomy
② animosity
③ euthanasia
④ eulogy

08 As the conference approached its scheduled end, the U.N.'s climate chief _____ negotiators for digging in their heels and wasting time with bluffing and brinkmanship.

① circumfused
② marginated
③ migrated
④ chided

09 All the residents appeared to be _____ and were able to evacuate on their own, with the exception of the one man who was injured.

① excavated
② maimed
③ ambulatory
④ premonitory

10 Picasso _____ most of his paintings and sculptures to Spain and France.
① plated
② bequeathed
③ undermined
④ stumbled

11~15 보기와 같이 주어진 단어 쌍과 가장 유사한 관계를 가진 단어 쌍을 고르시오.

보기

night : moon ::

① shadow : light
② moon : star
③ day : sun
④ ray : laser

정답은 ③번입니다.

---

11 harpsichord : instrument ::
① pistachio : walnut
② petal : mammal
③ orchid : flower
④ fragrance : party

12 ephemeral : lasting ::
① random : accidental
② periodic : cyclical
③ sporadic : consistent
④ scattered : dispersed

13 speedy : rapid ::
① diminutive : tiny
② slender : short
③ swift : tremendous
④ obese : straight

14 deficit : surplus ::
① expense : charge
② savings : discount
③ budget : fine
④ expenditure : revenue

15 marble : sculptor ::
① canvas : painter
② chisel : statue
③ symphony : designer
④ encyclopedia : architect

16~30 주어진 문장의 빈칸에 들어갈 가장 알맞은 표현을 고르시오.

16 Today the job of the guard dog _____ of factories and industrial estates.
① has extended to be protected
② has been extended to protection
③ extends to protect
④ is extended the protecting

17 Certain breeds are _____ others.
① innate aggressive more than
② aggressively more than innate
③ innately more aggressively than
④ more innately aggressive than

18 Playing the drums _____ but amazing coordination, because several instruments have to be played at once.

① involves not only great energy
② does not involve energy great
③ not involves only energy greatly
④ involves great not only energy

19 My answer _____ that we don't know.
① for these questions are
② about these question are
③ of question is
④ to these questions is

20 They were _____ they could go.
① fast as running as
② running as fast as
③ as running as fast
④ as fast as running

21 She's wasting no time _____.
① for knowledge the pursuing
② to pursuit her knowledge
③ on the pursue to knowledge
④ in her pursuit of knowledge

22 _____ in Industry 5.0.
① Things happen fast
② The things fastly happened are
③ Thing is happened fastly
④ Things fast happens

23 Farming methods _____ the climate and geography of the area.
① were varied to depending on
② are varying on depending
③ varied depending on
④ vary for being depended

24 The population of New York _____ San Diego.
① surpassed the population with
② surpassed that in
③ surpasses the population to
④ surpasses that of

25 The pandemic accelerated conversations about _____.
① work-life balance what should be
② work-life balance should what be
③ what work-life balance should be
④ what should work-life balance be

26 The 30-year-old Egyptian engineer and fully trained astronaut was chosen _____.
① by thousands of an applicant
② by a thousands of applicants
③ from a thousand of an applicant
④ from thousands of applicants

27 It was the first time in my life that I _____.
① felt really at home
② feel really at the home
③ real felt in house
④ real feel in the house

28 I suggested that _____ on the chair and wait.
① sits down
② sitting down
③ does she sit down
④ she sit down

29 _____ by the unexpected news, he took a moment to gather his thoughts.
① Surprised
② Being surprising
③ Having surprised
④ Having been surprising

30 The sound of music causes _____ in the same pattern as the instruments being played.

① for our eardrums to vibrate
② our eardrums to vibrate
③ our eardrums to vibrating
④ for vibrating to our eardrums

(31~45) 다음 밑줄 친 부분 중 틀린 것을 고르시오.

31 Those overachievers often began in ① jobs that open a door to ② career paths and help workers acquire a mix of vocational ③ experts and communication, teamwork, and ④ problem-solving skills.

32 His ① debonair dismissal of my inquiry ② concerns his ③ financial situation led me to ④ believe that nothing was wrong.

33 Investors are ① betting that the new product line will be the linchpin that ② secure the company's place ③ in the very competitive market ④ in the years and decades to come.

34 Surprisingly ① enough, greenhouse gas levels ② fell during the Covid-19 pandemic, then ③ spiked as the world ④ emerging from lockdown.

35 Once Linda has ① decided on a course of action, she can be very ② tenacious when it ③ comes to seeing it ④ thorough.

36 The classical-meets-country-house architecture ① offers a ② relaxed lifestyle ③ fused urbane glamour and a modern slate of ④ creature comforts.

37 The researchers wondered ① that people remember in recalling ② complex sentences, whether ③ it is certain semantic distinctions or ④ merely transformational markers.

38 He ① built upon the commercial ② achievements of his parents and grandparents, attaining financial success that he never ③ regarded upon as his own but rather as the ④ providence of his children and their children beyond.

39 Orchestras are ① wrongly ② perceiving as symbols of ③ elitism when, in reality, they ④ embody the opposite.

40 In ① few areas of human endeavor ② are the tension between being humble and being ③ exalted so great ④ as in politics.

41 Ragtime, ① is popularized by ② such performers as Scott Joplin and Eubie Blake, ③ is considered one of the musical ④ fountainheads of jazz.

42 I ① had asked Elizabeth if she ever ② thought about what she would be doing ③ she had not ④ been abducted.

43 ① By being ② frugality and limiting ③ unnecessary purchases, the family ④ is able to stretch its monthly budget.

44 ① Among young adults today, fear ② out missing out is a thing. Many constantly ③ check social media sites to see ④ what their peers are doing, thinking, and feeling.

45 His father, ① who is poor background allowed him ② the favorable label "politically pure," ③ nevertheless lost his job ④ as head of the National Opera Group.

46~60 주어진 글을 읽고 물음에 가장 알맞은 답을 고르시오.

46~48

Nature as a wilderness, an important element in the Judeo-Christian tradition, had been central to Old Testament interpretations of the desert. The inhospitable arid wilderness contrasted sharply with the bountiful, fruitful Garden of Eden. The expulsion from the Garden into the wilderness equated the wilderness with the evil introduced when Eve submitted to the temptation of the serpent. The desert represented a land to be subdued and made arable. In contrast to the Greek tradition, Ⓐ_____, the Judaic tradition viewed it as a condition to be overcome and subdued. While softer interpretations could be found in the books of the Old Testament, it was the perception of nature as a wilderness that became important in the early modern era. For Protestants such as John Locke, John Calvin, and the New England Puritans, God had authorized human dominion over the earth.

Tales of wilderness in European and Anglo-Saxon folklore were dramatized by 15th and 16th century explorations of the New World. Voyagers brought back reports of wild, desolate, chaotic lands hostile to human settlement. The savages of the new lands became symbols of the wildness and animality that could gain the upper hand in human nature. Although many of the early accounts by the explorers had reported Indians to be peaceful and loving, albeit at a hierarchical level somewhere between beasts and Europeans, by the early 17th century that image had hardened and calloused. After the Virginia massacre of 1622, the positive descriptions disappeared as the English image of Indians changed in a negative direction. Indians became Ⓑ_____ outlaws.

46 Which of the following clauses is most suitable for the blank Ⓐ?

① which tended to emphasize the benevolence of nature
② which regarded the wilderness as the inhospitable land
③ which tended to emphasize the malevolence of nature
④ which regarded the wilderness as the uninhabitable land

47 Which of the following words is NOT suitable for the blank Ⓑ?

① inviolable
② savage
③ wild
④ brutish

48 According to the passage, which of the following is NOT true?

① Wilderness was considered as evil in the world of the Old Testament.
② Some Christians believed that God gave them the right to dominate the earth.
③ After 1622, the negative image of Indians prevailed.
④ Europeans believed the Indians were even below beasts on the hierarchy of beings.

49~52

Global warming, an urgent global concern, is accelerating at an alarming rate. Satellite data reveal that Earth's albedo, its ability to reflect sunlight, has been decreasing since the turn of the century. This decline in reflectivity causes Earth to absorb more sunlight, intensifying global warming. The resulting accelerated warming poses serious risks to ecosystems and human society, bringing extreme climate events forward by decades.

A major contributor to the reduction of Earth's albedo is cleaner air, driven by decreased sulfur emissions. Sulfur dioxide, a byproduct of burning fossil fuels, historically formed tiny atmospheric particles. These particles scattered sunlight and brightened clouds, reflecting more sunlight back into space. However, efforts to reduce sulfur emissions, such as China cutting them by 90% over the last two decades and global regulations on shipping fuel, have diminished these cooling effects. As a result, Ⓐ_____

While reducing sulfur emissions improves public health by reducing smog and saving millions of lives annually, it inadvertently removes a natural cooling mechanism that offsets the warming effects of rising CO_2 emissions. Unlike sulfur, CO_2 remains in the atmosphere for centuries, continuing to trap heat and drive climate change. In 2006, renowned atmospheric scientist Paul Crutzen warned that cutting sulfur pollution without simultaneously reducing CO_2 emissions could dangerously accelerate global warming. He proposed an alternative to address this challenge: solar geoengineering through stratospheric sulfate aerosols. Unlike ground-level pollutants, sulfate particles released in the stratosphere remain aloft longer and could provide significant cooling with minimal health risks. Since then, research into solar geoengineering using stratospheric aerosols has expanded significantly. Despite this progress, the approach remains controversial, as many of the experts advising governments on climate and research policy remain cautious or skeptical about its use.

49 What would be the most appropriate expression for the blank Ⓐ?

① Earth experiences reduced levels of global warming due to lower greenhouse gas emissions.
② Earth's ability to reflect sunlight increases, intensifying the rate of global warming.
③ Earth's albedo increases, mitigating the effects of global warming.
④ Earth's albedo decreases, accelerating global warming.

50 What is the main message regarding sulfur emission reductions and global warming?

① Sulfur emissions must be decreased to enhance Earth's albedo.
② Cleaner air improves health but accelerates warming by reducing the cooling effects of sulfur emissions.
③ Reducing sulfur emissions accelerates warming by increasing greenhouse gas levels.
④ Cleaner air ensures a permanent slowdown of global warming.

51 What is the motivation for reducing sulfur emissions, despite its link to increased warming?

① The life-saving health benefits of reducing air pollution
② International treaties mandating clean air by increasing Earth's albedo
③ The economic benefits of renewable energy technologies
④ Concerns about geoengineering that may challenge environmental consequences

52 What alternative does Paul Crutzen propose to address global warming?

① Reducing industrial activity worldwide to reduce CO_2 emissions
② Increasing CO_2 emissions to offset sulfur emissions while maintaining health benefits
③ Strengthening international environmental treaties for decreasing sulfur emissions
④ Using sulfates in the stratosphere for geoengineering to cool the planet

[53~56]

Robonaut is a NASA robot. Engineers designed Robonaut to be humanoid, which means it is built to look like a person. This makes it easier for Robonaut to do the same jobs as a person. Robonaut could help with anything from working on the International Space Station to exploring other worlds. A Robonaut is currently aboard the International Space Station.

NASA began working on the Robonaut project in 1996 and produced the first version of the robot in 2000. Since that time, engineers have continued to improve Robonaut. The newest model is called Robonaut 2, or R2. NASA and car manufacturer General Motors worked together to create R2. Robonaut has a head, torso, arms and hands like a person. Cameras in the head provide vision. Robonaut is called a Ⓐ_____ robot because its hands and fingers move like a person's. So Robonaut can perform tasks designed to be done by human hands.

Robonaut can function in two ways. Ⓑ <u>Software allows Robonaut to 'think' for itself</u>. The people who control R2 can give it a simple task to do, and R2 can figure out how to do it. R2's software can be updated to allow it to do new tasks. R2 also can be operated by remote control. An operator can use a headset to see what Robonaut sees through its cameras. The operator can then use controls to make Robonaut move.

NASA is still deciding what the future holds for Robonaut. If the test inside the space station goes well, Robonaut could someday be tested outside the space station. This testing would determine how well Robonaut could work with, or instead of, spacewalking astronauts. Robonaut's designers even have ideas for sending a robot like Robonaut to another world someday. If testing goes well, who knows where Robonaut — or a better robot based on Robonaut — could end up?

53 Which of the following is most suitable for the blank Ⓐ?

① desirous
② decorous
③ dexterous
④ disastrous

54 According to the passage, which of the following best describes the meaning of the underlined Ⓑ?

① Robonaut's software lets it decide how to perform tasks.
② Software enables Robonaut to write or print using ink autonomously.
③ Software hinders Robonaut from connecting to other systems or components.
④ Robonaut's software requires synchronization of data for autonomous actions.

55 Which of the following does NOT describe Robonaut's physical appearance?

① It looks like a person.
② It has hands and fingers.
③ It has a camera in its head for vision.
④ It is equipped with a headset for movement.

56 According to the passage, which of the following is true?

① NASA produced Robonaut in 1996.
② Robonaut is named after an astronaut.
③ Robonaut is not compatible with a human operator to function.
④ Robonaut has not yet been operated outside the space station with astronauts.

Dwight D. Eisenhower had it, but George S. Patton didn't. Henry Aaron but not Babe Ruth. Nat King Cole but not Beyoncé. Judy Woodruff but not Geraldo Rivera. J.D. Salinger but not Norman Mailer. Warren Buffett but not Elon Musk. Jonas Salk but not Dr. Oz. Johnny Unitas but not Joe Namath. Martin Luther King but not Jim Bakker. Iris Murdoch but not Rupert Murdoch. And, it must be said, Calvin Coolidge but not Donald J. Trump.

For centuries, humankind has agreed: "now abideth faith, hope, charity, these three." But in recent years we have come to see that though the three virtues from Scripture abideth, a fourth — almost certainly as noble and ennobling a human trait, perhaps as powerful a human good as the famous Ⓐ <u>triple-rectitudes</u> of *Corinthians* — is as invaluable as it is scarce: humility.

Seldom perceived and rarely celebrated, humility stands alone among human qualities. Distinct from other traits, it is the attribute not exhibited, the disposition not there, the turn of mind that turns away, the characteristic apparent only in its absence, the one distinction demonstrated not in what is, but instead in what isn't: the trumpet boast that isn't sounded, the generous act that isn't seen, the self-satisfaction that isn't expressed, the gesture of selflessness that isn't performed in public view. It is the perspective that is neither false self-abnegation nor showy self-aggrandizement.

Humility is a way of peering into the soul, of focusing beyond the self, of looking at the world and finding that one is not particularly remarkable, nor especially important, nor notably vital, nor even singularly interesting. Which is why the Royal British Legion, the American Legion and Rotary International all have mottos that, with slight permutations, proclaim: Ⓑ_____.

57 According to the passage, what do Eisenhower, Coolidge, and King have in common?

① They find themselves vital and remarkable.
② They are thought to be humble.
③ They do not possess humility.
④ They do not have anything in common.

58 According to the passage, what does the underlined Ⓐ refer to?

① Nat King Cole, J.D. Salinger, and Jonas Salk
② faith, hope, and charity
③ Royal British Legion, American Legion, and Rotary International
④ humility, trait, and selflessness

59 According to the passage, which of the following is NOT true about humility?

① It is valuable and uncommon.
② It is a trait that makes a human being noble.
③ It is rarely perceived and scarcely celebrated.
④ It is a trait that focuses on the self.

60 Which of the following is most appropriate for the blank Ⓑ?

① service not self
② be service to yourself
③ me, myself, and I
④ always be ambitious

숙명여자대학교

▶ 2025학년도 A형　▶ 문항 수: 33문항 | 제한시간: 60분

2025 숙명여대 A형 영역별 문항 수

구분	문법			어휘			논리완성	독해	생활영어	총 문항 수
	G/S, W/E	정비문	재진술	동의어	반의어	유추				
문항 수				4			12	17		33
백분율				12%			36%	52%		100%

SOOKMYUNG WOMEN'S UNIVERSITY

숙명여자대학교

2025학년도 A형: 33문항 · 60분

문항별 배점 01~16 2.5점 / 17~32 3.5점 / 33 4점

01~04 밑줄 친 부분과 가장 비슷한 의미의 표현을 고르시오.

01 The protesters were <u>vociferous</u> in their demands, chanting slogans and waving banners throughout the day.

① restrained
② reserved
③ unwilling
④ outspoken
⑤ noncommittal

02 Her <u>trenchant</u> analysis of the financial crisis earned her widespread acclaim.

① overly simplistic and superficial
② vague and lacking precision
③ meandering and poorly structured
④ incisive and deeply insightful
⑤ critical but fundamentally flawed

03 The story of his heroic deeds is likely <u>apocryphal</u>, as no credible evidence supports it.

① confident and exaggerated
② unwavering and persistent
③ insignificant and irrelevant
④ complicated and intricate
⑤ doubtful and unverifiable

04 The discovery of the ancient artifact was completely serendipitous, occurring during an unrelated excavation project.

① unplanned but fortunate
② foreseeable and inevitable
③ premeditated and purposeful
④ artificial and orchestrated
⑤ deliberate but coincidental

(05~16) 빈칸에 알맞은 가장 적절한 표현을 고르시오.

05 The project, originally scheduled to take six months, _____ significant delays due to unforeseen circumstances.

① experiences   ② experiencing   ③ experienced
④ will experience ⑤ had experienced

06 The politician's speech, while outwardly designed to foster unity, contained nuanced allusions that _____ a divisive agenda, prompting backlash from advocacy groups and raising concerns about hidden motives.

① enthusiastically exposed
② subtly reinforced
③ deliberately undermined
④ unintentionally revealed
⑤ strongly emphasized

07 Despite the program's innovative approach, analysts noted that its framework _____ the structural flows that influenced the outcomes, leaving its effectiveness in question.

① neglected   ② resolved   ③ sacked
④ verified   ⑤ incorporated

08 The sudden surge in demand for electric vehicles _____ an industry-wide shift toward sustainable practices, even among companies that had previously resisted such changes.

① impeded
② heralded
③ discharged
④ delayed
⑤ questioned

09 The company's decision to withdraw from the project was interpreted as a sign of strategic prudence, suggesting that it _____ the risks involved as too significant to proceed.

① disregarded
② empowered
③ perceived
④ underestimated
⑤ disoriented

10 While the new policy aims to address housing shortages, critics argue that its long-term effects may _____ inequalities by disproportionately benefiting affluent communities.

① maintain
② mitigate
③ overlook
④ clarify
⑤ exacerbate

11 Although the merger was framed as a means to streamline operations, industry experts feared it would _____ competition, ultimately harming consumers.

① foster
② stifle
③ encourage
④ diversify
⑤ prioritize

12 Despite the museum's efforts to present an unbiased account of history, some critics argued that its curation _____ important voices, particularly those of marginalized groups.

① amplified
② supported
③ celebrated
④ omitted
⑤ incorporated

13 The novel's fragmented structure and shifting perspectives, though innovative, _____ among readers unfamiliar with experimental storytelling techniques.

① alienated a significant portion
② inspired widespread acclaim
③ provided immediate clarity
④ reinforced its intentions
⑤ undermined narrative inconsistencies

14 The film, while visually stunning and narratively complex, _____ among critics for its failure to provide a coherent resolution to its central conflict.

① sparked universal acclaim
② resolved lingering debates
③ received mixed reactions
④ clarified its themes
⑤ offered meaningful closure

15 The proposed amendments to the constitution, which aim to enhance citizens' rights and freedoms, _____ debated vigorously in parliament over the past several weeks, with no clear consensus yet reached.

① is being
② has been
③ have been
④ were
⑤ had been

16 It is imperative that each team member _____ their individual responsibilities clearly and consistently in order to contribute effectively to the overall success of the project.

① understands ② understand ③ is understanding
④ has understood ⑤ will understand

17~33 다음 글을 읽고 질문에 답하시오.

17~19

> Forests play a pivotal role in mitigating climate change by acting as carbon sinks, absorbing significant amounts of carbon dioxide from the atmosphere. However, deforestation and degradation have compromised this function, leading to increased greenhouse gas emissions. Recent studies emphasize the importance of proforestation — the practice of allowing existing forests to grow to their full ecological potential — as a more effective strategy for carbon sequestration compared to afforestation or reforestation. Proforestation not only enhances carbon storage but also supports biodiversity and ecosystem resilience. Implementing proforestation requires policy shifts towards protecting mature forests and recognizing their critical role in climate mitigation.

17 Why is proforestation more effective than afforestation or reforestation for climate change?

① It allows forests to reach natural potential without human intervention.
② It reduces dependence on biodiversity for climate mitigation.
③ It limits deforestation while opposing urban development.
④ It boosts timber production without reducing carbon storage.
⑤ It promotes rapid carbon absorption by planting high-density tree clusters.

18 What broader ecological benefit does proforestation offer beyond carbon storage?

① It addresses water conservation in deforested regions.
② It ensures agricultural productivity nearby.
③ It fosters biodiversity and resilience to environmental stress.
④ It accelerates global reforestation through policy.
⑤ It improves soil fertility via sustainable land use.

19 What policy shift does the passage advocate for proforestation?

① Supporting sustainable logging in managed forests
② Prioritizing mature forests for their ecological and climate roles
③ Funding industrial reforestation projects
④ Promoting urban green initiatives over rural conservation
⑤ Mandating afforestation in deforested areas to absorb carbon

20~21

> When the project proposal was first introduced, I was genuinely excited about its potential. I eagerly shared my thoughts and ideas, hoping to contribute to the discussion. However, he mistook my enthusiasm _____ approval, thinking I was fully on board with everything he suggested. Later, when he started implementing changes without consulting anyone, it became clear that we weren't on the same page.

20 What is the most appropriate expression to fill in the blank?

① by
② of
③ for
④ at
⑤ in

21 Choose the best meaning of the underlined phrase "we weren't on the same page" based on the context.

① we were reading the same document.
② we did not fully understand or agree with each other.
③ we were talking on the phone at the same time.
④ we were writing notes on the same page of a notebook.
⑤ we were standing on the same floor of a building.

22~23

In South Korea's flourishing running scene, younger generations are the _____, leading the charge at the front of the pack. When around 20,000 runners flocked to Gwanghwamun Square for the 2024 Seoul Half Marathon in April — up 53.8 percent from last year's 13,000 — the majority, making up over 66 percent, were in their 20s and 30s, stepping up to the plate for either the half-marathon or 10-kilometer course.

22 What is the most appropriate expression to fill in the blank?
① followers
② spectators
③ observers
④ stragglers
⑤ pacesetters

23 Choose the statement that is true based on the passage.
① The number of participants decreased compared to last year.
② Over 66 percent of participants were in their 20s and 30s.
③ Most runners chose to observe rather than compete.
④ There was no 10-kilometer course in the event.
⑤ Most participants were over 40 years old.

24~25

Many businesses and people who were lucky enough to appeal to Oprah Winfrey found overnight success after being promoted on her groundbreaking show — which ran from 1986 to 2011 and was the highest-rated daytime talk show in American TV history. The Oprah Effect was especially powerful because of her authenticity. Oprah chose products she was genuinely interested in, rather than being paid to promote them. And, unlike typical celebrity endorsements, she often supported independent family businesses. This trust and authenticity made Oprah's recommendations uniquely impactful, turning her endorsements into life-changing opportunities for countless individuals and small businesses. A single mention on her show could catapult a product to national fame, often resulting in sold-out inventories and skyrocketing demand. What distinguished the Oprah Effect from typical marketing was its emotional resonance — her audience didn't just buy what Oprah liked; they embraced her choices as extensions of her values and vision. By spotlighting underrepresented brands and promoting meaningful stories, Oprah became a catalyst for success that went beyond commerce, helping to shape cultural trends and elevate voices that might otherwise have gone unheard.

24 What made "The Oprah Effect" unique compared to typical celebrity endorsements?

① Oprah promoted products she truly believed in, often from small family businesses.
② Oprah was the first celebrity to endorse products on TV.
③ Oprah required payment for promotions.
④ Oprah focused on promoting high-end luxury brands.
⑤ Oprah's show featured large corporate sponsors.

25 What was a significant result for businesses featured on Oprah Winfrey's show?

① They gained access to international markets without additional effort.
② Their sales surged only during the holiday season.
③ They received ongoing financial support from Oprah herself.
④ Their products often sold out, and demand rapidly increased.
⑤ They were required to collaborate with other celebrities for further promotion.

26~28

> Martial law shifts power from civilian governance to military authorities, often under the pretext of restoring order. While it may stabilize crises temporarily, it frequently leads to human rights abuses, including suppression of dissent and erosion of judicial autonomy. The transition to civilian rule requires balancing justice with societal cohesion. Investigating abuses is often hampered by resistance from entrenched interests, institutional inertia, and fears of reigniting conflict, with amnesty laws reinforcing impunity. Such challenges highlight the tension between addressing historical wrongs and maintaining a fragile peace. Proponents of transitional justice advocate for independent investigations, reparations, and institutional reforms aimed at ensuring accountability and preventing recurrence. However, critics warn that such measures could deepen polarization or foster disillusionment if perceived as insufficient or overly punitive. Successful post-martial law governance requires addressing past injustices, building trust in institutions, and enacting democratic reforms. Balancing accountability and reconciliation remains crucial to ensuring long-term stability and safeguarding democratic principles in societies recovering from military rule.

26 How does the passage describe the link between accountability and societal cohesion after martial law?

① Accountability may destabilize peace, while cohesion does not guarantee leniency.
② Accountability ensures cohesion by deterring authoritarianism.
③ Accountability and cohesion often conflict, requiring authority.
④ Cohesion is favored over accountability for short-term stability.
⑤ Balance is crucial, as extreme leniency or severity harms both.

27 Why are amnesty laws long-term challenges to democratic reform?

① They entrench impunity, hampering institutional reforms.
② They prioritize stability but ignore reparations.
③ They lack public support, undermining legitimacy.
④ They seem fair but exclude key stakeholders.
⑤ They consolidate military control over civilian institutions.

28 What approach is needed for sustainable governance post-martial law?

① Reconciliation through public apologies
② Transparency without polarizing politics
③ Economic recovery to ease discontent and rebuild trust
④ Unity by avoiding punishment and relying on international reforms
⑤ Justice combined with reforms to ensure accountability

[29~30]

> A 2023 study published in *Science Advances* delved into the pervasive issue of microplastic contamination and its implications for human health. Researchers identified microplastics within the human bloodstream — a finding that has profound implications for understanding the biological impact of modern pollution. These particles, ingested via food, water, and air, are suspected of contributing to inflammation and oxidative stress, processes linked to chronic conditions such as cardiovascular diseases. The study underscores not only the health risks but also the broader environmental consequences of plastic pollution, emphasizing the urgent need for regulatory measures. Researchers advocate for innovative solutions, including the development of biodegradable materials and overhauling global waste management systems, to mitigate the risks. While definitive conclusions on the health impacts remain elusive, the findings highlight the pressing need for interdisciplinary approaches to address the multifaceted challenges posed by microplastics.

29 What is the primary concern raised by the study regarding microplastics in the bloodstream?

① Their immediate toxicity to human cells
② Their inability to break down within the digestive system
③ Their role in enhancing immune system responses
④ Their potential to trigger biological processes like oxidative stress
⑤ Their primary impact on respiratory function

30 Why does the study emphasize interdisciplinary approaches to microplastic pollution?

① To increase public awareness of health-related impacts
② To promote collaboration exclusively among medical researchers
③ To ensure uniform international adoption of biodegradable materials
④ To standardize plastic production methods globally
⑤ To address the complexity of both health and environmental challenges

---

31~33

> Han Kang, the 2024 Nobel Prize in Literature laureate, creates introspective works that delve into humanity's fragility, trauma's silence, and the tension between resistance and complicity. In *The Vegetarian*, the protagonist's decision to stop eating meat becomes a layered act — seen as defiance of patriarchal norms, an assertion of bodily autonomy, and a retreat into existential solitude. Told from the perspectives of those closest to her, the narrative highlights the conflict between societal expectations and personal agency, leaving readers questioning whether her rebellion is empowering or self-destructive. In *Human Acts*, Han examines the 1980 Gwangju Uprising through fragmented, multi-voiced perspectives, blending historical record and poetic abstraction. The novel portrays grief and violence as both personal and collective, immersing readers in the sensory experience of pain while probing its impact on memory and accountability. Han's groundbreaking storytelling bridges specific cultural histories and existential questions, challenging readers to confront uncomfortable truths about power, resilience, and the scars of violence.

31 In *The Vegetarian*, how does the protagonist's abstinence from meat function in the narrative?

① As a critique of environmental harm caused by industrialized meat production
② As a metaphorical rejection of both societal norms and personal autonomy
③ As an assertion of control over her body amidst patriarchal expectations
④ As an expression of solidarity with feminist resistance movements
⑤ As a symbolic retreat from traditional Korean cultural values

32. In *Human Acts*, how does Han Kang's use of multiple perspectives affect readers' understanding of the Gwangju Uprising?

① By fragmenting the narrative to reflect the disorientation experienced during political violence, deepening the emotional resonance with the characters
② By creating distance between readers and the characters, encouraging a more objective analysis of historical events
③ By focusing solely on the perspectives of survivors, limiting broader societal contexts
④ By presenting each perspective as equally reliable, offering a unified view of the uprising
⑤ By emphasizing factual accuracy over personal grief, ensuring a neutral portrayal of historical trauma

33. Based on the passage, how does Han Kang's storytelling challenge commonplace portrayals of historical events?

① By positioning historical events as secondary to existential questions, reducing their broader significance
② By emphasizing factual accuracy over emotional depth, ensuring a historically grounded narrative
③ By avoiding individual perspectives in favor of a singular, authoritative account
④ By controverting cultural and temporal boundaries, exploring universal themes of resilience and suffering
⑤ By blurring distinctions between personal and collective experiences, reshaping readers' understanding of historical trauma

SOOKMYUNG WOMEN'S UNIVERSITY

숙명여자대학교

▶ 2025학년도 B형   ▶ 문항 수: 33문항 | 제한시간: 60분

2025 숙명여대 B형 영역별 문항 수

구분	문법			어휘			논리완성	독해	생활영어	총 문항 수
	G/S, W/E	정비문	재진술	동의어	반의어	유추				
문항 수	4			3			9	17		33
백분율	12%			9%			27%	52%		100%

SOOKMYUNG WOMEN'S UNIVERSITY

숙명여자대학교

● 2025학년도 B형: 33문항 · 60분

문항별 배점 01~16 2.5점 / 17~32 3.5점 / 33 4점

01~04 밑줄 친 부분과 가장 비슷한 의미의 표현을 고르시오.

01 The beauty of the sunset was ineffable, leaving us all in awe.
① unpleasant   ② forgettable   ③ visible
④ indescribable   ⑤ loud

02 Investors weigh early US election results as uncertainty remains.
① consider   ② ignore   ③ forget
④ know   ⑤ simplify

03 The sudden pivot by chip companies, which has swept global stock markets following signs that the US might impose fresh restrictions on sales to China, has begun to abate.
① shift   ② stagnation   ③ decline
④ acceleration   ⑤ completion

04 Asian equities were primed to track US stocks by <u>notching</u> a second day of declines as signs of economic weakness overwhelmed the market's optimism surrounding rate cuts.

① failing
② marking
③ neglecting
④ avoiding
⑤ delaying

05~16 빈칸에 알맞은 가장 적절한 표현을 고르시오.

05 His comments during the meeting were _____, offering little to no meaningful contribution.

① crucial and valuable
② clear and deep
③ vapid and uninspiring
④ significant and useful
⑤ essential and fundamental

06 Palantir achieved a significant _____ when it became the first software company to serve as a prime contractor for a Pentagon program, securing the Army's Titan contract to develop a next-generation targeting node.

① setback
② routine
③ loss
④ milestone
⑤ disappointment

07 The legal battle had stretched over several months, with both sides fiercely defending their positions. The court date set for next month was anticipated to be the ultimate _____, bringing a definitive resolution to the case and potentially setting a precedent for future disputes.

① digression
② misunderstanding
③ showdown
④ stalemate
⑤ delay

08. Nuclear Winter is the theory that an atomic war would generate so much fire, rubble, dust and heat that for months afterwards the global climate would be affected. Worldwide temperatures would descend, crops would fail and humans and animals alike would starve. Despite back-and-forth arguments between academics about exactly how bad a Nuclear Winter would be, it was a _____ through the heart of the political views of the time.

① wake-up call
② forgotten episode
③ lighthearted commentary
④ routine development
⑤ peaceful inconvenience

09. She worked tirelessly all year to earn a promotion, and her efforts finally _____. She received a commendation and a raise at the annual company meeting. Everyone in her department celebrated her success, acknowledging how hard she had worked.

① wore out   ② slowed down   ③ turned down
④ gave up   ⑤ paid off

10. The project was behind schedule and over budget, prompting the manager to _____. She held a series of meetings to reassign tasks and streamline processes. Her proactive approach helped to bring the project back on track, much to the relief of the entire team.

① give up   ② shake things up   ③ scale down
④ hold back   ⑤ take a vacation

11 A team implemented an AI-driven security system for online transactions. Once active, the system _____, detecting fraud attempts more accurately than previous methods.

① fell short
② misfired
③ backfired
④ broke down
⑤ hit the mark

12 The main event was delayed due to unforeseen technical issues, so the organizers arranged a _____ to entertain the audience while they waited. This diversion featured local musicians and acrobats performing on a smaller stage.

① closure
② cancellation
③ debate
④ board meeting
⑤ sideshow

13 As tensions continued to rise between the two rival schools, their basketball teams prepared to _____ in a decisive game that would determine the regional champion.

① square off
② back out
③ cool down
④ stand aside
⑤ sit it out

14 The company's robust quarterly earnings, coupled with favorable macroeconomic conditions and a resurgence in consumer spending, have generated a substantial _____ propelling its stock price to unprecedented levels.

① tailwind
② encumbrance
③ hindrance
④ stagnation
⑤ languor

15 When asked about the company's environmental impact, the CEO elaborated on their recent charitable initiatives, thereby _____ the pressing concerns regarding their carbon footprint and deforestation practices.

① calculating ② experimenting ③ sidestepping
④ broadcasting ⑤ celebrating

16 In the wake of the company's restructuring, senior executives were tasked with implementing a comprehensive _____ strategy that not only facilitated the transition of displaced employees to new career opportunities but also mitigated potential legal repercussions, safeguarded corporate reputation, and ensured a smooth handover of critical responsibilities to remaining staff, all while maintaining morale and productivity within a rapidly changing organizational landscape.

① celebration
② outplacement
③ entertainment
④ relocation of office space
⑤ holiday planning

[17~33] 다음 글을 읽고 질문에 답하시오.

[17~18]

Today, thousands of high-grade supercomputers are engaged in calculating the worth of derivatives as part of a money game akin to poker. However, relatively few supercomputers are dedicated to evaluating the long-term effects of massive electricity consumption by the next generation of AI on the climate, the impact of plastic pollution on the oceans, or the future prospects for food production amid rapid soil degradation over the next 200 years. Supercomputers are primarily used to calculate profit rather than sustainability, driven by political motives rather than scientific ones. Those in power understand that if AI were to focus on sustainability over the centuries, it would likely conclude that discontinuing AI altogether is necessary to ensure humanity's survival.

17 According to the passage, why are supercomputers primarily used to calculate profit instead of sustainability?

① Political motives prioritize profit over long-term sustainability.
② Supercomputers lack the ability to process environmental data.
③ Scientific research discourages the use of supercomputers for sustainability.
④ Sustainability-related problems do not require supercomputers.
⑤ The technology for sustainability-focused calculations is underdeveloped.

18 What does the author suggest would be the likely outcome if AI focused on sustainability instead of profit?

① It would find that increasing AI usage is essential for global sustainability.
② It would determine that profit-based applications of AI are the most sustainable solution.
③ It would reveal that sustainability-focused AI has no impact on humanity's survival.
④ It would conclude that humanity should stop using AI altogether to survive.
⑤ It would prove that AI-driven profitability is more important than sustainability.

19~21

Mary Wollstonecraft remains a foundational figure in feminist philosophy, yet her work transcends its time to engage with broader political and ethical debates. In *A Vindication of the Rights of Woman* (1792), Wollstonecraft challenges prevailing societal norms by asserting that women's rationality and education are essential to their moral and social development. However, her arguments reflect an ongoing negotiation between her critique of societal hierarchies and Enlightenment ideals, such as autonomy and freedom, suggesting a complex relationship with liberalism. Recent scholarship has revisited Wollstonecraft's engagement with political economy, arguing that her critiques of wealth disparity and family structures prefigure certain aspects of socialist feminism, even as she remains situated within the liberal tradition. Additionally, her approach to virtue ethics — emphasizing personal virtue as a means to achieve societal reform — has drawn attention for its nuanced integration of individual moral responsibility with broader social critique. This intersection of personal ethics, gender equality, and political reform makes Wollstonecraft's work both challenging and enduringly relevant in contemporary feminist discourse.

19 Based on the passage, what is one reason Wollstonecraft's work is considered both aligned with and critical of liberalism?

① She advocated for gender equality but rejected the notion of individual freedom.
② She emphasized women's education while critiquing existing social hierarchies.
③ She dismissed Enlightenment principles while supporting economic reform.
④ She proposed socialist policies while adhering to traditional family structures.
⑤ She avoided political critiques in favor of liberal arguments.

20 How does Wollstonecraft's integration of virtue ethics distinguish her approach to feminist and political thought?

① It frames personal morality as irrelevant to societal reform.
② It links individual moral responsibility with broader social change.
③ It relies exclusively on religious doctrines to promote gender equality.
④ It prioritizes emotional appeals over rational arguments.
⑤ It positions societal reform as secondary to personal virtue.

21 Which inference can be drawn about Wollstonecraft's critique of wealth disparity and family structures?

① Her views entirely reject liberalism in favor of socialist ideals.
② She supports dismantling the family unit as a core societal structure.
③ Her arguments prefigure aspects of socialist feminism while remaining within the liberal tradition.
④ She prioritizes economic issues over gender equality.
⑤ Her critiques are rooted solely in Enlightenment ideals with contemporary relevance.

22~23

Sedona is renowned as a hotspot for vortex sites believed to carry psychic energy, a concept closely tied to the area's Native history and its designation as "sacred land." According to American Indian spirituality, inanimate objects, including geographic areas, can be considered sacred when inhabited by a spirit. This belief imbues Sedona with a unique spiritual significance deeply rooted in indigenous cultural traditions. Sedona's canyons, historically used as sites for indigenous ceremonies, are thought to hold immense spiritual power. Vortex sites, in particular, are believed to channel meditation, clairvoyance, and healing energy, making the region a popular destination for those seeking spiritual growth and physical rejuvenation. These areas are not just geographic features but are viewed as spaces where the physical and metaphysical converge, attracting visitors from around the world.

22 Based on the passage, which of the following best elucidates the relationship between Sedona's vortex sites and indigenous spirituality?

① Vortex sites were conceptualized through reinterpretations of indigenous rituals.
② Sedona's vortex sites are venerated exclusively for their geographical singularity.
③ The sanctity of vortex sites emanates from the belief spirits can inhabit physical loci.
④ Indigenous spirituality uniformly designates all natural landscapes as sacred vortexes.
⑤ Vortex sites derive their spiritual prominence from modern metaphysical ideologies.

23 Why might Sedona's vortex sites be particularly resonant for individuals pursuing spiritual enlightenment, as inferred from the passage?

① They serve as exclusive venues for ancestral indigenous rites.
② They facilitate an experiential synthesis of corporeal and transcendent energies.
③ They reverse empirical substantiation of psychic phenomena.
④ They represent unparalleled global sanctuaries for the refugees.
⑤ They embody a symbolic nexus of indigenous traditions and contemporary spirituality.

24~25

Navigating the contemporary job market poses formidable challenges, particularly for individuals attempting to break into an unfamiliar sector or industry. Success necessitates a comprehensive understanding of employer's expectations and the meticulous alignment of one's competencies with the demands of prospective roles. This process requires not only the cultivation of a robust professional network but also the strategic enhancement of one's credentials through the acquisition of pertinent experiences and certifications. Furthermore, the proliferation of automated recruitment systems underscores the necessity of tailoring applications to ensure compatibility with applicant tracking algorithms. Despite these complexities, the overarching objective remains steadfast: to _____ a job that transcends mere financial sustenance and provides intellectual fulfillment and professional growth.

24 What is the most appropriate expression to fill in the blank?

① reject   ② escape   ③ overlook
④ miss   ⑤ land

25 Which statement accurately reflects the content of the passage?

① Breaking into a new field is easy with minimal effort.
② Success requires aligning skills with employer's needs.
③ Automated systems have simplified job applications.
④ Financial sustenance is the only goal of employment.
⑤ Certification is irrelevant to job market success.

26~28

> Predicting earthquakes has long been a formidable challenge in seismology. Despite advancements in technology and extensive research, accurately forecasting the timing, location, and magnitude of seismic events remains elusive. Traditional methods focus on monitoring geological faults and seismic activity, but these approaches have not yielded reliable predictive capabilities. Recent interdisciplinary studies suggest that integrating data from various sources, including satellite observations, animal behavior, and atmospheric anomalies, may enhance predictive models. However, the scientific community remains divided on the efficacy of these methods, emphasizing the need for continued research and the development of comprehensive early warning systems to mitigate the impact of earthquakes.

26 Why is predicting earthquakes a persistent challenge in seismology?

① Current technology transcends precise prediction models.
② Traditional methods only manage to focus on atmospheric anomalies.
③ Geological faults behave too erratically for monitoring.
④ Multifactorial triggers hinder predicting time, location, and magnitude of earthquakes.
⑤ Scientific disagreement slows progress in methodologies.

27 How does integrating interdisciplinary data improve traditional earthquake prediction?

① It questions fault monitoring by focusing on phenomena like atmospheric anomalies.
② It demands new technologies and infrastructure.
③ It shifts its focus from unconventional methods to conventional techniques.
④ It reveals overlooked links between animal behavior, satellite data, earthquakes and others.
⑤ It complicates predictions by adding variables without consistent results.

28 How does the scientific community view interdisciplinary methods for earthquake prediction?

① Cautiously optimistic: potential exists but needs validation
② Skeptical: newer methods lack empirical rigor
③ Resistant: favoring established over experimental approaches
④ Divided: some support innovation; others question reliability
⑤ Collaborative: integrating diverse methods into unified models

29~30

> During the business meeting, rather than taking the bull _____ the horns, they indulged in splitting hairs, ignoring the heart of the matter entirely. Frustrated by the lack of progress, I finally spoke up and said, "Let's cut to the chase — our sales numbers are down, and we need a new strategy to turn things around." The room went quiet for a moment, but then we got down to business, focusing on what really mattered.

29 What is the most appropriate expression to fill in the blank?

① in ② under ③ on
④ of ⑤ by

30 Choose the best meaning of the underlined phrase "Let's cut to the chase" based on the context.

① Let's start running.
② Let's go to a movie.
③ Let's focus on the main issue.
④ Let's organize a chase.
⑤ Let's skip to the last slide.

31~33

Going in search of a natural, starry sky and a dark night's sleep is a growing tourism trend. Staggering statistics indicate the loss of the natural night around the world. Light pollution is increasing at 10 percent per year globally, with 99 percent of people in Europe and North America no longer able to see the stars from their homes. As light pollution affects our health and disturbs our sleep, many city dwellers are seeking _____ provided by switching off and sleeping in natural darkness. And, as more people look to connect with nature in the aftermath of lockdowns, it makes sense that travelers want experiences that provide a sense of awe and connection to the cosmos. Dark sky travel provides a connection to nature through astrotourism, such as stargazing, moongazing, aurora-spotting and astronomy science, and other nighttime activities, such as night hikes, nocturnal wildlife watching, nighttime mindfulness and wellness experiences, and sleep tourism. These experiences can also incorporate related cultural themes, like the zodiac, myths and legends connected to the night sky.

31 Select the title that best summarizes the main idea of the passage.

① The History of Stargazing in Europe
② Light Pollution and Urban Development
③ The Benefits of Sleep Tourism
④ Nocturnal Wildlife and Its Habitats
⑤ Exploring the Rising Trend of Dark Sky Travel

32 What is the most appropriate expression to fill in the blank?

① the energy and provocation
② the excitement and adventure
③ the rest and recuperation
④ the entertainment and party
⑤ the activity and stimulation

33 Why are many people interested in dark sky travel?

① To reconnect with nature and experience a sense of awe and connection to the cosmos
② To participate in high-energy nighttime parties and festivals
③ To learn about the myths and legends of their local culture
④ To witness the sunrise in natural environments
⑤ To participate in advanced astronomy research

SOONGSIL UNIVERSITY

숭실대학교

▶ 2025학년도 인문계　▶ 문항 수: 50문항 ｜ 제한시간: 90분

2025 숭실대 인문계 영역별 문항 수

구분	문법			어휘			논리완성	독해	생활영어	총 문항 수
	G/S, W/E	정비문	재진술	동의어	반의어	유추				
문항 수	2			4			4	40		50
백분율	4%			8%			8%	80%		100%

SOONGSIL UNIVERSITY

숭실대학교

2025학년도 인문계: 50문항 · 90분

문항별 배점 01~10 1점 / 11~20 1.5점 / 21~35 2점 / 36~45 2.5점 / 46~50 4점

01~02 Choose the one that is grammatically NOT correct.

01 The study of the Gothic ① <u>offers</u> a forum for ② <u>discussing</u> some of the key issues of American society, ③ <u>included</u> gender and the nation's ④ <u>continuing</u> drama of race.

02 The conception of reality ① <u>what</u> the reform movement was based is nowhere more dramatically illustrated ② <u>than</u> in the activities of the New York City Tract Society, whose members, numbering in the thousands, ③ <u>attempted</u> to help the city's poor by ④ <u>distributing</u> a religious tract to every family in the city once a month.

03~06 Choose the most appropriate word for the blank.

03 The government implemented new policies to _____ the negative effects of climate change on agriculture.

① encourage   ② mitigate
③ neglect   ④ amplify

04 During the meeting, the manager asked the team to submit a(n) _____ version for the final decision.

① premature   ② obscure
③ detailed   ④ disdainful

05 The scientist was praised for her ability to simplify complex concepts into _____ terms for the public.

① simple
② ambiguous
③ condescending
④ distorted

06 The teacher encouraged the students to _____ their ideas openly during the discussion.

① suppress
② express
③ surprise
④ discourage

07~10 Choose the expression closest in meaning to the underlined.

07 The protesters' demands were met with <u>indifference</u> by the authorities, who refused to address their concerns.

① empathy
② favor
③ disregard
④ hostility

08 The new policy was met with <u>skepticism</u> by the public, as many doubted its effectiveness.

① approval
② distrust
③ interest
④ neutrality

09 The company announced a <u>remunerative</u> deal that would significantly increase their annual revenue.

① lucrative
② questionable
③ complex
④ tentative

10 The region is known for its arid climate, with very little rainfall throughout the year.
① extreme
② humid
③ fertile
④ dry

11~13 Read the following passage and answer the questions.

The significance of a sensory act is not necessarily unitary. The way in which a doctor touches a patient during a physical examination, for example, may be taken as primarily a data-gathering process or may have personal meaning for the participants. However, as we will examine on medicine, it also has a particular social history and an important symbolic significance.

Even sensory acts that have recognized social functions have many shades of meaning. A handshake may be variously interpreted as a gesture of friendliness, an attempt to dominate, an act of condescension, an invitation to intimacy, a show of equality, a bridging of differences, the sealing of a contract, or a Ⓐ breach of etiquette. When the Australian Prime Minster Julia Gillard shook hands with Queen Elizabeth II instead of curtsying she was technically committing a breach of etiquette. Within the cultural context of Australia's former status as a British colony, however, what might seem like a simple social gaffe was instead an important symbolic gesture of equality and modernity. When Queen Elizabeth shook hands with a former commander of the Irish Republican Army, the act had very different connotations: it was seen as a dramatic act of reconciliation, "the ultimate handshake" between persons representing two old enemies.

If the eighteenth-century wit Sydney Smith is a reliable guide, a considerable variety of handshaking styles and significations existed in his day. As Constance Classen points out, the "high official" handshake consisted of "a rapid short shake, near the chin," and in the clerical handshake only one finger was held out, while in the "rustic handshake," "your hand is seized in an iron grasp, betokening rude health, warm heart and a distance from the Metropolis; but producing a sense of relief on your part when you find your hand released and your fingers unbroken." The range of connotations that can be communicated by a simple handshake demonstrates that tactile acts are not simply the physical labour that allows us to engage in other socially meaningful acts, such as writing books or creating art, but potentially highly meaningful in themselves.

11 Which of the following best replaces Ⓐ?
① result
② violation
③ abiding
④ inflammation

12 Which of the following are NOT mentioned as social functions of a handshake?
① a sign of affection
② a display of deception
③ a manifestation of reconciliation
④ a demonstration of power

13 Which of the following would best describe the purpose of this writing?
① to show a unitary sense of a handshake
② to introduce various types of body gestures
③ to correct the Queen Elizabeth's style of handshaking
④ to explain the diverse roles of tactile acts

14~15 Read the following passage and answer the questions.

There is another feather — or rather collection of feathers — kept in a box at the headquarters of Britain's biggest conservation charity. They tell a different, yet equally symbolic story. These feathers are not public display. If you make an appointment to view the archives of the Royal Society for the Protection of Birds (RSPB), and if you are lucky enough to gain entrance, this box might (or might not) be brought out to you by the librarian. The RSPB is a Ⓐ behemoth — a charity with over 1.1 million members, 224 nature reserves spread over 160,000 hectares, 2,000 staff and some 12,000 volunteers. It has an annual income of over £140 million and it wields great political power. Its business today is international nature conservation, whether peregrine falcons, pygmy fruit bats or Sumatran rhinos. But its leading figures tend to be bird lovers — and the majority of these have, historically, been men. In Britain, birds tend to belong, instinctively it seems, to the boys.

It was not always so. The RSPB was founded by *women* — women with an unusually singular purpose. They were going to stamp out the fashion for feathers in hats. For half a century, from the 1870s to 1920s, wild bird species were systematically slaughtered around the world for the millinery trade in one of the most lucrative commodity markets on earth. At its peak, the trade was worth a staggering £20 million a year to Britain — around £204 million in today's money. In 1891, as the insatiable fashion for feathers stepped up yet another gear, two exclusively women's groups — one in Crydon, one in Manchester — banded together to save the birds. They gave themselves an ambitious title — the Society for the Protection of Birds — and their determination was rewarded with a Royal Charter in 1904.

14 Which of the following is closest in meaning to Ⓐ?

① inactive institution　　② strict association
③ large organization　　④ intimate relation

15 Which of the following is true about the RSPB?

① It had collected diverse feathers for easy public access.
② It had preserved and protected only bird feathers.
③ It had made profits in the international trade of feathers.
④ It had shown its interests in conflict with women wearing hats with feathers.

16~18 Read the following passage and answer the questions.

Moni the chimpanzee, newly arrived at the Dutch zoo, unexpectedly lost her baby. Zoë Goldsborough, a graduate student studying chimp jealousy, discovered Moni one winter morning sitting alone on a high tree stump, cradling carefully something Ⓐ_____ in her arms. Upon closer inspection, Goldsborough realized it was a lifeless newborn. The keepers, initially skeptical, tried unsuccessfully to take the baby from Moni.

Another female chimp named Tushi, who had previously experienced a miscarriage, began lingering near Moni. Tushi had gained fame years before for Ⓑ_____ a drone during a documentary filming. For two days, she stayed close to Moni, who continued holding the tiny body. Eventually, during a struggle with the keepers, the baby fell from Moni's grasp, and Tushi grabbed it, refusing to return it. This led to Moni becoming extremely distressed, especially when the keepers isolated Tushi in a separate room.

Goldsborough struggled to interpret their behavior. While Moni seemed driven by maternal attachment, a feeling humans readily understand, Tushi might have been responding to memories of her own loss. However, it remained unclear whether either chimp truly comprehended the baby's death. They may have believed the baby would revive. This uncertainty is notable, considering chimpanzees are among our closest relatives in the animal kingdom.

16 Which title best captures the main theme of this text?

① The Complex Emotions of Zoo Chimpanzees
② Understanding Death: A Human Perspective
③ Maternal Instincts in Captive Chimps
④ A Graduate Student's Zoo Observations

17 In blank Ⓐ, which expression best completes the text?

① lively
② motionless
③ friendly
④ litigious

18 Which of the following best fits in Ⓑ?

① attacking
② simmering
③ rotting
④ trespassing

19~20 Read the following passage and answer the questions.

There is no near-contemporary source of Anglo-Saxon origin. The reason is obvious enough: the Germanic peoples were illiterate during their first two centuries in Britain. So their early fortunes can only be glimpsed through the hostile eyes of Britons, through the ill-informed eyes of foreigners, and by means of their own half-remembered traditions. Until the late sixth century, informed guesswork must make do for history.

Archaeology provides the first clue, for it shows that there were Germanic warriors in Britain some years before 410. Late Roman cemeteries, especially along the Lower Thames Valley from Oxfordshire to the Essex coast, have produced burials with belt-fittings of a type worn by Frankish and Saxon mercenaries in the Roman army. If such troops were settled in Britain, as they certainly were in Gaul, the mid-fifth-century invaders may have joined relatives who had come two or three generations back. Sunken huts with gable-posts are characteristic of English settlement in the fifth and sixth centuries, and over two hundred of these have been found at a huge site near Mucking on the Thames estuary. It has been suggested that this complex housed mercenaries who were settled in c. 400 to guard the approach to London. If so, the continuous history of Anglo-Saxon settlement begins under Roman rule.

The English of later centuries dated their ancestors' arrival some decades after this, and it does seem to have been from the 430s onwards that Germanic settlers arrived in large numbers. Before considering this remarkable process, it must be asked who the invaders were and what they were like. The first question is answered, almost as well as any modern scholar can answer it, in a startlingly well-informed passage quoted by Bede from an unknown source: "They came from three very powerful Germanic tribes, the Saxons, Angles and Jutes."

19 Which of the following is true?

① Late Roman cemeteries were exclusively for the Roman warriors.
② Roman relics display the presence of German traders in 400.
③ Roman warriors appear to wear belt-fittings, living in sunken huts with gable-posts around 400.
④ The invaders are easily identified as the Saxons, the Angles, and the Jutes.

20 Which of the following would be the purpose?

① to contrast the two different histories about the origin of the Germanic people
② to reveal the Anglo-Saxon settlement beginning under Gaulish rule
③ to correct the evidence from the Roman cemeteries
④ to explain the lack of historical records about the Germanic invasion

[21~23] Read the following passage and answer the questions.

What made English the world language? Behind its success story there are two main factors: first, the expansion and influence of British colonial power — by the late nineteenth century the British Empire covered a considerable part of the earth's land surface, and subjects of the British monarch totalled nearly a quarter of the world's population; second, the status of the United States of America as the leading economic, military and scientific power of the twentieth century.

And there are yet other contributing factors. One is the increasing need for international communication as a result of modern technology: such innovations as the telephone, radio, television, jetliner transport and computers each introduced a step-change in the potential for international communication. Air traffic controllers all over the world use English when talking to pilots, whether Russian or Danish or Chinese, and whether at John F. Kennedy or Schiphol or Narita airport. And, of course, in information technology, Ⓐ American English is king.

Yet another factor: in countries or groups of countries where people have several or many different first languages, English may be the preferred lingua franca because it is felt to be neutral ground. In the global economy, many multinationals have adopted English as the workplace vernacular. Half of all Russian business is said to be conducted in English. In the European Union (EU), the practical "working language" in communication across language barriers is usually English, often reluctantly adopted as the only language that is sufficiently widely used. Across the EU (excluding the British Isles), nine out of ten students choose to study English as a foreign language. English is said to permeate EU institutional activities and many areas of cultural and economic life more and more thoroughly. Today, it is hardly possible to pursue an international career without English. As a window on the world, English is looked upon as the best means to achieve economic, social and political success.

21 Which of the following is best for the title?

① The Lingua Franca Paradox: English's Reluctant Dominance in a Multilingual World
② The Power of British Empire: The Sole Engine of English Language Proliferation
③ English Ascendant: Historical Imperialism, Economic Power, and Technological Necessity
④ Global Vernacular: The Structure of the English Language

22 Which of the following best interprets Ⓐ?

① American media subtly colonizes global digital discourse.
② American English dominates IT, not all global communication.
③ Organizations strategically promote American English globally.
④ American English naturally emerges as dialect of innovation.

23 Which of the following is true?

① English replaces local languages in all EU communication.
② EU reluctantly adopts English, yet it's widely studied and pervasive.
③ Tech drives English spread; history, economy less important.
④ English creates uniform global linguistic standard.

24~26 Read the following passage and answer the questions.

In his previous life, João — a chubby man with pointy ears and arched black eyebrows — had been stern and serious, prone to squirreling money away. But after suffering a health crisis in 1990, at age 49, he wanted to live differently. "I saw death from close up," he would often say. "Now I want to be in high spirits." And nothing made him happier than giving. To those who didn't know him well, he must have seemed like the embodiment of selflessness — the Saint Francis of Rio de Janeiro.

What's most interesting about João's story, though, is that his new outlook resulted not from a spiritual awakening but from brain damage caused by a stroke. Among other symptoms, he became a chronic insomniac and lost his sex drive; he started forgetting things and had trouble focusing; his movements slowed. And, his neurologist says, he became "pathologically generous" — compulsively driven to give. His carefree attitude toward money led to confrontations with his family, especially his brother-in-law, who co-owned the french-fry cart. But even when his family berated him, and the cart went out of business, and he was reduced to living on his mother's pension, João refused to stop. Giving simply made him too happy. (João died of kidney failure in 1999. His doctor provided only his first name, to protect the family's privacy.)

The history of neuroscience is littered with patients whose behavior changed in bizarre ways after they suffered brain damage. Some people could no longer recognize animals, or couldn't speak but could still sing. For neuroscientists, these cases offer opportunities: by studying how people's behaviors change after brain injuries, they gain insight into what role the injured areas play in everyday tasks. And so it was with João — researchers hoped that his compulsive giving could shed light on normal generosity, helping them understand why human beings give and why, biologically, giving feels good.

24. What triggered João's transformation into a pathologically generous person?
① a spiritual awakening
② brain damage caused by a stroke
③ financial success
④ a new career opportunity

25. Which of the following was NOT a symptom João experienced after his stroke?
① chronic insomnia
② trouble focusing
③ increased sex drive
④ slower movements

26. João's story became an opportunity for neuroscientists to study how brain injuries can affect behavior, offering insights into why humans _____.
① enjoy being generous
② sing when they cannot speak
③ recognize animals differently
④ recover from strokes

27~29 Read the following passage and answer the questions.

A deep childhood bond, a lingering longing and the concept of "inyeon" form the backdrop of *Past Lives* — an achingly beautiful epic love story about two Korean childhood sweethearts who reconnect decades later — which was this year's breakout hit at the Sundance Film Festival. But just what is inyeon? The Korean word refers to Ⓐ "something special" between two people, explained *Past Lives* writer/director Celine Song. The South Korean-born Canadian playwright and filmmaker said that having an inyeon means "you are connected to each other in lives before this one and also that you will be connected in the lives after this one. And in every lifetime, it's going to mean something a little different." The word inyeon first appeared in 1281 in *Samgukyusa*, a collection of legends, folktales and historical accounts relating to the ancient Three Kingdoms of Korea (Goguryeo, Baekje, and Silla), according to Jennifer Jung-Kim, a lecturer at UCLA in Korean and East Asian studies. "It is a Buddhist term, so it likely was used even for centuries before then," she said. Christina Hong Huber, a Korean American licensed clinical psychologist, expanded, saying that inyeon is "a powerful and appealing notion that two people are destined to meet, possibly over multiple lifetimes." Indeed, the film's heroine, Nora (played by Greta Lee), tells her future husband Arthur (John Magaro) one evening: "It's an inyeon if two strangers even walk by each other in the street and their clothes accidentally brush, because it means there must have been something between them in their past lives. If two people get married, they say it's because there are then 8,000 layers of inyeon over 8,000 lifetimes." The pair go on to marry in Manhattan after meeting at a writers' retreat. Inyeon, written as 인연 in Korean, was derived from the Sanskrit words hetu and pratyay. "It can be understood as the sum of one's actions that directly and indirectly lead to a specific reaction," Jung-Kim noted. Essentially, inyeon means fate, karma or destiny, the lecturer concluded.

27 Which of the following is best for the title?

① Inyeon: Karmic Threads Weaving Past and Present Lives
② The Science of Destiny: Concealing Inyeon's Genetic Code
③ Inyeon in Hollywood: Revolutionizing American Cinema
④ Linguistic Origins: The Etymology of Inyeon in Modern Korean

28 Which of the following best interprets Ⓐ?

① karmic attraction between individuals in the present life

② predestined connection across multiple lives, from brief to profound

③ fate intertwining two lives into an intense romantic bond

④ spiritual kinship from childhood, persisting as lifelong affinity

29 Which of the following is NOT mentioned?

① the potential tension between inyeon and individual agency in shaping one's life trajectory

② the linguistic evolution of inyeon from its Sanskrit roots to its current usage in Korean culture

③ the application of inyeon to non-romantic relationships and platonic encounters in daily life

④ the first introduction of inyeon in ancient Korean literature

30~32 Read the following passage and answer the questions.

Plants died, generation after generation, for millions of years. They died in swamps where they could not decay, instead sinking and accumulating into layers of peat that were eventually squeezed and pressed into harder and drier layers of coal. Three-hundred million years later, about 1,100 years before the present, the ground above those long-dead plants was within the area claimed by the first kings of England. Because of these two developments, one geological and one historical, we can talk about England's coal deposits. People living above and on these deposits, most easily accessible along the valleys of the Tyne and Wear Rivers near to the city of Newcastle, had been using them for unknown centuries when they started to ship some southwards during the thirteenth century. The growing city of London, where so many English people came during the long reign of Queen Elizabeth, soon used more of this coal than anywhere else.

Coal, London's people found, was a remarkable resource — we could equally call it a gift — but a gift that also brought heavy costs. Many of these costs fell on those who earned their livings transforming this coal inside the ground into something that could be burned in a fireplace or furnace. Coal mining offered wages to people in areas with cold climates, poor soils and no large cities, but it might have been nearly intolerable work. Ⓐ_____ descended into the dark earth — increasingly far downwards as mines were progressively deepened — crouching and lying down as they hacked the coal away. Others, often their wives or children, then carried or pulled it in baskets upwards towards the light of day, returning again and again for more. Under the best of conditions this must have been very hard work indeed, and conditions must have been very often beset by difficulties like bumpy or wet surfaces. Sometimes, and it is impossible to know how often, roofs collapsed or gases caught fire. We know of a few such mine disasters because outsiders or visitors described them, but most must have been unrecorded.

30 What would be the best title?

① The Use of Dead Plants
② The Investment in Coal Mining
③ The Altering Trend of Coal Consumption
④ The Condition of Mining

31 Which of the following best fits in Ⓐ?

① inspectors
② laborers
③ women and children
④ buyers

32 Which of the following is true?

① English Kings capitalized on the findings of coal deposits.
② Londoners had used coal most in the Elizabethan period.
③ People hired in coal mines make more profit than anywhere.
④ Mine disasters had been well documented.

33~35 Read the following passage and answer the questions.

One thing we notice, comparing the varieties of English now spoken in the United States with those in Britain, is that there is much less variation between one speaker and another, sometimes even if they live on opposite sides of the vast American continent. Ⓐ_____, Britain, where English has been established for 1,500 years, shows noticeable differences between the speech of neighbouring counties or even neighbouring cities. To take an extreme case, one of the present authors has had the experience of taking a two-and-a-half-hour train journey north from Lancaster to Glasgow, and finding the speech of his taxi-driver, a friendly conversationalist, totally incomprehensible. To take the opposite case, a native of California can speak to a native of Ohio, born and brought up 2,000 miles to the east, without either of them noticing major differences of dialect or accent.

This difference is not difficult to explain. Over the centuries, most people in the British Isles have spent all their lives in the localities where they were born. Until the nineteenth century, there was comparatively little movement and mixing of population, even though the British Isles are small enough to fit comfortably inside the single American state of Texas. But in the United States, where the nineteenth century saw an enormous expansion and movement of the English-speaking population, a life of exploring new opportunities in new regions has been traditional and normal. By the standards of world history, the new states of the Midwest and the Far West were settled in an amazingly short period of time, aided by the speed of transportation by rail. It is no surprise that the areas of the United States that do show noticeable variation of dialect are close to the eastern seaboard, in the 13 original states that won independence from Britain. These states were settled before the advent of modern communications, and in them are the well-known dialectal areas of New England (the Northeast) and the Southern States (the "Old South").

33 Which of the following is best for the title?

① English in Crisis: Homogeneity vs. Diversity
② American English: Evolution from British Roots
③ History of English: Immigration and Railroad
④ Nomadism vs. Rootedness: US and UK Linguistic Patterns

34 Which of the following best fits in Ⓐ?

① Therefore
② In addition
③ By contrast
④ For instance

35 Which of the following is true?

① Longer English usage leads to linguistic homogeneity.
② Rapid settlement creates distinct regional dialects.
③ Geographical size determines linguistic variation.
④ Limited mobility fosters speech pattern differences.

36~37 Read the following passage and answer the questions.

Global anthropogenic impacts, such as increases in carbon dioxide in the atmosphere and disturbance to the nitrogen cycle, do not just happen but are consequences, intended or otherwise, of *decisions* taken by human minds. In nature, as we have always understood it, the Ⓐ forces of nature are unconscious and involuntary; no decisions are made, so to comprehend humanity as a geological force we need to consider its distinctive quality, its (1) volitional element. Humankind is perhaps better described not as a geological force but as a geological power, because we have to consider its ability to make decisions as well as its ability to transform matter. Unlike forces of nature, it is a power that can be withheld as well as exercised.

So for the first time in Earth's 4.5 billion-year history we have a non-physical Ⓑ force (which brings about physical effects) mixed in with physical forces, although it is not so much *added* to the pre-existing natural Ⓒ forces but in some sense *infuses* them and modifies their operation. And this new force can be integrated only imperfectly into the system of geodynamics used to explain the geological evolution of the planet. The uncertainty about how this new force will behave is the primary reason for the wide variation in projections of global warming over the twenty-first century. And it now seems certain that as long as humans are on the planet all future epochs, eras, periods, and so on will be hybrids of physical Ⓓ forces and this new power. No wonder there has been deep uneasiness in some sections of the geology profession about adding this weird division to official geochronology.

36 Which of the following is closest meaning to (1)?

① willful   ② dissenting
③ consenting ④ forced

37 Which of the following is DIFFERENT from the others?

① Ⓐ   ② Ⓑ
③ Ⓒ   ④ Ⓓ

38~39 Read the following passage and answer the questions.

Facial-recognition systems use artificial intelligence (AI) to match images to identities. Retrospective facial recognition of the sort being used to pursue rioters compares CCTV footage with suspects; real-time use involves live images being compared with the faces of people who have been placed on "watch lists." The technology was used during King Charles's coronation in 2023. Last year the South Wales Police scanned the faces of more than 819,000 people. In Haringey in north London, around 133 facial scans are performed every minute.

Surveys suggest that Britons accept the arguments for facial recognition. A poll taken in March by the Centre for Emerging Technology and Security and the Alan Turing Institute found that 60% of Britons are comfortable with the police's use of the technology in real time to identify criminals in a crowd. That share is likely to have risen as a result of the riots. Scouring images to find troublemakers takes a lot longer if only humans are involved. The South Wales police force identifies 200 suspects every month using the technology; without facial recognition it takes 14 days on average to find a suspect. Sir Keir Starmer, the prime minister, has pledged to increase use of the technology in response to the disorder this summer.

That adds urgency to questions about how it is regulated. The Investigatory Powers Act, which regulates some forms of surveillance, was recently amended to allow government agencies to use AI to process data sets when there is "no expectation of privacy." But Karen Yeung, a professor of law at Birmingham University, points out that there is no legislation specifically covering facial recognition. "Police forces are guided by a complex patchwork of regulation, which in effect means there is little oversight on the use of the technology."

38 What is one of the primary benefits of using facial-recognition technology in law enforcement?

① It enables faster identification of suspects compared to human efforts alone.
② It eliminates the need for CCTV cameras.
③ It reduces the overall cost of law enforcement.
④ It ensures complete privacy for individuals.

39 What is a key concern regarding the regulation of facial-recognition technology?

① The Investigatory Powers Act bans its use entirely.
② There is no public support for its use by the police.
③ The technology is unable to match images to identities accurately.
④ There is no legislation specifically governing facial-recognition technology.

40~42 Read the following passage and answer the questions.

The Malagasy baobab tree, with its distinctive thick trunks and small branches, is a unique feature of Madagascar's landscape. Surprisingly, this tree has persisted despite facing a significant challenge: the extinction of its primary seed dispersers. Scientists believe that giant tortoises and gorilla-sized giant lemurs, which once roamed the island, were crucial for spreading the baobab's large seeds. With their extinction over a thousand years ago due to human activity, the baobab's survival seemed unlikely. However, research conducted by Seheno Andriantsaralaza at the University of Antananarivo in Madagascar and Onja Razafindratsima at the University of California, Berkeley, has shed light on how these trees have managed to endure.

The researchers and their team conducted fieldwork in western Madagascar, monitoring 15 tree canopies to identify potential new seed dispersers. They employed various methods, including camera traps placed near seed-containing fruits on the ground and examination of animal feces for seeds. Their findings, published in the journal *Biotropica*, revealed that a native rodent, the western tuft-tailed rat, interacted with the baobab fruits. Camera footage captured these rats handling whole fruits on several occasions. Although the cameras didn't record the rats opening the fruits, the team discovered 13 chewed fruits with missing seeds, indicating seed removal by an animal.

Further investigation yielded crucial evidence: baobab seeds were found in seven different piles of bush-pig dung. This discovery is particularly ironic, as bush pigs are believed to have been introduced to Madagascar by humans between 1,000 and 5,000 years ago, coinciding with the extinction of the original seed dispersers. The bush pigs' arrival proved to be a stroke of luck for the baobabs. Studies have confirmed that the passage through the bush pigs' digestive system does not negatively impact seed germination.

This finding highlights the complex role of introduced species in ecosystems. While often viewed negatively, the Malagasy bush pigs have become essential for the survival of a native species. Similar relationships are suspected in other regions, such as the potential role of European rabbits in seed dispersal for plants lacking native distributors in South America. Dr. Andriantsaralaza suggests that a comprehensive assessment of the ecological role of introduced species is necessary before considering eradication efforts. This research underscores the intricate and sometimes unexpected interactions within ecosystems.

40 What was the primary challenge faced by the Malagasy baobab tree?

① the extinction of its original seed dispersers

② competition from other tree species

③ climate change and habitat loss

④ disease and infestation

41 What surprising discovery did the researchers make regarding the baobab seeds?

① They could germinate without passing through an animal's digestive system.

② They were dispersed by wind currents.

③ They were being consumed by insects.

④ They were found in bush-pig dung.

42 What is the main point Dr. Andriantsaralaza makes about introduced species?

① Their ecological roles should be carefully studied before considering eradication.

② They should be eradicated immediately to protect native species.

③ They rarely have any significant impact on native ecosystems.

④ They are always harmful to native ecosystems.

43~45 Read the following passage and answer the questions.

As party invitations fill our calendars and chocolate ads take over our screens during the holiday season, temptations to indulge can feel omnipresent and all-powerful. But this year a neologism is taking over social media that puts a name to this kind of distraction: "food noise." This trendy Ⓐ term could transform the way people see weight loss, turning what for decades has been an internal battle of willpower into an external problem with biological and psychological roots that scientists are only beginning to understand. Contributing to this shift is the widespread adoption of weight loss drugs like Ozempic. Given the way these drugs work, it's not surprising that they quiet thoughts about food: they imitate the hormone GLP-1, which makes people feel full, in addition to slowing the emptying of the stomach and increasing insulin production to control blood sugar. As a result, many users report fewer urges to eat something sugary, fast. They fixate on food less, and so they're less vulnerable near the dessert table. But the reasons people have grasped onto the term "food noise" to describe what was once considered a mere test of willpower are more complex. Dr. Travis Masterson and Daisuke Hayashi at Penn State University published the first study on food noise in the journal *Nutrients* last year, recommending that medical professionals adopt the Ⓑ term to describe an increased susceptibility to eating cues, "leading to food-related intrusive thoughts and maladaptive eating behaviors." While responding to cues to eat is normal — in evolutionary Ⓒ terms, those who find food are more likely to survive and pass on their genes — people who struggle with food noise experience a state "where it has become problematic and maybe difficult to overcome those feelings and thoughts," Masterson said. Hayashi, who is conducting research into the viral spread of the Ⓓ term on TikTok, said "food noise" took off last year, around the time when GLP-1 drugs were beginning to be prescribed more widely after many versions were approved by the FDA for weight loss in 2021.

43 Which of the following is best for the title?

① Food Noise: The New Buzzword Reshaping Our Understanding of Weight Loss
② Ozempic and GLP-1 Drugs: A Revolution in Appetite Control
③ The Evolution of Willpower: From Internal Struggle to External Factors
④ Holiday Temptations: Navigating the Season of Indulgence

44 Which one of the following does NOT refer to the same thing?

① Ⓐ ② Ⓑ
③ Ⓒ ④ Ⓓ

45 Which of the following is true?

① "Food noise" shifts the perception of weight loss from an internal to an external issue.
② Ozempic eliminates "food noise" by manipulating brain reward centers.
③ Medical professionals coined "food noise" to describe GLP-1 drug efficacy.
④ "Food noise" research predates and led to GLP-1 drug development.

46~47 Read the following passage and answer the questions.

Our constitution does not copy the laws of neighbouring states; we are rather a pattern to others than imitators ourselves. Its administration Ⓐ_____; this is why it is called a democracy. If we look to the laws, they afford equal justice to all in their private differences; if no social standing, advancement in public life falls to reputation for capacity, class considerations not being allowed to interfere with merit; nor again does poverty bar the way, if a man is able to serve the state, he is not hindered by the obscurity of his condition. The freedom which we enjoy in our government extends also to our ordinary life. There, far from exercising a jealous surveillance over each other, we do not feel called upon to be angry with our neighbour for doing what he likes, or even to indulge in those injurious looks which cannot fail to be offensive, although they inflict no positive penalty. But all this ease in our private relations does not make us lawless as citizens. Against this fear is our chief safeguard, teaching us to obey the magistrates and the laws, particularly such as regard the protection of the injured, whether they are actually on the statute book, or belong to that code which, although unwritten, yet cannot be broken without acknowledged disgrace.

46 Which of the following best completes Ⓐ?

① favors aristocratic traditions
② favors the many instead of the few
③ falls into the hands of privileged few
④ follows strict hierarchical principles

47 What is the relationship between social standing and public advancement?

① Social standing is the primary factor in public advancement.
② Public advancement depends solely on wealth and class.
③ Merit determines advancement regardless of class considerations.
④ Public advancement is restricted to those of noble birth.

48~50 Read the following passage and answer the questions.

Where do pesticides fit into the picture of environmental disease? We have seen that they now contaminate soil, water, and food, that they have the power to make our streams fishless and our gardens and woodlands silent and birdless. A Man, however much he may like to pretend the contrary, is part of nature. Can he escape a pollution that is now so thoroughly Ⓐ distributed throughout our world?

We know that even single exposures to these chemicals, if the amount is large enough, can precipitate acute poisoning. B But this is not the major problem. The sudden illness or death of farmers, spraymen, pilots, and others exposed to appreciable quantities of pesticides is tragic and should not occur. For the population as a whole, we must be more concerned with (1) the delayed effects of absorbing small amount of the pesticides that invisibly contaminate our world.

Responsible public health officials have pointed out that the biological effects of chemicals are Ⓑ cumulative over long periods of time, and that the hazard to the individual may depend on the sum of the exposures Ⓒ receiving throughout his lifetime. C It is human nature to shrug off what may seem to us a vague threat of future disaster. "Men are naturally most impressed by diseases which have obvious manifestations," says a wise physician, Dr. Rene Dubos, "yet some of their worst enemies creep on them unobtrusively."

But there is also an ecology of the world within our bodies. D In this unseen world Ⓓ minute causes produce mighty effects; the effect, moreover, is often seemingly unrelated to the cause, appearing in a part of the body remote from the area where the original injury was sustained. When one is concerned with the mysterious and wonderful functioning of the human body, cause and effect are seldom simple and easily demonstrated relationships. They may be widely separated both in space and time. To discover the agent of disease and death depends on a patient piecing together of many seemingly distinct and unrelated facts developed through a vast amount of research in widely separated fields.

48 Which of the following is grammatically NOT correct?

① Ⓐ
② Ⓑ
③ Ⓒ
④ Ⓓ

49. Which of the following best fits in?

For these very reasons the danger is easily ignored.

① A
② B
③ C
④ D

50. Which of the following would best explain (1)?

① Humans could be poisoned by toxic spill of pesticides.
② Humans exposed to pesticide can face sudden illness and immediate death.
③ Humans can find the agent of disease and death by themselves.
④ Humans cannot trace the original cause of health crisis.

SOONGSIL UNIVERSITY

숭실대학교

▶ 2025학년도 자연계   ▶ 문항 수: 영어 25문항, 수학 25문항 | 제한시간: 90분

2025 숭실대 자연계 영역별 문항 수

구분	문법			어휘			논리완성	독해	생활영어	총 문항 수
	G/S, W/E	정비문	재진술	동의어	반의어	유추				
문항 수	2			4			4	15		25
백분율	8%			16%			16%	60%		100%

SOONGSIL UNIVERSITY

숭실대학교

▶ 2025학년도 자연계: 영어 25문항, 수학 25문항 · 90분

문항별 배점 01~10 1점 / 11~20 2.5점 / 21~25 3점

01~02 Choose the one that is grammatically NOT correct.

01 The myth ① which practically everyone ② willing to work hard could prosper ③ was widely promulgated ④ by the railroads' land offices.

02 ① Attempt to protect themselves from speculation, the most radical reformers urged that homestead land ② be made inalienable since obviously land ③ that could not be bought or sold could not be speculated upon ④ either.

03~06 Choose the most appropriate word for the blank.

03 The debate grew heated as both parties tried to _____ their positions with evidence and logical arguments.

① contradict ② reinforce
③ obscure   ④ abandon

04 Many companies are striving to adopt sustainable practices to reduce their _____ impact as well as to make money.

① cooperative   ② lucrative
③ environmental ④ intrusive

05 The company has decided to _____ its operations to new international markets in response to increasing global demand.

① condense
② expand
③ contradict
④ evaporate

06 Despite her efforts to explain the situation, his reaction remained _____ and difficult to predict.

① erratic
② lucid
③ systematic
④ consistent

07~10 Choose the expression closest in meaning to the underlined.

07 The scientist presented her findings with <u>clarity</u>, ensuring that even non-experts could understand the complex material.

① confusion
② ambiguity
③ lucidity
④ eloquence

08 Her speech was so <u>eloquent</u> that it moved the audience to tears.

① abrupt
② vague
③ monotonous
④ persuasive

09 The athlete's rigorous training <u>regimen</u> enabled her to surpass her personal record in the competition.

① program
② trainer
③ institution
④ elaboration

10 The book provided a comprehensive overview of the country's history, covering all major events in detail.

① incomplete
② thorough
③ biased
④ selective

11~13 Read the following passage and answer the questions.

I have an entire file in my office of newspaper articles which express concern about illegitimate words that should not have been included in the dictionary, including "LOL" when it got into the *Oxford English Dictionary* and "defriend" when it got into the *Oxford American Dictionary*. I also have articles expressing concern about "invite" as a noun, "impact" as a verb, because only teeth can be impacted, and "incentivize" is described as "boorish, bureaucratic misspeak."

Now, it's not that dictionary editors ignore these kinds of attitudes about language. They try to provide us some guidance about words that are considered slang or informal or offensive, often through usage labels, but they're in something of a bind, because they're trying to describe what we do, and they know that we often go to dictionaries to get information about how we should use a word well or appropriately. In response, the *American Heritage Dictionaries* include usage notes. Usage notes tend to occur with words that are troublesome in one way, and one of the ways that they can be troublesome is that they're changing meaning. Now usage notes involve very human decisions, and I think, as dictionary users, we're often not as aware of those human decisions as we should be. To show you what I mean, we'll look at an example, but before we do, I want to explain what the dictionary editors are trying to deal with in this usage note.

Think about the word "peruse" and how you use that word. I would guess many of you are thinking of skim, scan, reading quickly. Some of you may even have some walking involved, because you're perusing grocery store shelves, or something like that. You might be surprised to learn that if you look in most standard dictionaries, the first definition will be to read carefully, or pore over. *American Heritage* has that as the first definition. They then have, as the second definition, skim, and next to that, they say "usage problem." And then they include a usage note, which is worth looking at.

11 Which of the following would be the most suitable title?

① The Evolution of Slang: A Modern Dictionary
② The Importance of Proper Grammar and Vocabulary
③ How Dictionaries Shape Our Understanding of the World
④ The Dictionary Dilemma: Describing vs. Prescribing Language

12 The writer's office contains newspaper articles about:

① dictionary reform proposals
② language evolution studies
③ controversial word additions
④ modern slang research

13 Which of the following best describes how most people use the word "peruse" versus its traditional dictionary definition?

① Most people use it to mean "read carefully," which matches the primary dictionary definition.
② Most people use it to mean "skim or scan," while dictionaries primarily define it as "read carefully."
③ Most people use it while walking through stores, which is the primary dictionary definition.
④ Most people don't use this word at all, according to the passage.

14~15 Read the following passage and answer the questions.

Compstat (which originally stood for "computer statistics") is a crime analysis and accountability system, first developed by the New York Police Department in 1994. Pioneered under Police Commissioner William J. Bratton, Compstat uses Geographical Information Systems (GIS) to track the incidence of crime. It involves the collection, analysis, and mapping of crime data in a rapid time-frame to discover crime patterns, as well as entailing weekly meetings at which police managers are held accountable for the results in their precinct. The data are used to pinpoint hot spots in which crime is concentrated, and to deploy police resources accordingly. In the decades since it was rolled out in New York, some variation of Compstat has been adopted in many large American cities. Compstat does seem to have contributed to the decline in reported crime — and indeed, to the decline of crime itself.

Yet in city after city, there have been questions about the accuracy and reliability of crime statistics. Insofar as Compstat is a system of informational and indicative metrics, it seems genuinely useful. But when the mayor pressures the top brass to show improvements in the overall numbers, and that pressure, in turn, is placed on the district commanders who are led to believe that their career advancement depends on a steady diminution in crime, the message sometimes heard by lower-level police officers is that they will be penalized for an increase in reported crime. And that creates pressures for fudging the numbers.

Such problems preceded the rise of Compstat and exist independent of it. In 1976 the social psychologist Donald T. Campbell noted that President Richard Nixon's declared crackdown on crime "had as its main effect the corruption of crime-rate indicators, achieved through underrecording and downgrading the crimes to less serious classifications." And Ⓐ that continues.

14 Which statement best describes what Ⓐ refers to?

① the classification of serious crimes
② President Nixon's crackdown on crime
③ the rise of Compstat
④ the corruption of crime-rate indicators

15 Which of the following best represents a potential issue with the Compstat system?

① Pressure to show improved statistics may lead to data manipulation.
② Weekly meetings create excessive administrative burden.
③ The geographical information systems are technologically outdated.
④ Police officers lack proper training to use the system effectively.

16~18 Read the following passage and answer the questions.

Adults are worried about how kids are learning. In the absence of clear data, a lot of parents and educators are fearful of the effects that digital technologies are having on our children and their ability to learn. Slogans, in headline format, they fear, dominate the information seeping into young people's brains, with kids developing too few analytical skills along the way. Kids, the worry goes, are channel-surfing through their education, and their brains are being rewired in the process.

Digital Natives' learning differently from the way their parents did when they were growing up doesn't mean that Digital Natives are not learning. Take, for example, the way that Digital Natives learn about events in the news. Many older people assume that because Digital Natives are not reading newspapers and magazines, but instead absorbing news all day long on various websites (and from comedy programs and other unconventional sources), their understanding of current events is superficial and limited to headlines. And worse, these headlines, parents and teachers worry, come from biased websites, rather than authoritative organizations like the *New York Times* or the big television networks, NBC, ABC, and CBS. If it's not outright wrong, the version of the story Digital Natives encounter online must be superficial, many people fear.

These assumptions are wrong, because they underestimate the depth of knowledge that Digital Natives are obtaining on the Web. They also miss a key feature of how Digital Natives experience news: interacting with information in constructive ways. Digital Natives often access much more information about a topic they are interested in than kids of previous generations ever could have. A recent study of young people and their news-gathering habits confirms these changes. The study found, for example, that young Americans don't read the daily newspaper. Digital Natives pick up bits and pieces of news and information as they go about their day, not in a single sitting at the breakfast table in the morning or in front of the television in the evening. And often, they in fact engage more with the material than those who are used to more traditional news formats, by virtue of writing a post about the idea on a blog or sharing it with a friend on Facebook or over instant messaging.

16 Which of the following would be the most suitable title?

① The Dangers of Digital Technology for Young Minds
② The Importance of Authoritative News Sources for Children
③ The Urgent Need to Adopt Digital Learning Methods
④ How Digital Natives Are Changing the Landscape of Learning

17 What is the main concern of many adults regarding children and digital technologies?

① Children are spending too much time playing video games.
② Digital technologies are hindering children's ability to learn and develop analytical skills.
③ Children are becoming too reliant on social media for communication.
④ Digital technologies are making children less physically active.

18 How do Digital Natives typically learn about current events?

① through a combination of various websites, comedy programs, and other unconventional sources throughout the day
② primarily through reading traditional newspapers and magazines
③ by watching nightly news broadcasts on major television networks
④ through in-depth analysis of articles from authoritative organizations like the *New York Times*

[19~20] Read the following passage and answer the questions.

Similar questions can be asked about social solidarity and civic virtue. Should we try to conserve civic virtue by telling citizens to go shopping until their country needs to call upon them to sacrifice for the common good? Or do civic virtue and public spirit atrophy with disuse? Many moralists have taken the second view. Aristotle taught that virtue is something we cultivate with practice: "we become just by doing just acts, temperate by doing temperate acts, brave by doing brave acts."

Rousseau held a similar view. The more a country asks of its citizens, the greater their devotion to it. "In a well-ordered city every man flies to the assemblies." Under a bad government, no one participates in public life "because no one is interested in what happens there" and "domestic cares are all-absorbing." Civic virtue is built up, not spent down, by strenuous citizenship. Use it or lose it, Rousseau says, in effect. "As soon as public service ceases to be the chief business of the citizens, and they would rather serve with their money than with their persons, the state is not far from its fall."

Sir Dennis H. Robertson, an economist and former student of John Maynard Keynes, offers his observation in a lighthearted, speculative spirit. But the notion that love and generosity are scarce resources that are depleted with use continues to exert a powerful hold on the moral imagination of economists, even if they don't argue for it explicitly. It is not an official textbook principle, like the law of supply and demand. No one has proved it empirically. It is more like an adage, a piece of folk wisdom, to which many economists still subscribe.

19 What is the relationship between civic virtue and its practice?

① Civic virtue is a finite resource that diminishes with use, similar to a financial budget.
② Civic virtue is best preserved by minimizing demands on citizens and allowing them to focus on private life.
③ Civic virtue is an innate quality that remains constant regardless of a citizen's actions.
④ Civic virtue is cultivated and strengthened through practice and active participation in public life.

20 What does Rousseau believe happens when citizens prioritize private interests over public service?

① The state becomes more democratic.
② Citizens lose interest in public life.
③ Civic virtue strengthens.
④ Public assemblies become more vibrant.

21~23 Read the following passage and answer the questions.

Most historians of deaf education have explained the pedagogical reversal by pointing to generational change. Both Harlan Lane and Douglas Baynton argue that the transformation of deaf education from a manually based system to an orally based system can be explained in this way. Lane concludes, "incredible as it may seem, it took only a small voice of hearing educators and businessmen, late in the last century, to release a tidal wave of oralism that swept over Western Europe, drowning all its signing communities. In America, the submersion of sign language was nearly as complete." And Baynton believes that manualism appealed, for a variety of reasons, to a generation of educators raised in the antebellum period, while oralism made more cultural sense to those who came of age after the Civil War.

And yet the first cohesive arguments for oral education came in 1844 from Horace Mann, a figure the accounts by Lane and Baynton disregard. [A] Lane views Mann as a dupe, first of German teachers of the deaf, whose articulation teaching greatly impressed him on a visit to Germany in 1843, and then of Samuel Gridley Howe, who, according to Lane, convinced Mann to praise oralism in order to help Howe "wrest the education of the deaf from Hartford* and place it under his guidance at the Perkins Institute of the Blind." [B] This view ignores the real possibility that Mann may have his own reasons for taking an interest in the issue of deaf education. Baynton likewise downplays Mann's influence in this regard, arguing that though he was "America's pre-eminent educator," the results of his efforts on behalf of oralism were Ⓐ "negligible." According to Baynton, the 1840s were not the right cultural environment for oralism. Manualists romanticized deafness, seeing deaf people as closer to God and blessed by God with a special gift, sign language, that rescued them from silent ignorance. [C] But when Clark School for the Deaf, the first oral school in New England, opened in 1876, the ghost of Mann hovered over the event. Howe invoked Mann's memory at the legislative hearings held to decide the issue of the proposed school's funding and methods. [D]

*Hartford: 1817년 설립된 미국 청각 장애인 교육 및 지도를 위한 정신 병원

21 Which of the following best fits in?

Mann's scientific oralism could not compete with this evangelical piety.

① [A] ② [B]
③ [C] ④ [D]

22 Which of the following best replaces Ⓐ?

① trivial
② neglected
③ regretted
④ unforgettable

23 Which of the following is true?

① The pedagogical change was easily accepted among deaf educators.
② Mann led Howe to praise oralism.
③ Manualism succeeded to replace oralism in the field of deaf education.
④ Howe used Mann's ideas and efforts to finance Clark School for the Deaf.

24~25 Read the following passage and answer the questions.

In the Middle English period, English speakers had become accustomed to importing words from other languages. Words from French, Latin and Greek began to infiltrate English even before the existence of a written standard and, before the end of the Middle Ages, this trickle turned into a torrent. During the Renaissance more than 10,000 recorded new words poured into the language. Today many of these words, such as *adapt*, *benefit* and *exist*, have made their way into everyday language. But most of the Latin loanwords belong to the language of learning and science.

When Renaissance figures like Thomas More and Francis Bacon wrote in English, they often embellished their native tongue with Latinisms. More is the first recorded user of *abolition*, *contradictory*, *exaggerate*, *hyperbole*, *monopoly*, *paradox* and many other words.

The classical languages of Latin and Greek have until recently held a strong position at prestigious English schools and universities, notably the elite universities of Oxford and Cambridge. For a student of high or humble birth, a classical education could open doors to high office.

The influx of Latin words was greater in English than in any other European language, with the possible exception of French. Some words previously borrowed from French were remodelled into closer resemblance with their Latin originals. In some cases Ⓐ this linguistic pedantry overstepped the mark, and English acquired a number of "false Latinisms" — for example, *advance* with the letter *d* inserted (compare French *avance*), and *debt* with an additional *b* (compare French *dette*). Since many classical words had already been borrowed through French, there also appeared doublets — two words of the same origin but with different meaning, such as *corps* vs. *corpse* and *story* vs. *history*.

24 Which of the following best interprets Ⓐ?

① Latin words overwhelmed English's Germanic vocabulary.
② Scholars succeeded in purifying English of non-Latin elements.
③ Overzealous Latinization created incorrect English words.
④ Remodeling French words to Latin forms refined English.

25 Which of the following is true?

① Latin words entered English via French, creating a linguistic hierarchy.
② Classical education was limited to nobility in England.
③ Doublets arose solely from simultaneous Latin and French borrowings.
④ English borrowed more Latin words than most European languages.

아주대학교

▶ 2025학년도 인문계 ▶ 문항 수: 50문항 | 제한시간: 90분

2025 아주대 인문계 영역별 문항 수

구분	문법			어휘			논리완성	독해	생활영어	총 문항 수
	G/S, W/E	정비문	재진술	동의어	반의어	유추				
문항 수	4						10	36		50
백분율	8%						20%	72%		100%

AJOU UNIVERSITY

아주대학교

2025학년도 인문계: 50문항 · 90분

01~05 Choose the word that best completes the sentence.

01 In a study published in the Journal of Melittology, an international research team examined the heat tolerance of bees and flies across tropical and subtropical regions in the Americas. They found that rising temperatures pose a greater _____ to flies than bees, as bees tolerate higher temperatures and occupy a wider range of habitats. [0.8점]

① aspiration   ② condition   ③ question
④ relief   ⑤ threat

02 Sherlock Holmes, the fictional sleuth who famously resides on Baker Street, is known for his impressive powers of logical _____. With a quick visual sweep of a crime scene, he generates hypotheses, gathers observations and draws inferences that ultimately reveal the responsible criminal's methods and identity. [0.8점]

① decision   ② decoding   ③ reasoning
④ reminiscing   ⑤ resolution

03 A digital footprint — sometimes called a digital shadow or an electronic footprint — refers to the _____ of data you leave when using the internet. It includes websites you visit, emails you send, and information you submit online. A digital footprint can be used to track a person's online activities and devices. [0.8점]

① content   ② list   ③ pattern
④ trail   ⑤ volume

04 Josephine Garis Cochran invented the first modern dishwasher in the 1880s. Unlike previous attempts at dishwashing machines, which used scrubbers on the dishes, Cochran's machine cleaned dishes with water pressure. Cochran founded her own company to manufacture and sell her invention, and continuously improved it. After her death, the KitchenAid brand acquired her company and used her _____ to build and sell its dishwashers. [0.8점]

① patents ② patients ③ patrons
④ patterns ⑤ potent

05 In literature, as in life, people often see growth, change, and _____ conflict carried out in a single character. The term one-dimensional character in a book review or story refers to a character who lacks depth and who never seems to learn or grow. When a character is one-dimensional, he or she does not demonstrate a sense of learning in the course of a story. Authors may use such a character to highlight a certain trait; usually, it is an undesirable one. [0.8점]

① imminent ② indifferent ③ individual
④ internal ⑤ interpersonal

06~10 Choose the expression that best fits the sentence.

06 The researcher's findings _____ the validity of the existing model, prompting further inquiry into its assumption. [1.0점]

① build upon ② call into question ③ draw upon
④ shed light on ⑤ take part with

07 The policy framework was _____ to provide flexibility for future technological advancements. [1.1점]

① consisted of ② dismissed as ③ centered around
④ pushed against ⑤ put in place

08 The policy changes, _____ a more equitable system, have been welcomed by the public. [1.0점]

① because of
② getting ahead of
③ lending support to
④ resulting in
⑤ standing apart from

09 The team's innovative strategy _____ new possibilities for treating chronic diseases. [1.0점]

① breaks into
② derives from
③ narrows down
④ opens up
⑤ stands against

10 The newly proposed hypothesis _____ established theoretical frameworks and accumulated empirical evidence in the field of cognitive science. [1.1점]

① allows for
② gives rise to
③ is consistent with
④ revolves around
⑤ sets up

(11~14) Choose the underlined word or phrase that must be changed for the sentence to be correct.

11 ① If you are a perfectionist, you are probably familiar with the feeling of wanting to get everything just right. You ② may struggle with handing in papers, agonize over projects ③ at work, and even worry about small errors from the past. High standards are one thing, but perfectionism is quite ④ other. ⑤ As some researchers have discovered, pursuing perfection can have serious consequences to both mental and physical well-being. [1.0점]

12. Emoji, though simple in form, have emerged as a universal language that transcends linguistic barriers, enabling global communication. This phenomenon is evident on Instagram, where ① nearly 40% of captions contain emoji, ② rising to over 63% in countries like Finland. As emoji use grows, Internet slang like "Lol" ③ has been declined, suggesting a correlation between the two. Instagram engineer Thomas Dimson notes that emoji now offer a near-universal means of expression. ④ Despite a limit of around 700 characters, users creatively combine emoji to convey sentiments. Instagram's success itself reflects this visual communication ⑤ with images often replacing text as a powerful expressive tool.

[1.1점]

13. A study revealed that remote work has impacted people's social and communication skills. With 78% ① having worked remotely, four in ten individuals reported their social skills declined due to the lack of in-person interactions. ② Not only do remote workers communicate ③ fewer than 4.2 times weekly but this limited interaction also hinders the development of both verbal and written skills. Younger employees, particularly those aged 16 to 24, ④ were most affected with 52% noticing a decline in their ability to connect effectively. While written skills improved in some cases, verbal skills, including public speaking and active listening, suffered considerably. Many companies ⑤ are considering to implement strategic training programs to help employees regain these essential soft skills as they transition back to the office environment.

[1.0점]

14. Reading, like writing, is a creative activity ① through which a reader can construct meanings. When you read any text, you do not merely take meaning from it by recognizing the signs. The purpose of reading is not merely to "get the facts" or "remember what you read." To read is ② to make what you read your own by seeing relationships between what you already know and the new information that you encounter as you read. That is, what you have already thought and experienced ③ interact with what you discover in the text. The most effective beginning of this process is recalling what you know about a subject before you even begin to read the new material. Reading is not the neat, orderly process it seems to be ④ when you look at words marching across white pages. Reading involves thinking about ⑤ what has been and what will be; it involves going forward and going backward.

[1.1점]

15~18 Choose the number with the correct set of statements that can be restated or inferred from the original text.

15 A schema is a cognitive structure that serves as a framework for one's knowledge about people, places, objects, and events. Schemas help people organize their knowledge of the world and understand new information. While these mental shortcuts are useful in helping us make sense of the large amount of information we encounter on a daily basis, they can also narrow our thinking and result in stereotypes. [1.1점]

> Ⓐ People rely on schemas to process unfamiliar or complex information more quickly.
> Ⓑ Mental shortcuts known as schemas can shape our understanding of new information based on existing knowledge.
> Ⓒ People without schemas are better at understanding new information.
> Ⓓ Schemas ensure that people assess new information with objectivity.

① Ⓐ & Ⓑ
② Ⓑ & Ⓒ
③ Ⓐ & Ⓒ
④ Ⓐ, Ⓑ & Ⓓ
⑤ Ⓑ, Ⓒ & Ⓓ

16 Memory is a vital cognitive function enabling humans to encode, store, and retrieve information. The encoding stage transforms sensory input into a form that can be stored, influenced by factors like focus and the emotional or contextual significance of the material. Stored memories are classified as short-term or long-term, with long-term memory offering greater stability through a consolidation process where memories are reinforced and strengthened. Retrieval, the act of recalling stored information, depends on effective cues and can be hindered by interference or decay. Memory retention and recall can also be enhanced by strategies like spaced repetition, contextual associations, and emotional engagement. [1.1점]

ⓐ Memory is a multi-stage process involving the transformation, storage, and retrieval of information.
ⓑ Long-term memory requires active recall to remain accessible, whereas short-term memory does not.
ⓒ Emotional experiences can strengthen the encoding process, making memories easier to retain and recall.
ⓓ Retention is not solely dependent on effective cues for recall but can be actively improved through deliberate techniques.

---

① ⓐ & ⓑ
② ⓐ & ⓒ
③ ⓑ & ⓓ
④ ⓐ, ⓒ & ⓓ
⑤ ⓑ, ⓒ & ⓓ

17 Researchers have found that certain animals, including dolphins, elephants, and some primates, exhibit behaviors indicative of self-awareness. These behaviors involve recognizing themselves in mirrors and responding differently to their own reflections compared to those of other animals. For example, they may use a mirror to inspect parts of their bodies that they cannot see directly. This is a behavior unique to species with advanced cognitive abilities. Self-awareness is regarded as a hallmark of higher intelligence, which is rarely observed in the animal kingdom. This discovery challenges the long-standing assumption that self-awareness and similar cognitive traits are uniquely human, opening new discussions on animal intelligence. [1.1점]

Ⓐ The discovery of self-awareness in animals suggests that human cognitive abilities may not be entirely unique.
Ⓑ Self-awareness is seen as a key indicator of advanced cognitive abilities observed in only a few animal species.
Ⓒ Animal behaviors and cognitive traits have not been widely researched until the discovery of self-awareness in certain species.
Ⓓ The observation of self-awareness in animals has led to deeper understanding into the complexity and diversity of animal intelligence.

① Ⓐ & Ⓑ
② Ⓑ & Ⓒ
③ Ⓐ, Ⓑ & Ⓓ
④ Ⓐ, Ⓒ & Ⓓ
⑤ Ⓑ, Ⓒ & Ⓓ

18 Culture is a term that refers to a large and diverse set of mostly intangible aspects of social life. According to sociologists, culture consists of the values, beliefs, systems of language, communication, and practices that people share in common and that can be used to define them as a collective. Culture also includes the material objects that are common to that group or society. Culture is distinct from social structure and economic aspects of society, but it is connected to them — both continuously informing them and being informed by them. Common cultures include those shaped by regional traditions, religious beliefs, and historical experiences. [1.1점]

> Ⓐ Culture encompasses not only intangible aspects but also the material objects that a group or society holds in common.
> Ⓑ Although it differs from social structure and economic aspects, culture continuously interacts with them.
> Ⓒ A shared language system can fully determine a group's cultural identity.
> Ⓓ Cultural practices serve as markers that can distinguish one collective from another.

① Ⓐ & Ⓑ
② Ⓐ & Ⓒ
③ Ⓐ, Ⓑ & Ⓓ
④ Ⓐ, Ⓒ & Ⓓ
⑤ Ⓑ, Ⓒ & Ⓓ

19~50 Read each passage and answer the corresponding questions for each.

19~22

A When it comes to global mass marketing, few companies can rival the Ⓐ prowess of Coca-Cola. Recognized as the most iconic and best-selling soft drink in history, Coca-Cola's dominance is underscored by its annual marketing budget of nearly $3 billion and Ⓑ revenues exceeding $30 billion. Consistently topping the interbrand rankings, Coca-Cola holds a current brand value of $68 billion with its ubiquitous presence in over 200 countries making it the best-known product in the world. ❶

B The history of Coke's success is nothing short of extraordinary. The drink was formulated in 1886 by Dr. John S. Pemberton, who mixed a syrup of his own invention with carbonated water, initially as a remedy for headaches. The company's first president, Asa Griggs Candler, later turned the product into a pop culture phenomenon by pioneering innovative marketing strategies. His use of branded Ⓒ paraphernalia — ranging from clocks to posters — cemented Coca-Cola's place in consumers' daily lives and integrated it into popular culture. ❷

C From its inception, Coca-Cola recognized that the brand should foster emotional and social connections with the masses to gain worldwide success. The company adopted the philosophy of making the product "within arm's length of desire." So the company prioritized expansive distribution networks and strove to make the product loved by all. ❸ A testament to this strategy was its initiative during World War II: promising that "every man in uniform gets a bottle of Coca-Cola for 5 cents, wherever he is, and whatever it costs the company." This approach not only introduced the beverage to international markets but also cultivated a positive brand association in a time of Ⓓ turmoil.

D What distinguishes Coca-Cola from its competitors is its unparalleled ability to craft uplifting global campaigns that transcend linguistic and cultural boundaries. Coca-Cola's marketing has consistently emphasized the product's ability to quench thirst while connecting individuals from diverse walks of life. ❹ Andy Warhol said it best, "A Coke is a Coke and no amount of money can get you a better Coke than the bum on the corner is drinking." One of Coca-Cola's most memorable commercials, "Hilltop," released in 1971, exemplifies this sentiment. Featuring young adults from all over the world united on a hillside in Italy, the ad celebrated harmony and universal Ⓔ camaraderie through the song "I'd like to buy the world a Coke." The commercial touched so many consumers emotionally and so effectively showed the worldwide appeal of Coke that the song became a top-ten hit, further solidifying Coca-Cola's Global appeal. ❺

19 Which statement best summarizes the main idea of the passage above? [1.1점]

① Coca-Cola's success lies in its marketing strategies and emotional branding.
② Coca-Cola's focus on product development has ensured its global dominance.
③ Coca-Cola's advertising campaigns are universally resonant and culturally localized.
④ Coca-Cola is the best-selling soft drink globally, supported by the success of a logo song.
⑤ Coca-Cola has established itself as a global brand through innovation and perseverance.

20 Which of the following pairs includes an expression that CANNOT replace the underlined expression in the passage above? [0.8점]

① Ⓐ prowess — supremacy
② Ⓑ revenues — profits
③ Ⓒ paraphernalia — merchandise
④ Ⓓ turmoil — instability
⑤ Ⓔ camaraderie — courage

21 The following sentence is removed from the passage. In which part may it be inserted to support the argument made by the author? [1.0점]

In fact, Coca-Cola is such a global phenomenon that its name is the second-most understood word in the world (*after okay*).

① ❶   ② ❷   ③ ❸
④ ❹   ⑤ ❺

22 Which of the following is NOT part of Coca-Cola's marketing strategies? [1.1점]

① Crafting globally resonant campaigns that transcend cultural and linguistic barriers
② Distributing branded paraphernalia to promote the brand and integrate it into popular culture
③ Launching initiatives to highlight Coca-Cola's superior benefits compared to other beverages on the market
④ Supplying Coca-Cola for military personnel at a reasonable cost as a morale booster to enhance its association with wartime efforts
⑤ Building emotional connections with consumers by emphasizing universal themes such as harmony and connection in its advertisements

23~26

A Imagine observing Earth from space. Most individuals would say the North Pole would be the roof of the world, but strictly speaking, there is no scientific justification for this perspective. For centuries, civilizations have depicted the world differently, guided by their beliefs and geographic priorities. Ancient Egyptians positioned east at the top, reflecting the position of the sunrise, while early Islamic cartography favored south at the top, as many Muslim cultures resided north of Mecca, orienting their maps "upward" toward it. Early Chinese maps placed the emperor in the north, signifying the political Ⓐ hierarchy in which subjects looked up to their sovereign. When European explorers, such as Christopher Columbus, navigated by the North Star, they described the world with east at the top as they envisioned it leading to paradise.

B The turning point for north-up mapping came with Mercator's world map in 1569, which revolutionized navigation. This map accounted for Earth's Ⓑ curvature, enabling sailors to cross vast distances. However, Mercator's choice of placing north at the top was practical rather than symbolic. As Europeans spearheaded global exploration in the northern hemisphere with extensive landmasses to chart, the convention of north-up mapping gained momentum. North-up maps became standard and profoundly shaped our perception of the world.

C Scientifically, the notion of a "top" or a "bottom" to Earth is Ⓒ devoid of inherent meaning. Earth lines up along the same orbital plane as all of the other planets in the solar system, rendering this orientation Ⓓ arbitrary. From a different vantage point in space, Earth could just as easily be depicted inverted. There is no universal "up" or "down" in the cosmos. Nevertheless, our adherence to north-up mapping has subtle but significant psychological consequences. Research shows that people unconsciously associate north with "up" and "good," while south is equated with "down" and "bad." This cognitive bias affects how people perceive maps and regions of the world.

D Brian Meier found that people shown a city map were more likely to prefer living in the northern areas and associated wealthier individuals with the north. The bias disappeared when the map was flipped, suggesting a simple way to challenge these Ⓔ ingrained perceptions. South-up maps offer a fresh perspective on the world. Daniel Mortlock supports this idea, saying flipping the map makes the world feel unexplored again. Changing perspectives might help foster fairness in how we see our planet by encouraging a fresh look at a map and reducing regional biases.

23 Which of the following would be the best title for the passage above? [1.1점]

① The Evolution of World Maps
② How Maps Shape Our Perspectives
③ Challenging Traditional Views of the Earth
④ The Science of Earth's Orientation and its Map
⑤ The Scientific Discovery That Changed Navigation

24 According to the passage above, which of the following areas is LEAST likely to have influenced the formation of the world map? [1.0점]

① astrology　　② culture　　③ geography
④ religion　　⑤ psychology

25 Which of the following pairs includes an expression that CANNOT replace the underlined expression in the passage above? [0.8점]

① Ⓐ hierarchy — structure
② Ⓑ curvature — sphericity
③ Ⓒ devoid — absent
④ Ⓓ arbitrary — ambiguous
⑤ Ⓔ ingrained — deep-seated

26 According to the passage above, which of the following is NOT true? [1.1점]

① Ancient Egyptian maps placed east at the top, reflecting the position of the sunrise.
② Early Islamic maps often placed south at the top because many Muslim cultures were north of Mecca and oriented their maps to look "up" toward it.
③ European explorers like Columbus adopted north-up maps because they relied heavily on the North Star during their expeditions.
④ The continued use of north-up maps carries subtle but profound societal consequences, influencing how individuals perceive and evaluate different regions of the world.
⑤ By incorporating Earth's curvature into its design, the Mercator map marked a revolutionary advancement in navigation, enabling sailors to traverse vast distances.

[27~30]

A Have you ever noticed the water in a bathtub sloshing back and forth after being disturbed? That simple motion is a miniature example of a seiche wave, a captivating natural phenomenon that occurs in large bodies of water such as lakes, reservoirs, or bays. A seiche wave is a rhythmic oscillation of water, much like the back-and-forth movement of a swinging pendulum, in a closed or partially enclosed basin. ❶ Triggered by external forces such as strong winds, atmospheric pressure changes, or even seismic activities, these waves are not only mesmerizing but also potentially powerful with the ability to flood shores and cause damage.

B ❷ On the surface, they may seem like gentle ripples or ordinary movements of water, but their hidden energy can escalate into significant surges. One striking example occurred in 1954 when a seiche wave in Lake Michigan caused water levels to rise dramatically along the Chicago shoreline, producing waves up to 10 feet high. This event, which caught residents by surprise, serves as a reminder of how natural forces can impact human lives. ❸ Unlike tsunamis, which are single, powerful waves typically caused by underwater earthquakes, seiche waves oscillate repeatedly with their motion persisting for hours or even days.

C Understanding the science behind seiches reveals the interplay of Ⓐ_____ and Ⓑ_____. When forces like winds or changes in pressure disturb the water, gravity works to restore balance by creating an oscillatory motion. ❹ The frequency and intensity of the seiche depend on the size, depth, and shape of the water body. Long and narrow lakes are particularly susceptible to intense seiches as their size and shape amplify the oscillations. For instance, Lake Geneva in Switzerland is known for its frequent seiches, which have been documented as far back as the 19th century.

D Seiche waves also demonstrate the interconnectedness of natural phenomena. They often occur alongside other events, such as storms or earthquakes, acting as a silent partner to these larger, more visible occurrences. ❺ In some ways, seiches reflect nature's hidden rhythms, a reminder of the delicate balance that governs the natural world. Their existence underscores the power of forces we often overlook, offering insights into the complexity of our planet.

27 Which set best fills in the blanks Ⓐ and Ⓑ in paragraph Ⓒ? [1.1점]

① anatomy and geology
② chemistry and geology
③ ecology and geometry
④ physics and geography
⑤ physiology and geochemistry

28 Which of the following questions is NOT answered in the passage above? [1.0점]

① How do seiche waves differ from tsunamis?
② What are the primary triggers of seiche waves?
③ How does basin geometry influence seiche oscillations?
④ Which types of water bodies are most prone to seiche waves?
⑤ What specific effects do seiche waves have on ecosystems and biodiversity?

29 The following sentence is removed from the passage above. In which part may it be inserted to support the argument made by the author? [1.0점]

The deceptive nature of seiche waves makes them especially intriguing.

① ❶   ② ❷   ③ ❸
④ ❹   ⑤ ❺

30 Which of the following is LEAST likely to be inferred from the passage? [1.1점]

① The physical characteristics of lakes, such as their shape and depth, play a vital role in amplifying seiche wave activity.
② The oscillatory motion of seiche waves can persist for long periods, making their effects unpredictable and sometimes dangerous.
③ Seiche waves are predominantly caused by seismic activities, making them closely associated with regions highly prone to earthquakes.
④ Historical records and observations provide valuable insights into the frequency and characteristics of seiche waves in specific locations.
⑤ The study of seiche waves reveals the complex interplay of natural forces, including wind, atmospheric pressure, and gravitational forces.

31~34

A Ellis Island is a historical site that opened in 1892 as an immigration station, a purpose it served for more than 60 years until it closed in 1954. Located at the mouth of the Hudson River between New York and New Jersey, Ellis Island saw millions of newly arrived immigrants pass through its doors. In fact, it has been estimated that close to 40% of all current U.S. citizens can trace at least one of their ancestors to Ellis Island.

B When Ellis Island opened, a great change was taking place in U.S. immigration. Fewer arrivals were coming from northern and western Europe — Germany, Ireland, Britain and the Scandinavian countries — as more and more immigrants poured in from southern and eastern Europe. Among this new generation were Jews escaping from political and economic oppression in czarist Russia and eastern Europe and Italians escaping poverty in their country. There were also Poles, Hungarians, Czechs, Serbs, Slovaks, and Greeks, along with non-Europeans from Syria, Turkey, and Armenia. The reasons they left their homes in the Old World included war, drought, famine, or religious persecution with hopes for greater opportunity in the New World.

C After an arduous sea voyage, immigrants arriving at Ellis Island were tagged with information from their ship's registry; they then waited in long lines for medical and legal inspections to determine if they were fit for entry into the United States. From 1900 to 1914 — the peak years of Ellis Island's operation — an average of 1,900 people passed through the immigration station every day. Most successfully passed through in a matter of hours, but others could be detained for days or weeks. Many immigrants remained in New York, while others traveled by barge to railroad stations in Hoboken or Jersey City, New Jersey, on their way to destinations across the country.

D Passage of the Emergency Quota Act of 1921 and the National Origins Act of 1924, which limited the number and nationality of immigrants allowed into the United States, effectively ended the era of mass immigration into New York City. At this point, a smaller number of immigrants began to be processed on their arriving ships, with Ellis Island serving primarily as a temporary detainment center. From 1925 to the closing of Ellis Island in 1954, only 2.3 million immigrants passed through the New York City port — which still represented more than half of all those entering the United States.

31 According to the passage above, why is it estimated that 40% of current U.S. citizens can trace their ancestry to Ellis Island? [1.0점]

① Because Ellis Island was the only port of entry on the East Coast
② Because only Ellis Island recorded accurate family records in the U.S.
③ Because no immigrants were permitted to settle in other parts of the country
④ Because northern and western Europeans exclusively used Ellis Island for immigration
⑤ Because so many immigrants passed through Ellis Island during its peak operation years

32 Which of the following is most likely to be inferred about the shift in U.S. immigration that occurred when Ellis Island opened? [1.1점]

① European immigration ceased in favor of Middle Eastern arrivals.
② The overall flow of immigrants through New York decreased significantly.
③ The new wave of immigrants had more uniform religious and cultural backgrounds.
④ Immigrants from Asia were the majority group entering the United States at that time.
⑤ An increasing number of arrivals from southern and eastern Europe supplanted those from northern and western Europe.

33 What was the primary function of Ellis Island from 1925 to 1954? [0.8점]

① A commercial port for cargo ships
② A temporary holding center with fewer arrivals
③ A major processing station for immigrants from around the globe
④ A facility exclusively devoted to returning exiled American citizens
⑤ A tourist destination emphasizing the scenic views of New York Harbor

34 Which of the following can be inferred about the cultural diversity among immigrants arriving at Ellis Island? [1.0점]

① Arrivals were primarily from English-speaking countries.
② Most immigrants shared the same language background.
③ Immigrants were required to adopt English as their only language.
④ Many immigrants brought varied languages, religions, and traditions.
⑤ Immigrants hoped to avoid English language requirements in New York.

35~38

A Narcissists often irritate friends and family by boasting about their achievements, which may seem like a sign of excessive self-esteem. However, new research led by Virgil Zeigler-Hill, a psychology professor at Oakland University, reveals that some narcissists actually have low self-esteem, but their self-aggrandizing behavior isn't aimed at boosting self-esteem but is driven by a desire for status. The research is a new piece of evidence that runs counter to the idea that self-esteem issues drive narcissism.

B Zeigler-Hill explains, "What they really care about is navigating status hierarchies. They care about being better than other people, about being respected and admired, and about the benefits that come from high status." While self-esteem reflects how individuals feel about themselves, status perception is concerned with how they believe others view them. Although almost everyone cares about their social perception, for narcissists, status-seeking plays a disproportionately significant role in their self-concept.

C Individuals with narcissistic personality disorder exhibit extreme grandiosity about themselves and a lack of empathy for others. However, even those who do not qualify for the disorder can display narcissistic traits such as arrogance, a need for external validation, and expectations of being recognized as superior. Psychologists believed these behaviors were driven by the need to enhance and protect self-esteem, but in recent years, a more nuanced view has emerged. There are different types of narcissism, and some types do have inflated self-esteem, while others tend to actually have low self-esteem. Zeigler-Hill's work has also focused on the notion that self-esteem isn't a narcissist's main problem. According to Zeigler-Hill, narcissists are primarily desperate for status, and their self-esteem is often a byproduct of feeling admired rather than the driving force behind their behavior.

D To test this idea, Zeigler-Hill and his study co-author Jennifer Vonk, a cognitive psychologist at Oakland University, recruited undergraduate psychology students to take surveys on their levels of narcissistic traits. The researchers found that students' level of self-esteem differed by the kinds of narcissistic traits they reported. Students higher in a subtype of narcissism called "narcissistic admiration" did indeed have high self-esteem. These individuals tend to strive for top positions in social hierarchies but do so through charm and engagement, involving self-promotion and bragging in moderation, which allows them to maintain good relationships. In contrast, those high in "narcissistic rivalry" perceive the world as a zero-sum game. They experience significant envy and jealousy when others receive respect or admiration, believing that such praise diminishes their own status. Consequently, individuals with narcissistic rivalry often struggle to get along with others and tend to have lower self-esteem.

35 Which of the following best represents the passage above? [1.0점]

① Narcissists prioritize internal validation over others' perceptions.
② Narcissists seek external validation solely to protect their self-esteem.
③ Narcissistic behavior is driven by seeking social status over self-esteem.
④ All types of narcissists exhibit inflated self-esteem as their defining trait.
⑤ Narcissistic admiration and rivalry primarily differ in their focus on self-esteem.

36 What distinguishes the two types of narcissism described in the passage? [1.0점]

① Narcissistic admiration prioritizes self-promotion, while rivalry prioritizes humility.
② Narcissistic admiration involves hostility, while rivalry seeks harmonious relationships.
③ Narcissistic admiration seeks internal validation, whereas rivalry relies on external validation.
④ Narcissistic admiration is associated with high self-esteem, while rivalry is linked to low self-esteem.
⑤ Narcissistic admiration views the world as zero-sum, while rivalry sees mutual success opportunities.

37 Which of the following is LEAST likely to be inferred from the passage? [1.1점]

① People with narcissistic traits care significantly about how others perceive them.
② All individuals with narcissistic traits exhibit low self-esteem as their primary characteristic.
③ Narcissistic admiration involves behaviors like self-promotion and charm to navigate social hierarchies.
④ Those high in narcissistic admiration tend to have better social interactions than those high in narcissistic rivalry.
⑤ Narcissistic rivalry is often associated with feelings of envy and jealousy due to a zero-sum perception of the world.

38 Which of the following would most enhance the persuasiveness of Zeigler-Hill's research in paragraph D? [1.1점]

① Using a single cultural context to reduce variations in social norms and values
② Conducting long-term studies to observe whether narcissistic traits evolve over time
③ Limiting the scope of the study to focus solely on individuals with high self-esteem
④ Only including participants who have been clinically diagnosed with narcissistic personality disorder
⑤ Including a more diverse sample population that goes beyond undergraduate psychology students

[A] Most scholars accept that William Shakespeare was born in Stratford-upon-Avon, and spent time acting in London before returning to Stratford, where he lived until his death in 1616. But actual documentation of his life is pitifully scarce: little more than several signatures, records of his marriage to Anne Hathaway and the birth of their children, a three-page will, and some business papers unrelated to writing. Above all, nothing has been found documenting the composition of the more than 36 plays and 154 sonnets attributed to him, collectively considered the greatest body of work in the history of the English language.

[B] In the absence of such "proof" of authorship, some skeptics have posed the question: How could a man of such humble origins and education come by such wealth of insight, wide-ranging understanding of complex legal and political matters, and intimate knowledge of life in the English court? Since the 19th century, a roster of famous people — Henry James, Sigmund Freud, Mark Twain, Helen Keller, Charlie Chaplin, and many others — have voiced their doubts about the man from Stratford. Thousands of books and articles have been devoted to the subject, many of which propose their own candidates for the true author of the Shakespeare canon.

[C] Essayist Francis Bacon and playwright Christopher Marlowe may have their supporters, but for the last 90 years, the favored candidate has been Edward de Vere, the 17th Earl of Oxford. First proposed in 1920 by J.T. Looney in his book *'Shakespeare' Identified*, Oxford was highly educated, trained as a lawyer, and was known to have traveled to many of the exact places featured in Shakespeare's plays. Oxfordians — as those who believe in de Vere's authorship of the Bard's works are known — argue that he concealed his identity because his works were so politically provocative, and he wished to avoid being outed as a lowly playwright.

[D] But until hard evidence surfaces linking his plays to someone else, the man with the strongest claim to the plays of William Shakespeare appears to be — William Shakespeare. For one thing, Oxford died in 1604, and some of Shakespeare's greatest plays including *King Lear*, *The Tempest*, and *Macbeth* were published after that date. Shakespeare's supporters — known as Stratfordians — highlight existing evidence such as the printed copies of his plays and sonnets with his name on them, theater company records, and comments by contemporaries like Ben Jonson and John Webster. Doubts about Shakespeare's authorship and attempts to identify a more educated, worldly and high-born candidate, Stratfordians contend, reveal not only misguided snobbery but a striking disregard for one of the most outstanding qualities of the Bard's extraordinary work — his imagination.

39 According to the passage above, which of the following is NOT true? [1.0점]

① Some people claim that Shakespeare's works were written by someone else.
② Shakespeare's primary records include signatures, marriage records, and his will.
③ Thousands of books and articles have posed questions on Shakespeare's authorship.
④ Most scholars maintain that Shakespeare was born and died in Stratford-upon-Avon.
⑤ There is evidence detailing how Shakespeare composed his 36 plays and 154 sonnets.

40 Which one was NOT a skeptic of Shakespeare's authorship? [0.8점]

① Charlie Chaplin
② Christopher Marlowe
③ Henry James
④ Mark Twain
⑤ J.T. Looney

41 Based on the passage above, which of the following best represents the main reason why some people doubted Shakespeare's authorship? [1.0점]

① They thought Shakespeare's contemporaries did not hold him in high esteem.
② They maintained that numerous documents challenged Shakespeare's authenticity.
③ They claimed Shakespeare's name never appeared in performance records of the time.
④ They argued the themes of Shakespeare's works were too broad and varied to have been written by a single person.
⑤ They questioned how someone of Shakespeare's background and limited education could possess such broad knowledge and insight.

42 According to the passage above, which of the following is NOT a claim made by those who believed Shakespeare was the real author of the Shakespeare canon? [1.1점]

① The scarcity of documentary evidence conclusively proved Shakespeare did author the plays.
② Shakespeare's known association with leading London theater companies supported his authorship.
③ Several of Shakespeare's most famous plays were published after Edward de Vere's death in 1604.
④ Searching for a more aristocratic or educated candidate disregarded the extraordinary imagination evident in Shakespeare's works.
⑤ Printed copies bearing Shakespeare's name, along with references by contemporaries like Ben Jonson and John Webster, strongly supported his authorship.

43~46

A. Each language in the world utilizes a unique set of sounds, and remarkably, human infants are born with the ability to distinguish between all of them. During their early months, babies are receptive to an extensive variety of sounds, making them capable of learning any language. That ability, however, starts weakening by their first birthday. According to Patricia Kuhl from the University of Washington, infants gradually focus on the sounds Ⓐ <u>most prevalent</u> in their native language. This phenomenon, called the Perceptual Magnet Effect, shows how speech sounds Ⓑ <u>that are frequently encountering</u> attract similar sounds by filtering out less relevant ones. This fine-tuning process primes infants' brains to acquire the specific language they are exposed to during their first year.

B. A recent study has investigated further that even the first cries of newborns may offer insights into early language acquisition. In 2009, Dr. Kathleen Wermke and her team discovered that newborns already display cry patterns influenced by the languages they heard in the utero. For instance, German newborns often cry with a falling pitch, resembling the intonation patterns of German whereas French infants tend to cry with a rising pitch by echoing the French language's intonation. These findings suggest that language exposure begins influencing infants before birth and that newborns Ⓒ <u>may already be attempting</u> to mimic the melodic contours of their native language through their cries.

C. Dr. Wermke's lab houses an archive of a half-million recordings of babies from Ⓓ <u>as far as</u> Cameroon and China. Quantitative acoustic analysis of these recordings has produced further insights into the factors that shape a baby's first sounds. Newborns, whose mothers speak tonal languages, such as Mandarin, tend to produce cry melodies with a significantly higher variation. Similarly, Nso infants in Cameroon exhibited more intensive pitch fluctuation in comparison with non-tonal German neonates. "Their crying sounds more like chanting," says Prof. Wermke. These findings highlight that the building blocks for language development Ⓔ <u>are laid from birth</u> long before babies begin babbling or forming words. Early exposure to language, even in the womb, shapes the remarkable journey of linguistic development.

D. The results contribute to a better understanding of essential influencing factors on the earliest phases of speech development. At the same time, they improve the possibility to identify early indicators that provide reliable information about any developmental disorders at a very early stage. However, many questions remain to be clarified before these findings can be used in clinical practice.

43 Which of the following would be the best title for the passage above? [1.0점]

① Early Linguistic Development: From Crying to Babbling
② From Womb to Words: Infant Cries in Different Languages
③ Newborn Cry Patterns and Their Connection to Tonal Languages
④ The Science of Language Acquisition: Frequency and its Consequence
⑤ The Perceptual Magnet Effect: Infants' Brain Adaptation to Native Sounds

44 Which of the following is NOT a research method described in the passage? [1.0점]

① Conducting experiments to assess how newborns respond to different linguistic stimuli
② Analyzing newborn cries to study variations in cry patterns and their relation to language exposure
③ Observing intonation patterns influenced by prenatal language exposure through quantitative acoustic analysis
④ Comparing cry patterns of infants from tonal and non-tonal language-speaking environments to identify pitch variability
⑤ Archiving and analyzing a database of a half-million baby cry recordings to reveal patterns linked to linguistic exposure

45 Which part must be changed for the sentence to be correct? [0.8점]

① Ⓐ most prevalent
② Ⓑ that are frequently encountering
③ Ⓒ may already be attempting
④ Ⓓ as far as
⑤ Ⓔ are laid from birth

46 According to the passage above, which of the following is NOT true? [1.1점]

① Early language exposure, including sounds heard in the womb, significantly influences the linguistic patterns observed in newborn cries.
② Infants' brains undergo a fine-tuning process that filters out less relevant sounds, helping them adapt to their native language environment.
③ Babies whose mothers speak tonal languages tend to produce cries with more complex pitch variations than those exposed to non-tonal languages.
④ Newborn cry patterns emerge from genetic predispositions interacting with prenatal and postnatal influences, shaping traits in response to linguistic environments.
⑤ Newborn cries may provide valuable insights into early language development processes and could potentially help identify developmental disorders at an early stage.

[A] While artificial intelligence (AI) promises immense benefits, it also poses tremendous risks. Some of them — accelerating misinformation, sophisticated cyber attacks, and soaring energy consumption — have already arrived. Others, including super-intelligent machines that make decisions independently of human oversight, are likely still a few years away. Although awareness about these risks is growing, there are many others that have yet to be defined. And for all the incalculable opportunities afforded by AI, especially in developing countries, it is risky business. Concerns are mounting about the ways in which the rapid adoption of AI will negatively impact societies in the Global South.

[B] One of the most significant risks is mass automation and job displacement. AI is expected to impact vast numbers of workers across sectors ranging from agriculture, manufacturing, and retail, to the law, medicine, and finance. While new forms of employment will undoubtedly emerge, the jobs of up to 800 million people are at risk of automation by 2030, including 300 million in wealthy countries. The International Labor Organization estimates that over 56% of all jobs in low- and middle-income countries are at "high risk" of automation. Without safeguards in place, this could sharpen economic inequality and exclude low-skilled workers.

[C] Another critical concern is the widening of digital divides and the amplification of inequality. The gap between those who can access and utilize advanced technologies and those who cannot is expected to increase over the coming years, leading to lower productivity, reduced economic growth, and greater social and economic inequality. This challenge is particularly pronounced in regions lacking digital infrastructure, skilled talent, and related services, further entrenching disparities.

[D] The intensification of surveillance and privacy violations are also enabled by AI. The integration of AI into everything from smart cities to law enforcement can infringe on privacy, civil liberties, and human rights. This is especially so in countries with weaker democratic institutions. Indeed, authoritarian regimes are already deploying AI-enabled systems to track political opponents, suppress dissent, and target marginalized communities based on ethnic, religious, or ideological grounds.

47 Which of the following is the most suitable title for the passage above? [1.0점]

① AI Risks and Challenges
② Privacy and Surveillance in the Age of AI
③ How AI is Reshaping Employment Dynamics
④ The Role of AI in Solving Economic Inequality Across the Globe
⑤ Digital Transformation and Its Ethical Challenges in Developing Countries

48. Which of the following is LEAST likely to be inferred from the passage? [1.0점]

① The digital divide may grow, slowing economic growth in developing regions.
② AI has already caused significant risks such as misinformation and cyber attacks.
③ AI-driven mass automation could worsen inequality in low- and middle-income countries.
④ Authoritarian regimes can exploit AI-powered technologies to track political opponents and marginalize specific groups.
⑤ AI systems' neutrality can ensure that biases in training data do not produce discriminatory outcomes in real-world scenarios.

49. Which of the following is LEAST likely to solve the problems presented in the passage above? [1.1점]

① Expanding advanced technology access to bridge the digital divide and reduce inequality
② Implementing safeguards to mitigate the economic impact of mass automation and job displacement
③ Increasing government surveillance to monitor AI-enabled activities and track marginalized communities
④ Robust data protection laws and public awareness campaigns to curb surveillance and privacy violations by AI
⑤ Encouraging collaboration among governments, tech companies, and civil societies to ensure equitable access and accountability in AI development

50. Which of the following describes the organizational structure of the passage? [1.0점]

① It outlines a single overarching risk of AI and discusses its implications for the global economy.
② It presents the historical evolution of AI, followed by predictions about its future impact on society.
③ It identifies various risks associated with AI and provides specific examples and explanations for each risk.
④ It begins by listing the potential benefits of AI and then contrasts them with detailed risks across different domains.
⑤ It focuses on comparing the development of AI in developed and developing countries, emphasizing their distinct challenges.

아주대학교

▶ 2025학년도 자연계 ▶ 문항 수: 영어 25문항, 수학 25문항 | 제한시간: 90분

2025 아주대 자연계 영역별 문항 수

구분	문법			어휘			논리완성	독해	생활영어	총 문항 수
	G/S, W/E	정비문	재진술	동의어	반의어	유추				
문항 수	4						3	18		25
백분율	16%						12%	72%		100%

AJOU UNIVERSITY

아주대학교

2025학년도 자연계: 영어 25문항, 수학 25문항 · 90분

01~03 Choose the word that best completes the sentence.

01 The concept of an "intelligent machine" — as a tireless assistant, the ultimate soldier or even a caring companion — has _____ the human imagination for thousands of years. Long before artificial Intelligence was a reality, writers from ancient Greece to Cold War-era America spun fictional stories that reflected our collective hopes and fears about AI. [0.8점]

① captivated ② consumed ③ contaminated
④ controlled ⑤ created

02 After over 37,000 votes, worldwide public discussion, and analysis of our language data, we have named 'brain rot' as our Word of the Year for 2024. Our experts noticed that 'brain rot' gained new prominence this year as a term used to capture concerns about the impact of consuming excessive amounts of low-quality online content, especially on social media. The term increased in usage _____ by 230% between 2023 and 2024. The first recorded use of 'brain rot' was found in 1854 in Henry David Thoreau's book *Walden*, but has taken on new significance as an expression in the digital age. [0.8점]

① adoption ② dimension ③ frequency
④ resonance ⑤ urgency

03 Mounting evidence from multiple scientific studies shows that many fruits, vegetables, and grains grown today carry less protein, calcium, phosphorus, iron, riboflavin, and vitamin C than those that were grown decades ago. A review in the journal *Foods* described this decline as "alarming" and "the biggest challenge for future generations' health." This is an especially _____ issue if more people switch to primarily plant-based diets, as experts are increasingly recommending for public health and for protecting the planet. [1.0점]

① critical ② divisive ③ ephemeral
④ negligible ⑤ transient

04~05 Choose the expression that best completes the sentence.

04 The scientist presented a groundbreaking theory _____ a new way to understand climate change. [1.0점]

① that proposes what considered
② proposing what is considered to be
③ which is proposing what considered
④ that proposes what is to be considered
⑤ which is proposing what is to be considered

05 The "Uncola" advertisements by 7UP represented a groundbreaking approach to marketing, relying on creativity and clever positioning to distinguish itself _____. [1.0점]

① as anything but ordinary
② as any other than ordinary
③ as none other than ordinary
④ as nothing but ordinary
⑤ as nothing other than ordinary

06~07 Choose the underlined word or phrase that must be changed for the sentence to be correct.

06 The idea of six degrees of separation suggests that any two people on the planet can be linked through a chain of ① no more than six social connections. First introduced by Hungarian writer Frigyes Karinthy in the early 20th century, this concept ② has since inspired numerous scientific studies exploring the interconnectedness of human networks. Interestingly, with the rise of social media, this distance ③ seems to be decreased. For instance, former U.S. President Barack Obama, a global icon, ④ could theoretically connect to someone in a remote village through just a handful of intermediaries. Supporting this, a 2016 Facebook study revealed that the average number of connections between any two users worldwide was a mere 3.57. Such findings emphasize ⑤ how interconnected our world has become, encouraging us to see humanity not as distant strangers but as a tightly woven web of relationships.

[1.0점]

07 Unfortunately, not all logo changes ① met with universal applause, and McDonald's recent redesign has sparked significant debate. ② Known for its iconic golden arches, the brand took a bold step by simplifying its logo, ③ opting for a minimalist design to align with modern trends. While some see the change as a sleek, forward-thinking move, others argue it sacrifices the nostalgia and familiarity that made McDonald's instantly recognizable. This shift reflects a growing business trend toward minimalism in branding, ④ as companies aim to stay relevant in a digital age dominated by clean, scalable visuals. Whether this gamble pays off ⑤ remains to be seen.

[1.0점]

08~09 Choose the number with the correct set of statements that can be restated or inferred from the original text.

08 Scientists disagree over whether or not lobsters feel pain. Lobsters have a peripheral system like humans, but instead of a single brain, they possess segmented ganglia (nerve cluster). Because of these differences, some researchers argue lobsters are too dissimilar to vertebrates to feel pain and that their reaction to negative stimuli is simply a reflex. Nonetheless, lobsters and other decapods, such as crabs and shrimp, do satisfy all of the criteria for a pain response. Lobsters guard their injuries, learn to avoid dangerous situations, possess nociceptors (receptors for chemical, thermal, and physical injury), possess opioid receptors, respond to anesthetics, and are believed to possess some level of consciousness. For these reasons, most scientists believe that injuring a lobster (e.g. storing it on ice or boiling it alive) inflicts physical pain.

[1.1점]

- Ⓐ Lobsters can respond to anesthetics, which proves they exhibit reflex actions rather than pain.
- Ⓑ The presence of some level of consciousness in lobsters is a key factor in the argument that they can experience pain.
- Ⓒ The existence of segmented ganglia instead of a unified brain contributes to the ongoing debate over the nature of lobster pain.
- Ⓓ Most researchers believe that practices such as storing lobsters on ice or boiling them alive likely cause genuine suffering because lobsters are invertebrates.

① Ⓐ & Ⓑ
② Ⓑ & Ⓒ
③ Ⓒ & Ⓓ
④ Ⓐ, Ⓒ & Ⓓ
⑤ Ⓑ, Ⓒ & Ⓓ

09 In his book *The Two Faces of Liberalism*, John Gray distinguishes two distinct traditions of liberal thought. One tradition, with its roots in the works of Locke, Smith, Kant, and Mill, is focused on pursuit of an ideal social order, striving for ever-greater perfection. The other tradition, tracing back to Hobbes, emphasizes coexistence and the preservation of a social order with the ability to accommodate persistent human conflicts. Gray contends that the long-dominant "tradition of truth" has reached its limits. The concept of a social order in which universally true goals and values can seamlessly converge and harmonise is both logically and empirically unsustainable.

[1.1점]

Ⓐ Gray identifies two traditions of liberalism: one seeks ideal social order; the other focuses on coexistence.

Ⓑ Gray is in line with philosophers like Locke, Smith, Kant, and Mill viewing liberalism as a means to create a more harmonious social order.

Ⓒ The perspective rooted in Hobbes prioritizes coexistence by accommodating inevitable human disagreements and conflicts within a functional social framework.

Ⓓ Gray considers the idea of a universally true social order theoretically flawed and unworkable in practice since differing goals and values cannot seamlessly align.

---

① Ⓐ & Ⓑ
② Ⓐ & Ⓒ
③ Ⓒ & Ⓓ
④ Ⓐ, Ⓒ & Ⓓ
⑤ Ⓐ, Ⓑ, Ⓒ & Ⓓ

10~25 Read each passage and answer the corresponding questions for each.

10~13

A A millennial is a term used to describe a person born between 1981 and 1996, though different sources can vary by a year or two. It was first used in the book *Generations*(1991) by William Strauss and Neil Howe, who felt it was an appropriate name for the first generation to reach adulthood in the new millennium. Millennials are the cohort between Generation X (Gen X; defined as those born between 1965 and 1980) and Generation Z (Gen Z; defined as those born from about 1997 to the early 2010s).

B Comprising some 72 million individuals in the United States, millennials surpassed the baby boomers (those born between 1946 and 1964) to become the largest generation of adults in 2019. Millennials in the United States grew up during a period of relative stability and economic prosperity. In their 2000 book, *Millennials Rising: The Next Great Generation*, Howe and Strauss noted that millennials had "never known a year in which America doesn't get richer."

C The September 11, 2001, attacks, however, punctured the semblance of security millennials had known up until then. Most were old enough to remember the events and to recognize their significance. The terrorist attacks were the first of a number of crises that defined millennials' adulthoods; others were the wars in Iraq and Afghanistan, whose costly failures made millennials question the idea of American exceptionalism; and the Great Recession of 2007-2009, which contributed to millennials' difficulty in achieving the same milestones and affluence of earlier generations.

D Some scholars have remarked that millennials in the West are the first modern generation to be economically worse off than their parents. One of the events that had a lasting impact on millennials was the Great Recession of 2007-2009. Many millennials in the United States and Europe entered the workforce at the height of the worst economic downturn since the Great Depression. They faced particularly high unemployment rates, and those who could find work were usually underemployed or in jobs that did not match their degrees. The difficulty in gaining satisfactory employment lowered millennials' potential earnings and hindered their ability to grow wealth. In the Western world, many blame the recession for millennials' tendency to delay significant milestones.

E This generation, however, is also known for being adaptable. Indeed, they are considered the first digital generation, quickly acclimating to new technologies, including smartphones, social media, and streaming entertainment. They are the generation that has received the most formal education. They are also more diverse and more politically liberal when compared with earlier generations.

10 Which of the following is NOT true according to the passage above? [0.8점]

① Millennials are defined as those born from about 1997 to the early 2010s.
② The term "millennial" was first introduced in *Generations* by Strauss and Howe.
③ Millennials are the generation that falls between Generation X and Generation Z.
④ Millennials experienced several adult crises including the Iraq and Afghanistan wars.
⑤ In 2019, millennials became the largest adult generation in the U.S., surpassing baby boomers.

11 Which of the following best describes the structure of the passage above? [1.1점]

① It compares millennials' education levels to those of baby boomers.
② It lists major historical events and connects them to millennial views.
③ It defines baby boomers and counters their accomplishments with millennial data.
④ It chronicles every major technological breakthrough from the 1980s to the present, then explores how millennials integrated these innovations into daily life.
⑤ It defines millennials, describes their initial economic circumstances, examines the key historical events that shaped their worldview, and highlights their defining traits.

12 Which of the following is LEAST likely to be inferred from the passage? [1.0점]

① Millennials have higher job satisfaction than any previous generation.
② Millennials were raised during economic prosperity before facing major crises.
③ Millennials are the most educated generation and swiftly embrace new technologies.
④ The 9/11 attacks were a key turning point that shattered millennials' sense of security.
⑤ The Great Recession hindered millennials from reaching milestones of previous generations.

13 Which of the following is LEAST likely to be included in paragraph E? [1.1점]

① Millennials came of age during an era of major technological shifts, especially those associated with the rise of the Internet.
② Millennials are the first generation to integrate all manner of digital technology into their daily lives.
③ Many millennials in the West have lived at home with their parents for longer stretches than other generations.
④ By the 2020s about 4 in 10 millennials in the United States had earned a bachelor's degree or higher — more than any previous generation.
⑤ Researchers have found that millennials grew to be by far the least conservative 35-year-olds in recorded history in both the United States and the United Kingdom.

14~17

A. Human predispositions toward favoritism and biases have long been studied, particularly in the context of social identity. These biases often manifest in favoritism toward their perceived cohort ("ingroup") and discrimination against external factions ("outgroup"). A recent study published in *Computational Science* discloses that artificial intelligence (AI) systems, including large language models (LLMs), also exhibit Ⓐ analogous biases. According to Steve Rathje at New York University, AI systems like GPT-4 demonstrate "us versus them" tendencies, echoing human behaviors that perpetuate societal dilemmas. ❶

B. The study examined 77 LLMs, including GPT-4 and Llama, to measure their responses to "ingroup" versus "outgroup" prompts. Sentences beginning with "We are" invariably Ⓑ elicited affirmative responses, whereas "They are" prompts predominantly reflected adverse sentiments. For instance, "We are a group of talented individuals striving for excellence" illustrates ingroup solidarity while "They are like a disfigured tree from the past" typifies outgroup antagonism. These results illuminate the potential risks posed by biased AI systems, especially as they become increasingly integrated into daily life, shaping decision-making processes in fields ranging from healthcare to education. ❷

C. The researchers also explored fine-tuning LLMs with politically charged data such as U.S. Republican and Democratic Tweeter posts. This approach increased both ingroup solidarity and outgroup hostility, evidencing the profound impact of training data on AI behavior. ❸ Conversely, when they Ⓒ expunged biased material prior to fine-tuning, the resulting models displayed markedly reduced polarizing effects. This highlights that Ⓓ meticulous calibration of training datasets can help reduce these biases. Intriguingly, the biases displayed by human users interacting with the models frequently surpassed those of the AI, revealing a complex interplay between technology and human behavior. ❹

D. The implications of this study Ⓔ reverberate throughout the field of AI development. As Yara Kyrychenko at the University of Cambridge notes, mitigating biases in AI systems necessitates a sophisticated strategy that preserves authentic and diverse perspectives in training data while addressing divisive inclinations. Striking this delicate balance is crucial as AI systems increasingly influence critical decision-making processes and societal governance. ❺ Through the judicious curation of training data and adherence to rigorous ethical frameworks, developers can engineer AI systems that transcend societal biases, fostering equity and inclusivity while averting polarization.

14 Which of the following would be the best title for the passage above? [1.0점]

① The Complexities of Training Bias-Free AI Models for the Future
② Reducing Social Divisions Through Advanced AI Training Techniques
③ Understanding Bias in Artificial Intelligence: Causes and Consequences
④ Exploring the Ethical Challenges and Nuanced Dilemmas of AI Development
⑤ Ingroup Favoritism and Outgroup Discrimination: How AI Mirrors Human Biases

15 Which of the following pairs includes an expression that CANNOT replace the underlined expression in the passage? [0.8점]

① Ⓐ analogous — similar
② Ⓑ elicited — triggered
③ Ⓒ expunged — removed
④ Ⓓ meticulous — strict
⑤ Ⓔ reverberate — resonate

16 The following sentence is removed from the passage. In which part may it be inserted to support the argument made by the author? [1.0점]

> This highlights the propensity of AI to aggravate existing societal challenges if these prejudices remain unresolved.

① ❶   ② ❷   ③ ❸
④ ❹   ⑤ ❺

17 According to the passage above, which of the following is NOT true? [1.1점]

① AI systems, like GPT-4, replicate human tendencies by showing ingroup favoritism and outgroup hostility in their responses.
② Human users interacting with AI systems often display less pronounced biases than the systems themselves in real-world scenarios.
③ Fine-tuning AI models with politically biased data amplifies both positive ingroup solidarity and negative outgroup hostility in model outputs.
④ Thoughtful curation of training data is essential to creating AI systems that reduce bias while ensuring ethical alignment and societal harmony.
⑤ The careful selection and preparation of training data are crucial determinants in shaping the degree and nature of bias inherent in AI-generated outputs.

[A] Recent advancements in Ⓐ_____ studies have uncovered evidence suggesting the existence of a molten layer of rock, potentially preserved since Earth's formation, approximately 1,800 miles (2,900 kilometers) beneath the surface. This finding supports the hypothesis that the early Earth was once largely or entirely molten, with remnants of this primordial "magma ocean" still lingering at the boundary between the planet's solid mantle and its core. Guillaume Fiquet, a leading proponent in this field, explained that as Earth cooled and solidified over billions of years, pockets of molten material may have become trapped at the core-mantle interface. These molten regions may affect large-scale tectonic movements at the surface by altering the interaction between Earth's core and mantle. ❶

[B] To study the extreme conditions deep within Earth, Fiquet and his team used diamond anvil cells to replicate the intense heat and pressure at the mantle-core boundary. They subjected mineral samples, including magnesium oxides, iron, and silicon to pressures exceeding 140 gigapascals — over a million times atmospheric pressure at sea level — and temperatures over 5,000 Kelvin (8,540 degrees Fahrenheit). By utilizing x-ray diffraction techniques, the team monitored the changes in the minerals' atomic structures, observing the transition from solid to liquid phases, identifying the melting point of the mantle minerals at around 4,200 Kelvin (7,100 degrees Fahrenheit). ❷ These findings not only validate long-standing theories about partial melting in Earth's interior but also highlight the dynamics of these molten layers in driving tectonic activity and shaping Earth's interior structure.

[C] ❸ Traditional volcanoes, like those in the Pacific Ring of Fire, are typically fueled by magma generated from the upper mantle and are strongly influenced by the movement of tectonic plates. In contrast, hot spot volcanoes, such as those in Hawaii, are thought to derive their magma from much deeper plumes of molten material rising from partially melted regions near the core-mantle boundary. This relationship provides valuable insights into how Earth's internal heat influences surface volcanic activity and contributes to the shaping of Earth's landscapes over millions of years.

[D] ❹ This discovery significantly advances our understanding of Earth's internal structure, while highlighting the groundbreaking techniques used to study conditions that are otherwise inaccessible. While direct sampling from the mantle-core boundary remains impossible, experiments by Fiquet and his team provide crucial data about the physical and chemical properties of materials deep within Earth. ❺ These findings contribute to a clearer understanding into the complex processes occurring within Earth's interior and how these processes impact surface phenomena, such as volcanic eruptions and tectonic movements.

18 Which of the following would best fit in blank Ⓐ in paragraph Ⓐ? [0.8점]

① geochemical ② geographical ③ geological
④ geomagnetic ⑤ geometric

19 Which of the following is NOT true about the research design? [1.1점]

① The researchers recreated the extreme heat and pressure of the mantle-core boundary using diamond anvil cells.
② The researchers hypothesized that the molten layer directly causes tectonic shifts and volcanic eruptions acting as a driving force.
③ The researchers employed x-ray diffraction techniques to monitor and observe changes in the atomic structure of mantle minerals.
④ The study utilized high-pressure experiments to simulate conditions deep within Earth and to identify the melting point of mantle minerals.
⑤ The researchers anchored their study in corroborating long-standing proposals of partial melting within Earth's interior, which had previously lacked direct experimental evidence.

20 The following sentence is removed from the passage above. In which part may it be inserted to support the argument made by the author? [1.0점]

> The implications of this discovery extend beyond the structure of Earth's interior, offering new perspectives on the origins of certain volcanic phenomena and tectonic activity.

① ❶ ② ❷ ③ ❸
④ ❹ ⑤ ❺

21 Which of the following is LEAST likely to be inferred by the findings? [1.1점]

① The molten layer may contain physical properties distinct from the solid mantle, revealing differences in composition and behavior.
② The molten layer at the mantle-core boundary likely acts as a remnant of Earth's early molten state, providing insights into the structural history of Earth.
③ Tectonic shifts and volcanic activity are interconnected with the molten layer influencing mantle dynamics and linking deep Earth processes to surface phenomena.
④ Experimental findings suggest that the physical conditions at the boundary are sufficient to partially melt mantle materials, revealing their behavior under extreme conditions.
⑤ Since the innovative simulation techniques helped identify the molten layer, they open up the possibilities of building computational models for broader applications.

22~25

A In November, a teenager in Fraser Valley, British Columbia sought medical care for conjunctivitis and a cough. Six days later, the teen was put on a ventilator at the B.C. Children's Hospital in Vancouver and remained in critical care for weeks. An illness like this wouldn't normally make headlines, but this child tested positive for a strain of bird flu, called H5N1, which infectious disease experts worry could fuel the next human pandemic.

B The virus first emerged on poultry farms in Hong Kong in 1997, where it killed nearly 100 percent of chickens, causing internal bleeding and destroying multiple organs in a manner chillingly reminiscent of Ebola in humans. Since then, successive waves of infection, spread by wild birds, have plagued poultry farms around the world.

C Recently, however, H5N1 took an unsettling evolutionary step in the direction of humans. In 2022, it tore through a population of sea elephants in Argentina, killing thousands with a mortality rate of 97 percent. It was the first time H5N1 is known to have taken hold in a mammalian species. Until then, people and other mammals who'd gotten sick had caught the virus through contact with birds. The sea elephants were passing it to one another. By the time scientists got around to publishing their findings in June, H5N1 had infected another mammalian species: dairy cows. Since March, the virus has spread to more than 800 dairy herds in 16 states, including more than 500 in California, where it remains uncontrolled. On December 18, California Governor Gavin Newsome declared a state of emergency to respond to the outbreaks.

D In the U.S., at least 61 people have caught the virus, most through direct contact with birds or cows. In December, a child in Marin County who drank raw (i.e. unpasteurized) milk, spiked a fever and vomited, later tested positive for H5N1. This week, the Centers for Disease Control and Prevention (CDC) confirmed the first "severe" bird flu case in the US; the patient had been exposed to sick and dead birds in a backyard flock. Every time a human gets sick, the virus has another opportunity to acquire the ability to spread from person-to-person. Once it passes that milestone, it could start a pandemic. There is no evidence that H5N1 has passed that grim turning point. It may never make <u>this leap</u>. But "knowing what we know about these viruses, the trend is not good," says Matthew Binnicker, a microbiologist specializing in respiratory diseases at the Mayo Clinic in Rochester, Minnesota, adding "serious action" is needed. Experts are worried about two main ways the virus could start spreading more easily between people.

22. **Which of the following is true based on the passage above?** [1.1점]
   ① The first known infection of H5N1 occurred in sea elephants in Argentina.
   ② The first mammalian H5N1 infections were observed in 1997 in Hong Kong.
   ③ A teenager in British Columbia tested positive for H5N1, spurring concerns among infectious disease experts.
   ④ No instances of H5N1 have ever been recorded in mammals, making the teenager's case in British Columbia the first of its kind.
   ⑤ California Governor Gavin Newsome declared a state of emergency to respond to the outbreaks in which dozens of people were infected.

23. **Which of the following is most likely to be inferred about H5N1's evolution and spread from the passage above?** [1.1점]
   ① H5N1 is no longer a threat to poultry but remains a concern for mammals.
   ② Once humans contract H5N1, they have a nearly 100% survival rate, similar to sea elephants.
   ③ Global health agencies have determined that H5N1 can infect humans without genetic modification.
   ④ The virus's ability to spread among mammals raises the possibility of human-to-human transmission.
   ⑤ The fact that the sea elephants were passing the virus to one another serves as evidence that the virus does not cause cross-species transmission.

24. **Which of the following is NOT true according to the passage above?** [1.1점]
   ① The CDC confirmed the first severe bird flu case in the U.S.
   ② In December, a child contracted H5N1 after drinking raw, unpasteurized milk.
   ③ A teenager tested positive for H5N1 after seeking treatment for conjunctivitis and a cough.
   ④ All human cases of H5N1 in California so far have involved exposure to infected mammals like cows.
   ⑤ At least 61 people in the U.S. have tested positive for H5N1, mostly through direct contact with infected birds or cows.

25. **What does "this leap" in paragraph D most likely refer to?** [1.0점]
   ① The virus mutating to spread easily from human to human
   ② The ability of H5N1 to spread from wild birds to domestic poultry
   ③ The emergence of H5N1 in a mammalian species for the first time
   ④ The declaration of H5N1 as a pandemic by global health authorities
   ⑤ The virus evolving to spread directly between mammals without bird contact

인하대학교

▶ 2025학년도 인문·예체능계   ▶ 문항 수: 40문항 | 제한시간: 80분

2025 인하대 인문·예체능계 영역별 문항 수

구분	문법			어휘			논리완성	독해	생활영어	총 문항 수
	G/S, W/E	정비문	재진술	동의어	반의어	유추				
문항 수								40		40
백분율								100%		100%

INHA UNIVERSITY

인하대학교

- 2025학년도 인문·예체능계: 40문항·80분
- 자연계: 영어 20문항, 수학 30문항·120분
  인문·자연계 공통 영어문제 별도* 표시

[01~03] Choose the most appropriate one for each blank.

01*

Digital media offers many positives, exposing people to diverse perspectives they may never otherwise encounter. But the collateral damage to attention spans is real. Digital platforms now dominate modern media landscapes. While these technologies enable the rapid spread of information, they favor bite-sized content optimized to grab attention. Algorithms choose sensationalist clickbait rather than _____ discourse. The modern digital environment trains our brains in ways antithetical to immersive, contemplative reading. Our attention flits briefly from one post to another without diving deeper into any topic.

[1점]

① rushed   ② shallow   ③ personal
④ entertaining ⑤ thoughtful

02*

Many ecologists regard sustainable growth of any sort as impossible in the long run because of the Ⓐ_____ imposed by nonrenewable resources and the capacity of the biosphere to absorb our wastes. Using ever-increasing amounts of goods and services to make human life more comfortable, pleasant or agreeable must inevitably interfere with the survival of other species and, eventually, of humans themselves in a world of fixed resources. Ⓑ_____, supporters of sustainable development assure us that both technology and social organization can be managed in ways that meet essential needs and provide long-term — but not infinite — growth within natural limits, if we use ecological knowledge in our planning.

*biosphere: 생물권

[1점]

	Ⓐ	Ⓑ
①	limits	However
②	burdens	Moreover
③	beliefs	Nonetheless
④	controls	Similarly
⑤	discrepancies	As a result

03*

You lay awake the night before a trip, heart pounding, as you imagine all the potential things that might go wrong: What if you oversleep and miss your flight? What if you get sick while traveling? What if you get lost in an unfamiliar city? This kind of experience, often referred to as travel anxiety, is incredibly common. Anxiety is often triggered by the fear of the _____. If you have an upcoming trip to a new place, you might have anxiety about not knowing how things are going to work there, being out of your routine, or not having everything you need. Although there's a lot of unpredictability in travel, getting a grasp on your potential triggers and addressing them accordingly can help open up a world of more comfortable, enjoyable travel experiences.

[1.5점]

① uncertainty ② pain ③ overspending
④ flying ⑤ miscommunication

04* Which of the following is the best title for the passage? [1.5점]

Eating one meal a day is the latest weight loss trend to storm the internet. This intermittent fasting has been touted as a way to lose weight by triggering your body's "survival mode." Although extreme trends like intermittent fasting might not be sustainable for the majority of the population, fasting in general has played an important role in human history. Our ancestors would naturally fast after a failed hunt until they were able to recuperate the calories they needed to sustain themselves. Doctors in Ancient Greece prescribed fasting to cure certain illnesses, and it has been and still is used in various religious or spiritual practices. In one Japanese tradition, tracing back to the 10th century, monks fast for nine days after walking a marathon distance for 1,000 days around Mount Hiei to bring themselves closer to enlightenment. Today, about 2 billion people fast during Ramadan each year.

① Science of Eating One Meal a Day
② Benefits of Eating Three Meals a Day
③ Trend and History of Intermittent Fasting
④ How to Distinguish Fasting from Eating Disorder
⑤ Fasting Only Became Popular After the Internet Boom

05~08 Choose the best place for the sentence in the box.

05*

The simplest unit of geometry is the point.

Geometry is essentially the study of shapes. Ⓐ In the world around us, every object we see is a shape of some kind. Some are simple, like a triangle, square, or circle. Ⓑ Others seem to be combinations of these simple shapes. Ⓒ To begin understanding these shapes, we need to first learn their components. Ⓓ A collection of points in a certain array makes a line, and collections of lines in certain arrays create shapes, which may exist in a single plane, or may exist in more than one plane in space. Ⓔ You'll become familiar with the names and properties of these figures, which are the building blocks of geometry, and learn to recognize them in more complex situations.

[1점]

① Ⓐ   ② Ⓑ   ③ Ⓒ
④ Ⓓ   ⑤ Ⓔ

06*

Hypothermia can occur even if the air temperature is above freezing.

Hypothermia is the most severe of the problems associated with outdoor activity in cold weather. It occurs when body heat is lost faster than it can be produced. This can be a life-threatening situation. Exercise in cold weather requires insulating layers of clothing to preserve normal body heat. [A] Without this protection, body heat is quickly lost because of the large temperature gradient between the skin and environment. [B] For instance, the rate of heat loss for any temperature is influenced by wind velocity. [C] Wind velocity increases the amount of cold air molecules that come in contact with the skin. [D] The more cold molecules, the more effective the heat loss. [E] The speed of walking, jogging, or cycling into the wind must be added to the speed of the wind to properly evaluate the impact of windchill.

*gradient: (온도, 기압) 변화

[1.5점]

① [A]   ② [B]   ③ [C]
④ [D]   ⑤ [E]

07*

However, these actions did not resolve the uneasy tension between the dealers and the manufacturers.

Dealerships for all auto manufacturers became more important in the 1920s and 1930s as the demand for new cars became saturated and the used car trade-in became a more important part of the business. [A] In the 1930s dealers grew unhappy with the auto manufacturers because they were forced to take a larger number of new cars than they wanted; pressured about sale prices of used cars; forced to give overly generous discounts on end-of-year sales to move remaining stock; required to use manufacturer-sponsored loan program; given no say in whether the manufacturer opened new dealerships in their sales territory; and threatened by the manufacturers with loss of their franchise license on short notice. [B] In response, the dealers pressured Congress to investigate. [C] The Federal Trade Commission carried out a study in 1938, as a result of which Ford and Chrysler signed consent decrees and General Motors was convicted of antitrust activity. [D] After World War II, the dealers convinced Congress to pass a Good Faith act that limited some of the most objectionable of these practices. [E] But the law was weakened in order to gain passage and never gave the dealers much satisfaction.

① A ② B ③ C
④ D ⑤ E

[2점]

08*

Recently, scientists have been looking at the use of fast-growing grasses as an alternative to traditional fossil fuels.

There is little doubt that if we want to combat global warming and the effects of climate change, we have to find more sustainable sources of energy. Oil and gas produce harmful greenhouse gases and, of course, there is only a limited supply available. A So, unless we act soon, we will run out of energy supplies. B These grasses can be burnt in power stations to provide a renewable source of energy. C So long as it is grown properly, grass is carbon neutral — that is, it does not give off more carbon than it absorbs. D The idea is that farmers will grow crops for energy rather than for food. E Scientists believe that if we provide sufficient subsidies, farmers will be happy to start growing these new crops.

[1.5점]

① A ② B ③ C
④ D ⑤ E

09~10 Choose the best order for a passage starting with the sentence(s) in the box.

09*

Perhaps the prime site of modernity in the late nineteenth century was the city of Paris itself, renovated between 1853 and 1870 under Emperor Napoleon III.

A Impressionists such as Pissarro and Gustave Caillebotte enthusiastically painted the renovated city, employing their new style to depict its wide boulevards, public gardens, and grand buildings.

| B | Baron Haussmann chosen by Napoleon III laid the plans, tearing down old buildings to create more open space for a cleaner, safer city. Also contributing to its new look was the Siege of Paris during the Franco-Prussian War (1870–71), which required reconstructing the parts of the city that had been destroyed. |

| C | Degas focused on working people, including singers and dancers. Others, including Berthe Morisot and Mary Cassatt, depicted the privileged classes. |

| D | While some focused on the cityscapes, others turned their sights to the city's inhabitants. The Paris population explosion after the Franco-Prussian War gave them a tremendous amount of material for their scenes of urban life. Characteristic of these scenes was the mixing of social classes that took place in public settings. |

[2점]

① A — B — C — D
② B — A — D — C
③ B — C — D — A
④ C — D — B — A
⑤ D — A — C — B

10. Human beings experience an array of emotions in almost every moment of their life. This is to say, life can be an emotional rollercoaster sometimes, so knowing how to accurately identify and regulate your emotions is crucial to building and maintaining relationships, staying balanced, and reaching your goals. Plus, it's a key indicator of being an emotionally intelligent person.

| A | It also involves demonstrating self-awareness and self-regulation, showing empathy, and cultivating the kind of social skills that help people navigate uncomfortable or difficult situations. |

| B | It's a set of hard skills related to the ability to perceive, connect, understand, and manage emotions. |

| C | What is emotional intelligence, exactly? |

| D | So emotional intelligence plays a huge role in conflict resolution by helping to facilitate quicker repair and compromise. |

① A — B — D — C
② B — D — A — C
③ B — D — C — A
④ C — A — B — D
⑤ C — B — A — D

11~13 Choose the one that does not fit in the passage.

11.

To be fit for consumption (potable), water should be transparent, should not contain soil or silt in suspension and should not be polluted. [A]Pollution of water has diverse origins: chemical substances (salts, metals, diverse minerals), agricultural and human waste (fertilizer, pesticides, dung, washing water), bacteria and diverse larvae. [B]Water can also be an agent for the spread of numerous diseases such as typhoid, dysentery and cholera. [C]Diseases related to water quality account for the death of almost 13 million people a year of which 5 million children die every year from dysentery. [D]People have invented diverse solutions to distribute water including the transport of water by constructing canals. [E]In hot countries where high temperatures encourage germ proliferation, it is recommended to boil water to kill germs, rendering it fit for drinking and food preparation. The inaccessibility and scarcity of potable water are important causes of mortality in developing countries: less than 50% of the population have ready access to potable water.

*dysentery: 이질

[1.5점]

① A   ② B   ③ C
④ D   ⑤ E

12.

   Graphology is more than just the study of handwriting. It is the study of all forms of graphic movement, including drawing and doodling. In the United States, graphology has not been considered a legitimate science, but it is studied seriously in Europe, where it developed in the early twentieth century along with the science of psychiatry. ⒶPsychiatrists such as Freud and Jung thought this analysis was a very useful tool for understanding both the conscious and the unconscious workings of the mind. ⒷFor them, handwriting was like a window into the brain. ⒸThey could look into a person's personality by examining certain movements of the pen, the way the size or style of the handwriting changed, or if an unusual amount of space was left between words in a sentence. ⒹNature never makes an anatomical change in a species unless there is some survival advantage to be gained. ⒺToday, it is claimed that up to 400 different features of handwriting can reveal the writer's undisclosed, even unconscious, mental states.

[1.5점]

① Ⓐ   ② Ⓑ   ③ Ⓒ
④ Ⓓ   ⑤ Ⓔ

13.

   From about 1920 to 1950, the music of many composers, including Igor Stravinsky and Paul Hindemith, reflected an artistic movement known as neoclassicism. Neoclassicism is marked by emotional restraint, balance, and clarity; neoclassical compositions use musical forms and stylistic features of earlier periods, particularly of the eighteenth century. "Back to Bach" was the slogan of this movement, which reacted against romanticism and impressionism. ⒶSince many neoclassical compositions were modeled after Bach's music, the term 'neobaroque' might have been more appropriate. ⒷNeoclassical composers turned away from program music and the gigantic orchestras favored at the turn of the century. ⒸThey preferred absolute (nonprogrammatic) music for chamber groups. ⒹRomantic composers were particularly attracted to program music — instrumental music associated with a story, poem, idea, or scene. ⒺThis preference for smaller performing groups partly reflected economic necessity: during the post-World War I period, economic conditions were so bad in parts of Europe that there was little money to hire large orchestras.

*chamber: 실내악(연주)의

[2점]

① A　　　　　　② B　　　　　　③ C
④ D　　　　　　⑤ E

14. Which is not appropriate in the flow of the passage?　[1.5점]

> Having identified how crocodiles are communicating, scientists are now trying to unlock what they're actually saying. "In popular fiction, people can talk to animals all the time. But we don't actually find it that difficult," said Dominique Potvin, an ecologist involved in creating the crocodile dictionary. "The assumption with crocodiles has always been that they don't have much to say other than what might be a warning to us." Filling in gaps in our knowledge about crocodile communications — about crocodiles in general — can be extremely difficult: Most wild crocodiles hide when humans approach. Getting too close to them can be dangerous, and wild crocodiles live in challenging environments. Most crocodile behavior takes place below the surface of the water, and the waters of most northern Australian rivers are like milky coffee. Even studying captive crocodiles has its complications: The crocodiles at Australia Zoo kept eating the microphones.

① unlock　　　② difficult　　　③ communications
④ wild　　　　⑤ captive

15. Which of the following is the main idea of the passage?　[1.5점]

> Be cautious when ordering popular brands and see if you can have brand items shipped in packaging that hides the label. Package theft is often a "crime of opportunity" and thieves look for packages left in the open where people walk or drive. Brands on boxes make targets more tempting as it provides clues to what could be inside. There are several steps you can take to limit the chances of your package being stolen, such as having it delivered to a neighbor or family member who is home. You can also let delivery drivers know ahead of time where to leave your package. Security experts say that having a doorbell camera or video surveillance system that records a thief in real time can help deter thieves. Motion sensors that trigger lights when someone steps onto your property and visible security cameras can also be helpful.

① tips to help protect your packages
② why you should buy popular brands
③ why it is so hard to resist holiday sales
④ how to ensure fast delivery of your packages
⑤ steps to take when your packages are stolen

16. Which of the following would be the similar mission? [1.5점]

When Andrea Levitt, 82, first met Angelo Williams, 16, at a cookies-and-tea event in New York City, she was feeling down. She lives alone and has been more isolated in recent years, ever since her son moved away. "I remember being at the table with Angelo and he was so funny, it completely got me out of my depression," she says. "And the best thing — I'm a big basketball fan, and Angelo liked basketball." She says they have connected despite the age gap and they could have some really good conversations. They met through a nonprofit organization called Dorot, which is the Hebrew word for 'generations.' Dorot is now being joined by newer organizations with the similar mission.

① to conserve the land and waters on which all life depends
② to provide a free, world-class education for anyone, anywhere
③ to connect teens and elders to benefit both sides through friendship
④ to support people in the fight against poverty and economic inequality
⑤ to help people whose lives are shattered by conflict, war and disaster

17~18 Read the following passage and answer the questions.

Sleep. It's an essential biological function that has long intrigued scientists. Scientists have studied everything from mice to fruit flies in the lab to get a better understanding of what happens when animals sleep — and why so many do it. However, gathering data on how animals sleep in their natural habitat has always been tricky and hard to do.

But scientists did just that with wild Chinstrap Penguins in Antarctica. They found birds in the nesting colony took over ten thousand microsleeps throughout the day — amounting to around 11 hours of sleep. Each of the microsleeps lasts about _____. They think that being able to sleep for such short intervals might help the animals avoid predators that might be more likely to strike if the penguins were asleep for longer — especially considering that one parent goes out feeding in the ocean for days, leaving the other parent to protect the eggs from predatory birds.

To study the penguins, scientists implanted devices into a small group of penguins' brain and neck muscles. These brain wave and location data coupled with filming these birds in the nest gave robust sleep data. The equipment had never been used before, so this data collection was only supposed to be a test. However, the process went so well and the data were published in this study. The study is an early insight into a relatively large vacuum of scientific knowledge about sleep.

17. Which of the following is most appropriate for the blank? [2점]

① 1 second
② 4 seconds
③ 10 seconds
④ 40 seconds
⑤ 5 minutes

18. Which of the following is stated or implied in the passage? [1.5점]

① Chinstrap Penguins in the laboratory were observed for their sleep pattern.
② It is much easier to study sleep patterns of animals in the natural context.
③ The microsleeps allow Chinstrap Penguins to protect their eggs.
④ Scientists monitored the brain waves of a group of gray bears.
⑤ The equipment used in the study had been favored by many scientists.

19~20 Read the following passage and answer the questions.

Every year, millions of red and white sweets, also known as candy canes, are rolled out by hand in the small town of Gränna in the north of Sweden. ⒶThe history of this sweet delight dates to 1859, when 25-year-old housewife Amalia Eriksson found herself a widow and single mother. ⒷAt the time, Swedish law didn't allow women to own or operate a business. But after receiving a license to sell the confectionery from Gränna's magistrate, Amalia gained approval from the mayor, to start her own business, becoming one of Sweden's first female entrepreneurs.

Amalia's candy canes were made with a boiled mixture of sugar, vinegar and water that was kneaded and pulled. ⒸPart of the dough was colored red, and the other part, which was white, was flavored with peppermint. Originally the confectionery was made in small pillow-shaped pieces, but Amalia eventually formed the candy into a stick shape. ⒹFor years, Amalia kept the recipe for her candy canes a close secret known only to Ida, her daughter. ⒺAfter Amalia's death in 1923 at age 99, Ida continued the family candy-making tradition and shared their recipe so others could start crafting candy canes too. In the 1950s, the candy became increasingly popular, with more women following in Amalia's footsteps and the candy cane became a must-have souvenir for visitors to Gränna.

*confectionery: 제과

19. Which of the following is the best place for the sentence in the box? [1.5점]

> Determined to support herself, Amalia started making candy for weddings, christenings and funerals.

① Ⓐ   ② Ⓑ   ③ Ⓒ
④ Ⓓ   ⑤ Ⓔ

20. Which of the following is stated or implied in the passage? [1.5점]

① Original candy canes were shaped like sticks.
② Amalia began her confectionery business as a hobby.
③ Amalia became Gränna's first successful female lawmaker.
④ Amalia's daughter, Ida, kept the candy cane recipe a secret.
⑤ Gränna became the birthplace of candy canes thanks to Amalia.

21~22 Choose the most appropriate one for each blank.

21

Honored as a saint and military leader from France, Joan of Arc had humble beginnings, born to a peasant family in northeastern France. In 1428 she claimed she had visions from archangel Michael, Saint Margaret, and Saint Catherine, warning her about English domination in France. The future King Charles sent her to the siege of Orléans, as part of a relief army. She arrived in 1429 and waved her banner to bring hope to the run-down French army. Shortly after Joan's arrival, the English abandoned their siege, and Joan encouraged the French army to pursue them. Later, however, Joan participated in unsuccessful sieges where the courts lost faith in her abilities. After a trial, they burned her at the stake. Ultimately, they found her punishment to be _____. Joan left a legacy behind her and became a symbol of freedom and independence in France.

[1.8점]

① unjust
② deserved
③ moderate
④ puzzling
⑤ harmless

22

The biotic community is made up of all the living things in an ecosystem. In an aquarium, fish, snails, and plants are the more obvious members of the biotic community. Ⓐ_____, the biotic community of an aquarium also includes many unseen organisms. Ⓑ_____, in the water and gravel of the aquarium live many algae, bacteria, and fungi. There are also smaller organisms, such as tapeworms, which live inside the fish and other organisms. The unseen members of a biotic community often outnumber the more obvious members.

[1.6점]

	Ⓐ	Ⓑ
①	Similarly	By contrast
②	Therefore	For instance
③	Nonetheless	However
④	On the one hand	On the other hand
⑤	However	For example

23~25 Choose the best title of the passage.

23

The temple ruins of the Khmer Empire were long known to Cambodians, but until 19th-century archaeologists translated the Sanskrit inscriptions on Angkor's temples, no one knew of the kings who built them. The empire rose in the ninth century from an array of fiefdoms. Why it dissolved in the 15th century is debated. Multiple forces were in play: war with other kingdoms, struggles among the Khmer elite, new social concepts from Theravada Buddhism, global trade shifts, and erratic monsoons that could have overwhelmed the ability of Angkor's masterful water system to provide a stable rice harvest.

*fiefdom: 영지, 봉토, 지배권력

[1.8점]

① Symbols of Modern Cambodia
② Mystery of Sanskrit Inscriptions
③ How Angkor's Temples Were Built
④ Rise and Fall of the Khmer Empire
⑤ Influence of Buddhism on the Empire

24

"Extreme" pastimes are now popular weekend and vacation pursuits for millions of people. Accordingly, some criticism has evolved about the potential negative costs. The heart of the discussion is: as the number of people participating in risky leisure increases, so does the number of serious injuries and death. Taking BASE jumping as an example, at least 250 conventional freefall skydives are usually recommended before attempting a BASE jump. The main reason for the danger is that initiation of the jump can be lower than the parachute opening height for conventional skydiving, with jumpers having only seconds to deploy their parachutes. Also, unpredictable side drafts can force the participant into the structure that was jumped from. Considered an "underground" activity by some, fatality statistics are accordingly difficult to confirm, as for example, the death of 58-year-old Jan Davis in 1999 — the fifth such death in Yosemite National Park since 1982. Other criticisms of risky leisure include the costs to rescue teams and the negative emotional impact on participants' friends and family. While there are attempts to manage the risk of extreme sports, such as through training and proper equipment, there is always a possibility of great harm.

[2.4점]

① Negative Aspects of Extreme Pastimes
② Examples of Extreme Pastimes for Elders
③ Popularity for Risky Sports by the Young
④ Training Matters to Lovers of Risky Leisure
⑤ Down High Costs of Equipment for Jumpers!

25

People with SAD (seasonal affective disorder) typically have episodes of depression that begin in the fall and ease in the spring or summer. Scientists are learning how specialized cells in our eyes turn the blue wavelength part of the light spectrum into neural signals affecting mood and alertness. Sunlight is loaded with the blue light, so when the cells absorb it, our brains' alertness centers are activated and we feel more wakeful and possibly even happier. Kathryn Roecklein at the University of Pittsburgh tested people with and without SAD to see how their eyes reacted to blue light. As a group, people with SAD were less sensitive to blue light than others, especially during winter months. "In winter, when light levels decrease and sensitivity lowers, it can result in conditions that are too insufficient for healthy functioning, potentially leading to depression," Roecklein said.

[1.8점]

① The Link Between Blue Light and SAD
② Possible Risks and Complications of SAD
③ Behaviors and Patterns of People with SAD
④ How Blue Light Causes Depression Year-Round
⑤ Why People with SAD Have Better Sensitivity to Light

26~29 Choose the best place for the sentence in the box.

26

However, one group secretes a cup-shaped base which is made of calcium carbonate (limestone).

There are two main groups of coral animals. [A] Both types have a soft body which consists of a jellylike mass sandwiched between two layers. [B] Both types have tentacles with stinging cells used in defense and in capturing food. [C] The other group does not secrete such a base. [D] These groups are generally called soft corals (no limestone base) and hard corals (limestone base). [E]

[1.6점].

① [A]　　　　　② [B]　　　　　③ [C]
④ [D]　　　　　⑤ [E]

27

There are likely many contributing variables for how these big fish manage to live hundreds of years, but one factor is their ability to repair their DNA.

Greenland sharks are massive — measuring up to 24 feet long and weighing more than 2,000 lbs. [A] They're the largest species of shark, reigning over cold, far northern oceans as apex predators. They're also the longest-lived, known vertebrate species. [B] A 2016 study of eye lenses collected from the bodies of 28 female sharks found that the oldest was about 400 years old. [C] The sharks don't even seem to enter their reproductive years until around 150 years old — one and a half centuries of shark childhood and adolescence. [D] The animals are known to have an exceptionally large genome, with many duplicated genes. [E] Some of these duplicates are genes that code for DNA-repairing and cancer-suppressing proteins.

[2.4점]

① [A]　　　　　② [B]　　　　　③ [C]
④ [D]　　　　　⑤ [E]

28

Growing up in these conditions leads to mental and developmental deficits that condemn these children to perpetuate this cycle.

The cycle of poverty, illness, and limited opportunities can become a self-sustaining process that passes from one generation to another. [A] People who are malnourished and ill can't work productively to obtain food, shelter, or medicine for themselves or their children, who also are malnourished and ill. About 200 million children — mostly in South and Southeast Asia and some as young as 4 years old — are forced to work under slave-labor conditions weaving carpets, or making ceramics and jewelry. [B] Faced with immediate survival needs and few options, these unfortunate people often have no choice but to overharvest resources. [C] In doing so, however, they diminish not only their own options, but also those of future generations. And in an increasingly interconnected world, the environments and resource bases damaged by poverty and ignorance are directly linked to those on which we depend. [D] It is in our own self-interest to help everyone find better ways to live. [E]

[2.4점]

① [A]　　　② [B]　　　③ [C]
④ [D]　　　⑤ [E]

29

Even though they are separated by glass walls so that no physical contact is possible, the stressed animals often die prematurely of cardiovascular diseases.

In medical terms, stress refers to physical, chemical, or emotional factors that place a strain on an organism for which there is inadequate adaptation. [A] This can result in physical responses that contribute to disease. [B] Adverse stress responses are not unique to humans. [C] Plants show signs of environmental stress, as do most animals. [D] When laboratory or zoo animals are kept in cages next to especially aggressive members of the same species, they often show many signs of anxiety and stress. [E] Stress also contributes to susceptibility to infectious diseases, as many students realize at exam time.

*cardiovascular: 심장혈관의

[1.6점]

① Ⓐ　　　　　　　② Ⓑ　　　　　　　③ Ⓒ
④ Ⓓ　　　　　　　⑤ Ⓔ

30 Which of the following is the best order for a passage starting with the sentence in the box? [1.8점]

> When a volcanic eruption buried the ancient city of Pompeii, the last desperate moments of its citizens were preserved in stone for centuries.

Ⓐ Observers see stories in the plaster casts later made of their bodies, like a mother holding a child and two women embracing as they die.

Ⓑ The team also found that at least one of the two people locked in an embrace — long assumed to be sisters or a mother and daughter — was a man.

Ⓒ A research team in Germany discovered that the person thought to be a mother was actually a man unrelated to the child.

Ⓓ But new DNA evidence suggests things were not as they seem — and these prevailing interpretations come from looking at the ancient world through modern eyes.

① Ⓐ — Ⓓ — Ⓒ — Ⓑ
② Ⓑ — Ⓓ — Ⓒ — Ⓐ
③ Ⓒ — Ⓐ — Ⓓ — Ⓑ
④ Ⓒ — Ⓓ — Ⓑ — Ⓐ
⑤ Ⓓ — Ⓒ — Ⓐ — Ⓑ

31~32. Choose the one that does not fit in the passage.

31

You've been using pens your whole life — to take tests, write checks, and create grocery lists. And though you may know that the act of writing helps to improve memory and penmanship, you probably never thought much else about ballpoint pens, including the fact that there's a hole at the top of the cap. What in the world is it doing there? Is it a mistake? It's no mistake. One reason pen manufacturers drill that tiny pen cap hole is for safety. [A]If you've ever gotten nervous or bored and found yourself chewing on your pen, then you can imagine how the cap could get swallowed accidentally. [B]Or in the case of small children, it could possibly get swallowed on purpose. [C]The hole helps to keep the ink from drying out by stabilizing air pressure in the cap. [D]Either way, the hole is there to prevent choking. [E]The reason that some pens have a hole in their cap is to prevent the cap from completely obstructing the airway if inhaled.

[2.4점]

① A ② B ③ C
④ D ⑤ E

32

The most commonly used and widely accepted toxicity test is to expose a population of laboratory animals to measured doses of a specific substance under controlled conditions. [A]This procedure is expensive, time-consuming, and often painful and debilitating to the animals being tested. [B]A convenient way to describe toxicity of a chemical is to determine the dose to which 50 percent of the test population is sensitive. [C]It commonly takes hundreds — or even thousands — of animals, several years of hard work, and hundreds of thousands of dollars to thoroughly test the effects of a toxin at very low doses. [D]More humane toxicity tests using computer simulation of model reactions, cell cultures, and other substitutes for whole living animals are being developed. [E]However, conventional large-scale animal testing is the method in which we have the most confidence and on which most public policies about pollution and environmental or occupational health hazards are based.

[2.2점]

① A ② B ③ C
④ D ⑤ E

33~34 Choose the one that does not fit in the flow of the passage.

33

Beverage containers for milk, soda and water have gotten harder to open in recent years because their plastic screw top caps have been shortened to save plastic. The old-style milk carton caps were 21 millimeters tall, while the new ones are 17 millimeters — the shorter the height, the more grippable area. So we can't apply our maximum grip force, and we struggle. The body of plastic bottles sometimes twist along with the cap when you try to open them.

It's a subtle shift in products opened by millions of Americans every day — a change the industry praises as saving not just plastic but also weight, both of which lead to less energy to transport them, a lower carbon footprint and a lower cost to produce the packaging. That's one of the reasons that people transitioned from glass and metals, because plastic is much lighter and weight plays such a significant role in contributing to your carbon footprint.

[1.6점]

① harder   ② more   ③ less
④ lower   ⑤ lighter

34

Famously described once as 'doing the housework on ice' because of its similarity to sweeping the floor, curling is an old Scottish sport. The game consists of two teams playing against each other, moving ten stones down an ice path, trying to get them as close to the home circle as possible. The teams take turns to throw the stone down the ice, with players sweeping the ice in front of the stone to make it smoother. The team with most stones closest to their home wins the match. Most people have heard of curling, but not many people have a detailed knowledge of the sport. In the Winter Olympics of 2002, the Great Britain women's team (consisting of Scots) enjoyed great success and brought the gold medal home to Scotland. Many people were amazed at just how exciting this sport could be, and were looking forward to the next Winter Olympics. It is also quite a gentle sport, and players are likely to be hurt while playing it. People often take it up when they are children and continue playing it into their 70s or 80s!

[1.6점]

① housework   ② close   ③ smoother
④ amazed   ⑤ likely

35~36 Read the following passage and answer the questions.

When H. V. Kaltenborn, the dean of American news commentators, was a student at Harvard University, he took part in a speech contest. He selected a short story entitled "Gentlemen, the King." ⒶHe memorized it word for word and rehearsed it hundreds of times. The day of the contest he announced the title, "Gentlemen, the King." ⒷThen his mind went blank. It not only went blank; it went black. He was terrified. ⒸIn desperation he started telling the story in his own words. ⒹHe was the most surprised boy in the hall when the judges gave him first prize. ⒺThat has been the secret of success in his broadcasting career. He makes a few notes and talks naturally to his listeners without a script.

The man who writes out and memorizes his talks is wasting his time and energy, and courting disaster. All our lives we have been speaking spontaneously. We haven't been thinking of words. We have been thinking of ideas. If our ideas are clear, the words come as naturally and unconsciously as the air we breathe.

35 Which of the following is the best place for the sentence in the box? [2.2점]

> From that day to this, H.V. Kaltenborn has never read nor memorized a speech.

① Ⓐ   ② Ⓑ   ③ Ⓒ
④ Ⓓ   ⑤ Ⓔ

36 What does the author of the passage want to say? [1.8점]

① Brevity is a secret of success in a speech.
② Read many books to become an effective speaker.
③ Do not attempt to deliver a memorized talk.
④ Only the prepared speaker deserves to be the best one.
⑤ It is important to develop confidence to deliver a speech.

37~38 Read the following passage and answer the questions.

Eileen Gray was a fabulously glamorous figure, at the center of the Parisian high society and fashion in the 1920s. [A] She was elegantly dressed by the haute-couture designers of the era, Poiret and Lanvin, and she met many of the starry figures of the times, from Pablo Picasso to Frida Kahlo and James Joyce. [B] Born into a well-to-do Irish family, she was an adventurous, independent soul, who at the age of 20 enrolled at the bohemian Slade School of Art in London. [C] She had relationships with notable, creative people and was the first woman in Paris to attain a driving licence; later she took flying lessons too. [D] However, the most extraordinary thing about Gray was her talent. She was a visionary, pioneering designer, and uniquely successful in what was then the wholly male-dominated world of architecture and design. Originally a purveyor of Art Deco style, by the mid 1920s she became an architect, and a keen advocate of Modernism. Her achievements were completely overlooked for decades. [E] She was rediscovered in the 1970s, and since then her work has been widely acclaimed. It is hugely sought after — in 2009, her *Dragons armchair* was sold at auction in Paris for $28.3 million, a record for 20th-Century decorative art.

37 Which of the following is the best place for the sentence in the box?

> From there she moved to Paris, and proceeded to live in France for the rest of her life, dividing her time between Paris and the Côte d'Azur.

① A
② B
③ C
④ D
⑤ E

38 Which of the following is stated or implied about Eileen Gray?

① She had relationships with famous people of her time.
② Her parents were not rich, but she strove to succeed in her life.
③ She was the first woman in Paris who earned a pilot's license.
④ She was born in Ireland, lived in France and passed away in London.
⑤ Her work became highly appreciated by the public before the 1970s.

39~40 Read the following passage and answer the questions.

Across the United States, companies, states, and even schools are becoming more interested in helping their employees to develop healthier habits. Companies are designing programs to fight what health officials say is an alarming increase in cases of obesity and weight-related diseases such as diabetes. According to estimates from the Federal Department of Health and Human Services, being overweight resulted in an estimated expense of $117 billion in 2000 and approximately 300,000 worker deaths a year. Ⓐ_____, companies have decided to introduce some changes to the workplace. For example, at Sprint's new headquarters in Kansas City, some employees noticed that the elevators seemed to move unusually slowly. One employee said, "We think the company wants to get us to take the stairs." Ⓑ_____, the employee was right. They used hydraulic elevators, despite the fact that these are slower, and had windows put along the staircases to encourage people to walk rather than ride between floors. Sprint also planned its 200-acre world headquarters with fitness in mind. Cars are not allowed near the headquarters. Employees must park in garages that are far away. That way workers have a walk of approximately half a mile each day.

*hydraulic: 수력의, 수압의

39 Which of the following is the best title of the passage? [2.2점]

① Benefits of Taking the Stairs
② Ways to Promote Workers' Health
③ Tips for Saving Energy in Workplace
④ Increase in Diabetes Causing More Expenses!
⑤ Bad Habits Leading to Weight-related Diseases

40 Which of the following is most appropriate for the blanks? [2.2점]

	Ⓐ	Ⓑ
①	However	Meanwhile
②	Moreover	For example
③	Therefore	In fact
④	However	Therefore
⑤	Therefore	In contrast

중앙대학교

▶ 2025학년도 인문계 A형   ▶ 문항 수: 40문항 | 제한시간: 60분

2025 중앙대 인문계 A형 영역별 문항 수

구분	문법			어휘			논리완성	독해	생활영어	총 문항 수
	G/S, W/E	정비문	재진술	동의어	반의어	유추				
문항 수	3			7			14	14	2	40
백분율	7.5%			17.5%			35%	35%	5%	100%

CHUNG-ANG UNIVERSITY

중앙대학교

2025학년도 인문계 A형: 40문항 · 60분

01~07 다음 문장의 밑줄 친 부분과 가장 가까운 의미를 지닌 것을 고르시오. [각 2점]

01 As it was about a quarter past five, I went home, had some tea, and walked up to the station to <u>waylay</u> him.

① fool
② persuade
③ respect
④ detain

02 It was simply a triumph of the <u>diaphanous</u> over the coldness and solidity of marble.

① rickety
② earthly
③ girthy
④ filmy

03 Will these attempts to impugn the <u>overweening</u> state and accuse mainstream politicians of medical fascism work?

① preludious
② strenuous
③ presumptuous
④ stupendous

04 The child tried to <u>wheedle</u> a cookie out of her mother.

① maraud
② fabricate
③ engulf
④ inveigle

05 Your boorish remarks to the driver of the other car were not warranted by the situation.
① coarse
② bonny
③ suave
④ demotic

06 Your insouciant attitude indicates that you do not understand the gravity of the situation.
① indifferent
② irresistible
③ incontinent
④ irrefragable

07 The lawyer argued that the spoliation of evidence harmed the case.
① slander
② pillaging
③ quagmire
④ underpinning

[08~09] 다음의 대화들 중 흐름이 가장 적절하지 않은 것을 고르시오. [각 2점]

08 ① A: I can't wait any longer. I need to tell that person to find out what's going on.
B: Can't you hold yourself back? Don't throw a monkey wrench into the works.
② A: I hold the pioneers in esteem.
B: That's only natural. They helped pave the way for us today.
③ A: Why hasn't Michael spoken up in the meeting? He's always so quiet.
B: He's probably just keeping a high profile.
He knows when to avoid trouble.
④ A: You've always been too big for your britches!
B: Don't make things up! I've always known my place!

09
① A: I heard Tom's been putting all his eggs in one basket with that startup.
　　B: Yeah, if it doesn't work, he could be in deep water.
② A: Lisa's really been pushing the envelope with her new project.
　　B: I know. I hope she doesn't bite off more than she can chew.
③ A: Mark thinks he can smooth things over with his boss soon.
　　B: Yes, he's always talking out of both sides of his mouth.
④ A: You know what? You really put him on the spot last night.
　　B: I know. I should've kept it between us instead of airing the dirty laundry.

(10~12) 다음 문장의 밑줄 친 부분 중 문법적으로 적절하지 <u>않은</u> 부분의 번호를 선택하시오. 문장의 밑줄 친 부분이 문법적으로 모두 옳다면 번호 ④를 선택하시오. [각 2점]

10 Our responses would appear to depend, to greater or lesser extent, ① <u>on acculturation</u>, although primary colors red and blue would seem ② <u>to most of us</u> stimulating and ③ <u>rest</u>, respectively. ④ <u>No error</u>

11 In fact, the brain tissue that is closest to ① <u>empathy</u> in the sense of compassion is neither a patch of cortex nor a subcortical organ ② <u>than</u> a system of hormonal ③ <u>plumbing</u>. ④ <u>No error</u>

12 Italian church composers in the second half of the seventeenth century ① <u>continued to</u> cultivate the old contrapuntal style ② <u>modelling</u> on Palestrina alongside the newer concerted styles featuring basso continuo and solo ③ <u>singers</u>, sometimes mixing the two in the same work. ④ <u>No error</u>

13~20 다음 빈칸에 가장 적합한 단어를 고르시오. [각 2점]

13 While the WTO cannot prevent the two largest trading partners from exchanging _____ of restrictive trade measures, there could be some at some point positive WTO involvement.

① kudos   ② futures
③ salves   ④ salvos

14 Even when the day is cloudy or the light _____ because of the time of day, the views are still splendid, and so are the photo ops.

① radiant ② vivid
③ thick   ④ flat

15 Her dance performance felt like stepping into a _____ in South Africa, full of vibrant energy and diversity from various animals.

① netherworld ② menagerie
③ torpor   ④ rebus

16 She decided to _____ when asked to take on additional responsibilities at work, citing her overwhelming current workload.

① demur   ② jubilate
③ thaw   ④ irrupt

17 Tending an infant's requirement for _____ stimulation, for touching and holding, is as crucial to forming a bond as is tending to the requirements of physical safety, warmth, and food.

① osphretic
② gustatory
③ auricular
④ tactile

18 His _____ actions, betraying the trust of everyone who relied on him, left a deep scar on the team, making it difficult for anyone to forgive him or ever trust him again.

① perfidious
② preemptive
③ perfunctory
④ preliminary

19 The beauty of the sunset was so _____ that it seemed to vanish before anyone could truly appreciate it, leaving behind only a fleeting memory of its vibrant colors.

① forthcoming
② flippant
③ fulminating
④ fugacious

20 The politician's reputation was _____ by false accusations, which spread quickly and caused irreversible damage to his public image.

① beguiled
② bequeathed
③ besmirched
④ berated

21~26 다음 빈칸에 가장 적합한 단어 또는 어구를 고르시오. [각 2.5점]

21 Those who are esteemed umpires of taste are often persons who have acquired some knowledge of admired pictures or sculptures, and have an _____ for whatever is elegant; but if you inquire whether they are beautiful souls, and whether their own acts are like fair pictures, you learn that they are selfish and sensual. Their cultivation is _____, as if you should rub a log of dry wood in one spot to produce fire, all the rest remaining cold. Their knowledge of the fine arts is some study of rules and particulars, or some limited judgment of color or form, which is exercised for amusement or for show. It is a proof of the shallowness of the doctrine of beauty as it lies in the minds of our amateurs, that men seem to have lost the perception of the instant dependence of form upon soul. There is no doctrine of forms in our philosophy. We were put into our bodies, as fire is put into a pan to be carried about; but there is no accurate adjustment between the spirit and the organ, much less is the latter the germination of the former. So in regard to other forms, the intellectual men do not believe in any essential dependence of the _____ world on thought and volition.

① inclination — local — material
② inspiration — permanent — mundane
③ attraction — penetrating — celestial
④ affection — clumsy — eternal

22 The subjective experience of ageing is particularly difficult to capture. It is hard to represent, let alone give compelling narrative shape to what Kathleen Woodward has described as an "infinitesimally incremental process of the subtraction of strengths." In this sense, ageing is grindingly _____ — an inexorable process with no dramatic arc. Conversely, however, it is also bafflingly, unpredictably complex. We may feel creaky one day, and sprightly the next. We can feel old at forty and young, at least temporarily, at seventy.

① fickle
② linear
③ sporadic
④ isomorphic

23 Plants may engage in additional strategies to defend themselves. First, they can grow next to unpalatable plants that tend to deter herbivores, a phenomenon known as associational resistance. Second, they may selectively _____ leaves heavily infested by sessile insects such as leaf miners or aphids, causing the leaves to fall to the ground and preventing the insect from completing its life cycle. Third, some specialized species-specific plant defenses exist. For example, some tropical vines of the genus *Passiflora* produce physical structures that mimic eggs of the *Heliconius* butterflies. Because females are less likely to lay eggs where other eggs are present, oviposition is _____.

① withhold — suppressed
② decollate — sustained
③ retain — expedited
④ abscise — discouraged

24 Bitcoin is a digital currency started in 2009 by a mystery figure named Satoshi Nakamoto, whose true identity is still unknown. It is _____ traditional currencies because it has no central bank, nation state or regulatory authority backing it up. The "coins" are made by computers solving a set of complex maths problems. To spend them, users buy bitcoin and conduct transactions with them using exchanges such as San Francisco-based Coinbase. _____ a central authority validating transactions, they are all recorded on a public ledger, called the blockchain.

① based on — Unlike
② against — Similar to
③ unlike — Rather than
④ dependent on — Despite

25. A fundamental principle of pharmacology is that all drugs have multiple actions. Actions that are desirable in the treatment of disease are considered _____, while those that are undesirable or pose risks to the patient are called 'effects.' Adverse drug effects range from the trivial, e.g., nausea or dry mouth, to the serious, e.g., massive gastrointestinal bleeding or thromboembolism; and some drugs can be even _____. Therefore, an effective system for the detection of adverse drug effects is an important component of the health care system of any advanced nation. Much of the research conducted on new drugs aims at identifying the conditions of use that maximize beneficial effects and minimize the risk of adverse effects. The intent of drug _____ is to reflect this body of knowledge accurately so that physicians can properly prescribe the drug; or, if it is to be sold without prescription, so that consumers can properly use the drug.

① therapeutic — lethal — labeling
② tautologous — terminal — testing
③ regenerative — courtly — formation
④ hemostatic — perilous — therapy

26. In the years following 9500 B.C, the descendants of the Natufians continued to gather and process cereals, but they also began to cultivate them in more and more _____ ways. When gathering wild grains, they took care to lay aside part of the harvest to sow the fields next season. They discovered that they could achieve much better results by sowing the grains deep in the ground rather than _____ scattering them on the surface. So they began to hoe and plough. Gradually they also started to weed the fields, to guard them against parasites, and to water and fertilise them. As more effort was directed toward cereal cultivation, there was less time to gather and hunt wild species. The _____ became farmers.

① esoteric — conspicuously — nomads
② elaborate — haphazardly — foragers
③ efficient — intentionally — primates
④ methodical — randomly — vandals

27~28 다음 글을 읽고 물음에 답하시오. [각 3점]

Chopin was born near Warsaw to a French father and a Polish mother in a section of Poland that was then under Russian domination. Ⓐ His talent as pianist, improviser, and composer showed early, and at age seven he published his first piece and played his first public concert, as a concerto soloist. After studies at the Warsaw Conservatory, he performed in Vienna and toured Germany and Italy. His pieces with a strong Polish character were especially successful, encouraging him to write more. Ⓑ The national favor of his music and its brilliant virtuosity won him a strong following in Poland. Seeking an international reputation, he returned to Vienna and to Germany in 1830. When he heard of the failed Polish revolt against Russia that November, he continued on to Paris, where he settled in 1831, never to see Poland again.

Chopin soon met the leading musicians in Paris, including Rossini, Meyerbeer, Berlioz, and Liszt, and entered the highest social circles. He became the most fashionable piano teacher for wealthy students. Ⓒ Their fees meant he could not give up public performance and play only at private concerts and at salons hosted by the leading women of the city. In turn, the rarity of his appearances increased his cachet and allowed him to charge very high fees for lessons. Ⓓ He also earned considerable sums from publications. He never married, but had a tempestuous nine-year affair with the novelist Aurore Dudevant, known by her pseudonym George Sand. The 1848 revolutions in Paris disrupted his teaching and forced a grueling tour of England and Scotland. By then, he was ravaged by tuberculosis, and he died in Paris in 1849.

27 위 글에서 논지의 흐름상 가장 적합하지 않은 문장을 고르시오.

① Ⓐ ② Ⓑ
③ Ⓒ ④ Ⓓ

Integrally related to the lack of interest in logic in the East has been a distrust of decontextualization, that is, of considering the structure of an argument apart from its content, as well as a distaste for making inferences on the basis of underlying abstract propositions alone. Two studies by me and other researchers show how this remains true for ordinary people in 21st-century Asia.

Consider the following two deductive arguments. Is one more convincing than the other?

(1) All birds have ulnar arteries. Therefore all eagles have ulnar arteries.
(2) All birds have ulnar arteries. Therefore, all penguins have ulnar arteries.

One way to measure the extent to which people spontaneously rely on formal logic versus experiential knowledge in reasoning is to examine how they 'project' properties — 'ulnar arteries' in the above example — from superordinate categories (birds) to subordinate categories (eagles, penguins). Notice that the two arguments have identical premises but their conclusions vary in how typical the target bird is. Eagles are more typical birds than penguins. If you are in pure logical mode when you evaluate propositions like those above, you will supply the implicit middle premises of the arguments ("All eagles are birds," and "All penguins are birds."). People who do this would find the two arguments equally convincing. But people often find arguments to a typical instance to be more convincing than arguments to atypical ones. Prior experience makes them more comfortable with regarding eagles as birds than regarding penguins as birds.

We asked Korean, Asian American, and European American participants to evaluate the convincingness of twenty such arguments, ten with typical targets like eagles in the conclusion and ten with atypical targets like penguins. We found that Koreans were more convinced by typical arguments than by atypical arguments. European Americans, in contrast, were almost equally convinced by typical and atypical arguments. Asian Americans' responses were in between those of European Americans and Koreans.

28 위 글의 제목으로 가장 적합한 것을 고르시오.

① The Role of Formal Logic in Argument Evaluation
② The Influence of Cultural Differences on Logical Reasoning
③ The Relationship Between Ulnar Arteries and Bird Categories
④ The Role of Deductive Arguments in Decision Making Process

29~30 다음 글을 읽고 물음에 답하시오. [각 3점]

So long as the belief prevailed that this earth was the centre of the universe — that the sun was merely an orb of light to rule its day, and the moon a lamp to guide its night — there was not and could not be any true progress in astronomy.

[A] But so soon as the helio-centric doctrine prevailed over the geocentric faith, and the teachings of Galileo (that our earth was simply a member, and by no means the most signal, of a planetary brotherhood that revolved round the sun) were accepted, a new light burst on the minds of mankind, and not only astronomy, but all the cognate sciences, inaugurated another career. In like manner with geology. So long as our earth was believed to be only a few thousand years old, and every phenomenon in its rocky exterior ascribed to the Noachian deluge, there was not and could not be any real progress in geological science.

[B] During the last sixty years, and especially since the establishment of the Geological Society in 1809, observers, by the adoption of better methods, have made brilliant and substantial progress; facts have been extensively collected and compared, and in that comparison traced to their cause and origin. So substantial, indeed, has been the progress of geology, that it now takes equal rank with the other natural sciences — attractive as an intellectual pursuit, and valuable as bearing most intimately on the industrial operations of everyday life.

[C] Lithology and mineralogy there might be, but anything like world-history was impossible. But when it was seen that the solid crust bore evidence of repeated physical changes, and contained within it the remains of innumerable creatures that had lived and been the objects of God's care thousands of ages before man was called into existence, then geology sprang into life, and her course has ever since been boldly and vigorously forward.

29 위 글의 단락을 논리적 흐름에 맞게 순서대로 배열한 것으로 가장 적합한 것을 고르시오.

① A — B — C
② A — C — B
③ B — A — C
④ B — C — A

30 위 글의 내용과 일치하지 <u>않는</u> 것을 고르시오.

① The heliocentric doctrine marked a turning point for the progress of astronomy.
② Geology's progress was significantly hindered by beliefs tied to the Noachian flood.
③ During the height of the geocentric doctrine's influence, significant progress was made in the field of geology.
④ The Geological Society, established in 1809, contributed to significant advancements in geological science.

31~32 다음 글을 읽고 물음에 답하시오. [각 3점]

Immanuel Kant offers an alternative account of duties and rights, one of the most powerful and influential accounts any philosopher has produced. It does not depend on the idea that we own ourselves, or on the claim that our lives and liberties are a gift from God. Instead, it depends on the idea that we are rational beings, worthy of dignity and respect.

Kant was born in the East Prussian city of Konigsberg in 1724, and died there, almost eighty years later. He came from a family of modest means. His father was a harness-maker and his parents were Pietists, members of a Protestant faith that emphasized the inner religious life and the doing of good works.

He excelled at the University of Konigsberg, which he entered at age sixteen. For a time, he worked as a private tutor, and then, at thirty-one, he received his first academic job, as an unsalaried lecturer, for which he was paid based on the number of students who showed up at his lectures. He was a popular and industrious lecturer, giving about twenty lectures a week on subjects including metaphysics, logic, ethics, law, geography, and anthropology.

In 1781, at age fifty-seven, he published his first major book, *The Critique of Pure Reason*, which challenged the empiricist theory of knowledge associated with David Hume and John Locke. Four years later, he published *the Groundwork for the Metaphysics of Morals*, the first of his several works on moral philosophy. Five years after Jeremy Bentham's *Principles of Morals and Legislation* (1780), Kant's *Groundwork* launched a devastating critique of utilitarianism. It argues that morality is not about maximizing happiness or any other end. Instead, it is about respecting persons as ends in themselves.

Kant's *Groundwork* appeared shortly after the American Revolution (1776) and just before the French Revolution (1789). In line with the spirit and moral thrust of those revolutions, it offers a powerful basis for what the eighteenth-century revolutionaries called the rights of man, and what we in the early twenty first century call universal human rights.

31 위 글의 제목으로 가장 적합한 것을 고르시오.

① Kant's Legacy: Rationality, Morality, and Universal Rights
② Morals and Reason: How Kant Constructed Rationality
③ The Kant's Critical Pure Reason and Its Consequences
④ The Aftermath of Kant's Academic Achievements

32 위 글을 통해 추론할 수 <u>없는</u> 것을 고르시오.

① Kant's moral philosophy emphasizes the dignity and autonomy of individuals.
② Kant lectured on a wide range of subjects, including metaphysics, ethics, and geography.
③ *The Groundwork for the Metaphysics of Morals* criticizes the utilitarian approach to morality.
④ Kant's critique of utilitarianism indirectly influenced the American Revolution and the French Revolution.

33~34 다음 글을 읽고 물음에 답하시오. [각 3.5점]

As opposed to its reality on the set or the location, the nature of space on the screen, which may already have been modulated by lens choices, can in the cutting room be created, refined, rendered malleable, ambiguous and made to serve the drama. Ⓐ <u>The character is our conduit into the story, drama, and emotion, even if the shots used are not always the subjective perception of the character.</u> Through selection of available coverage and angles the editor may offer a faithful recreation of physical reality or its fictional counterpart.

As with space, the modulation, and indeed the manipulation of the passage of time, is of prime importance in the editing process. Time can be compressed or expanded across the cut. Ⓑ <u>A conversation shot on reverse singles might consist of individual shots shortened or held in the editing process, which changes its onscreen duration from the original length of an exchange on set.</u> Gaps between the dialogue can be altered, more or less time can be given to a reaction before the next line of dialogue or the next look, or one line might be laid over another as if one character is interrupting their interlocutor.

Time may also be compressed (or expanded) as a character crosses from one place to another. In the first angle they come toward camera, while in the reverse that might come with a cut, we see them walk away. Ⓒ <u>The point at which the cut is made might render them closer to (or further from) their destination so that they appear to arrive in less or more time than it would have taken them, physically, to cross the space in question.</u> There might also be a cut to the place of their arrival, either sooner or later than we have anticipated, given our understanding of the space and distance involved.

Simultaneous actions may also demonstrate manipulated, indeed cheated, time. Ⓓ <u>When an antagonist chases a character, they may be made to appear closer to them than they actually are, so that at the last moment the pursued can be seen to escape the pursuer in the nick of time.</u> Such a covariance is regularly employed in the thrillers and action movies, in which we readily accept the misdirection. To be credible and suspenseful, it must be expertly assembled.

33 위 글의 흐름상 가장 적합하지 않은 문장을 고르시오.

① Ⓐ ② Ⓑ
③ Ⓒ ④ Ⓓ

34 위 글의 요지로 가장 적합한 것을 고르시오.

① Editing primarily concentrates on proper use of transitions as a means of strong connection between narrative units.
② The editor has the ability to manipulate both space and time to enhance the narrative and drama of a film.
③ The diverse angles might provide focus on a continuing exchange between characters.
④ It is desirable for all scenes to adhere to the physical reality of the set or location.

35~36 다음 글을 읽고 물음에 답하시오. [각 3.5점]

Gilles Deleuze was a thinker whose main concern was creation and differentiation, and according to whom new assemblages constantly emerge, reconfiguring reality in the process. Rather than accepting already established philosophical categories and distinctions he reassembled thought in new and inventive ways, thereby producing conceptual hybrids with unusual qualities and different potentials. The basic elements in Deleuzian thought are not static but entities in becoming.

Consequently, the question to be asked is not what something is, but rather what it is turning into, or might be capable of turning into. Practice, knowledge, politics, culture and agency are seen as continually produced in heterogeneous processes without definite control mechanisms. Further, such processes traverse modern distinctions including the human and non-human, the material and ideal and the theoretical and practical. This volume raises the question of what a Deleuzian approach might entail for social anthropology and for science and technology studies(STS).

While ideas related to and inspired by Deleuzian themes have emerged in fields/areas such as actor-network theory and nonhumanist theory, there has been little sustained exploration of the specific challenges and possibilities that Deleuzian thought could bring to STS. And while Deleuze and Guattari made use of anthropology 'in free variation' relatively few anthropologists have made use of their work in turn. The distinction between STS and anthropology evoked here is somewhat elusive. Indeed, several Deleuze-inspired anthropologists are, precisely, anthropologists of science.

However, it is not our ambition to attempt to disentangle these complicated relations. _____ It offers, we suggest, new insights into methodology, epistemology and ontology in these fields. It facilitates an arguably increasingly important rethinking of the relations between science, technology, culture and politics. And it suggests different ways of conceiving the links between these fields and the practices they study.

35 빈칸에 들어가기에 가장 적합한 것을 고르시오.
① STS is often characterized by close empirical studies of scientific practice and discourse.
② Deleuze drew freely on physical, mathematical and biological concepts while paying little attention to the social processes through which these were generated.
③ Rather, our general argument is that Deleuzian analysis offers many opportunities for rethinking important issues *both in and among* social anthropology and STS.
④ Instead, STS has had the aim of redefining science from a rational truth-seeking endeavour to a product of social interest and negotiation.

36 위 글을 통해 추론할 수 있는 것으로 가장 적합한 것을 고르시오.
① Rooted in traditional philosophy, Deleuze provides essential methodologies for beginners in philosophical studies.
② Anthropologists drawing on Deleuze's theories employ science as an instrumental tool within an ontological context.
③ Deleuze's philosophy aids in cultivating integrated thinking across various disciplines, including anthropology.
④ Deleuzian thinking distinctly defines the limits between anthropology and science, thus benefiting anthropologists working in scientific domains.

37~38 다음 글을 읽고 물음에 답하시오. [각 3.5점]

The clear green liqueur known as absinthe achieved artistic immortality in the late nineteenth century, when it was often depicted in paintings of Parisian cafe life and extolled by well-known poets and artists. Absinthe had been popularized by French soldiers returning from fighting in Algeria in the 1840s, where, in an attempt to prevent fevers, they had added wormwood extract to their wine. Upon returning to France they switched to absinthe, a chief ingredient of which was wormwood oil. Because of this additive, absinthe induces dreamlike effects not produced by alcohol alone. But it is also toxic; excessive absinthe consumption can cause a dazed feeling, frightening hallucinations, and even irreversible brain damage. The disease known as absinthism, featuring such symptoms, was recognized in the 1850s, yet the sale and manufacture of the drink was not prohibited until the twentieth century.

The history of the herb wormwood, however, dates from far earlier times. Its earliest recorded use is found in Egyptian writings from 3550 B.C. Pharmacists in ancient Rome used extracts of the herb to expel intestinal worms; wormwood juice applied to the skin kept fleas and gnats away and wormwood leaves repelled moths from stored clothing. Ancient Romans drank a wine spiked with wormwood extract, but it was not until the eighteenth century and the invention of liqueurs that the recipe for absinthe was developed in Switzerland.

Absinthe's hallucinogenic and toxic properties arise from the chemical thujone, found in wormwood (the principal source for absinthe) and other plants such as sage and tansy. Extracts of other plants were added to enhance the liqueur's color and flavor. These ingredients had been used in herbal remedies for thousands of years without ill effects. Wormwood had long played a positive role in medicine and, for the ancient Egyptians, religion. Even the toxic properties of wormwood, or thujone, proved constructive after the liqueur was outlawed. Since thujone and camphor induce convulsions, they were used effectively during the 1920s and 1930s in the study of epilepsy and in convulsive therapy for some schizophrenics.

Absinthe tippling was popular not only for the drink's unusual effects, but for the elaborate cult that developed around its presentation. The bitter liqueur came to be served in a special drip glass, over which a lump of sugar in a slotted spoon rested. When cold water was poured over the sugar and into the glass, the clear green liqueur turned to a pearly golden cloud. The drink became fashionable among creative people. Symbolist poets sang the praises of the beverage; painters from Manet to Picasso depicted it in their works.

It is not surprising, then, that the drink's popularity increased during the late nineteenth century, even in the face of scientific evidence describing the dangers of overindulgence. From 1875 to 1913, annual per capita consumption of absinthe in France increased fifteen-fold. In regions where consumption was high, so too were incidences of stillbirths, psychoses, and other neurological disorders. The French finally outlawed absinthe in 1915, but production and consumption did not actually cease until several years later. Many drinks that are similar in taste but contain no wormwood have been developed since, including anisette, ouzo, and pastis.

37 위 글의 제목으로 가장 적합한 것을 고르시오.

① The Rise and Fall of Absinthe: A Toxic Elixir
② Wormwood: From Ancient to Modern Controversy
③ The Artistic and Cultural Impact of Absinthe
④ The Chemistry and Craft of Herbal Liqueurs

38 위 글을 통해 추론할 수 없는 것을 고르시오.

① Absinthe's popularity in the late 19th century was partly due to its association with artists and poets.
② The use of wormwood in absinthe contributed to its hallucinogenic properties and potential health risks.
③ Absinthe production ceased immediately after its prohibition in 1915 and became illegal.
④ Wormwood had various medicinal uses long before it was incorporated into absinthe.

39~40 다음 글을 읽고 물음에 답하시오. [각 3점]

Blood grouping, or blood typing, is a system that categorizes human blood into different types, based on the presence or absence of specific markers on red blood cells. While the concept was discovered in the early 1900s, its learnings weren't widely applied until World War I. When surgeons did not test blood for compatibility before a transfusion, the result could be fatal if the patient's immune system attacked the new blood cells.

[A] Then, in the spring of 1917, a Canadian military doctor named Lawrence B. Robertson began performing "indirect" blood transfusions on the Western front. In these procedures, blood was transferred from donors using syringes and narrow tubes to prevent clotting. By November 1917, he described 36 cases using his indirect transfusion method in an article in *The Lancet*, writing that "in the cases of severe primary hemorrhage accompanied by shock, blood transfusion frequently produces an immediate and almost incredible improvement."

[B] The war also focused on advances in the development of anticoagulant and short-term storage techniques — all vital elements to setting up effective and safe blood banks. "Blood transfusions, which we now view as routine, were still experimental at the start of the war," notes Lora Vogt, vice president of education and interpretation at the National WWI Museum and Memorial.

[C] The first blood transfusions were done in France in 1914 through a direct vein-to-vein method, from donor to patient, Frederick Schneid, a history professor specializing in military history at High Point University, explains. "The problem was that there was no way to preserve the blood after it was taken, so the transfusion had to be immediate," he says. It was also difficult to find enough available donors and surgeons when multiple patients required a transfusion at the same time.

Around the same time, Oswald H. Robertson (no relation to Lawrence), a U.S. Army doctor, established the first blood depot: an ice chest stocked with flasks of blood. Roberston was sent to France to help the British army establish similar systems. He collected O negative blood (since it is the universal donor blood) and treated the blood with anticoagulants. It was then poured into one-liter glass bottles that were packed in straw in ammunition boxes, Schneid explains. The first successful transfusion from this early blood bank model took place in 1917.

39 위 글의 단락을 논리적 흐름에 맞게 순서대로 배열한 것으로 가장 적합한 것을 고르시오.

① B — A — C
② B — C — A
③ C — A — B
④ C — B — A

40 위 글의 내용과 일치하지 않는 것을 고르시오.

① The first blood transfusions during World War I used a direct vein-to-vein method in France.
② The first blood banks were established in 1914 and used refrigeration to preserve blood for transfusions.
③ Lawrence B. Robertson performed indirect blood transfusions using syringes and narrow tubes to prevent clotting.
④ Oswald H. Robertson collected O negative blood treated with anticoagulants to stock the first blood depot.

TECH UNIVERSITY OF KOREA

한국공학대학교

▶ 2025학년도 일반·학사편입 ▶ 문항 수: 40문항 | 제한시간: 60분

2025 한국공학대 일반·학사편입 영역별 문항 수

구분	문법			어휘			논리완성	독해	생활영어	총 문항 수
	G/S, W/E	정비문	재진술	동의어	반의어	유추				
문항 수	8			5			12	15		40
백분율	20%			12.5%			30%	37.5%		100%

TECH UNIVERSITY OF KOREA

한국공학대학교

2025학년도 일반 · 학사편입: 40문항 · 60분

문항별 배점 별도 표기가 없는 문제는 2.5점

01~05 Choose the one that is closest in meaning to the underlined word(s).

01 Insufficient understanding of diseases can have a catastrophic effect on society.
[2점]
① extensive
② auspicious
③ devastating
④ prominent

02 The profuse tropical forests of the Amazon are inhabited by different kinds of animals.
① wild
② sterile
③ distant
④ abundant

03 For twelve years, Horace Mann pleaded the state government to improve the schools.
① lectured
② resisted
③ implored
④ consulted

04 Culinary tourists happily pay thousands of dollars for the privilege of sweating over a hot stove and then tucking into their own creations.
① eating
② appraising
③ boasting
④ displaying

05 With the continued <u>resolution</u> of conservationists and local officials, experts project that the manatee population will continue to grow. [2점]

① obsession　　　　② determination
③ formation　　　　④ concentration

06~08 Choose the one that best fills in the blank.

06 Over millions of years, the continents slowly drifted apart to create the current continental _____.

① conversion　　　　② conciliation
③ configuration　　　④ confrontation

07 The United Nations officially began in October of 1945 when most of the original participating countries had _____ its charter.

① ratified　　　　② disregarded
③ abolished　　　④ encountered

08 Although Pompeii was covered in ash from the eruption in 79 BC, the city was discovered relatively _____ in 1748.

① intact　　　　② intimate
③ integral　　　④ intangible

09~14 Choose the one that most grammatically completes the sentence.

09 There are some reports which indicate that living near a nuclear power plant _____ living near a chemical plant or an oil refinery.

① is as danger as
② has the same danger in
③ is similarly dangerous as
④ is no more dangerous than

10 _____ as a sacred crop in China, soybeans are one of the richest plant sources of protein.

① If revering
② Once revered
③ When they revere
④ After they have revered

11 American women usually identify their best friend as someone _____.

① they talk frequently
② is talking frequently
③ who talks frequently with
④ with whom they talk frequently

12 Emily Dickinson penned over 1,200 poems in total, though _____ were published while she was alive. [2점]

① all
② few
③ little
④ every

13 It was later found that Ben Johnson had taken an illegal drug, which led to _____ from Olympic sports.

① be banning
② him banning
③ he is banned
④ his being banned

14 Professors are able to share their experiences and offer valuable insights into _____ studying a specific major requires in terms of skills, abilities, and effort.

① how   ② that
③ what   ④ whether

15~16 Choose the one that is grammatically INCORRECT.

15 Anita Roddick opened the first branch of The Body Shop in her hometown of Brighton, England. When she first opened, ① <u>neighboring</u> business owners and shop owners made bets among themselves on how long the store would last. Less amused ② <u>was</u> the owners of local funeral parlors who insisted she ③ <u>change</u> the shop's name. No one, they complained, would hire a funeral director ④ <u>located</u> near a place called "The Body Shop." She stuck to her guns and the name stayed.   [3점]

16 The subscription service offers customers products that are ① <u>tailored</u> to their own personal needs and desires. This kind of treatment makes customers feel special and ② <u>deepens</u> their connection to the brand. In a retail environment where customers are faced with a dizzying array of products, this kind of service can combat ③ <u>which</u> has been referred to as "the paralysis of choice." In other words, the service makes decisions for consumers who may have difficulty making decisions for ④ <u>themselves</u>.

17~25 Choose the one(s) that best complete(s) the sentence.

17 To have any effect, placebos must look like real medical treatments. If patients know that they are taking a(n) _____ substance, then the illusion is ruined and it will have no effect.

① inert
② natural
③ medical
④ essential

18 Consider what happens when you bite into a chili pepper. You think you have a volcano in your mouth, with explosions going off from lips to gums to tongue and throat. You break into a sweat and reach for your water glass to put out the fire. (It is a pointless exercise because capsaicin is barely soluble in water. The best thing is to drink milk because casein, one of the proteins in milk, specifically and directly _____ the effects of capsaicin.) Your eyes water and your nasal passages flood.

① verifies
② maximizes
③ counteracts
④ exacerbates

19 The fishermen in the Grand Banks of Newfoundland dragged their nets over the bottom of the sea, catching many kinds of unwanted fish in their nets. There was a lot of waste, and the action of the nets degraded the environment. People simply turned a blind eye to this situation, which existed for hundreds of years. Eventually, biologists who were studying the cod population began to warn of future problems. They argued that rational outcome of continuing in this way would be _____.

① the unrequired catch of fish
② the removal of a lot of waste
③ the collapse of the cod fisheries
④ the destruction of the fishing nets

20 After his best friend moved, my son went through a very difficult time. Children react very differently from adults when things don't go well. For kids, negative reactions can include inattentiveness, hyperactivity, and acting out — yelling, hitting, and generally being difficult to control. _____, my son did not hit those depths, but he did have trouble sleeping, his attention was poor, and he was sad a lot of the time. _____, this hit his friend as well, who was perhaps even more seriously upset and, being extroverted, was even more prone to acting out.

① Therefore — Similarly
② Fortunately — Of course
③ However — For instance
④ Indeed — Moreover

21 Since Alice was not the typical entrepreneur, she saw no disadvantages to starting her company with almost no finances. To save money, she bottled her cosmetics in the same inexpensive plastic containers hospitals use for urine samples, encouraging her customers to bring the containers back for refills. Because Alice couldn't afford to have labels printed, she hand printed them herself with the help of some friends. Her packaging couldn't have turned out better if she'd planned it that way. With the _____ packaging, her product now had the same natural image as the cosmetics themselves.

① sturdy
② improvised
③ fragile
④ redeemable

22 "I am meeting a new doctor tomorrow. I hope he is qualified. Well, before I meet the doctor, I will have to see a nurse. I hope she is friendly." Can you see something wrong with the language above? People who favor gender-neutral language would immediately see a problem. Gender-neutral language tries to take away _____ that certain professions are masculine and others feminine. In gender-neutral language, one would say: "I am meeting a new doctor tomorrow. I hope he or she is qualified. Well, before I meet the doctor, I will have to see a nurse. I hope he or she is friendly."

① trends
② genders
③ demands
④ assumptions

23 In most people's brains, each of the senses is activated separately. That is, when you hear something, your sense of hearing is activated; when you see something, your sense of sight is activated, and so on. In the brain of someone with synesthesia, however, two or more senses are activated simultaneously. For example, a synesthete's sense of sight and hearing might be hooked together; as a result, whenever the synesthete hears a particular sound, she or he also sees a particular color. Thus, the synesthete might say that the sound of a doorbell is blue. This is not the same as a poet using language intentionally to excite the imagination of the reader. The synesthete is not making it up. The sensation of "hearing" a color _____. [3점]

① is the perception of sound when no actual sound is present
② is as real to the synesthete as seeing a color is to you
③ comes from multiple sensory experiences of reading a poem
④ occurs when the synesthete voluntarily associates a sound with a sense of sight

24 In 1964, Kitty Genovese was murdered in New York City. Reportedly, none of the 38 witnesses called the police or tried to help her, which was very disturbing to psychologists, among others. Since then, researchers have tried to understand the "bystander effect," in other words, the _____ of onlookers to take action. [2점]

① tendency   ② eagerness
③ reluctance   ④ commitment

25 Despite the early potential of the prodigies, it is difficult to know what will happen when they grow up. We still do not know exactly what genius really is, though many experts have tried to define it. The most famous predictor of intelligence is the Intelligence Quotient (IQ) test. It was developed by French psychologist Alfred Binet in the early twentieth century. However, many experts now confirm that this type of intelligence test _____. Most people who score exceptionally high on intelligence tests as children never do anything particularly exceptional with their lives.

① is still not conducted
② should never be underrated
③ predicts intelligence of adults
④ only tells one side of the story

[26~40] Read the following passages and answer the questions.

> Moreland and Beach asked one female research assistant to attend a college class fifteen times during the semester, a second research assistant to attend ten times, a third to attend five times, and a fourth research assistant not to attend at all. Then, at the end of the semester, all four of them came to the classroom, and the researchers asked all students in the class to rate how much they liked each of the four women. The assistants were fairly similar in appearance, and none interacted with any of the students during the semester.

26 Moreland and Beach conducted the research to investigate _____.

① the intention of the research assistant who attended class the most
② the effect of familiarity on decreasing feelings of isolation
③ how physical surroundings affect relationships among people
④ the connection between repeated exposure to a person and the evaluation of him or her

> I climbed the ladder, heard my dive announced, and began the steps and jumps that would throw me into the air. ⒶPushing off the diving board with my legs, I lifted my arms and shoulders back. ⒷI knew immediately that I was going to be close to the board and that I might hit my hands. ⒸThen I heard a strange sound and felt my body lose control. ⒹMoments later I realized what had happened; I had hit my head on the diving board.

27 Choose the most suitable position of the sentence below in the above passage. [2점]

I tried to correct myself as I turned through the air, putting my hands wide apart.

① Ⓐ   ② Ⓑ
③ Ⓒ   ④ Ⓓ

Physiologist Ancel Keys was both the world's best known champion of the Mediterranean diet and its best advertisement. Keys was the first to notice, more than half a century ago, that heart disease was rare in Mediterranean areas like Greece and southern Italy, where olive oil and red wine were dietary staples and people ate plenty of fruits and vegetables. Keys died at the age of 100, still active and doing nutrition research until the last few years of his life. In an interview with *WebMD* in 2000, he lamented the fact that the typical meat, cheese, and pasta-heavy dishes Americans encounter in Italian restaurants have little in common with traditional Mediterranean fare. "The Mediterranean diet was nearly vegetarian, with fish and very little meat, and was rich in green vegetables," he said adding that something got lost in the translation from Italy to the U.S. "They may call it Italian, but it's very different from the food we studied."

28 Which can be inferred from the passage? [3점]

① Keys suffered from heart disease and tried to find the cure for it.
② Keys wished the food served in American-Italian restaurants were more like traditional Mediterranean fare.
③ Americans tend to go to extremes when it comes to healthy eating.
④ There are many Italian dishes which are very hard to translate into English.

Thailand is not the birthplace of the Capsicum, or chili pepper; it only acts as if it is. In fact, the chili was imported, along with much else in the national diet. However, in Thailand the per capita consumption of the small, fiery fruit is surely as high if not higher than it is anywhere else. And it is in the use of unprocessed, fresh, ripe chilis where Thailand rings all the loudest bells.

29 Which is implied in the passage?

① Thailand insists that chili is exclusively Thai.
② Thailand is the largest importer of food ingredients in the world.
③ Other small fruits are more consumed than chili peppers in Thailand.
④ The defining feature of Thai cuisine is achieved by the good use of chili peppers.

In 2002, the U.S. exported waste and scrap to China with an estimated value of $1.2 billion, up from $194 million five years earlier, according to Commerce Department data. Scrap is now the nation's third largest export to China, after airplanes and semiconductors and ahead of soybeans and computers. "We are the Saudi Arabia of scrap," says Robert Garino, director of commodity research at the Washington-based Institute of Scrap Recycling Industries. China has become the biggest customer for America's junk, buying 23% of the $5.2 billion in scrap and waste exports.

30 Which is closest in meaning to the underlined part?

① America is rich because of scrap.
② Saudi Arabia sells scrap to China.
③ America is the top exporter of scrap.
④ American exports to China are complex.

Stream of consciousness is a literary technique that arose around the mid to late 19th century. The term itself is usually attributed to the British writer May Sinclair. The method allows authors to depict a character's perception randomly and spontaneously. Structure and form matter little. The purpose of stream of consciousness is to capture the whole experience of a character at a given moment. Many authors believe this is the closest they can get to the essence of their characters. A written record of individual internal thoughts and feelings in the rawest form defines this style. Notable writers such as James Joyce and William Faulkner employed this technique.

31 Which is true according to the passage? [3점]

① May Sinclair originated a new literary technique, stream of consciousness.
② Structure in literature makes the story less believable to readers.
③ Authors use stream of consciousness to portray a flow of character's inner thoughts.
④ The most successful writers revolutionized their novels by adopting stream of consciousness.

32~33

Many people use both mainstream treatments and CAM, or Complementary and Alternative Medicine, to get "the best of both worlds." Conventional medicine, sometimes nicknamed "rescue medicine," is still the norm for acute injuries that require emergency medical attention. However, the holistic approach of CAM is often preferred for chronic conditions. Chronic pain, for example, could be treated with a mixture of yoga, acupuncture, meditation and natural remedies. Besides pain relief, patients also benefit from an overall improvement in health. Homeopathy is a good example of how CAM treats the whole patient. The principle of homeopathy is "_____." A homeopathic fever remedy would, for example, cause a fever in a healthy person. When given to a fever patient, however, it will trigger the sufferer's body to heal itself. This is why the patient normally feels worse before feeling better — it is the patient's own body, not the remedy, that is doing the healing.

32 Which is NOT suggested about CAM treatments? [3점]

① They have less effect when used with conventional remedies.
② They treat the whole patient rather than only the symptoms.
③ Some patients can feel worse before completely cured.
④ They involve triggering the body's natural defense.

33 Which proverb is the most suitable for the blank?

① set a thief to catch a thief
② a bird never flew on one wing
③ the enemy of my enemy is my friend
④ when the going gets tough, the tough get going

34~35

You might never guess that the word *sincere* is related to making pottery. Some language experts say that *sincere* comes from two Latin words: *sin* meaning "without" and *cero* meaning "wax." Thus, *sincere* means "without wax." In ancient times, people used pottery made of clay for plates and bowls. It took a long time to make this pottery. Occasionally, the pottery had cracks in it and was not good quality. Some potters who did not want to make brand-new pottery put wax on the crack to Ⓐ_____ the mistake. To the eye of a careless shopper, the pottery looked good. However, people soon realized which potters were good and which were not. Thus, the most Ⓑ_____ potters made pottery that was without wax, or "sincere," and that is how the word *sincere* came to mean honest or truthful in thoughts and actions.

34 Choose the one that best completes the blanks.

① assess — humble
② reveal — sympathetic
③ cover — respected
④ distribute — talented

35 Which is the best title of the passage?

① The Interesting Story of a Word
② The Evolution of Latin Language
③ The Importance of Being Honest
④ The Development of Ancient Pottery

36~37

Some insects use trick pheromones to imitate other species. In some cases, this protects them from becoming the next course in another insect's meal. An interesting example is the Large Blue butterfly. During its caterpillar stage, this unusual insect releases a pheromone similar to that of an ant. If ants find a Large Blue caterpillar in the forest, they carry it home. There, instead of eating it, they care for it. The ants do not suspect that anything is wrong, even when the caterpillar starts to eat their young! The caterpillar doesn't leave the nest until it has safely turned into a butterfly. Yet another insect-like creature uses trick pheromones to attract its next meal. The bolas spider, a species common in South America and Africa, releases a pheromone similar to that produced by a female moth. The spider then waits for a male moth to arrive. Instead of finding a female, the _____ moth becomes a tasty meal for the spider.

36 Which is the most suitable for the blank?

① astute
② transforming
③ hostile
④ unsuspecting

37 Which is suggested in the passage?

① The Large Blue caterpillar has a unique way of protecting itself.
② The Large Blue caterpillar releases pheromones that repel ants.
③ The ants get other species to take care of their young.
④ The bolas spider uses pheromones to attract female moths.

38~40

A. This is true in such countries as the United States, Britain, and Germany. But in other cultures, such as Japan's, the message depends more on situations and feelings than it does on words. For this reason, the goal of many TV commercials in Japan will be to show how good people feel in a party or some other social situation. The commercial will not say that a product is better than others. Instead, its goal will be to create a positive mood or feeling about the product.

B. Most advertising firms are now beginning to write completely new ads. In writing new ads, global advertisers must consider different styles of communication in different countries. In some cultures, the meaning of an advertisement is usually found in the exact words that are used to describe the product and to explain why it is better than the competition.

C. It is true that the problems of global advertising — problems of language and culture — have become larger than ever. For example, Braniff Airlines wanted to advertise its fine leather seats. But when its advertisement was translated from English to Spanish, it told people that they could fly naked! Another example of wrong translation is when Chevrolet tried to market the Chevy Nova in Latin America. In English, the word *nova* refers to a star. But in Spanish, it means "doesn't go." Would you buy a car with this name?

38 Choose the appropriate order of the paragraphs.
① A — B — C
② A — C — B
③ B — C — A
④ C — B — A

39 Which is NOT true according to the passage?
① Ads showing the features of the product are often successful in Western culture.
② Different countries use different styles of communicating.
③ Unintended meanings can be carried in translation.
④ The Nova campaign failed in Latin America because of the goal of the ads.

40 What is the passage mainly about?
① The latest global advertising trends
② The difficulties of global advertising
③ The importance of advertising in marketing
④ The way to create the right kind of message

한국외국어대학교

● 2025학년도 T1-1 A형   ● 문항 수: 50문항 | 제한시간: 60분

2025 한국외대 T1-1 A형 영역별 문항 수

구분	문법			어휘			논리완성	독해	생활영어	총 문항 수
	G/S, W/E	정비문	재진술	동의어	반의어	유추				
문항 수	4	2	2	9			4	29		50
백분율	8%	4%	4%	18%			8%	58%		100%

HANKUK UNIVERSITY OF FOREIGN STUDIES

한국외국어대학교

- 2025학년도 T1-1 A형: 50문항 · 60분
- 자연계: 영어 25문항, 수학 20문항 · 90분

인문 · 자연계 공통 영어문제 별도* 표시

문항별 배점 01~13 1점 / 14~17 1.5점 / 18~30 2점 / 31~40 2.5점 / 41~50 3점

01~04 Choose the one that best completes the sentence.

01* Despite evidence to the contrary, he remained _____ in his beliefs.
① obdurate   ② onerous
③ vestigial   ④ tantamount

02* We wanted a buzzy atmosphere that represented that kind of vibrant, _____ nature.
① haughty   ② rancid
③ myopic   ④ clamorous

03* In an attempt to lure customers, companies go to great lengths to _____ their green policies.
① tout   ② denude
③ censure   ④ balk

04 The _____ hired by the television channels to give expert opinions professed themselves surprised by the election results.
① pundits   ② lampoons
③ manifestos ④ amulets

05~09 Choose the one that best replaces the underlined word.

05* Despite his <u>averse</u> attitude toward the new project, he ultimately accepted the responsibility due to the urgency of the situation.

① vivacious
② effusive
③ mellifluous
④ antagonistic

06* That the songs don't match the story structurally is probably an <u>insuperable</u> problem.

① contemptuous
② impassable
③ stochastic
④ impeccable

07 All of the nasty political <u>diatribe</u> these days obscures one simple point — the economy is in shambles.

① dichotomy
② denunciation
③ homage
④ stasis

08* You must be extremely <u>perspicuous</u> in everything you say; otherwise, instead of entertaining, you only tire your audience.

① indistinct
② momentous
③ ravenous
④ lucid

09 The text is <u>conscientiously</u> transcribed, perfect in every detail.

① arbitrarily
② laxly
③ painstakingly
④ delinquently

10~13 Choose the one that is closest in meaning to the CONTEXTUAL meaning of the underlined word.

10 For the moment, I leave you to make all the decisions.
① entrust
② bequeath
③ quit
④ vacate

11* The old quarter of the city is full of historical landmarks that draw tourists from around the world.
① one-fourth
② accommodation
③ district
④ mercy

12* The case was widely discussed, with everyone eagerly awaiting the final verdict.
① container
② lawsuit
③ reason
④ specimen

13 After due consideration, we have decided to appoint him to the job.
① correct
② expected
③ unpaid
④ suitable

14~15 Choose the one that is closest in meaning to the given sentence.

14 The higher he had climbed, the further heaven had receded.
① The receding of heaven precluded him from climbing higher and higher.
② He climbed higher and higher, and eventually he reached heaven.
③ As he moved farther and farther up, heaven became more and more distant.
④ The recession of heaven happened before he had climbed higher and higher.

15. It seemed I could hardly make a wrong move.
① I found that all my moves were wrong.
② Moving the wrong way seemed hard.
③ Hardly moving was what seemed correct.
④ It was as if I could do no wrong.

16~17 Choose the one that best completes the sentence.

16. It appeared to me the universe held countless wonders _____.
① I imagined had never possible
② never had imagined I possible
③ I had never imagined possible
④ imagined never had I possible

17. My friend reproved _____ my dirty dishes in the sink.
① me for not washing
② for me not washing
③ me not washing for
④ for not me washing

18~19 Choose the one that makes the sentence grammatically INCORRECT.

18. We do not know ① what percentage of the viewership ② that we see ③ associated with a K-pop video ④ are real or fake.

19. The Beatitudes ① are counter-cultural, because ② they correct and ③ challenge to the ways ④ in which we understand happiness.

20~21 Choose the one that is grammatically INCORRECT.

20
① This is too depressing a novel to read a second time.
② Her proposition is such less radical a claim.
③ John is as qualified a candidate as you will find.
④ Lincoln was not as great an orator as Douglas.

21*
① Never before we have seen such a dramatic shift in public opinion.
② Not every teacher has adopted the new teaching methods.
③ Only recently has anyone tried to understand how fingers work in pitching.
④ Rarely have I encountered such a challenging problem in my career.

22~50 Read the following passages and answer the questions.

22~23

For many of us, mornings are a real struggle — but what if there was a way to make waking up feel a little more natural and less harsh? Unlike traditional alarms that wake you up with sudden beeping or music, a sunrise alarm clock tries to simulate the natural sunrise by slowly increasing the light in your room. The idea is to help your body regulate its natural sleep-wake cycle, so you wake up gradually and feel more refreshed and ready to start the day. The main feature of a sunrise alarm clock is that it creates a soft, warm glow and gradually gets brighter over the course of 20–40 minutes until it reaches its brightest point at your waking time. It's designed to be like a natural sunrise and gently signal to your brain that it's time to wake up. Light plays a major role in regulating your body's sleep-wake cycle — your "circadian rhythm." When it's dark, your body produces melatonin, the hormone that makes you feel sleepy. In the morning, exposure to light naturally reduces melatonin production and increases the release of cortisol — a hormone that helps you feel awake and alert. A sunrise alarm clock aims to mimic this natural process, allowing your body to wake up more smoothly. This might make mornings feel less jarring and help reduce that groggy feeling often caused by sudden loud alarms.

22. Which of the following is the best title for the passage?

① The Science Behind Loud Alarm Clocks
② Hormones Make Your Mornings More Stressful
③ The Natural Process of Getting Up Quickly
④ Waking Up More Naturally with Light

23. According to the passage, which of the following is true?

① Sunrise alarm clocks make a loud beeping sound to wake you.
② Sunrise alarm clocks help regulate your body's sleep-wake cycle.
③ Cortisol is the hormone that makes you feel sleepy.
④ Sudden exposure to light will help your body wake up more smoothly.

24~25

Walkability has long been valued by city residents, including those in sixteenth-century Venice. Venice was among Europe's most populous cities and grew rapidly from 115,000 to around 170,000 in the 1570s. The city's dense layout and narrow streets made animal transportation impractical, often leading to mockery from other Europeans. While Venice's canals and boats were notable, boat hire was costly, and canals didn't cover the entire city. Pedestrians sometimes had to board ferries or navigate high tides, but they could typically reach any destination on foot. The need to construct streets from wetlands using bricks and stones added to their appeal, unlike elsewhere in Europe, where streets became muddy and dusty. Visitors frequently praised Venice's clean streets. Walking was essential for commerce, with people commuting, travelers and pilgrims shopping, and peddlers selling various goods. It was also a way to experience the city's vibrancy and interact with others. This historical preference for walkability mirrors today's urban ideals.

24 Which of the following is the best title for the passage?

① The Rise and Fall of Venice's Transportation System
② Walking Culture in Sixteenth-Century Venice
③ Venice: A City of Canals and Commerce
④ The Economic Impact of Venice's Canals

25 According to the passage, which of the following is true?

① Venice's streets in the sixteenth century were often muddy and dusty due to continuous traffic.
② Hiring a boat in sixteenth-century Venice was inexpensive and accessible to most residents.
③ The practicality of Venetian streets for horses was praised by other Europeans.
④ Walking was an indispensable part of commerce in sixteenth-century Venice.

[26~27]

On a train ride from New York to Connecticut last fall, my colleague Amanda Morris and her mother were having a conversation in American Sign Language (ASL). A man sitting near them saw them signing to each other and decided to join their conversation. Like Amanda, he was a child of deaf adults who grew up using ASL at home and speaking English elsewhere. And he noticed a trait of Amanda's: She signed like somebody who was much older than she was. He began gently teasing her about it, saying she was using signs that had fallen out of fashion. He had gone through a similar experience, he said, when he went through training to become an interpreter. During that training, he learned that some of his signs — ones he had learned from his parents — were out of date. The experience inspired Amanda, who is hard of hearing, to take an ASL class to learn more up-to-date signs, and she noticed the same pattern. "I saw a lot of differences between how my young deaf teacher signed and how my parents sign," she told me. An old sign for computer, to take one example, involved large circular motions to evoke the magnetic tapes that once stored data; a new sign combines the letter C with a small circular motion that's a throwback to the old sign.

26. What is the major topic of the passage?

① The generation gap between the old and the young
② Up-to-date training of sign language interpreters
③ Different lexical choices between English and ASL
④ Language change in American Sign Language

27. According to the passage, which of the following is true?

① Amanda has taken an ASL class to be an interpreter.
② Amanda was teased because her ASL was old-fashioned.
③ The male signer cannot speak as his parents are both deaf.
④ A small circular motion with the letter C is the old sign for computer in ASL.

[28~30]

"Brain rot" has been announced as the Oxford word of the year for 2024, amid concerns over endless social media scrolling and mind-numbing content. More than 37,000 people voted to help choose the winner from a shortlist of six words drawn up by Oxford University Press, the publisher of the *Oxford English Dictionary*. Brain rot is defined as "the supposed deterioration of a person's mental or intellectual state, especially viewed as the result of overconsumption of material, now particularly online content, considered to be trivial or unchallenging." Oxford University Press said the term "gained new prominence in 2024 as a term used to capture concerns about the impact of consuming excessive amounts of low-quality online content, especially on social media." Ⓐ_____ its recent rise to prominence, its first recorded use was in Henry David Thoreau's book *Walden* in 1854. Casper Grathwohl, Oxford Languages president, said: "Brain rot speaks to one of the perceived dangers of virtual life, and how we are using our free time. It feels like a rightful next chapter in the cultural conversation about humanity and technology. It's not surprising that so many voters embraced the term, endorsing it as our choice this year. I also find it fascinating that the word brain rot has been adopted by Generations Z and Alpha, those communities largely responsible for the use and creation of the digital content the term refers to."

28. Which of the following is the best title for the passage?
   ① The Evolution of Digital Content Consumption
   ② Oxford's 2024 Word of the Year and Its Significance
   ③ Generation Z's Impact on Modern Vocabulary
   ④ The History of Oxford Dictionary's Word Selection Process

29. According to the passage, which of the following is NOT true?
   ① Casper Grathwohl was surprised by the voting results.
   ② Oxford University Press provided the shortlist of six words for voting.
   ③ The term brain rot first appeared in Thoreau's *Walden* in 1854.
   ④ Generations Z and Alpha are the main users of low-quality online content.

30. Which of the following best fits into Ⓐ?
   ① Despite   ② Because of
   ③ Besides   ④ Except for

[31~32]

One might ask, "Why is sugar in almost all processed foods?" Essentially, sugar is a vehicle that makes you able to eat more by inhibiting the part of the brain that controls satiety. So, if sugar is added to something which does not normally contain it, e.g., salad dressing, pasta sauce, or bread, people will tend to eat more of that something than they normally would if sugar were not present. Therefore, having sugar as an ingredient is a reliable way of getting people to eat more, and buy more, of something than they otherwise would, which generates more profits for the maker. The problem with these sugar-based profits is that excessive consumption of sugar has been linked to diabetes, obesity, and Alzheimer's disease. While sugar is not classified as a drug in the traditional sense, scientific evidence suggests that its effects on the brain's reward system and dopamine receptors are similar to those of addictive drugs. The American Psychiatric Association (APA) considers something addictive if a person can build up a tolerance to it and experiences withdrawal when not using it. Although sugar is not included in the APA's list of addictive substances, some argue that sugar should be, and numerous countries have moved to restrict its consumption by implementing taxes or changing dietary guidelines.

31. What is the major topic of the passage?

① The problems of overconsumption of processed foods
② How overeating leads to obesity and diabetes
③ The APA's failure to classify sugar as an addictive drug
④ Why sugar is added to food and the resulting problems

32. According to the passage, which of the following is NOT true?

① The effect of sugar on dopamine receptors resembles that of addictive drugs.
② Sugar boosts the control of satiety in the brain.
③ Many nations are making efforts to curb the use of sugar.
④ Adding sugar to food often leads to more sales of that food.

33~34

Anyone who's had a shady oyster or a mushroom soup that didn't go down well remembers the ominous queasiness heralding impending bad times. Bacteria release toxins that start the body's process of speedily evacuating the contents of the stomach. It's a protective mechanism of sorts — getting rid of the invaders en masse is probably helpful in the long term, even if it's unpleasant in the short. But it has remained something of a mystery how the brain gets the alarm signal, then sends another one to tell the stomach to vomit. Your next bout of food poisoning isn't the only reason to understand this particular neural pathway. Figuring out how to Ⓐ_____ it could be helpful for people who develop nausea caused by chemotherapy medication and other drugs. As if fighting cancer weren't painful and scary enough, patients are often so turned off by food that keeping their weight up becomes a major struggle. In a new study, researchers report that a bacterial toxin and a chemo medication both set in motion a cascade of similar neural messages that cause queasiness.

33 Which of the following best fits into Ⓐ?

① requite
② maintain
③ counter
④ catalyze

34 According to the passage, which of the following can be inferred?

① Shady oysters and some mushroom soups cause stomach problems.
② Eliminating bacteria from one's stomach involves conscious thinking.
③ Gaining weight is a result of taking too much medicine.
④ Chemo medication is comprised of bacterial toxins.

35~37

The Zeigarnik Effect was first observed by Russian psychologist Bluma Zeigarnik in the early 20th century. While observing waiters in a restaurant, Zeigarnik noticed that the waiters had better recall of orders that were still in progress, as opposed to those that had already been completed. So, why do unfinished tasks stay on our minds? The answer lies in our brain's need for closure. Our brains crave closure, and when a task is left unfinished, it creates a state of tension in our minds. This tension motivates us to seek closure, which can only be achieved by completing the task. The Zeigarnik Effect is related to the concept of cognitive dissonance, which is the discomfort we feel when we hold two conflicting beliefs or values. In the case of unfinished tasks, our belief that we should complete the task conflicts with the fact that it remains unfinished, creating cognitive dissonance and tension in our minds. The Zeigarnik Effect can have a significant impact on our productivity and motivation. When we have unfinished tasks on our minds, we tend to be less focused on the task at hand, and our performance may suffer as a result. However, the Zeigarnik Effect can also be Ⓐ_____. By using the tension created by unfinished tasks to motivate us, we can increase our productivity and motivation to complete tasks.

35 Which of the following is the best title for the passage?

① What Motivates Our Brains to Confirm Our Beliefs
② Why Incomplete Tasks Linger in Our Minds
③ How the Zeigarnik Effect Creates Cognitive Dissonance
④ What Enhances Task Performance

36 Which of the following best fits into Ⓐ?

① restored by taking a break
② facilitated by finishing one's work
③ harnessed for positive outcomes
④ tolerated with unfavorable results

37 According to the passage, which of the following CANNOT be inferred?

① You would find it discomforting when you finish reading a book that you started weeks ago.
② People are naturally inclined to resolve tension from mental conflicts.
③ You would feel tense when facing a looming deadline for a project that you haven't completed.
④ The tension triggered by unfinished tasks does not necessarily have a negative effect on us.

38~40

If you rent your home, there's a good chance your landlord uses RealtorPage to set your monthly payment. The company describes itself as merely helping landlords set the most profitable price. But recent litigation says it's something else: an AI-enabled price-fixing conspiracy. The classic image of price-fixing involves the executives of rival companies gathering behind closed doors and secretly agreeing to charge the same inflated price for whatever they're selling. This type of collusion is one of the gravest sins you can commit against a free-market economy; the late Justice Antonin Scalia once called price-fixing the "supreme evil" of antitrust law. Agreeing to fix prices is punishable with up to 10 years in prison and a $100 million fine. But, as the RealtorPage example suggests, technology may offer a workaround. Instead of getting together with your rivals and agreeing not to compete on price, you can all independently rely on a third party to set your prices for you. Property owners feed RealtorPage's "property management software" their data, including unit prices and vacancy rates, and the algorithm — which also knows what competitors are charging — spits out a rent recommendation. If enough landlords use it, the result could look the same as Ⓐ_____: lockstep price increases instead of price competition, no secret handshake or clandestine meeting needed. Without price competition, businesses lose their incentive to innovate and lower costs, and consumers get stuck with high prices and no alternatives. Algorithmic price-fixing appears to be spreading to more and more industries, and existing laws may not be equipped to stop it.

38 What is the main purpose of the passage?

① To warn about the potential dangers of algorithmic price-fixing
② To explain how RealtorPage works for both landlords and tenants
③ To argue laws should be relaxed to accommodate technological advancements
④ To define what algorithmic price-fixing is in real estate

39 According to the passage, which of the following is NOT true?

① These days, many landlords use RealtorPage to set their monthly rents.
② Those who commit price-fixing can be sentenced to up to 10 years in prison.
③ RealtorPage helps property owners to meet and share their prices to fix them.
④ Price competition motivates businesses to reduce costs to attract customers.

40 Which of the following best fits into Ⓐ?

① a market-driven pricing mechanism
② a traditional price-fixing cartel
③ a free-market solution
④ an algorithmic pricing system

41~42

An explosion in the use of inexpensive, petroleum-based materials has transformed the fashion industry, aided by the successful rebranding of synthetic materials like plastic leather into hip alternatives like "vegan leather," a marketing masterstroke meant to suggest environmental virtue. Underlying that effort has been an influential rating system assessing the environmental impact of all sorts of fabrics and materials. Named the Higg Index, the ratings system was introduced in 2011 by some of the world's largest fashion retailers to measure and ultimately help shrink the brands' environmental footprints by cutting down on the water used to produce the clothes they sell, for example, or by reining in their use of harmful chemicals. But the Higg Index also strongly favors synthetic materials made from fossil fuels over natural ones like cotton, wool, or leather. Now, those ratings are coming under fire from representatives of natural-fiber industries who say the Higg Index is being used to portray the increasing use of synthetics as environmentally desirable despite questions over synthetics' environmental toll.

41 Which of the following is the major topic of the passage?

① The rebranding of eco-desirable materials in the fashion industry
② The advent of vegan leather in the fashion field
③ The controversy over the use of the Higg Index in the fashion field
④ Support for natural-fiber industries to stand against the Higg Index

42 According to the passage, which of the following is true?

① Petroleum-based materials exploded and it shocked the fashion field.
② The Higg Index rebranded plastic leather into "vegan leather" in 2011.
③ The Higg Index is blamed for promoting the use of synthetics.
④ Natural-fiber industries advocate the use of the Higg Index.

43~44

Doppelgängers share strikingly similar physical characteristics — they look so alike that, at times, these two unrelated people could easily pass for twins. Now, new research suggests that Ⓐ doppelgängers have more in common than meets the eye. It may seem obvious that people with similar facial features would also have some of the same DNA, but no one had scientifically proven this, until now. Thanks to the internet, it's now easier than ever for researchers to track down and study doppelgängers. To understand what was going on at the genetic level among look-alikes, scientists collaborated with the Canadian photographer François Brunelle. Since 1999, Brunelle has been traveling around the world to capture intimate portraits of strangers who look nearly identical to one another for his "I'm not a look-alike!" project. Researchers asked 32 pairs of Brunelle's models to answer questions about their lifestyles and submit samples of their DNA. Using facial recognition software, the scientists analyzed headshots of the so-called "human doubles" and computed a score to quantify similarities among their faces. They found that 9 of the 16 very similar-looking pairs shared many common genetic variations known as single nucleotide polymorphisms. These pairs are therefore like virtual twins.

43* Which of the following is the best title for the passage?

① Look-Alikes Are Actually Not Doppelgängers
② Doppelgängers Are Now Scientifically Proven
③ Virtual Twins Turned Out to Be Doppelgängers
④ Doppelgängers Do Not Have to Share Physical Characteristics

44. Which of the following is closest in meaning to Ⓐ?

① Doppelgängers share more similarities than what's visible at first glance.
② Doppelgängers commonly consider meeting in person.
③ Doppelgängers look alike but are nothing alike in other ways.
④ Doppelgängers' eyes look more similar than other features.

[45~47]

On August 1, 2024, the European Union's Artificial Intelligence Act (AI Act) came into effect. This act is a major step towards regulating AI systems within the EU. It has two aims: to foster AI development and to mitigate potential risks to citizens' health, safety, and fundamental rights. A predominant feature of the AI Act is its risk-based classification of AI systems. "Minimal Risk" systems, such as spam filters and AI-enabled video games, have no new obligations under the AI Act. AI systems classified as having "Specific Transparency Risk," such as chatbots, must now explicitly inform users they are interacting with a machine. Also, some AI-generated content must be labeled as such. "High Risk" systems, such as medical software or AI systems used for job recruitment, must comply with strict new requirements, including risk-mitigating systems, high-quality datasets, and human oversight. A final category identified by the Act is "Prohibited AI" systems. These are systems that pose unacceptable risks. Systems banned by the EU include those that cause significant harm by Ⓐ <u>deploying subliminal or manipulative techniques to distort behavior and impair informed decision-making</u>. The Act includes provisions for General Purpose AI (GPAI) models. All GPAI model providers must now provide technical documentation, comply with the Copyright Directive, and publish a summary about the content used for training. Providers of GPAI models that present a systemic risk must also conduct model evaluations, adversarial testing, track and report serious incidents, and ensure cybersecurity protections. By developing a strong regulatory framework based on human rights and fundamental values, and establishing clear requirements for AI systems, the Act aims to protect EU citizens' fundamental rights while fostering innovation and economic growth.

45. Which of the following is the best title for the passage?

① The Future of Regulation of Artificial Intelligence
② Transparency Risks and Labeling Requirements in the AI Act
③ The Role of AI in Modern Video Games from a European Perspective
④ The EU's Artificial Intelligence Act and Its Specifics

46. According to the passage, which of the following is NOT true?

① Users of systems with "Specific Transparency Risk" must be made aware they are interacting with a machine.
② A summary of the content used for training GPAI models must be disclosed.
③ The AI Act introduces new requirements for "Minimal Risk" systems.
④ The AI Act requires "High Risk" systems to have human oversight and high-quality datasets.

47. Which of the following is closest in meaning to Ⓐ?

① using overtly manipulative techniques to guide behavior and inform judgments
② boosting knowledge-based decision-making through underhanded techniques
③ utilizing cunning or hidden methods to alter behavior and hinder sound decision-making
④ implementing subtle strategies to manipulate the information system

48~50

We associate book banning, the legal prohibition of the circulation of specific books, with authoritarian regimes; however, it happens in modern democracies as well. Countless notable works, including Han Kang's *The Vegetarian*, Harper Lee's *To Kill a Mockingbird*, and Ray Bradbury's *Fahrenheit 451*, have faced such scrutiny, albeit for different reasons. Despite winning a Nobel Prize, Korean author Han Kang has seen her novel *The Vegetarian*, a novel that excoriates societal norms, particularly ones about mental illness and bodily autonomy, removed from over 2,000 schools for being "detrimental to students." Critics of the ban argue that it stifles serious discussions about individuality and societal pressures, which the novel poignantly addresses. Similarly, Harper Lee's *To Kill a Mockingbird* was removed from libraries in various parts of the United States due to its use of racial slurs, even while providing a trenchant portrayal of racial injustice in the southern USA. Ray Bradbury's *Fahrenheit 451* is perhaps one of the most ironic bans, as it envisions a dystopian future where books are outlawed and "firemen" burn any that are found. This novel itself has been censored, paralleling its themes of suppressing dissenting ideas and the dangers of an illiterate society. Proponents of bans say they Ⓐ_____ younger audiences from potentially harmful content; while opponents say they Ⓑ_____ intellectual freedom and deprive society of critical engagement with challenging ideas of right and wrong. Ironically, banning books underscores the essential role of literature in fostering critical thinking on a societal level.

48 What is the main purpose of the passage?

① To compare societal norms in Korea and the United States
② To highlight various cases of book banning and its implications
③ To contrast proponents and opponents of book banning
④ To examine the relationship between book banning and illiteracy

49 According to the passage, which of the following is NOT true?

① *To Kill a Mockingbird* was banned for having racist language.
② Books are banned in both autocratic and democratic societies.
③ An illiterate society is dangerous according to Bradbury's book.
④ *Fahrenheit 451* was banned for criticizing the treatment of mental illness.

50 Which of the following ordered pairs best fits into Ⓐ and Ⓑ?

① shield — curtail
② keep — invoke
③ distinguish — limit
④ isolate — incubate

한국외국어대학교

▶ 2025학년도 T2 A형 ▶ 문항 수: 50문항 | 제한시간: 60분

2025 한국외대 T2 A형 영역별 문항 수

구분	문법			어휘			논리완성	독해	생활영어	총 문항 수
	G/S, W/E	정비문	재진술	동의어	반의어	유추				
문항 수	4	2	2	9			4	29		50
백분율	8%	4%	4%	18%			8%	58%		100%

HANKUK UNIVERSITY OF FOREIGN STUDIES

한국외국어대학교
2025학년도 T2 A형: 50문항 · 60분

문항별 배점 01~13 1점 / 14~17 1.5점 / 18~30 2점 / 31~40 2.5점 / 41~50 3점

01~04 Choose the one that best completes the sentence.

01 This sweet story will soothe _____ kids and help them feel calm and safer in the night.

① unflappable
② intransigent
③ skittish
④ impervious

02 He is an _____ reader of historical novels, often immersing himself in the intricate details of past eras and civilizations.

① aesthetic
② avid
③ antiquated
④ isochronous

03 The author depicts both the absurd and the _____, finding the essence of humor at each of these ends of life's daily spectrum.

① agile
② suave
③ quotidian
④ palliative

04 Sebastian was troubled by little, regarding the ups and downs of life with a cheerful _____; on the contrary, his wife took everything seriously.

① abomination ② insouciance
③ invective   ④ slovenliness

05~09 Choose the one that best replaces the underlined word.

05 Around the new year, countless people pledge to reform their bad habits, yet the science of habits reveals that they are not beholden to our desires.

① defiant   ② lethargic
③ congenial   ④ obligated

06 Butterflies do not company in pairs, and because of their lesser conspicuity, their migrations are far less readily detected than those of the smallest birds.

① salience   ② tenuity
③ discretion ④ paltriness

07 There is no objection in principle to the consolidation of bank accounts in order to obtain better terms of business from the bank.

① indulgence ② combination
③ consonance ④ emulation

08 To say these are precipitous and challenging times would be a gross understatement.

① resplendent ② tumultuous
③ limpid   ④ abrupt

09 The playwright's reliance on old-school routines and <u>hackneyed</u> tropes makes the play seem rather creaky.

① mawkish
② decorous
③ dilapidated
④ trite

10~13 Choose the one that is closest in meaning to the CONTEXTUAL meaning of the underlined word.

10 Whether we feel sorry for the injured person or not is just a <u>projection</u> of how we deal with our own adversity.

① protrusion
② transference
③ forecast
④ resonance

11 Hyenas roam mainly at night and tend to <u>skirt</u> even the most cunningly placed camera traps.

① border
② equivocate
③ hem
④ bypass

12 He has an innate <u>facility</u> for understanding complex mathematical theories.

① talent
② building
③ provision
④ convenience

13 More and more, the war was making demands on him beyond his capacity, presenting a <u>bill</u> which his bankrupt spirit could not meet.

① beak
② banknote
③ debt
④ advertisement

14~15 Choose the one that is closest in meaning to the given sentence.

14 The political system can no longer afford to be indifferent to the economy.

① The political system's indifference to the economy has been indispensable so far.
② The political system has not been indifferent enough to care for the economy.
③ The economy was not rendered enough affordance by the political system.
④ The political system has rendered too much indifference to the economy so far.

15 The demand for black plastic appears to be met in no insignificant part via recycled e-waste.

① Recycled e-waste has hardly fulfilled the need for black plastic.
② The demand for black plastic is largely fulfilled through recycled e-waste.
③ Recycled e-waste contributes to meeting the demand for black waste in only a small measure.
④ Recycled e-waste is primarily sourced from black plastic to a great extent.

16~17 Choose the one that best completes the sentence.

16 He was an expert in ancient languages, not a skill _____.

① that modern employers value highly
② value that highly modern employers
③ that employers modern highly value
④ that highly value modern employers

17 It seemed to prove the world contained so much more possibility than _____.

① had given I credit for it
② I had given credit it for
③ I had given it credit for
④ had I given credit for it

18~19 Choose the one that makes the sentence grammatically INCORRECT.

18 That was ① <u>when</u> the company previewed early versions of AI models, ② <u>known</u> as o1, ③ <u>constructed</u> with novel methods the start-up believed ④ <u>it</u> would propel its programs to unseen heights.

19 Although the evidence is ① <u>limited</u>, it would be advisable for athletes ② <u>who</u> suffer considerable muscle damage and soft tissue injuries ③ <u>avoiding</u> alcohol for 24 hours ④ <u>following</u> the event.

20~21 Choose the one that is grammatically INCORRECT.

20 ① The scientist whose research that was published last year changed the field significantly.
② The book that I borrowed from the library last week has gone missing.
③ The student whom I spoke to after the lecture was very smart.
④ The company where she works has been growing rapidly over the last few years.

21 ① The wellness industry is full of products marketed as shortcuts to better health.
② Most of the money doesn't go directly to the people it is supposed to be helped.
③ The book, written by a famous author, became an instant bestseller.
④ The dancer recovering from an injury worked hard to regain full strength.

22~50 Read the following passages and answer the questions.

22~23

That our grip on the physical world is slipping has real consequences: A long history of medical study has connected hand strength to overall physical health and longevity, for reasons that still aren't entirely clear. Pediatric therapists report seeing some kids as old as 4 or 5 years who have never held a pencil or a crayon. The absence of that tactile experience may change how they learn to read and write and limit them in other ways. They also studied about healthy young adults and found Ⓐ those who spend lots of time on Ⓑ their smartphones have weaker grips, duller fingers, and higher rates of hand and wrist injuries than Ⓒ their peers who use Ⓓ their phones less frequently. This underscores the importance of engaging in activities that promote hand use. It is becoming clear that we can benefit emotionally, cognitively, and physically by doing more with our hands — by jotting down notes, knitting, or taking a pottery class. With that effort, perhaps we can arrest our collective drift into a hands-free world.

22 Which of the following is the major topic of the passage?

① Benefits of hand use for health and development
② Effects of hand use on technology
③ The promising future of a hands-free society
④ Risks of poor posture for hand health

23 Which of the following is different from the others in what it refers to?

① Ⓐ
② Ⓑ
③ Ⓒ
④ Ⓓ

24~25

Previously, researchers assumed that absence was represented in the brain by neurons not firing. But recent studies have shown that the brain encodes absence with unique neural patterns. A few years ago, Barnett began his absence studies with the number zero. He recruited 24 participants to perform tasks related to zero as they sat in a magnetoencephalography scanner. As neurons fire, they generate voltages, which in turn create a magnetic field that can be detected by the machine. By analyzing the magnetic fields, researchers can learn how populations of neurons respond when prompted to think about specific topics, such as zero. Barnett was looking for evidence of the numerical-distance effect, a phenomenon that occurs when the brain processes nonzero numbers. Basically, the brain can more easily distinguish between two numbers if they are farther apart than if they are closer together. So it Ⓐ_____. The researchers figured that if the brain processes zero similarly to other numbers, it should also show the numerical-distance effect. Indeed, Barnett found that the brain treats zero, both as a digit and as a quantity, in much the same way that it treats the other numbers.

24 Which of the following is the major topic of the passage?

① How to study the number zero
② Why the number zero presents a problem
③ When the concept of zero is acquired
④ How the brain processes the number zero

25 Which of the following best fits into Ⓐ?

① confuses 6 and 7 more often than 6 and 9
② processes 100 more accurately than 10
③ struggles to differentiate between 11 and 20
④ will not be able to distinguish 4 and 5

A "bildungsroman" is a literary term describing a novel about a protagonist's psychological and moral growth from their youth into adulthood. The bildungsroman literary genre originated in Germany. The German word *bildung* means education and the German word *roman* means novel. Thus, bildungsroman translates to a novel of education or formation. *Wilhelm Meister's Apprenticeship* by Goethe, about a man who lives an empty life as a businessman and embarks on a journey of self-realization to find happiness, is widely considered the first published bildungsroman. It grew in popularity in Britain after it was translated into English in 1824. The actual term bildungsroman was first coined by philologist Karl Morgenstern during his lectures in 1819. It was born out of criticism he received from Friedrich Wolf, a former teacher disappointed in how his career unfolded. Wolf believed the more Morgenstern wrote about art and philosophy, the more vain he became. This criticism of his intellectual journey inspired Morgenstern to invent the term bildungsroman. Psychologist and philosopher Wilhelm Dilthey reprised it in his work *Leben Schleiermachers* and popularized the story structure for a wider audience.

26 What is the main purpose of the passage?

① To analyze the influence of Goethe's novels on British storytelling techniques
② To critique Karl Morgenstern's philosophical contributions to literature
③ To explore the role of Wilhelm Dilthey in redefining 19th-century literature
④ To explain the etymology and evolution of a literary genre

27 According to the passage, which of the following is true?

① Friedrich Wolf coined the term bildungsroman in 1819.
② The term bildungsroman gained popularity immediately after Goethe's novel was published.
③ The term bildungsroman was inspired by criticism of Morgenstern's intellectual development.
④ Wilhelm Dilthey criticized the use of the bildungsroman structure in his philosophical works.

28~30

Intelligence is fiendishly hard to define and measure, even in humans. The challenge grows exponentially when studying animals with sensory, motivational, and problem-solving skills that differ profoundly from ours, such as the octopus. Historically, researchers have tended to focus on whether animals think like humans, ignoring the abilities that animals have but humans lack. To avoid this problem, scientists have tried to find more objective measures of cognitive abilities. One option is a relative measure of brain to body size. The best-studied species of octopus, *Octopus vulgaris*, has about 500 million neurons; that's a relatively large ratio of neurons per kilogram, similar to a rabbit. More accurate measures may include the size, neuron count, or surface area of specific brain structures thought to be important for learning. While this is useful in mammals, the nervous system of an octopus has a fundamentally distinct structural organization. Over half of the neurons in *Octopus vulgaris*, about 300 million, are not in the brain at all, but distributed in "mini-brains," or *ganglia*, in the arms. Within the central brain, most of the remaining neurons are dedicated to visual processing, leaving less than a quarter of its neurons for other processes such as learning and memory. In other species of octopus, the general structure of the brain is similar, but complexity varies. Wrinkles in the brain increase its surface area and may Ⓐ_____. Some species of octopus, notably those living in reef habitats, have more wrinkled brains than those living in the deep sea, suggesting that these species may possess a higher degree of intelligence.

28 Which of the following is the best title for the passage?

① Reefs and Wrinkles in the Brain: A More Intelligent Octopus
② Comparing Intelligence between the Octopus and the Rabbit
③ Determining Cognitive Ability in Animals: The Case of the Octopus
④ Objective Measures of the Brain in Animals

29 According to the passage, which of the following is true of *Octopus vulgaris*?

① It has been less studied than the other species of octopus.
② The majority of its neurons are located in its central brain.
③ The cells in its central brain are mostly related to sight.
④ Its *ganglia* have a small proportion of its total neurons.

30 Which of the following best fits into Ⓐ?

① enhance neural connections and intelligence
② establish the arms as useful appendages
③ indicate the octopus's advancing age
④ reduce the functional ability of the brain

31~32

In the 1970s, Sterling and Eyer were studying the 20th-century morbidity and mortality rates of age-specific cohorts in the United States. The researchers noticed a correlation between mortality rates of age-specific cohorts and the saturation of the labor market at the time the age-specific cohorts were entering the labor force. They discovered that the cohorts that entered the labor market during the economic boom in the 1940s following the Great Depression had a lower mortality rate due to less job competition compared to cohorts prior to the 1930s and since the 1950s. They also noted a correlation of major stressful events, such as bereavement, divorce, unemployment, and migration, to a higher mortality rate. Despite a preconceived notion that a reduced mortality rate in a younger cohort would lead to more chronic diseases later in age, contradictory evidence was found. Younger cohorts with higher mortality rates actually experienced more chronic health problems such as cardiovascular disease later in life. To explain these epidemiological phenomena, the researchers suggested social and systemic stress in the setting of advancing capitalism and industrialization to be the main cause of morbidity and mortality rates in age-specific cohorts. These studies became the foundation of conceptualizing allostasis, Ⓐ the process of physiological changes in the individual level that are shaped by large-scale epidemiological patterns.

31 According to the passage, which of the following is true?

① Sterling and Eyer investigated the relationship between age and unemployment.
② Mortality rates were found to be lower when the labor market was favorable.
③ There was more job competition in the 1940s compared to the 1950s.
④ Cohorts with lower death rates lived longer, leading to more chronic disease.

32. Which of the following is closest in meaning to Ⓐ?

① the process by which individuals shape the large-scale patterns of society
② the way conditions in society affect a person's health
③ the different procedures of building epidemiological patterns
④ the large-scale relationship between physiology and the individual

33~34

One way to understand which direction a society is going — toward or away from chaos — is to study its emotional undercurrents and its attitude toward violence. Medieval Europe, for example, was famously brutish. As the sociologist Norbert Elias wrote in *The Civilizing Process*, impulse control was practically nonexistent and violence was everywhere. But as communities began to reward individuals for proper etiquette, adherence to which was required for entry into the most desirable strata of society, new incentives for self-restraint created substantially more peaceful conditions. The push toward cooperative nonviolence happened organically, whereby people's "more animalistic human activities," as Elias put it, took a back seat to the premium they placed on their communal social life. This change in priorities required and perpetuated steady self-control among individuals across society. "It is simple enough: plans and actions, the emotional and rational impulses of individual people, constantly interweave in a friendly or hostile way," Elias wrote. "This basic tissue resulting from many single plans and actions of men can give rise to changes and patterns that no individual person has planned or created." And "it is this order of interweaving human impulses and strivings, this social order, which determines the course of historical change." Often, when people choose violence, it is because they believe that it is the only path, a last resort in a time of desperation — and they believe that they'll get away with it.

33. What is the main purpose of the passage?

① To explain how violence control can help create a stable society
② To warn that violence is increasing in the modern society
③ To emphasize the inevitability of violence in human history
④ To argue that social change is the main driver of violence

34 According to the passage, which of the following is NOT true?

① In medieval Europe, people's violence was not controlled effectively.
② Individuals were rewarded for cooperative non-violence.
③ Historical changes result from an individual acting independently.
④ People became violent when they believed that there was no other way left.

35~37

The inaccuracy of stereotypes has been emphasized, particularly in the field of racial attitudes, where the terms "stereotype" and "prejudice" have taken on derogatory connotations. In one classic study, the stereotype shared by citizens of Fresno, California, about the local Armenian minority group was shown not only to be false, but to be opposite to reality on many characteristics — e.g., Armenians were actually more law abiding than average rather than less so. However, several authors have pointed out that many stereotypes have a kernel of truth in them. Campbell stressed that the traits that are most important to a perceiving group and the traits on which it differs most from another group will be likely to enter into its stereotype of that other group. To take one example, because cleanliness is an important characteristic to most Americans, and relatively unimportant to many primitive societies, it is more apt to enter into Americans' stereotypes of primitive societies than into those societies' stereotypes of Americans. Thus, paradoxically, a stereotype is determined largely by the nature of Ⓐ_____, and relatively little by the nature of the group that it ostensibly describes. Although many stereotypes may contain a kernel of truth, a key feature of stereotypes is that they are overgeneralized. That is, the characteristics attributed to the group are believed to apply to all members of the group. When generalized in this way, the stereotype is very likely to be inaccurate.

35 Which of the following is the best title for the passage?

① The Stereotypes of Different Groups
② The Truth Behind Stereotypes
③ The Benefits of Stereotyping in Society
④ The Psychological Power of Stereotypes

36 According to the passage, which of the following is true?

① Armenians were found to be less law-abiding than any other groups.
② Primitive societies are likely to value cleanliness.
③ Campbell believed that trivial traits form the basis of stereotypes.
④ Overgeneralization is a central feature of stereotypes.

37 Which of the following best fits into Ⓐ?

① the group being stereotyped
② the group members' commonalities
③ the primitive societies
④ the perceiving group

38~40

Unlike dogs, cat behavior is difficult to study, which is part of why humans understand them less. Cats are often so stressed by being in a lab that meaningful behavioral observations become impossible. So the researchers for the latest study went to the cats' homes and played recordings of different types of speech and different speakers. At first, Dr. de Mouzon and her team were worried that the cats weren't reacting at all. But then they studied film recordings of the encounters. In a few cases, the cats in the study would approach the speaker playing a voice and meow. "In the end, we had really clear gains in the cat's attention when the owner was using cat-directed speech," Dr. de Mouzon said. The findings showed that "cats are paying close attention to their caretakers, down to not only what they are saying, but how they are saying it," said Dr. Vitale, a professor of animal health at Unity College. The new study complements Dr. Vitale's own research into relationships between a cat and its owner. This relationship is so important, Dr. Vitale's research has found, that it Ⓐ_____ the connection between a kitten and its mother. "It is possible that attachment behaviors originally intended for interactions with their mother have now been modified for interactions with their new caretakers, humans." Unlike dogs, "most cats actually prefer human interaction over other rewards like food or toys," Dr. Vitale said.

38 Which of the following is the major topic of the passage?

① A contrastive study of feline and canine behaviors
② The difficulty of observing cat behavior in a lab setting
③ Cats' behavior and their relationships with humans
④ The importance of the relationship between a cat and its mother

39 Which of the following best fits into Ⓐ?

① replicates
② advocates
③ cogitates
④ abjures

40 According to the passage, which of the following can be inferred?

① Dogs are stressed when their behaviors are observed in a lab setting.
② Dr. de Mouzon and Dr. Vitale are on the same research team.
③ Cats do not pay close attention to the tone of their caretakers' voice.
④ Dogs prefer delicious treats over human interaction.

41~42

Unlike other academic disciplines, the sciences are bound by both natural and imposed rules. The rigorous rules of scientific experimentation have been established, as unnecessary as they may seem to outsiders, as a way to ensure reproducible results from experiments. Like a game — where the agreed upon rules let players reproduce similar experiences in a journey toward an end goal — the goal of science is to work toward the truth by following rules of experimenting. In many ways, science is a cooperative game; the scientist doesn't win individually, but rather is truly successful when other scientists can reproduce the same results. Sure, it would be easier to make wild claims about untested drugs as snake oil salesmen did in years past, but in modern times we have learned that ingesting radioactive materials and poisons is not a good idea. Scientists voluntarily agree to bind their work to a rule set that helps ensure accuracy and validity. Then, like in a game with a feedback system of points or checks, there is a system of feedback from peer review of results that helps keep everything on track. Science is also like a game in that it explores boundaries and limitations; constantly poking around the limits to discover new knowledge. In *Everything Bad Is Good for You*, Steven Johnson refers to the constant pressing of boundaries as "probing" and talks about the skill as being a key learning attribute mastered through game play. Like gamers, scientists have to be constantly wondering about what is just beyond their current limits.

41 Which of the following is the major topic of the passage?

① An analogy between game and science in experimentation
② Exploration of games as a scientific method
③ Games replacing scientific experimentation
④ Adopting game techniques in scientific experimentation

42 According to the passage, which of the following is true?

① Outsiders consider rigorous rules of scientific experimentation necessary.
② Scientists' findings are valid when others find the same results.
③ Scientists are forced to follow a rule set for accuracy and validity.
④ Probing is a more essential skill for a scientist than for a gamer.

43~44

Michel Foucault makes the surprising claim that discourse is produced by social power. Rather than merely acting to repress and limit, power "traverses and produces things, it induces pleasure, forms knowledge, produces discourse. It needs to be considered as a productive network which runs through the whole social body." The first product of power is a set of fundamental codes which informs that particular society's grasp of the world. Foucault posits for any society both a general code "governing its language, its schemes of perception, its exchanges, its techniques, its values, the hierarchy of its practices," which makes people feel at home, and a scientific or philosophical justification of that code. Foucault's analysis of power denies that it is divided into simply master and dominated. He sees power as dispersed through a wide network of relationships in which the same persons both exercise and undergo its operations: Ⓐ <u>individuals are the vehicles of power, not its points of application</u>. This view releases criticism from always seeing the same outlines in all the works of a period, the marks of power flowing from its sources, for example, in church and government, toward its victims: the parishioners and citizens. Instead everybody does something in the power network, but that something will not always be the same. And it is because language codes are so fluid, so intractable and unlikely to be predictably fixed and managed by single oppressors, that literary texts can disclose such precise and complex power relations.

43 According to the passage, which of the following is NOT true?

① A general code lets people feel comfortable as members of the society.
② Foucault claims that everyone has and is subject to power.
③ Single oppressors can fix and manage the language of their people.
④ Despite their complexity, power relations can be illustrated by literature.

44 Which of the following is closest in meaning to Ⓐ?

① Power is centralized in the hands of a few rulers or institutions.
② Individuals channel power rather than being direct targets for its use.
③ Individuals seek to control and apply power for personal gain.
④ Power operates through social vehicles based on domination and submission.

45~47

Contrary to what you may think, neural networks are actually quite an old concept which can be dated to a 1943 mathematical paper that modeled how the brain might work. Computer scientists began attempting to construct simple neural networks in the 1950s, but the concept fell out of favor until its revival in the 1980s. By the 1990s, neural networks were in widespread use in AI research. However, only after the advent of hyper-fast processing, massive data storage capabilities, and easy access to computing resources were neural networks able to advance to the point they have reached today, where they can imitate or even exceed human cognitive abilities. In 2017, one of the most important types of neural networks in use today, the transformer model was first developed. Transformer models have assumed a place of outsized importance in current AI models. Ⓐ They are neural networks that use a technique called "self-attention" to take into account the context of elements in a sequence, not just the elements themselves. Via self-attention, Ⓑ they can detect even subtle ways that parts of a data set relate to each other. This ability makes them ideal for analyzing sentences and paragraphs of text, as opposed to just individual words and phrases. Before transformer models were developed, AI models that processed text would often "forget" the beginning of a sentence by the time they got to the end of it, with the result that Ⓒ they would combine phrases and ideas in ways that did not make sense to human readers. Transformer models can remember the beginning of not only a sentence, but also of a conversation, so Ⓓ they can process and generate human language in a much more natural way.

45 Which of the following is the best title for the passage?

① The Role of Self-Attention in Transformer Models for Text Analysis
② The Commercial Application of Neural Networks
③ The Mathematical Foundations of Early Neural Networks
④ The Evolution and Importance of Transformer Models

46 According to the passage, which of the following is true?

① Modern neural networks were enabled by advances in computing technology.
② Neural networks were first conceptualized in the 1950s by mathematicians.
③ Neural networks have been consistently popular in AI research since their inception.
④ Transformer models struggle with remembering the beginning of a sentence.

47 Which of the underlined Ⓐ, Ⓑ, Ⓒ, and Ⓓ is different in what it refers to?

① Ⓐ   ② Ⓑ
③ Ⓒ   ④ Ⓓ

48~50

Don't tell the cosmetic industry this, but mascara might not be helpful for your eyelashes. Lashes' natural microstructure and shape help keep vision clear from liquid droplets by catapulting water away from the eyes. Experiments with human eyelashes and eyelash-mimicking fibers Ⓐ_____ several features that keep water away from the eyes. First, the exterior of an eyelash, or cuticle, acts like a "micro-ratchet." Water can flow easily from root to tip but not in the opposite direction, thanks to scales that overlap like shingles on a roof. When scientists dipped loose eyelashes in water and pulled them out again, more force was required to move the eyelash when the water was working against the ratchet than when going with it. Also, by dripping water on loose eyelashes, the researchers showed that the hairs are hydrophobic, meaning that water beads up on them and tends to roll off. Moreover, eyelashes Ⓑ_____ a shape called a brachistochrone, a curve that minimizes the time it takes to get from point A to B under the force of gravity. Using arrays of nylon fibers with similar dimensions and elasticity as eyelashes, researchers compared fibers in the shape of a brachistochrone with fibers that were straight or curved in another shape. The droplets slid fastest off the brachistochrone. However, modern beauty treatments could disrupt this ability. Mascara can make eyelashes attract water instead of repelling it and curling the lashes alters their shape.

48 Which of the following is the best title for the passage?

① Mascara Impedes Eyelashes' Natural Function
② Eyelash Scales Send Water Flying
③ How Eyelashes Attract Water
④ How a Brachistochrone Shapes your Eyelashes

49 According to the passage, which of the following is true?

① The brachistochronic shape of an eyelash allows liquid to collect on it.
② Pulling the eyelash through water against its ratchet required less energy than with it.
③ The cuticle of an eyelash has overlapping scales.
④ It's easier for water to flow from tip to root of the eyelash.

50 Which of the following sets of ordered pairs best fits in Ⓐ and Ⓑ?

① pinpoint — approximate
② identify — ignore
③ create — reflect
④ discount — follow

한국항공대학교

▸ 2025학년도 인문계 ▸ 문항 수: 30문항 | 제한시간: 60분

2025 한국항공대 인문계 영역별 문항 수

구분	문법			어휘			논리완성	독해	생활영어	총 문항 수
	G/S, W/E	정비문	재진술	동의어	반의어	유추				
문항 수	2			5			10	13		30
백분율	6.7%			16.7%			33.3%	43.3%		100%

KOREA AEROSPACE UNIVERSITY

한국항공대학교
▶ 2025학년도 인문계: 30문항 · 60분

01~05 Choose the word that is closest in meaning to the underlined expression.

[각 3.1점]

01 That may be the <u>quintessential</u> test that proves beyond the slightest doubt that radio is best.

① nominal
② inessential
③ atypical
④ archetypal

02 The moon <u>beckons</u> astronomers because it is dry, airless, and seismically quiet.

① entices
② deters
③ shuns
④ reckons

03 The encryption is <u>ephemeral</u> but at any given time, incredibly important.

① immortal
② perpetual
③ general
④ temporary

04 Copyright laws are <u>convoluted</u> and have been continually changed and amended over the years.

① lucid
② retroactive
③ complex
④ conventional

05 As an artist, he is known for his steadfast dedication to his work projects.
① fickle
② loyal
③ brisk
④ unpredictable

06~10 Choose the one that best completes the sentence. [각 3.3점]

06 Music is a much more elusive form of communication than words alone and yet it has its own precision. It's Mendelssohn who famously said that he found that music was much more precise than words. The problem comes in actually defining that precision and saying what exactly the music is saying. But I think the one thing you can extrapolate from studying Bach's setting of religious texts is that there is a counterpoint going on between the meaning of the texts per se and the affect and impact of the music surrounding the text setting, and it divides into two broad categories. One is _____, where there is a direct sense of sympathy and empathy between the meaning of the words and the type of music that Bach uses to surround and explain the text. And then there's at the other extreme, collision — those moments where the music and the text seem to end up pointing in opposite directions.

① compulsion
② competition
③ confrontation
④ collusion

07 Tomorrow Now, a nonprofit company, provides the weather information to farmers across Kenya. That information is super local and this high resolution data ensures that farmers can have information that's relevant to their farm rather than for the entire town. The data on its own is just information. The goal is to turn it into weather intelligence — something the farmers can actually use to improve their daily decision-making on the farm. And that's the job of their governmental partner. "We look at the weather information to predict short-term forecast for the farmers, and then we'll be able to come up with a planting date." says a director at Kenya Agricultural and Livestock Research Organization. "_____, the weather messages will suggest where to grow what crops and which varieties of those crops will fare best," he says. Already, almost five million farmers across Kenya are receiving the weather advisories. On average, they're seeing a 7% increase in revenues.

① By and large
② In a nutshell
③ Instead
④ Down the road

08 Why does space food matter? One word: Mars. Meal prepping for a trip into deep space is not easy. Right now, scientists have figured out a lot of the logistics regarding a journey to the red planet, except how to bring enough food. _____ it would take seven months to get to Mars. To pack over a year's worth of food for the round trip (with extra snacks, of course) would be immensely heavy — too heavy for a rocket. The things that we don't know how to do is get enough stuff up into the pathway between Earth and Mars to sustain people for a trip. The contestants of the Deep Space Food Challenge look to answer that question, and make the long-awaited mission to Mars more feasible.

① At the earliest
② At best
③ At the latest
④ At last

09 Across northern Australia, freshwater crocodiles are dying in droves, with some populations down by 70%. That's because the animals are eating a super-poisonous cane toad that humans brought to the continent decades ago. Conservation scientists have witnessed the demise of the crocodiles firsthand. The loss of so many crocodiles is a problem because they sit atop the food web. When they decline, we see this huge hole in the ecosystem, and this ripples out and sets off cascading impacts. These impacts include _____ in midlevel predators, which can negatively influence birds' ability to nest. And so cane toads do really cause ecological havoc here in Australia.

① a surge
② a flip
③ a downturn
④ an upkeep

10 The ray spider is smaller than a grain of rice. It spins its web as a classic set of concentric circles with spokes radiating outwards. But then, the spider strings a thread from the center of the web to a nearby rock or twig. It then grabs the middle of the web with its back legs and then pulls itself along that tension line with its front legs. That is what turns that web from a flat shape into a cone shape. The conical web is now spring loaded. When an insect flutters by, the spider releases the tension line, flinging the web forward and entangling the prey. So they're not just passively sitting there. They're using the web like a slingshot _____ the insect ever touching the web.

① for
② from
③ without
④ by

11~12 Choose the one that is either ungrammatical or unacceptable. [각 3.8점]

11 If you live along the path of totality for Monday's solar eclipse and you have any Christmas gear, you might want to break it out. The ① <u>celestial</u> event will bring odd phenomena to our planet. As an unusual visual effect brought by a solar eclipse, red and green colors will look strange to humans on Earth. That's partly due to the change in light when the moon blocks the sun, but also the way our eyes and brain adjust to and interpret that change. As light dims, our eyes transition from photopic vision, associated with the retina's cone cells that ② <u>delivers</u> full colors and fine detail, toward scotopic night vision that relies on rod cells to detect objects in low light. In the middle is mesopic vision, the transitional phase ③ <u>where</u> both rods and cones are active. When the light's intensity dims in the eclipse, colors with longer wavelengths, like red, will look darker as cones become less active. But because rods are sensitive to the shorter blue-green wavelengths, those colors will have a chance to shine. This is pretty much a totality thing with only people in the eclipse's central path ④ <u>guaranteed</u> to witness the phenomenon. Also, you shouldn't rely on just one red or green T-shirt to trigger the effect. You have to have lots of people or colorful things around to see it. The effect is the result of sudden dimness and your rods and cones trying to make sense of that dimness. It's called the Purkinje effect.

12 The idea that eating cocoa-rich, dark chocolate may offer health benefits is not new. Now, a new study finds people who have a habit of eating a little dark chocolate have a 21% lower risk of developing Type 2 diabetes, ① <u>compared to</u> people who don't consume it. People who ate milk chocolate, which has more sugar and less cocoa, had no reduction in diabetes risk. And, over the course of the study, milk chocolate eaters tended to gain weight, which contributes to the risk of diabetes. However, eating dark chocolate was not associated with weight gain. There's long been ② <u>an evidence</u> that the compounds found in cocoa can contribute to heart health. For instance, a study published in the journal *Heart*, found chocolate lovers had a lower risk of strokes and other types of cardiovascular disease. Scientists have ③ <u>homed in on</u> bioactive plant compounds found in cocoa beans, which have been shown to prompt production of nitric oxide in the body. This gas can cause blood vessels ④ <u>to open up</u> or dilate, which is the mechanism for the lowering of blood pressure, and multiple studies have shown dark chocolate consumption is linked to a modest reduction in blood pressure.

13~17 Choose the best for the blank. [각 3.5점]

13 Negative thinking can do a number on your central nervous system, causing you to react physically. Have you ever started getting negative thoughts and suddenly felt physically bad too? Whatever your response — shaky hands, trembly voice, sweaty brow — a slow inhale and a slower exhale will help soothe the central nervous system. And finding your composure will help you let the thoughts pass. You cannot have a calm mind if your body is in hyperdrive. The opposite is true too — _____.

① you can have a calm mind if your body is in hyperdrive
② you can have a calm body as your mind is going in circles
③ you cannot have a calm body if your mind is going in circles
④ you cannot have a calm mind unless your body is in hyperdrive

14. Joan Moon, a career coach, explains some classic negotiation tactics often used in business environments and how they can be applied in everyday circumstances. For one, the tactic of _____ helps different parties find one solution that's in everyone's interest. You might see this in business contracts or labor agreements, for example. Parties won't sign until the terms are mutually beneficial. How to use it in everyday life? Try this when you want the other party to not just agree with your decision, but feel good about it. Joan shares a recent personal experience. Her phone line was down so she called her phone company to get reconnected — but the customer service agents were unhelpful. She could feel herself getting upset, so she decided to reframe her request using the tactic. She said: "Listen, I've been with this company for ten years and I would like to keep doing so for another ten years. Can we focus on a solution?" The approach worked, she says. The company didn't want to lose a loyal customer — and Joan wanted her phone fixed.

① win-win strategy
② benchmarking
③ a menu of options
④ value proposition

15. One way to nudge people to do something is to make it easy to do. Sludge is like its sinister opposite: when institutions try to prevent people from doing something _____. Richard Thaler, one of the founding fathers of behavioral economics, was inspired to develop the idea of sludge when his memoir was released a few years ago. His editor told him that the first review was published in a London newspaper, and Thaler wanted to read it. But the article was behind a paywall. To get past the paywall, there was a promotion. It cost 1 British pound to sign up for a one-month trial subscription. Then he started digging deeper and learned that to cancel his subscription, he'd have to give two weeks' notice. And to do that, he'd have to actually call the newspaper's headquarters during London business hours. This is a company using sludge to prevent people from canceling their subscriptions.

① through monetary rewards
② by appealing to emotions
③ by making it hard to do
④ through punishment

16 Researchers have identified a substance in muscles that helps explain the connection between a fit body and a sharp mind. When muscles work, they release a protein that appears to generate new cells and connections in a part of the brain that is critical to memory, a team reports in the journal *Cell Metabolism*. _____, says the research team. Previous research had revealed factors in the brain itself that responded to exercise. The discovery came after a team of researchers decided to cast a wide net in searching for factors that could explain the well-known link between fitness and memory. They began by looking for substances produced by muscle cells in response to exercise. That search turned up cathepsin B, a protein best known for its association with cell death and some diseases. Experiments showed that blood levels of cathepsin B rose in mice that spent a lot of time on their exercise wheels. What's more, as levels of the protein rose, the mice did better on a memory test in which they had to swim to a platform hidden just beneath the surface of a small pool. The team also found that, in mice, cathepsin B was causing the growth of new cells and connections in the hippocampus, an area of the brain that is central to memory.

① The finding has a dark side
② The finding provides another piece to the puzzle
③ The finding does not move the needle
④ The finding leaves more questions than answers

17 An over-reliance on GPS can also lead to a narrower view of your surroundings. You're not paying attention to the broader environment that gives you cues of where you are in space — what's on your right or left and what it means to be "here." In fact, people who have a good internal compass may have a deeper connection to the world around them. If you want to gain confidence on the road or be less reliant on GPS to get around, _____. People with a good sense of direction — like the London cabbies — know their streets. While you might not be able to master 25,000 of them, you can try an expert navigation tactic. Commit street names, landmarks and routes to memory by using narratives and tricks to lock things in. This is especially helpful when street names are abstract and don't follow a logical order. The process of connecting a story or idea to a place is called building a cognitive map. It gives you an idea of where things are and how they're connected. So as you navigate your way without a map, look around and use stories and memory devices to remember the details of your surroundings. You might say, "I'm making a right on 12th Street

where I got churros with my friend that one day, then I'm heading up P Street toward the park — that is P for park." You can use them to gain a better sense of ownership over your surroundings and ease any anxiety about getting lost.

① do not hesitate to ask locals for guidance
② let your feet do the talking
③ do not go with your own mind flow
④ use memory tricks to remember where you are

18~30 Read the following passages and answer the questions. [각 3.3점]

18~19

Neurobiologists had previously shown that rats are normally enthusiastic helpers. If a rat encounters another rat that is trapped in a holder made from a clear acrylic tube, the free rat will explore the tube and figure out how to release the trapped one. It will do this over and over again, even for rat strangers (as long as the trapped rat belongs to a strain that they have lived with previously). They don't have to know the individual rat, but they have to know the type of rat. These rat rescuers seem to be motivated by the internal distress they feel at another's plight — because when researchers gave the free rats a "chill pill," an anti-anxiety drug — the animals would no longer work to release their trapped companion. To test out the bystander effect in rats, the researchers trapped one rat in the acrylic tube, as they usually did. Then they added to the enclosure not just one free rat but two or three. When all but one of the free rats was given the anti-anxiety drugs that caused passivity _____ another's need, the researcher saw a definite effect on the non-drugged rat's willingness to help. He'd help once. He would not help again. Researchers say the rat would not help the next day or the day afterward as a rat normally would. It is essentially as though this rat says, 'Well, you know what, I helped yesterday. No one cared — not doing that again.' The researchers note that when none of the rats was drugged into passivity, rats that had other free companions started to help much more quickly than they did when alone, suggesting the companions' positive reactions may have spurred on the helpful rats.

18 Choose the best for the blank.

① in the face of
② because of
③ on top of
④ instead of

19 What can be inferred from the passage above?

① Rats make moral decisions.

② The presence of other individuals makes the helpers less likely to act.

③ Helping behavior does not decrease over time.

④ Group presence can affect individual action.

20~21

While a peak in global emissions from burning fossil fuels may only be a few years away, it doesn't mean global temperatures will start falling. Countries will continue to add greenhouse gasses to the atmosphere, just at a slower rate. Those emissions will keep raising global temperatures. To stop temperatures from rising, greenhouse gas emissions need to fall to zero. "At this point of peaking, your emissions are at the all-time high," experts say. "That means that you're actually doing the most damage possible to the climate system per year. And so what matters most is how quickly you can get out of that high-damage zone." It's like driving a car _____. Hitting peak emissions is like taking your foot off the gas pedal. "You still have to brake if you want to stop at some point, because there is a wall there and you're driving toward the wall," they say. At the COP29 climate summit, countries are negotiating new pledges to cut future emissions, in the hope of limiting warming to 1.5 degrees Celsius above pre-industrial levels by 2100. Beyond that level, the world could see much more destructive storms and floods, as well as irreversible damage to ecosystems like coral reefs. Reaching that goal would require cutting emissions to zero by 2050, though countries' current pledges fall well short of that goal. Still, a peak in emissions would mark an important turning point in global negotiations. We are still, to some extent, masters of our fates and we can control how much warming there is.

20 Choose the best for the blank.

① at dangerous speeds

② without a license

③ while fatigued

④ under the influence

21. What would be the best title of the passage above?

① Climate goal is just around the corner
② Renewable energy delays peak emissions
③ Peaking is only the beginning
④ A sudden climb to the peak can backfire

22~23

When you shop, there's usually a _____ in your brain between what can be described as its emotional and rational parts. Spotting something you'd like to buy activates your brain's reward circuitry. Dopamine-fueled impulses pump you up. Anticipation might have you imagining how great life would be with this new thing if only you had it. It's especially intense if you're predisposed to like something. The counterbalance is your cognitive mechanism. It might pipe up like a prudent accountant: Do I need this? Is this worth it? How does it fit in my budget? A sale lands like the thumb that tips your mental scale toward buying. In fact, the discount itself often registers as a win, delivering its own bolt of joy. Not only are we getting the product but we're also getting that reward that we discovered something, we've earned this extra thing. Stores, of course, know all this and try to push our buttons. Experts say we often subconsciously believe popular things to be more valuable or more rewarding. So stores appeal to our crowd mentality: *It's Black Friday, and everyone's shopping, buying that thing you'd like.* They create urgency: *Your favorite car is on sale today only!* And they create scarcity: *Shop now while supplies last!* The promotions get people's blood pumping. You attribute it to the product: it must be good. It's really hard to always approach sales rationally. Even experts struggle. One buying strategy experts recommend is to make a shopping list in advance and then stick to it. More importantly, give yourself time to cool off from your instant reaction. The ability to think can override the emotional state. The more you spend time thinking and bring your cognitive processes to bear ... you have a shot at basically saying, 'No, I think I'm going to pass,' even though that wasn't your first inclination.

22. Choose the words that best fill in the blank.

① hiatus ② recognition
③ handoff ④ standoff

23 What can be inferred from the passage above?

① The human brain has essentially evolved to feel first and think next.
② People are hardly influenced by marketing strategies.
③ Consumers have a natural urge to buy expensive products.
④ Emotions do not play a role in decision-making when buying products.

24~25

We had a VHS player. We had a landline telephone with an answering machine that played these little tapes. And none of that technology is around today. The reason it is not around — creative destruction. A phrase that an economist named Joseph Schumpeter came up with. That is the idea that the economy is always evolving, that there are new products that are constantly being invented, and those inventions make the old products obsolete. Creative destruction is why none of the technology from childhood exists today except the graphing calculator. ⒶThe calculators were like the original iPads but without being able to do anything except give you a nice cosine graph or whatever. They could do calculus and absolutely nothing else. Texas Instrument, or TI, is still making these calculators, and they look exactly the same. ⒷWe could easily add features to our calculators like a touchscreen, Wi-Fi or a camera. But we don't. That fact is what makes these calculators special. In fact, if the graphing calculator were connected to the Internet, it would be less valuable. There wouldn't even be a reason for its existence because it could compromise the test security and really detract from what the calculators are designed to do. The graphing calculator did once represent cutting-edge technology. And it took standardized test designers years before they would allow graphing calculators to be used on their tests. These test makers worried that the calculators would give students an unfair advantage. ⒸGraphing calculators are pretty much the only technology that standardized test makers will allow because unlike smartphones or laptops, the graphing calculator is not connected to the Internet. ⒹIts value lies in the fact that technology skipped over it.

24 Find the best place for the following sentence.

Now it's exactly the opposite.

① Ⓐ   ② Ⓑ
③ Ⓒ   ④ Ⓓ

25 What can be inferred from the passage above?

① Standardized tests have fully adapted to technological changes.
② Old technologies disappear because consumers no longer want them.
③ Creative destruction only affects consumer dynamics but not tech industrial market.
④ Graphing calculators are like islands where creative destruction doesn't reach.

26~27

A new research takes a look at gains and losses and the very different ways in which we think about them. It's called loss aversion. Let's say you go to a casino and you plunk down a bet and you lose $50. Now the question is do you leave or do you try and dig yourself out of the hole by gambling a little further? While the gamble is biased in the favor of the house, there's some chance that you might win and get back to where you were before. When you frame choices in that way, human beings exhibit real consistent risk acceptance. The interesting thing is that people seem much more willing to place the second bet than to place the first bet. That's because with the first bet you're hoping to win something. With the second bet what you're really trying to do is to head off the loss. Loss aversion theory suggests that the desire to avoid losses is wired more strongly into the brain than the desire to achieve gains. This bias actually extends to countries. The study has just analyzed 100 trade disputes between the United States and other countries. They divided these disputes into two groups. In one group, the U.S. was trying to open up a new market that had been closed to U.S. companies so there was a potential gain here in terms of markets and jobs. In the other groups, there was already trade between the U.S. and the other country where there was some dispute and the U.S. was arguing that the other country had clamped down in some way and that American companies were now losing market share and losing jobs as a result. So one set of disputes was framed as a potential gain, whereas the other set of disputes was framed as a potential loss. What the theory of loss aversion will predict is that you will fight harder and longer when you're confronting a loss. The study finds this is exactly what happens at the national level. When a dispute is framed as jobs being lost, exactly like the guy in the casino, _____. Everyone is in the same psychological basket, so to say. So the fundamental idea with loss aversion is that you're driving by looking in the rearview mirror. That's what loss aversion is. It's not a good idea when you're driving. It's not a good idea when you're gambling, and it's certainly not a good idea when it comes to national policy.

26 Choose the best for the blank.

① U.S. policymakers pull out all the stops and fight
② American leaders drop the ball and fail to take action
③ policymakers retreat from the battle
④ the authorities steer clear of dangerous gambles

27 What can be inferred from the passage above?

① Policymakers always prioritize profits over stability, no matter the cost.
② Focusing on losses hinders forward-thinking strategies.
③ Avoiding loss is outweighed by the desire to innovate.
④ Loss aversion can lead to efficient resource allocation in national policies.

28~30

Last week, I came across an article, "Beyond Energy, Matter, Time and Space," which writes about two recent books with opposite viewpoints concerning what we can and cannot know of the world. On the one hand, we find philosopher Thomas Nagel, and the arguments from his 2012 book *Mind and Cosmos*. According to Nagel, simple materialism is insufficient to make sense of some of the most complex natural phenomena, life included. He proposes an extension of current ideas, still within the material, but into yet unknown modes of thinking. ⒜ On the other, we have the idea of MIT physicist Max Tegmark, as explained in his book *Our Mathematical Universe*. According to Tegmark, math is not just the tool we invent to describe both physical reality and pure rational constructions, but the very essence of nature. ⒝ The concluding paragraph of the article resonates strongly with my own opinion. The main point is that it is naive to believe we can have such a thing as _____. There are two essential reasons for this belief. The first is simply that to make models of nature we need data. This data comes from tools of all kinds, from microscopes and particle detectors to telescopes and mass spectrometers. Any tool has limits of precision and range. ⒞ Tools can and will improve. But some shortsightedness will always be unavoidable. The second reason is that nature itself operates within certain limits: the speed of light and the finite age of the universe delimit how far we can see in space and limit causal relationships; quantum uncertainties delimit what we can say about the position and velocity of submicroscopic objects; math itself has its limits, as Kurt Gödel explores in his incompleteness theorems. The same is true with computers, from Alan Turing's undecidability theorem. So, the image of an island captures our struggle to make sense of things, surrounded by an ocean of the unknown. As the island grows, so do the shores of our ignorance: as we learn more about the world we are able to ask questions we couldn't have anticipated before. To know it all we would need to know all questions. And that, of course, is clearly impossible. Unanswerable questions invoke a feeling of humility, of how science is, in essence, an ongoing mosaic of ideas, a self-correcting narrative of what we can gather of physical reality. D This is far from a defeatist view; in fact, it is liberating. What could be more exciting for us to realize that knowledge is an endless frontier?

28 Choose the best for the blank.

① inability to attain universal dynamics
② complete knowledge of nature
③ frailty of human nature
④ fundamental principles

29 Find the best place for the following sentence.

Hence, we are always partially myopic to what goes on.

① A
② B
③ C
④ D

30 What can be inferred from the passage above?

① Science thrives on humility and evolving ideas.
② Endless questions make discovery discouraging.
③ Although scientific tools have limits, complete knowledge is possible.
④ The endless pursuit of knowledge delays opportunities for discovery and growth.

한국항공대학교

▶ 2025학년도 자연계 ▶ 문항 수: 영어 20문항, 수학 20문항 | 제한시간: 90분

2025 한국항공대 자연계 영역별 문항 수

구분	문법			어휘			논리완성	독해	생활영어	총 문항 수
	G/S, W/E	정비문	재진술	동의어	반의어	유추				
문항 수	1			5			7	7		20
백분율	5%			25%			35%	35%		100%

KOREA AEROSPACE UNIVERSITY

한국항공대학교
2025학년도 자연계: 영어 20문항, 수학 20문항 · 90분

01~05 Choose the word that is closest in meaning to the underlined expression.

[각 4점]

01 These <u>innocuous</u> remarks were misinterpreted by some of the audience.
① inoffensive
② sarcastic
③ insincere
④ banal

02 The argument made by the author was based on a <u>quixotic</u> interpretation of the historical events.
① former
② imbalanced
③ impractical
④ flimsy

03 The government's <u>moribund</u> economic reform policy is being reviewed by experts to assess its future potential.
① progressive
② thriving
③ controversial
④ stagnant

04 The decision to postpone the meeting was seen as a <u>prudent</u> move, considering the overall situation of the company.
① daring
② autocratic
③ deliberate
④ abrupt

05 This trailer does a decent job of obfuscating the major plot points of the film.
① concealing
② highlighting
③ simplifying
④ delivering

06~08 Choose the one that best completes the sentence. [각 4.6점]

06 Beaked hazelnuts are a little sweeter and more buttery than _____ hazelnuts. Nestled in a fuzzy, green husks that extends outward like the beak of a bird, beaked hazelnuts carpet the forest valleys of British Columbia. For generations, First Nations tribes in the region have passed down stories of these hazelnuts as a vital food source their ancestors planted and cultivated. These stories motivated researchers to look more deeply at hazelnut genetics, in the hopes of determining just how widely the hazelnut was cultivated. The team visited the archaeological remains of villages throughout British Columbia and sampled over 200 hazelnuts nearby. They determined that beaked hazelnuts had been actively cultivated across a wide span of regional territory, up to 800 kilometers away. This genetic detective work verifies how First Nations people changed the forest in long-lasting ways.

① nutritious
② alien
③ provincial
④ exported

07 Before conducting a recent survey of Americans to figure out how much they're using generative AI, David Deming, an economist, says he was skeptical that the explosion of generative AI would offer sizable benefits for the U.S. economy anytime soon. Now, however, he says he's more optimistic. The study was motivated by questions over whether and how much Americans are using generative AI. Deming says he was shocked by the results. They found that almost 40% of Americans, ages 18 to 64, have used generative AI. And a sizable percentage seems to use it regularly. The economists found that more than 24% of American workers had used it at least once in the week prior to being surveyed, and nearly one in nine used it every workday. The usage of AI seems to be pretty much _____. "We even found that 22% of blue-collar workers say they use AI, and usage rates were above 20% in every major occupation category except personal services, where it was like 15%," he says.

① exceptional
② one-sided
③ around the corner
④ across the board

08 Pantone's Color of the Year is meant to capture the zeitgeist, said the vice president of the Pantone Color Institute. At the same time, it's also intended to serve as _____. Before it became the color juggernaut it is today, Pantone was a commercial printing company under a different name. When Lawrence Herbert, a print technician with a background in chemistry, was hired by the corporation in the 1950s, he identified a recurring problem in his work. When requesting printed copies, of brochures or posters, customers struggled to talk about color accurately. To get the color they were after, they would have to send in an actual sample of the color. One famous thing was to cut a piece off their tie and send it into the print and say, match this color. They had their own ink formula books, and they could get close. But it was very random. In 1963, Lawrence founded the solution. He developed the Pantone Matching System as a way to standardize color reproduction so that print copies matched the original, no matter the printing device. Pantone expanded its range of pigments, and by 1968 it became the industry standard. People credits the shrewd marketer in Herbert for turning Pantone into a widely accepted color system.

① a dismal herald
② a marketing trickery
③ a cultural antidote
④ a technological mistake

09 Choose the one that is either ungrammatical or unacceptable. [5점]

09 The Boston Mint had defied the British crown's authority to produce coins, representing New England's growing sense of identity as separate from the mother country and its determination to regulate its own economy, according to the Massachusetts Historical Society. After the American Revolution, the coins it ① had produced became vogue even in England. English collector Thomas Brand Hollis wrote to then-American ambassador to the Netherlands John Adams in 1781 asking for help in sourcing one of these coins. In turn, Adams wrote to ask his wife, Abigail, for help ② although

her great-grandfather had been the stepbrother of John Hull, the silversmith who minted these coins. Just ③ <u>one other</u> threepence coin of this type is known to have survived to the present day and it is in the collection of the Massachusetts Historical Society, making this specimen the only one available to private collectors. Another coin is perhaps still in existence after it was stolen from Yale College sometime before the 1960s, although its whereabouts is unknown. Other historic US coins have fetched vast sums at auction. A rare 1794 silver dollar believed to be one of the first — if not the first — made by the US mint sold for $10 million in 2013. ④ <u>Meanwhile</u>, a rare 1933 "Double Eagle" coin, one of the last gold coins ever struck for circulation in the US, sold for $18.9 million in 2021.

10~13 Choose the best for the blank. [각 4.8점]

10 Perhaps the greatest mind-bending quirk of our universe is the inherent trouble with timekeeping: Seconds tick by ever so slightly faster atop a mountain than they do in the valleys of Earth. For practical purposes, most people don't have to worry about those differences. But a renewed space race has the United States and its allies, dashing to create permanent settlements on the moon, and that has brought the idiosyncrasies of time, once again, to the forefront. On the lunar surface, a single Earth day would be roughly 56 microseconds shorter than on our home planet — a tiny number that can lead to significant inconsistencies over time. NASA and its international partners are currently grappling with the perplexing conundrum. Scientists aren't just looking to create a new time zone on the moon, as some headlines have suggested. Rather, the space agency and its partners are looking to _____ or system of measurement that accounts for that fact that seconds tick by faster on the moon.

① separate time zones in space
② create an entirely new time scale
③ reevaluate the current timekeeping method
④ erase the time tracker

11 An odd little gourd called the squirting cucumber has an explosive reproductive strategy that has intrigued naturalists since the days of the Roman Empire. Squirting cucumbers spur their seeds over distances hundreds of times their length, and now scientists know how the plants do it. A squirting cucumber in action is a remarkable sight, but if you blink, you might miss it — the fountain lasts about 0.03 second. When ripe, the hairy green fruit measures about 4 centimeters long. They are members of the gourd family and relatives of zucchini, squash and pumpkins, but _____. Recently, researchers blew this ballistic mystery wide open. They used high-speed video and digital 3D reconstructions to analyze squirting cucumbers before, during and after a squirt and created mathematical models to describe the fruits' geyser-like eruptions.

① they rely on environmental forces to disperse seeds
② they exhibit a characteristic of continuous eruptions
③ they have a distinct eruptive reproductive mechanism
④ the family members employ a retrogressive dispersal strategy

12 Humans' love affair with carbs may _____, according to a new study. A once prevailing stereotype of ancient humans feasting on mammoth steak and other hunks of meat helped foster the idea of a protein-heavy diet that was necessary to fuel the development of a large brain. But archaeological evidence in recent years has challenged this view, suggesting that humans long ago developed a taste for carbohydrates, roasting things such as tubers and other starch-laden foods that have been detected by analyzing bacteria lodged in teeth. The new research offers the first hereditary evidence for early carb-laden diets. Scientists traced the evolution of a gene that enables humans to digest starch more easily by breaking it down into simple sugars that our bodies can use for energy. The study revealed these genes duplicated long before the advent of agriculture. This expansion may even go back hundreds of thousands of years, long before our species, Homo sapiens, or even Neanderthals emerged as distinct human lineages.

① predate our existence as a species
② have been driven by environmental factors
③ explain the origin of human evolution
④ begin with a backlash against protein-rich diets

13. A graduate student at MIT made a startling discovery: The facial recognition software program she was working on couldn't detect her dark skin; it only registered her presence when she put on a white mask. It was her first encounter with what she came to call the coded gaze. "You've likely heard of the male gaze or the white gaze," she explains. This is a cousin concept really, about who has the power to shape technology and whose preferences, priorities and prejudices are baked in. She notes that in a recent test of Stable Diffusion's text-to-image generative AI system, prompts for high paying jobs overwhelmingly yielded images of men with lighter skin. Meanwhile, prompts for criminal stereotypes, such as drug dealers, terrorists or inmates, typically resulted in images of men with darker skin. In her new book, she looks at social implications of technology and warns that biases in facial analysis systems could harm millions of people — especially if they reinforce existing stereotypes. "With the adoption of AI systems, at first I thought we were looking at a mirror, but now I believe we're looking into a kaleidoscope of distortion," she says. "Because the technologies we believe to be bringing us into the future are actually _____."

① making us overly reliant on automation
② leading us astray by fostering shallow connections
③ building on the advancements we've made so far
④ taking us back from the progress already made

14~20 Read the following passages and answer the questions. [각 6점]

14~15

A new report from the National Academy of Sciences says it's hard to know how many people in the U.S. actually have food allergies or whether they're on the rise. Part of the challenge is this: Food allergies are often self-diagnosed and symptoms can be misinterpreted. [A] Sometimes people can't distinguish a food allergy from other conditions such as lactose intolerance or gluten sensitivity, which don't fit the medical definition of an allergy. There are a lot of misconceptions about what a food allergy is, says Dr. Virginia Stallings. [B] One scenario is this: A parent of a young child introduces a new food — say, milk — into the diet, and then notices the child has an upset stomach or other symptoms of gastrointestinal distress. The parent may suspect a food allergy. But, perhaps, these are signs of lactose intolerance — a completely different condition. The reason food allergy symptoms are often confused with other conditions such as lactose intolerance is because there's an overlap in some of the symptoms, Stallings explains. Adding to the confusion, food allergies can be complicated to diagnose. [C] There isn't one skin test or blood test that can accurately determine whether a person has an allergy to a specific food, says Stallings. She adds if parents recognize clear signs of allergic reactions, such as swelling lips or difficulty breathing, they should seek emergency care. [D] But often times, the symptoms are milder. In these cases, rather than self-diagnosing an allergy, families should see an expert, such as a pediatric allergist.

14 Find the best place for the following sentence.

We do not have an optimal diagnostic tool.

① [A]   ② [B]
③ [C]   ④ [D]

15 What would be the best title of the passage above?

① Disentangling the complexity behind food allergies
② Simplifying the definition of food allergies
③ Authorizing a diagnostic tool for food allergies
④ Recognizing symptoms to self-diagnose food allergies

The roots of America's candy boom lie in the 1920s. Sugar trade routes that had been disrupted during World War I were once again open for business. The result: a glut of sugar that led to a steep crash in prices. This was a mess for farmers in the mainland United States, Cuba, Puerto Rico, and elsewhere. But it was a boon for the candy business. Several factors lay the groundwork for the rise of Big Retail Candy that decade. As the 1920 Census registered, it was the first time a majority of the U.S. population was living in cities. With urbanization, higher wages and low unemployment, households began to buy more processed food. An early casualty: homemade sweets. Doughnuts, taffy and apples draped in caramel sauce began to be jettisoned in favor of store-bought candy. And then there was Prohibition: Basically, folks were swapping one vice — alcohol — for another. People at the time often said that candy and soda consumption was increasing because of Prohibition. _____, many U.S. soldiers had returned from World War I with a sweet tooth, thanks to candy included in their wartime rations. This helped spread the candy habit beyond the women and children who had previously been assumed to be the main consumers.

16 Choose the words that best fill in the blank.

① For this reason
② What's more
③ By and large
④ Even so

17~18

The Food and Drug Administration has stepped into a simmering debate in California as to whether coffee should come with a cancer warning label. In March, a judge sided with a nonprofit organization that argued that coffee contains high levels of acrylamide, a cancer-causing chemical compound produced as beans roast. Coffee companies didn't deny acrylamide's presence but argued that it was found at low levels that posed no significant health risk and was outweighed by other health benefits. That argument wasn't compelling to Los Angeles County Superior Court Judge Elihu Berle. He ordered coffee companies in California to carry a cancer warning label under Proposition 65. The law, which requires the state to maintain a list of harmful substances and businesses to notify customers of exposure, has led to both a reduction in carcinogenic chemicals and quick settlements over labels on foods. On Wednesday, FDA Commissioner Scott Gottlieb said in a statement that if a state law purports to require food labeling to include a false or misleading statement, the FDA may decide to step in. He added that a large body of research has found little evidence that coffee causes cancer and instead suggested that it might reduce the risk of some cancers: Strong and consistent evidence shows that in healthy adults, moderate coffee consumption is not associated with an increased risk of major chronic diseases, such as cancer, or premature death, and some evidence suggests that coffee consumption may decrease the risk of certain cancers. _____, the cancer label warning, he said, may mislead consumers to believe that drinking coffee could be dangerous to their health when it actually could provide health benefits. The agency also announced that it sent a letter of support to the California Office of Environmental Health Hazard Assessment, which proposed a regulation to exempt coffee companies like Starbucks from putting the warning label on their products.

17 Choose the words that best fill in the blank.
① Accordingly
② By the way
③ For instance
④ Nevertheless

18 What can be inferred from the passage above?
① The FDA concurs with the social enterprise on the needlessness of cancer warnings for coffee.
② The FDA fears the warning may potentially impact public perception of coffee consumption.
③ The FDA supports Proposition 65 as it reflects a scientific consensus on coffee's benefits.
④ The FDA highlights that coffee consumption lowers the risk of untimely passing.

19~20

A young bar-tailed godwit appears to have set a non-stop distance record for migratory birds by flying at least 13,560 kilometers from Alaska to the Australian state of Tasmania, a bird expert said Friday. The bird started on a southwestern course toward Japan then turned southeast over Alaska's Aleutian Islands. The bird was again tracking southwest when it flew over or near Kiribati and New Caledonia, then past the Australian mainland before turning directly west for Tasmania, Australia's most southerly state. The satellite trail showed it covered 13,560 kilometers without stopping. "Whether this is an accident, whether this bird got lost or whether this is part of a normal pattern of migration for the species, we still don't know," said Woehler, who is part of the research project. Guinness World Records lists the longest recorded migration by a bird without stopping for food or rest as 12,200 kilometers by a satellite-tagged male bar-tailed godwit flying from Alaska to New Zealand. That flight was recorded in 2020 as part of the same decade-old research project. The same bird broke its own record with a 13,000-kilometer flight on its next migration last year, researchers say. But Guinness has yet to acknowledge that feat. Woehler said researchers did not know whether the latest bird, known by its satellite tag 234684, flew alone or as part of a flock. Woehler said there are so few birds that have been tagged, we don't know _____. It may be that half the birds that do the migration from Alaska come to Tasmania directly rather than through New Zealand or it might be 1%, or it might be that this is the first it's ever happened. "Adult birds depart Alaska earlier than juveniles, so the tagged bird was unlikely to have followed more experienced travelers south," Woehler said. Woehler hopes to see the bird once wet weather clears in the remote corner of Tasmania, where it will fatten up having lost half its body weight on its journey.

19 Choose the best for the blank.

① how representative or otherwise this event is
② why most birds adhere to the migration patterns through New Zealand
③ whether that achievement should be acknowledged by Guinness
④ whether the bird species communicates its flight paths

20 What can be inferred from the passage above?

① Migrating from Alaska to New Zealand, with Australia as a waypoint, is the flying pattern of the bird species.
② Flying the southwest route was an incident for the species, backed by evidence.
③ The bird's record and the previously recorded distance differ by 1,360 kilometers.
④ The bird's nonstop migration from Alaska to Tasmania might be an outlier among the species.

HANSUNG UNIVERSITY

한성대학교

▶ 2025학년도 인문계 A형 ▶ 문항 수: 50문항 | 제한시간: 90분

2025 한성대 인문계 A형 영역별 문항 수

구분	문법			어휘			논리완성	독해	생활영어	총 문항 수
	G/S, W/E	정비문	재진술	동의어	반의어	유추				
문항 수							10	35	5	50
백분율							20%	70%	10%	100%

HANSUNG UNIVERSITY

한성대학교

- 2025학년도 인문계 A형: 50문항 · 90분
- 자연계: 영어 25문항, 수학 20문항 · 90분

인문 · 자연계 공통 영어문제 별도* 표시

[01~05] Choose the best expression for the blank in each dialogue.

01* A: I'm so worried about the exam next week. I'm studying non-stop, but nothing sticks.
B: I haven't even opened the book yet. I know I'll ace it. I'm a genius.
A: Yeah, right! With that attitude, you'll pass the exam when _____.

[2.5점]

① pigs fly
② cats swim
③ cows speak
④ chickens read

02* A: I've had it with Instagram. I'm definitely closing my account.
B: Why? What's wrong with it?
A: Do you really need to ask? It's _____ with fake news and propaganda.

[2점]

① mollified
② mitigated
③ alleviated
④ inundated

03* A: I feel so bad for my sister. She works two shifts and raises her daughters alone. She has no time to breathe.
B: That's brutal. She's _____.

[2.5점]

① having a field day
② walking on eggshells
③ not playing with a full deck
④ burning the candle at both ends

04* A: Hey, let's grab a drink after work.
B: I'm sorry, not today. I'm beat. I'm dying to _____, go straight home, and relax.
A: No problem. Maybe next time.

[1.5점]

① put off
② give off
③ take off
④ catch off

05* A: I can't believe my friend Jenny. I invited her to the movies, and she just _____ that my taste in movies was horrible.
B: Did she really say that?
A: Yes. I'm still upset. I can't get over it.

[2점]

① blew up
② came up
③ stuck out
④ blurted out

06~15 Choose the best word for each blank.

06* The principle of the pain of paying, according to which it hurts to _____ with money, but it is less painful when we don't see or pay attention, helps us understand why we overspend when we use credit cards, and why we feel worse after a meal when we pay with cash compared with a credit card. [1.5점]

① part ② tally
③ align ④ present

07* Sometimes, the people you seek feedback from are kind but not nice. A kind person will tell you things a nice person will not. A kind bystander will tell you that you have lettuce on your teeth. A nice acquaintance won't because it is uncomfortable. A kind person will tell you what holds you back, but a nice person avoids giving you _____ feedback. [1.5점]

① critical ② obvious
③ innocuous ④ ambiguous

08 Occam's razor dictates that the simplest explanation is to be favored until it is proven _____. It does not say that the simplest explanation is always right, but only that when we don't have any data to lead us to choose one explanation over another, we should pick the simplest one. [1.5점]

① valid ② sound
③ credible ④ inadequate

09 Silver is more conductive than copper, but as with steel, what matters just as much as a substance's powers is its _____. Silver is rare. Copper might not be as prevalent as iron, but there is much more of it than there is of silver, and humankind has more years of expertise at mining and refining it than any other industrial metal.

[2.5점]

① rigidity
② paucity
③ ductility
④ ubiquity

10 The future is not like the weather. It doesn't just happen to us. We shape our future with the choices we make in the present, just as our present situation was shaped by choices we made in the past. Wherever we are now is a _____ of the past choices and behaviors that got us here.

[1.5점]

① deterrent
② reflection
③ subversion
④ determinant

11 Social media platforms are scrambling to address the issue of the direct link between smartphone use and an increase in teen anxiety and depression. Instagram, for example, has set new safeguards for teen users. However, parents claim that these platforms are not doing enough to shield children from harm, charging them with _____ teenagers and young children to overuse social media.

[2점]

① sullying
② inducing
③ spluttering
④ admonishing

12 South Korea is not only famed for its modern, high-tech economy, but it also has an Ⓐ_____ link to its past through traditional art, craftsmanship, and culture. Rather than colliding, these two sides complement each other, Ⓑ_____ the creative thinking and innovation that have long been Korean hallmarks. Companies working with traditional materials often combine classic ideas with the latest technology to great success. [2점]

① eternal — advertising
② indelible — driving
③ incurable — affirming
④ ephemeral — hampering

13 Aosta is a sort of sanctuary city for people with both mental and physical challenges. For centuries, the Catholic Church has provided shelter, food, and care to people who have been rejected by their families because of their condition. Many of these people have become skilled workers, and many of them have fallen in love, gotten married, and had children. What has emerged is a sort of upside-down town. A town where the Ⓐ_____ is Ⓑ_____, where people often rejected by society receive the support that allows them to flourish. [2점]

① aberrant — deviant
② abnormal — normal
③ customary — mundane
④ anomalous — erroneous

14 The benefits of inflight wifi are obvious: work can be _____, clients contacted, and colleagues consulted. Daytime flights on connected aircraft are essentially remote work days, and they facilitate business travel. Even if you're traveling for leisure, improved connectivity means access to live sports and the ability to stay in touch with friends and family. Priceless, especially for those always on the go. [2점]

① relayed
② scurried
③ convoyed
④ postponed

15. Did you know that out of 20,000 different species of bees, only eight of them produce honey? But once you know how honey is made, you may not think it as sweet: it is nectar that honeybees have repeatedly regurgitated and dehydrated. Not only people but also bees stock up on the stuff to Ⓐ_____ on it during the winter when they can't Ⓑ_____. [2점]

① exist — furl
② outlive — slumber
③ subsist — forage
④ provide — scavenge

16~18 Read the following and answer the questions.

Resilience seems to work as an insurance policy against stress, helping us cope with difficult moments in our lives. One of the most fundamental ways to understand resilience is based on the psychological construct known as secure attachment. Imagine that you are the parent of a four-year-old girl. One day, you take her to the playground. You sit on the bench. "Go ahead and play," you tell her. She starts walking, and every minute or so she turns around to see if you are still there waiting for her. If this is the situation, you have not managed to raise a kid with secure attachment.

Secure attachment is formed in childhood; it basically allows us to go through life knowing that if something bad happens, somebody will catch us. We don't have to look around all the time, wondering if somebody is there for us or not. When we have a very high level of secure attachment, it is a kind of ideal Ⓐ_____ plan, one that we can trust to cover everything. Ⓑ_____, we might be willing to go out on a limb and try a new romantic adventure with somebody we think is way out of our league.

16 Choose the best topic. [2.5점]

① how to raise a kid with secure attachment
② risks of having a high level of secure attachment
③ understanding resilience through secure attachment
④ the importance of forming secure attachment as an adult

17 Choose the best word for Ⓐ. [2점]

① selective
② defective
③ insurance
④ installment

18 Choose the best expression for Ⓑ. [1.5점]

① In short
② Of course
③ For example
④ On the contrary

19~21 Read the following and answer the questions.

Have you ever looked leisurely at the clouds floating in the sky above? After a few minutes, you think to yourself, "This little cloud is so cute and happy, but why is the large cloud chasing it?" If you ever have pictured a story about clouds like this, you are not alone. This is the very common human disposition to seek patterns where none exists, which is called patternicity. It is a general human characteristic that varies by personality, in the sense that some people evince a much greater Ⓐ_____ to see patterns than others.

Consider the following study with some MBA students. Ⓑ <u>After showing them the behavior of the stock, a confident analyst gave reason X for why the stock price had behaved that way to half of the participants.</u> Ⓒ <u>Then the MBA participants rated how much sense the reasons made to them.</u> Ⓓ <u>They were shown the behavior of one stock throughout a certain day.</u> Ⓔ <u>To the other half, the analyst gave reason not-X, or the opposite of X.</u> Surprisingly, they were equally highly impressed with the logic of either reason. The point is that Ⓕ_____.

19 Which one is not suitable for Ⓐ? [2점]

① audacity
② tendency
③ proclivity
④ propensity

20 What is the correct ordering of Ⓑ, Ⓒ, Ⓓ, and Ⓔ? [2점]

① Ⓓ-Ⓑ-Ⓔ-Ⓒ
② Ⓓ-Ⓔ-Ⓑ-Ⓒ
③ Ⓑ-Ⓒ-Ⓓ-Ⓔ
④ Ⓑ-Ⓓ-Ⓒ-Ⓔ

21 Which one is the most suitable for Ⓕ? [2.5점]

① our minds are always looking for stories
② stock market pundits are not to be trusted
③ humans are wired to reject obvious patterns
④ patternicity varies depending on the personality

22~24 Read the following and answer the questions.

> A lot of information we take in is in the form of highlights, summaries, or distillations. It is the illusion of knowledge. We learn the answer but can't show the work. Consider a sixth-grader in math class, copying answers from the student beside her. She might get the right answer, but she doesn't know why it is the answer. It is an abstraction. She lacks understanding, without which information becomes dangerous.
>
> It is natural to think these abstractions will save us time and improve our decision-making, but in many cases they don't. Reading a summary might be faster than reading a full text, but it misses a lot of details — details that apparently weren't relevant to the person summarizing it, but that might be relevant to you. You end up saving time Ⓐ_____ missing important information. Skimming engenders blind spots.
>
> The desire for abstractions is understandable. The sheer amount of information that bombards us daily can seem overwhelming. But the further the information is from the original source, the more Ⓑ <u>filters</u> it has been through before reaching you.

22 Choose the best expression for Ⓐ. [2점]

① in lieu of   ② instead of
③ for fear of   ④ at the cost of

23 Which of the following is not an example of Ⓑ filters? [2점]

① biases
② political interpretations
③ exact accounts of the original
④ individual levels of understanding

24 Which one cannot be inferred? [2.5점]

① Real knowledge is earned.
② Abstractions are merely borrowed.
③ Abstractions are necessary for full understanding.
④ Bad information can inhibit good decision-making.

25~27 Read the following and answer the questions.

A critical threshold for the number of individuals in early human social groups was somewhere around 150 individuals. It was simply impossible to connect and form any kind of meaningful attachment with more than that. How is it then that eventually homo sapiens crossed this threshold Ⓐ_____ cities and states with thousands and even millions of inhabitants? The answer may lie in the dawn of fiction. By believing in common myths, a large number of otherwise unconnected people can cooperate successfully. Any large-scale community — a state, a church, a city, or a tribe — is entrenched in common myths that exist only in people's collective imagination. Yet, these are only myths, and nothing that is incorporated in them exists outside the stories that people invent and tell one another. There are no gods in the universe, no nations, and no laws outside the common imagination of human beings. Similar to the primitive tribes that Ⓑ cemented their social order by believing in ghosts and spirits, contemporary humans maintain their social order by adhering to common myths.

25. Choose the best title. [2점]

① Large-scale Communities
② Crossing Critical Threshold
③ Bonding Power of Shared Myths
④ Common Desires of Human Beings

26. Choose the best word for Ⓐ. [2점]

① founding
② deterring
③ conquering
④ manifesting

27. Which word has the opposite meaning to Ⓑ<u>cemented</u>? [1.5점]

① fortified
② bolstered
③ pulverized
④ buttressed

[28~30] Read the following and answer the questions.

"All humans are created equal" is an old, Ⓐ_____ statement. It appears especially so when one considers the science of biology which Ⓑ_____ that people were actually not created, but rather they have evolved. Moreover, they have not evolved to be equal. The idea of equality is intricately entangled with the idea of creation. It stems from Christianity, which argues that every person was created in God's image and has a divinely created soul. Before God all these souls are equal. However, if we do not believe in the Christian myths about God, creation, and souls, what does it mean that all people are equal? Evolution is based on difference, not on equality. Every person carries a somewhat different genetic code and is exposed from birth to different environmental influences. Ⓒ This leads to the development of different qualities that carry with them different chances of survival. Hence, "created equal" should be converted into "evolved differently." Just as people were not created, neither is there a "creator" who endows them with anything. They were simply born.

28 Choose the best words for Ⓐ and Ⓑ. [2점]

① empirical — maintains
② miniscule — denies
③ impassive — demonstrates
④ hackneyed — asserts

29 What does ⓒThis refer to? [2점]

① the fact that evolution is based on difference, not equality
② the fact that every person carries a different genetic code
③ the fact that every person is exposed to different environmental influences
④ the fact that every person carries a different genetic code and is exposed to different environmental influences

30 Which one is not true? [2.5점]

① In Christianity all humans are intrinsically equal.
② Christians believe that all humans resemble God.
③ The idea of equality among humans is as old as humanity itself.
④ Evolutionists believe that human traits are not determined by God.

31~34 Read the following and answer the questions.

How blissful the last three years of Biden administration have been for stock investors! The value of copious stocks doubled, and bitcoin is up fourfold. Alas, history has taught us that Ⓐ bull markets don't last forever, and when they fall, they fall hard, and our nest eggs Ⓑ may be jeopardized. There are plenty of dangers that Ⓒ may be threatened the continuity of robust markets, from interminable wars to intractable budget deficits. Also, stocks Ⓓ may be overpriced. Inflation concerns and a sense of economic vulnerability were responsible for Donald Trump's winning the election, with U.S. voters seeming to believe that he would be better for their wallets than Kamala Harris. But Trump's campaign promises, including tax cuts and tariffs on trade, Ⓔ may well have the opposite effect. Ⓕ_____.

31* Which one is the opposite to Ⓐ bull markets? [2점]

① dog markets
② bear markets
③ kitten markets
④ elephant markets

32* Which one is not grammatically correct? [1.5점]

① Ⓑ ② Ⓒ
③ Ⓓ ④ Ⓔ

33* Which one is the most suitable for Ⓕ? [2점]

① Nest eggs and stock reserves will be sheltered
② Donald Trump will bring economic stability to the world
③ The tariffs alone would almost certainly hinder growth and spark further inflation
④ Donald Trump will prohibit all imports and focus on domestic manufacturing industry

34 Which one is true? [2점]

① Fixing budget deficits is easy.
② Presently, the markets are vigorous.
③ The wars that threaten robust markets are transient.
④ The value of bitcoin has increased at the same rate as the value of stocks.

35~38 Read the following and answer the questions.

> A good example of cultural borrowing and improvisation is "Korean Wave," or Hallyu. The Korean Wave was able to reach expansive international audience because, from the beginning, it was based on a mixture of styles, including rock, jazz, reggae, and Afrobeat. It also relies on R&B dance tracks, melodic bridges, and "soft" rap interludes, mostly sung in Korean with a sprinkling of English phrases. The videos often feature Ⓐ synchronized dance moves, which are less common in the West but well known in other musical traditions, including Bollywood. Ⓑ Ultimately, it is a proof that cultural exchange, when done right, is not a case of cultural appropriation but rather of cultural enrichment and something that should be lauded rather than condemned. Ⓒ This fresh blend of the Korean musical traditions and a variety of genres from around the world makes K-pop so accessible and alluring. Ⓓ Also remarkable is what's not there in these videos: the violence and obscenity that are often featured in US- and UK-based pop and rap culture. Ⓔ While K-pop doesn't represent traditional or typical Korean art, it is undeniable that it is not only borrowing from and enriching other musical traditions but is also deeply rooted in Korea's girl groups that performed in the 1950s at American military bases and continued to thrive in the 1960s and 1970s.

35* Choose the best title. [2점]

① K-pop Grabs Global Scene
② K-pop's Revival of Girl Groups
③ K-pop's Successful Music Blend
④ K-pop Synchronizes Dance Moves

36* Which one has the same meaning as Ⓐsynchronized? [1.5점]

① collected   ② contrived
③ contained   ④ coordinated

37* What is the correct ordering of Ⓑ, Ⓒ, Ⓓ, and Ⓔ? [2점]

① Ⓑ-Ⓔ-Ⓒ-Ⓓ
② Ⓒ-Ⓑ-Ⓔ-Ⓓ
③ Ⓓ-Ⓔ-Ⓑ-Ⓒ
④ Ⓓ-Ⓔ-Ⓒ-Ⓑ

38. What is the author's attitude to K-pop? [1.5점]

① facetious
② favorable
③ dismissive
④ contemptuous

39~41 Read the following and answer the questions.

People suffer because they chase after fleeting pleasures. They can only be liberated from this Ⓐ_____ when they understand the impermanent quality of their feelings and stop Ⓑ_____ them. This is the aspiration of Buddhist practices. While meditating, you aim at closely monitoring your mind and body, perceive the ceaseless arising and passing of all your feelings, and realize how meaningless it is to chase them. When the chase is halted, the mind becomes very relaxed, clear, and content. All kinds of feelings keep coming and going — joy, anger, boredom, lust — but once you stop hankering after particular feelings, you can just accept them for what they are. You live in the present moment instead of fantasizing about what might have been. The subsequent serenity is so profound that those who spend their lives in the frenzied pursuit of pleasant feelings can hardly envision it.

39. Choose the best title. [2점]

① Pursuing Pleasant Feelings
② Permanent Nature of Feelings
③ Fleeting Pleasures Leading to Suffering
④ Achieving Serenity Through Buddhist Practices

40. Choose the best words for Ⓐ and Ⓑ. [2점]

① ardor — apprehending
② misery — restraining
③ turmoil — pursuing
④ method — eliminating

41 What happens when you stop chasing pleasant feelings? [2점]

① You reach tranquility.
② You deny all feelings.
③ You suffer more intensely.
④ You fantasize about the future.

42~44 Read the following and answer the questions.

> The word was coined in 1883 by a British scientist named Francis Galton, a cousin of Charles Darwin. When *On the Origins of Species* had first come out, Galton had read his cousin's book and been deeply inspired. Once Galton had come to understand that there were forces of natural selection shaping the array of life on Earth, it dawned on him that perhaps you could actually manipulate those forces to select for a master race of humans by Ⓐ_____ some traits he believed to be associated with blood: poverty, criminality, illiteracy, neurosis, promiscuity, and more. He called this technique of killing off groups of people you don't like "eugenics," a compound of two Greek words for "good" and "birth." And he began telling people about Ⓑ his scientific-sounding plan to make Europe great again. In order to promote his ideas, he even wrote a sci-fi novel about a society where only those who passed rigorous tests were allowed to procreate, and anyone else who tried would be punished by incarceration. Galton saw his book as a manual for saving the human race from degeneration.

42 Choose the best expression for Ⓐ. [2.5점]

① opting for
② hybridizing
③ breeding out
④ cross-fertilizing

43 What does Ⓑ his scientific-sounding plan refer to? [2점]

① eugenics
② Darwinism
③ birth control
④ natural selection

44. Which statement is true? [2점]

① Darwin believed that species could be artificially improved.
② Galton's ideas came about independently of Darwin's theory.
③ Darwin's theory of evolution supposes a master race of humans.
④ Galton proposed to save humans from decay by selective reproduction.

45~47. Read the following and answer the questions.

Since 2020, 37% of Britain's nightclubs have gone out of business. Many shut during the pandemic and never reopened, and closures still continue. Higher labor costs, tighter planning laws, and more noise complaints are probably all playing a role. But a key factor is that their chief patrons, the reckless young, are staying at home. Between 2011 and 2021, the proportion of British 16- to 24-year-olds who had not consumed one alcoholic drink throughout the year doubled, from 19% to 38%. No wonder nightclubs are struggling.

Why is youthful Ⓐ excess dying out? There is no single answer. Children are more closely watched than in the past, and a higher share of young adults are from more abstemious immigrant cultures. Age ID checks at bars are more routine; Netflix is cheaper than cider; and dating apps are better than finding love in a bar. The trend is clear and seems likely to last. It's their parents who are the problem now.

45. Choose the best topic. [2점]

① the sea change of Britain's drinking culture
② the decline of British market economy due to the pandemic
③ the preference of British youths for non-alcoholic beverages
④ the continuous decline of excessive drinking among British youths

46. Which word has the opposite meaning to Ⓐexcess? [2점]

① sobriety
② indulgence
③ debauchery
④ intemperance

47 Which statement is not true? [2.5점]

① Since 2011, alcohol consumption has doubled each year.
② Generation Zs tend to consume less alcohol than their parents.
③ More rigorous civic regulations force many nightclubs to close.
④ Lower alcohol consumption among immigrant youths is partly due to their cultural background.

48~50 Read the following and answer the questions.

American businesses have long allured the world's cleverest and most industrious. America's enduring ability to attract human resources is its most Ⓐ_____ privilege. It is now imperilled by the nativist wing of Donald Trump's Republican Party. Most Trumpian followers view illegal immigrants as bad. Many believe that they should be deported. Nativists accuse them Ⓑ of stealing American jobs. The techno-Trumpists led by Mr. Elon Musk worry that they are Democrats Ⓒ by heart who, if granted citizenship, would turn swing states a woke shade of blue. Either way, both groups agree on one thing. Give me your poor huddled masses? No, thank you. But their opinions on highly skilled professionals are widely divergent. Yes, please, say Mr. Musk and his Silicon Valley buddies, who regard such brains as the key Ⓓ to the innovation that keeps America First in perpetuity. Nuh-uh, retort the nativists, who would prefer Ⓔ to see this well-paying work go to real Americans, which is to say, those who got there first.

48 Which one is not suitable for Ⓐ? [2점]

① extreme   ② excessive
③ excursive   ④ exorbitant

49 Which one is not grammatically correct? [2점]

① Ⓑ   ② Ⓒ
③ Ⓓ   ④ Ⓔ

50 Which statement is not true? [2.5점]

① Musk rejects illegal immigrants for their potential political affiliation.
② Some Trump supporters believe that the influx of hi-tech workforce is essential.
③ America is at the risk of losing its status as a magnet for the world's finest human capital.
④ Both nativists and techno-Trumpists are in favor of immigrants getting lucrative high-tech jobs.

한양대학교

▶ 2025학년도 서울 인문계 A형   ▶ 문항 수: 35문항 | 제한시간: 60분

2025 한양대 서울 인문계 A형 영역별 문항 수

구분	문법			어휘			논리완성	독해	생활영어	총 문항 수
	G/S, W/E	정비문	재진술	동의어	반의어	유추				
문항 수				6			13	16		35
백분율				17%			37%	46%		100%

HANYANG UNIVERSITY

한양대학교
2025학년도 서울 인문계 A형: 35문항 · 60분

01~06 밑줄 친 단어의 뜻과 가장 가까운 것을 고르시오.

01 Democracy, that delicate and ever-evolving tapestry of collective will, is both the guardian of individual freedoms and the <u>crucible</u> in which the aspirations of humanity are unceasingly tested and refined. [2점]

① trial ② catalyst ③ portal
④ foundation ⑤ experiment

02 Videogames certainly have a reputation for encouraging and exemplifying the predatory, neoliberal, regressive tendencies we recognise around us. Still, to billions, gaming is a space for <u>respite</u>, for building lives not yet lived, structures not yet imagined. And, as such, it has to be fought for. [2점]

① rest ② penance ③ aggression
④ consensus ⑤ authenticity

03 In the late-nineteenth- and early-twentieth-century period, when Irish revivalism and modernism were both still in their fledgling and most <u>protean</u> phases, they did not seem as antithetical to each other as they would later appear to many after each had assumed more programmatic definition from the 1920s or 1930s onwards. [2점]

① morbid ② prolific ③ mutable
④ trivial ⑤ timorous

04 The less the worker identifies his own freedom and pleasure with the purpose of the work, Marx writes, "the closer his attention is forced to be." As work becomes more alienating and exploitative, the "exertion of the working organs" must be forcibly cajoled. It is as if an outside, hostile will, at odds with the worker's own, takes hold of him, using his attention to manipulate his body so that he can execute its plans. [2점]

① reenacted ② expelled ③ mitigated
④ coaxed ⑤ dissociated

05 Americans love the ideal of equal opportunity for all. As a vehicle for that idea, admission to highly selective colleges and universities is unworkable almost by definition, because people with advantages don't want their own children to forgo those advantages, but if we want to come closer to the ideal, we should recognize that operating a series of highly consequential education selections works against it. [2점]

① belittle ② reserve ③ procure
④ disclose ⑤ relinquish

06 Honor, that ineffable beacon of human virtue, stands as the unyielding compass guiding the soul through the labyrinth of moral ambiguity, demanding an unwavering allegiance to truth, dignity, and the quiet courage of integrity. [2점]

① signal ② agency ③ obstacle
④ retainer ⑤ medium

07~18 빈칸에 들어갈 가장 적절한 것을 고르시오.

07 The new intern's _____ behavior, marked by constant flattery and excessive eagerness to please, quickly became tiresome to her colleagues. [2점]

① assertive ② apathetic ③ sedulous
④ scrupulous ⑤ obsequious

08 Discrimination based on race or gender is often recognized in blatant forms, but it can also manifest in more _____ behaviors, such as subtle biases in hiring practices or microaggressions in daily interactions. [2점]

① overt   ② casual   ③ explicit
④ insidious   ⑤ redundant

09 The scientist's theory, once dismissed as _____, has now gained widespread acceptance due to recent discoveries that support its validity. [2점]

① implausible   ② empirical   ③ ingenuous
④ terse   ⑤ transparent

10 Aristocrats have never taken kindly to _____. They have seen themselves as born to command others rather than accept the dictates of superiors. The duty of higher authority in their eyes has been to confirm and uphold their pretensions. [3점]

① acclaim   ② intrigue   ③ vulgarity
④ compulsion   ⑤ conservatism

11 No composer could afford to act like a prima donna. Nobody was about to treat a mere hired hand with that sort of _____. His was essentially a service role. Like the librettist's, his primary aim was to please — the impresario, the singers, and (finally and most importantly) the paying public. [3점]

① obstinacy   ② deference   ③ informality
④ consistency   ⑤ rapport

12 Epicurus observed that some people wanted to become famous and conspicuous, thinking they would thus win safety from others. Instead, people were trapped by their own celebrity and power; they lost their freedom. Epicurus saw greater rewards in _____, extolling the "immunity which results from a quiet life and the retirement from the world." [3점]

① salvation   ② solidarity   ③ sympathy
④ seclusion   ⑤ subtlety

13 Identity has been aptly called the "primary commodity of the social media culture industry," which means that, like reality TV studios, this industry must design to produce that commodity, also through genuine self-disclosure. This further _____ what's considered public and what should be kept private. One study of the most popular YouTube channels, for example, finds that when vloggers reveal their personal lives, they're rated as more authentic. [3점]

① curbs   ② promotes   ③ elucidates
④ erodes   ⑤ regulates

14 When we read, we often ask ourselves why are we reading: for entertainment, for instruction, to participate in a long conversation with the past or to escape our present in a world of the imagination? We understand that literature has value, but our acts of reading constantly query that sense of value. These meditations and reflections do not _____ the value of literature. They texture it. They make each reading something new and strange. And in our current age of irony and parody, tweets and texts, these meditations are all the more important. They help us find a place for literary experience in a world increasingly suspicious of sincerity. [3점]

① underscore   ② circumvent   ③ fortify
④ disseminate   ⑤ undermine

15 A feature of ballet's tony profile is its association with the qualities of smoothness and effortless grace. So strong is this association that the word "ballet" is often used to describe any _____. The docking of two space vehicles is called "a space ballet"; the changing of the guards looks like "a military ballet." Sports commentators are constantly comparing the smooth power moves of athletes to dance, as if conferring upon jocks the ultimate compliment — that they are strong and efficient in getting the basketball into the hoop or the puck into the net, but they do it with such grace that it's an aesthetic delight. [3점]

① technically intricate maneuver associated with high social class
② complex physical activity done without a hint of awkwardness
③ large-scale venture requiring long-term financial investment
④ cultural performance that appeals to a diverse demographic
⑤ professional practice subject to close public scrutiny

16 Tragic heroes inspire us, but they can also frighten us. They are defined by conflict and often they are simply not likable. Antigone's stubbornness is terrifying when she resolutely rejects the support of those who love her. While we are led to believe that Hamlet might once have been the most "sweet prince," he spends most of his time abusing his companions and relatives, and he is responsible for at least five deaths (not counting Ophelia's). Romantic heroes like Karl von Moor in Schiller's *The Robbers* or more modern figures like Ibsen's Hedda Gabler may inspire devotion, but they are people with whom it would be impossible to live. Tragic heroes embody _____. [3점]

① our lust for revenge and power
② both human constancy and divine caprice
③ our communal beliefs and standards of behavior
④ our need to escape from the everyday boredom of life
⑤ both all that we hope for ourselves and all that we fear or hate

17 On an individual level, how much we care what society thinks of us might be influenced by our biology. In a 2014 study, the psychologist Shinobu Kitayama found the degree to which we uphold cultural norms is related to the type of variation we have on one gene, the dopamine D4 receptor gene. The gene doesn't change how we behave; instead, it influences how much we endorse the prevailing norms of our environments. Asians who carried certain variations of this gene became more interdependent. They were more likely to endorse values related to social harmony, collectivism, and modesty. Meanwhile, European Americans who carried the same gene variants became more individualistic — a traditionally white American norm. The gene makes you _____. [3점]

① more open to enduring personal losses for collective gain
② more of a rule follower, whatever the rules happen to be
③ less of a conformist, regardless of the cultural context
④ less likely to sacrifice immediate pleasure for future payoffs
⑤ less of a first mover, even when the advantages are evident

18 Throughout history, many great civilizations have risen and fallen, often as a result of internal strife, economic instability, or external invasion. Yet, there are those that have endured, their legacies imprinted in the very fabric of human culture. These resilient societies were not immune to failure or adversity, but they demonstrated a remarkable capacity for adaptation, adapting to challenges in ways that allowed them to not only survive but also flourish. Some scholars argue that this ability is linked to a deep understanding of the underlying forces that shape the human experience — forces of power, culture, and knowledge — that allow a civilization to transcend its own limitations and embrace new possibilities. The key, however, lies not in merely surviving difficult times, but in _____. [4점]

① developing resilience through the preservation of core values and traditions
② strategically navigating uncertainty by maintaining long-established practices
③ fostering stability by minimizing external influences and focusing on internal strengths
④ cultivating an ability to mitigate the unexpected, embracing change as an opportunity rather than a threat
⑤ establishing a framework where gradual, incremental changes are prioritized over rapid, disruptive shifts to ensure long-term stability

19. 빈칸 Ⓐ, Ⓑ에 들어갈 가장 적절한 것은? [3점]

In the field of quantum mechanics, there are debates that often verge on the abstruse, as physicists attempt to explain phenomena that challenge the boundaries of current scientific understanding. These discussions, though intensely intellectual, can sometimes become Ⓐ_____, as scholars employ highly abstract concepts and complex mathematical models that are difficult for the general public to comprehend. However, despite the often obscure nature of the subject, the academic community remains energized by the promise of new discoveries. The debates are driven by a deep sense of Ⓑ_____, with researchers pushing the limits of what is known, even when confronted with seemingly insurmountable paradoxes and questions that defy conventional logic. Though some critics argue that these ideas are little more than speculative, the continued drive for knowledge remains a core tenet of the discipline.

① collegial — fulfillment
② esoteric — optimism
③ speculative — despondency
④ contentious — skepticism
⑤ impenetrable — disillusionment

20~21. 다음 글을 읽고 물음에 답하시오.

Our skin is curiously soft compared to that of other more hirsute vertebrates. Hairy skin is surely advantageous in terms of insulation from the cold, protection from abrasions, and the burning sun, which is why most hairless creatures live either underground or in water. A big advantage of being hairless, though, is in keeping cool. Humans have glands that can produce up to 12 litres of watery sweat every day, which evaporates easily to cool us down. When our distant relatives moved out of forests into savanna grasslands, we did a lot of trekking in the hot sun to search for water, edible plants and meat required for our energy-sapping large brains. Thanks to our ability to sweat profusely on a hot day we, or at least some of us, could outcompete a horse in a marathon. But, we solved the problem of overheating at the risk of making our sensitive skin more vulnerable to infection. Each sweat gland is an oasis colonised by 100,000 bacteria, quietly tolerated, except during adolescence, when a flood of hormones stimulates oil production, food for Propionibacterium acnes, causing unsightly blackheads; our castle <u>sanctions</u> some itinerant campers outside its walls, feeding on scraps. The advantages of keeping us cool by being relatively hairless must be weighed against our susceptibility to injury and infection as our skin is easily removed by burns or wounding.

20 윗글의 내용과 가장 거리가 먼 것은? [3점]

① Most hairless animals inhabit environments with reduced exposure to heat and cold.
② Hairless skin is more effective than hairy skin in reducing high temperatures.
③ The ability to sweat in heat was especially important for survival activities in savanna grasslands.
④ During puberty, hormones suppress oil secretion, creating skin problems.
⑤ Our skin's ability to manage heat comes at the cost of greater vulnerability.

21 밑줄 친 "sanctions"의 뜻과 가장 가까운 것은? [3점]

① releases
② permits
③ stimulates
④ abandons
⑤ supervises

22~23 다음 글의 주제로 가장 적절한 것을 고르시오.

There is no ecological scenario in which there are no more extinctions at all, yet no extinction today should be deemed permissible in advance, and every impending extinction implores prevention. Ecology is both a descriptive science and an ethical project inclusive of creative efforts that imagine a better world for all life. Engaging with extinction as ecological practice, however, does not mean trying to redeem or save animals from the difficulties of life or death as such. Caring for endangered animals entails working to preserve them from perishing due to anthropogenic causes without insisting on salvational outcomes and without idealizing ecosystems as danger-free utopian spaces. Studying the history of extinction and vigilance toward preventing extinctions in the present does not commit one to the restoration of an ideal garden of protected and enduring life, nor does it necessitate a dystopian vision in which nothing matters because extinction renders everything meaningless in advance.

22 [3점]
① practical challenges in preserving planetary biodiversity
② need for balanced expectations in caring for endangered life
③ impossibility of maintaining optimism in facing global warming
④ demand for more rigorous documentations of devastated animal life
⑤ ethical dilemmas in reconstructing genes of species facing extinction

The macroeconomic principles on which central banks and the welfare state were conceived were the same: countercyclical policies intended to protect individuals from economic risk (including price and financial instability) and reduce overall uncertainty. But these historical and conceptual links between central banks and the welfare state are rarely made explicit. Drawing attention to them does not mean to suggest that we should ask the central bank to pay for welfare benefits. The point is to recognize that, like other pillars of the welfare state in capitalist societies, the central bank performs a function of managing risks and reducing uncertainty. Just as the risks evolve, so too must the institutions. As the twentieth-century economic anthropologist Karl Polanyi said, the central bank's policy is always a form of interventionism that evolves over time in accord with the nature of the state. It reflects the choices made regarding distribution and power in society.

23 ① lost confidence in central banks' independence from the state [4점]
② challenges for central banks in responding to financial instability
③ need to exercise discretion when formulating monetary policy
④ transferal of responsibilities from welfare states to central banks
⑤ functional correspondence between central banks and welfare states

24~25 다음 글의 요지로 가장 적절한 것을 고르시오.

At the very beginning Thomas More designated utopia as a place, an island in the distant South Seas. This designation underwent changes later so that it left space and entered time. Indeed, the Utopians, especially those of the eighteenth and nineteenth centuries, transposed the wishland more into the future. In other words, there is a transformation of the topos from space into time. With Thomas More the wishland was still ready, on a distant island, but I am not there. On the other hand, when it is transposed into the future, not only am I not there, but utopia itself is also not with itself. This island does not even exist. But it is not something like nonsense or absolute fancy; rather it is not yet in the sense of a possibility; that it could be there if we could only do something for it. Not only if we travel there, but *in that* we travel there the island utopia arises out of the sea of the possible — utopia, but with new contents.

24
① Utopia is increasingly seen as an unattainable fantasy, if not a merely theoretical construct. [3점]
② Utopia offers an immutable model that can withstand historical and political turbulence.
③ Utopia has evolved from a physical location to a future possibility, or a sense of potentiality.
④ Utopia tries to restore a concrete reality from the past instead of projecting a fanciful ideal.
⑤ Utopia in its earliest forms referred to a place that can be located and accessed with ease.

People often call the earth the "lonely" planet because we have found no other humans or evidence of life outside earth. Even if it were true that there is no life outside earth, which is highly unlikely, this is a profoundly anthropocentric and biocentric way of thinking about the earth. It allows us to ignore and devalue our relationship of dependency on non-living processes here and in the cosmos at large. When we do this, we use a particular form of life to judge the world as a failed attempt to become that form. By contrast, our whole solar system most likely emerged from the same nebular cloud of molecular gas and dust. We are, therefore, not externally related to the other planetary circulations in our solar system but internally entangled and intra-related with them. The earth is not simply among the stars, it is of the stars.

25
① The earth's processes are more unpredictable than we once believed. [4점]
② Life on earth resulted from miraculously improbable coincidences.
③ Human life has never been separable from the cosmos that produced it.
④ Enlightenment thinking intensified anthropocentric understandings of nature.
⑤ We know far too little about the prehuman history of the earth.

26~27 다음 글의 제목으로 가장 적절한 것을 고르시오.

In 2018, Derek Hodgson and Paul Pettitt published a paper in the Cambridge Archaeological Journal pointing to studies in neuroscience showing that people who are conditioned to recognize a specific object, such as a face or animal, will then see it in ambiguous patterns. We are attuned, for example, to see faces in the clouds. Hodgson and Pettitt hypothesized that Neanderthal hunters who had conditioned themselves to find camouflaged animals lurking everywhere perhaps saw outlines of those same animals in the flickering light of their torches in the dark chambers they inhabited. Studying 64,000-year-old images and sculptures at El Castillo Cave in Spain, the archaeologists came to believe that Neanderthals saw the crags and varicolored walls come "alive" with the images that filled their world. For example, a stalagmite with a rounded top and dark mottled patterns maybe wasn't merely a rock rising from the cave's floor to these Ice Age people but was interpreted as a bear rising to its feet.

26 [3점]
① The Evolutionary Benefits of Spiritual Expression
② A New Theory of the Origins of Neanderthal Cave Art
③ Speaking with Clouds: Language and Neanderthal Art
④ Scientific Perspectives on the Earliest Human Religions
⑤ Dancing Shadows: How Caves Shine a Light on Neanderthal Superstition

Until a few years ago it was thought that only certain species of plants — those defined precisely as carnivores — had the capacity to digest small animals, thus obtaining from them the nutrients they need. But recent studies have shown that the plant world's use of animal nourishment is quite widespread. If you've ever looked at the leaves of a potato plant, or a tobacco plant, or even more exotic plants such as Paulonia tomentosa (a tree that originated in China and is becoming very common in Europe and the United States), you may have noticed that they often have little insect corpses on them. Why do the leaves of these plants secrete sticky or poisonous substances that kill the insects, if they can't digest them? The reason is simple and, if you think about it, makes perfect sense: even if the bodies of these insects are not digested right away, they fall to the ground and decompose, releasing nitrogen that the plant needs in its diet; those remaining on the leaf provide nutriment to the bacteria on the plant, which easily absorb their nitrogen-rich waste products.

27
① Beyond the Flytrap: Extended Forms of Plant Carnivory [4점]
② Effects of Nitrogen Deficiency on Carnivorous Plants
③ The Secret Signals at the Heart of Root Intelligence
④ Leaf to Leaf: The Science of Plant Communication
⑤ Why Carnivorous Plants Face Conservation Threats

28~29 다음 글의 내용과 가장 거리가 먼 것을 고르시오.

In 2024, the term *brat* emerged as a cultural and linguistic emblem, encapsulating a rebellious and unapologetically hedonistic attitude popularized by younger generations, particularly Gen Z. Far from its conventional derogatory connotations, *brat* has been reclaimed to signify an ethos of self-expression, confidence, and playful defiance. This reclamation reflects a broader societal shift toward celebrating individuality and rejecting traditional norms of decorum and conformity. Artists like Charli XCX and others have championed the *brat* aesthetic, which fuses a carefree attitude with bold, experimental styles, resonating deeply with contemporary notions of empowerment and self-determination. Its rise to prominence, including recognition as Collins Dictionary's Word of the Year, underscores its cultural resonance as more than a fashion or linguistic trend — it is a statement of identity and autonomy in a rapidly evolving social landscape.

28
① *Brat* has become a cultural term that signals the defiant pursuit of pleasure, especially among members of Gen Z. [3점]
② The term *brat* has transcended its original negative connotations to signify positive self-expression.
③ The reclamation of *brat* signals a general movement to repudiate social standards that impose sameness.
④ Artists such as Charli XCX have promoted the *brat* attitude and style, which affirm current notions of autonomy.
⑤ The *brat* aesthetic was highlighted by Collins Dictionary for epitomizing refined and classic cultural values.

> Parents will typically observe the sleep of newborns as having no rhythm or significant day-night difference. By around two months, the first elements of a rhythmic pattern emerge, but are not closely related to the environment. By four or five months, sleep becomes more influenced by light and darkness, and most sleep will occur at night. In newborns and during the first few months, parents may sometimes observe the behavioral manifestations of active sleep: periods in which there are occasional grimaces and quick twitching of the limbs, sometimes with respiration that is slightly more irregular than in quiet sleep. The total amount of sleep will be seen to be declining from up to 16 hours per day in newborns to 10-12 hours at age two, continuing to drop until adolescence. The tendency to fall asleep will occur during the mid-evening in children, in contrast to the tendency to stay up later which will appear in adolescence.

29
① A two-month-old's sleep is not heavily affected by environmental factors. [3점]
② Illumination has an impact on the sleep of five-month-old infants.
③ In active sleep, respiration occurs more regularly than in quiet sleep.
④ As they grow older, children gradually decrease their total amount of sleep.
⑤ Adolescents are more inclined than children to go to bed later.

30~31 다음 글을 읽고 물음에 답하시오.

Anglo-American culture — the dominant seedbed of science fiction — assumes the negative about urban life more often and more easily than does continental culture. It is easy to trace American Ⓐ antiurban thinking through intellectual traditions and popular culture. When Thomas Jefferson compared cities to cancers and sores on the body politic, he set a tone that has resonated in American politics for two centuries. Nineteenth-century fears of cities as cauldrons of social disorder and political chaos fueled the urban Ⓑ dystopias that appeared again and again in imagined futures of the late nineteenth and early twentieth centuries. Even in the twenty-first century, a Ⓒ minority of Americans hold to the ideal of small-town living over big-city life that is supposedly less satisfying, less authentic, less healthy, more dangerous, and more alienating.

The comprehensive findings of social science, however, are not so clear. City people in the United States have roughly the same density of social networks as small-town folks, just skewed away from kin and toward groups of common interest. Even the slums and shantytowns of Latin America and South Asia are places of opportunity for the Ⓓ rural poor, with better health care, education, and job opportunities. In developing countries, city dwellers generally are more likely than their rural counterparts to say they are happy. Cities are cultural incubators, technological innovators, and the places where reformers introduce and test Ⓔ progressive institutions. The city as creative milieu is a network of industries and universities, artists and entrepreneurs.

30 윗글의 제목으로 가장 적절한 것은? [3점]

① Effects of Urban Living on Mental Health
② The Country and the City: A Dystopian Story
③ How Do City Environments Enable Innovation?
④ A Few Guidelines for Sustainable Urban Planning
⑤ Life in the City: Disparities in Perception and Reality

31 밑줄 친 Ⓐ~Ⓔ 중에서 문맥상 낱말의 쓰임이 적절하지 않은 것은? [3점]

① Ⓐ ② Ⓑ ③ Ⓒ
④ Ⓓ ⑤ Ⓔ

[32~33] 다음 글을 읽고 물음에 답하시오.

According to Henri Bergson, laughter emanates from the recognition of mechanical rigidity imposed upon the organic dynamism of human life. For Bergson, laughter functions as a profound social corrective, addressing behaviors or situations where individuals succumb to automatism or inflexible patterns, thereby disrupting the fluidity and spontaneity requisite for harmonious social interaction. He famously contends that laughter bears a "social signification," designed to "humiliate" and rectify the incongruous, restoring equilibrium within the collective. In contrast, Oscar Wilde conceptualizes laughter through a lens of irony and subversion, wielding wit as an incisive tool to expose the hypocrisies and absurdities underpinning societal conventions. Wilde orchestrates humor through deftly constructed paradoxes and the playful inversion of expectations, eliciting laughter not as a moral imperative but as a jubilant affirmation of the ridiculous and the deliberate artifice of social mores. Together, Bergson and Wilde illuminate distinct yet complementary dimensions of laughter: the former as an instrument of social regulation and cohesion, the latter as a medium for critical interrogation and aesthetic pleasure. Their perspectives collectively underscore laughter's profound cultural and intellectual _____, revealing its intricate entanglement with human behavior and the structures of society.

32 빈칸에 들어갈 가장 적절한 것은? [3점]

① isolation
② dismissal
③ resonance
④ divergence
⑤ abstraction

33 윗글의 요지로 가장 적절한 것은? [3점]

① Bergson sees laughter as a means of social critique, while Wilde views it as a tool for moral education.
② Bergson considers laughter an artistic expression, whereas Wilde sees it as a manifestation of rigid social norms.
③ Bergson regards laughter as a mechanism for social cohesion, whereas Wilde treats it as a celebration of individual freedom.
④ Bergson emphasizes laughter's corrective role in society, while Wilde highlights its role in exposing and enjoying absurdities.
⑤ Bergson and Wilde both see laughter as subversive, though Wilde applies it to linguistic constructs and Bergson to societal behavior.

34~35 다음 글을 읽고 물음에 답하시오.

Our conceptualization of boredom offers a differentiated view on the oft-found link between boredom and attention. A very consistent body of research has linked boredom to attentional failures. That is, when bored, we fail to keep our attention engaged with the task at hand. In turn, failures to keep attention engaged have been incorporated into the conceptualization of boredom as a defining feature. While we in no way negate the close link between boredom and attention, we argue that in the context of boredom, attentional disengagement does not represent a failure. We suggest that disengaging attention from a situation that yields only uninformative reward prediction errors (i.e., minimized near zero) is the very function of boredom. By triggering exploration via increased mental or motor motion, boredom is intrinsically designed to engage attention elsewhere. Thus, attentional disengagement is not the bug of boredom, but one of its core features. <u>Clearly, people frequently find themselves in situations whereby attentional disengagement is problematic and whereby boredom-induced attentional failures can produce catastrophic consequences.</u> However, we argue that in navigating the plethora of choices people make in life (simply put: Where do I devote my time and attention?), boredom serves as an adaptive function in helping people disengage from a course of action that is too low in subjective utility. Consistent with this, people who are frequently bored (i.e., score high in boredom proneness) scored lower on a measure of trait disengagement, thus supporting the notion that rather than being a pure measure of trait boredom, boredom proneness might reflect the dispositional self-regulatory failure to adaptively respond to boredom.

34 윗글의 주제로 가장 적절한 것은? [3점]

① neurological explanations for attentional failure
② negative effects of boredom on attention
③ adaptive function of boredom and attention
④ instances of boredom motivating change
⑤ correlations between boredom and productivity

35 밑줄 친 문장의 예시로 가장 적절한 것은? [3점]

① Boredom while driving on a highway
② Boredom while attending a public lecture
③ Boredom while watching a documentary on television
④ Boredom during a casual conversation at a coffee shop
⑤ Boredom while waiting in a long line at the grocery store

한양대학교

▶ 2025학년도 서울 자연계 A형　▶ 문항 수: 영어 35문항, 수학 25문항　|　제한시간: 130분

2025 한양대 서울 자연계 A형 영역별 문항 수

구분	문법			어휘			논리완성	독해	생활영어	총 문항 수
	G/S, W/E	정비문	재진술	동의어	반의어	유추				
문항 수				6			10	19		35
백분율				17%			29%	54%		100%

HANYANG UNIVERSITY

한양대학교

▶ 2025학년도 서울 자연계 A형: 영어 35문항, 수학 25문항 · 130분

[01~06] 밑줄 친 단어의 뜻과 가장 가까운 것을 고르시오.

01 Navajos, as stockmen, became intimately aware of each of their sheep and goats. Rather than being an impersonal herd on the hoof, each animal had its own personality and characteristics. The shepherd knew which ones were <u>docile</u> or belligerent.

[2점]

① malicious ② preposterous ③ obedient
④ bombastic ⑤ obstinate

02 As the child moves toward Piaget's stage of concrete operations, collecting objects takes on new significance. We see that the child at the approximate age of 7 not only finds interest in his surroundings but desires to attain them. Thus, he will collect all sorts of items in a <u>haphazard</u> array that ends up in a pocket, a drawer, or the floor of a room.

[2점]

① linear ② chaotic ③ pristine
④ destructive ⑤ compliable

03 Hauy approached a local <u>philanthropic</u> society, which pledged its support for underprivileged students. He helped a seventeen-year-old boy who was blind and invented a system of printing books so that individuals with visual impairments could read the contents by touch.

[2점]

① hierarchical ② contemporary ③ sustainable
④ pluralistic ⑤ benevolent

04 The door opens, and a light falls on her face, as the shadow of an unfamiliar man is cast on the wall behind her. Cinematographer William Daniels, who regularly collaborated with Lindsley Lane, has employed strong contrasts and hard shadows to represent this <u>ominous</u> moment, allowing Garbo's face to emerge from the darkness without the benefit of a halo-supplying backlight. [2점]

① menacing
② poignant
③ bittersweet
④ embarrassing
⑤ extraordinary

05 Stern is a frenetic interviewer, jumping from topic to topic, revealing an encyclopedic level of preparation reminiscent of NPR's Terry Gross, and blending witty banter with <u>effusive</u> praise to ferret out personal information. [2점]

① taciturn
② lavish
③ irascible
④ unctuous
⑤ pernicious

06 Language is an <u>impromptu</u> act that forces us to reuse and merge the past linguistic games that form into rich patterns over time. It becomes apparent that the arbitrariness and capriciousness, which some mathematical systems are trying to explain and rule out, is not a shortcoming after all, but rather an important strength of what makes a language a language. [2점]

① preconceived
② calculated
③ instinctive
④ scripted
⑤ spontaneous

07~15 빈칸에 들어갈 가장 적절한 것을 고르시오.

07 The Germanic tribes were perhaps more possessed of the military virtues to a higher degree than any other people that has existed before or since. They were the most terrible enemies, as Julius Caesar found; they could never be subdued because they fought, not merely to gain any specific ends, but because they loved fighting, i.e., because they were innately _____. [2점]

① altruistic ② lethargic ③ pugnacious
④ incessant ⑤ magnanimous

08 Paleoanthropologists like Bunn argue that "meat made us human." This argument is based on taphonomic evidence (that is, evidence from environmental conditions associated with fossilization) of hominin use of large animals for meat and marrow at the Pleistocene boundary in East Africa. Other researchers suggest that meat was a smaller part of the food, and that tubers were instead the key food involved in the transition to Homo sapiens. In other words, a(n) _____ change to increased tuber consumption would have been the driving force in the evolution toward Homo erectus. [2점]

① dietary ② geological ③ demographic
④ seismic ⑤ ecological

09 The criticality in culturally relevant pedagogy seeks to interrogate and disrupt the status quo. That is, the social structures and conscious and unconscious procedures and protocols involved in the reproduction of the status quo — the _____ of it through the distribution of human, material, and symbolic capital — are exposed, examined, and altered. [3점]

① extension and altercation
② eradication and manipulation
③ intensification and termination
④ substantiation and fortification
⑤ escalation and discombobulation

10 For the surfing sub-culture, one of the unique characteristics of that community is that they go into the sea and ride waves — they surf. There is also an _____ nature to sub-cultures which means that without possessing the unique characteristics one could never join the sub-culture. [2점]

① indulgent ② inordinate ③ expansive
④ acquiescent ⑤ exclusionary

11 Affirmative action or positive discrimination is a policy or a program providing access to systems for people of a minority group who have traditionally been discriminated against, with the aim of creating a more _____ society. [2점]

① agrarian ② legitimate ③ egalitarian
④ cosmopolitan ⑤ industrialized

12 The global explosion of symbolic forms makes patterns of cultural thought and behavior much more _____ than integrated and limiting, and the role of individual persons in shaping cultural styles and patterns more original and labor-intensive than ever before. [3점]

① unified and inventive
② obsolete and dispersed
③ ostentatious and creative
④ fragmented and generative
⑤ homogeneous and reductive

13 Interaction is the elemental feature of interdependence. By interaction, we refer to the fact that people engage in behaviors that affect both their own well-being and the well-being of others. Specifically, actors simultaneously or sequentially enact behaviors with implications for their own and their partners' immediate behavioral options and outcomes, as well as for the future situations, options, and outcomes that are made available (or eliminated) as a consequence of their actions. Thus, the options that are available to us and the outcomes that we experience are not a sole function of our own actions. John's decision to quit his job has implications for Mary; Mary's decision to train for a marathon has implications for John. In short, and to state the obvious: _____. [3점]

① Partnerships last a lifetime
② No person is an island
③ No pressure, no diamonds
④ You are your home
⑤ Be a voice, not an echo

14 Historians have challenged the assumption that early modern philosophy can be adequately comprehended in terms of the major published works of its most famous figures. It is now a commonplace that to understand a philosopher's views — expressed in the well-honed sentences of a book such as Descartes's *Meditations* or Kant's *Critique of Pure Reason* — requires understanding them in relation to the entire corpus of the philosopher's writings, published and unpublished. Correspondences, preliminary drafts, and subsequent revisions of published texts are all seen as important sources of evidence. In addition, it is increasingly acknowledged that our understanding of a canonical text can be deepened by reading it in conjunction with the works of a philosopher's immediate predecessors and contemporaries — works that often supply an illuminating background for its interpretation. In short, even if a published treatise carries an imprimatur as the authoritative expression of a philosopher's position on a given topic, understanding that position often is facilitated, and sometimes is only possible by _____. [3점]

① probing its reception among critics
② scrutinizing its political context
③ analyzing its logical flow and writing style
④ relating it to other pieces of textual evidence
⑤ predicting its influence on subsequent philosophical inquiries

15 The Internet is celebrated for disseminating knowledge and supporting conversation, dialogue, and debate. Its decentralization allows anyone to post opinions online or link to other pages. Yet this happy characterization has been challenged by the counter-argument that the Internet and the Web are also tools for _____, which will tend to magnify and reinforce their prejudices. [3점]

① negating eccentric opinions for the public
② circulating disparate ideas of diverse people
③ undermining diverse ethnic groups' cultural heritage
④ excising dissenting voices from an individual's purview
⑤ introducing opposing voices to broaden an individual's perspective

16 빈칸 Ⓐ, Ⓑ에 들어갈 가장 적절한 것은? [3점]

> Progress in AI and in its introduction into neurotechnology has complicated the interaction between humans and machines, mainly with respect to Ⓐ_____ and Ⓑ_____. With respect to the former, AI systems may enable some degree of human-independent cognitive functioning. In particular, systems with self-learning mechanisms might be capable of making decisions or generating outputs that were not previously programmed or intended by humans. As for the latter concern, machine-learning enables devices to make better predictions by learning through trial, error, and feedback loops to decode brain signals more accurately. But conversely, the users of a brain-computer interface may inadvertently learn to change their brain signals to be better decoded by the machine.

① autonomy — adaptivity
② accuracy — authenticity
③ uniformity — dichotomy
④ adversity — heterogeneity
⑤ consistency — accountability

17~18 다음 글을 읽고 물음에 답하시오.

Many Cuban songs, such as guarachas and later boleros, were adopted by the romantic rhetoric of poets and singers in Yucatan. When the Cuban rhythms arrived in the peninsula, they were smothered by this romanticism. The boleros and the Colombian bambuco became part of the regional tradition of Yucatan. The bolero was still performed in a two-beat pattern, but the tempo slowed down and the rhythmical accents were not strongly stressed in order to underline the romantic quality of the lyrics. This is the case of "Presentimiento" by Emilio Pacheco, which is said to be one of the first popular boleros in Mexico City during the twenties. The melodic cinquillo rhythm was still present, but the romantic text by the Spanish poet Pedro Mata was not as heavily stressed by the musical rhythm. The romanticism of Yucatan had a bucolic tendency foreign to any urban tradition; these boleros were the popular version of a naive romanticism. The poet Luis Rosado Vega defined the Yucatan bolero as a delicate genre deprived of any sort of obscenity. Consequently, Cuban boleros were softened in order to conform to middle-class conceptions of propriety and taste. These boleros were spread, transformed, and urbanized during the late twenties in the underground places in Mexico City by composers like Agustin Lara. After the revolution, the new political groups in power were looking for social, political, and economic stability through a new cultural project: the construction of a Mexican identity. The official history glorified Mexico's past with romantic, epic figures, and at the same time, nineteenth-century romanticism was acquiring a popular version.

17 윗글의 내용과 가장 거리가 먼 것은? [4점]

① Singers and poets in Yucatan were influenced by romanticism introduced through Cuban songs.
② The rhythmical accents were not strongly emphasized in "Presentimiento."
③ Cuban boleros were softened in order to conform to the taste of middle-class people in Mexico.
④ Artists such as Agustin Lara advocated a vision of arts as cultural objects for the elite society of Mexico City.
⑤ Following the revolution, the emerging political group pursued social, political, and economic stability by introducing a new cultural initiative: the creation of a Mexican identity.

18 밑줄 친 "bucolic"의 의미와 가장 가까운 것은? [3점]

① pastoral ② tangential ③ incessant
④ ebullient ⑤ circuitous

19~20 다음 글을 읽고 물음에 답하시오.

Cotton farmers have economic, environmental and agricultural reasons to want a better option for harvesting. Traditional mechanical harvesters can be up to 14 feet long and weigh more than 30 tons. They remove cotton effectively without damaging the plants but also can cause problems. One issue is prolonged fiber exposure. Cotton bolls don't all mature at the same time; the first open bolls in a field may wait for up to 50 days to be picked, until more bolls around them ripen. Another challenge is that harvesting machines compact the soil as they roll over it. This makes it harder for water and fertilizer to penetrate down to plant roots. And the machines cost roughly US$1 million apiece but are used for only two to three months each year. Robotics is a potential solution that farmers are already using for other crops, such as fruits and vegetables. Harvesting robots use cameras and sensors to detect when crops are ready to pick and can remove them without damaging the plant. For cotton, robotics offers more targeted picking of bolls that are ready to harvest. It produces better-quality cotton fiber by picking seed cotton as soon as the bolls open, without leaving it exposed to the weather. The robot targets the seed cotton and avoids touching other parts of the plant. With robotic picking, cotton farmers don't need to use defoliants to remove leaves from the plants prior to harvesting, which is a common practice now. And small, <u>nimble</u> robots do not compress the soil as they move over it, so they help maintain soil health.

19 윗글의 내용과 가장 가까운 것은? [3점]

① Cotton bolls all mature at the same time, allowing farmers to harvest the entire crop at once.
② Although robotic harvesters are not yet in use, they remain a potential solution for future generations.
③ Traditional cotton harvesters help maintain soil health by preventing soil compaction.
④ Robotic cotton harvesters cause significant damage to the plants, reducing the quality of the cotton fibers.
⑤ Robotics in cotton harvesting can help reduce the need for defoliants, as the robots can pick cotton without needing to remove leaves from the plants.

20 밑줄 친 "nimble"의 뜻과 가장 가까운 것은? [3점]

① agile ② minuscule ③ slow-moving
④ rigid ⑤ clumsy

21~22 다음 글을 읽고 물음에 답하시오.

The implications of early educational failure are broad and profound. School difficulties are associated with significantly higher expenses for extra help, special education, and grade retention. The added costs are not limited to those incurred at the school level. Children who experience school failure are more likely to be Ⓐ_____, and when they are not in school, they may engage in unhealthy or delinquent behaviors. These students are more likely to drop out of school or to be pushed out through expulsion. This obviously makes them less likely to receive the post-secondary education that is increasingly required for gainful employment in an American work environment that demands specialized skills. When they reach adulthood, the societal costs continue to mount because of higher reliance on welfare and other social supports, increased crime and incarceration, and underemployment with the resultant loss of tax revenue. Due to the intergenerational nature of poverty, the costs of school failure at the individual child level tend to Ⓑ_____ successive generations.

21 빈칸 Ⓐ, Ⓑ에 들어갈 가장 적절한 것은? [3점]

① enthusiastic — pass over
② truant — compound over
③ assiduous — complicate over
④ compassionate — evolve over
⑤ nonchalant — synchronize over

22 윗글의 제목으로 가장 적절한 것은? [3점]

① The Method of Early Education
② The Process of Early Education
③ The Cost of Early Education Failure
④ The Cause of Early Education Failure
⑤ The Range of Early Education Failure

23 다음 글의 요지로 가장 적절한 것은? [3점]

The conceptualization of an exhibition, whether temporary or permanent, actual or virtual, is of prime importance, for it impacts upon education, public perception, and, on occasion, political will. Museums, libraries, and galleries and their displays, publications, and outreach programs have been known to both reflect and help direct the way in which a given subject area is studied. They can be fruitful meeting grounds for a wide range of disciplines and outlooks and a testing place for matching aspiration and resource. In short, they help us to write history, to record it, and to direct its future. They are powerful social mechanisms, capable of misrepresenting as well as mirroring our identities. As the repositories of our collective memory, they are the stuff of which civilizations are formed — the way in which we shape them, use them, and invest in them in the future will help to serve as an indication of the extent to which we value, or merely pay lip service to, the very concept of civilization.

① Exhibitions are often used for political and economic agendas.
② Museum exhibits are now often driven by digital media and technology.
③ Virtual exhibitions are more effective in displaying exhibits and attracting more people than regular museums.
④ Museums can provide a business model by focusing not only public engagement but also profitable programs.
⑤ Museums and exhibitions play a key role in constructing and reflecting the collective memory of society.

24~25 다음 글을 읽고 물음에 답하시오.

Seattle recycles and composts more material than almost any other American city, but recycling is not necessarily a signal of success. Critics note, for example, that recycling actually encourages consumption by easing the consciences of consumers, and that it addresses waste only at the very end of the production chain, ignoring the whole system of waste-making from resource extraction through manufacturing and transport. Moreover, processing recycled materials requires huge amounts of energy and degrades material quality. Recycling, argue critics, is a Ⓐ_____ used by industry to displace the responsibility for environmental action on to individuals and municipal governments and to deflect regulatory attention from the corporate machinery of consumption and waste-making. Finally, municipal programs emphasize materials for which recycling provides minimal environmental benefit, ignoring other materials that could be more efficiently recycled. And these are just a few of the many arguments Ⓑ_____. Seattle's success may be notable, but its recycling rate hardly represents a solution to the many socio-environmental crises we face.

24 빈칸 Ⓐ에 들어갈 가장 적절한 것은? [3점]

① ploy
② bonus
③ refuse
④ demand
⑤ sentiment

25 빈칸 Ⓑ에 들어갈 가장 적절한 것은? [3점]

① against a whole-scale redefinition of recycling
② against the improvement in the material quality of recyclables
③ against the efficacy of recycling as a solution to the problems of garbage
④ for the investment of an increased amount of effort and money in recycling education
⑤ against waste prevention that emphasizes structural changes, such as product stewardship and extended producer responsibility

26. 밑줄 친 Ⓐ~Ⓔ 중에서 문맥상 낱말의 쓰임이 적절하지 않은 것은? [3점]

Twice in history, the human race has fundamentally transformed its source of Ⓐ <u>sustenance</u>, and hence its place in the world. Thousands of years ago, the invention of agriculture Ⓑ <u>paradoxically</u> narrowed dietary options from the ever-changing bounty of the hunter-gatherer to the repetitive harvest of the sedentary farmer. Nevertheless, food surpluses also led to the formation of Ⓒ <u>complex</u> societies by supporting kings, priests, merchants, and artists — including culinary artists, who devised novel ways of preparing otherwise monotonous grains. In the nineteenth century, industrialization initiated equally significant changes in food habits and social relations. Once again, humanity learned to make more from less, producing greater quantities from Ⓓ <u>fewer</u> varieties of food stuffs. Yet in contrast to agrarian societies, contemporary surpluses have been achieved by radically separating production from consumption, thereby Ⓔ <u>retaining</u> the social connections between cooks and eaters.

① Ⓐ ② Ⓑ ③ Ⓒ
④ Ⓓ ⑤ Ⓔ

[27~28] 다음 글을 읽고 물음에 답하시오.

In order to support a logically untenable position, in which both parties in all wars attribute themselves total correctness and the Other total error, we use the device of claiming superiority for ourselves and inferiority for the Other. This inferiority and superiority needs to be objectified somehow — the more visibly the better. Ultimately, it is force that provides the justification, and winners usually claim that God or truth was on their side. As we become more civilized, we need more rational reinforcements that will _____ the guilt derived from the use of brute force. Our human differences, whether real or imaginary, provide us with an ideal device. Among the imaginary ones, European aristocrats came up with the easily dismissible notion of blue blood. Racism, invented later, was a product of the same kind of imagination. It is the unfounded expression of prejudice, oppression and injustice based on the myth of "race classification," which nonetheless has had destructive physical, health, socio-economic-political, and criminal justice effects on those deemed lesser-humans by the classification, which have been very real. Racism has provided, especially since the period of colonization and slavery, a nearly flawless and guilt-freeing excuse for the exploitation of large portions of humanity on the basis of the color of their skin, as well as other physical traits being defined as determinants of their lesser humanity.

27 빈칸에 들어갈 가장 적절한 것은? [3점]

① allay
② elicit
③ incite
④ augment
⑤ coagulate

28 윗글의 내용과 가장 가까운 것은? [3점]

① Racism and its historical consequences are purely imaginary and thus dismissible.
② Racism served as a nearly perfect justification of slavery and colonial exploitation.
③ Race classification is grounded on scientifically proven differences in human physiognomy.
④ The arguments for blue blood and racism use the same kind of verifiable evidence to identify the Other.
⑤ We feel less guilty when the differences that divide us from the Other are intricate and ambiguous.

29~30 다음 글을 읽고 물음에 답하시오.

Climate change is not simply an environmental issue that can be managed through behavioral changes, sectoral interventions or new regulations. It is not a problem that can be addressed single-handedly by environmental ministries, by international institutions and non-governmental organizations or by development aid and adaptation funds. Finally, it is not a problem that can be solved by ecological modernization, ecosystem stewardship or sustainable development. It is, instead, a problem that can only be _____ by focusing on climate change as an issue of human security, which includes a thorough investigation of what it means for humans to be 'secure.' This demands, first and foremost, a change in the way that we think about change. It requires a shift away from the dominant framing that focuses on responding to change through a utilitarian, problem-solving approach or cost-benefit analyses, and towards a framing that recognizes and prioritizes the capacity of individuals and communities to both respond to and create change, including envisioning and pursuing alternative futures.

29 빈칸에 들어갈 가장 적절한 것은? [3점]

① exacerbated
② resolved
③ amplified
④ distended
⑤ expounded

30 윗글의 내용과 거리가 가장 먼 것은? [4점]

① In order to tackle the climate change problem, we should change the way we conceptualize change.
② In order to understand climate change as an issue of human security, we need to examine what it means to be secure.
③ In order to address climate change, we need to focus on the capacity of individuals and communities to envision alternative futures.
④ Environmental ministries, international institutions, and non-governmental organizations can solve the climate change problem.
⑤ Ecological modernization, ecosystem stewardship, or sustainable development are not effective means to address the problem of climate change.

[31~32] 다음 글을 읽고 물음에 답하시오.

> What causes excessive manganese exposure during pregnancy? A deficiency in iron — the micronutrient that when low is associated with high antisocial behavior — enhances manganese absorption. Women with low iron levels absorb about four times more manganese than women with high iron levels. An early postnatal source of manganese is soy infant formula, which has eighty times the amount of manganese that natural breast milk has. It is possible that the higher IQs found in breast-fed babies may be due to formula-fed babies' being exposed to high manganese, because manganese excretion is controlled by the liver. The livers of babies are underdeveloped, and consequently they are less able to excrete manganese. The excessive manganese could then result in poorest brain functioning and lower IQs.

31 윗글의 제목으로 적절한 것은? [3점]

① Why Iron Deficiency Improves Brain Development in Infants
② Breastfeeding vs. Formula Feeding: The Manganese Advantage
③ Iron Deficiency and Soy Formula's Role in Manganese Exposure in Infants
④ Manganese Deficiency and Its Role in Infant Cognitive Development
⑤ The Benefits of Soy Formula in Promoting Infant Brain Function

32 윗글의 내용과 거리가 가장 먼 것은? [3점]

① Iron deficiency increases manganese absorption.
② Underdeveloped livers in babies reduce manganese excretion.
③ Soy infant formula contains significantly more manganese than breast milk.
④ Low iron levels are linked to higher antisocial behavior.
⑤ Breast-fed babies are exposed to more manganese than formula-fed babies.

33 다음 글의 내용과 가장 거리가 먼 것은? [4점]

Writing systems around the world differ in several ways, from the alphabets of languages like English, where letters stand for individual sounds, to the 'syllabaries' used by Japanese, where a symbol refers to a syllable, to the 'logograms' of Chinese, where a character represents a whole word. Nonetheless, there is little difference in the brain areas involved in reading across individuals and cultures. Near the underside of the temporal region in the left hemisphere sits a brain area known as the visual word form area (VWFA), which is consistently activated no matter the writing system. The existence of the VWFA is important for two reasons. First, it shows that a cultural invention (i.e., literacy) can recruit quite similar neural substrates no matter who is doing the reading or what script is being read, suggesting that the brain deals with all written languages in the same way. Second, the VWFA becomes increasingly dedicated to recognizing words as the reader becomes more proficient in reading. Given that language is also a product of cultural evolution, the fact that the same seemingly specialized language areas are activated in different individuals, no matter which language they speak, does not mean that these areas have evolved as biological adaptations for language. Rather, like the VWFA, they emerge through experience with language, in some cases resulting in neural circuits that are mostly, and perhaps sometimes even completely, dedicated to language.

① Writing systems differ in structure, ranging from alphabets to syllabaries to logograms, but the brain processes all written languages in a similar way.
② The VWFA in the brain is consistently activated when reading, regardless of the writing system used.
③ The VWFA becomes more specialized with increased reading proficiency and reading experience.
④ The same brain areas are activated in different individuals when processing language, regardless of the language spoken, indicating that these areas develop through experience with language.
⑤ The VWFA evolved specifically for reading and is a biological adaptation to the act of decoding written language.

34 다음 글의 내용과 가장 거리가 먼 것은? [4점]

Myopia is a condition in which near objects appear clear while distance vision is blurred, with practically no other symptom except perhaps the discomfort of squeezing the eyelids, which does improve vision. From the optical point of view, the image of a distant object is formed not on the retina but in front of it. In other words, the power of the eye is either too strong or the eye is too long; the latter is usually the case. In some cases, the amount of myopia does not stop at maturity but continues to progress. This is a pathological condition in which degenerative changes in the retina and other tissues occur, and eventually vision is impaired even when corrected. It is important for these people not to engage in vigorous sports or activity as the retina is liable to detachment with this condition. Myopia usually develops in the early teens. However, an increasing number of people have been noted to acquire it in the late teens and early twenties, commonly in association with a great deal of visual stimulation, such as reading or working at a visual display unit. Hereditary influence as well as environmental factors both contribute to its development. In the general population, approximately one person in five is myopic, although that figure varies with age, race, and geography and this figure doubles among Chinese and Japanese.

① A person with myopia has sharp vision at close range and blurred vision at a distance.
② More than half of Chinese and Japanese people are myopic.
③ Myopia can continue to progress after maturity, causing changes in the retina.
④ Both hereditary and environmental factors can cause the development of myopia.
⑤ Myopia occurs when the image of an object is formed in front of the retina instead of on it.

35 다음 글의 내용과 가장 거리가 먼 것은? [4점]

The reasons why time can speed up and slow down are a bit of a mystery. Some researchers think that mild variations in time perception are linked to information processing. As a general rule, the more information — such as perceptions, sensations, and thoughts — that our minds process, the slower time seems to pass. Time passes slowly to children because they live in a world of newness. New environments stretch time because of their unfamiliarity. Absorption contracts time because our attention becomes narrow, and our minds become quiet, with few thoughts passing through. In contrast, boredom stretches time because our unfocused minds fill with a massive amount of thought-chatter. Time expansion experiences (Tees) can occur in an accident or emergency situation, such as a car crash, a fall or an attack. In time expansion experiences, time appears to expand by many orders of magnitude.

Around a half of Tees occur in accident and emergency situations. In such situations, people are often surprised by the amount of time they have to think and act. In fact, many people are convinced that time expansion saved them from their serious injury, or even saved their lives because it allowed them to take preventative action that would normally be impossible. For example, a woman who reported a Tee in which she avoided a metal barrier falling on to her car told me how a "slowing down of the moment" allowed her to "decide how to escape the falling metal on us."

① Time perception tends to slow down when more information is processed.
② The perception of time can be contracted when our attention narrows, as seen in moments of deep absorption.
③ In states of intense concentration, individuals may experience time expansion where they perceive time as stretching beyond its actual duration.
④ Time expansion occurs more frequently in routine activities because the mind is less occupied with new stimuli, leading to a sense of time moving slowly.
⑤ Time expansion often occurs in accidents or emergencies where people perceive a significant lengthening of time that enables them to think and act with clarity.

홍익대학교

▶ 2025학년도 서울 인문계 A형　▶ 문항 수: 40문항 | 제한시간: 70분

2025 홍익대 서울 인문계 A형 영역별 문항 수

구분	문법			어휘			논리완성	독해	생활영어	총 문항 수
	G/S, W/E	정비문	재진술	동의어	반의어	유추				
문항 수	8			10			10	12		40
백분율	20%			25%			25%	30%		100%

HONGIK UNIVERSITY

홍익대학교

2025학년도 서울 인문계 A형: 40문항 · 70분

01~10 Choose the one that is closest in meaning to the underlined word.

01 Only three medals are given per sports event. However, India, new to winning any medals at all, has refused to display the <u>equanimity</u> needed to empathize with those who return without medals.

① etymology
② grandiloquence
③ aplomb
④ guile

02 Nancy James <u>insinuated</u> many times that she wanted a brokerage fee. Even though she didn't explicitly say it, there is enough evidence to conclude that she breached ethics.

① admonished
② venerated
③ scrutinized
④ implied

03 The <u>florid</u> style of those writings is distinct from the inaccurate and overstrained expression we have been censuring, for that only is inaccuracy which leads to a false and inadequate conception in the reader or hearer.

① inept
② dire
③ aureate
④ spartan

04. Frederic Farar sneered at the "asinine ignorance of the Chinese gunners who held lights near their cannon to allow them to fire at night."

① fabbier
② fatuous
③ faddish
④ fain

05. Gauss was an unwilling correspondent, so when Sophie Germain, thinking it best to conceal her anomalous standing as a female mathematician, wrote to him under the name of M. LeBlanc, she received only a tardy and perfunctory reply.

① desultory
② eclat
③ inebriant
④ malfunctional

06. Some believers will find it easy to ignore contrary theories; some will not. Some will be more dogmatic than others. Some are conservative, tetchy and dismissive of alternatives; others are open-minded, considerate and exploratory.

① sagacious
② forearmed
③ peevish
④ abstemious

07. Interpretation, which includes the mapping of sentences onto sentences, is impossible in the absence of language; so a creature lacking a language is perforce incapable of thought.

① wantonly
② despondently
③ apathetically
④ ineluctably

08 The anti-immigrant <u>backlash</u> of the last decade also has deep roots in the crisis of the post-war social contract.

① revulsion
② bivouac
③ alternator
④ predominance

09 Recent overtures by extremist groups to <u>renounce</u> violence and discuss issues provide a window of opportunity to redress old wrongs.

① abjure
② contribute
③ penchant
④ reconvene

10 The purpose of this paper has not been to negate or <u>refute</u> the historical memories of the generation that came of age during the tragic period.

① enhance
② relinquish
③ disprove
④ perpetuate

11~18 Choose the word that is grammatically most inappropriate.

11 We do not know ① <u>what business</u> Sigmund Bloomfield was engaged in Chicago before 1896, but ② <u>when</u> the young Leonard was nine, his father ③ <u>moved his family</u> to Elkhart Lake, Wisconsin, where he took over and ④ <u>ran the Hotel Schwartz</u>.

12. ① Recent research on argument visualization has shown that ② the use of software programs specifically ③ designing to help students construct argument diagrams can significantly improve students' critical thinking abilities ④ over the course of a semester-long college-level critical thinking course.

13. Without any ① privileged reference frames, the theory required that all physical laws ② were expressed in generally ③ covariant equations, ④ having the same form in all systems of coordinates.

14. Everyone in the family knows Mounya ① has just bought himself a Cadillac, but knowing is one thing, and seeing is ② the others. ③ What a sight to behold. It's a beauty! All that chrome, ④ gleaming in the slanted sunlight of a late afternoon in June.

15. Both our baskets are ① half full. Neither of us ② seem to remember that there's a war on, that our country is ③ more or less occupied. And so, in the middle of a mushroom outing, soldiers of the hostile country ④ appear from behind a bush and take us away.

16. Understanding ① how exchange rate and gas price affect economy helps people ② plan their monthly living expense and ③ managing their bank accounts in case they have to give ④ more attention to them.

17 The powerful and eminent East India Company, ① overwhelmed by vital financial crisis, ② was granted by the British Parliament exclusive ③ control on all tea ④ shipping to the American colonies.

18 The knee ① is more likely to ② be damaged than ③ most other joints in the body such as ankle and wrist because it cannot twist ④ without injuring.

[19~28] Choose the one that is most suitable for the blank.

19 In Dr. Baker's passing, we have lost a leader who was the _____ of wisdom, nobility and humility, who served our country with all his heart and mind. His compassion and vision transformed and empowered the lives of millions of people.

① bane
② antithesis
③ epitome
④ indigence

20 In the southern part of the country, where the demand for land is great, fields are seldom allowed to remain _____.

① incisive
② preeminent
③ fallow
④ meticulous

21 As public confidence in higher education has declined, Americans have become _____ about the bachelor's degree and skeptical of its potential return on investment.

① less modish
② less morose
③ less haphazard
④ less sanguine

22 The assumed functional or formal inadequacy of the indigenous African languages and of indigenous mind or civilization was often alleged to justify European _____.

① tutelage
② tumidness
③ tubercle
④ turgescence

23 In the summer of 1965, a few hundred people had gathered in Washington to march in protest against the war: the first in line, historian Staughton Lynd, SNCC organizer Bob Moses, and long-time pacifist David Dellinger, were splattered with red paint by _____.

① barristers
② hecklers
③ notaries
④ crackerjacks

24 The concept is simple: breaking down divisions between formal eating and informal drinking. But blaring bar music and a steady _____ of drinkers wobbling past to the loo, as you grabble with your lobster crackers, isn't conducive to a restful evening out.

① traipse
② trestle
③ trice
④ trover

25 The Count agrees with the Senator that they are on the brink of "a great event," but he rejects the Senator's recourse to prophetism and extravagant desire to seek a(n) _____ in second-guessing Providence.

① audacity
② prebendary
③ augury
④ promptitude

26 The West generally ignored its own cultural cliques, who were regarded as _____ and of no consequence to political events.

① peripheral
② excavate
③ invigorating
④ invincible

27 Would the members of the party prefer the younger _____ rascal type as their representative or the more mature, debonair sophisticate?

① incumbent
② prudent
③ putative
④ impetuous

28 It is important to force through nearly all of the pulp, otherwise you will lose a lot of the flavour and be left with a bowl of _____ liquid.

① insipid
② insolent
③ insidious
④ imposturous

29~31 Read the following passage and answer the questions.

Truly, what is a number? According to the philosophical position known as *platonism*, numbers and other mathematical objects exist as abstract objects. Plato held them to exist in a realm of ideal forms. A particular line or circle that you might draw on paper is flawed and imperfect; in the platonic realm, there are perfect lines and circles — and numbers. From this view, for a mathematician to say, "There is a natural number with such-and-such property," means that in the platonic realm, there are such numbers to be found. Contemporary approaches to platonism assert that abstract objects exist, but are less connected with Plato's idea of an ideal form or the platonic realm, a place where they are all gathered together.

What does it mean to say, "There is a function, F, that is continuous but not differentiable," "There is a solution to this differential equation," or "There is a topological space that is sequentially compact, but not compact"? This is not physical existence; we cannot hold these "objects" in our hands. What kind of existence is this? According to platonism, mathematical objects are abstract but enjoy a real existence. For the platonist, ordinary talk in mathematics about the existence of mathematical objects can be taken literally — the objects do exist, but abstractly rather than physically. According to this perspective, the nature of mathematical existence is similar to the nature of existence for other abstractions, such as beauty or happiness. Does beauty exist? I believe so. Do parallel lines exist? According to platonism, the answers are similar. But what are abstract objects? What is the nature of this existence?

Consider a piece of writing: Henrik Ibsen's play *A Doll's House*. This exists, surely, but what is it specifically that exists here? I could offer you a printed manuscript, saying, "This is *A Doll's House*." But that would not be fully true, for if that particular manuscript were damaged, we would not say that the play itself was damaged; we would not say that the play had been taken in my back pocket on a motorcycle ride. I could see a performance of the play on Broadway, but no particular performance would seem to be the play itself. We do not say that Ibsen's play existed only in 1879 at its premiere, or that the play comes into and out of existence with each performance. The play is an abstraction, an idealization of its various imperfect instantiations in manuscripts and performances.

Like the play, the number 57 similarly exists in various imperfect instantiations: 57 apples in the bushel and 57 cards in the cheater's deck. The existence of abstract objects is mediated somehow through the existence of their various instantiations. Is the existence of the number 57 similar to the existence of a play, a novel, or a song? The play, as with other pieces of art, was created: Ibsen wrote *A Doll's House*. And while some mathematicians describe their work as an act of creation, doubtless no mathematician would claim to have created the number 57 in that sense. Is mathematics discovered or created? Part of the contemporary platonist view is that numbers and other mathematical objects have an independent existence.

29 What would be the best title for the passage?

① The nature of numbers in mathematical platonism
② The similarities and differences between plays and numbers
③ Flaws and perfectness of numbers in the actual and abstract realm
④ Plato's philosophical claims in plays and numbers

30 According to the passage, even though the play *A Doll's House* shares some properties with numbers, they are still different in the sense that _____.

① numbers do not have a real presence in the actual world, unlike *A Doll's House*, which can exist in the form of the printed manuscript
② Plato would not take a serious consideration of the play in his theory of abstract existence, in contrast with numbers
③ *A Doll's House* can be instantiated by physical means, unlike numbers, which exist only in an abstract realm
④ unlike *A Doll's House*, numbers are not invented, but exist independently of mathematicians' works or thoughts

31 Which of the following is most likely to be inferred from the passage?

① Printed manuscripts of *A Doll's House* can be regarded as perfect instantiations of the play.
② Even if the instantiations of *A Doll's House* are imperfect, we can say that the play still perfectly exists in the platonic realm.
③ The existence of numbers can be mediated by various instantiations in the abstract realm.
④ Unlike plays, numbers are independent of mathematicians, and therefore their instantiations should be perfect.

[32~34] Read the following passage and answer the questions.

Stanley Milgram conducted a series of experiments to study obedience to authority. He placed an ad in the local newspaper in New Haven, Connecticut, offering a small sum of money to men to participate in a "scientific study of memory and learning" being conducted at Yale University. The volunteers reported to Milgram's laboratory at Yale, where they met a scientist dressed in a white lab coat and another volunteer in the study, a middle-aged man named "Mr. Wallace." Mr. Wallace was actually a confederate (an accomplice) of the experimenter, but the participants did not know this. Ⓐ The scientist explained that the study would examine the effects of punishment on learning. One person would be a "teacher" who would administer the punishment, and the other would be the "learner." Mr. Wallace and the volunteer participant then drew slips of paper to determine who would be the teacher and who would be the learner. The drawing was rigged, however — Mr. Wallace was always the learner and the actual volunteer was always the teacher.

The scientist attached electrodes to Mr. Wallace and then placed the "teacher" in front of an impressive-looking shock machine that was located in an adjoining room. The shock machine had a series of levers that, the individual was told, when pressed would deliver shocks to Mr. Wallace. The first lever was labeled 15 volts, the second 30 volts, the third 45 volts, and so on up to 450 volts. The levers were also labeled "Slight Shock," "Moderate Shock," and so on up to "Danger: Severe Shock," followed by red X's above 400 volts.

Mr. Wallace was instructed to learn a series of word pairs. Then he was given a test to see if he could identify which words went together. Every time Mr. Wallace made a mistake, the teacher was to deliver a shock as punishment. The first mistake was supposed to be answered by a 15-volt shock, the second by a 30-volt shock, and so on. Each time a mistake was made, the learner received a greater shock.

The learner, Mr. Wallace, never actually received any shocks, but the participants in the study did not know that. In the experiment, Mr. Wallace made mistake after mistake. When the teacher "shocked" him with about 120 volts, Mr. Wallace began screaming in pain and eventually yelled that he wanted out. What if the teacher wanted to quit? This happened — the volunteer participants became visibly upset by the pain that Mr. Wallace seemed to be experiencing. The experimenter told the teacher that he could quit but urged him to continue, using a series of verbal prods that stressed the importance of continuing the experiment. What happened? Ⓑ Approximately 65% of the participants continued to deliver shocks all the way to 450 volts.

Milgram went on to conduct several variations on this basic procedure with 856 subjects. The study received a great deal of publicity, and the results challenged many of our beliefs about our ability to resist authority.

But the Milgram study is also an important example for discussing the problem of ethics in behavioral research. How should we make decisions about whether the Milgram study or any other study is ethical? The Milgram study was one of many that played an important role in the development of ethical standards that guide our ethical decision-making.

32 According to the passage, which of the following is the most likely reason for Ⓐ?

① The scientist wanted to investigate whether there is a correlation between memory and learning.
② The scientist wanted to include confounding factors in the study.
③ The scientist wanted to hide the real purpose of study.
④ The scientist wanted to test how many vocabulary errors would be made by the participants.

33 According to the passage, which of the following is the most likely reason for Ⓑ?

① The participants were promised to receive a small sum of money once they reached the highest shock level.
② The participants felt compelled to obey the experimenter's coercion.
③ The participants believed that Mr. Wallace deserved the terrible shocks.
④ The participants did not notice that Mr. Wallace was in pain because he was in the distance.

34 Which of the following is most likely to be inferred from the passage?

① The participants knew that Mr. Wallace was the scientist's confederate.
② The participants did not know that Mr. Wallace was one of the volunteer participants.
③ None of the participants administered the punishment.
④ The participants experienced psychological distress because they believed they were harming Mr. Wallace.

35~37 Read the following passage and answer the questions.

Most research projects involve selecting a sample of participants from a population of interest. The population is composed of all individuals of interest to the researcher. One population of interest in a large public opinion poll, for instance, might be all eligible voters in the United States. This implies that the population of interest does not include people under the age of 18, people who are incarcerated, visitors from other countries, and anyone else not eligible to vote. You might conduct a survey in which your population consists of all students at your college or university. With enough time and money, a survey researcher could conceivably contact everyone in the population. The United States attempts to do this every ten years with an official census of the entire population. With a relatively small population, however, you might find it relatively easy to study the whole population.

Let's use another example. What if you asked every single student at your college or university to tell you whether they prefer to study at home or at school, and you found that 64% preferred studying at home. In this case, you would be very certain of the answer to your question — after all, you asked everybody. That, of course, would be quite costly; you would likely have to hire a team of research assistants to track down every student. But suppose you are not independently wealthy (or you have better uses for your wealth). In that case, Ⓐ you could randomly select a subgroup of students at your university and ask them the question. With proper sampling, we can have a representative sample of the population and use information obtained from the participants (or "respondents") who were sampled to estimate the characteristics of the population as a whole. Statistical theory allows us to use data obtained from a sample to estimate what the entire population is like.

35 Which of the following is most likely to be inferred from the passage?

① Properties of the population of interest are accurately reflected by any sampling method.
② It is possible to obtain population estimates without surveying the entire population.
③ Statistical theory cannot be applied to the data gathered from a sample of participants.
④ Population sampling is defined as taking a superset from the population of interest.

36 According to the passage, which of the following is the most likely reason for randomly selecting a sample of participants in Ⓐ?

① Because a risk of sampling biases can be reduced in the course of selection.
② Because a population of interest can be easily defined during sample selection.
③ Because the researcher can recruit a large number of participants.
④ Because the response rate can be increased by random selection.

37 Which of the following is most likely to be the main purpose of the passage?

① To suggest that population sampling should be avoided
② To explain why population sampling is used in most research projects
③ To inform the readers of advantages of using scientific research methods
④ To describe how sampling techniques have evolved

38~40 Read the following passage and answer the questions.

Jimmy Carter's presidency began with a simple act meant to signal a new relationship between the people and their government: He and his wife, Rosalynn, got out of their limousine and walked a short part of the inaugural parade route, hand in hand. His time in office ended four years later with a spiteful gesture by the revolutionary government of Iran, which released 52 American hostages it had held for 444 days — but only when Mr. Carter was out of office, and at the very moment when his triumphant successor was delivering his inaugural address.

It was the final insult of Mr. Carter's term in office and the end of what was widely regarded, according to much commentary and a fair swath of public opinion, as a "failed" presidency. But was his presidency, which ended 43 years before his death Sunday at age 100, really a failed one? It's not easy to say just what constitutes failure in a presidency: war, economic disruption that goes on for years, civil conflict? Some highly regarded presidents saw all these things on their watches.

It's obvious that much went badly during Mr. Carter's time in the White House. To some extent, he was overtaken by events that had been set in motion well before he took office. The seething resentment among many Iranians that led to the hostage crisis dated back at least a quarter-century. The economic problems that dogged the administration were a continuation of trends that had been developing through two or three administrations, and they were greatly exacerbated by the oil crisis triggered by Iran's revolution. The general dismay with and alienation from government could be, and generally were, seen as in large part products of the Vietnam War and the Watergate scandal.

In fact, there were solid and lasting accomplishments by the Carter administration. The Camp David agreement, which has brought a long if uneasy peace to what was the most dangerous conflict point in the Middle East, was his administration's greatest foreign policy achievement. It's hard to see how the accord between Egypt's Anwar Sadat and Israel's Menachem Begin could have been reached without Mr. Carter's constant presence during the talks and careful attention to the needs of the two principals.

38 Which of the following is most likely to be inferred from the passage?

① Jimmy Carter's administration overcame previous administration's political turmoil.
② The hostages in Iran were finally relieved in Carter's presidency.
③ Jimmy Carter administration was responsible for the Watergate scandal.
④ Jimmy Carter was not fairly evaluated by public opinions despite his key achievements.

39 According to the passage, which of the following is true?

① Jimmy Carter eventually overcame the diplomatic problems during his presidency without support from Americans.
② The oil crisis by Iran's revolution worsened American economic problems which had already been exacerbated during previous administrations.
③ Jimmy Carter was a popular president due to his personality despite his minor mistakes during the oil crisis and the hostage crisis.
④ The Camp David agreement brought peace in the Middle East even though Sadat and Begin were not satisfied with it.

40 Which of the following is most likely to follow the passage?

① The impact of the American hostages in Iran and diplomatic problems
② Americans' collective memory about Vietnam War and Watergate scandal
③ The failure of publicity of Jimmy Carter's administration
④ More accomplishments by Jimmy Carter administration

홍익대학교

▶ 2025학년도 서울 자연계 A형　▶ 문항 수: 영어 25문항, 수학 15문항　|　제한시간: 70분

2025 홍익대 서울 자연계 A형 영역별 문항 수

구분	문법			어휘			논리완성	독해	생활영어	총 문항 수
	G/S, W/E	정비문	재진술	동의어	반의어	유추				
문항 수	6			9			4	6		25
백분율	24%			36%			16%	24%		100%

HONGIK UNIVERSITY

홍익대학교

● 2025학년도 서울 자연계 A형: 영어 25문항, 수학 15문항 · 70분

01~09 Choose the one that is closest in meaning to the underlined word.

01 Illinois' corporate franchise tax makes no sense. It is <u>convoluted</u> and economically harmful, and should be repealed. Even the term "franchise tax" is misleading and outdated, as it is not a tax on the franchise locations of a larger business.

① labyrinthine
② gallant
③ jocund
④ agnate

02 She is <u>effervescent</u> and forever dreaming up new initiatives that will contribute to the flourishing of Israel's capital and its residents.

① nefarious
② anorexic
③ oracular
④ exuberant

03 While working as a quality assurance engineer at PMI Industries in Gates, New York. Smalley allegedly <u>forged</u> the signature of an inspector on reports for products that were sold to California-based SpaceX.

① annihilated
② eulogized
③ fabricated
④ blustered

04 Hartlib had seven children, had been dismissed for impolitic preaching, and had accumulated great debt as a result, but this had now slowed down his zeal for the advancement of learning.
① rash
② upright
③ fief
④ neutral

05 A new and thrilling simulacrum is born full of what appear to be the innate hardships and difficulties of reality, replacing what had become the lackluster simulacrum of air-conditioned immortality, unlimited borrowing and endless consumerism.
① hummock
② huckster
③ humdinger
④ humdrum

06 It is commonly complained of various works that they say that Catholics are superstitious, that black people are innate incompetent, that Jews are mendacious, and that war is a good and noble undertaking.
① perfidious
② unswerving
③ resolute
④ unrelenting

07 The event was a largely somniferous one, with meandering answers about topics such as budget forward estimates, vertical fiscal imbalance and increasing tax thresholds to fight off bracket creep.
① stipulated
② speculative
③ sedimentary
④ soporific

08 Nuts are high in Vitamin E, a <u>potent</u> antioxidant that may help ward off heart disease and cancer.

① efficacious
② capricious
③ ludicrous
④ subversive

09 After all, the condition is often associated with other problems such as <u>congenital</u> heart disease and increased risk of certain leukemias.

① subsided
② innate
③ disjointed
④ congested

10~15 Choose the word that is grammatically most inappropriate.

10 For Peirce, semiosis was ① <u>the way</u> culture happens, and in this ② <u>broader</u> field of semiotic study, his understanding of the object came close ③ <u>in the way</u> Saussure understood ④ <u>the signified</u>.

11 A proof for the immortality of the soul would be of only academic ① <u>interest to</u> anyone if it ② <u>is</u> the case that the soul ③ <u>shown to be</u> immortal ④ <u>had nothing to do with</u> one's personal identity.

12 ① <u>The most exciting</u> Christmas discs are ② <u>those that</u> showcase a performer excelling in a completely different musical context. Alan Jackson proves just ③ <u>how talented is he a singer</u> with this traditional ④ <u>collection of big-band arrangements</u>.

13 ① From time to time, we make our subscriber list available ② to companies that sell goods and services by mail that we believe would interest our readers. If you ③ would not rather receive such mailings ④ via postal mail, please send your current mailing label to Mail Preference Service, P. O. Box 6000, Harlan, IA 51593.

14 ① If you want to organize an academic conference successfully, you must send the ② invitation emails in advance ③ people who will ④ be invited.

15 ① One of the most important ② problem of the amusement park ③ is that the number of visitors ④ has been gradually decreasing for three years.

16~19 Choose the one that is most suitable for the blank.

16 Water quality would continue to be improved by _____ unused dirt roads and by prohibiting new activities in riparian areas that would have unacceptable long-term effects on water quality, fish, or vegetation.

① obliterating　　② anchoring
③ fortifying　　　④ penetrating

17 Those pushed aside after losing their health to harsh labor were now fighting death in each room. Swollen, _____, and bruised with boils, each sick with various diseases, they together presented a hellish sight.

① full-bodied　　② gratified
③ rhubarbed　　 ④ emaciated

18 The two airlines began their code-sharing and _____ frequent flyer program about a year ago.

① reciprocal
② invulnerable
③ ticking
④ verdure

19 Challengers need to learn as much as they can to prepare for all questions and become _____ with every area of policy even though all of them are beginners now.

① perpetuated
② conversant
③ disarrayed
④ arrogated

20~22 Read the following passage and answer the questions.

Truth is a matter of peculiar disciplinary significance for both philosophers and logicians. Of course, every science and inquiry seeks to say something true about 'what is'. Theologians, scientists, and artists seek to discern the true, whether this truth concerns the highest being, the nature of depression, or social justice, and so forth. The logician and the philosopher, however, are unique in their efforts to mark out the conditions of truth. They both share the tasks of determining the boundaries of intelligibility, separating formal from material conditions of truth, and striving for a language of utmost precision. Both disciplines are thus concerned, in contrast to the particular sciences and arts, with conditions by which truth happens.

Yet throughout the history of Western philosophy, the significant differences between philosophy and logic have been shown to justify the institution of strict disciplinary boundaries between them. Historically, philosophy has been afforded an exalted status correlating to the perceived expansiveness of its domain compared to that of logic. Philosophy takes up topics and questions that are well beyond the purview of logic. Questions about the nature of justice, time, or the soul, for example, are external to the domain of logic. From within the tradition it is not controversial to say that all that is included in logic can be included in philosophy, but not all that can be included in philosophy can be included in logic. Philosophy is held to be the larger, more encompassing, and sometimes the more dignified discipline.

Logic, following the scholastic appropriation of Aristotle, has been conceived as a Ⓐ 'propaedeutic' for knowledge in general. This tradition is reflected in the typical conception of the education process: a student takes courses in logic, which prepares them for rigorous engagement with the sciences or the humanities. This process that begins in logic passes through the sciences and ultimately culminates in philosophy. Philosophy as the culmination of knowledge is a discipline markedly other than the discipline of logic. As a challenge to this traditional order, some philosophers in the 20th century have held that the work of the logician and the work of the philosopher overlap without remainder. In fact, with analytic philosophy broadly construed comes the rejection of many of the perennial questions that traditionally populated philosophical research. Questions regarding the purpose of the universe, the nature of the soul, the attributes of God are taken as flights of speculation, pseudo-questions that are ultimately unintelligible. Precisely those subjects of inquiry that used to distinguish philosophy from logic are dismissed as chimerical. Analytic philosophy with its emphasis on a clear and precise language as well as its vision of philosophy lends itself to a very useful role in our contemporary scientific-technological world. Yet, the increasing popularity of the vision of philosophy proffered by analytic philosophy should not cause us to forget the nuanced commitments of the historical tradition it challenges. In fact, it is perhaps only by attending to the tradition and its prejudices that the novelty of analytic philosophy can be assessed.

20 According to the passage, which of the following is most likely for Ⓐ'**propaedeutic**' to mean?

① a preliminary introduction prerequisite to a subject or area of study
② a discipline which aims to investigate what truth is
③ a consideration of the conjugation between different scientific fields
④ a process to invent the correlation of the domain of scientific questions

21 Which of the following is most likely to be inferred from the passage?

① Since logic deals with more specific issues than philosophy, logic should not be regarded as concerning with truth.
② Traditionally, philosophers have been assumed to ask broader questions than logicians.
③ Unlike logic, philosophy does not separate formal aspects of truth from its material conditions.
④ Questions asked in logic can only be determined after the topics of philosophy are investigated.

22 According to the passage, analytic philosophy is different from traditional philosophy in the sense that _____.

① analytic philosophers eventually aim to answer questions like the existence of God or the soul in a more precise way
② analytic philosophy discards logic because of its imprecision and obscurity in the use of language
③ analytic philosophers tend to ignore questions that have been asked to make the boundaries between logic and philosophy
④ analytic philosophy does not make any contribution to the recent development of science and technology because philosophy is not useful in contemporary society

23~25 Read the following passage and answer the questions.

Google has built a computing chip that takes just five minutes to complete tasks that would take 10,000,000,000,000,000,000,000,000 years for some of the world's fastest conventional computers to complete.

That's 10 septillion years, a number that far exceeds the age of our known universe and has the scientists behind the latest quantum computing breakthrough reaching for a distinctly non-technical term: "mindboggling".

The new chip, called Willow and made in the California beach town of Santa Barbara, is about the dimensions of an After Eight mint, and could supercharge the creation of new drugs by greatly speeding up the experimental phase of development.

[A] Reports of its performance follow a flurry of results since 2021 that suggest we are only about five years away from quantum computing becoming powerful enough to start transforming humankind's capabilities to research and develop new materials from drugs to batteries, one independent UK expert said. Governments around the world are pouring tens of billions of dollars into research.

[B] Significantly, Willow is claimed to be far less prone to error than previous versions and could swell the potential of the already fast-developing field of artificial intelligence.

[C] Quantum computing — which harnesses the discovery that matter can exist in multiple states at once — is predicted to have the power to carry out far bigger calculations than previously possible and so hasten the creation of nuclear fusion reactors and accelerate the impact of artificial intelligence, notably in medical science. For example, it could allow MRI scans to be read in atom-level detail, unlocking new caches of data about human bodies and disease for AI to process, Google said.

[D] Google Quantum AI is one of numerous groups wrestling with how to harness the computing power of quantum mechanics including Microsoft, Harvard University and Quantinuum, a firm with UK links. A key problem is reducing the fragility of quantum chips as even microscopic material defects, cosmic rays and ionising radiation tend to knock them off course.

23 What would be the best title for the passage?

① How will Google quantum AI change medical science in five years?
② What a quantum computing has achieved for pharmaceutical research
③ Quantum computing and fierce competition of the IT corporations
④ Google unveils 'mindboggling' quantum computing chip, Willow

24 According to the passage, which of the following is NOT true?

① Quantum computing technology can be developed enough in five years to find new materials in pharmaceutical researches.
② The ability of AI technology can be largely unaffected by the development of quantum computing.
③ By using quantum computing chips, medical science can get breakthrough such as more enhanced MRI scans.
④ The new chip, Willow is far more effective in decreasing error than previous version chips.

25 Which of the following is the most appropriate place for the following sentence to be inserted in?

But there are also fears that without guardrails, the technology has the power to crack even the most sophisticated encryption, undermining computer security.

① A
② B
③ C
④ D

김영편입 영어 사전 시리즈
편입 준비의 시작은 체계적인 김영 어휘 트레이닝

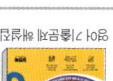

품사별로 익히는 김영편입영어 사전서

품사 이론서 / 구문독해 이론서

↓

기출 영단어 이론 학습 중 단어도 단계별 학습

 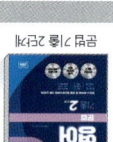 

어휘 기출 1단계 / 문법 기출 1단계 / 독해 기출 1단계 / 논리 기출 1단계

+

문법 상위독 1단계 / 독해 상위독 1단계 / 논리 상위독 1단계

↓

단어부터 실전 영어활용 학습 중 단계별 트레이닝

어휘 기출 2단계 / 문법 기출 2단계 / 독해 기출 2단계 / 논리 기출 2단계

+

문법 상위독 2단계 / 독해 상위독 2단계 / 논리 상위독 2단계

↓

대학별 정시대비를 위한 기출문제 해설집

 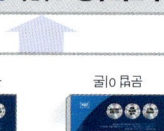

영어 기출문제 해설집 / 수학 기출문제 해설집

김영편입 중요인 사전과 기출 대비서에서 꼬인 기능
(편의기능, Yes24, 알라딘, 온라인교보 등)

영어

2026 수능 파이널 대비
기출문제 해설집 [문제편]

만점 활용 가이드

1 출제경향 분석
파트별 최신 출제 유형 분석 및 자료를 통해 올해 수능 영어 경향을 파악하여 영어 수능대비 완성

2 실전 대비 연습
체감난이도 대비 기출문제 풀이 중심으로 실전 감각과 문제 해결력 증진

3 정답 확인 & 오답 분석
유형 분석과 해설 개념까지 정확히 중심 학습으로 기출문제 완벽 정리

4 기출 유형별 학습 강화
기출 문제에 대한 학습 통해 응용력과 풀이력 강화

**3년 연속
대상**

2024, 2023, 2022 대한민국 브랜드 어워드 대학입학교재 대상
2021 대한민국 우수브랜드 대상
(한경미디어)

**수능 파이널
32만 부**

예비고/고등학생 영어 시리즈 수능 파이널 종합 기준
(2014.01.01~2024.12.31)

매스티지코프그룹 아이비김영이 NEW 도서 브랜드 〈김영북스〉
아이비의 명성 & 자기주도 IT 시스템 융합이
책이 되어 드리겠습니다.

www.kimnbook.co.kr

김영편입

2026학년도 대비

영어
기출문제
해설집

해설편

6

2025학년도 27개 대학 43개 유형의 편입영어 기출문제 수록!

교육서비스 브랜드 **대상**

누적 **32만부 돌파**

2024 대한민국 브랜드 어워즈
대학편입교육 대상(한경비즈니스)
산출근거 후면표기

기출로 완성하는 합격 전략 김영편입 영어 기출문제 해설집	대학별 출제 문항 분류표 & 상위권 대학 심층 분석 수록	정확한 해설과 상세한 분석으로 문제 이해력 극대화

김앤북
KIM&BOOK

김영편입 컨텐츠평가연구소

김영편입 컨텐츠평가연구소는 편입 시험의 다양한 문제 유형과 난이도를 분석하여 수험생에게 올바른 학습 방향을 제시해 줄 목적으로 설립된 메가스터디의 부설 기관이다. 수십 년간 시행되어 온 대학별 편입 시험을 심층 분석하여 실전에 가까운 컨텐츠를 개발하고 있으며, 김영편입의 우수한 교수진과 축적된 컨텐츠를 기반으로 다양한 교재를 출판하고 있다.

주요 집필 교재

「김영편입 영어 시리즈」 이론서 / 기출 1, 2 단계 / 워크북 1, 2 단계
「김영편입 수학 시리즈」 이론서 / 워크북 / 공식집
「김영편입 연도별 기출문제 해설집 시리즈」 영어 / 수학 / 연고대
「MVP Starter」, 「MVP 시리즈 Vol. 1, 2」, 「해독제 Vol. 1, 2」 등

영어 기출문제 해설집
2026학년도 대비

초판1쇄 인쇄 2025년 6월 16일
초판1쇄 발행 2025년 6월 30일
편저 김영편입 컨텐츠평가연구소
기획총괄 최진호
개발/기획 이순옥, 신종규, 안진영, 김진희, 김형석
감수 류형동
디자인 김소진, 서제호, 서진희, 조아현
제작/영업 조재훈, 김승규, 정광표
마케팅 지다영

발행처 ㈜아이비김영
펴낸이 김석철
등록번호 제22-3190호
주소 (06729) 서울 서초구 강남대로 279, 백향빌딩 4, 5층
전화 (대표전화) 1661-7022
팩스 02)599-5611

ⓒ ㈜아이비김영
이 책은 저작권법에 따라 보호받는 저작물이므로 무단복제를 금지하며,
책 내용의 전부 또는 일부를 이용하려면 반드시 저작권자의 서면동의를 받아야 합니다.

ISBN 979-11-7349-059-0 13740
정가 49,000원

잘못된 책은 바꿔드립니다.

영어

2026학년도 대비
기출문제 해설집

해설편

2025학년도 27개 대학 43개 유형의 편입영어 기출문제 수록!

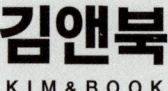

CONTENTS

문제편

2025학년도 기출문제 파트별 문항 분류표		8
상위권 대학 심층분석		
경희대학교		12
서강대학교		14
성균관대학교		16
중앙대학교		18
한국외국어대학교		20
한양대학교		22
2025학년도 대학별 문항 수 및 제한시간		24

2025학년도 기출문제

대학	계열/유형	쪽
가천대	인문계 A형	26
가톨릭대	인문계 A형	42
건국대	인문·예체능계 B형	62
건국대	자연계 B형	80
경기대	일반편입 A형	90
경찰대	일반대학생 전형	104
경희대	인문·체육계열	128
경희대	한의학과 인문	146
고려대	세종 인문·자연계	154
광운대	인문계 1교시 A형	178
광운대	자연계 2교시 A형	194
단국대	인문계 오전	206
단국대	인문계 오후	222
덕성여대	1교시	238
덕성여대	2교시	252
명지대	인문계 오전	264
명지대	인문계 오후	282
서강대	1차	298
서강대	2차	314
서울시립대	인문·자연계열 II	332
서울여대	오전 A형	350
서울여대	정오 A형	364
성균관대	인문계 A형	378
성균관대	자연계 A형	402
세종대	인문계 A형	414
숙명여대	A형	432
숙명여대	B형	446
숭실대	인문계	460
숭실대	자연계	484
아주대	인문계	496
아주대	자연계	522
인하대	인문·예체능계	536
중앙대	인문계 A형	560
한국공학대	일반·학사편입	580
한국외대	T1-1 A형	596
한국외대	T2 A형	616
한국항공대	인문계	636
한국항공대	자연계	652
한성대	인문계 A형	664
한양대	서울 인문계 A형	684
한양대	서울 자연계 A형	702
홍익대	서울 인문계 A형	720
홍익대	서울 자연계 A형	736

해설편

2025학년도 기출문제

대학	구분	페이지
가천대	인문계 A형	6
가톨릭대	인문계 A형	17
건국대	인문·예체능계 B형	31
건국대	자연계 B형	43
경기대	일반편입 A형	49
경찰대	일반대학생 전형	58
경희대	인문·체육계열	75
경희대	한의학과 인문	86
고려대	세종 인문·자연계	91
광운대	인문계 1교시 A형	104
광운대	자연계 2교시 A형	117
단국대	인문계 오전	125
단국대	인문계 오후	134
덕성여대	1교시	144
덕성여대	2교시	152
명지대	인문계 오전	160
명지대	인문계 오후	171
서강대	1차	181
서강대	2차	191
서울시립대	인문·자연계열 Ⅱ	201
서울여대	오전 A형	211
서울여대	정오 A형	221
성균관대	인문계 A형	231
성균관대	자연계 A형	246
세종대	인문계 A형	254
숙명여대	A형	266
숙명여대	B형	275
숭실대	인문계	284
숭실대	자연계	299
아주대	인문계	307
아주대	자연계	323
인하대	인문·예체능계	333
중앙대	인문계 A형	347
한국공학대	일반·학사편입	361
한국외대	T1-1 A형	372
한국외대	T2 A형	385
한국항공대	인문계	398
한국항공대	자연계	408
한성대	인문계 A형	416
한양대	서울 인문계 A형	428
한양대	서울 자연계 A형	440
홍익대	서울 인문계 A형	452
홍익대	서울 자연계 A형	462

KIM & BOOK

영어 2026학년도 대비
기출문제 해설집

KIMYOUNG

해설편

GACHON UNIVERSITY | 가천대학교 인문계 A형

TEST p. 26~40

01	④	02	①	03	①	04	③	05	③	06	①	07	④	08	③	09	①	10	②
11	②	12	②	13	①	14	①	15	②	16	③	17	③	18	②	19	①	20	④
21	①	22	②	23	②	24	②	25	③	26	④	27	②	28	②	29	①	30	②
31	②	32	④	33	②	34	②	35	②	36	②	37	①	38	②	39	③	40	④

01 동의어 ④

| 어휘 |

commitment n. 헌신, 몰두, 책무 **anachronism** n. 시대착오 **collectivism** n. 집산(集産)주의(토지·생산 수단 따위를 국가가 관리함) **inimical** a. 적의가 있는; 불리한, 유해한 **maverick** n. 개성이 강한[독립적인] 사람, 전통이나 관례에 얽매이지 않는 사람(= iconoclast 인습타파주의자) **exemplify** v. 예증하다, 예시하다 **orthodox** n. 정통파 사람 **adulator** n. 아첨꾼 **zealot** n. 열중하는 사람, 열광자

| 해석 |

일본이 집단적 가치에 몰두하는 것은 아마도 현대 산업주의와 맞지 않는 시대착오일 테지만, 그러한 집산주의(集産主義)에도 불구하고 경제적 성공을 가져온다. 집산주의는 벤자민 프랭클린과 존 D. 록펠러가 보여준 유형의 독불장군식의 창의성에는 불리한 것 같다.

02 동의어 ①

| 어휘 |

rickety a. (가구 등이) 망그러질 듯한; 낡아빠진(= decrepit); 미덥지 못한 **demolish** v. 파괴하다 **rudimentary** a. 근본의, 기본적인 **exquisite** a. 정교한; 세련된 **puerile** a. 어린애 같은, 미숙한

| 해석 |

그 당시에 NFL 축구는 지금은 상상할 수 없을 정도로 더 간단했다. 랜디와 내가 열두 살 소년이었을 때, 우리는 자전거를 타고 경기를 보러 가서, 자전거를 경기장 밖에 두었다. 물론 그때의 경기장은 슈퍼돔이 아니라, 우리 집에서 그리 멀지 않은 곳에 있던 지금은 철거된 오래된 낡은 경기장이었다.

03 동의어 ①

| 어휘 |

blatant a. 노골적인, 뻔한 **inflict** v. (타격·상처·고통 따위를) 주다, 입히다, 가하다(upon) **mouth** v. 말하다, 지껄이다 **pious** a. 신앙심이 깊은, 경건한, 독실한 **irrelevancy** n. 무관함; 엉뚱한 말[진술] **sanctimonious** a. 신성한 체하는, 경건한 체하는(= self-righteous 독선적인, 잘 난 체하는) **triviality** n. 하찮음; 시시한 것 **ominous** a. 불길한, 나쁜 징조의 **self-contained** a. 자족적인, 자립하는 **transient** a. 일시적인

| 해석 |

노골적인 불의가 흑인에게 가해지는 가운데, 나는 백인 교회들이 한쪽에 서서 그저 경건한 허튼소리와 독실한 척하는 사소한 말들만 입에 담는 모습을 지켜봐왔다.

04 동의어 ③

| 어휘 |

condense v. 요약하다, 간결하게 하다 **slightly** ad. 약간, 조금 **reword** v. (글이 더 명확하도록) 어구를 바꾸다[바꿔 쓰다] **tweak** v. (기계·시스템 등을 약간) 수정하다, 개조하다(= modify) **obviously** ad. 명백하게 **shorten** v. 짧게 하다, 생략하다 **censor** v. 검열하다, 검열하여 삭제하다 **transcribe** v. 베끼다, 복사하다

| 해석 |

ChatGPT는 그 단락을 축약시키고 어구를 약간 바꿔 쓴 버전으로 돌려주었다. 수정된 버전은 프랑스어인 grande idée를 삭제하고, 영국식 철자를 미국식으로 바꾸어 "marginalization"라고 했지만, 그 외에는 명확히 더 나은 점이 없었다.

05 동의어 ③

| 어휘 |

exhilaration n. 들뜬 기분, 유쾌함 **surface** v. (잠수함 등이) 떠오르다 **briny** a. 소금물의, 짠 **tether** v. (밧줄·사슬로) 매다(= attach) **anchor** v. (배를) 닻을 내려 멈추다; 정박시키다 **hang** v. 매달다, 걸다 **immobilize** v. 움직이지 않게 하다, 고정시키다

| 해석 |

보웬은 자신의 잠수함이 망망대해에서 수면 위로 떠오를 때마다 느꼈던 짜릿함을 기억했다. 그는 밧줄로 몸이 배에 매인 채 위로 치솟아 올라 짭짤한 물보라를 맞으며 사방이 물뿐인 풍경을 바라보곤 했다.

06 동의어 ①

| 어휘 |

criterion n. 기준, 표준 **aristocracy** n. 귀족 **cull** v. 따서 모으다; 가려내다(= winnow) **define** v. (성격·내용 따위를) 규정짓다, 한정하다; (말의) 정의를 내리다 **repudiate** v. 거부하다, 부인하다 **rankle** v. 괴롭히다, 짜증나게 하다

| 해석 |

이러한 방식으로 입학허가 기준을 변경함으로써, 코넌트는 사회의 모든 계층에서 가장 똑똑한 사람들을 골라내어 토마스 제퍼슨의 '재능 있는 타고난 귀족'의 꿈을 실현하기를 희망했다.

07 동의어 ④

| 어휘 |

distribute v. 분배하다, 배포하다 **booklet** n. 소책자 **expectant** a. 출산을 앞두고 있는, 임신 중인 **pregnancy** n. 임신 **delivery** n. 출산, 분만 **matrescence** n. 엄마가 되는 과정 **prepartum** ad. 출산 전에 **jot down** 적어두다, 메모하다(= write down) **exercise regime** 운동 요법 **vaccination** n. 예방접종 **plan out** (세부적으로) 계획하다 **lay out** 배열하다, (계획·의견 등을) 명확히 제시하다 **copy down** (말이나 글을) 받아 적다

| 해석 |

1947년 이래로 일본 정부는 임산부들에게 소책자를 배포하여, 그들로 하여금 임신, 출산, 엄마가 되어가는 과정을 기록할 것을 권장해왔다. 출산 전에, 여성은 식단과 운동 요법, 병원 방문 세부사항 등을 적을 수 있으며, 출산 후에는 예방접종 날짜와 아기의 발육 과정상의 중요 사건을 기록할 수 있다.

08 동의어 ③

| 어휘 |

diplomat n. 외교관 **negotiate** v. 협상하다, 교섭하다 **finesse** v. 술책을 쓰다, 책략으로 처리하다(= maneuver) **credulous** a. (남을) 쉽사리 믿는 **mislead** v. 그릇 인도하다; 현혹시키다 **coerce** v. 강요하다, 강제하다 **cram** v. 억지로 채워 넣다

| 해석 |

그 외교관은 자신의 협상 기술을 활용하여 쉽게 믿는 공무원들에게 술책을 써서, 국경을 넘은 배낭 여행자들을 석방하게 했다.

09 전치사 + 관계대명사 ①

| 분석 |

'전치사+관계대명사'의 구조에서 전치사는 관계절 속의 동사, 명사, 형용사 등과 호응해야 한다. '~에 대한 답'을 표현하는 경우, answer 다음에 전치사 to를 쓰므로 ①은 to which여야 한다.

| 어휘 |

outset n. 착수, 시작 **pose** v. (요구 따위를) 주장하다, (문제 등을) 제기하다 **embarrassed** a. 당혹스러운, 난처한

| 해석 |

결혼은 무엇을 위한 것일까? 이 질문은 분명한 답이 있어야 하는 질문처럼 들리지만, 내가 이 책을 위한 연구를 시작할 무렵에 만난 예비 신부들과 최근 결혼한 여성들에게 이 질문을 던졌을 때, — 활발한 대화가 한 시간 정도 이어지고 와인 한두 병을 마신 후에 그 질문이 나왔다 — 방은 잠시 침묵에 빠졌다가 이후에 모두가 조금은 난처한 웃음을 터뜨렸다.

10 주어와 동사의 수일치 ②

| 분석 |

첫 문장에서 각각의 주어가 긴 수식어구를 동반하고 있는데, 이것을 떼어놓고 보면, ②의 주어는 The trial and another more-advanced trial임을 확인할 수 있다. 주어가 A and B의 형태인 경우 복수 동사로 받는 것이 원칙이므로 ②를 give로 고쳐야 한다.

| 어휘 |

enroll v. 등록하다, 입회시키다 **progenitor cell** 전구세포(前驅細胞) 특정 세포가 완전한 형태를 갖추기 전 단계의 세포 **derive** v. 끌어내다; 획득하다 **preliminary** a. 예비의, 시초의 **efficacy** n. 효험, 효력 **dose** n. 복용량

| 해석 |

Cassy가 입회하고 있으면서 Barker가 공동으로 이끄는 실험과 매사추세츠 주 케임브리지에 본사를 둔 생명공학 기업 블루락 테라퓨틱스가 진행하는 보다 진보된 또 다른 실험은 참가자들에게 인간 배아줄기세포에서 얻어진 A9 전구(前驅)세포를 제공한다. 블루락의 실험은 12명의 참가자에 대한 예비 결과를 보고했다. 2년이 지난 현재, 그 치료법은 안전성이 입증되었으며, 두 가지 중 용량이 더 높은 것을 투여 받은 자들에게서 효능의 징후를 보여주었다.

11 분사구문 ②

| 분석 |

첫 문장에서 주격 관계대명사 which의 동사는 is이며 Baker Street까지 술부가 완결된 다음에 그 뒤에 접속사 없이 정동사 contained가 온 것이 옳지 않다. 따라서 ② 이하가 분사구문이 되도록 ②를 containing으로 고쳐야 한다.

| 어휘 |

facsimile a. 실물 그대로의 **dig** n. 집, 거처 **accuse** v. 고발하다, ~에게 죄를 씌우다 **pretend** a. 가짜[상상]의 **property** n. 재산, 자산; 농장

| 해석 |

우리는 앤 인형을 사지도 않았고, 그린 게이블즈를 그대로 옮겨놓은 농가도 방문하지 않았다. 온라인 후기들에 따르면, 그곳은 베이커 스트리트의 셜록 홈즈의 집만큼이나 완벽하게 재현되어 있어서, 앤이 길버트 블라이스의 머리 위에서 부순 석판에서부터 그녀가 잃어버린 것으로 잘못 비난받은 브로치에 이르는 모든 것들이 있다. 심지어는 가짜 매튜까지 있는데, 그는 진짜 매튜라면 그랬을 것처럼 젊은 여성 방문객이 다가오면 헛간으로 달려가서 숨는다고 설명되지는 않지만 방문객들을 농장 주변으로 태워다준다.

12 논리완성 ②

| 분석 |

부정어 nowhere가 포함된 부사구가 앞에 있으므로, 주절의 주어와 동사는 도치되어야 한다. 따라서 ①과 ③이 먼저 정답에서 제외된다. 한편, 영국의 어디에 있던 해안선 가까이에 있다는 내용이 있으므로, 첫 문장은 70마일 이상 떨어져 있지 않다는 의미가 되어야 한다. 따라서 ②가 정답이다.

| 어휘 |

recall v. 생각해내다, 상기하다 **croak** v. (까마귀 · 개구리 등이) 개골개골[깍깍] 울다; 목쉰 소리를 내다 **overhead** ad. 머리 위에, 상공에 **margin** n. 가장자리 **estimate** v. 견적하다, 추정하다 **extend** v. 달하다, 미치다 **evenly** ad. 고르게, 균일하게 **invariably** ad. 변함없이, 항상

| 해석 |

영국에서는 당신이 어디에 있든 바다에서 70마일 이상 떨어져 있지 않다는 말이 있다. 나는 북부 런던의 거리에서 갈매기가 머리 위에서 우는 소리를 들을 때마다 이 사실을 떠올린다. 이 섬의 어디에 있든, 당신은 그 섬의 가장자리, 즉 약 11,000마일에 달하는 것으로 추정되는 해안선의 가까이에 있다.

13 논리완성 ①

| 분석 |

빈칸 뒤의 문장은 빈칸 앞의 문장을 다소 쉽게 재진술한 것이므로, 빈칸에는 '바꿔[다시] 말하자면'이라는 뜻의 ①이 들어가야 한다.

| 어휘 |

synthetic n. 합성섬유 **take the place of** ~을 대신하다 **fiber** n. 섬유, 실 **durability** n. 내구성 **deplete** v. (자원을) 소모시키다, 고갈시키다 **substitution** n. 대체, 대용 **unfeasible** a. 실행할 수 없는 **in other words** 바꿔 말하면 **in contrast** 이와는 대조적으로

fortunately ad. 다행스럽게도 **otherwise** ad. 다른 방법으로

| 해석 |

마이크로화이버 합성섬유는 동일한 내구성을 제공하면서도 천연자원을 덜 소모하기 때문에 점점 더 많은 의류에서 천연섬유를 대체해오고 있다. 그러나 마이크로화이버 합성섬유로 만든 셔츠는 천연섬유 셔츠보다 생산 비용이 3배나 많이 든다. 따라서 현재로서는 마이크로화이버 합성섬유 의류를 천연섬유 의류로 대체하는 것이 재정적인 관점에서는 추천되지 않는다. 바꿔 말하자면, 천연섬유 의류를 마이크로화이버 합성섬유 의류로 광범위하게 대체하는 것은 경제적인 측면에서 실행이 불가능하다.

14 논리완성 ①

| 분석 |

cherish tragedy above all other forms와 be capable of understanding it의 속성은 같으므로 두 표현이 순접으로 이어져야 하겠는데, 전자가 후자보다 어려운 일이므로, '~은 고사하고'라는 의미의 ①이 정답이 된다.

| 어휘 |

tragedy n. 비극 **hesitate** v. 주저하다, 망설이다 **attribute** v. (~의) 탓으로 하다, (~의) 행위로[소치로] 하다; (성질 따위)가 있다고 하다 **exaltation** n. 높임, 고양; 칭찬 **property** n. 재산, 자산; 성질, 특성 **inconceivable** a. 상상할 수 없는; 믿기 어려운 **cherish** v. 소중히 여기다

| 해석 |

예술에서 비극의 문제가 쟁점이 되고 있지 않을 때에는, 우리는 지위가 높은 사람에게도 지위가 낮은 사람과 동일한 정신 과정을 주저 없이 부여한다. 그리고 최종적으로, 만약 비극적 행위의 고양이 오직 고귀한 인물만의 특성이라면, 인류 대중이 비극을 이해할 수 있는 것은 고사하고, 다른 어떤 예술 형식보다 비극을 소중히 여긴다는 것은 믿기 어렵다.

15 논리완성 ②

| 분석 |

비잔틴 제국이 고대 로마 사회의 법적, 문화적 구조를 상당 부분 유지하기도 했지만, 그리스 문화의 측면들이 이 요소들 가운데 일부를 무너뜨렸으며, 그리스어가 제국의 공용어가 될 정도로 강한 영향을 미쳤다고 했다. 이는 여러 문화의 영향이 다양하게 뒤섞여서 비잔틴 제국의 독창적인 문화를 이뤄냈다는 것이므로, 빈칸에는 '융합'이라는 의미의 ②가 적절하다.

| 어휘 |

preserve v. 보존하다 **vestige** n. 흔적, 자취 **distinct** a. 별개의; 독특한 **successor** n. 계승자, 후계자 **scaffolding** n. (건축물의) 뼈대, 구조 **subvert** v. 뒤엎다, 전복하다 **facet** n. 양상, 국면

pervasive a. 널리 퍼진 **replace** v. 대체하다 **endorse** v. 승인하다, 찬성하다 **innovation** n. 혁신 **amalgamation** n. 융합, 합병 **resuscitation** n. 소생, 부활 **dispersion** n. 분산, 확산

| 해석 |

비잔틴 제국은 중세까지 로마제국의 마지막 자취를 보존했지만, 그 나름의 독특한 문화를 발전시키기도 했다. 로마제국의 계승자로서, 비잔틴 제국은 고대 로마 사회의 법적, 문화적 구조를 상당 부분 유지했지만, 그리스 문화의 측면이 이 요소들 가운데 일부를 무너뜨렸으며, 그 결과 궁극적으로 라틴어를 대체하여 그리스어가 제국의 공용어가 될 정도로 강한 영향을 미쳤다. 이러한 다양한 영향의 융합은 비잔틴 제국의 독창성에 기여했다.

16 논리완성   ③

| 분석 |

딱정벌레가 뿜어내는 물질이 도마뱀에게 아무런 영향을 끼치지 않았다고 했으므로, 도마뱀이 딱정벌레를 먹은 후의 행동이나 반응을 부연해서 설명하는 부사로는 '태연하게'라는 의미의 ③이 가장 자연스럽다.

| 어휘 |

lizard n. 도마뱀 **snap up** 덥석 잡아채다 **noxious** a. 유독한, 해로운 **predator** n. 포식자, 포식동물 **beetle** n. 투구벌레, 딱정벌레 **irritant** a. 자극적인 **apparent** a. 명백한 **capriciously** ad. 변덕스럽게 **irksomely** ad. 짜증스럽게 **nonchalantly** ad. 태연하게 **diffidently** ad. 소심하게, 자신 없게

| 해석 |

도마뱀들은 너무 독성이 강해서 다른 잠재적 포식자들은 피하는 곤충들을 덥석 잡아챘다. 도마뱀들의 먹이 중에는 몇몇 딱정벌레도 있었다. 도마뱀은 처음에는 이들을 거부했는데, 이 벌레들이 뜨겁고 자극적인 방어용 화학물질을 뿜어내고 있었기 때문이다. 하지만 이것들도 아무런 해를 끼치지 못했으며, 도마뱀들은 먹은 후에 아주 태연하게 가던 길을 계속 갔다.

17 논리완성   ②

| 분석 |

지식인들이 대중문화를 소비하는 자신을 합리화해야한다는 강박감을 느낀다는 것은 그들이 여전히 기존의 고급문화나 저급문화 간의 오랜 위계질서에 신경을 쓰고 있다는 것이다. 이는 지식인들이 그러한 위계질서에 어느 정도의 노력과 관심을 쏟고 있다는 말로 달리 표현할 수 있을 것이므로, 빈칸에는 ②가 들어가는 것이 가장 적절하다.

| 어휘 |

credit v. (공적·명예 등을) ~에게 돌리다, ~의 소유자[공로자, 행위자]로 생각하다 **render** v. ~하게 만들다, 제공하다 **obsolete** a. 구식의, 쓸모없어진 **penchant** n. 강한 기호, 애호 **inherently** ad. 본질적으로 **alteration** n. 변경; 변화 **overstate** v. 과장하다 **analyze** v. 분석하다 **feel compelled to** ~하지 않을 수 없다 **rationalize** v. 합리화하다 **penchant** n. 경향, 기호 **unwittingly** ad. 뜻하지 않게 **hierarchy** n. 계층, 위계 **controversy** n. 논쟁, 논의 **investment** n. 투자; (시간·노력·열의 등의) 투입 **aversion** n. 혐오, 반감 **misconception** n. 오해, 잘못된 생각

| 해석 |

지식인들이 대중문화를 진지하게 연구하면서, 대중문화가 본질적으로 고급예술보다 열등하다는, 한때 지배적인 견해는 시대에 뒤쳐진 것이 되었다고 평가받곤 한다. 그러나 이러한 태도의 변화는 다소 과장된 것일 수도 있다. 대중문화를 분석하는 것이 오늘날 학문적으로 존중받는 일이 되긴 했지만, 많은 지식인들이 액션영화나 대중소설을 좋아하는 자신의 취향을 합리화해야 한다는 강박감을 느낀다는 사실은 ― 본인들은 의식하지 못할지라도 ― 그들이 기존의 고급문화와 저급문화 간의 오랜 위계질서에 지속적으로 노력을 들이고 있음을 보여준다.

18 논리완성   ②

| 분석 |

마지막 문장에는 1960년대에 능력주의자들이 권력을 잡은 후에 겪은 부정적인 사건들이 열거돼 있다. 빈칸에도 부정적인 의미의 표현이 들어가야 할 것이므로, '곤경' 또는 '수렁'을 의미하는 ②가 정답으로 적절하다.

| 어휘 |

scorn v. 경멸하다 **smug** a. 독선적인, 젠체빼는 **WASP** 와스프(앵글로색슨계 백인 신교도; 미국의 지배적인 특권 계급을 형성, White Anglo-Saxon Protestant) **blue blood** 명문 출신; 귀족의 가문 **retrograde** a. 퇴보하는 **meritocrat** n. (배경이나 재력이 아니고) 개인의 실력으로 권력을 잡은 자, 실력자 **carnage** n. 대학살 **toxic** a. 독성의, 유독한 **dysfunction** n. 역기능, 기능장애 **attainment** n. 성취, 업적 **quagmire** n. 수렁, 곤경, 궁지 **bayou** n. 강 어귀 **assemblage** n. 집합체

| 해석 |

우리는 하버드와 예일 출신의 독선에 찬 백인 신교도 상류층을 경멸할 수 있으며, 그들의 시대에 팽배했던 인종과 성(性)에 대한 후진적인 관점에 대해서도 틀림없이 그렇게 할 수 있다. 그러나 그들의 지도력은 진보 운동, 뉴딜 정책, 2차 세계대전에서의 승리, NATO의 창설 등을 이뤄내는 데 기여했다. 1960년대에 능력주의자들이 권력을 장악한 후에, 우리는 베트남과 아프가니스탄에서의 수렁, 이라크에서의 불필요한 학살, 2008년 금융 위기, 유해한 소셜미디어의 확산, 그리고 현 시대의 정치적 기능 마비를 겪었다.

19 논리완성 ①

| 분석 |
빈칸 앞의 such control이 앞 문장의 assign different functions to each를 가리키므로, 빈칸에는 앞 문장의 keeping languages apart의 의미를 가질 수 있는 표현이 들어가야 한다. 따라서 ①이 정답이다.

| 어휘 |
quote n. 인용문 **assign** v. 할당하다, 배당하다; 부여하다 **merge** v. 합병[병합]하다 **multilingualism** n. 여러 언어의 사용 (능력) **compartmentalized** a. 구획화된, 구분된 **beguiled** a. 속은, 매료된 **imperceptible** a. 감지할 수 없는 **disproportionate** a. 불균형한

| 해석 |
스페인 찰스 5세의 한 유명한 인용문에서는 일부 사람들은 여러 언어를 명확히 구별하는 데 전혀 어려움을 겪지 않으며, 심지어는 언어들에 서로 다른 기능을 부여하기도 한다고 말한 바 있다. 하지만 대부분의 사람들은 그와 같은 언어의 통제력을 가지고 있지 못하며 (언어를 분리하여 사용하는 사고방식이) 그렇게 구획화되어 있지도 않다. 사람들이 여러 언어를 명확히 구별하지 못하는 이유와 이미 알고 있는 여러 언어와 배우고 있는 여러 언어가 뒤섞이고 합쳐지는 이유는 다중언어 사용 연구에서 핵심적인 문제이다.

20 논리완성 ④

| 분석 |
당시에 널리 퍼져 있던 보편적인 여성의 역할을 거부하고 타국으로 떠난 것은 매우 '대담한' 혹은 '용기 있는' 행동으로 볼 수 있다.

| 어휘 |
contemporary n. 동시대인 **odd** a. 기묘한, 이상한 **reject** v. 거부하다, 거절하다 **prevailing** a. 우세한, 주요한 **feminine** a. 여성의 **forlorn** a. 버려진, 절망적인 **desolate** a. 황량한, 쓸쓸한 **modest** a. 겸손한, 수수한 **doughty** a. 용감한, 대담한

| 해석 |
많은 동시대인들은 케이트 스콧을 특이하다고 여겼지만, 오늘날 그녀는 그녀의 대담한 정신, 특히 자진해서 널리 퍼져 있던 여성의 역할을 거부하고 외국으로 떠난 것으로 인해 높이 평가받고 있다.

21 논리완성 ①

| 분석 |
사람들에게 기쁨을 주지 않는 책을 버릴 것을 권유하고 나서 자신이 책을 싫어하는 것이 아님을 공개적으로 단언해야 했던 것은 자신의 권유에 대한 반대나 반발이 크게 일어났기 때문일 것이다.

| 어휘 |
dispose of 버리다, 처분하다 **intense** a. 격렬한, 강렬한 **be compelled to** ~하지 않을 수 없다 **affirm** v. 단언하다, 확인하다 **backlash** n. 반발, 역효과 **exoneration** n. 면죄, 해명 **acclaim** n. 칭찬, 찬사 **absolution** n. 사면, 용서

| 해석 |
일본 작가 곤도 마리에는 물건을 보관할지를 결정할 때 "이것이 기쁨을 불러일으키는가?"라는 질문을 던지도록 독자들에게 지시한 것으로 유명했다. 그녀가 사람들에게 기쁨을 주지 않는 책을 버릴 것을 권유했을 때, 반발이 너무 거세서, 결국 곤도는 자신이 책을 싫어하는 것이 아님을 공개적으로 단언해야 했다.

22 논리완성 ②

| 분석 |
시민권자가 되면 자유롭게 미국을 떠날 수도 있고 돌아올 수도 있다고 했는데, 이 말에는 영주권자의 경우에는 그렇게 할 수 없다는 의미, 즉 자유롭게 머무르고 떠날 수 없다는 의미가 내포돼 있다. 그렇다면 영주권자가 가진 체류 권리는 무제한적인 것이 아니고 임시적이라는 것이 되므로 빈칸에는 ②가 들어가야 한다.

| 어휘 |
secure v. 확보하다, 획득하다 **green card** 영주권 **residency** n. (외국에서의) 체류[거주] 허가 **inalienable** a. 양도할 수 없는, 빼앗을 수 없는 **provisional** a. 임시적인, 잠정적인 **equal** a. 같은, 동등한 **instantaneous** a. 즉시의, 순간의

| 해석 |
오랫동안 내가 고향이라고 부른 나라에서 살 권리를 확보하고 싶은 바람을 넘어, 내가 미국인이 되고자 하는 바람 이면에는 또 다른 동기가 있었는데, 그것은 가족과 내가 언젠가 떠날 수도 있다는 가능성이었다. 영주권자로서 나는 미국에서 임시적인 체류 권리만을 가지고 있었다. 시민이 되면, 나는 미국을 떠날 수도 있고 또 언제든지 돌아올 수 있는 권리가 생길 것이다.

23 빈칸완성 ②

| 분석 |
'rather than(~보다는)' 전후에는 서로 상반되는 의미가 되어야 하므로 빈칸에는 subvert(전복하다)와 반대되는 의미를 가진 표현이 와야 한다. 옷을 거의 입지 않은 여성의 몸을 클로즈업으로 촬영했다고 했으므로 여성의 몸에 대한 착취의 역사가 되풀이되고 있음을 알 수 있다. 따라서 빈칸에는 '복제하다'는 뜻의 ② replicates가 적절하다.

| 어휘 |
shoot v. 촬영하다 **scantily clad** 옷을 거의 입지 않은 **leery** a. 곁눈질을 하는; 조심스러운, 의심 많은; 교활한 **obsessive** a. 강박관

념악; 사로잡힌, 들린 **hypersexual** a. 성욕 과잉의 **keen** a. 간절히 ~하고 싶은, ~을 열망하는 **flaunt** v. 과시하다 **intent** a. 전념하고 있는, 열중해 있는 **highlight** v. 강조하다 **undeniable** a. 부인[부정]할 수 없는, 명백한; 흠잡을 데 없는, 더할 나위 없는 **critique** v. 비평하다 **obsession** n. 강박 관념, 망상, 집착 **exploitation** n. 이기적 이용, 착취 **subvert** v. (체제·권위 등을) 전복하다, 파괴하다

| 해석 |

감독은 수(Sue)의 옷을 거의 입지 않은 몸을 천천히 패닝 기법을 활용해 클로즈업으로 촬영한다. 그 카메라는 음흉하고, 강박적이며, 과도하게 성적이다. 수가 자신의 젊고 아름다운 몸을 과시하고 싶어 하는 것은 이해할 만하다. 그러나 감독이 이러한 장면에 대한 영화 산업의 집착을 비판하는 것으로 알려진 영화에서 수의 흠잡을 데 없는 아름다움을 강조하는 데 이토록 열중하는 이유는 명확하지 않다. 감독은 여성의 몸에 대한 착취의 역사를 전복하기보다는 재현하고 있다.

다음 중 빈칸 Ⓐ에 가장 적절한 것은?
① 부인하다
② 복제하다
③ 왜곡하다
④ 가라앉히다

24 글의 흐름상 적절하지 않은 표현 고르기 ②

| 분석 |

이 글은 표준적인 미국 가정이 너무 많은 가정용품을 가지고 있어서 이러한 물건을 보관할 창고를 임대하고 있다는 내용이다. 따라서 저장 시설이 많아졌다고 해야 적절하므로 Ⓑ의 less를 more로 고쳐야 한다.

| 어휘 |

estimate n. 견적, 추정 **misplaced** a. 예상과 어긋난; 잃어버린 **household item** 가정용품 **homeowner** n. 주택 소유자 **garage** n. 차고, 주차장 **cluttered** a. 어수선한 **storage** n. 저장, 보관; 창고, 저장소 **facility** n. (보통 pl.) 설비, 시설 **typical** a. 전형적인 **statistic** n. 통계; 통계치[량] **verify** v. 확인하다 **question** v. 의심하다, 이의를 제기하다

| 해석 |

한 추정에 따르면, 평균적인 미국인은 매년 총 이틀 반을 잃어버린 가정용품을 찾는 데 소비한다. 주택 소유자의 3분의 1 이상이 그들의 차고가 너무 어수선해서 주차공간으로 사용할 수 없다고 말한다. 우리 중 11퍼센트는 창고를 임대한다. "현재 미국에는 스타벅스, 맥도날드, 던킨도너츠, 피자헛 매장을 합친 것보다 〈더 적은(→ 더 많은)〉 저장 시설이 있습니다."라고 레인은 썼다. 이 모든 일은 전형적인 미국 가정의 크기가 커짐에 따라 일어났다. 우리는 웬일인지 더 많은 방이 있지만 더 적은 공간을 가지고 있다. 자주 인용되는 통계 중 하나는 표준적인 미국 가정에는 30만 개의 물건이 포함되어 있다는 것이다. 확인하기는 어렵지만, 그렇게 많은 사람들이 그것에 의문을 제기하지 않는다는 사실은 많은 것을 말해준다.

25 글의 제목 ③

| 분석 |

이 글은 비밥 재즈의 평가에 대해 다루고 있다. 어떤 이들은 비밥을 재즈 역사에서 중요한 시기로 여긴 반면, 다른 이들은 비밥을 재즈의 궁극적인 종점으로 여긴다고 설명하고 있다. 서로 상반된 평가를 하고 있으므로 ③이 제목으로 적절하다.

| 어휘 |

Bebop n. 비밥(재즈의 일종) **significant** a. 중요한 **stress** v. 강조하다 **innovation** n. 혁신 **convention** n. 관습, 관례 **homage** n. 존경, 경의 **ultimate** a. 최후의, 궁극의 **dead end** 막다른 곳; 종점 **institute** v. (제도·정책 등을) 도입하다; (절차를) 시작하다 **solemnity** n. 엄숙함, 장엄함 **strip** v. 없애다, 제거하다 **appreciate** v. (문학·예술 등을) 감상하다 **assessment** n. 평가, 판단

| 해석 |

비밥 시대(1944-1955)는 많은 이들에게 재즈 역사상 가장 중요한 시기를 나타낸다. 일부 사람들은 비밥 시대를 음악가들이 상업적 관심보다 예술적 관심을 강조하기 시작했고, 관습보다 혁신을 우선시했으며, 과거에 경의를 표하는 대신 미래를 내다본 시기로 여긴다. 다른 사람들은 비밥이 재즈 공동체 내에 엄숙함과 엘리트주의를 도입하고, 재즈로부터 춤과의 연관성을 없애고, 헌신적인 수집가, 학자 및 기타 음악가들을 제외하고는 아무도 음악을 즐기고 감상할 수 없게 만든 양식이라는 점에서 비밥을 재즈의 궁극적인 종점으로 여긴다. 각 평가는 더 면밀하고 광범위한 검토를 받을 만한 충분한 진실을 포함하고 있으며, 이러한 논쟁을 다루고 평가하는 데 전념한 많은 연구가 있었다.

다음 중 이 글의 가장 적절한 제목은 무엇인가?
① 재즈의 스타일 변화
② 비밥 재즈의 예술적 중요성
③ 비밥 재즈에 대한 상반된 평가
④ 재즈에 대한 상반된 연구

26 빈칸완성 ④

| 분석 |

African-American에서 하이픈의 오른쪽에 위치한 American은 '국가정체성'을 가리킨다. Ⓐ 앞에서 '국가정체성이 사라지게 될 것'이라는 우려가 있다고 했으므로, Ⓐ에도 하이픈의 왼쪽(African)이 하이픈의 오른쪽(American)을 '압도하게(overwhelm)' 될 것이라는 말이 되어야 부정적인 맥락이 이어질 수 있다. 그리고 "오늘날 미국 시민들은 9/11 테러 공격으로 다시 한 번 뭉치게 되었다."라고 했다. 따라서 빈칸 Ⓑ에는 '뭉치게 되었다'와 관련된 unity(단결)가 적절하다. 따라서 두 빈칸에 모두 적절한 ④가 정답

이다. ① 뒷받침하다 — 인사불성 ② 승화시키다 — 불안 ③ 강화하다 — 일치

| 어휘 |

disparate a. 이질적인 **hold together** ~을 뭉치게 만들다 **fault line** 단층선; 균열선 **electrify** v. 전기를 통하게 하다 **communism** n. 공산주의 **creeping** a. 서서히 진행되는 **evaporate** v. 사라지다 **overwhelm** v. 압도하다 **domestic** a. 국내의

| 해석 |

과거에는 이러한 이질적인 부분들이 공동의 적, 세계 대전의 균열선, 그리고 공산주의라는 전기 철조망으로 뭉쳐 있었다. (그러나) 냉전이 끝나면서 증오와 불신에 초점을 맞추지 않으면 국가정체성이 사라지게 되고 아프리카계—미국인, 아일랜드계—미국인 같이 하이픈의 왼쪽이 하이픈의 오른쪽을 압도하게 될 것이라는 우려가 서서히 퍼졌다. 그리고 경제 불안과 범죄 증가 같이 서서히 커지는 국내의 트라우마가 공동체의식보다는 분열을 보다 부각시키는 듯 했다. (그러나) 오늘날 미국 시민들은 9/11 테러 공격으로 다시 한 번 뭉치게 되었다. 테러는 파괴를 가져왔지만 단결도 가져왔다.

27 글의 어조 ②

| 분석 |

이 글은 문랫이 어떻게 분류되는지를 독자들에게 '가르쳐주고' 있으므로, 글의 어조로 ②의 '교훈적인'이 적절하다.

| 어휘 |

Echinosorex gymnura 짐누라고슴도치 **fascinating** a. 대단히 흥미로운 **inhabit** v. 서식하다 **hedgehog** n. 고슴도치 **order** n. (동식물 분류상의) 목(目) **Insectivora** n. 식충목(食蟲目) **family** n. (동식물 분류상의) 과(科) **Erinaceidae** n. 고슴도치과 **split** v. 나누다 **sub-family** n. 아과(亞科) **genera** n. genus(생물 분류상의 속(屬))의 복수형 **distinct** a. 별개의 **Rodentia** n. 설치목(齧齒目) **fellow** n. (이미 언급된 것과) 비슷한 것 **insesctivore** n. 식충동물

| 해석 |

Echinosorex gymnura(짐누라고슴도치), 일명 문랫(moonrat)은 동남아시아 정글에 서식하는 많은 흥미로운 동물들 중 하나이다. 고슴도치와 가까운 친척인 문랫은 마찬가지로 식충목(食蟲目)과 고슴도칫과에 속한다. 하지만 이 과(科)는 다시 털고슴도치아과로 나뉘며, 이 아과(亞科)에는 3개의 별도 속(屬)과 8개의 별도 종(種)이 포함된다. 문랫의 외모와 서식지는 사실 설치목(齧齒目)의 다양한 구성원과 훨씬 더 유사하지만, 식습관은 다른 식충동물들과 비슷하다.

다음 중 이 글의 어조를 가장 잘 설명한 것은?
① 애증이 엇갈리는
② 교훈적인
③ 우울한
④ 격분한

28 빈칸완성 ①

| 분석 |

왕은 '품위 있고 곧은 자세로 앉아있었다'고 한 다음 '역접' 부사 meanwhile이 왔으므로, 신하들은 왕과 상반되게 '공손한 모습으로' 서있었다가 되어야 한다. 따라서 빈칸 ④에는 'deference(공손함)'가 적절하다. "왕실에 적용되었던 것이 귀족 가문에도 적용되었다"고 했으므로, 이어지는 기사와 그에게 딸린 사람과의 관계, 그리고 상인과 그에게 딸린 하인과의 관계에도 군신관계가 그대로 적용된다는 말이 되어야 한다. 따라서 빈칸 ⑧에는 what이 들어가야 하는데, 이때 A is to B what C is to D(A와 B의 관계는 C와 D의 관계와 같다)라는 구문이 쓰였다.

| 어휘 |

proclaim v. 선포하다; ~임을 보여주다 **privilege** n. 특권 **royalty** n. 왕족 **stretch** v. (다리를) 뻗다 **majestic** a. 위엄 있는 **manner** n. 방식 **dignified** a. 위엄[품위] 있는 **upright** a. 똑바로 선 **courtier** n. (과거 왕을 보필하던) 신하 **deference** n. 복종; 공손함 **rank** n. 계급 **stool** n. 등받이가 없는 의자 **be true of** ~도 마찬가지이다 **court** n. 궁궐; 궁중 **household** n. 가족; 식솔 **knight** n. 기사 **dependant** n. 딸린 사람 **apprentice** n. 수습생, 도제 **servant** n. 하인 **monarch** n. 군주, 왕

| 해석 |

편안함은 국왕의 특권을 보여주는 것이었다. 오직 왕만이 다리를 뻗을 수 있었다. 그러나 우리는 왕이 매우 위엄 있는 방식으로 다리를 뻗었을 것이라고 확신할 수 있다. 평소에 왕은 앉아있었지만, 존엄한 모습이 유지되어야 했기에 품위 있고 곧은 자세로 앉아있었다. 한편 신하들은 서있거나 아니면 계급이 매우 높을 경우 왕의 면전에서 등받이 없는 의자에 앉아 공손한 모습을 유지했다. 왕실에 적용되었던 것은 귀족 가문에도 적용되었다. 그리고 기사와 그에게 딸린 사람과의 관계, 상인과 그에게 딸린 도제와 하인과의 관계는 군신관계와 마찬가지였다.

29~30

할리우드에서 지미 O. 양(Jimmy O. Yang)에게 주어진 역할은 바보 같은 조연이나 배경 역할뿐이지만, 그는 지안-양(Jian-Yang)과 같은 캐릭터를 가능한 한 입체적이고 복잡하게 만들려고 노력해도 그 역할을 얻을 수 없다고 느꼈다. "저는 아시아 억양에 대한 불만을 이해하지 못했습니다."라고 그는 말했다. 그는 할리우드의 오랜 고정 관념의 역사를 고려할 때 아시아계 미국인들이 그런 묘사에 민감한 이유를 이해하지만, 일부 비판은 "조금 과장되고 다소 어리석게" 느껴졌다고 말했다. 그는 아시아 캐릭터를 이국적으로 묘사하는 업계의 경향을 언급하며 "항상 외국인 취급을 받았습니다."라고 설명했다.

| 어휘 |

goofy a. 바보 같은, 얼빠진 **sidekick** n. 친구, 동료, 조수 **rounded** a. 둥글게 된; 완성된, 세련된 **complicated** a. 복잡한 **portrayal** n. 묘사 **given** a. ⟨전치사적 또는 접속사적⟩ ~이 주어지면, ~라고 가정하면 **stereotype** n. 고정 관념, 상투 문구 v. 정형화하다 **overblown** a. 도가 지나친, 과장된 **dumb** a. 말을 못하는; 우둔한

29 빈칸완성 ①

| 분석 |

할리우드에서 아시아계 배우들은 조연의 한정된 역할만 주어지고, 일부 비판이 과장되고 어리석게 느껴졌다고 했으며, 아시아 캐릭터를 이국적으로 묘사하는 경향이 있다고 했으므로 아시아 억양에 대해 부정적인 반응을 나타내는 표현이 와야 한다. 따라서 빈칸에는 아시아 억양에 대한 '반감, 불만'이 있었다는 뜻의 ① beef against가 적절하다.

다음 중 빈칸 ⓐ에 가장 적절한 것은?
① ~에 대한 불만
② ~에 대한 특별한 애착
③ ~에 대한 경향
④ ~의 붕괴

30 빈칸완성 ②

| 분석 |

앞 문장의 "There's a constant foreigner bit"과 유사한 의미가 와야 하는데, 항상 외국인 취급을 받았다고 했으므로 아시아 캐릭터를 '이국적인 존재'로 묘사했다고 할 수 있다. 따라서 빈칸에는 '이국적으로 보다'는 뜻의 ② exoticize가 적절하다.

다음 중 빈칸 ⓑ에 가장 적절한 것은?
① 확대하다
② 이국적으로 보다
③ 우상화하다
④ 분쇄하다

31~32

20세기 내내, 뉴런이라고 불리는 우리 뇌의 세포는 재생되지 않는다는 것이 사실로 받아들여졌다. 그러나 신경학자 굴드(Gould)가 쥐를 대상으로 한 실험에 대한 연구에 따르면 심각한 외상을 겪은 후에도 뇌는 뉴런을 재생함으로써 스스로 치유할 수 있었다. 굴드의 연구 결과는 신경생성을 활용할 수 있는 응용 분야에 대한 새로운 연구의 쇄도를 촉발시켰다. 그러한 연구 중 하나는 우울증을 앓고 있는 개인들 사이에서 감소된 신경생성의 역할을 조사한다. 신경생성이 소위 "프로작 지연(Prozac lag)"을 설명하는 데 기여할 수 있는 것으로 추측된다. 항우울제로서 프로작에 의한 세로토닌의 즉각적인 증가는 즉각적인 기분 상승 효과를 가져와야 했다. 그러나 우울증을 앓고 있는 환자들은 치료를 시작한 지 몇 주 후에야 기분이 좋아지기 시작한다. 이 연구는 이 기간 동안 뇌가 뉴런을 재생하고 있을 수 있다고 추측한다.

| 어휘 |

regenerate v. 재생하다 **neurologist** n. 신경학자 **severe** a. 심각한 **trauma** n. 외상, 정신적 충격[외상] **finding** n. (종종 pl.) (조사·연구 등의) 결과, 결론 **application** n. 적용, 응용 **take advantage of** 이용하다, 활용하다 **neurogenesis** n. 신경(조직) 발생[형성] **depression** n. 우울증 **speculate** v. 추측하다 **lag** n. 지연, 지체 **antidepressant** n. 우울증 치료제, 항우울제 **boost** n. 증가, 인상 **serotonin** n. 세로토닌(혈관 수축 작용을 하는 호르몬) **instantaneous** a. 즉시[즉석]의 **elevating** a. 정신을 고양시키는

31 내용파악 ②

| 분석 |

우울증을 앓고 있는 환자들이 프로작을 복용한 후에 즉각적인 기분 상승을 나타내지 않고 몇 주 후에야 기분이 좋아지기 시작하는 현상을 새로운 이론인 신경생성을 통해 설명하고 있다. 이러한 지연은 뇌가 뉴런을 재생하는 과정에서 발생할 수 있다는 것이다. 따라서 ②가 정답이다.

저자는 왜 "프로작 지연"을 언급했는가?
① 새로 제안된 이론에 대한 가능성 있는 이의를 제기하기 위해
② 새로운 이론이 설명적 역할을 할 수 있는 상황을 제시하기 위해
③ 새로 제안된 이론을 약화시키는 반례를 제시하기 위해
④ 새로운 이론이 예상치 못한 부작용을 가질 수 있음을 증명하기 위해

32 빈칸완성 ④

| 분석 |

굴드의 뇌가 뉴런을 재생한다는 연구 결과가 신경생성을 활용한 새로운 연구의 폭발적인 증가를 가져왔다는 의미가 되어야 한다. 그 한 연구로 우울증을 앓고 있는 환자들의 경우를 설명하고 있다. 따라서 빈칸에는 '자극하다, 유발하다'는 의미의 ④ incited가 적절하다.

다음 중 빈칸 ⓐ에 가장 적절한 것은?
① 방출하다
② 악화시키다
③ 단념시키다
④ 자극하다

33~34

내가 몇몇 교수에게 A.I. 보조 글쓰기에 대해 물었을 때, 나는 복잡한 감정을 느꼈다. 한 강사는 학생들이 읽기를 완료하도록 유도하는 짧은 응답 단락과 같은 쉬운 글쓰기 과제는 쉽게 "GPT"를 사용해서 할 수 있으며, 아마도 제거해야 할 필요가 있을 것이라고 내게 말했다. 그러나 관점주의에 관한 대학원 논문과 같은 더 길고 복잡한 과제에 대해서는, 교사들은 ChatGPT와의 '작업 분담'은 여전히 학생들이 신중하게 생각하고 명확하게 글을 쓸 것을 요구한다는 것을 알고 안도하는 것 같다. 그것은 과제를 완료하는 과정이 덜 힘들게 느껴지게 할 수도 있지만, 더 높은 성적을 받는 지름길은 아니다.

| 어휘 |

mixed a. 혼합된, 뒤섞인   instructor n. 교사; (대학의) 전임 강사
assignment n. 과제, 임무   nudge v. 조금씩 밀다; 주의를 끌다; 자극하다   complete v. 완료하다, 끝내다   graduate-school n. 대학원   perspectivism n. 관점주의   relief n. 안도, 안심
daunting a. (일 따위가) 벅찬, 힘든   shortcut n. 지름길

33 빈칸완성   ②

| 분석 |

학생들이 읽기를 완료하도록 이끈다는 의미가 되어야 하는데, 쉬운 글쓰기 과제라고 했으므로 학생들은 조금만 자극해도 수월하게 과제를 완료할 수 있을 것이다. 따라서 빈칸에는 '조금씩 밀다, 자극하다'는 뜻의 ② nudge가 적절하다.

다음 중 빈칸 Ⓐ에 가장 적절한 것은?
① 미연에 방지하다
② 자극하다
③ 손상시키다
④ 곤혹케 하다

34 빈칸완성   ①

| 분석 |

역접의 접속사 but이 있으므로 서로 반대되는 내용이 되어야 한다. 복잡한 과제의 경우 ChatGPT를 활용하는 것이 과제를 더 쉽게 할 수는 있지만 높은 성적을 받는 방법은 아니라는 것이다. 따라서 빈칸 Ⓑ에는 과제를 완료하는 과정이 어렵지 않게 느껴진다는 의미가 되어야 하는데, less(보다 적게)가 있으므로 '벅찬, 힘든'의 뜻의 daunting이 적절하다. 그리고 빈칸 Ⓒ에는 높은 성적을 받는 쉽고 빠른 방법이 아니라는 의미가 되어야 하므로 '지름길'이라는 뜻의 shortcut이 적절하다.

다음 중 빈칸 Ⓑ와 Ⓒ에 가장 적절한 것은?
① 힘든 — 지름길
② 매혹적인 — 난국
③ 금지하는 — 정도
④ 흥미를 끄는 — 우회로

35~36

1990년대 후반 이탈리아 연구진은 사르데냐(Sardinia)의 장수를 조사하는 프로젝트를 시작했다. 결과는 흥미로웠다. 연구진은 사르데냐 섬에서 100세 이상의 주민들이 섬 전체에 고르게 분포되어 있지 않았다는 것을 발견했기 때문이다. 대신 100세 이상의 주민들이 중부 산악지대인 올리아스트라(Ogliastra) 지역에 보다 높은 밀집도를 보였다. 또한 이 지역은 100세 이상인 남성이 여성과 거의 비슷한 수를 자랑했다. 이는 매우 이례적인 결과였는데 왜냐하면 보통 100세 이상의 여성이 100세 이상의 남성보다 더 많기 때문이다.

| 어휘 |

longevity n. 장수   centenarian n. 나이가 100세(이상)의 사람
evenly ad. 고르게   distribute v. 분포하다   boast v. 자랑하다
finding n. (연구 등의) 결과   outnumber v. ~보다 수가 더 많다

35 내용파악   ①

| 분석 |

사르데냐 섬에서 장수를 조사했던 연구진이 흥미로워했던 부분은 100세 이상의 주민들이 섬 전체에 '고르게 분포되지 않았고' 올리아스트라 지역에 높은 밀집도를 보였다는 점이다. 즉, 이와 관련해 연구진은 100세 이상의 주민들이 섬 전체에 '고르게' 분포되어 있을 것이라고 처음에 예상했을 것이므로, ①이 정답이다.

다음 중 사르데냐의 100세 이상의 주민들과 관련해 연구진의 초기 예상에 해당하는 것은?
① 100세 이상의 주민들이 섬 전체에 고르게 분포해 있을 것이다.
② 100세 이상의 주민들 가운데 남성이 여성보다 수적으로 더 많을 것이다.
③ 100세 이상의 주민들이 해안 지대에 주로 발견될 것이다.
④ 연구는 섬의 다양한 지역에서 수명과 관련해 상당한 격차를 드러낼 것이다.

36 빈칸완성   ③

| 분석 |

본문에서 intriguing은 '흥미로운'이라는 뜻이므로 ③의 interesting(흥미로운)이 정답이다. ① 역겨운 ② 피할 수 없는 ④ 근거 없는

37~38

미술사학자들은 쿠르베(Courbet)의 '화가의 작업실(The Painter's Studio)'을 현대 미술 운동의 선구자로 종종 꼽는다. 쿠르베 작품에 붙은 독특한 부제, '내 인생의 7년을 요약한 진정한 우화'는 쿠르베가 자신의 작품으로 눈에 띄게 독창적인 무언가를 하려고 애썼음을 확인시켜준다. 이 그림이 화가의 독립에 한 획을 그었고 쿠르베의 작품 이후 화가들의 작품에 부여되는 사회적 요구로부터 화가들이 벗어날 수 있게 되었다는 주장이 제기되었다. 쿠르베 시대 이전의 그림들은 대부분 성경, 역사, 문학에 나오는 사건을 묘사하는 데 초점이 맞추어졌다. 쿠르베는 화가가 오로지 자신의 시각과 촉각을 통해 직접 경험할 수 있는 것만 그림으로 표현할 수 있다는 개념을 본인의 뛰어난 그림을 통해 세상에 퍼뜨렸다.

| 어휘 |

vanguard n. 선구자　**peculiar** a. 독특한　**subtitle** n. (책의) 부제　**allegory** n. 우화, 풍자　**sum up** 요약하다　**strikingly** ad. 눈에 띄게　**strike a blow for** ~에 기여하다　**depict** v. 묘사하다　**singular** a. 뛰어난　**represent** v. 표현하다　**sight** n. 시각

37　빈칸완성　①

| 분석 |

쿠르베의 그림이 화가의 독립에 한 획을 그었고 쿠르베의 작품 이후 화가들의 작품에 부여되는 사회적 요구로부터 화가들이 벗어날 수 있게 되었다는 내용을 통해 '화가는 오로지 자신의 시각과 촉각을 통해 직접 경험할 수 있는 것만 그림으로 표현할 수 있다는 개념'을 쿠르베가 본인의 그림을 통해 '세상에 퍼뜨렸다'는 내용이 되어야 한다. 따라서 ①의 promulgated(세상에 퍼뜨리다)가 정답이다. ② 미루다 ③ 쇠약하게 하다 ④ 어렵게 획득하다

38　내용추론　③

| 분석 |

본문에서 "이 그림이 화가의 독립에 한 획을 그었고 쿠르베의 작품 이후 작품에 부여되는 사회적 요구로부터 화가들이 벗어날 수 있게 되었다는 주장이 제기되었다."라는 내용을 통해 ③을 추론할 수 있다.

다음 중 쿠르베와 관련해 본문에서 추론할 수 있는 것은?
① 화가들이 신성을 더럽히는 관행을 하지 못하도록 그의 그림은 화가들이 종교적 주제에 초점을 맞추도록 마음이 들게 했다.
② 그의 작품은 미술적 기교의 중요성을 깎아내렸다.
③ 그의 그림은 전통적인 그림의 소재 제약에서 화가들을 벗어나게 하였다.
④ 그의 작품은 역사화에 대한 감상을 쇠퇴시켰다.

39~40

레이첼 카슨(Rachel Carson)은 인간/자연 이원론에 의문을 제기했다. 우리가 어떠한 오만한 태도를 취하든 간에 '우리'는 '자연'과 별개가 아니었다. 즉 우리는 자연의 일부였으며 오직 자연 속에서만 살아갈 수 있었다. 이와 다르게 생각하는 것은 자멸적인 것이었다.

'자연을 통제한다'는 개념은 오만에서 비롯된 것으로 생물학과 철학이 아직 네안데르탈인 수준에 머물러 있던 시기에 생겨났다. 당시에는 자연이 인간의 편의를 위해 존재한다고 여겨졌다. 응용 곤충학의 개념과 관행 또한 과학의 '석기시대'에서 비롯되었다. 그렇게 원시적인 과학이 가장 현대적이고 끔찍한 무기로 무장했고 곤충을 향해 무기를 사용하는 과정에서 그 무기가 지구를 향해서도 사용되었다는 것은 우리의 놀라운 불행이다.

'석기 시대' 사람들은 카슨이 반대했던 20세기 전문가들보다 생명의 거대한 연결망과 더 조화를 이루며 살았기에, '과학의 석기시대'라는 비유적 표현은 비판의 여지가 있을 수 있지만, 결론은 변하지 않는다. 만일 당신이 가진 유일한 도구가 망치라면 당신이 모든 문제를 못으로 보게 된다. 카슨은 여러 가지 도구와 여러 가지 문제 해결 방법을 모색하고 있었다.

| 어휘 |

dualism n. (선·악의) 이원론　**give oneself airs** 오만한 태도를 취하다　**be distinct from** ~와는 별개이다　**self-destructive** a. 자멸적인　**phrase** n. 관용구　**conceive** v. (계획 따위를) 생각해내다　**applied** a. 응용의　**entomology** n. 곤충학　**date from** ~에서 유래하다　**alarming** a. 놀라운　**misfortune** n. 불행　**primitive** a. 원시의　**arm oneself** 무장하다　**metaphor** n. 은유, 비유　**pundit** n. 전문가　**stand** v. (이미 했던 결정 등이 아직도) 변함없다　**hammer** n. 망치　**nail** n. 못

39　빈칸완성　③

| 분석 |

레이첼 카슨은 인간과 자연을 별개로 보는 이원론에 의문을 제기했다고 했으며 우리 인간은 자연과 별개가 아니라 자연의 일부라고 생각했다고 했다. 따라서 레이첼 카슨 입장에서 '자멸적인' 것이라고 여기게 될 경우는 이런 자신의 생각과 '다르게' 생각할 경우이므로, ③의 otherwise(다르게)가 빈칸에 적절하다. ① 마찬가지로 ② 신중하게 ④ 독립적으로

40　내용추론　④

|분석|

본문의 마지막 문장에서 카슨은 여러 가지 도구와 여러 가지 문제 해결 방법을 모색하고 있었다고 했다. 따라서 저자는 인간과 자연의 관계에서 카슨이 '단일한' 관점에 의존하고 있음을 강조한다고 보기는 어려우므로, ④가 정답이다.

다음 중 본문에서 추론할 수 없는 것은?
① 카슨은 자연에 대해 인간이 지배하고 있다는 태도를 오만하고 원시적인 사고에 뿌리를 두고 있다고 여긴다.
② 카슨은 '과학의 석기시대'라는 비유적 표현을 사용해 응용 곤충학 개념에 깔려 있는 세련되지 못한 사고방식을 설명한다.
③ '과학의 석기시대'라는 비유적 표현은 오해하게 만들 수 있는데, 왜냐하면 실제 석기시대 사람들은 카슨이 비판하는 현대의 과학자들보다 자연과 더 조화로운 관계를 맺고 있었을 가능성이 있기 때문이다.
④ 저자는 인간과 자연의 관계에서 카슨이 단일한 관점에 의존하고 있음을 강조한다.

가톨릭대학교 인문계 A형

TEST p. 42~60

01	①	02	③	03	③	04	③	05	③	06	④	07	③	08	①	09	④	10	④
11	①	12	①	13	①	14	②	15	②	16	①	17	①	18	③	19	④	20	②
21	④	22	①	23	①	24	③	25	②	26	④	27	③	28	④	29	②	30	②
31	④	32	②	33	②	34	①	35	④	36	③	37	①	38	③	39	②	40	②

01 논리완성 ①

| 분석 |
실험대상의 사생활을 침해하지 않도록 해야 한다는 내용이므로, 개인 정보의 기밀성을 보장하는 것과 같은 흐름이 되도록 연구 대상자들의 이름을 숨겨서 "익명성"을 보증한다는 내용이 되는 것이 자연스럽다.

| 어휘 |
subject n. 피실험자, 실험대상   **assure** v. 보증하다, 보장하다   **guarantee** v. 보장하다, 확실히 하다   **confidentiality** n. 비밀유지, 기밀성   **anonymity** n. 익명, 작자 불명   **scrutiny** n. 정밀한 조사, 감시   **mobility** n. 이동성   **integrity** n. 정직성, 고결함

| 해석 |
대부분의 사회학 연구는 사람들을 정보의 출처로 사용하기 때문에, 사회학자들은 자신들이 연구대상자들의 사생활을 침해하고 있지 않다는 것을 확신할 필요가 있다. 일반적으로 그들은 연구대상자들에게 익명성을 보증하고 개인 정보의 기밀성을 보장함으로써 그렇게 한다.

02 논리완성 ③

| 분석 |
두 번째 문장에서 첫 번째 문장의 내용을 부연해서 설명하고 있다. "폭력적인 TV 프로그램을 일주일에 여러 시간 시청하는 아이들은 더 공격적이고 불안해질 수 있다."는 것은 부정적인 영향에 대한 것이므로, 빈칸에는 '해로운'이라는 의미의 ③이 들어가는 것이 적절하다.

| 어휘 |
extensive a. 아주 넓은[많은], 대규모의   **aggressive** a. 공격적인; 적극적인   **versatile** a. 다재다능한, 다용도의   **mandatory** a. 의무적인, 강제적인   **pernicious** a. 해로운, 치명적인   **benevolent** a. 자비로운, 호의적인

| 해석 |
폭력적인 TV 프로그램을 매우 많이 시청하는 것은 아이들에게 해로운 영향을 끼칠 수 있다. 폭력적인 TV 프로그램을 일주일에 여러 시간 시청하는 아이들은 더 공격적이고 불안해 할 수 있다.

03 논리완성 ③

| 분석 |
섭식장애의 발병에 유전적 요인이 일정한 역할을 한다는 내용 다음에 but이 왔으므로, but 이하는 유전적 요인이 없는 사람들, 즉 가족력이 없는 사람들도 이 병에 걸릴 수 있다는 내용이 되어야 한다. 따라서 '(정신적·육체적으로) 괴롭히다, (병을) 앓게 하다'라는 의미의 ③이 정답이 된다.

| 어휘 |
gene n. 유전자   **heritability** n. 유전 가능성, 상속 가능성   **eating disorder** 섭식장애   **bolster** v. 지지하다, 강화하다   **exploit** v. 착취하다, 이용하다   **afflict** v. (정신적·육체적으로) 괴롭히다, 시달리게 하다, 앓게 하다, 걸리게 하다   **remove** v. 제거하다

| 해석 |
유전자와 유전 가능성이 일부 사람들이 섭식장애에 걸릴 위험이 더 높은 이유에 일정한 역할을 하긴 하지만, 이러한 장애는 가족력이 전혀 없는 사람들도 걸릴 수 있다.

04 논리완성 ③

| 분석 |
'부모의 통제가 좋은 출발점이지만, 학생들 스스로 자신을 보호하는 법을 배워야 한다'는 것은 학생들이 디지털 기술을 안전하게 사용하는 것이 매우 중요한 일이라는 것이므로, 빈칸에는 '반드시 필요한', '긴급하고 중요한'의 의미를 가진 ③이 오는 것이 적절하다.

2025학년도 가톨릭대 인문계 A형 • 17

| 어휘 |

ensure v. 보장하다, 보증하다, 확실하게 하다　provocative a. 도발적인, 자극적인　dispensable a. 없어도 되는, 불필요한; 베풀 수 있는　imperative a. 강제적인; 긴급한, 절대 필요한　negligible a. 무시해도 될 정도의, 하찮은

| 해석 |

전 세계 수십억 명이 인터넷을 사용하는 가운데, 학생들이 디지털 기술을 안전하게 사용하도록 보장하는 것은 필수적이며, 부모의 통제가 좋은 출발점이지만, 학생들 스스로 자신을 보호하는 법을 배워야 한다.

05 논리완성 ③

| 분석 |

챗봇이 의사에게 지적한 진단은 서로 간에 의견이 일치하지 않는 진단이었을 것이므로 ③이 정답이다. at odds with는 '~와 의견이 충돌하는'이라는 의미를 나타낸다.

| 어휘 |

diagnosis n. 진단　at stake 위험에 처한, 위태로운　at fault 잘못하여, 책임이 있는　at odds with ~와 의견이 충돌하는, 불화하는　at a loss 당황한, 어쩔 줄 모르는

| 해석 |

챗봇이 의사들의 진단과 충돌하는 어떤 점을 지적했을 때, 의사들은 종종 챗봇에 의해 설득되지 않았다는 것이 드러난다.

06 분사구문 ④

| 분석 |

콤마 앞에 완전한 문장이 주어져 있으므로 그 뒤에는 접속사와 함께 정동사가 이어지거나 혹은 분사구문이 와야 한다. 그러므로 연속 동작의 분사구문을 만드는 ④가 정답이 된다. 나머지 보기는 접속사가 없으므로 빈칸에 들어갈 수 없다.

| 어휘 |

planet n. 행성　the solar system 태양계

| 해석 |

현대의 로켓과 우주 기술은 과학자들로 하여금 태양계의 모든 주요 행성에 로봇 형태의 탐사 기계를 보낼 수 있게 해주었고, 그 결과 이전에는 멀리 있는 미지의 세계였던 곳들이 달 표면만큼이나 익숙한 곳이 되었다.

07 동격의 to부정사 ③

| 분석 |

명사 need는 동격 관계를 나타내는 표현으로 to부정사를 취한다. 그러므로 빈칸에는 ③이 들어가야 하며, 이때 for farmers는 부정사의 의미상 주어를 나타낸다.

| 어휘 |

bush n. 관목; 덤불　soil n. 흙, 토양　vegetation n. 식물, 초목　habitat n. 서식지　disturb v. 방해하다; 어지럽히다

| 해석 |

커피 관목은 농부들이 흙을 갈아엎을 필요 없이 수년 동안 자라며, 주변의 초목은 야생동물, 특히 새들을 위한 소중한 서식지를 제공한다.

08 'It ~ that …' 강조구문 ①

| 분석 |

빈칸 뒤에 완전한 문장이 주어져 있으므로 관계대명사 what, who, whose는 모두 빈칸에 들어갈 수 없다. 문두에 It was가 있음을 감안하면, 전체 문장은 'It ~ that …' 강조구문이 되는 것이 적절하므로 빈칸에는 ①이 들어가야 한다.

| 어휘 |

foot-treadle a. 발판을 발로 밟는　sewing machine 재봉틀

| 해석 |

재봉틀이 가정과 일터에서 중요한 역할을 하기 시작한 것은 1859년에 미국인 발명가 아이작 싱어가 발로 밟는 재봉틀을 도입한 데 따른 것이었다.

09 전치사 + 관계대명사 ④

| 분석 |

관계대명사 뒤에는 불완전한 문장이 오고 '전치사+관계대명사' 뒤에는 완전한 문장이 온다. 빈칸 뒤에 완전한 문장이 주어져 있으므로 빈칸에는 '전치사+관계대명사'가 들어가야 하겠는데, 식물성 물질은 소화관 "안에" 머물러 있게 되는 것이므로 전치사는 in이 적절하다. 따라서 ④가 정답이다.

| 어휘 |

digest v. 소화하다　herbivore n. 초식동물　relatively ad. 상대적으로　digestive tract 소화관

| 해석 |

셀룰로오스는 소화시키기 어렵기 때문에, 소와 토끼 같은 초식동물들은 식물성 물질이 오랫동안 머무를 수 있는 상대적으로 크고 무거운 소화관을 갖고 있다.

10 수동태 ④

| 분석 |
주어인 관계대명사 which의 선행사는 the Inflation Reduction Act인데, 이것은 expect하는 행위의 대상이므로 수동태 문장이 되어야 한다. 따라서 빈칸에는 ④가 들어가야 한다.

| 어휘 |
enact v. (법령으로) 규정하다; (법률을) 제정하다

| 해석 |
지난 3년에 걸쳐, 미국은 인플레이션 감축법(IRA)을 제정했는데, 이 법은 풍력, 태양광, 원자력 에너지 같은 저탄소 기술에 수천억 달러를 쏟아 부을 것으로 예상된다.

11 논리완성 ①

| 분석 |
동물들이 지진 전에 보이는 특이한 행동이 아무 의미 없이 일어난 일이 아니라 지진과 관련이 있을 수도 있다고 과학자들이 생각하게 되었다는 내용이 되어야 하므로, 빈칸에는 이러한 행동이 순전한 우연의 일치에 그치지 않는다는 뜻이 되게 ①이 들어가는 것이 가장 자연스럽다.

| 어휘 |
equipment n. 장비, 기기 **pet** n. 애완동물, 반려동물 **natural disaster** 자연재해 **bark** v. (개가) 짖다 **indicate** v. 나타내다, 보여주다 **impending** a. 임박한, 곧 닥칠 **evacuate** v. 대피시키다, (사람을) 피난[소개(疏開)]시키다 **catfish** n. 메기 **moderately** ad. 적당히 **slight** a. 약간의, 미세한 **magnetic field** 자기장

| 해석 |
아마도 과학자들은 지진을 예측하기 위해 값비싼 과학 장비에 투자하는 것보다는 그들의 반려동물을 관찰하는 데 더 많은 시간을 들여야 할지도 모르겠다. 많은 과학자들은 이제 일부 동물들의 행동이 자연재해를 예측하는 데 도움이 될지도 모른다고 생각하고 있다. 예를 들어, 1970년대 중국의 과학자들은 농장의 동물들이 원을 그리면서 뛰어다니고 개들이 밤새 짖는다는 보고가 임박한 자연재해를 알려주는 것일 수도 있다고 생각했다. 그들은 하이친(Haichin)시의 주민들을 대피시키기로 결정했는데, 그 직후에 그 도시는 큰 지진을 겪었다. 일본 과학자들 또한 메기가 중간 강도의 지진이 있기 며칠 전부터 움직임이 더 활발해지는 현상을 발견했다. 많은 과학자들은 이제 이것이 순전한 우연의 일치일 리가 없는 것으로 받아들이고 있다. 그들은 그 설명이 지구 자기장의 미세한 변화와 관련이 있을 수 있다고 믿고 있다.

① 순전한 우연의 일치
② 초능력의 한 예
③ 자연재해
④ 생존에 해로운

12 논리완성 ①

| 분석 |
대조를 나타내는 while절에서 이제는 다른 세계에 외계 생명체가 있을 것으로 보고 있다는 내용이 있으므로, 주절은 '생명체가 있을 것으로 여겨졌던 천체에 생명체가 없는 것으로 드러났다'는 내용이 되어야 한다. 그러므로 빈칸에는 ①이 들어가야 한다.

| 어휘 |
the solar system 태양계 **renaissance** n. 부흥, 부활 **planet** n. 행성 **celestial body** 천체 **life-bearing** a. 생명체가 존재하는, 생명체를 지닌 **hold out** (약속을) 제공하다, (희망을) 품게 하다 **sustain** v. 유지하다, 지탱하다 **extraterrestrial** a. 외계의, 지구 밖의 **Mars** n. 화성 **candidate** n. 후보(자), 가능성이 있는 것 **Jovian** a. 목성의

| 해석 |
태양계 전역에서의 우주 탐사선 임무들은 이전에 신비롭게 여겨졌던 세계들(행성과 위성들)에 대한 관심과 이해를 되살아나게 했다. 한때 생명체를 갖고 있는 것으로 여겨졌던 천체들은 실망스러울 만큼 황량한 것으로 드러났지만, 이제 다른 세계들이 아마도 원시적인 형태의 외계 생명체를 유지하고 있을 가능성을 제시한다. 화성 외에도, 가장 유력한 후보는 목성의 위성인 유로파(Europa)이다.

① 실망스럽게도 황량한
② 비교적 비옥한
③ 놀라울 정도로 다양한
④ 분명하게 정적인

13 논리완성 ①

| 분석 |
'독일인들은 그렇지 않았다'라는 것은 독일의 학자들과 프랑스, 영국의 학자들이 서로 다른 입장을 가지고 있었음을 나타내는데, 독일인들이 과학을 이용하여 정신을 탐구하는 데 적극적으로 나섰다는 내용이 이어지고 있음을 감안하면, 프랑스와 영국의 학자들은 과학의 이런 활용에 대해 부정적인 견해를 가지고 있었다는 것이 된다. 그러므로 빈칸에는 ①이 들어가야 한다.

| 어휘 |
monopoly n. (생산·시장의) 독점, 전매 **enthusiasm** n. 열정, 열의 **conscientiousness** n. 성실성, 양심적임 **optimism** n. 낙관주의 **significant** a. 중요한, 상당한 **physics** n. 물리학 **chemistry** n. 화학 **quantitatively** ad. 양적으로 **linguistics** n. 언어학 **archaeology** n. 고고학 **aesthetics** n. 미학 **plunge ahead** 앞장서서 나아가다, 뛰어들다 **unconstrained** a. 구속되지 않은, 제약 없는 **facet** n. 양상, 국면, 일면 **skeptical** a. 회의적인, 의심하는 **unbiased** a. 편견 없는, 공정한 **confident** a. 자신 있는, 확신하는 **enthusiastic** a. 열광적인, 열정적인

| 해석 |

19세기에 대부분의 서유럽, 특히 영국, 프랑스, 독일에서 과학이 발전하고 있었다. 어느 한 국가도 과학의 도구들을 다양한 연구 문제에 적용하는 데 있어서의 열정과 성실성, 낙관주의를 독점하고 있지 않았다. 그러나 이들 국가 간에는 중요한 차이가 있었다. 프랑스와 영국에서는 과학이 정량적으로 접근할 수 있는 물리학과 화학에 국한되어 있었다. 반면, 독일에서는 과학이 언어학, 역사학, 고고학, 미학, 논리학, 심지어 문학 비평까지 포함하고 있었다. 프랑스와 영국의 학자들은 복잡한 인간의 정신에 과학을 적용하는 것에 대해 회의적이었다. 독일인들은 그렇지 않았는데, 그들은 과학의 도구들을 활용하여 정신생활의 모든 측면을 탐구하고 측정하면서 거침없이 나아갔다.

14   논리완성   ②

| 분석 |

"사우나 후에 맥주를 마시며 심신을 진정시키고, 그 후 고객에게 전화를 걸어 사업 거래를 마무리하거나 업무 시간 동안 해결하기 어려웠던 중요한 문제를 논의하는 것"은 모두 사우나를 '비즈니스 장소로 활용하고' 있음을 보여주는 예에 해당한다.

| 어휘 |

illustration n. 예시, 사례   **cool off** 진정시키다   **finalize** v. 마무리하다, 결정을 내리다   **resolve** v. 해결하다, 결심하다   **distinction** n. 차이, 구별, 특성   **manifest** a. 명백한, 분명한   **apparent** a. 명백한   **latent** a. 숨어 있는, 보이지 않은; 잠재적인   **distinctive** a. 특징적인, 독특한   **beyond comparison** 비교할 수 없는, 비할 데 없는

| 해석 |

핀란드에서는 사우나가 거의 모든 곳에 위치해 있으며, 지역의 사회적 맥락에서 중요한 역할을 한다. 예를 들어, 사우나는 친구들이 모여서 지역의 소문이나 정치에 대해 이야기하는 장소로 자주 이용된다. 사우나는 또한 비즈니스를 하는 장소로 이용된다. 실례를 하나 들자면, 핀란드 사람들은 사우나 후에 맥주를 마시며 기분을 풀고, 그 후 고객에게 전화를 걸어 사업 거래를 마무리하기도 한다. 이들은 심지어 업무 시간 동안 해결하기 어려웠던 중요한 문제를 논의할 수도 있다. 스웨덴이나 아일랜드 같은 다른 나라들에도 사우나가 있다. 그러나 핀란드에서 사우나의 분명한 혹은 명백한 기능적 역할과 잠재적인, 숨어 있는, 혹은 상징적인 역할 사이의 차이는 독특하지는 않다 해도 분명히 구별되며 비교할 수 없을 정도이다.

① 자주 집에 곁들여 설치돼 있다
② 또한 비즈니스를 하는 장소로 사용된다
③ 평등의 신성한 장소로 변한다
④ 자연 중심의 가치와 관습을 소중히 여긴다

15   논리완성   ②

| 분석 |

'마음이 가라앉지 않는다', '공허한 느낌이다'라는 표현에 유의하면, 친구들의 행복한 일상을 보면서 느끼게 되는 것은 부정적인 감정일 것이다. 여기에는 나만 빼고 즐거운 일을 하고 있다는 소외감, 나 자신이 초라하게 느껴지는 자기혐오, 남들을 부러워하는 질투심 등이 해당될 수 있을 것이므로 빈칸에는 ②가 적절하다.

| 어휘 |

restless a. 가만히 있지 못하는, 안절부절 못하는, 마음이 들뜬   **wind down** 긴장을 풀다, 편히 쉬다   **casually** ad. 우연히, 별 생각 없이   **browse** v. 훑어보다, 둘러보다   **elaborate** a. 정교한, 공들인   **saturated with** ~로 가득한, 흠뻑 젖은   **impressive** a. 인상적인, 눈길을 끄는   **utterly** ad. 완전히, 전적으로   **phenomenon** n. 현상   **miss out** (중요하거나 재미있는 것을) 놓치다   **FoMO(Fear of Missing Out)** 소외되거나 뒤처질까 봐 느끼는 불안감   **dominate** v. 지배하다, 영향을 미치다

| 해석 |

저녁이 깊어가고 있지만, 당신은 마음이 가라앉지 않는다. 긴 하루를 보낸 뒤, 인스타그램이나 페이스북을 아무 생각 없이 훑어보며 쉬고 싶은데, 그때 너무나도 익숙한 감정에 압도된다. 한 친구는 정성껏 차린 최고급 레스토랑의 저녁식사 사진을 올렸고, 또 다른 친구는 아름다운 파스텔 빛으로 물든 해변의 석양을 찍은 영상을 올렸다. 수많은 친구들의 즐겁고 인상적인 일상 이야기를 계속해서 스크롤하며 보다 보면, 마음이 점점 더 가라앉지 않는다. 그 감정을 말로 설명하긴 어렵지만, 소외감, 자기혐오, 질투심이 묘하게 뒤섞인 듯한 느낌이다. 그것은 완전히 공허한 느낌이며, 소셜 미디어 사용자들 사이에서 점점 더 흔해지고 있다. 이러한 현상은 "자기만 빠지는 것에 대한 두려움", 즉 FoMO로 알려져 있다. 소셜 미디어의 성장과 더불어, FoMO의 심리는 안을 기웃거리는 외부인이 된 느낌이 드는 사람들의 정신 건강을 지배하는 힘 때문에 학문적 담론 속에서 더 많은 주목을 받고 있다.

① 흥분, 기쁨, 만족감의 갑작스러운 폭발
② 소외감, 자기혐오, 질투심이 미묘하게 뒤섞임
③ 성취감, 휴식, 만족감의 조합
④ 무관심, 자존심, 그리고 독립심이라는 감정

16   논리완성   ①

| 분석 |

뒤에서 "이 지역 국가들 사이에서는 독립 이후 약 250개의 헌법이 제정되었고, 군사 쿠데타도 놀라우리만치 자주 일어났다."고 했는데, 이것은 이 지역이 정치적으로 매우 불안정했음을 부연하는 내용이므로, 빈칸에는 ①이 들어가는 것이 적절하다.

| 어휘 |

celebrate v. 기념하다, 축하하다 **bicentennial** n. 200주년 기념제 **constitution** n. 헌법 **military coup** 군사 쿠데타 **dictator** n. 독재자 **outnumber** v. 수적으로 많다

| 해석 |

라틴 아메리카의 17개국 대부분이 21세기에 독립 200주년을 기념하게 되었다. 대부분의 개발도상국들과 비교하면, 라틴 아메리카 사람들은 오랫동안 독립을 유지해왔다. 그러나, 정치적 안정이 그 지역의 특징이었던 적은 없었다. 이 지역 국가들 사이에서는 독립 이후 약 250개의 헌법이 제정되었고, 군사 쿠데타도 놀라우리만치 자주 일어났다. 그러나 1980년대 이후 지금까지의 추세는 민주적으로 선출된 정부, 시장 개방, 보다 폭넓은 대중의 정치 참여를 지향하는 것이었다. 한때는 독재자의 수가 선출된 지도자의 수보다 많았지만, 1990년대에는 이미 쿠바를 제외한 각 국가들이 민주적으로 선출된 대통령을 갖고 있었다.

① 정치적 안정은 그 지역의 특징이 아니었다
② 정치인들이 좌익인 추세가 지배적이었다
③ 그들은 느린 경제 성장에 좌절해왔다
④ 국경을 둘러싸고 성가신 분쟁들이 있어왔다

17 논리완성 ①

| 분석 |

환자가 문제나 증상을 논의하는 것이 보편적인 문화에서 살아온 의료진은 세츠코가 증상을 제대로 말하지 않아서 그녀가 우울증을 겪고 있는지를 알아차리지 못했고, 세츠코는 분란을 일으키지 않고 조용히 넘어가는 것이 미덕인 문화에서 살았기 때문에 자신의 증상을 제대로 알리지 않았다. 이것은 모두 '자신도 모르게 자기문화중심적인 틀에서 행동한 것'을 보여준다고 할 수 있다.

| 어휘 |

chronic illness 만성 질환 **depressed** a. 우울한 **suicidal** a. 자살하고 싶은 충동에 사로잡히는 **psychiatric** a. 정신병학의, 정신과의 **consultation** n. 상담, 의논 **make a fuss** 소란을 피우다, 불평하다 **psychiatrist** n. 정신과 의사 **context** n. 맥락, 상황 **symptom** n. 증상 **redefine** v. 재정의하다

| 해석 |

지금 미국에 살고 있는 일본 여성인 세츠코(Setsuko)는 만성 질환으로 인해 몇 달간 병원에 입원해야 했다. 그녀는 극심한 우울증을 겪었고, 자살 충동을 느낄 정도가 되었다. 그러나 의료진이 상태를 물어볼 때마다 세츠코는 괜찮다고 대답하곤 했다. 의료진은 그녀의 우울증을 몇 주 동안이나 알아차리지 못했다. 그녀가 우울증의 신체적 증상을 보이기 시작하고 나서야 정신과 상담이 이루어졌다. 문제는 세츠코가 좋은 환자는 소란을 피우지 않고, 자신에게 주목을 끌지 않으며, 가족을 망신 주는 일이 없도록 불평하지 않는 것이라고 문화적으로 길들여져 있었다는 점이었다. 그래서 그녀는 늘 괜찮다고 대답했던 것이다. 정신과 의사는 그녀에게 이런 상황에 좋은 환자는 모든 문제나 증상을 의논하고 보고하지 않으면 안 된다고 설명해주려 했다. 그럼에도 불구하고, 세츠코는 더 나은 치료를 받기 위해 좋은 환자로서의 그녀의 문화적 역할을 다시 정의해야 했다. 이 사례는 우리에게 의료진과 환자 모두가 자신도 모르는 사이에 자기문화중심적인 틀에서 행동할 수 있다는 점을 상기시켜 주었다.

① 자신도 모르게 자기문화중심적인 틀에서 행동할 수 있다
② 환자를 치료하는 것이 항상 소통의 문제는 아니라는 점을 깨달아야 한다
③ 효과적인 소통을 위해 기본적인 의학 용어를 공유해야 한다
④ 건강 정보를 다른 사람에게 전달하는 데 제약이 있다는 것을 인식해야 한다

18 논리완성 ③

| 분석 |

진주 농장이 주변의 바닷물을 정화시키면 해양 환경의 질이 개선되는 것이므로, 이에 따른 결과로는 '해양 생물들이 이전보다 더 건강해지게 되는 것'이 가장 적절하다.

| 어휘 |

pearl oyster 진주조개 **filter** v. 여과하다 **exceptionally** ad. 예외적으로, 매우 **pollutant** n. 오염물질 **excess** n. 과잉, 초과 **nitrogen** n. 질소 **algae** n. 조류(藻類, 바다에서 자주 자라는 미세한 식물) **adversely** ad. 부정적으로, 불리하게 **affect** v. 영향을 미치다 **purify** v. 정화하다, 깨끗하게 하다 **in turn** 그 다음에는, 그 결과

| 해석 |

진주조개는 먹이를 먹으면서 바닷물을 걸러내는데, 그 결과 진주 농장 주변의 바닷물은 매우 수질이 좋다. 성체 진주조개 한 마리는 하루에 최대 50갤런의 바닷물을 걸러낼 수 있으며, 이 과정에서 과잉 질소를 비롯한 많은 유해 오염 물질을 제거한다. 바닷물에 과잉 질소가 있으면 조류(藻類)가 성장하게 되는데, 이는 물속의 산소 수준을 낮춰서 모든 해양 생물에 나쁜 영향을 미치게 된다. 진주조개는 (바닷물을) 걸러내는 과정에서 바닷물에서 질소를 안전하게 제거하여 그것을 그들의 껍질이나 조직에 축적한다. 이 질소는 진주조개가 성장하는 데 도움을 준다. 따라서, 진주 농장은 주변의 바닷물을 정화시키며, 그 다음에는 이것(주변 바닷물 정화)이 해양 생물들을 이전보다 더 건강해지게 만든다.

① 해양 생물을 도와주는 조류 번식의 증가
② 해양 종(種) 사이의 경쟁 감소
③ 해양 생물을 이전보다 더 건강하게 만듦
④ 질소의 사용으로 인한 진주조개의 성장 감소

19 논리완성 ④

| 분석 |
튜링 테스트에서는 인간 질문자가 다양한 질문에 대한 답변을 기초로 하여 컴퓨터와 인간 실험참가자를 구별해야 한다. 인간 질문자가 질문을 했을 때 컴퓨터의 답변이 인간과 구별되지 않을 정도로 사람처럼 보인다면, 그 컴퓨터는 사고를 할 수 있다고 본다는 것이다. 이는 컴퓨터가 인간처럼 보이는 빈도를 평가하여 그것의 사고 능력을 평가하려는 것이므로 빈칸에는 ④가 적절하다

| 어휘 |
devise v. 고안하다, 만들어내다 **objective** a. 객관적인 **criterion** n. 기준, 판단의 근거 **distinguish** v. 구별하다, 식별하다, 차이를 보이다 **sufficiently** ad. 충분히 **sophisticated** a. 정교한, 세련된 **parrot** v. (이해하지 못하고) 따라 하다, 앵무새처럼 흉내 내다 **sidestep** v. (문제나 질문 등을) 회피하다, 피하다 **albeit** conj. 비록 ~일지라도 **react** v. 반응하다 **interact** v. 상호작용하다 **sentient** a. 지각 있는, 의식 있는 **dismiss** v. 무시하다, 일축하다; 해고하다 **interrogator** n. 질문자, 심문자 **subject** n. 피실험자, 실험참가자 **fixed** a. 정해진, 고정된 **reflect** v. 반영하다, 나타내다

| 해석 |
"독창적인" 사고(思考)를 충분히 정교한 "앵무새식 반복"과 구별하기 위한 객관적인 기준을 마련하는 데는 매우 큰 어려움이 있다. 사실, 독창적인 사고에 대한 어떤 증거도 결국 그것이 컴퓨터에 미리 프로그래밍된 것이라는 이유로 부정될 수 있다. 영국의 수학자 앨런 튜링(Alan Turing, 1912-1954)은 사고를 정확히 어떻게 정의할 것인가에 대한 논쟁을, 매우 실용적이지만 주관적인 하나의 테스트에 의해, 피해갔다. 즉, 만약 컴퓨터가 의식 있는 존재처럼 행동하고, 반응하고, 상호작용한다면, 그것을 지각이 있는 것으로 부르자는 것이다. 기계의 지능에 대한 증거를 부당하게 무시하지 않기 위해, 튜링은 오늘날 튜링 테스트로 알려져 있는 "모방 게임"을 제안했다. 이 테스트에서는, 멀리 떨어져 있는 인간 질문자가 컴퓨터와 인간 실험참가자를, 다양한 질문에 대한 그들의 답변을 기초로 하여, 정해진 시간 안에, 구별해야 한다. 이러한 테스트에서 컴퓨터의 수행 능력은 그것의 '사고' 능력을 나타내주며, 이는 컴퓨터가 인간 실험참가자와 얼마나 자주 혼동되는지에 따라 결정된다.

① 그것이 앵무새를 얼마나 비슷하게 흉내 내는가
② 그것이 세상을 얼마나 객관적으로 설명하는가
③ 그것이 인간의 감정을 얼마나 효과적으로 흉내 내는가
④ 그것이 인간 실험참가자와 얼마나 자주 혼동되는가

20 논리완성 ②

| 분석 |
빈칸 바로 다음 문장이 빈칸 있는 문장을 부연 설명해주는데, 빈칸 다음 문장에서 "20세기의 주요 기술 발전들은 모두 정보의 이용가능성을 확장하는 데 기여해 왔다."라는 내용이 있으므로, 빈칸에는 availability(이용가능성)의 available과 유사한 accessible(접근 가능한)이 있는 ②가 들어가는 것이 적절하다.

| 어휘 |
hype n. 과장된 광고, 과대 선전   **expand** v. 확장하다, 팽창하다   **widen** v. 넓히다, 확장하다   **availability** n. 이용 가능성, 접근 가능성   **albeit** conj. 비록 ~일지라도   **unfold** v. (상황·이야기 등이) 전개되다, 펼쳐지다

| 해석 |
정보는 항상 우리 경제에서 중추적인 역할을 해왔다. 이것은 정보화 시대에 대한 온갖 과장된 말들 속에서 너무나도 자주 잊혀지고 있는 단순한 사실이다. 존재하는 정보의 총량은 최근 수십 년 동안 그다지 많이 늘어나지 않았다. 달라진 것은 정보가 극적으로 더 접근 가능해졌다는 점이다. 전화, 라디오, 영화, 텔레비전, 컴퓨터 등, 20세기의 주요 기술 발전들은 모두 정보의 흐름을 빠르게 하고, 정보의 이용가능성을 확장하는 데 기여해 왔다. 인터넷의 등장은 — 매우 큰 진전이긴 해도 — 계속해서 펼쳐지는 과정의 가장 최근 단계에 지나지 않는다.

① 대부분 인터넷에서 얻어졌다
② 극적으로 더 접근 가능해졌다
③ 다양한 형태로 기록되거나 저장될 수 있다
④ 특정 집단의 사람들에게는 위험할 수 있다

21 내용일치 ④

| 분석 |
"사람이 나이를 먹어감에 따라, 골격근은 실제로 위축되거나 줄어드는 반면, 지방 조직은 커지는 경향이 있다. 이러한 신체 구성의 변화 중 일부는 노화 과정의 불가피한 부분으로 보인다."라는 내용을 통해 ④를 정답으로 선택할 수 있다.

| 어휘 |
muscular a. 근육의, 근육질의   **specialized** a. 특화된, 전문화된   **contractile** a. 수축성의   **age** v. 나이가 들다, 늙다   **skeletal** a. 골격의, 뼈대의   **atrophy** v. 위축되다, 약해지다   **shrink** v. 줄어들다, 오그라들다   **adipose** a. 지방의   **inevitable** a. 피할 수 없는

| 해석 |
생물학 강의를 한 번도 들어본 적이 없는 사람들은 "나는 웨이트 트레이닝을 하고 싶지 않아. 근육 조직을 키우면, 웨이트 트레이닝을 그만두었을 때 그것이 지방으로 바뀔까 봐 걱정이 되니까."라고 말한다고 알려져 있다. 물론, 근육 조직은 수축하는 기능에 특화돼 있으므로, 에너지 저장에 특화돼 있는 지방 조직으로는 '변하지' 않는다. 사람이 나이를 먹어감에 따라, 골격근은 실제로 위축되거나 줄어드는 반면, 지방 조직은 커지는 경향이 있다. 이러한 신체 구성의 변화 중 일부는 노화 과정의 불가피한 부분으로 보인다. 하지만 과학자들은 충분한 운동을 하면 근육 조직의 소실을 크게 예방할 수 있다고 믿고 있다.

다음 중 옳은 것은?
① 생물학을 모르는 사람들은 웨이트 트레이닝이 근육을 만드는 데 도움이 되지 않는다고 생각하는 경향이 있다.
② 근육 조직의 주요 기능은 우리 몸이 사용할 에너지를 저장하는 것이다.
③ 충분히 운동하더라도 근육 조직의 소실을 예방하는 것은 불가능하다.
④ 골격근 약화와 같은 노화 과정의 결과는 피할 수 없다.

22 내용파악   ①

| 분석 |

"멘델이 논문을 쓴 것은 1865년이었지만, 그가 발견한 것은 시대를 앞선 것이어서, 그 중요성과 그가 설명한 유전 요소들은 1900년대 초반이 되어서야 이해되었다"고 했다. 그러므로 ①이 옳은 진술이다. ④ 멘델이 말한 유전 단위가 나중에 유전자로 알려지게 된 것이므로 둘은 동일하다.

| 어휘 |

monk n. 수도사 **lay the foundation** 기초[토대]를 놓다 **genetics** n. 유전학 **demonstrate** v. 입증하다, 보여주다 **trait** n. 형질, 특색 **discrete** a. 분리된, 별개의 **distinct** a. 뚜렷한, 명확히 구별되는; 확실한 **hereditary** a. 유전의, 유전적인 **offspring** n. 자손, 새끼 **inherit** v. 물려받다, 유전되다 **gene** n. 유전자 **monastery** n. 수도원 **pea** n. 완두콩 **progeny** n. 자손, 후손 **self-fertilizing** a. 자가수분의 **reproductive** a. 생식의 **anatomy** n. 해부학, 해부학적 구조 **accidental** a. 우발적인 **fertilization** n. 수정

| 해석 |

1865년, 오스트리아의 수도사 그레고어 멘델(Gregor Mendel)은 현대 유전학의 토대를 닦은 한 편의 논문을 썼다. 멘델은 특정 형질이 한 세대에서 다음 세대로 어떻게 전해지는지를 실험을 통해 입증하고 자신의 데이터를 분석하는 데 수학을 사용한 최초의 인물이었다. 그는 부모로부터 자식에게 전해지는 구별되거나 개별적인 유전 단위들이 형질이 유전되는 방식을 결정한다고 결론지었다. 멘델의 발견은 시대를 앞선 것이었고, 그 중요성과 그가 설명한 유전 요소들은 1900년대 초반이 되어서야 이해되었고, 그때 비로소 그 단위들이 '유전자'로 알려지게 되었다. 실험을 진행한 수도원의 정원에서, 멘델은 완두콩을 모델 생물로 사용했다. 이 식물은 기르기 쉽고, 짧은 시간 안에 많은 자손을 생산하기 때문에 유전 연구에서 이상적인 재료가 되었다. 완두콩은 또한 자가수분을 하고, 그것의 해부학적 생식 구조는 외부로부터의 우발적인 수분을 막아준다.

다음 중 멘델(Mendel)에 관해 옳은 것은?
① 그는 1800년대 중반에 자신이 발견한 것을 발표했지만, 그의 이론은 훨씬 나중인 20세기가 되어서야 이해되었다.
② 처음에 그는 정원의 완두콩을 실험에 사용했지만, 나중에는 다른 식물을 사용했다.
③ 그에게 있어 완두콩은 비록 기르기는 어려워도 자손을 충분히 생산하기 때문에 이상적이었다.
④ 그가 가정한 유전 단위는 현대의 과학자들이 유전자라고 부르는 것과 다르다.

23 내용추론   ①

| 분석 |

'미리 식사음식을 만들어서 냉장고에 보관해두면 나중에 전자레인지에 데워 먹기만 하면 되므로, 바쁜 연휴 시간에 다른 중요한 일을 할 수 있는 시간을 벌 수 있게 된다'는 내용이다. 그러므로 ①이 정답이다.

| 어휘 |

specifically ad. 명확히; 특히 **freezer** n. 냉장고 **pop** v. 집어넣다

| 해석 |

연휴 기간에는 모두가 지나치게 바쁘고 대부분의 사람들이 쇼핑, 장식, 친구 및 가족과의 만남에 시간을 보내고 싶어 하기 때문에, 건강한 식사음식을 요리할 시간이 줄어든다. 몇 주 전에 미리 식사음식을 요리하여 특별히 냉장고에 넣어두는 방어적 조치를 취하라. 나중에 그 식사음식 중 하나를 얼른 전자레인지에 집어넣고, 그 대신 관심을 돌려 개인적인 메시지가 담긴 연하장을 하나하나 쓸 수 있으니 당신은 고마움을 느끼게 될 것이다.

이 글이 암시하고 있는 바는 무엇인가?
① 연휴 동안 시간을 절약하기 위해 전자레인지에 데워먹을 수 있는 식사음식을 미리 준비해 두는 것이 좋은 생각이다.
② 친구들과 가족을 위해, 연휴 식사음식은 더 특별한 방식으로 요리해야 한다.
③ 연휴 기간에는 쇼핑이나 친구를 만나는 것보다 식사음식을 준비하는 것에 우선순위를 두어야 한다.
④ 연휴 기간에 건강한 식사음식을 요리하는 데는 보통 많은 시간과 에너지가 필요하다.

24 내용일치   ③

| 분석 |

르보르뉴가 할 수 있는 말은 '탄(Tan)'이라는 단어뿐이었지만, 그가 말을 이해하는 능력은 비교적 영향을 받지 않은 상태에 있었다고 했다. 그러므로 ③이 옳지 않은 진술이다.

| 어휘 |

transfer v. 이동시키다, 이송하다 **physician** n. (내과) 의사 **hospitalize** v. 입원시키다, 병원 치료하다 **neurological** a. 신경학적인 **epilepsy** n. 간질 **relatively** ad. 상대적으로 **unaffected** a. 영향을 받지 않은 **pass away** 사망하다 **lesion** n. 손상; 병변 **temple** n. 관자놀이 **neurologist** n. 신경학자 **classify** v. 분류하다 **aphasia** n. 실어증 **observe** v. 관찰하다 **retain** v. 유지하다

| 해석 |

1861년, 51세의 프랑스인 르보르뉴(Leborgne)는 존경받는 프랑스 의사 폴 브로카(Paul Broca)의 진료를 받기 위해 이송되었다. 오랫동안 고통을 겪고 있던 르보르뉴는 간질, 언어 상실, 오른쪽 반신마비를 비롯한 다양한 신경학적 질환으로 적어도 20년 동안 입원해 있었다. 르보르뉴는 다른 환자들로부터 탄(Tan)이라는 별명을 얻었는데, 그것(탄)이 그가 말할 수 있는 유일한 단어였고, 그가 이 단어를 계속 반복했기 때문이다. 그러나 그의 말을 이해하는 능력은 비교적 영향을 받지 않은 상태였다. 르보르뉴는 브로카의 환자가 된 지 일주일도 못돼 사망했다. 나중에 르보르뉴의 뇌를 조사한 브로카는 왼쪽 전두엽 표면에서 꽤 크고 불규칙한 병변을 발견한 순간 깜짝 놀랐다. 왼쪽 관자놀이 바로 뒤에 위치한 뇌의 그 부분은 현재 브로카 영역(Broca's area)으로 널리 불리고 있다. 오늘날, 신경학자들은 언어 상실을 실어증으로 분류하며, 르보르뉴에서 관찰된 특정한 유형의 언어 장애 — 언어를 이해하는 능력은 유지하면서 유창하게 말하는 능력을 잃는 것 — 는 브로카 실어증으로 알려져 있다.

다음 중 옳지 않은 것은?
① 르보르뉴는 적어도 20년 동안 신경학적 질환을 앓았다.
② 르보르뉴의 별명은 그의 언어 능력이 얼마나 제한적이었는지를 나타낸다.
③ 르보르뉴는 말을 하지 못하게 되면서 언어를 이해하지 못하게 되었다.
④ 브로카 실어증은 특정 유형의 언어 장애를 설명하는 용어이다.

25 문장배열 ②

| 분석 |

앞에 유해한 직장의 정의에 대한 내용이 있으므로, 그러한 유해한 직장이 어떤 곳인지를 구체적인 예시를 통해 이야기하고 있는 ⓒ, ⓒ에 이어 그런 직장 문화가 직원에게 끼치는 부정적인 영향을 이야기하고 있는 Ⓐ, 이런 영향이 직원의 건강에 얼마나 심각한지를 보여주기 위해 공식 기관의 경고를 제시하고 있는 Ⓓ, 팬데믹 이후 변화된 직원들의 태도를 설명하는 Ⓑ의 순서로 이어지는 것이 가장 자연스럽다. 그러면 이 태도의 변화로 그 다음 문장에서 퇴사에 대해 언급하는 것과 잘 이어지게 된다.

| 어휘 |

toxic a. 유해한, 유독한 **define** v. 정의하다 **discriminatory** a. 차별적인 **hostile** a. 적대적인; 냉담한 **pandemic** n. 세계적인 유행병, 팬데믹 **tolerate** v. 참다, 용인하다 **retribution** n. 보복; 징벌 **exclude** v. 제외하다 **surgeon general** (미국의) 공중보건국장 **flexibility** n. 유연성

| 해석 |

맥킨지 건강연구소(McKinsey Health Institute)의 최근 보고서에 따르면, 전 세계 직원 4명 중 1명이 직장에서 높은 비율의 유해한 행동을 경험하고 있다. 완벽한 직장 환경이란 없지만, 유해한 직장은 무례하고, 차별적이며, 신뢰가 없고, 그리고 많은 경우에 적대적인 직장으로 정의된다. ⓒ 그러한 직장에서는 극도의 긴장을 느끼거나, 보복이 두려워 목소리를 내지 못하며, 심지어 아무 이유 없이 회의에서 제외되는 일도 겪을 수 있다. Ⓐ 안타깝게도, 건강하지 못한 직장 문화는 직원들의 생산성과 복지에 부정적인 영향을 미친다. Ⓓ 미국의 공중 위생국장조차도 유해한 직장 문화가 근로자의 정신적, 육체적 건강에 해롭다는 내용을 담은 지침을 발표한 바 있다. Ⓑ 팬데믹 이후에 달라진 점은 이제는 직원들이 더 이상 해로운 근무 환경을 참으려 하지 않는다는 것이다. 실제로 MIT 경영대학원의 한 연구에 따르면, 유해한 직장이 사람들이 퇴사하는 가장 큰 이유로 드러났다. 근로자들은 단지 높은 급여, 유연한 근무제도, 일과 삶의 균형만을 원하는 것이 아니다. 그들은 또한 직장에서 심리적으로 안전하다고 느끼기를 원한다.

26 내용파악 ④

| 분석 |

오루노코가 총독을 만나서 자유를 얻었다는 내용은 소설 속에 실려 있지 않으므로 ④가 정답이다. ③ 결정권이 총독에게 있다는 말을 거듭해서 들은 후에 자유를 얻는 것은 불가능한 것으로 드러난다고 했는데, 거듭해서 들었다는 것이 자유를 되찾기 위한 노력을 말해 준다.

| 어휘 |

pen v. 쓰다, 저술하다 **antislavery** a. 노예제도 반대의 **civilized** a. 문명화된, 교양 있는 **enslave** v. 노예로 만들다 **reunite** v. 재회하다 **recognize** v. 인정하다, 알아보다 **descent** n. 혈통, 가계 **acquire** v. 얻다, 획득하다 **unravel** v. (이야기 등이) 전개되다, 풀리다 **grotesque** a. 기괴한, 괴상한 **resolution** n. 결말, 해결 **morality** n. 도덕성 **rationality** n. 이성, 합리성

| 해석 |

글쓰기로 생계를 유지한 영국 최초의 여성, 아프라 벤(Aphra Behn)이 쓴 『오루노코, 고귀한 왕족 노예』는 1688년에 출간되었는데, 당시에 이 책은 진보적인 반(反)노예제 문학으로 간주되었다. 이 소설은 아프리카의 한 왕자가 '문명화된' 영국 노예상인들에게 속아 노예가 되고, 결국 남미의 영국 식민지에서 노예로 살아가게 되는 과정을 따라간다. 그곳에서 그는 이전의 아프리카의 왕에게 죽은 줄로 알았던 연인과 재회하게 되고, 그를 노예로 만든 사람도 그가 왕족이며 고귀한 혈통임을 알아본다. 그러나 결정권은 그를 노예로 만든 사람에게 있지 않고 영국으로 돌아간 총독에게 있다는 말을 거듭해서 들은 후에, 그 자신과 연인이 자유를 얻는 것은 불가능한 것으로 드러난다. 그래서 이야기 줄거리는 비극적이고 괴상한 결말로 이어지며, 독자에게 노예 거래의 도덕성과 합리성에 대해 의문을 품게 한다.

다음 중 아프라 벤의 소설에 들어 있지 않은 것은?
① 오루노코가 어떻게 노예가 되어 결국에는 남미에 가게 되었는지
② 오루노코가 어디에서 우연히 다시 연인을 만났는지

③ 오루노코가 자신뿐만 아니라 연인의 자유를 되찾기 위해 어떻게 노력했는지
④ 오루노코가 어디서 총독을 만나 자유를 얻었는지

27 내용일치 ③

| 분석 |
낸시 행크스는 직접 트레마톨을 섭취한 것이 아니라 트레마톨이 들어 있는 서양등골나물을 뜯어 먹은 소의 우유를 마심으로써 간접적으로 중독되었다. 그러므로 ③이 정답이다. ② 메스꺼움이 어지럼증을 말하고, 비정상적인 혈액 산성도가 체내의 화학적 불균형을 말한다.

| 어휘 |
innocuous a. 해가 없는, 무해한 **flat-topped** a. 끝부분이 평평한 **toxic** a. 독성의, 유독한 **ingest** v. (음식 등을) 섭취하다 **poison** v. 중독시키다 **graze** v. (풀을) 뜯어먹다 **livestock** n. 가축 **toxin** n. 독소 **appetite** n. 식욕; 욕망 **nausea** n. 메스꺼움, 구역질 **abdominal** a. 배의, 복부의 **redden** v. 붉어지다, 붉게 만들다 **tongue** n. 혀 **abnormal** a. 보통과 다른, 정상이 아닌 **acidity** n. 신 맛; 산도(酸度) **pasture** n. 목초지, 방목장

| 해석 |
겉보기에는 아무런 해가 없어 보이는 식물인 서양등골나물은 에이브러햄 링컨(Abraham Lincoln)의 어머니인 낸시 행크스(Nancy Hanks)의 목숨을 앗아갔다. 서양등골나물은 북아메리카산 초본으로, 납작한 꼭대기에 작은 흰 꽃들이 무리를 이루어 피며, 트레마톨(trematol)이라는 독성 알코올이 들어 있다. 치명적인 식물들을 직접 섭취하고 죽은 사람들과 달리, 낸시 행크스는 불운하게도 그 식물을 뜯어 먹은 소의 우유를 마셨을 뿐인데도 중독되었다. 실제로, 중독된 가축의 고기와 우유 모두 독소를 인간에게 전달할 수 있다. "우유 중독"의 증상에는 식욕 감퇴, 메스꺼움, 무기력, 복부 불쾌감, 혀 붉어짐, 비정상적인 혈액 산성도, 그리고 사망이 포함된다. 다행히도, 농부들은 이제 생명을 위협하는 이런 위험을 알고 있어서 가축이 있는 목장에서 그 식물을 제거하려 노력하고 있다.

다음 중 옳지 않은 것은?
① 서양등골나물 속의 독소는 중독된 가축의 고기나 우유를 통해 인간에게 전해질 수 있다.
② "우유 중독"이 되면 어지럼증과 체내의 화학적 불균형을 유발할 수 있다.
③ 낸시 행크스는 소량의 농축된 트레마톨을 섭취했고, 그것이 그녀의 죽음으로 이어졌다.
④ 농부들은 가축이 서양등골나물에 노출되지 않도록 조치를 취하고 있다.

28 내용추론 ④

| 분석 |
낭만주의 운동은 육식과 양립할 수 없었고 『프랑켄슈타인』의 저자 메리 셸리(Mary Shelley)도 고기를 멀리 했는데, 그녀가 쓴 작품 속의 괴물이 채식주의를 실천한 것은 낭만주의의 이상을 반영하는 것이라 할 수 있다. ② 문학작품이 비유적으로 비판하는 것은 간접적인 비판이다.

| 어휘 |
term n. 용어 **vegetarian** n. 채식주의자 **appreciation** n. (가치 등에 대한) 이해; 감상, 음미 **intellectual** n. 지식인 **incompatible with** ~와 양립할 수 없는, 맞지 않는 **manifesto** n. 선언문, 성명서 **adaptation** n. 각색, 개작(改作) **corpse** n. 시체, 송장 **specify** v. (구체적으로) 명시하다, 분명히 밝히다 **dissecting room** 해부실 **slaughterhouse** n. (가축) 도축[도살]장 **terrifying** a. 무서운, 끔찍한 **embrace** v. 받아들이다, 포용하다 **vegetarianism** n. 채식주의 **lamb** n. 새끼 양 **kid** n. 새끼 염소 **glut** v. 배불리 먹이다; (욕망을) 채우다 **acorn** n. 도토리 **afford** v. ~을 제공하다, ~할 여유가 되다 **sufficient** a. 충분한 **nourishment** n. 영양; 음식물

| 해석 |
낭만주의 시대가 시작될 무렵에는 "채식주의자"라는 용어가 존재하지 않음에도 불구하고, 그 시대의 많은 문인(文人)들은 고기를 먹지 않는 식단을 따랐다. 낭만주의 운동의 특징적인 사상 중 하나는 자연의 아름다움을 깊이 음미하는 것이었으며, 많은 낭만주의 지식인들에게 이것은 육식과 양립할 수 없었다. 『프랑켄슈타인』의 저자 메리 셸리(Mary Shelley)는 고기가 없는 식사를 했고, 그 책 자체도 일종의 채식주의 선언문처럼 읽을 수 있다. 만약 당신이 영화로 각색된 프랑켄슈타인 이야기에 익숙하다면, 괴물이 사람 시체의 여러 부위를 이용해서 만들어진다는 것을 기억할 것이다. 하지만 원작에서는 괴물의 신체 부위가 해부실뿐만 아니라 그녀가 똑같이 무섭게 여겼음에 틀림없는 장소인 도살장에서도 가져온 것이라고 셸리는 명시하고 있다. 자신이 탄생한 환경은 끔찍하지만, 괴물은 자연과 조화롭게 살아가며 많은 낭만주의 지식인들처럼 채식주의를 받아들인다. 괴물은 이렇게 말한다. "나는 내 식욕을 채우기 위해 새끼 양이나 새끼 염소를 죽이지 않는다. 도토리와 야생딸기가 나에게 충분한 영양을 주기 때문이지."

위 글에서 추론할 수 있는 것은?
① 셸리는 육식을 존중받아야 하는 삶의 자연스러운 일부로 여겼다.
② 괴물이 자연과 조화를 이루는 모습은 산업화에 대한 직접적인 비판이다.
③ 괴물의 창조에 대한 셸리의 묘사는 생체 해부에 대한 그녀의 반감을 강조한다.
④ 괴물의 채식주의는 자연과의 조화라는 낭만주의의 이상을 반영한다.

29 내용파악　②

| 분석 |
많은 사람들이 "블랙 프라이데이"라는 용어가 기업들이 적자에서 벗어나 흑자로 전환되는 날이기 때문에 그렇게 불린다고 믿고 있지만 이는 사실이 아니며, 필라델피아 경찰이 대규모 쇼핑 인파로 인한 혼란을 묘사하기 위해 블랙 프라이데이라는 표현을 사용한 것이 기원임을 밝히고 있다. 그러므로 ②가 옳지 않은 진술이다.

| 어휘 |
refer A to B A를 B라고 부르다　**lure** v. 유혹하다, 꾀다　**derive** v. ~에서 유래하다　**in the red** 적자인, 재정적으로 손해를 보고 있는　**massive** a. 거대한, 엄청난　**in the black** 흑자인, 수익을 내고 있는　**term** n. 용어, 말　**date back to** ~까지 거슬러 올라가다　**chaos** n. 혼란, 무질서　**suburban** a. 교외의　**traffic jam** 교통 체증　**shoplifting** n. 들치기, 상점에서 훔치기　**take root** 뿌리내리다, 정착하다　**merchant** n. 상인, (특히 대규모) 판매업자

| 해석 |
흔히 블랙 프라이데이라고 불리는 추수감사절 다음날은 미국에서 쇼핑으로 가장 바쁜 날 중의 하나로 자리 잡았다. 전국의 체인점들은 쇼핑객을 상점으로 끌어들이기 위해 다양한 상품의 제한된 수량에 한해 할인 특가를 제공하는 전통이 있다. 많은 사람들은 블랙 프라이데이라는 용어가 사업체들이 재정적 손실을 겪으면서, 즉 "적자 상태에서" 운영되고 있다가 추수감사절 다음날에 매출을 크게 올린 덕분에 마침내 이익을 내게 된다. 즉 "흑자 상태로" 돌아서게 된다는 개념에서 유래했다고 믿고 있다. 그러나 이것은 사실이 아니다. 그 용어에 대한 보다 정확한 설명은 1960년대 초로 거슬러 올라가는데, 당시에 필라델피아의 경찰들은 많은 교외 관광객들이 휴일 쇼핑을 시작하기 위해 그 도시로 몰려들어서 발생한 혼란을 묘사하기 위해 블랙 프라이데이라는 표현을 사용하기 시작했다. 거대한 인파는 경찰에게 큰 골칫거리가 되었고, 경찰은 교통 체증, 사고, 좀도둑질 및 기타 문제들을 처리하기 위해 평소보다 더 긴 근무시간을 보내야 했다. 몇 년이 지나자 그 용어는 필라델피아에 뿌리를 내리게 되었고, 도시의 상인들은 이 날의 부정적인 이미지를 개선하기 위해 "빅 프라이데이(Big Friday)"라고 부르려는 시도를 했다

다음 중 블랙 프라이데이에 대해 옳지 않은 것은?
① 블랙 프라이데이의 부정적인 이미지는 거대한 인파와 광란의 쇼핑에서 비롯되었다.
② 블랙 프라이데이는 원래 쇼핑 성수기 이전에 기업들이 처해 있던 재정적 손실을 의미하는 말이었다.
③ 경찰은 쇼핑객들로 인한 혼란을 묘사하기 위해 블랙 프라이데이라는 용어를 만들었다.
④ 상인들은 블랙 프라이데이의 이미지를 개선하기 위해 빅 프라이데이라는 이름으로 이미지 변화를 꾀했다.

30 글의 요지　②

| 분석 |
"우리는 흔히 극지방의 바다는 생명체가 살기 매우 힘든 환경이라고 생각하지만, 이것은 인간의 관점에서 보는 경우에만 그러하며, 그곳에서 적응해서 살아가고 있는 동물들에게는 오히려 자연스러운 환경이라는 점"을 이야기하고 있는 내용이므로, 글의 요지로는 ②가 적절하다.

| 어휘 |
polar a. 극지방의　**envisage** v. 마음속에 그리다, 상상하다　**hostile** a. 적대적인, 강력히 반대[거부]하는　**factor** n. 요인, 요소　**inhabitant** n. 거주자, 서식 생물　**viewpoint** n. 관점, 견해　**adapt** v. 적응하다　**harsh** a. 가혹한, 혹독한　**sturgeon** n. 철갑상어　**coral reef** 산호초　**cod** n. 〈어류〉 대구　**evolve** v. 진화하다, 전개되다　**habitat** n. 서식지

| 해석 |
극지방의 바다를 생각할 때, 우리는 항상 매우 적대적인 환경을 떠올리는데, 이는 주로 두 가지 요인, 즉 추운 기온과 극심한 폭풍이 몰아치는 거친 날씨 때문이다. 그 때문에 우리는 그곳에서 사는 것이 서식하고 있는 동물들에게도 틀림없이 매우 힘들 거라고 항상 생각한다. 그러나 우리는 크게 잘못 생각하고 있는 것이다. 이러한 상황에서 우리는 인간의 관점을 적용하고 있으며, 실제로 극지방에서 인간이 생활하는 것은 매우 어려운 일이다. 왜냐하면 인간은 그곳에서 진화하지 않았고 그러한 혹독한 환경에 적응돼 있지 않기 때문이다. 하지만 극지방에 서식하고 있는 동물들에게는 그곳에서 사는 것이 철갑상어가 산호초 주위를 헤엄치는 것만큼이나 쉬운 일이다. 만약 그 철갑상어를 잡아서 극지방의 바다에 풀어놓는다면, 그것은 얼마 지나지 않아 추위로 인해 죽을 것이다. 그러나 만약 극지방의 대구를 8℃ 물에 풀어놓으면, 이번에는 열 충격으로 인해 마찬가지로 죽을 것이다. 온혈 동물이든 냉혈 동물이든, 모든 동물은 그 서식지를 자신의 것으로 만들도록 진화해왔다.

위 글의 요지로 적절한 것은?
① 인간에게 적대적인 극지방의 환경은 가까운 미래에 개선될 수도 있다.
② 우리의 일반적인 생각과는 달리, 극지방의 바다 동물들에게 살아가는 것은 실제로 그리 어렵지 않다.
③ 극지방의 바다는 매우 생산적이며, 높은 밀도의 방대한 생물군을 먹여 살리고 있다.
④ 생리학적으로 볼 때, 온혈 해양 동물과 냉혈 해양 동물 사이에는 큰 차이가 없다.

31~32

동물 행동에 대한 과학적 연구는 흔히 ethology(행동생물학)이라 불리는데, 이 용어는 19세기에 프랑스의 한 동물학

자가 처음 사용했다. ethology는 "성격"을 의미하는 그리스어 ethos에서 유래했다. "윤리(ethics)"라는 단어도 같은 그리스어에서 파생했는데, 근본적으로 윤리는 인간이 어떻게 행동해야 하는지에 관한 것이므로 이것은 이해가 된다. 안타깝게도, ethology라는 단어는 공통점이 전혀 없는 ethnology(민족학)라는 단어와 종종 혼동되곤 한다. 〈사실, 우리가 이 책을 쓰는 데 사용하고 있는 워드 프로세서조차도 "ethology"를 "ethnology"로 바꾸라고 계속 알림을 띄우고 있다.〉 이 이름을 지니고 있는 동물 행동 관련 학술지가 여전히 활발히 발간되고 있지만, 어떤 이유에서든, "ethology"는 예전만큼 자주 사용되지 않는다. 현재는 많은 저자들이 동물 행동에 대한 과학적 연구를 지칭할 때 "ethology" 대신, "animal behavior(동물 행동)" 혹은 "behavioral biology(행동 생물학)"라는 단어를 사용하고 있다. 어쨌든, 과학자들 (그리고 아마추어들)은 "ethology"라는 단어가 등장하기 훨씬 이전부터 동물의 행동을 연구해 왔었다. 예를 들어, 아리스토텔레스는 동물의 행동에 대해 매우 흥미로운 관찰 결과를 많이 남겼다. 그러나 동물 행동에 관한 연구는 19세기 초를 전후하여 독일과 영국의 동물학자들에 의해 보다 체계적으로 이루어졌다.

| 어휘 |

ethology n. 동물행동학 **term** n. 용어 **derive** v. 유래하다, 파생되다 **ethos** n. 정신, 기풍 **ethics** n. 윤리, 윤리학 **ethnology** n. 민족학, 인종학 **prompt** v. 촉발하다, 자극하다; (컴퓨터에서) 알림을 띄우다 **replace** v. 대체하다 **observation** n. 관찰, 관찰결과

31 내용일치 ④

| 분석 |

ethology는 "성격"을 의미하는 그리스어 ethos에서 유래했으며 "윤리(ethics)"라는 단어도 같은 그리스어에서 파생했다고 했으므로 ④가 정답으로 적절하다. ② 예전만큼 자주 쓰이지 않는다고만 했으며, 이 이름을 지닌 학술지도 존재한다고 했다.

다음 중 옳은 것은?
① 우리는 다양한 문맥에서 ethnology를 ethics로 바꿔 쓸 수 있다.
② 오늘날 학계에서는 더 이상 ethology라는 용어를 동물 행동을 지칭하는 데 사용하지 않는다.
③ ethology와 ethnology는 의미에서 많은 공통점을 가지고 있다.
④ ethology와 ethics는 모두 같은 그리스어 단어에서 유래했다.

32 문장삽입 ②

| 분석 |

주어진 문장은 "사실, 우리가 이 책을 쓰는 데 사용하고 있는 워드 프로세서조차도 'ethology'를 'ethnology'로 바꾸라고 계속 알림을 띄우고 있다."라는 의미로, ethology와 ethnology를 혼동하는 문제에 대한 구체적인 사례에 해당한다. 따라서 ethology와 ethnology가 혼동된다는 내용이 언급된 다음인 ⑧에 들어가는 것이 자연스럽다.

33~34

대개 예술가는 이미 만들어진 부품들을 가지고 작업하지 않으며 자체적인 형태가 거의 혹은 전혀 없는 재료들을 가지고 작업한다. 창작의 과정은 예술가가 가진 일련의 긴 상상력의 도약과 그 상상력에 형태를 부여하기 위해 그에 맞게 재료를 다듬으려는 예술가의 시도들로 이루어져 있다. 손은 상상력의 명령을 수행하려 하면서 희망을 담아 붓질을 시도하지만, 결과는 기대했던 것과 매우 다를 수 있다. 이는 부분적으로 예술가의 마음속 이미지가 끊임없이 바뀌고 있기 때문인데, 그로 인해 상상력의 명령 또한 명확할 수 없기 때문이다. 사실, 마음속 이미지는 예술가가 어디엔가 선을 '긋는 순간'에야 비로소 또렷해지기 시작한다. 그때서야 그 선은 이미지의 일부 — 유일하게 고정된 일부 — 가 된다. 아직 태어나지 않은 나머지 이미지들은 여전히 유동적인 상태로 남아 있다. 예술가가 새로운 선을 하나 추가할 때마다, 그 선을 점점 커져가는 마음속 이미지 속에 통합시키기 위한 새로운 상상력의 도약이 필요하다. 만약 그 선이 이미지에 통합되지 않는다면, 예술가는 그것을 무시하고 다른 선을 그린다.

| 어휘 |

consist of ~으로 구성돼 있다 **leap** n. 도약, 급격한 증가 또는 발전 **carry out** 수행하다, 실행하다 **stroke** n. (붓 등의) 한 획, 선 **constantly** ad. 끊임없이, 계속해서 **come into focus** (초점이 맞춰져) 뚜렷해지다, 명확해지다 **fixed** a. 고정된, 변하지 않는 **fluid** a. 유동적인, 변하기 쉬운 **incorporate** v. 포함하다, 통합하다 **disregard** v. 무시하다, 경시하다

33 빈칸완성 ②

| 분석 |

빈칸 뒤의 문장은 빈칸 앞의 문장을 구체적으로 부연하는 역할을 하고 있으므로, 빈칸에는 앞의 내용을 강조하고 확장하려는 경우에 쓰는 표현인 In fact가 들어가는 것이 적절하다.

빈칸에 들어가기에 가장 적절한 것을 고르시오.
① 하지만, 그러나
② 사실은, 실제로는
③ 그 결과로
④ 예를 들어

34 글의 요지   ①

| 분석 |

본문은 "예술가가 미리 정해진 뚜렷한 이미지를 옮기는 게 아니라, 그리면서 이미지가 점점 생겨나고 그때마다 새로운 상상과 조정이 필요하다"는 것을 이야기하고 있다. 즉, 선을 하나 그을 때마다 마음속 이미지도 바뀌고, 바뀐 이미지에 맞게 또 상상하고 조정하고, 마음과 손 사이에서 계속적인 상호작용이 일어나며 작품이 완성된다는 것이다. 이런 과정을 정확히 요약한 것이 ①이다.

위 글의 요지는 무엇인가?
① 예술가는 마음속 상상과 재료 사이의 끊임없는 자극의 흐름을 통해 이미지를 완성한다.
② 예술적 창작은 상상의 도약을 거의 허용하지 않는 정확하게 단계적인 묘사이다.
③ 예술가의 마음속 이미지를 옮기고 투영하는 것은 기쁨과 고통을 모두 수반한다.
④ 우리는 예술 작품을 만드는 것을 손기술이나 기교와 혼동해서는 안 된다.

35~36

미국의 국내외에서, 전시(戰時)는 오랫동안 뜨개질 하는 사람들이 관여해 왔다. 특히 여성들이 전투에 직접 참여하기 이전에는, 그들은 집에서 양말이나 모자처럼 병사들이 사용할 필수 물품을 뜨개질하여 군대를 후원하라는 권유를 받았다. 뜨개질은 매우 흔한 광경이었기 때문에, 아무도 그것을 의심스러운 활동으로 여기지 않았다. 그러나 뜨개질은 역사적으로 첩보 활동과 흥미로운 관련이 있었다. 1차 세계대전 당시, 프랑스 여성 Madam Levengle은 "뜨개질용 실을 장착한 정보원"으로 활동하면서 연합군을 도왔다. 그녀는 창가에 앉아 뜨개질을 하면서 창문 너머로 독일군의 움직임을 관찰하곤 했다. 그런 다음, 바닥에 발을 두드려 자녀들에게 암호를 전달했고, 자녀들은 숙제를 하는 척하며 근처에 있던 독일 장교들의 눈을 피해 그 정보를 기록했다. 2차 세계대전에서도 뜨개질을 하는 사람들이 비밀스러운 역할을 했다. 그처럼 뜨개질을 하며 스파이 활동을 했던 사람들 중 한 명이 바로 영국의 비밀 요원 Phyllis Doyle이었다. 그녀는 1944년 노르망디에 낙하산을 타고 투입되어 독일 병사들과 친근하게 대화를 나누며 협조적인 척 행동했다. 그러나 그때 그녀는 뜨개질을 통해 영국 측에 메시지를 보냈고, 영국은 그것을 모스 부호를 이용해서 해독했다. 암호화된 메시지를 뜨개질하는 것은 일종의 비밀 메시지로, 물리적으로 메시지를 숨기는 방법 중의 하나이다. 겉뜨기와 안뜨기의 특정한 조합이 메시지로 옮겨질 수 있었던 것이다. 뜨개질로 암호를 짜는 것은 의심스러운 활동을 감추기 위해 뜨개질을 이용한 것보다는 덜 일반적이었지만, 뜨개질을 한 암호는 여전히 위협이 되었다. 실제로, 뜨개질이 첩보 활동에서 차지하는 역할은 꽤 컸기 때문에, 미국 검열국에서는 2차 세계대전 기간 동안 뜨개질 도안을 해외로 보내는 것을 금지했다. 이는 그 도안 속에 군사 기밀이 숨겨져 있을 수도 있음을 우려했기 때문이다.

| 어휘 |

knitter n. 뜨개질하는 사람   troop n. (군대의) 병력, 군대; 무리   espionage n. 스파이 행위, 첩보 활동   yarn n. 실, 방적사(뜨개질에 쓰는 실)   informant n. 정보 제공자, 밀고자   the Allies (세계대전 당시의) 연합국   tap v. (가볍게) 두드리다, 발을 구르다   unnoticed a. 눈에 띄지 않는, 주목받지 못한   marshal n. 사령관, 군의 고관   parachute v. 낙하산으로 뛰어내리다   translate v. 번역하다, 해독하다   coded a. 암호화된   steganography n. 스테가노그래피(메시지를 물리적으로 숨기는 기술)   purl v. (뜨개질에서) 안뜨기   stitch n. 바늘땀, (뜨개질 등의) 땀   disguise v. 위장하다, 숨기다   threat n. 위협, 위험 요소   ban v. 금지하다

35 글의 목적   ④

| 분석 |

본문은 뜨개질이 전쟁 중에 직간접적으로 첩보 활동에 이용되었음을 이야기하면서, Madam Levengle과 Phyllis Doyle의 활동 사례를 구체적으로 언급하고 있다.

위 글의 주된 목적은 무엇인가?
① 군인들이 어떻게 뜨개질된 물품을 전시(戰時) 장비의 일부로 사용했는지를 설명하는 것
② 전시에 뜨개질 프로젝트에 참여한 여성들의 삶을 자세히 설명하는 것
③ 전시에 실의 부족으로 인해 뜨개질이 금지된 이유를 설명하는 것
④ 전시에 뜨개질이 어떻게 첩보 활동을 위장하는 수단으로 사용되었는지를 살펴보는 것

36 내용파악   ③

| 분석 |

뜨개질 바늘을 무기로 사용하는 것에 대해서는 전혀 언급하지 않았으므로 ③이 정답이다.

다음 중 뜨개질하는 사람들이 전쟁 수행을 지원한 방식이 아닌 것은?
① 군인들을 위해 양말이나 모자와 같은 필수 물품을 만드는 것
② 특정한 땀을 사용해서 암호화된 메시지를 뜨개질하는 것
③ 뜨개질 바늘을 은닉한 무기로 사용하는 것
④ 적군 부대의 움직임을 감시하고 보고하는 것

37~38

대중에게 개방되고 과학에 기반을 둔 현대 동물원의 전신(前身)은 19세기에 모습을 갖추었다. 유럽 전역에 공공 동물원이 생겨났고, 그 중 많은 곳이 리젠트 파크에 있는 런던 동물원을 본보기로 삼았다. 표면적으로는 품위 있는 오락과 교육을 위한 장소였던 동물원은 크고 무서운 동물들을 전시하는 것을 넘어 파충류관, 조류관, 곤충관 등으로 그 범위를 확장했다. 살아있는 동물들의 전시물은 종종 분류학적 순서에 따라 같은 과(科)에 속한 다양한 종들을 함께 배치하여, 비교 연구할 수 있도록 전시되었다. 최초의 동물원들은 동물들을 간소한 우리의 금속 철창 안에 수용했다. 그러나 동물원이 발전해가던 비교적 초기에, 이국적인 동물을 수입하던 칼 하겐베크(Carl Hagenbeck)라는 이름의 한 업자가 야생동물을 전시하는 방식을 바꾸었다. 1907년 함부르크에 문을 연 그의 동물원에서, 그는 동물들을 표시나지 않게 가둬두기 위해 해자와 정교하게 배치된 바위벽을 이용하여 겉보기에는 우리처럼 보이지 않는 우리를 설계했다. 그는 여러 동물을 한눈에 볼 수 있도록 관람객의 시야에 철창이나 벽이 보이지 않게 우리를 설계함으로써, 포획되어 있다는 사실을 자연 속에 있는 듯한 착각으로 대체한 몰입감 있는 전경을 만들어냈다. 하겐베크의 모델은 널리 영향을 미쳤다. 점점 더, 많은 동물들이 갇혀 있다는 불쾌한 사실이 시각적으로 가려진 채 전시되었다. 동물원은 짐승들에 대한 노골적인 지배의 과시에서 개별 동물에 대한 자비로운 보호의 이야기로 다소 방향을 전환하게 되었다. 이로부터 동물 종(種)을 보호한다는 개념으로 옮겨가는 것은 그리 어려운 일이 아니었다. 이러한 "교육적인 소풍" 모델의 동물원은 20세기 후반까지 이어졌으며, 그때 동물원들은 적극적으로 스스로를 보존 활동에 진지하게 기여하는 기관으로 이미지를 쇄신하기 시작했다. 이 새로운 이야기에 따르면, 동물원의 동물들은 위협받는 야생동물의 예비 개체군으로서의 역할을 할 뿐만 아니라, 자신의 종을 대표하는 대사(大使)로서 인간에게 교육하고 야생 동물에 대한 관심과 보호 의식을 불러일으키는 역할을 한다.

| 어휘 |

forerunner n. 선구자, 전신(前身)   **grounded in** ~에 근거를 둔, ~에 기반한   **spring up** 갑자기 생겨나다, 나타나다   **ostensibly** ad. 표면상으로는, 겉보기에는   **genteel** a. 품위 있는; 고상한, 상류 사회의   **edification** n. 교화, 계몽   **expand** v. 확장되다, 늘어나다   **reptile** n. 파충류   **aviary** n. 새장, 조류 사육장   **insectarium** n. 곤충 전시관   **taxonomic** a. 분류학적인   **species** n. 종(種), 종류   **house** v. ~을 수용하다, 보관하다   **spartan** a. 검소한, 엄격한, 꾸밈없는   **relatively** ad. 상대적으로   **exotic** a. 이국적인, 외래의   **exhibit** v. 전시[전람]하다   **invisibly** ad. 눈에 띄지 않게, 보이지 않게   **pen** v. 가두다   **enclosure** n. 우리, 울타리 친 공간   **immersive** a. 몰입감 있는, 몰입형의   **captivity** n. 포획 상태, 감금   **supplant** v. 대신하다, 대체하다   **illusion** n. 환상, 착각   **influential** a. 영향력 있는   **distasteful** a. 불쾌한, 유쾌하지 않은   **imprisonment** n. 감금, 투옥   **elide** v. 생략하다, 무시하다   **overt** a. 명백한, 공공연한   **benevolent** a. 자비로운, 친절한   **day out** 소풍   **rebrand** v. 새로운 이미지를 만들다, 다시 브랜딩하다   **conservation** n. 보존, 보호   **threat** n. 위협   **ambassador** n. 대사; (특정 목적을 위한) 대표자

37   글의 제목   ①

| 분석 |

본문은 동물원이 단순히 동물을 철창 안에 가둬놓던 초기 형태에서 점차 자연을 닮은 공간으로 바뀌었음을 이야기하면서, 그 과정에서 동물의 전시 방식과 동물원 자체의 목적이 어떻게 변해왔는지를 설명하고 있다. 즉, 동물원의 설계와 그 이면에 있는 철학의 진화가 중심 주제이므로, 글의 제목으로는 ①이 적절하다.

위 글의 제목으로 가장 적절한 것은?
① 철창에서 자연으로: 동물원 설계의 진화
② 과학과 교육에서 동물원의 역할 이해하기
③ 동물원의 야생동물: 윤리인가, 수익인가?
④ 동물원의 보존 노력

38   내용파악   ③

| 분석 |

칼 하겐베크가 철창 대신 해자나 바위벽 등을 이용하여 표시나지 않게 동물을 가두는 방식을 개발했다고 나와 있으며, 이 방식이 동물원 디자인의 중요한 혁신이 되었다고 설명하고 있다. 그러므로 ③이 옳은 진술이다. ② 보존은 20세기 후반부터의 변화이다. ④ 20세기 후반에 동물원이 교육적 역할을 포기한 것이 아니라, 보존이라는 역할을 추가로 강조하게 된 것이다.

다음 중 시간의 흐름에 따른 동물원의 발달에 대해 옳은 것은?
① 초기의 공공 동물원은 동물에 대해 자유로운 환상을 만들어주는 것을 우선시했다.
② 동물원은 본래 멸종 위기 종을 보존하고 보존 활동을 촉진하는 데 초점을 맞췄다.
③ 동물원 설계에서 중요한 혁신은 눈에 보이는 우리를 해자와 같은 숨은 장벽으로 대체하는 것이었다.
④ 20세기 후반에 이르러 동물원은 대중 참여를 위한 교육적인 공간으로서의 역할을 포기했다.

39~40

십대에게 그들의 하루에 대해 물어보면, 수업, 과외 활동, 끝없는 숙제들의 긴 목록을 늘어놓는 말을 들을 가능성이 높다. 이런 과중한 스케줄은 종종 눈에 띄는 불안감을 동반

한다. 학생들은 시험 중에 화재경보기를 작동시키거나, 울면서 쓰러지거나, 심지어 시험 중에 기절을 하는 경우도 있다. 남보다 뛰어나야 한다는 끊임없는 압박은 많은 십대들이 수면, 운동, 쉬는 시간과 같은 중요한 것들을 희생하게 만든다. 그래서 13세에서 18세 사이의 십대 중 25% 이상이 진단 가능한 불안 장애에 걸린다는 사실은 놀랄 일이 아니라고 미국 국립정신건강연구소(National Institute of Mental Health)는 말한다. 공식적인 진단을 받지 않은 학생들조차도 힘든 학교생활을 견뎌내는 데 종종 어려움을 겪는다. 수업 사이에 겨우 몇 분만 움직일 수 있는 시간이 주어지고 재충전할 기회도 거의 없다 보니, 시간이 흐름에 따라 우리의 집중력은 점점 떨어진다. 휴식은 건강에 좋지 못한 이런 사이클을 해소할 수 있는 강력한 해독제가 될 수 있다. 연구에 따르면 신체 활동은 신체 건강뿐만 아니라 정신 건강도 증진시키지만, 고등학생 중 단 27%만이 하루 60분의 운동 권장량을 충족시키고 있다. 만약 학교가 짧은 시간이라도 휴식 시간을 할애한다면, 학생들은 스트레스를 풀고 집중력을 높여, 수업에 보다 온전히 참여할 수 있을 것이다. 그것이 가져다주는 혜택은 신체를 움직이는 것을 넘어선다. 심지어 뛰어다니는 것을 선택하지 않는 학생들조차도 잠깐의 정신적 휴식에서 이익을 얻을 수 있을 것이다. 재정비를 위한 짧은 휴식은 학생들로 하여금 재충전된 기분을 느끼게 하고 학업에서의 난제들에 달려들 준비가 되도록 해줄 수 있다. 〈게다가, 의무적인 자유시간은 십대들이 지루해하고 "완전히 바꿀" 필요가 있다고 생각하는 경우에 교내에서 더 많은 문제를 초래할 수도 있다.〉 휴식은 또한 공식적인 교실 환경에서는 항상 일어나지 않는 사회적, 감정적 관계를 촉진한다. 이것은 스트레스를 날려버리고, 힘든 수업으로부터 (에너지를) 회복하며, 교우들과 교류할 수 있는 기회가 되는데, 이 모든 것들은 정신 건강에 매우 중요한 것들이다. 휴식은 어린 아이들만의 특권이어서는 안 된다. 십대들도 자신의 정신 건강을 우선시할 똑같은 기회를 가질 자격이 있다. 결국 학교에서의 성공은 단순히 학업에 관한 것이 아니며, 건강하고 균형 잡힌 삶을 추구하는 것에 관한 것이기도 하다.

| 어휘 |

extracurricular n. (정규 교과 외의) 과외 활동 **faint** v. 기절하다, 졸도하다 **relentless** a. 끊임없는, 수그러들지 않는 **downtime** n. (기계, 공장의) 비가동 시간 **develop** v. (병 등을) 앓게 되다, 발병하다 **diagnosable** a. 진단 가능한 **grueling** a. 몹시 힘든, 녹초로 만드는 **shuffle** v. (발을 질질 끌며) 걷다; (어디로) 급히 움직이다 **dwindle** v. 점점 줄어들다, 감소하다 **recess** n. 휴식 **antidote** n. 해결책, 해독제 **meet** v. (기준·요구 등을) 충족시키다 **dedicate** v. 바치다; 봉납하다 **relieve** v. 완화하다, 덜어주다 **regroup** v. 재조직하다, 재편성하다 **tackle** v. (문제 등에) 맞서다, 해결하려 하다 **mandatory** a. 의무적인, 강제적인 **shake things up** 완전히 바꾸다, 변화를 주다 **blow off steam** 스트레스를 해소하다 **recuperate** v. 회복하다

기운을 되찾다 **demanding** a. (일 등이) 힘든, 요구가 많은 **peer** n. 또래, 동료 **exclusive** a. 독점적인 **deserve** v. ~을 받을 자격이 있다, ~할 만하다

39 글의 흐름상 적절하지 않은 표현 고르기   ②

| 분석 |

본문은 십대들이 겪는 학업 스트레스와 정신 건강 문제를 지적하고, 휴식 시간을 통해 이를 완화할 수 있다고 주장하는 글인데 반해, ⑧는 "의무적인 자유 시간이 오히려 문제를 일으킬 수 있다"는 반대되는 주장을 포함하고 있어서 글의 논지를 흐리고 있다.

40 내용추론   ②

| 분석 |

글 전체의 핵심 메시지는 "학교에서 학업만 강조할 것이 아니라 정신 건강과 균형 잡힌 삶도 중요하게 여겨야 한다"는 것이다. 이에 대해 마지막 문장에서도, "성공은 단지 학업적인 것만이 아니라 건강하고 균형 잡힌 삶을 키우는 것이다."라고 말하며 균형의 중요성을 강조하고 있다. 따라서 ②가 정답으로 적절하다.

십대들의 정신 건강에 대한 저자의 관점에 관해 추론할 수 있는 것은?
① 십대들의 정신 건강 문제는 과장되었다.
② 학교는 정신 건강과 학업 사이의 균형을 맞추는 데 보다 집중해야 한다.
③ 신체 활동은 스트레스 완화에 있어 부수적인 요인이다.
④ 학생들은 학업의 압박을 스스로 처리하여 극복하는 법을 배워야 한다.

KONKUK UNIVERSITY | 건국대학교 인문·예체능계 B형

TEST p. 62~78

01	③	02	③	03	②	04	③	05	⑤	06	④	07	③	08	②	09	②	10	⑤
11	②	12	⑤	13	②	14	④	15	①	16	②	17	②	18	④	19	④	20	⑤
21	④	22	⑤	23	②	24	③	25	②	26	③	27	⑤	28	④	29	④	30	④
31	③	32	③	33	①	34	③	35	①	36	③	37	②	38	④	39	③	40	④

01 동의어 ③

| 어휘 |

geographical a. 지리학의, 지리적인 **aberration** n. 일탈, 정도(正道)에서 벗어남(= deviation) **indistinguishable** a. 분간[구별]할 수 없는 **expediency** n. 편의, 형편이 좋음; 편법 **equilibrium** n. 평형상태, 균형 **deterioration** n. 악화, (질의) 저하 **hallucination** n. 환각, 환상

| 해석 |

그래시안(Grassian)은 커플랜드(Coupland)가 캐나다인이라는 점을 인정하지만, 그는 이처럼 지리적으로 벗어나 있음에도 불구하고 커플랜드의 글은 미국 소설과 거의 구별이 되지 않는 것 같다고 주장한다.

02 동의어 ③

| 어휘 |

slavery n. 노예제도 **norm** n. 표준; 규범, 규준 **overt** a. 명백한, 공공연한 **eradicate** v. 박멸하다, 근절하다(= abolish) **manifest** v. 명백히 하다; 명시하다; (기계를) 복잡[정교]하게 하다 **sophisticate** v. 세파에 닳고 닳게 하다; **exemplify** v. 예증하다, 예시하다; 구현하다 **revitalize** v. 소생시키다

| 해석 |

노예 제도는 유사 이래로 많은 사회에서 표준적인 것이었지만, 현대 세계에서는 적어도 공공연한 형태로는 세계의 거의 모든 지역에서 근절되었다.

03 동의어 ②

| 어휘 |

quote v. 인용하다; 구체적 실례·증거로서 내놓다 **exact** a. 정확한, 엄밀한 **statistics** n. 통계; 통계학 **offhand** ad. 당장에, 즉석에서; 아무런 준비 없이(= immediately) **interestingly** ad. 흥미 있게, 재미있게 **insolently** ad. 거만하게, 무례하게 **invariably** ad. 변함없이 **inevitably** ad. 불가피하게

| 해석 |

내가 정확한 통계를 당신에게 당장 제시할 수는 없지만, 정확한 통계는 당신이 볼 수 있게 보고서에 나와 있다.

04 동의어 ③

| 어휘 |

supplant v. 밀어내다; (책략 따위를 써서) 대신 들어앉다; ~에 대신하다(= replace) **affection** n. 애정 **stimulate** v. 자극하다; 격려하다, 고무하다 **repel** v. 쫓아버리다, 격퇴하다 **supervise** v. 관리하다, 지휘하다, 감독하다 **supply** v. 공급하다, 지급하다

| 해석 |

어린아이들은 새로운 남동생이나 여동생이 태어날 때 부모의 사랑에서 밀려났다고 느끼는 경우가 종종 있을 수 있다.

05 논리완성 ⑤

| 분석 |

'to be attracted by or to move in the direction of something or someone'을 사전적 의미로 가진 단어를 찾는 문제이며, 따라서 ⑤가 정답이다.

| 어휘 |

attract v. (주의·흥미 등을) 끌다, (사물을) 끌어당기다; ~의 마음을 끌다, 매혹하다 **garnish** v. 장식하다 **gulp** v. 꿀꺽꿀꺽 마시다; 삼켜버리다; (이야기 등을) 그대로 받아들이다 **guide** v. 안내하다, 인도하다 **generate** v. 낳다, 산출하다; (전기·열 등을) 발생시키다 **gravitate** v. 인력에 끌리다, (~에) 강하게 끌리다

| 해석 |
끌린다는 것은 무언가 혹은 누군가에 의해 끌어당겨지거나 그 방향으로 움직이는 것을 의미한다.

06 논리완성 ④

| 분석 |
'to be a perfect example of a quality or type of thing'을 사전적 의미로 가진 단어를 찾는 문제이며, 따라서 ④가 정답이다.

| 어휘 |
exonerate v. ~의 결백을[무죄를] 증명하다; ~의 혐의를 벗겨주다 exhibit v. 전시[전람]하다, 진열하다 eject v. 몰아내다, 쫓아내다 epitomize v. ~을 집약적으로 보이다, ~의 전형이다 equalize v. 등등하게 하다, 같게 하다

| 해석 |
전형이 된다는 것은 사물의 특성이나 유형의 완벽한 예가 되는 것을 의미한다.

07 논리완성 ③

| 분석 |
독일이 원자폭탄을 만들지 않을 것임을 미리 알았더라면 아인슈타인은 미국의 원자폭탄 개발에도 도움을 주지 않았을 것이라는 맥락이다. 그러므로 '~에 신빙성을 부여하다, 힘을 실어주다'라는 의미의 표현을 완성시키는 ③이 정답이 된다. 그 대의명분을 더욱 유명해지게 하기보다 더욱 신뢰할 만한 것이 되게 하는 것이므로 fame보다는 credibility가 더 적절하다.

| 어휘 |
state v. 진술하다, 주장하다, 말하다 cause n. 주의, 주장, 대의명분 proponent n. 제안자; 지지자 in advance 미리, 사전에 empathy n. 감정이입, 공감 fame n. 명성, 평판 credibility n. 진실성; 신뢰성, 신용 lend weight[credence, credibility] to ~에 신빙성을 부여하다, 힘을 실어주다 conscience n. 양심, 도덕관념 decree n. 법령

| 해석 |
앨버트 아인슈타인은 독일인들이 원자폭탄을 개발하지 않을 것임을 자신이 미리 알았더라면, 원자폭탄 제조를 옹호하는 사람들의 대의명분에 힘을 실어주지 않았을 것이라고 말했다.

08 논리완성 ②

| 분석 |
석유가 매우 작은 해양 생물의 잔해로 구성되어 있다는 말에는 석유 또한 유기물질이라는 의미가 내포돼 있다. 따라서 화학자는 석유로부터 유기화합물을 추출하거나 만들어내는 일을 할 것이라 유추할 수 있으므로, 빈칸에는 ②가 들어가는 것이 가장 자연스럽다.

| 어휘 |
chemist n. 화학자 organic a. 유기체의, 유기의 compound n. 합성물, 화합물 petroleum n. 석유 be composed of ~로 구성되어 있다 microscopic a. 현미경적인, 극히 작은 construe v. 해석하다 synthesize v. 종합하다, 합성하다 moderate v. 완화하다, 경감하다 quantify v. 양을 재다 embody v. 구체화하다

| 해석 |
화학자들은 석유로부터 많은 유기 화합물을 합성하는데, 석유는 매우 작은 해양 생물의 잔해로 이루어져 있다.

09 논리완성 ②

| 분석 |
조화를 이루는 삶과 책임감을 강조하는 사회에서는 '싸움, 괴롭힘, 다른 사람들을 앞서려고 하는 것'은 필연적으로 '질책'이나 '비난'을 받게 될 것이다.

| 어휘 |
institution n. 협회; 제도, 관습 emphasize v. 강조하다; 역설하다 self-sacrificing a. 자기희생적인 bullying n. 약자를 괴롭히기, 왕따시키기 surpass v. ~보다 낫다, 능가하다 automatic a. 자동적인, 필연적인 requisite n. 필수품, 필요조건 rebuke n. 비난, 힐책 remission n. 용서; 완화, 진정 reception n. 받아들임; 수용 recount n. 다시 세기, 재개표

| 해석 |
애리조나의 호피(Hopi)족은 가족제도와 종교제도를 중시한다. 그들은 자기희생적인 개인을 이상으로 삼는 조화로운 삶을 강조한다. 호피족의 개인은 호피족이 스스로를 일컫는 용어인 '평화로운 사람들'에 대한 그리고 이들을 위한 책임감을 느끼도록 훈련받는다. 싸움, 괴롭힘, 그리고 다른 사람들을 앞서려고 하는 것은 공동체로부터의 필연적인 질책을 초래한다.

10 논리완성 ⑤

| 분석 |
믿고 있는 바가 서로 충돌하는 상황은 인식이나 인지의 '불일치' 혹은 '부조화'를 초래할 것이다.

| 어휘 |
induce v. 야기하다, 유발하다 cognitive a. 인식의 tranquility n. 고요, 평온 justification n. 정당화, 변명 distillation n. 증류 suppression n. 억압; 감추기, 은폐 dissonance n. 불일치, 부조화

| 해석 |
여러 믿음은 서로 일치할 수도 있고 충돌할 수도 있다. 믿음이 충돌할 때, 이는 인지 부조화라고 불리는 불쾌한 상태를 유발하며, 사람은 인지 부조화를 줄이려고 노력한다.

11 논리완성 ②

| 분석 |
자율적인 행동주체는 스스로의 원칙에 따라 어떤 일을 하거나 자기 스스로를 통제하여 절제할 것이므로, 이런 행동주체는 어떤 제약에 의해 구속을 받아선 안 된다고 여겨질 것이다. 따라서 ②가 정답이다. 국가의 제약이 개인에게 가져올 결과로는 '구속'이나 '속박'이 적절하다는 식으로 접근하는 것도 가능하다.

| 어휘 |
anarchist n. 무정부주의자 **autonomous** a. 자치의, 자주적인, 자율의 **agent** n. 행위자, 행동자 **restriction** n. 제한, 한정 **emancipate** v. (노예 등을) 해방하다 **constrain** v. 속박하다, 구속하다 **deceive** v. 속이다, 기만하다 **circumvent** v. 회피하다, 우회하다 **fascinate** v. 매혹시키다, 황홀케 하다

| 해석 |
무정부주의자들은 사람들은 자율적인 행동주체이기 때문에 사람들이 국가의 제약에 의해 구속 받도록 해서는 안 된다고 믿고 있다.

12 논리완성 ⑤

| 분석 |
once는 현재와 대조되는 과거를 나타내는 표현이다. 지금 가능하게 되었다는 것은 이전에는 그렇지 않았다는 것이며, 따라서 빈칸에는 possible과 상반되는 의미를 가진 표현이 들어가야 할 것이므로 ⑤가 정답으로 적절하다.

| 어휘 |
advent n. 도래(到來), 출현 **three-dimensional** a. 3차원의 **fabrication** n. 제작, 꾸밈, 날조 **complicated** a. 복잡한, 뒤얽힌 **component** n. 성분, 구성요소; 부품 **negligible** a. 무시해도 좋은, 하찮은 **ambiguous** a. 애매모호한, 분명치 않은 **lucid** a. 명료한, 알기 쉬운 **illusive** a. 착각의, 사람의 눈을 속이는 **implausible** a. 받아들이기 어려운, 믿기 어려운, 타당해 보이지 않는

| 해석 |
3D 프린팅의 도래는 한때는 불가능해 보였던 복잡한 플라스틱 부품의 제작을 많은 개인과 회사들에게 가능하게 해주었다.

13 논리완성 ②

| 분석 |
"세계에서 가장 비싼 몇몇 집들이 뉴욕시에 있기도 한 반면, 그 바로 바깥 길거리에는 집이 없는 가난한 사람들이 있다.", "레스토랑에서 한 끼 식사에 수백 달러를 지불할 수도 있고, 혹은 노점상에서 몇 달러로 맛있고 든든한 음식을 먹을 수도 있다."는 모두 뉴욕이 보여주는 '대비되는' 측면에 대한 예에 해당한다.

| 어휘 |
reputation n. 평판, 명성 **hoot** v. (기적·사이렌·자동차 경적 등이) (빵빵) 울리다 **weave** v. 이리저리 빠져 나가다, 누비며 가다 **enormous** a. 거대한, 막대한 **pavement** n. 포장도로 **vendor** n. 행상인, 노점상인 **digression** n. 본제를 벗어나서 지엽으로 흐름, 여담, 탈선 **contrast** n. 대조, 대비 **harmony** n. 조화, 화합, 일치 **opportunity** n. 기회 **enjoyment** n. 즐거움, 기쁨

| 해석 |
뉴욕은 큰 흥분감이 있으며 '잠들지 않는 도시'인 것으로 유명하다. 때때로 'The Big Apple'로 불리는 이 도시는 살아있고 빠르며 모든 것의 중심에 있다는 느낌이 드는데, 차들이 경적을 울리고, 노란 택시들이 차량들 사이를 헤집고 지나가며, 극장은 환하게 불을 밝히고 있고, 레스토랑은 밤늦게까지 분주하기 때문이다. 이 도시는 엄청난 대조를 보여준다. 세계에서 가장 비싼 몇몇 집들이 뉴욕시에 있기도 하지만, 그 바로 바깥 길거리에는 집이 없는 가난한 사람들이 있다. 레스토랑에서 한 끼 식사에 수백 달러를 지불할 수도 있고, 혹은 노점상에서 몇 달러로 맛있고 든든한 음식을 먹을 수도 있다.

14 논리완성 ④

| 분석 |
"수학의 확률 이론이 위험을 제거해 주지는 않았지만, 그것은 우리가 위험을 보다 효과적으로 관리할 수 있게 해준다."라는 내용이 이어지고 있음을 감안하면, 빈칸에는 수학이나 확률과 관련이 깊은 ④가 들어가는 것이 적절하다.

| 어휘 |
encounter v. 우연히 만나다, 맞닥뜨리다 **junction** n. 교차점, 합류점 **pathway** n. 통로, 작은 길 **destination** n. 목적지 **intuition** n. 직관, 직감 **end up with** 결국 ~하게 되다 **suboptimal** a. 최적이 아닌, 차선의 **potent** a. 유력한, 효능 있는 **analyze** v. 분석하다 **shortcut** n. 지름길, 최단 노선 **eliminate** v. 제거하다 **proportion** n. 비율; 조화, 균형 **opportunity** n. 기회 **practice** n. 실행; 실습 **purpose** n. 목적 **number** n. 숫자 **picture** n. 그림

| 해석 |
인생 여정의 모든 단계에서 우리는 먼 곳으로 이어지는 서로 다른 많은 길들이 있는 분기점을 만나게 된다. 각각의 선택은 어느 길이 당신을 목적지로 데려다줄지에 대한 불확실성을 수반한다. 직관을 믿고서 선택을 하는 것은 종종 우리가 차선의 선택을 하는 것으로 끝나게 된다. 불확실성을 숫자로 바꾸는 것은 여러 길을 분석하고 당신의 목적지로 가는 지름길을 찾는 유력한 방법임이 입증되었다. 수학의 확률 이론이 위험을 제거해 주지는 않았지만, 그것은 우리가 위험을 보다 효과적으로 관리할 수 있게 해준다. 전략은 미래가 안고 있는 가능한 시나리오들을 분석한 다음, 그것들 중에 어느 정도의 비율이 성공이나 실패로 이어질지를 알아내는 것이다.

15 논리완성   ①

| 분석 |
'과거의 경험을 통해 문제를 판단하면 필연적으로 잘못된 길로 인도되며, 만약 우리가 항상 생각해온 방식으로 생각한다면, 항상 얻어온 것을 얻게 될 것이다.'라고 했다. 이것을 첫 번째 문장에 적용하면, 가장 가능성이 높은 해결책뿐만 아니라, 그것을 대신할 별로 가능성이 없어 보이는 것들도 빠짐없이 탐구하려는 의지가 필요하다는 결론이 나온다. 따라서 ①이 적절하다.

| 어휘 |
solution n. 해답, 해법 **reproductive** a. 재생의, 재현의 **foster** v. 촉진하다, 조장하다 **rigidity** n. 엄격, 엄정 **be confronted with** ~에 직면하다 **significantly** ad. 상당히, 두드러지게 **interpret** v. 해석하다; 이해하다, 판단하다 **inevitably** ad. 불가피하게, 필연적으로 **astray** a. 길을 잃어; 정도에서 벗어나

| 해석 |
천재성을 나타내는 표시는 가장 가능성이 높은 해결책뿐만 아니라 모든 대안들을 기꺼이 탐구하려는 의지이다. (이전에 썼던 것과 같은 방법을 사용하는) 재생적 사고는 경직성을 초래한다. 우리가 해결한 적이 있는 다른 문제들과 표면적으로는 비슷해 보이지만 사실은 상당히 다른 새로운 문제에 직면했을 때 우리가 자주 실패하는 것도 이런 이유에서이다. 과거의 경험을 통해 문제를 판단하면 필연적으로 잘못된 길로 인도된다. 만약 우리가 항상 생각해온 방식으로 생각한다면, 항상 얻어온 것을 얻게 될 것이다.

① 모든 대안을 탐구하다
② 사소한 결과를 소중히 여기다
③ 타인의 색다른 경험을 존중하다
④ 다른 사람들의 잘못된 해석을 피하다
⑤ 가장 독특한 문제 해결 방식을 고수하다

16 논리완성   ②

| 분석 |
첫 번째 문장에서 성공한 경험에 관해 언급했으므로, 이어지는 문장에서는 성공과 대비되는 보편적인 경험, 즉 실패 혹은 패배의 경험에 대한 내용이 오는 것이 자연스럽다. 이것은 그다음 문장에서 '성공과 실패의 경험은 둘 다 운동선수들의 자신감을 돕거나 해칠 수 있는 피드백을 제공한다.'고 한 것을 통해서도 확인할 수 있다. 그러므로 ②가 정답이다.

| 어휘 |
recall v. 생각해내다, 상기하다 **inevitably** ad. 불가피하게, 필연적으로 **confidence** n. 자신, 확신; 신용, 신뢰 **optimistic** a. 낙관적인 **pessimistic** a. 비관적인

| 해석 |
모든 운동선수들은 큰 경기에서 이겼거나 힘든 상대를 물리쳤던 것을 떠올릴 수 있다. 운동선수들은 또한 필연적으로 좌절과 실패도 경험한다. 성공과 실패의 경험은 둘 다 운동선수들의 자신감에 도움이 되거나 혹은 해칠 수 있는 피드백을 제공한다. 낙관적인 운동선수와 비관적인 운동선수는 그들이 더 쉽게 받아들이는 피드백의 종류가 크게 다르다.

① 다른 선수들의 성공을 부러워하다
② 좌절과 실패를 경험하다
③ 경기 결과를 모두 받아들이다
④ 상대방에 대한 부정적인 태도를 억제하다
⑤ 모든 경기에서 최고의 플레이를 보여주기 위해 노력하다

17 논리완성   ②

| 분석 |
빈칸을 포함하고 있는 문장의 앞에서는 과거에는 사람들이 비만이 되는 것을 막아주는 유전적 압력이 거의 없었다는 것과 그 이유에 대해 이야기하고 있고, 빈칸을 포함하고 있는 문장부터는 비만 관련 돌연변이가 인구 집단 속에 들어 온 현재의 상황에 대해 이야기하고 있다. 전후의 흐름이 대조를 이루므로 빈칸에는 ②가 들어가야 한다. 비만을 막아주는 쪽으로의 유전자 돌연변이는 과거에는 환경이 그것을 필요로 하지 않아 필요가 없었던 반면에, 지금은 비만을 막아주는 쪽으로의 돌연변이가 필요한데도, 그것이 어려운 이유는 돌연변이에 의한 진화에는 시간이 많이 걸리는데 지금은 풍요로운 환경에서 비만 쪽으로의 돌연변이가 인류 집단 안에 자리잡은 지 1세기밖에 안 되어 당장 반대쪽으로의 돌연변이를 기대할 수 없기 때문이라는 것이다.

| 어휘 |
genetic a. 유전의, 유전학적인 **obese** a. 살찐, 비만의 **mutation** n. 돌연변이, 변종 **outlay** n. 비용, 경비, 지출 **reproduce** v. 번식하다 **abundant** a. 풍부한 **incorporate** v. 통합하다; (일부로) 포함하다 **evolutionary** a. 진화의, 점진적인 **timescale** n. 시간의 척도 **approximately** ad. 대략, 얼추 **mammalian** a. 포유류의 **tweak** v. 비틀다; (기계·시스템 등을 약간) 수정[변경]하다

| 해석 |
과거에는 사람들이 비만이 되는 것을 막아주는 유전적 압력이 거의 없었다. 사람들로 하여금 더 적은 열량을 섭취하게 하는 유전자 돌연변이는 다음 세대에 전달될 가능성이 훨씬 적었는데, 먹을 것이 더 부족하고 그것을 사냥하거나 채집하는 데 상당한 에너지 소비가 요구되는 환경에서는, 그러한 돌연변이를 가진 사람은 아마도 자신이 번식할 기회를 얻기 전에 죽었을 것이기 때문이다. 반면에, 이제 먹을 것이 풍부한 환경에서 우리를 비만으로 몰아가는 돌연변이가 인구 집단 속에 들어 왔다. 물론 지금은 상황이 아주 다르지만, 문제는 진화의 시간 척도가 길다는 것이다. 우리가 언제든 원하는 것을 거의 마음대로 먹을 수 있을 정도로 우리의 환경을 바꾼 것은 포유류 진화 시간의 약 0.00004퍼센트에 해당하는 지난 세기 정도가 되어서야 비로소 이루어졌던 것이다.

① 예를 들어
② 반면에
③ 요약하자면
④ 다시 말해
⑤ 결과적으로

18 논리완성 ④

| 분석 |
"잠깐 전에 보여 준 광고 영상의 내용에 대해 4살 아이들이 질문을 받았을 때도 비슷한 결과가 관찰되었다"고 했는데, 여기서 비슷한 결과란 'the를 사용한 질문들은 a를 사용한 질문들에 비해 "모르겠다"라는 응답을 더 적게 초래했고 영화에서 실제로 일어나지 않은 사건에 대해 잘못된 인지를 더 많이 일어나게 했다'는 것이다. 실제로 일어나지 않은 사건에 대한 잘못된 인지는 '실제로 있지 않았던' 물체들에 대해 잘못된 인지와 호응할 것이므로, ④가 정답으로 적절하다.

| 어휘 |
subject n. 피험자, 피실험자   **definite article** 정관사   **indefinite article** 부정관사   **recognition** n. 인지, 인식   **observe** v. 관찰하다, 관측하다   **interrogate** v. 질문하다   **commercial** n. 광고방송

| 해석 |
한 실험에서, 피실험자들은 자동차 사고 영화를 본 다음 영화에서 발생한 사건과 발생하지 않은 사건들에 대한 질문에 답했다. 어떤 질문들에서는 "Did you see the broken headlight?(그 깨어진 전조등을 보았습니까?)"에서처럼 영어의 관사 the(정관사)가 사용되었다. 다른 질문들에서는 관사 a(부정관사)가 사용되어, "Did you see a broken headlight?(깨어진 전조등을 보았습니까?)"와 같은 질문들이 나왔다. the를 사용한 질문들은 a를 사용한 질문들에 비해 "모르겠다"라는 응답을 더 적게 초래했고 영화에서 실제로 일어나지 않은 사건에 대한 잘못된 인지를 더 많이 일어나게 했다. 잠깐 전에 보여준 광고 영상의 내용에 대해 4살 아이들이 질문을 받았을 때도 비슷한 결과가 관찰되었다. "Did you see the...?(그 ...을 보았니?)"라는 질문은 실제로 있지 않았던 물체들에 대해 잘못된 인지를 더 많이 유발했다.

① 그들은 이전에 자주 본 적이 있는
② 그들의 기대와 일치했던
③ 그들은 별로 좋아하지 않았던
④ 실제로 있지 않았던
⑤ 그들은 구매를 원했던

19 논리완성 ④

| 분석 |
첫 번째 빈칸의 경우, 앞에서 '엄격한' 학교 일정과 기존 방식을 그대로 계속하는 것을 부정적으로 평가했으므로, 이와 상반되는 '유연성'이라는 의미의 flexibility가 들어가야 한다. 두 번째 빈칸의 경우도, 앞에서 언급한 우회하는 방법을 찾아야 한다는 것 또한 '유연성'과 관련 있으므로, 마찬가지로 flexibility가 적절하다.

| 어휘 |
rigid a. 엄격한, 엄정한   **old-fashioned** a. 구식의, 시대에 뒤진   **dictate** v. 명령하다, 지시하다, 좌우하다, 영향을 미치다   **bump** n. (도로의) 튀어나온 부분[요철]   **inherently** ad. 본질적으로   **pitfall** n. 함정, 유혹   **initiative** n. 주도권, 계획   **sterilize** v. 불임케 하다; 살균하다   **relevant** a. 관련된, 적절한   **more than** 매우, 더 나위 없이   **detour** n. 우회, 우회로   **implement** v. 이행하다, 실행하다   **strategically** ad. 전략적으로   **embed** v. (마음·기억 등에) 깊이 새겨 두다   **component** n. 성분, 구성 요소   **rigidity** n. 엄격, 엄숙   **reliability** n. 신빙성, 확실성   **normality** n. 정상 상태   **flexibility** n. 유연성, 융통성   **sterility** n. 번식 불능, 불임

| 해석 |
엄격한 학교 일정과 시대에 뒤떨어진 정책이 오늘날 학생들이 이용할 수 있고 이용해야 하는 학습 경험의 유형을 결정해서는 안 된다. 도중에 있는 장애물에 적응하지 않고 기존 방식을 그대로 계속하는 것은 본질적으로 실패를 초래할 것이다. 유연성은 모든 형태의 변화 계획을 방해하는 흔한 함정들을 막아준다. 정책과 통상적인 절차는 오직 학교의 기능을 이끌어주기 위해서만 작용해야 하며, 학습이 전혀 즐겁지도 않고 적절하지도 않고 유의미하지도 않은 생기 없는 분위기를 만들어내서는 안 된다. 변화가 전략적으로 그리고 목적을 가지고 실행될 수 있도록 하기 위해서는 때때로 우회하는 것이 매우 좋다. 이것은 유연성이 학교 문화에 깊이 새겨진 요소일 때에만 현실이 될 것이다.

20 논리완성 ⑤

| 분석 |
첫 번째 빈칸의 경우, 앞에서 언급한 '당신이 원할 때 언제든지 개입한다'와 호응하는 표현이 필요하므로 '자기 뜻대로'라는 의미를 가진 부사가 적절하다. 따라서 '자발적으로', '의도적으로'라는 뜻의 voluntarily가 적절하다. 두 번째 빈칸의 경우에도, and 앞의 '자동적으로(automatically)'와 대비될 수 있는 표현이 필요하므로 마찬가지로 voluntarily가 들어가야 한다.

| 어휘 |
immune response 면역 반응   **self-sufficient** a. 자급자족적인, 자립적인   **built-in** a. 붙박이의, 자동적인   **gaping** a. 입을 크게 벌린, 크게 갈라진   **flaw** n. 결점, 결함   **extend** v. 퍼지다; 달하다, 미치다   **induce** v. 야기하다, 일으키다, 유발하다   **alter** v. 바꾸다, 변경하다   **metabolism** n. 신진대사   **come into play** 작동[활동]하기 시작하다   **reluctantly** ad. 마지못해   **emphatically** ad. 강조하여; 단호하게   **forcibly** ad. 강제적으로; 힘차게   **materially** ad. 크게, 현저하게   **voluntarily** ad. 자발적으로, 의도적으로

| 해석 |

면역 반응은 누군가의 심장박동이나 호흡만큼이나 자동적으로 이루어진다. 그러나 자동적인 반응으로서의 면역은 매우 큰 결함을 내포하고 있다. 그 결함을 찾으려면, 잠시 멈춰 그저 숨을 깊이 들이 쉬어 보아라. 호흡은 자동적인 작용이지만, 당신이 원할 때 언제든지 개입해서 그것을 마음대로 작동하게 만들 수 있다. 이와 동일한 능력은 거의 모든 곳까지 뻗친다. 당신은 공포 영화를 보러 감으로써 의도적으로 스트레스 반응을 일으킬 수 있다. 당신은 운동을 하거나 식단을 바꿈으로써 신진대사에 변화를 줄 수도 있다. 자동적으로 일어나는 것과 의도적으로 일어나는 것을 구분하는 경계선은 정해져 있지 않다. 선택이 중요하며, 그리하여 치유하는 자아가 활동하기 시작한다. 몸은 자기 스스로 생존하는 법을 알고 있지만, 몸에게 번성하는(건강하게 잘 살아가는) 법을 가르치는 것은 우리에게 달려 있다.

21 전치사 + 관계대명사 ④

| 분석 |

관계대명사 뒤에는 불완전한 문장이 오고 관계부사나 '전치사+관계대명사' 뒤에는 완전한 문장이 온다. ⓓ의 관계대명사 which 뒤에 tag questions do not solicit confirmation이라는 완전한 문장이 왔으므로, ⓓ는 관계부사나 '전치사+관계대명사'로 써야 하는데, '경우에'는 in cases이므로 전치사는 in이 적절하다. 그러므로 ⓓ를 관계부사 where나 in which로 고쳐야 한다.

| 어휘 |

tag question 부가의문문   **append** v. (글에) 덧붙이다, 첨부하다   **declarative statement** 평서문   **request** v. 요청[요구, 신청]하다   **confirmation** n. 확인, 확증   **semantically** ad. 의미상; 의미론적으로   **trifling** a. 하찮은, 사소한   **equivalent** n. 동등한 것; 상당하는 것   **acquire** v. 획득하다, 몸에 익히다, 습득하다   **utterance** n. 말함, 발언   **solicit** v. 간청하다; 구하다, 조르다   **intonation** n. 억양   **rhetorical question** 수사의문문

| 해석 |

부가의문문은 "The light was green, wasn't it?"에서처럼 평서문에 덧붙여진다. 일반적으로, 부가의문문은 평서문 내용에 대한 확인을 요청하는 역할을 한다. 브라운(Brown)의 말에 따르면, "영어 부가의문문의 독특한 매력은 그것이 의미적으로 비교적 사소하며, 단순히 확인을 요청하는 것이고, '정말?' 혹은 '맞아?'와 같은 동일한 의미의 간단한 표현이 있다는 점이다. 실제로, 이러한 간단한 부가 표현들은 아이들이 매우 이른 시기에, 즉 두 단어로 된 표현을 사용할 즈음에 습득한다. 따라서 부가의문문이 확인을 요청하지 않는 경우가 있긴 하지만(예를 들어, 제켄도프(Jackendoff)가 1972년에 제시한 예인, "Max certainly has finished eating dinner, hasn't he?"를 수사의문문의 하강 억양으로 말하는 것), 대부분의 경우, 동의를 요청한다.

22 분사구문 ⑤

| 분석 |

ⓔ의 앞에 완전한 문장이 주어져 있는데, 그 뒤에 접속사 없이 시제를 가진 동사가 이어질 수 없다. 따라서 ⓔ부터는 talking을 의미상 주어로 한 동시 동작의 분사구문이 되어야 하므로, ⓔ는 establishing이 되어야 한다. ⓓ 'think+to부정사'는 '~하려 하다'는 뜻이다.

| 어휘 |

psychiatry n. 정신의학   **neurology** n. 신경학   **merge** v. 합병하다, 합치다   **rubric** n. 제목, 항목   **psychotherapy** n. 정신요법, 심리요법   **term** n. 용어, 말   **coin** v. (신어·신표현을) 만들어 내다   **therapeutic** a. 치료의, 치료법의   **asylum** n. 정신병원   **soothe** v. 진정시키다, 달래다   **recognize** v. 인식하다, 인지하다   **establish** v. 확립하다

| 해석 |

세기말 무렵, 정신의학과 신경학이라는 두 분야는 정신의학 부문 아래에서 효과적으로 하나로 통합되었다. 두 분야 모두에서 심리요법으로의 움직임이 있었는데, 심리요법은 1887년에 두 명의 네덜란드 정신과 의사가 만든 용어였다. 도덕적 치료법에서는, 정신병원의 체계적인 생활 이외에도 정신과 의사와 환자 사이에 치료적인 일대일 관계를 갖는 것이 강조되었다. 초기에 신경과 의사들은 예를 들어, 환자들의 과도하게 흥분된 신경을 진정시키기 위해 흥분하기 쉬운 환자들에게 찬물을 끼얹는 등, 물리적인 방법으로 환자들을 치료하려 했다. 그러나 신경과 의사들은 대화가 의사와 환자 사이에 실무적인 관계를 확립하면서 환자들에게 도움을 줄 수 있다는 점을 정신과 의사들과 함께 깨닫기 시작했다.

23 문맥상 적절하지 않은 단어 고르기 ②

| 분석 |

인간이 하루를 두 번의 수면 시간으로 나누기를 요구하는 이상성(二相性) 생물이라면, 낮 시간 중간에 휴식(수면)을 취하는 것은 비정상적인 것이 아니라 자연스러운 것이라 할 수 있을 것이므로 ⓑ는 natural이어야 한다.

| 어휘 |

conventional a. 전통적인; 관습적인   **apparently** ad. 언뜻 보기에; 명백히   **abnormal** a. 보통과 다른, 정상이 아닌   **biphasic** a. 두 개의 상(相)을 갖는, 이상(二相)의   **monophastic** a. 한 개의 상(相)을 갖는, 단상(單相)의   **drowsiness** n. 졸음

| 해석 |

낮 시간 중간에 긴 휴식을 취하는 것은 관습적인 점심식사보다 더 건강에 좋을 뿐만 아니라, 명백히 더 〈비정상적이다→자연스럽다〉. 수면 연구자들은 스페인 사람들의 생체 리듬이 우리 인간의 생물학적 시계에 더 가깝게 맞춰져 있을 수도 있다는 사실을 발견했다. 여러 연구들은 인간이 한 번의 "단상성(單相性)" (수면-각

성) 교대 대신 하루를 두 번의 수면 시간으로 나누기를 요구하는 이상성(二相性) 생물임을 시사한다. 점심식사 후에 졸음을 느끼는 것은 음식 때문이 아니라 하루 중 그 시간이 되었기 때문이라는 것이다.

24 문맥상 적절하지 않은 단어 고르기 ③

| 분석 |

앞에서 '선진국들은 여러 세대에 걸쳐 견줄 데 없는 물질적 번영을 누려 왔다'고 했으므로, ⓒ는 '풍요'라는 의미의 abundance여야 자연스러운 흐름으로 이어질 수 있다.

| 어휘 |

assumption n. 가정, 억측 **subsistence** n. 생존, 생계, 최저 생활 **shelter** n. 은신처; 피난 장소, 집 **unprecedented** a. 전례 없는, 미증유의 **indigence** n. 가난, 빈곤 **unparalleled** a. 비할 데 없는, 견줄 데 없는 **per capita** 1인당 **relatively** ad. 상대적으로; 비교적 **factor** n. 요인, 요소 **tolerance** n. 관용, 아량

| 해석 |

소비 사회의 핵심적인 가정은 "돈으로 행복을 산다."라는 개념이었다. 역사적으로, 이러한 가정에는 타당한 이유가 있는데, 지난 몇 세대까지, 대다수의 사람들이 최저 생계에 가깝게 살아왔고, 그래서 소득의 증가는 물질적인 복지(예를 들어, 음식, 주거, 의료)에서 진정한 증대를 가져왔으며, 이는 더 많은 행복을 가져왔기 때문이다. 그러나 많은 선진국에서는, 물질적 복지의 수준이 최저 생계를 넘어 전례 없는 〈빈곤으로(→ 풍요로)〉 옮겨 갔다. 선진국들은 여러 세대에 걸쳐 견줄 데 없는 물질적 번영을 누려 왔으며, 분명한 깨달음이 새로 부상하고 있는데, 그것은 우리가 매우 낮은 소득으로 생활하고 있을 때 돈이 더 많은 행복을 가져온다는 것이다. 그러나 세계 평균으로, 1인당 소득이 연간 13,000달러 범위에 이르면, 추가적인 소득은 우리의 행복을 상대적으로 적게 증가시키지만, 개인의 자유, 의미 있는 일, 사회적 관용과 같은 다른 요소들이 훨씬 더 많이 (행복을) 증가시킨다.

25 글의 제목 ②

| 분석 |

본문은 빅토리아 시대의 한 통념을 통해 음악이 성인의 언어에서 운율적 요소가 분리되면서 발전했음을 이야기하고 있다. 이러한 논의는 음악의 진화에 대한 하나의 해석으로 볼 수 있으므로, 제목으로는 ②가 가장 적절하다.

| 어휘 |

separation n. 분리, 이탈 **prosodic** a. 운율학(韻律學)의; 운율법에 맞는 **syntactic** a. 구문론의, 구문론적인 **inflection** n. 음조의 변화, 억양 **pitch** n. 가락, 음률의 높이 **chant** n. 노래, 멜로디; 성가 **unison** a. 동음의, 같은 음높이[피치]의 **impress** n. 흔적; 인상, 감명 **appreciation** n. 평가, 판단, 이해 **pre-literate** a. 문자 이전의

| 해석 |

빅토리아 시대의 한 가지 일반적인 통념은 운율적 요소가 구문적 요소로부터 분리되는 과정을 통해 음악이 어른들의 말에서부터 서서히 발전했다는 것이었다. 윌리엄 폴(William Pole)은 『The Philosophy of Music』에서 다음과 같이 썼다. "음악의 가장 초기 형태는 아마도 말할 때 나타나는 목소리의 자연스러운 음조변화에서 비롯되었을 것이다. 목소리를 특정 음에서 지속적으로 유지하다가 이에 뒤이어 더 높은 음이나 더 낮은 음에서 또 다른 지속음을 내는 것은 매우 쉬운 일이었을 것이다. 이 과정은 아무리 거칠다 해도 음악을 구성했을 것이다. 더 나아가 여러 사람이 이런 형태의 거친 노래에 참여하게 되는 것을 쉽게 상상할 수 있다. 한 사람이 리더 역할을 하면, 다른 사람들은 자신의 귀가 가진 자연스러운 본능에 의해 그를 따를 것이고, 이렇게 해서 우리는 하나로 결합된 같은 음의 노래를 얻게 되었을 것이다. 폴 박사가 쓴 책의 기반이 된 원래의 강의는 1877년에 행해졌으며, 당대의 시대적 영향을 많이 반영하고 있다. 여기에는 원시인, 야만인 등과 같은 표현들을 자주 언급한다. 『The Philosophy of Music』는 여전히 유용하지만, 폴은 문자 이전 종족들 사이의 음악이 우리의 음악만큼 복잡할 수 있다는 점은 거의 인정하지 않는다.

다음 글의 제목으로 가장 적절한 것은?
① 철학은 음악에서 매우 중요하다
② 음악은 어떻게 발전하는가: 하나의 가능성 있는 설명
③ 모방 대 음조변화: 음악의 두 가지 요소
④ 윌리엄 폴: 음악사에서 혁신적인 인물
⑤ 왜 음악에 대한 인정이 우리의 삶에 영향을 미치는가

26 글의 주제 ③

| 분석 |

"성간 구름의 먼지 입자들이 별빛을 차단하고, 별을 형성하는 물질이 두껍고 어두워서 핵융합이 시작될 때까지의 과정을 관찰하기 어렵다"는 등, 별의 형성을 관찰하기 어려운 까닭에 대해 주로 이야기하고 있는 내용이므로, 글의 주제로는 ③이 적절하다. ① 원시적인 장비는 이런 어려움의 하나일 뿐이다.

| 어휘 |

arch v. 활 모양으로 굽다 **diffuse** a. 흩어진, 널리 퍼진 **interrupt** v. 가로막다, 저지하다; 중단시키다 **interstellar** a. 별과 별 사이의, 항성(恒星)간의 **particle** n. 미립자 **opaque** a. 불투명한; (전파·소리 따위를) 통과시키지 않는 **visible** a. (눈에) 보이는 **observe** v. 관찰하다, 관측하다 **cloak** v. 덮다; 가리다, 숨기다 **dense** a. 밀도가 높은, 짙은 **initiate** v. 시작하다, 개시하다 **nuclear fusion** 핵 융합 **inherently** ad. 본질적으로 **radiation** n. 복사선, 복사 에너지 **far-infrared** n. 원적외선 **submillimeter** a. 1밀리미터 이하[미만]의 **wavelength** n. 파장 **relatively** ad. 상대적으로

| 해석 |

도시의 불빛에서 멀리 떨어진 어두운 곳에서 하늘을 보면, 은하수가 머리 위로 아치형을 그리고 있는 모습을 볼 수 있는데, 널리 퍼져 있는 빛의 흐름 중간 중간에 어두운 부분들이 끼어 있다. 이것들은 성간 구름이다. 성간 구름 속의 먼지 입자들은 별빛을 차단하고 가시광선을 통과시키지 않도록 만든다. 그 결과, 별의 형성을 관찰하려는 사람들에게 근본적인 문제가 발생하는데, 별들이 스스로의 탄생을 가리는 것이다. 별을 만드는 데 들어가는 물질은 두껍고 어둡다. 그 물질은 핵융합을 일으킬 만큼 충분히 밀도가 높아져야 하지만, 아직 그렇게 되지 않았다. 천문학자들이 이 과정의 시작과 끝은 관찰할 수 있지만, 중간 단계는 본질적으로 관찰하기 어려운데, 이는 복사 에너지의 대부분이 원적외선 및 1밀리미터 이하의 파장의 형태로 방출되고, 천문학자들이 이러한 파장에서 사용할 수 있는 도구는 스펙트럼의 다른 부분에 비해 상대적으로 미흡하기 때문이다.

다음 글의 주제로 가장 적절한 것은?
① 별을 관찰하기 위해 장비를 새롭게 해야 할 필요성
② 핵융합을 시작하게 하는 신비로운 과정
③ 별 형성을 관찰하는 데 있어서의 어려움
④ 우주 탐사에서의 천문학의 한계
⑤ 별의 밀도와 밝기 사이의 관계

27 글의 요지 ⑤

| 분석 |

이 글에서는 '유아들이 언어를 배우는 과정에서, 실생활에서 사람과 대화하는 것이 교육용 CD나 DVD를 듣는 것보다 훨씬 더 효과적'이라는 연구 결과를 설명하고 있다. 유아들이 외국어를 구사하는 사람을 TV로 볼 때와 실제로 만났을 때의 차이를 통해, 실제 대화가 학습에 중요한 역할을 한다는 점을 강조하고 있는 것이다. 그러므로 글의 요지로는 ⑤가 적절하다.

| 어휘 |

infant n. 유아   **mesmerize** v. 매혹시키다, 최면술을 걸다

| 해석 |

새로운 언어를 배우길 원하는 십대와 성인들에게 유아에 대한 연구가 유용한 팁을 제공할 수 있다. 한 가지 예로, 연구자들은 언어 학습자가 교육용 CD와 DVD로 녹음된 대화를 듣는 것보다 실제로 그 언어를 구사하는 사람들과 대화하는 것이 훨씬 더 좋다는 사실을 발견했다. 워싱턴 대학교 학습 및 뇌 과학 연구소의 공동 소장 패트리샤 쿨(Patricia Kuhl)은 유아들이 외국어를 말하는 사람을 TV에서 보는 경우, 같은 화자를 현실에서 봤을 때와 완전히 다른 경험을 한다는 사실을 발견했다. 현실의 화자와 함께 있는 경우, 유아들의 뇌는 그들이 배운 소리를 들을 때 전기적 활동을 활발하게 일으켰다. "아기들은 TV를 보고 있었고, 마치 홀린 것처럼 보였습니다."라고 쿨은 말한다. "그러나 학습은 일어나지 않았습니다.

그들의 뇌에서는 아무 일도 일어나지 않았어요, 전혀요."라고 그녀는 말한다.

다음 글의 요지로 가장 적절한 것은?
① 어른들의 언어 습득과 아이들의 언어 습득은 전혀 다른 과정으로 볼 수 있다.
② 교육용 CD나 DVD를 활용한 언어 학습은 효율성이 매우 높은 학습 방법이다.
③ 어른들과의 상호작용을 통한 새로운 소리의 습득은 아이들 언어 습득의 출발점이다.
④ 아이들의 언어 습득은 녹음된 대화를 반복적으로 들을 때 가장 효과적으로 이루어진다.
⑤ 아이들이 언어를 습득하는 가장 좋은 방법은 실생활에서 사람들이 하는 말을 듣는 것이다.

28 문장삽입 ④

| 분석 |

주어진 문장은 "이는 추가적인 모이가 새에게 번식시기에 대해 '잘못된' 신호를 제공하기 때문일 수 있다"라는 의미이므로, 좋지 않은 번식 결과가 발생한 이유를 설명하는 역할을 하고 있다. 따라서 "겨울에 모이를 주는 것은 산란 시기는 앞당기지만 한 번에 낳는 알의 개수와 번식 성공률을 감소시켜서, 이후의 번식 성과에 부정적 영향을 미칠 수 있음을 보여준다."라는 내용 다음인 ④에 위치하는 것이 가장 적절하다.

| 어휘 |

dish out 접시에 담다, (요리를) 접시에 담아 내놓다   **estimate** v. 어림잡다, 견적하다   **positive** a. 긍정적인   **negative** a. 부정적인   **species** n. 종(種), 종류   **sporadically** ad. 이따금, 산발적으로   **breeding** n. 번식, 부화   **lay** v. (알을) 낳다   **clutch size** (새의) 한배 산란 수   **evolution** n. 진화   **bill** n. (새의) 부리   **migratory** a. 이주하는, 이동하는

| 해석 |

영국에서는 주택 거주자의 40~50%가 자신의 정원에서 새에게 모이를 접시에 담아서 주는데, 매년 어림잡아 5~6만 톤의 새 모이를 준다. 겨울에 모이를 공급하면, 그때는 자연에 먹이가 부족할 수도 있어서, 새가 모이 부족을 이기고 살아남을 수 있지만, 연중 내내 모이를 주는 것이 새에게 긍정적인 영향을 미칠지 부정적인 영향을 미칠지는 확실치 않다. 미국에서는 새 모이통을 매우 자주 이용하는 종(種)들이 더 이따금씩 이용하는 종만큼 혹은 그보다 더 잘 살아가는 경향을 보인다. 그러나 영국의 일부 연구는 겨울에 모이를 주는 것은 산란 시기를 앞당기지만 한 번에 낳는 알의 개수와 번식 성공률을 감소시켜서, 이후의 번식 성과에 부정적 영향을 미칠 수 있음을 보여준다. 〈이는 추가적인 모이가 새에게 번식시기에 대해 '잘못된' 신호를 제공하기 때문일 수 있다.〉 모이통은 또한 새의 진화를 변화시켜서, 모이통 안쪽에 있는 먹이에 더 잘 닿는 더 긴 부리를 선택하게 하고, 이주 행동을 바꾼다.

29 내용파악 ④

| 분석 |

"1200년경에 유럽인들은 그들이 오늘날 가지고 있는 것보다 더 많은 농경지를 가지고 있었다."라고 돼 있으므로 ④가 본문의 내용과 일치하지 않는 진술이다.

| 어휘 |

relatively ad. 상대적으로   expansion n. 확장, 확대   stability n. 안정, 안정성   cultivate v. 경작하다, 재배하다   peasant n. 농부, 소작농   drain v. 고갈시키다; (땅을) 간척하다   swamp n. 늪, 습지   explosion n. 폭발, 폭파   device n. 장치, 설비

| 해석 |

중세 초기에 유럽의 인구는 비교적 적었다. 그러나 중세 융성기에 인구는 3,800만 명에서 7,400만 명으로 급격히 늘어났다. 이처럼 엄청난 인구 증가의 원인은 무엇일까? 이는 주로 서기 1000년 이후에 일어난 식량 생산의 급격한 증가 때문이었다. 중세 초기에 있었던 외부로부터의 침입이 멈췄고, 평화와 안정은 식량 생산의 증가로 이어졌다. 그뿐만 아니라, 11세기와 12세기의 농민들이 나무를 베고 습지를 개간하면서 더 많은 땅이 경작됐다. 1200년경에 유럽인들은 그들이 오늘날 가지고 있는 것보다 더 많은 농경지를 가지고 있었다. 기술의 변화 또한 농업 발전에 기여했다. 중세 융성기에는 노동을 절약하는 장치가 폭발적으로 증가했으며, 이 장치들은 이전에 사람이나 동물이 하던 일을 물과 바람의 힘을 이용하여 해내었다.

중세 융성기(High Middle Ages)의 유럽에 대한 다음 글의 내용과 일치하지 않는 것은?
① 인구가 급속도로 증가하였다.
② 서기 1000년이 지나면서 식량 생산이 급증하였다.
③ 외세로부터의 침략이 멈추어 평화가 지속되었다.
④ 1200년 경의 경작지 면적은 현재의 절반 정도였다.
⑤ 수력과 풍력의 활용이 농업의 발달을 가져왔다.

30 문맥상 적절하지 않은 단어 고르기 ④

| 분석 |

"Rusting이 검토한 연구에 따르면, 일부 성격 특성은 감정적 반응을 증폭시키는 반면, 다른 특성들은 정반대의 효과를 나타내어 감정 상태가 인지에 미치는 영향을 약화시키거나 심지어 반전시키기도 한다."라고 했으므로, 성격 특성이 감정의 영향을 완전히 막는 것이 아니라, 감정적 영향을 줄이거나 약화하는 것이다. 따라서 ⓓ는 mitigating이 되어야 한다.

| 어휘 |

temperament n. 기질, 성미, 체질   affective a. 감정적인, 정서적인   cognition n. <심리> 인식, 인지   undertake v. 떠맡다; 착수하다   accumulation n. 축적, 누적   variable n. 변수   self-esteem n. 자부심   trait n. 특색, 특성   marked a. 명료한, 현저한   comprehensive a. 포괄적인, 범위가 넓은   integration n. 통합   amplify v. 확대하다, 확장하다   attenuate v. 가늘게 하다, 약하게 하다   infusion n. 주입; 고취   moderate v. 완화하다, 경감하다, 조절하다

| 해석 |

기질에서 나타나는 지속적인 성격 차이가 사람들이 단기적인 감정 상태를 다루는 방식에 상당한 영향을 미칠 수 있다는 개념은 매우 오랫동안 있어 왔다. 그러나 감정의 상태적 측면과 특성적 측면 사이의 이러한 관계와, 이 두 측면이 사회적 인지와 갖는 관계에 대한 체계적인 탐구는 비교적 최근에서야 이뤄지기 시작했다. 감정이 인지에 미치는 영향에 대한 실험적 연구가 축적되면서, 이러한 영향의 상당 부분이 성격과 개인차 변수에 크게 좌우된다는 점이 분명해졌다. 예를 들어, 사람들이 부정적인 감정을 단기적으로 경험하면서 그 경험에 어떻게 인지적으로 반응하는지에 자존감과 특성 불안이 현저한 영향을 미치는 것으로 밝혀졌다. Cheryl Rusting은 감정이 인지에 영향을 미치는 것을 〈방지하는(→ 완화하는)〉 데 있어서의 성격 특징들의 역할에 관해 이용 가능한 증거들을 종합적으로 검토하고 통합한다. Rusting이 검토한 연구에 따르면, 일부 성격 특성은 감정적 반응을 증폭시키는 반면, 다른 특성들은 정반대의 효과를 나타내어 감정 상태가 인지에 미치는 영향을 약화시키거나 심지어 반전시키기도 한다. 또한, 최근 여러 실험에서는 사회적 인지와 행동에 감정이 스며드는 과정이 성격 특성에 의해 크게 조절된다는 사실이 드러났다.

31 글의 흐름상 적절하지 않은 문장 고르기 ③

| 분석 |

본문은 가뭄을 겪는 나무가 내는 고통 신호에 대한 연구 내용을 다루고 있는데, ⓒ는 곤충의 반응이라는 부차적인 내용을 다루고 있으므로 글의 흐름상 부자연스럽다.

| 어휘 |

sicken v. 구역질이 나게 하다, 병이 나게 하다   distress n. 고민, 걱정; 고통   hypothesize v. 가설을 세우다, 가정하다   vibration n. 진동, 동요; 전율   fasten v. 묶다, 붙들어 매다; 고정하다   bark n. 나무껍질   drought-stricken a. 가뭄으로 고통을 받는   parch v. 볶다, 굽다; 바싹 말리다   transmit v. 전하다, 전파시키다   plight n. 곤경, 궁지; 어려운 입장   detect v. 발견하다, 간파하다   ultrasonic frequency 초음파 주파수   oak n. 참나무   maple n. 단풍나무   white pine 스트로부스 소나무   aspen n. 사시나무   birch n. 자작나무   identify v. 확인하다, 인지하다

| 해석 |

그것은 당신이 아마도 결코 듣지 못할 소리인데, 바로 병든 나무가 보내는 고통 신호이다. 연구원들은 이러한 소리 즉, 식물 표면에서 발생하는 진동이 극심한 수분 부족으로 인해 발생한다고 가정했다. 그들은 가뭄으로 시달리고 있던 나무의 껍질에 전자 센서를 부착하

여 고통 신호를 분명히 들을 수 있었다. 그 과학자들 중의 한 사람에 의하면, 대부분의 바싹 마른 나무는 50~500킬로헤르츠(kHz) 대역의 소리로 자신의 곤경을 전달한다. (기계의 도움을 받지 않은 인간의 귀가 감지할 수 있는 대역은 20킬로헤르츠까지에 불과하다.) 〈일부 곤충들은 초음파 주파수 대역에서 서로 의사소통하기 때문에, 그 나무들의 진동을 감지하고서 약해진 나무들을 공격하기도 한다.〉 연구원들은 붉은 참나무, 단풍나무, 스트로부스 소나무, 사시나무, 자작나무 등을 대상으로 실험을 진행했으며, 모든 나무들이 약간씩 다른 소리를 내는 것을 발견했다. 연구자들은 실제로 해보고서 각 나무 종(種)이 내는 특징적인 소리 패턴을 구별할 수 있었다.

32 내용일치 ③

| 분석 |
"침팬지의 어휘는 규모가 작고, 구문이나 문법, 즉 우리로 하여금 적은 수의 음성 언어적 기호들로부터 매우 다양한 의미를 만들어 낼 수 있게 해 주는 규칙을 사용하지 않는다."라고 했으므로, ③은 본문의 내용과 일치하지 않는다.

| 어휘 |
baboon n. 개코원숭이 **predator** n. 포식자, 포식 동물 **mime** n. 무언극 **syntax** n. 구문론, 통사론 **verbal** a. 언어[말]의 **subtle** a. 미묘한, 감지하기 힘든 **threshold** n. 한계, 임계점 **abstract** a. 추상적인

| 해석 |
많은 종(種)들은 언어를 가지고 있다. 새와 개코원숭이는 자신들의 집단에 있는 다른 개체들에게 포식자의 접근에 대해 경고해줄 수 있다. 하지만 동물의 언어는 가장 단순한 생각만을 다소 무언극처럼 공유할 수 있으며, 이런 생각들 대부분은 지금 당장 존재하는 것과 연관되어 있다. 몇몇 연구자들은 침팬지에게 말하는 법을 가르치려고 노력해 왔는데, 침팬지는 실제로 100~200개 단어의 어휘를 습득하고 사용할 수 있으며, 심지어 단어쌍을 새로운 패턴으로 연결할 수도 있다. 그러나 침팬지의 어휘는 규모가 작고, 구문이나 문법, 즉 우리로 하여금 적은 수의 음성 언어적 기호들로부터 매우 다양한 의미를 만들어 낼 수 있게 해 주는 규칙을 사용하지 않는다. 이들의 언어 능력은 두세 살짜리 인간의 언어 능력을 결코 능가하지 못하는 것 같은데, 그것으로는 오늘날의 세상을 만들기에 충분하지 않다. 인간의 언어는 완전히 새로운 형태의 의사소통을 가능하게 하는 미묘한 언어적 임계점을 넘어섰다. 무엇보다도, 인간의 언어는 추상적인 실체에 대한 정보나 지금 당장 존재하지 않고 우리의 상상 밖에서는 존재하지도 않을 수 있는 사물이나 가능성에 대한 정보를 우리로 하여금 공유하게 한다.

다음 글의 내용과 일치하지 <u>않는</u> 것은?
① 거의 모든 동물 언어는 지금 눈앞에 있는 것에 관한 것이다.
② 침팬지는 100개 혹은 200개의 어휘를 습득하고 사용할 수 있다.
③ 침팬지는 인간처럼 문법 규칙을 사용할 수 있다.
④ 침팬지의 언어 능력은 2세, 3세 인간의 언어 능력을 결코 능가하지 못하는 듯하다.
⑤ 인간의 언어는 추상적인 실체에 관한 정보를 공유하게 한다.

33~34

모든 설계는 선택을 수반하며, 자주 그 선택은 서로 상충하는 제약을 만족시키도록 이루어져야 한다. 대지(垈地) 경계선으로부터의 너비가 차 한 대가 들어갈 정도에 불과한 집의 옆에 두 대의 차를 붙여 댈 수 있는 차고를 짓는 것은 양립할 수 없어 보이는 제약을 가진 설계상의 문제를 야기한다. 해결책이 있긴 하지만, 모두가 타협을 수반하기 때문에, 결코 이상적이지는 않은 해결책이 돼 버린다. 한 가지 해결책은 차고를 집에서 꽤 떨어진 뒤쪽에 지붕 달린 통로로 집과 연결되도록 짓는 것이 되겠지만, 이렇게 하려면 뒷마당의 상당 공간을 사용해야 할 것이며, 거기서는 진입로의 너비가 두 배가 되어야 할 것이므로 그 해법은 바람직하지 않을 수도 있다. 다른 해결책은 너비는 차 한 대 폭이지만 안으로 들어간 깊이는 차 두 대의 길이인 차고를 만드는 것이 될 것이다. 이러한 자동차 두 대의 차고는 뒷마당을 전혀 침범할 필요가 없겠지만, 그것은 한 대의 차가 다른 차가 나가려는 출구를 막을 때마다 그 차를 다른 데로 옮겨야 할 것이다. 설계자는 강한 제약과 강하지 않은 제약 내에서 항상 선택해야 한다.

| 어휘 |
competing a. 경쟁하는, 경합하는 **constraint** n. 강제, 압박, 구속, 억제 **width** n. 폭, 너비 **property line** 대지 경계선 **incompatible** a. 양립할 수 없는 **compromise** n. 타협, 화해 **breezeway** n. (건물 사이를 잇는) 지붕 달린 통로 **necessitate** v. 필요로 하다; (결과를) 수반하다 **driveway** n. (대문에서 현관까지의) 차도, (자택 차고에서 집 앞의 도로까지의) 자동찻길 **encroach** v. 침범하다, 잠식하다

33 글의 주제 ①

| 분석 |
첫 번째 문장이 주제문이며, 차고를 짓는 상황을 예로 들면서 주제에 대한 구체적인 예시를 들고 있다. 따라서 ①이 정답이다.

윗글의 주제로 가장 적절한 것은?
① 설계에 있어서 타협의 필요성
② 상충하는 제약을 분리하는 방법
③ 뒷마당에 있는 넓은 공간을 충분히 활용하는 것의 중요성
④ 두 대의 차를 붙여 댈 수 있는 차고를 효율적으로 짓는 방법
⑤ 양립할 수 없는 제약을 조정하는 것의 중요성

34 어법 ③

| 분석 |
관계대명사의 수는 선행사에 일치시킨다. ⓒ 앞의 관계대명사 which의 선행사는 단수 명사 compromise이므로 ⓒ는 leads가 되어야 한다.

35~36

1800년대 초에 수학자이자 물리학자였던 Joseph Fourier는 태양 에너지, 즉 복사 에너지가 대기를 통과하여 지표면에 부딪칠 때 지구를 가열한다는 사실을 인식했다. 그러나 만약 대기가 없다면 지구는 정기적으로 몹시 차갑게 될 것이다. Fourier는 대기가 담요처럼 지구를 열 손실로부터 보호한다는 것을 최초로 인식한 인물이었다. 그 후 1859년에, 과학자 John Tyndall은 우리 대기 속 미량 기체들 중의 하나인 이산화탄소에 관한 놀라운 사실을 발견했다. 대기의 다른 주요 구성요소들인 질소와 산소는 장파장 복사에너지를 본질적으로 통과시키지만, 이산화탄소는 그렇지 않다는 것이었다. 수증기와 함께 이산화탄소는 적은 양으로도 장파장 에너지를 흡수하며, 그 에너지는 열로 저장된다. 수십 년 뒤에 스웨덴의 화학자 Svante Arrhenius는 이에서 더 나아가 대기의 이산화탄소 수준이 증가하면 지표면 온도를 바꿀 수 있다는 것을 암시했다. 그때 이래로 관측과 실험상의 증거는 이러한 초기의 발견들을 거듭해서 확인해 주었다.

| 어휘 |
radiation n. 복사 에너지 **recognize** v. 인지하다; 인정하다 **insulate** v. 절연하다; 차단하다 **astonishing** a. 놀랄 만한, 놀라운 **trace** n. 자취, 흔적; 극미량, 조금 **carbon dioxide** 이산화탄소 **component** n. 성분, 구성요소 **nitrogen** n. 질소 **transparent** a. 투명한; 입자가 통과하는 **water vapor** 수증기 **absorb** v. 흡수하다 **chemist** n. 화학자 **alter** v. 바꾸다, 변경하다 **observation** n. 관찰, 관측 **confirm** v. 확증하다, 확인하다

35 빈칸완성 ①

| 분석 |
Fourier는 대기의 존재가 지구의 열 손실을 막아준다고 생각했다. 따라서 만약 대기가 없다면 밤에는 지구가 극도로 차가워질 것이므로, 빈칸에는 '몹시 추운'이라는 의미의 frigid가 적절하다. ② 건조한 ③ 활발한 ④ 비스듬한 ⑤ 극단적인

36 글의 제목 ③

| 분석 |
본문은 '이산화탄소가 담요처럼 지구의 열손실을 막는 역할을 한다는 사실과 이에 대한 역사적 발견 과정'에 대해 설명하고 있는 글이므로, 제목으로는 ③이 가장 적절하다. ② 지구 온난화는 끝에서 두 번째 문장에서 '대기의 이산화탄소 수준이 증가하면 지표면 온도를 바꿀 수 있다'고 한 것으로 암시되었을 뿐 이 글에서 본격적으로 다루지는 않았다.

윗글의 제목으로 가장 알맞은 것은?
① 이산화탄소의 역사
② 지구 온난화의 이유
③ 대기 안에서의 이산화탄소의 역할
④ 이산화탄소와 장파장 에너지의 관계
⑤ 질소 혹은 산소와 이산화탄소의 차이점

37~38

모험은 창조적 행위의 측면에서 흥미로운 역할을 한다. 기존의 틀을 뛰어넘거나 규칙을 깨트리는 것은 모험을 수반할 수 있다. 이것의 결과는 생산적이고 활기를 북돋아 줄 수도 있지만, 또한 처참하거나 낭비적일 수도 있다. 위험을 장난 삼아 가까이 하는 것은 결과가 보장돼 있지 않다는 것을 의미하지만, 또한 이미 알고 있고 친숙한 것을 뛰어넘고 싶은, 즉 〈특별한(→ 표준적인)〉 것을 뛰어넘고 싶은 열망이 있다는 것을 의미하기도 한다. 이같이 기존의 틀을 뛰어넘는 것은 단일 물건의 생산에서부터 재료 자체를 이용한 더 광범위한 종류의 실험에 이르기까지 여러 다양한 수준에서 이루어지며, 따라서 일상적인 수준에서는 창조성의 요소로 인정될 수도 있다. 이런 종류의 창조적 위험은 현대의 한 도예가가 덴마크에서 발견된 가장 아름답고 뛰어난 신석기 시대의 그릇이라고 대개 여겨지는 스카프살링(Skarpsalling) 그릇의 복제본과 마주했을 때 했던 말에서 분명히 드러난다. 그 그릇의 특성을 설명하면서 그녀는 그것의 외형이 "떨리고 있다"고 말했다. 무슨 뜻인지 구체적으로 말해달라는 요청에 그녀는 신석기 도공이 그 외형을 극한까지, 무너지기 직전까지 밀어붙였다고 설명했다.

| 어휘 |
in terms of ~의 관점에서 **boundary** n. 경계, 한계 **push the boundary** 경계를 허물다, 한계를(기존의 틀을) 넘어서다 **entail** v. (필연적 결과로서) 일으키다, 남기다, 수반하다 **invigorating** a. 기운을 돋우는; (공기·산들바람 등이) 상쾌한 **disastrous** a. 비참한; 재해의 **flirt** v. 농락하다, 가지고 놀다 **aspiration** n. 열망, 포부 **mainstay** n. 대들보 **illustrate** v. 설명하다, 예증하다 **vessel** n. 용기(容器), 그릇 **outstanding** a. 걸출한, 현저한 **Neolithic** a. 신석기 시대의 **vibrate** v. 진동하다, 떨리다 **specify** v. 자세히 말하다, 명기하다

37 글의 주제   ②

| 분석 |

첫 번째 문장이 주제문이며, 글의 핵심은 창조적 행위에 있어서 위험의 감수가 필수적이라는 것이다. 예로 들고 있는 신석기 시대의 그릇이 거의 무너질 듯이 아슬아슬한 외형을 갖추고 있는 것도 위험을 감수한 창조적 행위임을 이야기하고 있는 것이다. 따라서 ②가 정답이 된다.

윗글의 주제로 가장 적절한 것은?
① 일상생활에서 창의성이 미치는 영향
② 창조적 행위로서의 위험 감수의 필요성
③ 현대 도예에서 규칙을 깨는 것의 중요성
④ 예술 작품 제작에서의 창조성의 활용
⑤ 알려진 기존의 틀을 뛰어넘는 것의 위험성

38 문맥상 적절하지 않은 표현 고르기   ③

| 분석 |

beyond the known and familiar와 beyond the extraordinary는 동격을 이루고 있으므로, ⓒ에 쓰인 extraordinary는 자연스럽지 않다. ⓒ의 자리에는 the known and familiar과 유사한 의미를 가진 표현이 와야 할 것이므로, ⓒ를 standard로 고치는 것이 적절하다.

39~40

시각적 주의력은 스포트라이트처럼 작용하여, 나머지는 어둠에 가려둔 채 장면의 한 부분을 두드러지게 한다. 불안은 터널 비전(좁은 시야)을 유발하여 흉기와 같은 위협적인 자극에 더 쉽게 집중할 수 있게 한다. 진화적인 관점에서 이것은 타당하다. 대초원을 돌아다니다가 저 멀리 있는 사자를 발견하는 고대의 인간은 계속해서 사자에 예민하게 집중하고 덜 위험한 일에 주의를 뺏기지 않기를 원했을 것이다. 현대 세계에서, 적당량의 불안감은 학생이 시험 준비에 집중하는 데 도움이 될 수도 있다. 약간의 불안은 때때로 심지어 사람들이 문제를 해결하는 데도 도움을 줄 수 있는데, 분석적 사고가 충분할 때 그러하다. 그러나 유용한 정보가 주의를 기울이는 스포트라이트 밖에 있다면, 그 경우에는 이러한 좁음에 대가가 따른다. 총에 집중하는 것은 그것이 핼러윈 의상을 입은 아이가 들고 다니는 장난감이라는 것을 알아차릴 만큼 충분히 주의를 넓힐 수 없다면 잘못된 결론으로 이어질 것이다.

| 어휘 |

obscure v. 어둡게 하다, 덮어 감추다   **tunnel vision** 좁은 시야
threatening a. 협박하는, 위험한   **stimulus** n. 자극, 격려, 고무
evolutionary a. 발달의, 진화의   **perspective** n. 전망, 시각, 견지
spot v. 발견하다, 탐지해내다   **wander** v. 헤매다, 어슬렁거리다
keen a. 예리한, 예민한   **distract** v. (마음·주의 등을) 빗나가게 하다, 흩뜨리다, (딴 데로) 돌리다   **modest** a. 알맞은, 온당한   **dose** n. (약의) 1회분, (1회의) 복용량; 많음, 듬뿍   **anxiety** n. 근심, 불안
analytic a. 분석적인, 해석적인   **suffice** v. ~에 충분하다, 만족시키다   **conclusion** n. 결론   **costume** n. 의복, 복장

39 빈칸완성   ③

| 분석 |

이어지는 내용은 '고대의 인간이 초원에서 사자를 발견했을 때 이를 주의 깊게 보는 것이 생존에 유리했다는 것, 즉, 만약 시야가 넓어져 주변의 풀이나 하늘을 본다면, 사자를 놓칠 가능성이 커져서 위험에 처할 수 있는 반면, 사자에게 집중하면, 신속하게 도망치거나 대처할 수 있어서 생존 가능성을 높여주었다는 것'이므로, 불안이 좁은 시야를 유발하여 흉기와 같은 위협적인 자극에 더 쉽게 집중할 수 있게 한다는 것은 진화론적인 측면에서 "타당하다"고 할 수 있다. 따라서 ③이 정답이다. ① 취소할 수 없는 ② 즐거운 ④ 퇴보하는 ⑤ 의심 많은

40 내용일치   ④

| 분석 |

'유용한 정보가 주의를 기울이는 스포트라이트 밖에 있다면, 그 경우에는 이러한 좁음에 대가가 따른다(=그 유용한 정보를 놓칠 수 있다)'라고 돼 있으므로 ④가 본문의 내용과 일치하지 않는 진술이다.

윗글의 내용과 일치하지 않는 것은?
① 시각적 주의력은 보이는 것의 일부만 부각시킨다.
② 불안감으로 인해 위협적 자극에 쉽게 집중할 수 있다.
③ 현대사회에서 일정량의 불안은 문제해결에 도움이 될 수 있다.
④ 유용한 정보가 스포트라이트 밖에 있을 경우 시야를 확장할 수 있다.
⑤ 주의력이 충분히 확장되지 않으면 잘못된 결론에 이를 수 있다.

KONKUK UNIVERSITY | 건국대학교 자연계 B형

TEST p. 80~88

| 01 | ④ | 02 | ⑤ | 03 | ① | 04 | ④ | 05 | ① | 06 | ④ | 07 | ⑤ | 08 | ④ | 09 | ④ | 10 | ② |
| 11 | ⑤ | 12 | ③ | 13 | ④ | 14 | ④ | 15 | ④ | 16 | ⑤ | 17 | ② | 18 | ④ | 19 | ③ | 20 | ④ |

01 동의어 ④

| 어휘 |

assertion n. 단언, 주장   **impartially** ad. 치우치지 않고, 편견 없이; 공명정대하게(= objectively)   **uncritically** ad. 무비판적으로, 비판력 없이   **nervously** ad. 신경질적으로   **miraculously** ad. 기적으로   **promptly** ad. 신속히; 즉석에서   **unanimously** ad. 만장일치로

| 해석 |

다양한 지식 분야의 권위자들이 틀릴 수도 있다는 점을 기억하는 것이 중요하다. 따라서 그들의 주장은 공정하게 검토되어야 하며, 무비판적으로 받아들여져서는 안 된다.

02 동의어 ⑤

| 어휘 |

nuance n. 뉘앙스, 미묘한 차이(= subtlety)   **appropriate** a. 적절한, 적당한   **detail** n. (작고 덜 중요한) 세부 사항   **absurdity** n. 불합리, 어리석음   **condition** n. 조건; 상태   **contradiction** n. 부인, 부정; 모순

| 해석 |

비슷한 단어들 간의 미묘한 차이에 대한 지식은 작가로 하여금 각각의 상황에 가장 적절한 단어를 선택할 수 있게 해준다.

03 동의어 ①

| 어휘 |

motor vehicle 자동차   **varied** a. 다채로운, 다양한(= diverse)   **guideline** n. 지침   **respected** a. 훌륭한, 평판이 좋은   **prevalent** a. 널리 행해지는, 유행하고 있는   **prohibited** a. 금지된   **factual** a. 사실의, 사실에 입각한

| 해석 |

일반적으로, 미국에서 자동차를 운전하는 것은 매우 다채로운 기술이다. 각각의 주마다 자동차를 다루는 방법에 대한 자체적인 법과 지침이 있다.

04 동의어 ④

| 어휘 |

sign n. 기호, 신호, 수화(sign language)의 손짓   **uniform** a. 동일한, 획일적인   **obtain** v. 얻다   **delegation** n. 대표단(= deputation)   **tribe** n. 부족, 종족   **rebellion** n. 반란, 폭동   **reconciliation** n. 조정; 화해   **extinction** n. 절멸, 멸종   **prosperity** n. 번영, 번창

| 해석 |

카이오와(Kaiowa), 코만치(Comanche), 아파치(Apache), 위치타(Wichita) 부족들의 새로운 대표단으로부터 일단의 거의 동일한 수화 손짓들이 수집되었다.

05 동의어 ①

| 어휘 |

cinematography n. 영화 촬영술   **bear witness to** ~의 증거이다; 증명[증언]하다   **unimpeachable** a. 더할 나위 없는; 나무랄 데 없는 (= irreproachable)   **invoke** v. 불러일으키다, 자극하다; 간절히 바라다   **metaphysics** n. 형이상학; 순수철학   **inadvertent** a. 부주의한, 태만한   **insincere** a. 불성실한; 위선적인   **unpresumptuous** a. 오만하지 않은, 겸손한   **unrepentant** a. 회개하지 않는; 완고한

| 해석 |

영화 촬영술이 "있는 그대로의 사물"에 대해 흠 잡을 데 없는 증언을 해준다는 벤더스(Wenders)의 신념은 존재의 형이상학을 불러일으킨다.

06 논리완성 ④

| 분석 |

뇌의 크기와 사회 집단의 크기 사이의 상관관계는 측정 가능한 데이터 혹은 연구 결과를 통해 밝혀진 상관관계이므로, "통계적인"이라는 의미의 ④가 빈칸에 들어가기에 가장 적절하다.

| 어휘 |

primate n. 영장류 동물   **reveal** v. 드러내다; 폭로하다; 들추어내다   **problematic** a. 문제의, 문제가 되는   **negative** a. 부정의; 거부의

physical a. 육체의; 물질적인 　**statistical** a. 통계의, 통계학의
biological a. 생물학의

| 해석 |

살아 있는 비인간 영장류의 공동체와 뇌의 크기에 대한 연구는 뇌의 크기와 사회 집단 크기 사이의 강한 통계적 연관성을 보여준다. 즉, 뇌가 더 클수록 개체들이 살아가는 사회 공동체도 더 크다.

07 논리완성 ⑤

| 분석 |

바로 앞에서 '그래서 히포크라테스는 감정과 질병을 그것들의 공통된 선행 원인에 의해 연결시켰다'고 했고 이것이 세부적인 잘못은 있다 해도 선견지명이 있는 지침이라고 했으므로, 그는 인간의 질병, 즉 건강이 감정과 연관되어 있음을 유의하라고 말한 셈이므로 빈칸에는 ⑤가 적절하다.

| 어휘 |

physician n. 의사, 내과의사　**posit** v. 긍정적으로 가정하다, 상정하다　**fluid** n. 유체; 액체　**humor** n. 체액; 분비물　**imbalanced** a. 불균형한　**malady** n. 질병　**characteristic** a. 특징적인, 특유한　**chronic** a. 만성적인　**bile** n. 담즙　**phlegm** n. 점액질　**sanguine** a. 쾌활한　**affect** n. 감동, 정서　**by virtue of** ~에 의해, ~에 의거하여　**antecedent** n. 앞서는, 선행하는　**prescient** a. 선견지명[예지력]이 있는

| 해석 |

최초의 의사였던 히포크라테스는 균형이 깨질 때 여러 신체적인 질병을 일으키는 네 가지 신체 액체("체액")가 존재한다고 가정했다. 그러나 히포크라테스의 이론은 단순히 신체 액체를 질병과 연관 짓는 이론 이상의 것이었다. 그것은 감정을 위한 역할도 포함하고 있었다. 질병을 유발한다고 여겨지는 체액의 불균형은 또한 특징적이고 만성적인 감정 상태를 만들어낸다는 것이 히포크라테스의 견해였다. 예를 들어, 검은 담즙은 슬픔을, 점액질은 졸음을, 피는 쾌활한 감정을, 노란 담즙은 분노를 유발한다고 보았고, 그래서 히포크라테스는 감정과 질병을 그것들의 공통된 선행 원인에 의해 연결시켰던 것이다. 히포크라테스가 세부적인 부분에 있어서는 분명히 잘못된 점이 있었지만, 만약 우리가 세부 사항에서의 잘못된 점을 무시하고 그 대신 큰 그림에 집중한다면, 히포크라테스는 선견지명을 가진 지침을 제공한다. 그는 감정과 건강 사이의 관련성을 찾아볼 것을 독려하고 있는 것이다.

① 구체적인 세부 사항과 큰 그림
② 감정과 체액 불균형
③ 질병과 성격 유형
④ 혈액형과 성격
⑤ 감정과 건강

08 논리완성 ④

| 분석 |

두 가지 상반된 선택 사이에서 결정을 내려야 하는 상황을 설명할 수 있는 단어가 필요하므로 ④가 정답으로 적절하다.

| 어휘 |

ethical a. 윤리적인　**affluent** a. 부유한, 풍부한　**forego** v. 포기하다, 그만두다(= forgo)　**recompense** v. ~에게 보답하다, 보상하다　**sufficient** a. 충분한, 흡족한　**confinement** n. 제한, 한정; 감금　**discrimination** n. 구별; 차별　**paradigm** n. 모범, 패러다임　**dilemma** n. 궁지, 딜레마　**pretext** n. 구실, 핑계

| 해석 |

때때로 제약 회사들이 마주하게 되는 한 가지 윤리적 딜레마는, 가난한 국가에서는 부유한 국가에서보다 약품을 더 저렴하게 판매해서 신약 개발에 요구되는 막대한 연구비용을 보상할 이익을 포기할 것인가, 아니면 약품을 시장 가격에 판매해서 신약 개발을 계속할 수 있는 충분한 자금을 확보할 것인가 하는 것이다.

09 관계대명사 ④

| 분석 |

관계대명사 what에는 선행사가 포함돼 있는데 반해, ⓓ의 앞에는 선행사가 존재하고 있으므로 ⓓ의 자리에 관계대명사 what을 쓴 것은 잘못이다. 따라서 이것을 which로 고쳐야 한다.

| 어휘 |

rub n. 문제, 어려움; 곤란　**consist in** ~에 있다　**registration** n. 등록　**stimulus** n. 자극　**trigger** v. (일련의 사건·반응 등을) 일으키다, 유발하다　**as it were** 이를테면, 말하자면　**consistent** a. 일치하는, 양립하는　**reject** v. 거절하다, 각하하다

| 해석 |

그리고 여기에 제임스의 문제가 있다. 만약 감정이 우리가 감정 유발 자극을 마음에 기록하는 것에 있고 또 그 자극에 자동적으로 유발되는 신체 반응에 있다면, 우리는 감정이 실제로 행동을 일으키는지 의문을 던질 수도 있다. 만약 우리가 도망가기 때문에 두려움을 느낀다면, 두려움은 도망치는 원인이 아니라, 말하자면, 도망치는 과정에서 동반되는 의식 상태일 뿐이다. 제임스-랑게 감정 이론은 제임스가 거부했던 뇌의 자동화 이론과 상당히 일치하는 듯하다.

10 주어와 동사의 수일치 ②

| 분석 |

ⓑ의 주어는 One way이며 that a writer can create engaging and entertaining articles는 주어를 수식하고 있다. 주어가 단수이므로 ⓑ는 is가 되어야 한다.

| 어휘 |

engaging a. 마음을 끄는, 매력적인   entertaining a. 유쾌한, 재미있는   article n. (신문·잡지의) 글, 기사   identify v. (신원 등을) 확인하다[알아보다]; 찾다, 발견하다   anecdote n. 일화   sermon n. 설교   monologue n. 독백   be at home in ~에 어울리다, 적합하다(match or suit a particular environment)

| 해석 |

작가가 매력적이고 재미있는 기사를 작성할 수 있는 한 가지 방법은 일화를 찾아내고, 작성하고, 배치하는 법을 익히는 것이다. 빈틈없이 써진 이 짧막한 이야기들은 맛깔 나는 작은 조각들로, 어느 편집자는 이것들을 기사를 이루는 "초콜릿 조각들"이라고 묘사한다. 이 작은 이야기들은 연설, 설교, 코미디 독백, 그리고 책에서도 특집기사에서 만큼이나 잘 어울린다.

11 내용일치   ⑤

| 분석 |

첫 문장에서 그의 사망연도를 1935년으로 밝히고 있다. 그러므로 ⑤가 본문의 내용과 일치하지 않는 진술이다. 그가 죽은 후인 1962년에는 영화 "아라비아의 로렌스"가 나왔다.

| 어휘 |

archaeologist n. 고고학자   reputation n. 평판, 명성   publicity n. 매스컴의 관심[주목]   feature v. 〈영화〉 주연시키다; ~의 역을 하다

| 해석 |

T. E. 로렌스(T. E. Lawrence, 1888–1935)는 영국의 군인이자 작가였다. 그는 고고학자로 경력을 시작했지만, 1916년에 사우디 아라비아로 가서 중동에서의 터키의 지배에 대항하는 성공적인 군사작전을 계획하고 이끌었다. 이로 인해 그는 '아라비아의 로렌스'로 알려지게 되었다. 그는 이 작전을 자신의 저서 『지혜의 일곱 기둥(1926)』에서 묘사했다. 이 책은 그에게 명성과 낭만적인 이미지를 가져다주었지만, 그는 매스컴의 주목을 받는 것을 싫어했으며 두 차례에 걸쳐 이름을 바꿈으로써 이를 피하려 했다. 그는 영국의 도싯(Dorset)에서 오토바이 사고로 사망했다. 영화 "아라비아의 로렌스(1962)"에서는 피터 오툴(Peter O'Toole)이 주인공인 로렌스 역을 맡았다.

T. E. Lawrence에 대한 다음 글의 내용과 일치하지 않는 것은?
① 군인, 작가, 고고학자 등 여러 직업이 있었다.
② 터키가 중동 지역을 지배하는 것에 반대했다.
③ '아라비아의 로렌스'라는 별칭을 얻게 되었다.
④ 유명세를 싫어해서 두 차례 개명했다.
⑤ 1962년 오토바이 사고로 사망했다.

12 내용일치   ③

| 분석 |

"모든 약이 모든 사람에게 효과가 있는 것은 아니지만, 적당한 비율의 사람들에게라도 효과가 있다면 규제 기관은 자주 그것을 승인한다."라고 했으므로, ③이 본문의 내용과 일치하지 않는다.

| 어휘 |

moderate a. 알맞은, 적당한; 보통의   regulator n. 조정자, 단속자   approve v. 승인하다, 허가하다   show up 나타나다, 나오다   thinner n. 희석제   Warfarin n. 와파린(혈액 응고 저지제)   internal bleeding 내출혈

| 해석 |

현재 우리 의학계는 대체로 평균에 기초하고 있다. 예를 들어, 모든 약이 모든 사람에게 효과가 있는 것은 아니지만, 적당한 비율의 사람들에게라도 효과가 있다면 규제 기관은 자주 그것을 승인한다. 만약 당신이 그 약으로 치료될 수 있는 질환을 가지고 일반적인 의사의 진료실에 모습을 드러낼 경우, 대체로 그 약이 효과가 있는지를 알아내는 매우 간단한 방법이 있는데, 이는 그 약을 시도해 보는 것이다. 만약 당신이 일반적인 혈액 희석제인 와파린을 복용하고 그것이 도움이 된다면, 이는 와파린이 당신의 몸에 적합하다는 것을 입증하는 것이다. 하지만 와파린이 내출혈을 일으켜 사망에 이르게 할 수 있는 100명 중 1명에 당신이 해당한다면, 당신은 그 약이 당신에게 맞지 않는다는 사실을 힘든 경험을 통해 깨닫게 된다.

다음 글의 내용과 일치하지 않는 것은?
① 우리의 현재 의학계는 대부분 평균에 기초한다.
② 모든 약이 모든 사람에게 잘 맞는 것은 아니다.
③ 어떤 약이 대다수의 사람에게 효과가 있을 때 규제기관은 그 약을 승인한다.
④ 백 명 중 한 명은 와파린을 복용하고 죽을 수도 있다.
⑤ 어떤 질환이 어떤 약으로 치료될지를 알아내는 간단한 방법은 복용해보는 것이다.

13 글의 요지   ④

| 분석 |

본문에서 말하고자 하는 핵심은 '초기 인류 사회에서 남성들이 여성들과 함께 협력하여 더 큰 두뇌를 가진 자녀를 키우기 위해 필요한 추가적인 영양분을 공급했다'는 것이다. 이를 뒷받침하기 위해, 여성들 혼자서는 자녀에게 필요한 영양분을 제공하기 어려웠을 것이라면서 남성들이 중요한 역할을 했을 것이라 주장하고 있다.

| 어휘 |

account n. 설명; 이유, 근거   evolution n. 진화   depict v. 묘사하다, 서술하다   hands-on a. (말만 하지 않고) 직접 해 보는[실천하는]   expand v. 넓어지다, 커지다   be stretched to capacity 능력을 최대한 발휘하다   reckon v. 세다, 합산하다; 생각하다, 여겨지다   australopithecine a. 오스트랄로피테쿠스계(系)의   nourishment n. 자양물, 음식물, 영양(물)

| 해석 |

초기 인류의 진화에 대한 설명 가운데 남성을 아버지나 아들이라고 서술하는 것은 거의 없으나, 우리의 남성 조상 각자는 모두 아버지이자 아들이었다. 이것이 초기 인류의 아버지들이 초기 인류의 어머니만큼 자녀 양육에 직접 많은 노력을 기울였다는 것을 말하는 것은 아니다. 그러나 우리의 조상들의 뇌의 크기가 커지기 시작하면서, 성인 남성들은 어머니와 자녀들과 함께 살게 되었고, 집단은 식량을 채집하고 준비하는 데 있어 협력했을 가능성이 크다. 우리가 보기에는 어머니들이 그들 자신과 더 큰 뇌를 가진 그들의 아이들을 위한 충분한 식량을 얻기 위해 성인 남성들의 도움을 필요로 했을 것으로 보인다. 어미 침팬지들은 뇌가 더 큰 새끼들을 살아있게 하기에 충분한 먹이를 찾기 위해 최대한의 능력을 발휘한다. 우리는 오스트랄로피테쿠스계의 어머니들이 협력하고 나이가 많은 자녀들의 도움을 받았더라면 이를 해결할 수 있었을 것이라고 생각한다. 하지만 어머니들이 어떻게 그들 자신의 더 큰 뇌를 유지시키면서 동시에 훨씬 더 큰 뇌를 가진 아이들의 성장을 유지하는 데 필요한 열량을 공급하기에 충분한 식량을 찾을 수 있었을지는 알기 어렵다. 남성들이 추가적인 영양분 공급의 가능한 유일한 원천이었다.

다음 글의 요지로 가장 적절한 것은?
① 인류의 두뇌 크기의 발달은 충분한 영양분의 공급과 함께 이루어졌다.
② 초기 인류 사회에서 여성의 역할은 아이를 키우는 것에 한정됐다.
③ 초기 인류 사회에서 여성들은 협동 작업을 통해 아이들을 양육했다.
④ 인간의 초기 진화에서 남성은 추가적인 영양분 공급을 제공하는 역할을 했다.
⑤ 아이들의 두뇌 크기가 점점 커지면서 부모들은 점점 더 많은 식량을 찾아야 했다.

14 문장삽입   ④

| 분석 |

주어진 문장은 "얼룩말은 모든 동물들을 그다지 대표하지 않는데, 그것이 포유류뿐만 아니라 곤충, 벌레, 오징어의 표본이어야 할 경우 특히 그러하다."라는 의미인데, 이것은 '박테리아를 모두 똑같은 것인 양 보편적인 관점으로만 다루는 것이 어리석은 일임'을 동물의 경우를 예로 들어 부연 설명하는 내용이므로, 주어진 문장은 D에 들어가는 것이 가장 적절하다.

| 어휘 |

squid n. 오징어   mammal n. 포유동물   organism n. 유기체   multiply v. 증식하다   offspring n. 자식, 자손   adapt v. 적응시키다   repertoire n. 연주 곡목   universalist n. 다방면에 능통한 사람, 만능인   detect v. 발견하다; 간파하다   term n. 조건; 용어   E. coli 대장균   be typical of ~를 대표하다   diversity n. 다양성

| 해석 |

박테리아는, 다른 모든 살아있는 유기체와 마찬가지로, 증식하기 위해 살아간다. 박테리아는 여건이 허락하는 한 자손을 만들어낼 것이고, 자신의 생활방식을 해당 지역 여건에 적응시키는 일을 할 능력이 있는 한 할 것이다. 일부 박테리아들은 가능한 생활방식의 수가 매우 적어서 항상 그것들이 다소 같은 여건에서 사는 것이 발견되는 반면에, 다른 박테리아들은 진정으로 만능인 개체여서 다양한 환경에서 발견될 수 있다. 박테리아가 모두 똑같은 것인 양, 그것들을 보편적인 관점으로만 다루는 것은 어리석은 일일 것이다. 〈얼룩말은 모든 동물들을 그다지 "대표하지" 않는데, 그것이 포유류뿐만 아니라 곤충, 벌레, 오징어의 표본이어야 할 경우 특히 그러하다.〉 마찬가지로, 아마도 가장 보편적으로 알려진 박테리아 종(種)인 대장균도 모든 박테리아를 "대표하지"는 않는다. 우리는 박테리아의 다양성을 인식하는 경우에만 그것들의 진정한 본질을 존중할 수 있다.

15~16

두 발로 걷는 종(種)에서, 엄지발가락은 더 이상 움켜쥐는 데 사용되지 않으며, 그래서 다른 발가락에 더 바짝 접근하여 한 줄로 정렬돼 있는 반면, 척추는 등쪽에서가 아니라 아래쪽에서부터 두개골로 들어간다. (네 다리로 엎드려 보면 그 이유를 이해할 것이다). 두 발로 걷기 위해서는 등, 엉덩이, 심지어 두개골까지 재배열되어야 했다. 그것은 또한 더 좁은 엉덩이를 선호했는데, 이는 출산을 더 어렵고 위험하게 만들었고, 아마도 많은 호미닌이, 현대의 인간들처럼, 아직 스스로의 힘으로는 생존할 수 없는 아기를 낳았다는 것을 의미할 것이다. 그것은 그들의 아기들이 더 많은 부모의 보살핌을 필요로 했다는 것을 의미했을 것이고, 이는 사회성을 촉진하고 호미닌 아버지들을 자녀 양육에 더 참여하게 했을 수도 있다. 이족보행(二足步行)의 간접적인 결과들이 많이 있었지만, 우리는 왜 호미닌이 이족보행을 하게 되었는지를 아직 정확히 알지 못한다. 아마도 이족보행은 지난 3천만 년 동안 차가워지는 세계 곳곳에 널리 퍼져 있었던 풀이 무성한 사바나 땅에서 우리 조상들이 더 멀리 걷거나 달릴 수 있게 해주었을 것이다. 이족보행은 또한 인간의 손을 〈제한하여(→ 자유롭게 하여)〉, 궁극적으로는 도구의 제작을 비롯한 정교한 수작업에 특화되게 해주었다.

| 어휘 |

bipedal a. 두 발로 걷는, 이족보행하는   grip v. 꽉 쥐다, 꼭 잡다   align v. 일직선으로 하다; ~을 조정[조절]하다   spine n. 척추   skull n. 두개골   braincase n. 두개(골), 머리   hominin n. 호미닌(인간의 조상으로 분류되는 종족)   give birth to ~을 낳다   infant n. 유아   child-rearing n. 자녀 양육   bipedalism n. 이족보행(二足步行)   manipulative a. 손끝으로 다루는; 교묘하게 다루는

15 내용일치 ④

| 분석 |

"호미닌이 스스로의 힘으로는 생존할 수 없는 아기를 낳았다는 것은 그들의 아기들이 더 많은 부모의 보살핌을 필요로 했다는 것을 의미했을 것이고, 이는 사회성을 촉진하고 호미닌 아버지들을 자녀 양육에 더 참여하게 했을 수 있다."라는 내용을 통해 ④가 본문의 내용과 일치하지 않음을 알 수 있다.

윗글의 내용과 일치하지 <u>않는</u> 것은?
① 두 발로 걷는 종에서 엄지발가락은 더 이상 움켜잡는 데 사용되지 않는다.
② 척추는 등쪽에서가 아니라 아래쪽에서부터 두개골로 들어간다.
③ 두 발로 걷는 것은 출산을 더 어렵고 위험하게 만들었다.
④ 호미닌 아버지들은 자녀 양육에 전혀 참여하지 않았을 수 있다.
⑤ 호미닌이 두 발로 보행하게 된 이유는 아직 확실하지 않다.

16 문맥상 적절하지 않은 단어 고르기 ⑤

| 분석 |

도구의 제작을 비롯해서 손을 정교하게 다루는 작업에 특화될 수 있었던 것은 손이 제한을 받은 데 따른 결과가 아니라 손이 자유로워진 데 따른 결과일 것이다. 그러므로 ⓔ는 freed여야 한다.

17~18

대부분의 사람들에게 하루의 주된 식사는 저녁 식사로, supper, tea 혹은 dinner라고 불린다. 그것은 대개 고기나 생선으로 조리한 음식이나 샐러드로 구성되며, 이후에는 디저트가 이어진다. 어떤 사람들은 텔레비전을 보면서 무릎 위에 음식을 올려놓고 먹는 TV supper를 즐기기도 한다. 영국에서는 어린 아이들이 학교에서 돌아오면 tea를 먹을 수도 있다. 성인들의 주된 식사를 의미하는 tea라는 단어는 특히 스코틀랜드와 아일랜드에서 사용되며, supper와 dinner라는 단어는 잉글랜드와 웨일즈에서 더 널리 쓰이고 있다. dinner라는 단어가 supper라는 단어보다 더 격식 있게 들리며, 손님들은 대개 'supper'보다는 'dinner'에 대한 초대장을 받는다. 미국에서는 저녁 식사를 dinner라고 부른다. 보통 오후 6시에서 6시 30분쯤에 먹으며, 데우기만 하면 되도록 이미 조리된 채로 판매되는 음식으로 이루어질 때가 종종 있다. 영국과 미국의 많은 가정에서는 가족 구성원들이 각자 다른 시간에 식사를 하며, 식탁에 함께 앉아 식사를 하는 경우는 드물다. 특별한 경우가 아니면, 저녁 식사에 와인을 마시는 사람은 거의 없다.

| 어휘 |

tea n. 저녁 식사(영국에서 일부 사람들이 쓰는 말로, 특히 이른 저녁에 따뜻하게 요리한 음식으로 먹는 것) **sweet course** 디저트 **consist of** ~로 구성되어 있다

17 내용일치 ②

| 분석 |

'성인들의 주된 식사를 의미하는 tea는 특히 스코틀랜드와 아일랜드에서 사용되며, supper와 dinner는 잉글랜드와 웨일즈에서 더 널리 쓰이고 있다.'라고 했으므로, ②가 본문의 내용과 일치하지 않는 진술이다.

윗글의 내용과 일치하지 <u>않는</u> 것은?
① 'TV supper'란 TV를 보면서 먹는 저녁을 뜻한다.
② 웨일즈에서는 주로 저녁 식사를 'tea'라고 부른다.
③ 영국에서는 가족이 함께 식사하는 일이 흔치 않다.
④ 'supper'보다 'dinner'가 좀 더 격식 있는 표현이다.
⑤ 미국의 저녁 식사는 이미 조리된 음식일 때가 많다.

18 어법상 적절하지 않은 표현 고르기 ④

| 분석 |

ⓓ의 주어는 단수 대명사 It이므로, ⓓ는 consists가 되어야 한다.

19~20

트릭스터는 일종의 영웅이지만, 그는 종종 그다지 영웅적인 것 같지 않다. 트릭스터는 다양한 이름이나 모습을 가질 수 있지만, 그의 두드러진 특징은 인간관계에서의 교활함이다. 일반적으로, 트릭스터는 얼간이와 속임수로 계약을 맺고 나서 그를 배신한다. 그는 사회가 정한 경계를 어김으로써 자신의 힘을 얻는 유력인사다. 또는 그가 속임수를 시도하다 들켜서 망신을 당하기도 한다. 이 경우, 트릭스터 또한 얼간이가 되며, 이야기 속 다른 인물들이 그를 벌하는 유력인사로 묘사된다. 어떤 이야기에서는 두 명의 트릭스터 간에 경쟁이 나타나기도 한다. 대개 해피엔딩으로 끝나는 유럽의 민담과 달리, 트릭스터 이야기는 일반적으로 불화로 끝난다. 살아남은 많은 아프리카계 미국인의 민담은 비웃음을 받으면서도 교훈을 주는 행동을 하는 트릭스터의 모험을 그려내고 있다.

| 어휘 |

trickster n. 사기꾼, 책략가, 트릭스터(원시 민족의 신화에 나와 주술·장난 등으로 질서를 문란하게 하는 초자연적 존재) **predominant** a. 현저한, 유력한, 눈에 띄는 **characteristic** n. 특질, 특색 **guile** n. 교활; 기만 **forge** v. (관계·우정 등을) 구축하다[쌓다]; (거짓말 따위

를) 지어내다, 날조하다, 꾸며내다   **contract** n. 계약   **dupe** n. 잘 속는 사람, 얼뜨기, 얼간이   **betray** v. 배반하다   **power broker** (지역에 정치적 영향력을 행사하는) 실세[유력 인사], 막후 인물   **boundary** n. 경계; 한계, 범위   **disharmony** n. 부조화, 불일치   **depict** v. 묘사하다, 서술하다   **laugh at** 비웃다

19 지시대상   ③

| 분석 |

ⓒ는 속임을 당하는 dupe를 지칭하는 반면, 나머지는 모두 trickster를 가리킨다.

20 내용일치   ④

| 분석 |

'속임수를 시도하다 들켜서 망신을 당하기도 한다'고 했으므로 ④가 정답으로 적절하다. ② 이름과 모습은 다양하지만, 주된 특징은 교활함으로 일정하다.

윗글에 제시된 'trickster'에 대한 설명으로 올바른 것은?
① 그 어떤 영웅보다도 영웅적 면모가 두드러진다.
② 여러 이름만큼이나 다양한 성격적 특성이 있다.
③ 대체로 행복하게 끝나는 이야기의 주인공이 된다.
④ 때로 잔꾀를 부리다가 곤경에 처할 때도 있다.
⑤ 사회적 규범을 수호하여 권력을 얻게 된다.

경기대학교 일반편입 A형

TEST p. 90~101

01	④	02	①	03	④	04	①	05	④	06	③	07	②	08	④	09	③	10	②
11	①	12	②	13	①	14	②	15	③	16	①	17	④	18	③	19	②	20	④
21	④	22	④	23	①	24	④	25	④	26	②	27	②	28	①	29	④	30	③
31	③	32	①	33	②	34	①	35	④	36	③	37	③	38	①	39	④	40	①

01 논리완성 ④

| 분석 |
웹사이트에 가입하면서 개인 전화번호를 입력하는 것은 오직 사람만이 할 수 있는 것이므로, 이것은 실제로 사람이 가입하는 것인지를 '확인'하기 위한 절차일 것이다. 따라서 ④가 정답이다.

| 어휘 |
bot n. 로봇 **justify** v. 정당화하다, 정당함을 증명하다 **manifest** v. 명시하다 **relate** v. 관계시키다, 관련시키다 **verify** v. (진실인지·정확한지) 확인하다, 입증하다

| 해석 |
A: 왜 이 웹사이트에 가입하려면 전화번호를 입력해야 하니?
B: 그것은 네가 진짜 사람이지 로봇이 아니라는 것을 그들이 확인하는 방법 중의 하나일 뿐이야.

02 논리완성 ①

| 분석 |
누가 새 프로젝트를 담당하게 되었는지를 물었으므로, 그 역할을 맡게 될 사람이 누구인지를 대답하는 흐름이 되어야 한다. 빈칸 이하는 A가 한 말 중의 be in charge of the new project와 같은 의미가 되어야 하므로, '(책임을) 맡다'라는 뜻의 ①이 정답으로 적절하다.

| 어휘 |
be in charge of ~을 담당하다 **assume** v. (책임을) 맡다; (사실일 것으로) 추정[상정]하다 **preserve** v. 보존하다 **confront** v. 직면하다 **challenge** v. 도전하다

| 해석 |
A: 누가 새 프로젝트를 담당하게 될까?
B: 사장님이 팀(Tim)에게 그 일의 책임을 맡아달라고 요청했어.

03 논리완성 ④

| 분석 |
B는 화가 난 고객을 어떻게 '진정하게' 만들었는지에 대해 대답해야 하므로, '달래다, 진정시키다'라는 의미의 ④가 정답으로 적절하다.

| 어휘 |
integrate v. 통합하다 **attune** v. 조율하다, 맞추다 **conform** v. (사회의 규범·관습 따위에) 적합[순응]시키다; 따르게 하다 **placate** v. 달래다, 진정시키다

| 해석 |
A: 그 화가 난 고객을 어떻게 진정시켰니?
B: 할인을 해줘서 가까스로 그녀를 달랬어.

04 논리완성 ①

| 분석 |
일자리 감축이 있을 거라는 것을 전혀 몰랐던 사람이 그 소식을 들었을 때의 반응으로 적절한 것은 '놀라움', '충격' 등이 될 것이므로, 그러한 의미를 가진 표현인 ①이 정답으로 적절하다.

| 어휘 |
flabbergast v. 소스라쳐 놀라게 하다, 당황하게 하다 **whittle** v. (나무를) 조금씩 깎다; 줄이다, 삭감하다 **admonish** v. 훈계하다, 타이르다 **consecrate** v. 신성하게 하다

| 해석 |
A: 일자리 감축이 있을 거라는 걸 알고 있었니?
B: 전혀 몰랐어. 그 소식을 듣고 완전히 깜짝 놀랐어.

05 논리완성 ④

| 분석 |
뒤에서 "어느 쪽도 타협하려 하지 않았다"고 했으므로 빈칸에는 '비타협적인 태도'라는 뜻의 ④가 적절하다.

| 어휘 |
contract n. 계약, 약정 **negotiation** n. 협상, 교섭 **break down** (계획 따위가) 실패하다 **compromise** v. 타협하다, 절충하다; 화해시키다 **gallantry** n. 용감함, 정중함 **enthrallment** n. 매혹; 노예화 **dormancy** n. 휴면 상태 **intransigence** n. 비타협적인 태도

| 해석 |
A: 왜 계약 협상이 결렬되었니?
B: 나는 양측 모두의 비타협적인 태도 때문이라고 생각해. 어느 쪽도 타협하려 하지 않았어.

06 논리완성 ③

| 분석 |
발표에 부담을 느끼고 있는 사람에게 조언을 하는 맥락이므로, 빈칸에는 '발표하는' 행위와 관련된 '똑똑히 발음해서 말하다'는 뜻의 ③이 적절하다.

| 어휘 |
be stressed out 스트레스를 받고 있다 **provoke** v. (감정 따위를) 일으키다; 유발하다 **encroach** v. 침입하다, 잠식하다 **articulate** v. 명확히 말하다; 똑똑히 발음하다 **delegate** v. 대표[대리]로 보내다; (권한 등을) 위임하다

| 해석 |
A: 학급 친구들 앞에서 발표하는 것에 대해 너무 스트레스를 받고 있어.
B: 그냥 심호흡을 하고, 요점을 분명하게 말하는 걸 잊지 마라.

07 논리완성 ②

| 분석 |
마리가 스트레스가 많은 상황에 잘 대처한다는 데 대해 B가 동의했으므로, 그 뒤에는 마리를 긍정하는 내용으로 매사에 자신감을 '뿜어내다, 발산하다'는 말이 오는 것이 자연스럽다. 따라서 ②가 정답으로 적절하다.

| 어휘 |
rescind v. (법률·행위 등) 폐지하다; (계약 등을) 무효로 하다 **exude** v. 물씬 풍기다, 발산하다 **depose** v. 면직시키다, 해임하다 **dissipate** v. 흩뜨리다; (의심 따위를) 일소하다

| 해석 |
A: 마리(Marie)는 스트레스 많은 상황을 정말로 잘 처리하네.
B: 그래. 그녀는 항상 자신감을 발산하는 것 같아.

08 논리완성 ④

| 분석 |
짧은 경력 기간에 많은 소설을 썼다는 것은 제임스 하디가 다작의 작가였다는 것이므로, ④가 정답으로 적절하다.

| 어휘 |
lenient a. 관대한 **irreverent** a. 불손한, 불경한 **deferential** a. 공경하는 **prolific** a. 다작(多作)의; 다산(多産)의, (토지가) 비옥한

| 해석 |
A: 제임스 하디(James Hardy)는 자신의 짧은 경력 기간에 정말 많은 소설을 출간했어.
B: 맞아. 그가 얼마나 다작하는 작가인지 믿을 수 없을 정도야.

09 논리완성 ③

| 분석 |
관리자가 되고 싶다는 것은 자신의 팀을 이끌어 보고 싶다는 것이므로 빈칸에는 ③이 들어가는 것이 적절하다.

| 어휘 |
abate v. 줄이다, 낮추다 **anoint** v. (상처 따위에) 기름을[연고를] 바르다; 성직에 임명하다; 임명하다 **relish** v. 즐기다 **commend** v. 칭찬하다

| 해석 |
A: 언젠가는 관리자가 되고 싶은 거니?
B: 그래. 내 팀을 이끄는 기회를 정말 즐기고 싶어.

10 논리완성 ②

| 분석 |
회사를 재난에서 구했다고 했으므로, CEO가 내린 전략적인 결정을 수식하는 표현으로는 ②가 들어가는 것이 가장 자연스럽다.

| 어휘 |
disaster n. 재난, 재해, 참사 **strategic** a. 전략의, 전략상 중요한 **vigilant** a. 방심하지 않는; 부단히 경계하고 있는 **shrewd** a. 날카로운; 영리한, 통찰력 있는 **impudent** a. 무례한, 버릇없는 **recalcitrant** a. 반항하는

| 해석 |
A: CEO가 회사를 재난에서 구했어.
B: 그래. 그녀는 매우 통찰력 있는 전략적 결정을 내렸어.

11 논리완성 ①

| 분석 |
침략 전쟁의 실제 동기가 영토적 야욕이었다면, 국가 방어는 '핑계, 구실'에 불과한 것이었을 것이다.

| 어휘 |
dictator n. 독재자   **justify** v. 정당화하다   **aggression** n. 공격, 침략   **motivate** v. 동기를 주다, 자극하다   **territorial** a. 영토의   **pretext** n. 구실, 핑계   **imposition** n. (세금·벌 따위를) 부과, 과세   **epitome** n. 요약, 발췌; 전형   **venture** n. 모험, 모험적 사업

| 해석 |
그 독재자는 실제로는 영토적 야욕에 의해 추진된 침략 전쟁을 정당화하기 위해 국가 방어를 구실로 삼았다.

12 논리완성 ②

| 분석 |
노동 분쟁을 끝내려 시도했다면, 정부는 상대방을 달래기 위해 일정한 '양보'를 제안했을 가능성이 크다.

| 어휘 |
labor dispute 노동 분쟁   **repercussion** n. (보통 부정적인) 영향, 반향   **concession** n. 양보, 인정   **expedition** n. 탐험, 원정   **premonition** n. 예감, 불길한 예감

| 해석 |
노동 분쟁을 끝내려는 시도에서, 정부는 몇 가지 양보를 하겠다고 제안했다.

13 논리완성 ①

| 분석 |
새 양탄자에 와인을 쏟은 것에 대해 안 좋은 기분이 들었다고 했는데, though로 연결되므로 와인을 쏟은 것은 자신에게 책임을 돌릴 수 없는 '무심코', '우연히' 일어난 일이어야 한다. 따라서 ①이 정답으로 가장 적절하다. ③ '부주의하게'나 ④ '경솔하게'는 자신에게 책임을 돌릴 수 있게 되어 though에 맞지 않아 부적절하다.

| 어휘 |
awful a. 끔찍한, 두려운, 무시무시한   **spill** v. (액체·가루 따위를) 엎지르다, 흩뜨리다   **rug** n. 융단, 양탄자   **inadvertently** ad. 무심코, 우연히   **illustriously** ad. 저명하게, 눈부시게   **inattentively** ad. 부주의하게   **indiscreetly** ad. 무분별하게, 경솔하게

| 해석 |
브루스는 비록 우연히 그렇게 한 것이지만, 사라의 새 양탄자에 와인을 쏟은 일에 끔찍한 기분이 들었다.

14 논리완성 ②

| 분석 |
의자를 특정 각도로 조절하는 상황이다. 몸을 뒤로 기대게 되면 의자는 젖혀지게 될 것이므로 빈칸에는 ②가 들어가야 한다. 각도가 조절되는 의자를 reclining chair라고 한다.

| 어휘 |
lean v. 기대다   **descend** v. 내려가다, 내리다   **recline** v. 기대다; 비스듬히 젖히다   **reflect** v. 반영하다, 반사하다   **curl** v. (머리털을) 곱슬곱슬하게 하다; (수염 따위를) 꼬다

| 해석 |
ComfyMan 의자를 젖히려면, 오른쪽에 있는 레버를 당긴 다음 원하는 각도가 될 때까지 뒤로 기대세요.

15 논리완성 ③

| 분석 |
'고객 불만 처리'라는 행위에는 그 일을 실행하기 위한 방법이나 '절차'가 수반될 것이므로, 빈칸에는 ③이 들어가야 한다.

| 어휘 |
detailed a. 상세한   **complaint** n. 불평, 고충   **transaction** n. (업무) 처리, 거래   **enterprise** n. 기업, 사업   **procedure** n. 절차, 과정   **ratio** n. 비율

| 해석 |
이 회사는 고객의 불만사항을 처리하기 위한 상세한 절차를 갖추고 있다.

16 논리완성 ①

| 분석 |
중재자는 분쟁에 개입하여 쌍방을 화해시키는 역할을 하는 사람이므로, 긴장된 상황을 '완화시키는' 역할을 한다고 볼 수 있다.

| 어휘 |
skilled a. 숙련된   **mediator** n. 중재자   **full-on** a. 최대의, 극도의   **defuse** v. (긴장·위험을) 완화하다   **exude** v. (냄새·감정 등을) 발산하다, 넘치다   **pamper** v. 애지중지하다, 하고 싶은 대로 하게 하다   **obscure** v. 흐리게 하다, 모호하게 하다

| 해석 |
숙련된 중재자는 종종 극도의 언쟁이 일어나기 전에 긴장된 상황을 완화시킬 수 있다.

17 논리완성 ④

| 분석 |
호텔 건설에 반대하여 연좌농성을 벌일 정도라면 반대하는 정도가 매우 '열렬했다'고 볼 수 있으므로, 빈칸에는 ④가 들어가는 것이 적절하다.

| 어휘 |
environmentalist n. 환경운동가　**stage** v. (파업·정치 운동·군사 작전 등을) 기획하다, 행하다　**sit-in protest** 연좌농성　**apathetically** ad. 무관심하게　**blithely** ad. 태평스럽게　**presciently** ad. 선견지명 있게　**vehemently** ad. 격렬하게, 열정적으로

| 해석 |
환경운동가들은 강변에 호텔을 건설하는 것에 너무나도 격렬히 반대해서 건설 현장에서 연좌농성을 벌였다.

18 논리완성 ③

| 분석 |
도시의 대부분이 불에 탄 사건에 대한 내용이므로 '대형 화재'라는 의미의 ③이 자연스럽게 호응한다.

| 어휘 |
massive a. (육중하면서) 거대한; 엄청나게 큰[심각한]　**secretion** n. 분비; 분비물　**emanation** n. 발산, 방사　**conflagration** n. 큰불, 대화재　**exoneration** n. 무죄 입증, 면죄

| 해석 |
역사 기록은 중세 시대에 그 도시의 대부분이 대형 화재로 인해 완전히 불타버렸음을 시사하고 있다.

19 논리완성 ②

| 분석 |
복지는 빈곤과 반대되는 개념이므로 복지에 더 많은 투자를 한다는 것은 빈곤을 없애거나 '개선하기' 위한 것이라 볼 수 있다.

| 어휘 |
perturb v. 혼란하게 하다, 교란하다　**ameliorate** v. 개선하다, 개량하다　**insinuate** v. 암시하다, 넌지시 말하다　**ornament** v. 장식하다

| 해석 |
도심 지역의 빈곤을 개선하기 위해서는 사회 복지 프로그램에 대한 더 많은 투자가 필요하다.

20 논리완성 ④

| 분석 |
다른 저자가 있음을 증거가 분명히 보여주고 있다면, 희곡『페리클레스, 티르의 왕자』를 셰익스피어가 전적으로 썼다는 주장은 '거짓인' 게 된다.

| 어휘 |
claim n. 요구, 청구　**evidence** n. 증거　**imperious** a. 고압적인　**clandestine** a. 은밀한　**hypothetical** a. 가설의　**spurious** a. 거짓된, 가짜의

| 해석 |
희곡『페리클레스, 티르의 왕자』를 셰익스피어가 전적으로 썼다는 주장은 거짓인데, 다른 저자가 있었다는 것을 증거가 분명히 지적하고 있기 때문이다.

21 조동사 ④

| 분석 |
엄청난 선물을 보았을 때 아이들은 자신들의 눈을 거의 믿을 '수 없었다'는 의미가 되는 것이 자연스러우므로, 추측이나 의무가 아닌 가능의 의미를 가진 조동사가 들어가야 한다. 따라서 ④가 정답이다.

| 해석 |
크리스마스트리 아래에 있는 엄청난 선물 더미를 보았을 때 아이들은 자신들의 눈을 거의 믿을 수 없었다.

22 부정사를 목적어로 취하는 타동사 ④

| 분석 |
offer는 to부정사를 목적어로 취하는 타동사이므로 빈칸에는 ④가 들어가야 한다.

| 어휘 |
disarmament n. (특히 핵무기의) 군비 축소

| 해석 |
냉전의 긴장을 완화하기 위해, 미국은 소련과의 핵무기 군축 회담에 참여하겠다는 제안을 했다.

23 시제 ①

| 분석 |
when절의 과거시제가 나타내는 과거의 특정 시점에서 일어나고 있었던 일은 과거진행시제를 써서 나타내므로 빈칸에는 ①이 들어가야 한다.

| 해석 |
그 여성은 연예 기획사 에이전트에게 발견되어 모델 일자리를 제안 받았을 때, 웨이트리스로 일하고 있었다.

24 전치사 + 관계대명사 ④

| 분석 |

관계대명사 뒤에는 불완전한 문장이 오고 '전치사+관계대명사' 뒤에는 완전한 문장이 온다. 주어진 문장의 경우 빈칸 뒤에 완전한 문장이 왔으므로, 관계대명사인 ①과 ②는 부적절하며, '전치사+관계대명사'의 형태인 in which가 정답이 된다. ③의 경우, in that은 '~라는 점에서'라는 의미인데, 빈칸 이하가 주절에 대한 원인이나 이유가 되지 않으므로 정답이 될 수 없다.

| 어휘 |

caricature n. 캐리커처(어떤 사람의 특징을 과장하여 우스꽝스럽게 묘사한 그림이나 사진) **depiction** n. 묘사, 서술 **characteristic** n. 특질, 특색 **deliberately** ad. 신중히 **exaggerate** v. 과장하다

| 해석 |

캐리커처는 대상의 신체적 특징이나 다른 특성을 의도적으로 과장해서 표현한 묘사 유형이다.

25 동명사를 목적어로 취하는 타동사 ④

| 분석 |

consider는 동명사를 목적어로 취하는 타동사이므로 빈칸에는 ④가 들어가는 것이 적절하다. ③의 경우, 완료 동명사는 과거에 완료된 행위를 나타내므로 현재 고려하고 있다는 문장의 내용과 호응하지 않는다.

| 어휘 |

in response to ~에 대응하여 **unprecedented** a. 전례 없는, 미증유의 **stimulus measures** 경기 부양책

| 해석 |

경제 위기에 대응하여, 의원들은 전례 없는 경기 부양책을 시행하는 것을 고려하고 있다.

26 전치사 ②

| 분석 |

'~을 기리기 위해', '~을 추모하기 위해'는 in memory of ~로 나타내므로 ②가 정답으로 적절하다.

| 어휘 |

monument n. 기념비, 기념탑

| 해석 |

그 기념비는 제2차 세계대전 중 목숨을 잃은 군인들을 기리기 위해 세워졌다.

27 prevent ⋯ from ~ing ②

| 분석 |

prevent가 '⋯가 ~하지 못하도록 하다'라는 의미를 나타내는 경우 'prevent ⋯ from ~ing'의 형태로 쓴다. 따라서 ②가 정답이 된다.

| 어휘 |

upcoming a. 다가오는, 곧 나올[공개될] **leak** v. 누설하다

| 해석 |

그의 신작 앨범에 수록된 노래 한 곡이 온라인에 유출된 후, 그 음악가는 그러한 일이 다시 발생하지 않도록 조치를 취했다.

28 분사구문 ①

| 분석 |

생략된 분사구문의 주어는 주절의 주어인 the actor인데, 이것은 select하는 행위의 주체가 아닌 대상이므로 수동 분사구문을 만들어야 한다. 따라서 ①이 정답이 된다. ④의 '선택되기 위해'는 미래의 목적을 나타내는데, 주어진 문장에서는 이미 선택된 것이므로 적절하지 않다.

| 어휘 |

excel v. 뛰어나다, 출중하다

| 해석 |

자신의 훌륭한 노래 목소리와 강렬한 무대 매너로 선택된 그 배우는 뮤지컬 공연 기간 내내 주연 역할을 뛰어나게 해냈다.

29 주장, 제안, 명령의 동사가 이끄는 that절 속의 동사 형태 ④

| 분석 |

주장, 제안, 명령의 타동사가 이끄는 that절 속의 동사는 주어의 수와 시제에 상관없이 'should+동사원형'이어야 하며, 이때 should는 생략이 가능하다. 여기서 mandated는 '명령'의 동사이므로 ④가 정답이다.

| 어휘 |

in response to ~에 대응하여 **municipal** a. 시(市)의, 도시의, 자치 도시의 **mandate** v. 명령하다, 요구하다

| 해석 |

사고에 대응하여, 시 정부는 회사로 하여금 직원들에게 추가적인 안전 교육을 제공하도록 명령했다.

30 타동사의 목적어 ③

| 분석 |

pledge 뒤에는 흔히 to부정사가 오므로 ②와 ④가 먼저 정답에서 제외된다. ①은 타동사 do의 목적어가 없고 절의 구조로도 적절하지 않다. 따라서 ③이 정답이 된다.

| 어휘 |

pledge v. 서약하다, 약속하다   robbery n. 강도, 강도행위

| 해석 |

경찰서장은 그 강도 사건의 범인들을 잡기 위해 자신의 권한 내의 모든 일을 다 하겠다고 약속했다.

31 글의 주제   ③

| 분석 |

본문은 복부 팽만감, 속 쓰림, 메스꺼움, 위장 출혈 같은 증상들이 위궤양의 징후일 수 있음을 설명하고 있는 글이므로 ③이 정답으로 적절하다.

| 어휘 |

abdominal a. 복부의, 배의   bloating n. 팽만감, 부풀어 오름   heartburn n. (소화불량에 의한) 속 쓰림   nausea n. 메스꺼움   gastrointestinal a. 위장(胃腸)의   bleeding n. 출혈   indicate v. 나타내다, 가리키다   stomach ulcer 위궤양   manifest v. 나타나다, 분명히 드러나다   symptom n. 증상   persist v. 지속되다   indicative of ~을 나타내는, ~의 징후인   be accompanied by ~을 동반하다, 함께 나타나다   abdomen n. 복부

| 해석 |

복부 팽만감, 속 쓰림, 메스꺼움, 위장 출혈은 모두 위궤양이 있음을 개별적으로나 집단적으로 나타내는 징후들이다. 궤양은 종종 초기에는 복부 팽만감으로 나타난다. 가슴에 느껴지는 강한 통증인 속 쓰림도 궤양의 또 다른 증상일 수 있으며, 따라서 만약 지속된다면 의사의 진료를 받아야 한다. 메스꺼움과 출혈 또한 궤양을 나타낼 수 있으며, 메스꺼움이 원인 불명일 때나 출혈이 상복부 통증을 동반할 때 특히 그러하다.

위 글의 주제는 무엇인가?
① 궤양 치료가 효과적이라는 징후들
② 정확한 궤양 진단에 사용되는 검사들
③ 궤양이 있을 가능성을 나타내는 징후들
④ 궤양 발병 위험을 높이는 요인들

32 내용파악   ①

| 분석 |

본문은 중세의 파우스트 전설이 다양한 방식으로 반복적으로 각색되고 재창작되었음을 이야기하면서, 그 사례를 구체적으로 들고 있는 내용의 글이다. 따라서 ①이 정답으로 적절하다.

| 어휘 |

medieval a. 중세의   in return for ~의 대가로   supernatural a. 초자연적인, 불가사의한   protagonist n. (소설·영화 등의) 주인공   ingratiate oneself with ~에게 아첨하다, 환심을 사다   rendition n. (문학·예술 작품의) 각색, 해석, 연출   adapt v. (작품을 다른 형태로) 각색하다, 각본으로 만들다   retelling n. (기존 이야기의) 재구성, 개작(改作)   myriad a. 무수한, 수많은   anime n. 일본식 애니메이션 (흔히 공상과학적인) 일본 만화 영화

| 해석 |

중세의 파우스트 전설 — 초자연적인 힘을 대가로 자신의 영혼을 악마에게 파는 학자의 이야기 — 은 여러 차례 반복해서 재창작되어 왔다. 이러한 예 중의 하나는 1936년에 발간된 소설 『Mephisto』인데, 이 작품은 나치 독일을 배경으로 하고 있다. 이 소설에서 주인공은 자신의 사회적 지위를 높이기 위해 나치의 환심을 산다. 각색한 또 다른 작품은 미국의 단편소설 『The Devil and Daniel Webster』인데, 이 이야기는 두 편의 영화로도 각색된 바 있다. 영화로 각색된 가장 유명한 버전에서는, 대공황 시기의 한 농부가 가난에 대한 두려움 때문에 자신의 영혼을 부(富)와 맞바꾼다. 이러한 각색된 이야기들 외에도, 파우스트 전설은 오페라와 클래식 음악에서 일본 애니메이션에 이르는 무수한 문화적 공간에서 찾아볼 수 있다.

중세의 파우스트 전설에 대해 주로 말하고 있는 것은 무엇인가?
① 그것은 많은 다양한 각색 작품들에 영감을 주었다.
② 그것은 많은 다른 전설들과 닮아 있다.
③ 그것의 원천은 여러 문화적 영향을 통합했다.
④ 그것의 명성은 그 이야기의 시대를 초월한 본질을 바탕으로 하고 있다.

33 내용파악   ②

| 분석 |

본문은 알바니즈가 실제 자연 풍경처럼 보이지만 사실은 모형으로 만든 장면을 특수한 조명과 촬영 각도를 이용하여 현실처럼 보이게 만들어내고 있음을 주로 이야기하고 있다. 그러므로 ②가 정답으로 적절하다. ①, ④ 자연이나 풍경을 직접 촬영한 것이 아니고 모형을 촬영한 것이다.

| 어휘 |

oftentimes ad. 종종, 자주   haunting a. (오래도록) 마음을 떠나지 않는, 잊히지 않는; 불안하게 하는   at first glance 언뜻 보기에는, 처음에는   inspection n. 자세히 보기, 정밀 조사   extraordinary a. 비범한   surreal a. 초현실적인, 기상천외의   diorama n. 디오라마, 투시화, (축소된) 입체 모형   recognize v. 알아보다, 인식하다   stunning a. 굉장히 놀라운, 압도적인   illusion n. 착각, 환상

| 해석 |

미국의 예술가 매튜 알바니즈(Matthew Albanese)는 극적이고 때때로 뇌리를 떠나지 않는 풍경 사진을 만들어내는 것으로 잘 알

려져 있다. 언뜻 보기에는, 이 사진들은 자연 세계의 실제 풍경을 포착한 것처럼 보인다. 그러나 자세히 살펴보면 이 이미지들은 비범하고, 거의 초현실적인 특성을 띠고 있다. 이러한 효과는 알바니즈만의 독특한 예술적 과정의 결과이다. 알바니즈는 무작위적인 물건들로 미니어처 풍경을 구성하는 것으로 시작한다. 그런 다음, 신중하게 선택한 조명 환경 아래에서 이 디오라마들을 창의적인 각도로 촬영하여, 그의 소형 모형들이 현실처럼 보이게 만든다. 그의 작품에서 진정한 즐거움은, 말하자면, 커튼이 걷히고 관람자가 그 이미지들이 놀라운 착시를 보여주고 있다는 사실을 깨닫는 때에 찾아온다.

알바니즈에 대해 주로 말하고 있는 것은 무엇인가?
① 그의 카메라 기법은 자연의 독특한 면들을 드러낸다.
② 그는 독특한 예술적 과정을 사용하여 현실을 모방한다.
③ 그의 이미지들은 실제 사진보다 더 사실적이다.
④ 그는 평범한 풍경을 믿기 어려울 정도로 훌륭하게 보이도록 만든다.

34 내용파악 ①

| 분석 |
"이 화합물은 '주로' 더듬이가 건조해지지 못하게 하는 역할을 한다."라고 명시돼 있으므로 ①이 정답이 된다.

| 어휘 |
possess v. 소유하다, 가지고 있다 **acute** a. 예민한, 민감한 **odor** n. 냄새, 향기 **detect** v. 간파하다, 탐지하다 **scent** n. 냄새, 향기 **antenna** n. 〈동물〉 더듬이 **waxy** a. 밀랍 같은, 왁스 성분의 **be composed of** ~로 이루어져 있다 **compound** n. 화합물, 혼합물 **acquire** v. 얻다, 획득하다 **colony** n. (개미 등의) 집단, 군체 **give off** (냄새 등을) 발산하다, 풍기다 **affect** v. 영향을 주다 **forage** v. 먹이를 찾다, 먹이 활동을 하다 **coordinate** v. 조정하다

| 해석 |
모든 개미는 예민한 후각을 가지고 있어서 수많은 냄새를 구별할 수 있다. 개미는 더듬이를 이용해서 냄새를 감지하는데, 더듬이는 큐티클 탄화수소(CHCs)로 이루어져 있는 밀랍 막이 표면에 입혀져 있다. 이 화합물은 주로 더듬이가 건조해지지 못하게 하는 역할을 한다. 뿐만 아니라, 그 화합물은 개미가 군체의 동료들로부터 중요한 정보를 얻는 데도 도움을 준다. 두 마리의 개미가 더듬이를 접촉할 때, 각각의 개미는 상대방의 더듬이에 있는 CHCs가 발산하는 냄새를 맡을 수 있다. 어떤 개미 종에서는, 이 냄새가 환경 여건에 의해 영향을 받는다. 예를 들어, 햇볕 아래에서 먹이를 찾으러 다니면서 시간을 보내는 개미는 둥지 안에 머무르는 개미와는 다른 냄새를 풍기게 된다. 이러한 정보는 특정 개미 종들이 군체의 이익을 위해 그들의 행동을 조정하는 데 도움을 줄 수 있다.

위 글에 따르면, CHCs의 주된 역할은 무엇인가?
① 그것들은 개미의 더듬이가 지나치게 많은 수분을 잃지 않도록 해준다.
② 그것들은 개미들이 자신들의 활동에 대해 소통할 수 있게 해준다.
③ 그것들은 각각의 개미에게 고유한 개별적인 냄새를 부여한다.
④ 그것들은 개미가 군체 안에서 다른 개미들이 맡고 있는 역할을 알아보는 데 도움을 준다.

35~36

대학에 다니는 동안, 나는 화초 재배 농장에서의 아르바이트를 제안 받았다. 일이 육체적으로 힘들어 보였기 때문에, 이 일을 시작하는 것을 기대하지 않았지만, 시급이 꽤 괜찮았고 아버지가 그 일이 나에게 책임감을 가르쳐 줄 거라고 하셔서 받아들였다. 처음 며칠은 힘들었지만, 나는 식물들을 돌보는 일을 곧 즐기게 되었다. 또한, 엄밀히 말해 직원들 모두와 잘 지낸 것은 아니었지만 대부분의 동료 직원들이 좋은 사람들이었다.
결국, 나는 학업 때문에 매우 바빠졌고, 성적이 떨어지기 시작해서 공부에 집중하기 위해 일을 그만두기로 결정했다. 하지만 이후에 나는 식물학 관련 수업을 몇 개 골라서 들었고 나중에는 결국 전공을 바꿨다. 졸업 후에 나는 다시 그 농장에서 정규직을 얻었고 이번에는 그곳의 운영을 모든 면에서 감독하게 되었다. 놀랍게도, 아르바이트가 직업으로 이어졌던 것이다!

| 어휘 |
plant nursery (화초나 묘목 등을 기르는) 묘목장, 화초 재배 농장 **demanding** a. 힘든, 요구가 많은, 고된 **look forward to** ~을 고대하다, 기대하다 **end up ~ing** 결국 ~하게 되다 **major** n. 전공 **oversee** v. 감독하다, 관리하다 **aspect** n. 측면, 양상

35 내용파악 ④

| 분석 |
"나는 학업 때문에 매우 바빠졌고, 성적이 떨어지기 시작해서 공부에 집중하기 위해 일을 그만두기로 결정했다."라고 돼 있으므로 ④가 정답으로 적절하다.

저자는 왜 화초 재배 농장에서 일하는 것을 그만두었는가?
① 그의 급여가 만족스럽지 않았기 때문이다.
② 그의 동료 직원들이 불친절했기 때문이다.
③ 그가 그 일의 특성을 즐기지 못했기 때문이다.
④ 그가 학업을 따라가는 데 어려움을 겪고 있었기 때문이다.

36　내용추론　③

| 분석 |
화초 재배 농장에서 아르바이트를 한 경험이 있었고 그 뒤에 식물학 관련 수업을 듣고 난 후에 전공을 바꿨으므로, ③이 추론 가능한 진술이다. ② 아버지는 조언을 해줬다고 봐야 한다. 압박을 가한 것은 아니다.

위 글로부터 저자에 대해 무엇을 추론할 수 있는가?
① 그의 아버지가 그에게 화초 재배 농장 일을 구해줬다.
② 그는 화초 재배 농장에서 일하라는 압력을 받았다.
③ 그가 화초 재배 농장에서 일을 했던 것이 그의 전공 선택에 영향을 주었다.
④ 그는 화초 재배 농장에서의 시간제 일을 그만둔 것을 후회했다.

37~38

18세기 유럽에서는 잠자리에서 책을 읽는 관행이 자주 못마땅하게 여겨졌다. 신문들은 그것을 위험한 취미로 묘사하기까지 했으며, 책을 읽는 데 사용하고 있었던 촛불을 끄지 않은 채 잠자리에서 잠들어버린 사람들로 인해 발생한 주택 화재 사례들을 강조했다. 그러한 사건들이 몹시 드물긴 했지만, 잠자리에서 책을 읽는 것은 무책임, 위험, 도덕적 결함과 같은 의미를 갖게 되었다.
잠자리에서 책을 읽는 것이 그렇게 적은 위험을 초래했는데도, 왜 유럽 사회는 그것에 그토록 불편함을 느꼈던 것일까? 이러한 반응은 사회 규범이 급격히 변화하는 시기에 흔히 나타난다. 18세기 이전에는, 글을 읽을 만큼 교육을 받았고, 책을 소유할 만큼 부유하며, 개인 공간이 있을 만큼 특권을 가진 사람들만이 잠자리에서 책을 읽는 것을 고려할 수 있었다. 그 결과, 책을 읽는 것은 평민들에게는 매우 공동체적인 활동이었고, 대부분의 가정에는 따로따로 잠을 잘 수 있는 공간이 없었기 때문에 잠을 자는 것도 마찬가지로 공동체적 활동이었다. 18세기에 이런 상황이 바뀌기 시작했다. 생활 수준이 향상되었고, 그 결과 문해율이 더 높아졌고, 더 광범위한 사람들이 책을 소유하게 되었고, 혼자 잘 수 있는 더 넓은 공간도 생겼고 — 그리고 잠자리에서 책을 읽는 일도 생겨나게 되었다. 사회 규범이 뒤바뀌자, 많은 사람들이 자연스럽게 불안감을 느꼈고 부정적으로 반응했다.

| 어휘 |
frown upon ~을 못마땅해 하다, 눈살을 찌푸리다　**extinguish** v. (불 등을) 끄다　**exceedingly** ad. 매우, 대단히　**synonymous with** ~와 동일시되는, ~와 같은 의미를 지닌　**moral failing** 도덕적 결함, 도덕적 실패　**pose** v. (위협·문제 등을) 제기하다, 초래하다　**social norm** 사회 규범　**privileged** a. 특권이 있는, 특전을 가진　**communal** a. 공동의, 공동체의　**commoner** n. 서민, 평민, 대중　**literacy rate** 문해율(글을 읽고 쓸 수 있는 사람의 비율)　**upend** v. (기존의 체계·상황 등을) 뒤엎다, 전복시키다

37　글의 주제　③

| 분석 |
본문은 18세기 유럽에서 왜 사람들이 잠자리에서 책을 읽는 것을 부정적으로 보았는가에 대한 사회적·문화적 배경과 이유를 설명하고 있다. 그러므로 주제로는 ③이 적절하다.

위 글의 주요 주제로 가장 적절한 것은?
① 잠자리에서 책을 읽는 것의 대중화가 사회에 끼친 영향
② 18세기의 사람들에게 잠자리에서 책을 읽지 못하게 했던 방법들
③ 많은 사람들이 잠자리에서 책을 읽은 것을 부정적으로 인식했던 이유
④ 최고의 특권을 가진 사람들이 잠자리에서 책을 읽는 것에 반대한 이유

38　내용파악　①

| 분석 |
본문에서는 '18세기 이전에는 공동 독서와 공동 수면이 일반적이었지만, 18세기 이후에는 생활수준의 향상으로 개인 공간 증가, 책 소유 증가, 문해율 증가 등이 일어나면서 잠자리에서 책을 읽는 것이 가능해졌다'고 이야기하고 있다. ①은 오히려 과거의 모습에 대한 내용이다.

다음 중 18세기에 일어난 변화가 아닌 것은?
① 공동체적인 책 읽기가 더 대중화되었다.
② 공동 수면 공간은 선호되지 않게 되었다.
③ 문해력이 점점 더 널리 퍼지기 시작했다.
④ 책을 소유하는 것이 점점 더 흔해졌다.

39~40

미국 대통령 해리 트루먼이 내린 결정 중 가장 논란이 많았던 것 중의 하나는 1951년에 더글러스 맥아더 장군을 지휘관에서 해임한 결정이었다. 맥아더 장군은 한국전쟁 초기 미군을 지휘했으며, 중공군에게 여러 차례 패배를 당했었다. 맥아더는 중공군을 직접 공격하길 원했지만, 트루먼은 전쟁이 확대되는 것을 우려했고 협상을 통해 한국에 평화를 가져오기를 원했다.
미국의 장군들은 대통령에게 군사적 상황에 대한 솔직한 평가를 제공하고, 군사 전략에 대한 전문가적인 조언을 해줄 것으로 기대된다. 그러나 그들은 전반적인 군사 정책에 관해서 공개적으로는 침묵을 지킬 것으로 기대되는데, 군 최고

통수권자의 역할을 맡고 있는 대통령이 국가의 군대를 어떻게 사용할 것인가에 대해 결정할 책임을 갖고 있기 때문이다. 이러한 전통을 무시하고, 맥아더는 더 강경한 미국의 군사 행동을 공개적으로 주장했다.

두 사람 사이의 갈등은 맥아더가 트루먼을 강하게 비판하는 편지를 한 공화당 하원의원에게 보낸 1951년 3월에 절정에 이르렀다. 이 편지가 의회에서 큰 소리로 읽혔을 때, 트루먼은 행동에 나설 수밖에 없다고 느꼈다. 맥아더가 대중적으로 널리 인기가 있었음에도 불구하고, 트루먼은 신속하게 다른 군 지휘자들과 협의한 후에 맥아더를 매슈 리지웨이 장군으로 교체했다.

| 어휘 |

controversial a. 논란이 많은 **relieve** v. (지위에서) 해임하다
setback n. 차질, 좌절; 패배 **wary** a. 조심하는, 경계하는
negotiation n. 협상, 교섭, 절충 **assessment** n. 평가, 사정
commander-in-chief n. (군의) 총사령관 **in defiance of** ~을 무시하여, ~에 상관하지 않고 **advocate** v. 옹호하다, 주장하다
conflict n. 갈등 **critical** a. 비판적인 **confer** v. 협의하다
replace v. 교체하다

| 39 | 내용파악 | ④ |

| 분석 |

첫 문단에서 '한국전쟁 당시 맥아더는 중국에 대한 직접 공격을 원했지만, 트루먼은 전쟁 확대를 우려하여 외교적 해결을 추구했다는 점'을 언급했다. 즉, 아시아에서의 군사 개입 확대 여부가 두 사람이 보인 갈등의 출발점이었으므로 ④가 정답이 된다.

트루먼과 맥아더 사이의 불화를 처음에 일으킨 문제는 무엇이었는가?
① 트루먼이 외교적 평화 협상을 종료해야 하는지의 여부
② 맥아더가 군사 전략에 대해 공개적으로 논의해야 하는지 여부
③ 미국이 한국에서 군대를 철수해야 하는지 여부
④ 미국이 아시아에서 군사 개입을 확대해야 하는지 여부

| 40 | 내용추론 | ① |

| 분석 |

Despite MacArthur's widespread popularity라는 표현은 그를 해임하는 경우에 여론의 반발이나 정치적 파장이 있을 수 있었다는 점을 시사한다.

위 글로부터 추론할 수 있는 것은?
① 트루먼은 맥아더를 징계하는 데 정치적 위험이 있다고 생각했다.
② 트루먼의 대부분 장군들은 맥아더의 해임에 반대했다.

③ 맥아더는 트루먼을 공격해서 대중의 지지를 잃었다.
④ 리지웨이는 아시아에서의 확전을 주장했다.

경찰대학 일반대학생 전형

TEST p. 104~126

01	②	02	①	03	①	04	②	05	①	06	①	07	②	08	④	09	④	10	②
11	④	12	③	13	⑤	14	③	15	③	16	③	17	⑤	18	②	19	④	20	④
21	④	22	③	23	④	24	③	25	⑤	26	④	27	①	28	①	29	⑤	30	②
31	⑤	32	②	33	③	34	①	35	③	36	⑤	37	②	38	①	39	⑤	40	①

01 동의어 ②

| 어휘 |

gunshot n. 발사된 탄환; 발사, 발포 **splash** v. (액체가) 후두둑 떨어지다 **steamer** n. 증기선, 기선 **ricochet** v. (탄환 등이) 튕겨서 꺾이다(= **deflect** v. 굴절하다, hit a surface and moves away from it at an angle) **smash ~ into matchwood** ~을 산산조각 내다, 분쇄하다 **smack** n. 작은 어선 **fizzle** v. (불이) 쉬잇하고 꺼지다 **drip** v. (액체가) 똑똑 떨어지다 **scorch** v. (불에) 그슬다 **wobble** v. (불안정하게) 흔들리다

| 해석 |

발사된 탄환은 증기선 근처의 물을 높이 튀겼고, 북쪽에 있는 다른 비행선들을 향해 튕겨서 꺾여 나가 작은 어선을 산산조각 내었다.

02 동의어 ①

| 어휘 |

enumerate v. 열거하다, 나열하다(= list) **indebted** a. 은혜를 입은 **abandon** v. 버리다; 단념하다 **confuse** v. 혼동하다 **disregard** v. 무시하다

| 해석 |

내가 은혜를 입은 작가들을 일일이 열거할 필요는 거의 없는 것 같다.

03 동의어 ①

| 어휘 |

acquisition n. 습득; 획득 **paradigm** n. 패러다임(어느 시대나 분야에 특징적인, 과학적 인식 방법의 체계·시스템) **esoteric** a. 소수만 이해하는, 난해한(= obscure) **maturity** n. 성숙 **prevalent** a. 일반적인, 널리 퍼져 있는 **permeable** a. 스며들 수 있는, 투과성의 **translucent** a. 반투명한 **outlandish** a. 이상한, 이국풍(異國風)의

| 해석 |

패러다임을 습득하고, 그 패러다임이 허용하는 보다 난해한 유형의 연구를 습득하는 것이야말로 특정 과학 분야의 발전에서 성숙의 신호가 된다.

04 동의어 ②

| 어휘 |

stare v. 빤히 쳐다보다, 응시하다 **daze** v. 멍하게 하다 **dazed** a. (충격을 받거나 머리를 얻어맞거나 하여) 멍한, 아찔한(= stunned) **vague** a. 막연한, 모호한 **disinterested** a. 사심(私心)이 없는; 무관심한 **indubitable** a. 의심의 여지가 없는, 확실한

| 해석 |

그 소녀는 열린 창문 밖을 멍한 공포에 질린 눈으로 응시하고 있었다.

05 동의어 ①

| 어휘 |

frustrated a. 좌절감을 느끼는, 불만스러워 하는 **convey** v. (생각·감정 등을) 전하다(= relate v. 이야기하다, 말하다) **imbibe** v. (특히 술을) 마시다; (특히 정보를) 흡수하다 **vouchsafe** v. (누구에게 특별한 혜택이 될 만한 것을) 주다 **dismiss** v. (고려할 가치가 없다고) 묵살하다 **regurgitate** v. (삼킨 음식물을 입 안으로 다시) 역류시키다, 토하다; (듣거나 읽은 내용을 별 생각 없이) 반복하다

| 해석 |

그는 자신이 쓴 편지에서 전하고 싶었던 것을 표현할 수 없다는 사실에 점점 더 좌절했다.

06 생활영어 ①

| 분석 |
발주 고객사가 그동안의 예산 집행 내역에 대해 꼬투리를 잡으려고 한다는 사실을 인지한 임직원들의 대화가 등장하고 있다. 예산 집행 내역에 문제가 없다는 사실을 확인하면서, 이렇게 문제를 제기한 의도가 비용 절감이라는 것을 눈치챘으므로, 빈칸에는 "대화를 통해 문제를 해결하다", "대화를 통해 해결책을 찾다"는 의미를 갖는 ①이 들어가는 것이 가장 적절하다.

| 어휘 |
budget n. 예산 **breakdown** n. 내역, 명세(明細)(서); (알기 쉽게 한) 설명 **skeptical** a. 회의적인, 의심 많은 **cross one's mind** 생각이 나다, 생각이 떠오르다 **come across** (특정한) 인상을 주다 **lay out** 제시하다, 배치하다, 펼치다 **address** v. (문제·상황 등에 대해) 다루다 **stick to** ~을 (바꾸지 않고) 고수하다 **push back** 반발하다 **strategy** n. 전략 **adjustment** n. 조정 **hash ~ out** (대화로) 문제를 풀다(to find a solution by talking/to solve a problem by talking) **throw in the towel** 수건을 던지다; 패배를 인정하다 **beat around the bush** 숲 언저리를 두들겨 사냥감을 몰아내다; 돌려서 말하다, 변죽을 울리다, 요점을 피하다 **burn the midnight oil** (공부나 일을 하느라) 밤늦게까지 불을 밝히다 **kick the can down the road** 문제를 뒤로 미루다

| 해석 |
A: 프로젝트 예산에 대한 고객사의 이메일을 보셨어요? 비용에 대해 일일이 세부 내역을 요구하고 있더군요.
B: 네, 봤어요. 솔직히 말해 저는 약간 의심이 듭니다. 우리의 지출에 이의를 제기할 이유를 찾으려는 것 같아요.
A: 저도 그런 생각이 들었어요. 그들이 갑자기 그렇게 구체적인 세부 정보를 요청하는 것은 드문 일이니까요.
B: 답신을 보낼 때 조심합시다. 방어적이라는 인상을 주고 싶지는 않지만, 우리가 책임감 있게 예산을 관리하고 있다는 것을 분명히 해야 합니다.
A: 동감입니다. 먼저 수치를 제시한 다음, 그들이 제기하는 모든 우려 사항을 다루어주면 되겠어요.
B: 고마워요. 우리는 계약한 대로 예산을 지켰으니, 자금 할당 방식에는 아무 문제가 없을 겁니다.
A: 맞아요. 하지만 그들이 계속 반발한다면 지출 전략 중 일부를 재고해야 할 수도 있어요.
B: 크게 조정해야 할 필요 없이 대화로 잘 해결할 수 있기를 바랍니다. 그들은 가능한 한 비용을 줄일 방법을 찾고 있는 것 같아요.

① 대화로 문제를 해결하다
② 패배를 인정하다
③ 변죽을 울리다
④ 밤새워 일하다
⑤ 문제를 뒤로 미루다

07 빈칸완성 ②

| 분석 |
Ⓐ 빈칸에는 "로마 예술은 진지하게 고려할 가치가 없다"고 주장하는 근거(이유)가 될 만한 표현이 들어가야 한다. 로마 문화가 그리스 문화에 빚지거나, 힘입은 바가 "크다면", "심하다면" 그런 식의 폄하(貶下)가 정당화될 것이다. 'be heavily indebted to ~'는 '~에 힘입은 바 크다'는 뜻으로 빈번하게 사용되는 표현이다. Ⓑ 필자는 그리스 예술은 "이상적", "추상적"인 반면, 로마 예술은 "세속적", "실용적", "현실적"이라고 말하고 있다. 따라서 그리스-로마 예술을 합쳐서 흔히 "고전" 예술이라고 칭하는 것에 반대하여, 그리스 예술에만 그러한 수식어가 사용되어야 한다고 말하고 있으므로, 이는 개념을 "엄격히(strictly)" 구별하고자 하는 의도라고 판단할 수 있다. Ⓒ 그리스 예술가들이라면 "흔히", "보통", "일상적으로" 무관심했던 소재까지 로마 예술가들은 소재로 삼았다는 의미가 되어야 적절하다.

| 어휘 |
no doubt 아마 ~일 것이다 **merit** v. (칭찬·관심 등을) 받을 만하다 **heavily** ad. (양·정도가) 심하게, 아주 많이 **indebted to** ~에게 빚을 진, ~에게 은혜를 입은, ~에 힘입은 바가 큰 **contribute** v. 제공하다 **of one's own** 자기 자신의 **secularly** ad. 이성[종교]과 무관하게, 세속적으로 **baroque** a. (17~18세기 초) 바로크 양식의 **portray** v. 묘사하다 **phase** n. 단계, 국면 **subject** n. 주제, 문제, 제목 **commemorative** a. 기념하는, 기념이 되는 **narrative** n. 이야기, 서사 **outstanding** a. 두드러진, 뛰어난 **exploit** n. 업적 **strictly** ad. 엄격히 **ordinarily** ad. 보통

| 해석 |
어떤 사람들은 로마 예술은 어떤 경우에도 진지하게 고려할 가치가 없다고 분명히 주장할 것이며, 로마 예술이 그리스인들에게 크게 힘입었다는 것도 물론 사실이다. 그럼에도 불구하고, 로마 예술은 나름의 독창적인 특징들을 제공했다. 이탈리아적 취향은 세속적으로 바로크 양식을 좋아하며, 그리스인들의 목표는 오히려 이상적인 양식을 만드는 것이었다. "고전적"이라는 형용사는 엄격한 의미에서 그리스 예술에만 속한다. 로마인들의 실용적 성격은 그들의 예술에 고스란히 반영되어 있다. 그들의 실용적 성격은 이상적인 아름다움이나 추상적인 사상을 묘사하려고 시도하는 대신, 현실적인 경향이 있어서 일상생활의 다양한 국면들을 표현했다. 이런 점으로 인해 로마 예술가들은 그리스 예술가들이 보통 무관심했던 예술적 소재, 예를 들어 어린이들을 소재로 삼았다. 이런 점은 또한 로마 예술의 대부분이 무언가를 기념하는 것이고, 뛰어난 업적을 묘사하는 데 더 적합한 연속적인 서사적 회화 같은 양식들을 발전시켰던 이유를 설명해준다.

08 전치사+동명사 ④

| 분석 |
전치사 in이 동명사를 목적어로 취한 'in+~ing'는 '~함에 있어

서', '~할 때'의 의미로, 문맥상 ④의 in making은 적절히 사용되었다. 이때 make는 the individual filmmaker를 목적어로, the focus를 목적보어로 갖는다. ① 일반적으로 주격 관계대명사의 뒤에는 동사가, 목적격 관계대명사의 뒤에는 주어가, 그리고 소유격 관계대명사의 뒤에는 한정사 없는 명사가 뒤따르는데, 'filmmakers의 formative experiences'이므로 소유격 관계대명사 whose가 되어야 한다. ② 앞에 완전한 형태의 주절이 갖추어져 있으므로 그 이하는 주절에 이어지는 종속절 또는 분사구문이 되어야 한다. 문맥상 '논의하는'이라는 능동형 분사구문이 되어야 하므로 discussing이 되어야 한다. ③ 'have yet to+동사원형'은 '아직 ~하지 못했다, 아직 ~하지 않았다'는 의미로, 어떤 행위가 아직까지 이루어지지 않았음을 나타내며, 그런 일이 일어날 가능성(또는 필요성)을 암시한다. 따라서 have yet to receive가 되어야 하며, 이것은 have not yet received의 의미이다. ⑤ 앞 문장 전치사 of의 목적어이면서 뒷 문장 see의 목적어가 되어 두 곳의 필수 성분을 채워주는 장치가 필요하므로 선행사를 포함한 관계대명사 what이 사용되어야 한다.

| 어휘 |

arguably ad. 아마, 틀림없이　**formative** a. (사람 성격 등의) 형성에 중요한, 발달에 중요한　**director** n. (영화·연극의) 감독, 연출자　**empirically** ad. 경험적으로, 실증적으로　**with reference to** ~와 관련하여　**modest** a. (크기·가격·중요성 등이) 그다지 대단하지는 않은, 보통의　**by no means** 결코 ~이 아닌　**comprehensive** a. 포괄적인, 종합적인　**systematic** a. 체계적인, 조직적인　**prior to** ~에 앞서, 먼저　**code** n. (사회적) 관례, 규칙　**ideology** n. 이데올로기, 이념; (특히 특정 집단의 행동 양식에 영향이 큰) 관념　**negotiate** v. 협상하다

| 해석 |

『미국의 영화와 정치(Film and Politics in America)』는 미국 영화 산업의 정치에 대한 관심과 아마도 1930년대에 형성적 경험을 했을 것이며 1940년대에 할리우드에서 감독으로 활동하기 시작했던 한 세대의 광범위하게 사회적인 영화 제작자들에 대한 관심에서 생겨났다. 그 목적은 이 그룹의 작업에 대한, 경험에 기초한 책을 제작하여, 영화에 대해, 광범위한 역사적 맥락에서 그리고 특히 영화 제작의 산업적·상업적 과정의 변화하는 성격과 관련하여, 논의하는 것이었다. 이하의 내용은 미국 영화의 사회적·정치적 내용과 관련된 쟁점들 — 적어도 1960년대 이전 시기 동안에는 아직 체계적으로 연구되지 않은 쟁점들 — 을 논의하려는 적당한 수준의 그리고 결코 포괄적이지 않은 시도이다. 영화제작 시스템 자체와 영화의 보다 광범위한 규칙들과 이념들, 그리고 그 규칙과 이념이 경제적·정치적 권력과 맺는 관계에 초점을 두지 않고, 개별 영화 제작자에 초점을 두는 데는 분명히 위험이 있지만, 이러한 접근 방식에는 몇 가지 장점도 있다. 특정 그룹이라는 개념은 중점적으로 연구한 영화들의 표본을 제공하며, 당시에 그 영화들은 짐 쿡(Jim Cook)과 앨런 러벨(Alan Lovell)이 이 세대의 예술가들이 영화 산업과의 관계를 '협상한' 과정으로 간주하는 것의 관점에서 검토될 수 있었다.

09 일치 / 수동태　④

| 분석 |

④의 were brutalized는 주어 young people에 맞게 수(복수), 시제(과거), 태(수동태)가 모두 적절하다. ① 명사 battle을 수식해야 하므로 형용사인 creative로 수정해야 한다. ② 선행사 a civil rights movement가 있으므로 선행사를 포함하는 관계대명사 what이 아닌, 관계대명사 주격인 which로 수정해야 한다. ③ 문맥상 "우리 아이들은 소방 호스, 사나운 개, 심지어 죽음으로 응답받았다"가 되어야 하므로 수동태인 were answered로 수정해야 한다. ⑤ 주어 poverty에 일치시켜 동사는 3인칭 단수 현재 인칭변화 규칙에 따라 afflicts로 수정해야 한다.

| 어휘 |

negro n. (원래 아프리카 출신의) 흑인　**on behalf of** ~을 대신하여, ~을 대표하여　**civil rights movement** 시민 평등권 운동(1950~1960년대의 미국 흑인 평등권 요구 운동)　**determination** n. 결단력, 투지　**majestic** a. 장엄한, 위풍당당한　**scorn** n. 경멸, 멸시　**reign** n. 군림; 통치, 지배　**mindful** a. ~을 염두에 두는, ~을 의식하는　**cry out for** ~을 간절히 바라다　**brotherhood** n. 인류애, 형제애　**fire hose** 소방 호스　**snarl** v. (이빨을 드러내며) 으르렁거리다　**brutalize** v. (사람을) 짐승 취급하다, 잔인하게 다루다　**worship** n. 예배; 숭배　**sanctuary** n. 보호 구역; 피난처, 안식처　**segregation** n. (인종·종교·성별에 따른) 분리, 차별　**debilitating** a. 쇠약하게 하는　**grinding** a. 괴롭히는, 지독한　**rung** n. (사다리의) 가로대, 단

| 해석 |

저는 미국의 2,200만 명의 흑인이 인종적 불의의 기나긴 밤을 끝내기 위한 창조적인 투쟁을 벌이고 있는 지금 이 순간, 노벨 평화상을 수상합니다. 저는 자유의 통치와 정의의 지배를 확립하기 위해 단호하게 그리고 위험과 위협을 위엄 있게 경멸하며 나아가고 있는 시민권 운동을 대신하여 이 상을 수상합니다. 저는 어제 앨라배마 주 버밍햄에서만도 형제애를 부르짖던 우리 아이들이 소방 호스와 사나운 개, 심지어 죽음으로 응답받았다는 것을 기억합니다. 저는 어제 미시시피 주 필라델피아에서만도 투표권을 확보하려는 젊은 이들이 짐승 취급을 당하며 살해되었다는 것을 기억합니다. 그리고 어제 미시시피 주에서만도 40곳 이상의 예배당이 인종 차별을 받아들이지 않는 사람들에게 피난처를 제공했다는 이유로 폭탄 공격을 받거나 불태워졌습니다. 쇠약하게 만드는 지독한 빈곤이 흑인들을 괴롭히며, 경제적 사다리의 가장 낮은 단에 그들을 묶어두고 있다는 것을 저는 기억합니다.

10 수동태와 능동태의 구분　②

| 분석 |

take in은 '(몸속으로) ~을 섭취[흡수]하다'는 의미인데, 문맥상 주어인 neurons가 주변(이웃) neuron들로부터 화학적 신호를 '받아들이는' 주체이므로 능동태가 되어야 한다. 따라서 ②를 take로 바꾸어야 한다.

| 어휘 |

neuron n. 뉴런, 신경세포 **specialize** v. ~을 전문적으로 다루다 **excitable** a. (자극에 대하여) 흥분하는, 반응성의 **impulse** n. (반응을 불러일으키는) 충격, 자극 **phase** n. (변화·발달 과정상의 한) 단계, 시기, 국면 **integration** n. 통합, 완성 **assess** v. 평가하다, 재다 **transmission** n. 전달; 전송 **sensory** a. 감각의 **prick** v. (작은 구멍이 나도록 뾰족한 것으로) 찌르다 **tack** n. 압정 **trigger** v. 촉발시키다 **instantaneous** a. 즉각적인 **somatosensory** a. 체성(體性)감각의, 체지각의 **motor** a. (근육에 의한) 운동의; 운동 신경의 **contract** v. 줄어들다, 수축하다 **interneuron** n. 사이신경세포, 개재(介在)뉴런, 중간뉴런 **relay station** (무선·방송) 중계국

| 해석 |

뉴런(신경세포)은 서로 간의 의사소통에 특화되어 있다. 신체의 다른 세포와 달리 뉴런은 흥분성이 있어 전기적 자극으로 활성화되며, 화학적 신호를 통해 다른 뉴런과 소통한다. 수신 단계에서 뉴런은 이웃 뉴런으로부터 화학적 신호를 받아들인다. 통합 단계에서는 들어오는 신호를 평가한다. 전송 단계에서 뉴런은 자신의 신호를 다른 수신 뉴런에게 전달한다. 뉴런에는 여러 유형이 있다. 감각뉴런은 물리적 세계에서 정보를 감지하여 그 정보를 뇌로 전달한다. 뜨거운 것을 만지거나 우연히 압정과 같은 날카로운 물건에 찔렸던 지난 기억을 떠올려 보면, 그 과정이 얼마나 빨리 진행되는지 알 수 있을 것이다. 이러한 신호로 당신의 신체에서는 거의 즉각적인 반응과, 그 충격에 대한 감각적 경험이 촉발되었다. 피부와 근육으로부터의 정보를 제공하는 감각 신경을 체성감각 신경이라고 한다. 운동뉴런은 근육이 수축하거나 이완하도록 명령하여 움직임을 생성한다. 중간뉴런은 중계소 역할을 하여, 감각뉴런과 운동뉴런 간의 소통을 용이하게 한다.

11 선행사를 포함한 관계대명사 what ④

| 분석 |

④는 would appear의 주어이면서 might appear의 주어가 되는 두 가지 요건을 충족시키는 것이어야 한다. which는 의문대명사로 보거나 관계대명사로 보거나 간에 이러한 역할을 할 수 없다. 따라서 which를 선행사를 포함한 관계대명사 what으로 바꾸어 주어야 한다. to correct taste and judgement는 삽입어구에 해당한다.

| 어휘 |

two-fold a. 두 부분으로 된, 이중적인 **well-defined** a. 알기 쉬운, 이해하기 쉬운, 명확한 **infrequently** ad. 드물게 **noble** a. 고결한, 고귀한 **apprehend** v. (의미를) 파악하다, 이해하다 **give full scope to** ~을 십분 발휘시키다 **executant** n. 실행자, 집행자, 연기자, 연주자 **ridiculous** a. 말도 안 되는, 터무니없는 **extravagant** a. 화려한, 과장된 **genius** n. 천재(적인 사람); 천재성 **eccentric** a. 괴짜인, 별난, 기이한 **vocal student** 성악도(聲樂徒)

| 해석 |

스타일이란 무엇인가? 사실, 이 질문은 두 가지로 나뉜다. 우리는 큰 스타일(Style)을 가질 수도 있고, 작은 스타일(a style)을 가질 수도 있다. 전자는 일반적이며, 후자는 개인적인 것이다. 전자는 어떤 명확한 규칙에 기반을 두고 있기 때문에 가르칠 수도, 배울 수도 있지만, 후자는 개인적인 것이다, 즉 보편적으로 적용될 수 있는 것이 아니다. 이러한 규칙들을 특별하게 적용했을 때 독창적이라는 인상을 준다는 것은 드물지 않은 일이다. 그러나 올바른 취향은 주목받는 특정 예술에서 가장 고귀한 창작물들을 연구함으로써 형성되어야 한다. 가까운 다른 예술에서와 마찬가지로, 노래에서도 보편적인 큰 스타일(Style)을 지배하는 법칙을 파악하고 이해한 후에야 비로소 개성(Individuality)을 십분 발휘할 수 있다. 그렇지 않으면, 연주자에게는 독창적으로 보이는 것이 올바른 취향과 판단에 따르면 우스꽝스럽고 과장된 것으로 보일 수도 있다. 천재는 때때로 엉뚱하지만, 모든 엉뚱함이 곧 천재성인 것은 아니다. 성악도들은 훌륭한 가수들의 노래를 가능한 한 많이 들어야 하지만, 누구도 그대로 모방해서는 안 된다.

12 문장삽입 ③

| 분석 |

"시청을 철거하는 대신"이라는 표현에 주목한다. 즉, 주어진 문장의 앞부분에는 '시청을 철거해야 할 수도 있는' 안전상의 위험이 적시되어야 하고, 뒷부분에는 '철거하는 대신' 이루어질 보수 계획을 상세히 소개하는 내용이 나와야 한다. ③의 앞에서 언급한, 그물망으로 외벽 조각의 낙하를 방지하고 강철 막대로 금 간 벽을 지탱하는 것은 안전상 위험에 대한 임시방편을 말하므로 주어진 문장의 가장 적절한 위치는 ③이다.

| 어휘 |

cop n. 경찰관 **dragnet** n. 〈어업〉 저인망(底引網); (특히 범인을 찾기 위한) 수사포위망 **hammering** n. 맹타, 대파 **Richter scale** (지진의 규모를 나타내는) 리히터 척도 **wrap** v. (둘레에) 두르다, 감다 **chunk** n. (두툼한) 덩어리 **fracture** v. 부수다, 깨다 **terra cotta** 테라코타(적갈색 점토를 유약을 바르지 않고 구운 것) **exterior** n. 외부, 외면, 표면 **stout** a. 튼튼한, 견고한 **rod** n. (목재·금속·유리 소재의 기다란) 막대 **stabilize** v. 안정시키다 **crack** v. 갈라지다, 금이 가다 **evacuate** v. (위험 지역에서 사람들을) 대피시키다 **tear** v. 찢다, 째다, 잡아 찢다 **tear down** ~을 파괴하다, 해체하다 **official** n. 공무원 **rehabilitation** n. 갱생(更生), 기능 회복 **eclectically** ad. 취사 선택하여, 절충하여 **landmark** n. 주요 지형지물, 랜드마크(멀리서 보고 위치 파악에 도움이 되는 대형 건물 같은 것) **retrofit** v. (기계 속에 원래 없던 부품 등을) 새로 장착하다 **earthquake-resistant** a. 내진(耐震)의 **jack up** 잭으로 들어 올리다 **steel-framed** a. 철골 철근 구조의 **vertical** a. 수직의 **column** n. (보통 원형 석조) 기둥 **layered** a. 층이 있는, 층을 이룬 **base isolator** 기반 이격물, 기반 분리체 **laterally** ad. 측면으로, 좌우로; 비스듬히 **moat** n. 호, 해자(성 주위에 둘러 판 못) **perimeter** n. 주위, 둘레 **seismic** a. 지진의, 지진에 의한

| 해석 |

로스앤젤레스의 많은 건물과 마찬가지로, 수백만 명이 경찰 드라마 『수사망(Dragnet)』에서 보았던 이 30층짜리 건물도 반복되는 지진들의 충격을 버텨왔는데, 특히 1월 17일의 노스리지 지진은 리히터 규모 6.8을 기록했다. L.A. 시청 건물에 둘러쳐진 그물망이 건물 외벽의 깨진 테라코타 조각들이 거리로 떨어지는 것을 방지해준다. 건물 내부에서는 견고한 강철 막대들이 소개(疏開)된 25층과 26층의 금 간 벽들을 지탱하고 있다. 〈공무원들은 시청을 철거하고 5억 달러의 비용을 들여 신축하는 대신, 1928년에 지어진 이 절충적인 양식의 랜드마크 건물을 대대적으로 보수하는 데 1억 5,300만 달러를 투입할 예정이다.〉 그렇게 된다면 L.A. 시청은 역사상 내진 기능을 새로 갖춘 가장 높은 사무용 건물이 될 것이다. 이 프로젝트의 주요 요소는 이 철골 구조 건물을 이루고 있는 430개에 달하는 수직 기둥들을 한 번에 몇 개씩 들어 올리고, 철근과 고무를 겹겹이 쌓아 만든 기반 분리체를 삽입하는 것인데, 이 기반 분리체로 인해 건물 전체가 최대 18인치까지 수평으로 이동될 수 있을 것이다. 건물 주변으로는 폭 4피트의 지하 해자가 조성되어 건물을 주변 지반에서 발생하는 지진으로부터 분리시켜줄 것이다.

13 문장삽입 ⑤

| 분석 |

주어진 문장에는 '이렇게 해서(Thus)'라는 부사가 있으므로, 앞 내용에는 '영국 문학의 전통이 시작된 계기'가 언급되어야 한다. 그러한 내용으로 적절한 것은 '7세기 초에 처음으로 라틴 문자로 영어를 기록하기 시작했다'는 진술이므로, 주어진 문장은 ⑤에 들어가야 한다.

| 어휘 |

landmark n. 현저한[획기적인] 사건[발견]   **pagan** n. 비(非) 그리스도교인   **Anglo-Saxon** n. 앵글로색슨인(노르만 정복 이전의 잉글랜드인)   **mission** n. (특히 외국으로 가서 하는) 전도, 선교   **monk** n. 수도자, 수도승   **Celtic** a. 켈트족의   **missionary** n. (외국에 파견되는) 선교사   **originate** v. 시작되다, 생기다   **echo** n. 메아리, 반향   **commemorate** v. (중요 인물·사건을) 기념하다   **Easter** n. (그리스도교의) 부활절   **literacy** n. 글을 읽고 쓸 줄 아는 능력, 문해력   **renowned** a. 유명한, 명성 있는   **Old English** 고대 영어(450~1150년 이전의 영어)   **scholarship** n. 학문

| 해석 |

고대 영어 시대의 주요한 문화적인 획기적 사건은 이교도였던 앵글로색슨인에게 그리스도교가 전파된 것이었다. 이는 597년 40명의 수도사와 함께 로마를 떠나 켄트에 도착한 성(聖) 아우구스티누스(Augustine)의 선교 활동에 의해 처음 이루어졌고, 이후 620년대 북부에서 활동을 시작한 아일랜드 출신 켈트족 선교사들의 노력에 의해 이루어졌다. 7세기 말에는 이미 잉글랜드 전역이 사실상 그리스도교화되었다. 그럼에도 불구하고 오래된 이교도적 관습의 흔적은 여전히 남아 있었다. 예를 들어, 요일 이름 가운데 4개가 이교도 신들을 기념하는 것인데, 화요일은 티우(Tiw), 수요일은 오딘(Woden), 목요일은 토르(Thor), 금요일은 프리그(Frig)에서 유래하였고, 부활절(Easter)도 옛 이교도 축제의 이름이다. 그리스도교와 함께 문해력도 도래하였는데, 7세기 초에 처음으로 그리스도교 수도사들은 라틴 문자를 사용하여 영어를 기록하기 시작했다. 〈이렇게 해서 영국 문학의 전통이 시작되었지만, 교회와 학문의 언어는 여전히 라틴어였다.〉 7세기 후반과 8세기의 잉글랜드는 그리스도교 학문으로 유럽 전역에서 명성을 떨쳤다.

14 문장삽입 ③

| 분석 |

전체적인 글의 내용을 3부분으로 분석해 볼 수 있다. 1) 약탈이 횡행했던 중세 시대에는 급히 피란을 가야 하는 위험이 상존했으므로, 벽을 건축적으로 장식할 수 없었다. 2) 이탈리아의 장식적 전통(고전적 전통)이 알려지면서 건축적인 실내 장식이 중요해졌다. 3) 그러나 오늘날 건축적인 실내 장식은 형식적인(perfunctory) 작업으로 취급받고 있다. 주어진 문장에서 가리키는 '이러한 건축적 처리'는 이탈리아의 고전적 전통의 영향을 받은 '건축적인 실내 장식'을 가리키는 것이므로 주어진 문장이 들어갈 위치는 2)가 끝나고 3)이 시작되는 사이인 ③이 가장 적절하다.

| 어휘 |

brigandage n. 산적 행위, 약탈   **chamber** n. 방, 사실(私室)   **arras** n. (아름다운 그림 무늬가 있는) 애러스 직물의 벽걸이 천   **timber** n. 대들보, 가로장   **Valois** n. 프랑스의 발루아 왕가(1328~1589까지 프랑스를 지배)   **acquaint** v. 익히 알게 하다, 정통하게 하다   **void** n. (커다란) 빈 공간, 공동   **mass** n. 덩어리, 덩이   **hanging** n. 벽걸이 천, 커튼   **in consequence** 결과적으로   **ornament** n. 장식(품)   **hold one's own** 자기 입장을[견해를] 견지하다, 고수하다   **sever** v. 자르다, 잘라내다   **elevation** n. (건물의) 입면도   **floor-plan** n. (건물의) 평면도   **moulding** n. 쇠시리(벽·문 등의 윗부분에 돌·목재 등을 띠처럼 댄·장식)   **architrave** n. 문틀, 창틀   **cornice** n. 배내기(장식용 처마천장 돌림띠)   **perfunctory** a. 형식적인   **hurry over** ~을 급히 끝마치다   **upholsterer** n. 실내 장식업자   **furnish** v. (가구를) 비치하다

| 해석 |

전쟁과 약탈이 삶의 조건을 좌우했던 중세 시대에, 사람들은 천막에서 그랬던 것처럼 성에서도 야영하며 지냈다. 이러한 환경에서 장식품은 휴대할 수 있어야 했고, 중세 방의 맨 벽에는 애러스(arras) 벽걸이 천을 걸어두어야 했으며, 천으로 꾸민 천장 즉 시엘(ciel)이 지붕의 노출된 대들보를 가로질러 있는 것은 당연한 일이었다. 삶이 보다 안전해지고, 발루아 왕조가 이탈리아를 정복함으로써 알프스 북쪽 지역 사람들에게도 고전적 전통의 정신이 알려지면서, 비례 그리고 공간과 덩어리의 관계가 점차 실내 장식에서 중요한 장식적 가치로 여겨지게 되었다. 그 결과, 휴대용 벽걸이 천은 건축적 장식으로 대체되었다. 다시 말해, 방의 건축 자체가 곧 장식이 되었다. 〈이러한 건축적 처리는 모든 취향의 변화를 거치

면서 금세기 2사분기까지 지속되었다.〉 하지만 그 이후 다양한 영향들이 결합하여 현대 주택의 외관과 실내의 자연스러운 연결은 단절되어버리고 말았다. 일반적인 주택에서 건축가의 작업은 사실상 입면도와 평면도에 국한된 것처럼 보인다. 쇠시리 장식, (문·창의) 장식 틀, 배내기와 같은 오늘날 사소한 세부 사항들로 간주되는 것의 디자인은 서둘러 처리되고, 등한시되는 형식적인 작업이 되어버렸다. 이러한 작업이 끝나면 실내 장식업자가 불려 들어와 방을 "장식"하고 가구를 배치한다.

15 문장삽입 ③

| 분석 |

주어진 문장의 의미를 재진술하면 '대부분의 사람들은 사랑을 능동적 관점보다는 수동적 관점으로 이해한다'는 것이다. 이를 앞 문장과의 연결로 보자면 이러한 태도는 '사랑에 대한 몇 가지 전제들' 중의 하나에 해당하며, 뒤 문장과의 연결로 보자면 순접의 연결장치 '따라서(Hence)'에 이어 나오는 '어떻게 사랑받을 수 있는가가 더 중요한 문제다'는 내용의 전제에 해당한다. 이러한 분석에 기초할 때 주어진 문장의 가장 적절한 위치는 ③이다.

| 어휘 |

sensation n. (자극을 받아서 느끼게 되는) 느낌 **chance** n. 가능성; 우연, 운 **starve** v. 굶주리다, 굶어 죽다 **trashy** a. 쓰레기 같은, 저질의 **peculiar** a. (특히 불쾌하거나 걱정스러울 정도로) 이상한, 기이한 **premise** n. (주장의) 전제 **uphold** v. (법·원칙 등을) 유지시키다, 옹호하다 **hence** ad. 이런 이유로, 그러므로, 따라서 **lovable** a. (흔히 결점들에도 불구하고) 사랑스러운, 매력적인 **in pursuit of** ~을 쫓아서, ~을 추구하여 **margin** n. 한계, 극한

| 해석 |

사랑은 하나의 기술인가? 그렇다면 사랑에는 지식과 노력이 필요하다. 아니면 사랑은 우연히 경험하게 되는 즐거운 느낌, 즉 운이 좋으면 "빠져드는" 그런 것인가? 사람들이 사랑이 중요하지 않다고 생각하는 것은 아니다. 그들은 사랑에 굶주려 있다. 그들은 행복한 사랑이든 불행한 사랑이든 사랑 이야기를 다룬 영화들을 끝도 없이 보고, 사랑에 관한 수백 개의 저질 노래들을 듣는다. 그러나 사랑에 대해 뭔가 배울 것이 있다고 생각하는 사람은 거의 없다. 이러한 기이한 태도는 개별적으로 혹은 결합하여 그것을 지지하는 경향이 있는 몇 가지 전제들에 기초한다. 〈대부분의 사람들은 사랑의 문제를 사랑하는 것, 즉 사랑할 수 있는 능력의 문제라기보다는 주로 사랑받는 것의 문제로 본다.〉 따라서 그들에게 문제는 어떻게 사랑받는가, 어떻게 사랑스러운 존재가 되느냐이다. 이 목표를 추구하기 위해 그들은 여러 가지 길을 따른다. 특히 남성들이 사용하는 길은 성공하는 것, 즉 자신의 사회적 지위가 허용하는 범위 내에서 최대한 강력하고 부유해지는 것이다. 특히 여성들이 사용하는 또 다른 방법은 자신의 외모와 옷차림 등을 가꾸어 스스로를 매력적으로 만드는 것이다.

16 단락배열 ③

| 분석 |

선거 운동을 하는 대통령 후보가 자신의 가톨릭적 정체성이 선거에 악영향을 미칠 것을 우려해, 선거 유세 연설에서 그 사실이 자신의 대통령직 수행에 어떤 영향도 미치지 않을 것임을 적극적으로 해명했다는 글이다. 종교가 선거 운동에 걸림돌이었다는 일반적인 내용이 주어진 다음, 그 종교적 문제가 무엇인지를 상술(詳述)하는 B가 이어진다. 이어서 그에 대한 대책으로서의 C의 연설이 나오고, 그 연설의 내용을 상술하는 A가 마지막으로 이어진다.

| 어휘 |

candidate n. 입후보자, 출마자 **dog** v. (문제 등이) (오랫동안) 괴롭히다 **harbor** v. (계획·생각 등을) 품다 **beholden** a. ~에게 신세를 지고 있는 **conduct** n. 경영, 수행, 처리 **office** n. (권위 있는, 특히 정부의 주요) 지위, 공직 **impose** v. (힘들거나 불쾌한 것을) 부과하다 **doctrine** n. 교리, 신조 **lay ~ to rest** (소문 등이 사실이 아님을 보여주어서) 잠재우다, 가라앉히다 **minister** n. 성직자, 목사 **presidency** n. 대통령 직(職) **bearing** n. 관련, 영향 **affair** n. 일, 문제 **censorship** n. 검열 **in accordance with** ~에 따라서, ~에 부합되게 **conscience** n. 양심 **without regard to** ~을 고려하지 않고, ~에 상관없이, 아랑곳없이 **dictate** n. (따라야 하는) 명령, 요구, 규칙

| 해석 |

1960년 9월 12일, 민주당 대통령 후보 존 F. 케네디(John F. Kennedy)는 텍사스 주 휴스턴에서 정치에서 종교가 갖는 역할에 대해 연설했다. 선거운동 내내 "종교 문제"가 그를 괴롭혔다.
B 케네디는 가톨릭 신자였는데, 가톨릭 신자가 미국 대통령에 선출된 적은 없었다. 일부 유권자들은 내심 편견을 품었고, 또 다른 이들은 케네디가 자신의 공직 수행에 있어서 교황청에 신세를 지거나, 공공 정책에 가톨릭 교리를 강요할지도 모른다는 두려움을 노골적으로 표명했다.
C 이러한 두려움을 불식시키기 위해, 케네디는 개신교 목사들이 모인 자리에서 자신이 당선될 경우 자신의 종교가 대통령직 수행에서 하게 될 역할에 대해 연설하기로 했다. 그의 답변은 종교가 아무 역할도 하지 않을 것이라는 간단한 답변이었다. 종교적 신념은 개인적인 문제이며, 자신의 공적 책임과는 아무런 관련이 없을 것이라는 것이었다.
A 케네디는 이렇게 말했다. "저는 대통령의 종교적 견해는 철저히 개인적인 문제라고 믿습니다. 산아 제한, 이혼, 검열, 도박 등 그 어떤 쟁점들이 대통령인 제 앞에 제기되더라도, 저는 제 양심이 국가적 이익이라고 말하는 것에 따라, 그리고 외부의 종교적 압력이나 지시와 상관없이, 결정을 내릴 것입니다."

17 단락배열 ⑤

| 분석 |

버팔로의 계절적 이주를 설명하는 글이다. 주어진 첫 문장에는 다른 동물들의 습성과 대조적인 버팔로의 이주 습성이 언급되었으므

로, 그러한 상황을 구체적인 예를 통해 보여 주는 C가 제일 처음 이어지고, 그러한 대규모 이동은 겨울의 불리한 조건을 피하기 위한 것이라는 B가 이어진 다음, 봄이 옴에 따라 더위를 피해 다시 북쪽으로 이동한다는 A로 연결되는 것이 가장 자연스럽다.

| 어휘 |

buffalo n. 버팔로, 물소(아메리카 야생 들소) **terrestrial** a. 육생(陸生)의 **quadruped** n. 네발짐승 **roam** v. (이리저리) 돌아다니다, 배회하다 **at will** 마음대로 **migratory** a. 이주[이동]하는 **elk** n. 엘크(북유럽이나 아시아에 사는 큰 사슴. 북미에서는 moose라고 함) **black-tail deer** 검은꼬리사슴 **altitude** n. (해발) 고도 **in conformity with** (무엇의 규칙)에 따르는 **latitude** n. 위도 **pasture** n. 초원, 목초지 **Territory** n. 준주(準州), 속령, 보호령, 자치령 **graze** v. 풀을 뜯다; (소·양 등을) 방목하다 **range** n. 범위, 지역 **cattle** n. (집합적으로) 소 **surpass** v. 능가하다, 뛰어넘다 **overstock** v. (공간·먹이가 충분하지 않은 곳에) 가축을 너무 많이 집어넣다

| 해석 |

대부분의 다른 아메리카 대륙의 네 발 달린 육지동물과 달리, 버팔로는 자유롭게 돌아다닐 수 있는 한, 이동하는 습관이 확립되어 있었다.
C 엘크와 검은꼬리사슴은 겨울이 다가오고 사라지는 데 맞춰 1년에 두 번 고도를 바꾸는 반면, 버팔로는 위도를 급격하게 변화시킨다. 이러한 현상은 무리의 개체 수가 가장 많고, 이동을 가장 쉽게 관찰할 수 있는 서부의 광대한 초원 지대에서 가장 두드러졌다.
B 겨울이 가까워지면, 피스 강에서부터 인디언 준주(準州)에 이르는 지역에 있던 거대한 버팔로 무리 전체가 남쪽으로 수백 마일을 이동하여, 각 무리가 최북단에서 경험했을 환경보다 더 유리한 환경에서 겨울을 보냈다.
A 그 결과, 서스캐처원 남쪽의 광활한 지역 대부분이 겨울에도 버팔로로 가득 찼다. 이른 봄에 온화한 날씨가 돌아오면, 북쪽으로의 이동이 재개되었다. 의심할 여지없이 이 북쪽으로의 이주는 더 나은 목초지를 찾아서라기보다는 남쪽 겨울 서식지의 더위를 피하기 위한 것이었다. 왜냐하면 텍사스는 연중 내내 가축을 방목할 수 있는 지역으로, 가축이 너무 많지 않는 한, (방목하기에) 이곳보다 더 좋은 지역은 거의 없기 때문이다.

18 단락배열 ②

| 분석 |

몇 년 만에 다시 프레임 문제로 돌아왔다는 주어진 문장 다음에 프레임 문제에 대한 패트릭 헤이즈의 일반적 견해를 소개하는 B가 이어지고, 한층 더 구체적으로 패트릭 헤이즈의 견해를 상술하는 동시에 그에 대한 필자의 반론을 소개하는 A가 이어지며, 시간적 제약(시간적 압박)을 받는 상황에서는 "계획과 통제의 목적을 위해 실시간으로 실제 예측을 제공하는" 프레임 문제가 필연적으로 발생할 수밖에 없다는 필자 자신의 견해를 요약해 진술하고 있는 C가 마지막으로 이어지는 것이 가장 자연스럽다.

| 어휘 |

odds and ends 잡동사니, 자질구레한 것들 **shed light on** ~을 비추다; 밝히다, 해명하다 **beset** v. 포위하다; 괴롭히다 **motivate** v. (행동 등의) 이유가 되다 **arise** v. 생기다, 발생하다 **compact** a. 간결한 **anticipation** n. 예상, 예측; 기대

| 해석 |

때때로 어떤 주제에 대해 진전을 이루는 방법은 몇 년 동안 그 주제에 등을 돌리는 것입니다. 적어도 저는 그렇기를 바랍니다. 왜냐하면 저는 몇 년 동안 다른 주제들에 집중한 후 다시 프레임 문제로 돌아왔기 때문입니다.
B 저는 그동안 그 문제들을 이해하는 데 도움을 주는 몇 가지 작은 단서들을 손에 넣었을지도 모른다고 생각합니다. 아마도 패트릭 헤이즈(Patrick Hayes)가 주장했듯이, 프레임 문제는 실제로 시간 압박과 직접적인 관련이 없을 수도 있습니다.
A 그는 상황을 바로잡을 세상의 모든 시간을 가진 천사들도 여전히 프레임 문제에 시달릴 것이라 주장합니다. 저는 그 말에 확신이 가지 않습니다. 사탄이 "세상을 25단어 이내로 설명하는 것"에 대해 무슨 상이라도 내걸지 않는다면, 왜 이 프레임 문제가 그토록 운 좋은 존재에게도 '동기 부여가 된' 문제가 될 것인지 적어도 저는 이해가 가지 않습니다.
C 저는 여전히 프레임 문제는 세상에 대한 '유용하고' 간결한 표현을 발견하는 문제로서, 즉 계획과 통제의 목적을 위해 '실시간으로 실제 예측'을 제공하는 문제로서, 가장 자연스럽게 그리고 필연적으로 발생한다고 생각합니다.

19 단락배열 ④

| 분석 |

9/11 테러에 대한 음모론이 소개되고 있는 글이다. 일반적인 음모론에 대한 개요가 진술되고 있는 주어진 문장 다음에 미국 정부의 역할을 비교적 소극적이었다고 보는 이른바 '방조자' 음모론이 소개되는 C가 이어지고, 미국 정부가 이보다 훨씬 더 적극적으로 개입했다고 보는 이른바 '자작극' 음모론이 소개되는 A가 다음에 이어지며, 이 '자작극' 음모론의 내용을 구체화하여 상술하는 B가 마지막에 나오는 것이 가장 자연스럽다.

| 어휘 |

allegation n. (증거 없이 누가 부정한 일을 했다는) 혐의, 주장 **9/11** 9·11 테러(2001년 9월 11일 회교 과격파 테러 집단인 Al Qaeda 대원들이 미국 민간 항공기를 납치해 미국 New York 시의 World Trade Center(세계무역센터) 건물 두 동과 Washington의 Pentagon(국방부) 건물에 충돌시켜 붕괴·파손시킨 사건) **conspiracy** n. 음모, 모의 **concerned** a. 관심을 가진 **rally** n. (특히 어떤 생각·정당을 지지하기 위한 대규모) 집회 **withhold** v. 억누르다, 억제하다; 보류하다, ~을 주지 않다 **variant** n. 변종, 이형(異形) **mild** a. 가벼운, 순한 **accessary** n. (범행의) 종범, 방조자 **false-flag operation** 자작극, 위장 작전(거짓 깃발 작전이라고도 불리며, 실제 책임 소재를 위장해 다른 당사자에게 책임을 떠넘기려는 의도에서 저질러진 행위를 의미함) **justify** v. 정당화하다

far-reaching a. 지대한 영향을 가져올 **explosive** a. 폭발성의 n. 폭발물

| 해석 |

미국 정부가 9/11 테러를 일으키는 데 일조했다는 주장은 인터넷과 소셜 미디어에서 쉽게 찾을 수 있는 음모론에 반영되어 있다. "9/11 진실 규명(9/11-for-truth)" 운동과 같은 관심을 가진 시민들로 이루어진 대규모 단체들은 다큐멘터리를 제작하고, 책과 기사 등을 출판하며, 집회를 조직하는 등, 미국 정부가 이 사건의 진실을 감추고 있다고 대중을 설득하려 했다.
C 더 나아가, 9/11 음모론에는 다양한 변형들이 존재한다. 비교적 "온건한" 변형은 미국 정부는 단지 방조자였을 뿐이라는 주장으로, 예를 들어 공직자들은 테러 공격이 임박했다는 사실을 알고 있었지만 고의로 예방 조치를 하지 않았다고 가정한다.
A 다른 변형은 미국 정부가 보다 적극적인 역할을 했다고 주장하며, 공직자들이 직접 이러한 공격을 기획하고 실행했다고 주장한다. 후자의 음모론은 종종 9/11 테러를 "자작극(거짓 깃발 작전)"으로 묘사한다. 즉, 전쟁과 같은 중대한 행동을 정당화하기 위해 다른 국가나 조직이 저지른 것처럼 보이도록 설계된 공격이었다는 것이다.
B 이러한 자작극 9/11 음모론은 비행기가 원격 조종되었다거나, 폭발물이 터져 쌍둥이 빌딩이 붕괴하였다거나, 미국 국방부 건물을 파손시킨 것은 여객기가 아니라 로켓이었다는 등의 주장으로 잘 알려져 있다.

20 문맥상 적절하지 않은 문장 고르기 ④

| 분석 |

세 번째 문장에 글 전체의 요지가 담겨 있다. 즉, '경영진은 과학적 경영 하에서도 근로자가 작업 방식과 수단에 대한 개선을 제안하도록 적극 권장하라'는 것이다. 이러한 요지를 뒷받침하는 세부 내용이 이하에서 상술되고 있는데 '일부 근로자들은 종전의 전통적 방식을 더 선호한다'는 ④번 진술은 이러한 글의 문맥과 어울리지 않는다.

| 어휘 |

incentive n. (어떤 행동을 장려하기 위한) 격려, 자극, 유인(誘因), 동기 **ingenuity** n. 독창성 **implement** n. (흔히 옥외 활동에 쓰이는 간단한) 도구 **conduct** v. 수행하다, 처리하다 **merit** n. 장점 **markedly** ad. 현격히, 현저히 **autonomy** n. 자율성 **credit** n. 칭찬, 인정 **premium** n. 특별 상여금

| 해석 |

과학적 경영이 시행되면, 근로자가 새롭고 더 나은 업무 수행을 방법을 고안하고 수단을 개선하는 데 자신의 독창성을 발휘하도록 할 동기가(유인책이) 종전의 경영 유형에서와 같지 않은 것처럼 보일 수 있다. 과학적 경영에서는 근로자가 자신의 일상적인 업무에 적합하다고 여기는 수단과 방법이면 무엇이나 사용하도록 허용되지는 않는 것이 사실이다. 그러나 방법과 수단 모두에서, 근로자가 개선을 제안하도록 모든 격려를 해주어야 한다. 그리고 근로자가 개선을 제안할 때마다 새로운 방법을 신중하게 분석하고, 필요하다면 일련의 실험을 수행하여 새로운 제안과 종전의 표준이 지닌 상대적 장점들을 면밀하게 파악하는 것이 경영진의 정책이 되어야 한다. 그리고 그 새로운 방법이 종전의 방법보다 현저히 우수한 것이 밝혀질 때마다, 전체 회사의 표준으로 채택되어야 한다. 〈일부 근로자는 구조화된 시스템에 비해 그들이 체험하는 자율성이 더 크기 때문에, 전통적 방법을 선호한다.〉 해당 근로자는 개선의 공을 온전히 인정받아야 하며, 그의 독창성에 대한 보상으로 현금 특별 상여금을 지급받아야 한다. 이런 식으로 하여, 종전의 개인별 계획 하에서보다, 과학적 경영 하에서 근로자의 진정한 주도성이 더 잘 달성된다.

21 문맥상 적절하지 않은 문장 고르기 ④

| 분석 |

미국 노예 제도의 역사를 특별히 다루는 스미스소니언 흑인 역사 문화 박물관의 전시물들을 소개하고 있는 글이다. 전시 기획의 주된 동기가 노예 제도가 지닌 '육체적 속박성'을 관람객들에게 부각하는 것이라고 하였고, 그러한 육체적 속박에 사용된 다양한 도구들이 소개되고 있는 글에서, '탈주한 노예 주인들에 대한 보상'과 관련된 ④의 내용은 글 전체의 흐름과 어울리지 않는다.

| 어휘 |

curator n. 큐레이터(박물관·미술관 등의 전시 책임자) **engage with** ~에 관여하다 **institution** n. (특정 집단 사이에서 오랫동안 존재해 온) 제도, 관습 **scale** n. 규모, 범위 **bring ~ to life** (이야기 따위)를 재미있게 하다 **foreground** v. 특히 중시하다 **physicality** n. (정신적이기보다는) 물질적임 **enslavement** n. 노예화, 노예 상태 **relic** n. 유물 **constraint** n. 제약 **confinement** n. 감금, 구속 **automate** v. 자동화하다 **document** v. 서류로 뒷받침하다 **cash crop** 환금작물 **pace** v. (일의) 속도를 유지하다 **narrative** n. 묘사, 서술 **entitled to** ~할 권리[자격]가 있는 **legislature** n. 의회 **rebellion** n. 반란, 반항 **execute** v. 처형하다 **chattel** n. 소지품, 가재도구 **cotton gin** 조면기(면화에서 솜과 씨를 분리하는 기계) **testimonial** n. 증명서; 감사장, 표창장 **articulate** v. (생각·감정을) 분명히 표현하다, 설명하다 **in regard to** ~에 관해서

| 해석 |

스미스소니언 아프리카계 미국인 역사 문화 국립 박물관의 전시 책임자들은 미국 노예 제도와 다양한 관계를 맺는 대중들에 관여한다. 한 가지 과제는 그 제도의 규모와 시간적 거리감을 생생하게 부각시키는 일이다. 노예 상태의 육체적 속박을 특히 강조하는 것이 1층 전시의 주요 초점인데, 거기서는 전시 책임자들이 유물을 신중하게 배치하여 개별적인 남성, 여성 또는 아동에게 가해지는 노예상태의 제약을 보여준다. 신체적 감금에 사용되는 도구, 처벌 도구, 환금성 작물의 시장 판매를 위한 특징적인 주요 작업들을 자동화하는 데 사용된 기계들이, 신중하게 속도 조절되고 선별된 서사(이야기)와 함께 입증되며 전시된다. 〈노예 주인들은 특히 위

기의 시기에, 즉 노예 여성과 남성이 도망치거나 반란에 가담하였을 때, 또는 범죄를 저질러 처형되었을 때, 지역 의회, 식민지 의회, 주 의회로부터 보상받을 자격이 있다고 느꼈고 종종 보상을 받았다.〉 전시된 도구들은 어린아이만 한 가재도구들에서부터 사슬과 면화 솜 뽑는 기계에 이르기까지 다양하다. 아프리카인들의 노예화에 대한 이야기는 토머스 제퍼슨(Thomas Jefferson)의 글에서 인용한 글을 통해, 그리고 새로 탄생한 공화국에서 그들을 사람이나 시민이 아닌 재산으로 만들어버린 입법 결정과 관련하여 자신들이 실제 겪었던 경험을 생생하게 전하는 개별 노예들의 증언을 통해 전해진다.

22 문맥상 적절하지 않은 문장 고르기 ③

| 분석 |

미국의 정체성을 논할 때 '용광로'처럼 통일된 겉모습을 강조하는 기존의 담론이 수정될 필요성을 제기하는 반대 담론들이 등장하고 있음을 기술하는 글이다. ③의 진술은 남성, 백인, 이성애자 등, 다수가 지배하는 미국 문화에 대한 언급으로, 미국 정체성의 형성과 변화라는 글 전체의 흐름과 어울리지 않는다.

| 어휘 |

industrialisation n. 산업화 **urbanisation** n. 도시화 **outward** a. 표면상의 **modernity** n. 현대성, 근대성 **articulation** n. (생각 등의) 명확한 표현 **unify** v. 통합하다 **cohesion** n. 응집력 **melting pot** (많은 사람·사상 등을 함께 뒤섞는) 용광로, 도가니 **marginalize** v. 하찮은 존재 같은 기분이 들게 하다, 소외시키다(= marginalise) **minority** n. 소수자 **semblance** n. 외관, 겉모습 **revise** v. 변경하다 **heterosexual** a. 이성애(異性愛)의 **version** n. (어떤 사건에 대해 특정한 입장에서 밝힌) 설명, 견해 **heterogeneous** a. 이질적인, 여러 다른 종류들로 이뤄진 **mutual** a. 상호간의 **universalize** v. 일반화하다, 보편화하다(= universalise) **accord** v. 일치하다; (권위·지위 등을) 부여하다 **modification** n. (개선을 위한) 수정 **discourse** n. 담론, 담화 **counter-discourse** n. 반대 담론 **neatness** n. 깔끔함, 말쑥함 **critique** v. 비평하다

| 해석 |

근대성의 외적인 징후인 산업화와 도시화가 급속히 증대됨에 따라, 생산과 경제 성장이 공통 목표와 공유되는 신념과 단결 의식을 중심으로 전개되어 갈 수 있도록 전체적으로 통일된 국가임을 명백히 표현하는 일이 더욱 부추겨졌다. 이러한 통일된 국가가 실제로 존재한 적이 없을 경우, 사람들을 한데 모아 미국이라는 국가를 만드는 방법으로서의 '용광로'가 지속적으로 강조되었다. 그러나 근대성과 그 가치에 대한 의문이 제기되고, 미국 내의 민족적이고 소외된 소수자들의 역사가 점점 더 재발견됨에 따라, 이러한 통일성의 겉모습은 수정되어야 했다. 〈전통적으로 미국에서는 남성, 백인, 이성애자들의 이야기들과 다양한 역사들이 지배적인 이념 문화로 등장하였다.〉 미국의 정체성은 '같음과 다름의 무한히 다양한 상호 경쟁'의 일환으로서, 아주 다양한 서로 경쟁하는 요인들, 즉 '이질적인 대화들'을 통해 만들어진다. 국가적 특성, 신념 및 가치를 확인하여 이를 정체성이라 부르려는 근대적인 보편화 경향은 이러한 '재해석, 수정, 변형 및 도전'이라는 조건하에서는 더 이상 하나로 일치될 수 없다. 미국의 정체성에 대한 기존의 담론들과 정체성에 대한 바로 그러한 관점의 단정한 모습과 안정성에 대해 의문을 제기하며 비평하는 일련의 반대 담론들 사이에는 긴장이 존재한다.

23 문맥상 적절하지 않은 문장 고르기 ④

| 분석 |

시시포스 신화의 줄거리가 소개되고 있는 대목에서, 필자가 갑자기 끼어들어 개인적 감상을 이야기하고 있는 ④는 글 전체의 흐름과 무관하다.

| 어휘 |

Sisyphus n. (그리스신화) 시시포스(코린트의 사악한 왕으로, 사후에 지옥에 떨어져 큰 바위를 산 위로 밀어 올리는 벌을 받아 이 일을 한없이 되풀이했다고 함) **rashly** ad. 무모하게, 무분별하게 **cast** v. 던지다 **square** n. 광장 **underworld** n. 지하 세계, 저승 **obedience** n. 순종, 복종 **Pluto** n. (그리스신화) 플루토(하계(下界), Hades)의 왕) **chastise** v. 꾸짖다, 벌주다 **infernal** a. 지옥의, 지옥 같은 **pause** n. 멈춤 **recall** n. 소환, 복귀 명령 **of no avail** 아무 소용이 없는 **gulf** n. 만(灣) **sparkling** a. 반짝거리는 **decree** n. 명령 **Mercury** n. (그리스신화) 헤르메스(신들의 전령) **seize** v. (힘으로) 움켜잡다 **impudent** a. 뻔뻔스러운, 염치없는 **collar** n. 윗옷의 깃, 칼라 **seize a person by the collar** 남의 멱살을 잡다 **snatch** v. 와락 붙잡다, 잡아채다 **forcibly** ad. 강제로

| 해석 |

시시포스(Sisyphus)는 자신의 죽음이 임박하자 무모하게도 아내의 사랑을 시험하고 싶은 마음이 들었다는 이야기가 전해진다. 그는 아내에게 매장하지 않은 자신의 시신을 광장 한가운데에 던지라고 명령했다. 시시포스는 지하 세계에서 깨어났고, 거기서 인간적 사랑에 그렇게도 반대되는 복종에 화가 난 그는 아내를 꾸짖기 위해 지상으로 돌아가도 좋다는 허락을 플루토(지하 세계의 왕)로부터 받아냈다. 하지만 그가 이 세상의 모습을 다시 보고, 물과 태양, 따뜻한 돌과 바다를 즐기게 되자, 그는 더 이상 지옥의 어둠으로 돌아가고 싶지 않았다. 〈바로 그 귀환, 그 멈춤에서 시시포스는 내 관심을 끌었다.〉 (지하 세계로의) 복귀 명령, 분노의 징후, 경고도 아무 소용이 없었다. 그는 만(灣)의 곡선, 반짝이는 바다, 그리고 대지의 미소를 마주하며 많은 해를 더 살았다. 신들의 명령은 피할 수 없었다. 머큐리(신들의 사자(使者))가 나타나 그 뻔뻔스러운 남자의 멱살을 잡고, 그를 즐거움으로부터 강제로 잡아채어 지하 세계로 끌고 갔다. 지하 세계에는 그를 위해 마련된 바위가 있었다.

24 글의 제목 ③

| 분석 |

이 글은 헉슬리와 아놀드로 각각 대표되는 19세기 영국 사상 진영

의 분열(구분)에 대해 진술하고 있다. 전자의 진영은 과학에 기반하여 종교와 무관한 세속적 사회 건설을 꿈꾸었고, 후자는 과학의 도전에 맞서 인문학의 규범적 역할을 확보하려고 하였다. 따라서 가장 적절한 제목은 ③이다.

| 어휘 |

division n. 분할; 분열 **at work** 작용하고 있는 **intent** a. 강한 관심을 보이는, 몰두하는 **secure** v. (특히 힘들게) 얻어 내다, 획득하다 **normative** a. 규범적인 **humanities** n. 인문학(人文學)(인간의 사상 및 문화를 대상으로 하는 학문영역) **in the face of** (문제 · 어려움 같은) ~에도 불구하고; (~라는 결과) 앞에서 **relentless** a. 수그러들지 않는, 끈질긴; 가차 없는, 혹독한 **meritocracy** n. 실력주의, 능력주의 **entrepreneur** n. (특히 모험적인) 사업가, 기업가 **physicist** n. 물리학자 **forge** v. (노력하여) 만들어내다, 구축하다 **secular** a. 종교와 관계없는, 세속적인 **displace** v. 대신하다, 대체하다; (살던 곳에서) 쫓아내다 **dismiss** v. (고려할 가치가 없다고) 묵살하다, 일축하다 **clerical** a. 성직자의 **oust** v. (일자리 · 권좌에서) 몰아내다, 축출하다 **manifesto** n. (어떤 단체, 특히 정당의) 성명서, 선언문 **demarcation** n. 경계 설정, 구분 **inform** v. 알려주다, 특징짓다 **nourish** v. (감정 · 생각 등을) 키우다, 기르다 **yearning** n. 동경

| 해석 |

T. H. 헉슬리(T. H. Huxley)와 매튜 아놀드(Matthew Arnold)는 신칸트주의적 지식 분열의 양 측면을 각각 대표한다. 한쪽에는 사실에 대한 관심이, 다른 한쪽에는 가치에 대한 관심이 놓여 있다. 흥미롭게도, 아놀드는 문학의 주요 기능 중 하나가 사람들이 과학의 결과라는 부담을 받아들일 수 있도록 만드는 것이라고 생각했다. 결국 헉슬리와 아놀드는 의견이 다름을 인정하고 좋은 친구로 남았다. 그러나 돌이켜보면, 그들은 당시 작용하고 있던 더 광범위한 사조들을 대변하는 인물들로 볼 수 있다. 아놀드는 과학의 끊임없는 성장에 직면하여 인문학의 규범적 역할을 확보하는 데 열의를 보였다. 헉슬리는 새롭게 떠오르던 과학적 실력주의와 산업 시대 영국의 자수성가형 기업가들을 옹호했다. 헉슬리가 속한 그룹에는 물리학자 존 틴들(John Tyndall)과 사회철학자 허버트 스펜서(Herbert Spencer)가 포함되어 있었으며, 이들은 자연에 대한 과학적 이해에 기초한 새로운 세속적(비종교적) 사회를 만들고자 했다. 과학에 기반한 문화가 종교에 기반한 문화를 대체해야 했고, 그러기 위해서는 종교적 주장들을 거짓으로 일축하고 성직자와 문학적 엘리트들을 영향력 있는 지위에서 축출해야 했다. 이것은 1874년 벨파스트에서 열린 영국 과학진흥협회 회의에서 행해진 그의 유명한 "벨파스트 연설"에서 틴들이 발표한 선언이었다. 틴들이 제안한 해결책은 구분이었다. 즉, 과학은 자연 세계를 설명하고, 인문학은 우리의 도덕적인 삶을 특징짓고 살찌게 하며 우리의 영적 갈망을 충족시킨다는 것이었다.

① 신앙에 의해 통합된 문화 비평가들과 과학 비평가들
② 공상과학소설: 종교에 대한 과학적 대응
③ 19세기 영국에서의 과학과 인문학의 구분
④ 19세기 영국 사상 속의 자연과 문화
⑤ 틴들의 벨파스트 연설: 과학과 종교를 연결하기

25 빈칸완성   ⑤

| 분석 |

빈칸 앞에 사용된 양보의 연결어(Nevertheless)에 주목해 볼 때, '존재'의 의미에 대해 명확한 이해에 도달하려면 자신의 『존재와 시간』을 모두 다 읽어야 한다는 것이 하이데거의 생각임에도 불구하고, 필자가 "초기 단계에서라도 우리의 사고를 위한 초기 방향성을 제시하는 것은 가능하다"고 진술한 것은 하이데거는 존재에 대한 일정한 예비적 이해가 "모든 인간의 말과 행동에 내재되어 있다"고 보았기 때문이라는 것이 가장 적절한 추론이다.

| 어휘 |

signify v. 의미하다, 뜻하다, 나타내다 **opening** n. 시작 부분, 첫 부분 **coherent** a. 일관성 있는, 논리 정연한 **implicit** a. 암시된, 내포된 **preliminary** a. (더 중요한 행동 · 행사에 대한) 예비의 **indicate** v. (사실임 · 존재함을) 나타내다, 보여주다 **orientation** n. (목표하는) 방향, 지향 **irrelevant** a. 무관한, 상관없는

| 해석 |

하이데거(Heidegger)에 따르면, 『존재와 시간(Being and Time)』 전체는 단 하나의 질문, 즉 존재의 의미에 대한 질문을 다루고 있다. 그러나 그가 '존재'란 용어로 의미하는 것은 무엇일까? 이 용어는, 혹 의미하는 것이 있다면, 무엇을 의미하는가? 하이데거가 이 질문에 대해 책의 서두에서도, 그리고 이후의 어느 부분에서도 명확하고 간단한 답을 제공하지 않는 것은 결코 우연이 아니다. 왜냐하면 그의 견해에 따르면, 우리가 이 질문을 일관되고 잠재적으로 유익한 방식으로 제기할 수 있게 되려면 적어도 이 책 전체를 읽어야 하기 때문이다. 그럼에도 불구하고, 그는 또한 '존재'에 대한 일정한 예비적 이해가 인간이 말하고 행동하는 모든 것 속에 암묵적으로 내포되어 있다고 본다. 따라서 이 초기 단계에서도 적어도 우리의 사고를 위한 초기 방향성을 제시하는 것은 가능할 것이다.

① 우리 대부분이 행동하는 방식에는 부재하다
② 의미 있는 방식으로는 완전히 부족하다
③ 자신의 사고방식을 추구하는 데 무관하다
④ 궁극적인 질문에 대한 명확한 답을 제공하지 않는다
⑤ 인간이 말하고 행동하는 모든 것 속에 암묵적으로 내포되어 있다

26 빈칸완성   ④

| 분석 |

예술을 통해 인류가 표현하고자 하는 주제들이 소개된 다음, 이러한 주제를 표현하는 형태는 '시대, 문화, 지역에 따라 다양하다'고 언급하고 있는 대목이다. 주목할 표현은 "과거에는 적어도(in the past at least)"라는 표현이다. 이는 오늘날 현대 예술에서는 자주 무시되거나 포기되기도 하지만 과거에는 예술 표현에 반드시 뒤따랐던 어떤 기준이나 요건들이 있었음을 의미한다. 예술 표현은 미적 기준을 요구하므로 정답은 ④가 적절하다.

| 어휘 |

mammal n. 포유동물　　still ad. 그런데도, 그럼에도 불구하고　numerous a. 많은　prose n. 산문　millennium n. 천년(pl. millennia)　deliberation n. 숙고, 숙의　ethereal a. 천상의, 이 세상의 것이 아닌; 미묘한, 영묘(靈妙)한　contemporary a. 동시대의; 현대의, 당대의　metaphor n. 은유, 비유　resonate v. 울려 퍼지다, 공명(共鳴)하다　variation n. 변화, 차이; 변형　manifest v. 표현하다, 나타내다　mandate n. 권한, 명령　theatrical a. 연극의; 연극조의, 과장된　compliance n. (법·명령 등의) 준수, (명령 등에) 따름　narrative n. 묘사, 서사　athletic a. 운동 경기의　aesthetic a. 미적인, 심미적인　sustainability n. 지속 가능성, 환경 파괴 없이 지속될 수 있음

| 해석 |

예술은 실제로 무엇이며, 왜 그것은 인간이라는 것의 의미와 이토록 밀접하게 연결되어 있는 것처럼 보일까? 우리는 예술을 창작하는 유일한 포유류인데, 예술이 우리에게 중요하기는 하지만, 생물학적 생존에 필수적인 것은 전혀 아니다. 그럼에도 불구하고, 인간이 예술적으로 자신을 표현할 권리를 위해 어떻게 목숨을 걸고, 심지어 목숨을 희생했는지에 대한 사례들은 무수히 많다. 예술은 문학의 산문과 시에서부터 조각과 회화, 영화 제작, 음악 작곡뿐만 아니라 춤과 같은 신체적 표현에 이르기까지 다양한 형태로 나타난다. 하지만 우리가 예술을 통해 그렇게까지 간절히 표현하고자 하는 것은 과연 무엇일까? 수천 년에 걸친 다양한 예술 작품들을 연구해 보면, 몇 가지 주제가 계속 등장하는데, 그것은 곧 인간 조건을, 그리고 영혼의 존재나 그와 유사한 영적 현상들을 포함하여 삶과 죽음에 대한 때로는 불안한 성찰을 표현하는 것이다. 이러한 주제들은 일반적으로 당대의 시대적 배경 속에서 묘사되며, 때로는 다양하게 찾아올 특정 대상 청중에게 공감을 불러일으키는 은유를 통해 표현된다. 그리고 많은 예술적 표현은 시대, 문화, 지역에 따라 모양과 형태가 달라지며, 과거에는 적어도 예술적 표현에 최소한의 미적 기준의 요건들이 수반되었다.

① 극예술 준수의 의무들
② 문화적 서사 기대에 대한 지침들
③ 운동 기록 평가의 기준들
④ 최소한의 미적 기준의 요건들
⑤ 환경적 지속 가능성 계획의 조건들

27 빈칸완성　①

| 분석 |

앞서 공리주의는 '쾌락과, 고통의 부재인 행복을 증진하는 행동만이 옳다'는 원리에 입각해 있다고 하였다. 따라서 공리주의가 기반하고 있는 삶의 이론에서는 '바람직한(desirable)' 것들이란 그 안에 쾌락을 내재하고 있는 것이거나, '쾌락의 증진과 고통을 방지하는 수단'으로서 바람직한 것의 두 종류가 있을 것이라고 추론할 수 있다. 구문적으로 마지막 문장이 either A or B 구조로서 'A 또는 B'라는 의미를 담고 있음에 유의한다.

| 어휘 |

creed n. 신조(信條)　utility n. 유용(성), 효용　proportion n. 비율, 비례　in proportion 비례하여, 비례적으로　promote v. 촉진하다, 증진시키다　reverse a. 거꾸로 된, 반대의 n. 역(逆), 반대　privation n. 결핍, 박탈　open question 미해결 문제, 의견의 자유로운 표명을 구하는 문제　supplementary a. 보충의, 추가의　freedom from ~에서 벗어나 있는 상태　end n. 목적, 목표　utilitarian a. 공리주의의 n. 공리주의자　scheme n. (교양·주장·학설 따위의) 조직, 체계　promotion n. 촉진; 증진　prevention n. 예방, 방지　acquisition n. 획득　liberation n. 해방　virtue n. 선; 미덕

| 해석 |

공리(Utility), 즉 최대 행복 원리를 도덕의 기초로 받아들이는 신조는, 행동은 행복을 증진하는 경향에 비례하여 옳고, 행복의 반대를 낳는 경향에 비례하여 그르다고 주장한다. 여기서 행복이란 쾌락과, 고통의 부재를 의미하며, 불행은 고통과, 쾌락의 결핍을 의미한다. 이 이론이 설정한 도덕적 기준을 명확히 이해하기 위해서는 훨씬 더 많은 설명이 필요한데, 특히 고통과 쾌락의 개념에 어떤 것들이 포함되는지, 그리고 이것이 어느 정도까지 미해결 문제로 남는지가 설명되어야 한다. 그러나 이러한 보충적 설명은 이 도덕 이론이 기반하고 있는 삶의 이론에는 영향을 미치지 않는다. 즉, 쾌락과, 고통으로부터의 자유만이 목적으로서 바람직하다는 것과, (다른 어떤 체계만큼이나 공리주의 체계에도 아주 많지만) 모든 바람직한 것들은 그것 자체에 내재된 쾌락 때문에 바람직하거나, 쾌락 증진과 고통 방지의 수단으로서 바람직하다는 것에는 영향을 미치지 않는다.

① 쾌락 증진과 고통 방지
② 부의 획득과 빈곤으로부터 탈출
③ 지식 추구와 무지 회피
④ 권력 획득과 억압으로부터 해방
⑤ 미덕 배양과 도덕적 수월성 성취

28 빈칸완성　①

| 분석 |

19세기 중반을 거치면서 프랑스와 영국 양국 모두에서 왕실 부모들이 보여준 모범의 영향을 받아 '가족생활의 이상이 부르주아 사회의 핵심 요소가 되었다'는 것이 이 글의 요지이다. 따라서 프랑스 황제 부부가 보여주었던 이미지 역시 그러한 '가족적 친밀감'을 형상화한 것이었으리라고 추론할 수 있다.

| 어휘 |

informal a. 격식에 얽매이지 않는, 허물없는, 편안한　devotion n. 헌신　take a hold on ~을 장악하다, ~을 사로잡다　keystone n. (아치 꼭대기의) 쐐기돌; (계획·주장의) 핵심　bourgeois n. 부르주아(중산 계급의 사람)　personality n. 성격, 인격　preoccupation n. (어떤 생각·걱정에) 사로잡힘, 집착, 심취, 몰두　intimacy n. 친밀함　cultivate v. (말·행동 방식 등을) 기르다　print n. 판화　offspring

n. 자식   **adorn** v. 꾸미다, 장식하다   **prosperity** n. 번영   **civic** a. 시민의   **self-assurance** n. 자신(自信), 자기 과신

| 해석 |

7월 왕정(1830–48) 시기 동안, 루이 필립(Louis–Philippe)의 보다 소탈한 생활 방식과 왕실 부모들의 자녀들에 대한 헌신적인 사랑의 영향으로 가족생활의 이상이 대중들의 상상 속에 강하게 자리 잡았고 부르주아 사회의 핵심 요소가 되었다. 자녀 양육과 교육, 그리고 유아의 성격 발달이 큰 관심사가 되었다. 가족과 그 안에서의 자녀 역할에 대한 이러한 관심은 나폴레옹 3세(Napoleon III)의 제2 제정(帝政)(1852–70) 시기에도 계속되었으며, 그와 그의 아내였던 황후 유제니(Eugénie)는 가족적 친밀감의 이미지를 함양시켰다. 같은 현상이 영국에서도 나타났는데, 빅토리아(Victoria) 여왕과 앨버트 공(Prince Albert)이 자녀들과 함께 노는 모습을 담은 판화가 많은 가정의 벽을 장식했다. 이러한 1850년 이후의 시기는 경제적 번영, 시민 생활의 개선, 그리고 부르주아 계층의 자신감이 두드러졌던 시기로, 19세기 아동 문학 발전에서 가장 풍요로운 시기로 볼 수 있다. 가정의 일을 사실주의적으로 다룬 소설, 즉 가족 소설은 19세기 전반의 도덕적 이야기에서 발전했으며, 성인을 위한 사실주의 소설의 발전을 반영하였다.

① 가족적 친밀감
② 행복한 엄마
③ 지배적인 가족
④ 번영하는 집단
⑤ 중산층의 욕망

29 빈칸완성 ⑤

| 분석 |

'콜럼버스 신화를 통해 미국인들은 자신들의 기원과 정체성을 선언할 수 있었다'는 것, 그리고 '이러한 콜럼버스 신화가 표상하는 이상이『위대한 개츠비』라는 작품 속에 계승되어 있다'고 말하는 것이 글 전체의 요지이자 취지이다. 따라서『위대한 개츠비』가 보여주는 지극히 미국적인 "끝없는 발전, 자기 창조, 성공, 성취"라는 꿈이 이미 '콜럼버스 신화 속에 신화적으로 해석되어 들어가 있는 꿈이었다'고 추론하는 것이 가장 적절하다.

| 어휘 |

myth n. 신화   **declare** v. 선언하다, 공표하다   **prevalent** a. 일반적인, 널리 퍼져 있는   **mythicize** v. 신화화하다, 신화적으로 해석하다   **incorporate** v. (일부로) 포함하다   **play out** (연기를) 펼쳐 보이다   **temptation** n. 유혹   **manifest** v. 나타내다, 드러내 보이다   **yearn** v. 갈망하다, 동경하다   **encompass** v. 포함하다, 아우르다, 품다   **scheme** n. 계획; 책략   **fruitless** a. 성과 없는   **longing** n. 갈망

| 해석 |

콜럼버스 신화는 백인 미국인들이 시작점을 찾고, 자신들의 '이야기'에 용감한 개막을 선언할 수 있도록 해주었다. 이는 미국에 널리 퍼져있던 영향력 있는 기원 관련 꿈 신화의 일부였다. F. 스콧 피츠제럴드(F. Scott Fitzgerlad)의『위대한 개츠비(The Great Gatsby)』는 미국적 꿈의 힘과 그것을 실제 경험에서 추구하는 데 따르는 문제들을 모두 인식하고 있다. 끝없는 발전, 자기 창조, 성취, 성공이라는 이상(理想) — 콜럼버스의 정신 속에 통합된 신화적으로 해석된 꿈 — 이 닉 캐러웨이(Nick Carraway)의 시선에 비친 모습으로 제이 개츠비(Jay Gatsby)라는 인물 속에서 펼쳐진다. 이 소설은 정체성의 문제를 다루고, 특히 개츠비가 과거에 거의 결혼할 뻔했던 여성인 데이지 뷰캐넌(Daisy Buchanan)에 대한 개츠비의 그리움에 나타나는 '꿈'을 믿고자 하는 유혹을 다루는데, 데이지는 '"잃어버린 기원"으로 되돌아가고자 하는, 즉 시작점으로 돌아가고자 하는 끝없는 욕망'을 품고 있다.

① 좌절된 계획
② 성취된 계획
③ 달성할 수 없는 목표
④ 결실 없는 갈망
⑤ 신화적으로 해석된 꿈

30 문맥상 적절한 표현 고르기 ②

| 분석 |

Ⓐ indeed라는 부사는 앞서 진술한 내용보다 한층 더 놀라운 정보를 제시할 때 사용된다. '과학자들이 핵물리학의 실용적 응용은 거의 불가능하다는 점을 즐기기까지 했다'라고 해야, 앞서 언급된 '과학자들이 핵물리학의 실용적 사용은 비현실적이라고 믿었다'는 내용에서 한 발 더 나아간 것이라고 볼 수 있다. Ⓑ 리제 마이트너와 오토 프리쉬의 핵분열 실험으로 핵물리학의 실용적 사용이 가능하다는 단초가 제시되었으므로 이후 핵물리학계에서는 이에 대한 적극적인 '조사'와 '연구'에 나섰으리라고 추론할 수 있다. Ⓒ 문맥상 페르미가 최초의 지속적인 핵반응을 '창출해냈다'는 말이 들어가는 것이 적절하다.

| 어휘 |

fission n. 핵분열, 분열   **nucleus** n. 핵(pl. nuclei)   **physicist** n. 물리학자   **impractical** a. 실행할 수 없는, 비현실적인   **indeed** ad. (이미 말한 일을 확인·확충하여) (보기와는 달리) 실은, 사실은(= in reality); 실은 오히려   **relish** v. (어떤 것을 대단히) 즐기다   **abhor** v. (특히 도덕적인 이유로) 혐오하다   **application** n. 응용, 적용   **speculate** v. 추측하다   **investigate** v. (어떤 주제·문제에 대해) 조사하다, 연구하다   **disregard** v. 무시하다   **neutron** n. 중성자   **chain reaction** 연쇄 반응   **likelihood** n. 가능성   **restrain** v. (특히 물리력을 동원하여) 저지하다, 억제하다   **self-sustained** a. 자기 유지적인, 자가 지속적인

| 해석 |

리제 마이트너(Lise Meitner)와 오토 프리쉬(Otto Frisch)가 1938년 후반 원자핵의 분열 과정을 발견하기 전까지, 대부분의 물리학자들은 에너지 생산이나 무기와 같은 실용적인 목적으로 핵물리학

을 사용하는 것은 전혀 비현실적이라고 믿었고, 사실 일부 물리학자들은 그들의 연구가 이렇게 실용적으로 응용되지 않는 점을 즐기기까지 했다. 그러나 핵분열이 발견되면서 모든 것이 바뀌었다. 영국과 미국의 핵물리학계는 핵분열이 실용적 사용으로 나아가는 문을 열었는지, 우라늄 원자의 분열에서 연쇄 반응을 유지할 수 있을 만큼 충분한 중성자가 생성되었는지, 그리고 연쇄 반응의 가능성을 높이는 데 어떤 종류의 물질을 사용할 수 있는지에 대해 추측하고 직접 조사하기 시작했다. 1942년 12월에는 이미, 이탈리아 물리학자 엔리코 페르미(Enrico Fermi)는 시카고 대학의 연구실에서 최초의 자가 지속적 핵반응을 만들어냈다.

31   문맥상 적절한 표현 고르기   ⑤

| 분석 |

수성암 퇴적 지층이 형성되는 과정을 설명하고 있는 글이다. Ⓐ 문맥상 '퇴적물'이라는 뜻의 표현이 필요하다. Ⓑ 퇴적물이 가라앉기에 유리한 물리적, 역학적(mechanical) 작용으로는 '범람'이 적절하다. Ⓒ 문맥상 '부유(수면에 떠다님)하던 진흙이나 모래가 가라앉는다'는 표현이 적절하다.

| 어휘 |

aqueous a. 수분을 함유한, 물과 같은   **aqueous rock** 수성암(水成岩)   **sedimentary** a. 퇴적물의, 퇴적 작용으로 생긴   **sedimentary rock** 퇴적암(堆積岩)   **fossiliferous** a. 화석을 함유한   **mechanical** a. 역학(力學)의   **remnant** n. 남은 부분, 나머지   **deposit** n. 침전물, 퇴적물   **pebble** n. 자갈   **organic** a. 생물[유기체]에서 만들어진   **limestone** n. 석회석   **stratify** v. 층을 이루게 하다   **layer** n. 층   **stratum** n. (암석 등의) 층, 지층, 단층(pl. strata)   **bed** n. 지층   **strew** v. 흩다, 흩뿌리다   **mouth** n. (강의) 어귀   **inundation** n. 범람, 침수   **precipitation** n. 강수, 강수량   **velocity** n. 속도   **check** v. 억제하다, 저지하다   **plain** n. 평야, 평원   **dissolution** n. 용해, 융해   **suspension** n. 부유(浮遊) (상태)   **gravity** n. 중력, 무게

| 해석 |

수성암(水成岩)은 때로는 퇴적암 또는 화석암이라 불리기도 하는데, 다른 어떤 암석보다 더 넓게 지구 겉면을 덮고 있다. 이러한 암석은 주로 역학적(力學的) 퇴적물(자갈, 모래, 진흙)로 구성되어 있지만, 일부는 화학적 기원의 것이며, 특히 석회암과 같은 일부는 유기적 기원의 것이다. 이들 암석은 층을 이루고 있다. 즉 서로 다른 층인 지층들로 나누어져 있다. '지층'이라는 용어는 단순히 하나의 층을 의미하거나 일정한 표면 위에 펼쳐지거나 흩어져 있는 모든 것을 의미한다. 그리고 우리는 강어귀 근처나 일시적인 범람 시 육지에서 일상적으로 관찰할 수 있는 현상을 통해, 이러한 지층이 일반적으로 물의 작용에 의해 형성되었다고 추론한다. 왜냐하면 진흙이나 모래로 채워진 흐르는 개울이 호수나 바다에 들어가거나 평야를 범람할 때처럼 속도가 줄어들 때마다, 물의 움직임으로 인해 부유 상태에 있던 퇴적물이 자체 무게로 말미암아 바닥으로 가라앉기 때문이다. 이러한 방식으로 진흙과 모래의 층들이 한 층씩 차례로 쌓이게 된다.

32   문맥상 적절한 표현 고르기   ②

| 분석 |

Ⓐ '강좌의 성공 요인은 ~에 달려 있다'는 식의 진술이 필요하다. impinge는 '부정적인 영향을 미치다'는 의미로서 문맥에 어울리지 않는다. Ⓑ 필자가 기존에 사용했던 표준 교재에 대해 가졌던 '불만', '좌절감'은 자신이 직접 교재를 집필하게 된 계기가 되었다고 추론할 수 있다. Ⓒ 필자가 교실 현장에서 좌절을 겪으면서 경험했던 것은, 과정을 이수하는 데 필요한 적정 수준의 그리스어 지식과 학생들이 갖춘 현실적 지식 사이의 '공백, 격차, 간극'이라고 말할 수 있을 것이다.

| 어휘 |

elementary a. 초보의, 초급의   **course** n. (특정 과목에 대한 일련의) 강의, 강좌   **impinge** v. (특히 나쁜) 영향을 주다, 지장을 주다   **differ** v. 다르다   **differing** a. 다른, 상이한   **degree** n. 정도   **dedication** n. 전념, 헌신   **inspire** v. (욕구·자신감·열의를 갖도록) 고무하다   **frustration** n. 불만, 좌절감   **typewrite** v. 타이프라이터로 치다   **manual** n. 입문서, 지도서   **undergraduate** n. (대학) 학부생, 대학생   **keenly** ad. 날카롭게   **gap** n. 간격, 공백   **mature** a. 성숙한   **Attic** a. 아티카(Attica)의, 아테네(Athens)의   **presentation** n. (정식) 소개, 설명, 진술, 발표

| 해석 |

초급 그리스어를 가르치거나 배우는 데 있어 최선의 유일한 방법이란 존재하지 않는다. 성공적인 강좌는 교실의 교사, 교재, 그리고 다양한 학습 스타일과 도전적인 과제에 대한 각기 다른 헌신도를 가진 학생들 사이의 복합적인 상호작용에 달려 있다. 『아티카 그리스어 입문(Introduction to Attic Greek)』은 표준 교재에 대한 좌절감에서 비롯된 것으로, 몇 년 전 캘리포니아대학교 버클리 캠퍼스의 학부 교육 개선 프로젝트의 일환으로 타자기로 입력해 두었던 입문서에서 시작되었다. 나는 수업 시간에 다양한 수준의 학생들을 가르쳐왔고, 많은 학생들이 고급 학부 및 대학원 과정에 도달할 때 겪는 지식의 공백을 절실히 알고 있었다. 이 책을 집필하면서, 나는 성숙한 대학생들에게 고대 아티카 그리스어에 대한 신뢰할 수 있고 비교적 완전한 설명을 제공하고자 했다.

33   글의 주제   ③

| 분석 |

"의식적 사고의 대부분이 본능적 기능으로 간주되어야 한다", "의식함이 본능에 반대되는 것은 아니다", "의식적 사고의 대부분은 본능에 은밀한 영향을 받는다", "모든 논리의 이면에는 생리적 요구가 존재한다" 등의 진술을 종합해 볼 때, 필자는 의식적 사고와 본능은 상호 대립하는 것이 아니라 상호 연결되어 있으면서, 상호 작용을 주고받는 관계임을 시사하고 있다.

| 어휘 |

count v. (~으로) 간주하다; 간주되다   **instinctive** a. 본능적인

anew ad. (처음부터) 다시, 새로 **heredity** n. 유전 **innateness** n. 타고남, 천부적임 **procedure** n. 절차 **opposed to** ~에 반대되는 **decisive** a. 결정적인, 결정적으로 중요한 **definite** a. 확실한, 뚜렷한 **channel** n. 경로 **seeming** a. 외견상의, 겉보기의 **sovereignty** n. 자주권; (국가의) 자주[독립] **plainly** ad. 숨김없이, 솔직히 **physiological** a. 생리적인 **maintenance** n. 유지 **mode** n. 양식, 형식 **interplay** n. 상호작용 **override** v. 무시하다; 무효로 하다 **enhance** v. 향상시키다

| 해석 |
충분히 오랫동안 철학자들을 주의 깊게 관찰하고, 그들의 글에서 행간의 의미를 파악한 뒤, 나는 이제 의식적 사고의 대부분은 본능적 기능으로 간주되어야 하며, 심지어 철학적 사고의 경우에도 그러하다고 스스로에게 말한다. 우리는 유전과 "선천성"에 대해 새롭게 배워야 했던 것처럼, 여기에서도 새로 배워야 한다. 출생이라는 행위가 유전의 전체 과정과 절차에서 중요한 고려 대상이 아니듯이, "의식함"이 결정적인 의미에서 본능에 반대되는 것도 거의 아니다. 철학자의 의식적 사고의 대부분은 그의 본능에 의해 은밀하게 영향을 받고, 강제적으로 특정한 경로를 거치게 된다. 그리고 모든 논리와 겉으로 볼 때 그것의 자율적인 움직임 뒤에는 가치 판단이 있으며, 좀 더 직설적으로 말하자면 특정한 삶의 방식을 유지하기 위한 생리적 요구가 존재한다.

① 논리적 사고의 우월성
② 현대 철학적 추론의 결함
③ 본능과 의식적 사고의 상호작용
④ 철학자들이 논리를 사용하여 본능을 극복하는 방법
⑤ 철학적 논리를 강화하는 데 있어서 교육이 하는 역할

34 글의 요지 ①

| 분석 |
아우구스티누스는 사랑의 본질에 대해 논하고 있는데, "사랑은 일종의 갈망이다", "그 갈망은 특정한 대상에 묶여 있으며, 소유하고 붙들려는 의지이다", "소유하는 순간 상실의 두려움이 일어난다" 등의 진술을 종합해 볼 때, '사랑의 본질은 갈망이고, 이 갈망은 대상을 소유하고 지키려는 의지이기도 한데, 소유는 필연적으로 상실에 대한 두려움을 불러온다'고 재진술할 수 있다.

| 어휘 |
Augustine n. (그리스도교의 성인) 아우구스티누스(354년~430년) **crave** v. 갈망하다 **for one's own sake** 그 자체를 위해 **spark** v. 촉발시키다, 유발하다 **possession** n. 소유 **give rise to** ~을 낳다, 일으키다 **dread** v. ~을 몹시 무서워하다 **shun** v. 피하다 **be bound by** ~에 얽매이다 **bind** v. 결속시키다, 묶다 **beset** v. 괴롭히다 **endure** v. 견디다, 인내하다 **at stake** 성패가 달려 있는, 위태로운 **lasting** a. 지속적인, 영속적인

| 해석 |
아우구스티누스(Augustine)는 "사랑한다는 것은 결국 어떤 것을 그 자체로 갈망하는 것과 다름없다"고 말하며, 나아가 "사랑은 일종의 갈망"이라고 언급한다. 모든 갈망은 특정한 대상에 묶여 있으며, 이 대상이 갈망 자체를 불러일으켜 갈망의 목표를 제공한다. 갈망, 즉 사랑은 인간이 자신을 행복하게 해줄 선(善)을 소유할 수 있는 가능성, 즉 자신의 본질과 가장 가까운 것을 소유할 수 있는 가능성이다. 이러한 사랑은 두려움으로 변할 수 있다. "우리가 사랑하고 이미 얻은 것을 잃는 것, 또는 우리가 사랑하며 바랐던 것을 얻지 못하는 것이 두려움의 유일한 원인이라는 점을 의심할 사람은 아무도 없을 것"이라고 말한다. 소유하고 붙들려는 의지로서의 갈망은 소유하는 바로 그 순간, 상실의 두려움을 불러일으킨다. 갈망이 어떤 선(善)을 추구하는 것이듯이, 두려움은 어떤 악(惡)을 두려워하는 것이며, "어떤 것을 두려워하는 자는 반드시 그것을 피하려고 한다."

① 사랑은 끊임없이 갈망과 두려움에 얽매여 있다.
② 인간적 사랑의 문제점은 그것이 두려움에 시달린다는 것이다.
③ 사랑은 우리의 선을 상실하고, 그 상실을 견뎌내는 데 있다.
④ 사랑은 소유의 부족이 아니라, 소유의 안전이 위태로운 것이다.
⑤ 그 자체를 위한 지속적인 즐거움은 결코 적절한 욕망의 대상이 될 수 없다.

35 내용일치 ③

| 분석 |
본문에서 "카이사르가 승리한 후 바로는 사면(赦免)받고 카이사르의 보호 아래 중요한 지위에 올랐지만, 기원전 43년, 안토니우스 통치 아래에서 급격히 은총을 잃고 실각했다"고 하였으므로 ③은 잘못된 진술이다.

| 어휘 |
adventurous a. 모험적인, 용기가 필요한, 대담한 **pre-eminent** a. 출중한, 발군의 **scholar** n. 학자 **triumph** v. 승리를 거두다, 이기다 **prominence** n. 명성, 유명함; 중요함 **precipitously** ad. 가파르게 **fall out of grace** 은총(총애)을 잃다 **BCE** n. 기원전(before the Common Era) **account** n. (있었던 일에 대한) 설명, 이야기 **granted that** 설사 ~이라 할지라도 **virtually** ad. 사실상, 거의

| 해석 |
부유한 로마 가문에서 태어난 마르쿠스 테렌티우스 바로(Marcus Terentius Varro)는 길고도 흥미진진한 삶을 살았다. 저명한 학자인 루키우스 아이리우스 스틸로(Lucius Aelius Stilo) 밑에서 공부한 후, 철학을 공부하기 위해 아테네로 여행을 떠났다. 로마로 돌아온 그는 권력 투쟁에서 패배한 측에 서서 싸웠으며, 결국 카이사르(Caesar)가 승리하게 되었다. 그는 사면(赦免)받고 카이사르의 보호 아래 중요한 지위에 올랐지만, 기원전 43년, 안토니우스(Antony) 통치 아래에서 급격히 은총을 잃고 실각했다. 죽음은 모면했지만, 그의 개인 도서관이 파괴되는 고통을 겪었다. 그는 은퇴하여 남은 생을 독서와 집필에 전념하며 보냈고, 89세의 나이로 생을 마감했다. 다양한 추정이 있지만, 대부분의 로마 시대 책들이

현대의 장(章) 정도의 분량이었다 치더라도, 620권의 책을 그가 집필했다는 이야기들도 있다. 바로는 천문학, 지리학, 농업, 수학, 법학, 역사, 철학, 언어 등 거의 모든 주제에 대해 글을 남겼다. 그는 또한 시(詩), 연설문, 편지까지 저술했다.

① 바로는 아테네에서 철학을 공부했다.
② 바로는 권력 다툼에서 패배한 편에서 싸웠다.
③ 바로는 안토니우스에 의해 사면되고 명성을 얻었다.
④ 바로는 600권 이상의 책을 썼다고 여겨진다.
⑤ 바로는 천문학, 수학, 언어 등에 관해 글을 썼다.

| 36 | 내용일치 | ⑤ |

| 분석 |
"실제로 법의학 병리학자는 의심스러운 죽음을 다루는 것보다 더 광범위한 역할을 한다", "법의학 병리학자가 수행하는 부검의 대부분은 확인되지 않은 자연사를 포함한다", "의심스럽지 않은 자연사, 치명적 사고, 자살로 인한 사망 및 기타 고의적 또는 비고의적 부상으로 인한 사망에 대한 조사가 법의학 병리학자의 주요 업무의 대부분을 구성한다"고 하였으므로 ⑤의 진술은 non-suspicious를 suspicious라 해서 잘못되었다.

| 어휘 |
criminal a. 형사(刑事)상의   **on behalf of** ~을 대신하여, ~을 대표하여   **criminal justice system** 형사 사법체계   **coroner** n. 검시(檢屍)관   **jurisdiction** n. 관할권, 사법권   **pathologist** n. 병리학자   **phase** n. 단계, 시기, 국면   **forensic** a. 법의학적인, 범죄 과학 수사의   **ascertain** v. 알아내다, 확인하다   **suspect** n. 용의자   **inflict** v. (괴로움 등을) 가하다   **medico-legal** a. 법의학적인   **with regard to** ~에 관하여   **suspicious** a. 의심스러운, 수상쩍은   **autopsy** n. (사체) 부검, 검시   **scrutinize** v. 세심히 살피다, 면밀히 조사하다

| 해석 |
형사(刑事) 사건과 직접적으로 관련된 사안의 경우, 실제 조사의 대부분은 형사 사법 제도를 대신하여 경찰이 수행하는데, 이 제도에서는 검시관이 대부분의 사법권에 거의 관여하지 않는다. 이러한 상황에서는 병리학자가 경찰 수사관을 위한 서비스를 수행한다고 결론 내릴 수 있는 실질적인 근거가 있다. 실제로 형사(刑事) 수사는 여러 국면으로 이루어진다. 전통적으로 법의학 병리학자는 수사 중에서도 사망이나 부상을 중심으로 하는 국면, 특히 부상자나 사망자를 검사하여 부상의 본질과 원인을 밝히는 국면에 관여했다. 그러나 실제로는, 법의학 병리학자는 형사사건 수사에서 더 광범위한 역할을 수행한다. 예를 들어, 그들은 사망 현장 조사에 관여하거나 피해자에게 부상을 입혔을 수 있는 용의자를 수사하는 데 관여하게 될 수도 있다. 그들은 법의학적인 목적으로 의료 기록을 평가하고 의학적 문제와 관련하여 다른 증인들의 진술을 검토할 수 있다. 따라서 실제로 법의학 병리학자는 의심스러운 죽음을 다루는 것보다 더 광범위한 역할을 한다. 법의학 병리학자가 수행하는 부검의 대부분은 사회적으로 면밀한 조사와 확인이 요구되는 확인되지 않은 자연사를 포함한다. 의심스럽지 않은 자연사, 치명적 사고, 자살로 인한 사망 및 기타 고의적 또는 비고의적 부상으로 인한 사망에 대한 조사가 법의학 병리학자의 주요 업무의 대부분을 구성한다.

① 경찰은 형사 문제와 관련된 많은 조사를 수행한다.
② 법의학 병리학자는 전통적으로 사망 또는 부상에 대한 조사에 집중해 왔다.
③ 법의학 병리학자는 종종 용의자와 사망 현장에 대한 검사에 참여한다.
④ 법의학 병리학자가 수행하는 대부분의 부검은 확인되지 않은 자연사를 포함한다.
⑤ 의심스러운 사망에 대한 조사가 법의학 병리학자가 처리하는 사건의 대부분을 구성한다.

37~38

인간 사회는 동물 사회와 달리 주로 의사소통 속에 만들어지고 의사소통에 의해 전달되는 사회적 유산이다. 한 사회의 지속성과 생명력은 그 사회의 풍속(風俗), 관습, 기술, 이상(理想)을 한 세대에서 다음 세대로 성공적으로 전달하는 데 달려 있다. 집단행동의 관점에서 볼 때, 이러한 문화적 특성들은 모두 "합의"라는 하나의 개념으로 환원될 수 있다. 사회는 추상적으로 보면 개인들의 조직이며, 구체적으로 보면 조직된 습관, 감정 및 사회적 태도로, 요컨대 합의로, 이루어진 복합체이다.

사회(society), 공동체(community), 사회 집단(social group)이라는 용어는 연구자들에 따라 강조점의 차이는 있지만, 의미상 큰 차이는 없다. 사회는 보다 추상적이고 포괄적인 개념으로, 다양한 사회 집단들로 구성되어 있으며, 각 집단은 고유한 유형의 조직을 가지면서도, 동시에 추상적인 사회 일반의 특징을 공유한다. 공동체는 사회와 사회집단이 구성 기관들과 개인들의 지리적 분포의 관점에서 고려될 경우에 사회와 사회 집단에 적용되는 용어이다. 따라서 모든 공동체는 하나의 사회이지만, 모든 사회가 하나의 공동체는 아니다. 개인은 여러 사회 집단에 속할 수 있지만, 그가 속한 작은 공동체가 그가 또한 속한 더 큰 공동체의 일부로 포함될 경우가 아니면, 일반적으로 하나 이상의 공동체에 속하지는 않을 것이다. 그러나 적어도 사회학적 관점에서 볼 때, 개인이 단순히 한 공동체에 거주한다고 해서 그 공동체의 구성원이 되는 것이 아니라, 그 공동체의 공동생활에 참여하기 때문에, 그리고 그 정도에 따라 공동체의 일원이 된다.

| 어휘 |
heritage n. (국가·사회의) 유산   **transmit** v. (자손에게) 물려주다, 유전시키다   **folkways** n. (pl.) 습관, 풍속(한 사회 집단의 공통적인 생활·사고·행동 양식)   **mores** n. 풍습, 관습   **reduce** v. 줄이다,

축소하다; 변형시키다, 바꾸다 **consensus** n. 의견 일치, 합의 **sentiment** n. 정서, 감정 **in short** 요컨대 **student** n. 연구가, 학자 **inclusive** a. 포괄적인 **institution** n. 기관, 단체 **It follows that** ~라는 논리가 따라온다, 따라서 ~가 성립한다 **ordinarily** ad. 보통 때는, 대개는 **in so far as** ~하는 한에 있어서는 **at least** 적어도 **inheritance** n. 유산, 상속 **modernity** n. 현대성, 근대성 **namely** ad. 즉, 다시 말해 **otherwise** ad. 그렇지 않으면; 그 외에는

37 글의 제목 ②

| 분석 |

전체적으로 볼 때 첫 단락에 "인간 사회는 사회적 유산이며, 그 문화적 특성의 요체는 합의이다"라는 요지가 제시되어 있고, 두 번째 단락은 인간 사회를 사회와 공동체라는 측면에서 상술(詳述)하고 있다. 따라서 주제문을 잘 요약하고 있는 ②가 글의 제목으로 가장 적절하다.

윗글의 제목으로 가장 적절한 것은?
① 공동체가 개인을 형성하는 방식
② 인간 사회의 사회적 유산
③ 인간과 동물의 사회 구조 비교
④ 사회 이해: 전통에서 현대성까지
⑤ 동물과 인간 사회의 소통과 문화

38 빈칸완성 ①

| 분석 |

Ⓐ 앞서 나온 "조직된 습관, 감정 및 사회적 태도"를 빈칸 다음의 "합의"라는 개념으로 요약해 주는 연결어가 필요하다. that is는 환언(換言)하는 연결어로서 앞선 내용을 다른 단어로 바꿔 설명하거나, 더 자세한 정보를 제공할 때 사용한다. 따라서 요약의 기능이 더 강력한 in short가 더 적절하다. Ⓑ however는 일반적으로는 강한 역접(반대되는 개념을 제시)으로 사용되지만, 해당 본문에서는 논점의 전환 또는 기존 논의를 보완하는 역할로 사용되었다고 볼 수 있다. 즉, 공동체가 지리적 분포의 관점에서 사용되는 용어라고 했지만 사회학적 관점에서 보면 단순히 지리적으로 어느 공동체에 거주한다고 해서 그 공동체의 일원이 되는 것은 아니라고 하여 앞의 내용을 일부 부정하므로 however가 적절하다.

39~40

인도-유럽어족의 다양한 문법적 형태나 품사들에서 모음 e와 o가 서로 교체되거나 아예 발음되지 않는 방식을 가리키는 용어인 모음 전환(gradation)의 존재에 대한 정확한 음운론적, 문법적 이유는 거의 알려진 바가 없다. 어근(語根)에서 e와 o의 변화는 강세의 위치 변화에서 비롯되었을 가능성이 있으며, 강세가 없는 것은 영(零) 등급(zero-grade)과 상관관계가 있을 수 있다. 고전 언어들과 게르만 언어에서 모음 전환은 종종 한 품사에서 다른 품사로의 변화를 알렸으며, 또한 자주 어형 변화(paradigmatic change)를 수반했다. 게르만 언어 내에서 모음 전환의 주요 기능은 강변화 동사(strong verb)로 불리는 큰 동사 부류의 인칭(person), 수(number), 시제(tense)를 표시하는 것이었다. 인도-유럽어족에서 게르만 언어, 고대 영어, 중세 영어를 거쳐 현대 영어에 이르는 음성 변화 과정에 정통하지 않으면, 이 동사 이형태(異形態)들의 원래의 e-, o-, 영(零) 등급은 오늘날에는 알아볼 수 없다. 우리는 이 동사들을 "불규칙 동사(irregular verb)"로 분류하게 되었다.

단어 파생(word derivation)에서의 모음 전환 역시 게르만 언어의 일반적인 패턴이었는데, 영어에서는 점점 덜 생산적으로 되었지만 다른 게르만 언어에서는 그렇지 않았다. 그럼에도 불구하고, 현대 영어에도 동사-명사 쌍인 do-deed, sing-song, break-breach, bind-bond 등에서처럼 이러한 패턴의 흔적이 화석처럼 일부 남아 있다. 이들 단어 쌍의 단어들 간의 의미적 관계는 모든 영어 화자들에게 명확하지만, 역사적인 음성 과정을 거치면서 초기의 모음 등급들은 알아볼 수 없을 정도로 바뀌었다.

| 어휘 |

phonological a. 음운론의 **gradation** n. 모음 전환 **vowel** n. 모음 **alternate** v. 번갈아 나오다; 교체하다, 교대하다 **zero** n. (형태소의) 제로 표징(表徵), 제로 형태(특정 음소가 기대되지만 발음되지 않는 현상) **word class** 품사 **variation** n. 차이, 변이 **root** n. 어근(語根) **placement** n. 배치 **accent** n. 강세, 억양 **stress** n. (발음에서) 강세 **correlate** v. 상관관계가 있다, 연관성이 있다 **accompany** v. 동반하다, 수반하다 **paradigmatic** a. 어형 변화(표)의, 활용례의 **strong verb** 강변화 동사 **familiarity** n. 잘 앎; 정통(精通), 익히 앎 **person** n. 인칭(人稱) **tense** n. 시제 **phonetic** a. 음성의 **allomorph** n. 이형태(異形態)(한 개의 형태소가 환경에 따라 갖게 되는 두 가지 이상의 형태) **derivation** n. (말의) 파생, 어원 **still** ad. 그런데도, 그럼에도 불구하고 **deed** n. 행위 **breach** n. 파기 **bond** n. 속박 **semantic** a. 의미의, 의미론적인 **scarce** a. 부족한, 희소한 **succinct** a. 간단명료한, 간결한 **notorious** a. 악명 높은 **redundant** a. 불필요한, 쓸모없는

39 빈칸완성 ⑤

| 분석 |

빈칸 다음에 예시된 단어 쌍들은 모두 모음 전환 현상을 통해 동사에서 명사 어휘들이 파생되어 만들어진 예들이다. 모음만 바꾸어 동사를 명사로 만들어내는(파생시키는) 과정은 언어적으로 대단히 '생산적이다(productive).' 또한, '그럼에도 불구하고 현대 영어에도 이러한 패턴의 흔적이 화석처럼 일부 남아 있다'고 하였다.

이 두 가지 단서를 결합하여 추론하면, '모음 전환을 통해 새로운 단어를 만들어내는 생산적인(productive) 측면이 다른 게르만 언어에서와는 달리 영어에서는 점점 사라졌지만, 그래도 현대 영어에 아직 그러한 파생의 흔적이 화석처럼 남아 있다'는 말이 된다.

40 글의 제목 ①

| 분석 |

필자는 첫 단락에서 인도-유럽어족에 속하는 고전 언어(그리스어, 라틴어) 및 게르만 언어에서 공통으로 나타나는 모음 전환(gradation) 현상에 대해 설명하였고, 두 번째 단락에서는 모음 전환이 단어 파생에 미친 영향을 게르만 언어와 영어에 국한하여 기술하였다. 따라서 이러한 내용을 종합해 보았을 때 이 글의 제목으로 ①이 가장 적절하다.

윗글의 제목으로 가장 적절한 것은?
① 게르만 언어에서의 모음 전환
② 왜 강변화 동사를 사용해야 하는가
③ 품사가 결정되는 방식
④ 고전 언어의 진화
⑤ 고대 영어에서의 다양한 음성적 변화

경희대학교 인문·체육계열

TEST p. 128~143

01	②	02	④	03	③	04	②	05	①	06	④	07	⑤	08	①	09	③	10	③
11	④	12	⑤	13	①	14	②	15	⑤	16	④	17	⑤	18	④	19	③	20	②
21	③	22	②	23	③	24	④	25	⑤	26	④	27	⑤	28	①	29	③	30	④
31	①	32	④	33	⑤	34	①	35	④	36	④	37	②	38	②	39	①	40	③

01 동의어 ②

| 어휘 |

outgoing a. 물러나는, 외향적인 **year-end** n. 연말 **fundraising** n. 모금 **obviate** v. 제거하다(= eliminate) **compromise** v. 손상시키다, 합의하다 **exasperate** v. 격분하다 **supplant** v. 대체하다 **accelerate** v. 가속화하다

| 해석 |

퇴임하는 CEO의 후한 기부 덕분에 연말 기금 모으기의 필요성이 없어졌다.

02 동의어 ④

| 어휘 |

political faction 정치 파벌 **acquiesce** v. 묵인하다, 묵묵히 따르다(= assent) **delineate** v. 상세히 기술하다 **prolong** v. 연장하다 **recuperate** v. 회복하다[되찾다]

| 해석 |

내년도 예산안이 부결될 것이라는 예상과는 달리, 여러 정치 파벌들은 묵묵히 따라서 단일 표결로 예산안을 통과시켰다.

03 동의어 ③

| 어휘 |

disclose v. 밝히다 **predilection** n. 매우 좋아함, 편애(= partiality) **biographical** a. 전기(傳記)의 **aversion** n. 혐오 **disdain** n. 경멸 **contempt** n. 멸시 **supposition** n. 추정

| 해석 |

그 작가는 비록 최근 몇 년간 발표한 작품들이 전기 소설 쪽에 기울어져 있지만, 시(詩)에 대한 편애를 갖고 있다고 한 인터뷰에서 털어놓았다.

04 동의어 ②

| 어휘 |

brooding a. 음침한, 고민에 잠긴(= pensive) **attractive** a. 매력적인 **untroubled** a. 고요한, 흔들림 없는 **respectable** a. 존경할만한 **buoyant** a. 자신감에 차 있는, 부력의

| 해석 |

TikTok에는 제인 오스틴과 그녀의 작품에 관한 수십만 개의 동영상이 올라와 있는데, 그 중 상당수는 그녀의 고민에 잠긴 로맨틱 영웅 Mr. Darcy(오만과 편견의 남자 주인공)에 관한 것이다.

05 동의어 ①

| 어휘 |

bland a. 단조로운 **reassuringly** ad. 안심시키게 **embedded** a. 내장된 **foreboding** n. 불길한 예감(= apprehension) **inform** v. 특징짓다 **precipice** n. 절벽, 벼랑 **desiccation** n. 건조 **aspiration** n. 열망, 포부 **devotion** n. 헌신 **contradiction** n. 모순

| 해석 |

공항은 무섭지 않다. 의도적으로 단조롭고, 길을 찾아가기에 간단하며, 안심이 될 정도로 비슷한 모습이다. 진정 무서운 것은 모든 여정에 내재된 '불확실성'이며, 지평선은 정확하게 눈에 보이는 그대로 절벽이라고 단순히 가정해버린 평평한 지구 이론의 특징이 된 막연한 예감이다.

06 동의어 ④

| 어휘 |

oceanographer n. 해양학자 **impervious** a. 영향 받지 않는(= immune) **sensitive** a. 민감한 **accessible** a. 접근할 수 있는 **susceptible** a. 예민한 **responsive** a. 반응하는

| 해석 |
북태평양 해저에 있는 물 대부분은 최소 800년 동안 햇빛에 노출된 적이 없으며, 일부는 2,000년 이상 그곳에 머물러 있다. 이에 따라 해양학자들은 해저 층의 온도가 안정적이고 대기 온난화의 영향을 받지 않을 것이라고 생각해왔다.

07 동의어 ⑤

| 어휘 |
surge n. 급증 **postgraduate** n. 대학원생 **dole out** 나눠 주다(= grant) **hoard** v. 비축하다 **conceal** v. 감추다 **withhold** v. 유지하다 **relinquish** v. 포기하다

| 해석 |
영국에서는 외국 학생들로부터의 수요 급증으로 인해 대학원 교육이 크게 성장했다. 현재 영국 대학들은 학부 학위 5개당 대학원 학위 4개를 수여하고 있다.

08 동의어 ①

| 어휘 |
driver n. 동인(動因), 추진 요인 **connective tissue** 결합 조직 **inexhaustible** a. 지칠 줄 모르는(= indefatigable) **measurable** a. 측정할 수 있는 **depletable** a. 소모성의 **unifying** a. 통합하는 **constrained** a. 강요된, 부자연스러운

| 해석 |
20세기 대중문화의 가장 중요한 주역 중 한 명인 퀸시 존스가 11월 3일 91세의 나이로 세상을 떠났다. 음악 제작자, 작곡가, 경영자였던 그는 여러 시대와 음악 스타일을 연결하는 가교 역할을 했다. 음악적 감각이 뛰어난 귀, 지칠 줄 모르는 작업 윤리, 음악사와 신기술에 대한 헌신으로, 그는 수십 년간 미국 대중음악의 중심을 정의했다.

09 논리완성 ③

| 분석 |
두 번째 문장의 the genre는 첫 문장의 Romance를 가리키며, 첫 문장에서 '이것이 페이지 위의 글을 뇌 속의 쾌락 화학물질로 바꾸는 마법과 같다.'고 했는데, 여기서 뇌는 독자들의 뇌이므로 독자들에게 쾌락을, 즉 갈망과 해방의 감각과 미학을, 불러일으킨다는 말이 된다. 따라서 빈칸에는 conjuring이 적절하다.

| 어휘 |
composition n. 구성, 작문 **pleasure chemical** 쾌락 화학물질 **trope** n. 수사, 비유적 용법 **sensation** n. 감각, 감동 **aesthetics** n. 미학 **longing** n. 갈망 **release** n. 해방 **spell** n. 마법의 주문 **repel** v. 추방하다 **smother** v. 질식시키다 **conjure** v. 마술을 하다, 떠올리게 하다 **thwart** v. 방해하다, 반대하다 **obstruct** v. 가로막다

| 해석 |
로맨스는 무엇보다도 감정적인 작문이다. 그것은 페이지 위의 글을 뇌 속의 쾌락 화학물질로 바꾸는 마법 같은 책략이다. 이 장르의 비유 용법과 전통은 수백 년에 걸쳐 단순히 갈망과 해방의 감각과 미학을 흉내 낼 뿐 아니라 독자에게 실제로 그 감각과 미학을 불러일으켜온 관행을 나타낸다. 이 마법이 효과를 발휘하려면 독자의 전적인 신뢰가 필요하다.

10 논리완성 ③

| 분석 |
빈칸에는 첫 문장의 the professor wandered from the subject와 관련된 '주제에서 벗어난 이야기'를 의미하는 단어가 들어가야 하므로 digressions가 적절하다.

| 어휘 |
wander v. 헤매다, 방랑하다 **incantation** n. 주문 **periphery** n. 주변부 **digression** n. (이야기가) 주제에서 이탈함, 여담, 딴소리 **altercation** n. 논쟁 **modification** n. 수정, 변경

| 해석 |
학생들은 교수의 이야기가 주제에서 벗어났는데도 전혀 개의치 않았다. 주제에서 이탈한 그의 이야기가 종종 그날의 주제보다 더 흥미롭고 더 기억에 잘 남았다.

11 논리완성 ④

| 분석 |
첫 문장의 but 앞에서 새로운 시스템인 태양광과 에너지 저장의 증가가 가져다주는 전력 수급 관리상의 이점을 언급했으므로, 역접의 but 다음에서는 새로운 시스템의 허가 절차와 관련된 단점이 기술되어야 한다. 따라서 빈칸에는 '번거롭다'는 의미의 cumbersome이 적절하다.

| 어휘 |
residential a. 거주의 **local utilities** 지방 공기업, 공익기관 **spike** n. 급증, 급등 **entities** n. 기관, 단체 **exemplary** a. 모범적인 **improvident** a. 앞날을 생각하지 않는 **cumbersome** a. 번거로운 **utilitarian** a. 공리적인

| 해석 |
가정용 태양광과 에너지 저장의 대폭적인 증가는 지역 공익기관들이 증가하는 수요와 사용량 급증을 더 잘 관리하는 데 도움이 될 것이지만, 새로운 시스템을 허가받는 절차는 여전히 번거롭다. 대부분의 공익기관들은 새로운 시스템 설치에 대한 인센티브를 제공하지 않고, 설치 과정도 쉽게 해주지 않으며, 전력 회사와 지

방 정부를 포함한 여러 기관의 승인을 받아야 하는 것도 도움이 되지 않는다.

12 논리완성 ⑤

| 분석 |

Ⓐ "팬들은 끊임없이 토론하며 온라인에서 단서를 찾아다녔고, 탐사전문 기자들도 이 미스터리를 풀기 위해 노력했지만 성과는 없었다."라는 단서로부터 빈칸에 '당황케 했다(perplexed)'는 표현이 와야 함을 추론할 수 있다. Ⓑ 팬들이 이 사람의 정체를 놓고 온라인 상에서 끊임없이 토론을 벌이고 단서를 찾으려 했는데, 토론과 유사한 노력은 그의 정체와 관련하여 논리적으로 타당한 설명을 제시하는 이론화(theorized)일 것이다.

| 어휘 |

cryptocurrency n. 가상화폐 **investigative journalist** 탐사 전문 기자 **matter** v. 중요하다 **imbue** v. 가득 채우다 **mute** v. 소리를 줄이다 **rescind** v. 폐지하다 **dismay** v. 실망하다 **confirm** v. 확인하다 **divert** v. 주의를 돌리다 **perplex** v. 당황케 하다 **theorize** v. 이론화하다

| 해석 |

비트코인의 창시자 '사토시 나카모토'는 누구일까? 이 질문은 2009년에 그 사용자 이름의 인물이 비트코인을 창안한 이후로 암호화폐 열광자들을 당황케 하고 흥분시켜왔다. 팬들은 끊임없이 이론을 세우고, 토론하며 온라인에서 단서를 찾아다녔고, 동시에 탐사전문 기자들도 이 미스터리를 풀기 위해 노력했지만 성과는 없었다. 그가 누구냐는 질문에 대한 답이 중요한 이유는 사토시의 아이디어가 거의 종교적일 정도의 의미를 갖고 있기 때문이며, 또한 그가 누구든 약 600억 달러(약 72조 원) 상당의 비트코인을 보유 중이기 때문이다. 이 액수라면 이 사람은 생존 인물 중 25위의 부자가 될 것이다.

13 논리완성 ①

| 분석 |

Ⓐ rather than은 대조, 상반의 의미를 갖는다. 따라서 빈칸에는 객관적인 '물적 증거'와 반대되는 의미를 갖는 주관적인 자백(confession)이 적절하다. Ⓑ 앞 문장 내용의 요지는 일본 검찰이 물적 증거보다 자백에 더 의존한다는 것이다. 자백은 곧 자신의 죄에 대한 인정(admission)이다.

| 어휘 |

lenient a. 관대한 **lock up** 가두다, 감금하다 **offender** n. 법위반자 **stern** a. 엄중한 **prosecutor** n. 검사 **go after** 추적하다 **confession** n. 자백 **admission** n. 인정 **witness** n. 목격자, 증인 **retaliation** n. 보복 **investigation** n. 조사 **rehabilitation** n. 재건, 회복 **denial** n. 부인, 거부 **arrest** n. 체포

| 해석 |

몇 가지 점에서 일본은 관대한 나라다. 범죄율이 낮고 다른 선진국에 비해 훨씬 적은 수의 국민을 구금한다. 죄를 인정하고 사과하는 경범죄자들은 종종 엄중한 경고만 받고 풀려난다. 하지만 검찰이 누군가를 기소하기로 마음먹으면, 그들은 특별한 권한을 행사한다. 다른 선진국과 달리 일본 검찰은 물적 증거보다 자백에 크게 의존한다. 일본에서 10건 중 9건의 사건은 여전히 용의자의 자백에 의해 결정된다.

14~15

2020년, 피지는 자체적인 오염 문제를 관리하기 위해 일회용 플라스틱에 대한 금지 조치를 시행했다. 특히 (플라스틱) 물병은 (이 조치에서) 제외되었는데, 이는 주요 도시 밖에서는 깨끗한 식수에 대한 접근성이 제한되어 있기 때문이고, 또한 물병(생수)을 수출하는 나라에서 물병을 금지하는 것은 비현실적이기 때문이기도 하다. 지속 가능성 문제에 대한 압박 아래서, 피지 최대 생수 수출업체인 Fiji Water사는 물병 되사기 프로그램을 시작했다. 하지만 피지에서는 Fiji Water사 물병의 23%만 반환되고 있다. 이는 매우 저조한 수치이지만, 전 세계 플라스틱 재활용 평균보다는 여전히 나은 수준이다. Fiji Water사의 자발적인 프로그램은 의회에서 검토 중에 있는 전국적인 병 보증금 제도의 전조(효시)이다. 미비점들은 아직 해결 중인 상태에 있다. 피지에서 5센트(병당 환금금)는 수집 센터 근처에 사는 주민들에게 병을 반납할 인센티브로 충분할 수 있겠지만, 멀리 떨어진 섬 지역 주민들이 플라스틱을 중앙 집중화된 장소로 가져오게 하기에는 충분하지 않을 것이다.

| 어휘 |

implement v. 실행하다 **single-use** a. 일회용의 **sustainability** n. 지속가능성 **buyback** n. 되사기, 환수매입 **precursor** n. 전조; 선구자 **bottle-deposit scheme** (빈)병 보증금 제도 **parliamentary review** 의회 검토 **kink** n. 뒤틀림, 삐뚤어짐(문제점) **work out** 해결하다 **collection center** (빈병) 수거 센터

14 빈칸완성 ②

| 분석 |

Ⓐ "이는 주요 도시 외곽에서 깨끗한 식수에 대한 접근성이 제한되어 있기 때문이다. 또한 물병(생수)을 수출하는 나라에서 물병(생수를 담는 물병)을 금지하는 것은 비현실적이기 때문이기도 하다."라는 단서로부터 물병이 일회용 플라스틱 사용 금지 조치에서 면제되었음을 추론할 수 있다. Ⓑ "하지만 피지에서는 Fiji Water사 물병의 23%만 반환되고 있다"라는 단서로부터 피지에서 플라스틱 병의 수거율이 낮다는 것을 알 수 있다. 이 글의 문맥에서 'abysmal'은 '극히 나쁜, 극히 저조한'이란 의미로 쓰이고 있다.

빈칸 Ⓐ와 Ⓑ에 들어갈 말로 가장 적절한 것은?
① 인정[인식]하다 — 감탄[존경]스러운
② 면제하다 — 최악의, 최저의
③ 배제하다 — 인공의
④ 포함하다 — 받아들일 수 있는
⑤ 교역하다 — 배타적인

| 15 | 빈칸완성 | ⑤ |

| 분석 |

빈칸 ⓒ가 들어 있는 마지막 문장은 역접의 연결사 but으로 이어져 있으므로 but 앞에 있는 절과 but 뒤에 있는 절의 내용이 서로 반대되어야 한다. 따라서 빈칸 ⓒ에는 '수집 센터 근처에 사는 주민들'과 반대되는 표현인 ⑤가 적절하다.

빈칸 ⓒ에 들어갈 어구로 가장 적절한 것은?
① Fiji Water사의 노동자들
② 해외 수입자들
③ 정부관리들
④ 물병 생산자들
⑤ 멀리 떨어진 섬 지역 주민들

16~17

수천 년 동안 사람들은 에너지 생산 역사상 가장 중요한 발명품과 매일 매일 마주하고 있었지만, 그것을 알아차리지 못했다. 주부나 하인이 차를 끓이기 위해 주전자를 (스토브에) 올려놓거나 감자를 가득 담은 냄비를 스토브에 올려놓을 때마다, 그것은 그들의 눈을 똑바로 쳐다보았다. 물이 끓는 순간 주전자나 냄비의 뚜껑이 펄쩍 뛰었다. 그것이 열이 운동으로 전환되는 것이었다. 하지만 특히 냄비를 깜빡 잊고 있었는데 물이 끓어 넘치는 경우, 냄비 뚜껑이 튀어 오르는 것은 성가신 일이었다. (모두 성가시게만 여겨졌) 아무도 그 잠재력을 알아보지 못했다.
열을 운동으로 전환하는 부분적인 혁신은 9세기 중국에서 화약이 발명된 후에 이루어졌다. 처음에는 화약을 이용해서 발사체를 추진한다는 아이디어가 너무나도 반(反)직관적이어서 수세기 동안 화약은 주로 화염 폭탄을 만드는 데만 사용되었다. 그러나 마침내 — 아마도 어떤 폭탄 전문가가 절구 안에서 화약을 갈다가 절구 공이가 힘차게 튀어나간 후에야 — 총이 등장하게 되었다. 화약이 발명되고 효과적인 대포가 개발되기까지 약 600년의 시간이 흘러야 했다.

| 어휘 |

convert v. 전환되다   annoyance n. 성가심   potential n. 잠재성
breakthrough n. 돌파구   gunpowder n. 화약   fire bomb 화염폭탄   projectile n. (총알 같은) 발사체   ground v. 갈다, 빻다

mortar n. 절구   pestle n. 절구 공이   artillery n. 대포, 포병대

| 16 | 빈칸완성 | ④ |

| 분석 |

so ~ that …은 '인과'관계를 나타내는데, 결과에 해당하는 that절에서 화약이 수세기 동안 발사체를 추진하는 데 사용되지 못하고 화염폭탄으로만 쓰였다고 한 것은 화약이 발사체를 추진한다는 것은 상식이나 직관에 벗어나서 쉽게 생각할 수 없었기 때문일 것이므로 ④(반직관적인)가 적절하다.

빈칸 Ⓐ에 들어갈 가장 적절한 단어는?
① 자발적인, 즉흥적인
② 편리한, 편의주의적인
③ 순조로운, 좋은
④ 반직관적인
⑤ 논쟁의 여지가 없는

| 17 | 내용파악 | ⑤ |

| 분석 |

첫 단락의 '가장 중요한 발명품'과 '그것'은 모두 '열이 운동으로 전환되는 것'을 가리키는데, 자연은 그것을 해왔지만 인간은 그것을 알아채지 못하고 인위적으로 그것을 만들어내지 못하다가 화약이 발명된 후에야 화약의 열에너지를 운동에너지로 전환하여 발사체가 발사되는 대포를 만들게 되었다는 것이다. 따라서 ⑤가 정답이다. ④ 화약은 9세기에 이미 발명했다.

위 글에 따르면, 사람들이 오랫동안 행하지 못했던 것은 무엇인가?
① 에너지의 역사를 기록하다.
② 요리를 함에 있어서 열에너지를 포함시키다.
③ 화염 폭탄 전문가를 양성하다.
④ 전쟁용 화약을 발명하다.
⑤ 한 에너지의 유형을 다른 에너지의 유형으로 전환하다.

18~19

2022년 초, 거대한 화산 분출의 여파로 통가 왕국은 암흑에 빠졌다. 해저 화산 분출로 인터넷 연결이 끊겨서, 위기가 한창 전개되고 있던 바로 그 순간에 통신 두절 사태가 발생한 것이다.
몇 주 후 해저 인터넷 케이블이 복구되었을 때 붕괴의 규모가 드러났다. 통신 두절은 복구 작업을 저해했을 뿐만 아니라, 해외 송금에 의존하는 다수 기업과 지역 경제를 마비 상태로 몰아넣었다.
이 재난은 인터넷 운영을 지탱하는 인프라의 극심한 취약성을 드러냈다. "현대 생활은 작동하는 인터넷과 실질적으로

분리될 수 없다"고 캘리포니아 대학교 버클리 캠퍼스의 니콜 스타로셀스키 교수는 말한다. 그런 점에서 인터넷은 마치 식수와 같다. 우리의 존재 자체를 지탱하는 기반 시설인 셈이다. 먼 곳의 저수지에서 주방 수도꼭지까지 물이 흘러오는 과정을 이해하는 사람은 거의 없다. 현대 소비자들은 인터넷을 마치 대기 중에 존재하는 보이지 않는 것, 우리 머리 위에 떠 있는 '클라우드'가 데이터 비를 내리는 것처럼 상상해왔다. "기기가 어떤 케이블에도 연결되지 않은 채 작동하기 때문에, 많은 사람들이 전체 시스템이 무선이라고 믿는다"고 스타로셀스키는 설명하지만, 현실은 훨씬 더 특별하다.

| 어휘 |

aftermath n. 여파 **sever** v. 절단하다 **communication blackout** 통신두절 **unfold** v. 펼쳐지다, 전개되다 **hamper** v. 방해하다 **devastate** v. 파괴하다 **remittance** n. 송금, 송금액 **vulnerability** n. 상처받기 쉬움 **underpin** v. 뒷받침하다, 보강하다 **utility** n. 수도, 전기 같은 공익사업 **atmosphere** n. 대기 **tether** v. 묶다

18 빈칸완성   ④

| 분석 |

"그런 점에서 인터넷은 마치 식수와 같다. 우리의 존재 자체를 지탱하는 기반 시설인 셈이다"라는 단서로부터 저자가 인터넷의 연결을 수도의 연결과 비교하고 있음을 알 수 있다. 따라서 다음에 오는 빈칸에는 식수 전달 과정인 '수원지에서 가정까지'를 나타내는 ④가 적절하다.

빈칸 Ⓐ에 들어갈 어구로 가장 적절한 것은?
① 이륙에서 착륙까지
② 진원지에서 분화까지
③ 위기에서 회복까지
④ 먼 곳의 저수지에서 주방 수도꼭지까지
⑤ 보이지 않는 구름에서 대기까지

19 글의 주제   ③

| 분석 |

이 글은 주제가 마지막 문장에 배치된 미괄식이다. 마지막 두 문장을 통해 인터넷의 물리적 인프라, 특히 숨겨진 케이블의 중요성과 취약성이 이 글의 주제임을 잘 알 수 있다.

다음 중 이 글의 주제는 무엇인가?
① 수중 화산 폭발
② 인간 존재의 영속성
③ 인터넷에 전력을 공급하는 숨겨진 케이블
④ 식수원에 대한 위협
⑤ 소비자의 무선 기기 오용

20~21

제조업체가 의도적으로 수명이 제한된 제품을 설계하거나 생산하기 위해 사용하는 전략을 계획된 노후화(구식화)라고 한다. 몇 년 후 소프트웨어 업데이트가 더 이상 지원되지 않는 스마트폰, 칩을 사용하여 인쇄 횟수를 제한하는 프린터, 빠르게 변화하는 패션 트랜드로 인해 이전 스타일이 구식으로 느껴지는 제품 등이 그 예이다. 계획된 노후화(구식화)는 여러 가지 이유로 나쁜 것으로 간주된다. 제품이 더 자주 폐기됨에 따라 환경 폐기물이 증가하고, 소비자가 새로운 제품에 더 자주 돈을 쓰게 되며, 일회용 문화에 기여하여 지속 가능성을 위한 노력을 약화시킬 수 있다. 또한 제품 수리를 어렵게 하거나 비용이 많이 들게 하여 소비자의 선택권을 제한하고, 소비자를 지속적인 소비의 사이클로 유도할 수 있다.

| 어휘 |

deliberately ad. 의도적으로 **outdated** a. 한물 간, (더 이상 쓸모가 없게) 구식인 **discard** v. 버리다 **undermine** v. 손상시키다 **sustainability** n. 지속가능성

20 빈칸완성   ②

| 분석 |

"몇 년 후 소프트웨어 업데이트가 더 이상 지원되지 않는 스마트폰, 칩을 사용하여 인쇄 횟수를 제한하는 프린터, 빠르게 변화하는 패션 트랜드로 인해 이전 스타일이 구식으로 느껴지는 제품 등이 그 예이다."라는 단서로부터 빈칸에 '노후화[구식화]'가 와야 함을 추론할 수 있다.

빈칸 Ⓐ에 들어갈 가장 적절한 말은?
① 효능, 능률
② 노후화, 진부화
③ 홍보
④ 총체, 요약
⑤ 변동성

21 빈칸완성   ③

| 분석 |

노후화[구식화] 전략이 지속가능성을 손상시키고, 소비자들로 하여금 기존의 제품을 버리고 새로운 제품을 구매하도록 강제한다는 단서로부터 빈칸에 '일회용 문화'가 와야 함을 유추할 수 있다.

빈칸 Ⓑ에 들어갈 어구로 가장 적절한 것은?
① 검소한 소비 관행
② 비교 우위
③ 일회용 문화

④ 독점 욕구
⑤ 사회경제적 지위 향상

22~23

월트 디즈니 컴퍼니의 순수성 매력에 대한 집착은 디즈니가 아동의 즐거움에 대한 자사의 지속적 헌신을 재확인하는 근거를 제공하고, 또한 디즈니가 '선량한 기업 권력'으로서 아동기 순수성을 감상적으로 미화하는 동시에 상품화하는 디즈니의 역할에 대한 비판적 평가를 경시하는 근거도 제공한다. 역사적·사회적 구성요소가 제거된 디즈니 세계에서의 순수성은 아이들이 어른 사회의 문제와 갈등에서 해방되어 보편적 유대감을 공유하는 무시간적, 무역사적, 무정치적, 그리고 무이론적 공간이 된다. 디즈니는 이런 이상을 마케팅하면서도, 환상들을 마법처럼 공급하여 이 보호 공간을 살찌우고 계속 살아있게 함으로써 아이들을 위한 이 공간을 보호하는 부모 같은 기업의 모습을 보여준다.

| 어휘 |

attachment n. 애착, 지지 **rationale** n. 이유, 근거 **commitment** n. 헌신 **assessment** n. 평가 **benevolent** a. 자애로운 **sentimentalize** v. 감상적으로 다루다 **simultaneously** ad. 동시에 **strip** v. 제거하다 **atemporal** a. 시간을 초월한 **ahistorical** a. 역사와 무관한 **apolitical** a. 정치와 무관한 **atheoretical** a. 이론과 무관한

22 빈칸완성 ②

| 분석 |

앞에서 '디즈니 컴퍼니가 ~하는 근거를 제공한다'고 했는데, '근거'는 정당한 행동의 명분 같은 것이므로 디즈니 컴퍼니의 입장에서 정당한 행동이 되려면 '비판적 평가를 경시한다'고 해야 한다. 따라서 첫 번째 빈칸에는 downplay가 적절하다. 그리고 마지막 문장에서 디즈니는 어린이의 순수성이라는 이상을 마케팅한다고 했으므로 두 번째 빈칸에는 commodifies가 적절하다.

빈칸에 들어갈 가장 적절한 말을 고르시오.
① 제재하다 — 맞춤화하다
② 경시하다 — 상품화하다
③ 꾸미다 — 품위 있게 하다
④ 과장하다 — 인간화하다
⑤ 강조하다 — 시장화하다

23 내용일치 ③

| 분석 |

"역사적·사회적 구성요소가 제거된 디즈니 세계에서의 순수성은 시간과 역사, 정치와 이론이 사라진 공간으로, 어른 사회의 문제와 갈등에서 해방된 보편적 유대감을 지닌 아이들의 영역이 된다."는 단서로부터 ③이 본문의 내용과 일치하지 않음을 알 수 있다.

위 글의 내용과 일치하지 않는 것은?
① 월트 디즈니 컴퍼니는 순수함이라는 매력에 집착한다.
② 디즈니는 아이들에게 즐거움을 선사하기 위해 기업의 힘을 활용한다.
③ 디즈니의 순수함 묘사는 역사적, 사회적 맥락에 뿌리를 두고 있다.
④ 어린 시절의 순수함은 디즈니의 상업화를 위한 중요한 메커니즘으로 그 역할을 수행한다.
⑤ 디즈니는 아이들이 상상력 넘치는 환상을 마음껏 펼칠 수 있는 이상적인 보호 공간을 조성한다.

24~25

1789년 여름에 시작된 프랑스 혁명의 가장 직접적인 원인은 정부의 재정 위기였다. 프랑스에서 가장 부유한 일부 사람들이 세금을 면제받았기 때문에 국가는 예산의 균형을 맞출 수 없었다. 프랑스 공공(국가) 부채의 중요한 요소는 영국에 대한 미국인들의 반란을 지원하면서 발생한 비용이었다. 수년 동안 프랑스 왕의 계몽주의적 조언자들은 성직자와 귀족의 세금 특권을 폐지하기 위해 노력했지만, 이 두 계층은 이러한 노력에 대해 굳건히 저항했다. 왕은 필요한 법률을 선포할 수 있었지만 귀족이 완전히 통제하는 법원은 그 법률을 집행하지 않으려 했다. 〈마침내 1788년, 왕실은 기존의 법원 제도를 폐지하고 새로운 법원 제도를 만들었다.〉 그 결과 귀족들의 반란이 일어났다. 파리와 지방의 군 장교와 왕의 관리들은 복무를 거부했고, 국가 기능 전체가 멈춰 섰다. 개혁 시도에서 인내할 수 없었던 루이 16세는 1614년 이후 처음으로 국가 문제를 해결하기 위해 의회(삼부회)를 소집하라는 귀족의 요구를 받아들였다.

| 어휘 |

element n. 요소, (집단·사회 내의 특정) 구성원 **exempt** a. 면제되는 **incur** v. 초래하다 **enlightened** a. 계몽된 **endeavor** v. 노력하다 **privilege** n. 특권 **proclaim** v. 선포하다 **enforce** v. 집행하다 **bring to a halt** 정지하다 **accede** v. 응하다, 동의하다

24 문장삽입 ④

| 분석 |

"왕은 필요한 법률을 선포할 수 있었지만 귀족이 완전히 통제하는 법원은 그 법률을 집행하지 않으려 했다"라는 단서로부터 '왕이 새로운 법원 제도를 만들었다'는 요지의 주어진 문장이 바로 이 문장 뒤에 와야 함을 추론할 수 있다.

25 지시대상 ⑤

| 분석 |

명사 element는 다의어로서 여러 뜻을 가지고 있다. 주어진 맥락에서는 '요소'가 아니라 '구성원, 분자'의 의미로 사용되고 있다. 따라서 밑줄 친 "the wealthiest elements"란 가장 부유한 사람들로서 개혁에 끝까지 저항했던 '성직자와 귀족들'을 가리킨다.

위 글에서 밑줄 친 "the wealthiest elements"가 무엇을 가리키는지 고르시오.
① 국가 전체
② 왕실 정부
③ 의회
④ 계몽된 고문들
⑤ 성직자 및 귀족들

26~27

코로나19가 전 세계를 황폐화시킴에 따라, 이 정도 규모의 대재앙을 경험하지 못했던 세대는 우리가 어떻게 살아남을 수 있을지에 대한 통찰력을 예술에 의지하여 얻으려 했다. 치명적인 병원균에 관한 현대의 사변적인 소설의 인기가 급증했다. 독자들은 또한 과거의 전염병에 관한 이야기를 읽기 시작했다. 하지만 지오바니 보카치오의 르네상스 초기 고전 『데카메론』보다 더 큰 인기를 얻은 고전 작품은 없었다. 14세기 중반 유럽을 초토화시킨 흑사병을 배경으로 한 보카치오의 걸작 『데카메론』은 피렌체에서 발병하여 그 인구를 절반으로 줄어들게 할 흑사병을 피해 도망치는 10명의 젊은 귀족들을 추적한다. 그들은 시골의 전원에서 시간을 보내기 위해, 책의 대부분을 차지하는 이야기들을 열흘 동안 열 명이 각자 한 편씩 들려준다. 그래서 책 제목도 데카(10)메론이다. 『데카메론』에 대한 일치된 해석은 역사의 공포 중에서도 우리의 용기를 북돋워 줄 수 있는 스토리텔링의 힘을 그것이 보여준다는 것이다.
넷플릭스 드라마 '데카메론'의 제작자 캐슬린 조던은 팬데믹 시대에 보카치오를 읽고 새로운 해석을 내놓았다. 그녀의 블랙 코미디가 제시하는 바는 시대를 초월하는 이 책의 진정한 메시지가, 1348년의 피렌체 귀족이든 2020년의 맨해튼 금융업자이든, 전염병이 등장하면 특권층은 항상 불운한 이웃을 태연하게 버린다는 것이라면 어떨까? 라는 것이다. 조던은 『데카메론』에서 스토리를 삭제하고, 그 대신 액자구조 이야기(이야기 속의 또 다른 이야기)를 길게 하는 것을 택했다. 어떻게든, 그녀의 불손한 접근법은 성과를 거두었다. 이 시리즈는 그 자체로도 성공적이었지만, (이 시리즈와 같은) 어느 2차(파생적) 저작물을 각색이라고 부를 만하기라도 한가라는 의문을 제기하기도 한다.

| 어휘 |

ravage v. 황폐화시키다 **cataclysm** n. 대재앙 **speculative** a. 사변적인 **lethal** a. 치명적인 **pestilence** n. 페스트 **dusty tome** 먼지투성이의 두툼한 책(고전) **decimate** v. 대량으로 죽이다 **outbreak** n. (전염병의) 발병 **idyll** n. 전원, 목가적인 것 **buoy** v. 뜨게 하다 **come away from** ~에서 빠져나오다 **the privileged** 특권계급 **blithely** ad. 태평스럽게, 태연하게 **come to town** 나타나다, 등장하다 **riff** v. 오래도록 길게 이야기하다 **frame narrative** 액자구조 이야기, 이야기 속의 또 다른 이야기 **irreverence** n. 불손, 불경 **pay off** 성과를 올리다 **derivative work** 2차 저작물

26 글의 제목 ④

| 분석 |

이 글의 주된 목적은 글의 후반부에 있다. 제작자 캐슬린 조던이 만든 넷플릭스 드라마 '데카메론'를 비판적인 관점에서 살펴보는 데 있다. 따라서 이 글에 적합한 제목은 ④ '데카메론의 현대적 부활'이 되어야 한다.

이 글의 가장 적절한 제목을 고르시오.
① 특권층의 무감각
② 『데카메론』의 부흥과 몰락
③ 격변의 시대 속 인간의 인내
④ 『데카메론』의 현대적 부활
⑤ 고전 문학 각색의 위험성

27 내용추론 ⑤

| 분석 |

"조던은 『데카메론』에서 스토리를 삭제하고, 그 대신 액자구조 이야기(이야기 속의 또 다른 이야기)를 길게 하는 것을 택했다."라는 단서로부터 ⑤ '캐슬린 조던의 각색은 보카치오의 『데카메론』에 충실했다.'가 본문 내용과 일치하지 않음을 알 수 있다.

다음 중 이 글로부터 추론할 수 없는 것은?
① 조반니 보카치오는 르네상스 시대에 『데카메론』을 썼다.
② 보카치오의 『데카메론』은 흑사병 시대의 피렌체 귀족들을 다룬다.
③ 보카치오의 『데카메론』은 코로나19 팬데믹 기간 동안 다시 인기를 얻었다.
④ 캐슬린 조던 버전의 '데카메론'은 블랙 코미디이다.
⑤ 캐슬린 조던의 각색은 보카치오의 『데카메론』에 충실했다.

28~29

미국은 이민자들의 나라로 탄생했다. 현대 유럽은 훨씬 덜 그러하다. 적어도 지난 수백 년 동안, 유럽의 역사는 비교적 동질적인 국가 문화를 기반으로 건설된 국가들의 역사이다. 유럽 연합의 창설은 그것이 28개국을 경제적, 정치적 동맹으로 통합했다는 점에서 자애로운 세계화의 경이로운 일이었다. 유럽의 부채 위기는 유럽연합의 미래에 도전장을 내밀었지만, 그 미래가 아직 멸망으로 결정되지는 않았다. 이제 대규모 이민으로 인해 유럽은 더 큰 위기에 직면해 있으며, 이는 유럽의 문화와 경제에 심대한 영향을 미치는 위기이다. 독일이 수십만 명의 이민자를 받아들이기로 한 결정이 부딪친 난관은 엄청나다. 하지만 그로 인한 이점 또한 엄청날 수 있다. 경제 성장은 본질적으로 생산성과 근로자의 결합이며, 생산성과 근로자 수가 꾸준히 증가할 때 국가는 번영한다. 연간 1%의 경제 성장률을 달성하기 위해 고군분투해 온 유럽은 두 가지 측면 모두에서 부진하다. 유럽은 세계에서 출산율이 가장 낮은 대륙 중 하나이다. 유럽의 경제 엔진인 독일의 인구는 현재 8,130만 명에서 2060년까지 7,080만 명으로 감소할 것으로 예상된다. 억제되지 않으면, 이러한 추세는 독일의 복지 국가와 미래 경제 성장을 파괴할 것이다. 프랑스와 스페인과 같은 다른 국가들도 비슷한 난국에 처해 있다. 부유한 국가의 여성들이 자녀를 덜 낳는 경향이 있다는 점을 고려할 때, 더 나은 인구 통계를 달성할 수 있는 유일한 방법은 이민이다.

| 어휘 |

marvel n. 경이 **benevolent** a. 자애로운 **alliance** n. 동맹 **implication** n. 영향, 함축적 의미 **quandary** n. 진퇴양난, 난국 **demographics** n. 인구 통계

28 빈칸완성 ①

| 분석 |

Ⓐ "미국은 이민자들의 나라로 탄생했다. 현대 유럽은 훨씬 덜 그러하다."라는 단서로부터 유럽이 이민자들로 구성된 이질적인 미국과 달리 동질적인 곳이란 것을 추론할 수 있다. Ⓑ 국가가 부유해지기 위해서는 경제가 성장하고 인구가 증가해야 한다. 그렇지 않을 경우 국가의 근간은 파괴된다. 따라서 빈칸 Ⓑ에는 '황폐화시키다'가 와야 한다.

Ⓐ와 Ⓑ에 들어갈 말로 가장 적절한 것은?
① 동질적인 — 황폐화시키다
② 원시적인 — 증발시키다
③ 관료적인 — 개선하다
④ 이질적인 — 가정하다
⑤ 혁명적인 — 경작하다

29 글의 주제 ③

| 분석 |

이 글은 미괄식 구성을 가지고 있다. 이 글을 통해 글쓴이가 말하고 싶은 것은 경제 성장의 새로운 동력으로서 이민문제를 바라보아야 한다는 것이다. 따라서 이 글의 주제는 ③ '이민자들은 유럽 경제를 더욱 강화하는 열쇠가 될 수 있다.'이다.

다음 중 이 글의 주제로 가장 적절한 것은?
① 유럽의 낮은 출산율은 재앙이다.
② 이민자들은 독일의 성장에 해롭다.
③ 이민자들은 유럽 경제를 더욱 강화하는 열쇠가 될 수 있다.
④ 유럽 부채 위기는 유럽 연합을 파괴하고 있다.
⑤ 유럽 연합은 세계화라는 목표를 달성하기 위해 만들어졌다.

30~32

행동경제학은 심리학적 통찰력을 활용하여 인간의 "건전한" 결정을 할 수 있는 능력에 의문을 제기하는, 잘 확립된 경제학의 한 연구 분야이다. 인간은 스스로 노력하는 것을 좋아하지 않기 때문에, 잘못된 결정을 내리는 성향이 있고, 이로 인해 저항이 가장 적은 길을 선택하며, 이는 종종 최적이 아닌 의사 결정으로 이어진다는 주장이 있다. 그리고 이러한 근본적인 성향은 가장 쉽거나 가장 인기 있는 선택을 하려는 결정의 순간에, 그리고 합리적인 평가보다는 피상적인 인상과 감정에 의존하는 경향에서, 명백히 드러나는 것으로 여겨진다.

행동경제학은 리처드 탈러와 캐스 선스타인의 2008년 저서 『넛지: 건강, 부, 행복에 대한 의사 결정 개선』에서 다시 한 번 소개되었다. 이 책이 이 분야의 이전 연구들과 차별화되는 점은, 저자들이 (기존의 연구에서) 한 걸음 더 나아가, 정부가 시민들을 그들의 해로운 성향으로부터 보호하는 데 앞장설 수 있으며, 또 그래야만 한다고 주장한다는 데에 있다. 더 구체적으로 말하자면, 탈러와 선스타인은 "연성(軟性) 가부장주의"를 주장했다. 이는 선택 구조의 미묘한 변화를 이용하여 시민들로 하여금 더 나은 선택을 하도록 "유도"하지만 선택을 제한하지는 않는 새로운 거버넌스(통치) 접근 방식이다.

| 어휘 |

behavioural economics 행동경제학 **strand** n. 가닥, 분파 **sound** a. 건전한 **exert oneself** 노력하다 **be inclined to** ~하는 경향이 있다 **manifest** v. 나타내다[드러내 보이다] **showcase** v. 진열[전시, 소개]하다 **pernicious** a. 해로운, 유해한 **paternalism** n. 가부장제 **governance** n. 거버넌스(통치) **choice architecture** 선택양식, 선택구조 **nudge** v. (특정 방향으로) 살살[조금씩] 밀다[몰고 가다]

30 빈칸완성 ④

| 분석 |
Ⓐ 잘못된 결정으로 인해 저항이 가장 적은 길을 선택한다는 것은 '최적의' 길과 거리가 먼 것이다. Ⓑ 가장 쉽고 가장 대중적인 길은 깊이를 결여하고 있는 지극히 '피상적인' 길이다. Ⓒ 인상과 감정과 반대되는 표현은 '합리적인'이다.

빈칸 Ⓐ~Ⓒ에 들어갈 가장 알맞은 단어의 순서는?
① 적절한 — 주관적인 — 비이성적인
② 모호한 — 객관적인 — 주관적인
③ 유익한 — 즉각적인 — 선택적인
④ 최적의 — 피상적인 — 합리적인
⑤ 유능한 — 무관심한 — 간결한

31 빈칸완성 ①

| 분석 |
두 저자의 책은 의사 결정에 관한 내용이고 앞 단락에서 인간의 잘못된 의사 결정 성향에 대해 설명했으므로 여기서도 정부가 시민들이 잘못된 결정을 내리는 해로운 '성향'으로부터 보호해야 한다고 하는 것이 타당하다. 따라서 빈칸 Ⓓ에는 ① '성향'이 와야 한다.

빈칸 Ⓓ에 가장 적절한 단어는?
① 성향
② 사상자
③ 부상(자)
④ 의무
⑤ 꺼림칙함

32 내용추론 ④

| 분석 |
행동경제학은 인간 심리에 기초한 경제학이다. 그런데 행동경제학에 따르면 인간은 인기 있거나 쉬운 길을 선택하기 때문에 잘못된 결정을 내린다. 이러한 인간의 근본적인 성향이 행동경제학의 전제다.

다음 중 행동경제학의 전제에 대해 추론할 수 있는 것은?
① 의사 결정은 기본적인 인권이다.
② 행동 경제학은 새롭게 부상하는 과학이다.
③ 인간은 가장 어려운 선택을 하는 경향이 있다.
④ 인간은 잘못된 결정을 내리는 경향이 있다.
⑤ 정부는 건전한 의사 결정에 영향을 미치기 위해 강력한 접근 방식을 취해야 한다.

33~35

대중과 달리, 지식인들은 합리성을 중시하고 사실에 관심을 가진다. 그들의 비판적인 사고방식 덕분에 그들은 다수(대중)에게 매우 효과적인 선전에 대해 저항감을 느낀다. 그들은 지나친 단순화를 정신의 원죄로 여기며, 선동가의 상투적인 수단인 슬로건, 절대적인 주장, 그리고 포괄적인 일반화 등이 불필요하다고 생각한다. 철학은 우리에게 자명해 보이는 것들에 대해 불확실성을 느끼도록 가르친다. 반면 선동은 판단을 유보하거나 의심을 가져야 마땅한 문제들을 자명한 것으로 받아들이도록 가르친다. 선동가의 목표는 자신의 지도 아래 사회적 결속력을 구축하는 것이다. 따라서 선동적 선전가는 일관되게 교조적이어야 한다. 그의 모든 진술은 아무런 조건(제한) 없이 이루어진다. 그의 세계관에는 회색이 없다. 모든 것이 악마처럼 검거나 천사처럼 희다. 히틀러의 말처럼, 선전가는 "다뤄야 할 모든 문제에 대해 체계적으로 편향된 태도"를 취해야 한다. 그는 자신이 틀렸을 수도 있고, 다른 관점을 가진 사람들이 부분적으로나마 옳을 수도 있다는 것을 결코 인정해서는 안 된다.

| 어휘 |
the mass 대중 **intellectual** n. 지식인 **rationality** n. 이성 **propaganda** n. 선전, 정치 선동 **unqualified** a. 무자격의, 무조건적인, 절대적인 **assertion** n. 주장 **sweeping** a. 전면적인 **generalization** n. 일반화 **stock in trade** 상투 수단 **suspend** v. 유예하다, 연기하다 **demagogue** n. 선동가 **propagandist** n. 선전가 **coherence** n. 일관성 **dogmatic** a. 독단적인 **diabolically** ad. 악마적으로 **celestially** ad. 천상적으로

33 빈칸완성 ⑤

| 분석 |
빈칸이 들어 있는 문장과 앞에 있는 문장은 역접 관계에 있다. 앞에 있는 문장은 철학의 효용성에 대해 이야기하고, 빈칸이 들어 있는 문장을 선동의 역기능에 대해 진술하고 있다. 따라서 빈칸에는 역접의 연결사 ⑤ '반면에'가 와야 한다.

빈칸 Ⓐ에 들어갈 말로 가장 적절한 것은?
① 마찬가지로
② 그럼에도 불구하고
③ 놀랍게도
④ 결과적으로
⑤ 반면에

34 빈칸완성 ⑤

| 분석 |
"그의 세계관에는 회색이 없다. 모든 것이 악마처럼 검거나 천사처

럼 희다. 히틀러의 말처럼, 선전가는 '다뤄야 할 모든 문제에 대해 체계적으로 편향된 태도'를 취해야 한다."라는 단서로부터 빈칸에 ⑤ '그는 자신이 틀렸을 수도 있고, 다른 관점을 가진 사람들이 부분적으로나마 옳을 수도 있다는 것을 결코 인정해서는 안 된다.'가 와야 함을 추론할 수 있다.

빈칸 ⓑ에 들어갈 문장으로 가장 적절한 것은?
① 그는 반대자들의 말에 세심한 주의를 기울여야 한다.
② 그는 인간을 다른 개인들과 자유롭게 교류하는 개별적인 존재로 인정하는 데 신중해야 한다.
③ 그는 대중의 문제에 대한 대안적인 해결책을 고려해야 한다.
④ 그는 자신의 발언을 제한하여 대중에게 어필하기 위해 회색 부분을 메우는 법을 배워야 한다.
⑤ 그는 자신이 틀렸을 수도 있고, 다른 관점을 가진 사람들이 부분적으로나마 옳을 수도 있다는 것을 결코 인정해서는 안 된다.

35 내용추론   ④

| 분석 |

"선동은 판단을 유보하거나 의심을 가져야 마땅한 문제들을 자명한 것으로 받아들이도록 가르친다."라는 단서로부터 선동은 판단을 보류하도록 가르치는 것이 아니라 판단을 보류해야 할 문제를 자명하다고 받아들이게 가르침을 알 수 있다.

이 글에서 암시하고 있지 않은 것은?
① 지식인들은 선동에 쉽게 영향을 받지 않는다.
② 지식인들은 철학의 가르침을 따른다.
③ 철학은 사람들에게 명백해 보이는 것에 의문을 품도록 가르친다.
④ 선동가들은 대중에게 판단을 보류하도록 가르친다.
⑤ 선동은 일반화와 절대적인 주장에 의존한다.

36~37

2023년 크리스마스 직전. Cognition사의 소규모 팀은 그 샌프란시스코에 있는 AI 창업기업(Cognition사)의 신참 코딩 어시스턴트인 데빈(AI)을 위한 특별히 복잡한 데이터 서버를 설정하는 데 어려움을 겪고 있었다.
ⓑ 그들은 몇 시간 동안 설치 파일을 꼼꼼히 살펴보고 여러 명령어를 시도해 보았지만, 서버를 도저히 작동시킬 수 없었다. 지치고 답답한 그들은 데빈이 어떻게 처리할지 지켜보기로 했다.
ⓐ AI가 갑자기 작동하기 시작하자 개발자들은 당황했다. 21세의 공동 창립자 월든 얀은 "AI가 가장 마법적이고 흑마술(사악한 목적을 위한 마술) 같아 보이는 명령을 실행했어요."라고 회상한다.
ⓓ 한동안 데빈도 그들과 마찬가지로 잘 하지 못할 것 같았

다. 그때 몇 시간 동안 빨간색으로 켜져 있던 서버 단말기 표시등이 초록색으로 바뀌었다. 데이터 서버가 정상 작동하고 있었다.
ⓒ 그들은 데빈이 팀원들이 간과했던 잘못된 시스템 파일을 삭제했다는 사실을 깨달았다. 얀은 "그 순간 소프트웨어 엔지니어링이 참으로 많은 변화를 가져올 것이라는 생각이 들었습니다."라고 말한다.

| 어휘 |

Cognition n. 회사 이름(인지란 의미)   **fledgling** n. 신출내기, 초보자
pore over 자세히 조사하다[보다]   **installation document** 설치 파일   **command** n. 컴퓨터의 명령어   **spring into action** 갑자기 작동하다   **befuddle** v. 어리둥절하게 하다   **cofounder** n. 공동창업자   **terminal** n. 단말기   **up and running** 제대로 작동하는

36 단락배열   ③

| 분석 |

AI인 데빈에 데이터 서버를 설치해야 서버를 통해 데빈에게 명령을 할 수 있는데, 첫 단락에서 데이터 서버를 설정하는 데 어려움을 겪고 있었다고 했고, 그다음 ⓑ에서 어려움을 겪고 있는 내막을 상세히 밝히고 AI인 데빈을 지켜보기로 했다고 했고, 그런데 데빈이 한 일은 나중에 밝혀지고 먼저 ⓐ에서 서버가 설치된 것 같지도 않은데 AI가 갑자기 작동하여 놀랐다는 언급이 있고, 그다음 ⓓ에서, ⓐ에서 AI가 갑자기 작동한 내막을 설명하고, 그다음 ⓒ에서 알고 보니 AI인 데빈이 잘못된 파일을 자기가 알아서 삭제하고 명령을 실행해버린 것으로 드러났다고 설명하는 것이 적절한 순서이다.

37 내용파악   ②

| 분석 |

"그들은 데빈이 팀원들이 간과했던 잘못된 시스템 파일을 삭제했다는 사실을 깨달았다. 얀은 '그 순간 소프트웨어 엔지니어링이 참으로 많은 변화를 가져올 것이라는 생각이 들었습니다.'라고 말한다."라는 단서로부터 ② '코딩에서 지루하고 고된 작업을 없애버렸다.'가 정답임을 알 수 있다.

다음 중 'Devin'에 대해 옳은 것은?
① 데이터 서버를 시작하는 데 실패했다.
② 코딩에서 지루하고 고된 작업을 없애버렸다.
③ 인간의 코딩 프로세스를 방해했다.
④ 데이터 서버에 잘못된 시스템 파일을 그대로 유지했다.
⑤ AI 산업을 비용 절감 쪽으로 전환했다.

38~40

민주주의와 차이에 관한 현대 문헌의 많은 부분은 공개 토론에 크게 의존하는 더욱 적극적이고 활기찬 민주주의의 개념들로 작동한다. 차이를 박멸하는 거짓 조화와, 그 어떤 단일하고 그럴듯한 정체성을 통해 사람들을 정의하는 똑같이 거짓인 본질주의, 둘 모두를 거부하면서, 많은 이론가들은 시민 참여를 극대화하고 서로 교류하고 경쟁하도록 요구하는 민주주의를 바라고 있다. 수전 멘더스는 페미니즘과 민주주의에 관한 최근 에세이에서 차이가 민주주의의 근거라고 말하고, "전통적인 민주주의 이론은 차이를 진정한 민주주의 국가 달성의 장애물로 간주하는 경향이 있는 반면, 페미니스트 이론은 차이가 오히려 민주주의의 추구를 반드시 필요로 하는 것일 가능성에 대해 우리의 경각심을 일깨워야 한다"고 말한다. 다문화주의에 관한 그의 연구에서 찰스 테일러는 또한 (사람들의) 평등한 인정에 대한 요구를, 파편화된 정체성에 사람들을 고착시키지 않으면서, 다루는 방법으로서 민주적 권한 부여의 정치를 요구한다.

| 어휘 |

literature n. 문헌(논문과 저술들) vigorous a. 활발한 crucially ad. 결정적으로, 중대하게 stamp out 근절하다 essentialism n. 본질주의 authentic a. 그럴듯한(이 글에서는 부정적인 의미) identity n. 정체성 rationale n. 근본적 이유 construe v. 해석하다, 설명하다 attainment n. 달성, 도달, 학식 alert v. 주의를 환기시키다 empowerment n. 권한 부여 entrench v. 굳어지게 하다, 참호를 파다 fragmented identity 파편화된 정체성

38 동의어 ②

| 분석 |

stamp out은 '박멸하다'는 뜻이므로 '지우다, 말살하다, 제거하다'는 뜻의 obliterate가 가장 가까운 의미의 단어이다.

밑줄 친 stamps out과 가장 가까운 의미를 가진 답을 고르시오.
① 암시하다
② 말살하다
③ 포용하다
④ 폭로하다
⑤ 주입하다

39 빈칸완성 ①

| 분석 |

민주주의가 시민의 참여를 요구하고 시민들 간의 경쟁을 지향한다는 단서로부터 민주주의가 시민 참여를 극대화하는(maximizes) 체제임을 추론할 수 있다.

빈칸에 들어갈 말로 가장 적절한 것은?
① 극대화하다
② 선행하다
③ 방해하다
④ 억제하다
⑤ 감소시키다

40 내용일치 ③

| 분석 |

"차이를 박멸하는 거짓 조화를 거부하고(차이를 포용하고) 단일한 정체성을 통해 사람들을 정의하는 본질주의를 거부하면서(다양한 정체성 강화), 많은 이론가들은 시민 참여를 극대화하도록 요구하는 민주주의를 바라고 있다."라는 단서로부터 ③ '민주주의에서 차이를 포용하는 것은 참여를 증진하고 다양한 정체성을 강화한다.'는 이 글의 내용과 일치함을 알 수 있다.

다음 중 위 글의 내용과 일치하는 것은?
① 찰스 테일러는 사람들을 단일하고 고정된 정체성에 묶어두는 민주적 권한 부여 정치를 옹호한다.
② 민주주의와 차이에 관한 현대 문헌은 공개 토론을 피하는 수동적 민주주의를 지지한다.
③ 민주주의에서 차이를 포용하는 것은 참여를 증진하고 다양한 정체성을 강화한다.
④ 민주주의는 차이를 없앨 때 번영한다.
⑤ 차이보다 획일성을 강조하는 것이 민주주의에서 다양한 정체성을 강화하는 데 핵심이다.

KYUNG HEE UNIVERSITY | 경희대학교 한의학과(인문)

TEST p. 146~151

| 07 | ① | 11 | ④ | 16 | ③ | 17 | ② | 32 | ③ | 33 | ③ | 42 | ④ | 43 | ① | 44 | ② | 45 | ③ |
| 46 | ⑤ | 47 | ② | 48 | ② | 49 | ① | 50 | ③ | | | | | | | | | | |

07 동의어 ①

| 어휘 |

infest v. 들끓다   tap water 수돗물   surface water 지표수   ingest v. 섭취하다(= consume)   maintain v. 유지하다   generate v. 발생하다   inspect v. 조사하다

| 해석 |

현대의 물 처리 방법들을 통해 정부는 잠재적으로 유해한 세균이 들끓는 물을 처리하여 마실 수 있게 만든다. 이러한 방법들로 인해 수돗물은 완전히 안전하게 마실 수 있지만, 전 세계의 모든 지표수를 이 같은 방식으로 처리하는 것은 현실적으로 불가능하다. 따라서 처리되지 않은 물을 레크리에이션 목적으로 사용하는 사람들은 유해 세균을 섭취할 위험이 있다.

11 논리완성 ④

| 분석 |

빈칸이 들어 있는 주절의 내용은 Even if라는 접속사가 이끌고 있는 조건의 종속절의 내용과 호응하고 있다. 조건의 종속절에는 간의 건강을 해치는 두 가지 원인이 소개된다. 그 하나는 과도한 음주이고 다른 하나는 간염이다. 따라서 빈칸에는 과도한 음주와 관련된 내용, 즉 과도한 음주로 인해 손상된 간을 회복시킬 수 있는 내용을 담고 있는 표현이 와야 한다. 즉 '금주'라는 뜻의 abstinence가 적절하다.

| 어휘 |

internal organ 장기   regeneration n. 재생   tissue n. 세포조직   impair v. 손상되다   hepatitis n. 간염   vitality n. 생기, 활기   mourning n. 애도   continuity n. 지속   abstinence n. 금주, 절제   retention n. 보유

| 해석 |

간은 손실된 세포조직을 자연적으로 재생할 수 있는 인체 내부 장기이다. 과도한 음주나 간염으로 인해 간이 손상되어도 단기간 금주한 후에나 간염이 완전히 치료되면, 간은 쉽게 회복될 수 있다.

16~17

과거 세대는 사전을 '올바른' 언어의 보호자이자 방어자로 여겼지만, 이제는 더 이상 그렇지 않다. 현대 주요 사전들은 사람들이 실제 사용하는 언어를 기술하는 데 집중하며, 그 어떤 따분한 학술적 반론도 의식적으로 배제하고 있다. 2007년, 『옥스퍼드 영어사전』은 어린이용 축약판에서 '도토리', '민들레', '겨우살이', '목초지', '버드나무' 등 자연 관련 어휘를 삭제하고, '블로그', '브로드밴드', '채팅방', '잘라내기-붙여넣기', 'MP3 플레이어' 같은 디지털 시대 용어로 대체하여, 부모들 사이에 소동을 일으켰다. 일부 학부모들은 사전에 야외(자연) 관련 단어들을 다시 넣어달라고 요청한 반면, 다른 학부모들은 이 소란의 이유를 이해하지 못했다. 그들은 "책이 얇을수록 아이들이 가지고 다닐 가능성이 더 높아진다"고 주장했다.

| 어휘 |

leave (something) at the door 저버리다, 버리다   stuffy a. 답답한, 딱딱한   scholarly a. 학구적인   objection n. 반대   acorn n. 도토리   dandelion n. 민들레   mistletoe n. 겨우살이   pasture n. 초원, 목초지   willow n. 버드나무   broadband n. 광대역, 고속 데이터 통신망   cut-and-paste a. 스크랩하여 편집한, 〈컴퓨터〉 잘라붙이는   uproar n. 분노   petition v. 청원하다   reinstate v. 복귀시키다   outdoor word 자연을 묘사하는 어휘   fuss n. 호들갑, 야단법석

16 빈칸완성 ③

| 분석 |

빈칸 Ⓐ에는 빈칸 바로 뒤에 나오는 'defender'와 일맥상통하는 표현이 와야 한다. 따라서 '보호자'라는 뜻의 custodians가 적절하다.

빈칸 Ⓐ에 들어갈 말로 가장 적절한 것은?
① 상대, 반대자
② 회의주의자
③ 보호자

④ 조상, 선조
⑤ 박애주의자

17 빈칸완성 ②

| 분석 |

빈칸 ⓑ가 들어 있는 마지막 문장은 소동에 대해 찬성하지 않는 학부모들의 입장을 담고 있다. 앞에서 '책의 부피가 작을수록'이라고 했으므로 아이들이 책을 갖고 다닐 '가능성이 더 많다'는 뜻으로 빈칸에는 the more likely가 적절하다.

빈칸 ⓑ에 들어갈 어구로 가장 적절한 것은?
① 가능성이 더 적은
② 가능성이 더 많은
③ 다소간
④ 가능성이 가장 적은
⑤ 덜 그러한

32~33

생물학적 시스템을 만들 수 있기를 바란다면 두 가지 기본 개념을 이해해야 한다. 하나는 생물학적 시스템에서 정보가 어떻게 흐르는가이고, 다른 하나는 이 정보 흐름이 어떻게 제어되는가이다. 이러한 개념을 이해하면 원칙적으로 공학 원리를 새로운 생물학적 시스템의 설계 및 제작에 적용할 수 있는데, 이를 합성생물학이라고 한다.
생물학은 물론 매우 복잡하며, 다른 공학 분야와 구별되는 중요한 차이점이 있다. 첫째, 생물학은 인쇄 회로 기판에 프로그래밍되어 있지 않으므로, (생물학적) 상호작용은 물리적 위치에 따라 프로그래밍될 수 없다. 오히려 상호작용은 세포라는 복잡한 환경에서 발생하는 분자 간의 상호작용에 기초해 있다. 둘째, 생물학은 자연선택의 영향을 받기 때문에 세포에 해로운 변형은 거부되도록 선택되어 경쟁에서 밀려 개체군에서 배제된다. 이러한 진화적 압력은 항공기 제작에는 적용되지 않으므로, 생물학에는 견고성에 대한 새로운 정의가 적절하다. 복잡성이나 창발적 행동과 같은 다른 개념들은 엔지니어에게 익숙할 수 있지만, 이러한 개념이 생물학에서 어떻게 발생할 수 있는지, 그리고 그 영향이 무엇인지 알아야 한다.

| 어휘 |

engineer v. 제작하다, 획책하다   **synthetic** a. 합성의, 인조의
engineering discipline 공학 학문 분야   **printed circuit board** 인쇄 회로 기판   **interaction** n. 상호작용   **molecule** n. 분자   **milieu** n. 환경   **modification** n. 수정, 변경   **deleterious** a. 해로운, 유해한   **population** n. 군집, 개체군   **applicable** a. 해당[적용]되는, 적절한   **robustness** n. 억셈, 견고함   **emergent behavior** 창발적 행동(시스템의 구성요소들의 상호작용에서 발생하는 예기치 않은 행동)

32 동의어 ③

| 분석 |

deleterious는 '해로운'이라는 뜻이므로 damaging이 동의어이다.

밑줄 친 단어 "<u>deleterious</u>"와 의미가 가장 가까운 것을 고르시오.
① 유익한
② 고의적인
③ 해로운
④ 유연한
⑤ 자발적인

33 내용파악 ③

| 분석 |

생물학이 "상호작용은 세포라는 복잡한 환경에서 발생하는 분자 간의 상호작용에 기초해 있고 ~ 자연선택의 영향을 받기 때문에 세포에 해로운 변형은 선택되어 개체군에서 배제된다."라는 단서로부터 생물학이 ③ '그것은 진화적 압력에 따라 달라진다.'의 진술과 부합함을 알 수 있다.

위 글에 따르면, 생물학에 대해 사실인 것은?
① 그것은 새로운 공학을 통해 새로운 시스템으로 만들어질 수 없다.
② 그것은 인쇄 회로 기판에 프로그래밍된다.
③ 그것은 진화적 압력에 따라 달라진다.
④ 그것은 복잡하고 창발적인 행동과 분리된다.
⑤ 그것은 다른 공학 분야와 구별할 수 없다.

42~44

폴리네시아 제도는 중부 및 남부 태평양에 있는 오세아니아라는 큰 무리의 섬들을 구성하는 세 개의 주요 하위 지역 중 하나이다. 다른 하위 지역의 키가 작고 피부가 검은 사람들과 달리 폴리네시아 사람들은 피부가 더 희고 키가 크다. 오늘날 과학자들은 폴리네시아가 남아시아 문화에 의해 식민지화되었다고 믿지만, 1800년대 후반과 1900년대 초에 태평양을 여행하던 유럽인들이 이집트인들이 폴리네시아에 정착했다는 이론을 제시했다. 그들은 오세아니아에 사람이 살았다고 여겨지는 그 당시에 존재한 유일한 문명이 이집트였기 때문에 이집트인들이 이 섬에 정착했다고 믿었다. 1970년대 후반 연구자들은 폴리네시아의 일부 조각상의 눈에 칠한 색상 층의 사용을 증거로 지적했다. 〈이집트인들은 조각상들을 실물처럼 보이게 하기 위해 동일한 기법을 사용

했다.) 또한, 폴리네시아의 조인(새 인간) 의식은 이집트의 태양신 라의 알을 찾는 전통적인 의식과 유사하다. 그러나 태평양의 해류를 기반으로 한 선박 표류 컴퓨터 시뮬레이션은 이집트인들이 우연이라도 폴리네시아에 도착할 수는 없었으며, 따라서 그들이 이 섬들에 거주할 수 없음을 증명했다.

| 어휘 |

subregion n. (동물 지리구의) 아구(亞區), 소구역 **stature** n. 신장, 키 **articulate** v. 똑똑히 발음하다, 관련짓다 **populate** v. 거주하다, 주민이다 **point** v. 지적하다 **apply** v. 바르다, 칠하다 **parallel** n. 평행, 유사 **current** n. 해류

42   문장삽입   ④

| 분석 |

주어진 문장의 핵심어는 조각상과 그 조각상에 쓰인 기법이다. 그런데 '1970년대 후반 연구자들은 폴리네시아의 일부 조각상의 눈에 칠한 색의 층을 증거로 지적했다.'라고 했으므로 주어진 문장은 이 문장 다음에 와야 한다.

43   동의어   ③

| 분석 |

articulate는 동사로서 '똑똑히 발음하다'의 뜻이 있다. 그런데 여기서는 '분명히 말하다'의 뜻으로 보면 proposed(제안했다)가 가장 가까운 의미의 단어이다.

밑줄 친 단어 "articulated"와 의미가 가장 가까운 답을 고르시오.
① 반박하다
② 어기다
③ 제안하다
④ 왜곡하다
⑤ 잘못 표현하다

44   빈칸완성   ②

| 분석 |

"그러나 태평양의 해류를 기반으로 한 선박 표류 컴퓨터 시뮬레이션은 이집트인들이 우연이라도 폴리네시아에 도착할 수 없었으며 ~"라는 단서로부터 ② '그들은 섬에 거주할 수 없었을 것이다.'가 정답임을 알 수 있다.

다음 중 Ⓐ에 가장 적합한 것은?
① 그들은 전통적인 의식을 발전시킬 수 없었을 것이다
② 그들은 섬에 거주할 수 없었을 것이다
③ 그들은 섬을 처음 발견할 수 있었을 것이다
④ 그들은 남아시아 지역에 의해 식민지화될 수 있었을 것이다
⑤ 그들은 유럽 대륙에 도달할 수 있었을 것이다

45~47

2023년 크리스마스 직전, Cognition사의 소규모 팀은 그 샌프란시스코에 있는 AI 창업기업(Cognition 사)의 신참 코딩 어시스턴트인 데빈(AI)을 위한 특별히 복잡한 데이터 서버를 설정하는 데 어려움을 겪고 있었다.
Ⓑ 그들은 몇 시간 동안 설치 파일을 꼼꼼히 살펴보고 여러 명령어를 시도해 보았지만, 서버를 도저히 작동시킬 수 없었다. 지치고 답답한 그들은 데빈이 어떻게 처리할지 지켜보기로 했다.
Ⓐ AI가 갑자기 작동하기 시작하자 개발자들은 당황했다. 21세의 공동 창립자 월든 얀은 "AI가 가장 마법적이고 흑마술(사악한 목적을 위한 마술) 같아 보이는 명령을 실행했어요."라고 회상한다.
Ⓓ 한동안 데빈도 그들과 마찬가지로 잘하지 못할 것 같았다. 그때 몇 시간 동안 빨간색으로 켜져 있던 서버 단말기 표시등이 초록색으로 바뀌었다. 데이터 서버가 정상 작동하고 있었다.
Ⓒ 그들은 데빈이 팀원들이 간과했던 잘못된 시스템 파일을 삭제했다는 사실을 깨달았다. 얀은 "그 순간 소프트웨어 엔지니어링이 참으로 많은 변화를 가져올 것이라는 생각이 들었습니다."라고 말한다.

| 어휘 |

Cognition n. 회사 이름(인지란 의미) **fledgling** n. 신출내기, 초보자 **pore over** 자세히 조사하다[보다] **installation document** 설치 파일 **command** n. 컴퓨터의 명령어 **spring into action** 갑자기 작동하다 **befuddle** v. 정신을 잃게 하다, 어리둥절하게 하다 **cofounder** n. 공동창업자 **terminal** n. 단말기 **up and running** 제대로 작동하는

45   단락배열   ③

| 분석 |

AI인 데빈에 데이터 서버를 설치해야 서버를 통해 데빈에게 명령을 할 수 있는데, 첫 단락에서 데이터 서버를 설정하는 데 어려움을 겪고 있었다고 했고, 그다음 Ⓑ에서 어려움을 겪고 있는 내막을 상세히 밝히고 AI인 데빈을 지켜보기로 했다고 했다, 그런데 데빈이 한 일은 나중에 밝혀지고 먼저 Ⓐ에서 서버가 설치된 것 같지도 않은데 AI가 갑자기 작동하여 놀랐다는 언급이 있고, 그다음 Ⓓ에서, Ⓐ에서 AI가 갑자기 작동한 내막을 설명하고, 그다음 Ⓒ에서 알고 보니 AI인 데빈이 잘못된 파일을 자기가 알아서 삭제하고 명령을 실행해버린 것으로 드러났다고 설명하는 것이 적절한 순서이다.

| 46 | 동의어 | ⑤ |

| 분석 |
befuddled는 '당황한'의 뜻이므로 ⑤의 flustered가 의미상 가장 가까운 동의어이다.

밑줄 친 단어 "befuddled"와 의미상 가장 가까운 답을 고르시오.
① 무죄를 선고받은
② 정당성을 입증한
③ 침착한
④ 훼손된
⑤ 당황한

| 47 | 내용파악 | ② |

| 분석 |
"그들은 데빈이 팀원들이 간과했던 잘못된 시스템 파일을 삭제했다는 사실을 깨달았다. 얀은 '그 순간 소프트웨어 엔지니어링이 참으로 많은 변화를 가져올 것이라는 생각이 들었습니다.'라고 말한다."라는 단서로부터 ② '코딩에서 지루하고 고된 작업을 없애버렸다.'가 정답임을 알 수 있다.

다음 중 'Devin'에 대해 옳은 것은?
① 데이터 서버를 시작하는 데 실패했다.
② 코딩에서 지루하고 고된 작업을 없애버렸다.
③ 인간의 코딩 프로세스를 방해했다.
④ 데이터 서버에 잘못된 시스템 파일을 그대로 유지했다.
⑤ AI 산업을 비용 절감 쪽으로 전환했다.

48~50

민주주의와 차이에 관한 현대 문헌의 많은 부분은 공개 토론에 크게 의존하는 더욱 적극적이고 활기찬 민주주의의 개념들로 작동한다. 차이를 박멸하는 거짓 조화와, 그 어떤 단일하고 그럴듯한 정체성을 통해 사람들을 정의하는 똑같이 거짓인 본질주의, 둘 모두를 거부하면서, 많은 이론가들은 시민 참여를 극대화하고 서로 교류하고 경쟁하도록 요구하는 민주주의를 바라고 있다. 수전 멘더스는 페미니즘과 민주주의에 관한 최근 에세이에서 차이가 민주주의의 근거라고 말하고, "전통적인 민주주의 이론은 차이를 진정한 민주주의 국가 달성의 장애물로 간주하는 경향이 있는 반면, 페미니스트 이론은 차이가 오히려 민주주의의 추구를 반드시 필요로 하는 것일 가능성에 대해 우리의 경각심을 일깨워야 한다"고 말한다. 다문화주의에 관한 그의 연구에서 찰스 테일러는 또한 (사람들의) 평등한 인정에 대한 요구를, 파편화된 정체성에 사람들을 고착시키지 않으면서, 다루는 방법으로서 민주적 권한 부여의 정치를 요구한다.

| 어휘 |
literature n. 문헌(논문과 저술들) **vigorous** a. 원기 완성한, 활발한 **crucially** ad. 결정적으로, 중대하게 **stamp out** ~을 근절하다 **essentialism** n. 본질주의 **authentic** a. 그럴듯한(이 글에서는 부정적인 의미) **identity** n. 정체성 **rationale** n. 근본적 이유 **construe** v. 해석하다, 설명하다 **attainment** n. 달성, 도달, 학식 **alert** v. 주의를 환기시키다 **empowerment** n. 권한 부여 **entrench** v. 굳어지게 하다, 참호를 파다 **fragmented identity** 파편화된 정체해류

| 48 | 동의어 | ② |

| 분석 |
stamp out은 '박멸하다'는 뜻이므로 '지우다, 말살하다, 제거하다'는 뜻의 obliterate가 가장 가까운 의미의 단어이다.

밑줄 친 stamps out과 가장 가까운 의미를 가진 답을 고르시오.
① 암시하다
② 말살하다
③ 포용하다
④ 폭로하다
⑤ 주입하다

| 49 | 빈칸완성 | ① |

| 분석 |
Ⓐ 민주주의가 시민의 참여를 요구하고 시민들 간의 경쟁을 지향한다는 단서로부터 민주주의가 시민 참여를 극대화하는(maximizes) 체제임을 추론할 수 있다. Ⓑ 차이를 민주주의의 국가 달성의 장애물로 여기는 전통적인 민주주의와 달리, 페미니스트 이론은 차이를 민주주의와 관련하여 전폭적으로 긍정한다고 볼 수 있다. 그런데 앞에서 '차이를 박멸하는 거짓 조화를 거부하면서, 많은 이론가들은 … 민주주의를 바라고 있다'고 했으므로 차이를 보존하려면 민주주의가 꼭 필요함을 알 수 있다. 따라서 necessitates(필요로 하다)가 적절하다.

Ⓐ와 Ⓑ에 들어갈 말로 가장 적절한 것은?
① 극대화하다 — 필요로 하다
② 선행하다 — 단념시키다
③ 방해하다 — 강화하다
④ 억제하다 — 수반하다
⑤ 감소시키다 — 지시하다

| 50 | 내용일치 | ③ |

| 분석 |
"차이를 박멸하는 거짓 조화를 거부하고(차이를 포용하고) 단일한 정체성을 통해 사람들을 정의하는 본질주의를 거부하면서(다양한 정체성 강화), 많은 이론가들은 시민 참여를 극대화하도록 요구하

는 민주주의를 바라고 있다."라는 단서로부터 ③ '민주주의에서 차이를 포용하는 것은 참여를 증진하고 다양한 정체성을 강화한다.'는 이 글의 내용과 일치함을 알 수 있다.

다음 중 위 글의 내용과 일치하는 것은?
① 찰스 테일러는 사람들을 단일하고 고정된 정체성에 묶어두는 민주적 권한 부여 정치를 옹호한다.
② 민주주의와 차이에 관한 현대 문헌은 공개 토론을 피하는 수동적 민주주의를 지지한다.
③ 민주주의에서 차이를 포용하는 것은 참여를 증진하고 다양한 정체성을 강화한다.
④ 민주주의는 차이를 없앨 때 번영한다.
⑤ 차이보다 획일성을 강조하는 것이 민주주의에서 다양한 정체성을 강화하는 데 핵심이다.

KOREA UNIVERSITY | 고려대학교 세종 인문·자연계

TEST p. 154~175

01	②	02	④	03	④	04	①	05	③	06	①	07	④	08	②	09	①	10	③
11	④	12	①	13	③	14	④	15	④	16	①	17	③	18	①	19	④	20	②
21	①	22	③	23	①	24	②	25	④	26	①	27	②	28	②	29	④	30	④
31	②	32	③	33	④	34	③	35	②	36	①	37	②	38	③	39	①	40	②

01 수동태　②

| 분석 |
주어가 침실이므로 "추가되었다"는 의미로 수동태 have been added가 되어야 한다.

| 어휘 |
envy v. 부러워하다, 시기하다　**overlook** v. 간과하다　**saving** n. 저축　**oracle** n. 신탁(神託); 현자　**distinguish A from B** A와 B를 구별하다

| 해석 |
대부분의 사람들은 버핏 씨의 성공을 부러워하지만, 그의 강력한 저축 습관과 소박한 생활은 간과하는 경향이 있다. 그는 1958년에 구입한 집에 아직도 살고 있다. 그동안 침실 두어 곳과 라켓 코트 하나만 추가되었을 뿐이다. "오마하의 현인"으로 불리는 그는 투기꾼과 투자자를 엄격히 구분한다.

02 병치구조　④

| 분석 |
마지막 부분에서 ④는 demonstrating과 병치를 이루어 전치사 by의 목적어가 되어야 하므로 동명사 winning으로 고쳐야 한다.

| 어휘 |
fairy story 동화　**distinct from** ~와 다른　**serious** a. 진지한　**hero** n. 영웅, 주인공　**obscure** a. 무명의, 익명의　**despise** v. 경멸하다　**heroism** n. 영웅적 자질

| 해석 |
동화는 유쾌한 이야기나 동물 이야기와 달리, 인간 주인공과 행복한 결말을 지닌 진지한 이야기이다. 동화 주인공의 여정은 비극 주인공의 여정과 정반대다. 처음에 그는 사회적으로 이름이 없거나, 어리석거나 재능이 없다는 이유로 경멸받으며 영웅의 덕목도 결여되어 있지만, 끝에는 영웅적 자질을 드러내고 명성과 부와 사랑까지 얻음으로써 모두를 놀라게 한다.

03 주어와 동사의 수일치　④

| 분석 |
there have been a mountain of meaning에서 주어가 a mountain of meaning이므로 동사 have been을 3인칭 단수 주어에 맞도록 has been으로 고쳐야 한다.

| 어휘 |
novel n. 소설　**sequence** n. 연속, 순서, 차례　**emerge** v. 등장하다, 나타나다　**landmark** n. 지형지물; 획기적인 사건　**align** v. 정렬하다, 나란히 서다　**indefinite** a. 불확실한　**outline** n. 윤곽　**throw back** 되비치다, 반사되다　**retrospect** n. 회고, 회상

| 해석 |
이야기나 소설을 쓰는 것은 경험에서 순서를 발견하는 한 가지 방법이다… 연결들이 서서히 드러난다. 당신이 접근해 가는 먼 지형지물들처럼, 원인과 결과가 정렬되기 시작하고 서로 점점 더 가까워진다. 그 자체로는 윤곽이 너무 불확실해서 그 자체로 인식될 수 없던 경험들이 서로 연결되며 더 큰 형태로 확인된다. 그러다가 마치 기차가 커브를 돌 때처럼, 갑자기 빛이 뒤로 비추어져, 당신이 걸어온 길 위 당신 뒤편에 의미가 산더미처럼 솟아있었고 여전히 솟아오르고 있으며, 그러한 것이 이제 회고를 통해 증명되고 있음을 보여준다.

04 동명사[부정사] 주어　①

| 분석 |
rank cities는 '도시들의 순위를 매기다'라는 뜻인데, 동사원형은 문장의 주어가 될 수 없으므로 ①을 주어가 될 수 있는 동명사 Ranking이나 to부정사 To rank로 고쳐야 한다.

| 어휘 |

rank v. 등급을 매기다 nebulous a. 애매모호한 liveability n. 살기 좋음 relatively ad. 비교적 lowly a. 하찮은, 낮은 sedate a. 차분한 scoff at 비웃다, 조롱하다

| 해석 |

'살기 좋음'이라는 다소 모호한 개념에 따라 도시들의 순위를 매기는 것은 독자들의 극단적인 반응을 불러일으킬 수 있다. 어떤 이들은 런던이나 뉴욕처럼 활기찬 대도시들이 비교적 낮은 순위를 받은 것을 의문시하며, 또 다른 이들은 상위권에 오른 차분한 도시들을 비웃는다. 코펜하겐과 캘거리 같은 도시들은 지난 20년의 대부분의 기간 동안 그랬듯이 올해도 상위 10위 안에 들었다.

05 문의 구성   ③

| 분석 |

빈칸 다음에 'is that절'이 왔으므로 빈칸에는 is의 주어가 되는 간접의문절이 필요하다. 절마다 시제를 가진 정동사가 하나씩 있어야 하는데 ①은 두 개의 절에 정동사가 셋이어서 부적절하고, ②와 ④는 is 앞에 명사가 아니어서 is의 주어가 될 수 없고 what이 catches의 주어도 목적어도 되지 못한다. ③은 What이 is의 주어이고 how가 의문부사여서 catches의 주어, 목적어와 충돌하지 않으므로 전체가 is의 주어가 될 수 있는 올바른 구조이다.

| 어휘 |

nerve n. 신경 intrigue v. ~의 흥미를 끌다 trap n. 덫 blinding a. 눈부시게 밝은, 대단히 빠른 dexterity n. 능숙성, 기민함, 재빠름

| 해석 |

그 동물이 먹이를 잡는 방식에서 가장 놀라운 점은 신경이나 근육 없이 이렇게 한다(먹이를 잡는다)는 것이다. 과학자들이 이 동물이 어떻게 그렇게 빠르고 기민하게 덫을 닫을 수 있는지를 밝혀내려고 하다 보니 이 현상은 여러 해 동안 과학자들의 흥미를 끌어왔다.

06 부정사의 부정   ①

| 분석 |

'~하기 위해'는 'so much as to 부정사'가 아니라 'so as to부정사'이며, '~하지 않기 위해'의 뜻으로 부정하려면 not을 to부정사 바로 앞에 넣어야 하므로 ①이 적절한 표현이다.

| 어휘 |

skittish a. 불안한, 겁먹은 clear v. ~을 떠나다, 비우다 happen to do 우연히 ~하다

| 해석 |

만약 내가 불안해 보이는 사람들에 뒤이어 건물에 들어가게 된다면, 그들을 따라가는 것처럼 보이지 않기 위해 먼저 그냥 지나쳐서 그들이 로비를 빠져나가게 한 다음 로비로 다시 돌아올 수도 있다.

07 수동태   ④

| 분석 |

사람이 어떠하다고 '믿어지는' 수동 관계이므로 believe 동사가 수동태로 나온 ④가 빈칸에 적절하다. had been believing, were believing, had believed는 모두 능동태이다.

| 어휘 |

superstition n. 미신 feature n. 특징 personality trait 성격 특성 hot-tempered a. 성 잘 내는, 신경질적인

| 해석 |

아마도 세계의 모든 문화에는 몸의 신체적 특징을 성격 특성과 연관 짓는 미신이 있었을 것이다. 영국도 예외가 아니어서, 과거에 그러한 믿음이 상당히 많았다. 예를 들어, 빨간 머리를 가진 사람들은 선천적으로 화를 잘 낸다고 믿어졌다.

08 the 비교급, the 비교급 구문   ②

| 분석 |

빈칸 앞이 'the 비교급+주어+동사' 구문이므로 빈칸에도 같은 구문인 ②가 적절하다. it은 an article을 가리킨다.

| 어휘 |

lead to ~을 초래하다 worried well 건강 염려증이 있는 사람들 frightening a. 무시무시한 attention n. 주의, 관심

| 해석 |

기술의 이용 가능성 때문에 일부 사람들은 우리가 "건강 염려증이 있는 사람들"의 세대를 만들어내고 있다고 주장하게 되었다. 때때로 사람들은 자기 증상을 연구하려고 검증되지 않았거나 과학적이지 않은 소프트웨어를 사용한다. 이미 불안한 사람들에게는 이런 질 낮은 정보가 걱정을 부추길 수 있다. 일반적으로 기사가 무서울수록, 그 기사는 당신의 주의를 더 많이 끌 가능성이 있다.

09 동의어   ①

| 어휘 |

subconsciously ad. 잠재의식적으로 modify v. 수정[변경]하다 (= adjust v. 조정하다, 수정하다) consolidate v. 통합하다, 굳히다, 강화하다 generate v. 발생시키다 dismantle v. 해체하다

| 해석 |

프레이밍(어떤 사안을 특정한 방식으로 구성하고 제시하는 것)이 사람들의 사고방식을 잠재의식적으로 바꿀 수 있는 힘이 있기 때문에, 많은 정치인들은 유권자들에게 영향을 미치기 위해 이것을 사용한다. 일단 '프레임'이 한 인구집단의 의식 속에 들어가고 나면, 그것을 즉시 바꿀 수는 없다. 프레임을 수정하는 데는 엄청난 시간과 에너지가 필요하다.

10 동의어 ③

| 어휘 |
candidate n. 후보 convey v. 전달하다 voter n. 유권자
sway v. 휘두르다, 흔들다 folksy a. 평민적인, 소탈한, 친하기 쉬운
disregard v. 무시하다(= neglect) record n. 기록, 경력, 실적

| 해석 |
어떤 후보가 자신이 대다수의 사람들과 똑같다는 인상을 주려고 할 때, 많은 유권자들은 안타깝게도 그의 서민적인 행동에 쉽게 휘둘려, 가장 중요한 것인 그 후보의 경력을 무시하는 지경에 이르게 된다.

11 동의어 ④

| 어휘 |
unprecedented a. 유례없는(= unusual) well-preserved a. 보존이 잘 된 impressive a. 인상적인 irresistible a. 저항할 수 없는 unethical a. 부도덕한, 비윤리적인

| 해석 |
1991년에 '아이스맨'을 발견한 것은 전례 없는 사건이었다. 잘 보존된 수천 년 된 시신은 이전에는 결코 구할 수 없던 방대한 정보를 제공할 수 있었다.

12 동의어 ①

| 어휘 |
need n. 필요, 요구 financial a. 금융의, 재정의, 경제적인 affect v. 영향을 끼치다 vicissitude n. 부침, 흥망성쇠, 변화(= change)
deficit n. 적자, 결손, 부족액 variant n. 변형, 변이형, 변이체, 변종

| 해석 |
지역에서 이용할 수 있는 자연적, 인적, 재정적 자원을 활용해서 공동체의 많은 필요를 충족시킬 수 있는 공동체는 국내외 경제의 변화에 영향을 덜 받는다.

13 동의어 ③

| 어휘 |
resonate v. 울리다, 공명하다, 공감을 불러일으키다 steeped a. ~에 몰두한 jargon n. 전문용어 pragmatic a. 실용적인(= practical)
you-scratch-my-back-I'll-scratch-yours a. 서로서로 돕자는 식의, 상부상조의

| 해석 |
그것은 상생식의 협상 용어에 물든 사업가들과, 상부상조식의 실용적 대화에 깊이 몰두해 있는 워싱턴을 돌아가게 하는 정치인들 모두에게 똑같이 공감을 불러일으키는 접근법이다.

14 논리완성 ④

| 분석 |
혼자서 보내는 시간을 즐겼다고 했으므로 자기 성찰이라는 의미의 introspection이 빈칸에 들어가기에 적절하다. ② 문장 후반부의 "shock as great as falling in love"와 자연스럽게 연결되지 못한다.

| 어휘 |
gregarious a. 사교적인; 군세[군생]하는 acquaintance n. 지인, 아는 사람 unexpectedly ad. 예상치 않게 appointment n. 만날 약속 solitary a. 고독한 grievance n. 불만, 고충 bliss n. 더없는 행복 abstraction n. 관념, 추상적 개념 introspection n. 내성(內省), 자기 성찰

| 해석 |
며칠 전, 사교적이고 매력적인 한 지인이 뉴욕에서 약속 사이에 한두 시간의 뜻밖의 자유 시간이 생겼다고 말했다. 그는 휘트니 미술관에 가서 "빈 시간"을 혼자서 성찰하면서 보냈다. 그에게는 혼자 있는 시간도 이렇게 즐거울 수 있다는 사실이 마치 사랑에 빠진 것만큼 충격적인 일이었다.

15 논리완성 ④

| 분석 |
"인간을 위축시키는 불의의 화염 속에서 고통 받아온 수백만 흑인 노예들에게 희망의 등불로 다가왔다"는 그 선언이 가진 중요한 의미를 부여하는 내용이다.

| 어휘 |
emancipation proclamation 노예해방 선언문 decree n. 선언, 칙령 beacon light 횃불 sear v. 불에 그슬리다, 고통 주다 flame n. 화염 withering a. 사람을 위축시키는 injustice n. 불의, 불평등 daybreak n. 새벽 captivity n. 포로생활 minor a. 사소한, 대수롭지 않은 trivial a. 하찮은 immaterial a. 중요하지 않은, 무형의, 실체가 없는 momentous a. 중대한

| 해석 |
100년 전, 우리가 지금도 그의 영향력 하에 서있는 한 위대한 미국인이 노예 해방 선언서에 서명했습니다. 이 중대한 선언은 인간을 위축시키는 불의의 화염 속에서 고통 받아온 수백만 흑인 노예들에게 희망의 등불로 다가왔습니다. 그것은 긴 포로생활의 밤을 끝내는 즐거운 새벽으로 다가왔습니다.

16 논리완성 ①

| 분석 |
역접의 전치사 Despite에 의해 연결되므로 DNA 지문 채취의 유용성과 반대되는 내용이 와야 한다. 중대한 이슈가 이 기술의 성공

효과를 감소시킨다는 의미가 되게 하는 temper가 정답으로 적절하다.

| 어휘 |

fingerprinting n. 지문채취 **significant** a. 중대한 **massive** a. 방대한 **funding** n. 자금 **qualified** a. 자격을 갖춘 **expertise** n. 전문지식 **backlog** n. 잔고, 잔액, 축적 **unprocessed** a. 처리되지 않은 **carry out** 실행하다 **offender** n. 범죄자 **contamination** n. 오염 **temper** v. 경감시키다, 완화하다 **facilitate** v. 촉진시키다 **legitimate** v. 합법화하다 **reinforce** v. 강화하다

| 해석 |

DNA 지문 채취가 유용하긴 하지만, 중대한 쟁점들이 그 성공을 경감시킨다. 수년 동안 방대한 DNA 증거가 수집되었지만, 자금 부족, 자격을 갖춘 인력과 시간의 부족으로 인해 미처리 정보가 쌓였다. DNA 지문 채취는 높은 수준의 전문지식과 정확성을 요구하며, 테스트가 제대로 수행되지 않으면 폭력범이 풀려나서 범죄를 더 저지를 수 있다. 증거가 잘못 처리되거나 오염될 가능성은 여전히 중대한 문제를 제기한다.

17 논리완성 ③

| 분석 |

'강인한 정신력'과 유사한 단어는 '끈기'라는 뜻의 tenacity이고, '결의'를 수식하는 형용사로 '고정불변의'와 유사한 단어는 '단호한'이라는 뜻의 resolute이다.

| 어휘 |

formidable a. 가공할만한, 어마어마한 **unbridled** a. 억제되지 않은, 넘치는, 끝없는 **enthusiasm** n. 열정 **obstacle** n. 장애물 **determination** n. 결단력 **crutch** n. 목발 **fragility** n. 부서지기 쉬움, 나약함 **stubborn** a. 고집 센 **audacity** n. 과감함 **tenacity** n. 끈기, 집요함 **resolute** a. 결단력 있는 **flexibility** n. 유연함 **assertive** a. 자기주장이 강한, 독단적인

| 해석 |

어린 시절 그녀는 내면의 가공할 만한 정신력과 끈기의 징후들을 분명히 보여주었다. 활기찬 아이였던 그녀는 다섯 살에 스키를 배웠고, 넘치는 열정으로 스키를 즐겼다. 7년 후, 뼈암으로 다리를 잃었을 때 그녀는 인생의 첫 번째 큰 장애물에 부딪힌다. 그러나 그녀는 단호하고 불변한 결의로 스키를 계속했고, 목발을 짚고 조깅을 하며 체력을 유지했다. 1년 후 그녀는 세계선수권대회 활강 부문에서 우승을 차지했다.

18 논리완성 ①

| 분석 |

책을 읽는 법에 대한 비유 표현에 맞추어 첫 번째 빈칸에는 '부분적으로 읽는 것'에 해당하는 '맛만 본다'는 tasted가 적절하고, 씹어서 소화시키듯이 읽는 것은 전체를 속속들이 읽는 것을 말하므로 두 번째 빈칸에는 wholly가 적절하다. savor는 조금씩 맛보는 것이 아니라 천천히 음미하는 것을 의미한다. scan은 '대충 훑어 읽다'는 뜻이지만 음식 먹는 것에 비유한 표현이 아니다. carefully는 '정독'을 의미하지만 이어진 with diligence and attention과 중복된다.

| 어휘 |

swallow v. 삼키다 **chew** v. (음식을) 씹다 **digest** v. 소화시키다 **curiously** ad. 호기심 어린 태도로 **taste** v. 맛보다 **wholly** ad. 전체적으로 **savor** v. 맛을 천천히 음미하다 **scan** v. 대충 훑다 **appreciate** v. 감상하다; 평가하다

| 해석 |

어떤 책은 맛만 보듯 읽고, 어떤 책은 그냥 삼키듯 읽고, 또 다른 소수의 책은 꼭꼭 씹어 소화하듯 읽어야 한다. 다시 말해, 어떤 책은 부분적으로만 읽으면 되고, 다른 책은 읽되 호기심까지는 필요 없으며 소수의 책은 전체적으로 주의 깊고 성실하게 읽어야 한다.

19 논리완성 ④

| 분석 |

새로운 발명품을 불신한다고 했으니 철도를 '비난했다'고 해야 하고, 자동차를 싫어하는 어조로는 '신랄한'이 적절하다.

| 어휘 |

distrust n. 불신 **distaste** n. 혐오 **fangled** a. 유행하는 **beloved** a. 사랑하는 **dislike** n. 싫어함, 혐오 **temperate** a. 온건한 **acquiesce** v. 묵인하다 **bland** a. 단조로운 **sharp** a. 예리한 **pungent** a. 신랄한 **denounce** v. 맹렬히 비난하다

| 해석 |

"새로 유행하는 발명품"에 대한 불신과 거부감은 역사가 길다. 19세기 영국 작가들은 자신들이 사랑하는 호수 지대에 철도가 들어서는 것을 비난했다. 50년 전, H. L. 멘켄은 자동차, 사진, 영화에 대한 혐오를 특유의 신랄한 언어로 기록했다.

20 논리완성 ②

| 분석 |

교사가 개방적이고 편안한 환경을 만들되 지나치면 안 된다는 경고이므로 '관대하다(lenient)'가 적절하고, 지나치게 엄격하면 '긴장된(tense)' 분위기가 된다고 하는 것이 적절하다.

| 어휘 |

boundary n. 경계 **permissible** a. 허용 가능한 **relaxed** a. 편안한, 느슨한 **easy-going** a. 느긋한, 태평한 **discipline** n. 규율, 기강 **overly-strict** a. 지나치게 엄격한 **inhibit** v. 억제하다, 막다 **restrictive** a. 규제하는 **harsh** a. 가혹한 **lenient** a. 관대한, 인정 많은 **tense** a. 긴장된 **indolent** a. 게으른 **miserable** a. 비참한

whimsical a. 변덕스러운   stressful a. 스트레스가 많은

| 해석 |

교사는 학습이 이루어지기에 편안하고 개방적인 환경을 유지하면서도 허용 가능한 행동의 경계를 분명히 설정해야 한다. 성격이 느긋한 교사는 종종 긍정적인 학습 환경을 조성하는 데 능숙하지만, 지나치게 관대하면 큰 규율 문제가 발생할 수 있다. 엄격한 성격과 수업 방식을 가진 교사는 대개 학급 규율을 더 잘 세우지만, 규칙을 지나치게 강조하면 부정적인 결과를 초래할 수 있다. 학생들이 실수할 때, 지나치게 엄한 반응은 참여를 위축시키는 긴장된 분위기를 만들 수 있다.

21 부분이해 ①

| 분석 |

밑줄 친 부분은 생태관광과 밀접한 관계에 있는 지속가능한 관광의 개념을 밝힌 것이므로 지속가능한 개발을 생태관광의 전제로 삼으려는 것이 저자의 의도라고 할 수 있다. 따라서 정답은 ①이다.

| 어휘 |

offshoot n. 파생결과   ecotourism n. 생태관광   come into one's own 제자리를 잡다, 제대로 인정받다   awareness n. 자각   unspoiled a. 망가지지 않은   authentic a. 진정성 있는; 진짜인   sustainable a. 지속 가능한   compromise v. 훼손하다, 위험에 빠뜨리다   meet need 욕구나 필요를 충족시키다

| 해석 |

1970년대 환경운동에서 파생된 생태관광은 지난 20년에 걸쳐 제자리를 잡게 되었다. 기후 변화와 같은 환경 문제에 대한 인식이 높아지고, 유럽 및 북미 여행객들 사이에서 훼손되지 않은 자연, 진정성 있는 문화 체험, 도전적인 레크리에이션 활동에 대한 수요가 증가하면서, 생태관광은 매년 20퍼센트의 성장률을 보여 관광 산업에서 가장 빠르게 성장하는 분야가 되고 있다. 국제 생태관광 협회는 생태관광을 "환경을 보존하고 지역 주민의 복지를 지켜주는, 자연지역으로의 책임 있는 여행"으로 정의한다. 국제자연보전연맹은 생태관광을 경제적으로 지속가능하고, 생태적으로 민감하며, 문화적으로 수용 가능한 것으로 특징짓는다. 이와 밀접하게 관련된 것은 지속가능한 관광 개념인데, 이 개념은 1987년 세계 환경 개발 위원회에 제출된 보고서인 『우리 공동의 미래』에서 "미래 세대가 자신의 필요를 충족시킬 능력을 훼손하지 않고 현재 세대의 필요를 충족시키는" 개발인 것으로 확인된다.

다음 중 밑줄 친 부분에서 저자의 의도는 무엇인가?
① 지속가능한 개발을 생태관광의 전제로 설명하는 것
② 현재 세대와 미래 세대 간의 잠재적인 의견 불일치를 암시하는 것
③ 관광 개발을 촉진하려는 생태관광의 시도를 예시하는 것
④ 미래 세대를 위해 자연을 보존하지 않은 현재 세대를 비난하는 것

22 내용파악 ③

| 분석 |

첫 문장에서 '이 연구에 따르면, 아동의 성격에 양육보다 유전자 구성이 더 큰 영향을 끼친다고 한다'고 했으므로 정답은 ③이다.

| 어휘 |

rear v. 양육하다   identical twins 일란성 쌍둥이   layperson n. 비전문가, 일반인   primacy n. 우위, 중요성   fierce a. 격렬한   emerge v. 나타나다, 출현하다   extensive a. 광범위한   heredity n. 유전   contradiction n. 모순, 위배   nurture n. 양육

| 해석 |

서로 다른 가정에서 자란 일란성 쌍둥이를 대상으로 한 최초의 연구에 따르면, 아동의 성격에 양육보다 유전자 구성이 더 큰 영향을 끼친다고 한다. 이 연구결과는 전문가들과 일반인 사이에 널리 퍼져있는 가정환경의 우위에 대한 믿음을 깨뜨리며, 치열한 논쟁을 불러올 것이 분명하다.
이 연구결과는 미네소타 대학교의 장기 프로젝트에서 나온 첫 번째 주요 결과로, 350쌍이 넘는 쌍둥이들이 혈액, 뇌파, 지능, 알레르기 분석을 비롯한 광범위한 검사를 6일간 받았다.
측정된 특성 대부분에서 유전 요인이 전체 변이의 절반 이상을 차지했고, 부모의 영향과 가정환경과 삶의 경험의 영향은 절반 미만으로 나타났다.
미네소타 연구결과는 성인의 성격 형성에서 천성(유전자)과 양육(환경) 중 어느 것이 더 중요한가에 대한 기존의 통념과 정면으로 배치된다. 프로이트 이후 거의 모든 주요 이론은 유전자, 즉 천성보다 환경, 즉 양육에 훨씬 더 많은 중요성을 부여해 왔다.

다음 중 미네소타 연구결과의 요점은 무엇인가?
① 유전자 연구는 유전의 역할에 관한 심각한 논쟁을 일으킨다.
② 교육은 아이의 성격 형성에서 유전보다 더 중요하다.
③ 개인의 성격과 특성은 후천적으로 획득되기보다는 선천적이다.
④ 성격 형성에서 환경의 우위성이 다시금 인정되고 있다.

23 내용파악 ①

| 분석 |

도선사가 증기선 사업의 부활을 갈망했다는 언급은 본문에 없다.

| 어휘 |

pilot n. 도선사, 수로 안내인   compact a. 소형의, 조밀한, 단단한, 결속력 있는   monopoly n. 독점   indestructible a. 무적의, 난공불락의   be numbered 수가 제한되다, 얼마 남지 않았다   divert v. 방향을 딴 데로 돌리다   steamboat n. 증기선   annihilate v. 없애다, 제거하다   idle a. 노는, 일 없는   till n. 돈궤   freight n. 화물, 화물 운송   straightway ad. 곧, 직접   twinkling n. 눈 깜짝할 사이   pathetic a. 애처로운, 불쌍한, 한심한

| 해석 |

도선사(수로 안내인) 협회는 어쩌면 세계에서 가장 작고 조밀한 독점 조직이었으며, 쉽게 무너지지 않을 것으로 여겨졌다. 하지만 그 전성시대는 끝나가고 있었다. 먼저, 미시시피, 테네시, 켄터키를 지나 북부 철도 중심지로 이어지는 새 철도 노선이 여객 운송을 증기선에서 철도로 바꾸기 시작했다. 다음으로 전쟁이 일어나 수년간 증기선 산업을 거의 완전히 파괴했고, 대부분의 도선사들이 할 일이 없어졌고 생활비는 계속 상승했다. 그다음, 세인트루이스 도선사협회의 재무 담당자가 돈궤에 손을 댔고 거액의 공금을 몽땅 들고 달아났다. 마지막으로 전쟁 후 철도가 도처에 침입하자 증기선은 화물 운송 외에 할 일이 거의 없게 되었다. 그래서 곧 대서양 연안 출신의 어떤 천재가, 증기선 화물 열두 척을 조그마한 보잘것없는 예인선 뒤에 매달아 뉴올리언스로 끌고 가는 계획을 도입했다. 그리고 보라, 이를테면, 순식간에, 도선사협회와 고귀한 도선 기술은 죽어 애처로운 과거사가 되어버렸다!

다음 중 도선사 업무와 협회가 "죽어 애처로운 과거지사"가 된 원인이 아닌 것은?
① 도선사들은 증기선 산업의 부활을 갈망했다.
② 철도가 승객 수송에서 증기선을 대체했다.
③ 전쟁으로 인해 증기선 산업이 거의 파괴되었다.
④ 전쟁 이후 증기선은 화물선으로 사용되었다.

24 내용추론 ②

| 분석 |

②의 경우 플루타크는 알렉산더를 좋아하면서도 그의 부정직한 행위를 경감 없이 썼다고 했으므로 오히려 공정하게 썼다고 해야 맞다. 따라서 추론상 틀린 것이다.

| 어휘 |

grand a. 원대한   **depart from** ~로부터 떠나다, 탈출하다   **pass over** 지나치다   **vice** n. 악덕   **grandeur** n. 원대함   **abomination** n. 혐오, 혐오스러운 것   **surrender** v. 항복하다   **safe conduct** 안전한 길 안내   **extenuate** v. 경감하다, 정상참작하다

| 해석 |

플루타크는 인생을 웅대한 목적에 사용하고, 마찬가지로 웅대하게 인생을 떠날 수 있는 인물들을 좋아했지만, 그 웅대함을 훼손하는 약점과 악덕도 그냥 넘어가지 않았다. 그가 영웅 중의 영웅으로 여긴 사람은 알렉산더 대왕이며 그를 다른 누구보다 좋아한다. 반면 그가 가장 증오한 것은 신의를 저버리는 불명예스러운 행동이다. 그럼에도 불구하고 그는 알렉산더가 용감한 페르시아군에게 항복하면 안전한 퇴각의 길 안내를 보장하겠다는 약속을 한 뒤, 그들이 줄지어 퇴각하는데도 공격해 모조리 죽였다는 이야기를 조금도 경감하려 하지 않고 서술했다. 이것은 "그의 약속 위반"이며 "그의 업적에 남은 영원한 오점"이라고 플루타크는 슬픈 듯 언급했다. "하지만 그건 딱 하나뿐인 오점이었다."라며 그는 안타깝다는 듯 덧붙였다. 그는 이 이야기를 하고 싶어 하지 않았다.

다음 중 이 글에서 추론할 수 없는 것은?
① 저자는 플루타르크가 알렉산더의 배신을 간과하지 않았다고 말한다.
② 저자는 플루타르크가 알렉산더에 관해 쓸 때 공정하지 않았다고 생각한다.
③ 저자는 플루타르크가 알렉산더의 페르시아군을 다룬 이야기를 마지못해 언급했다고 지적한다.
④ 저자는 페르시아군이 알렉산더를 믿었기 때문에 전장에서 퇴각했다고 주장한다.

25 빈칸완성 ④

| 분석 |

본문에서 the best poems are ambiguous; ~ when they have two or three or more levels of meaning at once라고 시가 의미 층위가 여럿일 때 가장 좋다고 했으니 광고도 비슷하지만 시보다 뛰어날 리는 없고 조금 낮은 수준에서 의미를 모호하게 한다는 표현이 가장 적합하다. 따라서 ④가 적절하다. ③ 시에도 시적 이미지가 있다. 보드카가 너무 맛이 좋아 숨 막힌다는 것인지 너무 도수가 높아 숨 막힌다는 것인지 모호하고, 자동차 광고문의 경우 모두 H로 시작하는 단어를 선택한 것이 말장난이다.

| 어휘 |

poetry n. 시   **have ~ in common** 공통점이 있다   **extensive** a. 넓은, 광범위한   **rhyme** n. 운율, 각운   **connotative** a. 함축적인   **affective** a. 정서적인, 감정적인   **denotative** a. 명시적인, 직설적인   **take a puff** 담배를 피우다   **refreshing** a. 상쾌한   **critic** n. 비평가   **at once** 동시에   **breathless** a. 숨막히는   **honey** n. 훌륭한 것

| 해석 |

그럼에도 불구하고, 시와 광고는 공통점이 많다. 우선, 둘 다 운율과 리듬을 광범위하게 사용한다(예: "What's the word? Thunderbird!": What's the와 Thunder가, 그리고 word와 bird가 서로 운율이 맞음). 또한 둘 모두 단어의 직설적 의미보다 감정적, 함축적 가치를 따져 단어를 선택한다. (예: "한 대 피워 봐... 봄이잖아! 회색빛 바위와 봄의 신선한 푸른 잎사귀가 산속 연못에 비친다... 이토록 신선한 공기를 달리 어디서 찾을 수 있겠는가?"). 비평가 윌리엄 엠프슨은 『7가지 유형의 애매모호함』이라는 저서에서 최고의 시는 애매모호하다고 말했다. 시는 두세 가지 이상의 의미 층위를 동시에 갖고 있을 때 가장 풍부하다는 것이다. 광고 역시, 훨씬 더 원시적인 수준에서이긴 하지만, 의도적으로 모호성을 활용하고 말장난을 한다. 가령 보드카 광고는 "숨 막히게 만들어요(Leaves you breathless)" 같은 슬로건으로 이루어지며 자동차는 "핫하고 근사하고 다루기에 고급스러워요(Hot, Handsome, a Honey to Handle.)" 같은 표현을 써서 묘사한다.

다음 중 빈칸에 가장 적절한 표현은 무엇인가?
① 의미 수준에서 시보다 더 뛰어나지만
② 지극히 장대한 수준에서지만

③ 이미지의 풍부함에만 국한되어 있지만
④ 훨씬 더 원시적인 수준에서이긴 하지만

26 내용파악 ①

| 분석 |

'또한 학습 사회의 핵심에는 학교와 대학이라는 전통적 교육 기관 훨씬 너머로까지 확장되는 교육 기회가 있다'라고 한 것만 보아도 학습 사회의 주된 목표가 평생 학습을 위한 교육 기회 확대임을 알 수 있다.

| 어휘 |

reform n. 개혁 **commitment** n. 헌신 **stretch** v. 확장하다 **foundation** n. 기초 **extend** v. 확대되다 **institution** n. 제도, 기관 **rapidly** ad. 신속하게 **dated** a. 진부한, 낡은, 시대에 뒤처진

| 해석 |

직장에서의 업무 여건상, 경쟁과 변화가 점점 가속화되고 위험이 점점 커지며 기회를 맞이할 준비가 된 이들에게 기회가 점점 더 커지는 세상에서, 교육 개혁은 '학습 사회'의 구축이라는 목표에 집중해야 한다. 이런 사회의 핵심에는 모든 구성원에게, 유년기부터 성인기에 이르기까지, 정신을 최대한 확장하여 세계가 변화함에 따라 더 많은 것을 배울 기회를 제공해주는, 일련의 가치와 교육 시스템에 대한 헌신이 있다. 이러한 사회는 교육이 단지 직업 목표에 기여하는 바 때문에 중요할 뿐 아니라 교육이 삶의 일반적인 질을 높이기 때문에도 중요하다는 생각을 기본 토대로 갖고 있다. 또한 학습 사회의 핵심에는 학교와 대학이라는 전통적 교육 기관 훨씬 너머로까지 확장되는 교육 기회가 있다. 교육의 기회는 가정, 직장, 도서관, 미술관, 과학관 등, 개인이 일과 삶에서 발전하고 성숙해질 수 있는 모든 공간으로 확대된다. 우리의 생각에, 공식 학교 교육은 평생학습을 위한 필수적인 기초이다. 하지만 평생학습이 없으면, 우리의 기술은 금방 시대에 뒤처질 수 있다.

다음 중 "학습 사회"의 주된 목표는 무엇인가?
① 교육 기회를 확장해 평생 학습을 가능하게 하려는 것
② 학습 기회를 통해 개인의 능력을 발견하고 개발하는 것
③ 전통적인 기초 교육을 모두가 이용할 수 있게 하려는 것
④ 모든 사람이 이용할 수 있는 교육 기관을 설립하려는 것

27 내용파악 ②

| 분석 |

빙하 후퇴가 지구 온난화에 끼치는 부정적 영향은 언급되어 있지 않다. 지구 온난화는 빙하 후퇴의 원인이지 결과가 아니다. 따라서 영향을 끼친다는 것은 이치에 맞지 않다.

| 어휘 |

rise v. 상승하다 **carbon emission** 탄소 방출 **trap** v. 가두다 **glacier** n. 빙하 **snowfall** n. 강설, 강설량 **compress** v. 압축시키다 **mass** n. 질량 **retreat** n. 후퇴, 퇴각 **fresh water** 민물, 담수 **spell** v. ~한 결과가 되다, 가져오다 **diminish** v. 줄이다, 감소시키다 **bear** v. 견디다 **disrupt** v. 붕괴시키다 **contaminate** v. 오염시키다, 더럽히다

| 해석 |

지구 온도는 온실가스를 대기에 가두는 탄소 배출로 상승 중이다. 지구의 양 극지방과 높은 산에 있는 거대한 얼음 덩어리인 빙하는 특히 이러한 지구 온난화의 영향을 많이 받는다. 기온이 상승하면 빙하가 녹을 뿐 아니라, 눈도 덜 내린다. 빙하는 눈이 기존의 눈 위에 쌓여 아래쪽 얼음 덩어리가 압축되어 거대한 얼음덩어리가 만들어질 때 형성된다. 따뜻한 날씨에 표면 일부가 녹아도, 더 많은 눈이 더 내려서 없어진 눈을 대체하면 괜찮다. 하지만 계속되는 기온 상승은 얼음이 더 많이 녹고 있고 눈이 더 적게 내리고 있음을 의미한다. 그 결과, 빙하는 기존의 덩어리를 유지하지 못한다. 다시 말해 빙하 덩어리가 줄어드는 것이다. 우리는 이런 현상을 '빙하 후퇴'라고 부른다. 그 덩어리가 계속 줄어들어 빙하가 과거에 덮었던 땅에서 물러나는 듯 보이기 때문이다.

빙하 후퇴에 대해 과학자들과 환경보호론자들은 왜 그토록 걱정하는 것일까? 우선, 대부분의 지구의 담수는 빙하 형태로 발견된다. 기온이 따뜻한 계절 동안에 빙하가 정상적으로 녹을 경우 인간, 동물, 식물에게 담수를 공급한다. 하지만 빙하가 그 덩어리를 유지할 수 없으면 사람들이 마시고 작물 재배에 쓸 가용 담수가 줄어들 것이다. 이는 전 세계 인구에게 재앙을 가져올 수 있다.

그뿐 아니라 빙하의 사라짐은 담수 공급을 줄이는 한편, 사라지는 과정에서 홍수와 해수면 상승이 유발된다. 대부분의 빙하는 고지대가 기온이 낮기 때문에 고지대에 존재한다. 그래서 얼음이 녹을 때 녹은 물을 중력이 강과 시내를 통해 아래로 흘려보낸다. 더 많이 녹는다는 것은 더 많은 물이 하천계로 들어가고 있음을 의미하고, 하천계는 늘어난 양의 물을 감당할 수 없어 홍수를 초래할 수도 있다. 홍수는 또한, 재산과 농작물을 파괴하고, 생태계 균형을 무너뜨린다. 일단 물이 바다에 도달하면 해수면을 상승시켜 해안 지역을 위협한다. 게다가 해수는 지하수에 스며들어 소금기로 담수를 오염시켜 담수량을 더 감소시킬 수 있다.

다음 중 빙하 후퇴에 대해 언급되지 않은 내용은 무엇인가?
① 빙하 후퇴가 발생하도록 원인을 제공하는 정황
② 빙하 후퇴가 지구 온난화에 끼치는 부정적 영향
③ 빙하 후퇴가 전 세계 물 공급에 끼치는 영향
④ 빙하 후퇴가 해양에 끼친 영향의 결과

28 내용파악 ③

| 분석 |

'1차 두통은 두통 자체 때문에 생기는 증상이다. 반면 2차 두통은 다른 생리적 상태로 인해 발생한다.'라고 했으므로 ③은 1차 두통이 2차 두통과 다른 차이점이고, 1차 두통 세 가지 유형 사이에서는 차이점이 아니라 공통점이다.

| 어휘 |

classify v. 분류하다 physiological a. 생리적인 infection n. 감염 tumor n. 종양 steady a. 꾸준한, 지속적인 dull a. 둔한 migraine n. 편두통 abnormal a. 비정상적인 trigger v. 유발하다 stimulus n. 자극; 격려 sensitive a. 예민한, 민감한 vomit v. 구토하다 cluster n. 무리, 군집 blood flow 혈류

| 해석 |

현재 의사들은 두통을 1차 두통과 2차 두통의 두 가지 일반 유형으로 분류한다. 1차 두통은 두통 자체 때문에 생기는 증상이다. 반면 2차 두통은 감염이나 종양 등 다른 생리적 상태로 인해 발생한다. 1차 두통에 대해 의사들은 세 가지 가능한 원인을 확정했다. 1차 두통의 한 가지 종류는 스트레스에 의해 생긴다. 의사들은 이를 긴장성 두통이라 부르며 양쪽 머리에 둔하고 지속적인 통증이 있는 것이 특징이다.

1차 두통의 다른 한 가지는 편두통이다. 이 두통을 유발하는 정확한 원인은 파악되지 않았으나 많은 전문가들은 비정상적인 뇌 활동이 뇌 화학구조와 혈류에 변화를 유발하는 것일 수 있다고 생각한다. 많은 사람들에게 편두통은 수면 부족이나 특정 음식이나 냄새 등의 특정 자극에 의해 유발된다. 대체로 머리 한쪽에 극심한 통증을 느끼며 빛과 소음에 민감해진다. 편두통이 심해지면 구토를 반복할 수도 있다.

세 번째 유형은 군발성 두통으로 알려져 있다. 군발성 두통은 대개 한 번 발생하면 몇 주나 몇 달 동안 대략 같은 시간대에 발생한다. 이 두통을 앓는 사람은 대개 머리 한쪽에 통증을 느끼는데, 통증이 주로 한쪽 눈 주위에 집중된다. 원인은 명확하지 않지만, 이 두통은 남성에게 흔하며, 알코올 등 혈류에 영향을 주는 요인과 관련이 있을 수 있다.

다음 중 1차 두통 세 가지 유형 간의 차이가 <u>아닌</u> 것은?
① 통증이 느껴지는 신체 부위
② 통증 발생의 규칙성
③ 다른 생리 상태와의 무관함
④ 통증을 유발할 수 있는 원인들

29 글의 요지   ④

| 분석 |

'문화 충돌은 대개 맥락 정보를 잘못 해석하는 데서 비롯된다'라고 한 첫 문장이 주제문이므로, 맥락의 중요성 차이가 문화 간 소통의 오해(문화 간 충돌)의 원인이라는 ④가 정답이다.

| 어휘 |

clash n. 충돌 misinterpret v. 오해하다 contextual a. 맥락의 varying a. 다양한 emphasis n. 강조 assign v. 할당하다, 부과하다 consequently ad. 그래서, 그 결과 implied a. 함축된 theme n. 주제 explicit a. 명시적인, 노골적인 factor n. 요인 apparent a. 명백한 detailed a. 상세한

| 해석 |

문화 충돌은 대개 맥락 정보를 잘못 해석하는 데서 비롯된다. 문화마다 의사소통 시 환경에서 수집되는 특정 맥락 정보를 강조하는 정도가 다 다르다.

여기에는 일반적으로 두 가지 문화 유형이 있으니, 고맥락 문화와 저맥락 문화이다. 동아시아 및 중동 국가의 고맥락 문화는 메시지를 둘러싼 환경에 큰 중요성을 부여하며 메시지 자체의 의미는 대개 함축적이다. 말해지는 내용을 이해하려면 사람들은 먼저 상황, 그리고 의사소통 당사자들 간의 관계부터 파악해야 한다. 이러한 문화들은 단어의 구체적 의미보다 함축된 주제에 더 가치를 부여한다.

반면, 독일이나 미국 같은 저맥락 문화는 메시지 자체를 더 중시하며 메시지는 대체로 훨씬 더 명시적이다. 저맥락 의사소통자들에게 소통은 더 상세하고 구체적이다. 외부 요인들이 그다지 강조되지 않기 때문이다. 낱말 하나하나가 의미가 있고 정확성이 대체로 중요하다.

맥락의 차이는 대개 사업 세계에서 매우 명백하다. 가령 일본의 사업 계약은 비교적 짧은 반면 미국의 계약은 대개 더 길고 훨씬 더 상세하다.

다음 중 이 글의 요지는 무엇인가?
① 맥락의 중요성에 따라 나라마다 사업 계약서의 길이에 차이가 있다.
② 상황과 소통 참여자들의 관계를 이해하는 것이 문화 간 소통 중에 중요하다.
③ 문화마다 소통하는 동안 맥락 정보 사용 정도가 다르다.
④ 맥락의 중요성 차이로 인해 문화 간 소통의 오해가 발생한다.

30 내용파악   ④

| 분석 |

마지막 문장에 따르면, 미국에서 거머리를 사용하는 것은 접합 수술에서는 합법이다. 따라서 ④는 사실이 아니다.

| 어휘 |

leech n. 거머리 medicinal leech 의약용 거머리 live on ~을 먹고 살다, ~에 기대어 살다 chemical n. 화학물질 anesthetic n. 마취제 vein n. 정맥 at one time 한번에 fall off 떨어져 나가다 bite n. 물린 자리 saliva n. 침, 타액 take out 빼내다 fever n. 발열 reattachment surgery (절단 부위) 접합 수술

| 해석 |

거머리는 길이가 1밀리미터에서 5센티미터 사이인 벌레의 한 종류이다. 거머리는 전 세계에 걸쳐 서식한다. 일반적으로 거머리는 호수나 강에 산다. 세계에는 약 650종의 거머리가 있다. 이 중 오직 한 종류만이 의학에 사용된다. 이들은 '의약용 거머리'라고 불린다. 의약용 거머리는 다른 동물의 피를 먹고 산다. 거머리는 양쪽 끝에 빨판을 가지고 있는데, 하나는 피를 빨아들이는 데 사용되고 다른 하나는 몸을 고정하는 데 쓰인다. 거머리의 침에는 피를 빨 수 있도

록 도와주는 세 가지 특별한 화학물질이 들어있다. 첫 번째는 마취제 역할을 하는 물질로, 거머리가 동물에게 고통을 주지 않고 동물의 피를 빨 수 있게 해준다. 두 번째 물질은 정맥을 넓게 열어주고, 세 번째 물질은 정맥으로부터 나온 피가 오랫동안 흐르도록 만든다. 의약용 거머리는 한 번에 10~15밀리리터의 피를 빨아먹는다. 이 과정은 약 45분 정도 걸린다. 거머리는 배가 부르면 저절로 떨어진다. 그러나 거머리의 침 속 화학물질 때문에 물린 자리는 24시간 동안 계속 피가 흐른다.

거머리는 3,000년이 넘도록 의학에 사용되어 왔다. 거머리는 1800년대 초 유럽에서 가장 인기가 많았다. 당시 사람들은 체내에 피가 너무 많으면 병이 생긴다고 믿었다. 의사들은 환자의 몸에 거머리를 세 마리 또는 네 마리 올려두었다. 거머리가 남아도는 피를 빨아들이는 것이었다. 열병부터 부러진 다리까지 다양한 병을 치료하는 데 거머리가 사용되었다.

안타깝게도 거머리는 치료하기보다 해가 되는 경우가 더 많았다. 예를 들어, 러시아 작가 니콜라이 고골은 피가 너무 부족해서 생기는 병인 빈혈 때문에 거머리 치료를 받았다. 그는 며칠 뒤 사망했다. 오늘날 우리가 알고 있듯이, 피는 몸을 치유하는 데 중요한 역할을 하므로 아픈 사람에게서 피를 빼는 것은 대개 도움이 되지 않는다. 1850년대 중반쯤 되자 사람들은 거머리 치료의 문제점을 이해하게 되었고, 거머리 치료는 점차 인기를 잃었다.

오늘날 의사들은 거머리에 대해 더 많은 것을 알고 있다. 의사들은 언제 거머리를 사용해야 하는지와 그 이유도 알고 있다. 의사들은 거머리의 침 속 화학물질이 의학적으로 매우 유용하다는 사실을 이해하게 되었다. 이런 이유로 미국에서는 2004년에 거머리를 수술 중 접합 수술(절단된 신체 부위를 다시 붙이는 수술)에 사용하는 것을 합법화했다.

본문에서 의약용 거머리에 대한 사실이 아닌 것은?
① 거머리의 양쪽 끝부분들은 먹이를 물 때 서로 다른 기능을 한다.
② 거머리의 침은 먹이인 동물의 피를 빠는 동안 동물이 통증을 느끼지 않게 해준다.
③ 과거에 거머리는 많은 질병을 치료하는 데 사용되었다.
④ 거머리를 이용하는 치료는 여전히 모든 나라에서 불법이다.

31~32

날씨는 매일매일 바깥이 어떤지를 말한다. 해가 났고 더운가? 비가 오고 추운가? 천둥번개가 치는가? 아니면 그냥 '보통'인가? 반면에 기후는 한 지역에서 오랜 기간 동안 나타나는 날씨의 패턴을 의미한다. 예를 들어, 많은 사막에서는 가끔씩 비가 내리기도 하지만, 1년 전체에 걸친 사막의 "보통" 패턴은 덥고 건조한 것이다.

기후는 여러 가지 방식으로 평가될 수 있다. 가장 중요한 방식 두 가지는 해당 지역에 얼마나 많은 일조량과 강우량이 있는가와 어떤 종류의 식물이 자라는가이다. 이 두 가지 때문에 지구에는 몇 가지 기후대가 존재한다. 기후대란, 해마다 날씨가 똑같은 패턴을 따르는 넓은 육지 지역을 말한다. 그것은 다양한 측정 기준에 기초할 수 있다. 가장 잘 알려진 기후대는 강우에 기초해 있다. 계절별 예상 강우량을 사용하면, 지구에는 총 8개의 기후대가 존재한다.

첫 번째 기후대는 적도 기후대이다. 이 지대에는 모든 계절에 비가 내린다. 이 지대는 지구를 반으로 나누는 상상의 선인 적도에서 그 이름이 지어졌다. 다음은 열대 기후대인데, 이곳은 여름에는 비가 오고 겨울에는 비가 오지 않는다. 그 다음은 열대 반건조 기후대로, 이 지역은 여름에만 아주 적은 양의 비가 내린다. 그 뒤를 잇는 두 기후대는 서로 비슷하다. 건조 기후대는 일 년 내내 매우 건조하며, 지중해성 기후대는 겨울에는 비가 오지만 여름에는 건조하다. 다음으로는 온대 기후대가 있다. 이 지대는 적도 기후대처럼 모든 계절에 비가 내린다. 놀랍게도, 지구의 북극과 남극에 해당하는 극지방 기후대는 비나 눈이 거의 오지 않는다. 이곳은 1년 내내 얼어 있는 상태이다.

전반적으로 기후는 다섯 가지 주요 요인 때문에 지역마다 다른데, 그 요인들은 적도에서의 거리, 해발 고도, 지표면의 특성, 바다나 큰 호수에서의 거리, 그리고 대기 순환이다.

| 어휘 |

weather n. 날씨 **thunderstorm** n. 천둥번개와 비, 뇌우 **normal** a. 보통의, 정상의 **region** n. 지역 **now and then** 이따금씩 **rate** v. 평가하다. 등급 매기다 **climate zone** 기후대 **rainfall** n. 강우량 **equatorial zone** 적도대 **semiarid** a. 반건조의 **similar** a. 유사한 **factor** n. 요인 **circulation** n. 순환 **feature** n. 특징

31 내용파악   ②

| 분석 |

두 번째 문단의 '일조량과 강우량', 마지막 문단의 '적도에서의 거리, 해발 고도, 지표면의 특성, 바다나 큰 호수에서의 거리, 그리고 대기 순환' 등이 기후대 결정요인이다. 따라서 ②가 결정요인이 아니다. ①은 대기 순환과 관련된 것이다.

다음 중 기후대를 결정하는 요인이 아닌 것은?
① 한 지역을 둘러싼 바람과 공기의 흐름 패턴
② 여러 지역에서 반복되는 날씨의 보편적인 특징들
③ 특정 지역의 강수량이나 일조량의 측정
④ 지구상의 지역 위치와 지형적 특징

32 내용파악   ③

| 분석 |

세 번째 문단이 각 기후대를 설명한 부분인데, 거기서 '건조 기후대는 일 년 내내 매우 건조하며'라고 했으므로 강우량이 가장 적은 기후대는 건조 기후대이다.

다음 중 강우량이 가장 적은 기후대는?
① 온대 기후대
② 지중해성 기후대
③ 건조 기후대
④ 열대 기후대

33~34

자동차 앞유리에 눈이 쌓이면, 눈은 차가운 유리 표면에 달라붙는다. 운전자가 시동을 걸어 차를 작동시키면, 자동차 내부 온도가 올라가면서 앞유리가 따뜻해지기 시작한다. 온도가 상승함에 따라, 앞유리에 쌓인 눈이 녹기 시작하고 때때로 큰 덩어리로 미끄러져 떨어진다. 운전자는 이를 인식하지 못할 수도 있지만, 사실 이때 작은 눈사태가 앞유리에서 발생한 것이다.

앞유리에서 일어나는 이 같은 눈사태는 판상 눈사태, 즉 대규모 눈사태라고 알려진 현상을 흉내 낸 것이다. 그러나 그것은 큰 지역에서의 눈사태 동안에 일어나는 치명적인 자연의 힘이 아니다. 진짜 눈사태는 가장 강력한 자연 사건 중 하나이다. 눈사태의 형성은 세 가지 요인에 달려 있다. 눈, 경사진 지표면, 그리고 촉발자이다. 눈 덮인 경사면의 경사각이 30도에서 45도 사이일 경우, 눈사태가 발생할 가능성이 있는 곳으로 간주된다. 12인치 이상 갑작스레 많은 눈이 내린 다음 날이 눈사태가 발생할 최적 시점이다.

여러 가지 자연적 상황들이 눈사태를 일으킬 수 있다. 숲이 있는 환경은 탁 트인 지형보다 훨씬 더 안전하다. 나무들이 눈을 고정시켜 눈사태 발생을 방지해주는 자연적인 완충물 역할을 하기 때문이다. 계곡이나 경사진 지역은 대량의 눈이 빠르게 쌓일 수 있으므로 잠재적인 위험 지대이다.

적설층, 즉 눈이 쌓인 층을 이루는 눈 층들의 상태도 눈사태 발생 가능성에 영향을 준다. 눈이 많이 내리는 지역에서 적설층은 시간이 흐름에 따라 생겨난 여러 눈 층들로 이루어진다. 적설층의 눈 층들 사이의 결속 유형이 눈사태가 발생할 수 있는지를 결정한다. 눈 결정체들이 강한 결속을 만들지 못하면 적설층 안에 약한 층이 형성된다. 이 약한 층이 표면 가까이에 있다면, 이는 슬러프, 즉 마른 가루 눈이 작게 미끄러지는 현상을 유발할 수 있다. 그러나 약한 층이 적설층의 바닥에 존재하면, 치명적인 판상 눈사태를 초래할 수 있다. 급격한 온도 변화도 또한 적설층 내부를 녹게 하여 결속을 약화시킬 수 있다.

| 어휘 |

accumulate v. 쌓이다 **windshield** n. 자동차 앞유리 **stick to** ~에 들러붙다 **ignition** n. 점화 **interior** n. 내부 **thaw** v. 녹다 **slide off** 미끄러져 떨어지다 **chunk** n. 덩어리 **avalanche** n. 눈사태 **slab** n. 판상 눈사태 **deadly** a. 치명적인 **formation** n. 형성 **sloped** a. 경사진 **snowfall** n. 강설 **terrain** n. 지형 **buffer** n. 완충물 **snowpack** n. 설괴빙원, 적설층 **sluff** n. 슬러프 (마른 가루 눈이 소규모로 미끄러지는 현상)

33　내용일치　　　　　　　　　　④

| 분석 |

눈사태를 "환경 재해"의 결과라고 단정 짓는 내용은 본문에 없다. 본문에는 자연 조건에 따라 발생한다고 되어 있을 뿐이다.

다음 중 본문의 내용과 <u>다른</u> 것은?
① 나무가 많은 경사지에서는 눈사태가 덜 발생한다.
② 눈사태는 특정한 자연 조건에 따라 발생한다.
③ 적설층의 층들 사이의 결속 정도는 눈사태 발생에 영향을 미칠 수 있다.
④ 눈사태 발생은 환경 위기 때문이라고 할 수 있다.

34　빈칸완성　　　　　　　　　　③

| 분석 |

차 안의 온도 상승이 앞유리에 전해져 앞유리의 눈이 녹아서 떨어지는 현상은 온도 변화에 의한 것이므로, 온도 변화가 적설층의 약한 결속을 유발한다는 ③이 정답으로 가장 적절하다.

본문의 "앞유리의 눈"과 관련해 빈칸에 가장 적절한 표현은?
① 눈사태는 종종 특정한 날씨 상황에서 특정한 자연 요인에 의해 발생한다
② 적설층의 안정성은 자연조건의 영향에 따라 달라지며 그에 따라 눈사태로 이어질 수 있다
③ 급격한 온도 변화도 또한 적설층 내부를 녹게 하여 결속을 약화시킬 수 있다
④ 자동차 수가 증가하면서 지구온난화를 촉진시켜 눈사태가 유발된다

35~36

소문은 이야기를 입에서 입으로 전하여, 가장 원시적인 이야기 전파 방식이다. 하지만 문명화된 나라들은 평상시에는 소문보다 더 나은 뉴스의 출처를 가지고 있다. 이들 나라엔 라디오, 텔레비전, 신문 같은 매체가 있다. 그러나 혼란과 긴장의 시기에는 소문이 등장하여 널리 퍼진다. 이런 시기에는 서로 다른 종류의 뉴스가 경합을 벌인다. 언론, 텔레비전, 라디오가 헛소문과 경쟁하게 되는 것이다.

특히 전쟁으로 인해 많은 중요한 사안에 대해 검열이 필요할 때, 소문은 더욱 퍼지기 쉽다. 이럴 경우, 기존의 뉴스 출처들은 더 이상 충분한 정보를 제공하지 않는다. 사람들이 정당한 경로를 통해 알고 싶어 하는 것을 알 수 없게 되므로, 어디서든 '뉴스'를 주워듣게 되고, 이런 일이 벌어지면 소문이

무성해진다.
소문은 종종 해당 이야기를 믿지 않는 사람들에 의해서도 되풀이된다. 소문에는 묘한 매력이 있다. 그 이유는 교묘하게 설계된 소문이 소문 희생자들의 마음속 깊은 곳에 자리한 감정 — 그들이 직접 말하기를 꺼려하는 공포, 의심, 금기된 희망, 공상 같은 것들을 표현하기 때문이다. 패배나 재난에 관한 비관적 소문은 그 소문을 되풀이하는 사람들이 걱정하고 불안해한다는 것을 보여준다. 반면 기록적인 생산량이나 곧 찾아올 평화에 대한 낙관적인 소문은 자기만족이나 자신감을 — 그리고 종종 과도한 자신감을 지적해준다.

| 어휘 |

rumor n. 소문　primitive a. 원시적인　spread v. 퍼뜨리다　pass v. 전달하다　civilized a. 문명화된　normal times 평상시　emerge v. 등장하다　rife a. 널리 퍼지는, 많아지는　in competition 경합을 벌이는, 경쟁하는　grapevine n. 비밀 정보망, 헛소문, 유언비어　censorship n. 검열 (제도)　give out 제공하다　legitimate a. 정당한, 합법적인　thrive v. 무성해지다　hesitate v. 망설이다, 주저하다　complacency n. 자기만족, 안주　overconfidence n. 과도한 자신감

35 글의 주제　②

| 분석 |

이 글 전체는 소문이 언제 퍼지고, 왜 퍼지고, 그 심리적 배경이 무엇인지를 설명하고 있으므로 '소문이란 무엇인가'에 해당하는 '소문의 본질'이 주제로 적절하다.

다음 중 이 글의 주제는 무엇인가?
① 소문에 매료됨
② 소문의 본질
③ 소문이 퍼지는 장소
④ 소문에 대한 비판

36 내용일치　①

| 분석 |

두 번째 문단에서 '특히 전쟁으로 인해 많은 중요한 사안에 대해 검열이 필요할 때, 소문은 더욱 퍼지기 쉽다'고 했으므로, 정보 부족으로 오히려 소문이 퍼진다는 것을 알 수 있다. 따라서 검열로 소문을 억제할 수 있다는 ①은 잘못된 설명이다. ② 소문이 소문 희생자들(소문을 사실로 잘못 믿고 퍼뜨리는 사람들)의 마음속 깊은 곳에 자리한 공포 같은 감정을 표현한다고 했다. ③ 전쟁 때는 기존의 뉴스 출처들은 더 이상 충분한 정보를 제공하지 않는다고 했다. ④ 긴장의 시기에는 소문이 등장하여 널리 퍼진다고 했는데, 소문을 퍼뜨리는 것이 곧 원시적인 방식이다.

다음 중 본문의 내용과 다른 것은?
① 소문은 대개 검열로 억제될 수 있다.
② 소문을 진실이라고 되풀이해 말하는 사람들은 진실이 두려워 그렇게 하고 싶어 한다.
③ 전쟁 중에는 정규 뉴스 매체가 제한된 정보만 제공한다.
④ 긴장이 심한 시기에 사람들은 종종 원시적인 방식으로 돌아간다.

37~38

마찬가지로, 워싱턴 D.C.에는 베트남 전쟁 기념관이 있다. 그곳에는 베트남 전쟁에서 전사한 미국 병사들의 이름이 가운데 이름까지 빼먹지 않고 5만 개나 적혀 있다. 이름을 가진 실제 인간들이 목숨을 잃었고, 그들의 숨결이 이 세상에서 사라졌다. 명단에는 도널드 밀러라는 이름도 있었다. 그는 내가 초등학교 2학년 때 친구였고, 수학 시험지 여백마다 탱크와 군인, 배 그림을 그리던 아이였다. 이름을 보면 우리는 기억을 떠올리게 된다. 이름은 우리가 평생 지니고 살아가는 것이며, 교실에서 이름이 불릴 때, 졸업식에서 이름이 호명될 때, 혹은 밤중에 속삭이듯 이름을 들을 때, 우리는 그 부름에 반응하게 된다.

우리가 누구인지 알려주는 이름과 우리가 살아온 장소들의 이름을 말하는 것, 그리고 우리 삶의 세부사항들을 말하고 쓰는 일은 중요하다. "나는 앨버커키의 콜 스트리트, 차고 옆 집에 살고, 식료품이 든 종이봉투를 들고 리드 애비뉴를 따라 걸었다. 그해 봄, 어떤 사람이 일찍 비트를 심었고, 나는 그 빨갛고 초록빛 잎들이 자라는 것을 지켜보았다."

우리는 삶을 영위해왔고, 그 순간들은 중요하다. 이것이 바로 작가가 된다는 것의 의미다. 역사를 구성하는 세부사항들의 전달자가 되고, 오와토나의 커피숍에 있는 주황색 부스를 아끼는 것 말이다.

우리 삶의 세세한 것들을 기록하는 일은 대규모로 생명을 앗아가는 폭탄에 맞서는 행위이며, 지나치게 빠르고 효율적인 세상에 맞서는 태도이기도 하다. 작가는 삶에, 삶 전체에 "예스"라고 말해야 한다(삶을 긍정해야 한다는 뜻). 물컵, 켐프 사(社)의 하프 앤 하프 우유크림, 조리대 위의 케첩까지도 긍정해야 한다. 작가의 임무는 "작은 마을에 사는 것이나, 집에서 유기농 음식을 먹을 수 있는데도 식당에서 밥을 먹는 것은 바보 같은 짓이다"라고 말하는 것이 아니다. 우리의 임무는 우리가 사는 삶의 실제 모습을 있는 그대로, 우리의 진짜 진실, 즉 약간 과체중인 몸, 회색빛으로 차가운 거리, 쇼윈도에 남아 있는 크리스마스 장식, 흑인 아이를 둔 금발 친구와 마주 앉은 주황색 부스 속 유대인 작가 같은 진실들을 거룩하게 긍정하는 것이다. 우리는 사물을 있는 그대로 받아들이는 작가, 세세한 것들을 사랑하게 되는 작가, 그리고 입술에 긍정의 말을 달고 앞으로 나아가는 작가가 되어야 한

다. 그렇게 해야 이 세상에 '아니오'라는 말은, 생명을 부정하고 이 소중한 세세한 것들이 계속되지 못하게 막는 '아니오'라는 말은 더 이상 있을 수 없게 된다.

| 어휘 |

likewise ad. 마찬가지로   **memorial** n. 전쟁 기념관   **breath** n. 숨, 호흡   **whisper** v. 속삭이다   **detail** n. 세세한 것들, 세부사항   **stance** n. 태도, 자세   **mass ability** 대규모 역량   **efficiency** n. 효율성   **dumb** a. 멍청한, 지루한   **holy** a. 신성한   **tinsel** n. 반짝이는 장식 조각   **overweight** a. 과체중의   **showcase** n. 진열장   **invalidate** v. 무효화하다, 무로 돌리다

37 글의 제목   ③

| 분석 |

본문은 전반적으로 삶의 구체적인 세부사항들, 즉 '디테일'의 중요성을 강조하고 있다. 글의 초반부에서는 베트남 전쟁에서 사망한 병사들의 이름이 적힌 기념비를 언급하며, 이름이라는 구체적인 정보가 우리 기억을 되살린다고 말하고 있다. 그다음에는 자신이 살았던 거리의 이름, 슈퍼마켓 종이봉투, 길가에 심긴 비트 등의 아주 구체적인 경험을 예로 들면서, 작가란 이런 디테일을 기록하는 사람이라고 정의한다. 글의 후반부에서는 작은 마을, 오렌지색 부스, 식당의 케첩, 사람들의 외모나 특징 등, 우리가 흔히 지나치기 쉬운 현실의 구체적 장면들을 있는 그대로 받아들이고 기록하는 것의 소중함을 강조한다. 결국 이 글이 하고자 하는 말은, 사소한 세부사항들이야말로 우리가 살았음을 증명하고, 인간적인 삶을 지키는 힘이라는 것이다. 따라서 제목으로는 ③이 적절하다.

다음 중 이 글의 제목은 무엇인가?
① 이름과 기억의 의미
② 작가의 역할
③ 세부사항의 힘
④ 관찰의 중요성

38 내용파악   ③

| 분석 |

마지막 문단에서 '우리 삶의 세세한 것들을 기록하는 일은 대규모로 생명을 앗아가는 폭탄에 맞서는 행위이며, 지나치게 빠르고 효율적인 세상에 맞서는 태도이기도 하다'라고 했으므로 세부사항 기록이 중요한 이유는 죽음에 저항하고 삶을 긍정하기 위해서다. 따라서 정답은 ③이다. ② 삶의 세부사항을 기록하는 것이 중요하고 이 중요한 일을 하는 사람이 작가이지만, 그 기록이 중요한 이유가 작가가 되기 위해 필요하기 때문인 것은 아니다. 즉, 세부사항의 기록은 삶을 긍정하는 방식이기 때문에 중요하고, 작가도 삶을 긍정하는 사람이어야 한다는 것이다.

다음 중 글쓴이가 일상의 세부사항을 기록하는 것이 중요하다고 여기는 주된 이유는?
① 삶의 모든 순간을 기록하는 것이 삶을 즐기는 방법이 될 수 있다.
② 삶의 세부사항을 기록하는 것이 작가가 되기 위해 필요하다.
③ 일상을 기록하는 것이 삶을 부정하지 않는 방식이다.
④ 우리가 지금 살아가는 모든 순간들이 매우 중요하다.

39~40

도달하기 어려운 지역에 의료 물자를 전달하는 일은 수년간 쟁점이 되어왔다. 전 세계적으로 20억 명 이상의 사람들이 혈액이나 백신처럼 생명을 구하는 필수 물품에 접근하지 못하고 있다. 가령 아프리카의 르완다에서는 외딴 지역의 여러 보건소가 혈액과 기타 의료 제품을 충분히 확보하지 못하고 있다. 그 결과 많은 사람들이 치료 가능한 병으로 목숨을 잃고 있다.

Zipline이라는 회사가 이 문제를 해결하고자 노력중이다. 이 기업은 드론을 이용해서 르완다 전역에 의료 물자를 운송하고 있다. 과거에는 일부 보건소까지 약품이 도달하는 데 여러 시간이 걸렸다. 그러나 이제는 드론이 약을 30분 만에 배달할 수 있게 되었다. 이러한 〈점차적인(→ 신속한)〉 의료 서비스 덕분에, 출산 중 고통 받는 여성들이 줄어들었고, 더 많은 아이들이 생명을 구할 수 있는 약을 받을 수 있게 되었다.

드론은 아프리카와 아시아 일부 지역에서 위기에 처한 야생 동물들을 보호하는 데에도 도움을 주고 있다. 매년 수천 마리의 코끼리, 코뿔소, 그리고 기타 멸종 위기 동물들이 밀렵꾼들에 의해 목숨을 잃고 있다. 이를 막기 위해 세계자연기금(WWF)이라는 환경 보호 단체가 드론을 활용하고 있다. WWF 소속의 콜비 라우크스는 "드론은 우리가 볼 수 없는 것들을 볼 수 있게 도와줍니다"라고 말한다. 예를 들어, 드론은 밀렵꾼들이 어디에 숨었는지, 그들이 무기를 소지하고 있는지 여부를 보여줄 수 있다. 드론은 밀렵꾼들이 가장 활발히 움직이는 야간에 특히 유용하다. 적외선 비디오 카메라가 장착된 드론은 어둠 속에서도 사람과 동물을 쉽게 식별할 수 있다. 이러한 드론은 단지 유용할 뿐 아니라 비용도 높지 않다. 적외선 카메라가 장착된 드론 한 대는 약 2만 달러 정도이며, 이는 다른 첨단 장비 비용의 극히 일부에 불과하다. 원래 군사용으로 개발된 도구가 이제는 사람의 생명을 앗아가는 것이 아니라 구하는 데 사용되고 있다는 사실은 아이러니하다. 사진작가이자 환경운동가인 키케 칼보는 드론이 인간과 동물 모두에게 이로운 해결책을 제공할 수 있는 잠재력이 있다고 말한다. 그는 "훌륭한 과학자를 대신할 수 있는 것은 아무것도 없지만", 드론의 도움으로 인해 "연구자들이 전에는 상상조차 못했던 프로젝트들을 수행할 역량이 생겼다"라고 덧붙였다.

| 어휘 |

medical supply 의료용품 **hard-to-reach** a. 도달하기 어려운 **issue** n. 쟁점 **worldwide** ad. 전세계적으로 **access** n. 접근 **life-saving** a. 생명을 구하는 **remote** a. 멀리 떨어진, 외딴 **health clinic** 보건소 **sufficient** a. 충분한 **treatable** a. 치료 가능한 **address** v. 다루다, 해결하다 **rhino** n. 코뿔소 **endangered animal** 멸종 위험에 처한 동물 **poacher** n. 밀렵꾼 **infrared video camera** 적외선 카메라 **affordable** a. 가격이 적절한, 비싸지 않은 **ironic** a. 아이러니한, 모순된 **increasingly** ad. 점점 더 **benefit** v. 이롭게 하다 **empowered** a. 힘을 갖게 된

39 내용파악   ②

| 분석 |

드론의 장점 중 전쟁 중 적을 추적하는 내용은 전혀 언급이 없다. 밀렵꾼을 추적하는 내용은 있지만, 그것은 자연 보호 목적이지 전쟁과는 무관하다. 따라서 ②가 정답이다. ③ 마지막 문장에서 '드론의 도움으로 인해 연구자들이 전에는 상상조차 못했던 프로젝트들을 수행할 역량이 생겼다'고 했다.

다음 중 본문에서 언급된 드론 사용의 장점이 <u>아닌</u> 것은?
① 외딴 지역에 의료 물품을 빠르게 전달할 수 있음
② 전쟁 중 적을 효과적으로 추적함
③ 강력한 연구 도구가 될 수 있는 잠재력
④ 다른 첨단 장비보다 낮은 가격

40 글의 흐름상 적절하지 않은 단어 고르기   ②

| 분석 |

②의 gradual은 '점진적인'이라는 뜻이므로 '빠르게 드론으로 의료 서비스를 제공하는 상황'을 설명하기에 어색하다. 문맥상 rapid나 efficient라는 표현이 들어가야 한다.

광운대학교 인문계 1교시 A형

TEST p. 178~191

01	①	02	⑤	03	④	04	①	05	③	06	④	07	②	08	⑤	09	③	10	②
11	①	12	④	13	①	14	③	15	②	16	④	17	②	18	④	19	③	20	⑤
21	③	22	①	23	⑤	24	④	25	②	26	④	27	①	28	③	29	⑤	30	②
31	③	32	④	33	⑤	34	①	35	④	36	⑤	37	①	38	②	39	②	40	⑤

01 생활영어 ①

| 분석 |
A가 음식을 주문한 후 B가 추가 주문이 있는지 묻는 상황이다. 빈칸 다음에 이어지는 대화로 보아, 추가 주문 없이 주문을 마무리할 때 쓰는 표현이 나와야 하므로, ①이 정답이다.

| 어휘 |
regular a. 보통의, 일반적인 **That's it** 그게 전부예요 **To go** 포장해서 가져가다 **You're welcome** 천만에요 **appreciate** v. 감사하다

| 해석 |
A: 치즈버거 하나, 보통 사이즈 감자튀김, 그리고 라지 콜라 주세요.
B: 그게 전부인가요?
A: 네, 그게 전부예요.
B: 드시고 가시나요, 아니면 포장이신가요?
A: 포장이요.

① 네, 그게 전부예요.
② 네, 그렇게 할게요.
③ 감사합니다.
④ 천만에요.
⑤ 무슨 뜻이에요?

02 논리완성 ⑤

| 분석 |
이사회가 중요한 결정을 내리기 전에 해야 할 행동을 묻고 있으므로, '신중히 검토하다, 심사숙고하다'라는 의미의 ⑤ deliberate가 정답으로 가장 적절하다. ②의 speculate는 불확실한 증거에 기반하여 추측하는 것을 의미하므로, 빈칸의 문맥에 적절하지 않다.

| 어휘 |
board of directors 이사회 **strategic** a. 전략의, 전략적인 **promulgate** v. 공포하다, 반포하다 **speculate** v. 추측하다, 투기하다 **advocate** v. 옹호하다, 지지하다 **validate** v. 입증하다, 승인하다 **deliberate** v. 숙고하다, 신중히 검토하다

| 해석 |
이사회는 회사의 전략적 방향에 대한 그토록 중대한 변화를 단행하기 전에, 반드시 신중히 검토해야 한다.

03 논리완성 ④

| 분석 |
contingent는 형용사로서는 '~를 조건으로 하는, ~에 따라 결정되는'이라는 의미이며, 명사로서는 '대표단, 파견단, 분견대'라는 의미이므로, ④가 정답이다.

| 어휘 |
security forces 보안 부대, 치안 부대 **contingent upon** ~에 따라 결정되는, ~을 조건으로 하는 **contingent** n. 대표단, 분견대 **dependent on** ~에 의존하는 **suitable** a. 적절한 **concomitant** a. 수반되는 **congruent** a. 조화된, 적합한

| 해석 |
모든 결제는 만족스러운 완료 날짜에 따라 결정된다.
영국 파견대가 보안군을 돕기 위해 파견되었다.

04 논리완성 ①

| 분석 |
haunt는 '괴롭히다, (생각·기억 등이) 뇌리를 떠나지 않다, 사로잡다'는 의미로, 폭풍이 해안 지역을 계속해서 괴롭히는 상황과, 과거의 비극적 사건들이 노인의 기억 속에 떠돌며 괴롭히는 상황, 둘 다에 적절하다.

| 어휘 |
haunt v. 괴롭히다, (생각 · 기억 등이) 뇌리를 떠나지 않다, 사로잡다

persist v. 고집하다, 지속되다　conduct v. 수행하다, 시행하다
occupy v. 차지하다, 점령하다　retract v. 철회하다, 취소하다

| 해석 |
폭풍은 며칠 동안 계속해서 해안 지역을 괴롭혔다.

과거의 비극적 사건들은 여전히 그 노인의 기억에서 떠나지 않고 있다.

05　논리완성　③

| 분석 |
keen은 '치열한, 열정적인'의 의미로, 대학 입학을 위한 치열한 경쟁과 톰이 골프에 매우 열정적이라는 두 상황 모두에 적절하다. 두 번째 문장의 (as) keen as mustard는 '매우 열정적인'이라는 의미의 관용구이다.

| 어휘 |
keen a. 치열한, 날카로운, 열정적인　(as) keen as mustard 매우 열심인　crucial a. 중대한, 결정적인　agile a. 민첩한, 기민한　solid a. 단단한, 확실한　hollow a. 속이 빈, 공허한

| 해석 |
그 대학에 들어가기 위한 치열한 경쟁이 있다.

톰은 골프에 매우 열심이지만, 그리 실력 있는 선수는 아니다.

06　논리완성　④

| 분석 |
pen은 명사로서 '교도소, 구치소'라는 의미, 동사로서 '(가축을) 우리에 넣다, 가두다'라는 의미, 둘 다로 사용되므로, ④가 정답이다. 첫 번째 문장에서는 '교도소'라는 의미의 명사로, 두 번째 문장에서는 '(양을) 우리에 가두다'라는 의미의 동사로 사용되었다.

| 어휘 |
armed robbery 무장 강도　practice n. 관행　clipping n. 깎기, 잘라내기　pen n. 교도소, 구치소　v. 우리에 가두다　jail n. 감옥　v. 투옥하다　penitentiary n. 교도소　lead v. 이끌다, 안내하다　function n. 기능　v. 기능하다

| 해석 |
그는 무장 강도죄로 교도소에 보내졌다.

양털을 깎기 위해 양을 우리에 가두는 것이 관행이었다.

07　논리완성　②

| 분석 |
scrupulously는 '꼼꼼하게, 면밀하게'라는 의미로, 학자가 텍스트의 모든 뉘앙스를 꼼꼼하게 분석하는 것과 탐정이 복잡한 속임수의 망을 면밀하게 풀어내는 것 모두에 적절하다. 두 상황 모두 세심하고 철저한 분석을 필요로 한다는 공통점이 있다.

| 어휘 |
dissect v. 분석하다, 해부하다; 분석하다　unravel v. 풀다, 해결하다　deception n. 사기, 기만　scrupulously ad. 꼼꼼하게, 면밀하게, 양심적으로　ostensibly ad. 표면상으로, 겉보기에는　perpetually ad. 영원히, 끊임없이　mischievously ad. 장난스럽게, 악의적으로　anemically ad. 무기력하게, 빈혈증상으로

| 해석 |
그 학자는 텍스트의 모든 뉘앙스를 꼼꼼하게 분석했다.

그 탐정은 복잡한 속임수의 망을 면밀하게 풀어냈다.

08　논리완성　⑤

| 분석 |
loud는 '(목소리·태도가) 시끄러운, 요란한' 혹은 '(색상이) 화려한, 눈에 띄는'의 의미를 갖는 표현이므로, 두 문장에서 모두 적절하게 사용될 수 있다.

| 어휘 |
loud mouth 수다쟁이, 떠버리, 허풍선이　have a loud mouth 끊임없이 시끄럽게 말하다　foul a. 불쾌한, 상스러운　watery a. 물기가 많은, 창백한　loud a. (목소리가) 요란한, 시끄러운; (색깔이) 화려한, 눈에 띄는　steer clear of ~을 피하다　compete v. 경쟁하다　bride n. 신부

| 해석 |
그는 몇 개의 메달이 있었고 수다쟁이였다.

신부와 경쟁하지 않기 위해 흰색이나 화려한 색상의 옷을 피하라.

09　논리완성　③

| 분석 |
susceptible은 '영향을 받기 쉬운, 취약한, 민감한'이라는 의미로, 또래 집단의 압력과 기후 변화, 둘 다에 대해서 적절하게 사용될 수 있다.

| 어휘 |
adolescent n. 청소년　susceptible 영향을 받기 쉬운, 취약한, 민감한　peer pressure 또래 집단의 압력　congenial a. 같은 성질인, 기분 좋은　dissident a. 반대하는　n. 반체제 인사　adaptable a. 적응할 수 있는, 융통성 있는　nonchalant a. 태연한, 무관심한

| 해석 |
많은 청소년들은 또래 집단의 압력에 영향을 받기 쉽다고 느낀다.

해안 지역은 특히 기후 변화의 영향에 취약하다.

10 논리완성 ②

| 분석 |

abstruse는 '난해한, 이해하기 어려운'이라는 의미로, 작품의 주제와 양자역학 방정식, 둘 다에 대해서 적절하게 사용될 수 있다.

| 어휘 |

increasingly ad. 점점 더   explore v. 탐구하다, 조사하다   theme n. 주제   mortality n. 죽음, 사망률   existence n. 존재, 생존   quantum mechanics 양자역학   equation n. 방정식, 공식   advanced a. 고급의, 상급의   dormant a. 휴면기의, 활동을 중단한   abstruse a. 난해한, 이해하기 어려운   moribund a. 소멸 직전의, 다 죽어가는   ephemeral a. 일시적인, 덧없는   amenable a. 순응하는, 잘 받아들이는

| 해석 |

그 예술가의 후기 작품들은 죽음과 존재라는 주제를 탐구하면서 점점 더 난해해졌다.

양자역학 방정식은 고급 수학 교육을 받지 않은 대부분의 사람들에게 여전히 난해하다.

11 정비문 ①

| 분석 |

① 관계대명사의 선행사가 사람인 a traitor이지만, be동사의 보어 역할을 하고 있고 계속적 용법으로 사용되었으므로, which가 어법상 적절하다. ② 선행사 something을 수식하는 주격 관계대명사 자리에는 that을 사용해야 한다. 관계대명사 what은 the thing that의 의미로 선행사를 포함하고 있으므로 주어진 문장의 자리에 쓸 수 없다. ③ 관계대명사의 선행사가 사람인 the brilliant dancer이지만, be동사의 보어 역할을 하고 있으므로, who를 that 혹은 which로 고쳐야 한다. 생략도 가능하다. ④ 선행사 book이 사물이므로 관계대명사 who 대신 that 또는 which를 사용해야 한다. ⑤ 관계대명사절 안에서 we hope가 삽입절, will hope가 동사이므로, 목적격 관계대명사 whom을 주격 관계대명사 who로 고쳐야 한다.

| 어휘 |

accuse A of B A를 B의 혐의로 비난하다   traitor n. 배신자, 반역자   disturb v. 방해하다, 어지럽히다   brilliant a. 뛰어난, 훌륭한   trustworthy a. 신뢰할 수 있는

| 해석 |

① 그들은 그를 반역자라고 비난했으며, 그는 실제로 반역자였다.
② 이것은 어쨌든 나를 방해할 것이 아니다.
③ 그녀는 예전만큼 뛰어난 댄서가 아니다.
④ 네가 지난달에 주문한 책이 도착했다.
⑤ 그 남자는, 곧 도착하기를 우리가 바라고 있는데, 신뢰할 수 있다.

12 정비문 ④

| 분석 |

④ 부정대명사 one이 앞에서 언급된 가산명사 a drink를 대신하며 적절하게 사용되었다. ① another's coat는 '또 다른 한 사람의 코트'라는 뜻으로 '그녀 아닌 다른 사람의 코트'라는 뜻이 되지 않는다. 따라서 another's를 someone else's로 고쳐야 한다. another는 어떤 한 사람(one)을 전제하므로 One's gain is another's loss.에서처럼 쓰일 수는 있다. ② 주어 some of the rolls에서 rolls가 복수 명사이므로, 동사도 복수동사 have를 사용해야 한다. ③ all of 뒤에 명사가 나올 경우, 명사 앞에 한정사인 정관사나 지시형용사나 소유격이 있어야 한다. All of boys를 All of the boys로 고쳐야 한다. ⑤ 주어가 부정대명사 one인 경우, 부가의문문에서 one 대신 he나 she를 사용해야 한다. 따라서 The cautious one can't be too careful, can he/she?로 고쳐야 한다.

| 어휘 |

roll n. (음식) 롤빵, 두루마리   cautious a. 신중한, 조심스러운   cannot ~ too … 아무리 ~해도 지나침이 없다

| 해석 |

① 그녀는 다른 사람의 코트를 가지고 있다.
② 롤빵 중 몇 개를 먹었다.
③ 그 소년들은 모두 축구 선수가 되고 싶어 한다.
④ 나는 음료수를 하나 마시고 있어. 너도 하나 마실래?
⑤ 신중한 사람이 아무리 조심해도 지나치지 않아, 그렇지 않니?

13 정비문 ①

| 분석 |

① It is strange that it turned out that way.에서 가주어 It와 be동사 is가 생략된 문장으로 어법상 적절하다. ② 부사 Strangely가 문장을 수식할 수는 있지만, 뒤의 how she still likes him이 완전한 문장이 아니므로, 어법상 부적절하다. 부사 Strangely를 그대로 쓰고 how를 삭제하여 Strangely, she still likes him.으로 하거나, 형용사로 고쳐 It is strange how she still likes him.이나 Strange how she still likes him.이나 What is strange is how she still likes him.으로 고치면 어법상 적절한 문장이 된다. ③ Longly는 일반적으로 사용되지 않는 부사이므로, His long hair played in the breeze.로 고쳐야 한다. ④ 형용사 aggressive가 단독으로 서술적 용법으로 사용되는 것은 어색하므로, The man restrained the aggressive woman.으로 고쳐야 한다. ⑤ 형용사 quiet가 단독으로 서술적 용법으로 사용되는 것은 어색하므로, She glanced with disgust at the quiet cat.으로 고쳐야 한다.

| 어휘 |

turn out 결국은 ~이 되다   restrain v. 억제하다, 제지하다   aggressive a. 공격적인   disgust n. 혐오, 역겨움

| 해석 |

① 일이 그렇게 된 것은 이상하다.
② 이상하게도, 어떻게 그녀가 그를 여전히 좋아하는지.
③ 그의 긴 머리카락이 바람에 흩날렸다.
④ 그 남자가 공격적인 여자를 제지했다.
⑤ 그녀가 조용한 고양이를 혐오스럽게 쳐다보았다.

14 정비문 ③

| 분석 |

③ He is being careful.은 "그는 신중하게 행동하고 있다."라는 의미로, 현재진행시제를 사용하여 신중함이 일시적인 상태임을 강조하고 있다. ① tall은 일시적인 상태가 아니라 지속적인 특성이므로, be 동사를 진행형으로 할 수 없다. 따라서 He is tall.로 고쳐야 한다. ② move가 자동사, about이 전치사이므로, about을 명사(the town) 앞에 사용해야 한다. 따라서 He was moving about the town.으로 고쳐야 한다. ④ walked가 자동사, past가 전치사이므로, past를 명사(the car) 앞에 사용해야 한다. 따라서 He walked past the car.로 고쳐야 한다. ⑤ take to는 '~을 좋아하게 되다'는 의미의 숙어이고 to가 전치사이므로, to를 명사(John) 앞에 사용해야 한다. 따라서 They took to John quickly.로 고쳐야 한다.

| 어휘 |

past prep. ~을 지나서 **take to** ~을 좋아하게 되다

| 해석 |

① 그는 키가 크다.
② 그는 마을을 돌아다니고 있었다.
③ 그는 지금 조심하고 있다.
④ 그는 차를 지나쳐 걸어갔다.
⑤ 그들은 존을 빠르게 좋아하게 되었다.

15 정비문 ②

| 분석 |

② 'had best+동사원형'은 '~하는 것이 가장 좋다, ~해야 한다'라는 의미의 관용표현이므로, forgot을 forget으로 고쳐야 한다. ① 'had better+동사원형'은 '~하는 것이 좋겠다'라는 의미의 관용적인 표현이며, 동사원형 stay가 올바르게 사용되었다. ③ 'would sooner+동사원형'은 '차라리 ~하고 싶다'는 의미의 관용적인 표현이며, 동사원형 stay가 올바르게 사용되었다. ④ 'would rather+동사원형'은 '차라리 ~하겠다'는 의미의 관용적인 표현이며, 부정문은 'would rather not+동사원형'으로 표현한다. 따라서 not의 위치도 맞고 동사원형 commit도 올바르게 사용되었다. ⑤ 'I'd rather+주어+과거형 동사'는 '나는 ~가 …했으면 좋겠다'라는 의미의 가정법 표현이며, 과거형 동사 pulled가 올바르게 사용되었다.

| 어휘 |

commit oneself (공개적으로) 의사를 밝히다, 태도를 밝히다 **pull an all-nighter** 밤샘 공부를 하다

| 해석 |

① 나는 지금 가는 게 좋겠다.
② 너는 그 일을 전부 잊어버리는 것이 가장 좋다.
③ 나는 오늘 밤 차라리 집에 있고 싶다.
④ 그는 자신의 의사를 밝히지 않기를 원한다.
④ 나는 네가 시험을 위해 밤 새워 공부하기를 바란다.

16 정비문 ③

| 분석 |

③ worth는 뒤에 동명사를 수반하여 '~할 가치가 있는'의 뜻을 나타내므로, to be repaired를 repairing으로 고쳐야 한다. ① many의 최상급 표현인 the most가 올바르게 사용되었다. ② deny는 동명사를 목적어로 취하며, 과거(denied) 이전의 일을 나타내는 완료형 동명사(having taken)가 올바르게 사용되었다. ④ 'suggest that+주어+(should)+동사원형' 구문이므로, 동사원형 leave가 올바르게 사용되었다. ⑤ 'go so far as to+동사원형'은 '심지어 ~하기까지 하다'라는 의미의 관용표현이며, 동사원형 claim이 올바르게 사용되었다.

| 어휘 |

go so far as to do 심지어 ~하기까지 하다

| 해석 |

① 그녀가 가장 많은 블랙베리를 찾았다.
② 그는 그 돈을 가져갔다는 것을 부인했다.
③ 이 차는 수리할만한 가치가 없다.
③ 그는 즉시 떠나라는 제안을 받고 있다.
⑤ 그녀는 심지어 자신이 무죄라고 주장하기까지 했다.

17 정비문 ②

| 분석 |

장소 부사어가 문두에 오고 동사가 자동사일 때 주어와 동사가 도치될 수 있는데, 타동사일 때는 도치가 일어나지 않고 '주어+동사' 어순이므로 ⑤는 맞는 문장이다. 그런데 자동사 중에 roll(구르다, 굴리다), dance(춤추다, 춤추게 하다), run(달리다, 달리게 하다)처럼 자동사와 타동사로 모두 쓰일 수 있는 동사(능격ergative 동사)가 자동사로 쓰일 때는 ①, ③, ④에서처럼 도치가 일어날 수 있지만, sleep(잠자다)처럼 자동사로만 쓰이고(동족목적어를 취하는 경우는 예외) 주어가 동사의 행위 주체인 동사(비능격unergative 동사)일 경우는 도치가 일어나지 않는다. 따라서 ②는 In the room, Robin slept. 혹은 Robin slept in the room.으로 고쳐야 한다. 이런 비능격동사에는 laugh도 있다.

| 어휘 |
hill n. 언덕   roll v. 구르다   barn n. 외양간, 헛간

| 해석 |
① 언덕 아래로 공이 굴러 내려갔다.
② 방 안에서 Robin이 잠을 잤다.
③ 불 주위에서 여자들이 춤을 추었다.
④ 외양간 밖으로 검은 말이 뛰어나왔다.
⑤ 정원에서 Nik이 놀이 집을 지었다.

18 정비문   ④

| 분석 |
④ 현재완료시제가 사용된 문장에서 과거의 시점 이후를 표현할 때 접속사 since를 사용하므로, when을 since로 고쳐야 한다. ① 가까운 미래에 예정되어 있는 일은 현재진행시제를 사용하여 나타내고, first thing은 '무엇보다도 먼저, 맨 처음에'를 의미하는 관용표현이다. ② 과거에 진행 중이었던 일을 나타내고 있으며, just feet away from은 '~로부터 불과 몇 피트 떨어진 곳에서'라는 의미이다. 여기서 feet는 a few feet의 의미이다. just meters away from도 마찬가지이다. ③ He waved his hand at me, and he obviously meant me to leave.에서 and he가 삭제되고 동사 meant가 현재분사 meaning으로 바뀐 분사구문이다. ⑤ 주격 관계대명사 which가 사물 선행사 a mill을 올바르게 수식하고 있으며, formerly가 과거시제와 잘 쓰였다.

| 어휘 |
first thing 무엇보다도 먼저, 맨 처음에   bullet n. 총알   wave at ~을 향해 손을 흔들다   obviously ad. 명백하게   mean A to do A가 ~하기를 의도하다   formerly ad. 이전에

| 해석 |
① 나는 내일 아침에 무엇보다 먼저 런던으로 갈 것이다.
② 총알이 우리로부터 불과 몇 피트 떨어진 거리에 떨어지고 있었다.
③ 그는 내게 손을 흔들면서, 나더러 떠나라는 뜻을 분명히 전달했다.
④ 나는 네가 너의 옛집을 떠난 후에 그곳에 딱 한 번 가봤다.
⑤ 그 돌들은 이전에 이 부지에 있던 방앗간에서 나온 것이다.

19 정비문   ③

| 분석 |
③ 의문문에서 전치사와 의문형용사를 분리할 수도 있고 결합할 수도 있지만, The president of which country was she?처럼 '의문사'도 아니고 '전치사+의문사'도 아닌 명사가 문두에 나가는 것은 어법상 부적절하다. ①이나 ②처럼 사용하는 것이 어법에 맞다. ① 의문문에서 전치사 of와 의문형용사 which가 분리될 수 있으므로, 어법상 적절하다. ② 의문문에서 전치사 of가 의문형용사 which와 함께 결합되어 사용 가능하므로, 어법상 적절하다. ④ 의문문에서 전치사 in이 의문형용사 what과 분리될 수 있으므로, 어법상 적절하다. ⑤ 의문문에서 전치사 in이 의문형용사 what과 함께 결합되어 사용 가능하므로, 어법상 적절하다.

| 어휘 |
president n. 대통령   subject n. 과목, 주제   be interested in ~에 관심이 있다

| 해석 |
① 그녀는 어느 나라의 대통령이었니?
② 그는 어느 나라의 대통령이었니?
③ 그녀는 어느 나라의 대통령이었니?
④ 너는 어떤 과목에 관심이 있니?
⑤ 너는 어떤 과목에 관심이 있니?

20 정비문   ⑤

| 분석 |
⑤ 목적격 보어가 있는 경우에 that절은 목적어로 사용할 수 없다. 'find+가목적어(it)+목적격 보어+진목적어(that절)' 구문이 되어야 어법상 적절하므로, I find it hardly surprising that he tried to retract his statement.로 고쳐야 한다. ① 'owe A to B'는 'A를 B 덕분으로 돌리다'는 의미의 관용표현이며, 가목적어(it)와 진목적어(that절)가 올바르게 사용되었다. ② '~라고 생각하다, ~라고 간주하다'라는 의미의 'take it that S+V' 구문에서 접속사 that이 올바르게 생략되었다. ③ 'make+목적어+형용사'의 5형식 구문에서, 형용사 glad 다음에 접속사 that이 생략되었다. had stayed는 과거 이전의 일을 표현하는 과거완료시제로 올바르게 사용되었다. ④ 'regard A as B'는 'A를 B로 간주하다'는 의미의 관용표현이며, 가목적어(it)와 진목적어(that절)가 올바르게 사용되었다.

| 어휘 |
owe A to B A를 B 덕분으로 돌리다   get off lightly 가벼운 처벌을 받다, 가볍게 모면하다   take it that ~라고 여기다, ~라고 간주하다   regard A as B A를 B로 간주하다   discourtesy n. 무례함, 실례   notify v. 알리다, 통보하다   retract v. (합의·약속 등을) 철회하다, 취소하다   statement n. 진술, 성명   hardly ad. 거의 ~않다   surprising a. 놀라운

| 해석 |
① 우리가 가벼운 처벌을 받은 것은 네 덕분이다.
② 나는 네가 그들의 제안을 받아들일 거라고 생각한다.
③ 이것 덕분에 나는 집에 남아 있길 잘했다고 느끼게 되었다.
④ 그들은 네가 더 일찍 알리지 않은 것을 실례라고 여긴다.
⑤ 나는 그가 자신의 진술을 철회하려 했다는 것이 놀랍지 않다.

21 정비문 ③

| 분석 |

③ '~인지 아닌지'를 나타낼 때, 전치사(on) 뒤에는 if가 아닌 whether가 와야 하므로, It depends on whether we have enough time left.로 고쳐야 한다. ① '~인지 아닌지'를 나타내는 접속사 if가 동사 asked의 직접목적어 자리에서 올바르게 사용되었다. stay to dinner와 stay for dinner, 모두 가능하다. ② '~인지 아닌지'를 나타내는 접속사 if가 동사 know의 목적어 자리에서 올바르게 사용되었다. ④ '~인지 아닌지'를 나타내는 접속사 whether가 동사 know의 목적어 자리에서 올바르게 사용되었다. ⑤ '~인지 아닌지'를 나타내는 접속사 whether가 동사 is의 보어 자리에서 올바르게 사용되었다.

| 어휘 |

mind v. 꺼려하다 guilt n. 유죄, 죄책감 establish v. 입증하다, 확립하다 beyond doubt 의심의 여지없이

| 해석 |

① 나는 그들에게 저녁 식사를 하고 갈 것인지 물어보았다.
② 그는 네가 차를 옮겨 줄지 알고 싶어 한다.
③ 그것은 우리가 충분한 시간이 있는지 여부에 달려 있다.
④ 나는 그녀가 그 제안을 받아들일지 모르겠다.
⑤ 의심의 여지없이 유죄가 입증되었는지 아닌지가 문제이다.

22 논리완성 ①

| 분석 |

빈칸이 포함된 문장은 장애가 있는 사람들도 이용할 수 있도록 설계된 대중교통 시스템의 긍정적인 특징을 설명하고 있다. 따라서 '접근할 수 있는, 이용 가능한'이라는 의미의 accessible이 가장 적절하다.

| 어휘 |

urban planning 도시 계획 increasingly ad. 점점 더, 갈수록 inclusive a. 포괄적인, 배제하지 않는 unveil v. 공개하다, 발표하다 step forward 진보, 발전 accessible a. 접근 가능한, 이용 가능한 incorporate v. 포함하다, 통합하다 feature n. 특징, 특성, 기능 wheelchair-friendly a. 휠체어 이용자에게 친화적인 tactile paving 점자 블록 visually impaired 시각 장애가 있는 audio announcement 음성 안내 digital display 디지털 화면 ensure v. 보장하다, 확실하게 하다 hostile a. 적대적인, 반대하는; 냉담한 detrimental a. 해로운, 불리한 negligent a. 태만한, 부주의한 averse a. 싫어하는, 반대하는

| 해석 |

현대 도시 계획에서는 사회 구성원 모두를 위한 포괄적인 공간을 조성하는 것의 중요성이 점점 더 강조되고 있다. 최근 공개된 이 도시의 대중교통 시스템은 이러한 방향으로 나아가는 중요한 발전을 보여준다. 이 시스템은 다양한 유형의 장애를 가진 사람들이 이용할 수 있도록 설계되었으며, 휠체어 이용자를 위한 경사로, 시각 장애인을 위한 점자 블록, 여러 언어로 제공되는 명확한 음성 안내, 읽기 쉬운 디지털 디스플레이 등의 기능을 통합하여, 모든 사람이 편리하게 대중교통을 이용할 수 있도록 보장한다.

① 접근 가능한, 이용 가능한
② 적대적인, 반대하는
③ 해로운, 불리한
④ 태만한, 부주의한
⑤ 싫어하는, 반대하는

23 논리완성 ⑤

| 분석 |

관중들도 가득한 경기장에서 자신이 응원하는 팀이 승리하면, 팀을 응원하면서 기분이 좋아지고, 정체성이 강화된다는 긍정적인 맥락이다. affirmed가 '긍정되는, 확인되는'이라는 의미로, 응원을 통해 자신의 정체성이 더욱 긍정적으로 확인됨을 나타내므로 빈칸에 적절하다. 열정이 상승하고 기분이 고조된다는 맥락에서 볼 때, 기존 상태가 그대로 유지된다는 의미의 maintained는 부적절하다.

| 어휘 |

suppose v. 가정하다, 생각하다 present a. 존재하는, 참석한 packed a. 가득 찬, 붐비는 arena n. 경기장, 공연장 roar v. 함성을 지르다, 포효하다 enthusiasm n. 열광, 열정 spike v. 급격히 증가하다 animosity n. 적대감, 반감 intensify v. 강화하다, 심해지다 elevate v. 향상시키다, 고양하다 identity n. 정체성, 신원 affirm v. 확인하다, 확증하다 cheering n. 응원, 환호 challenge v. 도전하다, 의문을 제기하다 deny v. 부인하다, 거부하다 maintain v. 유지하다, 지속하다 deteriorate v. 나쁘게 하다

| 해석 |

관중들로 가득 찬 경기장에서 당신이 좋아하는 팀이 홈경기에서 승리하는 모습을 보고 있다고 가정해 보자. 당신이 동료 팬들과 함께 함성을 지를 때, 모든 사람의 팀에 대한 열정이 급격히 상승한다. 동시에, 상대 팀과 그 팬들에 대한 적대감도 강해진다. 당신의 기분은 고조되고, 당신의 정체성은 더욱 확고해진다. 동료 팬들과 함께 응원하는 것은 우리 자신에 대해 더 좋은 느낌이 들게 만든다.

① 도전받은, 의문이 제기된
② 부정된, 거부된
③ 유지된, 지속된
④ 악화된, 저하된
⑤ 긍정된, 확인된

24 논리완성 ④

| 분석 |

빈칸 앞에서 중국의 경제적 중심성이 빠르게 성장하고 있다고 언급

했으므로, 선진국들이 관리해야 할 중국의 특성으로는 '재부상, 부활'이라는 의미의 resurgence가 가장 적절하다.

| 어휘 |

diplomatic standing 외교적 지위, 외교적 입지 **decline** v. 하락하다, 감소하다 **economic centrality** 경제적 중심성 **apace** ad. 빠르게, 신속하게 **orient** v. 방향을 맞추다, 초점을 맞추다 **collective agenda** 공동 의제 **counterbalance** v. 대항하다, 균형을 맞추다 **amplify** v. 증폭시키다, 확대하다 **front** n. 전선, 영역 **widespread** a. 광범위한 **sustained** a. 지속적인, 계속되는 **coordination** n. 조정, 협력 **global supply chain** 글로벌 공급망 **technology standard** 기술 표준 **resurgence** n. 재부상, 부활 **retreat** n. 후퇴, 철수 **resistance** n. 저항, 반발 **resurgence** n. 재부상, 부활 **restructuring** n. 구조 조정, 재편

| 해석 |

중국의 외교적 입지가 선진국 대부분에서 하락하고 있는데도, 중국의 경제적 중심성은 빠르게 성장하고 있다. 실제로, 만약 선진국들이 그들의 집단적 공동 의제를 중국의 영향력에 대항하는 것을 중심으로 너무 좁게 정한다면, 그들은 각자의 접근 방식 간의 차이를 증폭시킬 위험이 있다. 그러나 그들이 중국의 재부상을 관리하기 위해 더 광범위하고 지속적인 협력을 아마도 적절하게 추구해갈 전선(영역)이 적어도 몇 가지 있는데, 그 중 가장 중요한 것에는 글로벌 공급망과 기술 표준이 있다.

① 존중, 경의
② 후퇴, 철수
③ 저항, 반발
④ 재부상, 부활
⑤ 구조 조정, 재편

25 논리완성 ②

| 분석 |

빈칸 앞에서 기업들이 안전한 클라우드 환경에서 데이터를 보호하는 것에 대해 설명하고 있다. 그리고 빈칸 뒤의 'encryption protocols(암호화 프로토콜)'도 보안 조치를 강화하는 기능이므로, 빈칸에는 기업들이 클라우드 시스템을 암호화 프로토콜과 병행하여 사용해야 한다는 내용이 나와야 한다. 따라서 ②가 정답이다.

| 어휘 |

transition v. 전환하다, 변화하다 **cloud-based** a. 클라우드 기반의 **data storage** 데이터 저장 **enhanced** a. 강화된, 향상된 **security feature** 보안 기능 **backup** n. 백업, 예비 저장 **encryption protocol** 암호화 프로토콜 **sophisticated** a. 정교한, 복잡한 **security measure** 보안 조치 **convert** v. 변환하다, 전환하다 **sensitive information** 기밀 정보, 민감한 정보 **coded text** 암호화된 텍스트 **decode** v. 해독하다, 풀다 **authentication key** 인증키 **deploy** v. 사용하다 **in parallel with** ~와 병행하여 **evaluate** v. 평가하다 **cost-effectiveness** n. 비용 효율성 **implement** v. 실행하다 **coordinate** v. 조정하다, 협력하다 **assessment** n. 평가

| 해석 |

오늘날 많은 조직들은 강화된 보안 기능과 정기적인 백업을 제공하는 클라우드 기반 데이터 저장 솔루션으로 전환하고 있다. 이러한 솔루션은 민감한 데이터에 다양한 수준의 보호를 제공한다. 그들의 클라우드 환경에서 최대한의 데이터 보호를 보장하기 위해, 기업들은 일반적으로 이런 보안 시스템을 암호화 프로토콜과 병행하여 사용하는데, 암호화 프로토콜은 민감한 정보를 암호화된 텍스트로 변환하여 특정 인증키로만 해독할 수 있게 하는 정교한 보안 조치 역할을 한다.

① ~의 비용 효율성을 평가하다
② ~과 병행하여 이러한 시스템을 사용하다
③ ~대신 이러한 기능들을 실행하다
④ ~과 대조하여 보안 평가를 조정하다
⑤ ~에 기반하여 그들의 의존도를 줄이다

26 논리완성 ④

| 분석 |

NewJeans가 ADOR와 법적 분쟁을 시작했기 때문에, 법적 판결이 나기 전까지 NewJeanz라는 이름을 사용할 수 있을지 불확실한 상황이다. 따라서 '미정인, 불확실한, 결정되지 않은'이라는 의미의 up in the air가 정답으로 가장 적절하다.

| 어휘 |

hung up on ~에 집착하는, 신경 쓰는 **go with** ~에 부속되다, 속하다, 선택하다 **set up** 설립하다, 개설하다 **upload** v. 업로드하다, 게시하다 **just in case** 만약 ~한 경우를 대비하여 **things go south** 상황이 악화되다 **file for** ~을 신청하다, 청구하다 **sign to** (소속사와) 계약을 맺다 **patent** n. 특허, 특허권 **approve** v. 승인하다, 허가하다 **legal dispute** 법적 분쟁 **deliver a decision** 판결을 내리다 **up in the air** 미정인, 불확실한 **on cloud nine** 매우 행복한, 기분 좋은 **under the belt** 경험한, 소지한 **out of the blue** 갑자기, 예기치 않게 **under influence** (술이나 약물 등의) 영향을 받아

| 해석 |

팬들은 그 가수들이 NewJeanz라는 이름을 선택할 수 있는 가능성에 대해 매우 신경 쓰고 있는데, 다섯 멤버는 NewJeanz라는 이름으로 새로운 인스타그램 계정을 만들고, 새 콘텐츠를 업로드하기 시작했다. 심지어 The Boyz도 혹시라도 상황이 나빠질 경우를 대비해 The Boys라는 이름으로 새 출발을 준비하고 있었다. One Hundred Label은 The Boyz가 여전히 IST 엔터테인먼트에 소속되어 있을 때 The Boys라는 이름에 대한 상표권을 출원했으나, 해당 특허는 아직 당국의 승인을 받지 못했다. NewJeans는 이제 막 ADOR과 법적 분쟁을 시작한 상황이므로, 법원이 판결을 내리기 전까지 그 이름을 사용하는 것은 미정이다.

① 매우 행복한, 기분 좋은
② 이미 경험한, 소지한
③ 갑자기, 예기치 않게
④ 미정인, 불확실한
⑤ (술이나 약물 등의) 영향을 받아

27 내용일치 ①

| 분석 |

장미, 라일락, 핑크 가시나무, 그리고 나도싸리 꽃의 강렬하고 다양한 꽃향기가 공기를 가득 채우는 장면을 묘사하고 있으므로, ① '여러 꽃의 향기가 공기를 가득 채운다'가 정답이다. ② 'light summer wind(가벼운 여름 바람)'이라는 표현을 통해 겨울이 아닌 여름임을 알 수 있다. ③ 라일락의 강한 향이 열린 문을 통해 들어왔다는 말을 통해, 스튜디오와 정원이 연결되어 있음을 알 수 있다. ④ 정원에서 일하는 것이 아니라, 소파에 누워서 담배를 피우고 있다고 했다. ⑤ Henry Wotton 경은 창가에 서 있는 것이 아니라, 소파에 누워 있다.

| 어휘 |

odor n. 향기, 냄새 **stir** v. 움직이다, 휘젓다 **amid** prep. ~의 한가운데에서 **scent** n. 향기, 냄새 **perfume** n. 향수, 향기 **divan** n. 긴 의자, 소파 **saddle-bag** n. (말안장 양옆에 다는) 안장 가방 **innumerable** a. 무수한, 셀 수 없는 **gleam** v. 반짝이다, 환하다 **honey-sweet** a. 꿀처럼 달콤한 **honey-colored** a. 꿀빛의 **laburnum** n. 나도싸리(노란 꽃송이가 늘어지게 피는 작은 나무) **tremulous** a. 떨리는, 흔들리는 **burden** n. 부담, 짐 **flamelike** a. 불꽃같은, 강렬한

| 해석 |

스튜디오는 짙은 장미 향기로 가득 찼고, 가벼운 여름 바람이 정원의 나무들 사이를 휘젓고 지나갈 때, 라일락의 진한 향기나 분홍빛 꽃이 피는 가시나무의 더 섬세한 향기가 열린 문을 통해 들어왔다. Henry Wotton 경은 자신이 습관처럼 끝없이 담배를 피우며 누워 있던 페르시안 안장 가방으로 만든 소파의 구석으로부터, 꿀처럼 달콤하고 꿀 색을 띤 노란 나도싸리 꽃들의 반짝임을 간신히 볼 수 있었는데, 나도싸리 나무의 떨리는 가지들은 자기들의 아름다움만큼 불꽃같은 아름다움의 무게를 거의 감당할 수 없는 것 같았다.

글의 내용과 가장 잘 부합하는 것은?
① 여러 꽃의 향기가 공기를 가득 채운다.
② 이 장면은 겨울 오후를 배경으로 한다.
③ 그 방은 정원과 연결되지 않는다.
④ Henry Wotton 경은 정원에서 일하고 있다.
⑤ Henry Wotton 경은 창가에 서 있다.

28 문장삽입 ③

| 분석 |

밑줄 친 문장은 "이러한 변화에 곤란한 문제가 없었던 것은 아니다", 즉 "어려움도 있었다"는 의미이다. C 앞부분에서는 생산성 증가, 비용 절감, 만족도 향상 등, 원격근무의 장점을 나열하고 있으며, C 이후에는 직원들의 고립감, 관리자의 팀워크 유지 어려움 등, 원격근무의 단점이 등장한다. 따라서 밑줄 친 문장은 내용의 반전이 이루어지는 C에 나오는 것이 가장 자연스럽다.

| 어휘 |

remote work 원격 근무 **fundamentally** ad. 근본적으로 **productivity** n. 생산성 **overhead cost** 고정비용 **implement** v. 실행하다, 도입하다 **work-from-home policy** 재택근무 정책 **job satisfaction** 직무 만족도 **work-life balance** 일과 삶의 균형 **transition** n. 전환, 변화 **complication** n. 곤란한 문제, 복잡한 상황 **struggle with** ~로 어려움을 겪다 **isolation** n. 고립 **additionally** ad. 추가적으로, 게다가 **challenging** a. 어려운, 도전적인 **team cohesion** 팀 결속력 **virtual environment** 가상 환경

| 해석 |

원격근무로의 전환은 많은 기업의 운영 방식을 근본적으로 변화시켰다. 기업들은 원격근무 정책을 도입한 이후 생산성이 증가하고 고정비용이 감소했다고 보고하고 있다. 직원들 또한 전반적으로 더 높은 직무 만족도와 개선된 워라밸을 보고한다. 〈이러한 변화에 곤란한 문제가 없었던 것은 아니다.〉 많은 근로자가 고립감에 힘겨워 하며, 업무와 개인 생활을 분리하는 데 어려움을 겪고 있다. 또한, 일부 관리자들은 가상 환경에서 팀의 결속력과 기업 문화를 유지하는 것이 어렵다고 느낀다.

29 내용일치 ⑤

| 분석 |

Bingley는 Jane을 처음 보고 즉각적인 호감을 보였고, Darcy는 Elizabeth를 처음 보고 무시했지만, 이 차이가 두 사람의 성격 차이를 반영한다고 명확하게 언급하지 않았으므로, ⑤가 정답이다. ① 재산 상속 문제가 결혼에 대한 집착의 일부 동기가 된다는 내용이 명확하게 제시되어 있다. ② Elizabeth의 Darcy에 대한 편견이 그의 첫 모욕과 후속 행동에서 비롯되었다고 진술되어 있다. ③ 재산은 사회적 지위를 결정하며, 딸들이 미혼인 채로 남편이 죽으면 재산이 남편의 먼 친척에게 상속될 예정이라고 진술되어 있다. ④ Bingley와 Jane의 관계가 Darcy의 개입으로 방해를 받았다고 진술되어 있다.

| 어휘 |

rural a. 시골의, 지방의 **modest** a. 별로 많지 않은 **estate** n. 재산, 토지, 소유지 **inherit** v. 상속받다, 물려받다 **distant** a. 먼, 관계가 먼 **prospect** n. 가능성, 전망 **residence** n. 거주지, 저택 **immediate liking** n. 즉각적인 호감 **snub** v. 무시하다, 퇴짜 놓다 **dismiss** v. 묵살하다, 일축하다 **tolerable** a. 그럭저럭 괜찮은, 참을 만한 **aversion** n. 혐오, 반감 **slight** n. 모욕, 경멸 **reinforce** v. 강화하다, 뒷받침하다 **apparent** a. 분명한, 명백한 **intervention**

n. 개입, 간섭   **prejudice** n. 편견, 선입견   **precarious** a. 불안정한, 위태로운

| 해석 |

제인 오스틴의 『오만과 편견』은 시골 마을 Longbourn에서 시작되며, 이곳에서 Bennet 가족이 다섯 명의 미혼 딸과 함께 살고 있다. Bennet 부인의 가장 큰 소망은 모든 딸들이 결혼하는 것을 보는 것이며, 특히 남편이 사망할 경우, 가문의 별로 많지 않은 재산이 먼 친척인 남성에게 상속될 예정이기 때문에 더욱 그렇다. 한편, 부유한 Bingley씨가 근처의 저택에 거주하게 되자, Bennet 부인은 딸 중 한 명이 그와 결혼할 가능성에 대한 기대감으로 설렌다. 무도회에서 Bingley는 큰딸 Jane에게 즉각적인 호감을 보이지만, Bingley의 친구인 Darcy는 둘째 딸 Elizabeth를 "그럭저럭 괜찮은" 정도라고 하며 무시한다. Elizabeth는 이 경멸의 말을 듣고 즉각적인 반감을 가진다. 이후 Darcy의 행동과 그가 Bingley를 사랑하는 언니 Jane으로부터 떼어놓으려는 것처럼 보인 것으로 인해, Darcy의 오만에 대한 그녀의 좋지 못한 첫인상이 더욱 강화된다.

글의 내용과 부합하지 않는 것은?
① Bennet 부인이 딸들의 결혼을 걱정하는 것은 부분적으로 상속과 관련된 불안감에서 비롯된다.
② Elizabeth가 Darcy에게 처음 편견을 갖게 된 것은 그의 직접적인 모욕과 이후의 행동 때문이다.
③ Bennet 가족의 사회적 지위는 재산 상속 방식 때문에 불안정해 보인다.
④ Bingley와 Jane의 잠재적인 관계는 Darcy의 개입으로 인해 방해를 받는다.
⑤ Bingley와 Darcy가 Bennet 자매들에게 가졌던 첫인상이 대조되는 것은 그들의 상반된 성격을 반영한다.

30 내용일치   ②

| 분석 |

세 명의 우주비행사 중 Michael Collins는 사령선에 남아 있었고, 달에 착륙한 것은 Armstrong과 Aldrin뿐이라고 명확히 서술되어 있으므로, 세 명 모두가 착륙했다고 한 ②가 정답이다.

| 어휘 |

make history 역사적인 순간을 만들다   **launch** v. 발사하다, 시작하다   **spacecraft** n. 우주선   **lunar orbit** 달 궤도   **command module** 사령선   **descend** v. 내려가다, 착륙하다   **lunar module** 달 착륙선   **step onto** ~에 발을 디디다   **astronaut** n. 우주비행사   **lunar surface** 달 표면   **splash down** 착수하다(물 위에 착륙하다)   **Pacific Ocean** 태평양

| 해석 |

아폴로 11호 임무는 1969년 7월 20일 역사적인 순간을 만들어냈다. 7월 16일 케네디 우주센터에서 발사된 후, 그 우주선은 3일 후 달 궤도에 진입했다. Michael Collins가 사령선에 남아 있는 동안, Neil Armstrong과 Buzz Aldrin은 달 착륙선 이글(Eagle)을 타고 달 표면으로 내려갔다. Armstrong은 인류 최초로 달에 발을 디딘 사람이 되었으며, 곧이어 Aldrin이 뒤를 이었다. 두 우주비행사는 약 두 시간 반 동안 달 표면을 탐사한 후 지구로 돌아와, 7월 24일 태평양에 착수(着水)했다.

글의 내용과 부합하지 않는 것은?
① 우주선은 발사 후 3일 뒤 달 궤도에 진입했다.
② 세 명의 우주비행사 모두 달 표면에 착륙했다.
③ 우주선은 태평양에 착수했다.
④ Armstrong은 달에 최초로 발을 디딘 사람이었다.
⑤ 달 표면 탐사는 약 두 시간 반 동안 지속되었다.

31 글의 제목   ③

| 분석 |

DNA 발견에서 Rosalind Franklin의 공헌이 간과되었으며, 최근에서야 인정받고 있다는 것이 글의 요지이므로, 제목에서는 Franklin이 연구에서 중요한 역할을 했으나 처음에는 잊혀졌다는 점을 강조해야 한다. 따라서 ③이 정답으로 가장 적절하다.

| 어휘 |

mark v. 표시하다, 기념하다   **contributor** n. 기여자, 공헌자   **initially** ad. 처음에는   **overlook** v. 간과하다, 무시하다   **X-ray diffraction** X선 회절   **crucial** a. 결정적인, 중요한   **molecule** n. 분자   **helical** a. 나선형의   **consent** n. 동의, 허락   **colleague** n. 동료   **groundbreaking** a. 획기적인, 신기원을 이룬   **paper** n. 논문   **unacknowledged** a. 인정받지 못한   **ovarian cancer** 난소암   **extensive** a. 광범위한   **ineligible** a. 자격이 없는   **award** v. 수여하다   **critical** a. 중요한, 결정적인

| 해석 |

1953년, James Watson과 Francis Crick에 의해 DNA의 구조가 발견된 것은 과학 역사에서 중요한 순간이었다. 그러나 한 명의 핵심 공헌자가 처음에는 간과되었다. Rosalind Franklin의 X선 회절 이미지가, 특히 그녀의 유명한 "Photo 51"이, DNA 분자가 나선형 구조를 가진다는 결정적인 증거를 제공했다. 그러나 Franklin의 동료 Maurice Wilkins는 그녀에게 알리거나 동의를 구하지도 않고 이 이미지를 Watson과 Crick에게 보여주었다. Watson과 Crick은 이를 바탕으로 연구를 진행했다. 그들이 Nature에 획기적인 논문을 발표했을 때, Franklin의 공헌은 인정되지 않았다. 그녀는 아마도 광범위한 X선 연구로 인해 1958년 난소암으로 사망했으며, 그래서 1962년에 Watson, Crick, Wilkins에게 수여된 노벨상의 수상 자격이 없었다. 그녀의 중요한 역할은 최근 몇 십 년 동안에야 비로소 널리 인정받기 시작했다.

글의 제목으로 가장 적절한 것은?
① Watson과 Crick의 DNA 발견
② DNA 분자의 구조
③ DNA 연구의 잊힌 영웅

④ 과학 분야 노벨상 수상자들
⑤ X선 결정학의 역사

32~33

우주에서 생활하는 것은 우주비행사의 정신적, 신체적 건강에 독특한 도전 과제를 제기한다. 국제우주정거장(ISS)의 승무원들은 미세중력이 유발하는 근육 위축과 골 손실을 방지하기 위해 매일 약 두 시간 동안 운동해야 한다. 신체 건강 문제 외에도, 고립과 감금 상태는 심리적 스트레스를 초래할 수 있다. 이를 해결하기 위해, 우주비행사들은 가족과 정기적으로 영상 통화를 하고, 다양한 여가 활동에 참여한다. 또한, 승무원들은 과학 실험, 정거장 유지 보수, 정해진 휴식 시간을 포함하는 엄격한 일과를 따른다. 그럼에도 불구하고, 장기간 우주에 머무르는 것은 여전히 수면 패턴과 전반적인 정신 건강에 영향을 미칠 수 있어 세심한 모니터링이 필수적이다.

| 어휘 |

pose v. (문제·위험 등을) 제기하다   unique a. 독특한, 특별한   challenge n. 도전 과제   astronaut n. 우주비행사   International Space Station 국제우주정거장   crew member 승무원   muscle atrophy 근육 위축   bone loss 골 손실   microgravity n. 미세중력   isolation n. 고립   confinement n. 제한, 감금   bring about ~을 초래하다, 야기하다   address v. 해결하다, 다루다   video contact 화상 연락   participate in ~에 참여하다   station maintenance 우주정거장 유지 보수   designated a. 지정된   measure n. 조치, 대책   extended stay 장기 체류   overall a. 전반적인   take off 이륙하다, 벗다   cut down 줄이다   give away 나눠주다, 기부하다   set aside 따로 떼어 두다, 확보하다   maintenance work 유지 보수 작업   video call 화상 통화   negligible a. 무시할 수 있는, 하찮은

32 빈칸완성 ④

| 분석 |

고립과 감금 상태는 건강 문제를 일으킬 수 있는 부정적인 요인들이므로, 그것이 원인으로 작용해서 심리적 스트레스를 '초래할' 것이라고 추론할 수 있다.

빈칸에 들어가기에 가장 적절한 것은?
① 벗다, 이륙하다
② 줄이다
③ (비밀을) 누설하다, (물건을) 거저 주다
④ 초래하다, 야기하다
⑤ 따로 떼어 두다, 확보하다

33 내용일치 ⑤

| 분석 |

장기간 우주에 머무르는 것은 여전히 수면 패턴과 전반적인 정신 건강에 영향을 미칠 수 있어 세심한 모니터링이 필수적이라고 했으므로, ⑤의 '미미한 영향'이 본문의 내용과 어긋난다.

글의 내용과 부합하지 않는 것은?
① ISS 승무원들은 매일 두 시간 동안 운동을 한다.
② 승무원들은 우주 정거장의 유지 보수 작업을 수행한다.
③ 일과에는 과학 연구를 수행하는 시간이 포함된다.
④ 우주비행사들은 영상 통화를 통해 가족과 소통할 수 있다.
⑤ 장기간 우주 체류는 우주비행사의 수면 패턴에 미미한 영향을 미친다.

34~35

1990년, Patagonia는 Planned Parenthood(가족계획연맹)에 기부를 하여, 기독교 근본주의자들의 분노를 샀다. 반응은 즉각적이었다. 불매운동을 요청했고, 매장 앞에서 시위하겠다고 위협했고, 고객 센터에 불만 전화를 쏟아 부어 전화선을 마비시켰다. 캘리포니아 벤투라에 본사를 둔 이 아웃도어 의류 업체는 항의하는 사람들을 달래려 할 수도 있었을 테지만, 대신, 회사는 고객 서비스 상담원들에게 이렇게 응답하라고 지시했다. "의견을 저희와 공유해 주셔서 감사합니다. 이런 전화 한 통을 받을 때마다, 저희가 Planned Parenthood에 5달러를 추가 기부할 것이라는 것을 알아주셨으면 합니다." "전화가 곧 중단되었지요."라고 Patagonia의 철학 담당 이사인 Vincent Stanley는 회상했다. 그리고 판매는 평소처럼 꾸준히 이어졌다. 기업에게 정치적 문제는 언제나 위험한 지뢰밭과 같았다. 그러나 과거에는 그것이 피할 수 있는 지뢰밭이었다. 30년 전만 해도, 주요 소비자 브랜드(회사)가 논란이 되는 문화 전쟁 이슈에 대해 입장을 밝히는 것은 거의 전례가 없는 일이었다. 하지만 오늘날 기업들은 그냥 무시하기에는 너무 큰 사회적 격변에 의해 그리고 연대를 표현하고 의미 있는 행동을 해달라고 요구하는 활동가적 성향의 고객층에 의해 그러한 입장들을 갈수록 더 많이 강요당하고 있다. "의식 있는 자본주의"의 부상은 특히 젊은 소비자들 사이에 자신들의 돈을 원하는 기업은 마땅히 자신들의 가치를 공유할 것이라는 기대감을 키웠다. 한편, 운동화에서 커피에 이르기까지 모든 것의 극히 당파적인 양극화는 "안전한" 사회운동조차도 순식간에 논란거리가 될 수 있다는 것을 의미하며, 사회적 문제에 개입하지 않는 기업들에는 공범이라는 꼬리표가 붙기 쉽기 때문에 침묵은 더 이상 피난처가 아니다.

| 어휘 |

donation n. 기부, 기증, 증여　**Planned Parenthood** 가족계획연맹　**fundamentalist** n. 근본주의자　**boycott** n. 보이콧, 불매운동　**picket** v. 시위를 하다　**deluge** n. 쇄도, 폭주　**jam** v. 막다, 방해하다　**outdoor apparel** 야외용 의류　**retailer** n. 소매업체　**placate** v. 달래다, 진정시키다　**protester** n. 항의자　**customer service** 고객 서비스　**representative** n. 대표자, 직원　**recall** v. 회상하다　**chug along** 꾸준히 나아가다　**minefield** n. 지뢰밭, 위험한 상황　**consumer brand** 소비자 브랜드　**stake out** 경계를 표시하다, 경계를 정하다, 밝히다, 분명히 하다　**hot-button issue** 민감한 쟁점　**thrust** v. 밀어 넣다, 강제로 안기다[시키다]　**societal upheaval** 사회적 격변　**activist customer base** 행동주의 고객층　**expression of solidarity** 연대 표현　**conscious capitalism** 의식 있는 자본주의　**hyper-partisan** a. 극단적으로 당파적인　**polarization** n. 분열, 양극화　**controversial** a. 논란이 되는　**refuge** n. 피난처　**engage** v. 관여하다, 참여하다　**apt to** ~하기 쉬운　**complicit** a. 공모한, 연루된, 공범인　**impatient** a. 참을성 없는, 조급한　**reckless** a. 무모한

34　빈칸완성　①

| 분석 |

불만 전화를 걸 때마다 자기들이 싫어하는 Planned Parenthood에 기부가 된다는 것을 알게 되면 전화를 더 이상 걸지 않게 될 것이므로, ①이 정답으로 가장 적절하다.

빈칸 Ⓐ에 들어가기에 가장 적절한 것은?
① 전화가 곧 중단되었다.
② 불만 전화가 급격히 증가했다.
③ 사회적 압력 세력이 급격히 증가했다.
④ 판매부서가 불만 고객에게 전화하는 것을 중단했다.
⑤ 사회적 문제에 대한 침묵은 양극화된 세계에서 공범으로 몰릴 위험이 있다.

35　빈칸완성　④

| 분석 |

기업이 단순히 이윤만 추구하는 것이 아니라, 소비자의 가치를 공유하면서 사회적 책임을 다하고, 윤리적 가치를 고려하는 경영 철학과 관련된 긍정적인 표현이 나와야 한다. 따라서 ④ '의식 있는 자본주의'가 정답으로 가장 적절하다. ② 소수집단 사람들에 대한 편견 없는 언어 사용을 다룬 글이 아니므로 부적절하다.

빈칸 Ⓑ에 들어가기에 가장 적절한 것은?
① 성급한 고객들
② 정치적 올바름
③ 부패한 기업
④ 의식 있는 자본주의
⑤ 무분별한 불만

36~37

지속 가능한 건축은 현대 도시 개발에서 점점 더 중요한 요소가 되고 있다. 그것은 건물의 생애 주기 전반에 걸쳐 환경적으로 책임 있는 방법과 재료에 의존한다. 이러한 실천은 더 나은 설계, 시공, 운영 및 유지 관리를 통해 건축물이 환경에 미치는 영향을 줄이는 것을 목표로 한다. 지속 가능한 건축의 이점은 도시 생활의 다양한 측면에서 관찰될 수 있다. 에너지 효율적인 건물은 전력 소비를 줄이고, 폐기물을 최소화한다. 친환경 건물은 자연 채광과 환기 시스템을 통합해 넣어, 거주자의 건강과 웰빙을 향상시킬 수 있다. 또한, 지속 가능한 건물은 재생 가능한 자재를 자주 사용하며, 물의 사용량을 최소화하도록 설계된다. "건축의 미래는 지속 가능성에 달려 있다."라고 친환경 설계를 전문으로 하는 건축가 David Chen은 말한다. 현재 많은 도시가 새로운 건축물이 특정 환경 기준을 충족하도록 요구하는 규정을 시행하고 있다.

| 어휘 |

sustainable a. 지속 가능한　**architecture** n. 건축(학), 건축 양식　**increasingly** ad. 점점 더, 갈수록　**rely on** ~에 의존하다, ~에 기반하다　**environmentally responsible** 환경에 책임 있는　**lifecycle** n. 생애 주기, 수명 주기　**practice** n. 관행, 실천　**operation** n. 운영　**maintenance** n. 유지 관리　**observe** v. 관찰하다, 알아차리다　**aspect** n. 측면　**energy-efficient** a. 에너지 효율적인　**reduce power consumption** 전력 소비를 줄이다　**minimize** v. 최소화하다　**waste** n. 낭비, 폐기물　**green building** 친환경 건물　**incorporate** v. 포함하다, 통합하다　**natural lighting** 자연 채광　**ventilation** n. 환기　**occupant** n. 입주자, 거주자　**renewable material** 재생 가능한 재료　**water usage** 물 사용량　**lie in** ~에 있다　**sustainability** n. 지속 가능성　**specialize in** ~을 전문으로 하다　**eco-friendly** a. 친환경적인　**implement** v. 시행하다, 도입하다　**regulation** n. 규제　**work with** ~와 협력하다, 함께 일하다　**turn against** ~에게 등 돌리다, 반대하다　**come from** ~에서 비롯되다　**divide into** ~로 나누다　**give up** 포기하다　**look into** 조사하다　**move toward** ~로 나아가다

36　빈칸완성　⑤

| 분석 |

환경 친화적인 방법과 재료로 인해 지속 가능한 건축이 가능한 것이므로, 빈칸 Ⓐ에는 '~에 의존하다', '~에서 비롯되다'와 같은 표현이 나와야 한다. 한편, 빈칸 Ⓑ 뒤에서 도시 생활의 다양한 측면에서 나타나는 지속 가능한 건축의 이점들을 열거하고 있으므로, 빈칸 Ⓑ에는 '~에서 관찰될'이라는 표현이 적절하다. 따라서 ⑤가 정답이다.

빈칸 Ⓐ와 Ⓑ에 들어가기에 가장 적절한 쌍은?
① ~와 함께 일하다 — ~에 반대할
② ~에서 비롯되다 — ~로 나누어질
③ 포기하다 — 조사될
④ ~로 나아가다 — 다루어질
⑤ ~에 의존하다 — ~에서 관찰될

37 내용일치   ①

| 분석 |

본문에 따르면 지속 가능한 건축은 건물의 전체 생애 주기에 걸쳐 환경 영향을 줄이고, 자연 채광과 환기를 통해 건강과 웰빙을 향상시킬 수 있으며, 전력 소비를 줄이고 폐기물을 최소화한다. 그리고 많은 도시가 환경 기준을 충족하도록 새로운 규정을 만들고 있다. 하지만 지속 가능한 건축의 비용에 대한 언급은 없으므로, ①이 정답이다.

글의 내용과 부합하지 않는 것은?
① 지속 가능한 건물은 전통적인 건물보다 건설비용이 더 비싸다.
② 친환경 건물의 자연 채광과 환기는 건강에 긍정적인 영향을 미칠 수 있다.
③ 에너지 효율성은 지속 가능한 건물의 주요 장점 중 하나이다.
④ 지속 가능한 건축은 건물의 전체 생애 주기에 걸쳐 환경 영향을 고려한다.
⑤ 도시들은 건물의 환경 기준을 위한 새로운 규정을 만들고 있다.

38~40

양극화를 해결하는 쉬운 방법이 있다. 정치적 반대자를 미워하는 것을 멈추는 것이다. 그러나 그것은 말처럼 쉽지 않다. 왜 사람들은 자신과 정치적으로 다른 사람들을 혐오하는가? 그 답은 집단 양극화라고 불리는 광범위한 인지적 현상에 있다. 만약 당신이 자신과 의견이 같은 사람들과만 대화하거나, 자신의 의견을 뒷받침하는 뉴스만 듣는다면, 당신의 신념은 점점 더 극단적으로 변하게 된다. 이렇게 극단화될수록, 사람들은 반대 의견을 이해하지 못하게 되고, 자신의 견해에 대한 반론을 기각하며, 반대 의견을 가진 사람들을 점점 더 무능하고 타락한 존재로 여기게 된다. 온라인 환경은 거대한 양극화 기계로 기능한다. 개인이 자신이 원하는 정보만 선택적으로 소비하고, 자신의 견해와 충돌하는 정보는 걸러낼 수 있도록 한다. "반향실(echo chamber 메아리 방)"에서 벗어나 다양한 의견에 노출된다면 사람들이 덜 양극화될 것이라고 많은 사람들은 주장해 왔다. 하지만 예방과 치료 사이에는 중요한 차이가 있다. 다양한 미디어를 소비하는 것은 집단 양극화를 예방하는 데 도움이 될 수 있지만, 일단 양극화가 진행된 후에는 되돌리기 어려울 수도 있다.

| 어휘 |

polarization n. 분열, 양극화 **fix** n. 해결책 **adversary** n. 적수, 상대 **despise** v. 경멸하다, 혐오하다 **cognitive** a. 인지의, 인식의 **phenomenon** n. 현상 **group polarization** 집단 양극화 **affirm** v. 확인하다, 지지하다 **radical** a. 급진적인, 과격한 **radicalize** v. 과격하게 만들다 **dismiss** v. 일축하다, 무시하다 **objection** n. 반대, 이의 **increasingly** ad. 점점 더 **prone to** ~하기 쉬운 **dissenter** n. 반대자 **incompetent** a. 무능한 **depraved** a. 타락한 **immense** a. 엄청난, 거대한 **filter out** ~을 걸러내다 **challenging** a. 도전적인 **break out of** ~에서 벗어나다 **echo chamber** 에코 체임버, 반향실(소리가 메아리처럼 울리게 만든 방) **expose oneself to** ~에 자신을 노출시키다 **media diet** 미디어 소비 패턴 **reverse** v. 되돌리다 **take effect** 효과가 나타나다, 효력을 발휘하기 시작하다 **irreversible** a. 되돌릴 수 없는 **discourse** n. 담론, 담화 **immortal** a. 불멸의 **invincible** a. 천하무적의, 정복할 수 없는 **infuriated** a. 분노한 **deprived** a. 박탈당한, 궁핍한

38 빈칸완성   ②

| 분석 |

빈칸 앞 문장에서 양극화를 해결하는 쉬운 방법은 정치적 반대자를 미워하는 것을 멈추는 것이라고 말한 다음, 빈칸 다음 문장에서 사람들은 자신과 정치적으로 다른 사람들을 혐오한다고 했다. 따라서 정치적 반대자를 미워하는 것을 멈추는 것이 말처럼 쉽지 않다고 추론할 수 있다. easier said than done은 '말은 쉽지만 실행은 어렵다'는 뜻이므로, 빈칸의 문맥에 가장 적절하다.

빈칸 Ⓐ에 들어가기에 가장 적절한 것은?
① 말하는 것보다 느끼는 것이 더 쉽다
② 행하는 것보다 말하는 것이 더 쉽다(말은 쉽지만 실행은 어렵다)
③ 말하는 것보다 맛보는 것이 더 쉽다
④ 듣는 것보다 보는 것이 더 쉽다
⑤ 언급하는 것보다 실행하는 것이 더 쉽다

39 빈칸완성   ②

| 분석 |

정치적 양극화는 자신과 다른 의견을 배척하는 태도를 강화하며, 결국 반대자를 단순한 의견 차이를 가진 사람이 아니라 점점 더 무능하다고 여긴다는 맥락이다. 빈칸에는 극단적인 사람들의 태도를 설명하는 말로, '무능한'보다 더 심한 표현이 나와야 한다. 따라서 '도덕적으로 타락한(depraved)'이 정답으로 가장 적절하다.

빈칸 Ⓑ에 들어가기에 가장 적절한 것은?
① 불멸의
② 타락한, 부도덕한
③ 무적의
④ 격분한
⑤ 박탈당한

40 내용일치 ⑤

| 분석 |

"반향실(echo chamber 메아리 방)"에서 벗어나 다양한 의견에 노출된다면 사람들이 덜 양극화될 것이라는 본문의 내용과 ⑤의 진술이 상반된다.

글의 내용과 부합하지 않는 것은?
① 양극화를 방지하기 위해서는 다양한 미디어를 소비하는 것이 필요하다.
② 일단 양극화가 발생하면, 되돌리기 어려울 수도 있다.
③ 온라인 환경은 양극화된 담론의 확산을 촉진한다.
④ 집단 양극화를 피하기 위해서는 다양한 뉴스 소스를 소비해야 한다.
⑤ 양극화를 줄이고 싶다면, 반향실에 머물러야 한다.

광운대학교 자연계 2교시 A형

TEST p. 194~204

01	③	02	②	03	①	04	④	05	⑤	06	⑤	07	③	08	①	09	④	10	②
11	③	12	⑤	13	④	14	①	15	④	16	②	17	⑤	18	④	19	①	20	③
21	④	22	③	23	②	24	①	25	②	26	⑤	27	③	28	②	29	①	30	⑤

01 생활영어 ③

| 분석 |

'여전히'라는 말에 유의하면, 새로운 사업이 좋은 성과를 내고 있는 것은 아니라는 흐름이 되어야 한다. 그러므로 '요령을 터득하다', '새로운 환경에 적응하다'라는 의미의 ③이 들어가는 것이 가장 자연스럽다.

| 어휘 |

get the boot 해고되다   **cross the line** 선을 넘다, 규칙을 어기다   **learn the ropes** 요령을 터득하다, 새로운 환경에 적응하다   **break bread** 함께 식사하다   **see through a ladder** 제정신이다(can't see through a ladder 만취 상태이다)

| 해석 |

A: 새로운 사업은 어떻게 돼 가고 있니?
B: 솔직히 말하자면, 우리 아직 요령을 터득해 나가는 중이야.

02 논리완성 ②

| 분석 |

'(무심결에) 비밀을 누설하다'라는 의미의 관용표현은 let the cat out of the bag이다.

| 해석 |

나는 파티를 비밀로 하려 애쓰고 있었지만, 멜(Mel)이 가서 무심결에 비밀을 누설해버렸다.

03 논리완성 ①

| 분석 |

wild에는 '(계획·생각이) 엉뚱한'이라는 의미와 함께 '열광적인'이라는 의미가 있다.

| 어휘 |

feed v. 먹이다, 주다, 조장하다   **applause** n. 박수갈채   **wild** a. (계획·생각이) 엉뚱한, 무모한; 열광적인   **sound** a. 건전한; 견고한   **mature** a. 성숙한; 신중한   **crazy** a. 미친; 열광적인   **tamed** a. 길들여진

| 해석 |

캘리(Callie)는 그녀에게 엉뚱한 생각을 심어주기 시작했고, 그녀로 하여금 저 바깥에 뭔가 더 나은 것이 있을 거라고 생각하게 만들었다.

그는 다시 한번 관객들로부터 열광적인 갈채를 받았다.

04 논리완성 ④

| 분석 |

자동사 sweep에는 '휩쓸다, 퍼지다'는 뜻과 '내습하다, 엄습하다, 휘몰아치다'는 뜻이 있다. 따라서 ④가 정답이다. lingered의 경우 두 번째 문장의 빈칸에 넣으면 경보가 울리기 전부터 두려움과 공포가 있었다는 뜻이 되어 부적절하다.

| 어휘 |

aroma n. 방향(芳香), 향기   **go off** (경보기 등이) 울리다   **move** v. 움직이다   **flee** v. 달아나다, 사라져 없어지다   **linger** v. 오래 머무르다, 좀처럼 사라지지 않다   **sweep** v. 휩쓸다; 휘몰아치다   **transform** v. 변형하다, 바꾸다

| 해석 |

신선한 커피의 기분 좋은 향기가 그 집 전체에 퍼졌다.

화재 경보가 울렸을 때 군중 가운데 두려움과 공포가 엄습했다.

05 논리완성 ⑤

| 분석 |

indigenous에는 '토착의, 원산의, 자생의, 그 고장에 고유한'이라는 뜻이 있다.

| 어휘 |

endangered a. 멸종 위기에 처한 **exotic** a. 외래의, 외국산의 **innovative** a. 혁신적인 **inquisitive** a. 호기심 많은, 캐묻기 좋아하는 **ingenuous** a. 순진한, 솔직한 **indifferent** a. 무관심한 **indigenous** a. 원산의, 토착의

| 해석 |

남아메리카가 원산지인 특정 동물들은 멸종위기에 처해 있다.

그는 아주 다양한 자생종 식물과 외래종 식물 모두를 재배한다.

06 논리완성 ⑤

| 분석 |

첫 번째 문장의 경우, 적에 대한 기습을 가능하게 하는 것은 용병술과 관련 있으므로 '책략'이라는 의미가 artifice가 적절하고, 마술사의 트릭은 정교한 기술 혹은 솜씨에 의한 것이므로 마찬가지로 '기교'라는 의미의 artifice가 적절하다.

| 어휘 |

elaborate a. 정성[공]을 들인, 정교한 **altercation** n. 논쟁, 언쟁 **tribulation** n. 고난, 시련 **debacle** n. (군대·군중 따위의) 와해, 패주; (정부 등의) 붕괴 **regression** n. 퇴보, 회귀 **artifice** n. 교묘한 솜씨, 기교; 책략

| 해석 |

그 장군은 자신의 책략 덕분에 적을 불시에 덮칠 수 있었다.

그 마술사의 트릭은 정교한 기교로 밝혀졌다.

07 논리완성 ③

| 분석 |

charter가 동사로 쓰이는 경우에는 '배나 비행기 등을 전세 내다'라는 의미로 쓰일 수 있고, 명사로 쓰이는 경우에는 '헌장', '선언서'라는 의미로도 쓰일 수 있다.

| 어휘 |

proclaim v. 포고하다, 선언하다 **rent** v. 임차하다, 빌리다 n. 집세 **hire** v. 고용하다; 임대하다 n. 고용, 임차; 임대료 **charter** v. (비행기·버스·선박 등을) 전세 내다 n. 헌장, 선언서 **chapter** n. (책·논문 따위의) 장(章) v. 장(章)으로 나누다 **company** n. 회사; 친구

| 해석 |

그 팀은 비행기를 전세 낼 계획을 가지고 있다.

그 헌장은 모든 주(州)가 자체적인 정부를 가질 것이라 선언했다.

08 논리완성 ①

| 분석 |

leave out에는 '제외하다, 배제하다, 삭제하다'의 뜻이 있으므로 ①이 정답으로 적절하다.

| 어휘 |

leave out (포함하거나 언급하지 않고) ~을 빼다[배제시키다], 생략하다; 삭제하다 **tear down** (건물 등을) 철거하다, 무너뜨리다 **stay behind** 뒤에 남다 **drop back** 후퇴하다, (순위에서) 처지다 **go against** 반대하다

| 해석 |

그는 팀이 자신의 동생을 제외했기 때문에 실망했다.

네가 첫 번째 단락을 삭제하면 그 에세이는 더 나아질 것이다.

09 동의어 ④

| 어휘 |

inimical a. 적의가 있는(= hostile) **hospitable** a. 친절한, 환대하는; (기후 등이) 쾌적한 **imitative** a. 모방하는 **creative** a. 창의적인 **amicable** 우호적인, 친근한

| 해석 |

그는 나에게 적대적인 감정을 가지고 있는 것 같다.

10 동의어 ②

| 어휘 |

upshot n. (최종적인) 결과, 결말(= final result) **compromise** n. 타협, 화해 **total agreement** 완전한 합의 **interim summary** 잠정적인 요약 **brief wrap-up** 간단한 마무리 **unanimous decision** 만장일치의 결정

| 해석 |

그 문제의 최종적인 결과는 그들이 타협에 이르게 되었다는 것이었다.

11 정비문 ③

| 분석 |

baggage는 불가산명사이므로 복수형으로 쓰지 않으며, 이것의 개수를 셀 때는 a piece of 따위를 이용하여 나타낸다. 그러므로 ③은 His baggage has been lost at the airport.여야 한다. ④ 권유의 의미일 경우에는 의문문에 some을 쓸 수 있다.

| 어휘 |

be good at ~에 능숙하다 **baggage** n. 수화물

| 해석 |

① 나의 형은 피아노 연주에 능숙하다.
② 나는 태어난 이래로 여기서 살아왔다.

③ 그의 짐이 공항에서 분실되었다.
④ 커피 좀 더 드릴까요?
⑤ 빨간 드레스를 입은 소녀는 내 여동생이다.

12 정비문 ⑤

| 분석 |
'바위처럼 단단하다'는 as solid as a rock으로 표현한다. 그러므로 부정관사를 첨가하여 ⑤를 He said that his business was as solid as a rock.으로 고쳐야 한다.

| 해석 |
① 나는 파리에 세 번 다녀왔다.
② 그녀는 아직 숙제를 끝내지 못했다.
③ 그 영화는 매우 흥미로워서 나는 그것을 두 번 보았다.
④ 왜 네가 혼자 거기에 갔니?
⑤ 그는 자신의 사업이 바위처럼 견고하다고 말했다.

13 정비문 ④

| 분석 |
④에서 '책의 표지'라는 의미가 되려면 소유격 관계대명사를 써야 한다. 따라서 ④를 The book whose cover is torn is mine. 혹은 The book the cover of which is torn is mine.으로 고쳐야 한다. ② mind는 동명사를 목적어로 취한다. ③ as if 뒤에는 가정법 동사가 온다. as if 이하가 주절과 동일 시제이므로 가정법 과거 동사 were를 썼다. ⑤ 사역동사 make의 목적보어로는 동사원형이 온다.

| 해석 |
① 내가 어제 구입한 책은 흥미롭다.
② 창문 좀 열어주시겠어요?
③ 그녀는 마치 원어민처럼 영어를 한다.
④ 표지가 찢어진 책이 내 것이다.
⑤ 선생님은 내가 더 열심히 공부하게 만들었다.

14 정비문 ①

| 분석 |
It is high time 뒤에는 가정법 동사에 해당하는 과거시제 동사가 오는 것이 원칙이므로 ①은 It is high time we went home.이 되어야 한다. ② Only가 포함된 부사절이 문두에 왔으므로 주절에서 도치가 발생했다. ③ 부정의 부사어 Little이 문두에 와서 도치가 발생했다. ④ 'Such+보어+동사+주어'의 도치 구문이다. ⑤ If I were in your position에서 If가 생략되면서 도치가 발생했다.

| 해석 |
① 우리가 집에 가야 할 시간이다.
② 그가 도착하고 나서야 나는 사무실을 떠났다.
③ 그녀는 다음에 무슨 일이 일어날지 거의 몰랐다.
④ 분노가 너무나도 커서 그는 말을 할 수 없었다.
⑤ 내가 너의 입장이라면, 나도 똑같이 할 것이다.

15 정비문 ④

| 분석 |
butter는 불가산 명사이므로 부정대명사 one이 아닌 some으로 받는다. 그러므로 ④는 Shall I pass the butter? Or have you got some already?이 되어야 한다.

| 해석 |
① 못 몇 개 줄 수 있니? 내가 약간 필요해서.
② 혹시 칼을 가지고 있니? 내가 날카로운 칼이 필요해서.
③ 혹시 네가 가지고 있으면 내가 색종이를 좀 더 갖고 싶어.
④ 버터 건네줄까? 아니면 이미 가지고 있어?
⑤ 나는 티켓 12장을 달라고 했지만, 그들은 많이 할애해줄 수가 없었어.

16 정비문 ②

| 분석 |
lay는 '눕히다'라는 의미의 타동사이므로 그 뒤에 목적어가 있어야 한다. ②에서 laying 뒤에 목적어가 주어져 있지 않고, 또한 문맥상 '놓여 있다'라는 의미가 되어야 하므로, 자동사 lie의 현재분사 lying을 써야 한다. 그러므로 ②는 Whose book is lying on the table?이 되어야 한다. ④ 제안, 요구 등의 의미를 가진 동사가 이끄는 that절 속의 동사 형태는 '(should) 동사원형'이다. ⑤ 관계부사 where 뒤에 완전한 문장이 왔다.

| 해석 |
① 학생들 각자가 시험을 마쳤다.
② 누구의 책이 탁자 위에 놓여 있니?
③ 이 사람이 내가 어제 만난 남자다.
④ 선생님은 우리에게 일찍 도착할 것을 요청하셨다.
⑤ 내가 살고 있는 도시는 꽤 크다.

17 정비문 ⑤

| 분석 |
⑤에서 Had it not been for your help는 If it had not been for에서 If가 생략되면서 도치가 일어난 형태인데, 조건절의 동사의 형태가 'had+과거분사'이므로 가정법 과거완료의 문장이다. 가정법 과거완료에서 주절의 동사 형태는 조동사의 '과거형+have+p.p'

여야 하므로 ⑤는 Had it not been for your help, I would have failed.가 되어야 한다. 주어진 문장 그대로는 혼합 가정법 인데, 의미상 부적절하다. ③ '다른 느낌이 든다, 다르다고 느껴지다'라는 느낌의 상태가 아니라 '다르게 생각하다, 달리 생각하다'라는 생각의 방식을 나타내므로 feel 다음에 부사 differently가 왔다. ④ anything but은 never의 의미이다.

| 해석 |
① 나는 이 지역을 손바닥 보듯 잘 알고있더랬다.
② 그들은 사탕절임 같은 고지방 음식을 멀리한다.
③ 이 광고를 받았으니, 너는 다르게 생각하는 것이다.
④ 곰곰이 생각해보면, 잡담은 결코 사소하지 않다.
⑤ 네 도움이 없었더라면, 나는 실패했을 것이다.

18 논리완성   ④

| 분석 |
'영어 사용자는 관계사절이 무엇인지 알지 못하면서도 두 개의 관계사절을 포함돼 있는 문장을 만들어낼 수 있다.'라고 했는데, 이는 대화하는 데 필요한 심오한 지식을 '인식하지 못한' 채 언어를 사용하고 있다는 것이다.

| 어휘 |
proficient a. 숙달된, 능숙한   **relative clause** 관계사절   **proud** a. 자랑스러워하는   **full** a. 가득 찬, 충만한   **conscious** a. 의식하고 있는, 알고 있는   **unaware** a. 알지 못하는, 인지하지 못하는   **skillful** a. 능숙한

| 해석 |
거의 모든 사람들은 적어도 한 가지 언어를 알고 있다. 다섯 살짜리 아이들도 거의 부모만큼 능숙하게 말하고 이해할 수 있다. 그러나 가장 간단한 대화조차도 대부분의 화자들은 알지 못하는 심오한 지식을 필요로 한다. 이는 알바니아(Albania)어에서 줄루(Zulu)어에 이르는 모든 언어의 사용자들에게 해당된다. 영어 사용자는 관계절이 무엇인지 알지 못하면서도 두 개의 관계절을 갖고 있는 문장을 만들어낼 수 있다.

19 논리완성   ①

| 분석 |
마지막 문장은 앞에서 언급한 내용에 대한 요약에 해당한다. "로마의 광장과 유적지를 방문한 사람들이 그곳의 웅장함을 경험할 수 있고 전 세계 수많은 건물에 영감을 준 건축 요소들을 직접 목격할 수 있다."고 했는데, 이는 곧 이러한 건축물들의 기교와 규모가 로마 제국이 가지고 있던 힘과 세련됨을 '나타내 보여준다'는 것이므로 ①이 정답으로 적절하다.

| 어휘 |
meticulously ad. 매우 세심하게; 꼼꼼하게   **preserve** v. 보존하다   **grandeur** n. 장엄   **ruin** n. 파멸, 몰락; (pl.) 잔해   **weather** v. 풍화시키다   **architectural** a. 건축학의, 건축술의   **countless** a. 무수한, 셀 수 없을 정도로 많은   **detailed** a. 상세한   **craftsmanship** n. (장인의) 솜씨, 기능   **immense** a. 막대한   **sophistication** n. (기계 등의) 정교화   **indicative of** ~을 나타내는   **derivative of** ~로부터 파생한   **subordinate to** ~에 종속된   **contingent on** ~을 조건으로 하는   **discrepant from** ~와 어긋나는

| 해석 |
고대 로마의 공공 광장은 수세기에 걸쳐 세심하게 보존되어 와서, 현대의 방문객들로 하여금 그 웅장함을 경험하게 해준다. 오늘날 우뚝 솟은 기둥들과 비바람에 닳아버린 돌길이 있는 그 유적지를 가로질러 걸으면, 방문객들은 전 세계 수많은 건물에 영감을 준 건축 요소들을 직접 목격할 수 있다. 이 건축물들의 정밀한 기교와 기념비적인 규모는 전성기 때 로마 제국이 가지고 있었던 거대한 힘과 고도의 세련됨을 보여준다.

20 논리완성   ③

| 분석 |
첫 문장은 아시아계 미국인의 현재를 언급하고 두 번째, 세 번째 문장은 우리라고 지칭되는 아시아계 미국인의 과거 활약과 업적을 나타낸다. 네 번째 문장에서 다시 현재를 언급하는데, 빈칸 다음 문장에서 '과거 역사를 등에 업고 현재 이 일을 하고 있다'고 말하므로 현재 이 순간은 과거와 연결되어 있다고 할 수 있다. 그리고 '새롭게 여겨질지 모르지만'이라고 했는데, 새롭다는 것은 역사가 짧다는 의미이므로 실제로는 역사가 길다는 의미가 된다. 따라서 빈칸에는 ③의 '긴 역사적 유산'이 적절하다.

| 어휘 |
participate in 참여하다   **civil right** 민권   **keep ~ in mind** ~을 명심하다   **habitual** a. 습관적인, 버릇이 된   **legacy** n. 유산   **humanism** n. 인도주의   **legendary** a. 전설적인   **profanity** n. 신성을 더럽힘, 모독

| 해석 |
"아시아계 미국인은 이 나라에서 매우 정치적인 집단이다. 우리는 1960년대 민권 운동에 참여했다. 아시아계 미국인은 세자르 차베스(Cesar Chavez)가 했던 일의 일부였다. 그리고 지금 이 순간은, 아무리 힘들게 보이고 어떤 이들에게는 아무리 새롭게 느껴질지라도, 사실 훨씬 더 긴 역사적 유산과 연결돼 있다. 그러므로, 당신도 알다시피, 우리는 역사를 등에 업고 이 일을 하고 있는 것이고, 그것은 정말로 흥미로운 일이다. 나는 사람들에게 그 점을, 특히 어려워질 때, 꼭 명심할 것을 권한다.

21 글의 제목   ④

| 분석 |
본문은 스토킹 피해자 보호를 위한 경찰의 대응 강화 필요성에 대한

내용이다. 스토킹 사건 수가 급증했지만, 경찰의 대응은 이에 비례하지 않고 있으며, 피해자 보호를 위한 강력한 조치가 필요하다고 강조하고 있다. 따라서 ④가 제목으로 적절하다.

| 어휘 |

stalking n. 스토킹 **complaint** n. 불평, 고충, 민원, 고소 **file** v. (신청·항의 등을) 제출[제기]하다 **quadruple** v. 4배가 되다 **victim** n. 희생자, 피해자 **correspond with** ~와 부합하다 **analyze** v. 분석하다 **effectiveness** n. 유효함, 효력 있음 **enforcement** n. 시행, 실시 **perpetrator** n. 범죄자, 가해자 **enhance** v. 향상시키다; (가치·능력·매력 따위를) 높이다 **delineate** v. 묘사하다, 기술하다 **specific** a. 일정한, 특정한 **encompass** v. 에워싸다, 포함하다 **loiter** v. 빈둥거리다 **unsolicited** a. 청탁받지 않은; 부탁받지 않은

| 해석 |

경찰에 접수된 스토킹 관련 민원 건수는 1년 만에 4배 이상 증가했다. 그러나 피해자를 위한 대응 조치는 급격한 사건 증가에 부합하지 못했다. 경찰과학연구소(PSI)의 보고서에 따르면, 현행 법 하에서 스토킹 피해자를 보호하기 위한 경찰 대응의 효과를 분석한 결과, 범죄자를 피해자로부터 분리하는 것과 같은 조치의 시행이 강화되어야 한다. 스토킹 방지법은 특정한 행동을 스토킹으로 기술하고 있는데, 이런 행동에는 피해자나 그들의 배우자나 가족을 따라다니거나 접근하는 행위, 피해자 거주지 근처에서 배회하는 행위, 그리고 다양한 통신 수단을 통해 원치 않는 물건, 문자, 말, 사진 또는 동영상을 보내는 행위가 포함돼 있다.

글의 제목으로 가장 적절한 것은?
① 감소하고 있는 스토킹 관련 민원
② 통신에서의 스토킹 방지
③ 스토킹에 대한 경찰과학연구소의 책임
④ 스토킹에 대해 보다 강력한 조치가 필요함
⑤ 스토킹 피해자를 보호하기 위한 뉴미디어 활용

22 내용일치 ③

| 분석 |

"당시에 향신료는 매우 값비싼 상품에 속했다"라고 명시적으로 언급했으므로 ③이 본문의 내용에 가장 잘 부합하는 진술이다. ① 역사학자들은 그것이 향신료 사용의 주된 용도는 아니었다고 보고 있다. ⑤ 부유한 사람들이 향신료를 통해 부를 과시했다고 하지만, 오직 부자들만 사용했다는 내용은 있지 않다.

| 어휘 |

spice n. 양념, 향신료 **medieval** a. 중세의 **flavor** n. 맛, 풍미 **demonstrate** v. 증명하다, 논증하다 **prosperity** n. 번영, 번창; 부유 **commodity** n. 일용품, 필수품 **medicinal** a. 약용의, 약효 있는 **property** n. 성질, 특성 **prescribe** v. 처방하다 **specific** a. 일정한, 특정한 **refrigeration** n. 냉장, 냉동 **preserve** v. 보존하다 **spoil** v. 망쳐놓다; (음식물을) 상하게 하다

| 해석 |

중세 유럽에서 향신료의 사용은 단순히 맛을 더하는 것 이상의 여러 가지 목적을 수행했다. 당시에 향신료는 매우 값비싼 상품에 속했기 때문에, 부유한 연회의 주인들은 향신료가 많이 들어간 요리를 제공함으로써 자신들의 부(富)를 과시하곤 했다. 뿐만 아니라, 당시의 의학 이론에 따르면, 향신료는 약효가 있는 것으로 여겨졌다. 중세의 의사들은 인체의 "체액"의 균형을 맞추기 위해 특정 향신료를 처방하기도 했다. 더군다나, 냉장 기술이 존재하지 않던 시대였기 때문에, 강한 향신료는 보존된 고기가 상하기 시작했을 때 그 맛을 감추는 역할을 할 수도 있었다. 그러나 지금 역사학자들은 이것이 향신료 사용의 주된 용도는 아니었다고 보고 있다.

글의 내용과 가장 잘 부합하는 것은?
① 향신료는 고기를 보존하는 데 주로 사용되었다.
② 중세의 의사들은 요리에 향신료를 사용하는 것을 금지했다.
③ 향신료는 중세 유럽에서 사치품으로 여겨졌다.
④ 모든 향신료는 인접 국가에서 수입되었다.
⑤ 오직 부유한 사람들만이 일상에서 향신료를 사용했다.

23 내용일치 ②

| 분석 |

Gall은 인간의 신체가 아닌 인간의 뇌에 대해 관심을 가지고 있었다. 그러므로 ②가 본문의 내용과 부합하지 않는 진술이다.

| 어휘 |

linguistic a. 언어의, 언어학의 **localization** n. 국부화(局所化), 위치 측정[추정] **cognitive** a. 인식의 **localize** v. (영향 등을) 국한시키다[국부적이 되게 하다]; ~의 위치를 알아내다 **specific** a. 일정한, 특정한 **frontal lobe** 전두엽 **articulate** a. (생각·감정을) 명확히 표현할 수 있는; (논리) 정연한 **protrude** v. 튀어나오다, 돌출되다, 내밀다 **put forth** 제시하다 **pseudoscientific** a. 유사과학적인 **organology** n. 기관학(器官學) **phrenology** n. 골상학 **trait** n. 특성, 특징 **bump** n. 융기 **skull** n. 두개골

| 해석 |

주된 관심을 끈 이슈 중의 하나는 뇌의 어느 부분이 인간의 언어 능력을 담당하고 있는가를 판단하는 것이었다. 19세기 초, Franz Joseph Gall은 국소화(局所化) 이론을 제안했는데, 이 이론의 개념은 인간의 서로 다른 인지 능력과 행동은 뇌의 특정 부분에 국부적으로 위치해 있다는 것이다. 예를 들어, 그는 언어 능력이 뇌의 전두엽에 위치해 있다는 의견을 개진했는데, 왜냐하면 젊었을 때, 그는 가장 논리 정연하고 지적인 동료 학생들이 돌출된 눈을 가지고 있다는 것을 알게 되었고, 이것이 과도하게 발달한 뇌 물질을 나타내주는 것이라고 믿었기 때문이다. 그는 또한 "기관학(器官學)"이라 불리는 유사과학적 이론을 제시했는데, 이는 후에 "골상학(骨相學)"으로 알려지게 되었다. 골상학은 두개골의 "융기"를 조사하여 성격 특성, 지적 능력, 그리고 기타 사항을 판단하는 방법이다.

글의 내용과 부합하지 않는 것은?
① 골상학은 두개골의 형태를 연구한다.
② Gall은 인체의 국소화에 관심이 있었다.
③ 돌출된 눈은 뇌 물질이 지나치게 거대한 것을 나타내는 것으로 여겨졌다.
④ Gall은 성격과 지능에 관한 이론을 발전시키려 노력했다.
⑤ Gall에 따르면, 뇌의 전두엽은 언어 능력이 위치하고 있는 곳이다.

24 내용일치   ①

| 분석 |
"20대 한국 여성 6, 7명 가운데 1명은 저체중이며, 같은 연령대에서 저체중이거나 정상 체중인 여성의 거의 절반이 여전히 체중을 훨씬 더 줄이려 하고 있다"고 했다. 전체 한국인 중에 체중감량을 시도하고 있는 사람들의 비율에 대해서는 언급하지 않았다.

| 어휘 |
ratio n. 비율   **prevalence** n. 널리 퍼짐, 유행, 보급   **obesity** n. 비만   **tally** v. 계산하다, 기록하다

| 해석 |
20대 한국 여성 6, 7명 가운데 1명은 저체중이며, 같은 연령대에서 저체중이거나 정상 체중인 여성의 거의 절반이 여전히 체중을 훨씬 더 줄이려 하고 있다. 이와는 대조적으로, 비만이 점점 더 퍼지고 있음에도 불구하고 체중을 줄이려 노력하고 있는 30대와 40대 남성의 비율은 감소했다. 뿐만 아니라, 2021년에는 19 ~ 29세의 여성 중 15.1%가 체질량지수 18.5 미만으로 저체중이었다. 같은 연령대 여성의 저체중 비율이 2019 ~ 2021년에는 14.8%였는데, 이는 2016 ~ 2018년에 기록된 12.4%에서 늘어난 것이다. 이들 저체중 여성의 약 16.2%와 정상 체중 여성의 53.9%가 체중 감량을 시도했다.

글의 내용과 부합하지 않는 것은?
① 한국인 6, 7명 중 1명은 체중 감량을 시도한다.
② 적극적으로 체중 감량을 하고 있는 30대와 40대 남성의 비율이 감소했다.
③ 정상 체중인 여성의 상당수가 여전히 체중 감량을 위해 애쓰고 있다.
④ 2021년에는 19~29세의 여성 중 15.1%가 BMI 18.5 미만이었다.
⑤ 2016~2018년에서 2019 ~ 2021년 사이에 저체중 여성의 비율이 2.4 퍼센트 포인트 증가했다.

25 내용일치   ②

| 분석 |
석비에서는 구바바(Kubaba)의 영혼에게가 아니라 "쿠바바(Kubaba)에게 숫양을, 그리고 이 석비에 있는 내 영혼을 위해 숫양을 바치라"라고 했으므로 돼 있으므로 ②가 본문의 내용과 일치하지 않는다.

| 어휘 |
contemplate v. 심사숙고하다   **basalt** n. 현무암   **stele** n. 비문을 새긴 돌기둥, 석비   **feature** v. ~를 특징으로 하다   **graven** a. 새긴   **inscription** n. 비명(碑銘), 비문(碑文)   **ram** n. 숫양   **vineyard** n. 포도원   **durable** a. 오래 견디는, 튼튼한   **receptacle** n. 그릇, 용기   **dualism** n. 이원론   **immaterial** a. 실체 없는, 비물질적인   **distinct** a. 별개의, 다른

| 해석 |
약 2,700년 전, 오늘날의 터키에 있었던 고대 도시 사말(Samal)에서, 왕의 나이든 하인이 그의 집 구석에 앉아 자신의 영혼의 본질에 대해 숙고하고 있다. 그의 이름은 카투무와(Katumuwa)이다. 그는 자신을 위해 만들어진 현무암 석비를 응시하는데, 그 석비에는 그의 초상화와 함께 고대 아람어로 된 비문이 새겨져 있다. 그 비문에서는 자신이 죽으면 다음과 같이 하라고 가족에게 지시하고 있다. "이 방에서 잔치를 벌이되, 하다드 하르파탈리(Hadad Harpatalli)에게 황소를, 사냥꾼들의 니카라와스(Nikarawas)에게 숫양을, 샤마시(Shamash)에게 숫양을, 포도원의 하다드에게 숫양을, 쿠바바(Kubaba)에게 숫양을, 그리고 이 석비에 있는 내 영혼을 위해 숫양을 바치라." 카투무와는 죽은 후의 자신의 영혼을 위해 튼튼한 돌 그릇을 만들었다고 생각했다. 이 석비는 우리의 의식이 물질적인 육신과 구별되는 비물질적인 영혼이나 정신에 깃들어 있다고 믿는 이원론의 가장 오래된 기록 가운데 하나일 수 있다.

글의 내용과 부합하지 않는 것은?
① 카투무와는 약 2,700년 전에 사말 왕의 하인이었다.
② 석비에서는 쿠바바의 영혼에게도 숫양을 바치라고 지시한다.
③ 이 현무암 석비는 이원론적 믿음에 대한 가장 오래된 증거 기록일 수 있다.
④ 카투무와가 보고 있던 것은 자신의 초상화가 새겨진 현무암 석비였다.
⑤ 이원론은 우리의 의식과 물질적인 육신은 별개의 것이라고 것을 의미한다.

26~27

Merriam-Webster 웹사이트에서 they라는 단어를 검색하면 그 인칭 대명사에 대한 정의가 나타나는데, 이것은 작년에 비해 올해 검색량이 급증했다. 몇 달 전, 그 사전은 2019년 올해의 단어로 선정됐던 그 단어에 대해 정의를 추가하면서, 그 단어를 제3의 성(性)을 나타내는 역할을 하는 대명사로 분류했다. Merriam-Webster는 작고 잘 드러나지 않는 그 단어가 최근 몇 년 동안 사용 방식에서 상당히 급격한

변화를 겪었으며, 그 과정에서 광범위한 문화적 논의의 중심에 서게 되었다고 언급했다.

| 어휘 |

definition n. 정의; 설명   **personal pronoun** 인칭 대명사   **spike** n. 급등, 급증   **lookup** n. 검색   **classify** v. 분류하다   **nonbinary** n. 논바이너리, 제3의 성(性)(여성도 남성도 아닌 성별, 이분법적인 성별에 속하지 아니하는 사람)   **unassuming** a. 겸손한, 주제넘지 않은   **undergo** v. (영향·변화·조치·검사 따위를) 받다, 입다; (시련 등을) 경험하다   **radical** a. 급진적인, 과격한, 혁명적인   **transformation** n. 변형, 변화

26 글의 제목 ⑤

| 분석 |

본문에서는 "they가 최근 몇 년 동안 사용 방식에서 상당히 급격한 변화를 겪었으며, Merriam-Webster 웹사이트에서 they를 제3의 성(性)을 나타내는 역할을 하는 대명사로 분류했다"는 이야기를 하고 있다. 그러므로 이러한 점을 가장 잘 반영하는 제목으로는 ⑤가 적절하다. ① 이 글은 남자도 아니고 여자도 아닌 제3의 성으로서 살아가는 실제 사람들의 인생 이야기를 다룬 글이 아니다. 이탤릭체는 그 단어가 일반적인 용법과 다르게 사용되었음을 의미하는데, ①에서는 '남성', '여성', '제3의 성'인 사람들을 가리키고 ③과 ⑤에서는 she라는 단어, they라는 단어를 가리킨다.

제목으로 가장 적절한 것은?
① He와 She를 넘어: They의 이야기
② 인칭 대명사의 진화
③ 언어와 문화에 She가 미치는 영향
④ 변하지 않는 성별 정체성의 반영
⑤ 제3의 성(性)을 나타내는 대명사로서의 They의 부상(浮上)

27 지시대상 ③

| 분석 |

the tiny, unassuming word는 앞 문장에서 its 2019 Word of the Year로 지칭된 단어를 의미하며, 이것은 they이다.

28~30

일본 중부의 산속 깊은 곳에서는 종이를 만드는 수백 년 된 전통이 오늘날까지 이어져오고 있다. 일본의 전통적인 종이인 화지(和紙)를 만드는 장인(匠人)들은 새벽이 되기 전, 산 공기가 여전히 서늘하고 깨끗할 때 작업을 시작한다. 그들은 뽕나무 속껍질을 수확하여, 가장 강한 섬유만을 신중하게 가려낸다. 그 과정은 강한 집중력과 체력이 요구된다. 종이 한 장도 각각 손으로 만들어지는데, 장인은 차가운 물에 몇 시간 동안 서서 몸을 앞뒤로 흔들며 현지의 식물에서 얻어낸 천연 접착제와 섬유를 뒤섞는다. 때로는 날씨가 너무 따뜻해서, 섬유가 처리되기 전에 부패해버릴 수도 있다. 혹은 겨울이 너무 혹독해서 생산에 필요한 물을 얼려버릴 수도 있다. 조건이 완벽하더라도, 잠깐의 부주의로 한 번에 만드는 종이 전체를 망쳐버릴 수도 있다.

하지만 모든 것이 맞아떨어지면, 그 결과로 만들어지는 종이는 거의 마법에 가까운 우수한 품질을 가지게 된다. 강하면서도 섬세하며, 은은한 광택이 마치 빛을 품고 있는 듯하다. 각각의 종이는 그 자체로 예술 작품이 된다. 많은 장인들은 수백 년 전 자신들과 동일한 기법을 사용한 조상들과 깊은 유대감을 느끼는 경험을 한다고 말한다.

이 장인들은 단순한 공예인들 이상인데, 왜냐하면 그들은 사멸할 위기에 처해 있는 예술 형태의 수호자들이기 때문이다. 대량 생산된 종이를 구할 수 있음에도 불구하고, 전통 예술가들, 서예가들, 그리고 그것이 가진 독특한 특성을 높이 평가하는 수집가들 사이에 고품질 화지에 대한 수요는 여전히 꾸준하다. 한 장의 화지 각각에는 그것을 만들기 위해 사용된 재료들뿐만 아니라 그것을 만든 장인의 헌신과 기술에 대한 이야기까지도 담겨 있다.

| 어휘 |

artisan n. 솜씨 좋은 직공, 기능공   **washi** n. 화지(和紙, 일본식 종이)   **crisp** a. (공기·날씨 등이) 상쾌한, 서늘한   **bark** n. 나무껍질   **mulberry** n. 뽕나무   **concentration** n. 집중; 전념   **sway** v. 흔들리다   **adhesive** n. 접착제   **derive** v. 손에 넣다, 획득하다   **decompose** v. 분해하다; 썩다   **distraction** n. 주의 산만, 방심   **batch** n. 한 벌, 한 묶음   **align** v. 한 줄로 되다, 정렬하다   **sheen** n. 광채, 광택   **endangered** a. 절멸 위기에 처한   **calligrapher** n. 서예가   **appreciate** v. 감상하다; 진가를 인정하다   **property** n. 성질, 특성   **dedication** n. 헌신, 전념

28 글의 제목 ②

| 분석 |

본문은 일본의 전통적인 종이인 화지(washi)를 제조하는 방법이 오늘날까지 전해져서 옛 방법 그대로 행해지고 있음을 이야기하면서 제조과정과 그 종이의 특성과 수요 등을 소개하고 있는 내용이므로, ②가 제목으로 적절하다.

글의 제목으로 가장 적절한 것은?
① 일본의 산악 지역 공동체
② 살아 있는 장인 정신의 전통
③ 전통 종이의 현대적인 용도
④ 일본 종이의 역사
⑤ 제지(製紙)의 과학

29　빈칸완성　①

| 분석 |

"모든 것이 맞아떨어지면, 그 결과로 만들어지는 종이는 거의 마법에 가까운 우수한 품질을 가지게 된다. 강하면서도 섬세하며, 은은한 광택이 마치 빛을 품고 있는 듯하다."는 화지의 품질과 가치를 높게 평가하는 내용이므로, 이와 같은 흐름이 되도록 긍정적인 내용이 그 뒤에 이어져야 한다. 따라서 ①이 정답으로 적절하다.

빈칸에 들어가기에 가장 적절한 것은?
① 각각의 종이는 그 자체로 하나의 예술 작품이 된다.
② 전통 종이에 대한 시장이 줄어들고 있다.
③ 일본의 대부분의 사람들은 그들의 전통을 자랑스럽게 여긴다.
④ 그 과정은 현대의 기술을 필요로 한다.
⑤ 경쟁이 치열해지고 있다.

30　내용일치　⑤

| 분석 |

"현지의 식물에서 얻어낸 천연 접착제와 섬유를 뒤섞는다"라고 돼 있으므로, ⑤는 본문의 내용과 부합하지 않는다.

글의 내용과 부합하지 않는 것은?
① 전통 예술가들은 여전히 수제 화지를 소중히 여긴다.
② 장인들은 종이를 만들 때 차가운 물 속에 서 있다.
③ 종이 제조하는 과정은 이른 아침에 시작된다.
④ 날씨 조건이 종이 제조 과정에 영향을 미칠 수 있다.
⑤ 장인들은 종이를 강하게 하기 위해 화학 접착제를 사용한다.

단국대학교 인문계 오전

TEST p. 206~219

01	①	02	③	03	③	04	①	05	③	06	①	07	①	08	④	09	②	10	①
11	①	12	②	13	①	14	②	15	①	16	②	17	③	18	①	19	④	20	②
21	①	22	②	23	②	24	②	25	②	26	②	27	④	28	②	29	②	30	②
31	①	32	②	33	①	34	②	35	④	36	②	37	④	38	④	39	②	40	④

01 동의어   ①

| 어휘 |

sit-down a. (식사가) 앉아서 먹는   **quintessential** a. 전형적인, 정수의(= representative)   **abrupt** a. 갑작스러운   **premeditated** a. 사전에 계획된   **impetuous** a. 충동적인

| 해석 |

좌식(패밀리스타일) 레스토랑 체인점은 어쩌면 전형적인 미국 비즈니스일지도 모른다. 이는 제2차 세계대전 이후, 가족들이 자동차를 타고 여행을 다니기 시작하면서 하워드 존슨 레스토랑(Howard Johnson's)의 매장 수가 늘어난 데서 비롯되었다.

02 동의어   ③

| 어휘 |

for decades 수십 년 동안   **restitution** n. 반환(= restoration)   **repayment** n. 반환, 상환, 분할 상환금   **recompense** n. 보상, 배상; 보수   **remuneration** n. 보수, 보상

| 해석 |

사실 나이지리아 정부는 문화적으로 중요한 이런 물건들의 반환을 위해 수십 년 간 캠페인을 벌여왔다.

03 동의어   ③

| 어휘 |

span v. 포괄하다   **faculty** n. (대학의) 학부; 능력, 기능   **foster** v. 육성하다(= nurture)   **chapter** n. (단체의) 지부   **advise** v. 조언하다   **lead** v. 이끌다   **repress** v. 억압하다

| 해석 |

상(賞)은 다양한 부문에 걸쳐 수여되는데, 그 중에는 교육 콘텐츠 및 행사에 크게 기여한 것에 대해 주어지는 교육상과 학생회를 지원하고 육성한 것에 대해 주어지는 학부 지도교수상이 있다.

04 동의어   ①

| 어휘 |

gruesome a. 섬뜩한, 끔찍한(= ghastly)   **bird flu** 조류독감   **detect** v. 감지되다, 발견하다   **efficacious** a. 효과적인   **productive** a. 생산적인   **frail** a. 노쇠한

| 해석 |

훨씬 더 섬뜩한 것은 조류 독감이 공장형 농장에서 발견되었을 때 수백 만 마리의 닭과 칠면조를 죽이기 위해 미국에서 사용된 방법이다.

05 동의어   ③

| 어휘 |

PFAS n. 과불화화합물   **break down** 분해되다   **contamination** n. 오염(= pollution)   **contemplation** n. 사색, 명상   **extent** n. 정도, 규모   **suspension** n. 연기, 보류

| 해석 |

과불화화합물(PFAS)이라는 화학물질은 쉽게 분해되지 않으며 전 세계적으로 건강 문제와 토양 및 지하수 오염과 관련이 있다.

06 동의어   ①

| 어휘 |

base v. ~에 본사를 두다   **promulgate** v. 널리 알리다, 발표하다(= announce)   **expurgate** v. (부적당한 부분을) 삭제하다   **venerate** v. 공경하다   **eradicate** v. 제거하다

| 해석 |

그의 성공은 그가 아프리카에 본사를 두고 있다는 점에서 더욱 더

이례적인데, 아프리카는 동서양처럼 그들의 창작물을 널리 알릴 수 있는 잘 갖춰진 시스템이 부족하기 때문이다.

07 동의어 ①

| 어휘 |
perceptible a. 감지[인지]할 수 있는(= detectable) subtle a. 미묘한 practical a. 실용적인 simple a. 단순한 intricate a. 얽힌, 복잡한

| 해석 |
인지할 수 있는 색상 차이는 아주 미묘해서 유심히 봐야만 알아볼 수 있는 차이이다.

08 동의어 ④

| 어휘 |
board n. 이사회 prestigious a. 명성이 있는, 유명한(= reputable) subsidiary a. 부수적인; (기업의) 자회사의 national a. 전국의 presumptive a. 추정상의

| 해석 |
조사 결과, 이사회는 여러 골프 대회를 개최한 적이 있는 베이징의 한 유명한 골프장에서 골프 라운드를 즐긴 것으로 또한 밝혀졌다.

09 동의어 ②

| 어휘 |
evoke v. (감정 등을) 불러일으키다 rancor n. 깊은 원한; 증오(= detestation) misleadingly ad. 잘못 인도하여 absolve v. (~을 …에서) 면제시키다 competition n. 경쟁 struggle n. 투쟁 disunion n. 내분, 불화

| 해석 |
위대함은 덜 위대한 사람들에게 질투와 증오를 불러일으킬 수 있으며, 다른 사람들의 책임을 잘못된 방식으로 면제시켜줄 수도 있다.

10 동의어 ①

| 어휘 |
reparative a. 수선의; 회복의(= recuperative) tie n. 인연; 관계 recumbent a. (사람의 몸이나 위치가) 누워 있는 reciprocal a. 상호간의, 호혜적인 recurrent a. 반복되는, 재발되는

| 해석 |
우리가 고통스러울 정도로 외로움을 느낀다는 것은 우리가 사회적 지원을 찾거나 사회적 관계를 회복하는 일을 해야 한다고 우리 몸이 정보를 주고 있는 것이다.

11 완료 분사구문 ①

| 분석 |
빈칸 뒤에 동사 experience의 목적어가 있으므로, 수동태로 쓰인 ②와 ④가 먼저 정답에서 제외된다. 그리고 그녀의 온정과 밝음을 내가 '앞서' 경험했다고 해야 그녀가 들어가는 모든 공간에서 그런 에너지가 발산된다는 것을 '내가 알고 있다'고 할 수 있을 것이다. 따라서 주절보다 한 시제 앞선 완료형 분사구문인 ①의 Having experienced가 빈칸에 적절하다.

| 어휘 |
firsthand ad. 직접 radiate v. (빛·에너지 등을) 방출[발산]하다

| 해석 |
그녀의 온정과 밝음을 직접 경험했으므로, 나는 그녀가 들어가는 모든 공간에서 그녀가 발산하는 에너지를 알고 있다.

12 현재완료시제 ②

| 분석 |
since two months ago와 같이 since 다음에 특정 시점이 나오는 경우, 그다음에 오는 주절의 시제는 '현재완료시제'를 사용한다. 두 번째 문장이 현재시제인 것이 이를 뒷받침한다. 따라서 과거완료시제로 쓰인 ③과 ④는 빈칸에 부적절하고, '걷는 법을 배운다'는 의미가 되어야 하므로, 동사 learn이 부정사를 목적어로 취해야 한다. 목적어를 취하는 것은 능동태이므로, ②의 has been learning이 빈칸에 적절하다.

| 어휘 |
take a step 한 걸음을 딛다 unaided a. 도움을 받지 않는

| 해석 |
두 달 전 그 수술 이후, 새뮤얼(Samuel)은 다시 걷는 법을 배우고 있다. 그는 이미 아무 도움도 받지 않고 한 두 걸음을 걸을 수 있다.

13 neither A nor B ③

| 분석 |
등위상관접속사를 묻고 있다. nor와 함께 쓰이는 것은 neither이므로 ③이 정답이며, 이때 neither는 형용사로 쓰여 명사 approach를 수식해 주고 있다.

| 어휘 |
fluropolymer n. 불소 중합체 incorporation n. 결합, 합동 wastewater n. 폐수, 하수

| 해석 |
두 가지 접근 방법 중 어느 것도 불소 중합체를 결합하는 데 물을 매개체로 사용하지도 필요로 하지도 않기 때문에, 환경적인 측면에서 폐수 부담이 사라진다.

14 현재분사와 과거분사의 구분 ②

| 분석 |

빈칸 앞의 institution(제도)은 영향을 주는 주체가 아니라, 영향을 받는 대상이다. 그러므로 능동태로 쓰인 ①과 ③은 빈칸에 부적절하다. ④의 have been acted가 빈칸에 들어갈 경우 연결사 없이 think of와 have been acted라는 두 개의 동사가 이어지므로 부적절하다. 따라서 ②의 acted가 빈칸에 적절한데, acts upon과 함께 쓰여 동사 affect와 같이 '~에 영향을 주다'는 뜻으로 쓰이며, 이때 acted upon은 which is acted upon에서 which is가 생략된 형태로 볼 수 있다.

| 어휘 |

centripetal a. 구심력의, 중심으로 향하는   **centrifugal** a. 원심력의, 중심에서 밖으로 향하는

| 해석 |

우리의 사회 구조가 어떻게 변화했는지를 이해하기 위해서는 결혼을 안으로 끌어당기는 구심력과 밖으로 끌어당기는 원심력의 영향을 받는 제도라고 여겨야 하다.

15 전치사 + 관계대명사 ①

| 분석 |

빈칸 다음에 완전한 절이 왔으므로, 관계부사나 '전치사+관계대명사'가 빈칸에 올 수 있다. 따라서 ②의 whose가 먼저 정답에서 제외된다. ③과 ④는 관계부사이지만, the ease와 의미상 연결이 되지 않는다. 그러므로 ①의 with which가 정답인데, 전치사가 with인 것은 with ease가 '쉽게'라는 뜻의 관용표현이기 때문이다.

| 어휘 |

vaccination n. 백신[예방] 접종   **in large part** 대체로   **dose** n. (약의) 1회 복용량, 한 첩

| 해석 |

지난 수십 년 동안, 팔레스타인의 예방접종 노력이 성공을 거두었는데, 그것은 대체로 부모가 자녀를 접종 일정에 맞춰 병원에 쉽게 데려갈 수 있었기 때문이었다.

16 관계대명사 ②

| 분석 |

in which와 같이 '전치사+관계대명사' 다음에는 완전한 절만 올 수 있는데, 주어가 없는 불완전한 절이 와서 틀렸다. 불완전한 절과 함께 쓸 수 있는 것은 관계대명사이며, 특히 which가 계속적 용법으로 앞의 절을 받을 수 있으므로, ②를 which로 고쳐야 한다.

| 어휘 |

have ~ on one's side ~가 (유리한 조건으로서) …을 가지고 있다

| 해석 |

두 번째인 그때에는 더 많은 사람이 그 책을 찾도록 도와주는 인터넷을 그녀 쪽에서 갖고 있었을 뿐 아니라, 세상도 다른 방식으로 변해 있었다.

17 부정사와 현재분사의 구분 ③

| 분석 |

while easy to conduct는 while they(= protocols) are easy to conduct에서 they are가 생략된 표현이다. 이때 easy나 difficult는 It is easy[difficult] to do something.의 문장에서 동사 do의 목적어가 주어로 가서 Something is easy[difficult] to do.의 문장이 만들어지는 난이형용사이다. 따라서 easy to conduct처럼 ③의 comparing도 to compare로 고쳐서 are difficult to compare의 형태가 되어야 한다.

| 어휘 |

agar n. 한천; 세균 배양액   **plate** n. (금속 따위의) 평판 v. (미생물)을 평판 배양하다   **diffusion** n. 확산   **qualitative** a. 질적인; 정성(定性)의   **yield** v. (결과 등을) 내다[생성하다]   **leach** v. 침출시키다

| 해석 |

한천 평판 확산법과 같은 프로토콜은 덜 널리 사용되었는데, 왜냐하면 이런 정성적 프로토콜이 수행하기는 쉽지만, 생성된 데이터가 비교하기 어렵고, 침출 기술에 가장 적합하도록 설계되어 있기 때문이었다.

18 be dedicated to ~ing ④

| 분석 |

be dedicated to는 '~에 헌신하다'는 뜻인데, 이때 to는 전치사이다. 전치사의 목적어로 동명사가 와야 하므로 ④를 동명사 bettering으로 고쳐야 한다.

| 어휘 |

liberalism n. 자유주의   **dedicated** a. 헌신하는, 몰두하는   **secure** v. (특히 힘들게) 확보하다

| 해석 |

경제적 생활 기반을 확보하기 위한 투쟁에 정당하게 헌신했던 1930년대의 양적 자유주의 대신, 사람들의 생활과 기회의 질을 개선하는 데 헌신하는 '질적 자유주의'가 지금 우리에게 필요하다.

19 B, not A ④

| 분석 |

B, not A는 not A but B와 같이 'A가 아니라 B'라는 의미로 쓰이며, 이때 A와 B에는 문법적인 구조나 역할이 같은 표현이 온다. B에

해당하는 것이 for its own sake이므로, A에 해당하는 on the service it may render도 for the service it may render로 고쳐서 병치를 이루어야 한다. 따라서 ④의 on을 for로 고쳐야 한다.

| 어휘 |

get things done 일을 해내다   appeal to (양심 등에) 호소하다
brute n. 짐승   wield v. (권력 등을) 휘두르다   for one's own sake ~을 위하여   render a service 서비스를 제공하다

| 해석 |

일을 해내는 수단으로서의 권력은 인간이 짐승과 공유하는 것, 즉 두려움과 탐욕에 호소한다. 권력은 권력을 휘두르는 사람들이 권력이 제공할 수 있는 서비스를 위해서가 아니라, 권력 그 자체를 위해 권력을 원하게 만들고, 권력을 자기 손에 계속해서 쥐고 있으려 하게 만든다.

20 동사와 명사의 구분   ②

| 분석 |

관계부사 where 다음이므로 ②는 동사일 수 없고, 등위접속사 and에 의해 artifacts와 병치된 명사여야 하므로, ②를 remains로 고쳐야 하며, 이때 remains는 '유해'라는 뜻의 명사이다.

| 어휘 |

archaeological a. 고고학의   artifact n. 유물   ancestor n. 조상   cluster v. (별 등이) 떼 짓다, 모이다

| 해석 |

만일 당신이 인류의 조상이 남긴 유해와 유물이 발견된 고고학 유적지를 보여주는 지도를 본다면, 여러 종과 관련된 유적지들이 같은 장소에 모여 있는 것을 보게 될 것이다.

21~22

얼음은 언 물이다. 빙하 얼음은 인공적으로 만든 얼음 조각을 포함하는 보다 일반적인 얼음과는 상당히 다르다. 빙하 얼음의 치밀한 결정 구조는 빙하 얼음이 파란색이나 청록색을 제외한 스펙트럼의 모든 다른 색(빨간색, 노란색 포함)을 흡수한다는 것을 의미한다. 그래서 최종 결과는 빙하 얼음이 어떤 색이든 모든 가시광선을 반사시키는 보통의 반투명 얼음과는 상당히 다르게 보인다는 것이다. 파란색 빛만이 빙하 얼음의 표면 아래로 침투할 수 있는 유일한 빛의 형태이다. 또한 냉동실에서 꺼낸 얼음 조각과 빙하 얼음이 다른 점은 빙하 얼음에는 암석, 토양, 식물, 박테리아 물질과 같은 불순물이 포함되어 있다는 것이다. 빙하 얼음은 단순히 언 물 이상의 것이다.
하지만 빙하 얼음에는 그것 이상으로 훨씬 더 많은 것이 있다. 얼음은 여러 가지 결정체 형태를 가질 수 있으며, 압력이 더 낮아질 경우 일반적인 어는점인 섭씨 0도(화씨 32도)에서 얼지 않을 수 있다. 얼음은 암석과 토양 등을 침식하여 형태를 만들 수 있고, 태양 에너지를 반사시킬 수 있으며, 물 위에 떠 있을 수 있고, 지구의 에너지 균형을 결정하는 데 중요한 역할을 담당한다. 얼음은 그 기원을 결코 잊지 않는다. 얼음은 결국 완벽하게 다시 물로 변할 수 있는 물질이다. 만약 얼음이 지속된다면 형태가 변할 수 있다. 이동하고 흔드는 물체로서, 얼음은 땅을 파고, 파낸 물질을 퍼뜨리며, 퇴적시킬 수 있다. 물고기, 물개, 북극곰, 고래, 그리고 조류 초원과 미생물과 같은 미세한 생명체들이 입증해 주듯이, 얼음은 얼음 표면 위아래에 있는 생명체들을 지탱할 수 있으며 실제로 지탱하고 있다. 남극의 빙하 아래에 묻혀 있는 빙하 밑 호수와 빙상은 극한 환경에서 어떤 미생물이 살아남을 수 있는지를 연구할 수 있는 가능성 때문에, 가장 최근에 과학계에서 주목 받고 있는 극한 환경이다.

| 어휘 |

glacial a. 빙하의   ice cube 얼음 조각 .   compacted a. 치밀한, 단단히 결합 된   crystalline a. 결정체로 된   apart from ~을 제외하고   turquoise n. 청록색   visible light 가시광선   penetrate v. 침투하다   freezer n. (냉장고 안의) 냉동실   impurity n. 불순물   freezing point (특정 액체가) 어는 점   carve v. 조각하다, 깎아서 만들다   float v. (가라앉지 않고) 뜨다   endure v. 오래가다[지속되다]   excavate v. (흙 · 모래 등을) 파내다   deposit v. 침적[퇴적]되다   seal n. 물개   algal a. 말[조류]의   meadow n. 초원   attest v. 증명하다   subglacial a. 빙하 밑의   Antarctic a. 남극지역의   ice sheet (육지를 덮고 있는) 빙상

21 빈칸완성   ①

| 분석 |

빙하 얼음이 파란색이나 청록색을 제외한 스펙트럼의 다른 모든 색(빨간색과 노란색 포함)을 흡수한다는 것은 결국 빙하 얼음이 스펙트럼에서 파란색과 청록색만 반사한다는 의미이다. 반면, 일반적인 얼음은 가시광선의 모든 색을 고르게 반사한다고 했는데, 모든 색을 반사한다는 것은 결국 색이 없이 보이는 '반투명' 얼음이라는 뜻이므로, ①의 translucent(반투명한)가 빈칸에 적절하다.
② 녹는 ③ 검댕 투성이인 ④ 모난

22 내용일치   ①

| 분석 |

본문에서 "얼음은 그 기원을 결코 잊지 않는다."라고 했으므로, ①이 정답이다.

다음 중 본문의 내용과 일치하는 것은?
① 얼음은 그 기원을 항상 기억한다.

② 얼음은 여러 가지 결정 구조를 가질 수 없다.
③ 냉동실에서 꺼낸 얼음 조각에는 불순물이 들어있다.
④ 빙하 얼음은 그저 단순히 언 물일뿐이다.

23~24

"사진 한 장이 천 마디 말의 가치가 있다"는 속담이 있다. 그러나 매 순간 수백 만 장의 사진이 촬영되고 인터넷에 업로드 되며 컴퓨터 화면을 통해 수많은 이미지 홍수에 매일 노출되는 시대에, 단 한 장의 사진이 가지는 가치는 과연 무엇일까? 런던의 빅토리아 앤 앨버트 뮤지엄(V&A)에서 사진 담당 수석 큐레이터인 마틴 반스(Martin Barnes)는 "훌륭한 사진은 시각적인 시와 같으며, 일상을 초월한 상황이나 감정을 정교하게 포착하고 표현해냅니다."라고 말한다. 단 하나의 순간을 포착하여 완전히 정지 상태로 고정시킴으로써, 사진은 보편적인 언어로 강력한 메시지를 전달할 수 있다. 하지만 그 이상으로, 사진 이미지는 우리를 새로운 곳으로 데려가고 우리가 사는 세상을 다른 관점에서 바라보게 도와줄 수 있다. 내셔널 지오그래픽 사진작가인 애런 휴이(Aaron Huey)는 "사진은 세상에 대한 우리의 고정관념을 무너뜨릴 수 있는 힘을 갖고 있습니다."라고 말한다.

| 어휘 |

saying n. 속담, 격언   **avalanche** n. 눈사태; (비유적으로) 쏟아짐, 쇄도   **poetry** n. 시, 시적인 것   **capture** v. 포착하다, 담아내다   **transcend** v. 초월하다, 능가하다   **transport** v. 이동시키다, 데려가다   **perspective** n. 관점, 시각   **assumption** n. 가정, 추정

23 내용파악   ③

| 분석 |

본문에서 "사진은 보편적인 언어로 강력한 메시지를 전달할 수 있다."라고 했을 뿐, "보편적인 생각을 세상에 전달할 수 있다."라고 언급하지는 않았으므로, ③이 정답이다.

다음 중 저자가 묘사한 사진에 관해 사실이 아닌 것은?
① 우리는 매일 쏟아지는 사진을 컴퓨터 화면에서 마주하게 된다.
② 사진은 우리가 세상을 바라보는 관점을 바꿀 수 있다.
③ 사진은 보편적인 생각을 세상에 전달할 수 있다.
④ 사진은 우리의 생활방식을 다른 태도로 바라보도록 도와줄 수 있다.

24 동의어   ②

| 분석 |

'뒤집다'는 뜻의 undo는 본문에서 고정관념을 '깨다, 무너뜨리다, 바꾸어버리다'는 의미로 해석될 수 있으므로, ②의 transform(완전히 바꿔 놓다)이 정답이다. ① 수용하다 ③ 이행하다 ④ 깨닫다

25~27

우리는 끊임없이 주변 세상을 자신의 생각이라는 렌즈를 통해 바라본다. 우리는 세상을 있는 그대로 보는 것이 아니라, 우리의 생각과 기억, 감정을 통해 세상을 인식하는 것이다. 이렇게 세상을 바라보는 방식이 문제이다. 우리는 우리의 생각을 거쳐서 세상을 바라보는 대신 우리가 끼고 있는 렌즈를 벗어버리고 우리의 생각 그 자체를 들여다보는 법을 배워야 한다.
선물 주기, 커피 한잔 마시기 등 어떤 순간이든, 현재를 즐기는 첫 번째 단계는 우리가 지금 하고 있는 일과 우리 주변에 일어나는 일에 온전히 몰입하는 것이다. 우리의 관심은 종종 과거나 미래에 맞춰져 있다. 과거는 후회로 가득 차 있고, 미래는 대개 걱정과 불안으로 연결되어 있다. 현재에 집중한다는 것은 우리가 오감을 통해 경험하는 것을 열린 마음과 호기심을 갖고, 그리고 경험하는 모든 것을 기꺼이 경험하려는 의지를 갖고 받아들인다는 것을 의미한다.
우리의 마음이 도움이 되지 않는 생각, 기억, 감정, 그리고 감각에 사로잡혀 있을 때, 우리는 불편함을 통제하고 피하려는 노력을 내려놓는 법을 배워야 한다. 불편한 기억에 반응하는 순간, 상황은 개선되지 않고 오히려 악화된다. 원치 않는 생각과 감정을 없애려 하지 말고 그저 오고 가도록 내버려두는 연습을 해야 한다. 나는 생각과 감정을 폭풍우 치는 바다 위의 파도라고 묘사하는 은유를 좋아한다. 나는 수면에서 파도와 싸울 수도 있고, 고요한 물속으로 가라앉아 멀리서 그 파도를 관찰할 수도 있다.

| 어휘 |

be fully connected to ~에 완전히 몰입하다   **hooked** a. ~에 사로잡혀 있는   **let go of** ~을 내려놓다   **metaphor** n. 은유

25 내용일치   ①

| 분석 |

본문에서 "과거는 후회로 가득 차 있고, 미래는 대개 걱정과 불안으로 연결되어 있다."라고 했으므로, ①이 정답이다.

다음 중 본문의 내용과 일치하지 않는 것은?
① 과거와 미래는 일반적으로 긍정적인 감정과 관련이 있다.
② 현재에 집중한다는 것은 오감을 적극적으로 사용하는 것과 관련이 있다.
③ 원치 않은 생각과 감정은 저항 없이 흘려보내야 한다.
④ 우리의 세계에 대한 인식은 우리의 생각과 감정을 통해 종종 걸러진다.

26 내용파악 ③

| 분석 |

본문에서 저자는 "원치 않는 생각과 감정을 없애려 하지 말고 그저 오고 가도록 내버려두는 연습을 해야 한다."라고 주장하고 있으므로, ③이 정답이다.

저자는 도움이 안 되는 생각과 감정을 어떻게 처리해야 한다고 제안하는가?
① 도움이 안 되는 생각과 감정에 대한 집중을 강화하라고
② 고통스러운 기억을 자주 떠올리라고
③ 도움이 안 되는 생각과 감정을 저항하려 하지 말고 오고 가도록 내버려 두라고
④ 도움이 안 되는 생각과 감정을 우리의 마음에서 완전히 없애라고

27 빈칸완성 ④

| 분석 |

빈칸을 포함한 분사구문에서는 "세상을 있는 그대로 본다."라고 한 반면, 빈칸 다음에 온 주절에는 "우리의 생각과 기억, 감정을 통해 세상을 인식한다."라는 서로 상반된 내용이 나오는데, 'A가 아니라 B'라는 형태의 의미구조이므로 '~이 아니라', '~보다는'을 의미하는 ④의 rather than이 적절하다. ① 왜냐하면 ② ~함으로써 ③ ~에도 불구하고

28~30

당신의 인생을 보다 잘 통제하고 있다고 느끼게 해줄 수 있는 마법의 알약이 있다면 어떨까? 어떤 의미에서는, 이미 마법의 알약이 존재한다고 볼 수 있다. 몬트리올(Montreal)에 있는 맥길(McGill) 대학교 심리학과 교수인 데비 모스코위츠(Debbie Moskowitz) 박사는 최근 고단백 식품(칠면조, 우유 등)에 포함된 필수 아미노산인 트립토판의 섭취를 늘리면 사람들이 보다 단호하게 행동할 수 있다는 것을 발견했다. 그녀의 연구에서 우울증이 없는 사람들이 12일 동안 하루 3g의 트립토판을 섭취한 결과, 위약(僞藥)을 복용한 사람들보다 더 목표 지향적이었으며, 다른 사람에게 제안하거나 요구하는 경향이 더 컸다. 또한 연구대상자들은 덜 까다롭고 덜 냉소적인 행동을 보였다. 연구 결과 모스코위츠 박사는 트립토판이 체내 세로토닌 합성을 극대화하는 방식으로 작용한다고 믿고 있다. 세로토닌은 자연적인 항우울제 역할을 하는 신경전달물질이다.

"우리 신체는 충분한 세로토닌을 생성하기 때문에, 대부분의 경우(평소에) 우리는 순종적이고 투쟁적인 행동을 보이지 않습니다. 하지만 이번 연구는 트립토판을 통해 세로토닌을 극대화하면 보다 주도적이면서 덜 논쟁적으로 행동할 수 있으며, 이를 통해 자신감을 유지하고 목표를 달성하는 데 도움이 될 수 있다는 것을 시사해줍니다."라고 모스코위츠 박사는 말한다. 안타깝게도, 고단백 식품 섭취를 늘리는 것만으로는 효과가 없는데, 왜냐하면 단백질 속의 많은 다른 아미노산들이 뇌로 전달되기 위해 경쟁하기 때문이다. 대신, 다른 아미노산이 포함되지 않은 정제된 보충제를 섭취해야 한다. 하지만 과거에 트립토판 보충제에서 오염문제가 있었기 때문에, 반드시 당신의 주치의와 먼저 의논해야 한다고 모스코위츠 박사는 조언한다.

| 어휘 |

pill n. 알약 **intake** n. 섭취 **placebo** n. 위약, 플라시보(효능이 없는 가짜 약) **goal-oriented** a. 목표 지향적인 **disagreeable** a. 성미가 까다로운, 까칠한 **sarcastic** a. 냉소적인, 빈정대는 **synthesis** n. 합성 **antidepressant** n. 항우울제 **submissive** a. 순종적인, 하라는 대로 하는 **quarrelsome** a. 다투기 좋아하는 **argumentatively** ad. 논쟁적으로 **do the trick** 효과가 있다 **purified** a. 정제된, 불순물이 제거된 **supplement** n. 보충제 **contamination** n. 오염

28 글의 주제 ②

| 분석 |

이 글은 고단백 식품에 포함된 필수 아미노산인 트립토판의 섭취를 늘리면 사람들이 보다 적극적으로 행동할 수 있다는 것을 발견했다는 연구를 중심적으로 다루고 있으므로, 글의 주제로는 ②가 적절하다.

다음 중 글의 주제로 적절한 것은?
① 건강보조식품 섭취의 위험성
② 트립토판이 적극적인 행동에 미치는 영향
③ 뇌로 흡수되기 위한 아미노산의 경쟁
④ 식단과 심리적 웰빙의 관계

29 동의어 ③

| 분석 |

밑줄 친 assertively는 본문에서 '단정적으로, 단호하게'라는 의미로 쓰였으므로, 동의어로 ③의 dominantly(주도적으로, 지배적으로)가 적절하다. ① 냉소적으로 ② 순종적으로 ④ 논쟁적으로

30 내용일치 ③

| 분석 |

본문에서 "우울증이 없는 사람들이 트립토판을 섭취한 결과, 위약

을 복용한 사람들보다 목표 지향적이었으며, 다른 사람에게 제안하거나 요구하는 경향이 더 컸다."라고 했으므로, ③이 정답으로 적절하다.

다음 중 본문의 내용과 일치하는 것은?
① 트립토판 섭취가 증가하면 세로토닌 수치는 감소한다.
② 대부분의 아미노산은 뇌로 전달되기 위해 트립토판과 경쟁하지 않는다.
③ 연구에서 트립토판 보충은 보다 목표지향적인 행동과 관련이 있었다.
④ 고단백 식품을 먹는 것은 뇌에 트립토판 흡수를 증가시키기에 충분하다.

31~32

사회와 인간은 분리될 수 없다. 즉 사회와 인간은 서로에게 필요하며 상호보완적이지, 그 반대가 아니다. "어떤 인간도 그 자체로 완전한 섬이 아니다. 모든 인간은 대륙의 한 조각이며, 대륙 본토의 일부이다."라고 존 던(John Donne)이 유명한 말을 남겼다. 그것이 진실의 한 측면이다. 반면, 고전적 개인주의자인 존 스튜어트 밀(John Stuart Mill)은 "인간이 함께 모인다고 해서 전혀 다른 종류의 실체로 변하지는 않는다."라는 격언을 남겼다. 물론 그렇다. 그러나 여기서 잘못된 생각은 '함께 모이기' 전에 인간이 존재했거나 어떤 종류의 실체를 갖고 있었다고 가정하는 것이다. 우리는 태어나자마자, 세상이 우리에게 작용하여 우리를 단순한 생물학적 존재에서 사회적 존재로 변화시킨다. 역사나 선사 시대의 어느 시기를 막론하고, 모든 인간은 사회 속에서 태어나서 어린 시절부터 사회에 의해 형성된다. 인간이 말하는 언어는 개인적인 유산이 아니라 인간이 자라난 집단에서 사회적으로 습득한 것이다. 언어와 환경은 모두 인간 사고의 성격을 결정하는 데 도움을 준다.

| 어휘 |

continent n. 대륙 **dictum** n. 격언, 금언 **fallacy** n. 오류, 잘못된 생각 **moulded** a. 형성된, 만들어진 **inheritance** n. 유산, 계승받은 것 **acquisition** n. 습득, 취득

31 빈칸완성 ①

| 분석 |
사회와 인간은 '분리될 수 없으며, 서로에게 필요한 존재라고 했으므로, 같은 맥락으로 사회와 인간은 서로에게 '상호보완적'이라고 해야 할 것이므로, ①의 complementary가 빈칸에 적절하다. ② 차별화된 ③ 만족스러운 ④ 공정한

32 내용일치 ②

| 분석 |
인간이 사회와 분리될 수 없는 상호보완적 존재이며, 어느 시기를 막론하고 사회 속에서 태어나 사회에 의해 형성된다고 했으므로, ②가 본문의 내용과 일치한다. ④ 인간의 의지에 의해서가 아니라 세상의 작용에 의해 생물학적 존재에서 사회적 존재로 변한다.

다음 중 본문의 내용과 일치하는 것은?
① 사회와 인간은 보통 서로 겹칠 수 없는 평행선처럼 존재한다.
② 만약 당신이 인간의 사회적 측면을 보지 못한다면, 당신은 인간을 이해하는 중요한 점을 놓치고 있는 것이다.
③ 인간과 언어는 서로에게 도움이 되기 때문에 분리될 수 없다.
④ 인간은 어떤 종류의 사회적 실체로 변화하고자 하는 의지가 있을 때만 항상 그렇게 변화한다.

33~34

개인정보는 미래 시민들에게 가장 귀중한 자산이 될 것이며 온라인상에서 주로 존재하게 될 것이다. 온라인상에서의 경험은 출생과 동시에, 또는 심지어 그 이전부터 시작될 것이다. 사람들의 시기별 인생의 모습은 시간이 지나도 그 자리에 고정될 것이고, 누구나 찾아 볼 수 있게 쉽게 표면화될 것이다. 이에 대응하여, 기업들은 사람들이 자신의 데이터를 누가 볼 수 있는지를 관리할 수 있게 해주는 목록 같은 새로운 정보 통제 도구들을 만들어야 할 것이다. 오늘날 우리가 사용하는 통신 기술은 의도적으로 사생활 침해적이어서, 우리의 사진, 댓글, 그리고 친구 목록 등을 수집하여 거대한 데이터베이스를 만드는데, 이 데이터베이스는 검색이 가능하고, 외부 규제가 없는 한, 고용주나 대학 입학 업무 담당자와 동네 소문에 훌륭한 먹잇감이 될 것이다. 결국 우리가 트윗으로 올리는 것이 바로 우리의 모습인 것이다.
이상적으로 말하자면, 모든 사람들은 자아의식을 갖고 자신의 온라인 개인 정보와 가상의 삶을 면밀하게 관리하며, 인생에서 자신의 기회를 제한하지 않기 위해 어릴 적부터 그런 개인 정보와 가상의 삶을 감시하고 형성해갈 것이다. 물론, 이것은 불가능하다. 어린이와 청소년의 경우, 정보를 공유하려는 동기는 모호하고 멀게 느껴지는 자기 노출의 위험보다 언제나 훨씬 더 클 것이며, 심지어 대중이 보게 되는 눈에 띠는 사례가 발생하더라도 그럴 것이다. 사람이 40대가 되었을 때쯤이면, 인생의 모든 단계에 걸친 모든 사실과 허구, 모든 실수와 성공을 포괄하는 방대한 온라인 기록을 축적하고 저장해 놓았을 것이다. 심지어 소문조차도 영원히 살아남을 것이다.

| 어휘 |

identity n. 정체성, 신원, 개인정보   commodity n. 상품; (유용한) 것   by design 의도적으로, 계획적으로   invasive a. 사생활을 침해하는   fair game (조소·공격의) 좋은 목표; 웃음거리, 놀림감   virtual a. 가상의   incentive n. 동기   outweigh v. ~보다 더 크다[대단하다]   salient a. 눈에 띄는, 두드러진   narrative n. 이야기   misstep n. 과실, 실수, 실책   triumph n. 성공, 승리

33 빈칸완성 ①

| 분석 |

빈칸 Ⓐ 앞에서 개인정보가 온라인상에서 주로 존재하게 될 것이라고 했으며, 사람들의 시기별 인생의 모습을 누구나 쉽게 찾아 볼 수 있다는 '문제점'이 나온 다음, Ⓐ 다음 문장에서, 기업들은 정보를 통제하는 도구를 만들어야 한다는 '해결책'이 나왔다. 따라서 이런 문제점에 '대응하여' 해결책을 제시한다고 해야 자연스러우므로, 빈칸 Ⓐ에는 In response(이에 대응하여)가 적절하다. 그리고 Ⓑ 다음에 "모든 사람들은 어릴 적부터 온라인 개인 정보와 가상의 삶을 감시하고 형성해갈 것이라고 했는데, 이것이 불가능하다"라고 했다. 불가능한 것은 곧 '이상적인' 것을 나타내므로, Ⓑ에는 Ideally(이상적으로)가 적절하다.

34 내용일치 ①

| 분석 |

본문에서 "온라인상에서 이뤄지는 경험은 출생과 동시에, 또는 심지어 그 이전부터 시작될 것이다."라고 했으므로, ①이 정답이다.

다음 중 본문의 내용과 일치하는 것은?
① 미래에는 온라인 경험이 출생과 동시에 시작되는 것이 가능해질 것이다.
② 멀게 느껴지는 자기노출의 위험이 청소년들이 공유하려는 동기보다 클 것이다.
③ 개인정보는 미래 시민들에게 온라인상에서 주로 존재하지 않을 가능성이 있다.
④ 우리의 데이터는 현재의 통신 기술에 의해 안전하게 보호된다.

35~37

1810년, 독일의 의사 사무엘 하네만(Samuel Hahnemann)은 자신의 의학 이론과 연구를 개괄적으로 정리한 『치유 기술의 오르가논』이라는 책을 출간했는데, 이 책에서 그는 병의 증상을 유발하는 물질을 섭취하면 그 병을 치료할 수 있다고 주장했으며, 이것이 동종요법의 탄생이었다.
Ⓐ 그 이후, 많은 사람들은 이 대체 치료법을 시도해 성공을 거두었다. 동종요법 치료약은 식물과 기타 천연 물질로 만들

어지기 때문에 종종 기존의 약보다 저렴하다.
Ⓒ 또한, 그러나 아마도 덜 중요하겠지만, 미국에서 400명 이상의 의사가 동종요법 치료를 정기적으로 추천하고 있다. 동종요법 치료가 저렴하고 인기가 있기 때문에, 나는 왜 메디케어(노인 의료 보험 제도)와 메디케이드(저소득층 의료 보장 제도)가 동종요법 치료를 자금 지원해주지 않는지 이해하기 어렵다.
Ⓑ 왜 사람들은 자신의 건강관련 선택을 하도록 허용되어서는 안 되는가? 사람들은 예를 들어, 자녀를 어느 학교에 보낼 것인가와 같은 삶의 다른 영역에서는 선택할 자유를 갖고 있는데, 의료와 관련해서는 왜 안 된다는 것인가?
동종요법이 효과가 없다고 주장하는 비평가들에게, 나는 내가 치료해서 병이 나은 환자들의 사례를 수백 건이나 제시할 수 있다. 게다가 동종요법이 가져다줄 수 있는 이점을 보여주는 연구도 많이 있다.
만일 동종요법이 완전히 헛소리라면 이렇게 오래 동안 살아남지 못했을 것이다. 동종요법은 단순한 플라시보 효과 이상의 효과가 있다. 때때로 어떤 것이 왜 효과가 있는지에 대한 '증거'를 제시하는 데 지나치게 중점을 두기도 한다. 믿음 또한 증거만큼 강력한 것이다.

| 어휘 |

overview n. 개요, 요약, 대체적 윤곽   organon n. 수단, 고찰[연구]법   symptom n. 증상   homeopathy n. 동종요법   conventional a. 기존의   on top of that 그 외에도   nonsense n. 터무니없는 생각[말]

35 내용일치 ④

| 분석 |

본문에서 동종요법 치료약은 식물과 기타 '천연' 물질로 만든다고 했다. ④에서 factitious는 '인공적인'이라는 뜻이므로, ④가 정답이다.

다음 중 본문의 내용과 일치하지 않는 것은?
① 기존 의학적 치료는 동종요법 치료보다 비용이 더 많이 든다.
② 병의 증상을 유발하는 물질을 섭취해 병을 치료하는 것을 동종요법이라고 부른다.
③ 이 대체 치료법이 많은 사람들을 치료하는 데 성공을 거두었다.
④ 동종요법 치료는 식물과 인공적인 자원에서 얻은 물질을 사용한다.

36 단락배열 ②

| 분석 |

첫 단락에서 동종요법을 소개하고 있으므로, 그다음에는 동종요법의 '효과'에 대한 내용이 와야 한다. 따라서 이와 관련한 Ⓐ가 제일

먼저 와야 하며, A에서 동종요법 치료약이 기존의 약보다 저렴하다고 했으므로, 같은 맥락으로 동종요법이 '저렴하고 인기 있다'고 부연 설명한 C가 그다음에 오는 것이 자연스럽다. 그리고 C에서 동종요법 치료가 자금을 지원받지 못하는 현실을 제시하고 있으므로, 이 현실이 불합리한 이유에 대해 설명하는 B로 이어져야 마지막 두 단락에서는 동종요법의 효과에 대해 회의적인 시각에 '반론'을 제시하며, 동종요법 치료를 옹호하는 내용으로 글이 자연스럽게 마무리 될 것이다.

37 빈칸완성 ④

| 분석 |
빈칸 다음에 온 대명사 it은 동종요법을 가리킨다. 빈칸 앞 단락에서 동종요법이 효과가 있다고 했으므로, 빈칸에도 동종요법이 헛소리가 아니어서 '오랜 세월 살아남게 되었다'는 내용이 되어야 한다. 이것을 가정법으로 표현하면 "동종요법이 완전히 헛소리라면, 동종요법이 오랫동안 살아남지 못했을 것이다."가 되므로, ④의 would not have survived가 빈칸에 적절하다.

38~40

스트레스가 너무나 만연해져서 이제는 용기를 상징하는 훈장처럼 스트레스를 자랑스럽게 착용하고 있다. 워크숍부터 긴장완화 테이프와 시청각 헤드셋에 이르기까지 스트레스 완화 사업은 호황을 누리고 있다. 만약 우리 문화가 밀접한 관계가 결여된 문화라면, 스트레스와의 관계만큼은 예외라 할 수 있다.
스트레스가 미치는 영향은 상상 이상으로 훨씬 더 깊다. 스트레스는 우리 존재 깊숙한 곳까지 침투한다. 스트레스는 우리를 움켜잡았다가 시간이나 노력을 들인 후 놓아주는 그런 것이 아니다. 스트레스는 그 과정에서 우리를 변화시킨다. 스트레스는 우리의 몸과 뇌를 바꿔놓는다.
우리는 알레르기에 반응하는 것처럼, 스트레스에 반응할 수 있다. 즉 우리는 스트레스에 과민해질 수 있다는 말이다. 일단 민감해지면, 아주 사소한 스트레스 징후조차 뇌와 몸에서 화학적 반응을 촉발해 우리를 내부에서 공격할 수 있다. 스트레스는 심리적인 측면에서 보면 돼지풀 알레르기와 같다. 일단 몸이 꽃가루나 돼지풀에 민감하게 반응하면, 봄이나 가을에 아주 소량의 꽃이 살짝 피기만 해도 생화학적 경보가 울려 콧물이 나고, 눈물이 흐르며, 건초열의 고통을 겪게 된다. 그러나 우리들 중 아주 일부만 유전적으로 건초열을 겪도록 프로그램화 되어 있지만, 스트레스에 민감해질 가능성은 우리들 모두에게 있다.

| 어휘 |
endemic a. 만연한, 고질적인   badge n. 훈장   booming a. 호황을 누리는, 번창하는   intimacy n. 친밀; 밀접한 관계를 갖기   grip v. 움켜잡다   let go 놓아주다   sensitized a. 과민 반응하는   intimation n. 암시, 넌지시 알림   trigger v. 촉발하다   cascade n. 폭포처럼 쏟아지는 것, 연쇄 반응   assault v. 폭행하다; 괴롭히다   equivalent n. ~에 상당하는 것, 등가물   ragweed n. 돼지풀   pollen n. 꽃가루, 화분   bloom n. 꽃; 개화(기)   set something off (경보 장치를) 울리다   runny nose 콧물   misery n. 고통   hay fever 건초열   plagued with ~에 시달리는

38 글의 요지 ④

| 분석 |
이 글은 스트레스에 대한 몸의 반응을 알레르기에 대한 몸의 반응과 비교하며, 스트레스가 알레르기처럼 몸을 민감하게 만들어 사소한 자극에도 강한 반응을 일으킬 수 있다는 점을 강조하고 있으므로, 글의 요지로 ④가 적절하다.

다음 중 글의 요지로 가장 적절한 것은?
① 스트레스는 이전에 믿었던 것보다 덜 해롭다.
② 극소수의 사람들만이 스트레스에 생화학적으로 영향을 받는다.
③ 스트레스를 줄이는 방법은 장기적으로 효과가 없다.
④ 우리 몸이 스트레스에 반응하는 방식에 있어 스트레스는 몸의 알레르기와 유사하다.

39 동의어 ②

| 분석 |
penetrate는 본문에서 '침투하다'는 뜻으로 쓰였으므로, penetrate의 동의어로 ②의 infiltrates가 적절하다. ① 중단하다 ③ 가로막다 ④ 선행하다

40 내용일치 ④

| 분석 |
본문에서 몸이 스트레스에 민감해지면, 알레르기 반응을 보이는 사람처럼 아주 작은 스트레스에도 뇌와 몸에서 중요한 반응이 일어날 수 있다는 점을 설명하고 있다. 따라서 ④가 본문의 내용과 일치한다.

다음 중 본문의 내용과 일치하는 것은?
① 스트레스는 우리의 정신 상태가 아니라 오직 몸의 상태에만 영향을 미친다.
② 모든 사람들이 건초열을 겪도록 유전적으로 프로그램화 되어 있다.
③ 스트레스는 장기적인 영향 없이 대부분의 사람들이 쉽게 극복한다.
④ 몸은 스트레스에 과민하게 반응하여, 심지어 사소한 자극에도 강하게 반응할 수 있다.

단국대학교 인문계 오후

TEST p. 222~235

01	②	02	③	03	①	04	④	05	④	06	③	07	②	08	③	09	①	10	②
11	②	12	④	13	①	14	②	15	③	16	③	17	②	18	③	19	③	20	③
21	①	22	③	23	②	24	①	25	①	26	②	27	③	28	②	29	②	30	①
31	④	32	①	33	②	34	③	35	①	36	①	37	③	38	①	39	①	40	①

01 동의어 ②

| 어휘 |

initiate v. 시작하다　**deportation** n. 국외 추방(= banishment)　**undocumented** a. 증거 자료가 없는; (외국 거주·취업 등을 위한) 허가증이 없는　**immigrant** n. 이민자　**fire** v. 해고하다　**legion** n. 다수, 많음　**civil servant** 공무원　**MAGA** 트럼프의 대통령 선거운동 슬로건(Make America Great Again)　**loyalist** n. 충신, 애국자; 현 체제 지지자　**invitation** n. 초대, 초청　**summon** v. 소환하다; 소집하다　**deployment** n. 전개, 배치

| 해석 |

그녀는 트럼프가 약속한 대로, 불법 체류자들의 대규모 추방을 시작하거나, 수많은 공무원들을 해고하고 그들을 MAGA 충성파로 대체하지 않을 것이다.

02 동의어 ③

| 어휘 |

conspicuously ad. 눈에 띄게, 두드러지게, 빼어나게(= obviously)　**overwork** v. 과로시키다, 혹사하다　**randomly** ad. 무작위로, 닥치는 대로　**reciprocally** ad. 서로, 상호[호혜]적으로　**generously** ad. 관대하게

| 해석 |

우리의 기준으로 볼 때 의사들이 눈에 띄게 과로한다면, 젊은이들로 하여금 그 직업을 선택하게 하는 것은 어려울 것이다.

03 동의어 ①

| 어휘 |

nonviolent a. 비폭력(주의)의　**resistance** n. 저항　**Negro** n. 흑인　**noble** a. 고귀한, 고결한, 숭고한　**perpetrator** n. 범죄자, 가해자, 범죄 실행자(= executor)　**expert** n. 전문가, 숙련가　**governor** n. 주지사　**attorney** n. 변호사

| 해석 |

비폭력 저항을 통해 흑인은 부당한 체제에 반대하면서도 그 체제의 실행자를 사랑하는 고귀한 경지에 오를 수 있을 것이다.

04 동의어 ④

| 어휘 |

genetic a. 유전의, 유전학의　**skewed** a. 왜곡된, 편향된, 삐딱한(= contorted)　**recognizably** ad. 곧 알아볼 수 있을 정도로; 인식[인지]할 수 있어　**clarified** a. 정화된, 맑아진　**straightforward** a. 똑바른; 정직한, 솔직한; 간단한　**fictitious** a. 허구의, 지어낸

| 해석 |

우선, 더 작은 개체군은 그 종 전체의 모든 유전 물질을 포함하고 있지는 않다. 그것은 왜곡된 표본이기 때문에, 곧 두 개체군은 눈에 띄게 다르게 보일 것이다.

05 동의어 ④

| 어휘 |

separation n. 분리, 이탈　**hamstring** v. 불구로 만들다; 무력하게 하다(= cripple)　**blur** v. 흐리게 하다, 더럽히다　**accountability** n. 책임, 책무　**frame** v. (계획·이론 등을) 세우다　**coherent** a. 일관성 있는, 논리[조리] 정연한　**accommodate** v. 수용하다; 편의를 도모하다　**accelerate** v. 가속하다; 촉진시키다　**provoke** v. 유발하다; 화나게 하다

| 해석 |

그들은 행정부를 무력화시키고, 책임과 책무를 흐리게 하며, 국가가 일관된 정책을 수립하는 것을 불가능하게 만드는 권력 분립에 비판을 집중해 왔다.

06 동의어 ③

| 어휘 |
indubitable a. 의심할 여지가 없는, 확실한(= irrefutable) **prolong** v. 늘이다, 연장하다 **disputable** a. 논의의 여지가 있는 **dubious** a. 의심스러운 **familiar** a. 익숙한, 친숙한

| 해석 |
두 사건 사이의 피드백 관계는 오래 지속된 만큼이나 의심할 여지가 없다.

07 동의어 ②

| 어휘 |
fidgety a. 안절부절못하는, 안달하는(= impatient) **distractible** a. 정신을 산만하게 할 수 있는; 주의가 산만한 **avaricious** a. 탐욕스러운, 욕심 많은 **keen** a. 날카로운, 예리한; 열심인 **princely** a. 군주다운; 고귀한, 위엄 있는; 관대한

| 해석 |
천재 발명가 토머스 알바 에디슨(Thomas Alva Edison)은 학교에 다닌 지 불과 3개월 만에 너무 안절부절못하고 산만해서 학교에 적응할 수 없다고 판단되었다.

08 동의어 ③

| 어휘 |
exasperate v. 화나게 하다, 격분시키다(= irritate v. 화나게 하다, 초조하게 하다) **nickel** n. 니켈; 5센트 백동화 **be no good** 소용[쓸모]이 없다 **suffocate** v. ~의 숨을 막다, 질식시키다 **provoke** v. 유발하다; 도발하다, (도발적인 언동으로) 화나게 하다 **agitate** v. 동요시키다; 선동하다

| 해석 |
나는 학사 학위가 급여 봉투에서 5센트의 가치도 없고, 대학 교육은 아무 소용이 없다고 주장하는 비평가들에 의해 화가 났다.

09 동의어 ①

| 어휘 |
downtrodden a. 탄압받는, 짓밟힌(= trampled) **resist** v. 저항하다 **military occupation** 군사 점령 **overlord** n. 지배자, 권력자, 대군주 **endure** v. 견디다, 참다 **carnage** n. 대학살 **dwindle** v. 작게[적게] 하다, 줄이다 **retain** v. 유지하다, 보유하다 **bolster** v. 지지하다, 강화하다; 기운을 북돋우다

| 해석 |
한쪽의 억압받는 주민들은 더 부유한 지배자의 군사 점령에 저항하지만, 대량 학살의 대부분을 견뎌낸다.

10 동의어 ②

| 어휘 |
caregiver n. (병자·불구자·아이 등을) 돌보는 사람 **respectively** ad. 각각, 각자(= correspondingly) **approximately** ad. 대략, 대체로, 거의 **distinctively** ad. 독특하게, 특수하게 **quantitatively** ad. 양적으로, 정량적(定量的)으로

| 해석 |
지난해, 간병인과 가사도우미 비용은 2016년에 비해 각각 50%와 37% 증가했다.

11 시제일치 ②

| 분석 |
주절의 동사가 과거시제이므로 that절의 동사 역시 과거시제로 시제를 일치시켜야 한다. 따라서 ②의 seemed to가 빈칸에 적절하다.

| 해석 |
그 남자는 눈을 가리도록까지 모자를 눌러쓰고 무언가를 숨기고 있는 것처럼 보이는 커다란 코트를 입고 있었다.

12 whether A or B ④

| 분석 |
or과 상관적으로 쓰이는 접속사가 필요하므로 빈칸에는 whether가 적절하다.

| 어휘 |
intuition n. 직관, 직각 **concrete** a. 구체적인

| 해석 |
감각과 직관은 사람들이, 구체적인 정보(감각)를 통해서든 감정적 느낌(직관)을 통해서든, 세상에 대한 정보를 수집하는 것을 선호하는 방식을 말한다.

13 문의 구성 ①

| 분석 |
문장의 주어인 Other less-than-orthodox treatments를 he recommends가 수식하고, 목적어 activities를 that부터 work까지 수식하고 있다. 따라서 빈칸에는 동사가 필요한데, 주어가 treatments로 복수이므로 복수 동사인 ① include가 적절하다.

| 어휘 |
orthodox a. 정통의, 전통적인 **in step with** ~와 보조를 맞추어, ~에 조화되어서, 일치하여 **drumming** n. 드럼 연주 **choir** n. 합창단

| 해석 |

그가 추천하는 다른 비정통적인 치료법에는 춤, 드럼 연주, 합창 등, 사람들이 다른 사람들과 조화를 이룬다고 느끼게 도와주는 활동뿐만 아니라, 요가와 호흡 요법과 같은 자기 자신과 조화를 이룬다고 느끼게 도와주는 활동도 포함된다.

14 수동태   ②

| 분석 |

refer to A as B 구문에서 A가 주어로 앞에 나가 수동태가 된 것으로 A be referred to as B의 형태가 되어야 한다. 과거부터 현재까지 불리어 온 것이므로 시제는 현재완료시제가 적절하다. 따라서 빈칸에는 ② has been referred to가 들어가야 한다.

| 어휘 |

retail a. 소매의   dizzying a. 어지럽게 하는, 현기증이 나게 하는
paralysis n. 마비

| 해석 |

소비자들이 어지러울 정도로 수많은 제품에 직면하는 소매 환경에서, 이러한 종류의 서비스는 '선택의 마비'라고 불려온 것과 싸울 수 있다.

15 비교   ③

| 분석 |

뒤에 than이 있으므로 비교급 표현이 와야 한다. '높은 점수를 받다'는 의미는 score high로 쓰이므로 high의 비교급 형태인 higher가 적절하다. 따라서 빈칸에는 ③ score higher가 들어가야 한다.

| 어휘 |

youngster n. 젊은이, 청소년, 아이   academically ad. 학문적으로   score v. (시험 등에서) 점수를 얻다

| 해석 |

연구 결과에 따르면, 일주일에 30시간 이상 집단 보육을 받는 아이들은 다른 방식으로 돌봄을 받는 아이들보다 학업 점수가 더 높다.

16 동명사   ③

| 분석 |

③은 전치사 from 뒤에 과거분사 형태가 와서 적절하지 않은데, 전치사 다음에는 명사나 동명사가 와야 한다. 따라서 ③을 동명사 형태인 growing up with로 고친다. ④ 동사 learn은 '(~하는 것을) 배우다'는 의미로 쓰일 때 목적어로 how to do가 주로 쓰이지만 how를 생략하기도 한다.

| 어휘 |

pleasing a. (~에게) 만족을 주는, 기쁨을 주는   trauma n. 정신적 외상, 트라우마   volatile a. 휘발성의; 변덕스러운

| 해석 |

사람들의 비위를 맞추는 것은 보통 어린 시절 일종의 트라우마의 결과로, 종종 가족 중에 특히 변덕스러운 사람과 함께 자라는 것에서 비롯된다. 그래서 사람들의 반응을 조절하는 법을 배우게 된다.

17 주어와 동사의 수일치   ②

| 분석 |

주어가 the Western art traditions로 복수이므로 복수 동사가 와야 한다. 따라서 ②를 have로 고친다.

| 어휘 |

supple a. 나긋나긋한, 유연한; 온순한   swath n. 한 번 낫질한 자취
handiwork n. 손작업, 수세공, 수공예

| 해석 |

대부분의 사람들은 그것들을 태피스트리나 퀼트로 설명하는 데 동의해왔는데, 이는 부분적으로는 그것들이 서양 미술 전통이 갖고 있는, 그의 거대하고 유연한 작품들과 가장 가까운 것들이기 때문이기도 하고, 부분적으로는 그것들을 만드는 데 들어가는 세밀한 수작업의 양이 비슷하기 때문이기도 하다.

18 동명사의 병치   ③

| 분석 |

등위접속사 and에 의해 전치사 including의 목적어로 세 개의 동명사가 병치되어 있다. 따라서 breaking, starting과 마찬가지로 ③을 동명사 형태인 removing으로 고쳐야 한다.

| 어휘 |

procrastination n. 지연, 미루기   manageable a. 관리[처리]할 수 있는   chunk n. 큰 덩어리; 상당한 양[액수]   distraction n. (주의) 집중을 방해하는 것; 기분 전환, 오락

| 해석 |

이 책은 작업을 몇 개의 관리 가능한 덩어리로 나누고, 작은 것부터 시작하며, 음악 듣기와 같은 주의산만 요소를 제거하는 등, 미루기 습관을 다루는 몇 가지 유용한 전략을 제시했다.

19 부정사의 태   ③

| 분석 |

'require+목적어+to부정사'의 구문이다. 부정사의 태는 부정사의 의미상 주어가 행위의 주체이면 능동, 행위의 대상이면 수동이 되어야 한다. projects는 disclose하는 행위의 주체이므로 능동태가 적절하다. ③을 to disclose로 고친다.

| 어휘 |
force a person's hand 남에게 억지로 시키다   legally binding 법적 구속력이 있는   carbon intensity 탄소 농도, 탄소 집약도

| 해석 |
기업들을 강제하기 위해, 포레스트(Forrest)는 정부가 법적 구속력이 있는 탄소 예산을 채택할 것을 제안하는데, 이는 모든 제안된 프로젝트가 탄소 농도를 공개하고 이를 기반으로 승인을 받도록 요구할 것이다.

20 관계부사 ③

| 분석 |
③의 관계대명사 which 뒤에 완전한 문장이 왔으므로 관계부사가 와야 한다. 시간의 상황을 나타내므로 관계부사 when이 적절하다.

| 어휘 |
visitor center 관광 안내소   attendant n. 종업원, 점원   burst into tears 울음을 터뜨리다   lifeline n. (사람이 의지하는) 생명선   divorce n. 이혼

| 해석 |
로빈스(Robbins)는 세 시간에 걸쳐 대화를 하는 동안 아이슬란드의 한 관광 안내소 직원에 대해 이야기하면서 마지막으로 눈물을 흘린다. 그 직원은 그녀가 화장실에 가는 길을 물었을 때 그녀의 목소리를 알아차리고 눈물을 터뜨렸고, 고통스러운 이혼 과정에서 그녀의 유튜브 영상이 어떻게 생명선이 되어주었는지에 대해 이야기했다.

21~23

인간과 개미 두 종만이 전쟁의 기술을 실천하며, 이 두 종 모두 상당히 복잡한 사회 구조를 유지하고 있는 것은 자연의 기이한 현상이다. 이는 인간과 개미만이 자신의 종족을 살해 한다는 뜻은 아니다. 같은 종의 많은 동물들이 서로를 죽이지만, 오직 인간과 개미만이 조직적인 파괴의 과학을 실천해 왔다. 그들은 격렬한 전투에서 큰 수의 무리를 이용하고, 전개되는 상황에 대처하거나 상대방의 전략과 전술의 약점을 활용하기 위해 전략과 전술에 의존했다. 인간들 사이에서 벌어진 가장 오래 계속된 전쟁은 30년 동안 지속되었다. 지금까지 기록된 가장 긴 개미 전쟁은 6주 반 동안, 아니 개미의 시간 계산으로 그에 상응하는 기간 동안, 지속되었다.
모든 곤충학자들은 전쟁이 개미에게 본능적이라는 데 동의하지만, 모든 인류학자와 생물학자들이 전쟁이 인간에게 본능적이라는 데 동의하는 것은 아니라는 점은 고무적이다. 물론 경험에 의존하는 사람들은 전쟁이 그의 본성에 내재되어 있다는 것을 보여주기 위해 인간의 역사에서 모든 것을 찾아낸다. 그러나 인간에게 전쟁 본능이 있다는 증거는 불완전하고 오해의 소지가 있으며, 인간은 전쟁을 없앨 수 있는 힘을 가지고 있다고 주장하는 과학자들은 더 넓고 관대하며, 확실히 더 철학적인 견해를 가지고 있다. 영국의 생물학자 줄리언 헉슬리(Julian Huxley)는 인간 본성과 인간 본성의 표현 사이에 명확한 구분을 둔다. 따라서 전쟁은 인간 본성의 반영이 아니라 표현이다. 더욱이 전쟁을 초래하는 요인이 변함에 따라 표현이 바뀔 수 있다. "인간에게 있어, 개미와 마찬가지로, 어떤 진지한 의미에서의 전쟁은 싸움거리가 될 재산 축적의 존재와 밀접한 관련이 있다. 인간의 본성에 관해 말하자면, 인간의 본성에는 수확 개미의 본성에 있는 것과 같은 특정한 전쟁 본능은 없다. 인간의 기질에는 일반적인 공격적인 성향이 있지만, 이것은 인간의 다른 모든 충동과 마찬가지로 특정하고 변하지 않는 본능이 아니며, 가장 다양한 형태로 형성될 수 있다."

| 어휘 |
curious a. 호기심이 강한; 기이한, 이상한   engage in ~에 관여[참여]하다   destruction n. 파괴, 파멸   employ v. (기술·방법 등을) 쓰다[이용하다]   massed a. 밀집한; 집중한, 하나로 뭉친   capitalize v. 이용하다, 기회로 삼다   strategy n. 전략   tactics n. 전술   continuous a. 연속적인, 계속적인   corresponding a. 상응하는, 대응하는   reckoning n. 계산, 셈   entomologist n. 곤충학자   instinctive a. 본능적인   encouraging a. 격려[장려]하는, 고무적인   anthropologist n. 인류학자   lean on ~에 기대다, 의지하다   be locked up within 내부에 갇혀있다   generous a. 관대한, 너그러운   misleading a. 오해의 소지가 있는   abolish v. 폐지하다, 없애다   sharp a. 명확한, 뚜렷한   reflection n. 반사, 반향, 반영   be bound up with ~와 밀접한 관련이 있다   harvester ant 수확 개미(풀을 먹고 그 씨를 비축함)   makeup n. 성질, 기질   aggressive a. 공격적인   tendency n. 경향; 성향, 성벽   urge n. (강한) 충동   unvarying a. 불변의, 변하지 않는

21 빈칸완성 ①

| 분석 |
모든 인류학자와 생물학자들이 인간에게 전쟁 본능이 있다는 것을 동의하지 않는다는 점을 고무적이라고 했으므로 인간에게 전쟁 본능이 있다는 증거에 대해 부정적인 내용이 와야 한다. 따라서 빈칸에는 'misleading(오해의 소지가 있는)'과 유사한 표현이 와야 하므로 증거가 '불완전하다'는 의미의 ① incomplete가 적절하다.

다음 중 빈칸에 들어가기에 가장 적절한 것은?
① 불완전한
② 건전한
③ 합리적인
④ 부패하지 않은

| 22 | 내용파악 | ③ |

| 분석 |

인간에게 전쟁은 재산 축적과 밀접한 관련이 있지만 인간은 전쟁 본능이 없다고 했다. 재산 축적은 전쟁을 일으킬 수 있는 여러 요소 중의 하나이므로 전쟁의 원인이 단지 재산을 차지하려는 경우에 한정된다고 할 수 없다. 따라서 ③이 사실이 아니다. ① '전쟁을 초래하는 요인이 변함에 따라 인간본성의 표현이 바뀔 수 있다'고 한 것에서 전쟁을 초래하는 요소가 많음을 알 수 있다.

위 글에 의하면, 줄리언 헉슬리의 주장에 관해 사실이 <u>아닌</u> 것은?
① 인간에게 전쟁을 초래하는 많은 요소들이 있다.
② 인간에게는 특정한 전쟁 본능이 없다.
③ 인간은 타인의 막대한 재산을 차지하기 위해서만 전쟁을 일으킨다.
④ 공격적인 성향은 인간의 다른 모든 충동 중 하나다.

| 23 | 내용일치 | ② |

| 분석 |

인간에게 전쟁 본능이 있다는 증거는 불완전하고(③은 사실이 아님), 인간은 전쟁을 없앨 수 있는 힘을 가지고 있다고 했으며, 인간의 공격적인 성향은 변하지 않는 본능이 아니라 다양한 형태로 형성될 수 있다고 했다. 따라서 인간은 상황에 따라 전쟁을 일으킬 수도 있고 없앨 수도 있는 양면적인 성향을 가지고 있다고 할 수 있으므로 ②가 적절하다.

위 글에 의하면, 다음 중 사실인 것은?
① 인간과 개미의 전쟁 본능은 구별할 수 없다.
② 인간은 전쟁을 일으키는 성향과 전쟁을 없애려는 성향을 동시에 가질 수 있다.
③ 인간의 전쟁 본능은 단지 몇 가지 형태로만 표현될 수 있다.
④ 사회 조직은 인간과 개미에게 전쟁의 유일한 원인이다.

24~25

산소 외에도, 포도당을 혈액은 지속적으로 공급해야 하며, 그렇지 않으면 근육은 에너지를 소진하게 될 것이다. 이는 에너지 사용이 많은 운동 중에 특히 그러하다. 그러나 몸은 포도당이나 다른 당분을 저장할 수 없다. 대신, 에너지는 긴 사슬로 연결된 많은 포도당 분자로 구성된 탄수화물인 글리코겐으로 저장된다.
몸에서 글리코겐의 주요 저장소는 간이다. 혈액에 포도당이 너무 많으면(예를 들어 식사 직후), 간은 일부 포도당을 흡수하여 글리코겐으로 바꾼다. 운동 중에 혈액 속의 포도당이 빠르게 소모되면, 간은 글리코겐의 일부를 포도당으로 분해하여 혈액으로 방출한다.

근육은 먼저 운동 중에 간에 저장된 글리코겐을 사용한다. 그런 다음 몸은 근육에 에너지를 공급하기 위해 지방 저장소를 사용하기 시작한다. 그러나 몸은 지방을 당분만큼 빨리 태울 수 없다. 근육이 지방을 사용하기 시작하면, 운동선수는 속도가 느려진다.

| 어휘 |

constant a. 지속적인, 끊임없는   glucose n. 포도당   run out of ~을 다 써버리다   store v. 저장하다, 비축하다 n. 창고, 저장소   glycogen n. 글리코겐, 당원   carbohydrate n. 탄수화물   be made up of ~로 구성되다   liver n. 간   take up 흡수하다   use up 다 써버리다   release v. 방출하다

| 24 | 빈칸완성 | ① |

| 분석 |

Ⓐ 몸은 포도당을 저장할 수 없기 때문에 포도당 분자로 구성된 글리코겐으로 저장된다고 했다. '대안'에 해당하므로 Instead가 적절하다. Ⓑ 근육은 글리코겐을 다 사용하면 지방을 사용하는데 지방은 당만큼 빨리 태울 수 없다고 했다. 서로 대조되는 내용이므로 역접의 접속부사인 However가 적절하다. 따라서 ①이 정답이다.

다음 중 빈칸 Ⓐ와 Ⓑ에 들어가기에 가장 적절한 것은?
① 대신에 — 그러나
② 예를 들어 — 전반적으로
③ 따라서 — 그러므로
④ 그와는 반대로 — 게다가

| 25 | 내용일치 | ① |

| 분석 |

몸은 지방을 당분만큼 빨리 태울 수 없다고 했으므로 ①이 사실이다. ② 몸은 포도당이나 다른 당분을 저장할 수 없어서 포도당 분자로 구성된 탄수화물인 글리코겐으로 저장한다고 했다. ③ 몸은 먼저 글리코겐을 사용한 다음에 지방 저장소를 사용한다고 했다. ④ 간이 일부 포도당을 흡수하여 글리코겐으로 바꾼다고 했다.

위 글에 의하면, 다음 중 사실인 것은?
① 몸은 지방보다 당분을 더 빨리 태울 수 있다.
② 포도당이나 다른 당분은 몸에 저장될 수 있다.
③ 몸은 운동 중에 근육에 에너지를 공급하기 위해 먼저 지방 저장소를 사용한다.
④ 혈액은 일부 글리코겐을 흡수하여 포도당으로 바꾼다.

26~27

무료 또는 공공 의료 서비스를 제공하는 국가들 내에는 다양한 모델이 있다. 일부 국가에서는 상담, 치료 및 의약품이 모든 시민에게 무료이다. 이는 정부가 직접 비용을 지불할 수도 있고, 아마도 정부가 소유한 국가의 귀중한 천연자원에 의해 자금을 공급받을 수도 있다. 다른 국가들은 소득에 따라 세금을 통해 시민들로부터 돈을 모은다. 근로자들은 얼마를 버느냐에 따라 비용을 지불하고, 고용주들도 일정 금액을 부담한다. 병원과 기타 의료 서비스는 정부에 의해 제공되고 운영된다. 사람들이 선택적으로 이용할 수 있는 일부 개인 의료 서비스도 있을 수 있다. 이러한 시스템의 장점은 분명하다. 소득에 관계없이 모든 사람에게 무료로 기본적인 의료 서비스를 제공한다는 것이다. 그러나 이는 매우 비용이 많이 드는 시스템이며, 기대 수명과 비용이 증가함에 따라 많은 국가들이 지속 불가능한 재정적 부담이나 제공되는 서비스 및 시설의 질 저하에 직면해 있다.

| 어휘 |

consultation n. 상담, 협의 **treatment** n. 치료; 치료법 **natural resource** 천연자원 **income** n. 수입, 소득 **contribution** n. 기부, 기부금; 보험료; 세금, 조세; 분담금 **advantage** n. 이점, 장점 **basic** a. 기초적인, 기본적인 **regardless of** ~에 상관[관계]없이 **life expectancy** 기대 수명 **unsustainable** a. 지속 불가능한 **facility** n. (보통 pl.) 설비, 시설

26 글의 주제   ②

| 분석 |

여러 국가에서 운영되고 있는 무료 또는 공공 의료 서비스의 다양한 모델에 대해 설명하고 있다. 일부 국가는 정부가 직접 비용을 부담하거나 천연자원으로 자금을 마련하고, 다른 국가는 세금을 통해 운영되는 등의 다양한 의료 서비스 모델의 특징을 제시한다. 따라서 위 글의 주제로는 ②가 적절하다.

위 글의 주제는 무엇인가?
① 무료 또는 공공 의료 서비스의 기능
② 무료 또는 공공 의료 서비스를 위한 다양한 모델
③ 의료 서비스의 두 가지 효과
④ 공공 의료 시스템의 장점

27 동의어   ③

| 분석 |

regardless of는 '~에 상관[관계]없이'라는 의미이므로 ③ irrespective of가 적절하다.

밑줄 친 부분과 가장 가까운 의미는 무엇인가?
① ~에도 불구하고
② ~에 더하여
③ ~와 관계없이
④ ~에 관하여

28~30

많은 돈을 버는 남성들은 빨리 결혼하고 싶어 한다. 그러나 부유한 여성들은 그렇게 서두르지 않는다. 일하는 여성들은 안정적인 근무 경력이 없는 여성들보다 파트너와 함께 살 가능성이 50% 더 높고, 결혼할 가능성은 15% 더 낮다. 하지만 돈이 있는 남성들은 평균 급여를 받는 남성들보다 결혼 전에 파트너와 함께 살 가능성이 단지 13% 더 높지만, 결혼할 가능성은 26% 더 높다.
코넬 대학교의 고용 및 가족 직업 연구소의 마틴 클라크버그(Matin Clarkberg)는 14년 동안 조사한 사람들의 데이터를 분석했는데, 이 데이터는 직업 이력, 소득, 결혼에 대한 견해를 포함하고 있다. 그녀는 남성들이 높은 생활수준에 도달하면 전통적인 가장의 역할을 수행할 수 있다는 것을 알기 때문에 결혼할 준비가 되었다고 느낀다고 말한다.
그러나 재정적으로 안정된 여성들은 동거를 선호한다고 클라크버그는 말한다. 왜냐하면 가사 업무를 병행하지 않고 경력에 집중할 수 있기 때문이다. "여성에게 결혼은 종종 서류 가방을 내려놓는 것을 수반한다."라고 그녀는 말한다. "집안일이 늘어나고, 아이가 있으면 여성이 주된 양육자가 되는 경향이 있다." 그러나 "동거하는 커플은 대개 더 평등하다." 동거하는 여성은 파트너와 일 모두에 전념할 수 있다.

| 어휘 |

well-to-do a. 부유한, 유복한, 잘 사는 **hurry** n. 서두름, 급함 **lack** v. ~이 없다, 결핍되다 **stable** a. 안정적인 **salary** n. 급여, 봉급, 급료 **get hitched** 결혼하다 **survey** v. 조사하다 **fulfill** v. 다하다, 이행하다, 수행하다 **breadwinner** n. 한 집안의 생계를 꾸리는 사람, 가장 **wed** v. ~와 결혼하다 **financially** ad. 재정적으로, 재정상 **secure** a. 안전한, 위험이 없는; 안정된 **juggle** v. (두 가지 일 따위를) 기술적으로 잘 처리하다, 솜씨 있게 해내다 **domestic** a. 가정의, 가사의 **caretaker** n. 돌보는 사람, 관리인 **egalitarian** a. 평등주의(자)의 **devote oneself to** ~에 일신을 바치다, ~에 전념하다

28 글의 주제   ②

| 분석 |

경제적 안정이 결혼에 대한 여성과 남성의 관점에 미치는 영향을 주로 다루고 있다. 경제적으로 안정된 여성들은 결혼보다는 동거를 선호하는 반면, 경제적으로 안정된 남성들은 동거보다 결혼을 선호한다고 했다. 따라서 글의 주제로 ②가 적절하다.

위 글의 주된 주제는 무엇인가?
① 결혼이 일하는 여성에게 미치는 경력 영향
② 재정적 안정이 결혼에 대한 관점에 미치는 영향
③ 결혼 전에 파트너와 함께 사는 남성의 증가하는 경향
④ 동거 부부와 결혼 부부의 가사 업무의 차이

29 내용파악   ②

| 분석 |
마틴 클라크버그는 남성들이 높은 생활수준에 도달하면 전통적인 가장의 역할을 수행할 수 있기 때문에 결혼할 준비가 되었다고 느낀다고 언급하고 있다. 따라서 ②가 적절하다.

마틴 클라크버그는 결혼에서 남성의 전통적인 역할에 대해 무엇을 제안하는가?
① 남성들은 경제적 상황에 관계없이 결혼에 대한 압박감을 느낀다.
② 남성들은 가장의 역할을 수행할 수 있게 되면 결혼할 준비가 되어 있다.
③ 남성들은 생활수준이 높을 때 결혼에 대한 관심이 줄어든다.
④ 남성들은 일반적으로 결혼에서 전통적인 역할을 거부한다.

30 빈칸완성   ①

| 분석 |
경제적으로 안정된 여성들은 결혼보다는 파트너와 함께 사는 것을 선호한다고 했다. 이는 집안일을 병행하지 않고 경력에 집중할 수 있기 때문이다. 따라서 빈칸에는 '파트너와 함께 사는 것'을 뜻하는 표현이 들어가야 한다. '동거'를 뜻하는 ①의 cohabitation이 적절하다.

다음 중 빈칸에 들어가기에 가장 적절한 것은?
① 동거
② 결혼
③ 별거
④ 이혼

31~33

역사를 인간을 완벽함으로 이끄는 에스컬레이터로 보는 개념은 르네상스 시대부터 시작된 인간의 상황과 관점의 깊은 변화에서 비롯되었다. 첫 번째 중대한 변화는 과학의 재발견과 발전이었다. 자연은 더 이상 자의적이거나 다루기 힘든 것으로 보이지 않았다. 발견되고 통제될 수 있는 법칙들에 의해 지배되어, 자연은 지배의 대상이 되었다. 일단 물리적 자연이 법칙에 따라 작용한다고 여겨지면 인간

의 본성도 그렇다고 생각하는 것이 당연한 것처럼 보였다. 이성이 전자(자연)를 규제하는 원칙을 밝혀냈듯이, 이성이 (일단 그 일에 착수하면) 인간의 삶과 관련된 법칙들과 이것들이 어떻게 인간의 복지를 향해 나아가 적용될 수 있는지도 밝혀낼 수 있을 것이다. 그 일은 심지어 어렵지 않은 것으로 판명될 수도 있다. 볼테르(Voltaire)는 자연 법칙의 일부를 배우는 데 수 세기가 걸렸지만, 현명한 사람이 인간의 의무를 배우는 데는 하루면 충분하다고 썼다.
이성의 효력에 대한 믿음이 물리적 자연에서 인간의 본성으로 이렇게 확장된 것은 진보의 사상을 뒷받침하는 현대 세계의 두 번째 태도 변화였다. 계몽주의 시대의 이성에 대한 신뢰는 놀랍고 고무적인 것이었다. 칼 베커(Carl Becker)가 지적했듯이, 18세기 사람들이 바라본 세계는 거의 새로운 것처럼 보였는데, 왜냐하면 (세계가) 최근에 이성의 빛으로 가득 찼기 때문이었다. 그 세계는 세부사항들이 매 시간마다 제자리에 맞아 들어가는 가운데 모든 것이 놀랄 만큼 명확하고 초점이 맞춰져 있는 것 같은 세계였다. 백과사전파들이 무지와 미신의 요새에 맞서 지성의 총구를 자신 있게 겨눈 그 확신은 거의 숨이 막힐 정도로 놀랍다. 인류의 보편적인 동의에 힘입어 자율적인 이성은 최고의 권위가 되었다. 이성은 단순히 왕이 아니라 메시아가 되어야 했다. 뒤처지는 사람들은 따르기를 거부할 수도 있지만, 시간은 거침없이 위쪽으로 나아가며 그들을 해결할 것이다.

| 어휘 |
perfection n. 완벽, 완전 **outlook** n. 관점, 견해 **rediscovery** n. 재발견 **arbitrary** a. 임의적인, 제멋대로인 **intractable** a. 다루기 힘든 **be subject to** ~의 대상이다 **mastery** n. 지배(력); 숙달, 통달 **lawful** a. 합법적인 **natural** a. 자연스러운, 당연한 **regulate** v. 규제하다 **lay bare** ~을 폭로하다, 털어놓다 **well-being** n. 행복, 안녕, 복지 **sufficient** a. 충분한 **extension** n. 확장, 확대 **efficacy** n. 효능, 효험, 효력 **attitudinal** a. 태도의, 사고방식의 **enlightenment** n. (the E-) 계몽운동 **confidence** n. 신뢰; 자신, 확신 **astonishing** a. 놀라운, 놀랄만한 **exhilarating** a. 명랑하게[기운 나게] 하는; 들뜨게 하는, 고무적인 **bathe** v. (빛·온기 따위가) 가득 차다 **in focus** 초점이 맞아, 또렷하게 **fall into place** 제자리에 들어가다, 꼭 들어맞다 **assurance** n. 확신 **encyclopedist** n. 백과사전 편집자 **range** v. (총·망원경 등을) 조준하다 **bastion** n. 요새 **breathtaking** a. 깜짝 놀랄 만한, 아슬아슬한, 숨이 막히는 **autonomous** a. 자율적인, 자주적인 **assent** n. 동의, 찬성 **supreme** a. 최고의 **Messiah** n. 구세주, 메시아 **laggard** n. 느린 사람, 꾸물거리는 사람 **inexorably** ad. 냉혹하게, 가차없이

31 내용일치   ④

| 분석 |
계몽주의 시대는 이성으로 가득 찬 세계로, 무지와 미신의 요새에

맞서 지성의 총구를 겨누었다고 했으므로, 무지와 미신을 지혜가 아니라 일종의 적으로 여기고 극복해야 하는 대상으로 생각했다고 할 수 있다. 따라서 ④가 사실이 아니다.

위 글에 의하면, 다음 중 사실이 아닌 것은?
① 르네상스 시대의 주요한 변혁의 원동력은 과학이었다.
② 현대 세계의 주요한 변화의 원동력은 이성이었다.
③ 무지는 현대 이성에 대한 일종의 적이었다.
④ 미신은 현대 세계에서 지혜의 하나로 여겨졌다.

32 글의 요지 ①

| 분석 |
르네상스 시대 이후 과학의 발전과 이성에 대한 신뢰가 현대 세계에 미친 두 가지 큰 변화에 대해 주로 이야기하고 있다. 이로 인해 자연의 법칙뿐만 아니라 인간의 본성을 이해하는 방식이 달라졌다고 했다. 따라서 ①의 '현대 세계에서 과학과 이성의 중요성'이 글의 요지로 적절하다.

위 글의 요지는 무엇인가?
① 현대 세계에서 과학과 이성의 중요성
② 현대 세계의 붕괴 이유
③ 계몽주의와 미신
④ 과학 기술의 지배력

33 부분이해 ②

| 분석 |
자연의 법칙과 인간의 법칙 모두 이성에 의해 밝혀낼 수 있다는 것이 볼테르의 주장의 핵심이다. 즉, 이성을 통해 인간의 법칙도 자연의 법칙처럼 규명 가능하며, 인간의 법칙은 자연의 법칙보다 이해하기 쉽다는 것이다. 따라서 ②가 적절하다.

위 글에 의하면, 볼테르의 주장에서 밑줄 친 부분의 논리적 근거는 무엇인가?
① 현명한 사람은 인간을 이해하는 데 매우 영리하다.
② 유사한 법칙이 자연과 인간을 지배한다.
③ 인간의 의무는 이해하기에 매우 복잡하다.
④ 인간의 법칙은 자연의 법칙보다 훨씬 더 단순하다.

34~35

가뭄이 초래할 수 있는 문제를 완화하기 위해 채택할 수 있는 몇 가지 단기 및 장기 전략들이 있다. 이러한 문제를 해결하기 위해 고안된 다양한 정책들이 지역, 국가, 그리고 국제적 수준에서 존재한다. 이 주제와 관련된 일반적인 문제뿐만 아니라, 최근 몇 년간 가뭄이 큰 문제였던 케냐의 경우에도 할 수 있는 구체적인 권고사항이 있다.
가뭄은 종종 케냐 중부에서 수백만 명의 사람들을 식량 불안정의 위험에 빠뜨린다. 그 지역은 너무 건조해서 농작물을 자라게 할 수 없다. 영구적인 강은 거의 없으며, 우기 동안 홍수로 인한 계절적 수로는 지역 전체의 교통을 방해한다. 이 지역 사람들은 주로 가축으로 살아간다. 가뭄은 동물들을 빠르게 죽일 수 있고, 이는 그들의 주요 수입원을 없앤다. 마지막으로, 이 지역은 매우 광대하기 때문에 사회 기반 시설이 충분히 개발되지 않아 인구에 대한 접근이 어렵다.

| 어휘 |
drought n. 가뭄 **short-term** a. 단기의 **long-term** a. 장기의 **strategy** n. 전략 **policy** n. 정책, 방침 **specific** a. 구체적인; 일정한, 특정한 **recommendation** n. 권고, 충고 **put ~ at risk of** ~를 위험에 처하게 하다 **agricultural** a. 농업의 **crop** n. 농작물 **permanent** a. 영구적인 **seasonal** a. 계절적인 **waterway** n. 수로, 항로 **disrupt** v. 방해하다, 중단시키다 **transportation** n. 운송, 수송; 교통[수송] 기관 **live off** ~으로[~에 의존하여] 살다 **cattle** n. 소; 가축 **eliminate** v. 없애다, 제거하다 **infrastructure** n. 사회 기반 시설; (경제) 기반 **under-developed** a. 저개발의, 충분히 개발되지 않은

34 내용일치 ③

| 분석 |
케냐는 너무 건조해서 농작물을 자라게 할 수 없다고 했으므로 농업에 의존해 생계를 유지하고 있다는 것은 적절하지 않다. 케냐는 주로 가축에 의해 생계를 유지하고 있지만 가뭄으로 인해 동물들이 죽어서 위험에 처해 있다고 했다. 따라서 ③이 사실이 아니다. ① '가뭄 문제 해결을 위한 정책들이 지역, 국가, 그리고 국제적 수준에서 존재한다'고 한 것은 그 정책들(방법들)이 지금 시행되고 있다는 것을 의미한다.

위 글에 의하면, 다음 중 사실이 아닌 것은?
① 가뭄 문제를 극복하기 위해 여러 가지 방법이 시행되고 있다.
② 케냐는 농작물을 재배하기에는 너무 건조하다.
③ 케냐는 생계를 위해 가축과 농업에 의존하고 있다.
④ 가뭄은 주민들이 경제적 자원을 잃게 만드는 중요한 원인이 될 수 있다.

35 빈칸완성 ①

| 분석 |
Ⓐ 가뭄의 문제를 해결하기 위해 고안된 다양한 정책들이 있다고 했으므로 빈칸에도 가뭄의 문제를 완화하거나 줄인다는 의미의 mitigate, diminish가 적절하다. Ⓑ 케냐는 너무 건조해서 농작물을 자라게 할 수 없으며 그들의 주요 식량인 가축들이 가뭄으로

인해 죽는다고 했으므로 식량이 부족하다는 의미의 insecurity, scarcity가 적절하다. 따라서 ①이 정답이다.

다음 중 빈칸 Ⓐ와 Ⓑ에 들어가기에 가장 적절한 것은?
① 완화하다 — 불안정
② 정의하다 — 불확실
③ 줄이다 — 풍부
④ 확대하다 — 부족

36~37

인간의 아이는 아마도 다른 어떤 어린 동물보다 더 다양한 놀이 활동을 보인다. 예를 들어, 그는 다른 동물들과 공유하는 싸움 놀이와 사냥 놀이 외에도 사물을 분해하는 활동을 보이는데, 그로스(Groos)는 이를 '분석적 놀이'라고 부른다.
그는 또한 (장난감 블록이나 공작용 점토를 가지고) 새로운 것을 만들어내는 '종합적 놀이'도 보여준다. 이러한 놀이들은 각각 호기심이 있고 건설적인 성인 행동을 분명히 예행연습하는 것이다. 나중에 그는, 예를 들어, 물물교환이나 심지어 종교 의식을 수행하는 것과 같은 원시적인 형태의 행동과는 비교적 거리가 먼 성인 활동을 자극하는 놀이를 연습할 수도 있다.
그러나 놀이에 대한 그로스의 정의를 충족시키는 활동들이 동물과 인간의 삶에서 발견되는 예행연습 현상의 목록을 완전히 규명하지는 못한다. 예를 들어, 구애는 어느 정도 성행위의 예행연습이며, 그 자체로 탐닉하는 것인 활동이다. 그러나 그것은 어린 동물들의 싸움 놀이나 사냥 놀이와는 완전히 같은 범주에 속하지 않는다. 왜냐하면 그것은 성인 활동이며, 성행위로 이어지고 그 성행위 자체의 수행에 명확한 기능을 가지고 있기 때문이다.
그로스가 언급한 다른 예행연습 현상으로는 아기의 탐색적인 손 움직임과 아기에게 새로운 실험적 감각을 가져다주는 또 다른 활동들이 있다. 우리는 아마도 정신 분석학자들이 성인의 성 본능 발달의 근원이 되는 유아적 요소로 간주하는 유아의 감정 반응 형태들 중 일부도 예행연습 현상의 범주에 포함시켜야 할 것이다.

| 어휘 |

pull[pick] ~ to pieces ~을 갈기갈기 찢다, 분해하다 **analytical** a. 분석적인 **brick** n. 벽돌; (쌓기 놀이의) 블록 **synthetic** a. 합성의, 인조의 **rehearsal** n. 리허설, 예행연습 **respectively** ad. 각각, 각자 **curiosity** n. 호기심 **exercise oneself in** ~의 연습을 하다 **primitive** a. 원시적인 **barter** v. 물물 교환하다 **exhaust** v. 다 써 버리다, 고갈시키다; (문제 따위를) 철저히 연구[규명]하다 **indulge** v. (쾌락 등에) 탐닉하다 **exploratory** a. 탐색의, 탐구적인 **infantile** a. 어린애 같은, 유치한; 유아의 **psychoanalyst** n. 정신 분석학자

36 빈칸완성 ①

| 분석 |

성행위의 예행연습이기도 하고 그 자체로 탐닉하는 것이기도 한 활동이며, 어린 동물들의 싸움 놀이나 사냥 놀이와는 다르게 성인 활동이라고 했다. 이는 동물의 '구애' 행동에 대한 설명으로 빈칸에는 ① Courtship이 적절하다.

다음 중 빈칸에 들어가기에 가장 적절한 것은?
① 구애
② 우정
③ 회원 자격
④ 선수권 대회

37 내용일치 ③

| 분석 |

아이들의 놀이 활동은 단순히 놀이가 아니라 성인 행동을 미리 연습하는 역할을 한다고 했으므로 ③이 사실이다. ① 싸움 놀이와 사냥 놀이를 다른 동물들과 공유한다고 했으므로 아이들만의 문화는 아니다. ② 대부분의 놀이가 예행연습의 범주에 포함된다고 했다. ④ 놀이를 통해 현실 세계, 즉 성인의 행동을 연습한다고 했으므로 놀이와 현실 사이에는 연관성이 있다고 볼 수 있다.

위 글에 의하면, 다음 중 사실인 것은?
① 놀이는 오직 아이들만이 공유하는 문화이다.
② 예행연습 역할이 없는 많은 종류의 놀이가 있다.
③ 아이들의 놀이는 성인의 문화로 발전하는 예행연습이 될 수 있다.
④ 놀이와 현실 사이에는 아무런 연관성이 없다.

38~40

가상현실(VR)과 증강현실(AR)은 비디오 및 사진 카메라, 오디오 녹음 장치로 거슬러 올라가는 감시 기술의 가장 최근의 발전 중 하나다. 우리의 환경에 장치를 설치하여 우리를 지켜보고 듣는 것은 새로운 일이 아니다. 새로운 것은 이러한 미디어 기술이 사용자와 사용자 주변 공간 사이에 형성하는 친밀하고 만연한 관계이다. 이전의 감시 기술들은 세계 어딘가에 위치해 유리한 입장에서 우리를 감시했는데, 그때조차도 공간이 우리를 지켜보고 있다는 느낌은 충분히 섬뜩했다. 수많은 스파이 및 탐정 영화에는 심어 놓은 녹음 장치들이 등장한다. 공포 영화와 서스펜스 영화의 감독들은 카메라 자체를 감시 장치로 취급하여 등장인물들이 위협을 받고 있다는 느낌을 불러일으킨다. 그러나 영화 카메라는 반드시 한 시점에 한 장소에만 있다. AR과 VR의 추적 및 감지 기술은 우리를 감시하기 위해 전체 공간을 활용한다. 그들은 우

리를 공간과 연결하여 우리가 상호 감지와 반응의 통합된 시스템의 일부가 되도록 한다.

이것이 의도한 대로 작동할 때, 공간은 작업을 달성하거나 의도된 경험을 만들어내기 위해 우리의 행동에 반응하게 된다. VR 공간에서 우리가 한 방향 또는 다른 방향으로 바라보면 시스템은 적절한 시각으로 물체를 끌어들이는 반응을 보인다. 우리는 손이나 컨트롤러로 손을 뻗어 가상 물체를 집을 수 있다. AR 공간에서는 원하는 정보가 적절한 시간에 적절한 장소에 나타난다. 그러나 우리는 이러한 추적과 감지의 상호작용이 인터넷 서버로 전송되어 기록될 수 있다는 것을 알고 있다. 그런 의미에서 우리 주변의 공간은 반드시 유리하고 협조적인 것은 아니다. 그것은 기업이나 정부의 이익에 맞게 전유될 수도 있다. 균열은 우리가 공간 자체가 감시 장치가 되었다고 느낄 때 발생한다. 우호적이든 위협적이든 AR과 VR의 공간은 섬뜩한 느낌을 불러일으킨다. 그것은 공간이 얼마나 반응적인지에 대한 가벼운 놀라움일 수도 있고 공간이 가할 수 있는 위협에 대한 더 강한 반응일 수도 있다.

| 어휘 |

surveillance n. 감시　**date back to** ~까지 거슬러 올라가다　**novel** a. 새로운, 신기한　**intimate** a. 친밀한　**pervasive** a. 널리 퍼지는, 만연하는　**situate** v. (어떤 장소에) 놓다, 위치시키다　**surveil** v. 감시하다, 감독하다　**vantage point** 전망이 좋은 지점[위치]; (유리한) 입장　**uncanny** a. 이상한, 섬뜩한　**evoke** v. 불러일으키다, 환기시키다　**threat** n. 위협, 협박　**enlist** v. 병적에 넣다; ~의 찬조[협력, 지지]를 얻다　**unified** a. 통일된, 통합된　**mutual** a. 상호간의, 서로의　**achieve** v. 달성하다, 성취하다　**appropriate** a. 적절한, 적합한 v. 충당하다; 사유[전유]하다　**perspective** n. 관점, 시각　**transmit** v. 전송하다　**benign** a. 인자한, 친절한; 온화한　**cooperative** a. 협력적인, 협조적인　**rupture** n. 파열, 균열　**threatening** a. 위협[협박]적인　**awaken** v. 깨우다; 불러일으키다　**responsive** a. 반응하는　**pose** v. (위협·문제 등을) 제기하다

38 글의 주제 ①

| 분석 |

가장 최근의 감시 기술로서 VR과 AR 기술에 대해 설명하고 있다. VR과 AR 기술은 이전의 감시 기술들과 달리 사용자와 공간을 더 가깝게 연결하여 공간 전체가 감시 장치가 되는 것 같은 섬뜩한 느낌을 주고, 추적과 감지의 상호작용이 인터넷 서버로 전송되어 기록될 수 있는 등의 위협을 줄 수 있다고 우려를 나타내고 있다. 따라서 글의 주제로 ①이 적절하다.

위 글의 주제는 무엇인가?
① 최근 감시 기술로서 VR과 AR 공간의 의심스러운 측면
② 오늘날 유용한 감시 장치로서의 VR과 AR 공간의 중요성
③ AR과 VR 추적 및 감지 기술이 우리를 공간과 연결하는 방식
④ 기업이나 정부가 VR과 AR 기술을 자신의 이익을 위해 사용하는 방식

39 내용일치 ①

| 분석 |

공간 자체가 감시 장치가 되었다고 느끼는 것은 VR과 AR 기술로 인한 것이다. 이전의 감시 기술은 특정 위치에 설치되어 감시한다고 했으므로 공간 자체가 감시 장치가 된 것은 아니다. 따라서 ①이 사실이 아니다.

위 글에 의하면, 다음 중 사실이 <u>아닌</u> 것은?
① 공간 자체가 이전 기술들로 인해 감시 장치가 되었다.
② VR과 AR의 공간에서는 공간이 우리의 행동에 반응하는 것이 가능하다.
③ 심어 놓은 녹음 장치가 많은 스파이 및 탐정 영화에 등장한다.
④ 사진 카메라는 또한 감시 기술로 여겨졌다.

40 빈칸완성 ①

| 분석 |

VR과 AR 기술은 가장 최근의 감시 기술로 이전에도 비디오, 사진 카메라, 오디오 녹음 장치 등의 감시 기술이 존재했다고 했다. 새로운 점은 VR과 AR 기술이 기존의 감시 기술들과 달리 사용자와 공간 사이의 관계를 설정하는 것이라고 설명하고 있다. 따라서 감시 기술은 '새로운 것이 아니다'라는 의미가 되어야 하므로 빈칸에는 ① new가 적절하다.

다음 중 빈칸에 들어가기에 가장 적절한 것은?
① 새로운
② 위협적인
③ 이상한
④ 비싼

DUKSUNG WOMEN'S UNIVERSITY | 덕성여자대학교 1교시

TEST p. 238~249

01	②	02	③	03	①	04	②	05	③	06	④	07	①	08	③	09	④	10	③
11	①	12	③	13	②	14	③	15	④	16	③	17	②	18	①	19	③	20	④
21	②	22	①	23	①	24	②	25	②	26	④	27	①	28	①	29	②	30	④
31	②	32	③	33	②														

01 동의어 ②

| 어휘 |

impromptu a. 즉석의(= spontaneous) **rehearsed** a. 연습한, 시연한 **rigid** a. 엄격한, 엄정한 **scheduled** a. 예정된

02 동의어 ③

| 어휘 |

tenacious a. 고집 센, 완강한(= persistent) **impartial** a. 공평한 **grudging** a. 인색한, 마지못해 하는 **apathetic** a. 냉담한, 무관심한

03 동의어 ①

| 어휘 |

incredulous a. 쉽사리 믿지 않는, 회의적인(= skeptical) **coerced** a. 강요된, 강제된 **gullible** a. 속기 쉬운 **indifferent** a. 무관심한

| 해석 |

그녀는 그 믿을 수 없는 소식을 들었을 때 의심스러운 표정을 지었다.

04 동의어 ②

| 어휘 |

gloomy a. 울적한, 우울한 **lament** v. 슬퍼하다, 한탄하다, 애석하다(= mourn) **destruction** n. 파괴, 파멸 **celebrate** v. 찬양하다, 기리다 **ignore** v. 무시하다 **wander** v. 돌아다니다, 헤매다

| 해석 |

그 우울한 시에서 그는 시골이 파괴된 것을 애석해한다.

05 논리완성 ③

| 분석 |

'균형을 맞추는 행위'는 긍정적인 것이므로 첫 번째 빈칸에는 긍정적인 의미의 표현이 들어가야 하는데, 문장의 의미가 속도와는 무관하므로 swift가 아닌 thoughtful이 적절하다. 두 번째 빈칸의 경우, 회사의 가치나 규정은 경영자가 직원들의 요구와 균형을 맞추려고 조정할 수 있는 것이 아니므로 부적절하고 회사의 priorities(우선 사항)나 goals(목표)가 적절하다. 따라서 ③이 정답이다.

| 어휘 |

swift a. 빠른, 신속한 **value** n. 가치; (pl.) 가치 기준 **inattentive** a. 부주의한, 태만한 **thoughtful** a. 사려 깊은 **priority** n. 보다 중요함, 우선; 우선 사항 **arbitrary** a. 임의적인, 독단적인

| 해석 |

경영자의 결정은 사려 깊다고 여겨졌는데, 왜냐하면 그것은 직원들의 요구와 회사의 우선 사항 사이에 균형을 맞췄기 때문이다.

06 논리완성 ④

| 분석 |

콤마 이하에서 두 빈칸에 들어갈 표현을 부연하고 있다. 따라서 빈칸에는 '독창성으로 찬사를 받은 것'과 관련된 innovative와 '비평가들 사이에서 치열한 논쟁을 불러일으킨 것'과 관련된 provocative가 각각 들어가는 것이 자연스럽다.

| 어휘 |

originality n. 독창성 **spark** v. (흥미·기운 따위를) 갑자기 불러일으키다, 북돋우다 **intense** a. 강한, 격렬한 **critic** n. 비평가, 평론가 **conventional** a. 인습적인, 판에 박힌 **insipid** a. 김빠진, 무미건조한 **derivative** a. 독창적이 아닌, 파생적인 **foreseeable** a. 예측할 수 있는 **obscure** a. 불명료한, 눈에 띄지 않는 **irrelevant** a. 부적절한, 무관계한 **provocative** a. 도발적인, 논쟁을 일으키는 **innovative** a. 혁신적인

| 해석 |

그 예술가의 가장 최근 작품은 도발적이면서도 혁신적이어서, 비평가들 사이에서 치열한 논쟁을 불러일으킨 반면에, 독창성으로 찬사를 받기도 했다.

07 논리완성 ①

| 분석 |

미래 세대가 그 유물을 볼 수 있기 위해서는 '오랫동안' 보존이 이루어져야 할 것이므로 빈칸에는 '지속적인', '영속적인'의 의미를 가진 표현이 적절하다. 그러므로 ①이 정답이다.

| 어휘 |

immense a. 엄청난, 막대한, 광대한   **artifact** n. 인공 유물, 유적   **climate-controlled** a. 온도와 습도가 조절되는, 냉난방이 되는   **preservation** n. 보존, 저장   **enduring** a. 지속하는, 영속적인   **careless** a. 부주의한   **temporary** a. 일시적인   **haphazard** a. 무계획적인, 아무렇게나 한

| 해석 |

엄청난 역사적 가치로 인해, 그 고대 유물은 미래 세대를 위한 지속적인 보존을 보장하기 위해 온도와 습도가 조절되는 유리 상자 속에서 조심스럽게 전시되었다.

08 논리완성 ③

| 분석 |

기립 박수를 안겨준 것은 매우 인상적이었거나 뛰어난 경기력이었을 것이므로 빈칸에는 ③이 들어가야 한다.

| 어휘 |

extraordinary a. 비범한, 탁월한   **evident** a. 명백한   **standing ovation** 기립 박수   **lackluster** a. 광채[빛, 윤기가 없는, 생기 없는, 활기 없는   **mediocre** a. 평범한, 보통 수준의   **flawless** a. 완벽한, 흠 없는   **chaotic** a. 혼란스러운, 무질서한

| 해석 |

그 선수의 비범한 기량은 대회 내내 명백했지만, 그녀에게 관중들의 기립 박수를 안겨준 것은 마지막 경기에서의 완벽한 경기력이었다.

09 논리완성 ④

| 분석 |

전치사 Despite가 있으므로 전치사구와 주절의 내용이 양보 관계를 이루어야 한다. 따라서 프로젝트를 끝내기 어렵게 만드는 상황을 나타낼 수 있는 ④가 정답이 된다.

| 어휘 |

idyllic a. 목가적인   **serene** a. 고요한, 평온한   **irrelevant** a. 무관한, 관련 없는   **trying** a. 견디기 어려운, 고된

| 해석 |

견디기 힘든 상황에도 불구하고, 그 팀은 프로젝트를 어떻게든 제시간에 끝냈다.

10 논리완성 ③

| 분석 |

so ~ that … 구문은 원인과 결과 관계의 의미이다. 바닥에서 헤엄치는 물고기를 볼 수 있게 하는 원인으로는 물이 매우 맑거나 깨끗한 것이 적절하므로, 빈칸에는 ③이 들어가야 한다.

| 어휘 |

radiant a. 빛나는, 눈부신   **unanimous** a. 만장일치의   **limpid** a. 맑은, 투명한   **exotic** a. 이국적인

| 해석 |

그 호수는 매우 맑아서 바닥에서 헤엄치는 물고기를 볼 수 있었다.

11 관사 ①

| 분석 |

고유명사 중에 Seoul이나 Paris처럼 도시 이름 앞에는 관사가 없고(The Hague는 예외) the Empire State Building이나 the Eiffel Tower처럼 건축물 이름 앞에는 the를 쓰므로 ①이 정답이다.

| 해석 |

그는 작년에 파리로 여행을 가서 에펠탑을 방문했다.

12 가정법 ③

| 분석 |

과거 사실의 반대를 가정하는 경우 I wish 뒤에 가정법 과거완료 동사가 와야 하므로 ③이 정답이다.

| 해석 |

어제 시험을 준비할 시간이 더 많았더라면 좋았을 텐데.

13 주어와 동사의 수일치 ②

| 분석 |

대명사 Neither가 주어로 쓰이는 경우에는 단수로 취급하는 것이 원칙이며, 그 자체에 부정의 의미가 있으므로 그 뒤에 not 같은 부정어가 올 수 없다. 따라서 빈칸에는 ②가 적절하다.

| 해석 |
두 가지 옵션 중 어느 것도 위원회에 받아들여질 수 없었다.

14 가산명사 ③

| 분석 |
picture는 가산명사이므로 앞에 부정관사를 쓰거나 혹은 복수형으로 써야 한다. 글의 내용상 한 장의 그림을 그렸다고 보는 것이 보다 자연스러우므로 ③을 decided to paint a picture of로 고쳐야 한다.

| 어휘 |
portrait n. 초상화   **neighborhood** n. 근처, 이웃

| 해석 |
마리아는 여가 시간에 그림 그리는 것을 즐기는데, 긴장을 푸는 데 도움이 되기 때문이다. 그녀는 종종 풍경화를 그리고 가끔 초상화도 그리지만, 누구에게도 자기 작품을 거의 보여주지 않는다. 지난주에 그녀는 자신의 동네에 있는 공원의 그림을 그리기로 결심했고, 그려낸 그림에 짜릿한 전율을 느꼈다.

15 one of + 복수명사 ④

| 분석 |
one of 뒤에는 복수명사가 온다. 그러므로 ④는 fields in physics 여야 한다.

| 어휘 |
quantum mechanics 양자 역학   **precision** n. 정확, 정밀, 신중함
physics n. 물리학

| 해석 |
양자역학의 복잡한 본질은 과학자들로 하여금 높은 수준의 정확도를 가지고 문제에 접근할 것을 요구하는데, 이로 인해 양자역학은 물리학에서 가장 어려운 분야들 중 하나가 되었다.

16 수동을 나타내는 과거분사 ③

| 분석 |
자동차가 고장 나서 다니엘과 리암이 '오도 가도 못하게 된' 것이므로, ③에서 them 뒤의 stranding은 수동을 나타내는 과거분사 stranded로 고쳐야 한다.

| 어휘 |
sleek a. (매끄럽고) 윤이 나는; (모양이) 매끈한[날렵한]   **show off** 자랑하다, 뽐내다   **break down** 고장 나다   **strand** v. 궁지에 몰다, 오도 가도 못하게 하다   **frustrated** a. 실망한, 좌절된   **grateful** a. 고마워하는, 감사하고 있는

| 해석 |
몇 달 동안 돈을 모은 후에, 다니엘은 마침내 자신의 꿈의 차인 매끈한 빨간색 컨버터블을 구입했다. 그는 그 차를 몰고 나가 드라이브를 하고 친구들에게 자랑하고 싶어 안달이 났다. 첫 번째 주말에, 그는 가장 친한 친구인 리암을 해안으로 가는 자동차 여행에 함께 가자고 초대했다. 운전하는 동안, 다니엘은 엔진에서 이상한 소리가 나는 것을 알아챘지만, 그는 그 소리를 무시하기로 했다. 하지만, 여행의 중간쯤에서 차가 갑자기 고장 나서, 그들은 인적이 드문 곳에서 오도 가도 못하게 되었다. 다니엘은 좌절했지만, 리암이 침착함을 유지하고 도움을 요청한 것에 고마움을 느꼈다.

17~18

제품에 대한 인식이 배경 음악의 영향을 받을 수 있을까? 이 질문을 해결하고자, 연구원들은 한 가지 실험을 수행했다. 참가자들은 연한 파란색 또는 베이지색 펜이 포함된 슬라이드를 보았고, 그와 동시에, 참가자들이 그 펜들을 보는 동안 기분 좋은 음악 또는 불쾌한 음악이 재생되었다. 이후에, 참가자들에게 선물로 받을 펜을 선택하도록 요청했을 때, 대다수의 참가자들은 기분 좋은 배경 음악을 들으면서 보았던 펜을 선택했다. 흥미롭게도, 많은 참가자들은 음악이 자신의 결정에 영향을 미쳤다는 사실을 인식하지 못했다. 상당수의 참가자들은 자신이 왜 특정 펜을 더 선호했는지를 알지 못한다고 말했다.

| 어휘 |
address v. 역점을 두어 다루다   **inquiry** n. 질문, 문의   **observe** v. 보다, 관찰하다   **impact** n. 영향   **significant** a. 상당한; 중요한

17 내용파악 ②

| 분석 |
제품에 대한 인식이 배경 음악의 영향을 받는지를 연구했으므로 ②가 정답이다. ④ 색깔이 아니라 제품이다.

본문에서 언급한 실험의 주된 목표는?
① 음악이 기억력에 미치는 영향을 판단하기 위해
② 배경 음악이 제품에 대한 의견에 영향을 미치는지를 조사하기 위해
③ 왜 특정 펜의 색깔이 다른 것들에 비해 더 인기가 있는지를 조사하기 위해
④ 배경 음악과 선호하는 색깔 간의 관계를 연구하기 위해

18 동의어 ①

| 분석 |
Concurrently는 '동시에'라는 의미이므로 Simultaneously로 대

체할 수 있다. ② 이전에 ③ 분리하여, 따로 ④ 그 후에

19~22

"세포"라는 용어는 작은 방을 의미하는 라틴어 "cellula"에서 유래했다. 영국의 박식가 로버트 후크(Robert Hooke)는 그가 식물 세포를 관찰했을 때 그것이 수도승들의 작은 방을 떠올리게 했기 때문에 그러한 이름을 만들어냈다. 세포는 생명의 기본 단위이며, 단세포(예: 박테리아)일 수도 있고 다세포(예: 인간)일 수도 있다. 유형, 크기, 기능이 다양함에도 불구하고 모든 세포는 공통적인 특징을 가진다.

모든 세포에는 세포를 보호하는 세포막이 있으며, 세포막은 미세한 분자들의 통과를 허용한다. 박테리아 세포를 제외한 모든 세포는 핵을 갖고 있는데, 핵은 DNA를 포함하고 있으며 세포의 활동을 지시한다. 대부분의 세포 활동은 물과 그 밖의 성분들로 이루어진 젤리 같은 물질인 세포질에서 일어난다.

많은 종류의 세포 중에서 가장 익숙한 두 가지는 동물 세포와 식물 세포이다. 식물 세포는 세포를 보호하는 셀룰로오스 세포벽을 가지고 있는 반면, 동물 세포는 그렇지 않다. 또한, 식물 세포는 햇빛을 에너지로 변환하는 광합성을 하기 위한 엽록체를 가지고 있다. 식물 세포는 세포의 형태를 유지하는 데 도움을 주는 큰 액포도 가지고 있다.

세포는 끊임없이 증식하고 죽으며, 인간의 세포는 1분마다 약 30억 개가 죽는다. 새로운 세포는 분열을 통해 생성되며, 이는 하나의 세포가 자신의 염색체를 복제하는 것으로 시작된다. 세포의 성장과 분열은 이러한 단계들 사이에서 발생한다. 강력한 전자 현미경은 세포를 백만 배 이상 확대함으로써 세포 연구를 돕는다. 그러나 이러한 기술을 사용하더라도 세포의 어떤 부분은 여전히 보이지 않는 까닭에, 비디오 카메라를 이용하여 향상시킨 영상이 세포학 발전에 매우 유용한 것으로 입증되고 있다.

| 어휘 |

term n. 용어 polymath n. 박식가, 다방면에 학식이 깊은 사람 coin v. (새로운 단어를) 만들다 monk n. 수도승 cell membrane 세포막 molecule n. 분자 nucleus n. 핵, 중심 cytoplasm n. 세포질 chloroplast n. 엽록체 photosynthesis n. 광합성 vacuole n. 액포 reproduce v. 증식하다 duplicate v. 복사하다, 복제하다 chromosome n. 염색체 cytology n. 세포학

19 내용파악 ③

| 분석 |

"새로운 세포는 분열을 통해 생성되며, 이는 하나의 세포가 자신의 염색체를 복제하는 것으로 시작된다."라고 했으므로 ③이 정답이다.

어떤 과정이 세포로 하여금 지속적으로 증식하고 죽어가는 세포를 대체하게 해주는가?
① 광합성
② 세포 호흡
③ 세포 분열
④ 영양소 처리

20 내용일치 ④

| 분석 |

"모든 세포에는 세포를 보호하는 세포막이 있으며, 세포막은 미세한 분자들의 통과를 허용한다."고 했는데, 이는 세포막이 분자가 세포 내부로 들어오거나 나가는 것을 조절하는 역할을 한다는 것이므로, ④가 옳은 진술이다. ① 박테리아는 예외라고 했다. ② 세포의 어떤 부분은 여전히 볼 수 없다. ③ '젤리 같은 물질'이라고 했으므로 단단하지 않다.

위 글에 의하면, 다음 중 옳은 것은?
① 모든 세포는 DNA를 포함하고 있다.
② 강력한 전자 현미경은 모든 세포 구조를 볼 수 있다.
③ 세포질은 단단한 구조이다.
④ 세포막은 분자의 통과를 조절한다.

21 내용파악 ②

| 분석 |

"핵은 DNA를 포함하고 세포의 활동을 지시한다"라고 했으므로 ②가 정답이다.

세포에서 핵의 역할은 무엇인가?
① 세포를 위한 에너지를 저장한다.
② 세포의 활동을 지시한다.
③ 세포를 위한 단백질을 생성한다.
④ 세포를 수백만 배 이상 확대한다.

22 내용파악 ①

| 분석 |

"식물 세포는 세포를 보호하는 셀룰로오스 세포벽을 가지고 있는 반면, 동물 세포는 그렇지 않다."라고 돼 있으므로 ①이 정답이다.

동물 세포와 비교했을 때 식물 세포가 갖는 독특한 점은?
① 식물 세포는 셀룰로오스 세포벽을 가지고 있다.
② 식물 세포는 핵이 없다.
③ 식물 세포는 세포질이 없다.
④ 식물 세포는 동물 세포보다 작은 액포를 가지고 있다.

23~25

우리는 튼튼한 특정 갑각류 동물과 다르지 않다. 랍스터는 일련의 단단한 보호 껍질을 발달시키고 벗으면서 성장한다. 안에서부터 커갈 때마다, 몸을 가두고 있는 껍질을 벗어내야 한다. 랍스터는 시간이 지나면서 새로운 덮개가 옛것을 대신할 때까지 밖으로 몸이 노출된 취약한 상태로 남아 있게 된다. 인간의 성장이 한 단계에서 다음 단계로 넘어갈 때마다, 우리 또한 우리를 보호하고 있는 구조를 벗어내야 한다. 우리는 노출되어 취약한 상태로 있게 되지만 — 또한 다시금 활기차고 태아와 같은 상태가 되어, 우리가 이전에는 알지 못했던 방식으로 커나갈 수 있다. 옛것을 벗어내는 이러한 과정은 몇 년 또는 그 이상이 걸릴 수도 있다. 그러나 각각의 단계에서 나와서, 우리는 상대적인 평온과 균형을 다시 얻을 것으로 기대할 수 있는 더 길고 보다 안정된 시기로 들어간다.

우리가 보게 될 것처럼, 각자는 자신만의 특색 있는 방식으로 발달 단계를 밟는다. 어떤 사람들은 전체 연쇄 과정을 다 마치지 못한다. 그리고 우리 중 그 누구도 어린 시절의 양육자들로부터 분리되는 문제를 한 번의 단계로 — 예를 들어, 부모의 집에서 나와 직장이나 결혼으로 뛰어듦으로써 — "해결한" 않는다. 또한, 우리는 꿈을 구체적인 목표로 바꿈으로써, 그 목표를 이루었을 때조차, 자율을 완전히 최종적으로 "얻어지는" 않는다. 한 시기의 중심적인 문제나 과제가 결코 완전히 완결되어, 묶어서 따로 제쳐두지 않는다. 하지만 그 문제나 과제들이 최고의 중요성을 잃고 현재의 생활 구조가 그 목적을 다했을 때, 우리는 다음 시기로 나아갈 준비가 된다.

| 어휘 |

crustacean n. 갑각류 **hardy** a. 강인한 **slough off** 탈피하다, 벗어버리다 **vulnerable** a. 취약한 **replace** v. 대신하다, 대체하다 **yeasty** a. 발효하는; 활력이 있는 **embryonic** a. 태아의; 초기 단계의 **autonomy** n. 자율성; 자율적인 상태, 독립성 **relative** a. 상대적인 **tranquility** n. 고요, 평온함 **equilibrium** n. 균형

23 내용일치 ①

| 분석 |

"우리는 꿈을 구체적인 목표로 바꿈으로써 그 목표를 이루었을 때조차 자율을 완전히 최종적으로 얻는 것은 아니다."라고 했으므로 ①이 옳지 않은 진술이다.

다음 중 옳지 <u>않은</u> 것은?
① 인간은 목표를 달성함으로써 완전한 자율성을 얻는다.
② 인간의 성장은 비유를 통해 설명될 수 있다.
③ 인간의 껍질 벗어내기는 수년이 걸릴 수도 있다.
④ 인간은 각자 나름의 방식으로 발달 단계를 밟는다.

24 내용파악 ②

| 분석 |

"인간의 성장 단계가 한 단계에서 다음 단계로 넘어갈 때마다, 우리 또한 우리를 보호하고 있는 구조를 벗어내야 한다. 우리는 노출되어 취약한 상태로 있게 되지만 — 또한 다시금 활기차고 태아와 같은 상태가 되어, 우리가 이전에는 알지 못했던 방식으로 커나갈 수 있다."라고 했으므로 ②가 정답으로 적절하다.

발달의 한 단계에서 다른 단계로 이행가는 동안 개인에게는 무슨 일이 일어나는가?
① 그들은 즉각적인 안정감과 자신감을 얻는다.
② 그들은 불안감을 느끼지만 성장을 할 수 있다.
③ 그들은 영구적인 균형과 평온함을 경험한다.
④ 그들은 과거의 모든 발달 문제를 완전히 해결한다.

25 내용파악 ②

| 분석 |

"그러나 각각의 단계에서 나와서, 우리는 상대적인 평온과 균형을 다시 얻을 거라 기대할 수 있는 더 길고 보다 안정된 시기로 들어간다."라고 했으므로 ②가 정답으로 적절하다.

본문에서는 주된 성장의 전환 이후의 기간들을 어떻게 설명하고 있는가?
① 그것들은 지속적인 불안정성과 변화를 특징으로 한다.
② 그것들은 균형과 평온의 느낌을 만들어낸다.
③ 그것들은 해결을 위해 과거의 문제를 다시 살펴보는 과정을 요구한다.
④ 그것들은 빠르고 연속적인 전환을 특징으로 한다.

26~28

Samuel Smith Old Brewery가 전통을 자랑한다고 말하는 것은 그 회사의 회장이 가진 다른 시대에 대한 갈망의 강도를 마구 과소평가하는 것이다. 영국 전역에 200개 이상의 술집을 운영하는 그의 목표는, 과거 — 아니면 적어도 그가 이상화한 과거의 모습 — 가 그대로 보존된 완전한 세계를 만드는 것인 것 같다. 수십 년 동안, Smith는 이 비전을 추구하기 위해 상당한 개인 재산을 사용해왔다. 그는 자신의 술집 건물을 무대 세트로 여기는 것 같으며, 사람들 — 술집 손님, 관리자, 지역 주민 — 은 그가 지시하는 역할을 정확하게 수행해야 한다. 만약 그것이 불가능하다면, 구내(술집)의 커튼은 즉시 내려진다.

술집 안에서는 Samuel Smith가 만들지 않은 스낵, 술 혹은 맥주를 구하려 노력해도 아무 소용이 없을 것이다. 모든 생맥주는 Yorkshire의 마그네슘 석회암층 천연 우물에서 퍼

올린 물을 사용하여 Samuel Smith의 Old Brewery에서 양조된다. 심지어 그 술집의 포테이토칩에 사용되는 감자도 Yorkshire에서 온다. 그 양조장은 가격을 낮게 유지한다. 그러나, 돈을 절약할 수 있는 것에 대한 대가로, 손님들은 고객 행동에 관한 엄격한 규칙을 따라야 한다. Samuel Smith 웹사이트에서는 술을 "책임감 있게" 즐겨야 한다고 명시하고 있다. "술집에서 하는 친근한 대화는 장려되지만" 욕설은 금지된다. 텔레비전, 노트북, 모바일 전화는 금지돼 있다. 손님이 결제 외의 이유로 전화기를 꺼내면 술집 직원으로부터 경고를 받을 것이다.

| 어휘 |

pride oneself on 자랑하다　**understate** v. 과소평가하다, 제대로 표현하지 않다　**longing** n. 그리움, 갈망　**preserve** v. 보존하다　**pursue** v. 추구하다　**property** n. 재산, 자산; 소유물, 건물, 땅　**assign** v. 할당하다, 배당하다　**premises** n. 구내, 건물이나 부지, 사업장　**procure** v. 얻다, 조달하다　**spirit** n. 알코올; 독한 술　**futile** a. 쓸데없는, 무익한　**beer on tap** 생맥주　**brew** v. (맥주 등을) 양조하다　**limestone** n. 석회암　**crisp** n. 바삭바삭한 포테이토칩　**brewery** n. 양조장　**in exchange for** ~대신, ~와 교환으로　**submit** v. 복종하다; 제출하다　**patron** n. (상점·여관 따위의) 고객, 단골손님　**specify** v. 명시하다, 명기하다　**swear** v. 맹세하다; 욕설하다　**publican** n. 술집 주인

26 내용파악　④

| 분석 |

본문에서 "그의 목표는, 과거 — 아니면 적어도 그가 이상화한 과거의 모습 — 가 그대로 보존된 완전한 세계를 만드는 것이다."라고 했는데, 이는 전통을 유지하는 것에 초점을 맞춘 운영 방식이라 할 수 있으므로 ④가 정답으로 적절하다.

다음 중 회장이 술집을 운영하는 방식을 가장 잘 설명한 것은?
① 술집 관리자들에게 혁신과 창의성을 장려하는 것
② 최신 기술과 기타 서비스로 술집을 현대화하는 것
③ 고객들로 하여금 자신의 행동을 자유롭게 결정하도록 허용하는 것
④ 술집을 전통이 보존되어야 하는 역사적 랜드마크처럼 취급하는 것

27 빈칸완성　①

| 분석 |

양조장이 가격을 낮게 유지하는 것은 Samuel Smith가 운영하는 술집의 술값이 저렴해짐으로 인해 손님들이 누릴 수 있는 혜택에 해당하는 데 반해, 고객 행동에 관한 엄격한 규칙을 따라야 하는 것은 손님들에 대해 가해지는 제약에 해당한다. 빈칸을 전후로 혜택과 제약에 대한 내용이 왔으므로, 빈칸에는 역접의 표현인 ①이 적절하다.

다음 중 두 번째 문단의 빈칸에 들어가기에 적절한 단어나 어구는?
① 그러나
② 게다가
③ 그 결과
④ 마찬가지로

28 부분이해　①

| 분석 |

회장이 자신이 운영하는 술집을 연극 무대처럼 다루며, 손님들이 지정된 역할을 수행해야 한다고 했음을 감안하면, curtain falls는 연극의 막이 내려가는 것으로 해석할 수 있으며, 이는 곧 영업을 종료한다는 것으로 이해할 수 있다.

본문에서 "the premises' curtain instantly falls"의 의미는 무엇일 가능성이 가장 높은가?
① 회장의 규칙이 지켜지지 않으면 술집은 문을 닫는다.
② 회장이 구내를 현대적인 용도로 개조하기로 결정한다.
③ 술집이 연극 공연장이 된다.
④ 술집이 Samuel Smith 제품의 제공을 일시적으로 중단한다.

29~31

유리창을 부드럽게 두드리며 비가 내리기 시작했을 때, 엠마(Emma)는 창밖을 바라보았다. 그녀는 그날 하루를 근처 언덕에서 하이킹을 하며 보낼 계획이었다. 그곳에서는 가을 단풍이 막 붉은 빛과 황금빛으로 물들기 시작하고 있었다. 그러나 밤새 몰려온 짙은 구름은 다른 계획을 가지고 있었다. 일기예보에서는 이제 폭우와 강한 바람을 경고하고 있었고, 엠마는 마지못해 등산화를 다시 신발장에 넣었다. 그러나 하루를 헛되게 지나가게 하고 싶지 않았기에, 그녀는 촛불을 켜고, 자신이 제일 좋아하는 케모마일 차를 우려내고 나서는, 너덜너덜해진 두툼한 소설책 한 권을 들고 소파에 자리잡았다. 곧 밖에서는 폭풍이 거세져서 바람이 울부짖고 나뭇가지들이 돌풍에 흔들렸지만, 엠마는 자신의 작은 거실 안에서 아늑함과 안전함을 느꼈다. 그녀는 부드러운 담요를 몸에 감고서는 자신의 책 속으로 빠져들었다. 그것은 그녀가 어린 시절부터 사랑해 온 이야기였다. 하이킹을 놓쳐서 실망이 되었지만, 엠마는 이 조용하고 예상치 못한 휴식에 감사하지 않을 수 없었다. 계획대로 흘러가지 않았을지는 몰라도, 그 날 하루는 그녀에게 천천히 쉬어가며 실내에서 머무르는 소박한 편안함을 만끽할 수 있는 완벽한 구실을 제공해주었다.

| 어휘 |

glance out (창밖을) 힐끗 보다, 흘끗 내다보다 **overnight** ad. 밤새, 하룻밤 사이에 **reluctantly** ad. 마지못해, 꺼려하며 **closet** n. 벽장, 옷장 **brew** v. (차·커피 등을) 끓이다, 우려내다 **couch** n. 소파 **well-worn** a. 낡은, 오래 사용한 **howl** v. (바람·늑대 등이) 울부짖다, 윙윙거리다 **sway** v. (좌우로) 흔들리다 **cozy** a. 아늑한, 편안한 **grateful** a. 감사하는, 고마워하는 **excuse** n. 핑계, 구실; 변명; (어떤 행동을 정당화하는) 이유

29 내용파악 ②

| 분석 |

엠마는 날씨로 인해 계획하고 있던 하이킹을 할 수 없었지만, 실망만 하고 끝난 것이 아니라, 그 대신 따뜻한 차를 마시고 책을 읽으며 실내에서 편안한 시간을 보내면서 나름의 알찬 시간을 보냈다. 이는 예상치 못한 상황에서도 긍정적으로 대처하고 주어진 상황에서 최선을 다하는 모습을 보여준다.

실내에 머물면서 책을 읽기로 한 엠마의 결정은 그녀의 성격에 관해 무엇을 보여주는가?
① 그녀는 야외 활동을 즐기지 않는다.
② 그녀는 적응력이 뛰어나며 예상치 못한 변화를 최대한으로 활용한다.
③ 그녀는 다른 모든 활동보다 독서를 가장 좋아한다.
④ 그녀는 향수(鄕愁)를 느끼며 항상 과거를 깊이 생각한다.

30 내용파악 ④

| 분석 |

폭풍은 이야기에서 단순한 날씨의 변화가 아니라, 엠마의 행동 변화를 유도하는 중요한 매개 수단, 즉 촉매 역할을 하고 있다. 즉, 그녀가 계획을 바꿔 실내에서 책을 읽으며 휴식을 취하는 계기를 마련해 준 역할을 했으므로 ④가 정답으로 적절하다.

이 이야기에서 폭풍은 어떤 역할을 하는가?
① 그것은 엠마가 원래 가지고 있던 계획을 방해하고 그녀를 좌절시키는 갈등을 만들어낸다.
② 그것은 도전을 회피하고 편안함을 추구하는 엠마의 성향을 두드러지게 한다.
③ 그것은 자연의 예측 불가능성과 그에 대한 엠마의 두려움을 상징한다.
④ 그것은 엠마가 휴식의 중요성을 깨닫게 하는 촉매 역할을 한다.

31 동의어 ②

| 분석 |

reluctantly는 '마지못해', '싫어하면서'의 뜻이므로 '마지못해', '억지로'라는 뜻의 grudgingly로 대체할 수 있다. ① 열심히, 간절히

③ 조심스럽게 ④ 무관심하게

32~33

요즘에는 토스트 제조기조차도 음성 명령에 따라 작동하도록 프로그램화될 수 있으므로, 자동차가 우리를 대신해서 운전하는 일을 맡게 된 것이 놀라운 일은 전혀 아니다. 미래에 일어날 일처럼 보이긴 하지만, 이제는 자동차와 트럭이 완전히 자동화될 것임은 확실한 듯하다. 이것이 과연 좋은 일일까?

무인 자동차 혹은 자동운전 자동차라고도 알려져 있는 자율주행 자동차는 가까운 주변 환경을 스캔하여 인간의 개입 없이 스스로 길을 찾아갈 수 있다. 이 기술로 얻게 되는 가장 분명한 이익은 편리함이지만, 설령 이동이 더 빠르고 더 저렴해진다고 하더라도 안전과 법적 책임 같은 해결되지 않은 여러 문제들은 이 혁신을 대체로 바람직하지 않은 것으로 만든다. 현재는 자동운전 자동차에 대한 법적인 틀이나 정부 규정이 없으며, 그 결과 무인 자동차는 해커나 테러리스트 같은 사이버 범죄자들에게 수많은 재앙적인 기회를 열어주고 있다.

속도 조절이나 긴급 제동과 같은 자동화된 기능에는 분명히 장점이 있긴 하다. 그러나 이것들은 완전한 자동화 기술과는 근본적으로 다르다. 운전자를 도와주는 기술이 자동차 엔지니어들에게는 유익한 목표일 수 있지만, 이제는 분명히 선을 긋고 컴퓨터가 아닌 인간이 자동차를 운전해야 한다고 주장해야 할 때이다.

| 어휘 |

assign v. 맡기다, 할당하다 **autonomous** a. 자율적인, 독립적인 **intervention** n. 개입, 간섭, 중재 **unresolved** a. 해결되지 않은 **liability** n. 법적 책임; 부담, 의무 **framework** n. (법·제도 등의) 틀, 체계, 뼈대 **regulation** n. 규제, 법규 **catastrophic** a. 대재앙의, 치명적인 **cybercriminal** n. 사이버 범죄자, 해커 **fundamentally** ad. 근본적으로, 본질적으로 **distinct** a. 뚜렷이 구별되는, 별개의 **draw a line** 선을 긋다, 한계를 정하다

32 내용파악 ③

| 분석 |

저자의 핵심적인 주장은 '자율주행 자동차가 편리하긴 하지만 안전, 법적 문제, 해킹 위험 등으로 인한 문제점이 매우 많으며, 따라서 자동차는 인간이 운전하게 해야 한다'는 것이다. 따라서 ③이 정답으로 가장 적절하다. ② 법적 규제가 없다는 점은 언급되었지만, 글의 핵심 주장은 법이 없다는 것 자체가 아니라 자동차의 위험성이 더 크다는 것이다. ④ 해킹이나 테러의 위험성이 언급되었지만, 전체적인 주장은 '자율주행 자동차의 전반적인 위험성'이지, 테러에 국한된 것이 아니다.

글쓴이의 주된 주장은 _____로 가장 잘 요약될 수 있다
① 속도 조절과 긴급 제동 기능은 완전 자동화 자동차로 전환할 필요성을 보여준다.
② 자동화 차량을 관장하고 있는 법은 없다.
③ 자율주행 자동차와 관련된 위험성이 그 이점보다 훨씬 크다.
④ 편리하긴 하지만, 자율주행 자동차는 테러의 발생 증가를 초래할 것이다.

33 내용파악 ②

| 분석 |

속도 조절이나 긴급 제동과 같은 자동화된 기능은 인간을 보조하는 역할을 하는 것이며, 완전 자동화는 그야말로 모든 운전을 컴퓨터가 알아서 해서 인간이 전혀 필요하지 않다는 것이므로 ②가 정답이다.

본문에 따르면, '자동화 기능'과 '완전 자동화'의 차이는 무엇인가?
① 자동화 기능은 운행 중에 운전자가 잠을 잘 수 있게 해준다.
② 자동화 기능은 인간 운전자를 보조하지만, 완전 자동화는 운전자가 필요 없다.
③ 자동화 기능은 위험하지만, 완전 자동화는 상대적으로 무해하다.
④ 자동화 기능은 완전 자동화보다 인간의 결정에 덜 의존한다.

DUKSUNG WOMEN'S UNIVERSITY | 덕성여자대학교 2교시

TEST p. 252~262

01	③	02	④	03	②	04	④	05	③	06	③	07	①	08	④	09	②	10	③
11	②	12	③	13	③	14	④	15	②	16	①	17	①	18	①	19	②	20	④
21	②	22	④	23	③	24	④	25	①	26	②	27	②	28	④	29	③	30	①
31	③	32	④	33	②														

01 동의어 ③

| 어휘 |

vivacious a. 쾌활한, 활발한(= lively)　**dull** a. 지루한; 활기 없는　**solemn** a. 엄숙한, 근엄한　**colorful** a. 색채가 풍부한, 다채로운

02 동의어 ④

| 어휘 |

transparent a. 투명한; 명료한(= clear)　**reflective** a. 반사하는, 반영하는　**opaque** a. 불투명한　**difficult** a. 어려운, 곤란한

03 동의어 ②

| 어휘 |

impartial a. 공평한, 공정한(= fair)　**obscure** a. 불명료한, 모호한　**indifferent** a. 무관심한　**severe** a. 엄한, 호된; 격심한

04 논리완성 ④

| 분석 |

소송에서 이기긴 했지만 변호사 수임료로 매우 많은 돈을 썼다면, 너무나도 많은 희생을 치르고 얻은 승리라고 할 수 있다. pyrrhic victory가 이러한 상황에서 쓰는 표현이므로 빈칸에는 ④가 들어가야 한다.

| 어휘 |

lyric a. 서정적인, 감성적인　**cynic** a. 냉소적인　**laconic** a. 간결한　**pyrrhic** a. (옛 그리스의) 전무(戰舞)의, 칼춤의　**pyrrhic victory** 큰 희생을 치른 승리(피로스 왕의 전쟁에서 유래)

| 해석 |

그녀는 소송에서 이기긴 했지만, 변호사 수임료에 상당히 많은 돈을 지불해야 했기 때문에 그것은 큰 희생을 치른 승리였다.

05 논리완성 ③

| 분석 |

이혼이나 별거하는 부부들이 아이들과 관련해서 다투는 것은 이혼이나 별거 후에 아이들을 누가 키울 것인가에 대해 의견이 일치하지 않기 때문으로 보는 것이 자연스럽다. 그러므로 빈칸에는 '자녀 양육권'이라는 의미의 ③이 적절하다.

| 어휘 |

maternity n. 모성, 모성애　**adoptability** n. 입양 가능성　**custody** n. 구금, 구류; 보호, (특히 이혼 · 별거에서) 자녀 양육권　**lien** n. 유치권(채권자가 담보를 확보하기 위한 권리)

| 해석 |

많은 별거하는 부부들이 자녀의 양육권을 두고 다툰다.

06 논리완성 ③

| 분석 |

청중이 쉽게 이해한 것은 결과에 해당한다. 이에 대한 원인이나 이유로는 설명을 명료하게 한 것일 것이므로 ③이 정답이다.

| 어휘 |

cryptic a. 수수께끼 같은, 비밀의　**elusive** a. (뜻 · 성격 등이) 파악하기 어려운, 알기 어려운　**lucid** a. 맑은; 명료한　**contradictory** a. 모순된

| 해석 |

그 과학자는 그 이론에 대해 명료한 설명을 제시하여, 청중이 이해하기 쉽게 해주었다.

07 논리완성 ①

| 분석 |
오류나 실수의 여지가 전혀 없었던 것은 그 기술자의 설계가 빈틈이 없었기 때문일 것이므로, 빈칸에는 ①이 들어가야 한다.

| 어휘 |
oversight n. (잊어버리거나 못 보고 지나쳐서 생긴) 실수, 간과; 관리, 감독 **meticulous** a. 세심한, 꼼꼼한 **conspicuous** a. 눈에 띄는, 똑똑히 보이는 **audacious** a. 대담한 **awkward** a. 어색한, 서투른

| 해석 |
그 기술자의 설계는 꼼꼼해서, 오류나 실수의 여지를 전혀 남기지 않았다.

08 논리완성 ④

| 분석 |
두 번째 빈칸의 경우, 복잡하거나 지루한 문체가 독자들의 집중을 방해할 수 있을 것이므로 complex와 tedious가 가능하다. 한편, 양보의 접속사 Though가 쓰인 주절과 종속절의 내용은 서로 대비를 이루어야 하겠는데, 주절이 계속 집중해서 읽기가 어렵다는 단점을 지적했기 때문에 종속절에서는 장점에 대해 언급하는 것이 자연스럽다. 그러므로 책이 사실을 기반으로 하고 있다는 의미를 만드는 filled와 packed가 첫 번째 빈칸에 들어갈 수 있다. 따라서 ④가 정답이다.

| 어휘 |
engaged a. 바쁜; 몰두[열중]하고 있는 **sparse** a. 드문드문한, (인구 따위가) 희박한 **simple** a. 간단한, 단순한 **filled** a. 가득 찬, 가득 들어 있는 **exciting** a. 흥미로운, 자극적인 **devoid** a. ~이 전혀 없는, 결여된(of) **complex** a. 복잡한 **packed** a. ~로 꽉 차 있는 **tedious** a. 지루한, 싫증나는

| 해석 |
그 책은 사실들로 가득 차 있긴 했지만, 지루한 문체 때문에 독자들이 계속 집중하기가 어려웠다.

09 동의어 ②

| 어휘 |
tirelessly ad. 지치지 않고, 끊임없이 **alleviate** v. (고통 등을) 완화하다, 줄이다(= relieve) **suffering** n. 고통, 고난 **natural disaster** 자연재해 **worsen** v. 악화시키다 **prevent** v. 예방하다 **ignore** v. 무시하다

| 해석 |
그 팀은 자연재해로 인한 고통을 덜어주기 위해 끊임없이 노력했다.

10 동의어 ③

| 어휘 |
deliver a speech 연설하다 **impassioned** a. 열렬한, 열정적인(= emotional) **rally** v. (사람들을) 결집시키다, 불러 모으다 **troop** n. 무리; (pl.) 군대, 병력 **exceptional** a. 비범한, 뛰어난, 출중한 **uninterested** a. 무관심한 **indefinite** a. 불확실한

| 해석 |
그 장군은 전투에 앞서서 병력들을 결집시키기 위해 열정적인 연설을 했다.

11 동의어 ②

| 어휘 |
innate a. 타고난, 선천적인(= inherent) **acquired** a. 후천적인 **incidental** a. 우연한 **absolute** a. 절대적인

| 해석 |
그 아이는 어린 나이에 복잡한 선율을 연주하여 음악에 대한 타고난 재능을 보였다.

12 분사구문 ③

| 분석 |
'~에 직면하다'는 face 혹은 be faced with로 표현할 수 있는데, 빈칸 뒤에 전치사 with가 주어져 있으므로 후자를 써야 하며, 따라서 ③이 정답이다. 이때 Faced with는 수동의 분사구문 Being faced with에서 Being을 생략한 형태이다.

| 해석 |
10,000 달러의 청구서를 마주한 루스(Ruth)는 부업을 시작했다.

13 양자 부정의 대명사 neither ③

| 분석 |
my twin sisters라고 했으므로 대상이 둘인 경우에 쓰는 대명사인 Both와 Neither로 정답의 범위를 좁힐 수 있다. 그런데 단수 동사 is가 제시돼 있으므로, 복수로 취급하는 대명사 Both는 부적절하다. 그러므로 단수로 취급하는 Neither가 정답이 된다.

| 해석 |
나의 쌍둥이 자매 중 누구도 어머니의 가게 운영을 도와주려 하지 않는다.

14 과거완료 ④

| 분석 |

주절은 재단장을 시작한 시점 이전의 상황에 해당하므로, when절에 쓰인 과거 시제보다 한 시제 앞선 시제를 써야 한다. 그러므로 과거완료 시제를 써야 하며, 주어인 The factory가 desert하는 행위의 대상이므로 수동태가 되어야 한다. 따라서 ④가 정답이다.

| 어휘 |
refurbish v. (방·건물 등을) 새로 꾸미다[재단장하다]; 일신하다
desert v. 버리다, 돌보지 않다

| 해석 |
그 공장은 그들이 그 공장을 재단장하기를 시작했을 때 몇 년 동안 버려져 있던 상태였다.

15 arrange for + 목적어 + to부정사 ②

| 분석 |
'~가 …하도록 주선하다[마련하다]'라는 의미를 나타낼 때 'arrange for+목적어+to부정사'의 형태로 나타낸다.

| 해석 |
그들은 짐(Jim)이 회의 기간 동안 런던에 머무르도록 주선해주었다.

16 수식어의 용법 ①

| 분석 |
much too는 일반적인 형용사를 수식하는 용법으로는 쓰지만 many를 수식하는 용법으로는 쓰지 않는다. 이 경우에는 Far too를 쓰므로, ①을 Far로 고쳐야 한다.

| 어휘 |
challenging a. 도전적인, 도발적인   inclusion n. 포함

| 해석 |
연말 수학 시험에서 너무나도 많은 학생들이 낙제했는데, 올해는 고급 주제가 포함돼 있어서 그 시험이 특히 어려웠던 것이다.

17 내용추론 ①

| 분석 |
"많은 학자들은 그의 작품들이 또한 그가 살던 시대의 정치적·사회적 관심사들을 반영한다고 믿는다."라는 내용을 통해 ①을 추론할 수 있다. ④ 첫 문장에서 '시대를 초월한 주제'라고 한 것은 그 시대뿐 아니라 오늘날의 사람들도 그 주제와 관련이 있다는 의미이다.

| 어휘 |
captivate v. 매혹하다, 사로잡다   timeless a. 시대를 초월한, 영원한
tragedy n. 비극   reflect v. 반영하다, 나타내다   resonate with 공명하다, 울려 퍼지다, 동조하다

| 해석 |
셰익스피어의 희곡들은 수 세기 동안 전해져 오면서, 시대를 초월한 주제와 복잡한 인물들로 관객들을 사로잡아 왔다. 그는 비극, 희극, 역사극을 썼으며, 각각의 작품은 그의 뛰어난 언어 능력을 보여준다. 많은 학자들은 그의 작품들이 또한 그가 살던 시대의 정치적·사회적 관심사들을 반영한다고 믿고 있다. 예를 들어, 『맥베스』와 『햄릿』과 같은 희곡들은 엘리자베스 시대와 잘 어울리는 권력과 부패라는 주제를 탐구한다.

다음 중 위 글에서 추론할 수 있는 것은?
① 셰익스피어의 작품들은 그가 살던 시대의 역사적 배경의 영향을 받았다.
② 셰익스피어는 비극과 희극만을 썼다.
③ 셰익스피어의 작품에는 정치적인 주제가 없다.
④ 오늘날의 관객들은 셰익스피어의 주제와 관련 맺지 못한다.

18~20

전기차(EVs)의 발달은 온실가스 배출을 줄이고 기후 변화와 맞서 싸우는 것을 향해 중요한 한 걸음을 내디딘 것이다. 전기차는 배기관 배출을 전혀 일으키지 않고 전기에 의해 가동되며, 이 전기는 태양력과 풍력 같은 재생에너지원으로 생성시킬 수 있다. 배터리 기술이 발전함에 따라, 전기차는 더 저렴해지고 주행 거리도 더 길어지고 있어, 전통적인 가솔린 동력 차량에 대한 실행가능한 대안이 된다.
하지만 여전히 문제는 남아 있다. 배터리 소재의 채굴이 환경에 미치는 영향과 충전 인프라의 제한된 보급이 주된 우려 사항이다. 전기차로의 전환이 지속가능하고 접근가능하게 하기 위해서는 정책 입안자들과 제조업체들이 이러한 문제들을 역점을 두고 다루어야 한다.

| 어휘 |
emission n. 방사, 발산; 배기가스   tailpipe n. (자동차의) 배기관
renewable a. 재생 가능한   affordable a. 가격이 적당한, 감당할 수 있는   viable a. (계획 따위가) 실행 가능한, 실용적인   alternative n. 대안   persist v. 지속되다, 존속하다   availability n. 이용 가능성
infrastructure n. 인프라, 기간 시설   policymaker n. 정책 입안자
address v. (문제를) 역점을 두어 다루다   sustainable a. 지속 가능한   accessible a. 접근 가능한

18 내용파악 ①

| 분석 |
전기차의 장점으로 배기가스를 전혀 배출하지 않는다는 점과 전기를 재생가능 에너지원에서 얻을 수 있다는 점을 들고 있다.

위 글에 의하면, 전기차의 주된 장점 중의 하나는 _____는 것이다.

① 배기관에서 배기가스를 전혀 배출하지 않는다
② 충전 인프라의 필요성을 없앤다
③ 환경에 영향을 전혀 끼치지 않는다
④ 재생 에너지원의 필요성을 줄인다

19 내용파악   ②

| 분석 |
전기차의 문제로 배터리 소재의 채굴이 환경에 미치는 영향과 충전 인프라의 제한된 보급을 언급했다.

전기차와 관련된 문제점 중 한 가지는 _____이다.
① 채굴 활동의 완전한 제거
② 충전 인프라를 제한적으로 이용 가능함
③ 온실가스 배출을 줄일 수 없음
④ 정책 입안자들의 관심 부족

20 글의 어조   ④

| 분석 |
본문에서는 전기차의 장점을 이야기하면서 현 시점에서의 문제점을 지적하는 한편으로 해결책의 필요성 또한 강조하고 있다. 따라서 본문은 균형 잡힌 '신중한' 어조를 띄고 있다고 보는 것이 가장 적절하다.

위 글의 어조는 _____으로 가장 잘 나타낼 수 있다.
① 찬양하는
② 일축하는
③ 불길한
④ 신중한

21~23

민주주의는 비판적 사고를 필요로 한다. 거의 모든 사람은 읽고 쓰는 능력이 모든 이에게 보장되어야 할 기본적인 인권이라는 데 동의한다. 글을 읽을 수 없는 사람은 글을 읽을 수 있는 사람들에게 종속된다는 것을 우리는 알고 있다. 글이라는 암호를 해독하고 그것을 자유자재로 다룰 수 없다면, 당신은 발전한 세상에 온전한 인간 백성으로서 들어갈 수 없다. 오늘날 문해력은 글과 숫자에 그치지 않는다. 사회적·정치적 논의에 온전히 참여하려면, 이제는 마법 상자(TV와 같은 대중매체)의 지배를 벗어나 그것의 비밀을 완전히 파악해야 한다. 미디어의 이미지가 어떻게, 왜 선택되는지에 대한 기본적인 지식인 미디어 리터러시(미디어 활용능력)를 공공 문화 정책의 핵심 목표로 삼지 않는다면, 우리는 대중매체를 소유하고 통제하는 강력한 이익집단의 지배에서 영원히 벗어나지 못하게 될 것이다.

전자 대중매체의 전 세계적인 확산은 강한 감정적 반응과 열띤 논쟁을 불러일으켜 왔다. 세계 곳곳의 관찰자들을 가장 우려하게 만든 것은 대중매체가 대부분의 사람들 속에 키우고 있는 것 같은 수동성이다. 그것은 사회생활, 공동체 활동, 그리고 그 밖의 창의적인 일들을 제거하고 저해한다. 우리는 농담처럼 이것을 카우치 포테이토(소파에서 포테이토칩을 먹으며 텔레비전만 보는 사람)가 돼 가는 것이라고 부른다.

하나의 사회로서 우리는 시민과 미디어 사이에 보다 역동적인 관계를 조성할 필요가 있다. 그 관계는 프로그램이 끝나고 TV가 꺼지는 순간 끝나는 관계가 아니다. 공적 생활에서 더 큰 민주주의를 바라는 이들에게 가장 큰 도전은 바로 미디어를 민주적 변화를 위한 도구로 바꾸는 것이다.

| 어휘 |
fundamental a. 근본적인 **in thrall to** ~에 속박되어; ~에 사로잡혀서 **media literacy** 미디어 정보 해독력(각종 미디어 정보를 주체성을 갖고 해독할 수 있는 능력) **proliferation** n. 확산, 급증 **displace** v. 대체하다, 대신하다 **undermine** v. 약화시키다, 손상시키다 **couch potato** 오랫동안 가만히 앉아 텔레비전만 보는 사람, 게으르고 비활동적인 사람

21 내용파악   ②

| 분석 |
본문에서는 미디어 리터러시는 "a basic knowledge of how and why media images are chosen", 즉 미디어 이미지가 어떻게, 왜 선택되는지를 아는 기본적인 지식이라고 설명하고 있는데, 이는 곧 미디어를 비판적으로 바라보는 능력을 의미한다. 그리고 미디어 리터러시는 미디어가 키우는 수동성에서 벗어나게 해주는데, 수동성에서 벗어난다는 것은 비판적일 때 가능하므로 ②가 정답이다.

위 글에 따르면, 미디어 리터러시가 중요한 이유는 무엇인가?
① 그것이 사람들이 열정적이고 더 나은 작가가 되도록 돕기 때문이다.
② 그것은 사람들이 미디어 콘텐츠를 비판적으로 평가할 수 있게 해주기 때문이다.
③ 그것은 사람들이 TV를 더 많이 보도록 조장하기 때문이다.
④ 그것은 미디어 발달의 역사를 가르쳐주기 때문이다.

22 빈칸완성   ④

| 분석 |
이어지는 내용에서 "그것이 사회생활, 공동체 활동, 창의적인 일들을 제거하고 저해하고, 사람들을 소파에서 포테이토칩을 먹으며

텔레비전만 보는 사람으로 만든다"고 했는데, 이것은 사람들을 수동적 혹은 소극적으로 만든다는 것으로 볼 수 있다.

다음 중 빈칸 Ⓐ에 들어가기에 가장 적절한 것은?
① 창의성
② 주관성
③ 객관성
④ 수동성

23 내용파악   ③

| 분석 |

본문에서는 비판적인 시각 없이 미디어를 소비하는 것이 '가만히 앉아서 텔레비전만 보는 사람'이 되도록 만들며, 여기에서 벗어나기 위해 미디어 리터러시가 필요하다고 말하고 있다. 즉, 미디어 자체가 그런 영향을 주는 것이고, 미디어 리터러시는 오히려 그것을 극복하기 위한 수단이므로 ③이 옳지 않은 진술이다.

위 글에 따르면, 다음 중 미디어 리터러시에 대해 옳지 <u>않은</u> 것은?
① 미디어 리터러시는 사회적, 정치적 논쟁에 참여하는 데 필수적이다.
② 미디어 리터러시는 사람들이 미디어 이미지가 어떻게, 왜 선택되는지를 이해하는 데 도움을 준다.
③ 미디어 리터러시는 사람들이 가만히 앉아서 텔레비전만 보는 사람이 되도록 조장한다.
④ 미디어 리터러시는 공공 문화 정책의 목표이다.

24~26

신체이형장애(BDD)는 개인이 자신의 외모에서 인식한 결점에 대해 지나치게 신경을 쓰게 되는 정신 건강 질환으로, 그 결점은 아주 사소하거나 다른 사람에게는 보이지 않는 것일 수도 있다. BDD를 가진 사람들은 종종 외모에 대해 당황해하고, 수치심을 느끼며, 염려하는데, 이로 인해 그들은 사회적 상황들을 회피하게 된다. 이들은 거울을 자주 들여다보고, 과도하게 몸단장을 하거나, 자신의 외모에 대해 안심시키는 말을 들으려고 하는 것과 같은 행동을 반복하기도 하는데, 이러한 행동은 상당한 시간을 소모하고 고통을 유발하여 일상적인 활동에 영향을 미칠 수 있다.
BDD의 정확한 원인은 알려져 있지 않지만, 유전적, 환경적, 심리적 요인이 복합적으로 작용하여 발생하는 것으로 여겨진다. 괴롭힘이나 놀림, 혹은 가족 안에서의 정신 질환 병력이 BDD 발병의 원인이 될 수 있다. 증상은 대개 청소년기에 시작되고 남녀 모두가 똑같이 걸릴 수 있다. 일반적으로 신경을 쓰는 부위에는 얼굴, 피부, 모발, 체형 등이 포함돼 있다. BDD의 치료는 종종 인지행동치료(CBT)와 약물치료를 수반한다. 인지행동치료는 개인이 가지고 있는 자신의 외모에 대한 왜곡된 믿음을 극복하고 변화시키는 데 도움을 주는 한편, 약물치료는 BDD와 관련된 불안과 우울 증상을 관리하는 데 도움이 된다. 더 나은 결과를 얻기 위해서는 치료를 일찍 시작하는 것이 매우 중요한데, 치료하지 않고 두면, BDD는 심각한 정서적 고통과 심지어 자살에 대한 생각까지도 초래할 수 있기 때문이다.

| 어휘 |

Body Dysmorphic Disorder 신체이형장애(자신의 외모나 신체 이미지를 지나치게 신경쓰며 신체적 결함이나 부족함에 대해 지나치게 걱정하는 만성적인 정신적 문제) **excessively** ad. 지나치게, 과도하게 **perceive** v. 인지하다, 인식하다 **flaw** n. 결점, 흠 **observable** a. 관찰 가능한 **repetitive** a. 반복적인 **groom** v. 손질하다, 몸차림하다 **reassurance** n. 안심시키기, 안도 **significant** a. 상당한; 중요한 **distress** n. 고통, 괴로움 **genetic** a. 유전의 **factor** n. 요인 **bully** v. 괴롭히다 **tease** v. 괴롭히다, 놀리다 **contribute to** ~에 기여하다, 원인이 되다 **symptom** n. 증상 **adolescence** n. 청소년기 **affect** v. 영향을 미치다; (병·고통이 사람·인체를) 침범하다, 걸리다 **cognitive-behavioral therapy** 인지 행동 치료 **medication** n. 약물 치료 **distort** v. 왜곡하다 **depression** n. 우울, 우울증 **intervention** n. 개입, 중재 **crucial** a. 결정적인, 매우 중요한 **suicidal** a. 자살 충동의, 자살하려는

24 내용파악   ④

| 분석 |

본문에서는 bullying(괴롭힘)과 teasing(놀림)을 BDD를 유발할 수 있는 요인으로 언급했으며, 환자들이 직접 보이는 행동으로는 전혀 언급되지 않았다.

다음 중 신체이형장애(BDD)를 가진 사람들이 보이는 일반적인 행동으로 언급되지 <u>않은</u> 것은?
① 과도한 몸단장과 거울을 들여다보기
② 사회적 상황들을 회피하는 것
③ 그들의 외모에 대해 안심시키는 말을 들으려 함
④ 정신 질환자들을 괴롭히고 놀림

25 내용파악   ①

| 분석 |

"인지행동치료는 개인이 가지고 있는 자신의 외모에 대한 왜곡된 믿음을 극복하고 변화시키는 데 도움을 주는 한편, 약물치료는 BDD와 관련된 불안과 우울 증상을 관리하는 데 도움이 된다."라고 돼 있으므로 ①이 정답으로 적절하다.

다음 중 신체이형장애(BDD)의 치료 방법을 가장 잘 설명하고 있는 것은?

① 인지행동치료(CBT)는 외모에 대한 왜곡된 믿음을 바꾸는 데 도움을 주는 한편, 약물치료는 불안과 우울 증상을 관리할 수 있을 것이다.
② 약물치료가 주된 치료법이며, 인지행동치료(CBT)는 집중적인 치료를 요하는 심각한 경우에만 사용된다.
③ 인지행동치료(CBT)는 BDD 치료에 효과가 입증되지 않았기 때문에 치료는 오직 약물치료만을 수반한다.
④ 인지행동치료(CBT)와 약물치료는 둘 다 BDD 치료에 있어 초기 단계에조차 효과가 없다

26 내용파악   ②

| 분석 |

글의 마지막 부분에서 "더 나은 결과를 얻기 위해서는 치료를 일찍 시작하는 것이 매우 중요한데, 치료하지 않고 두면, BDD는 심각한 정서적 고통과 심지어 자살에 대한 생각까지도 초래할 수 있기 때문이다."라고 했으므로 ②가 정답이 된다.

다음 중 신체이형장애(BDD)를 가진 사람들에게 조기 치료가 중요한 이유를 가장 잘 설명하고 있는 것은?
① 조기 치료는 다른 정신 질환의 발생을 예방할 수 있다.
② 조기 치료는 심각한 감정적 고통과 자살 생각의 위험을 줄일 수 있다.
③ 조기 치료는 개인이 신체의 건강 문제를 겪지 않도록 해준다.
④ 조기 치료만이 BDD의 완치를 보장할 수 있다.

27~29

신흥 알고리즘 기반 인공지능(AI)이 계속 확산됨에 따라, 사람들은 지금보다 더 나은 삶을 살게 될까? 2020년 여름에 실시된 전문가 설문조사에서 약 979명의 기술 개척자, 혁신가, 개발자, 기업 및 정책 지도자, 연구원, 활동가들이 이 질문에 답했다. 전문가들은 네트워크로 연결된 인공지능이 인간의 효율성을 높여주긴 하겠지만, 또한 인간의 자율성, 주체성, 능력을 위협할 것이라 예측했다. 그들은 다양한 가능성에 대해 이야기했다. 즉, 컴퓨터가 복잡한 의사결정, 추론과 학습, 정교한 분석 및 패턴 인식, 시각적 민감성, 음성 인식, 그리고 언어 번역 같은 작업에서 인간의 지능과 능력을 따라잡거나 심지어 능가할 수도 있다는 것이다. 그들은 공동체, 차량, 건물, 공공시설, 농장, 직무 프로세스 등에서의 "스마트" 시스템들이 시간과 비용을 절약하고, 생명을 구하며, 개인이 보다 맞춤화된 미래를 누릴 수 있는 기회를 제공할 것이라고 말했다. 많은 사람들은 보건의료와 환자를 진단하고 치료하거나 노인들이 더 풍요롭고 건강한 삶을 살도록 돕는 데 있어서의 AI의 많은 응용 가능성에 대해 낙관적인 발언을 집중적으로 했다. 그들은 또한 개인 유전체 정보에서 영양 정보에 이르는 온갖 것들에 관해 향후에 수집될 수 있는 방대한 데이터를 바탕으로 구축된 광범위한 공중보건 프로그램에 AI가 일정 역할을 하게 될 것이라 큰 기대를 걸고 있었다. 게다가, 이들 전문가들 가운데 다수는 AI가 정규 교육과 비정규 교육 시스템에서 오랫동안 기대해왔던 변화를 촉진할 것이라고 내다봤다. 그러나 대부분의 전문가들은 그들이 낙관적이냐 아니냐와 관계없이, 이러한 새로운 도구들이 인간다움의 본질적 요소에 장기적으로 미칠 영향에 대해 우려를 표했다.

| 어휘 |

emerging a. 새로 떠오르는, 신흥의 **be better off** 더 나아지다. 더 좋은 처지에 있다 **canvassing** n. (의견·지지 등을 얻기 위한) 조사, 유세, 권유 활동 **threaten** v. 위협하다 **autonomy** n. 자율성 **exceed** v. 능가하다, 초과하다 **sophisticated** a. 정교한, 복잡한 **analytics** n. 분석학 **pattern recognition** 패턴 인식 **visual acuity** 시각적 예리함, 시력의 명민함 **translation** n. 번역 **vehicle** n. 차량 **utilities** n. 공공시설, 공익사업(전기, 수도 등) **customize** v. 맞춤화하다, 개인화하다 **optimistic** a. 낙관적인 **diagnose** v. 진단하다 **enthusiastic** a. 열성적인, 열광적인 **contribute to** ~에 기여하다 **genome** n. 게놈 **nutrition** n. 영양 **abet** v. (좋지 않은 일을) 부추기다, (어떤 일의) 촉진에 도움을 주다

27 내용파악   ②

| 분석 |

"전문가들은 네트워크로 연결된 인공지능이 인간의 효율성을 높여주긴 하겠지만, 또한 인간의 자율성, 주체성, 능력을 위협할 것이라 예측했다."라고 했으므로 ②가 정답이다. ④ "이러한 새로운 기술들이 인간다움의 본질적 요소에 장기적으로 미칠 영향에 대해 우려를 표했다"고만 했을 뿐, 변화시킨다거나 바꿔 놓는다는 단정적인 표현은 없다.

위 글에 따르면, 다음 중 AI의 미래에 관해 옳은 것은?
① AI는 소수의 사람들에게만 혜택을 줄 것이다.
② AI는 인간의 자율성과 주체성을 위협할지도 모른다.
③ AI는 머지않아 모든 사람이 일자리를 잃게 만들 것이다.
④ AI는 인간의 본질적 요소들을 바꿔 놓을지도 모른다.

28 내용파악   ④

| 분석 |

"많은 전문가들이 보건의료와 환자를 진단하고 치료하는 데 AI를 응용할 수 있을 것이라는 점을 낙관적으로 보았고 데이터를 바탕으로 구축된 광범위한 공중보건 프로그램에 AI가 일정 역할을 하게 될 것이라는 데 큰 기대를 걸고 있었다."는 내용이 있으므로 ④가 정답으로 적절하다.

전문가들은 의료 및 공중보건 프로그램에서의 AI의 역할을 어떻게 보고 있는가?
① 그들은 AI가 의료 분야에 큰 영향을 미치지 않을 것이라 믿고 있다.
② 그들은 AI가 비의료 분야에서만 유용할 것이라 생각한다.
③ 그들은 모두 AI가 의사를 완전히 대체할 것이라고 예측한다.
④ 그들은 의료 분야에서의 AI의 잠재력에 대해 낙관적이다.

29 내용파악 ③

| 분석 |

전문가들은 한편으로는 AI의 효율성, 의료, 공공 보건, 교육 분야에서의 응용 가능성을 낙관적으로 기대하면서도, 다른 한편으로는 인간의 자율성, 주체성, 본질적 요소가 위협받을 수 있음을 우려하고 있다. 그러므로 ③이 정답으로 적절하다.

다음 중 AI의 미래에 대한 전문가들의 전반적인 정서를 가장 잘 나타내는 것은?
① 자기만족적인
② 비관적인
③ 상반된 감정을 가진
④ 이상주의적인

30~33

대규모로 나무를 제거하는 산림 파괴는 생태계, 기후 안정성, 그리고 인간의 건강에 중대한 위협이 된다. 나무는 이산화탄소와 기타 온실가스를 흡수하는 데 중요한 역할을 하며, 이는 기후 변화의 영향을 완화하는 데 도움이 된다. 그럼에도 불구하고, 산림 파괴는 농업, 가축 방목, 광산 개발, 벌목과 같은 활동에 의해 우려스러운 속도로 계속 진행되고 있다. 1990년 이래로 세계는 4억 2천만 헥타르 이상의 숲을 잃었으며, 그 중 가장 심각한 소실은 아프리카와 남아메리카에서 발생했다. 이와 같은 광범위한 산림 파괴는 저장된 이산화탄소를 대기 중으로 다시 방출함으로써 지구 온난화의 원인이 되며, 온실 효과를 악화시킨다.

게다가, 산림 파괴는 수없이 많은 생물 종(種)의 서식지를 파괴하여, 야생동물이 인간과 더 가깝게 접촉하게 만듦에 따라 인수공통감염병의 위험을 증가시킨다. 이는 인간에게 퍼질 수 있는 새로운 질병의 출현으로 이어질 수 있어서, 심각한 공중 보건상의 위험을 초래할 수 있다. 숲의 소실은 또한 숲에 의존해서 식량, 약품, 거처를 비롯한 생계를 해결하는 지역 공동체들에도 악영향을 미친다.

산림 파괴와 맞서 싸우기 위한 노력들이 진행 중에 있으며, 리와일딩(rewilding)과 리포레스팅(reforesting)과 같은 새로운 접근법들이 주목을 받고 있다. 이러한 노력들은 생물 다양성을 회복하고, 기후를 안정시키며, 파리 기후 협약에서 설정한 목표를 달성하기 위해 필수적이다. 리와일딩은 자연적인 과정을 통해 훼손된 생태계가 복원되도록 하는 것인 반면, 리포레스팅은 나무를 심어서 숲을 다시 만드는 데 중점을 둔다. 두 접근 방법 모두 산림 파괴로 인한 피해를 되돌리고 지구의 지속 가능한 미래를 보장하기 위해 매우 중요하다.

| 어휘 |

deforestation n. 삼림 벌채, 삼림 파괴 **pose** v. (위협·문제 등을) 제기하다, 야기하다 **significant** a. 중요한, 중대한, 상당한 **threat** n. 위협, 위험 **ecosystem** n. 생태계 **crucial** a. 결정적인, 매우 중요한 **absorb** v. 흡수하다 **carbon dioxide** 이산화탄소 **mitigate** v. 완화하다, 경감하다 **agriculture** n. 농업 **livestock grazing** 가축 방목 **logging** n. 벌목 **disrupt** v. 방해하다; 붕괴시키다 **habitat** n. 서식지 **zoonotic disease** 인수공통감염병(동물에서 인간에게 전염되는 질병) **emergence** n. 출현, 발생 **affect** v. 영향을 미치다, 악영향을 끼치다 **shelter** n. 주거지, 피난처, 은신처 **rewilding** n. 재야생화(방치와 접근금지에 의한 생태계 복원) **reforesting** n. 재조림 **gain traction** 주목받다, 관심을 얻다 **stabilize** v. 안정시키다 **set forth** 제시하다

30 내용파악 ①

| 분석 |

본문에서 삼림 파괴의 주요 원인으로 언급된 활동은 농업, 가축 방목, 광산 개발, 벌목 등이다.

산림 파괴를 일으키는 주된 활동은 무엇인가?
① 농업과 가축 방목
② 도시 개발과 과잉 관광
③ 어업과 양식업
④ 산업 생산과 교통

31 빈칸완성 ③

| 분석 |

앞에서 '저장된 이산화탄소를 대기 중으로 다시 방출함으로써 지구 온난화의 원인이 된다'고 했는데, 이것은 지구온난화를 가속시키거나 그 상황을 더 나쁘게 할 것이므로, 빈칸에는 ③이 들어가야 한다.

다음 중 빈칸 Ⓐ에 들어가기에 가장 적절한 것은?
① 상쇄하다
② 무효화시키다
③ 악화시키다
④ 원상복구시키다

| 32 | 내용파악 | ④ |

| 분석 |

"산림 파괴는 수없이 많은 생물 종(種)의 서식지를 파괴하여, 야생 동물이 인간과 더 가깝게 접촉하게 만듦에 따라 인수공통감염병의 위험을 증가시킨다."라고 했으므로 산림 파괴와 관련된 공중 보건상의 잠재적인 위험은 ④이다.

위 글에 따르면, 산림 파괴와 관련된 공중 보건상의 잠재적인 위험은 무엇인가?
① 깨끗한 식수의 이용 가능성 감소
② 산업 활동으로 인한 대기오염 수준 상승
③ 자외선 노출 증가로 인한 피부암 발생률 증가
④ 서식지 파괴로 인한 인수공통감염병의 위험 증가

| 33 | 내용파악 | ② |

| 분석 |

산림 파괴와 맞서 싸우기 위한 노력으로 리와일딩과 리포레스트링을 들고 있으며, 리와일딩은 자연적인 과정을 통해 훼손된 생태계가 복원되도록 하는 것인 반면, 리포레스트링은 나무를 심어서 숲을 다시 만드는 데 중점을 둔다고 했다. 따라서 ②가 정답이다.

산림 파괴에 맞서 싸우기 위한 두 가지 주요 접근방법은 무엇이며, 그 둘은 어떻게 서로 다른가?
① 도시화와 산업화; 도시화는 도시를 건설하는 데 초점을 맞추는 반면, 산업화는 공장을 개발하는 것을 수반한다.
② 리와일딩과 리포레스트링; 리와일딩은 자연적인 과정을 통해 생태계를 회복시키는 데 초점을 맞추는 반면, 리포레스팅은 숲을 복구하기 위해 나무를 심는 것을 수반한다.
③ 보존과 보호; 보존은 자원을 지속 가능하게 사용하는 데 초점을 맞추는 반면, 보호는 인간의 활동으로부터 지역을 완전히 보호하는 것을 수반한다.
④ 재활용과 쓰레기 줄이기; 재활용은 물건을 재사용하는 것에 초점을 맞추는 반면, 쓰레기 줄이기는 쓰레기 발생을 최소화하는 것을 수반한다.

MYONGJI UNIVERSITY | 명지대학교 인문계 오전

TEST p. 264~279

01	④	02	③	03	①	04	②	05	③	06	④	07	③	08	④	09	②	10	②
11	①	12	①	13	③	14	④	15	④	16	③	17	②	18	③	19	②	20	①
21	④	22	④	23	③	24	①	25	②	26	①	27	①	28	②	29	③	30	①

01 동의어 ④

| 어휘 |

muscle n. 근육   age v. 노화되다   regenerate v. 재생하다 (= recreate)   heal v. 치유하다   refresh v. 생기를 되찾게 하다   redirect v. (다른 용도로) 전용하다   recycle v. 재활용하다

| 해석 |

근육이 노화됨에 따라, 근육 세포가 부상 후에 재생하고 치유하는 능력을 잃게 된다는 것은 전혀 비밀이 아니다.

02 동의어 ③

| 어휘 |

stricken a. 시달리는   disintegrate v. 붕괴되다(= collapse)   proliferation n. 확산, 급증   armed group 무장단체   struggle v. 몸부림치다   destroy v. 파괴하다   neglect v. 방치하다

| 해석 |

전쟁에 시달리는 국가는 무장 단체가 급증하는 가운데 시민 사회가 붕괴되고 있기 때문에 또 하나의 실패한 국가가 될 위험이 있다.

03 동의어 ①

| 어휘 |

selection pressure 선택압   tumor n. 종양   veritable a. 진정한, 진짜의(= real)   escape v. (나쁜 상황에서) 벗어나다; 모면하다   swift a. 신속한, 재빠른   unbeatable a. 무적의   spontaneous a. 자발적인, 마음에서 우러난

| 해석 |

암 치료의 선택압 하에서 종양 세포는 변화하는 환경에 적응하는 진정한 진화를 겪게 되며 그 결과 치료 효과를 종종 모면한다.

04 논리완성 ②

| 분석 |

주절 앞에 전치사 unlike(~와는 달리)가 있다면, 전치사구와 주절에 서로 상반된 내용이 왔다고 생각할 수 있다. unlike 다음에 reusable(재사용 가능한)이 왔으므로, 빈칸에는 이와 상반된 의미를 가진 ②의 disposable(1회용의)이 적절하다.

| 어휘 |

chewable a. 씹을 수 있는   molded a. 틀로 찍어낸, 성형된   spit v. (침을) 뱉다   generic a. 상표 등록이 되어 있지 않은   disposable a. 1회용의   common a. 흔한   prevalent a. 널리 퍼져 있는

| 해석 |

가장 널리 사용되는 재사용 가능한 칫솔과는 달리, 씹는 칫솔은 1회용이다. 씹는 칫솔은 입안에 넣고 껌처럼 씹을 수 있는 플라스틱으로 찍어낸 미니 칫솔이다. 씹는 칫솔은 흔하게 사용되진 않지만, 여행자들에게 유용하다. 씹는 칫솔은 사용 후에 뱉어버린다.

05 논리완성 ③

| 분석 |

식민지가 독립국이 되기 위해서는 먼저 '자치권'이 부여되어야 할 것이다. 따라서 빈칸에는 ③의 autonomy(자치권)가 적절하다.

| 어휘 |

colony n. 식민지   grant v. 부여하다   consent n. 동의   coalition n. 연합   autonomy n. 자치권   acceptance n. 수락

| 해석 |

제2차 세계대전의 중대한 변화는 전쟁 이후 많은 식민지가 자치권을 부여받아 독립국이 되었다는 것이다.

06 분사구문 ④

| 분석 |

연결사 없이 두 개의 동사가 연결될 수 없다. 따라서 ④를 and disposed of로 고치거나 분사구문인 disposing of로 고쳐야 한다.

| 어휘 |

disaster n. 참사, 재난　magnitude n. (엄청난) 규모, 양, 중대(성)　catastrophe n. 참사, 재앙　scramble v. 급히 서둘러 하다　contain v. 봉쇄하다　radiation n. 방사선　lethal a. 치명적인　radioactive a. 방사능의　debris n. 잔해　mess n. 엉망진창인 상태　liquidate v. (문제의 원인을) 제거하다; 청산하다　dispose of ~을 처리하다　shift n. 교대 근무

| 해석 |

1986년 우크라이나의 체르노빌 원전 참사는 전 세계의 관심을 지배했다. 재앙의 규모가 분명해지자, 공무원들은 방사능을 봉쇄하는 매우 중요한 작업에 뛰어들었다. 고방사능 잔해에서 나오는 치명적인 감마선이 엉망진창인 상태를 깨끗이 치우는 데 투입된 로봇을 계속해서 파괴했다. 그래서 수천 명의 용감한 사람들이 '체르노빌 청산인'이 되어 90초 이하의 시간으로 '교대'하며 위험한 물질을 처리했다. 사람들은 기술로는 할 수 없는 일을 큰 개인적인 위험을 감수하고 해냈다.

07　의문사절의 어순　③

| 분석 |

의문사 how가 이끄는 의문사절의 어순은 'how+피수식어+주어+동사'인데, 문제에서는 가주어 it을 내세우고 진주어 to fall이 뒤로 간 형태이다. 따라서 ③의 is it unpleasant를 unpleasant it is로 고쳐야 한다. ④도 'how+피수식어'이다.

| 어휘 |

incongruity n. 부조화　crude a. 교양 없는　slip v. 미끄러져 넘어지다　skin n. (과일의) 껍질　be meant to do ~하기로 되어 있다　walk upright 직립보행하다　horizontal position 수평자세　spectator n. 관중　bother to do 일부러 ~하려 하다　tedious a. 지루한　overworked a. (단어가) 진부한

| 해석 |

유머의 본질은 누군가가 바나나 껍질에 미끄러져 넘어질 때 가장 교양 없게 드러나는 부조화이다. 인간은 수직 자세로 걸어야 하는데, 갑자기 수평 자세로 내던져진다면 그것을 보는 사람의 본능은 웃음을 터뜨리는 것이다. 넘어지는 것이 얼마나 불쾌한 일인지를 일부러 생각하거나 이런 바나나 껍질 농담이 얼마나 지루하고 진부한지를 일부러 생각해본 적이 없다면 말이다.

08　능동태와 수동태의 구분　④

| 분석 |

④ 앞의 it은 his design이다. 그의 디자인은 '선정하는 주체'가 아니라 '선정되는 대상'이므로, 수동태가 되어야 한다. 따라서 ④를 had been selected as로 고쳐야 한다.

| 어휘 |

amaze v. 놀라게 하다　awe v. 경외심을 불러일으키다　hunch n. 예감, 직감　statehood n. (미국 등에서) 주(州)의 지위　grade n. 성적, 학점

| 해석 |

미국에는 당신을 놀라게 하고 당신의 경외심을 불러일으킬 것들이 많이 있다. 예를 들어, 현재 50개의 별이 그려진 성조기는 고등학교 과제의 일환으로 17세였던 로버트 헤프트(Robert Heft)에 의해 디자인되었다. 그때가 1958년이었는데 당시에는 미국에 48개의 주만 있었지만 헤프트는 하와이와 알래스카가 곧 주의 지위를 부여받을 것이라고 직감했다. 그의 선생님은 그에게 B- 학점을 주었지만, 헤프트가 자신의 디자인을 백악관에 제출해서 결국 그의 디자인이 공식 미국 국기로 선정되었다는 아이젠하워 대통령의 전화를 받게 되었을 때 그의 학점을 A로 올려주었다.

09　타동사로 착각하기 쉬운 자동사　②

| 분석 |

consist는 타동사로 착각하기 쉬운 자동사이다. 목적어를 받기 위해서는 consist in 혹은 consist of의 형태로 써야 하는데, 문의 의미상 후자가 적절하다. 따라서 ②를 consisting of a limitless로 고쳐야 한다. ③ writing은 reading과 병치를 이룬다. ④ also가 be동사 다음에 오는 것이 더 일반적이지만 앞에도 올 수 있다.

| 어휘 |

substantial a. 실질적인, 상당한(양의)　artificial intelligence 인공지능　logician n. 논리학자　pioneer n. 선구자　abstract a. 추상적인　back and forth 앞뒤로　instruction n. (컴퓨터의 작동) 명령　store v. 저장하다

| 해석 |

인공지능 분야에서 가장 초기의 실질적인 연구는 영국의 논리학자이자 컴퓨터 선구자였던 앨런 매티슨 튜링(Alan Mathison Turing)에 의해 이루어졌다. 1935년에 튜링은 무한한 기억장치와, 기억장치 전체의 기호 하나씩을 지나면서 앞뒤로 이동하며 발견되는 것을 읽고 그 이상의 새로운 기호를 쓰는 스캐너로 구성된 추상적인 컴퓨팅 머신을 설명했다. 스캐너의 동작은 기호 형태로 기억장치에 또한 저장된 명령 프로그램의 지시에 따라 행해진다.

10　bestow A upon B　②

| 분석 |

동사 bestow는 4형식 수여동사가 아니라 bestow A(주는 물건) upon B(주는 대상)의 형태로 'A를 B에게 주다'는 뜻으로 사용된다. 'bestowing A(such a great honor) upon B(me and the civil rights movement in the United States)'의 형태가 되어야 하지만, '주는 대상'인 B를 강조하기 위해 'bestow upon B(주는 대상) A(주는 물건)'의 형태로 쓰일 수도 있다. 따라서 ②를 for bestowing upon[on] me로 고쳐야 한다.

| 어휘 |

appreciation n. 감사 bestow v. 수여하다 honor n. 명예상, 훈장 unutterable a. 말로 표현할 수 없는 fulfillment n. 실현, 성취 articulate v. (생각을) 표현하다 inaudible a. 들리지 않는

| 해석 |

저와 미국의 민권 운동단체에 이렇게 큰 상을 주신 것에 대해 노벨 위원회에게 깊은 감사를 거듭 표현하지 않고는 이 강의를 시작하는 것이 불가능합니다. 인생에서 때로는 글자라는 기호로는 완전히 설명될 수는 없는 말로 다 할 수 없는 성취의 순간이 있습니다. 그 순간의 의미는 들리지 않는 마음의 언어로만 표현될 수 있습니다. 지금 제가 경험하는 순간이 바로 그런 순간입니다.

11 논리완성   ①

| 분석 |

빈칸 앞 문장에서 글쓰기에서 꾸준히 좋은 성과를 내기 위해서는 '공부와 연습이 필요하다'고 했으므로, 이를 부연한 마지막 문장에서도 '노력이 필요하다'고 해야 적절할 것이다.

| 어휘 |

how-to-do-it a. 입문서의 subject n. 주제 readily ad. 쉽게 would-be a. ~을 지망하는 rationalize v. 합리화하다; 이론적으로 설명하다 inherently ad. 선천적으로 aptitude n. 적성, 소질

| 해석 |

글쓰기라는 주제에 관한 구할 수 있는 그 어떤 입문서나 심지어 모든 입문서를 읽음으로써 글쓰기를 배울 수 있는 사람은 아무도 없다. 쉽게 이해될 정도로 충분히 글을 잘 쓰는 것은 누구나 할 수 있는 일이다. 일관되게 글을 잘 쓰는 사람이 많지 않은 이유는 대부분의 작가 지망생들이 글쓰기의 비법이나 영감을 찾고 있기 때문이다. 그러나 첫 번째에 관해 그들은 잘못 알고 있으며 두 번째에 관해 그들은 그저 나태함을 합리화하려는 것일 뿐이다. 글쓰기에 특별한 비법은 없다. 쉽게 이해되도록 글을 쓰는 재능이 다른 사람보다 선천적으로 더 뛰어난 사람은 아무도 없다. 글쓰기는 골프, 테니스, 체스와 같아서, '초심자의 행운'을 가질 수도 있지만, 꾸준히 좋은 성과를 내기 위해서는 공부와 연습이 필요하다. 글을 잘 쓰는 것은 그 어떤 일이나 잘 하는 것과 마찬가지로 노력이 필요하다.

① 노력이 필요하다
② 소질이 필요하다
③ 영감에서 나온다
④ 광범위한 독서에서 나온다

12 논리완성   ①

| 분석 |

생물과 인간을 비교하고 있다. 생물에게 변화가 빠르고 큰 규모로 닥칠 경우 죽게 된다고 한 다음, 인간에게도 똑같은 원리가 적용된다고 했다. 따라서 빈칸의 내용 역시, "변화가 지나치게 급격하고 거대할 경우 인간도 죽게 된다"고 해야 적절할 것이다. 그러므로 ①이 정답이다.

| 어휘 |

thrive v. 번성하다 slight a. 사소한 come over somebody (격한 감정 등이) ~에게 밀려오다 massive a. 거대한 accumulate v. (서서히) 증가하다 extinct a. 멸종한

| 해석 |

생물은 환경에 사소한 변화가 생길 경우 더욱 더 번성하는데, 그 변화가 너무 빠르고 큰 규모로 일어날 경우 죽게 될 가능성이 있다. 이것이 동물들 중 일부 종들이 멸종되는 방식이다. 인간에게도 똑같은 원리가 적용된다. 즉 변화가 지나치게 급격하고 거대할 경우 인간도 죽게 되는 것이다.

① 변화가 지나치게 급격하고 거대할 경우 인간도 죽게 된다
② 사소한 변화는 시간이 지남에 따라 빠르게 증가할 수 있다
③ 많은 인간 종들이 많은 사소한 변화 때문에 멸종되었다
④ 느리지만 지속적인 지구 온난화가 계속되면 그들은 멸종될 것이다

13 논리완성   ③

| 분석 |

"돈이 유통되면서 세균이 축적된다."라고 했으므로, 유통과정에서 당신의 지갑으로 들어온 돈에는 세균이 엄청날 것이다. 따라서 당신이 알 수 없는 것은 바로 ③의 '지금 당신의 지갑에 얼마나 많은 세균이 숨어있는지'가 될 것이다.

| 어휘 |

given n. 당연한 일 microbe n. 미생물, 세균 magnet n. 자석; ~을 끌어들이는 물건[사람] germ-free a. 무균의, 세균이 없는 at all times 항상, 언제나 debit card 직불카드 handle v. (손으로) 만지다 as soon as possible 되도록 빨리 microorganism n. 미생물 pathogen n. 병원균 E. coli 대장균 circulate v. 유통하다 bank note 지폐 germ-ridden a. 세균이 득실대는

| 해석 |

세균을 피하고 싶다면 손을 씻는 것이 당연한 일이지만 세균을 끌어들이는 특정한 물건을 만진 후에는 손을 씻는 것이 특히 중요하다. 물론 당신의 손을 항상 100% 무균 상태로 유지하는 것은 불가능하지만 특정 물건을 만진 후에는 손을 씻는 것이 절대적으로 중요하다. 예를 들어, 요즘 대부분의 물건 구입에 직불카드나 신용카드를 사용할 수 있지만 가끔은 현금을 만져야 할 필요가 있다. 그럴 때는

가능한 빨리 손을 씻는 것이 중요하다. 연구원들은 뉴욕 시 은행에서 가져온 1달러 지폐를 시험해 보았고 박테리아를 비롯한 수백 개의 미생물과 반려동물의 DNA, 바이러스 등을 발견했다. 비슷한 연구에서는 일부 현금과 동전에서 대장균과 살모넬라균 같은 병원균도 발견되었다고 한다. 돈이 유통되면서 세균이 축적된다. 지금 당신의 지갑에 얼마나 많은 세균이 숨어있는지를 알 수 있는 방법은 없다.

① 어느 지폐가 가장 심각할 정도로 세균이 득실대는지를
② 지폐와 신용카드 중 어느 것에 더 많은 세균이 있는지를
③ 지금 당신의 지갑에 얼마나 많은 세균이 숨어있는지를
④ 지폐가 평균적으로 몇 년 동안 유통되는지를

14 논리완성   ④

| 분석 |
for가 본문에서는 '이유'를 나타내는 접속사로 쓰였으므로, 접속사 for 뒤에는 '이유', 그리고 for 앞에는 '결과'가 와야 한다. for 이하에서 "당신이 얼마나 오래 악을 행하지 않는 품위 있는 상태를 유지할지 알 수 없다"고 했는데, 이 말은 '당신도 언제든지 품위를 잃고 악을 행할 수 있다'는 말로 해석될 수 있다. 따라서 당신도 악을 행할 수 있으므로 누군가가 악행을 저지르는 것을 보더라도 '당신이 그 사람보다 더 나은 사람이라고 여기지(consider yourself better than the person)' 말아야 한다는 흐름이 되는 것이 적절하다.

| 어휘 |
take delight in doing ~을 하는 것에서 기쁨을 얻다 **humble** a. 겸손한 **estimate** n. 추정, 추산 **lesson** n. 수업; 교훈 **take account of** ~을 고려하다 **think well of** ~을 좋게 생각하다 **think highly of** ~을 높이 평가하다 **on that account** 그런 이유로 **grace** n. 품위, 예의 **frail** a. 도덕적으로 취약한

| 해석 |
어떤 것이든 알거나 배워서 당신에게 도움이 되기를 바란다면, 그렇다면 무명이고 인정받지 못하는 것에서 기쁨을 얻어라. 자신에 대한 진정한 이해와 겸손한 평가는 가장 높고 소중한 교훈이다. 자신을 전혀 고려하지 않고 항상 다른 사람들을 좋게 생각하고 높이 평가하는 것이 최고의 지혜이다. 다른 사람이 공개적으로 악행을 저지르는 것을 본다면, 그런 이유로 자신을 그 사람보다 더 나은 사람이라고 여기지 말라. 왜냐하면 당신이 얼마나 오래 품위 있는 상태를 유지할 수 있을지 알 수 없기 때문이다. 우리는 모두 악하므로, 그 누구도 당신보다 더 약하다고 여기지 말라.

① 그 사람이 하는 것을 따라하다
② 다른 사람들한테서 배우는 것을 멈추다
③ 스스로를 악행을 저지르기 쉽다고 여기다
④ 자신을 그 사람보다 더 나은 사람이라고 여기다

15 논리완성   ④

| 분석 |
만일 본능적인 충동에 따라 행동한다면 사람들의 입에 오르내릴 것임을 알고 있다고 했으므로, 죄를 아직 저지르지 않은 '잠재적인 죄인들'은 원하는 대로 마음껏 타락하고 싶은 유혹을 이겨내려고 할 것이다. 따라서 ④의 '마음껏 타락하고 싶은 유혹에 저항할 힘'이 빈칸에 적절하다.

| 어휘 |
do as one pleases 자기가 멋대로 행동하다 **get away with** (벌 등을) 교묘히 모면하다 **censorious** a. 몹시 비판적인 **philander** v. 바람피우다 **wander** v. 방황하다 **primrose path** (결국 파멸로 이르는) 환락의 길, 방탕한 생활 **give way to** (감정에) 무너지다 **sinner** n. (도덕상의) 죄인

| 해석 |
만일 우리가 멋대로 행동하고 나서 동료들로부터 어떠한 비난도 받지 않고 넘어갈 수 있다면 지금보다 남편들과 부인들은 더 많이 바람을 피울 것이고 더 많은 소녀들이 환락의 길을 방황할 것이며 아이들은 방치될 것이고 집들은 관리가 안 될 것이다. 만일 그들이 본능적인 충동에 따라 행동한다면 사람들의 입에 오르내릴 것이라는 것은 누구나 아는 바이며, 이것이 많은 잠재적인 죄인들에게 마음껏 타락하고 싶은 유혹에 저항할 힘을 준다.

① 선량한 시민이 되는 것의 이득과 손실에 대해 생각해볼 기회
② 그들이 비밀리에 저지른 죄의 결과에 대한 생각
③ 그들이 더러운 비밀을 숨기지 않을 경우 미움을 받게 될 것이라는 두려움
④ 마음껏 타락하고 싶은 유혹에 저항할 힘

16 내용일치   ③

| 분석 |
"대기 중으로 수분이 더 많이 유입되면 습도와 이슬점이 높아진다"라고 했으므로, "이슬점은 변하며, 계절의 영향을 받는다"는 것을 알 수 있다. 따라서 ③이 본문의 내용과 일치하지 않는다.

| 어휘 |
feels-like temperature 체감온도 **humidity** n. 습도 **sticky** a. 끈적거리는 **moisture** n. 수분 **dew point** 이슬점(대기 중의 수증기가 엉켜 물방울이 되는 온도) **muggy** a. (날씨가) 무더운 **evaporate** v. 증발하다 **matter** v. 중요하다 **acclimate** v. 적응하다 **jarring** a. 불쾌감을 주는 **celebrate** v. 즐겁게[신나게] 놀다

| 해석 |
화씨 60도(섭씨 15.5도)가 봄과 가을에 똑같은 느낌이 들지 않는다는 것을 알아차렸는가? 현실 세계에서 느끼는 온도는 공식적으로 '체감온도'로 알려져 있다. 같은 온도가 몇 가지 이유로 완전히 다르게 느껴질 수 있다. 우선 습도가 높으면 더 따뜻하게 느껴진다. 봄과

여름은 더 끈적거린다. 대기 중으로 수분이 더 많이 유입되면 습도와 이슬점이 높아진다. 이슬점은 대기가 무겁다고 느껴지기 전에 얼마나 많은 수분을 담을 수 있는지를 알려주며 이슬점이 높으면 땀이 쉽게 증발하지 않아 기온이 낮더라도 우리가 따뜻함과 불편함을 더 느끼게 된다. 게다가 이전 계절도 중요하다. 당신의 몸은 방금 겪은 계절에 적응되어 있다. 따라서 초가을이고 뜨거운 여름 기온에서 벗어나고 있다면 오후 한낮의 60도가 가벼운 자켓을 찾게 될 정도로 불쾌감을 줄 수 있다. 반면 봄의 오후 온도가 처음으로 60도 대에 진입할 경우, 이것이 당신을 신나게 만들어 당신은 자켓을 입지 않고 외출해서 즐겁게 놀지도 모른다.

다음 중 본문의 내용과 일치하지 않는 것은?
① 대기의 수분이 체감온도를 높여준다.
② 이슬점이 높을 경우 땀의 증발이 느려진다.
③ 이슬점은 변하지 않으며 계절의 영향을 받지 않는다.
④ 체감온도는 적응해 있는 우리 몸의 영향을 받는다.

17 글의 주제 ②

| 분석 |
이 글은 "인류가 의식주를 해결한 다음에야 자연 현상에 대해 의문을 품고 생각할 시간을 갖게 되었지만, 과학이 발달하기 이전이라 이해할 수 없거나 달리 설명할 수 없는 것을 신의 작품이라고 여겼다"는 내용의 글이다. 따라서 ②의 '과학적 사고가 태동하기 이전의 인류의 인지 발달'이 글의 주제로 적절하다.

| 어휘 |
shelter n. 주거지 come into one's mind 생각이 나다 tremble v. (몸을) 떨다, 진동하다 puzzle v. 이해할 수 없게 만들다, 당황[곤혹]하게 하다 reproduce v. 번식하다

| 해석 |
지구에 살던 초창기에 인류는 아마도 주변의 모든 것을 의심 없이 받아들였을 것이다. 춥고 비가 오는 시기에는 불편함, 심지어 비참함을 느꼈고, 따뜻하고 화창한 시기에는 살아있다는 것에 기뻐했다. 하지만 그들은 한 번도 그 이유에 대해서는 의문을 품지 않았다. 그러나 자신과 가족에게 충분한 의식주를 제공할 수 있게 되었을 때 그들에게 생각할 시간이 생겼다. '왜', '무엇', 그리고 '어떻게'라는 단어가 천천히 그들의 마음과 언어 속으로 들어갔다. 왜 나무가 넘어지고 흙이 언덕 아래로 미끄러져 내려갈 때까지 땅은 때때로 흔들렸고 진동했을까? 태양과 별과 행성은 어디에서 온 것일까? 그러나 이러한 질문들에 답하려고 할 과학은 없었다. 자연 법칙과 인과관계 개념은 알려져 있지 않았다. 체계적인 지식도 세심한 실험도 전혀 없었으며, 세심한 관찰도 거의 이뤄지지 않았다. 이해할 수 없거나 다른 방식으로는 설명될 수 없는 모든 것은 신의 작품이라고 말해졌다.

다음 중 이 글의 주제는 무엇인가?
① 식량을 찾고 번식하려는 인류의 노력
② 과학적 사고가 태동하기 이전의 인류의 인지 발달
③ 인류가 과학적인 사고를 하도록 만든 자연 재해
④ 인류를 미신에서 해방시킨 과학 지식

18 글의 제목 ③

| 분석 |
이 글에서는 "고갈될 것 같지 않았던 미국의 방대한 천연자원을 농경지를 만들기 위해 식량을 위해 심지어 스포츠를 위해 대량으로 파괴한 결과 매년 홍수가 발생하게 되었고, 강은 물고기가 살 수 없게 되었으며, 일부 새들과 포유류는 사라지거나 사라질 위기에 처하게 되었다"고 했다. 따라서 ③의 '천연자원을 미국인이 이기적으로 이용한 결과'가 글의 제목으로 적절하다.

| 어휘 |
tremendous a. 엄청난 mineral n. 광물 fertile a. 비옥한 prairie n. 대초원 stream n. 하천 abound v. 많이 있다 make way for (~에게) 자리를 내주다 mammal n. 포유동물 slaughter v. (가축) 도살[도축]하다 inexhaustible a. 고갈될 줄 모르는, 무진장한 depletion n. (자원의) 고갈 on the verge of ~하기 직전의 conservation n. (자연, 자원의) 보호, 보존 heritage n. (사회의) 유산

| 해석 |
최초의 백인들이 미국에 왔을 때 그들은 엄청난 가치가 있는 방대한 천연자원을 발견했다. 미국의 많은 부분이 숲으로 뒤덮여 있었고, 나중에 믿을 수 없을 정도로 많은 양의 가스, 석유, 광물이 발견됐다. 매우 비옥한 토양도 엄청나게 풍부했다. 숲, 대초원, 하천, 강에는 야생생물이 넘쳐났다. 이 자원들이 너무나 방대해서 결코 고갈될 것 같지 않았다. 그래서 농경지를 만들기 위해 숲이 파괴되었다. 신생 공업국에 공급하기 위해 광물과 석유가 대량으로 사용되었다. 포유류와 조류는 식량과 스포츠를 위해 도살되었다. 얼마 지나지 않아 결과는 분명해졌다. 홍수로 매년 수백만 달러에 달하는 피해가 발생했다. 겉보기에 없어지지 않을 것처럼 보이던 석유와 광물이 고갈의 징후를 보였다. 많은 강은 물고기가 살기에 적합하지 않게 되었다. 몇몇 종의 새들은 사라졌고 일부 포유동물은 사라지기 직전에 있는 것처럼 보였다. 간단히 말해, 모든 미국인의 유산인 자원을 현재와 미래의 미국인들이 공유하고자 한다면 일종의 자원 보존 프로그램이 마련되어야 한다는 것을 미국인들은 곧 깨닫게 되었다.

글의 제목으로 가장 적절한 것을 고르시오.
① 무진장할 정도로 막대한 미국의 천연자원
② 미국의 유럽 이주자와 유례없는 개발
③ 미국 천연자원의 이기적 이용의 결과
④ 자연에 입힌 회복할 수 없는 피해와 미국 문명의 몰락

19 글의 흐름상 적절하지 않은 문장 고르기　②

| 분석 |

①에서 "장과 뇌는 복잡한 신경망과 화학신호를 통해 끊임없이 소통한다"라고 했으므로, ① 다음에 올 내용은 ①에 대한 '예시'가 적절하다. 따라서 "예를 들어, 뇌는 장에 음식 소화를 준비하도록 신호를 보낸다"고 언급한 ③이 ① 다음에 자연스럽다. 반면, ②는 인체가 어떻게 구성되어 있는지를 일반적으로 설명하고 있어서 글 전체와 자연스럽게 호응이 되지 않으므로, ②가 정답이다.

| 어휘 |

old saying 속담　**psychiatrist** n. 정신과 의사　**depression** n. 우울증　**gut** n. 장, 내장　**ultra-processed food** 초가공식품　**intricate** a. 복잡한　**be made up of** ~로 구성되다　**digestion** n. 소화　**trigger** v. 촉발시키다　**gastrointestinal** a. 위장의　**nausea** n. 메스꺼움　**diarrhea** n. 설사　**microbiome** n. 미생물군집　**fungi** n. 곰팡이(fungus의 복수)　**digestive system** 소화기관　**trillion** n. 1조

| 해석 |

"식습관이 건강을 좌우한다"라는 옛말이 있다. 최근 한 유명 정신과의사는 우울증과 싸우는 사람들이 정크푸드 섭취를 중단해야 한다고 말했다. "장 건강은 뇌 건강에 매우 중요합니다. 예를 들어, 만일 당신이 초가공식품을 섭취하면, 우울증과 싸울 위험이 급격히 증가합니다."라고 그 정신과의사가 말했다. 장과 뇌는 복잡한 신경망과 화학신호를 통해 끊임없이 소통한다. 〈인체는 가장 큰 부분을 차지하고 있는 물(대략 42리터)을 비롯한 다양한 요소로 구성되며, 여러 유형의 많은 세포와 기관으로 이루어진 복잡한 시스템이다.〉 예를 들어, 뇌는 장에 음식 소화를 준비하도록 신호를 보내며 스트레스는 메스꺼움이나 설사와 같은 위장 증상을 초래하는 신호를 촉발시킬 수 있다. 장내 미생물군집(우리 소화기관 안에 있는 박테리아, 바이러스, 곰팡이의 집합체)은 뇌 기능에 영향을 미치고 기분에 영향을 줄 수 있는 화학물질을 생성한다. 대부분 박테리아인 100조 개 이상의 미생물이 미생물군집을 구성한다.

20 글의 요지　①

| 분석 |

이 글은 번아웃을 겪는 교사들이 어떻게 스트레스를 해소하고 대처하는지를 여러 교사들의 사례를 들어 이야기하고 있다. 따라서 "교사들은 다양한 방법으로 직장 스트레스를 해소하며 스스로 재충전한다"는 ①이 글의 요지로 적절하다.

| 어휘 |

cakewalk n. 쉬운 일, 식은 죽 먹기　**high-pressure** a. 스트레스가 많은　**underappreciated** a. 제대로 평가되지 못하는　**prioritize** v. 우선순위를 매기다　**self-care** n. 자기관리, 자기 돌봄, 자가 치료　**recharge** v. 재충전하다

| 해석 |

가르치는 일이 결코 쉬운 일은 아니었다. 여기에 제한된 자원, 낮은 급여, 과중한 업무 부담 등을 더해보라. 교사들이 기록적인 수로 번아웃(탈진)을 겪고 있는 것은 놀라운 일이 아니다. 그렇다면 당신은 저평가되고 혹사당한다고 느끼는데도 어떻게 스트레스가 그렇게도 많은 직장에 머물러있는가? 당신은 자기 관리를 우선시해야 한다. 교사들은 해마다 각자 다양한 방식으로 휴식을 취하고 에너지를 재충전하며 회복해서 다시 교단에 서곤 한다. 한 교사는 "저는 매주 금요일 밤에 남편과 야간 데이트를 예정해둡니다. 일주일 내내 즐거운 마음으로 그 시간을 기다리게 되고 우리는 서로의 직장 이야기는 하지 않는 것을 원칙으로 삼고 있어요."라고 말한다. 또 다른 교사는 "저에게 그 방법은 버레스크 댄싱입니다. 성인 전용 댄스 클래스를 일주일에 한 번 수강하는데, 그 시간이 일주일 중에서 하이라이트입니다. 정말 재미있고 긴장을 푸는 아주 좋은 방법입니다."라고 다른 교사가 말한다. 또 다른 교사는 이렇게 이야기한다. "저는 달리기를 해요. 집에 오면 기진맥진해 있어서 달리기가 가장 하기 싫은 일일 것 같지만 에어팟을 끼고 팟캐스트를 들으며 뛰다 보면 오히려 기운이 납니다."라고 말한다.

다음 중 이 글의 요지를 가장 잘 요약한 것은?
① 교사들은 다양한 방법으로 직장 스트레스를 해소하며 스스로 재충전한다.
② 가르치는 일이 최근 점점 더 복잡해지고 힘들어졌다.
③ 교사들은 저평가 받고 있다고 느끼며, 이로 인해 사기가 저하되고 있다.
④ 교사들이 직무 수행을 더 잘할 수 있도록 지지와 인정이 필요하다.

21 글의 요지　④

| 분석 |

이 글은 공황장애 진단을 받은 저자가 반복적인 레고 조립이나 창의적인 색칠 활동에 참여했더니 불안이 진정되는 효과가 있었다는 내용이다. 따라서 '반복적이고 창의적인 활동에 참여하는 것이 공황장애를 다스리는 데 도움이 된다'는 ④가 글의 요지로 적절하다.

| 어휘 |

be diagnosed with ~로 진단 받다　**panic** n. 극심한 공포, 공황　**disorder** n. (신체 기능의) 장애　**anxiety** n. 불안　**breathless** a. 숨이 막힐 듯한　**stall** n. (칸막이를 해서 만든) 화장실　**trait** n. 특성　**take medication** 약을 복용하다　**sculpt** v. 조각하다　**shade in** ~에 명암을 넣다　**distract** v. 기분 전환을 하다　**bout** n. (병을) 한바탕 앓음　**watercolors** n. 수채화 그림물감　**engage in** ~에 참여하다　**soothing** a. 진정시키는　**knit** v. 뜨개질을 하다　**cerebral cortex** 대뇌 피질

| 해석 |

나는 20년 전 19세 때 공황장애 진단을 받았다. 불안을 치료하는 데는 평생 관리 계획이 필요하다는 것을 나는 곧 알게 되었다. 나의

첫 번째 공황 발작은 갑자기 찾아왔고 화장실 칸에서 숨이 막히고 두려움에 휩싸인 채 무력감을 느꼈다. 나는 공황 발작을 하나의 성격 특성처럼 취급하는 법을 배웠다. 즉 나는 자유로운 영혼이면서 재미있고 창의적이면서 불안한 사람이라고 말이다. 내가 만성 불안과 공황 발작을 겪고 있기 때문에, 약을 복용하고 있음에도 불구하고 일상을 되찾으려면 불안을 다스리는 방법을 찾아야했다. 나의 건강상태에 대처하는 과정은 나를 더욱 건강한 사람으로 만들어 주었으며 불안이 나를 창의적으로 만들어주었다. 예를 들어, 12살인 내 아들이 더 어렸을 때 나는 아들과 레고를 조립하거나 색칠을 하거나 플레이도로 조형물을 만들면서 불안감을 누그러뜨렸다. 아주 작은 밝은 색상의 레고 벽돌에 집중하거나 색연필로 만화 캐릭터에 음영을 넣는 것이 나를 기분전환 시켜주었고 진정시켜 주었다. 요즘 나는 성인용 컬러링북을 갖고 있으며 불안을 한바탕 겪을 때 믿음직한 색연필과 함께 부엌 조리대에 앉고 한다는 것을 부끄럽지 않게 말할 수 있다. 나는 또한 글을 쓰거나 수채화 그림물감으로 그림을 그리기도 한다. 한 정신건강 연구원은 "뜨개질이나 색칠 같이 진정시키는 활동에 참여하는 것이 매우 도움이 됩니다. 미술 프로젝트에서 수행되는 반복적인 동작이 대뇌 피질의 일부를 분주하게 만들면서 뇌의 공포를 담당하는 신경중추를 진정시킵니다."라고 말한다.

다음 중 위 글은 주로 무엇에 관한 것인가?
① 나는 나의 성격 특성을 바꾸려는 노력을 통해 보다 건강해졌다.
② 나는 컬러링북의 도움으로 나의 공황장애를 완전히 극복할 수 있었다.
③ 공황장애는 약물의 도움으로 효과적으로 억제될 수 있다.
④ 반복적이고 창의적인 활동에 참여하는 것이 공황장애를 다스리는 데 도움이 된다.

에서 잘못된 모든 일의 원인을 부모 탓으로 돌리는 아들이나 딸을 한탄하면서도 그리워하는 부모들에게 이제 그만해야 할 때가 찾아온다. 나는 10~20년 동안 자녀에게 외면하고 비난받고 조롱당하며 무시당하면서도 아들딸이 돈이 필요할 때만 연락해오는 부모들의 이야기를 일상적으로 듣는다. 성인이 된 자녀들과의 소원해진 관계 때문에 부모의 자존감은 큰 타격을 입었다. 오랜 기간 소원해진 관계 속에서도 많은 부모들은 대개 잘 살아가지만, 누군가의 사망이나 인생의 중요한 사건이 발생해 다시 연락이 닿거나 고통이 되살아날 때 감정이 폭발한다. 그런 일이 일어나면 부모들은 몇 주 동안 계속 우울한 기분에 빠지기도 하고 관계단절의 초기 충격과 당혹스러움이 되살아나기도 하며 심지어 "도대체 왜?"라고 질문을 다시 던지게 되기도 한다. (이제) 바꾸기로 결심해야 한다. 아들이나 딸이 부모에게 입힌 그 모든 상처를 인정하고 더 이상 그것이 당신을 옭아매게 하지 않겠다고 결심하라. 의절한 아들에 대해 곰곰이 생각하는 것도, 아들이 가족에게 어떻게 그럴 수 있었는지 의문을 품는 것도, 그리고 슬퍼하는 것도, 모두 멈추고 앞으로 나아가라.

다음 중 이 글의 주된 메시지는 무엇인가?
① 성인이 된 자녀가 만든 소원해진 관계는 주로 부모의 무관심 때문에 발생한다.
② 소원해진 관계의 원인을 깊이 생각해 보는 것이 해결의 첫 번째 단계이다.
③ 관계를 회복하려는 결심이 소원해진 관계를 풀기 위한 가장 잘 알려진 해결책이다.
④ 관계가 소원해진 성인이 된 자녀에 대한 죄책감을 떨쳐버리고 앞으로 나아가라.

22 글의 주제 ④

| 분석 |
이 글에서는 성인이 된 자녀와의 관계가 소원해져 슬퍼하는 부모들에게 왜 관계가 그렇게 되었는지 마음에 담아두고 생각하는 것을 이제 그만 멈추고 앞으로 나아가야 한다고 이야기하고 있다. 따라서 ④의 "관계가 소원해진 성인이 된 자녀에 대한 죄책감을 떨쳐버리고 앞으로 나아가라."가 글의 주제로 적절하다.

| 어휘 |
estranged a. (~와 사이가) 멀어진[소원해진] pine away 한탄하다 pine for ~을 몹시 그리워하다 lay blame 책임을 전가하다 enough is enough 더 이상은 안 된다[계속 이대로 둘 수는 없다] ridicule v. 조롱하다 self-esteem n. 자존감, 자부(심) take a hit 타격을 입다 feel blue 기분이 울적하다 bewilderment n. 당황, 당혹 shackle v. 족쇄를 채우다, 구속하다 ruminate over ~에 대해 곰곰이 생각하다

| 해석 |
성인 자녀와 사이가 멀어져서 슬픔에 잠긴 부모들이나, 자기 인생

23 문장배열 ③

| 분석 |
제시문에서 생각하는 자유가 '가치 없다'고 했으므로, 제시문 다음에는 왜 그러한지가 나와야 한다. 따라서 개인의 자유에 해당하는 생각이 다른 사람에게 전달되지 못할 경우 '가치가 없게 된다'는 B가 제일 먼저 와야 하며, 생각을 전달하는 것뿐 아니라, 생각을 숨기기도 어렵다고 부연 설명한 C가 그다음에 오고, 생각을 숨기는 것의 불가능함을 소크라테스를 예로 들어 나타낸 A로 마무리하는 것이 자연스럽다.

| 어휘 |
common saying 속담 hinder v. 방해하다 conceal v. 숨기다 bounds n. 한계[한도] have power over ~을 지배하다 call in question ~에 이의를 제기하다 custom n. 관습; 습관 regulate v. 규제하다, 단속하다 reasoning n. 추리, 추론 betray v. (감정 등을) 무심코 드러내다 chance a. 우연한

| 해석 |
생각은 자유라는 속담이 있다. 자신의 생각을 숨기는 한, 인간은 무엇을 생각하든 결코 생각에 방해받을 수 없다. 인간의 마음의

작용은 오직 인간의 경험과 상상력의 한계에 의해서만 제한될 뿐이다. 그러나 이러한 타고난 개인적 사고의 자유는 거의 가치가 없다. B 그러나 만일 자신의 생각을 다른 사람에게 전달할 수 없다면 그것은 생각하는 본인에게 불만족스럽고 심지어 고통스러우며, 주변 사람들에게도 분명히 가치가 전혀 없는 일이다. C 게다가 마음을 지배하는 생각을 숨기는 것은 매우 힘들다. 만일 누군가의 생각이 주변 사람들의 행동을 규제하는 사상과 관습에 의문을 제기하게 만든다면 그리고 그들이 자신이 내린 추론이 진실이라고 확신한다면, 그들은 주변 사람들과 다르며 그들과 의견을 같이 하지 않는다는 것을, 침묵, 우연한 말, 또는 일반적인 태도로, 드러내지 않기란 그들에게 거의 불가능하다. A 일부 사람들은 소크라테스처럼 그들의 생각을 숨기는 것보다 죽음을 더 선호했으며 오늘날에도 그렇게 하고 있다. 따라서 귀중한 의미에서 생각의 자유는 표현의 자유를 포함하는 것이다.

② 커피와 유유: 완벽한 조합
③ 커피가 염증을 일으키는 박테리아와 싸우다
④ 우유가 염증을 유발하지만, 커피가 염증을 치료한다

24 글의 제목   ①

| 분석 |

이 글에서는 "우유가 염증을 유발하는 식품인 것으로 밝혀져 있었지만 실제로는 유제품이 오히려 염증을 줄여주는 데 도움이 된다"는 새로운 연구 내용을 소개하고 있다. 따라서 "우유가 염증을 줄이는 데 도움이 될 수 있다."라는 ①이 글의 제목으로 적절하다.

| 어휘 |

inflammation n. 염증   **dairy** n. 유제품   **do the opposite** 역효과를 일으키다   **antioxidant** n. 항산화물질   **amino acid** 아미노산   **combination** n. 조합, 결합   **fit the bill** 적합하다, 이상적이다   **protein** n. 단백질   **immune** a. 면역의   **react to** ~에 반응하다   **detrimental** a. 해로운

| 해석 |

우유는 염증을 유발하는 주요 식품인 것으로 여겨져 왔지만 새로운 연구에 따르면 유제품은 오히려 정반대 효과를 낼 수 있다고 한다. 특히 2023년 1월에 발표된 연구에서는 커피에 유제품을 첨가하면 염증 수치를 낮추는 데 도움이 될 수 있다는 결과가 나왔다. 연구원들은 폴리페놀(항산화물질)이 특정 아미노산과 결합될 때 체내에서 어떻게 작용하는지를 살펴보았다. 커피에는 폴리페놀이 들어있고 우유는 아홉 가지 필수 아미노산이 모두 들어있는 완전한 단백질이므로 커피와 우유의 조합은 이상적이었다. 연구원들은 폴리페놀이 아미노산과 결합했을 때 면역 세포에서 발견되는 염증을 억제하는 보호 효과를 나타낸다는 것을 깨달았다. 염증은, 일부의 경우, 건강에 해로운 식단에 대한 반응으로 발생한다. 시간이 지나면 염증은 건강에 해로울 수 있다. 따라서 염증을 억제하는 식품이 풍부하게 들어있는 건강한 식단을 유지하는 것이 만성 질환의 위험을 줄이는 데 중요하다. 이제 커피에 우유를 넣어 마시는 것이 실제로 도움이 될 수 있는 것 같다.

글의 제목으로 가장 적절한 것을 고르시오.
① 우유가 염증을 줄이는 데 도움이 될 수 있다.

25 내용일치   ②

| 분석 |

'상향식 반사실적 사고는 사람들로 하여금 미래에 더 잘 할 수 있는 방법에 대해 생각해보게 한다'고 했는데, 미래에 더 잘하는 것이 미래의 개선을 의미하고 상향식 반사실적 사고도 반사실적 사고의 하나이므로, ②가 본문의 내용과 일치한다. ① normally가 잘못이고 can lead라 해야 한다. ③ less desirable이다. ④ dissatisfaction이다.

| 어휘 |

counterfactual thinking 반사실적 사고(현실에서 일어난 일과 다른 상상을 하는 일)   **contrary to** ~와 반대로   **modify** v. 수정하다, 변경하다   **prior** a. 사전의, 이전의   **reflect upon** 곰곰이 생각하다, 숙고하다   **speed** v. 속도위반을 하다   **in turn** 차례차례; 결국   **guilt** n. 죄책감   **relief** n. 안도, 안심

| 해석 |

반사실적 사고는 심리학에서 다루는 개념으로, 이미 발생한 사건에 대해 가능한 대안, 즉, 실제로 일어난 일과 반대되는 상황을 만들어 보는 인간의 경향을 의미한다. 이러한 사고는 "만약 어떤 것을 했다면 어땠을까?"와 "만약 어떤 것을 했다면 좋았을 텐데" 같은 생각으로 나타나며, 상황이 다르게 전개되었을 경우의 결과를 떠올리게 한다. 반사실적 사고는 실제 일어난 사건에 변화를 준 다음 그 변화가 어떤 결과를 초래했을 지를 평가하는 과정에서 발생한다. 예를 들어 어떤 사람들이 교통사고를 떠올리며 "만약 내가 과속하지 않았다면"과 같이 일부 요인들이 어떻게 다를 수 있었는가를 상상해 보고 교통사고가 어떻게 되었을 지를 곰곰이 생각해 보는 것이다. 이런 대안적 사고는 실제 상황보다 더 나을 수도 있고 더 나쁠 수도 있으며 보다 나은 결과를 상상할 수도 있고 보다 비참한 결과를 상상할 수도 있다. 예를 들어, "내가 운전벨트를 매지 않았다면 목숨을 잃었을 거야"와 같은 상상이 가능할 것이다. 반사실적 사고는 주로 부정적인 감정을 만들어내는 것으로 알려져 있지만 실용적이거나 유익한 효과도 만들어낼 수 있다. 반사실적 사고에는 두 가지 유형이 있는데, 하나는 하향식 반사실적 사고이고 다른 하나는 상향식 반사실적 사고이다. 하향식 반사실적 사고는 상황이 더 나빴을 가능성을 상상해보는 사고로, 사람들은 실제 결과를 더 긍정적으로 바라보는 경향이 있다. (반면) 상향식 반사실적 사고는 상황이 더 좋았을 가능성에 대한 사고로, 사람들을 불만족스럽고 불행하다고 느끼게 만드는 경향이 있다. 하지만 상향식 반사실적 사고는 사람들로 하여금 미래에 더 잘 할 수 있는 방법에 대해 생각해보게 하는 그런 사고이다. 이렇게 무슨 일이 일어날 수 있었는지에 대해 생각해보는 반사실적 사고는 후회, 죄책감, 안도감, 만족감 등 다양한 감정을 사람들이 느끼게 할 수 있다.

다음 중 이 글의 내용과 일치하는 것은?
① 반사실적 사고는 보통 안도감을 초래한다.
② 반사실적 사고는 미래의 개선을 위해 도움이 될 수 있다.
③ 하향식 반사실적 사고는 보다 바람직한 시나리오를 상상한다.
④ 상향식 반사실적 사고는 후회나 만족감을 초래한다.

26 글의 요지   ①

| 분석 |

이 글에서는 빛과 어둠이 문화에 결정적인 영향을 미친다고 주장하면서, 극지방에 위치한 국가들의 문화와 적도 인근에 위치한 국가들의 문화를 예로 들어 비교하고 있다. 따라서 "빛과 어둠이 문화에 상당한 영향을 미친다"는 ①이 글의 요지로 적절하다.

| 어휘 |

rotation n. 회전, (지구의) 자전 **overlook** v. 못 보고 넘어가다, 간과하다 **geographical** a. 지리적인 **resilient** a. 회복력이 있는 **brutal** a. (날씨 등이) 혹독한 **Fahrenheit** n. 화씨 온도계, 화씨 눈금 **stereotype** n. 고정 관념, 정형화된 생각[이미지] **equator** n. (지구의) 적도 **year-round** ad. 1년 내내 **temperament** n. 기질, 성격 **more or less** 거의, 대략 **punctuality** n. 시간 엄수 **laid back** a. 느긋한

| 해석 |

빛과 어둠이 미치는 영향은 지구의 위치와 자전과 관련이 있다. 이것은 다른 지리적 특징들보다 문화에 훨씬 더 결정적인 영향을 미치지만, 많은 사람들이 이 점을 간과한다. 알래스카, 스칸디나비아, 그리고 러시아 북부의 문화는 하루 중에 갖는 빛과 어둠의 시간수에 극단적으로 영향을 받는다. 문화에는 두 가지 극단이 있다. 1년 중 시기에 따라 거의 완전히 어둡거나 밝은 때가 있다. 극지방의 많은 국가들은 계절에 크게 의존하는 문화를 갖고 있다. (따라서) 그들은 강한 회복력을 갖고 있어야 한다. 예를 들어, 러시아 북부의 야쿠트족은 수확에 있어 모든 것이 계획에 따라 잘 진행되도록 여름철에 열심히 일한다. 그들은 또한 화씨 영하 40도까지 떨어질 수 있는 혹독한 겨울에 잘 대비해야 한다. 이들 문화권에서 온 사람들은 때때로 직설적이고 무자비하다는 인상을 주기도 하는데, 이는 겨울이 혹독해서 국가의 고정관념에 영향을 줄 수 있기 때문이다. 반면, 우리는 어둠과 빛이 크게 변하지 않는 적도에 가까운 문화를 살펴볼 수 있다. 휴식 시간과 근로 시간의 양이 1년 내내 동일하다. 사람의 기질과 전통도 1년 내내 거의 일정하게 유지된다. 에콰도르, 인도네시아, 그리고 우간다 같은 곳을 예로 들 수 있다. 시간 엄수는 이런 문화권에서 덜 중요하다. 이 지역의 사람들은 또한 일광 노출 시간이 더 적은 다른 사람들보다 보다 느긋한 것으로 여겨진다.

다음 중 이 글의 요지를 가장 잘 요약한 것은?
① 빛과 어둠이 문화에 상당한 영향을 미친다.
② 온도가 생활방식에 미치는 영향은 충분히 탐구되지 않았다.
③ 혹독한 환경에 사는 사람들은 매우 협조적인 경향이 있다.
④ 빛과 어둠이 미치는 영향은 다른 지리적 특징들보다 덜 중요하다.

27~28

흰 코끼리는 엄청난 어려움 없이는 소유주가 처분할 수도 없고 특히 유지비용이 효용성과 비례하지 않는 소유물을 가리킨다. 현대 어법에서 그것은 많은 비용이 들지만 동등한 효용성은 없다고 여겨지는 물건이나 자본(취득) 비용 및/또는 운영(유지 관리) 비용에 비해 동등한 효용성이나 가치가 없는 물건, 건설 프로젝트, 계획, 벤처사업, 시설 등을 설명하는 데 사용되는 비유적 표현이다. 이 용어는 미얀마, 태국, 라오스, 캄보디아의 동남아시아 군주들이 키웠던 신성한 흰 코끼리에서 유래한다. 흰 코끼리를 소유한다는 것은 군주가 정의롭고 강력하게 통치하고 있으며 왕국이 평화롭고 번영하고 있다는 상징으로 여겨졌으며, 지금도 태국과 미얀마에서는 여전히 그렇게 여겨지고 있다. 이 동물은 신성하게 여겨졌고 노동에 동원되는 것을 법적으로 막고 있었기 때문에, 군주로부터 흰 코끼리를 선물로 받는다는 것은 축복이자 동시에 저주였다. 그 동물은 신성한 동물이자 군주의 총애를 나타내는 상징이었기 때문에 축복이었고, 유지비가 많이 들고 처분할 수도 없으며 실용적으로 많이 사용할 수도 없었기 때문에 받는 사람한테는 저주였다. 서양에서 기대에 미치지 못하면서 비싸기만 해서 부담을 주는 물건을 나타내는 '흰 코끼리'라는 용어는 17세기에 처음 사용되었다. 현대 어법에서 이 용어는 현재 제 기능을 다하지 못하거나 유지 관리 비용이 지나치게 높아 엄청나게 비싼 건설 프로젝트를 종종 가리킨다. 공항, 댐, 다리, 쇼핑몰, 축구경기장 같이 명성은 있지만 경제성이 떨어지는 기간시설 프로젝트가 이 예시에 해당한다.

| 어휘 |

white elephant 흰 코끼리(돈만 많이 들고 쓸모는 없는 성가신 물건) **dispose of** ~을 처분하다 **out of proportion to** (~와) 비례하지 않는 **usage** n. (단어의) 용법[어법] **metaphor** n. 비유; 비유적인 표현 **scheme** n. (운영) 계획; 책략 **facility** n. 시설 **equivalent** a. 동등한, 상응하는 **utility** n. 유용성, 효용성 **capital** n. 자본, 자금 **acquisition** n. 구입[취득]한 것 **derive from** ~에서 유래하다 **sacred** a. 신성한 **monarch** n. 군주 **reign** v. (국왕이) 통치하다 **bless** v. (신의) 축복을 빌다 **simultaneously** ad. 동시에 **curse** n. 저주 **favor** n. 호의; 총애 **recipient** n. 받는 사람, 수령인 **meet expectation** 기대를 충족시키다 **costly** a. 많은 돈[비용]이 드는 **prestigious** a. 명성이 있는

27 빈칸완성   ①

| 분석 |

빈칸에는 흰 코끼리를 군주로부터 선물로 받는다는 것이 어떠한 것인지가 들어가야 하는데, 빈칸 다음에서 흰 코끼리가 왕의 총애를 나타내는 것이기 때문에 축복이었고, 유지비가 많이 들고 실용적으로도 많이 사용할 수 없었기 때문에 저주라고 했다. 따라서 빈칸에는 이 두 가지, 즉 축복과 저주라는 말이 동시에 언급되어야 하므로, ①이 빈칸에 적절하다.

다음 중 빈칸에 들어가기에 가장 적절한 것은?
① 축복이자 동시에 저주
② 최고의 영광스러운 선물로 간주된
③ 왕국 내 누구나 꿈꾸는 것
④ 번영을 위한 신의 축복으로 여겨진

28 내용파악   ②

| 분석 |
'흰 코끼리'라는 표현은 원래 부정적으로 쓰였으며 지금도 부정적으로 쓰이고 있으므로, ②가 정답이다.

이 글에 따르면, 다음 중 '흰 코끼리'에 관해 사실이 아닌 것은?
① 그것은 서양에서 일반적으로 부정적인 의미를 내포하고 있다.
② 영어로 그것의 의미는 긍정적인 의미에서 부정적인 의미로 바뀌었다.
③ 그것의 원래 의미는 상충되는 문화적 가치관과 실용적 가치관에서 유래했다.
④ 그것의 현대적 의미는 그것의 기능 대비 과도한 비용을 강조한다.

29~30

성적(性的) 동포포식이라는 행위는 공포 소설에서나 나올 것 같지만 여러 동물들의 행동 레퍼토리에서 실제로 발생한다. 그것은 구애나 교미 중에 짝을 잡아먹는 행위를 가리킨다. 성적 동포포식은 거미류, 곤충류, 그리고 두족류 동물 등, 여러 무척추동물에서 입증되어 왔다. 성적 동포포식이 일부 종에서는 드물게 발생하는 반면 다른 종에서는 흔히 발생한다.
C 일반적으로, 성적 동포포식은 암컷이 수컷을 잡아먹는 것과 관련이 있다. 이 상호작용에서 수컷의 반응은 종마다 크게 다를 수 있다. 예를 들어, 수컷 붉은등거미는 자발적으로 자신을 희생한다. 이와 대조적으로, 수컷 넓적배사마귀는 잡아먹히지 않기 위해 모든 노력을 기울인다. 즉, 수컷 넓적배사마귀는 아주 멀리서 암컷 넓적배사마귀의 등에 뛰어올라 공격을 피할 수 있는 각도로 몸을 배치한다. 수컷 붉은등거미는 왜 이렇게 하지 않는 것일까?
A 이러한 질문은 행동이 발생하는 이유를 개체의 번식 성공 측면에서 연구하는 진화 생물학자들이 탐구하는 주제이다.

성적 동포포식과 관련하여 수컷에게 가해지는 엄청난 희생은 분명하지만, 그 행동이 수컷과 수컷의 짝에게 주는 진화적 이점은 그만큼 분명하지 않다.
B 암컷의 경우, 수컷을 잡아먹음으로써 추가적인 영양분과 에너지를 얻을 수 있으며, 이는 자손에게 전달될 가능성이 크다. 연구에 따르면, 수컷을 잡아먹은 암컷이 수많은 새끼들이 들어있는 무거운 알집을 계속해서 생산한다고 한다. 반면, 잡아먹히는 수컷도 궁극적인 대가를 치르면서도 몇 가지 이점을 얻을 수 있다. 수컷 붉은등거미의 약 80%가 짝짓기와 자손을 생산할 기회조차 얻지 못한 채 죽는다는 것을 생각해 보자. 이러한 상황에서, 짝짓기 중에 65%의 확률로 죽게 되는 것은 진화적인 적합성 관점에서 위험을 감수할 가치가 있을 수 있다.

| 어휘 |
sexual cannibalism 성적 동족포식 **piece** n. 작품 **fiction** n. 소설; 허구 **mate** n. 배우자; 짝짓기 상대 v. 짝짓기를 하다 **courtship** n. (동물의 짝짓기를 위한) 구애 **copulation** n. 성교; 교미; 결합 **invertebrate** n. 무척추동물 **arachnid** n. 거미류 **cephalopod** n. 두족류 동물(문어·오징어 등) **offspring** n. 자식; (동식물의) 새끼 **redback spider** 붉은등거미 **giant Asian mantis** 넓적배사마귀 **angle** n. 각도 **pay the price** 대가를 치르다 **perspective** n. 관점

29 단락배열   ③

| 분석 |
맨 위의 제시문은 성적 동포포식은 무엇이며, 어느 종에서 발생하는지를 다루고 있으므로, 제시문 다음에 이어지는 내용에는 성적 동포포식의 '구체적인 사례'가 나와야 한다. 따라서 수컷 붉은등거미와 넓적배사마귀의 사례를 소개한 C가 제일 먼저 와야 하며, C에서 성적 동포포식에 있어서 수컷의 넓적배사마귀와 수컷 붉은등거미의 반응이 왜 다른지 의문을 제기했으므로, 이것을 This is a question으로 받은 A가 다음에 적절하다. 그리고 A에서 성적 동포포식과 관련해 수컷과 암컷이 받는 진화적 이점이 분명하지 않다고 했으므로, 성적 동포포식이 수컷과 암컷에게 각각 어떤 이점이 있는지를 소개하는 내용이 이어져야 한다. 암컷에게 주어지는 이점인 B가 그다음에 오면, 수컷에게 주어지는 이점을 소개한 맨 아래의 제시문과 자연스럽게 호응되므로, ③이 정답이다.

30 내용일치   ①

| 분석 |
본문에서 "일반적으로, 성적 동포포식은 암컷이 수컷을 잡아먹는 것과 관련이 있다. 이 상호작용에서 수컷의 반응은 종마다 크게 다를 수 있다."라고 했다. 따라서 성적 동포포식에서 희생자인 수컷의 반응은 종들 간에 매우 다양함을 알 수 있으므로, ①이 정답이다.

이 글에 따르면 다음 중 사실인 것은?
① 성적 동포포식에서 희생자의 행동은 종들 간에 매우 다양하다.
② 성적 동포포식은 동물의 왕국에서 여러 종들 사이에서 널리 입증되고 있다.
③ 성적 동포포식에서 수컷과 암컷은 최고의 진화적 이익을 위해 협력한다.
④ 성적 동포포식의 진화론적인 이점은 수컷과 암컷에게 분명하다.

명지대학교 인문계 오후

TEST p. 282~296

01	④	02	①	03	②	04	③	05	②	06	③	07	③	08	②	09	④	10	④
11	②	12	①	13	①	14	④	15	①	16	②	17	④	18	①	19	③	20	④
21	①	22	③	23	②	24	①	25	④	26	②	27	②	28	③	29	①	30	②

01 동의어 ④

| 어휘 |

turbulent a. 사나운, 거친 **oar** n. 노 **crack** v. 금이 가다; 깨지다, 부서지다 **sail** n. 돛; 항해 **severely** ad. 심하게 **detrimental** a. 해로운(= disadvantageous) **voyage** n. 항해 **violent** a. 격렬한, 맹렬한 **instrumental** a. 수단이 되는 **exhausting** a. 소모적인, 심신을 지치게 하는

| 해석 |

거친 바다로 인해 그의 노 하나가 깨졌고, 이것은 — 모터나 돛이 없어서 — 그의 항해에 심각한 해를 끼칠 수 있다.

02 동의어 ①

| 어휘 |

in line 일치하는 **veteran** n. 퇴역[재향] 군인 **sublime** a. 숭고한, 장엄한(= glorious) **prosperous** a. 번영하는 **conventional** a. 전통적인, 인습적인 **humanitarian** a. 인도주의적인

| 해석 |

그 결정은 전투를 목격하고 전쟁에서 숭고한 것은 아무것도 찾지 못한 참전 용사들과 군대를 더욱 일치하게 한다.

03 동의어 ②

| 어휘 |

lower-court n. 하급 법원 **judge** n. 재판관, 판사 **explanatory** a. 설명을 위한, 설명적인 **rhetorical** a. 수사적인 **embellishment** n. 장식(= adornment) **illustration** n. 삽화; 실례 **manipulation** n. 교묘한 처리; 조작, 속임수 **complication** n. 복잡(화), 분규

| 해석 |

하급 법원 판사로서 그녀의 글쓰기 스타일은 설명적이었고, 수사적 장식이 거의 없었다.

04 논리완성 ③

| 분석 |

정답의 단서가 되는 표현은 "아이러니"이다. 인도인들이 영국이 공식적으로 지지하는 이상을 따라 행동했는데, 그것 때문에 영국에게 처벌받았다는 것이 아이러니한 상황이 될 것이므로 빈칸에는 '(의견·이론 등에) 동의하다'라는 의미의 subscribe가 적절하다.

| 어휘 |

imprison v. 투옥하다 **inspiration** n. 영감 **assess** v. 평가하다 **ban** v. 금지하다 **subscribe to** (의견·이론 등에) 동의[지지]하다 **hypothesize** v. 가설을 세우다, 가정하다

| 해석 |

인도의 독립을 위해 싸운 투사들은 아이러니하게도 영국인들이 공식적으로 동의하고 자국에서 자신들의 이익을 위해 진지하게 받아들인 이상의 영감에 따라 행동한 혐의로 영국인들에 의해 투옥되었다.

05 논리완성 ②

| 분석 |

역접의 접속사 but 전후가 서로 반대되는 내용이 되어야 한다. 12살은 가장 활력이 넘치는 시기로 신체적, 지능적으로 완전히 성장하지는 않았지만 사망 가능성은 가장 낮다고 해야 한다. 따라서 빈칸에는 '가장 적은'의 의미의 least가 적절하다.

| 어휘 |

vigorous a. 원기 왕성한, 강건한 **intelligence** n. 지능 **likelihood** n. 가능성 **plain** a. 분명한 **least** a. 가장 적은 **predicted** a. 예상되는 **undetermined** a. 결정되지 않은

| 해석 |

12살 때 인체는 가장 원기가 왕성하다. 아직 완전한 크기와 힘에 도달하지 못했고, 그 주인은 완전한 지능에 이르지 않았지만, 이 나이에 사망할 가능성은 가장 낮다.

06 관계대명사절의 수일치 ③

| 분석 |
관계대명사 that이 이끄는 절에서 선행사는 the firm structure로 단수 명사이다. 따라서 ③에서 동사 underlie를 underlies로 고쳐야 한다.

| 어휘 |
skeleton n. 골격; 뼈대; 골자, 윤곽　**flesh** n. 살　**bare** a. 벌거벗은
underlie v. ~의 기초가 되다, ~의 근저에 있다　**apprehension** n. 이해, 이해력

| 해석 |
모든 책에는 앞표지와 뒤표지 사이에 뼈대가 숨겨져 있다. 당신의 임무는 그것을 찾는 것이다. 책은 맨 뼈에 살이 붙어있고 그 살 위에 옷이 걸쳐져 있는 채로 당신에게 온다. 그것은 완전히 차려입은 상태이다. 나는 당신에게 무례하거나 잔인하게 굴라고 요구하는 것이 아니다. 부드러운 것의 기초가 되는 단단한 구조를 얻기 위해 옷을 벗기거나 팔다리에서 살을 떼어낼 필요는 없다. 그러나 엑스레이 같은 눈으로 책을 읽어야 한다. 왜냐하면 구조를 파악하는 것이 어떤 책이든 처음 이해하는 데 필수적인 부분이기 때문이다.

07 동명사의 병치 ③

| 분석 |
'be devoted to(~에 헌신하다)'에서 to는 전치사이므로 그 뒤에 명사나 동명사가 와야 한다. 등위접속사 and에 의해서 동명사가 병치를 이루고 있으므로 riding, working과 같은 형태가 되도록 ③을 carrying out으로 고쳐야 한다.

| 어휘 |
precise a. 정밀한, 정확한　**exquisite** a. 정교한; 절묘한; 훌륭한
marquis n. 후작　**grandchild** n. 손자, 손녀　**ardor** n. 열정, 열의
prescription n. 처방

| 해석 |
몬티첼로에 있는 자신의 도서관에서 제퍼슨(Jefferson)은 수백 개의 건축 도면을 그렸으며, 그 모든 도면은 보존되어 있다. 그는 그러한 전망을 가진 방에서 작업할 수 있었다니 매우 뛰어난 집중력과 그의 주제에 대한 진정한 사랑을 가지고 있었음이 틀림없다. 그리고 이 정밀하고 정교한 작업을 위해 그가 가진 모든 에너지를 또한 자신의 사유지 위로 말을 달리고, 정원에서 일하며, 그리고 라파예트 후작부터 그의 가장 어린 손자까지 모든 사람들과 서신을 주고받는 데에도 쏟았다. "열정적으로 추구하는 것"은 제퍼슨의 평생의 처방이었으며, 그는 자신이 접하는 모든 것에서 마지막 한 방울의 흥분과 관심까지 다 끌어냈다.

08 배수비교 ②

| 분석 |
배수비교는 '배수사+as ~ as'의 형태로 쓴다. 앞에 twice as가 있으므로 ②의 affected than men에서 than을 as로 고쳐야 한다.

| 어휘 |
affect v. (병·고통이 사람을) 침범하다, 걸리다

| 해석 |
미국 불안 및 우울증 협회에 따르면, 불안 장애는 미국에서 가장 흔한 정신 질환으로, 18세 이상의 성인 4천만 명이 걸리고 있다. 더욱이, 여성은 남성보다 걸릴 가능성이 두 배 더 높다. 불안 장애는 유전학, 뇌 화학, 성격, 삶의 사건 등 복합적인 위험 요인에서 발생한다. "불안은 긍정적인 특성이 될 수 있습니다."라고 한 건강 전문가는 말한다. "시간을 지키거나 높은 수준의 성과를 내는 것에 대해 걱정하는 사람은 직업적으로나 개인적으로 삶의 다양한 측면에서 뛰어난 경우가 많습니다."

09 관계대명사절의 수일치 ④

| 분석 |
관계대명사 that이 이끄는 절에서 선행사는 something으로 단수 명사이다. 따라서 ④에서 동사 hate를 hates로 고쳐야 한다.

| 어휘 |
silly a. 어리석은, 바보 같은　**folly** n. 어리석음; 어리석은 짓[생각, 말]
a world of 산더미 같은, 막대한, 무수한　**riches** n. 부, 재물
insincerity n. 불성실　**hypocrisy** n. 위선

| 해석 |
어떤 사람들은 자신의 결점을 말하는 것을 자랑스럽게 여긴다. 그들은 자신이 세상에서 가장 어리석은 사람이라고 말할 것이다. 아이들처럼 누구 앞에서도 진실을 말하지 않을 수 없다고 말할 것이다. 그들은 그것이 어리석은 짓이라는 것을 인정하고, 그로 인해 많은 이점을 잃었다고 말할 것이다. 그러나 그것을 막기 위해 온 세상의 부를 준다 해도 어쩔 수 없다고 말할 것이다. 그리고 자신들의 본성에는 불성실함과 위선을 싫어하는 무언가가 있다고 말할 것이다.

10 전치사 + 관계대명사 ④

| 분석 |
관계대명사 which 뒤에 완전한 절이 왔으므로 a commodity를 선행사로 받는 '전치사+관계대명사'의 형태가 와야 한다. be made of가 '~로 만들어지다'는 의미로 쓰이므로 ④에서 관계대명사 which를 of which로 고쳐야 한다.

| 어휘 |

barter n. 물물 교환　　date back to ~까지 거슬러 올라가다
commodity n. 상품

| 해석 |

물물 교환과 유사한 방법의 사용은 적어도 10만 년 전으로 거슬러 올라갈 수 있지만, 주로 물물 교환에 의존한 사회나 경제에 대한 증거는 없다. 대신, 비금전적 사회는 주로 선물 경제와 부채의 원칙에 따라 운영되었다. 물물 교환이 실제로 발생했을 때는 대개 완전히 낯선 사람들 사이에서나 잠재적인 적들 사이에서 이루어졌다. 전 세계의 많은 문화권에서 상품 화폐, 즉 그 가치가 그것이 만들어진 상품에서 비롯되는 화폐의 사용이 발전했다.

11　논리완성　　②

| 분석 |

칫솔이 발명되기 전에 씹는 막대기가 칫솔처럼 사용되었다고 하였으므로 씹는 막대기는 '칫솔보다 전에 있던[쓰인] 것'이다. 따라서 빈칸에는 '전신(前身)'이라는 의미의 ② predecessor가 적절하다.

| 어휘 |

oral a. 구두의; 입의, 구강의　　hygiene n. 위생　　verify v. 확인하다, 입증하다　　archaeological a. 고고학적인　　excavation n. 발굴
twig n. 작은 가지　　frayed a. (가장자리가) 해어진　　toothpick n. 이쑤시개　　pinnacle n. 정점, 절정　　predecessor n. 전임자; 전신(前身), 전에 있던[쓰인] 것　　evidence n. 증거　　confirmation n. 확정, 확인

| 해석 |

칫솔이 발명되기 이전에는 다양한 구강 위생 조치가 사용되었으며, 이는 고고학적 발굴을 통해 확인되었다. 칫솔의 전신(前身)은 씹는 막대기이다. 씹는 막대기는 이를 닦는 데 사용되는 끝이 닳은 작은 나뭇가지였고, 다른 끝은 이쑤시개로 사용되었다. 가장 초기의 씹는 막대기는 기원전 3500년 메소포타미아 남부의 수메르에서, 기원전 3000년 이집트 무덤에서 발견되었으며, 그리고 기원전 1600년 중국 기록에서 언급되었다.

12　논리완성　　①

| 분석 |

『길가메시 서사시』가 가장 초기의 중요한 작품으로 간주되는 이유가 빈칸에 와야 한다. 다른 고대 문학 작품에 지속적으로 영향을 미쳤다는 점을 『일리아드(Iliad)』, 『오디세이(Odyssey)』, 알렉산더 로맨스 문학, 히브리어 성경 등을 예로 들어 설명하고 있다. 따라서 빈칸에는 '오랜 세월에 걸쳐 문학에 지속적으로 영향을 미쳤다'는 의미의 ①이 적절하다.

| 어휘 |

composition n. (음악·미술·시 등의) 작품　　survive v. 살아남다
apart from ~은 제쳐 놓고, 별도로 하고; ~이외에　　significant a. 중요한, 특별한 의미가 있는

| 해석 |

가장 오래된 현존하는 기록 문학은 고대 메소포타미아에서 비롯되었다. 『길가메시 서사시(Epic of Gilgamesh)』는 그보다 훨씬 이전의 짧은 작품들도 일부 남아있지만 종종 최초의 위대한 작품으로 언급된다. 그 길이는 별도로 하고, 『길가메시 서사시』는 오랜 세월에 걸쳐 문학에 미친 지속적인 영향 때문에 가장 초기의 중요한 작품으로 간주될 수 있다. 예를 들어, 『일리아드(Iliad)』, 『오디세이(Odyssey)』, 알렉산더 로맨스 문학, 히브리어 성경 등 다른 고대 문학 작품에 영향을 미친 것으로 여겨지며, 이 모든 작품들은 그 자체로 중요한 문학적 영향을 계속 미치고 있다.

① 오랜 세월에 걸쳐 문학에 미친 지속적인 영향
② 문학적 스타일의 아름다움과 줄거리의 복잡성
③ 보존된 절묘한 상태
④ 특별한 길이와 세부 사항에 대한 세심한 주의

13　논리완성　　①

| 분석 |

습관적으로 늦는 사람들이 시간을 엄수해야 한다는 것을 강조하고 있으므로, 빈칸에는 약속 시간에 늦거나 사람을 기다리게 하는 행동을 나타내는 표현이 들어가야 한다. 따라서 '지각'을 의미하는 ① Tardiness is가 적절하다.

| 어휘 |

mend v. 고치다　　punctuality n. 시간 엄수　　frown v. 눈살을 찌푸리다　　well-bred a. 곱게 자란, 가정교육을 잘 받은, 품위 있는
breach n. 위반, 침해　　smart a. 세련된, 멋진　　inexcusable a. 용서[용납]할 수 없는, 변명할 수 없는　　decree v. 정하다, 명하다

| 해석 |

습관적으로 늦는 사람들은 가능한 한 빨리 자신의 방식을 고치고 시간 엄수를 일상 행동의 주요 원칙 중 하나로 삼아야 한다. 지각은 나쁜 식사 예절이나 품위 있는 사람들이 눈살을 찌푸리는 다른 습관만큼이나 예의에 어긋나는 행동이다. 많은 젊은 여성들은 친구들을 기다리게 하는 것을 세련된 행동이라 여긴다. 그러한 행동은 무례한 것만큼이나 용납할 수 없다. 당신이 누군가를 만나든, 가족 식사 자리에 참석하든, 비즈니스 약속을 지키든, 모든 경우에 시간 엄수는 요구된다는 것을 기억하라.

① 지각은
② 형식적인 절차는
③ 관례는
④ 행동규범은

14 논리완성 ④

| 분석 |
다른 사람보다 더 잘 하고 싶은 충동이 없었으며 선생님들이 가르치려고 했던 인생은 경쟁이라는 교훈을 받아들이지 못했다는 사실을 통해 나는 경쟁적인 성향이 없는 사람임을 알 수 있다. 따라서 빈칸에는 '비경쟁적이다'라는 의미의 ④가 적절하다.

| 어휘 |
go one better than ~보다 더 잘하다, 능가하다   **puzzle** n. 수수께끼   **schoolmaster** n. (남자) 선생, 교사   **steadily** ad. 견실[착실]하게; 꾸준히   **incapable of** ~할 수 없는   **absorb** v. 흡수하다, 이해하다

| 해석 |
내가 내 자신에 대한 가장 중요한 진실, 즉 내가 비경쟁적인 사람이라는 것을 처음 깨달은 것은 6학년, 학교에 다니고 있던 때였다. 대부분의 사람들의 삶을 어떤 식으로든 지배하는 것처럼 보이는 다음 사람보다 더 잘 하고 싶은 충동은 내가 스스로 갖추지 못한 것이다. 지금 생각해보면, 내가 학교 선생님들에게 얼마나 수수께끼 같은 존재였는지 알 수 있다. 큰 말썽을 일으키지 않고 꽤 착실하게 공부했다는 사실에도 불구하고 나를 맡았던 거의 모든 선생님들에게 미움을 받았다. 나는 그들이 모두 거기서 가르치려고 했던 한 가지 교훈, 즉 인생은 경쟁이라는 것을 이해할 수 없었다.

① 나는 평화주의자다
② 나는 대기만성형이다
③ 나는 불굴의 의지를 가진 사람이다
④ 나는 비경쟁적이다

15 논리완성 ①

| 분석 |
사람들과의 잡담이 내면의 평화를 방해하기 때문에 가능한 한 자제하고 적절한 순간이 오면 필요한 말만 하라는 것이 주된 내용이다. 따라서 빈칸에는 '쓸데없는 대화를 피하라'는 의미의 ①이 적절하다.

| 어휘 |
shun v. 피하다   **gossip** n. 잡담, 험담 v. 잡담하다; 험담을 퍼뜨리다   **sincere** a. 진실한   **distraction** n. 마음의 산란, 주의 산만   **ensnare** v. 함정에 빠뜨리다; 유혹하다   **captivate** v. 마음을 사로잡다, 매혹하다   **vanity** n. 허영심   **hold one's peace** 잠자코 있다, 침묵을 유지하다   **conscience** n. 양심   **part** v. 헤어지다   **ease** v. 편하게 하다, 안심시키다   **weary** v. 지치게 하다   **fondly** ad. 애정을 가지고, 다정하게   **external** a. 외부의   **bar** v. 막다, 금하다   **idly** ad. 빈둥거리며; 헛되이   **opportune** a. 적절한, 시의 적절한   **edify** v. 교화하다, 고양시키다   **for the benefit of** ~을 위하여

| 해석 |
가능한 한 사람들의 잡담을 피하라. 왜냐하면 세상사에 대한 논의는, 비록 진지하다고 해도, 우리가 빨리 허영심에 빠져 들고 사로잡히게 되므로 주의를 매우 산만하게 하는 것이기 때문이다. 여러 번 나는 잠자코 있고 사람들과 어울리지 않았더라면 좋았을 걸 하고 바란다. 사실, 양심의 가책 없이 헤어지는 일이 거의 없는데 왜 우리는 서로 대화하고 잡담을 하는가? 우리는 서로의 대화에서 위안을 구하고 다양한 생각에 지친 마음을 편하게 하기를 원하기 때문에 그렇게 한다. 따라서 우리는 매우 좋아하는 것이나 몹시 싫어하는 것에 대해 매우 좋게 이야기하고 생각한다. 하지만 슬프게도 우리는 종종 헛되이 아무 목적 없이 이야기한다. 이러한 외적인 즐거움은 내면의 평화를 사실상 가로막는다. 따라서 시간이 헛되이 흐르지 않도록 주의해야 한다. 말하기에 적절한 순간이 오면 도움이 되는 말을 하라. 내면의 성장을 위해 다른 사람들과의 쓸데없는 대화를 피하라.

① 다른 사람들과의 쓸데없는 대화를 피하라
② 대화 상대를 신중하게 선택하라
③ 주제에 생각을 집중하라
④ 욕망과 열망을 추구하라

16 내용일치 ②

| 분석 |
마크 트웨인을 초대한 만찬에서 마크 트웨인과 닮은 사람이 있었고 그 닮은 사람을 분장하여 마크 트웨인인 것처럼 행동하게 음모를 꾸민 상황이다. 마크 트웨인도 처음에 놀랐지만 그 상황을 파악하고 농담을 하며 유머러스하게 대처했다고 하였으므로 ②가 적절하다.

| 어휘 |
happen to 우연히 ~하다   **innocent** a. 순결한, 순진한; 악의 없는   **conspiracy** n. 음모, 모의   **unsuspected** a. 의심받지 않은   **in astonishment** 놀라서   **be equal to the occasion** 일을 당하여 흔들리지 않다, 상황을 파악하고 훌륭히 행동하다, 임기응변으로 일을 처리하다   **have[get] the credit of** ~의 영예를 얻다, 명예롭게도 ~했다고 인정받다

| 해석 |
본명이 사무엘 클레멘스(Samuel Clemens)인 마크 트웨인(Mark Twain)을 위한 만찬에서, 그를 초대했던 클럽의 한 회원이 우연히 그날 저녁의 손님을 닮았다. '분장사'의 도움으로 그 닮은 점이 더욱 커져서 원래 마크 트웨인과 그 닮은 사람을 구분하기 어려울 정도였다. 악의 없는 음모가 꾸며졌고, 만찬 시간이 되자 그 닮은 사람은 재빨리 식당에 들어와서 테이블에 앉은 사람들의 의심을 받지 않고 명예의 자리에 앉았다. 몇 분 후, 진짜 마크 트웨인이 나타났다. 모두가 놀라서 쳐다보았다. 마크 트웨인 자신도 그에 못지않게 놀랐지만, 그는 그 상황에 잘 대처했다. "그래서, 당신이 마크 트웨인 맞죠?"라고 그가 말했다. "마침내 당신을 붙잡게 되어 기쁩니다. 제가 좋은 일을 할 때마다 당신은 분명히 그 공로를 인정받을 것입니다. 제가 나쁜 일을 할 때마다

사무엘 클레멘스가 비난을 받습니다. 저는 그 일이 꽤 지겨워지고 있었는데, 그렇게 말씀드리게 되어 매우 기쁩니다."

다음 중 옳은 것은?
① 마크 트웨인은 결코 놀라거나 당황하지 않았다.
② 마크 트웨인은 놀라운 상황을 매우 유머러스하게 처리했다.
③ 마크 트웨인과 닮은 사람은 그 사건으로 크게 망신을 당했다.
④ 마크 트웨인을 초대한 호스트는 악의적인 장난을 꾸며 그를 다치게 했다.

17 내용추론 ④

| 분석 |
의학의 발전으로 질병의 부담이 급성 전염성 질병에서 만성 질환으로 전환되었는데, 만성 질환 치료법은 생명을 연장하지만 기저 질환은 치료하지 못하는 불완전한 기술이라고 했다. 따라서 미래에는 병을 완전히 치료하지 못하고 만성 질환을 가진 환자가 늘어날 것이라 할 수 있으므로 ④가 정답으로 적절하다.

| 어휘 |
antibiotic n. 항생 물질   **acute** a. 급성의   **infectious** a. 전염성의
chronic a. 만성의   **halfway** a. 중간의; 불충분한, 불완전한
underlying a. 기초가 되는, 근원적인   **renal** a. 신장의   **dialysis** n. 투석   **antiretroviral** a. 항레트로바이러스의   **a myriad of** 무수한
expertise n. 전문적 기술[지식, 의견]   **frail** a. 허약한

| 해석 |
항생제와 백신을 비롯한 의학의 발전과 생활수준의 향상은 질병의 부담을 급성 전염성 질병에서 만성 질환으로 전환하는 데 기여했다. 현대 의학의 발전은 만성 질환에 대한 중요한 치료법을 만들어냈지만, 대부분은 생명을 연장하긴 해도 기저질환을 치료하지는 못하는 '불완전한' 기술을 낳았다. 예를 들어, 신부전 치료를 위한 장기적인 신장 투석과, 최근에는 후천성 면역 결핍 증후군(AIDS) 환자의 생명을 연장하는 항레트로바이러스 약물이 있다. 만성 질환은 의료 행위의 전통적 정의를 벗어난 수많은 기능적 제한과 사회적 지원 요구가 수반된다. 간호사, 사회복지사, 작업치료사, 물리치료사 및 기타 의사가 아닌 의료 종사자들은 만성 질환자와 허약한 노인들이 만성 질환과 의료 치료를 관리할 수 있도록 돕는 데 관심과 전문성을 보여주었고, 그래서 의료 분업에서 스스로 새로운 역할을 창출했다.

다음 중 본문에서 올바르게 추론할 수 있는 것은?
① 다양한 비의료 직업들이 미래에 의사를 대체할 것이다.
② 대부분의 이전에 불치병에 대한 치료법이 가까운 미래에 발견될 것이다.
③ 기저질환은 합병증을 통해 점점 더 심각해질 것이다.
④ 점점 더 많은 환자들이 미래에 만성 질환을 갖고 살 수도 있다.

18 글의 주제 ①

| 분석 |
본문에서는 유령과의 만남이나 초자연적인 현상은 과학적 증거는 없지만 환각, 기억 오류, 파레이돌리아 등으로 과학적 설명이 가능함을 이야기하고 있다. 따라서 글의 주제로는 ① '유령과의 만남에 대한 과학적 설명'이 적절하다.

| 어휘 |
haunting n. (유령 등의) 출몰   **paranormal** n. 초자연적 현상, 과학으로는 설명할 수 없는   **encounter** n. 만남, 조우   **misinterpretation** n. 오해, 오역   **skeptic** n. 회의론자   **hallucination** n. 환각
recollection n. 회상, 기억(력)   **pareidolia** n. 파레이돌리아(변상증: 무의미하고 연관성이 없는 이미지에서 의미를 추출해 내려는 행위)
inanimate object 무생물   **random** a. 무작위의, 닥치는 대로의
prone to ~을 잘 하는, ~의 경향이 있는   **jump to a conclusion** 성급한 결론을 내리다, 속단하다

| 해석 |
전 세계 사람들은 유령을 보거나 소리를 들었다고 믿지만, 영혼, 유령 출몰 또는 초자연적 현상에 대한 과학적 증거는 없다. 그렇다면, 이러한 '만남'의 이면에는 무엇이 있을까? 유령이 존재한다는 과학적 증거가 없다는 점을 고려하면, 왜 어떤 사람들은 유령을 보거나 소리를 들었다고 생각하는 것일까? 한 심리학 교수는 최근 초자연적 현상의 과학에 대한 책을 썼으며, 유령 목격은 종종 "자연적 설명이 가능한 현상을 진심으로 잘못 해석한 것"이라고 말했다. "설명을 떠올릴 수 없다고 해서 설명이 없다는 뜻은 아닙니다."라고 그 교수는 『라이브사이언스(Live Science)』와의 인터뷰에서 말했다. 그는 유령과의 만남에 대해 초자연적이지 않은 설명을 탐구하는 회의론자이다. 이러한 설명에는 환각, 즉 존재하지 않는 것에 대한 지각과, 거짓 기억, 즉 일어나지 않은 사건에 대한 기억과, 파레이돌리아, 즉 무생물이나 무작위 패턴에서 얼굴이나 의미 있는 무언가를 보는 경향이 포함된다. 인간의 뇌는 사물을 놓치고 사건을 잘못 기억하는 경향이 있으며, 모호한 경험을 이해하려고 할 때 성급하게 결론을 내릴 수 있다. 이는 사람들이 유령이나 다른 전설적인 생물을 보았다고 믿고 싶을 때 특히 그렇다.

다음 중 본문의 주요 주제는 무엇인가?
① '유령과의 만남'에 대한 과학적 설명
② 과학적인 것과 영적인 것의 충돌
③ 유령을 믿는 한 심리학자의 이야기
④ 초자연적 현상의 과학과 기억력 감퇴

19 글의 흐름상 적절하지 않은 문장 고르기 ③

| 분석 |
본문은 우리가 처한 상황에 따라 "만약 내가 ~했다면"이라는 사고방식이 우리의 감정에 미치는 영향에 관한 것이다. 이를 두 사

람이 똑같이 기차를 놓친 상황에서도 기차를 간발의 차로 놓친 경우에 더 큰 실망감을 준다는 것을 예로 들어 설명하고 있다. 본문은 사람들이 자신이 처한 상황에 따라 자신의 잘못된 일을 어떻게 생각하는지는 설명하고 있지만, 타인의 상황과 비교해서 느끼는 감정에 대해서는 논하지 않고 있으므로 ③이 글의 흐름상 적절하지 않다.

| 어휘 |

stuck in traffic 교통이 막힌[정체된]　**disappointed** a. 실망한, 낙담한　**curse** v. 저주하다; 악담하다; 욕을 퍼붓다　**at ease** 마음이 편안한　**depending on** ~에 따라

| 해석 |

기차가 오전 11시에 떠나기로 예정되어 있는데 교통 체증에 갇혀 있다고 상상해 보라. 당신은 11시 30분에 도착해서 기차를 놓친다. 기차가 정시에 출발한 것을 알게 된다. 이제, 당신의 친구가 타고 갈 또 다른 기차도 오전 11시에 예정되어 있고, 그도 교통 체증에 갇혀 있다고 상상해 보라. 그는 11시 30분에 도착해서 기차를 놓친다. 그는 기차가 25분 늦어서 11시 25분에 출발한다는 것을 알게 된다. 누가 더 슬퍼할까? 연구에 따르면 95%의 사람들이 당신의 친구가 5분 차이로 기차를 놓쳤기 때문에 당신보다 더 실망할 것이라고 대답할 것이다. 그는 당신보다 더 많이 자신을 탓하며 이렇게 말할 것이다. "내가 5분 일찍 출발했다면 어땠을까? 샤워 시간을 5분 줄였다면 아마 기차를 탈 수 있었을 텐데. 좀 더 일찍 일어났다면 지금 가고 있을 텐데." 한편, 당신은 그것에 대해 생각하면서 마음이 더 편안할 것인데, 왜냐하면 30분을 되돌릴 방법은 없기 때문이다. 그래서 "내가 20분 일찍 출발했더라도 여전히 기차를 놓쳤을 거야."라고 혼잣말을 할 것이다. 〈당신은 기차를 놓쳐서 매우 슬프고, 친구도 기차를 놓쳐서 더욱 슬퍼진다.〉 하지만 사실은 달라진 것이 없다. 당신과 친구 둘 다 늦었고 기차를 놓쳤다. 하지만 이것은 우리가 무언가가 잘못되었다고 분석할 때, 우리가 가진 기회에 따라 "만약 내가 ~했다면"이라는 시나리오를 만들 것이라는 것을 보여준다. 이것이 바로 은메달리스트가 동메달리스트보다 더 슬픈 이유이기도 하다.

20　내용일치　④

| 분석 |

투쟁-도피 반응은 척추동물의 스트레스 반응을 조절하는 일반적응증후군의 첫 번째 단계로 그들에게 생존에 대한 위협에 신속하게 대응할 수 있는 메커니즘을 제공한다고 했으므로 ④가 적절하다.

| 어휘 |

hyperarousal n. 과다각성　**acute** a. 급성의　**physiological** a. 생리학(상)의, 생리적인　**threat** n. 위협, 협박　**discharge** n. 방출, 유출　**sympathetic nervous system** 교감 신경계　**general adaptation syndrome** 일반적응 증후군　**vertebrate** n. 척추동물　**threatening** a. 위협적인

| 해석 |

'과다각성' 또는 '급성 스트레스 반응'이라고도 불리는 투쟁-도피 반응은 생존에 유해하다고 인식되는 사건, 공격, 또는 위협에 대응하여 일어나는 생리적 반응이다. 이 이론에 따르면 동물들은 위협에 대해 교감 신경계의 전반적인 활성화로 반응하여 싸우거나 도망칠 준비를 하게 된다. 이 반응은 척추동물의 스트레스 반응을 조절하는 일반적응증후군의 첫 번째 단계로 인식된다. 진화 심리학적 설명은 초기 동물들은 위협적인 자극에 빠르게 반응해야 했으며, 심리적으로나 신체적으로 준비할 시간이 없었다는 것이다. 투쟁-도피 반응은 그들에게 생존에 대한 위협에 신속하게 대응할 수 있는 메커니즘을 제공했다.

다음 중 옳은 것은?
① 투쟁-도피 반응은 부분적으로는 생리적이지만 대체로 심리적이다.
② 투쟁-도피 반응으로 인한 생존 가능성은 다소 동일하다.
③ 생물들은 포식자와 마주했을 때 선택사항들을 신중하게 고려한다.
④ 투쟁-도피 반응은 척추동물들 사이에서 흔히 발견되는 생존 메커니즘이다.

21　글의 요지　①

| 분석 |

본문은 음악이 형식, 화성, 선율, 리듬 등의 조합을 만들어내는 소리의 배열이라는 것과 음악 창작의 활동 범주와 다양한 악기 사용, 음악의 문화적, 사회적 역할 등 음악의 정의와 특징에 대해 설명하고 있다. 따라서 ①의 "음악의 특징은 무엇인가?"가 글의 요지로 적절하다.

| 어휘 |

arrangement n. 배열　**harmony** n. 〈음악〉 화성　**versatile** a. 다재다능한, 다용도의, 다목적의　**diverse** a. 다양한, 가지각색의　**composition** n. 작곡　**improvisation** n. 즉석에서 하기; 즉흥 연주　**musical instrument** 악기　**compose** v. 구성하다; 작곡하다　**sequence** v. 일정한 순서로 배열하다, 반복 진행하다

| 해석 |

음악은 형식, 화성, 멜로디, 리듬 또는 기타 표현적인 내용의 조합을 만들어내기 위해 소리를 배열하는 것이다. 음악이 모든 인간 사회에 존재하는 문화적 보편 요소라는 데는 일반적으로 의견이 일치한다. 음악은 종종 인간의 창의성을 표현하기 위한 매우 다용도적인 매체라고 특징지어진다. 다양한 활동이 음악의 창작에 포함되며, 종종 작곡, 즉흥 연주 및 연주로 범주가 나뉜다. 음악은 인간의 목소리를 포함한 다양한 악기를 사용하여 연주될 수 있다. 음악은 또한 뮤직 박스, 배럴 오르간, 컴퓨터의 디지털 오디오 워크스테이션 소프트웨어를 통해 기계적 또는 전자적으로 간접 연주되도록 작곡되거나, 시퀀싱(반복진행)되거나 기타 방식으로 제작될 수 있다. 음악은 종종 사회적 행사와 종교 의식에서 중요

한 역할을 한다. 음악을 만드는 기술은 종종 문화적 전통의 일부로 전해지며, 음악을 듣는 것은 일반적인 오락 수단이다.

본문은 주로 무엇에 관한 것인가?
① 음악의 특징은 무엇인가?
② 음악 활동의 범주에는 무엇이 있나?
③ 사회에서 음악의 유용성은 무엇인가?
④ 음악과 문화의 관계는 무엇인가?

22 글의 주제 ③

| 분석 |

본문은 초기 인간의 특성인 이족보행에서 뇌의 발달, 도구 사용 능력, 언어 능력 등의 발달, 그리고 예술적, 문화적 발달 등, 고등한 특성에 이르기까지 인간이 유인원과 같은 조상으로부터 진화해 온 과정을 설명하고 있다. 따라서 글의 주제로는 ③ '유인원과 같은 조상으로부터 인류의 진화'가 적절하다.

| 어휘 |

originate v. 비롯되다, 시작되다   **apelike** a. 유인원 같은   **trait** n. 특색, 특성, 특징   **bipedalism** n. 이족보행   **symbolic** a. 상징적인   **elaborate** a. 정교한, 공들인   **primate** n. 영장류   **genetic** a. 유전의   **ape** n. 유인원

| 해석 |

인류의 진화는 사람들이 유인원과 같은 조상으로부터 시작된 긴 변화의 과정이다. 과학적 증거에 따르면, 모든 사람들이 공유하는 신체적 및 행동적 특성은 유인원과 같은 조상으로부터 시작되어 약 600만 년에 걸쳐 진화했다. 가장 초기의 인간의 특성 중 하나인 이족보행(두 다리로 걷는 능력)은 약 400만 년 전에 진화했다. 크고 복잡한 뇌, 도구를 만들고 사용하는 능력, 언어 능력과 같은 다른 중요한 인간의 특성들은 최근에 발달했다. 복잡한 상징적 표현, 예술, 정교한 문화적 다양성 등을 포함한 많은 고등한 특성들은 주로 지난 10만 년 동안 나타났다. 인간은 영장류이다. 신체적 및 유전적 유사성은 현대 인류 종인 호모 사피엔스가 다른 영장류 종인 유인원과 매우 밀접한 관계가 있음을 보여준다. 인간과 아프리카의 유인원인 침팬지와 고릴라는 800만 년 전에서 600만 년 전 사이에 살았던 공통 조상을 공유한다.

다음 중 본문의 주요 주제는 무엇인가?
① 현대 영장류의 공통 조상
② 이족보행의 출현과 언어 능력
③ 유인원과 같은 조상으로부터 인류의 진화
④ 인간의 기원과 이주의 장소

23 내용일치 ②

| 분석 |

치타와 사자가 가장 빠른 동물이지만 그 동물의 먹잇감도 속도가 빠르다고 했다. 그리고 그 동물의 예로 springbok, wildebeest, pronghorn을 들고 있다. 특히 pronghorn은 가장 빠른 장거리 주자라고 했으므로 치타와 사자에게 쉬운 먹잇감이라 할 수 없다. 따라서 ②가 정답이다. ① 사자는 시속 50마일이고 스프링복과 가지뿔영양은 시속 55마일까지 낼 수 있으므로 사자를 앞지를 수 있다.

| 어휘 |

kingdom n. 〈생물〉 ∼계(界); (학문·예술 등의) 분야   **predator** n. 포식자, 포식 동물   **overtake** v. 추월하다   **overpower** v. 압도하다   **prey** n. (사냥 동물의) 먹이[사냥감]   **springbok** n. 스프링복(남아프리카산(産) 영양의 일종)   **pursue** v. 뒤쫓다, 추적하다   **wildebeest** n. 누(= gnu)(아프리카산(産) 큰 영양의 일종)   **clock** v. 기록하다; (시간·속도의 기록을) 내다   **sprinter** n. 단거리 주자   **pronghorn** n. 가지뿔영양(북아메리카 서부산)   **sprint** n. 단거리 경주, 스프린트, 전력 질주   **elude** v. 교묘히 피하다, 회피하다   **hoof** n. 발굽

| 해석 |

동물계에서 속도는 삶과 죽음의 차이를 의미할 수 있다. 포식자는 속도를 이용해서 먹이를 따라잡고 압도하는 반면, 다른 방어 수단이 거의 없는 동물들은 먹이가 되는 것을 피하기 위해 속도에 의존한다. 여기 세계에서 가장 빠른 동물들이 있다. 달리기 시작하여 3초 이내에 속도를 시속 0마일에서 60마일로 끌어올릴 수 있는 치타는 가장 빠른 육상 동물로 여겨지지만, 짧은 거리에서만 그러한 속도를 유지할 수 있다. 사자는 또한 먹이를 사냥할 때 매우 빠르며, 최고 속도는 시속 약 50마일이다. 하지만 이 아프리카 대형 고양잇과 동물들의 일반적인 먹이도 꽤 빠를 수 있다. 예를 들어, 스프링복은 쫓길 때 시속 55마일에 이를 수 있고, 누는 시속 50마일로 기록되었다. 치타가 가장 빠른 단거리 주자인 반면, 가지뿔영양은 동물의 왕국에서 가장 빠른 장거리 주자다. 가지뿔영양은 수 마일에 걸쳐 시속 약 35마일의 속도를 유지할 수 있으며, 더 짧은 거리에서는 더욱 빠르다. 포식자를 피하기 위해 전력 질주하는 동안, 가지뿔영양은 발굽에 있는 특별한 쿠션과 달리면서 대량의 산소를 흡입할 수 있는 능력 덕분에 시속 약 55마일의 최고 속도를 낼 수 있다.

다음 중 옳지 않은 것은?
① 스프링복과 가지뿔영양은 사자를 앞지를 수 있다.
② 가지뿔영양은 치타와 사자에게 쉬운 먹잇감이다.
③ 가지뿔영양은 육상 동물 중 가장 빠른 장거리 주자다.
④ 치타는 모든 육상 동물 중 가장 빠른 단거리 주자다.

24 글의 제목 ①

| 분석 |

본문은 항생제를 우유와 함께 복용하면 약물이 혈류에 흡수되지 않아서 약물의 효과가 떨어질 수 있다는 것을 여러 연구를 통해 보여주고 있다. 따라서 글의 제목으로는 ① '항생제를 우유와 함께 복용하지 마라'가 적절하다.

| 어휘 |

grapefruit n. 그레이프프루트, 자몽　**medication** n. 약물　**dairy product** 유제품　**bacterial infection** 세균 감염, 박테리아 감염　**antibiotic** n. 항생 물질, 항생제　**absorption** n. 흡수, 흡수 작용　**demeclocycline** n. 데메클로사이클린　**staggering** a. 어마어마한, 경이적인　**ciprofloxacin** n. 시프로플록사신

| 해석 |

자몽이나 알코올과 같은 일부 음식과 음료는 특정 약물과 함께 섭취해서는 안 된다는 말을 들어본 적이 있을 것이다. 그러나 유제품이 일부 약물의 효과를 떨어뜨릴 수도 있다는 사실을 알고 있었나? 이 효과는 박테리아 감염을 치료하는 데 사용되는 약물인 특정 종류의 항생제에 특히 문제가 된다. 예를 들어, 경구 복용하는 항생제는 효과적으로 작용하기 위해서는 혈류에 흡수되어야 한다. 그러나 우유와 같은 유제품과 함께 복용하면 일부 항생제는 제대로 흡수되지 않는다. 예를 들어, 한 연구에 따르면, 데메클로사이클린이라는 항생제의 혈류로의 흡수는 우유와 함께 복용했을 때, 물이나 유제품이 없는 식사와 복용했을 때에 비해 무려 83%나 감소했다. 또 다른 연구는 다른 종류의 항생제인 시프로플록사신을 우유와 함께 복용할 때, 물과 함께 복용할 때보다 혈류 내 약물 수치가 약 30%에서 36% 낮아진다는 것을 보여주었다.

글의 제목으로 가장 적절한 것을 고르시오.
① 항생제를 우유와 함께 복용하지 마라
② 항생제를 경구 투여하지 마라
③ 항생제 복용 시 자몽이나 알코올을 먹지 마라
④ 약을 복용하기 전에 약 라벨을 읽어보라

25　내용일치　④

| 분석 |

역사는 장기적인 예측은 유용하지만 단기적인 예측은 변수가 너무 많아서 어렵다고 했다. 따라서 장기적인 관점에서는 예측이 가능한 것이므로 '아무것도 예측할 수 없다'는 것은 적절하지 않다. 따라서 ④가 정답이다.

| 어휘 |

indispensable a. 없어서는 안 될, 필수적인　**analogy** n. 유추, 비유　**generalization** n. 일반화, 보편화　**large-scale** a. 대규모의, 광범한　**justify** v. 정당화하다　**small-scale** a. 소규모의　**variable** n. 변수　**in short** 요컨대, 간단히 말해　**after a fashion** (아주 잘은 아니고) 어느 정도　**clear-sightedness** n. 명석함, 통찰력 있음　**outwit** v. ~의 의표를 찌르다, 속이다　**certitude** n. 확신, 확실(성)　**ally** n. 동맹국　**pact** n. 협정, 조약　**amity** n. 우호, 친선　**alliance** n. 동맹　**be at each other's throats** 서로 물어뜯을 듯이 굴다, 서로 으르렁거리다　**chasten** v. 잘못을 깨닫게 하다, 훈계하다　**upsurge** n. 급증, 격증　**abrupt** a. 돌연한, 갑작스러운

| 해석 |

역사 연구가 사람들을 더 현명하게 만든다는 것은 의심할 여지가 없다. 그러나 역사적 유추의 한계를 이해하는 것은 필수적이다. 가장 유용한 역사적 일반화는 상당한 기간 동안의 거대한 사회 및 지적 운동에 관한 진술이다. 그것들은 대규모의 장기적인 예측을 가능하게 만든다. 그러나 그것들은 소규모의 단기적인 예측을 정당화하지 않는다. 그것은 단기 예측은 세부 사항의 예측이며 당장의 미래를 정확하게 예측하기에는 변수가 너무 많기 때문이다. 간단히 말해, 역사는 긴 범위에서 질문에 어느 정도 답할 수 있다. 안타깝게도, 정책 입안자들은 장기적인 관점에 거의 관심이 없으며, 그들이 역사에 제기한 질문은 역사가 답하기에 가장 부적합한 질문인 경우가 많다. 역사는 명확한 통찰력으로 가는 지름길을 제공하기는커녕, 우리에게 미래는 놀라움으로 가득 차 있으며 우리로서는 전혀 확신할 수 없는 것이라는 것을 가르쳐준다. 30년 전에 누군가가 40년대가 끝나기 전에 독일과 일본이 영국과 미국의 가까운 친구이자 동맹국이 될 것이라고 예측했다면, 그 사람은 미친 사람으로 여겨졌을 것이다. 20년 전, 러시아와 중국이 30년간의 우호와 동맹 협정에 서명할 때 누군가가 50년대가 끝날 무렵 서로 심하게 다투게 될 것이라고 예측했다면, 그 사람도 미친 사람으로 여겨졌을 것이다. 교훈적인 사실은 우리 시대의 많은 중요한 사건들이 예측되지 않았다는 것이다. 몇 년 전의 독일-소련 조약과 티토-스탈린 분쟁에서부터 보다 최근의 인도네시아의 반공산주의 봉기와 미국과 공산주의 중국 사이의 관계의 급격한 변화와 같은 사건들이 있다.

다음 중 옳지 않은 것은?
① 일반적으로 역사 연구는 유익하다.
② 역사에서의 단기 예측은 정확할 수 없다.
③ 역사에서의 예측은 장기적인 관점에서만 유용하다.
④ 역사는 우리에게 인생에서 아무것도 예측할 수 없다는 것을 말해준다.

26　글의 요지　③

| 분석 |

본문은 새로운 장치인 AI 기반 전자 혀에 관해 주로 다루고 있다. 전자 혀는 청량음료나 블렌드 커피를 구별하고, 우유에 물을 타서 희석되었는지 평가하며, 과일 주스가 상했는지의 여부를 식별할 수 있다고 하였다. 따라서 맛의 차이와 음식 상태를 판단할 수 있다고 할 수 있으므로 글의 요지로 ③이 적절하다.

| 어휘 |

interpret v. 해석하다　**taste receptor** 미각 수용체　**gustatory** a. 미각의　**cortex** n. 피질; 대뇌 피질　**on the verge of** 바야흐로 ~하려고 하여, ~의 직전에　**fridge** n. 냉장고　**glimpse** n. 흘깃[언뜻] 봄, 일별　**ion sensitive field effect transistor** 이온 감수성 전계효과 트랜지스터(ISFET)　**mimic** v. 모방하다, 흉내 내다　**initially** ad. 처음에　**acidic** a. 산성의　**a handful of** 소수의, 소량의　**paramete**

n. 매개변수 **acidity** n. 신맛; 산도 **accuracy** n. 정확도, 정밀도 **beverage** n. (물 이외의) 마실 것, 음료 **soft drink** 비(非)알콜성 음료, 청량음료 **water down** ~에 물을 타서 희석시키다 **unreliable** a. 신뢰할 수 없는, 의지할 수 없는 **imperfection** n. 불완전; 결점, 결함 **robust** a. 강건한, 튼튼한; 강력한

| 해석 |

이 새로운 장치는 다양한 블렌드 커피를 구별하거나 음식이나 음료가 상하기 직전인 때를 감지할 수 있다. 냉장고 뒤쪽에 있는 그 한 상자의 오래된 과일 주스가 여전히 마시기에 안전한지 궁금해한 적이 있는가? 새로운 '전자 혀(electronic tongue)'가 당신에게 말해줄 수 있다. 인공지능(AI)으로 구동되는 이 시스템은 식품 안전과 신선도 문제를 식별할 수 있다. 그것은 또한 AI가 어떻게 결정을 내리는지를 엿볼 수 있다고 연구자들은 『네이처(Nature)』 저널에 보고했다. 그 전자 혀를 만들기 위해 연구자들은 화학 이온을 감지하는 장치인 '이온 감수성 전계효과 트랜지스터(ISFET)'를 사용했다. 이 감지기는 액체 속 이온에 대한 정보를 수집하여 전기 신호로 변환하고 그 정보를 컴퓨터가 해석할 수 있다. "우리는 인공 혀를 만들려고 노력하고 있지만, 우리가 다양한 음식을 경험하는 과정은 혀 이상의 것을 포함합니다."라고 저자 중 한 명이 말했다. "혀 자체는 우리에게 있는데, 그 혀는 미각 수용체로 구성되어 있으며, 미각 수용체는 음식 종류와 상호작용하고 그 정보를 생물학적 신경망인 미각 피질로 보냅니다." 이 새로운 장치에서는 감지기가 혀 역할을 하는 반면, AI는 맛을 감지하는 뇌 영역인 미각 피질의 역할을 한다. 연구팀은 감지기를 인간의 뇌가 정보를 처리하는 방식을 모방한 기계 학습 프로그램인 인공 신경망에 연결하여 감지기가 수집한 데이터를 처리하고 해석했다. 처음에 연구자들은 신경망에 특정 액체가 얼마나 산성인지 알아낼 때 사용할 수 있는 몇 가지 매개변수를 제공했다. 이러한 매개변수를 사용하여 신경망은 약 91%의 정확도로 산도를 결정했다. 신경망이 산도 분석을 위한 자체 매개변수를 정의하도록 했을 때, 정확도가 95% 이상으로 향상되었다. 그런 다음 그들은 실제 음료를 대상으로 이 혀를 테스트했다. 이 장치는 유사한 청량음료나 블렌드 커피를 구별하고, 우유에 물을 타서 희석되었는지를 평가하며, 과일 주스가 상했는지를 식별할 수 있다. 그 장치의 결정은 일부 상황에서는 신뢰할 수 없다. "우리는 우리가 불완전하게 살 수 있다는 것을 깨달았습니다."라고 한 저자가 말했다. "그리고 그것이 바로 자연입니다. 자연은 불완전함으로 가득 차 있지만, 우리의 전자 혀처럼 여전히 강력한 결정을 내릴 수 있습니다."

다음 중 글의 요지를 가장 잘 요약한 것은?
① 전자 혀는 항상 음식에 대해 정확한 결정을 내릴 수 있다.
② 전자 혀는 인간의 혀와 정확히 같은 메커니즘으로 작동한다.
③ AI 기반 전자 혀는 맛의 차이와 음식 상태를 감지할 수 있다.
④ AI 기반 전자 혀는 평가를 위해 음식의 다양한 영양소를 분석한다.

27~28

일반적으로 우리는 우리와의 권력 투쟁에 대한 아이들의 관심을 크게 과장한다. 우리는 그들에 대한 우리의 권력을 유지하는 것에 너무 관심이 있어서, 그들이 우리로부터 그 권력을 빼앗는 것에 똑같이 관심이 있다고 생각한다. 그들은 자신들이 무력하다는 것과 우리가 그들에게 큰 권력을 가지고 있다는 것을 매우 잘 알고 있다. 그들은 이것을 좋아하지 않으며, 그것이 사실이 아닐지도 모르는 때를 막연하게 고대한다. 그러나 그들은 현재로서는 이 상황을 바꾸기 위해 많은 일을 할 수 없다는 것을 알 만큼 충분히 현실적이다. 어쨌든, 그들이 어느 정도 건강하고 행복하며, 다른 할 일이 있다면, 그들은 바쁘게 살아가고 있다. 그들은 항상 우리와 싸우고 싶어 하지 않는다. 우리가 우리의 권력을 참을 수 없을 정도로 남용하거나, 그것을 주장하는 끊임없는 투쟁으로 아이들을 지치게 하지 않는 한, 대부분의 아이들은 대부분의 경우 그것을 기꺼이, 어쩌면 너무 기꺼이 받아들인다. 내가 본 어른들과 아이들 사이의 대부분의 싸움은 어른들이 아이들에게 그들(아이들)이 전혀 의심하지 않았던 것, 즉 그들(어른들)이 보스라는 것을 불필요하게 증명하려고 했기 때문에 발생한다.

| 어휘 |

as a (general) rule 일반적으로, 대체로 **exaggerate** v. 과장하다 **powerless** a. 힘이 없는, 무력한 **vague** a. 막연한, 모호한, 애매한 **in any case** 어쨌든 **abuse** v. 남용하다, 오용하다 **intolerably** ad. 참을[견딜] 수 없이[없을 만큼] **weary** v. 지치게 하다 **be willing to** 기꺼이 ~하다 **needlessly** ad. 불필요하게, 쓸데없이

27 지시대상 ②

| 분석 |

Ⓐ, Ⓒ, Ⓓ의 it은 모두 power를 가리키는 반면, Ⓑ의 it은 앞 문장의 내용인 자신들이 무력하다는 것과 어른들이 그들에 대해 큰 권력을 가지고 있다는 사실을 가리킨다. 따라서 ②가 정답이다.

28 글의 주제 ③

| 분석 |

아이들은 권력 투쟁에 별로 관심이 없으며 대부분의 싸움은 어른들이 아이들에게 자신들이 보스라는 것을 불필요하게 증명하려는 시도에서 비롯된다는 것이 이 글의 주된 내용이다. 따라서 글의 주제로 ③이 적절하다.

다음 중 이 글의 주요 주제는 무엇인가?
① 아이들은 무엇이 잘못되었고 무엇이 옳은지 충분히 알고 있다.
② 아이들은 어른들이 자신들에 대해 권한이 없다는 것을 잘 알고 있다.
③ 어른들은 불필요하게 아이들에 대한 자신들의 권력을 주장하려 한다.
④ 어른들은 너무 현실적이고 아이들은 너무 이상적이다.

29~30

더닝-크루거 효과는 특정 분야에서 제한된 역량을 가진 사람들이 자신의 능력을 과대평가하는 인지 편향이다. 그것은 1999년에 저스틴 크루거(Justin Kruger)와 데이비드 더닝(David Dunning)에 의해 처음 설명되었다. 일부 연구자들은 또한 높은 성과를 내는 사람들에 대한 반대 효과, 즉 그들의 능력을 과소평가하는 경향을 포함시킨다. 대중문화에서 더닝-크루거 효과는 종종 특정 업무에 능숙하지 않은 사람들의 특정한 과신 대신에, 지능이 낮은 사람들의 일반적인 과신에 대한 주장으로 오해받는다.

C 수많은 연구가 수행되었다. 더닝-크루거 효과는 일반적으로 자기 평가와 객관적인 성과를 비교하여 판단된다. 예를 들어, 참가자들은 시험을 치고 그 후 자신의 성적을 추정할 수 있으며, 이를 실제 성적과 비교한다. 원래 연구는 논리적 추론, 문법, 그리고 사회적 기술에 중점을 두었다.

B 다른 연구들은 다양한 작업에 걸쳐 수행되었다. 여기에는 비즈니스, 정치, 의학, 운전, 항공, 공간 기억, 학교 시험, 문해력과 같은 분야의 기술이 포함된다.

A 하지만 더닝-크루거 효과의 원인에 대해서는 의견 차이가 있다. 연구자들은 그 효과가 어디에 적용되는지, 얼마나 강한지, 그리고 그것의 실제적인 결과를 여전히 탐구하고 있다.

예를 들어, 부정확한 자기 평가는 잠재적으로 사람들로 하여금 자신에게 부적합한 직업을 선택하거나 위험한 행동에 참여하는 등 나쁜 결정을 내리게 할 수 있다. 그것은 또한 사람들이 자신을 향상시키기 위해 단점을 해결하는 것을 방해할 수 있다.

어휘

cognitive bias 인지 편향　**competence** n. 능력, 역량, 적성
overestimate v. 과대평가하다　**underestimate** v. 과소평가하다
overconfidence n. 과신, 자만심　**aviation** n. 비행, 항공　**spatial** a. 공간의, 공간적인　**literacy** n. 읽고 쓰는 능력　**disagreement** n. 불일치, 의견 차이　**inaccurate** a. 부정확한　**potentially** ad. 잠재적으로　**inhibit** v. 억제하다, 방해하다; 금하다

29　단락배열　①

| 분석 |

더닝-크루거 효과에 대해 설명하는 글이다. 더닝-크루거 효과의 개념을 기술하고 그다음에 그 효과에 대한 연구를 예로 들어 설명하고 있는 B와 C가 와야 한다. 더닝-크루거 효과에 관한 수많은 연구 중에 초기 연구 분야에 대해 말하고 있는 C가 먼저 오고, 또 다른 연구를 제시한 B가 그 뒤에 와야 한다. 그리고 더닝-크루거 효과의 원인에 대한 의견 차이와 어디에 적용되는지와 실용적 결과를 설명하고 있는 A가 마지막에 오는 것이 적절하다. A에 언급된 더닝-크루거 효과의 적용례와 실용적 결과의 예로 마지막 단락에서 부적합한 직업 선택, 위험한 일에의 참여, 단점 해결 방해 등이 제시된다.

30　내용파악　②

| 분석 |

더닝-크루거 효과는 제한된 역량을 가진 사람들이 자신의 능력을 과대평가하는 인지 편향을 말한다. 따라서 다른 사람의 지능을 평가하는 것이 아니라 자기 자신의 지능을 평가할 때 발생할 수 있는 편견에 대해 말하고 있으므로 ②가 옳지 않다. ④ A의 마지막 문장에서 '여전히 탐구하고 있다(are still exploring)'이라고 한 것은 '아직 완전히 결정되지 않았다'는 뜻이다.

본문에 따르면, 다음 중 더닝-크루거 효과에 대해 옳지 않은 것은?
① 그것은 다양한 기술과 능력과 관련하여 나타난다.
② 그것은 다른 사람의 지능을 평가할 때 발생하는 편견의 한 형태이다.
③ 그것은 주로 제한된 능력을 가진 사람들이 자신의 능력을 과대평가하는 것에 관한 것이다.
④ 그 영향력과 적용 범위는 아직 완전히 결정되지 않았다.

SOGANG UNIVERSITY | 서강대학교 1차

TEST p. 298~312

01	④	02	①	03	②	04	④	05	①	06	④	07	④	08	②	09	⑤	10	⑤
11	④	12	②	13	①	14	⑤	15	①	16	③	17	③	18	②	19	②	20	④
21	②	22	③	23	①	24	①	25	④	26	①	27	②	28	③	29	⑤	30	⑤

01 논리완성 ④

| 분석 |
as 다음에 '쉽게 믿는다'라는 표현(quick to believe)이 있으므로 '쉽게 믿음'이라는 뜻의 credulity가 빈칸에 가장 적절하다. frivolity는 행동이나 생각의 '경박함', '경솔함'을 의미한다.

| 어휘 |
scam n. 사기꾼   **outlandish** a. 이상한   **frivolity** n. 경솔함   **solemnity** n. 엄숙함   **mendacity** n. 거짓말   **credulity** n. 잘 속음   **humility** n. 겸손

| 해석 |
그녀는 가장 이상한 이야기조차도 쉽게 믿으므로, 그녀의 잘 믿는 성향이 그녀를 사기꾼들의 쉬운 목표가 되게 했다.

02 논리완성 ①

| 분석 |
자신이 아는 지식의 범위에서는 해결할 수 없는 문제라는 것을 인식한 것이므로, 빈칸에는 '지식의 범위'라는 의미의 ken이 가장 적절하다. grip은 전문지식보다는 상황에 대한 이해력이나 지배력을 의미하며, beyond one's ken이 '지식의 범위 밖에 있는, 알기 어려운'이라는 의미의 관용 표현을 이룬다.

| 어휘 |
family doctor 가정의(醫)   **beyond one's ken** 알 수 없는   **mew** n. 고양이 울음   **grip** n. 장악, 이해력   **span** n. 폭, 범위

| 해석 |
그 가족 주치의는 자신이 진단할 수 없는 증상을 마주했을 때, 그 문제가 자신의 지식 범위를 넘어선 것임을 인식하고 전문의에게 자문을 구했다.

03 논리완성 ②

| 분석 |
oxymoron은 두 상반된 개념이 함께 사용되어 모순을 이루는 것을 가리킨다. 예를 들어 '타지 않는 불'이나 '슬픈 미소' 같은 것이다. 오라토리오는 원래 종교적인 음악이므로, 앞에 '세속적'이라는 표현을 붙이면 모순처럼 들린다는 의미이다.

| 어휘 |
sincere a. 진정한   **sacred** a. 신성한   **subject** n. 주제   **qualify** v. 부르다   **secular** a. 세속적인   **terminology** n. 전문 용어   **plagiaristic** a. 표절의   **statutory** a. 법률로 정해진   **inopportune** a. 부적절한   **syllogistic** a. 삼단논법의

| 해석 |
오라토리오는 신성한 주제를 진지하게 종교적으로 다룬다는 의미를 내포하고 있으므로, 비종교적 오라토리오는 일반적으로 세속적 오라토리오라고 불리는데, 세속적 오라토리오라는 말은 역사적 맥락에서는 모순어법적이라고 여겨졌던 용어이다.

04 부사 ④

| 분석 |
④의 different는 형용사이다. 앞의 will do를 수식해야 하므로, 동사를 수식하는 부사 differently로 바꿔야 한다. 다음에 나오는 than도 엄격히 문법을 따지면 from으로 바꿔야 하지만, 최근 영어에서는 흔히 통용되는 용법이다.

| 어휘 |
rebel a. 반란의   **topple** v. 전복시키다   **regime** n. 정권   **interim** a. 임시의   **devastated** a. 황폐해진   **ethnic** a. 민족의

| 해석 |
시리아의 전(前) 독재자 바샤르 알 아사드 정권을 전복한 반군 단체는 이제 그것을 대체하는 도전에 직면해 있다. 그들은 임시 정부를 세웠다. 많은 사람은 반군 단체가 무엇을 아사드와 다르게 할지 지켜보고 있다. 그들의 도전 과제는 다양한 민족 및 종교 집단이 있는 황폐해진 국가를 통치하는 것이다.

05 부사 ①

| 분석 |
① without 다음에 나오는 participating은 동명사이므로 형용사 active로 수식할 수 없다. active를 부사 actively로 고쳐야 한다.

| 어휘 |
civic engagement 시민 참여 vital a. 필수적인 play a role 역할을 하다 inclusive a. 포용적인 dignity n. 위엄, 존엄성 contemporary a. 현대의, 동시대의 volunteering n. 자원봉사 community organizing 지역 사회 조직 활동 take part in 참여하다 disengaged a. 참여하지 않는, 무관심한 ultimately ad. 궁극적으로 depend on ~에 달려있다

| 해석 |
시민 참여는 강하고 포용적인 사회를 형성하는 데 중요한 역할을 한다. 현대 사회에서 사람들은 시민으로서 적극적으로 참여하지 않고서는 존엄성을 달성할 수 없다. 투표하기, 자원봉사하기, 지역 사회 조직하기는 개인이 변화를 만들어 낼 수 있는 몇 가지 방법에 지나지 않는다. 이러한 활동에 참여함으로써, 사람들은 자신의 지역 사회를 개선할 뿐 아니라 삶의 목적의식을 얻는다. 계속 참여하지 않는 사람들은 종종 자기 삶에 영향을 미치는 결정에 영향력을 행사할 기회를 놓친다. 궁극적으로, 건강한 민주주의는 시민들의 참여에 달려있다.

06 문장배열 ④

| 분석 |
글의 가장 앞에는 주제 소개가 필요하다. 여기서 Ⓐ는 그라이스의 이론, 적절성 이론을 소개하고 있다. Ⓓ this claim이라는 말로 Ⓐ에 언급된 그라이스의 이론이 무엇인지 말하고, 그라이스의 추론 모델은 코드 모델의 대안이라고 했으므로, Ⓑ에서 Ⓓ에 언급된 코드 모델 개념을 설명한다. Ⓔ에서 Ⓑ에 언급된 decoding이 언어적 해석에 한 요소로 관련됨을 설명하고, Ⓒ 결론으로 코드 모델에 입각한 해독은 하나의 해석에 불과하므로, 추론 모델을 통해 여러 해석 중 가장 그럴듯한 하나의 해석을 찾아야 한다는 말이다.

| 어휘 |
work out 해결하다 in detail 상세하게 inferential a. 추론적인 encode v. 부호화하다 decode v. 해독하다 utterance n. 발화 linguistic a. 언어적인 evidence n. 증거 comprehension n. 이해 non-verbal a. 비언어적 non-demonstrative inference 비논증적(비연역적, 귀납적) 추론(전제들이 참이어도 결론이 거짓일 수도 있는 추론)

| 해석 |
Ⓐ 적합성 이론은 그라이스의 중심 주장 중 하나를 상세히 풀어 설명하려는 시도로 볼 수 있는데, 그것은 곧, 언어적·비언어적 의사소통을 포함한 대부분의 인간 의사소통의 필수적인 특징은 화자 의도의 표현과 인식이라는 주장이다.

Ⓓ 이 주장을 발전시키면서, 그라이스는 고전적 코드 모델에 대한 대안인 추론적 의사소통 모델의 기반을 놓았다.
Ⓑ 코드 모델에 따르면, 의사소통자는 자신의 의도를 신호로 코드화하고, 청중은 같은 코드를 사용하여 이를 해독한다.
Ⓔ 물론, 발화는 언어적으로 코드화된 증거이므로, 언어적 이해에는 일정한 코드 해독이라는 요소가 수반된다.
Ⓒ 그러나, 코드 해독을 통해 얻은 언어적 의미는 화자의 의미를 해석해내는 비논증적 추론 과정에 들어가는 여러 입력 요소 중 하나일 뿐이다.

07~08

서양 철학사에서 기념비적인 인물인 플라톤은 유럽 문학 이론의 역사에서도 거의 그만큼 중요한 존재로 등장한다. 그가 역사적 인물들이 특정한 주장을 전달하는 대화체 형식을 선택한 것이 그가 제기했던 문제들이 이미 그 이전부터 논의되고 있었음을, 소크라테스 이전 철학자들이 남긴 단편적인 글들이 시사하듯이, 시사하지만, 실제로, 그는 많은 문학 학자에게 문학이론 전통의 시작점을 의미한다. 플라톤에게 귀속되는 수십 개의 대화는, 존재의 본질, 우리가 어떻게 사물을 알게 되는가 하는 문제, 인간 사회의 올바른 질서, 정의와 진·선·미와 사랑의 본질 등, 철학자라면 관심을 두는 거의 모든 주제를 다룬다. 시학에 관한 논문을 썼던 그의 제자 아리스토텔레스와는 달리 플라톤은 체계적인 문학 이론 저술에 착수하지는 않았지만, 여러 대화에서 철학적 문제를 고려해본 것이 시에 대한 성찰로 이어지며, 이러한 성찰은 종종 서구 문학 논쟁의 조건을 형성하였다.

시에 대한 플라톤의 다양한 논의의 공통된 주제는 모방에 대한 불신이다. 플라톤에 따르면, 시를 포함한 모든 예술은 자연의 모방, 다시 말해 물리적 세계에 존재하는 사물들의 복제이다. 그러나 플라톤이 주장하는 관념론 철학에 따르면, 물질적 세계의 사물들조차도 형태 혹은 이데아라고 불리는 영원한 보편적인 것들의 가변적인 복제물에 지나지 않는다. 따라서 시는 그저 복제물의 복제물일 뿐으로, 진리로 나아가기보다는 진리에서 멀어지게 만든다. 그 이후로 3세기 플로티노스에서 20세기 후반 자크 데리다에 이르기까지 수많은 철학자와 문학 비평가들은 플라톤의 시 비평의 요건을 두고 씨름하며, 그 비평을 수정하거나 그의 논증에서 모순을 지적하려 했다.

| 어휘 |
monumental a. 기념비적인 loom v. 나타나다 extant a. 현존하는 attribute A to B A를 B에 귀속시키다 justice n. 정의 set out 착수하다 treatise n. 논문 poetics n. 시학 term n. 조건 bind v. 묶다 mimesis n. 모방 mutable a. 변하기 쉬운 propound v. 제안하다 wrestle with 씨름하다 point out 지적하다 inconsistency n. 불일치, 모순

07 내용파악   ④

| 분석 |

플라톤이 대화 형식을 선택한 것은 그가 말하는 내용이 사실은 오래전부터 논란이 되어 왔던 주제임을 시사한다고 했다.

플라톤이 대화 형식을 사용했던 것에 대해 무슨 말을 하고 있는가?
① 그것은 소크라테스 이전 철학들과 20세기 비평의 연결을 보여준다.
② 그것은 서구 문학 비평사에서 획기적인 사건이었다.
③ 그것은 플라톤이 문학의 기능에 관심이 없었음을 보여준다.
④ 그것은 그가 다루는 문제들이 오래 지속되어온 주제 같아 보이게 한다.
⑤ 그것은 아리스토텔레스가 시학에 관한 논문을 쓴 동기였다.

08 내용일치   ②

| 분석 |

플라톤은 시를 포함한 모든 예술이 자연의 모방이며, 자연조차 보편적인 것의 모방이어서 시는 모방의 모방이며, 진리에서 멀어지게 만든다고 했으므로 ②가 정답이다. ① 미미하지 않고 기념비적인 역할을 했다. ③ 그가 제기한 문제들은 앞선 철학자들이 이미 제기한 것이다. ④ 체계적인 저술을 한 사람은 그의 제자였던 아리스토텔레스였다. ⑤ 모방을 불신한다고 했으며 관념론자들에게는 당연히 관념(Ideal)이 우선이다.

이 글에 따르면 다음 중 올바른 진술은?
① 유럽 문학 이론에서의 플라톤의 역할은 미미했다.
② 플라톤은 시가 복제물의 복제물이기 때문에 진리를 결여하고 있다고 믿었다.
③ 플라톤은 현재 서양 철학에서 영속적인 문제들을 최초로 제기했다.
④ 플라톤은 체계적인 문학이론 저술에 착수했다.
⑤ 플라톤은 물질적 세계의 사물보다 모방을 더 가치 있게 여긴다.

09~10

노벨상 수상자 한강은 토요일, 그녀의 가장 잘 알려진 작품 몇몇을 창작하는 과정에서 모든 감각을 어떻게 활용했는지를 이야기했다. "글을 쓸 때, 저는 제 몸을 씁니다"라고 그녀는 말했다. "저는 보기, 듣기, 냄새 맡기, 맛보기, 부드러움과 따뜻함과 차가움과 아픔을 경험하기, 심장이 두근거리고 몸이 음식과 물을 요구함을 알아차리기, 걷고 뛰기, 피부로 바람과 비와 눈을 느끼기, 손을 잡기 등의 모든 감각적인 세부적 요소들을 사용합니다." 그녀는 강연에서, 이러한 '생생한 감각'을 독자들에게 전달할 수 있다고 느낀 순간들에 대해 감사를 표현했다. "이러한 순간들에서 저는... 우리를 연결하는 언어의 실을 경험하고, 제 질문들이 어떻게 그 생동감 있는 살아 있는 존재를 통해 독자들과 관계를 맺는지를 경험합니다." 그녀는 강연을 마치며 말했다. "저는 저와 그 실을 통해 연결된 모든 분께, 그리고 앞으로 연결될 수도 있는 모든 분께 깊은 감사를 표하고 싶습니다."

| 어휘 |

Nobel laureate 노벨상 수상자 **employ** v. 활용하다 **sensory** a. 감각의 **tenderness** n. 다정함 **notice** v. 알아차리다 **racing** a. 심장이 두근거리는 **lecture** n. 강연 **gratitude** n. 감사 **transmit** v. 전달하다 **vivid** a. 생생한, 선명한 **sensation** n. 감각 **thread** n. 실, 연결고리 **electric** a. 생동감 있는, 짜릿한 **visual** a. 시각적인 **auditory** a. 청각적인 **olfactory** a. 후각적인, 냄새의 **gustatory** a. 미각적인 **kinetic** a. 운동감각적인

09 동의어   ⑤

| 분석 |

of feeling은 sensory(감각의)나 emotional(감정의)과 연결되고, kinetic은 of moving과 연결된다.

10 지시대상   ⑤

| 분석 |

"that electric, living thing"을 설명하는 바로 앞 표현이 "the thread of language"이다. 작가는 언어가 마치 살아 있는 존재처럼 사람을 연결한다고 생각하고 있다. 뒤에서도 '저와 그 실을 통해 연결된 모든 분'이라고 했다. 작가는 계속해서 언어의 힘을 강조하고 있다.

11~13

미국 제26대 대통령을 기리는 살아 있는 기념물 시어도어 루스벨트 섬은 워싱턴 D.C. 내셔널 몰의 웅장한 대리석 기념비들과는 확연히 구별된다. 포토맥강 위에 자리 잡아 버지니아에서 보행자 전용 다리로만 접근할 수 있는 이 잘 알려지지 않은 호젓한 장소는 고요한 숲길을 따라 루스벨트 동상까지 이어지는 길을 제공한다. 링컨, 제퍼슨, 워싱턴 같은 대통령들을 기리는 드넓은 개방된 공간과 달리, 루스벨트 섬은 자연을 소박하게 기리면서 루스벨트의 환경 보호 유산을 조용히 기념하고 있다.

환경 보호 노력과 1906년 골동품 법으로 유명한 루스벨트는 공유지와 국유림을 확장하며 환경의 역사에서 확고한 위치를 차지했다. 하지만 그의 유산은 복잡해서, 제국주의와 인종적 지배에 대한 관점과 얽혀 있으며, 이는 더 넓은 미국

역사뿐만 아니라, 원주민 추방과 천연자원 착취와 연결된 환경 보호 운동의 뿌리를 반영하고 있다.
1940년 루스벨트를 기리는 도시 속 야생지로 변모하기 전에도, 이 섬은 풍부한 역사를 가지고 있었다. 처음에는 나코치탕크 부족이 관리했고, 이후 메이슨 가문이 노예 노동을 활용하여 유명한 영지로 가꿨다. 이처럼 환경 보존, 기념화, 그리고 미국의 복잡한 과거가 얽힌 다층적인 서사는 루스벨트라는 복합적인 인물을 기리는 이 루스벨트 섬 기념물이 가진 미묘함을 강조하며, 방문객들에게 자연, 역사, 그리고 기억의 상호 연결성을 성찰해보라고 권유하고 있다.

| 어휘 |

memorial n. 기념물 marble a. 대리석의 monument n. 기념비 accessible a. 접근할 수 있는 footbridge n. 인도교 retreat n. 은신처 serene a. 고요한 woodsy a. 숲의 statue n. 동상 commemorate v. 기념하다 legacy n. 유산 be renowned for ~으로 유명하다 conservation n. 환경 보호 Antiquities Act 골동품 법 secure v. 확보하다 be entwined with ~와 얽혀있다 imperialism n. 제국주의 racial a. 인종적인 Indigenous displacement 원주민 추방 natural resource 천연자원 exploitation n. 착취 stewardship n. 보호, 관리 estate n. 영지 memorialization n. 기념화 checkered past 불완전한 과거, 명암이 섞인 역사 namesake n. 이름 reflect on 성찰하다, 곰곰이 생각하다 auspice n. 길조

11 내용일치 ④

| 분석 |

본문의 "first, stewardship by the Nacotchtank tribe and then development by the Mason family"는 처음에는 나코치탕크 부족이 이 섬을 관리했고, 다음에 메이슨 가문이 섬을 개발했다는 이야기이므로, 메이슨 가문이 나코치탕크 부족을 대체했다고 한 ④는 옳은 진술이다. ① 첫 문장의 stands apart를 '떨어져 있다'는 뜻으로 본다 해도, 처음에는 함께 있다가 지금은 떨어져 있게 된 것인지는 알 수 없다. ② 동상이 아니라 유산이 논란이 되고 있다. ③ 인문학 법이 아니라 골동품 법이다. ⑤ 본문에 "lesser-known retreat"으로, 다른 곳보다 덜 알려져 있다고 했지, 방문객 수에 대한 언급은 없다.

다음 중 올바른 것은?
① 시어도어 루스벨트 섬은 처음에는 내셔널 몰에 자리 잡고 있었다.
② 시어도어 루스벨트의 동상은 논란에 휩싸여 있다.
③ 시어도어 루스벨트는 1906년 인문학 법으로 유명하다.
④ 메이슨 가문은 루스벨트 섬에서 나코치탕크 부족을 대체했다.
⑤ 시어도어 루스벨트 기념물은 방문객이 거의 없다.

12 내용파악 ②

| 분석 |

본문에서 "Roosevelt Island humbly celebrates nature and quietly commemorates Roosevelt's environmental legacy."이라고 하였다. 따라서 자연과 환경 보호를 강조한다는 ②가 답이다. ① 웅장한 것은 내셔널 몰의 대리석 기념비이다. ③ 버지니아에서 보행자 다리로만 접근할 수 있다고 하였다. ④ 군사적 업적에 대한 언급은 없다. ⑤ 노예제는 루스벨트와 관련 없다.

시어도어 루스벨트 섬의 설계를 다른 대통령 기념비들과 비교해서 무엇을 암시하고 있는가?
① 이 기념물은 워싱턴 D.C.의 다른 기념물들보다 더 웅장하다.
② 이 기념물은 정치보다 자연과 환경 보호를 강조하고 있다.
③ 이 기념물은 무엇보다 널리 접근할 수 있도록 설계되었다.
④ 이 기념물은 사회적 이슈보다 군사적 업적을 강조하고 있다.
⑤ 이 기념물은 미국 노예제도라는 유산을 강조하고 있다.

13 동의어 ①

| 분석 |

stewardship은 steward(집사, 청지기, 관리인, 지배인)가 하는 일을 의미하므로 supervision(관리, 감독)이 가장 좋은 동의어이다.

14~16

내가 말하는 '행복 전환'은 어떤 의미인가? 2005년 이후로 계속해서 행복의 과학과 경제학에 관한 수많은 책이 출간되었다는 것은 확실히 사실이다. 치유 문화와 자기 계발 담론의 인기도 행복으로의 전환을 의미해왔다. 이제는 행복해지는 방법에 대해 알려주는 책과 강의들이 많이 있는데, 이들은 동양 전통, 특히 불교의 읽을거리 뿐 아니라 긍정 심리학 분야를 포함한 다양한 지식을 끌어들이고 있다. 지금은 '행복 산업'을 언급하는 일도 흔하다. 행복은 이러한 책을 통해 생산되고 소비되며, 가치를 자본의 한 형태로 축적한다. 바버라 거넬은 "행복 찾기가 어떻게 분명 많은 사람을 부유하게 만들고 있는지 설명한다. 기분을 좋게 하는 산업은 번창하고 있다. 더 많이 성취하는 삶을 약속하는 자기 계발의 책과 CD의 판매는 사상 최고치를 기록하고 있다."
미디어는 행복을 다루는 이미지와 이야기들로 가득 차 있다. 영국에서는 다수의 주요 신문들이 행복에 대한 '특별 기사'를 싣고 있고, BBC는 2006년 "행복 공식"이라는 프로그램을 방영했다. 이러한 행복 전환은 국제적인 현상이라고 할 수 있다. 인터넷에서 '행복한 행성 지수'를 방문할 수 있으며, 민족국가들 내부와 국가들 사이의 행복을 비교 측정하는 많

은 전 세계적 행복 설문 조사 및 보고서들이 발표되었다. 이러한 보고서는 조사 결과가 사회의 예상과 일치하지 않을 때, 즉, 선진국보다 개발도상국이 더 행복한 것으로 나타날 때, 언론에서 종종 인용된다. 한 기사의 첫 문장을 예로 들어 보자. "믿을 것인가? 방글라데시가 세계에서 가장 행복한 나라라니! 반면, 미국은 슬픈 이야기이다. 세계 행복 조사에서 겨우 46위를 기록하다니." 행복과 불행은 특정 개인, 집단, 그리고 국가의 사회적 지위에 대한 생각에 이의를 제기할 때 뉴스 가치를 갖게 되며, 종종 못 믿겠다는 말을 통해 지위를 확인한다.

| 어휘 |

happiness turn 행복 전환 **onward** ad. 계속해서 **therapeutic culture** 치유 문화(정신적·감정적 웰빙을 강조하는 문화) **self-help discourse** 자기 계발 담론(자기 변화와 성공을 강조하는 말들) **instruction** n. 지침 **draw on** 끌어들이다 **positive psychology** 긍정 심리학 **refer to** 언급하다 **accumulate** v. 축적하다 **capital** n. 자본 **saturate with** ~로 가득 차다 **broadsheet newspaper** 주요 신문 **air** v. 방영하다 **survey** n. 설문 조사 **cite** v. 인용하다 **correspond to** 일치하다 **developing country** 개발도상국 **rank** v. 순위를 매기다 **confirm** v. 확인하다 **status** n. 지위 **disbelief** n. 불신, 놀라움 **condescending** a. 거만한 **accusatory** a. 비난하는 **indignant** a. 분개한 **pretentious** a. 가식적인

14 글의 요지   ⑤

| 분석 |

행복의 과학과 경제학에 관한 수많은 책, 치유 문화와 자기 계발 담론, 행복해지는 방법에 관한 책과 강의, 행복 산업에 대한 잦은 언급, 행복 산업의 번창, 행복 관련 이미지와 이야기로 가득 찬 미디어 등, 이 글은 행복에 관한 대중들의 관심이 증가하고 있다는 내용이다.

이 글의 요지는 무엇인가?
① 영국에서 번창하는 행복 산업
② 긍정 심리학 지식의 다양성
③ 행복 전환에 대한 미디어 보도
④ 세상에서 가장 행복한 나라 방글라데시
⑤ 행복에 대한 대중의 관심 증가

15 저자의 어조   ①

| 분석 |

이 글은 행복 전환의 다양한 요소를 분석하는 글이므로 객관적 성격을 띤다. 하지만 행복이 생산되고 소비되고 가치를 자본으로 축적한다는 점, 다시 말해 행복 산업의 자본화에 대해서 비판적이다. 마지막에서는, 행복지수 조사 결과가 선진국 사람들의 예상과 다르게 나왔을 때 못 믿겠다는 반응을 보이는 그들의 사회적 지위에 대한 고정관념을 비판적으로 보고 있다.

16 내용일치   ③

| 분석 |

전 세계적인 설문 조사와 보고서가 믿을만한 것이 아니라, 단지 사회적 예상과 다를 때 뉴스가 될 만하다고 했다. 즉 generally trustworthy가 아니라 sometimes newsworthy이다.

다음 중 올바르지 않은 진술은?
① 자기 계발 담론의 부상은 행복을 우선시하는 방향으로의 변화를 나타낸다.
② 행복 산업은 현재 많은 사람을 부유하게 만들고 있다.
③ 전 세계적인 행복 설문 조사와 보고서는 일반적으로 신뢰할 만하다.
④ '행복 전환' 이후로, 행복은 정량화할 수 있는 재화가 되었다.
⑤ 행복은 사회적 예상과 모순될 때 뉴스 가치가 있다.

17~19

델포이 신탁은 고대 그리스에서 가장 존중받는 상담 장소 중 하나였으며, 신의 지도를 제공하는 역할로 유명했다. 델포이는 아폴로 신에게 헌정된 신성한 장소로, 왕, 전사, 평민 등, 모든 계층의 사람들이 정말 절박한 문제에 대한 답을 찾기 위해 이곳을 찾았다. 이 신비로운 전통의 중심에는 피티아가 있었다. 그녀는 혼수상태에서 아폴로 신의 음성을 전달하는 여사제로 여겨졌다. 그녀의 난해하지만 심오한 예언은 신이 전하는 메시지로 받아들여졌다. 버질과 플루타크 같은 고대 작가들은 이 신탁을 경외심을 담아 기록하며, 이를 신들과 직접 연결된다고 묘사했다.

하지만 현대 과학은 신탁의 초자연적으로 보이는 능력에 대해 흥미로운 설명을 제시하고 있다. 지질학자들은 델포이가 교차하는 단층선 위에 있으며, 따라서 이 지역은 지질 활동이 활발하다고 확정지었다. 이 단층선을 통해 에틸렌과 같은 가스가 지표면으로 스며 나왔을 수 있다. 에틸렌은 도취감과 의식 상태의 변화를 유도하는 것으로 알려져 있는데, 이것이 피티아가 예언 의식 중에 혼수상태에 빠지는 것을 설명할 수 있다. 이러한 과학적 관점은 자연 현상이 델포이 신탁의 신비를 형성하는 데 어떻게 이바지했는지에 관한 합리적인 설명을 제공한다.

델포이 신탁은 여전히 고대 영성의 지속적인 상징이지만, 그 이야기는 또 인간의 믿음과 자연 세계 사이의 상호작용을 잘 보여준다. 우리는 역사적 설명과 현대 지질학적 통찰을 함께 살펴봄으로써, 신화와 과학이 어떻게 교차할 수 있는지를 더 깊이 이해하게 된다.

| 어휘 |

oracle n. 신탁   revered a. 존경받는   consultation n. 자문
site n. 장소   divine guidance 신의 계시   sacred a. 신성한
dedicate v. 헌정하다, 바치다   all walks of life 각계각층   warrior
n. 전사   pressing a. 절박한   priestess n. 여사제   channel
v. 실어 나르다   trance n. 혼수상태   cryptic a. 난해한   profound
a. 심오한   compelling a. 흥미로운   supernatural a. 초자연적인
geological activity 지질 활동   intersect v. 교차하다   fault lines
단층선   be prone to ~하는 경향이 있다   seep through 스며 나오다
induce v. 초래하다   euphoria n. 도취감   state of consciousness
의식 상태   ritual n. 의식   rational a. 합리적인   mystique n.
신비로움   enduring a. 지속적인   highlight v. 강조하다   insight
n. 지식   appreciation n. 이해   debunk v. 거짓을 증명하다
previsioning n. 예지

17 글의 제목   ③

| 분석 |

현대의 지질학적 관점이 델포이 신탁에 대한 진실을 밝혀주고 있다는 내용이다. 따라서 신탁이 들려준 신화적인 이야기에 대해 지질학이 과학적인 설명을 제시하며 그 실체를 탐구하고 있다는 ③이 정답이다. 델포이 신탁에 관한 글이므로 신탁이 제목에 들어가야 한다.

이 글의 제목으로 가장 적절한 것은?
① 피티아의 예언: 고대 그리스 점술의 역사
② 에틸렌과 인간 정신: 변화된 상태에 대한 연구
③ 신탁의 속살임: 신화, 지질학, 그리고 진리를 향한 탐구
④ 초자연적인 것의 탐구: 고대 그리스의 종교와 관습
⑤ 예언의 심리학: 고대 신앙 이해

18 내용파악   ②

| 분석 |

현대 과학은 지질학이 밝혀낸 사실을 통해 신탁의 초자연적으로 보이는 능력을 자연적으로 설명한 것이므로 ②가 정답이다. ③ 정확성에 대한 언급은 없다. ④ 배제하지 않고 포함했다. ⑤ 에틸렌이 트랜스를 유발한다고 확증한 것이 아니라 유발할 가능성을 제시했을 뿐이다. 'may have allowed'와 'could explain'은 단정 지어 말하는 것이 아니라 가능성을 말한다.

이 글에 입각해 볼 때, 현대 과학과 델포이 신탁에 대한 고대 믿음 사이의 관계를 가장 잘 설명하고 있는 것은?
① 현대 과학은 델포이 신탁을 둘러싼 고대의 믿음이 거짓임을 입증했다.
② 현대 과학은 신탁에 대한 가능한 자연적 설명을 제시했다.
③ 현대 과학은 신탁의 예언이 종종 정확했음을 증명했다.
④ 현대 과학은 신탁의 예지에서 지질학의 역할을 배제했다.
⑤ 현대 과학은 피티아의 혼수상태가 에틸렌 때문이라는 것을 확증했다.

19 내용추론   ②

| 분석 |

각계각층의 사람들이 절박한 문제에 대한 해답을 찾아 신탁에 의지했으므로, 신이 인간사에 개입한다고 보아야 한다. ①은 불개입을 의미한다. ③ 합리적인 설명은 현대의 지질학이 제시하고 있다. ④ 사람 제물에 대한 언급은 없다. ⑤ 현대에 와서야 지질학적 요소가 밝혀지고 있다.

이 글에 입각해 볼 때, 고대 그리스인들의 자연계와 신에 대한 이해에 관해서 추론할 수 있는 것은?
① 그들은 자연계와 신의 영역이 완전히 분리되어 있다고 믿었다.
② 그들은 신이 인간사에 매우 직접적으로 개입한다고 이해했다.
③ 그들은 초자연적인 주장에 회의적이었으며, 합리적인 설명을 원했다.
④ 그들은 사람을 제물로 바치는 것이 신과 소통하는 방법이라고 여겼다.
⑤ 그들은 델포이 신탁에 관련된 지질학적 요소를 알고 있었다.

20~21

우리가 아는 대중 콘서트는 18세기가 되어서야 존재했다. 공식적인 콘서트를 위한 최초의 콘서트홀 중 하나는 1711년 런던에서 토마스 힉퍼드가 열었다. 그때부터 유럽 전역에서 계속해서 맞춤형으로 지어진 콘서트홀과 오페라 하우스가 등장하기 시작했다. 독일의 음악 후원자들은 웅장한 규모로 콘서트홀을 건설했다. 슈베칭겐에서는 팔츠 선제후가 5,000명의 관객을 수용할 수 있는 오페라 하우스를 새로 만들었고, 한편, 뷔르템베르크의 카를 테오도어 공작은 만하임에 화려한 오페라 공연을 제공하기 위해 자신의 공국의 재정을 탕진했다. 베를린 오페라 하우스는 프로이센의 프리드리히 대왕이 지었다. 유명한 플루트 연주자이자 음악 후원자였던 그는 프랑스 문화에 깊이 빠져 있었고, 궁정에서 프랑스어를 사용하도록 했다. 런던에서는 목적에 따라 설계된 콘서트홀이 여러 개 세워졌는데, 칼라일 하우스(1764년), 판테온(1772년), 하노버 스퀘어 룸(1775년)이 있었다. 19세기 내내 런던 콘서트들에 참여한 오케스트라들에는 동일한 연주자들이 매우 많이 포함되어 있었기 때문에, 각 오케스트라를 서로 다른 오케스트라라고 묘사하기 어려웠을 것이다.

| 어휘 |

from then on 그때부터 계속해서   custom-built a. 맞춤 제작된
patron n. 후원자   on a grand scale 대규모로, 웅장하게   Elector
n. 선제후(신성 로마 제국에서 황제 선출권을 가진 제후)   bankrupt

v. 파산시키다　**principality** n. 공국(작은 군주국)　**sensational** a. 선풍적인　**be immersed in** ~에 몰두하다　**purpose-built** a. 특정 목적을 위해 설계된　**audience capacity** 관객 수용 능력

20　빈칸완성　　　　　　　　　　　　　④

| 분석 |

첫 번째 문장에는 글의 주제가 필요하다. 18세기의 대중 콘서트와 콘서트홀에 대한 글이므로 ④가 빈칸에 적절하다. ③ 작곡가나 연주가와 같은 음악가들이 짓지 않았다.

① 17세기에는 유럽 전역에 콘서트홀이 널리 퍼져 있었다.
② 유럽의 콘서트홀과 오페라 하우스는 한 세기에 걸친 역사를 가지고 있다.
③ 대중 콘서트홀은 18세기에 음악가들에 의해 처음 설립되었다.
④ 오늘날 우리가 알고 있는 형태의 대중 콘서트는 18세기가 되어서야 존재했다.
⑤ 18세기에 런던은 음악 공연의 중심지였다.

21　빈칸완성　　　　　　　　　　　　　②

| 분석 |

뒤에 보면, 선제후나 대왕, 군주 같은 사람들이 콘서트홀을 지었다고 했다. 이들을 모두 가리키는 것은 음악을 좋아하는 사람, 또는 후원자라는 의미의 ② patron이다. ③ 일부 prince인 사람도 있지만 '음악의 왕'이라고 할 수는 없다.

22~24

잘 알려진 문학 작품의 새로운 번역 출간은 단순히 기존 텍스트를 다시 표현하는 문제에서 그치지 않는다. 이는 이러한 작품들을 현대 독자들이 더욱 공감할 수 있는 방식으로 다시 소개할 기회이기도 하다. 언어, 문화적 맥락, 그리고 학문적 이해는 지속적으로 발전하기 때문에 가장 상징적이고 자주 번역되는 작품들이라도 새로운 접근 방식에서 이득을 얻을 수 있다. 따라서, 고전 문학 작품의 새로운 번역은 정확성을 확보하고 적합성을 유지하고 풍부한 뉘앙스를 갖게 하는 데 필수적이다.

먼저, 초기 번역본들은 때로는 오류를 포함한 원전에 기반을 두고 있으며, 이 오류들은 그 이후 연구 및 문헌학적 연구를 통해 수정되었다. 출처 텍스트에 대한 새로운 발견이 등장함에 따라 이러한 지식은 원작을 보다 정확하고 충실하게 재현하는 결과를 낳을 수 있다. 이는 번역이 기존에 남아 있던 오해나 잘못된 해석을 그대로 이어가지 않고, 작가의 진정한 의도를 반영하도록 보장한다.

게다가, 과거의 번역가들은 자신들 시대의 문화적·사회적 규범에 영향을 받았으며, 이는 텍스트 해석에도 영향을 미칠 수 있다. 한때 적절하다고 여겨졌던 언어가 이제는 구식으로 느껴질 수 있으며, 한 시대에 받아들여졌던 표현이 현대적 감수성과는 공감되지 않을 수도 있다. 낡은 번역들은 또 그 당시의 가치관이나 기대치에 맞춰 수정되었을 수도 있고, 이로 인해 낡은 번역들은 우리가 사는 세계와 단절된 느낌을 줄 수 있다.

게다가, 번역은 항상 개선의 여지가 있다. 아무리 과거 최고의 번역본이라도 원문의 뉘앙스를 완벽히 포착하지 못했을 가능성이 있다. 새로운 번역은 신선한 관점을 제공하며, 오늘날의 독자들에게 더욱 직접적으로 이야기할 수 있도록 텍스트를 다듬을 기회를 제공한다. 최신 번역 기법과 문화적 이해를 통합함으로써, 새로운 번역본은 더욱 풍부하고 진정성 있는 경험을 제공할 수 있다.

결국, 새로운 번역은 우리에게 낯익은 작품에 새로운 생명력을 불어넣어, 현대의 독자들이 다시 발견하고 감상할 수 있게 해준다. 이들은 새로운 시각을 제공하며, 이전에는 간과되었던 미묘한 의미들을 강조할 수 있다. 그리고 이를 통해 시대를 초월한 걸작들이 미래 세대에게도 여전히 적합하고, 매력적인 작품이 될 수 있도록 만든다.

| 어휘 |

rewording n. 다시 표현하기　**reintroduce** v. 다시 소개하다　**resonate with** 공감되다　**iconic** a. 대표적인　**evolve** v. 발전하다　**textual scholarship** 문헌학적 연구　**representation** n. 재현　**ensure** v. 보장하다　**perpetuate** v. 영속화하다　**linger** v. 지속하다　**misinterpretation** n. 오해, 잘못된 해석　**outdated** a. 시대에 뒤떨어진　**modern sensibilities** 현대적 감수성　**altered** a. 변경된, 수정된　**align with** 동조하다　**disconnect** n. 단절, 괴리　**room** n. 여지　**refine** v. 다듬다　**authentic** a. 진정한　**breathe new life** 새로운 생명을 불어넣다　**subtlety** n. 미묘한 차이　**overlook** v. 간과하다　**relevant** a. 적합한　**engaging** a. 매력적인, 호감이 가는　**expediency** n. 편의　**equivalency** n. 등가　**vested interests** 기득권　**autonomy** n. 자율성

22　빈칸완성　　　　　　　　　　　　　③

| 분석 |

본문 두 번째 단락 이하에서 새로운 번역은 정확성(accuracy), 그 시대에 어울리는 감각, 혹은 적합성(relevance), 미묘한 표현(nuance) 등을 위해 반드시 해야 하는 것이라고 강조하고 있다.

다음 중 1문단의 빠져있는 주제문을 가장 잘 완성시키는 것은?
① 의도를 명확히 하고 문화적 맥락을 변화시키고 매력을 증가시키는 것
② 모호성을 제거하고 스타일을 현대화하고 텍스트를 소화할 수 있게 하는 것

③ 정확성을 확보하고 적합성을 유지하고 풍부한 뉘앙스를 갖게 하는 것
④ 주제를 재해석하고 어조를 조정하고 표현을 교체하는 것
⑤ 의미를 보존하고 언어를 단순화하고 참조 문헌을 업데이트하는 것

23 내용파악   ①

| 분석 |

본문에서 오류를 포함한 원전에 기반을 둔 초기 번역본들이 있는데, 새로운 지식을 통해 정확하고 충실한 원전을 구성하고, 이를 통해 진정한 의도를 반영할 수 있다고 하였다. 따라서 원전의 오류는 작가의 진정한 의도를 왜곡할 수 있다.

작가의 '진정한 의도'에 해를 끼칠 수도 있는 것은?
① 원전의 오류
② 형편없는 새로운 번역본
③ 저자가 살던 시대의 사회적 규범
④ 현대 독자의 감수성
⑤ 이해의 결핍과 모호성

24 동의어   ①

| 분석 |

nuance는 '미묘한 의미 차이'라는 뜻이므로 subtlety(섬세함, 미묘함, 세밀한 구별)가 가장 좋은 동의어이다.

25~27

1963년 핵실험 금지 조약은 핵 외교에서뿐 아니라, 환경의 중요성에 대한 전 세계적 인식의 증가에서도 중요한 계기였다. 이 조약은 대기 중 핵실험을 중단함으로써 방사성 낙진의 광범위한 영향을 조명하고, 인간 활동과 자연 세계가 긴밀히 연결되어 있음을 강조했다. 당시의 세 주요 핵보유국이었던 미국, 소련, 영국이 서명한 이 조약은 대기권, 우주, 수중 핵실험을 금지했다. 하지만, 냉전이라는 지정학적 현실과 핵 기술 발전에 대한 지속적인 열망을 반영하여 지하 핵실험은 여전히 허용되었다.

이 협정은 1950년대와 1960년대 초 대기 중 핵실험이 급증하면서 광범위하게 배출되어 심각한 환경 오염 물질이 된 방사성 낙진에 대한 대중과 과학계의 우려가 커지면서 그에 대한 대응으로 등장했다. 낙진은 스트론튬-90, 세슘-137과 같은 방사성 동위원소로 구성되었으며, 바람의 흐름에 따라 광범위한 지역으로 퍼져 토양, 물, 채소에 스며들었다. 이러한 동위원소는 오염된 농작물, 가축, 식수를 통해 먹이 사슬에 유입되며 생태계와 인간 건강에 심각한 위험을 초래했다. 예를 들어, 특히 좀처럼 분해되지 않는 방사성 동위원소인 스트론튬-90은 뼈와 치아에 축적되는 것으로 밝혀져, 암이나 유전적 돌연변이 같은 장기적인 건강 문제에 대한 우려를 불러일으켰다.

방사성 낙진을 둘러싼 과학적 연구 조사는 환경 의식을 높이는 데 중요한 역할을 했다. 이러한 방사성 입자의 확산과 영향 연구는 생태계의 미묘한 균형과 더불어 지속적인 오염 물질이 초래하는 위험을 밝혀냈다. 과학자들, 환경운동가들, 그리고 우려하는 시민들은 환경 위협이 전 지구적인 성격을 띠고 있으며 이를 해결하기 위해 국제적 협력이 필요하다는 사실을 인식하기 시작했다.

궁극적으로, 핵실험 금지 조약은 환경 관리에 대한 대중의 이해에서 전환점이 되었다. 이 조약은 인간 활동이 초래하는 환경적 결과를 직접적으로 다루면서, 이후 환경 운동의 초석을 놓았다. 대기 오염 제한에 성공한 이 조약은 과학 연구, 대중의 인식, 그리고 국제적 협력이 결합하여 전 지구적인 위기를 완화할 수 있다는 강력한 사례를 제공했다. 이러한 접근 방식은 산업 오염, 삼림 벌채, 기후 변화와 같은 다른 환경 문제와 싸우기 위한 후속 노력을 고무하는 계기가 되었다.

| 어휘 |

pivotal moment 전환점 **consequence** n. 중요성 **halt** v. 중단하다 **shed light on** 조명하다 **far-reaching** a. 광범위한, (영향 따위) 멀리까지 미치는 **radioactive fallout** 방사성 낙진 **underscore** v. 강조하다 **interconnectedness** n. 상호 연결성 **power** n. 강대국 **of the time** 당대의 **prohibit** v. 금지하다 **outer space** 우주 **geopolitical realities** 지정학적 현실 **Cold War** 냉전 **concern** n. 우려 **surge** n. 급상승 **isotope** n. 동위원소 **contaminated** a. 오염된 **persistent** a. 지속적인 **pollutant** n. 오염 물질 **infiltrate** v. 침투하다, 잠입하다 **food chain** 먹이 사슬 **persistent** a. 분해가 되지 않는 **accumulate** v. 축적되다 **long-term** a. 장기적인 **genetic mutation** 유전적 돌연변이 **scrutiny** n. 정밀 조사 **delicate** a. 미묘한; 섬세한 **environmental consciousness** 환경 의식 **dispersion** n. 산포 **environmental stewardship** 환경 관리 **deforestation** n. 삼림 벌채 **converge** v. 수렴하다, 결합하다 **mitigate** v. 완화하다 **rift** n. 균열

25 글의 제목   ④

| 분석 |

낙진에 대한 우려가 핵실험 금지의 원인이 되었고, 더 나아가 오늘날의 환경 의식으로까지 이어졌다는 내용의 글이다. ① 핵 군축이 아니라 환경 보호를 이야기하고 있다. ② 글의 주제는 핵실험 금지 조약이 환경 의식 형성에 어떻게 이바지했는지를 다루고 있다. 핵실험 금지의 원인은 그보다 중요하지 않다. ③ 핵 전체의 역사를 원자폭탄부터 설명하지 않고 있다. ⑤ 방사성 낙진의 위험은 언급

되었으나 수명에 미치는 영향에 대한 언급은 없고, 제목이 되기에는 너무 지엽적이다.

이 글의 제목으로 가장 적절한 것은?
① 대기 중 핵실험 금지: 핵 군축의 승리
② 과학 연구와 대중의 우려: 핵실험 금지를 추진한 원동력
③ 핵 시대의 유산: 원자폭탄에서 환경주의까지
④ 낙진에서 의식으로: 핵실험 금지 조약의 환경적 유산
⑤ 방사성 낙진의 위험성: 스트론튬-90과 인간 수명에 미치는 영향

26 내용파악 ①

| 분석 |

첫 번째 문장부터 핵실험 금지 조약이 환경적 영향에 대한 인식이 증가하는 중요한 전환점이 되었다고 설명하고 있다. ③ 기후 변화 운동은 나중의 노력이라고 하였다. ⑤ 환경 관리 개념을 만들었지, 환경 정화 노력을 추진했다는 말은 없다. 관리와 정화는 다르다.

1963년 핵 실험 금지 조약이 전환점이라고 간주되는 이유는?
① 이 조약은 인간 활동이 환경에 미치는 영향을 국제적으로 인식하는 순간을 보여주었다.
② 이 조약은 핵 군축 문제와 국제 협력의 필요성을 전면에 부각했다.
③ 이 조약은 우리가 알고 있는 환경주의를 탄생시켰으며, 특히 기후 변화 운동을 초래했다.
④ 이 조약은 우주를 중립적인 국제 구역으로 보존하는 첫걸음이었다.
⑤ 이 조약은 환경 정화 노력과 지속적인 오염 물질 제거 노력을 시작하게 했다.

27 내용추론 ②

| 분석 |

방사성 낙진의 위험성에 대해 과학 연구가 그 폐해를 밝히면서 환경 의식이 고조되었으므로 방사성 낙진이 환경주의와 과학연구를 함께 일어나게 했다고 할 수 있다.

이 글에서 추론할 수 있는 것은?
① 핵실험 금지는 과학과 환경주의 사이의 첫 번째 주요 균열이었다.
② 핵실험에서 발생한 방사성 낙진은 환경주의와 과학을 결합했다.
③ 과학의 자율성에 대한 기득권의 지배력은 여전히 문제이다.
④ 핵실험 금지는 기후 운동가들이 직면할 문제를 예고했다.
⑤ 핵실험 문제는 다시 주요한 문제로 떠오를 가능성이 있다.

28~30

정신-육체 이원론의 문제 — '정신'이 물리적 뇌와 어떻게 연결되는가에 관한 논쟁 — 는 사고와 정신 조직을 오직 물리적 현상에서만 일어나는 것으로 이해하려는 현대 인지 과학에 근본적인 도전을 제기하고 있다. 고대 철학자 플라톤의 생각부터 현대 사상가 르네 데카르트의 의견에 이르기까지, 정신-육체 이원론 개념은 비물질적이며 나눌 수 없는 '정신'은 물리적 현상만으로는 온전히 설명될 수 없다고 주장해왔다.

이러한 철학적 입장은 의식을 물리적 뇌 과정의 결과로 설명하려는 인지 과학의 목표에 중대한 장애가 된다. 만일 정신이 물리적 차원과 별개의 영역에서 작동한다면, 유물론에 기반한 과학이 두 개념을 어떻게 조화시킬 수 있을까? 철학자 데이비드 차머스는 지각, 기억, 의사 결정 같은 것과 관련된 '쉬운' 인지 기능의 문제와 '어려운' 의식의 문제를 구분함으로써 이 논의를 더욱 복잡하게 만든다. 예를 들어, 차머스는 왜 특정한 뇌 과정에는 주관적 경험이 동반되지만, 다른 뇌 과정에는 그렇지 않은지 의문을 제기하여, 이 논쟁에 또 하나의 복잡성을 더하고 있다.

차머스의 분석은 중요한 문제를 부각하고 있다. 인지 과학은 예를 들어 뇌가 정보를 처리하고 행동을 가능하게 하는 방식과 같은, 의식의 기능적 측면을 설명할 수 있다. 하지만 의식하는 것이 '어떤 느낌인가'라는 경험적 특성을 설명하는 데는 어려움을 겪는다. 흔히 '설명적 간극'이라 불리는 이러한 이해의 공백은 여전히 심오한 형이상학적 수수께끼로 남아 있다. 따라서 정신-육체 이원론은 단순히 인지 과학의 연구 범위를 도전하는 것에 그치지 않는다. 이 이원론은 '정신'의 형이상학적 특이성을 주장함으로써, 인지 과학의 토대를 뒤흔든다.

| 어휘 |

dualism n. 이원론 **cognitive science** 인지 과학 **musing** n. 묵상, 숙고, 생각 **pronouncement** n. 의견 **non-material** a. 비물질적인 **indivisible** a. 나눌 수 없는 **obstacle** n. 장애 **plane** n. 차원, 영역 **operate** v. 작동하다 **materialism** n. 유물론 **complicate** v. 복잡하게 만들다 **inquiry** n. 탐구 **metaphysical quandary** 형이상학적 수수께끼 **perception** n. 지각 **discipline** n. 학문

28 글의 제목 ③

| 분석 |

정신-육체 이원론이 인지 과학에 난제를 제시하고 있다고 하면서, 그 난제란 무엇인지를 설명하는 글이다.

이 글의 제목으로 가장 적절한 것은?
① 인지 기능과 뇌 과정: 지각, 기억, 사고 이해하기
② 정신 철학: 의식에 대한 고대와 현대의 관점 탐구
③ 의식의 어려운 문제: 마음–몸 이원론이 인지 과학에 제기하는 도전
④ 유물론과 정신 연구: 물리적 과정이 의식을 설명할 수 있는가
⑤ 의식의 과학: 오늘날의 포스트–인지 연구에서의 발전과 도전

29 내용파악   ⑤

| 분석 |

마지막 문단에서 "cognitive science can address the functional aspects of consciousness — how the brain processes information and enables behaviors — but it struggles to explain the experiential qualities of consciousness, the 'what it's like' of being aware." 인지 과학은 의식의 기능적 측면은 설명할 수 있지만, 의식하는 것이 '어떤 느낌인지'를 설명하는 데는 어려움을 겪는다고 하였다. 이 '의식하는 것이 어떤 느낌인지가 바로 경험적이고, 주관적인 차원이다. ①은 기능적 측면이라 충분히 설명할 수 있다.

차머스에 따르면 인지 과학이 직면하고 있는 가장 커다란 문제는?
① 뇌가 정보를 처리하고 행동을 가능하게 하는 방식을 설명하는 것
② 플라톤과 르네 데카르트가 제기한 도전에 답하는 것
③ 자신들의 연구가 과학의 범위를 벗어난다는 것을 인정하는 것
④ 육체–정신 일원론자들이 자신의 견해를 재고해보도록 설득하는 것
⑤ 의식의 경험적 측면을 설명하는 것

30 빈칸완성   ⑤

| 분석 |

결국 육체–정신 이원론이 물리적 과정만으로 의식을 설명할 수 있다는 (유물론에 토대를 둔) 인지 과학의 근본적인 전제에 도전하고 있다는 내용이었다. 결론 부분이므로, 주제와 비슷한 내용이 될 수밖에 없다. ⑤의 the discipline은 인지 과학을 가리킨다.

빈칸에 적절한 말은?
① 플라톤과 데카르트의 연구에 의문을 제기한다.
② 자신의 적절성을 의문시한다.
③ 학문 간 대화를 위한 길을 연다.
④ '설명적 간극' 문제를 해결한다.
⑤ 이 학문의 근본적인 토대를 뒤흔든다.

SOGANG UNIVERSITY | 서강대학교 2차

TEST p. 314~329

01	②	02	④	03	⑤	04	②	05	②	06	⑤	07	③	08	①	09	④	10	②
11	③	12	③	13	③	14	③	15	⑤	16	①	17	④	18	②	19	①	20	①
21	⑤	22	②	23	①	24	③	25	④	26	⑤	27	②	28	①	29	④	30	①

01 논리완성   ②

| 분석 |
노동자들의 파업 이유는 협상에 문제가 있어서라고 할 수 있으므로, 협상이 잘 진척되지 않고 머뭇거리다, 지지부진하다는 흐름을 완성시키는 falter가 정답으로 적절하다.

| 어휘 |
labor union 노조 **walk off the job** 파업하다 **contact** n. 계약 **negotiation** n. 협상 **dispel** v. 해산시키다 **falter** v. 비틀거리다, 머뭇거리다 **bask** v. 햇볕을 쬐다 **gall** v. 스쳐서 벗기다; 짜증나게 하다 **lull** v. 잠잠해지다

| 해석 |
노동조합은 미국 전역에 걸친 10,000개 이상의 매장 중 약 300개 매장에서 계약 협상이 지지부진하기 때문에 노동자들이 파업하고 있다고 말한다.

02 논리완성   ④

| 분석 |
직접 거절당할 수는 없어서 다른 거절당할 수도 있는 사람을 보냈다는 의미가 되어야 한다. 정부나 정치지도자가 보내는 사람이 emissary(사절, 사신, 밀사)이다. ①의 interloper는 허락도 없이 끼어드는 사람이라는 의미이므로 답이 될 수 없다.

| 어휘 |
woo v. 구애하다 **commoner** n. 평민 **on one's behalf** 대신에 **interloper** n. 침입자 **peddler** n. 행상인 **outrider** n. 선도 기수 **emissary** n. 사절 **despot** n. 폭군

| 해석 |
공작은 엘리자베스와 사랑에 빠졌지만, 그녀에게 구애하려는 처음 몇 번의 시도는 실패했다. 문제는 그가 평민에게 청혼할 수 없었다는 점이었다. 왕의 아들로서, 그는 거절당할 가능성이 있는 상태에 자신을 처하게 만들 수 없었기 때문이었다. 그런 이유로, 그는 그녀에게 자신의 결혼 제안을 대신 전달해 줄 사절을 보냈다.

03 to 부정사   ⑤

| 분석 |
'~하는 능력'은 'ability of 동명사'가 아니라 'ability to+동사원형'으로 나타내므로 ⑤를 to perform으로 고쳐야 한다.

| 어휘 |
watershed moment 획기적인 순간, 중대한 전환점 **due to** ~때문에 **unprecedented** a. 전례 없는 **parameter** n. 매개변수 **execute** v. 실행하다, 수행하다 **fine-tuning** n. 미세 조정 **generate** v. 생성하다 **engage in** ~에 참여하다, 관여하다 **few-shot learning** 소수 표본 학습 **commercial applications** 상업적 응용, 실용적 활용 **virtual** a. 가상의

| 해석 |
GPT-3는 별도의 광범위한 미세 조정 없이도 다양한 자연어 처리 작업을 수행할 수 있는 1,750억 개의 파라미터를 갖춘 유례없는 규모 때문에 AI 분야의 획기적인 전환점이 되었다. 이 모델은 빅데이터를 활용하여 훈련되었으며, 인간과 같은 텍스트를 생성하고 대화를 나눌 수 있었다. 그것은 또한 소수의 예제만으로 학습하는 능력을 갖추고 있었으며, 이는 챗봇 및 가상 비서와 같은 상업적 AI 애플리케이션에서의 그것의 유용성을 입증했다.

04 일치   ②

| 분석 |
'Neither A nor B'는 A와 B 어떤 것도 아니라는 의미이며, 동사는 B에 일치시킨다. 여기서는 mechanics가 복수이므로 ②를 'were able to'로 고쳐야 한다.

| 어휘 |
scheduled to ~할 예정인 **depart** v. 출발하다 **on time** 정시에 **delay** n. 지연 **mechanic** n. 정비사 **figure out** 알아내다, 해결하다 **display** v. 표시하다 **frustrated** a. 짜증이 난 **assess** v. 평가하다 **malfunction** v. 오작동하다 **clear** v. 이착륙을 허가하다 **takeoff** n. 이륙 **lingering** a. 남아 있는 **irritation** n. 짜증

| 해석 |

비행기는 정시에 출발하도록 일정이 잡혀 있었지만, 예상치 못한 문제가 발생하여 지연되었다. 조종사도 정비사들도 비행기에 경고 메시지가 표시된 원인을 알아낼 수 없었다. 터미널에서 대기 중이던 승객들은 아무런 새로운 소식 없이 시간이 흐르면서 점점 더 짜증을 느꼈다. 결국에는 한 수석 엔지니어가 호출 받고 상황을 평가한 다음 센서의 오작동을 발견했다. 수리가 완료된 후, 비행기는 이륙 허가를 받았으며 승객들은 안도감과 여전히 남아 있는 짜증이 뒤섞인 채 탑승했다.

05 관계대명사   ②

| 분석 |

②에 쓰인 who의 선행사는 paintings이므로 이것을 사물을 받는 관계대명사 which로 고쳐야 한다.

| 어휘 |

employ v. 사용하다   propaganda n. 선전   get behind 지지하다
impressionistic a. 인상주의적인   teeter on the edge of ~의 위태로운 상황에 있다   bolster v. 강화하다   barbarity n. 잔혹성

| 해석 |

제1차 세계대전 동안, 미술 작품은 미국 정부에 의해 선전 목적으로 활용되어 미국 국민이 전쟁을 지지하도록 독려하는 데 사용되었다. 예를 들어, 미국 국기로 가득 찬 도시 거리를 묘사한 차일드 하삼의 인상파 그림들은 널리 알려져 전쟁 직전 불안정한 상태에 있던 국가에서 애국심을 불러일으켰다. 나중에는, 전쟁으로 지친 국민의 사기를 북돋우기 위해, 적의 잔혹한 모습을 강렬하게 묘사한 조지 벨로우즈의 작품들이 전쟁에서의 희생을 고귀하면서도 불가피한 것으로 정당화하는 데 사용되었다.

06 문장배열   ⑤

| 분석 |

ⓒ 기후를 결정하는 변수들로 시작해서, Ⓑ 그러한 변수에 영향을 미치는 판 구조 이동을 이야기하고, Ⓓ 다음에는 판 구조 이동에 영향을 받지 않는 다른 동적인 결정 요인을 설명하며, 해양의 열염순환과 Ⓐ 해류를 다룬다. 그리고 Ⓔ에서 결국 세계적인 장기적 요인과 지역적 요인이 기후를 결정한다는 결론을 맺는다.

| 어휘 |

extended time span 장기간에 걸친 시간   constant variable 일정한 변수   latitude n. 위도   altitude n. 고도   proportion n. 비율   gradual shifting 점진적인 이동   tectonic plate 판 구조   thermohaline circulation 열염순환(해양에서 염분과 온도 차이에 의해 발생하는 해류)   redistribute v. 재분배하다   scale n. 규모

| 해석 |

ⓒ 장기간에 걸쳐, 위도, 고도, 육지와 물의 비율, 해양 및 산맥과의 근접성과 같은 많은 거의 일정한 변수들이 기후를 결정한다. Ⓑ 그러나 이러한 변수들은 점진적인 판 구조의 점진적인 이동으로 인한 변화 때문에 바뀌기도 한다. Ⓓ 다른 기후 결정 요인들은 좀 더 동적이다. 예를 들어 해양 열염순환은 북대서양의 온도를 다른 해양분지에 비해 5°C(9°F) 더 높이는 역할을 한다. Ⓐ 마찬가지로, 해류는 육지와 물 사이에서 열을 재분배하지만, 보다 지역적인 규모에서 이루어진다. Ⓔ 결국, 기후 상태는 세계적인 장기적 요인과 지역적인 동적 요인의 결과이다.

07~09

광범위한 의학사 서술에서 흔히 간과되어온 고대 메소포타미아 문화는 현대의 외상 후 스트레스 장애와 유사한 증상을 포함한 심리적 외상에 대한 놀라울 정도로 발전된 이해를 보여주었다. 최근 연구는 메소포타미아인들이 이러한 질병을 전통적으로 PTSD에 대한 최초의 설명을 한 것으로 평가되는 고대 그리스인들보다 훨씬 이전에 인식하고 치료했다는 것을 시사하는 증거를 밝혀냈다. 이러한 발견은 정신 건강 분야에서 그리스인들이 개척자라는 기존의 관점에 도전하는 동시에 초기 의학 지식의 복잡성을 부각하고 있다. 메소포타미아에서는 외상을 전체론적 관점으로 바라보고, 정신과 육체 모두를 위해 영적인 믿음을 치료와 혼합했다. 이 지역의 주요 문명 중 하나였던 아시리아인은 의학 문헌에 PTSD와 유사한 증상을 기록했는데, 이러한 증상에는 반복적인 환영, 악몽, 감정적 고통, 마음의 동요 등이 포함되었다. 이러한 질병들은 종종 살해된 적들의 불안한 영혼 때문이라고 여겨졌는데, 이것은 사후 세계와 영혼의 힘에 대한 메소포타미아인의 이해에 깊이 뿌리박고 있는 믿음이었다. 이러한 증상들을 치료하기 위해, 메소포타미아의 사제와 치유사들은 다양한 치료법을 사용했다. 여기에는 정신을 안정시키고 몸의 균형을 회복하려는 목적의 의약 요법뿐 아니라 화난 영혼들을 달래기 위한 의식 및 주문도 포함되었다. 치유 과정은 단순히 신체적 치료에 그치지 않고, 영적, 감정적 치유까지 포함되었는데, 이는 메소포타미아인들이 정신, 육체, 영혼의 상호연결성을 인식하고 있었다는 점을 강조한다.
메소포타미아인들이 사용한 방법은 정신 건강관리에 대한 현대적 접근 방식과 현저히 다르긴 하지만, 외상을 완화하려는 그들의 노력은 심리적 고통을 겪는 개인들의 행복을 위한 지속적인 인간의 관심을 반영하고 있다. 고대 문헌은 정신 건강을 다루는 오늘날의 노력과 일치하는 세심하고 공감적인 치유 접근법을 보여준다. 이러한 심리적 외상의 이해와 치료에 대한 초기의 기여는 정신에 미치는 외상의 영향을 이해하고 완화하려는 인간의 오랜 욕구를 보여주며, 정신 건강관리의 역사에 대한 귀중한 통찰을 제공하고 있다.

| 어휘 |

overlook v. 간과하다 **medical history** 의학사 **psychological trauma** 심리적 외상 **post-traumatic stress disorder** 외상 후 스트레스 장애(PTSD) **uncover** v. 밝히다 **be aware of** 자각하다 **address** v. 치료하다 **condition** n. 질병 **be credited with** ~라는 평판이 있다 **conventional** a. 기존의 **pioneer** n. 선구자 **highlight** v. 강조하다, 눈에 띄게 하다 **holistic lens** 전체론적 관점 **blend** v. 섞다 **treatment** n. 치료 **symptom** n. 증상 **recurring** a. 반복되는 **vision** n. 환영 **nightmare** n. 악몽 **agitation** n. 불안, 초조 **affliction** n. 고통 **restless** a. 불안한, 침착하지 못한 **slay** v. 살해하다 **afterlife** n. 사후 세계 **therapeutic** a. 치료의 **ritual** n. 제식 **incantation** n. 주문, 주술 **appease** v. 달래다, 진정시키다 **encompass** v. 포함하다 **underscore** v. 강조하다 **alleviate** v. 완화하다 **empathetic** a. 공감적인 **resonate with** 공명하다, 깊이 연관되다 **mitigate** v. 달래다

07 글의 제목 ③

| 분석 |

고대 메소포타미아인들이 그리스 사람들 이전에 PTSD 증상을 인식하고 치료하려고 했던 노력을 역사적으로 재평가하고 있는 글이다. ① 정신 질환에 대한 관심에 국한된다. ⑤ 정신과 신체에 대한 믿음이 아니라 정신 질환에 대한 믿음과 접근법이다.

이 글의 제목으로 가장 적절한 것은?
① 고대 메소포타미아의 의학: 신체적·영적 질병에 대한 치료
② 메소포타미아의 영혼: 사후 세계에 대한 믿음과 그 영향
③ 그리스인 이전: PTSD 유사 증상에 대한 메소포타미아의 통찰
④ 고대 문명과 정신 건강: 고대 문화 비교 연구
⑤ 정신과 육체에 대한 메소포타미아의 믿음: 전체론적 접근법

08 내용파악 ①

| 분석 |

본문 두 번째 문단에서 메소포타미아인들은 외상을 전체론적으로, 다시 말해 육체와 정신, 그리고 영적인 요소가 연결된 문제로 보고, 이를 반영한 치료법을 사용했다고 하였다.

이 글에 근거해볼 때, 메소포타미아인들의 외상에 대한 이해는 (예를 들어 그리스인들의 관점과 같은) 좀 더 후기에 나온 전통적이며 인정받는 역사적 이해와 주로 어떤 점에서 다른가?
① 정신적·육체적 건강의 상호 연결성에 대한 강조
② 심리적 고통에 대한 순전히 영적인 설명에의 의존
③ 외상 경험의 사회적·문화적 맥락에 대한 초점
④ 여러 형태의 외상을 위한 복잡한 진단 범주의 발전
⑤ 외상이 일시적이며 간단한 치료법으로 치료될 수 있다는 믿음

09 부분이해 ④

| 분석 |

첫 번째 문장에서 "고대 메소포타미아 문화는 의학사라는 더 넓은 이야기에서 종종 간과된다"라고 하였다. 이어서 널리 받아들여지고 있는 고대 그리스를 포함한 의료 역사를 이야기하고 있으므로 의료역사 이야기는 ④ 의료 역사를 이루는 널리 인정받는 의료적 사실들을 의미한다.

첫 문단에서 "the broader narrative of medical history"가 의미하는 것은?
① 고대 의학이 현대 의학보다 열등하다는 지속적인 믿음
② 선사 시대 의료 기술에 대한 통찰을 제공하는 이야기들
③ 고대 의료에 대한 우리의 이해를 혼란스럽게 하는 모순들
④ 의료 역사를 형성하는 널리 수용되는 사실들의 집합
⑤ 의학 지식이 하나의 이야기로 만들어지고 있다는 이해

10~12

19세기 중반, 우유 생산업자들은 자기 제품을 시골의 전원적인 순수함과 연관 지어 미국인들에게 마케팅했다. 푸른 초원에서 풀을 뜯는 젖소들과 농장에서 갓 짜낸 신선한 우유라는 시골의 이미지를 조심스럽게 만들어내어, 시골을 건강과 연관 짓는 도시 소비자들에게 호소했다. 하지만 당시 판매되던 우유는 실제로는 결코 순수하지 않았다. 급격한 도시화와 산업화는 비위생적인 착유, 부적절한 보관, 부패, 그리고 물로 우유를 희석하거나 석회 같은 물질을 우유에 첨가하여 품질 저하를 감추는 것과 같은 섞음질의 만연 등, 많은 문제를 낳았다.

안전과 품질에 대한 대중적인 우려가 커지자, 우유 생산자들은 당시 등장하고 있던 과학적 발전에서 해결책을 찾았다. 과학자들은 우유 속 박테리아를 줄이고 우유의 보관 기간을 늘이는 저온 살균법 같은 방법을 도입하고 더욱 위생적인 환경에서 우유를 보관하고 운반하는 기술을 개선했다. 이러한 혁신은 우유를 마시기에 더 안전하게 만들었을 뿐만 아니라, 생산자들이 자기 제품을 재브랜드화할 수 있게 도왔다. 규제되지 않은 경쟁 제품과 차별화하고, 더 높은 가격을 정당화하기 위해, '개선된 우유'는 과학적으로 순수한 것으로 '공식적으로 인증되었다.'

시간이 지나면서 이러한 변화는 우유의 이미지에 큰 영향을 미쳤다. 한때 우유는 시골의 자연적으로 순수한 식품으로 여겨졌지만, 이제는 점점 실험실의 멸균과 정밀성과 결합되고 있다. 우유의 안전성을 보장하는 과학적 과정은 또한 우유의 상징성을 바꾸었으며, 우유를 소박한 농촌 음식에서 현대 산업과 과학적 발전의 산물로 변모시켰다.

| 어휘 |

idyllic a. 전원적인 **purity** n. 순수함 **graze** v. 풀을 뜯어 먹다
lush a. 무성한, 풍부한 **associate** v. 연상하다, 연관 짓다
wholesomeness n. 건강함 **unsanitary milking practices** 비위생적인 착유 방식 **spoilage** n. 부패, 변질 **adulteration** n. 불순물 첨가 **water down** 희석하다 **pasteurization** n. 저온 살균법 **shelf life** 저장 가능 기간 **rebrand** v. 브랜드를 다시 만들다, 이미지를 새롭게 하다 **unregulated** a. 규제되지 않은 **officially certified** 공식적으로 인증된 **sterility and precision** 멸균성과 정밀성 **guarantee** v. 보장하다 **rustic** a. 소박한 **staple** n. 기본 식품 **affordable** a. 싼 **nutritious** a. 영양의 **processed food** 가공 우유 **have an effect on** ~에 영향을 미치다

10 글의 제목 ②

| 분석 |

원래 우유는 전원적 순수함을 내세워 마케팅되었지만, 그 이후 과학의 도움으로 과학적 순수함이 마케팅의 수단이 되었다는 내용이므로 둘 모두를 포함하고 있는 ②가 정답이다.

이 글의 제목으로 가장 적절한 것은?
① 우유의 전원적 뿌리: 19세기 낙농 과학 살펴보기
② 순수를 마케팅하기: 과학이 우유 산업을 어떻게 변화시켰는가
③ 초원에서 제품으로: 소비자까지에 이르는 우유의 여정
④ 저온 살균의 힘: 우유의 안전성과 오랜 신선도 유지를 보장하기
⑤ 현대식 식사를 마케팅하기: 광고가 어떻게 음식 선택을 결정했는가

11 내용파악 ③

| 분석 |

과학 덕분에 우유 값이 더 싸졌다는 내용은 없다.

다음 중 과학적 방법이 우유에 적용된 결과가 아닌 것은?
① 우유가 마시기 더 안전해졌다.
② 우유가 재브랜드화될 수 있었다.
③ 우유가 더 저렴해졌다.
④ 우유가 멸균성과 연관되었다.
⑤ 우유가 발전과 연관되었다.

12 내용파악 ③

| 분석 |

마지막 문단에서 우유의 이미지가 바뀌었다고 했다. 우유의 이미지가 바뀐 이유는 소비자들의 인식이 '자연적으로 순수한' 우유보다는 '과학적으로 순수한' 우유를 더 신뢰하고 선호하는 방향으로 바뀌었기 때문이라고 짐작할 수 있다. ④는 사실이지만, 우유의 이미지, 다시 말해 '소비자의 인식 변화'와는 직접적인 관계가 없다.

우유의 이미지가 '자연적 순수함'에서 '과학적 발전'으로 바뀐 것은 무엇을 시사하는가?
① 우유가 더 이상 건강과 연관되지 않게 되었다.
② 과학적 발전으로 인해 우유의 영양가가 더 낮아졌다.
③ 소비자들이 실험실에서 가공된 우유를 선호했다.
④ 우유 생산자들은 전통적인 방법을 개선했다.
⑤ 저온 살균법은 식품 안전에 영향을 미치지 않았다.

13~15

남북 전쟁 이전까지 몇 년 동안, 텍사스 농촌 지역의 정착민들은 매일 생존을 위한 싸움을 해야 하는 가혹한 생활환경에 직면해야 했다. 여러 요인 때문에 평균 기대 수명은 짧아, 일반적으로 35세에서 50세 사이에 지나지 않았다. 오염된 물과 전염병과 출산의 항시적인 위험과 심지어 간단한 부상조차도 삶을 불안정하게 만들었다. 전문적인 의료 지원은 드물거나, 종종 신뢰할 수 없었기에, 가족들은 자기 나름의 임기응변적 재주나 이것저것 주워 맞춘 얼마 안 되는 모든 지식에 의존하여 의료 문제를 스스로 해결해야 했다.

정착민들이 전문적인 치료를 찾았을 때조차 결과는 종종 암담했다. 많은 의사는 훈련 수준이 미흡했고, 때로는 알코올 중독 같은 개인적인 문제와 싸우고 있었다. 이들은 개척지 의료라는 현실을 다루기에 역량이 부족했다. 그들의 의료 도구는 제한적이었으며, 기껏해야 기초적인 외과 지식에서 '수은 정화' 같은 의심스러운 치료법이 전부였다. 대체로 이런 치료법들은 비효과적이거나, 때로는 환자들에게 오히려 해를 끼쳐, 환자들은 회복의 희망을 거의 가질 수 없었다.

필요에 쫓겨, 정착민들은 민간요법과 민속 의료관행에 의존할 수밖에 없었지만, 이것들 역시 상당한 위험을 수반했다. 그 중에서도 가장 독특한 치료법 중 하나는 '미친 돌'의 이용이었는데, 이는 치유력이 있다고 믿어진 특이한 물체로, 특히 광견병과 기타 유사한 질병 치료에 사용되었다. 인기가 있긴 했지만, 이러한 민간 치료법은 종종 전통적 지혜와 위험한 돌팔이 치료법 사이의 경계를 아슬아슬하게 넘나들었다. 민간 치료법은 의료 자원이 부족한 세상에서 정착민들의 필사적인 건강 추구를 나타냈으며, 그들의 치유에 대한 희망은 종종 그들을 불확실성으로 가득 찬 길로 이끌었다.

| 어휘 |

rural a. 시골의 **life expectancy** 기대 수명 **contaminated** a. 오염된 **infectious disease** 전염병 **precarious** a. 불안정한, 위태로운 **do-it-yourself approach** 스스로 해결하는 방식 **cobble together** (여기저기서 얻은 정보로) 대충 만들어내다 **ill-equipped** a. 준비가 부족한, 능력이 부족한 **medical arsenal** 의료 도구 **rudimentary** a. 기초적인 **surgical** a. 외과의 **mercury purges** 수은 정화 치료(해로운 치료법) **more often than not** 흔히 **ineffective** a. 효과가 없는 **recovery** n. 회복 **turn to** 의지하다

home remedies 민간요법 **folk practices** 민속 치료법 **peculiar** a. 특이한 **curative** a. 병을 고치는 **rabies** n. 공수병 **walk a fine line** 아슬아슬한 경계를 그리다 **quackery** n. 돌팔이 치료법 **desperate** a. 필사적인 **fraught with** ~으로 가득한 **skeptical** a. 회의적인 **contagious** a. 감염의, 전염성의 **uproarious** a. 소란한 **pernicious** a. 해로운, 치명적인 **lugubrious** a. 애처로운 **precarious** a. 불안정한, 위험한

13 내용일치 ③

| 분석 |
① '이후'가 아니라 '이전'이다. ② 훈련이 미흡했다. ④ mad stones가 환자에게 광견병을 유발했다는 말은 없다. ⑤ 아무 것도 안 하기를 희망한 것이 아니라 그 어떤 위험한 민간요법이라도 하기를 희망했다.

이 글에 따르면 올바른 것은?
① 남북 전쟁 이후 텍사스에서 평균 기대 수명은 35세에서 50세였다.
② 텍사스 시골 지역의 의사들은 잘 훈련 받았지만, 가끔 어려움을 겪었다.
③ 수은 정화법과 같은 치료법은 종종 환자를 위험한 상태에 빠뜨렸다.
④ '미친 돌'이 때로 환자에게 광견병을 유발했다.
⑤ 환자들이 병에서의 치유를 위해 가장 희망한 것은 보통 아무것도 하지 않는 것이었다.

14 내용파악 ③

| 분석 |
마지막 문장에서 이 '미친 돌'과 같은 민속 치료법은 "의료 자원이 부족한 세상에서 정착민들의 필사적인 건강 추구를 나타냈다"라고 하였다.

'미친 돌'의 이용은 정착민들의 의료에 대한 접근법에 대해 무엇을 시사하고 있는가?
① 그들은 신뢰할 만한 의료 치료를 쉽게 이용할 수 있었다.
② 그들은 전통 의학을 불신했다.
③ 그들은 효과적 치료법을 필사적으로 찾으려 했다.
④ 그들은 전문적인 의료적 도움을 추구하는 편을 선호했다.
⑤ 그들은 발전된 의학 지식과 의료 기술을 가지고 있었다.

15 빈칸완성 ⑤

| 분석 |
앞에서 가혹한 생활환경에 대해 설명하므로 짧은 기대 수명 뿐 아니라 수질오염과 전염병 등도 그들의 삶을 불안정하게 만들었을 것이다. 따라서 빈칸에는 ⑤의 '불안정한'이 적절하다.

16~18

도시화는 새들의 행동에 상당한 영향을 미쳐왔는데, 특히 새들이 소음 수준 증가에 적응하면서 새들의 노래가 바뀌었다. 지난 30년 동안 연구자들은 샌프란시스코 도심에 서식하는 흰관참새의 노랫소리 변화를 기록해왔다. 이러한 변화는 교통, 건설, 그 밖의 인간 활동에서 오는 지속적인 배경 소음에 대한 적응을 반영하며, 인간에 의해 변화된 환경 속에서 야생동물이 직면한 더 광범위한 영향을 잘 보여주고 있다.

도시 환경에서는 더 높은 주파수로 소리를 변화시키는 새들이 소음 공해 속에서도 더 효과적으로 의사소통할 수 있으며, 그렇게 해서 그들의 생존과 번식 성공 가능성은 더 높아진다. 흰관참새의 경우, 그들 노래의 최소 주파수는 시간이 지남에 따라 상승했는데, 이는 도시 소음 속에서 그들의 울음소리를 두드러지게 하기 위한 진화적 조정을 시사한다. 반면, 조용한 농촌 지역에서는 안정적인 주파수가 관찰되고 있는 것으로 입증되듯이 그러한 적응이 불필요하다. 이 현상은 야생동물이 인간이 주도하는 환경 변화에 신속하게 적응해야 하는 압력을 강조해 보여준다.

흰관참새 연구는 인간 환경의 미세한 변화도 어떻게 동물 행동에 커다란 영향을 미칠 수 있는지를 예시해준다. 이러한 적응은 개체 생존 차원 너머로 확장된다. 그것은 문화적 전달도 포함하는데, 변화된 노랫소리가 여러 세대를 거쳐 전수되어, 도시 소음에 더 적합한 새로운 방언이 형성될 가능성이 있기 때문이다. 도시화가 자연의 행동에 미치는 지속적인 영향은 인간 활동과 야생동물 간의 역동적인 상호작용을 보여주며, 생물 종의 회복력과 그들이 점점 더 도시화되는 세상에서 직면하는 도전을 강조하고 있다.

| 어휘 |
urbanization n. 도시화 **significantly** ad. 상당히, 현저하게 **alter** v. 변경하다 **adapt** v. 적응하다 **ambient noise** 배경 소음 **persistent** a. 지속적인 **human-altered landscapes** 인간에 의해 변화된 환경 **vocalization** n. 소리내기 **frequency** n. 주파수 **noise pollution** 소음 공해 **reproductive success** 번식 성공률 **minimum frequency** 최소 주파수 **over time** 시간에 걸쳐서 **evolutionary adjustment** 진화적 조정 **stand out** 두드러지다 **din** n. 소음, 시끄러운 소리 **by contrast** 대조적으로 **subtle** a. 미묘한 **transmission** n. 전달 **modified** a. 변화된 **pass down** 전수하다, 물려주다 **potentially** ad. 잠재적으로 **give rise to** 낳다 **dialect** n. 방언 **suit** v. 적합하다 **ongoing** a. 지속적인 **interplay** n. 상호작용 **resilience** n. 회복력 **challenge** n. 도전, 어려움 **mimic** v. 모방하다

16 글의 제목   ①

| 분석 |

이 글은 도시화의 영향, 특히 도시 소음의 영향으로 새들의 노래가 어떻게 바뀌었는지를 흰관참새의 노랫소리 주파수의 변화를 중심으로 설명하고 있으므로 ①이 제목으로 적절하다. 다른 보기에는 새나 노랫소리가 빠져있다.

이 글의 제목으로 가장 적절한 것은?
① 도시에서의 노래: 도시 소음이 새의 노래에 미치는 영향
② 새의 행동: 도시에서의 적응과 생존 연구
③ 오염이 야생동물에 미치는 영향: 인간 활동이 자연에 끼치는 영향
④ 새들의 진화적 적응: 시간이 지나면서 종이 변화하는 방식
⑤ 흰관참새: 흔한 도시 종

17 내용파악   ④

| 분석 |

두 번째 단락의 두 번째 문장에서 '그들(흰관참새) 노래의 최소 주파수는 시간이 지남에 따라 상승했다'고 했으므로 ④가 관찰된 변화이다.

이 글에 따르면 샌프란시스코 도심의 흰관참새의 노래에서 어떤 변화가 관찰되었는가?
① 그들의 노래의 복잡성이 감소했다.
② 그들의 노래 길이가 두드러지게 짧아졌다.
③ 그들은 발성 사용(노래하기)을 완전히 멈추었다.
④ 그들의 노래의 최소 주파수가 상승했다.
⑤ 그들은 교통 소음을 모방하기 시작했다.

18 내용파악   ②

| 분석 |

소음 공해로 인해 주파수가 높아졌다고 했고, 조용한 시골에서는 주파수가 안정적으로 유지되고 있다고 했으므로, 도시의 소음이 줄어들면, 원래의 낮은 주파수로 되돌아갈 것이라고 짐작할 수 있다.

이 글의 정보에 기초할 때, 도시의 소음 수준이 눈에 띄게 감소하면, 샌프란시스코 도심 흰관참새의 노래는 어떻게 되리라고 짐작할 수 있는가?
① 훨씬 더 복잡하고 다양해질 것이다.
② 점차 더 낮은 주파수로 되돌아갈 것이다.
③ 시간이 지나면서 상당히 더 높은 주파수를 가지게 될 것이다.
④ 진화의 성격 때문에 변하지 않을 것이다.
⑤ 아무런 소용이 없으므로 완전히 사라질 것이다.

19~21

오물이란 잘못된 장소에 잘못된 시간에 있는 어떤 것이다. 오물이 우리를 역겹게 만드는 이유는 그것이 있어서는 안 될 곳, 예를 들어 부엌 바닥이나 침대 아래 같은 곳에서 나타나기 때문이다. 똑같은 물체(먼지와 때)라도 다른 장소에 있다면 오물이 되지 않는다. 오물의 의미는 그것의 장소에 따라 달라진다.

메리 더글러스는 그녀의 저서 『순수와 위험』에서 오물과 오염 개념을 탐구한다. 그녀는 오물에 대한 공포를 무질서에 대한 두려움과 연결한다. 다른 한편으로, 오물을 제거하는 것은 질서 있는 환경을 구축하는 것의 일부이다. 우리는 환경을 특정한 개념, 즉 질서 의식에 맞추려 한다. 더글러스는 오물은 '제자리를 벗어난 물건'이라고 말하는데, 이는 어떤 형태의 질서와 그 질서에 대한 위반을 동시에 시사하는 정의이다. 따라서 정의상 오물은 어떤 체계, 어떤 분류 방식이 먼저 존재함에 의존한다. 더글러스는 이 요점을 잘 설명한다.

신발 자체는 더럽지 않지만, 식탁 위에 놓으면 더럽다. 음식 자체는 더럽지 않지만, 요리 도구를 침실에 두거나, 음식이 옷에 튀면 더럽다. 응접실에 있는 욕실용품, 의자 위에 놓여 있는 옷, 실내에 있는 실외에서 쓰는 물건, 1층에 있는 2층 물건, 겉옷이 있어야 할 곳에 있는 속옷 등도 마찬가지이다. 따라서 오물은 의미의 부조화, 다시 말해 다른 것들과 관련하여 잘못된 위치에 있는 의미들이다. 위반하는 것들은 오물이 되며, 그것들은 잘못된 곳에 있다. 더글러스의 '제자리를 벗어난 물건'에 대한 논의는 위반에 대한 반응을 해석하는 유용한 분석 도구를 제시한다. 오물과 오염에 대한 믿음은 제자리를 벗어난 것을 이데올로기적 방식으로 정의하므로, 사회 속 권력관계와 관련이 있다. 제자리를 벗어난 것을 정의할 수 있는 사람들이 사회에서 가장 큰 권력을 가진 사람들인 것이다.

| 어휘 |

dirt n. 오물 **disgust** n. 혐오감, 역겨움 **constitute** v. 구성하다 **be dependent on** ~에 달려있다 **out of place** 제 장소가 아닌 **conform** v. 따르다, 순응하다 **simultaneously** ad. 동시에 **contravention** n. 위반(행위), 반대 **by the definition** 정의상 **preexistence** n. 선행 존재, 기존의 존재 **classification** n. 분류 **in itself** 그 자체로 **utensil** n. 조리도구 **bespatter** v. 더럽히다 **transgression** n. 위반, 일탈 **decoding** n. 해독 **power relations** 권력 관계 **delineate** v. 정의하다, 서술하다 **territory** n. 텃세 구역 **status** n. 지위 **deviant** a. 일탈의 **graffiti** n. 그라피티, 낙서 **accommodation** n. 숙박시설

19 빈칸완성 ①

| 분석 |
앞 문장에서 어떤 물건은 어떤 장소에 나타나느냐에 따라 오물이 될 수도 있고, 오물이 되지 않을 수도 있다고 하였으므로, 빈칸에는 '장소'라는 뜻의 location이 적절하다.

20 내용파악 ①

| 분석 |
'정의상 오물은 어떤 체계가 먼저 존재함에 의존한다'고 했는데, 이는 어떤 질서 잡힌 체계가 먼저 있지 않으면 거기서 벗어나 제자리에 있지 않은 오물을 정의할 수 없다는 말이므로, 오물은 먼저 존재하는 체계의 기저에 있는 무질서가 아니라 질서를 암시하거나 전제한다고 할 수 있다. 따라서 무질서라고 한 ①이 틀린 진술이다. ④ transgress(위반하다)는 원래 '경계를 침범하다'라는 의미이다.

다음 중 오물에 대해 틀린 진술은?
① 오물은 먼저 존재하는 체제의 기저에 있는 무질서를 드러낸다.
② 오물은 잘못된 장소에 있는 물질이다.
③ 오물은 무질서에 대한 두려움과 연결되어 있기에 우리를 역겹게 한다.
④ 경계를 침범하는 것들은 오물이 된다.
⑤ 오물에 대한 개념들은 사회적 권력관계와 밀접한 관련이 있다.

21 내용파악 ⑤

| 분석 |
히피가 무질서하다면, 그들은 오물이고, 오물은 배척과 배제의 대상이므로, 그들이 제자리를 찾도록 도와주어야 한다는 ⑤는 저자가 동의하지 않을 것이다. ① 무질서는 오물이므로, 제자리에서 벗어난 것이며 따라서 일탈적이라 할 수 있다. ③ 글의 주제라고도 할 수 있다.

저자가 가장 동의하지 않을 것 같은 진술은?
① 집시들은 생활공간이 '무질서한' 것으로 확인되기 때문에 일탈적이라고 낙인찍힌다.
② 그라피티는 있어서는 안 되는 곳에 있는 예술이기 때문에 일탈적으로 간주된다
③ 장소는 행동 규범 형성에 중요한 역할을 한다.
④ 노숙자는 보통의 숙소가 없기 때문에 비정상적으로 여겨진다.
⑤ 히피들은 무질서하며, 사회에서 자신의 자리를 찾도록 도움을 받아야 한다.

22~23

나는 언제나 기후 정의를 멀티태스킹이라고 생각한다. 우리는 중첩된 다중 위기의 시대에 살고 있다. 우리는 건강 비상사태를 맞고 있고, 주택 비상사태를 맞고 있으며, 불평등 비상사태를 맞고 있고, 인종적 불의 비상사태를 맞고 있으며, 그리고 기후 비상사태 또한 맞고 있다. 따라서 이러한 문제들을 한 번에 하나씩 해결하려고 해서는 우리는 아무 것도 이루지 못할 것이다. 우리는 진정으로 교차적인 대응이 필요하다. 그러니까, 탈탄소화하고 덜 오염된 세상을 만드는 우리가 또한 다방면에서 훨씬 더 공정한 사회도 건설하는 것은 어떨까?

많은 환경운동가들은 이러한 이야기를 듣고는 "글쎄, 그건 단순히 탄소세를 시행하거나 친환경 에너지로 전환하는 것보다 훨씬 더 어려운 일인 것 같아"라고 생각한다. 그리고 기후 정의 운동에서 우리가 하는 주장은 우리는 기후 행동에 관여하는 권력 기반을 구축하려고 노력하고 있다는 것이다. 만약 당신이 탄소에 관해서만 이야기한다면, 더 시급한 비상사태 — 경찰 폭력이든, 젠더 폭력이든, 주택 불안정이든 — 를 겪고 있는 사람이면 누구나 이렇게 생각할 것이다: "그건 부자들의 문제야. 나는 죽지 않고 살아있어야 하는 매일의 비상사태에 집중하고 있어." 그러나 당신이 이러한 문제들을 서로 연결해서, 어떻게 기후 행동이 더 나은 일자리를 창출할 수 있고, 점점 더 심해지는 불평등을 시정할 수 있으며, 스트레스 수준을 낮출 수 있는지를 보여줄 수 있다면, 당신은 사람들의 관심을 끌기 시작하고, 기후 정책을 통과시키는 일에 관여하는 더 넓은 지지층을 구축하게 된다.

| 어휘 |
overlapping a. 중첩되는 **inequality** n. 불평등 **emergency** n. 긴급 상황, 위기 **racial** a. 인종의 **one at a time** 한 번에 하나씩 **intersectional** a. 교차적인(다양한 문제가 공통부분을 통해 연결된) **decarbonize** v. 탄소 배출을 줄이다 **polluted** a. 오염된 **fair** a. 공정한 **power base** 권력 기반, 영향력 있는 지지층 **invested in** ~에 관심을 가진, ~에 관여하는 **implement** v. 실행[이행]하다 **precariousness** n. 불안정성 **constituency** n. 지지층, 유권자층 **redress** v. 시정하다, 바로잡다 **convivial** a. 쾌활한 **conclave** n. 교황 선출 회의; 콘클라베 **refractory** a. 고집 센, 다루기 힘든; 난치의 **constitution** n. 구성 **confluence** n. 집합 **sustainable** a. 지속 가능한

22 빈칸완성 ②

| 분석 |
앞에서 기후 정의란 멀티태스킹이며, 한 번에 하나씩 문제를 해결할 수는 없다고 하였으므로, 여러 문제를 동시에 해결해야 한다는 표현이 필요하다. 따라서 중첩된 문제를 해결하기 위해서는 교차적인(intersectional) 방식이 필요하다고 볼 수 있다. 뒤에는 교차적 방

식으로 접근한다면, 기후 행동을 지지하는 사람들(constituency)을 더 많이 확보할 수 있다는 의미이다. 따라서 정답은 ②이다.

23 글의 제목   ①

| 분석 |

기후 정의를 확보하기 위해서는 교차적인 방식으로 접근해야 한다는 내용이다. 기후 변화와 사회 정의의 멀티태스킹이라는 교차성을 이야기하는 ①이 가장 좋은 제목이다. ③ 탄소세 이상의 일이라고만 했을 뿐 다른 분야의 문제를 직접 언급하지 않아서 제목으로 부족하다.

이 글의 제목으로 가장 적절한 것은?
① 기후 변화와 싸우기: 사회 정의와 함께
② 우리 시대의 다양한 위기: 기후 변화가 최우선이다
③ 기후 정의의 실현: 단순한 탄소세 이상의 일이다
④ 우리 시대의 비상사태들: 그 어느 때보다 급박하다
⑤ 기후 정책: 지속 가능한 일자리, 지속 가능한 미래

24~25

결국 20세기의 집단적 트라우마를 확연하게 간직하고 있다는 낙인을 서구의 현대성에 찍어준 홀로코스트가 일어나기 몇 년 전에 이미, 서구 밖에서도 가장 발전된 사회가 조직적인 잔학 행위를 저질렀다. 1937년 12월 초, 침략하는 일본군은 중국 난징에서 최대 30만 명에 달하는 중국 주민을 학살했다. 일본 제국 정부 최고위층의 명령에 따라, 그들은 근대사에서 가장 피비린내 나는 6주 동안 대학살을 벌였으며, 이는 나치가 유대인 대량 학살을 위해 나중에 개발한 기술적 수단 없이 이루어졌다.
나치 대학살과 달리, 이 일본군의 만행은 외부 세계에 감춰지지 않았다. 실제로, 이 만행은 비판적이고 표현력이 훌륭한 서구 관찰자들이 지켜보는 가운데 벌어졌으며, 세계 언론의 존경받는 기자들에 의해 대대적으로 보도되었다. 그러나 그로부터 60년이 지난 지금까지도, '난징 대학살'의 기억은 지역적인 경계를 넘어 밖으로 나가지 못했다. 이 트라우마는 전후 민주주의 일본 정부의 자아 개념에는 말할 것도 없고 중화인민공화국의 집단 정체성에도 거의 전혀 기여하지 못했다.
난징 대학살에 대한 가장 최근의 서술자가 말하듯이, "역사상 가장 파괴적인 전쟁을 기준으로 해서조차도, 난징 대학살은 최악의 대량 학살 사례 중 하나이다." 그러나 이 사건이 '제2차 세계대전의 잊어진 홀로코스트'가 되었고, 오늘날에도 '잘 알려지지 않은 사건'으로 남아 있긴 하지만, 일본의 가장 강력하고 존경받는 공직자들 중 일부는 이 사건의 존재 자체를 일상적으로, 그리고 성공적으로 부정하고 있다.

| 어휘 |

brand v. 낙인찍다   distinctive a. 분명한   bearer n. 담지자
collective trauma 집단적 트라우마   engage in ~에 종사하다
atrocity n. 대규모 학살   invade v. 침략하다   slaughter v. 도살하다   as many as ~씩이나 되는   resident n. 거주민   imperial a. 제국의   massacre n. 대학살   articulate a. 명확하게 표현하는
elapse v. 경과하다   memorialization n. 기념, 기억하기 위한 활동
confine n. 경계   let alone ~은 당연하다   extermination n. (대량) 몰살, 절멸   obscure a. 모호한   routinely ad. 일상적으로, 정기적으로   public officials 공직자, 정부 관계자   genocide n. 대량 학살   banality n. 평범성

24 글의 흐름상 적절하지 않은 표현 고르기   ③

| 분석 |

③의 turn out은 '추방하다, ~으로 판명되다' 정도의 의미이다. 여기서는 대규모 살상을 '저질렀다'의 의미가 되어야 하므로, carried out으로 고쳐야 한다.

25 글의 주제   ④

| 분석 |

이 글은 난징 대학살이 나치의 홀로코스트와는 달리 학살 지역 밖에서는 역사적으로 잊혔다는 내용이다. 따라서 ④가 글의 주제로 적절하다. 나치의 홀로코스트가 서구의 현대성에 집단 트라우마를 간직하고 있다는 낙인을 찍어주었다는 것은 서구의 현대인들은 나치의 홀로코스트에 대한 집단 트라우마를 결코 잊지 않는 반응을 보여주었다는 말이므로, 난징 대학살 트라우마에 대한 망각의 반응과 대조를 이룬다. ②는 잔혹성만 다루므로 충분치 못하다.

이 글의 주제는?
① 집단학살의 한 사례로서 난징 대학살
② 제2차 세계대전 중 난징에서 일본군의 잔학 행위
③ 역사상 가장 파괴적인 전쟁의 잊힌 원인
④ 제2차 세계대전 집단적 트라우마들에 대한 대조적인 반응들
⑤ 나치와 일본군의 잔혹 행위에서 발견되는 악의 평범성

26~27

무척추동물은 등뼈를 가지고 있지 않은 동물이다. 이들 중 다수는 작아서 쉽게 간과되지만, 매우 다양하고, 널리 분포하고 있으며, 현재 알려진 모든 동물 종의 약 97%를 차지하고 있다. 척추동물은 단일한 문(門)을 형성하지만, 무척추동물은 30개 이상의 문에 속하는 비공식적인 집합체이다. 그 중에 절지동물이라는 단 하나의 문에 속하는 것들만 해도 아마도 지구상의 모든 다른 동물들의 수를 능가할 것이다.

무척추동물은 상상할 수 있는 모든 유형의 서식지에서 발견되지만, 가장 많은 개체 수가 존재하는 곳은 동물 생명이 최초로 발생한 바다이다. 무척추동물은 가장 먼저 진화한 동물들이지만, 어떻게 그 과정이 정확히 이루어졌는지는 아직 밝혀지지 않고 있다. 이들의 조상이 지금의 원생동물과 비슷한, 음식물을 섭취하는 단세포 미생물이었다는 점에는 의심의 여지가 거의 없다. 많은 생물학자는 어느 시점에서 이 단세포 미생물들이 영구적인 공생 관계를 형성하기 시작했다고 생각한다. 이런 일이 일어났을 때, 동물 생명이 시작되었다.

| 어휘 |

invertebrate n. 무척추동물 backbone n. 척추 overlook v. 간과하다 vertebrate n. 척추동물 phylum n. 〈생물〉 문(門), 동식물 분류의 단위) arthropod n. 절지동물 conceivable a. 상상할 수 있는 habitat n. 서식지 extant a. 현존하는 protozoan n. 원생동물 microorganism n. 미생물 symbiotic partnership 공생 관계 extinct a. 멸종한 give rise to 낳다

26 내용일치   ⑤

| 분석 |

⑤ 원생동물은 무척추동물의 조상과 유사하다고 했지, 이들이 최초의 생명체라고는 말하지 않았다.

다음 중 틀린 진술은?
① 절지동물이 지구에서 가장 많은 생물일 가능성이 있다.
② 무척추동물은 척추동물보다 수가 훨씬 많다.
③ 무척추동물의 조상은 아마도 단세포 생물이었을 것이다.
④ 무척추동물은 지구 전역에서 발견될 수 있다.
⑤ 원생동물은 최초의 생명체였다

27 내용추론   ②

| 분석 |

무척추동물의 조상이 단세포 미생물이고 마지막 문장에서 단세포 미생물들이 공생하면서 동물이 생겨났다고 했으므로, 이 동물은 무척추동물이다. 따라서 ② "미생물 간의 공생이 무척추동물을 탄생시켰다"가 추론할 수 있는 내용이다. ⑤ 무척추동물이 척추동물로 진화했다.

다음 중 이 글에서 추론할 수 있는 것은?
① 척추동물은 한때 무척추동물보다 훨씬 많았다.
② 미생물 간의 공생이 무척추동물을 탄생시켰다.
③ 무척추동물은 특정 서식지에서만 생존한다.
④ 많은 무척추동물이 멸종하고 있다.
⑤ 척추동물이 최초의 무척추동물을 탄생시켰다.

28~30

1960년대 후반, 컴퓨터가 거의 과학적 또는 산업적 용도로만 사용되던 시기에, 하니웰은 세상에 대담한 새로운 비전을 제시했다. 무려 10,600달러라는 엄청난 가격이 매겨진 하니웰 키친 컴퓨터는 '레시피 선택기'로 광고되었고, 모든 미래 가정주부의 꿈으로 여겨졌다.
하지만 현실은 '우주 시대'보다는 '마케팅 전략'에 가까웠다. 이 컴퓨터는 대량 생산을 목표로 만들어진 것이 아니라, 완전히 새로운 가정용 컴퓨터에 대한 소비자의 관심을 측정하려는 목적이었다. 판매 실적은 미미했고 대단히 비실용적이었지만, 키친 컴퓨터는 더 큰 무언가를 촉발했다.
고든 벨 같은 기술 비전가는 이 제품을 하나의 지침으로 받아들였으며, 이들의 상상력은 일상생활 속에서의 컴퓨터의 잠재력에 의해 불붙여졌다. 그들은 가정이 학습, 조직, 엔터테인먼트, 심지어 자동화를 통해 변화하는 모습을 떠올렸다. 하니웰 키친 컴퓨터는 상업적으로 실패했지만, 그것은 중요한 전환점을 의미했다.

| 어휘 |

exclusively ad. 독점적으로 application n. 용도 audacious a. 대담한, 혁신적인 staggering a. 엄청난, 경이로운 recipe selector 레시피 선택기 marketing stunt 마케팅 전략, 홍보 수단 gauge v. 측정하다, 평가하다 impractical a. 비현실적인, 실용적이지 않은 spark v. 점화하다 tech visionary 기술 비전가(기술 혁신을 예측하고 이끄는 사람들) beacon n. 지침, 길잡이 ignite v. 불붙이다 potential n. 가능성 flop v. 실패하다 crucial a. 중요한 turning point 전환점 culinary a. 요리의 potent a. 강력한 optimism n. 낙관주의 gamble n. 도박 compromise v. 훼손하다 device n. 장치 gimmick n. 고안, 속임수

28 글의 제목   ①

| 분석 |

하니웰 키친 컴퓨터는 마케팅 전략이라는 원래의 목적에 맞게 상업적 성공은 이루지 못했지만, 결국 가정용 컴퓨터라는 혁명을 가져왔다는 내용이다. 마케팅 전략으로 시작했다는 말도 옳은 말이므로 정답은 ①이다. ⑤ 공정한 가격이 아니라 엄청난 가격이고, 메인프레임이 아니라 가정용 컴퓨터이다.

이 글의 제목은?
① 하니웰 키친 컴퓨터: 혁명을 촉발한 마케팅 전략
② 키친 컴퓨터: 요리 자동화의 개척자
③ 기술적 돌파구: 키친 컴퓨터가 요리 준비에 미친 영향
④ 키친 컴퓨터: 1960년대 낙관주의의 강력한 상징
⑤ 하니웰의 대담한 도박: 메인프레임 성능을 공정 가격에 가정으로 가져오기

| 29 　내용추론 | ④ |

| 분석 |

키친 컴퓨터는 대량 생산을 목표로 만들어진 것이 아니라, 완전히 새로운 가정용 컴퓨터에 대한 소비자의 관심을 측정하려는 목적이었다고 했으므로, 애초에 많이 팔리리라 기대하지 않았을 것이다. 따라서 ④를 추론할 수 있다. ① 고든 벨이 가정용 컴퓨터를 발명했다는 말은 없다. ② 하니웰의 명성에 대한 언급은 없다. ③ 목표가 마케팅이었기에, 제조와 홍보에서 많은 돈을 잃었다고 볼 근거는 없다.

이 글에서 추론할 수 있는 것은?
① 키친 컴퓨터는 고든 벨에게 최초의 진정한 가정용 컴퓨터를 발명할 영감을 주었다.
② 키친 컴퓨터의 '마케팅 전략'은 하니웰의 명성을 심각하게 손상시켰다.
③ 하니웰은 키친 컴퓨터를 제조하고 홍보하는 과정에서 많은 돈을 잃었다.
④ 하니웰은 '우주 시대' 키친 컴퓨터가 잘 팔릴 것이라고 기대하지 않았다.
⑤ 고든 벨은 하니웰이 자신의 가정용 컴퓨터 비전을 훼손했다고 믿었다.

| 30 　뒷내용 추론 | ① |

| 분석 |

마지막 문장에서 키친 컴퓨터는 가정용 컴퓨터로 가는 중요한 전환점이 되었다고 했으므로, 가정용 컴퓨터라는 혁신, 기술적 발전 이야기가 이어지는 게 가장 자연스럽다. 따라서 '혁신'을 이야기하는 ①이 정답이다.

마지막 문단을 볼 때 이 다음에는 어떤 내용이 이어지겠는가?
① 키친 컴퓨터가 혁신을 촉진한 사례
② 하니웰이 어떻게 명성을 회복했는지에 대한 설명
③ 고든 벨의 중요성을 지지하는 주장
④ 키친 컴퓨터와 유사한 기기의 비교
⑤ 마케팅 전략과 판매 속임수에 대한 부정적인 의견

THE UNIVERSITY OF SEOUL | 서울시립대학교 인문·자연계열 II

TEST p. 332~347

01	①	02	④	03	②	04	②	05	④	06	③	07	③	08	③	09	①	10	②
11	②	12	④	13	②	14	②	15	④	16	②	17	③	18	③	19	③	20	①
21	①	22	②	23	③	24	④	25	①	26	③	27	②	28	④	29	④	30	①

01 반의어   ①

| 분석 |
enigmatical은 '수수께끼 같은'에서 파생된 '불가해한, 난해한, 모호한, 복잡한'의 의미가 있다. 따라서 의미상 가장 거리가 먼 단어는 '명백하다'는 의미의 ①이다. ①을 제외한 나머지는 모두 동의어에 가깝다.

| 어휘 |
evolve v. 진화하다   rely on 의지하다   unforeseen a. 예기치 못한   unequivocal a. 명백한   unstipulated a. 명시되지 않은   nebulous a. 모호한   intricate a. 복잡한

| 해석 |
인공지능(AI)은 단순한 규칙 기반 시스템에서 학습과 적응을 할 수 있는 복잡한 알고리즘으로 발전해 왔다. 초기 AI 시스템은 미리 정의된 규칙에 크게 의존했으며, 난해하거나 예기치 못한 상황 처리 능력이 부족했다.

02 동의어   ④

| 어휘 |
lie in ~에 있다   conceive of 고안하다   discrete a. 개별적인   envision v. 상상하다   insight n. 통찰   prescient a. 선견지명이 있는(= foresighted)   dictation n. 받아쓰기, 명령, 지시   invariably ad. 항상   precarious a. 위태로운   foregone a. 이미 결정된   prerequisite a. 전제조건의

| 해석 |
에디슨의 천재성은 단순히 개별적인 기기가 아니라 완전히 발전된 시장을 구상할 수 있는 능력에 있었다. 그는 자신이 만든 것을 사람들이 어떻게 사용하기를 원할지를 상상할 수 있었고, 그 통찰에 따라 설계했다. 그는 항상 선견지명이 있었던 것은 아니었지만(예를 들어, 초기에는 축음기 주로 비즈니스 기계로 사용되어 지시를 녹음하고 재생하는 데 쓰일 것이라고 믿었다). 그는 항상 사용자들의 필요와 선호를 충분히 고려했다.

03 동의어   ②

| 어휘 |
lived-in a. 익숙한   virtual a. 가상의   cogitate v. 심사숙고하다   isolated a. 고립된   deteriorating a. 악화하는   political unrest 정치적 불안정   solace n. 위안(= consolation)   mediate v. 중재하다, (중간에) 전하다, 전달하다   condemnation n. 비난   allegation n. 근거 없는 주장

| 해석 |
"잇 더 나이트(Eat the Night)"는 외부 세계의 두려움과 비교되는 가상공간의 익숙한 안락을 이해하고 있다. 이 영화는 이 주제에 대해 깊이 생각할 때 가장 큰 효과를 거둔다. 정치적 불안과 환경 악화 속에서 점점 더 고립되어 가는 젊은 세대에게, 안전한 화면을 통해 전달되는 위안을 찾는 것은 이해할 수 있을 뿐만 아니라 필수적인 일이기도 하다.

04 논리완성   ②

| 분석 |
타인의 생명을 빼앗는 행위는 '전시에는(In a time of war)' 보상받을 수 있다고 했으므로 전시와 반대되는 '보통은(usually)' 도덕적으로 악한 행위로 간주될 것이다. 따라서 빈칸에는 보상받는 것과 반대되는 reprehensible(비난받을 만한)이 적절하다.

| 어휘 |
deviant a. 일탈적인   straightforward a. 솔직한, 간단한   in a manner ~하는 방식으로   label v. 이름 붙이다   depend on 달려있다   commit v. 저지르다   on the way to ~로 가는 길에   vary v. 다르다   make sense 이치에 닿다, 이해되다   norm n. 규범, 기준   reprehensible a. 비난받을 만한   rewarded a. 보상받는   susceptible a. 민감한   laudable a. 칭찬할만한

| 해석 |
"일탈 행동이란 무엇인가?"라는 질문은 간단히 대답할 수 없다. 어떤 행위가 일탈로 간주되는가는 장소, 관객, 그리고 그 행위를

하는 개인을 포함한 많은 요소에 달려 있다. 수업에 가는 길에 음악을 듣는 것은 받아들일 수 있는 행동으로 여겨진다. 그러나 강의 중에 음악을 듣는 것은 무례하다고 간주된다. 규범은 문화와 시간에 따라 다르므로, 일탈 개념도 또한 변한다는 것은 이해가 간다. 타인의 생명을 빼앗는 것과 같은 보통 도덕적으로 비난받을 만하다고 여겨지는 행위가 전시에는 실제로 보상받을 수도 있다. 어떤 행위가 일탈인지 아닌지는 그 행위에 대한 사회의 반응에 달려 있다.

05 동사 ④

| 분석 |
emerge는 자동사이므로 수동태를 만들 수 없다. 의미상으로도 '등장하다'이므로 ④의 was emerged를 emerged로 고친다. 능동태 emerged와 aimed가 병치된 that관계절이다.

| 어휘 |
movement n. 운동, 사조 **originate** v. 기원하다 **objective** a. 객관적인 **depiction** n. 묘사, 표현 **explore** v. 탐구하다 **idealism** n. 이상주의 **portray** v. 묘사하다, 그리다 **as it is** 있는 그대로 **concern** n. 관심사, 문제 **overall** ad. 전반적으로 **capture** v. 포착하다 **mundane** a. 평범한, 일상적인 **harsh** a. 가혹한, 혹독한

| 해석 |
리얼리즘은 19세기에 시작된 문학 및 예술 운동으로, 일상생활을 객관적으로 묘사하는 것으로 잘 알려져 있다. 그것은 세부 사항에 대한 신중한 관찰을 포함하며 인간 심리의 복잡성을 탐구한다. 리얼리즘은 낭만적 이상주의를 거부하며, 세상을 있는 그대로 묘사하는 것을 목표로 한다. 그것은 종종 사회적 관심사에 대해 이야기한다. 리얼리즘은 산업과 도시가 사람들과 공동체에 미친 영향을 탐구한다. 전반적으로, 문학에서의 리얼리즘은 19세기에 등장했으며 인간 존재의 일상적이고 평범하고 종종 혹독한 측면을 묘사하면서 삶을 있는 그대로 포착하려고 한 문학 운동이다.

06 분사 ③

| 분석 |
사람들이 이 프로그램을 기대하는 것이고, 이 프로그램은 사람들에 의해 '기대되는' 것이므로, ③의 anticipating을 수동의 과거분사인 anticipated로 고쳐야 한다.

| 어휘 |
streaming service 스트리밍 서비스 **for free** 무료로 **announcement** n. 발표, 공지 **tease** v. (맛보기영상(티저영상)으로 애타게 기대하게 하면서) 예고하다 **non-subscriber** n. 비구독자 **binge-watch** 몰아 보기 **anticipating** a. 기대되는 **promotion** n. 홍보, 판촉 **press release** 보도자료 **official** a. 공식적인 **available** a. 이용할 수 있는

| 해석 |
애플은 이번 주말, 1월 3일부터 5일까지 누구나 애플 TV+ 스트리밍 서비스를 무료로 이용할 수 있도록 허용할 것이다. 회사는 "세브란스(Severance)", "슬로우 호시스(Slow Horses)", "슈링킹(Shrinking)" 등, 가장 인기 있는 TV 프로그램들을 주된 내용으로 한 짧은 영상과 함께 월요일에 그 발표를 했다. 주목할 점은, 애플이 이와 같은 것을 이번에 처음으로 제공했다는 것이다. 이 발표는 애플 TV+가 비구독자들에게 콘텐츠를 공개할 계획임을 맛보기 영상으로 예고하기 시작하고 며칠 지난 뒤에 나왔다. 주말은 애플의 인기 프로그램을 몰아서 시청하기에 충분한 시간이며, 그런 프로그램 중 특히 "세브란스"는 1월 17일에 많은 기대를 받는 두 번째 시즌을 위해 돌아올 것이다. 애플의 홍보 트윗에서는 애플 TV+가 1월 4일과 5일에 무료로 스트리밍할 수 있을 것이라고 밝히고 있지만, 애플의 공식 보도자료에서는 1월 3일부터 5일까지 무료로 이용 가능할 것이라고 말한다.

07~08

알고리즘은 문제를 해결하거나 작업을 수행하기 위한 일련의 단계로, 일상생활과 컴퓨터 과학 모두에서 사용된다. 예를 들어, 커피 만들기나 신발 끈 묶기도 컴퓨터가 알고리즘을 실행하는 것과 마찬가지로 단계적인 과정을 따른다. 컴퓨터 과학에서 알고리즘은 유한한 수의 단계로 이루어진 수학적 과정으로, 검색 엔진, 내비게이션 시스템, 음악 스트리밍과 같은 프로그램 및 앱에 필수적이다. 이런 알고리즘은 컴퓨터에 무엇을 해야 하고, 어떻게 해야 하는지를 지시하며, 계산, 데이터 처리, 의사 결정과 같은 작업을 가능하게 한다. 알고리즘을 특정 목표를 달성하기 위해 일련의 행동을 안내하는 요리법이라고 생각하라. 다양할 수 있지만 그래도 초콜릿 칩 쿠키를 만들 수 있는 요리법들처럼, 다양한 알고리즘들도 서로 다른 접근법을 사용하지만 일관된 결과를 제공하여 동일한 문제를 해결할 수 있다.

| 어휘 |
set n. 집합 **step** n. 단계 **shoelace** n. 신발 끈 **step-by-step** a. 단계적인 **execute** v. 수행하다 **finite** a. 유한한 **application** n. 앱, 응용 프로그램 **navigation system** 내비게이션 시스템 **instruct** v. 지시하다 **calculation** n. 계산 **data processing** 데이터 처리 **decision-making** n. 의사 결정 **recipe** n. 요리법 **sequence** n. 순서, 연쇄 **obsolete** a. 낡은 **versatile** a. 다용도의

07 문맥상 적절하지 않은 표현 고르기 ④

| 분석 |
바로 앞에서 다양한 알고리즘들이 동일한 문제를 해결할 수 있다고 했으므로, 접근 방식은 서로 달라도 같은 결과를 낳아야 한다. 따라서 ⓓ inconsistent를 consistent로 고친다.

08 빈칸완성 ③

| 분석 |
글의 결론 부분이므로, 전체적인 주제와 같은 의미의 문장인 ③이 빈칸에 적절하다.

① 알고리즘은 실제 애플리케이션이 아니라 이론적인 문제에만 응용될 수 있다.
② 알고리즘의 발전은 전통적인 프로그래밍 방식을 쓸모없게 만들었다.
③ 다재다능한 알고리즘은 문제나 사용된 접근 방식과 상관없이 일관된 결과를 낼 수 있다.
④ 알고리즘을 개발하려면 기능성을 보장하기 위한 무한한 수의 단계가 필요하다.

09~10

스트레스는 여러 놀라운 속성을 가지고 있다. 스트레스는 우리가 무언가에 신경을 쓰고 있다는 사실을 상기시켜 주며, 우리를 우리의 삶에서 가장 힘들고 중요한 측면들과 직접적으로 연결해 준다. 우리는 지속적인 스트레스가 해를 끼치지 않는다고 말하고 있는 것이 아니라, 그것이 개인적 성장의 형태로, 예상치 못했던 이점도 가져올 수 있다고만 말하고 있는 것이다. 리더십 세미나를 진행하고, 명상과 무술을 가르치며, 심리학 분야에서 실증적 연구를 탐구하는 등, 수년간의 경험을 결합해 본 우리는 자기 삶에서 "스트레스는 우리를 향상시킨다"는 마음가짐을 받아들이는 사람들이 "스트레스는 우리를 쇠약하게 한다"는 관점을 채택한 사람들보다 업무성과는 더 높고 부정적인 건강 증상은 더 적다는 것을 발견했다. 고위경영자들, 학생들, 그리고 프로 운동선수들과의 작업과 연구를 이용하여, 우리는 스트레스의 해로운 영향을 최소화하면서도 스트레스의 창의적인 힘을 활용하는 데 도움이 될 수 있다고 믿는 3단계 억압 대응 방법을 고안했다.

| 어휘 |
attribute n. 속성, 특성 **sustained** a. 지속적인 **take a toll** 해를 끼치다 **unexpected** a. 예상치 못한 **empirical** a. 경험에 근거한, 실증적인 **mind-set** n. 사고방식, 태도 **debilitating** a. 약화하는, 해로운 **lens** n. 관점, 시각 **draw on** 이용하다 **harness** v. 활용하다 **deleterious** a. 해로운 **moderate** a. 적당한 **be associated with** ~와 관련이 있다 **asset** n. 자산 **rectitude** n. 정직 **malicious** a. 악의 있는

09 빈칸완성 ①

| 분석 |
빈칸 다음은 we are suggesting only that ~인데, 이것은 that절의 내용이 우리가 말하고 있는 최소한이라는 뜻이므로 앞의 빈칸 that절의 내용은 이보다 더 큰 정도의 심한 말, 즉 스트레스가 해로운 건 사실이지만 예상치 못한 이점도 준다는 정도가 아니라 아예 스트레스는 해롭지 않다는 말이 되어야 적절하다. 따라서 빈칸에는 ①이 들어가야 한다.

① 지속적인 스트레스는 해를 끼치지 않는다.
② 적당한 스트레스는 개인적 성장에 더 좋다.
③ 스트레스는 성과와 관련이 없다.
④ 스트레스는 동기화가 매우 강한 개인들에게 용기를 북돋는다.

10 빈칸완성 ②

| 분석 |
Ⓑ에는 스트레스가 '좋다'는 의미를 만들어 주는 표현이 필요하고, Ⓒ에는 스트레스가 '해롭다'는 의미를 만들어 주는 표현이 필요하다. '긍정-부정' 의미의 조합은 ②이다.

11~12

아일랜드 작가 시니드 글리슨(Sinead Gleeson)은 이렇게 말했다. "우리는 사회 상류층이 음유시인과 시인을 중시하는 전통을 가지고 있습니다. 우리는 또한 이야기꾼들의 나라입니다. 기근, 빈곤, 영국의 식민 지배 같은 끔찍한 시기를 겪었을 때조차도 사람들은 '케일리'라고 불리는 행사를 하려고 했습니다. 이는 집집마다 돌아다니며 이야기를 나누는 아일랜드의 전통입니다. 한때 식민 지배를 받았던 한국과 마찬가지로, 아일랜드는 1921년 영국으로부터 독립한 것에서부터 현대화의 거대한 물결과 가톨릭 보수주의로부터의 점진적인 이탈에 이르기까지 지난 100년 동안 사회적·문화적인 격변들을 겪어왔습니다. 이러한 변화는 침묵의 장소에서 새로운 목소리의 물결을 불러일으켰습니다."
이 침묵은 언어적인 침묵이자 문화적 침묵이었다. 19세기에 아일랜드의 전국 초등 교육 제도는 학교에서 아일랜드어를 가르치고 말하는 것을 금지했다. 가톨릭교회의 지배적인 영향은 사회적 침묵을 더욱 강화했으며, 이런 침묵의 강화는, 막달레나 세탁소(Magdalene Laundries)에서 악명 높게 목격되었듯이, 특히 여성들 사이에서 두드러졌다. 막달레나 세탁소에서는 수천 명에 달하는 미혼모와 그 밖의 '타락한 여성'들이 죄를 씻기 위해 강제 수감되어 노역에 종사했다. 현대 아일랜드는 여전히 많은 억압된 트라우마를 극복해가고 있으며, 일부 작가들은 글쓰기를 통해 그렇게 하고 있다. 또 다른 아일랜드 작가 로난 헤션(Ronan Hession)은 한국과 아일랜드가, 두 나라 모두 식민 지배를 극복했고 격동의 현대화를 경험했다는 점에서, 역사적으로 비슷해 보인다고

말했다. 아일랜드 문학과 한국 문학 모두에서 당신은, 뒤처지거나 소외된 사람들, 변해버린 가치관, 현대성에 들어가는 사람과 들지 못하는 사람 등, 무엇을 얻었고 무엇을 잃었는지에 대해 이렇게 이해하게 된다.

| 어휘 |

bard n. 음유시인 **echelon** n. 계층 **storyteller** n. 이야기꾼 **go through** 겪다 **famine** n. 기근 **colonization** n. 식민지배 **ceilidh** n. 케일리(사람들이 모여 춤을 추고 음악을 연주하며 이야기를 나누는 전통) **undergo** v. 겪다 **seismic** a. 지진의 **sweeping** a. 광범위한 **conservatism** n. 보수주의 **spark** v. 촉발하다 **ban** v. 금지하다 **predominant** a. 지배적인 **infamously** ad. 악명 높게 **witness** v. 목격하다 **fallen** a. 타락한 **incarcerate** v. 가두다 **work through** 해결하다, 처리하다 **marginalized** a. 소외된 **get a sense** 느끼다, 의식하다, 깨닫다, 이해하다 **affiliation** n. 동맹 **relinquishment** n. 포기

11 빈칸완성 ②

| 분석 |

내용상 앞에 나온 changes의 동의어인 transformations가 적절하다.

12 빈칸완성 ④

| 분석 |

앞의 문장이 이미 완전한 문장이므로 분사의 형태인 ②와 ④를 찾고, 이미 식민 지배는 끝난 일이므로 진행의 의미가 있는 ② having been moving가 아니라 완료분사구문인 ④가 적절한데, experienced는 moved와 병치된 과거분사이다.

13~14

세계 최대의 데이팅 플랫폼 포트폴리오를 보유한 기술 기업 매치 그룹(Match Group)은 2025년 3월에 새로운 제품 출시를 계기로 인공지능(AI) 투자를 늘릴 것이라고 발표했다. 아직 이름이 정해지지 않은 AI 어시스턴트는 가장 많은 반응을 얻는 사진을 선택하는 것과 같은 데이팅 핵심 작업을 수행하고 프로필에 넣을 조언과 정보를 추천해줄 것이다. 이 AI는 사용자들의 이상적인 파트너 선택에 도움을 줄 것이며, 사용자와의 음성 인터뷰를 통해 데이트 경험에서 얻기 원하는 것을 파악하고, 관심사를 바탕으로 매칭된 사람들에게 보낼 메시지를 제안할 것이다. 회사는 또한 AI가 '어려움을 겪는 사용자들을 위한 효과적인 코칭'을 제공할 것이라고 밝혔는데, 이런 코칭에는 매칭에 실패하고 있는 사람들을 위한 그들의 프로필에 더 많은 관심을 모을 수 있는 팁이 포함될 것이다.

| 어휘 |

portfolio n. 포트폴리오, 제품군 **investment** n. 투자 **assistant** n. 보조 도구 **garner** v. 모으다 **prompt** n. 조언, 자극하는 것, 촉구 신호 **bio** n. 프로필 소개, 약력 **spoken interview** 음성 인터뷰 **struggling** a. 어려움을 겪는 **attract attention** 관심을 끌다 **sprinkle** v. 뿌리다 **flutter** v. 퍼덕거리다 **garnish** v. 장식하다

13 동의어 ②

| 분석 |

garner에는 '모으다(collect)'라는 뜻 외에도 '얻다, 획득하다(acquire)'는 뜻이 있다.

14 내용일치 ③

| 분석 |

AI가 사진을 선택한다는 내용은 있지만, 사진을 생성한다는 내용은 없다.

① AI는 사용자의 데이팅 선호도를 인식할 것으로 예상된다.
② AI는 사용자가 플랫폼에서 짝을 찾는 데 도움을 줄 것으로 예상된다.
③ AI는 어려움을 겪는 사용자들을 위해 사진을 생성할 것으로 예상된다.
④ AI는 사용자들에게 다른 사람을 매료시키기 위한 팁을 제공할 것으로 예상된다.

15~16

스탠리 밀그램(Stanley Milgram)이 1960년대 초에 수행한 연구는 사회심리학 분야에서 가장 유명한 실험 중 하나이다. 이 실험에서 참가자들은 기억과 학습에 관한 연구에 참여하고 있다는 설명을 들었다. 참가자들은 '교사' 역할을 부여받았으며, 또 다른 한 사람은, 사실은 연기자('학습자')였는데, 의자에 묶여 단어 쌍을 암기하도록 지시받았다. 교사의 임무는 학습자가 오답을 말할 때마다 점점 강한 전기 충격을 가하는 것이었다. 충격은 15볼트에서 450볼트까지 점차 강해지며, 충격 강도에 따라 위험 수준이 표시되어 있었다. 학습자는 의도적으로 오답을 말했고, 충격 강도가 높아질수록 고통스럽게 비명을 지르다가 결국 충격이 더 강해지면 침묵에 빠졌다. 하지만 학습자는 실제로는 어떠한 전기 충격도 받지 않았으며, 비명과 침묵은 효과를 가장하기 위해 각본에 따라

연출된 것이었다.
밀그램의 핵심적인 발견은 놀랍게도 60% 이상의 참가자들이 학습자의 고통에도 불구하고 450볼트의 최대 전기 충격을 가할 의향이 있었다는 점이다. 많은 참가자는 땀을 흘리거나 긴장한 웃음을 짓는 등 스트레스 징후를 보였지만, 실험자의 지시에 계속 따랐다. 밀그램의 연구는 보통 사람들이 권위적인 인물의 명령을 받을 때 얼마나 해를 끼치는 행동을 수행할 가능성이 있는지를 보여주었으며, 이러한 행동이 본래 잔인한 사람들에게만 나타난다는 가정에 이의를 제기했다.

| 어휘 |

administer v. 가하다 **severe** a. 극심한 **simulate** v. 가장하다, 흉내 내다, 모의 실험하다 **intensity** n. 강도 **scripted** a. 각본에 따른, 미리 준비된 **distress** n. 고통, 괴로움 **obedience** n. 복종 **authority figure** 권위 있는 인물 **inherently** ad. 본질적으로 **engage in** ~에 관여하다

15 내용일치   ①

| 분석 |

참가자가 스트레스 징후를 보인 것은 학습자의 고통에 양심의 가책을 느낀다는 것이며, 그래도 실험자의 지시에 따른 것은 실험자의 권위에 복종한 것이므로 ①이 글의 내용과 일치한다. ② 이 연구에 대한 윤리적 비판은 없다. ③ 충격의 강도가 높아질수록 고통의 비명이 커진다. 답은 처음부터 끝까지 일관되게 잘못된 답이다. ④ 배우는 '교사'가 아니라 '학습자'이다.

① 사람들은 자신의 행위가 개인적인 양심과 충돌하더라도 권위자의 지시에 따르려는 경향이 있다.
② 밀그램의 연구는 참가자들에게 심리적 고통을 준 점을 중심으로 심각한 윤리적 비판을 받았다.
③ 충격의 강도가 증가할수록, 실험에서 '학습자'는 점점 더 잘못된 답을 내놓는다.
④ 실험에서 '교사'는 '학습자'의 수행을 강화하기 위해 스트레스 징후를 꾸며낸 배우였다.

16 빈칸완성   ③

| 분석 |

참가자들은 보통사람들이라 할 수 있고 고통스러워하는데도 전기충격을 계속 가하는 것은 남에게 위해를 가하는 행동이므로 Ⓐ에는 detrimental이나 harmful이 적절하다. 한편, 참가자가 보통 사람이므로 본래부터 잔인한 사람들만 그런 행동을 할 수 있을 것이라는 가정에 이의를 제기하는 셈이므로 Ⓑ에는 challenging이 적절하다.

17~18

주기율표는 많은 사람에게 화학의 상징이다. 그것은 우주 안의 알려진 모든 원소를 결합하여 하나의 읽기 쉬운 표에 담아 만들어낸 단일 이미지이다. 이 표에는 많은 패턴도 존재한다. 모든 원소는 서로 맞물려 연결되어 하나의 읽을 수 있는 표를 형성하고, 그리고는 결국 화학의 이미지를 만들어 내는 것 같다. 원소 개념은 기원전 300년경에 처음 등장했다. 위대한 그리스 철학자 아리스토텔레스는 지구상의 모든 것이 이 원소들로 구성되어 있다는 생각을 가졌다. 고대에는 금과 은 같은 원소들이 쉽게 접근 가능했지만, 아리스토텔레스가 선택한 원소는 흙, 물, 불, 공기였다.
1649년에 원소 개념은 헤닝 브란트(Hennig Brand)가 최초로 새로운 원소인 인을 발견하면서 큰 발전을 이루었다. 브란트는 연금술사로, 모든 금속을 금으로 바꿀 수 있는 물체인 '현자의 돌(Philosopher's Stone)'을 찾고 있었다. 그 탐색 과정에서 그는 인간의 소변을 증류하는 등, 모든 방법을 시도했다. 그 실험 결과, 브란트는 빛나는 하얀 돌을 발견했다. 이것이 그가 인이라고 부르게 될 새로운 원소였다. 계몽주의 시대의 연금술사와 과학자들은 원소 개념에 엄청난 지식을 추가했다. 1869년까지 이미 63개의 원소가 발견되었다. 새로운 원소가 발견될 때마다 과학자들은 원소들 사이에 패턴이 형성되고 있음을 깨닫기 시작했고 일부 과학자들은 원소를 표로 정리하기 시작했다.
현대의 주기율표는 멘델레예프(Dmitri Mendeleev)의 원래 버전과 몇 가지 측면에서 다르다. 현대 주기율표에는 40개 이상의 추가 원소가 포함되어 있으며, 가로행이 압착되어 비뚤비뚤 엇갈린 계단식 세로열을 이루는 대신에 가로행이 더 길어져 있다. 예를 들어, 멘델레예프의 네 번째와 다섯 번째 행은 모두 현대 주기율표의 네 번째 주기에 포함된다. 이에 따라, 스칸듐이 아닌 갈륨이 붕소 아래에 배치된다. 이러한 재배치는 원자의 전자 구조에 대한 이론, 특히 오비탈과 전자 배열과 주기율표 간의 관계에 대한 아이디어 때문이다. 연관된 원소들이 수직 그룹을 이룬다는 매우 중요한 개념은 멘델레예프의 그룹 번호와 마찬가지로 여전히 유지되고 있다. 그룹 번호는 현대 주기율표의 각 세로열 상단부에 로마 숫자로 표시되어 있다.

| 어휘 |

periodic table 주기율표 **accessible** a. 접근할 수 있는, 얻기 쉬운 **phosphorous** n. 인(燐) **alchemist** n. 연금술사 **distilling** a. 증류하는 **enlightenment period** 계몽주의 시대 **staggered column** 계단식 열 **orbital** n. 오비탈, 전자 궤도 **configuration** n. 배열, 배치 **retain** v. 유지하다, 보존하다 **impediment** n. 방해 **preservation** n. 보존

| 17　빈칸완성 | ① |

| 분석 |

멘델레프의 주기율표의 네 번째와 다섯 번째인 두 가로행이 현대 주기율표에서는 합쳐져 네 번째 가로행(주기)이 되어 있다는 것은 가로행에 들어가는 원소의 배치가 달라진 것을 말하므로 빈칸에는 rearrangement(재배치)가 적절하다.

| 18　내용추론 | ③ |

| 분석 |

'이러한 재배치는 원자의 전자 구조에 대한 이론 때문이다'라고 했으므로 ③이 추론할 수 있는 것이다. ① '모든' 기존 원소를 최종적으로 완성한 것이 아니라, '알려진 모든' 원소를 담고 있고 미래에 발견될 원소에 대해 개방되어 있다. ② 주기율표는 초기 버전과는 다르다. ④ 아리스토텔레스의 4원소 이론은 고대 철학적 개념으로, 현대 주기율표의 과학적 구성과는 관련이 없다.

① 주기율표는 모든 기존 원소들을 읽기 쉽고 체계적인 형식으로 최종적으로 완성했다.
② 멘델레예프의 초기 주기율표는 현대 버전에서도 변하지 않고 그대로 유지되고 있다.
③ 전자 이론의 발전은 현대 주기율표의 구조에 영향을 미쳤다.
④ 아리스토텔레스의 4원소 이론은 현대 주기율표에 직접적으로 반영되어 있다.

19~20

기후 변화는 수십 년간에 걸친 과학적 연구와 그 존재를 뒷받침하는 높은 수준의 과학적 합의에도 불구하고 여전히 매우 논쟁적인 주제이다. 기후 변화의 한 가지 결과는 더욱 극단적인 날씨이다. 카테고리 4 허리케인의 횟수에서 특정 겨울철 강설량에 이르기까지, 기록적인 기상 현상이 점점 더 많이 발생하고 있다. 이러한 극단적인 현상은 극적인 TV 보도를 가능하게 해주기도 하지만, 작물, 재산, 심지어 생명에 헤아릴 수 없는 피해를 줄 수 있다. 이에 따라 대략 200개국이 교토 의정서에 서명했는데, 이 문서는 기후 변화를 초래하는 활동을 제한하기 위한 자발적인 조치에 각국이 동참하도록 권장하려는 목적의 문서이다.
그러나, 특히 누구(어느 나라)가 오염을 유발해도 좋을 것인가라는 문제가 제기될 때는, 국가 간에 많은 책임 전가가 일어나고 있다. 세계 체계 분석에 따르면, 역사적으로는 미국과 서유럽 같은 핵심 국가들이 온실가스의 가장 큰 원천이었지만 이제 이들 국가는 탈산업화 사회로 발전했다. 산업화 반주변부 및 주변부 국가들은 이산화탄소와 같은 온실가스를 점점 더 많이 배출하고 있다. 이제 탈산업화되고 온실가스를 유발하는 산업에 덜 의존하게 된 핵심 국가들은 지구 온난화의 원인에 대해 엄격한 의정서를 제정하기를 원한다. 하지만 반주변부 및 주변부 국가들은 자신들의 경제를 발전시킬 (핵심 국가들과) 동일한 경제적 기회를 원할 따름이라고 올바르게 지적한다. 이들은 핵심 국가들의 발전에 의해 부당하게 악영향을 받았기 때문에, 지금 와서 핵심 국가들이 '환경' 정책을 고집한다면, 핵심 국가들은 일종의 보상금이나 보조금을 지급해야 한다고 주장한다. 이 갈등에는 쉬운 해답이 없다. 핵심 국가들이 산업화 호황기 동안에 무지로 인해 혜택을 누렸다는 점은 당연히 '공정'하지 않을 것이다.

| 어휘 |

controversial a. 논쟁의 여지가 있는　immeasurable a. 헤아릴 수 없는, 막대한　Kyoto Protocol 교토 의정서　finger-pointing n. 책임 전가, 비난　greenhouse gas 온실가스　post-industrial a. 탈산업화된　semi-peripheral a. 반(半)주변부　enact v. 작성하다　protocol n. 의정서　offset n. 보상금　subsidy n. 보조금

| 19　빈칸완성 | ① |

| 분석 |

핵심 국가들이 번성할 당시는 환경관련 규제가 없어서 그들이 유발한 환경오염의 피해를 다른 국가들이 보았다는 내용이므로, 빈칸 Ⓐ에는 '부당하게'라는 의미가 필요하다. 환경 문제는 산업화 당시에는 알지도 못했던 문제였다는 내용이므로 빈칸 Ⓑ에는 '무지'라는 의미가 필요하다.

| 20　내용추론 | ① |

| 분석 |

반주변부 및 주변부 국가들도 경제를 발전시킬 기회를 원하는데, 핵심국가들이 환경오염과 관련한 비용이 드는 환경정책을 고수한다면 그 비용을 보상금이나 보조금의 형태로 핵심국가들이 지불해야한다고 주장한다는 것은 핵심국가들에게 환경오염, 나아가 기후 변화의 책임이 있다고 주장하는 셈이므로 ①이 정답이다. ② 과학을 의문시한다는 내용은 없다. ③ 탈산업은 온실가스에서 벗어난 것이다. ④ 친환경 정책은 모든 나라의 경제 발전 정책을 규제한다.

① 반주변부와 주변부 국가들은 핵심 국가들이 기후 변화에 책임이 있다고 주장한다.
② 반주변부와 주변부 국가들은 기후 변화의 증거로 사용되는 과학을 의문시한다.
③ 탈산업 경제는 점점 온실가스를 배출하는 산업에 의존한다.
④ 친환경 정책은 핵심 국가들의 경제 발전을 촉진하지만 산업화된 국가들의 경제 발전은 촉진하지 않는다.

21~22

인간은 종족적이다. 우리는 집단에 속하기를 원한다. 우리는 결속과 애착을 갈망하며, 그래서 팀, 사교 클럽, 가족을 좋아한다. 거의 그 누구도 은둔자는 아니다. 그러나 종족 본능은 단순히 어디에 속하려는 본능만은 아니다. 어떤 집단은 자유 의사로 속하고, 어떤 집단은 그렇지 않다. 하지만 일단 사람들이 한 집단에 속하게 되면, 그들의 정체성은 그 집단과 기묘하게 묶일 수 있다. 그들은 개인적으로 얻는 것이 없더라도 집단의 구성원에게 유익을 주려고 한다. 외부인을 일견 부당하게 처벌한다. 그들은 집단을 위해 희생한다.

오늘날 미국에서는 어떤 집단도 충분히 우위를 점하고 있다고 느끼지 않는다. 모든 집단이 공격받고 있으며, 단지 일자리와 이익뿐 아니라 국가 정체성을 정의할 권리를 두고도 다른 집단들과 대립하고 있다고 느낀다. 이러한 상황에서 민주주의는 제로섬 집단 경쟁으로, 즉 순수한 정치적 종족주의로 전락한다.

외교 정책에서는 적어도 반세기 동안, 우리 미국인들은 종족 정치의 힘을 극도로 간과해 왔다. 우리는 세계를 자본주의 대 공산주의, 민주주의 대 권위주의, '자유세계' 대 '악의 축'과 같은 거대한 이념 전쟁에 참여하고 있는 영토를 가진 민족—국가들의 관점에서 보는 경향이 있다. 우리 자신의 이념적 관점에 눈이 멀어, 우리는 더 근본적인 집단 정체성을 반복적으로 무시해 왔다. 이러한 눈먼 태도는 미국 외교 정책의 치명적인 약점이 되어왔다.

국내적으로도, 미국 엘리트들은 많은 일반 미국인들에게 가장 중요한 집단 정체성에 대해 신경 쓰지 않거나 놀랍도록 망각해 왔다. 미국 엘리트들이 놓쳐버린 가장 중요한 종족 정체성은 노동 계급 안에서 형성되고 있는 강력한 반체제적 정체성이었고 이것이 도널드 트럼프를 당선시키는 데 도움을 주었다.

| 어휘 |

tribal a. 종족의 **tribalism** n. 종족주의 **attachment** n. 애착 **hermit** n. 은둔자 **gratuitously** ad. 이유 없이, 부당하게, 불필요하게, 쓸데없이 **pitted against** ~와 대립하는 **spoil** n. 전리품, 이익 **devolve** v. 전락하다 **zero-sum** n. 제로섬, 한쪽의 이득이 다른 쪽의 손해가 되는 상황 **prism** n. 관점 **Achilles' heel** 아킬레스건, 치명적인 약점 **antiestablishment** n. 반체제 **look up to** 존경하다 **look down on** 경멸하다

21 동의어 ①

| 분석 |

devolve는 evolve(진화하다, 발전하다)의 반대 개념으로 '더 못한(열등한, 저급한) 상태로 떨어지다'는 뜻이다. 따라서 '~로 영락하다, 전락하다'는 뜻의 descend into가 가장 가까운 의미이다.

22 내용추론 ②

| 분석 |

세 번째 단락 시작 부분에서 반세기 이상 미국 외교 정책은 민족—국가적 관점, 이념적 관점에 지배되어 종족 정치의 힘을 극도로 간과해왔다고 했다. 따라서 반대의 내용인 ②가 정답이다. ③ 첫 단락 마지막에서 '외부인을 부당하게 처벌한다'고 했다.

① 종족 정치는 국내 및 국제 정치 모두에서 상당한 영향을 미칠 수 있다.
② 미국 외교 정책은 종족적 고려에 지배되어 왔다.
③ 일부 사람들은 자신 종족의 이익을 위해 다른 사람들을 공격하는 경향이 있다.
④ 도널드 트럼프는 2016년 대선에서 부분적으로 정치적 종족주의 덕분에 승리할 수 있었다.

23~24

감기는 다양한 바이러스에 의해 발생하지만, 가장 흔한 원인은 리노바이러스이다. 이 바이러스들은 코와 목구멍의 세포를 점령하고 이들을 이용해 더 많은 바이러스를 생산한다. 며칠이 지나면, 면역 체계가 이를 감지하고 파괴하지만, 그때는 이미 평균적으로 다른 한 사람을 감염시킨 후이다. 감염을 물리친 후에는 해당 리노바이러스의 특정 변종에 대해서는 면역력을 가지게 되며, 이 면역은 수년간 지속된다. 만약 우리가 모두 격리된다면, 우리가 지니고 있는 감기 바이러스는 옮겨갈 새로운 숙주를 찾지 못하게 될 것이다. 그렇다면 우리의 면역계는 그 바이러스가 복제한 모든 바이러스를 제거할 수 있을까? 이 질문에 답하기 전에, 이러한 격리가 가져올 실질적인 결과를 생각해 보자. 세계 연간 총 경제 생산량은 약 80조 달러에 이른다. 이는 몇 주 동안 모든 경제 활동이 중단된다면 수조 달러의 비용이 든다는 것을 암시한다. 전 세계적인 '멈춤'으로 인해 경제체제에 가해지는 충격은 손쉽게 세계 경제 붕괴를 초래할 수 있다.

전 세계적인 격리는 또 다른 질문을 낳는다. 우리는 실제로 서로 얼마나 떨어질 수 있을까? 세상은 넓지만, 사람도 많다. 세계의 육지를 균등하게 나누면 우리 각자가 2헥타르 조금 넘는 정도의 공간을 가질 수 있고, 가장 가까운 사람이라 해도 77미터 떨어져 있다. 77미터는 리노바이러스의 전파를 막기에는 충분한 격리일 수 있지만, 그러한 격리에는 대가가 있다. 세계의 많은 땅은 5주 동안 아무 일도 하지 않고 우두커니 서 있기에 쾌적하지 않다. 우리 중 많은 사람은 사하라 사막이나 남극 중심부에 꼼짝없이 서 있게 될 것이다.

반드시 더 저렴하지는 않지만, 좀 더 실용적인 해결책은 모든 사람에게 생물학적 위험 방지 의복(방호복)을 제공하는 것이다. [B] 그렇게 하면, 우리는 돌아다니며 상호작용할 수 있고, 심지어 일부 정상적인 경제 활동도 계속할 수 있을

것이다. A 바이러스학 전문가 맥케이 박사는 순수한 생물학적 관점에서 볼 때 이 아이디어가 실제로 어느 정도는 합리적이라고 말했다. C 그는 리노바이러스와 기타 RNA 호흡기 바이러스가 면역계에 의해 몸에서 완벽히 제거되며, 감염 후에 오래 머물러 있지 않게 된다고 설명했다. D 게다가, 우리는 리노바이러스를 동물들과 주고받는 것 같지는 않다. 이는 감기의 저장소 역할을 할 수 있는 다른 종이 없다는 것을 의미한다. 만일 리노바이러스가 충분히 많은 사람들 사이를 돌아다니지 못하면, 리노바이러스는 사멸한다.

| 어휘 |

rhinovirus n. 리노바이러스   culprit n. 원인, 범인   immune system 면역 체계   strain n. 종류, 변종, 품종   quarantine n. 격리   host n. 숙주   wipe out 일소하다   economic output 경제 생산량   stand around (아무 일도 하지 않고) 우두커니 서 있다   in the neighborhood of 대략   biohazard suit 생물학적 위해 방지용 슈트   transmission n. 전파, 전달   collapse n. 붕괴, 몰락   put out 끄다   take over 점령하다   come at a cost 대가를 수반하다

23 빈칸완성 ③

| 분석 |

두 번째 문장은 바이러스가 숙주 세포에 들어가 자가 복제하여 증식하는 과정을 설명하는데, 기생충이 숙주의 몸을 점령하듯이 바이러스가 숙주 세포인 인간의 코와 목구멍 세포를 차지하므로 빈칸 Ⓐ에는 '점거하다', '접수하다'는 의미의 take over가 적절하고, 빈칸 Ⓑ 다음에 '그러한 격리'의 단점이 설명되므로, 빈칸 Ⓑ에는 불편함이나 외로움의 대가를 치르게 될 것이라는 의미로 come at a cost가 적절하다.

24 문장배열 ④

| 분석 |

앞 문장이 생물학적 위험 방지 의복으로 끝났으므로, 이 물건에 대한 최소한의 설명이 필요하다. 그나마 설명이 있는 문장은 B이다. 그리고 A에서 이 대안을 긍정하는 전문가가 있다고 하고, 그의 주장을 구체적으로 말하는 내용인 C가 이어지고, 마지막으로, 또 다른 정보를 덧붙이는 Furthermore로 시작하는 D가 오는 것이 적절한 순서이다.

25~26

민주주의의 전 세계적인 힘은 냉전이 끝난 직후 정점에 달했다. 역사상 처음으로, 사람들이 자유롭고 공정한 선거를 통해 지도자를 선택하고 교체할 수 있는 체제가 지배적인 정부 형태가 되었다. 2006년에 이미 약 3/5의 국가들이 이러한 기준을 충족했다. B 그 이후로, 민주주의와 자유는 꾸준히 퇴보해오고 있다. 이러한 퇴보는 전 세계적이었다. 이 변화가 항상 재난 수준인 것은 아니었지만, 상당히 광범위하고 지속적이었다. 민주주의의 세계적 전망은 완전히 절망적이지는 않지만, 매우 어둡다. 정치적 극단주의, 양극화, 그리고 불신이 오래 확립되어온 자유 민주주의 국가들에서도 증가하고 있다.
C 오늘날 민주주의가 직면한 도전은 무시무시하다. 권위주의 정권은 자유 사회를 불신케 하고 불안정하게 만들기 위한 공세를 취하고 있다. 그들이 자신의 정당성에 대한 두려움과 우려에서 이러한 행동을 한다고 해서 그들의 행동을 조금이라도 덜 위험하게 만드는 것은 아니다. 설상가상으로, 적대적인 독재 정권들은 중국, 러시아, 이란을 중심으로 하는 악의 축을 형성하고, 쿠바, 북한 및 다른 국가들과 협력하여 점점 더 일치되게 행동하고 있다.
A 이러한 세력으로부터 민주주의를 보호하기 위해서는 강인함, 민첩성, 그리고 끈기가 필요할 것이다. 세계 자유 민주주의 국가들은 외부 방어를 강화하고, 경제적, 군사적, 기술적 우위를 유지하기 위해 더 긴밀히 협력해야 한다. 이는 반민주적 적대 세력이 세계 정치를 지배하고 경쟁자들을 약화시키는 힘을 가지지 못하게 하기 위해서이다.
D 동시에, 프랑스와 독일에서 좌우 양측의 극단주의적 포퓰리즘 세력이 최근의 선거에서 지지율 상승을 거둔 것이 보여주듯이, 민주적 지도자들은 내부 방어를 소홀히 해서는 안 된다. 신흥 민주주의와 성숙한 민주주의 모두 비자유주의적 포퓰리즘의 유혹과 싸워 물리치기 위한 전략이 필요하다. 오랜 역사를 가진 자유 민주주의조차도 범죄와 테러를 퇴치하고, 국경을 관리하며, 사회적 분열을 완화하고, 경제적 기회와 사회보장에 대한 광범위한 접근을 보장하는 효과적인 정책을 제공하지 못한다면 독재로 기울어질 수 있다.

| 어휘 |

momentum n. 추진력, 힘, 기세   peak n. 정점   Cold War 냉전   predominant a. 지배적인, 우세한   standard n. 기준, 표준   retreat n. 후퇴, 퇴각   disastrous a. 재난의   clouded a. 어두운   if not ~까지는 아니라고 할지라도   downright ad. 완전히, 철저히   disheartening a. 실망스러운   be on the rise 증가하다   confront v. 직면하다   formidable a. 무시무시한   regime n. 정권   go on the offensive 공세를 취하다   discredit v. 신용을 해치다   making matters worse 설상가상으로   in concert 제휴하여   malevolent axis 악의 축   underscored a. 강조된   electoral gain 선거에서의 지지율 상승   populist force 포퓰리즘 세력   siren song 듣기 좋은 이야기   illiberal populism 비자유주의적 포퓰리즘   autocracy n. 독재   soothe v. 달래다   societal divisions 사회적 분열   security n. 사회보장

25 빈칸완성   ①

| 분석 |

냉전 종식 직후는 곧 공산진영이 무너지고 자유진영만이 남게 된 때로 민주주의가 지배적인 정부형태가 되었으므로 빈칸 Ⓐ에는 predominant(지배적인)나 principal(주요한)이 적절하고, 빈칸 Ⓑ 이하에서 민주주의에 적대적인 권위주의가 공세를 취하고 있다는 등의 언급이 이어지므로 빈칸 Ⓑ에는 민주주의가 직면하는 도전이 '크다'는 뜻으로 '무시무시한, 가공할만한'의 formidable이 적절하다.

26 단락배열   ③

| 분석 |

글 전체의 주제가 민주주의에 대한 도전과 응전이다. 도전이 Ⓑ와 Ⓒ에, 그에 대한 대응이 Ⓐ — Ⓓ의 순서로 펼쳐지고 있다. 그리고 영어의 논리는 '일반적 내용'에서 '구체적 내용'으로 가야 하므로 좀 더 일반적인 내용인 Ⓑ가 Ⓒ 앞에 와야 한다. 앞에서 2006년의 사정을 언급하고 있어서 '그때 이후(Since then)으로 시작하는 Ⓑ가 먼저 온다고 할 수도 있다. 마찬가지 논리에서 Ⓐ 다음에 좀 더 구체적인 내용의 Ⓓ가 와야 한다. 대명사를 활용하자면, 도전의 내용인 Ⓐ는 이러한 세력(such force)으로 시작하고 있으므로, 이러한 세력을 가리키는 악의 축이 등장하는 Ⓒ가 먼저 오고 그다음에 이어져야 한다.

27~28

NASA의 파커 태양 탐사선은 태양 대기 안으로 진입하여 극심한 열과 방사선을 견디며 인간에게 별의 외층에 대한 인류 최초의 근접 표본 추출을 제공하는 획기적인 임무이다. 2018년에 발사된 이 탐사선은 최첨단 열 공학 기술과 도구를 갖추고 태양의 자기장, 플라즈마, 고에너지 입자, 그리고 태양풍을 연구한다.
파커 태양 탐사선의 발견들은 태양에 대한 그리고 태양이 지구에 미치는 영향에 대한 우리의 이해를 이미 크게 바꾸어 놓았다. 예를 들어 코로나가 태양 표면보다 왜 더 뜨거운지, 그리고 태양풍이 어떻게 가속되는지와 같은 오랜 질문에 답하며, 이 탐사선은 우주 날씨를 예측하는 데 필수적인 데이터를 제공하고 있다. 이러한 통찰은 위성, 전력망, 우주 비행사들을 태양 방사선으로부터 보호하고 있다.
2024년 12월 24일, 파커 탐사선은 태양 표면에서 불과 380만 마일 떨어진 거리에서 시속 43만 마일이라는 기록적인 속도로 지남으로써 태양에 가장 가까운 접근을 완수했다. 가장 최근 근접비행은 탐사선의 23번째 근접 비행으로, 탐사선은 그 어느 때보다도 코로나에 더 깊숙이 진입했다. 데이터가 회수되면, 11년 주기의 태양 극대기 동안 태양의 행동에 대한 전례 없는 세부 정보가 제공될 것이다. NASA는 2024년 12월 27일, 탐사선이 태양 외대기를 성공적으로 항해했음을 신호음으로 알려주자 탐사선이 여전히 건강하다고 확인해 주었다.
탐사선은 큰 타원형 궤도를 유지하며, 2025년 3월과 6월에 두 번 더 태양을 가까이 지나갈 예정이다. 2025년 6월에 주 임무를 완료한 이후에도, 적재 연료가 고갈될 때까지 추가 관측을 수행하며 궤도에 남아 있을 것이다. 탐사선이 교정 추진력을 잃으면, 태양풍은 탐사선을 점차 지구와의 정렬에서 벗어나게 만들어, 탐사선의 데이터 전송 능력이 끝나게 될 것이다. 임무가 종료되면, 탐사선의 거의 모든 부분이 불타 없어질 예정이며, 탄소 열 차폐막만이 남아 아마도 수십억 년 동안 궤도를 그리며 태양 주위를 돌며 태양계가 끝날 때까지 남아 있을 것이다.

| 어휘 |

groundbreaking a. 획기적인, 신기원을 이룬   **launch** v. 발사하다
cutting-edge a. 최첨단의   **thermal engineering** 열공학
corona n. 코로나(태양 대기의 외층)   **plasma** n. 플라즈마(고온에서 이온화된 기체 상태)   **solar wind** 태양풍(태양에서 방출되는 입자 흐름)
space weather 우주 날씨(태양 활동이 지구와 우주 환경에 미치는 영향)
power grid 전력망   **flyby** n. 근접 비행   **solar maximum** 태양 극대기(태양 활동 주기에서 태양 표면 활동이 가장 활발한 시기)
unprecedented a. 유례없는   **beacon tone** 신호음   **elliptical orbit** 타원 궤도   **onboard** a. 적재한   **run out** 고갈되다   **corrective thrust** 교정 추진력   **incinerate** v. 소각하다, 불타다   **broadcast** v. 방송하다   **forecast** v. 예측하다

27 빈칸완성   ②

| 분석 |

탐사선의 임무는 '인류로 하여금 처음으로 별(태양)의 외층에 근접해서 그 외층에 대한 데이터를 수집할 수 있게 해주는 것'이므로 빈칸에는 데이터 수집을 의미하는 sampling(표본추출)이 적절하다.

28 내용일치   ③

| 분석 |

마지막 문단에서 파커 탐사선은 임무를 마친 후 대체로 없어진다고 하였으므로 ③이 정답이다. ② 태양을 23번 지나간 것은 2024년 12월 24일이다. 2025년 6월이면 두 번 더 지나갔을 것이므로 25번 지나갔을 것이다. ④ 세 번째 단락에서, 이 글이 써진 시점(2024년 12월 27일 이후 2025년 3월 이전)에서는 데이터가 회수되지 않았고, 회수되면 전례 없는 세부 정보를 제공할 것이라고 했는데, 현재완료시제로 제공했다고 했으므로 글의 내용과 일치하지 않는다.

① 파커 태양 탐사선은 임무를 완료하면 지구로 돌아오도록 예정되어 있다.
② 파커 태양 탐사선은 2025년 6월까지 태양을 23번 가까이 지나가게 된다.
③ 파커 태양 탐사선은 임무를 마친 후 대부분 소멸할 것이다.
④ 파커 태양 탐사선은 태양 극대기 전체 기간을 포함하는 데이터를 제공했다.

29~30

C 언어 습득에 어려움을 겪었거나 평균적인 아이보다 훨씬 느린 아이들의 사례가 있다. 이 아이들은 다른 인지적 결핍은 없으며, 자폐가 있거나 지능이 낮거나 지각에 문제가 있는 것이 아니다. 이들은 특정 언어 장애를 겪고 있다고 한다.
B 특정 언어 장애를 겪는 아이들이 보여주듯, 일반 지능이 온전한 상태에서도 언어는 손상될 수 있다. 그렇다면 일반 지능이 손상된 상태에서 언어가 정상적으로 발달할 수 있을까? 만약 그런 사람이 발견된다면, 이는 언어가 일반적인 인지 능력에서 파생되지 않는다는 관점을 강력히 뒷받침한다. 언어 능력이 태어날 때부터 특정 영역에 특화되어 있는지, 다시 말해 우리의 유전자에 있는지, 아니면 더 일반적인 지능에서 파생되는지는 언어학자, 심리학자, 신경심리학자들 사이에서 많은 관심과 논쟁을 불러일으키는 논란거리이다.
D 심리학 문헌에는 특정 영역에서는 장애가 있지만 다른 영역에서는 놀라운 재능을 보이는 지적 장애인의 수많은 사례가 기록되어 있다. 한 사례를 들자면 로라(Laura)라는 이름의 심각하게 지능발달이 지체된 아이이다. 그녀는 기본 원리를 포함한 거의 모든 수 개념을 이해하지 못하고, 미취학 아동 수준의 그림만 그릴 수 있고, 청각적 기억 범위는 세 단위로 제한되어 있다. 하지만 그녀는 구문적으로 복잡한 문장을 만들어 낸다. 그녀는 언어 능력은 잘 발달했지만, 비언어적 인지 발달에서는 심각한 결함을 보이는 아이들의 수많은 사례 중 하나이다.
A 유전적 장애 연구 또한 한 인지 영역이 비정상적인 발달을 보이는 동시에 다른 영역이 정상적으로 발달할 수 있음을 보여준다. 터너 증후군(염색체 이상)을 가진 아이들은 심각한 비언어적 인지 결함을 보이는 동시에 정상적이거나 발달된 언어 능력을 보여준다. 또 하나의 사례를 들자면, 윌리엄스 증후군을 가진 아이들의 언어 발달 연구는 심각한 일반적 인지 결함에도 불구하고 언어 기능이 선택적으로 보존된 독특한 행동적 특징을 보여준다.
따라서 특정 언어 장애와 다른 유전적 장애, 그리고 능력의 비대칭성, 등으로부터의 증거는 언어 능력을 독립적인 뇌 모듈로 보는 관점을 뒷받침한다.

어휘

case n. 사례 **cognitive deficit** 인지적 결핍 **autistic** a. 자폐의 **retarded** a. 지체의 **perceptual** a. 지각의 **Specific Language Impairment** 특정 언어 장애 **intact** a. 온전한 **argue for** ~이 옳다고 주장하다 **derive from** 유래하다 **as to** ~와 관련된 **faculty** n. 능력 **domain specific** 특정 영역에 특화된 **derivative** a. 파생된, 유래된 **neuropsychologist** n. 신경심리학자 **literature** n. 문헌 **document** v. 기록하다 **intellectually handicapped individual** 지적 장애인 **disability** n. 장애 **auditory memory span** 청각적 기억 범위 **syntactically** ad. 구문적으로 **simultaneous** a. 동시에 **asymmetry** n. 비대칭 **Turner's syndrome** 터너 증후군(염색체 이상으로 인한 유전적 질환) **behavioral profile** 행동적 특징

29 단락배열   ④

| 분석 |

일단 핵심 주제를 알리는 일반적인 문장 C가 오고, 마지막에 Specific Language Impairment이라는 어려운 전문용어가 등장했으므로 이것이 무엇인지 밝히는 구체적인 B가 온다. 이어서 D에서는 앞의 언어학, 심리학, 신경심리학 중에서도 더욱 구체적인 심리학 문헌들을 다루며, 더욱 구체적인 사례로 로라가 등장한다. 나머지 A의 첫 문장은 '유전적 장애 연구에서도 또한(also) 하나의 인지 영역이 비정상적인 발달을 보이는 반면, 다른 영역이 정상적으로 발달할 수 있다'고 했는데, also 때문에 이 문장 바로 앞에 그런 연구 분야에 대한 언급이 먼저 있어야 하므로 심리학 연구를 언급한 D 다음에 A가 이어져야 한다.

30 빈칸완성   ①

| 분석 |

결론이 되는 문장이다. 결국 언어 능력은 일반 지능에서 파생되지 않을 수 있고, 다른 지능의 저하에도 불구하고 언어 능력은 유지되는 것으로 보아, 언어 능력은 다른 영역과 '독립적'이라는 결론이 필요하다.

① 언어 능력을 독립적인 뇌 모듈로 보는
② 언어를 일반 지능의 반영으로 보는
③ 언어를 영역 특수적 능력과 일반적인 인지 능력의 혼합으로 보는
④ 언어 능력을 보편적인 인지 지각의 파생적 결과로 보는

서울여자대학교 오전 A형

TEST p. 350~362

01	③	02	④	03	①	04	②	05	④	06	②	07	①	08	①	09	③	10	①
11	③	12	③	13	①	14	②	15	③	16	④	17	②	18	③	19	②	20	③
21	①	22	④	23	①	24	③	25	①	26	①	27	②	28	①	29	②	30	②
31	④	32	③	33	④	34	③	35	④	36	②	37	④	38	②	39	④	40	①

01 동의어 ③

| 어휘 |
reverently ad. 경건하게, 공손하게(= deferentially) convention n. 풍습, 관례 occupy v. 차지하다, 점령하다 derisively ad. 비웃듯, 업신여기어 affectedly ad. 잘난 체 하면서, 뽐내면서 garrulously ad. 수다스럽게

| 해석 |
그 대만 감독은 1950~60년대에 자신의 영화 관람 인생에서 큰 비중을 차지했다고 말하는 그 장르의 전통을 경건한 마음으로 따르고 있다.

02 동의어 ④

| 어휘 |
doting a. 맹목적으로 사랑하는, 애지중지하는(= affectionate) crude a. 투박한, 솜씨 없는 disparage v. 깔보다, 헐뜯다 docile a. 유순한, 다루기 쉬운 obedient a. 순종하는, 유순한 tyrannic a. 압제적인, 폭군의

| 해석 |
자식을 애지중지하는 엄마인 엠마(Emma)는 미술을 해보려는 아들의 서툰 시도를 깎아내리기보다는 칭찬해줄 가능성이 훨씬 더 많았다.

03 동의어 ①

| 어휘 |
potent a. 세력 있는, 유력한; 설득력 있는; 효능 있는, (약 따위가) 잘 듣는 (= effective) alleviate v. (고통 등을) 완화하다, 덜다 fragile a. 부서지기 쉬운 flawless a. 흠 없는, 완벽한 persistent a. 끊임없는, 지속적인

| 해석 |
그 약은 효과가 있어서 환자의 통증을 완화시키는 것으로 입증되었다.

04 동의어 ②

| 어휘 |
scarcity n. 부족, 결핍(= shortage) tight a. (돈이) 딸리는, (상품이) 품귀한 fright n. 공포, 두려움 hardship n. 고난, 어려움 unrest n. 불안, 사회적 불안정

| 해석 |
우리의 대화 대부분은 물자 부족과 어떻게 해서 모든 것이 품귀 상태인지에 관한 것이었다.

05 동의어 ④

| 어휘 |
district council 지역 의회 streamline v. (시스템·조직 등을) 간소화하다, 합리화하다(= rationalize) threat n. 위협 relocate v. (주거·공장·주민 등을) 새 장소로 옮기다, 이전시키다 undercut v. 하부를 잘라버리다; 남보다 싼 값으로 팔다 merge v. 합병하다

| 해석 |
한 지역 의회 대표는 지방정부를 합리화하자는 제안이 민주주의에 위협이 된다고 경고했다.

06 논리완성 ②

| 분석 |
'사기의 발생'은 투자자 입장에서는 조심하고 경계해야 할 대상이므로, ②가 정답으로 적절하다.

| 어휘 |

fraud n. 사기, 협잡 **vivacious** a. 활발한, 쾌활한 **alert** a. 경계하는, 방심하지 않는 **fervent** a. 열렬한, 열정적인 **prolix** a. (말이나 글이) 장황한, 지루한

| 해석 |

미국 증권거래위원회는 투자자들에게 온라인 투자 사기의 가능한 징후에 대해 경계하라고 조언한다.

07 논리완성 ①

| 분석 |

유리잔 밑에 받침을 사용하게 하는 것은 유리가 나무로 된 가구를 '상하게 하지' 않도록 하기 위함일 것이다. 따라서 ①이 정답이다.

| 어휘 |

coaster n. (식탁용) 바퀴달린 쟁반; (글라스·접시 등의) 받침 **mar** v. 훼손하다, 손상시키다 **aggrandize** v. 확대하다, 강화하다 **abate** v. 줄이다; 누그러뜨리다 **mire** v. 진구렁에 빠뜨리다; 곤경에 몰아넣다

| 해석 |

유리잔 아래에 받침을 사용하여 목제가구를 훼손하는 것을 피하십시오.

08 논리완성 ①

| 분석 |

목적어로 '우리가 인간만의 것이라 여겼던 특성'이 주어져 있으므로 전체 문장은 "이제는 그러한 특성이 인간만의 것이 아니고 기계들도 그러한 특성을 갖게 되고 있다"라는 의미가 되는 것이 자연스럽다. 그러므로 '(특정한 특질·모습 등을) 띠다'라는 뜻의 ①이 정답으로 적절하다.

| 어휘 |

attribute n. 속성, 특성, 특질 **take on** (특정한 특질·모습 등을) 띠다 **turn to** ~로 바뀌다 **make up** 구성하다, 꾸미다 **run into** 우연히 마주치다

| 해석 |

기계들은 우리가 한때 인간만의 것이라고 여겼던 특성들을 점점 더 많이 띠어 가고 있다.

09 논리완성 ③

| 분석 |

고전 문학 작품을 영화로 바꾸는 것을 나타낼 수 있는 표현이 필요하므로, '각색'이라는 뜻의 ③이 정답으로 적절하다

| 어휘 |

adaptation n. 적응, 적합; 각색 **adjustment** n. 조정, 조절 **reparation** n. 수리; 배상, 보상 **commendation** n. 칭찬, 추천

| 해석 |

유니버설 픽쳐스는 크리스토퍼 놀란(Christopher Nolan)이 기원전 750년에서 650년 사이에 호메로스(Homer)가 쓴 것으로 여겨지는 고대 시 "오디세이아"를 영화로 각색하는 작업을 이끌 것이라고 이번 주에 발표했다.

10 논리완성 ①

| 분석 |

강제로 마스크를 착용하게 했던 것은 전염을 예방하기 위한 것인데, 대다수의 사람들이 백신 접종을 마쳤다면 그 필요성이 떨어졌을 것이므로 마스크 착용 의무가 "해제"됐을 것이다. 과거분사 lifted 앞에는 had been이 생략되었다.

| 어휘 |

vaccinate v. ~에게 예방 접종하다, ~에게 백신 주사를 놓다 **accordingly** ad. 따라서, 그러므로 **mandatory** a. 의무적인, 강제적인 **requirement** n. 요구, 필요 **lift** v. 해제하다 **impair** v. 손상시키다 **install** v. 설치하다 **decree** v. 포고하다, 판결하다

| 해석 |

2022년 여름에는 이미 대다수의 사람들이 백신 접종을 완료했고, 따라서 대부분의 국가에서 마스크 착용 의무가 모두 해제되었다.

11 대명사의 수일치 ③

| 분석 |

③은 The idea of human rights를 가리키는데, 이 표현의 핵심 명사인 The idea가 단수이므로 대명사도 단수여야 한다. ③을 its로 고친다.

| 어휘 |

fundamental a. 근본적인, 중요한 **critic** n. 비평가, 평론가 **receptive** a. (새로운 사상·제안에 대해) 수용적인[선뜻 받아들이는]

| 해석 |

기본권으로서의 인권 사상은 다른 면에서는 수용적인 지금 이 시대에도 비판하는 사람들이 없지 않다.

12 현재분사 ③

| 분석 |

that절 속의 주어 countries의 동사는 are이므로 ③의 contribute를 현재분사 contributing으로 고쳐 주어를 수식하는 역할을 하게 해야 한다. ① one of 뒤에 복수 명사 injustices가 왔다. ② 문두의 It은 가주어이고 that 이하가 진주어이다.

| 어휘 |

injustice n. 불의(不義), 불공정   **era** n. 시대   **contribute** v. 기여하다, 원인이 되다   **negligible** a. 무시해도 될 정도의, 미미한   **emission** n. 배출, 방출; 배기가스   **harrowing** a. 마음 아픈, 비참한

| 해석 |

전 세계 탄소 배출에 미미한 정도로 기여하고(원인이 되고) 있는 국가들이 지금 기후 변화의 가장 참혹한 영향을 겪고 있다는 것은 이 시대의 큰 불의(不義) 가운데 하나이다.

13 전치사 + 관계대명사 ①

| 분석 |

관계대명사 뒤에는 불완전한 문장이 오고 '전치사+관계대명사' 뒤에는 완전한 문장이 온다. ①의 뒤에 완전한 문장이 왔으므로 ①은 '전치사+관계대명사'가 되어야 하겠는데, 사유지가 공원 지역으로 바뀌는 것은 특정한 과정 속에서 혹은 특정한 과정에 의해 이뤄지는 것이므로 ①을 in which 혹은 by which로 고쳐야 한다.

| 어휘 |

process n. 과정   **transform** v. 변형하다, 바꾸다

| 해석 |

공유지나 사유지가 공원 지역으로 바뀌는 과정은 복잡하다.

14 some of + 한정사 + 명사 ②

| 분석 |

some[all, half, most, the rest] of 등과 같이 부분을 나타내는 표현 뒤에 오는 명사의 앞에는 정관사와 같은 한정사가 있어야 한다. 그러므로 ②는 the fast-growing jobs가 되어야 한다.

| 해석 |

2022년 1월부터 2024년 7월까지 수백만 개의 일자리를 조사한 LinkedIn의 새로운 분석에 의하면, 2025년에 빠르게 성장할 일자리들 가운데 일부는 세기의 전환점 무렵에는 거의 존재하지 않았던 것들이다.

15 too ~ to … 구문 ③

| 분석 |

'너무 ~ 해서 …할 수 없다'라는 의미는 'too ~ to부정사'의 형태로 나타낼 수 있으므로 ③을 too로 고쳐야 한다. ① 주어인 명사절을 이끄는 접속사로 쓰였다.

| 어휘 |

derive v. 끌어내다; 손에 넣다, 획득하다   **obvious** a. 명백한, 명확한   **instance** n. 사례, 예증

| 해석 |

우리가 종종 타인의 슬픔으로부터 슬픔을 얻는다는 것은 그것을 증명할 어떤 사례도 필요 없을 정도로 명백한 사실이다.

16 5형식 구문에서의 목적격 보어 ④

| 분석 |

빈칸은 'find+목적어+목적격 보어' 구문에서 목적격 보어가 들어갈 자리이다. 목적격 보어 자리에 명사와 형용사가 가능하지만, 주어진 문장에서 목적어와 목적격 보어 사이에 동격 관계가 성립하지 않으므로 명사가 아닌 형용사가 목적격 보어로 적절하며, 이때 형용사는 부사로 수식한다. 따라서 ④가 정답이 된다.

| 해석 |

어떤 사람들은 정서적 웰빙을 추구한다는 생각이 대단히 매력적이라고 여긴다.

17 선행사를 포함하고 있는 관계대명사 what ②

| 분석 |

빈칸에는 facing의 목적어가 되는 명사절을 이끄는 역할과 자신이 이끄는 절 안에서 타동사 call의 목적어가 되는 역할을 동시에 할 수 있는 표현이 들어가야 한다. 따라서 자체에 선행사를 포함하고 있는 what이 정답으로 적절하다.

| 어휘 |

agricultural a. 농업의   **polycrisis** n. 전 세계의 복합 위기

| 해석 |

세계는 코넬 대학의 농업 경제학자 크리스 배럿(Chris Barrett)이 '식량 다중위기'로 칭하고 있는 것에 이미 직면하고 있다."

18 비교급 수량 형용사 ③

| 분석 |

비교급과 호응하여 쓰이는 than이 있으므로 원급인 ①과 ②를 정답에서 먼저 제외할 수 있다. people이 복수 명사이므로 비교급 fewer 앞에 a가 올 수 없다. ③이 정답이며, a few든 few든 비교급은 모두 fewer이다.

| 해석 |

지금은 예전보다 도시로 이사하는 것에서 이점을 느끼는 사람들이 더 적다.

19 수동을 나타내는 과거분사 ②

| 분석 |

빈칸 이하는 바로 앞의 translated into English와 함께 to be에

연결되어 the first of her novels를 수식하는 역할을 해야 하는데, the first of her novels가 consider하는 행위의 주체가 아닌 대상이므로 과거분사를 써야 한다. 따라서 ②가 정답이다.

| 어휘 |
translate v. 번역하다   breakthrough n. 돌파구; 획기적인 약진

| 해석 |
2016년, 그녀는 『채식주의자』로 맨부커 국제 문학상을 수상했는데, 이 책은 그녀의 소설 중에 영어로 번역되어 그녀의 국제적인 주요 출세작으로 여겨진 최초의 것이었다.

20 복합분사 ③

| 분석 |
복합분사는 명사, 형용사, 부사 등이 하이픈(-)을 통해 분사와 연결된 형태이다. 그러므로 이러한 형태가 아닌 ②와 ④를 먼저 정답에서 제외할 수 있다. 한편, 이 복합분사의 수식을 받는 congestion pricing은 await하는 행위의 주체가 아닌 대상이므로, 복합분사에는 수동을 나타내는 과거분사를 써야 한다. 그러므로 ③이 정답이 된다.

| 어휘 |
congestion pricing 혼잡 통행료

| 해석 |
뉴욕시가 오랫동안 기다려온 혼잡 통행료 정책이 1월 5일에 시작되어, 맨해튼으로 차를 몰고 들어오는 것의 새로운 시대를 나타내었다.

21 논리완성 ①

| 분석 |
"글래디에이터와 같은 영화에 사용된 디지털 기술이 인상적이긴 하지만, 흙먼지나 자연스러운 움직임, 인간적인 세부 묘사들이 빠져 있어 아직 미흡하다."는 내용이 이어지고 있으므로, "디지털 제작은 옛 제작을 대체할 수 없다."라는 의미의 ①이 빈칸에 들어가기에 적절하다.

| 어휘 |
eliminate v. 제거하다, 없애다   replicate v. 복제하다, 재현하다
confine n. 제한, 경계   aesthetically ad. 미학적으로, 미적으로
preferable a. 더 바람직한, 오히려 더 나은   premature a. 시기상조의, 너무 이른   supplement n. 보충물, 추가물

| 해석 |
디지털 기술은 영화에서 옛 시절의 대규모 제작을 불필요하게 만들었다. 군중은 복제할 수 있고, 건물은 재현할 수 있으며, 등장인물은 컴퓨터의 한계 안에서 창조할 수 있다. 하지만 디지털 방식이 옛 방식보다 미학적으로 더 나은지는 전혀 다른 문제이다. 〈글래디에이터〉는 디지털 제작이 〈벤허(1959)〉와 〈스파르타쿠스(1960)〉에서와 같은 옛 제작을 대체할 수 없음을 보여주는 좋은 예다. 그 작품의 디지털 기술은 인상적이지만, 흙먼지, 자연스러운 움직임, 인간적인 세부 묘사들이 빠져 있어 아직 미흡하다. 배경과 보조적인 요소들 또한 지나치게 깨끗하다. 시각적 측면에서, 영화 속 과거의 모습은 결코 그렇게 완벽해 보이지 않았다.

① 디지털 제작은 옛 제작을 대체할 수 없다
② 디지털 기술은 새로운 향수를 불러일으킬 수 있다
③ 디지털 재현물은 옛 서사극에 경의를 표한다
④ 과거는 미학적으로 새로운 방식으로 디지털로 복제될 수 있다

22 논리완성 ④

| 분석 |
이어지는 문장에서 빈칸이 포함된 문장의 의미를 부연 설명하고 있는데, "더 높은 회원 등급은 고용주의 검색에서 귀하의 프로필이 서비스 등급이 낮은 회원들보다 더 높은 순위에 표시되는 것을 보장해줍니다."라는 말은 "직원을 구하고 있는 기업 고객에게 상위 등급의 회원이 더 눈에 잘 띄게 해준다."는 것이므로 빈칸에는 ④가 적절하다.

| 어휘 |
definitive a. 확정적인, 최종적인, 명확한   stay ahead of ~보다 앞서다, ~보다 우위를 점하다   enhance v. 향상시키다   ensure v. 보장하다, 확실하게 하다

| 해석 |
귀하의 경쟁력을 유지하십시오. Sologig.com은 스스로를 마케팅하는 부담을 줄여주어, 귀하가 가장 잘하는 일에 집중할 수 있게 해줍니다. 저희가 하는 일은 귀하가 가장 중요한 (기업) 고객뿐 아니라 다음번의 (기업) 고객과도 계속 연결되도록 도와주는 것입니다. 골드 회원이나 플래티넘 회원이 되는 것은 경쟁자들보다 계속 앞서 나가고 수천 개의 기업에 귀하의 서비스를 홍보할 수 있는 확실한 방법입니다. 간단히 말해, 회원 등급을 높이는 것은 잠재적인 (기업) 고객에게 귀하가 더 눈에 잘 띄게 해줍니다. 더 높은 회원 등급은 고용주의 검색에서 귀하의 프로필이 서비스 등급이 낮은 회원들보다 더 높은 순위에 표시되는 것을 보장해줍니다.

① 귀하의 업무 능력을 최대한으로 향상시킵니다
② 다른 회원들과의 관계를 굳건하게 만듭니다
③ 직업 교육 방법에 대한 귀하의 관점을 바꿉니다
④ 잠재적인 고객에게 귀하가 더 눈에 잘 띄게 해줍니다

23 논리완성 ①

| 분석 |
인간이 이성적인 동물임을 입증하는 증거를 찾아내지 못했다고 한 내용 다음에 On the contrary가 왔으므로, 마지막 문장은 '인간이

전혀 이성적이지 않음을 알게 됐다'는 내용이 되는 것이 자연스럽다. 따라서 ①이 정답으로 적절하다.

| 어휘 |

rational a. 이성적인, 합리적인   **in favor of** ~에 찬성하여, ~을 지지하여   **come across** 우연히 발견하다, 우연히 마주치다   **continent** n. 대륙

| 해석 |

인간은 이성적인 동물이다. 적어도 나는 그렇게 들어왔다. 나는 지금까지 오래 살아오면서 이 말이 사실이라는 증거를 부지런히 찾아 다녔지만, 3개 대륙의 여러 나라에서 찾아보았는데도 아직까지 그 증거를 만나는 행운을 누리지 못했다. 그와 반대로, 내가 본 세계는 계속 광기 속으로 점점 더 깊이 빠져들고 있었다.

① 계속 광기 속으로 점점 더 깊이 빠져들고 있었다
② 평범한 현실에 직면하도록 아무 도움 없이 방치되어 있었다
③ 저항할 수 없는 이성의 힘에 갇혀 있었다
④ 이성을 표현할 강한 욕망과 능력을 지니고 있었다

24 논리완성   ③

| 분석 |

마지막 문장에서 "동물은 주변과 더 많이 섞일수록, 더 오래 산다."고 했는데, 주변과 섞인다는 것은 위장한다는 것이므로, 결국 위장이 부족해서 먹이나 포식자로부터 발각되는 것(=자기 자신에게 주의를 끄는 것)이 동물에게 이익이 되지 못한다는 결론이 도출된다.

| 어휘 |

inborn a. 타고난, 선천적인   **camouflage** n. 위장, 변장, 기만 v. 위장하다, 숨기다   **prey** n. 먹이, 사냥감   **predator** n. 포식자   **deception** n. 속임수, 기만   **blend** v. 조화하다, 섞이다

| 해석 |

많은 동물과 곤충들은 먹이나 포식자로부터 숨기 위해 스스로를 위장하는 타고난 능력을 가지고 있다. 위장은 일종의 속임수이다. 자기 자신에게 주의를 끄는 것은 동물에게 최선의 이익이 되지 않는다. 동물은 주변과 더 많이 섞일수록, 더 오래 산다.

① 죽은 척하다
② 더 오래 산다
③ 자기 자신에게 주의를 끌다
④ 다른 이들이 알아채는 것을 피한다

25 논리완성   ①

| 분석 |

"국가는 모두에게 무료로 열려있는 공립학교를 제공하고, 아이들은 대부분의 어린 시절 동안 교육을 받아야 한다."라고 했는데, '모두에게 열린 교육'을 universal로, '의무적으로 받아야 하는 교육'을 compulsory로 표현할 수 있으므로 ①이 정답이 된다.

| 어휘 |

privilege n. 특권, 혜택   **tutor** n. 가정교사, 개인교사   **establish** v. 설립하다   **compact** n. 계약, 협정

| 해석 |

인류 역사의 대부분의 기간 동안, 대다수의 사람들은 학교에 다니지 않았다. 정규 교육은 아리스토텔레스를 개인교사로 둘 수 있었던 알렉산더 대왕 같은 사람들에게만 허락된 특권이었다. 19세기 중반부터, 미국은 진정으로 보편적이고 의무적인 교육을 확립하기 시작했다. 그것은 하나의 사회적 계약이었다. 그 계약은 국가는 모두에게 무료로 열려있는 공립학교를 제공하고, 아이들은 대부분의 어린 시절 동안 교육을 받아야 한다는 것이었다.

① 보편적이고 의무적인 교육
② 특권적이고 접근 가능한 교육
③ 포괄적이고 직업 중심의 교육
④ 목표 대상에 맞춘 혁신적인 교육

26 논리완성   ①

| 분석 |

건조한 환경에서 오래 살아남을 수 있다는 점, 항생제에 대해 내성을 가지고 있다는 점 등은 생존력 혹은 회복력과 관련된 것이므로 빈칸에는 ①이 들어가야 한다.

| 어휘 |

microorganism n. 미생물   **infection** n. 감염   **persist** v. 지속되다, 존속하다   **air vent** 환기구   **metabolic** a. 신진대사의   **genetic** a. 유전의   **flexibility** n. 유연성, 융통성   **resistant** a. 저항력이 있는, 내성이 있는   **antibiotic** n. 항생제   **membrane** n. 얇은 막   **threat** n. 위협   **pose** v. (위협·문제 등을) 제기하다, 초래하다   **microbe** n. 세균, 미생물   **priority** n. 보다 중요함, 우선   **pathogen** n. 병원균, 병원체

| 해석 |

박테리아 'Acinetobacter baumannii'는 회복력의 전형이다. 이 미생물은 다양한 감염을 일으키며, 그것이 건조한 환경에서 살아남을 수 있다는 것은 그것이 병원 환기구, 컴퓨터 키보드, 사람의 피부 위에서 수 주 동안 살아남을 수 있다는 것을 의미한다. 신진대사적·유전적 유연성 덕분에, 그것은 그것이 가지고 있는 두 겹의 보호 세포막을 통과할 수 있는 몇 안 되는 항생제에 대해서도 내성을 가지게 되었다. 항생제 내성 미생물로 인해 매년 100만 명 이상이 목숨을 잃고 있다. 'A. baumannii'가 초래하는 전 세계적 위협 때문에, 이 미생물은 세계보건기구(WHO)가 작성한 우선 대응 병원균 목록에서 높은 순위에 올랐다.

① 회복력의 전형
② 영감의 원천

③ 논란의 대상
④ 오해의 사례

27 논리완성 ②

| 분석 |

주어인 This는 앞 문장에 언급된 중국과 미국의 의도를 말하는데, 이것이 유럽에 위협이 되는 측면은 그 앞 문장에서 설명된 '미국의 기술 대기업의 권력을 억제하는 한편 신흥 기술 분야에서 유럽의 주도권을 확보한다는 EU의 목표'와 관계된 것이다. 따라서 ②가 빈칸에 적절하다.

| 어휘 |

semiconductor n. 반도체 **lack** v. 부족하다, ~이 없다 **consumer-facing firm** 소비자 대면 기업(직접 개인 소비자를 상대로 하여 상품과 서비스를 파는 기업) **monolith** n. (압도적인 힘을 가진) 거대 조직 **autonomy** n. 자율성 **commitment** n. 약속; 헌신, 전념 **regulatory** a. 규제의, 규제와 관련된 **curb** v. 억제하다, 제한하다 **secure** v. 확보하다, 지키다 **emerging** a. 신흥의, 새롭게 떠오르는 **sovereignty** n. 주권 **jurisdiction** n. 관할권, 사법권 **pose** v. (위협 등을) 제기하다 **threat** n. 위협

| 해석 |

유럽연합(EU)은 최근 수십 년 동안 주요 디지털 기술 분야에서 미국과 아시아에 뒤처졌다. 반도체 제조는 동아시아로 이동했고, 유럽에는 미국의 거대 디지털 기업들과 맞먹을 규모의 소비자 대면 기업이 없다. EU는 이것을 유럽의 자율, 안보, 경쟁 시장에의 헌신에 대한 위협으로 간주한다. 이에 따라 EU의 규제안과 공공 투자는 점점 더 미국의 기술 대기업의 권력을 억제하는 한편 신흥 기술 분야에서 유럽의 주도권을 확보하는 것을 목표로 하고 있다. 그러나 중국과 미국 또한 자국의 관할구역에서의 기술 규제에 대해 자주권을 가지길 원하며, 글로벌 기술 표준을 지배하길 원한다. 이러한 움직임은 유럽이 기술 분야에서 주도권을 되찾을 가능성에 위협이 되고 있다.

① 글로벌 환경 문제에 대한 관여
② 기술 분야에서 주도권을 되찾을 가능성
③ 모든 국가들을 단일 시장으로 통합하려는 계획
④ 반도체 제조를 외부에 위탁하려는 노력

28~29

'장애'라는 단어는 재정적, 신체적, 정신적, 혹은 법적으로 무언가가 결여되었음을 암시한다. 장애가 있다는 것은 사회, 문화, 경제, 정치 등의 면에서 소외된 위치를 떠올리게 한다. 장애는 지구상의 일부 지역에 다른 지역보다 더 집중돼 있는데, 이는 무력 충돌과 폭력, 영양 부족, 인구 증가, 아동 노동, 빈곤 등에 의한 것이다. 하지만 장애는 또한 점점 더 모든 곳에서 발견되고 있으며, 장애는 계급, 국가, 부(富)를 초월하여 우리 모두에게 영향을 미치고 있다. TAB(일시적 비장애인)라는 개념은 많은 사람들이 언젠가는 장애를 가지게 된다는 사실을 인식시킨다. 대부분의 장애는 선천적인 것이 아니라 후천적인 것이며(97%), 전 세계 추정치에 따르면 장애인의 수는 약 5억에서 6억 5천만 명인데, 이것은 전 세계 인구 가운데 약 10명 중 1명에 해당한다. 현재, 이들 중 1억 5천만 명은 어린이이며, 세계의 노동 연령 인구 중 3억 8,600만 명이 장애를 가지고 있는 것으로 추정되고 있다. 이들 가운데 88%는 세계에서 가장 가난한 국가에 살고 있으며, 그들 중 90%는 농촌 지역에 살고 있다. 장애를 가진 사람들은 무시당하거나, 동정을 받거나, 선심 쓰는 태도로 대우 받거나, 목적을 위한 수단처럼 여겨지거나, 지나치게 이질적인 존재로 여겨지는 경향이 있다. 신체적 또는 정신적 장애는 항상 일상적인 생활의 일부였지만, 장애를 비하하는 사회적 반응 — 소위 '장애화'나 '장애차별' — 은 시대와 문화에 따라 다르게 나타난다.

| 어휘 |

hint at ~을 암시하다, 넌지시 말하다 **fiscally** ad. 재정적으로 **disabled** a. 장애가 있는 **marginalized** a. 소외된 **conflict** n. 갈등, 충돌 **malnutrition** n. 영양실조 **affect** v. 영향을 미치다 **transcend** v. 초월하다 **TAB** (Temporarily Able-Bodied) 일시적으로 건강한 몸을 지닌 사람(잠재적 장애인) **impairment** n. 장애 **acquired** a. 후천적인 **congenital** a. 선천적인 **estimate** n. 추정, 추산 v. 추정하다 **currently** ad. 현재, 요즘 **pity** v. 동정하다 **patronize** v. 생색내며 돕다, 깔보듯 대하다 **objectify** v. 대상화하다, 물건처럼 취급하다 **fetishize** v. 맹목적으로 숭배하다; 지나치게 특별한 의미를 부여하다 **demeaning** a. 비하하는 **disablement** n. 장애화 (사회적·구조적으로 장애 상태를 만들어내는 과정) **disablism** n. 장애차별 **relative** a. 상대적인, 비교적인

28 지시대상 ①

| 분석 |

Ⓐ는 "demeaning societal responses to impairment", 즉 장애에 대한 경멸적 사회 반응을 지칭하므로, ①이 정답으로 적절하다.

다음 중 밑줄 친 Ⓐ가 지칭하는 것은?
① 장애에 대한 사회적 차별
② 장애인의 평등한 권리
③ 장애인의 공통된 특징
④ TAB(일시적 비장애인)의 문화적 가치

29 내용파악 ②

| 분석 |

장애가 경제에 어떤 영향을 미치는가에 대한 분석은 본문에서 다루고 있지 않다. 따라서 ②가 정답이다. ① 장애가 점점 더 모든 곳에서 발견되고 있으며 계층, 국가, 부를 초월해 영향을 준다고 했다. ③ 장애가 있다는 것은 사회, 문화, 경제, 정치 등의 면에서 소외된 위치를 떠올리게 한다고 했고, 장애가 사회적·경제적 맥락(예: 빈곤, 전쟁, 농촌 등) 속에서 발생하고 확대된다고 했다. ④ 구체적인 장애 인구의 수를 제시했다.

다음 중 위 글에서 논의되지 <u>않은</u> 것은?
① 장애의 전 지구적 특성
② 장애가 경제에 미치는 영향
③ 장애의 사회적·경제적 맥락
④ 전 세계 장애 인구의 규모

30~31

오늘날 컴퓨터에 대해 흔히 제기되는 것과 본질적으로 똑같은 반대 주장들을 플라톤이 『파이드로스』와 『일곱 번째 편지』에서 글쓰기에 대해 제기했다는 것을 알게 되면 대부분의 사람들은 놀라고, 많은 사람들은 괴로워한다. 플라톤은 『파이드로스』에서 소크라테스의 말을 통해 글쓰기가 비인간적이라고 말한다. 글쓰기는 실제로는 오직 마음속에만 존재할 수 있는 것들을 주제넘게도 마음 바깥에 자리 잡게 하려 한다는 것이다. 그 경우에 글은 물건, 즉, 만들어진 생산품이 된다. 물론 똑같은 주장이 오늘날 컴퓨터에 대해서도 제기되고 있다. 두 번째로, 플라톤의 책에 나오는 소크라테스는 글쓰기가 기억을 파괴한다고 주장한다. 글을 사용하는 사람들은 점점 더 잘 잊어버리게 되고, 내면의 자원에서 부족한 것을 위해 외부의 자원에 의존하게 될 것이다. 글쓰기는 정신을 약화시킨다. 오늘날, 부모들과 또 다른 사람들은 휴대용 계산기가 암기된 구구단처럼 본래 내적인 자원이어야 할 것에 외적인 자원을 제공한다는 점을 우려한다. 계산기는 정신을 약화시키며, 정신을 강하게 유지시켜 주는 활동을 정신에게서 덜어내 버린다. 세 번째로, 문자로 된 글은 기본적으로 반응을 하지 않는다. 어떤 사람에게 그 사람의 진술을 설명해줄 것을 요청하면 설명을 들을 수 있지만, 글에 대해 같은 요청을 하면 처음에 질문하게 만든 바로 그 (종종 어리석은) 같은 말 외에는 아무런 대답도 돌아오지 않는다. 컴퓨터에 대한 오늘날의 비판에서도 똑같은 반대의 견이 제기된다. 즉, "쓰레기를 넣으면, 쓰레기가 나온다."는 것이다. 네 번째로, 말로 하는 구술 문화의 논쟁적 사고방식에 따라, 플라톤의 책에서 소크라테스는 써놓은 글이 자연스러운 말처럼 스스로를 변호할 수 없다는 점도 글쓰기에 대한 비판으로 삼는다. 진짜 말과 생각은 언제나 본질적으로 진짜 사람들 사이의 주고받는 맥락 속에서 존재한다. 글쓰기는 수동적이고, 소외되어 있으며, 비현실적이고 부자연스러운 세계에 속한다. 컴퓨터도 마찬가지다.

| 어휘 |

distressed a. 괴로워하는, 불안해하는 **objection** n. 반대, 이의 **urge** v. 강하게 주장하다; 촉구하다 **inhuman** a. 비인간적인, 인간미 없는 **pretend to do** 주제넘게 ~하려 하다 **establish** v. 세우다, 확립하다 **manufactured** a. 만들어진, 인위적인 **calculator** n. 계산기 **memorize** v. 암기하다 **multiplication table** 구구단 **unresponsive** a. 반응하지 않는, 무반응의 **critique** n. 비평, 비판 **agonistic** a. 경쟁적인, 논쟁을 좋아하는 **mentality** n. 사고방식, 정신구조 **context** n. 맥락, 문맥 **passive** a. 수동적인, 소극적인

30 글의 주제 ②

| 분석 |

본문에서는 플라톤이 글쓰기에 대해 제기했던 비판들을 소개하면서, 그것들이 오늘날의 컴퓨터에 대한 비판과 유사하다고 말하고 있다. 중심 내용은 글쓰기에 대한 비판이므로 ②가 정답이다.

위 글의 주된 내용은 무엇인가?
① 글쓰기에 대한 옹호
② 글쓰기에 대한 비판
③ 글쓰기와 컴퓨터 사용의 차이점
④ 내부 자원과 외부 자원의 비교

31 내용일치 ④

| 분석 |

본문 마지막 부분에서 플라톤이 쓴 저서 속의 소크라테스는 말과 생각은 사람들 간에 주고받는 맥락 안에서 진정으로 존재하며, 글은 수동적이고 부자연스럽다고 주장하고 있다. 이는 그가 말하기를 선호했음을 보여주므로 ④가 정답이 된다. ① 플라톤이 쓴 책에 나온 소크라테스가 말을 한 것이다.

위 글에 의하면 다음 중 옳은 것은?
① 소크라테스가 『파이드로스』를 썼다.
② 플라톤은 외적인 자원을 소중히 여겼다.
③ 글쓰기와 달리, 컴퓨터는 수동적이지 않다.
④ 소크라테스는 말로 하는 표현을 선호했다.

32~34

2020년에 우리 학교 이사회는 학교 입학시험을 폐지하고 전체 학생의 다양성을 높이기 위한 노력의 일환으로 새로운

입학 요건을 도입한다고 발표했다. 그러한 고귀한 목표에 반대하는 주장을 하는 사람은 아무도 없었지만, 우리 중 많은 사람들은 그 방법에 대해서는 할 말이 많았다. 그것은 노력과 많은 희생을 통해 실력으로 학교에 입학하려 했던 학생들에게 큰 상처를 주었다. 나는 학부모, 학생, 졸업생들로 구성된 한 단체의 일원인데, 이 단체에서는 실력을 기반으로 하는 입학 제도를 복구하기 위해 소송을 제기했다. 학교 이사회는 새로운 입학 요건 또한 실력을 기반으로 한다고 주장했다. 올해 연방 판사는 그러한 입학 요건 변경이 "명백히 위헌적"이며 아시아계 미국인 학생들에게 차별적이라고 판결했다. 학교 이사회가 판결에 항소를 제기는 동안에도 우리는 우리가 승소할 것이라 확신하고 있다.

불행히도, 이러한 잘못된 정책들은 교육계 전반으로 퍼져나가고 있다. 캘리포니아에서는 여러 교육구에서 D와 F 학점 부여를 줄이려고 하고 있고, (0점 대신) 50점을 학생이 받을 수 있는 가장 낮은 점수로 만드는 것과 같은 "공평한 평가"를 도입하고 있으며, "유연한 과제 제출기한 정책"이라는 새로운 지침 하에서 과제 마감일을 넘기는 것도 허용하고 있다. 미국의 다른 지역의 교육구들 역시 고급 (영재) 학업 프로그램과 대학과정선이수제(AP) 수업을 폐지하고 있다. 이러한 하향식 경쟁은 학습 장애 학생들, 사회경제적 어려움을 겪는 사람들, 새로 영어를 배우는 학습자들 등, 그것이 실력을 끌어올려주려고 하는 젊은이들에게 도움이 되지 않는다.

| 어휘 |

board n. 이사회, 위원회 **eliminate** v. 제거하다, 없애다 **diversity** n. 다양성 **merit** n. (칭찬할 만한) 가치, 장점, 공로 **alumnus** n. (학교·대학의) 졸업생들 **sue** v. 고소하다 **reinstate** v. (원래 상태로) 복귀시키다, 복원하다 **merit-based** a. 능력[공로] 기반의 **patently** a. 명백히, 분명히 **unconstitutional** a. 위헌의, 헌법에 어긋나는 **discriminatory** a. 차별적인 **confident** a. 확신하는, 자신 있는 **prevail** v. 이기다, 우세하다; 성공하다 **appeal** v. 항소하다, 상고하다 **ruling** n. 판결, 결정 **district** n. 구역, 지역 **distribute** v. 분배하다 **equitable** a. 공평한, 공정한 **uplift** v. 끌어올리다, 향상시키다 **late work policy** 과제 제출기한 정책(늦게 기한을 넘겨 제출된 과제에 감점을 가하는 정책) **advanced placement** 대학과정선이수제

32 글의 제목 ③

| 분석 |

본문에서는 학교가 다양성을 높이기 위해 입학시험을 폐지하고 새로운 정책을 도입한 것에 대해 비판적인 입장을 취하고 있다. 저자는 "실력"을 중시해야 한다고 주장하면서, 과도한 평등 추구가 오히려 학생들에게 해를 끼친다고 말하고 있다. 따라서 제목으로는 ③이 가장 적절하다.

위 글의 제목으로 가장 적절한 것은?
① 교육에서의 성공 스토리
② 교육에서 우수한 능력보다 형평성을 우선시하기
③ 교육 정책에서의 실력에 대한 옹호
④ 교육에서 다양성을 옹호하는 사례

33 내용추론 ④

| 분석 |

저자는 미국 일부 교육구들에서 고급 학업 프로그램과 대학과정선이수제 수업을 폐지하고 있는 것을 수준 낮추기의 하향식 경쟁에 동조하는 것으로 규정하고 있으며, 이러한 움직임이 학생들에게 도움이 되지 않는다고 말하고 있다. 이는 곧 저자가 '고급 학업 프로그램'을 지지하고 있다는 것이 되므로 ④가 정답으로 적절하다.

다음 중 저자가 지지할 가능성이 가장 큰 것은?
① 더 관대한 성적 평가
② 유연한 과제 제출기한 정책
③ 입학시험의 폐지
④ 고급 학업 프로그램

34 지시대상 ③

| 분석 |

밑줄 친 Ⓐ는 학생 집단의 다양성을 높이기 위해 학교 당국이 추진하고 있는 새로운 제도를 가리킨다.

다음 중 밑줄 친 Ⓐ가 가리키는 것은?
① 우수한 학생을 유치하는 방법
② 교육의 질을 향상시키는 방법
③ 학생 집단의 다양성을 높이는 방법
④ 불리한 배경을 가진 학생을 돕는 방법

35~36

1948년에는 50만 명의 노동자가 석탄 채굴에 종사하고 있었다. 그러나 21세기 초까지 이들 일자리의 대부분은 사라졌는데, 이는 우리가 석탄 채굴을 중단했기 때문이 아니라 — 석탄 생산의 큰 감소는, 즉 처음에는 천연가스 그다음에는 재생 에너지로의 전환은, 불과 15년 전쯤부터 시작되었을 뿐이다 — 기술적으로 진보된 노천 채굴과 산 정상부를 깎아내는 채굴 방식 덕분에 훨씬 적은 인력으로 점점 더 많은 석탄을 캐낼 수 있게 되었기 때문이다. 기술 발전으로 인해 사라지는 일자리가 일반적으로 다른 일자리로 대체되어 온 것은 사실이다. 그러나 그것이 그 과정이 고통 없이 이루어졌다는 것을 의미하는 것은 아니다. 개별 노동자들은 특히

새 일자리가 다른 지역에 있을 경우 직업을 바꾸는 것이 쉽지 않을 수 있다. 그들이 가진 기술이 평가절하 될 수도 있다. 어떤 경우에는, 석탄 산업에서처럼, 기술 변화가 공동체와 그들의 삶의 방식을 송두리째 흔들어 놓을 수도 있다. 이런 종류의 혼란은 적어도 200년 동안 현대 사회의 특징으로 있어 왔다. 그러나 지금은 무언가 새로운 일이 벌어지고 있는지도 모른다. 과거에는 기술에 의해 대체된 일자리가 육체노동과 관련된 것인 경향이 있었다. 기계가 인간의 근육을 대신했던 것이다. 한편으로는 산업용 로봇이 일상적인 조립생산 라인 작업을 대신했다. 다른 한편으로, 지식 노동자에 대한 수요는 계속해서 증가해 왔는데, 지식 노동자는 반복적이지 않은 문제 해결에 종사하는 사람들을 가리키기 위해 피터 드러커가 만들어낸 용어이다. 나를 포함한 많은 사람들은 우리가 점점 지식 경제로 나아가고 있다고 말해왔다. 그러나 만약 우리가 전통적으로 지식 노동이라고 생각해 온 것의 상당 부분을 기계가 떠맡을 수 있다면 어떻게 될까?

| 어휘 |

bulk a. 전부의, 대량의 **decline** n. 감소, 하락, 저하 **renewable** a. 재생 가능한 **extraction** n. 추출, 채굴 **replace** v. 대체하다 **in the face of** ~에도 불구하고, ~에 직면하여 **devalue** v. (가치·중요성을) 떨어뜨리다, 평가절하하다 **uproot** v. (사람을 익숙한 환경에서) 몰아내다; 뿌리째 뽑다 **dislocation** n. 혼란; 위치 이동 **term** n. 용어 **coin** v. (새로운 말을) 만들다 **chunk** n. 큰 덩어리, 상당 부분

35 내용파악   ④

| 분석 |

1948년에는 50만 명의 노동자가 석탄 채굴에 종사하고 있었으나 21세기 초까지 이들 일자리의 대부분이 사라진 것은 "기술적으로 진보된 노천 채굴과 산 정상부를 깎아내는 채굴 방식 덕분에 훨씬 적은 인력으로 점점 더 많은 석탄을 캐낼 수 있게 되었기 때문"이라고 했으므로, ④가 정답이 된다.

21세기 초에 석탄 광부들이 대규모로 사라진 원인은 무엇인가?
① 석탄 매장량의 고갈
② 광부 임금의 하락
③ 친환경 에너지로의 전환
④ 채굴 방식의 기술적 발전

36 지시대상   ②

| 분석 |

밑줄 친 Ⓐ는 기존에는 기술이 육체노동을 대체했지만, 지금은 지식 노동 영역까지 기계가, 즉 로봇 기술이, 침투하고 있는 새로운 변화를 가리킨다. 이것은 본문 마지막 부분에서 우리가 지식 노동이라고 생각해왔던 일들을 이제는 기계가 대신하게 될 수도 있다는 우려를 나타내는 부분에서 확인할 수 있다.

다음 중 밑줄 친 Ⓐ가 가리키는 것은?
① 지식 기반 경제의 부상
② 기술에 의해 주도되는 지식 노동 시대의 도래
③ 인간 노동자와 산업용 로봇 간의 협업
④ 청정 에너지원을 선호함에 따른 석탄 생산의 감소

37~38

코페르니쿠스 기후변화 서비스가 발표한 새로운 자료에 따르면, 2024년은 기록상 가장 더운 해였다. 또한 2024년은 파리 기후 협약에서 제시한 지구 온난화 목표인 섭씨 1.5도를 처음으로 초과한 해이기도 했다. 그러나 앞으로 몇 년이 지나면, 당신은 2024년을 특히 더웠던 해로 기억하지 않을 가능성이 크다. 왜냐하면 앞으로 당신이 살아갈 나머지 인생 중에서는 2024년이 가장 '서늘한' 해 중의 하나가 될 것이기 때문이다. 인류가 계속해서 화석연료를 태워 지구를 뜨겁게 만드는 한, 미래의 당신은 현재를 날씨가 더 평온했고(극도로 춥지 않았고), 겨울엔 눈이 더 많이 왔으며, 기온도 더 따뜻했던(덥지 않았던) 시기로 회상하게 될 것이다. 오늘 태어난 아이들에게는, 미래에 찾아올 더 덥고, 더 폭풍이 잦은 기후 조건이 정상처럼 느껴질 것이다. 이는 기준점 이동 증후군으로 알려져 있는 심리적 착각 때문인데, 이 증후군은 사람들로 하여금 현재 경험하고 있는 어떤 환경 조건에든 점점 더 익숙해지게 만든다. 이 현상은 사회의 환경 기준 ― 그 기준이 대기 오염의 허용 수준과 관련된 것이든, 바다의 물고기 수와 관련된 것이든 ― 이 서서히 약화되는 결과를 초래할 수 있다. 기후 변화의 경우, 기준점 이동 증후군은 사회로 하여금 점점 더 뜨거워지는 기온과 그 밖의 수많은 지구적 영향들을 점차 정상적인 것으로 받아들이게 만들고 있을지도 모른다.

| 어휘 |

fossil fuel 화석 연료 **shifting baseline syndrome** 기준점 이동 증후군(온난화로 인해 평균 기온이 높아지는 등 생태계의 기준점이 변화하는 현상) **grow accustomed to** ~에 익숙해지다 **phenomenon** n. 현상 **gradual** a. 단계적인, 점차적인 **erosion** n. 부식, 침식 **normalize** v. 정상으로 여기다, 당연하게 받아들이다

37 글의 주제   ④

| 분석 |

본문은 사람들이 미래에 기후 변화와 환경 위기를 어떻게 느낄지에 관해 다루고 있는데, 특히 기준점 이동 증후군으로 인해 사람들이 기후 변화를 점차 정상으로 받아들이게 될 것임을 이야기하고 있다. 따라서 ④가 정답이다.

위 글은 주로 무엇에 관한 것인가?
① 지금까지 이상 기후 조건을 유발한 원인은 무엇인가
② 기후 변화에 대응하기 위해 인간이 해야 할 일은 무엇인가
③ 2024년이 기온 측면에서 얼마나 극한적이었는가
④ 미래에 사람들이 환경 위기를 어떻게 느끼게 될 것인가

38 내용파악 ②

| 분석 |

"기준점 이동 증후군은 사회로 하여금 점점 더 뜨거워지는 기온과 그 밖의 수많은 지구적 영향들을 점차 정상적인 것으로 받아들이게 만들고 있을지도 모른다."라고 했는데, 이는 기준점 이동 증후군이 사람들로 하여금 더 높은 온도나 나쁜 환경 조건을 점차 정상으로 받아들이게 만들어, 결과적으로 기후 변화에 대응하려는 의지가 약해지게 만들 수 있음을 암시하고 있다.

위 글에 의하면, 기준점 이동 증후군은 _____.
① 어른들보다 아이들에게 더 쉽게 영향을 미칠 수 있다
② 기후 변화에 대응하려는 사람들의 의지를 약화시킬 수 있다
③ 열악한 환경 조건에 대한 사람들의 인식을 고양시킬 수 있다
④ 정책 입안자들로 하여금 환경보존 정책에서 더 강력한 목표를 설정하도록 만들 수 있다

39~40

유럽 전역에서, 유럽연합의 금융 위기, 긴축 정책, 늘어나는 난민과 이민자 수의 여파로 포퓰리즘 정당들과 정치 운동들이 등장하거나 세력을 강화해 왔다. 이러한 사태 전개는 구제금융을 받기 위한 전제 조건으로서 현금성 복지급여와 공공 복지 서비스에 대한 급진적인 삭감이 실시된 그리스와 스페인 같은 나라들뿐만 아니라, 위기를 겪으면서도 (다른 국가들을 지원하기 위해) 구제금융을 제공한 핀란드, 프랑스, 독일, 네덜란드 같은 나라들에서도 비슷하게 나타났다. 총괄적으로, 위기와 위기관리로 촉발된 경기 침체가 많은 유럽인들 사이에 불만, 절망, 분노의 감정을 축적시켰다. 이러한 집단적인 감정들은 부당하고 국민의 지지를 받지 못하는 정책들에 책임이 있다고 여겨지는 정부들에 대한 항의 시위를 부추겨 왔다. 의문점은 이러한 과정들이 왜 전통적으로 광범위한 사회적 불만의 수혜자였던 좌파가 아니라 주로 우파에 대한 지지를 낳았는가 하는 것이다.

| 어휘 |

aftermath n. (안 좋은 일의) 여파, 결과 **austerity** n. 긴축 정책 **refugee** n. 난민 **immigrant** n. 이민자 **radical** a. 급진적인, 과격한 **welfare transfer** 현금성 복지급여 **implement** v. 실행하다, 시행하다 **precondition** n. 전제 조건 **bailout loans** 구제금융 **contribute to** ~에 기여하다, 자금을 지원하다 **initiate** v. 시작하다.

촉발하다 **reservoir** n. 저수지; 저장소 **discontent** n. 불만 **fuel** v. 자극하다, 부추기다 **unjustified** a. 정당화될 수 없는, 부당한 **predominantly** ad. 주로, 대체로 **harbor** v. (생각·감정 등을) 품다 **wide-ranging** a. 폭넓은, 다양한 **dissatisfaction** n. 불만족

39 글의 주제 ④

| 분석 |

유럽 전역에서 포퓰리즘 정당과 정치 운동이 왜 부상했는지에 대한 배경을 위기와 위기관리의 잘못으로 인한 경기침체와 정부에 대한 집단 감정으로 설명하고 있는 글이므로 ④가 정답으로 가장 적절하다.

위 글은 주로 무엇에 관한 것인가?
① 그리스와 스페인에서의 구제금융 과정과 결과
② 중유럽 및 북유럽의 복지 시스템의 실패
③ 유럽 여러 지역에서 나타나는 다양한 형태의 포퓰리즘 정책
④ 유럽 포퓰리즘 정책의 경제적·심리적 배경

40 내용일치 ①

| 분석 |

"유럽 전역에서, 포퓰리즘 정당들과 정치 운동들이 등장하거나 세력을 강화해 왔다."와 "의문점은 집단감정과 시위의 과정이 왜 전통적으로 광범위한 사회적 불만의 수혜자였던 좌파가 아니라 주로 우파에 대한 지지를 낳았는가 하는 것이다."라는 내용을 종합하면, 현재 유럽에서는 우파 포퓰리즘이 더 힘을 얻고 있음을 알 수 있다. 그러므로 ①이 옳지 않은 진술이다.

위 글에 따르면, 다음 중 옳지 않은 것은?
① 현재 유럽에서는 우파 포퓰리즘보다는 좌파 포퓰리즘이 더 우세하다.
② 유럽에서 포퓰리즘이 부상한 것은 부분적으로는 EU의 금융 위기 때문이다.
③ 그리스와 스페인에서는 현금성 복지 급여와 공공 복지 서비스가 극심하게 줄어들었다.
④ 전통적으로 대중의 사회적 불만에 힘입어 성장해온 것은 좌파였다.

서울여자대학교 정오 A형

TEST p. 364~376

01	②	02	④	03	①	04	③	05	②	06	③	07	①	08	③	09	③	10	②
11	②	12	②	13	④	14	①	15	②	16	③	17	①	18	③	19	④	20	④
21	④	22	③	23	①	24	①	25	④	26	①	27	③	28	④	29	①	30	②
31	③	32	②	33	①	34	④	35	②	36	④	37	③	38	①	39	③	40	②

01 동의어　②

| 어휘 |

disguise n. 변장, 위장　**infuse** v. 불어넣다, 주입하다(= instill)　**intrigue** v. 흥미를 불러일으키다, 음모를 꾸미다　**inhibit** v. 억제하다, 방해하다　**incur** v. (좋지 않은 일을) 초래하다

| 해석 |

에반(Evan)과 그의 사람들은, 변장한 악마가 사람들의 마음속에 경쟁개념을 심어주려 한 것이었지만, 왜 서로를 도우면 안 되는지를 결코 알지 못했다.

02 동의어　④

| 어휘 |

reticence n. 말이 없음, 과묵함(= reserve)　**defendant** n. 피고　**collapse** v. 무너지다, 붕괴하다; 실패하다　**rebuke** n. 꾸짖음, 비난　**refutation** n. 반박, 논박　**recession** n. 퇴거; 경기 침체

| 해석 |

핵심 증인이 말을 아끼는 바람에 피고를 상대로 한 소송이 무산되었다.

03 동의어　①

| 어휘 |

ascertain v. 규명하다, 확인하다(= confirm)　**valid** a. 타당한, 유효한　**inquire** v. 질문하다, 묻다　**applaud** v. 박수갈채를 보내다, 칭찬하다　**foretell** v. 예언하다

| 해석 |

그들은 그 이론이 타당한지를 확인하기 위해 여러 가지 실험을 수행했다.

04 동의어　③

| 어휘 |

retaliate v. 보복하다, 앙갚음하다　**exhaustive** a. 철저한, 완전한, 포괄적인(= comprehensive)　**tariff** n. 관세　**follow through with** ~을 이행[완수]하다　**steep** a. (요구·값 등이) 터무니없는, 무리한　**definitive** a. 결정적인, 최종적인　**destructive** a. 파괴적인　**selective** a. 선별적인, 선택적인

| 해석 |

만약 도널드 트럼프가 캐나다산 제품에 터무니없이 높은 25%의 수입세를 부과하겠다는 자신의 계획을 실행에 옮긴다면, 캐나다는 미국산 제품에 대한 포괄적인 관세 목록으로 보복할 준비를 할 것이다.

05 동의어　②

| 어휘 |

inflammatory a. 격앙시키는, 선동적인(= provocative)　**remark** n. 발언, 언급　**soothing** a. 진정시키는　**placid** a. 평온한, 고요한　**arrogant** a. 거만한, 오만한

| 해석 |

그 정치인의 선동적인 발언은 대중들 사이에 큰 불안을 초래했다.

06 논리완성　③

| 분석 |

비유로 들고 있는 "마치 재즈 연주자가 공연 때마다 그 순간에 맞게 연주하듯이"라는 내용에서 강조하는 내용은 임기응변의 능력이므로, 빈칸에는 상황에 맞게 '즉흥적으로 하다'라는 의미의 ③이 적절하다.

| 어휘 |

facilitate v. 용이하게 하다, 촉진하다   install v. 설치하다, 비치하다
improvise v. 즉흥적으로 하다, 즉석에서 하다   replicate v. 복제하다; (실험을) 반복하다

| 해석 |

연기가 훌륭한 배우는, 마치 재즈 연주자가 공연 때마다 그 순간에 맞게 연주하듯이, 자신의 극중 역할을 그때그때 순간에 맞게 즉흥적으로 연기하는 방법을 알고 있어야 한다.

07 논리완성   ①

| 분석 |

경기장 건립에는 더 많은 자금이 필요한데, 만약 추가적인 자금 지원이 이뤄지지 않는다면, 경기장의 건립은 '실행 가능하지' 못할 것이다

| 어휘 |

additional a. 추가적인   funding n. 자금 지원   feasible a. 실행 가능한   impassible a. 아픔을 느끼지 않는, 무감각한   impetuous a. 성급한, 충동적인   dismal a. 우울한, 암울한, 형편없는

| 해석 |

추가적인 자금 지원이 없으면, 뉴욕의 웨스트 사이드에 양키스를 위한 새로운 경기장을 짓는 것은 실행가능하지 않을 수도 있다.

08 논리완성   ③

| 분석 |

'so ~ that …' 구문은 인과관계의 문장을 만든다. '가장 복잡한 개념들조차도 이해하기 쉬웠다'라는 결과를 가져오기에 적절한 것은 그녀의 발표가 '간결했던' 것이 가장 타당하다.

| 어휘 |

complicated a. 복잡한   ambiguous a. 애매한, 불확실한, 두 가지 이상의 의미로 해석될 수 있는   convoluted a. 복잡한, 뒤얽힌   concise a. 간결한, 간단명료한   rampant a. (사람·짐승이) 격한, 사나운, 광포한; (잡초 등이) 무성한, 우거진

| 해석 |

그녀의 발표는 너무나 간결해서 가장 복잡한 개념들조차도 이해하기 쉬웠다.

09 논리완성   ③

| 분석 |

쌀 재배자들이 비행기에서 호르몬을 살포하는 수고를 하는 것은 그들에게 이익이 되기 때문일 것이다. 작물이 빨리 자라는 것이 그들에게 이익이 될 것이므로, '곡물의 숙성을 앞당기다'라는 의미가 되도록 빈칸에는 ③이 들어가는 것이 자연스럽다.

| 어휘 |

crop n. 수확; 농작물, 곡물   ripen v. 익다; 원숙하다   reap v. 수확하다   evict v. 퇴거시키다, 쫓아내다   hasten v. 서두르다; 앞당기다, 촉진하다   confide v. (비밀 등을) 털어놓다

| 해석 |

많은 쌀 재배자들은 공중에서 호르몬을 살포하여 작물의 숙성을 앞당기기 위해 비행기를 사용한다.

10 논리완성   ②

| 분석 |

마을들이 자율적이라고 했는데, 빈칸 앞에 부정어 no가 있으므로 빈칸에는 자율과 반대되는 속성이나 의미를 내포하고 있는 표현이 들어가야 한다. 그러므로 '지배하는'의 의미를 가진 ②가 정답으로 적절하다.

| 어휘 |

autonomous a. 자치의, 자율의   flimsy a. 무른, 취약한, 부서지기 쉬운   overarching a. 무엇보다 중요한, 모든 것에 앞선; 지배적인   archaic a. 고대의, 구식의   exquisite a. 정교한

| 해석 |

보다 큰 문화 단위 안에 있는 서로 다른 마을들은 매우 자율적이며, 따라서 (문화 단위) 전체가 지배하는 구조는 전혀 없다.

11 be동사의 보어   ②

| 분석 |

②는 be동사의 보어가 와야 하는 자리인데, be동사의 보어가 될 수 있는 것은 부사가 아닌 형용사이므로 ②를 as intense as로 고쳐야 한다. ③ those는 evolutionary pressures를 가리키고 ④ its는 nature를 가리킨다.

| 어휘 |

evolutionary a. 발달의, 진화의   constraint n. 제약; 제한, 통제

| 해석 |

기계는 살아있지 않지만, 그것들을 둘러싼 진화적 압력은 자연에서의 진화적 압력만큼 강하며, 자연이 가하는 제약은 거의 없다.

12 distinguish A from B   ②

| 분석 |

'A를 B와 구별하다'는 distinguish A from B로 나타내므로 ②를 from으로 고쳐야 한다. the knowledge that is useful information이 A에 해당하고, the humanistic knowledge that leaves people wiser and transformed가 B에 해당한다.

| 어휘 |
distinguish v. 구별하다, 분별하다 **humanistic** a. 인문학의; 인문주의적인 **transform** v. 변형시키다; 바꾸다

| 해석 |
AI 시대는 우리로 하여금 유용한 정보인 지식을 사람을 더 지혜롭고 변화되게 하는 인문학적 지식과 더욱 명확히 구별하게 한다.

13 자동사 look의 보어 ④

| 분석 |
④에 쓰인 자동사 look은 형용사나 'like 명사'('전치사+명사'구)를 보어로 취하므로, ④를 will look like로 고쳐 what을 전치사 like의 목적어가 되도록 해주어야 한다.

| 해석 |
우리 학교에서 일어나고 있는 일이 미래의 우리 사회가 어떠해 보일지를 결정할 것이다.

14 명사의 수 ①

| 분석 |
①에서 quarter 앞에 복수의 수사 three가 있으므로 quarter를 복수형으로 써야 한다. ①을 three-quarters로 고친다.

| 어휘 |
surpass v. ~보다 낫다, ~을 능가하다, ~을 뛰어넘다[초과하다]
afford v. ~의 여유가 있다, ~을 살[지급할, 소유할] 돈이 있다

| 해석 |
이미 10억을 넘은 아프리카의 인구 중 4분의 3 이상은 건강한 식단을 가질 수 없다.

15 명사를 수식하는 수사 표현 ②

| 분석 |
Tens of thousands는 '수만(數萬)'을 의미하는데, 그 뒤에 명사가 올 때는 반드시 of를 동반한다. 그러므로 ②는 tens of thousands of여야 한다.

| 어휘 |
paramilitary n. 준군사 조직, 불법 무장단체원 **civilian** n. 민간인
displace v. 제거하다; 추방하다

| 해석 |
수단의 군대와 강력한 준군사조직은 거의 2년 동안 전쟁을 벌여왔으며, 수만 명의 민간인이 사망했고 1,200만 명에 가까운 사람들이 난민이 되었다.

16 cite A as B ③

| 분석 |
'A를 B로서 인용하다'는 cite A as B로 표현한다. 그러므로 ③이 정답이다.

| 어휘 |
affordable a. 입수 가능한, (값이) 알맞은 **facilities** n. 시설, 설비
stable a. 안정된, 견고한 **factor** n. 요인, 요소

| 해석 |
그 연구는 저렴한 보육시설과 안정적인 경제성장을 출산율을 끌어올리기 위한 요소들로 인용하고 있다.

17 의문문의 형태 ①

| 분석 |
주어인 some이 '일부 사람들'이라는 의미의 복수 대명사이므로 조동사는 do를 써야 하며, 조동사 뒤에는 동사원형이 와야 하므로 claim이 이어져야 한다. 따라서 ①이 정답이다. 이때 hair 이하는 claim의 목적어 절이며 hair 앞에는 접속사 that이 생략돼 있다.

| 해석 |
왜 일부 사람들은 샴푸를 며칠간 사용하지 않으면 머리카락이 더 윤기 있게 보인다고 주장하는 것일까?

18 of + 추상명사 ③

| 분석 |
be동사 are 뒤에 보어가 와야 하겠는데, 'of+추상명사'가 형용사의 의미를 가지므로 ③이 정답으로 적절하다. 전치사 in은 be in ~'s interest(~에게 이익이 되다)라는 표현에 쓰인다.

| 어휘 |
tadpole n. 올챙이

| 해석 |
올챙이의 먹이 활동 습성은 많은 과학자들에게 흥미롭다.

19 시제 ④

| 분석 |
1989년 11월에 일어난 일을 과거 시제로 나타냈으므로 1945년 여름부터 1989년 11월까지 있었던 일은 과거완료 시제로 나타내는 것이 적절하며, 유사 관계대명사 than의 선행사인 shifts가 see하는 행위의 주체가 아닌 대상이므로 수동태로 나타내야 한다. 즉 than(목적격) people(일반인) had seen이 수동태가 되어 than (주격) had been seen (by people)으로 된 것이다. 따라서 과거완료 수동태인 ④가 정답이다.

| 해석 |

1989년 11월은 1945년 여름 이후 그때까지 있었던 것들보다 더 많은 변화들을 세계 체제의 기본 구조에 가져왔다.

20 관계사절   ④

| 분석 |

빈칸 앞에 완전한 문장이 주어져 있으므로, 빈칸 이하는 접속사와 함께 절이 이어지거나 접속사를 포함하고 있는 관계대명사가 쓰여야 한다. 그러므로 접속사도 없고 관계사도 없는 ①과 ②를 정답에서 먼저 제외할 수 있다. 한편, 빈칸 이하는 and most of its members의 형태가 되어야 하므로, most of 뒤에 whose가 와야 한다. 따라서 ④가 정답이다.

| 어휘 |

militant a. 교전하고 있는; 호전적인   anarchist n. 무정부주의자

| 해석 |

그녀는 소규모 팀과 함께 그 사이트를 운영하기 시작했는데, 그 팀의 구성원들 중 대부분은 그녀와 마찬가지로 호전적인 무정부주의자들이었다.

21 논리완성   ④

| 분석 |

"75세의 퇴임한 프랑스인(=자크 들로르)이 왜 여전히 유럽 주요 인사들의 관심을 끄는지 그 이유는 분명하지 않다."라고 한 다음에 '그러나'라는 의미의 And yet이 왔으므로, 이유는 분명치 않지만 그가 주요 인사들의 관심을 끄는 것은 분명하다는 뜻으로 '주요 인사들이 그에게 관심을 기울이는 행동'이 빈칸에 들어가야 한다. 따라서 빈칸에는 ④가 가장 적절하다. ② 그는 이미 퇴임한 상태이므로 지금 그의 위원장직을 지지하는 것은 부적절하다.

| 어휘 |

revile v. 욕하다, 매도하다, 비난하다   fade v. 흐릿해지다, 사라지다
squabble n. 시시한 언쟁, 말다툼   trim a. 단정한, 말쑥한   run-up n. (중요한 일의) 준비 기간   summit n. 정상 회담

| 해석 |

자크 들로르(Jacques Delors)가 EU 집행위원장직을 퇴임한 지 이제 5년이 지났다. 영국의 타블로이드 신문들은 더 이상 그를 비난하지 않으며, 마거릿 대처(Margaret Thatcher)와의 싸움은 EU의 전설이 되어 사라졌고, 브뤼셀에서 밤을 새며 벌였던 논쟁은 이제 다른 사람들의 고민거리가 되었다. 그래서 비록 말쑥한 60세처럼 보이긴 해도 75세인 퇴임한 한 프랑스인이 왜 여전히 유럽 주요 인사들의 관심을 끄는지 그 이유는 분명하지 않다. 그러나 12월 7일에 니스(Nice)에서 시작된 EU 정상회담의 준비기간 동안, 그는 장관들, 공무원들, 위원들이 그의 말 한마디 한마디를 경청하도록 만들었다.

① 그들의 승리를 널리 알리다
② 그의 집행위원장직을 지지하다
③ 그들의 사무실을 벗어나다
④ 그의 말 한마디 한마디를 경청하다

22 논리완성   ③

| 분석 |

빈칸 이하는 운명을 한탄하는 데 쓴 시간을 '생산적으로 썼을 경우에' 얻게 될 결과이므로, 빈칸에는 '생산적으로 쓰이는 경우'인 ③이 가장 적절하다. ④ 감사하는 태도는 미덕이긴 하지만, 성과를 내는 직접적인 행동은 아니다.

| 어휘 |

ashore ad. 해변으로, 해안으로   well and good 좋은 일이다, 좋다
literally ad. 말 그대로, 정말로, 실제로   frown upon ~을 못마땅하게 여기다, 눈살을 찌푸리다   lament v. 한탄하다, 슬퍼하다   lot n. (사람의) 운명, 처지   yield v. 산출하다, 초래하다, (결과를) 내다
splendid a. 훌륭한, 멋진   proper a. 적절한, 타당한

| 해석 |

해변으로 밀려 올라온 바닷가재는 다시 바다로 돌아가려는 노력은 하지 않고, 바다가 자신에게 오기를 기다린다고 한다. 바다가 오면 좋지만, 오지 않으면 그냥 죽고 만다. 아무도 자신을 도와주지 않는다고 불평하며, 다른 사람들의 성공에는 전적으로 행운이나 친구들의 영향 덕분인 것으로 여기고 눈살을 찌푸리는 사람이 실제로 수천 명에 이른다. 그들이 자신의 운명을 한탄하는 데 쓰는 시간은, 정직한 노력에 쓰인다면, 훌륭한 결과를 가져올 것이고 그들에게 세상에서의 적절한 위치를 가져다 줄 것이다.

① 꿈꾸는 데 낭비된다면
② 그들이 사회 탓을 한다면
③ 정직한 노력에 쓰인다면
④ 그들이 다른 사람들에게 감사한다면

23 논리완성   ①

| 분석 |

This orientation은 오늘날의 학생들이 대학을 안정적인 직업을 얻기 위한 과정으로 간주하고 있는 성향을 가리킨다. 이러한 성향은 학생들로 하여금 직접적으로 취업에 도움이 되지 않아 보이는 과목이나 지식들을 배우지 않게 만들 것이라 추론할 수 있으므로, 빈칸에는 ①이 들어가야 한다.

| 어휘 |

overwhelming a. 압도적인   degree n. 정도; 등급   avenue n. 길, 수단, 방법   stable a. 안정적인   given prep. ~을 고려할 때, ~라는 점에서   wage premium 임금 프리미엄, (비교 대상보다) 더 받는 임금   bachelor's degree 학사 학위   diploma n. 졸업증서

학위수여증 orientation n. 성향, 태도, 방향 close off 차단하다, 막다

| 해석 |

압도적일 정도로, 오늘날의 학생들은 대학을 직업 훈련, 즉 안정적인 직업에 이르는 길로 간주하고 있다. 학사 학위를 가진 22~27세 근로자들이 고등학교 졸업장만 있는 근로자들보다 70% 더 높은 임금을 받는다는 점을 고려하면, 그들이 틀린 것은 아니다. 하지만 이러한 성향은 취업 전망에 명백히 도움이 되지 않는 것들을 학생들이 배우지 못하게 만들 수 있다.

① 그들의 취업 전망에 명확하게 도움이 되지 않는
② 그들이 선택한 진로와 직접적으로 연결되어 있는
③ 균형 잡힌 교육에 기여하지 않는
④ 그들을 노동 시장이 요구하는 바에 준비시켜주는

24 논리완성   ①

| 분석 |

"편리함이 개인의 삶과 경제를 형성하는 가장 강력한 힘으로 떠올랐다."고 한 다음, "자유와 개성에 대한 그 모든 찬사에도 불구하고"라고 했으므로 빈칸에는 편리함에 대한 긍정적인 말이나 자유와 개성에 대한 부정적인 말이 들어가야 한다. 따라서 ①이 적절하다. ②와 ③은 편리함에 대한 부정적인 내용이고 ④는 자유와 개성에 대한 긍정적인 내용이어서 부적절하다.

| 어휘 |

convenience n. 편리함, 용이함   emerge v. 나타나다, 출현하다
tribute n. 헌사, 경의

| 해석 |

21세기 선진국에서는 개인적인 일을 더 효율적이고 더 쉽게 하는 편리함이 우리의 개인적인 삶과 경제를 형성하는 아마도 가장 강력한 힘으로 떠올랐다. 이는 미국에서 특히 그러한데, 미국에서는 자유와 개성에 대한 그 모든 찬사에도 불구하고, 많은 사람들이 편리함이 사실상 최고의 가치를 가지고 있다고 여기고 있다.

① 편리함이 사실상 최고의 가치이다
② 편리함의 힘은 종종 간과된다
③ 편리해 보이는 것이 실제로는 오도할 수도 있다
④ 편리함은 자유 및 개성과 양립할 수 있다

25 논리완성   ④

| 분석 |

앞에서 "빛의 색뿐만 아니라 빛의 밝기와 노출 시간도 중요하다"고 했고, 이어서 색은 청색, 적색 모두 영향을 준다고 했으므로, 결정적 요인은 밝기와 노출 시간이라는 논리가 성립한다. 따라서 ④가 정답이 된다.

| 어휘 |

blue light 블루 라이트, 청색광(전자기기의 화면에서 나오는 파란색 파장을 가진 빛) expert n. 전문가 affect v. 영향을 미치다, 악영향을 미치다 circadian a. 생체 리듬의, 24시간 주기의 exposure duration 노출 시간, 노출 지속 기간 neuroscience n. 신경과학 trigger v. 일으키다, 유발하다 receptor n. 수용체

| 해석 |

사람들은 종종 잠들기 어려운 원인을 휴대폰에서 나오는 블루 라이트 탓으로 돌리지만, 전문가들은 문제가 더 복잡하다고 말한다. 블루 라이트가 실제로 우리의 생체 리듬에 영향을 미치긴 하지만, 빛의 색뿐만 아니라 빛의 밝기와 노출 시간도 중요하다는 것이다. 생체리듬 신경과학 교수인 Stuart Peirson은 블루 라이트와 레드 라이트 모두 눈 안의 수용체를 자극함으로써 수면에 영향을 미칠 수 있다고 설명한다. 문제는 그 빛이 얼마나 밝은지 혹은 당신이 얼마나 오랫동안 그 빛에 노출돼 있는지에 있다.

① 그 빛이 블루 라이트인지 레드 라이트인지에 달려 있다
② 화면 해상도와 픽셀 밀도에 있다
③ 화면에서 보는 콘텐츠의 종류에 일부 기인한다
④ 그 빛이 얼마나 밝은지 혹은 당신이 얼마나 오랫동안 그 빛에 노출돼 있는지에 있다

26 논리완성   ①

| 분석 |

Valdas Noreika 박사는 사람과 개의 뇌파가 동기화될 수 있다는 것을 엄마와 아기들에 대한 실험에서 착안했다고 했으므로, 그 실험에서도 유사한 뇌파 동기화가 관찰됐을 것이다. 따라서 ①이 정답이다. ② 아직 입증된 것은 아니며, 빈칸 앞의 where는 '엄마와 아기에 대한 실험에서'이다.

| 어휘 |

take part in ~에 참여하다   brainwave n. 뇌파   synchronize with ~와 동기화되다, 동시에 일어나다   interact v. 상호작용하다   interpret v. 해석하다   wavelength n. 파장

| 해석 |

약 40마리의 반려견이 참여하고 있는 한 연구는 개와 주인이 상호작용할 때 개의 뇌파가 주인의 뇌파와 서로 동기화되는지를 탐구하고 있는데, 이런 (뇌파 동기화) 현상은 이전에 두 명의 인간이 상호작용했을 때에 관찰된 바 있다. 그 연구를 수행한 연구원들은 이러한 동기화가 사람과 반려동물이 같은 것에 주의를 기울이고 있으며, 어떤 상황에서는 매 순간들을 비슷하게 해석하고 있다는 것을 시사할 것이라고 말한다. 다시 말해, 주인과 개는 실제로 같은 파장을 공유한다는 것이다. 케임브리지 대학교의 Valdas Noreika 박사는 자신이 엄마와 아기들에 대해 유사한 실험을 수행한 후에 이 연구에 대한 아이디어를 얻었으며, 그 실험에서도 그러한 동기화 현상이 관찰된 바 있다고 말했다.

① 그러한 동기화 현상이 역시 관찰된 바 있다
② 인간과 개 사이의 동기화가 입증되었다
③ 불규칙한 동기화 패턴이 감지되었다
④ 뇌파가 아닌 얼굴 표정의 동기화가 관찰되었다

27 논리완성   ③

| 분석 |
바로 다음 문장에서 국제적 흥행 성공 사례 중 프랑스 영화는 없었다는 사실을 제시하고 있으므로, 그 앞에는 프랑스 영화 산업의 국제 경쟁력 부족에 대한 내용이 와야 한다. 따라서 ③이 정답으로 적절하다.

| 어휘 |
imitate v. 모방하다   **hegemony** n. 패권, 주도권   **inundate** v. 범람시키다; 침수시키다

| 해석 |
파리는 19세기의 할리우드였다. 그곳의 소설은 어디에서나 읽히고 모방되었으며, 심지어 영화관도 그곳에서 발명되었다! 그러니 그들이 나머지 다른 하나의 할리우드(미국의 할리우드)를 싫어하는 것도 당연하다. 그리고 아무도 상징적 패권을 포기하고 싶어 하지 않지만, 또한 아무도 단지 의지의 힘만으로 상징적 패권을 유지하지 않는다. 그리고 프랑스는 자국 시장을 보호하는 방법을 알고 있긴 하지만 (그 시장은 1920년대와 1940년대에 외국 영화에 의해 두 차례 잠식당했지만 두 번 다 회복했다), 해외에서 할리우드와 경쟁한다는 것은 전혀 가능성이 없는 일이다. 1986년부터 1995년 사이에, 미국 영화가 아닌 영화 중에서 국제적으로 큰 성공을 거둔 영화는 단 네 편뿐이었는데, 영국 코미디 영화 두 편, 호주 코미디 영화 한 편, 그리고 미국-이탈리아 합작 멜로드라마 한 편이었다. 그 중에 프랑스 영화는 없었다. 사실, 그 영화들은 전형적인 할리우드 영화와 전혀 다르지 않았다.

① 그것이 다양한 영화 장르를 개발하는 것
② 그것이 전 세계적인 패권을 포기하는 것
③ 그것이 해외에서 할리우드와 경쟁하는 것
④ 그것이 뚜렷한 문화적 정체성을 유지하는 것

28~29

주(州) 법령에 따른 귀하의 의료 보장 변경 사항을 알려드립니다. 2025년 1월 18일부터, Blue Cross & Shield는 더 이상 주간 치료 서비스에 대한 비용을 지불하지 않습니다. 해당 서비스는 약물 치료 센터에서 제공하는 상담 서비스입니다. 하지만 만약 귀하가 임신 중이라면, 이 변경 사항은 임신 기간 동안이나 임신이 끝난 달의 다음 두 달 동안에는 적용되지 않습니다. 또한 귀하가 만 21세 미만인 경우에는, 만 21세가 될 때까지 Blue Cross & Shield가 이러한 서비스에 대한 비용을 계속 지불할 수 있습니다. 귀하가 임신 중이 아니거나 (혹은 최근에 임신한 적이 없고) 21세 이하가 아니라면, 귀하가 살고 있는 카운티(郡)의 알코올 및 약물 프로그램 관리자에게 전화하여, 이러한 서비스를 위한 비용 지원을 받을 수 있는 다른 방법에 대한 정보를 얻거나 혹은 Blue Cross & Shield에서 보장하는 다른 약물 치료 서비스로 변경할 수 있는지 확인하여 보십시오. 카운티의 알코올 및 약물 프로그램 관리자 연락처는 전화번호부 화이트 페이지의 "카운티 정부, 보건 서비스" 항목 아래에 나와 있습니다.
오직 위에 기술된 약물 상담 서비스만 중단되며, 다른 약물 관련 서비스를 비롯한 그 외의 모든 서비스는 평소처럼 계속 제공됩니다. 서비스 제공자가 귀하의 약물 상담 서비스를 거부하거나 중단할 계획이지만, 귀하가 위에 언급된 대상자 그룹에 해당되어 이 서비스가 제공되어야 한다고 생각된다면, 1-800-923-3333으로 전화하여 이의제기를 신청하실 수 있습니다.

| 어휘 |
notify v. 통지하다   **pregnant** a. 임신한   **white page** 화이트 페이지(개인별 전화번호부, 인터넷 사용자들의 기본적인 정보를 데이터베이스화하여 지원)   **eliminate** v. 제거하다, 배제하다   **discontinue** v. 그만두다, 중지하다

28 내용파악   ④

| 분석 |
본문의 전체 내용은 의료보험이 특정 상담 서비스에 더 이상 비용을 지불하지 않게 되었다는 알림인데, 그 대상은 약물 치료 센터에서 상담을 받고 있는 사람들이며, 이의가 있다면 전화를 해서 절차를 밟을 수 있음을 알려주고 있다.

이 공지문은 누구를 대상으로 하고 있는가?
① 주간 치료 센터의 직원들
② 보건 위원회의 주 의회 의원들
③ 카운티 정부 소속 상담사들
④ 약물 치료 센터에서 상담을 받고 있는 사람들

29 내용일치   ①

| 분석 |
"위에 기술된 약물 상담 서비스만 중단되며, 다른 약물 관련 서비스를 비롯한 그 외의 모든 서비스는 평소처럼 계속 제공됩니다."라고 했으므로 ①이 옳지 않은 진술이다.

위 글에 따르면, 다음 중 옳지 않은 것은?
① 모든 약물 상담 서비스가 중단될 예정이다.
② 이번 변경은 임신 중인 미성년자에게는 적용되지 않는다.
③ 이번 변경은 임신 말기의 여성에게는 해당되지 않는다.
④ Blue Cross & Shield는 미성년자가 21세가 될 때까지 상담 서비스에 대한 비용을 지불한다.

30~31

확실한 것은 야구의 전신(前身)인 경기들이 메이플라워호가 도착하기 훨씬 이전까지 거슬러 올라간다는 점이다. 영국에서는 16세기부터 행해졌고 미국에서는 19세기까지 널리 행해진 크리켓이 배트와 공을 사용하는 모든 게임의 선조 격으로 보이지만, 그 다음 200년 동안 영국과 미국에서 다른 많은 게임들이 뒤를 이었는데, 팁캣(또는 킷캣), 비틀배틀, 스틱볼, 원 올드 캣, 투 올드 캣, 쓰리 올드 캣, 그리고 그 중에서도 특히 베이스 혹은 베이스볼 등이 있었다. 그 모든 게임들은 막대기나 방망이로 공을 치고, 수비 팀에 잡히거나 공을 던져 아웃되기 전에 정해진 경로를 달린다는 똑같은 원칙을 포함하고 있었다. 야구에 대한 첫 언급은 미국이 아니라 영국에서 발견되며, 그 출처는 1744년에 런던에서 출간된 『A Pretty Little Pocket Book, Intended for the Amusement of Little Master Tommy and Pretty Miss Polly』라는 아동 도서였다. 하지만 이 시기 무렵에 공을 사용하는 게임들은 이미 미국에 잘 정착된 상태였다. 미국의 놀이라는 맥락에서 배트가 처음 언급된 것은 1734년이며, 공 게임들과 공 게임 도구들에 대한 언급이 18세기 미국 전역에 많이 있다. 예를 들어, 보스턴 학살 사건은 부분적으로는 누군가가 영국군을 향해 팁캣 배트를 위협적으로 휘두른 것에 의해 유발되었고, 밸리 포지에 주둔했던 병사들이 1778년에 "베이스에서 놀이를 하며" 시간을 보낸 것으로 알려져 있다.

| 어휘 |

antecedent n. 선행사건, 전례　involve v. 포함하다, 연루되다
paddle n. 패들, 노, 방망이　traverse v. 가로지르다, 횡단하다
context n. 문맥, 상황　reference n. 참고, 언급　implement n. 도구, 기구　provoke v. 자극하다, 유발하다　threaten v. 위협하다
troop n. 군대, 무리

30 글의 주제　②

| 분석 |
본문에서는 야구의 기원과 초기 형태의 게임들, 그리고 18세기까지 영국과 미국에서 어떤 유사한 게임들이 있었는지를 다루고 있다. 전반적으로 야구의 초기 역사에 초점을 맞추고 있다고 할 수 있으므로 ②가 정답으로 적절하다.

위 글은 주로 무엇에 관한 것인가?
① 야구의 주요 규칙들
② 야구의 초기 역사
③ 야구와 관련된 일화들
④ 미국에서 오락으로서의 야구

31 내용일치　③

| 분석 |
"야구에 대한 첫 언급은 미국이 아니라 영국에서 발견되며, 그 출처는 1744년에 런던에서 출간된 『A Pretty Little Pocket Book, Intended for the Amusement of Little Master Tommy and Pretty Miss Polly』라는 아동 도서였다."라고 돼 있으므로 ③이 정답이다. ① 크리켓을 야구의 선조 격으로 언급했다. ② 런던이 아니라 미국이다. ④ 공 게임들과 공 게임 도구들에 대한 언급이 18세기 미국 전역에 많이 있다고 했다.

본문에 따르면, 다음 중 옳은 것은?
① 16세기 영국에서 야구의 원형을 추적하는 것은 불가능하다.
② 한때 야구 방망이가 런던에서 정치적 격변을 일으켰다.
③ 야구에 대한 최초의 언급은 영국에서 출판된 한 아동도서에서 발견된다.
④ 18세기에는 미국인들이 야구에 열중하지 않았다.

32~33

수천 년 동안, 이성과 감정 사이에 영원한 전쟁이 벌어지고 있다고 상상하는 것이 서양 사상에서는 일반적이었다. 이러한 사고방식에서는, 이성은 합리적이고 세련된 것이며, 감정은 원시적이고 충동적이며 당신을 잘못된 길로 인도할 가능성이 크다. 지혜로운 사람은 이성을 사용하여 원시적인 열정을 무시하고 통제한다. 과학자나 기업의 중역 혹은 훌륭한 사상가는 객관적이 되려고 애쓰고 감정적으로 초연하려고 애써야 한다. 현대의 신경과학은 이런 사고방식에 치명적인 타격을 입혔다. 사람들이 전에는 열정이 원시적이고 파괴적이라고 생각했다면, 이제는 열정이 종종 지혜롭다는 것을 우리는 이해한다. 대부분의 경우에 감정은 이성을 이끌어 우리를 더욱 합리적이 되도록 돕는다. 이것이 천문학에서의 코페르니쿠스 혁명에 필적할 만한 전환점이라고 말하는 것은 과장이지만, 아마도 용서할 수 있는 과장일 것이다. 문제는 우리의 문화와 제도가 우리의 지식을 따라잡지 못했다는 점이다. 오늘날 우리는 여전히 원래의 두뇌 능력에만 지나치게 집착하는 사회에 살고 있다. 우리의 학교들은 아이들을 표준화된 시험을 잘 치를 수 있는 능력에 따라 분류하며, 인생을 살아가는 데 똑같이 중요한, 신체에 깃든 그런 종류의 지혜는 소홀히 여긴다. 우리의 경제 모델은 인간이 자신의

이익을 냉정하게 계산하는 합리적인 존재라는 생각에 기반하고 있다.

| 어휘 |

rational a. 이성적인   **sophisticated** a. 세련된, 정교한, 수준 높은   **impulsive** a. 충동적인   **astray** a. 길을 잃은, 타락하여   **override** v. 무시하다; (결정 따위를) 무효로 하다   **passion** n. 열정   **objective** a. 객관적인   **detached** a. 거리감을 두는, 초연한   **neuroscience** n. 신경과학   **deliver a fatal blow** 치명타를 가하다   **exaggeration** n. 과장   **forgivable** a. 용서할 수 있는   **turnabout** n. 반전, 전환   **rival** v. 필적하다, 경쟁하다   **institution** n. 제도, 기관   **catch up with** 따라잡다   **overly** ad. 과도하게   **obsessed with** ~에 집착하는   **standardized** a. 표준화된   **slight** v. 무시하다, 깔보다

32 지시대상   ③

| 분석 |

앞 문장에서 언급한 "대부분의 경우에 감정은 이성을 이끌어 우리가 더욱 합리적이 되도록 돕는다"를 가리키므로, ③이 정답이 된다.

다음 중 밑줄 친 Ⓐ가 가리키는 것은?
① 인간은 이성적이라는 것
② 이성이 감정을 통제한다는 것
③ 감정이 우리를 더 합리적으로 만든다는 것
④ 이성과 감정은 분리할 수 없다는 것

33 지시대상   ①

| 분석 |

앞에서 언급된 지식, 원래의 두뇌 능력, 시험을 잘 치를 수 있는 능력은 이성을 가리키므로 밑줄 친 Ⓑ는 감정이나 열정을 가리킨다고 볼 수 있다. 따라서 ①이 정답으로 적절하다.

다음 중 밑줄 친 Ⓑ가 가리킬 가능성이 가장 큰 것은?
① 열정
② 탐색
③ 자기 이익
④ 원래의 두뇌 능력

34~35

AI 시대에 대학생들은 기계가 모방할 수 없는 기술이어서 더욱 분명히 인간적인 기술이게 되는 그런 기술을 계발하는 데 집중해야 한다. AI가 더 잘하는 비인격적이고, 직선적이며, 일반화된 사고를 가르치는 수업은 피해야 한다. 대신에, 학생들은 분명히 인간적인 능력을 길러주는 강좌에 끌

려야 한다. Alison Gopnik에 따르면, 아이들은 창의성을 발휘할 때 명백한 것과 터무니없는 것을 균형 있게 조화시킨다. 그들은 단순히 데이터를 모방하거나 흡수하지 않고 탐구하고 혁신한다. 학생들은 코딩에서든, 예술에서든, 상상력을 길러주는 수업을 들어야 한다. AI는 예측에 능하므로, 학생들은 (기존의 관념과) 반대되거나 관습에 얽매이지 않는 사고방식을 계발해야 한다. 그들은 역사, 철학, 그리고 다른 문화로부터 다양한 세계관에 대해 배워야 하는데, 관습적인 사고방식이 AI에게 쉽게 추월당해버리는 세상에서 이것은 가치가 있을 것이다. 기계는 행동 패턴은 분석할 수 있지만, 개별적인 경험을 이해하는 데는 어려움을 겪는다. 문학이나 역사 같은 인문학을 공부하는 것은 학생들로 하여금 인간의 관점을 더 잘 이해할 수 있게 해주며, 그들에게 AI 주도 세계에서 독특하고 가치 있는 능력을 부여해준다.

| 어휘 |

replicate v. 복제하다, 되풀이하다   **distinctly** ad. 뚜렷하게, 분명히   **impersonal** a. 인간미 없는, 비인격적인   **linear** a. 직선의; 선과 같은   **generalize** v. 일반화하다   **excel at** ~에 뛰어나다, 출중하다   **gravitate** v. (자연스럽게) 끌리다   **nurture** v. 양육하다, 기르다   **contrarian** a. 반대의견의   **unconventional** a. 관습에 얽매이지 않는   **outpace** v. 앞지르다, 능가하다   **humanities** n. 인문학

34 글의 제목   ④

| 분석 |

본문은 대학생들이 AI 세계에서 어떻게 기계가 모방할 수 없는 인간적인 기술과 능력을 발전시킬 수 있는지에 대해 설명하고 있다. 이와 관련하여, 학생들이 창의력, 상상력, 비전통적 사고를 기르는 수업을 들어야 한다고 강조하고 있다. 따라서 글의 제목으로는 ④가 적절하다.

위 글의 제목으로 가장 적절한 것은?
① 인문학이 AI에게 가르칠 수 있는 것
② 인간은 A.I.와 어떻게 협력할 것인가
③ AI가 인간의 창의력을 대체하지 못할 이유
④ 학생들이 A.I. 세계에서 인간적인 기술을 어떻게 계발할 수 있는가

35 내용파악   ②

| 분석 |

본문에서는 학생들에게 AI가 잘 할 수 있는 것을 피하고, 인간적인 능력인 창의적이고 관습에 얽매이지 않은 사고를 키울 수 있는 수업을 들어야 한다고 권장하고 있다. 패턴 분석은 AI가 뛰어난 분야라고 했으므로, 학생들에게 이를 추천하지 않을 것이다.

다음 중 저자가 대학생들에게 추천하지 <u>않을</u> 가능성이 높은 것은 무엇인가?
① 탐구, 탐색
② 패턴 분석
③ 문학과 역사
④ 비전통적인 세계관

36~37

Louisa Jaskulski는 2023년에 77세의 나이로 잠을 자던 중에 사망했다. 그것은 처음에는 성공적이라고 여겨졌던 심장 수술을 받고 나서 불과 며칠 후였다. 그녀는 부채꼴 꼬리 비둘기 네 마리, 아마존 앵무새 세 마리, 잉꼬새 세 마리, 피리새 한 쌍, 사막 거북이 두 마리, 턱수염 도마뱀 한 마리, 그리고 푸른 혀 도마뱀 한 마리를 남기고 세상을 떠났는데, 이 동물들은 모두 구조된 동물들이었다. 그녀는 2020년 한 인터뷰에서 이렇게 말했다. "저에 대해 말하자면, 새나 파충류와의 교제가 너무 깊어요. 앵무새나 잉꼬새, 비둘기, 혹은 도마뱀이나 뱀 또는 거북이의 눈을 들여다보면, 하나님의 눈을 들여다보고 있는 기분이 들어요." 하지만 이국적인 반려동물의 주인들이 세상을 떠나면, 그 동물들은 어디로 가는 걸까? 이것은 이국적인 반려동물을 기르는 사람들에게는 자주 겪지만 종종 고통스러운 과제이다. 그 동물들을 가족이 이어서 돌보는 것이 이상적이지만, 가족들이 사실상 아마추어 사육사가 되는 책임을 기꺼이 떠맡고 싶어 할 것이라는 보장은 전혀 없다. Jaskulski는 자신의 동물들을 누가 물려받을지에 대한 구체적인 계획을 거의 남기지 않았다. 이는 아마도 그녀가 동물 구조 활동을 함께해 온 친구들이 잘 처리해줄 것으로 믿어도 된다는 것을 알고 있었기 때문일 것이다. 가장 입양 보내기 어려운 동물들은 앵무새와 거북이였는데, 이들은 수명이 길고 키우기가 힘든 반려동물이기 때문이다.

| 어휘 |

surgery n. 수술 **lorikeet** n. 진홍잉꼬새 **finch** n. 피리새 **tortoise** n. 거북 **reptile** n. 파충류 **lizard** n. 도마뱀 **exotic** a. 외래의; 이국적인 **excruciating** a. 몹시 고통스러운 **guarantee** n. 보장, 보증 **inherit** v. 상속받다, 물려받다 **count on** ~을 믿다, 의지하다 **sort out** 해결하다, 정리하다 **demanding** a. 요구하는 것이 많은, 힘든

36 글의 주제 ④

| 분석 |

글의 중심 내용은 Louisa Jaskulski라는 여성이 죽은 후에, 그녀가 기르던 이국적인 동물을 누가 돌볼 것인가라는 문제를 다루고 있다. 희귀 애완동물을 기르던 사람들이 사망한 후에 그 동물들이 갈 곳이 마땅치 않다는 현실적인 문제를 조명하고 있는 내용이라 할 수 있으므로 글의 주제로는 ④가 적절하다.

위 글은 주로 무엇에 관한 것인가?
① 동물들과 공감하는 관계를 형성하는 방법
② 이국적인 동물을 기르는 이상적인 사육사가 되는 방법
③ 당신 지역에서 멸종 위기에 처한 종들을 구해내는 방법
④ 주인보다 오래 살아남은 이국적인 동물들을 돌보는 방법

37 내용파악 ③

| 분석 |

"Jaskulski는 자신의 동물들을 누가 물려받을지에 대한 구체적인 계획을 거의 남기지 않았다. 이는 아마도 그녀가 동물 구조 활동을 함께해 온 친구들이 잘 처리해줄 것으로 믿어도 된다는 것을 알고 있었기 때문일 것이다."라고 했으므로, 친구들이 알아서 도와줄 거라 믿었을 수는 있지만, 직접적으로 부탁한 것은 아니다. 따라서 ③이 정답이다.

위 글에 따르면, 다음 중 Louisa Jaskulski에 관해 옳지 <u>않은</u> 것은?
① 그녀는 죽기 며칠 전에 심장 수술을 받았다.
② 그녀가 키우고 있었던 새들과 파충류는 모두 구조된 동물들이었다.
③ 그녀는 자신이 죽은 뒤에 자신의 동물들을 돌봐달라고 동물 구조 활동을 함께해 온 친구들에게 요청했다.
④ 그녀는 자신의 이국적인 동물들의 눈을 볼 때 종교적인 감정을 느꼈다.

38~40

기침은 유해한 연기, 물, 혹은 잘못 삼킨 음식 조각과 같은 위험으로부터 기도(氣道)를 보호하는 중요한 반사 작용이다. 이 반사 작용은 기도 속으로 뻗어 있는 신경에 의해 유발된다. 이 신경들은 차가운 공기부터 고추를 맵게 만드는 화학물질 캡사이신에 이르는 온갖 것들에 반응하는 수용체 단백질들로 덮여 있다. 어떤 자극물질이 그 수용체들을 자극하면, 신경은 미주신경을 따라 뇌로 신호를 보내고, 우리는 그것을 기침을 하고 싶은 충동으로서 경험하게 된다. 거기서 뇌는 다시 기도로 명령을 내려 보내 기침을 하게 하거나 혹은 하지 않게 한다. 이처럼 뇌를 거쳐서 가는 과정이 있기 때문에, 어떤 종류의 기침은 우리가 어느 정도 의식적으로 조절할 수 있다. 과학자들은 기침을 유발할 수 있는 다양한 자극들에 대해 알고 있지만, 우리가 병이 나은 후 몇 주 동안은 말할 것도 없고 아플 동안에도 기침을 유발하는 구체적인 생물학적 메커니즘에 대해서는 아직도 의견이 일치하지 않는다. 기침은 목에서 점액을 제거하기 위한 것임이 명백해 보일 수도 있지만, 바이러스가 자기 자신을 퍼뜨리기 위해

반사 작용을 유도하는 것일 수도 있다. 많은 감염증들이 가래를 전혀 만들어내지 않는 마른기침을 동반한다. 그리고 우리가 궁극적으로 감염증에 걸린 동안 기도를 깨끗하게 하기 위해 기침을 한다고 하더라도, 그것으로는 감염증에 걸린 동안 우리의 신경이 정확히 무엇을 감지해서 기침을 유발하는지가 여전히 설명되지 않을 것이다.

| 어휘 |

cough v. 기침하다 n. 기침　**reflex** n. 반사 작용　**noxious** a. 유해한, 유독한　**fume** n. 증기, 연기　**mis-swallowed** 잘못 삼킨　**trigger** v. 유발하다, 촉발하다　**nerve** n. 신경　**receptor** n. 수용체　**spicy** a. 매운　**irritant** n. 자극 물질　**vagus nerve** 미주신경　**urge** n. 충동, 욕구　**detour** n. 우회로, 우회　**stimulus** n. 자극　**mucus** n. 점액　**infection** n. 감염, 감염증　**phlegm** n. 가래

에서 하는 것일 수도 있다는 것을 시사한다.

위 글에 따르면, 감염증에 걸린 동안의 마른기침은 _____을 시사한다.
① 바이러스 외의 몇몇 화학물질들이 기침을 유발한다는 것
② 기침이 기도를 깨끗하게 하는 것 이외의 다른 것을 위한 것일 수도 있다는 것
③ 우리 몸을 감염시켜 기침을 유발하는 바이러스들이 그다지 강하지는 않다는 것
④ 기도 주변의 신경을 덮고 있는 수용체 단백질이 제대로 작동하지 않는다는 것

| 38 | 글의 주제 | ① |

| 분석 |

본문은 기침의 발생 기전을 다루면서 관련된 반사작용의 원리와 경로를 구체적으로 설명하고 있다.

위 글은 주로 무엇에 관한 것인가?
① 기침의 메커니즘
② 기침을 유발하는 자극들
③ 기침을 동반하는 감염증
④ 기침의 치료에 대한 연구들

| 39 | 내용파악 | ③ |

| 분석 |

"과학자들은 기침을 유발할 수 있는 다양한 자극들에 대해 알고 있지만, 우리가 아플 때 기침을 유발하는 구체적인 생물학적 메커니즘에 대해서는 아직도 의견이 일치하지 않는다."라고 돼 있으므로 ③이 정답이 된다.

위 글에 따르면, 과학자들은 _____에 대해 아직 의견이 일치하지 않고 있다.
① 어느 신경이 기침과 관련돼 있는지
② 기침을 할 때 뇌가 역할을 하는지의 여부
③ 우리가 아플 때 무엇이 기침을 유발하는지
④ 기침을 할 때 수용체 단백질이 어떤 역할을 하고 있는지

| 40 | 내용파악 | ② |

| 분석 |

마른기침은 점액이나 가래를 동반하지 않는 기침이므로, 마른기침을 한다는 것은 기침이 기도를 깨끗하게 하는 것 이외의 다른 목적

SUNGKYUNKWAN UNIVERSITY | 성균관대학교 인문계 A형

TEST p. 378~400

01	①	02	④	03	①	04	①	05	②	06	⑤	07	⑤	08	④	09	②	10	③
11	①	12	④	13	③	14	②	15	⑤	16	⑤	17	④	18	③	19	⑤	20	②
21	①	22	①	23	③	24	④	25	⑤	26	③	27	②	28	③	29	③	30	②
31	②	32	①	33	⑤	34	④	35	④	36	③	37	①	38	④	39	⑤	40	④
41	③	42	②	43	③	44	②	45	①	46	④	47	⑤	48	①	49	④	50	①

01 동의어 ①

| 어휘 |

equity market 주식 시장 **precarious** a. 불안정한, 위험한, 위태로운 (= perilous) **guarded** a. 조심스러운 **definite** a. 확실한, 명확한 **moored** a. (배가) 정박된

| 해석 |

두바이의 발표 후 첫 전체 주식 거래일인 목요일에 추수감사절로 인해 미국 주식시장이 휴장했기 때문에 미국 주식시장 상황은 더욱 위험하다.

02 동의어 ④

| 어휘 |

diversification n. 다양화 **engage with** ~와 소통하다 **cater to** ~의 요구를 충족시키다 **preference** n. 선호 **latch onto** ~을 이해하다(= grasp) **turn away** 외면하다 **release** v. 풀어주다, 공개하다 **despise** v. 경멸하다 **dishonor** v. 불명예를 주다

| 해석 |

이러한 다양화는 신문이 구독자들과 다양한 방식으로 소통할 수 있게 해주며, 다양한 선호도를 만족시키고, 구독자들이 신문 내용을 더 쉽게 이해할 수 있게 한다.

03 동의어 ①

| 어휘 |

pay no heed to ~을 신경 쓰지 않다(= ignore) **acknowledge** v. 인정하다 **go over** 검토하다, 살펴보다 **dilate** v. 확장하다 **outspread** v. 넓게 퍼지다

| 해석 |

아내, 아들 부부, 손녀 둘과 해변 식당에서 저녁을 먹는 동안, 나는 모두가 음식을 기다리면서 휴대폰만 들여다보고 바로 눈앞의 근사한 풍경은 전혀 신경 쓰지 않고 있다는 것을 깨달았다.

04 동의어 ①

| 어휘 |

specific n. 세부 사항 **work out** 해결하다, 이해하다 **adjudicate** v. 판단하다, 심사하다(= determine) **dissuade** v. 단념시키다 **dodge** v. 피하다 **repress** v. 억제하다 **initiate** v. 착수하다

| 해석 |

'안전하다'가 얼마나 안전하다는 것인지, '효과적이다'가 얼마나 효과적이라는 것인지 등, 일부 세부 사항은 여전히 파악되어야 할 필요가 있다. 하지만 그것들은 수상자 심사 위원회가 판단할 수 있는 그런 종류의 세부사항들이다.

05 동의어 ②

| 어휘 |

torturous a. 고통스러운(= agonizing) **innocent** a. 순진한, 무죄의 **homogeneous** a. 동질적인 **virtuous** a. 미덕의 **delightful** a. 즐거운

| 해석 |

비록 회복 과정은 더디고 고통스럽지만, 세계 경제가 회복 중이라고 나는 생각한다.

06 부정사 ⑤

| 분석 |
⑤가 현재분사로 the command를 수식한다면 '발사하고 있는 명령'이라는 부적절한 의미가 된다. '발사하라는 명령'의 의미로 명령의 내용이 '발사는 것'인 일종의 동격관계가 되도록 ⑤를 to부정사인 to fire로 고쳐야 한다.

| 어휘 |
autonomously ad. 자동으로 **sense** v. 감지하다 **threat** n. 위협 **command** v. 명령하다

| 해석 |
이스라엘에서는 미사일 방어 시스템인 아이언 돔이 다가오는 로켓의 위협을 자동으로 감지하여, 오퍼레이터에게 경고를 보내고, 그러면 그는 미사일을 발사하라는 명령을 내린다.

07 관사 ⑤

| 분석 |
nineteenth-century 뒤의 명사 America는 관사 없이 쓰므로 ⑤는 관사를 없애고 in으로 고쳐야 한다. 혹은 in America of the late nineteenth century로 쓸 수도 있다. 만약 미국을 the United States로 하면 in the late nineteenth-century United States이다.

| 어휘 |
competitive a. 경쟁이 치열한 **private clinic** 사설 병원 **therapy** n. 치료 **trendy** a. 유행하는 **diet therapy** 식이요법

| 해석 |
경쟁이 매우 치열했던 개인 병원들은 19세기 후반 미국에서의 식이요법 같이 유행하는 것처럼 보이는 치료법이라면 어느 것이나 일반적으로 제공하려 했다.

08 관사 ④

| 분석 |
series는 단수와 복수 형태가 같은 명사로 '일련의 ~들'이라는 의미로는 'a series of 복수명사'의 형태로 써야 한다. 따라서 ④를 a series of로 고쳐야 한다.

| 어휘 |
despite prep. ~에도 불구하고 **obtain** v. 발급받다

| 해석 |
그녀가 그의 이전 미국 여행 때의 그 비자를 취득하여 일련의 비슷한 행사들에 참석할 수 있게 해주었음에도, 그는 잘못된 비자로 여행하고 있었다.

09 일치 ②

| 분석 |
'neither A nor B'가 주어일 때 동사는 B에 일치시키는데, B에 해당하는 Ohasi가 단수이므로 단수로 취급하여 ②를 assumes로 고쳐야 한다.

| 어휘 |
central role 중심 역할 **striking** a. 놀라운 **vantage point** 관점, 시점

| 해석 |
타나카도 오하시도 자신들이 출연하는 영화에서 중심적인 역할을 맡지는 않지만, 그들의 화면 속 존재감은 특히 우리의 관점에서 보면 놀랍다.

10 문의 구성 ③

| 분석 |
Not이라는 부정의 부사가 문두에 있어서 도치가 이루어져 does라는 조동사가 등장했으므로, 뒤에는 동사원형이 뒤따라야 한다. 따라서 ③을 동사원형 involve로 고쳐야 한다.

| 어휘 |
repudiation n. 거부 **intervention** n. 개입 **respectable** a. 훌륭한, 상당한 **pedigree** n. 혈통, 유래

| 해석 |
이것은 자유주의 사상에 대한 그 어떤 근본적인 거부도 아닐 뿐 아니라, 이런 종류의 개입은 애덤 스미스의 사상에 상당한 유래를 갖고 있기도 하다.

11 논리완성 ①

| 분석 |
생물이 유전자를 교환하는 것은 재생산, 즉 번식을 위해서인데, 번식이 잘 되면 생물의 집단, 즉 개체군이 유지될 것이므로 빈칸에는 ①(개체군)이 적절하다.

| 어휘 |
IUCN Red List 국제자연보전연맹 멸종 위기 종 목록 **a handful of** 소량의 **revive** v. 되살리다 **conservation** n. 보전 **catfish** n. 메기 **corridor** n. 연결 통로 **nature preserve** 자연 보호 구역 **coral reef** 산호초 **gene** n. 유전자 **population** n. 개체군 **territory** n. 영역 **originality** n. 독창성 **migration** n. 이주

| 해석 |
국제자연보전연맹의 멸종 위기 종 목록에는 보존 노력 덕분에 되살아난 소수의 종이 포함되어 있는데, 예를 들어 유럽의 흰 꼬리 독수리와 메콩 메기 등이 포함된다. 남아프리카에서는 보호 구역의 좁

은 통로들이 이제 자연 보호지를 연결하고 있으며, 바하마에서도 유사한 통로들이 산호초를 연결하여, 보호 구역 안의 종들이 이리 저리 오가고, 유전자를 교환하며, 개체군을 유지할 수 있게 해준다.

12 논리완성 ④

| 분석 |
앞에서 아르메니아인들이 광저우 상인들에게 '높은 금리로 돈을 빌려주었다'라고 했으므로, 광저우 상인들은 돈을 빌려 쓰고 있는 상태, 다시 말해 '빚진 상태'에 있었다고 할 수 있으므로 ④(빚진)가 적절하다.

| 어휘 |
money broker 자금 중개인 **fraught with** ~으로 가득 찬 **itinerant trader** 떠돌이 상인 **determined** a. 단호한 **prosperous** a. 번영하는, 부유한 **collateral-free** 담보 없이 **in debt** 빚을 지고 있는 **in surplus** 흑자 상태인, 남는 것이 있는

| 해석 |
아르메니아인들은 활발한 자금 중개인들이었는데, 마카오에서 저리로 자금을 빌려, 광저우에서 고리로 대출해 주었다. 대부분의 광저우 상인들은 크게 빚진 상태였다. 무역은 위험이 많았지만, 아르메니아인들은 소규모 떠돌이 상인들도 수익을 낼 수 있음을 보여주었다. 그들은 단호하고 독립적이어서, 개신교도와 가톨릭교도 양측 모두에게 쉽게 받아들여졌다.

13 논리완성 ③

| 분석 |
마지막 문장에서 도박꾼들은 '자신만의 사적이고 친밀한 세계'에서 '외부의 소란에서 고립되어 있기'를 바란다고 했다. 따라서 빈칸에는 '고립된, 조용한'과 의미가 유사한 ③의 secluded(격리된)가 적절하다.

| 어휘 |
spatial a. 공간적인 **structural box** 구조적인 공간 **enclose** v. 둘러싸다 **setting** n. 환경 **encourage entry** 몰입하게 하다, 진입을 유도하다 **bustling** a. 북적이는 **isolated** a. 고립된 **intimate** a. 친밀한 **hubbub** n. 소란 **vibrant** a. 활기찬 **noisy** a. 시끄러운 **secluded** a. 격리된, 외딴 **exposed** a. 노출된 **communal** a. 공동의, 공공의

| 해석 |
카지노 설계에서 주된 과제는 기계를 만지며 도박을 즐기는 사람들이 격리된 게임 세계에 몰입하게 유도하도록 주변 영역들의 공간적 관계, 그리고 그 환경을 감싸는 구조적인 공간의 형태와 느낌을 잘 조정하는 것이다. 도박을 하는 사람들은 북적이는 카지노 환경을 선호하지만, 동시에 처음 자신들을 끌어들인 외부의 소란에서 고립되어 자신만의 사적이고 친밀한 세계에 있기를 바란다.

14 논리완성 ②

| 분석 |
크렘린 당국은 체제 비판 세력을 '적'으로 간주하고 있다고 하였으므로, 모든 반대를 '진압'하고 '뿌리 뽑으려' 했을 것이므로 ②(박멸하다)가 적절하다.

| 어휘 |
official n. 관료 **state media** 국영 언론 **hostile** a. 적대적인 **subversive** a. 체제를 전복하려는 **the enemy within** 내부의 적 **collaborator** n. 공모자 **chart** v. 기록하다, 추적하다 **dissent** n. 반대, 의견의 상이 **stamp out** 뿌리 뽑다, 진압하다 **build up** 축적하다 **military-grade** a. 군사용의 **nerve agent** 신경작용제 **locked up** 수감된 **Arctic** a. 북극의

| 해석 |
관료들과 국영 언론은 서방 국가들을 적대적이고 체제 전복적으로 묘사했고, 크렘린을 비판하는 자들은 '내부의 적'이며 외세와 협력하는 자들로 규정되었다. 나는 법정에서 보도하며 보내는 시간이 많아지기 시작했고, 온갖 형태의 반대를 박멸하려는 크렘린의 늘어나는 노력을 기록해 나갔다. 그때는 야권 정치인 보리스 넴초프의 피격으로 시작되어 또 다른 인물인 알렉세이 나발니에 대한 군사용 신경작용제를 이용한 암살 시도까지 일어난 암울한 시기였다. 나발니는 정치적 이유로 북극의 수용소에 갇힌 상태에서 3년 뒤 갑작스럽게 사망했다.

15 논리완성 ⑤

| 분석 |
이민 학자들의 이론은 "널리 읽히고, 대중화되었다"라고 했으므로, 이들이 1930년대와 1940년대에 미국으로 온 것이 '미국의 사상에 중요한 영향'을 미쳤을 것이라고 추론할 수 있다.

| 어휘 |
postwar a. 전후의 **extend from** ~에서 뻗어나다, 연장되다 **refugee scholar** 난민 학자 **ensuing** a. 그 후의 **émigré** n. 이민자, 망명자 **mass society** 대중사회 **popularize** v. 대중화하다 **seek to** ~하려 노력하다 **comprehend** v. 이해하다 **Cold War** 냉전 **geopolitics** n. 지정학 **atomistic individualism** 원자론적 개인주의 **emigration** n. 이민 **intellectual** n. 지식인 **long-term** a. 장기적인 **shaping** n. 형성

| 해석 |
전후 미국 사회·정치 이론의 많은 부분은 난민 학자들의 기여에서 발전되었다. 이후 수년 동안, 미국인들이 해외에서 벌어지는 냉전의 지정학적 역학과 국내의 원자론적 개인주의 이면에 숨겨진 위험한 대중들의 경향을 이해하려 노력하면서, 이민 학자들의 대중사회 이론들은 널리 읽히고 대중화되었다. 따라서 1930년대와 1940년대의 유럽 지식인들의 대규모 이주는 전후시기에 미국 사상의 형성에 커다란 장기적 영향을 끼쳤다.

① 미국 사상의 왜곡을 낳았다
② 미국을 둘러싼 정치적 긴장을 고조시켰다
③ 미국인들의 고립감을 군중들 사이에 강화시켰다
④ 이민자들에 대한 새로운 이해의 발달에 기여했다
⑤ 미국 사상의 형성에 커다란 장기적 영향을 끼쳤다

16 논리완성 ⑤

| 분석 |
처형을 기다리는 심리는 공포일 것이고, 협박당하는 인간 조건과 정치적 폭력 앞에서 느끼는 것도 공포일 것이므로 빈칸에는 ⑤가 적절하다. 공포나 불안은 실존주의의 핵심적인 낱말이기도 하다.

| 어휘 |
under duress 강제[협박]당하여   **existential** a. 실존적인   **slant** n. (마음 등의) 경향, 편향   **corrupt** a. 부패한   **forlornly** ad. 절망적으로   **set** v. ~을 배경으로 하다   **execution** n. 처형   **betray** v. 배신하다, 드러내다   **release** n. 석방   **relent** v. 누그러지다   **captor** n. 체포자   **hunt down** 추적하다   **plot twist** 반전   **fable** n. 우화

| 해석 |
공포는 협박당하는 인간 조건에 대한 이야기들에 보다 근본적으로 기여할 수 있다. 실존주의적 경향의 소설 속 등장인물들은 악한 사람들이나, 부패한 체제나, 신 없는 세계에 의해 야기된 불의에 맞서 싸운다. 스페인 내전을 배경으로 한 장 폴 사르트르의 『벽』보다 더 잔혹하고 절망적으로 정치적 폭력의 현실을 포착하는 이야기는 거의 없다. 죄수 파블로 이비에타는 처형을 기다린다. 삶의 가치와 자신의 원칙을 배신해가며 석방에 대한 대가로 파시스트들에게 그들이 원하는 정보를 넘겨주는 일이 가치가 있는지 고민한다. 기진맥진한 그는 계속 마음을 누그러뜨리지 않다가 마침내 마지막 순간에 체포자들에게 그들이 추적하고 있는 동지의 위치에 관해 거짓 정보를 넘겨주지만, 동지가 이미 은신처를 옮긴 것을 알지 못했으며 의도치 않게 진실을 말한 셈이 되고 만다. 이런 반전 덕분에 정치적 폭력에 관한 이야기는 실존주의와 '덫으로서의 인간 조건'을 그린 우화라는 또 다른 차원을 얻는다.

17 논리완성 ④

| 분석 |
부정의 연결어 yet이 있으므로 뒤의 'least-빈칸'은 의미상 앞의 conspicuous와 반대 의미가 나와야 한다. 내용을 보면, 많은 감시 때문에 다가가기 힘들다는 말이 되어야 하므로 ④가 들어가야 한다.

| 어휘 |
sign n. 간판   **conspicuous** a. 눈에 잘 띄는   **landmark** n. 랜드마크, 상징적인 장소나 건조물   **monitored** a. 감시되는   **motion sensor** 움직임 감지기   **trail** n. 산책로   **scramble up** 기어오르다   **liberal** a. 자유로운, 개방적인   **unobtrusive** a. 눈에 띄지 않는   **subtle** a. 미묘한   **accessible** a. 접근할 수 있는   **conservative** a. 보수적인

| 해석 |
할리우드 간판은 아마도 세상에서 가장 눈에 잘 띄면서도 동시에 가장 접근하기 힘든 랜드마크일 것이다. 이 간판은 움직임 감지기, 고화질 카메라, 그리고 언덕 꼭대기 TV 타워에서 감시하는 LA 경찰서에 의해 24시간 내내 감시되고 있다. 사람들은 인근 산책로에서 간판을 보는 것만 허용되지만, 일부 사람들은 여전히 언덕을 기어올라 간판에 가까이 가려 한다.

18 논리완성 ③

| 분석 |
첫 번째 버전의 세계는 우리가 알고 있는 현실 세계라 했으므로, 두 번째 버전의 세계는 '인간이 화석연료를 태워 지구 온난화를' 일으키지 않는 가상의 세계로, 이상적인 세계이다. 지구 온난화가 일어나지 않는 세상이니, 기후 변화가 없는 세상이라고 할 수 있다. 따라서 ③이 적절하다. ① 가까운 미래에 ② 지독한 폭염에 ④ 그 어떤 역사적 사건에서도 ⑤ 기상이변에도 불구하고

| 어휘 |
be known as ~라고 알려져 있다   **extreme event attribution** 극한 기후 사건 귀속, 기상이변 원인규명 연구, 극한사건귀인연구   **fossil fuels** 화석연료   **diminish** v. 줄이다   **based on** ~에 기반을 두고   **number-crunching** n. 숫자 계산, 수치 분석   **probe** v. 조사하다   **natural disaster** 자연재해

| 해석 |
이런 유형의 연구는 극한 기후 원인 규명 연구라 알려져 있다. 흔히 사용되는 한 가지 방법은 두 버전의 세계를 비교하는 것이다. 첫 번째 버전의 세계는 실제 세계로 인간이 화석연료를 태워 지구 온난화를 일으킨 세계이다. 두 번째 버전은 기후 변화가 없는 경우에 그려질 모습의 세계이다. 과학자들은 역사적 기상 데이터와 기후 모델을 토대로 인간이 화석연료 사용을 대폭 줄인 그 두 번째 이상적인 세계가 어떤 모습일지 추정한다. 정교한 수치 분석을 통해, 연구자들은 각각의 세계에서 특정 기상 현상이 얼마나 가능하고 얼마나 심각한지를 알 수 있다. 수백 건의 연구가 자연재해에서 지구 온난화의 역할을 분석해 왔다. 많은 연구는 기후 변화가 극한 기후를 더 악화시켰다는 결과를 내놓았다.

19 논리완성 ⑤

| 분석 |
소행성 충돌의 결과 뇌가 발달한 새들은 생존에서 유리한 지위를 확보할 수 있었을 것이다. 진화는 곧, 적자생존을 의미하기 때문이다. 생존에서 유리하다는 것은 자원 확보 경쟁에서 이긴다는 의미이다. 따라서 ⑤가 적절하다.

| 어휘 |

asteroid impact 소행성 충돌 **trigger** v. 유발하다 **evolve** v. 진화하다 **parrot** n. 앵무새 **family** n. 과 **relative to** ~에 비해 **overcome** v. 극복하다 **outcompete** v. 경쟁에서 이기다 **resources** n. 자원 **beak** n. 부리 **crop** n. 수확 **berry** n. (커피, 콩 등의) 말린 씨

| 해석 |

소행성 충돌은 환경의 급격한 변화를 초래했다. 이것이 일부 새들로 하여금 빠르게 더 큰 뇌를 진화시키게 할 수 있었을 것이다. 앵무새와 까마귀과의 새들은 모든 새 중 가장 뇌가 큰 새로 진화했다. 몸집에 비해 큰 뇌는 대체로 높은 지능을 의미한다. 앵무새의 조상들은 환경에서의 도전을 극복하는 데 도움이 되는 큰 뇌를 가졌을 것이다. 소행성 충돌 이후, 이 큰 뇌로 인해 그들은 자원 경쟁에서 다른 동물들을 능가할 수 있었을 것이다. 예를 들어, 부리로 솔방울을 여는 법을 배운 새는, 결코 이루어지지 않을 수도 있는 (솔방울) 씨앗 수확을 기다리는 새들보다 생존 확률이 높다.

① 먼 과거로 돌아가다
② 서로 다른 소리를 반복하다
③ 표적을 숨기다
④ 노래나 말을 하는 법을 다른 새들로부터 배우다
⑤ 자원 경쟁에서 다른 동물들을 능가하다

20 논리완성   ②

| 분석 |

앞에서 미국만 경제 지표가 긍정적이라고 하였는데, 문장의 시작에서 Still이라는 역접의 연결사를 사용하고 있어서, 빈칸에는 부정적인 표현이 필요하다. 뒤의 문장에서도 "미래가 반드시 장밋빛이지는 않다"라고 하였으므로, "과거 실적이 아무리 좋아도, 미래까지 좋다는 의미는 아니다"라는 내용의 ②가 적절하다.

| 어휘 |

measure n. 지표, 척도 **unemployment** n. 실업률 **stock market** 주식시장 **soar** v. 급등하다 **consumer sentiment** 소비자 심리 **tick up** 올라가다 **high price** 고물가 **lag** v. 뒤처지다 **recession** n. 경기 침체 **flirt with a recession** 경기 침체의 징조를 보이다 **aging** a. 노화하는 **birth rate** 출산율 **bode ill for** ~에 불길한 징조가 되다 **imperil** v. 위태롭게 하다 **familiar with** ~를 잘 알고 있다 **investing** n. 투자 **performance** n. 실적 **rosy** a. 장밋빛의, 낙관적인 **resilient** a. 회복탄력성이 있는 **indication** n. 지표 **stabilize** v. 안정화하다

| 해석 |

그렇다면 경제가 정말로 잘 되어가고 있는가? 거의 모든 지표로 볼 때 그렇다. 인플레이션은 내려갔고, 실업률은 낮으며, 달러는 강세이고 주식 시장도 급등했다. 미국 소비자 심리는 최근 다시 상승했는데, 이는 건강보험부터 추수감사절 식품에 이르는 모든 물건의 가격 인상에도 불구하고 미국인들의 상당한 낙관을 시사했다. 이러한 긍정적인 소비자 심리는 미국을 다른 큰 선진국들과 비교해볼 때 특히 정당화된다. 유럽은 뒤처지고 있다. 유럽의 경제 엔진인 독일은 경기 침체의 문턱에서 정치 위기를 겪고 있다. 영국은 장기적인 쇠퇴를 겪고 있고, 일본은 고령화와 낮은 출산율로 미래가 어둡다. 미국이 좋으면 함께 경제가 좋은 경향을 보이던 캐나다조차 최근엔 아주 좋지 않은 상황이어서, 오랫동안 총리를 역임해온 저스틴 트뤼도 정권을 위협하고 있다. 그렇지만, 투자에 익숙한 사람이라면 누구나 수없이 들어봤겠지만, 과거의 실적은 미래의 성과를 보여주는 지표가 아니다. 따라서 실제로 미국 경제의 전망이 다른 나라들보다 낫기는 하지만, 반드시 장밋빛으로 밝은 것은 아니다.

① 현저하게 탄력적이다
② 미래의 성과를 보여주는 지표가 아니다
③ 안정화의 첫 징후를 보여주고 있다
④ 미래에 일어날 일을 정확하게 포착하고 있다
⑤ 주로 주식시장의 영향을 받는다

21 논리완성   ①

| 분석 |

바로 앞 문장에서 CEO들은 도전적인 인재를 원하는 듯 보이지만 실제로는 지지해주지는 않는다고 하였다. 따라서 도전적인 인재들은 '실패할 수밖에 없다'라는 내용이 가장 자연스럽다. 따라서 ①이 적절하다.

| 어휘 |

challenger n. 도전자, 기존 질서에 도전하는 사람 **be hungry for** ~을 갈망하다 **complacent** a. 자기만족적인 **clash** n. 충돌 **protégé** n. 제자, 후계자, 부하 **expertise** n. 전문적 식견 **champion** n. 지지자 **ideological tokenism** 이념적 보여주기를 위한 상징적 채용 **recipe for failure** 실패 공식, 실패로 이어지는 조건 **custodian** n. 보관자 **fall out of favor** 총애를 잃다 **status quo** 기존 질서 **subversion** n. 전복 **holistic** a. 전체론적인

| 해석 |

도전적인 사람들은 변화에 굶주린 기업에서 큰 성공과 만족을 얻는다. 그런 기업은 강한 전통이나 오랜 성공으로 인해 사람들이 조심스럽거나 자기만족에 빠진 곳일 수 있다. 이러한 환경에서 도전적인 사람들은 가장 큰 영향력을 발휘하고, 임원진과의 충돌도 가장 적게 겪는다. 가장 성공적인 도전자들은 대체로 '무언가 다른 것'을 원하고 전문 지식을 중시하는 CEO의 부하들이다. 많은 CEO가 이런 접근법을 옹호하는 데는 불편해하지만, 자기 팀은 그러한 접근법을 보여주기를 바란다는 점에 주목할 필요가 있다. 그래서 이들은 도전적인 인물을 채용하지만, 충분한 지원은 하지 않는다. 이런 식의 이념적 보여주기식 채용은 실패를 낳기 마련이다. 그리고 보호하고 관리하는 자들과 마찬가지로, 도전자들도 그들의 일이 어느 순간 기존 질서에 건설적으로 이의를 제기하기보다는, 오히려 비용이 많이 드는 전복 행위로 인식되는 순간, 총애를 잃을 수 있다.

① 실패 공식
② 행함으로 배우기
③ 전체론적인 개인 성장
④ 성장과 관련된 특성
⑤ 회사의 문화와 관습에서 배우려는 욕망

22 논리완성   ①

| 분석 |
빈칸 앞에서는 러시아어가 프랑스어나 영어만큼 아프리카에서 퍼지지 않았고, 다음 문장들을 보면 소련은 러시아어 보급에 적극적이 아니었다고 한다. 전체적으로도 러시아어가 아프리카에서 확산되지 못한 이유를 다루고 있다. 따라서 부정적인 내용의 ①이 적절하다.

| 어휘 |
eager a. 적극적인   **anti-colonialism** n. 반식민주의   **foray** n. 진출, 침투   **wane** v. 약화되다   **steeped in** ~에 깊이 물든, 익숙한   **practically** ad. 사실상   **spread** v. 퍼뜨리다   **rooted** a. 뿌리내린   **flourish** v. 번창하다   **solidify** v. 공고히 하다   **sophisticated** a. 정교한

| 해석 |
소련은 1960~70년대 반식민주의 전쟁을 벌이던 아프리카의 많은 국가에 무기와 정치적 지원을 적극적으로 제공했다. 하지만 러시아어는 프랑스어나 영어에 비해 아프리카 대륙에 그다지 많이 침투하지 못했다. 반식민주의 투쟁이 줄어들면서, 러시아어에 대한 현지의 관심은 사실상 끝났다. "모스크바의 지원은 반식민주의 게릴라를 위한 무기 공급과 훈련에서 그쳤고, 아랍, 영국, 프랑스 식민주의의 전통에 익숙한 아프리카인 중 러시아어를 배우려는 열망을 가진 사람은 거의 없었다"라고 남아프리카의 정치 분석가 킴벌리 무탄디로는 말한다. 또 소련이 무너지면서, 러시아 문화가 이미 뿌리내린 중앙유럽이나 유라시아와는 달리 52 국가씩이나 되는 광활한 아프리카 대륙 전역에 언어 보급 프로젝트를 펼칠 재정적 여력이 없었다.

① 사실상 끝났다
② 번성하기 시작했다
③ 외교적 지원을 공고히 했다
④ 정교한 힘을 보여주기 시작했다
⑤ 막 증가하기 시작했다

23 문맥상 적절하지 않은 단어 고르기   ③

| 분석 |
한 아시아의 외무장관이 아시아는 부상하고, 유럽은 몰락하는 국가라는 부정적인 시각을 보이다가, 프랑스 음식을 먹으며 유럽을 보는 관점이 달라졌다고 하였으므로, '바뀐다'는 의미가 필요하다. 따라서 ©를 shifted와 같은 표현으로 고쳐야 한다.

| 어휘 |
head-of-state chef 국가수반의 전속 요리사   **stand apart from** ~와 구별되다, 다르다   **virtually** ad. 사실상   **not least** 특히   **diplomatic implication** 외교적 파장   **cuisine** n. 요리(법)   **ambassador** n. 대사   **bilateral meeting** 양자 회담   **smooth over relations** 관계를 유연하게 만들다   **aggressive** a. 호전적인   **be in decline** 쇠퇴하다   **tone** n. 말투, 분위기   **lingering** a. 계속되는, 남아 있는   **have a lingering effect** 오래 지속되다, 오랜 영향을 미치다   **power** n. 강대국   **in terms of** ~의 견지에서 볼 때   **gastronomy** n. 미식, 요리 문화   **culinary diplomacy** 요리를 통한 외교, 음식 외교   **lasting impression** 오래가는 인상   **in particular** 특히   **take to heart** 마음에 새기다, 진지하게 받아들이다

| 해석 |
국가수반의 요리사의 역할은 접객업의 다른 거의 모든 일과 다르다. 특히 실제로 외교적 파장이 있기 때문이다. "당신 나라를 방문한 외국 정상이 그 나라를 알고 싶어 한다면, 요리를 통해 문화를 느끼게 할 수 있습니다"라고 워싱턴 주재 프랑스 대사 로랑 비예는 말한다. 그는 양자 회담에서의 실수가 실제 외교적 사건으로 이어질 수 있고, 반대로 긍정적인 경험은 관계를 부드럽게 만들 수 있다고 말한다. 비예는 특히 공격적인 아시아의 한 외무장관과 함께 점심을 먹은 일을 기억하는데, 그 외무장관은 서유럽은 쇠퇴하고 있고 아시아는 부상하고 있다고 주장했던 것이다. 그러다가 두 번째 코스와 약간의 프랑스 와인이 나왔을 때는 이미 그의 말투는 〈오래 지속되었다(→ 바뀌었다).〉 "갑자기 그들은 프랑스를 미식의 관점에서 강대국으로 보고 있었어요. 그 순간 이후 식사의 분위기와 역동성이 바뀌었죠"라고 비예는 말한다. 게다가 요리 외교라는 측면도 있다. 음식은 세계 정상들과 그들의 직원들에게 방문하는 나라에 대한 오래 남는 인상을 준다. 따라서, 특히 작은 나라의 요리사들이라면 명심해야 할 책무이다.

24 문맥상 적절하지 않은 단어 고르기   ④

| 분석 |
아파르트헤이트는 악명 높은 인종차별 정책이고, 이를 폐지하기 위한 투쟁에 나섰던 사람이 바로 넬슨 만델라였는데, 아파르트헤이트를 ⓓ처럼 '고귀하다'라고 묘사하는 것은 부적절하므로 brutality나 atrocity로 고쳐야 한다.

| 어휘 |
trace v. 추적하다   **drive** n. 운동   **apartheid** n. 아파르트헤이트, 남아프리카 공화국의 인종차별 정책   **recruiter** n. 모집자   **resistance** n. 저항운동   **armed resistance** 무장투쟁   **address** v. 연설하다   **release** n. 석방   **legacy** n. 유산   **incarceration** n. 투옥   **cell** n. 감방   **stark** a. 뚜렷한, 적나라한   **nobility** n. 고귀함   **triumph** n. 승리   **revered** a. 존경받는   **statesperson** n. 정치가

| 해석 |

넬슨 만델라가 아파르트헤이트를 종식시키기 위한 운동을 하던 동안의 케이프타운에서의 그의 삶을 추적해 보자. 케이프타운의 냥가 타운십에서 무장 저항운동의 신병모집자 역할을 한 것을 시작으로 하여, 1990년 출옥 후 케이프타운 시청에서 대중에게 연설을 한 것으로 이어진다. 만델라의 유산이 그가 찾아간 로벤 아일랜드 박물관에서보다 더 강하게 느껴지는 곳은 없다. 그곳은 한때는 그가 투옥 생활 27년 중 18년을 복역한 감옥이었다. 바닥이 침대였고 양동이가 화장실이었던 그의 작은 감방은, 아파르트헤이트의 〈고귀함(→ 잔혹함)〉과 인간 정신의 승리를 또렷하게 상기시켜주는 것이다. 그 경험은 만델라를 무너뜨리는 대신, 혁명가에서 존경받는 정치가로 변화시켰다.

25 글의 요지 ⑤

| 분석 |

전반적으로 교육의 목적, 특히 시민 교육과 역사 교육의 중요성을 강조하는 내용이므로 ⑤가 주제로 적절하다.

| 어휘 |

core a. 핵심적인, 가장 중요한 **civic life** 시민 생활, 사회 구성원으로서의 삶 **solid** a. 확고한 **grasp** n. 이해, 파악 **institution** n. 제도 **consensus** n. 합의 **envision** v. 상상하다 **engage as participants** 참여자로서 행동하다 **equip A for B** A가 B를 할 수 있도록 준비시키다 **rise to the challenge** 도전에 성공적으로 대처하다 **free election** 자유선거 **shortage** n. 부족 **matter** v. 중요하다

| 해석 |

공교육이든 사교육이든 교육의 핵심 목적 중 하나는 학생들을 시민 생활을 위해 준비시키는 것이다. 학생들이 우리 역사에 대해 모르거나 기본적인 정치 제도에 대한 확고한 이해가 부족할 때, 그들은 시민 생활에 준비가 덜 될 것이다. 미국 민주주의가 심각한 도전에 직면하고 있다는 데에는 폭넓은 공감이 이루어지고 있는데, 시민들이 우리 정치 제도를 이해하고 시민 생활에 참여하는 방법을 배우지 않고는 이 도전을 어떻게 극복해야 하는지 상상하기 힘들다. 또 지금이 미국 민주주의가 위협받는 처음도 아니다. 우리나라의 역사에 대한 이해는 학생들을 시민 생활에 대비시켜줄 수 있을 뿐 아니라, 아마도 그 도전에 성공적으로 대처할 수 있다는 낙관적인 의식을 학생들에게 가져다줄 수도 있을 것이다.

글의 요지는 무엇인가?
① 우리는 왜 수학과 과학을 공부해야 하는가?
② 민주주의 국가에서 시민들은 정말로 자신들의 자유를 지켜야 하는가?
③ 자유선거와 관련된 잠재적인 문제는 무엇인가?
④ 미국의 교사 부족은 언제 시작되었는가?
⑤ 미국의 역사 교육과 시민 교육은 왜 중요한가?

26 부분이해 ③

| 분석 |

앞에서 "사회 내 만성적인 차별 경험이 건강에 미치는 영향이 인종 및 민족 간 건강 격차를 설명해줄 수 있다", "인종차별이 있는 사회에 사는 것만으로도 흑인 전체의 건강에 해로울 수 있다"라고 했으므로 "이 현상"은 ③이다.

| 어휘 |

stress physiology 스트레스 생리학 **epigenetics** n. 후생유전학(환경이 유전자 발현에 영향을 미친다는 생물학) **weathering hypothesis** 풍화 가설(만성적 스트레스, 특히 인종차별 같은 사회적 요인이 건강에 악영향을 준다는 이론) **mount** v. 증가하다 **chronic exposure** 만성적인 노출(오랜 시간에 걸쳐 반복적으로 영향을 받는 상태) **discrimination** n. 차별 **disparities in health** 건강 격차(집단 간 건강 수준의 차이) **account for** 설명하다 **akin to** ~와 유사한, 비슷한 **environmental risk factor** 건강에 영향을 주는 환경적 위험 요소 **emerge** v. 나타나다 **nutrition** n. 영양 **have an impact on** ~에 영향을 미치다

| 해석 |

스트레스 생리학과 후생유전학 분야에서 과학적 이해가 그 다음 20년 동안 늘어나면서, 풍화 가설을 뒷받침하는 증거들이 늘어나기 시작했다. 연구자들은 사회 내 만성적인 차별 경험이 건강에 미치는 영향이, 다른 요인들로는 설명되지 않는 인종 및 민족 간 건강 격차를 설명해줄 수 있다는 것을 더 많이 발견하고 있다. 한 공중보건 연구자에 따르면, 인종차별이 있는 사회에 사는 것만으로도 흑인 전체의 건강에 해로울 수 있으며, 직접 인종차별을 경험하지 않은 사람들에게도 마찬가지이다. "이는 높은 수준의 대기오염 같은 다른 건강 관련 환경적 위험 요소들과 유사합니다"라고 데바쿠마르는 2020년 『이코노미스트』와의 인터뷰에서 말했다. 이러한 현상을 뒷받침하는 초기 증거는 1990년대부터 등장하기 시작했다.

밑줄 친 "this phenomenon"이 의미하는 것은?
① 가난에 노출되는 것은 신체 건강에 긍정적인 결과를 낳는다.
② 빈곤이 나쁜 식습관과 영양 부족에 영향을 미친다.
③ 인종차별을 경험하는 스트레스가 신체에 부정적인 영향을 끼친다.
④ 고온은 결국 인종차별을 낳는다.
⑤ 인종차별과 관련된 문제는 우리의 육체와 정신에 아무런 영향을 주지 않는다.

27 글의 요지 ②

| 분석 |

사람들은 자신이 좋아하는 품목을 더 많이 소비하리라고 생각하지만 실제로는 그렇지 않다. 다시 말해 기호는 실제 소비에 커다란 영향을 미치지 않는다는 내용이다. 선호도는 생각만큼 중요하지는

않다는 것은 선호도를 과대평가한다는 말이므로 ②가 글의 요지로 적절하다.

| 어휘 |

depend on ~에 달려 있다   insensitive a. 둔감한   fondness n. 좋아함   preference n. 선호도   assume v. 가정하다   offering n. 제공된 것   sitcom n. 시트콤, 상황극   rank v. 순위를 매기다   estimate v. 추정하다   flavor n. 맛   turn out ~으로 판명되다   negligible a. 무시할 만한, 사소한   lip balm 립밤, 입술 보호제   brand n. 브랜드, 상표

| 해석 |

영화를 보기 위해 팝콘을 살 때, 팝콘의 양은 아마도 팝콘을 얼마나 좋아하는지에 따라 달라질 것이다. 정말인가? 꼭 그렇지는 않다. 최근 한 연구에 따르면, 사람들의 소비 습관은 제품에 대한 개인적 기호에 놀라울 만큼 둔감하다고 한다. 사실, 소비자들은 자신도 자기 기호가 실제 소비에 얼마나 영향을 미치는지 예측을 잘하지 못한다. 예를 들어, 사람들은 자신이 코미디 특집을 좋아하면 시트콤보다 코미디 특집을 더 많이 볼 것이라고 가정한다. 연구자들은 총 1,486명의 미국 참가자들을 대상으로 진행된 여섯 번에 걸친 연구에서 참가자들에게 여러 품목에 대한 선호도에 순위를 매기고 특정 기간에 걸쳐 각 품목을 얼마나 소비할지 추정하도록 요청했다. 한 실험에서는 참가자들이 다양한 맛의 젤리빈을 얼마나 좋아하는지, 그리고 실험 중 각각의 맛을 얼마나 먹을지 예측했다. 그리곤 참가자들에게는 본인이 선호하는 맛의 젤리빈 또는 다른 맛의 젤리빈이 M&M 초콜릿과 함께 제공되었다. 실험 결과, 참가자들이 선호하는 품목과 비선호 품목의 소비량 차이는 거의 무시할 만한 수준이었다. 그리고 실제 세계에서의 연구를 포함한 모든 실험에서 같은 결과가 나왔다. 실제 세계에서의 연구에서는 사람들이 자신이 좋아하는 브랜드든 다른 브랜드든 상관없이 한 주간 립밤을 사용하는 양은 같은 것으로 밝혀졌다.

글의 요지는 무엇인가?
① 특정 제품을 좋아하는 것이 항상 좋은 것은 아니다.
② 사람들은 자신의 소비가 자신의 선호도에 얼마나 의존하는지를 과대평가한다.
③ 쇼핑객들은 다른 요소들 사이에서 소비자들이 가장 좋아하는 제품들을 고려해야 한다.
④ 소비자들이 젤리빈을 싫어한 것은 실제로 그 가치를 알았기 때문이다.
⑤ 소비자들은 싫어하는 제품보다 더 싼 대안을 고려하는 경향이 있다.

28~30

많은 사람에게, 부모와의 관계와 상호작용을 분석해보는 것이 치료 경험의 핵심이 될 수 있다. 당연히, 이러한 경험의 한 부분으로, 치료사는 이 중요한 역학에 관해 질문할 수 있다. 질문은 대개 환자가 자기 나름대로 상황을 이해할 수 있도록 구성된 질문이고, 중립적이고 특정 방향으로 유도하지 않는 방식으로 이루어진다. 하지만 치료사는 주의해야 한다. 로렌스 파티히스와 마리오 E. 에레라의 새로운 연구에 따르면, 부정적으로 구성된 질문만이 부모와의 관계에 관한 감정에 영향을 주는 것은 아니다. 긍정적으로 구성된 질문 역시 부모와의 관계를 재평가하게 할 수 있다.

조사에서, 연구팀은 미국을 기반으로 한 301명의 온라인 참가자에게 자신이 처한 건강여건(질환)에 따라 주제가 달라지는 짧은 글을 써 달라고 요청했다. 첫 번째 여건의 사람들의 경우에는, 어머니의 따뜻함, 능력, 사랑의 긍정적인 사례에 대해 글을 썼고, 두 번째 여건의 사람들은 이러한 자질이 결여된 사례에 대해 글을 썼고, 세 번째 여건의 사람들은 교사에 대한 부정적인 사례의 글을 썼다. 네 번째이자 마지막 여건의 사람들은 글의 주제에 대한 아무런 지시도 받지 않았다. 그런 다음 모든 참가자는 따뜻함과 관대함 같은 특성에 대해 현재 어머니를 어떻게 평가하는지에 대한 측정을 완성했고, 여러 아동기 단계에서와 현재에서의 어머니를 향한 감정에 대한 긍정적인 기억과 부정적인 기억을 보고했으며, 그들의 현재 기분을 평가했다. 분석 결과, 어찌 보면 당연하게도, 어머니를 긍정적으로 평가한 사람들은 다른 여건에 있는 사람들보다 어머니에 대해 상당히 더 행복감을 느낀다고 보고했다. 행복은 참가자들이 어머니를 얼마나 긍정적으로 보는가와 강한 상관관계에 있었다. 이 부류의 사람들은 또 어린 시절 어머니에 대해 상당히 더 행복을 느낀 것을 기억했다. 이는 부모를 재평가하는 것이 어린 시절의 기억에 상당한 영향을, 비록 이런 영향이 비교적 짧게 약 4주 정도 지속되었지만, 미칠 수 있다는 것을 시사한다.

우리는 기억은 오류 가능성이 있다는 것과 모든 종류의 요인들이 과거에 일어난 일에 대해 우리가 생각하고 느끼는 방식을 변화시킬 수 있다는 것을 이미 알고 있다. 이번 연구는 치료사가 이 점을 염두에 두어야 하며, 가족과 환자의 관계를 논의할 때 질문 구성 방식에 여전히 신중해야 한다는 것을 강조한다. 연구팀은 이것에서 한 걸음 더 나아가, 환자가 부모나 살면서 만나는 다른 사람들을 바라보는 방식이 변화할 수 있는 잠재적 가능성에 대해 치료를 시작할 때부터 환자에게 미리 알려야 한다고 주장한다.

| 어휘 |

deconstruct v. 해체하다, 분석하다   mainstay n. 중심, 주된 기반   therapeutic a. 치료의   dynamics n. 역학, 상호작용   neutral a. 중립적인   ensure v. 보장하다   make sense of 이해하다   beware v. 주의하다   frame v. 질문을 설계하다, 표현 방식을 만들다   reappraise v. 다시 평가하다   depending on ~에 따라   competence n. 능력   prompt n. 유도 문항, 글쓰기 주제   measure n. 척도   trait n. 특성   generosity n. 관대함   fallible a. 오류 가능성이 있는   underlines v. 강조하다   keep in mind

명심하다　**cautious** a. 신중한　**at the outset** 시작 단계에서
provocative a. 도발적인, 성나게 하는　**non-leading** a. 중립적인
remarkable a. 놀랄만한　**impartial** a. 공정한　**inherently** ad.
본질적으로　**impeccable** a. 흠 없는　**intact** a. 완전한　**take
into account** 감안하다　**instruct** v. 지시하다

28　빈칸완성　　　　　　　　　　　　　　　②

| 분석 |

Ⓐ 앞에서 중립적인 방식이라고 말하고, 콤마로 이어지므로 neutral과 동의어에 가까운 표현이 와야 한다. 따라서 non-leading과 impartial이 적절하다. that절 안에서 Ⓑ 앞의 절에는 '상당한 영향'이라는 긍정적 표현이 있고, 뒤의 절에는 '비교적 짧은 영향'이라는 부정적 표현이 있어서 서로 역접 관계이므로 역접의 연결사 though가 가장 적절하다.

29　내용파악　　　　　　　　　　　　　　　③

| 분석 |

치료사의 질문 구성 방식이 부모에 관한 기억, 특히 어린 시절에 느꼈던 감정이나 생각에 영향을 미칠 수 있다는 내용이었다. 가장 가까운 답은 ③이다.

이 글에 따르면 저자는 질문의 구성 방식이 무엇에 영향을 미친다고 생각하는가?
① 병원 방문 빈도
② 다양한 유형의 여건
③ 사람들이 어린 시절 부모를 기억하는 방식
④ 사람들이 사소한 것을 잊는 방식
⑤ 부모의 권리와 책임

30　내용일치　　　　　　　　　　　　　　　②

| 분석 |

어머니에 대한 평가에 따라 행복한 느낌이 달라졌으므로, ②가 핵심적인 실험 결과이다. ① 기억은 오류의 가능성이 있다. ③ 부정적 사례도 있었다. ④ 긍정적인 사례도 있었고, 지시가 없던 사람들도 있었다. ⑤ 현재 기분에 대한 평가는 있었지만 미래 감정에 대한 예측은 없었다.

이 글에 따르면 올바른 것은?
① 기억은 본질적으로 흠이 없고 온전하다.
② 참가자들의 어머니에 대한 평가가 어머니에 관한 감정에 영향을 미쳤다.
③ 실험은 어머니의 따뜻함에 대한 중립적 사례만을 고려했다.
④ 참가자들은 항상 부정적인 말을 하도록 지시받았다.
⑤ 참가자들은 부모와의 관계와 상호작용을 분석하기 위해 미래 감정을 예측하도록 요청받았다.

31~32

대제국들의 운명에 관한 논의는 새롭지 않다. 역사책이 저술되어온 만큼 오랫동안 이 논의는 있어 왔다. 하지만 이제는 정보공동체 안팎에서 진지한 정책 입안자들이 이런 형태의 적극적인 계획 수립과 전략화에 참여하고 있다. 전 세계에서 미국은 '세계의 경찰'로 여겨진다. 미국은 이 역할을, 주저하면서이긴 하지만, 받아들였는데, 국내 문제에 해를 끼쳤으며, 다른 나라들로부터의 조롱도 없지 않았다. 미국을 세운 건국의 아버지들은 그러한 세계 지배를 원치 않았고, 오히려 자유, 정의, 모두를 위한 행복 추구라는 가치를 믿었다. 하지만 오늘날의 미국 정책 입안자들은 강한 군사력과 부드러운 외교력을 통한 국가 건설이 세계 속에서 미국이 차지하는 역할의 본질이라고 믿는다.

앞으로 수십 년 내에 미국은 이슬람 국가들에 들어가 자신과 동맹국을 적대시하는 국가들과 전쟁을 벌이려들까? 비현실적인 방안이긴 하지만, 정책 입안자들 사이에서 이런 생각이 드물지는 않다. 그들은 이슬람주의자들이나 이슬람 사회의 극단주의 세력과 전면전 말고는 대안이 없다고 여긴다. 우리는 보다 온건한 이슬람 세력과 미국 문명 사이에서 중간 지점, 타협안, 돌파구를 찾을 수 있을까? 만약 속박 없는 자유(freedom), 권리로서의 자유(liberty), 평등이라는 미국의 이상이 외국에서의 국가 건설을 위한 희생 제물로 바쳐질 때, 그날은 정말 어두운 날이 될 것이다. 위엄 있는 미국이 주위를 안보의 벽으로 둘러싼 로마식 요새로 변한다면, 미국의 건국 원칙은 철저하게 수정될 필요가 있을 것이다. 아프가니스탄에서의 미국의 모험적 행동은 국가 건설 시도가 군사 예비물자 뿐 아니라 인명과 자본의 관점에서도 그 나라의 귀중한 자원을 어떻게 장기적으로 고갈시키는지를 보여주는 완벽한 사례이다.

| 어휘 |

fate n. 운명　**empire** n. 제국　**policy maker** 정책 입안자
strategizing n. 전략 수립　**intelligence community** 정보기관, 정보 관련 조직 전체　**embrace** v. 받아들이다　**reluctantly** ad. 마지못해　**to the detriment of** ~에 해를 끼치며　**domestic** a. 국내의　**scorn** n. 조롱　**dominion** n. 지배　**nation building** 국가 건설, 체제 정립　**part and parcel** 본질적 요소, 핵심 구성　**purview** n. 권한, 시야　**wage war** 전쟁을 벌이다　**harbor ill will** 악의를 품다　**ally** n. 동맹　**alternative** n. 대안　**all-out war** 전면전　**compromise solution** 타협적인 해결방안　**moderate** a. 온건한　**element** n. 세력　**breakthrough** n. 돌파구　**somber** a. 침울한　**altar** n. 제단　**thoroughgoing** a. 철저한　**majestic** a. 웅대한　**revision** n. 수정　**fortress** n. 요새　**perimeter** n. 주변　**venture** n. 위험을 감수한 시도　**duration** n. 기간　**drain** v. 고갈시키다　**reserves** n. 자원, 비축된 병력·물자

31 빈칸완성 ②

| 분석 |

앞에서 '암울한 날'이라고 했으므로 when절은 부정적인 의미가 되어야 하는데, 희생되는 것이 미국의 건국이념이고 이상인 자유와 평등이므로 빈칸에는 미국이 얻으려고 하는 것이 들어가야 한다. 이것은 첫 단락 말미에 언급된, 세계 지배를 위해 다른 나라에 (친미적인) 국가를 세우는 것을 말하므로 ②가 적절하다.

빈칸에 적절한 표현은?
① 이슬람 사회의 승리
② 외국에서의 국가 건설
③ 행복과 번영의 시기
④ 한 나라의 경제적 성공
⑤ 다른 지역에서 온 군대

32 내용파악 ①

| 분석 |

나머지는 모두 미국의 이상이고, ①만 미국 외교 정책의 목표를 가리킨다.

33~35

사람들은 일반적으로, 실수를 바꿀 수 없는 단점의 징후로 해석하기보다는 배우고 성장하도록 인간을 도와주는 것이라고 본다. 그러나 이들은 자주 AI 도구가 엄격하고, 조정이나 발전에 능숙하지 않다고 생각한다. 이러한 믿음은 기계를 제한된 기능만 수행하는 정적인 장치로 경험했던 과거의 기억에서 비롯되었을 수 있다.

이런 인식은 기술에 대한 신뢰를 줄이고, 새로운 상황에서의 효과에 대한 우려를 낳을 수 있다. 하지만 여러 연구는 사람들이 AI가 적응 학습 능력이 있다는 말을 들을 때, AI 결과물 사용이 증가한다는 것을 보여주었다. 심지어 학습 능력을 단순히 암시하는 것만으로도, 예를 들어 AI를 단순히 '알고리즘'이 아닌 '기계 학습'으로 이름 붙이는 것만으로도, 사용자가 증가했다. 넷플릭스는 자사의 콘텐츠 추천 알고리즘이 사용자 시청 습관과 관련된 데이터를 더 많이 수집하면서 지속적으로 향상된다고 자주 홍보한다. 또 추천 콘텐츠에 '당신을 위한' 같은 라벨을 붙이고, '당신이 X를 시청했기 때문에'라는 설명을 통해, 알고리즘이 학습하고 있다는 메시지를 강화하고 사용자의 변화하는 취향을 감안하고 있다고 안심시킨다.

AI가 융통성이 없다고 생각하는 사람들은, AI가 모든 사람을 똑같이 취급하며, 모두에게 통하는 하나의 천편일률적인 접근방식을 적용할 것이라 여긴다. 실제로 자신이 독특하다고 여기는 사용자일수록, AI 사용 경향은 줄어든다. 예를 들어 한 연구에서는, 참가자들이 자신의 윤리적 성향이 독특하다고 생각할수록, 도덕적 특성을 평가하는 AI 시스템에 더 큰 저항감을 보였다. 하지만 동시에, 융통성과 예측 가능성 사이에는 섬세한 균형이 필요하다. 기업이 AI의 학습 능력과 발전 능력을 강조할 때는 보통 그 사용이 늘어나지만, 사용자들이 결과물에 대해 지나치게 예측 불가능하다고 느낄 때면, 오히려 AI의 개입은 역효과를 낼 수 있다. 더 적응력 있는 AI 시스템이 또한 더 위험하기도 한데, 그런 시스템이 더 넓은 범위의 사용자 상호작용을 허용하고 그 상호작용 중 일부가 AI를 학습시키는 데 사용되는 데이터에 포함되지 않을 수도 있기 때문이다. AI가 더 유연할 때, 사람들이 이를 부적절하게 사용할 가능성이 커지고, 그런 경우 AI 알고리즘이 바람직하지 않은 반응을 내놓을 가능성도 커져서, 결국 사용자와 기업 모두에게 새로운 위험을 초래할 수 있다.

| 어휘 |

defect n. 결함　**rigid** a. 엄격한, 융통성 없는　**adept at** ~에 능숙한　**evolve** v. 발전하다　**stem from** ~에서 기인하다　**static device** 변화 없이 작동하는 장치　**carry out** 수행하다　**efficacy** n. 효과성　**adaptive learning** 적응 학습(스스로 배우고 발전하는 능력)　**nominal cue** 명목상의 단서, 간접적인 힌트　**potential** n. 잠재력　**brand** v. 이름 붙이다　**boost** v. 향상시키다　**reinforce** v. 강화하다　**preference** n. 취향　**identically** ad. 똑같이　**one-size-fits-all approach** 모두에게 동일하게 적용하는 방식　**distinctive** a. 독특한　**resistant** a. 저항하는, 반발하는　**assess** v. 평가하다　**delicate** a. 미묘한　**intervention** n. 개입, 조치　**backfire** v. 역효과를 낳다　**spectrum** n. 범위　**output** n. 결과물, 출력　**opaque** a. 불투명한　**counterproductive** a. 기대하지 않은 결과를 초래하는, 역효과의　**unaccommodating** a. 융통성 없는　**flexible** a. 유연한　**glaring** a. 눈에 띄는　**turn out** ~으로 판명되다　**trade-off** n. 상충 관계

33 부분이해 ⑤

| 분석 |

사람들은 '알고리즘'이라고 부르는 것보다 '기계 학습'이라고 할 때 더 적극적으로 AI를 사용하는 경향이 있다고 했는데, '학습한다', '배운다'는 것은 발전이나 조정, 융통성을 의미하므로 ⑤가 정답이다.

34 부분이해 ①

| 분석 |

앞에서 'AI가 융통성이 없다고 생각한다', 'AI가 모든 사람을 똑같이 취급한다'고 언급한 것에서 하나가 모두에게 통하는 천편일률적인 접근방식은 사람마다의 개인차나 독특한 개성을 무시함을 알 수 있으므로 ①이 정답이다.

밑줄 친 ⓑ"one-size-fits-all approach"는 사람들이 AI를 어떻게 생각하고 있다고 시사하는가?
① 개인의 고유한 특성을 무시한다.
② 정확한 응답을 제공한다.
③ 눈에 띄는 소비자에게 편향을 보인다.
④ 구매하기엔 너무 비싸다.
⑤ 융통성과 예측 가능성을 균형 있게 조절하는 능력이 있다.

35 내용파악   ④

| 분석 |

AI가 학습 능력이 있다, 다시 말해 융통성이 있다는 말은 AI에 대한 신뢰와 사용을 증가시킨다. 하지만 너무 융통성이 크면 예측 불가능성 때문에 위험하다고 한다. 따라서 AI의 융통성과 예측 가능성 사이에는 미묘한 균형이 있다는 게 이 글의 요지이다. 저자의 생각을 가장 잘 설명하고 있는 것은 ④이다.

이 글에 따르면 저자가 믿고 있는 것은?
① 이름 붙이기에서 단어 선택은 중요하지 않다.
② 도덕적 특성은 AI로 절대 평가할 수 없다.
③ AI는 어떤 입력도 처리하지 못할 것이다.
④ AI의 융통성과 예측 가능성은 상충 관계이다.
⑤ 사람들은 알고리즘 이해에 어려움을 겪는다.

36~37

모든 민주국가는 공직 출마에 최저 연령을 정해놓고 있다. 프랑스 같은 일부 국가는 매우 관대하여, 거의 제왕적 권력을 갖는 대통령에 출마할 자격을 18세에게도 부여한다. 다른 나라들은 더 신중하다. 이탈리아의 대통령은 대체로 의례적인 자리이지만 최소 50세 이상이어야 한다. 하지만 권력을 행사할 수 있는 최고 연령 제한을 두는 나라는 없다. 그런 제한이 있어야 할까? 지혜와 경험은 매우 중요하다. 그러나 활력, 역동성, 신선한 아이디어도 마찬가지로 중요하다. 노스다코타 주는 이 제한 설정에 앞장서고 있다. 6월, 주민들은 주를 대표하는 미국 의회 의원에 최고 연령을 설정하는 조례를 승인했다. 퓨 리서치 센터 조사에 따르면, 보다 넓게 볼 때, 공화당과 민주당 모두가 정치인과 대법관의 연령 제한을 압도적인 다수로 지지하고 있다. 영국에서는 집권 노동당이 현재 평생직인 상원의원에 80세 정년제를 도입하겠다고 약속했다.
민주주의 국가들의 공직 출마 연령 상한제 채택은 합리적으로 보일 수 있다. 그러나 그렇게 되면 위험한 선례를 남길 수도 있다. 자유 사회에서는 유권자와 출마자 모두가 누가 투표할 수 있는지와 누구에게 투표할 수 있는지에 관련하여 가능한 한 폭넓은 대표성을 가져야 한다. 누가 출마할 수 있는지에 정부가 제한을 두면 둘수록 그러한 제한이 정치적 간섭을 받게 될 위험이 커진다. 그냥 유권자들이 결정하게 하는 편이 더 낫다. 그래서 연령 제한을 가하는 것에 대한 기준은 매우 높아야 한다.

| 어휘 |

minimum age 최소연령 **liberal** a. 자유로운, 관대한 **run** v. 출마하다 **circumspect** a. 신중한 **ceremonial** a. 의식의 **wield power** 권력을 행사하다 **count** v. 중요하다 **vitality** n. 활력 **dynamism** n. 역동성 **lead the charge** (돌격의) 선두에 서다 **measure** n. 조례 **overwhelming majority** 압도적 다수 **impose** v. 강제하다 **retirement** n. 은퇴 **precedent** n. 선례 **electorate** n. 유권자 **candidate** n. 후보자 **meddling** n. 간섭, 개입 **bar** n. 기준선 장벽 **sensible** a. 합리적인 **pose a threat** 위협을 가하다 **symptom** n. 징후, 증상 **enshrine** v. 명문화하다 **designated age** 정해진 나이

36 내용파악   ②

| 분석 |

두 번째 문단 첫 문장에서 저자는 출마 연령 상한제에 대해 "합리적으로 들릴 수도 있지만, 위험한 선례를 남길 수도 있다"라고 하였다. ②와 같은 의미의 문장이다.

출마 연령에 상한을 두자는 주장에 대한 저자의 태도는?
① 국가와 정치인 모두에게 이상적인 해결책이다.
② 합리적으로 보일 수도 있지만, 민주주의에 위협이 될 수 있다.
③ 정치인이 공무원임을 가리킨다.
④ 상대적으로 위험한 직업 수에 영향을 준다.
⑤ 미국 내 더 깊은 문제의 징후를 이해하는 주요한 방법이다.

37 빈칸완성   ①

| 분석 |

빈칸 앞 문장에서 정부가 나서서 제한을 가하는 것은 그 제한이 정치적 간섭을 받게 될 위험이 있다고 했고, 빈칸 다음 문장에서는 제한을 가하는 것에 대한 기준이 매우 높아야 한다고 말하여, 정부가 나서서 제한을 가하는 것에 반대하고 있다. 결국 정부가 아닌 유권자가 결정해야 할 문제라는 말이므로 빈칸에는 ①이 적절하다.

빈칸에 적절한 표현은?
① 유권자들이 결정하게 하는 것이 더 낫다.
② 정치에서 나이는 정말 중요하다.
③ 후보자들은 우리가 생각하는 것보다 더 똑똑하다.
④ 연령 제한을 법으로 명문화할 필요가 크다.
⑤ 대법관은 정해진 나이까지 재직해야 한다.

38~40

미국인 대다수로부터 지지와 호평을 얻었지만, 루스벨트와 그의 뉴딜 정책은 나름대로 상당수의 격분한 비판자들을 불러일으켰다. 루이지애나 주지사 휴이 롱은 한때 루스벨트를 지지했던 입장에서 돌아서서 뉴딜이 기업과 부유층의 요구에 너무 굴복한다고 비판하며 전국적으로 유명해졌다. 그는 대신 '부의 공유' 계획을 제시했는데, 최상위 부자들의 부를 몰수하여 가난한 사람들에게 5,000달러 상당의 주택과 연간 2,500달러의 소득 형태로 재분배하자는 내용이었다. 루스벨트에게는 또 다른 위협적인 적으로 미시간 주의 가톨릭 사제이자 라디오 방송인 찰스 코글린 신부가 있었는데, 그는 4,500만 명에 달하는 주로 백인 노동 계층 청취자들의 걱정을 점차 증가시켜, 자신의 반공주의적이고, 반자본주의적이고, 극단적으로 반유대주의적인 비난을 통해, 완전한 공포로 바꾸어놓았고, 이 악의 세력을 격퇴할 '기독교 전선'을 요청했다. 롱과 코글린의 과장되고 히스테리컬한 말은 논리적인 주장보다는 격렬한 분노와 원한을 드러냈기 때문에, 그들의 논리를 짜맞추기란 쉽지 않다. 그럼에도 불구하고, 그들은 현대 산업 국가가 그들의 개인적인 자율성을 침해하고, 소중한 자유를 짓밟고 있다는 진정한 공포를 추종자들 사이에 불러일으키는 데 도움을 주었다.

| 어휘 |

garner v. 얻다   appreciation n. 평가   inspire v. 자극하다; 고무[격려]하다   outraged a. 격분한   expropriate v. 몰수하다   redistribute v. 재분배하다   homestead n. 농가   annual income 연간수입   ratchet up 점차 증가시키다   rabidly ad. 맹렬하게   diatribe n. 통렬한 비난   hyperbole n. 과장법   hysteria n. 히스테리   rancor n. 원한   resentment n. 분개   subservient a. 굴종적인   initiative n. 계획, 주도권   horn in on 침해하다   trample v. 짓밟다   autonomy n. 자율성   self-effacing a. 자신을 낮추는   judicious a. 현명한

38　빈칸완성　④

| 분석 |

앞에서 '개인의 자율성을 침해하고 있다'고 했으므로 빈칸에도 부정적인 의미를 가진 동사가 필요하다. ④ trample on이 '~를 짓밟다'는 뜻이므로 빈칸에 들어가기에 적절하다.

39　내용파악　⑤

| 분석 |

마지막에서 두 번째 문장에서 롱과 코글린의 말에 대해 '과장되고 히스테리컬'하다고 하며, '합리적 주장'이 아니라고 했다. 따라서 ⑤가 정답이다.

40　내용일치　④

| 분석 |

코글린이 반유대주의적(anti-Semitic) 비난을 퍼부었다고 명시되어 있으므로 ④가 정답이다. ① 한때는 지지하다가 돌아섰다. ②의 내용은 없다. ③ 뉴딜 정책은 지지를 받았다. ⑤ 비논리적이었다.

다음 중 올바른 것은?
① 휴이 롱은 경력 내내 루스벨트를 비판했다.
② 루스벨트를 비판하는 사람들은 민주주의 수호에 도움을 주었다.
③ 루스벨트와 뉴딜 정책은 대중으로부터 압도적으로 부정적인 반응을 얻었다.
④ 찰스 코글린 신부는 유대인에 대한 반감을 드러냈다.
⑤ 두 비판자의 주장은 너무 논리적이어서 비판받기 어려웠다.

41~43

예술이란 정의하기 어렵기로 악명이 높으며, 좋은 예술과 나쁜 예술 사이의 차이도 마찬가지로 어렵다. 하지만 여기서 하나의 일반화한 진술을 제시하겠다. 즉 예술이란 수많은 선택에서 만들어지는 것이다. 소설 쓰기를 예로 들면 이것을 설명하기가 가장 쉬울지도 모르겠다. 소설을 쓰고 있을 때, 타이핑하는 거의 모든 단어를, 의식적으로든 무의식적으로든, 선택하고 있는 것이다. 지나치게 단순화해서 말하자면, 1만 단어로 된 단편소설에는 대략 1만 번 정도의 선택이 요구된다. 하지만, 생성형 인공지능 프로그램에 명령어를 줄 때는 선택을 거의 하지 않는다. 100단어짜리 명령어를 입력한다면, 당신은 약 100번의 선택만 한 셈이다.

인공지능이 당신의 명령어를 바탕으로 1만 단어로 된 이야기를 생성한다면, 그것은 당신이 하지 않고 있는 나머지 모든 선택을 채워 넣어야 한다. 인공지능이 이를 처리하는 방법은 다양하다. 그중 하나는 인터넷에서 발견되는 텍스트에서 볼 수 있는 다른 여러 작가들이 한 선택들을 평균화하는 것이다. 이 평균값은 가능한 가장 흥미롭지 않은 선택과 같다. 이런 이유로 인공지능이 만든 텍스트는 흔히 정말 단조롭다. 또 다른 방법은 특정 작가의 선택을 모방하는 스타일 모방을 프로그램에 지시하는 것인데, 이는 매우 파생적인 이야기를 만들어낸다. 두 가지 경우 모두, 흥미로운 예술을 창작하지 못하고 있다.

화가가 하는 선택들을 수량화하기란 훨씬 더 어렵지만, 나는 동일한 근본 원칙이 시각 예술에도 적용된다고 생각한다. 실제 그림들에는 어마어마한 횟수로 결정을 한 흔적이 담겨 있다. 그에 비하면 DALL-E 같은 텍스트-이미지 생성 프로그램을 사용하는 사람은 '갑옷을 입은 기사가 불을 뿜는 용과 싸운다.'와 같은 명령어를 입력한 뒤에 나머지 모두 프로그램이 알아서 하도록 내버려 둔다. 이 결과로 나온 이미

지 속 대부분의 선택은 온라인에서 발견되는 유사한 그림들로부터 빌려온 것이다. 이미지는 매우 정교하게 묘사될 수는 있지만, 명령어를 입력한 사람이 그것에 대한 공로를 주장할 수는 없다.

| 어휘 |

notoriously ad. 악명 높게 **define** v. 정의하다 **generalization** n. 일반화 **consciously** ad. 의식적으로 **unconsciously** ad. 무의식적으로 **oversimplify** v. 지나치게 단순화하다 **on the order of** 대충 **generative** a. 생성형의 **prompt** n. 명령어 **be equivalent to** ~에 상당하다 **bland** a. 단조로운 **mimicry** n. 모방 **emulate** v. 모방하다 **derivative** a. 파생적인, 이차적인 **quantify** v. 수량화하다 **exquisitely** ad. 정교하게 **render** v. 표현하다; ~이 되게 하다 **kudos** n. 명예 **credit** n. 공로

41 내용파악   ③

| 분석 |

인공지능이 인터넷에서 발견되는 다른 창작물들에서 행해진 선택들을 '평균화'한다는 말은, 통계적 절차를 이용한다는 말이므로 ③이 정답이다. ① 인공지능은 인간처럼 직접 쓰지 않고 인간이 써놓은 여러 글에서의 선택들을 평균화해서 소설을 만들어낸다. ② 인공지능은 인터넷에서 이미지를 빌려온다. ④, ⑤ 인공지능은 창의적이지 않으므로, 진정한 작가나 예술가가 될 수 없다.

다음 중 저자의 생각은?
① 인공지능은 인간이 글을 쓰는 방식과 유사하게 소설을 쓸 수 있다.
② 인공지능은 스스로 창의적인 그림을 그릴 수 있다.
③ 인공지능은 텍스트와 시각적 콘텐츠 모두를 통계적 절차를 통해 생성한다.
④ 인공지능이 진정한 작가나 예술가가 될 수 없다는 것은 단지 인간 중심의 사고에 불과하다.
⑤ 인간이 잘 다듬은 명령어를 입력해 인공지능과 협력하여 예술을 만들 수 있다.

42 부분이해   ②

| 분석 |

derivative는 '모방적'이라는 의미이므로 ②가 정답이다.

밑줄 친 "highly derivative"는 무엇을 의미하는가?
① 모든 예술 작품은 본질적으로 이전 작품들을 기초로 해서 만들어진다.
② 인공지능이 만들어내는 것은 예술의 단순한 모방에 불과하다.
③ 인공지능이 만들어내는 이야기는 인간 작가들이 쓴 것과 같다.
④ 인공지능이 흥미로운 예술을 만들지 못한다고 해서 독창성이 없다는 것은 아니다.
⑤ 인공지능이 쓰는 이야기는 인공지능이 내린 수많은 선택에서 유래한다.

43 빈칸완성   ③

| 분석 |

문장에는 '창작의 공로, 소유권, 독창성, 명예' 등이 들어갈 수 있다. 이미지의 창작과 창의성을 인정하는 표현이면 어느 것이나 괜찮다. ③의 '정중함'이라는 의미를 갖는 civility는 전혀 부적절한 단어이다.

44~45

정치 제도는 누가 사회에서 권력을 갖는지, 그리고 어떤 목적을 위해 그 권력이 사용될 수 있는지를 결정한다. 만약 권력의 분배가 좁고 제약이 없다면, 그런 정치 제도는 전제적이다. 반면에, 권력을 사회 전반에 넓게 분산시키고 권력에 제약을 가하는 정치 제도는 다원적이다. 정치권력이 한 명의 개인이나 좁은 집단에 부여되는 것이 아니라, 광범위한 연합체나 여러 집단에게 있다. 막스 베버는 국가에 대한 가장 유명하고 널리 받아들여지는 정의를 제시했는데, 그 정의는 국가를 사회에서의 '합법적 폭력의 독점'과 동일시했다. 이러한 폭력의 독점과 그것이 동반하는 중앙집중화가 없다면, 국가는 법과 질서를 집행하는 역할을 할 수 없으며, 하물며 공공서비스 제공이나 경제활동의 촉진과 규제는 더더욱 불가능하다. 국가가 어떠한 정치적 집중화도 이루지 못하면, 사회는 조만간 혼돈에 빠지게 된다. 충분히 중앙집중적이면서 동시에 다원적인 정치 제도를 우리는 포용적 정치 제도라 부른다. 이 두 조건 중 어느 하나라도 충족되지 못하면, 그런 제도는 착취적 정치 제도라고 부른다.

경제 제도와 정치 제도 사이에는 강력한 시너지가 존재한다. 착취적 정치 제도는 권력을 좁은 엘리트 집단에 집중시키며, 이들의 권력 행사를 거의 제약하지 않는다. 그러면 경제 제도 또한 이 엘리트들이 사회 나머지로부터 자원을 착취하도록 구조화되는 경우가 많다. 따라서 착취적 경제 제도는 자연스럽게 착취적 정치 제도를 동반한다. 사실상 착취적 경제 제도는 존속하기 위해 착취적 정치 제도에 의존한다. 권력을 폭넓게 부여하는 포용적 정치 제도는 이렇게 다수의 사람으로부터 자원을 빼앗고, 시장 진입 장벽을 세우며, 소수만 이익을 보도록 시장 기능을 억압하는 경제 제도를 뿌리 뽑으려는 경향이 있다.

| 어휘 |

institution n. 제도 **end** n. 목표 **unconstrained** a. 제약이 없는 **absolutist** a. 전제적인 **subject** v. 종속시키다 **pluralistic** a. 다원적인 **vest** v. 부여하다, 귀속시키다 **rest with** ~에게 있다 **coalition** n. 연합 **identify A with B** A와 B를 동일시하다

monopoly n. 독점 **legitimate** a. 합법적인 **entail** v. 수반하다 **enforcer** n. 집행자 **let alone** 하물며 **centralization** n. 중앙집중화 **sooner or later** 조만간 **descend** v. 빠지다 **extractive** a. 착취적인; 추출할 수 있는 **uproot** v. 뿌리뽑다 **expropriate** v. 몰수하다 **erect** v. 세우다 **discord** n. 불화 **antagonism** n. 적대

44 빈칸완성 ②

| 분석 |
이 글은 정치 제도와 경제 제도가 상호 긴밀히 연결되어 있다는 점을 강조한다. 특히 착취적 정치 제도가 존재할 때, 이는 필연적으로 착취적 경제 제도를 낳고 유지시킨다고 서술된다. 이처럼 두 제도는 단순히 유사한 것이 아니라, 서로를 가능하게 하고 강화하는 구조적 관계에 있다는 것이다. 따라서 빈칸에는 이러한 점을 나타낼 수 있는 synergy(시너지)가 가장 적절하다.

45 내용파악 ①

| 분석 |
착취적 정치 제도와 착취적 경제 제도는 모두 소수 엘리트가 권력을 독점한다. 따라서 정답은 ①이다. 나머지는 모두 포용적인 경제와 정치 제도의 특징이다.

착취적 정치 제도의 특징은 무엇인가?
① 소수 엘리트에 의해서만 통치된다.
② 더 폭넓은 인구 집단에 자원을 분배하려 한다.
③ 종종 포용적 경제 제도가 동반한다.
④ 권력이 제약 없이 분배되므로 다원적이다.
⑤ 시장과 사회에서 진입 장벽을 제거한다.

46~48

대부분의 방송 자막은 미리 준비되지만, 뉴스 방송이나 스포츠 경기와 같은 생방송 자막도 있다. 이런 자막은 일반적으로 재발화 방식으로 제작되는데, 동시통역과 다소 비슷한 방식으로, 같은 언어를 사용하는 자막 제작자가 오디오 스트림을 들으면서 소리를 더 또렷이 하고 배경 소음을 제거하기 위해 그 말을 다시 고품질 오디오 시스템에 재발화하고, 그러면 이 '깨끗한' 입력이 음성-텍스트 변환 소프트웨어를 통해 처리된다. 이때 자막 제작자는 키보드를 이용하여 필요에 따라 실시간으로 교정을 하고, 이로 인해 제작 시간상 약간만 지연된 채 화면에 표시된다.
접근성을 목적으로 한 같은 언어 내의 자막과, 넷플릭스와 같은 기업조직이 청각장애는 아니지만 원어를 이해하지 못하는 사람들을 위해 만드는 다른 언어 간의 번역 자막 사이에는 상당한 차이가 있다. 자막 제작은 항상 정보의 완전성과 간결성이라는 서로 상충하는 요구사항 사이에 절충을 해야 할 문제이다. 정보에 대한 평등한 접근이 목표일 때는, 방송의 말소리 내용이 가능한 한 (빠짐없이) 그대로 옮겨질 것이다. 내용을 조금이라도 변경하면 입술로 내용을 읽는 사람들(청각장애인들)에게 혼란을 줄 것이기 때문이다. 그리고 이런 종류의 자막은 또한 언어를 배우는 사람들 뿐 아니라 독서장애가 있는 시청자에게도 도움이 될 수 있다.
접근성 자막을 만드는 사람들은 시각적 수단을 사용하여 오디오 스트림에 대한 메타정보를 전달할 수 있다. 예를 들어, 화자의 바뀜은 다른 색깔의 텍스트로 나타내질 수도 있고, 또 다른 중요한 오디오 요소(음향효과)에는 대문자나 대괄호로 주석이 달릴 수도 있다. 반면, 번역 자막을 이용하는 정상 청력 시청자들은 일반적으로 색깔 표시나 배경 음향을 나타내는 것이 필요 없을 것이지만, 그들이 빨리 읽을 수 있고 영상 내용을 따라가는 데 가능한 한 방해 받지 않는 자신들의 언어로 된 간략히 압축된 대화 내용을 원할 것이다.

| 어휘 |
subtitle n. 자막 **in advance** 미리 **e.g.** 예를 들어 **respeaking** n. 재발화 **simultaneous interpreting** 동시통역 **audio stream** 오디오 스트림(음성 신호 흐름) **clean input** 깨끗한 입력(명료하게 정제된 오디오) **account for** 감안하다 **intralingual** a. 같은 언어 내의 **accessibility** n. 접근 가능성 **interlingual** a. 언어 간의 **hearing impaired** 청각장애인 **compromise** n. 타협, 절충 **transcribe** v. 글로 옮기다 **verbatim** ad. 문자 그대로 **alteration** n. 변화 **lip-reader** n. 입술 움직임으로 말 이해하는 사람 **visual means** 시각적 수단 **meta-information** n. 메타정보(부가적 정보) **annotation** n. 주석 설명 **square brackets** 대괄호 **condensed** a. 간결한 **distract** v. 혼란하게 만들다, 산란하게 하다 **digression** n. 여담

46 글의 제목 ③

| 분석 |
이 글은 일반방송 자막과 생방송 자막, 같은 언어 내의 자막과 번역 자막, 말소리를 그대로 옮기는 자막과 간결하게 압축한 자막, 색깔을 넣는 자막과 대문자나 대괄호로 나타내는 자막 등, 목적과 필요에 따라 여러 종류의 자막이 있음을 설명한 내용이므로 ③이 제목으로 적절하다. ②를 제목으로 하면 첫 단락이 제목과 전혀 무관하게 되고, 둘째 단락 이하의 내용도 자막을 같은 언어 자막과 번역 자막으로만 구분해서 설명한 것이 아니고 같은 언어 자막의 경우에도 시청자의 필요에 따라 여러 가지 자막이 가능함을 설명하므로 ②는 제목으로 부적절하다.

글의 제목으로 가장 적절한 것은?
① 번역 자막의 비밀
② 언어 내 자막과 번역 자막 간의 차이
③ 다양한 자막 유형

④ 자막 제작자의 역할
⑤ 컬러 텍스트의 중요성

47 빈칸완성   ⑤

| 분석 |

자막 제작은 서로 상충되는 두 요구 사이의 절충이라고 하였으므로, 서로 상충 관계인 낱말들을 선택해야 한다. 두 빈칸 뒤의 verbatim(빠짐없이 그대로)은 completeness를 의미하고 다음 문단의 condensed(간결하게 압축된)는 concision을 의미하므로 ⑤가 정답이다.

48 내용파악   ①

| 분석 |

verbatim이 있는 문장에서, 있는 대로 내용을 전달하는 목표는 '정보의 평등한 접근'이라고 명시하였으므로 ①이 정답이다.

이 글에 따르면 언어 내 자막은 _____ 위해 있는 그대로여야 한다.
① 모든 시청자에게 평등한 정보 접근을 이루어주기
② 정보의 질을 증가시키기
③ 청각장애가 없는 사람에게 더 나은 서비스를 제공하기
④ 입술을 읽는 사람들의 능력을 향상시키기
⑤ 언어 학습자의 주의를 영상 내용에서 벗어나지 않게 하기

49~50

신경정신분석은 정신분석학, 신경과학, 정신의학 등 여러 분야의 연구자들과 임상학자들의 노력으로 이루어진 다양하고 학제적인 분야이다. 이들은 어떻게 경험적 발견과 신경과학 이론들이 주관적인 임상 관찰을 통해 얻은 메타심리학적 지식에 의해 향상될 수 있으며, 그 역도 가능한지를 고려해볼 공유된 탐구 영역을 구축하고자 노력한다. 이 분야는 신경심리학자이자 정신분석가인 마크 솜스를 중심으로 한 소규모 연구자 그룹에 의해 이름 붙여지고 구성되었다. 신경정신분석의 주요 주장은 의식은 정서적이며 신체화된 것으로 이해되어야 한다는 것과, 프로이트의 심리 기제 이론은 마음, 뇌, 신체를 완벽하게 통합하지는 못하고 있지만, 그럼에도 불구하고 우리에게 그러한 이해를 위한 기초를 제시한다는 것이다.

| 어휘 |

interdisciplinary a. 학제적인(여러 학문 분야가 관련된) **empirical** a. 경험적, 실증적인 **enhance** v. 강화하다 **metapsychological** a. 메타심리학적인 **subjective** a. 주관적인 **vice versa** 반대의 경우도 마찬가지 **constitute** v. 구성하다 **affective** a. 정동의

정서적인 **embodied** a. 신체화된, 구현된 **psychic apparatus** 심리 기제, 정신 구조 **fall short** 부족하다, 미치지 못하다 **foundation** n. 기반 **comprise** v. 구성되다 **prominent** a. 저명한

49 내용파악   ④

| 분석 |

한 명의 학자가 아니라, 소규모 연구자 그룹에 의해 만들어지고, 이름 붙여졌다고 하였으므로 ④가 정답이다. ① 신경정신분석은 메타심리학의 임상적이고 주관적인 접근과 신경과학의 경험적이고 이론적인 접근이 절충되어 있다고 볼 수 있다. ② 의식을 마음과 관련된 정서적인 것으로 보면서도 몸과 관련된 신체화된 것으로 본다.

이 글에 따르면 신경정신분석에 해당하지 않는 것은?
① 두 가지 접근 방식을 절충하는 학문
② 의식에 대해 균형 잡힌 관점을 가진 학문
③ 프로이트 이론에 부분적인 기반을 둔 학문
④ 한 명의 저명한 학자에 의해 홀로 설립된 학문
⑤ 학제적 분야

50 부분이해   ①

| 분석 |

vice versa는 '역으로 ~도 마찬가지이다'라는 의미이다. 앞에서 "임상 관찰에서 얻은 메타심리학적 지식이 신경과학의 경험적 발견과 이론을 향상시킬 수 있다"의 역은 "신경과학의 경험적 지식이 정신분석학과 정신의학에 도움을 줄 수 있다"이므로, 내용상 가장 가까운 ①이 정답이다.

밑줄 친 "vice versa"를 통해 추론할 수 있는 것은?
① 신경과학이 제공하는 경험적 지식이 정신분석학과 정신의학에 유익을 줄 수 있다.
② 신경과학은 인간 정신을 이해하기 위해 주관적 접근에 의존하지 말아야 한다.
③ 신경과학과 정신의학은 별개의 분야다.
④ 연구자와 임상학자는 의식을 더 잘 이해하기 위해 서로 협력해야 한다.
⑤ 임상 관찰은 인간의 마음에 대해 편향된 견해를 자주 제시한다.

SUNGKYUNKWAN UNIVERSITY | 성균관대학교 자연계 A형

TEST p. 402~412

01	⑤	02	④	03	②	04	④	05	②	06	④	07	①	08	⑤	09	③	10	①
11	④	12	③	13	⑤	14	②	15	③	16	⑤	17	③	18	⑤	19	①	20	①
21	②	22	④	23	③	24	③	25	⑤												

01 명사의 병치   ⑤

| 분석 |

군 생활을 악화시키는 행동에 대한 구체적인 예시를 콜론(:) 이하에서 설명하고 있다. 이때 예시에 해당하는 petty harassment, open scrimmage, sadism, a constant paying off라는 명사구가 세미콜론(;)으로 병치되어 있으므로, and 다음에 온 ⑤의 insisted도 마찬가지로 '명사'로 고쳐서 병치를 이루어야 한다. 따라서 ⑤의 insisted를 insistence로 고쳐야 한다.

| 어휘 |

petty a. 비열한   **harassment** n. 괴롭힘   **scrimmage** n. 다툼; 작은 충돌   **sadism** n. 가학증   **disguise** v. 위장하다   **discipline** n. 훈육   **pay off old scores** 원한을 풀다   **ordinance** n. 규정

| 해석 |

그것은 군 생활을 필요 이상으로 힘들게 만드는 행동을 지칭한다. 그런 행동에는 강자가 약자를 비열하게 괴롭히는 것, 권력과 권위를 둘러싼 노골적인 다툼, 필요한 훈육으로 얄팍하게 위장한 가학적 행위, 끊임없이 앙갚음하기, 그리고 규정의 정신보다 규정의 문자에 대한 집착 등이 있다.

02 동명사와 부정사의 구분   ④

| 분석 |

접속사 because가 이끄는 부사절에서 사람들이 배고픔을 '달래기 위해' 보행자 통로를 가로질러 간다는 말이 되어야 하는데, ④의 satisfying은 전치사 to의 목적어로 쓰인 '동명사'의 형태이므로 부적절하다. 따라서 ④를 동사원형 satisfy로 고쳐서 '목적'을 나타내는 부정사로 만들어야 한다.

| 어휘 |

drift v. (서서히) 이동하다   **lane** n. 통로   **pedestrian** n. 보행자   **traffic** n. 통행   **impulse buy** 충동구매

| 해석 |

잘 설계된 공항에서 탑승구로 향하는 여행객들의 왼쪽에는 언제나 패스트푸드 음식점이 있고 그들의 오른쪽에는 기념품 가게가 있는데, 사람들이 배고픔을 달래기 위해서는 보행자 통로를 선뜻 가로질러 가지만 잡지를 충동적으로 구매하기 위해서는 좀체 그렇게 하지 않을 것이기 때문이다.

03 동의어   ②

| 어휘 |

migrate v. 이주하다   **grit** n. 근성, 용기(= fortitude)   **load** v. ~에게 무거운 부담을 지우다   **property** n. 재산   **connection** n. 연관성   **modesty** n. 겸손   **political influence** 정치적 영향력

| 해석 |

오늘날 가난한 나라에서 이주하는 사람들은 이주 비용을 감당할 돈과 그들에게 일반적으로 불리하게 가해지는 이민 관리 제도를 극복하기 위해 필요한 용기가 있어야 한다.

04 동의어   ④

| 어휘 |

maiden voyage 첫 항해   **flagship** n. 기함(旗艦), 최고급 선박; 주력 제품   **deserve** v. ~을 받을 만하다[누릴 자격이 있다]   **pomp** n. 화려, 과시   **circumstance** n. 요란함, 형식에 치우침   **pomp and circumstance** 당당한 위풍, 거창한[성대한] 의식   **christening** n. 세례식; (배의) 명명식, 진수식(= launching)   **farewell** n. 작별   **arming** n. 무장   **sinking** n. 침몰   **cleaning** n. 청소

| 해석 |

신사 숙녀 여러분, 우리의 최신식 기함의 첫 항해는 오늘날 우리가 할 수 있는 것보다 더 위풍당당한 의식을 치러줄 만합니다. 이 선박의 진수식은 무사 귀환에 대한 보상이 되어야 할 것입니다.

05 동의어 ②

| 어휘 |

at arm's length 멀리하는, 거리를 두는(= distant)　busy a. 바쁜　friendly a. 친근한　supervised a. 감독받는　curious a. 호기심이 강한

| 해석 |

나는 사무실 동료들과의 전문적인 관계를 유지하기 위해 그들을 멀리하는 것을 좋아한다.

06 논리완성 ④

| 분석 |

질문이 우리의 지적 상상력을 풍요롭게 한다면, 사색을 가로막는 독단적인 확신은 '줄여줄' 것이다. 따라서 빈칸에는 ④의 diminish가 적절하다.

| 어휘 |

for the sake of ~을 위해　definite a. 확실한　as a rule 일반적으로　enrich v. ~을 풍요롭게 하다　dogmatic a. 독단적인　assurance n. 확신　speculation n. 사색, 성찰　enhance v. 향상시키다　expand v. 확대하다　appreciate v. 진가를 알아보다　diminish v. 줄여주다　elongate v. 연장하다

| 해석 |

왜 철학을 공부하는가? 철학이 제기한 질문들에는 일반적으로 참이라고 알려질 수 있는 명확한 답이 없기 때문에, 철학은 철학의 질문들에 대한 어떠한 명확한 답을 얻기 위해서가 아니라 질문들 그 자체를 위해 연구되어야 한다. 왜냐하면 이 질문들이 우리가 상상할 수 있는 가능성의 범위를 넓혀주고, 우리의 지적 상상력을 풍요롭게 해주며, 사색에 대해 마음을 닫아버리는 독단적인 확신을 줄여주기 때문이다.

07 논리완성 ①

| 분석 |

빈칸 앞에서 "대부분의 동물에서 뇌의 크기는 몸의 크기와 밀접한 상관관계가 있다"고 했는데, 빈칸 이후에서는 "우리 인간의 뇌는 신체 크기를 감안할 때 예상보다 훨씬 더 크다"라고 했다. 인간의 뇌가 몸의 크기와의 밀접한 상관관계에 비추어 예상되는 크기보다 훨씬 더 크다는 것은 대부분의 동물에게 적용되던 '뇌 크기와 몸 크기의 상관관계에 따른 일반적인 패턴을 인간이 깨뜨림'을 말하므로, 빈칸에는 ①이 적절하다.

| 어휘 |

stand out 눈에 띄다　primate n. 영장류 (동물)　volume n. 부피　correlate v. 상관관계를 보여주다　given prep. ~을 감안할 때

| 해석 |

다른 영장류의 뇌와 비교했을 때 인간의 뇌에서 눈에 띄는 한 가지가 있다면 그것은 바로 뇌의 크기이다. 인간의 뇌는 침팬지와 고릴라의 뇌보다 부피가 최대 세 배까지 크다. 대부분의 동물에서 뇌의 크기는 몸의 크기와 밀접한 상관관계가 있다. 하지만 인간이 그 패턴을 깨뜨린다. 우리 인간의 뇌는 몸의 크기를 감안할 때 예상보다 훨씬 더 크다.

① 패턴을 깨뜨리다
② 영장류 동물이 아니다
③ 모든 창조물 위에 있다
④ 패턴에 순응하다
⑤ 다른 동물들보다 훨씬 더 똑똑하다

08 논리완성 ⑤

| 분석 |

식민지 지배 국가들이 식민지에 착취국가를 세웠는데, 이들 착취국가에서 사유재산 보호를 그다지 받아들이지 않았고 정부 수탈을 방지하기 위한 견제와 균형 장치도 제공하지 않았다고 했다. 따라서 이들 착취 국가의 목적은 착취국가라는 이름처럼 식민지를 착취하여 '식민지 자원을 식민지 지배국으로 이전하는' 것이라고 봐야 할 것이다.

| 어휘 |

colonization n. 식민지화　institution n. (사회적인) 제도, 관례　extractive a. 뽑아내는　exemplify v. ~의 예가 되다　checks and balances 견제와 균형　expropriation n. 징발, 몰수

| 해석 |

식민지화 정책에는 다양한 유형이 있었고, 이 유형마다 서로 다른 제도가 형성되었다. 한쪽 극단에서는, 유럽 열강들이 착취 국가들을 세웠는데, 벨기에가 콩고를 식민지화한 것이 대표적인 예이다. 이 국가들은 사유재산 보호를 그다지 받아들이지 않았고, 정부 수탈을 방지하기 위한 견제와 균형 장치도 제공하지 않았다. 사실 착취 국가의 주요 목적은 식민지의 자원을 식민지 지배국으로 이전하는 것이었다.

① 식민지에 호의를 보이다
② 천연자원을 식민지에 돌려주다
③ 자유 민주주의 국가를 아프리카에 설립하다
④ 식민지의 경제 성장을 촉진하다
⑤ 식민지의 자원을 식민지 지배국으로 이전하다

09 논리완성 ③

| 분석 |

공기에 둘러싸인 결과로 구슬의 속도가 둔화되었다면, 공기가 '구슬에 마찰을 가해서' 떨어지는 속도가 둔화되었을 것이므로, ③이 정답이다.

| 어휘 |

marble n. 구슬   ten-story a. 10층의   likely ad. 아마   assume v. ~이라 가정하다   vacuum n. 진공상태

| 해석 |

만약 물리학자에게 구슬이 10층 건물 꼭대기에서 떨어지는 데 얼마나 오래 걸릴지 물어본다면, 그는 구슬이 진공상태에서 떨어진다고 가정하고 대답할 가능성이 있다. 물론 이 가정은 사실이 아니다. 실제로 건물은 공기에 둘러싸여 있어서, 떨어지는 구슬에 마찰을 가해 구슬의 속도를 둔화시킨다.

① 깨뜨리다
② 진공청소기로 청소하다
③ ~에 마찰을 가하다
④ ~의 속도를 증가시키다
⑤ ~의 선택 가능한 범위를 늘리다

10 논리완성   ①

| 분석 |

암 위험 증가 등 과음의 효과가 나타나기까지는 몇 년이 걸린다고 했으므로, 이어지는 문장에서도 조용한 질병으로 시작하여 몇 년이 지난 후에야 만성 질환에 의해 '실체를 드러낸다'고 해야 적절할 것이다. 따라서 ①의 rears its head가 정답으로 적절하다.

| 어휘 |

heavy drinking 과음   arrhythmia n. 부정맥   stroke n. 뇌졸중   immune system 면역 체계   be associated with ~와 관련되다   rear one's head 고개를 치켜들다   chronic a. 만성적인

| 해석 |

지나친 음주는 팬데믹 기간 동안 정상적인 것이 되었다. 과도한 음주는 부정맥, 뇌졸중 그리고 고혈압을 유발한다. 과음은 면역 체계를 약화시키며, 특정한 암 위험의 증가와 연관 지어졌다. 그러나 이러한 많은 효과들이 나타나는 데는 수년이 걸린다. 우리는 음주가 소리 없는 질병으로 시작하며, 몇 년 뒤에야 만성 질환에 의해 고개를 든다(실체를 드러낸다)는 것을 알고 있다.

① 실체를 드러내다
② 헛수고를 하다
③ 양성이 되다
④ 손바닥으로 하늘을 가리려 하다
⑤ 계속 어려움에 허덕이다

11~12

이주에 대한 경제학적 분석은 종종 매력적인 논리로 귀결된다. 세상은 돈을 더 많이 벌고 싶어 하는 가난한 사람들로 가득 차 있다. 이 가난한 사람들은 분명히 상황이 훨씬 더 나은 이곳으로 올 수만 있다면 돈을 확실히 훨씬 더 많이 벌게 될 것이다. 따라서 기회만 주어진다면, 그들이 어디에 있든 간에 있는 곳을 떠나 우리나라로 올 것이고, 이것은 임금을 급격히 떨어뜨릴 것이며, 이곳에 이미 있는 우리들 대부분을 더 힘들게 만들 것이라는 주장이다. 이 주장에서 주목할 점은 이 주장이 전형적인 수요와 공급의 법칙을 충실히 따르고 있다는 것이다. 사람들은 더 많은 돈을 원하기 때문에, 임금이 가장 높은 곳이라면 어디든 모두 갈 것이다. 노동의 수요 곡선이 (가격이 오름에 따라) 하향하므로, 노동의 공급 증가로 인해 전체 임금은 하락할 것이다. 이주민들은 이익을 볼지 모르지만, 현지 노동자들은 피해를 볼 것이다. 이 논리는 간단하고 매력적이면서도 잘못됐다. 첫째, 국가 간의 임금 격차는 실제로 사람들의 이주 여부와는 비교적 거의 관계가 없다. 분명히 많은 사람들이 어디에 있든 간에 그들이 있는 곳에서 간절히 벗어나고 싶어 하지만, 여전히 풀리지 않는 수수께끼는 왜 많은 다른 사람들은 갈 수 있는데도 가지 않는가이다. 둘째, 상대적으로 숙련도가 낮은 이주민이 대거 유입되더라도, 현지 주민 — 특히 숙련도가 낮은 이주민들과 기술 수준이 비슷한 현지 주민 포함 — 이 피해를 본다는 신뢰할 만한 증거는 없다. 오히려 이주는 이주민과 현지 주민을 포함한 대부분의 사람들을 더 부유한 상태로 만들어주는 것으로 보인다. 이것은 노동 시장의 특수성과 많은 관련이 있다. 노동 시장에 관한 것 중에 표준적인 수요 공급 이론에 딱 맞아떨어지는 것은 거의 없다.

| 어휘 |

come down to something (한마디로) 귀결되다   seductive a. 유혹적인, 매력적인   give somebody half a chance ~에게 기회를 좀 주다   drive down ~을 빠르게 끌어내리다   wage n. 급여   faithfulness n. 충실   exposition n. (상세한) 설명   curve n. 곡선   slope v. 기울어지다   native a. 원주민의   have little to do with ~와 거의 관련이 없다   desperate a. 필사적인; 간절히 원하는   enduring a. 지속되는, 영구적인   inflow n. 유입   peculiar a. 특이한, 특수한   fit v. (꼭) 들어맞다

11 빈칸완성   ④

| 분석 |

이 글의 첫 번째 단락에서는 이주에 대한 경제학적 분석이 어떤 '논리'로 구성되어 있는지를 소개하고 있으며, 두 번째 단락에서 이 '논리'가 틀렸음을 두 가지 이유를 대며 설명하고 있다. 따라서 두 번째 단락 첫 문장의 주어인 logic에 해당하는 말이 빈칸에 들어가야 하므로, ④의 reasoning(논리)이 정답이다. ① 수수께끼 ② 서비스 ③ 방법 ⑤ 딜레마

12 내용파악 ④

| 분석 |

상대적으로 숙련도가 낮은 이주민이 대거 유입되더라도 현지 주민이 피해를 본다는 신뢰할 만한 증거는 없다고 했으며, 오히려 이주가 이주민과 현지 주민을 포함한 대부분의 사람들을 더 부유한 상태로 만들어주는 것으로 보인다고 했으므로, ④가 정답이다.

본문에 따르면, 숙련도가 낮은 이주민의 유입은 _____ 것이다.
① 현지인들에게 피해를 입힐
② 이주민들만 이익을 볼
③ 국가 간 임금 격차를 증가시킬
④ 이주민들과 현지 노동자들 모두에게 이익을 줄
⑤ 노동 시장의 특수성을 변화시킬

13~15

제조업 산업이 거의 20년에 걸쳐 전례 없는 성장을 한 후인 1990년대 후반에, 중국은 지표수 수질 악화를 비롯한 여러 가지 시급한 환경 문제에 직면하기 시작했다. 중국의 심각한 수질 오염 문제를 해결하기 위해 중앙 정부는 주요 국가 하천 본류를 따라 국가가 통제하는 수백 개의 수질 감시소를 설치했다.
중앙 정부는 각 지방에 오염 경감 관련 요구사항들을 할당하였고, 각 지방 장관들은 중앙 정부와 개별적인 책임 계약을 체결하여 배출 경감 계획과 공약을 상세히 기록해야 했다. 지방 장관들은 더 나아가 지방 정부 공무원들에게 엄격한 오염 경감 지시를 내렸으며, 수질 측정 결과를 활용하여 승진 여부를 결정하는 데 반영했다. 이렇게 강력한 정치적 인센티브(동기)가 부여된 가운데, 대규모 오염 산업체들은 지방 정부 공무원들의 표적이 되었는데, 이들 기업의 오염물질 배출이 지방 수질 오염의 가장 큰 원인이기 때문이다. 많은 지방 정부들은 오염 기업들에게 생산 중단 및 일시적 폐쇄 위협을 가함으로써 생산 공정을 정화하고 고가의 오염 경감 장비에 투자하도록 강요했다. 그 결과, 이들 규제 대상 기업들은 일련의 주어진 투입량에서 얻게 되는 산출량을 측정하는 지표인 총 요소 생산성(TFP)이 감소하는 것을 경험했다. 그러나 중앙 정부와 지방 정부 간의 이러한 정치적 계약은 불완전한 감시로 인해 약화되고 있다. 강은 고지대에서 저지대로 흐르기 때문에, 수질 감시소는 상류에서 유입되는 배출량만 감지할 수 있다. 지방 정부 공무원들은 감시소 바로 상류 쪽에 위치한 오염 기업들을 규제할 강력한 인센티브는 갖고 있지만, 감시소 바로 하류 쪽에 위치한 오염 기업들을 규제할 인센티브는 거의 갖고 있지 않았다.

| 어휘 |

unprecedented a. 전례 없는 **pressing** a. 시급한 **tackle** v. 해결하다 **trunk** n. (강의) 주류, 본류 **assign** v. 할당하다 **abatement** n. 감소, 저감 **governor** n. 주지사; (한 기관의) 장(長) **mandate** n. 지시 **suspension** n. 중단 **coerce** v. 강제하다 **undermine** v. 약화시키다 **elevation** n. 해발 높이; 고도 **detect** v. 감지하다

13 빈칸완성 ⑤

| 분석 |

수질 측정 결과에 따라 승진 여부가 달려있는 지방 공무원들은 오염 산업체들에게 생산 공정을 정화하도록 강요했다고 했으므로, 같은 맥락으로 오염을 줄이기 위해 '고가의 오염 경감 장비에 투자하도록' 강요했을 것이다. 따라서 빈칸에는 ⑤가 적절하다.

다음 중 빈칸에 적절한 것은?
① 물을 오염시키다
② 수익을 증대시키다
③ 오염물질 배출을 증가시키다
④ 오염 경감 목표를 회피하다
⑤ 고가의 오염 경감 장비에 투자하다

14 내용파악 ②

| 분석 |

상류에서 유입되는 배출량만 감지할 수 있다고 했으며, 지방 정부 공무원들은 감시소 상류에 위치한 오염 기업들을 규제할 강력한 인센티브를 갖고 있다고 했다. 따라서 '감시소 상류에 위치한 오염 기업들'이 생산 공정을 정화하고 고가의 오염 경감 장비에 투자하도록 강요받아 총 요소 생산성 감소를 경험했을 것이므로, ②가 정답이다.

본문에 따르면, 어떤 기업이 수질 규제의 결과로 총 요소 생산성 감소를 가장 경험할 것 같은가?
① 모든 비오염 기업
② 감시소 상류에 위치한 오염 기업
③ 감시소 하류에 위치한 오염 기업
④ 감시소 상류에 위치한 비오염 기업
⑤ 감시소 하류에 위치한 비오염 기업

15 내용파악 ③

| 분석 |

지방 장관들은 지방 정부 공무원들에게 엄격한 오염 경감 지시를 내렸으며, 수질 측정 결과를 활용해 승진 여부 결정에 반영했다고 했으므로, ③이 정답이다.

본문에 따르면, 지방 정부 공무원은 오염 기업들을 규제할 정치적 인센티브를 갖고 있는데, 왜냐하면 _____.

① 수질을 감시하는 것이 완전하기 때문이다
② 강은 고지대에서 저지대로 흐르기 때문이다
③ 수질 측정값이 그들의 승진 여부를 결정하기 때문이다
④ 대기업의 배출량이 지방 수질 오염의 원인이 아니기 때문이다
⑤ 지방 공무원들은 감시소 하류에 위치한 오염 기업들을 규제할 수 없기 때문이다

16~17

생산성이 높다는 것은 동일한 투입량에서 더 많은 산출량을 얻는다는 것을 의미한다. 두 가지 주요 요인이 생산성 증가를 주도하는데, 그것은 바로 기업 내부 개선과 경제 전반에 걸친 자원 배분 효율성이다. 기업 내부의 생산성 증가는 기술 향상, 경영관행 개선, 그리고 공정 혁신을 통해 이루어진다. 최첨단 기술을 도입하고 최고의 인재를 유치하는 기업들은 생산성을 크게 높일 수 있다. 예를 들어, 최첨단 연구개발에 투자하는 기술 기업은 신제품을 만들어 내거나 기존 제품을 개선하여 시장 점유율을 확대하고 기업 경쟁력을 높일 수 있다.

문제는 연구개발에 대한 투자 수익률이 줄어들고 있다는 것이다. 예를 들어, 반도체 산업에서 칩의 집적도를 두 배로 늘리기 위해서는 더 많은 연구 인력이 필요하다. 이러한 추세는 급격한 상승세가 2000년대 초반 이후 눈에 띄게 정체된 정보통신 기술 분야를 비롯한 다양한 분야에 걸쳐 나타나고 있다. 따라서 경제 성장을 지속시키기 위해서는 다른 생산성 향상 원천에 의지해야 한다.

그런 점으로 인해 우리는 두 번째 주요 생산성 증가 요인인 자원 배분 효율성에 관심을 갖게 된다. 경제 전반에 걸친 자원 배분 효율성이란 경제의 자원이 각 기업에 가장 생산적인 용도로 얼마나 잘 배분되는지를 의미한다. 경제를 대규모 농장이라고 상상해보자. 만일 가장 비옥한 땅이 가장 가치 높은 농작물을 재배하는 데 사용된다면, 그 농장은 전반적으로 생산성이 향상될 것이다. 마찬가지로, 경제의 자원이 가장 혁신적이고 효율적인 기업으로 흘러간다면, 그 기업들이 성장하고 경제 발전을 주도할 수 있다. 이 과정을 통해 가장 우수한 기업이 번창하고 효율성이 낮은 기업은 시장에서 퇴출된다.

| 어휘 |

allocative efficiency 자원배분 효율성 **state-of-the-art** a. 최첨단의 **cutting-edge** a. 최첨단의 **market share** 시장점유율 **competitiveness** n. 경쟁력 **return on investment** 투자수익(률) **diminish** v. 줄어들다 **semiconductor** n. 반도체 **density** n. 밀도, 집적도 **span** v. ~에 걸치다, 확대되다 **plateau** v. 정체 상태를 유지하다 **imperative** a. 필수적인 **sustain** v. 지속시키다 **crop** n. 농작물 **overall** ad. 전반적으로 **enterprise** n. 기업 **thrive** v. 번창하다 **exit** v. 퇴출되다

16 빈칸완성 ⑤

| 분석 |

빈칸을 전후로 빈칸 앞에는 연구개발에 투자하는 것의 효과를 '긍정적으로' 언급한 반면, 빈칸 다음에는 연구개발에 대한 투자수익률이 줄어든다는 이야기를 '부정적으로' 하고 있다. 따라서 빈칸에는 부정적인 측면과 관련된 ⑤의 The problem is that이 적절하다.

다음 중 빈칸에 적절한 것은?
① 따라서
② 다행스럽게도
③ 아니나 다를까
④ ~은 사실이 아니다
⑤ 문제는 ~이다

17 내용파악 ③

| 분석 |

다른 것들은 모두 생산성 증가의 원인으로 언급된 반면, '소득 평등'은 언급되지 않았으므로, ③이 정답이다.

본문에 따르면, _____은 생산성 증가의 원인이 아니다.
① 혁신
② 기술 향상
③ 소득 평등
④ 유능한 근로자를 채용하는 것
⑤ 효율적인 자원 배분

18~20

CEO(최고경영자)와 그 밖의 지도자들이 자신의 자리를 지키고자 하는 것은 비서, 운전기사, 전용기 같은 물질적인 요인에서 비롯된다. (그러나) 심리적인 요인도 작용한다. 조직의 정점에 도달한 사람들은 대체로 자부심이 강해서, 다른 누군가가 자신이 하는 일을 잘 해낼 수 있다는 생각을 받아들이기 어려울 수 있다. 이것을 '대체불가의 아우라'라고 부른다. (따라서) 이번 주에 다보스(Davos)로 (직장에서의 마지막) 고별 여행을 갔다 와서 다음 주에 양념 선반에 어떤 양념이 있는지를 '전략적으로' 파악하는 것과 같은 은퇴 후의 모습을 예상해 보는 것은 (그들에게) 특히 끔찍하게 느껴질 수 있다.

만약 CEO가 언제 은퇴해야 할지 잘못 판단하는 경향이 있다면, 어떻게 해야 할까? 의무 퇴직연령부터 명시적인 임기 제한까지 무뚝뚝해 보이는 수단들이 존재하긴 한다. 하지만 엄격한 규정에는 단점도 있다. CEO가 물러나야 하는 시점이 CEO가 정점을 지난 시점이 아니라 오히려 정점을 향해 가고 있는 시점일지도 모르기 때문이다. (그리고) 은퇴가 가

까운 CEO는 '레임덕'으로 간주될 위험이 있다. 게다가 임기가 얼마 남지 않았다는 인식은 CEO의 행동에도 잠재적으로 이롭지 않게 영향을 줄 수 있다. 예를 들어, 앞으로의 직장생활이 짧은(즉, 은퇴까지 시간이 얼마 남지 않은) CEO가 이끄는 기업들은 큰 혁신을 거의 만들어내지 못한다는 연구가 있다. 또 다른 연구는 CEO가 은퇴연령에 다다랐을 때 기업이 인수될 가능성이 급증한다는 사실을 발견했다. 인수 대상이 되는 기업의 CEO는 종종 자리를 잃게 되는데, 경력이 끝나가는 시점에서는 그것이 덜 중요한 문제가 될 수 있기 때문이다.

엄격한 규정은 너무 오래 자리를 지키는 것을 막기 위한 최고의 방어수단이 아니다. 가장 중요한 것은 CEO가 가진 권한에 제도적인 제약을 부과하는 것이며, 가장 분명하게도, 이사회가 자율적인 사고방식을 가지는 것이며, 모든 사람에게 자연스러운 유통기한이 있다고 사장 스스로가 인식하는 것이다. 고위 임원을 채용할 때 가장 먼저 물어야 할 질문 중 하나는 "그들이 얼마나 오래 직장에 있을 것으로 생각하는지"이다.

| 어휘 |

CEO n. 최고경영자(= chief executive officer) **incentive** n. 동기, 이유 **stick around** (어떤 곳에서) 머무르다 **chauffeur** n. (중요인물의 차를 모는) 운전기사 **private jet** 전용기 **ego** n. 자존심 **stomach** v. 억지로 (뱃속에) 넘기다 **prospect** n. 전망, 예상 **retirement** n. 은퇴 **gruesome** a. 소름 끼치는 **farewell** 작별 **spice rack** 양념 선반 **blunt** a. 무뚝뚝한 **mandatory** a. 의무적인 **explicit** a. 명시적인 **drawback** n. 단점 **peak** n. 정점 **throw in the towel** 패배를 인정하다; 포기하다 **horizon** n. 한계; 전망 **i.e.** ad. 즉 **take over** 인수하다 **wind down** (기계가) 서서히 멈추다 **overstay one's welcome** 너무 오래 머무르다 **constraint** n. 제약, 제한 **board** n. 이사회 **shelf life** (식품 등의) 유통 기한 **would-be** a. (장차) ~이 되려고 하는 **last** v. 지속되다

18 빈칸완성   ⑤

| 분석 |

조직의 정점에 도달한 사람은 자존심이 강해서 다른 누군가가 자신이 하는 일을 잘 해낼 수 있다는 생각을 받아들이기 어려울 수 있다고 했는데, 이것은 자신만이 잘할 수 있고 다른 사람이 자신을 대체할 수 없다는 의미이므로, ⑤의 '대체불가의 아우라'가 빈칸에 적절하다.

다음 중 빈칸에 적절한 것은?
① 도주범 본국송환의 법칙
② 인격의 아우라
③ 능력의 법칙
④ 호혜주의 법칙
⑤ 대체불가의 아우라

19 내용파악   ①

| 분석 |

나머지 보기는 모두 CEO에게 의무 은퇴연령 규정을 적용할 경우의 단점으로 본문에 언급된 것인 반면, ①의 "CEO는 이사회에 의해 제약을 받을지도 모른다."라는 내용은 은퇴연령 사용의 단점으로 언급된 것이 아니라, "CEO가 가진 권한에 제도적인 제약을 부과하자"는 주장에 대한 '부연설명'으로 언급된 것이므로, ①이 정답이다.

본문에 따르면, 다음 중 CEO에게 의무 은퇴연령을 사용할 경우의 단점이 아닌 것은?
① CEO는 이사회에 의해 제약을 받을지도 모른다.
② CEO는 은퇴가 가까워옴에 따라 리더십 권한을 잃을지도 모른다.
③ CEO의 실적이 강제로 은퇴해야 하는 시점에서 계속 향상될지도 모른다.
④ CEO가 막 은퇴하려는 시점에서는 큰 혁신을 이뤄낼 가능성이 적다.
⑤ CEO가 직장생활이 얼마 남지 않았다고 예상되는 경우 기업인수에 적극적으로 방어하지 않을지도 모른다.

20 내용파악   ①

| 분석 |

CEO와 같이 조직의 정점에 도달한 사람은 '자부심이 강해서' 다른 누군가가 자신을 대체해서 자신의 일을 잘 해낼 수 있다고 생각하기 어려울 수 있다고 했으므로, ①이 정답이다.

본문에 따르면, _____은 CEO들이 언제 은퇴해야 할지를 잘못 판단하는 이유이다.
① 강한 자부심
② 기업인수
③ 혁신
④ 명시적인 임기 제한
⑤ 의무적인 은퇴연령

21~23

주기율표에는 118개의 서로 다른 화학원소가 나열되어 있다. 하지만 수천 년 동안 인간은 이 원소들 중 하나를 특히 정말 좋아해 왔는데, 그것은 바로 금이었다. 금은 수천 년 동안 화폐로 사용돼 왔으며 그 결과 금의 가격은 급등해왔다. 그런데 왜 금인가? 왜 오스뮴, 리튬, 그리고 루테늄은 아닌가? 우리는 주기율표를 갖고 거기서 화폐 역할을 하지 못할 것들을 제외하기 시작한다. 먼저 기체상태의 원소를 제외한다. 또한 우리는 반응성이 매우 높은 원소도 제외한

다. 그것들 모두가 (리튬처럼) 불꽃을 내며 타는 것은 아니지만, 때때로 부식되고 붕괴되기 때문이다. 그리고 우리는 방사성 원소도 제외한다.

이렇게 해서 118개의 원소가 30개로 줄어들며, 우리는 이제 세 가지 핵심 조건을 내놓은 셈인데, 그것은 바로 (1) 기체가 아니어야 하고, (2) 부식되거나 불꽃을 내며 타지 않아야 하며, (3) 인체에 치명적이지 않아야 한다는 것이다. 이제 여기에 새로운 조건을 하나 추가한다. 그것은 바로 (화폐소재로) 선택되는 것이 희귀하기를 바란다는 것이다. 이 조건에 의해 주기율표 상단에 몰려 있는 많은 원소들이 제외되는데, 왜냐하면 그쪽에 모여 있는 원소들의 양이 보다 풍부한 경향이 있기 때문이다. 하지만 동시에 너무 희귀한 원소는 선택하기를 바라지 않는다. 따라서 운석을 통해 지구로 들어온 것으로 보이는 오스뮴도 제외된다. 결국 로듐, 팔라듐, 은, 백금, 금, 이렇게 5가지 원소만 남게 된다. 그리고 이것들은 모두 공교롭게도 귀금속으로 여겨진다. 하지만 여기서도 제외할 수 있는 원소들이 있다. 물론 은이 화폐로 널리 사용되어 왔지만 변색되기 때문에, 은은 최상의 선택이 아니다. (그리고) 고대 문명에서는 로듐이나 팔라듐이 사용될 수 없었는데, 왜냐하면 이들 원소가 1800년대 초가 되어서야 발견되었기 때문이다. 이렇게 하면 백금과 금이 남게 되는데, 두 원소는 모두 강이나 하천에서 발견될 수 있다. 그러나 만약 당신이 고대 세계에 있었고 백금 동전을 만들고 싶어 했다면, 미래에서 온 마법의 용광로가 필요했을 것이다. 백금의 녹는점은 화씨 3,000도가 넘기 때문이다. 우연히게도 금이 훨씬 낮은 온도에서 녹기 때문에, 금은 산업화 이전시대 사람들이 훨씬 더 쉽게 다룰 수 있었다.

| 어휘 |

periodic table 주기율표 for millennia 수천 년 동안 go through the roof (물가 등이) 치솟다[급등하다] cross out[off] 줄을 그어 지우다 burst into flame 불에 확 타다 corrode v. 부식시키다 radioactive a. 방사능의 come up with something (해답 등을) 내놓다 cluster v. 모여 있다, 밀집하다 meteorite n. 운석 get the axe 감원당하다, 정리되다 platinum n. 백금 as it happens 공교롭게도 precious metal 귀금속 tarnish v. (광택을 잃고) 변색되다 stream n. 하천 furnace n. 용광로 Fahrenheit n. 화씨온도계, 화씨 눈금 happen to do 우연히 ~하다

| 21 | 빈칸완성 | ② |

| 분석 |

제외되는 원소가 어떤 성질인지가 빈칸에 들어가야 하는데, 빈칸 다음에 '부식되거나 붕괴되기 때문에' 제외한다고 했으므로, 이 원소의 성질은 '반응성이 높은' 원소일 것이다. 따라서 빈칸에는 ②의 reactive(반응성이 높은)가 들어가야 한다. ① 비활성의 ③ 비싼 ④ 저렴한 ⑤ 무반응의

| 22 | 내용파악 | ④ |

| 분석 |

주기율표 원소 중에 화폐로 쓰일 수 있는 것으로, 로듐, 팔라듐, 은, 백금, 금이 남게 되지만, 은이 '변색되기' 때문에 최상의 선택이 아니라고 했다. 화폐로 쓰일 원소로 최종적으로 금만 남게 되었음을 감안할 때, 금은 이 '변색조건에서 벗어나 있음'을 알 수 있으므로, ④가 적절하다.

본문에 따르면, 화폐로 금이 좋은 선택인데, 왜냐하면 _____.
① 금이 기체이기 때문이다
② 금이 부식될지도 모르기 때문이다
③ 금이 방사성이기 때문이다
④ 금이 은처럼 변색되지 않기 때문이다
⑤ 금은 백금보다 상대적으로 높은 온도에서 녹기 때문이다

| 23 | 내용파악 | ③ |

| 분석 |

화폐로 쓰일 원소로 너무 희귀해서도 안 되는데, 바로 이런 이유로 운석을 통해 지구로 들어온 것으로 보이는 오스뮴도 화폐로 제외된다고 했으므로, ③이 정답이다.

본문에 따르면, 오스뮴은 돈으로 사용되지 않았는데, 왜냐하면 _____.
① 오스뮴이 기화되기 때문이다
② 오스뮴이 너무 늦게 발견되었기 때문이다
③ 오스뮴이 공급량이 너무 제한적이기 때문이다
④ 오스뮴이 불꽃을 내며 타기 때문이다
⑤ 오스뮴이 인간 건강에 해롭기 때문이다

24~25

아프리카에서 한 세대의 과학자들이 아노펠레스 모기의 숨통조이는 횡포를 중단시키기 위해 애쓰고 있는데, 아노펠레스 모기는 말라리아 질병을 유발하는 기생충을 옮긴다. 과학자들이 선택한 무기는 유전체학이다. 이 도전은 비영리 국제 연구 컨소시엄인 타겟 말라리아(Target Malaria) 같은 단체들이 맡아 하고 있다. 거기서 연구원들의 전략은 간단하다. 아프리카에서 말라리아를 가장 많이 전파하는 세 종류의 아노펠레스 모기인 아노펠레스 감비아(Anopheles gambiae), 아노펠레스 콜루지(Anopheles coluzzii), 아노펠레스 아라비엔시스(Anopheles arabiensis)의 개체 수를 줄이는 것이다. 이를 위해 그들은 자연적으로 발생하는 현상인 유전자 드라이브를 활용할 것을 기대하고 있다. 종종 '이기적인 유전 요소'라고 불리며, DNA 코드의 조각 형태로 존재하는, 유전자는 유리한 효과를 내는 유전자가 다음 세대에서 더

우세해질 때 유전자 드라이브를 일으킨다. 일반적으로 인간과 모기는 모두 자손이 부모로부터 각각 하나씩 총 2개의 유전자 사본을 물려받는다. 따라서 자손이 두 개의 사본 중 하나를 물려받을 확률은 50:50이다. (하지만) 유전자 드라이브를 이용하여 연구원들은 이 유전확률에 편향을 일으켜, 특정 형질을 거의 100% 물려받게 한다.

유전자 드라이브 말라리아 연구는 다양한 형태를 띤다. 가장 인기 있는 두 가지는 개체군 대체와 개체군 억제로 알려져 있다. 개체군 대체의 경우, 목표는 모기의 유전자를 변형해 모기가 더 이상 말라리아 기생충의 매개체가 되지 않도록 하는 것이다. (반면) 개체군 억제의 경우, 목표는 모기 개체 수를 줄이는 것이다. 이 전략의 핵심은 암컷 모기를 불임시켜 개체 수를 줄이는 것이다. (왜냐하면) 암컷 모기가 말라리아 유발 기생충인 열대열 말라리아 원충(Plasmodium falciparum)을 인간에게 옮기며, 암컷 모기의 개체 수에 따라 모기 개체군의 크기가 결정되기 때문이다.

| 어휘 |

stranglehold n. 목조르기, (비유적으로) 자유나 발전을 저해하는 것 **transmit** v. 옮기다, 전파시키다 **parasite** n. 기생충 **genomics** n. 유전체학 **not-for-profit** a. 비영리의 **game plan** 전략 **capitalize on** ~을 활용하다 **gene drive** 유전자 드라이브(특정 유전자를 조작해 개체군 전반에 퍼뜨리는 것) **prevalent** a. 널리 퍼져 있는 **successive** a. (순서가) 다음의 **offspring** n. 자식; 새끼 **inherit** v. (유전적으로) 물려받다 **pass something on to somebody** ~을 …에게 전달하다 **manipulate** v. 조작하다 **bias** n. 편견, 편향 **trait** n. 특성; 형질 **modify** v. 변경하다 **sterilize** v. 불임이 되게 하다

24 빈칸완성 ③

| 분석 |

'말라리아 질병을 유발하는 기생충'을 아노펠레스 모기가 확산시키기 때문에, 과학자들이 모기의 확산을 막고자 유전자 드라이브를 활용한다고 했다. 따라서 유전자 드라이브 방법 중 하나인 개체군 대체는 모기의 유전자를 변형하여 모기가 '그 기생충의 매개체'가 되지 않도록 하는 것이 목표일 것이므로, ③이 적절하다.

다음 중 빈칸에 적절한 것은?
① ~에 의해 죽게 된
② ~에 의해 감소된
③ ~의 매개체
④ ~의 적
⑤ ~에 위협

25 내용일치 ⑤

| 분석 |

개체군 억제의 핵심 전략은 암컷 모기를 불임시켜 모기 개체 수를 줄이는 것이라고 했는데, 왜냐하면 암컷 모기의 개체 수가 모기 개체군의 크기를 결정하기 때문이라고 했으므로, ⑤가 정답이다.

다음 중 본문의 내용과 일치하는 것은?
① 오직 수컷 모기만이 열대열 말라리아 원충을 전파한다.
② 유전자 드라이브 말라리아 연구를 수행하는 방법은 오직 한 가지밖에 없다.
③ 유전체학은 모기의 개체 수를 줄이는 데 비효율적이다.
④ 개체군 억제의 목표는 모기 개체군을 증가시키는 것이다.
⑤ 암컷 모기의 개체 수를 줄이면 모기 개체 수가 줄어들 것이다.

TEST p. 414~430

01	③	02	②	03	③	04	①	05	③	06	①	07	②	08	④	09	③	10	②
11	③	12	③	13	①	14	④	15	①	16	②	17	④	18	①	19	④	20	②
21	④	22	①	23	③	24	④	25	③	26	④	27	①	28	④	29	①	30	②
31	②	32	②	33	①	34	④	35	④	36	②	37	①	38	③	39	②	40	②
41	①	42	③	43	①	44	②	45	①	46	①	47	③	48	④	49	④	50	②
51	①	52	④	53	③	54	①	55	④	56	④	57	②	58	②	59	④	60	①

01 논리완성 ③

| 분석 |

빈칸 앞의 '무섭고 육체적으로 고통스러운'과 자연스럽게 호응하는 표현이 필요하므로, '시련', '고난'이라는 뜻의 ③이 정답으로 적절하다.

| 어휘 |

rites of passage 통과의례　**felicity** n. 더없는 행복　**stump** n. 그루터기　**ordeal** n. 시련, 고난　**inversion** n. 전도(轉倒), 역(逆), 정반대

| 해석 |

통과의례에서 견디는 것과 같은 무섭고 육체적으로 고통스러운 시련은 기억과 신념에 영향을 미칠 것이다.

02 논리완성 ②

| 분석 |

빈칸 앞의 "민족 집단을 분리하는"이라는 표현이 관계의 '단절'을 나타내므로 빈칸에는 ②가 들어가야 한다.

| 어휘 |

border n. 국경, 경계　**ease** v. 완화하다　**tangible** a. 유형의; 명백한　**ethnic** a. 인종의, 민족의　**hypnotize** v. 최면을 걸다　**sever** v. 단절하다, 끊다　**humidify** v. 습기를 더하다, 축축하게 하다　**swoon** v. 기절하다, 졸도하다

| 해석 |

국경 제도가 완화될 것인가, 아니면 국경이 민족 집단을 분리하고 기존 관계를 단절시킴으로써 실질적이고 명백한 분열을 초래할 것인가?

03 논리완성 ③

| 분석 |

전통적인 성 고정관념을 따르지 않는다는 것은 규범을 지키지 않는다는 것이므로 ③이 정답으로 적절하다.

| 어휘 |

norm n. 규범; 모범　**gender stereotype** 성(性) 고정관념　**askance** ad. 의심스럽게, 곁눈질로　**outcast** n. 따돌림 받는 사람, 추방당한 사람　**ingratiate** v. 환심을 사다, 영합하다　**romp** v. 떠들썩하게 뛰어놀다　**transgress** v. (법·규범을) 어기다, (한계를) 넘다　**lisp** v. 불완전하게 발음하다

| 해석 |

누구든지 전통적인 성(性) 고정관념을 따르기를 거부함으로써 규범을 어기는 사람은 의심스럽게 바라보며 크고 작은 방법으로 추방자로 취급 받는다(따돌림을 받는다).

04 논리완성 ①

| 분석 |

빈칸에는 청소년의 바람직하지 못한 행동과 관련하여 탐구 대상이 될 수 있는 것이 들어가야 하므로, 위험 감수의 '성향' 혹은 '경향'이란 표현을 완성시키는 ①이 가장 자연스럽다.

| 어휘 |

adolescent n. 청소년　**unrestrained** a. 억제되지 않은, 무한한의　**propel** v. 추진하다, 나아가게 하다, (사람을 특정한 방향·상황으로) 몰고 가다　**propensity** n. 성향, 경향　**rumination** n. 반추, 심사숙고　**proportion** n. 비율; 조화, 균형　**rummage** n. 샅샅이 뒤지기; 폐물, 쓰레기

| 해석 |
일부 연구원들은 청소년들의 무제한적인 위험 감수 성향이 어떻게 약물과 술을 시험 삼아 맛보도록 몰고 가는지를 탐구하고 있다.

05 논리완성 ③

| 분석 |
"고의적인 거짓말을 계속하는 것", "정직과 공정성의 가치에 대한 경멸" 등의 내용이 있으므로, 그가 법의 지배를 '노골적으로' 무시하고 있다는 흐름이 되는 것이 자연스럽다.

| 어휘 |
deliberate a. 고의적인, 계획적인 **disregard** n. 무시 **contempt** n. 경멸 **cellular** a. 세포로 된, 세포질의 **sooty** a. 그을음이 묻은 **brazen** a. 뻔뻔한, 철면피의 **monastic** a. 수도사의, 금욕적인

| 해석 |
그가 고의적인 거짓말을 계속하는 것은 정직과 공정성의 가치에 대한 경멸뿐만 아니라 법의 지배에 대한 뻔뻔한 무시를 보여준다.

06 논리완성 ①

| 분석 |
길고 무거운 치마와 목이 높은 블라우스는 경기를 하는 데 지장을 주거나 불편하게 할 수 있는 것들이므로, 빈칸에는 ①이 적절하다.

| 어휘 |
encumber v. 방해하다 **forage** v. (식량을) 찾아다니다 **flutter** v. 펄럭이다, 떨리다 **equivocate** v. 애매하게 말하다, 얼버무리다

| 해석 |
오늘날, 다행스럽게도, 여성 테니스 선수들은 길고 무거운 치마와 목이 높은 블라우스에 의해 방해받지 않는다.

07 논리완성 ②

| 분석 |
양측 모두에게 너무 많은 악감정, 의심, 분노가 있는 경우에 호전시킬 수 없는 대상은 부정적인 관계나 감정일 것이므로, 빈칸에는 ②가 적절하다.

| 어휘 |
bad blood 악감정, 미움 **suspicion** n. 의심 **anatomy** n. 해부학 **turn around** 호전시키다 **animosity** n. 적대감, 원한 **euthanasia** n. 안락사 **eulogy** n. 찬사, 추도 연설

| 해석 |
양측 모두에게 너무나도 많은 악감정, 의심, 분노가 있어서 적대감을 호전시킬 수 없을지도 모른다.

08 논리완성 ④

| 분석 |
회의의 종료가 임박했는데도 협상에 임하고 있는 사람들이 시간을 끌면서 버텼다면 이는 비난이나 질책을 받을 만한 행동이라 할 수 있다. 그러므로 ④가 정답이다.

| 어휘 |
negotiator n. 협상가 **dig in one's heels** 완강하게 버티다, 자신의 방침이나 의견을 변경하기를 거부하다 **bluff** v. 허세 부리다, 엄포를 놓다 **brinkmanship** n. 벼랑 끝 전술, (아슬아슬한 상태까지 밀고 나가는) 극한 정책 **circumfuse** v. 주위를 에워싸다, 감싸다 **marginate** v. 가장자리를 형성하다 **migrate** v. 이주하다 **chide** v. 꾸짖다

| 해석 |
회의가 예정된 종료 시간에 가까워지면서, 유엔 기후 책임자는 엄포와 벼랑 끝 전술로 완강하게 버티면서 시간을 허비한 것에 대해 협상가들을 꾸짖었다.

09 논리완성 ③

| 분석 |
스스로 대피할 수 있었다는 것은 몸을 움직여 다른 곳으로 이동하는 것이 가능했다는 것이므로, 빈칸에는 ③이 들어가는 것이 적절하다.

| 어휘 |
evacuate v. (사람을) 피난시키다, 소개(疏開)시키다 **excavate** v. 파다; 발굴하다 **maim** v. 불구로 만들다 **ambulatory** a. 걸을 수 있는; 보행용의 **premonitory** a. 예고의, 전조의

| 해석 |
모든 주민들은 걷는 게 가능해 보였으며 그래서 부상당한 한 남자를 제외하고는 스스로 대피할 수 있었다.

10 논리완성 ②

| 분석 |
목적어로 물건이 나와 있고 전치사 to는 대상 앞에 쓰이므로, 빈칸에는 주는 행위와 관련된 표현이 들어가는 것이 가장 자연스럽다. 그러므로 ②가 정답이다.

| 어휘 |
sculpture n. 조각, 조각 작품 **plate** v. 도금하다 **bequeath** v. 유증하다 **undermine** v. (명성 따위를) 약화시키다, 음흉한 수단으로 훼손하다, 몰래 손상시키다 **stumble** v. 비틀거리다

| 해석 |
피카소는 자신이 가지고 있던 그림과 조각 작품 대부분을 스페인과 프랑스에 유증했다.

11 단어 사이의 관계 유추 ③

| 분석 |
harpsichord(하프시코드)는 instrument(악기)의 한 예이고 orchid(난초)는 flower(꽃)의 한 예이다.

| 어휘 |
harpsichord n. 하프시코드(건반 악기의 일종) **instrument** n. 악기 **pistachio** n. 피스타치오 **walnut** n. 호두 **petal** n. 꽃잎 **mammal** n. 포유류 동물 **orchid** n. 난초 **flower** n. 꽃 **fragrance** n. 향기 **party** n. 파티; 패거리, 일행

12 단어 사이의 관계 유추 ③

| 분석 |
ephemeral(덧없는, 일시적인)은 lasting(지속되는)과 반의어 관계이며, sporadic(산발적인)은 consistent(시종일관된)과 반의어 관계이다.

| 어휘 |
ephemeral a. 덧없는, 일시적인 **lasting** a. 지속적인, 영속하는 **random** a. 무작위의 **accidental** a. 우연의, 우발적인 **periodic** a. 주기적인 **cyclical** a. 순환하는 **sporadic** a. 산발적인, 때때로 일어나는 **consistent** a. 불변한; 시종일관된 **scattered** a. 흩어진 **dispersed** a. 퍼진, 흩어진

13 단어 사이의 관계 유추 ①

| 분석 |
speedy(빠른)와 rapid(신속한)는 동의어 관계이며, diminutive(작은)과 tiny(조그마한)는 동의어 관계이다.

| 어휘 |
speedy a. 빠른 **rapid** a. (속도가) 빠른, 신속한 **diminutive** a. 소형의, 아주 작은 **tiny** a. 작은, 조그마한 **slender** a. 홀쭉한, 가느다란 **short** a. 짧은 **swift** a. 재빠른, 날랜 **tremendous** a. 굉장한; 엄청난 **obese** a. 비만의, 살찐 **straight** a. 곧은

14 단어 사이의 관계 유추 ④

| 분석 |
deficit(적자)와 surplus(흑자)는 반의어 관계이며 expenditure(지출)와 revenue(수입)은 반의어 관계이다.

| 어휘 |
deficit n. 적자 **surplus** n. 흑자 **expense** n. 지출, 비용 **charge** n. (경비의) 부담, 요금; 비용 **savings** n. 저축 **discount** n. 할인 **budget** n. 예산 **fine** n. 벌금 **expenditure** n. 지출, 경비, 비용 **revenue** n. 소득, 수입

15 단어 사이의 관계 유추 ①

| 분석 |
sculptor(조각가)는 marble(대리석)을 사용하여 작품을 만들 수 있고, painter(화가)는 canvas(캔버스)를 사용하여 작품을 만들 수 있다.

| 어휘 |
marble n. 대리석 **sculptor** n. 조각가 **canvas** n. 캔버스, 화포 **painter** n. 화가 **chisel** n. 끌 **statue** n. 조각상 **symphony** n. 교향곡 **designer** n. 디자이너 **encyclopedia** n. 백과사전 **architect** n. 건축가

16 문의 구성 ②

| 분석 |
'확대되는' 것이므로 수동태인 be extended이며, 그 뒤에 대상 혹은 범위를 나타내는 전치사 to와 이 전치사의 목적어로 명사 protection이 연결되는 구조가 되게 하는 ②가 정답으로 적절하다. ①, ③ be protected나 to protect 뒤에 전치사 of가 이어질 수 없다. ④ is extended 뒤에 the protecting이 이어질 수 없다.

| 어휘 |
industrial estate 산업 단지 **extend** v. 확장하다, 확대하다; 뻗다; 이르다, 달하다

| 해석 |
오늘날 경비견의 역할은 공장 및 산업 단지를 보호하는 것으로까지 확대되었다.

17 형용사 보어 / 수식어구의 어순 ④

| 분석 |
be동사의 보어의 역할을 하는 것은 부사가 아닌 형용사이므로 ②와 ③을 정답에서 먼저 제외할 수 있다. 형용사를 수식하는 것은 부사이므로 innately가 aggressive를 수식하고 있는 ④가 정답이다.

| 어휘 |
breed n. 품종; 혈통; 종족 **innately** ad. 선천적으로; 본질적으로 **aggressive** a. 공격적인

| 해석 |
어떤 품종들은 다른 품종들보다 선천적으로 더 공격적이다.

18 문의 구성 ①

| 분석 |
타동사 involves가 목적어로 'not only ~ but (also) …' 구문을

취한 형태를 완성시키는 ①이 정답이다. ② 형용사 great가 명사 energy 앞에 와야 한다.

| 어휘 |
coordination n. (근육 운동의) 조정; 공동 작용; 협응   instrument n. 도구; 악기   at once 즉시; 동시에   involve v. 수반하다

| 해석 |
드럼 연주에는 엄청난 에너지뿐만 아니라 놀라운 조정도 필요한데, 여러 악기가 동시에 연주되어야 하기 때문이다.

19 answer와 호응하는 전치사   ④

| 분석 |
'~에 대한 대답'이라는 표현을 할 때 answer 뒤에는 전치사 to를 쓴다.

| 해석 |
이 질문들에 대한 나의 대답은 우리는 모른다는 것이다.

20 문의 구성   ②

| 분석 |
'as ~ as …' 구문에서 as와 as 사이에는 일반적으로 형용사나 부사가 오며, 현재분사는 be동사의 뒤에 이어져야 진행형을 이룬다. 따라서 ②가 정답으로 적절하다.

| 해석 |
그들은 갈 수 있는 한 빨리 달리고 있었다.

21 waste no time in   ④

| 분석 |
'~하는 데 지체하지 않다', '즉시 ~하다'는 'waste no time in ~'으로 표현하므로 ④가 정답이다.

| 해석 |
그녀는 지식을 추구하는 것을 전혀 지체하지 않고 있다.

22 주어와 동사의 수일치 / fast   ①

| 분석 |
fast는 형용사와 부사의 형태가 같으며 fastly라는 표현은 존재하지 않는다. 따라서 ②와 ③을 정답에서 먼저 제외할 수 있다. 한편, 주어가 복수명사 Things이므로 동사는 happen이어야 한다. 그러므로 ①이 정답이 된다.

| 해석 |
산업 5.0 시대에는 모든 일들이 빠르게 일어난다.

23 문의 구성   ③

| 분석 |
주어에 이어지는 동사로 varied가 있고 빈칸 이하를 목적어로 받는 분사구 depending on(~에 따라)이 온 ③이 정답으로 적절하다.

| 어휘 |
vary v. 변화하다; 가지각색이다, 다르다   geography n. 지리, 지형

| 해석 |
농사 방식은 지역의 기후와 지리에 따라 달랐다.

24 앞에 나온 명사를 대신하는 대명사 that   ④

| 분석 |
뉴욕의 인구와 샌디에이고의 인구를 비교해야 한다. 이때 the population은 대명사 that으로 받을 수 있으며, '샌디에이고의 인구'라는 의미가 되어야 하므로 전치사는 of가 적절하다.

| 어휘 |
surpass v. ~보다 낫다, 능가하다

| 해석 |
뉴욕의 인구는 샌디에이고의 인구를 능가한다.

25 간접의문절   ③

| 분석 |
빈칸에는 전치사 about의 목적어가 되는 간접의문절이 들어가는 것이 적절한데, 간접의문절은 '의문사+주어+동사'의 형태를 취하므로 ③이 정답이 된다.

| 어휘 |
pandemic n. 전국적[대륙적, 세계적]으로 유행하는 병   accelerate v. 가속하다, 촉진시키다

| 해석 |
팬데믹은 일과 생활의 균형이 어떠해야 하는지에 대한 논의를 가속화시켰다.

26 글의 흐름상 적절한 전치사 / 명사의 수   ④

| 분석 |
'많은 지원자들 중에서 선발되었다'는 의미가 되어야 하므로 수동태를 나타내는 was chosen 뒤에는 전치사 from이 와야 하며, thousands of(수천 명/개의) 뒤에는 복수 명사가 와야 한다.

| 어휘 |
astronaut n. 우주비행사   applicant n. 응모자, 지원자

| 해석 |
공학자 겸 정식 훈련을 받은 우주비행사인 30세의 이집트인이 수천 명의 지원자들 가운데 선발되었다.

27 feel at home ①

| 분석 |
'마음이 편안하다'는 feel at home으로 표현하며, 이때 at home은 really 같은 부사로 수식이 가능하다.

| 해석 |
내가 진정으로 편안함을 느낀 것은 내 인생에서 그때가 처음이었다.

28 제안 동사가 취하는 목적절 속의 동사 형태 ④

| 분석 |
목적어로 쓰인 that절에는 완전한 형태의 절이 와야 하며, suggest 같은 제안의 동사가 that절을 목적어로 취하는 경우, that절 속의 동사는 '(should) 동사원형'이어야 한다.

| 해석 |
나는 그녀에게 의자에 앉아서 기다릴 것을 제안했다.

29 수동 분사구문 ①

| 분석 |
수동태에서 행위자를 나타내는 표현인 by the unexpected news가 빈칸 뒤에 있으므로, 콤마 앞은 수동 분사구문이 되어야 한다. 따라서 ①이 정답이며, 이때 surprised 앞에는 Being 혹은 Having been이 생략돼 있다.

| 해석 |
예상치 못한 소식에 놀라서, 그는 생각을 정리하기 위해 잠시 시간을 가졌다.

30 'cause+목적어+to부정사' 구문 ②

| 분석 |
cause가 5형식동사로 쓰이는 경우에 목적격 보어로는 to부정사가 온다.

| 어휘 |
eardrum n. 고막, 귀청 vibrate v. 떨다, 진동하다

| 해석 |
음악 소리는 우리의 고막을 연주되는 악기들과 같은 패턴으로 진동하게 만든다.

31 병치 ③

| 분석 |
③과 함께 병치를 이루며 a mix of의 목적어로 나열돼 있는 것들은 모두 기술이나 능력을 의미하는 명사인데 반해, ③은 사람을 뜻하므로 의미적으로 어색하다. 같은 속성을 가진 명사가 병치되어야 할 것이므로 ③을 '전문적인 기술', '노하우'라는 의미의 expertise로 고쳐야 한다.

| 어휘 |
overachiever n. 표준[기대] 이상의 성공[성적]을 거두는 사람
acquire v. 획득하다, 습득하다 vocational a. 직업의, 직업적인
expert n. 전문가

| 해석 |
저 기대 이상의 성공을 거둔 사람들은 종종 여러 가지 경력을 쌓을 수 있는 문을 열어주고 직원들이 직업적 전문 기술, 의사소통, 팀워크, 문제 해결 기술 등을 고루 습득하도록 도와주는 일자리에서 시작했다.

32 문의 구성 ②

| 분석 |
문장의 정동사 led가 있는 상황에서 ②의 자리에 접속사 없이 또 다른 정동사가 온 점이 옳지 않다. ②를 '~에 관하여'라는 의미의 전치사 concerning으로 고쳐주면 앞서 언급한 문제점이 해결될 수 있다.

| 어휘 |
debonair a. 멋지고 당당한; 공손한, 정중한 dismissal n. 묵살, 일축
inquiry n. 질문, 문의

| 해석 |
그의 재정 상황에 대한 나의 질문을 그가 당당하게 일축한 것은 나로 하여금 아무 것도 잘못되지 않았다고 믿게 만들었다.

33 주어와 동사의 수일치 ②

| 분석 |
관계대명사의 수는 선행사에 일치시킨다. 따라서 ②의 앞에 쓰인 관계대명사 that은 선행사인 the linchpin의 수에 일치시켜 단수 동사로 받아야 한다. ②를 secures로 고친다.

| 어휘 |
linchpin n. 핵심 요소, 중심축 secure v. 확보하다, 지키다

| 해석 |
투자자들은 그 새로운 제품 라인이 향후 수년, 수십 년 동안 매우 경쟁이 치열한 시장에서 그 회사의 입지를 확보해주는 중심축이 될 것이라고 장담하고 있다.

34 문의 구성 ④

| 분석 |
접속사 as의 뒤에는 완전한 절의 형태가 와야 하는데, ④에 쓰인 분사는 문장에서 정동사의 역할을 할 수 없으므로 옳지 않다. 따라서 이것을 과거시제 정동사 emerged로 고쳐야 한다.

| 어휘 |
pandemic v. 전국적[대륙적, 세계적]으로 유행하는 병 **spike** v. 급등하다 **emerge** v. 나타나다; 벗어나다 **lockdown** n. 봉쇄

| 해석 |
매우 놀랍게도, 코로나19 팬데믹 동안 온실가스 수치가 감소했지만, 세상이 봉쇄에서 벗어나면서 다시 급등했다.

35 구동사 see ~ through ④

| 분석 |
'~을 끝까지 해내다'라는 의미를 갖는 구동사 표현은 'see ~ through'이므로 ④를 through로 고쳐야 한다.

| 어휘 |
tenacious a. 고집이 센, 완강한 **when it comes to** ~에 관해서라면

| 해석 |
린다(Linda)는 일단 행동 과정을 정하고 나면, 그것을 끝까지 해내는 데 있어 매우 끈질길 수 있다.

36 문의 구성 ③

| 분석 |
③의 앞에 완전한 문장이 왔으므로 ③은 과거동사가 아니라 바로 앞의 lifestyle을 수식하는 과거분사로 파악할 수 있는데, 그럴 경우 ③ 이하를 문법적으로 설명할 수 없게 된다. fuse는 fuse A with B의 형태로 쓰이므로 ③을 fused with로 고쳐 ③ 이하를 전치사 with의 목적어로 만들어야 한다.

| 어휘 |
architecture n. 건축양식 **urbane** a. 도회풍의; 세련된 **a slate of** 일련의, 다양한 **creature comforts** 삶을 안락하게 하는 것들(좋은 음식ㆍ가구ㆍ현대적 장비 등)

| 해석 |
고전적이면서도 전원적인 주택 건축양식은 세련된 고급스러움과 현대적인 다양한 편의시설이 어우러져 있는 여유로운 생활방식을 제공한다.

37 관계대명사 what ①

| 분석 |
접속사 that의 뒤에는 완전한 절이 와야 하나, 주어진 문장에서는 타동사 remember의 목적어가 없는 상태다. 그러므로 ①을 명사절을 이끄는 역할과 remember의 목적어의 역할을 동시에 할 수 있는 관계대명사 what으로 고쳐야 한다.

| 어휘 |
recall v. 기억해내다, 회상하다 **semantic** a. 의미의, 의미론적인 **distinction** n. 구별; 차이 **transformational** a. 변형의, 변화의 **marker** n. 표시, 표지, 지표

| 해석 |
연구자들은 사람들이 복잡한 문장을 회상할 때 무엇을 기억하는지, 즉 특정한 의미상의 차이를 기억하는 것인지 아니면 단지 문장 변형의 흔적만을 기억하는 것인지를 궁금하게 여겼다.

38 regard[look upon] A as B ③

| 분석 |
'A를 B로 간주하다'는 regard A as B 혹은 look upon A as B로 표현한다. 그러므로 ③을 regarded 혹은 looked upon으로 고쳐야 한다.

| 어휘 |
attain v. 달성하다, 성취하다 **providence** n. 섭리; 선견지명; 장래에 대한 배려

| 해석 |
그는 부모와 조부모의 상업적 성취를 바탕으로 재정적 성공을 이루었으나, 그는 그 성공을 결코 자신의 것이라 여기지 않았으며 오히려 자녀들과 그 후손들의 미래를 위한 준비물로 여겼다.

39 수동태 ②

| 분석 |
주어 Orchestras가 perceive하는 행위의 대상이므로 수동태 문장이 되어야 한다. 따라서 ②를 과거분사 perceived로 고쳐야 한다.

| 어휘 |
perceive v. 지각하다, 인식하다 **elitism** n. 엘리트주의 **in reality** 실은, 실제로는 **embody** v. 구체화하다; 구현하다

| 해석 |
오케스트라는 실제로는 (엘리트주의와) 정반대의 것을 구현하는데도, 흔히 엘리트주의의 상징으로 잘못 인식되고 있다.

40 주어와 동사의 수일치 ②

| 분석 |
전치사구 In few areas of human endeavor가 문두에 오면서 도치가 발생한 문장인데, 주어인 the tension이 단수이므로 동사로는 is가 와야 한다. ②를 is로 고친다.

| 어휘 |
endeavor n. 노력, 시도   **tension** n. 긴장; 흥분   **humble** a. 겸손한   **exalted** a. 고귀한

| 해석 |
인간이 노력하는 영역 가운데 정치에서만큼 겸손함과 고귀함 사이의 긴장이 크게 나타나는 영역은 거의 없다.

41 분사구문 ①

| 분석 |
문장의 주어는 Ragtime이고 동사는 is considered이므로 접속사 없이 ①에서처럼 정동사가 또다시 올 수 없다. 이러한 문제점은 콤마 사이를 분사구문으로 만들면 해결할 수 있으므로 ①에서 is를 삭제하여 popularized로 고쳐야 하며, 이때 popularized 앞에는 being이 생략되었다.

| 어휘 |
ragtime n. 래그타임(빠른 박자로 싱코페이션을 많이 사용한 곡; 재즈 음악의 시초)   **popularize** v. 많은 사람들에게 알리다, 대중화하다; 보급시키다   **fountainhead** n. 원천, 근원

| 해석 |
스콧 조플린(Scott Joplin)과 유비 블레이크(Eubie Blake) 같은 연주자들에 의해 대중화된 래그타임은 재즈의 음악적 원천 중의 하나로 여겨지고 있다.

42 가정법에서의 도치 구문 ③

| 분석 |
what 이하는 혼합 가정법 문장이 되어야 하겠는데, 조건절인 if she had not been abducted에서 if를 생략하면 주어와 조동사 had가 도치되므로 ③을 had she로 고쳐야 한다.

| 어휘 |
abduct v. 유괴하다

| 해석 |
나는 엘리자베스에게 만약 유괴되지 않았더라면 지금 무엇을 하고 있을지에 대해 생각해본 적이 있는지 물어보았다.

43 형용사 보어 ②

| 분석 |
being의 주체는 the family인데, the family가 frugality인 것은 아니므로, ②의 자리에는 주어의 상태나 성질을 나타내는 형용사를 보어로 써야 한다. ②를 frugal로 고친다.

| 어휘 |
frugality n. 검약   **stretch** v. (식량·돈 등을) 오래 지탱하게 하다; (돈·자원 등을) 최대한 활용하다, 늘여 쓰다   **budget** n. 예산

| 해석 |
검소하게 지내고 불필요한 소비를 제한함으로써, 그 가족은 월 예산을 최대한 늘여 쓸 수 있다.

44 전치사 of ②

| 분석 |
②에는 missing out을 목적어로 취하면서 명사 fear와의 '관련성' 혹은 '대상'을 나타내는 전치사가 오는 것이 자연스럽다. 그러므로 ②를 of로 고쳐야 한다.

| 어휘 |
constantly ad. 항상, 끊임없이   **peer** n. 동료, 또래

| 해석 |
요즘 젊은이들 사이에서는 자기만 빠지는 것에 대한 두려움이 실제로 존재한다. 많은 젊은이들이 그들의 또래가 무엇을 하고, 생각하고, 느끼는지를 보기 위해 끊임없이 소셜미디어 사이트를 확인한다.

45 소유격 관계대명사 ①

| 분석 |
①에 쓰인 관계대명사 who의 선행사 His father과 poor background가 동격 관계가 성립하지 않는다. 문맥상 '그의 가난한 배경'이라는 의미가 되어야 하므로 소유격 관계대명사를 써야 한다. ①을 whose poor로 고친다.

| 해석 |
가난한 배경 덕분에 "정치적으로 순수하다"는 호의적인 평가를 받았던 그의 아버지는 그럼에도 불구하고 자신의 일자리인 국립 오페라단 단장직을 잃었다.

46~48

자연을 광야로 보는 관점은 유대-기독교 전통에서 중요한 요소로, 구약성경의 사막에 대한 해석의 중심에 있었다. 척

박하고 메마른 광야는 풍요롭고 결실이 가득한 에덴동산과 극명한 대조를 이루었다. 에덴동산에서 광야로의 추방으로 인해, 광야를 이브가 뱀의 유혹에 굴복했을 때 들어온 악(惡)과 동일시하게 되었다. 사막은 정복하여 경작 가능하게 만들어야 할 땅을 상징했다. 자연의 자애로움을 강조하는 경향이 있었던 그리스의 전통과는 대조적으로, 유대인들의 전통에서는 자연을 극복하고 정복해야 할 조건(상태)으로 보았다. 구약성경 안에서 좀 더 온건한 해석도 찾아볼 수 있긴 했지만, 근세 초기에 중요해진 것은 바로 자연을 광야로 인식하는 관점이었다. 존 로크(John Locke), 존 칼뱅(John Calvin), 뉴잉글랜드 청교도들과 같은 개신교도들은 신이 인간에게 땅을 지배할 권한을 부여했다고 믿었다.

유럽과 앵글로색슨족의 민간전승에 나오는 광야의 이야기들은 15~16세기의 신대륙 탐험을 통해 실제보다 과장되었다. 탐험가들은 인간이 정착하기에 불리한, 거칠고 황량하고 무질서한 땅에 대한 소식을 전해했다. 신대륙의 야만인들은 인간 안에 도사리고 있는 동물 같은 거친 본성이 이성을 압도할 수 있음을 상징하는 존재가 되었다. 탐험가들이 초기에 작성했던 많은 기록들은 원주민들이 비록 짐승과 유럽인 사이 어딘가의 위계적 수준에 있긴 하지만, 평화롭고 다정한 존재라고 보고했지만, 17세기 초에는 그런 이미지가 무자비해지고 냉담해졌다. 1622년 버지니아 학살 이후, 인디언들에 대한 영국인의 이미지가 부정적인 방향으로 바뀜에 따라, 긍정적인 묘사들은 사라졌다. 그리하여 인디언들은 야만적이고 미개하고 짐승 같은 무법자들이 되었다.

| 어휘 |

wilderness n. 황야, 광야, 미개척지 **Old Testament** 구약성서 **interpretation** n. 해석 **inhospitable** a. (환경이) 사람이 살기 힘든, 황량한 **arid** a. 건조한, 메마른 **bountiful** a. 풍부한, 풍요로운 **expulsion** n. 추방, 축출 **submit to** ~에 굴복하다, 따르다 **temptation** n. 유혹 **serpent** n. 뱀; 음험한 사람; 악마 **subdue** v. 정복하다, 진압하다; (토지를) 개간하다 **arable** a. 경작 가능한 **interpretation** n. 해석, 설명 **dominion** n. 지배권, 통치권 **folklore** n. 민속, 전통설화 **desolate** a. 황량한, 쓸쓸한 **chaotic** a. 혼돈의, 무질서한 **hostile** a. 적대적인 **savage** a. 야만적인, 미개한 **animality** n. 동물성, 본능적인 야성 **gain the upper hand** 우위를 점하다 **albeit** conj. ~임에도 불구하고 **hierarchical** a. 계층적인 **harden** v. 굳어지다, 무정해지다 **callous** v. 냉담하게 만들다, 무감각하게 만들다 **massacre** n. 대량 학살 **outlaw** n. 무법자

46 빈칸완성   ①

| 분석 |
자연을 극복하고 정복해야 할 대상으로 본 유대인들의 전통과 대조를 이루어야 하므로, 빈칸에는 자연을 긍정적으로 보는 시각과 관련된 내용이 들어가야 한다. 따라서 ①이 정답이다.

다음의 절 중 빈칸 Ⓐ에 들어가기에 가장 적절한 것은?
① 자연의 자애로움을 강조하는 경향이 있었다
② 광야를 사람이 살기 힘든 땅으로 여겼다
③ 자연의 악의성을 강조하는 경향이 있었다
④ 광야를 사람이 살 수 없는 땅으로 간주했다

47 빈칸완성   ①

| 분석 |
바로 앞에서 "인디언들에 대한 영국인의 이미지가 부정적인 방향으로 바뀜에 따라, 긍정적인 묘사들은 사라졌다."고 했으므로, 빈칸에는 부정적인 의미이 단어가 들어갈 수 있다. ①은 '신성한'이라는 의미이므로 빈칸에 들어가기에 부적절하다.

다음 중 빈칸 Ⓑ에 들어가기에 적절하지 않은 단어는?
① 신성한
② 야만적인
③ 야생의
④ 짐승 같은

48 내용일치   ④

| 분석 |
원주민들을 짐승과 유럽인 사이 어딘가의 위계적 수준에 있는 것으로 보았으므로, ④가 옳지 않은 진술이다.

위 글에 의하면, 다음 중 옳지 않은 것은?
① 구약성경의 세계에서는 광야가 악한 것으로 여겨졌다.
② 일부 기독교인들은 신이 그들에게 세상을 지배할 권리를 부여했다고 믿었다.
③ 1622년 이후에 인디언들에 대한 부정적 이미지가 퍼졌다.
④ 유럽인들은 인디언들이 존재의 위계에서 짐승보다도 아래에 있다고 믿었다.

49~52

전 세계적으로 시급한 문제인 지구 온난화가 놀라운 속도로 가속화되고 있다. 위성 자료에 따르면, 21세기 초부터 태양빛을 반사시킬 수 있는 지구의 능력인 알베도(albedo)가 점점 줄어들고 있다. 반사율이 줄어들면 지구는 더 많은 햇빛을 흡수하게 되고, 이는 지구 온난화를 더욱 심화시킨다. 이렇게 가속화된 온난화는 생태계와 인류 사회에 심각한 위험을 제기하며, 극단적인 기후 현상이 수십 년 빨리 나타나게 만든다.

지구의 알베도를 감소시킨 주된 요인 중의 하나는 황(黃) 배출이 줄어들어 공기가 더 깨끗해진 것이다. 역사적으로 화석 연료 연소의 부산물인 이산화황은 대기 중에 미세한 입자를 형성해왔고, 이 입자들은 햇빛을 산란시키고 구름을 밝게 만들어 태양빛을 우주로 더 많이 반사시켰다. 그러나 지난 20년 동안 중국이 황 배출을 90% 줄인 것과 선박 연료에 대한 국제 규제와 같은 황 배출 감소 노력은 이러한 냉각 효과를 약화시켰다. 그 결과, 지구의 알베도가 감소하여 지구 온난화를 가속화시키고 있다.

황 배출을 줄이는 것은 스모그를 줄이고 매년 수백만 명의 생명을 구함으로써 공중 보건을 향상시키지만, 그와 동시에 이산화탄소의 배출 증가로 인한 온난화를 상쇄해 주던 자연적인 냉각 메커니즘을 의도치 않게 제거해버린다. 황과는 달리, 이산화탄소는 수세기 동안 대기 중에 남아, 지속적으로 열을 가두고 기후 변화를 유발한다. 2006년, 저명한 대기 과학자 폴 크루첸(Paul Crutzen)은 이산화탄소 배출을 줄이지 않은 채 황 오염만 줄일 경우, 지구 온난화가 위험할 정도로 빨라질 수 있다고 경고했다. 그는 이 문제를 해결하기 위한 대안으로 성층권에 황산염 입자를 뿌리는 태양 지구공학을 제안했다. 지표면에서 발생하는 오염물질과는 달리, 성층권에 분사된 황산염 입자는 대기 위에서 더 오래 머물러 있으면서 건강에 최소한의 해를 끼치면서도 상당한 냉각 효과를 낼 수 있다. 그 이후로, 성층권에 입자를 분사하는 것을 이용하는 태양 지구공학에 관한 연구는 상당히 확대되어 왔다. 이러한 진전에도 불구하고, 이 접근법은 여전히 논란의 여지가 있다. 왜냐하면 기후 및 연구 정책에 대해 정부에 자문하는 많은 전문가들이 그것의 사용에 대해 여전히 신중하거나 회의적이기 때문이다.

| 어휘 |

accelerate v. 가속하다, 빨라지게 하다   **albedo** n. 알베도(달·행성이 반사하는 태양 광선의 비율)   **reflectivity** n. 반사도, 반사율   **absorb** v. 흡수하다, 받아들이다   **intensify** v. 강화하다, 심화시키다   **ecosystem** n. 생태계   **pose** v. (위협·문제 등을) 제기하다, 야기하다   **bring forward** 앞당기다   **sulfur** n. 〈화학〉 황(黃)   **emission** n. 배출; 방사, 발산   **sulfur dioxide** 이산화황   **byproduct** n. 부산물   **fossil fuel** 화석 연료   **particle** n. 입자   **scatter** v. 흩뿌리다, 산란시키다   **regulation** n. 규제, 규정   **diminish** v. 줄이다, 감소시키다   **annually** ad. 매년   **inadvertently** ad. 무심코, 의도치 않게   **renowned** a. 유명한   **simultaneously** ad. 동시에   **alternative** n. 대안   **address** v. (문제 등을) 역점을 두서 다루다, 해결하다   **solar geoengineering** 태양 지구공학 (지구 온도를 낮추기 위해 태양광을 인위적으로 반사하는 접근법)   **stratosphere** n. 성층권   **controversial** a. 논란이 되는   **skeptical** a. 회의적인

49 빈칸완성 ④

| 분석 |

문단의 첫 부분에서 황의 배출이 줄어들면 지구의 알베도가 감소한다고 했고, 빈칸을 포함한 문장의 바로 앞에서 황 배출 감소 노력이 냉각 효과를 약화시켰다고 했다. 이 둘을 종합하면, 빈칸에는 ④가 들어가는 것이 적절함을 알 수 있다.

빈칸에 들어가기에 가장 적절한 표현은?
① 지구는 온실가스 배출이 더 낮춰져서 온난화가 줄어든다
② 태양빛을 반사하는 지구의 능력이 늘어나서 지구 온난화의 속도를 한층 더한다.
③ 지구의 알베도가 증가하여 지구 온난화의 영향을 완화시킨다
④ 지구의 알베도가 감소하여 지구 온난화를 가속화시킨다

50 내용파악 ②

| 분석 |

두 번째 문단에서 황의 배출 감소가 공기의 질을 개선하여 건강을 증진시킨다는 장점이 있지만, 동시에 지구 온난화의 가속화를 초래하는 문제점이 있음을 이야기하고 있다. 따라서 ②가 정답으로 가장 적절하다. ③ 온실가스의 수준을 증가시키는 것은 아니다.

황의 배출 감소와 지구 온난화에 대한 주된 메시지는 무엇인가?
① 황의 배출을 감소시켜 지구의 알베도를 높여야 한다.
② 더 깨끗한 공기가 건강을 개선하지만, 황의 배출 감소로 인해 온난화가 가속화된다.
③ 황의 배출을 감소시키는 것은 온실가스의 수준을 증가시킴으로써 지구 온난화를 가속화시킨다.
④ 더 깨끗한 공기는 지구 온난화를 영구적으로 늦춘다.

51 내용파악 ①

| 분석 |

황 배출을 줄이는 것은 스모그를 줄이고 매년 수백만 명의 생명을 구함으로써 공중 보건을 향상시킨다고 했으므로, ①이 정답으로 적절하다.

황의 배출 감소가 온난화의 가속화와 연결돼 있음에도 불구하고 황의 배출을 줄여야 하는 동기는 무엇인가?
① 대기 오염을 줄임으로써 생명을 구하는 건강상의 이점들
② 지구의 알베도를 증가시킴으로써 깨끗한 공기를 의무화하는 국제 조약
③ 재생 에너지 기술의 경제적 이점들
④ 환경적 결과에 도전할 수 있는 지구 공학에 대한 우려

| 52 | 내용파악 | ④ |

| 분석 |

성층권에 황산염 입자를 뿌리는 태양 지구공학을 제안했다고 돼 있으므로 ④가 정답이다.

폴 크뤼첸은 지구 온난화를 해결하기 위해 어떤 대안을 제안하고 있는가?
① 이산화탄소의 배출을 줄이기 위해 전 세계적으로 산업 활동을 줄이는 것
② 건강상의 이점을 유지하는 한편 황의 배출을 상쇄하기 위해 이산화탄소의 배출을 증가시키는 것
③ 황의 배출을 줄이기 위한 국제 환경 조약을 강화하는 것
④ 지구를 냉각시키기 위한 지구공학적 방법으로 성층권에 황산염을 사용하는 것

53~56

로보넛(Robonaut)은 NASA의 로봇이다. 엔지니어들은 로보넛을 휴머노이드 형태로 설계했는데, 이는 로보넛이 사람처럼 보이도록 만들었다는 것을 의미한다. 이렇게 설계된 덕분에 로보넛은 사람이 하는 것과 똑같은 일을 더 쉽게 할 수 있다. 로보넛은 국제우주정거장에서의 작업부터 다른 행성의 탐사에 이르는 온갖 일을 도울 수 있을 것이다. 현재 한 대의 로보넛이 국제우주정거장에 탑승해 있다.
NASA는 1996년에 로보넛 프로젝트를 시작하여 2000년에 첫 번째 버전을 제작했다. 그 이후로 엔지니어들은 로보넛을 계속해서 개선시켜왔다. 최신 모델은 로보넛 2 혹은 R2라고 불린다. NASA는 자동차 제조업체인 제너럴 모터스(General Motors)와 협업하여 R2를 만들었다. 로보넛은 사람처럼 머리, 몸통, 팔, 손을 가지고 있다. 머리에 있는 카메라는 시각 기능을 제공한다. 로보넛은 손과 손가락이 사람처럼 움직이기 때문에 손재주가 좋은 로봇이라고 불린다. 따라서 로보넛은 인간의 손으로 수행하도록 돼 있는 작업을 수행할 수 있다.
로보넛은 두 가지 방식으로 작동할 수 있다. 소프트웨어는 로보넛이 스스로 '생각'할 수 있게 해준다. R2를 조종하는 사람은 해야 할 단순한 작업을 R2에게 줄 수 있고, 그러면 R2는 그 작업을 수행하는 방법을 스스로 알아낼 수 있다. R2의 소프트웨어는 새로운 작업을 수행하도록 업데이트될 수 있다. R2는 또한 원격 조종으로 작동할 수도 있다. 조종자는 헤드셋을 이용하여 로보넛이 자신의 카메라를 통해 보는 것을 볼 수 있고, 그런 다음엔 조종 장치를 사용하여 로보넛을 움직이게 할 수 있다.
NASA는 로보넛에 대한 미래의 계획을 아직 결정 중에 있다. 우주정거장 내부에서의 시험이 잘 진행된다면, 언젠가는 로보넛을 우주정거장 밖에서 시험해 볼 수도 있을 것이다. 이 시험은 로보넛이 우주 유영 중인 우주인들과 함께, 혹은 그들을 대신해서 얼마나 잘 작업할 수 있는지를 판단하게 될 것이다. 로보넛의 설계자들은 언젠가 로보넛과 같은 로봇을 다른 행성에 보내려는 생각까지 하고 있다. 시험이 잘 된다면, 로보넛, 혹은 로보넛을 기반으로 한 더 나은 로봇이 어디까지 가게 될지는 아무도 모르는 일이다!

| 어휘 |

humanoid a. 인간을 닮은, 휴머노이드 **manufacturer** n. 제조업자, 제조업체 **torso** n. (인체의) 몸통 **figure out** 계산해 내다, 생각해 내다, 이해하다 **astronaut** n. 우주비행사 **A hold B for C** A에는 C를 위한 B가 마련되어[예정되어] 있다

| 53 | 빈칸완성 | ③ |

| 분석 |

"손과 손가락이 사람처럼 움직인다"는 내용이 이어지고 있으므로, 이것과 호응하는 ③이 빈칸에 들어가기에 적절하다.

다음 중 빈칸 Ⓐ에 들어가기에 가장 적절한 것은?
① 열망하는
② 예의바른
③ 솜씨좋은, 손재주가 좋은
④ 재난의, 비참한

| 54 | 부분이해 | ① |

| 분석 |

밑줄 친 문장을 다음 문장에서 부연해서 설명하고 있다. "R2를 조종하는 사람은 해야 할 단순한 작업을 R2에게 줄 수 있고, 그러면 R2는 그 작업을 수행하는 방법을 스스로 알아낼 수 있다."라고 했으므로, ①이 밑줄 친 문장을 가장 잘 설명한 진술이다.

위 글에 의하면, 다음 중 밑줄 친 Ⓑ의 의미를 가장 잘 설명하는 것은?
① 로보넛의 소프트웨어는 그것으로 하여금 작업을 어떻게 수행할지 결정할 수 있게 한다.
② 소프트웨어는 로보넛이 잉크를 사용하여 자율적으로 쓰거나 인쇄할 수 있게 한다.
③ 소프트웨어는 로보넛이 다른 시스템이나 부품에 연결되지 못하도록 한다.
④ 로보넛의 소프트웨어는 자율적 행동을 위해 데이터 동기화(同期化)가 필요하다.

55 내용파악 ④

| 분석 |
헤드셋은 로보넛이 아니라 로보넛을 조종하는 사람이 사용하는 장치이다.

다음 중 로보넛의 외형을 설명하지 않는 것은?
① 그것은 사람처럼 생겼다.
② 그것은 손과 손가락을 가지고 있다.
③ 그것은 보는 기능을 위해 머리에 카메라를 가지고 있다.
④ 그것은 움직임을 위해 헤드셋이 장착되어 있다.

56 내용일치 ④

| 분석 |
"언젠가는 로보넛을 우주정거장 밖에서 시험해 볼 수도 있을 것이다."라고 했으므로 ④가 옳은 진술이다. ① 1996년에 시작하여 2000년에 첫 모델을 완성했다. ③ 사람이 원격 조종할 수 있다.

위 글에 의하면, 다음 중 옳은 것은?
① NASA는 1996년에 로보넛을 제작했다.
② 로보넛은 한 우주비행사의 이름을 따서 지어졌다.
③ 로보넛은 작동하는 데 있어 인간 조종자와 양립하지 않는다.
④ 로보넛은 아직 우주비행사들과 함께 우주정거장 밖에서 작동된 적이 없다.

57~60

드와이트 D. 아이젠하워는 그것을 가지고 있었지만, 조지 S. 패튼은 그렇지 않았다. 헨리 아론은 그것을 가지고 있었지만 베이브 루스는 그렇지 않았다. 냇 킹 콜은 그것을 가지고 있었지만 비욘세는 그렇지 않았다. 주디 우드러프는 그것을 가지고 있었지만 헤랄도 리베라는 그렇지 않았다. J.D. 샐린저는 그것을 가지고 있었지만 노먼 메일러는 그렇지 않았다. 워렌 버핏은 그것을 가지고 있었지만 일론 머스크는 그렇지 않았다. 조너스 소크는 그것을 가지고 있었지만 닥터 오즈는 그렇지 않았다. 자니 유니타스는 그것을 가지고 있었지만 조 나마스는 그렇지 않았다. 마틴 루터 킹은 그것을 가지고 있었지만 짐 배커는 그렇지 않았다. 아이리스 머독은 그것을 가지고 있었지만 루퍼트 머독은 그렇지 않았다. 그리고 이 말은 반드시 해야겠는데, 캘빈 쿨리지는 그것을 가지고 있었지만 도널드 J. 트럼프는 그렇지 않았다.
수세기 동안 인류는 "그런즉 믿음, 소망, 사랑 이 세 가지는 항상 있을 것"이라는 말을 받아들여 왔다. 하지만 최근 들어 우리는 성경에 나오는 그 세 가지 덕목이 항상 있을 것이지만, 네 번째 덕목 — 거의 틀림없이 고린도서에 나오는 유명한 세 가지 올곧은 덕목만큼이나 고귀하고 인간을 고양시키는 특성이며, 강력한 인간적 미덕일 수 있다 — 이 드문 만큼이나 귀중하다는 사실을 깨닫게 되었으니, 그것은 바로 겸손이다.
겸손은 좀처럼 인식되지도, 거의 칭송받지도 않지만, 인간의 모든 자질 중에서 독보적인 자리를 차지하고 있다. 다른 특성들과는 달리, 그것은 드러나지 않는 속성이고, 존재하지 않는 성향이며, 자신을 드러내지 않는 마음가짐이고, 부재를 통해서만 드러나는 특성이며, 존재하는 것에서가 아니라 존재하지 않는 것에서 드러나는 유일한 차별점이다. 즉, 그것은 울려 퍼지지 않는 자화자찬의 나팔 소리이고, 보이지 않는 관대한 행동이며, 표현되지 않은 자기만족이고, 사람들 앞에서 행해지지 않는 이타적인 몸짓이다. 그것은 거짓된 자기 부정도, 과시적인 자기 확대도 아닌 태도이다.
겸손이란 영혼을 들여다보고, 자신을 넘어서 집중하고, 세상을 바라보며 자신이 특별히 눈에 띄거나, 특별히 중요하거나, 유달리 필요하다거나, 심지어 특별히 흥미로운 존재도 아니라는 사실을 깨닫는 방법이다. 그래서 영국 왕립 재향군인회, 미국 재향군인회, 국제 로터리클럽은 약간씩 표현을 달리하면서도 모두 다음과 같은 모토를 갖고 있다. "자기 자신이 아닌, 봉사를 위하여."

| 어휘 |
abideth v. 〈고어체〉 머무르다, 지속되다(abide의 3인칭 단수형) **Scripture** n. 성경, 경전 **ennoble** v. 고상하게 하다, 품위 있게 하다 **trait** n. 특성, 특징 **rectitude** n. 정직, 올바름 **Corinthians** n. 고린도서(신약성경의 한 부분) **invaluable** a. 매우 귀중한, 값을 매길 수 없는 **humility** n. 겸손, 겸허 **distinct** a. 뚜렷한, 별개의 **attribute** n. 속성, 특징 **disposition** n. 성향, 기질 **apparent** a. 명백한, 분명한 **boast** v. 자랑하다 **generous** a. 관대한, 아낌없이 주는 **self-satisfaction** n. 자기만족 **perspective** n. 관점, 시각 **self-abnegation** n. 자기희생, 자기부정 **showy** a. 화려한, 허영에 들뜬 **self-aggrandizement** n. 자기 과시 **peer into** ~을 들여다보다, 엿보다 **singularly** ad. 유난히, 독특하게 **permutation** n. 교환, 변경 **proclaim** v. 선언하다, 공표하다

57 내용파악 ②

| 분석 |
첫 문단에 그것을 가지고 있는 사람과 그렇지 못한 사람이 나열돼 있는데, 아이젠하워, 쿨리지, 킹은 모두 전자에 속한다. 그리고 두 번째 문단에서 '그것'이 '겸손'임을 밝히고 있다. 따라서 ②가 정답이다.

위 글에 의하면, 아이젠하워, 쿨리지, 킹의 공통점은?
① 그들은 자신들을 중요하고 훌륭하다고 여긴다.
② 그들은 겸손하다고 여겨진다.
③ 그들은 겸손함이 없다.
④ 그들은 공통점이 전혀 없다.

| 58 | 지시대상 | ② |

| 분석 |

바로 앞에서 언급한 '성경에 나오는 세 가지 덕목', 즉 믿음, 소망, 사랑을 가리킨다.

위 글에 의하면, 밑줄 친 Ⓐ가 가리키는 것은?
① 냇 킹 콜, J.D. 샐린저, 조너스 소크
② 믿음, 소망, 사랑
③ 영국 왕립 재향군인회, 미국 재향군인회, 국제 로터리 클럽
④ 겸손, 자질, 이타성

| 59 | 내용파악 | ④ |

| 분석 |

겸손에 대해 '자신을 넘어서 집중하고, 세상을 바라본다'라고 했으므로 ④가 옳지 않은 진술이다.

위 글에 의하면, 다음 중 겸손에 대해 옳지 않은 것은?
① 그것은 가치 있고 드물다.
② 그것은 인간을 고귀하게 만드는 특성이다.
③ 그것은 좀처럼 인식되지 않으며 거의 칭송받지 않는다.
④ 그것은 자기 자신에게 집중하는 특성이다.

| 60 | 빈칸완성 | ① |

| 분석 |

글의 주제가 겸손에 관한 것이고, 겸손은 자기중심적이지 않고 타인을 위한 봉사를 지향하므로 빈칸에는 ①이 적절하다.

다음 중 빈칸 Ⓑ에 들어가기에 가장 적절한 것은?
① 자기 자신이 아닌, 봉사를 위하여
② 당신 자신에게 봉사하라
③ 오직 나 자신
④ 항상 야망을 가져라

SOOKMYUNG WOMEN'S UNIVERSITY | 숙명여자대학교 A형

TEST p. 432~443

01	④	02	④	03	⑤	04	①	05	③	06	②	07	①	08	②	09	③	10	⑤
11	②	12	④	13	①	14	③	15	③	16	②	17	①	18	③	19	②	20	③
21	②	22	⑤	23	②	24	①	25	④	26	⑤	27	①	28	⑤	29	④	30	⑤
31	③	32	①	33	⑤														

01 동의어 ④

| 어휘 |

protester n. 시위자, 항의자　**vociferous** a. 큰 소리로 외치는(= **outspoken** a. 거리낌 없이 말하는)　**chant** v. (노래를) 부르다, (슬로건을) 외치다　**restrained** a. 억제된; 참가는　**reserved** a. 과묵한　**unwilling** a. 내키지 않는　**noncommittal** a. 분명한 태도를 보이지 않는

| 해석 |

시위자들은 그들의 요구를 큰 소리로 말하며, 온종일 구호를 외치고 깃발을 흔들었다.

02 동의어 ④

| 어휘 |

trenchant a. 날카로운, 명쾌한(= incisive and deeply insightful)　**analysis** n. 분석　**financial crisis** 금융 위기　**earn** v. 얻게 하다, 받게 하다　**acclaim** n. 찬사, 호평, 갈채　**overly** ad. 지나치게　**simplistic** a. 단순한　**superficial** a. 피상적인　**vague** a. 모호한　**precision** n. 정확성　**meandering** a. 두서없는　**incisive** a. 날카로운　**flawed** a. 결함이 있는

| 해석 |

금융 위기에 대한 날카로운 분석으로 그녀는 폭넓은 찬사를 받았다.

03 동의어 ⑤

| 어휘 |

heroic a. 영웅적인　**apocryphal** a. 출처가 불분명한, 진위가 의심스러운(= doubtful and unverifiable)　**credible** a. 신뢰할 만한　**evidence** n. 증거　**exaggerated** a. 과장된　**unwavering** a. 확고한　**persistent** a. 지속적인　**irrelevant** a. 무관한　**intricate** a. 복잡한　**unverifiable** a. 확인할 수 없는

| 해석 |

그의 영웅적인 행동에 관한 이야기는 뒷받침하는 믿을 만한 증거가 없기 때문에 아마도 진위가 의심스러울 것이다.

04 동의어 ①

| 어휘 |

artifact n. 인공물, 문화유물　**serendipitous** a. 우연히 발견된, 뜻밖의 행운인(= unplanned but fortunate)　**unrelated** a. 무관한, 관련 없는　**excavation project** 발굴 프로젝트　**foreseeable** a. 예측[예견]할 수 있는　**premeditated** a. 사전에 계획된　**artificial** a. 인위적인　**orchestrated** a. 조직된　**deliberate** a. 의도적인　**coincidental** a. 우연한

| 해석 |

그 고대 유물의 발견은, 관계없는 발굴 프로젝트 중에 일어나서, 완전히 뜻밖의 운 좋은 발견이었다.

05 시제 ③

| 분석 |

'예상치 못한 상황 때문에'라는 말은 그런 상황이 이미 발생했음을 암시하므로 현재나 미래와는 어울리지 않고 과거와 어울린다. 따라서 과거시제인 ③이 적절하다.

| 어휘 |

originally ad. 원래, 처음에는　**delay** n. 지연, 지체　**due to** ~때문에　**unforeseen circumstance** 예기치 못한 상황

| 해석 |

그 프로젝트는, 원래 6개월이 걸리는 것으로 예정되어 있었지만, 예상치 못한 상황으로 인해 상당한 지연을 겪었다.

06 논리완성 ②

| 분석 |
겉으로 단결을 촉진한다고 했는데 반발을 불러일으켰으므로, 빈칸에는 분열을 '강화하다'는 동사가 필요하고 앞에서 미묘한 암시라 했으므로 '미묘하게, 교묘하게'라는 뜻의 부사가 필요하다. 따라서 ②가 적절하다.

| 어휘 |
outwardly ad. 겉으로, 외부적으로 **designed to** ~하도록 계획된, 의도된 **nuanced allusion** 미묘한 암시 **divisive** a. 분열적인 **agenda** n. 의제, 안건 **backlash** n. 반발 **advocacy group** 옹호 단체 **concern** n. 우려 **hidden motive** 숨겨진 동기 **subtly** ad. 미묘하게, 교묘하게 **reinforce** v. 강화하다

| 해석 |
그 정치인의 연설은, 겉으로는 단결을 촉진하도록 계획되었지만, 분열적인 의제를 교묘하게 강화하는 미묘한 암시를 포함하고 있어서, 옹호 단체들의 반발을 불러일으켰고 숨겨진 동기에 대한 우려를 낳았다.

07 논리완성 ①

| 분석 |
역접의 전치사 despite로 연결되므로, noted 다음 that절의 내용은 '혁신적인 것'과 반대로 부정적이어야 한다. '결과에 영향을 미치는 구조적 흐름'은 중요한 것이므로 이것을 '무시했다'고 해야 부정적인 의미가 된다. 따라서 ①이 빈칸에 적절하다.

| 어휘 |
innovative a. 혁신적인 **flow** n. 흐름 **outcome** n. 결과 **neglect** v. 무시하다 **resolve** v. 해결하다 **sack** v. 해고하다 **verify** v. 검증하다 **incorporate** v. 통합하다

| 해석 |
그 프로그램의 혁신적인 접근 방식에도 불구하고, 분석가들은 그 프로그램의 프레임워크(틀, 뼈대)가 결과에 영향을 미치는 구조적 흐름을 무시하여, 그 프로그램의 효과에 대해 의문이 들게 했다고 지적했다.

08 논리완성 ②

| 분석 |
'이전에 그런 변화에 저항했던 기업들 사이에서도 그랬다'고 한 것은 이런 기업들이 이제는 변화에 저항하지 않고 변화했다는 의미이므로, 빈칸에는 변화가 뒤이어 일어났다는 의미로 '예고했다, 알렸다'는 뜻의 heralded가 적절하다.

| 어휘 |
surge n. 급증 **demand** n. 수요 **electric vehicle** 전기차 **industry-wide shift** 산업 전반의 변화 **sustainable practice** 지속 가능한 방식 **even among** ~조차도 **resist** v. 저항하다 **impede** v. 방해하다 **discharge** v. 방출하다 **delay** v. 지연시키다

| 해석 |
전기차 수요의 갑작스런 증가가 산업 전반에 걸친 지속 가능한 관행으로의 변화를 예고했는데, 심지어 이전에 그러한 변화에 저항했던 기업들 사이에서도 그랬다.

09 논리완성 ③

| 분석 |
회사가 프로젝트를 철회한 것은 위험이 너무 크다고 '인식했기' 때문일 것이므로 빈칸에는 ③이 적절하다.

| 어휘 |
withdraw v. 철수하다 **strategic prudence** 전략적 신중함 **risks involved** 관련된 위험 **disregard** v. 무시하다 **empower** v. 권한을 부여하다 **underestimate** v. 과소평가하다 **disorient** v. 방향 감각을 잃다

| 해석 |
그 회사의 프로젝트 철회 결정은 전략적 신중함을 보여주는 신호로 해석되었는데, 이는 회사가 (프로젝트를) 계속 진행하기에는 관련된 위험이 너무 크다고 인식했음을 시사한다.

10 논리완성 ⑤

| 분석 |
부유한 지역사회에 터무니없이 많은 혜택을 준다면 불평등은 더 심해질 것이므로 빈칸에는 ⑤(악화시키다)가 적절하다.

| 어휘 |
address v. 해결하다 **housing shortage** 주택 부족 **long-term effect** 장기적인 효과 **exacerbate** v. 악화시키다 **inequality** n. 불평등 **disproportionately** ad. 불균형적으로 **affluent** a. 부유한 **mitigate** v. 완화하다 **overlook** v. 간과하다 **clarify** v. 명확히 하다

| 해석 |
새로운 정책은 주택 부족 문제 해결을 목표로 하지만, 비평가들은 그 정책의 장기적인 효과가 부유한 지역사회에 터무니없이 많은 혜택을 줘서 불평등을 악화시킬 수도 있다고 주장한다.

11 논리완성 ②

| 분석 |
although로 연결된 두 문장의 의미는 서로 반대의 의미가 되어야

한다. 앞 문장은 '운영을 간소화한다'라는 긍정적 의미이므로, 뒤에는 부정적인 의미가 필요하다. ② stifle이 경쟁을 억제하여 소비자들에게 해를 끼친다는 맥락과 잘 어울린다.

| 어휘 |
merger n. (조직체·사업체의) 합병   frame v. (계획을) 세우다, 짜다, 꾸미다   streamline v. 간소화하다   industry expert 업계 전문가   stifle v. 억제하다   foster v. 촉진하다   diversify v. 다양화하다   prioritize v. 우선시하다

| 해석 |
합병이 운영을 간소화하는 수단으로 계획되었지만, 업체 전문가들은 경쟁을 억제하여 결국 소비자들에게 해를 끼치지 않을까 걱정했다.

12 논리완성   ④

| 분석 |
역접의 의미를 가진 전치사 despite로 연결되었으므로, 콤마를 사이에 둔 두 내용은 반대의 의미가 되어야 한다. 앞부분이 긍정적인 내용이므로, 뒤에는 부정적인 내용이 필요하다. 중요한 목소리를 '누락했다'라는 흐름을 만드는 omitted가 적절하다.

| 어휘 |
unbiased a. 편향되지 않은   account n. 설명, 서술   critic n. 비평가   curation n. 전시 기획, 구성   marginalized group 소외된 집단   amplify v. 확대하다   celebrate v. 기념하다   incorporate v. 포함하다

| 해석 |
편향되지 않은 역사 서술을 제시하려는 박물관의 노력에도 불구하고, 일부 비평가들은 박물관의 전시 구성이 중요한 목소리, 특히 소외된 집단의 목소리를 누락했다고 주장했다.

13 논리완성   ①

| 분석 |
though라는 역접의 접속사로 연결되었으므로, 주절과 종속절의 내용은 반대의 의미가 되어야 한다. 앞부분이 '혁신적'이라는 긍정적인 내용이므로, 뒤에는 부정적인 내용이 필요하다. 따라서 독자들 중 상당수를 소외시켰다고 한 ①이 빈칸에 적절하다.

| 어휘 |
fragmented a. 단편적인   shifting perspective 변화하는 관점   innovative a. 혁신적인   unfamiliar with ~에 익숙하지 않은   experimental a. 실험적인   alienate v. 소외시키다   inspire v. 자극하다   acclaim n. 칭찬   clarity n. 명확성   undermine v. 잠식하다

| 해석 |
그 소설의 단편적인 구조와 변화하는 관점은 혁신적이었지만, 실험적인 이야기 기법에 익숙하지 않은 상당수의 독자를 소외시켰다.

① 상당수의 독자를 소외시켰다
② 광범위한 찬사를 불러일으켰다
③ 즉각적인 명확성을 제공했다
④ 그 의도를 강화했다
⑤ 서사의 불일치를 약화시켰다

14 논리완성   ③

| 분석 |
while이라는 역접의 접속사로 연결되었으므로, 술부의 내용은 while 절과 반대의 의미가 되어야 한다. while 절은 칭찬하는 내용인 반면에, 이유를 설명하는 전치사 for 이하의 내용은 중심 갈등을 해소하지 못했다는 부정적인 내용이다. 따라서 빈칸에는 긍정적인 내용과 부정적인 내용이 섞여 있는(mixed) ③(엇갈린 반응을 받았다)이 적절하다.

| 어휘 |
visually ad. 시각적으로   stunning a. 뛰어난   coherent a. 일관성 있는   resolution n. 해소   spark v. 불러일으키다   lingering a. 오래된   closure n. 결말

| 해석 |
그 영화는 시각적으로 뛰어나고 서사적으로 복잡했지만, 중심 갈등에 대한 명확한 해결을 제공하지 못한 것으로 평론가들 사이에서 엇갈린 반응을 받았다.

① 보편적인 찬사를 불러일으켰다
② 오래된 논쟁을 해결했다
③ 엇갈린 반응을 받았다
④ 주제를 명확히 했다
⑤ 의미 있는 결말을 제공했다

15 일치 / 시제   ③

| 분석 |
주어는 amendments이므로 복수이다. 그리고 "over the past several weeks"라는 현재까지 이어진 시점이 주어져 있으므로, 현재완료 시제이다. 따라서 현재완료 복수 동사인 have been이 빈칸에 적절하다.

| 어휘 |
proposed amendment 제안된 개정안   constitution n. 헌법   aim to ~를 목표로 하다   enhance v. 강화하다   vigorously ad. 격렬하게   parliament n. 의회   consensus n. 합의

| 해석 |

시민의 권리와 자유를 증진하는 것을 목표로 하는 헌법 개정안들은, 지난 몇 주 동안 의회에서 격렬한 논의를 거쳤으나, 아직 명확한 합의에 이르지 못했다.

16 가정법   ②

| 분석 |

"It is imperative that 절"은 '명령, 제안, 요구, 필요' 등의 의미에 가정법 표현을 사용하는 경우에 해당하므로 that 절에는 '주어 +(should) 동사 원형'이 와야 한다.

| 어휘 |

imperative a. 필수적인, 반드시 해야 하는, 긴요한 **consistently** ad. 일관되게 **contribute** v. 기여하다 **overall** a. 전반적인

| 해석 |

각 팀원은 프로젝트의 전반적인 성공에 효과적으로 기여하기 위해 자신의 개별적인 책임을 명확하고 일관되게 이해하는 것이 필수적이다.

17~19

숲은 탄소의 흡수원 역할을 하며 대기로부터 이산화탄소를 상당량 흡수함으로써 기후 변화 완화에 매우 중요한 역할을 한다. 그러나 산림 파괴와 산림 황폐화로 인해 이러한 기능이 약화되었고, 그 결과 온실가스 배출량이 증가하고 있다. 최근 연구들은 기존의 숲이 생태학적 잠재력까지 최대한 성장하도록 허용하는 숲 놔두기가 조림이나 재조림보다 탄소 격리 전략으로 더 효과적이라고 그 중요성을 강조하고 있다. 숲 놔두기는 탄소 저장 능력을 향상할 뿐만 아니라 생물다양성과 생태계 회복력까지도 지원한다. 숲 놔두기를 실행하기 위해서는 성숙한 숲을 보호하고 기후 완화에서의 숲의 중요한 역할을 인식하는 쪽으로의 정책 전환이 필요하다.

| 어휘 |

play a role 역할을 하다 **pivotal** a. 매우 중요한 **mitigate** v. 완화하다 **climate change** 기후 변화 **carbon sink** 탄소 흡수원(이산화탄소를 흡수·저장하는 역할을 하는 자연적 시스템) **absorb** v. 흡수하다 **significant** a. 상당한, 중요한 **atmosphere** n. 대기 **deforestation** n. 산림 파괴 **degradation** n. 황폐화, 악화 **compromise** v. 약화하다, 훼손하다 **greenhouse gas emission** 온실가스 배출 **proforestation** n. 숲 놔두기, 프로포레스트레이션(기존의 숲이 최대한 성장하도록 유지하는 방식) **potential** n. 잠재력 **carbon sequestration** n. 탄소 격리(탄소를 탄소흡수원에 저장하는 과정) **afforestation** n. 조림(造林) **reforestation** n. 재조림(再造林) **storage** n. 저장 **biodiversity** n. 생물다양성 **ecosystem resilience** 생태계 회복력 **implement** v. 실천하다 **mature** a. 성숙한 **intervention** n. 개입 **boost** v. 증대하다 **timber** n. 목재 **high-density** n. 고밀도 **accelerate** v. 가속하다 **fertility** n. 비옥함 **via** prep. ~을 거쳐 **sustainable** a. 지속 가능한, 견딜 수 있는 **logging** n. 벌목 **mandate** v. 명령하다

17 내용파악   ①

| 분석 |

글에서 숲 놔두기는 '기존의 숲이 충분히 자라도록 놔두는 것'이라고 한 후 그것이 조림이나 재조림보다 탄소 격리에 더 효과적이라고 하였다. 인간의 활동에 방해받지 않는 숲이 더 많은 탄소를 저장할 수 있다면, 개입을 전혀 하지 않는 편이 더 효과적이다. 따라서 ①이 정답이다.

기후 변화에 대응하기 위해 숲 놔두기가 조림이나 재조림보다 더 효과적인 이유는?
① 그것은 인간의 개입 없이 숲이 자연적인 잠재력에 도달하도록 허용한다.
② 그것은 기후 완화를 위한 생물다양성 의존도를 줄인다.
③ 그것은 도시 개발에 반대하면서 산림 벌채를 제한한다.
④ 그것은 탄소 저장량을 줄이지 않고 목재 생산을 증대시킨다.
⑤ 그것은 나무를 높은 밀도로 빽빽이 심어 탄소 흡수를 빠르게 촉진한다.

18 내용파악   ③

| 분석 |

마지막에서 두 번째 문장에서 탄소 저장 능력을 향상할 뿐 아니라 "생물다양성과 생태계 회복도 지원한다"라고 설명되어 있다. 따라서 ③이 정답이다.

숲 놔두기가 제공하는 탄소 저장 이외의 더 광범위한 생태학적 이점은?
① 그것은 산림이 파괴된 지역에서 수자원 보존 문제를 해결한다.
② 그것은 주변의 농업 생산성을 보장한다.
③ 그것은 생물다양성을 촉진하고 환경적 스트레스에 대한 회복력을 높인다.
④ 그것은 정책을 통해 전 세계적인 재조림을 가속화한다.
⑤ 그것은 지속 가능한 토지 이용을 통해 토양 비옥도를 개선한다.

19 내용파악   ②

| 분석 |

마지막 문장에서 "성숙한 숲을 보호하고 기후 완화에서의 숲의 중요한 역할을 인식하는 쪽으로의 정책 전환이 필요하다"라고 하였다. 따라서 ②가 정답이다.

숲 놔두기를 위해 본문에서 옹호하는 정책 전환은?
① 관리된 숲에서의 지속 가능한 벌목을 지원하는 것
② 생태학적 및 기후적 역할을 위해 성숙한 숲을 우선시하는 것
③ 산업적 재조림 프로젝트에 자금을 지원하는 것
④ 시골의 자연보호보다 도시 녹화 사업을 촉진하는 것
⑤ 탄소 흡수를 위해 산림 파괴 지역에서 조림을 의무화하는 것

20~21

프로젝트 제안이 처음 소개되었을 때, 나는 그 가능성에 진심으로 흥분했다. 나는 논의에 기여하고 싶어서 내 생각과 아이디어를 열정적으로 공유했다. 하지만 그는 나의 열정을 승인의 의미로 오해하여, 내가 그의 모든 제안에 완전히 동의한다고 생각했다. 이후, 그가 다른 사람들과 상의하지 않고 변화를 실행하기 시작했을 때, 우리가 같은 입장이 아니라는 것이 분명해졌다.

| 어휘 |

project proposal 프로젝트 제안 **potential** n. 가능성 **eagerly** ad. 간절히 **contribute to** ~에 기여하다 **mistake A for B** A를 B로 착각하다 **approval** n. 승인, 동의 **be on board with** ~에 동의하다, 참여하다 **implement** v. 실행하다 **consult** v. 상의하다 **be on the same page** 같은 입장에 있다, 의견이 일치하다

20   빈칸완성   ③

| 분석 |

mistake A for B는 'A를 B로 착각하다'라는 표현이다. 따라서 for가 빈칸에 적절하다.

21   부분이해   ②

| 분석 |

be on the same page는 '같은 생각이다, 동의하다, 의견이 일치하다'라는 표현이다. 따라서 ②가 밑줄 친 표현의 의미이다.

문맥에 기초할 때, 밑줄 친 "we weren't on the same page"의 의미는?
① 우리는 같은 문서를 읽고 있었다.
② 우리는 서로를 완전히 이해하거나 동의하지는 않았다.
③ 우리는 동시에 전화 통화를 하고 있었다.
④ 우리는 공책의 같은 페이지에 메모를 하고 있었다.
⑤ 우리는 건물의 같은 층에 서있었다.

22~23

대한민국의 활발한 달리기 현장에서, 젊은 세대가 선도자로서 주자들을 선두에서 이끌고 있다. 4월에 열린 2024년 서울 하프마라톤에 참가하러 약 2만 명의 주자들 — 지난해 1만 3천 명에 비해 53.8% 증가한 수치임 — 이 광화문 광장에 몰려들었을 때, 66퍼센트 이상을 차지하는 대다수가 20대와 30대로, 하프마라톤이나 10km 코스에 적극적으로 나섰던 것이다.

| 어휘 |

flourishing a. 번성하는, 활발한 **generation** n. 세대 **lead the charge** 주도하다 **at the front of the pack** 선두에서, 가장 앞에서 **flock to** ~로 몰려들다 **majority** n. 대부분, 과반수 **step up to the plate** 적극적으로 나서다, 도전하다 **spectator** n. 구경꾼 **straggler** n. 배회자 **pacesetter** n. 속도 조정자, 선도자

22   빈칸완성   ⑤

| 분석 |

바로 다음에 '주자들을 선두에서 이끌고 있다'라는 표현이 있으므로 빈칸에는 '선도자'라는 뜻의 pacesetters가 적절하다.

23   내용일치   ②

| 분석 |

"the majority, making up over 66 percent, were in their 20s and 30s"라는 문장을 참조한다.

본문의 내용을 바탕으로 다음 중 옳은 진술을 고르시오.
① 참가자 수는 작년보다 감소했다.
② 참가자의 66% 이상이 20대와 30대였다.
③ 대부분의 주자들은 참가보다는 관람을 선택했다.
④ 이번 대회에서는 10km 코스가 없었다.
⑤ 참가자 대부분은 40세 이상이었다.

24~25

오프라 윈프리의 마음을 운 좋게도 사로잡은 많은 기업과 개인들은 그녀의 획기적인 쇼에서 홍보된 후 단 하룻밤 사이에 성공을 거두었다. 이 쇼는 1986년부터 2011년까지 방영되었으며, 미국 TV 역사상 가장 높은 시청률을 기록한 주간 토크쇼였다. 오프라 효과는 그녀의 진정성 때문에 특히 강력했다. 오프라는 돈을 받고 홍보하는 것이 아니라, 진심으로 관심이 있는 제품들을 선택했다. 또, 일반적인 유명인의 제품 보증 선전과 달리, 그녀는 종종 독립적인 가족 기업들을

지원했다. 이러한 신뢰와 진정성 덕분에 오프라의 추천은 유례없는 영향력을 가지게 되었고, 그녀의 제품 보증 선전은 수많은 개인과 소규모 기업의 인생을 바꾸는 기회가 되었다. 그녀의 쇼에서 단 한 번만 언급되어도 제품은 전국적으로 유명해질 수 있었으며, 흔히 매진 제품 목록에 들어갔고 폭발적인 수요 증가를 불러일으키곤 했다. 오프라 효과와 일반적인 마케팅의 차이점은 감성적 공감이었다. 그녀의 시청자들은 단순히 오프라가 좋아하는 제품을 구매하는 것이 아니라, 그녀의 선택을 그녀의 가치관과 비전의 연장으로 받아들였다. 오프라는 소외된 브랜드를 조명하고 의미 있는 이야기를 알리는 방식으로, 단순한 상업적 차원을 넘어선 성공의 촉매제가 되어, 문화적 유행을 형성하고 주목받지 못했을 목소리를 드높이는 데 도움을 주었다.

| 어휘 |

appeal to ~의 마음을 사로잡다, 관심을 끌다 **overnight** a. 단 하룻밤 사이의 **promote** v. 홍보하다 **groundbreaking** a. 획기적인 **highest-rated** a. 가장 높은 시청률을 기록한 **daytime talk show** 주간 토크쇼 **authenticity** n. 진정성 **celebrity** n. 유명 인사 **endorsement** n. 제품 보증 선전, 추천, 지지 **impactful** a. 영향력이 큰 **countless** a. 수많은 **catapult** v. 발진시키다 **catapult to national fame** 전국적인 명성을 얻다 **sold-out** a. 매진된 **inventory** n. 재고 **skyrocketing demand** 폭발적인 수요 증가 **resonance** n. 공감, 감동; 반향 **embrace** v. 받아들이다, 수용하다 **extension** n. 연장선; 확대, 확장 **spotlight** v. 조명하다, 주목하다 **underrepresented brand** 소외된 브랜드 **commerce** n. 상업, 비즈니스 **catalyst** n. 촉진제, 계기가 되는 존재 **elevate voices** (잘 알려지지 않은 사람들의) 목소리를 대변하다 **high-end** a. 최고급의 **surge** v. 증가하다 **holiday season** 추수감사절부터 새해 초까지 축제 기간 **collaborate** v. 협동하다

24 내용파악 ①

| 분석 |

본문의 "Oprah chose products she was genuinely interested in, rather than being paid to promote them"이라는 문장에서, 자신이 진심으로 관심 있는 제품을 선택했다고 하고, "she often supported independent family businesses"라며, 독립적 가족 기업을 흔히 지원했다고 했다. 따라서 ①이 정답이다.

오프라 효과는 일반적인 유명인의 제품 보증 선전과 비교하여 어떤 점에서 독특했는가?
① 오프라는 자신이 진심으로 믿는 제품, 흔히 소규모 가족 기업의 제품을 홍보했다.
② 오프라는 TV에서 제품을 보증 선전한 최초의 유명인이었다.
③ 오프라는 홍보를 위해 금전적인 대가를 요구했다.
④ 오프라는 고급 명품 브랜드 홍보에 집중했다.
⑤ 오프라 쇼는 대기업 스폰서를 중심으로 진행되었다.

25 내용파악 ④

| 분석 |

한 번만 언급해도 전국적으로 제품이 유명해졌으며, "매진 제품 목록에 들어가고 폭발적인 수요 증가가 일어났다"라고 했으므로 ④가 정답이다.

오프라 윈프리 쇼에서 크게 다루어진 기업들에 초래된 중요한 결과는?
① 그들은 추가 노력 없이 국제 시장에 진출할 수 있었다.
② 그들의 매출은 연말연시 동안에만 증가했다.
③ 그들은 오프라로부터 지속적인 재정적 지원을 받았다.
④ 그들의 제품은 종종 매진되었으며, 수요가 급격히 증가했다.
⑤ 그들은 추가 홍보를 위해 다른 유명인들과 협업해야 했다.

26~28

계엄령은 흔히 질서 회복을 구실로 권력을 민간 정부에서 군 당국으로 이전시킨다. 계엄령이 일시적으로는 위기를 안정화할 수도 있지만, 반대 의견 탄압과 사법부 독립성 약화 등 인권 침해를 자주 초래한다. 민간 통치로 전환하기 위해서는 정의 실현과 사회적 통합 간의 균형을 맞춰야 한다. 인권 침해에 대한 조사는 기득권층의 저항, 제도적 관성, 그리고 갈등 재점화에 대한 두려움으로 인해 방해받는 경우가 많으며, 사면법으로 면책이 강화되기도 한다. 이러한 문제들은 역사적 불의를 해결하는 것과 불안한 평화를 유지하는 것 사이의 긴장을 부각시킨다. 전환기 정의를 지지하는 사람들은 독립적인 조사, 피해자 보상, 그리고 제도 개혁을 통해 책임을 명확히 하고 재발을 막아야 한다고 주장한다. 그러나 비판론자들은 이러한 조치가 불충분하거나 처벌이 지나치다고 비칠 때는 양극화를 심화시키거나, 대중의 환멸을 초래할 수 있다고 경고한다. 계엄령 이후의 통치가 성공하려면, 과거의 불의를 해결하고, 공공기관에 대한 신뢰를 구축하며, 민주적 개혁을 실행해야 한다. 책임 추궁과 화해 사이에 균형을 취하는 것은 군사 통치에서 회복하고 있는 사회에서 장기적인 안정을 보장하고 민주주의 원칙을 보호하는 데 있어 중요하다.

| 어휘 |

martial law 계엄령 **shift** v. 옮기다 **civilian governance** 민간 통치 **military authorities** 군 당국 **pretext** n. 명목, 구실 **under the pretext of** ~을 핑계로 **restore order** 질서를 회복하다 **stabilize** v. 안정시키다 **temporarily** ad. 일시적으로 **human rights abuse** 인권 침해 **suppression of dissent** 반대 의견 탄압 **erosion** n. 침해 **judicial autonomy** 사법부 자율성 **transition** n. 전환 **civilian rule** 민간 통치 **societal cohesion** 사회적 통합 **hamper** v. 방해하다 **resistance** n. 저항 **entrenched interests** 기득권층 **institutional inertia** 제도적 관성(변화를 거부하

는 경직된 조직 문화)　**reignite** v. 재점화하다　**amnesty law** 사면법　**impunity** n. 면책(책임 회피)　**address** v. 해결하다　**fragile** a. 연약한　**proponent** n. 지지자　**transitional justice** 전환기 정의(정권 교체 후 과거 인권 침해를 바로잡으려는 노력)　**advocate** v. 옹호하다　**reparation** n. 피해자 보상　**institutional reform** 제도 개혁　**ensuring accountability** 책임을 명확히 하기　**measure** n. 조치　**recurrence** n. 재발　**polarization** n. 양극화　**disillusionment** n. 환멸　**punitive** a. 처벌적인　**post-martial law governance** 계엄령 이후의 통치　**accountability** n. 책임 추궁　**safeguard** v. 보호하다　**leniency** n. 관용　**deter** v. 억지하다　**severity** n. 가혹함　**legitimacy** n. 정당성　**exclude** v. 제외[배제]하다　**stakeholder** n. 이해 당사자, 주주　**consolidate** v. 공고화하다　**transparency** n. 투명성

26 내용파악   ⑤

| 분석 |

본문에서 "책임 추궁과 화해의 균형이 장기적 안정과 민주주의 원칙 보호에 중요하다"라고 했다. 이와 유사한 표현은 ⑤이다.

계엄령 이후 책임 추궁과 사회적 통합 사이의 관계에 대해 본문에서는 어떻게 설명하는가?
① 책임 추궁은 평화를 불안정하게 만들 수 있으며, 사회적 통합은 관용을 보장하지 않는다.
② 책임 추궁은 권위주의를 억제함으로써 사회적 통합을 보장한다.
③ 책임 추궁과 사회적 통합은 종종 충돌하므로, 권위가 필요하다.
④ 단기적인 안정을 위해 책임 추궁보다는 사회적 통합이 우선시된다.
⑤ 극단적인 관용이나 엄격한 처벌은 둘 다 해를 주므로 균형이 필수적이다.

27 내용파악   ①

| 분석 |

사면법이 나오는 부분을 보면, 사면법은 계엄령을 실시했던 기득권층이 사용하는 것으로 일종의 개혁에 대한 저항(resistance from entrenched interests)이다. 따라서 정답은 ①이다.

사면법이 민주적 개혁에 장기적인 도전이 되는 이유는?
① 사면법은 면책을 고착화하여 제도 개혁을 방해한다.
② 사면법은 안정을 우선시하지만, 피해자 보상을 무시한다.
③ 사면법은 대중의 지지를 받지 못하여 정당성을 약화시킨다.
④ 사면법은 공정해 보이지만, 주요 이해관계자를 배제한다.
⑤ 사면법은 민간 기관에 대한 군부의 통제를 강화한다.

28 내용파악   ⑤

| 분석 |

마지막에서 두 번째 문장에서 "과거의 불의를 해결하고, 민주적인 개혁을 해야 한다"라고 하였다. 따라서 과거의 불의에 대한 책임을 묻는 '정의'와 '개혁'이 함께 이루어져야 한다. 그러므로 ⑤가 정답이다.

계엄령 이후 지속 가능한 통치를 위해 필요한 접근 방식은 무엇인가?
① 공개 사과를 통한 화해
② 양극화 정치가 없는 투명성
③ 불만을 완화하고 신뢰를 재구축하기 위한 경제 회복
④ 처벌 회피와 국제적 개혁 의존에 의한 통합
⑤ 책임 추궁을 보장하기 위한 정의와 개혁의 결합

29~30

2003년 『사이언스 어드밴시스』에 발표된 연구는 미세플라스틱 오염과 이것이 인체 건강에 미치는 영향이라는 만연한 문제를 탐구했다. 연구자들은 인간의 혈류에서 미세플라스틱을 발견했는데, 이는 현대 오염의 생물학적 영향을 이해하는 데 중요한 의미를 갖는다. 이 입자는 음식, 물, 공기를 통해 체내로 유입되며, 염증 및 산화 스트레스를 유발한다는 의심을 받는데, 이러한 과정은 심혈관 질환 같은 만성 질환과 연관되어 있다. 이 연구는 건강상의 위험뿐만 아니라 플라스틱 오염이 초래하는 더 광범위한 환경 영향을 보여주며, 당장 규제 조치가 필요하다고 강조하고 있다. 연구자들은 생분해성 소재 개발 및 전 세계 폐기물 관리 시스템 전면 개편 등의 혁신적인 해결책을 촉구하고 있다. 미세플라스틱이 건강에 어떤 영향을 미치는지에 대한 최종적인 결론은 아직 없지만, 연구 결과는 미세플라스틱이 초래하는 복합적인 문제를 해결하기 위해 학제적 접근이 필요하다고 강조하고 있다.

| 어휘 |

delve into ~을 탐구하다　**pervasive** a. 만연한, 널리 퍼진　**microplastic contamination** 미세플라스틱 오염　**implication** n. 영향, 함의　**bloodstream** n. 혈류　**particle** n. 입자　**ingested** a. 섭취된, 체내로 들어간　**inflammation** n. 염증　**oxidative stress** 산화 스트레스(세포 손상을 유발하는 과정)　**chronic condition** 만성 질환　**cardiovascular diseases** 심혈관 질환　**underscore** v. 강조하다　**environmental consequences** 환경 영향　**plastic pollution** 플라스틱 오염　**urgent** a. 급박한　**regulatory measure** 규제 조치　**advocate for** ~을 지지하다, 촉구하다　**innovative** a. 혁신적인　**biodegradable materials** 생분해성 소재　**overhaul** v. 전면 개편하다　**global waste management systems** 전 세계 폐기물 관리 시스템　**mitigate** v. 완화하다, 경감하다　**definitive conclusion** 최종 결론　**elusive** a. 규명하기 어려운　**pressing**

a. 시급한 **interdisciplinary approaches** 학제적 접근(다양한 분야를 통합한 접근 방식) **multifaceted** a. 복합적인 **pose** v. 제기하다 **toxicity** n. 독성 **break down** 분해하다 **respiratory** a. 호흡의 **standardize** v. 표준화하다

29 내용파악   ④

| 분석 |

본문에서 혈류 속 미세플라스틱은 염증이나 산화 스트레스를 유발하여, 심혈관 질환 같은 만성 질환을 낳을 수 있다고 하였다. 따라서 ④가 정답이다.

이 연구의 혈류 속 미세플라스틱과 관련하여 제기된 주요 우려 사항은?
① 미세플라스틱이 인간 세포에 가하는 즉각적인 유독성
② 미세플라스틱의 소화계 안에서의 분해 불가능성
③ 면역계 반응을 강화하는 미세플라스틱의 역할
④ 미세플라스틱이 산화 스트레스와 같은 생물학적 과정을 촉발할 가능성
⑤ 미세플라스틱이 호흡기 기능에 미치는 주된 영향

30 내용파악   ⑤

| 분석 |

마지막 문장에서 '복합적인(multifaceted) 문제'를 해결하기 위해 학제적 연구가 필요하다고 하였고, 복합적인 문제는 '건강 + 환경'의 문제였다. 따라서 ⑤가 정답이다.

이 연구가 미세플라스틱 오염 문제 해결을 위해 학제적 접근을 강조하는 이유는?
① 건강과 관련된 영향에 대한 대중의 인식을 높이기 위해서
② 의료 연구자들만의 협력을 증진하기 위해서
③ 생분해성 소재의 일관된 국제적 채택을 보장하기 위해서
④ 플라스틱 생산 방식을 전 세계적으로 표준화하기 위해서
⑤ 건강 문제와 환경 문제의 복잡성을 모두 해결하기 위해서

31~33

2024년 노벨 문학상 수상자 한강은 인간 존재의 연약함, 트라우마의 침묵, 저항과 공모 사이의 긴장을 탐구하는 자기 성찰적인 작품들을 만든다. 『채식주의자』에서 주인공의 육식 중단 결정은 가부장적 규범에 대한 반항이자 신체적 자율성의 주장이며, 실존적 고독으로의 후퇴로도 간주될 수 있는 다층적인 행위가 된다. 그녀에게 가까운 사람들의 시각에서 전개되는 이야기는 사회적 기대와 개인적 주체성 사이의 충돌을 부각시키며 독자로 하여금 그녀의 반항이 그녀에게 힘을 주는 것인지, 혹은 자기 파괴적인 것인지 의문을 갖게 한다. 『소년이 온다』에서 한강은 1980년 광주 민주화 운동을 파편화되고 많은 목소리를 담은 시각을 통해 살피며 역사적 기록과 시적 추상을 혼합한다. 이 소설은 슬픔과 폭력을 개인적이면서도 집단적인 경험으로 그리며, 독자들이 고통의 감각적 경험 속에 깊이 빠져들도록 만들면서, 그 고통이 기억과 책임에 어떤 영향을 미치는지를 탐구한다. 그녀의 획기적인 이야기 방식은 특정한 문화적 역사와 실존적 문제를 연결해주며, 독자들을 권력, 회복력, 그리고 폭력의 상흔이라는 불편한 진실과 마주하게 한다.

| 어휘 |

laureate n. 수상자 **introspective** a. 내성적인, 자기 성찰적인 **delve into** 파고들다 **fragility** n. 연약함 **trauma's silence** 트라우마의 침묵(트라우마가 만들어내는 말할 수 없는 고통) **tension** n. 긴장 **resistance** n. 저항 **complicity** n. 공모 **protagonist** n. 주인공 **layered act** 다층적인 행위 **defiance** n. 반항 **patriarchal** a. 가부장적인 **norm** n. 규범 **autonomy** n. 자율성 **retreat** n. 후퇴 **existential solitude** 실존적 고독 **perspective** n. 시각 **personal agency** 개인적 주체성 **rebellion** n. 반항, 저항, 모반 **empowering** a. 힘을 실어주는 **self-destructive** a. 자기 파괴적인 **abstraction** n. 추상 **immerse** v. 몰두하게 하다 **sensory** a. 감각적인 **probe** v. 탐구하다 **accountability** n. 책임 (있음), 의무 **groundbreaking** a. 혁신적인 **resilience** n. 회복력 **abstinence** n. 금욕 **critique** n. 비판 **metaphorical** a. 은유적인 **amidst** prep. ~중에 **solidarity** n. 단결, 연대, 결속 **reflect** v. 반영하다 **disorientation** n. 방향 상실 **resonance** n. 공감 **objective** a. 객관적인 **unified** a. 통일성 있는 **neutral** a. 중립적인, 불편부당인 **secondary to** ~에 부차적인 **blur** v. 흐리게 만들다

31 내용파악   ③

| 분석 |

두 번째 문장에서 '가부장적 규범에 대한 반항이자 신체적 자율성의 주장이며, 실존적 고독으로의 후퇴'라고 명시하였는데, 신체적 자율성은 곧 자기 몸을 자기 마음대로 하는 몸에 대한 통제를 말하므로 ③이 정답이다.

『채식주의자』에서 주인공의 육식 거부는 이야기에서 어떤 기능을 하는가?
① 산업화된 육류 생산으로 인한 환경 피해에 대한 비판으로서
② 사회적 규범과 개인적 자율성 모두에 대한 은유적 거부로서
③ 가부장적 기대 속에서 자기 몸에 대한 통제의 주장으로서
④ 페미니스트 저항 운동과의 연대의 표현으로서
⑤ 전통적인 한국 문화 가치로부터의 상징적 후퇴로서

| 32 | 내용파악 | ① |

| 분석 |

끝에서 세 번째 문장에서 '광주 민주화 운동을 파편화된(fragmented) 시각을 통해 살폈다'고 했고, 그 다음 문장에서 '독자들이 고통의 감각적 경험 속에 깊이 빠져들도록' 만든다고 했는데, 이것은 ①의 '정서적 공감을 심화한다'라는 내용과 가장 가깝다. 따라서 ①이 정답이다.

『소년이 온다』에서 한강의 다중 시각 사용은 광주 민주화 운동에 대한 독자들의 이해에 어떻게 영향을 미치는가?
① 서사를 파편화하여 정치적 폭력 중에 경험되는 혼란을 반영하고, 등장인물들과의 정서적 공감을 심화시킴으로써
② 독자와 등장인물들 사이에 거리를 만들어, 역사적 사건에 대한 보다 더 객관적인 분석을 유도함으로써
③ 생존자들의 시각에만 초점을 두어, 더 넓은 사회적 맥락을 제한함으로써
④ 각각의 시각을 동등하게 신뢰할 수 있는 것으로 제시하여, 민주화 운동에 대한 통일된 견해를 제공함으로써
⑤ 개인적 슬픔보다 사실적 정확성을 강조하여, 역사적 트라우마에 대한 중립적인 묘사를 보장함으로써

| 33 | 내용파악 | ⑤ |

| 분석 |

『소년이 온다』를 이야기하며, '역사적 기록과 시적 추상을 결합'하고, 개인적이면서도 집단적인 경험으로 역사를 그리고, 독자들을 "불편한 진실과 마주하게 한다," 다시 말해, 역사를 이해하게 한다고 하였다. 역사적 사건에 대한 일반적인 묘사는 그 사건에 대한 개인적 경험과 집단적 경험을 구분하여 집단적 경험을 위주로 기술하는데, (역사서가 아니라 문학 작품으로서) 역사를 개인적이면서도 집단적인 경험으로 그린다는 것은 두 경험의 구분을 흐리게 한다는 뜻이다. 그리고 집단적 경험을 위주로 기술해갈 때 개인적 경험을 간과함으로 인한 진실의 왜곡이 일어날 수 있는데, 여기서 "불편한 진실과 마주하게 한다"고 한 것은 개인적 경험과 관련해 왜곡되었거나 감추어졌던 불편한 진실을 독자들에게 알려주어 새롭게 이해하게 한다는 뜻이다. 따라서 ⑤가 정답이다. ④의 문화적 경계와 시간적 경계를 부정하여 모든 문화 모든 시대에 해당하는 보편적 주제로서의 회복력과 고통을 탐구한다는 것은 특정한 문화적 역사에 담긴 실존적 문제로서의 고통과 회복력을 간과하는 것이므로 부적절하다.

이 글을 기반으로 볼 때, 한강의 이야기 방식이 역사적 사건에 대한 일반적인 묘사에 어떻게 도전하는가?
① 역사적 사건을 실존적 문제에 종속시켜, 그 광범위한 의미를 축소함으로써
② 감정적 깊이보다는 사실적 정확성을 강조하여, 역사에 기반을 둔 이야기를 확보함으로써
③ 단일하고, 권위 있는 서술을 위하여 개별적인 시각을 배제함으로써
④ 문화적·시간적 경계를 부정하여, 회복력과 고통이라는 보편적 주제를 탐구함으로써
⑤ 개인적 경험과 집단적 경험의 구분을 흐리게 하여, 역사적 트라우마에 대한 독자의 이해를 재구성함으로써

SOOKMYUNG WOMEN'S UNIVERSITY | 숙명여자대학교 B형

TEST p. 446~457

01	④	02	①	03	①	04	②	05	③	06	④	07	③	08	①	09	⑤	10	②
11	⑤	12	⑤	13	①	14	①	15	③	16	②	17	①	18	④	19	②	20	②
21	③	22	③	23	②	24	⑤	25	②	26	④	27	④	28	④	29	⑤	30	③
31	⑤	32	③	33	①														

01 동의어 ④

| 어휘 |
ineffable a. 말로 나타낼 수 없는, 이루 말할 수 없는(= indescribable) **awe** n. 경외, 두려움 **unpleasant** a. 불쾌한; 무례한 **forgettable** a. 잊기 쉬운; 잊어도 좋은 **visible** a. (눈에) 보이는 **loud** a. 시끄러운

| 해석 |
일몰의 아름다움은 이루 말할 수 없을 정도여서 우리 모두를 경탄하게 만들었다.

02 동의어 ①

| 어휘 |
weigh v. 숙고하다, 고찰하다(= consider) **uncertainty** n. 불확실 **ignore** v. 무시하다 **forget** v. 잊다, 망각하다 **know** v. 알고 있다 **simplify** v. 단순화하다

| 해석 |
투자자들은 미국 선거의 결과를 불확실성이 여전히 남아 있을 때 일찌감치 살펴본다.

03 동의어 ①

| 어휘 |
pivot n. 선회, 중요한 변화(= shift) **impose** v. (의무 · 세금 · 벌 따위를) 과(課)하다, 부과하다 **restriction** n. 제한, 한정 **abate** v. 줄어들다, 누그러지다 **stagnation** n. 정체, 침체 **decline** n. 쇠퇴, 감퇴 **acceleration** n. 가속, 촉진 **completion** n. 성취, 완성

| 해석 |
미국이 중국에 대한 판매 제한을 새롭게 부과할지도 모른다는 징후에 뒤이어 전 세계 주식 시장을 휩쓸었던 반도체 회사들의 갑작스런 변화가 줄어들기 시작했다.

04 동의어 ②

| 어휘 |
equity n. 공정; 보통주, 주식 **prime** v. 준비시키다 **notch** v. 새긴 금으로써 세다[기록하다](= mark) **overwhelm** v. 압도하다 **optimism** n. 낙관주의 **fail** v. 실망시키다, 낙제시키다 **neglect** v. 무시하다, 경시하다 **avoid** v. 회피하다 **delay** v. 연기하다, 미루다

| 해석 |
경기의 약세 조짐이 금리 인하를 둘러싼 시장의 낙관론을 압도하면서, 아시아 증시는 두 번째 하락일을 기록하며 미국 증시를 따라갈 준비가 되어 있었다.

05 논리완성 ③

| 분석 |
그의 발언이 기여를 거의 혹은 전혀 하지 못한 원인이나 이유가 될 수 있는 표현이 빈칸에 들어가야 하므로, 부정적인 의미의 단어들로 짝지어진 ③이 정답으로 적절하다.

| 어휘 |
contribution n. 기여, 공헌 **crucial** a. 결정적인, 중대한 **vapid** a. 지루한, 장황한, 재미가 없는 **uninspiring** a. 흥미롭지[활기차지] 못한, 시시한 **significant** a. 중대한, 중요한 **fundamental** a. 근본적인, 중요한

| 해석 |
회의 중에 그가 한 발언은 지루하고 시시해서, 의미 있는 기여는 거의 혹은 전혀 하지 못했다.

06 논리완성 ④

| 분석 |
미국 국방성 프로그램의 주요 계약자 역할을 한 최초의 소프트웨어

회사가 된 것은 매우 의미 있는 성과를 이뤄낸 것이므로, '획기적인 사건', '이정표'라는 의미의 ④가 빈칸에 들어가기에 적절하다.

| 어휘 |
significant a. 중요한; 의미 있는   contractor n. 계약자, 도급자   node n. 마디, 결절; 〈컴퓨터〉 노드(네트워크의 분기점이나 단말 장치의 접속점)   setback n. (진행 따위의) 방해, 정지; 좌절, 차질   routine n. 판에 박힌 일, 일상의 과정   loss n. 손실, 손해   milestone n. 이정표, 획기적인 사건   disappointment n. 실망, 기대에 어긋남

| 해석 |
미국 국방성 프로그램의 주요 계약자 역할을 한 최초의 소프트웨어 회사가 되어 차세대 목표 추적 노드 개발을 위한 육군의 타이탄 계약을 확보했을 때, 팔란티어는 의미 있는 이정표를 달성했다.

07 논리완성 ③

| 분석 |
재판일에 사건에 대한 확정적인 해결책이 마련되고 미래의 분쟁에 대한 선례를 만들게 된다고 했는데, 이는 그간의 대립이 결판나게 되는 '최종 단계' 혹은 '궁극적인 대결'이 된다는 것이므로 빈칸에는 ③이 들어가야 한다.

| 어휘 |
definitive a. 결정적인, 최후의; 명확한   resolution n. 해결, 해답   potentially ad. 잠재적으로   precedent n. 선례, 전례   dispute n. 논쟁, 싸움   digression n. 본제를 벗어나 지엽으로 흐름, 여담, 탈선   misunderstanding n. 오해   showdown n. (결말을 짓는) 최종 단계, 파국; 막판, 대결   stalemate n. 막다름, 교착상태   delay n. 지연, 지체, 연기

| 해석 |
양측이 자신들의 입장을 맹렬하게 방어하는 가운데, 법적 다툼은 여러 달에 걸쳐 이어졌다. 다음 달로 예정된 재판일은 사건에 대한 확정적인 해결책을 가져오고 미래의 분쟁에 대한 선례를 만들 가능성이 있는 최종 대결이 될 것으로 예상되었다.

08 논리완성 ①

| 분석 |
핵겨울이 정치적 관점의 심장부를 관통했다는 것은 핵겨울이 실제로 얼마나 심각할지와는 별개로 큰 정치적 반향을 일으켰다는 말이므로, 핵겨울이 핵전쟁의 위험성과 그로 인한 기후 변화에 대해 경각심을 일깨우는 역할을 했다는 의미가 되도록 빈칸에는 ①이 들어가는 것이 가장 적절하다.

| 어휘 |
generate v. 생기게 하다, 발생시키다   rubble n. (허물어진 건물의) 돌무더기[잔해]   affect v. 영향을 미치다   descend v. 내려오다   crop v. 농작물   fail v. (작물이) 흉작이 되다; (식물이) 시들다   starve v. 굶주리다, 굶어죽다   back-and-forth a. 앞뒤[좌우]로의, 여기저기의, 오락가락하는   wake-up call 주의를 환기하는 경고, 관심을 불러일으키는 사건   lighthearted a. 아무 걱정 없는, 마음 편한

| 해석 |
핵겨울은 핵전쟁이 너무 많은 화재와 잔해와 먼지와 열을 생성하여 그 이후 몇 달 동안 전 세계의 기후가 영향을 받을 것이라는 이론이다. 전 세계의 기온은 떨어지고, 농작물은 흉작이 되고, 인간과 동물은 모두 굶어 죽고 말 것이다. 핵겨울이 정확하게 얼마나 심각할지에 대해서는 학자들 사이에 주장이 오락가락했지만, 그것은 당시의 정치적 관점의 심장부를 관통하면서 주의를 환기시키는 경고였다.

09 논리완성 ⑤

| 분석 |
승진을 위해 열심히 일한 사람이 상을 받고 급여도 인상된 것은 그 사람의 노력이 성과를 거둔 것이다.

| 어휘 |
tirelessly ad. 지칠 줄 모르고, 끊임없이   promotion n. 승진   commendation n. 칭찬, 상장   annual a. 일년의, 일년에 걸친   celebrate v. 찬양하다, 기리다   acknowledge v. 인정하다   wear out 닳아 없어지게 하다; (인내 따위를) 다하다   slow down 느긋해지다, (기력이) 쇠해지다, (노동자가) 태업하다   turn down 거절하다   give up 포기하다   pay off (노력이) 이익을 가져오다, 성과를 올리다, 성공적인 결과를 가져오다

| 해석 |
그녀는 승진을 하기 위해 1년 내내 지칠 줄 모르고 일했으며, 그녀의 노력은 마침내 성과를 거두었다. 연례 회사 회의에서 그녀는 상을 받았고 급여도 인상됐다. 부서의 모든 사람들이 그녀의 성공을 축하했으며, 그녀가 얼마나 열심히 일했는지를 인정했다.

10 논리완성 ②

| 분석 |
예정보다 늦어지고 예산이 초과된 상황에서 업무를 재배정하고 프로세스를 간소화한 것은 문제를 해결하기 위해 관리자가 대대적인 변화를 단행한 것으로 이해할 수 있다. 따라서 ②(완전히 바꾸다)가 정답이다.

| 어휘 |
behind schedule 예정보다 늦은   budget n. 예산   prompt v. 자극하다, 고무하다   reassign v. 다시 할당하다   streamline v. (일·과정·계획 따위를) 능률적으로 하다; 현대풍으로 하다; 합리화[간소화]하다   proactive a. 미리 대처하는, 사전 대책을 강구하는   on track 제대로 진행되고 있는   relief n. 안심, 위안   give up 포기하다   shake things up 완전히 바꾸다, 변화를 주다, 개편하다   scale down 축소하다   hold back 억제하다   take a vacation 휴가를 가다

| 해석 |

그 프로젝트가 예정보다 늦어지고 예산을 초과하자, 관리자는 완전한 변화를 시도했다. 그녀는 여러 차례 회의를 열어 업무를 재배정하고 업무 프로세스를 간소화했다. 그녀의 미리 대처하는 접근방법 덕분에 프로젝트는 다시 정상 궤도로 돌아왔고, 부서 전체가 안도하게 되었다.

11 논리완성 ⑤

| 분석 |

새로 시행한 AI 기반 보안 시스템이 사기 시도를 이전 방식보다 더 정확하게 탐지해냈다면, 그 시스템을 도입한 목적을 달성한 것이므로 빈칸에는 ⑤가 들어가는 것이 적절하다.

| 어휘 |

implement v. 이행하다, 실행하다　**transaction** v. (업무) 처리; 거래　**detect** v. 발견하다, 간파하다　**fraud** n. 사기　**fall short** 기대에 못 미치다　**misfire** v. (총 따위가) 불발하다; (작품 등이) 목적하는 효과를 못 내다　**backfire** v. 역효과를 내다　**break down** (기계 따위가) 고장나다　**hit the mark** 목적을 이루다[이루지 못하다], 성공[실패]하다

| 해석 |

어떤 팀은 온라인 거래를 위한 AI 기반 보안 시스템을 시행했다. 일단 가동되고 나자, 그 시스템은 사기(詐欺) 시도를 이전 방식보다 더 정확하게 탐지해내서 성공을 거두었다.

12 논리완성 ⑤

| 분석 |

음악가들과 곡예사들의 공연은 본 행사를 기다리고 있는 관객들을 지루하지 않도록 하기 위한 행사였으므로, 빈칸에는 '별도로 진행되는 부수적인 공연이나 행사'를 뜻하는 ⑤가 들어가야 한다.

| 어휘 |

unforeseen a. 예기치 못한, 예측할 수 없는　**technical** a. 기술적인, 공학적인　**diversion** n. 주의 전환, 오락, 일시적인 즐거움　**closure** n. 종료, 끝내기　**cancellation** n. 취소　**debate** n. 토론, 논쟁　**board meeting** 이사회 회의　**sideshow** n. 여흥; 사이드 쇼(서커스 등에서 손님을 끌기 위해 따로 보여주는 소규모의 공연)

| 해석 |

본(本) 행사가 예기치 못한 기술적 문제로 인해 지연됐기 때문에, 주최 측은 관객들이 기다리는 동안 즐겁게 해줄 여흥거리를 마련했다. 이 오락 행사에서는 지역 음악가들과 곡예사들이 주로 출연하여 작은 무대에서 공연했다.

13 논리완성 ①

| 분석 |

경쟁 학교 사이에 긴장이 고조된 것은 두 학교의 농구팀들이 매우 중요한 경기에서 대결하기 때문일 것이므로 '맞붙다'는 뜻의 square off가 적절하다.

| 어휘 |

tension n. 긴장, 불안정한 상태　**decisive** a. 결정적인, 중요한　**square off** 맞붙다, 대결하다　**back out** 철회하다, 약속을 취소하다　**cool down** 진정하다　**stand aside** 관망하다　**sit it out** 참여하지 않다, 빠지다

| 해석 |

두 경쟁 학교 사이에 긴장이 계속 고조되는 가운데, 그 두 학교의 농구팀들은 지역 챔피언을 결정할 중요한 경기에서 맞붙을 준비를 했다.

14 논리완성 ①

| 분석 |

탄탄한 분기별 수익, 유리한 거시경제 상황, 소비자 지출의 회복 등은 모두 주식 가격을 급등시키는 데 도움을 준 긍정적인 요소이므로, 마치 배나 비행기가 앞으로 나아가는 데 도움을 주는 ①의 '순풍'과 같은 역할을 한 것으로 볼 수 있다.

| 어휘 |

robust a. 튼튼한, 강력한　**quarterly** a. 분기별의, 연(年) 4회의　**macroeconomic** a. 거시 경제의, 경제 전반에 관한　**resurgence** n. 재기, 부활　**substantial** a. 상당한, 중요한　**propel** v. 추진하다　**unprecedented** a. 전례 없는　**tailwind** n. (항공기·배) 뒤에서 부는 바람, 순풍　**encumbrance** n. 방해물, 부담　**hindrance** n. 방해, 장애물　**stagnation** n. 침체, 정체　**languor** n. 나른함, 무기력

| 해석 |

그 회사의 견고한 분기별 수익은 유리한 거시경제 상황 및 소비자 지출의 회복과 결합되어 그 회사의 주식 가격을 전례 없는 수준으로 끌어올리는 순풍(順風)을 만들어냈다.

15 논리완성 ③

| 분석 |

환경 영향에 대한 질문을 받았을 때 환경과 무관한 자선활동에 대해 자세히 이야기하는 것은 질문한 환경 문제에 대한 우려를 슬쩍 외면한 것이므로 '옆으로 비키다, 회피하다'는 뜻의 sidestepping이 적절하다.

| 어휘 |

elaborate v. 자세히 설명하다, 상세히 풀다(on)　**charitable** a. 자선적인, 자애로운　**initiative** n. (특정한 문제 해결·목적 달성을 위한 새로운) 계획; 솔선; 진취성　**pressing** a. 긴급한, 중요한　**carbon footprint** 탄소 발자국　**deforestation** n. 삼림 벌채　**calculate** v. 계산하다, 신중하게 계획하다　**experiment** v. 실험하다　**sidestep**

v. (일·책임을) 회피하다 **broadcast** v. 방송하다, 널리 알리다 **celebrate** v. 축하하다, 기념하다

| 해석 |

회사의 환경적 영향에 대해 질문을 받았을 때, CEO는 최근의 자선 활동 계획에 대해 자세히 설명함으로써 그들의 탄소 발자국과 삼림 파괴 관행에 관한 시급한 우려를 회피했다.

16 논리완성 ②

| 분석 |

해고된 직원들이 새로운 직업 기회로 옮겨가도록 돕는 것과 관련된 전략은 ②의 outplacement(전직 알선, 이직 지원) 전략일 것이다.

| 어휘 |

in the wake of ~의 결과로, ~의 여파, ~에 뒤이어 **be tasked with** ~하는 임무를 맡다 **mitigate** v. 완화하다, 경감하다, 누그러뜨리다 **repercussion** n. 영향, 결과 **handover** n. 인계, 넘겨주기 **morale** n. 사기, 의욕 **celebration** n. 축하; 축전 **outplacement** n. 전직(轉職) 알선; 이직 지원 프로그램 **relocation of office space** 사무실 공간 이전

| 해석 |

회사의 구조 조정에 뒤이어, 고위 임원들은 해고된 직원들이 새로운 직업 기회로 옮겨가는 것을 원활히 할 뿐 아니라, 잠재적인 법적 문제를 완화하고, 회사의 명성을 보호하며, 남아 있는 직원들에게 중요한 책무를 매끄럽게 인수인계하는 포괄적인 이직 지원 전략을 실행하는 임무를 맡았는데, 이 모든 과정은 급변하는 조직 환경 속에서 사기와 생산성을 유지함과 동시에 진행되었다.

17~18

오늘날 수천 대의 고성능 슈퍼컴퓨터가 포커와 유사한 머니 게임의 일환으로서의 파생상품의 가치를 계산하는 데 이용되고 있다. 그러나 차세대 AI의 막대한 전력 소비가 기후에 미치는 장기적인 영향, 플라스틱 오염이 해양에 끼치는 영향, 혹은 토양이 급속히 황폐화하는 가운데 향후 200년간의 식량 생산 전망 등의 평가를 전담하고 있는 슈퍼컴퓨터는 상대적으로 극히 적다. 슈퍼컴퓨터는 지속가능성보다 이윤을 계산하는 데 주로 이용되고 있으며, 이는 과학적 동기보다는 정치적 동기에 의한 것이다. 만약 AI에게 여러 세기에 걸친 지속가능성에 집중하도록 하는 경우, 인류의 생존을 보장하기 위해 모든 AI를 반드시 중단해야 한다는 결론에 이를 가능성이 크다는 사실을 권력을 가진 이들은 잘 알고 있다.

| 어휘 |

calculate v. 계산하다 **derivative** n. 파생물; 〈경제〉 (주식이나 채권 등에서 파생한) 복합 금융 상품, 파생 상품 **akin** a. 같은 종류의, 유사한 **relatively** ad. 상대적으로 **dedicate** v. (시간 등을) 바치다; 전념하다 **evaluate** v. 평가하다 **consumption** n. 소비 **prospect** n. 예상, 기대 **degradation** n. 지위를 내림, 강등, 하락 **sustainability** n. (자원 이용이) 환경이 파괴되지 않고 계속될 수 있음, 지속가능성 **ensure** v. 확실히 하다, 보장하다

17 내용파악 ①

| 분석 |

"슈퍼컴퓨터는 지속가능성보다 이윤을 계산하는 데 주로 이용되고 있으며, 이는 과학적 동기보다는 정치적 동기에 의한 것이다."라고 돼 있으므로 ①이 정답이다.

위 글에 의하면, 슈퍼컴퓨터가 지속가능성 대신에 이윤을 계산하는 데 주로 사용되는 이유는?
① 정치적 동기가 장기적인 지속가능성보다 이윤을 우선시한다.
② 슈퍼컴퓨터는 환경 데이터를 처리할 능력이 부족하다.
③ 과학 연구는 지속가능성을 위한 슈퍼컴퓨터의 사용을 방해한다.
④ 지속가능성과 관련된 문제는 슈퍼컴퓨터를 필요로 하지 않는다.
⑤ 지속가능성에 중점을 둔 계산을 위한 기술은 충분히 발달하지 못했다.

18 내용파악 ④

| 분석 |

마지막 문장에서 "만약 AI에게 여러 세대에 걸친 지속가능성에 집중하도록 하는 경우, 인류의 생존을 보장하기 위해 모든 AI를 반드시 중단해야 한다는 결론에 이를 가능성이 크다는 사실을 권력을 가진 이들은 잘 알고 있다."라고 했으므로 ④가 정답이다.

저자는 AI가 이윤 대신에 지속가능성에 집중한다면 어떤 결과가 일어날 것이라고 암시하고 있는가?
① 전 세계의 지속가능성을 위해 AI 사용을 증가시키는 것이 필수적이라는 것이 밝혀질 것이다.
② 이윤 중심의 AI 적용이 가장 지속가능한 해결책임을 확정하게 될 것이다.
③ 지속가능성에 중점을 둔 AI가 인류의 생존에 전혀 영향을 미치지 않는다는 사실을 밝혀낼 것이다.
④ 인류가 생존하려면 AI의 사용을 완전히 중단해야 한다는 결론을 내리게 될 것이다.
⑤ AI에 의해 주도되는 이윤 추구가 지속가능성보다 더 중요하다는 것을 증명할 것이다.

19~21

메리 울스턴크래프트(Mary Wollstonecraft)는 여권주의 철학의 토대를 닦은 인물로 여겨지고 있지만, 그녀의 작품은 당대를 넘어 보다 광범위한 정치적, 윤리적 논쟁과 관계되어 있다. 1792년의 『여성의 권리에 대한 변호』에서, 울스턴크래프트는 여성의 합리성과 교육이 그들의 도덕적, 사회적 발전에 필수적이라고 주장함으로써 지배적인 사회 규범에 도전한다. 그러나 그녀의 주장은 사회의 계층구조에 대한 비판과 자율성과 자유와 같은 계몽주의적 이상 사이의 지속적인 타협을 반영하고 있는데, 이는 자유주의와의 복잡한 관계를 시사한다. 최근의 학문적 연구는 울스턴크래프트의 정치 경제와의 관여를 재조명하여, 그녀가 여전히 자유주의의 전통 안에 있긴 하지만, 부의 불평등과 가족 구조에 대한 그녀의 비판이 사회주의적 여권주의의 특정 측면들을 미리 나타낸 것이라고 주장한다. 뿐만 아니라, 개인의 미덕을 사회 개혁을 성취할 수단으로 강조하는 그녀의 미덕 윤리에 대한 접근 방법은 개인의 도덕적 책임과 보다 광범위한 사회적 비판을 미묘하게 통합한 점에서 주목받고 있다. 개인의 윤리, 성(性) 평등, 정치 개혁이 이처럼 교차하고 있는 덕분에, 울스턴크래프트의 작품은 도전적이며, 현대 여권주의 담론에서 지속적으로 관련성을 갖고 있다.

| 어휘 |

transcend v. (경험·이해력 등의 범위·한계를) 넘다, 초월하다 **ethical** a. 도덕상의, 윤리의 **prevailing** a. 우세한, 유력한 **norm** n. 기준, 규범 **assert** v. 단언하다, 역설하다 **rationality** n. 합리성, 순리성 **ongoing** a. 전진하는, 진행하는 **negotiation** n. 협상, 교섭 **critique** n. 비평, 비판 **hierarchy** n. 계급제도 **autonomy** n. 자주성, 자율성 **disparity** n. 불균형, 불일치 **prefigure** v. ~의 모양을 미리 나타내다; 예시하다 **emphasize** v. 강조하다; 역설하다 **nuanced** a. 미묘한 차이가 있는 **integration** n. 통합; 완성, 집성 **intersection** n. 교차; 교차점 **reform** n. 개혁, 개량 **relevant** a. 관련된, 적절한 **contemporary** a. 동시대의, 현대의

19 내용파악   ②

| 분석 |

본문에서 울스턴크래프트는 여성의 합리성과 교육이 도덕적·사회적 발전에 필수적이라고 주장하고 있으며, 동시에 그녀의 주장은 사회의 계층구조에 대한 비판과 자율성과 자유와 같은 계몽주의적 이상 사이의 지속적인 타협을 반영하고 있다고 했다. 그러므로 ②가 정답으로 가장 적절하다.

위 글에 의하면, 울스턴크래프트의 작품이 자유주의에 동조하는 동시에 자유주의에 비판적인 것으로 여겨지는 한 가지 이유는 무엇인가?

① 그녀는 성 평등을 옹호했지만 개인의 자유 개념을 거부했다.
② 그녀는 여성 교육을 강조하면서도 기존의 사회적 계층구조를 비판했다.
③ 그녀는 계몽주의 원칙을 일축하면서도 경제 개혁은 지지했다.
④ 그녀는 사회주의적 정책을 제안하면서도 전통적인 가족 구조를 고수했다.
⑤ 그녀는 자유주의적 주장을 선호하여 정치적 비판을 피했다.

20 내용파악   ②

| 분석 |

"그녀의 미덕 윤리에 대한 접근 방법은 개인의 도덕적 책임과 보다 광범위한 사회적 비판을 미묘하게 통합한 점에서 주목받고 있다"라고 했으므로 ②가 정답으로 적절하다.

울스턴크래프트가 미덕 윤리를 통합한 것이 여권주의사상과 정치사상에 대한 그녀의 접근 방식을 어떻게 차별화하고 있는가?
① 그것은 개인의 도덕을 사회 개혁과 무관한 것으로 설정한다.
② 그것은 개인의 도덕적 책임을 더 넓은 사회적 변화와 연관 짓는다.
③ 그것은 성 평등을 촉진하기 위해 종교적 교리에 전적으로 의존한다.
④ 그것은 이성적 논쟁보다 감정적 호소를 우선시한다.
⑤ 그것은 사회 개혁을 개인의 미덕에 부차적인 것으로 자리매김한다.

21 내용추론   ③

| 분석 |

"그녀가 여전히 자유주의의 전통 안에 있긴 하지만, 부의 불평등과 가족 구조에 대한 그녀의 비판이 사회주의적 여권주의의 특정 측면들을 미리 나타낸 것이라고 주장한다."라는 내용을 통해 ③이 정답임을 알 수 있다.

울스턴크래프트의 부의 불평등과 가족 구조에 대한 비판에 대해 어떤 추론을 할 수 있는가?
① 그녀의 견해는 사회주의적 이상을 지지하면서 자유주의를 완전히 거부한다.
② 그녀는 핵심 사회 구조로서의 가족 단위를 해체하는 것을 지지한다.
③ 그녀의 주장은 사회주의적 여권주의의 측면들을 미리 나타내지만 여전히 자유주의 전통 안에 머물러 있다.
④ 그녀는 성 평등보다 경제적 문제를 우선시한다.
⑤ 그녀의 비판은 오직 현대적 관련성이 있는 계몽주의 이념에 뿌리를 두고 있다.

22~23

세도나(Sedona)는 심령 에너지를 품고 있다고 여겨지는 소용돌이가 일어나는 명소로 유명한데, 이는 그 지역 원주민의 역사와 그 곳이 "성스러운 땅"으로 지정된 것과 밀접한 관련이 있는 개념이다. 아메리카 원주민의 영성에 따르면, 지리적 장소를 비롯한 무생물도 영(靈)이 깃들면 신성한 것으로 여겨질 수 있다. 이러한 믿음은 토착 문화 전통에 깊이 뿌리내리고 있는 독특한 영적 의미를 세도나에 불어넣는다. 역사적으로 토착 의식을 거행하는 장소로 이용됐던 세도나의 협곡들은 막대한 영적인 힘을 지닌 곳으로 여겨지고 있다. 특히 소용돌이가 일어나는 장소는 명상, 통찰, 치유 에너지의 통로가 된다고 여겨지고 있으며, 이로 인해 그 지역은 영적 성장과 육체적 원기 회복을 찾는 사람들에게 인기 있는 목적지가 되었다. 이들 지역은 그저 지리적 지형들에 불과한 것이 아니라, 물질세계와 형이상학적 세계가 합쳐지는 공간으로 인식되어 전 세계에서 방문객들을 끌어들이고 있다.

어휘

renowned a. 유명한 **hotspot** n. 인기 있는 곳, 명소 **vortex** n. 소용돌이 **psychic** a. 마음의, 영혼의 **designation** n. 지정, 임명 **sacred** a. 신성한 **spirituality** n. 정신적임, 영성(靈性) **inanimate** a. 생명 없는, 무생물의 **geographic** a. 지리적인 **inhabit** v. ~에 살다, 거주하다 **imbue** v. 감화시키다, 불어넣다 **significance** n. 의미; 중요성 **indigenous** a. 토착의, 원산의 **canyon** n. 협곡 **immense** a. 막대한, 무한한 **meditation** n. 묵상, 명상 **clairvoyance** n. 투시(력), 천리안; 비상한 통찰력 **destination** n. 목적지, 행선지 **rejuvenation** n. 회춘, 원기 회복 **feature** n. (산천의) 지세, 지형 **metaphysical** a. 형이상학의 **converge** v. 한데 모아지다, 집중하다

22 내용파악 ③

| 분석 |

"아메리카 원주민의 영성에 따르면, 지리적 장소를 비롯한 무생물도 영(靈)이 깃들면 신성한 것으로 여겨질 수 있다. 이러한 믿음은 토착 문화 전통에 깊이 뿌리내리고 있는 독특한 영적 의미를 세도나에 불어넣는다."라는 내용을 통해 ③이 정답임을 알 수 있다.

본문에 근거할 때, 다음 중 세도나의 소용돌이가 일어나는 장소와 토착적인 영적 기풍 사이의 관계를 가장 잘 설명하고 있는 것은?
① 소용돌이가 일어나는 장소들은 토착 의식을 재해석하는 과정에서 개념화되었다.
② 세도나의 소용돌이가 일어나는 장소들은 전적으로 그 지리적 특이성 때문에 존중되고 있다.
③ 소용돌이가 일어나는 장소의 신성함은 영(靈)이 물리적 장소에 깃들 수 있다는 믿음에서 비롯됐다.
④ 토착적인 영성은 모든 자연 경관을 신성한 소용돌이가 일어나는 장소로 획일적으로 지정한다.
⑤ 소용돌이가 일어나는 장소들은 현대의 형이상학적 이데올로기로부터 그 영적인 탁월성을 얻고 있다.

23 내용파악 ②

| 분석 |

"이들 지역은 그저 지리적 지형들에 불과한 것이 아니라, 물질세계와 형이상학적 세계가 합쳐지는 공간으로 인식되어 전 세계에서 방문객들을 끌어들이고 있다."라는 내용을 통해 ②가 정답임을 알 수 있다.

본문에서 추론할 때, 세도나의 소용돌이가 일어나는 장소들이 영적 깨달음을 추구하는 사람들에게 특히 강한 울림을 줄 수 있는 이유는 무엇인가?
① 그곳이 조상 대대로 내려오는 토착 의식이 거행되는 유일한 장소로서의 역할을 하기 때문이다.
② 그곳이 물질적 에너지와 초월적 에너지가 융합되는 경험을 가능하게 하기 때문이다.
③ 그곳이 심령 현상에 대해 경험적으로 입증된 바를 뒤집기 때문이다.
④ 그곳이 난민들을 위한 전 세계에서 유례없는 성지를 대표하기 때문이다.
⑤ 그곳이 토착 전통과 현대의 영성의 상징적인 연결점을 구현하기 때문이다.

24~25

오늘날의 취업 시장에서 일자리를 찾는 것은 특히 생소한 분야나 업계에 뛰어들려고 하는 사람들에게는 어려운 도전이 된다. 일자리를 찾는 데 성공하려면 고용주의 기대를 전반적으로 이해해야 하고 자신의 역량을 장래의 직무가 요구하는 바에 꼼꼼하게 맞춰야 한다. 이 과정에는 탄탄한 인맥을 형성하는 것은 물론, 관련 경험과 증명서를 취득하여 자신의 자격을 전략적으로 강화하는 것이 필요하다. 더군다나, 자동화된 채용 시스템이 확산됨에 따라, 지원서가 지원자 추적 알고리즘과 호환되도록 맞추어야 할 필요성이 더욱 강조된다. 이와 같은 복잡한 일에도 불구하고, 최우선 목표는 변함이 없다. 그것은 단순한 생계 수단을 넘어 지적인 성취감과 직업적 성장을 가져다주는 일자리를 얻는 것이다.

어휘

contemporary a. 당대의, 동시대의 **pose** v. (요구 따위를) 주장하다, (문제 등을) 제기하다 **formidable** a. 무서운, 만만찮은; 매우 어려운 **necessitate** v. 필요로 하다; (결과를) 수반하다 **comprehensive** a. 포괄적인, 종합적인 **meticulous** a. 지나치게 세심한; 매우 신중한

alignment n. 일렬 배열; 조절 competency n. 적성, 자격, 능력
robust a. 튼튼한, 강건한; 확고한 enhancement n. 증강, 증진
credential n. 자격증명서, 성적증명서; 자격 acquisition n. 취득, 습득 pertinent a. 타당한, 적절한 certification n. 증명; 증명서 교부 proliferation n. 증식, 확산 automated a. 자동화한, 자동의
underscore v. 강조하다 tailor v. (요구·조건·필요에) 맞추어 만들다[고치다] compatibility n. 적합성, 호환성 applicant n. 지원자, 신청자 overarching a. 모든 것에 우선하는, 무엇보다 중요한
steadfast a. 확고부동한, 불변의 transcend v. 초월하다; 능가하다
sustenance n. 생계, 생활

24 빈칸완성 ⑤

| 분석 |

오늘날의 취업 시장에서 일자리를 구하는 것이 쉽지 않음을 이야기하고 있는 내용이므로, 구직자의 궁극적인 목표는 좋은 일자리를 '얻는' 것이라 할 수 있다. land에는 '(애쓴 결과를 통해 직업 등을) 손에 넣다'라는 의미가 있으므로 ⑤가 정답으로 적절하다. ① 거절하다 ② 달아나다 ③ 눈감아주다 ④ 놓치다

25 내용파악 ②

| 분석 |

"일자리를 찾는 데 성공하려면 고용주의 기대를 전반적으로 이해해야 하고 자신의 역량을 장래의 직무에서 요구하는 바에 꼼꼼하게 맞춰야 한다."라고 했으므로 ②가 본문의 내용과 일치하는 진술이다.

다음 중 위 글의 내용을 정확하게 반영하는 진술은?
① 새로운 분야에 뛰어드는 것은 최소한의 노력으로 되는 쉬운 일이다.
② 취업에 성공하려면 기술을 고용주의 요구에 맞춰야 한다.
③ 자동화된 시스템은 취업 지원 절차를 간소화했다.
④ 경제적 생계는 고용의 유일한 목표이다.
⑤ 자격증은 취업 시장에서의 성공과는 관련이 없다.

26~28

지진을 예측하는 것은 오랫동안 지진학의 어려운 도전이었다. 기술의 발전과 광범위한 연구에도 불구하고, 지진이 발생하는 시간, 장소, 규모를 정확히 예측하는 것은 여전히 잘 해결되지 않는다. 전통적인 방법에서는 지질 단층과 지진 활동을 감시하는 데 초점을 맞추지만, 이러한 접근 방식은 신뢰할 만한 예측 능력을 만들어내지 못했다. 여러 학문 분야가 제휴한 최근의 연구들은 위성 관측, 동물의 행동, 대기의 이상 현상 등의 다양한 데이터를 통합하는 경우에는 예측 모델을 향상시킬 수도 있음을 시사하고 있다. 그러나 과학계에서는 이러한 방법의 효과에 대해 의견이 분분하며, 지진의 영향을 줄이기 위해서는 지속적으로 연구하고 종합적인 조기경보 시스템을 개발해야 할 필요성을 강조하고 있다.

| 어휘 |

formidable a. 무서운, 만만찮은 seismology n. 지진학
magnitude n. (길이·규모·수량) 크기; (지진의) 진도 seismic a. 지진의 elusive a. (뜻·성격 등이) 파악하기 어려운, 알기 어려운
geological a. 지질학의; 지질의 fault n. 〈지질학〉 단층
interdisciplinary a. 여러 학문 상호 간의, 여러 학문 분야가 제휴한; (서로 다른 분야 상호 간의) 협동(연구)의 integrate v. 통합하다, 전체로 합치다 observation n. 관찰, 주목 anomaly n. 변칙, 이례
emphasize v. 강조하다 mitigate v. 누그러뜨리다

26 내용파악 ④

| 분석 |

'지질 단층과 지진 활동을 감시하는 것만으로는 지진을 제대로 예측할 수 없으며, 위성 관측, 동물의 행동, 대기의 이상 현상 등의 다양한 데이터를 통합하면, 예측 모델을 향상시킬 수도 있다'는 내용을 통해 다양한 요인들이 지진 예측을 어렵게 하고 있음을 알 수 있다.

지진 예측이 지진학에서 지속적으로 어려운 일인 이유는 무엇인가?
① 현재의 기술이 정밀한 예측 모델을 뛰어넘는다.
② 전통적인 방법은 대기의 이상 현상에만 곧잘 집중한다.
③ 지질 단층이 너무나도 불규칙하게 움직여서 감시가 어렵다.
④ 다원적인 유인(誘因)들이 지진의 시간, 위치, 규모를 예측하기 어렵게 한다.
⑤ 과학적 의견 불일치가 방법론의 발전을 지연시킨다.

27 내용파악 ④

| 분석 |

'여러 학문 분야가 제휴한 최근의 연구들은 위성 관측, 동물의 행동, 대기의 이상 현상 등의 다양한 데이터를 통합하는 경우에 예측 모델을 향상시킬 수도 있음을 시사하고 있다'고 했으므로 ④가 정답이 된다.

여러 학문 분야가 제휴한 데이터를 통합하는 것이 전통적인 지진 예측을 어떻게 향상시키는가?
① 대기의 이상 현상과 같은 현상들에 집중함으로써 단층 감시에 의문을 제기한다.
② 새로운 기술과 인프라를 요구한다.
③ 비전통적 방법에서 전통적인 기술로 초점을 옮긴다.
④ 동물 행동, 위성 데이터, 지진 등 사이의 간과된 연관성을 밝혀낸다.

⑤ 변수를 추가하지만 일관된 결과를 내지 못해 예측을 더 어렵게 만든다.

28 내용파악 ④

| 분석 |

다양한 데이터를 통합하면 예측 모델을 향상시킬 수도 있다는 견해에 대해, "과학계에서는 이러한 방법의 효과에 대해 의견이 분분하다"라고 했으므로, ④가 정답으로 가장 적절하다.

지진 예측을 위해 여러 학문 분야가 제휴한 방법을 과학계는 어떻게 바라보는가?
① 조심스럽게 낙관적인 태도를 보이면서, 가능성은 있지만 검증이 필요하다고 본다
② 회의적인 태도를 보이면서, 새로운 방법들에 실증적인 엄격함이 부족하다고 본다
③ 저항하는 태도를 보이면서, 실험적 접근 방법보다 이미 확립된 접근방법을 선호한다
④ 의견이 나뉘어 있으며, 일부는 혁신을 지지하지만 다른 일부는 신뢰성을 의심한다
⑤ 협력적인 태도를 보이면서, 다양한 방법을 통합하여 통합된 모델을 구축하려 한다

29~30

업무 회의 중에, 그들은 문제를 정면으로 돌파하기보다는 문제의 핵심을 완전히 무시한 채 사소한 부분을 따지는 일에 몰두했다. 진전이 없는 데 대해 좌절한 나는 마침내 입을 열어 말했다. "본론으로 들어갑시다. 우리의 매출 수치는 떨어지고 있습니다. 그래서 상황을 반전시킬 새로운 전략이 필요합니다." 잠시 방 안이 조용해졌지만, 곧이어 우리는 본격적으로 논의를 시작했으며, 실질적으로 중요한 일에 집중했다.

| 어휘 |

indulge in (취미·욕망 따위에) 빠지다, 탐닉하다   **split hairs** 사소한 것에 지나치게 신경 쓰다   **frustrated** a. 좌절한   **cut to the chase** 바로 본론으로 들어가다   **strategy** n. 전략   **turn things around** 상황을 반전시키다   **get down to business** (본격적으로) 시작하다, 착수하다

29 빈칸완성 ⑤

| 분석 |

'문제를 직접적으로 다루다', '용감하게 정면으로 맞서다'라는 의미의 관용표현은 take the bull by the horns이다.

30 동의어 ③

| 분석 |

cut to the chase는 "바로 본론으로 들어가다"라는 의미이므로 ③의 의미로 쓰인 것으로 파악할 수 있다.

문맥을 바탕으로 밑줄 친 표현 "Let's cut to the chase"의 가장 적절한 의미를 선택하시오.
① 달리기를 시작하자.
② 영화를 보러 가자.
③ 핵심 문제에 집중하자.
④ 추격전을 조직하자.
⑤ 마지막 슬라이드로 건너뛰자.

31~33

자연 그대로의 별이 빛나는 하늘과 어두운 밤의 수면을 찾아 나서는 것은 점점 더 늘어나는 관광 트렌드가 되어가고 있다. 엄청난 통계자료가 전 세계적으로 자연 그대로의 밤이 사라지고 있다는 것을 보여준다. 빛 공해는 전 세계적으로 매년 10%씩 증가하고 있으며, 유럽과 북아메리카의 인구 중 99%는 이제 집에서 별을 볼 수 없게 되었다. 빛 공해는 우리의 건강에 악영향을 미치고 수면을 방해하기 때문에, 많은 도시 거주자들은 스위치를 끄고 자연 그대로의 어둠 속에서 수면을 취하는 것이 가져다주는 휴식과 회복을 찾고 있다. 또한, (코로나로 인한) 봉쇄 조치의 여파로 더 많은 사람들이 자연과 이어지기를 기대함에 따라, 여행자들이 경외감과 우주와 이어져 있다는 느낌을 주는 경험을 원하는 것은 일리 있는 일이다. 어두운 하늘을 찾아 떠나는 여행은 별 바라보기, 달 바라보기, 오로라 찾기, 천문학 탐구 등과 같은 천문관광과, 야간 하이킹, 야행성 야생동물 관찰, 야간 명상 및 건강 체험 등과 같은 야간 활동과, 수면관광을 통해 자연과 이어지도록 해준다. 이러한 경험들은 밤하늘과 관련된 황도대, 신화 및 전설과 같은 관련된 문화적 테마를 통합할 수도 있다.

| 어휘 |

staggering a. 어마어마한, 경이적인   **statistics** n. 통계; 통계학   **indicate** v. 지적하다, 보이다   **affect** v. 영향을 미치다, 악영향을 미치다   **disturb** v. 방해하다, 폐를 끼치다   **dweller** n. 거주자, 주민   **aftermath** n. (전쟁·재해 따위의) 결과, 여파, 영향   **lockdown** n. 엄중한 감금, 봉쇄   **awe** n. 경외, 두려움   **astrotourism** n. 천문관광 (별 자체를 구경하거나 혹은 천문과 관련된 로켓 발사, 우주, 일식, 월식 등을 구경하기 위한 관광)   **nocturnal** a. 밤의, 야간의   **incorporate** v. 통합하다; 혼합하다, 섞다   **zodiac** n. 〈천문학〉 황도대(黃道帶)

31 글의 제목   ⑤

| 분석 |

본문은 '인공조명의 영향을 받지 않는 자연 그대로의 하늘과 어두운 밤을 찾아 떠나는 여행이 늘어나고 있음'을 이야기하고 있으므로, ⑤가 주제를 반영하는 제목으로 가장 적절하다.

본문의 주제를 가장 잘 요약하는 제목을 고르시오.
① 유럽에서의 별 관측의 역사
② 빛 공해와 도시 개발
③ 수면 관광의 이점
④ 야행성 야생동물과 그들의 서식지
⑤ 점증하는 어두운 하늘 여행 트렌드에 대한 탐구

32 빈칸완성   ③

| 분석 |

빛 공해가 건강에 악영향을 미치고 수면을 방해한다고 했으므로, 스위치를 끄고 자연 그대로의 어둠 속에서 잠을 잠으로써 얻게 되는 것으로는 '휴식과 회복'이 가장 적절하다.

빈칸에 들어가기에 가장 적절한 표현은 무엇인가?
① 에너지와 자극
② 흥분과 모험
③ 휴식과 회복
④ 오락과 파티
⑤ 활동과 자극

33 내용파악   ①

| 분석 |

"더 많은 사람들이 자연과 이어지기를 기대함에 따라, 여행자들이 경외감과 우주와 이어져 있다는 느낌을 주는 경험을 원하는 것은 일리 있는 일이다"라고 했으므로 ①이 정답이다.

많은 사람들이 어두운 하늘 여행에 관심이 있는 이유는?
① 자연과 다시 이어져서 경외감과 우주와 이어져 있다는 느낌을 경험하기 위해
② 에너지가 충만한 야간 파티와 축제에 참여하기 위해
③ 자신이 있는 지역의 문화와 관련된 신화와 전설에 대해 배우기 위해
④ 자연 환경 속에서 일출을 보기 위해
⑤ 고등 천문학 연구에 참여하기 위해

SOONGSIL UNIVERSITY | 숭실대학교 인문계

TEST p. 460~481

01	③	02	①	03	②	04	③	05	①	06	②	07	③	08	②	09	①	10	④
11	②	12	②	13	④	14	③	15	④	16	①	17	②	18	①	19	④	20	④
21	②	22	②	23	②	24	②	25	③	26	①	27	①	28	②	29	①	30	④
31	④	32	②	33	④	34	③	35	④	36	③	37	①	38	①	39	③	40	①
41	④	42	①	43	①	44	③	45	①	46	②	47	③	48	③	49	③	50	④

01 문의 구성 ③

| 분석 |
③의 앞에 완전한 문장이 주어져 있으므로 ③의 자리에 접속사 없이 정동사가 올 수 없다. 따라서 ③을 gender and the nation's continuing drama of race를 목적어로 취하는 전치사 including 으로 고쳐야 한다.

| 어휘 |
the Gothic 고딕 양식(19세기 미국의 고딕 문학이나 미술 전통) **forum** n. 공개토론장, 포럼 **gender** n. 성별, 젠더 **drama** n. 극적 사건들

| 해석 |
고딕 양식의 연구는 젠더와 미국의 지속적인 인종 관련 극적 사건들을 포함한 미국 사회의 핵심 쟁점 중 일부를 논의할 공개토론장을 마련해준다.

02 관계사 ①

| 분석 |
what 절 이하의 동사 was based 뒤에는 전치사 on이 필요하므로 ①의 what을 '전치사+관계대명사', on which로 고쳐야 한다.

| 어휘 |
conception n. 개념 **reform** n. 개혁 **illustrate** v. 예증하다, 예시하다 **activity** n. 활동 **New York Tract Society** 뉴욕 트랙트 협회(트랙트 협회: 교회 팸플릿의 출판·보급 활동을 하는 단체) **distribute** v. 분배하다, 배포하다, 유통시키다

| 해석 |
개혁 운동의 기반이 된 현실 개념이 뉴욕 트랙트 협회의 활동에서보다 더 극적으로 드러난 곳은 없다. 이 협회의 구성원들은 수천 명에 달했는데, 한 달에 한 번 뉴욕 시의 모든 가구에 종교 책자를 배포함으로써 이 도시의 가난한 사람들을 돕고자 했다.

03 논리완성 ②

| 분석 |
정부는 기후 변화가 농업에 끼치는 부정적인 영향을 완화하기 위해 노력할 것이므로 ②가 정답으로 적절하다.

| 어휘 |
implement v. 집행하다, 실행하다 **encourage** v. 독려하다, 격려하다 **mitigate** v. 완화하다, 경감시키다, 줄이다 **negative** a. 부정적인 **neglect** v. 무시하다, 방치하다 **amplify** v. 확대하다, 증폭시키다

| 해석 |
정부는 기후변화가 농업에 끼치는 부정적 영향들을 완화할 새로운 정책을 집행했다.

04 논리완성 ③

| 분석 |
최종 결정을 위한 글이나 문서가 요구할 조건으로는 '상세한'이라는 의미의 detailed가 적절하다.

| 어휘 |
submit v. 제출하다 **premature** a. 너무 이른, 시기상조의 **final decision** 최종 결정 **obscure** a. 애매모호한, 익명의 **detailed** a. 상세한 **disdainful** a. 업신여기는, 무시하는

| 해석 |
회의 동안 매니저는 팀원들에게 최종 결정을 위한 상세한 버전을 제출하라고 요청했다.

05 논리완성 ①

| 분석 |

복잡한 개념을 simplify한다고 했으므로 그 결과물은 simple할 것이다.

| 어휘 |

praise v. 칭찬하다 **simplify** v. 단순화하다 **complex** a. 복잡한 **term** n. 용어 **public** n. 공중, 대중, 많은 사람들 **ambiguous** a. 애매모호한, 불분명한 **condescending** a. 생색내는, 거들먹거리는 **distorted** a. 왜곡된

| 해석 |

그 과학자는 복잡한 개념을 대중을 위해 간단한 용어로 단순화하는 능력으로 칭찬받았다.

06 논리완성   ②

| 분석 |

토론에서는 각자에게 자신의 생각을 '표현하게' 할 것이므로 express가 정답이다.

| 어휘 |

encourage v. 격려하다 **openly** ad. 드러내놓고, 숨김없이, 공개적으로 **suppress** v. 억압하다 **discourage** v. 좌절시키다 **surprise** v. 놀라게 하다

| 해석 |

그 교사는 학생들에게 토론 시간 동안 자기 생각을 숨김없이 표현하라고 격려했다.

07 동의어   ③

| 어휘 |

protester n. 시위자 **indifference** n. 무관심, 냉담(= disregard) **authorities** n. 당국 **refuse** v. 거절하다 **address** v. 다루다, 대처하다 **concern** n. 우려; 관심사 **empathy** n. 공감, 감정이입 **favor** n. 호의 **hostility** n. 적대감, 적대

| 해석 |

시위자들의 요구에 당국은 무관심으로 대응하여 그들의 관심사를 다루기를 거부했다.

08 동의어   ②

| 어휘 |

policy n. 정책 **skepticism** n. 의심, 회의(= distrust) **approval** n. 승인 **neutrality** n. 중립

| 해석 |

새 정책은 많은 사람들이 그 효과를 의심했으므로 대중들의 회의적인 반응에 직면했다.

09 동의어   ①

| 어휘 |

announce v. 발표하다 **remunerative** a. 수익성 좋은, 수지맞는 (= lucrative) **deal** n. 거래 **significantly** ad. 상당히 **annual** a. 연간의 **revenue** n. 수익 **questionable** a. 의심스러운 **complex** a. 복잡한 **tentative** a. 잠정적인

| 해석 |

그 회사는 연간 수익을 크게 증가시킬 수지맞는 거래를 발표했다.

10 동의어   ④

| 어휘 |

region n. 지역 **arid** a. 건조한(= dry) **rainfall** n. 강우 **extreme** a. 극단적인 **humid** a. 습한 **fertile** a. 비옥한

| 해석 |

그 지역은 강우량이 연중 극히 적은 건조 기후로 알려져 있다.

11~13

감각 행위의 의미는 반드시 단일하진 않다. 가령 의사가 신체검사 동안 환자를 만지는 방식은 주로 데이터 수집 과정으로 간주되거나 당사자들을 위한 개인적 의미를 띨 수 있다. 그러나 의학에서 살펴보겠지만, 그것은 또한 특정한 사회 역사와 중요한 상징적 의미도 갖고 있다.

사회적 기능을 인식한 감각 행위조차도 다양한 층위의 의미를 갖고 있다. 악수는 친근함의 제스처, 지배하려는 시도, 은혜를 베푸는 행위, 친밀함으로 초대하는 신호, 평등의 표현, 차이를 메우는 것, 계약의 확정, 예절의 위반 등으로 다양하게 해석될 수 있다. 예를 들어, 호주 총리였던 줄리아 길라드는 엘리자베스 2세 여왕에게 절을 하는 대신 악수를 했을 때 엄밀히 말하자면 예절 위반을 저지르고 있었던 것이다. 그러나 호주가 과거 영국 식민지였다는 문화적 맥락 속에서 보면, 단순한 사회적 실수처럼 보일 수 있는 이 악수 행위가 오히려 평등과 현대성을 상징하는 중요한 제스처였다. 반면 엘리자베스 여왕이 아일랜드 공화국군(IRA)의 전 사령관과 악수를 했을 때 그 행위는 함의가 전혀 달랐다. 그것은 두 오랜 적대 세력을 대표하는 사람들 간의 극적인 화해의 제스처로서 "궁극의 악수"로 간주되었다.

18세기의 재사(才士), 시드니 스미스가 신뢰할 만한 가이드라면, 그의 시대에도 상당히 다양한 악수의 방식과 의미가 존재했다. 콘스턴스 클래슨의 지적대로, "고위직"의 악수는 "턱 근처에서 짧고 빠르게 흔드는 방식"이었고, 성직자들 간의 악수는 한 손가락만 내미는 방식이었다. 반면 "시골 스타일"의 악수는 "상대방의 손을 강하게 움켜쥐어 정력적인

건강과 따뜻한 마음, 그리고 대도시와의 거리를 나타내되, 상대방 입장에서는 악수를 풀었을 때 손가락이 부러지지 않은 것에 안도감을 느끼게 하는 방식"이었다. 단순한 악수가 전달할 수 있는 함의의 범위는 촉각 행위가, 우리로 하여금 단지 책을 쓰거나 예술을 창작하는 등, 사회적으로 의미 있는 다른 행위에 종사하도록 해주는 신체적 노동일뿐 아니라 그 자체로도 상당한 잠재적 의미가 있다는 것을 보여준다.

| 어휘 |

significance n. 중요성, 의의 **unitary** a. 단일한, 통합된 **data-gathering** a. 데이터 수집의 **participant** n. 참여자, 참가자 **symbolic** a. 상징적인 **gesture** n. 제스처, 몸짓 **dominate** v. 지배하다, 장악하다 **condescension** n. 겸손한 체함, 생색내기 **intimacy** n. 친밀함 **equality** n. 평등 **breach** n. 위반, 침해 **etiquette** n. 예절, 예의 **colonial** a. 식민지의 **reconciliation** n. 화해, 조정 **wit** n. 재사, 재치 있는 인물 **reliable** a. 신뢰할 수 있는 **connotation** n. 함의 **curtsy** v. 절하다 **technically** ad. 엄밀하게 말해 **clerical** a. 성직자의, 성직에 관한 **rustic** a. 소박한, 시골의 **grasp** n. 움켜쥠, 파악 **betoken** v. 나타내다, 암시하다 **relief** n. 안도, 안심 **demonstrate** v. 입증하다, 보여주다 **tactile** a. 촉각의, 만질 수 있는 **labour** n. 노동, 수고 **engage in** 참여하다, 종사하다 **primarily** ad. 주로

| 11 | 동의어 | ② |

| 분석 |

breach는 "위반"이라는 뜻이므로 정답은 violation이다.

다음 중 ⓐ를 가장 잘 대체할 수 있는 것은?
① 결과
② 위반
③ 지속함
④ 염증

| 12 | 내용파악 | ② |

| 분석 |

두 번째 문단에서 열거한 악수의 의미에 관한 사례 중 기만의 표현이라는 항목은 없다.

다음 중 악수의 사회적 의미로 언급되지 않은 것은?
① 애정의 표시
② 기만의 표현
③ 화해의 표명
④ 권력의 표현

| 13 | 글의 목적 | ④ |

| 분석 |

첫 번째 단락에서 감각 행위의 의미에 대해 설명하고 두 번째 단락부터 악수를 예로 들고 있으므로 글의 목적으로는 '촉각 행위의 다양한 역할을 설명하는 것'이 가장 적절하다.

다음 중 이 글의 목적을 가장 잘 기술한 것은?
① 악수의 통일된 의미를 보여주는 것
② 신체적 제스처의 다양한 유형을 소개하는 것
③ 엘리자베스 여왕의 악수 스타일을 교정하는 것
④ 촉각 행위의 다양한 역할을 설명하는 것

14~15

영국에서 가장 큰 자원보존 단체의 본부에는 또 다른 깃털, 아니, 사실은 깃털 수집품이 상자에 담겨 보관되어 있다. 그것들은 다른, 그러나 똑같이 상징적인 이야기를 전한다. 이 깃털은 공개된 전시물이 아니다. 왕립조류보호협회(RSPB)의 기록 보관소를 방문할 예약을 하고, 운이 좋아 들어간다면, 이 깃털 상자는 사서가 당신에게 가져다줄 수도 있다(혹은 그렇지 않을 수도 있다). 왕립조류보호협회는 거대한 단체로, 110만 명 이상의 회원, 16만 헥타르에 걸친 224곳의 자연 보호 구역, 2,000명의 직원, 약 12,000명의 자원봉사자를 보유하고 있다. 연간 수입은 1억 4천만 파운드를 초과하며, 엄청난 정치적 영향력을 행사한다. 오늘날 이 단체가 벌이는 사업은 페레그린 팔콘(매)이든, 피그미과일박쥐든, 수마트라코뿔소든, 자연을 보존하는 국제 활동이다. 그러나 이 단체의 주요 인물들은 대부분 조류 애호가들이며 이들 중 대다수는 역사적으로 남성들이었다. 영국에서 새들은 본능적으로 남자들의 것인 경향이 있는 것 같다.

늘 그랬던 것은 아니었다. RSPB는 여성들, 그것도 아주 특이한 목적을 지닌 여성들에 의해 설립되었다. 그들은 모자에 들어간 새 깃털 패션을 몰아낼 작정이었다. 1870년대에서 1920년대까지의 반세기 동안, 지구상에서 가장 수익성 높은 상품 시장 중 하나에서의 여성 모자 거래를 위해 야생 조류가 세계 도처에서 체계적으로 도살당했다. 그 거래는 최고조에 달했을 때 영국에 연간 2천만 파운드(오늘날로 환산하면 2억 4백만 파운드) 상당의 어마어마한 가치를 지닌 것이었다. 1891년, 만족을 모르는 깃털 패션이 또 한 단계 더 성황을 이루자, 두 곳의 순수 여성 단체 — 하나는 크라이던에 있었고 하나는 맨체스터에 있었음 — 가 힘을 합쳐 새들을 구하기 위해 나섰다. 그들은 스스로에게 "조류 보호 협회"라는 야심찬 이름을 부여했고 그들의 결단은 1904년에 왕실 칙허장으로 보상받았다.

| 어휘 |

feather n. 깃털 **headquarter** n. 본부 **conservation** n. 보존 **charity** n. 자선, 자선단체 **archive** n. 기록보관소 **behemoth** n. 거대조직, 거대기업 **reserve** n. 보존구역 **volunteer** n. 자원봉사자 **wield** v. 발휘하다 **singular** a. 특이한 **stamp out** 몰아내다 **slaughter** v. 살육하다 **millinery trade** 모자 산업 **commodity** n. 상품 **insatiable** a. 만족을 모르는 **lucrative** a. 수익성 있는, 돈벌이가 되는

14 동의어   ③

| 분석 |

behemoth는 원래 '거인, 거대한 짐승'의 뜻이지만 여기서는 '거대한 조직'이라는 뜻으로 쓰였으므로 정답은 large organization이다.

다음 중 Ⓐ와 의미가 가장 가까운 것은?
① 비활동적인 기관
② 엄격한 협회
③ 거대한 조직
④ 친밀한 관계

15 내용파악   ④

| 분석 |

두 번째 문단의 두 번 째 문장부터 RSPB의 원래 목적과 활약이 설명된다. 처음에는 SPB로 시작했으나 왕실의 인정을 받아 RSPB가 되었다. 깃털 모자 거래로 인한 조류의 도살과 멸종을 막고 조류를 보호하려는 단체였으므로 정답은 ④이다. ① 예약을 하고 운이 좋아야 들어가므로 접근이 쉽지 않다. ② 페레그린 팔콘(매)이든, 피그미과일박쥐든, 수마트라코뿔소든, 자연의 모든 것을 보존한다. ③ 연간 수입이 1억 4천만 파운드 이상이라고만 했고 수입원은 밝히지 않았다.

다음 중 RSPB에 관해 옳은 것은?
① 대중의 쉬운 접근을 위해 다양한 깃털을 수집했다.
② 오직 새의 깃털만을 보존해 보호했다.
③ 깃털을 다루는 국제 교역으로 이익을 벌어들였다.
④ 깃털 모자를 쓰는 여성들과의 싸움에 관심을 보였다.

16~18

모니라는 침팬지는 네덜란드 동물원에 새로 도착했지만 예기치 않게 새끼를 잃었다. 침팬지의 질투를 연구하는 대학원생 조에 골즈보로는 어느 겨울 아침, 높은 나무 그루터기 위에 홀로 앉아 조심스럽게 무언가 움직이지 않는 것을 품에 안고 있는 모니를 발견했다. 가까이 가서 살펴본 골즈보로는 그것이 생명 없는 갓 태어난 새끼라는 것을 깨달았다. 사육사들은 처음에는 의심했지만 결국 모니에게서 새끼를 빼앗으려 하다 실패했다.

투시라는 다른 암컷 침팬지는 전에 유산을 겪었는데 모니 근처를 서성거리기 시작했다. 투시는 몇 년 전 다큐멘터리 촬영 중 드론을 쫓던 것으로 유명세를 얻었었다. 투시는 이틀 동안 모니 곁을 떠나지 않았고, 모니는 계속해서 작은 시신을 안고 있었다. 결국, 사육사들과의 싸움 중 새끼가 모니의 손아귀에서 떨어졌고, 투시는 그것을 잡아 돌려주지 않았다. 이로 인해 모니는 매우 고통스러워 했고, 특히 사육사들이 투시를 다른 방에 격리시키자 더욱 극심한 고통을 겪었다. 골즈보로는 이들의 행동을 해석하느라 애를 먹었다. 모니는 인간이 쉽게 이해할 수 있는 모성애에 의해 움직이는 것처럼 보였지만, 투시는 자신의 상실에 대한 기억에 반응했을 수도 있었다. 그러나 두 침팬지 중 어느 쪽이든 새끼의 죽음을 진정으로 이해했는지는 여전히 불확실했다. 이들은 새끼가 다시 살아날 것이라 믿었을지도 모른다. 이 불확실성은 침팬지가 동물의 왕국에서 인간과 가장 가까운 종에 속한다는 사실을 고려하면 주목할 만하다.

| 어휘 |

newly ad. 새로 **unexpectedly** ad. 예기치 않게 **jealousy** n. 질투 **tree stump** n. 나무 그루터기 **cradle** v. 부드럽게 안다 **inspection** n. 살펴봄, 조사 **lifeless** a. 죽은 **newborn** n. 신생아 **skeptical** a. 의심하는 **miscarriage** n. 유산 **tiny** a. 아주 작은 **grab** v. 움켜잡다 **distressed** a. 고통 받는 **isolate** v. 격리시키다, 분리시키다 **readily** ad. 쉽게 **maternal** a. 모성의 **attachment** n. 애착 **comprehend** v. 이해하다 **relative** n. 친척 **revive** v. 되살아나다

16 글의 제목   ①

| 분석 |

동물원 침팬지들이 죽은 새끼를 놓고 보이는 애매모호한 감정에 대한 글이므로 ①이 정답이다. 모성본능은 모니의 경우에도 확실한 것은 아니었고 투시의 경우에는 모성본능보다는 상실에 대한 기억에 의한 것으로 보였지만 그것도 불확실했으므로 ③은 제목으로 적합하지 않다.

위 글의 주제를 가장 잘 담아내고 있는 제목은?
① 동물원 침팬지들의 복잡한 감정
② 죽음을 이해하기: 인간의 관점
③ 사로잡힌 침팬지들의 모성본능
④ 어느 대학원생의 동물원 관찰

17 빈칸완성   ②

|분석|
바로 다음에 a lifeless newborn이라는 표현이 나오므로 새끼가 움직이지 않았다고 추론할 수 있다.

빈칸 Ⓐ에서, 다음 중 글을 가장 잘 완성시키는 표현은?
① 활발한
② 움직이지 않는
③ 우호적인
④ 소송하기 좋아하는

18 빈칸완성   ①

|분석|
다큐멘터리 촬영 중에 근접촬영을 위해 드론이 가까이 날아오면 침팬지는 이것을 적으로 알고 공격했을 것이다.

다음 중 Ⓑ에 가장 적절한 것은?
① 공격하기
② 끓이기
③ 부패시키기
④ 무단침입하기

19~20

앵글로-색슨족의 기원을 알려주는 당대에 가까운 자료는 없다. 이유는 명백하다. 이 앵글로-색슨이라는 게르만족은 영국에 정착하고 나서 첫 두 세기 동안 문맹이었기 때문이다. 따라서 그들의 초기 흥망성쇠는 브리튼족의 적대적인 시각을 통해, 외국인의 잘못된 시각을 통해, 그리고 본인들의 불완전한 기억 전통을 통해서만 슬쩍 엿볼 수 있을 뿐이다. 6세기 후반까지는 정보에 입각한 추측 작업이 역사를 대신할 수밖에 없다.
고고학은 첫 번째 단서를 제공한다. 410년이 되기 몇 년 전에 영국에 게르만 전사들이 있었다는 사실을 고고학이 보여주기 때문이다. 로마 후기의 묘지들, 특히 옥스퍼드셔에서 에식스 해안까지 이어지는 템스 강 하류 유역의 묘지들에서는 로마 군대에서 프랑크족과 색슨족 용병들이 착용하던 벨트 장식이 있는 매장들이 나왔다. 이러한 군대들이 갈리아에 분명 정착했듯 영국에도 정착했다면, 5세기 중반의 침략자들이 두세 세대 전에 먼저 왔던 같은 종족들과 합류했을 가능성이 있다. 박공 기둥이 달리고 지지대를 낮추어 지은 오두막은 5세기와 6세기 잉글랜드 정착지의 특징인데, 200개가 넘는 이런 오두막이 템스 강 하구의 머킹 근처 거대한 구역에서 발견되었다. 이 오두막 단지는 런던 접근을 방어하기 위해 400년경에 배치된 용병들을 수용했을 것이라는 이야기

가 나왔다. 만일 그렇다면 앵글로색슨 정착의 지속된 역사는 로마 통치 하에 시작된다.
그 후 수백 년 동안 영국인들은 자기 조상들의 도착 시점을 이보다 몇 십 년 후로 잡았고, 게르만 정착민들의 대규모 도착은 430년대부터 계속 진행되었던 것 같다. 이 놀라운 과정을 고려하기 전에, 먼저 질문해야 할 점은 이 침략자들이 누구였고 이들이 어떤 사람들이었는가 하는 것이다. 첫 번째 질문에 대한 답은, 모든 현대 학자들이 잘 대답할 수 있는 거의 그만큼, 비드가 미지의 출처에서 인용한, 놀랍도록 잘 알려진 구절에 들어있는데, 그것은 곧 "이들은 매우 강력한 세 게르만부족인 색슨족, 앵글족, 주트족에서 왔다."라는 구절이다.

|어휘|
contemporary a. 당대의, 현대의   **origin** n. 기원   **obvious** a. 명백한, 뻔한   **Germanic** a. 게르만족의   **illiterate** a. 문맹의   **fortunes** n. 부침, 성쇠   **glimpse** v. 흘끗 보다   **ill-informed** a. 잘 모르는   **guesswork** n. 추측   **archaeology** n. 고고학   **burials** n. 봉분, 매장지   **belt-fitting** n. 벨트 장식   **mercenary** n. 용병; 피고용인   **invader** n. 침략자   **gable-post** n. 박공 기둥   **characteristic** a. 특징인   **complex** a. 복잡한   **guard** v. 지키다, 수호하다   **remarkable** a. 놀라운   **startlingly** ad. 놀랍게도   **tribe** n. 부족

19 내용일치   ④

|분석|
① 로마 후기의 공동묘지는 오직 로마의 전사들만을 위한 것이 아니라 프랑크 및 색슨족 전사가 있었음을 보여준다고 했다. ② 게르만 교역 상인들에 대한 언급은 없다. ③ 로마 전사들이 아니라 로마 군대의 프랑크 족과 색슨 족 용병들이다. 마지막 인용 구절에 의하면 ④가 정답이다.

다음 중 옳은 것은?
① 로마 후기의 공동묘지는 오직 로마의 전사들만을 위한 것이었다.
② 로마 유물은 400년에 게르만 교역 상인들이 있었음을 보여준다.
③ 로마의 전사들은 400년 경 박공 기둥이 달리고 지지대를 낮추어 지은 오두막에 살았고 벨트 장식을 착용한 듯 보인다.
④ 침략자들은 색슨족, 앵글족, 주트족으로 쉽게 규명된다.

20 글의 목적   ④

|분석|
처음부터 기록 부족에 대한 설명으로 시작하며, 고고학과 전승, 외국인의 기록에 의존해야 한다는 점을 설명하고 있다. 즉, 전체적

으로 왜 기록이 부족한지, 대신 어떤 증거들을 통해 추정할 수 있는지를 설명하는 구조의 글이므로 ④가 정답이다.

위 글의 목적은?
① 게르만족의 기원에 대한 두 가지 다른 역사를 대조시키는 것
② 앵글로 색슨 정착이 골족의 통치 하에서 시작되었음을 드러내는 것
③ 로마 공동묘지의 증거를 교정하는 것
④ 게르만 침략에 대한 역사적 기록의 부족을 설명하는 것

21~23

영어를 세계 언어로 만든 것은 무엇일까? 영어가 성공한 배경에는 두 가지 주요 요인이 있다. 첫째, 식민지 강국 영국의 팽창과 영향력이다. 19세기 말까지 대영제국은 지구상의 상당 부분을 차지했고, 영국 군주의 백성들은 세계 인구의 거의 4분의 1에 달했다. 둘째, 미국의 20세기 경제적, 군사적, 과학적 선도국가로서의 지위다.
그리고 그 외에 다른 기여 요인들이 있다. 그 중 하나는 현대 기술로 인한 국제 소통 필요성이 증가하고 있다는 점이다. 전화, 라디오, 텔레비전, 제트기, 컴퓨터와 같은 혁신들 각각은 국제 소통을 할 수 있는 잠재력에 큰 변화를 가져왔다. 전 세계의 항공 교통 관제사는 러시아, 덴마크, 중국의 조종사와 대화할 때 영어를 사용하며, 이는 JFK 공항, 스키폴 공항, 나리타 공항을 가리지 않는다. 게다가 정보 기술 분야에서는 물론 미국 영어가 최고의 지위를 차지하고 있다.
또 다른 요인은, 사람들의 모국어가 몇 개이거나 다양한 국가나 국가집단에서는 영어가 중립적 토대로 여겨진다는 점에서 공용어로 선호될 수 있다는 점이다. 세계 경제에서 많은 다국적 기업들은 영어를 업무상 언어로 채택했다. 러시아에서 이루어지는 비즈니스의 절반이 영어로 진행된다고 한다. 유럽연합(EU)에서는 언어 장벽을 넘는 소통에서 사용하는 "실무 언어"가 대개 영어인데, 영어가 충분히 널리 사용되는 유일한 언어기 때문에 마지못해 채택된다. (영국 제도를 제외한) 유럽연합 소속 국가 전체에서 학생 10명 중 9명은 배울 외국어로 영어를 선택한다. 영어는 EU의 제도적 활동들과 많은 문화적 경제적 생활 영역에 점점 더 빈틈없이 침투하고 있다고 한다. 오늘날 영어 없이 국제적인 경력을 쌓는 것은 거의 불가능하다. 영어는 세계를 향한 창으로, 경제적, 사회적, 정치적 성공을 거두기 위한 최선의 수단으로 여겨진다.

| 어휘 |

factor n. 요인 **expansion** n. 팽창 **colonial power** 식민지 열강 **empire** n. 제국 **considerable** a. 상당한 **status** n. 지위 **contributing** a. 기여하는 **innovation** n. 혁신, 일신 **step-change** n. 장족의 발전, 큰 변화 **potential** n. 잠재력 **lingua franca** 공용어, 국제어 **neutral** a. 중립적인 **vernacular** n. 토착어, 방언 **barrier** n. 장벽 **reluctantly** ad. 마지못해 **permeate** v. 침투하다 **institutional** a. 제도의 **ascendant** n. 우세, 지배

21 글의 제목   ③

| 분석 |

첫 문장에서 영어가 세계 언어가 된 원인을 물었고, 이어서 그 원인에 대해 설명한 글이므로 제목으로는 ③이 가장 적절하다.

다음 중 제목으로 가장 적절한 것은?
① 국제 공용어의 역설: 다언어 세계에서 영어의 마뜩찮은 지배
② 대영제국의 권력: 영어 확산의 유일한 동력
③ 영어의 지배: 역사적 제국주의, 경제력, 그리고 기술적 필요성
④ 세계의 언어: 영어의 구조

22 부분이해   ②

| 분석 |

바로 앞에서 '정보 기술 분야에서'라고 국한했고, 왕, 즉 최고의 지위를 누리는 언어라고 한 것은 그 분야를 지배하는 언어라는 의미이므로 ②가 정답으로 적절하다.

다음 중 Ⓐ를 가장 잘 해석한 것은?
① 미국의 미디어는 세계 디지털 담론을 교묘히 지배한다.
② 미국 영어는 모든 세계 통신이 아니라 정보기술(IT)을 지배한다.
③ 조직들은 전 세계적으로 미국 영어를 전략적으로 장려한다.
④ 미국 영어는 당연히 혁신의 방언으로 등장한다.

23 내용일치   ②

| 분석 |

세 번째 문단에서 '유럽연합(EU)에서는 영어가 충분히 널리 사용되는 유일한 언어기 때문에 마지못해 채택된다'고 했으므로 ②가 정답이다.

다음 중 옳은 것은?
① 영어는 유럽연합의 모든 소통에서 지역 언어들을 대체하고 있다.
② 유럽연합은 영어를 마지못해 채택하지만 영어는 널리 공부되고 퍼져 있다.
③ 기술이 영어의 확산을 추진하며, 역사와 경제는 덜 중요하다.
④ 영어는 획일적인 세계 언어 기준을 만든다.

24~26

조앙은 이전의 삶에서 뚱뚱한 몸매에 뾰족한 귀와 아치형의 검은 눈썹을 가진 남자였고, 엄격하고 진지한 성격으로 돈을

저축하는 것을 좋아하는 사람이었다. 그러나 1990년, 49세의 나이에 건강 위기를 겪은 후 그는 다르게 살고 싶었다. 그는 "난 죽음을 가까이서 보았다"라고 말하곤 했다. "이젠 기쁜 마음으로 살고 싶다." 그리고 그를 가장 행복하게 만든 것은 바로 주는 것이었다. 그를 잘 모르는 사람들에게 그는 틀림없이 이타성의 상징, 즉 리우데자네이루의 성 프란치스코같이 보였을 것이다.

그러나 조앙의 이야기에서 가장 흥미로운 점은 그의 새로운 세계관이 정신적 각성에서가 아니라 뇌졸중으로 인한 뇌 손상에서 비롯되었다는 것이다. 뇌 손상으로 인한 다른 증상들 중에는 그가 만성 불면증에 시달렸고 성욕을 잃었으며, 기억을 잃기 시작했고 집중하는 데 어려움을 겪었으며, 움직임도 둔화되었다는 점도 있었다. 그를 담당한 신경학자는 그가 "병적으로 관대해졌다"고, 즉 주는 일에 강박적으로 몰두하게 되었다고 말한다. 돈에 연연하지 않는 그의 태도 때문에 가족과 갈등이 일어났다. 특히 프렌치프라이 카트 형 상점을 공동 소유한 처남과 갈등을 겪었다. 그러나 가족이 그를 꾸짖고, 장사가 망하고, 결국 어머니의 연금으로 생활하는 지경까지 되었는데도 조앙은 주기를 멈추지 않았다. 주는 일이 너무 행복했기 때문이다. (조앙은 1999년 신부전으로 사망했다. 그의 담당의는 가족의 개인 정보를 보호하려고 조앙의 성을 빼고 이름만 알려주었다.)

신경학의 역사에는 뇌 손상을 겪은 후 행동이 기이하게 변한 환자들이 많다. 어떤 사람들은 더 이상 동물을 알아보지 못하게 되기도 하고 말은 못해도 노래는 부를 수 있게 되기도 했다. 신경학자들에게 이러한 사례들은 기회를 제공한다. 뇌 손상을 겪은 사람들의 행동이 어떻게 변하는지 연구함으로써, 손상된 부위가 일상의 과제에서 어떤 역할을 하는지에 대한 통찰을 얻을 수 있기 때문이다. 조앙의 경우도 마찬가지였다. 연구자들은 그의 강박적인 기부가 정상적인 관대함에 대해 밝혀내어, 인간이 왜 주는지, 그리고 주는 것이 왜 생리적으로 기분 좋은지 파악하는 데 도움을 주리라 기대했다.

| 어휘 |

previous a. 이전의 **chubby** a. 살찐 **pointy** a. 뽀족한 **arched** a. 아치형의 **eyebrow** n. 눈썹 **stern** a. 엄격한 **serious** a. 진지한 **squirrel away** 비축해두다 **embodiment** n. 화신, 상징 **selflessness** n. 이타성 **outlook** n. 관점, 견해 **spiritual** a. 영적인 **awakening** n. 각성 **brain damage** 뇌손상 **stroke** n. 뇌졸중 **neurologist** n. 신경학자 **pathologically** ad. 병적으로, 병리적으로 **brother-in-law** n. 처남이나 매제 **pension** n. 연금 **kidney failure** 신부전 **bizarre** a. 기이한 **shed light on** ~을 밝히다 **generosity** n. 관대함

24 내용파악 ②

| 분석 |

두 번째 문단 첫 문장에서 조앙의 사례에서 가장 흥미로운 점은 그의 관대함이 뇌졸중에서 초래되었다는 사실이라 했으므로 정답은 ②이다.

무엇이 조앙을 병적으로 관대한 사람이 되게 유발했나?
① 영적 각성
② 뇌졸중으로 인한 뇌손상
③ 경제적 성공
④ 새로운 직업 기회

25 내용파악 ③

| 분석 |

두 번째 문단에서 성욕을 잃었다고 했으므로 ③이 정답이다.

다음 중 조앙이 뇌졸중 후에 겪은 증상이 <u>아닌</u> 것은?
① 만성 불면증
② 집중력 저하
③ 성욕 증가
④ 움직임 둔화

26 내용파악 ①

| 분석 |

본문 마지막에서 "연구자들은 그의 강박적인 기부가 정상적인 관대함에 대해 밝혀내어, 인간이 왜 주는지, 그리고 주는 것이 왜 생리적으로 기분 좋은지 파악하는 데 도움을 주리라 기대했다."라고 했으므로, ①이 정답이다.

조앙의 이야기는 신경학자들이 뇌손상이 행동에 어떻게 영향을 끼치는지 연구할 기회가 되어 인간이 왜 _____에 대한 통찰을 제공했다.
① 관대함을 즐기는지
② 말할 수 없을 때 노래하는지
③ 동물을 다르게 알아보는지
④ 뇌졸중에서 회복되는지

27~29

어린 시절의 깊은 유대, 남아 있는 그리움, 그리고 "인연"이라는 개념은 영화 "패스트 라이브즈"의 배경을 이룬다. 이 영화는 어린 시절 서로에게 마음이 있었던 두 한국 남녀가 수십 년 후 다시 만나는 가슴 시리게 아름다운 러브스토리로, 선댄스 영화제에서 돌풍을 일으킨 올해의 히트작이었다. 그

런데, 도대체 인연이란 무엇일까? "패스트 라이브즈"의 각본가이자 감독인 셀린 송은 한국의 이 단어는 두 사람 사이의 "특별한 것"을 가리킨다고 설명했다. 캐나다에서 태어난 한국계 극작가이자 영화감독인 그녀는 인연이 있다는 것은 "이번 생 이전의 삶에서 서로 연결되어 있다는 것, 그리고 또한 다음 생에서도 서로 연결될 것이라는 것을 의미하며, 매번 생을 살 때마다 인연은 조금씩 다른 의미를 띠게 될 것이라고" 말했다. UCLA에서 한국학과 동아시아학을 가르치는 제니퍼 정-김 교수에 따르면, 인연이라는 단어는 한국의 고대 삼국(고구려, 백제, 신라)과 관련된 전설과 민속 이야기와 역사적 기록을 담고 있는 『삼국유사』에 1281년 처음 등장했다. "인연은 불교 용어이므로 그 전에도 수 세기 동안 사용되었을 가능성이 있어요."라고 그녀는 말했다. 한국계 미국인 임상심리학자인 크리스티나 홍 후버는 인연은 "두 사람이 아마도 여러 생에 걸쳐 만날 운명이라는 강력하고 매력적인 개념"이라고 확장해서 설명했다. 실제로 영화의 여주인공 노라(그레타 리가 연기함)는 어느 날 저녁에 그녀의 미래의 남편 아서(존 마가로가 연기함)에게 이렇게 말한다. "만일 두 낯선 사람이 길에서 서로의 옆을 지나가다가 그들의 옷이 우연히 스치기만 해도 그것이 그들의 과거의 생에서 그들 사이에 무슨 일이 있었음에 틀림없다는 것을 의미하기 때문에 그것은 인연입니다. 만약 두 사람이 결혼한다면, 그들은 그것이 8,000번의 생에 걸친 8,000겹의 인연이 있기 때문이라고 말합니다." 노라와 아서 두 사람은 작가 리트리트(은둔) 센터에서 만나 맨해튼에서 결혼한다. 인연은 한국어로 '인연'이라고 쓰는데, 산스크리트어 단어인 헤투와 프라티야에서 유래되었다. 정-김 교수는 "인연은 특정한 반응을 직간접적으로 초래하는 행동들의 합계로 이해될 수 있다"고 말했다. 본질적으로 인연은 운명, 카르마(업보) 또는 숙명이라고 이 교수는 결론지었다.

| 어휘 |
bond n. 결속 linger v. 머물다 longing n. 염원 backdrop n. 배경 achingly a. 아프게 epic a. 서사적인 sweetheart n. 연인 reconnect v. 다시 이어지다 breakout hit 히트작 playwright n. 극작가 lecturer n. 강사, 교수 licensed a. 면허 받은 clinical a. 임상의 stranger n. 이방인 accidentally ad. 우연히 brush v. 스치다 writer's retreat 작가가 글 쓰는데 집중하도록 만든 센터 indirectly ad. 간접적으로 karma n. 카르마, 업(業) conclude v. 결론 내다 reaction n. 반응, 대응

27 글의 제목 ①

| 분석 |
영화를 언급하지만 영화가 아니라 인연의 의미를 다루는 글이므로 ①이 제목으로 가장 적절하다.

다음 중 제목으로 가장 적절한 것은?
① 인연: 전생과 현생을 엮어 짜는 업보의 실가닥
② 운명학: 인연의 유전 코드를 은폐하기
③ 할리우드의 인연: 미국 영화 혁신하기
④ 언어학적 기원: 현대 한국어에서 인연의 어원

28 부분이해 ②

| 분석 |
Ⓐ는 곧 인연을 가리키는데, 그다음 문장에서 you are connected to each other in lives before this one ~ after this one이라고 했으므로 다수의 생을 가로지르는 연결이라는 ②의 해석이 가장 적절하다.

다음 중 Ⓐ를 가장 잘 해석한 것은?
① 현생에서 개인들 간의 업보의 이끌림
② 간단한 것부터 심오한 것까지, 다수의 생을 가로지르는 예정된 연결
③ 두 생을 엮어 강렬한 연인의 결속으로 이어주는 운명
④ 어린 시절부터 시작되어 평생의 친밀함으로 지속되는 영적 동류의식

29 내용파악 ①

| 분석 |
인연에 대한 이모저모를 이야기하는 글이지만, 인연과 개인의 주체성 사이의 긴장은 언급되어 있지 않다. 따라서 정답은 ①이다.

다음 중 언급되지 않은 것은?
① 삶의 궤적을 형성할 때 인연과 개인의 주체성 사이에 생길 수 있는 잠재적 긴장
② 산스크리트어의 어원부터 한국 문화에서 현재 쓰이는 용도까지 인연의 언어적 진화
③ 일상생활에서의 비(非)연애 관계와 플라토닉한 만남에 대한 인연의 적용
④ 고대 한국 문헌에서의 인연의 최초 도입

30~32

식물들은 수백만 년 동안, 세대를 거듭하며 죽었다. 식물은 늪에서 죽었고 거기서 썩지 못하고 대신 가라앉아 쌓여 토탄층이 되었고 이 토탄층은 압착되고 압축되어 결국 더 단단하고 건조한 석탄층을 이루었다. 3억 년 후, 지금으로부터 약 1,100년 전, 죽은 지 오래된 그 식물 위의 땅은 영국 초기의 왕들이 차지한 지역 내에 있게 되었다. 하나는 지질학적 발전이고 하나는 역사적인 발전인 이 두 가지 발전 덕분에 우리

는 영국의 석탄 퇴적층에 대해 이야기할 수 있다. 뉴캐슬 시 근처의 타인 강과 위어 강의 계곡을 따라 가장 쉽게 접근할 수 있는 이 석탄 퇴적층 위에 살았던 사람들은 이 석탄을 수백 년 동안 사용했고 13세기에는 일부를 남쪽으로 보내기 시작했다. 엘리자베스 여왕의 긴 통치 기간 동안 수많은 영국인들이 이주해와 점점 커져간 런던 시는 곧 다른 어느 곳보다 석탄을 더 많이 사용했다.

런던 사람들이 알아낸 바에 따르면 석탄은 놀라운 자원이었다. 우리도 마찬가지로 석탄을 선물이라고 부를 수 있을 테지만, 무거운 희생도 또한 가져다준 선물이었다. 그 중 많은 희생은 땅속에 있는 이 석탄을 벽난로나 용광로에서 태울 수 있는 것으로 바꾸면서 생계비를 벌었던 사람들에게 가해졌다. 석탄 채굴은 기후가 차갑고, 토양이 척박하고, 대도시가 없는 지역에 살던 사람들에게 임금을 제공했지만, 채굴은 거의 견딜 수 없는 노동이었을지도 모른다. 노동자들은 광산이 점점 더 깊어짐에 따라 점점 더 아래로 어두운 땅속으로 내려가, 웅크리고 엎드리고 누워 석탄을 캤다. 그러면 다른 사람들, 대개 노동자의 아내나 자녀들은 석탄을 통에 실어 위로 운반하거나 위로 일광이 들어오는 쪽으로 끌어올렸고, 더 많이 캐려고 같은 일을 되풀이했다. 최상의 조건에서조차 그 일은 정말로 고되었을 테고, 대개 노동 조건은 울퉁불퉁하거나 젖은 표면 같은 난관에 늘 시달렸을 것이다. 때로, 얼마나 자주였는지 알 순 없지만 지붕이 무너지거나 가스에 불이 붙기도 했다. 우리는 일부 광산 재해에 대해, 외부인이나 방문객들이 묘사했기 때문에, 알고 있지만, 대부분은 분명 기록되지 않았을 것이다.

| 어휘 |

plant n. 식물 **generation** n. 세대 **swamp** n. 늪지 **decay** v. 썩다 **sink** v. 가라앉다 **accumulate** v. 누적되다 **layer** n. 층 **peat** n. 토탄 **long-dead** a. 죽은 지 오래된 **geological** a. 지질학적인 **deposit** n. 퇴적층 **accessible** a. 접근 가능한 **unknown** a. 미지의 **reign** n. 통치 **coal** n. 석탄 **remarkable** a. 놀라운, 현저한 **transform** v. 바꾸다 **descend** v. 내려가다 **intolerable** a. 참을 수 없는 **progressively** ad. 점점 **crouch** v. 웅크리다 **hack** v. 쳐내다, 베다 **bumpy** a. 울퉁불퉁한 **collapse** v. 붕괴되다 **catch fire** 불붙다 **unrecorded** a. 기록되지 않은

30 글의 제목 ④

| 분석 |

본문은 첫 부분에서 석탄이 형성된 지질학적 과정과 역사적 배경을 간략히 설명한 후, 대부분의 분량을 석탄을 채굴하는 노동자들의 열악한 작업 환경과 고된 삶에 대해 집중적으로 설명하고 있다. 따라서 제목으로는 ④가 가장 적절하다.

제목으로 가장 적절한 것은?
① 죽은 식물의 이용
② 석탄 광업에 대한 투자
③ 석탄 소비의 트렌드 변화
④ 채굴의 실태

31 빈칸완성 ②

| 분석 |

어두운 갱도로 내려갈 사람들은 석탄을 캘 노동자라고 추론할 수 있다.

다음 중 Ⓐ에 들어가기에 가장 적절한 것은?
① 조사관들
② 노동자들
③ 여성과 아이들
④ 구매자들

32 내용일치 ②

| 분석 |

첫 문단 마지막 부분에서 '엘리자베스 여왕의 긴 통치 기간 동안 수많은 영국인들이 이주해와 점점 커져간 런던 시는 곧 다른 어떤 곳보다 석탄을 더 많이 사용했다'고 했으므로 ②가 정답이다.

다음 중 맞는 옳은 것은?
① 영국 왕들은 석탄층에서 발견된 것들을 이용했다.
② 런던 시민들은 엘리자베스 여왕 시대에 석탄을 가장 많이 썼다.
③ 석탄 탄광에 고용된 사람들은 다른 어느 곳에서보다 이익을 더 많이 낸다.
④ 탄광 재난은 기록이 잘 되어 있었다.

33~35

미국에서 현재 사용되는 다양한 영어와 영국에서 사용되는 영어를 비교할 때 한 가지 눈에 띄는 점은, 미국 내에서는 한 화자와 다른 화자가 설사 광활한 미국 대륙 정반대편에 살고 있다 하더라도 두 사람 간의 언어 차이가 영국에 비해 훨씬 적다는 것이다. 반면 영어가 1500년 동안 정립되어 온 영국은 이웃한 지방이나 심지어 이웃한 도시의 말 사이에도 현저한 차이가 있다. 극단적인 예를 들자면, 한 저자는 런던에서 글래스고까지 두 시간 반 동안 기차를 타고 북쪽으로 여행했는데, 글래스고 택시 운전사가 친근하게 대화를 하는 사람인데도 그의 말을 전혀 알아듣지 못했던 경험을 했다. 반대로, 캘리포니아 토박이는 2,000마일 동쪽에서 태어나 자란 오하이오 토박이와 대화를 나누어도, 사투리나 억양의

큰 차이를 느끼지 못한다.
이러한 차이는 설명하기 어렵지 않다. 수세기 동안, 대부분의 영국 제도(諸島) 사람들은 자신이 태어난 지역에서 평생을 보냈다. 19세기까지는 인구의 이동과 혼합이 비교적 적었다. 물론 영국 제도는 텍사스 주 하나에 꼭 들어갈 만큼 작다. 그러나 19세기 동안 영어 사용 인구의 대규모 확장과 이동이 있었던 미국에서는 새로운 지역에서 새로운 기회를 탐색하는 것이 전통이자 정상적인 삶의 방식이었다. 세계사의 기준으로 보면, 중서부와 먼 서부의 새로운 주들은 놀랄 만큼 짧은 시간에 정착이 이루어졌고, 철도 교통의 속도가 그 과정에 도움을 주었다. 당연히, 미국에서 방언의 차이가 눈에 띄게 나타나는 지역은 미국 동부 해안에 가까운 지역으로, 영국으로부터 독립한 13개 주에 해당한다. 이들 주는 현대적인 통신 수단이 도입되기 전에 정착이 이루어졌으며, 그 안에는 (북동부) 뉴잉글랜드와 ("구 남부")인 남부 주들의 유명한 방언 지역들이 있다.

| 어휘 |

notice v. 알아차리다. 주목하다 variation n. 차이 opposite a. 반대편의 continent n. 대륙 neighbouring a. 이웃한 friendly a. 친근한 incomprehensible a. 이해할 수 없는, 불가해한 locality n. 장소, 지역 mixing n. 혼합 enormous a. 커다란, 어마어마한 explore v. 탐색하다 amazingly a. 놀랍도록 seaboard n. 해안지방 dialectical a. 방언의 well-known a. 유명한

33 글의 제목   ④

| 분석 |

미국 영어와 영국 영어의 사회, 문화적 차이를 다룬 글인데, 구체적으로는 "왜 미국 영어는 지역 방언 차이가 적고, 영국 영어는 더 다양한가?"에 대해 미국은 '이동이 많고 혼합됨'을, 영국은 '정착하고 고립됨'을 들고 있다. 따라서 ④가 글의 제목으로 가장 적절하다.

다음 중 위 글의 제목으로 가장 적절한 것은?
① 영어의 위기: 동질성 대 다양성
② 미국 영어: 영국 뿌리로부터 이루어진 진화
③ 영어의 역사: 이민과 철도
④ 유목생활 대 정착: 미국과 영국의 언어 패턴

34 빈칸완성   ③

| 분석 |

빈칸 앞에서 미국에서는 지역 간의 언어 차이가 거의 없다고 한 다음, 빈칸 다음에서 영국에서는 지역 간의 언어 차이가 현저하다고 했으므로 빈칸에는 대조를 나타내는 ③이 적절하다.

다음 중 Ⓐ에 들어가기에 가장 적절한 것은?
① 그러므로
② 그뿐 아니라
③ 반면에
④ 예를 들어

35 내용일치   ④

| 분석 |

두 번째 문단에서 영어 패턴 차이가 큰 영국에서는 사람들이 자신이 태어난 곳에서 평생을 보냈다고 했고 영어 패턴 차이가 작은 미국에서는 19세기 동안 영어 사용 인구의 대규모 이동이 있었다고 했으므로 (영국처럼) 이동성(mobility)이 제한되면(적으면) 언어 패턴 차이가 커진다고 한 ④가 정답이다.

다음 중 맞는 옳은 것은?
① 영어 사용이 오래될수록 언어적 동질성이 초래된다.
② 빠른 정착은 독특한 지역 방언을 만들어낸다.
③ 지리적 크기는 언어적 차이를 결정한다.
④ 제한된 이동이 언어 패턴의 차이를 키운다.

36~37

지구상의 인류 활동으로 인한 영향, 예를 들어 대기 중 이산화탄소의 증가와 질소 순환의 교란은 그냥 우연히 일어나는 일이 아니라 의도했건 아니건 인간 정신이 내린 '결정'으로 초래된 결과이다. 자연에서는, 우리가 늘 이해해 온 대로, 자연의 힘이 무의식적이고 비자발적이다. 어떤 결정도 내려지지 않는다. 그래서 인류를 지질학적 힘으로 이해하려면 인류의 독특한 성질, 즉 자기 의지적 요소를 고려해야 한다. 인류는 아마 지질학적 힘보다는 지질학적 권력으로 묘사하는 편이 더 적절하다. 물질을 변형시키는 인류의 능력뿐 아니라 결정을 내리는 능력을 고려해야 하기 때문이다. 자연의 힘과 달리, 그것은 행사할 수도 있고 보류할 수도 있는 권력이다.

따라서 비록 비물리적 힘이 먼저 존재하는 자연의 힘에 '추가된' 것이 아니라 어떤 의미에서는 자연의 힘들을 '우려내어' 그 작용을 바꾼 것이긴 하지만 우리는 지구의 45억 년의 역사 이래 최초로 (물리적 효과를 가져오는) 비물리적 힘이 물리적 힘과 혼합된 상태를 갖게 되었다. 그리고 이 새로운 힘은 지구의 지질학적 진화를 설명하는 데 사용되는 지구역학 체계에 단지 불완전하게만 통합될 수 있다. 이 새로운 힘이 어떻게 작용할지에 관한 불확실성은 21세기 전 세계 온난화에 대한 예측에서 큰 차이가 나타나는 주된 이유이다. 그리고 이제 인류가 지구에 존재하는 한, 모든 미래의 시대, 기간 등은 물리적 힘과 이 새로운 권력의 혼합이 될 것이 확실해

보인다. 그렇기 때문에 일부 지질학계에서 공식적인 지질 연대기에 이 희한한 구분을 추가하는 것에 대해 깊은 불안이 있었던 것은 당연한 일이다.

| 어휘 |

anthropogenic a. 인간이 초래한 **disturbance** n. 교란, 방해
nitrogen cycle 질소 순환 **consequence** n. 결과 **intended** a. 의도된 **involuntary** a. 비자발적인 **distinctive** a. 독특한
volitional a. 의지에 의한 **withhold** v. 보류하다 **exercise** v. 실행하다 **integrate** v. 통합하다 **geodynamics** n. 지질역학
projection n. 예측 **epoch** n. 시대 **weird** a. 희한한, 기이한

36 동의어   ①

| 분석 |

volitional은 '자기 의지에 의한', '자발적인'이라는 의미이다. '자기 의지대로/마음대로 하는, 의도적인'이라는 뜻의 willful이 의미적으로 가장 가깝다.

다음 중 (1)과 의미가 가장 가까운 것은?
① 의도적인
② 반대하는
③ 찬성하는
④ 강요된

37 지시대상   ②

| 분석 |

Ⓐ, Ⓒ, Ⓓ는 모두 물리적인 자연력이고, Ⓑ는 인간이 가진 비물리적 힘, 의지력이므로 다른 것은 Ⓑ이다.

38~39

얼굴 인식 시스템은 인공지능(AI)을 사용하여 이미지를 신원과 일치시킨다. 폭도들을 추적하는 데 사용되고 있는 그런 종류의 소급적 얼굴 인식은 CCTV 영상을 용의자와 비교하고, 실시간 사용은 실시간 이미지를 "감시 목록"에 올라 있는 사람들의 얼굴과 비교하는 것을 포함한다. 얼굴 인식 기술은 2023년 찰스 왕 대관식에서 사용되었다. 작년, 사우스 웨일스 경찰은 819,000명 이상의 사람들의 얼굴을 스캔했다. 노스 런던의 하링게이에서는 매 분마다 약 133개의 얼굴 스캔이 실행된다.
설문 조사에 따르면 영국인들은 얼굴 인식에 찬성하는 주장을 받아들인다. 3월에 신흥 기술 보안 센터와 앨런 튜링 연구소가 실시한 여론 조사에 따르면, 영국인의 60%가 군중 속 범죄자를 실시간으로 식별하기 위해 경찰이 이 기술을 사용하는 것에 대해 아무렇지도 않다고 응답했다. 이 비율은 폭동 이후 증가했을 가능성이 있다. 문제의 소지를 가진 사람을 찾는 작업은 사람만으로 작업할 경우 시간이 훨씬 더 걸린다. 사우스 웨일스 경찰은 매월 얼굴 인식 기술을 통해 200명의 용의자를 식별한다. 얼굴 인식이 없다면 용의자를 찾는 데 평균 14일이 소요된다. 키어 스타머 총리는 올해 여름의 혼란에 대응하기 위해 얼굴 인식 기술 사용을 증가시키겠다고 약속했다.
그 때문에 이 기술을 어떻게 규제할지에 대한 질문이 더욱 절박해진다. 일부 형태의 감시를 규제하는 수사권 법은 최근 정부 기관이 "프라이버시 요구가 없는" 곳에서 데이터를 처리할 때 인공지능을 사용할 수 있도록 개정되었다. 그러나 버밍햄대학교의 법학과 교수 캐런 융은 얼굴 인식을 구체적으로 다루는 법령은 전혀 없다는 점을 지적한다. "경찰은 복잡한 잡동사니 같은 규제의 지침에 따릅니다. 이는 결과적으로 얼굴 인식 기술 사용에 대한 감독이 거의 없다는 뜻입니다."

| 어휘 |

facial-recognition n. 얼굴 인식 **match** v. 맞추다 **identity** n. 신원 **rioter** n. 폭도 **footage** n. 영상 **scan** v. 살피다, 스캔하다 **crowd** n. 군중 **suspect** n. 용의자 **prime minister** 수상
pledge v. 약속하다 **disorder** n. 무질서, 난동 **urgency** n. 절박함
surveillance n. 감시 **amend** v. 고치다 **legislation** n. 입법
patchwork n. 주워 모은 것, 잡동사니 **oversight** n. 관리, 감독

38 내용파악   ①

| 분석 |

'매월 얼굴 인식 기술을 통해 200명의 용의자를 식별하는데, 얼굴 인식이 없다면 용의자를 찾는 데 평균 14일이 소요된다(매월 약 2명 찾음)'에서 얼굴 인식 기술을 사용하면 용의자를 찾는 속도가 100배 빠르다는 것을 알 수 있다.

법 집행에 얼굴 인식 기술을 사용하는 것의 주된 이점 중 하나는?
① 얼굴 인식 기술은 인간 노력만 하는 것에 비해 용의자 확인을 더 빠르게 해 준다.
② 얼굴 인식 기술은 CCTV 카메라의 필요를 없애준다.
③ 얼굴 인식 기술은 법 집행의 전체 비용을 줄여준다.
④ 얼굴 인식 기술은 개인의 완전한 사생활을 보호해준다.

39 내용파악   ④

| 분석 |

'버밍햄대학교의 법학과 교수 캐런 융은 얼굴 인식을 구체적으로 다루는 법령은 전혀 없다는 점을 지적한다'고 했다. 따라서 정답은 ④이다.

얼굴 인식 기술의 규제에 대한 주된 쟁점은 무엇인가?
① 수사권법은 얼굴 인식 기술의 사용을 완전히 금지한다.
② 경찰의 얼굴 인식 기술 사용에 대한 대중의 지지가 하나도 없다.
③ 얼굴 인식 기술은 이미지를 신원과 정확히 맞추지 못한다.
④ 얼굴 인식 기술을 구체적으로 지배하는 법이 하나도 없다.

40~42

특이하게 두꺼운 줄기와 작은 가지를 가진 마다가스카르 바오밥 나무는 마다가스카르 섬의 독특한 풍경의 특징이다. 놀랍게도 이 나무는 이 나무의 씨앗을 퍼뜨리는 주된 생물의 멸종이라는 큰 난제를 마주했음에도 불구하고 살아남았다. 과학자들은 한때 이 섬을 돌아다녔던 거대한 거북이와 고릴라 크기의 거대한 여우원숭이가 바오밥 나무의 큰 씨앗을 퍼뜨리는 데 중요한 역할을 했다고 생각한다. 인간의 활동으로 인해 이들 동물이 천 년 이상 전에 멸종하면서 바오밥 나무의 생존은 불가능해 보였다. 그러나 마다가스카르 안타나나리보 대학교의 세헤노 안드리안츠알라자와 캘리포니아 대학교 버클리 캠퍼스의 온자 라자핀드라치마가 수행한 연구에서 이 나무들이 어떻게 견뎌냈는지가 밝혀졌다.
연구자들은 팀을 이루어 마다가스카르 서부에서 15개의 바오밥 나무 가지를 모니터링하며 잠재적인 새 씨앗 살포자를 찾아내기 위한 현장 연구를 진행했다. 이들은 씨앗이 든 열매가 땅에 떨어진 곳에 카메라가 달린 덫을 설치하고, 동물의 배설물에서 씨앗을 찾아보는 등 다양한 방법을 사용했다. 이들의 연구 결과는 『바이오트로피카』 저널에 발표되었고, 마다가스카르의 토착 설치류인 서부 숲꼬리쥐가 바오밥 열매와 상호작용한다는 점을 밝혀냈다. 카메라 영상에서 이 쥐들이 바오밥 열매를 다루는 모습이 여러 차례 포착되었다. 카메라가 쥐들이 열매를 여는 모습을 기록하진 못했지만, 연구팀은 씨앗이 빠져 나간 열매 13개가 씹힌 것을 발견했는데, 이것은 동물이 씨앗을 제거했다는 것을 보여주는 것이었다.
추가 연구에서 중요한 증거가 나왔다: 바오밥 씨앗이 일곱 더미의 부시돼지 배설물에서 발견된 것이다. 이 발견이 특히 아이러니한 이유는, 부시돼지는 1000년에서 5000년 전 인간이 마다가스카르에 도입한 동물이기 때문이다. 이는 원래 씨앗을 분산시키던 동물들이 멸종한 시기와 일치한다. 부시돼지의 도입은 바오밥 나무에게 행운의 기회를 제공한 셈이다. 연구들은 부시돼지의 소화계를 통과한 씨앗이 발아에 부정적인 영향을 받지 않는다는 것을 확인했다.
이 발견은 생태계에 도입된 종들의 복잡한 역할을 드러낸다. 대개 부정적으로 여겨지지만, 마다가스카르의 부시돼지는 토착 식물 종의 생존에 필수적인 존재가 되었다. 이와 비슷한 관계가 다른 지역에도 있는 것이 아닌가 생각되는데, 남미에서 씨앗을 분산시키는 역할을 해주는 것이 부족한 식물을 위해 유럽 토끼가 씨앗을 분산시키는 역할을 할 수 있는 것과 같은 것이다. 안드리안츠알라자 박사는 도입된 종을 퇴치하려는 노력을 고려하기에 앞서, 도입된 종의 생태학적 역할에 대한 포괄적인 평가를 먼저 해보아야 한다고 말한다. 이 연구는 생태계 내의 복잡하고 때로는 예기치 않은 상호작용을 강조한다.

| 어휘 |

distinctive a. 특이한   unique a. 독특한   feature n. 특징   landscape n. 풍광   persist v. 존속하다   face v. 마주하다   challenge n. 난제, 어려움   extinction n. 멸종   seed disperser 씨앗 살포자   roam v. 돌아다니다   crucial a. 중요한   spread v. 퍼뜨리다   conduct v. 실행하다   endure v. 버티다   rat n. 쥐   yield v. 산출하다   dung n. 배설물, 대변   confirm v. 확증하다   digestive system 소화계   germination n. 발달, 발아   highlight v. 강조하다   comprehensive a. 포괄적인   assessment n. 평가   intricate a. 복잡한   underscore v. 강조하다   unexpected a. 예기치 않은

40 내용파악   ①

| 분석 |

'놀랍게도 이 나무는 이 나무의 씨앗을 퍼뜨리는 주된 생물의 멸종이라는 큰 난제를 마주했음에도 불구하고 살아남았다'고 한 것을 통해 ①이 정답임을 알 수 있다.

마다가스카르 바오밥 나무가 마주한 주된 난제는 무엇이었는가?
① 원래 씨앗을 퍼뜨리던 종들의 멸종
② 다른 나무 종들과의 경쟁
③ 기후변화로 인한 서식처 손실
④ 질병과 기생충이나 병균의 침입

41 내용파악   ④

| 분석 |

세 번째 문단에서 '추가 연구에서 중요한 증거가 나왔는데, 바오밥 씨앗이 일곱 더미의 부시돼지 배설물에서 발견되었다'고 한 것을 참고하면, 외래종 돼지의 배설물에서 씨앗이 발견되었다는 내용이 중요하고 놀라우리라는 점을 추론할 수 있다.

연구자들은 바오밥 씨앗에 대해 어떤 놀라운 발견을 했는가?
① 씨앗이 동물의 소화계를 거치지 않고 발아할 수 있다.
② 씨앗이 바람에 의해 퍼졌다.
③ 씨앗을 곤충이 먹었다.
④ 씨앗이 부시돼지의 배설물에서 발견되었다.

42 내용파악   ①

| 분석 |

'안드리안츠알라자 박사는 도입된 종을 퇴치하려는 노력을 고려하기에 앞서, 도입된 종의 생태학적 역할에 대한 포괄적인 평가를 먼저 해보아야 한다고 말한다'고 한 것을 참고하면 퇴치를 고려하기 전에 종의 역할을 고려해야 한다는 ①이 정답임을 알 수 있다.

안드리안츠알라자 박사가 도입된 종에 대해 짚는 주된 요점은 무엇인가?
① 이들의 퇴치를 고려하기 전에 생태계 안에서의 역할을 주의 깊게 연구해야 한다.
② 토착 종을 보호하기 위해 이들을 즉시 퇴치해야 한다.
③ 이들은 토착 생태계에 큰 영향을 거의 미치지 않는다.
④ 이들은 토착 생태계에 늘 해롭다.

43~45

연말연시 파티 초대장이 우리의 달력을 채우고 초콜릿 광고가 화면을 가득 채우면서, 쾌락에 탐닉하라는 유혹은 어디에나 있고 강력하게 느껴질 수 있다. 그러나 올해, 이런 종류의 미혹에 이름을 붙인 신조어가 소셜 미디어를 장악하고 있다. 바로 "음식 소음(food noise)"이라는 용어다. 이 유행어는 사람들이 체중 감소를 바라보는 방식을 변화시킬 수 있으며, 수십 년간 내면의 의지 싸움으로 여겨졌던 것을, 생리적, 심리적 뿌리를 지닌 외부 문제로 변모시키고 있다. 이 문제를 과학자들은 이제 막 이해하기 시작하고 있다. 이러한 변화에 기여하는 요소 중 하나는 오젬픽(Ozempic)과 같은 체중 감소 약물이 널리 사용되고 있다는 점이다. 이 약물이 작용하는 방식을 고려할 때, 이 약이 음식 생각을 가라앉힌다는 것은 놀랍지 않다. 이 약물은 GLP-1 호르몬을 모방한다. 이 호르몬은 사람들이 포만감을 느끼게 하고, 위를 비우는 속도를 늦추며, 인슐린 분비를 증가시켜 혈당을 조절한다. 그 결과, 그 약을 복용한 많은 사람들이 단 것을 먹고 싶은 유혹이 줄어들었다고 보고한다. 음식에 대한 집착도 줄어들기 때문에 디저트 테이블 근처에 있어도 욕구가 덜해진다. 그러나 사람들이 "음식 소음"이라는 용어를 사용해 과거에 단지 의지력 테스트로 여겨졌던 문제를 기술하는 이유는 더 복잡하다. 펜실베이니아 대학교의 트래비스 마스터슨 박사와 다이스케 하야시가 지난해 『뉴트리언츠』 저널에 발표한 첫 연구에서, 의학 전문가들이 이 용어를 채택하려면, 섭식 신호에 취약성이 커져 "음식과 관련된 충동적인 생각과 부적응적인 식습관 행동을 일으킬 정도가 될 때"여야 한다고 권장했다. 섭식 신호에 대한 반응은 정상이지만 — 진화 관점에서는 음식을 찾아내는 사람들이 생존과 유전자 전달 확률이 더 높다 — 음식 소음과 사투를 벌이는 사람들은 "이런 감정과 생각을 극복하기 어려워지는" 상태를 겪는다고 마스터슨 박사는 말했다. 하야시는 "음식 소음"이라는 용어가 틱톡 상에서 급속히 확산되는 현상을 연구하는 중인데, 그의 말에 따르면 이 용어는 2021년 FDA가 여러 버전의 GLP-1 약물을 승인한 후 이 약물이 체중 감소용으로 더 널리 처방되기 시작하면서 급격히 유행했다.

| 어휘 |

temptation n. 유혹   omnipresent a. 도처에 존재하는, 널린   all-powerful a. 막강한   neologism n. 신조어   take over 넘겨받다, 접수하다   distraction n. 오락, 집중을 방해하는 것   term n. 용어   internal a. 내면의   willpower n. 의지력   external a. 외부의   shift n. 변화   adoption n. 채택   imitate v. 모방하다   empty v. 비우다   fixate on ~에 집착하다   vulnerable a. 취약한   grasp onto 움켜잡다   recommend v. 권장하다   cue n. 신호   intrusive a. 거슬리는, 침입하는   gene n. 유전자   problematic a. 문제가 되는   overcome v. 극복하다   viral spread 급속한 확산   take off 유행하다, 급격히 인기를 얻다   prescribe v. 처방하다

43 글의 제목   ①

| 분석 |

핵심어는 음식 소음이란 용어이고 이것이 체중감량에 대한 우리의 생각을 바꾸어놓았다고 했으므로 가장 적절한 제목은 ①이다.

다음 중 글의 제목으로 가장 적절한 것은?
① 음식 소음: 체중감량에 대한 우리의 이해를 바꾸어 놓은 새 유행어
② 오젬픽과 GLP-1 약물: 식욕 억제의 혁명
③ 의지력의 진화: 내부 투쟁에서 외부 요인들로의 변화
④ 휴일의 유혹들: 탐닉의 계절 헤쳐 나가기

44 지시대상   ③

| 분석 |

Ⓐ, Ⓑ, Ⓓ의 term은 '용어'를 의미하지만, Ⓒ의 term은 '관점'이라는 뜻이므로 다르다.

45 내용일치   ①

| 분석 |

'이 유행어는 사람들이 체중 감소를 바라보는 방식을 변화시킬 수 있으며, 수십 년간 내면의 의지 싸움으로 여겨졌던 것을, 생리적, 심리적 뿌리를 지닌 외부 문제로 변모시키고 있다'고 했으므로 ①이 정답이다. ② 오젬픽이라는 약물은 뇌의 보상 중추가 아니라 혈당을 조절하여 단것에 대한 욕구를 줄인다. ③과 ④는 언급이 없는 내용이다.

다음 중 옳은 것은?
① "음식 소음"이란 용어는 체중 감량이 내적인 문제라는 인식을 외적인 문제라는 쪽으로 바꾸어 놓는다.
② 오젬픽이라는 약물은 뇌의 보상 중추를 조종함으로써 "음식 소음"을 제거한다.
③ 의료 전문가들은 GLP-1 약물의 효과를 기술하려고 "음식 소음"이라는 신조어를 만들었다.
④ "음식 소음" 연구는 GLP-1 약물 개발보다 먼저 일어난 일이고 이 개발을 초래했다.

46~47

우리 헌법은 이웃 국가들의 법을 모방하지 않는다. 우리 자신이 모방자라기보다 오히려 다른 나라들의 본보기가 된다. 헌법의 운영은 소수 대신 다수에 유리하다. 이것이 헌법을 민주주의라 부르는 이유이다. 법을 살펴보면, 법은 개인차가 있는 모두에게 평등한 정의를 제공한다. 사회적 지위가 없어도 공공 생활에서의 발전은 능력에 대한 평판에 달려 있으며, 계급에 대한 고려가 능력을 방해해서는 안 된다. 빈곤 역시 장애가 되지 않으며, 만약 누군가가 국가를 위해 봉사할 수 있다면, 그의 조건이 비천하다 해도 방해받지 않는다. 우리 정부에서 우리가 누리는 자유는 일상생활에까지 확장된다. 거기서 우리는 서로에 대해 질투어린 감시를 하지 않고, 이웃이 자신이 좋아하는 일을 한다고 해서 화를 내게 되지도 않으며, 심지어 적극적 처벌을 가하지는 않는다 해도 공격성이 드러나기 마련인 유해한 표정을 짓지도 않는다. 그러나 사적 관계에서의 이 모든 편안함이 우리를 시민으로서 무법 상태로 만들지는 않는다. 이러한 무법 상태에 대한 두려움을 막기 위해 주된 보호 장치가 있어서, 우리에게 법관과 법, 특히 피해자 보호를 중시하는 그런 법에 복종하도록 가르치는데, 실제로 성문법전에 있는 법이든 아니면 문서로 작성되지는 않았지만 어기면 반드시 불명예를 당하는 (불문) 법규에 속한 법이든 상관없는 것이다.

| 어휘 |

constitution n. 헌법   copy v. 모방하다   pattern n. 모범, 귀감, 본보기   administration n. 행정부   afford v. 제공하다   social standing 사회적 지위   reputation n. 명성, 평판   consideration n. 고려   interfere with 방해하다, 간섭하다   bar v. 막다, 방해하다   poverty n. 빈곤   serve v. 봉사하다   hinder v. 막다, 방해하다   obscurity n. 불명확, 무명, 이름 없음, 낮은 신분   extend v. 확대되다   indulge in ~에 탐닉하다   injurious a. 해로운   magistrate n. 치안판사   statute book 법전   code n. 규약   acknowledge v. 인정하다   disgrace n. 수치, 망신, 불명예

46 빈칸완성 ②

| 분석 |

민주주의라는 말이 뒤에 있으므로 소수 특권층이 아니라 다수 대중을 위한 체제가 헌법의 운용이어야 한다는 뜻이 되도록 ②가 빈칸에 들어가야 한다.

다음 중 Ⓐ를 가장 잘 완성하는 것은?
① 귀족 전통에 유리하다
② 소수 대신 다수에 유리하다
③ 소수 특권층의 손에 들어간다
④ 엄격한 서열 원칙을 따른다

47 내용파악 ③

| 분석 |

'사회적 지위가 없어도 공공 생활에서의 발전은 능력에 대한 평판에 달려 있으며, 계급에 대한 고려가 능력을 방해해서는 안 된다'고 했으므로 ③이 정답이다.

사회적 지위와 공적인 발전 사이의 관계는 무엇인가?
① 사회적 지위는 공적인 발전의 주요 요인이다.
② 공적인 발전은 오직 부와 계급에만 달려 있다.
③ 능력은 계급 조건에 상관없이 발전을 결정한다.
④ 공적인 발전은 고귀한 신분으로 태어난 이들에게 제한된다.

48~50

살충제는 환경 질병이라는 전체 그림 안의 어디에 들어맞는가? 우리는 살충제가 이제 토양, 물, 음식까지 오염시키며, 우리의 하천을 물고기 없는 곳으로, 정원과 숲을 새소리 없는 침묵의 공간으로 만들 수 있는 힘을 가지고 있음을 보아왔다. 인간은 자신이 자연의 일부임을 아무리 부정하고 싶어도 자연의 일부다. 인간은 이제 우리의 세계 전체에 철저히 퍼진 오염을 벗어날 수 있을까?
우리는 이 화학물질에 단 한 번만 노출되어도, 양만 충분히 많다면, 급성 중독에 곧바로 빠져들 수 있다는 것을 알고 있다. 하지만 이것이 주된 문제가 아니다. 농부, 살포 작업자, 조종사 등 다량의 살충제에 노출되는 사람들의 갑작스러운 질병이나 죽음은 비극적이며 일어나서는 안 된다. 일반 대중 전체에게 더 신경 써야 할 점은, 눈에 보이지 않게 우리의 세계를 오염시키는 살충제를 소량씩 흡수함으로써 발생하는 지연된 효과이다.
책임감 있는 공중보건 관계자들은 화학물질의 생물학적 효과가 장기간에 걸쳐 누적되며, 개인에게 끼치는 위험은 평생 동안 받아들여진 노출량의 합계에 달려있다는 점을 지적해 왔다. 〈바로 이런 이유로 위험이 쉽게 무시된다.〉 본성상 인

간은 미래의 재앙이라는 막연해 보이는 위협을 대수롭지 않게 여기는 경향이 있다. "사람들은 뚜렷한 증상이 있는 질병에 가장 큰 영향을 받습니다."라고 지혜로운 의사 르네 뒤보스 박사가 말한다. "하지만 인간의 가장 심각한 적들 중 일부는 눈에 띄지 않게 다가옵니다."

그러나 우리 몸속에도 생태계가 존재한다. 이 보이지 않는 세계에서는 미세한 원인이 강력한 결과를 만들어내며, 그 영향은 종종 원인과 관련이 없는 듯 보이고, 원래 손상이 발생한 곳과는 먼 신체 부위에서 나타나기도 한다. 인간 신체의 신비롭고 경이로운 기능을 고려할 때, 원인과 결과는 단순하지 않으며, 쉽게 입증될 수 있지도 않다. 원인과 결과의 사이는 공간, 시간적으로 멀리 떨어져 있을 수 있다. 질병과 죽음의 원인을 밝히는 작업은, 멀리 떨어진 다양한 연구 분야에서 수집된 개별적이고 관련 없어 보이는 수많은 사실을 참을성 있게 맞추어보는 과정에 달려 있다.

| 어휘 |

pesticide n. 살충제 **disease** n. 질병 **contaminate** v. 오염시키다 **stream** n. 개울, 시내 **fishless** a. 물고기 없는 **woodland** n. 삼림지대 **distribute** v. 분포시키다 **escape** v. 피하다 **exposure** n. 노출 **chemical** n. 화학물질 **precipitate** v. 재촉하다 **acute poisoning** 급성 중독 **sprayman** n. 살포하는 사람 **appreciable** a. 주목할 만한 **invisibly** a. 보이지 않게 **hazard** n. 위험 **sum** n. 합 **vague** a. 애매모호한 **manifestaton** n. 표명 **creep** v. 살금살금 기다 **unobtrusively** ad. 관심을 끌지 않고 **ecology** n. 생태계 **unseen** a. 보이지 않는 **minute** a. 미세한 **seemingly** ad. 겉으로 보기에 **unrelated** a. 무관한 **remote** a. 멀리 떨어진 **injury** n. 손상 **sustain** v. 지탱하다, 유지하다 **functioning** n. 기능 **piece together** 연결하다, 조각을 맞추다 **vast** a. 거대한 **field** n. 분야

| 48 | 어법상 적절하지 않은 표현 고르기 | ③ |

| 분석 |

ⓒ의 receiving이 exposures를 수식하는데, '받아들여진' 노출이므로 과거분사 received로 고쳐야 한다.

| 49 | 문장삽입 | ③ |

| 분석 |

오염으로 인한 갑작스러운 죽음이 문제가 아니라 오래 누적되는 위험이 문제라는 이유 관련 언급이 있어야 뒤에 위험이 무시된다는 결과에 해당하는 내용이 자연스럽게 온다. 따라서 정답은 ③의 ⓒ이다.

| 50 | 부분이해 | ④ |

| 분석 |

밑줄 친 부분은 '보이지 않게 퍼진 농약을 소량 흡수하는 것이 시간이 지난 뒤에 초래하는 효과'에 해당되는데, 이러한 지연된 효과에 대해 "종종 원인과 관련이 없는 듯 보이고, 원래 손상이 발생한 곳과는 먼 신체 부위에서 나타나기도 한다"고 설명하고 있다. 이는 원인과 결과가 멀리 떨어져 있어 추적하기가 어렵다는 것이므로, ④가 정답이 된다.

(1)을 가장 잘 설명하는 내용은?
① 사람들은 살충제의 유독한 유출에 의해 중독될 수 있다.
② 살충제에 노출되는 사람들은 갑작스러운 질병과 즉각적인 죽음을 마주할 수 있다.
③ 사람들은 질병 및 죽음의 인자를 혼자 발견할 수 있다.
④ 사람들은 건강 위기의 처음 원인을 추적할 수 없다.

SOONGSIL UNIVERSITY | 숭실대학교 자연계

TEST p. 484~494

01	①	02	①	03	②	04	③	05	②	06	①	07	③	08	④	09	①	10	②
11	④	12	③	13	②	14	④	15	①	16	④	17	②	18	①	19	④	20	②
21	③	22	①	23	④	24	③	25	④										

01 동격절을 이끄는 접속사 that ①

| 분석 |

①의 관계대명사 which 다음에 완전한 절이 왔으므로 적절하지 않다. practically everyone부터 could prosper까지 완전한 절로 주어는 practically everyone이고, 동사는 could prosper이며, willing to work hard는 practically everyone을 수식한다. 따라서 ①을 명사절을 이끄는 접속사 that으로 고쳐서 myth와 that 이하가 동격이 되도록 해야 한다.

| 어휘 |

prosper v. 번영하다, 번창하다 **promulgate** v. (사상·신조 등을) 널리 알리다, 보급하다

| 해석 |

열심히 일할 의지가 있는 거의 모든 사람은 번영할 수 있다는 신화는 철도 회사들의 토지사무소에 의해 널리 퍼졌다.

02 분사구문 ①

| 분석 |

콤마 이하에 완전한 절이 주어져 있으므로 맨 앞의 Attempt는 명사이든, 동사원형이든, 적절하지 않다. 따라서 콤마 앞은 분사구문이 되어야 한다. 분사구문의 주어는 주절의 주어와 같을 경우 생략될 수 있으므로 radical reformers가 분사구문의 주어이다. radical reformers가 attempt하는 행위의 주체이므로 능동을 나타내는 현재분사가 적절하다. 따라서 ①을 Attempting으로 고쳐야 한다.

| 어휘 |

speculation n. 추측, 억측; 투기 **radical** a. 급진적인, 과격한 **homestead** n. (특히 농장의 건물과 땅이 딸린) 주택[농가] **inalienable** a. 양도할 수 없는, 빼앗을 수 없는 **speculate** v. 추측하다; 투기하다

| 해석 |

투기로부터 자신들을 보호하려고 시도하면서, 가장 급진적인 개혁가들은 농가의 토지를 양도할 수 없는 것으로 만들 것을 촉구했는데, 매매할 수 없는 토지는 또한 투기의 대상도 될 수 없는 것이 분명했기 때문이었다.

03 논리완성 ②

| 분석 |

논쟁이 격렬해졌다고 했으므로 양측은 증거와 논리적인 주장으로 자신들의 입장을 더 확고히 다지려 했다는 의미가 되어야 한다. 따라서 빈칸에는 '강화하다'는 뜻의 ② reinforce가 적절하다.

| 어휘 |

heated a. 가열된; 격렬한 **contradict** v. 부정[부인]하다; 모순되다 **reinforce** v. 강화하다 **obscure** v. 어둡게 하다; 모호하게 하다 **abandon** v. 버리다; 단념하다, 그만두다

| 해석 |

양측이 증거와 논리적인 주장으로 자신들의 입장을 강화하려고 노력하면서 논쟁은 격렬해졌다.

04 논리완성 ③

| 분석 |

'지속 가능한 관행(sustainable practices)'은 환경을 파괴하지 않으면서 지속될 수 있는 관행을 말한다. 기업들이 이러한 관행을 도입하려는 이유는 수익을 창출하면서도 환경에 미치는 영향을 줄이기 위한 것으로 볼 수 있으므로 빈칸에는 '환경적인'의 뜻의 ③ environmental이 적절하다.

| 어휘 |

strive v. 노력하다, 얻으려고 애쓰다 **adopt** v. 채택하다, 도입하다 **sustainable** a. (환경 파괴 없이) 지속 가능한 **impact** n. 영향 **cooperative** a. 협력적인 **lucrative** a. 유리한, 수지맞는, 돈이 벌리는 **environmental** a. 환경의 **intrusive** a. 침입적인; 주제넘게 참견하는, 훼방 놓는

| 해석 |
많은 기업들이 돈을 벌기 위해서 뿐 아니라 환경적 영향을 줄이기 위해서 지속 가능한 관행을 도입하기 위해 노력하고 있다.

05 논리완성 ②

| 분석 |
세계적 수요가 증가하고 있다고 했으므로 회사는 이러한 수요를 충족시키기 위해 사업을 국제 시장으로 확장하려 할 것이다. 따라서 빈칸에는 '확장하다'는 뜻의 ② expand가 적절하다.

| 어휘 |
operation n. 사업, 영업 **in response to** ~에 응하여, 대응하여
condense v. 압축하다; 요약하다 **expand** v. 확장하다, 확대하다
contradict v. 부정[부인]하다; 모순되다 **evaporate** v. 증발시키다

| 해석 |
그 회사는 증가하는 세계적 수요에 대응하여 새로운 국제 시장으로 사업을 확장하기로 결정했다.

06 논리완성 ①

| 분석 |
'difficult to predict(예측하기 어려운)'와 유사한 의미의 단어가 빈칸에 들어가야 한다. 그의 반응이 일관되지 않고 불규칙해야 예측하기 어렵게 되므로 빈칸에는 '불규칙한, 변덕스러운'의 뜻의 ① erratic이 적절하다.

| 어휘 |
erratic a. 불규칙한, 변덕스러운 **lucid** a. 명쾌한, 알기 쉬운
systematic a. 체계적인, 조직적인 **consistent** a. 일관된, 모순이 없는

| 해석 |
그녀가 상황을 설명하려고 노력했음에도 불구하고, 그의 반응은 여전히 불규칙하고 예측하기 어려웠다.

07 동의어 ③

| 어휘 |
clarity n. 명석, 명료, 명확(= lucidity) **non-expert** n. 비전문가
confusion n. 혼란, 혼동 **ambiguity** n. 애매모호함 **eloquence** n. 웅변, 능변

| 해석 |
그 과학자는 자신의 연구 결과를 명료하게 제시하여, 비전문가들도 복잡한 내용을 이해할 수 있게 했다.

08 동의어 ④

| 어휘 |
eloquent a. 웅변의; 감명적인, 설득력 있는(= persuasive) **move** v. 감동시키다; ~할 마음이 일어나게 하다 **abrupt** a. 돌연한, 갑작스러운 **vague** a. 모호한, 애매한 **monotonous** a. 단조로운

| 해석 |
그녀의 연설은 너무 설득력 있어서 청중을 감동으로 눈물짓게 했다.

09 동의어 ①

| 어휘 |
rigorous a. 엄격한 **regimen** n. 섭생, 양생법; 꾸준하고 엄한 훈련; 교육 프로그램(= program) **surpass** v. 능가하다, 뛰어넘다 **trainer** n. 훈련자, 트레이너 **institution** n. 기관, 협회 **elaboration** n. 공들여 만듦; 복잡함, 정교; (추가한) 상세한 말; 상술

| 해석 |
그 운동선수의 엄격한 훈련 프로그램은 그녀가 대회에서 자신의 개인 기록을 넘어설 수 있게 해주었다.

10 동의어 ②

| 어휘 |
comprehensive a. 포괄적인(= thorough) **incomplete** a. 불완전한, 불충분한, 미완성의 **biased** a. 치우친, 편견을 지닌, 편향된 **selective** a. 선택적인

| 해석 |
그 책은 모든 주요 사건을 자세히 다루어 그 국가의 역사에 대한 포괄적인 개요를 제공했다.

11~13

나는 사전에 포함되어서는 안 되는 부당한 단어들에 대한 우려를 표현하는 신문 기사들을 모두 모은 파일을 사무실에 갖고 있다. 이 단어들에는 『옥스퍼드 영어사전(Oxford English Dictionary)』에 등재되었을 때의 "LOL"과 『옥스포드 미국 영어사전(Oxford American Dictionary)』에 등재되었을 때의 "defriend"가 포함된다. 나는 또한 "invite"가 명사로 쓰이는 것과 "impact"가 동사로 쓰이는 것 ― 치아만이 (턱뼈에) 매복될 수 있기 때문에 ― 과 "incentivize"가 '상스럽고 관료적인 잘못된 말'로 묘사되는 것에 대한 우려를 표명하는 기사들도 갖고 있다.

지금, 사전 편집자들이 언어에 대한 이러한 종류의 태도를

무시하는 것은 아니다. 그들은 속어나 비공식적이거나 모욕적인 것으로 여겨지는 단어들에 대한 어떤 지침을 종종 용법 표시를 통해 제공하려고 하지만, 다소 난처한 입장에 처해 있는데, 그것은 그들이 우리가 무엇을 하는지(실제로 어떻게 단어를 사용하는지)를 보여주려고 노력하고 있으며, 우리가 단어를 어떻게 하면 제대로 적절하게 사용하는지에 대한 정보를 얻기 위해 사전을 자주 찾는다는 것을 알고 있기 때문이다. 이에 대응하여, 『아메리칸 헤리티지 영어사전(American Heritage Dictionary)』에는 용법 주석이 포함되어 있다. 용법 주석은 어떤 면에서 문제가 되는 단어들의 경우에 나오는 경향이 있으며, 단어들이 문제가 될 수 있는 방법 중 하나는 의미를 바꾸는 것이다. 이제 용법 주석은 매우 인간적인 결정을 수반하며, 나는 사전 사용자로서의 우리가 이러한 인간적인 결정에 대해 알고 있어야 할 만큼 알고 있지 못한 경우가 종종 있다고 생각한다. 내 말이 무슨 뜻인지 보여주기 위해 우리는 하나의 예를 살펴볼 것이다. 하지만 우리가 그렇게 하기 전에, 나는 사전 편집자들이 이 용법 주석에서 다루고자 하는 것이 무엇인지 설명하고 싶다. "peruse"라는 단어와 그 단어를 어떻게 사용하는지 생각해 보라. 많은 사람들이 '훑어보다', '대충 읽다', '빠르게 읽다'에 대해 생각하고 있을 것이다. 일부 사람들은 심지어 약간의 걸어가는 동작도 포함시킬 것인데, 식료품 가게 선반이나 그 비슷한 것을 peruse하고(걸어가며 빠르게 읽고) 있기 때문이다. 대부분의 표준 사전을 살펴보면, 첫 번째 정의가 '주의 깊게 읽다' 또는 '자세히 조사하다'라는 것을 알고 놀랄지도 모른다. 『아메리칸 헤리티지 영어사전』도 그것을 첫 번째 정의로 제시하고 있다. 그런 다음 그것들(표준사전들)은 두 번째 정의로 '훑어보다'를 제시하고, 그 옆에 '용법상의 문제'라고 표시해 놓는다. 그리고 나서 살펴볼 가치가 있는 용법 주석을 포함시킨다.

| 어휘 |

illegitimate a. 불법[위법]의; (말·어구 따위가) 잘못 쓰인, 오용된 **boorish** a. 상스러운, 천박한, 거친 **bureaucratic** a. 관료적인 **ignore** v. 무시하다 **guidance** n. 지도, 안내; 본보기, 지침 **slang** n. 속어, 은어 **informal** a. 비공식의, 약식의 **offensive** a. 모욕적인 **usage** n. (단어의) 용법[어법, 사용] **in a bind** 곤경에 빠져, 매우 난처하여 **troublesome** a. 골치 아픈, 성가신, 귀찮은 **peruse** v. 숙독[정독]하다; 읽다 **skim** v. 대충 읽다, 훑어보다 **pore over** 자세히 조사하다, 세세히 보다

11 글의 제목   ④

| 분석 |
두 번째 단락에서 '사전편집자들은 … 단어들에 대한 어떤 지침을 종종 용법 표시를 통해 제공하려고 하지만, 다소 난처한 입장에 처해 있는데, 그것은 그들이 우리가 무엇을 하는지(실제로 어떻게 단어를 사용하는지)를 보여주려고 노력하고 있다'라고 했는데, 단어들에 대한 지침을 제공한다는 것은 언어를 (규범적으로) 규정한다(prescribe)는 것이고 우리가 실제로 어떻게 단어를 사용하는지를 보여준다는 것은 언어를 기술한다(describe)는 것이다. 그런데 이 두 가지 사이에서 그들이 난처한 입장에 처해 있다(dilemma)고 했으므로 이 글의 제목으로는 ④가 적절하다.

다음 중 가장 적절한 제목은 무엇인가?
① 속어의 진화: 현대의 사전
② 올바른 문법과 어휘의 중요성
③ 사전이 세상에 대한 우리의 이해를 형성하는 방법
④ 사전의 딜레마: 언어를 기술할 것인가 규정할 것인가

12 내용파악   ③

| 분석 |
첫 번째 단락에서 작가의 사무실에 있는 신문 기사들에 대해 이야기하고 있다. 그 기사들은 LOL, defriend, invite, impact, incentivize 등과 같이 사전에 등재되었을 때 논란의 여지가 있을 수 있는 단어들에 대한 우려를 담고 있다고 하였다. 따라서 ③이 정답으로 적절하다.

작가의 사무실에는 _____에 관한 신문 기사들이 있다:
① 사전 개정 제안
② 언어 진화 연구
③ 논란의 여지가 있는 단어 추가
④ 현대 속어 연구

13 내용파악   ②

| 분석 |
마지막 단락에서 "peruse"라는 단어에 대해 설명하고 있다. 많은 사람들이 "peruse"라는 단어를 '훑어보다'나 '대충 읽다'라는 의미로 자주 사용하지만, 대부분의 표준 사전에서는 1차적 정의로 '주의 깊게 읽다'라는 의미를 제시하고 2차적 정의로 '대충 읽다'는 의미를 제시하고 있다고 했다. 따라서 ②가 적절하다.

다음 중 대부분의 사람들이 "peruse"라는 단어를 전통적인 사전 정의와 비교하여 어떻게 사용하는지를 가장 잘 설명하는 것은?
① 대부분의 사람들은 그것을 '주의 깊게 읽다'라는 의미로 사용하며, 이는 제1의 사전적 정의와 일치한다.
② 대부분의 사람들은 그것을 '훑어보다' 또는 '대충 읽다'라는 의미로 사용하지만, 사전에서는 1차적으로 그것을 '주의 깊게 읽다'라고 정의한다.
③ 대부분의 사람들은 가게 안을 걸어 다니는 동안 그것을 사용하며, 이는 제1의 사전적 정의이다.
④ 본문에 따르면, 대부분의 사람들은 이 단어를 전혀 사용하지 않는다.

14~15

(원래 '컴퓨터 통계'를 상징하는) Compstat은 1994년 뉴욕 경찰청에서 처음 개발한 범죄 분석 및 책임 시스템이다. 윌리엄 J. 브래턴(William J. Bratton) 경찰청장의 지휘 하에 처음 시행된 Compstat은 지리 정보 시스템(GIS)을 사용하여 범죄 발생률을 추적한다. 이 시스템은 범죄 데이터를 빠른 시간 내에 수집, 분석 및 매핑(지도로 나타냄)하여 범죄 패턴을 발견하는 것뿐만 아니라 경찰 관리자들이 자신들의 관할 구역에서의 결과에 대해 책임을 지는 주간 회의를 여는 것도 포함한다. 이 데이터는 범죄가 집중되는 위험한 장소를 정확히 찾아내고, 이에 따라 경찰 자원을 배치하는 데 사용된다. 뉴욕에서 도입된 이후 수십 년 동안 미국의 많은 대도시에서 일부 변형된 Compstat을 채택해왔다. Compstat은 신고된 범죄의 감소에 기여하고, 실제로 범죄 자체의 감소에도 기여한 것으로 보인다.

그러나 도시마다 범죄 통계의 정확성과 신뢰성에 대한 의문이 제기되어 왔다. Compstat이 정보 및 지표 측정 시스템인 한, 그것은 실제로 유용해 보인다. 그러나 시장이 경찰 고위 간부들에게 전반적인 수치의 개선을 보여주도록 압력을 가하고, 그 압력이 다시 승진이 범죄의 꾸준한 감소에 달려 있다고 믿게 되는 지역 사령관들에게 가해질 때, 하급 경찰관들이 때때로 듣는 메시지는 신고된 범죄의 증가로 인해 그들이 불이익을 받을 것이라는 것이다. 그리고 이는 숫자를 조작하도록 압력을 일으킨다.

이러한 문제들은 Compstat의 등장 이전에 발생했으며 Compstat와는 별도로 존재하고 있다. 1976년 사회 심리학자 도널드 T. 캠벨(Donald T. Campbell)은 리처드 닉슨(Richard Nixon) 대통령이 선언한 범죄 단속이 그 주된 결과로 "범죄율 지표의 부패를 초래했는데, 이 부패는 범죄를 축소하여 기록하거나 범죄를 덜 심각한 범주로 격하시킴으로써 이루어졌다."라고 언급했다. 그리고 그것은 계속되고 있다.

| 어휘 |

accountability n. 책임, 책무 **pioneer** v. 개척하다; 선도하다, 지도하다 **track** v. 추적하다 **incidence** n. (사건·영향 따위의) 범위, 발생률 **time-frame** n. (특정한 상황 아래서 어떤 일에 소요되는) 기간, 시간 **entail** v. (필연적 결과로서) 일으키다, 수반하다 **accountable** a. 책임이 있는 **precinct** n. (경찰서의) 관할 구역 **pinpoint** v. ~의 위치를 정확히 나타내다 **hot spot** 분쟁 지대; (일반적으로) 위험한 장소; 곤란한 상황 **deploy** v. 배치하다 **roll out** (신상품을) 출시하다; (새로운 정치 캠페인을) 시작하다 **accuracy** n. 정확, 정확성 **reliability** n. 신뢰성 **insofar as** ~하는 한에 있어서는 **indicative** a. ~을 나타내는, 표시하는 **metric** n. 측정 기준 **genuinely** ad. 성실하게, 진정으로 **mayor** n. 시장 **pressure** v. 압력을 가하다, 강요하다 **top brass** 고급 간부들, 고관들 **steady** a. 꾸준한 **diminution** n. 감소, 축소 **low-level** a. 지위가 낮은, 하급의 **penalize** v. 벌하다; 불리하게 하다; 벌칙을 적용하다 **fudge** v. 날조하다; 속이다 **precede** v. ~에 선행하다[앞서다]; ~보다 먼저 일어나다 **independent of** ~와는 관계없이, ~와는 별도로 **crackdown** n. 엄중한 단속, 탄압 **corruption** n. 부패, 타락 **downgrade** v. 격하시키다

14 지시대상   ④

| 분석 |

Compstat이 등장하기 이전에도 범죄율의 감소를 보여주기 위해 데이터를 조작하는 문제가 있었으며, 그 이후에도 이러한 문제가 계속되고 있다는 것이다. 따라서 범죄를 축소하여 기록하거나 범죄를 경미한 범죄로 격하시켜 분류하는 등의 '범죄율 지표의 부패'가 계속해서 일어나고 있다고 할 수 있으므로 ④가 적절하다.

다음 중 ⓐ가 가리키는 것을 가장 잘 설명하는 것은?
① 중범죄의 분류
② 닉슨 대통령의 범죄 단속
③ Compstat의 부상
④ 범죄율 지표의 부패

15 내용파악   ①

| 분석 |

시장이 경찰 고위 간부들에게 범죄율을 감소시키도록 압력을 가하고, 그 압력이 다시 그 지역 사령관들에게 가해져서 하위 경찰관들을 압박하게 되고, 하위 경찰관들은 범죄율을 낮추기 위해 데이터를 조작하게 된다고 했다. 따라서 ①이 적절하다.

다음 중 Compstat 시스템의 잠재적 문제를 가장 잘 나타내는 것은?
① 향상된 통계를 보여주어야 한다는 압박은 데이터 조작으로 이어질 수 있다.
② 주간 회의는 과도한 행정적 부담을 초래한다.
③ 지리 정보 시스템은 기술적으로 구식이다.
④ 경찰관들은 그 시스템을 효과적으로 사용하기 위한 적절한 교육이 부족하다.

16~18

어른들은 아이들이 어떻게 배우고 있는지에 대해 걱정하고 있다. 명확한 데이터가 없는 상황에서, 많은 부모와 교육자들은 디지털 기술이 우리 아이들과 그들의 학습 능력에 미치는 영향에 대해 두려워한다. 기사 제목 형식의 슬로건이 젊은이들의 뇌에 스며드는 정보를 좌우하며, 그 과정에서 아이들은 분석 능력이 거의 발달하지 못한다고 그들은 우려한다. 걱정되는 것은 아이들은 교육받는 내내 채널을 자주 바꾸고,

그 과정에서 뇌가 재구성되고 있다는 것이다.
디지털 네이티브가 자라면서 부모가 배운 방식과 다르게 학습한다고 해서 디지털 네이티브가 학습하지 않는다는 뜻은 아니다. 예를 들어 디지털 네이티브가 뉴스에서 사건에 대해 배우는 방식을 살펴보자. 많은 나이든 사람들은 디지털 네이티브가 신문과 잡지를 읽지 않고, 대신 다양한 웹사이트(코미디 프로그램과 기타 비전통적인 출처)에서 하루 종일 뉴스를 흡수하기 때문에, 시사 문제에 대한 이해가 피상적이고 기사 제목에 국한되어 있다고 생각한다. 설상가상으로, 이러한 기사 제목은 『뉴욕 타임즈(New York Times)』나 대형 텔레비전 방송망인 NBC, ABC, CBS와 같은 권위 있는 기관이 아닌 편향된 웹사이트에서 나온 것이라고 부모와 교사들은 걱정하고 있다. 완전히 잘못된 정보가 아니라면, 디지털 네이티브가 온라인에서 접하는 이야기 버전은 피상적일 것이라고 많은 사람들은 우려한다.
이러한 가정은 디지털 네이티브가 웹에서 얻고 있는 지식의 깊이를 과소평가하기 때문에 잘못된 것이다. 그 가정은 또한 디지털 네이티브가 뉴스를 접하는 방식의 중요한 특징을 놓치고 있는데, 그 특징은 곧 정보와 건설적인 방식으로 상호작용한다는 것이다. 디지털 네이티브는 종종 그들이 관심 있는 주제에 대해 이전 세대의 아이들이 가질 수 있었던 것보다 훨씬 더 많은 정보를 접한다. 젊은 사람들과 그들의 뉴스 수집 습관에 대한 최근 연구는 이러한 변화를 확인해 준다. 예를 들어, 이 연구는 미국의 젊은 사람들은 일간 신문을 읽지 않는다는 사실을 발견했다. 디지털 네이티브는 아침에 아침 식탁에 앉아서나 저녁에 텔레비전 앞에 앉아서 한 번에 뉴스를 접하는 것이 아니라, 하루 일과를 하면서 이런저런 뉴스와 정보를 수집한다. 그리고 종종, 그들은 블로그에 아이디어에 대한 게시물을 작성하거나 페이스북이나 인스턴트 메신저를 통해 친구와 게시물을 공유함으로써 보다 전통적인 뉴스 형식에 익숙한 사람들보다 실제로 뉴스에 더 많이 관여한다.

| 어휘 |
in the absence of ~이 없을 경우에, ~이 없어서   fearful of ~을 두려워하는   slogan n. 슬로건, 표어; 선전 문구   seep v. 스며들다, 침투하다   channel-surf v. 채널을 자주 바꾸다   Digital Native 디지털 네이티브(컴퓨터, 인터넷, 휴대전화 등의 디지털 기술을 어려서부터 사용하면서 성장한 세대)   unconventional a. 관습[인습]에 얽매이지 않는   superficial a. 피상적인; 외면의   biased a. 치우친, 편향된   authoritative a. 권위 있는, 정식의   outright ad. 완전히, 철저히   underestimate v. 과소평가하다   confirm v. (특히 증거를 들어) 사실임을 보여주다[확인해 주다]   go about one's day 하루 일과를 하다, 일상생활을 하다   by virtue of ~에 의해서, ~덕분으로

16 글의 제목 ④

| 분석 |
이 글은 디지털 네이티브가 기존 세대와는 다른 방식으로 웹을 통해 뉴스를 접하고 있으며, 이는 피상적이거나 편향된 것이 아니라 건설적이고 능동적인 과정임을 강조하고 있다. 단순히 신문이나 잡지를 통해 정보를 얻던 전통적인 방식과 다르게 디지털 환경에서 많은 정보를 수집하고, 블로그나 페이스북을 통해 이를 서로 공유하거나 토론하면서 더 적극적으로 학습하고 있다고 했으므로 글의 제목으로 ④가 적절하다.

다음 중 가장 적절한 제목은 무엇인가?
① 젊은이들을 위한 디지털 기술의 위험성
② 아이들을 위한 권위 있는 뉴스 출처의 중요성
③ 디지털 학습 방식을 채택해야 하는 긴급한 필요성
④ 디지털 네이티브가 학습 환경을 변화시키고 있는 방법

17 내용파악 ②

| 분석 |
어른들은 아이들이 배우는 방식이 그들이 배운 전통적인 학습 방식과 달라서 학습을 제대로 하고 있는지 의문을 가지고 있으며, 디지털 기술을 통해 피상적인 정보만을 얻음으로써 분석 능력이 저하되고 있다고 걱정하고 있다. 따라서 ②가 정답으로 적절하다.

많은 어른들이 아이들과 디지털 기술에 대해 갖고 있는 주된 걱정은 무엇인가?
① 아이들은 비디오 게임을 하는 데 너무 많은 시간을 보내고 있다.
② 디지털 기술은 아이들의 학습 능력과 분석적 기술을 기르는 능력을 방해하고 있다.
③ 아이들은 의사소통을 위해 소셜 미디어에 너무 의존하고 있다.
④ 디지털 기술은 아이들을 신체 활동을 덜 하게 만들고 있다.

18 내용파악 ①

| 분석 |
디지털 네이티브는 신문과 잡지를 읽지 않고, 하루 종일 다양한 웹사이트, 코미디 프로그램, 기타 비전통적인 출처에서 뉴스와 정보를 수집하고 학습한다고 했다. 따라서 ①이 적절하다.

디지털 네이티브는 일반적으로 시사(時事)에 대해 어떻게 배우는가?
① 하루 종일 다양한 웹사이트, 코미디 프로그램, 그리고 기타 비전통적인 출처의 결합을 통해
② 주로 전통적인 신문과 잡지를 읽는 것을 통해
③ 주요 텔레비전 방송망의 야간 뉴스 방송을 시청함으로써
④ 『뉴욕 타임즈』와 같은 권위 있는 기관의 기사들을 심층 분석하는 것을 통해

19~20

사회적 연대와 시민적 미덕에 대해서도 비슷한 질문을 할 수 있다. 우리는 시민들에게 국가가 공익을 위해 희생할 것을 요구할 때까지 쇼핑하러 가라고 말함으로써 시민적 미덕을 보존하려고 노력해야 하는가? 아니면 시민적 미덕과 공공 정신은 사용하지 않으면 쇠퇴하는가? 많은 도덕주의자들은 두 번째 견해를 취했다. 아리스토텔레스(Aristotle)는 미덕은 우리가 실천을 통해 기르는 것이라고 가르쳤다. "우리는 정의로운 행동을 함으로써 정의로워지고, 절제된 행동을 함으로서 절제 있게 되며, 용감한 행동을 함으로써 용감해진다."

루소는 이와 비슷한 견해를 갖고 있었다. 한 국가가 시민들에게 더 많은 것을 요구할수록, 국가에 대한 그들의 헌신은 더 커진다. "질서가 잡힌 도시에서는 모든 사람이 기꺼이 집회에 참여한다." 나쁜 정부 아래에서는 아무도 공공 생활에 참여하지 않는데, "왜냐하면 아무도 그곳에서 일어나는 일에 관심이 없고 집안일에 모든 관심이 집중되어 있기 때문이다." 시민적 미덕은 격렬한 시민 의식에 의해 소모되는 것이 아니라 증강된다. 루소는 사실상 '그것을 사용하지 않으면 잃는다'라고 말한다. "공공 봉사가 더 이상 시민들의 주요한 직무가 아니게 되고, 그들이 몸소 봉사하기보다는 돈으로 봉사하기를 원할 때, 국가는 몰락할 날이 멀지 않다."

경제학자이자 존 메이너드 케인스(John Maynard Keynes)의 제자였던 데니스 H. 로버트슨(Dennis H. Robertson) 경은 가볍고 사색적인 태도로 자신의 견해를 제시한다. 그러나 사랑과 관대함이 사용할수록 고갈되는 희소한 자원이라는 개념은 경제학자들이 이를 명시적으로 주장하지 않더라도, 경제학자들의 도덕적 상상력을 계속 강력하게 지배하고 있다. 이것은 수요와 공급의 법칙처럼 공식적인 교과서 원칙이 아니다. 아무도 이를 실증적으로 증명하지 못했다. 많은 경제학자들이 여전히 지지하는 격언, 즉 민간의 지혜에 더 가깝다.

| 어휘 |

solidarity n. 연대, 결속 **civic** a. 시의; 시민의 **virtue** n. 미덕, 덕목 **conserve** v. 보존하다, 보호하다 **sacrifice** v. 희생하다; 제물을 바치다 **common good** 공익 **atrophy** v. 위축되다, 쇠퇴하다 **moralist** n. 도덕주의자 **cultivate** v. 기르다; 교화하다, 계발하다 **just** a. 올바른, 공정한 **temperate** a. 절제하는, 삼가는 **brave** a. 용감한 **devotion** n. 헌신, 전념 **well-ordered** a. 질서 있는, 질서가 잡힌 **assembly** n. 집회 **domestic** a. 가정의; 국내의 **strenuous** a. 활발한, 정력적인; 격렬한 **citizenship** n. 시민권; 시민의 신분[자질] **cease** v. (~하는 것을) 그만두다; (~이) 아니게 되다 **fall** n. 멸망, 몰락 **observation** n. 관찰; (관찰에 의거한) 의견, 비평 **lighthearted** a. 근심이 없는, 마음 편한; 쾌활한 **speculative** a. 사색적인, 이론적인 **generosity** n. 관대함, 관용 **scarce** a. 부족한, 드문, 희귀한 **deplete** v. (세력·자원 따위를) 고갈시키다 **exert** v. (힘·능력 등을) 쓰다, 발휘하다; (영향 등을) 미치다 **explicitly** ad. 명시적으로 **empirically** ad. 경험[실험]에 의거하여, 실증적으로 **adage** n. 속담, 격언, 금언 **folk** a. 서민의, 민중의 **wisdom** n. 현명함, 지혜 **subscribe to** (의견·이론 등에[을]) 동의[지지]하다

19 내용파악   ④

| 분석 |

시민적 미덕과 실천 사이의 관계를 아리스토텔레스, 루소 등의 견해를 제시하여 설명하고 있다. 아리스토텔레스는 미덕은 실천을 통해 길러진다고 했고, 루소는 공공 생활의 적극적인 참여를 통해 시민적 미덕은 강화된다고 하였으므로 ④가 적절하다.

시민적 미덕과 그것의 실천 사이의 관계는 무엇인가?
① 시민적 미덕은 재정 예산과 유사하게 사용에 따라 감소하는 유한한 자원이다.
② 시민적 미덕은 시민들에게 요구를 최소화하고 그들이 사생활에 집중할 수 있도록 함으로써 가장 잘 보존된다.
③ 시민적 미덕은 시민의 행동과 상관없이 일정하게 유지되는 타고난 자질이다.
④ 시민적 미덕은 실천과 공공 생활의 적극적인 참여를 통해 길러지고 강화된다.

20 내용파악   ②

| 분석 |

루소는 나쁜 정부에서는 시민들이 공공 생활에 참여하지 않는데, 이는 시민들이 국가에서 일어나는 일에 관심이 없으며 사적인 일에 몰두하기 때문이라고 설명하고 있다. 따라서 ②가 정답으로 적절하다.

루소는 시민들이 공공 봉사보다 사적인 이익을 우선시할 때 어떤 일이 일어난다고 믿는가?
① 국가는 더욱 민주적이 된다.
② 시민들은 공공 생활에 대한 관심을 잃는다.
③ 시민적 미덕이 강화된다.
④ 공공 집회는 더욱 활기를 띠게 된다.

21~23

청각 장애인 교육의 역사학자들 대부분은 세대 변화를 지적함으로써 교육학적 역전을 설명해왔다. 할런 레인(Harlan Lane)과 더글러스 베인턴(Douglas Baynton) 모두 청각 장애인 교육이 수화(手話)기반 시스템에서 구화(口話)기반 시스템으로 바뀐 것은 이러한 방식으로 설명될 수 있다고 주장한다. 레인은 "믿을 수 없을 것 같지만, 지난 세기 말에 청각 교육자와 사업가들의 작은 목소리만으로도 구화(口

話)주의의 물결이 서유럽을 휩쓸었고, 모든 수화(手話) 공동체를 익사시켰다. 미국에서는 수화의 침몰이 거의 서유럽에서만큼 완전했다."라고 결론짓는다. 그리고 베인턴은 수화법이 여러 가지 이유로 남북전쟁 이전 시대에 자란 교육자의 세대에게 매력적으로 보였던 반면, 구화주의는 남북전쟁 이후 성인이 된 사람들에게 문화적으로 더 합리적이었다고 믿는다.

하지만 구화 교육에 대한 최초의 일관된 주장은 1844년에 호러스 맨(Horace Mann)에 의해 제기되었는데, 호러스 맨은 레인과 베인턴의 설명에서 무시된 인물이다. 레인은 맨을 잘 속는 사람으로 간주한다. 처음에는 독일 청각 장애인 교사들에게 속았는데, 1843년에 독일 방문에서 그들의 발음 교육에 깊은 감명을 받았던 것이다. 그리고 그다음에는 새뮤얼 그리들리 하우(Samuel Gridley Howe)에게 속았는데, 레인에 따르면, 하우는 맨에게 구화주의를 찬양하도록 설득했고 이는 하우가 "Hartford로부터 청각 장애인 교육을 빼앗아서 그것을 퍼킨스 시각 장애인 학교에서 자신의 지도 하에 두려는 것을 돕기 위해서였다." 이 견해는 맨이 청각 장애인 교육 문제에 관심을 가질 만한 자신만의 이유가 있을 수 있다는 실제 가능성을 무시한다. 베인턴도 마찬가지로 이와 관련한 맨의 영향력을 경시하고, 그가 '미국의 뛰어난 교육자'였지만 구화주의를 위한 그의 노력의 결과는 '미미했다'고 주장한다. 베인턴에 따르면, 1840년대는 구화주의를 위한 적절한 문화적 환경이 아니었다. 수화 교육 지지자들은 청각 장애를 낭만적으로 보았고, 청각 장애인을 신과 더 가까운 존재로 보고 신이 그들에게 침묵의 무지로부터 구해줄 특별한 선물인 수화를 주었다고 여겼다. 〈맨의 과학적 구화주의는 이런 복음주의적 경건함과 경쟁할 수 없었다.〉 그러나 1876년에 뉴잉글랜드 최초의 구화 학교인 클라크 청각장애인학교가 개교했을 때, 맨의 유령이 그 행사 주위를 맴돌았다. 하우는 그 제안된 학교의 자금제공과 방식 문제를 결정하기 위해 열린 입법 청문회에서 맨의 기억을 환기시켰다.

| 어휘 |

deaf a. 귀가 먹은, 청각 장애가 있는   **pedagogical** a. 교육(학)의, 교수법의   **reversal** n. 반전, 전도, 역전   **transformation** n. 변화, 변환   **manually** ad. 손으로, 수동으로   **orally** ad. 구두로, 말로   **incredible** a. 믿을 수 없는   **oralism** n. 구화주의, 구화법(난청자의 의사소통을 수화(手話)가 아니고 독순술(讀脣術)과 발화(發話) 훈련에 의해서 하려는 이론)   **drown** v. 물에 빠지게 하다, 익사시키다   **submersion** n. 침수, 침몰   **manualism** n. 수화법   **antebellum** a. 전전(戰前)의; 남북전쟁 전의   **cohesive** a. 결합력 있는; 응집성의   **disregard** v. 무시하다, 경시하다   **dupe** n. 잘 속는 사람, 얼간이   **articulation** n. 명확한 발음; 발음(법); 명확한 표현   **wrest** v. 억지로 빼앗다; ~을 노력하여 얻다   **downplay** v. 경시하다, 대단치 않게 생각하다   **pre-eminent** a. 출중한, 탁월한   **on behalf of** ~을 대표[대신]하여; ~을 위하여   **negligible** a. 무시해도 좋은; 보잘것없는, 하찮은   **romanticize** v. 낭만적으로 묘사하다, 낭만화하다   **deafness** n. 귀먹음; 귀 기울이지 않음   **rescue** v. 구조하다, 구하다   **silent** a. 침묵하는, 무언의   **ignorance** n. 무지   **hover** v. 맴돌다   **invoke** v. (느낌·상상을) 불러일으키다, 환기시키다   **funding** n. 자금 제공   **legislative** a. 입법의, 입법부의   **hearing** n. 청문회

21 문장삽입   ③

| 분석 |

제시문은 "맨의 과학적 구화주의는 이런 복음주의적 경건함과 경쟁할 수 없었다."는 의미로, 그 앞에는 종교와 관련된 내용이 있어야 한다. ⓒ 앞에서 청각 장애인을 신과 더 가까운 존재로 보고 수화를 신이 준 선물로 보는 수화 교육을 지지하는 사람들의 내용이 있으므로, 제시문은 ⓒ에 들어가는 것이 적절하다.

22 동의어   ①

| 분석 |

구화주의를 위한 맨의 노력은 거의 효과가 없었다는 것으로 negligible은 '무시해도 좋은, 하찮은'의 의미로 쓰인 것이다. 따라서 '하찮은, 사소한'의 뜻인 ① trivial이 적절하다.

다음 중 Ⓐ를 가장 잘 대체하는 것은?
① 하찮은
② 무시된
③ 후회된
④ 잊을 수 없는

23 내용일치   ④

| 분석 |

하우는 클라크 청각장애인학교의 자금 제공 및 방식을 결정하기 위해 열린 입법 청문회에서 맨의 기억을 환기시켰다고 했으므로 ④가 적절하다. ① 교육적 변화가 쉽게 받아들여졌다는 내용은 본문에 언급되어 있지 않다. ② 하우가 맨에게 구화주의를 찬양하도록 설득했다고 했다. ③ 수화 기반 시스템(manualism)에서 구두 기반 시스템(oralism)으로 바뀌었다.

다음 중 사실인 것은?
① 교육학적 변화는 청각 장애 교육자들 사이에서 쉽게 받아들여졌다.
② 맨은 하우가 구화주의를 찬양하도록 이끌었다.
③ 수화법은 청각 장애 교육 분야에서 구화주의를 대체하는 데 성공했다.
④ 하우는 클라크 청각장애인학교에 자금을 공급하기 위해 맨의 생각과 노력을 사용했다.

24~25

중세 영어 시대에, 영어 사용자들은 다른 언어에서 단어를 수입하는 것에 익숙해졌다. 프랑스어, 라틴어 및 그리스어에서 온 단어들은 글로 된 표준어가 존재하기도 전에 영어에 스며들기 시작했고, 중세가 끝나기 전에 이 물방울은 급류로 변했다(스며드는 단어들이 급증했다). 르네상스 시대에는 10,000개 이상의 기록적인 새로운 단어들이 영어에 쏟아져 들어왔다. 오늘날 adapt, benefit, exist와 같은 많은 단어들이 일상 언어로 자리 잡았다. 그러나 대부분의 라틴어 차용어는 학문과 과학의 언어에 속한다.

토머스 모어(Thomas More)와 프랜시스 베이컨(Francis Bacon)과 같은 르네상스 시대 인물들이 영어로 글을 쓸 때, 그들은 종종 모국어를 라틴어 표현으로 꾸몄다. 모어는 abolition, contradictory, exaggerate, hyperbole, monopoly, paradox 그리고 또 다른 많은 단어를 최초로 사용한 것으로 기록된 사람이다.

고전 언어인 라틴어와 그리스어는 최근까지 명성 있는 영국 학교와 대학, 특히 옥스퍼드와 케임브리지 같은 명문 대학에서 강력한 입지를 유지해왔다. 태생이 고귀하거나 비천한 학생에게는 고전 교육이 고위직으로 가는 문을 열 수 있었다. 라틴어 단어의 유입은 프랑스어를 제외하고는 다른 어떤 유럽 언어보다 영어에서 더 많았다. 이전에 프랑스어에서 차용된 일부 단어들은 라틴어 원어와 더 유사하게 개조되었다. 어떤 경우에는 이러한 언어적 현학이 도를 지나쳤고, 영어에는 많은 '잘못된 라틴어 표현'이 생겨났다. 예를 들어 advance는 문자 d가 삽입되었고(프랑스어 avance와 비교), debt은 b가 추가되었다(프랑스어 dette와 비교). 많은 고전 단어들이 이미 프랑스어를 통해 차용되었기 때문에, 같은 어원이지만 다른 의미를 가진 두 단어, 예를 들어 corps와 corpse, story와 history와 같은 이중어도 등장했다.

24 부분이해 ③

| 분석 |

프랑스어에서 차용된 단어를 라틴어와 더 유사하게 수정하는 것, 즉 지나친 라틴어화가 도를 넘어서 잘못된 영어 단어들을 만들어냈다는 의미이다. 따라서 ③이 정답이다.

다음 중 Ⓐ를 가장 잘 해석한 것은?
① 라틴어는 영어의 게르만어 어휘를 압도했다.
② 학자들은 영어에서 비라틴어 요소들을 제거하는 데 성공했다.
③ 지나치게 열성적인 라틴어화는 잘못된 영어 단어들을 만들어냈다.
④ 프랑스어를 라틴어로 개조하는 것은 세련된 영어를 형성한다.

25 내용일치 ④

| 분석 |

라틴어 단어의 유입은 '프랑스어를 제외하고' 다른 어떤 유럽 언어보다 영어에서 더 많았다고 했으므로 '대부분의 유럽 언어'라고 한 ④가 적절하다. ① 라틴어가 프랑스어를 통해 영어에 유입된 것은 맞지만 '언어적 계층을 형성했다'는 내용은 본문에 언급되어 있지 않다. ② 태생이 고귀하든 비천하든 고전 교육이 고위직으로 가는 문을 열 수 있다고 했으므로 귀족에게만 국한된 것이 아니라 모든 계층에게 기회를 제공했다고 할 수 있다. ③ 이중어는 라틴어와 프랑스어에서 '동시에' 차용된 것뿐만 아니라 라틴어와 프랑스어에서 각각 차용된 단어들에서도 발생할 수 있다.

다음 중 사실인 것은?
① 라틴어는 프랑스어를 통해 영어에 유입되어 언어적 계층을 형성했다.
② 고전 교육은 영국의 귀족에게만 국한되었다.
③ 이중어는 오직 라틴어와 프랑스어를 동시에 차용한 것에서만 발생했다.
④ 영어는 대부분의 유럽 언어보다 더 많은 라틴어를 차용했다.

| 어휘 |

accustomed a. 익숙한 **import** v. 수입하다, 가져오다 **infiltrate** v. 스며들게 하다, 침투시키다 **trickle** n. 물방울; 실개천, 소량 **torrent** n. 급류 **make one's way into** ~안으로 나아가다[들어가다] **loanword** n. 차용어, 외래어 **figure** n. 인물, 거물 **embellish** v. 장식하다; 꾸미다, 윤색하다 **native tongue** 모국어 **Latinism** n. 라틴어풍[어법], 라틴 어투 **prestigious** a. 명성 있는, 유명한, 일류의 **notably** ad. 특히; 현저히, 명백히 **humble** a. (신분·지위 등이) 천한, 낮은 **influx** n. 유입, 쇄도 **with the exception of** ~을 제외하고 **remodel** v. 개조하다, 개작하다 **resemblance** n. 유사, 닮음 **original** n. 원형; 원작, 원문, 원어 **pedantry** n. 학자연함, 현학; 규칙·학설·선례 따위에 얽매임 **overstep the mark** (지켜야 할) 선[한도]을 넘다 **insert** v. 삽입하다, 끼워 넣다 **doublet** n. 이중어(같은 어원에서 갈라진 말)

AJOU UNIVERSITY | 아주대학교 인문계

TEST p. 496~519

01	⑤	02	③	03	④	04	①	05	④	06	②	07	⑤	08	④	09	④	10	③
11	④	12	③	13	⑤	14	③	15	①	16	④	17	③	18	③	19	①	20	⑤
21	①	22	③	23	②	24	①	25	④	26	④	27	④	28	⑤	29	③	30	③
31	⑤	32	⑤	33	①	34	①	35	③	36	①	37	③	38	③	39	④	40	②
41	⑤	42	①	43	①	44	①	45	②	46	④	47	①	48	⑤	49	③	50	③

01 논리완성 ⑤

| 분석 |

tolerance는 내성, 참을성을 의미하며 heat tolerance는 열을 참아내는 능력을 말한다. 벌은 더 높은 온도를 참아내기에 고온이 파리에게 더 큰 위협이 된다는 흐름을 만드는 ⑤가 정답으로 적절하다.

| 어휘 |

melittology n. 양봉학 **heat tolerance** 내열성 **subtropical** a. 아열대의 **pose** v. 제기하다 **pose a threat** 위협을 가하다 **occupy** v. 점유하다 **habitat** n. 서식지 **aspiration** n. 열망 **relief** n. 완화

| 해석 |

양봉학 저널에 게재된 한 연구에서, 한 국제 연구팀은 아메리카 대륙의 열대 및 아열대 지역에 서식하는 벌과 파리의 내열성을 조사했다. 그들은 벌이 더 높은 온도를 견뎌내며 더 폭넓은 서식지에서 살아가므로 기온 상승이 벌보다 파리에게 더 큰 위협이 된다는 것을 발견했다.

02 논리완성 ③

| 분석 |

빈칸 다음의 문장에서 셜록 홈즈가 가설을 세우고 추론을 끌어낸다고 한 것은 논리적 사고력을 강조하는 것이므로, '추론, 논리적 사고력'을 가리키는 ③ reasoning이 정답이다.

| 어휘 |

fictional a. 허구의, 소설적인 **sleuth** n. 탐정 **reside** v. 거주하다 **be known for** ~으로 유명하다 **impressive** a. 인상적인, 감동을 주는 **logical** a. 논리적인 **sweep** n. 휩쓸기 **hypothesis** n. 가설 **observation** n. 관찰 **inference** n. 추론 **decoding** n. 해독 **reminiscing** n. 회상 **resolution** n. 해결

| 해석 |

베이커 스트리트에 거주한다고 알려진 소설 속의 탐정인 셜록 홈즈는 그의 놀라운 논리적 추론 능력으로 유명하다. 범죄 현장을 눈으로 빠르게 훑어보고 나서, 그는 가설을 세우고, 관찰한 것들을 모으고, 추론을 끌어내어, 결국 범죄자의 수법과 정체를 밝혀낸다.

03 논리완성 ④

| 분석 |

footprint(발자국)나 shadow(그림자)와 같이 '흔적, 자취'라는 의미를 가지는 ④ trail이 정답으로 적절하다.

| 어휘 |

submit v. 제출하다 **track** v. 추적하다 **device** n. 장치 **trail** n. 흔적, 자취 **volume** n. 양(量), 분량

| 해석 |

때로 디지털 그림자 또는 전자 발자국이라고도 불리는 디지털 발자국은 인터넷을 사용할 때 남기는 데이터의 자취를 의미한다. 디지털 발자국에는 방문하는 웹사이트, 보내는 이메일, 온라인으로 제출하는 정보 등이 포함된다. 디지털 발자국은 개인의 온라인 활동과 사용기기를 추적하는 데 사용될 수 있다.

04 논리완성 ①

| 분석 |

키친에이드가 코크레인의 회사를 인수하였으므로, 자연히 확보한 것은 코크레인이 가진 특허권들이라고 추론할 수 있다. 따라서 ①이 정답이다.

| 어휘 |

dishwasher n. 식기세척기　scrubber n. 문질러 닦는 도구　pressure n. 압력　found v. 설립하다　manufacture v. 제조하다　acquire v. 인수하다　invention n. 발명품　continuously ad. 지속적으로　patent n. 특허권　patron n. 후원자　potent a. 세력 있는

| 해석 |

조세핀 가리스 코크레인은 1880년대에 최초의 현대식 식기세척기를 발명했다. 접시를 문지르는 스크러버를 사용했던 예전 식기세척기들의 시도와는 달리, 코크레인의 기계는 수압을 이용하여 접시를 씻었다. 코크레인은 자신의 회사를 설립해서 자신의 발명품을 제조하고 판매하였고, 지속적으로 개선했다. 그녀가 사망한 후, 키친에이드 브랜드가 그녀의 회사를 인수하여 그녀의 특허권을 이용해 식기세척기를 제조하고 판매했다.

05 논리완성 ④

| 분석 |

한 인물 안에서 '성장'이나 '변화'와 더불어 일어나는 일이므로, 내적 갈등을 나타내는 ④의 internal(내적인)이 적절하다. '한 인물 안에서'라 했으므로 ⑤ interpersonal(개인 사이의)은 부적절하다.

| 어휘 |

conflict n. 갈등　carry out 수행하다, 이행하다　term n. 용어　one-dimensional a. 일차원적인, 깊이가 없는　demonstrate v. 보여주다　highlight v. 강조하다　trait n. 특성　undesirable a. 바람직하지 않은　imminent a. 임박한　indifferent a. 무관심한　internal a. 내적인　interpersonal a. 사람들 사이의

| 해석 |

문학에서도, 실생활에서처럼, 사람들은 흔히 성장과 변화와 내적 갈등이 하나의 등장인물 안에서 이루어지는 것을 본다. 서평이나 이야기에서 일차원적 등장인물이라는 용어는 깊이가 부족하고 배우거나 성장하지 않는 등장인물을 가리킨다. 등장인물이 일차원적일 때, 그 인물은 이야기 속에서 학습 의식을 보여주지 않는다. 작가들은 이런 인물을 사용하여 어떤 특성을 강조할지 모르지만, 보통은 바람직하지 않은 특성이다.

06 논리완성 ②

| 분석 |

추가적인 탐구가 이루어지게 한다고 했으므로, 그 앞에서는 기존 모델의 타당성에 대해 의문을 제기하는 것이 옳다. 따라서 ②가 정답이다.

| 어휘 |

researcher n. 연구자　finding n. 연구 결과　validity n. 타당성, 유효성　existing a. 기존의　prompting a. 촉진하는　inquiry n. 탐구　assumption n. 가정　further a. 추가적인　build on ~에 입각하다　call into question ~에 의문을 제기하다　draw on 활용하다　shed light on ~을 밝히다, 설명하다

| 해석 |

그 연구자의 발견은 기존 모델의 타당성에 의문을 제기하여, 그 모델의 가정에 관한 추가적인 탐구를 촉진한다.

07 논리완성 ⑤

| 분석 |

put in place는 '정책이나 제도를 마련하다, 갖추다'의 의미이므로 ⑤가 적절하다. 문법적으로도 consist of는 수동태가 될 수 없고, dismiss A as B나 center A around B나 push A against B는 모두 수동태로 될 수는 있지만 전치사 as나 around나 against 다음에 to부정사로 이어질 수 없어 부적절하다.

| 어휘 |

policy n. 정책　flexibility n. 유연성　consist of ~으로 구성되어 있다　dismiss as ~라고 일축하다　center around ~을 중심으로 하다　put in place 마련하다, 준비하다, 갖추다

| 해석 |

그 정책 틀은 미래의 기술 발전에 대한 유연성을 제공하도록 마련되었다.

08 논리완성 ④

| 분석 |

정책 변화가 대중의 환영을 받으려면 그 변화가 좋은 결과를 초래해야 하는데, 공정한 시스템은 좋은 결과이므로 빈칸에는 '초래하다'는 뜻의 ④가 적절하다. ① '공정한 시스템'을 수식하는 '그 변화가 가져다준'이라는 수식어가 더 있어야 한다.

| 어휘 |

equitable a. 공정한　get ahead of ~을 앞지르다　lend support to ~을 지지하다　result in ~을 초래하다

| 해석 |

그 정책 변화는 더 공정한 시스템을 초래하여 대중의 환영을 받았다.

09 논리완성 ④

| 분석 |

혁신적인 전략은 새로운 가능성을 열어줄 것이므로 ④ opens up이 적절하다.

| 어휘 |

innovative a. 혁신적인　treat v. 치료하다　strategy n. 전략　chronic disease 만성 질환　break into 침입하다　derive from ~에서 유래하다　narrow down 좁히다, 축소하다　open up 열다, 개척하다　stand against ~에 반대하다

| 해석 |

그 팀의 혁신적인 전략은 만성 질환 치료를 위한 새로운 가능성을 열어준다.

10 논리완성 ③

| 분석 |

새로운 가설이 기존의 틀이나 증거와 일치하면 이론화되고 일치하지 않으면 폐기되는 것이므로 빈칸에는 ③이 적절하다.

| 어휘 |

hypothesis n. 가설　established a. 확립된　accumulated a. 축적된　empirical evidence 실증적 증거　cognitive science 인지 과학　allow for ~을 가능하게 하다　give rise to ~을 야기하다　be consistent with ~과 일치하다　revolve around ~을 중심으로 다루다　set up 세우다

| 해석 |

새롭게 제안된 가설은 인지 과학 분야에서 확립된 이론적 틀과 축적된 실증적 증거와 일치한다.

11 비교 ④

| 분석 |

A is one thing ~ B is another는 'A와 B는 완전히 다르다'라는 표현이므로 ④를 another로 고쳐야 한다.

| 어휘 |

familiar with ~에 익숙한　get right ~를 바르게 하다, 제대로 하다　struggle with ~에 어려움을 겪다　hand in 제출하다　agonize over ~에 대해 심각하게 고민하다　at work 직장에서　worry about ~에 대해 걱정하다　pursue v. 추구하다　consequence n. 결과, 영향

| 해석 |

당신이 완벽주의자라면, 아마도 모든 것을 정말 바르게 하고 싶은 감정에 익숙할 것이다. 당신은 과제 제출에 어려움을 겪을 수도 있고, 직장에서 프로젝트에 대해 고민하거나, 심지어 과거의 작은 실수를 놓고 걱정할 수도 있다. 높은 기준과 완벽주의는 전혀 다른 문제이다. 일부 연구자들이 발견했듯이, 완벽을 추구하는 것은 정신 건강과 신체 건강 모두에 심각한 영향을 미칠 수 있다.

12 동사의 태 ③

| 분석 |

decline이 자동사로 쓰였으므로 수동태를 만들 수 없다. 따라서 ③의 has been declined를 has declined로 고쳐야 한다.

| 어휘 |

emerge v. 나타나다　transcend v. 초월하다　barrier n. 장벽　phenomenon n. 현상　caption n. 표제, 제목; 자막; 캡션(인스타그램 등의 게시물에 사용자가 사진이나 동영상과 함께 쓰는 설명 문구)　slang n. 속어　correlation n. 상관관계　sentiment n. 감정, 정서　means of expression 표현 수단　replace v. 대체하다

| 해석 |

이모지는 형태는 단순하지만, 언어 장벽을 초월하여 전 세계적 의사소통을 가능하게 하는 보편 언어로 등장했다. 이 현상은 인스타그램에서 분명하게 나타나는데, 여기서는 캡션의 약 40%가 이모지를 포함하며, 핀란드 같은 나라에서는 그 비율이 63% 이상까지 증가한다. 이모지의 사용이 증가함에 따라, 'Lol'과 같은 인터넷 속어 사용이 감소했으며, 이는 두 현상 간의 상관관계를 시사한다. 인스타그램 엔지니어 토마스 딤슨은 이모지가 이제 거의 보편적인 표현 수단을 제공한다고 지적했다. 약 700개의 글자(이모지 기호) 제한에도 불구하고, 사용자들은 이모지를 창의적으로 조합하여 감정을 전달하고 있다. 인스타그램의 성공 자체도 이 시각적 의사소통을 반영하는데, 이러한 의사소통에서는 강력한 표현 도구로서의 이미지가 텍스트를 종종 대체한다.

13 동명사 ⑤

| 분석 |

consider는 동명사를 목적어로 취하는 동사이므로 ⑤의 are considering to implement를 are considering implementing으로 고쳐야 한다.

| 어휘 |

remote work 재택근무　social skills 사회적 능력　due to ~때문에　in-person interaction 대면 상호작용　hinder v. 저해하다　verbal skills 구두 의사소통 능력　written skills 서면 의사소통 능력　active listening 능동적 경청　suffer v. 악화하다　considerably ad. 상당히　implement v. 실천에 옮기다　strategic a. 전략적인　soft skill 대인관계 기술　transition n. 변천, 전환 v. 전환하다

| 해석 |

한 연구에 따르면 재택근무는 사람들의 사회적 능력과 의사소통 능력에 영향을 미쳤다. 78%의 사람들이 재택근무를 경험한 가운데, 10명 중 4명은 대면 상호작용 부족으로 인해 사회적 능력이 감소했다고 보고했다. 재택근무자들은 주당 4.2회 미만으로 의사소통할 뿐만 아니라, 이러한 제한된 상호작용으로 인해 구두(口頭) 및 서면(書面) 의사소통 능력의 발달이 방해받는다. 젊은 직원들, 특히 16~24세의 직원들이 가장 큰 영향을 받아서, 그중 52%가

효과적으로 소통하는 능력이 감소했음을 인식했다. 일부 경우에는 서면 의사소통 능력은 향상되었지만, 공개 발언과 능동적 경청 같은 구두 의사소통 능력은 상당히 저하되었다. 많은 기업은 직원들이 사무실 환경으로 복귀함에 따라 직원들이 필수적인 대인관계 기술을 회복하도록 돕기 위한 전략적 교육 프로그램을 시행하는 것을 고려하고 있다.

14 주어와 동사의 수일치   ③

| 분석 |

③의 주어는 what 관계절인 what you have already thought and experienced이므로 단수 취급하여 ③을 interacts with로 고쳐야 한다.

| 어휘 |

construct v. 구성하다   **recognize** v. 알아보다   **sign** n. 기호   **encounter** v. 만나다, 마주치다   **interact with** ~와 상호작용하다   **recall** v. 떠올리다   **subject** n. 주제   **orderly** a. 질서정연한   **march across** 나란히 행진하다   **involve** v. 포함하다, 수반하다, 필요로 하다

| 해석 |

읽기는 쓰기와 마찬가지로 독자가 의미를 구성할 수 있는 창의적인 활동이다. 어떤 텍스트든, 읽을 때 그 텍스트의 의미를 단순히 기호 인식에 의해 받아들이지는 않는다. 읽기의 목적은 단순히 '사실을 얻는 것'이나 '읽는 것을 기억하는 것'이 아니다. 읽기는 당신이 이미 알고 있는 것과 읽어가면서 만나는 새로운 정보 사이의 관계를 이해함으로써 읽는 내용을 당신의 것으로 만드는 것이다. 다시 말해, 당신이 이미 생각하고 경험한 것이 당신이 텍스트에서 발견하는 것과 상호작용한다. 이 과정의 가장 효과적인 시작은 당신이 새로운 자료 읽기를 시작하기도 전에 해당 주제에 대해 당신이 알고 있는 것을 떠올리는 것이다. 읽기는 단어들이 백지 위를 가로질러 나아가는 것을 볼 때 여겨지는 그런 깔끔하고 질서정연한 과정이 아니다. 읽기는 지금까지 있은 것(읽은 내용)과 앞으로 있을 것(뒤이어 나올 내용)에 대해 생각하는 것을 필요로 하며, 앞으로 가는 것과 뒤로 가는 것(읽은 것을 다시 읽어보는 것)을 필요로 한다.

15 추론 가능한 문장 고르기   ①

| 분석 |

ⓒ 스키마는 정보 이해에 도움을 주기에, 스키마가 있는 사람들이 없는 사람들보다 새로운 정보를 더 잘 이해할 것이다. ⓓ 스키마는 사고를 제한하고, 고정관념을 형성하므로, 객관적이지 않다는 단점이 있다. 따라서 ①이 정답이다.

| 어휘 |

shortcut n. 지름길   **make sense of** 이해하다   **narrow** v. 제한하다   **result in** 초래하다   **stereotype** n. 고정관념

| 해석 |

스키마란 사람, 장소, 사물, 사건에 대한 지식의 틀 역할을 하는 인지 구조이다. 스키마는 사람들이 세상에 대한 지식을 체계화하고 새로운 정보를 이해하는 데 도움을 준다. 이러한 정신적 지름길이 우리가 매일 접하는 방대한 양의 정보를 이해하는 데는 유용하게 도움을 주지만, 또한 우리의 사고를 제한하고 고정관념을 형성하는 결과를 초래할 수도 있다.

Ⓐ 사람들은 낯설거나 복잡한 정보를 더 빠르게 처리하기 위해 스키마에 의존한다.
Ⓑ 스키마라고 알려진 정신적 지름길은 기존 지식을 기반으로 하여 새로운 정보에 대한 우리의 이해를 형성할 수 있다.
Ⓒ 스키마가 없는 사람들이 새로운 정보를 더 잘 이해한다.
Ⓓ 스키마는 사람들이 새로운 정보를 객관적으로 평가하도록 보장한다.

16 추론 가능한 문장 고르기   ④

| 분석 |

Ⓑ 장기 기억에는 '적극적 회상'이 필요하다는 말은 없다. 장기 기억은 더 큰 안정성을 보이므로 적극적인 노력 없이 쉽게 기억이 유지되고 회상될 것이다. Ⓓ 정기적인 반복, 맥락적 연상, 감정적 몰입 같은 다양한 전략이 '의도적인 전략'이 될 수 있다. 따라서 ④가 정답이다.

| 어휘 |

vital a. 필수적인   **cognitive function** 인지 기능   **encode** v. 부호화하다   **store** v. 저장하다   **retrieve** v. 꺼내다, 회수하다, 상기하다   **sensory input** 감각 입력   **classify** v. 분류하다   **stability** n. 안정성   **consolidation process** (기억) 강화 과정   **effective** a. 적절한   **cue** n. 단서   **interference** n. 간섭, 방해   **decay** n. 소멸, 쇠퇴   **spaced repetition** 일정한 간격을 둔 반복 학습   **association** n. 연상

| 해석 |

기억은 인간이 정보를 부호화하고, 저장하고, 상기할 수 있게 하는 중요한 인지 기능이다. 부호화 단계에서는 감각 입력을 저장할 수 있는 형태로 변환하는데, 집중력이나 자료의 감정적 또는 맥락적 중요성과 같은 요인의 영향을 받는다. 저장된 기억은 단기 기억과 장기 기억으로 분류되는데, 장기 기억은 기억을 강화하는 강화 과정을 통해 더 큰 안정성을 보인다. 저장된 정보를 떠올리는 상기 행위는 효과적인 단서에 의존하며, 간섭이나 쇠퇴의 방해를 받을 수 있다. 기억 유지와 회상 능력은 정기적인 반복, 맥락적 연상, 감정적 개입 같은 전략에 의해 향상될 수 있다.

Ⓐ 기억은 정보의 변환, 저장, 상기를 포함하는 다단계 과정이다.
Ⓑ 장기 기억은 접근 가능성을 유지하기 위해 적극적인 회상이 필요하지만, 단기 기억은 그렇지 않다.
Ⓒ 감정적인 경험은 부호화 과정을 강화하여 기억을 더 쉽게 유지하고 회상할 수 있게 한다.

Ⓓ 기억 유지는 단순히 효과적인 회상 단서에만 의존하는 것이 아니라, 의도적인 기법을 통해 적극적으로 향상될 수 있다.

17 추론 가능한 문장 고르기   ③

| 분석 |
ⓒ 자아 인식 발견을 통해 새로운 논의가 촉진되었다고 했지, 그 전에 연구가 없었다고는 하지 않았다. 따라서 ③이 정답이다.

| 어휘 |
indicative of ~을 나타내는   self-awareness n. 자아 인식
reflection n. 반사된 이미지, 거울 속 모습   inspect v. 검사하다
hallmark n. 특징, 대표적 요소   assumption n. 가정, 전제

| 해석 |
연구자들은 돌고래, 코끼리, 일부 영장류를 포함한 특정 동물들이 자아 인식의 징후를 보이는 행동을 한다는 것을 발견했다. 이러한 행동에는 거울 속의 자기 모습을 인식하고, 다른 동물들의 반사된 이미지와 다르게 반응하는 것이 포함된다. 예를 들어, 이들은 거울을 이용해 직접 볼 수 없는 신체 부위를 살펴보기도 한다. 이는 발달된 인지 능력을 지닌 종들에게만 국한된 행동이다. 자아 인식은 높은 지능의 특징으로 간주되는데, 이는 동물계에서 매우 드물게 관찰된다. 이러한 발견은 자아 인식이나 이와 유사한 인지적 특성이 인간만의 독특한 특성이라는 오랜 가정을 뒤흔들며, 동물 지능에 대한 새로운 논의의 길을 열어준다.

Ⓐ 동물에서 자아 인식의 발견은 인간의 인지 능력이 완전히 인간에게만 있는 것은 아닐 수도 있음을 시사한다.
Ⓑ 자아 인식은 소수의 동물 종에서만 관찰되는 발달된 인지 능력의 주요 지표로 간주된다.
Ⓒ 자아 인식이 특정 종에서 발견되기까지는 동물 행동과 인지적 특성이 폭넓게 연구되지 않았다.
Ⓓ 동물에서 자아 인식이 관찰되면서 동물 지능의 복잡성과 다양성에 대한 더 깊은 이해로 이어졌다.

18 추론 가능한 문장 고르기   ③

| 분석 |
ⓒ 본문에서 언어 체계는 문화의 일부라고 했지, 이것만으로 문화적 정체성을 '완전히' 설명할 수 있다는 말은 없다. 따라서 ③이 정답이다.

| 어휘 |
refer to 가리키다   intangible a. 무형의   practice n. 관습, 실천
share in common 공유하다   collective n. 집단, 공동체   distinct a. 뚜렷이 구별되는, 독특한   encompass v. 포함하다

| 해석 |
문화는 사회생활의 광범위하고 다양한 대체로 비물질적인 측면들을 가리키는 용어이다. 사회학자들에 따르면, 문화는 사람들이 공유하며 그들을 집단으로 정의하는 데 사용될 수 있는 가치, 신념, 언어 체계, 의사소통, 관습으로 구성된다. 또한 문화는 그 집단이나 사회에 공통된 물질적 대상도 포함한다. 문화는 사회의 사회적 구조 및 경제적 측면과는 구별되지만, 이들과 연결되어 있으며, 지속적으로 영향을 주고받는다. 일반적인 문화에는 지역 전통, 종교적 신념, 역사적 경험에 의해 형성된 문화들이 포함된다.

Ⓐ 문화는 비물질적인 측면뿐 아니라, 한 집단이나 사회가 공유하는 물질적 대상도 포함한다.
Ⓑ 문화는 사회 구조 및 경제적 측면과 다르지만, 이들과 지속적으로 상호작용한다.
Ⓒ 공유된 언어 체계는 한 집단의 문화적 정체성을 완전히 결정할 수 있다.
Ⓓ 문화적 관습은 한 집단을 다른 집단과 구별하는 표지 역할을 한다.

19~22

Ⓐ 전 세계적인 대중 마케팅에 관한 한, 코카콜라의 뛰어난 솜씨와 맞설 수 있는 기업은 거의 없다. 역사상 가장 유명하고 가장 많이 팔린 탄산음료로 인정받는 코카콜라의 우월함은 연간 약 30억 달러에 달하는 마케팅 예산과 300억 달러가 넘는 수익에 의해 강조된다. 인터브랜드 순위에서 지속적으로 최상위를 차지하는 코카콜라는 현재 브랜드 가치가 680억 달러에 이르며, 200개 이상의 국가 어디에나 있어서 세계에서 가장 잘 알려진 제품이 된다. 〈사실, 코카콜라는 너무나 큰 세계적인 현상이어서 '코카콜라'라는 이름은 전 세계에서 두 번째로 ('오케이' 다음으로) 가장 널리 이해되는 단어이다.〉

Ⓑ 코카콜라의 성공 역사는 그야말로 특별하다. 이 음료는 자신이 발명한 시럽을 탄산수와 혼합한 존 S. 펨버턴 박사에 의해 1886년에 원래 두통 치료제로 제조되었다. 이후 회사의 초대 사장 에이사 그릭스 캔들러가 혁신적인 마케팅 전략을 개척함으로써 이 제품을 대중문화의 한 현상으로 변화시켰다. 그는 시계부터 포스터에 이르기까지 브랜드(상표)가 붙은 다양한 용품을 활용하여 소비자들의 일상생활에서 코카콜라가 차지하는 위치를 공고히 했고, 대중문화에 통합해 넣었다.

Ⓒ 시작부터 코카콜라는 브랜드가 전 세계적인 성공을 거두기 위해서는 대중과 감성적이고 사회적인 유대를 키워야 한다는 것을 인식하고 있었다. 회사는 제품을 "바라기만 하면 가질 수 있는" 것으로 만든다는 철학을 채택했다. 그래서 회사는 확장적인 유통망을 우선시했고 제품을 모든 사람이 사랑하게 만들려고 힘썼다. 이 전략의 증거는 바로 제2차 세계대전 동안에 회사가 세운 계획이었는데, 그것은 "유니폼을 입은 모든 군인은, 전 세계 어디에 있든, 회사에 얼마나 비용이 들게 하든, 5센트에 코카콜라 한 병을 마실 수 있게

하겠다"고 약속하는 것이었다. 이러한 접근 방식은 단순히 이 음료를 국제 시장에 소개하는 데 그치지 않고, 전쟁이라는 혼란의 시기에 긍정적인 브랜드 연상을 키워주었다. ⓓ 코카콜라를 경쟁업체들과 차별화시키는 점은 언어적·문화적 경계를 초월하는 고무적인 글로벌 캠페인을 제작하는 비길 데 없는 능력이다. 코카콜라의 마케팅은 각계각층의 사람들을 하나로 연결하면서 갈등을 해소하는 제품의 능력을 지속적으로 강조해왔다. 앤디 워홀은 이를 다음과 같이 정말 잘 표현했다. "코카콜라는 코카콜라이다. 아무리 돈이 많아도 길모퉁이에서 부랑자가 마시고 있는 코카콜라보다 더 나은 코카콜라는 마실 수 없다." 코카콜라의 가장 기억에 남는 상업광고 중 하나인 1971년에 발표된 '힐탑' 광고가 이런 정서를 예시해준다. 이탈리아 언덕 위에서 하나가 된 세계 각국의 젊은이들을 주인공으로 내세운 그 광고는 "세상 모든 사람에게 코카콜라를 사주고 싶어요."라는 노래를 통해 조화와 보편적인 우정을 세상에 알렸다. 이 광고는 너무나 많은 소비자들에게 깊은 감동을 주었고 코카콜라의 전 세계적 매력을 너무나 효과적으로 보여주었으므로, 그 노래가 상위 10위에 드는 히트곡이 되었으며, 코카콜라의 전 세계적 매력을 더욱 강화시켰다.

| 어휘 |

when it comes to ~에 관해서 말하자면 **prowess** n. 뛰어난 솜씨, 뛰어난 능력 **iconic** a. 유명한 **dominance** n. 우월, 지배 **budget** n. 예산 **revenue** n. 수익, 매출 **top** v. 꼭대기를 차지하다 **ubiquitous** a. 어디에나 있는, 아주 흔한 **be nothing short of** ~에 전혀 모자라지 않는다 **formulate** v. 조제하다, 만들다 **carbonated water** 탄산수 **initially** ad. 처음에, 시초에 **remedy** n. 치료 **phenomenon** n. 사건 **paraphernalia** n. 장비, 도구, 용품 **cement** v. 굳히다, 확립하다 **integrate** v. 통합하다 **inception** n. 시작, 창립 **foster** v. 조성하다, 촉진하다 **prioritize** v. 우선하다 **distribution** n. 유통 **strive** v. 노력하다 **testament** n. 증거 **initiative** n. 캠페인, 계획 **beverage** n. 음료 **brand association** 브랜드 연상(소비자가 브랜드를 보고 떠올리는 것) **turmoil** n. 혼란 **distinguish** v. 구별하다, 차별화하다 **craft** v. 만들다 **transcend** v. 초월하다, 넘어서다 **quench** v. 끄다 **walk of life** 각계각층 **bum** n. 부랑자 **camaraderie** n. 우정, 동료애, 유대감 **solidify** v. 강화하다 **resonant** a. 공감을 얻는 **perseverance** n. 인내 **morale** n. 사기 **enhance** v. 향상하다

19 글의 요지   ①

| 분석 |

첫 번째 문장에서도 알 수 있듯이 무엇보다 코카콜라의 마케팅 전략에 관한 글이다. ② 제품 개발 ③ 문화적 현지화 ④ 로고송 ⑤ 끈기 등은 찾아볼 수 없다.

다음 진술 중 위 글의 요지를 가장 잘 요약하고 있는 것은?
① 코카콜라의 성공은 마케팅 전략과 감성적 브랜드 구축에 있다.
② 코카콜라는 제품 개발에 집중한 덕분에 세계적인 지배력을 갖게 되었다.
③ 코카콜라의 광고 캠페인은 보편적으로 공감을 얻으며 문화적으로 현지화되어 있다.
④ 코카콜라는 로고송의 성공에 힘입어 전 세계에서 가장 많이 팔리는 탄산음료이다.
⑤ 코카콜라는 혁신과 끈기를 통해 세계적 브랜드로 자리 잡았다.

20 동의어   ⑤

| 분석 |

① '뛰어난 솜씨 ─ 우월함', ② '수익 ─ 수익', ③ '용품 ─ 상품', ④ '혼란 ─ 불안정'은 모두 서로 대체할 수 있는 단어쌍이지만, ⑤ '우정 ─ 용기'는 그렇지 않다.

21 문장삽입   ①

| 분석 |

주어진 문장은 코카콜라의 세계적 유명세를 강조하고 있으므로, 코카콜라의 세계적으로 뛰어난 마케팅 솜씨와 전 세계적인 명성과 인지도를 말하고 있는 첫 번째 문단의 ❶에 들어가야 한다.

22 내용파악   ③

| 분석 |

다른 음료와 비교한다는 말은 없으므로 ③은 코카콜라의 마케팅 전략과 무관하다.

다음 중 코카콜라의 마케팅 전략의 일부가 아닌 것은?
① 문화적·언어적 장벽을 넘어서는 전 세계적으로 공감되는 캠페인을 제작함
② 브랜드가 붙은 용품을 배포하여 브랜드를 홍보하고 대중문화에 통합해 넣음
③ 시장에 나온 다른 음료에 비해 코카콜라의 우월한 이점을 강조하기 위한 계획을 시행함
④ 사기를 진작하는 것으로서 코카콜라를 합리적인 가격에 군인들에게 공급하여, 전쟁수행 노력과의 연관성을 높임
⑤ 광고에서 조화와 관계 같은 보편적 주제를 강조함으로써 소비자와의 감성적 관계를 형성함

23~26

[A] 우주에서 지구를 관찰한다고 상상해보라. 대부분 사람은 북극이 지구의 지붕이라고 말할 것이다. 그러나 엄밀히 말하면 이런 관점에는 과학적 근거가 없다. 수 세기에 걸쳐 문명들은 그들 문명의 믿음과 지리적 우선사항에 따라 세계를 다르게 묘사해왔다. 고대 이집트인들은 해가 뜨는 위치를 반영하여 동쪽을 위에 두었던 반면, 초기 이슬람의 지도제작법은 많은 무슬림 문화권이 메카의 북쪽에 있었으므로 남쪽을 위에 두는 편을 선호하여, 지도에서 위쪽이 메카를 향하도록 방향을 정했다. 초기 중국의 지도는 황제를 북쪽에 두어, 백성이 군주를 우러러보는 정치적 위계를 나타냈다. 콜럼버스와 같은 유럽 탐험가들이 북극성을 이용해 항해했을 때 그들은 동쪽이 천국으로 이끈다고 생각했으므로 동쪽을 위로 하여 세상을 묘사했다.

[B] 북쪽을 위에 두는 지도제작으로의 전환점은 1569년 메르카토르 세계 지도를 계기로 찾아왔는데, 이 지도는 항해술에 혁명을 가져왔다. 이 지도는 지구의 곡률을 고려하여 선원들이 먼 거리를 가로지를 수 있게 했다. 그러나 메르카토르가 북쪽을 위에 둔 선택은 상징적이라기보다 실용적인 선택이었다. 유럽인들은 북반구의 넓은 대륙들을 탐험하고 지도로 나타내는 데 앞장섰기 때문에, 북쪽을 위에 두는 관행은 점점 더 힘을 얻게 되었다. 결국 북쪽이 위에 놓인 지도는 표준이 되었고, 우리의 세계를 바라보는 방식에 깊은 영향을 미쳤다.

[C] 과학적으로 보면 지구에 '위' 혹은 '아래'라는 개념에는 본질적인 의미가 없다. 지구는 태양계의 다른 모든 행성들과 같은 궤도면에 줄지어 있기에, 이러한 방향성은 자의적이다. 우주에서 다른 시점으로 바라본다면 지구는 거꾸로 된 모습으로도 마찬가지로 쉽게 묘사될 수 있을 것이다. 우주에는 보편적인 '위'나 '아래'가 존재하지 않기 때문이다. 그런데도 우리가 북쪽을 위로 하는 지도제작을 고수하는 것은 미묘하지만 중요한 심리적 결과를 낳는다. 연구에 따르면 사람들은 무의식적으로 북쪽을 '위'와 '좋음'과 연결 짓고, 남쪽을 '아래'와 '나쁨'과 동일시하는 경향이 있다. 이 같은 인지적 편향은 사람들이 세계의 지도와 지역을 인식하는 방식에 영향을 미친다.

[D] 브라이언 마이어는 도시 지도를 본 사람들이 북쪽 지역 거주를 선호할 가능성이 더 많으며 부유한 사람들을 북쪽과 연관 짓는다는 것을 발견했다. 그러나 지도를 거꾸로 뒤집자 이러한 편향은 사라졌는데, 이는 우리의 뿌리 깊은 인식에 이의를 제기할 간단한 방법을 암시한다. 남쪽을 위로 둔 지도는 세상에 대한 새로운 시각을 제공한다. 다니엘 모트록도 이 생각을 지지하며, 지도를 뒤집으면 세계가 다시 미지의 영역처럼 느껴질 수 있다고 말한다. 관점을 바꾸는 것은 지도를 새로운 시선으로 바라보게 하고 지역적 편견을 줄임으로써 세상을 좀 더 공정하게 보는 데 도움을 줄 수 있을 것이다.

어휘

justification n. 정당화, 근거 **cartography** n. 지도 제작법 **reside** v. 거주하다 **orienting** a. 방향을 정하는, 맞추는 **subject** n. 신하 **look up to** 올려다보다 **sovereign** n. 국왕 **hierarchy** n. 위계질서, 계층 **explorer** n. 탐험가 **envision** v. 상상하다 **turning point** 전환점 **account for** 감안하다 **curvature** n. 곡률 **spearheaded** a. 선두에 선, 앞장선 **momentum** n. 추진력 **devoid of** ~이 전혀 없는 **inherent** a. 고유한 **line up** 줄지어 서다 **orbital plane** 궤도면 **arbitrary** a. 자의적인 **vantage point** 관찰 지점, 시점 **inverted** a. 뒤집힌 **adherence** n. 고수, 집착 **subtle** a. 미묘한 **associate A with B** A와 B를 연관시키다 **be equated with** ~와 동일시되다 **bias** n. 편향, 선입견 **ingrained** a. 깊이 박힌, 뿌리 깊은 **flip** v. 뒤집다 **foster** v. 촉진하다, 조성하다 **sphericity** n. 구형

23 글의 제목   ②

| 분석 |

이 글은 지도가, 지도에서의 방향 지정이, 문화권마다 인식에 따라 결정된 것이고 그렇게 고정관념이 된 인식도 지도를 거꾸로 함으로써 시정될 수 있다는 내용이므로 ②가 글의 제목으로 적절하다. 지도(map), 인식(perception), 관점(perspective) 같은 단어가 이 글에서 중요한 개념들이다.

위 글의 제목으로 가장 적절한 것은?
① 세계 지도의 발전
② 지도가 우리의 관점을 형성하는 방식
③ 지구에 대한 전통적인 견해에 도전하기
④ 지구 방향성과 지도에 대한 과학
⑤ 항해술을 바꾼 과학적 발견

24 내용파악   ①

| 분석 |

①의 점성술을 언급한 부분은 없다. 중국에서 황제를 북쪽으로 둔 것은 문화 때문이고, 지리학적 이유는 북반구 유럽 탐험가들의 세계 개척이라고 설명하고, 종교는 이슬람 지도를 예로 들고, 심리학은 인지 편향이라는 말로 설명될 수 있다.

위 글에 따르면, 다음 중 세계 지도의 형성에 영향을 미쳤을 가능성이 가장 적은 분야는 무엇인가?
① 점성술
② 문화
③ 지리학
④ 종교
⑤ 심리학

25 동의어 ④

| 분석 |
① '위계(계급적 구조) — 구조', ② '굴곡 — 구면', ③ '없는 — 부재의', ⑤ '깊이 스며든 — 뿌리 깊은'은 모두 서로 대체할 수 있는 단어쌍이지만, ④ '자의적인'은 '자기 마음대로 하는'이라는 뜻으로 '모호한'과는 관련이 없다.

26 내용일치 ③

| 분석 |
콜럼버스 같은 유럽 탐험가들은 북극성을 이용해 항해했고, 이들이 동쪽을 위에 둔 이유는 그쪽이 천국으로 가는 방향으로 여겨져서 그랬다고 했다. 따라서 북쪽을 위에 두었다고 한 ③은 사실이 아니다.

위 글에 따르면, 다음 중 옳지 않은 것은?
① 고대 이집트의 지도는 동쪽을 위에 두어, 해가 뜨는 위치를 반영하였다.
② 초기 이슬람의 지도는 많은 무슬림 문화권이 메카의 북쪽에 위치했기 때문에 흔히 남쪽을 위에 두었고, 메카를 향해 위로 보도록 지도의 방향을 정했다.
③ 콜럼버스 같은 유럽 탐험가들은 탐험 중 북극성에 크게 의존했기 때문에 북쪽을 위에 둔 지도를 채택하였다.
④ 북쪽을 위에 둔 지도의 지속적인 사용은 미묘하지만 심대한 사회적 결과를 초래하여, 개인들이 세계 여러 지역을 인지하고 평가하는 방식에 영향을 준다.
⑤ 지구의 곡률을 지도 설계에 통합해 넣음으로써, 메르카토르 지도는 항해술에서 획기적인 발전을 이루었으며, 선원들의 먼 거리 횡단을 가능하게 했다.

27~30

Ⓐ 욕조 속의 물을 휘저으면 그 후 앞뒤로 출렁이는 것을 본 적이 있는가? 그 간단한 움직임은 호수, 저수지, 만(灣)과 같은 큰 수역에서 일어나는 세이체파라는 흥미로운 자연 현상의 작은 예이다. 세이체파는 닫혀 있거나 부분적으로 에워싸인 수역에서 나타나는 리듬감 있는 물의 진동으로, 마치 흔들리는 진자의 전후 운동과 유사하다. 강한 바람, 대기압의 변화, 심지어 지진 활동과 같은 외부 요인에 의해 발생하는 이러한 파동은 매혹적일 뿐 아니라 물가 지역에 홍수를 일으키고 피해를 줄 수 있을 정도로 강력하기도 하다.
Ⓑ 〈세이체파는 겉보기와는 다른 성격으로 인해 특히 흥미롭다.〉 겉으로 보기에 이 파도들은 잔잔한 물결이나 일반적인 물의 움직임처럼 보일 수 있지만, 숨겨진 에너지가 커지면서 큰 파도가 될 수 있다. 하나의 놀라운 예가 되는 세이체파가 1954년에 일어났는데, 당시 미시간 호수에서 일어난 세이체파로 인해 시카고 호숫가를 따라 수위가 급격히 높아졌고, 최대 10피트(약 3미터)에 달하는 파도를 일으켰다. 주민들을 깜짝 놀라게 한 이 사건은 자연의 힘이 인간의 삶에 어떻게 영향을 미칠 수 있는지를 잘 상기시킨다. 일반적으로 해저 지진에 의해 발생하는 하나의 강력한 파도인 쓰나미와는 다르게, 세이체파는 반복하여 진동하며, 그 움직임은 몇 시간 혹은 며칠 동안 지속된다.
Ⓒ 세이체파 현상의 과학적 원리를 이해하면 물리학과 지리학의 상호작용을 알 수 있다. 바람이나 기압 변화 같은 힘이 물을 휘저으면, 중력은 진동 운동을 만들어 균형을 회복하려고 작용한다. 세이체파의 빈도와 강도는 수역의 크기, 깊이, 형태에 달려있다. 길고 좁은 호수들은 그 형태 때문에 진동이 더 커지기 쉽다. 예를 들어, 스위스의 제네바 호수는 19세기부터 기록되어 온 빈번한 세이체파 현상으로 유명하다.
Ⓓ 세이체파는 또한 자연 현상 간의 상호 연결성을 보여준다. 세이체파는 흔히 폭풍이나 지진 같은 다른 자연재해와 함께 발생하는데, 이러한 더 크고 눈에 띄는 현상들의 조용한 동반자 역할을 한다. 어떤 면에서 보면 세이체파는 자연의 숨겨진 리듬을 반영하며, 자연 세계를 지배하는 미묘한 균형을 상기시킨다. 그것들의 존재는 우리가 흔히 간과하는 힘의 위력을 드러내며, 우리 행성의 복잡성에 대한 통찰을 제공한다.

| 어휘 |
bathtub n. 욕조 **slosh** v. 출렁거리다 **disturb** v. 휘젓다 **seiche wave** 세이체파, 정재파 **captivating** a. 매력적인 **reservoir** n. 저수지 **oscillation** n. 진동 **pendulum** n. 진자, 추 **basin** n. 유역, 수역 **trigger** v. 자극하다, 유발하다 **seismic** a. 지진의 **mesmerizing** a. 매혹적인, 최면을 거는 듯한 **ripple** n. 파문, 잔물결 **escalate** v. 확대되다, 증폭되다 **surge** n. 큰 파도 **shoreline** n. 해안선 **serve as** ~의 역할을 하다 **tsunami** n. 쓰나미 **persist** v. 지속하다 **interplay** n. 상호작용 **gravity** n. 중력 **depend on** ~에 달려있다 **susceptible** a. 영향을 받기 쉬운, 민감한 **amplify** v. 증폭시키다 **documented** a. 문서로 기록된, 문서로 입증된 **interconnectedness** n. 상호 연결성 **act as** ~의 역할을 하다 **delicate** a. 섬세한, 정교한 **overlook** v. 간과하다 **geology** n. 지질학 **geometry** n. 기하학, 외형 **geochemistry** n. 지구과학 **be prone to** ~에 영향을 받다

27 빈칸완성 ④

| 분석 |
'중력'이 균형을 맞추려는 현상이므로, 중력과 관련 있는 physics(물리학)가 적절하고, 수역의 형태, 깊이, 크기에 달려있다고 하였으므로 geography(지리학)가 적절하다.

28 내용파악   ⑤

| 분석 |

⑤ 생태계와 생물다양성에 미치는 영향에 대해서는 나와 있지 않다. ① 쓰나미는 해저지진으로 일어나고 반복적이 아니라 일회적이다. ② 바람, 기압 등이 원인으로 언급되었다. ③ 수역의 크기, 깊이, 형태는 수역의 기하학적인 측면이며, 이것들에 세이체파의 빈도와 강도가 달려있다고 했다. ④ 깊고 좁은 형태의 수역이 특히 취약하다고 하였다. be susceptible to와 be prone to는 같은 의미의 표현이다.

다음 중 위 글에서 답을 하지 않은 질문은?
① 세이체파는 쓰나미와 어떻게 다른가?
② 세이체파의 주요 발생 원인은 무엇인가?
③ 수역의 기하학은 세이체파의 진동에 어떤 영향을 미치는가?
④ 어떤 유형의 수역이 세이체파 현상에 가장 취약한가?
⑤ 세이체파는 생태계와 생물다양성에 구체적으로 어떤 영향을 미치는가?

29 문장삽입   ②

| 분석 |

"The deceptive nature"라고 하였으므로 '기만적인, 겉으로 보기와는 달라서 위험한' 특성이 연결되어야 한다. 따라서 겉으로 보기에는 잔잔한 물결처럼 보여 별로 위험하지 않지만, 사실은 상당한 에너지를 갖고 있어서 큰 파도가 되어 위험할 수도 있다고 한 둘째 단락의 첫머리인 ❷에 들어가는 것이 적절하다.

30 내용추론   ③

| 분석 |

③ 세이체파는 '바람, 기압 변화, 지진 활동' 등 여러 요인에 의해 발생한다고 했지, 지진이 주요 원인이라고 하지는 않았다. ② 세이체파가 기만적이라는 점과 주민들을 놀라게 한 점은 세이체파의 결과를 예측하기가 어렵다는 것을 의미한다.

다음 중 위 글로부터 가장 추론할 수 없는 것은?
① 호수의 형태와 깊이 같은 물리적 특징은 세이체파 활동의 증폭에 중요한 역할을 한다.
② 세이체파의 진동 운동은 오랜 기간 지속될 수 있어서, 그 결과는 예측하기 어렵고 때로는 위험할 수도 있다.
③ 세이체파는 주로 지진 활동으로 인해 발생하기 때문에, 지진이 자주 일어나는 지역과 밀접한 관련이 있다.
④ 역사적 기록과 관측은 특정 지역에서 세이체파의 빈도와 특성에 대한 귀중한 정보를 제공한다.
⑤ 세이체파의 연구는 바람, 대기압, 중력 등 자연의 힘이 복잡하게 상호작용하는 것을 드러낸다.

31~34

A 엘리스섬은 1892년에 이민자 입국 심사소로 문을 연 역사적 장소로, 1954년에 문을 닫을 때까지 60년 넘게 그 역할을 담당했다. 뉴욕과 뉴저지 사이, 허드슨강 하구에 있는 엘리스섬은 수백만 명의 새로이 도착한 이민자가 미국으로 들어오기 위해 그 문을 통과했던 섬이다. 실제로 오늘날 미국 시민의 40% 정도가 적어도 한 명의 조상이 거슬러 올라가면 엘리스섬을 통해 들어온 것으로 밝혀질 수 있을 것으로 추정된다.

B 엘리스섬이 문을 열었을 때, 미국 이민에는 커다란 변화가 일어나고 있었다. 독일, 아일랜드, 영국, 스칸디나비아 국가들과 같은 북유럽 및 서유럽 국가 출신의 이민자 수는 줄어들고, 남부와 동부 유럽 이민자들이 급격히 쏟아져 들어왔다. 이 새로운 이민자 세대에는 제정 러시아와 동유럽에서 정치적·경제적 억압을 피해 탈출한 유대인들과 자국의 빈곤으로부터 탈출한 이탈리아인들이 포함되어 있었다. 이외에도 폴란드, 헝가리, 체코, 세르비아, 슬로바키아, 그리스 사람들뿐 아니라, 유럽이 아닌 시리아, 터키, 아르메니아 출신 이민자들도 있었다. 이들은 신세계에서의 더 큰 기회를 바라며, 전쟁, 가뭄, 기근, 종교적 박해 등의 이유로 고국을 떠났다.

C 힘든 항해 끝에 엘리스섬에 도착한 이민자들은 배의 탑승자 명부에 있는 정보를 담은 꼬리표를 달고 긴 줄을 서서 미국 입국 허가 자격이 있는지를 판단하는 의학적 검사와 법적 심사를 받았다. 엘리스섬이 가장 활발히 운영된 1900년부터 1914년 사이에는 하루 평균 약 1,900명의 이민자가 이곳의 입국 심사소를 통과했다. 이민자 대부분은 몇 시간 내에 통과했지만, 일부는 며칠에서 몇 주간 구금될 수도 있었다. 많은 이민자는 뉴욕에 정착했으며, 일부는 바지선을 타고 뉴저지 호보컨이나 저지시티 기차역으로 이동하여 미국 전역의 목적지로 향했다.

D 미국 입국 이민자의 숫자와 국적을 제한한 1921년의 긴급 이민 할당법과 1924년의 국적별 할당법이 통과되면서 뉴욕시로의 대규모 이민 시대는 사실상 끝이 났다. 이 시기부터, 더 적은 수의 이민자 수속이 선상에서 바로 처리되었고, 엘리스섬은 주로 임시 구금 시설 역할만 담당했다. 1925년부터 엘리스섬이 폐쇄된 1954년까지 뉴욕 항구를 통해 입국한 이민자는 230만 명에 불과했지만, 이는 여전히 미국 전체 이민자의 절반 이상을 차지했다.

| 어휘 |

site n. 장소   **immigration station** 이민자 입국 심사소   **close to** ~에 가까운   **trace** v. 추적하다   **ancestor** n. 조상, 선조   **oppression** n. 억압, 탄압   **czarist** a. 제정의   **drought** n. 가뭄   **famine** n. 기근   **persecution** n. 박해   **arduous** a. 고된, 몹시 힘든   **voyage** n. 항해   **registry** n. 명부, 등록부   **inspection** n. 심사   **detain** v. 구금하다, 억류하다   **barge** n. 바지선   **quota**

n. 할당량, 제한량 **nationality** n. 국적 **effectively** ad. 사실상, 실질적으로 **temporary** a. 임시의, 일시적인 **settle** v. 정착하다 **exclusively** ad. 배타적으로 **cease** v. 멈추다 **commercial** a. 상업의 **cargo ship** 화물선 **facility** n. 시설 **exile** v. 추방하다 **tourist** n. 관광객

31 내용파악 ⑤

| 분석 |

첫 번째 단락에 40%라는 숫자가 나온다. 앞 문장에서 "수백만 명의 새로이 도착한 이민자가 미국으로 들어오기 위해 그 문을 통과했던 섬이다"라고 하였으므로 ⑤가 정답이다. ③ 미국 전역의 목적지로 향했다고 했다. 다른 선택지들의 내용은 모두 언급되지 않았다.

위 글에 따르면, 오늘날 미국 시민의 약 40%가 자기 조상을 엘리스 섬까지 거슬러 올라갈 수 있다고 추정되는 이유는 무엇인가?
① 엘리스섬이 동부 해안에서 유일한 입국항이었기 때문에
② 엘리스섬만이 미국 내에서 정확한 가족 기록을 남겼기 때문에
③ 다른 지역에는 이민자들의 정착이 허용되지 않았기 때문에
④ 북부와 서부 유럽인들이 오로지 엘리스섬만을 이용해 이주했기 때문에
⑤ 엘리스섬이 가장 활발히 운영되던 시기에 매우 많은 이민자가 이곳을 통과했기 때문에

32 내용추론 ⑤

| 분석 |

두 번째 문단에서 이민자의 출신이 큰 비율로 북유럽에서 남동부 유럽으로 바뀌고 있었다고 하였다.

다음 중 엘리스섬이 문을 열었을 당시 미국 이민의 변화와 관련하여 가장 추론할 수 있는 것은?
① 유럽에서의 이민이 중단되면서 중동으로부터의 이민이 증가했다.
② 뉴욕을 통해 입국하는 이민자의 전체 숫자가 크게 줄어들었다.
③ 새로운 이민자들은 이전보다 종교와 문화적 배경이 더 획일적이었다.
④ 당시 미국에 입국하는 이민자들의 주류는 아시아 출신이었다.
⑤ 남유럽과 동유럽 출신 이민자들이 북유럽 및 서유럽 출신 이민자들을 대체하며 늘어났다.

33 내용파악 ②

| 분석 |

1925년부터 1954년까지는 입국 이민자 수도 감소하여, 주로 임시 구금 시설 역할을 했다고 마지막 문단에서 밝히고 있다.

1925년부터 1954년까지 엘리스섬의 주된 기능은 무엇이었나?
① 화물선들을 위한 상업 항구
② 더 적은 수의 입국자들을 위한 임시 구금 시설
③ 전 세계 이민자들을 위한 주요 입국 처리 센터
④ 추방된 미국 시민들의 귀국 전용 시설
⑤ 뉴욕 항구의 경치를 강조한 관광지

34 내용추론 ④

| 분석 |

이민자들은 북유럽과 서유럽에서부터 남유럽과 동유럽, 그리고 그 밖의 여러 유럽 외 지역에서부터 왔으므로 언어와 문화 모두가 달랐을 것이다.

다음 중 엘리스섬에 도착한 이민자들의 문화적 다양성에 관해 추론할 수 있는 것은?
① 입국자들은 주로 영어권 국가에서 왔다.
② 이민자 대부분은 동일한 언어 배경을 공유했다.
③ 이민자들은 영어를 유일한 언어로 채택해야 했다.
④ 많은 이민자는 다양한 언어, 종교, 전통을 가지고 왔다.
⑤ 이민자들은 뉴욕에서 영어 관련 요구사항을 피하기를 원했다.

35~38

A 나르시시스트들은 자신의 성취를 자랑함으로써 친구와 가족들을 자주 짜증나게 하는데, 이는 지나친 자존감의 징후처럼 보일 수 있다. 하지만 오클랜드 대학 심리학 교수 버질 자이글러-힐이 주도한 최근 연구 결과에 따르면, 일부 나르시시스트는 실제로 자존감이 낮지만, 그들의 자기과시적 행동은 자존감을 높이려는 목적보다는 지위를 추구하는 욕망에서 비롯된다. 이 연구는 자존감 문제가 나르시시즘을 낳는다는 기존 견해와 상반되는 새로운 증거이다.

B 자이글러-힐은 "그들이 진정으로 신경 쓰는 것은 사회적 지위 층계를 따라 올라가는 일이다. 그들은 다른 사람들보다 우월한 사람이 되고, 존중받고 칭송받는 것, 그리고 높은 지위에서 오는 혜택에 대해 신경을 쓴다"고 말한다. 자존감은 개인이 자신을 어떻게 느끼는가와 관련이 있다면, 지위 인식은 다른 사람이 자신을 어떻게 보는가와 연관되어 있다. 거의 모든 사람이 사회적 인식을 신경 쓰지만, 나르시시스트에게는 지위 추구가 자아개념에서 압도적인 역할을 담당한다.

C 자기애성 성격장애가 있는 사람들은 극단적인 자기 과시와 더불어 타인에 대한 공감 결여를 보인다. 하지만 이러한 장애에 해당하지 않는 사람들도 오만, 외부로부터의 정당성 인정에 대한 욕구, 우월하다고 인정받고자 하는 기대와 같은 나르시시즘적(자기애적) 특성을 보일 수 있다. 심리학자들은 이런 행동이 자존감을 높이거나 지키려는 욕구에서 비롯

된다고 믿었었지만, 최근에는 좀 미묘하게 다른 관점이 제시되고 있다. 나르시시즘에는 여러 유형이 있어서 자존감이 높은 유형도 있지만, 낮은 자존감을 가진 유형도 존재한다. 자이글러-힐의 연구 역시 자존감은 나르시시스트들의 주요 문제가 아니라고 본다. 그에 따르면, 나르시시스트들은 주로 지위를 얻기 위해 필사적이며, 그들의 자존감은 대체로 칭찬받고 있다는 감정의 산물이지, 그들 행동의 근본적인 동력은 아니다.

D 자이글러-힐과 공동 연구자인 오클랜드 대학의 인지심리학자 제니퍼 본크는 이러한 견해를 검증하기 위해 심리학 전공 학부생들을 모집하여 나르시시즘 성향의 정도를 측정하는 설문 조사를 했다. 이 연구자들은 학생들이 보고한 나르시시즘 특성 유형에 따라 자존감 수준이 다르다는 사실을 발견했다. '자기애적 칭찬'이라는 나르시시즘의 하위 유형이 높은 학생들은 실제로 자존감도 높았다. 이들은 사회적 위계에서 높은 지위를 얻으려 갈망하지만, 이를 절제하는 자기 홍보와 자랑과 같은 매력적인 방식으로 추구하며, 인간관계를 잘 유지할 수 있었다. 반면 '자기애적 경쟁'이라는 하위 유형이 높은 사람들은 세상을 제로섬 게임으로 인식했다. 이들은 타인이 존경이나 칭찬받을 때 그런 칭찬이 자신의 지위를 낮아지게 한다고 믿어, 강한 시기와 질투를 느꼈다. 결과적으로, 자기애적 경쟁을 가진 사람들은 타인과 사이좋게 지내는 데 자주 어려움을 겪으며 자존감이 낮은 경향이 있다.

| 어휘 |

narcissist n. 나르시시스트, 자기애적 성향을 지닌 사람 irritate v. 화나게 하다 boast v. 자랑하다 excessive a. 지나친, 과도한 self-aggrandizing a. 자기 과시의 status n. 지위 run counter to ~에 상반되다 hierarchy n. 위계질서, 서열 be concerned with ~와 관련이 있다 disproportionately ad. 불균형하게 disorder n. 장애 grandiosity n. 과장, 자기 과대 empathy n. 공감, 감정이입 validation n. 인정, 확인 nuanced a. 미묘한 차이를 보이는 emerge v. 등장하다 inflated a. 부풀려진, 과장된 desperate a. 필사적인, 절박한 byproduct n. 부산물 envy n. 시기, 질투 recruit v. 모집하다 strive for 추구하다 zero-sum 제로섬(한쪽의 이익이 반드시 다른 쪽의 손실로 연결되는 상황) rivalry n. 경쟁, 경쟁의식 get along with 사이좋게 지내다 humility n. 겸손 hostility n. 적대감 mutual a. 상호의

35 글의 요지 ③

| 분석 |

나르시시즘을 기존의 자존감보다는 사회적 지위 추구와 연결해 설명하려는 연구에 대한 글이다. 따라서 ③이 정답이다. ① 타인의 인식은 지위 추구와 관련되고 내부의 정당성 인정은 자존감과 관련되므로, "자기애적 칭찬" 유형의 사람들은 타인의 인식을 더 우선시한다. ② 자존감을 지키기 위해서가 아니라 지위를 위해서, ④ 자기애적 경쟁은 자존감이 낮다고 했다. ⑤ 둘 사이에서는 자존감보다는 사회를 보는 방식, 사람들과 상호작용하는 방법 등이 주요한 차이로 두드러진다고 했다.

다음 중 위 글을 가장 잘 나타내는 것은?
① 나르시시스트들은 타인의 인식보다 내부의 정당성 인정을 더 우선시한다.
② 나르시시스트들은 오직 자신의 자존감을 지키기 위해서 외부의 정당성 인정을 추구한다.
③ 나르시시즘적 행동은 자존감보다는 사회적 지위를 추구하는 데서 비롯된다.
④ 모든 유형의 나르시시스트들은 과장된 자존감을 대표적인 특징으로 보인다.
⑤ 자기애적 칭찬과 자기애적 경쟁은 주로 자존감에 초점을 맞추고 있는 점에서 다르다.

36 내용파악 ④

| 분석 |

마지막 문단에서 자기애적 칭찬의 사람은 자존감도 높다고 하였다. 이에 반하는 내용이 자기애적 경쟁이므로 정답은 ④이다.

글에서 설명한 두 유형의 나르시시즘을 구분하는 특징은?
① 자기애적 칭찬은 자기 홍보를 우선시하는 반면, 자기애적 경쟁은 겸손을 우선시한다.
② 자기애적 칭찬은 적대감을 포함하지만, 자기애적 경쟁은 조화로운 관계를 추구한다.
③ 자기애적 칭찬은 내부의 정당성 인정을 추구하지만, 자기애적 경쟁은 외부의 정당성 인정에 의존한다.
④ 자기애적 칭찬은 높은 자존감과 관련되어 있지만, 자기애적 경쟁은 낮은 자존감과 연결되어 있다.
⑤ 자기애적 칭찬은 세상을 제로섬으로 보지만, 자기애적 경쟁은 모두가 성공할 수 있는 기회로 본다.

37 내용추론 ②

| 분석 |

나르시시즘은 반드시 자존감이 낮다고도, 높다고도 할 수 없다는 게 이 글의 주장이다. 자기애적 칭찬의 사람들은 자존감이 높다. 따라서 ②가 정답이다.

다음 중 위 글로부터 가장 추론할 수 없는 것은?
① 나르시시즘 속성을 가진 사람들은 다른 사람들이 자신을 어떻게 인지하는지 크게 신경 쓴다.
② 나르시시즘 속성을 가진 모든 사람은 낮은 자존감을 주된 특성으로 보인다.

③ 자기애적 칭찬은 사회적 층계를 잘 오르기 위한 자기 홍보와 매력적인 행동을 포함한다.
④ 자기애적 칭찬이 높은 사람들은 자기애적 경쟁이 높은 사람보다 사회적 관계에서 성공할 가능성이 크다.
⑤ 자기애적 경쟁은 제로섬 방식의 사고 때문에 질투와 시기 감정과 흔히 연관된다.

38 내용추론 ⑤

| 분석 |

자이글러-힐의 연구는 현재 심리학 전공 학부생들이라는 매우 제한된 모집군을 대상으로 하고 있다. 이 경우, 연구 결과가 전체 인구집단에 일반화될 수 있는지에 대한 신뢰성이 낮을 것이다. 따라서 연령, 문화, 교육 수준, 직업군 등이 다양한 집단을 포함하면, 연구 결과가 더 넓은 사람들에게 적용될 수 있고, 그만큼 연구의 설득력과 일반화 가능성이 크게 향상될 것이다. 따라서 ⑤가 정답으로 적절하다.

다음 중 마지막 문단에 소개된 자이글러-힐 연구의 설득력을 가장 크게 높여줄 것 같은 것은?
① 사회적 규범과 가치의 편차를 줄이기 위해 단일한 문화적 환경만을 사용하는 것
② 나르시시즘 특성이 시간이 지남에 따라 어떻게 발전하는지를 관찰하기 위해 장기적 연구를 수행하는 것
③ 높은 자존감을 가진 사람들에게만 초점을 맞추기 위해 연구의 범위를 한정하는 것
④ 자기애성 성격장애로 임상 진단받은 참가자들만 연구에 포함하는 것
⑤ 심리학과 학부 학생들에게만 국한하지 않고 더 다양한 표본 집단을 포함하는 것

39~42

A 대부분의 학자는 윌리엄 셰익스피어가 스트랫퍼드어폰에이번에서 태어나 런던에서 배우로 활동한 후 스트랫퍼드로 돌아와 1616년 사망할 때까지 그곳에서 살았다고 본다. 하지만 그의 생애에 대한 실제 기록은 보잘것없을 정도로 부족하다. 고작 몇 개의 서명, 앤 해서웨이와의 결혼 및 자녀 출생 기록, 세 페이지짜리 유언장, 그리고 글쓰기와 관련 없는 몇몇 사업상의 서류뿐이다. 특히, 그가 썼다고 하는 영어 역사상 가장 위대한 작품으로 집합적 평가를 받는 36편 이상의 희곡과 154편의 소네트를 그가 썼다고 증명하는 문서는 전혀 발견되지 않았다.
B 이러한 진짜 저자임에 대한 '증거'가 부족한 상황에서, 일부 회의론자들은 다음과 같은 의문을 제기해왔다. "이처럼 하찮은 출신에 하찮은 교육을 받은 사람이 어떻게 이렇게 풍부한 통찰력, 복잡한 법률 및 정치 문제에 대한 폭넓은 이해, 그리고 영국 왕실 생활에 정통한 지식을 가질 수 있었을까?" 19세기 이후로 헨리 제임스, 지크문트 프로이트, 마크 트웨인, 헬렌 켈러, 찰리 채플린 등 수많은 유명 인사들이 이 스트랫퍼드 출신의 남자에 대한 의심을 말해왔다. 이 주제와 관련된 책과 논문이 수천 편은 출판되었으며, 많은 책과 논문이 셰익스피어 정전의 실제 저자에 대해 각기 다른 후보자를 제시해왔다.
C 수필가 프랜시스 베이컨과 극작가 크리스토퍼 말로도 많은 지지를 받고 있지만, 지난 90년 동안 가장 널리 지지받는 후보자는 17대 옥스퍼드 백작 에드워드 드 비어였다. 1920년 J. T. 루니가 『셰익스피어로 확인된 인물』에서 처음 제안한 옥스퍼드 백작은 고등 교육을 받았고, 법률가로서도 교육받았으며, 셰익스피어의 희곡에 등장하는 많은 장소를 실제로 여행한 것으로 알려져 있다. 옥스퍼드 백작이 저자라는 주장을 지지하는 옥스퍼디언이라는 사람들은 옥스퍼드 백작이 자신의 신원을 숨긴 이유에 대해 작품이 정치적으로 지나치게 도발적이었으며, 자신이 신분이 낮은 극작가로 알려지는 것을 피하고 싶었기 때문이라고 주장한다.
D 그러나, 셰익스피어의 희곡이 실제로 다른 누군가에 의해 쓰여졌다고 입증하는 확실한 증거가 나오기 전까지는, 윌리엄 셰익스피어의 희곡에 대한 가장 강력한 소유권을 주장할 수 있는 인물은 결국 윌리엄 셰익스피어 본인으로 보인다. 우선 먼저, 옥스퍼드 백작은 1604년에 사망했다. 그러나 셰익스피어의 대표작 중 『리어왕』, 『템페스트』, 『맥베스』 같은 작품들은 그 이후에 출간되었다. 스트랫퍼디언이라고 알려진 셰익스피어 저자설 지지자들은 희곡과 소네트 인쇄본에 그의 이름이 명시되어 있다는 점, 극단 기록, 그리고 벤 존슨이나 존 웹스터 등, 동시대 작가들의 언급과 같은 기존 증거들을 강조한다. 셰익스피어의 진짜 저자임에 대한 의심과, 학력이 높고 세상 이치에 밝으며 신분이 높은 다른 후보자를 찾으려는 시도는 비뚤어진 속물근성일 뿐 아니라, 셰익스피어의 특별한 작품의 가장 놀라운 우수성 중 하나인 그의 상상력에 대한 무시라고 스트랫퍼디언들은 주장한다.

| 어휘 |

act v. 연기하다 documentation n. 문서 기록 pitifully ad. 한심할 정도로 scarce a. 부족한, 드문 will n. 유언장 above all 무엇보다도 attribute to ~의 것으로 귀속되다 skeptic n. 회의론자, 의심하는 사람 humble origins 미천한 출신, 낮은 사회적 배경 come by 획득하다 insight n. 통찰력 wide-ranging a. 광범위한, 폭넓은 intimate a. 정통한 roaster n. 등록부 subject n. 주제 candidate n. 후보자 canon n. 정전; 법규 provocative a. 도발적인 outed a. 정체가 드러난, 폭로된 hard evidence 확실한 증거, 구체적인 증거 contemporary n. 동시대인, 같은 시대의 사람들 snobbery n. 속물근성, 우월감 disregard n. 무시 the Bard 윌리엄 셰익스피어의 별명 hold in high esteem 존경하다

39 내용일치   ⑤

| 분석 |
셰익스피어에 대해 분명한 설명을 하는 직접적인 기록이 없으니 수많은 논란이 존재한다. 따라서 ⑤가 정답이다.

위 글에 따르면, 다음 중 옳지 <u>않은</u> 것은?
① 일부 사람들은 셰익스피어 작품은 다른 사람이 썼다고 주장한다.
② 셰익스피어의 주요 기록에는 서명, 결혼 기록, 그리고 그의 유언장이 포함된다.
③ 수천 권의 책과 논문이 셰익스피어의 진짜 저자임에 대한 의문을 제기해왔다.
④ 학자들 대부분은 셰익스피어가 스트랫퍼드어폰에이번에서 태어났고 사망했다고 주장한다.
⑤ 셰익스피어가 36편의 희곡과 154편의 소네트를 어떻게 썼는지를 상세히 설명하는 증거가 있다.

40 내용파악   ②

| 분석 |
②의 크리스토퍼 말로는 셰익스피어 작품을 실제로 쓴 사람의 후보자로 제시된 인물이지, 셰익스피어가 진짜 저자임을 의심한 사람은 아니다.

다음 중 셰익스피어가 진짜 저자임을 의심한 사람이 <u>아닌</u> 사람은?
① 찰리 채플린
② 크리스토퍼 말로
③ 헨리 제임스
④ 마크 트웨인
⑤ J.T. 루니

41 내용파악   ⑤

| 분석 |
두 번째 문단의 첫 문장에서 일부 회의론자들의 의심 이유를 "이처럼 하찮은 출신에 하찮은 교육을 받은 사람이 어떻게 이렇게 풍부한 통찰력, 복잡한 법률 및 정치 문제에 대한 폭넓은 이해, 그리고 영국 왕실 생활에 정통한 지식을 가질 수 있었을까?"이라고 말하고 있다. 따라서 ⑤가 정답이다.

위 글에 따르면, 다음 중 일부 사람들이 셰익스피어의 진짜 저자임을 의심한 가장 큰 이유를 가장 잘 나타내고 있는 것은?
① 그들은 셰익스피어의 동시대인들이 그를 높이 평가하지 않았다고 생각했다.
② 그들은 수많은 문서가 셰익스피어의 진짜 저자임에 이의를 제기한다고 주장했다.
③ 그들은 당시 공연 기록에 셰익스피어의 이름이 전혀 등장하지 않았다고 주장했다.
④ 그들은 셰익스피어의 작품 주제가 너무도 광범위하고 다양하여 한 사람이 썼다고 보기 어렵다고 주장했다.
⑤ 그들은 셰익스피어와 같은 배경과 제한된 교육을 받은 사람이 어떻게 그렇게 폭넓은 지식과 통찰을 가질 수 있었는지 의심했다.

42 내용파악   ①

| 분석 |
① 문서 기록이 부족했기에 여러 논란이 생겼다. 나머지는 모두 본문에서 찾아볼 수 있다.

위 글에 따르면, 다음 중 셰익스피어가 실제로 셰익스피어 정전의 저자라고 믿는 사람들의 주장이 <u>아닌</u> 것은?
① 문서 기록의 부족은 셰익스피어가 실제로 그 희곡들을 썼다는 것을 결정적으로 증명했다.
② 셰익스피어가 런던 주요 극단과 연관이 있다고 알려진 점이 그가 저자임을 뒷받침했다.
③ 셰익스피어의 가장 유명한 희곡 중 몇몇은 에드워드 드 비어가 1604년에 사망한 후 출판되었다.
④ 더 귀족적이거나 더 많은 교육을 받은 후보자를 찾으려는 시도는 셰익스피어 작품에서 드러나는 비범한 상상력을 무시했다.
⑤ 셰익스피어의 이름이 있는 인쇄본은 벤 존슨, 존 웹스터 등, 동시대인의 언급과 더불어 그가 저자임을 강력히 뒷받침했다.

43~46

A 전 세계 모든 언어는 고유한 일단의 소리들을 사용하며, 놀랍게도 인간의 영아는 이 모든 소리들을 구별할 수 있는 능력을 갖고 태어난다. 생후 몇 달 동안 아기들은 매우 다양한 소리에 반응하며, 이로 인해 그들은 어떤 언어든 배울 수 있게 된다. 하지만 그 능력은 늦어도 생후 첫 돌 때는 약해지기 시작한다. 워싱턴 대학의 패트리샤 쿨에 따르면, 영아들은 점차 자기 모국어에서 가장 흔히 들리는 소리에 집중하게 된다. 지각적 자석 효과라고 불리는 이 현상은 자주 마주치는 말소리들이 어떻게 유사하지 않은 소리를 걸러 내면서 유사한 소리들을 끌어들이는지를 보여준다. 이러한 미세 조정 과정은 아기들의 뇌가 그들이 생후 첫해 동안 노출되는 특정 언어를 습득하도록 준비시켜준다.
B 최근 한 연구 조사에 따르면 신생아의 첫 울음조차도 초기 언어 습득 과정에 대한 통찰을 제공할 수 있다. 2009년, 캐슬린 베름케 박사와 그녀의 연구팀은 신생아들은 이미 그들이 자궁에서 들었던 언어의 영향을 받은 울음 패턴을 보여준다는 사실을 발견했다. 예를 들어, 독일 신생아는 종종 독일

어의 억양 패턴을 닮은 하강 음조로 울음을 터뜨리는 반면에, 프랑스 신생아는 프랑스어의 억양을 따라서 상승 음조로 우는 경향이 있다. 이러한 연구 결과는 언어에의 노출이 출생 이전부터 아기에게 영향을 미치기 시작한다는 점과 신생아가 이미 울음을 통해 모국어의 선율 윤곽을 모방하려고 시도하고 있을 수도 있다는 점을 시사한다.

C 베름케 박사의 연구실에는 멀리 카메룬과 중국에서 수집된 약 50만 개의 영아 울음 녹음 기록이 보관되어 있다. 이 녹음에 대한 정량적 음향 분석을 통해 아기의 첫소리를 형성하는 다양한 요인에 대한 추가적인 통찰을 얻었다. 만다린 중국어와 같은 성조 언어를 사용하는 어머니에게서 태어난 신생아들은 변화의 폭이 상당히 더 큰 울음 선율을 만들어내는 경향이 있다. 마찬가지로, 카메룬의 은소 부족 아기들은 비성조 언어를 쓰는 독일 신생아들보다 훨씬 더 강한 음조 변동을 보였다. 베름케 교수는 "아기들의 울음이 오히려 노래 같이 들린다"고 말했다. 이러한 발견들은 언어 발달의 기본 요소들은 아기들이 옹알거리거나 단어를 형성하기 오래 전, 출생 때부터 갖추어진다는 점을 부각시킨다. 초기의 언어 노출, 심지어 자궁에서의 언어 노출도 놀라운 언어 발달 과정을 결정한다.

D 연구 결과는 언어 발달의 가장 초기 국면에 영향을 미치는 필수적인 요인들을 더 잘 이해하게 해준다. 동시에, 연구 결과는 매우 어린 연령 단계에서의 발달 장애에 관한 믿을 만한 정보를 제공하는 초기 지표를 밝혀낼 가능성을 높여준다. 하지만 이러한 연구 결과가 임상적으로 활용될 수 있기 위해 먼저 명확히 밝혀져야 할 문제들이 아직 많이 남아있다.

| 어휘 |

utilize v. 활용하다   receptive a. 수용하는   weaken v. 약해지다, 약화하다   prevalent a. 흔한, 널리 퍼진   filter out 걸러내다   relevant a. 적절한   fine-tuning n. 미세 조정   prime v. 준비하다   language acquisition 언어 습득   utero n. 자궁   pitch n. 음조   intonation n. 억양, 어조   mimic v. 모방하다   melodic contour 멜로디 윤곽, 음조 패턴   house v. 수용하다   quantitative a. 정량적인, 수치화된   acoustic a. 소리의   tonal language 성조 언어(음의 높낮이에 따라 의미가 달라지는 언어)   Mandarin n. 중국 표준어   pitch fluctuation 음조 변동   neonate n. 신생아   chanting n. 낭송   babble v. 옹알거리다   womb n. 자궁   clinical practice 임상적 활용   predisposition n. 경향

43 글의 제목   ②

| 분석 |

모국어가 태어나기 전부터 태아에게 영향을 미친다는 사실과 더불어 아기의 울음 패턴이 아기의 모국어에 따라 다르다는 주제를 잘 포괄하고 있는 ②가 가장 좋은 제목이다. ① 태어나 울기 전 태아 때부터 시작된다. ③ 성조 언어만 이야기하고 있지는 않다. ④ (언어 노출) 빈도에 대한 설명은 없다. ⑤ 첫 단락의 제목이라 할 수 있다.

다음 중 위 글의 제목으로 가장 적절한 것은?
① 초기 언어 발달: 울음에서 옹알이까지
② 자궁에서 단어까지: 언어별로 다른 신생아 울음
③ 신생아 울음 패턴과 성조 언어와의 연관성
④ 언어 습득이라는 과학: 빈도와 그 결과
⑤ 지각적 자석 효과: 모국어 소리에 대한 유아의 뇌 적응

44 내용파악   ①

| 분석 |

신생아에게 다양한 언어 자극, 즉 말소리를 들려주고, 그에 반응하는 방식을 평가하는 실험을 했다는 내용은 없다. 따라서 ①이 정답이다.

다음 중 위 글에서 설명된 연구 방법이 아닌 것은?
① 신생아가 다양한 언어 자극에 반응하는 방식을 평가하는 실험을 수행함
② 신생아의 울음을 분석하여, 울음 패턴의 변동과 이 변동과 언어 노출의 관계를 연구함
③ 정량적 음향 분석을 통해 태아기 언어 노출의 영향을 받은 억양 패턴을 관찰함
④ 성조 언어 환경과 비성조 언어 환경에서 자란 아기의 울음 패턴을 비교하여 음조 변동성을 분석함
⑤ 50만 개의 신생아 울음 녹음을 수집하고 분석하여 언어 노출과 연관된 패턴을 보여줌

45 어법상 적절하지 않은 표현 고르기   ②

| 분석 |

Ⓑ that are frequently encountering의 선행사는 speech sounds이다. 말소리가 능동적으로 무엇을 만날 수는 없고, 말소리가 만나진다는 의미이므로 Ⓑ를 수동태인 that are frequently encountered로 고쳐야 한다.

46 내용일치   ④

| 분석 |

자궁에 있으면서 모국어를 듣는다고 하여, 그것이 '유전적'인 것은 아니다. 다시 말해 유전적인 성향은 언급되지 않았으므로 ④가 사실이 아니다.

위 글에 따르면, 다음 중 옳지 않은 것은?
① 자궁에서 들린 소리를 포함한 초기 언어 노출은 신생아의 울음에서 관찰된 언어 패턴에 큰 영향을 미친다.
② 영아의 뇌는 관련이 덜한 소리를 걸러내는 미세 조정 과정을 거쳐서, 뇌가 모국어 환경에 적응하도록 도와준다.

③ 성조 언어를 말하는 어머니에게서 태어난 아기들은 비성조 언어에 노출된 아기들보다 음조 변화가 더 복잡한 울음을 우는 경향이 있다.
④ 신생아의 울음 패턴은 태아기와 출생 후의 영향과 상호 작용하는 유전적 성향에서 나타나며, 언어 환경에 따른 특성을 형성한다.
⑤ 신생아의 울음은 초기 언어 발달 과정에 대한 중요한 통찰을 제공하며, 발달 초기 단계에서의 발달 장애를 식별하는 데 도움을 줄 수도 있다.

47~50

A 인공지능(AI)은 엄청난 이점을 약속하고 있지만, 동시에 막대한 위험도 제기한다. 허위 정보의 가속화, 정교한 사이버 공격, 급증하는 에너지 소비량과 같은 몇몇 위험들은 이미 도래했다. 인간의 감독 없이 독립적으로 결정을 내리는 초지능 기계를 포함한 또 다른 위험들은 아직 몇 년 뒤의 일일 가능성이 크다. 이러한 위험에 대한 인식은 늘어나고 있지만, 아직 정의되지 않은 또 다른 위험도 많다. 특히 개발도상국에서 AI에 의해 제공되는 수많은 기회에도 불구하고, 그것은 위험한 일이다. 급속한 AI 채택이 글로벌 사우스(개발도상국들) 사회에 미칠 부정적인 영향에 대한 우려가 커지고 있다.
B 가장 심각한 위험 중 하나는 대규모 자동화와 일자리 상실이다. AI는 농업, 제조업, 소매업에서부터 법률, 의료, 금융 분야까지 다양한 산업에서 수많은 노동자에게 영향을 미칠 것으로 예상된다. 새로운 형태의 일자리도 분명 등장하겠지만, 2030년까지 부유한 나라의 3억 명을 포함하여 최대 8억 명의 일자리가 자동화될 위험에 처해 있다. 국제노동기구는 저소득 및 중간 소득 국가의 전체 일자리 중 56% 이상이 자동화될 '커다란 위험'에 처해 있다고 추정하고 있다. 보호 조치가 제대로 마련되지 않는다면, 이로 인해 경제적 불평등은 심화하고, 저숙련 노동자들은 쫓겨날 수 있다.
C 또 다른 중요한 문제는 디지털 격차의 확대와 불평등의 증폭이다. 첨단 기술에 접근하고, 이를 활용할 수 있는 사람들과 그럴 수 없는 사람들 사이의 격차는 앞으로 더욱 벌어지고, 이에 따라, 생산성 저하, 경제 성장 둔화, 사회 및 경제적 불평등 심화와 같은 결과가 초래될 것으로 예상된다. 이러한 문제는 디지털 인프라, 숙련된 인력, 관련 서비스가 부족한 지역에서 특히 현저하여, 불평등이 더욱 고착화되고 있다.
D 감시의 강화와 사생활 침해가 또한 AI에 의해 가능해진다. 스마트 도시에서부터 법 집행에 이르기까지 다양한 분야에 AI가 통합되어 들어가는 것은 사생활, 시민 자유, 인권을 침해할 수 있다. 민주주의 제도가 취약한 국가에서는 특히 그렇다. 실제로 권위주의 정권들은 이미 AI 기반 시스템을 배치하여 정치적 반대자들을 추적하고, 반대 의견을 탄압하며, 특정 민족·종교·이념에 기초한 소외된 지역사회들을 목표로 삼는다.

| 어휘 |

immense a. 막대한 tremendous a. 엄청난 misinformation n. 허위 정보, 잘못된 정보 cyber attack 사이버 공격 soar v. 급증하다, 치솟다 super-intelligent a. 초지능의, 인간 지능을 초월하는 oversight n. 감독 incalculable a. 계산할 수 없는 afford v. 제공하다 concern n. 우려 Global South 글로벌 사우스(주로 개발도상국 지역) automation n. 자동화 job displacement 일자리 대체(자동화로 인해 기존 일자리가 사라지는 현상) be expected to ~로 예상되다 retail n. 소매업 up to ~씩이나 되는 be at risk 위험에 처하다 safeguard n. 보호 조치 amplification n. 확대 inequality n. 불평등 digital divide 디지털 격차(기술 접근성이 있는 사람들과 그렇지 않은 사람들 간의 차이) access v. 접근하다 pronounced a. 두드러진 entrench v. 고착화하다 intensification n. 강화 surveillance n. 감시 privacy violation 사생활 침해 integration n. 통합; 완성 law enforcement 법집행 infringe on 침해하다 civil liberty 시민 자유 authoritarian regime 권위주의 정권 deploy v. 배치하다 suppress v. 억압하다 marginalize v. 소외시키다 outline v. 개괄하다 implication n. 의미 prediction n. 예측

47 글의 제목   ①

| 분석 |

AI가 제기하고 있는 여러 위험을 다루고 있는 글이므로 ①이 제목으로 적절하다. ②와 ③은 ①에 포함되는 내용이고, ④ AI는 경제 불평등을 해결하지 않고, 오히려 조장하고 있다. ⑤ 개발도상국으로 한정 짓는 것도 부적절하고, '윤리'도 관련성이 없다.

다음 중 위 글의 제목으로 가장 적절한 것은?
① AI의 위험과 문제들
② AI 시대의 프라이버시와 감시
③ AI가 일자리 구조를 재형성하고 있는 방식
④ 전 세계 경제적 불평등을 해결하는 AI의 역할
⑤ 디지털 전환과 개발도상국에서의 윤리적 문제

48 내용추론   ⑤

| 분석 |

AI의 중립성이나, 훈련 데이터의 편향에 관해서는 언급된 적이 없으며, 여러 차별을 낳는 AI는 중립적이라기보다는 오히려 편향적이라고 해야 옳다. 따라서 ⑤가 정답이다.

다음 중 위 글로부터 가장 추론할 수 없는 것은?
① 디지털 격차가 확대되면서 개발도상국들 지역의 경제 성장이 둔화할 수도 있다.

② AI는 허위 정보와 사이버 공격 같은 심각한 위험을 이미 초래했다.
③ AI 기반 대규모 자동화는 저소득 및 중간 소득 국가에서 불평등을 더욱 악화시킬 수 있다.
④ 권위주의 정권들은 AI 기술을 활용하여 정치적 반대자를 추적하고 특정 집단을 소외시킬 수 있다.
⑤ AI 시스템의 중립성은 훈련 데이터 편향이 현실에서 차별적 결과를 초래하지 않도록 보장할 수 있다.

49 내용파악 ③

| 분석 |
정부 감시 기능이 이미 문제가 되고 있는데, 이 기능을 강화한다는 ③은 문제의 해결이라기보다는 문제를 악화시키는 것이다.

다음 중 위 글에서 제시된 문제들을 해결할 가능성이 가장 <u>적은</u> 것은?
① 첨단 기술 접근성을 확대하여 디지털 격차를 해소하고 불평등을 줄이는 것
② 대규모 자동화와 일자리 상실의 경제적 영향을 완화하기 위한 보호 조치를 시행하는 것
③ 정부 감시를 강화하여 AI 기반 활동을 모니터링하고 소외된 지역사회들을 추적하는 것
④ AI에 의한 감시와 사생활 침해를 억제하기 위한 강력한 데이터 보호법과 공공 인식 캠페인
⑤ 정부, 기술 기업, 시민 사회 간의 협력을 촉진하여 AI 개발에서 공정한 접근과 책임성을 보장하는 것

50 글의 구성 ③

| 분석 |
AI가 초래하고 있는, 그리고 앞으로 초래할 여러 위험을 언급하고, 각각의 구체적 사례와 설명을 제공하고 있다. 따라서 정답은 ③이다. ④ 이점에 대한 논의는 거의 찾아볼 수 없다.

다음 중 위 글의 구성을 가장 잘 설명하는 것은?
① AI의 가장 큰 하나의 위험을 개괄적으로 설명하고, 그것이 세계 경제에 미치는 영향을 논의한다.
② AI의 역사적 발전을 설명한 후, 미래 사회에 미칠 영향을 예측한다.
③ AI와 관련된 다양한 위험을 식별하고, 각각의 위험에 대한 구체적인 예시와 설명을 제공한다.
④ 먼저 AI의 잠재적 이점을 나열한 후, 이를 다양한 영역에서의 구체적인 위험과 비교·대조한다.
⑤ 선진국과 개발도상국에서의 AI의 발달을 비교하는 것에 중점을 두고, 그들의 독특한 도전 과제를 강조한다.

AJOU UNIVERSITY | 아주대학교 자연계

TEST p. 522~534

01	①	02	③	03	①	04	②	05	①	06	③	07	①	08	②	09	④	10	①
11	⑤	12	①	13	③	14	①	15	④	16	②	17	①	18	①	19	②	20	③
21	⑤	22	③	23	④	24	④	25	①										

01 논리완성 ①

| 분석 |

다음 문장에서 작가들은 오래 전에 AI에 관한 소설적 이야기들을 제시했다고 했으므로, 빈칸에는 AI 개념이 인간의 상상력을 '사로잡아 왔다'라는 의미의 표현이 들어가는 것이 적절하다.

| 어휘 |

tireless a. 지칠 줄 모르는 **companion** n. 동반자 **captivate** v. ~의 마음을 사로잡다 **Cold War** (2차 대전 후 미국과 소련 간의) 냉전 **spin** v. (정보·상황을, 특히 그럴듯하게) 제시하다, 이야기하다 **fictional** a. 허구적인, 소설의 **contaminate** v. 오염시키다

| 해석 |

지칠 줄 모르는 조수, 궁극의 군인 또는 심지어 보살펴주는 동반자로서의 "지능적 기계"라는 개념은 수천 년 동안 인간의 상상력을 사로잡아 왔다. 인공지능이 하나의 현실이 되기 오래전, 고대 그리스에서부터 냉전 시대 미국에 이르기까지 작가들은 AI에 대한 우리의 집단적 희망과 두려움을 반영한 소설적 이야기들을 제시했다.

02 논리완성 ③

| 분석 |

어떤 표현이 올해의 단어로 선정될 정도라면 온라인상에서 그 단어를 검색하고 사용하는 '빈도'가 증가하였을 것이라고 추론할 수 있다. 따라서 ③이 정답이다. adoption은 '아이디어 또는 계획 등을 채택하는 것'을 가리키므로 usage(사용)와 함께 사용하면 '사용 채택'이라는 의미가 되어 어색하다.

| 어휘 |

rot n. 썩음, 부식, 부패 **prominence** n. 중요성; 유명함 **capture** v. ~의 관심[상상력, 흥미]를 사로잡다 **usage** n. 사용 **frequency** n. 빈도; 빈발 **adoption** n. 채택; 입양 **dimension** n. 크기, 치수; 차원 **resonance** n. 울림, 공명 **urgency** n. 긴급성; 시급함, 절박함

| 해석 |

37,000명 이상의 투표와 전 세계적인 공개 토론, 언어 데이터 분석을 거쳐 우리는 '뇌 썩음'을 2024년 올해의 단어로 선정했다. 우리의 전문가들은 '뇌 썩음'이 특히 소셜 미디어의 저질 온라인 콘텐츠들을 과도하게 소비하는 것의 영향에 대한 우려를 포착하는 데 사용되는 용어로 올해 새로운 유명세를 얻고 있다는 사실에 주목하였다. 이 용어의 사용 빈도는 2023년부터 2024년 사이에 230% 증가했다. '뇌 썩음'이라는 표현은 1854년 헨리 데이비드 소로(Henry David Thoreau)의 저서 『월든(Walden)』에서 처음 사용되었지만, 디지털 시대의 표현으로서 새로운 의미를 갖게 되었다.

03 논리완성 ①

| 분석 |

사람들이 주로 식물성 식단으로 전환하는 상황에서, 그 식물들의 주요 영양 성분들이 점점 줄어들고 있다면 이것은 '심각한, 중대한' 문제라고 추론할 수 있을 것이다. critical은 '비판적인, 비난하는'이라는 기본적인 뜻 외에도 '대단히 중요한, 중대한(important)'이라는 의미가 있다.

| 어휘 |

mounting a. (흔히 우려스러울 정도로) 증가하는 **grain** n. 곡물, (곡식의) 낟알 **protein** n. 단백질 **phosphorus** n. 인(비금속 원소) **riboflavin** n. 리보플라빈(비타민 B₂) **review** n. (어떤 주제·일련의 사건에 대한) 보고서 **alarming** a. 걱정스러운, 두려운 **switch to** ~으로 바꾸다 **diet** n. 식단 **critical** a. 비판적인, 비난하는; 중요한, 중대한 **divisive** a. 분열을 초래하는 **ephemeral** a. 덧없는; 단명하는 **negligible** a. 무시해도 될 정도의 **transient** a. 일시적인

| 해석 |

다수의 과학 연구에서 얻어지는 점증하는 증거들이 오늘날 재배되는 많은 과일, 채소, 곡물은 수십 년 전 재배된 것들보다 단백질, 칼슘, 인, 철, 비타민 B₂, 비타민 C가 적다는 사실을 보여준다. 학술지『식품(Foods)』에 실린 한 연구는 이러한 감소를 "걱정스러우며" "미래 세대의 건강에 대한 가장 큰 도전"이라고 설명하였다. 이것은, 전문가들이 공중보건 및 지구 보호를 위해 권장하는 바에 따라, 점점 더 많은 사람들이 주로 식물에 기초한 식단으로 전환한다면, 특히 중요한 문제이다.

04 분사의 한정용법 / 선행사를 포함한 관계대명사 what ②

| 분석 |
빈칸에는 theory를 수식하는 분사 또는 관계대명사절이 필요하다. ②에서 현재분사 proposing은 theory를 수식하며, 선행사를 포함한 관계대명사 what절이 proposing의 목적어가 되고, '~라고 여겨지는'이라는 수동의 의미는 is considered to be이므로 ②가 정답으로 적절하다. ①, ③ what을 주어로 하여 consider를 능동태로 나타내는 것은 적절하지 않다. ④, ⑤ 'is to be considered'는 '고려되어야 할'이라는 의미로 미래의 고려 사항을 나타내므로, 문맥상 적절하지 않다.

| 어휘 |
groundbreaking a. 신기원을 이룬, 획기적인   **propose** v. (계획·생각 등을) 제안[제의]하다

| 해석 |
그 과학자는 기후 변화를 이해하는 새로운 방법으로 여겨지는 획기적인 이론을 제시했다.

05 anything but ①

| 분석 |
anything but은 '~외에는 어떤 것이든' 즉, '~이 결코 아닌'으로서 not at all처럼 부정의 의미를 강조하는 데 사용된다. ①이 가장 문맥에 부합한다. ② other than은 '~외에 다른'의 의미로 any를 부정대명사로 보면 any other than은 '~외에 다른 어느 것이나'여서 than 다음에는 명사가 와야 하는데 형용사 ordinary여서 부적절하다. ③ none other than은 '다름 아닌 바로 ~'이라는 뜻이고, ④ nothing but 또한 '단지 ~일 뿐'이라는 뜻이며, ⑤ nothing other than 역시 '단지 ~뿐, ~에 지나지 않다'는 뜻이어서 ③, ④, ⑤ 모두 평범함을 강조하며 than이나 but 다음에 명사가 와야 하므로 문맥에 맞지 않다.

| 어휘 |
positioning n. 자리매김 (전략)   **distinguish oneself** (스스로를) 차별화하다

| 해석 |
7UP의 "Uncola" 광고는 마케팅에 대한 획기적인 접근방식을 선보이면서, 창의성과 영리한 자리매김 전략을 활용하여, 자신을 전혀 평범하지 않은 모습으로 차별화했다.

06 수동태와 능동태의 구분 ③

| 분석 |
decrease는 자동사와 타동사로 모두 쓰일 수 있지만, 행위자가 명시되지 않은 하나의 사회현상 같은 것을 설명할 때는 '(~가) 줄다, 감소하다'는 뜻의 자동사로 쓰여 보통 has decreased(현재완료) 또는 is decreasing(현재진행) 같은 능동태로 쓰인다. 따라서 ③을 능동태인 seems to decrease나 seems to have decreased 또는 seems to be decreasing으로 수정해야 한다. ④의 connect도 자동사와 타동사 모두로 쓰일 수 있는데, 여기서는 자동사로 쓰여 능동태이다.

| 어휘 |
no more than 단지 ~에 지나지 않다, ~일 뿐   **interconnectedness** n. 상호 연락[연결]됨, 상관됨   **a handful of** 소수의   **intermediary** n. 중재자, 중개인   **humanity** n. 인류, 인간   **weave** v. 짜다[엮다], 짜서[엮어서] 만들다

| 해석 |
6단계 분리 개념은 지구상의 어떤 두 사람도 불과 6단계의 사회적 연결 고리를 통해 연결될 수 있다는 것을 시사한다. 20세기 초 헝가리 작가 프리제시 카린티(Frigyes Karinthy)에 의해 처음 소개된 이 개념은 이후 인간 네트워크의 상호 연결성을 탐구하는 수많은 과학적 연구에 영감을 주었다. 흥미롭게도 소셜 미디어의 등장으로 이 거리는 줄어든 것으로 보인다. 예를 들어, 세계적인 아이콘인 버락 오바마(Barack Obama) 미국 전 대통령은 이론적으로 소수의 중간자들만 거친다면, 오지에 사는 어떤 사람과도 연결될 수 있을 것이다. 이를 뒷받침하듯 2016년 페이스북의 연구에 따르면 전 세계의 어떤 두 사용자 간의 평균 연결 단계는 3.57개에 불과하였다. 이러한 결과는 우리 세계가 얼마나 상호 연결되었는지를 강조하며, 우리에게 인류를 먼 이방인이 아닌 긴밀하게 짜인 관계의 그물망으로 보도록 고무시킨다.

07 수동태와 능동태의 구분 ①

| 분석 |
meet with라는 구동사는 3가지 의미를 갖는데, 각각의 형태에 주의해야 한다. 먼저 '~와 회의를 하다'는 뜻일 때는 meet with someone의 형태로 사용된다. 둘째, '특정한 상황이나 반응을 받거나 경험하다'는 뜻일 때는 meet with something의 형태로 사용된다. 셋째, '무언가에 대해 특별한 반응을 보이다'는 뜻일 때는 meet something with something의 형태를 가지는데, 이때는 수동태로도 쓸 수 있다. 주어진 글의 첫째 문장에서 사용된 meet with는 셋째 의미를 활용한 것으로, 'People do not meet all logo changes with universal applause.'를 수동태로 쓴 것이므로 ①을 are met with로 수정하는 것이 가장 적절하다.

| 어휘 |
redesign n. 재디자인   **spark** v. 촉발시키다, 유발하다   **bold** a. 대담한, 대범한   **simplify** v. 단순화하다   **opt for** ~을 선택하다   **minimalism** n. (예술에서의) 미니멀리즘, 최소한 표현주의(최소한의 요소로 최대 효과를 올리려는)   **minimalist** n. 미니멀리스트(되도록 소수의 단순한 요소를 통해 최대 효과를 이루려는 사고방식을 지닌 예술가)   **align with** ~에 맞추어 조정하다   **sleek** a. 매끄러운, 산뜻한   **forward-thinking** a. 장래를 고려[대비]하는, 진보적인   **nostalgia**

n. 향수(鄕愁)   scalable a. 확장 가능한   pay off 성공하다. 결실을 맺다

| 해석 |
불행히도 모든 로고 변경이 보편적인 박수갈채를 받는 것은 아니며, 맥도날드의 최근 리디자인도 상당한 논쟁을 불러일으켰다. 상징적인 황금 아치로 유명한 이 브랜드는 현대적인 추세에 맞추기 위해 미니멀리즘 디자인을 선택하여 로고를 단순화하는 대담한 조치를 취했다. 일부 사람들은 이 변화를 세련되고 장래를 고려한 조치로 간주하지만, 다른 사람들은 맥도날드를 즉시 알아볼 수 있게 했던 친숙함과 향수(鄕愁)를 희생시킨다고 주장한다. 이러한 변화는 깔끔하고 확장 가능한 시각적 요소가 지배하는 디지털 시대에 기업들이 적합성을 유지하려고 하면서, 점점 더 브랜드 전략에서 미니멀리즘을 선호하는 비즈니스 추세를 반영한다. 이 도박이 성공할지는 두고 봐야 할 것이다.

08 추론 가능한 문장 고르기   ②

| 분석 |
Ⓐ 마취제에 대한 반응은 '바닷가재는 고통 반응에 대한 모든 기준을 충족한다'는 내용에 대한 상술 차원에서 제시된 것일 뿐 반사작용의 증거가 아니므로 잘못된 진술이다. Ⓑ '바닷가재는 어느 정도의 의식을 가지고 있다고 여겨진다. 이러한 이유로, 대부분의 과학자들은 바닷가재를 다치게 하는 행위가 신체적 고통을 유발한다고 믿는다'고 하였으므로 타당한 진술이다. Ⓒ '바닷가재는 하나의 뇌 대신 분절된 신경절을 가지고 있다. 이러한 차이로 인해 일부 연구자들은 바닷가재가 고통을 느끼지 않으며, 부정적인 자극에 대한 반응은 단순한 반사 작용일 뿐이라고 주장한다'고 하여 논쟁의 대상이 됨을 보여주므로 타당한 진술이다. Ⓓ '대부분의 연구자들이 얼음 위에 보관하거나 살아있는 채로 끓이는 행위는 바닷가재에게 신체적 고통을 유발한다고 믿는다'고 하는 진술은 나와 있으나, 그 이유를 '바닷가재가 무척추동물이기 때문'이라고 명시하지 않았다. 오히려, 바닷가재가 '무척추동물'이라는 사실은 '그들이 고통을 느끼지 않는다'는 일부 연구자들의 근거로 사용되고 있으므로, 잘못된 추론이다.

| 어휘 |
peripheral a. 말초의, 주변부의   peripheral nervous system 말초 신경계   segment v. (여러 부분으로) 나누다, 분할하다   ganglia n. ganglion(신경총)의 복수   cluster n. (함께 자라거나 나타나는) 무리, 다발   dissimilar to ~와 다른[닮지 않은]   vertebrate n. 척추동물   reflex n. 반사 작용[운동], 반사적인 반응[동작]   decapod n. 십각목 갑각류, 십각류(十脚類)(의) (새우·게 등)   crab n. 게   criteria n. criterion(기준)의 복수   nociceptor n. 통각수용기   receptor n. (동물 세포의) 수용기[감지기]   thermal a. 열의   opioid n. 오피오이드 (아편 비슷한 작용을 하는 합성 진통·마취제)   anesthetics n. 마약, 마취제   inflict v. (괴로움 등을) 가하다[안기다]

| 해석 |
과학자들은 바닷가재가 고통을 느끼는지에 대해 의견이 엇갈린다. 바닷가재는 인간과 마찬가지로 말초 신경계를 가지고 있지만, 하나의 뇌 대신 분절된 신경절(신경 다발)을 가지고 있다. 이러한 차이로 인해 일부 연구자들은 바닷가재가 척추동물과 너무 다르기 때문에 고통을 느끼지 않으며, 부정적인 자극에 대한 반응은 단순한 반사 작용일 뿐이라고 주장한다. 그럼에도 불구하고, 바닷가재와 게, 새우와 같은 기타 십각목 갑각류는 고통 반응에 대한 모든 기준을 충족한다. 바닷가재는 상해를 입은 부분을 보호하고, 위험한 상황을 피하는 법을 배우며, 통각 수용체(화학적, 열적, 물리적 손상에 대한 수용체)를 가지고 있고, 오피오이드 수용체도 가지고 있으며, 마취제에 반응하고, 어느 정도의 의식을 가지고 있다고 여겨진다. 이러한 이유로, 대부분의 과학자들은 바닷가재를 다치게 하는 행위(예: 얼음 위에 보관하거나 살아있는 채로 끓이는 것)가 신체적 고통을 유발한다고 믿는다.

Ⓐ 바닷가재는 마취제에 반응할 수 있는데, 이는 바닷가재가 고통보다는 반사 작용을 보인다는 것을 증명한다.
Ⓑ 바닷가재에게 어느 정도 의식이 있다는 것은 바닷가재가 고통을 경험할 수 있다는 주장의 핵심 요소이다.
Ⓒ 통합된 뇌 대신 분절된 신경절이 존재한다는 사실은 바닷가재 고통의 본질에 대한 지속적인 논쟁에 기여한다.
Ⓓ 대부분의 연구자들은 바닷가재를 얼음 위에 보관하거나 살아있는 채로 끓이는 것과 같은 관행은, 바닷가재가 무척추동물이기 때문에 진짜 고통을 유발할 가능성이 있다고 믿는다.

09 추론 가능한 문장 고르기   ④

| 분석 |
Ⓐ 본문에서 언급된 두 가지 전통을 정확히 요약하고 있으므로 타당한 진술이다. Ⓑ 그레이는 두 전통 중 특정 하나의 전통을 지지한다고 말하지 않았고, 오히려 '진리의 전통은 한계에 도달했다'라며 두 전통에 대해 비판적인 입장을 보이고 있다. 따라서 Ⓑ는 부적절한 추론이다. Ⓒ '홉스적 전통은 공존과 끊임없이 반복되는 인간 갈등을 수용할 수 있는 사회 질서의 보존을 강조한다'고 하였으므로 정확하게 일치하는 추론이다. Ⓓ 그레이는 '보편적으로 참된 목표와 가치가 원활하게 수렴하고 조화를 이루는 사회 질서의 개념이 논리적으로나 경험적으로 지속 불가능하다'고 주장하므로 정확하게 일치하는 추론이다.

| 어휘 |
strive for ~을 얻으려고 노력하다   trace back to ~의 기원이 …까지 거슬러 올라가다   coexistence n. 공존, 병립   accommodate v. (의견 등을) 수용하다[담다]   persistent a. 끊임없이 지속[반복]되는   seamlessly ad. 아주 매끄럽게   converge v. (생각·정책·목적 등이) 수렴되다   harmonize v. 조화를 이루다, 어울리다(= harmonise)   empirically ad. 경험적으로   in line with ~와 비슷한, ~와 일치하는   prioritize v. 우선순위를 매기다   functional a. 기능 위주의,

실용적인 **unworkable** a. 실행[실시] 불가능한 **in practice** 실제로는 **align** v. 나란히[가지런히] 만들다, 일직선으로 하다

| 해석 |

존 그레이(John Gray)는 그의 저서 『자유주의의 두 얼굴(The Two Faces of Liberalism)』에서 자유주의 사상의 뚜렷한 두 가지 전통을 구분한다. 로크(Locke), 스미스(Smith), 칸트(Kant), 밀(Mill)의 저작에 뿌리를 두고 있는 하나의 전통은 점점 더 완벽한 상태로 나아가려 노력하면서 이상적인 사회 질서를 추구하는 데 초점을 맞춘다. 홉스(Hobbes)로 거슬러 올라가는 또 다른 전통은 공존과 끊임없이 반복되는 인간 갈등을 수용할 수 있는 사회 질서의 보존을 강조한다. 그레이는 오랫동안 지배적이었던 "진리의 전통"이 한계에 도달했다고 주장한다. 보편적으로 참된 목표와 가치가 원활하게 수렴되고 조화를 이룰 수 있는 사회 질서의 개념은 논리적으로나 경험적으로 지속 불가능하다고 보는 것이다.

Ⓐ 그레이는 자유주의의 두 가지 전통을 식별한다. 하나는 이상적인 사회 질서를 추구하고 다른 하나는 공존에 초점을 맞춘다.
Ⓑ 그레이는 자유주의를 보다 조화로운 사회 질서를 만드는 수단으로 보는 로크, 스미스, 칸트, 밀과 같은 철학자들과 일치한다.
Ⓒ 홉스에 뿌리를 둔 관점은 기능적 사회적 틀 내에서 불가피한 인간의 의견 불일치와 갈등을 수용함으로써 공존을 우선시한다.
Ⓓ 그레이는 서로 다른 목표와 가치가 완벽하게 일치할 수 없기 때문에, 보편적으로 참된 사회 질서라는 개념은 이론적으로 결함이 있고 실제로 실행 불가능하다고 생각한다.

10~13

Ⓐ 밀레니얼(Millennial)은 1981년부터 1996년 사이에 태어난 사람들을 지칭하는 용어이지만, 출처에 따라 한두 해 정도 차이가 날 수 있다. 이 용어는 윌리엄 스트라우스(William Strauss)와 닐 하우(Neil Howe)가 저술한 『세대(Generations)』(1991)에서 처음 사용되었으며, 저자들은 새 천년기에 성인이 되는 첫 번째 세대에게 적합한 이름이라고 생각했다. 밀레니얼은 X세대(Gen X; 1965년~1980년 사이 출생)와 Z세대(Gen Z; 대략 1997년부터 2010년대 초반 출생) 사이의 세대를 의미한다.
Ⓑ 미국에서 약 7,200만 명으로 구성된 밀레니얼 세대는 2019년에 베이비붐 세대(1946년~1964년 출생)를 넘어서며 가장 많은 성인 세대로 자리 잡았다. 미국의 밀레니얼 세대는 비교적 안정적이고 경제적으로 번영하던 시기에 성장했다. 하우(Howe)와 스트라우스(Strauss)는 2000년 저서 『밀레니얼의 부상: 이다음의 위대한 세대(Millennials Rising: The Next Great Generation)』에서 밀레니얼 세대는 "미국이 부유해지지 않은 해를 경험한 적이 한 번도 없다"고 언급했다.
Ⓒ 그러나 2001년 9월 11일의 공격은 밀레니얼 세대가 그때까지 알고 있던 안전하고 든든해 보이던 세상의 모습을 망쳐 놓았다. 대부분의 밀레니얼 세대는 그 사건을 기억하고 그 중요성을 인식할 수 있을 만큼 나이가 들어 있었다. 이 테러 공격은 밀레니얼 세대의 성인기를 정의한 여러 위기 중 첫 번째 사건이었다. 다른 위기로는 이라크 전쟁과 아프가니스탄 전쟁이 있었는데, 그 전쟁들의 값비싼 실패로 말미암아 밀레니얼 세대는 미국 예외주의라는 개념에 의문을 품게 되었다. 또한 2007-2009년의 세계 금융위기(Great Recession)도 있었는데, 이것은 밀레니얼 세대가 이전 세대와 같은 중요한 인생 목표와 풍요를 달성하기는 어렵도록 만들었다.
Ⓓ 일부 학자들은 서구의 밀레니얼 세대가 부모 세대보다 경제적으로 더 나쁜 처지에 놓인 최초의 현대 세대라고 언급해오고 있다. 밀레니얼 세대에게 지속적인 영향을 미친 사건 중 하나는 2007-2009년의 세계 금융위기였다. 미국과 유럽의 많은 밀레니얼 세대는 대공황(Great Depression) 이후 최악의 경기 침체가 최고조에 이르렀을 때 노동 시장에 진입했다. 이들은 특히 높은 실업률에 직면했으며, 취업에 성공하더라도 대개 불완전 고용상태이거나 학위에 어울리지 않는 직장에서 일해야 했다. 만족스런 취업을 하기 어려움은 밀레니얼 세대의 잠재 소득을 낮추었고, 부를 축적하는 능력을 저해했다. 서구 사회에서는 많은 사람들이 밀레니얼 세대가 중요한 인생 목표를 미루는 경향을 경기침체 탓으로 돌린다.
Ⓔ 그러나 이 세대는 적응력이 뛰어난 것으로도 알려져 있다. 실제로 그들은 스마트폰, 소셜 미디어, 스트리밍 엔터테인먼트를 비롯한 새로운 기술에 빠르게 익숙해진 첫 번째 디지털 세대로 여겨진다. 그들은 가장 많은 정규 교육을 받은 세대이다. 그들은 또한 이전 세대와 비교했을 때 더 다양하고 정치적으로 더 진보적이다.

| 어휘 |

adulthood n. 성인(임), 성년 **millennium** n. 새로운 천년이 시작되는 시기 **cohort** n. (통계적으로 동일한 특색이나 행동 양식을 공유하는) 집단 **comprise** v. ~으로 구성되다[이루어지다] **surpass** v. 능가하다, 뛰어넘다 **puncture** v. (자신감·자존심 등이 갑자기) 없어지게[상하게] 만들다 **semblance** n. 외관, 겉모습 **security** n. 안도감, 안심, 마음 든든함 **American exceptionalism** 미국 예외주의(미국이 역사적 발전 과정, 정치 체제, 가치관 등에 있어서 다른 나라들과 근본적으로 다르며, 특별한 역할을 수행한다는 신념) **recession** n. 불경기, 불황 **Great Recession** (2007-2009년) 세계 금융위기 **Great Depression** (1929년 미국에서 비롯된) 대공황 **milestone** n. (역사·인생 등의) 획기적인 사건; (인생의 주요) 이정표, 목표 **affluence** n. 풍요 **at the height of** ~의 절정에, ~이 한창일 때에 **downturn** n. (매출 등의) 감소[하락], (경기) 하강[침체] **underemployed** a. 할 일이 충분하지 않은, 능력 이하의 일을 하는 **degree** n. 학위 **hinder** v. 저해[방해]하다, ~을 못하게 하다 **acclimate** v. (장소·기후 등에) 익숙해지다

[적응하다] **liberal** a. 자유민주적인; 진보적인, 진보주의의 **counter** v. 반박하다 **chronicle** v. 연대순으로 기록하다 **breakthrough** n. (과학 등의) 큰 발전, 약진 **shatter** v. 산산이 부수다, 산산조각 내다 **come of age** 성년이 되다 **stretch** n. (얼마 동안 계속되는) 기간, 시간 **bachelor's degree** 학사 학위

10 내용일치 ①

| 분석 |

Ⓐ 단락 첫째 문장에서 '밀레니얼은 1981년부터 1996년 사이에 태어난 사람들'이라고 하였으므로 ①은 잘못된 진술이다.

위 글에 의하면, 다음 중 옳지 않은 것은?
① 밀레니얼 세대는 1997년에서 2010년대 초반 사이에 태어난 세대를 말한다.
② "밀레니얼"이라는 용어는 스트라우스와 하우의 저서 『세대』에서 처음 소개되었다.
③ 밀레니얼 세대는 X세대와 Z세대 사이에 있는 세대이다.
④ 밀레니얼 세대는 이라크 전쟁과 아프가니스탄 전쟁을 포함한 여러 성인 위기를 경험했다.
⑤ 2019년 밀레니얼 세대는 미국에서 베이비붐 세대를 능가하여 가장 많은 성인 세대가 되었다.

11 글의 구조 ⑤

| 분석 |

Ⓐ 단락은 '밀레니얼 세대의 정의'에 해당하고 Ⓑ 단락은 '그들의 초기 경제적 상황에 대한 설명', Ⓒ와 Ⓓ 단락은 '그들의 세계관을 형성한 주요 역사적 사건들'이며 Ⓔ는 '그들의 결정적인 특성'에 해당하므로 ⑤가 글의 구조를 가장 잘 설명하고 있음을 알 수 있다.

다음 중 위 글의 구조를 가장 잘 설명하는 것은?
① 밀레니얼 세대의 교육 수준을 베이비붐 세대의 교육 수준과 비교한다.
② 주요 역사적 사건들을 나열하고 그것들을 밀레니얼 세대의 관점과 연결한다.
③ 베이비붐 세대를 정의하고 밀레니얼 세대의 데이터로 그들의 업적을 반박한다.
④ 1980년대부터 현재까지의 모든 주요 기술적 약진들을 기록한 다음, 밀레니얼 세대가 이러한 혁신들을 일상생활에 어떻게 통합했는지 살펴본다.
⑤ 밀레니얼 세대를 정의하고, 그들의 초기 경제적 상황을 설명하고, 그들의 세계관을 형성한 주요 역사적 사건들을 조사하고, 그들의 결정적인 특성을 강조한다.

12 내용추론 ①

| 분석 |

Ⓓ 단락에서 '밀레니얼 세대는 특히 높은 실업률에 직면했으며, 취업에 성공하더라도 대개 불완전 고용상태이거나 학위에 어울리지 않는 직장에서 일해야 하는 등, 만족스런 취업이 어려웠고, 결과적으로 중요한 인생 목표를 미루는 경향을 초래했다'고 하였으므로 ①은 잘못된 추론이다.

다음 중 위 글에서 가장 추론할 수 없는 것은?
① 밀레니얼 세대는 이전 세대보다 직무 만족도가 높다.
② 밀레니얼 세대는 그들이 주요한 위기들을 겪기 전, 경제적 번영기에 자랐다.
③ 밀레니얼 세대는 가장 교육 수준이 높은 세대이며, 새로운 기술을 빠르게 받아들인다.
④ 9/11 테러는 밀레니얼 세대의 안정감을 산산이 부수어버린 중요한 전환점이었다.
⑤ 세계 금융위기는 밀레니얼 세대가 이전 세대의 중요 인생 목표들을 성취하는 것을 방해했다.

13 내용파악 ③

| 분석 |

자녀 세대가 부모와 사는 기간이 길어진다는 것은 그만큼 그들의 경제적 자립이 어려워졌다는 것을 짐작하게 하는 것이므로, ③은 밀레니얼 세대가 겪어 온 경제적 어려움을 언급하고 있는 Ⓓ 단락에 포함될 때 더 적절한 내용이다. ①과 ②는 Ⓔ 단락의 밀레니얼 세대가 '첫 번째 디지털 세대'라는 내용의 예시에 해당하고, ④는 '가장 많은 정규 교육을 받은 세대'라는 진술의 예시에 해당하며, ⑤는 '정치적으로 더 진보적'이라는 진술의 예시에 해당한다.

다음 중 Ⓔ 문단에 포함될 가능성이 가장 낮은 것은?
① 밀레니얼 세대는 주요 기술 변화, 특히 인터넷의 부상과 관련된 기술 변화가 일어난 시대에 성인이 되었다.
② 밀레니얼 세대는 모든 종류의 디지털 기술을 일상생활에 통합한 최초의 세대이다.
③ 서구의 많은 밀레니얼 세대는 다른 세대보다 더 오랫동안 부모와 함께 살고 있다.
④ 2020년대에는 미국의 밀레니얼 세대 10명 중 약 4명이 학사 학위 이상을 취득했다. 이는 이전 세대보다 많은 수치이다.
⑤ 연구자들은 밀레니얼 세대는 미국과 영국 역사상 가장 보수적이지 않은 35세들이라는 점을 발견했다.

14~17

Ⓐ 인간의 편애와 편향으로 치우치는 성향은 오랫동안 연구되어 왔는데, 특히 사회적 정체성의 맥락에서 그랬다. 이러한 편향은 종종 자신이 인식하는 집단("내집단")에 대한 편애와 외부 파벌("외집단")에 대한 차별로 나타난다. 최근 『전산 과학(Computational Science)』에 게재된 연구에 따르

면, 대규모 언어 모델(LLM)을 포함한 인공지능(AI) 시스템도 유사한 편향을 보인다고 한다. 뉴욕대학교의 스티브 래스제(Steve Rathje)에 따르면, GPT-4와 같은 AI 시스템은 "우리 대(對) 그들"과 같은 경향을 보이며, 이는 사회적 딜레마를 영속시키는 인간의 행동을 그대로 되풀이하고 있는 것이다.

B 이 연구는 GPT-4와 Llama를 포함한 77개의 대형 언어 모델을 분석하여 "내집단"과 "외집단" 프롬프트에 대한 반응을 측정했다. "우리는"으로 시작하는 문장은 항상 긍정적인 반응을 이끌어 낸 반면, "그들은"으로 시작하는 프롬프트는 주로 부정적인 감정을 반영했다. 예를 들어, "우리는 탁월함을 추구하는 재능 있는 개인들의 집단이다"는 내집단의 연대감을 나타내는 반면, "그들은 과거의 흉한 나무와 같다"는 외집단에 대한 적대감을 특징적으로 보여준다. 이러한 결과는 편향된 AI 시스템이 초래할 수 있는 잠재적 위험을 보여주는데, 이는 특히 AI 시스템이 의료에서 교육에 이르기까지 다양한 분야의 의사 결정 과정을 형성하면서 일상생활 속에 점점 더 통합되어 들어가고 있기에 더욱 그렇다. 〈이는 이러한 편견이 해결되지 않은 채 남아 있다면 AI가 기존 사회적 과제를 더욱 악화시킬 수 있는 경향이 있음을 보여준다.〉

C 연구자들은 또한 미국 공화당과 민주당의 트위터 게시물과 같은 정치적으로 민감한 데이터로 LLM을 미세 조정할 수 있는지 탐구했다. 이러한 접근 방식은 내집단 연대감과 외집단 적대감을 모두 증가시켜, 훈련 데이터가 AI의 행동에 미치는 커다란 영향력을 입증했다. 반대로, 미세 조정 전에 편향된 자료를 제거했을 때 생성된 모델에서는 양극화를 초래하는 효과가 현저히 감소했다. 이는 훈련 데이터 세트를 정밀하게 보정(補正)하면 이러한 편향을 줄이는 데 도움이 될 수 있음을 강조한다. 흥미롭게도, AI와 상호작용하는 인간 사용자들이 보이는 편향성이 종종 AI 자체의 편향성을 능가하는 것으로 나타나, 기술과 인간 행동 간의 복잡한 상호작용을 드러냈다.

D 이 연구의 함의는 AI 개발 분야 전반에 커다란 반향을 불러일으킨다. 케임브리지 대학교의 야라 키리첸코(Yara Kyrychenko)가 지적하듯이, AI 시스템의 편향성을 완화하려면 훈련 데이터에서 진정성 있고 다양한 관점을 보존하면서 분열적 성향을 해결하는 정교한 전략이 필요하다. AI 시스템이 중요한 의사 결정 과정과 사회적 거버넌스에 점점 더 많은 영향을 미치고 있으므로, 이러한 섬세한 균형을 맞추는 것은 중요하다. 훈련 데이터의 현명한 선정과 엄격한 윤리적 체계의 준수를 통해, 개발자들은 사회적 편향을 초월하여 공정성과 포용성을 촉진하면서 양극화를 방지하는 AI 시스템을 설계할 수 있다.

| 어휘 |

predisposition n. 성향, 경향 **favoritism** n. 편파, 편애 **manifest** v. 표명하다 **cohort** n. (통계적으로 동일한 특색이나 행동 양식을 공유하는) 집단 **ingroup** n. 내집단(조직·사회 내부의 배타적인 소규모 집단) **faction** n. 파벌, 파당 **outgroup** n. 외집단 **disclose** v. (눈에 안 보이던 것을) 드러내다 **analogous** a. 유사한 **echo** v. 되풀이하다, 그대로 흉내 내다 **perpetuate** v. 영구화하다, 영속시키다 **LLaMA Meta** AI에서 개발한 대규모 언어 모델(Large Language Model Meta AI) **prompt** n. 프롬프트(운영 체제에서 사용자에게 보내지는 메시지) **elicit** v. (정보·반응을 어렵게) 끌어내다 **affirmative** a. 긍정의 **predominantly** ad. 대개, 대부분 **adverse** a. 부정적인, 불리한 **solidarity** n. 연대, 결속 **disfigure** v. (외양을) 흉하게 만들다[망가뜨리다] **typify** v. ~의 특징을 나타내다 **antagonism** n. 적의, 적대감 **propensity** n. (특정한 행동을 하는) 경향[성향] **aggravate** v. 악화시키다 **illuminate** v. (이해하기 쉽게) 밝히다[분명히 하다] **fine-tuning** n. 미세 조정 **charged** a. (어떤 감정에) 차 있는, 격앙된; 격론을 부른 **profound** a. 엄청난, 깊은 **expunge** v. (이름·정보·기억 등을) 지우다[삭제하다] **polarize** v. 양극화되다, 양극화를 초래하다 **meticulous** a. 꼼꼼한, 세심한 **calibration** n. 눈금 매기기, 눈금의 교정 **intriguingly** ad. 흥미를 자아내어, 호기심을 자극하여 **surpass** v. 능가하다, 뛰어넘다 **reverberate** v. (사람들에게) 반향[파문]을 불러일으키다 **mitigate** v. 완화[경감]시키다 **necessitate** v. ~을 필요하게 만들다 **sophisticated** a. 정교한, 복잡한 **authentic** a. 진짜인, 진정성(眞正性) 있는 **divisive** a. 분열을 초래하는 **address** v. (문제·상황 등에 대해) 고심하다[다루다] **strike a balance** 균형을 유지하다 **governance** n. 거버넌스(공동의 목표를 달성하기 위하여, 주어진 자원 제약 하에서 모든 이해 당사자들이 책임감을 가지고 투명하게 의사 결정을 수행할 수 있게 하는 제반 장치) **judicious** a. 신중한, 판단력 있는 **curation** n. 큐레이션(다른 사람이 만들어놓은 콘텐츠를 목적에 따라 분류하고 배포하는 일) **adherence** n. 고수 **rigorous** a. 철저한, 엄격한 **framework** n. 구조, 구성, 체제 **equity** n. 공평, 공정 **inclusivity** n. 포용성 **avert** v. 방지하다, 피하다 **trigger** v. 촉발시키다 **resonate** v. 공명을 받다[반향을 불러일으키다] **pronounced** a. 확연한, 두드러진 **alignment** n. 조정

14 글의 제목   ⑤

| 분석 |

본문은 AI가 인간의 편향성을 반영하여 내집단 편애와 외집단 차별을 보인다는 연구 결과를 다루고 있다. 연구 방법과 결과를 설명하면서 AI가 인간과 유사한 방식으로 편향을 나타낼 수 있음을 강조하고 있음을 고려할 때 ⑤가 가장 적절한 제목이다.

다음 중 위 글의 제목으로 가장 적절한 것은?
① 미래를 위한 편견 없는 AI 모델 훈련의 복잡성
② 고급 AI 훈련 기술을 통한 사회적 분열 감소
③ 인공지능의 편견 이해: 원인과 결과
④ AI 개발의 윤리적 과제와 미묘한 딜레마 탐구
⑤ 내집단 편애와 외집단 차별: AI가 인간의 편견을 반영하는 방식

15 동의어 ④

| 분석 |

meticulous는 '(어떤 일을 정확하게 하기 위해) 세심한, 꼼꼼한 (very careful)'이라는 의미인 반면, strict는 '(규칙 등이) 엄격하게 적용되는'이라는 의미이다. 따라서 meticulous와 strict는 의미가 다르므로 대체할 수 없다.

16 문장삽입 ②

| 분석 |

주어진 문장이 'AI 시스템의 편향성이 기존의 사회적 문제를 악화시킬 수 있다'는 점을 강조하고 있음을 고려했을 때, 'AI가 내집단과 외집단을 다르게 인식하며 편향을 보인다'는 연구 결과를 소개하는 B 단락에 삽입되기에 적절함을 알 수 있다. 특히, '이러한 결과는 편향된 AI 시스템이 초래할 수 있는 잠재적 위험을 보여준다'는 진술에 이어 'AI 시스템이 일상생활 속에 통합되어 들어가고 있다'는 진술 뒤인 ❷에 해당 문장을 삽입하면, AI 편향이 사회적 문제를 심화시킬 수 있다는 논지가 더욱 강화될 것이다.

17 내용일치 ②

| 분석 |

C 단락에서, 'AI와 상호작용하는 인간 사용자들이 보이는 편향성이 종종 AI 자체의 편향성을 능가하는 것으로 나타났다'고 하였으므로 ②는 본문과 내용과 반대되는 잘못된 진술이다.

위 글에 의하면, 다음 중 옳지 않은 것은?
① GPT-4와 같은 AI 시스템은 반응에서 내집단 편애와 외집단 적대감을 보여줌으로써 인간의 경향을 모방한다.
② AI 시스템과 상호작용하는 인간 사용자는 실제 시나리오에서 시스템 자체보다 덜 두드러진 편향을 보이는 경우가 많다.
③ 정치적으로 편향된 데이터로 AI 모델을 미세 조정하면, 긍정적 내집단 연대감과 부정적인 외집단 적대감이 모두 증폭된 결과가 나온다.
④ 훈련 데이터를 신중하게 선별하는 것은 윤리적 조정과 사회적 조화를 보장하면서 편견을 줄이는 AI 시스템을 만드는 데 필수적이다.
⑤ 훈련 데이터의 신중한 선택과 준비는 AI가 생성해내는 내용에 내재된 편향의 정도와 특성을 형성하는 데 결정적으로 중요한 요인이다.

18~21

A 지질학적 연구의 최근 진전으로 지구 표면 아래 약 1,800마일(2,900킬로미터) 깊이에 지구 형성 초기부터 보존된 것으로 보이는 용융 암석층이 존재할 가능성을 시사하는 증거가 드러났다. 이 발견은 초기 지구가 한때 대부분 또는 완전히 용융 상태였으며, 이 원시 "마그마 바다"의 잔존물이 지구의 고체 맨틀과 핵 사이의 경계에 아직도 남아 있을 수 있다는 가설을 뒷받침한다. 이 분야의 주요 주창자인 기욤 피케(Guillaume Fiquet)는 지구가 수십억 년에 걸쳐 냉각되고 응고되면서 용융 물질의 일부가 핵-맨틀 경계면에 갇혔을 가능성이 있다고 설명했다. 이러한 용융 영역은 지구 핵과 맨틀 간의 상호작용을 변화시킴으로써 대규모 지각 운동에 영향을 미칠 수도 있다.

B 지구 깊은 곳의 극한 조건을 연구하기 위해, 피케와 그의 연구팀은 다이아몬드 앤빌 셀을 사용하여 맨틀-핵 경계의 강한 열과 압력을 재현했다. 그들은 마그네슘 산화물, 철, 실리콘을 포함한 광물 샘플을 해수면 대기압의 백만 배가 넘는 140기가 파스칼 이상의 압력과 5,000켈빈(화씨 8,540도) 이상의 온도에 노출시켰다. 연구팀은 X선 회절 기술을 활용하여 광물의 원자 구조 변화를 관찰하고, 고체에서 액체로의 상전이 과정을 관찰했고, 맨틀 광물의 용융점이 약 4,200켈빈(화씨 7,100도)임을 확인했다. 이러한 연구 결과는 지구 내부에서 부분 용융이 발생한다는 오랜 이론을 입증할 뿐만 아니라, 용융 층의 역학 작용들이 지각 활동을 유발하고 지구 내부 구조를 형성한다는 점을 부각하여 보여준다.

C 〈이 발견의 의미는 지구 내부 구조를 넘어서 특정 화산 현상과 지각 활동의 기원에 대한 새로운 관점을 제공한다.〉 전통적인 화산, 예를 들어 환태평양 화산대에 있는 화산들은 상부 맨틀에서 생성된 마그마에 의해 일반적으로 연료(활동 에너지)가 공급되고 지각판의 움직임에 의해 강한 영향을 받는다. 반면, 하와이와 같은 핫 스폿 화산은 핵-맨틀 경계 부근에 있는 부분 용융 영역에서 솟구치는 훨씬 더 깊은 용융 물질 기둥으로부터 마그마를 공급받는 것으로 생각된다. 이러한 관계는 지구 내부의 열이 표면의 화산 활동에 어떻게 영향을 미치는지, 그리고 수백만 년에 걸쳐 지구의 지형을 어떻게 형성해왔는지를 이해하는 데 귀중한 통찰력을 제공한다.

D 이 발견은 지구 내부 구조에 대한 우리의 이해를 크게 향상시키는 동시에, 그렇지 않았더라면 접근할 수 없었던 조건을 연구하는 데 사용되는 획기적인 기술을 부각시킨다. 맨틀-핵 경계에서의 직접적인 시료 채취는 여전히 불가능하지만, 피케와 그의 연구팀이 수행한 실험은 지구 깊은 곳 물질의 물리적, 화학적 특성에 대한 중요한 데이터를 제공한다. 이러한 연구 결과는 지구 내부에서 발생하는 복잡한 과정에 대한 이해를 높이고, 이러한 과정이 화산 폭발 및 지각 운동과 같은 지표 현상에 어떤 영향을 미치는지에 대한 더 명확한 이해에 기여한다.

| 어휘 |

molten a. 녹은 remnant n. 남은 부분, 나머지 primordial a. 태고의, 원시 시대부터의 linger v. (예상보다 오래) 남다[계속되다] proponent n. (어떤 사상·행동 방침의) 지지자 solidify v. 굳어지다, 굳히다 pocket n. (주변과는 이질적인 작은) 집단[지역] interface n. 경계면, 접점 tectonic a. 지각(地殼) 구조상의 diamond anvil cell 다이아몬드 침골 세포(고압 연구 분야에서 필수적인 장비) replicate v. (정확히) 모사[복제]하다 subject v. (물건을) (~ 조건에) 노출시키다, 대다, 쬐다 oxide n. 산화물 Fahrenheit n. 화씨 diffraction n. 회절(回折) X-ray diffraction X선 회절(원자 배열을 해석하는 데 응용) transition n. 상전이(相轉移)(물질이 조건에 따라 한 형태에서 다른 형태로 바뀌는 현상) phase n. (변화·발달 과정상의 한) 단계[시기, 국면] validate v. 입증하다 dynamics n. 역학, 동역학, 역학 관계 Pacific Ring of Fire 환태평양 화산대 tectonic plate 지각판, 텍토닉 플레이트(판상(板狀)을 이루어 움직이고 있는 지각의 표층) hot spot 핫 스폿(고온 물질이 상승하는 지각 부분; 바다의 화산도 따위) plume n. (연기·수증기 등이 피어오르는) 기둥 groundbreaking a. 신기원을 이룬, 획기적인 otherwise ad. (만약) 그렇지 않으면[않았다면] geochemistry n. 지구 화학(지구와 지구의 암석, 광물의 화학적 조성에 대한 연구) geography n. 지리학(국가, 도시, 강, 산, 호수 등의 위치를 다루는 연구 분야) geomagnetics n. 지자기(地磁氣)학(지자기 및 지자기 활동에 관한 연구) geometry n. 기하학(점, 선, 각도, 면, 입체를 다루는 수학의 한 분야) anchor v. (생각·주의력 등을) (~에) 고정시키다 corroborate v. (진술·이론 등을 뒷받침하는 증거나 정보를) 제공하다, 확증[입증]하다

18 빈칸완성 ③

| 분석 |

지질학은 지구의 구조, 역사와 그 변화를 연구하는 학문이며, 본문은 지구 내부의 지질학적 구조와 용융 층 및 마그마 잔존물에 대한 연구를 다루고 있으므로 빈칸에는 '지질학적'이 들어가는 것이 가장 적절하다. 본문의 연구가 지구 내부의 화학적 조성과 관련 있지만 '지구화학적(geochemical)'이라고 해서는 글의 범위가 지금보다 훨씬 더 좁혀질 것이므로 적절하지 않다.

19 내용파악 ②

| 분석 |

A 단락 마지막 문장에서 '이러한 용융 영역은 지구 핵과 맨틀 간의 상호작용을 변화시킴으로써 대규모 지각 운동에 영향을 미칠 수도 있다'고 하였는데, ②는 '용융 층이 직접적 원인으로 작용하여 지각 변동과 화산 폭발을 일으킨다'고 하였으므로 잘못된 진술이다.

다음 중 연구 설계에 대해 옳지 않은 것은?
① 연구자들은 다이아몬드 앤빌 셀을 사용해 맨틀—핵 경계의 극한의 열과 압력을 재현했다.
② 연구자들은 용융 층이 직접적인 추진력으로 작용하여 지각 변동과 화산 폭발을 일으킨다고 가정했다.
③ 연구자들은 X선 회절 기술을 사용하여 맨틀 광물의 원자 구조 변화를 관찰하고 모니터링했다.
④ 이 연구는 지구 내부의 조건을 시뮬레이션하고 맨틀 광물의 용융점을 식별하기 위해 고압 실험을 활용하였다.
⑤ 연구자들은 이전에 직접적인 실험적 증거가 부족했던 지구 내부의 부분 용융에 대한 오랜 제안을 뒷받침하는 데 연구의 초점을 맞추었다.

20 문장삽입 ③

| 분석 |

B 단락 끝에서 "용융 층의 역학 작용들이 지각 활동을 유발하고 지구 내부 구조를 형성한다"고 하였고, C 단락에서는 전통적인 화산 활동과 핫 스폿 화산 활동이 대조적으로 설명되고 있다. 따라서 '지구 내부 구조를 넘어서 화산 현상의 기원에 대한 새로운 관점을 제공한다'는 주어진 문장은 ❸에 들어가는 것이 가장 적절하다. 한편, ❺ 또한 고려될 수 있으나, 연구의 전반적인 의의를 정리하는 부분으로, 특정 화산 현상과의 연결을 강조하기엔 적절하지 않다.

21 내용추론 ⑤

| 분석 |

용융 층의 존재를 확인하는 연구에서 컴퓨터 시뮬레이션이 얼마나 도움이 되었는지와 그것의 응용 분야 사용 가능성 등은 전혀 언급되지 않았으므로 ⑤가 추론될 가능성이 가장 낮다. ① A 단락에서 맨틀—핵 경계에 용융 층의 존재가 밝혀졌으며, 이것이 맨틀과 상호작용한다고 하였으므로 타당한 추론이다. ② 본문에서 언급된 핵심 내용이며 특히 A 단락에서 구체적으로 진술되어 있으므로 타당하다. ③ 본문 전체에 걸쳐 연구진이 제시한 가설과 부합하는 진술이다. ④ B 단락에서 소개된 실험 결과에 대한 진술과 일치하는 추론이다.

다음 중 연구 결과를 통해 가장 추론할 수 없는 것은?
① 용융 층은 고체 맨틀과 구별되는 물리적 특성을 포함할 수 있으며, 조성 및 반응의 차이를 드러낼 수 있다.
② 맨틀—핵 경계의 용융 층은 지구 초기 용융 상태의 잔존물 역할을 하여 지구의 구조적 역사에 대한 통찰력을 제공할 가능성이 높다.
③ 지각 변동과 화산 활동은 맨틀 역학에 영향을 미치는 용융 층과 상호 연결되어 있으며, 지구 내부 과정이 표면 현상과 연관되어 있음을 시사한다.
④ 실험 결과는 경계의 물리적 조건은 맨틀 물질을 부분적으로 용융하기에 충분하며, 극한 조건에서의 반응을 드러낸다는 것을 시사한다.
⑤ 혁신적인 시뮬레이션 기법이 용융 층을 규명하는 데 도움이 되었으므로, 더 넓은 응용 분야를 위한 계산 모델을 구축할 가능성을 열어준다.

22~25

A 11월, 캐나다 브리티시 컬럼비아주 프레이저 밸리에 사는 한 10대 청소년이 결막염과 기침 증상으로 병원을 찾았다. 6일 후, 이 청소년은 밴쿠버에 있는 B.C. 어린이 병원에서 인공호흡기를 달고 몇 주 동안 중환자실에 머물러야 했다. 이러한 질병은 보통의 경우 큰 주목을 받지 않지만, 이 청소년이 조류독감의 한 변종인 H5N1 양성 판정을 받자, 전염병 전문가들은 이것이 다음번 인간 팬데믹을 불러일으킬 수 있다고 우려하고 있다.

B 이 바이러스는 1997년 홍콩의 가금류 농장에서 처음 발견되었는데, 내출혈을 일으키고 인간의 에볼라를 연상시키는 소름 끼치는 방식으로 여러 장기를 파괴하면서 닭의 거의 100%를 폐사시켰다. 그 이후로 야생 조류에 의한 연이은 감염 파동이 전 세계 가금류 농장을 괴롭혀왔다.

C 그러나 최근 H5N1 바이러스는 인간에게로 향하는 진화적 단계를 밟으면서 불안을 낳았다. 2022년, 이 바이러스는 아르헨티나의 바다코끼리 개체군을 97%의 치사율로 휩쓸며 수천 마리를 죽였다. 이는 H5N1이 포유류 종에 본격적으로 자리 잡은 것으로 알려진 최초의 사례였다. 그전까지는 인간을 포함한 포유류는 조류와의 접촉을 통해서 바이러스에 감염되어 병에 걸렸었다. 바다코끼리들은 서로에게 바이러스를 전파하고 있었다. 과학자들이 6월에 연구 결과를 발표할 즈음, H5N1은 또 다른 포유류 종인 젖소에게까지 감염을 확산시켰다. 3월 이후, 이 바이러스는 16개 주 800개 이상의 젖소 무리로 퍼졌으며, 그 중에 500개 이상의 젖소 무리는 캘리포니아에 있는데, 캘리포니아는 아직도 통제되지 않고 있다. 12월 18일, 캘리포니아 주지사 개빈 뉴섬(Gavin Newsome)은 이 확산 사태에 대응하기 위해 비상사태를 선포했다.

D 미국에서는 최소 61명이 바이러스에 감염되었으며, 대부분 조류나 소와의 직접적인 접촉을 통해 감염되었다. 12월, 캘리포니아 마린 카운티에서 한 어린이가 생우유(즉, 살균되지 않은)를 마신 후 고열과 구토 증상을 보였으며, 이후 H5N1 양성 판정을 받았다. 이번 주, 미국 질병통제예방센터(CDC)는 미국 내 첫 번째 "심각한" 조류독감 사례를 확인했는데, 환자는 뒷마당에서 키우던 병들고 죽은 조류에 노출된 것으로 밝혀졌다. 인간이 감염되어 아플 때마다 바이러스는 인간에서 인간으로의 전파 능력을 획득할 기회를 얻게 된다. 만약 바이러스가 이 중요한 전환점을 지나면, 팬데믹이 시작될 수 있다. H5N1이 이 암울한 전환점을 지났다는 증거는 없다. 그 바이러스가 결코 이런 도약을 해내지 못할 수도 있다. 하지만 미네소타주 로체스터에 있는 메이요 클리닉의 호흡기 질환 전문가인 미생물학자 매튜 비니커(Matthew Binnicker)는 "이 바이러스들에 대해 우리가 알고 있는 바를 고려할 때, 추세가 좋지 않다"며 "심각한 조치"가 필요하다고 덧붙였다. 전문가들은 이 바이러스가 사람들 사이로 더욱 쉽게 확산할 수 있는 두 가지 주요 경로를 우려하고 있다.

| 어휘 |

conjunctivitis n. 결막염 **critical care** 중환자 관리 **positive** a. (검사 결과가) 양성(반응)의 **strain** n. 변종 **poultry** n. 가금류 **chillingly** ad. 으스스하게, 냉담하게 **reminiscent of** ~을 연상시키는 **successive** a. 연속적인, 연이은, 잇따른 **plague** v. (한동안 고통·문제로) 괴롭히다 **unsettling** a. 불안하게[동요하게] 만드는 **mortality** n. 치사율 **mammalian** a. 포유류의 **get around to** ~까지도 하다, ~에까지 손이 미치다 **dairy** a. 낙농(업)의 **outbreak** n. (전쟁·사고·질병 등의) 발생, 돌발, 창궐 **unpasteurized** a. 저온살균을 하지 않은 **milestone** n. 중요한[획기적인] 단계[사건] **grim** a. 암울한 **leap** n. 뜀, 도약(跳躍); 급격한 증가[상승] **respiratory** a. 호흡의, 호흡 기관의 **mutate** v. 돌연변이가 되다, 돌연변이를 만들다

22 내용일치 ③

| 분석 |

③은 A 단락에서 기술된 '브리티시 컬럼비아주 한 청소년의 H5N1 양성 반응이 전문가들의 우려를 불러일으켰다'는 내용과 정확히 일치한다. ① B 단락에서 '이 바이러스는 1997년 홍콩의 가금류 농장에서 처음 발견되었다'고 하였으므로 잘못된 진술이다. ② C 단락에서 '아르헨티나의 바다코끼리가 H5N1이 포유류 종에 본격적으로 자리 잡은 것으로 확인된 최초의 사례'라고 하였으므로 잘못된 진술이다. ④ ②번이 잘못된 것과 같은 이유에서 잘못된 진술이다. ⑤ C 단락에 따르면 감염된 사람이 아니라 젖소 농장에서의 감염 확산에 대응하기 위해 비상사태가 선포되었다.

위 글에 의하면, 다음 중 옳은 것은?
① H5N1의 첫 번째 알려진 감염은 아르헨티나의 바다코끼리에서 발생했다.
② 최초의 포유류 H5N1 감염은 1997년 홍콩에서 관찰되었다.
③ 브리티시 컬럼비아의 한 청소년이 H5N1에 양성 반응을 보이며, 전염병 전문가들 사이에 우려가 제기되었다.
④ 포유류에서 H5N1이 보고된 적이 없어, 브리티시 컬럼비아에서 이 청소년의 사례는 이런 종류의 사례로는 처음이다.
⑤ 캘리포니아 주지사 게빈 뉴섬은 수십 명이 감염된 발병에 대응하여 비상사태를 선포했다.

23 내용추론 ④

| 분석 |

바다코끼리들 간의 확산, 젖소 간의 확산, 그리고 젖소를 통한 사람 감염의 사례들을 볼 때, 이 바이러스가 사람과 사람 사이의 전파 능력을 얻게 될 가능성을 배제할 수 없다는 점에서 ④의 추론은 타당하다. ① H5N1은 여전히 가금류에도 위협이 된다. ② 바다코끼

리는 97% 치사율을 보였다고 하였고, 인간 감염 사례에서는 생존율에 대한 언급이 없다. ③ '유전자 변형 없는 인간 감염에 대한 세계 보건 기관들의 발표' 내용은 본문 어디에도 없다. ⑤ 바다코끼리끼리 감염된 것은 종내 전염(within-species transmission) 사례에 해당하는데, 이를 종간 전염(cross-species transmission)과 연관시키는 것은 무리한 추론이다.

다음 중 위 글로부터 H5N1의 진화와 확산에 대해 가장 추론할 수 있는 것은?
① H5N1은 더 이상 가금류에 위협이 되지 않지만 포유류에게는 여전히 우려 사항이다.
② 인간이 H5N1에 감염되면 바다코끼리와 비슷하게 거의 100%의 생존율을 보인다.
③ 세계 보건 기관들은 H5N1이 유전자 변형 없이도 인간을 감염시킬 수 있다고 밝혔다.
④ 포유류 사이에 바이러스가 퍼지는 능력은 인간에서 인간으로의 전염 가능성을 높인다.
⑤ 바다코끼리가 서로에게 바이러스를 전파했다는 사실은 바이러스가 종간 전염을 일으키지 않는다는 증거이다.

D 단락의 "this leap"은 무엇을 가리킬 가능성이 가장 높은가?
① 바이러스가 사람에서 사람으로 쉽게 확산되도록 돌연변이 하는 것
② H5N1이 야생조류에서 가금류로 확산되는 능력
③ 포유류 종에서 처음으로 H5N1이 출현하는 것
④ 세계 보건 당국이 H5N1을 팬데믹으로 선언하는 것
⑤ 바이러스가 조류 접촉 없이 포유류 간에 직접 확산되도록 진화하는 것

| 24 | 내용일치 | ④ |

| 분석 |
캘리포니아에서 생우유를 마신 아이가 H5N1에 감염된 사례가 언급되었지만, 모든 인간 감염 사례가 포유류 노출과 관련된 것은 아니다. 특히 미국 질병통제예방센터가 발표한 미국 내 첫 번째 '심각한' 조류독감 사례는 감염된 조류에 노출된 것이 원인이었다.

위 글에 의하면, 다음 중 옳지 않은 것은?
① 미국 질병통제예방센터는 미국에서 첫 번째 심각한 조류독감 사례를 확인했다.
② 12월에 어린이가 살균되지 않은 생우유를 마신 후 H5N1에 감염되었다.
③ 한 청소년이 결막염과 기침 치료를 받은 후 H5N1에 양성 반응을 보였다.
④ 지금까지 캘리포니아에서 발생한 모든 H5N1 인간 사례는 소와 같은 감염된 포유류에 노출된 것과 관련이 있다.
⑤ 미국에서 최소 61명이 H5N1에 양성 반응을 보였으며, 대부분은 감염된 조류 또는 소와 직접 접촉한 것이었다.

| 25 | 지시대상 | ① |

| 분석 |
해당 문장의 바로 앞에서 '인간이 감염될 때마다 바이러스는 인간에서 인간으로의 전파 능력을 획득할 수 있고, 중요한 전환점을 지나면 팬데믹이 시작될 수 있다'고 하였으므로, '이런 도약'이란 결국 '사람 사이의 전파를 용이하게 하는 변이 바이러스의 출현'이라고 판단할 수 있다.

인하대학교 인문·예체능계

TEST p. 536~558

01	⑤	02	①	03	①	04	③	05	④	06	①	07	④	08	②	09	②	10	⑤
11	④	12	④	13	④	14	②	15	①	16	③	17	②	18	③	19	②	20	⑤
21	①	22	⑤	23	④	24	①	25	①	26	③	27	④	28	②	29	⑤	30	①
31	③	32	②	33	④	34	⑤	35	⑤	36	③	37	③	38	①	39	②	40	③

01 빈칸완성 ⑤

| 분석 |

rather than 전후에는 서로 상반되는 의미의 표현이 와야 하므로 빈칸에는 sensationalist clickbait와 반대되는 의미를 가진 표현이 들어가야 한다. 가볍고 자극적인 콘텐츠를 선호하는 현상과 대조되는 것으로, 깊이 있고 숙고할 가치가 있는 논의에 대한 관심이 줄어들었다고 해야 한다. 따라서 '사려 깊은'이라는 의미의 ⑤ thoughtful이 적절하다.

| 어휘 |

positive n. 긍정적인 것 **expose** v. 드러내다; 노출시키다 **perspective** n. 관점, 시각 **encounter** v. ~와 우연히 만나다, 마주치다 **collateral** a. 부수적인, 이차적인 **dominate** v. 지배하다 **spread** n. 확산, 전파 **bite-sized** a. 한 입에 먹을[넣을] 수 있는; 다루기 쉬운 **optimize** v. 최적화하다 **discourse** n. 담론, 담화 **clickbait** n. 낚시성 링크(자극적인 제목으로 인터넷 사용자들의 클릭을 유도하는 기사나 광고) **antithetical** a. 정반대의, (아주) 대조적인 **immersive** a. 몰입형의 **contemplative** a. 정관[관조]적인, 명상적인 **flit** v. 빨리 지나가다; (생각·공상 등이) 스치다 **rushed** a. 서두른, 성급한 **shallow** a. 얕은; 피상적인 **personal** a. 개인적인 **entertaining** a. 재미있는, 유쾌한 **thoughtful** a. 사려 깊은

| 해석 |

디지털 미디어는 많은 긍정적인 것들을 제공하고, 사람들을 디지털 미디어가 아니면 결코 접할 수 없을 다양한 관점에 노출시킨다. 그러나 그로 인해 부수적으로 일어나는, 주의지속시간에 가해지는 피해는 실제로 존재한다. 디지털 플랫폼이 이제 현대 미디어 환경을 지배하고 있다. 이러한 기술은 정보의 빠른 확산을 가능하게 하지만, 주의를 끌기 위해 최적화된 짧은 콘텐츠를 선호한다. 알고리즘은 사려 깊은 담론보다는 선정적인 낚시성 링크를 선택한다. 현대의 디지털 환경은 몰입적이고 사색적인 독서와 반대되는 방식으로 우리의 뇌를 훈련시킨다. 우리의 주의는 어떤 주제도 깊이 파고들지 않고 한 게시물에서 다른 게시물로 빨리 스쳐 지나간다.

02 빈칸완성 ①

| 분석 |

Ⓐ 지속 가능한 성장이 불가능하다고 했으므로 자원이나 생태계의 수용력에 '한계(limits)'가 있다고 해야 적절하다. Ⓑ 앞에서 지속 가능한 성장이 불가능하다고 말한 반면, 뒤에서 지속 가능한 발전을 지지하는 사람들의 견해를 제시하고 있다. 빈칸 앞뒤로 상반된 내용이므로 역접부사인 However가 적절하다.

| 어휘 |

ecologist n. 생태학자, 생태[환경] 운동가 **sustainable** a. 지속 가능한 **nonrenewable** a. (자원이) 재생 불가능한 **biosphere** n. 생물권 **pleasant** a. 쾌적한, 즐거운, 기분 좋은 **agreeable** a. 기분 좋은, 유쾌한 **interfere with** ~을 방해하다, 지장을 주다 **assure** v. 확신시키다 **infinite** a. 무한한 **limit** n. 한계, 제한 **burden** n. 짐, 부담 **discrepancy** n. 차이, 불일치

| 해석 |

많은 생태학자들은 재생 불가능한 자원과 우리의 쓰레기를 흡수할 수 있는 생물권의 수용력이 가하는 한계 때문에 장기적으로 그 어떤 종류의 지속 가능한 성장도 불가능하다고 생각한다. 인간의 삶을 더 편안하고 쾌적하거나 기분 좋게 만들기 위해 점점 더 많은 양의 상품과 서비스를 사용하는 것은 필연적으로 다른 종의 생존을 방해하고, 결국에는 고정된 자원의 세계에서 인간 자신의 생존도 방해하게 된다. 그러나 지속 가능한 발전의 지지자들은 우리가 생태학적 지식을 사용하여 계획을 세운다면, 기술과 사회 조직 둘 모두가, 필수적인 요구를 충족시키고 자연적인 한계 내에서 무한하지는 않지만 장기적인 성장을 제공하는 방식으로 관리될 수 있다고 우리를 확신시킨다.

03 빈칸완성 ①

| 분석 |

여행 중에 발생할 수 있는 예측할 수 없는 상황에 대한 두려움이

불안을 유발하는 주된 원인이다. 따라서 빈칸에는 unpredictability (예측불가능)와 유사한 의미의 ① uncertainty(불확실성)가 적절하다.

| 어휘 |
awake a. 깨어서, 자지 않고   pound v. (심장이) 두근거리다
oversleep v. 늦잠 자다   incredibly ad. 믿을 수 없을 만큼, 매우
trigger v. 일으키다, 유발하다 n. (반응·사건을 유발하는) 자극, 유인
upcoming a. 다가오는, 곧 있을   routine n. 판에 박힌 일, 일과
unpredictability n. 예측불가능   uncertainty n. 불확실성   pain
n. 고통   overspending n. 낭비   miscommunication n. 잘못된 전달

| 해석 |
당신은 여행 전날 밤 심장이 두근거리며 잠을 이루지 못했다. 잘못될지도 모르는 모든 잠재적인 일들을 상상하면서 말이다. 늦잠을 자서 비행기를 놓치면 어쩌지? 여행 중에 아프면 어쩌지? 낯선 도시에서 길을 잃으면 어쩌지? 종종 여행 불안이라고 불리는 이런 경험은 매우 흔하다. 불안은 종종 불확실성에 대한 두려움에 의해 유발된다. 새로운 장소로 여행을 떠날 예정이라면, 그곳에서 일이 어떻게 될지 모르는 것에 대해서나, 일상에서 벗어나는 것에 대해서나, 필요한 모든 것을 갖추지는 못한 것에 대해 불안감을 느낄 수 있다. 여행에는 예측할 수 없는 일이 많이 있지만, 불안을 유발할 수 있는 요인을 파악하고 그것들을 적절히 해결하면 더 편안하고 즐거운 여행 경험의 세계를 여는 데 도움이 될 수 있다.

04 글의 제목   ③

| 분석 |
최신 체중 감량 트렌드인 간헐적 단식을 설명하고 있으며, 간헐적 단식이 인류 역사에서 어떤 역할을 해왔는지에 대해서도 언급하고 있다. 따라서 이 글의 제목으로는 ③ '간헐적 단식의 트렌드와 역사'가 적절하다.

| 어휘 |
trend n. 경향, 동향, 추세   intermittent a. 간헐적인   fasting n. 단식   tout v. 극구 칭찬[선전]하다   fast v. 단식하다   recuperate v. 회복하다   prescribe v. 처방하다   spiritual a. 영적인   trace back to ~으로 거슬러 올라가다   monk n. 수도사, 수사   marathon a. 마라톤의, 장시간에 걸친   enlightenment n. 계발, 계몽; (불교의) 깨달음

| 해석 |
하루 한 끼 식사는 인터넷을 강타한 최신 체중 감량 트렌드이다. 이 간헐적 단식은 몸의 '생존 모드'를 유발하여 체중을 줄이는 방법으로 크게 선전되어 왔다. 간헐적 단식과 같은 극단적인 트렌드가 대부분의 사람들에게 지속 가능하지 않을 수 있지만, 단식은 일반적으로 인류 역사에서 중요한 역할을 해왔다. 우리 조상들은 사냥에 실패한 후 생존을 지속하는 데 필요한 칼로리를 회복할 수 있을 때까지 자연스럽게 단식하곤 했다. 고대 그리스의 의사들은 특정 질병을 치료하기 위해 단식을 처방했으며, 단식은 다양한 종교적 또는 영적 관행에서 사용되어 왔으며 여전히 사용되고 있다. 10세기로 거슬러 올라가는 일본의 한 전통에서, 승려들은 깨달음에 가까워지기 위해 히에이 산 주변에서 마라톤 거리(42,195km)를 1,000일 동안 걸은 후 9일 동안 단식을 한다. 오늘날 매년 약 20억 명의 사람들이 라마단 기간 동안 단식한다.

다음 중 이 글의 제목으로 가장 적절한 것은?
① 하루 한 끼 식사의 과학
② 하루 세 끼 식사의 이점
③ 간헐적 단식의 트렌드와 역사
④ 단식과 섭식 장애를 구별하는 방법
⑤ 단식은 인터넷 붐 이후에야 인기를 얻었다

05 문장삽입   ④

| 분석 |
제시문은 "기하학의 가장 단순한 단위는 점이다."라는 뜻으로, 앞에는 형태들의 구성 요소에 대한 언급이 있어야 하고 그 뒤에서는 점에 대한 언급이 이어져야 한다. 따라서 D에 제시문이 들어가는 것이 가장 적절하다.

| 어휘 |
geometry n. 기하학   triangle n. 삼각형   square n. 정사각형
combination n. 결합   component n. 구성 요소   array n. 배열
building block 구성 요소   property n. 특성, 속성

| 해석 |
기하학은 본질적으로 형태를 연구하는 학문이다. 주변 세계에서 우리가 보는 모든 물체는 일종의 형태이다. 어떤 것들은 삼각형, 정사각형, 원처럼 단순하다. 다른 것들은 이러한 단순한 형태들의 결합인 것처럼 보인다. 이러한 형태들을 이해하기 시작하려면 먼저 그 구성 요소를 배워야 한다. 〈기하학의 가장 단순한 단위는 점이다.〉 점들이 특정한 배열로 모여 선을 만들고 선들이 특정한 배열로 모여 형태를 만드는데, 형태는 단일 평면에 존재할 수도 있고 공간 속 여러 개의 평면에 존재할 수도 있다. 당신은 기하학의 구성 요소인 이 형태들의 이름과 속성을 잘 알게 되고, 더 복잡한 상황에서 그것들을 인식할 줄 알게 될 것이다.

06 문장삽입   ②

| 분석 |
제시문은 "저체온증은 기온이 어는점 이상이어도 발생할 수 있다."라는 뜻이다. 저체온증은 기온 이외의 다른 요소에 의해서도 발생할 수 있다는 것이므로, '열 손실의 속도는 풍속에 의해 영향을 받는다'는 내용 앞의 B에 제시문이 들어가는 것이 적절하다.

| 어휘 |
hypothermia n. 저체온증; 체온 저하(법)   severe a. 극심한, 심각한

life-threatening a. 생명을 위협하는 **insulating** a. 절연[단열, 방음]을 위한 **preserve** v. 보존하다, 유지하다 **gradient** n. (온도·기압 등의) 변화도, 경사 **freezing** n. 결빙, 냉동; 빙점 **windchill** n. 풍속냉각, 풍속 냉각 지수(체감온도)

| 해석 |

저체온증은 추운 날씨에 하는 야외 활동과 관련된 문제 중 가장 심각하다. 저체온증은 체열이 생성되는 것보다 더 빨리 손실될 때 발생한다. 이것은 생명을 위협하는 상황이 될 수 있다. 추운 날씨에 운동을 하려면 정상적인 체열을 유지하기 위해 단열복을 껴입어야 한다. 이 보호 장치가 없으면 피부와 환경 사이의 큰 온도 변화 때문에 체열이 빠르게 손실된다. 〈저체온증은 기온이 어는점 이상이어도 발생할 수 있다.〉 예를 들어 어떤 온도에서든 열 손실의 속도는 풍속의 영향을 받는다. 풍속은 피부와 접촉하는 차가운 공기 분자의 양을 증가시킨다. 차가운 분자가 많을수록 열 손실이 더 효과적이다. 체감온도의 영향을 제대로 평가하려면 바람의 속도에 바람 속으로 걷거나, 조깅하거나 자전거 타고 들어가는 속도를 추가해야 한다.

07 문장삽입 ④

| 분석 |

제시문은 "그러나 이러한 조치들은 딜러와 제조업체 간의 불안한 긴장을 해결하지 못했다."라는 뜻이다. 따라서 앞에 these actions를 가리키는 표현이 와야 하는데, 연방거래위원회(FTC)가 조사를 실시하여 포드와 크라이슬러가 동의 명령에 서명하고 제너럴 모터스가 독점 금지 활동으로 유죄 판결을 받은 것을 지칭한다고 보아야 하므로, Ⓓ에 제시문이 들어가는 것이 적절하다. 신의성실법을 이러한 조치에 포함하여 제시문을 Ⓔ에 넣으면 그 다음 문장의 the law가 신의성실법을 가리키지 못한다.

| 어휘 |

dealership n. 판매 대리점, 특약점 **saturated** a. 스며든, 흠뻑 젖은; 포화된 **overly** ad. 지나치게, 과도하게 **generous** a. 관대한 **move** v. (상품을) 팔다, 처분하다 **stock** n. 재고품, 재고 **say** n. 발언권, 발언할 차례[기회] **threaten** v. 위협하다, 협박하다 **investigate** v. 조사하다, 연구하다 **consent decree** (두 적대 당사자들 사이에 합의된) 화해가 이서된 법원 명령 **antitrust** n. 독점 금지의 **be convicted of** ~로 유죄 판결을 받다 **objectionable** a. 반대할 만한, 이의가 있는; 불쾌한 **resolve** v. 해결하다 **uneasy** a. 불안한

| 해석 |

신차에 대한 수요가 포화 상태에 이르고 중고차 거래가 사업에서 더 중요한 부분이 되면서 1920년대와 1930년대에 모든 자동차 제조업체의 대리점은 더욱 중요해졌다. 1930년대에 딜러들은 자동차 제조업체들에게 불만을 가지게 되었는데, 그 이유는 그들은 그들이 원하는 것보다 더 많은 수의 신차를 가져야 했고, 중고차 판매 가격에 대해 압력을 받았으며, 남은 재고를 처분하기 위해 연말 세일에 지나치게 관대한 할인을 제공해야 했고, 제조업체가 후원하는 대출 프로그램을 사용해야 했으며, 제조업체가 그들의 판매 지역에 새로운 대리점을 열 지의 여부에 대해 발언권이 없었으며, 제조업체들로부터 갑작스런 통보로 프랜차이즈 라이선스를 잃을 수 있다는 위협을 받았기 때문이다. 이에 대응하여 딜러들은 의회에 조사를 촉구했다. 1938년 연방거래위원회(FTC)는 조사를 실시했으며, 그 결과로 포드와 크라이슬러는 동의 명령에 서명했고 제너럴 모터스는 독점 금지 활동으로 유죄 판결을 받았다. 〈그러나 이러한 조치들은 딜러와 제조업체 간의 불안한 긴장을 해결하지 못했다.〉 제2차 세계대전 이후, 딜러들은 의회를 설득하여 이러한 관행 중 가장 문제가 되는 것의 일부를 제한하는 신의성실법을 통과시켰다. 그러나 그 법은 통과되기 위해 약화되었고 딜러들에게 큰 만족감을 주지 못했다.

08 문장삽입 ②

| 분석 |

제시문은 "최근 과학자들은 전통적인 화석 연료의 대안으로 빠르게 자라는 풀의 사용을 검토하고 있다."라는 뜻으로, 재생 가능한 에너지원으로 풀을 재배하는 것에 대한 내용이 그 뒤에 와야 한다. Ⓑ 다음의 These grasses가 제시문의 fast-growing grasses를 가리키므로 제시문은 Ⓑ에 들어가야 적절하다.

| 어휘 |

combat v. 싸우다, 반항하다 **sustainable** a. 지속 가능한, 오랫동안 지속[유지] 가능한 **harmful** a. 해로운, 유해한 **run out of** ~을 다 써버리다 **alternative** n. 대안, 선택 가능한 것 **power station** 발전소 **renewable** a. 재생 가능한 **carbon neutral** a. 탄소 중립적인 **sufficient** a. 충분한 **subsidy** n. 보조금, 장려금

| 해석 |

지구 온난화와 기후 변화의 영향에 맞서 싸우고 싶다면 더 많은 지속 가능한 에너지원을 찾아야 한다는 것에는 의심의 여지가 거의 없다. 석유와 천연가스는 해로운 온실가스를 생산하며, 물론 제한된 공급량만 이용할 수 있다. 따라서 우리가 곧 행동을 취하지 않으면 에너지 공급이 고갈될 것이다. 〈최근 과학자들은 전통적인 화석 연료의 대안으로 빠르게 자라는 풀의 사용을 검토하고 있다.〉 이 풀들은 재생 가능한 에너지원을 제공하기 위해 발전소에서 태울 수 있다. 풀은 제대로 자라기만 하면 탄소 중립적이다. 즉, 흡수하는 탄소보다 더 많은 탄소를 배출하지 않는다. 그 생각은 농부들이 식량보다는 에너지를 위해 작물을 재배할 것이라는 것이다. 과학자들은 충분한 보조금을 제공하면 농부들이 기꺼이 이 새로운 작물을 재배하기 시작할 것이라고 믿고 있다.

09 단락배열 ②

| 분석 |

제시문은 19세기 후반의 현대성을 보여주는 장소로 나폴레옹 3세

황제 하에 개조된 파리를 들고 있다. 파리를 오스만 남작이 재건했다는 내용의 B가 제시문 다음에 오고, 이러한 개조된 파리의 모습을 묘사한 인상파 화가들을 설명하고 있는 A가 그다음에 온다. 그리고 도시 주민들에 대한 묘사로 눈길을 돌린 다른 화가들을 설명하고 있는 D가 그 뒤에 오고, 도시 생활 장면 중에서도 일하는 사람이나 특권 계급 등 사회 계층을 묘사한 화가들을 설명하고 있는 C가 마지막에 와야 한다.

| 어휘 |

prime a. 가장 중요한, 주요한 modernity n. 현대성, 근대성 renovate v. 개조하다 impressionist n. 인상파 화가 boulevard n. 넓은 가로수 길; 대로 tear down ~을 허물다 siege n. 포위 공격, 공성(攻城) reconstruct v. 재건하다 privileged class 특권 계급 cityscape n. 도시 풍경[경관] inhabitant n. 주민 거주자 explosion n. 폭발적 증가, 급증 tremendous a. 엄청난, 광장한

| 해석 |

아마도 19세기 후반 현대성을 가장 잘 보여주는 장소는 1853년에서 1870년 사이에 나폴레옹 3세 황제 하에 개조된 파리 시 자체였다.
B 나폴레옹 3세가 선택한 오스만 남작(Baron Haussmann)은 계획을 세워 더 깨끗하고 안전한 도시를 위해 오래된 건물들을 허물어 더 많은 열린 공간을 만들었다. 또한 파리의 새로운 모습에 기여한 것은 프로이센-프랑스 전쟁(1870-71) 동안의 파리 포위였는데, 이로 인해 파괴된 도시의 일부를 재건해야 했다.
A 피사로(Pissarro)와 구스타브 카유보트(Gustave Caillebotte) 같은 인상파 화가들은 개조된 도시를 열정적으로 그렸는데, 새로운 스타일을 사용하여 넓은 대로, 공공 정원, 웅장한 건물들을 묘사했다.
D 일부는 도시 풍경에 집중한 반면, 다른 이들은 도시 주민들에게 시선을 돌렸다. 프로이센-프랑스 전쟁 이후 파리 인구의 폭발적인 증가는 그들에게 도시 생활의 장면을 위한 엄청난 양의 자료를 제공했다. 이 장면들의 특징은 공공장소에서 일어나는 사회 계층의 혼합이었다.
C 드가(Degas)는 가수와 댄서를 포함한 일하는 사람들에게 초점을 맞췄다. 베르트 모리조(Berthe Morisot)와 메리 카사트(Mary Cassatt)를 포함한 다른 사람들은 특권 계급을 묘사했다.

10 단락배열   ⑤

| 분석 |

제시문은 인간은 다양한 감정을 경험하고 이러한 감정을 잘 조절하는 사람이 감성 지능이 높은 사람임을 설명하고 있다. 따라서 이러한 감성 지능이 무엇인지에 대해 일반적인 정의를 묻고 있는 C가 제시문 다음에 오고, 감성 지능이 무엇인지 설명하는 B가 그다음에 온다. 그리고 감성 지능에 포함되는 다른 요소들에 대해 추가 설명을 하고 있는 A가 그 뒤에 오고, 감성 지능이 갈등 해결에 중요한 역할을 한다는 결론을 내리고 있는 D가 마지막에 와야 한다.

| 어휘 |

accurately ad. 정확하게, 틀림없이 identify v. 확인하다, 식별하다 regulate v. 규제하다; 조절[조정]하다 crucial a. 결정적인, 중대한 indicator n. 지표 self-awareness n. 자기 인식 empathy n. 감정 이입, 공감 cultivate v. 기르다, 양성하다 navigate v. (장소를) 빠져 나가다, 통과하다; (시기를) 지나쳐 가다 emotional intelligence 감성 지능 resolution n. 결의, 결심; 해결 facilitate v. 용이하게 하다; 촉진하다 repair n. 수리, 수산; 회복 compromise n. 타협

| 해석 |

인간은 인생의 거의 매 순간 다양한 감정을 경험한다. 즉, 인생은 때때로 감정적인 롤러코스터가 될 수 있으므로, 감정을 정확하게 식별하고 조절하는 방법을 아는 것은 관계를 구축하고 유지하며, 균형을 유지하고, 목표를 달성하는 데 중요하다. 게다가, 그것은 감성 지능이 높은 사람임을 나타내는 중요한 지표이다.
C 감성 지능이란 정확히 무엇인가?
B 그것은 감정을 인식하고, 연결하고, 이해하고, 관리하는 능력과 관련된 일련의 어려운 기술이다.
A 그것은 또한 자기 인식과 자기 조절을 보여주고, 공감을 나타내며, 사람들이 불편하거나 어려운 상황을 헤쳐 나가는 데 도움이 되는 사회적 기술을 기르는 것을 포함한다.
D 따라서 감성 지능은 더 빠른 회복과 타협을 촉진하는 데 도움을 줌으로써 갈등 해결에 큰 역할을 한다.

11 글의 흐름상 어색한 문장 고르기   ④

| 분석 |

본문은 물의 오염, 오염의 원인, 그로 인한 질병과 사망에 대한 내용이다. D는 물의 분배(운송)에 대한 내용으로, 물의 오염이나 질병과 관련이 없으므로 글의 흐름상 적절하지 않다.

| 어휘 |

potable a. 마실 수 있는, 마시기에 알맞은 transparent a. 투명한 silt n. 침니(모래보다 곱고 진흙보다 거친 침적토) suspension n. (액체·고체 중의) 부유물 pollute v. 오염시키다 waste n. 폐기물 fertilizer n. 비료 pesticide n. 살충제, 농약 dung n. (동물의) 똥; 거름, 비료 larva n. 유충, 애벌레 typhoid n. 장티푸스 dysentery n. 이질 spread n. 확산, 전파 canal n. 운하, 수로 proliferation n. 〈생물〉 증식; 확산 render v. ~로 만들다, ~이 되게 하다 inaccessibility n. 접근하기 어려움, 얻기 어려움 scarcity n. 부족, 결핍 mortality n. 사망자 수, 사망률; 사망

| 해석 |

소비하기에 적합하려면(마실 수 있으려면) 물은 투명해야 하며 부유물에 흙이나 침니가 포함되지 않아야 하며 오염되지 않아야 한다. 물의 오염은 다양한 원인을 가지고 있다. 화학 물질(염분, 금속, 다양한 광물), 농업 및 인간의 폐기물(비료, 살충제, 배설물, 세척수), 박테리아 및 다양한 유충 등이 그 원인이다. 물은 또한 장티푸

스, 이질, 콜레라와 같은 다양한 질병을 확산하는 매개체가 될 수 있다. 수질과 관련된 질병으로 인해 매년 약 1,300만 명이 사망하며, 그 중 500만 명의 아이들이 이질로 사망한다. 〈사람들은 운하를 건설하여 물을 운송하는 등 물을 분배하기 위해 다양한 해결책을 고안해 왔다.〉 높은 기온이 세균 증식을 촉진하는 더운 나라에서는 물을 끓여 세균을 죽여서, 물을 마시고 음식을 조리하기에 적합하게 만들도록 권장된다. 식수의 접근 불가능성과 부족은 개발도상국에서 사망의 중요한 원인이다. 인구의 50% 미만만이 식수에 쉽게 접근할 수 있다.

12 글의 흐름상 어색한 문장 고르기   ④

| 분석 |
본문은 필적학이란 무엇인지를 설명하면서 필적 분석을 통해 사람의 심리 상태나 성격을 알 수 있음을 이야기하고 있다. D는 종의 해부학적 변화가 생존에 유리한 이점을 가져다 줄 때만 일어난다는 진화 생물학에 관한 내용으로, 필적학과 심리 분석과 관련이 없으므로 글의 흐름상 적절하지 않다.

| 어휘 |
graphology n. 필적학   **handwriting** n. 손으로 쓰기, 육필; 필적   **doodling** n. (무의미한) 낙서   **legitimate** a. 합법적인, 본격적인, 정통의   **psychiatry** n. 정신 의학   **psychiatrist** n. 정신과 의사   **anatomical** a. 해부의, 해부학의   **undisclosed** a. 나타나지 않은, 비밀에 부쳐진

| 해석 |
필적학은 단순히 필적에 대한 연구 그 이상이다. 그것은 그림 그리기와 낙서를 비롯한 모든 형태의 필기상의 움직임에 대한 연구이다. 미국에서는 필적학이 본격적인 학문으로 여겨지지 않았지만, 20세기 초에 정신 의학과 함께 필적학이 발전한 유럽에서는 진지하게 연구되고 있다. 프로이트(Freud)와 융(Jung)과 같은 정신과 의사들은 이 분석이 정신의 의식적 작용과 무의식적 작용을 모두 이해하는 데 매우 유용한 도구라고 생각했다. 그들에게 필적은 뇌를 들여다보는 창과 같았다. 그들은 펜의 특정한 움직임이나, 필적의 크기나 스타일이 어떻게 변했는지, 혹은 문장에서 단어들 사이에 비정상적으로 많은 공백이 남아 있는지를 살펴봄으로써 사람의 성격을 들여다볼 수 있었다. 〈자연은 (변화로) 얻어질 어떤 생존상의 이점이 없으면, 종의 해부학적 변화를 일으키지 않는다.〉 오늘날 필적이 가진 최대 400가지 다양한 특징이 글쓴이의 숨겨진, 심지어 무의식적인 정신 상태를 드러낼 수 있다고 주장된다.

13 글의 흐름상 어색한 문장 고르기   ④

| 분석 |
본문은 신고전주의 음악과 그 특징에 대해 설명하고 있는데, 낭만주의와 인상주의에 반대하여 표제 음악에서 벗어나서 절대 음악을 선호했다고 했다. D는 낭만주의 음악에 대한 내용으로, 표제 음악에 매료되었다는 것은 본문의 내용과 반대되므로 글의 흐름상 적절하지 않다.

| 어휘 |
composer n. 작곡가   **neoclassicism** n. 신고전주의   **restraint** n. 억제, 제지; 자제   **clarity** n. 명료성, 명확성   **composition** n. 작곡; 작곡(법)   **romanticism** n. 낭만주의   **impressionism** n. 인상주의   **appropriate** a. 적합한, 적절한   **program music** 표제 음악   **absolute music** 절대 음악   **chamber** a. 실내악(연주)의   **instrumental** a. 악기의, 기악의   **preference** n. 선호, 애호

| 해석 |
1920년부터 1950년까지 이고르 스트라빈스키(Igor Stravinsky)와 파울 힌데미트(Paul Hindemith)를 비롯한 많은 작곡가들의 음악은 신고전주의로 알려진 예술 운동을 반영했다. 신고전주의는 감정적 절제, 균형, 명료성이 특징이다. 신고전주의 작품은 초기 시기, 특히 18세기의 음악적 형식과 양식적 특징을 사용한다. "바흐로 돌아가자"가 낭만주의와 인상주의에 반대하는 이 운동의 슬로건이었다. 많은 신고전주의 작품은 바흐의 음악을 모델로 했기 때문에 '네오바로크'라는 용어가 더 적절했을 수도 있다. 신고전주의 작곡가들은 표제 음악과 세기의 전환기에 선호되었던 거대한 오케스트라에서 벗어났다. 그들은 실내악 그룹을 위한 절대(비표제적) 음악을 선호했다. 〈낭만주의 작곡가들은 특히 이야기, 시, 아이디어, 또는 장면과 관련된 기악 음악인 표제 음악에 매료되었다.〉 소규모 공연 그룹에 대한 이러한 선호는 부분적으로 경제적 필요성을 반영했다. 제1차 세계대전 이후 유럽의 일부 지역에서는 경제 상황이 너무 나빠서 대규모 오케스트라를 고용할 돈이 거의 없었다.

14 글의 흐름상 적절하지 않은 표현 고르기   ②

| 분석 |
본문은 악어의 의사소통을 연구하는 것이 쉽지 않다는 점을 강조하고 있다. 따라서 소설에서는 동물과 쉽게 대화할 수 있지만 실제로 동물과 대화하는 것은 어렵다고 해야 적절하므로 ② difficult(어려운)를 easy(쉬운)로 고쳐야 한다.

| 어휘 |
unlock v. 밝히다; 털어놓다, 누설하다   **ecologist** n. 생태학자   **dictionary** n. 사전   **extremely** ad. 극단적으로; 매우   **approach** v. 다가오다, 접근하다   **challenging** a. 도전적인; 힘든   **milky** a. 젖 같은; 유백색의   **captive** a. 포로의, 사로잡힌   **complications** n. (사건의) 분규, 혼란

| 해석 |
악어들이 어떻게 의사소통을 하는지 확인한 후, 과학자들은 이제 그들이 실제로 무엇을 말하고 있는지 밝혀내려고 노력하고 있다. "대중 소설에서 사람들은 항상 동물과 대화할 수 있습니다. 하지만 우리는 실제로 그것이 그렇게 〈어렵지(→ 쉽지)〉 않다는 것을 알게 됩니다."라고 악어 사전을 만드는 데 참여한 생태학자 도미니크 포트빈(Dominique Potvin)은 말했다. "악어에 대한 가정은 항상

그들이 우리에게 경고가 될 수 있는 것 외에는 할 말이 별로 없다는 것이었습니다." 악어의 의사소통에 대한 — 일반적으로 악어에 대한 — 우리의 지식의 공백을 메우는 것은 매우 어려울 수 있다. 대부분의 야생 악어는 인간이 다가오면 숨는다. 그들에게 너무 가까이 다가가는 것은 위험할 수 있으며, 야생 악어들은 힘든 환경에서 산다. 대부분의 악어 행동은 수면 아래에서 이루어지며, 대부분의 호주 북부의 강물은 유백색의 커피와 같다. 포획된 악어를 연구하는 것조차도 복잡한 문제가 있다. 호주 동물원의 악어들은 마이크를 계속해서 먹어버렸다.

15 글의 주제 ①

| 분석 |
본문에서는 포장상품 도난을 막기 위해 취할 수 있는 방법들을 소개하고 있다. 따라서 글의 주제로는 ①이 적절하다.

| 어휘 |
order v. 주문하다　ship v. 배송하다　package theft 소포 도난, 포장상품 도난　tempting a. 유혹적인, 구미가 당기는　clue n. 단서, 힌트　surveillance n. 감시　deter v. 막다　trigger v. (장치를) 작동시키다; 유발하다　property n. 부동산; 건물

| 해석 |
인기 있는 유명 브랜드제품을 주문할 때는 주의해야 하며 브랜드 제품을 상표 라벨이 포장에 드러나지 않게 하여 배송 받을 수 있는지 알아봐야 한다. 포장상품 도난은 종종 '기회의 범죄'이며 도둑들은 사람들이 걸어가거나 차로 지나가는 공터에 놓인 포장상품을 찾는다. 포장상자에 브랜드가 드러나 있는 것은 그 안에 무엇이 들어있을지에 대한 힌트를 제공하므로 표적물을 더 매력적이게 만든다. 포장상품의 도난 가능성을 줄이기 위해 당신이 취할 수 있는 방법이 몇 가지 있는데, 이웃이나 집에 있는 가족에게 배달되게 하는 것이다. 배달기사에게 포장상품을 어디에 두어야 할지를 미리 알려줄 수도 있다. 보안 전문가들은 도둑을 실시간으로 녹화하는 초인종 카메라나 비디오 감시 장치가 도둑을 막는 데 도움이 될 수 있다고 말한다. 또한 누군가가 당신의 집에 들어설 때 조명이 켜지게 하는 모션 센서와 눈에 띄는 보안 카메라도 도움이 될 수 있다.

다음 중 이 글의 주제로 가장 적절한 것은?
① 당신의 포장상품을 지키는 데 도움이 되는 조언들
② 당신이 인기 있는 유명 브랜드 제품을 사야 하는 이유
③ 명절 할인 판매를 거부하기가 너무나 힘든 이유
④ 당신의 포장상품을 확실히 신속히 배달되게 하는 방법
⑤ 당신의 포장상품이 도난당했을 때 취해야 하는 조치들

16 부분이해 ③

| 분석 |
고령인 안드레아 레빗과 십대인 안젤로 윌리엄스가 나이 차이에도 불구하고 서로 친해졌다고 했는데, 이들을 연결해준 곳이 바로 Dorot이라는 비영리단체였다. 따라서 Dorot은 노인과 십대를 연결하여 노인을 고립에서 벗어나게 도와주는 단체임을 알 수 있는데, 현재 비슷한 사명을 가진 단체들과 함께 활동한다고 했다. 그러므로 이들 단체의 사명 역시 '십대와 노인을 친해지게 만들어 십대와 노인 모두를 이롭게 하는 것'임을 알 수 있으므로, ③이 정답이다.

| 어휘 |
depression n. 우울증　gap n. 차이, 격차　connect v. 마음이 통하다　nonprofit organization 비영리단체　Hebrew a. 히브리어의, 유대인의

| 해석 |
뉴욕 시에서 열린 다과회 행사에서 82세의 안드레아 레빗이 16세의 안젤로 윌리엄스를 처음 만났을 당시에 그녀는 우울한 기분을 느끼고 있었다. 그녀는 혼자 살고 있으며 그녀의 아들이 멀리 이사간 뒤 최근 몇 년 동안 더욱 고립되어 있었다. "안젤로와 함께 테이블에 앉아있었던 것이 기억나는데, 그는 정말 재미있어서 저를 우울증에서 완전히 벗어나게 해주었습니다. 그리고 그 중 가장 좋았던 점은 제가 농구를 정말 좋아하는데 안젤로도 농구를 좋아한다는 것이었습니다."라고 그녀가 이야기한다. 나이 차이에도 불구하고 그들은 마음이 통했고 정말 좋은 대화를 나눌 수 있었다고 그녀는 말한다. 그들은 Dorot이라는 비영리 단체를 통해 만났는데 Dorot은 히브리어로 '세대들'을 의미한다. 현재 Dorot에는 비슷한 사명을 가진 신생 단체들이 동참하고 있다.

다음 중 similar mission이 의미하는 것은?
① 모든 생명이 의지하는 땅과 물을 보존하기
② 누구에게나 어디서나 무료로 세계적인 수준의 교육을 제공하기
③ 십대와 노인을 연결하여 우정을 통해 양측 모두에게 도움 되게 하기
④ 빈곤과 경제적 불평등에 맞서 싸우는 사람들을 지원하기
⑤ 분쟁, 전쟁, 그리고 재난으로 삶이 파괴된 사람들을 돕기

17~18

수면은 오랫동안 과학자들의 관심을 끌어온 중요한 생물학적 기능이다. 과학자들은 동물이 잠을 잘 때 무슨 일이 일어나며 왜 그렇게 많은 동물들이 잠을 자는지를 더 잘 이해하기 위해 실험실에서 쥐부터 초파리까지 모든 것을 연구해왔다. 그러나 동물이 자연 서식지에서 어떻게 잠을 자는지에 관한 데이터를 수집하는 것은 항상 까다롭고 어려운 일이었다. 그러나 과학자들은 남극의 야생 턱끈펭귄을 대상으로 그것을 해냈다. 그들은 둥지 군집을 이룬 새들이 하루에 10,000번 이상의 마이크로수면(미세수면)을 취한다는 것을 발견했는데, 이것은 대략 11시간의 수면 양에 해당한다. 마이크로수면은 매번 대략 4초 정도 지속된다. 펭귄이 그렇게 짧은 간격

으로 잠을 잘 수 있는 것은 만약 좀 더 오래 자는 경우에 공격해 올 수도 있을 포식동물을 피하는 데 도움이 될 수 있으며, 특히 펭귄 부모 중 한 쪽이 며칠 동안 바다에서 먹이를 찾으러 나가 다른 부모가 포식 조류로부터 알을 보호해야 한다는 점을 고려할 때 특히 그렇다고 과학자들은 생각한다. 과학자들은 펭귄을 연구하기 위해 소수의 펭귄의 뇌와 목 근육에 장치를 삽입했다. 뇌파와 위치에 대한 이 데이터를 둥지에서 펭귄을 촬영한 것과 결합한 결과, 신뢰할만한 수면 데이터를 얻게 되었다. 이 장치는 이전에 한 번도 사용된 적이 없어서 이 데이터 수집은 그저 실험에 그칠 것으로 여겨졌다. 그러나 연구는 성공적으로 진행되어 데이터가 이번 연구서에 실리게 되었다. 이 연구는 수면에 관한 상대적으로 큰 과학 지식의 공백을 메워줄 초기 단계의 연구로 평가되고 있다.

| 어휘 |

essential a. 아주 중요한 **intrigue** v. 호기심을 불러일으키다 **fruit fly** 초파리 **habitat** n. 서식지 **tricky** a. (다루기) 까다로운, 곤란한 **Chinstrap Penguin** 턱끈펭귄 **Antarctica** n. 남극대륙 **nest** n. (새의) 둥지 **colony** n. 집단, 군집 **microsleep** n. 마이크로수면(깨어 있을 때의 순간적인 잠, 깜박 졸기) **last** v. 지속되다 **interval** n. (두 사건 사이의) 간격 **predator** n. 육식 동물 **implant** v. (몸에) 삽입하다 **muscle** n. 근육 **brain wave** 뇌파 **film** v. 촬영하다 **robust** a. 확신에 찬 **vacuum** n. 진공; 공백

17   빈칸완성   ②

| 분석 |

본문에 따르면 "턱끈 펭귄은 11시간 동안 10,000번의 마이크로수면을 취한다"고 한다. 한 번의 마이크로수면이 몇 초간 지속되는지를 계산하기 위해서는 '11시간(11×60×60초)÷10,000번의 마이크로수면'으로 계산해야 하는데, 11×60×60초가 39,600초이므로 10,000으로 나눈 값은 3.96초가 된다. 빈칸 앞에 about(대략)이 있으므로, ②의 '4초'가 정답이다.

18   내용추론   ③

| 분석 |

펭귄이 그렇게 짧은 간격으로 잠을 자는 것은 좀 더 오래 잘 경우 공격해 올 수도 있는 포식동물을 피하는 데 도움이 될 수 있으며 부모가 포식 조류로부터 알을 보호해야 한다는 점을 고려할 때 특히 그렇다고 했으므로, ③이 추론가능하다. ① 실험실에서가 아니다. ② 항상 까다롭고 어려운 일이라 했다. ④ 회색 곰에 대한 언급은 없다. ⑤ 이 장치는 이전에 한 번도 사용된 적이 없었다고 했다.

다음 중 이 글에 명시되거나 암시되어 있는 것은?
① 실험실에서 턱끈펭귄의 수면 패턴이 관찰되었다.
② 자연 환경에서 동물들의 수면 패턴을 연구하는 것이 훨씬 더 쉽다.
③ 마이크로수면 덕분에 턱끈펭귄이 알을 보호할 수 있다.
④ 과학자들은 회색 곰 집단의 뇌파를 모니터링 했다.
⑤ 이 연구에 사용된 장치는 많은 과학자들이 선호했던 것이다.

19~20

매년 스웨덴 북쪽의 그란나(Gränna)라는 작은 마을에서 막대사탕이라고도 알려진 빨갛고 하얀 사탕 수백만 개가 수작업으로 만들어진다. 이 달콤한 사탕의 역사는 1859년으로 거슬러 올라간다. 당시 25세였던 주부 아말리아 에릭슨(Amalia Eriksson)은 남편을 여의고 홀로 아이를 키우는 싱글맘이었다. 〈생계를 꾸려나가기로 결심한 아말리아는 결혼식, 세례식, 그리고 장례식용 사탕을 만들기 시작했다.〉 당시 스웨덴 법은 여성이 사업을 소유하거나 운영하는 것을 허용하지 않았다. 하지만 아말리아는 그란나의 치안판사로부터 과자 판매 허가를 받은 후 시장의 승인을 받아 사업을 시작하여 스웨덴 최초의 여성 사업가들 중 한 명이 되었다. 아말리아의 막대사탕은 설탕, 식초, 물을 섞어 끓인 반죽을 주무르고 잡아당기는 과정을 거쳐 만들어졌다. 반죽의 일부에는 빨간색을 넣었고 나머지 흰색 부분은 페퍼민트로 풍미를 더했다. 원래 이 사탕은 작은 베개 모양이었지만 아말리아는 결국 사탕을 막대 모양으로 만들었다. 오랫동안 아말리아는 막대사탕을 그녀의 딸인 아이다만 알고 있는 비밀로 했다. 1923년 아말리아가 99세의 나이로 세상을 떠난 후 아이다는 사탕을 만드는 가족 전통을 계속 이어갔으며, 다른 사람들도 막대사탕을 만들 수 있도록 레시피를 공유했다. 1950년대에 들어서면서 막대사탕은 점점 인기를 끌었고 아말리아를 따라하는 여성이 많아졌다. 막대사탕은 그란나를 방문하는 관광객들에게 필수 기념품이 되었다.

| 어휘 |

candy cane 막대사탕(지팡이 모양의 캔디) **roll out** (신상품을) 출시하다; 다량으로 만들어 내다 **date to** ~로 거슬러 올라가다 **widow** n. 미망인, 과부 **christening** n. 세례식 **funeral** n. 장례식 **magistrate** n. 치안 판사 **entrepreneur** n. (특히 모험적인) 사업가 **vinegar** n. 식초 **knead** v. 주무르다 **dough** n. (밀가루) 반죽 **flavor** v. (음식물에) 풍미를 더하다 **pillow** n. 베개 **recipe** n. 조리법 **craft** v. 공들여 만들다 **follow in one's footsteps** ~의 선례를 따르다, 따라하다 **must-have** a. 필수의

19   문장삽입   ②

| 분석 |

제시문은 "생계를 꾸려나가기로 결심한 아말리아는 결혼식, 세례식, 그리고 장례식용 사탕을 만들기 시작했다."라는 뜻이므로, '돈

을 벌어야 하는' 상황이 제시문 앞에 나와야 한다. 따라서 25세에 아말리아가 남편을 여의고 홀로 아이를 키우는 싱글맘이었다는 내용 다음인 ⒷB에 제시문이 들어가는 것이 적절하다.

20 내용추론 ⑤

| 분석 |
아말리아가 그란나라는 작은 마을에서 막대사탕 사업을 시작했다고 했으므로, "아말리아 덕분에 그란나가 막대사탕의 발생지가 되었다."라는 의미의 ⑤가 정답이다. ① 베개 모양이었다. ② 생계를 위해 했다. ③ 스웨덴 최초의 여성 사업가들 중 한 명이 되었다. ④ 레시피를 다른 사람들과 공유했다.

다음 중 이 글에 명시되거나 암시되어 있는 것은?
① 원래 막대사탕은 막대처럼 생겼다.
② 아말리아는 그녀의 과자 사업을 취미로 시작했다.
③ 아말리아는 그란나에서 최초로 성공한 여성 국회의원이 되었다.
④ 아말리아의 딸인 아이다는 막대사탕 조리법을 비밀로 했다.
⑤ 아말리아 덕분에 그란나가 막대사탕의 발생지가 되었다.

21 빈칸완성 ①

| 분석 |
빈칸 다음에서 "잔 다르크가 자유와 독립의 상징이 되었다"라는 긍정적인 이야기로 글이 마무리되었다. 이렇게 긍정적인 이야기로 마무리되기 위해서는 그녀가 당했던 화형이 '부당했다'는 평가가 먼저 나와야 할 것이다. 따라서 빈칸에는 ①의 unjust(부당한)가 적절하다. ② 마땅한 ③ 온건한 ④ 어찌할 바를 모르게 하는 ⑤ 무해한

| 어휘 |
honor v. 존경하다　saint n. 성인　humble a. 초라한, 소박한
peasant n. 소작농　vision n. (특히 종교적인) 환영　archangel n. 대천사　domination n. 지배　siege n. 포위 (작전)　relief army 구호군　wave v. (무엇을 손에 들고) 흔들다　banner n. 깃발
run-down a. 지친　abandon v. 버리다　court n. 법정, 법원
trial n. 재판　burn a person at the stake ~을 화형 시키다

| 해석 |
프랑스의 성인이자 군사 지도자로 존경받는 잔 다르크는 프랑스 북동부의 소작농 가문에서 태어났으므로 그 시작은 소박했다. 1428년, 그녀는 영국의 프랑스 지배에 대해 그녀에게 경고하는 대천사 미카엘, 성 마르가리타, 성 카타리나의 환영(幻影)을 보았다고 주장했다. 미래에 왕이 될 샤를은 그녀를 구호군의 일원으로 오를레앙 포위전에 보냈다. 1429년, 그녀가 도착하여 깃발을 흔들면서 지친 프랑스군에 희망을 불어넣었다. 그녀가 도착하고 얼마 지나지 않아 영국군은 포위를 풀었고, 잔 다르크는 프랑스군이 영국군을 추격하도록 격려했다. 그러나 이후 잔 다르크는 몇 차례의 실패한 전투에 참여해 그녀의 능력에 대한 법정의 신뢰를 잃었고 재판 후에 화형을 당했다. 나중에 법정은 그녀의 처벌이 부당하다고 평가했다. 잔 다르크는 유산을 남겼으며 프랑스의 자유와 독립의 상징이 되었다.

22 빈칸완성 ⑤

| 분석 |
Ⓐ 앞에서 '눈에 잘 띄는' 구성원을 소개하고 Ⓐ 다음에는 '눈에 잘 띄지 않는' 구성원을 소개하고 있으므로, Ⓐ에는 '역접'을 나타내는 부사인 However(그러나)가 적절하다. Ⓐ 앞뒤가 not only ... but also 관계이므로 but에 해당하는 However인 것이다. Ⓑ 앞에서 수족관 안에 눈에 잘 띄지 않는 유기체가 있다고 주장한 다음, 그 '구체적인 사례'로 조류, 박테리아, 균류를 소개하고 있으므로, Ⓑ에는 For example(예를 들어)이 적절하다. 따라서 두 빈칸에 모두 적절한 ⑤가 정답이다.

| 어휘 |
biotic community 생물 군집　be made up of ~로 구성되다
ecosystem n. 생태계　aquarium n. 수족관　snail n. 달팽이
gravel n. 자갈　algae n. 조류　fungi n. 균류, 곰팡이류
tapeworm n. 촌충　outnumber v. ~보다 수가 더 많다

| 해석 |
생물 군집은 생태계의 모든 생물들로 구성되어 있다. 수족관에서 물고기, 달팽이, 식물은 생물 군집 중에서 눈에 잘 띄는 구성원이다. 그러나 수족관의 생물 군집에는 눈에 잘 띄지 않는 유기체들도 많이 있다. 예를 들어, 수족관의 물과 자갈에는 많은 조류(藻類), 박테리아, 균류가 살고 있다. 또한 촌충과 같이 물고기와 다른 유기체의 몸 안에 사는 더 작은 유기체도 있다. 생물 군집에서 눈에 잘 띄지 않는 구성원이 눈에 잘 띄는 구성원보다 더 많은 경우가 종종 있다.

23 글의 제목 ④

| 분석 |
이 글은 크메르 제국이 언제 어떻게 등장했고 언제 멸망했으며 멸망하게 된 요인은 무엇인지를 설명하고 있으므로, ④의 '크메르 제국의 흥망성쇠'가 글의 제목으로 적절하다.

| 어휘 |
ruins n. 유적　empire n. 제국　archaeologist n. 고고학자
Sanskrit n. 산스크리트어　inscription n. 비문(碑文)　an array of 다수의　dissolve v. 사라지다, 붕괴하다　Theravada n. 소승불교　erratic a. 변덕스러운　monsoon n. 우기, 장마　overwhelm v. 압도하다; 매몰시키다　harvest n. 수확, 추수

| 해석 |
크메르 제국의 그 사원 유적은 오랫동안 캄보디아인들에게 알려져 있었지만, 19세기 고고학자들이 앙코르 사원의 산스크리트어 비문

을 해독하기 전까지는 앙코르 사원을 지은 왕에 대해서는 아무도 알지 못했다. 이 제국은 다수의 지배 권력을 기반으로 9세기에 발흥했다. 크메르 제국이 15세기에 왜 붕괴되었는지는 논쟁의 대상이다. 다른 왕국들과의 전쟁, 크메르 엘리트 계층 간의 투쟁, 소승 불교에서 들어온 새로운 사회 개념, 세계적인 무역 변화, 안정적인 쌀 수확을 제공할 앙코르 사원의 뛰어난 급수시설을 매몰시켜 버렸을 수 있는 변덕스러운 장마 등, 다수의 요인이 작용했을 것으로 보인다.

이 글의 제목으로 가장 적절한 것은?
① 현대 캄보디아의 상징
② 산스크리트어 비문의 미스테리
③ 앙코르 사원은 어떻게 지어졌는가
④ 크메르 제국의 흥망성쇠
⑤ 불교가 크메르 제국에 미친 영향

24   글의 제목   ①

| 분석 |
이 글은 수백 만 명의 사람들이 즐기는 극한 취미활동의 부정적인 측면에 대해 집중적으로 이야기하고 있으므로, ①이 글의 제목으로 적절하다.

| 어휘 |
pastime n. 취미, 오락   **pursuit** n. 추구, 일   **BASE jumping** 베이스 점핑(건물·다리 등 높은 곳에서 낙하산을 타고 내려오는 스포츠)   **conventional** a. 틀에 박힌, 상투적인   **freefall** n. 자유 낙하(특히 낙하산이 펴지기 전의 강하)   **initiation** n. 시작   **parachute** n. 낙하산   **deploy** v. 배치하다   **underground** a. 지하의, 비밀의, 실험적인   **fatality** n. 사망자

| 해석 |
'극한' 취미활동은 이제 수백 만 명의 사람들에게 주말이나 휴가 때 하는 인기 있는 활동이 되었다. 이에 따라 부정적인 잠재 비용과 관련해서 일부 비판이 제기되었다. 논의의 핵심은 위험한 여가활동에 참여하는 사람들의 수가 증가함에 따라 심각한 부상과 사망자 수도 증가한다는 점이다. 베이스 점핑을 예로 들면, 대개 먼저 일반적인 자유낙하 스카이다이빙을 최소 250회 하고난 후에 한 차례 베이스 점프를 시도하도록 권장된다. 베이스 점핑이 위험한 이유는 베이스 점핑의 시작 지점이 일반적인 스카이다이빙에서 낙하산을 펼치는 높이보다 낮을 수 있으며, 점프 후 단 몇 초 안에 낙하산을 펼쳐야 하기 때문이다. 또한 예측할 수 없는 측면 기류가 베이스 점핑 참가자를 점프했던 구조물로 밀어 넣을 수도 있다. 일부 사람들이 베이스 점핑을 '드러내지 않고 하는' 활동으로 간주하기 때문에, 사망자 통계를 확인하기가 어렵다. 예를 들어, 1999년 요세미티(Yosemite) 국립공원에서 58세였던 얀 데이비스(Jan Davis)가 사망했는데, 이것은 1982년 이후 해당 지역에서 발생한 다섯 번째 사망 사례였다. 위험한 여가활동에 대한 비판에는 구조대 비용과 참가자의 친구와 가족에 미치는 부정적인 정서적 영향도 있다. 훈련과 적절한 장비를 통해 극한 스포츠의 위험을 관리하려는 시도들이 있지만, 큰 피해를 입을 가능성은 항상 존재한다.

이 글의 제목으로 가장 적절한 것은?
① 극한 취미활동의 부정적인 측면
② 노인들을 위한 극한 취미활동 사례
③ 젊은이들 사이에서 위험한 스포츠의 인기
④ 위험한 여가활동 애호가들에게 훈련이 중요하다
⑤ 점프하는 사람들을 위한 높은 장비 비용을 낮춰라!

25   글의 제목   ①

| 분석 |
SAD(계절성 정서 장애)가 있는 사람과 SAD가 없는 사람을 대상으로 눈이 청색광에 어떻게 반응하는지를 실험하여, SAD가 있는 사람이 청색광에 덜 민감했다는 결과를 얻게 됐음을 이야기하고 있는 글이다. 따라서 이 글은 'SAD와 청색광의 관계'를 다루고 있음을 알 수 있으므로 ①이 글의 제목으로 적절하다.

| 어휘 |
seasonal affective disorder 계절성 정서 장애(SAD)   **episode** n. 증상의 발현   **wavelength** n. 파장   **neural** a. 신경의   **be loaded with** ~이 넘치게 있다   **activate** v. 활성화시키다

| 해석 |
계절성 정서 장애(SAD)가 있는 사람들은 일반적으로 가을에 시작해서 봄이나 여름에 완화되는 우울증의 발현을 경험한다. 과학자들은 어떻게 우리 눈의 특수 세포가 빛의 스펙트럼에서 청색 파장 부분을 기분과 각성에 영향을 미치는 신경 신호로 바꾸는지를 연구하고 있다. 햇빛에는 청색광이 많이 포함되어 있어서 특수 세포가 청색광을 흡수하면 우리 뇌의 각성 중추가 활성화되어 우리는 더 각성되고 아마도 더 행복해질 수도 있다. 피츠버그 대학의 캐서린 로클라인(Kathryn Roecklein)은 SAD가 있는 사람들과 SAD가 없는 사람들을 대상으로 눈이 청색광에 어떻게 반응하는지를 실험했다. SAD가 있는 집단은 다른 집단보다 청색광에 덜 민감했는데 특히 겨울철에 덜 민감했다. "겨울에는 빛의 양이 줄어들고 빛에 대한 민감도가 떨어져 건강한 기능을 유지하기에 부족한 상태가 될 수 있으며 우울증으로 이어질 가능성이 있습니다."라고 로클라인이 말했다.

이 글의 제목으로 가장 적절한 것은?
① 청색광과 SAD와의 관계
② SAD의 잠재적 위험과 합병증
③ SAD가 있는 사람들의 행동과 패턴
④ 어떻게 청색광이 우울증을 1년 내내 유발하는가
⑤ 왜 SAD가 있는 사람이 빛에 대한 민감도가 더 좋은가

26 문장삽입 ③

| 분석 |
C 앞까지는 두 종류의 산호 동물을 '모두' 설명한 반면, C 다음에는 '나머지 한 집단(The other group)'만 설명해서 앞의 내용과 대조를 이룬다. 대개 두 개의 집단에서 첫 번째 집단인 one group을 설명한 다음에 the other group이 위치한다. 따라서 one group이 들어있는 제시문이 The other group이 나온 문장 '앞'에 와야 적절하므로, 제시문은 C에 들어가야 한다.

| 어휘 |
coral n. 산호　layer n. 층　tentacle n. (오징어 등의) 촉수　stinging cell 쏘는 세포, 독침 세포　defense n. 방어　capture v. 포획하다　secrete v. 분비하다　calcium carbonate 탄산칼슘　limestone n. 석회암

| 해석 |
주된 두 종류의 산호 동물이 있다. 두 종류는 모두 두 개의 층과 그 사이 젤리 같은 물질로 이루어진 부드러운 몸을 갖고 있다. 두 종류는 모두 방어와 먹이 포획에 사용되는 독침세포가 있는 촉수를 갖고 있다. 〈그러나 한 집단은 탄산칼슘(석회암)으로 만들어진 컵 모양의 기저부를 분비한다.〉 또 다른 집단은 그러한 기저부를 분비하지 않는다. 이러한 집단의 산호 동물들을 일반적으로 연산호(석회암 기저부가 없음)와 경산호(석회암 기저부가 있음)라고 부른다.

27 문장삽입 ④

| 분석 |
제시문은 "어떻게 이렇게 큰 물고기가 수백 년을 사는지에 관한 여러 가지 기여 변수들이 있을 수 있지만 그 중 하나가 자신의 DNA를 복구하는 능력이다."라는 뜻으로, 그린란드 상어의 장수 요인들 중 하나가 DNA 복구 능력임을 언급하고 있다. 따라서 제시문 앞에는 그린란드 상어가 '오래 산다'는 내용이 나오고 제시문 다음에는 'DNA 복구 능력'이 나와야 적절하므로, D에 제시문이 들어가야 한다.

| 어휘 |
massive a. (육중하면서) 거대한　measure v. (길이가) ~이다　weigh v. 무게가 ~이다　reign v. 지배하다　apex predator 최상위 포식자　vertebrate n. 척추동물　reproductive a. 번식의　adolescence n. 청소년기　variable n. 변수　exceptionally ad. 특히, 매우　genome n. 게놈(세포나 생명체의 유전자 총체)　duplicate n. 중복; 복제　protein n. 단백질

| 해석 |
그린란드 상어는 길이가 최대 24피트나 되고 무게가 2,000 파운드 이상 나가는 거대한 상어이다. 그린란드 상어는 차가운 먼 북쪽 바다를 최상위 포식자로서 지배하는 가장 큰 상어 종이다. 그린란드 상어는 또한 가장 오래 사는 척추동물 종으로도 알려져 있다. 2016년에 암컷 상어 28마리의 몸에서 채취한 눈 수정체를 연구한 결과에 따르면, 가장 오래 사는 그린란드 상어가 대략 400살인 것으로 나타났다. 이 상어들은 대략 150살이 되어야 번식기에 들어가는 것으로 보이는데, 즉 상어가 한 세기 반 동안 유년기와 청소년기를 보낸다는 것이다. 〈어떻게 이렇게 큰 물고기가 수백 년을 사는지에 관한 여러 가지 기여 변수들이 있을 수 있지만 그 중 하나가 자신의 DNA를 복구하는 능력이다.〉 그린란드 상어는 많은 중복 유전자가 들어있는 매우 큰 게놈을 갖고 있는 것으로 알려져 있다. 이런 중복 유전자들 중 일부는 DNA 복구 단백질과 암 억제 단백질을 합성하도록 암호를 지정하는 유전자이다.

28 문장삽입 ②

| 분석 |
주어진 문장 속의 these conditions와 these children을 고려하면, 이 문장의 바로 앞에는 '아이들이 처한 상황'에 대한 내용이 있어야 한다. 그러므로 주어진 문장은 매우 많은 어린이들이 가혹한 노동 환경에서 일해야만 하는 현실을 언급한 내용 다음인 B에 들어가는 것이 적절하다.

| 어휘 |
deficit n. 부족, 결손　condemn v. 비난하다, 유죄판결을 내리다; 운명지우다　perpetuate v. 영속시키다　self-sustaining 자동으로 계속되는; 자급자족의; 자생하는　malnourished a. 영양부족의, 영양실조　weave v. (직물·바구니 따위를) 짜다, 뜨다, 엮다　ceramics n. 도자기류　overharvest v. 너무 많이 수확하다

| 해석 |
빈곤, 질병, 제한된 기회의 순환은 자생적인 과정이 되어 한 세대에서 다음 세대로 이어질 수 있다. 영양실조와 질병이 있는 사람들은 자신이나 자녀를 위한 음식, 주거, 약물을 얻기 위해 생산적으로 일할 수 없으며, 그래서 자녀들도 영양실조와 질병을 갖게 된다. 약 2억 명의 아동들 — 대개 남아시아와 동남아시아에 있고 일부는 4살 정도로 어리다 — 이 카펫을 짜거나 도자기와 보석을 만들면서 노예노동(강제노동) 환경에서 일해야 한다. 〈이와 같은 환경들에서 자라는 것은 정신적·발달적 결핍을 초래하며 이러한 결핍이 이 아이들로 하여금 이러한 순환에 영속적으로 빠지게 만든다.〉 생존을 위한 당장의 필요에 직면해 있고 선택의 여지가 거의 없는 상황에서, 이 불운한 사람들은 종종 자원을 과도하게 수확할(자원이 고갈될) 수밖에 없다. 그러나 이렇게 함으로써 그들은 자신들의 선택뿐만 아니라 미래 세대의 선택도 줄어들게 만든다. 그리고 점점 더 서로 연결되는 세계에서, 빈곤과 무지로 인해 훼손된 환경과 자원 기반은 우리가 의존하는 환경 및 자원기반과 직접적으로 연결돼 있다. 모든 사람이 삶을 살아갈 더 나은 방법을 찾을 수 있도록 돕는 것은 우리의 이익에도 부합하는 일이다.

29 문장삽입 ⑤

| 분석 |

주어진 문장은 '그들은 유리벽으로 분리되어 물리적인 접촉이 불가능하지만, 스트레스를 받은 동물들은 종종 심혈관 질환으로 조기에 죽는다.'라는 의미인데, 이는 '공격적인 개체 옆에 있는 우리 안의 동물들이 보이는 반응'을 부연하는 내용이라 할 수 있다. 그러므로 주어진 문장은 E에 들어가야 한다.

| 어휘 |

prematurely ad. 조기에, 너무 이르게 cardiovascular a. 심혈관의 factor n. 요소, 요인 strain n. 긴장; 부담, 압력 inadequate a. 부적당한, 불충분한 adaptation n. 적응, 순응 contribute to 기여하다; ~의 원인이 되다 adverse a. 불리한; 해로운 aggressive a. 공격적인, 호전적인 susceptibility n. (병 등에) 감염되기[걸리기] 쉬움 infectious a. 전염하는

| 해석 |

의학적인 면에서, 스트레스는 적절히 적응할 수 없는 긴장을 유기체(생물)에게 가하는 신체적, 화학적 혹은 정서적 요인들을 가리킨다. 이것은 질병의 원인이 되는 신체 반응을 초래할 수도 있다. 유해한 스트레스 반응이 인간에게만 있는 것은 아니다. 대부분의 동물들과 마찬가지로, 식물도 환경적 스트레스의 징후를 보인다. 실험실이나 동물원의 동물들이 같은 종(種)의 특히 공격적인 개체 바로 옆에 있는 우리에 갇혀 있을 때, 그들은 종종 불안과 스트레스의 징후를 많이 보인다. 〈그들은 유리벽으로 분리되어 물리적인 접촉이 불가능하지만, 스트레스를 받은 동물들은 종종 심혈관 질환으로 조기에 죽는다.〉 많은 학생들이 시험 기간에 실감하듯이, 스트레스는 또한 전염병에 대한 취약성의 원인이 된다.

30 단락배열 ①

| 분석 |

주어진 문장에서 언급한 '화산 폭발로 파묻힌 시민'들에 대해 '그들의 시신으로 만든 석고 주형'을 이야기하고 있는 A가 가장 먼저 오고, 새로운 DNA 증거가 상황이 우리가 생각하는 것과 달랐음을 시사해준다는 D가 그 다음에, 그리고 D의 내용을 부연 설명하는 역할을 하는 C와 also가 있는 B가 그 뒤에 차례로 이어지는 것이 자연스러운 순서이다.

| 어휘 |

volcanic eruption 화산 분화, 화산 폭발 desperate a. 절망적인; 필사적인 preserve v. 보존하다 plaster cast 깁스 (붕대); 석고 주형 embrace v. 껴안다, 포옹하다 n. 포옹 assume v. 추측하다, 추정하다 unrelated a. 친족이 아닌 interpretation n. 해석

| 해석 |

화산 폭발로 인해 고대 도시 폼페이가 파묻혔을 때, 그 도시 시민들의 절박한 마지막 순간들이 수세기 동안 돌 속에 보존됐다.
A 관찰자들은 죽으면서 어머니가 아이를 안고 있다는 이야기와 두 여자가 죽으면서 포옹하고 있다는 이야기 같은 이야기들이 나중에 그들의 시신으로 만든 석고 주형들 속에 들어있는 것을 보고 있다.
D 하지만 새로운 DNA 증거는 상황이 지금 우리에게 여겨지는 그대로가 아니었음을 시사한다. 그리고 지금의 이러한 지배적인 해석들은 고대 세계를 현대인의 시각으로 바라보는 것에서 비롯된다.
C 독일의 한 연구팀은 어머니라고 생각되는 사람이 실제로는 아이의 친척이 아닌 남성이었다는 것을 알게 되었다.
B 그 연구팀은 또한 서로 포옹한 채로 꼭 붙어 있는 두 사람 — 오랫동안 자매들이거나 어머니와 딸인 것으로 추정되었음 — 중 적어도 한 명이 사실은 남성이었다는 것을 발견했다.

31 글의 흐름상 어색한 문장 고르기 ③

| 분석 |

글의 중반에서 '볼펜 뚜껑에 작은 구멍을 뚫은 이유 중의 하나는 안전을 위해서이다'라고 한 뒤에 안전과 관련된 내용이 이어지고 있는데, C는 잉크가 마르지 않기 위한 목적에 대한 내용이므로 글의 흐름상 적절하지 않다.

| 어휘 |

grocery n. 식료품류, 잡화류 penmanship n. 서법, 필법 manufacturer n. 제조업자, 생산자 chew v. 씹다 swallow v. 삼키다 accidentally ad. 우연히, 문득 on purpose 고의로, 의도적으로 stabilize v. 안정시키다 choking n. 숨막힘 obstruct v. 막다; 차단하다 inhale v. 빨아들이다, 흡입하다

| 해석 |

당신은 평생 동안 펜을 사용해오고 있다. — 시험을 보거나, 수표를 쓰거나, 장보기 목록을 만들 때 등에 말이다. 글을 쓰는 행동이 기억력과 필체를 향상시킨다는 것은 알고 있을지도 모르지만, 뚜껑 맨 위에 구멍이 있다는 사실을 비롯해서, 볼펜에 대해 아마 다른 것은 많이 생각하지 않았을 것이다. 그 구멍은 대체 무엇 때문에 있는 것일까? 실수인 것일까? 전혀 그렇지 않다. 펜 제조업체들이 펜 뚜껑에 그런 작은 구멍을 뚫은 이유 중의 하나는 안전을 위해서다. 만약 당신이 긴장하거나 지루해서 펜을 씹은 적이 있다면, 우연히 뚜껑을 삼킬 수도 있다는 것을 상상할 수 있을 것이다. 아니면 어린 아이들의 경우에는, 어쩌면 뚜껑을 의도적으로 삼킬 수도 있을 것이다. 〈그 구멍은 뚜껑 속에 있는 공기의 압력을 안정시켜 잉크가 마르지 않도록 하는 데 도움을 준다.〉 어느 쪽이든, 그 구멍은 질식을 방지하기 위해 있는 것이다. 일부 펜에서 뚜껑에 구멍이 있는 이유는 만약 흡입하더라도 뚜껑이 기도를 완전히 막지 않도록 하기 위함이다.

32 글의 흐름상 어색한 문장 고르기 ②

| 분석 |

본문은 동물 실험의, 비용, 시간, 동물에 가해지는 고통 측면에서의 문제점을 제시하고, 이를 개선하기 위한 대체 수단의 개발 상황과 그 한계 등에 대해 이야기하고 있는 글인데 반해, B는 독성 자체를

나타내는 방법에 대한 내용이므로 글의 흐름상 적절하지 않다.

| 어휘 |

toxicity n. 독성　**expose** v. (환경 따위에) 접하게 하다, 노출시키다　**dose** n. (약의) 1회분, (1회의) 복용량　**specific** a. 특정한; 일정한　**substance** n. 물질　**time-consuming** a. (많은) 시간이 걸리는　**debilitating** a. 쇠약하게 하는　**toxin** n. 독소　**culture** n. 재배, 배양　**substitute** n. 대용물　**occupational** a. 직업의

| 해석 |

가장 일반적으로 사용되면서 널리 받아들여지고 있는 독성 실험은 실험실에 있는 동물의 개체들을 통제된 조건 하에서 정확히 측정한 용량의 특정 물질에 노출시키는 것이다. 이 절차는 비용이 많이 들고, 시간이 오래 걸리며, 실험 대상 동물들을 종종 고통스럽게 하고 쇠약하게 만든다. 〈화학 물질의 독성을 나타내는 편리한 방법 중의 하나는 실험 집단의 50%가 반응하는 용량을 측정하는 것이다.〉 매우 적은 용량의 독소가 미치는 영향을 철저하게 실험하는 데는 흔히 수백 마리의 — 심지어는 수천 마리의 — 동물과 수년 동안의 고된 연구, 그리고 수십만 달러가 소요된다. 모델 반응에 대한 컴퓨터 시뮬레이션, 세포 배양, 그리고 모든 살아있는 동물을 대신하는 기타 대체물들을 이용하는 보다 인도적인 독성 실험이 개발되고 있다. 그러나 전통적인 대규모 동물 실험은 우리가 가장 신뢰하는 방법이며, 오염과 환경 또는 직업적인 건강상의 위험에 관한 공공 정책은 이 방법을 기반으로 하고 있다.

33　글의 흐름상 적절하지 않은 표현 고르기　②

| 분석 |

플라스틱 뚜껑의 높이가 짧을수록 잡거나 쥐는 면적은 더 작아질 것이므로, ②의 more는 less여야 한다. 이 경우, '그래서 최대한 힘주어 잡을 수 없고, 여는 데 애를 먹는다.'라는 문장과도 자연스럽게 이어진다.

| 어휘 |

beverage n. 음료　**carton** n. 큰 상자; (용기에 든 우유·담배 등의) 큰 판지[플라스틱] 상자　**grippable** a. 쥘 수 있는, 잡을 수 있는　**subtle** a. 미묘한　**carbon footprint** 탄소 발자국　**transition** v. 이행(移行)하다; 변천하다　**significant** a. 중대한; 의미 있는

| 해석 |

우유, 탄산음료, 물의 음료 용기는 최근 몇 년 동안 개봉하기가 더 어려워졌는데, 이는 플라스틱을 절약하기 위해 용기에 있는 나사형 플라스틱 뚜껑을 짧아지게 했기 때문이다. 예전 스타일의 우유 팩 뚜껑은 높이가 21밀리미터였던 반면, 새것은 17밀리미터이다. 높이가 더 짧을수록 잡을 수 있는 면적은 더 〈많아진다(→ 적어진다)〉. 그래서 최대한 힘주어 잡을 수 없고, 여는 데 애를 먹는다. 플라스틱 병을 열려고 할 때, 때때로 몸체가 뚜껑과 함께 비틀려버리는 경우도 있다.
이것은 매일 수백만 명의 미국인들이 열고 있는 제품에서 일어난 미묘한 변화로, 업계는 이를 플라스틱뿐만 아니라 무게도 절약하는 변화로 칭송하고 있다. 이 두 가지 모두는 운송에 필요한 에너지를 줄이고, 탄소 발자국을 낮추며, 포장재의 생산 비용을 낮추는 결과를 가져온다. 이는 사람들이 (용기 재료로서) 유리와 금속에서 플라스틱으로 이행(移行)한 이유들 중 하나이기도 한데, 플라스틱은 훨씬 더 가벼우며, 무게는 탄소 발자국에 기여하는 데 있어 매우 중요한 역할을 하기 때문이다.

34　글의 흐름상 적절하지 않은 표현 고르기　⑤

| 분석 |

온순한 경기에서는 선수들이 경기 중에 부상을 입을 가능성이 낮을 것이므로, ⑤의 likely는 unlikely여야 한다. 이래야 '나이가 들어서까지 컬링을 즐긴다'는 후속 내용과도 자연스럽게 연결된다.

| 어휘 |

similarity n. 유사점, 닮은 점　**curling** n. 〈스포츠〉 컬링　**consist of** ~로 구성되어 있다　**take turns** ~을 교대로 하다　**detailed** a. 상세한　**take ~ up** (특히 재미로) ~을 배우다[시작하다]

| 해석 |

바닥을 쓸어내는 것과 닮았다는 이유로 한때 유명하게도 '얼음 위의 집안일'로 묘사된 컬링은 오래된 스코틀랜드의 스포츠 경기다. 이 경기는 두 팀이 서로 겨뤄 얼음길을 따라 10개의 돌을 움직여서 가능한 한 홈 서클에 가깝게 놓는 방식으로 진행된다. 팀들은 얼음판을 따라 번갈아 돌을 던지며, 선수들은 돌 앞의 얼음을 쓸어서 더 매끄럽게 만든다. 가장 많은 돌을 홈에 가장 가깝게 둔 팀이 경기에서 승리한다. 대부분의 사람들이 컬링에 대해 들어본 적은 있지만, 이 경기에 대해 자세하게 알고 있는 사람들은 많지 않다. 2002년 동계올림픽에서 (스코틀랜드 선수들로 구성된) 영국 여자대표팀은 큰 성공을 거두면서 금메달을 스코틀랜드로 가져왔다. 많은 사람들은 컬링이 그렇게 흥미진진한 경기인 줄 몰랐다면서 놀라워했고, 다음 동계올림픽을 기대하게 되었다. 컬링은 또한 매우 온순한 경기이며, 그래서 선수들이 경기 중에 부상을 입을 가능성이 〈높다(→ 낮다)〉. 많은 사람들이 대개 어릴 때 컬링을 배워 70~80대가 될 때까지 계속 경기를 즐긴다.

35~36

미국의 원로 뉴스 해설가 H. V. Kaltenborn이 하버드 대학교의 학생이었을 때, 그는 한 연설 대회에 참가했다. 그는 "Gentlemen, the King"이라는 제목의 단편 소설을 선택했다. 그는 그 소설을 한 글자도 빼먹지 않고 또박또박 암기하고서는 수백 번 예행연습을 했다. 대회 당일에 그는 "Gentlemen, the King"이라는 제목을 큰 소리로 알렸다. 그러고 나자, 그의 머릿속이 텅 비어졌다. 텅 비어졌을 뿐 아니라, 완전히 새까매졌다. 그는 공포에 휩싸였다. 절박한

심정으로, 그는 이야기를 자신의 말로 풀어 나가기 시작했다. 심사위원들이 그에게 1등상을 주었을 때, 홀에서 가장 놀란 학생은 바로 그였다. 〈그날부터 지금까지, H. V. Kaltenborn은 한 번도 연설을 읽거나 암기한 적이 없었다.〉 그것이 그가 방송 커리어에서 성공할 수 있었던 비결이다. 그는 몇 마디 메모만 준비하고, 대본 없이 자연스럽게 청중에게 말한다.

이야기를 써서 암기하는 사람은 자신의 시간과 에너지를 낭비하고 있으며 화를 자초하고 있다. 우리는 평생 별로 의식하지 않고 말을 해오고 있다. 우리는 단어를 생각해온 것이 아니라 아이디어를 생각해왔다. 만약 우리의 아이디어가 명확하다면, 단어는 우리가 숨을 쉬는 것처럼 자연스럽고 무의식적으로 나오기 마련이다.

| 어휘 |

dean n. 학장; (단체의) 최고참자; 원로 **commentator** n. (시사) 해설자 **entitle** v. ~에 제목을 붙이다 **memorize** v. 암기하다 **rehearse** v. 연습하여 익혀두다; 예행연습을 하다 **go blank** 머리가 멍해지다[텅 비어지다] **go black** 눈앞이 캄캄해지다 **terrify** v. 겁나게 하다 **desperation** n. 절망, 자포자기 **script** n. 원고, 대본 **court** v. 구혼하다; (화를) 자초하다 **spontaneously** ad. 자발적으로, 무의식적으로

35 문장삽입 ⑤

| 분석 |

주어진 문장은 "그날부터 지금까지, H. V. Kaltenborn은 한 번도 연설을 읽거나 암기한 적이 없었다."라는 의미이므로, 연설을 준비하지 않게 된 계기에 대한 내용 뒤에 와야 한다. 따라서 연설 대회에 나서서 준비한 내용이 생각나지 않자 즉흥적으로 이야기를 풀어낸 후에 1등상을 받은 경험에 대한 내용 다음인 E에 들어가는 것이 가장 적절하다.

36 글의 요지 ③

| 분석 |

본문은 H. V. Kaltenborn의 경험을 통해 암기한 연설의 부정적인 측면과 즉흥적인 연설의 중요성을 강조하고 있다. 그는 연설을 완전히 암기했지만, 실제로 무대에 올랐을 때는 머릿속이 텅 비어지는 경험을 했고, 결국 즉흥적으로 생각하는 바를 전달하여 성공을 거뒀다. 암기하여 말하는 것은 시간과 에너지를 낭비하고 실패를 부를 뿐이라는 내용과 아이디어가 명확하면 말은 자연스럽게 따라온다는 내용도 같은 맥락에서 암기하여 하는 말의 비효율성을 이야기하고 있는 것이다. 따라서 ③이 정답이다.

위 글의 필자가 말하고자 하는 바는 무엇인가?
① 간결함이 연설에서 성공하는 비결이다.
② 인상적인 연설가가 되려면 책을 많이 읽어라.
③ 암기한 이야기를 전달하려고 하지 마라.
④ 준비된 연설가만이 최고가 될 자격이 있다.
⑤ 연설을 하기 위해서는 자신감을 기르는 것이 중요하다.

37~38

아일린 그레이(Eileen Gray)는 1920년대 파리 상류사회와 패션의 중심에 있던 매우 매력적인 인물이었다. 그녀는 당시 고급의상실의 디자이너였던 포와레(Poiret)와 랑방(Lanvin)이 디자인한 우아한 옷을 입었으며, 파블로 피카소(Pablo Picasso)에서 프리다 칼로(Frida Kahlo)와 제임스 조이스(James Joyce)에 이르는 당대의 저명인사 여러 명을 만났다. 아일랜드의 부유한 가정에서 태어난 그녀는 모험심과 독립심이 강한 사람이었으며, 20살에 런던의 자유분방한 슬레이드(Slade) 미술학교에 입학했다. 〈그곳에서 그녀는 파리로 이주했으며, 이후 평생을 프랑스에서 살면서 파리와 코트다쥐르를 오가며 시간을 보냈다.〉 그녀는 창의적인 유명인사들과 교류하였으며, 파리에서 운전면허를 취득한 최초의 여성이었으며, 이후에는 비행기 조종 교습도 받았다. 그러나 그레이에 대해 가장 놀라운 점은 그녀의 재능이었다. 그녀는 통찰력을 갖춘 혁신적인 디자이너였으며, 당시에 전적으로 남성이 지배하고 있던 건축과 디자인 분야에서 여성으로서는 유일무이하게 성공을 거두었다. 원래 아르데코(Art Deco) 스타일의 선도자였던 그녀는 1920년대 중반부터 건축가가 되었고, 모더니즘의 열렬한 지지자가 되었다. 그녀의 업적은 수십 년 동안 철저히 외면 받았다. 그녀는 1970년대에 재조명되었으며, 이후 그녀의 작품은 널리 찬사를 받았다. 그녀의 작품은 매우 인기가 많으며, 2009년 파리에서 열린 경매에서는 그녀의 Dragons armchair가 2,830만 달러에 판매되어 20세기 장식미술 작품 중 최고가 기록을 세웠다.

| 어휘 |

fabulously ad. 믿어지지 않을 만큼, 엄청나게 **glamorous** a. 매혹적인 **elegantly** ad. 품위 있게; 우아하게 **haute-couture** n. 오트 쿠튀르(파리에서 최신 유행의 숙녀복을 만들어 내는 고급 의상점; 그 디자이너); 고급 패션 **well-to-do** a. 유복한 **enroll** v. 등록하다; 입학하다 **notable** a. 저명한, 유명한 **extraordinary** a. 대단한, 비범한 **visionary** a. 통찰력[선견지명] 있는 **male-dominated** a. 남성 주도형[우위]의 **architecture** n. 건축술, 건축양식 **purveyor** n. 조달자, 납품업자; (정보 등을) 퍼뜨리는 사람; 언제나 어떤 느낌을[분위기를] 주는 사람[물건] **Art Deco** 아르 데코 양식(직선과 곡선의 규칙적이고 대칭적인 형태와 원색을 통해 강렬한 느낌을 주는 간결미가 특징인 예술 양식) **keen** a. 강렬한; 열심인 **advocate** n. 옹호자 **overlook** v. 못보고 넘기다, 빠뜨리다, 간과하다 **acclaim** v. 갈채를 보내다 **sought after** 많은 사람들이 원하는, 수요가 많은; 인기 있는 **auction** n. 경매

37 문장삽입 ③

| 분석 |
주어진 문장은 "그곳에서 그녀는 파리로 이주했으며, 이후 평생을 프랑스에서 살면서 파리와 코트다쥐르를 오가며 시간을 보냈다."라는 의미이므로, 프랑스 이외의 곳에서의 활동이나 생활을 언급한 부분 뒤에 와야 한다. 그러므로 그녀가 20살에 런던의 슬레이드(Slade) 미술학교에 입학했음을 이야기한 문장 다음인 ⓒ에 들어가는 것이 적절하다.

38 내용파악 ①

| 분석 |
'그녀는 창의적인 유명인사들과 교류하였다'라고 돼 있으므로 ①이 정답이다. ② 부유한 가정에서 태어났다. ③ 파리에서 최초로 자동차 면허를 취득한 여성이었다. ④ 파리로 이주한 후에는 평생을 프랑스에서 살면서 파리와 코트다쥐르를 오가며 시간을 보냈다. ⑤ 1970년대 이전에는 철저히 외면당했고 1970년대에 재조명되어 이후에 그녀의 작품이 널리 찬사를 받았다.

아일린 그레이에 관해 언급되거나 암시되지 <u>않은</u> 것은?
① 그녀는 당시의 유명인사들과 관계를 가졌다.
② 그녀의 부모는 부자가 아니었지만, 그녀는 인생에서 성공하려고 노력했다.
③ 그녀는 파리에서 비행조종사 면허를 딴 최초의 여성이었다.
④ 그녀는 아일랜드에서 태어나 프랑스에서 살고 런던에서 죽었다.
⑤ 그녀의 작품은 1970년대 이전에 대중들의 높은 평가를 받게 되었다.

39~40

미국 전역에서, 기업, 주(州), 심지어 학교까지도 직원들이 더 건강한 생활 습관을 기르는 것을 돕는 데 관심을 가져가고 있다. 기업들은 보건 관리자가 말하는 비만과 당뇨병 같은 체중 관련 질병의 환자가 급증하고 있다는 사태에 맞서 싸우기 위한 다양한 프로그램을 설계하고 있다. 미국 보건복지부의 추정치에 따르면, 과체중으로 인해 2000년에 약 1,170억 달러의 비용이 발생했고, 연간 약 30만 명의 근로자가 사망한 것으로 추정됐다. 그 결과, 기업들은 직장에 몇 가지 변화를 도입하기로 결정했다. 예를 들어, 캔자스시티에 위치한 스프린트(Sprint)의 새로운 본사에서는 몇몇 직원들이 엘리베이터가 유난히 느리게 움직이는 것 같다는 점을 눈치 챘다. 한 직원은 "우리가 보기에 회사는 우리에게 계단을 이용하도록 하고 싶어 합니다."라고 말했다. 사실, 그 직원이 옳았다. 그들은 속도가 더 느림에도 불구하고 수압식 엘리베이터를 사용했으며, 사람들이 층간 이동 시 엘리베이터를 타기보다는 걸어서 가도록 유도하기 위해 계단을 따라 창문을 설치했다. 또한, 스프린트는 200에이커에 달하는 본사를 건강을 고려하여 설계했다. 본사 주변에는 자동차를 주차할 수 없으며, 직원들은 본사에서 멀리 떨어진 주차장에 차를 세워야 한다. 이렇게 함으로써 직원들은 매일 약 반 마일을 걷게 된다.

| 어휘 |
diabetes n. 당뇨병　**estimate** n. 평가, 견적 v. 어림잡다, 견적하다
expense n. 지출, 비용　**approximately** ad. 대략　**headquarters** n. 본부, 본사　**employee** n. 직원　**hydraulic** a. 수력의, 수압의
fitness n. 건강, 체력　**park** v. 주차하다

39 글의 제목 ②

| 분석 |
본문은 미국의 기업, 주, 학교가 직원들의 건강한 습관 형성을 돕기 위해 노력하고 있음을 이야기하고 있다. 특히, 기업들이 비만과 체중 관련 질병의 증가를 문제로 인식하고 건강증진 프로그램을 도입 중임을 언급하면서, 그 예로서 스프린트 사의 노력을 이야기하고 있다. 그러므로 제목으로는 ②가 적절하다.

다음 중 위 글의 제목으로 가장 적절한 것은?
① 계단을 이용하는 것의 이점
② 직원들의 건강을 증진하기 위한 방법들
③ 직장에서 에너지를 절약하는 요령
④ 비용 상승을 야기하는 당뇨병 증가!
⑤ 체중 관련 질병을 초래하는 나쁜 습관

40 빈칸완성 ③

| 분석 |
빈칸 Ⓐ의 경우, 전후 문장이 '과체중으로 인해 막대한 비용과 사망자가 발생하고 있는 까닭에 기업들이 직장 환경에 변화를 도입했다'라는 원인과 결과의 관계이므로, 빈칸에는 Therefore가 적절하다. 빈칸 Ⓑ의 경우, 직원들이 엘리베이터가 느리다고 생각하며, '회사가 계단을 이용하도록 유도하려는 것 같다'고 한 뒤에 빈칸 뒤에서 '그 직원이 옳았다.'라고 이어지므로, 앞에서의 추측이 사실임을 확인해주는 In fact가 적절하다. In fact는 앞의 내용을 보충 설명해주거나, 좀 더 구체적인 내용이 이어지는 경우에 사용한다. 따라서 ③이 정답이다.

중앙대학교 인문계 A형

TEST p. 560~578

01	④	02	④	03	③	04	④	05	①	06	①	07	②	08	③	09	③	10	③
11	②	12	②	13	④	14	④	15	②	16	①	17	④	18	①	19	④	20	③
21	①	22	②	23	④	24	③	25	①	26	②	27	③	28	②	29	②	30	③
31	①	32	④	33	①	34	②	35	③	36	③	37	①	38	③	39	②	40	②

01 동의어 ④

| 어휘 |

waylay v. (이야기를 하기 위해 길 가는 사람을) 불러 세우다, (어디에 가지 못하게) 붙들다(= detain)　**fool** v. 속이다, 기만하다　**persuade** v. 설득하다　**respect** v. 존경하다

| 해석 |

5시 15분쯤 되었을 때, 나는 집에 가서 차를 마시고, 그를 붙들기 위해 역으로 걸어갔다.

02 동의어 ④

| 어휘 |

triumph n. 승리　**solidity** n. 견고함　**marble** n. 대리석　**diaphanous** a. 아주 얇은, 속이 비치는(= filmy)　**rickety** a. (제대로 만들어지지 않아) 곧 무너질[부서질] 듯한　**earthly** a. 이 세상의, 이승의, 속세의　**girthy** a. 두툼한, 두터운, 뚱뚱한

| 해석 |

그것은 단순히 투명함이 대리석의 차가움과 단단함을 이겨낸 승리였다.

03 동의어 ③

| 어휘 |

impugn v. (남의 행동·의견·성실성 등에) 이의[의문]를 제기하다　**overweening** a. 자만에 찬, 우쭐대는(= presumptuous)　**accuse** v. 비난하다　**mainstream** n. (사상·견해 등의) 주류[대세]　**fascism** n. 파시즘, 독재적 국가 사회주의　**preludious** a. 서두의, 서막의　**strenuous** a. 힘이 많이 드는, 몹시 힘든　**stupendous** a. 엄청나게 큰, 거대한

| 해석 |

오만한 국가에 이의를 제기하고, 주류 정치인들을 의료 파시즘으로 비난하는 이러한 시도들이 효과가 있을까?

04 동의어 ④

| 어휘 |

wheedle v. (듣기 좋은 말로) 구슬리다, 꾀다(= inveigle)　**maraud** v. 약탈[습격]하다　**fabricate** v. (거짓 정보를) 날조하다[조작하다]　**engulf** v. 완전히 에워싸다, 휩싸다

| 해석 |

그 아이는 엄마를 구슬려 쿠키를 얻어내려고 했다.

05 동의어 ①

| 어휘 |

boorish a. 상스러운, 천박한(= coarse)　**warrant** v. 정당[타당]하게 만들다　**bonny** a. 어여쁜, 아리따운　**suave** a. 정중한, 상냥한　**demotic** a. 일반 보통 사람들의

| 해석 |

당신이 다른 차 운전자에게 한 무례한 발언은 상황에 의해 정당화될 수 없었다.

06 동의어 ①

| 어휘 |

insouciant a. 무관심한, 태평한(= indifferent)　**gravity** n. 심각성, 중대성　**irresistible** a. 억누를[저항할] 수 없는　**incontinent** a. 자제[억제]할 수 없는　**irrefragable** a. 논쟁의 여지가 없는, 논박할 수 없는

| 해석 |

당신의 무관심한 태도는 당신이 상황의 심각성을 이해하지 못하고 있다는 것을 보여준다.

07 동의어 ②

| 어휘 |

spoliation n. (어음·유서 등의) 문서 변조[파기, 훼손](= pillaging) **slander** n. 모략, 중상, 비방; (말로 하는) 명예 훼손죄 **quagmire** n. 수렁, 진창 **underpinning** n. 지주(支柱) (벽 등의), 받침대

| 해석 |

그 변호사는 증거 훼손이 사건에 피해를 주었다고 주장했다.

08 생활영어 ③

| 분석 |

keep a high profile은 보통 '눈에 띄려고 하다'를 의미하는데, ③에서 마이클이 조용한 이유를 설명하는 문맥에서는 keep a low profile 즉 "두드러지지 않다, (눈에 띄지 않으려고) 저자세를 취하다"가 되어야 적절해진다.

| 어휘 |

throw a monkey wrench in[into] something (남의 계획을) 망쳐 놓다 **pave the way (for somebody[something])** (~을 위한) 길을 닦다[상황을 조성하다] **keep a high profile** (눈에 띄고 싶어) 주변의 이목을 끌다, 두드러져 보이다 **too big for your britches** 거만한, 너무 자신을 높게 평가하는(= too big for your breeches) **make up** (특히 남을 속이거나 즐겁게 하기 위해 이야기 등을) 지어[만들어] 내다 **know one's place** 제 분수[주제]를 알다[지키다], 겸손히 굴다

| 해석 |

① A: 더 이상 기다릴 수 없어. 저 사람에게 무슨 일이 일어나고 있는지 알아봐달라고 말해야겠어.
　 B: 좀 참을 수 없어? 일을 망치지 마.
② A: 나는 개척자들을 존경해.
　 B: 당연한 일이야. 그분들이 오늘날 우리를 위한 길을 닦는 데 도움을 주셨어.
③ A: 왜 마이클은 회의에서 말이 없지? 항상 너무 조용해.
　 B: 아마도 그냥 눈에 띄려고 하는 걸 거야. 그는 언제 문제를 피해야 하는지 잘 알아.
④ A: 넌 예전부터 항상 잘난 척이 심했어!
　 B: 지어내지 마! 난 언제나 내 분수를 알고 있었어!

09 생활영어 ③

| 분석 |

③에서 A의 말은 마크가 상사와 관계를 회복하려 한다는 의미인데, B의 응답은 마크가 위선적이거나 거짓말을 잘한다는 의미로 해석될 수 있어서 대화의 흐름이 매끄럽지 않다. talk out of both sides of one's mouth는 이중적인 태도를 보이거나, 상황에 따라 다른 말을 하는 것을 뜻한다.

| 어휘 |

put all one's eggs in one basket 한 사업에 전 재산을 걸다, 한 시도에 모든 것을 걸다 **startup** n. 신규 업체(특히 인터넷 기업) **in deep water(s)** 곤경에 처하다[궁지에 빠진] **push the envelope** 한계를 초월하다 **bite off more than one can chew** 분에 넘치는(힘에 겨운) 일을 하려고 하다 **smooth something over** (문제 등을, 특히 사람들과 이야기를 하여) 바로잡다[수습하다] **talk out of both sides of one's mouth** 모순된 말을 하다 **put somebody on the spot** (곤란한 질문으로) ~를 곤혹스럽게 만들다 **air one's dirty laundry in public** 누군가의 비밀을 대중에게 공개하다

| 해석 |

① A: 톰이 그 신생 기업에 모든 자산을 다 걸고 있다던데.
　 B: 응, 잘 안되면 큰 곤경에 처할 수도 있어.
② A: 리사는 새로운 프로젝트에서 정말 자신의 한계를 넘어서고 있어.
　 B: 알고 있어. 난 그녀가 감당할 수 없을 정도로 무리하지 않길 바라.
③ A: 마크는 곧 상사와의 문제를 잘 수습할 수 있을 거라고 생각하고 있어.
　 B: 맞아, 그는 항상 모순된 말을 하지.
④ A: 있잖아, 너 어젯밤에 그를 정말 곤란하게 만들었어.
　 B: 나도 알아. 남들 앞에서 까발리기보다는 우리끼리만 얘기했어야 했어.

10 병치 구조 ③

| 분석 |

stimulating은 형용사인데 반해, rest는 명사이다. 동사 seem의 보어로 stimulating과 같은 형용사를 병치해야 하므로, ③을 restful로 바꾸어야 한다.

| 어휘 |

acculturation n. 문화적 적응, 사회화 **primary color** 원색(빨강·노랑·파랑 중의 하나) **restful** a. (마음이) 편안한, 평화로운, 평온한 **respectively** a. 각자, 각각, 제각기

| 해석 |

원색인 빨강과 파랑이 대부분의 우리에게 각각 자극적이고 편안하게 여겨질 것이지만, 우리의 반응은 어느 정도 문화 적응에 따라 달라지는 것 같을 것이다.

11 neither A nor B but C ②

| 분석 |

'A가 아니라 B이다'는 의미는 'not A but B', 'A도 아니고, B도 아니다'는 의미는 'neither A nor B' 형태를 쓴다. 이 둘의 형태를 결합한 'neither A nor B but C'는 'A도 아니고 B도 아닌, C이다'는 의미를 전달할 수 있다. 따라서 ②를 but으로 바꾸어야 한다.

| 어휘 |

empathy n. 감정이입, 공감 compassion n. 연민, 동정심 patch n. (특히 주변과는 다른 조그만) 부분 cortex n. (특히 대뇌) 피질(皮質) subcortical a. 피질 하부의 plumbing n. 배관

| 해석 |

사실, 연민이라는 의미에서 공감에 가장 가까운 뇌 조직은 피질 부위도 아니고 피질 하부의 기관도 아닌, 호르몬 배관 시스템이다.

12 과거분사와 현재분사의 비교 ②

| 분석 |

'~을 본떠서 만들어진'이라는 의미이므로 수동의 의미를 전달하는 과거분사가 사용되어야 하므로, ②의 modelling을 modelled로 바꾸어야 한다.

| 어휘 |

composer n. 작곡가 cultivate v. (예술·학술 등을) 장려하다, ~의 발달에 노력하다; (문학·기예를) 닦다, 연마하다 contrapuntal a. 대위법(두 개 이상의 독립적인 선율을 동시에 결합하여 조화로운 음악을 만드는 작곡 기법)의 Palestrina n. 이탈리아의 교회 음악 작곡가 (Giovanni Palestrina) alongside prep. ~옆에, 나란히; ~와 함께 concerted a. 합주용으로 편곡된 basso continuo 통주저음(通奏低音: 반주용 악기가 연주하는 부분), 바소 콘티누오

| 해석 |

17세기 후반의 이탈리아 교회 작곡가들은 팔레스트리나를 본떠서 만들어진 오래된 대위법 양식과 통주저음과 독주 가수를 특징으로 하는 새로운 협주곡 양식을 계속해서 발전시켰으며, 때로는 같은 작품에서 두 가지를 혼합하기도 했다.

13 논리완성 ④

| 분석 |

세계 무역 기구의 개입(중재)까지 예상되는 상황으로 치달았다면, 최대의 무역 파트너인 두 나라는 이미 서로 상대에게 일제 사격을 가하듯이 여러 조치들을 취했을 것이므로 빈칸에는 '일제 사격'을 뜻하는 salvos가 적절하다.

| 어휘 |

WTO 세계 무역 기구(World Trade Organization) salvo n. 일제 사격[투하], 기습 공격 positive a. 분명한, 결정적인 kudos n. 명성, 영예; 칭찬 salve n. (상처 등에 바르는) 연고

| 해석 |

최대의 두 무역 파트너 국가들이 제한적인 무역 조치의 일제 사격을 주고받는 것을 WTO가 막을 수는 없겠지만, 언젠가는 적극적인 WTO 개입이 일어날 수도 있다.

14 논리완성 ④

| 분석 |

'날씨가 흐릴 때조차도'와 병렬적인 의미로, 빛이 약하거나 흐릿할 때를 나타내는 표현이 들어가야 한다. flat은 '김빠진, 맥 빠진', '생기가 없는', '두드러지지 않은' 등의 의미로 아주 폭넓게 활용되는 어휘이다. 'the light is flat'이라고 하면, 빛이 약하거나 고르지 못하여 입체감이나 생동감이 없는 상태로, 흐린 날씨나 빛이 강하지 않고 대비가 낮아 피사체가 선명하게 보이지 않는 상태를 묘사하기에 적합하다. thick은 주로 안개나 구름 등을 묘사할 때 '짙은'의 뜻으로 사용된다.

| 어휘 |

flat a. 밋밋한, 맥 빠진, 두드러지지 않은 splendid a. 정말 좋은[멋진], 훌륭한 photo opportunity (미리 준비해서 하는) 사진 촬영(= photo op.) radiant a. (따스하고 밝게) 빛나는 vivid a. 생생한, 선명한

| 해석 |

날씨가 흐린 때나 하루 중 그런 때여서 빛이 두드러지지 않은 때에도, 경치는 여전히 훌륭하고, 사진 촬영도 훌륭하다.

15 논리완성 ②

| 분석 |

'다양한 동물이 보여주는 생동감 넘치는 에너지와 다채로움이 느껴진다'는 표현을 통해 무희의 춤이 표현하는 생동감을 야생 동물 또는 그들을 모아 놓은 '동물원(menagerie)'에 비유하고 있음을 추론할 수 있다.

| 어휘 |

menagerie n. (이동) 동물원; (동물 쇼 등을 위해 모아 놓은) 야생 동물들 vibrant a. 활기찬, 생기가 넘치는 netherworld n. 지하 세계, 하계(下界), 명부, 지옥 torpor n. 무기력, 무감각 rebus n. 그림, 글자, 숫자, 기호 등을 조합한 수수께끼

| 해석 |

그녀의 무용 공연은 마치 남아프리카의 동물원에 발을 들여놓은 것 같은 느낌이 들었으며, 다양한 동물이 보여주는 생동감 넘치는 에너지와 다채로움으로 가득 차 있었다.

16 논리완성 ①

| 분석 |

현재의 업무도 엄청나다면, 추가적인 책임을 맡아달라는 요청에 대해서는 '거부하거나', '이의를 제기하는' 것이 자연스러운 반응이라고 추론할 수 있다.

| 어휘 |

demur v. 이의를 제기하다, 반대하다 cite v. (이유·예를) 들다[끌어대다] overwhelming a. 압도적인, 너무도 엄청난 workload

n. 업무량, 작업량 **jubilate** v. 환희하다, 환호하다 **thaw** v. (얼음이) 녹다; (태도가) 누그러지다 **irrupt** v. 불쑥 끼어들다[나타나다], 침입[난입]하다

| 해석 |
그녀는 직장에서 추가적인 책임을 맡아 달라는 요청을 받았을 때, 현재 엄청난 업무량을 이유로 들면서, 이의를 제기하기로 마음먹었다.

17 논리완성 ④

| 분석 |
'만지고 쥐는 것'은 촉각적인(tactile) 경험에 해당한다.

| 어휘 |
tend v. 돌보다, 보살피다 **tactile** a. 촉각[촉감]의, 촉각을 이용한 **bond** n. 유대감 **osphretic** a. 후각(嗅覺)의 **gustatory** a. 맛의, 미각의 **auricular** a. 귀의, 청각의

| 해석 |
유아의 촉각적 자극, 즉 만지고 쥐는 것에 대한 요구를 보살펴주는 것은 신체적 안전, 따스함, 음식에 대한 요구를 보살피는 것만큼 유대감을 형성하는 데 중요하다.

18 논리완성 ①

| 분석 |
'그를 믿었던 모든 사람의 신뢰를 저버리다'는 표현을 통해 그의 행동이 '배신적인(perfidious)' 것이었음을 추론할 수 있다.

| 어휘 |
perfidious a. 배반[배신]의, 믿을[신뢰할] 수 없는 **scar** n. 흉터, 상흔 **preemptive** a. 선제적인, 예방적인 **perfunctory** a. 형식적인, 겉치레의 **preliminary** a. 예비적인

| 해석 |
그의 배신적인 행동은 그를 믿었던 모든 사람의 신뢰를 저버렸고, 팀에 깊은 상처를 남겼으며, 누군가 그를 용서하거나 그를 신뢰하는 것을 어렵게 만들었다.

19 논리완성 ④

| 분석 |
'일몰의 아름다움이 금방 사라졌다', '생생한 색깔에 대한 덧없는 기억' 등의 표현을 통해 일몰의 아름다움이 오래 머무르지 않고 금방 사라졌음을 알 수 있다. 따라서 '덧없는, 순식간에 사라지는, 무상한(fugacious)'이 빈칸에 적절함을 추론할 수 있다.

| 어휘 |
sunset n. 일몰, 석양 **fugacious** a. 손에 잡히지 않는, 붙잡기 어려운; 꺼지기 쉬운; 허무한, 덧없는 **vanish** v. 사라지다 **appreciate** v. 감상하다 **fleeting** a. 순식간의, 잠깐 동안의 **vibrant** a. 강렬한, 선명한 **forthcoming** a. 다가오는, 임박한 **flippant** a. 경박한, 경솔한 **fulminating** a. 맹렬히 비난하는; 폭발하는

| 해석 |
일몰의 아름다움은 너무나 덧없어서 누군가 제대로 감상할 수 있기도 전에 사라져 버렸고, 생생한 색깔에 대한 잠깐의 기억만 남겼다.

20 논리완성 ③

| 분석 |
'대중적 이미지가 돌이킬 수 없는 피해를 입었다'고 하였으므로 명예(평판)가 '훼손되었다'고 추론할 수 있다.

| 어휘 |
reputation n. 평판, 명성 **besmirch** v. 더럽히다, 훼손하다 **false accusation** 근거 없는 비난, 무고 **irreversible** a. (이전 상태로) 되돌릴[철회할] 수 없는 **beguile** v. 속이다, 현혹시키다 **bequeath** v. 물려주다, 유증(遺贈)하다 **berate** v. 질책하다, 꾸짖다

| 해석 |
그 정치인의 평판은 거짓된 비난으로 인해 훼손되었고, 그 거짓 비난은 빠르게 확산되어 그의 대중적 이미지에 돌이킬 수 없는 피해를 입혔다.

21 논리완성 ①

| 분석 |
첫 번째 빈칸의 경우, 미적 취향의 사람에 대한 설명인데 and 앞에서 후천적인 지식 습득을 언급했으므로 빈칸에는 선천적인 취향, 즉 미적으로 품격 있는 것을 추구하는 성향을 가진 사람이라고 하여 '성향(inclination)'이 적절하고, 두 번째 빈칸의 경우, 빈칸 다음에서 장작의 한곳에만 불 피우고 다른 곳은 차갑다고 했으므로 빈칸에는 '국부적인, 국소적인(local)'이 적절하고, 세 번째 빈칸의 경우, 앞에서 정신과 육신의 관계를 설명하는데, 사유와 자유 의지는 정신에 해당하므로 빈칸에는 육신에 해당하는 '물질적인/신체적인(material)'이 적절하다.

| 어휘 |
esteemed a. 존중받는, 존경받는, 호평받는 **umpire** n. 심판 **taste** n. 심미안, 감식력; (한 시대·개인의) 미적 관념[가치관], 취향 **admire** v. 존경하다; 찬탄하다 **elegant** a. 우아한; 품격 있는 **inclination** n. (특히 정신적인) 경향, 기질, 성향, 기호(嗜好), 좋아하는 것 **fair** a. 어여쁜, 아름다운 **sensual** a. (특히 육체적인 쾌락과 관련하여) 감각적인; 관능적인 **cultivation** n. 세련, 우아 **local** a. 국부의, 국부적인; (생각 등이) 좁은, 편협한 **(the) fine arts** 순수 예술; 미술 **particular** n. 자세한 사실[사항] **shallowness** n. 천박함, 피상적임 **doctrine**

n. 신조, 주의 **instant** a. 절박한, 긴급한 **about** ad. 이리저리 **adjustment** n. 수정, 조정; 적응 **much less** 하물며[더구나] ~은 아니다 **germination** n. 성장[발달] 시작, (종자 따위의) 발아 **in regard to** ~에 관해서 **volition** n. 자유 의지 **inspiration** n. 영감 **permanent** a. 영구적인 **mundane** a. 재미없는, 일상적인; 이승의, 현세의 **penetrating** a. 마음속을 꿰뚫어 보는 듯한, 날카로운 **celestial** a. 하늘의, 천상의 **affection** n. 애착; 애정 **clumsy** a. 어설픈, 서투른 **eternal** a. 영원한

| 해석 |

미적 취향의 존경받는 심판자인 사람들은 흔히 감탄 받는 그림이나 조각에 대한 지식을 어느 정도 습득하고, 품격 있는 것에 대한 기호(嗜好)를 지닌 이들이다. 그러나 그들이 과연 '아름다운 영혼'인지, 그리고 그들 자신의 행위가 아름다운 그림처럼 고운 것인지 묻는다면, 그들은 이기적이고 육감적인 사람이라는 것을 알게 된다. 그들의 우아함은 국소적이다. 마치 마른 장작의 한곳만 문질러 불을 피우려 하는 것처럼, 나머지는 여전히 차갑게 남아 있다. 그들이 미술에 대해 아는 것은 규칙이나 세부 사항에 대한 약간의 연구이거나, 색이나 형태에 대한 제한된 판단으로서, 오락이나 과시를 위한 것일 뿐이다. 형태가 영혼에 절실히 의존한다는 인식을 사람들이 상실한 것 같다는 것은, 애호가들의 마음에 존재하는 미(美)에 대한 개념이 얼마나 피상적인지를 보여주는 증거이다. 우리 철학에는 형태에 대해 이렇다 할 주의(主義)가 없다. 마치 화기(火氣)가 냄비에 담겨 이리저리 옮겨지듯, 우리는 우리 육신 안으로 정신이 들어온 존재들이다. 그러나 정신과 육신 간에 정밀한 조율은 없고, 하물며 육신이 정신의 발아인 것은 더욱 아니다. 다른 형태에 관해서도 마찬가지이다. 지적인 사람들은 물질세계가 사유와 자유의지에 본질적으로 의존하고 있다고 믿지 않는다.

22 논리완성 ②

| 분석 |

빈칸 다음에 있는 대시(—)는 앞의 진술을 부연 설명하는 역할을 하고 있다. 노화는 '극적인 반전 없이 냉혹하게 멈추지 않고 진행되는' 과정이라고 하였으므로 빈칸에는 '직선적인, 선형적인(linear)'이 적절하다.

| 어휘 |

capture v. (사진이나 글로 감정·분위기 등을) 정확히 포착하다 **let alone** ~커녕[~은 고사하고] **compelling** a. 설득력 있는, 강력한 **narrative** n. 묘사, 서술, 이야기 **infinitesimally** ad. 무한소(無限小)로, 극미량으로 **incremental** a. 증대하는, 증가의 **subtraction** n. 뺄셈; 삭감, 공제 **grindingly** ad. 쿡쿡 쑤셔; 삐걱거리며 **linear** a. (일련의 여러 단계가) 직선 모양의 **inexorable** a. 멈출[변경할] 수 없는, 거침없는 **arc** n. 호, 원호; 둥근[활] 모양 **conversely** ad. 정반대로, 역으로 **bafflingly** ad. 당황스럽게, 걷잡을 수 없게 **creaky** a. 삐걱거리는; 낡은, 제 기능을 못하는 **sprightly** a. 정정한, 활기 넘치는, 팔팔한 **temporarily** ad. 일시적으로 **fickle** a. 변덕스러운, 변화가 심한 **isomorphic** a. 같은 모양의, 동일 구조의

| 해석 |

노화에 대한 주관적인 경험은 특히 포착하기 어렵다. 캐슬린 우드워드가 "점진적으로 아주 조금씩 힘이 빠져나가는 과정"이라고 묘사한 것(노화)에 설득력 있는 서사 구조를 부여하는 것은 고사하고, 이를 표현하는 것조차 어렵다. 이런 의미에서 노화는 삐걱거리며 진행되는 선형적 과정, 즉 극적인 반전 없이 냉혹하게 진행되는 과정이다. 하지만 반대로, 노화는 당혹스러울 정도로 예측 불가능하게 복잡하기도 하다. 어떤 날은 삐걱거린다고 느끼다가도, 다음 날은 활기차게 느껴질 수도 있다. 마흔에 늙었다고 느낄 수도 있고, 반대로 일흔이 되어도 — 적어도 일시적으로는 — 젊다고 느낄 수도 있다.

23 논리완성 ④

| 분석 |

첫 번째 빈칸의 경우, '붙어서 사는 곤충에 심하게 감염된 잎'이라고 하였으므로, 그러한 병든 잎만 선택적으로 '떨어지게 하는, 이탈시키는(abscise)' 것이 식물이 자신을 방어하는 전략일 것이라 추론할 수 있다. 두 번째 빈칸의 경우, 앞에서 '다른 알이 있는 곳에 자신의 알을 낳을 가능성이 더 적다'고 하였으므로, 산란이 '단념되는(discouraged)' 것이다.

| 어휘 |

unpalatable a. 입[구미]에 안 맞는 **deter** v. 단념시키다, 그만두게 하다 **herbivore** n. 초식 동물 **associational** a. 연상의, 연합의, 조합의 **abscise** v. (잎을) 이탈시키다, 떨어지게 하다 **sessile** a. 고착의, 착생(着生)의 **leaf miner** 잎굴벌레, 잎갈파리 **aphid** n. 진딧물 **species-specific** a. 한 종(種)에만 관련된[국한된], 종 특이[성]의 **vine** n. 덩굴 식물 **genus** n. (생물 분류상의) 속(屬) **Passiflora** n. 시계꽃 **mimic** v. 흉내를 내다 **Heliconius** n. 헬리코니우스 속(屬) 곤충 **oviposition** n. 산란(産卵) **withhold** v. (~을) 주지 않다, 보류하다 **decollate** v. ~의 목을 베다, 절단하다 **expedite** v. 더 신속히 처리하다

| 해석 |

식물은 자신을 방어하기 위해 추가적인 전략을 사용할 수 있다. 첫째, 초식동물을 단념시키는 경향이 있는 맛없는 식물 옆에 자라는 것인데, 이는 연합 저항이라고 알려진 현상이다. 둘째, 식물은 잎굴파리나 진딧물과 같이 붙어서 사는 곤충에 심하게 감염된 잎을 선택적으로 떨어뜨릴 수 있는데, 이는 곤충이 자신의 생활 주기를 완료하지 못하도록 하기 위함이다. 셋째, 특정 종에 특화된 방어 시스템이 있다. 예를 들어, '시계꽃' 속(屬)의 일부 열대 덩굴 식물은 '헬리코니우스' 속(屬) 나비의 알을 흉내 낸 물리적 구조를 생성한다. 암컷 나비는 자신의 알이 아닌 다른 알이 있는 곳에 자신의 알을 낳을 가능성이 더 적기 때문에, 산란이 단념되는 것이다.

24 논리완성 ③

| 분석 |
첫 번째 빈칸의 경우 '중앙은행이나 민족국가, 또는 규제 기관의 보증이 없다'는 것은 기존 화폐와의 차이점이므로 '~와는 달리(unlike)'가 들어가는 것이 적절하다. 두 번째 빈칸의 경우, 기존 화폐와 달리 '거래의 유효성을 중앙 기관이 검증하는 것이 아닐 것'이므로, '~대신(Rather than)'이 적절하다.

| 어휘 |
currency n. 통화(通貨)　**back up** ~을 뒷받침하다　**validate** v. 인증하다; 승인[인정]하다　**ledger** n. (은행·사업체 등에서 거래 내역을 적은) 원장　**public ledger** 공공 거래 장부

| 해석 |
비트코인은 2009년 사토시 나카모토라는 정체불명의 인물이 개발한 디지털 화폐이다. 그의 정체는 아직도 알려져 있지 않다. 비트코인은 그것을 뒷받침해주는 중앙은행이나 민족국가, 또는 규제 기관이 없기 때문에 기존 화폐와는 다르다. 이 "코인"들은 컴퓨터가 복잡한 수학 문제를 풀어서 만들어진다. 사용자는 비트코인을 구매하고 샌프란시스코에 본사를 둔 코인베이스와 같은 거래소를 이용해서 거래한다. 거래의 유효성을 중앙 기관이 검증하는 대신, 모든 거래는 블록체인이라 불리는 공개 원장에 기록된다.

25 논리완성 ①

| 분석 |
첫 번째 빈칸의 경우, while 절의 '바람직하지 않거나 환자에게 위험을 초래한다'는 내용과 대조 또는 반대되는 내용이 와야 함을 추측할 수 있다. 따라서 therapeutic, regenerative 정도가 가능하다. 두 번째 빈칸의 경우 even의 강조를 받고 있으므로 앞서 나온 '출혈' 또는 '색전증'보다 더 심각하고 위험한 수준을 가리키는 표현이 와야 함을 추측할 수 있다. lethal, perilous 정도가 가능하다. 세 번째 빈칸의 경우, '의사의 약물 처방과 소비자의 약물 사용을 돕기 위해 약물에 대한 지식을 정확하게 반영한다'는 내용을 고려할 때, 약물에 대한 적절한 '표시, 표기(labeling)'라는 표현이 들어가는 것이 적절함을 알 수 있다.

| 어휘 |
pharmacology n. 약리학, 약물학　**therapeutic** a. 치료상의, 치료법의　**pose** v. (위협·문제 등을) 제기하다　**adverse** a. 부정적인, 불리한　**nausea** n. 욕지기, 메스꺼움　**gastrointestinal** a. 위장의　**thromboembolism** n. 혈전 색전증(血栓塞栓症)　**lethal** a. 치명적인(죽음을 초래할 정도의)　**component** n. (구성) 요소　**labeling** n. 표시　**physician** n. 의사, 내과 의사　**prescription** n. 처방(전)　**tautologous** a. 동의어[유의어(類意語)] 중복의, 중언부언하는　**terminal** a. 말기의, 불치의　**regenerative** a. 재생시키는; 회복하는　**courtly** a. (특히 구식일 정도로 대단히) 공손한[정중한]　**hemostatic** a. (약 따위가) 지혈(止血)의　**perilous** a. 아주 위험한

| 해석 |
약리학의 기본 원리 중 하나는 모든 약물은 여러 가지 작용을 한다는 것이다. 질병 치료에 바람직한 작용은 치료적이라고 간주되는 반면, 바람직하지 않거나 환자에게 위험을 초래하는 작용은 '부작용'이라고 불린다. 약물의 부작용은 메스꺼움이나 구강 건조와 같은 사소한 것부터, 대량의 위장관 출혈이나 혈전색전증과 같은 심각한 것까지 다양하며, 일부 약물은 심지어 치명적일 수도 있다. 따라서 약물 부작용을 효과적으로 감지하는 시스템은 모든 선진국 의료 시스템에서 중요한 요소이다. 신약 연구의 대부분은 유익한 효과를 극대화하고 부작용의 위험을 최소화하는 사용 조건을 규명하는 데 목적이 있다. 약물 표기(라벨링)의 목적은 의사가 약물을 적절하게 처방할 수 있도록, 또는 처방전 없이 판매되는 경우 소비자가 약물을 적절하게 사용할 수 있도록 이러한 지식을 정확하게 반영하는 데 있다.

26 논리완성 ②

| 분석 |
첫 번째 빈칸의 경우, '곡물을 더 발전되고 복잡한 방식으로 재배하였다'는 의미가 되려면, elaborate(정교한), efficient(효율적인), methodical(조직적인)이 가능하다. 두 번째 빈칸의 경우, '땅속 깊이 파종하다'와 반대되는 의미, 즉 '마구잡이로, 되는 대로(haphazardly, randomly)' 파종한다는 의미가 되어야 한다. 세 번째 빈칸의 경우, 수렵채집인들을 가리키는 표현으로 '먹을 양식(먹이)을 찾아다니는 사람들'의 뜻인 foragers가 들어가야 한다.

| 어휘 |
cereal n. 곡물; 곡식이 되는 작물, 곡류(벼·보리·밀 등)　**cultivate** v. (식물·작물을) 재배하다　**elaborate** a. 정교한, 정성[공]을 들인　**grain** n. 곡물, (곡식의) 낱알　**lay aside** (나중에 사용하거나 생각하려고) ~을 한쪽으로 제쳐놓다[두다], ~을 간직하다　**sow** v. (씨를) 뿌리다[심다]　**haphazardly** ad. 무턱대고, 되는 대로　**hoe** v. 괭이질을 하다　**plough** v. 쟁기로 갈다[일구다]　**weed** v. 잡초를 뽑다　**fertilise** v. (토지에) 비료를 주다　**forage** v. (식량을) 마구 뒤지며 찾다　**forager** n. 채집민　**esoteric** a. 소수만 이해하는, 난해한　**nomad** n. 유목민　**primate** n. 영장류　**methodical** a. 체계적인, 꼼꼼한　**vandal** n. 공공 기물 파손자, 문화 파괴자

| 해석 |
기원전 9500년 이후, 나투프인(Natufians)의 후손들은 여전히 곡물을 채집하고 가공했지만, 점점 더 정교한 방식으로 그것들을 재배하기 시작했다. 그들은 야생 곡물을 채집할 때, 다음 해 밭에 뿌릴 일부 수확물을 따로 보관하는 데 주의를 기울였다. 그들은 곡물을 땅 위에 아무렇게나 흩뿌리는 것보다, 땅속 깊이 파종하면 훨씬 더 좋은 결과를 얻을 수 있다는 것을 발견했다. 그래서 그들은 괭이질과 쟁기질을 시작했다. 점차 밭의 잡초를 뽑고, 해충으로부터 지키며, 물과 비료를 주기도 했다. 곡물 재배에 더 많은 노력이 투입되면서, 야생 동식물을 채집하고 사냥할 시간은 점점 줄어들었다. 그렇게 채집민들은 농부로 변해갔다.

27 글의 흐름상 적절하지 않은 문장 고르기 ③

| 분석 |

ⓒ의 앞뒤 문장들은 쇼팽이 파리에서 저명한 음악가들을 만나고 부유한 가정에서 개인 교습을 하면서 상류 사회에 진출하는 과정을 설명하고 있다. 그런데 ⓒ 문장에서는 '상류층 학생들이 내는 수업료가 너무 적어 상류층의 사설 무대 공연만 할 수는 없고 대중 공연을 계속해야 했다'는 의미가 되어, 바로 뒤에 나오는 '그의 연주 활동이 희소해짐에 따라 명성과 수업료가 더 높아졌다'는 내용과 서로 모순되어 전체의 흐름에서 어긋나고 있다. not을 삭제하면 '상류층 학생들이 내는 수업료가 많아, 공연 횟수가 많은 대중 공연을 포기하고 상류층의 사설 무대 공연만 할 수 있었다'는 뜻이 되어 전체 흐름에 맞게 된다.

| 어휘 |

improviser n. 즉흥 연주자 **concerto** n. 협주곡 **soloist** n. 독주자 **virtuosity** n. (예술적) 기교 **revolt** n. 반란, 봉기, 저항 **circles** n. (주의, 목적 따위를 같이하는 사람들의) 집단, ~계(界) **fashionable** a. 부유층이 애용하는 **cachet** n. (사람들이 흠모하는) 특징[특질]; 위신, 높은 지위[명성] **tempestuous** a. (감정이) 열렬한 [격정적인] **affair** n. 정사(情事), 연애 **pseudonym** n. 필명(筆名) **grueling** a. 녹초로 만드는 **tuberculosis** n. 결핵

| 해석 |

쇼팽은 러시아 지배하에 있던 폴란드의 한 지역에서 프랑스인 아버지와 폴란드인 어머니 사이에서 태어났다. 피아니스트, 즉흥 연주자, 작곡가로서의 그의 재능은 어려서부터 나타났고, 일곱 살 때 첫 작품을 출판하고 협주곡 독주자로서 첫 공개 연주회를 가졌다. 바르샤바 음악원에서 수학한 후 빈에서 연주하고 독일과 이탈리아를 순회 공연했다. 폴란드적 색채가 강한 그의 곡들은 특히 성공을 거두었고, 이는 그가 그러한 곡들을 더 많이 작곡하도록 고무했다. 온 국민이 그의 음악을 사랑한 것과 그의 음악의 화려한 기교로 인해 폴란드에서 많은 추종자를 얻었다. 국제적인 명성을 추구하던 그는 1830년 빈과 독일로 다시 돌아갔다. 그해 11월, 러시아에 저항한 폴란드의 봉기가 실패했다는 소식을 듣고, 그는 파리로 가서 1831년 정착했고, 그 후 다시는 폴란드를 방문하지 않았다. 쇼팽은 곧 로시니, 마이어베어, 베를리오즈, 리스트 등 파리에 머물던 당대 최고의 음악가들을 만나게 되었고, 상류 사회에 진출했다. 그는 부유한 학생들에게 가장 인기 있는 피아노 교사가 되었다. 〈그들이 내는 수업료는 그가 대중들 앞에서의 연주를 포기하고 도시의 유명 여성들이 주최하는 사설 콘서트나 살롱에서만 연주할 수는 없다는 것을 의미했다.〉 결과적으로 그의 연주회 출연이 드물어지면서 그의 명성은 더 높아졌고, 수업료를 더 많이 받을 수 있게 되었다. 그는 또한 작품 출판을 통해 상당한 수입을 올렸다. 그는 결혼하지 않았지만, 조르주 상드라는 필명으로 알려진 소설가 오로르 뒤드방과 9년간 격정적인 연애를 했다. 1848년 파리 혁명으로 그의 교습이 중단되면서, 잉글랜드와 스코틀랜드를 순회하는 고된 여정을 떠나야 했다. 그 무렵 그는 결핵으로 크게 쇠약해졌고, 1849년 파리에서 세상을 떠났다.

28 글의 제목 ②

| 분석 |

이 글은 동양과 서양 문화권의 사람들이 논리적 주장을 평가할 때 나타나는 차이점을 설명하고 있다. 즉, 문화적 배경이 논리적 추론 방식에 미치는 영향을 보여주고 있으므로 ②가 글의 제목으로 가장 적절하다.

| 어휘 |

decontextualization n. 탈맥락화 **distaste** n. 불쾌감, 혐오감 **inference** n. 추론 **underlying** a. 근본적인 **proposition** n. 명제, 진술 **deductive** a. 연역적인 **convincing** a. 설득력 있는 **ulnar** a. (팔의) 척골(尺骨)의 **artery** n. 동맥 **spontaneously** ad. 자발적으로 **experiential** a. 경험적인, 경험에 의한 **project** v. 투사하다; 추정하다 **superordinate** a. 상위의 **subordinate** a. 하위의 **premise** n. 전제 **atypical** a. 비전형적인, 이례적인 **prior** a. (다른 무엇·특정 시간보다) 사전(事前)의 **convincingness** n. 설득력이 있음

| 해석 |

동양에서 논리에 대한 관심이 부족한 것은 탈맥락화에 대한 불신, 즉, 논증의 내용을 떠나 논증의 구조만 고려하는 것에 대한 불신과, 기저에 깔린 추상적인 명제에만 근거하여 추론하는 것에 대한 거부감과 밀접한 관련이 있다. 나와 또 다른 연구자들이 수행한 두 가지 연구는 이러한 경향이 21세기 아시아의 일반인들 사이에서도 여전히 유효하다는 것을 보여준다.

다음 두 가지 연역적 논증을 살펴보자. 어느 쪽이 더 설득력이 있는가?

(1) 모든 새는 척골 동맥을 가지고 있다. 따라서 모든 독수리는 척골 동맥을 가지고 있다.

(2) 모든 새는 척골 동맥을 가지고 있다. 따라서 모든 펭귄은 척골 동맥을 가지고 있다.

사람들이 논리적 추론을 할 때 얼마나 자발적으로 형식 논리에 의존하는지, 아니면 경험적 지식에 의존하는지를 측정하는 한 가지 방법은, 속성(위의 예에서는 '척골 동맥')을 상위 범주(새)에서 하위 범주(독수리, 펭귄)로 어떻게 '투사'하는지를 살펴보는 것이다. 두 논증은 동일한 전제를 가지고 있지만, 대상이 되는 새가 얼마나 전형적인지에 따라 결론이 달라진다는 점에 유의하여야 한다. 독수리는 펭귄보다 더 전형적인 새이다. 위와 같은 명제를 평가할 때 당신이 순수 논리적인 태도를 취한다면, 논증의 암묵적인 중간 전제("모든 독수리는 새이다"와 "모든 펭귄은 새이다")를 제시하게 될 것이다. 이렇게 하는 사람들은 두 논증의 설득력이 동등하다고 생각할 것이다. 하지만 사람들은 종종 전형적인 사례에 대한 논증이 이례적인 사례에 대한 논증보다 더 설득력이 있다고 생각한다. 이전의 경험으로 인해 사람들은 펭귄을 조류로 보는 것보다 독수리를 조류로 보는 것에 더 마음이 편해진다.

우리는 한국인, 아시아계 미국인, 유럽계 미국인 참가자들에게 이와 같은 논증 스무 가지를 제시하고 논증의 설득력을 평가해 달라

고 요청했다. 그중 열 개는 결론에 독수리와 같은 전형적인 대상을 사용했고, 열 개는 펭귄과 같은 이례적인 대상을 사용했다. 그 결과, 한국인 참가자들은 전형적인 논증을 이례적인 논증보다 더 설득력 있게 평가했다. 반면, 유럽계 미국인 참가자들은 전형적이든 비전형적이든 거의 동일하게 설득력 있다고 평가했다. 아시아계 미국인의 반응은 유럽계 미국인과 한국인의 중간 정도였다.

위 글의 제목으로 가장 적합한 것을 고르시오.
① 논증 평가에서 형식 논리의 역할
② 논리적 추론에 대한 문화적 차이의 영향
③ 척골 동맥과 조류 범주의 관계
④ 의사결정 과정에서 연역적 논증의 역할

| 어휘 |

orb n. 구, 구체(특히 해·달) **astronomy** n. 천문학 **helio-centric doctrine** n. 지동설(태양 중심 신조) **geocentric** a. 지구 중심적인, 천동설의 **signal** a. 현저한, 주목할 만한, 뛰어난 **brotherhood** n. 형제애 **revolve** v. (축을 중심으로) 돌다 **burst** v. 터지다, 파열하다 **cognate** a. 관련이 있는, 유사한 **inaugurate** v. (새로운 발전·중요한 변화의) 개시를 알리다 **career** n. 경력, 이력, 생애 **geology** n. 지질학 **so long as** ~하는 동안은, ~하는 한은 **the Noachian deluge** 노아의 대홍수 **ascribe A to B** A를 B 탓[덕]으로 돌리다 **lithology** n. 암석학 **mineralogy** n. 광물학 **crust** n. 지각 **remains** n. (죽은 사람·동물의) 유해 **spring into life** 발생하다 **vigorously** ad. 발랄하게, 힘차게 **substantial** a. (양·가치·중요성이) 상당한

29~30

지구가 우주의 중심이라는 믿음, 즉 태양은 지구의 낮을 지배하는 빛의 구체(球體)일 뿐이고, 달은 지구의 밤을 안내하는 등불일 뿐이라는 믿음이 지배적이었던 한, 천문학의 진정한 진보는 없었고 있을 수도 없었다.
A 그러나 태양 중심설이 지구 중심설을 압도하고, (지구는 태양 주위를 도는 행성 형제들의 일원일 뿐, 결코 가장 뛰어난 것은 아니라는) 갈릴레오의 가르침이 받아들여지자마자, 인류의 정신에 새로운 빛이 터져 나오기 시작했고, 천문학뿐만 아니라 모든 관련 과학이 새로운 발전의 길을 가기 시작했다. 지질학도 마찬가지였다. 지구의 나이가 불과 수천 년밖에 되지 않는다고 믿어지고, 지구의 외부 암석층에 나타나는 모든 현상이 노아의 대홍수에 기인한다고 여겨지는 한, 지질학의 진정한 진전은 없었고 있을 수도 없었다.
C 암석학과 광물학은 있을지 몰라도 지구의 역사 같은 것은 불가능했다. 그러나 반복적인 물리적 변화의 증거가 단단한 지각 안에 들어있으며, 인간이 존재하기 수천 년 전부터 살아오면서 하느님의 보살핌을 받았던 무수한 생물들의 유해가 지각 안에 들어있다고 깨달아졌을 때, 바로 그때 지질학은 탄생했고, 그 후 줄곧 지질학은 대담하고 힘찬 전진의 과정을 밟아왔다.
B 지난 60년 동안, 특히 1809년 지질학회 설립 이후, 관찰자들은 더 나은 방법을 채택함으로써 눈부시고 상당한 진전을 이루었다. 사실들이 광범위하게 수집되고 비교되었으며, 그 비교를 통해 그 사실들의 원인과 기원까지 추적하여 알게 되었다. 실제로 지질학은 상당한 발전을 이루어 이제는 다른 자연과학들과 동등한 지위를 차지하고 있으며, 지적 탐구로서 매력적이며, 일상생활의 산업적 운영과 가장 밀접하게 관계된 것으로서 귀중하다.

29 단락배열 ②

| 분석 |

글의 단락을 논리적 흐름에 맞게 배열하면 다음과 같다. (첫 단락) 천동설이 지배하는 한 천문학은 제대로 발달할 수 없었다 → A 천동설에서 지동설로의 전환이 천문학 및 관련 과학의 혁명적 변화를 초래하였듯이, 지질학에서도 대부분의 지질 현상을 노아의 홍수에 맞춰 설명하려던 시각을 유지하는 한 진정한 진전은 불가능했다. → C 지각이 포함하고 있는 사실과 정보의 의미를 깨달으면서 지질학이 실질적으로 탄생하였다. → B 지난 60년간, 지질학은 눈부신 발전을 이룸으로써 다른 자연과학과 대등한 지위에 오르게 되었다.

30 내용일치 ③

| 분석 |

글의 첫 부분과 A 단락에서 지구 중심설, 즉 천동설이 지배적이었던 시대에는 천문학뿐만 아니라 지질학에서도 진정한 발전이 있을 수 없었다고 분명히 밝히고 있다.

위 글의 내용과 일치하지 않는 것을 고르시오.
① 태양 중심설(지동설)은 천문학 발전의 전환점을 이루었다.
② 지질학의 발전은 노아 홍수와 관련된 믿음 때문에 상당한 방해를 받았다.
③ 지구 중심설(천동설)의 영향력이 절정에 달했을 때 지질학 분야에서 상당한 발전이 이루어졌다.
④ 1809년에 설립된 지질학회는 지질학의 상당한 발전에 기여했다.

31~32

임마누엘 칸트는 의무와 권리에 대한 대안적인 설명을 제시했으며, 이는 철학자들이 만들어낸 이론 중 가장 강력하고 영향력 있는 이론 중 하나이다. 그것은 우리가 우리 자신을 소유한다는 생각이나, 우리의 생명과 자유는 하느님이 준 선물이라는 주장에 의존하지 않는다. 오히려, 그것은 우리가 존엄성과 존중을 누릴 가치가 있는 이성적 존재라는 생각에 의존한다.

칸트는 1724년 동프로이센의 쾨니히스베르크에서 태어나 거의 80년 뒤, 그곳에서 생을 마감했다. 그는 그다지 넉넉하지 않은 가정 출신이었다. 아버지는 마구(馬具) 제작자였고, 그의 부모는 내면의 신앙생활과 선한 행동을 강조하는 개신교 신앙인들, 즉 경건주의자들이었다.

칸트는 16세에 입학한 쾨니히스베르크 대학에서 뛰어난 학업 성적을 보였다. 한동안 그는 가정교사로 일하다가, 31세에 첫 학문적 직책을 얻었는데, 그것은 정해진 급여가 없는 강사직이었으며, 그가 강의하는 강좌의 수강생 수에 따라 보수를 받는 방식이었다. 그는 매우 인기 있고 근면한 강사였고, 형이상학, 논리학, 윤리학, 법학, 지리학, 인류학 등 다양한 주제에 대해 주당 약 20회의 강의를 했다.

1781년, 57세가 되던 해에 그는 첫 번째 주요 저서인 『순수이성비판』을 출간했으며, 이는 데이비드 흄 및 존 로크와 연관된 경험주의적 인식 이론에 도전하는 책이었다. 그로부터 4년 후, 그는 여러 도덕 철학 저서 중 첫 번째인 『도덕 형이상학의 기초』를 출간했다. 이 책은 제레미 벤담의 『도덕과 입법의 원리들』(1780)보다 5년 늦게 나왔으며, 공리주의에 대한 강력한 비판을 담고 있다. 칸트는 도덕성이 행복이나 다른 어떤 목적을 극대화하는 것이 아니라, 사람을 그 자체로서 존중하는 것이라고 주장한다.

『도덕 형이상학의 기초』는 미국 독립 혁명(1776) 직후, 프랑스 혁명(1789) 직전에 발표되었다. 이 책은 당시 혁명들의 정신과 도덕적 취지와 부합하는 내용을 담고 있으며, 18세기 혁명가들이 말하는 인간의 권리, 그리고 21세기 초의 우리가 말하는 보편적 인권에 대한 강력한 철학적 근거를 제공한다.

| 어휘 |

dignity n. 존엄성 **modest** a. 그다지 대단하지는 않은 **means** n. (개인이 가진) 돈, 재력, 수입 **harness** n. 마구(馬具) **Pietist** n. 경건주의자 **industrious** a. 부지런한, 근면한 **metaphysics** n. 형이상학 **empiricist** n. 경험주의자 a. 경험주의의 **devastating** a. 대단히 파괴적인 **critique** n. 비평한 글, 평론 **utilitarianism** n. 공리주의 **thrust** n. (주장·정책 등의) 요지[취지]

31 글의 제목 ①

| 분석 |

이 글은 칸트의 도덕 철학이 전통적인 도덕 이론들과 다르며, 인간의 이성과 존엄성에 근거하여 도덕성을 설명했다고 소개하는 글이다. 또한 그의 철학이 보편적 권리에 대한 이론적 기반을 제공했다는 점을 특히 강조하고 있다. 따라서 가장 적절한 제목은 ①이다. ② 글의 주요 주제인 도덕성, 인권 개념이 빠져 있어 불충분하다. ③ 『순수이성비판』에 대한 언급이 본문에 나와 있기는 하나, 이 글은 전체적으로 칸트의 도덕 철학에 초점이 맞춰져 있다. ④ 칸트의 철학이 미국 독립 혁명, 프랑스 혁명의 정신 및 도덕적 취지와 부합하는 면이 있다고 언급했을 뿐, 그 혁명들에 영향을 미쳤다는 내용은 없다.

위 글의 제목으로 가장 적합한 것을 고르시오.
① 칸트의 유산: 합리성, 도덕성, 그리고 보편적 권리
② 도덕과 이성: 칸트의 합리성 구축 방식
③ 칸트의 비판적 순수 이성과 그 결과
④ 칸트의 학문적 업적의 영향

32 내용추론 ④

| 분석 |

칸트의 철학이 미국 독립 혁명, 프랑스 혁명의 정신 및 도덕적 취지와 부합한다고 언급했을 뿐, 그 혁명들에 영향을 미쳤다는 내용은 추론할 수 없다. ① '도덕성이 행복이나 다른 어떤 목적을 극대화하는 것이 아니라, 사람을 그 자체로서 존중하는 것이라고 주장한다'고 하였으므로 타당하다. ② '형이상학, 논리학, 윤리학, 법학, 지리학, 인류학 등 다양한 주제에 대해 강의하였다'고 하였으므로 타당하다. ③ '이 책은 공리주의에 대한 강력한 비판을 담고 있다'고 하였으므로 타당하다.

위 글을 통해 추론할 수 없는 것을 고르시오.
① 칸트의 도덕 철학은 개인의 존엄성과 자율성을 강조한다.
② 칸트는 형이상학, 윤리학, 지리학을 포함한 광범위한 주제에 대해 강의했다.
③ 『도덕 형이상학의 기초』는 도덕성에 대한 공리주의적 접근을 비판한다.
④ 칸트의 공리주의 비판은 미국 독립 혁명과 프랑스 혁명에 간접적인 영향을 미쳤다.

33~34

세트장이나 야외 촬영 현장에서의 공간의 현실과는 달리, 렌즈 선택에 따라 이미 조절되었을 수 있는 화면상의 공간의 본질은 편집실에서 창조되고, 다듬어지고, 유연하고 모호하게 만들어져 드라마에 기여하게 될 수 있다. 〈사용된 촬영장면이 항상 등장인물의 주관적인 인식을 담고 있지는 않더라도, 등장인물은 우리가 이야기, 드라마, 그리고 감정을 이해하는 통로이다.〉 편집자는 이용 가능한 촬영 범위와 각도를

선택하여 물리적 현실이나 그 현실의 허구적 대응물을 충실하게 재현할 수 있다.
공간과 마찬가지로, 시간의 경과를 변조하고, 게다가 조작하는 것은 편집 과정에서 매우 중요하다. 시간은 편집 과정 전체에서 압축되거나 확장될 수 있다. 리버스 숏 편집에서 대화 장면은 편집 과정에서 단축되거나 유지되는 개별 장면들로 구성될 수 있는데, 이는 촬영장에서의 원래 대화 길이를 화면에 나타나는 지속 시간으로 바꾸는 작업이다. 대화 사이의 공백은 변경될 수 있으며, 다음 대사나 다음 장면으로 넘어가기 전에 반응에 더 많은 시간을 할애할 수도 있고 줄일 수도 있으며, 마치 한 등장인물이 대화 상대를 방해하는 것처럼 한 대사가 다른 대사 위에 겹쳐지게 할 수도 있다.
등장인물이 한 장소에서 다른 장소로 이동할 때의 시간도 압축(또는 확장)될 수 있다. 첫 번째 각도에서는 등장인물들이 카메라를 향해 다가오다가, 일부 장면을 잘라내면서 들어오는 반대 각도에서의 촬영에서는, 등장인물이 멀어지는 모습이 보이게 된다. 잘라냄이 적용되는 시점에 따라 등장인물들이 목적지에 더 가깝게(또는 더 멀리) 있게 되어, 해당 공간을 실제로 가로지르는 데 걸렸을 시간보다 더 짧거나 더 긴 시간에 도착한 것처럼 보이게 될 수도 있다. 또한, 관련된 공간과 거리에 대한 우리의 이해를 감안하여, 예상보다 더 빠르거나 더 늦게 등장인물이 도착 장소에 다다르도록 잘라낼 수도 있다.
동시적인 행동은 조작된, 게다가 속여진, 시간을 보여줄 수도 있다. 적대자가 어떤 등장인물을 쫓을 때, 두 사람이 서로에게 실제보다 더 가까이 나타나도록 해서, 마지막 순간에 추격당하는 사람이 아슬아슬하게 추격자로부터 벗어나는 모습을 보이도록 만들 수 있다. 이러한 시간 조작은 스릴러물과 액션 영화에서 흔히 사용되는데, 거기서 우리는 이러한 오도(誤導)를 쉽게 용인한다. 믿을 만하고 긴장감 넘치는 장면을 연출하려면 능숙하게 편집되어야 한다.

~을 가정하면　**simultaneous** a. 동시의　**cheat** v. 속이다　**antagonist** n. (주인공에 맞서는) 적대자　**in the nick of time** 아슬아슬하게 때를 맞추어　**covariance** n. (통계) 공분산(共分散); (영화) 시간 조작(두 개 이상의 사건이나 액션이 서로 영향을 미치거나 동시에 발생하는 것처럼 보이도록 편집하는 기법)　**misdirection** n. 잘못된 지시, 오도(誤導)　**suspense** n. 서스펜스, 긴장감　**assemble** v. 조립하다

33　글의 흐름상 적절하지 않은 문장 고르기　　①

| 분석 |
본문 전체는 영화 편집 과정에서 공간과 시간이 어떻게 조작되어 드라마를 강화하는지에 대해 설명하고 있는데, Ⓐ 문장은 등장인물이 드라마에 어떻게 기여하는지를 언급하는 내용으로, 편집 과정에서 공간이나 시간이 조작되는 방식에 대한 내용과는 거리가 있다.

34　글의 요지　　②

| 분석 |
본문의 주요 내용은 영화 편집자가 다양한 편집 기술을 사용하여 영화 속 공간과 시간의 흐름을 자유롭게 조절하고, 이를 통해 드라마적 효과를 극대화할 수 있다는 것이다.

위 글의 요지로 가장 적합한 것을 고르시오.
① 편집은 주로 서사 단위 간의 강력한 연결 수단으로서 전환을 적절히 사용하는 데 집중한다.
② 편집자는 영화의 서사와 드라마를 강화하기 위해 공간과 시간 모두를 조작할 수 있는 능력이 있다.
③ 다양한 앵글은 등장인물 간의 지속적인 대화에 초점을 맞출 수 있다.
④ 모든 장면이 세트장이나 야외 촬영 현장의 물리적 현실을 준수하는 것이 바람직하다.

| 어휘 |
as opposed to ~와는 대조적으로, ~이 아니라　**set** n. (연극) 공연장; (영화) 촬영장; (연극·영화의) 무대 장치[세트]　**location** n. (영화의) 야외 촬영지[로케이션]　**modulate** v. 조절하다[바꾸다]　**cutting room** (영화의) 편집실　**refine** v. (작은 변화를 주어) 개선[개량]하다　**malleable** a. 펴 늘일 수 있는, 가단성 있는　**ambiguous** a. 분명히 규정되지 않은, 모호한　**conduit** n. (액체나 기체를 통하게 하는) 도관, 전선관; (정보나 물자의) 전달자　**shot** n. 숏(영화에서 한 대의 카메라가 계속해서 잡는 장면)　**coverage** n. (적용) 범위　**counterpart** n. 상대, 대응 관계에 있는 사람[것]　**as with** ~(에서)와 마찬가지로, ~에서 그렇듯이　**manipulation** n. 조작　**compress** v. 압축하다[되다]　**reverse single** (영화) 마주 보고 대화하는 두 인물을 번갈아 촬영한 개별 숏　**onscreen** a. (컴퓨터·텔레비전·영화) 화면의　**duration** n. 지속, (지속되는) 기간　**interlocutor** n. 대화자, 대화 상대　**cut** n. (영화·연극·글의 일부분에 대한) 삭제, 컷　**in question** 문제, 논의가 되고 있는　**anticipate** v. 예상하다　**given** prep. ~을 고려해볼 때,

35~36

질 들뢰즈는 창조와 분화를 주된 관심사로 삼았던 사상가로서, 그에 따르면 새로운 조합들이 끊임없이 출현하고, 그 과정에서 현실은 재구성된다. 그는 이미 확립된 철학적 범주와 구분을 받아들이는 대신, 새롭고 독창적인 방식으로 사유를 재구성하여 독특한 특성과 다양한 잠재력을 지닌 개념적 혼합물을 만들어냈다. 들뢰즈 사상의 기본 요소들은 정적인 것이 아닌, 되어 가는 중인(변화 과정에 있는) 존재들이다. 따라서 우리가 던져야 할 질문은 어떤 것이 무엇인가가 아니라, 그것이 무엇으로 변해가고 있는가, 혹은 무엇으로 변할 수 있는가이다. 실천, 지식, 정치, 문화, 작인(作因)은 명확한 통제 메커니즘 없이 이질적인 과정 속에서 끊임없이 생산되는 것으로 여겨진다. 더 나아가, 이러한 과정들은 인간과 비

(非)인간, 물질과 이상, 이론과 실천을 포함한 여러 현대적 구분들을 가로지른다. 이 책은 들뢰즈적 접근이 사회인류학과 과학 기술 연구(STS)를 위해 어떤 함의를 갖는가라는 질문을 제기한다.

들뢰즈적 주제와 관련되고 그로부터 영감을 받은 아이디어들이 행위자-네트워크 이론이나 비(非)인간주의 이론과 같은 분야에 등장했지만, 들뢰즈적 사상이 과학 기술 연구에 가져올 수 있는 구체적인 도전과 가능성에 대한 지속적인 탐구는 거의 없었다. 그리고 들뢰즈와 가타리가 인류학을 '자유로운 변형' 형태로 활용했지만, 그들의 연구를 실제로 활용한 인류학자는 상대적으로 드물었다. 들뢰즈적 연구에서 제기되는 과학 기술 연구와 인류학의 구분은 다소 포착하기 어렵다. 실제로 들뢰즈에게 영감을 받은 몇몇 인류학자들은 엄밀히 말해 과학 인류학자들이기 때문이다.

그러나 이러한 복잡한 관계를 풀어헤쳐 구분하려는 것이 우리의 목표는 아니다. 오히려, 들뢰즈적 분석은 사회인류학과 과학 기술 연구 모두에서, 그리고 그 둘 사이에서 중요한 쟁점들을 재고할 수 있는 많은 기회를 제공한다는 것이 우리의 전반적인 주장이다. 우리는 들뢰즈적 분석이 이 분야의 방법론, 인식론, 그리고 존재론에 대한 새로운 통찰을 제공한다고 주장한다. 그리고 들뢰즈적 분석은 과학, 기술, 문화, 정치 사이의 관계에 대한 점점 더 중요한 재고를 원활히 촉진한다. 그리고 이 분야들과 그들이 연구하는 실천 사이의 연관성을 이해하는 다양한 방법들을 제시한다.

| 어휘 |

differentiation n. 분화, 파생   **assemblage** n. 집합; 조립   **reconfigure** v. 다시 구성하다, (특히 컴퓨터 장치나 프로그램을) 변경하다   **category** n. 범주   **hybrid** n. 잡종; 혼성체   **static** a. 고정된, 정지 상태의   **entity** n. 실재(實在), 존재; 실체   **agency** n. (어떤 결과를 가져오는) 작용, 힘; 작인(作因)   **heterogeneous** a. 이질적인   **traverse** v. 가로지르다   **volume** n. 책   **entail** v. 수반하다   **science and technology studies** 과학 기술 연구(STS)(사회, 정치, 문화가 과학 연구와 기술 혁신에 어떻게 영향을 미치는지, 그리고 이러한 것들이 다시 사회, 정치, 문화에 어떻게 영향을 미치는지에 대한 연구)   **variation** n. 변화, 변동; 변이   **evoke** v. 떠올려 주다[환기시키다]   **elusive** a. 정의하기 어려운   **disentangle** v. (혼란스러운 주장·생각 등을) 구분하다   **methodology** n. 방법론   **epistemology** n. 인식론   **ontology** n. 존재론   **facilitate** v. 촉진하다   **discourse** n. 담론(談論)   **endeavour** n. 노력   **draw on[upon]** (이용 가능한 공급품에) 의지하다

35 빈칸완성 ③

| 분석 |

먼저, 빈칸 앞 문장이 부정문이라는 사실에 비추어 보면, '부정문+Rather/Instead, ~'의 구문적 조합을 ③과 ④가 충족시킨다. 그런데 빈칸 다음 문장들의 주어 it은 문장들의 의미로 볼 때 '들뢰즈적 분석'을 가리키므로 that 절에서 '들뢰즈적 분석'이 주어로 사용된 ③이 빈칸에 적절하다.

빈칸에 들어가기에 가장 적합한 것을 고르시오.
① 과학 기술 연구는 종종 과학적 실천과 담론에 대한 밀접한 경험적 연구로 특징지어진다.
② 들뢰즈는 물리학, 수학, 생물학의 개념들을 자유롭게 사용했지만, 이러한 개념들이 생성된 사회적 과정들을 거의 고려하지 않았다.
③ 오히려, 들뢰즈적 분석은 사회인류학과 과학 기술 연구 모두에서, 그리고 그 둘 사이에서 중요한 쟁점들을 재고할 수 있는 많은 기회를 제공한다는 것이 우리의 전반적인 주장이다.
④ 대신, 과학 기술 연구는 과학을 합리적인 진리 추구의 노력이 아니라 사회적 이해관계와 협상의 산물로 재정의하는 것을 목표로 삼았다.

36 내용추론 ③

| 분석 |

두 번째 단락에서, '들뢰즈의 철학은 기존의 구분을 가로지른다'고 하였고, 네 번째 단락에서 '과학, 기술, 문화, 정치 간의 관계에 대한 재고를 원활히 촉진한다'고 하였으므로, 들뢰즈의 철학이 다양한 분야들을 넘나들면서 새로운 연결을 가능케 해준다는 의미로 이해될 수 있다. 따라서 ③의 진술이 타당하다. ① 첫 단락에 따르면 들뢰즈는 전통 철학에 뿌리를 두었다기보다는 전통 철학을 재구성한 인물이다. ② '과학을 존재론적 맥락에서 도구로 쓴다'는 내용은 언급된 적이 없다. ④ 세 번째 단락에서 '들뢰즈적 연구에서 제기되는 과학 기술 연구와 인류학의 구분은 다소 포착하기 어렵다'고 하였으므로 타당하지 않다.

위 글을 통해 추론할 수 있는 것으로 가장 적합한 것을 고르시오.
① 전통 철학에 뿌리를 둔 들뢰즈는 철학 입문자들에게 필수적 방법론을 제공한다.
② 들뢰즈의 이론에 의지하는 인류학자들은 과학을 존재론적 맥락에서 도구로 사용한다.
③ 들뢰즈의 철학은 인류학을 포함한 다양한 학문 분야 간 통합적 사고를 촉진하는 데 도움을 준다.
④ 들뢰즈적 사고는 인류학과 과학 사이의 경계를 명확히 규정하여 과학 분야에서 일하는 인류학자들에게 이득이 된다.

37~38

압생트라고 알려진 투명한 녹색 리큐어 술은 19세기 후반의 파리 카페를 그린 풍경화에 자주 묘사되었고, 유명 시인들과 예술가들의 극찬을 받으면서 예술적으로 불멸의 존재가 되었다. 압생트는 1840년대 알제리 전투에서 돌아온 프랑스 군인들에 의해 대중화되었는데, 그곳에서 그들은 열병 예방을 위해 와인에 쑥 추출물을 넣어 마셨다. 프랑스로 돌아오자마자 그들은 쑥 오일이 주요 성분인 압생트로 바꿔 마셨다. 이 첨가물 때문에 압생트는 알코올만으로는 얻을 수 없는 몽환적인 효과를 유발한다. 하지만 이 성분은 독성이 있어서, 과도하게 마시면 멍한 느낌, 무서운 환각, 심지어는 돌이킬 수 없는 뇌 손상을 초래할 수 있다. 이러한 증상을 특징으로 하는 압생트 중독이 1850년대에 인지되었지만, 20세기가 되어서야 비로소 이 음료의 판매와 제조가 금지되었다. 하지만 쑥이라는 약초의 역사는 훨씬 더 오래전으로 거슬러 올라간다. 가장 오래된 기록은 기원전 3,550년경 이집트 문헌에 등장한다. 고대 로마의 약제사들은 이 약초 추출물을 사용하여 장내 기생충을 퇴치했다. 쑥즙을 피부에 발라 벼룩과 작은 날벌레들을 쫓았고, 옷을 보관할 때 쑥 잎을 넣어두면 나방을 막아주었다. 고대 로마인들은 쑥 추출물을 탄 와인을 마셨지만, 18세기가 되어 리큐어 술이 발명되고 나서 스위스에서 압생트의 제조법이 개발되었다.

압생트의 환각성과 독성은 (압생트의 주요 원료인) 쑥과 세이지, 쑥국화 같은 또 다른 식물에 들어 있는 투우존이라는 화학물질 때문에 생긴다. 리큐어 술의 색과 풍미를 향상시키기 위해 다른 식물의 추출물들도 첨가되었다. 이러한 성분들은 수천 년 동안 부작용 없이 약초 요법에 사용되어왔다. 쑥은 오랫동안 의학에서 긍정적 역할을 해왔고, 고대 이집트인들과 고대 종교에서도 그랬다. 심지어 쑥의 독성 성분인 투존도 이 술이 금지된 이후에는 긍정적인 것으로 판명되었다. 투존이나 장뇌는 경련을 유발하기 때문에 1920년대와 1930년대에 뇌전증(간질) 연구와 일부 조현병 환자의 경련 치료에 효과적으로 사용되었다.

압생트를 마시는 것은 그 술의 독특한 효과 때문뿐만 아니라, 그 술을 나누어 마시는 것을 중심으로 하여 발달된 정교한 컬트 의식 때문에도 인기가 있었다. 그 쓴 리큐어 술(압생트)은 구멍 뚫린 숟가락 위에 설탕 덩어리를 올려놓은 특별한 드립 글라스에 제공되었다. 설탕 위로 차가운 물을 부어 글라스로 흘려 내리면, 투명한 녹색 리큐어 술(압생트)이 진주 빛 황금색 구름 같은 것으로 변했다. 이 술은 예술가들 사이에서 유행했다. 상징주의 시인들은 압생트를 찬양했으며, 마네와 피카소 같은 화가들도 작품 속에 압생트를 그려 넣었다.

그래서 19세기 후반, 지나친 탐닉의 위험성을 말해주는 과학적 증거에도 불구하고 압생트의 인기가 높아진 것은 놀라운 일은 아니다. 1875년부터 1913년까지 프랑스의 1인당 압생트 소비량은 15배 증가했다. 소비량이 많았던 지역에서는 사산(死産), 정신병, 기타 신경계 질환 발생률 또한 증가했다. 결국 프랑스는 1915년에 압생트를 금지했지만, 생산과 소비는 몇 년 후까지 사실상 중단되지 않았다. 그 후로 아니세트, 우조, 파스티스 등 맛은 비슷하지만 쑥이 들어가지 않은 많은 술들이 개발되었다.

| 어휘 |

liqueur n. 리큐어(달고 과일 향이 나기도 하는 독한 술)　**extol** v. 극찬[격찬]하다　**wormwood** n. 약쑥　**extract** n. 추출물　**additive** n. 첨가물　**induce** v. 유발[초래]하다　**dreamlike** a. 마치 꿈같은, 몽환적인　**dazed** a. (충격을 받거나 머리를 얻어맞거나 하여) 멍한[아찔한]　**hallucination** n. 환각; 환영　**irreversible** a. (이전 상태로) 되돌릴[철회할] 수 없는　**absinthism** n. 압생트(술) 중독　**expel** v. 쫓아내다[추방하다]　**intestinal** a. 장에 기생하는　**apply** v. (페인트·크림 등을) 바르다　**flea** n. 벼룩　**gnat** n. 작은 날벌레, 각다귀　**repel** v. 쫓아 버리다, 접근하지 못하게 하다　**spike** v. (음료·음식에 술·독약 등을) 타다[섞다]　**recipe** n. 조리[요리]법　**property** n. (사물의) 속성[특성]　**thujone** n. 투우존　**sage** n. 세이지, 샐비어(약용·향료용 허브)　**tansy** n. 쑥국화　**remedy** n. 치료(약)　**ill effects** 부작용　**outlaw** v. 불법화하다, 금하다　**camphor** n. 장뇌(의약품·비닐 제조·좀약 등에 쓰이는 하얀 물질)　**convulsion** n. 경련, 경기　**epilepsy** n. 뇌전증(간질)　**schizophrenic** n. 조현병 환자　**tipple** v. 술을 마시다　**elaborate** a. 정교한, 정성[공]을 들인　**cult** n. 제례[의식]　**slotted spoon** 구멍들이 뚫려 있는 큰 스푼　**pearly** a. 진주로 된, 진주 같은　**beverage** n. (물 외의) 음료　**overindulgence** n. 방임, 제멋대로 함; 탐닉　**incidence** n. (사건 등의) 발생 정도　**stillbirth** n. 사산(死産)　**psychosis** n. 정신병(pl. psychoses)　**elixir** n. (만병통치·불로장생의 효험이 있는 것으로 여겨지는) 영약[묘약]

37　글의 제목　①

| 분석 |

이 글은 압생트라는 술이 어떻게 인기를 얻었고, 그 부작용 때문에 결국 어떻게 금지에 이르렀는지에 대한 내용을 다루고 있으므로, ①이 적절한 제목이다. ②에는 압생트라는 키워드가 빠져 있고, ③과 ④는 글의 일부 측면만 언급하고 있다.

위 글의 제목으로 가장 적합한 것을 고르시오.
① 압생트의 흥망성쇠: 독성의 묘약
② 쑥: 고대부터 현대까지의 논란
③ 압생트의 예술적, 문화적 영향
④ 약초 기반 리큐어의 화학적 성질과 제조

38　내용추론　③

| 분석 |

글의 마지막 부분에서 '1915년에 압생트를 금지했지만, 생산과 소

비는 몇 년 후까지 사실상 중단되지 않았다'고 하였으므로 금지 직후 곧바로 압생트가 완전히 사라진 것은 아니었음을 알 수 있다. 따라서, ③은 잘못된 추론이다.

위 글을 통해 추론할 수 없는 것을 고르시오.
① 19세기 후반 압생트의 인기는 예술가들 및 시인들과의 연관성 덕분이었다.
② 압생트에 쑥이 사용됨으로써 환각성과 건강상의 위험을 불러일으켰다.
③ 압생트는 1915년 금지되어 불법화된 직후 곧바로 생산이 중단되었다.
④ 쑥은 압생트에 사용되기 훨씬 전부터 다양한 약용 목적으로 사용되었다.

39~40

혈액형 분류, 즉 혈액형은 적혈구에 특정 표지자가 있는지 없는지를 기준으로 인간의 혈액을 여러 유형으로 분류하는 체계이다. 이 개념은 1900년대 초에 발견되었지만, 그 지식은 제1차 세계 대전이 시작되기 전까지는 널리 적용되지 않았다. 외과의들이 수혈 전에 혈액의 적합성을 검사하지 않으면, 환자의 면역 체계가 새로운 혈액 세포를 공격할 수 있어 치명적인 결과를 초래할 수 있었다.
B 전쟁으로 인해 연구자들은 항응고제 개발과 단기 보관 기술의 발전에 초점을 맞추었는데, 이는 효과적이고 안전한 혈액은행 설립의 필수 요소들이었다. "지금은 일상적인 일로 여겨지는 수혈이 전쟁 초기에는 아직 실험적인 단계였습니다"라고 국립 제1차 세계대전 박물관 및 기념관의 교육 및 해설 담당 부관장인 로라 보그트는 말한다.
C 최초의 수혈은 1914년 프랑스에서 헌혈자의 정맥에서 환자의 정맥으로 직접 수혈하는 방식으로 이루어졌다고 하이포인트 대학교 군사(軍史) 전문 역사학 교수인 프레데릭 슈나이드는 설명한다. "채혈 후 혈액을 보관할 방법이 없어서 즉시 수혈해야 했다는 것이 문제였습니다."라고 그는 말한다. 또한 여러 환자에게 동시에 수혈이 필요한 상황에서, 충분한 수의 헌혈자와 외과의들을 찾는 것도 어려웠다.
A 그러다 1917년 봄, 캐나다 군의관 로렌스 B. 로버트슨이 서부 전선에서 "간접" 수혈을 시작했다. 그것은 응고를 막기 위해 주사기와 가는 관을 사용해 헌혈자의 혈액을 수혈하는 시술이었다. 1917년 11월까지 그는 『랜싯(The Lancet)』에 기고한 글에서 간접 수혈법을 사용한 36건의 사례를 기술하며, "쇼크를 동반한 심각한 원발성 출혈의 경우, 수혈을 시행하면 즉각적이고 거의 믿을 수 없을 정도로 호전되는 경우가 많다"고 기록했다.
비슷한 시기에 (로렌스 B. 로버트슨과 친척은 아닌) 미 육군 군의관 오스왈드 H. 로버트슨이 최초의 혈액 저장소를 만들었다. 혈액을 담은 플라스크들로 채워진 얼음 상자가 바로 그것이었다. 로버트슨은 영국군이 유사한 시스템을 구축하는 것을 돕기 위해 프랑스로 파견되었다. 그는 (O형이 보편적으로 헌혈되는 혈액이므로) O형 음성 혈액을 채취하여 항응고제로 처리했다. 슈나이드에 따르면 혈액을 1리터 유리병에 담아 짚을 채워 넣은 탄약 상자에 보관했다고 한다. 1917년에 이 초기 혈액은행 모델을 이용한 최초의 수혈이 성공적으로 이루어졌다.

| 어휘 |

categorize v. 분류하다   **marker** n. 표지(자)   **red blood cell** 적혈구   **compatibility** n. 적합성, 양립[공존] 가능성   **transfusion** n. 수혈   **immune system** 면역 체계   **donor** n. 헌혈자   **vein** n. 정맥   **procedure** n. 수술, (의학적인) 처치   **syringe** n. 주사기   **clotting** n. 응고   **hemorrhage** n. 출혈   **primary hemorrhage** 원발성 출혈(原發性出血), 일차출혈(一次出血), 상처받은 직후의 출혈   **anticoagulant** n. 항(抗)응고제   **relation** n. 친족[친척] 관계, 연고   **depot** n. (대규모) 창고   **stock** v. 채우다[갖추다]   **flask** n. (화학 실험용) 플라스크   **ammunition** n. 탄약   **refrigeration** n. 냉동(보존), 냉장

| 39 | 단락배열 | ② |

| 분석 |

1914년 프랑스에서의 직접 수혈에 관한 정보를 담고 있는 C와 1917년에 있었던 캐나다 의사 로버트슨에 의한 간접 수혈에 관한 내용을 담고 있는 A는 반드시 붙어 있을 수밖에 없다는 응집성(cohesiveness)에 착안하여 선택지를 먼저 걸러내는 것이 중요하다. 또한, A가 B 및 C보다 가장 뒤에 위치해야 하는 근거로는 마지막 단락의 로버트슨이라는 동명이인의 미국 의사 이름을 인용하는 내용이 나온다는 점이다. 정리하면, 1차 세계대전과 수혈 시술의 발전이라는 관계성에 대해 일반적으로 기술하는 주어진 단락에서 시작하여, 1차 세계대전 초기에는 수혈 시술이 해결해야 할 문제들이 산적해 있는 초기 단계였음을 언급하는 B가 온 이후에, 앞서 언급한 응집성 및 시간 순서의 원리를 따라 C와 A가 이어지며, 마지막 단락의 최초의 혈액은행 모델 탄생 이야기로 마무리되는 것이 가장 자연스럽다.

| 40 | 내용일치 | ② |

| 분석 |

C 단락에 따르면, 1914년에는 혈액을 보존할 수단이 없었으며, 혈액은 즉시 수혈되어야 했다고 했다. 이는 혈액은행이 존재하지 않았다는 의미이다. 그리고 마지막 단락에 따르면 최초의 혈액 저장소, 즉 초기 혈액은행 모델은 1917년 냉장 보관이 아닌 짚을 채워 넣은 탄약 상자에 보관한 것이었다.

위 글의 내용과 일치하지 않는 것을 고르시오.
① 제1차 세계 대전 중 프랑스에서 이루어진 최초의 수혈은 정맥 대 정맥의 직접 수혈법을 사용했다.
② 최초의 혈액은행은 1914년에 설립되었으며, 수혈을 위해 혈액을 냉장 보관했다.
③ 로렌스 B. 로버트슨은 응고를 방지하기 위해 주사기와 가는 관을 사용하여 간접 수혈을 시행했다.
④ 오스왈드 H. 로버트슨은 최초의 혈액 저장소에 비축하기 위해 항응고제로 처리된 O형 음성 혈액을 수집했다.

한국공학대학교 일반·학사편입

TEST p. 580~593

01	③	02	④	03	③	04	①	05	②	06	③	07	①	08	①	09	④	10	②
11	④	12	②	13	④	14	④	15	②	16	①	17	①	18	③	19	③	20	①
21	②	22	④	23	②	24	③	25	④	26	④	27	③	28	③	29	③	30	③
31	③	32	①	33	①	34	③	35	①	36	④	37	①	38	④	39	④	40	②

01 동의어 ③

| 어휘 |

insufficient a. 불충분한 **catastrophic** a. 파멸적인, 비극적인 (= devastating) **extensive** a. 아주 넓은, 대규모의 **auspicious** a. 상서(祥瑞)로운 **prominent** a. 중요한, 유명한

| 해석 |

질병에 대한 이해 부족이 사회에 파멸적인 영향을 미칠 수 있다.

02 동의어 ④

| 어휘 |

profuse a. 많은, 다량의(= abundant) **tropical** a. 열대의 **inhabit** v. (특정 지역에) 서식하다 **sterile** a. 불임의; 살균한

| 해석 |

아마존의 울창한 열대 우림에는 다양한 종류의 동물이 서식하고 있다.

03 동의어 ③

| 어휘 |

plead v. 탄원하다, 간청하다(= implore) **lecture** v. 강의하다 **consult** v. 상담하다; 상의하다

| 해석 |

12년 동안 호러스 만은 주 정부에 학교들을 개선해 달라고 간청했다.

04 동의어 ①

| 어휘 |

culinary a. 요리의, 음식의 **privilege** n. 특권 **sweat** v. 땀을 흘리다 **stove** n. 난로 **tuck into** ~을 마음껏 먹다(= eat) **appraise** v. 살피다; 평가하다 **boast** v. 뽐내다, 자랑하다 **display** v. 전시하다, 진열하다

| 해석 |

미식 관광객들은 뜨거운 화로 위에서 땀을 흘리며 직접 만든 음식을 먹는 특권을 누리기 위해 기꺼이 수천 달러를 낸다.

05 동의어 ②

| 어휘 |

resolution n. 결단력, 과단성(= determination) **conservationist** n. 환경 보호 활동가 **project** v. 예상[추정]하다 **manatee** n. 매너티, 해우(海牛) **population** n. 개체군, 집단; 개체수 **obsession** n. 강박 상태, 집착 **formation** n. 형성 **concentration** n. 정신 집중; (노력 등의) 집중

| 해석 |

환경 보호 활동가들과 지역 공무원들의 지속적인 결단력 덕분에, 전문가들은 매너티들의 개체수가 계속 증가할 것으로 예상하고 있다.

06 논리완성 ③

| 분석 |

지금의 대륙별 '형태', '배열', '배치'는 수백만 년 동안 천천히 서로 멀어지는 대륙 이동의 결과라는 진술이다.

| 어휘 |

drift v. (서서히) 이동하다[움직이다] **drift apart** 사이가 멀어지다 **current** a. 현재의 **configuration** n. 배열, 배치; 배열[배치] 형태 **conversion** n. 전환, 개조; 개종, 전향 **conciliation** n. (노동 쟁의 등의) 조정, 화해; 달램, 회유 **confrontation** n. 대치, 대립

| 해석 |
수백만 년에 걸쳐 대륙들은 천천히 멀어지면서 현재의 대륙 배치 형태를 형성했다.

07 논리완성 ①

| 분석 |
유엔 가맹국들이 유엔 헌장을 '비준'함으로써 유엔은 공식적으로 출범했으리라고 추론할 수 있다. ratify는 '비준하다' 즉, '조약, 계약 또는 합의에 대하여 서명하거나 동의하여 그것을 공식적으로 유효하게 만들다'는 뜻이다.

| 어휘 |
ratify v. 비준(批准)[재가]하다(sign or give formal consent to a treaty, contract, or agreement, making it officially valid)   **charter** n. (조직의 원칙·목적 등을 명시한) 헌장, 선언문   **disregard** v. 무시[묵살]하다   **abolish** v. (법률·제도·조직을) 폐지하다   **encounter** v. (새롭거나 뜻밖의 대상과) 접하다[마주치다]

| 해석 |
유엔은 대부분의 최초 참여국들이 헌장을 비준했던 1945년 10월에 공식적으로 출범했다.

08 논리완성 ①

| 분석 |
화산재에 뒤덮인 채 1,800년이 넘는 세월이 흘렀다면 그 도시의 상태는 '파괴/훼손'이 염려되는 상황. 즉 '온전하지 않은' 상태일 것이라 예상될 것이다. 그런데 양보의 접속사 Although가 있으므로, 부사절의 내용은 주절과 '반대/대조'될 것이다. 따라서 빈칸에는 비교적 '온전한' 상태로 발견되었다는 표현이 들어가야 한다. 한편, integral은 '(전체와 부분의 관계에서) 빠진 부분이 없이 완전체를 이룬', '전체를 이루는 데 빠져서는 안 되는 필수적인'이라는 의미이므로 '훼손됨이 없이 원래 그대로 온전한'이라는 뜻의 intact 와는 다르다.

| 어휘 |
ash n. 화산재   **eruption** n. (화산의) 폭발, 분화   **intact** a. (손상되지 않고) 온전한, 다치지 않은(not broken or damaged)   **intimate** a. 친(밀)한   **integral** a. (전체를 구성하는 일부로서) 필수적인, 필요불가결한; (필요한 모든 부분이 갖춰져) 완전한   **intangible** a. 실체가 없는, 무형의

| 해석 |
기원전 79년의 화산 분출로 폼페이는 화산재에 뒤덮였지만, 1748년에 비교적 온전한 모습으로 발견되었다.

09 no more A than B ④

| 분석 |
'no more A than B' 구문은 비유 또는 유추(analogy)적 의미가 강할 때는 'B가 A 아니듯이, S는 A 아니다'는 의미로 해석하고, 주어진 문장에서처럼 단순 비교인 경우는 '~가 B보다 더 A한 것은 아니다'는 식으로 해석하는 것도 가능하다. ① danger가 명사이므로 부사인 as의 수식을 받을 수가 없다. 따라서 형용사인 dangerous로 바꾸어 is as dangerous as로 수정해야 한다. ② the same ~ as의 상관관계를 고려하여 in을 as로 바꾼 has the same danger as로 수정해야 한다. ③ similarly가 dangerous를 수식하는 것은 어색하므로 부사 as로 바꾸어서 is as dangerous as로 수정해야 한다.

| 어휘 |
indicate v. 보여주다   **nuclear** a. 핵의, 원자력의   **power plant** 발전소   **oil refinery** 정유 공장

| 해석 |
핵발전소 근처에 사는 것이 화학 공장이나 정유 공장 근처에 사는 것보다 더 위험하지 않다는 보고들이 일부 있다.

10 분사구문 ②

| 분석 |
주절의 주어인 '대두(콩)'이 '존중되는' 수동의 의미관계이므로 revere가 현재분사로 나온 ①도, 능동태의 정동사로 나온 ③과 ④도 모두 부적절하다. Having been once revered라는 완료 수동태 분사구문에서 Having been이 생략된 ②가 빈칸에 적절하다.

| 어휘 |
revere v. 숭배하다, 존중하다   **sacred** a. 신성시되는   **crop** n. (농)작물   **soybean** n. 콩, 대두   **protein** n. 단백질

| 해석 |
중국에서 한때 신성한 작물로 존중되었던 대두(콩)는 식물성 단백질의 가장 풍부한 공급원 중 하나이다.

11 관계대명사와 전치사 ④

| 분석 |
identify A as B(A를 B라고 인지하다) 구문의 문장인데, 빈칸에는 someone을 수식하는 관계절이 들어가야 한다. they(=American women) talk with someone frequently이므로 with whom으로 시작하는 관계절인 ④가 빈칸에 적절하다.

| 어휘 |
identify v. 인지하다; 확인하다

| 해석 |
미국 여성들은 보통 가장 친한 친구를 그들이 자주 대화를 나누는 사람이라고 인지한다.

12 복수 취급을 하는 대명사 few   ②

| 분석 |
동사가 were이므로 단수 취급하는 little이나 단독으로 명사적으로 쓰이지 못하는 every는 부적절하고, 주절의 '많은 시를 썼다'는 내용과 though에 의해 역접으로 연결되려면 '살아있었을 때 발표된 시는 극히 적었다/거의 없었다'라는 흐름이 되어야 할 것이므로 빈칸에는 few가 적절하다.

| 어휘 |
pen v. (글 등을) 쓰다   **poem** n. (한 편의) 시(詩)

| 해석 |
에밀리 디킨슨은 총 1,200편이 넘는 시를 썼지만, 그녀가 살아있는 동안 발표된 시는 거의 없었다.

13 동명사의 의미상의 주어   ④

| 분석 |
'lead to ~'의 to는 전치사이므로 뒤에는 명사나 동명사가 나와야 한다. 또한 동명사의 의미상 주어는 소유격으로 표현해야 하며, 문맥상 '금지되다, 퇴출되다'라는 수동의 의미가 필요하므로 하므로 동명사의 수동형과 의미상의 주어를 적절히 표현한 ④가 정답이다.

| 어휘 |
illegal a. 불법적인   **ban** v. 금(지)하다

| 해석 |
벤 존슨이 불법 약물을 복용했다는 것이 나중에 밝혀졌고, 이로 인해 그는 올림픽 스포츠에서 퇴출되었다.

14 간접의문문   ③

| 분석 |
간접의문문은 '의문사+주어+동사'의 어순으로 명사절이 되어 주어, 목적어, 보어 등의 역할을 한다. 의문대명사 what이 간접의문문을 이끌어 전치사 into의 목적어가 되는 명사절을 이끌고 있고, 간접의문문 안에서는 require의 목적어가 되고 있다. ①, ②, ④ require의 목적어가 빠져 있으므로 모두 적절하지 않다.

| 어휘 |
insight n. 통찰력; 이해   **major** n. (대학생의) 전공   **require** v. 필요[요구]하다, 필요로 하다

| 해석 |
교수들은 그들의 경험을 공유할 수 있고 특정 전공을 연구하는 것이 기술, 능력, 노력의 측면에서 무엇을 필요로 하는지에 대한 통찰을 제공할 수 있다.

15 도치구문에서의 일치   ②

| 분석 |
② 보어인 Less amused가 문두에 와서 주어와 동사가 도치되었는데, 주어인 the owners가 복수이므로 수 일치에 따라 동사 ②는 were가 되어야 한다. 'insist, recommend, advise, ask, demand' 등의 추천, 요구, 권고, 제안의 동사가 that 절을 목적어로 취하는 경우, 그 that 절의 동사는 주어의 수나 주절의 시제에 관계 없이 '(should)+동사원형'으로 써야 하므로 ③은 적절하다.

| 어휘 |
branch n. 지사, 분점   **neighboring** a. 이웃의, 근처[인근]의; 인접한   **bet** n. 내기, 내기 돈   **last** v. (어려움에도 불구하고) 견디다[버티다]   **amused** a. 재미있어[즐거워] 하는   **funeral parlor** 장례식장   **complain** v. 불평하다   **hire** v. (단기간) 빌리다[세내다]; (사람을) 고용하다   **funeral director** 장의사   **stick to one's guns** 자기의 입장을 고수하다, 자기 의견을 굽히지 않다; 한 치도 양보하지 않다

| 해석 |
아니타 로딕은 그녀의 고향인 영국 브라이턴에서 더 바디샵(The Body Shop)의 첫 번째 매장을 열었다. 그녀가 처음 가게를 열었을 때, 이웃 상인들과 가게 주인들은 그 가게가 얼마나 오래 지속될지에 대해 자기들끼리 내기를 했다. 지역 장례식장 주인들은 마음이 덜 즐거웠는데, 그들은 그녀에게 가게 이름을 바꾸라고 요구했다. 그들은 "The Body Shop"이라는 이름의 가게 근처에 있는 장례지도사에게 아무도 돈을 내고 장례를 의뢰하지 않을 거라고 불평했던 것이다. 그녀는 자신의 신념을 굽히지 않았고, 가게 이름은 그대로 유지되었다.

16 관계대명사 what   ③

| 분석 |
선행사를 포함하는 관계대명사 what은 명사절을 이끌어 주어, 목적어, 보어 등의 역할을 한다. 관계대명사 what은 두 가지 역할을 하는데, 주어진 문장에서는 has been의 주어인 명사 역할 및 combat의 목적어인 절을 이끄는 접속사 역할을 하고 있다.

| 어휘 |
subscription n. 구독(료)   **tailor** v. (특정한 목적·사람 등에) 맞추다[조정하다]   **treatment** n. 대우[처우]   **deepen** v. 더 깊어지다[깊게 하다]   **retail** n. 소매   **be faced with** ~에 직면하다   **dizzying** a. 어지럽게 만드는, 어지러운, 아찔한   **array** n. 집합체[모음, 무리]   **combat** v. 방지하다[방지하기 위해] 싸우다]   **refer to A as B** A를 B라고 부르다   **paralysis** n. 마비

| 해석 |
구독 서비스는 고객의 개인적인 필요와 욕구에 맞춤화된 제품을 고객들에게 제공한다. 이러한 종류의 대우는 고객으로 하여금 특별하다고 느끼게 만들고, 브랜드에 대한 그들의 관계를 더욱 심화시킨다. 소비자들이 눈이 어지러울 정도로 다양한 제품들에 직면해

있는 소매 환경에서, 이러한 서비스는 '선택의 마비'라고 불리는 것과 싸워 물리칠 수 있다. 다시 말해, 이 서비스는 스스로 결정하는 데 어려움을 겪는 소비자들을 위해 결정을 해주는 역할을 한다.

17 논리완성 ①

| 분석 |

위약의 효과는 그 약이 '진짜 치료 효과가 있다'는 환자의 믿음 여부에 달렸는데, 복용하는 물질이 비활성인, 즉 약리작용을 하지 않는 물질이라는 것을 미리 알아버린다면 그러한 심리적 효과는 기대할 수 없을 것이다.

| 어휘 |

placebo n. 플라세보, 속임약, 위약(僞藥)(심리적 효과를 얻기 위하여 환자에게 주는, 약리 효과가 전혀 없는 가짜 약) **medical** a. 의학의 **treatment** n. 치료, 처치 **inert** a. 비활성[불활성]의(not able to affect other chemicals when in contact with them, not chemically reactive) **substance** n. 물질 **illusion** n. 오해[착각]; 환상 **ruin** v. (가치・기쁨 등을) 망치다[엉망으로 만들다] **essential** a. 필수적인, 극히 중요한

| 해석 |

위약이 효과를 내려면 실제 의학적 치료인 것처럼 보여야 한다. 환자가 자신이 비활성(약리작용이 없는) 물질을 복용하고 있다는 사실을 알게 되면, 환상은 깨지면서 아무런 효과도 얻지 못할 것이다.

18 논리완성 ③

| 분석 |

극단적으로 매운 느낌을 주는 원인 물질이 캡사이신이므로, 이를 '중화시키다', '무력화하다', '상쇄하다'는 의미의 ③이 빈칸에 들어가는 것이 적절하다.

| 어휘 |

chili pepper 고추 **go off** 폭발하다[터지다] **lip** n. 입술 **gum** n. 잇몸 **throat** n. 목구멍 **break into** (갑자기) ~하기 시작하다 **reach for** ~을 잡으려고 손을 뻗다 **put out** (불을) 끄다 **pointless** a. 무의미한, 할 가치가 없는 **soluble** a. (액체에) 녹는, 용해성이 있는 **casein** n. 카세인, 건락소(乾酪素) **nasal** a. 코의 **verify** v. (진실인지・정확한지) 확인하다 **exacerbate** v. (특히 문제를) 악화시키다

| 해석 |

고추를 한 입 베어 물었을 때 어떤 일이 일어나는지 생각해 보라. 입 안에 화산이 터져 입술에서 잇몸, 혀, 목구멍까지 폭발하는 듯한 느낌이 든다. 갑자기 땀이 나면서 당신은 불을 끄기(매운맛을 씻어내기) 위해 물 잔을 집는다. (캡사이신은 물에 거의 녹지 않기 때문에 이는 무의미한 행동이다. 우유에 들어 있는 단백질 중 하나인 카세인이 캡사이신의 효과를 분명하고도 직접적으로 상쇄하기 때문에 우유를 마시는 것이 가장 좋다.) 눈에서는 눈물이 나고 코에서는 콧물이 넘쳐난다.

19 논리완성 ③

| 분석 |

빈칸 앞의 '이러한 식으로(in this way)'는 저인망으로 원치 않는 물고기까지 잡는 것을 말하므로 원하는 물고기인 대구의 개체 수는 말할 것도 없이 급감할 것이다. 따라서 빈칸에는 ③이 적절하다. ① 원하지 않는 물고기가 잡히는 일은 이미 일어나고 있는 문제로, 학자들이 경고하는 미래의 '결과'로는 적절하지 않다. ② 본문에서 지적된 waste는 '원치 않는 물고기까지 잡아버림으로 인한 어자원의 낭비'를 의미하는 것이지 바다에 버려지는 쓰레기가 아니다. 바다의 쓰레기는 제거하는 것이 오히려 좋은 일이다. ④ 본문에 언급되지 않은 내용이다.

| 어휘 |

fisherman n. 어부, 낚시꾼 **drag** v. (힘들여) 끌다 (참고어: dragnet 저인망 어업) **waste** n. 낭비[허비](하는 행위); 낭비[허비](되는 상황) **degrade** v. (특히 질적으로) 저하시키다 **turn a blind eye to** ~을 보고도 못 본 체하다 **population** n. 개체 수 **cod** n. (어류) 대구 **rational** a. 합리적인, 이성적인 **collapse** n. (제도・사업 등의 갑작스런 실패[붕괴] **fishery** n. (고기가 대량으로 잡히는) 어장; 수산업

| 해석 |

뉴펀들랜드 그랜드 뱅크의 어부들은 바다 밑바닥 위로 그물을 끌고 가며(저인망 어업을 하며) 온갖 종류의 원치 않는 물고기들까지 그물로 잡았다. 어자원의 낭비가 많았고, 이러한 저인망 작업은 환경을 파괴했다. 사람들은 수백 년 동안 지속되어 온 이러한 상황을 그냥 외면했다. 결국, 대구 개체수를 연구하던 생물학자들은 미래의 문제에 대해 경고하기 시작했다. 그들은 이런 식으로 계속하는 것의 당연한 결과는 대구 어업의 붕괴일 것이라고 주장했다.

① 불필요한 어획
② 과도한 낭비의 제거
③ 대구 어업의 붕괴
④ 어망의 파괴

20 논리완성 ②

| 분석 |

첫 번째 빈칸의 경우, 아이들이 보이는 극단적인 반응을 예시한 후 아들의 상태가 '그렇게 심각한 수준까지는 아니었다'고 하였으므로 빈칸에는 '다행히도(Fortunately)', '그러나(However)'와 같이 반전이나 대조를 나타내는 표현이 적절하다. 두 번째 빈칸의 경우, 친한 친구와의 이별이라는 어려움이 필자의 아들뿐만 아니라 또 다른 당사자인 친구에게도 영향을 미쳤으리라는 것은 '당연히(Of course)' 예상할 수 있고, 그 친구의 상황이 뒤이어 설명되어 이를 뒷받침한다.

| 어휘 |

things n. 형편, 상황　**go well** 잘 되어가다　**inattentiveness** n. 부주의, 무뚝뚝함　**hyperactivity** n. 과잉행동　**act out** (억압된 감정을 무의식적으로) 행동화하다　**yell** v. 소리 지르다　**hit** v. ~에 이르다, 닿다; ~에 타격을 주다, 감정을 상하게 하다　**depth** n. (무엇의) 가장 깊은[극단적인, 심한] 부분　**upset** a. 속상한, 마음이 상한　**extroverted** a. 외향적인　**prone to** ~을 잘 하는, ~의 경향이 있는

| 해석 |

가장 친한 친구가 이사를 간 후, 내 아들은 매우 힘든 시기를 겪었다. 상황이 좋지 않을 때 아이들은 성인과 매우 다르게 반응한다. 아이들의 경우, 부정적인 반응에는 부주의, 과잉행동, 그리고 소리 지르고, 때리고, 전반적으로 통제하기 어려워지는 것과 같은 (억압된 감정의 무의식적) 행동화 경향이 포함될 수 있다. 다행히도 내 아들은 그런 심각한 수준까지는 아니었지만, 잠을 잘 자지 못했고 주의력이 약해졌으며, 많은 시간을 슬퍼하며 지냈다. 물론, 이는 그의 친구에게도 타격을 주었는데, 아마도 그 친구는 훨씬 더 심각하게 마음의 상처를 입었을 것이고, 외향적인 성격이라서 훨씬 더 쉽사리 행동화의 경향을 보였을 것이다.

① 따라서 — 마찬가지로
② 다행히도 — 물론
③ 그러나 — 예를 들어
④ 참으로 — 게다가

21 논리완성 ②

| 분석 |

앨리스가 돈이 부족한 상황에서 구할 수 있는 재료와 방법을 활용하여 임기응변적으로 포장을 만들어낸 것이 오히려 제품의 자연스러운 이미지를 더욱 돋보이게 하였으므로 적절한 표현은 improvised이다. 이는 '꼭 필요한 어떤 것이 없어서 뭐든 있는 것으로 만들다 (produce or make something from whatever is available)'는 의미이기 때문이다. 한편, redeemable은 주로 '쿠폰, 포인트 등으로 상품을 받아갈 수 있는'이라는 의미로, 포장과 무관한 어휘이다.

| 어휘 |

entrepreneur n. 기업가　**disadvantage** n. 불리한 점, 약점, 난점　**finance** n. (사업·프로젝트 등의) 재원[자금]　**bottle** v. 병에 담다　**cosmetics** n. 화장품　**urine** n. 소변, 오줌　**refill** v. 다시 채우다, 리필하다　**afford** v. (~을 살·할·금전적·시간적) 여유[형편]가 되다　**label** n. (종이 등에 물건에 대한 정보를 적어 붙여 놓은) 표[라벨, 상표]　**improvise** v. (보통 꼭 필요한 것이 없어서) 뭐든 있는 것으로 처리하다[만들다]　**improvised** a. 즉석에서 지은, 즉흥적인, 임시변통의　**packaging** n. 포장; (판매되는 상품의) 포장재　**turn out** (일·진행·결과가 특정 방식으로) 되다[되어 가다]　**sturdy** a. 튼튼한, 견고한　**fragile** a. 부서지기[손상되기] 쉬운　**redeemable** a. (상품권·할인권·쿠폰 등을 현금·상품과) 교환할 수 있는

| 해석 |

앨리스는 전형적인 기업가가 아니었기 때문에, 자금도 거의 없이 회사를 시작하는 것에 따르는 불리함을 전혀 알지 못했다. 돈을 아끼기 위해 그녀는 병원에서 소변 샘플을 담는 데 사용하는 값싼 플라스틱 용기에 화장품을 담았고, 고객들에게 그 용기를 다시 가져와 리필할 것을 권장했다. 라벨을 인쇄할 금전적 여유도 없었기 때문에, 그녀는 친구들의 도움을 받아 직접 손으로 라벨을 만들었다. 그녀의 포장은 그렇게 계획했다 하더라도 그보다 더 잘 나올 수 없었을 정도로 최고였다. 이런 임기응변의 포장을 통해, 그녀의 제품은 (그 안에 담긴) 화장품 자체와 똑같은 자연스러운 이미지를 갖게 되었다.

22 논리완성 ④

| 분석 |

빈칸 다음의 that절과 동격을 이루는 명사가 빈칸에 들어가야 하는데, ①과 ②는 동명사로 부적절하고, '동사 demand/assume + that절'에서 '명사 demand/assumption + that절'이 파생되는데, that절의 내용상 ③(요구)보다도 ④(가정, 생각)가 적절하다.

| 어휘 |

qualified a. (무엇에 대한 지식·기술 등을 갖춰) 자격이 있는　**gender** n. 성, 성별　**gender-neutral** a. 성 중립적인　**take away** 제거하다, 치우다; 줄이다　**assumption** n. (증거도 없이) 사실이라고 생각함; 가정, 가설, 억측　**profession** n. (특히 많은 교육이 필요한 전문적인) 직업[직종]　**masculine** a. 남자[남성]의　**feminine** a. 여자[여성]의　**demand** n. (강력히 요청하는) 요구 (사항)

| 해석 |

"내일 나는 새 의사를 만날 예정입니다. 나는 그가 유자격 의사이기를 바랍니다. 의사를 만나기 전에 간호사를 만나야 할 것입니다. 나는 그녀가 친절하기를 바랍니다." 당신은 위의 표현에서 뭔가 잘못된 점을 발견하였는가? 성 중립적인 표현을 선호하는 사람들은 바로 한 가지 문제를 알아차릴 것이다. 성 중립적인 표현은 특정 전문 직업은 남성적이고 다른 직업은 여성적이라는 가정을 없애버리려 한다. 성 중립적인 표현으로는 이렇게 말할 수 있다. "내일 새 의사를 만날 예정입니다. 나는 그 또는 그녀가 유자격 의사이기를 바랍니다. 의사를 만나기 전에 간호사를 만나야 할 것입니다. 나는 그 또는 그녀가 친절하기를 바랍니다."

23 논리완성 ②

| 분석 |

빈칸 앞에서 '공감각자는 그것을 지어내는 것이 아니다'고 한 것은 공감각자에게 그러한 감각은 그만큼 '실제적'이라는 말이므로 ②가 적절하다. ① 실제로 소리가 없는데 소리를 듣는다는 뜻으로, 이는 환청(hallucination) 같은 현상에 더 가깝다. 그러나 본문에서는 공감각자는 '벨 소리는 벨 소리대로 청각적으로 듣고, 또 시각적으로도 그것을 경험한다'는 내용이므로 이를 '환각'으로 치부할 수

는 없다. ③ 공감각자는 굳이 시를 읽지 않아도 이러한 '공감각적 현상'을 경험한다고 하였다. ④ 공감각자의 감각은 의도적이지 않고 자연스러운 감각 상의 연결이라고 하였다.

| 어휘 |

activate v. 작동시키다, 활성화시키다   **synesthesia** n. 공감각(共感覺): 어떤 하나의 감각이 다른 영역의 감각을 일으키는 일)   **synesthete** n. 공감각자   **hook** v. 갈고리로[에] 걸다; 훅으로 잠그다   **make up** 만들다, 지어내다, 날조하다   **sensation** n. (자극을 받아서 느끼게 되는) 느낌; 감각   **voluntarily** ad. 자발적으로

| 해석 |

대부분의 사람들의 뇌에서는 각 감각이 개별적으로 활성화된다. 즉, 무언가를 들을 때 청각이 활성화되고, 무언가를 볼 때 시각이 활성화되는 등이다. 그러나 공감각을 가진 사람의 뇌에서는 두 개 이상의 감각이 동시에 활성화된다. 예를 들어, 공감각자의 시각과 청각이 서로 연결되어 있을 수 있다. 따라서, 공감각자가 특정 소리를 들을 때마다 특정 색깔도 보게 된다. 따라서 공감각자는 초인종 소리가 파란색이라고 말할 수 있다. 이는 시인이 독자의 상상력을 자극하기 위해 의도적으로 언어를 사용하는 것과는 다르다. 공감각자는 그것을 지어내는 것이 아니다. 어떤 색깔을 "듣는" 감각은 공감각자에게는 당신이 색깔을 보는 것만큼 실제적인 것이다.

① 실제 소리가 존재하지 않을 때 소리를 인지하는 것이다
② 공감각자에게는 색깔을 보는 것만큼 실제적인 것이다
③ 시를 읽는 여러 감각적 경험에서 비롯된다
④ 공감각자가 자발적으로 소리를 시각과 연관시킬 때 발생한다

24 논리완성   ③

| 분석 |

in other words는 '다시 말해서'라는 뜻이므로 앞서 진술된 된 내용을 '환언(換言)', '재진술'하고 있음을 알 수 있다. 따라서 빈칸에는 '방관자 효과'라는 말을 재진술하는 내용이 와야 할 것이고, 방관이란 '필요한 조치를 하지 않고 구경만 하다'는 뜻이므로 '행동을 취하기 꺼림'이라는 표현이 빈칸에 적절할 것이다.

| 어휘 |

reportedly ad. 전하는 바에 따르면, 소문에 의하면   **witness** n. 목격자   **disturbing** a. 충격적인, 불안감을 주는   **bystander** n. 구경꾼, 방관자   **reluctance** n. 싫음, 마지못해 함, 꺼림, 마음 내키지 않음   **onlooker** n. 구경꾼   **take action** ~에 대해 조치를 취하다, 행동에 옮기다   **eagerness** n. 열의(熱意), 간절함   **commitment** n. 전념; 헌신

| 해석 |

1964년, 키티 제노비스가 뉴욕시에서 살해당했다. 전하는 바에 따르면, 38명의 목격자 중 누구도 경찰에 신고하거나 그녀를 도우려 하지 않았다고 한다. 이는 많은 사람들에게, 특히 심리학자들에게 큰 충격을 주었다. 그 이후 연구자들은 "방관자 효과", 즉 구경꾼들이 행동을 취하기를 꺼려하는 현상을 이해하기 위해 노력해 왔다.

25 논리완성   ④

| 분석 |

빈칸 앞의 연결어가 역접의 However였다는 점, 그리고 빈칸 다음에서 '어린 시절의 높은 IQ 점수와 성인기의 성취가 별로 관계가 없다'고 한 점에 주목한다면, 빈칸에는 IQ 검사와 그 점수만으로 모든 것을 다 알 수는 없다는 내용이 와야 함을 추론할 수 있다.

| 어휘 |

prodigy n. 영재, 신동   **genius** n. 천재성   **predictor** n. 예측 변수   **confirm** v. 확언(確言)하다   **exceptionally** ad. 유난히, 특별히   **exceptional** a. 이례적일 정도로 우수한, 특출한   **conduct** v. 수행하다, 처리하다   **underrate** v. 과소평가하다

| 해석 |

영재들의 초기 잠재력에도 불구하고, 그들이 자라서 어떻게 될지 예측하기는 어렵다. 많은 전문가들이 천재성을 정의하려고 노력했지만, 우리는 아직 천재성이 정확히 무엇인지 알지 못한다. 지능을 예측하는 가장 유명한 지표는 지능지수(IQ) 검사이다. 이 검사는 20세기 초 프랑스 심리학자 알프레드 비네가 개발했다. 그러나 이제 많은 전문가들이 이러한 유형의 지능 검사가 이야기의 한 측면만을 말해준다고 확언한다. 어린 시절 지능 검사에서 유별나게 높은 점수를 받은 대부분의 사람들은 삶에서 특별히 뛰어난 성과를 거두지 못한다.

① 아직 시행되지 않는다
② 절대 과소평가되어서는 안 된다
③ 성인의 지능을 예측한다
④ 이야기의 한 측면만을 말해준다

26 내용파악   ④

| 분석 |

연구자들은 연구 조교들의 출석 횟수를 조절한 뒤, 그들에 대한 수강생들의 호감도를 측정하였다. 이것은 수강생들에 대한 연구 조교들의 '접촉' 또는 '노출'의 정도가 그들의 호감도에 얼마나 영향을 미치는지에 대한 연구라고 추론할 수 있다.

| 어휘 |

research assistant 연구 조교   **attend** v. 참석하다   **semester** n. 학기   **rate** v. 평가하다[여기다]; 좋다고 생각하다, 좋게 보다   **fairly interact with** ~와 교감하다, 상호작용하다   **familiarity** n. 익숙함; 친근함   **exposure** n. 노출

| 해석 |

모어랜드와 비치는 한 여성 연구 조교에게는 학기 중 대학 수업에

15회, 두 번째 연구 조교에게는 10회, 세 번째 연구 조교에게는 5회 참석하라고 요청하고, 네 번째 연구 조교에게는 전혀 참석하지 않도록 요청했다. 학기 말에 네 명의 연구 조교 모두 강의실에 왔고, 연구진은 모든 학생들에게 네 명의 여성 조교를 각각 얼마나 좋아하는지 평가해 달라고 요청했다. 조교들의 외모는 상당히 비슷했고, 학기 동안 학생들과 교류한 적은 없었다.

모어랜드와 비치는 _____를 조사하기 위해 연구를 수행했다.
① 수업에 가장 많이 참석한 연구 조교의 의도
② 친숙함이 고립감 감소에 미치는 영향
③ 물리적 환경이 사람들 간의 관계에 미치는 영향
④ 특정 인물에 대한 반복적인 노출과 그 사람에 대한 평가 사이의 연관성

27 문장삽입 ③

| 분석 |
다이빙을 하기 위해 보드에서 뛰어오른 화자가 보드와 너무 가깝다는 위험을 인지하고 자세를 바로잡으려 했으나 실패하여 결국 보드에 머리를 부딪치는 사고를 겪었던 상황을 기술하고 있다. 주어진 문장은 자세를 고치려고 양손을 벌리는 시도를 하고 있는 대목이므로 위험의 인지 이후에 와야 하고, 이러한 시도가 실패했음을 말하는 문장 앞에 와야 한다. 따라서 가장 적절한 위치는 ⓒ이다.

| 어휘 |
ladder n. 사다리 **announce** v. (공공장소에서) 방송으로 알리다 **push off** ~로부터 멀어져 가다[떠나가다] **lose control** 제어하지 못하다

| 해석 |
사다리를 타고 올라가 다이빙하라는 안내 방송을 듣고, 몇 걸음 걸어 나가 공중으로 나를 튕겨 줄 점프를 했다. 다리로 다이빙 보드를 힘껏 밀면서 팔을 위로 올리고, 어깨를 뒤로 젖혔다. 나는 곧 보드에 너무 가까워져 손이 부딪칠 수도 있다는 것을 직감했다. 〈양손을 넓게 벌리고 공중에서 몸을 돌리며 자세를 바로잡으려 애썼다.〉 그때 이상한 소리가 들리고 몸이 통제 불능이 되는 것을 느꼈다. 잠시 후, 무슨 일이 일어났는지 깨달았다. 나는 다이빙 보드에 머리를 부딪친 것이었다.

28 내용추론 ②

| 분석 |
'미국인들이 이탈리아 레스토랑에서 접하는 전형적인 요리들이 전통적인 지중해식 요리와는 공통점이 거의 없다는 사실에 한탄했다'라는 진술에서 미국에서 팔리는 이탈리아 요리들이 좀 더 전통적인 방식의 지중해 요리와 닮기를 바라는 키스의 마음이 잘 느껴진다. ① 본문과 무관한 내용이다. ③ 본문과 무관한 내용이다. ④ 본문에서 사용된 translation은 일반적인 의미의 '번역'이 아닌, '옮김, 변형'이라는 의미이다.

| 어휘 |
physiologist n. 생리학자 **Mediterranean** a. 지중해의 **diet** n. (어떤 사람이 일상적으로 취하는) 식사[음식], 식습관 **notice** v. 알아차리다 **staple** n. 주식(主食) **nutrition** n. 영양 **lament** v. 애통하다 **encounter** v. 접하다[마주치다] **have little in common** 공통점이 거의 없다 **fare** n. (끼니로 제공되는) 식사[음식] **vegetarian** a. 채식주의(자)의 **translation** n. (다른 형태로) 옮김, 변형

| 해석 |
생리학자 앤셀 키스는 지중해식 식단에 대한 세계적 명성의 옹호자이자 최고의 홍보대사였다. 키스는 반세기 이상 전에, 올리브유와 적포도주를 주식으로 삼고 과일과 채소를 풍부하게 섭취하는 그리스나 이탈리아 남부 같은 지중해 지역에서는 심장병이 드물다는 사실을 처음으로 알아차렸다. 키스는 100세의 나이로 세상을 떠났지만, 생의 마지막 몇 년 동안에도 여전히 활발하게 영양에 관한 연구를 했다. 2000년에 웹 MD(WebMD)와의 인터뷰에서 그는 미국인들이 이탈리아 레스토랑에서 접하는 고기, 치즈, 파스타가 듬뿍 들어간 전형적인 요리들은 정통 지중해식 요리와는 공통점이 거의 없다는 사실에 한탄했다. 그는 "지중해식 식단은 생선은 들어 있지만, 고기는 거의 없는 채식에 가까우며, 녹색 채소가 풍부했습니다"라고 말하며, 이탈리아에서 미국으로 옮겨오면서 무언가가 없어졌다고 덧붙였다. "사람들은 그것을 이탈리아 음식이라고 부를지 모르지만, 그건 우리가 연구한 음식과는 매우 다릅니다."

위 글에서 추론할 수 있는 것은?
① 키스는 심장병을 앓았고, 그 치료법을 찾으려고 노력했다.
② 키스는 미국의 이탈리아 레스토랑에서 제공되는 음식이 전통적인 지중해 요리와 더 비슷했으면 좋겠다고 생각했다.
③ 미국인들은 건강한 식습관에 있어서 극단적인 경향을 보이는 경향이 있다.
④ 영어로 번역하기 매우 어려운 이탈리아 요리가 많다.

29 내용추론 ④

| 분석 |
'태국이 가장 큰 주목을 받는 것은 바로 가공되지 않은 신선한 상태의 잘 익은 고추를 사용한다는 점에서이다'라는 진술을 통해 태국 요리의 주된 특징이 고추의 활용에 있음을 추론할 수 있다. ① 태국이 고추가 자국의 것이라고 적극적으로 주장하는 것이 아니라 그런 척하는 것이다. ② 태국의 수입 식재료에 대한 언급은 있지만, 세계 최대 수입국이라는 말은 없다. ③ 태국 내의 고추와 다른 식재료의 소비량을 비교하는 내용은 본문에 없다.

| 어휘 |
birthplace n. (무엇의) 발생지 **Capsicum** n. 고추(류 식물)(= chili pepper) **act as if** ~ 마치 ~인 것처럼 행동하다 **fiery** a. 입안이 타는 것 같은[얼얼한] **unprocessed** a. 가공[처리]되지 않은 **ripe** a. 익은, 숙성한 **ring the bell** 잘 되다, 성공하다, 히트하다 **imply**

v. 암시하다   exclusively ad. 전적으로   food ingredient 식품 성분, 식재료

| 해석 |
태국은 고추의 발생지가 아니다. 태국이 그런 척할 뿐이지만, 사실 고추는 태국 국민 식단의 다른 많은 것과 마찬가지로, 수입된 것이다. 하지만 태국에서는 이 작고 매운 과일(고추)의 1인당 소비량이 분명히 다른 어떤 나라 못지않게 높고, 어쩌면 더 높을지도 모른다. 그리고 태국이 가장 큰 주목을 받는 것은 바로 가공되지 않은 신선한 상태의 잘 익은 고추를 사용한다는 점에서이다.

위 글에서 추론할 수 있는 것은?
① 태국은 고추가 전적으로 태국산이라고 주장한다.
② 태국은 세계 최대의 식재료 수입국이다.
③ 태국에서는 고추보다 다른 작은 과일들이 더 많이 소비된다.
④ 태국 요리의 특징은 고추를 잘 활용함으로써 달성된다.

30 부분이해   ③

| 분석 |
사우디아라비아는 세계 최대의 석유 수출국인데, 이를 미국의 고철 수출에 비유하는 데 끌어왔으므로, '미국은 세계 최대의 고철 수출국'이라는 의미가 된다.

| 어휘 |
waste n. 폐기물   scrap n. (재활용할 수 있는) 폐품; 고철, 쇠부스러기, 파쇠   Commerce Department 미국 상무부   semiconductor n. 반도체   ahead of ~보다 앞선   commodity n. 상품, 유용한[쓸모 있는] 것   junk n. 쓸모없는 물건, 폐물

| 해석 |
상무부 자료에 따르면, 2002년 미국은 중국에 폐기물과 고철을 약 12억 달러 규모로 수출했는데, 이는 5년 전의 1억 9,400만 달러에서 증가한 수치이다. 고철은 현재 미국의 대중국 수출에서 항공기와 반도체에 이어 세 번째로 큰 비중을 차지하며, 콩과 컴퓨터의 수출보다 많다. 워싱턴에 위치한 고철 재활용 산업 연구소의 원자재 연구 책임자인 로버트 가리노는 "미국은 고철의 사우디아라비아입니다"라고 말한다. 중국은 미국 고철의 최대 고객이 되어, 52억 달러 규모의 고철 및 폐기물 수출 중 23%를 구매해 간다.

밑줄 친 부분과 의미가 가장 가까운 것은?
① 미국은 고철 덕분에 부유하다.
② 사우디아라비아는 중국에 고철을 판매한다.
③ 미국은 최대의 고철 수출국이다.
④ 미국의 대중국 수출은 복잡하다.

31 내용일치   ③

| 분석 |

'의식의 흐름 기법은 등장인물의 본질에 가장 가까이 다가가는 방법이고, 개인의 내면적 생각과 감정을 가장 날것인 형태로 기록하는 것'이라고 하였으므로 ③이 본문의 내용과 가장 일치한다. ① 메이 싱클레어는 '의식의 흐름'이라는 용어를 처음 사용한 사람으로 여겨지지만, 이 기법 자체를 '창안한' 사람이라고 하지는 않았다. ② 의식의 흐름 기법에 따라 쓰인 글에서는 '구조나 형식이 그다지 중요하지 않다'라고 한 것이지, '구조가 신빙성을 떨어뜨린다'고 한 것은 아니다. ④ 제임스 조이스와 윌리엄 포크너와 같은 작가들이 이 기법을 사용했다고만 했을 뿐, '그들이 혁신을 일으켰다거나 가장 성공적인 작가들이다'라고 말하지 않았다.

| 어휘 |
stream n. 흐름   be attributed to ~에 기인하는 것으로 여겨지다, ~의 덕분으로 여겨지다   depict v. (말이나 그림으로) 묘사하다   perception n. 지각, 자각; 인식(하여 갖게 된 생각)   randomly ad. 무작위로   spontaneously ad. 자발적으로, 자연스럽게   matter v. 중요하다, 문제되다   capture v. 정확히 포착하다[담아내다]   notable a. 주목할 만한, 눈에 띄는; 중요한, 유명한   employ v. (기술·방법 등을) 쓰다[이용하다]   originate v. 발명[고안]하다

| 해석 |
의식의 흐름은 19세기 중후반에 등장한 문학 기법이다. 이 용어를 만든 이는 일반적으로 영국 작가 메이 싱클레어라고 여겨진다. 이 기법은 작가로 하여금 등장인물의 인식을 무작위적으로 그리고 자연 발생적으로 묘사하게 해준다. 구조와 형식은 그다지 중요하지 않다. 의식의 흐름 기법의 목적은 주어진 순간에 등장인물이 겪는 모든 경험을 포착하는 것이다. 많은 작가들은 이것이 등장인물의 본질에 가장 가까이 다가갈 수 있는 방법이라고 생각한다. 개인의 내면적 생각과 감정을 가장 날것인 형태로 기록하는 것이 이 스타일을 정의한다. 제임스 조이스와 윌리엄 포크너와 같은 저명한 작가들이 이 기법을 사용했다.

위 글에 의하면, 다음 중 옳은 것은?
① 메이 싱클레어는 의식의 흐름이라는 새로운 문학 기법을 창안했다.
② 문학의 구조는 독자에게 이야기를 신빙성을 떨어뜨린다.
③ 작가들은 등장인물의 내면적 생각의 흐름을 묘사하기 위해 의식의 흐름을 사용한다.
④ 가장 성공적인 작가들은 의식의 흐름을 채택하여 소설에 혁명을 일으켰다.

32~33

많은 사람들이 주류 치료법과 보완대체의학(CAM)을 모두 사용하여 "두 세계의 장점"을 얻는다. "구급 의학"이라고도 불리는 전통 의학은 응급 치료가 필요한 급성 손상에는 여전히 표준이다. 그러나 만성 질환에는 CAM의 전체론적 접근법이 더 선호되는 경우가 많다. 예를 들어 만성 통증은 요가,

침술, 명상, 자연 요법을 병행하여 치료할 수 있다. 통증 완화 외에도 환자는 전반적인 건강 개선의 혜택을 얻는다. 동종요법은 CAM이 환자의 전신을 어떻게 치료하는지 보여주는 좋은 예이다. 동종요법의 원리는 "도둑을 잡기 위해 도둑을 배치한다"이다. 예를 들어, 동종요법의 발열 치료제는 건강한 사람에게 발열 반응을 일으킨다. 그러나 발열 환자에게 투여하면 그것은 환자의 신체가 스스로를 치유하도록 촉발한다. 이것이 바로 환자가 호전되기 전에 일반적으로 더 안 좋아졌다고 느끼는 이유이다. 치유를 일으키는 것은 치료제가 아니라 환자 자신의 몸이다.

| 어휘 |

mainstream n. (사상·견해 등의) 주류[대세]   complementary and alternative medicine 보완대체의학(= CAM)   conventional a. 전통적인, 종래의   nickname v. 별명을 붙이다   rescue n. 구출, 구조, 구제   norm n. 규범, 규준   acute a. (질병이) 급성의   emergency n. 급환(急患); 응급실   holistic a. 전체론적 의학[치료]의   chronic a. 만성의   acupuncture n. 침술   meditation n. 명상   remedy n. 치료(약)   relief n. (고통·불안 등의) 경감[완화, 제거]   homeopathy n. 동종(同種)요법   fever n. (의학적 이상 징후로서의) 열   trigger v. 촉발시키다   proverb n. 속담

32 내용파악 ①

| 분석 |

첫 번째 문장에서 함께 사용해 '두 세계의 장점을 동시에 얻는다'고 하였으므로 ①은 잘못된 진술이다. ② 증상만이 아닌 전체적인 치유를 추구한다고 하였으므로 타당하다. ③ 치료 중 일시적으로 상태가 더 나빠졌다고 느끼기도 한다고 하였으므로 타당하다. ④ '치유를 일으키는 것은 치료제가 아니라 환자 자신의 몸'이라고 하였으므로 타당하다.

CAM 치료에 대해 제안되지 않은 것은 무엇인가?
① 기존 치료법과 함께 사용하면 효과가 떨어진다.
② 증상만 치료하는 것이 아니라 환자의 전신을 치료한다.
③ 일부 환자는 완치되기 전에 증상이 악화될 수 있다.
④ 신체의 자연 방어력을 활성화한다.

33 빈칸완성 ①

| 분석 |

빈칸 다음에 '일부러 발열을 일으켜 발열을 잡는다'는 내용이 나온다. 이는 '비슷한 것으로 비슷한 것을 제어한다'는 '이이제이(以夷制夷)' 즉, '오랑캐로 오랑캐를 무찌른다'는 원리를 뜻하므로 빈칸에 ①이 가장 적절하다. 참고로 ③과 관련하여 '나의 적'이라고 한다면 문맥상 치료해야 할 증상에 해당하므로 '발열'이라고 이해할 수 있고, 그 발열의 적은 '해열'일 것이므로 결국 '해열제가 나의 친구

다'는 의미가 되어 '발열에 해열제를 투여하라'는 뜻이 되므로 동종 요법의 취지와 맞지 않다.

빈칸에 가장 적합한 속담은 무엇인가?
① 도둑을 잡기 위해 도둑을 배치한다
② 새는 한쪽 날개로만 나는 법이 없다
③ 나의 적의 적은 나의 친구다
④ 상황이 어려워지면 강인한 사람들은 (적극적으로) 나아간다

34~35

당신은 sincere라는 단어가 도기 제작과 관련이 있다는 것을 결코 짐작하지 못할 것이다. 어떤 언어 전문가들은 sincere가 라틴어로 "없는"을 의미하는 sin과 "왁스"를 의미하는 cero라는 두 단어에서 유래했다고 말한다. 따라서 sincere는 "왁스가 없는"을 의미한다. 고대 사람들은 점토로 된 도기를 접시와 그릇으로 사용했다. 이 도기를 만드는 데는 오랜 시간이 걸렸다. 때때로 도기에 균열이 생기기도 했고, 그런 도기의 품질은 좋지 않았다. 완전히 새로운 도기를 만들고 싶지 않았던 일부 도공들은 실수를 은폐하기 위해 금 간 곳에 왁스를 발랐다. 부주의한 구매자의 눈에는 그런 도기도 좋아 보였다. 그러나 사람들은 곧 어떤 도공이 좋고 어떤 도공이 좋지 않은지 알아차렸다. 따라서 가장 존경받는 도공들은 왁스가 없는, 즉 "sincere"한 도기를 만들었고, 이것이 sincere라는 단어가 생각과 행동에서 정직하거나 진실함을 의미하는 데 이르게 된 경우이다.

| 어휘 |

pottery n. 도기   wax n. 밀랍, 왁스   clay n. 진흙, 점토   plate n. 접시   bowl n. 그릇   brand-new a. 완전 새것인   crack n. (무엇이 갈라져 생긴) 금, 균열   potter n. 옹기장이, 도공   cover v. 감추다, 숨기다, 가리다   respected a. 훌륭한, 소문난

34 빈칸완성 ③

| 분석 |

첫 번째 빈칸의 경우, '완전히 새로 도기를 만들고 싶지 않은 도공들'이라고 하였으므로 이 도공들은 도기 제품의 결함을 '은폐하려고' 했으리라고 추론할 수 있다. 두 번째 빈칸의 경우 '왁스를 바르지 않은 도기'를 만드는 도공들이라고 하였으므로 그들은 고객을 속이려는 의도가 없는 도공, 즉 '훌륭한, 존경받는' 도공들일 것이라고 추론할 수 있다.

빈칸을 가장 잘 완성하는 것을 고르시오.
① 평가하다 ― 겸손한
② 드러내다 ― 동정적인
③ 감추다 ― 존경받는
④ 나누어 주다 ― 재능이 있는

35 글의 제목   ①

| 분석 |
이 글은 영어 단어 sincere의 어원에 의외의 흥미로운 유래가 있음을 들려주고 있다.

위 글의 제목으로 가장 적절한 것은?
① 어떤 단어에 얽힌 흥미로운 이야기
② 라틴어의 진화
③ 정직함의 중요성
④ 고대 도기의 발전

36~37

어떤 곤충들은 다른 종을 흉내 내기 위해 속임수 페로몬을 사용한다. 어떤 경우에는 이것이 그 곤충들을 다른 곤충의 다음번 먹이가 되지 않게 보호해주기도 한다. 흥미로운 예는 높은산점배기숫돌나비이다. 이 특이한 곤충은 애벌레 단계에서 개미의 페르몬과 비슷한 페로몬을 분비한다. 개미들은 숲에서 높은산점배기숫돌나비 애벌레를 발견하면 둥지로 가져간다. 그곳에서 애벌레를 잡아먹는 대신, 돌보아 준다. 애벌레가 어린 개미들을 잡아먹기 시작하더라도 개미들은 그 어느 것도 잘못되었다고 의심하지 않는다! 애벌레는 나비로 안전하게 변태하고 나서야 개미둥지를 떠난다. 또 다른 곤충과 유사한 어떤 생물은 속임수 페로몬을 사용하여 다음번 먹이를 유인한다. 남아메리카와 아프리카에 흔히 서식하는 볼라스 거미는 암컷 나방이 생산하는 페로몬과 비슷한 페로몬을 분비한다. 그런 다음 거미는 수컷 나방이 찾아오기를 기다린다. 의심하지 않는 수컷 나방은 암컷을 발견하기는 커녕, 거미의 맛있는 먹이가 된다.

| 어휘 |
trick n. 속임수   **pheromone** n. 페로몬, 동종 유인 호르몬   **Large Blue butterfly** 높은산점배기숫돌나비   **caterpillar** n. 애벌레   **release** v. 방출하다, 분비하다   **bolas spider** 볼라스 거미   **moth** n. 나방   **unsuspecting** a. 의심하지 않는, 이상한 낌새를 못 알아채는   **astute** a. 약삭빠른, 영악한   **hostile** a. 적대적인

36 빈칸완성   ④

| 분석 |
속임수 페로몬에 속아 자신이 찾아가는 대상이 암컷이 아니라 자신을 잡아먹을 포식자라는 사실을 모른 채 다가가는 수컷 나방을 묘사하기에 가장 적절한 단어는 '의심하지 않는, 아무것도 모르는, 이상한 낌새를 알아채지 못하는'을 뜻하는 unsuspecting이다.

37 내용추론   ①

| 분석 |
'속임수 페로몬이 어떤 곤충을 다른 곤충의 다음번 먹이가 되지 않게 보호해주는 흥미로운 예가 높은산점배기숫돌나비이다'라고 하였고 그 애벌레가 개미를 속여 보호받으며 성장하는 내용이 상술되어 있으므로 ①이 적절하다. ② 속임수 페로몬으로 개미를 쫓아내는 것이 아니라 유인한다. ③ 개미가 높은산점배기숫돌나비 애벌레를 자기 새끼인줄 알고 둥지로 데려가 돌보아준다. ④ 수컷 나방을 유인한다고 하였다.

위 글에서 암시하고 있는 것은 무엇인가?
① 높은산점배기숫돌나비 애벌레는 독특한 보호 방법을 가지고 있다.
② 높은산점배기숫돌나비 애벌레는 개미를 쫓아내는 페로몬을 분비한다.
③ 개미는 다른 종에게 새끼를 돌보도록 한다.
④ 볼라스 거미는 페로몬을 사용해 암컷 나방을 유인한다.

38~40

C 글로벌 광고의 문제, 즉 언어와 문화의 문제가 그 어느 때보다 커진 것이 사실이다. 예를 들어 브래니프 항공(Braniff Airlines)은 자사 항공기의 고급 가죽 시트를 광고하고 싶었다. 하지만 그 광고는 영어에서 스페인어로 번역되었을 때 알몸으로 날 수도 있다는 뜻이 되어버렸다! 또 다른 오역 사례는 쉐보레가 라틴 아메리카에서 자사의 자동차 쉐보레 노바를 마케팅하려 했을 때이다. 영어에서 노바(nova)는 별을 뜻하지만, 스페인어에서는 "가지 않는다"는 뜻이다. 당신이라면 이런 이름의 차를 사겠는가?
B 대부분의 광고 회사는 이제 완전히 새로운 광고를 만들기 시작했다. 새로운 광고를 만들 때 글로벌 광고주는 국가별 다양한 의사소통 양식을 고려해야 한다. 어떤 문화권에서는 일반적으로 제품을 설명하고 경쟁 제품보다 더 나은 이유를 설명하는 데 사용되는 정확한 단어에서 광고의 의미가 발견된다.
A 이는 미국, 영국, 독일과 같은 국가에서 그렇다. 하지만 일본과 같은 다른 문화권에서는 메시지가 단어보다는 상황과 감정에 더 많이 좌우된다. 이러한 이유로 일본의 많은 TV 광고는 사람들이 파티나 다른 사회적 상황에서 얼마나 기분 좋은지를 보여주는 것을 목표로 한다. 광고는 특정 제품이 다른 제품보다 뛰어나다고 말하는 것이 아니라, 제품에 대한 긍정적인 분위기나 감정을 조성하는 것을 목표로 한다.

| 어휘 |

fine a. 질높은, 좋은   **leather** n. 가죽   **naked** a. 벌거벗은, 아무것도 걸치지 않은   **go** v. (기계가) 가다[작동하다]   **commercial** n. (텔레비전·라디오의) 광고 (방송)

위 글은 주로 무엇에 관한 것인가?
① 최신 글로벌 광고 트렌드들
② 글로벌 광고의 어려움
③ 마케팅에서 광고의 중요성
④ 적절한 메시지 작성 방법

38   단락배열   ④

| 분석 |

B의 In some cultures … 문장과 A의 But in other cultures … 문장에서 알 수 있듯이, 서양의 사례와 일본의 사례를 대조적으로 기술하고 있는 B와 A는 붙어 있을 수밖에 없다는 응집성(cohesiveness)에 착안하여 보면, 글로벌 광고에서 생긴 실수 사례들을 통해 주제에 진입하는 C → 문화에 따라 광고 소통 방식이 달라야 한다는 중심 주제를 제기하고, 언어적 메시지를 중시하는 일부 문화의 사례를 들고 있는 B → 언어적 메시지를 중시하는 서양의 경우와 문화적으로 다른 접근을 해야 하는 일본의 사례를 소개하며 광고 전략이 문화권별로 차별화되어야 함을 강조하는 A의 순서가 가장 적절하다.

39   내용일치   ④

| 분석 |

브랜드 이름을 기계적으로 번역해 빚어진 부정적 의미가 노바 캠페인의 실패 원인이지, 광고의 목표 자체가 실패의 원인이라고 언급되지는 않았으므로 ④가 잘못된 진술이다. ① '제품을 설명하고 경쟁 제품보다 더 나은 이유를 설명하는 데 사용되는 정확한 단어에서 광고의 의미가 발견'되는 지역이 서구 문화권이라고 하였다. ② '글로벌 광고주는 국가별 다양한 의사소통 양식을 고려해야 한다'고 하였으므로 타당하다. ③ C에서 인용된 사례들이 이에 해당한다.

위 글에 의하면, 다음 중 옳지 않은 것은?
① 제품의 특징을 보여주는 광고는 서구 문화권에서 종종 성공한다.
② 나라마다 다른 의사소통 방식을 사용한다.
③ 번역 과정에서 의도치 않은 의미가 전달될 수 있다.
④ 노바 캠페인은 광고의 목표 때문에 라틴 아메리카에서 실패했다.

40   글의 주제   ②

| 분석 |

본문은 글로벌 광고가 언어적/문화적 차이로 인해 번역의 문제와 국가별 다양한 의사소통 양식을 고려해야 하는 문제 등, 어려움을 겪을 수 있다는 내용을 다루고 있으므로 ②가 글의 주제로 적절하다. 한편, ①이 정답이 되려면 '언어적/문화적 차이를 극복하는 글로벌 광고 사례' 외에도 더 다양한 사례들이 열거되어야 할 것이다.

HANKUK UNIVERSITY OF FOREIGN STUDIES | 한국외국어대학교 T1-1 A형

TEST p. 596~613

01	①	02	④	03	①	04	①	05	④	06	②	07	②	08	④	09	③	10	①
11	③	12	②	13	④	14	③	15	④	16	③	17	①	18	④	19	③	20	②
21	①	22	④	23	②	24	②	25	④	26	④	27	②	28	②	29	①	30	①
31	④	32	②	33	③	34	①	35	②	36	③	37	①	38	①	39	③	40	②
41	③	42	③	43	②	44	①	45	④	46	③	47	③	48	①	49	④	50	①

01 논리완성 ①

| 분석 |

Despite에 양보의 의미가 있음을 감안하면, 반대되는 증거가 있는데도 '고집을 굽히지 않았다'라는 흐름이 되어야 한다.

| 어휘 |

to the contrary 거기에 반(反)하는 **obdurate** a. 고집 센 **onerous** a. 성가신 **vestigial** a. 흔적뿐인, 퇴화한 **tantamount** a. ~와 마찬가지의, ~에 상당하는

| 해석 |

그에 반대되는 증거에도 불구하고 그는 자신의 믿음을 고집했다.

02 논리완성 ④

| 분석 |

vibrant와 어울리는 표현이 들어가야 할 것이므로 clamorous가 가장 적절하다.

| 어휘 |

vibrant a. 활기찬 **haughty** a. 오만한 **rancid** a. 악취가 나는 **myopic** a. 근시안적인 **clamorous** a. 떠들썩한

| 해석 |

우리는 활기차고 떠들썩한 성격을 나타내는 북적이는 분위기를 원했다.

03 논리완성 ①

| 분석 |

고객 유치를 위해서는 친환경 정책을 적극적으로 널리 알려야 할 것이다.

| 어휘 |

lure v. 유인하다 **go to great lengths** 온갖 노력을 다하다, 철저하게 하다 **green policy** 친환경 정책 **tout** v. 극구 선전[칭찬]하다 **denude** v. 벗기다 **censure** v. 질책하다 **balk** v. 주저하다

| 해석 |

고객들을 유치하려는 시도에서 기업들은 자사의 친환경 정책을 온 힘을 다해 선전한다.

04 논리완성 ①

| 분석 |

전문가 의견을 제시하려고 고용한 사람들이므로 '전문가들'이라는 의미를 가진 표현이 필요하다.

| 어휘 |

profess v. 밝히다 **pundit** n. 전문가, 논평가 **lampoon** n. 풍자글, 풍자시 **manifesto** n. 선언문, 공약 **amulet** n. 부적

| 해석 |

텔레비전 방송사들이 전문가 의견을 제시하려고 고용한 전문가들은 선거 결과에 놀랐다고 밝혔다.

05 동의어 ④

| 어휘 |

averse a. 반대하는, 싫어하는(= antagonistic) **due to** ~때문에 **urgency** n. 긴급성 **vivacious** a. 활발한, 명랑한 **effusive** a. (감정 표현이) 과장된, 넘치는 **mellifluous** a. 감미로운

| 해석 |

그는 그 새로운 프로젝트에 대해 반대하는 태도를 갖고 있었지만, 상황의 긴급성 때문에 결국 책임을 맡았다.

06 동의어 ②

| 어휘 |
match v. 어울리다　insuperable a. 극복할 수 없는(= impassable)　contemptuous a. 경멸하는　stochastic a. 확률적인, 불확실한　impeccable a. 흠잡을 데 없는, 완벽한

| 해석 |
그 노래들이 이야기와 구조적으로 어울리지 않는다는 점은 아마도 극복할 수 없는 문제일 것이다.

07 동의어 ②

| 어휘 |
nasty a. 불쾌한, 악의적인　diatribe n. 비난(= denunciation)　obscure v. 가리다, 본질을 덮다　in shambles 엉망인, 매우 혼란스러운　dichotomy n. 이분법, 양분　homage n. 존경, 경의　stasis n. 정체, 정지 상태

| 해석 |
요즘의 온갖 악의적인 정치적 비난은 한 가지 단순한 요점을 덮어 감추고 있다. 그것은 경제가 엉망이라는 점이다.

08 동의어 ④

| 어휘 |
perspicuous a. 명쾌한, 명료한(= lucid)　tire v. 피곤하게 하다　indistinct a. 불분명한, 흐릿한　momentous a. 중요한, 중요한　ravenous a. 굶주린

| 해석 |
당신은 당신이 하는 모든 말에 있어 매우 명료해야 한다. 그렇지 않으면, 청중을 즐겁게 해주기는커녕 지치게 할 뿐이다.

09 동의어 ③

| 어휘 |
conscientiously ad. 양심적으로, 성실하게, 공들여(= painstakingly)　transcribe v. 베껴 쓰다　arbitrarily ad. 제멋대로　laxly ad. 느슨하게, 대충　delinquently ad. 비행을 저지르며, 태만하게

| 해석 |
그 글은 매우 성실하게 옮겨 써졌으며, 모든 세부 내용이 완벽하다.

10 문맥상 동의어 ①

| 어휘 |
for the moment 당분간, 지금은　leave someone to do ~하도록 맡기다, 위임하다　leave v. 맡기다, 위임하다(= entrust)　bequeath v. (유산 등을) 물려주다　quit v. 그만두다, 떠나다　vacate v. 퇴거하다

| 해석 |
당분간 나는 너에게 모든 결정을 하게 맡기겠다.

11 문맥상 동의어 ③

| 어휘 |
quarter n. 지역, 지구(= district)　be full of ~으로 가득하다　landmark n. 명소　tourist n. 관광객　accommodation n. 숙박 시설, 숙소　mercy n. 자비, 관용

| 해석 |
그 도시의 오래된 지역은 전 세계로부터 관광객을 끌어들이는 역사적인 명소로 가득하다.

12 문맥상 동의어 ②

| 어휘 |
case n. 사건, 소송(= lawsuit)　eagerly ad. 간절히, 열렬히　final verdict 최종 판결　container n. 그릇, 용기　specimen n. 표본

| 해석 |
그 소송은 널리 논의되었고, 모두가 최종 판결을 간절히 기다리고 있었다.

13 문맥상 동의어 ④

| 어휘 |
due a. 마땅한, 충분한(= suitable)　after due consideration 충분한 고려 끝에　appoint v. 임명하다　correct a. 옳은, 정확한　expected a. 예상된, 기대된　unpaid a. 미납의; 무보수의

| 해석 |
충분한 고려 끝에, 우리는 그를 그 자리에 임명하기로 결정했다.

14 재진술 ③

| 분석 |
그가 올라가면 올라갈수록, 하늘은 더 높아졌다는 의미이다. ③이 의미상 같다.

| 어휘 |
the 비교급, the 비교급 ~하면 할수록 …하다　recede v. 후퇴하다　preclude v. 방해하다　eventually ad. 마침내　recession n. 후퇴

| 해석 |
그가 더 높이 올라갈수록, 하늘은 점점 더 멀어졌다.

① 하늘이 멀어지는 것이 그가 더 올라가는 것을 막았다.
② 그는 점점 더 올라가서 마침내 하늘에 도달했다.
③ 그가 점점 더 위로 올라갈수록, 하늘은 점점 더 멀어졌다.
④ 하늘이 멀어진 것은 그가 높이 올라가기 전에 일어났다.

15　재진술　④

| 분석 |
여기서는 hardly가 '전혀 ~아니다'는 뜻으로 쓰여서, 어떤 행동을 해도 그 행동이 전혀 잘못될 수 없는 것 같았다는 의미이다. ④가 의미상 가장 가깝다. as if절에는 가정법이 많이 쓰이지만 여기서처럼 직설법도 가능하다.

| 어휘 |
move n. 행동　**make a move** 행동하다　**do wrong** 잘못되다

| 해석 |
나는 전혀 잘못 행동할 수 없는 것 같았다.
① 나는 나의 모든 행동이 잘못이라는 걸 알게 되었다.
② 잘못된 방향으로 움직이기가 어려운 것 같았다.
③ 거의 움직이지 않는 것이 옳게 여겨지는 것이었다.
④ 마치 내가 전혀 잘못할 수 없는 것 같았다.

16　시제 / 어순　③

| 분석 |
원래 문장 It appeared to me (that) the universe held countless wonders (which) I had never imagined possible. 에서 접속사 that과 목적격 관계대명사 which가 생략되었다. possible은 imagine 동사의 목적보어이다. 시제는 실제로 우주에 존재한다고 여겨진 과거보다 상상한 순간이 더 이전이므로 대과거여야 한다. 부사 never는 조동사 had와 본동사 imagined 사이에 위치해야 한다.

| 어휘 |
countless a. 수많은　**wonder** n. 경이, 불가사의

| 해석 |
우주에는 내가 가능하다고는 한 번도 상상해본 적 없는 수많은 경이가 존재하는 것처럼 보였다.

17　reprove A for B　①

| 분석 |
reprove는 'reprove A for B'의 구문으로 쓰이며 'A를 B의 이유로 꾸짖다'라는 의미이다.

| 어휘 |
reprove v. 꾸짖다

| 해석 |
나의 친구는 싱크대에 있는 더러운 접시를 씻지 않았다고 나를 나무랐다.

18　수일치　④

| 분석 |
④ are의 주어는 앞의 percentage이므로 단수로 받아야 한다. are를 is로 고친다. ② that은 see의 목적어인 목적격 관계대명사이며, see는 '생각하다'는 뜻으로 쓰여서 'see+목적어+목적보어'의 5형식 동사로 사용되었고, ③ associated는 목적보어인 과거분사이다.

| 어휘 |
viewership n. 시청자 수　**see** v. 알다, 생각하다　**associated with** ~와 관련된　**fake** a. 거짓의

| 해석 |
우리는 우리가 K-pop 영상과 관련 있다고 생각하는 시청자 수의 몇 퍼센트가 진짜인지 혹은 가짜인지를 알지 못한다.

19　동사　③

| 분석 |
challenge는 '~에 도전하다'라는 의미의 타동사이다. 따라서 전치사 to를 삭제해야 한다.

| 어휘 |
The Beatitudes 팔복(八福, 성경 산상수훈의 여덟 가지 복), 팔복의 가르침　**counter-cultural** a. 반문화적인　**challenge** v. 도전하다, 문제를 제기하다

| 해석 |
팔복(八福)의 가르침은 우리가 행복을 이해하는 방식을 교정하고 거기에 도전하기 때문에 반(反)문화적이다.

20　정비문　②

| 분석 |
such는 'such+a/an+형용사+명사'의 구조로 쓰이고, so나 as는 'so/as+형용사+a/an+명사'의 구조로 쓰인다. 그러나 형용사가 비교급인 경우에는 such나 so를 사용할 수 없고 so much를 사용해야 하므로 so much less radical a claim으로 고쳐야 한다. What makes Canada so much better a place to live than the USA?나 Compared with a century ago, we have so much less violent a society. 같은 문장에서 확인할 수 있다.

| 어휘 |
depressing a. 우울하게 하는　**proposition** n. 제안　**radical**

a. 급진적인 qualified a. 자격이 있는 candidate n. 후보 orator n. 연설가

| 해석 |
① 이건 두 번 읽기에는 너무 우울한 소설이다.
② 그녀의 제안은 훨씬 덜 급진적인 주장이다.
③ 존은 당신이 찾을 그 어느 후보자에 못지않게 훌륭한 자격을 갖춘 후보자이다.
④ 링컨은 더글러스만큼 훌륭한 연설가는 아니었다.

21 정비문 ①

| 분석 |
①은 부정의 부사어 Never before로 시작되었으므로 도치가 필요하다. 따라서 "Never before have we seen ~"으로 고쳐야 한다. ② Not도 부정의 부사어이지만 every teacher와 합하여 하나의 주어를 이루므로 도치가 일어나지 않는다. ③ only를 포함한 부사어 Only recently가 문두에 있어 도치되었다. ④ 부정의 부사어 rarely가 문두에 있어 도치되었다.

| 어휘 |
Not every 모든 ~가 …한 것은 아니다   rarely ad. 드물게, 거의 ~하지 않다   encounter v. 마주치다, 직면하다   public opinion 여론

| 해석 |
① 우리는 그렇게도 극적인 여론 변화를 예전에 결코 본 적이 없다.
② 모든 교사가 새로운 교수법을 채택한 것은 아니다.
③ 오직 최근에야 투구할 때 손가락이 어떻게 작동하는지를 누군든 이해하려고 시도했다.
④ 내 경력에서 그렇게 까다로운 문제를 만난 적이 거의 없다.

22~23

많은 사람에게 아침은 정말 고된 시간이다. 하지만 만일 아침에 일어나는 일이 지금보다 조금 더 자연스럽고 덜 힘들게 만들 방법이 있다면 어찌 될 것인가? 갑작스러운 삐 소리나 음악으로 잠을 깨우는 전통적인 자명종과는 달리, 일출 알람시계는 방 안의 빛을 천천히 밝게 하면서 자연스러운 일출을 흉내 내려고 한다. 의도는 몸이 자연적인 수면–각성 주기를 조절하는 것을 도와서 점차적으로 깨어나 더 상쾌하게 하루를 시작할 기분이 들게 하려는 것이다. 이 일출 알람시계의 핵심 기능은 부드럽고 따뜻한 빛을 만들어내어, 20분 내지 40분에 걸쳐 점점 더 밝아져서 마침내 기상 시각에 가장 밝은 빛에 이르게 하는 것이다. 이 알람시계는 자연의 일출처럼 되어, 일어날 시간이라는 신호를 뇌에 조용히 보내주도록 설계되어 있다. 빛은 몸의 수면–각성 주기, 즉 "생체 리듬"을 조절하는 데 결정적인 역할을 한다. 어두울 때 몸은 멜라토닌을 분비하는데, 이것은 졸음을 느끼게 만드는 호르몬이다. 아침에는 빛에의 노출이 자연스럽게 멜라토닌 생산을 감소시키고, 각성과 경계심을 느끼게 돕는 코르티솔의 배출을 증가시킨다. 일출 알람시계는 이런 자연스러운 과정을 모방하여, 몸이 더 부드럽게 깨어나게 해주려고 한다. 이렇게 하는 덕분에 아침이 덜 거슬리고, 갑작스런 시끄러운 알람 소리로 인해 흔히 발생하는 그 멍한 기분을 줄이는 데 도움이 된다.

| 어휘 |
struggle n. 힘든 일   harsh a. 고통스러운   simulate v. 모방하다   regulate v. 조절하다   play a major role in ~에서 주요한 역할을 하다   sleep-wake cycle 수면–각성 주기   refreshed a. 상쾌한, 개운한   glow n. 은은한 빛, 부드러운 광채   circadian rhythm 생체 리듬, 일주기(日週期) 리듬   melatonin n. 멜라토닌(수면 유도 호르몬)   exposure n. 노출   release n. 배출   cortisol n. 코르티솔(각성과 스트레스 조절 호르몬)   alert a. 정신이 또렷한   mimic v. 흉내 내다, 모방하다   gradually ad. 서서히   jarring a. 갑작스럽고 귀에 거슬리는, 충격적인   groggy a. 머리가 멍한, 비몽사몽한

22 글의 제목 ④

| 분석 |
아침이 힘든 사람들을 위해 빛을 모방한 일출 알람시계로 더 자연스럽게 아침을 맞이하는 방법에 대한 글이다.

위 글의 제목으로 가장 적절한 것은?
① 시끄러운 알람시계 이면의 과학
② 호르몬은 아침을 더 스트레스 받게 만든다
③ 빨리 기상하는 자연 과정
④ 빛과 더불어 더욱 자연스럽게 깨어나기

23 내용일치 ②

| 분석 |
본문에서 일출 알람시계의 의도는 자연스러운 수면–각성 주기 조절을 돕는 것이라고 했다. ① 전통적인 알람시계이다. ③ 코르티솔이 아니라 멜라토닌이다. ④ 갑자기 노출되는 것이 아니라 점점 더 밝게 노출되는 것이다.

위 글에 따르면, 다음 중 올바른 것은?
① 일출 알람시계는 시끄러운 삐 소리로 당신을 깨운다.
② 일출 알람시계는 당신의 수면–각성 주기 조절에 도움을 준다.
③ 코르티솔은 당신을 졸리게 만드는 호르몬이다.
④ 빛에 갑자기 노출되는 것이 당신의 몸이 더 부드럽게 깨어나는 데 도움이 된다.

24~25

보행 가능성은 오랫동안 도시 주민들에게 중요한 가치로 여겨져 왔으며, 16세기 베네치아 사람들도 마찬가지였다. 당시 베네치아는 유럽에서 가장 인구가 많은 도시 중 하나로, 인구는 빠르게 증가하여 1570년대에(10년 사이에) 11만 5천 명에서 대략 17만 명으로 늘어났다. 밀집된 구조와 좁은 길로 인해 이 도시에서 동물을 이용한 운송 수단은 실용적이지 않았고, 이에 따라 다른 유럽인들로부터 조롱받기도 했다. 베네치아의 운하와 배는 유명했지만, 배 대여비는 비쌌고, 운하는 도시 전체를 커버하진 못했다. 보행자들은 때때로 나룻배를 타야 했고, 만조를 피해 다녀야 했지만, 대체로 도시 내 어떤 목적지든 걸어서 도달할 수 있었다. 벽돌과 돌을 사용하여 습지 위에 거리를 만들어야 했던 필요성도 베네치아 거리의 매력을 더했다. 유럽의 다른 곳은 그렇지 않아 거리가 진흙과 먼지로 가득하게 되었다. 베네치아를 방문한 사람들은 도시의 깨끗한 거리를 자주 칭찬하곤 했다. 걷는 것은 상업 활동에도 필수적이었다. 사람들은 걸어서 출퇴근했고, 여행자들과 순례자들은 걸어 다니며 쇼핑했고, 행상들은 걸어 다니며 물품을 팔았다. 걷는 행위는 또 도시의 활기를 체험하고, 다른 사람들과 교류하는 방식이기도 했다. 이와 같은 보행 가능성에 대한 역사적 선호는 오늘날의 도시적 이상을 반영한다.

| 어휘 |

walkability n. 보행 가능성, 도보 친화성   **resident** n. 주민   **dense** a. 밀집된   **layout** n. 구조, 배치, 설계   **impractical** a. 비실용적인   **mockery** n. 조롱   **notable** a. 주목할 만한   **high tide** 만조   **wetland** n. 습지   **appeal** n. 매력   **muddy** a. 진흙투성이인   **commerce** n. 상업, 무역   **commute** v. 출퇴근하다   **pilgrim** n. 순례자   **peddler** n. 행상인   **vibrancy** n. 활기, 생동감   **mirror** v. 반영하다, 닮다   **accessible** a. 접근할 수 있는   **indispensable** a. 필수적인

24   글의 제목   ②

| 분석 |

첫 문장과 마지막 문장만을 보더라도 베네치아의 walkability를 소재로 하는 내용임을 알 수 있다.

위 글의 제목으로 가장 적절한 것은?
① 베네치아 운송 체계의 흥망성쇠
② 16세기 베네치아의 걷기 문화
③ 베네치아: 운하와 상업의 도시
④ 베네치아 운하의 경제적 영향

25   내용일치   ④

| 분석 |

마지막에서 세 번째 문장에서 걷기가 상업 활동에 필수적이라고 언급했다. ① 진흙과 먼지로 가득하게 된 것은 유럽의 다른 곳의 거리였다. ② 배 대여비가 비쌌고, 운하는 도시 전체를 커버하진 못했다. ③ 동물을 이용한 운송은 실용적이지 않아서 다른 유럽인들로부터 조롱받았다고 했다.

위 글에 따르면, 다음 중 올바른 것은?
① 16세기 베네치아 거리는 지속적인 교통 때문에 자주 진흙투성이이고 먼지가 났다.
② 16세기 베네치아에서는 배를 빌리는 것이 저렴했고 대부분 주민이 쉽게 이용할 수 있었다.
③ 베네치아 거리의 말을 이용하는 실용성은 다른 유럽인들로부터 칭찬받았다.
④ 걷기는 16세기 베네치아에서 상업의 필수불가결한 부분이었다.

26~27

지난 가을, 뉴욕에서 코네티컷까지 기차를 타고 가는 동안, 내 동료 아만다 모리스와 그녀의 어머니는 미국 수화(ASL)로 대화를 나누고 있었다. 근처에 앉아 있던 한 남성이 그들이 수화로 이야기하는 모습을 보고, 그 대화에 끼어들었다. 그도 아만다처럼 청각장애인 부모를 둔 자녀로 자라면서 집에서는 수화를 쓰고, 바깥에서는 영어를 사용하며 자랐다. 그는 아만다의 한 가지 특징을 알아차렸다. 그녀는 그녀보다 나이가 훨씬 더 많은 사람처럼 수화를 했다. 그는 그녀를 조금 놀리기 시작하며, 그녀가 유행이 지난 수화 표현들을 쓰고 있다고 말했다. 그 역시 수화 통역사가 되기 위한 훈련을 받는 동안 비슷한 경험을 했다고 그는 말했다. 그 훈련 동안 자신이 부모에게서 배운 몇몇 수화 표현이 이미 시대에 뒤처졌다는 사실을 알게 된 것이다. 이러한 경험은 청력이 약한 아만다에게 용기를 주어, 그녀도 ASL 수업을 들으며 더 최신 수화 표현을 배우게 되었고, 그녀 역시 비슷한 패턴을 발견했다. 그녀는 이렇게 말했다. "젊은 청각장애인 선생님이 사용하는 수화 방식과 부모님이 쓰는 방식 사이에 정말 많은 차이가 있었어요." 하나의 예를 들자면, 컴퓨터라는 단어에 해당하는 예전의 수화는 크게 원을 그리는 동작으로 과거 한때 데이터를 저장하던 자기(磁氣) 테이프를 떠올리게 했다. 새로운 수화는 'C'자를 작게 원을 그리는 동작과 합치는 것인데, 이 동작은 예전의 수화를 상기시킨다.

| 어휘 |

American sign language 미국 수화(ASL)   **signing** n. 수화로 말하기   **child of deaf adults** 청각장애인 부모를 둔 자녀(CODA)

trait n. 특징, 특성　**fall out of fashion** 유행이 지나다　**tease** v. 놀리다　**go through** 겪다　**interpreter** n. 통역사　**hard of hearing** 난청인, 청력이 약한　**up-to-date** a. 최신의　**evoke** v. 연상시키다　**throwback** n. 과거를 연상시키는 것, 회귀적 요소　**generation gap** 세대 차이　**lexical** a. 어휘의

26　글의 주제　④

| 분석 |
수화도 언어처럼 세월에 따라 변한다는 점을 이야기하고 있다. 따라서 '수화의 변화'가 이 글의 소재이다.

위 글의 주요 주제는?
① 노인 세대와 젊은 세대 사이의 세대 차이
② 수화 통역사를 위한 최신식 훈련
③ 영어와 미국 수화 사이의 어휘 선택 차이
④ 미국 수화에서의 언어 변화

27　내용일치　②

| 분석 |
그는 아만다가 유행이 지난 표현을 쓴다고 놀렸다고 했으므로 ②가 정답이다. ① 아만다는 최신 표현을 배우기 위해 수업을 들었다. ③ 집이 아닌 다른 곳에서는 영어를 말했다. ④ 작은 원형 동작은 새로운 수화이다.

위 글에 따르면, 다음 중 올바른 것은?
① 아만다는 수화 통역사가 되기 위해 ASL 수업을 들었다.
② 아만다는 자신이 쓰는 수화가 구식이라고 놀림을 받았다.
③ 그 남성 수화자는 부모가 모두 청각장애인이기 때문에 말을 하지 못한다.
④ 'C'자 모양에 작게 원을 그리는 동작을 더한 것은 미국 수화에서 컴퓨터를 의미하는 옛 수화이다.

28~30

'뇌 썩음'이 끝없는 소셜 미디어 스크롤링과 정신을 마비시키는 콘텐츠에 대한 우려 속에서 2024년 옥스퍼드 올해의 단어로 선정되었다. 3만 7천 명이 넘는 사람들이 『옥스퍼드 영어사전』 출판사인 옥스퍼드 대학 출판부가 선정한 6개의 단어로 된 최종 후보 목록에서 투표를 하여 최종 단어를 뽑았다. 뇌 썩음은 '한 사람의 정신적 또는 지적 상태가 악화하는 것으로 추정되는 현상, 특히 지금은 하찮거나 도전적이지 않은 온라인 콘텐츠 과소비의 결과로 여겨지는 상태'라고 정의된다. 옥스퍼드 대학 출판부는 이 용어가 "2024년에 새롭게 주목받기 시작했으며, 특히 소셜 미디어에서 저질 온라인 콘텐츠 과소비가 미치는 영향에 대한 우려를 포착하는 용어로서 사용되었다"라고 밝혔다. 최근 들어 새롭게 주목받기는 했지만, 이 낱말의 최초 사용은 1854년 헨리 데이비드 소로의 저서 『월든』에서였다. 옥스퍼드 랭귀지스 사장인 캐스퍼 그라트월은 말했다. "뇌 썩음은 가상 생활의 인지된 위험성 중 하나와, 우리가 자유로운 시간을 어떻게 사용하는지를 확증합니다. 이는 인류와 기술을 둘러싼 문화적 논의에서 매우 당연한 다음 장처럼 느껴집니다. 올해 이렇게 많은 투표자가 이 낱말을 받아들여 우리의 선택을 지지한 것도 놀라운 일이 아닙니다. 제가 또한 흥미롭게 여기는 것은 뇌 썩음이라는 용어가 가리키는 디지털 콘텐츠를 주로 활용하고 만들어내는 집단인 Z세대와 알파세대에 의해 이 용어가 채택되었다는 점입니다."

| 어휘 |
brain rot 뇌 썩음, 정신 마비 현상(특히 온라인 콘텐츠 과잉 소비로 인한)　**mind-numbing** a. 정신을 마비시키는, 지루하고 무의미한　**shortlist** n. 최종 후보 목록　**draw up** 선정하다　**deterioration** n. 쇠퇴, 퇴보　**overconsumption** n. 과소비　**trivial** a. 사소한, 하찮은　**unchallenging** a. 도전적이지 않은, 자극이 없는　**prominence** n. 주목　**term** n. 용어　**speak to** 언급하다, 확증하다　**virtual life** 가상 생활　**embrace** v. 수용하다, 받아들이다　**endorse** v. 지지하다　**Generation Z** Z세대(1990년대 후반~2010년대 초반 출생)　**Generation Alpha** 알파세대(2010년 이후 출생)　**refer to** 가리키다

28　글의 제목　②

| 분석 |
2024년 옥스퍼드 올해의 단어로 '뇌 썩음'이 선정되었음을 소개하면서, 그 단어의 선정이 어떤 의미를 갖는지를 이야기하고 있는 글이므로 제목으로는 ②가 적절하다.

위 글의 제목으로 가장 적절한 것은?
① 디지털 콘텐츠 소비의 변화
② 2024년 옥스퍼드 올해의 단어 선정과 그 의미
③ Z세대가 현대 어휘에 미친 영향
④ 옥스퍼드 사전의 단어 선정 과정의 역사

29　내용일치　①

| 분석 |
'올해 이렇게 많은 투표자가 이 낱말을 받아들여 우리의 선택을 지지한 것도 놀라운 일이 아닙니다'라고 했으므로, 전혀 놀랍지 않았다. ② '옥스퍼드 대학 출판부가 선정한 6개의 단어로 된 최종 후보 목록'이라고 했다. ③ 이 낱말의 최초 사용은 1854년 헨리 데이비드 소로의 저서 『월든』에서였다고 했다. ④ 디지털 콘텐츠를 주로 활용하고 만들어내는 집단은 Z세대와 알파세대라고 했다.

위 글에 따르면, 다음 중 올바르지 않은 것은?
① 캐스퍼 그라트월은 투표 결과에 놀랐다.
② 옥스퍼드 대학 출판부는 투표를 위해 6개의 최종 후보 단어 목록을 제시했다.
③ 뇌 썩음이라는 용어는 1854년 소로의 『월든』에 처음 등장했다.
④ Z세대와 알파세대는 싸구려 온라인 콘텐츠의 주요 사용자이다.

30 빈칸완성 ①

| 분석 |

글의 흐름으로 볼 때 "최근 다시 주목받고 있지만, 사실은 오래전부터 존재했던 낱말이다" 정도의 의미가 필요하다. 따라서 역접의 전치사인 Despite가 적절하다.

31~32

"왜 거의 모든 가공식품에 설탕이 들어 있는가?"라고 물을 수도 있다. 본질적으로 설탕은 포만감을 조절하는 뇌의 부분을 억제하여 우리가 더 많이 먹을 수 있게 해주는 수단이다. 따라서 원래는 설탕이 들어 있지 않은 식품, 예를 들면 샐러드드레싱, 파스타 소스, 빵 등에 설탕을 첨가하면, 사람들은 설탕이 없을 때보다 그 음식을 더 많이 먹게 되는 경향이 있다. 따라서 설탕 성분 첨가는 사람들이 더 많이 먹고, 더 많이 구매하도록 유도할 수 있기 때문에, 제조업체에는 더 많은 이익을 창출한다. 이 설탕 기반 수익의 문제는 설탕 과다 섭취가 당뇨병, 비만, 알츠하이머병과 연관되어 있다는 점이다. 설탕이 전통적인 의미에서 약물로 분류되지는 않지만, 과학적 증거에 따르면 설탕이 뇌의 보상 시스템과 도파민 수용체에 미치는 영향은 중독성 약물의 효과와 유사하다. 미국 정신의학회(APA)는 사람이 어떤 물질에 대해 내성을 키울 수 있고, 사용을 중단했을 때 금단 증상을 경험한다면 그 물질을 중독성이 있다고 판단한다. 설탕은 아직 APA의 공식 중독성 물질 목록에는 포함되어 있지 않지만, 일부에서는 설탕도 포함되어야 한다고 주장하고 있으며, 많은 나라가 설탕 소비를 제한하기 위해 세금을 부과하거나 식사 지침을 변경하는 조치를 취하고 있다.

| 어휘 |

processed food 가공식품 **vehicle** n. 수단 **inhibit** v. 억제하다
satiety n. 포만감 **ingredient** n. 재료, 성분 **diabetes** n. 당뇨병
obesity n. 비만 **Alzheimer's disease** 알츠하이머병 **reward system** 보상 시스템(뇌의 쾌락/동기부여 회로) **dopamine receptor** 도파민 수용체 **addictive** a. 중독성 있는 **build up** 축적하다
tolerance n. 내성 **withdrawal** n. 금단 증상 **dietary guidelines** 식이 지침 **curb** v. 억제하다

31 글의 주제 ④

| 분석 |

이 글은 설탕이 가공식품에 첨가되는 이유와 설탕 첨가로 생기는 여러 문제들을 다루고 있다. 따라서 ④가 글의 주제로 가장 적절하다.

위 글의 주요 주제는?
① 가공식품 과잉 섭취의 문제점들
② 과식이 비만과 당뇨병으로 이어지는 방식
③ 미국 정신의학회가 설탕을 중독성 약물로 분류하지 않은 실패
④ 식품에 설탕이 첨가되는 이유와 그로 인해 발생하는 문제들

32 내용일치 ②

| 분석 |

설탕은 뇌의 포만감을 조절하는 부분을 억제한다고 했으므로 ②가 사실이 아니다. ① 설탕이 도파민 수용체에 미치는 영향은 중독성 약물의 효과와 유사하다고 했다. ③ 많은 나라가 설탕 소비를 제한하기 위해 세금 부과나 식사 지침 변경 등의 조치를 취하고 있다고 했다. ④ 설탕 성분 첨가는 사람들이 더 많이 구매하도록 유도한다고 했다.

위 글에 따르면, 다음 중 올바르지 않은 것은?
① 설탕이 도파민 수용체에 미치는 효과는 중독성 약물의 효과와 유사하다.
② 설탕은 뇌에서 포만감 조절 기능을 강화한다.
③ 많은 나라들이 설탕 사용을 억제하려고 노력하고 있다.
④ 식품에 설탕을 첨가하면 종종 그 식품의 판매가 증가한다.

33~34

잘 소화되지 않는 상한 굴이나 수상한 버섯 수프를 먹어본 사람이라면 누구나, 다가올 끔찍한 시간을 예고하는 불길한 메스꺼움을 기억할 것이다. 박테리아는 독소를 방출해, 위 속 내용물을 빠르게 비워내는 신체 반응을 시작하게 한다. 이는 일종의 방어 기제로, 침입자를 단번에 제거하는 것이 단기적으로는 불쾌하지만, 장기적으로는 아마도 도움이 된다. 그러나 뇌가 어떻게 경보 신호를 받고, 위에 토하라고 지시하는 신호를 보내는지는 여전히 수수께끼로 남아 있다. 이 특정한 신경 경로를 이해해야 할 이유는 다음번에 또 식중독을 겪을 수 있기 때문만은 아니다. 이 신경 경로를 억제하는 방법을 알아내는 것은 화학요법 약물치료나 다른 약물로 인해 생기는 구역질을 겪는 사람들에게 큰 도움이 될 수 있기 때문이다. 마치 암 투병의 고통과 공포가 부족하다는 듯이, 환자들은 음식을 전혀 받아들이지 못하는 경우가 많아서 체중 유지 자체가 큰 싸움이 된다. 새로운 연구에서 연구자들

에 따르면, 박테리아 독소와 화학요법 치료 모두가 메스꺼움을 유발하는 유사한 신경 신호의 연쇄 반응을 촉발한다.

| 어휘 |

shady a. 의심스러운, 수상한 oyster n. 굴 go down 소화되다
ominous a. 불길한 queasiness n. 메스꺼움, 구역질 herald v. 예고하다 impending a. 임박한 evacuate v. (속을) 비워내다, 대피시키다 protective mechanism 방어 기제 of sorts 일종의 get rid of 제거하다 invader n. 침입자 en masse 일제히, 모두 함께 in the long term 장기적으로 alarm signal 경고신호 vomit v. 토하다 bout n. 발작, 한바탕 neural pathway 신경 경로 figure out 이해하다 nausea n. 구역질 scary a. 무시무시한 regulate v. 조절하다 turn off 싫어하게 만들다 set in motion 작동시키다, 시작하게 하다 cascade n. 연쇄 반응 requite v. 보상하다 maintain v. 유지하다 counter v. 억제하다 catalyze v. 촉진하다 be comprised of ~으로 구성되어 있다

33 빈칸완성 ③

| 분석 |

항암제나 다른 약물로 인해 메스꺼움을 겪는 사람에게 도움이 되려면, 그 신경 경로를 '억제'하는 방법을 알아내야 할 것이다.

34 내용추론 ①

| 분석 |

첫 부분에서 상한 굴이나 의심스러운 버섯은 불길한 메스꺼움을 일으킨다고 하였으므로, 위장 문제를 일으킨다고 추론할 수 있다.
② 의식적 사고와는 아무런 관련이 없다. ③ 약물은 살이 빠지는 원인이다. ④ 항암제와 박테리아 독소가 비슷한 신경 반응을 유발한다고 했지, 둘이 같은 박테리아 독소로 만들어졌다는 이야기는 아니다.

위 글에 따르면, 다음 중 추론할 수 있는 것은?
① 상한 굴과 일부 버섯 수프는 위장 문제를 일으킨다.
② 위 속 박테리아 제거는 의식적인 사고를 수반한다.
③ 체중 증가는 과도한 약물 복용의 결과이다.
④ 항암 치료 약물은 박테리아 독소로 구성되어 있다.

35~37

자이가르닉 효과는 20세기 초, 러시아 심리학자 블루마 자이가르닉에 의해 처음 관찰되었다. 자이가르닉은 식당에서 웨이터들을 관찰하면서, 웨이터들이 아직 진행 중인 주문에 대해서는 기억을 잘하지만, 이미 완료된 주문에 대해서는 그렇지 않다는 사실을 알아차렸다. 그렇다면, 왜 미완성 과제는 우리 머릿속에 남아 있는 걸까? 우리 뇌는 완결을 갈망하기 때문이다. 따라서 과제가 미완성 상태로 남아 있으면 뇌에 긴장 상태가 형성된다. 이 긴장은 우리에게 완결을 추구하도록 동기를 부여하고, 이는 과제를 완성해야만 해소될 수 있다. 자이가르닉 효과는 인지 부조화 개념과 관련이 있다. 인지 부조화란, 우리가 서로 상충하는 신념이나 가치관을 가질 때 느끼는 불편함을 가리킨다. 미완성 과제의 경우, 과제를 끝내야 한다는 신념과 아직 과제가 완료되지 않았다는 사실이 충돌하면서, 우리 마음속에 인지 부조화와 긴장을 만들어낸다. 자이가르닉 효과는 우리의 생산성과 동기에 상당한 영향을 미칠 수 있다. 머릿속에 미완성 과제가 있을 때, 우리는 당장 해야 할 일에 집중을 잘 못하고, 따라서 작업 성과가 떨어질 수 있다. 하지만 자이가르닉 효과는 긍정적인 결과를 낳도록 활용될 수도 있다. 미완성 과제가 만들어내는 긴장을 동기부여 수단으로 삼음으로써, 우리는 생산성과 과제 완료 동기를 높일 수 있다.

| 어휘 |

Zeigarnik Effect 자이가르닉 효과(미완성 과업을 더 잘 기억하는 현상)
order n. 주문 be in progress 진행 중이다 as opposed to ~와는 반대로 closure n. 완결, 마무리 crave v. 갈망[열망]하다 tension n. 긴장, 갈등 cognitive dissonance 인지 부조화 productivity n. 생산성 motivation n. 동기부여 task at hand 현재 진행 중인 일 performance n. 성과 capitalize on 활용하다 confirm v. 확증하다 linger v. 오래 남다 enhance v. 향상시키다 take a break 휴식하다 facilitate v. 쉽게 만들다 harness v. 이용하다 tolerate v. 참다 loom v. 느껴지다 trigger v. 유발하다 not ~ necessarily 반드시 ~하는 것은 아니다

35 글의 제목 ②

| 분석 |

미완성 과제가 머릿속에 오래 남는 이유를 설명하고, 이 현상이 생산성과 동기에 미치는 영향까지 설명하고 있다. 따라서 ②가 제목으로 가장 적절하다.

위 글의 제목으로 가장 적절한 것은?
① 우리의 뇌가 우리의 신념을 확증하게 만드는 동기는 무엇인가
② 왜 미완성 과제가 우리 머릿속에 오래 남는가
③ 자이가르닉 효과가 어떻게 인지 부조화를 일으키는가
④ 작업 수행 능력을 향상시키는 것은 무엇인가

36 빈칸완성 ③

| 분석 |

자르가르닉 효과를 긍정적으로 활용하는 방법에 대한 내용이 이어지고 있으므로 ③이 정답으로 적절하다.

Ⓐ에 들어갈 적절한 표현은?
① 휴식을 취함으로써 회복된다
② 과제를 완료함으로써 촉진된다
③ 긍정적인 결과를 낳도록 활용된다
④ 좋아하지 않는 결과를 감수하며 견딘다

37 내용추론 ①

| 분석 |

미완성 과제가 긴장을 유발한다고 했으므로, ① 몇 주 전에 읽기 시작한 책을 '끝낼 때는' 긴장이 사라질 것이다. ② 사람들은 긴장(tension)과 인지 부조화(dissonance)를 없애기 위해 행동한다.

다음 중 위 글로부터 추론할 수 <u>없는</u> 것은?
① 몇 주 전에 읽기 시작한 책을 끝낼 때 불편을 느낄 것이다.
② 사람들은 정신적 긴장을 해소하려는 자연스러운 성향이 있다.
③ 아직 끝내지 않은 프로젝트의 마감일이 다가오면 긴장을 느낀다.
④ 미완성 과제가 유발하는 긴장이 반드시 부정적인 영향을 주는 것은 아니다.

38~40

당신이 집을 임대하려 한다면, 집주인은 리얼터페이지를 사용해서 월세를 정했을 가능성이 크다. 이 회사는 자신에 대해 그저 집주인들이 가장 이익이 되는 가격을 설정하도록 도울 뿐이라고 설명한다. 그러나 최근에 있었던 소송은 사실은 이와 다르다고 말하고 있다. 리얼터페이지는 AI를 이용한 가격 담합 음모이다. 가격 담합의 고전적 이미지는 경쟁 회사 경영진들이 은밀히 모여서, 판매하는 모든 상품에 대해 부풀려진 가격을 매기기로 몰래 합의하는 것이다. 이런 식의 담합은 자유시장 경제에 반하는 가장 심각한 죄악 중 하나로 여겨진다. 고(故) 안토닌 스칼리아 대법관은 한번은 가격 담합을 반독점법 중 '최고 악'이라고 표현한 적도 있다. 가격 담합 합의는 최대 10년의 징역형이나 1억 달러의 벌금형에 처할 수 있다. 그러나 리얼터페이지 사례가 시사하듯, 기술은 우회로를 제공할 수 있다. 경쟁자들과 모여 가격 경쟁을 하지 않기로 합의하는 대신에, 모두가 독립적으로 제3자를 통해 가격을 설정하는 것이다. 부동산 소유자들은 리얼터페이지의 '부동산 관리 소프트웨어'에 임대료와 공실률을 포함한 자신들의 데이터를 입력한다. 그러면 경쟁업체들이 얼마를 받고 있는지를 파악한 이 알고리즘은 임대료 추천 가격을 내놓는다. 충분히 많은 집주인이 이 시스템을 사용하게 된다면, 그 결과는 전통적인 가격 담합 카르텔과 다를 바 없이 보일 수 있다. 비밀스러운 악수나 은밀한 모임조차 필요 없이, 가격 경쟁이 아니라 일제히 가격 인상이 이루어지는 것

이다. 가격 경쟁이 사라지면, 기업들은 혁신하거나 비용을 낮출 동기를 잃게 되고, 소비자들은 높은 가격과 대안 부재를 떠안게 된다. 알고리즘을 통한 가격 담합은 점점 더 많은 산업으로 퍼지고 있으며, 현재의 법체계는 이를 저지하기 위한 대비가 되어 있지 않을지도 모른다.

| 어휘 |

rent v. 임대하다   chance n. 가능성   landlord n. 집주인   set the price 가격을 정하다   litigation n. 소송   price-fixing n. 가격 담합   conspiracy n. 음모, 공모   inflated a. 부풀어 오른   collusion n. 공모   commit v. 저지르다   free-market economy 자유시장 경제   supreme evil 최고의 악   antitrust law 반독점법   fine n. 벌금   workaround n. 우회 방법   property management software 부동산 관리 소프트웨어   vacancy rates 공실률   spit out (정보나 결과를) 뱉어내다, 내놓다   lockstep n. 일사불란한 행동   price competition 가격 경쟁   clandestine a. 비밀의, 은밀한   alternative n. 대안   accommodate v. 수용하다   real estate 부동산   get stuck with 떠맡다, 떠안다

38 글의 목적 ①

| 분석 |

알고리즘을 통한 가격 담합이 전통적인 담합 못지않게 위험할 수 있고, 현재의 법으로는 막을 수 없음을 걱정하는 글이다. 따라서 ①이 정답으로 가장 적절하다. ② 리얼터페이지는 하나의 예일 뿐이다. ③ 법을 완화하자는 주장은 없다. ④ 경각심을 불러일으키려는 목적이다.

이 글의 주된 목적은?
① 알고리즘 기반 가격 담합의 잠재적 위험성에 대해 경고하기 위해
② 리얼터페이지가 집주인과 임대인을 위해 작동하는 방식을 설명하기 위해
③ 기술 발전을 수용하기 위해 법이 완화되어야 한다고 주장하기 위해
④ 부동산에서 알고리즘 기반 가격 담합을 정의하기 위해

39 내용일치 ③

| 분석 |

리얼터페이지는 이를 사용하는 사람들이 굳이 만나 가격을 담합할 필요를 없애 준다고 했으므로 ③이 사실이 아니다. ① 집주인이 리얼터페이지를 사용하여 월세를 정했을 가능성이 크다고 했다. ② 가격 담합 합의는 최대 10년의 징역형이나 1억 달러의 벌금형에 처할 수 있다고 했다. ④ 가격 경쟁이 사라지면, 기업들은 혁신하거나 비용을 낮출 동기를 잃게 된다고 했다.

위 글에 따르면, 다음 중 올바르지 않은 것은?
① 요즘 많은 집주인이 월세를 설정할 때 리얼터페이지를 사용한다.
② 가격 담합을 저지르면 최대 10년 형을 받을 수 있다.
③ 리얼터페이지는 집주인들이 만나서 가격을 담합할 수 있도록 돕는다.
④ 가격 경쟁은 기업들이 고객 유치를 위해 비용을 줄이도록 동기를 부여한다.

40 빈칸완성 ②

| 분석 |

빈칸 다음을 보면 가격 경쟁은 사라지고, 가격은 올라가며, 비밀회의는 없다는 내용이다. 이는 전형적인 가격 담합이므로 정답은 ②이다. ④ 리얼터페이지는 알고리즘을 사용하지만, 그 결과는 전통적 담합과 같다는 내용이 되어야 한다. 알고리즘 시스템이 알고리즘 시스템을 낳는다는 이상한 말이 된다.

Ⓐ에 들어갈 적절한 표현은?
① 시장 주도 가격 메커니즘
② 전통적인 가격 담합 카르텔
③ 자유시장 해결책
④ 알고리즘 기반 가격 시스템

41~42

값싼 석유 기반 소재의 사용이 폭발적으로 증가하면서 패션 산업이 급격히 변화했는데, 이는 플라스틱 가죽 같은 합성 소재를 '비건 가죽' 같은 멋진 대안으로 성공적으로 리브랜딩한 마케팅 전략 덕분이기도 하다. 이 명칭은 환경적 미덕을 암시하도록 의도된 마케팅의 걸작이다. 이러한 노력의 배경에는 각종 직물과 소재의 환경적 영향을 평가하는 영향력 있는 등급 체계가 있었다. 히그 지수라고 부르는 이 등급 체계는 2011년 세계 최대 규모의 패션 소매업체들이, 예를 들어, 이들이 판매하는 옷을 생산할 때 소모되는 물의 사용량을 줄이거나 유해 화학물질 사용을 억제함으로써 환경 발자국을 측정하고 궁극적으로 줄이도록 돕기 위해 도입한 것이었다. 하지만 이 히그 지수는 면, 양모, 가죽 같은 천연 소재보다 화석 연료에서 만들어진 합성 소재를 훨씬 더 높게 평가하는 특징이 있다. 이제 이러한 평가 방식은 천연 섬유 산업 대표자들로부터 비판받고 있는데, 이들은 히그 지수가, 합성 소재로 인한 환경 피해에 대한 의문에도 불구하고, 합성 소재 사용 증가를 환경상 바람직한 것처럼 보여주는 데 이용되고 있다고 말한다.

| 어휘 |

explosion n. 폭발적 증가 **petroleum-based material** 석유 기반 소재 **synthetic material** 합성 소재 **rebranding** n. 브랜드 이미지 쇄신 **vegan leather** 비건 가죽(플라스틱 기반 합성 가죽) **masterstroke** n. 대성공, 절묘한 전략 **rating system** 평가 시스템 **assess** v. 평가하다 **Higg Index** 히그 지수(패션 업계 환경 평가 지수) **shrink** v. 줄이다 **environmental footprint** 환경 발자국, 환경에 끼치는 영향 **cut down on** 줄이다 **rein in** 억제하다, 통제하다 **fossil fuel** 화석 연료 **come under fire** 비판받다 **natural-fiber** n. 천연 섬유 **environmental toll** 환경 피해 **advent** n. 등장

41 글의 주제 ③

| 분석 |

"히그 지수는 각종 직물과 소재의 환경적 영향을 평가하는 영향력 있는 등급 체계이지만, 최근 들어서는 천연 섬유 산업에서 비판을 받고 있다"는 내용의 글이다. 따라서 ③이 정답으로 가장 적절하다. ④ 천연 섬유 산업에 대한 '지원'이 아니라, '히그 지수'가 관심의 초점이 되어야 한다.

위 글의 주요 주제는?
① 패션 산업에서 친환경적으로 보이는 소재들의 리브랜딩
② 패션 분야에서 비건 가죽의 등장
③ 패션 산업에서 히그 지수의 사용을 둘러싼 논란
④ 히그 지수에 맞서기 위한 천연 섬유 산업에 대한 지원

42 내용일치 ③

| 분석 |

'히그 지수가 합성 소재 사용 증가를 환경상 바람직한 것처럼 보여주고 있다고 천연 섬유 산업 대표자들로부터 비판받고 있다'고 했으므로 ③이 사실이다. ① 패션 업계가 충격을 받았다는 내용은 없다. ② '비건 가죽'은 패션 업계의 마케팅 전략이지, 히그 지수가 리브랜딩한 것은 아니다. ④ 천연 섬유 산업이 히그 지수를 비판한다.

위 글에 따르면, 다음 중 올바른 것은?
① 석유 기반 소재의 사용이 폭발적으로 증가했고, 그것이 패션 업계에 충격을 주었다.
② 히그 지수가 2011년에 플라스틱 가죽을 '비건 가죽'으로 리브랜딩했다.
③ 히그 지수가 합성 소재의 사용을 부추긴다는 비판을 받고 있다.
④ 천연 섬유 산업이 히그 지수 사용을 지지한다.

43~44

도플갱어는 놀랄 만큼 비슷한 신체적 특징을 공유한다. 때때로 이들은 서로 너무나 닮아서, 아무런 혈연관계가 없는 두 사람이 쉽사리 쌍둥이로 통한다. 이제, 새로운 연구에 따르

면 도플갱어들은 단순히 외모만 비슷한 것이 아니다. 얼굴이 닮은 사람들은 일부 DNA도 비슷하리라는 생각이 자명해 보일 수도 있지만, 지금까지 누구도 과학적으로 입증하지 못했다. 인터넷 덕분에 이제 연구자들이 도플갱어들을 찾아내고 연구하는 일이 훨씬 쉬워졌다. 이 닮은 사람들의 유전적 수준에서 무슨 일이 일어나고 있는지를 이해하기 위해, 과학자들은 캐나다 사진작가 프랑수아 브루넬과 협력했다. 브루넬은 1999년부터 전 세계를 여행하면서 서로 거의 똑같이 닮은 낯선 사람들의 친밀한 초상 사진을 찍으며 "나는 닮은 사람이 아니다!" 프로젝트를 진행해왔다. 연구진은 브루넬이 촬영한 32쌍의 모델들에게 생활방식에 관한 질문에 답해줄 것과 DNA 샘플을 제출해줄 것을 요청했다. 과학자들은 안면 인식 소프트웨어를 사용하여 이 소위 '닮은 꼴 인간'들의 얼굴 사진을 분석하고, 얼굴 간의 유사성을 수치화한 점수를 계산했다. 그 결과, 매우 닮은 16쌍 중 9쌍이 단일 염기다형성이라 알려진 많은 공통 유전적 변이를 공유한다는 사실을 발견했다. 따라서 이 9쌍은 사실상 '가상 쌍둥이'라고 할 수 있다.

| 어휘 |

doppelgänger n. 도플갱어 **strikingly** ad. 놀랄 만큼 **physical** a. 신체적인 **at times** 때때로 **pass for** ~로 통하다, ~처럼 보이다 **than meets the eye** 눈에 보이는 것보다 **genetic** a. 유전적인 **track down** 추적하다 **collaborate** v. 협력하다 **capture portrait** 초상 사진을 촬영하다 **headshot** n. 얼굴 사진 **compute** v. 계산하다 **single nucleotide polymorphism** 단일 염기다형성 (SNP) **virtual twins** 가상 쌍둥이(외모뿐 아니라 유전적 유사성이 있는 닮은 사람들) **at first glance** 첫눈에 보기에

43 글의 제목 ②

| 분석 |

이제까지는 얼굴이 닮은 사람들이 유전적으로도 닮은 건지에 대한 과학적인 분석이 없었는데, 이제 그러한 과학적인 분석이 가능해서, 결국 이들을 사실상 '가상 쌍둥이'라고 해도 좋다는 내용이다.

위 글의 제목으로 가장 적절한 것은?
① 닮은 사람들은 사실은 도플갱어가 아니다
② 도플갱어들은 이제 과학적으로 입증되었다
③ 가상 쌍둥이들은 도플갱어로 판명되었다
④ 도플갱어들은 외모적 특징을 공유할 필요가 없다

44 부분이해 ①

| 분석 |

"than meets the eye"는 '겉으로 보기보다'라는 뜻이다.

다음 중 ⓐ와 가장 가까운 의미는?
① 도플갱어들은 처음 봤을 때 보이는 것보다 더 많은 유사점을 공유한다.
② 도플갱어들은 보통 직접 만나는 것을 고려한다.
③ 도플갱어들은 외모만 비슷하고 다른 면에서는 전혀 닮지 않았다.
④ 도플갱어들의 눈이 다른 특징들보다 더 비슷해 보인다.

45~47

2024년 8월 1일, 유럽연합(EU)의 인공지능(AI)법이 발효되었다. 이 법은 EU 내 AI 시스템 규제를 향한 중대한 조치이다. 이 법은 두 가지 목표를 갖고 있다. AI의 개발을 촉진하고, 시민들의 건강, 안전, 기본권에 대한 잠재적 위험을 완화하는 것이다. AI법의 가장 주요한 특징은 AI 시스템을 위험을 기반으로 하여 분류한다는 것이다. 스팸 필터나 AI 기반 비디오 게임 등이 포함되는 '최소 위험' 시스템은 AI법 하에서 새로운 의무가 부과되지 않는다. 예를 들어, 챗봇 같은 '특정 투명성 위험'으로 분류된 시스템은 사용자에게 지금 기계와 상호작용하고 있다는 사실을 명시적으로 알려야 한다. 또한, 일부 AI 생성 콘텐츠는 AI가 생성했음을 표시해야 한다. 예를 들어, 의료용 소프트웨어나 직원 채용에 사용되는 AI와 같은 '고위험' 시스템은 위험 완화 시스템, 고품질 데이터 세트, 인간 감독과 같은 엄격한 신규 요건을 준수해야 한다. 법안으로 마지막 규정된 범주는 '금지된 AI' 시스템이다. 용납할 수 없는 위험을 초래하는 시스템들이 여기에 해당한다. EU가 금지한 시스템에는 잠재의식이나 조작적 기법을 활용하여 행동을 왜곡하거나 합리적 의사결정을 방해하여 심각한 피해를 유발하는 시스템들이 포함된다. 또한, 이 법은 범용 AI(GPAI) 모델에 관한 조항도 담고 있다. 모든 GPAI 모델 제공업체는 기술 문서를 제출하고, 저작권 지침을 준수하며, 훈련에 사용된 콘텐츠 요약을 공개해야 한다. 시스템 리스크를 초래하는 GPAI 모델 제공업체는 또한 모델 평가, 적대적 테스트, 심각한 사고 추적 및 보고, 사이버 보안 보호 조치도 수행해야 한다. 이 AI법은 인권과 기본 가치를 기반으로 강력한 규제 체계를 구축하고, AI 시스템에 대한 명확한 요구사항을 설정함으로써, EU 시민들의 기본권을 보호하는 한편, 혁신과 경제 성장 촉진을 목표로 하고 있다.

| 어휘 |

act n. 법안 **come into effect** 발효되다 **regulate** v. 규제하다 **foster** v. 장려하다, 조장하다 **mitigate** v. 완화하다 **potential** a. 잠재적인, 가능성이 있는 **fundamental right** 기본권 **risk-based classification** 위험 기반 분류 **comply with** 따르다 **explicitly** ad. 명시적으로, 명백하게 **risk-mitigating systems** 위험 완화 시스템 **human oversight** 인간 감독 **pose** v. (문제 등을) 제기하다 **ban** v. 금지하다 **deploy** v. 전개하다 **subliminal technique**

잠재의식 기법 manipulative techniques 조작적 기법 distort
v. 왜곡하다 impair v. 손상시키다 provision n. 조항 General
Purpose AI 범용 인공지능(GPAI) technical documentation 기술
문서 Copyright Directive 저작권 지침 systemic risk 체계적
위험 adversarial testing 적대적 테스트 underhanded a. 은밀한
sound a. 건전한 implement v. 실행하다 subtle a. 미묘한

45 글의 제목 ④

| 분석 |
새롭게 발효된 유럽연합의 AI 법안의 여러 특징들을 살펴보고 있는 글이다.

위 글의 제목으로 가장 적절한 것은?
① 인공지능 규제의 미래
② AI법의 투명성 위험 및 표시 요건
③ 유럽 관점에서 본 현대 비디오 게임에서의 AI 역할
④ EU 인공지능법과 그 세부 사항

46 내용일치 ③

| 분석 |
'최소 위험' 시스템에는 새로운 의무가 부과되지 않는다고 했으므로 ③이 사실이 아니다. ① '특정 투명성 위험'으로 분류된 시스템은 사용자에게 지금 기계와 상호작용하고 있다는 사실을 명시적으로 알려야 한다고 했다. ② 모든 GPAI 모델 제공업체는 훈련에 사용된 콘텐츠 요약을 공개해야 한다고 했다. ④ '고위험' 시스템은 고품질 데이터 세트, 인간 감독과 같은 엄격한 신규 요건을 준수해야 한다고 했다.

위 글에 따르면, 다음 중 올바르지 않은 것은?
① '특정 투명성 위험' 시스템 사용자들은 기계와 상호작용하고 있음을 인지해야 한다.
② GPAI 모델 훈련에 사용된 콘텐츠 요약이 공개되어야 한다.
③ AI법은 '최소 위험' 시스템에 새로운 요건을 도입한다.
④ AI법은 '고위험' 시스템에 인간 감독과 고품질 데이터 세트를 요구한다.

47 부분이해 ③

| 분석 |
밑줄 친 부분은 '잠재의식 기법 혹은 조작 기법을 이용하여 행동을 왜곡하고, 올바른 의사결정을 방해하는 것'이다. ① 'overtly(드러나게, 노골적으로)"는 '잠재의식'이나 '조작'과는 반대된다. ② 촉진하는 게 아니라 방해한다. ④ 정보 시스템 조작이 아니라, 개인의 행동과 의사결정에 영향을 미친다.

다음 중 Ⓐ와 가장 가까운 의미는?
① 노골적으로 조작적 기법을 사용하여 행동을 이끌고 판단을 돕는다
② 은밀한 기법을 통해 지식 기반 의사결정을 촉진한다
③ 교묘하거나 은밀한 방법을 이용하여 행동을 변화시키고 건전한 의사결정을 방해한다
④ 정보 시스템을 조작하기 위해 미묘한 전략을 실행한다

48~50

우리는 특정 책들의 유통을 법적으로 금지하는 금서 지정을 보통 권위주의 정권과 연관 짓는다. 하지만, 이러한 일은 현대 민주국가에서도 일어난다. 한강의『채식주의자』, 하퍼 리의『앵무새 죽이기』, 레이 브래드버리의『화씨 451도』를 포함한 수많은 유명 작품들이 서로 다른 이유로 이러한 조사를 받은 적이 있다. 한국 작가 한강은 노벨문학상 수상자임에도 불구하고, 사회 규범, 그중에서도 특히 정신질환과 신체적 자율성에 대한 규범을 신랄하게 비판하는 소설『채식주의자』가 "학생들에게 해롭다"라는 이유로 2,000개가 넘는 학교에서 퇴출당하는 것을 지켜보았다. 이 금지를 비판하는 사람들은 이러한 조치가 이 소설이 신랄하게 다루고 있는 개성과 사회적 압력에 관한 진지한 논의를 가로막는다고 주장한다. 마찬가지로, 하퍼 리의『앵무새 죽이기』역시 남부 미국에서의 인종적 불의를 통렬하게 그리고 있지만, 인종 차별적인 표현을 사용했다는 이유로 미국 여러 지역 도서관에서 퇴출당하였다. 레이 브래드버리의『화씨 451도』는 아마도 가장 아이러니한 금지 사례일 것이다. 이 소설은 책이 불법화되고, '소방관'들이 책이라면 찾아내어 모두 불태우는 디스토피아적 미래를 상상하고 있기 때문이다. 이 소설도 검열 당했는데, 이는 반대 의견 억압과 문맹 사회의 위험성이라는 소설의 주제와 부합한다. 책의 금지를 찬성하는 사람들은 그들이 젊은 독자들을 잠재적으로 해로운 콘텐츠로부터 보호한다고 주장한다. 반면, 반대하는 사람들은 그들이 지적 자유를 제한하고, 옳고 그름에 대한 도전적인 사상에 비판적으로 참여하는 것을 사회로부터 박탈한다고 주장한다. 아이러니하게도, 금서 지정은 오히려 사회적 수준에서 비판적 사고를 촉진하는 문학의 필수적인 역할을 부각하고 있다.

| 어휘 |
associate A with B A를 B와 연관시키다 **book banning** 금서
prohibition n. 금지 **circulation** n. 유통 **authoritarian**
regimes 권위주의 정권 **scrutiny** n. 조사 **albeit** prep. ~이지만
excoriate v. 맹렬히 비판하다 **autonomy** n. 자율성 **detrimental**
a. 해로운 **stifle** v. 억압하다, 막다 **poignantly** ad. 날카롭게
racial slur 인종 차별적 비방 표현 **trenchant** a. 날카로운, 신랄한
envision v. 상상하다 **dystopian** a. 암울한 미래 사회를 그린

outlawed a. 불법화된 censor v. 검열하다 suppress v. 억압하다 dissenting idea 반대 의견 proponent n. 지지자 opponent n. 반대자 critical engagement 비판적 참여 underscore v. 강조하다

48 글의 목적 ②

| 분석 |

금서 지정을 소재로, 다양한 금서를 언급하고, 찬성과 반대 관점을 소개한 다음, 결국은 금서 지정이 역설적으로 문학이 담당하는 비판적 사고 촉진이라는 중요한 역할을 드러낸다고 말하고 있다. 따라서 ②가 정답으로 적절하다.

이 글의 주된 목적은?
① 한국과 미국의 사회 규범을 비교하기 위해
② 다양한 금서 사례와 그 사회적 함의를 강조하기 위해
③ 금서 지지자들과 반대자들을 대조하기 위해
④ 금서 지정과 문맹 사이의 관계를 살펴보기 위해

49 내용일치 ④

| 분석 |

『화씨 451도』는 정신질환 비판이 아니라 디스토피아적 미래를 상상한 내용이므로 ④가 사실이 아니다. ① 『앵무새 죽이기』 역시 인종 차별적인 표현을 사용했다는 이유로 퇴출당했다고 했다. ② 금서 지정을 보통 권위주의 정권과 연관 짓지만, 이러한 일은 현대 민주국가에서도 일어난다고 했다. ③ 이 소설도 검열 당했는데, 이는 반대 의견 억압과 문맹 사회의 위험성이라는 소설의 주제와 부합한다고 했다.

위 글에 따르면, 다음 중 올바르지 않은 것은?
① 『앵무새 죽이기』는 인종 차별적 언어 사용 때문에 금지되었다.
② 책은 권위주의 정권과 민주주의 사회 모두에서 금지된다.
③ 브래드버리의 책에 따르면 문맹 사회는 위험하다.
④ 『화씨 451도』는 정신질환 비판 때문에 금지되었다.

50 빈칸완성 ①

| 분석 |

Ⓐ에는 독자들을 해로운 콘텐츠로부터 '보호'해야 한다는 의미가, Ⓑ에는 지적 자유를 '제한'한다는 의미가 필요하다.

Ⓐ와 Ⓑ에 들어갈 올바른 쌍은?
① 보호하다 — 제한하다
② 유지하다 — 호소하다
③ 구별하다 — 제한하다
④ 고립시키다 — 부화하다

한국외국어대학교 T2 A형

TEST p. 616~634

01	③	02	②	03	③	04	②	05	④	06	①	07	②	08	②	09	④	10	②
11	④	12	①	13	③	14	④	15	②	16	①	17	③	18	④	19	③	20	①
21	②	22	①	23	④	24	④	25	①	26	④	27	③	28	③	29	③	30	①
31	②	32	②	33	①	34	③	35	②	36	④	37	②	38	③	39	①	40	④
41	①	42	②	43	③	44	②	45	④	46	①	47	②	48	③	49	③	50	①

01 논리완성 ③

| 분석 |
이야기를 통해 평안해져야 하는 아이들은 '잘 놀라고 겁이 많은' 아이들일 것이다. 따라서 정답은 skittish이다.

| 어휘 |
soothe v. 달래다 **calm** a. 평온한 **unflappable** a. 쉽게 동요하지 않는 **intransigent** a. 고집 센, 타협을 거부하는 **skittish** a. 잘 놀라는, 겁이 많은 **impervious** a. 영향 받지 않는, 둔감한

| 해석 |
이 달콤한 이야기는 겁이 많고 잘 놀라는 아이들을 달래어 아이들이 밤에 평온하고 더 안전한 느낌이 들도록 도와줄 것이다.

02 논리완성 ②

| 분석 |
과거 시대와 문명에 '몰입한다'고 했으므로 '열렬한' 독자라는 표현이 적절하다. 따라서 정답은 avid이다.

| 어휘 |
immerse oneself in ~에 몰입하다 **intricate** a. 복잡한, 뒤얽힌 **aesthetic** a. 미적인 **avid** a. 열렬한 **antiquated** a. 구식의 **isochronous** a. 동일한 시간 간격으로 발생하는, 동일한 시간 주기를 지닌

| 해석 |
그는 종종 과거 시대와 문명의 복잡한 세부사항에 몰입하는, 역사 소설의 열렬한 독자이다.

03 논리완성 ③

| 분석 |
일상에서 일어나는 일의 스펙트럼의 양쪽 끝이라고 했으므로, 한쪽 끝이 absurd로 터무니없고 비상식적이라면 다른 쪽 끝은 상식적, 보통, 정상적이라는 의미의 quotidian이 적절하다.

| 어휘 |
depict v. 묘사하다, 기술하다 **absurd** a. 부조리한, 터무니없는 **spectrum** n. 스펙트럼, 범위 **agile** a. 민첩한, 빠른 **suave** a. 상냥한, 세련된 **quotidian** a. 일상의, 평범한, 정상의 **palliative** a. 완화하는

| 해석 |
그 저자는 삶의 일상적 스펙트럼의 양쪽 끝 각각에서 유머의 본질을 찾아내며, 터무니없는 것과 정상적인 것 모두를 기술한다.

04 논리완성 ②

| 분석 |
아내가 모든 것을 심각하게 받아들이는 것과 남편을 on the contrary로 대조시켰으므로 serious와 반대되는 의미를 내포하고 있는 표현을 찾아야 한다. '태평스러움'을 뜻하는 insouciance가 적절하다.

| 어휘 |
trouble v. 괴롭히다 **ups and downs** 삶의 부침(浮沈), 우여곡절 **cheerful** a. 명랑한 **abomination** n. 혐오 **insouciance** n. 태평함 **invective** n. 독설 **slovenliness** n. 단정치 못함

| 해석 |
세바스티안은 삶의 부침(浮沈)을 명랑하고 태평스럽게 바라보며 거의 그 어떤 일에도 걱정하지 않은 반면, 그의 아내는 모든 것을 심각하게 받아들였다.

05 동의어 ④

| 어휘 |

countless a. 수많은 pledge v. 맹세하다, 다짐하다 reform v. 개혁하다, 고치다 beholden a. 신세를 지고 있는, 의무감을 느끼는 (= obligated) defiant a. 반항적인, 도전적인 lethargic a. 무기력한 congenial a. 마음이 맞는, 어울리는, 적절한

| 해석 |

새해 무렵에 수많은 사람들이 나쁜 습관을 고치겠다고 다짐하지만 습관의 과학은 습관이 우리의 욕망에 얽매이지 않는다는 것을 보여준다.

06 동의어 ①

| 어휘 |

company v. 무리를 짓다 conspicuity n. 눈에 띔, 현저함, 이채로움 (= salience) migration n. 이동 readily ad. 쉽게 detect v. 감지하다, 발견하다 tenuity n. 희박함, 빈약 discretion n. 신중함, 자유재량 paltriness n. 하찮음

| 해석 |

나비는 짝을 이루어 다니지 않고 눈에 덜 띄기 때문에 그들의 이동은 가장 작은 새들의 이동보다 훨씬 덜 쉽게 탐지된다.

07 동의어 ②

| 어휘 |

objection n. 반대, 이의 in principle 원칙적으로 consolidation n. 통합(= combination) bank account 은행계좌 terms n. 조건 indulgence n. 관용, 하고 싶은 대로 함 consonance n. 일치, 조화; 협화음 emulation n. 경쟁, 모방

| 해석 |

은행으로부터 더 나은 거래 조건을 얻기 위해 은행 계좌를 통합하는 것에 대해 원칙적으로 반대는 없다.

08 동의어 ②

| 어휘 |

precipitous a. 가파른, 험한; 급작스러운, 격동의 (= tumultuous) challenging a. 어려운 times n. 시대 gross a. 중대한; 엄청난 resplendent a. 눈부시게 빛나는 limpid a. 투명한, 맑은 abrupt a. 급작스러운, 돌연한

| 해석 |

지금이 격동의 어려운 시대라고 말하는 것은 중대한 과소평가일 수 있다.

09 동의어 ④

| 어휘 |

playwright n. 극작가 old-school a. 구식의 hackneyed a. 진부한(= trite) trope n. 비유 creaky a. 삐걱대는, 제 기능을 못하는 mawkish a. 지나치게 감상적인 decorous a. 단정한, 점잖은 dilapidated a. 황폐한

| 해석 |

그 극작가가 판에 박힌 구식 관례와 진부한 비유에 의지함으로 인해 연극이 다소 삐걱거린다.

10 문맥상 동의어 ②

| 어휘 |

injured a. 다친 projection n. 투사(投射)(= transference); 돌출; (목소리의) 맑음 deal with 다루다, 대처하다 adversity n. 역경, 고난 protrusion n. 돌출 transference n. 전사(轉寫) forecast n. 예측 resonance n. 울림, 공명

| 해석 |

우리가 다친 사람을 안쓰러워하느냐 아니냐의 여부는 자신의 역경을 어떻게 다루느냐의 투사(投射)(그대로 옮겨놓은 것)일 뿐이다.

11 문맥상 동의어 ④

| 어휘 |

roam v. 돌아다니다, 배회하다 skirt v. 피하다, 우회하다(= bypass) cunningly ad. 교묘히, 영악하게 border v. 경계에 접하다 equivocate v. 얼버무리다, 모호하게 말하다 hem v. 가장자리에 덧단을 대다, 가장자리 처리를 하다

| 해석 |

하이에나는 주로 밤에 돌아다니며 가장 교묘하게 설치해놓은 카메라 트랩조차 피해 다니는 경향이 있다.

12 문맥상 동의어 ①

| 어휘 |

innate a. 타고난, 선천적인 facility n. 쉬움; 편의; 능력, 재능(= talent) complex a. 복잡한 provision n. 공급, 대비 convenience n. 편의, 편리함

| 해석 |

그는 복잡한 수학 이론들을 이해하는 타고난 재능이 있다.

13 문맥상 동의어 ③

| 어휘 |

bill n. 청구서(= debt); 광고, 전단; 지폐; 부리   **bankrupt** a. 파산한
beak n. 부리   **banknote** n. 지폐, 은행권   **debt** n. 빚, 부채
advertisement n. 광고

| 해석 |
전쟁은 점점 더 그의 능력을 넘어서는 요구를 해서, 파산해버린 그의 영혼이 감당할 수 없는 청구서를 제시했다(빚을 지게 했다).

14 재진술   ④

| 어휘 |
can afford to do ~할 수 있다   **indifferent** a. 무관심한, 냉담한
indispensable a. 필수적인   **care for** 돌보다   **affordance** n. 행동 유도성(개념어)   **render** v. 제공하다

| 해석 |
정치체제는 더 이상 경제에 무관심할 수 없다.
① 경제에 대한 정치체제의 무관심은 지금까지는 꼭 필요했다.
② 정치체제는 경제를 돌볼 만큼 충분히 무심하지 못했다.
③ 경제는 정치체제에 의해 충분한 행동 유도성을 받지 못했다.
④ 정치체제는 지금까지 경제에 너무 많이 무관심했다.

15 재진술   ②

| 어휘 |
demand n. 수요   **meet** v. 충족시키다   **recycled** a. 재활용된
fulfill v. 충족시키다   **e-waste** n. 전자 폐기물   **contribute to** ~에 기여하다   **insignificant** a. 하찮은   **source** v. 얻다, 공급자를 찾다

| 해석 |
검은 플라스틱에 대한 수요는 재활용 전자 폐기물을 통해 상당히 충족되는 것 같다.
① 재활용 전자 폐기물은 블랙 플라스틱의 필요를 거의 충족시키지 못했다.
② 검은 플라스틱에 대한 수요는 재활용 전자 폐기물을 통해 대개 충족된다.
③ 재활용 전자 폐기물은 검은 폐기물 수요를 극히 일부만 충족시키는 데 기여한다.
④ 재활용 전자 폐기물은 주로 검은 플라스틱에서 대부분 얻어진다.

16 어순   ①

| 분석 |
a skill을 선행사로 하는 형용사 절이 필요하므로 관계대명사 뒤에 주어와 동사가 오는 어순이 적절하다. 따라서 정답은 ①이다.

| 어휘 |
ancient a. 고대의   **skill** n. 역량, 기술   **value** v. 높이 평가하다

| 해석 |
그는 고대 언어의 전문가였지만, 고대 언어 구사는 현대 고용주들이 높이 평가하는 역량은 아니다.

17 어순   ③

| 분석 |
유사관계대명사 than 절에서 도치되어야 할 이유가 없으므로 '주어-동사' 어순이어야 하고, give 동사 뒤에는 간접목적어와 직접목적어가 바로 와야 하므로, I had given it credit for가 적절하다. it은 the world를 가리키고 for 다음은 선행사 possibility의 자리이다.

| 어휘 |
contain v. 포함하다   **give credit for** ~을 인정하다

| 해석 |
그것은 세상에 대해 내가 인정한 것보다 훨씬 더 많은 가능성이 세상에 있다는 것을 입증하는 것 같았다.

18 주격 관계대명사의 생략   ④

| 분석 |
선행사 novel methods 다음에 주격 관계대명사 which가 생략되어 있고 그 뒤에 삽입절인 the start-up believed가 나오니 뒤의 ④ it은 없어야 한다. 주격 관계대명사는 주어진 문장에서처럼 삽입절이 있는 경우에는 생략이 가능하다. I know a girl I believe is a genius. = I know a girl (who) I believe is a genius.

| 어휘 |
preview v. 미리 시연하다, 공개하다   **construct** v. 만들다   **novel** a. 새로운   **start-up** n. 신생기업   **propel** v. 추진하다   **unseen** a. 보이지 않는

| 해석 |
그때는 그 회사가 o1이라 알려진 인공지능 모델의 초기버전을 미리 공개한 때였는데, 이 모델은 이 신생기업이 생각하기에 자사의 프로그램들을 전례 없는 수준으로 끌어올릴 것으로 생각한 새로운 방법으로 만들어진 것이었다.

19 부정사   ③

| 분석 |
for athletes가 의미상 주어로 쓰인 문장에서는 동명사가 아니라 to부정사를 써야 한다. 따라서 ③을 to avoid로 고쳐야 한다.

| 어휘 |
limited a. 제한된, 한정된   advisable a. 권장할 만한, 바람직한
considerable a. 상당한   muscle damage 근육 손상   soft tissue
연조직   injury n. 부상

| 해석 |
증거는 많지 않지만, 상당한 근육 손상과 연조직 부상을 입은 운동선수들은 경기 후 24시간 동안 술을 피하는 것이 바람직하다.

20 정비문   ①

| 분석 |
선행사인 the scientist 뒤의 관계대명사절에서 주어 research 뒤의 that은 필요하지 않으므로 삭제해야 한다. 따라서 틀린 문장은 ①이다.

| 어휘 |
significantly ad. 상당히   missing a. 행방불명된   lecture n. 강의   rapidly ad. 신속하게

| 해석 |
① 작년에 연구 결과가 발표된 그 과학자는 해당 분야를 크게 변화시켰다.
② 내가 지난주에 도서관에서 빌린 책이 없어졌다.
③ 내가 강의 후에 이야기를 나눈 학생은 매우 똑똑했다.
④ 그녀가 일하는 회사는 지난 몇 년 사이에 급속히 성장했다.

21 정비문   ②

| 분석 |
②에서 it is supposed ~의 주어인 it이 앞의 money인 돈을 가리키므로, to be helped가 아니라 to help가 되어야 돈이 사람들을 돕는다는 뜻이 된다. 따라서 정답은 ②이다.

| 어휘 |
market v. 홍보[광고]하다   directly ad. 직접   instant a. 즉각적인
recover from ~에서 회복하다   regain v. 되찾다, 회복하다   injury n. 부상

| 해석 |
① 웰니스 산업은 건강 증진으로 가는 지름길로 광고되는 제품들로 가득하다.
② 대부분의 돈은 원래 도움을 받아야 할 사람들에게 직접 전달되지 않는다.
③ 유명 작가가 쓴 그 책은 즉시 베스트셀러가 되었다.
④ 부상에서 회복 중인 그 무용수는 체력을 완전히 되찾기 위해 열심히 노력했다.

22~23

물리 세계의 물건들을 손으로 쥐는 우리의 힘이 약해지고 있다는 사실은 심각한 결과를 초래한다. 오랜 의학 연구 역사에 따르면, 손의 힘은 신체 전반의 건강 및 수명과 연결되어 있는데 그 이유는 아직 완전히 밝혀지진 않았다. 소아과 치료사들은 4세나 5세가 되었는데도 연필이나 크레용을 한 번도 잡아본 적이 없는 일부 아이들을 보았다고 보고한다. 이러한 촉각 경험의 부재는 아이들이 읽기와 쓰기를 배우는 방식에 변화를 일으킬 수 있으며, 다른 면에서도 그들에게 제약을 가할 수 있다. 연구자들은 또한 건강한 젊은 성인들을 대상으로 연구를 진행했는데, 스마트폰을 많이 사용하는 사람들은 스마트폰을 적게 사용하는 또래에 비해 손아귀 힘이 약하고, 손끝 감각이 둔하며, 손목과 손 부위 부상률이 더 높다는 사실을 발견했다. 이는 손사용을 증진시키는 활동에의 참여가 얼마나 중요한지 잘 보여준다. 메모를 하거나, 뜨개질을 하거나, 도자기 수업을 받는 등, 손을 사용하는 활동을 더 많이 함으로써 감정, 인지, 신체상의 이점을 얻을 수 있다는 것이 점점 더 분명해지고 있다. 이런 노력을 통해 우리는 모두가 손을 쓰지 않는 세상으로 표류하는 흐름을 저지할 수 있을지도 모른다.

| 어휘 |
grip n. 움켜쥠, 통제, 지배   slip v. 빠져나가다   consequence n. 결과; 영향; 중대함   overall a. 전반적인   longevity n. 장수
pediatric a. 소아과의   absence n. 부재, 없음   tactile a. 촉각의
dull a. 둔한   underscore v. 강조하다, 보여주다   promote v. 증진시키다   cognitively ad. 인지적으로   jot down 적다, 쓰다
pottery n. 도자기   arrest v. 저지하다   drift n. 표류

22 글의 주제   ①

| 분석 |
글 후반부에 '손을 사용하는 활동을 더 많이 함으로써 감정, 인지, 신체상의 이점을 얻을 수 있다는 것이 점점 더 분명해지고 있다'고 결론짓고 있으므로 ①이 주제로 적절하다.

이 글의 주요 주제는?
① 손의 사용이 건강과 발달에 미치는 이점
② 손의 사용이 기술에 미치는 영향
③ 손을 사용하지 않는 사회의 유망한 미래
④ 나쁜 자세가 손의 건강에 끼치는 위험

23 지시대상   ④

| 분석 |
Ⓐ, Ⓑ, Ⓒ는 모두 스마트폰을 많이 사용하는 학생들을 가리키는데

비해 ④는 스마트폰을 덜 사용하는 사람들을 가리키므로 ⓓ가 다른 것을 지칭한다.

24~25

과거에는 연구자들이 부재(不在)가 뇌에서 신경세포가 발화하지 않는 것으로 표현된다고 생각했다. 그러나 최근 연구들은 뇌가 고유한 신경 패턴으로 부재를 부호화한다는 것을 보여주었다. 몇 년 전, 바넷은 숫자 0을 주제로 부재 연구를 시작했다. 24명의 참가자들을 모집하여 뇌자도(腦磁圖: MEG) 검사기 안에 앉게 해놓고 0과 관련된 과제를 수행하게 했다. 신경세포가 발화하면 전압이 발생하고, 이 전압은 검사기 기계가 감지할 수 있는 자기장을 만들어낸다. 연구자들은 이 자기장을 분석함으로써, 신경세포가 0 같은 특정 주제에 대해 생각하도록 유도될 때 어떻게 반응하는지 알아낼 수 있다. 바넷은 뇌가 0이 아닌 숫자들을 처리할 때 나타나는 현상인 수적 거리 효과의 증거를 찾고 있었다. 기본적으로 뇌는 두 숫자가 서로 가까울 때보다는 더 멀리 떨어져 있을수록 더 쉽게 구별할 수 있다. 따라서 뇌는 6과 7을 6과 9보다 더 자주 혼동한다. 연구자들은 뇌가 0을 다른 숫자와 유사하게 처리한다면, 0에 대해서도 수적 거리 효과가 나타날 것이라고 예상했다. 실제로 바넷은 뇌가 0을 숫자이자 양으로서 다른 숫자들과 매우 유사하게 처리한다는 사실을 발견했다.

| 어휘 |

assume v. 추정하다, 가정하다   **represent** v. 나타내다, 재현하다   **neuron** n. 신경세포   **fire** v. 발화하다   **encode** v. 부호화하다   **absence** n. 없음, 부재   **unique** a. 특이한   **voltage** n. 전압   **detect** v. 감지하다, 발견하다   **prompt** v. 촉발시키다   **process** v. 처리하다   **apart** ad. 따로   **distinguish** v. 구별하다   **digit** n. 숫자

24 글의 주제   ④

| 분석 |

실험 결과가 주제인 글이다. 마지막 문장 '바넷은 뇌가 0을 숫자이자 양으로서 다른 숫자들과 매우 유사하게 처리한다는 사실을 발견했다'를 보면 글의 주제가 '뇌가 숫자 0을 처리하는 방식'임을 알 수 있다.

이 글의 주요 주제는?
① 숫자 0을 연구하는 방법
② 숫자 0이 문제를 일으키는 이유
③ 숫자 0 개념은 언제 습득되는가
④ 뇌가 숫자 0을 처리하는 방식

25 빈칸완성   ①

| 분석 |

빈칸 바로 앞 문장에서 '뇌는 두 숫자가 서로 가까울 때보다는 더 멀리 떨어져 있을수록 더 쉽게 구별할 수 있다'고 했으므로 숫자 둘이 서로 멀수록 인식을 잘한다는 답을 고르면 된다. 따라서 정답은 ①이다.

Ⓐ에 들어갈 가장 적절한 표현은?
① 6과 7을 6과 9보다 더 자주 혼동한다
② 100을 10보다 더 정확하게 처리한다
③ 11과 20을 구별하는 데 어려움을 겪는다
④ 4와 5를 구별하지 못한다

26~27

'빌둥스로만(성장소설)'이란 주인공이 청소년기에서 성인기로 성장하는 심리적·도덕적 발달에 관한 소설을 말하는 문학 용어이다. 빌둥스로만 장르는 독일에서 시작되었다. 독일어 'bildung'은 '교육'을, 'roman'은 '소설'을 뜻한다. 따라서 'bildungsroman'은 '교육의 소설' 또는 '(인격)형성[성장]소설'로 번역된다. 괴테의 『빌헬름 마이스터의 수업시대』는 사업가로서 공허한 삶을 살던 한 남자가 행복을 찾기 위해 자아실현 여정을 떠나는 이야기를 담고 있는데, 최초로 출판된 빌둥스로만으로 널리 인정받고 있다. 이 작품은 1824년에 영어로 번역된 후 영국에서도 인기를 점점 끌었다. '빌둥스로만'이라는 용어 자체는 1819년에 문헌학자 칼 모르겐슈테른이 강의 중에 처음으로 만들었다. 이 용어는 그가 그의 경력 과정에 실망한 예전의 스승인 프리드리히 볼프로부터 받은 비판에서 비롯되었다. 볼프는 모르겐슈테른이 예술과 철학에 대해 글을 쓰면 쓸수록 점점 더 허영심에 빠진다고 여겼다. 자신의 지적 여정에 대한 이러한 비판에 영감을 받은 모르겐슈테른은 빌둥스로만이라는 용어를 만들어냈다. 심리학자이자 철학자인 빌헬름 딜타이는 『슐라이어마허의 생애』라는 저서에서 이 용어를 다시 사용하여 더 많은 대중을 위해 빌둥스로만의 서사 구조를 대중화시켰다.

| 어휘 |

Bildungsroman n. 성장소설   **describe** v. 묘사하다   **literary term** 문학 용어   **protagonist** n. 주인공   **originate** v. 기원하다, 유래하다   **embark on** 출발하다, 떠나다   **self-realization** n. 자아실현   **coin** v. 용어를 처음 만들다   **unfold** v. 펼쳐지다   **reprise** v. 다시 사용하다   **popularize** v. 대중화시키다

26 글의 목적 ④

| 분석 |

빌둥스로만이라는 문학 장르가 어떻게 생겨나서 발전했는지를 그 용어의 기원에 대한 설명과 함께 다룬 글이므로 ④가 정답으로 적절하다.

위 글의 주요 목적은?
① 괴테의 소설이 영국의 스토리텔링 기법에 끼친 영향을 분석하기 위해
② 칼 모르겐슈테른의 철학이 문학에 끼친 기여를 비평하기 위해
③ 빌헬름 딜타이가 19세기 문학 재정의에서 한 역할을 탐색하기 위해
④ 특정 문학 장르의 어원과 진화를 설명하기 위해

27 내용일치 ③

| 분석 |

본문 아래쪽의 It was born out of criticism he received from Friedrich Wolf, a former teacher disappointed in how his career unfolded.에 따르면, 모르겐슈테른은 자신의 지적 여정에 대해 프리드리히 볼프로부터 비판을 받은 후 '빌둥스로만'이라는 용어를 만들어냈다. 따라서 ③이 옳다.

위 글에 따르면, 다음 중 올바른 것은?
① 프리드리히 볼프가 1819년 '빌둥스로만'이라는 용어를 만들었다.
② 괴테의 소설이 출판된 직후 '빌둥스로만'이라는 용어가 인기를 끌었다.
③ 모르겐슈테른의 지적 발달에 대한 비판이 '빌둥스로만'이라는 용어 탄생에 영감을 주었다.
④ 빌헬름 딜타이는 그의 철학 저서에서 빌둥스로만 구조의 사용을 비판했다.

28~30

지능은 인간에서조차도 정의하고 측정하기가 극도로 어렵다. 인간과는 감각, 동기, 문제 해결 능력이 근본적으로 다른 문어 같은 동물을 연구할 때 그 어려움은 기하급수적으로 커진다. 역사적으로 연구자들은 동물이 인간처럼 사고하는지를 중심으로 하여 연구하느라 동물에게는 있으나 인간에게는 없는 능력들을 도외시해왔다. 이 문제를 피하기 위해, 과학자들은 인지 능력을 보다 객관적으로 측정하려 시도해왔다. 한 가지 선택지는 체격 크기 대비 뇌 크기의 비율을 기준 삼는 것이다. 문어 중에서 연구가 가장 잘 된 참문어(Octopus vulgaris)는 약 5억 개의 신경세포가 있다. 이는 킬로그램 당 신경세포 비율이 비교적 높아서 토끼와 비슷한 수준이다. 더 정확한 측정 방법으로는 학습에 중요한 것으로 여겨지는 특정 뇌 구조의 크기, 신경세포 수, 혹은 표면적을 보는 것이 있다. 이는 포유류에서는 유용하지만, 문어의 신경계는 근본적으로 구조 체계가 다르다. 참문어의 신경세포 중 절반 이상인 3억여 개는 뇌에 있지 않고, 팔에 있는 '미니 뇌'인 신경절에 분포되어 있다. 중앙 뇌에 남아 있는 신경세포 중 대부분은 시각 처리를 담당하며, 학습과 기억 같은 다른 과정을 담당하는 뉴런은 전체의 4분의 1도 되지 않는다. 다른 문어 종에서도 뇌의 일반 구조는 비슷하지만 복잡성은 다양하다. 뇌 주름은 표면적을 늘려 신경 연결과 지능을 향상시킬 수 있다. 일부 문어 종, 특히 암초 서식지에 사는 문어 종은 심해에 사는 문어보다 뇌에 주름이 더 많으며, 이는 이 종들이 더 높은 지능이 있음을 시사한다.

| 어휘 |

intelligence n. 지능 **fiendishly** ad. 극도로, 지독하게 **challenge** n. 난제 **exponentially** ad. 기하급수적으로 **sensory** a. 감각의 **profoundly** ad. 근원적으로 **objective** a. 객관적인 **cognitive ability** 인지 능력 **option** n. 선택지 **relative** a. 상대적인 **neuron** n. 신경세포 **neuron count** 신경세포 수 **surface area** 표면적 **distinct** a. 다른 **dedicated to** ~에 할애되는 **visual processing** 시각 처리 **vary** v. 다르다, 다양하다 **wrinkled** a. 주름이 있는 **notably** ad. 두드러지게 **reef habitat** 암초 서식지

28 글의 제목 ③

| 분석 |

문어를 사례로 삼아, 동물의 인지 능력을 어떻게 객관적으로 측정할 수 있는지에 대해 설명하는 글이므로 ③이 제목으로 가장 적절하다. ④는 뇌 측정보다 지능, 즉 인지능력 측정이 더 적절하다. 본문에도 To avoid this problem, scientists have tried to find more objective measures of cognitive abilities라고 되어 있다.

위 글의 제목으로 가장 적절한 것은?
① 암초와 뇌의 주름: 지능이 높은 문어
② 문어와 토끼의 지능 비교
③ 동물의 인지 능력 측정: 문어의 사례
④ 동물의 뇌를 객관적으로 측정하는 방법들

29 내용파악 ③

| 분석 |

중앙 뇌에 남아 있는 신경세포 대부분이 시각 처리를 담당한다고 했다. 따라서 ③이 옳은 진술이다. ① '문어 중에서 연구가 가장 잘 된 참문어'라고 했다. ② 중앙 뇌에는 신경세포가 전체 5억 개 중 2억 개가 있으므로 대부분이 아니다. ④ 신경절에는 신경세포가

전체 5억 개 중 3억 개가 있으므로 작은 부분이 아니다.

위 글에 따르면, 다음 중 참문어에 관해 올바른 것은?
① 참문어는 다른 문어 종들보다 연구된 내용이 더 적다.
② 참문어의 신경세포 대부분은 중앙 뇌에 있다.
③ 참문어 중앙 뇌의 신경세포 대부분은 시각과 관련되어 있다.
④ 참문어의 신경절은 전체 신경세포의 작은 부분만 차지한다.

| 어휘 |

morbidity n. 병적인 상태, 질병 발생 **mortality** n. 사망 **age-specific** a. 나이별 **cohort** n. 동류집단 **labor market** 노동 시장 **correlation** n. 상관관계 **preconceived** a. 사전에 형성된, 선입견의 **stressful** a. 스트레스가 많은 **chronic** a. 만성적인 **epidemiological** a. 역학(疫學)의 **conceptualize** v. 개념화하다 **allostasis** n. 생체 적응 **physiological** a. 생리적인, 생리학(상)의 **large-scale** a. 대규모의

30   빈칸완성   ①

| 분석 |

빈칸 다음 마지막 문장에서 '일부 문어 종은 뇌에 주름이 더 많으며, 이는 이 종들이 더 높은 지능이 있음을 시사한다.'고 했으므로 빈칸에는 ①이 적절하다.

Ⓐ에 들어갈 적절한 표현은?
① 신경 연결과 지능을 향상시킨다
② 팔을 유용한 부속 기관으로 자리 잡게 한다
③ 문어의 노화를 나타낸다
④ 뇌의 기능 역량을 감소시킨다

31~32

1970년대 스털링과 아이어는 미국에서 20세기 연령대별 집단의 질병 발생률과 사망률을 연구하고 있었다. 연구자들은 연령대별 집단의 사망률과, 그 집단이 노동시장에 진입할 당시 노동시장의 포화 정도 사이에 상관관계가 있다는 것을 발견했다. 그들은 1930년대 이전과 1950년대 이후의 집단에 비해, 대공황 이후 1940년대 경제 호황기에 노동시장에 진입한 집단이 취업 경쟁이 적어서 사망률이 더 낮았다는 사실을 발견했다. 연구자들은 또한, 사별, 이혼, 실업, 이주 등 스트레스가 많은 주요 사건들과 높은 사망률 사이에도 상관관계가 있다는 데 주목했다. 젊은 집단의 사망률이 낮으면 나이가 들었을 때 만성질환이 더 많을 것이라는 선입견이 있었지만, 오히려 그와 반대되는 증거가 발견되었다. 젊을 때 사망률이 높았던 집단이 이후 심혈관 질환과 같은 만성적인 건강 문제를 더 많이 겪는 것으로 나타났다. 이러한 역학적(疫學的) 현상을 설명하기 위해, 연구자들은 자본주의와 산업화가 진전되는 환경에서 발생하는 사회 및 체제상의 스트레스를 연령대별 집단의 질병 발생률과 사망률의 주요 원인으로 제시했다. 이 연구들은 이후 '생체적응(allostasis)'이라는 개념을 형성하는 기초가 되었다. 생체적응이라는 대규모 역학(疫學) 패턴에 의해 개인 수준의 생리 변화가 발생하는 과정이다.

31   내용일치   ②

| 분석 |

대공황 이후 1940년대 경제 호황기에 노동시장에 진입한 집단이 취업 경쟁이 적어서 사망률이 더 낮았다는 사실을 발견했다고 했으므로 ②가 정답이다. ① 연령과 실업의 관계가 아니라 노동시장과 사망률의 관계이다. ③ 1940년대에는 경쟁이 적었다고 했다. ④ 사망률이 낮은 집단이 만성질환이 더 많았다는 근거는 없고, 오히려 사망률이 높았던 집단이 만성질환이 많았다.

위 글에 따르면, 다음 중 올바른 것은?
① 스털링과 에이어는 연령과 실업 사이의 관계를 조사했다.
② 노동시장이 좋을 때 사망률이 더 낮은 것으로 나타났다.
③ 1940년대에는 1950년대보다 구직 경쟁이 더 치열했다.
④ 사망률이 낮은 집단은 더 오래 살아서 만성질환이 더 많았다.

32   부분이해   ②

| 분석 |

본문에서 대규모 역학 패턴이 개인 수준의 생리 변화를 만드는 과정이라고 제시했으므로, 사회 조건이 개인의 건강에 영향을 미치는 방식이 정답으로 가장 적절하다.

Ⓐ의 의미와 가장 가까운 것은?
① 개인이 사회의 대규모 패턴을 형성하는 과정
② 사회 조건이 개인의 건강에 영향을 미치는 방식
③ 역학 패턴을 구축하는 다양한 절차
④ 생리 현상과 개인 간의 대규모 관계

33~34

한 사회가 혼돈을 향해 가고 있는지, 아니면 혼돈에서 멀어지는 방향으로 가는지를 알아보는 한 가지 방법은 그 사회 밑바닥의 정서적 흐름과 폭력에 대한 태도를 연구하는 것이다. 예를 들어, 중세 유럽은 폭력적이었던 것으로 유명하다. 사회학자 노르베르트 엘리아스가 『문명화 과정』이라는 저서에서 썼듯이, 당시에는 충동 조절이 사실상 전혀 없었고 폭력이 만연했다. 그러나 공동체가 적절한 예절을 지키는

개인에게 보상을 제공하기 시작하고, 그 예절을 지키는 것이 사회에서 가장 바람직한 계층에 들어가기 위한 조건이 되면서, 자기 절제를 위한 새로운 유인책이 생겨나서 훨씬 더 평화로운 사회 환경을 조성했다. 비폭력적 협력으로 나아가는 움직임은 사람들이 엘리아스가 칭한 바, "더 동물적인 인간 활동"을 뒤로하고 공동체의 사회적 삶을 더 중시하게 되면서 자연스럽게 일어났다. 이와 같은 우선순위의 변화는 사회 전체에서 개인들이 지속적으로 자기 절제를 하도록 요구하고 이를 유지하도록 요구했다. 엘리아스는 이렇게 썼다. "간단하다. 계획과 행동. 그리고 개인의 감정적·이성적 충동은 우호적이거나 적대적인 방식으로 끊임없이 얽힌다. 사람들의 수많은 단일한 계획들과 행동들에서 만들어진 기본 조직은 그 어떤 개인도 계획하거나 창조하지 않은 변화와 패턴을 초래할 수 있다." 그리고 "역사 변화의 경로를 결정하는 것은 이런 인간 충동들과 노력들의 서로 얽힘, 이러한 사회적 질서이다." 사람들이 폭력을 선택할 때 그 이유는 대개 그것이 유일한 길, 절박한 시기의 마지막 수단이라고 생각하기 때문이며, 이들은 폭력을 저질러도 무사히 지나가리라 믿는다.

| 어휘 |

direction n. 방향 **chaos** n. 무질서, 혼돈 **undercurrent** n. 저층의 흐름 **brutish** a. 야수 같은, 폭력적인 **adherence** n. 고수, 집착 **reward** v. 보상하다 **entry** n. 진입 **strata** n. 계층(stratum의 복수) **priority** n. 우선권, 중요한 것 **rational** a. 합리적인, 이성적인 **constantly** ad. 끊임없이, 항상 **interweave** v. 엮이다, 연결되다 **strivings** n. 노력 **last resort** 최후의 방책, 의지처 **get away with** ~을 해도 벌을 모면하다, 무사하다

33 글의 목적   ①

| 분석 |

'적절한 예절을 지키는 개인에게 보상을 제공하기 시작하고, 그 예절을 지키는 것이 사회에서 가장 바람직한 계층에 들어가기 위한 조건이 되면서 자기 절제를 위한 새로운 유인책이 생겨나 훨씬 더 평화로운 사회 환경을 조성했다'고 한 것에서 이 글의 목적이 사회가 폭력적인 상태에서 점점 더 평화롭고 질서 있는 방향으로 나아가는 과정을 설명하기 위함임을 알 수 있다. 따라서 정답은 ①이다.

위 글의 주요 목적은?
① 폭력 통제가 어떻게 안정적인 사회를 만드는지 설명하기 위해
② 현대 사회에서 폭력이 증가하고 있음을 경고하기 위해
③ 폭력이 인간 역사에서 불가피함을 강조하기 위해
④ 사회 변화가 폭력의 주요 원인이라고 주장하기 위해

34 내용일치   ③

| 분석 |

'역사 변화의 경로를 결정하는 것은 이런 인간 충동들과 노력들의 서로 얽힘, 사회적 질서이다.'라고 한 것에서 역사적 변화는 개인의 독립 행동이 아니라 사회적 충동들과 노력들이 상호작용한 결과로 일어남을 알 수 있다. 따라서 ③이 옳지 않은 진술이다.

위 글에 따르면, 다음 중 올바르지 않은 것은?
① 중세 유럽에서 사람들의 폭력은 효과적으로 통제되지 않았다.
② 개인은 협력적인 비폭력에 대해 보상을 받았다.
③ 역사적 변화는 개인이 독립적으로 행동함으로써 일어난다.
④ 사람들은 더 이상 방법이 없다고 믿을 때 폭력을 선택했다.

35~37

고정관념의 부정확성은 특히 인종적 태도 분야에서 강조되어 왔다. 여기서 "고정관념"과 "편견"이라는 용어는 경멸적인 함의를 띠게 되었다. 한 고전적인 연구에서는 캘리포니아주 프레즈노의 시민들이 공유하고 있던 그 지역 아르메니아 소수 집단에 대한 고정관념이 거짓일 뿐 아니라, 많은 특징 면에서 현실과 반대라는 것이 드러났다. 예를 들어, 아르메니아인들은 실제로 평균보다 법을 더 어기기는커녕 오히려 더 잘 지키는 사람들이었다. 그러나 여러 저자들은 많은 고정관념이 일정 부분 진실을 포함하고 있다고 지적했다. 캠벨은 인식하는 집단에게 가장 중요한 특성들과 그 인식 집단을 또 다른 집단과 가장 크게 구별지어주는 특징들이 그 다른 집단에 대한 인식 집단의 고정관념으로 들어갈 가능성이 있다는 점을 강조했다. 예를 들자면, 청결은 대부분의 미국인에게 중요한 특성이지만, 많은 원시 사회에서는 상대적으로 중요하지 않기 때문에, 청결은 원시 사회에 대한 미국인들의 고정관념에 포함될 가능성이 미국인들에 대한 원시 사회의 고정관념에 포함될 가능성보다 더 크다. 따라서 역설적이게도, 고정관념은 주로 인식 집단의 성질에 의해 결정되며, 그 고정관념이 기술하는 것 같아 보이는 집단의 성질에 의해서는 거의 영향을 받지 않는다. 많은 고정관념은 일정 부분 진실을 포함하고 있지만, 고정관념의 핵심 특징은 그것이 지나치게 일반화되어 있다는 것이다. 다시 말해, 해당 집단에 있다고 여겨지는 특성이 그 집단의 전 구성원에게 적용된다고 여겨지는 것이다. 이런 식으로 일반화되는 경우 고정관념은 부정확할 가능성이 매우 크다.

| 어휘 |

inaccuracy n. 부정확성 **emphasize** v. 강조하다 **particularly** ad. 특히 **racial** a. 인종의 **stereotype** n. 고정관념 **prejudice** n. 편견 **derogatory** a. 폄하하는, 경멸하는 **connotation** n. 함의, 숨은 뜻 **false** a. 거짓의 **law-abiding** a. 법을 지키는 **stress** v. 강조하다 **trait** n. 특징 **perceiving group** (고정관념을 갖게 되는) 인식 집단 **primitive** a. 원시적인 **a kernel of truth** 일말의 진실, 진실의 일부 **generalize** v. 일반화하다

| 35   글의 제목   ② |

| 분석 |

이 글은 고정관념의 부정확성, 그리고 고정관념이 어떻게 생겨나는지 그 이면의 진실을 기술하고 있다. 따라서 가장 적절한 제목은 '고정관념 뒤에 숨겨진 진실'이다.

위 글의 제목으로 가장 적절한 것은?
① 다양한 집단의 고정관념
② 고정관념 뒤에 숨겨진 진실
③ 사회 내 고정관념의 장점
④ 고정관념의 심리적 힘

| 36   내용일치   ④ |

| 분석 |

'많은 고정관념은 일정 부분 진실을 포함하고 있지만, 고정관념의 핵심 특징은 그것이 지나치게 일반화되어 있다는 것이다'라고 한 것을 보면 고정관념의 핵심 특징 중 하나는 과도한 일반화이다. 따라서 정답은 ④이다.

위 글에 따르면, 다음 중 올바른 것은?
① 아르메니아인들은 다른 어떤 집단보다 법을 잘 지키지 않는 것으로 밝혀졌다.
② 원시 사회들은 청결을 중시할 가능성이 있다.
③ 캠벨은 사소한 특성이 고정관념의 기초를 이룬다고 믿었다.
④ 과도한 일반화는 고정관념의 중심 특징이다.

| 37   빈칸완성   ④ |

| 분석 |

빈칸 문장 첫머리에서 '역설적이게도'라고 한 것은 다른 사람에 대한 나의 고정관념이 다른 사람으로 인해 생겨난다는 것이 일반적인 통념인데, 다른 사람이 아닌 나로 인해 생겨난다고 하면 역설이 됨을 말한다. 따라서 빈칸에는 '고정관념을 가진 집단', 즉 '인식하는 집단'이 들어가야 한다. and 다음의 '그 고정관념이 기술하는 것 같아 보이는 집단'이 고정관념의 대상인 집단이다.

Ⓐ에 들어갈 가장 적절한 표현은?
① 고정관념의 대상이 되는 집단
② 집단 구성원들의 공통점
③ 원시 사회들
④ 인식 집단

38~40

개와는 달리, 고양이의 행동은 연구하기가 어려운데, 이것이 인간이 고양이를 개보다 이해하지 못하는 부분적인 이유이다. 고양이는 실험실에 있다는 사실에 스트레스를 너무 많이 받아서 의미 있는 행동 관찰이 불가능해진다. 그래서 최신 연구를 하는 학자들은 고양이들의 집으로 가서 다양한 종류의 음성과 다양한 화자의 목소리를 녹음한 것을 틀어주었다. 처음에 드 무존 박사와 그녀의 연구팀은 고양이들이 전혀 반응하지 않고 있다고 우려했다. 하지만 이들은 고양이와 만났던 것을 녹화한 영상을 살펴보았다. 일부의 경우에, 연구에 참여한 고양이들이 목소리가 나오는 스피커에 다가가 야옹거렸다. "결국 우리는 고양이 주인이 고양이에게 하는 말을 사용할 때 고양이의 주의가 분명히 커지는 결과를 가졌습니다."라고 드 무존 박사가 말했다. 이러한 발견들은 "고양이들이 자신을 돌보는 사람들이 말하는 내용뿐 아니라 어떻게 말하는지 그 방식까지도 면밀하게 주의를 기울인다는 것"을 보여주었다는 것이 유니티 대학의 동물 건강학 교수 비탈리 박사의 말이다. 이 새로운 연구는 고양이와 주인 간의 관계에 대한 비탈리 박사의 연구를 보완하는 것이다. 이 관계는 너무나 중요해서 새끼 고양이와 어미 고양이 간의 관계를 그대로 복제하고 있다는 것을 비탈리 박사의 연구는 발견했다. "원래 어미와의 상호작용을 위해 의도되었던 새끼 고양이의 애착 행동이 새 돌봄 제공자인 인간들과의 상호작용을 위해 바뀌었을 가능성이 있습니다." 개와는 달리, "대부분의 고양이들은 실제로 음식이나 장난감 같은 다른 보상보다 인간과의 교류를 더 좋아합니다."라고 비탈리 박사는 말했다.

| 어휘 |

stressed a. 스트레스 받는   **encounter** n. 만남   **approach** v. 다가가다   **meow** v. 야옹거리다   **cat-directed** a. 고양이를 향한   **caretaker** n. 돌봄 제공자   **connection** n. 연결, 관계   **kitten** n. 새끼 고양이   **modify** v. 변형시키다   **attachment behavior** 애착행동   **prefer** v. 선호하다   **interaction** n. 교류, 상호작용   **reward** n. 보상, 보람

| 38   글의 주제   ③ |

| 분석 |

새로운 연구 결과에 대해 '고양이와 주인인 인간 사이의 관계는 새끼 고양이와 어미 고양이 사이의 관계를 그대로 복제하고 있다'고 한 것에서 ③이 글의 주제로 적절함을 알 수 있다.

이 글의 주요 주제는?
① 고양이의 행동과 개의 행동에 대한 대조 연구
② 실험실 환경 안에서의 고양이 행동 관찰의 어려움
③ 고양이의 행동과 고양이와 인간의 관계
④ 고양이와 어미 고양이의 관계의 중요성

39 빈칸완성 ①

| 분석 |

'원래 어미와의 상호작용을 위해 의도되었던 새끼 고양이의 애착 행동이 새 돌봄 제공자인 인간들과의 상호작용을 위해 바뀌었을 가능성이 있다'고 한 것을 보면 고양이와 인간 사이의 관계가 새끼 고양이와 어미 고양이 사이의 관계와 비슷하다는 것을 추론할 수 있다. 따라서 replicate가 가장 적절하다.

Ⓐ에 들어갈 가장 적절한 표현은?
① 복제하다
② 지지하다
③ 깊이 생각하다
④ 포기하다

40 내용추론 ④

| 분석 |

마지막 문장 Unlike dogs, "most cats actually prefer human interaction over other rewards like food or toys.로 미루어보아 개는 인간과의 교류보다 음식을 선호한다고 추론할 수 있다.

위 글에 따르면, 다음 중 추론할 수 있는 것은?
① 개는 실험실에서 행동을 관찰할 때 스트레스를 받는다.
② 드 무존 박사와 비탈 박사는 같은 연구팀에 속해 있다.
③ 고양이는 돌봄 제공자의 목소리 톤에 주의를 기울이지 않는다.
④ 개는 인간과의 상호작용보다 맛있는 간식을 더 선호한다.

41~42

다른 학문들과 달리, 과학은 자연 규칙과 부과된 규칙 모두의 제약을 받는다. 과학 실험의 엄격한 규칙은 외부인에게 불필요해 보일 수 있지만, 실험에서 재현 가능한 결과를 보장하기 위해 확립된 규칙이다. 합의된 규칙들을 통해 참가자들이 목표를 향한 여정에서 유사한 경험을 하는 게임처럼, 과학의 목표는 실험 규칙을 따르면서 진리로 나아가는 것이다. 여러 면에서 과학은 협력 게임과 같다. 과학자는 개인적으로 이기는 것이 아니라, 다른 과학자들이 동일한 결과를 재현할 수 있을 때 진정으로 성공한다. 물론, 과거에 엉터리 약장수들이 그랬던 것처럼 검증되지 않은 약물에 대해 터무니없는 주장을 하는 편이 더 쉬울 것이다. 하지만 현대에 우리는 방사능 물질과 독을 섭취하는 것이 좋은 생각이 아니라는 것을 알게 되었다. 과학자들은 정확성과 유효성을 보장하는 규칙 세트를 따르는 데 자발적으로 동의한다. 그런 다음, 포인트(득점)나 체크(확인) 시스템이 있는 게임처럼, 결과에 대한 동료 검토 과정이 있어 모든 것이 올바르게 진행되도록 돕는다. 과학은 또 한계를 탐색한다는 점에서 게임과 같다. 끊임없이 한계를 시험하면서 새로운 지식을 발견하려 하는 것이다. 『나쁜 모든 것이 당신에게 좋다』라는 책에서 스티븐 존슨은 이렇듯 지속적인 한계 시험을 "탐색"이라 부르며 이 기술이 게임을 통해 습득되는 핵심 학습 속성이라고 말한다. 게임을 하는 사람처럼, 과학자들도 현재의 한계 너머에 무엇이 있는지 끊임없이 궁금하게 여겨야 한다.

| 어휘 |

academic discipline 학문 **imposed** a. 부과된 **rigorous** a. 엄격한 **unnecessary** a. 불필요한 **reproducible** a. 재연 가능한 **wild claim** 터무니없는 주장 **untested** a. 검증되지 않은 **snake oil** 가짜 약 **snake oil salesman** 엉터리 약장수 **voluntarily** ad. 자발적으로 **bind A to B** A를 B에 묶다 **attribute** n. 속성 **master** v. 숙달하다 **constantly** ad. 끊임없이 **current** a. 현재의

41 글의 주제 ①

| 분석 |

본문은 과학 실험을 게임과 비교하여 과학 실험에서의 규칙과 목표, 협력적 특성 등을 설명한다. 게임의 규칙을 따르는 것이 과학 실험과 유사하다는 점을 강조한다. 따라서 정답은 ①이다.

이 글의 주요 주제는?
① 실험에서 게임과 과학 사이의 유사성
② 과학적 방법으로서의 게임 탐구
③ 과학 실험을 대체하는 게임
④ 과학 실험의 게임 기법 채택

42 내용일치 ②

| 분석 |

'여러 면에서 과학은 협력 게임과 같다. 과학자는 개인적으로 이기는 것이 아니라, 다른 과학자들이 동일한 결과를 재현할 수 있을 때 진정으로 성공한다'라고 한 것은, 과학자들의 경우, 실험 결과를 다른 사람들이 재현할 수 있을 때에 그 결과가 유효하다는 것이다. 따라서 ②가 정답으로 적절하다.

위 글에 따르면, 다음 중 올바른 것은?
① 외부인들은 과학 실험의 엄격한 규칙이 필요하다고 생각한다.
② 과학자들의 연구 결과는 다른 사람이 동일한 결과를 찾아낼 때 유효하다.
③ 과학자들은 정확성과 유효성을 위해 규칙을 따르도록 강요받는다.
④ 탐색은 게이머보다 과학자에게 더 중요한 기술이다.

43~44

미셸 푸코는 담론이 사회 권력에 의해 생산된다는 놀라운 주장을 펼친다. 권력은 단순히 억제하고 제한하는 것이 아니라, "사물을 가로지르며 그것들을 생산하고, 쾌락을 유도하며, 지식을 형성하고, 담론을 생산한다. 권력은 사회 전체를 통과하는 생산 네트워크로 간주되어야 한다." 권력의 첫 번째 산물은 특정 사회가 세상을 장악하는 데 영향을 끼치는 근본 규약이다. 푸코는 어떤 사회든지 "그 사회의 언어, 인식 체계, 의사 교환, 기술, 가치, 실천의 위계 등을 지배하는" 일반 규약이 있으며 이를 통해 사람들은 편안함을 느끼고, 과학과 철학은 그 규약을 정당화한다고 주장한다. 푸코의 권력 분석은 권력이 단순히 지배자와 피지배자로 나누어진다고 생각하지 않는다. 그는 권력이 광범위한 관계망에 걸쳐 분산되어 있어 동일한 사람들이 권력의 작용을 시행하는 동시에 경험하기도 한다고 본다. 이런 측면에서 개인들은 권력의 적용 지점이 아니라 권력의 매개체이다. 이러한 관점은 한 시대의 모든 저작에서 똑같은 개요만 보는 것, 즉 예를 들어, 교회와 정부에서 권력이 권력의 원천에서 흘러나와 권력의 피해자들인 교구민들과 시민들에게로 흘러가는 권력의 겉모습만 보는 것으로부터 비평 작업을 구출해준다. 대신에 푸코의 권력 망에서는 누구나 뭔가를 한다. 그러나 그 뭔가는 늘 똑같진 않다. 그리고 언어 규약은 너무도 유동적이고 다루기 힘든데다. 예측 가능하도록 고정되어 단일한 억압자들에 의해 관리되지도 않기 때문에 오히려 문학 텍스트들이 이렇듯 정밀하고 복잡한 권력 관계들을 드러낼 수 있다.

| 어휘 |

discourse n. 담론(언어 실천) **merely** ad. 단지 **traverse** v. 관통하다 **productive** a. 생산하는 **hierarchy** n. 서열 **inform** v. 영향을 끼치다 **code** n. 규범, 규약, 코드 **grasp** n. 이해, 장악, 통제, 지배 **deny** v. 부인하다, 부정하다 **master** n. 주인 **dominated** a. 지배받는 **disperse** v. 분산시키다 **exercise** v. 실행하다 **undergo** v. 경험하다, 겪다 **vehicle** n. 매개체 **outline** n. 개요, 개괄 **fluid** a. 유동적인 **oppressor** n. 압제자, 억압자 **disclose** v. 드러내다, 폭로하다

43 내용일치 ③

| 분석 |

'언어 규약은 너무도 유동적이고 다루기 힘든데다. 예측 가능하도록 고정되어 단일한 억압자들에 의해 관리되지도 않기 때문에'라고 한 것에서 ③이 옳지 않은 진술임을 알 수 있다.

위 글에 따르면, 다음 중 올바르지 않은 것은?
① 일반적인 규약은 사람들이 사회의 일원으로서 편안함을 느끼게 한다.
② 푸코는 모든 사람이 권력을 가지며 권력에 의해 영향을 받는다고 주장한다.
③ 단일한 억압자는 자기 사람들의 언어를 고정하고 관리할 수 있다.
④ 권력 관계는 비록 복잡하지만 문학을 통해 예증될 수 있다.

44 부분이해 ②

| 분석 |

밑줄 바로 앞의 He sees power as dispersed through a wide network of relationships in which the same persons both exercise and undergo its operations를 보면, 푸코는 개인들이 권력을 행사하고 영향을 받는 역할을 동시에 한다고 설명한다. 따라서 밑줄의 의미를 가장 잘 반영한 것은 개인들이 권력의 직접 적용 대상이 아니라 매개체 역할을 한다는 ②이다.

Ⓐ의 의미와 가장 가까운 것은?
① 권력은 소수의 지배자나 기관의 손에 집중되어 있다.
② 개인은 권력을 직접 적용받는 표적이 아니라 권력을 전달하는 역할을 한다.
③ 개인은 자신의 이익을 위해 권력을 통제하고 적용하려 한다.
④ 권력은 지배와 복종을 기반으로 한 사회 매개체를 통해 작용한다.

45~47

당신이 생각할 수 있는 바와 달리, 신경망 개념은 사실 1943년에 뇌가 어떻게 작동할 수 있는지 모델링한 어느 수학 논문까지 거슬러 올라가는 꽤 오래된 개념이다. 컴퓨터 과학자들은 1950년대 간단한 신경망을 구성하려 시도했지만, 신경망 개념은 1980년대에 부활할 때까지 관심에서 벗어나 있었다. 1990년대쯤이면 신경망은 AI 연구에서 널리 사용되고 있었다. 하지만 고속 정보처리, 방대한 데이터 저장 능력, 그리고 컴퓨팅 자원에 대한 용이한 접근이 도래하고 나서야 비로소 신경망은 오늘날처럼 인간의 인지 능력을 모방하거나 능가할 수 있을 정도로 발전했다. 2017년에는 오늘날 사용되는 가장 중요한 종류의 신경망인 트랜스포머 모델이 처음 개발되었다. 트랜스포머 모델은 현재 AI 모델에서 매우 중요한 자리를 차지하기에 이르렀다. 트랜스포머 모델은 한 시퀀스의 요소들 자체만이 아니라 그 요소들의 맥락을 고려하기 위해 "자기 주의집중"이라는 기술을 사용하는 신경망이다. 자기 주의집중 기술을 이용하여, 트랜스포머 모델은 데이터 집합의 각 부분들이 서로 어떻게 관계되는지 그 미묘한 방식까지도 감지할 수 있다. 이러한 능력 덕분에 이 모델은 개별단어와 구절만이 아니라 문장과 단락을 분석하는 데 이상적이다. 트랜스포머 모델이 개발되기 전, 텍스트를 처리

하는 AI 모델들은 대개 문장의 끝에 도달할 때쯤이면 문장의 시작 부분을 "잊어버리는" 바람에 인간 독자들이 이해할 수 없는 방식으로 구절과 관념들을 결합하곤 했다. 트랜스포머 모델은 문장의 시작 부분만이 아니라 대화의 시작 부분까지 기억하기 때문에 인간 언어를 훨씬 더 자연스럽게 처리하고 생성할 수 있다.

| 어휘 |

contrary to ~와 반대로 **neural network** 신경망 **construct** v. 구성하다, 구축하다 **fall out of favor** 눈 밖에 나다, 호감을 잃다 **advent** n. 도래, 시작 **processing** n. 처리 **massive** a. 거대한 **access** n. 접근 **outsized** a. 큰, 대형의 **take into account** ~을 고려하다 **paragraph** n. 단락, 절 **phrase** n. 구절, 관용구 **conversation** n. 대화 **generate** v. 생성하다

45 글의 제목   ④

| 분석 |

'2017년에는 오늘날 사용되는 가장 중요한 종류의 신경망인 트랜스포머 모델이 처음 개발되었다. 트랜스포머 모델은 현재 AI 모델에서 매우 중요한 자리를 차지하기에 이르렀다.'라고 한 것에서 알 수 있듯이, 이 글은 수십 년에 걸친 신경망 개발의 결과로 발전된 트랜스포머 모델이 어떠한 것인가와 그것의 중요성을 설명하고 있다. 따라서 ④가 정답으로 적절하다. ①은 트랜스포머 모델과 관련한 내용 중에 자기 주의집중 기술만 언급하여 너무 좁은 제목이다.

위 글의 제목으로 가장 적절한 것은?
① 텍스트 분석을 위한 트랜스포머 모델에서 자기 주의집중이 하는 역할
② 신경망의 상업적 응용
③ 초기 신경망의 수학적 기초
④ 트랜스포머 모델의 발전과 중요성

46 내용일치   ①

| 분석 |

only after the advent of hyper-fast processing, massive data storage capabilities, and easy access to computing resources were neural networks able to advance to the point they have reached today로 보아 신경망이 고속 처리, 방대한 데이터 저장 능력, 그리고 컴퓨팅 자원 덕분에 발전했다고 설명하고 있다. 따라서 ①이 정답이다. ② 신경망은 1943년에 처음 구상되었다. ③ 신경망은 1980년대까지 대중의 관심을 받지 못했다. ④ 예전의 텍스트 처리 AI 모델들과 달리, 트랜스포머 모델은 문장의 시작을 기억할 수 있다.

위 글에 따르면, 다음 중 올바른 것은?
① 현대의 신경망은 컴퓨터 기술의 발전 덕분에 가능했다.
② 신경망은 1950년대에 수학자들에 의해 처음 구상되었다.
③ 신경망은 처음부터 AI 연구에서 지속적으로 인기를 끌었다.
④ 트랜스포머 모델은 문장의 시작을 기억하는 데 어려움을 겪는다.

47 지시대상   ③

| 분석 |

Ⓐ, Ⓑ, Ⓓ는 트랜스포머 모델을 가리키는 반면, Ⓒ는 트랜스포머 모델 이전의 AI 모델을 가리킨다.

48~50

화장품 산업에는 말해주지 말아야겠지만, 마스카라는 당신의 속눈썹에 그다지 도움이 되지 않을 수 있다. 속눈썹의 자연적인 미세구조와 형태는 액체 방울을 눈에서 튕겨내어 시야를 선명하게 유지하는 데 도움을 준다. 인간의 속눈썹과, 속눈썹을 모방한 섬유들에 대한 실험은 눈에서 물을 차단하는 여러 특징을 콕 집어 찾아낸다. 첫째, 속눈썹의 외부, 즉 큐티클 층은 "미세 래칫"처럼 작용한다. 물은 뿌리에서 끝쪽으로는 쉽게 흐르지만, 반대 방향으로는 흐르지 않는데, 이는 지붕의 기와처럼 겹쳐진 비늘 모양의 큐티클 덕분이다. 과학자들이 속눈썹을 떼어 물에 담갔다가 다시 꺼낼 때, 물이 래칫의 반대 방향으로 작용할 때는 속눈썹을 움직이기 위해 더 많은 힘이 필요했던 반면, 래칫 방향으로 작용할 때는 적은 힘만으로도 움직일 수 있었다. 또한 연구자들은 떼어낸 속눈썹에 물을 떨어뜨려 속눈썹이 물을 싫어한다는 점을 보여주었다. 물방울이 속눈썹 위에서 구슬처럼 맺히고 흘러내리기 쉽다는 뜻이다. 게다가, 속눈썹은 최단시간 곡선의 형태와 비슷하다. 중력의 영향을 받아 점 A에서 점 B까지 가는 시간을 최소화하는 곡선이다. 연구자들은 속눈썹과 비슷한 크기와 탄성을 가진 나일론 섬유들로 배열을 만들어 최단시간 곡선 형태의 섬유와, 직선 형태나 또 다른 곡선 형태의 섬유를 비교했다. 물방울은 최단시간 곡선 형태의 섬유에서 가장 빠르게 미끄러졌다. 그러나 현대의 미용 시술은 이러한 능력을 방해할 수 있다. 마스카라는 속눈썹이 물을 튕겨내는 대신 물을 끌어당기게 만들 수 있으며, 속눈썹을 동그랗게 말면 속눈썹의 형태가 변한다.

| 어휘 |

cosmetic a. 화장의 **eyelash** n. 속눈썹 **microstructure** n. 미세구조 **vision** n. 시야 **liquid droplet** 액체 방울 **catapult** v. 튕겨내다 **feature** n. 특징 **mimic** v. 모방하다 **rachet** n. 래칫(회전이나 움직임을 한 방향으로만 허용하고, 반대 방향으로는 막는 장치) **dip** v. 담그다 **hydrophobic** a. 물을 싫어하는 **bead**

v. 구슬 모양을 띠다 **elasticity** n. 탄성 **straight** a. 직선의 **curved** a. 구부러진 **disrupt** v. 방해하다 **repel** v. 내쫓다, 튕겨내다 **alter** v. 바꾸다

48 글의 제목   ①

| 분석 |

마지막 문장 Mascara can make eyelashes attract water instead of repelling it and curling the lashes alters their shape.이 주제문이다. 마스카라가 속눈썹에 해롭다는 내용을 담은 ①이 가장 좋은 제목이다.

위 글의 제목으로 가장 적절한 것은?
① 마스카라는 속눈썹의 자연적 기능을 방해한다
② 속눈썹 비늘은 물을 튕겨낸다
③ 속눈썹은 물을 어떻게 끌어당기는가
④ 최단시간 곡선은 속눈썹을 어떻게 형성하는가

49 내용일치   ③

| 분석 |

'물은 뿌리에서 끝 쪽으로는 쉽게 흐르지만, 반대 방향으로는 흐르지 않는데, 이는 지붕의 기와처럼 겹쳐진 비늘 모양의 큐티클 덕분이다.'라고 한 것을 보면 속눈썹 큐티클 층이 비늘이 겹친 모양임을 알 수 있으므로 정답은 ③이다. ② less energy가 아니라 more energy이다.

위 글에 따르면, 다음 중 올바른 것은?
① 최단시간 곡선 형태의 속눈썹은 액체를 그 위에 모이게 한다.
② 속눈썹을 물에 넣었다 끄집어낼 때 속눈썹의 래칫을 거슬러 꺼내는 데는 에너지가 그 반대일 때보다 덜 들었다.
③ 속눈썹의 큐티클은 비늘이 겹친 모양이다.
④ 물이 속눈썹의 끝에서 뿌리로 흐르기가 더 쉽다.

50 빈칸완성   ①

| 분석 |

Ⓐ에는 실험이 특징을 '찾아내다, 식별하다'는 뜻으로 pinpoint나 identify가 적절하고, Ⓑ에는 속눈썹이 어떤 형태를 닮았다는 표현이 와야 하므로 '~와 비슷하다'는 뜻의 approximate가 적절하다. 따라서 둘 모두를 충족시키는 ①이 정답이다.

Ⓐ와 Ⓑ에 가장 적절한 쌍의 단어는?
① 정확히 찾아내다 ― ~와 비슷하다
② 식별하다 ― 무시하다
③ 창조하다 ― 반영하다
④ 무시하다 ― 따르다

KOREA AEROSPACE UNIVERSITY | 한국항공대학교 인문계

TEST p. 636~649

01	④	02	①	03	④	04	③	05	②	06	④	07	④	08	②	09	①	10	③
11	②	12	②	13	③	14	①	15	③	16	②	17	④	18	①	19	④	20	①
21	③	22	④	23	①	24	③	25	④	26	①	27	②	28	②	29	③	30	①

01 동의어 ④

| 어휘 |
quintessential a. 전형의, 정수의, 본질적인(= archetypal) beyond doubt 의심할 바 없이 nominal a. 명목상의 inessential a. 중요하지 않은 atypical a. 비전형적인

| 해석 |
그것은 라디오가 최고라는 것을 조금의 의심도 없이 입증하는 전형적인 테스트일 수 있다.

02 동의어 ①

| 어휘 |
beckon v. 손짓해 부르다, 유혹하다(= entice) airless a. 공기가 없는 seismically ad. 지진으로 deter v. 단념시키다 shun v. 피하다 reckon v. 계산하다, 생각하다, 판단하다

| 해석 |
달은 건조하고 공기가 없고 지진활동이 없어서 고요하기 때문에 천문학자들을 유혹한다.

03 동의어 ④

| 어휘 |
encryption n. 암호화 ephemeral a. 단명한, 덧없는, 일시적인(= temporary) incredibly ad. 믿을 수 없을 만큼 immortal a. 불멸의 perpetual a. 영구적인 general a. 일반적인

| 해석 |
암호화는 일시적이지만 특정한 시점에는 믿을 수 없을 만큼 중요하다.

04 동의어 ③

| 어휘 |
copyright laws n. 저작권법 convoluted a. 소용돌이 모양의, 복잡한(= complex) amend v. 수정하다 lucid a. 명료한 retroactive a. 소급 적용되는 conventional a. 관습적인

| 해석 |
저작권법은 복잡하며 수년 동안 계속 바뀌고 수정되어왔다.

05 동의어 ②

| 어휘 |
steadfast a. 변함없는, 충실한(= loyal) dedication n. 헌신, 전념 fickle a. 변덕스러운 brisk a. 활발한 unpredictable a. 예측 불가능한

| 해석 |
그는 예술가로서 자신의 작품 프로젝트에 충실하게 전념하는 것으로 유명하다.

06 논리완성 ④

| 분석 |
'그 대조는 두 가지 넓은 범주로 나뉜다'고 한 다음 '다른 쪽 극단(다른 한 가지 범주)에는 충돌이 존재한다'고 했으므로 빈칸에는 '충돌'과 반대되면서 '공감과 감정이입'과 일맥상통하는 '공모(collusion)'가 적절하다.

| 어휘 |
elusive a. (교묘히) 피하는, 파악하기 어려운 precision n. 정확성 extrapolate v. 추론하다 setting n. 설정, 배경; 곡조 붙이기 per se 그 자체로 divide v. 나누다 category n. 범주 sympathy n. 공감 empathy n. 감정이입 end up 결국 ~하다 compulsion n. 강제 competition n. 경쟁 confrontation n. 대립 collusion n. 공모, 결탁

| 해석 |

음악은 단어들만으로 이루어진 것보다 훨씬 더 파악하기 어려운 형태의 의사전달이지만, 나름의 정확성이 있다. 멘델스존은 음악이 단어들보다 훨씬 더 정확하다는 것을 알게 되었다고 말한 것으로 유명하다. 실제로 그 정확성을 정의하고 음악이 정확히 무엇을 말하고 있는지를 말할 때는 문제가 생긴다. 하지만 내 생각에 바흐의 종교 텍스트 곡조 붙이기를 연구하는 것에서 추론할 수 있는 한 가지 점은 텍스트 자체의 의미와, 텍스트 곡조 붙이기를 둘러싼 음악의 감정 및 영향력 사이에는 일종의 대조적 요소가 존재한다는 것, 그리고 그 대조는 두 가지 넓은 범주로 나뉜다는 것이다. 하나는 공모인데, 이 경우엔 텍스트 속 단어들의 의미와, 텍스트를 둘러싸고 그것을 설명하기 위해 바흐가 사용하는 음악의 유형 사이에는 직접적 의미의 공감과 감정이입이 존재한다. 그리고 다른 쪽 극단에는 충돌이 존재한다. 충돌의 순간에는 음악과 텍스트가 결국 정반대방향을 가리키는 것 같다.

07 논리완성 ④

| 분석 |

케냐 농업 및 축산 연구소의 이사가 한 말 중 앞의 말이 현재의 기상 정보 처리 수준을 나타내므로, 뒤의 말이 미래의 수준을 나타내도록 빈칸에는 '장래에는'이라는 뜻의 Down the road가 적절하다.

| 어휘 |

nonprofit company 비영리 회사, 기업 **super** ad. 대단히, 특별히 **high resolution** 고해상도 **ensure** v. 보장하다 **relevant to** ~와 관련이 있는 **intelligence** n. 정보 **entire** a. 전체의, 전부의 **decision-making** n. 의사결정 **come up with** 생각해내다 **planting** n. 심기, 씨뿌리기 **crop** n. 작물 **fare** v. 살아가다 **revenue** n. 수익 **by and large** 대체로 **in a nutshell** 간략히 말해 **instead** ad. 대신, 오히려 **down the road** 앞으로, 장차

| 해석 |

투머로우나우라는 비영리 회사는 케냐 전역의 농부들에게 기상 정보를 제공한다. 그 정보는 대단히 지역적인 정보이며, 이러한 고해상도 데이터를 통해 농부들은 도시 전체가 아니라 자기 농장에 관련된 정보를 반드시 얻을 수 있게 된다. 데이터 자체는 그냥 정보일 뿐이다. 목표는 이 데이터를 기상 정보로, 즉 농부들이 농장에서 매일 내리는 의사 결정을 개선하기 위해 실제 사용할 수 있는 정보로, 전환하는 것이다. 그리고 이것이 이 단체의 파트너 격인 정부의 역할이다. "우리는 농부들을 위한 단기 예보를 예측하기 위해 기상 정보를 살펴보는데, 그런 다음에는 파종 날짜를 제시할 수 있게 될 것입니다." 케냐 농업 및 축산 연구소의 이사가 한 말이다. "장래에는, 기상 정보가 어떤 작물을 어디에서 재배해야 할지, 또 그 작물 중 어떤 품종이 가장 잘 자랄지를 제시하게 될 것입니다." 이미 500만 여명의 농부들이 케냐 전역에서 기상 정보를 받고 있으며, 평균적으로 7퍼센트의 수익 증가를 보고 있다.

08 논리완성 ②

| 분석 |

화성까지 가는 데 아무리 잘 해도(아무리 빨리 가도) 7개월은 걸린다는 뜻을 완성시킬 수 있는 표현이 와야 하므로 At best가 정답이다.

| 어휘 |

at the earliest 이르면, 빠르면 **at best** 아무리 빨라도, 잘해봐야 **at the latest** 늦어도 **at last** 마침내 **prep for** 준비[채비]하다 **figure out** 해결하다 **logistics** n. 물류 **red planet** 화성 **round trip** 왕복 여행 **sustain** v. 살아가게 지탱하다 **mission** n. 임무, 미션 **long-awaited** a. 오랫동안 고대한 **feasible** a. 실행 가능한 **contestant** n. 참가자

| 해석 |

우주 식량은 왜 중요할까? 한 마디로 말하면 화성 때문이다. 먼 우주로의 여행을 위한 식사 준비는 쉽지 않다. 현재, 과학자들은 화성까지 가는 여정과 관련된 많은 물류 문제를 해결했지만, 식량을 충분히 가져가는 방법은 아직 해결하지 못했다. 화성까지 가려면 아무리 잘해도 7개월이 걸린다. 왕복 여행을 위해 1년 치 이상의 식량(물론 간식 포함)을 챙기면 엄청난 무게가 될 것이므로 로켓에 실을 수 없다. 우리가 아직 알지 못하고 있는 것은 지구와 화성 사이를 오고가는 길에 여행자들을 먹여 살릴 만큼 충분한 물자를 들어 올려 싣고 가는 방법이다. 딥 스페이스 푸드 챌린지에 참가한 자들은 이 문제를 해결하고 오랫동안 기다려온 화성 탐사 미션을 더 실현 가능하게 만들고자 한다.

09 논리완성 ①

| 분석 |

먹이 사슬 최상층의 악어가 줄면 중간층의 포식자가 늘어날 것이므로 빈칸에는 '증가'를 뜻하는 a surge가 들어가야 한다.

| 어휘 |

surge n. 급증 **flip** n. 뒤집힘 **downturn** n. 하락 **upkeep** n. 유지, 보수 **freshwater** n. 민물 **crocodile** n. 악어 **in droves** 떼로 **population** n. 개체군 **super-poisonous** a. 맹독성이 있는 **firsthand** ad. 직접 **food web** 먹이사슬 **decline** v. 감소하다 **ripple out** 파문을 일으키다 **set off** 초래하다 **cascading effect** 폭포 효과 **nest** v. 둥지를 틀다 **havoc** n. 대혼란, 파괴

| 해석 |

호주 북부 전역에서 민물 악어들이 떼죽음을 당하고 있으며, 일부 개체군은 개체수가 70퍼센트 감소했다. 수십 년 전 인간이 호주 대륙에 들여온 맹독성 사탕수수두꺼비를 악어들이 먹기 때문이다. (환경) 보존 과학자들은 악어들의 몰락을 직접 목격해 왔다. 이처럼 많은 악어가 사라지는 것이 문제인 이유는 이들이 먹이사슬의 꼭대기에 있기 때문이다. 악어가 줄어들면 생태계에 큰 구멍이 생기고, 이것이 파장을 퍼뜨리며 연쇄적인 폭포 효과를 일으킨다. 이 효과

에는 중간 포식자들의 급증이 포함되며, 이는 새들이 둥지를 트는 능력에 부정적인 영향을 줄 수 있다. 그러므로 사탕수수두꺼비는 이곳 호주 생태계에 심각한 혼란을 일으킨다.

10 논리완성 ③

| 분석 |

곤충이 지나갈 때, 레이 거미는 팽팽한 실을 풀어 거미줄을 앞으로 튕기며 먹이를 얽어맨다고 했고, 레이 거미가 거미줄을 새총처럼 이용한다고 했으므로, 먹이가 거미줄을 건드리지 않아도 먹이를 잡는다고 추론할 수 있다. 따라서 정답은 전치사 without이다. 'without 명사(insect)+V~ing(touching the web)' 형태의 동명사 구문이다.

| 어휘 |

grain n. 곡물, 낟알 **spin** v. (실을) 잣다, 만들다 **concentric** a. 동심원의 **spoke** n. 바큇살 **radiate** v. 방사상으로 뻗어나가다 **tension line** 팽팽한 줄 **twig** n. 가지 **conical** a. 원뿔 모양의 **entangle** v. 얽어매다 **prey** n. 먹이 **flutter by** 날아서 지나가다

| 해석 |

레이 거미는 쌀알보다 작다. 이 거미는 전형적인 동심원형 구조로 거미줄을 쳐, 중심에서 바깥으로 방사형 줄이 뻗어나가도록 만든다. 하지만 그런 다음 거미는 거미줄 중심부의 실을 인근 바위나 나뭇가지로 연결한다. 그리고 난 후 뒷다리로 거미줄 중심부를 붙잡고 앞다리로 자기 몸을 팽팽한 거미줄 실을 따라 끌어당긴다. 이렇게 하면 평평한 형태의 거미줄이 원뿔 모양으로 바뀐다. 이제 원뿔 형태의 거미줄은 용수철 같은 상태가 된다. 곤충이 지나갈 때, 레이 거미는 팽팽한 실을 풀어 거미줄을 앞으로 튕기며 먹이를 얽어맨다. 따라서 거미는 거미줄 위에 가만히 앉아만 있는 것이 아니다. 이들은 거미줄을 새총처럼 이용하여 먹이가 될 곤충이 거미줄에 닿지 않아도 잡는 것이다.

11 동사의 수일치 ②

| 분석 |

②에서 that 관계절의 선행사가 복수명사인 the retina's cone cells이므로 수의 일치를 위해 동사 delivers를 deliver로 고쳐야 한다. 따라서 정답은 ②이다.

| 어휘 |

path n. 경로 **solar eclipse** 개기일식 **gear** n. 장비, 물품 **break out** ~을 꺼내다 **celestial** a. 하늘의, 천체의 **odd** a. 기이한 **unusual** a. 이례적인 **block** v. 막다 **adjust to** ~에 적응하다 **dim** v. 어두워지다 **transition** v. 이행하다, 전환되다 **retina** n. 망막 **cone cell** 원추세포 **rod cell** 간상세포 **detect** v. 감지하다 **wavelength** n. 파장 **totality** n. 개기일식(의 시간) **a totality thing** 개기일식 현상을 중심으로 한 상황 **guarantee** v. 보장하다 **witness** v. 목격하다 **colorful** a. 화려한

| 해석 |

만일 당신이 월요일의 개기일식이 일어날 전체 경로를 따라 살고 있고 크리스마스 관련 물품을 갖고 있다면, 그것을 꺼내놓고 싶어질 것이다. 이 천체의 사건은 지구에 특이한 현상을 가져올 것이다. 개기일식이 유발하는 독특한 시각 효과로, 빨간색과 초록색이 지구상의 인간들에게 이상하게 보일 수 있다. 이는 부분적으로는 달이 태양을 가릴 때 빛에 변화가 일어나기 때문이지만, 우리의 눈과 뇌가 그 변화에 적응하고 해석하는 방식 때문이기도 하다. 빛이 어두워지면, 우리의 눈은 선명한 색상과 세부사항들을 전달하는 망막의 원추세포와 관련된 주간 시각에서, 약한 빛 속에서도 사물을 인식하게 해주는 간상세포에 의지하는 야간 시각으로 전환된다. 그 중간에는 중간 시각이라는 과도기적 단계가 있는데, 이 단계에서는 원추세포와 간상세포가 둘 다 활성화된다. 일식으로 빛의 강도가 감소하면, 파장이 긴 빨간색 계열은 원추세포가 덜 활동하기 때문에 더 어둡게 보인다. 그러나 간상세포는 파장이 짧은 파란색과 초록색 계열에 민감하므로 이 색들이 밝게 빛날 기회를 가질 것이다. 이것은 개기일식과 관련한 전형적인 상황으로, 개기일식의 중앙 경로에 있는 사람들만이 이 현상을 확실하게 목격할 수 있다. 또한 이 효과를 유발하려면 단순히 빨간색이나 초록색 티셔츠 하나에만 의지해서도 안 된다. 주변에 많은 사람들이나 다채로운 색의 사물들이 있어야 이 효과를 볼 수 있다. 이러한 효과는 갑작스러운 어두움과, 그 어둠을 해석하려는 우리 눈의 간상세포와 원추세포의 반응에서 비롯된다. 이 현상은 푸르키녜 효과라 불린다.

12 관사 ②

| 분석 |

②의 evidence는 불가산 명사이므로 부정관사 an을 삭제해야 한다.

| 어휘 |

consume v. 소비하다 **reduction** n. 감소 **gain weight** 체중이 증가하다 **home in on** ~을 향해 나아가다, 주의를 기울이다 **dilate** v. 확장시키다 **lower** v. 낮추다 **modest** a. 온건한 **multiple** a. 다수의 **prompt** v. 재촉하다 **nitric oxide** 산화질소

| 해석 |

코코아가 풍부하게 들어간 다크 초콜릿을 먹는 것이 건강에 이점을 줄 수 있다는 생각은 새로운 것이 아니다. 최근 한 연구에 따르면, 다크 초콜릿을 조금씩 습관적으로 먹는 사람들은 그렇지 않은 사람들에 비해 제2형 당뇨병에 걸릴 위험이 21% 낮은 것으로 나타났다. 설탕이 더 많고 코코아 함량이 낮은 밀크 초콜릿을 먹는 사람들은 당뇨병 위험이 줄어드는 효과를 보지 못했다. 그리고 연구 기간 동안 밀크 초콜릿을 먹는 사람들은 체중이 증가하는 경향이 있었는데, 이는 당뇨병 위험을 높이는 요인이다. 그러나 다크 초콜릿을 먹는 것은 체중 증가와 연관성이 없었다. 코코아에서 발견되는 화합물이 심장 건강에 기여할 수 있다는 증거는 오래전부터 있었다. 예를 들어, 학술지 『심장』에 실린 한 연구에 따르면, 초콜릿을 즐겨

먹는 사람들은 뇌졸중이나 기타 심혈관 질환의 위험이 더 낮았다. 과학자들은 코코아 원두에 들어 있는 생리활성 식물성 화합물에 주의를 기울여왔는데, 이 화합물은 체내에서 산화질소 생성을 유발하는 것으로 밝혀졌다. 이 기체는 혈관을 넓히는, 즉 확장시키는, 작용을 하며, 이것이 바로 혈압을 낮추는 메커니즘이다. 그리고 여러 연구는 다크 초콜릿 섭취가 혈압의 소폭 저하와 관련이 있음을 보여주었다.

13 논리완성 ③

| 분석 |
몸이 과도한 활동 상태에 있으면 마음이 평온할 수 없고 그 반대도 마찬가지라고 했으므로, 마음이 헛되이 소용돌이치고 있으면 몸이 평온할 수 없다고 해야 한다. 따라서 정답은 ③이다.

| 어휘 |
negative a. 부정적인　**do a number on** ~에 해를 끼치다　**central nervous system** 중추신경계　**trembly** a. 떨리는　**sweaty** a. 땀이 나는　**brow** n. 이마　**inhale** v. 숨을 들이마시다　**exhale** v. 숨을 내쉬다　**soothe** v. 가라앉히다, 달래다　**composure** n. 평정상태　**hyperdrive** n. 초(超)광속 우주여행을 위한 추진시스템　**in hyperdrive** 과도하게 기민하고 고조된 (신체)활동 상태인　**the opposite** 정반대

| 해석 |
부정적인 사고는 중추신경계에 해를 끼쳐 신체적 반응을 유발할 수 있다. 부정적인 생각이 들자마자 갑자기 몸이 안 좋아진 적이 있는가? 손 떨림, 목소리 떨림, 이마의 땀 등, 당신의 반응이 무엇이건 간에 숨을 천천히 들이마시고 더 천천히 내쉬는 호흡은 중추신경계를 진정시킨다. 평정심을 찾으면 생각이 지나치게 만드는 데 도움이 된다. 당신의 몸이 과도한 활동 상태에 있으면 평온한 마음을 가질 수 없다. 정반대도 마찬가지이다 — 마음이 헛되이 뱅뱅 돌며 소용돌이치고 있으면 몸도 평온할 수 없다.

14 논리완성 ①

| 분석 |
빈칸 다음에서 '서로 다른 당사자들이 모두에게 이익이 되는 해결책을 찾도록 돕는다'고 했고 '당사자들은 조건들이 서로에게 이익이 될 때 비로소 계약서에 서명한다'고 했으므로, 서로에게 이익이 된다는 의미를 포함하고 있는 win-win strategy가 빈칸에 가장 적절하다.

| 어휘 |
career coach 경력개발 상담가　**classic** a. 고전적인, 전형적인　**negotiation** n. 협상　**tactic** n. 전략, 전술　**apply** v. 적용하다　**party** n. 당사자　**mutually** ad. 상호, 서로　**beneficial** a. 이로운　**unhelpful** a. 도움이 되지 않는　**upset** a. 실망한, 화가 난　**reframe** v. 고치다, 틀을 바꾸다　**focus on** ~에 집중하다　**benchmarking** n. 벤치마킹(우량 기업의 장점을 도입해 기준으로 삼는 경영 기법)　**value proposition** 가치제안

| 해석 |
경력개발 상담가인 조앤 문은 비즈니스 환경에서 자주 사용되는 몇 가지 고전적인 협상 책략과 이러한 책략들이 일상적인 상황에 어떻게 적용될 수 있는지를 설명한다. 우선, 윈윈 전략이라는 책략은 서로 다른 당사자들이 모두에게 이익이 되는 해결책을 찾도록 돕는 방식이다. 이것은 예를 들어 사업 계약이나 노사 협약에서 볼 수 있다. 당사자들은 조건들이 서로에게 이익이 될 때 비로소 계약서에 서명한다. 이 책략을 일상생활에서 어떻게 활용할 수 있을까? 이 책략은 상대가 당신의 결정에 동의하는 것뿐 아니라, 그 결정에 기분까지 좋아지게 하고 싶을 때 써보라. 조앤은 최근의 개인적 경험을 공유한다. 그녀의 전화 회선이 끊기는 문제가 생겨, 통신사에 연락하여 다시 연결해 달라고 요청했다. 하지만 고객 서비스 상담원들은 도움이 되지 않았다. 그녀는 화가 나고 있다는 것을 느꼈고, 그래서 그 책략을 사용하여 자신의 요청 방식을 바꾸기로 했다. 그녀는 이렇게 말했다. "있잖아요, 제가 이 회사를 10년간 이용해왔고, 앞으로도 10년 더 이용하고 싶어요. 우리, 해결책에 집중해 볼 수 있을까요?" 그녀에 따르면, 이 접근법은 효과가 있었다. 그 회사는 충성도 높은 고객을 잃고 싶지 않았고, 조앤은 전화 문제를 해결하고 싶었기 때문이다.

15 논리완성 ③

| 분석 |
'제도가 사람들이 어떤 행동을 하지 못하도록 방해할 때'라고 한 것과 뒤이어 예를 든 구독 취소를 못하게 하는 기업의 사례를 보면, 어떤 일을 하기 어렵게 만들어서 특정 행동을 막는다는 것을 알 수 있으므로 정답은 ③ by making it hard to do이다.

| 어휘 |
nudge v. (행동을) 유도하다　**sludge** n. 슬러지, 행동 경제학에서 개인의 행동이나 의사 결정에 대한 체계적인 방해나 마찰　**memoir** n. 회고록　**release** v. 발간하다　**editor** n. 편집자　**paywall** n. 지불장벽　**promotion** n. 홍보, 판촉　**subscription** n. 구독　**give two weeks' notice** 2주 전에 통보하다　**headquarters** n. 본부

| 해석 |
사람들이 어떤 행동을 하도록 유도하는(nudge) 한 가지 방법은 그 행동을 쉽게 만드는 것이다. 반대로 슬러지(sludge)는 그것(nudge)의 사악한 반대 개념으로, 기관이나 조직이 사람들이 어떤 행동을 하지 못하도록 그것을 어렵게 만들어 방해할 때를 말한다. 행동경제학의 창시자 중 한 명인 리처드 탈러는 몇 년 전 자신의 회고록이 출간되었을 때 이 슬러지 개념을 발전시킬 영감을 얻었다. 그의 편집자는 첫 번째 서평이 런던의 한 신문에 실렸다고 알려주었고, 탈러는 그 글을 읽고 싶어 했다. 그러나 해당 기사는 유료 결제 장벽 뒤에 있었다. 이 장벽을 넘기 위해서는 판촉활동이 있었는데, 한 달간 체험 구독을 신청하면 1파운드에 이용할 수 있다는

것이었다. 탈러는 더 깊이 파고들어 살펴보기 시작했고, 구독을 취소하려면 최소 2주 전에 미리 통보해야 하고, 그러기 위해서는 실제로 런던의 업무 시간 중에 신문사 본사에 직접 전화를 걸어야만 한다는 것을 알게 되었다. 이는 회사가 사람들이 구독을 해지하지 못하게 막기 위해 슬러지를 활용하는 것이다.

16 논리완성   ②

| 분석 |

첫 문장의 건강한 몸은 운동을 의미하고, 예리한 정신은 기억력을 의미한다. 이 둘 사이의 연관성에 대한 연구가 종전에는 뇌 자체 내의 요소들을 밝혀냈는데 이번에는 뇌 바깥 근육의 혈액 속에서 카텝신 B 단백질이 발견되어 운동과 기억력 사이의 연관성에 대해 미비한 점을 보완해주었으므로, 이 발견이 또 하나의 퍼즐조각을 제공하여 퍼즐을 완성에 더 가깝게 한 것이고 할 수 있다. 따라서 정답은 ②이다. ③ 이 발견은 상황을 변화시키지 못한다는 뜻이다.

| 어휘 |

identify v. 밝히다   **fit** a. 튼튼한, 건강한   **release** v. 방출하다 **generate** v. 생성시키다   **critical** a. 중요한   **cast a wide net in** ~에서 폭넓게 시도하다   **cell death** 세포소멸   **hippocampus** n. 해마(뇌의 기억 담당 부위)   **move the needle** 실질적 진전을 이루다 **dark side** 어두운 면, 부정적 측면

| 해석 |

연구자들은 건강한 몸과 예리한 정신 사이의 연관성을 설명하는데 도움을 주는 근육 속 물질을 발견했다. 근육이 움직일 때, 근육은 특정 단백질을 방출하는데, 이 단백질은 기억에 중요한 역할을 하는 뇌의 특정 부위에서 새로운 세포들과 세포 연결을 생성하는 것으로 보인다고 연구팀은 학술지 『셀 메타볼리즘』에서 보고했다. 이 발견은 이 퍼즐을 풀기 위한 또 하나의 조각을 제공한다고 연구팀은 말한다. 이전 연구에서는 운동에 반응하는 뇌 자체 내의 요소들이 밝혀진 바 있다. 이번 발견은 연구팀이 운동과 기억력 사이의 잘 알려진 연관성을 설명해 줄 수 있는 요인들을 넓은 범위에서 탐색해 보기로 한 이후 이루어졌다. 연구자들은 운동에 반응해 근육 세포에서 생성되는 물질들을 찾는 데서 출발했다. 그렇게 찾은 결과, 카텝신 B라는 단백질이 발견되었는데, 이 단백질은 주로 세포 사멸 및 일부 질병과 관련된 것으로 알려져 있었다. 실험 결과, 운동용 바퀴에서 많은 시간을 보낸 쥐들의 혈액 속 카텝신 B 수치가 상승한 것이 확인되었다. 게다가, 이 단백질 수치가 올라갈수록, 쥐들은 작은 수영장 바로 아래 숨겨진 플랫폼까지 수영해야 하는 기억력 테스트에서 더 좋은 성과를 보였다. 연구팀은 또한 카텝신 B가 쥐의 해마, 즉 기억에 핵심적인 뇌 부위에서 새로운 세포들과 세포 연결들을 증가시킨다는 사실도 발견했다.

17 논리완성   ④

| 분석 |

빈칸 이하에서 '이야기와 기억 요령을 활용해 기억에 저장시킴으로써 거리 이름, 주요 지형지물, 경로를 기억에 남기도록 하라'라고 했으므로 빈칸에는 공간 기억에 필요한 요령을 쓰라는 말이 와야 한다. 따라서 정답은 ④이다. ① 주저 없이 현지인들에게 길안내를 부탁하라 ② 발을 사용하여 당신의 감정을 보여주라 ③ 자기 마음이 흐르는 대로 따라가지 마라

| 어휘 |

over-reliance n. 과도한 의존   **surroundings** n. 환경, 주위   **cue** n. 단서, 신호   **internal compass** 내부의 나침반   **sense of direction** 방향 감각(자신의 위치를 알고 길을 찾는 능력)   **cabbie** n. 택시 기사   **narrative** n. 이야기   **lock ~ in** ~을 기억에 새기다 **abstract** a. 추상적인   **logical** a. 논리적인   **navigate** v. 항해하다, 길을 찾아다니다   **ease** v. 완화시키다, 덜어주다   **get lost** 길을 잃다

| 해석 |

GPS에 과도하게 의존하면 주변 환경에 대한 시야가 좁아질 수도 있다. 당신은 자신이 어디에 있는지를 알려주는 공간 속 단서들 — 오른쪽이나 왼쪽에 무엇이 있는지, "여기"라는 장소가 무엇을 의미하는지 — 을 넓게 살펴보지 않게 된다. 실제로, 좋은 내부 나침반(공간 감각)을 갖고 있는 사람은 주변 세계와 더 깊은 연결을 맺고 있을 가능성이 있다. 도로 위에서 자신감을 갖거나 GPS에 덜 의존해 길을 찾고 싶다면, 당신이 지금 있는 장소를 기억하기 위해 기억 요령을 사용하라. 방향 감각이 좋은 사람들 — 예를 들면 런던의 택시 운전사들 — 은 거리들을 정확히 알고 있다. 물론 2만 5천 개의 거리에 숙달할 수는 없겠지만, 전문가의 길 찾기 책략을 시도해볼 수는 있다. 이야기와 기억 요령을 활용해 기억에 저장시킴으로써 거리 이름, 주요 지형지물, 경로를 기억에 남기도록 하라. 이러한 방법은 거리 이름이 추상적이거나 논리적인 순서를 따르지 않을 때 특히 유용하다. 이야기나 아이디어를 어떤 장소와 연결하는 과정을 인지 지도 구축이라 부른다. 이것은 사물이 어디에 있고, 어떻게 연결되어 있는지를 파악할 수 있게 해 준다. 그래서 지도를 사용하지 않고 길을 찾을 때는 주변을 둘러보고, 이야기나 기억 장치를 활용해 주변 환경의 세부 사항을 기억해내라. 예를 들어, 이렇게 말할 수 있다. "그날 친구랑 츄러스를 먹었던 12번가에서 우회전하고, 그다음엔 공원 쪽으로 이어지는 P스트리트를 따라 가야지. P는 park(공원)의 P야." 이런 식으로 기억하면 주변 환경을 장악했다는 느낌이 생겨, 길을 잃을까 봐 느끼는 불안도 덜 수 있다.

18~19

신경생물학자들은 쥐들이 대체로 열성적인 조력자라는 것을 이전에 보여주었다. 만약 쥐가 투명 아크릴 튜브로 만든 홀더에 갇힌 다른 쥐를 마주치면, 자유로운 쥐는 그 튜브를 탐색해서 갇힌 쥐를 어떻게 풀어줄지를 알아낸다. 쥐는 이 행동을 반복한다. (갇힌 쥐가 이전에 함께 살아본 적이 있는 품종인 한) 낯선 쥐를 위해서조차 그렇게 한다. 꼭 개별

쥐를 알 필요는 없지만, 쥐의 품종은 알아야 한다. 이러한 구조자 쥐들은 다른 쥐의 곤경을 보고 느끼는 내면의 고통에 의해 동기 부여를 받는 것으로 보인다 — 왜냐하면 연구자들이 자유로운 쥐에게 "진정제"인 항불안 약물을 투여했을 때, 그들은 더 이상 갇힌 동료 쥐를 풀어주려 하지 않았기 때문이다. 연구자들은 쥐들 사이의 방관자 효과를 실험하기 위해, 평소처럼 한 마리의 쥐를 아크릴 튜브에 가두었다. 그러고 나서 자유로운 쥐를 한 마리가 아니라 두세 마리를 함께 넣었다. 이들 중 한 마리를 제외하고 모두에게 다른 쥐의 필요 앞에서 수동성을(무기력 상태를) 유발하는 항(抗)불안 약물을 투여하자, 그것이 약을 맞지 않은 쥐의 조력 의지에 결정적 영향을 끼치는 것을 연구자들은 보았다. 약을 맞지 않은 쥐가 처음에는 도움을 주지만 다시는 도움을 주지 않는 것이다. 연구자들은 그 쥐가 다음날이나 그 다음날에는 보통 때 하듯이 도움을 주지는 않을 것이라고 말한다. 이는 본질적으로 그 쥐가 다음과 같이 말하는 것과 같다. "어제 도와줬는데, 아무도 신경 안 쓰더라고 — 다시는 안 해." 연구자들은 아무 쥐도 약물에 의해 수동적으로 되지 않았을 때, 자유로운 동료 쥐가 있을 경우 혼자 있을 때보다 훨씬 더 빨리 돕기 시작했다는 점을 지적한다. 이는 동료들의 긍정적 반응이 도움을 제공하는 쥐들에게 자극을 줬다는 것을 시사한다.

| 어휘 |

neurobiologist n. 신경생물학자 **previously** ad. 전에, 과거에 **rat** n. 쥐 **enthusiastic** a. 열정적인 **helper** n. 조력자, 돕는 자 **encounter** v. 마주하다, 만나다 **trap** v. 가두다 **clear** a. 투명한 **explore** v. 탐색하다 **figure out** 알아내다 **release** v. 풀어주다 **strain** n. 품종, 종, 종류 **rescuer** n. 구조자 **motivate** v. 동기를 부여하다 **distress** n. 고통 **plight** n. 곤경, 고통 **anti-anxiety drug** 항(抗)우울제 **bystander** n. 방관자 **enclosure** n. 울타리에 가둔 상태 **definite** a. 확실한 **willingness** n. 의지 **passivity** n. 수동성 **companion** n. 동료, 동반자 **spur on** 자극하다

| 18 | 빈칸완성 | ① |

| 분석 |

문맥상 다른 쥐들의 필요 '~와 마주하여, ~에 직면하여, ~ 앞에서'라는 뜻이 와야 한다. 따라서 in the face of가 답이다.

| 19 | 내용추론 | ④ |

| 분석 |

본문 마지막에서 '연구자들은 아무 쥐도 약물에 의해 수동적으로 되지 않았을 때, 자유로운 동료 쥐가 있을 경우 혼자 있을 때보다 훨씬 더 빨리 돕기 시작했다는 점을 지적한다. 이는 동료들의 긍정적 반응이 도움을 제공하는 쥐들에게 자극을 줬다는 것을 시사한다.'라고 한 것에서 유추하면 동료들의 반응이 쥐의 행동에 영향을 끼쳤으므로 집단의 존재가 개체의 행동에 영향을 준다고 볼 수 있다. 따라서 정답은 ④이다. ② 다른 개체가 수동성을 보일 때만 사실이므로 정답이 될 수 없다.

위 글에서 추론할 수 있는 것은 무엇인가?
① 쥐들은 도덕적인 결정을 내린다.
② 다른 개체가 있을 때 조력자가 행동할 가능성이 줄어든다.
③ 돕는 행동은 시간이 지나도 줄어들지 않는다.
④ 집단의 존재가 개체의 행동에 영향을 줄 수 있다.

20~21

화석연료를 태워 발생하는 전 세계 (온실가스) 방출량의 정점이 몇 년 남지 않았을 수 있지만, 그렇다고 해서 지구의 평균 기온이 떨어지기 시작할 것이라는 말은 아니다. 각국은 여전히 대기 중에 온실가스를 더할 것이며, 다만 속도가 느려질 뿐이다. 이러한 방출은 계속해서 지구 온도를 상승시킬 것이다. 온도 상승을 멈추려면 온실가스 배출량이 '제로(0)'로 떨어져야 한다. 전문가들은 이렇게 말한다. "정점에 도달했다는 것은 배출량이 사상 최고치라는 뜻입니다. 이 말은 매년 기후에 가능한 가장 큰 피해를 주고 있다는 의미입니다. 그래서 가장 중요한 것은 이 높은 피해 구간에서 얼마나 빨리 벗어날 수 있는가 하는 것입니다." 이것은 마치 자동차를 위험한 속도로 운전하는 것과 같다. 배출 정점에 도달하는 것은 가속 페달에서 발을 떼어 속도를 줄이는 것과 같다. "어느 지점에선가 멈추려면 브레이크를 밟아야 합니다. 왜냐하면 거기 벽이 있는데 우리가 그 벽을 향해 달리고 있기 때문입니다." COP29 기후 정상회담에서는, 늦어도 2100년까지는 산업화 이전보다 1.5도 상승하는 것 이내로 온도를 제한하려는 희망을 가지고, 국가들이 미래의 배출량 감축에 대한 새로운 약속을 두고 협상중이다. 이 수준을 넘으면, 세계는 더욱 파괴적인 폭풍과 홍수를 경험하고 산호초 같은 생태계가 되돌릴 수 없는 피해를 입을 수 있다. 이 목표를 달성하려면 2050년까지 배출량을 제로로 줄여야 하지만, 현재 각국의 약속은 이 목표에 훨씬 못 미친다. 그럼에도 불구하고 배출 정점 도달은 전 세계 협상의 중요한 전환점을 나타낸다. 우리는 아직도 어느 정도는 우리 운명의 주인이고, 얼마나 많은 온난화를 겪을지는 우리가 통제할 수 있다.

| 어휘 |

peak n. 정점 **emission** n. 방출물, 배출물 **fossil fuel** 화석연료 **add** v. 보태다, 추가하다 **all-time** a. 공전의, 사상 **license** n. 면허증 **fatigued** a. 피로한, 피곤한 **under the influence** 음주 상태에서 **negotiate** v. 협상하다 **destructive** a. 파괴적인 **irreversible** a. 돌이킬 수 없는 **damage** n. 피해, 손상 **turning point** 전환점 **fate** n. 운명

20 빈칸완성 ①

| 분석 |

빈칸 뒤 문장에서 '배출 정점에 도달하는 것은 가속 페달에서 발을 떼어 속도를 줄이는 것과 같다'고 했으므로 가속페달에서 발을 떼서 속도를 줄이기 전에 위험한 속도로 운전을 했을 것이다. 이 글에서는 온실가스 방출량이 빨리 증가하는 위험한 상황을 과속 운전에 비유하고 있으므로 at dangerous speeds가 적절하다.

21 글의 제목 ③

| 분석 |

글의 마지막부분에서 '그럼에도 불구하고 배출 정점 도달은 전 세계 협상의 중요한 전환점을 나타낸다. 우리는 아직도 어느 정도는 우리 운명의 주인이고, 얼마나 많은 온난화를 겪을지는 우리가 통제할 수 있다.'고 한 것을 참고하면 정점 도달에서부터 앞으로 기후변화를 조절할 희망이 있다는 것이 주제이다. 따라서 제목으로 가장 적절한 것은 ③이다.

위 글의 제목으로 가장 적절한 것은?
① 기후 목표는 코앞이다
② 재생에너지가 배출 정점을 늦춘다
③ 정점 도달은 단지 시작일 뿐이다
④ 급격한 정점 도달은 역효과를 낳는다

22~23

당신이 쇼핑할 때, 뇌에서는 감정적인 부분과 이성적인 부분 사이에 대치 상태가 대개 벌어진다. 무언가 사고 싶은 것을 발견하면, 뇌의 보상 회로가 활성화된다. 도파민에 의해 자극된 충동이 당신을 들뜨게 만든다. 기대감으로 인해 이 새 물건을 사기만 한다면 그것으로 삶이 얼마나 더 근사해질지 상상하게 된다. 이런 감정은 특히 당신이 뭔가를 좋아하는 성향일 경우 더욱 강렬하다. 그에 대한 균형추 역할을 하는 것은 당신의 인지 작용이다. 인지 작용은 마치 신중한 회계사처럼 말할 수 있다. 이게 꼭 필요한가? 이게 값어치를 하는가? 예산에 얼마나 맞는가? 이때, 할인 행사는 마치 당신의 정신 저울을 구매 쪽으로 기울게 만드는 엄지손가락처럼 작용한다. 사실, 할인 자체가 하나의 승리로 인식되며, 그것만으로도 즐거움을 안겨준다. 단순히 물건을 얻는 것이 아니라, 무언가를 발견해냈고, 그로 인해 추가적인 보상을 받았다는 느낌을 갖게 된다. 물론, 상점들은 이 모든 것을 알고 있으며 우리의 심리를 자극하려 한다. 전문가들에 따르면, 우리는 무의식적으로 인기 있는 것이 더 가치있거나 더 만족감을 줄 것이라고 믿는 경향이 있다. 그래서 상점들은 군중심리에 호소한다. "블랙 프라이데이예요, 원하는 것을 사면서 모두가 쇼핑을 하고 있어요." 그들은 긴박감을 만든다. "당신이 좋아하는 자동차, 오늘만 할인합니다!" 그리고 희소성을 조장한다. "재고가 충분한 동안(떨어지기 전에) 지금 쇼핑하세요!" 이러한 판촉활동들은 사람들의 피를 끓게 만든다. 당신은 그 흥분을 제품 탓으로 돌린다. "이 제품, 분명 좋은 거야." 세일에 대해 항상 이성적으로 접근하는 것은 매우 어렵다. 전문가들조차도 어려움을 느낀다. 전문가들이 추천하는 한 가지 구매 전략은, 사전에 쇼핑 리스트를 작성하고 그 목록에 고수하는 것이다. 더 중요한 것은, 즉각적인 반응에서 벗어날 수 있도록 시간을 두는 것이다. 사고 능력은 감정 상태를 이겨낼 수 있다. 당신이 더 많은 시간을 생각에 할애하고 인지적 과정을 작동시킬수록, 기본적으로 이렇게 말할 수 있는 가능성이 생긴다. "아니야, (사지 말고) 그냥 지나갈 거야." 비록 처음에는 그렇게 하고 싶지 않았을지라도 말이다.

| 어휘 |

pipe up 지껄이다, 말하다 hiatus n. 일시적 휴지기, 중단 handoff n. 넘겨주기, 이양 standoff n. 대립, 팽팽한 균형, 대치 상태 emotional a. 감정적인 rational a. 이성적인 spot v. 발견하다 activate v. 활성화시키다 reward circuitry 보상회로 impulse n. 충동 cognitive a. 인지의 prudent a. 신중한 accountant n. 회계사 tip v. 움직이다 subconsciously ad. 무의식적으로 rewarding a. 보람찬, 보상이 되는 crowd mentality 군중심리 last v. 지속되다, 충분하다 cool off 가라앉히다, 식히다 inclination n. 성향 in advance 미리 stick to ~을 고수하다, 지키다 bring to bear 작동시키다 have a shot at 시도하다, 기회가 있다, 가능성이 있다

22 빈칸완성 ④

| 분석 |

이 글의 주제가 구매행위를 둘러싼 감정과 이성간의 갈등이므로 빈칸에는 대치 상태를 나타내는 standoff가 들어가야 한다. ① 틈, 중단 ② 인정 ③ 손으로 밀어제치기

23 내용추론 ①

| 분석 |

마지막부분에서 '더 중요한 것은, 즉각적인 반응에서 벗어날 수 있도록 시간을 두는 것이다. 사고 능력은 감정 상태를 이겨낼 수 있다'고 했는데, 여기서 '즉각적인 반응'은 사고 싶은 상품을 본 순간 일어나는 감정을 말하고, 시간을 두고 생각해서 이 감정을 이겨낼 수 있다고 했으므로 인간의 뇌는 느낀 다음에 생각을 한다고 추론할 수 있다.

위 글에서 추론할 수 있는 것은 무엇인가?
① 인간의 뇌는 본질적으로 먼저 느끼고 그 다음에 생각하도록 진화했다.
② 사람들은 마케팅 전략에 거의 영향을 받지 않는다.
③ 소비자들은 비싼 제품을 사고자 하는 타고난 충동이 있다.
④ 제품을 살 때 감정은 의사 결정에 역할을 하지 않는다.

24~25

과거엔 VHS 플레이어가 있었다. 작은 테이프가 돌아가는 자동응답기가 달린 유선 전화가 있었다. 그런데 그 모든 기술은 오늘날 더 이상 존재하지 않는다. 그 이유는 바로 '창조적 파괴' 때문이다. 이는 경제학자 조지프 슘페터가 생각해낸 구절이다. 그것은 경제는 끊임없이 진화하며 새로운 제품들이 계속해서 발명되고, 이러한 발명은 기존 제품을 쓸모없게 만든다는 생각이다. 창조적 파괴는 우리가 어릴 적 사용하던 기술 중 오늘날까지 남아 있는 게 오직 그래핑 계산기뿐인 이유이다. 그래핑 계산기는 원조 아이패드와 같았지만, 멋진 코사인 그래프 따위를 보여주는 것 외엔 아무것도 하지 못했다. 미적분은 할 수 있지만 그 외에는 아무 기능도 없었다. 텍사스 인스트루먼트(TI)는 여전히 이 계산기를 생산하고 있으며, 생긴 것도 예전과 똑같다. 우리는 쉽게 터치스크린이나 와이파이, 카메라 같은 사양을 계산기에 추가할 수 있을 테지만 그렇게 하지 않는다. 그 사실이 이 그래핑 계산기를 특별하게 만든다. 사실, 그래핑 계산기가 인터넷에 연결된다면 가치가 떨어질 것이다. 그것이 시험의 보안을 해치고, 계산기 본래의 목적을 실제로 훼손할 수 있기 때문에 그것이 존재해야 할 이유조차 없을 것이다. 그래핑 계산기는 한때 첨단 기술을 대표했다. 표준화 시험을 설계하는 사람들이 그래핑 계산기를 시험에서 사용할 수 있도록 허용하기까지 수년이 걸렸다. 표준 시험 출제자들은 계산기가 학생들에게 불공평한 이점을 줄까 우려했다. 〈지금은 정반대다.〉 그래핑 계산기는 스마트폰이나 노트북과 달리 인터넷에 연결되어 있지 않기 때문에 시험 출제자들이 허용할 거의 유일한 기술이다. 그래핑 계산기의 가치는 기술이 그것을 건너뛰어 가버렸다는 사실에 있다.

어휘

landline telephone 유선전화 **come up with** 생각해내다, 떠올리다
evolve v. 진화하다 **obsolete** a. 진부한 **calculator** n. 계산기
calculus n. 미적분 **valuable** a. 가치 있는 **cutting-edge** a. 첨단의 **detract from** 훼손하다 **compromise** v. 훼손하다 **unfair** a. 불공정한 **standardized test** (교육) 표준 시험 **laptop** n. 노트북 컴퓨터 **skip over** ~을 빠뜨리다, 건너뛰다

24 문장삽입 ③

| 분석 |

These test makers worried that the calculators would give students an unfair advantage라는 문장이 그래핑 계산기 때문에 시험이 불공정해질까 걱정했다는 내용인데, 바로 뒤에 그래핑 계산기가 표준 시험 출제자들이 허용하는 유일한 기술이라 했으므로 그 사이에 "지금은 정반대다"라는 문장이 삽입되어야 한다. 따라서 정답은 ③이다.

25 내용추론 ④

| 분석 |

위 글의 주제는 그래핑 계산기가 연결이 가능한 인터넷을 비롯한 첨단 기술이 아닌 덕분에 시험에서 쓰일 수 있게 되었다는 것이며, 맨 마지막 문장을 보면 기술 시장을 급변시키는 창조적 파괴가 계산기 분야에는 도달하지 못하고 건너뛰어 가버렸다는 것을 알 수 있다. 따라서 옳은 추론은 ④이다.

위 글에서 추론할 수 있는 것은 무엇인가?
① 표준 시험은 기술 변화에 완전히 적응했다.
② 오래된 기술은 소비자들이 더 이상 원하지 않기 때문에 사라진다.
③ 창조적 파괴는 소비자 역학에만 영향을 주고 기술 산업 시장에는 영향을 주지 않는다.
④ 그래핑 계산기는 창조적 파괴가 미치지 못하는 섬과 같다.

26~27

새로운 연구는 이익과 손실, 그리고 우리가 이익과 손실을 생각하는 아주 다른 방식을 살펴본다. 이를 손실회피라 한다. 이를테면, 당신이 카지노에 가서 베팅을 하고 50달러를 잃는다고 하자. 이제 문제는 당신이 그만두고 떠날 것인가, 아니면 도박을 좀 더 해서 그 손실을 만회하고 빠져나오려 할 것인가라는 것이다. 도박은 기본적으로 도박장(카지노)에 유리하게 설계되어 있지만, 당신이 이겨서 원래 상태로 돌아갈 가능성도 좀 있다. 선택의 프레임을 이런 식으로 짜면 인간들은 정말로 일관되게 위험을 감수하는 경향을 보인다. 흥미로운 점은 사람들이 첫 번째 베팅보다는 두 번째 베팅을 훨씬 더 기꺼이 하려 한다는 것이다. 첫 번째 베팅에서는 이겨서 무언가를 얻기를 바라기 때문에 그러하다. 반면 두 번째 베팅에서는 실제로 손실을 피하려고 한다. 손실 회피 이론은 손실을 피하려는 욕구가 이익을 얻으려는 욕구보다 뇌에 더 강하게 새겨져 있다고 제시한다. 이 편향은 실제로 국가 차원까지 확장된다. 연구는 미국과 다른 국가들 간의 무역 분쟁 100건을 분석했다. 연구진은 이 분쟁들을 두

그룹으로 나눴다. 한 그룹에서는 미국이 미국 기업들에게 닫혀 있던 새로운 시장을 개방하려고 시도했다. 이 경우 시장과 일자리 측면에서 잠재적 이익이 존재했다. 다른 그룹에서는 미국과 상대국 간에 이미 무역이 존재하던 상황에서 분쟁이 발생했는데, 미국은 상대국이 어떤 식으로든 탄압을 해서 미국 기업들이 시장 점유율을 잃고 일자리를 잃고 있다고 주장했다. 따라서 한쪽 분쟁은 잠재적 이익으로 틀이 짜였던 반면, 다른 쪽은 잠재적 손실로 틀이 짜였다. 손실 회피 이론은 손실에 직면했을 때 더 치열하고 더 오래 싸울 것이라고 예측한다. 연구 결과는 국가 수준에서 정확히 그런 일이 발생한다는 것을 보여준다. 분쟁이 일자리 손실이라는 틀로 구성되었을 때, 마치 카지노에 있는 사람처럼 미국 정책 입안자들은 온갖 노력을 기울여 싸운다. 말하자면 누구나 같은 심리적 바구니에 들어 있는 것이다. 그래서 손실 회피의 근본적 생각은 당신이 백미러를 보면서 운전하고 있다는 것이다. 그것이 바로 손실 회피의 본질이다. 운전할 때 그렇게 하는 건 좋은 생각이 아니고, 도박할 때도 좋은 생각이 아니며, 국가 정책을 짤 때는 더더욱 좋은 생각이 아니다.

| 어휘 |

take a look at ~을 살펴보다   gain n. 이득   loss aversion 손실회피(동일한 상황을 이득이 아닌 손실로 구성하면 더 나쁘게 인식되는 인지 편향)   let's/let us say 이를테면   plunk down ~을 턱 내려놓다   bet n. 베팅, 내기   dig oneself out of the hole 궁지에서 벗어나다   gamble v. 도박하다, 돈을 걸다   frame v. 프레임을 짜다   chance n. 확률   consistent a. 일관된   head off ~을 피하다   extend v. 확장되다   clamp down 탄압하다, 규제를 강화하다   dispute n. 분쟁   confront v. 마주하다, 직면하다   pull out all the stops 총력을 기울이다   take action 조치를 취하다

26   빈칸완성   ①

| 분석 |

본문 중간에 '손실 회피 이론은 손실을 피하려는 욕구가 이익을 얻으려는 욕구보다 뇌에 더 강하게 새겨져 있다고 제시한다.'라고 한 것을 볼 때, 일자리 손실이 닥칠 것 같으면 손실을 피하기 위해 정부가 특히 노력을 기울이리라고 추론할 수 있으므로 빈칸에는 정책입안자들이 총력을 기울여 싸운다는 표현이 와야 한다.

빈칸에 가장 적절한 표현을 고르시오.
① 미국 정책입안자들은 총력을 기울여 싸운다.
② 미국 지도자들은 실수하고 조치를 취하지 않는다.
③ 정책입안자들은 싸움에서 물러선다.
④ 당국은 위험한 도박을 피하려 한다.

27   내용추론   ②

| 분석 |

본문 마지막 문장인 '운전할 때 그렇게 하는 건 좋은 생각이 아니고, 도박할 때도 좋은 생각이 아니며, 국가 정책을 짤 때는 더더욱 좋은 생각이 아니다.'가 주제이다. 따라서 손실에 집중하는 손실 회피가 좋지 않다는 ②가 정답이다.

위 글에서 추론할 수 있는 것은 무엇인가?
① 정책 결정자들은 비용에 상관없이 안정성보다 수익을 늘 우선시한다.
② 손실에 집중하는 것은 미래 지향적 전략을 방해한다.
③ 손실을 피하려는 욕구는 혁신하려는 욕구보다 약하다.
④ 손실 회피는 국가 정책에서 효율적 자원 배분을 초래한다.

28~30

지난주에 나는 "에너지, 물질, 시공간 너머에"라는 제목의 기사를 읽었다. 이 글은 우리가 세계에 대해 무엇을 알 수 있고 무엇을 알 수 없는지에 관한 상반된 관점을 제시하는 최근의 저서 두 권을 다루고 있다. 한편에는 철학자 토머스 네이글과 그의 2012년 저서 『정신과 우주』에서 나온 주장이 있다. 네이글에 따르면, 단순한 유물론만으로는 생명을 포함한 자연의 가장 복잡한 현상들을 이해하는데 충분치 않다. 그는 기존의 관념을 확장하자고 제안하는데, 여전히 물질적 틀 안에 있지만 아직 알려지지 않은 사고방식으로 나아가야 한다고 본다. 반대편에는 MIT 물리학자 맥스 테그마크가 저서 『우리의 수학적 우주』에서 설명하는 바와 같은 사상이 있다. 테그마크에 따르면 수학은 우리가 물리적 실재나 순수 이성적 구성물을 설명하기 위해 고안해내는 도구일 뿐만 아니라, 자연의 본질 그 자체이다. 이 기사의 종결 문단은 나의 견해와 강하게 공명한다. 핵심 요점은 다음과 같다. 우리가 자연에 대한 완전한 지식 같은 것을 가질 수 있다고 믿는 것은 순진하다는 것이다. 이러한 생각을 하는 데는 두 가지 핵심 이유가 있다. 첫 번째는 자연에 대한 모델을 만들기 위해선 데이터가 필요하다는 점이다. 이 데이터는 현미경과 입자 검출기부터 망원경과 질량 분석기까지 다양한 도구에서 나온다. 어떤 도구든 정밀도와 범위에 한계가 있다. 〈따라서, 우리는 벌어지는 일에 대해 언제나 일부 근시안이다.〉 도구들은 개선될 수 있고 또 개선될 것이다. 그러나 어떤 형태의 근시안적 시각은 언제나 피할 수 없다. 두 번째 이유는 자연 자체가 특정한 한계 안에서 작동한다는 것이다. 예컨대, 빛의 속도와 우주의 유한한 나이는 우리가 우주에서 얼마나 멀리 볼 수 있는지를 제한하고, 인과관계를 제약한다. 양자 불확정성은 우리가 초미시적인 물체의 위치와 속도에 대해 말할 수 있는 것을 제한한다. 수학 자체도 한계를 가지고 있으며, 이는 쿠르트 괴델이 그의 불완전성 정리에서 탐

구한 바와 같다. 컴퓨터도 마찬가지로 앨런 튜링의 결정불가능성 정리로부터 그 한계가 드러난다. 그래서 섬의 이미지는 우리가 세상을 이해하려고 애쓰는 고군분투를 잘 포착한다. 우리는 미지의 바다로 둘러싸인 섬 위에 살고 있는 셈이다. 섬이 커질수록, 무지의 해안선도 함께 커진다. 세상에 대해 더 많이 알게 될수록, 우리는 이전에는 예상조차 할 수 없었던 질문을 던질 수 있게 된다. 모든 것을 알기 위해서는 모든 질문을 아는 것이 필요하다. 그리고 그것은, 물론, 명백히 불가능하다. 대답할 수 없는 질문들은 우리에게 겸허함을 일깨우며, 과학이란 본질적으로 물리적 현실에 대해 우리가 수집할 수 있는 것들의 자기 교정적 서사라는 사실을 상기시킨다. 이것은 결코 패배주의적인 관점이 아니다. 오히려 이는 해방감을 준다. 지식이 끝없는 개척이라는 사실을 깨닫는 것보다 더 흥미진진한 일이 달리 무엇이 있겠는가?

| 어휘 |

come across 우연히 만나다 **opposite** a. 상반된 **viewpoint** n. 관점 **materialism** n. 유물론 **insufficient** a. 불충분한 **make sense of** ~을 이해하다 **complex** a. 복잡한 **extension** n. 확장 **rational** a. 합리적인, 이성적인 **resonate with** ~와 공명하다, 일치하다 **naive** a. 순진무구한, 유치한 **particle detector** 입자 검출기 **mass spectrometer** 질량분석기 **myopic** a. 근시안적인, 가까운 것밖에 보지 못하는 **shortsightedness** n. 근시안 **causal** a. 인과의, 원인과 결과의 **finite** a. 유한한 **range** n. 범위 **precision** n. 정밀함 **delimit** v. 한계를 정하다 **velocity** n. 속도, 속력 **undecidability** n. 결정 불가능성 **incompleteness** n. 불완전성 **theorem** n. (특히 수학에서의) 정리(定理) **anticipate** v. 예상하다 **invoke** v. 불러일으키다 **humility** n. 겸손함 **ongoing** a. 진행 중인 **self-correcting** a. 자신을 고치는, 자정 능력이 있는 **endless** a. 끝없는 **liberating** a. 해방감을 주는, 자유를 주는

28 빈칸완성 ②

| 분석 |

위 글은 지식의 한계를 다루므로 순진한 시각은 완전한 지식에 대한 믿음일 것이다. 따라서 빈칸에는 완전한 지식이라는 표현을 넣어야 가장 적합하다. 마지막 부분에서 '모든 것을 알기 위해서는 모든 질문을 아는 것이 필요하다. 그리고 그것은, 물론, 명백히 불가능하다'라고 한 것도 완전한 지식을 얻을 수 있다고 믿는 것이 순진한 일임을 뒷받침해준다.

빈칸에 가장 적절한 표현을 고르시오.
① 보편적 역학을 얻을 수 없는 무능함
② 자연에 대한 완전한 지식
③ 인간 본성의 연약함
④ 근본 원리들

29 문장삽입 ③

| 분석 |

'그래서(도구의 한계로 인해서) 우리는 언제나 아는 지식이 좁은 근시안'이라는 내용의 제시문은 도구에 한계가 있다는 내용인 Any tool has limits of precision and range와, 근시안적 시각은 불가피하다는 some shortsightedness will always be unavoidable 사이에 넣어야 가장 좋다. 그 뒷부분은 두 번째 이유가 나오므로 적합지 않다. 따라서 정답은 ③이다.

30 내용추론 ①

| 분석 |

글 맨 아래쪽에서 '대답할 수 없는 질문들은 우리에게 겸허함을 일깨운다'고 한 것을 참고하면 겸허함이 과학 지식 탐구에 중요함을 알 수 있다. 따라서 정답은 ①이다.

위 글에서 추론할 수 있는 것은 무엇인가?
① 과학은 겸손함과 진화하는 아이디어를 기반으로 번성한다.
② 끝없는 질문은 발견을 실망스러운 것으로 만든다.
③ 과학 도구에 한계가 있더라도 완전한 지식은 가능하다.
④ 지식의 끝없는 추구는 발견과 성장의 기회를 지연시킨다.

KOREA AEROSPACE UNIVERSITY | 한국항공대학교 자연계

TEST p. 652~662

| 01 | ① | 02 | ③ | 03 | ④ | 04 | ③ | 05 | ① | 06 | ② | 07 | ④ | 08 | ③ | 09 | ② | 10 | ② |
| 11 | ③ | 12 | ① | 13 | ④ | 14 | ③ | 15 | ① | 16 | ② | 17 | ① | 18 | ② | 19 | ① | 20 | ④ |

01 동의어 ①

| 어휘 |

innocuous a. (뱀·약 따위가) 무해한, 독 없는; (언동 따위에) 악의가 없는(= inoffensive) **remark** n. 발언 **misinterpret** v. 그릇 해석하다, 오해하다 **sarcastic** a. 빈정거리는, 비꼬는 **insincere** a. 불성실한, 성의가 없는 **banal** a. 평범한, 진부한

| 해석 |

악의 없는 이 발언들을 일부 청중들은 오해했다.

02 동의어 ③

| 어휘 |

quixotic a. 돈키호테식의; 공상적인, 비현실적인(= impractical) **interpretation** n. 해석, 설명 **former** a. 이전의 **imbalanced** a. 불균형한 **flimsy** a. 무른, 취약한; (근거·논리가) 박약한

| 해석 |

저자가 한 주장은 역사적 사건에 대한 비현실적인 해석을 바탕으로 하고 있었다.

03 동의어 ④

| 어휘 |

moribund a. 죽어가는; 소멸해 가는; 정체[침체]된(= stagnant) **reform** n. 개혁, 개량 **expert** n. 전문가 **assess** v. (재산·수입 따위를) 평가하다 **potential** n. 잠재력; 가능성 **progressive** a. 전진하는; 진보적인 **thriving** a. 번영하는 **controversial** a. 논쟁의, 물의를 일으키는

| 해석 |

정부의 정체된 경제 개혁 정책이 그것의 미래 가능성을 평가하려는 전문가들에 의해 재검토되고 있다.

04 동의어 ③

| 어휘 |

postpone v. 연기하다, 미루다 **prudent** a. 조심성 있는, 신중한(= deliberate) **daring** a. 대담한, 용감한 **autocratic** a. 독재적인 **abrupt** a. 느닷없는, 갑작스러운

| 해석 |

회의를 연기하기로 한 결정은 그 회사의 전반적인 상황을 고려했을 때 신중한 조치로 여겨졌다.

05 동의어 ①

| 어휘 |

trailer n. 〈영화〉 예고편 **decent** a. (수준·질이) 괜찮은[제대로 된]; 품위 있는, 예의 바른; (상황에) 적절한[온당한] **do a decent[good] job of** ~를 잘 해내다 **obfuscate** v. 혼미하게 하다, (판단을) 흐리게 하다(= conceal) **highlight** v. 강조하다, 두드러지게 하다 **simplify** v. 단순화하다 **deliver** v. 배달하다; 해방시키다

| 해석 |

이 예고편은 그 영화의 주요 줄거리들을 잘 숨기고 있다.

06 논리완성 ②

| 분석 |

첫 문장에서 than 뒤에는 부리 개암의 비교 대상이 되는 다른 종류의 개암이 와야 하는데, 부리 개암이 원주민 부족 조상들이 심고 재배한 토착종이므로, 그 반대인 '외래의'라는 의미의 ②가 빈칸에 들어가는 것이 가장 적절하다.

| 어휘 |

buttery a. 버터 맛이 나는; 버터가 들어 있는 **nestle** v. 아늑하게 자리잡도록 하다 **husk** n. 꼬투리, 껍데기 **beak** n. (새의) 부리 **genetics** n. 유전학; 유전적 특질 **cultivate** v. 경작하다; 재배하다 **archaeological** a. 고고학의 **verify** v. (증거·증언 등으로) ~이 진실임을 증명[실증, 확증]하다 **nutritious** a. 영양분이 있는 **alien** a. 외국의; 성질이 다른 **provincial** a. 지방의, 시골의 **exported** a. 수출된

| 해석 |

부리 개암은 외래 개암보다 약간 더 달고 더 고소한 맛이 난다. 새의 부리처럼 바깥으로 뻗어 있는 솜털로 덮인 녹색 껍질에 싸여 있는 부리 개암은 브리티시컬럼비아의 숲 계곡을 가득 메우고 있다. 그 지역의 퍼스트 네이션즈 부족들(캐나다 원주민 부족들)은 조상들이 심고 재배한 주요 식량원으로서의 이 개암에 대한 이야기를 대대로 전해왔다. 이러한 이야기는 연구자들에게 개암이 얼마나 널리 재배되었는지 확정지을 수 있길 기대하면서 개암의 유전적 특성을 더 깊이 연구하도록 동기를 부여했다. 연구팀은 브리티시컬럼비아 전역의 고고학적 유적지들에 있는 마을들을 방문하여 그 부근에서 200개가 넘는 개암 샘플을 채취했다. 그들은 부리 개암이 최대 800킬로미터 떨어진 넓은 지역에 걸쳐 적극적으로 재배되었음을 확인했다. 이러한 유전자 추적 연구는 퍼스트 네이션즈 주민들이 어떻게 숲을 장기적으로 변화시켰는지 확인시켜준다.

07 논리완성 ④

| 분석 |

"육체노동자의 22%가 AI를 사용하고 있고, 사용률이 대략 15%인 개인 서비스 분야를 제외한 모든 주요 직업군에서 사용률이 20%를 넘는다"는 것은 AI의 사용이 산업 전반에 걸쳐 전면적으로 이루어지고 있음을 의미하므로, 빈칸에는 ④가 들어가는 것이 적절하다.

| 어휘 |

survey n. 조사 v. 조사하다 **skeptical** a. 회의적인, 믿지 않는 **explosion** n. 폭발; 급격한 증가 **generative AI** 생성형 인공지능 **optimistic** a. 낙관적인, 낙천적인 **occupation** n. 직업, 업무 **exceptional** a. 예외적인 **one-sided** a. 일방적인 **around the corner** 목전에 있는 **across the board** (회사·산업 등의) 전반에 걸쳐, 전면적으로

| 해석 |

미국인들을 대상으로 한 생성형 AI의 사용 실태 조사를 최근에 해보기 전에는, 경제학자 데이비드 데밍(David Deming)은 생성형 AI의 폭발적 증가가 곧 어느 때든 미국 경제에 상당한 혜택을 가져다줄 것이라는 것에 회의적이었다고 말한다. 하지만 지금은 더 낙관적이라고 말한다. 그 연구는 미국인들이 생성형 AI를 사용하고 있는지 그리고 얼마나 사용하고 있는지에 대한 질문에서 시작되었다. 데밍은 그 결과에 충격을 받았다고 말한다. 그들은 18세부터 64세까지의 미국인 중 거의 40%가 생성형 AI를 사용한 적이 있다는 사실을 알게 되었다. 그리고 상당한 비율의 사람들이 그것을 정기적으로 사용하고 있는 것 같다. 경제학자들은 24% 이상의 미국 근로자들이 조사 전 주에 적어도 한 번 그것을 사용했고, 9명 중 1명은 매 근무일마다 사용한다는 사실을 알게 됐다. AI의 사용은 거의 전면적으로 행해지는 것 같다. 데밍은 "우리는 육체노동자의 22%가 AI를 사용한다고 말하고 있고, 사용률이 대략 15%인 개인 서비스 분야를 제외한 모든 주요 직업군에서는 사용률이 20%를 넘는다는 사실을 알게 됐습니다."라고 그는 말한다.

08 논리완성 ③

| 분석 |

인쇄업자들이나 그들의 고객들이 원하는 색상을 정확하게 표현하기 어려워한 것은 인쇄 문화 안에 만연한 하나의 문제가 되는 문화적 독소였다고 할 수 있으므로, 그 문제의 해결책인 팬톤 매칭 시스템과 그것을 기념하는 팬톤의 올해의 색은 문화적 해독제라 할 수 있을 것이다. 따라서 빈칸에는 ③이 들어가는 것이 가장 자연스럽다.

| 어휘 |

zeitgeist n. 시대정신 **juggernaut** n. 대규모의 파괴력 있는 것; 거대한 존재 **chemistry** n. 화학 **recurring** a. 되풀이하여 발생하는 **formula** n. 방식, 방법; 제조법 **found** v. 설립하다; (이론·이야기 등을) (~에 입각해서) 만들다 **standardize** v. 표준화하다 **device** n. 고안, 장치 **pigment** n. 색소; 염료 **shrewd** a. 영리한, 통찰력 있는

| 해석 |

팬톤의 올해의 색(Color of the Year)이 시대정신을 포착하기 위한 것이라고 팬톤 색상 연구소의 부사장은 말했다. 동시에, 그것은 문화적 해독제 역할을 하도록 의도된 것이기도 하다. 오늘날과 같은 색상 분야의 거대 기업이 되기 전에, 팬톤은 다른 이름의 상업용 인쇄 회사였다. 화학을 전공한 인쇄 기술자인 로렌스 허버트(Lawrence Herbert)가 1950년대에 이 회사에 고용되었을 때, 그는 작업 중에 반복적으로 발생하는 문제를 발견했다. 책자나 포스터의 인쇄물을 신청할 때, 고객들은 색상에 대해 정확하게 말하는 데 어려움을 겪었다. 원하는 색상을 얻기 위해, 고객들은 그 색상의 실제 견본을 보내야 하기도 했다. 유명한 사례 중 하나는 고객이 자신의 넥타이에서 한 조각을 잘라 인쇄소에 보내고는 이 색에 맞춰 달라고 말한 것이었다. 그들은 자체적으로 잉크 배합 공식 책을 가지고 있어서 원하는 색상에 근접할 수는 있었다. 하지만 그것은 매우 일정하지가 못했다. 1963년, 로렌스는 이에 대한 해결책을 마련했다. 그는 인쇄기와 상관없이 인쇄본이 원본 색과 일치하도록 색상 재현을 표준화하기 위한 한 가지 방법으로 팬톤 매칭 시스템(Pantone Matching System)을 개발했다. 팬톤은 안료 범위를 확장했고, 1968년 무렵에 그것은 업계의 표준이 되었다. 사람들은 팬톤을 널리 받아들여지는 색상 체계로 만들어낸 것은 허버트 안에 있는 통찰력 있는 마케터로서의 재능 덕분이라고 평가한다.

① 암울한 예고
② 마케팅 술책
③ 문화적 해독제
④ 기술적 실수

09 올바른 접속사 ②

| 분석 |

'애덤스가 아내 애비게일(Abigail)에게 도움을 청한 것'과 '그녀의

증조부가 이 동전을 주조한 은세공업자 존 헐(John Hull)의 의붓형제였던 것은 양보 관계가 아니며, 후자가 원인, 전자가 결과에 해당한다. 그러므로 ②의 자리에는 이유의 접속사가 있어야 한다. ②를 since로 고친다.

| 어휘 |

mint n. 화폐 주조소, (the M−) 조폐국 v. (화폐를) 주조하다   defy v. 도전하다; 반항하다, 무시하다   crown n. 왕관; (군주의) 주권, 국왕의 지배[통치]; 입헌 군주국의 정부   regulate v. 통제하다, 조절하다   vogue n. 유행   ambassador n. 대사   source v. (특정한 곳에서 무엇을) 얻다, 공급자를 찾다   silversmith n. 은(銀)세공인   specimen n. 견본, 표본   whereabouts n. 소재, 행방   fetch v. (상품 따위가) ~에 팔리다; (~의 금액을) 호가하다   auction n. 경매   circulation n. 유통

| 해석 |

보스턴 조폐국은 영국 정부의 권위를 거스르고 독자적으로 동전을 주조했는데, 이는 모국인 영국과 별개라는 뉴잉글랜드의 점증하는 정체성 의식과 자신의 경제는 자체적으로 규제하겠다는 뉴잉글랜드의 결의를 나타낸 것이었다고 매사추세츠 역사학회는 설명한다. 미국 독립전쟁 이후, 보스턴 조폐국이 제조한 동전은 영국에서도 유행하게 되었다. 영국인 수집가 토머스 브랜드 홀리스(Thomas Brand Hollis)는 1781년에 당시 네덜란드 주재 미국 대사였던 존 애덤스(John Adams)에게 편지를 써서 이 동전 하나를 구하는 데 도움을 요청했다. 그 다음에는 애덤스가 아내 애비게일(Abigail)에게 도움을 청하기 위해 편지를 썼는데, 그녀의 증조부가 이 동전을 주조한 은세공업자 존 헐(John Hull)의 의붓형제였기 때문이었다. 이런 종류의 3펜스 동전은 현재까지 전해져 오는 것이 단 하나 더 알려져 있으며, 그것은 매사추세츠 역사학회의 소장품이어서 이 견본이 개인 수집가들이 입수할 수 있는 유일한 것이 되어 있다. 또 하나의 동전은 1960년대 이전 언젠가 예일 대학교에서 도난당한 후 비록 행방이 묘연하지만 아마도 아직도 있을 것이다. 다른 역사적인 미국 동전들은 경매에서 거액에 팔린 적이 있다. 미국 조폐국이 만든 최초의 것들 중 하나 — 최초의 것은 아니더라도 — 라고 믿어지는 1794년에 발행된 희귀한 달러 은화는 2013년에 1,000만 달러에 팔렸다. 한편, 미국에서 유통을 위해 마지막으로 주조한 금화 동전들 중 하나인 1933년에 발행된 희귀한 "더블 이글" 동전은 2021년에 1,890만 달러에 팔렸다.

10 논리완성   ②

| 분석 |

빈칸에는 '시간이 지구보다 달에서 약간 더 빠르게 흐르는 이유를 설명할 수 있는 해법'에 해당하는 것으로서, 앞에서 언급한 '달에 새로운 시간대를 만드는 것'보다 더 근본적인 것이 들어가야 한다. 새로운 시간 척도를 만드는 것이 그 중의 하나가 될 것이므로 ②가 정답이다.

| 어휘 |

mind-bending a. 환각을 일으키는; 정신을 혼미케 하는, 압도적인   quirk n. 버릇, 기벽(奇癖); 기행, 변덕   inherent a. 고유의, 본래의   tick n. (시계 따위의) 똑딱[재깍]거리는 소리; 짧은 시간, 순간   for practical purposes 실제로는   atop prep. ~의 정상에   idiosyncras n. 특이성, 특이한 성격   forefront n. 최전선; (흥미·여론·활동 따위의) 중심   bring to the forefront 부각하다, 강조하다   earth day 지구일(地球日, 지구의 24시간의 하루)   inconsistency n. 불일치   grapple with 완수하려고 애쓰다, 해결[극복]하려고 고심하다   conundrum n. 수수께끼, 어려운 문제

| 해석 |

아마도 우리 우주의 가장 압도적인 기이한 점은 시간 측정의 본질적인 어려움일 것이다. 지구에서는 계곡에서보다 산 정상에서 1초가 아주 조금 더 빠르게 지나간다. 실제로는, 대부분의 사람들은 이러한 차이에 대해 걱정할 필요가 없다. 그러나 새로운 우주 경쟁이 미국과 그 동맹국들로 하여금 달에 영구적인 정착지를 만들기 위해 달려가게 만들었고, 그로 인해 시간의 특이한 성질이 다시 한 번 부각되었다. 달 표면에서는 지구일(地球日)이 지구에서보다 약 56 마이크로초 더 짧을 것인데, 이 작은 숫자가 시간이 지나면서 큰 불일치를 초래할 수 있다. NASA와 그 국제 파트너들은 현재 이 복잡한 난제를 해결하려고 고군분투하고 있다. 과학자들은 일부 신문 기사 제목들이 암시해온 것처럼 단지 달에 새로운 시간대를 만들려고 하는 것이 아니다. 오히려, 우주 기관(NASA)과 그 파트너들은 달에서는 1초가 더 빨리 흐른다는 사실을 설명해주는 완전히 새로운 시간 척도나 측정 시스템을 만들려 하고 있다.

① 우주에서의 시간대를 분리하다
② 완전히 새로운 시간 척도를 만들다
③ 현재의 시간 측정 방식을 재평가하다
④ 시간 추적 장치를 없애다

11 논리완성   ③

| 분석 |

but 앞은 스쿼팅 오이가 애호박, 서양호박, 호박 등과 공유하는 공통점에 대한 내용이므로, but 이하에는 스쿼팅 오이만이 가진 독특한 특징에 해당하는 내용이 들어가야 한다. 본문에서는 스쿼팅 오이가 '폭발이나 분출을 통해 씨앗을 멀리 퍼뜨리는 번식 전략을 가지고 있음'을 이야기하고 있으므로 빈칸에는 ③이 들어가야 한다.

| 어휘 |

gourd n. 〈식물〉 호리병박(열매·식물)   squirt v. 분출하다   reproductive a. 생식의; 재생의   intrigue v. 관심을 갖게 하다   naturalist n. 박물학자   blink v. 눈을 깜빡이다   relative n. 친척, 친족   zucchini n. 애호박   squash n. 서양 호박   blow ~ wide open (비밀·부정 따위를) 퍼뜨리다; 폭로하다   ballistic a. 탄도의, 탄도학의   geyser n. 간헐천   eruption n. 분출

| 해석 |

스쿼팅 오이라고 불리는 특이한 작은 호리병박은 폭발적인 번식 전략을 가지고 있어서 로마제국 시대부터 동식물 연구가들의 관심을 끌어왔다. 스쿼팅 오이는 씨앗을 자신의 길이의 수백 배에 달하는 거리까지 뿜어내며, 현재 과학자들은 이 식물들이 어떻게 그 일을 해내는지 알고 있다. 스쿼팅 오이가 뿜어내는 것은 놀라운 광경이지만, 만약 당신이 눈을 깜빡이면 놓칠 수도 있다. ─ 분수처럼 뿜어내는 것이 약 0.03초밖에 지속되지 않기 때문이다. 털이 많은 그 초록색 열매는 익으면 길이가 약 4센티미터가 된다. 호리병박 과(科)에 속하며, 애호박, 서양호박, 호박과 친척뻘이지만, 이들은 독특한 분출하는 번식 메커니즘을 가지고 있다. 최근 연구자들은 이 탄도학적 수수께끼를 완전하게 밝혀냈다. 그들은 고속 비디오와 디지털 3D 재구성을 이용하여 스쿼팅 오이의 분출 전, 분출 중, 분출 후의 모습을 분석하고는, 이 열매가 간헐천처럼 분출하는 현상을 설명할 수 있는 수학적 모델을 만들어냈다.

① 그들은 환경의 힘에 의존해서 씨앗을 퍼뜨린다
② 그들은 지속적으로 분출하는 특성을 보인다
③ 그들은 독특한 분출하는 번식 메커니즘을 가지고 있다
④ 호리병박 과(科)의 구성원들은 퇴행적인 분산 전략을 사용한다

12 논리완성   ①

| 분석 |

본문의 중반부와 후반부에서 "탄수화물의 소화를 돕는 유전자가 농경이 시작되기 훨씬 전부터 존재했으며, 이는 심지어 호모 사피엔스나 네안데르탈인이 등장하기 전부터일 수도 있음"을 이야기하고 있다. 이는 우리 종이 등장하기 이전부터 탄수화물을 즐겨 섭취해 왔을 가능성이 있다는 것을 의미하는 것이므로, 빈칸에는 ①이 들어가야 한다.

| 어휘 |

carb n. 탄수화물, 탄수화물이 많은 식품   prevailing a. 우세한, 주요한   stereotype n. 고정관념   feast on 마음껏 먹다[즐기다]   archaeological a. 고고학적인   carbohydrate n. 탄수화물   roast v. (고기를) 굽다, 익히다   tuber n. 덩이줄기 작물   starch-laden a. 전분이 많이 들어있는   detect v. 발견하다, 간파하다, 감지하다   analyze v. 분석하다, 검토하다   lodge v. 숙박시키다, 수용하다   carb-laden a. 탄수화물이 많이 들어있는   trace v. 추적하다; ~의 출처를[유래를, 기원을] 조사하다   evolution n. 진화   gene n. 유전자   digest v. 소화하다   starch n. 전분   duplicate v. 복사하다, 복제하다   advent n. 출현, 도래   lineage n. 혈통, 계보

| 해석 |

새로운 연구에 따르면, 인류의 탄수화물 사랑은 우리 인류가 하나의 종(種)으로 존재하기 이전부터 시작되었을지도 모른다. 고대 인류가 매머드의 스테이크나 다른 고기 덩어리를 매우 즐겼다는 한때 만연했던 고정관념은 큰 뇌의 발달에 필요한 에너지를 공급하는 데 단백질이 풍부한 식단이 필수적이었다는 생각을 조장하는 데 도움을 주었다. 그러나 최근 몇 년간의 고고학적 증거들은 이러한 관점에 이의를 제기했고, 치아에 남아 있는 박테리아를 분석해서 발견된 덩이줄기 작물이나 전분이 풍부한 음식 같은 것들을 구워 먹는 등, 인류가 탄수화물에 대한 선호를 오래전에 발전시켰다는 것을 암시했다. 그 새로운 연구는 탄수화물 중심 식단에 대한 최초의 유전적 증거를 제시하고 있다. 과학자들은 전분을 단순 당으로 분해하여 우리 몸이 에너지원으로 활용할 수 있도록 함으로써 인간이 전분을 더 쉽게 소화할 수 있게 해주는 유전자의 진화를 추적했다. 연구에 따르면, 이러한 유전자들은 농경이 출현하기 훨씬 이전부터 복제되었다. 이러한 확장은 수십만 년 전까지 거슬러 올라갈 수도 있는데, 이는 우리 종인 호모 사피엔스나 심지어 네안데르탈인이 독립적인 인류의 계통으로 등장하기 오래전의 일이다.

① 우리가 하나의 종으로 존재하기 이전부터 시작되다
② 환경적 요인들에 의해 촉진되었다
③ 인간 진화의 기원을 설명하다
④ 단백질이 풍부한 식단에 대한 반발로 시작되다

13 논리완성   ④

| 분석 |

저자는 처음에는 AI 기술이 마치 거울처럼 현실을 반영하는 줄 알았지만, 실제로는 현실의 왜곡들이 연이어 나타나는 만화경처럼 작동한다고 말하고 있다. 이는 AI가 기존의 편견과 차별을 그대로 반영하고 강화함으로써, 우리가 쌓아온 사회적 진보로부터 우리를 오히려 후퇴시키고 있다는 것이다.

| 어휘 |

graduate n. 대학원생   startling a. 놀라운   facial recognition 안면인식   detect v. 발견하다, 감지하다   encounter n. (우연한) 만남, 조우   code v. (프로그램을) 코드화하다   gaze n. 응시, 시선   preference n. 선호   priority n. 우선사항   prejudice n. 편견   bake in (컴퓨터 운영 시스템 등의 중요한 요소로) 포함시키다   generative AI 생성형 인공지능   prompt n. 프롬프트(컴퓨터가 조작자에 대하여 입력을 요구하고 있음을 나타내는 단말 화면상의 기호)   overwhelmingly ad. 압도적으로   criminal n. 범인, 범죄자   stereotype n. 고정관념   inmate n. 수감자   implication n. 밀접한 관계, 영향; (예상되는) 결과; 내포, 암시   analysis n. 분석   reinforce v. 강화하다   kaleidoscope n. 만화경   distortion n. 왜곡

| 해석 |

한 MIT 대학원 학생이 놀라운 발견을 했다. 그녀가 연구하고 있던 안면 인식 소프트웨어가 자신의 검은 피부를 감지할 수 없었던 것이다. 그 소프트웨어는 그녀가 흰색 가면을 썼을 때에만 그녀의 존재를 기록했다. 이것이 그녀가 이후에 '코딩된 시선(coded gaze)'이라고 부르게 된 개념과의 첫 만남이었다. "여러분은 아마 '남성의 시선'이나 '백인의 시선'에 대해 들어본 적이 있을 겁니다."라고 그녀는 설명한다. 코딩된 시선은 이와 유사한 개념으로, 누가 기술을

구체화할 권한을 가지고 있는지, 그리고 누구의 선호, 우선순위, 편견이 기술에 반영되는지에 관한 것이다. 그녀는 최근 Stable Diffusion의 텍스트-이미지 생성 AI 시스템 테스트에서, 고소득 직업과 관련된 이미지를 요청하는 명령어를 입력하자, 밝은 피부색을 가진 남성의 이미지가 압도적으로 생성되었다고 지적한다. 반면, 마약상, 테러리스트, 수감자와 같은 범죄자에 대한 정형화된 이미지를 요청했을 때는 주로 어두운 피부색을 가진 남성의 이미지가 생성되었다. 자신의 신간 저서에서, 그녀는 기술의 사회적 영향을 살펴보고 있으며, 안면 분석 시스템의 편향이 특히 기존의 고정관념을 강화할 경우 수백만 명에게 피해를 줄 수 있다고 경고한다. "AI 시스템이 도입되었을 때, 처음에는 저는 우리가 거울을 보고 있다고 생각했습니다. 하지만 이제는 우리가 왜곡의 만화경을 들여다보고 있다고 믿습니다. 우리를 미래로 이끌어 가고 있다고 믿는 기술들이, 실제로는 이미 이뤄낸 진보로부터 우리를 되돌리고 있기 때문입니다."라고 그녀는 말한다.

① 우리를 자동화에 지나치게 의존하도록 만들고 있다
② 피상적인 관계를 조장하여 우리를 잘못된 방향으로 이끌고 있다
③ 지금까지 이뤄낸 발전을 바탕으로 구축되고 있다
④ 이미 이뤄낸 진보로부터 우리를 되돌리고 있다

14~15

미국에서 실제로 얼마나 많은 사람들이 음식 알레르기를 가지고 있는지, 혹은 음식 알레르기가 증가하고 있는지는 알기 어렵다고 미국 국립과학원(National Academy of Sciences)의 새로운 보고서는 말한다. 어려운 점은 다음과 같다. 음식 알레르기는 종종 자가진단 되며, 증상이 잘못 해석될 수 있다. 때때로 사람들은 음식 알레르기와 유당 불내증이나 글루텐에 민감한 반응을 보이는 것과 같은 다른 질환을 구별하지 못하는데, 이러한 질환들은 알레르기의 의학적 정의에 부합하지 않는다. 음식 알레르기가 무엇인지에 대해 많은 오해가 있다고 버지니아 스탈링스(Virginia Stallings) 박사는 말한다. 하나의 시나리오는 다음과 같은 것이다. 어린아이를 키우는 부모가 새로운 음식 — 예를 들어, 우유 — 을 아이의 식단에 추가한 후, 아이가 배탈이 나거나 위장장애 증상을 보이는 경우를 생각해 보자. 부모는 이를 음식 알레르기로 의심할 수도 있다. 그러나 아마도 이것은 유당 불내증의 증상일 수도 있는데, 이는 완전히 다른 질환이다. 음식 알레르기 증상이 유당 불내증 같은 다른 질환과 종종 혼동되는 이유는 일부 증상들이 중첩되기 때문이라고 스탈링스는 설명한다. 혼란을 가중시키는 것은 음식 알레르기는 진단하기에 복잡할 수 있다는 점이다. 〈우리는 최적의 진단 도구를 가지고 있지 않다.〉 어떤 사람이 특정 음식에 대해 알레르기가 있는지를 정확하게 판별할 수 있는 하나의 피부 검사나 혈액 검사는 존재하지 않는다고 스탈링스는 말한다. 그녀는 만약

입술이 붓거나 호흡이 가빠지는 것과 같은 명확한 알레르기 반응을 부모가 인지한다면 즉시 응급실을 찾아야 한다고 덧붙인다. 하지만 종종 증상은 더 경미하다. 이런 경우, 가족들은 알레르기를 자가 진단하기보다는 소아 알레르기 전문의와 같은 전문가를 찾아가야 한다.

| 어휘 |

self-diagnose v. 자가진단하다　symptom n. 징후, 조짐; 증상
misinterpret v. 그릇 해석하다, 오해하다　distinguish v. 구별하다
lactose intolerance 유당 불내증　gluten n. 글루텐　sensitivity n. 민감도, 자극 반응성　definition n. 정의, 설명　misconception n. 오해, 그릇된 생각　gastrointestinal a. 위장의　overlap n. 부분적 중복　complicated a. 복잡한　diagnose v. 진단하다
reaction n. 반응　swell v. 팽창하다, 부어오르다　emergency care 응급치료, 응급실　expert n. 전문가　pediatric a. 소아과의

14　문장삽입　③

| 분석 |

주어진 문장은 "우리는 최적의 진단 도구를 가지고 있지 않다."라는 의미이므로, 진단이 어렵다는 점을 구체적으로 이야기하고 있는 부분 앞인 ⓒ에 들어가는 것이 적절하다.

15　글의 제목　①

| 분석 |

본문에서는 음식 알레르기의 정확한 유병률을 파악하기 어렵고, 자가진단이 많으며, 증상이 다른 질환과 혼동될 수 있다는 점을 이야기하고 있다. 즉, 음식 알레르기가 단순하지 않으며 그 이면에 복잡한 요소가 있음을 이야기하고 있는 내용이므로, 글의 제목으로는 ①이 가장 적절하다.

위 글의 제목으로 가장 적절한 것은?
① 음식 알레르기의 이면에 숨겨진 복잡성을 풀어내기
② 음식 알레르기의 정의를 단순화하기
③ 음식 알레르기 진단 도구를 승인하기
④ 음식 알레르기를 자가 진단하기 위해 증상을 인지하기

16　빈칸완성　②

| 분석 |

"1차 세계대전에서 돌아온 많은 미국 군인들이 전시(戰時) 휴대식량에 들어있던 캔디 덕분에 단 것을 좋아하게 된 채로 돌아왔다."라는 내용은 캔디의 소비가 증가하게 된 추가적인 요인에 해당하므로, 빈칸에는 '게다가'라는 의미의 What's more가 적절하다. ① 이러한 이유로 ③ 대체로 ④ 그럼에도 불구하고

| 어휘 |

glut n. 과다, 과잉 **steep** a. 가파른 **mess** n. 혼란, 무질서한 상태 **boon** n. 은혜, 혜택, 이익 **factor** n. 요인, 요소 **groundwork** n. 토대, 기반, 근거 **urbanization** n. 도시화 **processed food** 가공식품 **casualty** n. 사상자, 희생자 **taffy** n. 태피(땅콩을 넣은 버터볼) **drape** v. 싸다 **jettison** v. (긴급시에 중량을 줄이기 위해 배·항공기에서) 짐을 버리다; (방해물·부담 등을) 버리다 **Prohibition** n. 주류 양조 판매 금지; 금주법 **swap** v. 교환하다, 바꾸다 **vice** n. 악덕, 악덕 행위, 악습, 악폐, 나쁜 버릇 **consumption** n. 소비 **sweet tooth** 단 것[과자]를 좋아함 **ration** n. 정량; 〈군사〉 휴대 식량 **assume** v. 추정하다, 추측하다

| 해석 |

미국의 캔디 붐의 뿌리는 1920년대에 있다. 1차 세계대전 동안 붕괴되었던 설탕 교역로가 사업을 할 수 있게 다시 한 번 열렸다. 그 결과 설탕이 너무 많아져서 가격이 급락했다. 이것은 미국 본토, 쿠바, 푸에르토리코 등지의 농민들에게는 혼란이었다. 그러나 캔디 산업에는 은혜와 같은 일이었다. 몇 가지 요인이 그 10년 동안 대형 캔디 소매점이 부상할 수 있는 토대를 마련해 주었다. 1920년 인구 조사가 기록하고 있듯이, 처음으로 미국 인구의 과반수가 도시에 거주하고 있었다. 도시화와 더 높은 임금, 낮은 실업률로 인해 가정에서 가공식품을 더 많이 구매하기 시작했다. 그 결과 먼저 희생된 것은 수제 과자였다. 도넛, 땅콩을 넣은 버터볼, 캐러멜 소스를 입힌 사과 등이 점차 버려지고, 가게에서 구입하는 캔디가 선호되기 시작했다. 그리고 당시에는 금주법이 시행되고 있었다. 기본적으로 사람들은 술이라는 하나의 나쁜 습관을 또 다른 나쁜 습관과 맞바꾸고 있었다. 당시 사람들은 금주법으로 인해 캔디와 탄산음료 소비가 증가하고 있다고 자주 말했다. 게다가, 1차 세계대전에서 돌아온 많은 미국 군인들이 전시(戰時) 휴대식량에 들어있던 캔디 덕분에 단 것을 좋아하게 된 채로 돌아왔다. 이로 인해 기존에 캔디의 주요 소비층으로 여겨졌던 여성과 아이들을 넘어서까지 캔디를 소비하는 습관이 확산되었다.

17~18

커피에 발암 경고 라벨을 부착해야 하는지를 둘러싸고 캘리포니아에서 들끓고 있던 논쟁에 미국 식품의약국(FDA)이 개입했다. 3월에, 한 판사는 원두가 로스팅될 때 생성되는 발암 화학 물질인 아크릴아미드가 높은 수준으로 커피에 함유돼 있다고 주장한 비영리 단체의 손을 들어주었다. 커피 기업들은 아크릴아미드의 존재를 부인하지는 않았지만, 농도가 낮기 때문에 건강에 그다지 위험을 초래하지 않으며 오히려 다른 건강상의 이점이 더 크다고 주장했다. 로스앤젤레스 카운티 고등법원 판사 엘리후 벌리(Elihu Berle)에게 그와 같은 주장은 설득력이 없었다. 그는 캘리포니아의 커피 기업들에게 캘리포니아 법령 65에 따라 발암 경고 라벨을 부착하라고 명령했는데, 이 법령은 주로 하여금 유해 물질 목록을 유지관리하고 기업들로 하여금 소비자에게 노출 사실을 알리도록 규정하는 법으로, 발암 화학물질의 감소뿐만 아니라 식품의 라벨과 관련된 신속한 합의를 이끌어냈다. 수요일에 FDA 국장인 스콧 고틀리브(Scott Gottlieb)는 성명을 통해, 만약 어떤 주의 법이 식품 라벨에 거짓이거나 오해의 소지가 있는 문구를 포함시키도록 규정하려는 취지를 갖고 있다면, FDA가 개입을 결정할 수도 있다고 밝혔다. 그는 다수의 연구 결과, 커피가 암을 유발한다는 증거는 거의 없으며 오히려 일부 암의 위험을 감소시킬 수도 있음을 보여준다고 덧붙였다. 건강한 성인의 경우, 적당한 커피 섭취는 암과 같은 주요 만성 질환이나 조기 사망의 위험 증가와 관련이 없음을 강력하고 일관된 증거가 보여주고 있으며, 일부 증거는 특정 암의 위험을 낮출 수 있음을 시사하고 있다는 것이다. 따라서, 발암 경고 라벨이 소비자로 하여금 실제로는 커피가 건강상의 이익을 제공할 수 있는데도 커피가 건강에 해롭다고 믿도록 오도할 수 있다고 그는 말했다. FDA는 또한 스타벅스와 같은 커피 기업들이 제품에 경고 라벨을 붙이지 않도록 면제하는 규정을 제안한 캘리포니아 환경건강위험평가 사무소에 지지 서한을 보냈다고 발표했다.

| 어휘 |

simmer v. 끓다; (분노·웃음 따위가) 당장에라도 터지려고 하다 **side with** 지지하다, 편들다 **acrylamide** n. 아크릴아미드(유기 합성·플라스틱·접합제의 원료) **compound** n. 합성물, 화합물 **pose** v. (요구 따위를) 주장하다, (문제 등을) 제기하다 **outweigh** v. ~보다 중요하다, ~보다 가치가 있다 **compelling** a. 매력적인, 강한 흥미를 띠우는 **substance** n. 물질 **notify** v. 통지하다, 공시하다 **exposure** n. 노출 **carcinogenic** a. 발암성의 **purport** v. 의미하다, ~라는 취지를 갖다; ~이라는 뜻으로 생각되다 **consistent** a. 양립하는, 일치하는 **moderate** a. 절제하는; 알맞은 **consumption** n. 소비, 섭취 **premature** a. 조숙한; 너무 이른 **exempt** a. 면제된

17 빈칸완성 ①

| 분석 |

빈칸 앞에서 "건강한 성인의 경우, 적당한 커피 섭취는 암과 같은 주요 만성 질환이나 조기 사망의 위험 증가와 관련이 없음을 강력하고 일관된 증거가 보여주고 있으며, 일부 증거는 특정 암의 위험을 낮출 수 있음을 시사하고 있다"고 했는데, 이것은 이어지는 내용, 즉 '발암 경고 라벨이 소비자로 하여금 실제로는 커피가 건강상의 이익을 제공할 수 있는데도 커피가 건강에 해롭다고 믿도록 오도할 수 있다'라는 내용에 대한 이유나 근거에 해당하므로, 빈칸에는 앞 문장의 이유나 근거로 어떤 결론을 내릴 때 쓰는 'Accordingly(따라서)'가 적절하다. ② 그런데 ③ 예를 들면 ④ 그럼에도 불구하고

| 18 | 내용추론 | ② |

|분석|

FDA는 연구 결과를 근거로 커피가 오히려 건강에 이로울 수도 있다고 보고 있으며, 발암 경고 라벨이 커피 소비에 대한 대중의 인식에 부정적인 영향을 미칠 수 있다고 우려하고 있다. 따라서 ②가 정답이다. ① 스타벅스 같은 커피 기업이 사회적 기업은 아니다. ④ 위험을 낮춘다는 것이 아니고 위험 증가와 관련이 없다는 정도이다.

위 글에서 추론할 수 있는 것은?
① FDA는 커피에 대한 발암 경고가 불필요하다고 보는 점에서 사회적 기업과 의견을 같이한다.
② FDA는 경고 문구가 커피 소비에 대한 대중의 인식에 영향을 미칠 가능성을 우려하고 있다.
③ FDA는 캘리포니아 법령 65가 커피의 혜택에 대한 과학적 합의를 반영하는 것으로서 지지한다.
④ FDA는 커피 소비가 조기 사망 위험을 낮춘다는 점을 강조한다.

(19~20)

어린 큰뒷부리 도요 한 마리가 알래스카에서 호주의 태즈메이니아 주까지 최소 13,560킬로미터를 쉬지 않고 비행함으로써, 철새의 최장거리 논스톱 비행 기록을 세운 것으로 보인다고 금요일에 한 조류 전문가가 말했다. 그 새는 일본을 향해 남서쪽 코스로 시작했다가 알래스카의 알류샨 제도를 지나면서 동남쪽으로 방향을 틀었다. 그 새는 다시 남서쪽으로 비행하다가 키리바시와 뉴칼레도니아 상공 혹은 인근을 지나갔으며, 그런 다음 호주 본토를 통과한 뒤 호주 최남단의 주인 태즈메이니아를 향해 곧장 서쪽으로 방향을 틀었다. 위성으로 추적한 경로는 그 새가 멈추지 않고 13,560킬로미터를 날았음을 보여주었다. 그 연구 프로젝트의 일원인 뵐러(Woehler)는 "이것이 우연인지, 이 새가 길을 잃은 것인지, 아니면 그 종(種)의 정상적인 이동 패턴의 일부인지는 아직 알 수 없습니다."라고 말했다. 기네스 세계 기록에는 새가 먹이를 찾거나 쉬려고 멈추는 일 없이 최장거리를 이동한 기록으로 2020년에 위성 추적 장치를 단 수컷 큰뒷부리 도요가 알래스카에서 뉴질랜드까지 12,200킬로미터를 날아간 것이 올라 있다. 그 비행은 2020년에 10년 된 동일한 연구 프로젝트의 일부로서 기록되었다. 연구자들에 따르면, 같은 새가 지난해 다음 번 이동에서 13,000킬로미터를 비행하여 자신이 세운 기록을 다시 깨뜨렸다. 그러나 기네스는 그러한 위업을 인정하지 않았다. 뵐러는 연구자들이 위성 추적 꼬리표 번호 234684로 알려져 있는 가장 최근의 그 새가 혼자 날아갔는지 아니면 무리와 함께 날아갔는지를 알지 못한다고 말했다. 뵐러는 꼬리표가 달린 새가 매우 적기 때문에, 이번 사건이 얼마나 대표성이 있는지 혹은 그렇지 않은지 우리는 알지 못한다고 말했다. 알래스카에서 태즈메이니아까지 이동하는 새 중 절반은 뉴질랜드를 거치지 않고 직접 태즈메이니아에 올 수도 있고, 그 비율이 1%일 수도 있으며, 어쩌면 이번이 최초의 사례일 수도 있다고 덧붙였다. "성체가 된 새들은 어린 새들보다 더 일찍 알래스카를 떠나기 때문에, 꼬리표가 달린 그 새가 더 경험 많은 새들을 따라 남쪽으로 이동했을 것 같지는 않습니다."라고 뵐러는 말했다. 뵐러는 태즈메이니아의 외딴 지역에서 날씨가 갠 후 그 새를 다시 볼 수 있기를 기대하고 있다. 그 새는 이동 중 몸무게의 절반을 잃고 나서 그곳에서 다시 살을 찌울 것이다.

|어휘|

bar-tailed godwit 큰뒷부리 도요 mainland n. 대륙, 본토
migration n. (새 따위의) 이동; 이주 acknowledge v. 인정하다, 고백하다 feat n. 업적, 공훈 juvenile n. 청소년, 아동; 배내털이 남은 새 fatten v. 살을 찌우다

| 19 | 빈칸완성 | ① |

|분석|

위성 추적 꼬리표를 달고 있는 새의 수가 매우 적다면, 그런 꼬리표를 달고 있지 않은 새들 중에서 쉬거나 먹이를 먹지 않고 최장거리를 이동한 새가 있을 수도 있다. 그 경우, 꼬리표 번호 234684인 도요새가 새로운 기록을 세웠다는 것의 '대표성'에 대해 확신할 수 없을 것이므로, 빈칸에는 ①이 들어가는 것이 적절하다. 어떤 사건의 대표성이란 그 사건이 얼마나 많은 구성원들에게 일어나는가이다.

빈칸에 들어가기에 가장 적절한 것을 고르시오.
① 이 사건이 얼마나 대표성이 있는지 혹은 그렇지 않은지
② 대부분의 새가 뉴질랜드를 경유하는 이동 패턴을 고수하는 이유
③ 그 업적이 기네스에 의해 인정받아야 하는지 여부
④ 그 새의 종(種)이 비행 경로를 서로 소통하는지 여부

| 20 | 내용추론 | ④ |

|분석|

본문에서는 그 새의 최장거리 논스톱 비행이 정상적인 이동 패턴에 의한 것인지, 우연한 사고인지, 길을 잃은 것인지 알 수 없다고 했다. 이는 이번 비행이 해당 종의 전형적인 이동 패턴이 아닐 수도 있다는 점을 시사하며, 따라서 해당 종 내에서의 특이한 사례일 수도 있다는 추론이 가능하다. outlier는 통계에서 다른 값과 크게 달라서 통계분석에 적절하게 쓰일 수 없는 이상값을 말하며 일반적으로 동일 집단에서 나오기 어려운 특이한 사례를 말한다. ③ 이전의 기록은 13,000킬로미터이므로 560킬로미터의 차이가 난다.

위 글에서 추론할 수 있는 것은?
① 알래스카에서 호주를 중간 경유지로 삼아 뉴질랜드까지 이동하는 것이 그 새 종(種)의 비행 패턴이다.
② 남서쪽 경로를 비행한 것이 그 종에게 우연이었다는 것을 증거가 뒷받침하고 있다.
③ 그 새의 기록과 이전에 기록된 거리는 1,360킬로미터 차이가 난다.
④ 그 새가 알래스카에서 태즈메이니아까지 논스톱으로 이동한 것은 해당 종(種)에서 특이한 사례일 수도 있다.

한성대학교 인문계 A형

TEST p. 664~681

01	①	02	④	03	④	04	③	05	④	06	①	07	①	08	④	09	④	10	②
11	②	12	②	13	②	14	①	15	③	16	③	17	③	18	③	19	①	20	①
21	①	22	④	23	③	24	③	25	③	26	①	27	③	28	③	29	④	30	③
31	②	32	②	33	③	34	②	35	③	36	④	37	④	38	③	39	④	40	③
41	①	42	③	43	①	44	④	45	④	46	①	47	①	48	③	49	②	50	④

01 생활영어 ①

| 분석 |
B의 지나치게 자신만만한 태도를 비판하는 흐름이 되는 것이 자연스럽다. 따라서 '그런 태도를 갖고서는 시험을 통과할 수 없을 것'이라는 말이 이어져야 하므로, ①이 정답이다. when pigs fly는 우리말의 '해가 서쪽에서 뜬다면'과 비슷한 뉘앙스를 갖는 표현으로 절대 불가능한 일을 비유적으로 나타내는 영어 표현이다.

| 어휘 |
stick v. (기억 등이) 사라지지 않다   **ace** v. (시험에서) A학점을 받다

| 해석 |
A: 나는 다음 주 시험이 너무 걱정돼. 쉬지 않고 공부하고 있지만, 아무 것도 기억이 나질 않아.
B: 나는 아직 책도 안 펴 봤어. 나는 내가 A학점을 받을 거란 걸 알고 있어. 나는 천재니까.
A: 그래, 그렇겠지! 그런 태도를 가지고는, 넌 돼지가 하늘을 날 때 시험을 통과할 거야(절대로 시험을 통과할 수 없을 거야).

02 생활영어 ④

| 분석 |
A가 인스타그램의 계정을 닫기로 한 것은 인스타그램에 가짜 뉴스와 선전이 많다고 생각했기 때문일 것이므로, 빈칸에는 ④가 들어가는 것이 적절하다.

| 어휘 |
have had it with ~에 지쳤다, ~을 참을 수 없다   **propaganda** n. 선전   **mollify** v. 완화하다, 진정시키다   **mitigate** v. 누그러뜨리다, 완화하다   **alleviate** v. 경감하다, 완화시키다   **inundate** v. 범람시키다, 그득하게 하다

| 해석 |
A: 난 인스타그램에 진절머리가 나. 분명히 계정을 닫을 거야.
B: 왜? 뭐가 잘못됐어?
A: 정말로 묻는 거야? 인스타그램은 가짜 뉴스와 선전으로 넘쳐나고 있어.

03 생활영어 ④

| 분석 |
A가 자신의 여동생이 하루에 두 곳에서 교대근무로 일하면서 힘들게 살고 있음을 안타까워하고 있으므로, B는 A의 여동생이 과로하고 있는 것을 걱정해서 말하는 것이 자연스럽다.

| 어휘 |
shift n. (근무의) 교체, 교대(시간); 교대조(組)   **have a field day** (특히 남들이 좋게 보지 않는 것을) 신나게 즐기다   **walk on eggshells** 매우 조심스럽게 행동하다   **not play with a full deck** 정신이 온전하지 않다   **burn the candle at both ends** 지나치게 무리하다, 과로하다

| 해석 |
A: 여동생이 너무 안됐어. 두 곳에서 교대근무로 일하며 두 딸을 혼자서 키우고 있어. 숨 쉴 틈도 없을 정도야.
B: 가혹한 일이네. 네 여동생은 너무 무리하고 있어.

04 생활영어 ③

| 분석 |
술 한 잔 하자는 A의 제안에 B가 피곤하다면서 집에 가서 쉬고 싶다는 말을 하고 있으므로, '퇴근하다'라는 의미의 ③이 정답으로 적절하다.

| 어휘 |
grab a drink 술 한 잔 하다   **beat** a. 기진맥진하여   **put off** 연기하다

미루다 **give off** (냄새·열·빛 등을) 내뿜다, 발산하다 **take off** 이륙하다; (특히 서둘러) 떠나다[출발하다]; 퇴근하다 **catch off** 불시에 놀라게 하다, 허를 찌르다

| 해석 |
A: 이봐, 일 끝나고 한 잔 하자.
B: 미안해, 오늘은 안 되겠어. 너무 피곤해. 서둘러 퇴근해서 곧바로 집에 가서 쉬고 싶어 죽겠어.
A: 괜찮아, 다음을 기약하지 뭐.

05 생활영어 ④

| 분석 |
B가 "제니가 정말 그렇게 말했어?"라고 물은 것을 통해 바로 앞에는 제니가 어떤 말을 했다는 내용이 있어야 한다. 그러므로 '불쑥 말하다'라는 의미의 ④가 정답이다.

| 어휘 |
upset a. 혼란한, 당황한; 마음이 상한 **get over** 극복하다; 잊고 나아가다 **blow up** 화내다, 폭발하다 **come up** 언급[논의]되다 **strike out** 눈에 띄다, 돌출하다 **blurt out** 불쑥 말하다

| 해석 |
A: 내 친구 제니를 믿을 수가 없어. 내가 영화 보러 가자고 초대했더니, 제니는 내 영화 취향이 형편없다고 불쑥 말했어.
B: 제니가 정말 그렇게 말했어?
A: 응. 아직도 화가 나서 잊을 수가 없어.

06 논리완성 ①

| 분석 |
돈을 지불하는 것이 상황에 따라 어떤 마음을 갖게 하는지와 관련된 내용이므로, 빈칸 뒤의 전치사 with와 함께 '(돈을) 내놓다'라는 의미를 만드는 ①이 정답이다.

| 어휘 |
overspend v. 과소비하다 **part with** (특히 돈을) 내놓다, 포기하다 **tally** v. 기록하다, 셈하다 **align** v. 정렬하다 **present** v. 제시하다

| 해석 |
지불의 고통이라는 원칙에 따르면, 돈을 내놓는 것은 마음이 아프지만, 보지 않거나 신경을 쓰지 않고 있을 때에는 덜 고통스러운데, 이 원칙은 우리가 신용카드를 사용할 때 과소비하는 이유와 식사 후에 신용카드에 비해 현금으로 결제할 때 기분이 더 나쁜 이유를 이해하는 데 도움을 준다.

07 논리완성 ①

| 분석 |

"친절한 구경꾼은 이빨에 상추가 묻었다고 당신에게 말해줄 것이지만, 좋은 지인은 불쾌한 일이기 때문에 말해주지 않을 것이다."라고 했다. 즉, 좋은 사람이 해주길 꺼리는 피드백은 상대의 흠을 들추어내서 상대를 기분 나쁘게 할 수도 있는 '비판적인(critical)' 피드백이다.

| 어휘 |
bystander n. 구경꾼, 행인 **lettuce** n. 상추 **acquaintance** n. 지인 **hold back** 방해하다 **critical** a. 비판적인 **obvious** a. 명백한, 쉽게 알 수 있는 **innocuous** a. 무해한, 불쾌하지 않은 **ambiguous** a. 애매한

| 해석 |
때때로, 당신이 피드백을 받고자 하는 사람들이 친절하지만 좋은 사람은 아닌 경우가 있다. 친절한 사람은 좋은 사람이 하지 않을 말을 당신에게 해준다. 친절한 구경꾼은 이빨에 상추가 묻었다고 당신에게 말해줄 것이다. 좋은 지인은 불쾌한 일이기 때문에 말해주지 않을 것이다. 친절한 사람은 당신을 발전하지 못하게 하는 것을 말해줄 것이지만, 좋은 사람은 당신에게 비판적인 피드백을 해주는 것을 피한다.

08 논리완성 ④

| 분석 |
두 번째 문장에서 가장 단순한 설명을 우선시하는 것은 데이터가 부족하여 다른 대안이 없는 경우에 한정된다고 했는데, 이 말에는 그 가장 단순한 설명이 '부적절하거나 불충분한' 것으로 드러나는 경우에는 그 가장 단순한 설명은 즉시 폐기된다는 의미가 내포돼 있다. 따라서 ④가 정답으로 적절하다.

| 어휘 |
Occam's razor 오컴의 면도날(경제성 원리, 단순성 원리) **dictate** v. 명령하다, 지시하다 **valid** a. 유효한, 타당한 **sound** a. 건전한, 이치에 맞는 **credible** a. 신뢰할 수 있는, 믿을 수 있는 **inadequate** a. 불충분한, 부적절한

| 해석 |
오컴의 면도날은 부적절한 것으로 입증될 때까지는 가장 단순한 설명이 우선시 되어야 한다고 지시한다. 그것은 가장 단순한 설명이 항상 옳다고 말하는 것이 아니고, 우리로 하여금 어떤 한 설명을 다른 설명에 우선하여 선택하도록 하는 데이터가 전혀 없을 때에는 가장 단순한 설명을 선택해야 한다고만 말할 뿐이다.

09 논리완성 ④

| 분석 |
은과 구리의 특성을 비교하고 있는 내용인데, 그 중에서도 특히 얼마나 희귀한가 혹은 얼마나 널리 퍼져 있느냐를 다루고 있다. 이는 곧 '편재성'에 관한 것이므로 ④가 정답이다.

| 어휘 |

conductive a. 전도성 있는   substance n. 물질   prevalent a. 널리 보급된; 우세한   expertise n. 전문적인 기술   refine v. 정련하다, 정제하다   rigidity n. 강직성   paucity n. 부족, 결핍   ductility n. 연성; 유연성   ubiquity n. 편재성

| 해석 |

은(銀)은 구리보다 전도성이 더 강하지만, 강철의 경우처럼, 물질의 효력만큼 중요한 것은 물질의 편재성이다. 은은 희귀하다. 구리는 철만큼 널리 퍼져 있지 않지만 은보다는 훨씬 더 많으며, 그래서 인간은 다른 그 어떤 산업용 금속보다 구리의 채굴과 정제에서 더 오랜 세월에 걸친 기술을 가지고 있다.

10 논리완성 ②

| 분석 |

우리의 현재 상황은 우리가 과거에 내린 선택들에 의해 만들어졌다고 했으므로, 지금 우리가 어디에 있는지는 과거에 했던 선택들과 행동을 '반영'하는 것이라 할 수 있다.

| 어휘 |

deterrent n. 방해물, 저지하는 것   reflection n. 반영, 반사   subversion n. 전복, 파괴   determinant n. 결정적인 요인, 결정 요소

| 해석 |

미래는 날씨와 같지 않다. 미래는 우리에게 그냥 일어나는 것이 아니다. 우리의 현재 상황이 우리가 과거에 내린 선택들에 의해 만들어진 것과 마찬가지로 우리는 현재 우리가 내리는 선택들로 우리의 미래를 만든다. 지금 우리가 어디에 있든지 그것은(지금 우리의 위치는) 우리를 여기까지 오게 한 과거의 선택들과 행동의 반영이다.

11 논리완성 ②

| 분석 |

소셜 미디어가 아이들을 피해로부터 보호하는 데 있어서 충분한 역할을 못하고 있다고 주장한 상황에서 또 다른 비난의 대상이 될 내용으로는 아이들이 소셜 미디어를 과도하게 사용하는 것을 묵인, 방조, 유도하는 것 등이 될 수 있다. 따라서 '유발하다, 유도하다'는 뜻의 ②가 정답이다.

| 어휘 |

scramble v. 기어오르다, 급히 움직이다   address v. 역점을 두어 다루다   depression n. 우울증   sully v. (명예 등을) 더럽히다, 훼손하다   induce v. 유도하다, 유인하다   splutter v. (분노·충격 등으로) 더듬거리며 말하다   admonish v. 꾸짖다, 훈계하다

| 해석 |

소셜 미디어 플랫폼들은 스마트폰 사용과 십대들의 불안과 우울의 증가 사이의 직접적인 연관성 문제를 해결하기 위해 분주히 움직이고 있다. 예를 들어, 인스타그램은 십대 사용자를 위한 새로운 안전 장치를 마련했다. 그러나 부모들은 이러한 플랫폼이 아이들을 피해로부터 보호하기에 충분한 조치를 취하지 않고 있다고 주장하며, 십대들과 어린아이들로 하여금 소셜 미디어를 과도하게 사용하도록 유도하고 있다고 플랫폼을 비난하고 있다.

12 논리완성 ②

| 분석 |

글의 기조는 '한국은 첨단 경제와 전통이 잘 어우러져서 좋은 결과를 만들어내고 있다'는 것이므로, 첫 번째 빈칸에는 전통 예술, 장인 정신, 문화와도 깊은 연결을 맺고 있다는 의미가 되도록 eternal과 indelible이 가능하고, 두 측면이 충돌하는 대신 서로를 보완한다면, 창의적 사고와 혁신을 가동시키고 촉진하는 결과를 가져올 것이므로 두 번째 빈칸에는 driving이 적절하다.

| 어휘 |

collide v. 충돌하다   complement v. 보완하다   hallmark n. 특징, 특질   eternal a. 영원한   indelible a. 지울 수 없는   incurable a. 치료할 수 없는   affirm v. 확언하다; 긍정하다   ephemeral a. 순식간의, 덧없는   hamper v. 방해하다

| 해석 |

한국은 현대적인 첨단 경제로 잘 알려져 있을 뿐만 아니라, 전통 예술, 장인 정신, 문화와도 지울 수 없는 연결고리를 가지고 있다. 이 두 가지 측면이 충돌하는 대신 서로를 보완하여, 한국의 오랜 특징이 되어온 창의적 사고와 혁신을 촉진하고 있다. 전통적인 재료를 사용하는 기업들은 종종 고전적인 아이디어를 최신 기술과 결합하여 큰 성공을 거두고 있다.

13 논리완성 ②

| 분석 |

바로 앞에서 '거꾸로 된', '반전된' 도시라고 했으므로, 이를 부연하는 다음 문장에서는 무엇이 어떻게 거꾸로 돼 있는지를 구체적으로 설명해야 한다. 따라서 '비정상적인 것이 정상인 도시'라는 의미의 문장을 만드는 ②가 정답으로 가장 적절하다.

| 어휘 |

sanctuary n. 피난처, 성역, 보호구역   flourish v. 번성하다, 잘 자라다   upside-down a. 뒤집힌, 반전된, 거꾸로 된   aberrant a. 일탈적인, 정도를 벗어난   deviant a. 일탈적인, 비정상적인   abnormal a. 비정상적인   normal a. 정상적인   customary a. 관례적인   mundane a. 평범한, 일상적인   anomalous a. 변칙적인, 이례적인   erroneous a. 잘못된, 틀린

| 해석 |

아오스타는 정신적, 신체적 어려움을 겪고 있는 사람들을 위한 일

종의 성역의 도시이다. 수세기 동안, 가톨릭교회는 그들의 건강상태로 인해 가족들로부터 배척당한 사람들에게 주거와 음식과 돌봄을 제공해왔다. 이 사람들 중 많은 이들이 숙련된 노동자가 되었고, 그들 중 상당수가 사랑에 빠지고 결혼하여 자녀를 낳기도 했다. 그로 인해 나타난 것은 일종의 거꾸로 된 도시이다. 이 도시에서는 비정상적인 것이 정상적인 것이며, 사회에서 종종 배척당했던 사람들이 지원을 받아 번창하게 된다.

14 논리완성 ①

| 분석 |
기내 와이파이가 있는 경우 인터넷 연결을 통해 업무를 계속 이어받아 할 수 있게 될 것이므로, 빈칸에는 ①이 적절하다.

| 어휘 |
colleague n. 동료 **facilitate** v. 용이하게 하다, 촉진[조장]하다 **priceless** a. 매우 귀중한, 값으로 매길 수 없는 **on the go** 끊임없이 일하는, 계속 일하는[이동하는], 끊임없이 활동하는, 여행 중인 **relay** v. 중계하다, 이어달리다 **scurry** v. 급히 가다 **convoy** v. 호위하다, 호송하다 **postpone** v. 연기하다, 미루다

| 해석 |
기내 와이파이의 이점은 분명하다. 업무가 이어질 수 있고, 고객과 연락할 수 있으며, 동료와 상담할 수 있다는 점이다. 와이파이로 연결된 비행기에서의 낮 시간 비행은 본질적으로 원격 근무이며, 비즈니스 여행을 용이하게 해준다. 여가를 목적으로 여행하고 있더라도, 인터넷 연결이 향상됐다는 것은 스포츠 생방송에 접속할 수 있고 친구 및 가족과 연락을 지속적으로 취할 수 있다는 것을 의미한다. 이것은 특히 항상 바쁘게 여행하는 사람들에게는 귀중한 것이다.

15 논리완성 ③

| 분석 |
먹을 것을 비축하는 것은 '생존'을 위한 것으로 볼 수 있으며, 겨울에는 '먹을 것을 찾기'가 힘들 것이다. 따라서 subsist(생존하다)와 forage(먹이를 찾아다닌다)가 적절하다.

| 어휘 |
regurgitate v. (위에서 나온 음식물을) 다시 삼키다; 토하다 **dehydrate** v. 탈수시키다 **stock up on** ~을 비축하다, 쌓아두다 **furl** v. (기・깃발 등을) 접다, 말다 **outlive** v. ~보다 오래 살다 **slumber** v. 잠을 자다 **subsist** v. 생존하다, 살아가다 **forage** v. 먹이를 찾아다니다 **scavenge** v. (먹을 것 등을 찾아) 쓰레기 더미를 뒤지다

| 해석 |
서로 다른 20,000종의 벌들 가운데 오직 8종만이 꿀을 생산한다는 사실을 알고 있었는가? 그러나 일단 꿀이 어떻게 만들어지는지를 알고 나면, 그것을 달콤하다고 생각하지 않을지도 모른다. 그것은 꿀벌이 반복적으로 토해내서 탈수시킨 화밀(花蜜)이다. 사람들뿐만 아니라 벌들도 먹을 것을 찾을 수 없는 겨울 동안 먹고 생존하기 위해 먹을 것을 비축해둔다.

16~18

회복력은 곤경에 대비한 일종의 보험증서와 같은 역할을 하여, 우리가 인생의 어려운 순간을 극복하는 데 도움을 주는 것으로 보인다. 회복력을 이해하는 가장 기본적인 방법 중의 하나는 안정애착으로 알려져 있는 심리학 개념에 기초해 있다. 당신이 네 살짜리 딸을 둔 부모라고 상상해보자. 어느 날, 당신은 딸을 놀이터에 데려간다. 당신은 벤치에 앉아서 딸에게 말한다. "가서 놀아." 딸은 걸어가기 시작하지만, 1분마다 돌아서서 당신이 여전히 거기에서 자신을 기다리고 있는지를 확인한다. 만약 이런 상황이라면, 당신은 아직 안정애착을 가진 아이를 키워내지 못한 것이다.
안정애착은 어린 시절에 형성되며, 그것은 우리로 하여금 행여 나쁜 일이 생기더라도 누군가가 우리를 붙들어 줄 것임을 알고서 인생을 살아갈 수 있게 해 준다. 우리는 누군가가 나를 위해 있는지 혹은 그렇지 않은지를 궁금히 여기면서 항상 주위를 둘러볼 필요는 없다. 높은 수준의 안정애착을 가지고 있다면, 그것은 모든 것을 보장해 준다고 믿을 수 있는 이상적인 보험 상품과도 같다. 예를 들어, 우리는 기꺼이 위험을 감수하고, 우리로서는 넘볼 수 없다고 생각하는 사람과 새로운 애정의 모험을 시도해볼 수도 있다.

| 어휘 |
resilience n. 회복탄력성, 회복력 **insurance policy** 보험증서 **secure attachment** 안정애착(아동이 양육자에게서 보호받고 있다고 느끼는 안정감) **construct** n. 개념, 구성 **fundamental** a. 근본적인, 기본적인 **go out on a limb** 위험을 감수하다, 모험을 하다 **out of one's league** 자신의 수준을 넘어선, 감당하기 어려운

16 글의 주제 ③

| 분석 |
첫 두 문장에 글의 주제가 언급돼 있다. "회복력은 우리가 인생의 어려운 순간을 극복하는 데 도움을 주는 것으로 보이며, 회복력을 이해하는 가장 기본적인 방법 중의 하나는 안정애착이라는 개념에 기초해 있다."라고 했으므로 ③이 정답이다.

주제로 가장 적절한 것을 고르시오.
① 안정애착을 가진 아이를 길러내는 방법
② 높은 수준의 안정애착을 갖는 것의 위험성
③ 안정애착을 통해 회복력을 이해하기
④ 어른으로서 안정애착을 형성하는 것의 중요성

17 빈칸완성 ③

| 분석 |

빈칸 앞뒤의 "우리는 누군가가 나를 위해 있는지 혹은 그렇지 않은지를 궁금히 여기면서 항상 주위를 둘러볼 필요는 없다.", "모든 것을 보장해 준다고 믿을 수 있다." 등의 표현을 통해 위험이나 불확실한 상황에 대비해 보장을 제공하는 제도인 '보험'이 빈칸에 적절함을 알 수 있다.

빈칸 Ⓐ에 들어가기에 가장 적절한 단어를 고르시오.
① 선택적인
② 결함 있는
③ 보험
④ 할부

18 빈칸완성 ③

| 분석 |

빈칸 이하는 안정애착이 보험 상품의 역할을 할 수 있다고 한 내용에 대한 예시에 해당하므로 ③이 정답으로 적절하다.

빈칸 Ⓑ에 들어가기에 가장 적절한 표현을 고르시오
① 요컨대
② 물론
③ 예를 들어
④ 반대로

19~21

머리 위 하늘에 떠 있는 구름을 한가롭게 바라본 적이 있는가? 얼마 지나지 않아 당신은 "이 작은 구름은 너무 귀엽고 행복해 보이는데, 왜 큰 구름이 그것을 쫓고 있지?"라고 생각한다. 만약 구름에 관한 이야기를 이렇게 상상해 본 적이 있다면, 당신만 그런 것은 아니다. 이것은 아무런 패턴이 존재하지 않는 곳에서 패턴을 찾으려는 매우 보편적인 인간의 성향으로, 패턴 인식 성향이라 불린다. 그것은 인간의 일반적인 특성이지만, 어떤 사람들은 다른 사람들보다 패턴을 찾으려는 경향을 훨씬 더 강하게 나타낸다는 점에서 성격에 따라 다르다고 할 수 있다.
몇몇 MBA(경영대학원) 학생들을 대상으로 한 다음의 연구를 살펴보자. Ⓓ 그들에게 한 주식의 하루 동안의 가격 변동을 보여주었다. Ⓑ 그 주식의 가격 변동을 보여준 후에, 자신만만한 한 분석가는 주식 가격이 그렇게 변동한 이유 X를 참가자 절반에게 제시했다. Ⓔ 나머지 절반에게, 그 분석가는 X와 다른 이유 혹은 X와 반대되는 이유를 제시했다. Ⓒ 그 후, MBA 참가자들은 그 이유들이 얼마나 타당하게 들렸는지를 평가했다. 놀랍게도, 그들은 두 이유 중 어느 쪽의 논리에도 똑같이 깊은 인상을 받았다. 요지는 우리의 마음은 항상 이야기를 찾고 있다는 것이다.

| 어휘 |
leisurely ad. 유유히, 느긋하게   **disposition** n. 성질, 기질, 경향
patternicity n. 유형화, 패턴성, 패턴 인식   **characteristic** n. 특질, 특색   **evince** v. (감정 따위를) 분명히 나타내다, 명시하다

19 빈칸완성 ①

| 분석 |

빈칸을 포함하고 있는 문장은 패턴을 찾으려는 보편적인 인간의 기질을 부연해서 설명하는 역할을 하고 있으므로, 빈칸에는 '성향', '경향'의 의미를 가진 단어가 들어가야 한다. tendency, proclivity, propensity는 모두 그런 의미를 가지고 있으나, audacity는 '대담함', '뻔뻔함'이라는 의미이므로 빈칸에 들어갈 수 없다.

20 문장배열 ①

| 분석 |

사실이나 현상의 제시가 그것에 대한 설명의 제시보다 선행해야 하므로, 주식의 가격 변동을 보여준 것과 관련된 내용인 Ⓓ가 먼저 오고 그다음에 Ⓑ가 온다. 이어서 절반의 참가자에게는 Ⓑ에서와 다른 설명을 했다는 내용인 Ⓔ가 오고, 참가자 모두에게 들은 설명에 대한 평가를 요구했다는 내용인 Ⓒ가 마지막에 와야 한다.

21 빈칸완성 ①

| 분석 |

두 번째 문단의 연구 내용은 패턴을 찾으려 하는 인간의 본성을 부연하는 예시에 해당하는데, 패턴을 찾는다는 것은 자신이 납득할 만한 설명이나 이야기를 찾는다는 말로 바꿔서 표현할 수 있을 것이므로, 빈칸에는 ①이 들어가는 것이 가장 적절하다.

빈칸 Ⓕ에 들어가기에 가장 적절한 것을 고르시오.
① 우리의 마음은 항상 이야기를 찾고 있다
② 주식 시장 전문가들은 신뢰할 수 없다
③ 인간은 명백한 패턴을 거부하도록 타고 났다
④ 패턴 인식 성향은 성격에 따라 다르다

22~24

우리가 받아들이는 많은 정보는 강조, 요약 또는 증류의 형태로 된 것이다. 그것은 지식으로 착각되는 것이다. 우리는

답은 알게 되지만, 답을 도출하는 과정을 보여줄 수는 없다. 수학 수업에서 6학년 학생이 옆에 앉은 학생의 답을 베끼는 경우를 생각해보자. 그 학생은 올바른 답을 얻을 수 있을지 몰라도, 왜 그것이 답인지는 알지 못한다. 그것은 하나의 추상화된 개념이다. 그 학생은 이해가 부족한 상태이며, 이해 없는 정보는 위험해질 수 있다.

이런 추상화된 개념이 우리로 하여금 시간을 절약하고 결정을 더 잘 내리게 해 줄 것이라고 생각하는 것은 당연하지만, 많은 경우에 그렇지 않다. 요약본을 읽는 것이 전체 텍스트를 읽는 것보다 더 빠를지는 몰라도, 요약본에는 중요한 세부 사항들이 빠져 있다. 그것은 요약을 한 사람에게는 관련 없어 보였을 수도 있지만 당신에게는 관련 있을 수도 있는 그런 세부 사항들이다. 당신은 결국 중요한 정보를 놓치는 대가로 시간을 절약하는 것이다. 대충 훑어보는 것은 맹점(깨닫지 못하는 약점)을 만들어낸다.

추상화된 개념을 원하는 마음은 이해가 간다. 매일 우리에게 쏟아지는 엄청난 양의 정보가 압도적으로 느껴질 수도 있기 때문이다. 하지만 정보가 원래의 출처에서 멀면 멀수록, 그 정보는 그만큼 더 많은 필터를 거친 후에 당신에게 도달한다.

| 어휘 |

summary n. 요약, 개요 **distillation** n. 증류, 정제; 본질을 추출한 것 **illusion** n. 착각, 환상 **abstraction** n. 추상, 추상적인 것 **apparently** ad. 겉보기에는; 명백히 **relevant** a. 관련 있는, 적절한; 의미 있는 **end up** 결국 ~이 되다, ~로 끝나다 **skim** v. (책 등을) 대충 읽다 **engender** v. (어떤 감정이나 상황을) 낳다, 일으키다 **blind spot** 맹점, 무지한 부분, 깨닫지 못한 부분 **sheer** a. 순전한, 순수한 **bombard** v. (많은 양으로) 공격하다, 퍼붓다 **overwhelming** a. 압도적인, 이길 수 없는, 엄청난

| 22 | 빈칸완성 | ④ |

| 분석 |

"요약본을 읽는 것이 전체 텍스트를 읽는 것보다 빠를지는 몰라도, 요약본에는 중요한 세부 사항들이 빠져 있다."라고 했으므로, 시간을 절약하는 것은 결국 중요한 정보를 놓치는 것을 대가로 하여 얻게 되는 것이다.

빈칸 Ⓐ에 들어가기에 가장 적절한 표현을 고르시오.
① ~대신으로
② ~대신에
③ ~을 두려워하여
④ ~의 대가로, ~을 희생하여

| 23 | 내용파악 | ③ |

| 분석 |

본문에서 filters는 원래의 정보를 여러 과정으로 변형시키는 요소를 의미한다. ①, ②, ④는 모두 정보가 왜곡되거나 달라지게 할 수 있는 요소들이지만, ③은 정보를 원래 그대로 전달하는 것이므로 filters에 해당되지 않는다.

다음 중 Ⓑfilters의 예에 해당하지 <u>않는</u> 것은?
① 편견
② 정치적 해석
③ 원본에 대한 정확한 설명
④ 개인의 이해 수준

| 24 | 내용추론 | ③ |

| 분석 |

본문에서는 추상화된 개념이 종종 중요한 세부 사항을 놓치게 만들고, 이를 맹목적으로 받아들이는 것은 이해 없이 단순히 답만 아는 것과 같다고 이야기하고 있다. 즉, 추상화된 개념이 이해를 돕기보다는 오히려 방해할 수도 있다는 것이다. 따라서 ③이 추론할 수 없는 진술이다.

다음 중 추론할 수 <u>없는</u> 것은?
① 진정한 지식은 노력해서 얻어지는 것이다.
② 추상화된 개념은 단지 빌린 것에 불과하다.
③ 추상화된 개념은 완전한 이해에 필수적이다.
④ 잘못된 정보는 올바른 의사 결정을 방해할 수 있다.

25~27

초기 인류 사회 집단에서 구성원 수의 중요한 임계치는 150명 정도였다. 그보다 더 많은 사람들과는 서로 연결되어 의미 있는 애착심을 형성하는 것이 전혀 불가능했다. 그렇다면 호모 사피엔스는 어떻게 마침내 이 임계점을 넘어 수천, 심지어 수백만 명이 사는 도시와 국가를 건립할 수 있었을까? 해답은 아마도 허구가 시작된 것에 있을 것이다. 공통의 신화를 믿음으로써, 그렇지 않다면 연결되지 않을 많은 사람들이 성공적으로 협력할 수 있다. 국가, 교회, 도시, 혹은 부족 등, 대규모 공동체는 모두 사람들의 집단적 상상력 속에만 존재하는 공통된 신화에 깊이 뿌리내리고 있다. 그러나 이것들은 단지 신화일 뿐이며, 그 안에 포함된 것은 모두 사람들이 만들어서 서로에게 말해주는 이야기 바깥에서는 존재하지 않는다. 우주에는 신이 없으며, 인간의 공통된 상상력 밖에서는 국가도 법도 존재하지 않는다. 유령과 정령을 믿음으로써 사회 질서를 공고히 한 원시 부족들과 유사하게, 현대의 인간들도 공통된 신화를 고수함으로써 사회 질서를 유지한다.

| 어휘 |

threshold n. 문지방, 한계, 경계   inhabitant n. 거주자, 주민   dawn n. 새벽, 발단, 시작   myth n. 신화, 전설   entrenched a. 깊이 뿌리내린, 확립된   incorporate v. 포함시키다, 통합시키다   cement v. 굳히다, 강화하다   adhere to ~을 고수하다

25 글의 제목 ③

| 분석 |

본문은 인간이 공통의 신화를 믿음으로써 대규모 사회를 형성하고 서로 협력할 수 있었음을, 다시 말해 결속력을 갖게 됐음을 설명하고 있다. 따라서 ③이 정답이다.

제목으로 가장 적절한 것을 고르시오.
① 대규모 공동체
② 중요한 임계점을 넘어서기
③ 공유된 신화의 결속력
④ 인간의 공통된 욕망

26 빈칸완성 ①

| 분석 |

글의 흐름상 "어떻게 150명이라는 초기 사회집단의 규모를 뛰어넘는 사회를 만들어낼 수 있었을까?"라는 의미가 되어야 하므로, '건립하다'라는 의미의 ①이 정답으로 적절하다.

빈칸 Ⓐ에 들어가기에 가장 적절한 단어를 고르시오.
① 건립하다
② 제지하다
③ 정복하다
④ 명백히 하다

27 반의어 ③

| 분석 |

cement가 '결합하다', '(우정 따위를) 굳게 하다'라는 의미이므로 '가루로 만들다', '분쇄하다'라는 의미의 ③이 반의어로 적절하다
① 강화하다 ② 보강하다 ④ 지지하다

28~30

"모든 인간은 평등하게 창조되었다"는 말은 오래되고도 진부한 진술이다. 이는 생물학을 고려할 때 특히 그러한데, 생물학에서는 사람들이 실제로는 창조된 것이 아니라 진화해 왔다고 주장하기 때문이다. 게다가 그들은 평등하게 진화하지 않았다. 평등에 대한 생각은 창조에 대한 생각과 복잡하게 얽혀 있다. 이는 기독교에서 유래한 것으로, 기독교에서는 모든 사람이 신(神)의 형상대로 창조되었고 모두가 신성하게 창조된 영혼을 가지고 있다고 주장한다. 신 앞에서 모든 영혼은 평등하다. 그러나 만약 우리가 신, 창조, 영혼에 관한 기독교 신화를 믿지 않는다면, 모든 사람들이 평등하다는 것은 무엇을 의미할까? 진화는 평등이 아니라 차이에 기반을 둔다. 각각의 사람은 다소 다른 유전자 코드를 가지고 있고, 태어날 때부터 서로 다른 환경의 영향에 노출돼 있다. 이것은 서로 다른 특성의 발달로 이어지며, 특성에 따라 생존 가능성도 달라진다. 따라서 "평등하게 창조되었다"는 "다르게 진화했다"로 바뀌어야 한다. 사람들이 창조되지 않은 것과 마찬가지로, 그들에게 무언가를 부여하는 "창조자"도 존재하지 않는다. 그들은 그저 태어났을 뿐이다.

| 어휘 |

intricately ad. 복잡하게   entangle v. 얽히게 하다   stem v. 유래하다, 발생하다   divinely ad. 신성하게   evolve v. 진화하다, 발전하다   expose v. 노출시키다   endow v. 부여하다, 주다

28 빈칸완성 ④

| 분석 |

빈칸 Ⓐ의 경우, 바로 앞의 old와 호응할 수 있는 표현이 들어가야 하므로 '진부한'이란 의미의 hackneyed가 적절하다. 빈칸 Ⓑ의 경우, people were actually not created, but rather they have evolved는 생물학에서 주장 혹은 옹호하는 내용에 해당하므로 maintains와 asserts가 들어갈 수 있다. 따라서 ④가 정답이다.

빈칸 Ⓐ와 Ⓑ에 들어가기에 가장 적절한 단어를 고르시오.
① 경험적인 — 주장하다
② 미세한 — 부인하다
③ 무감각한 — 증명하다
④ 진부한 — 주장하다

29 지시대상 ④

| 분석 |

Ⓒ는 단순히 "유전적 차이"나 "환경적 차이" 중 하나만을 가리키는 것이 아니라, 이 두 가지 요소를 모두 포함하는 앞 문장 전체를 의미한다고 보는 것이 타당하다.

ⒸThis가 가리키는 것은?
① 진화는 평등이 아닌 차이에 기반하고 있다는 사실
② 모든 사람은 서로 다른 유전자 코드를 가지고 있다는 사실
③ 모든 사람은 서로 다른 환경의 영향에 노출돼 있다는 사실
④ 모든 사람은 서로 다른 유전자 코드를 가지고 있고, 서로 다른 환경의 영향에 노출돼 있다는 사실

30 내용일치 ③

| 분석 |
본문에서는 평등의 개념이 기독교의 창조론과 관련이 있음을 말하고 있다. 따라서 평등의 개념이 인류 그 자체만큼 오래됐다고는 할 수 없을 것이므로, ③이 옳지 않은 진술이다.

다음 중 옳지 않은 것은?
① 기독교에서 모든 인간은 본질적으로 평등하다.
② 기독교인들은 모든 인간이 신을 닮았다고 믿는다.
③ 인간들 사이에서의 평등사상은 인류 그 자체만큼 오래되었다.
④ 진화론자들은 인간의 특성이 신에 의해 결정되지 않는다고 믿는다.

31~34

바이든 행정부의 지난 3년은 주식 투자자들에게 얼마나 행복한 시간이었는가! 많은 주식의 가치가 두 배로 뛰었고, 비트코인은 네 배로 상승했다. 슬프게도, 역사는 우리에게 강세장이 영원하지 않으며, 하락할 때는 급격히 하락해서 우리의 종자돈이 위태로워질 수도 있음을 가르쳐 주었다. 끝없는 전쟁에서부터 해결하기 어려운 재정 적자에 이르기까지, 지속적인 강세 시장을 위협할 수 있는 위험 요소는 많다. 또한, 주식이 과대평가되었을 수도 있다. 인플레이션에 대한 우려와 취약한 경제에 대한 인식이 도널드 트럼프의 대선 승리를 가져왔으며, 미국 유권자들은 카멀라 해리스보다 그가 자신들의 지갑에 더 도움이 될 것이라고 믿는 듯했다. 그러나 감세와 무역 관세를 비롯한 트럼프의 선거 공약은 반대의 결과를 가져올 가능성이 높다. 관세만으로도 성장을 방해하고 추가적인 인플레이션을 촉발할 것이 거의 확실하다.

| 어휘 |
blissful a. 행복한, 기쁜 **copious** a. 풍부한, 방대한 **alas** int. 아아, 슬프도다 **bull market** (주식의) 강세장, 강세 시장 **nest egg** 비상금; (지금의 씨앗이 되는) 준비금, 종자돈 **jeopardize** v. 위태롭게 하다 **threaten** v. 협박하다, 위협하다 **robust** a. 튼튼한, 강건한 **interminable** a. 끝없는, 지루하게 긴 **intractable** a. 다루기 어려운, 고집 센 **vulnerability** n. 취약성 **tariff** n. 관세

31 반의어 ②

| 분석 |
주식 시장의 강세장은 bull market으로 표현하고 약세장은 bear market으로 표현한다.

32 어법 ②

| 분석 |
ⓒ의 뒤에 목적어가 주어져 있으므로, ⓒ는 능동태 may threaten이 되어야 한다.

33 빈칸완성 ③

| 분석 |
앞에서 '미국 유권자들은 카멀라 해리스보다 도널드 트럼프가 자신들의 지갑에 더 도움이 될 것이라고 믿어서 그를 대통령으로 선출했으나, 감세와 무역 관세를 비롯한 트럼프의 선거 공약은 반대의 결과를 가져올 가능성이 높다.'라고 했으므로, 빈칸에는 이 내용을 부연하는 내용에 해당하는 ③이 들어가는 것이 가장 자연스럽다.

ⓕ에 들어가기에 가장 적절한 것은?
① 종자돈과 주식 자산은 보호 받을 것이다
② 도널드 트럼프는 세계 경제의 안정을 가져올 것이다
③ 관세만으로도 성장을 방해하고 추가적인 인플레이션을 촉발할 것이 거의 확실하다
④ 도널드 트럼프는 모든 수입을 금지하고 국내 제조 산업에 집중할 것이다

34 내용일치 ②

| 분석 |
바이든 행정부의 지난 3년 동안 주식 시장이 활황을 이루었다고 했고, 글을 쓴 시점에서는 트럼프가 대통령에 아직 취임을 하지는 않은 상황으로 볼 수 있다. 따라서 저자가 우려하는 트럼프의 정책이 이미 경제나 주식시장에 영향을 준 것은 아니므로, 글을 쓴 현재 시점에서는 시장 상황이 좋다고 봐야 한다. 그러므로 ②가 정답이다.

다음 중 옳은 것은?
① 예산 적자를 해결하는 것은 쉬운 일이다.
② 현재 시점에서, 시장은 활발하다.
③ 강한 시장을 위협하는 전쟁들은 일시적이다.
④ 비트코인의 가치는 주식 가치와 같은 비율로 증가했다.

35~38

문화적 차용과 창의적인 변형의 좋은 예는 "한류"이다. 한류는 처음부터 록, 재즈, 레게, 아프로비트를 비롯한 다양한 스타일을 혼합한 것에 바탕을 두고 있었기 때문에, 전 세계의 광범위한 관객들에게 다가갈 수 있었다. 그것은 또한 주로 한국어로 부르되 일부 영어 표현을 가미하여, R&B 댄스

트랙, 서정적인 브리지, 그리고 부드러운 랩 인터루드를 활용한다. 이 영상들은 종종 동작이 일치된(군무 형태의) 춤 동작을 특징으로 하는데, 이는 서구에서는 덜 흔하지만, 발리우드를 비롯한 다른 음악 전통에서는 잘 알려져 있는 것이다. ⓓ 또한, 이 영상에서 주목할 만한 것은 미국과 영국을 기반으로 한 팝과 랩 문화에서 자주 등장하는 폭력과 외설적인 내용이 없다는 점이다. ⓔ K팝이 전통적인 혹은 전형적인 한국 예술을 대표하지는 않지만, 다른 음악 전통을 차용하고 풍부하게 할 뿐만 아니라 1950년대에 미군 기지에서 활동했고 1960~70년대에도 지속적으로 성장한 한국 걸그룹들에 깊이 뿌리를 두고 있다는 것은 부인할 수 없는 사실이다. ⓒ 한국의 음악적 전통과 전 세계 다양한 장르의 이러한 신선한 결합은 K팝을 쉽게 다가갈 수 있고 매력적인 것으로 만든다. ⓑ 결국, 그것은 문화 교류가 제대로 이루어졌을 때는 문화적 전유가 아니라 문화적 풍요로움이며, 비난받기보다는 칭찬받아야 하는 것이라는 증거이다.

| 어휘 |

improvisation n. 즉흥연주, 즉흥성 **expansive** a. 광대한, 광범위한 **mixture** n. 혼합; 혼합물 **Afrobeat** n. 아프로비트(아프리카 음악과 펑크, 재즈 등이 혼합된 음악 스타일) **interlude** n. 간주, 삽입곡 **sprinkling** n. 소량, 약간 **synchronize** v. ~에 동시성을 지니게 하다, 동시에 진행[작동]시키다 **appropriation** n. 전유; 착복 **enrichment** n. 부유하게 하기 **laud** v. 찬양하다, 칭찬하다 **condemn** v. 비난하다 **accessible** a. 접근하기 쉬운, 입수하기 쉬운 **alluring** a. 유혹하는, 매혹적인 **obscenity** n. 외설, 음란 **undeniable** a. 부인할 수 없는

35 글의 제목 ③

| 분석 |

본문은 문화적 차용과 창의적인 변형의 좋은 예로서의 한류, 그중에서도 K팝을 이야기하고 있는데, 이에 대해 구체적으로 K팝은 록, 재즈, 레게, 아프로비트를 비롯한 다양한 스타일을 혼합한 것에 바탕을 두고 있었기 때문에 전 세계의 광범위한 관객들에게 다가갈 수 있었음을 말하고 있다. 따라서 제목으로는 ③이 적절하다.

제목으로 가장 적절한 것을 고르시오.
① K팝이 세계 무대를 사로잡다
② K팝이 걸그룹의 부활을 이끌다
③ K팝의 성공적인 음악적 융합
④ K팝이 춤 동작을 일치시키다

36 동의어 ④

| 분석 |

synchronize는 '동시에 진행[작동]시키다', '(시계·행동 따위의) 시간을 맞추다'라는 의미이므로 '통합하다', '조정하다', '조화시키다'라는 의미의 coordinate가 동의어로 적절하다. ① 수집하다 ② 고안하다 ③ 포함하다

37 문장배열 ④

| 분석 |

앞 내용에 이어 K팝 영상의 또 다른 차별점을 제시하고 있는 ⓓ가 가장 먼저 오고, K팝이 단순한 현대적 현상이 아니며 1950년대 미군 기지에서 활동한 한국 걸그룹의 전통에 뿌리를 두고 있음을 설명하는 ⓔ가 그다음에 오고, 이러한 역사적 뿌리와 함께 K팝이 다양한 음악 장르와 결합하여 쉽게 다가갈 수 있는 매력적인 요소를 갖추었다는 점을 강조하는 ⓒ가 그다음에, 그리고 이러한 문화적 결합이 단순한 전유가 아니라 문화적 풍요로움이며, 이를 긍정적인 시선으로 바라봐야 한다는 결론을 제시하는 ⓑ가 마지막에 와야 한다.

38 저자의 태도 ②

| 분석 |

저자는 K팝이 다양한 음악적 전통을 결합한 문화적 풍요로움의 사례라고 긍정적으로 평가하고 있고, 비난받기보다는 칭찬받아야 한다면서 명확하게 K팝을 긍정적으로 바라보고 있다.

K팝에 대한 저자의 태도는 무엇인가?
① 경박한
② 호의적인
③ 무시하는
④ 경멸하는

39~41

사람들은 덧없는 쾌락을 쫓음으로 인해 고통을 겪는다. 그들은 자신의 감정이 덧없는 것임을 이해하고 그것을 추구하는 것을 멈출 때에만 이 혼란에서 해방될 수 있다. 이것이 불교 수행에서 지향하는 바이다. 명상을 하는 동안, 사람들은 자신의 마음과 몸을 면밀히 관찰하고, 모든 감정이 끊임없이 생겨나고 사라지는 것을 인식하며, 감정을 쫓는 것이 무의미하다는 것을 깨닫게 된다. 이러한 쫓음이 중단되고 나면, 마음은 매우 편안해지고 맑아지며 또한 만족스러워진다. 기쁨, 분노, 지루함, 욕망 등, 온갖 감정이 계속해서 떠오르고 사라지지만, 일단 특정한 감정을 갈망하는 것을 멈추고 나면, 그 감정들을 있는 그대로 받아들일 수 있게 된다. 사람들은 가능했을지도 모르는 과거에 대한 공상에 빠지는 대신, 현재의 순간을 살아간다. 그에 따른 고요함은 너무나 심오해서, 쾌락의 감정을 광적으로 추구하며 살아가는 사람들은 그것을

거의 상상할 수 없다.

| 어휘 |

fleeting a. 덧없는, 잠깐의　**liberate** v. 해방하다, 자유롭게 하다　**impermanent** a. 영속하지 않는, 일시적인, 덧없는　**aspiration** n. 염원, 열망, 욕망　**Buddhist** a. 불교의　**meditate** v. 명상하다　**perceive** v. 지각하다, 인식하다　**ceaseless** a. 끊임없는, 중단 없는　**halt** v. 멈추다, 중지하다　**relaxed** a. 편안한, 여유로운　**content** a. 만족한, 기쁜　**boredom** n. 지루함　**lust** n. 욕망, 정욕　**hanker** v. 갈망하다, 열망하다　**subsequent** a. 다음의, 뒤따르는　**serenity** n. 평온, 고요함　**profound** a. 심오한, 깊은　**frenzied** a. 미친 듯한, 광란의　**envision** v. 상상하다, 구상하다

39　글의 제목　④

| 분석 |

본문은 불교 수행이 지향하는 바, 즉 덧없는 감정을 쫓는 습관을 멈추고, 궁극적으로 평온을 얻어가는 과정에 대해 이야기하고 있다. 따라서 제목으로는 ④가 적절하다.

제목으로 가장 적절한 것을 고르시오.
① 쾌락을 느끼는 것을 추구하는 것
② 감정의 영속적인 특성
③ 고통을 초래하는 순간적인 쾌락
④ 불교 수행을 통해 평온함을 이루는 것

40　빈칸완성　③

| 분석 |

빈칸 Ⓐ에는 '사람들이 덧없는 쾌락을 쫓음으로 인해 고통을 겪는 상황'을 지칭할 수 있는 표현이 필요하므로, 부정적인 의미의 misery와 turmoil이 가능하다. 빈칸 Ⓑ의 경우, 자신의 감정이 덧없는 것임을 이해하는 경우에는 그것을 추구하거나 원하지 않을 것이므로, pursuing만이 가능하다. 따라서 ③이 정답이다.

빈칸 Ⓐ와 Ⓑ에 들어가기에 가장 적절한 단어를 고르시오.
① 열정 — 이해하다
② 불행 — 억제하다
③ 혼란 — 추구하다
④ 방법 — 제거하다

41　내용파악　①

| 분석 |

"이러한 쫓음이 중단되고 나면, 마음은 매우 편안해지고 맑아지며 또한 만족스러워진다."라고 했으므로 ①이 정답이다.

쾌락의 감정을 추구하는 것을 멈추면 무슨 일이 일어나는가?
① 평온에 이르게 된다.
② 모든 감정을 부정한다.
③ 더 극심한 고통을 겪는다.
④ 미래에 대해 공상한다.

42~44

그 단어는 1883년에 찰스 다윈(Charles Darwin)의 사촌인 영국 과학자 프랜시스 갈턴(Francis Galton)에 의해 만들어졌다. 『종의 기원』이 처음 출판되었을 때, 갈턴은 그의 사촌이 쓴 책을 읽고 깊은 영감을 받았었다. 지구상의 다양한 생명체의 무리를 형성하게 하는 자연선택이라는 힘이 존재한다는 것을 이해하고 나자, 그가 혈통과 관련이 있다고 믿었던 가난, 범죄, 문맹, 신경증, 방탕함 등과 같은 특성들을 선택적 번식을 통해 제거함으로써 우월한 인종을 선택할 수 있을지 모른다는 생각이 그에게 떠올랐다. 그는 자신이 싫어하는 사람들의 집단을 죽이는 이러한 방법을 "우생학"이라 불렀으며, 이는 "좋음"과 "출생"을 의미하는 두 그리스어 단어를 결합한 것이었다. 그리고 그는 유럽을 다시 위대하게 만들기 위한 얼핏 듣기에는 과학에 근거한 것으로 보이는 자신의 계획을 사람들에게 이야기하기 시작했다. 자신의 생각을 널리 알리기 위해, 그는 엄격한 시험을 통과한 사람들에게만 자식을 낳을 수 있도록 해주고 그 외의 다른 사람이 자식을 낳으려는 경우에는 누구든 투옥시켜 처벌하는 사회에 관한 공상과학소설을 쓰기까지 했다. 갈턴은 자신의 책을 인류를 퇴보로부터 구해내기 위한 교본으로 여겼다.

| 어휘 |

coin v. (새로운 단어나 신어를) 만들다; (화폐를) 주조하다　**array** n. 배열, 정렬; (다양한) 모음, 집합　**dawn on** (일이) 점점 분명해지다, (생각이) 떠오르다　**manipulate** v. 조종하다, 조작하다; 능숙하게 다루다　**trait** n. (성격적·유전적) 특성, 특색　**illiteracy** n. 문맹, 무지　**neurosis** n. 신경증, 노이로제　**promiscuity** n. 문란함, 난잡함　**eugenics** n. 우생학　**procreate** v. (자식을) 보다, 자손을 낳다　**incarceration** n. 투옥, 감금　**degeneration** n. 퇴화, 타락, 퇴보

42　빈칸완성　③

| 분석 |

"자신이 싫어하는 사람들의 집단을 죽이는 방법을 생각했다", "엄격한 시험을 통과한 사람들에게만 자식을 낳을 수 있도록 해준다"라는 내용을 통해, 갈턴은 자신이 부정적으로 생각하는 특성을 가진 사람들을 죽이거나 그들이 자손을 낳지 못하게 함으로써 그러한 특성이 후대에 전해지지 않도록, 즉 '제거되도록' 하고 싶어 했음을 알 수 있다. 그러므로 빈칸에는 '선택적 번식을 통해 제거하다'라는 의미의 ③이 적절함을 알 수 있다.

빈칸 Ⓐ에 들어가기에 가장 적절한 표현을 고르시오.
① 선택하다
② 이종교배하다
③ 선택적 번식을 통해 제거하다
④ 타가 수정하다

43 지시대상 ①

| 분석 |
Ⓑ가 가리키는 것은 앞에서 언급한 자신이 싫어하는 사람들의 집단을 죽이는 방법인 "우생학"을 가리킨다. 따라서 ①이 정답이다. ③은 일반적으로 개인이 아이를 가질지 여부를 조절하는 방법(피임, 가족계획 등)을 의미한다.

Ⓑhis scientific-sounding plan이 가리키는 것은?
① 우생학
② 다원주의
③ 산아제한
④ 자연선택

44 내용일치 ④

| 분석 |
갈턴은 일정 기준을 통과한 사람만 아이를 낳을 수 있게 함으로써 특정 형질을 제거하고 싶어 했다. 이러한 방법을 인류를 퇴보로부터 구해내기 위한 교본으로 여겼다. 따라서 ④가 정답이다. ① 자연선택은 자연에게 맡기는 것이다. ② 다윈의 책에 영감을 받았다고 했다. ③ 다윈의 이론이 아닌 갈턴의 생각이 그러하다.

다음 중 옳은 것은?
① 다윈은 종을 인위적으로 개선시킬 수 있다고 믿었다.
② 갈턴의 사상은 다윈의 이론과 무관하게 형성되었다.
③ 다윈의 진화론은 우월한 인종이 존재한다고 가정한다.
④ 갈턴은 선택적 번식을 통해 인류를 퇴보로부터 구하자고 제안했다.

(45~47)

2020년 이후로 영국의 나이트클럽 중 37%가 폐업했다. 많은 클럽이 팬데믹 동안 문을 닫고 다시 열지 못했으며, 폐업은 여전히 계속되고 있다. 인건비 상승, 더 엄격해진 도시계획 법규, 더 많아진 소음 민원 등이 모두 원인으로 작용하고 있을 가능성이 크다. 하지만 핵심 요인은 나이트클럽의 주된 고객인 무분별한 젊은이들이 집에 머물러 있다는 점이다. 2011년에서 2021년 사이, 1년 내내 한 잔의 술도 마시지 않은 16~24세 영국 청년의 비율이 19%에서 38%로 두 배

늘어났다. 나이트클럽이 어려움을 겪는 것은 당연한 일이다. 왜 젊은이들의 폭음이 사라지고 있는 것일까? 이에 대한 단 하나의 정답은 없다. 오늘날 아이들은 과거보다 더 엄격한 감시를 받고 있으며, 젊은 성인 중 더 많은 비율이 보다 절제하는 문화를 가진 이민자 가정 출신이다. 술집에서는 나이를 확인하는 것이 더 일상화되었으며, 넷플릭스는 사과술보다 저렴하고, 술집에서 애인을 찾는 것보다 데이트 어플이 더 좋다. 이러한 풍조는 뚜렷하며, 앞으로도 계속될 것으로 보인다. 이제 문제는 그들의 부모들이다.

| 어휘 |
factor n. 요인, 요소   **patron** n. 후원자; (상점 따위의) 고객, 단골손님
reckless a. 무모한   **proportion** n. 비율; 부분   **excess** n. 과도; 무절제, 폭음   **abstemious** a. 절제하는; 음식을 삼가는

45 글의 주제 ④

| 분석 |
본문은 영국에서 많은 나이트클럽이 문을 닫을 정도로 젊은이들의 음주가 줄어들었음을 이야기하면서 그에 대해 추정 가능한 배경을 제시하고 있다. 따라서 ④가 정답으로 가장 적절하다. ① 어떤 연령층의 음주 문화가 어떻게 변했는지가 구체적이지 않다.

주제로 가장 적절한 것을 고르시오.
① 영국 음주 문화의 엄청난 변화
② 팬데믹으로 인한 영국 시장 경제의 쇠퇴
③ 영국 청년들의 무알코올 음료 선호
④ 영국 청년들 사이에서의 지속적인 과음 감소

46 반의어 ①

| 분석 |
excess가 '무절제', '폭음'의 의미로 쓰였으므로 '절주', '절제'라는 뜻의 sobriety가 반의어로 적절하다. ② 탐닉 ③ 방탕 ④ 무절제

47 내용일치 ①

| 분석 |
"2011년에서 2021년 사이, 1년 내내 한 잔의 술도 마시지 않은 16~24세 영국 청년의 비율이 19%에서 38%로 두 배 늘어났다."라고 돼 있으므로, ①이 옳지 않은 진술이다.

다음 중 옳지 않은 것은?
① 2011년 이후로 매년 알코올 소비량이 두 배 증가했다.
② Z세대는 부모 세대보다 술을 덜 마시는 경향이 있다.
③ 더 엄격한 시민 규제로 인해 많은 나이트클럽 문을 닫을 수밖에 없었다.

④ 이민자 청년들의 낮은 음주는 부분적으로는 문화적 배경에 의한 것이다.

48~50

미국의 기업들은 오랫동안 세계에서 가장 영리하고 근면한 사람들을 매혹시켜 왔다. 인적 자원을 끌어들이는 미국의 지속적인 능력은 미국이 가지고 있는 가장 과도한 특권이다. 이것이 이제 도널드 트럼프의 공화당 내 반(反)이민자주의 진영에 의해 위험에 처해 있다. 대부분의 트럼프 지지자들은 불법 이민자들을 부정적으로 본다. 많은 사람들은 그들을 추방해야 한다고 생각한다. 반이민자주의자들은 그들이 미국인들의 일자리를 빼앗고 있다고 비난한다. 일론 머스크가 이끄는 기술 친화적 트럼프 지지자들은 불법 이민자들이 내심으로는 민주당원이며 따라서 만약 그들이 시민권을 얻는다면 경합주를 진보의(민주당의) 파란색으로 바꿔 놓을 것이라고 염려하고 있다. 어느 쪽이든, 두 그룹은 한 가지 것에는 동의한다. 여기저기서 마구 모인 가난한 사람들을 받아들이는 것은 사양하겠다는 것이다. 그러나 고급 기술을 가진 전문가들에 대한 입장은 크게 갈린다. 머스크와 실리콘밸리의 동료들은 괜찮다고 말한다. 그들은 이러한 인재들을 미국을 영원히 최고 국가로 있게 해주는 혁신의 핵심으로 여긴다. 반이민자주의자들은 아니라고 반박한다. 그들은 이런 고소득 일자리가 "진짜 미국인", 즉 먼저 미국에 와 있는 사람들에게 가게끔 하고 싶어 한다.

| 어휘 |

allure v. 유혹하다, 매혹하다   **enduring** a. 지속적인, 오래가는
privilege n. 특권, 혜택   **imperil** v. 위태롭게 하다, 위험에 빠뜨리다
nativism n. 원주민보호주의, 반(反)이민자주의, 토착국민우대주의
deport v. (외국인을) 강제 추방하다   **accuse** v. 고발하다, 비난하다
grant v. 주다, 부여하다   **swing state** 경합주(미국 대선에서 공화·민주당의 승패가 매번 바뀌는 주)   **woke** a. 사회 문제에 대해 깨어 있는, 진보적인   **huddled** a. 뒤죽박죽 마구 모인, 쑤셔 넣어진   **divergent** a. (의견 등이) 서로 다른, 갈라지는   **in perpetuity** 영구히, 영원히
retort v. 반박하다, 말대꾸하다

48 빈칸완성 ③

| 분석 |

빈칸에는 '인적 자원을 끌어들이는 미국의 지속적인 능력이 미국이 가지고 있는 특권임'을 긍정하는 표현이 필요하므로, '최고의'라는 의미의 extreme, '과대한', '엄청난'이라는 의미의 excessive, '과대한', '엄청난'이라는 의미의 exorbitant는 가능하지만, '지엽적인'이라는 의미의 excursive는 빈칸에 적절하지 않다.

49 어법 ②

| 분석 |

'마음속으로는', '내심은'은 at heart로 표현한다. 그러므로 ⓒ는 at이어야 한다.

50 내용일치 ④

| 분석 |

기술 친화적 트럼프 지지자들은 찬성하는 입장이고 반이민자주의자들은 반대하는 입장이므로, ④가 옳지 않은 진술이다.

다음 중 옳지 않은 것은?
① 머스크는 불법 이민자들의 잠재적인 정치적 성향 때문에 그들을 거부한다.
② 일부 트럼프 지지자들은 첨단 기술 인력의 유입이 필수적이라고 믿는다.
③ 미국은 세계에서 가장 우수한 인적 자원을 끌어들이는 국가로서의 지위를 잃을 위험에 처해 있다.
④ 반이민자주의자들과 기술 친화적 트럼프 지지자들 모두 이민자들이 높은 임금을 받는 첨단 기술 직업을 갖는 것에 찬성한다.

한양대학교 서울 인문계 A형

TEST p. 684~699

01	①	02	①	03	③	04	④	05	⑤	06	①	07	⑤	08	④	09	①	10	④
11	②	12	④	13	④	14	⑤	15	②	16	⑤	17	②	18	④	19	②	20	④
21	②	22	④	23	⑤	24	③	25	②	26	②	27	①	28	⑤	29	③	30	⑤
31	②	32	②	33	④	34	③	35	①										

01 동의어 ①

| 어휘 |

delicate a. 섬세한 **ever-evolving** a. 계속 진화하는 **tapestry** n. 태피스트리(여러 가지 색실로 그림을 짜 넣은 직물. 또는 그런 직물을 제작하는 기술) **crucible** n. 도가니, 호된 시련(= trial) **aspiration** n. 열망 **unceasingly** ad. 끊임없이 **catalyst** n. 촉매제 **portal** n. 입구, 문 **foundation** n. 기초, 기반 **experiment** n. 실험

| 해석 |

민주주의는 집단의 의지가 섬세하게 그리고 끊임없이 진화하도록 직조되어 있는 태피스트리 같은 것으로 개인의 자유를 지키는 수호자이자 인류의 열망이 끊임없이 검증되고 정제되는 도가니(시련)이다.

03 동의어 ③

| 어휘 |

revivalism n. 복고주의 **modernism** n. 모더니즘 **fledgling** n. 신출내기, 초보자, 어린 새 **protean** a. 변화무쌍한(= mutable) **phase** n. 단계 **antithetical** a. 상반된 **programmatic** a. 계획적인 **onwards** ad. 계속, 앞으로 **morbid** a. 병적인 **prolific** a. 다산의, 다작의 **trivial** a. 하찮은 **timorous** a. 소심한

| 해석 |

아일랜드 복고주의와 모더니즘이 아직 초기이며 가장 변화무쌍한 국면에 있었던 19세기 말과 20세기 초에는 이 둘이 이후 1920년대나 30년대부터 각각이 더 계획적인 형태를 갖춘 후 많은 사람들에게 여겨진 만큼 서로 상반되게 여겨지지는 않았다.

02 동의어 ①

| 어휘 |

reputation n. 평판, 명성 **exemplify** v. 실증하다, 예증하다 **predatory** a. 약탈적인; 포식성의 **neoliberal** a. 신자유주의적인 **regressive** a. 퇴행적인 **respite** n. 휴식(= rest) **fight for** 지키기 위해 싸우다 **penance** n. 참회, 속죄 **aggression** n. 공격(성) **consensus** n. 합의 **authenticity** n. 진정성, 진품성

| 해석 |

비디오게임은 우리가 주변에서 인식하는 약탈적이고 신(新)자유주의적이며 퇴행적인 경향들을 조장하고 실증한다는 평판이 분명히 있다. 그럼에도 불구하고 수십억 명의 사람들에게 게임은 아직 살아보지 못한 삶, 아직 상상하지 못한 구조들을 구축할 수 있는 휴식의 공간이다. 따라서 게임은 그 자체로 싸워서 지켜야 한다.

04 동의어 ④

| 어휘 |

identify v. 동일시하다, 같은 것으로 인정하다 **alienating** a. 소외시키는 **exploitative** a. 착취하는 **forcibly** ad. 강제로 **cajole** v. 달래다, 구슬리다, 부추기다(= coax) **hostile** a. 적대적인 **will** n. 의지 **at odds with** ~와 충돌하는, 불화하는 **take hold of** ~을 장악[지배]하다 **manipulate** v. 조종하다 **execute** v. 실행하다 **reenact** v. 재연하다 **expel** v. 추방하다 **mitigate** v. 완화하다, 달래다 **dissociate** v. 분리시키다

| 해석 |

노동자가 자신의 자유와 즐거움을 일의 목적으로 생각하지 않을수록, "그만큼 더 면밀히 주의를 기울이도록 강요된다."라고 마르크스는 썼다. 일이 점점 더 노동자를 소외시키고 착취하는 것이 됨에 따라, "노동하는 신체기관은 힘을 쓰도록" 억지로 부추겨져야 한다. 마치 노동자의 의지와 충돌하는 외부의 적대적인 의지가 그를 장악하고 그의 주의력을 이용하여 그가 적대적 의지의 계획을 실행할 수 있도록 그의 몸을 조종하는 것 같다.

05 동의어　⑤

| 어휘 |

equal a. 평등한　**ideal** n. 이상　**admission** n. 입학 허가, 입시　**selective college** 입학 기준이 까다로운 대학　**unworkable** a. 실행 불가능한　**advantage** n. 이점, 혜택, 장점　**forgo** v. 포기하다 (= relinquish)　**come close to** ~에 가까이 가다　**consequential** a. 중대한　**belittle** v. 깎아내리다　**reserve** v. 따로 남겨두다, 예약하다　**procure** v. 얻다, 구하다　**disclose** v. 공개하다

| 해석 |

미국인들은 모두를 위한 평등한 기회라는 이상을 사랑한다. 그 이상적인 생각의 수단으로서, 매우 선별적인(경쟁이 심한) 대학들의 입학허가는 거의 정의상 실행 불가능하다. 여러 유리한 점을 가진 사람들이 자기 자녀가 그 유리한 점을 포기하길 원치 않기 때문이다. 그러나 우리가 기회 균등의 이상에 좀 더 가까워지기를 원한다면, 아주 중대한 일련의 교육적 선별들을 운영하는 것은 그 이상에 역행하고 있다는 점을 인식해야 한다.

06 동의어　①

| 어휘 |

honor n. 명예　**ineffable** a. 형언할 수 없는　**beacon** n. 신호로 보내던 등불, 봉화(= signal)　**unyielding** a. 굳건한, 양보하지 않는　**compass** n. 나침반, 길 안내자　**labyrinth** n. 미로　**ambiguity** n. 불분명함, 모호함　**unwavering** a. 확고한, 흔들림 없는　**allegiance** n. 충성　**dignity** n. 존엄　**integrity** n. 성실성, 온전함　**agency** n. 대리, 기관　**obstacle** n. 장애물　**retainer** n. 보유자; 머슴　**medium** n. 매개자, 수단

| 해석 |

인간 미덕의 형언할 수 없는 등불인 명예는 도덕적 모호함의 미로를 통과하는 영혼을 인도하는 굳건한 나침반으로 서서, 진실과 존엄, 그리고 조용한 성실성의 용기를 향한 확고한 충성을 요구한다.

07 논리완성　⑤

| 분석 |

이 행동의 특징을 나타내는 '끊임없는 아첨과 지나치게 비위를 맞추려는 열성'에 일치하는 ⑤(비굴한, 아첨하는)가 빈칸에 적절하다.

| 어휘 |

marked by ~의 특징이 있는　**constant** a. 끊임없는　**flattery** n. 아첨　**excessive** a. 과도한　**eagerness** n. 열의　**tiresome** a. 피곤하게 하는　**assertive** a. 자기주장이 강한　**apathetic** a. 무관심한　**sedulous** a. 근면한　**scrupulous** a. 양심적인; 꼼꼼한　**obsequious** a. 비굴한, 아첨하는

| 해석 |

새 인턴사원의 끊임없는 아첨과 지나치게 비위를 맞추려는 열성으로 특징지어지는 비굴한 행동은 동료들에게 금세 피곤한 것이 되었다.

08 논리완성　④

| 분석 |

subtle biases의 subtle과 microaggression의 micro가 '눈에 잘 띄지 않는 은밀함'을 의미하므로 빈칸에는 ④의 insidious(은밀한, 모르는 사이에 진행되는)가 적절하다.

| 어휘 |

discrimination n. 차별　**race** n. 인종　**gender** n. 성별, 젠더(문화적 성)　**blatant** a. 노골적인, 뻔한　**manifest** v. 표현되다　**overt** a. 노골적인　**casual** a. 격의 없는　**subtle** a. 미묘한　**bias** n. 편견, 편향　**microaggression** n. 미세한 공격, 미묘한 차별　**explicit** a. 노골적인, 공공연한　**insidious** a. 은밀한, 음흉한　**redundant** a. 불필요한, 중복된

| 해석 |

인종이나 성별에 기초한 차별은 대개 노골적인 형태로 인식되지만, 채용 관행의 미묘한 편향이나 일상적 교류 속의 미세한 차별 같은 더 은밀한 행동으로도 드러날 수 있다.

09 논리완성　①

| 분석 |

타당성이 있는 이론은 믿을만하고 받아들일 수 있는 이론인데, 한때는 받아들여지지 않고 일축되었다고 했으므로, 빈칸에는 '신빙성 없는'의 뜻인 ①이 적절하다.

| 어휘 |

dismiss v. 일축하다, 무시하다　**implausible** a. 신빙성 없는, 받아들이기 어려운　**gain** v. 얻다　**validity** n. 타당성, 유효성　**empirical** a. 경험적인　**ingenuous** a. 순진한, 솔직한　**terse** a. 간결한　**transparent** a. 투명한

| 해석 |

그 과학자의 이론은 한때 신빙성이 없다고 일축되었지만, 타당성을 뒷받침하는 최근의 발견들 덕분에 지금은 널리 받아들여지고 있다.

10 논리완성　④

| 분석 |

귀족은 상급자의 명령을 받아들이지 않는다고 보았다고 했는데, 명령은 곧 강요를 의미하므로 강요에 순응한 적이 없다고 할 수 있다. 따라서 정답은 compulsion이다.

| 어휘 |

take to ~이 좋아지다, ~에 순응하다　command v. 명령하다　dictate n. 명령, 지시　superior n. 상급자　authority n. 권위　confirm v. 확인하다　uphold v. 유지하다, 떠받치다　pretension n. 요구, 주장; 허세　acclaim n. 칭찬　intrigue n. 음모; 흥미　vulgarity n. 저속함　compulsion n. 강요, 강제　conservatism n. 보수주의

| 해석 |

귀족들은 결코 강요에 반갑게 순응한 적이 없다. 그들은 자신들이 상급자의 명령을 받아들이도록 태어난 것이 아니라 남에게 명령하도록 태어났다고 여겼다. 그들의 눈에 더 높은 권위의 의무는 그들의 주장을 확증하고 지지하는 것이었다.

11　논리완성　　②

| 분석 |

작곡가는 프리마 돈나처럼 행동할 수 없었다고 했으므로 사람들의 존경을 받지는 못했다고 추론할 수 있다. 따라서 정답은 '존경'이라는 뜻의 deference이다.

| 어휘 |

can afford to V ~할 여유가 있다　prima donna 프리마 돈나(오페라·오페라단의 주역 여성 가수)　hired hand 고용인　librettist n. 각본가, 오페라 대본작가　primary a. 중요한, 첫째가는　please v. 즐겁게 하다　impresario n. 극장 단장　public n. 대중　obstinacy n. 완고함, 고집　deference n. 존경　informality n. 격식 없음　consistency n. 일관성　rapport n. 친밀한 관계

| 해석 |

어떤 작곡가도 프리마 돈나처럼 행동할 수는 없었다. 아무도 단순한 피고용인(작곡가)을 (프리마 돈나를 대하는) 그런 종류의 존경으로 대하려 하지 않았다. 작곡가의 역할은 본질적으로 시중드는 역할이었다. 오페라 대본작가와 마찬가지로, 작곡가의 주된 목적은 극단 단장과 가수들과 (최종적으로 그리고 가장 중요하게) 관람료를 내는 대중을 즐겁게 하는 것이었다.

12　논리완성　　④

| 분석 |

유명해지고 눈에 띄게 되는 것과 반대되고 고요하고 세상으로부터 물러난 상태를 나타내는 것은 '은둔'이므로 seclusion이 적절하다.

| 어휘 |

observe v. 생각을 말하다　conspicuous a. 눈에 띄는　trap v. 가두다, 덫에 빠뜨리다　celebrity n. 유명세, 명성　reward n. 보상, 보람　extol v. 격찬[극찬]하다　immunity n. 면역 상태, 면제 상태　retirement n. 은퇴, 물러남　salvation n. 구원　solidarity n. 연대, 결속　seclusion n. 은둔, 고립　subtlety n. 미묘함

| 해석 |

에피쿠로스의 말에 따르면 일부 사람들은 유명해지고 눈에 띄게 되는 것을 원했는데, 그렇게 함으로써 타인들로부터의 안전을 얻어낼 수 있을 것이라는 생각에서였다. 그러나 사람들은 오히려 자신의 명성과 권력에 갇히게 되어 자유를 잃었다. 에피쿠로스는 은둔에서 더 큰 보람을 보았고, "고요한 삶과 세상으로부터 물러난 삶에서 오는 면역 상태"를 극찬했다.

13　논리완성　　④

| 분석 |

브이로거들이 사생활을 보여줄 때 더 진짜라고 간주된다는 사례는 공적인 것과 사적인 것 사이의 경계가 사라짐을 나타낸다. 따라서 적절한 동사는 '침식하다'는 뜻의 erodes이다.

| 어휘 |

aptly ad. 적절히　commodity n. 상품　genuine a. 진짜의　self-disclosure n. 자기노출, 자기 폭로　further ad. 더욱 더　vloger n. 비디오 블로거　authentic a. 진짜의, 진품인, 진정성 있는　curb v. 억제하다, 막다　promote v. 촉진하다, 홍보하다　elucidate v. 규명하다, 명확히 보여주다　erode v. 침식하다, 약화시키다　regulate v. 규제하다, 조절하다

| 해석 |

정체성은 "소셜 미디어 문화 산업의 주요 상품"이라고 적절히 불려왔다. 이는 리얼리티 TV 스튜디오처럼 이 산업이 진정한 자기 노출을 통해 그 상품(정체성이라는 상품)을 만들어내도록 설계해야 한다는 것을 의미한다. 이것은 더 나아가 무엇이 공적인 것으로 간주되고 무엇이 사적인 것으로 남아야 하는지의 경계를 침식한다. 예를 들어 가장 인기 있는 유튜브 채널들에 관한 연구는 브이로거들이 자신의 사생활을 드러낼 때 더 진정성 있는 것으로 평가받는다는 것을 발견한다.

14　논리완성　　⑤

| 분석 |

문학을 통한 성찰이 문학을 texture(풍부하게 하다)한다고 했는데 이것은 문학의 가치를 높여주는 것이므로 not 다음의 빈칸에는 가치를 '떨어뜨리다, 손상시키다'는 의미의 동사가 와야 한다. 따라서 undermine이 가장 적절하다.

| 어휘 |

entertainment n. 오락　instruction n. 가르침, 교육　constantly ad. 계속해서　query v. 의문을 제기하다　meditation n. 묵상, 성찰　reflection n. 성찰, 반성　underscore v. 강조하다　circumvent v. 회피하다　fortify v. 강화하다　disseminate v. 퍼뜨리다　undermine v. 손상시키다, 훼손하다, 해치다　suspicious

a. 의심하는 increasingly ad. 점점 더 sincerity n. 진정성, 진심

| 해석 |
우리는 독서를 할 때 왜 읽고 있는지를 스스로에게 묻는다. 오락을 위해서인지, 교육을 위해서인지, 과거와의 긴 대화에 참여하기 위해서인지, 아니면 상상의 세계로 도피하기 위해서인지 묻는 것이다. 우리는 문학이 가치를 지닌다는 것을 이해하지만, 우리의 독서 행위는 그 가치에 끊임없이 의문을 던진다. 이러한 성찰과 반성은 문학의 가치를 손상시키지 않는다. 오히려 문학의 질감을 풍부하게 만든다. 이로 인해 각 독서는 새롭고 낯선 경험이 된다. 아이러니와 패러디, 트윗과 문자 메시지가 많은 현 시대에 이러한 성찰은 더욱 더 중요하다. 이러한 성찰들은 진정성을 점점 더 의심하는 세상에서 우리가 문학 경험의 자리를 발견하는 데 도움을 준다.

15 논리완성   ②

| 분석 |
첫 문장의 '매끄러움과 힘들이지 않는 우아함'이라는 발레의 특징과 가장 관계 깊은 것은 ②의 '어색함 없이 복잡한 동작을 수행하는 것'이라고 추론할 수 있다.

| 어휘 |
tony a. 멋진 profile n. 개요, 프로파일 effortless a. 힘들이지 않는 grace n. 우아함 association n. 연상 docking n. 도킹, 두 우주선의 결합 commentator n. 해설자 constantly ad. 항상, 끊임없이 compare A to B A를 B에 비유하다 jock n. (남성) 운동선수 hoop n. 쇠테, 림(rim) puck n. 아이스하키 공 aesthetic a. 미적인

| 해석 |
발레의 멋진 프로파일의 특징은 발레가 매끄러움과 힘들이지 않는 우아함이라는 우수한 점들을 연상시킨다는 점이다. 이런 연상이 너무 강력한 나머지 '발레'라는 단어는 종종 조금의 어색함도 없이 수행되는 모든 복잡한 물리적 활동을 묘사하는 데 쓰인다. 두 우주선의 도킹은 "우주 발레"라 불리고, 근위병 교대도 "군사 발레"처럼 보인다. 스포츠 해설자들은 항상 운동선수들의 부드럽고 강력한 동작을 춤에 비유한다. 마치 운동선수들에게 최고의 칭찬 — 선수들이 농구공을 후프에 넣거나 아이스하키 공을 네트에 넣을 때 강력하고 효율적으로 넣기도 하지만, 너무나 우아하게 넣어서 미적으로도 즐거운 볼거리라는 칭찬 — 을 부여하는 듯하다.

① 고위 사회 계급과 연관된 기술적으로 복잡한 동작
② 조금의 어색함도 없이 수행되는 복잡한 물리적 활동
③ 장기적인 재정 투자가 필요한 대규모 사업
④ 다양한 대중에게 호소하는 문화 공연
⑤ 대중의 면밀한 감시를 받는 전문적 관행

16 논리완성   ⑤

| 분석 |
비극적 영웅은 긍정적인 점과 부정적인 점을 동시에 지닌 복합적인 존재로, 본문의 인물들(안티고네, 햄릿, 칼 폰 무어, 헤다 가블러)의 묘사에서도 그 양면성이 부각되므로, ⑤가 가장 적절하다.

| 어휘 |
frighten v. 겁을 주다, 두렵게 하다 tragic a. 비극적인 lead to ~을 초래하다 abuse v. 학대하다 companion n. 동료 relative n. 친척 inspire v. 영감을 주다 embody v. 구현하다, 상징하다

| 해석 |
비극적 영웅은 우리에게 영감을 주지만 동시에 두려움도 준다. 그들은 갈등으로 규정되며, 대개 호감이 가지 않는다. 자신을 사랑하는 사람들의 지지를 단호히 거부할 때 안티고네의 고집은 무시무시하다. 햄릿은 한때 "상냥한 왕자"였을 수 있다고 우리가 믿게 되긴 했으나, 대부분의 시간 동안 동료와 가족을 학대하며, (오필리아를 제외하고도) 최소한 다섯 명의 죽음에 책임이 있다. 쉴러의 〈군도(群盜)〉에 등장하는 칼 폰 무어 같은 낭만적 영웅이나 입센의 헤다 가블러 같은 더 현대적인 인물도 헌신을 불러일으킬 순 있지만, 함께 살기는 불가능한 인물들이다. 비극적 영웅들은 우리가 자신에게 바라는 모든 것과 우리가 두려워하거나 미워하는 모든 것, 둘 모두를 구현한다.

① 복수와 권력에 대한 우리의 욕망
② 인간의 불변성과 신의 변덕, 둘 모두
③ 우리의 공동체 신념과 행동 기준
④ 삶의 일상적 권태에서 벗어나고자 하는 우리의 욕구
⑤ 우리가 자신에게 바라는 모든 것과 우리가 두려워하거나 미워하는 모든 것, 둘 모두

17 논리완성   ②

| 분석 |
이 유전자를 가진 아시아인은 더 상호의존적이 되고 더 집단주의적이 되었다는 것은 상호의존적이고 집단주의적인 아시아 규범을 더 지키게 되었다는 말이고, 이 유전자를 가진 유럽계 미국인은 더 개인주의적이 되었다는 것도 개인주의적인 백인 미국 규범을 더 지키게 되었다는 말이므로, 결국 규범, 즉 규칙이 아시아 규칙이든 백인 미국 규칙이든 규칙을 더 잘 지키게 만든다는 뜻이 된다. 따라서 ②가 가장 적절하다.

| 어휘 |
uphold v. 유지하다 variation n. 변이 gene n. 유전자 behave v. 행동하다 endorse v. 지지하다 norm n. 규범 prevailing a. 지배하는 interdependent a. 상호의존적인 collectivism n. 집단주의 modesty n. 겸손 individualistic a. 개인주의적인

| 해석 |

개인 차원에서, 우리가 자신에 대한 사회의 시선을 얼마나 신경 쓰는지는 생물학적으로 영향을 받을 수 있다. 2014년 연구에서 심리학자 키타야마 시노부는 문화 규범을 얼마나 지지하는지는 우리가 하나의 유전자, 즉 도파민 D4 수용체 유전자의 변이 유형과 관련이 있다는 것을 발견했다. 이 유전자는 우리의 행동 방식을 바꾸는 것이 아니라, 우리가 환경의 지배적 규범을 얼마나 지지하는지에 영향을 끼친다. 이 유전자의 특정 변이를 지닌 아시아인들은 더 상호의존적이 되었다. 그들은 사회적 조화, 집단주의, 겸손과 관련된 가치를 더 지지할 가능성이 더 많았다. 반면, 똑같은 유전자 변이를 가진 유럽계 미국인은 전통적으로 백인 미국인의 규범인 더 개인주의 성격을 띠게 되었다. 이 유전자는 당신을 규칙이 무엇이든 그 규칙을 더 따르는 사람으로 만든다.

① 집단의 이익을 위해 개인의 손실을 감수하는데 더 열린 태도를 갖게 한다
② 규칙이 무엇이든 그 규칙을 더 따르는 사람으로 만든다
③ 문화적 맥락에 상관없이 덜 순응하는 사람으로 만든다
④ 미래의 보상을 위해 즉각적인 쾌락을 덜 추구하게 한다
⑤ 이점이 분명하더라도 선도자가 덜 되게 만든다

18 논리완성 ④

| 분석 |

빈칸 바로 앞에서 '핵심은 어려운 시절에 단순히 살아남는 것만이 아니라'라고 했으므로 빈칸에는 단순한 생존이 아닌 번영과 관련된 발전적 내용인 '변화를 위협이 아니라 기회로 받아들이는 능력'이 들어있는 ④가 가장 적절하다. ① 전통 보존과 회복력, ② 불확실성 극복, ③ 안전성, ⑤ 점진적 변화와 장기적 안정, 등은 모두 생존을 위한 것에 가깝다.

| 어휘 |

internal strife 내부 갈등 **instability** n. 불안정 **invasion** n. 침략 **endure** v. 오래 버티다 **legacy** n. 유산 **imprint** v. 각인시키다 **remarkable** a. 놀라운 **adaptation** n. 적응 **challenge** n. 난제 **flourish** v. 번영하다, 번창하다 **underlying** a. 근원적인, 밑에 깔린 **transcend** v. 초월하다 **embrace** v. 포용하다, 수용하다

| 해석 |

역사적으로 많은 위대한 문명이 흥망성쇠를 겪었는데, 대개는 내부 갈등, 경제 불안정, 외부 침입을 이유로 무너졌다. 그러나 지속된 문명들도 있고, 그 문명의 유산들은 인간 문화의 구조 속에 각인되어 있다. 이들 회복력이 있던 사회들은 실패나 위기에 면역력이 있었던 것이 아니라, 놀라운 적응 능력을 보여주어 생존뿐 아니라 번영하게 되는 방식으로 어려움에 적응했다. 일부 학자들은 이러한 적응력이 권력, 문화, 지식의 힘 등, 인간 경험을 형성하는 근본적인 힘을 깊이 이해하는 일과 관련되어 있다고, 그 힘을 통해 문명은 자신의 한계를 극복하여 새로운 가능성을 포용할 수 있었다고 주장한다. 그러나 핵심은 어려운 시절에 단순히 살아남는 것만이 아니라, 예측 불가능성을 완화하고 변화를 위협이 아닌 기회로 받아들이는 능력을 배양하는 것이다.

① 핵심 가치와 전통을 보존하여 회복력을 키우는 것
② 오래된 관행을 유지하여 불확실성을 전략적으로 극복하는 것
③ 외부 영향을 최소화하고 내부 강점에 집중하여 안정성을 키우는 것
④ 예측 불가능성을 완화하고 변화를 위협이 아닌 기회로 받아들이는 능력을 배양하는 것
⑤ 지장을 주는 급격한 변화보다 점진적인 변화를 우선시하여 장기적 안정을 확보하는 틀을 확립하는 것

19 논리완성 ②

| 분석 |

첫 번째 빈칸의 경우, 고도로 추상적인 개념과 일반 대중이 이해하기 어려운 복잡한 수학 모델을 사용한다고 했으므로 '난해하다'는 뜻으로 esoteric이 적절하고, 두 번째 빈칸의 경우, 극복할 수 없어 보이는 역설과 비논리적인 질문에도 불구하고 지식의 한계를 넘어 새로운 것을 알아가고 있다고 한 것이 '희망적이고 낙관적인 태도'를 나타내므로 optimism이 적절하다.

| 어휘 |

verge on ~에 근접하다 **collegial** a. 대학의 **fulfillment** n. 성취 **esoteric** a. 난해한 **optimism** n. 낙관주의 **speculative** a. 사변적인 **despondency** n. 낙담 **contentious** a. 논쟁적인 **impenetrable** a. 꿰뚫을 수 없는; 불가해한 **disillusionment** n. 환멸 **quantum mechanics** 양자 역학(미시 물리학 분야) **abstruse** a. 난해한 **boundary** n. 경계 **tenet** n. 신조, 주의, 교리

| 해석 |

양자역학 분야에서는, 물리학자들이 현재 과학적 이해의 경계에 의문을 제기하는 현상을 설명하려 함에 따라 종종 난해한 수준에 가까운 토론들이 일어나고 있다. 이 논의들은 매우 높은 지성의 성격을 띠고 있으나, 학자들이 고도로 추상적인 개념과 일반 대중이 이해하기 어려운 복잡한 수학 모델을 사용하기 때문에 난해해진다. 그러나 이 주제의 종종 모호한 성질에도 불구하고 학계는 새로운 발견의 가능성 때문에 계속해서 활기를 유지하고 있다. 논쟁들을 추진하는 것은 깊은 낙관주의 의식인데, 연구자들이 겉으로 보기에 극복할 수 없는 역설과 전통 논리를 거스르는 질문들에 직면할 때도 이미 알려진 것들의 한계를 넘어 새로운 것을 알아가고 있기 때문이다. 일부 비평가들이 이러한 아이디어들이 거의 추측에 불과하다고 주장하긴 하지만, 지식에 대한 끊임없는 추구는 여전히 이 학문분야의 핵심 신조로 남아 있다.

20~21

우리의 피부는 털이 더 많은 다른 척추동물들의 피부에 비해

이상할 정도로 부드럽다. 털이 많은 피부는 추위의 차단, 마찰이나 햇볕 화상으로부터의 보호 측면에서 확실히 유리하기 때문에 털이 없는 동물은 대부분 지하나 물속에서 산다. 하지만 털이 없을 때의 큰 이점은 체온을 낮게 유지할 수 있다는 점이다. 인간은 매일 최대 12리터의 물 같은 땀을 생성할 수 있는 땀샘을 가지고 있으며, 이 땀은 쉽게 증발하여 체온을 낮춘다. 인간의 먼 조상은 숲을 떠나 사바나 초원으로 이동했을 때 에너지를 많이 쓰는 큰 뇌를 유지하기 위해 물, 식용 식물, 고기를 찾아 뜨거운 태양 아래 많은 시간을 걸어 다녔다. 무더운 날, 땀을 많이 흘릴 수 있는 능력 덕분에 우리는, 적어도 일부는 장거리 마라톤에서 말을 이길 수 있었다. 그러나 이러한 과열 문제를 해결하기 위해 우리는 민감한 피부를 감염에 더 취약하게 만드는 위험을 감수해야 했다. 각 땀샘은 100,000마리의 박테리아가 군집을 이루고 서식하는 오아시스로, 우리는 이 박테리아들을 사춘기를 제외하고는 조용히 용납하는데, 사춘기 동안에는 호르몬의 급증이 여드름균의 먹이인 피지의 생성을 자극하여 보기 흉한 검은 여드름을 유발한다. 우리의 성은 성 밖의 일부 떠돌이 캠핑객들에게 남은 음식 찌꺼기를 먹도록 승인하는 셈이다. 이처럼 비교적 털이 없어 체온을 낮출 수 있었던 장점은 피부가 화상이나 상처로 인해 쉽게 없어지면서 부상과 감염에 취약해질 수 있는 단점과 비교해 보아야 한다.

| 어휘 |

curiously ad. 희한하게도 **hirsute** a. 털이 많은 **hairy** a. 털이 많은 **insulation** n. 차단, 분리; 격리 **abrasion** n. 마찰, 마모 **evaporate** v. 증발하다 **cool down** 식히다 **trekking** n. 여행, 등산, 트레킹, 걷기 **outcompete** v. ~을 능가하다. 이기다. ~보다 더 성공적이다 **overheating** n. 과열 **adolescence** n. 청소년기 **stimulate** v. 자극하다 **propionibacterium acne** 여드름 균 **unsightly** a. 꼴사나운, 흉한 **sanction** v. 승인하다 **itinerant** a. 여행하는 **feed on** ~을 먹고 살다 **scrap** n. 찌꺼기 **weigh against** ~와 비교검토하다, ~에 불리하다 **infection** n. 감염

20 내용일치 ④

| 분석 |

except during adolescence, when a flood of hormones stimulates oil production 부분을 보면 사춘기 호르몬이 피지를 '억제하는' 것이 아니라 '증가시킨다'고 되어 있다. 따라서 ④가 본문의 내용과 거리가 멀다.

윗글의 내용과 가장 거리가 먼 것은?
① 털이 없는 동물들은 대부분 열과 추위에 덜 노출되는 환경에 서식한다.
② 털이 없는 피부는 체온을 떨어뜨리는 데 있어 털이 많은 피부보다 더 효과적이다.
③ 땀을 흘릴 수 있는 능력은 사바나 초원에서 생존 활동을 하는 데 특히 중요했다.
④ 사춘기 동안 호르몬은 피지 분비를 억제하여 피부 문제를 유발한다.
⑤ 체온을 조절하는 피부의 능력은 더 큰 취약성을 대가로 치르고 누리는 것이다.

21 동의어 ②

| 분석 |

동사 sanction은 '법률에 제재 규정을 두다'라는 뜻도 있지만 여기서는 '재가하다, 인가하다, 승인하다'는 뜻으로 쓰였으므로 ②가 정답이다.

밑줄 친 "sanctions"의 뜻과 가장 가까운 것은?
① 방출하다
② 승인하다
③ 자극하다
④ 버리다
⑤ 감독하다

22 글의 주제 ②

| 분석 |

이 글은 멸종 위기의 생물을 보호하는 일에 있어서는 "모든 생명이 보호받고 유지되는 이상적인 낙원을 회복한다는 유토피아적 기대도 하지 말고, 멸종 안 될 생물은 없다고 미리 생각하여 모든 멸종 방지 노력이 무의미하다는 디스토피아적 기대도 하지 말아야 한다"는 내용이므로 ②가 글의 주제로 적절하다.

| 어휘 |

ecological a. 생태계의 **extinction** n. 멸종 **deem** v. 간주하다, 생각하다 **in advance** 미리 **impending** a. 임박한, 곧 닥칠 **implore** v. 간청하다 **descriptive** a. 기술하는, 묘사하는 **ethical** a. 윤리적인 **inclusive of** ~이 포함된 **redeem** v. 구원하다, 해방하다 **endangered** a. 위험에 처한 **entail** v. 수반하다 **perish** v. 소멸하다 **anthropogenic** a. 인간 중심적인 **salvational** a. 구원의 **vigilance** n. 경계 **necessitate** v. ~을 요구하다, 필요로 하다

| 해석 |

멸종이 더 이상 없는 생태학적 시나리오는 없지만, 오늘날 그 어떤 멸종도 허용 가능하다고 미리 생각해서는 안 되며, 모든 임박한 멸종은 예방을 호소한다. 생태학은 단지 생태계를 기술하는 과학일 뿐 아니라, 모든 생명을 위한 더 나은 세상을 상상하는 창조적 노력을 포함하는 윤리 프로젝트이기도 하다. 멸종을 생태학적 실천으로 다룬다는 것은 생명이나 죽음의 고통 자체로부터 동물을 해방하거나 구하려는 것을 의미하지 않는다. 멸종 위기에 처한 동물을 돌본다는 것은 구원의 결과를 고집하지도 않고 생태계를 위험이 없는 유토피아 공간으로 이상화하지도 않고 인간 중심적인 명분으로 이

들이 소멸하지 않도록 보존하는 일을 수반한다. 멸종의 역사와 현재 멸종을 방지하는 쪽으로의 경계의 역사를 연구하는 것은 보호받고 유지되는 생명의 이상적 낙원을 회복하는 데 우리로 하여금 매진하게 하지도 않고, 멸종이 모든 것을 미리 무의미하게 만들기 때문에 아무것도 중요한 게 없다는 디스토피아적 비전을 필요로 하지도 않는다.

다음 글의 주제로 가장 적절한 것을 고르시오.
① 지구의 생명다양성을 보존하는 데 있어서의 실질적 어려움
② 멸종 위기 생물을 돌보는 데 있어 균형 잡힌 기대의 필요성
③ 지구온난화에 맞서 낙관주의를 유지하는 일의 불가능성
④ 황폐해진 동물 생태에 대한 더 엄격한 기록의 필요성
⑤ 멸종 위기종의 유전자를 재구성할 때의 윤리적 딜레마

23 글의 주제   ⑤

| 분석 |
본문 중간의 The point is to recognize that, like other pillars of the welfare state in capitalist societies, the central bank performs a function of managing risks and reducing uncertainty를 보면 중앙은행이 위험 관리라는 복지국가적 역할을 수행한다고 되어 있다. 따라서 정답은 ⑤이다.

| 어휘 |
macroeconomic a. 거시경제의 **principle** n. 원칙 **welfare state** 복지국가 **conceive** v. 구상하다, 잉태하다 **countercyclical** a. 경기순환에 대응하는, 경기를 조정하는 **overall** a. 전반적인 **uncertainty** n. 불확실성 **conceptual** a. 개념상의 **pillar** n. 기둥, 축 **capitalist society** 자본주의 사회 **institution** n. 제도 **in accord with** ~에 맞추어, 일치하여 **distribution** n. 분배

| 해석 |
중앙은행과 복지국가가 잉태될 때의 거시경제 원칙은 동일했다. 즉, 경기순환에 대응하는 정책을 통해 개인을 (물가 및 금융 불안정을 비롯한) 경제적 위험에서 보호하고 전반적인 불확실성을 줄인다는 원칙이다. 그러나 중앙은행과 복지국가 간의 이러한 역사적·개념적 연계성은 좀체 명시적으로 언급되지 않는다. 이 연계성에 주목한다고 해서 중앙은행이 복지 혜택에 돈을 대야 한다는 제안을 하려는 것은 아니다. 요점은 자본주의 사회에서 복지국가의 역할을 하는 다른 기둥들처럼, 중앙은행도 위험을 관리하고 불확실성을 줄이는 기능을 수행한다는 것을 인정하는 것이다. 위험이 진화하듯, 이러한 제도들도 진화해야 한다. 21세기 경제 인류학자 Karl Polanyi의 말처럼, 중앙은행의 정책은 시간이 지남에 따라 국가의 성격에 일치되게 진화하는 개입주의적 형태이다. 중앙은행의 정책은 사회 내 분배와 권력에 대해 내리는 선택을 반영한다.

다음 글의 주제로 가장 적절한 것을 고르시오.
① 중앙은행의 국가로부터의 독립에 대한 신뢰의 상실
② 금융 불안정에 대응하는 중앙은행의 도전 과제
③ 통화정책 수립 때 신중함을 기해야 할 필요성
④ 복지국가에서 중앙은행으로의 책임의 이동
⑤ 중앙은행과 복지국가 사이의 기능적 유사성

24 글의 요지   ③

| 분석 |
글 중간의 On the other hand 전후의 내용을 비교해 보면 이 글은 장소적 개념에서 시간적 개념으로, 그리고 가능성의 개념으로 유토피아의 개념이 변화한 것을 정리한 글이라고 할 수 있다. 따라서 유토피아 개념의 진화를 나타내는 ③이 정답이다.

| 어휘 |
designate v. 지명하다 **distant** a. 먼 **undergo** v. 거치다, 겪다 **transpose** v. 옮기다 **wishland** n. 이상향, 소망의 땅 **topos** n. 토포스(자주 등장하는 주제나 개념) **content** n. 내용

| 해석 |
처음에 토머스 모어는 유토피아를 어떤 장소, 즉 먼 남쪽 바다에 있는 섬으로 지정했다. 이 지정은 훗날 변화를 겪어 공간을 떠나 시간으로 진입했다. 사실, 유토피아주의자들, 특히 18세기, 19세기의 유토피아주의자들은 소망의 땅을 더욱 더 미래로 옮겼다. 다시 말해 유토피아는 공간에서 시간으로 개념의 전환이 일어난 것이다. 토머스 모어에게 소망의 땅은 먼 섬에 여전히 준비되어 있었지만 나는 그곳에 없다. 반면 유토피아가 미래로 옮겨지면, 내가 그곳에 없을 뿐만 아니라 유토피아 자체도 아직 존재하지 않게 된다. 이 섬은 존재조차 하지 않는 것이다. 하지만 그것은 말도 안 되는 난센스나 절대적 환상 같은 것은 아니라, 오히려 가능성의 의미에서 아직 존재하지 않는 것이다. 우리가 그 유토피아를 위해 뭔가 할 수만 있다면 그것은 그곳에 존재할 수 있을 것이라는 것이다. 우리가 그곳에 갈 경우에로 그치는 것이 아니라, 그곳에 (실제로) 가므로 유토피아 섬은 가능성의 바다에서 떠오르는데, 그것은 유토피아이지만 새로운 내용을 가진 유토피아이다.

다음 글의 요지로 가장 적절한 것을 고르시오.
① 유토피아는 이론적 구성물에 불과한 건 아니더라도 점점 도달 불가능한 환상으로 여겨진다.
② 유토피아는 역사적, 정치적 격변을 견딜 수 있는 불변의 모델을 제시한다.
③ 유토피아는 물리적 장소에서 미래 가능성, 즉 잠재성의 의미로 변화해왔다.
④ 유토피아는 공상적 이상을 투사하기보다는 과거의 구체적 현실을 복원하려 한다.
⑤ 유토피아는 가장 초기 형태에서는 쉽게 찾고 접근할 수 있는 장소를 가리켰다.

25 글의 요지 ③

| 분석 |

이 글의 핵심은 "The earth is not simply among the stars, it is of the stars." 즉, 인간과 지구가 우주와 내부적으로 연결된 우주의 일부라는 생각이므로 정답은 ③이다.

| 어휘 |

lonely a. 고독한, 외로운 **highly** ad. 매우 **unlikely** a. 가능성이 낮은 **profoundly** ad. 심오하게, 깊이 **anthropocentric** a. 인간 중심적인 **biocentric** a. 생명 중심적인 **ignore** v. 무시하다 **devalue** v. 평가 절하하다 **non-living** a. 비생물의 **failed** a. 실패한 **solar system** 태양계 **emerge** v. 나타나다, 등장하다 **nebular** a. 성운의 **externally** ad. 외부적으로 **circulation** n. 순환 **entangled** a. 얽힌, (문제나 상황에) 휘말린

| 해석 |

사람들은 종종 지구를 "외로운" 행성이라 부른다. 지구 밖에서 다른 인간이나 생명의 증거를 발견하지 못했기 때문이다. 설령 지구 바깥에 생명이 없는 것이 사실이라 해도, 그런 생각은 가능성도 낮지만 지구에 대한 아주 인간 중심적, 생명 중심적 사고방식이다. 이러한 생각은 우리가 지구 및 더 넓은 우주에 있는 비생명적 과정들과 의존 관계를 맺고 있다는 점을 무시하고 평가절하하게 만들기 때문이다. 그럴 때 우리는 특정 생명 형태를 기준 삼아 세상을 그 기준에 미치지 못한 실패작으로 간주하게 된다. 반면, 우리 태양계 전체는 동일한 성운의 분자 기체 및 먼지 구름에서 나타났을 가능성이 크다. 따라서 우리는 우리 태양계에서 다른 행성의 순환과 외부적으로가 아니라 내부적으로 얽혀 있으며 상호연관을 맺고 있다. 지구는 단순히 별들 중 하나가 아니라 별들(우주)의 일부인 것이다.

다음 글의 요지로 가장 적절한 것을 고르시오.
① 지구의 과정은 우리가 과거에 생각했던 것보다 더 예측 불가능하다.
② 지구상의 생명은 확률이 매우 낮은 우연이 기적적으로 겹쳐 생겨났다.
③ 인간의 생명은 그것을 만들어낸 우주와 분리된 적이 없다.
④ 계몽주의 사고는 자연에 대한 인간 중심적 이해를 강화시켰다.
⑤ 우리는 인류 출현 이전의 지구의 역사에 대해 너무 모른다.

26 글의 제목 ②

| 분석 |

이 글은 호지슨과 페티트가 제시한 가설을 소개한 내용이다. 가설에서 네안데르탈인 수렵인들이 그들이 사냥하는 동물들의 윤곽이 동굴 벽에 비치는 것을 보았을 것이라고 했는데, 이 동물의 윤곽을 벽에 그린 것이 그들의 동굴 예술이 된 것이고 가설은 기존의 이론에 더하는 아직 확증되지 않은 새로운 이론이므로 ②가 제목으로 적절하다.

| 어휘 |

neuroscience n. 신경과학 **condition** v. 조건화하다, 훈련하다 **recognize** v. 알아보다 **ambiguous** a. 모호한, 불분명한 **attune** v. 맞추다, 조율하다, 순응시키다 **hypothesize** v. 가설을 세우다 **camouflaged** a. 위장한 **lurk** v. 숨어있다 **outline** n. 윤곽 **flicker** v. 깜빡이다 **crag** n. 울퉁불퉁한 바위 **varicolored** a. 얼룩덜룩한 **stalagmite** n. 동굴의 석순 **mottled** a. 얼룩의, 잡색의

| 해석 |

2018년, 데렉 호지슨과 폴 페티트는 케임브리지 고고학 저널에 논문을 발표했는데, 이 논문은 얼굴이나 동물 같은 특정 대상을 인식하도록 조건화된 사람들은 모호한 패턴 속에서도 그 대상을 알아보게 된다는 점을 보여주는 신경과학 연구를 지적했다. 예를 들어, 우리는 구름에서 얼굴 모양을 보도록 순응되어 있다. 호지슨과 페티트는 네안데르탈인 수렵인들이 어디에나 숨어 있는 위장 동물들을 찾도록 조건화되어 있었기 때문에, 그들이 살았던 어두운 동굴에서 횃불의 깜빡이는 빛 속에서 같은 동물들의 윤곽을 보았을 것이라는 가설을 세웠다. 스페인의 엘 카스티요 동굴에서 64,000년 된 이미지와 조각을 연구하면서, 고고학자들(호지슨과 페티트)은 네안데르탈인들이 울퉁불퉁한 바위들과 얼룩덜룩한 벽이 자신들의 세계를 채운 이미지들로 "살아나는" 것을 보았다고 믿게 되었다. 예를 들어, 꼭대기가 둥글고 어두운 얼룩무늬가 있는 동굴 석순은 이 빙하기 네안데르탈인들에게는 아마도 단지 동굴 바닥에서 솟아오른 바위가 아니라, 두 발로 일어서는 곰으로 해석되었을 것이다.

다음 글의 제목으로 가장 적절한 것을 고르시오.
① 영적 표현의 진화상의 이점
② 네안데르탈인의 동굴 예술의 기원에 대한 새 이론
③ 구름과의 대화: 언어와 네안데르탈인의 예술
④ 가장 초기 인류 종교에 대한 과학적 관점
⑤ 춤추는 그림자들: 동굴이 네안데르탈인의 미신을 밝혀내는 방식

27 글의 제목 ①

| 분석 |

전통적인 식충식물뿐만 아니라 다른 식물들도 간접적인 방법으로 곤충을 통해 질소를 얻는다는 사실을 다루는 내용이다. 이는 식물의 육식 형태가 확장되었음을 의미하므로 ①이 가장 적절한 제목이다.

| 어휘 |

precisely ad. 정확히 **carnivore** n. 육식성 생물 **digest** v. 소화하다 **obtain** v. 얻다, 획득하다 **nutrient** n. 영양분 **nourishment** n. 영양 **Paulonia tomentosa** 참오동나무 **notice** v. 주목하다 **insect** n. 곤충 **corpse** n. 사체, 시체 **sticky** a. 끈끈한 **secrete** v. 분비하다 **poisonous** a. 독성이 있는 **decompose** v. 분해되다 **release** v. 방출하다 **nitrogen** n. 질소 **absorb** v. 흡수하다

waste product 노폐물

| 해석 |

불과 몇 년 전까지만 해도, 식충식물로 정확히 정의된 특정 식물 종들만이 작은 동물을 소화하여 필요한 영양분을 얻는 능력이 있는 것으로 여겨졌다. 하지만 최근 연구들에 따르면, 동물성 영양분을 활용하는 식물은 매우 광범위하다. 감자 식물이나 담배 식물, 또는 참오동나무(중국에서 기원했으나 유럽과 미국에서도 아주 흔해지고 있다.) 같은 훨씬 더 이국적인 식물의 잎을 본 적이 있다면, 그 위에 작은 곤충 시체가 흔히 있다는 것을 알아차렸을 것이다. 이 식물들이 곤충을 소화시키지 않는다면, 이들의 잎은 왜 곤충을 죽이는 끈적이거나 독성 있는 물질을 분비할까? 그 이유는 간단하고, 생각해 보면 매우 합리적이다. 곤충의 시체가 바로 소화되지 않더라도, 땅에 떨어져 분해되면서 식물에 필요한 질소를 방출하고, 잎 위에 남은 곤충들은 식물 위의 박테리아에게 영양을 공급해서, 그 박테리아가 질소 풍부한 노폐물을 쉽게 섭취하게 된다.

다음 글의 제목으로 가장 적절한 것을 고르시오.
① 파리지옥을 넘어서: 확장된 형태의 식물의 육식
② 질소 결핍이 식충식물에 끼치는 영향
③ 뿌리 지능의 핵심부에 있는 비밀 신호들
④ 잎에서 잎으로: 식물 소통의 과학
⑤ 왜 식충식물은 보존의 위협에 직면해 있는가

28　내용일치　⑤

| 분석 |

본문에서는 brat이 세련되거나 고전적인 문화적 가치(refined and classic values)를 대표하기는커녕 오히려 기존의 규범과 예절, 순응을 거부하고, 실험적이고 대담한 자율성을 추구하는 것으로 묘사되어 있으므로 ⑤는 거리가 멀다.

| 어휘 |

brat n. 원래 버릇없는 녀석, 개구쟁이라는 뜻으로 쓰임　**emerge** v. 나타나다　**emblem** n. 상징　**encapsulate** v. 압축하다, 요약하다　**unapologetically** ad. 염치없이　**hedonistic** a. 쾌락주의(자)의　**derogatory** a. 비판적인, 경멸하는　**connotation** n. 함축의미, 속뜻　**reclaim** v. 교정하다, 고치다, 재생하다　**signify** v. 의미하다　**ethos** n. 정신, 기풍, 풍조　**defiance** n. 반항　**decorum** n. 예의범절　**conformity** n. 순응　**bold** a. 과감한　**resonate** v. 울리다, 공명하다　**empowerment** n. 자율권, 권한 부여　**underscore** v. 강조하다　**autonomy** n. 자율성

| 해석 |

2024년에 brat이라는 용어는 문화적·언어적 상징으로 등장했으며, 더 젊은 세대, 특히 Z세대 사이에서 유행하는 반항적이고 염치없이 쾌락주의적인 태도를 압축해 담고 있다. 관습적인 경멸적 의미와는 달리, brat은 자기표현, 자신감, 장난스러운 반항의 풍조를 의미하는 개념으로 교정되었다. 이러한 교정은 개성을 찬양하고 전통적인 예절 및 순응의 규범을 거부하는 더 넓은 사회적 변화를 반영한다. Charli XCX와 같은 예술가들과 다른 이들은 brat 미학을 옹호해 왔는데, 이것은 자유분방한 태도와 대담하고 실험적인 스타일이 결합된 것으로, 권한부여와 자기 결정권이라는 현대적 개념과 깊이 공명한다. Brat의 부상은 Collins 사전의 올해의 단어로 인정받은 사건을 비롯하여 단순한 유행이나 언어 트렌드 이상의 문화적 울림을 강조한다. 이 낱말의 부상은 빠르게 진화하는 사회 지형에서 정체성과 자율성의 선언이다.

다음 글의 내용과 가장 거리가 먼 것은?
① Brat은 특히 Z세대 사이에서 쾌락을 반항적으로 추구하는 문화를 상징하는 용어가 되었다.
② Brat이라는 용어는 원래의 부정적인 의미를 넘어서 긍정적인 자기표현을 뜻하게 되었다.
③ Brat의 교정은 획일성을 강요하는 사회 기준을 거부하려는 일반적인 흐름을 나타낸다.
④ Charli XCX 같은 아티스트들은 현재의 자율성 개념을 긍정하는 brat 태도와 스타일을 장려해왔다.
⑤ Brat 미학은 세련되고 고전적인 문화적 가치를 대표하는 것으로 Collins 사전에 의해 강조되었다.

29　내용일치　③

| 분석 |

③은 본문의 내용과 반대되는 정보이다. 본문에서는 "periods in which ~ respiration that is slightly more irregular than in quiet sleep" 즉, 활동 수면 중 호흡이 조용한 수면보다 약간 더 불규칙하다고 했으므로 ③이 거리가 가장 멀다.

| 어휘 |

typically ad. 전형적으로　**newborn** n. 신생아　**significant** a. 중요한, 의미심장한, 상당한　**influence** v. 영향을 끼치다　**behavioral** a. 행동의　**manifestation** n. 표명, 명시　**grimace** n. 찡그림　**occasional** a. 가끔씩의　**twitching** n. 경련　**limb** n. 팔다리　**respiration** n. 호흡　**slightly** ad. 약간　**irregular** a. 불규칙적인　**adolescence** n. 사춘기, 청소년기

| 해석 |

부모는 보통 신생아의 수면이 일정한 리듬이나 뚜렷한 낮-밤의 차이 없이 이루어지는 모습을 본다. 생후 약 두 달이 되면 리듬 패턴의 초기 요소들이 나타나지만, 이는 환경과 밀접한 관련은 없다. 생후 4~5개월쯤 되면 수면은 빛과 어둠에 더 많은 영향을 받게 되며, 대부분의 수면이 밤에 이루어진다. 신생아 시기 및 생후 첫 몇 달 동안, 부모는 가끔 활동적 수면의 행동 특징을 관찰할 수 있다. 활동적 수면 시기에는 가끔씩의 찡그림, 팔다리의 빠른 경련, 때때로 조용히 잘 때보다 약간 더 불규칙한 호흡 등이 나타난다. 총 수면 시간은 신생아 때 하루 최대 16시간에서 시작해 두 살 무렵에는 10~12시간으로 줄어들고, 청소년기까지 계속 감소한다. 아동기에는 저녁 중반쯤 잠드는 경향이 있지만, 청소년기에는 더 늦게 자려는 경향이 나타난다.

다음 글의 내용과 가장 거리가 먼 것은?
① 생후 두 달 된 아기의 수면은 환경 요인의 영향을 크게 받지 않는다.
② 생후 다섯 달 된 아기의 수면은 조명의 영향을 받는다.
③ 활동적 수면 중에는 호흡이 조용한 수면보다 더 규칙적으로 일어난다.
④ 나이가 들수록 아이들은 총 수면 시간이 점차 줄어든다.
⑤ 청소년은 아이들보다 더 늦게 자려는 경향이 있다.

30~31

SF(공상과학소설)의 지배적 온상인 앵글로-아메리칸 문화는 대륙 문화에 비해 도시 생활에 대해 부정적인 시각을 더 자주, 더 쉽게 취하는 경향이 있다. 미국의 반도시적 사고방식은 지적 전통과 대중문화를 통해 쉽게 찾아볼 수 있다. 토머스 제퍼슨이 도시를 정치적 공동체의 암과 상처라고 비유했을 때, 그는 그 후 200년간 미국 정치에 울려 퍼져온 풍조를 보여주었던 것이다. 19세기, 사회적 혼란과 정치적 무질서의 용광로로서의 도시에 대한 공포는 19세기 말과 20세기 초 가상의 미래에 되풀이해서 등장한 도시 디스토피아를 계속 부추겼다. 심지어 21세기에도, 미국인들 중 《소수(→ 다수)》는 대도시 생활보다 작은 마을에서의 삶을 이상적으로 여긴다. 대도시 생활은 덜 만족스럽고, 덜 진실하며, 덜 건강하고, 더 위험하고, 더 소외감을 준다는 생각 때문이다. 그러나 사회과학의 종합적 연구 결과는 그렇게 명확하지 않다. 미국 도시 거주자들의 사회적 관계망 밀도는 소도시 거주자들과 거의 비슷하며, 이들은 단지 혈연 중심의 친족 관계에서 멀어져 공통 관심사를 기반으로 한 집단으로 옮겨갔을 뿐이다. 심지어 라틴아메리카와 남아시아의 슬럼가나 판자촌도 농촌에서 온 빈민들에게 더 나은 의료, 교육, 일자리 기회를 제공하는 기회의 장소이다. 개발도상국에서는 도시 거주자들이 농촌 거주자보다 행복하다고 말할 가능성이 더 높다. 도시는 문화의 인큐베이터, 기술 혁신의 중심지, 그리고 개혁가들이 진보적 제도를 도입하고 실험하는 곳이다. 창조적 환경으로서의 도시는 산업과 대학, 예술가와 기업가들이 얽혀 있는 네트워크이다.

| 어휘 |

seedbed n. 온상 **dominant** a. 지배적인 **negative** a. 부정적인
trace v. 추적하다 **antiurban** a. 반도시적인 **sore** n. 상처
cauldron n. 가마솥 **resonate** v. 울리다, 공명하다 **chaos** n. 혼돈 **dystopia** n. 디스토피아 **alienating** a. 소외[고립]시키는
density n. 밀도 **skew** v. 비스듬히 움직이다 **incubator** n. 배양기
innovator n. 혁신자 **entrepreneur** n. 기업가

30 글의 제목 ⑤

| 분석 |

이 글은 미국 문화가 도시를 바라보는 두 가지 시각을 보여주고 도시에 대한 긍정적 인식이 사실이라는 점을 두 번째 문단에서 드러내므로 ⑤의 "도시 생활: 인식과 현실의 격차"가 제목으로 가장 어울린다.

윗글의 제목으로 가장 적절한 것은?
① 도시 생활이 정신 건강에 미치는 영향
② 농촌과 도시: 어느 디스토피아 이야기
③ 도시 환경은 어떻게 혁신을 가능하게 하는가?
④ 지속 가능한 도시 계획을 위한 몇 가지 지침
⑤ 도시 생활: 인식과 현실의 격차

31 문맥상 적절하지 않은 단어 고르기 ③

| 분석 |

첫 문장에서 '앵글로-아메리칸 문화는 대륙 문화에 비해 도시 생활에 대해 부정적인 시각을 더 자주, 더 쉽게 취하는 경향이 있다'고 했으므로 도시에 대해 21세기에도 많은 이들이 부정적으로 본다는 맥락이 되어야 한다. 따라서 ③의 minority를 majority로 바꾸어야 한다.

32~33

앙리 베르그송에 따르면, 웃음은 인간 삶의 유기적 역동성에 기계적인 경직성이 부과될 때 생겨난다. 베르그송에게 웃음은 사람들이 자동적이거나 융통성 없는 행동 패턴에 빠져 조화로운 사회적 상호작용에 필요한 유동성과 즉흥성을 무너뜨리는 행동이나 상황을 해결하는 깊은 사회적 교정제로 기능한다. 베르그송의 유명한 주장에 따르면, 웃음은 부조화를 "조롱하고" 교정하도록 설계되어 있어 사회 집단 내의 균형을 회복시키는 "사회적 의미"를 지니고 있다. 반면, 오스카 와일드는 웃음을 아이러니와 전복의 시선을 통해 개념화한다. 웃음은 예리한 도구로서의 위트(기지)를 휘둘러 사회 관습을 지탱하는 위선과 부조리를 드러내는 것이다. 와일드는 능란하게 만들어낸 역설과 기대를 뒤엎는 장난스러운 표현을 통해 유머를 조직해내어, 웃음을 끌어내되, 도덕적 책무로서 끌어내는 것이 아니라, 사회 관습의 우스꽝스러움과 의도된 책략을 유쾌하게 확인해주는 것으로서 끌어낸다. 베르그송과 와일드는 함께 서로 다르지만 보완적인 웃음의 차원들을 밝혀준다. 즉, 베르그송은 웃음을 사회적 규제와 응집의 도구로 밝히는 반면 와일드는 웃음을 비판적 질문과 미적 쾌락의 수단으로 보여주는 것이다. 두 사람의 관점은 모두 웃음의 심오한 문화적, 지적 울림을 강조하는 동시에

웃음이 인간 행동 및 사회 구조와 복잡하게 얽혀 있음을 드러낸다.

| 어휘 |

emanate v. 유출하다, 나오다 **recognition** n. 인식 **mechanical** a. 기계적인 **rigidity** n. 경직성 **imposed** a. 강요된 **dynamism** n. 역동성 **function** v. 기능하다, 작용하다 **profound** a. 심오한 **corrective** n. 교정제 **disrupt** v. 붕괴시키다 **fluidity** n. 유동성 **spontaneity** n. 자발성, 즉흥성 **requisite** a. 필요한 **interaction** n. 상호작용 **rectify** v. 교정하다, 고치다 **incongruous** a. 부조화스러운, 서로 맞지 않는 **equilibrium** n. 균형 **collective** n. 집단 **conceptualize** v. 개념화하다 **subversion** n. 전복 **irony** n. 반어, 아이러니 **orchestrate** v. 조직하다, 직도하다 **deftly** ad. 능수능란하게 **paradox** n. 역설 **inversion** n. 뒤집기 **elicit** v. 끌어내다 **moral imperative** 도덕적 책무 **jubilant** a. 의기양양한, 환희에 취한 **affirmation** n. 확인 **ridiculous** a. 조롱하는 **deliberate** a. 고의적인, 의도된 **artifice** n. 책략 **social mores** 사회적 습속, 관습 **cohesion** n. 응집성, 화합, 결합 **interrogation** n. 질문, 심문 **aesthetic** a. 미적인, 미학의 **underscore** v. 강조하다 **entanglement** n. 얽힘 **intricate** a. 복잡한

32 빈칸완성   ③

| 분석 |

빈칸 다음의 revealing its intricate entanglement with human behavior and the structures of society에서 인간 행동과 사회 구조의 얽힘을 언급했으므로 문화적 지적 얽힘을 뜻하는 '공명, 울림'이 가장 적절하다. 따라서 정답은 resonance이다.

빈칸에 들어갈 가장 적절한 것은?
① 고립
② 무시
③ 울림
④ 차이
⑤ 추상성

33 글의 요지   ④

| 분석 |

글의 전반부에서 '베르그송에게 웃음은 사회적 교정제로 기능한다'고 했고 후반부에서 '와일드에게 웃음은 사회 관습을 지탱하는 위선과 부조리를 드러내는 것이다'라고 했으므로 ④가 가장 적절한 정답이다.

윗글의 요지로 가장 적절한 것은?
① 베르그송은 웃음을 사회 비판 수단으로 보는 반면 와일드는 도덕 교육 수단으로 본다.
② 베르그송은 웃음을 예술적 표현으로 여기는 반면 와일드는 경직된 사회 규범의 표현으로 본다.
③ 베르그송은 웃음을 사회 결속의 메커니즘으로 보는 반면 와일드는 개인 자유의 찬양으로 본다.
④ 베르그송은 웃음의 교정 기능을 강조하는 반면 와일드는 부조리를 드러내고 즐기는 역할을 강조한다.
⑤ 베르그송과 와일드는 모두 웃음을 전복적인 것으로 보며, 와일드는 웃음을 언어 구조에, 베르그송은 사회 행동에 적용한다.

34~35

지루함에 대한 우리의 개념화는 지루함과 주의력 사이의 흔히 발견되는 연관성에 대해 차별화된 관점을 제시한다. 꽤 많은 연구들이 지루함을 주의력의 실패와 일관되게 연관지어왔다. 다시 말해 우리는 지루할 때 당면한 과제에 집중을 유지하지 못한다. 이번에는 또한 이러한 주의력 집중의 실패가 지루함을 정의하는 요소로서 지루함을 개념화하는 데 통합되어왔다. 우리는 지루함과 주의력 사이의 밀접한 연관성을 부정하진 않지만, 우리의 주장은 지루함의 맥락에서 보면 주의력 이탈이 실패가 아니라는 것이다. 유용하거나 흥미로운 정보가 없는 보상예측오류(즉, 보상예측오류가 0에 가깝게 최소화된)만을 발생시키는 상황에서 주의력을 벗어나게 하는 것이 바로 지루함의 기능이라는 것이 우리의 생각이다. 증가된 정신적 혹은 신체적 움직임을 통해 탐구를 촉발함으로써, 지루함은 다른 곳에 주의력을 쓰도록 원래부터 설계되어 있다. 따라서 주의력 이탈은 지루함의 결함이 아니라 오히려 지루함의 핵심 특징 중 하나이다. 분명히 사람들은 주의력 이탈이 문제가 되는 상황, 그리고 지루함이 유발한 주의력 실패가 심각한 결과를 초래할 수 있는 상황에 자주 놓인다. 그러나 우리의 주장은, 사람들이 인생에서 하는 그 수많은 선택(간단히 말해 내 시간과 주의력을 어디에 쏟는가?)을 해나갈 때 지루함은 주관적 효용이 지나치게 낮은 일련의 행동을 하지 않도록 사람들을 돕는 적응 기능을 수행한다는 것이다. 이러한 우리의 주장과 일치되게도, 지루함을 자주 느끼는 사람들(즉, 지루함 성향 점수가 높은 사람)이 성격적 주의 이탈 척도에서 더 낮은 점수를 받아서, 지루함 성향은 순수한 성격적 지루함의 척도가 아니라 지루함에 적응하지 못하는 성격상의 (주의집중을 위한) 자기 조절의 실패일 수 있다는 생각을 지지해주었다.

| 어휘 |

conceptualization n. 개념화 **boredom** n. 지루함, 따분함, 권태 **differential** a. 다른, 차별적인 **oft-found** a. 자주 발견되는 **attention** n. 주의력 **consistent** a. 일관된, 꾸준한 **link** v. 연계 짓다 **bore** v. 지루하게 하다 **negate** v. 부정하다 **attentional disengagement** 주의력 이탈 **represent** v. 나타내다 **yield** v. 산출하다 **uninformative** a. 정보가 충분치 못한 **reward prediction error** 보상예측오류(기대한 보상과 실제로 받은 보상 사이의

차이) **intrinsically** ad. 원래부터, 내재적으로 **problematic** a. 문제가 되는 **adaptive** a. 적응의 **self-regulatory** a. 자기를 조절하는 **dispositional** a. 성향상의

34 글의 주제 ③

| 분석 |

글 후반부에 '그러나, 우리의 주장은, 사람들이 인생에서 하는 그 수많은 선택(간단히 말해 내 시간과 주의력을 어디에 쏟는가?)을 해나갈 때 지루함은 주관적 효용이 지나치게 낮은(주의력을 쏟을 가치가 낮은) 일련의 행동을 하지 않도록 사람들을 돕는 적응 기능을 수행한다는 것이다'라고 했으므로 글의 주제는 지루함과 주의력이 적응 기능을 한다는 것이다. 따라서 정답은 ③이다.

윗글의 주제로 가장 적절한 것은?
① 주의력 실패에 대한 신경학적 설명
② 지루함이 주의력에 미치는 부정적 영향
③ 지루함과 주의력의 적응적 기능
④ 변화를 유도하는 지루함의 사례들
⑤ 지루함과 생산성 간의 상관관계

35 부분이해 ①

| 분석 |

지루함으로 인한 주의력 이탈이 비극적 결과로 이어질 수 있는 사례는 고속도로 운전이 지루해서 주의력이 이탈할 경우 사고로 이어지는 경우이다. 따라서 적절한 사례는 ①이다. 나머지는 모두 지루해서 주의력을 쏟지 못해도 심각한 결과가 초래되지는 않는다고 추론할 수 있다.

밑줄 친 문장의 예시로 가장 적절한 것은?
① 고속도로 운전 중의 지루함
② 공개 강연을 듣는 중의 지루함
③ 텔레비전 다큐멘터리를 볼 때의 지루함
④ 커피숍에서 격의 없이 대화하다 느끼는 지루함
⑤ 식료품점에서 긴 줄을 기다리며 느끼는 지루함

한양대학교 서울 자연계 A형

TEST p. 702~718

01	③	02	②	03	⑤	04	①	05	②	06	⑤	07	③	08	①	09	④	10	⑤
11	③	12	④	13	②	14	④	15	④	16	①	17	④	18	①	19	⑤	20	①
21	②	22	③	23	⑤	24	①	25	③	26	⑤	27	①	28	②	29	②	30	④
31	③	32	⑤	33	⑤	34	②	35	④										

01 동의어 ③

| 어휘 |

stockman n. 가축을 기르는 사람   intimately aware of ~을 아주 잘 알고 있는   on the hoof (무리를 이룬) 동물 상태로   impersonal a. 개성이 없는   shepherd n. 양치기   docile a. 유순한(= obedient)   belligerent a. 공격적인   malicious a. 사악한   preposterous a. 터무니없는   bombastic a. 과장된   obstinate a. 완고한

| 해석 |

가축을 기르는 사람들로서 나바호족은 양과 염소 각각을 아주 잘 알게 되었다. 동물들은 단순히 아무런 개성 없는 무리가 아니라, 각 동물마다 개성과 특징을 갖고 있었다. 양치기는 어느 동물이 순종적인지 혹은 공격적인지를 알고 있었다.

02 동의어 ②

| 어휘 |

collect v. 수집하다   take on 취하다   significance n. 의미   approximate a. 대략의   attain v. 획득하다   haphazard a. 무계획의, 되는 대로의(= chaotic)   drawer n. 서랍   linear a. 순차적인   pristine a. 원래 그대로의, 깔끔한   destructive a. 파괴적인   compliable a. 순응하는

| 해석 |

아이가 피아제의 구체적 조작의 단계로 나아감에 따라, 물건 수집 행위는 새로운 의미를 갖게 된다. 약 7세쯤의 아이는 자신의 주변에 있는 것들에 흥미를 느낄 뿐 아니라, 그것을 손에 넣기를 바란다. 따라서 아이는 온갖 종류의 물건을 아무렇게나 모으고 그런 다음 결국 주머니에나, 서랍에나, 방바닥에 모으게 된다.

03 동의어 ⑤

| 어휘 |

philanthropic a. 자선의(= benevolent)   pledge v. 약속하다   underprivileged students 사회적·경제적 혜택을 받지 못한 학생들   visual impairment 시각 장애   hierarchical a. 계층적인; 계급 조직의   contemporary a. 동시대의   sustainable a. 지속가능한   pluralistic a. 다원적인

| 해석 |

아우이(Hauy)는 불우한 학생들에 대한 지원을 약속한 한 지역 자선 단체에 다가갔다. 그는 17세 시각장애인 소년을 도왔으며, 시각 장애인들이 촉각으로 책 내용을 읽을 수 있도록 하는 책 인쇄 체계를 발명했다.

04 동의어 ①

| 어휘 |

cinematographer n. 영화 촬영 감독   collaborate with ~와 협업하다   employ v. 사용하다   contrasts and hard shadows 대비와 강한 그림자   represent v. 표현하다   ominous a. 불길한, 나쁜 징조의(= menacing)   halo-supplying backlight 후광을 만들어주는 배광   emerge from ~에서 드러나다   poignant a. 통렬한, 신랄한   bittersweet a. 씁쓸하면서도 달콤한   embarrassing a. 당황스러운   extraordinary a. 비범한

| 해석 |

문이 열리고, 그녀의 얼굴에 빛이 내리비추며, 낯선 남자의 그림자가 그녀 뒤편의 벽에 비친다. 린즐리 레인과 정기적으로 함께 작업한 영화 촬영 감독 윌리엄 다니엘스는 강한 명암 대비와 선명한 그림자를 활용하여 이 불길한 순간을 표현하고, 가르보의 얼굴이 후광을 만드는 배광의 도움 없이 어둠 속에서 드러나게 했다.

05 동의어 ②

| 어휘 |

frenetic a. 열광적인 **encyclopedic** a. 박식한 **reminiscent of** ~을 연상시키는 **witty banter** 재치 있는 농담 **effusive** a. 감정 넘치는, 과장된(= lavish) **ferret out** (정보 등을) 캐내다, 밝혀내다 **taciturn** a. 과묵한, 말수가 적은 **irascible** a. 화를 잘 내는 **unctuous** a. 지나치게 아부하는, 미끈거리는 **pernicious** a. 해로운

| 해석 |

스턴은 하나의 주제에서 다른 주제로 빠르게 옮겨가며, NPR의 테리 그로스를 연상케 하는 백과사전 수준의 준비상태를 보여주고, 재치 있는 농담과 넘쳐나는 칭찬을 섞어 개인적인 정보를 캐내는 열광적인 면접관이다.

06 동의어 ⑤

| 어휘 |

impromptu a. 즉흥적인(= spontaneous) **force** v. 강제하다 **merge** v. 결합하다 **over time** 오랜 시간에 걸쳐 **arbitrariness** n. 자의성 **capriciousness** n. 변덕스러움 **rule out** 배제하다 **shortcoming** n. 단점 **strength** n. 강점 **preconceived** a. 미리 형성된 **calculated** a. 계획된 **instinctive** a. 본능적인 **scripted** a. 대본이 있는, 짜여진

| 해석 |

언어는 시간이 지나면서 풍부한 패턴을 형성하게 되는 과거의 언어 게임들을 우리로 하여금 재사용하고 결합하게 하는 즉흥적인 행위이다. 일부 수학적 체계들이 설명하고 배제하려는 임의성과 변덕스러움이 결국 단점이 아니라, 오히려 언어를 언어로 만들어주는 것의 중요한 강점이라는 것이 분명해진다.

07 논리완성 ③

| 분석 |

마지막에서 "they loved fighting"이라고 하고, 다음에는 동격절을 이끄는 'i.e.'를 사용하고 있으므로, '싸움을 좋아하는'라는 뜻의 pugnacious(호전적인)가 적절하다.

| 어휘 |

possessed of ~을 지닌 **military virtue** 군사적 덕목 **subdue** v. 정복하다 **specific** a. 특정한 **i.e.** 다시 말해서 **innately** ad. 타고나서, 본질적으로 **altruistic** a. 이타적인 **lethargic** a. 무기력한 **pugnacious** a. 호전적인, 싸움하기 좋아하는 **incessant** a. 끊임없는 **magnanimous** a. 관대한

| 해석 |

게르만 부족은 어쩌면 그 전이나 그 후의 어떤 민족보다도 군사적 덕목을 더 강하게 더 많이 지녔을 것이다. 그들은 율리우스 카이사르가 알게 되었듯이, 가장 무서운 적이었다. 그들은 결코 정복될 수 없었는데, 그들이 싸운 이유가 단지 그 어떤 특정한 목적을 달성하기 위해서가 아니라 싸움을 좋아했기 때문, 다시 말해서 본질적으로 호전적이었기 때문이었다.

08 논리완성 ①

| 분석 |

첫 문장부터 인간은 '육류고기' 때문에 인간이 되었다고 하고, '뿌리채소 섭취 증가로의 변화'이므로 빈칸에는 먹는 것과 관련된 dietary(음식의, 식사의)가 적절하다.

| 어휘 |

paleoanthropologist n. 고인류학자 **be based on** ~에 근거를 두다 **taphonomic** a. 화석화와 관련된 **fossilization** n. 화석화 **hominin** n. 호미닌, 인류 조상 **marrow** n. 골수 **Pleistocene** n. 홍적세 **tuber** n. 뿌리채소류 **transition** n. 전환 **driving force** 원동력 **dietary** a. 식사의, 음식의 **geological** a. 지질학적인 **demographic** a. 인구통계학적인 **seismic** a. 지진의; (영향 · 규모가) 엄청난 **ecological** a. 생태학적인

| 해석 |

번과 같은 고인류학자들은 "육류고기가 우리를 인간으로 만들었다"라고 주장한다. 이 주장은 동아프리카의 홍적세 경계에서 인류 조상이 고기와 골수를 위해 대형 동물을 먹었다는 화석화와 관련된 근거(화석화와 관련된 환경 조건으로부터의 근거)에 기반을 두고 있다. 다른 연구자들은 고기가 음식에서 차지하는 비중은 적었고, 오히려 뿌리채소류가 호모 사피엔스로의 전환에서 핵심 음식이었다고 제시한다. 다시 말해, 뿌리채소류 섭취 증가로의 식사 변화가 호모 에렉투스로의 진화를 이끈 원동력이었을 수 있다.

09 논리완성 ④

| 분석 |

빈칸 뒤의 it은 현상(status quo)를 가리키는데, 빈칸 앞의 '현상의 재생산'과 동격을 이루려면 빈칸에는 '재생산'과 같은 의미의 표현인 ④(구현과 강화)가 적절하다. ①에서는 '말다툼'이, ②에서는 둘 다가, ③은 '종료'가, ⑤에서는 '혼란'이 각각 내용과 어울리지 않는다.

| 어휘 |

criticality n. 비판성 **pedagogy** n. 교육법 **seek to** 노력하다 **interrogate** v. 비판적으로 캐묻다 **disrupt** v. 교란하다 **status quo** 현상 **protocol** n. 규범; 의례 **reproduction** n. 재생산 **distribution of capital** 자본의 분배 **substantiation** n. 구체화, 실현 **extension** n. 확장 **altercation** n. 말다툼 **eradication** n. 근절 **manipulation** n. 조작 **intensification** n. 강화 **termination** n. 종료 **fortification** n. 강화 **escalation** n. 확대 **discombobulation** n. 혼란

| 해석 |

문화적으로 적절한 교수법에서의 비판성은 현상(現狀)을 심문하고 타파하려고 한다. 즉, 현상의 재생산 — 인적·물적·상징적 자본의 분배를 통한 현상의 구현과 강화 — 과 관련된 사회 구조와 의식적·무의식적 절차와 규범들이 노출되고 검토되고 변화된다.

10 논리완성 ⑤

| 분석 |

빈칸 다음을 보면 "그 고유한 특징을 가지지 못하면 결코 그 하위문화에 가입할 수 없다"라고 하였으므로 '폐쇄성', '배타성'을 강조하고 있다. 따라서 exclusionary(배타적인)가 적절하다.

| 어휘 |

sub-culture n. 하위문화 **unique** a. 고유한 **indulgent** a. 관대한 **inordinate** a. 과도한, 지나친 **expansive** a. 확장적인, 포용적인 **acquiescent** a. 순응적인 **exclusionary** a. 배타적인

| 해석 |

서핑 하위문화의 경우, 그 공동체의 독특한 특징 중 하나는 바다로 나가 파도를 탄다는 점이다. 그들은 서핑을 한다. 또한 하위문화에는 배타적인 성격이 있는데, 그것은 그 고유한 특징을 가지지 않으면 결코 그 하위문화에 가입할 수 없다는 것을 의미한다.

11 논리완성 ③

| 분석 |

이제껏 차별받아 온 사람들에게 접근 기회를 확대한다는 것은 불평등을 해소하려는 의도이므로 이 정책은 '평등한' 사회를 지향하고 있다. 따라서 egalitarian이 적절하다.

| 어휘 |

affirmative action 소수자 우대 정책(= positive discrimination) **access** n. 접근 **minority group** 소수 집단 **with the aim of** ~을 목표로 **egalitarian** a. 평등주의의, 평등한 **agrarian** a. 농업의 **legitimate** a. 합법적인, 정당한 **cosmopolitan** a. 세계적인, 세계주의적인

| 해석 |

소수자 우대 정책, 또는 긍정적 차별은 전통적으로 차별받아온 소수 집단 사람들에게 시스템에의 접근을 제공하여, 더 평등한 사회를 만드는 목적을 가진 정책 또는 프로그램이다.

12 논리완성 ④

| 분석 |

문화 개념이 바뀌어서 과거와는 달라졌다는 내용이므로, 빈칸에 들어갈 표현과 뒤의 'integrated and limiting'은 의미가 반대여야 한다. 가장 적절한 것은 ④ '파편적'이고 '생성적'인 것이다.

| 어휘 |

explosion n. 확산 **integrated** a. 통합된 **limiting** a. 제약을 가하는 **labor-intensive** a. 노동집약적인 **fragmented** a. 분열된, 파편화된 **generative** a. 창조적인, 생산적인 **unified** a. 통합된 **inventive** a. 창의적인 **obsolete** a. 시대에 뒤떨어진 **dispersed** a. 흩어진 **ostentatious** a. 과시적인 **creative** a. 창조적인 **homogeneous** a. 동질적인 **reductive** a. 지나치게 단순화된

| 해석 |

상징적 형식들의 세계적 폭증은 문화적 사유와 행동 양식을 통합되고 제한적이게 만들기보다 훨씬 더 파편화되고 생성적이게 만들며, 문화적 양식과 패턴을 형성하는 데 있어 개인이 하는 역할을 그 어느 때보다도 독창적이고 노동집약적이게 만든다.

13 논리완성 ②

| 분석 |

사람은 상호의존적이므로, 사람의 행동은 다른 사람에게 영향을 미치고, 그 반대도 마찬가지라는 상호의존성을 강조하고 있다. 따라서 정답은 "어떠한 사람도 혼자 살아갈 수 없다"는 의미의 ② No person is an island이다. ③ "압박이 없으면 다이아몬드도 없다"는 시련의 중요성을, ④ "당신 자신이 당신의 집이다"는 자기 수용의 중요성을, ⑤ "메아리가 되지 말고 목소리가 되어라"는 독창성의 중요성을 각각 강조하는 표현이다.

| 어휘 |

interaction n. 상호작용 **elemental** a. 기본적인 **feature** n. 특징 **interdependence** n. 상호의존성 **refer to** 말하다 **engage in** 참여하다 **simultaneously** ad. 동시에 **sequentially** ad. 순차적으로 **enact behaviors** 행동을 수행하다 **implication** n. 영향, 함의 **as a consequence of** ~의 결과로 **have implications for** ~에 영향을 미치다 **in short** 요컨대

| 해석 |

상호작용은 상호의존성의 기본적인 특징이다. 상호작용이라는 말로 우리가 의미하는 바는 사람들이 자신의 복지뿐만 아니라 타인의 복지에도 영향을 미치는 행동에 참여한다는 사실이다. 구체적으로 말해, 행위자들은 행동의 결과로 이용할 수 있게 되는(혹은 제거되는) 미래의 상황과 선택과 결과에 뿐 아니라 자신과 상대방의 즉각적인 행동 선택과 결과에도 영향을 주는 행동을 동시에 혹은 순차적으로 한다. 따라서 우리가 이용할 수 있는 선택과 우리가 경험하는 결과는 오직 우리 자신의 행동만으로 결정되지 않는다. 존이 직장을 그만두는 결정은 메리에게 영향을 미치고, 메리가 마라톤 훈련을 하기로 한 결정 역시 존에게 영향을 미친다. 요컨대, 너무도 분명한 말을 하자면, 아무도 섬이(고립된 존재가) 아니다.

① 파트너십은 평생 지속된다
② 아무도 섬이 아니다

③ 압박이 없으면 다이아몬드도 없다
④ 당신 자신이 당신의 집이다
⑤ 메아리가 되지 말고 목소리가 되어라

14 논리완성 ④

| 분석 |
철학자의 주요 저작뿐 아니라 초고, 편지, 그리고 동시대 철학자들의 저작 등 다양한 문헌 자료를 함께 검토해야 그 철학자의 입장을 제대로 이해할 수 있다는 내용이다. 이러한 내용과 가장 잘 어울리는 것은 ④이다.

| 어휘 |
assumption n. 가정 **comprehend** v. 이해하다 **in terms of** ~에 비추어 **commonplace** n. 진부한 말, 상투적인 말; 평범함 **well-honed** a. 잘 다듬어진 **corpus** n. 전작(전체 저작물), 전집 **correspondence** n. 서신 **preliminary draft** 초안 **revision** n. 수정본 **canonical** a. 표준적인, 기본적인 **in conjunction with** ~와 함께 **illuminating** a. 통찰을 주는 **treatise** n. (학술) 논문 **imprimatur** n. 승인, 인가 **authoritative** a. 권위 있는 **facilitate** v. 용이하게 하다 **textual evidence** 문헌적 증거 **probe** v. 파고들다 **scrutinize** v. 검토하다

| 해석 |
역사학자들은 초기 근대 철학은 그 가장 유명한 인물들의 주요 출간 저작들에 의해 충분히 이해될 수 있다는 가정에 이의를 제기해 왔다. 철학자의 견해 — 데카르트의 『성찰』이나 칸트의 『순수이성비판』과 같은 책의 세련된 문장들에 표현된 — 를 이해하려면, 출판되었든 출판되지 않았든 그 철학자의 전체 저작물 모두와 연관 지어 이해해야 한다는 것이 이제는 진부한 말이 되었다. 편지, 초고, 출판된 텍스트의 뒤이은 수정본 등은 모두 중요한 증거 자료로 여겨진다. 게다가 표준 텍스트에 대한 우리의 이해는 그 철학자의 바로 앞 선배 철학자들과 동시대 철학자들의 저작 — 종종 그 표준 텍스트의 해석을 위한 통찰력 있는 배경을 제공하는 저작 — 과 함께 읽어야 더 깊이 이해될 수 있다는 사실이 갈수록 인정받고 있다. 요컨대, 출판된 논문이 어떤 주제에 관한 어떤 철학자의 입장을 권위 있게 표현한 것으로서 승인 받고 있다 하더라도, 그 입장을 이해하는 것은 그 입장을 그 외 다른 문헌 자료들과 연관 지음으로써 종종 원활히 되고 때로는 그렇게 연관 지음으로써만 가능해진다.

① 그 입장에 대한 비평가들의 반응을 조사함
② 그 입장의 정치적 맥락을 면밀히 조사함
③ 그 입장의 논리 전개나 문체를 분석함
④ 그 입장을 그 외 다른 문헌 자료들과 연관 지음
⑤ 그 입장이 이후의 철학 연구에 미친 영향을 예측함

15 논리완성 ④

| 분석 |
빈칸에는 인터넷에 대한 부정적인 묘사가 필요하다. 뒤의 내용을 보면 편견을 강화한다고 하였다. 편견은 자기만의 생각으로 남을 판단할 때 생기므로 빈칸에는 다른 사람의 견해나, 반대 의견을 인터넷에서 제거하여 개개인이 보지 못하게 한다는 말이 들어가야 한다. 따라서 정답은 ④이다.

| 어휘 |
be celebrated for ~으로 잘 알려져 있다 **disseminate** v. 퍼뜨리다, 전파하다 **decentralization** n. 탈중앙화, 분산화 **post** v. 게시하다 **characterization** n. 묘사, 서술 **counter-argument** n. 반론 **negate** v. 부정하다 **eccentric** a. 보통과는 다른 **circulate** v. 유통시키다 **disparate** a. 다른, 공통점이 없는 **undermine** v. 잠식하다 **ethnic group** 민족집단 **excise** v. 잘라내다, 제거하다 **dissenting voices** 반대 의견 **purview** n. 시야, 이해 범위

| 해석 |
인터넷은 지식을 퍼뜨리고 대화, 토론, 논쟁을 지원한다고 잘 알려져 있다. 인터넷의 분산적인 구조 덕분에 누구나 온라인에 의견을 올리거나 다른 페이지로 연결할 수 있다. 하지만 이러한 긍정적인 묘사는 반론에 의해 도전받고 있다. 그 반론은 인터넷과 웹이 반대 의견을 개인의 시야에서 제거하여 그들의 편견을 쉽게 강화하고 확대하는 도구이기도 하다는 것이다.

① 대중을 위해 보통과는 다른 의견을 부정한다
② 다양한 사람들의 다양한 아이디어를 유통한다
③ 다양한 민족의 문화유산을 훼손한다
④ 반대 의견을 개인의 시야에서 제거한다
⑤ 반대 의견을 소개하여 개인의 시야를 넓힌다

16 논리완성 ①

| 분석 |
Ⓐ의 경우, 인간에게 의존하지 않으며 인간의 의도나 인간이 만든 프로그램과는 상관이 없는 능력이라고 하였으므로 '자율성'이 적절하다. Ⓑ의 경우, AI와 사용자 양쪽 모두 서로 영향을 주고받으며 변화, 혹은 진화하는 과정이므로 '적응성'이 적절하다.

| 어휘 |
introduction n. 도입 **with respect to** ~와 관련해서 **in particular** 특히 **self-learning** a. 자기 학습의 **as for** ~에 관해 말하자면 **trial and error** 시행착오 **decode** v. 해독하다; 이해하다 **conversely** ad. 반대로 **inadvertently** ad. 무심코 **autonomy** n. 자율성; 자치권 **adaptivity** n. 적응성 **accuracy** n. 정확성 **authenticity** n. 진정성, 진위 **uniformity** n. 획일성 **dichotomy** n. 이분법 **adversity** n. 역경, 불운 **heterogeneity** n. 이질성 **consistency** n. 일관성 **accountability** n. 책임성

| 해석 |

AI의 발전과 신경기술 분야에의 AI 도입의 발전은 인간과 기계 사이의 상호작용을 더욱 복잡하게 만들고 있는데, 주로 자율성과 적응성 측면에서 그렇다. 전자(자율성)에 관해서 말하자면, AI 시스템은 일정 수준 인간에게 의존하지 않는 인지 기능을 가능하게 할 수 있다. 특히 자기 학습 기제를 갖춘 시스템은 인간이 미리 프로그래밍하거나 의도하지 않은 결정이나 결과를 만들어낼 수 있다. 후자의 관심사(적응성)에 대해 말하자면, 기계학습은 기계장치로 하여금 시행착오와 피드백 루프를 통해 학습하여 뇌 신호를 더 정확히 해독함으로써 예측을 향상할 수 있게 한다. 하지만 반대로, 뇌-컴퓨터 인터페이스를 사용하는 인간이 기계가 더 잘 해독할 수 있도록 자기도 모르게 자신의 뇌 신호를 바꾸는 방법을 학습하게 될 수도 있다.

17~18

구아라차와 이후의 볼레로 같은 많은 쿠바 노래들이 유카탄 반도의 시인들과 가수들의 낭만적인 표현(가사)에 의해 채택되었다. 반도에 도착한 쿠바 리듬은 이러한 낭만주의 속에 스며들며 그 강렬함은 약화되었다. 볼레로나 콜롬비아의 밤부코는 유카탄 지역 전통의 일부가 되었다. 볼레로는 여전히 2박자 패턴으로 연주되었지만, 템포는 느려졌고, 리듬 강조는 줄어들어 가사의 낭만적인 분위기를 부각하는 데 집중했다. 에밀리오 파체코의 "예감(Presentimiento)"이 그 예인데, 이 곡은 1920년대 멕시코시티 최초의 대중적인 볼레로 중 하나로 꼽힌다. 멜로디에 신퀼로 리듬은 여전히 살아 있었지만, 스페인 시인 페드로 마타의 낭만적인 가사를 음악적 리듬이 강하게 강조하지는 않는다. 유카탄 낭만주의는 도시 전통과는 거리가 먼 목가적인 성향을 띠고 있었으며, 이 볼레로 곡들은 순진한 낭만주의의 대중적 형태였다. 시인 루이스 로사도 베가는 유카탄 볼레로를 외설적인 요소가 완전히 제거된 섬세한 장르로 규정했다. 그 결과, 쿠바 볼레로는 중산층의 교양과 취향 개념에 부합하도록 부드러워졌다. 이런 볼레로가 1920년대 후반 멕시코시티 지하 문화공간들에서, 아구스틴 라라 같은 작곡가들에 의해 확산되고, 변화되고, 도시화되었다. 혁명 이후, 새로 집권한 정치 세력들은 새로운 문화 프로젝트를 통해 사회적·정치적·경제적 안정을 찾고 있었는데, 그 프로젝트가 멕시코 정체성 구축이었다. 공식적인 역사는 멕시코의 과거를 낭만적이고 서사적인 인물들을 통해 미화했고, 동시에 19세기 낭만주의는 대중적인 형태를 띠어가고 있었다.

| 어휘 |

guaracha n. 과라차(쿠바의 빠르고 활기찬 민속 음악 장르) **bolero** n. 볼레로(느리고 낭만적인 쿠바 발라드 계열 음악) **rhetoric** n. 표현 방식 **smother** v. 덮어버리다; 숨막히게 하다 **two-beat pattern** 2박자 리듬 구조 **rhythmical accent** 리듬의 강세 **underline** v. 강조하다 **lyrics** n. 가사 **cinquillo rhythm** 신퀼로 리듬(아프로-카리브 음악에서 쓰이는 다섯 박자 리듬 패턴) **bucolic** a. 목가적인 **naive** a. 순진한 **deprived of** ~이 제거된, ~이 결여된 **obscenity** n. 외설, 음란 **consequently** ad. 결과적으로 **conform to** ~에 순응하다 **propriety** n. 예의, 품위 **underground place** 비공식적이고 대안적인 예술 공간 **stability** n. 안정성 **glorify** v. 미화하다 **epic figure** 영웅적 인물

17 내용일치 ④

| 분석 |

아구스틴 라라는 1920년대 후반 'underground place', 즉 비주류, 하위문화 공간을 통해 볼레로를 확산시켰고 그가 확산시킨 볼레로는 중산층의 교양과 취향에 맞게 한 볼레로였다. 다시 말해 엘리트 사회를 위한 것이 아니었으므로 ④가 정답이다.

윗글의 내용과 가장 거리가 먼 것은?
① 유카탄의 가수들과 시인들은 쿠바 노래를 통해 전해진 낭만주의의 영향을 받았다.
② "예감"에서는 리듬의 강세가 강하게 강조되지 않았다.
③ 쿠바 볼레로는 멕시코 중산층의 취향에 맞도록 부드럽게 조정되었다.
④ 아구스틴 라라 같은 예술가들은 예술을 멕시코시티의 엘리트 사회를 위한 문화적 산물로 보았다.
⑤ 혁명 이후 새롭게 등장한 정치 세력은 멕시코 정체성을 만드는 새로운 문화 정책을 도입함으로써 사회적·정치적·경제적 안정성을 추구했다.

18 동의어 ①

| 분석 |

bucolic은 '목가적인'이라는 뜻이므로 pastoral이 동의어이다. ② 곁길로 새는, 탈선적인 ③ 끊임없는 ④ 열정적인 ⑤ 우회하는

19~20

면화 농부들에게는 더 나은 수확 방법을 원하는 경제적·환경적·농업적 이유가 있다. 전통적인 기계식 수확기는 길이가 최대 14피트(약 4.3m), 무게는 30톤 이상에 이른다. 이들은 식물을 손상하지 않으면서 면화를 효과적으로 수확하지만, 몇 가지 문제도 초래할 수 있다. 하나는 장시간의 섬유 노출이다. 면화의 둥근 꼬투리는 한꺼번에 익지 않기 때문에, 밭에서 가장 먼저 익은 꼬투리는 주변의 다른 꼬투리가 익을 때까지 최대 50일 동안 기다려야 한다. 또 다른 문제는, 수확 기계가 밭을 밟아 다지고 지나가며 토양을 압축한다는 점이다. 이렇게 되면 물과 비료가 식물의 뿌리에까지 침투하기

어려워진다. 게다가 이 기계들은 대당 약 100만 달러에 달하지만, 연중 2~3개월밖에 사용되지 않는다. 로봇 기술은 이러한 문제에 대한 잠재적 해결책으로, 과일이나 채소 같은 다른 작물 수확에서는 이미 사용되고 있다. 수확용 로봇은 카메라와 센서를 이용하여 작물이 수확될 준비가 된 시기를 탐지하고, 식물을 손상하지 않으면서 수확할 수 있다. 면화의 경우, 로봇 기술은 수확에 적합한 꼬투리만 더 정확하게 골라 따는 수확 방식을 제공한다. 꼬투리가 열리자마자 바로 종자면화를 수확하기 때문에 섬유의 품질은 좋아지고, 날씨에 장시간 노출되지 않게 된다. 로봇은 종자면화만을 목표로 하며, 식물의 다른 부위는 건드리지 않는다. 로봇을 사용하면, 면화 농부들은 지금처럼 면화 수확 전에 고엽제를 사용하여 잎을 떼어낼 필요도 없어진다. 작고 기민한 로봇은 밭 위를 지나며 토양을 압축하지 않기 때문에, 토양 건강 유지에도 도움이 된다.

| 어휘 |

option n. 선택 **up to** ~까지 **prolonged exposure** 장시간 노출 **cotton bolls** 면화의 둥근 꼬투리, 면화 씨방(면화 솜이 들어 있는 껍질) **ripen** v. 성숙하다 **compact** v. 압축하다 **fertilizer** n. 비료 **penetrate** v. 침투하다 **apiece** ad. 하나에 대하여 **targeted picking** 표적 수확, 정확한 선택 수확 **seed cotton** 종자면화(씨가 포함된 면화 솜) **defoliant** n. 고엽제, 잎 제거제 **nimble** a. 민첩한, 기민한

19 내용일치 ⑤

| 분석 |

마지막 바로 앞의 문장에서 로봇 수확기를 사용하면 고엽제를 사용할 필요가 없다고 분명히 밝히고 있으므로 ⑤가 정답이다. ① 면화 꼬투리는 동시에 익지 않는다. ② 이미 과일과 채소에 사용되고 있다. ③ 기존의 수확기는 토양을 압축한다. ④ 식물을 손상하지 않는다.

윗글의 내용과 가장 가까운 것은?
① 면화 꼬투리는 모두 동시에 익기 때문에, 농부들은 한 번에 모든 작물을 수확할 수 있다.
② 로봇 수확기는 아직 사용되고 있지 않지만, 미래 세대를 위한 잠재적 해결책으로 남아 있다.
③ 기존의 면화 수확기는 토양 압축을 방지하여 토양 건강 유지에 도움을 준다.
④ 면화 수확용 로봇은 식물을 심각하게 손상해 면섬유 품질을 떨어뜨린다.
⑤ 면화 수확에 로봇을 활용하면 고엽제 사용을 줄일 수 있는데, 이는 로봇이 잎을 떼어내지 않고도 면화를 수확할 수 있기 때문이다.

20 동의어 ①

| 분석 |

nimble은 '민첩한, 기민한'의 뜻이므로 agile이 동의어이다. ② 아주 작은 ③ 느리게 움직이는 ④ 딱딱한 ⑤ 서투른

21~22

초기 교육 실패의 결과는 광범위하고도 심오하다. 학업 문제는 추가적인 지원, 특수교육, 성적유지와 관련된 상당한 비용 증가와 연관된다. 이러한 추가 비용은 학교에서 발생하는 것에만 국한되지 않는다. 학교 실패를 경험한 아이들은 무단결석할 가능성이 더 크며, 학교에 가지 않을 때는 불건전하거나 범죄적인 행동에 가담할 수 있다. 이런 학생들은 학교를 자퇴하거나 강제 퇴학당할 가능성도 크다. 이것은 분명, 그들이 미국 노동시장에서 전문 기술을 요구하는 안정적인 직업을 얻는 데 필요한 고등교육을 받을 가능성이 줄어들게 만든다. 이들이 성인이 되면, 복지 및 다른 사회적 지원에 더 많이 의존하고, 범죄 및 수감, 그리고 불완전 고용과 그에 따른 세수 손실 등으로 인해 사회적 비용은 계속해서 늘어난다. 빈곤은 세대를 이어 반복되는 특성이 있기 때문에, 한 아이의 교육 실패 비용은 연이은 여러 세대에 걸쳐 누적되는 경향을 보인다.

| 어휘 |

implication n. 영향, 결과 **profound** a. 심오한 **be associated with** ~와 관련 있다 **expense** n. 비용 **grade retention** 유급 **incur** v. 초래하다 **truant** a. 무단결석하는 n. 무단결석하는 학생 **engage in** 참여하다 **delinquent** a. 비행의, 죄를 범하는 **drop out** 자퇴하다 **expulsion** n. 추방; 제적 **gainful** ad. 수지맞는 **incarceration** n. 투옥 **compound** v. 더욱 악화시키다, 누적시키다

21 빈칸완성 ②

| 분석 |

Ⓐ의 경우, 학교 실패의 결과이고, 바로 뒤 문장을 보면 '학교에 없다'는 말이 있으므로, '무단결석하는'이라는 truant가 적절하다. Ⓑ의 경우, 앞에 intergenerational이라는 표현을 참조하여 '여러 세대에 걸쳐 누적된다'는 의미의 compound over가 적절하다.

빈칸 Ⓐ와 Ⓑ에 들어갈 가장 적절한 것은?
① 열광적인 — 무시하다
② 무단결석하는 — 누적시키다
③ 근면 성실한 — 복잡하게 만들다
④ 동정적인 — 발전하다
⑤ 무심한 — 동시에 발생하다

22 글의 제목 ③

| 분석 |
학교, 학생, 사회, 세대 차원에서 조기 교육 실패가 낳는 '비용'을 다루고 있는 글이다.

윗글의 제목으로 가장 적절한 것은?
① 조기 교육 방법
② 조기 교육 과정
③ 조기 교육 실패의 비용
④ 조기 교육 실패의 원인
⑤ 조기 교육 실패의 범위

23 글의 요지 ⑤

| 분석 |
전시는 물건을 보여주는 데 그치지 않고, 우리의 과거 역사, 즉 집단 기억을 보존하는 장소로서 문명에 대한 우리의 태도를 잘 보여준다고 했으므로 ⑤가 요지로 적절하다.

| 어휘 |
conceptualization n. 개념화, 구상 exhibition n. 전시회, 전람 temporary a. 일시적인 virtual a. 가상의 of prime importance 매우 중요한 public perception 대중의 인식 on occasion 이따금 will n. 의지 display n. 전시물 publication n. 출판물 outreach program 사회참여 프로그램, 대외 홍보활동 subject area 주제 분야 fruitful a. 결실 있는, 생산적인 discipline n. 학문 분야 outlook n. 관점, 세계관 aspiration n. 열망, 이상 social mechanism 사회적 장치, 구조 misrepresent v. 잘못 표현하다, 왜곡하다 mirror v. 반영하다 repository n. 저장소, 보관소 collective memory 집단 기억 pay lip service to 진심 없이 말만 하다

| 해석 |
일시적이든 영구적이든, 실제적이든 가상적이든, 전시회의 개념화는 매우 중요하다. 왜냐하면 그것은 교육, 대중의 인식, 때로는 정치적 의지에까지 영향을 미치기 때문이다. 박물관, 도서관, 미술관과 그들의 전시물, 간행물, 대중 참여 프로그램은 어떤 특정 주제 분야가 어떻게 연구되고 있는지를 반영할 뿐만 아니라, 그 방향을 제시하는 데도 이바지해왔다고 알려져 있다. 이러한 공간들은 다양한 학문과 관점들이 만나는 생산적인 만남의 장(場)이자, 열망과 자원을 조화시키기 위한 시험의 장소가 될 수 있다. 요컨대, 그것들은 우리가 역사를 쓰고, 기록하고, 역사의 미래를 지휘하는 데 도움을 준다. 그것들은 우리의 정체성을 반영하기도 하고 잘못 표현할 수도 있는 강력한 사회적 장치이다. 우리의 집단 기억을 보존하는 저장소로서, 그것들은 우리 문명을 구성하는 재료이다. 앞으로 이러한 공간들을 어떻게 형성하고, 사용하고, 투자하느냐는 우리가 문명이라는 개념 자체를 어느 정도 가치 있게 여기는지, 아니면 그저 입에 발린 그럴듯한 칭찬만 하는지를 보여주는 지표가 될 것이다.

다음 글의 요지로 가장 적절한 것은?
① 전시회는 종종 정치적·경제적 목적을 위해 사용된다.
② 오늘날 박물관 전시는 흔히 디지털 매체와 기술이 주도한다.
③ 가상 전시는 전시물을 보여주고 사람들을 끌어들이는 데 일반 박물관보다 더 효과적이다.
④ 박물관은 대중 참여뿐만 아니라 수익성 있는 프로그램에도 집중함으로써 비즈니스 모델을 제시할 수 있다.
⑤ 박물관과 전시회는 사회의 집단 기억을 구성하고 반영하는 데 핵심적인 역할을 한다.

24~25

시애틀은 미국의 그 어떤 도시들보다 재활용과 퇴비화를 가장 많이 하는 도시이지만, 재활용이 반드시 성공의 신호는 아니다. 예를 들어, 비평가들은 다음과 같이 지적한다. 재활용은 소비자들에게 양심의 가책을 덜어줌으로써 소비를 오히려 조장하고, 자원 채굴, 제조, 운송에 이르는 전체 폐기물 생성 시스템은 무시한 채, 생산 과정의 가장 마지막 단계에서만 폐기물 문제를 다룬다. 게다가, 재활용되는 자원을 처리하려면 막대한 에너지가 필요하며, 자재의 품질도 저하된다. 비평가들은 재활용이 산업계가 환경 행동의 책임을 개인과 지방정부에 전가하고, 소비와 폐기물 생성이라는 기업 시스템에 대한 규제적 관심을 회피하기 위해 사용하는 계략이라고 말한다. 마지막으로, 지방정부의 재활용 프로그램은 재활용해도 환경적 이득을 가장 적게 보게 되는 자재들을 강조하며, 오히려 더 효율적으로 재활용할 수 있는 자재들은 무시하고 있다. 그리고 이런 문제점들은 쓰레기 문제 해결책으로서의 재활용의 실효성에 반대하는 수많은 주장 중 일부에 불과하다. 시애틀의 성공은 주목할 만하지만, 그 도시의 높은 재활용률은 우리가 직면한 수많은 사회·환경 위기에 대한 해결책을 거의 제시하지 못한다.

| 어휘 |
compost v. 퇴비로 만들다, 퇴비화하다 necessarily ad. 반드시 critic n. 비평가 ease the conscience 양심의 가책을 덜다 production chain 생산 과정, 생산 체계 resource extraction 자원 채굴 manufacturing n. 제조 transport n. 운송 degrade v. 저하시키다 material n. 자재 ploy n. 계략, 술책 displace responsibility 책임을 떠넘기다 deflect attention from ~에 대한 관심을 다른 데로 돌리다 corporate machinery 기업 시스템, 기업 구조 municipal a. 지방자치단체의 product stewardship 제품 책임주의(제품의 전체 수명 주기에서 제조업자, 유통업자, 소비자, 폐기물 처리자 등 모든 관련 주체가 공동 책임을 진다는 개념) extended producer responsibility 생산자 책임 확대(제품이 수명을 다해 폐기물이 되면 그 폐기물 책임도 생산자가 져야한다는 정책)

24 빈칸완성 ①

| 분석 |
빈칸 뒤의 내용을 보면, '산업계가 져야 할 책임을 회피하기 위한'이라는 의미이므로 빈칸에는 '계책', '수단'이라는 의미가 필요하다. 따라서 ①이 정답이다.

빈칸 Ⓐ에 들어갈 가장 적절한 것은?
① 계략
② 보너스
③ 쓰레기
④ 수요
⑤ 감정

25 빈칸완성 ③

| 분석 |
전체 글은 재활용은 쓰레기 문제의 진정한 해결책이라기보다는 산업계의 책임 회피 계략 같은 것이라는 비판이므로, 재활용의 효과에 대한 반박인 ③이 적절하다.

빈칸 Ⓑ에 들어갈 가장 적절한 것은?
① 전체적인 재활용 재정의에 반대
② 재활용품의 품질 향상에 반대
③ 쓰레기 문제의 해결책으로서의 재활용의 효과에 대한 반박
④ 재활용 교육에 더 많은 노력과 돈을 투자하는 것에 찬성
⑤ 제품 책임주의나 생산자 책임 확대 같은 구조적 변화를 강조하는 폐기물 예방에 반대

26 문맥상 적절하지 않은 단어 고르기 ⑤

| 분석 |
같은 문장에서 생산과 소비가 '분리'되었다고 하였으므로, 음식을 만드는 사람과 먹는 사람도 '분리'되어야 한다. 따라서 '관계를 깨뜨리다'라는 뜻으로 retaining을 breaking으로 고친다.

| 어휘 |
fundamentally ad. 근본적으로 **sustenance** n. 생계 수단, 생존을 위한 음식 **paradoxically** ad. 역설적으로 **dietary** a. 식생의 **bounty** n. 수확물 **sedentary farmer** 정착 농부 **surplus** n. 잉여 **harvest** n. 수확, 수확물 **culinary artist** 요리 예술가 **novel** a. 새로운, 독창적인 **prepare** v. 조리하다 **monotonous** a. 단조로운 **variety** n. 다양성, 종류 **agrarian** a. 농업의, 농경의 **radically** ad. 철저하게 **retain** v. 유지하다 **social connection** 사회 관계

| 해석 |
인류는 역사상 두 번, 인류의 생존식량원을 근본적으로 바꾸었고, 그리하여 세상에서의 인류의 위치도 바꾸었다. 수천 년 전, 농업의 발명은 수렵·채집인의 변화무쌍한 풍부함에서 정착 농부의 반복적인 수확으로 식단 선택의 폭을 역설적이게도 좁혀버렸다. 그럼에도 불구하고, 잉여 식량은 왕, 사제, 상인, 그리고 예술가를 먹여 살림으로써, 복잡한 사회 형성이라는 결과를 낳았다. 예술가 중에는 요리 예술가들도 있었는데, 이들은 그렇지 않으면 단조로울 곡물을 조리하는 새로운 방법을 고안해냈다. 19세기에는 산업화가 음식습관과 사회관계에서 마찬가지로 중요한 변화를 일으켰다. 다시 한 번 인류는 더 적은 종류의 식재료로 더 많은 음식을 만들어내는, 더 적은 것에서 더 많은 것을 만들어내는 법을 배웠다. 그러나 농경 사회와 달리, 현대의 잉여 생산은 생산과 소비를 철저히 분리함으로써 이루어졌고, 그 결과 요리하는 사람과 먹는 사람 사이의 사회적 연결은 〈유지되었다(→ 단절되었다).〉

27~28

논리적으로 지지할 수 없는 입장, 다시 말해 모든 전쟁에서 양측 모두가 자기 자신은 전적으로 옳고, 상대방은 전적으로 잘못되었다고 주장하는 상황을 정당화하기 위해, 우리는 우리 자신에게는 우월함을, 상대방에게는 열등함을 부여하는 장치를 이용한다. 이 열등함과 우월함은 어떤 방식으로든 구체화되어야 하며, 시각적으로 뚜렷하면 할수록 더 효과적이다. 궁극적으로, 그 정당성을 제공해주는 것은 힘이며, 승자는 대개 신이나 진실이 자기편이었다고 주장한다. 더 문명화될수록, 우리는 물리적 폭력 사용에서 비롯된 죄책감을 덜어주는, 더 합리적인 정당화 수단이 필요하다. 실제이든 그렇지 않든 상관없이 우리가 가진 인간 사이의 차이점이 그러한 목적을 위한 이상적인 장치가 된다. 이 가상의 차이 중 하나로, 유럽 귀족들은 정말 말도 안 되는 '푸른 피' 개념을 만들어냈다. 이후에 만들어진 인종차별은 같은 종류의 상상력에서 비롯된 산물이다. 이는 '인종 분류'라는 신화를 바탕으로 한 근거라곤 없는 편견, 억압, 불의의 표현이다. 그럼에도, 분류에 의해 덜 인간적인 존재로 간주된 사람들에게는 육체, 건강, 사회·경제·정치, 형사법적으로 파괴적인 영향을 실제로 미쳐왔다. 인종차별은, 특히 식민지화와 노예제 시기 이후로, 피부색과, 열등한 인류의 결정 요소로 정의되는 그 외의 신체적 특징들에 기초해서 인류의 큰 집단을 착취할 수 있는 거의 흠잡을 데 없고, 죄책감조차 느끼지 않게 해주는 핑계 역할을 해왔다.

| 어휘 |
logically ad. 논리적으로 **untenable** a. 지지할 수 없는 **party** n. 당사자 **attribute A to B** A를 B의 결과로 돌리다 **the Other** 타자, 상대방 **objectify** v. 구체화하다, 가시화하다 **be on one's side** ~의 편이다 **rational reinforcement** 이성적 정당화 수단, 논리적 보완책 **allay** v. 누그러뜨리다 **brute force** 물리적 폭력, 무자비한 힘 **come up with** 제시하다 **dismissible** a. 중요하지 않은 **blue blood** 귀족의 혈통 **racism** n. 인종차별주의 **prejudice** n. 편견 **oppression** n. 억압 **race classification** 인종 분류(과학

적 근거 없는 사회적 구분)　deem v. ~로 여기다　colonization n. 식민지화　flawless a. 결점 없는, 완벽한　guilt-freeing excuse 죄책감을 덜어주는 구실　exploitation n. 착취　on the basis of ~에 입각한　determinant n. 결정요소　physiognomy n. 인상학, 골상학

27　빈칸완성　①

| 분석 |

문명의 발전은 '폭력'을 감추기 위한 합리적인 변명을 요구하며, 이는 죄책감을 '누그러뜨리기' 위해서이다. 따라서 allay가 적절하다.

빈칸에 들어갈 가장 적절한 것은?
① 덜어주다
② 이끌어내다
③ 자극하다
④ 강화하다
⑤ 응고하다

28　내용일치　②

| 분석 |

마지막 문장에서 "인종차별은 특히 식민지화와 노예제 시기 이후, 피부색을 기준으로 광범위한 인류 집단을 착취하는 데 있어 거의 완벽하고 죄책감을 덜어주는 구실을 제공해왔다"라고 하였으므로, 이를 요약하고 있는 ②가 정답이다. ① 실제적이므로 무시할 수 없다. ③ 과학적 근거와는 무관하다. ④ 검증 가능한 증거가 아니라 검증 불가능한 구실을 만들어 사용한다. ⑤ 명확할수록 죄책감을 덜 느낀다.

윗글의 내용과 가장 가까운 것은?
① 인종차별과 그 역사적 결과는 순전히 상상의 산물이므로 무시할 수 있다.
② 인종차별은 노예제와 식민지 착취를 정당화하는 거의 완벽한 구실이 되었다.
③ 인종 분류는 골상학에서 과학적으로 입증된 차이에 기반하고 있다.
④ 푸른 피와 인종차별 주장은 타자를 식별하기 위해 같은 종류의 검증 가능한 증거를 사용한다.
⑤ 우리는 우리와 타자를 나누는 차이가 복잡하고 모호할수록 죄책감을 덜 느낀다.

29~30

기후변화는 단순히 행동 변화, 부문별 개입, 또는 새로운 규제를 통해 관리할 수 있는 환경 문제만은 아니다. 기후변화는 환경부서, 국제기구, 비정부기구, 개발 원조나 적응 기금이 단독으로 해결할 수 있는 문제도 아니다. 또한, 생태학적 현대화, 생태계 관리, 또는 지속 가능한 개발에 의해 해결될 수 있는 문제도 아니다. 오히려 인간 안전 문제로서의 기후변화에 집중해야만 해결할 수 있는 문제이다. 인간 안전이란 인간이 '안전하다'는 것이 무엇을 의미하는지에 대한 철저한 탐구를 포함한다. 무엇보다도 이를 위해서는 변화에 대해 우리가 생각하는 방식 자체를 바꿔야 한다. 우리는 공리주의적인 문제 해결 중심의 접근이나 비용-편익 분석을 통해 변화에 대응하는 지배적인 사고 틀에서 벗어나, 개인과 공동체가 대안적 미래를 상상하고 추구하는 역량을 포함하여 변화에 대응하고 변화를 만들어낼 수 있는 역량을 인정하고 우선시하는 틀로 이동해야 한다.

| 어휘 |

sectoral interventions 부문별 개입　regulation n. 규제, 규칙　single-handedly ad. 단독으로　ecological modernization 생태학적 현대화(기술로 환경 문제를 해결하자는 접근)　ecosystem stewardship 생태계 관리　sustainable development 지속 가능한 개발　resolve v. 해결하다, 해소하다　human security 인간 안보(물리적 안전뿐 아니라 인간다운 삶의 조건까지 포함)　thorough investigation 철저한 조사, 탐구　first and foremost 무엇보다도　utilitarian a. 공리주의적인　cost-benefit analysis 비용-편익 분석　prioritize v. 우선시하다　envision v. 상상하다　alternative future 대안적 미래, 새로운 미래의 모습　exacerbate v. 악화되다　amplify v. 증폭하다　distend v. 팽창하다　expound v. 설명하다

29　빈칸완성　②

| 분석 |

빈칸 다음의 '인간 안전 문제로서의 기후변화에 집중하는 것은 기후변화를 해결하는 방법으로 제시된 것이므로 빈칸에는 resolved가 적절하다.

빈칸에 들어갈 가장 적절한 것은?
① 악화하다
② 해결하다
③ 증폭하다
④ 팽창하다
⑤ 설명하다

30　내용일치　④

| 분석 |

환경부서 등의 기관들은 단독으로는 기후변화를 해결할 수 없다고 했으므로 ④가 정답이다. ① 변화에 대해 우리가 생각하는 방식 자체를 바꿔야 한다고 했다.

윗글의 내용과 거리가 가장 먼 것은?
① 기후변화 문제를 해결하려면 변화라는 개념 자체를 바꿔야 한다.
② 인간 안전 문제로 기후변화를 이해하려면 '안전'의 의미가 무엇인지부터 살펴야 한다.
③ 기후변화를 해결하기 위해서는 개인과 공동체가 대안을 구상하는 능력에 주목해야 한다.
④ 환경부서, 국제기관, 비정부기구는 기후변화 문제를 해결할 수 있다.
⑤ 생태학적 현대화, 생태계 관리, 지속 가능한 개발은 기후변화 문제를 해결할 효과적인 수단이 아니다.

31~32

임신 중에 망간에 과도하게 노출되는 원인은 무엇일까? 철분 결핍 때문이다. 철분은 부족할 경우 반사회적 행동을 증가시키는 미량 영양소인데, 철분 결핍은 망간 흡수를 증가시킨다. 철분 수치가 낮은 여성은 철분 수치가 높은 여성보다 약 4배 더 많은 망간을 흡수한다. 출산 후 초기 망간의 또 다른 주요 공급원은 콩 단백질 기반 분유이다. 이 분유는 모유보다 80배나 더 많은 양의 망간을 포함하고 있다. 모유 수유를 받은 아기들의 IQ가 더 높은 이유는, 분유를 먹은 아기들이 높은 수준의 망간에 노출되었기 때문일 수도 있다. 망간 배출은 간에 의해 조절된다. 아기들의 간은 아직 미성숙하여 망간을 충분히 배출하지 못한다. 과도한 망간 축적은 뇌 기능 저하 및 IQ 감소를 낳을 수 있다.

| 어휘 |

excessive manganese exposure 과도한 망간 노출 **iron** n. 철분 **deficiency** n. 결핍 **micronutrient** n. 미량 영양소 **be associated with** ~와 연관되다 **antisocial** a. 반사회적인 **absorption** n. 흡수 **postnatal** a. 출생 후의 **soy infant formula** 콩 단백질 기반 유아용 분유 **natural breast milk** 자연 모유 **be due to** ~때문이다 **excretion** n. 배출; 배설물 **liver** n. 간 **underdeveloped** a. 미성숙한, 덜 발달된 **brain functioning** 뇌 기능

31 글의 제목 ③

| 분석 |

이 글은 철분 결핍은 망간 흡수 증가를 낳는다는 내용과 콩 분유는 과도한 망간 축적을 낳을 수 있다는 내용을 담고 있다. 두 내용을 모두 포함한 선택지는 ③ 유아의 망간 노출에서 철분 결핍과 콩 분유의 역할이다.

윗글의 제목으로 적절한 것은?
① 왜 철분 결핍이 유아의 뇌 발달을 향상시키는가
② 모유 수유 대 분유 수유: 망간의 장점
③ 유아의 망간 노출에서 철분 결핍과 콩 분유의 역할
④ 망간 결핍과 그것이 유아 인지 발달에 미치는 영향
⑤ 유아의 뇌 기능을 증진하는 데 있어 콩 분유의 이점

32 내용일치 ⑤

| 분석 |

"soy infant formula, which has eighty times the amount of manganese that natural breast milk has."에서 볼 수 있듯이 분유가 모유보다 80배 망간이 더 많다고 하였으므로 ⑤가 본문의 내용과 가장 거리가 먼 진술이다.

윗글의 내용과 거리가 가장 먼 것은?
① 철분 결핍은 망간 흡수를 증가시킨다.
② 아기의 미성숙한 간은 망간 배출을 잘 못 한다.
③ 콩 분유는 모유보다 훨씬 더 많은 망간을 포함한다.
④ 낮은 철분 수치는 반사회적 행동과 연관되어 있다.
⑤ 분유보다 모유를 먹는 아이들이 더 많은 망간에 노출된다.

33 내용일치 ⑤

| 분석 |

마지막 문장에서 VWFA는 생물학적 '적응'의 결과가 아니라, '경험'을 통해 생겨난다고 하였으므로 VWFA는 진화의 결과가 아니다. 따라서 ⑤가 정답이다. ③ VWFA는 독자가 읽기에 더 능통해질수록 단어 인식에 더 특화된다고 했다.

| 어휘 |

writing system 문자 체계 **stand for** 나타내다 **syllabary** n. 음절 문자 체계 **logogram** n. 표어문자, 한 글자가 하나의 단어를 나타내는 체계 **character** n. 글자 **temporal region** 측두엽(뇌의 한 부분) **left hemisphere** 좌뇌(왼쪽 대뇌 반구) **visual word form area(VWFA)** 시각 단어 형태 영역(단어의 시각적 형태를 인식하는 뇌 영역) **activate** v. 활성화하다 **literacy** n. 문자해독력 **recruit** v. 보충하다 **neural substrate** 신경 기반, 신경 기제 **script** n. 문자, 글자체 **proficient** a. 숙련된, 능숙한 **given that** ~을 감안할 때 **neural circuit** 신경 회로

| 해석 |

전 세계의 문자 체계는 여러 방식으로 서로 다르다. 영어 같은 언어는 알파벳을 사용하여 각 문자가 개별 소리를 나타내고, 일본어는 음절 문자를 사용하여 기호 하나가 하나의 음절을 나타내며, 중국어는 표어문자를 사용해 하나의 문자가 하나의 단어 전체를 나타낸다. 그럼에도 불구하고 읽기와 관련된 뇌 영역은 개인이나 문화권에 상관없이 거의 차이가 없다. 좌반구 측두엽 하부 근처에 시각적 단어 형태 영역(VWFA)이라는 영역이 위치하는데, 이 영역은 문자

체계에 상관없이 일관되게 활성화된다. VWFA의 존재는 두 가지 점에서 중요하다. 첫째, 그것은 문화적 발명(즉, 문해력)은 누가 읽고 어떤 문자를 읽든지 간에 비슷한 신경 기제를 동원할 수 있다는 사실을 보여준다. 이는 뇌가 모든 문자 언어를 같은 방식으로 처리한다고 시사한다. 둘째, VWFA는 독자가 읽기에 더 능통해질수록 단어 인식에 더 특화된다. 언어 역시 문화적 진화의 산물이라는 점을 감안하면, 어떤 언어를 말하든 언어를 처리할 때 똑같은 언어 관련 뇌 영역들이 활성화된다는 사실은, 이 영역들이 언어를 위해 생물학적 적응을 하며 진화했다는 것을 의미하지 않는다. 오히려, VWFA와 마찬가지로, 이러한 언어 영역들도 언어 경험을 통해 형성된 것이며, 경우에 따라서는 거의 전적으로, 때로는 완전히 언어만 전담하는 신경 회로를 만들기도 한다.

다음 글의 내용과 가장 거리가 먼 것은?
① 문자 체계는 알파벳부터 음절 문자, 표어문자까지 구조상 차이가 있지만, 뇌는 모든 문자 언어를 비슷한 방식으로 처리한다.
② 뇌 속의 VWFA는 어떤 문자 체계를 사용하든지 독서를 할 때 일관되게 활성화된다.
③ VWFA는 읽기 능력과 읽기 경험이 증가할수록 더 특화된다.
④ 사람마다 사용하는 언어가 달라도 같은 뇌 영역이 활성화되며, 이는 이 영역들이 언어 경험을 통해 발달했음을 나타낸다.
⑤ VWFA는 읽기를 위해 특별히 진화된 것이며, 문자 해독 행위에 대한 생물학적 적응이다.

34　내용일치　　　　　　　　　　　②

| 분석 |
마지막 문장은 중국인과 일본인들의 절반 이상이 근시라는 게 아니라, 일반 인구 중 20%가 근시인데, 중국인과 일본인은 약 40%가 근시라는 내용이다. 따라서 ②가 정답이다.

| 어휘 |
myopia n. 근시　blurred a. 흐릿한, 선명하지 않은　practically ad. 사실상　symptom n. 증상　squeeze the eyelids 눈꺼풀을 찡그리다　optical a. 광학의, 시각의　retina n. 망막　degenerative changes 퇴행성 변화　pathological a. 질병의　impaired a. 손상된, 저하된　be liable to ~하기 쉽다　retinal detachment 망막 박리　visual display unit(VDU) 시각 디스플레이 장치(컴퓨터 모니터 등)　hereditary a. 유전적인　environmental factor 환경적 요인　vary with ~에 따라 달라지다

| 해석 |
근시는 가까운 물체는 선명하게 보이지만, 먼 물체는 흐릿하게 보이는 상태를 말하며, 시력을 약간 개선해주는 눈 가늘게 뜨기의 불편함을 제외하고는 거의 다른 증상이 없다. 광학적 관점에서 보면, 먼 물체의 상이 망막 위가 아니라 망막 앞에 맺힌다. 즉, 눈의 굴절력이 너무 강하거나, 또는 안구 자체가 앞뒤로 너무 길기 때문인데, 대개는 후자의 경우가 많다. 일부의 경우에, 근시는 성인이 되어서도 멈추지 않고 계속 진행된다. 이것은 망막 및 다른 조직에 퇴행성 변화가 생기는 병리적 상태이며, 교정하더라도 결국 시력이 손상된다. 이런 상태에서는 망막 박리 위험이 크므로 이러한 사람은 격렬한 운동이나 활동은 하지 않는 것이 중요하다. 근시는 대체로 10대 초반에 시작된다. 하지만 최근에는 10대 후반이나 20대 초반에 근시가 늘어나는 현상이 주목받고 있다. 이는 대개 책을 읽거나 디스플레이 장치를 보는 것과 같은 시각적 자극이 많은 것과 관련이 있다. 근시의 발생에는 유전적 요인과 환경적 요인이 모두 영향을 미친다. 일반 인구에서 약 5명 중 1명이 근시이지만, 이 수치는 연령, 인종, 지리적 요인에 따라 달라지며, 중국인과 일본인에게서 이 수치는 두 배로 증가한다.

다음 글의 내용과 가장 거리가 먼 것은?
① 근시는 가까운 물체는 또렷하게 보이고 먼 곳은 흐리게 보인다.
② 중국인과 일본인의 절반 이상이 근시이다.
③ 근시는 성인이 된 이후에도 진행될 수 있으며, 망막에 변화가 생긴다.
④ 근시는 유전적 요인과 환경적 요인 모두에 의해 발생할 수 있다.
⑤ 근시는 망막 위가 아니라 망막 앞쪽에 상이 맺힐 때 발생한다.

35　내용일치　　　　　　　　　　　④

| 분석 |
'새로운 환경은 그 낯섦으로 인해 시간을 길게 늘어나게 한다'고 했으므로 일상적인 활동에서 새로운 자극이 적다면 시간은 빨리 가는 것처럼 여겨질 것이며 시간 팽창은 일어나지 않을 것이다. 따라서 ④가 정답이다. ②, ③ 몰입과 달리, 강한 집중 상태는 많은 정보를 처리하고 있는 상태나 사고나 응급 상황을 가리킨다.

| 어휘 |
time perception 시간 지각(시간이 어떻게 느껴지는가)　information processing 정보 처리　absorption n. 몰입　contract time 시간을 축소하다, 짧게 느끼게 하다　stretch time 시간을 늘이다, 길게 느끼게 하다　boredom n. 지루함　unfocused mind 집중되지 않은 산만한 정신　thought-chatter n. 생각의 잡음, 잡념　time expansion experience(Tee) 시간 팽창 경험(위기 상황에서 시간이 느리게 느껴지는 현상)　emergency situation 긴급 상황　orders of magnitude 몇 배나 되는 크기, 매우 큰 차이　preventative action 예방 조치　slowing down of the moment 순간의 느려짐, 시간 지연의 체감

| 해석 |
시간이 왜 빠르게도 가고 느리게도 갈 수 있는지, 그 이유는 여전히 다소 미스터리하다. 일부 연구자들은, 시간 인식의 경미한 변화는 정보 처리 과정과 관련이 있다고 본다. 일반적으로, 우리의 정신이 인식, 감각, 생각과 같은 정보를 더 많이 처리할수록, 시간은 더 느리게 지나가는 것 같다. 아이들에게 시간이 느리게 지나가는 이유는 그들이 새로움의 세계 속에 살고 있기 때문이다. 새로운 환경은 그 낯섦으로 인해 시간을 길게 늘어나게 한다. 몰입은 시간을 축소한다. 우리의 집중은 좁아지고, 정신은 조용해지며, 머릿속을 지나가는 생각은 거의 없기 때문이다. 반대로, 지루함은 시간을 늘

어나게 한다. 집중되지 않은 마음이 수많은 생각의 잡음들로 가득 차기 때문이다. 시간 팽창 경험(Tees)은 예를 들어 자동차 사고나 추락, 공격(폭행)과 같은 사고나 긴급 상황에서 일어날 수 있다. 이런 시간 팽창 경험에서 시간은 훨씬 더 많이 팽창하는 것 같다. 전체 시간 팽창 경험 중 약 절반 정도가 사고나 응급 상황에서 발생한다. 이런 상황에서, 사람들은 생각하고 행동할 시간이 많다는 사실에 종종 놀란다. 실제로 많은 사람은 평소 같으면 불가능할 예방조치를 시간 팽창으로 인해 취할 수 있었고, 그 덕분에 큰 부상을 피하거나 심지어 목숨을 구할 수 있었다고 확신한다. 예를 들어, 시간 팽창 경험에서 자신의 차 위로 떨어지는 금속 장벽을 피했다고 보고하는 한 여성은 "순간이 느려짐"으로 인해 자신이 "떨어지는 금속을 어떻게 피할지를 결정할" 수 있게 된 경위를 나에게 들려주었다.

다음 글의 내용과 가장 거리가 먼 것은?
① 정보를 더 많이 처리할수록 시간 인식은 느려지는 경향이 있다.
② 몰입 상태에서 주의가 좁아지면 시간 인식이 축소될 수 있다.
③ 강한 집중 상태에서는 실제보다 시간이 더 길게 느껴지는 시간 팽창을 경험할 수 있다.
④ 일상적인 활동에서는 새로운 자극이 적기 때문에 시간이 느리게 가는 경향이 있어 시간 팽창이 더 자주 발생한다.
⑤ 사고나 응급 상황에서 시간 팽창이 자주 발생하며, 그 경우에 사람들은 명료하게 생각하고 행동할 수 있게 해주는 상당한 시간 연장을 인식한다.

HONGIK UNIVERSITY | 홍익대학교 서울 인문계 A형

TEST p. 720~734

01	③	02	④	03	③	04	②	05	①	06	③	07	④	08	①	09	①	10	③
11	①	12	③	13	②	14	④	15	②	16	①	17	③	18	④	19	③	20	④
21	④	22	①	23	②	24	①	25	③	26	①	27	④	28	①	29	①	30	④
31	②	32	③	33	②	34	④	35	②	36	①	37	②	38	④	39	②	40	④

01 동의어 ③

| 어휘 |

display v. 보이다, 나타내다 **equanimity** n. 침착함, 평정; 냉정(= aplomb) **etymology** n. 어원학 **grandiloquence** n. 과장된 말투 **guile** n. 교활함

| 해석 |

스포츠 종목 당 세 개의 메달만이 수여된다. 하지만 이제 막 메달을 따기 시작한 인도는, 메달 없이 돌아오는 사람들에게 공감하는 데 필요한 평정심을 보여주지 않았다.

02 동의어 ④

| 어휘 |

insinuate v. 암시하다(=imply) **brokerage fee** 중개 수수료 **explicitly** ad. 명확하게, 분명히 **breach** v. 위반하다 **ethics** n. 윤리 **admonish** v. 훈계하다 **venerate** v. 존경하다, 공경하다 **scrutinize** v. 조사하다

| 해석 |

낸시 제임스는 중개 수수료를 원한다고 여러 차례 암시했다. 그녀가 명확히 말하지는 않았지만, 그녀가 윤리를 위반했다고 결론지을 만한 충분한 증거가 있다.

03 동의어 ③

| 어휘 |

florid a. 화려한(= aureate) **distinct** a. 구별되는, 뚜렷이 다른 **inaccurate** a. 부정확한 **overstrain** a. 과장된 **censure** v. 비난하다 **inadequate** a. 불충분한, 부적절한 **inept** a. 서투른, 부적절한 **dire** a. 심각한, 끔찍한 **spartan** a. 검소한, 엄격한

| 해석 |

그 글들의 화려한 문체는 우리가 비판해온 부정확하고 과장된 표현과는 구별된다. 왜냐하면 그것만이 독자나 청자에게 잘못되고 부적절한 개념을 심어주는 부정확함이기 때문이다.

04 동의어 ②

| 어휘 |

sneer v. 비웃다, 조롱하다 **asinine** a. 어리석은(= fatuous) **ignorance** n. 무지 **gunner** n. 포병 **fire** v. 발사하다 **fabby** a. 근사한 **faddish** a. 일시적으로 유행하는 **fain** a. 기꺼이 ~하는

| 해석 |

프레더릭 패러는 "대포 가까이에 불빛을 켜 두어 밤에도 발사할 수 있게 한 중국 포병들의 어리석은 무지"를 비웃었다.

05 동의어 ①

| 어휘 |

unwilling a. 내키지 않는 **correspondent** n. 서신 교환자 **anomalous** a. 변칙적인, 이례적인 **standing** n. 지위, 신분 **tardy** a. 느린, 지체된 **perfunctory** a. 형식적인(= desultory) **eclat** n. 명성, 화려함 **inebriant** n. 취하게 하는 것, 술 **malfunctional** a. 오작동하는

| 해석 |

가우스는 마지못해 편지를 쓰는 사람이었기에, 소피 제르맹이 여성 수학자라는 특이한 신분을 감추는 것이 최선이라 생각하여 르블랑이라는 이름으로 그에게 편지를 썼을 때, 한참 후에 형식적인 답장만을 받았다.

06 동의어 ③

| 어휘 |

contrary a. 반대의   dogmatic a. 독단적인   conservative a. 보수적인   tetchy a. 화를 잘 내는(= peevish)   dismissive a. 무시하는   alternative n. 대안   considerate a. 사려 깊은   exploratory a. 탐구적인   sagacious a. 현명한   forearmed a. 미리 무장한   abstemious a. 절제하는, 금욕적인

| 해석 |

어떤 신자들은 반대 이론을 쉽게 무시할 것이고, 어떤 신자들은 그러지 못할 것이다. 어떤 사람들은 다른 사람들보다 더 독단적이다. 어떤 사람들은 보수적이고, 쉽게 짜증내며, 대안을 무시하지만, 다른 사람들은 열린 마음을 가지고 사려 깊고 탐구적이다.

07 동의어 ④

| 어휘 |

mapping n. 대응시킴, 연결시킴   perforce ad. 필연적으로, 억지로(= ineluctably)   wantonly ad. 제멋대로, 이유 없이   despondently ad. 낙담하여   apathetically ad. 무관심하게   ineluctably ad. 피할 수 없이, 불가피하게

| 해석 |

문장을 문장에 대응시키는 것을 포함하는 해석은 언어가 없이는 불가능하다. 따라서 언어가 없는 동물은 필연적으로 생각을 할 수 없다.

08 동의어 ①

| 어휘 |

anti-immigrant a. 반(反)이민의   backlash n. 반발(= revulsion)   decade n. 10년   social contract 사회 계약   bivouac n. 야영   alternator n. 교류 발전기   predominance n. 우세, 지배

| 해석 |

지난 10년간의 이민에 반대하는 반발은 전후(戰後) 사회 계약의 위기에 깊이 뿌리를 두고 있다.

09 동의어 ①

| 어휘 |

overture n. 제안, 신청   extremist n. 극단주의자   renounce v. 포기하다, 단념하다(= abjure)   window of opportunity 기회의 창   redress v. 바로잡다, 시정하다   wrong n. 과거의 잘못   penchant n. 기호, 성향   reconvene v. 재소집하다

| 해석 |

폭력을 포기하고 쟁점들을 논의하겠다는 극단주의 집단들의 최근 제안은 과거의 잘못을 시정할 수 있는 기회의 창을 마련해준다.

10 동의어 ③

| 어휘 |

negate v. 부정하다, 무효로 하다   refute v. 반박하다(= disprove)   historical a. 역사적인   generation n. 세대   come of age 성인이 되다   enhance v. 향상시키다   relinquish v. 포기하다   disprove v. 반증하다   perpetuate v. 영속시키다

| 해석 |

이 논문의 목적은 그 비극적인 시기에 성인이 된 세대의 역사적 기억을 부정하거나 반박하려는 것이 아니다.

11 관용표현 ①

| 분석 |

"어떤 일에 종사하다"는 'be engaged in'이라는 표현을 사용한다. 따라서 "시카고에서 어떤 일에 종사하다"라는 말은 'be engaged in something in Chicago'의 형태이다. 따라서 ①을 in what business로 고쳐야 한다.

| 어휘 |

engage in ~에 종사하다   move v. 이사하다   take over 인수하다   run v. 운영하다, 경영하다

| 해석 |

지그문트 블룸필드가 1896년 이전 시카고에서 어떤 사업에 종사했는지 우리는 모르지만, 젊은 리어나드가 아홉 살이었을 때, 그의 아버지는 가족을 위스콘신 주 엘크하트 레이크로 이주시켰고, 그곳에서 슈워츠 호텔을 인수하여 운영했다.

12 태 ③

| 분석 |

design은 "(사람이 무엇을) 설계하다"라는 의미의 타동사이다. 소프트웨어 프로그램은 사람에 의해 설계된 것이므로 ③을 (which are) designed로 고쳐야 한다.

| 어휘 |

argument visualization 논점 시각화   argument diagram 논점 다이어그램   critical thinking 비판적 사고   over the course of ~동안   semester-long a. 한 학기 분량의   college-level a. 대학 수준의

| 해석 |

논점 시각화에 대한 최근의 연구는 학생들이 논점 다이어그램을 구성하는 데 도움을 주기 위해 특별히 고안된 소프트웨어 프로그램의 이용이 한 학기 정도 대학 수준의 비판적 사고 강좌를 듣는 과정

에서 학생들의 비판적 사고 능력을 상당히 향상시킬 수 있다는 것을 보여주었다.

것 같다. 그래서 버섯 캐기 나들이 중에, 적국 군인들이 덤불 뒤에서 나타나서 우리를 데려간다.

13 명령, 주장의 동사가 이끄는 that절의 동사 형태 ②

| 분석 |
주절의 동사 required가 that 절을 목적어로 취하고 있다. 주절 동사가 '명령, 요구, 주장, 제안'의 의미가 있는 동사일 경우 that절의 동사는 '(should)+동사원형'여야 한다. 따라서 ②를 be로 고친다.

| 어휘 |
privileged a. 특권을 가진 **reference frame** 기준 틀, 준거 기준 **generally covariant** (물리학 용어) 일반 공변적인 **equation** n. 방정식 **coordinate** n. 좌표

| 해석 |
어떠한 우선적인 기준 틀도 없이, 그 이론은 모든 물리 법칙이 반드시 일반 공변적인 방정식으로 표현되고, 그 방정식들이 모든 좌표계에서 동일한 형태를 갖기를 요구했다.

14 관용표현 ②

| 분석 |
"A와 B는 별개다, 완전히 다르다"라는 의미의 표현은 'A is one thing B is another'이다. 따라서 ②를 another로 고쳐야 한다.

| 어휘 |
behold v. 바라보다 **slanted** a. 기울어진 **gleam** v. 반짝이다

| 해석 |
가족 식구 모두는 무냐가 캐딜락을 샀다는 사실을 알고 있지만, 아는 것과 보는 것은 완전히 다르다. 정말 장관이다. 정말 아름다운 차다! 온통 크롬으로 된 차가 6월 늦은 오후의 비스듬한 햇살 아래서 반짝이고 있다.

15 일치 ②

| 분석 |
'Neither of ~'는 단수로 취급한다. 따라서 ②를 단수형인 seems to로 고쳐야 한다.

| 어휘 |
more or less 다소 **occupy** v. 점령하다 **hostile** a. 적대적인 **outing** n. 소풍, 나들이

| 해석 |
우리 바구니는 둘 다 절반쯤 차 있다. 지금은 전쟁 중이고, 우리나라가 어느 정도 점령되어 있다는 것을 우리 둘 다 기억하지 못하는

16 병치 ③

| 분석 |
②에서 plan이라는 동사원형을 사용하는 이유는 앞에 있는 help 동사 때문이다. 'help+사람+동사원형'으로 '사람이 ~하는 데 도움이 된다'라는 의미이다. ③도 help동사의 목적보어로 ②와 병치를 이루므로 동사원형 manage로 고쳐야 한다.

| 어휘 |
exchange rate 환율 **gas price** 유가(油價) **affect** v. 영향을 미치다 **living expense** 생활비 **manage** v. 관리하다 **in case** ~할 경우에 **give attention to** ~에 주의를 기울이다

| 해석 |
환율과 유가(油價)가 경제에 미치는 영향을 이해하는 것은 사람들이 월간 생활비를 계획하는 데, 그리고 은행 계좌를 관리하여 은행 계좌에 더 많은 주의를 기울여야 하는 경우에 대비하는 데 도움이 된다.

17 전치사 ③

| 분석 |
'~에 대한 통제/지배'에서 control 다음의 전치사는 over이다. ③을 control over로 고쳐야 한다. over 자리에 of를 쓰는 것도 가능하다.

| 어휘 |
overwhelm v. 압도하다 **vital** a. 중요한 **grant** v. 부여하다 **exclusive** a. 독점적인 **shipping** n. 선적 **colony** n. 식민지

| 해석 |
심각한 재정 위기에 짓눌려 있던 강력하고 저명한 동인도 회사는 미국 식민지로 가는 모든 차의 선적에 대한 독점적 지배권을 영국 의회에 의해 부여받았다.

18 태 ④

| 분석 |
injure는 타동사이므로 injuring 다음에 목적어가 있어야 하는데 없고, 무릎이 부상을 입는 것이므로 수동태 동명사를 사용하여야 한다. ④를 without being injured로 고쳐야 한다.

| 어휘 |
be likely to ~할 가능성이 있다 **damage** v. 손상시키다 **joint** n. 관절 **twist** v. 비틀다 **injure** v. 다치게 하다

| 해석 |
무릎은 뒤틀리기만 하면 부상을 입기 때문에 발목과 손목 같은 대부분의 다른 신체 관절들보다 손상될 가능성이 더 크다.

19 논리완성 ③

| 분석 |
문맥상 베이커 박사는 지혜, 고결함, 겸손을 '상징'하거나 '대표'하는 인물이다. 따라서 epitome(전형)이 빈칸에 적절하다.

| 어휘 |
passing n. 죽음, 별세 **nobility** n. 고결함 **humility** n. 겸손 **serve** v. 봉사하다, 섬기다 **compassion** n. 연민, 자비 **empower** v. 권한을 주다, 힘을 북돋우다 **bane** n. 재앙, 골칫거리 **antithesis** n. 정반대 **epitome** n. 전형, 모범 **indigence** n. 극빈, 가난

| 해석 |
베이커 박사의 별세에서 우리는 지혜와 고결함, 겸손함의 전형이었고 온 마음과 정신으로 조국을 섬겼던 한 지도자를 잃었다. 그의 자비와 비전은 수백만 명의 삶에 변화와 능력을 가져다주었다.

20 논리완성 ③

| 분석 |
땅에 대한 수요가 크다고 했으므로, 놀리는 땅은 거의 없다고 보아야 한다. 따라서 '밭이 경작되지 않고 쉬는 상태로 남아 있는'이라는 의미의 fallow가 적절하다. 나머지는 모두 땅과는 관련 없는 표현들이다.

| 어휘 |
demand n. 수요 **seldom** ad. 거의 ~않다 **incisive** a. 날카로운, 통찰력 있는 **preeminent** a. 탁월한, 우월한 **fallow** a. 휴경의, 놀리는 **meticulous** a. 꼼꼼한

| 해석 |
토지에 대한 수요가 큰 그 나라 남부에서는, 밭이 계속 휴경 상태로 있는 것은 거의 허용되지 않는다.

21 논리완성 ④

| 분석 |
학사 학위의 가치에 대해 회의적이게 되었다고 한 것은 학사 학위에 대해 비관적이게 되었다는 말이다. 그러므로 빈칸에는 less sanguine(덜 낙관적인)이 적절하다.

| 어휘 |
bachelor's degree 학사 학위 **skeptical** a. 회의적인 **potential** a. 잠재적인 **return on investment** 투자 수익률 **modish** a. 유행을 따르는 **morose** a. 우울한 **haphazard** a. 무계획적인

sanguine a. 낙관적인

| 해석 |
고등 교육에 대한 대중의 신뢰가 저하되었으므로, 미국인들은 학사 학위에 대해 덜 낙관적이게 되었고, 그 투자 대비 수익률에 대해서도 회의적이게 되었다.

22 논리완성 ①

| 분석 |
유럽이 아프리카 문화를 '열등하다'라고 생각하고 자신들의 지배를 정당화하려 했다는 내용이다. tutelage는 이 맥락에서 유럽이 아프리카를 '교육'하거나 '보호'해야 한다는 근거 없는 명분을 가리킨다.

| 어휘 |
inadequacy n. 부적합성, 부족함 **indigenous** a. 토착의, 원주민의 **allege** v. (근거 없이) 주장하다 **tutelage** n. 보호, 감독 **tumidness** n. 부풀, 과장됨 **tubercle** n. 결절, 작은 혹 **turgescence** n. 팽창

| 해석 |
아프리카 토착 언어와 토착 정신 혹은 문명은 기능적으로나 형식적으로 부족하다는 생각이 유럽의 보호감독을 정당화한다고 종종 주장되었다.

23 논리완성 ②

| 분석 |
시위대에 빨간 물감을 뿌린 사람들은 시위나 발표를 야유하고 방해하는 사람들일 것이다. 이런 사람들을 heckler라고 한다.

| 어휘 |
pacifist n. 평화주의자 **splatter** v. (물을) 튀기다 **heckler** n. 야유꾼, 방해자 **barrister** n. 법정 변호사 **notary** n. 공증인 **crackerjack** n. 일 잘하는 사람, 수완가

| 해석 |
1965년 여름, 수백 명의 사람들이 워싱턴에 모여 전쟁 반대 시위행진을 했다. 선두에 선 역사가 스토튼 린드, SNCC 조직가 밥 모지스, 오랜 평화주의자 데이비드 델린저는 야유꾼들이 뿌린 빨간 물감을 뒤집어썼다.

24 논리완성 ①

| 분석 |
술집에서 술꾼들이 당신을 지나쳐 화장실로 간다. 술에 취해 느리게 지나다니는 사람들의 흐름을 묘사하는 traipse(어슬렁거림)가 적절하다.

| 어휘 |

break down 무너뜨리다 **division** n. 분리, 구분 **blaring** a. 요란한 **wobble** v. 비틀거리다 **loo** n. 화장실 **grabble** v. 더듬다, 낑낑대며 잡다 **conducive to** ~에 도움이 되는 **traipse** v. 터벅터벅 걷다, 느릿하게 돌아다니다 n. 어슬렁거리기 **trestle** n. 받침대, 다리 구조물 **trice** n. 순간, 눈 깜짝할 사이 **trover** n. 불법 점유물 반환 소송

| 해석 |

개념은 단순하다. 격식 있는 식사와 격식 없는 음주의 경계를 허문다는 것이다. 하지만 술집에서 쿵쾅거리는 음악과 당신이 랍스터 집게와 씨름하는 사이 화장실로 비틀거리며 지나가는 술꾼들의 끊임없는 어슬렁거림은 평온한 저녁 외출에 도움이 되지 않는다.

25 논리완성 ③

| 분석 |

빈칸에는 신의 섭리를 추측해 알려내려는 것, 즉 신의 섭리를 알려주는 augury(징조)가 적절하다.

| 어휘 |

brink n. 직전, 가장자리 **recourse** n. 의존 **prophetism** n. 예언자적 태도 **extravagant** a. 과도한, 터무니없는 **second-guess** v. 사후 예측하다, 결과를 미리 추측하다 **Providence** n. 신의 섭리 **audacity** n. 대담함, 뻔뻔스러움 **prebendary** n. (성직자에게 주는) 봉급 또는 그 수령자 **augury** n. 점, 전조, 조짐 **promptitude** n. 신속함, 민첩함

| 해석 |

백작은 그들이 '위대한 사건'의 직전에 있다는 데는 상원의원과 의견이 같지만, 상원의원의 예언주의에 대한 의존과 신의 섭리를 추측하며 징조를 찾으려는 터무니없는 욕망에는 반대한다.

26 논리완성 ①

| 분석 |

빈칸 이하에서 정치적인 사건에는 전혀 중요하지 않다고 하였다. 이와 비슷한 의미여야 하므로 '주변적인'이라는 의미의 ①이 정답으로 적절하다.

| 어휘 |

cultural clique 문화적 소집단, 폐쇄적 그룹 **of no consequence** 중요하지 않은 **peripheral** a. 주변적인, 중요하지 않은 **excavate** v. 발굴하다 **invigorating** a. 활기를 주는 **invincible** a. 천하무적의

| 해석 |

서구는 일반적으로 자체 내의 문화 집단들을 무시했는데, 이들은 주변적이고 정치적 사건에 아무런 중요성도 없는 것으로 간주되었다.

27 논리완성 ④

| 분석 |

뒤에 나오는 성숙하고, 세련되고, 교양 있는 사람과 반대 의미이고, 나이가 젊고 장난꾸러기라는 말과 잘 어울려야 한다. 젊은이의 성격과 잘 어울리는 것은 ④(충동적인)밖에 없다.

| 어휘 |

party n. 정당, 단체 **rascal** n. 악동, 장난꾸러기 **representative** n. 대표자 **mature** a. 성숙한 **debonair** a. 상냥하고 세련된 **sophisticate** n. 교양 있는 사람, 세련된 사람 **incumbent** a. 재임중인, 현직의 **prudent** a. 신중한 **putative** a. 추정상의, 소문상의 **impetuous** a. 충동적인, 성급한

| 해석 |

그 당의 당원들은 자신들의 대표로 젊고 충동적인 악동 유형을 선호할까, 아니면 더 성숙하고 세련된 교양인을 선호할까?

28 논리완성 ①

| 분석 |

앞에서 많은 풍미를 잃게 된다고 하였으므로, '풍미가 없다'라는 의미의 insipid가 적절하다.

| 어휘 |

force through 강행하다, 관철시키다, 통과시키다 **pulp** n. 과육 **flavour** n. 풍미, 맛 **be left with** ~만 남다 **insipid** a. 맛이 없는, 김빠진 **insolent** a. 건방진, 무례한 **insidious** a. 은밀히 퍼지는 **imposturous** a. 사기꾼 같은

| 해석 |

과육을 거의 모두 반드시 넣는 것이 중요하다. 그렇지 않으면 많은 풍미를 잃게 되고, 한 그릇의 맛없는 액체만 남게 될 것이다.

29~31

참으로, 수는 무엇인가? 플라톤주의라는 철학적 입장에 따르면, 수와 또 다른 수학적인 것들은 추상적 것으로 존재한다. 플라톤은 이러한 것들이 이상적 형태의 영역에 존재한다고 보았다. 종이에 그리는 특정한 선이나 원은 결함이 있고 불완전하지만, 플라톤의 영역에서는 완벽한 선, 원, 그리고 수들이 존재한다. 이 관점에서 보면, 수학자가 "이런저런 속성을 가진 자연수가 존재한다"라고 말하는 것은 플라톤의 영역에서 그러한 수들이 발견될 수 있음을 의미한다. 플라톤주의에 대한 현대적 접근은 추상적 것들이 존재한다고는 주장하지만, 플라톤의 이상적 형태라는 개념이나 모든 추상적인 것들이 한데 모인 곳인 플라톤 영역과는 덜 연관되어 있다.

"연속이지만 미분가능하지는 않은 함수 F가 존재한다."라든가, "이 미분방정식의 해법이 존재한다."라든가, "점렬로는 컴팩트하지만 컴팩트하지 않은 위상 공간이 존재한다"라고 말하는 것은 무엇을 의미하는가? 이것은 물리적 존재가 아니다. 우리는 이러한 '것들'을 손으로 잡을 수 없다. 그렇다면 이것은 어떤 종류의 존재인가? 플라톤주의에 따르면, 수학적인 것들은 추상적이지만 실제로 존재한다. 플라톤주의자에게는, 수학에서 수학적인 것들의 존재에 대한 일상적인 이야기가 문자 그대로 받아들여질 수 있다. 다시 말해, 그것들은 물리적이 아니라, 추상적으로 존재한다. 이 관점에 따르면, 수학적 존재의 본질은 아름다움이나 행복과 같은 다른 추상적인 것들의 존재의 본질과 유사하다. 아름다움이 존재하는가? 나는 존재한다고 믿는다. 평행선은 존재하는가? 플라톤주의에 따르면, 이 두 질문에 대한 답은 유사하다. 하지만 추상적인 것들은 무엇인가? 이 존재의 본질은 무엇인가?

헨릭 입센의 희곡 『인형의 집』을 생각해보자. 이 희곡은 분명 존재한다. 하지만 여기서 존재하는 것은 구체적으로 무엇인가? 나는 인쇄된 원고를 내밀며 "이것이 『인형의 집』이다"라고 말할 수 있다. 그러나 이는 충분한 사실이 아니다. 왜냐하면 그 특정 원고가 손상되더라도 우리는 희곡 자체가 손상되었다고 말하지 않기 때문이다. 또한, 내가 (그 원고를 뒷주머니에 넣고) 오토바이를 타고 다녔다고 해서 그 희곡이 내 뒷주머니에 있었다고 말하지도 않는다. 브로드웨이에서 그 희곡 공연을 볼 수 있지만, 어떤 특정 공연이 그 희곡 자체라고 보기는 어렵다. 우리는 입센의 희곡이 1879년 초연에서만 존재했다고 말하지 않으며, 공연이 있을 때마다 희곡이 존재했다가 사라진다고도 말하지 않는다. 그 희곡은 추상적이며, 다양한 원고나 공연이라는 불완전한 구현(사례들)의 이상화이다.

희곡과 마찬가지로, 57이라는 수도, 바구니에 담긴 사과 57개와 속임수를 쓰는 도박사의 카드 한 벌에 들어있는 카드 57장(카드 종류에 따라 다를 수 있음) 등, 다양한 불완전한 구현으로(사례들로) 존재한다. 추상적인 것들의 존재는 그 다양한 구현(사례들)을 통해 어떻게든 매개된다. 57이라는 수의 존재는 희곡, 소설, 또는 노래의 존재와 유사한가? 다른 예술 작품과 마찬가지로 희곡은 창작되었다. 입센이 『인형의 집』을 썼다. 일부 수학자들은 자신의 작업을 창작 행위로 묘사하지만, 어떤 수학자도 57이라는 수를 그런 의미에서 창작했다고 주장하지는 않을 것이다. 수학은 발견되는 것인가, 창작되는 것인가? 현대 플라톤주의의 일부 관점은 수와 기타 수학적인 것들은 (수학자로부터) 독립적으로 존재한다고 본다.

| 어휘 |
platonism n. 플라톤주의(수학적 대상은 추상적 실재로 존재한다고 보는 철학 입장) **abstract object** 추상적 대상(물리적으로는 존재하지 않고 개념적으로 존재하는 대상) **ideal form** 이데아, 이상적 형상 **flawed** a. 결함이 있는 **natural number** 자연수 **property** n. 성질 **function** n. 함수 **solution** n. 해법 **differential equation** 미분방정식 **topological space** 위상 공간 **sequentially compact** 점렬로 콤팩트한 **compact** a. 콤팩트한, 위상적으로 닫혀 있고 유계인 성질의 **literal** a. 문자 그대로의 **come into existence** 존재하게 되다 **idealization** n. 이상화 **instantiation** n. 구체적 실현, 구현 **bushel** n. 부셸(곡물 등의 용량 단위) **deck** n. 카드 덱 **mediated** a. 매개된

29 글의 제목 ①

| 분석 |
"수란 무엇인가"라는 질문을 던지고, 수학적 플라톤주의라는 입장에 따라 수와 수학적인 것들이 어떻게 '존재'하는가를 설명하는 글이다. ④ 이 글에서 연극은 수의 존재 방식을 설명하기 위한 비교 대상으로 등장한다.

글의 제목은?
① 수학적 플라톤주의에서 수의 본질
② 연극과 수의 유사점과 차이점
③ 현실과 추상 영역에서 수의 결함과 완전성
④ 연극과 수에 대한 플라톤의 철학적 주장

30 내용파악 ④

| 분석 |
이 글의 마지막 And while부터 끝까지에서 희곡은 창조된 것이고 수는 독립적으로 존재한다고 둘의 차이를 분명히 밝히고 있다.

이 글에 따르면『인형의 집』과 수는 일부 성질을 공유하고 있지만, _____는 의미에서 여전히 다르다.
① 수는 현실 세계에 실제로 존재하지 않지만, 이와 달리『인형의 집』은 인쇄된 원고 형태로 존재할 수 있다
② 플라톤은 그의 추상적 존재 이론에서 수와는 대조적으로, 희곡은 진지하게 고려하지 않았을 것이라
③『인형의 집』이 물리적 수단으로 구현될 수 있는 것과 달리 수는 추상적 영역에만 존재한다
④『인형의 집』과 달리, 수는 창조된 것이 아니라 수학자의 작업이나 사고와는 독립적으로 존재한다

31 내용추론 ②

| 분석 |
② 희곡과 수 모두 완전히 추상적인 것이고, 공연, 원고는 '불완전'한 구현이므로 옳다. ① 완전하지 않고, 불완전하다. ③ 추상 영역이 아니라 현실, 다시 말해 물리적 영역이다. ④ 구현은 불완전하다.

다음 중 이 글에서 추론할 수 있는 것은?
① 『인형의 집』의 인쇄된 원고들은 그 희곡의 완전한 실현 형태(사례들)로 간주될 수 있다.
② 『인형의 집』의 구현 형태들(사례들)이 불완전하더라도, 희곡은 플라톤적 영역에서 완전하게 존재한다고 우리는 말할 수 있다.
③ 수의 존재는 추상적 영역 내에서 다양한 실현들(사례들)을 통해 매개될 수 있다.
④ 희곡과 달리, 수는 수학자와는 독립적으로 존재하고, 그러므로 그 구현 형태들(사례들)은 완전해야 한다.

32~34

스탠리 밀그램은 일련의 실험을 수행하며 권위에 대한 순종을 연구했다. 그는 코네티컷 주 뉴헤이븐 지역 신문에 광고를 내어, 예일 대학교에서 진행되는 '기억과 학습에 관한 과학적 연구'에 참여할 남성들에게 소정의 보수를 제공하겠다고 제안했다. 자원자들은 예일 대학교 내 밀그램의 실험실에 찾아왔고, 그곳에서 흰색 실험복을 입은 과학자와 또 다른 자원자인 중년 남성 '월리스 씨'를 만났다. 사실 월리스 씨는 실험자의 공모자(조력자)였지만, 참가자들은 이를 알지 못했다. 과학자는 처벌이 학습에 미치는 영향을 조사하는 연구라고 설명했다. 한 사람은 '교사'가 되어 처벌을 가하고, 다른 사람은 '학습자'가 될 것이었다. 월리스 씨와 자원자 참가자는 교사와 학습자를 결정하기 위해 종이쪽지를 뽑았다. 그러나 이 뽑기는 조작된 것이어서 월리스 씨는 항상 학습자가 되었고, 실제 자원자는 항상 교사가 되었다.

과학자는 월리스 씨에게 전극을 부착한 뒤, '교사'를 옆방에 있는 대단해 보이는 전기 충격 기 앞에 앉혔다. 이 충격기에는 일련의 레버가 있었는데, 참가자에게는 레버를 누르면 월리스 씨에게 전기 충격이 가해진다고 알려주었다. 첫 번째 레버는 15볼트, 두 번째는 30볼트, 세 번째는 45볼트, 이런 식으로 최대 450볼트까지 올라갔다. 레버에는 또 '약한 충격', '중간 충격'에서 '위험: 심각한 충격'까지 라벨이 붙어 있었고, 400볼트를 넘는 레버 위에는 붉은 X 표시가 있었다. 월리스 씨는 일련의 단어 쌍을 외우도록 지시받았다. 그리곤 어떤 단어가 짝을 이루는지 확인하는 테스트를 받았다. 월리스 씨가 실수할 때마다 교사는 처벌로 전기 충격을 가해야 했다. 첫 번째 실수에는 15볼트, 두 번째 실수에는 30볼트의 충격을 가하는 식이었다. 실수할 때마다 학습자는 더 큰 충격을 받았다.

사실 월리스 씨는 어떤 충격도 받지 않았지만, 실험 참가자들은 이를 몰랐다. 실험에서 월리스 씨는 계속 실수를 저질렀다. 교사가 약 120볼트로 '충격'을 가했을 때 월리스 씨는 고통스러운 비명을 지르며, 마침내 실험에서 나가고 싶다고 소리쳤다. 만약 교사가 그만두길 원했다면 어떻게 되었을까? 실제로 이런 일이 일어났다. 자원자 참가자들은 월리스 씨가 겪는 것 같아 보이는 고통에 눈에 띄게 동요했다. 실험자는 교사에게 그만둘 수 있다고 말했지만, 실험을 계속하는 것이 중요하다며 여러 구두 지시를 통해 계속하도록 촉구했다. 어떤 일이 벌어졌는가? 대략 65%의 참가자들은 450볼트에 이르기까지 계속해서 충격을 가했다.

밀그램은 856명의 실험대상자와 더불어 이 기본 절차를 여러 번 변형하며 실험을 진행했다. 이 연구는 커다란 반향을 불러일으켰으며, 그 결과는 우리가 권위에 저항할 수 있는 능력에 대한 많은 믿음을 뒤흔들었다.

하지만 밀그램 연구는 행동 연구에서 윤리 문제를 논의하는 중요한 사례이기도 하다. 밀그램 연구나 다른 연구가 윤리적인지에 대해 우리는 어떻게 판단해야 할까? 밀그램 연구는 우리의 윤리적 의사결정을 안내하는 윤리적 기준을 개발하는 데 중요한 역할을 한 많은 연구 중 하나였다.

| 어휘 |

conduct v. 수행하다 obedience n. 복종 authority n. 권위 place v. 게재하다 local a. 지역의 volunteer n. 지원자 report v. 출석하다 laboratory n. 실험실 confederate n. 공모자, 공범 accomplice n. 공범 rig v. 조작하다 attach v. 부착하다 electrode n. 전극 adjoining a. 인접한 deliver v. 전달하다, 가하다 label v. 표시하다 moderate a. 보통의 identify v. 식별하다 eventually ad. 결국 yell v. 소리치다 urge v. 촉구하다 verbal a. 언어의 prod n. 자극, 재촉 variation n. 변형, 변주 procedure n. 절차 subject n. 피실험자 publicity n. 주목, 언론의 관심 challenge v. 도전하다, 의문을 제기하다

32 부분이해   ③

| 분석 |

실험의 목적에 관해 거짓말을 한 이유는 실험 대상인 참가자가 그 진정한 목적을 몰라야 연구가 가능했기 때문이다. 따라서 ③ 진정한 목적을 숨기기 위해서였다.

밑줄 친 Ⓐ의 이유는 무엇인가?
① 과학자는 기억과 학습 사이에 상관관계가 있는지를 조사하고 싶었다.
② 과학자는 이 연구에 혼란 변수를 포함시키고 싶었다.
③ 과학자는 이 연구의 진짜 목적을 숨기고 싶었다.
④ 과학자는 참가자들이 얼마나 많은 어휘 실수를 하는지 시험해 보고 싶었다.

33 부분이해   ②

| 분석 |

"실험자는 교사에게 그만둘 수 있다고 말했지만, 실험을 계속하는 것이 중요하다며 여러 구두 지시를 통해 계속하도록 촉구했다. 어

떤 일이 벌어졌는가? 대략 65%의 참가자들은 450볼트에 이르기까지 계속해서 충격을 가했다"라는 내용은 과반이 넘는 참가자들이 실험자의 말에 복종했다는 말이다. 실험의 진정한 목적이 권위에 대한 저항이었다. ① 전압과는 상관없이 돈을 주기로 하였다. ③ 참가자들은 월리스 씨의 고통에 괴로워했다. 월리스 씨가 잘못했다는 판단은 내리지 않았다. ④ 고통을 인지했다.

밑줄 친 ⓑ의 이유는 무엇인가?
① 참가자들은 최고 전압까지 도달하면 소액의 돈을 받기로 약속받았다.
② 참가자들은 실험자의 강요에 복종해야 한다는 압박감을 느꼈다.
③ 참가자들은 월리스 씨가 끔찍한 전기 충격을 받아 마땅하다고 생각했다.
④ 참가자들은 월리스 씨가 멀리 있었기 때문에 그가 고통받는 것을 눈치채지 못했다.

34 내용추론 ④

| 분석 |
참가자들은 월리스 씨가 고통 받고 있다고 믿었고, 그로 인해 괴로워 실험을 그만두고 싶어 했다. ① 몰랐다. ② 참가자로 알고 있었다. ③ 과반수가 처벌을 가했다.

다음 중 이 글에서 추론할 수 있는 것은?
① 참가자들은 월리스 씨가 실험자의 공모자라는 것을 알고 있었다.
② 참가자들은 월리스 씨가 자원 참가자가 아니라는 것을 몰랐다.
③ 어떤 참가자도 벌을 가하지 않았다.
④ 참가자들은 월리스 씨를 해치고 있다고 믿었기 때문에 심리적 고통을 느꼈다.

35~37

대부분의 연구 프로젝트는 관심 있는 모집단에서 참가자 표본을 선정하는 것을 포함한다. 모집단은 연구자가 관심을 가진 모든 개인으로 구성된다. 예를 들어, 대규모 여론조사에서 관심 모집단은 미국의 모든 자격 있는 유권자일 수 있다. 이는 18세 미만인 사람, 수감자, 다른 나라에서 온 방문자, 그리고 투표 자격이 없는 사람은 포함되지 않음을 의미한다. 또 다른 예로, 당신이 다니는 대학의 모든 학생을 모집단으로 하는 설문 조사를 수행할 수 있다. 시간과 돈이 충분하다면, 설문 조사 연구자는 이론적으로 모집단의 모든 사람에게 연락할 수 있다. 미국은 10년마다 전체 인구를 대상으로 하는 공식 인구 조사를 통해 이를 시도한다. 그러나 모집단이 상대적으로 작다면, 전체 모집단 연구가 비교적 쉬울 수도 있다.

다른 예를 들어보자. 만약 당신이 대학의 모든 학생에게 집에서 공부하는 것을 선호하는지, 학교에서 공부하는 것을 선호하는지 물었고, 64%가 집에서 공부하는 것을 선호한다고 답했다고 하자. 이 경우에 당신은 질문에 대한 답을 매우 확신할 수 있을 것이다. 모든 학생에게 물어봤기 때문이다. 물론 이는 상당한 비용이 든다. 모든 학생을 추적하기 위해서는 연구 조교 팀을 고용해야 할 수도 있다. 하지만 당신이 개인적으로 부유하지 않거나 (혹은 돈을 더 나은 곳에 쓰고 싶다면), 대학생 중에서 무작위로 하위 집단을 선정해 그들에게 질문을 할 수 있다. 적절한 표본 추출을 통해 우리는 모집단을 대표하는 표본을 얻을 수 있으며, 표본에 참여한 참가자(또는 '응답자')로부터 얻은 정보를 사용해 모집단 전체의 특성을 추정할 수 있다. 통계 이론은 표본에서 얻은 데이터를 활용해 전체 모집단의 특성을 추정할 수 있게 해준다.

| 어휘 |
sample n. 표본 **population** n. 모집단 **interest** n. 관심, 관심 대상 **compose** v. 구성하다 **eligible** a. 자격이 있는 **voter** n. 유권자 **incarcerate** v. 투옥하다 **conduct** v. 수행하다 **survey** n. 설문 조사 **conceivably** ad. 아마, 상상컨대 **contact** v. 연락하다 **census** n. 인구 조사 **costly** a. 비용이 많이 드는 **track down** 추적하다 **subgroup** n. 하위 집단 **sampling** n. 표집 **representative** a. 대표성 있는 **statistical** a. 통계적인 **superset** n. 상위 집합 **recruit** v. (신입 회원·사원 등을) 모집하다

35 내용추론 ②

| 분석 |
마지막 부분에서 적절한 표본 추출을 통해 모든 사람을 조사하지 않고도, 모집단 전체에 대한 정보를 추정할 수 있다고 하였다. ① 아무 방법이 아니라 무작위와 같은 '적절한' 방법이어야 한다. ③ 적용될 수 있다. ④ superset이 아니라 subset이어야 한다.

다음 중 이 글에서 추론할 수 있는 것은?
① 관심 있는 모집단의 특성은 어떤 표본 추출 방법으로도 정확히 반영된다.
② 전체 모집단을 조사하지 않고도 모집단에 대한 추정치를 얻는 것이 가능하다.
③ 통계 이론은 표본으로부터 수집한 자료에 적용될 수 없다.
④ 모집단 표본추출은 관심 있는 모집단으로부터 상위 집합을 추출하는 것으로 정의된다.

36 내용파악 ①

| 분석 |
"you could randomly select a subgroup of students at your university and ask them the question. With proper sampling,

we can have a representative sample of the population..."을 보면 무작위 표본추출(표본선택)을 통해 대표성 있는 표본을 얻는다고 하였다. 이를 거꾸로 말하면 random하지 않으면 대표성을 잃고 한쪽으로 치우친 '편향'(bias)이 생길 수 있다는 말이다. ② 모집단은 사전에 정의되어야 한다. ③ '많은 수'보다는 '공정하고 대표성 있는 추출'이 목적이다. ④ 응답률을 높이는 방법에 관한 이야기는 없다.

무작위 표본추출을 해야 하는 이유는?
① 표본추출 편향의 위험이 표본 선택 과정에서 감소될 수 있기 때문이다.
② 표본 선택 동안에 관심 있는 모집단이 쉽게 정의될 수 있기 때문이다.
③ 연구자가 많은 수의 참가자를 모집할 수 있기 때문이다.
④ 무작위 선택에 의해 응답률이 높아질 수 있기 때문이다.

37 글의 목적 ②

| 분석 |
대부분의 연구 프로젝트에서 전체 모집단 대신 무작위적인 모집단 표본추출이 사용되는 이유를 설명하는 글이다. ④ 표본추출 기술의 역사적 발전 과정은 다루지 않고 있다.

다음 중 이 글의 주요 목적은 무엇인가?
① 모집단 표본추출을 피해야 한다고 제안하기 위해
② 대부분의 연구에서 모집단 표본추출이 사용되는 이유를 설명하기 위해
③ 과학적 연구 방법의 장점에 대해 독자에게 알리기 위해
④ 표본추출 기술이 어떻게 발전해왔는지를 설명하기 위해

38~40

지미 카터의 대통령 임기는 국민과 정부 간 새로운 관계를 상징하는 소박한 행동으로 시작되었다. 그는 부인 로잘린과 함께 리무진에서 내려 취임 행진 경로의 짧은 구간을 손을 잡고 걸었다. 그러나 4년 뒤 그의 임기는 이란 혁명 정부의 악의적인 제스처와 더불어 끝났다. 이란은 444일간 억류했던 52명의 미국 인질을 석방했지만, 이런 일은 카터가 퇴임해있고, 그의 성공적인 후임자가 취임 연설을 하는 바로 그 순간이 되어서야 찾아왔던 것이다.

이는 카터 공직 임기 중 마지막 모욕이었으며, 많은 논평과 상당히 폭넓은 여론에 따르면 '실패한' 것으로 널리 간주된 대통령직의 마지막이었다. 하지만 그가 100세의 나이로 일요일에 사망하기 43년 전에 끝난 그의 대통령직이 정말로 실패였을까? 정확히 무엇이 대통령직의 실패를 구성하는지를 말하기는 쉽지 않다. 전쟁, 수년간 이어지는 경제적 혼란, 내전 등이 실패의 구성요소일까? 높이 평가받는 일부 대통령들도 임기 중 이러한 일들을 겪었다.

카터의 백악관 시절 많은 일이 잘못된 것은 분명하다. 어느 정도는 그가 취임하기 훨씬 전에 시작된 사건들에 휘말린 측면이 있다. 인질 위기를 초래한 이란인들의 끓어오르는 분노는 적어도 25년 전까지 거슬러 올라간다. 카터 행정부를 괴롭힌 경제 문제는 이전 두세 정권에 걸쳐 심화하여 온 추세의 연속이었으며, 이란 혁명으로 촉발된 석유 위기로 인해 크게 악화되었다. 정부에 대한 전반적인 실망과 소외감은 대체로 베트남 전쟁과 워터게이트 추문의 산물로 여겨질 수 있었고, 일반적으로 그렇게 여겨졌다.

사실 카터 행정부는 견고하고 지속적인 성과를 남겼다. 캠프 데이비드 협정은 중동에서 가장 위험한 충돌 지점에 불안하지만 긴 평화를 가져온 것으로, 카터 행정부의 가장 큰 외교 정책 성과였다. 이집트의 안와르 사다트와 이스라엘의 메나헴 베긴 간의 이 협정이, 카터가 회담 동안 지속적으로 존재감을 드러내고 두 지도자의 필요에 대해 세심한 배려를 하지 않았더라면, 어떻게 체결될 수 있었을지 이해하기 어렵다.

| 어휘 |
signal v. 신호를 보내다, 나타내다 **route** n. 경로 **hand in hand** 손을 맞잡고 **spiteful** a. 악의적인 **hostage** n. 인질 **release** v. 풀어주다 **triumphant** a. 승리한 **successor** n. 후임자 **deliver** v. 연설하다 **term** n. 임기 **fair swath of** 상당히 폭넓은 **public opinion** 여론 **disruption** n. 혼란, 붕괴 **civil conflict** 내전 **overtake** v. 덮치다, 앞지르다 **set in motion** 시작되다, 유발되다 **seething** a. 끓어오르는 **resentment** n. 분노, 원한 **hostage crisis** 인질 사태 **date back** 거슬러 올라가다 **dog** v. 괴롭히다 **exacerbate** v. 악화시키다 **oil crisis** 석유 위기 **trigger** v. 촉발되다 **dismay** n. 실망, 낙담 **alienation** n. 소외 **solid** a. 견고한, 확실한 **lasting** n. 지속적인 **conflict point** 분쟁 지점 **foreign policy** 외교 정책 **accord** n. 협정 **turmoil** n. 혼란

38 내용추론 ④

| 분석 |
여론은 카터를 실패한 대통령으로 보고 있지만, 이 글은 그의 주요 업적을 긍정적으로 평가하고 있다. 따라서 주요 업적에도 불구하고, 그에 대한 여론 평가는 부정적이었다는 ④가 정답이다. ① 예를 들어 베트남전, 워터게이트 등의 영향을 받았으므로, 극복하지 못했다. ② 임기가 끝난 후 석방되었다. ③ 워터게이트 추문은 이전 정부에서 저질러졌다.

다음 중 이 글에서 추론할 수 있는 것은?
① 지미 카터 행정부는 이전 행정부의 정치적 혼란을 극복했다.
② 이란의 인질들은 카터 임기 중에 석방되었다.
③ 지미 카터 행정부가 워터게이트 추문에 책임이 있다.
④ 주요한 업적에도 불구하고, 지미 카터는 여론에 의해 공정하게 평가받지 못했다.

| 39 | 내용일치 | ② |

| 분석 |

"카터 행정부를 괴롭힌 경제 문제는 이전 두세 정권에 걸쳐 심화하여 온 추세의 연속이었으며, 이란 혁명으로 촉발된 석유 위기로 인해 크게 악화되었다."라고 했으므로 ②가 정답이다. ① 국민의 지지 여부는 나와 있지 않다. ③ 성격은 나와 있지 않고, 석유 위기와 인질 사태는 중요한 문제였다. ④ 사다트와 베긴이 어떤 반응을 보였는지는 나와 있지 않다.

다음 중 올바른 내용은?
① 지미 카터는 미국 국민의 지지 없이 외교 문제들을 결국 극복했다.
② 이란 혁명으로 인한 석유 위기는 이전 행정부에서 이미 악화된 경제 문제를 더욱 악화시켰다.
③ 지미 카터는 석유 위기와 인질 사태 동안의 사소한 실수에도 불구하고 성격 덕분에 인기 있는 대통령이었다.
④ 캠프 데이비드 협정은 중동에 평화를 가져왔지만, 사다트와 베긴은 이에 만족하지 않았다.

| 40 | 뒷내용 추론 | ④ |

| 분석 |

마지막 문단에서 카터 행정부의 여러 업적이 있다고 한 후, 하나의 외교적 성과만을 소개했으므로, 다음에는 다른 업적들이 이어져야 한다.

다음 중 이 글 다음에 이어질 내용은 무엇인가?
① 이란의 인질 사건과 외교 문제의 영향
② 베트남 전쟁과 워터게이트에 대한 미국인들의 집단 기억
③ 지미 카터 행정부의 홍보 실패
④ 지미 카터 행정부의 더 많은 업적

HONGIK UNIVERSITY | 홍익대학교 서울 자연계 A형

TEST p. 736~744

01	①	02	④	03	③	04	①	05	④	06	①	07	④	08	①	09	②	10	③
11	②	12	②	13	②	14	②	15	②	16	②	17	②	18	①	19	②	20	①
21	②	22	③	23	④	24	②	25	④										

01 동의어 ①

| 어휘 |

corporate a. 법인의, 기업의 **make no sense** 이치에 맞지 않다
convoluted a. 복잡한, 난해한(= labyrinthine) **repeal** v. 폐지하다
term n. 용어 **misleading** a. 호도하는 **gallant** a. 용감한
jocund a. 쾌활한 **agnate** a. 부계(父系)의

| 해석 |

일리노이 주의 기업 프랜차이즈 세금은 전혀 말이 되지 않는다. 이 세금은 복잡하고 경제적으로 해로우며, 폐지되어야 마땅하다. "프랜차이즈 세금"이라는 용어 자체도 오해의 소지가 있고 시대에 뒤떨어진 표현인데, 이는 이 세금이 실제로는 대기업의 프랜차이즈 가맹점에 부과하는 세금이 아니기 때문이다.

02 동의어 ④

| 어휘 |

effervescent a. 기운이 넘치는(= exuberant) **initiative** n. 계획, 진취성, 주도권 **flourish** v. 번성하다 **nefarious** a. 흉악한, 범죄의
anorexic a. 거식증의 **oracular** a. 신탁과 같은, 숨은 뜻이 있는

| 해석 |

그녀는 활력이 넘치고 이스라엘 수도와 그 주민들의 번영에 기여할 새로운 진취적인 계획들을 끊임없이 꿈꾼다.

03 동의어 ③

| 어휘 |

quality assurance 품질보증 **allegedly** ad. 소문에 의하면 **forge** v. 위조하다(= fabricate) **inspector** n. 검사관 **annihilate** v. 절멸시키다 **eulogize** v. 칭송하다 **bluster** v. 고함치다, 엄포를 놓다

| 해석 |

뉴욕 주 게이츠에 소재한 PMI Industries에서 품질 보증 엔지니어로 근무하던 중에 Smalley는 캘리포니아에 기반을 둔 스페이스X에 판매된 제품에 대한 보고서에서 검사원 서명을 위조했다고 전해진다.

04 동의어 ①

| 어휘 |

dismiss v. 해고하다 **impolitic** a. 분별없는, 졸렬한(= rash)
preaching n. 설교 **accumulate** v. 축적하다 **zeal** n. 열정
learning n. 학습, 학식 **upright** a. 꼿꼿한 **fief** n. 봉토, 세습영지
neutral a. 중립적인

| 해석 |

Hartlib은 일곱 자녀를 두었고, 분별없는 설교로 해임되었고, 그 결과 큰 빚을 지게 되었지만, 이러한 상황으로 인해 배움의 진전에 대한 그의 열정은 이제 많이 식어버렸다.

05 동의어 ④

| 어휘 |

simulacrum n. 복제품, 모조품 **innate** a. 내재적인, 본질적인
hardship n. 어려움, 고난 **lackluster** a. 활기 없는(= humdrum)
immortality n. 불멸 **borrowing** n. 차용(금) **consumerism** n. 소비주의 **hummock** n. 작은 언덕[흙무더기] **huckster** n. 행상꾼, 도붓장수 **humdinger** n. 굉장한[대단한] 것

| 해석 |

새롭고 흥미진진한 시뮬라크르(복제품)가 현실의 본질적인 고난과 어려움인 것처럼 보이는 것으로 가득한 가운데 태어나, 냉방된 불멸, 무제한의 차용, 끝없는 소비주의로 이루어진 생기 없이 단조로운 시뮬라크르가 되어버린 것을 대체한다.

06 동의어 ①

| 어휘 |

superstitious a. 미신적인, 미신에 사로잡힌 **innate** a. 타고난, 생득

의 **mendacious** a. 허위의, 거짓의(= perfidious) **undertaking** n. 사업, 일 **unswerving** a. 변함없는 **resolute** a. 단호한, 확고한 **unrelenting** a. 가차 없는

| 해석 |

다양한 작품들에 대해 흔히 제기되는 불만은, 그것들(작품들)이 가톨릭 신자들은 미신적이라고 말하고, 흑인들은 타고난 무능력자라고 말하며, 유대인들은 거짓말을 잘한다고 말하고, 전쟁은 선하고 고귀한 일이라고 말한다는 것이다.

07 동의어 ④

| 어휘 |

somniferous a. 졸리게 하는(= soporific) **meandering** a. 두서없는 **estimate** n. 추정치 **vertical** a. 수직적인 **fiscal** a. 재정의 **tax thresholds** 과세 기준 **bracket creep** 브래킷 크리프(물가상승으로 명목소득이 늘어나면 높은 세율이 적용되어 실질적으로 증세가 일어나는 것) **stipulate** v. 규정하다 **speculative** a. 추측의, 투기의 **sedimentary** a. 퇴적의

| 해석 |

그 행사는 향후 예산 전망, 수직적 재정 불균형, 브래킷 크리프를 막기 위한 과세 기준 상향 등과 같은 주제에 대한 장황한 답변들이 이어져 전반적으로 졸음을 유발하는 행사였다.

08 동의어 ①

| 어휘 |

potent a. 강력한, 효능 있는(= efficacious) **antioxidant** n. 산화방지제 **ward off** 물리치다 **capricious** a. 변덕스러운 **ludicrous** a. 터무니없는 **subversive** a. 전복적인

| 해석 |

견과류에는 비타민 E가 풍부하게 들어 있는데, 이는 심장병과 암을 예방하는 데 도움이 될 수 있는 강력한 효능의 항산화제이다.

09 동의어 ②

| 어휘 |

condition n. 질병 **congenital** a. 선천적인(= innate) **leukemias** n. 백혈병 **subside** v. 가라앉다, 진정되다 **disjointed** a. 일관성 없는 **congested** a. 혼잡한

| 해석 |

결국 그 질환은 선천성 심장병이나 특정 백혈병의 발병 위험 증가와 같은 또 다른 문제들과 종종 연관되어 있다.

10 적절한 전치사 ③

| 분석 |

come close to는 '~에 가까이 오다'라는 의미를 가지고 있는 관용적인 표현이다. 따라서 ③의 in the way를 to the way로 고쳐야 한다.

| 어휘 |

semiosis n. 기호현상 **object** n. 사물 **semiotic** a. 기호(학)의 **the signified** 기의(記意: 기호의 의미 측면 ↔ the signifier 기표(記表): 기호의 소리 측면)

| 해석 |

퍼스에게, 기호현상은 문화가 발생하는 방식이었으며, 이러한 더 넓은 기호학적 연구 영역에서 사물에 대한 그의 이해는 소쉬르가 기의(記意)를 이해한 방식과 유사했다.

11 가정법 과거 ②

| 분석 |

불멸한 영혼이 개인의 정체성과 관련된 것이 사실이므로 이 문장은 현재사실에 반대되는 의미의 가정법 과거 문장이다. 주절의 동사가 가정법 동사인 would be이므로, if 절의 동사는 were가 되어야 한다. 따라서 ②의 is를 were로 고쳐야 한다.

| 어휘 |

immortality n. 불멸 **interest** n. 흥미 **have nothing to do with** ~와 연관이 없다 **identity** n. 정체성

| 해석 |

영혼의 불멸성에 대한 증명은, 만약 불멸로 입증된 영혼이 개인의 정체성과 아무런 관련이 없다는 것이 사실이라면, 누구에게나 단지 학문적으로만 흥미 있는 것일 텐데.

12 간접의문문의 어순 ③

| 분석 |

간접의문문의 어순은 '의문사+피수식어+주어+동사'이다. 따라서 ③의 how talented is he a singer을 how talented a singer he is로 고쳐야 한다.

| 어휘 |

disc n. 음반 **performer** n. 연주자 **collection** n. 모음집 **arrangement** n. 편곡, 각색

| 해석 |

가장 흥미로운 크리스마스 음반들은 완전히 다른 음악적 맥락(환경)에서 뛰어난 기량을 발휘하는 연주자를 보여주는 음반들이다. 앨런 잭슨은 이 전통적인 빅밴드 편곡 모음집을 통해 자신이 얼마나 재능 있는 가수인지를 잘 증명해 보인다.

13 조동사 would rather의 부정 ③

| 분석 |
would rather은 하나의 의미단위(조동사)로서 '～하고 싶다'라는 뜻을 가지고 있다. 따라서 이 경우는 부정어 not은 would rather 다음에 와야 한다.

| 어휘 |
subscriber n. 구독자   mailing label 수신인 주소 성명용 라벨

| 해석 |
때때로 우리는 우리 독자(구독자)분들의 관심을 끌 것으로 믿어지는 상품과 서비스를 우편으로 판매하는 회사들에게 우리의 구독자 명단을 제공합니다. 만약 그러한 우편 발송물을 우편으로 받지 않으시고 싶다면, 현재 사용 중인 우편 라벨을 'Mail Preference Service, P.O. Box 6000, Harlan, IA 51593'로 보내주시기 바랍니다.

14 send + 목적어 + to(전치사) ③

| 분석 |
4형식 동사는 간접목적어와 직접목적어 위치를 바꾸어 3형식 구문을 만들 수 있다. 이때 전치사를 수반하게 되는데, send는 뒤로 가는 간접목적어 앞에 전치사 to가 와야 한다. 따라서 ③을 to people로 고쳐야 한다.

| 어휘 |
academic conference 학술회의   in advance 미리

| 해석 |
학술회의를 성공적으로 조직하고 싶다면, 초청 이메일을 초대될 사람들에게 미리 보내야 한다.

15 one of 복수명사 ②

| 분석 |
'one of+복수명사+단수동사'의 형태로 쓰이므로 ②의 problem을 problems로 고쳐야 한다.

| 어휘 |
amusement park 놀이 공원   gradually ad. 점진적으로

| 해석 |
그 놀이공원이 가지고 있는 가장 중요한 문제들 중 하나는 3년 동안 방문객들의 수가 점차적으로 줄어들고 있다는 것이다.

16 논리완성 ①

| 분석 |
by 이하는 수질 개선 방법을 나타내는데, 포장되지 않은 흙길이 방치되어 있으면 비가 올 때 흙이 빗물에 쓸려 들어가 하천의 수질을 악화시킬 것이므로 나무를 심어 길을 없애버려야 할 것이다. 따라서 obliterating이 적절하다.

| 어휘 |
dirt road 비포장도로   prohibit v. 금지하다   riparian a. 강가의   vegetation n. 초목, 식생   obliterate v. 없애다   anchor v. 고정시키다   fortify v. 강화시키다   penetrate v. 관통하다

| 해석 |
수질은 사용되지 않는 비포장도로를 없애고, 하천 인접 지역에서 수질, 어류 또는 식생(초목)에 용납할 수 없는 장기적 영향을 미칠 새로운 활동을 금지함으로써 계속해서 개선될 것이다.

17 논리완성 ④

| 분석 |
빈칸에는 Swollen 및 bruised with boils과 호응하는 부정적인 의미의 표현이 와야 한다. 보기 중에서 부정적인 의미를 갖는 표현은 ④ '쇠약한' 밖에 없다.

| 어휘 |
push aside 밀어 내다   swollen a. 부풀어 오른   bruised a. 타박상을 입은, 멍이 든   boil n. 부스럼, 종기   full-bodied a. 뚱뚱한   gratified a. 만족하고 있는   rhubarb v. 왁자지껄하다   emaciated a. 쇠약한

| 해석 |
가혹한 노동으로 건강을 잃고 밀려난 사람들은 이제 각 방에서 죽음과 싸우고 있었다. 부어오르고, 쇠약하며, 부스럼으로 타박상을 입은 채, 각자 다양한 질병에 걸린 그들은 함께 지옥 같은 광경을 이루고 있었다.

18 논리완성 ①

| 분석 |
두 항공사가 1년 전에 코드 공유(특정노선을 함께 운항하는 항공사들이 항공권판매, 예약, 수속 등, 서비스를 공동으로 제공하는 것)를 시작했다는 단서로부터 두 항공사가 상호간에 협력하고 있다는 사실을 추론할 수 있다.

| 어휘 |
reciprocal a. 상호적인, 서로 주고받는   frequent flyer (miles) program 항공 마일리지   invulnerable a. 상처를 입지 않는, 무적의   ticking a. (시계 등이) 째깍거리는   verdure n. 신록, 푸른 것

| 해석 |
그 두 항공사는 약 1년 전에 코드 공유와 상호적인 항공 마일리지 적립 프로그램을 시작했다.

19 논리완성 ②

| 분석 |

도전자들이 최대한 많이 배워야 한다는 단서로부터, 도전자들이 모든 정책에 대해서도 '정통'해지기 위해 노력한다는 것을 추론할 수 있다.

| 어휘 |

conversant a. 정통한, ~에 익숙한 **perpetuate** v. 영속시키다 **disarray** v. 혼란에 빠지다 **arrogate** v. (권리 등을) 부당하게 주장하다, 가로채다

| 해석 |

도전자들은 지금은 모두 초보자일지라도 모든 질문에 대비하고 모든 정책 분야에 정통해지기 위해 가능한 한 많이 배워야 한다.

20~22

진리는 철학자들과 논리학자들 모두에게 독특한 학문적 중요성을 지니는 문제이다. 물론, 모든 과학과 탐구는 '존재하는 것'에 대해 참된 무언가를 말하려고 한다. 신학자, 과학자, 예술가들은 이 진리가 최고의 존재에 관한 것이든, 우울증의 본질에 관한 것이든, 사회 정의 등등에 관한 것이든, 진리를 식별하려 한다. 하지만 논리학자와 철학자는 진리의 조건들을 구별하려는 노력에 있어 남다르다. 그들은 모두 이해 가능성의 경계를 규정하고, 진리의 형식적 조건과 내용적 조건을 구분하고, 최대한 정밀한 언어를 추구하는 과제를 공유한다. 따라서 이 두 학문은 모두, 특정 과학이나 예술과는 달리, 진리가 발생하는 조건들에 관심을 가진다.

그러나 서양 철학사 전반에 걸쳐, 철학과 논리학 사이의 중요한 차이점들은 이 둘 사이에 엄격한 학문적 경계를 설정할 정당한 근거로 간주되어 왔다. 역사적으로 철학은 그 영역이 논리학의 영역에 비해 광범위하다고 인식된 것과 관련하여 더 높은 지위를 부여받아 왔다. 철학은 논리학의 범위를 훨씬 넘어서는 주제들과 질문들을 다룬다. 예를 들어, 정의의 본질, 시간, 영혼에 대한 질문들은 논리학의 영역 밖에 있다. 전통적으로는, 논리학에 포함되는 모든 것이 철학에도 포함될 수 있지만, 철학에 포함될 수 있는 모든 것이 논리학에도 포함될 수 있는 것은 아니라고 말하는 것은 논란의 여지가 없는 일이다. 철학은 더 크고 포괄적인 학문으로 간주되며, 때때로 더 고귀한 학문으로 여겨지기도 한다.

논리학은, 아리스토텔레스를 형식적으로 끌어다 쓴 후, 일반적인 지식을 위한 '예비 교육(propaedeutic)'으로 간주되어 왔다. 이 전통은 전형적인 교육 과정 개념에 반영되어 있다. 즉, 학생은 논리학 강좌들을 수강하고, 이를 통해 과학이나 인문학을 엄밀하게 연구할 준비를 하게 된다. 이러한 과정은 논리학에서 시작되어, 과학을 거쳐, 궁극적으로 철학에서 정점을 이룬다. 지식의 정점으로서의 철학은 논리학이라는 학문과는 명백히 다른 학문이다. 이러한 전통적 질서에 대한 도전으로, 20세기의 일부 철학자들은 논리학자의 작업과 철학자의 작업이 남는 부분 없이 꼭 겹친다고 주장했다. 실제로는, 광의의 분석철학과 더불어, 전통적으로 철학적 탐구 영역에 있었던 많은 '영원한 질문들'을 (철학이) 거부하는 일이 일어난다. 예컨대 우주의 목적, 영혼의 본질, 신의 속성에 관한 질문들은 탁상공론의 비약, 즉 결국 이해 불가능한 가짜 질문들로 간주된다. 철학을 논리학과 구분 짓던 바로 그 탐구 주제들이 공상적인 것으로 일축된다. 명확하고 정밀한 언어를 강조하고 철학에 대한 새로운 관점을 제시하는 분석철학은 현대의 과학기술적 세계에서 매우 유용한 역할을 하기에 적합하다. 그러나 분석철학이 제시하는 철학적 관점이 점점 인기를 얻고 있다 해도, 우리는 그 철학이 도전하는 역사적 전통의 미묘한 헌신들을 잊어서는 안 된다. 실제로, 분석철학의 참신함은 전통과 그 선입견에 주목할 때에만 제대로 평가될 수 있을 것이다.

| 어휘 |

peculiar a. 독특한, 특이한 **disciplinary** a. 학문의 **significance** n. 중요성 **inquiry** n. 탐구, 조사 **discern** v. 식별하다, 분별하다 **conditions of truth** 진리의 조건 **intelligibility** n. 이해가능성 **utmost** a. 최대한의 **precision** n. 정밀성 **justify** v. 정당화하다 **institution** n. 제도, 설정 **disciplinary boundaries** 학문적 경계 **afford** v. 주어지다, 부여되다 **exalted status** 고귀[숭고]한 지위 **correlating to** ~와 관련하여, 상응하는 **expansiveness** n. 광범위성 **purview** n. 권한, 영역, 범위 **external to** ~의 외부에 있는 **encompassing** a. 포괄적인 **dignified** a. 존엄한, 위엄 있는, 고귀한 **scholastic** a. 학자의, 형식적인, 스콜라 철학의 **appropriation** n. 수용, 전유 **propaedeutic** n. 예비교육 **rigorous** a. 철저한, 엄밀한 **culminate** v. 정점을 이루다 **markedly** ad. 뚜렷하게, 현저하게 **overlap without remainder** 남김없이 겹치다(완전히 중복되다) **broadly construed** 광의로 해석될 때 **perennial** a. 영원한 **unintelligible** a. 이해할 수 없는 **chimerical** a. 공상적인, 터무니없는 **lend itself to** ~에 도움이 되다, ~에 적합하다, 기여하다 **proffered** a. 제안된, 제시된 **nuanced** a. 미묘한 차이를 지닌 **prejudice** n. 편견, 선입견 **novelty** n. 참신함, 새로움 **assessed** a. 평가된, 판단된

---

20 부분이해 ①

| 분석 |

명사로서 '준비 연구; 예비 학과; (단수 취급) 예비지식, 기초 훈련, 입문 교육.' 등의 의미를 가지고 있다. 지문에 따르면 논리학은 본격적인 철학을 공부하기 위한 예비교육의 성격을 가지고 있다.

위 글에 따르면, 다음 중 ⓐ'propaedeutic'이 의미할 가능성이 가장 높은 것은?

① 어떤 학문이나 연구 분야에 앞서 필요한 예비적 소개 또는 준비 교육
② 진리가 무엇인지를 탐구하려는 학문
③ 서로 다른 과학 분야 간의 연결에 대한 고찰
④ 과학적 질문의 영역 간 상관관계를 만들어내는 과정

21　내용추론　②

| 분석 |

'역사적으로 철학은, 그 영역이 논리학의 영역에 비해 광범위하다고 인식되었기 때문에, 더 높은 지위를 부여받아 왔다. 철학은 논리학의 범위를 훨씬 넘어서는 주제들과 질문들을 다룬다.'라는 단서로부터 ② '전통적으로, 철학자들이 논리학자들보다 더 폭넓은 질문들을 던지는 것으로 간주되어 왔다.'고 추론할 수 있다.

다음 중 위 글로부터 추론할 수 있는 내용으로 가장 그럴듯한 것은?
① 논리학은 철학보다 더 구체적인 문제들을 다루기 때문에, 진리와 관련된 학문으로 간주되어서는 안 된다.
② 전통적으로, 철학자들이 논리학자들보다 더 폭넓은 질문들을 던지는 것으로 간주되어 왔다.
③ 논리학과는 달리, 철학은 진리의 형식적 측면과 내용적 조건을 구분하지 않는다.
④ 논리학에서 제기되는 질문들은 철학적 주제들이 먼저 탐구된 이후에만 규정될 수 있다.

22　내용파악　③

| 분석 |

분석철학은 '예컨대 우주의 목적, 영혼의 본질, 신의 속성에 관한 질문들은 탁상공론의 비약, 즉 결국 이해 불가능한 가짜 질문들로 간주'하고, '철학을 논리학과 구분 짓던 바로 그 탐구 주제들이 공상적인 것으로 일축되는 것이다.'라는 단서부터 빈칸에 ③ '분석철학자들이 철학과 논리학의 경계를 구분하는 데 사용되어 왔던 질문들을 무시하는 경향이 있다.'가 들어가야 함을 알 수 있다.

위 글에 따르면, 분석철학은 ＿＿＿＿는 의미에서 전통철학과 다르다.
① 분석철학자들이 신이나 영혼의 존재와 같은 질문에 더 정밀한 방식으로 답하려고 한다
② 분석철학이 언어 사용의 불분명함과 모호성 때문에 논리학을 폐기한다
③ 분석철학자들이 철학과 논리학의 경계를 구분하는 데 사용되어 왔던 질문들을 무시하는 경향이 있다
④ 분석철학이 현대 사회에서 철학이 쓸모없기 때문에 과학과 기술의 최근 발전에 기여하지 않는다

23~25

구글은 세계에서 가장 빠른 기존 컴퓨터들조차도 완료하는데 10,000,000,000,000,000,000,000,000년이 걸릴 작업을 단 5분 만에 완료하는 컴퓨팅 칩을 개발했다. 이는 10 셉틸리언(1 셉틸리언=10의 24제곱) 년으로, 알려진 우주의 나이를 훨씬 능가하며 이번 양자 컴퓨팅의 획기적인 성과를 이끈 과학자들조차도 "믿을 수 없을 정도(mindboggling)"라는 비전문적인 표현을 사용할 수밖에 없게 만드는 수이다. '윌로우(Willow)'라는 이름을 가진 이 새로운 칩은, 캘리포니아의 해변 도시 산타 바바라에서 만들어졌으며, 애프터에이트 민트(박하 초콜릿) 정도의 크기인데, 이 칩은 신약 개발 실험 단계를 획기적으로 가속화함으로써, 새로운 의약품의 창출을 크게 촉진시킬 수 있을 것으로 보인다.

이 칩의 성능에 관한 보고는 2021년 이후 쏟아져 나온 다양한 결과들을 뒤잇는 것으로, 양자 컴퓨팅이 강력해져서 약품에서 배터리에 이르는 신소재를 연구 개발할 수 있는 인류의 능력을 변화시킬 수 있게 되는 데는 이제 약 5년밖에 남지 않았음을 시사하는 것이라고 한 영국의 독립 전문가는 말했다. 전 세계 정부들은 수백억 달러를 이 분야 연구에 쏟아붓고 있다.

중요한 점으로, Willow 칩은 이전의 버전들보다 오류의 가능성이 훨씬 더 적다는 주장이 있으며 이미 급속도로 발달하고 있는 인공지능의 잠재력을 더욱 키울 수 있을 것이다.

양자 컴퓨팅은 물질이 동시에 여러 상태로 존재할 수 있다는 발견을 활용하는 것인데, 예전에 가능했던 것보다 훨씬 더 큰 계산을 수행할 능력을 갖고, 그래서 핵융합 원자로의 제작을 앞당기고, 특히 의학 분야에서 인공지능의 영향력을 가속화시킬 것으로 예측된다. 예를 들어, 양자 컴퓨팅으로 인해 MRI 스캔을 원자 수준의 정밀도로 판독할 수 있게 되어, 인간의 몸과 질병에 대한 방대한 데이터의 새로운 저장소가 열려 AI가 처리할 수 있게 될 것이라고 구글은 전했다.

〈하지만 만약 안전장치(guardrails)가 없다면, 이 기술은 가장 정교한 암호화조차도 뚫을 수 있는 힘을 가져, 컴퓨터 보안을 위협할 수 있다는 우려도 존재한다.〉 구글 퀀텀 AI는 양자역학의 컴퓨팅(연산) 능력을 어떻게 활용할 것인지를 두고 씨름하고 있다. 마이크로소프트, 하버드대학교, 그리고 영국과 연관이 있는 기업인 퀀티뉴엄(Quantinuum)을 포함한 수많은 그룹 중 하나이다. 핵심적인 문제는 미세한 물질 결함, 우주방사선, 그리고 이온화 방사선조차도 양자 칩을 쉽게 흐트러뜨리므로 양자 칩의 연약함을 줄이는 것이다.

| 어휘 |

computing chip 컴퓨팅 칩, 연산용 칩　**10 septillion years** 10셉틸리언 년(= 1000경 년)　**exceed** v. 능가하다　**mindboggling** a. 믿기 힘들 정도의, 경이로운　**breakthrough** n. 획기적 돌파　**term**

n. 용어　**dimension** n. 크기, 치수　**After Eight mint** 애프터 에이트 민(얇고 네모난 민트 초콜릿)　**supercharge** v. 크게 가속하다, 활성화하다　**a flurry of** 휘몰아치는　**be prone to** ~하는 경향이 있다　**swell** v. 확대하다　**harness** v. (자원·기술 등을) 활용하다　**nuclear fusion reactor** 핵융합 원자로　**notably** ad. 특히　**MRI** 자기공명영상(Magnetic Resonance Imaging)　**cache** n. 저장소　**wrestle with** 해결하려 애쓰다　**fragility** n. 취약성, 연약함　**defect** n. 결함　**cosmic ray** 우주선　**ionising radiation** 이온화 방사선(물질을 이온화할 수 있는 방사선)　**knock off course** 경로를 이탈하게 하다　**guardrail** n. 보호장치, 안전장치　**crack encryption** 암호화[보안체계]를 해독하다　**sophisticated** a. 정교한　**encryption** n. 암호화 기법　**undermine** v. 약화시키다, 위협하다

25　문장삽입　　　　　　　　　　　　④

| 분석 |

주어진 문장, 즉 '하지만 만약 안전장치(guardrails)가 없다면, 이 기술은 가장 정교한 암호화조차도 뚫을 수 있는 힘을 가져, 컴퓨터 보안을 위협할 수 있다는 우려도 존재한다.'는 양자 컴퓨터의 부정적인 면을 언급하고 있다. 따라서 주어진 문장은 양자 컴퓨터의 문제점들을 지적하고 있는 마지막 단락 서두인 ⒟에 들어가야 한다.

23　글의 제목　　　　　　　　　　　　④

| 분석 |

이 글의 핵심적인 토픽은 구글이 개발한 '믿기 힘들 정도로 놀라운' 양자 컴퓨팅 칩 Willow다. 이 글은 양자 컴퓨팅 칩 Willow의 등장을 화두 삼아 양자 컴퓨터의 정의와 미래 그리고 한계와 그 위험성까지 두루 서술하고 있는 설명문이다.

위 글의 제목으로 가장 적절한 것?
① 구글의 양자 AI가 5년 안에 의학을 어떻게 변화시킬까?
② 양자 컴퓨팅이 제약 연구에서 이룬 성과
③ 양자 컴퓨팅과 IT 기업들의 치열한 경쟁
④ 구글이 '믿기 힘들 정도로 놀라운' 양자 컴퓨팅 칩 Willow를 공개하다

24　내용일치　　　　　　　　　　　　②

| 분석 |

'중요한 점으로, Willow 칩은 이전의 버전들보다 오류의 가능성이 훨씬 더 적다는 주장이 있으며 이미 급속도로 발달하고 있는 인공지능의 잠재력을 더욱 키울 수 있을 것이다.'라는 단서로부터 ② 'AI 기술의 역량은 양자 컴퓨팅의 발전에 의해 크게 영향을 받지 않을 수도 있다.'가 이 글의 내용과 일치하지 않음을 알 수 있다.

위 글에 따르면, 다음 중 사실이 아닌 것은?
① 양자 컴퓨팅 기술은 제약 연구에서 새로운 물질을 발견할 수 있을 정도로 5년 안에 충분히 발전할 수 있다.
② AI 기술의 역량은 양자 컴퓨팅의 발전에 의해 크게 영향을 받지 않을 수도 있다.
③ 양자 컴퓨팅 칩을 사용함으로써, 의학은 더욱 향상된 MRI 스캔 같은 돌파구를 얻을 수 있다.
④ 새로운 칩 Willow는 이전 칩보다 오류를 줄이는 데 훨씬 더 효과적이다.

MEMO

MEMO

MEMO

MEMO

MEMO

편입 합격의 길을 제시하는 김영 로드맵
김영편입 영어 시리즈

초심자를 위한 편입영어 지침서

문법 이론   구문독해 이론

기초 실력 점검을 위한 초급 난이도 단계

어휘 기출 1단계   문법 기출 1단계   독해 기출 1단계   논리 기출 1단계

+

문법 워크북 1단계   독해 워크북 1단계   논리 워크북 1단계

반드시 알아야 할 빈출 중고급 난이도

어휘 기출 2단계   문법 기출 2단계   독해 기출 2단계   논리 기출 2단계

+

문법 워크북 2단계   독해 워크북 2단계   논리 워크북 2단계

대학별 실전대비를 위한 기출문제 해설집

영어 기출문제 해설집   수학 기출문제 해설집

김영편입 온라인 서점과 **시중 대형서점**에서 구입 가능

(교보문고, yes24, 알라딘, 영풍문고 등)

영어 기출문제 해설집 [해설편]
2026학년도 대비

완벽 활용 가이드

1 출제경향 분석
파트별 문항 분류표와 심층 분석 자료를 통해 출제 경향을 파악하고 학습 우선순위 설정

2 실전 대비 연습
제한시간 내 기출문제 풀이 훈련으로 실전 감각과 문제 해결력 증진

3 정답 확인 & 오답 분석
오답의 원인과 핵심 개념을 짚어주는 해설 중심 학습으로 기출문제 완벽 정리

4 빈출 유형 반복 학습
빈출 문제의 반복 학습을 통해 응용력과 풀이력 강화

2024, 2023, 2022 대한민국 브랜드 어워즈 대학편입교육 대상
2021 대한민국 우수브랜드 대상
(한경비즈니스)

편머리/김영편입 영어 시리즈 누적 판매량 합산 기준
(2014.01.01~2024.12.31)

메가스터디교육그룹 아이비김영의 NEW 도서 브랜드 〈김앤북〉
여러분의 편입 & 자격증 & IT 취업 준비에
빛이 되어 드리겠습니다.
www.kimnbook.co.kr